W9-BAU-675

Sigelman

Life-Span Human Development, 8e

Life-Span
Human Development, 8e

Carol K. Sigelman
George Washington University

Elizabeth A. Rider
Elizabethtown College

CENGAGE
Learning

Australia • Brazil • Mexico • Singapore • United Kingdom • United States

**Life-Span Human Development,
Eighth Edition**
Carol K. Sigelman, Elizabeth A. Rider

Product Director: Jon-David Hague

Product Manager: Clayton Austin

Content Developer: Barbara Armentrout

Outsource Development Manager:
Jeremy Judson

Content Coordinator: Paige Leeds

Product Assistant: Nicole Richards

Media Developer: Audrey Espey

Art Director: Jennifer Wahi

Manufacturing Planner: Karen Hunt

Rights Acquisitions Specialist: Roberta Broyer

Production Service: PreMediaGlobal

Photo Researcher: Mrudula Ganeshan,
Carly Bergy

Text Researcher: Ganesh Kumar

Copy Editor: PreMediaGlobal

Text Designer: Jeanne Calabrese

Cover Designer: Jeff Bane

Cover Illustration: Jeff Bane

Compositor: PreMediaGlobal

For product information and technology assistance, contact us at
Cengage Learning Customer & Sales Support, 1-800-354-9706

For permission to use material from this text or product,
submit all requests online at **cengage.com/permissions**
Further permissions questions can be emailed to
permissionrequest@cengage.com

Library of Congress Control Number: 2013957520

ISBN-13: 978-1-285-45431-3

ISBN-10: 1-285-45431-6

Cengage Learning
200 First Stamford Place, 4th Floor
Stamford, CT 06902
USA

Cengage Learning is a leading provider of customized learning solutions with
office locations around the globe, including Singapore, the United Kingdom,
Australia, Mexico, Brazil, and Japan. Locate your local office at
www.cengage.com/global.

Cengage Learning products are represented in Canada by Nelson Education, Ltd.

To learn more about Cengage Learning Solutions, visit **www.cengage.com**.

Purchase any of our products at your local college store or at our preferred
online store **www.cengagebrain.com**.

Printed in Canada
1 2 3 4 5 6 7 18 17 16 15 14

To the students who have inspired us

Brief Contents

Contents

3 Genes, Environment, and Development 61

4 Prenatal Development and Birth 91

5 Body, Brain, and Health 129

6 Sensation, Perception, and Action 165

7 Cognition 199

8 Memory and Information Processing 231

9 Intelligence and Creativity 263

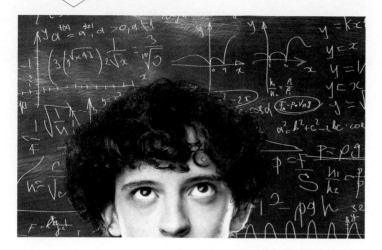

10 Language and Education 297

11 Self and Personality

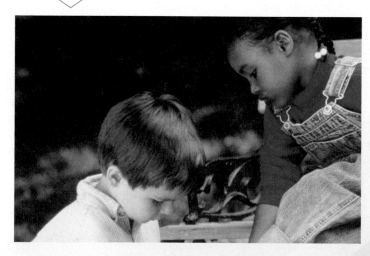

14 Emotions, Attachment, and Social Relationships 433

15 The Family 469

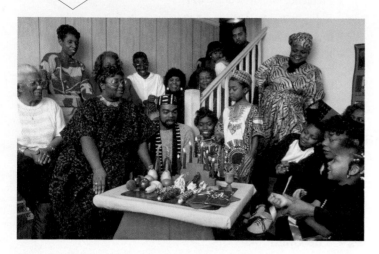

16 Developmental Psychopathology 505

17 The Final Challenge: Death and Dying 537

Preface

This book is about the development of human beings—from their days as fertilized eggs to their dying days. It explores regularities as well as differences in development, and it asks fundamental questions about why we humans develop as we do. The field of life-span human development is a dynamic one, and we attempt to keep up with the change in this, the eighth edition of *Life-Span Human Development*.

This new edition incorporates many exciting changes, yet it retains four core features valued by students and instructors over the years: (1) our unique integrated topical–chronological approach, (2) a presentation that is both research-based and relevant to students, (3) an emphasis on ideas—on the different theoretical perspectives that guide thinking about human development and research—and (4) an in-depth exploration of the all-important nature–nurture issue. In addition, we introduce new topics and controversies in life-span human development, update coverage throughout, and offer new pedagogical features and supplements to enhance the teaching–learning process.

Topical and Chronological Approach

The most distinctive feature of this book is its unique integrated topical–chronological approach. Almost all other life-span development textbooks adopt a chronological or "age–stage" approach, carving the life span into age ranges and describing the prominent characteristics of individuals within each age range. In contrast, we adopt a topical approach for the overall organization of the book blended with a chronological approach within chapters. Each chapter focuses on a domain of development, such as physical growth, cognition, or personality, and traces developmental trends and influences in that domain from infancy to old age. At the same time, each chapter highlights the special qualities of different age groups through major sections on infancy, childhood, adolescence, and adulthood.

Why Topical?

Why have we fought the tide? Like many other instructors, we have typically favored topically organized textbooks when teaching child, adolescent, or adult development. As a result, it seemed natural to use that same topical approach in introducing students to the whole life span. It also bothered us that chronologically organized texts often have to repeat themselves to remind readers of where development left off in an earlier age period that was covered in a previous chapter.

More important, a topic-by-topic organization conveys the flow of development in each area—the systematic, and often dramatic, transformations we undergo as well as the ways in which we continue to be the same individuals. The topical approach also helps us emphasize the processes behind development. Finally, a predominantly topical approach does justice to a life-span perspective on development, allowing us to view each period of life in relation to what comes before and what comes after. In chronologically organized textbooks, many topics are described only in connection with the age group to which they seem most relevant—for example, attachment in relation to infancy, or sexuality in relation to adolescence and adulthood. A topical organization stimulates us to ask intriguing questions we might otherwise not ask, such as these about close relationships:

- What do infants' attachments to their parents have in common with, and how do they differ from, attachments between childhood friends or between adult romantic partners?
- Do securely attached infants later have a greater capacity to form and sustain close relationships than infants whose early social experiences are less favorable?
- What are the consequences at different points in the life span of lacking a close relationship?

Attachments are important throughout the life span, and a topical organization helps make that clear.

Why Chronological?

We also appreciate the strengths of the chronological approach, particularly its ability to portray the whole person in each period of the life span. For this reason, we integrated the age–stage approach with the topical organization, aiming to have the best of both worlds.

Each topical chapter contains major sections on infancy, childhood, adolescence, and adulthood. The existence of these sections is proof that the chapters consider development in each of the domains covered across the whole life span. These age–stage sections call attention to the distinctive qualities of each phase of life and make it easier for students to find material on an age period of particular interest to them. In short, we believe that our integrated topical–chronological approach allows students to understand the flow of life-span development in particular areas and the factors influencing it while also appreciating the flavor of each developmental period.

Adaptability of the Integrated Topical–Chronological Approach

Even though links among chapters are noted throughout the book, instructors who are teaching short courses or who are otherwise pressed for time can omit a chapter without fear of rendering other chapters incomprehensible. For example:

- A cognitively oriented course might omit one or more of the socially oriented chapters (Chapters 11, 12, and 14–17).

- A socially oriented course might omit one or more of the cognitively oriented chapters (Chapters 6–10).

Moreover, this approach gives instructors the flexibility to cover infancy, childhood, and adolescence in the first portion of the course, if they prefer, and to save the material on adulthood for the end.

Research-Oriented and Relevant Coverage

We have worked hard to create a text that is rigorous yet readable—research-oriented yet "real" to students. The eighth edition of *Life-Span Human Development* tackles complex theoretical controversies and presents both classic and contemporary research from multiple disciplines. We aim to make developmental science accessible and relevant to students' lives and career goals but we refuse to "dumb it down."

Students need to understand how we know what we know about development—to appreciate the research process. With that in mind, we describe illustrative studies and present their data in graphs and tables, and we cite the authors and dates of publication for a large number of books and articles, all fully referenced in the bibliography at the end of the book. Some students may wonder why they are there. It is because we are committed to the value of systematic research, because we are bound to give credit where credit is due, and because we want students and their professors to have the resources they need to pursue their interests in human development during and after the course.

We also appreciate that solid scholarship is of little good to students unless they want to read it, can understand it, and see its relevance. To make the material more "real," we clarify developmental concepts through examples and analogies, connect topics in the text to topics in the news, and highlight the practical implications of research findings. We also incorporate applied material relevant to students' current and future roles as parents, teachers, psychologists, health professionals, and other human service professionals. And we help students see that major theories of human development do not just guide researchers but can guide them--for example, in raising, educating, or treating infants, children, or adolescents, understanding themselves and making important life decisions, appreciating that their parents and grandparents are also developing persons, and coping with challenges such as a death in the family.

Theoretical Grounding

Theories are critical in any science, telling scientists what to study, how to study it, and how to interpret their findings. We want students to leave the study of life-span human development with more than facts alone; we want them to appreciate the major issues of interest to developmental scientists and how the leading theories in the field have shaped our thinking about development. Most important, we want students to learn to use these theoretical perspectives to guide their thinking and action

when they encounter a question about human development outside the course.

With this in mind, we have devoted Chapter 2 to laying out in broad strokes the psychoanalytic, learning, cognitive developmental, and systems perspectives on human development, showing what they say, where they stand on key developmental issues, and how they explain developmental phenomena. In later chapters, we delve deeper into these and other perspectives and show what they have to say about various aspects of development; see, for example, treatment of the dynamic systems view of motor development in Chapter 6; Jean Piaget's groundbreaking cognitive-developmental theory in comparison to Lev Vygotsky's sociocultural perspective and Kurt Fischer's dynamic skill theory in Chapter 7; the information-processing perspective in Chapter 8; alternative views of intelligence in Chapter 9; nativist, learning, and interactionist theories of language development in Chapter 10; alternative theories of personality development in Chapter 11; theories of gender role in chapter 12; theories of moral development in Chapter 13; attachment theory in Chapter 14; and family systems theory and contrasting models of influence in the family in Chapter 15.

Nature–Nurture Theme

Finally, we want students to gain a deeper understanding of the nature–nurture issue and of the many interacting forces affecting the developing person. We want students to appreciate that human development is an incredibly complex process that grows out of transactions between a changing person and a changing world and out of dynamic relationships among biological, psychological, and social influences. No contributor to development—a gene, a temperament, a parent, a culture—acts alone and is unaffected by other influences on development.

We introduce the nature–nurture issue in Chapter 1, compare theorists' stands on the issue in Chapter 2, and give the issue extended treatment in Chapter 3 on genes and environment. Each subsequent chapter includes one or more illustrations of the intertwined contributions of nature and nurture to normal development and aging, and Chapter 16 looks at their roles in the development of psychological disorders. Along the way, we describe exciting studies that compare individuals with and without particular genes and with and without particular life experiences to bring home what it means to say that genes and environment interact to influence development—as when genes predisposing an individual to depression combine with stressful life events to produce depression. We also illustrate the many ways in which genes and environment affect one another—for instance, ways in which genetic makeup influences the experiences an individual has, and ways in which experience influences which of an individual's genes are activated or expressed.

In this edition, we have expanded coverage not only of genes, hormones, brain functions, and other biological forces in development but also of ways in which race and ethnicity, social class, and the larger cultural context modify development. Most important, we illuminate the complex interrelationships between biological and environmental influences that are at the heart of the developmental process—and that make it difficult to leave this course as either an extreme nativist or an extreme environmentalist.

Organization of the Text

Core Concepts: Chapters 1 to 4

The book begins by orienting students to the life-span perspective on human development and to approaches to the scientific study of development (Chapter 1), as well as to the central issues and theoretical perspectives that have dominated the field (Chapter 2). It then explores developmental processes in some depth, examining genetic and environmental influences on development (Chapter 3) and then focusing on important environmental influences during the prenatal and perinatal periods (Chapter 4).

Development of Basic Human Capacities: Chapters 5 to 10

Chapters on the growth and aging of the body and nervous system and on health (Chapter 5) and on the development of sensory, perceptual, and motor capacities (Chapter 6) launch our examination of the development of basic human capacities. Chapter 7 turns to cognitive development, with emphasis on the influential theories of Jean Piaget and Lev Vygotsky; Chapter 8 views memory and problem solving from an information-processing perspective; Chapter 9 highlights the psychometric approach to cognition, exploring individual differences in intelligence and creativity; and Chapter 10 explores language development and the roles of language, cognition, and motivation in educational achievement.

Development of Self in Society: Chapters 11 to 17

The next three chapters concern the development of the self: changes in self-conceptions and personality and their relationships to vocational identity and development (Chapter 11); in gender roles and sexuality (Chapter 12); and in social cognition, morality, and prosocial and antisocial behavior (Chapter 13). The self is set more squarely in a social context as we trace life-span changes in attachment relationships (Chapter 14) and in roles and relationships within the family (Chapter 15). Finally, we offer a life-span perspective on developmental problems and disorders (Chapter 16) and examine how humans of different ages cope with dying and bereavement (Chapter 17).

Getting the Big Picture

To help students pull together the "big picture" of life-span human development at the end of the course, we remind students of some of the major themes of the book at the end of Chapter 17 and offer a chart inside the back cover that summarizes major developments in each of the seven periods of the life span. Finally, an appendix, Careers in Human Development, lays out possibilities for translating an interest in human development into a career in research, teaching, or professional practice.

Engaging Students

The eighth edition provides learning objectives for each major numbered section and continues to use a variety of other strategies to increase students' engagement with the material and, more importantly, their learning.

Learning Objectives

Each major numbered section starts with two to five learning objectives to focus students' reading and give it purpose.

Checking Mastery Questions

To encourage students to actively check their command of the material as they progress through the chapter, we posed two to four Checking Mastery questions at the end of each numbered chapter section, the answers to which are in an appendix in this book.

Making Connections Questions

Also at the end of each major section, Making Connections questions invite students to reflect on the material—to weigh in on a debate in the field, evaluate the material's implications for public policy, apply the material to a case example, or explore the material's relevance to their own development. Many of these questions can serve as the basis for writing assignments, essay questions, or class discussions.

Boxes

The topics we address in boxes sprinkled throughout the chapters were chosen because they struck us as both interesting and important; they are not fluff to be skipped! This edition continues to include three kinds of boxes, each with a different purpose:

- **Exploration boxes** allow more in-depth investigation of research on a topic (for example, characteristics of the baby boom and millennial generations, effects of early experience on gene expression, secrets to a long life, characteristics of aging drivers, normal versus abnormal memory problems in old age, language acquisition among deaf children, the importance of self-control over the life span, and cultural differences in the meaning of good parenting).
- **Application boxes** examine how knowledge has been applied to optimize development (for instance, to prevent unwanted teenage pregnancy, promote healthy babies, improve cognitive functioning, combat the effects of negative stereotypes of aging, stop bullying, strengthen relationships, prevent family violence, treat children with psychological disorders, and support bereaved families).

- **Engagement boxes** provide opportunities for students to engage personally and actively with the material—to assess their own knowledge, beliefs, traits, and attitudes by completing personality scales, test items, surveys, and short quizzes (for example, by deciding where they stand on major issues in development, gauging their motivational style, completing a "Big Five" personality scale, determining their orientation toward romantic relationships, finding out if they might have characteristics associated with ADHD, or discovering whether they have experienced posttraumatic growth after a loss).

Content Updates in This Edition

As always, the book has been thoroughly updated to convey the most recent discoveries and insights developmentalists have to offer. We have added some exciting new topics and greatly revised, expanded, and updated coverage of other topics. A sampling:

Chapter 1. Understanding Life-Span Human Development

- Features all new research examples illustrating the use of case study, correlational, experimental, and cross-sectional as opposed to longitudinal approaches to study the implications of today's digital technologies for human development (for example, relationships between baby videos and infant language development, media use and adolescent development, and computer use and cognitive functioning in adulthood)

Chapter 2. Theories of Human Development

- New research on the nature and significance of observational learning across cultures
- Updates on application of major theories to explain school refusal in childhood and risky sexual behavior in adolescence
- Highlighting of Bronfenbrenner's bioecological theory to illustrate a systems perspective on development

Chapter 3. Genes, Environment, and Development

- Expanded coverage of exciting breakthroughs in the study of epigenetic effects--effects of early experience on gene expression and later development
- Bolstered discussion of how "genetically informed" studies can better establish that environmental influences such as good parenting truly affect development

Chapter 4. Prenatal Development and Birth

- New material on fetal programming and its implications for health over the life span

Chapter 5. Body, Brain, and Health

- Newly reorganized "Body, Brain, and Health" chapter.
- Greater emphasis on the development and aging of the brain, highlighting experience-guided growth in the prenatal period and infancy, the adolescent brain's role in adolescent risk taking, and the aging brain's compensation for decline
- Inclusion of theories of why we age and die and the nature-nurture issues they raise, including contributors to longevity among long-lived people
- More in-depth coverage of life-span health issues, especially of obesity as a major health concern

Chapter 6. Sensation, Perception, and Action

- Revised chapter now titled "Sensation, Perception, and Action" uses Gibson's ecological theory of perception to focus on synergistic relationships between perception and action.
- Material on motor development and the dynamic systems approach, formerly covered in Chapter 5, is now integrated in this chapter
- Coverage of vision in both infancy and adulthood has been significantly reorganized and updated

Chapter 7. Cognition

- Continues to cover the classic theories of Piaget and Vygotsky but adds Fischer's dynamic skill theory as a modern perspective that incorporates elements of both
- Introduces the concept of neuro-constructivism and brain research that fills holes in Piaget's explanation of cognitive development

Chapter 8. Memory and Information Processing

- Updated model of information processing reflecting current understandings of working memory
- A look at the neural bases of memory

Chapter 9. Intelligence and Creativity

- Expanded coverage of Sternberg's theory of successful intelligence
- Recent research on creativity, including the investment model of creativity

Chapter 10. Language and Education

- Integration of research on language into each of the age sections
- Research on the benefits of bilingualism

- Revamped coverage of research on education to focus more on the learner's perspective
- A closer look at how the brain changes in response to experience with language and education

Chapter 11. Self and Personality

- Expanded illustrations of differences in personality and self-concept in individualistic versus collectivist societies, including cultural differences in toddler self-recognition
- Use of Holland's influential person-environment fit model in discussing vocational choice
- New section on unemployment and its impacts on development
- More on gender differences in career development

Chapter 12. Gender Roles and Sexuality

- The latest research on sexuality across the lifespan
- Updated coverage of gender differences in media and technology use
- Discussion of how (and why) gender roles have changed in recent decades
- More on the interplay of genetic and environmental factors as they affect sexual and gender development

Chapter 13. Social Cognition and Moral Development

- New focus on the issue of whether human nature is basically prosocial or antisocial
- Exciting research by Michael Tomasello and others on early prosocial behavior as well as research on infant antisocial behavior
- Box on Mischel's famous "marshmallow study" on delay of gratification and the significance of early self-control for later development
- Coverage of bullying and its prevention
- Exploration of the positive youth development movement

Chapter 14. Emotions, Attachment, and Social Relationships

- New section on emotional development across the life span, including research on early emotions, cultural display rules, emotion regulation in adolescence, and emotional well-being in old age
- More on adolescent peer relations and dating, with attention to the different meanings of popularity and the role of relational aggression in peer relationships
- New research on the adaptiveness of different attachment styles in later life.

Chapter 15. The Family

- New box on Amy Chua, the Chinese "Tiger Mother," and the role of cultural context in defining good parenting
- Updates on changes in the American family, including new figures showing trends
- Discussion of likely effects of the Great Recession of 2008 on family life
- Updates on fathers—both those who are more involved than ever and those who are missing in action
- More on cohabitation and why it does not predict a more successful marriage

Chapter 16. Developmental Psychopathology

- Changes in diagnosis of psychological disorders associated with DSM-5, the 2013 *Diagnostic and Statistical Manual of Mental Disorders*
- Inclusion of ADHD from a life-span perspective
- New research on how genes and female hormones, not just social pressures, may contribute to the rise in eating disorders among females at puberty
- Introduction of the issue of socialization versus selection in the study of peer influence (that is, whether peers truly influence adolescents' behavior or adolescents merely select peers whose behavior matches their own)
- New table on leading forms of dementia (neurocognitive disorders) and updates on this critical topic in aging

Chapter 17. The Final Challenge: Death and Dying

- New research on attitudes toward euthanasia and other end-of-life interventions
- Box on higher mental functioning in some individuals presumed to lack consciousness
- New research on adolescents whose parents have died
- The concept of posttraumatic growth
- New research on the benefits of palliative care

Chapter Organization

The chapters of this book use a consistent format and contain the following:

- A chapter outline that orients students to what lies ahead
- A chapter opener that engages student interest
- Introductory material that lays out the plan for the chapter and introduces key concepts, theories, and issues relevant to the area of development to be explored
- Learning objectives at the start of each major numbered section
- Developmental sections (in Chapters 5–17) that describe and explain key changes and continuities during four developmental periods: infancy, childhood, adolescence, and adulthood

- Checking Mastery and Making Connections questions after each major section challenge students to test their understanding of the chapter material and to think about or apply it in new ways
- A Chapter Summary at the end of each chapter reviewing the chapter's main messages
- A Key Terms section listing new terms introduced in the chapter in the order in which they were introduced and with the page number on which they were introduced. These terms are printed in boldface, defined when they are first presented in a chapter, and included in the glossary at the end of the book

Supplements

The eighth edition of *Life-Span Human Development* is accompanied by a better array of supplements prepared for both the instructor and the student to create the best learning environment inside and outside the classroom. All the supplements have been thoroughly revised and updated. Especially noteworthy are the media and Internet-based supplements. We invite instructors and students to examine and take advantage of the teaching and learning tools available.

For the Instructor

Online Instructor's Manual with Test Bank. This manual contains chapter-specific outlines; a list of print, video, and online resources; and student learning objectives. The manual has a special emphasis on active learning with suggested student activities and projects for each chapter. The test bank, in computerized form, consists of approximately 135 multiple-choice, 20 true/false, 20 completion, and 10 essay questions for each chapter. Questions are marked with the correct answer, textbook section reference, and difficulty and are keyed to the Learning Objectives. ISBN-10: 1285454391; ISBN-13: 9781285454399

Online Powerpoint Slides. Microsoft® PowerPoint® lecture slides with graphics from the text allow you to bring together text-specific lecture outlines and art from the text or your own materials—culminating in a powerful, personalized, media-enhanced presentation. ISBN-10: 1285855442; ISBN-13: 9781285855448

For the Student

Internet-Based Supplements

MindTap for *Life-Span Human Development* puts everything you need for class in one, easy to navigate place. MindTap includes an integrated eBook, assignments, practice quizzes, videos, and more, all designed to help you be a more successful student. MindTap for *Life-Span Human Development* can be purchased at www.cengagebrain.com.

Instant Access Code:
ISBN-10: 1-285-74906-5   ISBN-13: 978-1-285-74906-8
Printed Access Card:
ISBN-10: 1-285-74897-2,   ISBN-13: 978-1-285-74897-9

Acknowledgments

We would like to express our continuing debt to David Shaffer of the University of Georgia for allowing his child development textbook to inform the first and second editions of this book.

Credit for excellent supplementary materials goes to Bradley Caskey, who revised the *Instructor's Manual with Test Bank*.

Producing this book required the joint efforts of Cengage Learning and PreMedia Global. We thank our editor, Jaime Perkins, for his leadership of the project, and Barbara Armentrout, our development editor, for her thoughtful readings of each chapter and superb efforts to make this edition the most visually appealing and pedagogically effective edition yet. We thank Sandra Mercado at PreMedia Global for outstanding management of the book's production and Mrudula Ganeshan and Carly Bergey for photo research. We are grateful, as well, for the able assistance of Rita Jaramillo, production project manager; Jennifer Wahi, art director; Roberta Broyer, rights acquisition specialist; Mary Noel and Audrey Espey, media developers; and Paige Leeds, content coordinator. We also appreciate the strong support of Angeline Lowe, marketing coordinator.

We remain deeply indebted to sponsoring editors past—to C. Deborah Laughton, who insisted that this project be undertaken, and to Vicki Knight, who skillfully shepherded the first edition through its final stages and oversaw the second edition. Finally, Katie Thompson deserves great thanks for her help with referencing, and Corby Rider deserves appreciation for his support and understanding of his workaholic mother.

Reviewers

We are very grateful to eight "cohorts" of reviewers for the constructive criticism and great suggestions that have helped us make each edition of this book better than the one before:

Barinder Bahvra, *Macomb Community College*
David Beach, *University of Wisconsin–Parkside*
Howard Bierenbaum, *College of William & Mary*
Fredda Blanchard-Fields, *Louisiana State University*
Cheryl Bluestone, *Queensborough Community College*
Tracie Blumentritt, *University of Wisconsin La Crosse*
Denise Ann Bodman, *Arizona State University*
Bob Bornstein, *Miami University–Oxford*
Janet Boseovski, *University of North Carolina at Greensboro*
Kim G. Brenneman, *Eastern Mennonite University*
Donna Brent, *Hartwick College*
Mary Ann Bush, *Western Michigan University*
Elaine H. Cassel, *Lord Fairfax Community College*
Yiwei Chen, *Bowling Green State University*
Bonny K. Dillon, *Bluefield College*

David R. Donnelly, *Monroe Community College, Rochester*
Shelley Drazen, *Binghamton University (SUNY)*
Michelle R. Dunlap, *Connecticut College*
Marion Eppler, *East Carolina University*
Dan Florell, *Eastern Kentucky University*
James N. Forbes, *Angelo State University*
Claire Ford, *Bridgewater State College*
Carie Forden, *Clarion University*
Jody S. Fournier, *Capital University*
Janet Fritz, *Colorado State University*
Rebecca J. Glover, *University of North Texas*
Cheryl Hale, *Jefferson College*
Charles Harris, *James Madison University*
Karen Hartlep, *California State University at Bakersfield*
Christina Hawkey, *Arizona Western College*
Jay E. Hillis, *Bevill State Community College, Brewer*
Debra L. Hollister, *Valencia Community College*
Amy Holmes, *Davidson County Community College*
Stephen Hoyer, *Pittsburg State University*
Malia Huchendorf, *Normandale Community College*
David P. Hurford, *Pittsburg State University*
Vivian Jenkins, *University of Southern Indiana*
Wayne G. Joosse, *Calvin College*
John Klein, *Castleton State College*
Franz Klutschkowski, *North Central Texas College*
Jim Korcuska, *University of San Diego*
Suzanne Krinsky, *University of Southern Colorado*
Brett Laursen, *Florida Atlantic University*
Sherry Loch, *Paradise Valley Community College*
Becky White Loewy, *San Francisco State University*
Rosanne Lorden, *Eastern Kentucky University*
Carolyn Cass Lorente, *Northern Virginia Community College, Alexandria*
Nancy Macdonald, *University of South Carolina–Sumter*
Susan Magun-Jackson, *University of Memphis*
Robert F. Marcus, *University of Maryland*

Gabriela A. Martorell, *Portland State University*
Rebecca Kang McGill, *Temple University*
Russell Miars, *Portland State University*
Ann K. Mullis, *Florida State University*
Ronald L. Mullis, *Florida State University*
Bridget C. Murphy-Kelsey, *Metropolitan State College*
Susan L. O'Donnell, *George Fox University*
Shirley M. Ogletree, *Southwest Texas State University*
Jim O'Neill, *Wayne State University*
Rob Palkovitz, *University of Delaware*
Suzanne Pasch, *University of Wisconsin at Milwaukee*
Louise Perry, *Florida Atlantic University*
Sharon Presley, *California State University East Bay*
Mark Rafter, *College of the Canyons*
Lakshmi Raman, *Oakland University*
Marjorie Reed, *Oregon State University*
Elizabeth Rhodes, *Florida International University*
Eileen Rogers, *University of Texas at San Antonio*
Mark Runco, *California State University at Fullerton*
Pamela Schuetze, *Buffalo State College*
Matt Scullin, *West Virginia University*
Lisa Sethre-Hofstad, *Concordia College*
Timothy Shearon, *Albertson College of Idaho*
Dawn Taylor-Wright, *Meridian Community College*
Luis Terrazas, *California State University at San Marcos*
Brooke Thompson, *Gardner-Webb University*
Polly Trnavsky, *Appalachian State University*
Katherine Van Giffen, *California State University at Long Beach*
Nancy L. Voorhees, *Ivy Tech Community College, Lafayette*
Catherine Weir, *Colorado College*
Kyle Weir, *California State University at Fresno*
Diane E. Wille, *Indiana University - Southeast*
Ruth Wilson, *Idaho State University*
Robin Yaure, *Penn State Mont Alto*

CAROL K. SIGELMAN is professor of psychology at George Washington University, where she also served as an associate vice president for 13 years. She earned her bachelor's degree from Carleton College and a double-major doctorate in English and psychology from George Peabody College for Teachers, now part of Vanderbilt University. She has been on the faculty at Texas Tech University, Eastern Kentucky University (where she won her college's outstanding teacher award), and the University of Arizona. She has taught courses in child, adolescent, adult, and life-span development and has published research on such topics as the communication skills of individuals with developmental disabilities, the development of stigmatizing reactions to children and adolescents who are different, and children's emerging understandings of diseases and psychological disorders. She is a Fellow of the Association for Psychological Science. For fun, she enjoys hiking, biking, and discovering good movies.

ELIZABETH A. RIDER is professor of psychology and associate provost at Elizabethtown College in Pennsylvania. She has also been on the faculty at the University of North Carolina at Asheville. She earned her undergraduate degree from Gettysburg College and her doctorate from Vanderbilt University. She has taught courses on child and life-span development, women and gender issues, applied developmental psychology, and genetic and environmental influences on development. She has published research on children's and adults' spatial perception, orientation, and ability to find their way. Through a grant from the Pennsylvania State System for Higher Education, she studied factors associated with academic success. The second edition of her text on the psychology of women, *Our Voices*, was published by John Wiley & Sons in 2005. When she is not working, her life revolves around her son and a fun-loving springer spaniel.

Sigelman

Life-Span Human Development, 8e

1 Understanding Life-Span Human Development

John Tatum thought he might be losing his edge, but he won three gold medals in swimming at the 2009 National Senior Games, competing for the first time in the 90–94 age group and avoiding head-to-head competition with his spry younger brother Brad, who snared five medals in the 85–89 age group (Hallett, 2009). They were among the 300,000 athletes age 50 and older who participate in the National Senior Games every 2 years—and yes, they were at it again in 2011, featured in a documentary film about the games.

John had always loved sports, starting when he and his brother had to teach themselves to swim in the Potomac River because city swimming pools were closed to blacks (Buerger, 2011). After retiring, he and his brother joined a senior swim team, swimming at least 2 hours three times a week, with workouts in between.

John grew up in Washington and remembers playing on the Lincoln Memorial just after it was built in 1922 (Parker, 2008). He attended segregated schools and served in an all-black regiment during World War II. He wanted to be a frogman (a combat diver or swimmer) but was told he could not because he was black, so he became a computer systems analyst with the Navy. He married in 1944 and had six children with his wife, Pearl. Pearl died of pancreatic cancer in 1978, but John has coped well with the challenge of caring for her and felt that he had done all he could (Parker, 2008). He suffered further blows when a daughter and a son both died of cancer in the early 1990s. He knows he's in excellent shape for a 90-year-old and he's determined to win: "None of this sappy 'for the team' stuff. We want medals, preferably gold ones" (Buerger, 2011, p. 19). But Brad recently had a bout with cancer, and John knows that he won't last forever either.

John Tatum, left, and his brother Brad at the National Senior Games.

Documentary Foundation

- how infants perceive the world,
- how preschool children think,
- how life events such as divorce affect a child's adjustment and later romantic relationships,
- why some college students have more trouble than others deciding on a major,
- whether most adults experience a midlife crisis, and
- how people typically change physically, mentally, and emotionally as they age.

We will also take on even more fundamental questions: How in the world does a single fertilized egg cell turn into a unique human being like John Tatum? And how can we use knowledge of the genetic and environmental forces that shape development to optimize it?

Do any of these questions intrigue you? Probably so, because we are all developing persons interested in ourselves and the other developing people around us. Most college students want to understand how they and those they know have been affected by their experiences, how they have changed over the years, and where they may be headed. Many students also have practical motivations for learning about human development—for example, a desire to be a good parent or to pursue a career as a psychologist, nurse, teacher, or other human services professional.

This introductory chapter lays the groundwork for the remainder of the book by addressing some basic questions: How should we think about development and the influences on it? What is the science of life-span development? How is development studied? And what are some of the special challenges in studying human development?

This book is about the development of humans like John Tatum—and you—from conception to death. Like any life, the life of John Tatum raises questions: Was his extraordinary physical fitness at age 90 mainly a matter of good genes, or was it the result of a life of physical activity and hours in the pool? What changes in physical functioning and fitness does aging entail, and are they inevitable? Going in a different direction, how were John and others of his generation affected by growing up black in a society that openly discriminated against them? And what allows some people to cope better than others with negative life events such as the death of a spouse or child?

We address questions like these and more in this book. Among other things, we'll ask

1.1 How Should We Think about Development?

LEARNING OBJECTIVES:

- Define development, aging, and their relationship to each other.

- Explain and illustrate the role played by age grades, age norms, and the social clock in making human development different in different historical, cultural, and subcultural contexts.

- Summarize the extreme positions one can take on the "nature–nurture" issue and the position most developmental scientists today take.

We begin by asking what it means to say that humans "develop" or "age" over the life span, how we can conceptualize the life span, and how we can approach the single biggest issue in the study of development, the nature–nurture issue, and understand developing humans in their ever-changing environments.

Defining Development

Development can be defined as systematic changes and continuities in the individual that occur between conception and death, or from "womb to tomb." By describing developmental changes as systematic, we imply that they are orderly, patterned, and relatively enduring—not fleeting and unpredictable like mood swings. The changes can be gains, losses, or just differences from what we were like before. Development also involves continuities, ways in which we remain the same or continue to reflect our past selves.

The systematic changes and continuities of interest to students of human development fall into three broad domains:

1. *Physical development.* The growth of the body and its organs, the functioning of physiological systems including the brain, physical signs of aging, changes in motor abilities, and so on.

2. *Cognitive development.* Changes and continuities in perception, language, learning, memory, problem solving, and other mental processes.
3. *Psychosocial development.* Changes and carryover in personal and interpersonal aspects of development, such as motives, emotions, personality traits, interpersonal skills and relationships, and roles played in the family and in the larger society.

Even though developmentalists often specialize in one of these three aspects of development, they appreciate that humans are whole beings and that changes in one area affect the others. The baby who develops the ability to crawl, for example, has new opportunities to develop her mind by exploring kitchen cabinets and to hone her social skills by trailing her parents from room to room. And for John Tatum, introduced at the start of the chapter, exercise through swimming may have sharpened his cognitive skills and enriched his social interactions.

How would you portray, as a line on a graph, typical changes from birth to old age? Many people picture tremendous positive gains in capacity from infancy to young adulthood, a flat line reflecting little change during early adulthood and middle age, and a steep decline of capacities in the later years. This stereotyped view of the life span is largely false, but it also has some truth in it, especially with respect to biological development. Traditionally, biologists have defined **growth** as the physical changes that occur from conception to maturity. We indeed become biologically mature and physically competent during the early part of the life span. **Biological aging** is the deterioration of organisms (including humans) that leads inevitably to their death. Biologically, then, development *does* involve growth in early life, stability in early and middle adulthood, and decline associated with now-accumulated effects of aging in later life.

Many aspects of development do not follow this "gain–stability–loss" model, however. Modern developmental scientists have come to appreciate that developmental change at any age involves both gains and losses. For example, although children gain many cognitive abilities as they get older, they also lose self-esteem and become more prone to **depression** (Gotlib & Hammen, 2002; Robins et al., 2002). Nor should we associate aging only with loss: Adults aged 60 and older score higher on vocabulary tests than adults aged 18–30 (Verhaeghen, 2003); some cognitive abilities and types of knowledge and expertise hold steady or even grow during adulthood (Ackerman, 2008; Alexander, Murphy, & Kulikowich, 2009). At age 68, gerontologist Margaret Cruikshank (2009) conveyed the positives of aging this way: "Decline is thought to be the main theme of aging, and yet for many old age is a time of ripening, of becoming most ourselves" (p. 207).

In addition, people do not always improve or worsen but instead just become different than they were (as when a child who once feared loud noises comes to fear hairy monsters under the bed instead). Development clearly means more than positive growth during infancy, childhood, and adolescence. And **aging,** as developmental scientists define it, involves more than biological aging (Ryff & Singer, 2009); it refers to a range of physical, cognitive, and psychosocial changes, *positive and negative,* in

the mature organism (Overton, 2010). In short, development involves gains, losses, neutral changes, and continuities in each phase of the life span, growth and aging are part of it.

Conceptualizing the Life Span

If you were to divide the human life span into periods, how would you do it?

● **Table 1.1** lists the periods that many of today's developmentalists regard as distinct. You will want to keep them in mind as you read this book, because we will constantly be speaking of infants, preschoolers, school-age children, adolescents, emerging adults, and young, middle-aged, and older adults. Note, however, that the given ages are approximate. Age is only a rough indicator of developmental status. Improvements in standards of living and health, for example, have meant that today's 65-year-olds are not as "old" physically, cognitively, or psychosocially as 65-year-olds a few decades ago were. There are also huge differences in functioning and personality among individuals of the same age; while some adults are bedridden at age 90, others like John Tatum are out swimming laps.

The most recent addition to this list of periods of the life span—the one you may not have heard of—is **emerging adulthood,** a transitional period between adolescence and full-fledged adulthood that extends from about age 18 to age 25 (maybe as late as 29). After World War II, it started taking youth longer to get to adulthood and its roles and responsibilities than it had in earlier eras as more adolescents began to attend college in large numbers to prepare for work and to postpone marriage and

● **Table 1.1** An Overview of Periods of the Life Span

Period of Life	Age Range
Prenatal period	Conception to birth
Infancy	First 2 years of life (the first month is the neonatal or newborn period)
Preschool period	2–5 or 6 years (some prefer to describe as *toddlers* children who have begun to walk and are age 1–3)
Middle childhood	6 to about 10 (or until the onset of puberty)
Adolescence	Approximately 10–18 (or from puberty to when the individual becomes relatively independent)
Emerging adulthood	18–25 or even later (transitional period between adolescence and adulthood)
Early adulthood	25–40 years (adult roles are established)
Middle adulthood	40–65 years
Late adulthood	65 years and older (some break out subcategories such as the young-old, old-old, and very old based on differences in functioning)

© Cengage Learning

What periods of the life span do these four females, representing four generations of the same family, fall in? What periods of the life span do you distinguish?

parenthood in the process (Furstenberg et al., 2004; Keniston, 1970). As a result, psychologist Jeffrey Arnett and others began to describe emerging adulthood as a distinct phase of the life span, in developed countries anyway, in which youth must spend years getting educated and accumulating wealth in order to make it as adults (Arnett, 2000, 2011; Arnett & Tanner, 2006; Tanner, Arnett, & Leis, 2009). According to Arnett, emerging adults (maybe you?):

- explore their identities;
- lead unstable lives filled with job changes, new relationships, and moves;
- are self-focused, relatively free of obligations to others, and therefore free to focus on their own psychological needs;
- feel in between—adultlike in some ways but not others; and
- believe they have limitless possibilities ahead (Arnett, 2000; Arnett & Tanner, 2006).

Not everyone agrees that emerging adulthood is a truly distinct period of development (Epstein, 2013), but it is clear that adolescents in modern societies are taking longer and longer to become adults. Do you view yourself as an adult? Why or why not? Sociologist Frank Furstenberg and his colleagues (2004) looked at five traditional, objective markers of adulthood: completing an education, being financially independent, leaving home, marrying, and having children. In 1960, 65% of men and 77% of women had achieved these milestones by age 30. By 2000, only 31% of 30-year-old men and 46% of 30-year-old women in the United States had achieved them.

Cultural Differences

Table 1.1 represents only one view of the periods of the life span. Age—like gender, race, and other significant human characteristics—means different things in different societies (Fry, 2009). Each society has its own ways of dividing the life span and of treating the people in different age groups. Each socially defined age group in a society—called an **age grade**

or age stratum—is assigned different statuses, roles, privileges, and responsibilities. Separating children into grades in school based on age is one form of age grading. Just as high schools have "elite" seniors and "lowly" freshmen, whole societies are layered into age grades.

Our society, for example, grants "adults" (18-year-olds by law in the United States) a voting privilege not granted to children. Legal definitions of the boundary between adolescence and adulthood vary, though. In most states in the United States, the legal age for marrying is lower than the legal age for voting or serving in the military, and the right to drink alcohol is granted last, commonly at age 21 (Settersten, 2005). Similarly, although we seem to define age 65 as the boundary between middle age and old age, in fact the ages at which people become eligible for Medicare, Social Security benefits, and "senior discounts" at restaurants and stores differ—and may change over time.

We define old age as age 65 or older, but the !Kung San of Botswana often don't know people's chronological ages and define old age instead in terms of functioning (Rosenberg, 2009). They distinguish between the *na* or "old" (an honorary title meaning big and great granted to all older people starting at around age 50); the "old/dead" (older but still able to function); and the "old to the point of helplessness," who are ailing and need care. The St. Lawrence Eskimo simply distinguish between boys and men (or between girls and women), whereas the Arusha people of East Africa devised six socially meaningful age grades for males: youths, junior warriors, senior warriors, junior elders, senior elders, and retired elders (Keith, 1985). In certain other cultures, the recognized periods of the life span include a period before birth and an afterlife, or the life span may be pictured as a circle that includes reincarnation or some other way of being "recycled" and born again (Fry, 1985; Kojima, 2003).

Cultures differ not only in the age grades they recognize but in how they mark the transition from one age grade to another (Fry, 2009). A **rite of passage** is a ritual that marks a person's "passage" from one status to another, usually in reference to the transition from childhood to adulthood. Rites of passage can involve such varied practices as body painting, circumcision, instruction by elders in adult sexual practices, tests of physical prowess, and gala celebrations (see Kottak, 2009). As the photo on the next page illustrates, Japan's rite of passage for 20-year-olds makes clear to all that they are now adults.

In the West, Jewish youth experience a clear rite of passage when they have their *bar* or *bat mitzvahs*, and 15-year-old Hispanic American girls in some communities participate in a *quinceañera* (meaning "fifteen years ceremony") to signify that they have become women. Unfortunately, one of the clearest rites of passage for adolescents in our society is a night of binge drinking at age 21. In one study, four of five college students reported that they drank on their 21st birthday to celebrate—12% of them an extremely dangerous 21 drinks (Rutledge, Park, & Sher, 2008). Perhaps because we lack a clear, society-wide rite of passage like Japan's, adolescents in our society end up less sure than adolescents in many other societies when they are adults.

Each January 15 in Japan, 20-year-olds are officially pronounced adults in a national celebration and enter a new age grade. Young women receive kimonos, young men receive suits, and all are reminded of their responsibilities to society. Young adults also gain the right to drink, smoke, and vote. The modern ceremony grew out of an ancient one in which young samurai became recognized as warriors (Reid, 1993). The age-grading system in Japanese culture clearly marks the beginning of adulthood with this rite of passage.

Once a society has established age grades, it defines what people should and should not do at different points in the life span (Elder & Shanahan, 2006). According to pioneering gerontologist Bernice Neugarten and her colleagues (Neugarten, Moore, & Lowe, 1965), these expectations, or **age norms**, are society's way of telling people how to act their age. In our culture, for example, most people agree that 6-year-olds are too young to date or drink beer but are old enough to attend school. We also tend to agree that adults should think about marrying around age 25 (although in some segments of society earlier or later is better) and should retire around age 65 (Neugarten, Moore, & Lowe, 1965; Settersten, 1998). In less industrialized countries, age norms often call for having children in one's teens and stopping work earlier than 65 in response to illness and disability (Shanahan, 2000).

Why are age norms important? First, they influence people's decisions about how to lead their lives. They are the basis for what Neugarten (1968) called the **social clock**—a person's sense of when things should be done and when he or she is ahead of or behind the schedule dictated by age norms. Prompted by the social clock, for example, an unmarried 30-year-old may feel that he should propose to his girlfriend before she gives up on him, or a 70-year-old who loves her job may feel she should start planning for retirement. Second, age norms affect how easily people adjust to life transitions. Normal life events such as having children typically tend to affect us more negatively when they occur "off time" than when they occur "on time," at socially appropriate ages (McLanahan & Sorensen, 1985). It can be challenging to experience puberty at either age 8 or age 18 or to become a new parent at 13 or 45. However, as Neugarten could see even in the 1960s, age norms in our society have been weakening for

some time. It's less clear now what one should be doing at what age and so people do things like marry and retire at a wide range of ages (Settersten & Trauten, 2009). Witness Madonna adopting a child at 50 and Elton John becoming a first-time father at 62 (Mayer, 2011).

Subcultural Differences

Age grades, age norms, and social clocks differ not only from **culture** to culture but also from subculture to subculture. Our own society is diverse with respect to race and **ethnicity,** or people's classification or affiliation with a group based on common heritage or traditions; and **socioeconomic status (SES),** or standing in society based on such indicators as occupational prestige, education, and income. African American, Hispanic American, Native American, Asian American, and European American individuals, and individuals of high and low SES, sometimes have quite different developmental experiences. Within these broad groups, of course, there are immense variations associated with a host of other factors. We must be careful not to overgeneralize.

Age norms tend to be different in higher-SES and lower-SES communities, and individuals from lower-income families tend to reach milestones of adulthood such as starting work, marrying, and having children earlier (Elder & Shanahan, 2006; Mollborn, 2009). When sociologist Linda Burton (1990, 1996) studied a low-SES African American community, she found it was common for young women to become mothers at about age 16—earlier than in most middle-class communities, white or black. Teenage mothers in this community looked to their own mothers and grandmothers to help them care for their children. Meanwhile, children were asked to grow up fast; they often tended younger siblings and helped their mothers with household tasks (Burton, 2007). Although age norms in middle-class communities in the United States call for postponing parenthood (Mollborn, 2009), it is not at all unusual in cultures around the world for females to become mothers in their teens and for grandmothers and older children to help them with child care responsibilities (Ochs & Izquierdo, 2009; Rogoff, 2003).

Perhaps the most important message about subcultural differences in development is that, regardless of race and ethnicity, poverty can be damaging to human development. In 2010, 15% of the U. S. population—but 22% of its children—lived below the poverty line, then $22,314 for a family of four (Macartney, 2011). Closer to one out of three African American and Hispanic American children are poor. Parents and children living in poverty experience more stress than higher-SES parents and children owing to noise, crowding, family disruption, hunger, exposure to violence, and other factors (Evans & Kim, 2012; Heymann, Penrose, & Earle, 2006; Huston & Bentley, 2010). And on average, although there are many exceptions, parents coping with poverty tend to provide less stable, stimulating, and supportive home environments than wealthier parents do (Bornstein & Bradley, 2003; and see Chapter 15). As a result, the developmental experiences and trajectories of children who grow up in poverty and children who grow up in affluence are significantly different. The damaging effects of poverty show themselves in lower academic achievement, poorer mental health and well-being, and even poorer physical health many years later (Aber, Morris, & Raver, 2012; Conger & Donnellan, 2007; Evans & Kim, 2012).

Historical Changes

The nature and meanings of periods of the life span also change from one historical period to another. In Europe and North America, they have changed along these lines:

- *Childhood.* Not until the 17th century in Western cultures did children come to be viewed as distinctly different from adults, as innocents to be protected and nurtured. In medieval Europe (A.D. 500–1500), for example, 6-year-olds were dressed in miniature versions of adult clothing, treated to some extent as "miniature adults" (Ariès, 1962), and expected to contribute to the family's survival as soon as possible (Cunningham, 1996; Hanawalt, 2003).

Although medieval children were pressured to abandon their childish ways as soon as possible and were dressed like miniature adults, it is doubtful that they were really viewed as miniature adults. Still, the modern concept of children as innocents to be nurtured and protected did not begin to take hold until the 17th century.

© Henry Lillie Pierce Fund/Museum of Fine Arts, Boston

- *Adolescence.* Not until the late 19th century and early 20th century was **adolescence**—the transitional period between childhood and adulthood that begins with puberty and involves significant physical, cognitive, and psychosocial changes—recognized as a distinct phase of the life span (Hine, 1999; Kett, 1977). As industrialization advanced, an educated labor force was needed, so laws were passed restricting child labor, making schooling compulsory, and separating youths attending school from the adult world (Furstenberg, 2000).

- *Emerging adulthood.* As you saw earlier, the transition period from childhood to adulthood has become so long in modern societies that a new period of the life span, *emerging adulthood*, has been defined in the late 20th and early 21st centuries.

- *Middle age.* Not until the 20th century did our society begin to define a period of middle age in which the nest is emptied of children. This distinct life phase emerged as 20th-century parents began to bear fewer children and live long enough to see their children grow up and leave home (Moen & Wethington, 1999). Sometimes characterized as a time of "crisis," sometimes as a time of hardly any change, middle age is now understood to be a time of good health, peak cognitive functioning, stable relationships, many responsibilities, and high satisfaction for most people (Whitbourne & Willis, 2006).

- *Old age.* Not until the 20th century did our society come to define old age as a period of retirement. There were not many old people in early eras, and they were not as healthy as old people today. Those who did survive to old age literally worked until they dropped. Starting in the last half of the 20th century, thanks to Social Security, pensions, Medicare, and other support programs, working adults began to retire in their 60s with many years ahead of them (Schulz & Binstock, 2006).

What will the life span look like in the future? In the early 21st century, the average **life expectancy** for a newborn in the United States—the average number of years a newborn who is born now can be expected to live—is 78 years, compared with 47 years in 1900 (National Center for Health Statistics, 2011). Life expectancy is 81 for a white female, 77 for a black female, 76 for a white male, and 70 for a black male. Overall, more and more people are reaching older and older ages in better health and with fewer disabilities (Kinsella, 2009; Satariano, 2006).

By 2030, when most members of the baby boom generation will have retired, adults 65 and older will represent not the 13% of the U.S. population they represent today but more like 20% (Satariano, 2006). As a result, an increasingly large group of elderly people will depend on a smaller generation of younger, working adults to support them (Wilmoth & Longino, 2006). Although these elders will be healthier, wealthier, and better educated than the generations that preceded them, they will also need a lot of services—and health and mental health professionals trained in aging to serve them—as more of them reach very old ages (Schaie, 2011; Schulz & Binstock, 2006; Treas & Hill, 2009). How will policy makers address these issues? Conflict between the generations over resources and resentful attitudes toward aging adults could become problems (North & Fiske, 2012).

Today's older adults are healthier, wealthier, and more educated than older adults of previous generations. However, as more of them reach advanced ages, they will need more services from people trained in gerontology and geriatrics.

This "graying of America," and indeed of the world's population, along with societal changes we cannot yet anticipate, will make the aging experience by the end of the 21st century different than it is today.

In sum, age—whether it is 7, 17, or 70—has had different meanings in different historical eras and most likely will mean something different in the 21st century than it did in the 20th. The broader message is clear: *We must view development in its historical, cultural, and subcultural context*. We must bear in mind that each social group settles on its own definitions of the life span, the age grades within it, and the age norms appropriate to each age range, and that each social group experiences development differently. We must also appreciate that in Western cultures it was only in the 17th century that children came to be seen as innocents; in the late 19th century that adolescence emerged as a distinct phase; and in the 20th century that our society recognized emerging adulthood, a middle-aged "empty nest" period, and an old age characterized by retirement. One of the most fascinating challenges in the study of human development is to understand which aspects of development are universal and which differ across social and historical contexts—and why (Norenzayan & Heine, 2005; Shweder et al., 2006).

Framing the Nature–Nurture Issue

Understanding human development means grappling with *the* major issue in the study of human development—the **nature–nurture issue,** or the question of how biological forces and environmental forces act and interact to make us what we are (see Goldhaber, 2012). We raised a nature–nurture question at the start of the chapter by asking whether 90-year-old John Tatum's swimming prowess was mainly attributable to good genes or good training, and we will highlight this central and always fascinating issue throughout this book.

Nature

On the nature side of the debate are those who emphasize the influence of heredity, universal maturational processes guided by the genes, biologically based or innate predispositions produced by evolution, and biological influences such as hormones and neurotransmitters. To those who emphasize nature, some aspects of development are inborn or innate, others are the product of **maturation,** the biological unfolding of the individual according to a blueprint contained in the **genes** (the hereditary material passed from parents to child at conception). Just as seeds turn into mature plants through a predictable process, humans "unfold" within the womb (assuming that they receive the necessary nourishment from their environment). Their genetic blueprint then makes it likely that they will walk and utter their first words at about 1 year of age, achieve sexual maturity between 12 and 14, and gray in their 40s and 50s. Maturational changes in the brain contribute to cognitive changes such as increased memory and problem-solving skills and to psychosocial changes such as increased understanding of other people's feelings. Genetically influenced maturational processes guide all of us through many of the same developmental changes at about the same points in our lives. Meanwhile, *individual* hereditary endowment is making each person's development unique.

Nurture

On the nurture side of the nature–nurture debate are those who emphasize change in response to **environment**—all the external physical and social conditions, stimuli, and events that can affect us, from crowded living quarters and polluted air, to social interactions with family members, peers, and teachers, to the neighborhood and broader cultural context in which we develop. We know that the physical environment matters—for example, that exposure to lead in the paint in old buildings can stunt children's intellectual development or that living near a noisy airport can interfere with their progress in learning to read (Evans, 2006). And we will see countless examples in this book of how the social environment—the behavior of other people—shapes development. Rather than seeing biological maturation as the process driving development, those on the nurture side of the nature–nurture debate emphasize **learning**—the process through which experience brings about relatively permanent changes in thoughts, feelings, or behavior. A certain degree of maturation is clearly necessary before a child can dribble a basketball, but careful instruction and long, hard hours of practice are just as clearly required if the child is to excel in basketball.

Nature plus Nurture

If nature is important in development, we would expect all children to have basically similar inborn capacities and to achieve similar developmental milestones at similar times because of maturation, and we would expect differences among individuals to be largely caused by differences in their genetic makeup. If nurture is important in development, we would generally expect human development to take a variety of pathways depending on each individual's life experiences. (See ● **Table 1.2** for the terms of the nature–nurture debate.)

● Table 1.2 The Language of Nature and Nurture

Nature	Nurture
Heredity	Environment
Maturation	Learning
Genes	Experience
Innate or biologically based predispositions	Cultural influences

© Cengage Learning

Let's settle the nature–nurture debate right now: Developmental changes are the products of a complex interplay between nature and nurture. It is not nature *or* nurture; it is nature *and* nurture (Goldhaber, 2012; Overton, 2010). To make matters more complex, it is nature affecting nurture and nurture affecting nature! For example, biology (nature) provides us with a brain that allows us to learn from our experiences (nurture), experiences that in turn change our brains by altering neural connections and can even change our genes by activating or deactivating them (see Chapter 3). Much of the fascination of studying human development comes from trying to understand more precisely how these two forces combine to make us what we are and become. It is appropriate, then, that we look next at the science of life-span human development and whether it is up to the challenge of answering questions like this.

Checking Mastery

1. How does the concept of aging differ from the concept of biological aging?
2. What is the difference between an age grade and an age norm?

Making Connections

1. Many observers, starting with Bernice Neugarten, believe that age norms for transitions in adult development such as marriage, parenthood, peak career achievement, and retirement have weakened in our society. Do you think such age norms could ever disappear entirely? Why or why not?
2. How might your life and development be different if you had been born in the United States in the late 19th century, before industrialization, rather than in the late 20th century?

1.2 What Is the Science of Life-Span Development?

LEARNING OBJECTIVES:

- Summarize the four goals of the science of life-span development and describe how the study of human development began.

- List and illustrate the seven key assumptions of the modern life-span perspective.

If development consists of systematic changes and continuities from conception to death, the science of development consists of the study of those changes and continuities and their causes. In this section we consider the goals of the science of life-span development, its origins, and the modern life-span perspective on development.

Goals and Uses of Studying Development

The goals driving the study of life-span development are:

> describing,
>
> predicting,
>
> explaining,
>
> and optimizing development (Baltes, Reese, & Lipsitt, 1980).

To achieve the goal of *description*, developmentalists characterize the functioning of humans of different ages and trace how it changes with age. They describe both normal development and individual differences, or variations, in development. Although average trends in human development across the life span can be described, it is clear that no two people (even identical twins) develop along precisely the same pathways.

Description is the starting point in any science, but scientists ultimately strive to achieve their second and third goals, *prediction* and *explanation*. Developmentalists seek to identify factors that predict development and establish that these factors actually cause humans to develop as they typically do or cause some individuals to develop differently than others. To do so, developmentalists often address nature–nurture issues. A first step is often finding a relationship between a possible influence on development and an aspect of development—for example, a relationship between whether or not an adolescent's friends use drugs and whether or not the adolescent does. If there is a relationship, knowing whether an adolescent's friends use drugs allows us to *predict* whether the adolescent uses drugs. But is this a causal relationship? That's what must be established before the goal of *explanation* is achieved. Maybe it's not that friends cause adolescents to use drugs by exposing them to drugs, encouraging them to try drugs, and so on. Maybe it's just that adolescents who use drugs pick friends who also use drugs (see Chapter 16 for evidence that both possibilities may be true).

The fourth goal of developmental science is *optimization* of human development. How can humans be helped to develop in positive directions? How can their capacities be enhanced, how can developmental difficulties be prevented, and how can any developmental problems that emerge be overcome? Pursuing the goal of optimizing development might involve evaluating ways to stimulate intellectual growth in preschool programs, to prevent binge drinking among college students, or to support elderly adults after the death of a spouse.

To those who are or aspire to be teachers, psychologists or counselors, nurses or occupational therapists, or other helping professionals, applied research aimed at optimizing development is especially relevant. Today's educators and human service and health professionals are being asked to engage in **evidence-based practice,** grounding what they do in research and ensuring that the curricula and treatments they provide have been demonstrated to be effective. Too often, these professionals go with what their personal experience tells them works rather than using what scientific research establishes to be the most effective approaches (Baker, McFall, & Shoham, 2009). Ensuring that the results of research are implemented faithfully and successfully in real schools, clinics, and treatment programs is challenging (McCall, 2009; Williams et al., 2012). However, we can all probably agree that we would rather have interventions of proven effectiveness than interventions that are ineffective or even harmful. If you seek a career dedicated to optimizing human development, you might want to consult the Appendix A of this book for information about career options related to life-span human development.

Early Beginnings

Just as human development has changed through the ages, attempts to understand it have evolved over time (Cairns & Cairns, 2006). Although philosophers have long expressed their views on the nature of humans and the proper methods of raising children, it was not until the late 19th century that the first scientific investigations of development were undertaken. Several scholars began to carefully observe the growth and development of their own children and to publish their findings in the form of **baby biographies.** Perhaps the most influential baby biographer was Charles Darwin (1809–1882), who made daily records of his son's development (Darwin, 1877; see also Dewsbury, 2009). Darwin's curiosity about child development stemmed from his interest in evolution. He believed that infants share many characteristics with their nonhuman ancestors and that understanding the development of the embryo and child can offer insights into the evolution of the species. Darwin's evolutionary perspective strongly influenced early theories of human development, which emphasized universal, biologically based maturational changes (Cairns & Cairns, 2006; Parke et al., 1994).

Baby biographies left much to be desired as works of science, however. Because different baby biographers emphasized

Charles Darwin's interest in evolution caused him to be interested in the development of his own children and to write a baby biography.

different aspects of their children's behavior, baby biographies were difficult to compare. Moreover, parents are not entirely objective observers of their own children, and early baby biographers may have let their assumptions about evolution bias their observations. Finally, because each baby biography was based on a single child—often the child of a distinguished family—its findings were not necessarily generalizable to other children.

Darwin greatly influenced the man most often cited as the founder of developmental psychology, G. Stanley Hall (1846–1924), the first president of the American Psychological Association (see Lepore, 2011, for an interesting view of the man). Well aware of the shortcomings of baby biographies, Hall attempted to collect more objective data from larger samples of individuals. He developed a now all-too-familiar research tool—the questionnaire—to explore "the contents of children's minds" at different ages (Hall, 1891).

Hall went on to write an influential book, *Adolescence* (1904). Inspired by Darwin's evolutionary theory, Hall drew parallels between adolescence and the turbulent period in the evolution of human society during which barbarism gave way to modern civilization. Adolescence, then, was a tempestuous period of the life span, a time of emotional ups and downs and rapid changes—a time of what Hall called **storm and stress**. Thus, we have Hall to thank for the notion that most teenagers are emotionally unstable—a largely inaccurate notion, as it turns out (see Chapter 16). Yet as this book will reveal, Hall was right to mark adolescence as a time of dramatic changes.

Hall capped his remarkable career by turning his attention to the end of the life span in *Senescence* (1922), an analysis of how society treats (or, really, mistreats) its older members. He deserves credit for recognizing that aging involves more than just decline (Thompson, 2009). By modern standards, Hall's developmental psychology was limited (Shanahan, Erickson, & Bauer, 2005). Yet he deserves much credit for stimulating scientific research on the entire human life span and for raising many important questions about it.

Developmentalist Paul Baltes is credited with increasing interest in the study of development from a life-span perspective.

Christine Windbichler

The Modern Life-Span Perspective

Although a few early pioneers of the study of human development like G. Stanley Hall viewed all phases of the life span as worthy of study, the science of human development began to break into age-group specialty areas during the 20th century. Some researchers focused on infant or child development, others specialized in adolescence, and still others formed the specialization of **gerontology**, the study of aging and old age. In the 1960s and 1970s, however, a true **life-span perspective** on human development began to emerge. In an influential paper, Paul Baltes (1939–2006) laid out seven key assumptions of the life-span perspective (Baltes, 1987; also see Baltes, Lindenberger, & Staudinger, 1998, 2006, for elaborations). These are important themes that you will see echoed throughout this book. They will also give you a good sense of the challenges facing researchers who study human development.

1. **Development is a lifelong process.** Today's developmentalists appreciate that human development is not just "kid stuff," that we change throughout the life span. They also believe that development in any period of life is best seen in the context of the whole life span. For instance, our understanding of adolescent career choices is bound to be richer if we concern ourselves with how those choices took shape during childhood and how they affect adult career development and success.

2. **Development is multidirectional.** To many pioneers of its study, development was a universal process leading in one direction—toward more "mature" functioning. Today's developmentalists recognize that different capacities show different patterns of change over time; for example, some intellectual abilities decline in late adulthood; some don't change much; and some even continue to improve (see Chapters 7, 8, and 9). Different aspects of human functioning have different trajectories of change.

3. **Development involves both gain and loss.** Building on the theme that development is multidirectional and that it is not all gain in childhood and loss in old age, Baltes maintained that both gain and loss are evident in each phase of the life span. Moreover, he believed that gain inevitably brings with it loss of some kind, and loss brings gain—that gain and loss occur jointly. Examples? As infants gain familiarity with the sounds of the language they hear spoken around them, they lose their ability to discriminate sounds used in other languages of the world (see Chapter 6). Gaining a capacity for logical thought as a school-age child means losing some of the capacity for fanciful, imaginative thinking one had as a preschooler (see Chapter 7). Choosing to hone certain skills in one's career can mean losing command of other skills (see Chapter 11).

4. **Development is characterized by lifelong plasticity.** **Plasticity** refers to the capacity to change in response to experience, whether positive or negative. Developmental scholars have long appreciated that child development can be damaged by a deprived environment and optimized by an enriched one. It is now understood that this plasticity continues into later life—that the aging process is not fixed but rather can be altered considerably depending on the individual's environment and experiences. For example, older adults can maintain or regain some of their intellectual abilities and even enhance them with the help of physical exercise (like John Tatum's swimming), a mentally and socially active lifestyle, or training designed to improve specific cognitive skills (Hertzog et al., 2009; Willis et al., 2006; and see Chapter 9). They may even be able to hold off Alzheimer's disease and other forms of dementia (Verghese et al., 2003). Studies of animals tell us such cognitive benefits are rooted in **neuroplasticity**, the brain's remarkable ability to change in response to experience throughout the life span. It is now clear that physical exercise and mental stimulation can result in changes in neurochemistry, the formation of new

Exploration 1.1

Growing Up Online

How is the adolescent experience affected by the fact that teens today spend many hours a week with everything from videos and email to Facebook, text messaging, Twitter, and Skype? When baby boomers grew up, there were no cell phones or home computers, much less an Internet (for example, Cotten et al., 2011). The Internet came into being in the early 1980s, around the time that home computers were becoming common. Facebook did not exist until 2004; Twitter was launched in 2006. And who knows what new technologies and uses of technologies will emerge next?

How are these technologies affecting human development? Researchers are beginning to address the question. For example, early research suggested that heavy Internet use was turning adolescents into social isolates with few friends and low well-being. However, that may have been because the first adolescent users were surfing the web and talking to strangers in chat rooms (Valkenberg & Peter, 2009). Now that most adolescents use the Internet and use it primarily to communicate with their friends through Facebook and other sites, studies seem to be showing more positive associations between Internet use and social adjustment and well-being; teens today are spending much of their time online talking to friends and disclosing their thoughts and feelings (Valkenberg & Peter, 2007, 2009).

However, the question of the effects of digital media on adolescents is far from resolved. For example, looking at a wide range of media, education professor Roy Pea and his colleagues (2012) found that heavy media use—especially spending large amounts of time watching videos, engaging in online communication, and multitasking by using multiple media at once—was negatively associated with feeling good about one's close relationships and social acceptance, whereas spending more time in face-to-face conversations was positively related to these aspects of social well-being. We have much to learn about how human development is being affected by digital media. In the meantime, maybe there is something to be said for talking to friends the old-fashioned way: offline.

The creation of the Internet is an historical change with many implications for the social lives of teens and for human development more generally.

---

connections among neurons, and, most remarkably, new neurons—even in aging brains (Doidge, 2007; Hertzog et al., 2009; Pereira et al., 2007; and see Chapter 5).

5. **Development is shaped by its historical–cultural context.** This theme was illustrated in Section 1.1 of this chapter and is illustrated beautifully by the pioneering work of sociology and psychology professor Glen Elder and his colleagues. They researched how the Great Depression of the 1930s affected the later life courses and development of the era's children and adolescents (Elder, 1998; Elder, Liker, & Cross, 1984)—work that is now very timely given the many families affected by the economic crisis called the Great Recession that began in 2008 (see Chapter 15). A few years after the stock market crashed in 1929, one of three workers was unemployed and many families were tossed into poverty (Rogler, 2002). Although many families survived the Great Depression nicely, this economic crisis proved to be especially difficult for children if their out-of-work and demoralized fathers became less affectionate and less consistent in disciplining them. When this happened, children displayed behavior problems and had low aspirations and poor records in school. They turned into men who had erratic careers and unstable marriages and women who were seen by their own children as ill tempered. Adolescents generally fared better than children did. Less dependent on their parents than children, adolescents were pushed into working to help support their families and developed a strong sense of responsibility from their experience. See **Exploration Box 1.1** for a look at how adolescent development is being changed by today's innovations in digital media and communication technologies.

6. **Development is multiply influenced.** Today's developmental scientists believe that human development is the product of nature and nurture, of many interacting causes both inside and outside the person, and both biological and environmental (see Chapter 3). It is the often-unpredictable outcome of ongoing interactions between a changing person and her changing world. Some influences are experienced by all humans at similar ages, others are common to people of a particular generation, and still others are unique to the individual (Baltes, 1987).

7. **Development must be studied by multiple disciplines.** Because human development is influenced by everything from biochemical reactions to historical events, it is impossible for one discipline to have all the answers. A full understanding of human development will come only when many disciplines, each with its own perspectives and tools of study, join forces (Lerner, 2006). Not only psychologists

but also biologists, neuroscientists, historians, economists, sociologists, anthropologists, and many others have something to contribute to our understanding. Some universities have established interdisciplinary human development programs that bring members of different disciplines together to forge more integrated perspectives on development.

In sum, Baltes's modern life-span perspective assumes that development occurs throughout the life span, is multidirectional, involves gains and interlinked losses at every age, is characterized by plasticity, is affected by its historical and cultural context, is influenced by multiple, interacting causes, and is best studied by multiple disciplines.

Checking Mastery

1. Focusing on the development over childhood of helpfulness, state a research question that illustrates each of four main goals of the study of life-span development.
2. Which three of the seven assumptions in Baltes's life-span perspective concern the nature–nurture issue?

Making Connections

1. How does the developmental psychology of Paul Baltes improve on the developmental psychology of Charles Darwin?
2. Create examples to show how four of the assumptions of the life-span perspective might apply to John Tatum, the 90-year-old swimmer introduced at the beginning of the chapter.

1.3 How Is Development Studied?

LEARNING OBJECTIVES:

- Summarize the scientific method and the choices involved in selecting a sample and choosing data collection methods.
- Evaluate the strengths and weaknesses of the case study, experimental, and correlational methods.
- Evaluate the strengths and weaknesses of the cross-sectional, longitudinal, and sequential designs.

How do developmental scholars gain understanding of the complexities of life-span development? Let us review for you, briefly, some basic concepts of scientific research and then turn to research strategies devised specifically for describing, predicting, explaining, and optimizing development (see Creasey, 2006; S. A. Miller, 2013). Even if you have no desire to do developmental research yourself, it is important for you to understand how the knowledge of development represented in this book was generated.

The Scientific Method

There is nothing mysterious about the **scientific method**. It is both a method and an attitude—a belief that investigators should allow their systematic observations (or data) to determine the merits of their thinking. For example, for every "expert" who believes that psychological differences between males and females are largely biological in origin, there is likely to be another expert who just as firmly insists that boys and girls differ because they are raised differently. Whom should we believe? It is in the spirit of the scientific method to believe the data—the findings of research. The scientist is willing to abandon a pet theory if the data contradict it. Ultimately, then, the scientific method can help the scientific community and society at large weed out flawed ideas.

The scientific method involves a process of generating ideas and testing them by making observations. Often, preliminary observations provide ideas for a **theory**—a set of concepts and propositions intended to describe and explain certain phenomena. Jean Piaget, for instance, formulated his influential theory of cognitive development by closely observing how French children of different ages responded to items on the Binet IQ test when he worked on the test's development, as well as by watching his own children's development (see Chapters 7 and 9).

Theories generate specific predictions, or **hypotheses**, regarding a particular set of observations. Consider, for example, a theory claiming that psychological differences between males and females are largely caused by differences in their experiences in the family. Based on this theory, a researcher might hypothesize that if parents grant boys and girls the same freedoms, the two sexes will be similarly independent, whereas if parents give boys more freedom than girls, boys will be more independent than girls. Suppose that the study designed to test this hypothesis indicates that boys are more independent than girls no matter how their parents treat them. Then the hypothesis would be disconfirmed by the findings, and the researcher would want to rethink this theory of gender differences. If other hypotheses based on this theory were inconsistent with the facts, the theory would have to be significantly revised or abandoned in favor of a better theory.

This, then, is the heart of the scientific method: Theories generate hypotheses, which are tested through observation of behavior, and new observations indicate which theories are worth keeping and which are not (■ Figure 1.1). It should be clear that theories are not just speculations, hunches, or unsupported opinions. A good theory should be:

Figure 1.1 The scientific method in action.

- *Internally consistent.* Its different parts and propositions should hang together and should not generate contradictory hypotheses.
- *Falsifiable.* It can be proved wrong; that is, it can generate specific hypotheses that can be tested and either supported or not supported by the data collected. If a theory is vague or does not generate clear hypotheses, it cannot be tested and will not be useful in advancing knowledge.
- *Supported by data.* A good theory should help us better describe, predict, and explain human development; that is, its hypotheses should be confirmed by research results.

Sample Selection

Any study of development focuses on a particular research **sample** (the group of individuals studied) with the intention of generalizing the results to a larger **population**, a well-defined group (such as premature infants, American high school students, or Chinese elders) from which the sample is drawn and about which we want to draw conclusions. Although it is advocated more than it is used, the best approach is to study a **random sample** of the population of interest—a sample formed by identifying all members of the larger population and then, by a random means (such as drawing names blindly), selecting a portion of that population to study. Random sampling increases confidence that the sample studied is representative of the larger population of interest and therefore that conclusions based on studying the sample will be true of the whole population.

In practice, developmentalists often draw their samples—sometimes random, sometimes not—from their local communities. Thus, researchers might survey students at a local high school about their drug use but then be unable to make statements about American teenagers in general if, for example, the school is in a suburb where drug-use patterns are different than they might be in an inner-city or rural area. They would certainly be unable to generalize about Kenyan or Brazilian high school students. All researchers must therefore be careful to describe the characteristics of the sample they studied and to avoid overgeneralizing their findings to populations that might be socioeconomically or culturally different from their research sample (Rogoff, 2003).

Data Collection

No matter what aspect of human development we are interested in, we must find appropriate ways to measure what interests us. The methods used to study human development are varied, depending on the age group and aspect of development of interest (Creasey, 2006; Miller, 2013). Here we will look at some pros and cons of three major methods of data collection used by developmental researchers: verbal reports, behavioral observations, and physiological measurements.

Verbal Reports

Interviews, written questionnaires or surveys, ability and achievement tests, and personality scales all involve asking people questions, either about themselves (self-report measures) or about someone else (for example, child behavior as reported by informants such as parents or teachers). These verbal report measures usually ask the same questions in precisely the same order of everyone so that the responses of different individuals can be directly compared. Increasingly, verbal report measures are administered via websites and smart phones (Wilt, Condon, & Revelle, 2012).

Although self-report and other verbal report methods are widely used to study human development, they have shortcomings. First, self-report measures typically cannot be used with infants, young children, cognitively impaired elders, or other individuals who cannot read or understand speech well. Informant surveys, questionnaires, or interviews are often used in these situations instead. Second, because individuals of different ages may not understand questions in the same way, age differences in responses may reflect age differences in comprehension or interpretation rather than age differences in the quality of interest to the researcher. Finally, respondents may try to present themselves (or those they are providing information about) in a positive or socially desirable light.

Behavioral Observations

Naturalistic observation involves observing people in their everyday (that is, natural) surroundings (Pellegrini, 1996). Ongoing behavior is observed in homes, schools, playgrounds, workplaces, nursing homes, or wherever people are going about their lives. Naturalistic observation has been used to study child development more often than adult development, largely because infants and young children often cannot be studied through

Physiological Measurements

Finally, developmental scientists sometimes take physiological measurements to assess variables of interest to them. For example, they use electrodes to measure electrical activity in the brain, chart changes in hormone levels in menopausal women, or measure heart rate and other indicators of arousal to assess emotions.

Today, exciting breakthroughs are being made in understanding relationships between brain and behavior through the use of **functional magnetic resonance imaging (fMRI)**, a brain-scanning technique that uses magnetic forces to measure the increase in blood flow to an area of the brain that occurs when that brain area is active. By having children and adults perform cognitive tasks while lying very still in an fMRI scanner, researchers can determine which parts of the brain are involved in particular cognitive activities. Sometimes fMRI studies reveal that children and adults, or young adults and older adults, rely on different areas of the brain to perform the same tasks, providing new insights into the development and aging of the brain and cognitive functions (see, for example, Dennis & Cabeza, 2008; O'Shaughnessy et al., 2008; Wittmann & D'Esposito, 2012; and see Chapter 5).

Physiological measurements have the advantage of being hard to fake; the person who tells you she is not angry may be physiologically aroused, and the adolescent who claims not to take drugs may be given away by a blood test. Physiological measurements are also particularly useful in the study of infants because infants cannot tell us verbally what they are thinking or feeling. The main limitation of physiological measurements is that it is not always clear exactly what they are assessing. For example, physiological arousal can signal other emotions besides anger.

These, then, are the most commonly used techniques of collecting data about human development: verbal report measures

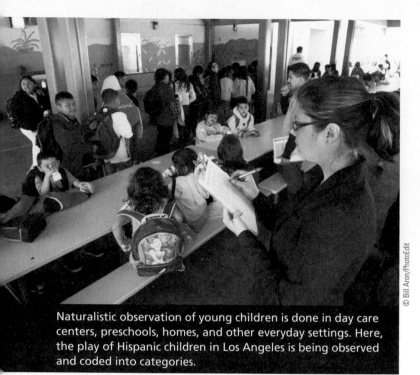

Naturalistic observation of young children is done in day care centers, preschools, homes, and other everyday settings. Here, the play of Hispanic children in Los Angeles is being observed and coded into categories.

self-report techniques that demand verbal skills. It is the only data collection technique that can reveal what children or adults do in everyday life.

However, naturalistic observation has its limitations as well. First, some behaviors (for example, heroic efforts to help in emergencies) occur too infrequently and unexpectedly to be studied through naturalistic observation. Second, it is difficult to pinpoint the causes of the behavior observed because in a natural setting many events are usually happening at the same time, any of which may affect behavior. Finally, the presence of an observer can sometimes make people behave differently than they otherwise would. Children may "ham it up" when they have an audience; parents may be on their best behavior. Therefore, researchers sometimes videotape the proceedings from a hidden location or spend time in the setting before they collect their "real" data so that the individuals they are observing become used to their presence and behave more naturally.

To achieve greater control over the conditions under which they gather behavioral data, and to capture rarely occurring events, researchers often use **structured observation**; that is, they create special stimuli, tasks, or situations designed to elicit the behavior of interest. To study moral development and cheating among college students, for example, researchers might arrange a situation in which students take a cognitive test after having been led to believe that any cheating on their part could not possibly be detected. By exposing all research participants to the same stimuli, this approach increases the investigator's ability to compare the effects of these stimuli on different individuals. Concerns about this method center on whether research participants will behave naturally and whether conclusions based on their behavior in specially designed settings will generalize to their behavior in the real world.

Functional magnetic resonance imaging is increasingly being used to study which parts of the brain are activated when humans of different ages perform various cognitive tasks. Testing children is challenging, however; they may fear entering the tube of the MRI and, once there, may have difficulty staying still as required.

Data Collection Methods in Action: Measuring Anger

We can illustrate the primary methods of data collection by considering a study by clinical psychologist Julie Hubbard and her colleagues (2002) that used all three approaches. Hubbard was interested in the relationship between anger and two styles of aggression in 8-year-olds, as determined by teachers' responses to questions about children's behavior in the classroom: a "hot" kind of aggression in which children hit, pinch, and otherwise abuse other children when provoked, and a cooler, more calculating style of aggression in which children use aggression to get what they want. The researchers hypothesized that aggressive children of the first type would be more likely than aggressive children of the second type to become angry in a laboratory situation in which another child (a confederate of the researchers) cheated shamelessly in a board game about astronauts and won. The researchers needed a way to measure anger. What would you suggest?

Behavioral observation. Hubbard used the structured observation approach by setting up the astronaut game situation, having the confederate cheat to provoke children's anger, and then observing signs of anger in facial expressions and nonverbal behavior. The confederate was carefully trained to behave the same way with each of the 272 participants in the study. Sessions were videotaped; trained graduate and undergraduate students then coded second by second whether the participants' facial expressions were angry, sad, happy, or neutral and whether they showed any nonverbal signs of anger (for example, slamming game pieces on the table). Two students independently coded a subsample of the videotapes to ensure that they could agree upon facial expressions and nonverbal behavior.

Verbal report. The researchers also had each participant watch a videotape of the game he or she played with the cheating confederate, stopped the tape at each turn in the game, and asked each child, "How angry did you feel now?" The child responded on a four-point scale ranging from 1 (not at all) to 4 (a lot). The researchers used these ratings to calculate for each child an average degree of self-reported anger over the entire game.

Physiological measure. The researchers collected data on two physiological indicators of anger by attaching electrodes to children's hands and chests (after convincing the children that astronauts normally wear sensors when they go into space!). Emotionally aroused people, including angry ones, often have sweaty palms and low electrical resistance of the skin, which can be measured by electrodes attached to their hands. Emotional arousal is also given away by a high heart rate, measured through electrodes on the chest.

Using these measures, Hubbard and her colleagues found that, as hypothesized, children who engaged in "hot" aggression in the classroom showed more anger during the game than "cool" aggressors. The difference was more evident in their skin resistance and nonverbal behavior than in their verbal self-reports and heart rates. Because all data collection methods have their weaknesses, and because different measures often yield different results, as in this study, use of multiple methods in the same study is a wise research strategy.

(interviews, questionnaires, and tests), behavioral observation (both naturalistic and structured), and physiological measures. **Exploration Box 1.2** provides an illustration of the use of the three techniques in a study of anger and aggression. Because each method has its limitations, knowledge is advanced the most when *multiple* methods and measures are used to study the same aspect of human development and these different methods lead to similar conclusions.

The Case Study, Experimental, and Correlational Methods

Once developmental scientists have formulated hypotheses, chosen a sample, and figured out what to measure and how to measure it, they can test their hypotheses. As we have seen, developmental science got its start with baby biographies, and on occasion today's researchers still study the development of individuals through case studies. More often they use the experimental and correlational methods to examine relationships between one variable and another—and, where possible, to establish that one variable causes another. We will illustrate these methods by sampling research on the implications of digital media for human development.

The Case Study

A **case study** is an in-depth examination of an individual (or a small number of individuals), typically carried out by compiling and analyzing information from a variety of sources, such as observation, testing, and interviewing the person or people who know her (see Flyvbjerg, 2011). The case study method can provide rich information about the complexities of an individual's development and the influences on it. It is particularly useful in studying people with rare conditions, disorders, and developmental experiences when it is not possible to assemble a large sample of people to study or when an unusual case can say something important about typical development. Recently, the case study method was used by forensic neuropsychologist Matthew Bowen and neuropsychiatrist Marvin Firestone (2011) to describe four individuals, all European American males, who have what some have called "Internet addiction." A new mental health condition termed "Internet use gaming disorder" is mentioned in the fifth edition of the American Psychiatric Association's (2013) *Diagnostic and Statistical Manual (DSM-5)* as a problem in need of further study to determine whether it should become an official diagnosable psychological disorder. One of the four individuals described in detail by Bowen and Firestone spent all afternoon and night until 8 or 9 AM online, mostly in chat rooms and at blogs or playing video games; all four men had psychological problems and difficulties in interpersonal relationships.

The case study method can complement correlational and experimental research (Flyvbjerg, 2011). It can be a good source of hypotheses that can be examined further in larger-scale studies and it can provide a rich picture of atypical development. However, conclusions based on a single case (or four) may not generalize to other individuals, and inferences about what may have caused the person to develop as he or she did often need further study.

The Experimental Method

In an **experiment**, an investigator manipulates or alters some aspect of the environment to see how this affects the behavior of the sample of individuals studied. Consider the effects of watching videos or DVDs on infants. Many of today's parents, wanting to get their children off to a great start, not only set their babies in front of *Sesame Street* and other television programs and let them play with iPhones and iPads but buy them special infant videos that claim they will advance babies' cognitive and language development—products made by Baby Einstein, Baby BumbleBee, and other companies. Do such infant videos actually speed infant development?

Judy DeLoache and her colleagues (2010) decided to find out by conducting an experiment with 72 infants ranging in age from 12 to 18 months. The DVD they studied showed scenes of a house and yard while a voice labeled 25 different household objects, each shown three different times. Each family in the study was randomly assigned to one of four experimental groups: (1) *parent teaching* (in this old-fashioned condition, no video was provided; rather, parents were given the 25 words featured in the video and asked to teach as many as possible to their babies however they wished), (2) *video-with-interaction* (child and parent watched the video together five or more times a week for four weeks and interacted as they did), (3) *video-with-no-interaction* (infants watched the video by themselves; their parents were usually nearby but did not interact with them), and (4) a *no-intervention* control (these babies got no video and no parent training; this control group was needed to determine how many words infants might learn naturally, without any training). After the training period, babies took a test of their knowledge of the target words. For example, an infant would be presented with replicas of a table (a target word in the video) and a fan (not a target word) and asked to point to the right object: "Can you show me the table?"

The goal of an experiment is to see whether the different treatments that form the **independent variable**—the variable manipulated so that its causal effects can be assessed—have different effects on the behavior expected to be affected, the **dependent variable** in the experiment. The independent variable in DeLoache's experiment was the type of training babies received, as defined by the four different experimental conditions. The dependent variable of interest was vocabulary learning (the percentage of words taught in the video that were correctly identified by the infant during the vocabulary test). When cause–effect relationships are studied in an experiment, the independent variable is the hypothesized cause and the

■ **Figure 1.2** Infants' mean scores on the vocabulary test after training in the DeLoache et al. (2010) experiment. Only infants taught words by their parents did better than chance on the test; exposure to baby videos that taught the words had no effect.

Source: Adapted from DeLoache, J. S. Chiong, C. S., Sherman, K. Islam, N., Vanderborght, M., Troseth, G. L., Strouse, G. A., & O'Doherty, K. (2010). Do babies learn from baby media? *Psychological Science, 21*, 1570–1574 (Figure 1 on p. 1572).

dependent variable is the effect. For example, if researchers were testing drugs to improve memory function in elderly adults with Alzheimer's disease, the type of drug administered (for example, a new drug versus a placebo with no active ingredients) would be the independent variable, and performance on a memory task would be the dependent variable.

So, in DeLoache's experiment, did vocabulary learning "depend on" the independent variable, the type of training received? Did infants learn from the baby video? The mean or average word learning scores for the four treatment groups are shown in ■ **Figure 1.2**. Babies did no better on the vocabulary learning test if they had seen the video than if they were in the control condition and received no training at all. The only group that did better on the test than what would be expected by chance was the group of babies taught the old-fashioned way—those in the parent teaching group. And it wasn't that babies or mothers were unenthusiastic about the video. As one mother exclaimed, "She loves the blasted thing. It's crack for babies!" (p. 1572). Other experimental studies seem to concur: infant videos do not speed language learning (Robb, Richert, & Wartella, 2009).

The DeLoache study has the three critical features shared by any true experiment:

1. *Random assignment.* **Random assignment** of participants to different experimental conditions (for example, by drawing names from a jar to determine who gets which treatment) helps ensure that the treatment groups are similar in all respects at the outset (for example, in the baby video study, similar in socioeconomic status, ethnicity, previous level of cognitive and language development, and any other characteristics that could affect infants' performance). Only if

experimental groups are similar in all respects initially can researchers be confident that differences among groups at the end of the experiment were caused by differences in which experimental treatment they received. Some studies, such as those evaluating already-started interventions, cannot randomly assign participants to groups; instead they compare the group receiving the intervention to a control group. Such studies are sometimes called "quasi experiments" because uncontrolled differences between the two groups could influence the results.

2. *Manipulation of the independent variable.* Investigators must arrange for different groups to have different experiences so that the effects of those experiences can be assessed. If investigators merely compare infants who already watch baby videos with infants who do not, they cannot establish whether video watching *causes* an increase in word knowledge. For example, it could be that more-educated parents buy these videos more often than less-educated parents and also talk and read more to their children.

3. *Experimental control.* In a true experiment with proper **experimental control**, all factors other than the independent variable are controlled or held constant so that they cannot contribute to differences among the treatment groups. In a laboratory study, for example, all experimental groups may be tested in the same room by the same experimenter reading the same instructions. It is hard in a field experiment like DeLoache's, where the experimental conditions are implemented in children's homes by their parents, to control all extraneous factors. However, DeLoache and her colleagues asked parents to keep a log of their use of the video (or of the time they spent teaching vocabulary words if they were in the parent teaching condition). This allowed the experimenters to check that parents were following instructions and not using other materials or departing from the study plan. They were trying their best to ensure that infants in the four treatment conditions were treated similarly except for the type of training they received.

The greatest strength of the experimental method is its ability to establish unambiguously that one thing causes another—that manipulating the independent variable causes a change in the dependent variable. When experiments are properly conducted, they contribute to our ability to *explain* human development and sometimes to *optimize* it. In the DeLoache study, the results suggest that parent–infant interaction may contribute more to vocabulary growth than baby videos. The results are consistent with other evidence that infants have a "video deficit" and do not learn as much from video presentations as they do from face-to-face presentations (Anderson & Pempek, 2005). They also support the American Academy of Pediatrics' recommendation that children younger than 2 not watch television or other media on the grounds that they are likely to develop better if they spend that time interacting with adults (Courage & Setliff, 2009).

Does the experimental method have limitations? Absolutely! First, because experiments are often conducted in laboratory settings or under unusual conditions, the results may not always hold true in the real world. The psychologist

Urie Bronfenbrenner (1979), who was critical of the fact that so many developmental studies are contrived experiments, once charged that developmental psychology had become "the science of the strange behavior of children in strange situations with strange adults" (p. 19). Experiments often show what can cause development but not necessarily what most strongly shapes development in natural settings (McCall, 1977).

A second limitation of the experimental method is that it often cannot be used for ethical reasons. How would you conduct a true experiment to determine how older women are affected by their husbands' deaths, for example? You would need to identify a sample of elderly women, randomly assign them to either the experimental group or the control group, and then manipulate the independent variable by killing the husbands of all the members of the experimental group! Ethical principles obviously demand that developmentalists use methods other than true experimental ones to study questions about the effect of widowhood—and a host of other significant questions about development.

The Correlational Method

Largely because it is unethical to manipulate people's lives, most developmental research is correlational rather than experimental. The **correlational method** generally involves determining whether two or more variables are related in a systematic way. Researchers do not randomly assign participants to treatment conditions and manipulate the independent variable as in an experiment. Instead, researchers take people as they are and attempt to determine whether there are relationships among their experiences, characteristics, and developmental outcomes.

Like DeLoache and her colleagues, public health professor Frederick Zimmerman and his colleagues (2007) were interested in the effects of media viewing on the language development of infants. They conducted a correlational study that involved telephone surveys with 1008 parents of children 8–24 months of age. They asked about infants' exposure to several types of media—not only videos and DVDs especially for babies, but children's educational programs, children's noneducational programs, and grownup TV. They used an established measure of language development in which parents report on their children's understanding of various words, and they correlated frequency of exposure to the different types of media with infants' vocabulary scores. Appreciating that there could be uncontrolled differences between families high and low in media use, they used statistical control techniques to adjust vocabulary scores to make it "as if" families were equal in potentially confounding characteristics such as race/ethnicity, parent education, family income, the presence of two parents in the home, day care participation, and other factors that they believed might be related to both media use and language development. They also asked about and controlled for the amount of time parents spent interacting with their infants by reading books and telling stories.

In correlational studies, researchers often determine the strength of the relationship between two variables of interest by calculating a **correlation coefficient**—an index of the extent to which individuals' scores on one variable are systematically associated with their scores on another variable. A correlation coefficient (symbolized as *r*) can range in value from −1.00 to +1.00. A positive correlation between video viewing time and language development would indicate that as time spent watching videos increases, so does an infant's language development score. (■ **Figure 1.3, Panel A**). A positive correlation of *r* = +.90 would indicate a stronger, more predictable positive relationship than a smaller positive correlation such as *r* = +.30. A negative correlation would result if the heaviest video viewers consistently had the lowest language development scores and the lightest viewers had the highest language development scores (■ **Figure 1.3, Panel B**). A correlation near 0.00 would be obtained if there was no relationship between the two variables—if one cannot predict how advanced in language development infants are based on knowing how much they watch baby videos (■ **Figure 1.3, Panel C**).

The findings of Zimmerman's study were quite surprising. Among the youngest infants (8–16 months), each hour of viewing baby DVDs or videos per day was associated with *fewer* words known; the correlation was negative. By contrast, parent reading and storytelling were positively correlated with language development scores. Among older infants (ages 17–24 months), baby video viewing was not associated one way or the other with language development scores, as the DeLoache et al. (2010) experimental study also found. However, reading and to a lesser extent storytelling continued to be positively correlated with language development.

Should we conclude from the Zimmerman study, then, that reading to infants and toddlers advances their language development but that giving babies under 17 months of age baby videos and DVDs impedes their language development? Not so fast. Because this is a correlational study, we cannot draw firm cause–effect conclusions the way we can in an experiment. Does watching baby videos really delay language development among young infants, or could there be other reasons for the negative relationship between watching baby videos and vocabulary?

One important rival interpretation in most correlational studies is the **directionality problem**: The direction of the cause–effect relationship could be the reverse of what the researcher thinks it is. That is, exposure to baby videos may not *cause* infants to be delayed in language development; rather, as Zimmerman et al. (2007) acknowledge, slow language development could cause video viewing. That is, parents who fear that their infant is delayed in language development may buy baby videos in the belief that the videos will speed language development.

A second rival interpretation in correlational studies is the **third variable problem**: The association between the two variables of interest may be caused by some third variable. Zimmerman and his colleagues measured and tried to control for a number of possible third variables. For example, it could be that parents who are not very motivated to interact with their babies rely more on videos to entertain or babysit them and that it is the lack of parent–infant interaction, not increased time watching baby videos, that hurts young infants' language development. To rule out this possibility, Zimmerman and his colleagues showed that babies' video watching was negatively correlated with vocabulary score even when amount of parent interaction through reading and storytelling, as well as a number of other potential "third variables," were controlled. However, as they admit, they did not control for the quality of parent–infant interactions and for additional, unmeasured factors that could explain both why some infants both watch more baby videos than other infants and have lower language development scores.

Thus, the correlational method has one major limitation: It cannot unambiguously establish a causal relationship between one variable and another the way an experiment can. Correlational studies can only *suggest* that a causal relationship exists. Although Zimmerman's team used statistical control techniques to make it as if other factors were equal, they could not completely rule out the directionality problem and the third variable problem to establish a cause–effect relationship between baby video viewing and delayed language development. It's a rule every researcher knows by heart: "Correlation is not causation."

Despite this key limitation, the correlational method is extremely valuable. First, as already noted, most important questions about human development can be addressed only through

■ **Figure 1.3** Plots of hypothetical correlations between the time babies spend watching infant videos and their knowledge of vocabulary words. Each dot represents a specific child who watches a certain amount of baby videos and has a certain score on a vocabulary test. Panel A shows a positive correlation between video watching and vocabulary: the more infants watch infant videos, the more vocabulary words they know. Panel B shows a negative correlation: the more infants watch videos, the fewer vocabulary words they know. Finally, Panel C shows zero correlation: the amount of time watching baby videos is unrelated to an infant's knowledge of vocabulary words.

Table 1.3 A Comparison of the Experimental Method and the Correlational Method

Experimental Method	Correlational Method
Manipulation by the investigator of an independent variable to observe effect on a dependent variable	Study of the relationship between one variable and another (without investigator manipulation and control of people's experiences)
Random assignment to treatment groups (to ensure similarity of groups except for the experimental manipulation)	No random assignment (so comparison groups may not be similar in all respects)
Experimental control of extraneous variables	Lack of control over extraneous variables
Can establish a cause–effect relationship between independent variable and dependent variable	Can suggest but not firmly establish that one variable causes another owing to directionality and third variable problems
May not be possible for ethical reasons	Can be used to study many important issues that cannot be studied experimentally for ethical reasons
May be artificial (findings from contrived experiments may not generalize to the "real world")	Can study multiple influences operating in natural settings (findings may generalize better to the "real world")

© Cengage Learning

the correlational method because it would be unethical to manipulate people's experiences in experiments. Second, complex correlational studies and statistical analyses allow researchers to learn about how multiple factors operating in the "real world" may combine to influence development. We just have to be on the lookout for the directionality problem and the third variable problem as rival interpretations of correlational relationships. See ● **Table 1.3** for a comparison of experimental and correlational methods.

Meta-analysis

Overall, the understanding of why humans develop as they do is best advanced when the results of different kinds of studies *converge*—when experiments demonstrate a clear cause–effect relationship and correlational studies reveal that the same relationship seems to be operating in everyday life. The results of multiple studies addressing the same question can be synthesized to produce overall conclusions through the research method of **meta-analysis** (Glass, McGaw, & Smith, 1981; van IJzendoorn, Bakermans-Kranenburg, & Alink, 2012). We do not yet have enough studies to say whether baby videos have an effect one way or the other on language development. But consider the effects of media violence on children and adolescents. A number of meta-analyses of many studies of the link between watching violence on television and aggression have been conducted. They show a reliable, although small, average correlation between the two, between about +.10 and +.30 (Bushman & Anderson, 2001; Ferguson & Savage, 2012). Although it is small, the relationship shows up in studies using the correlational method as well as in studies using the experimental method, and in both laboratory and naturalistic settings (Huesmann & Taylor, 2006). When meta-analyses are done and the results of many studies agree like this, we can be more confident in the finding, assuming that the quality of the studies that went into the meta-analysis is high (see Ferguson & Savage, 2012, though, on issues in studies of media violence and their interpretation).

Developmental Research Designs

Along with the experimental and correlational methods used by all kinds of researchers to study relationships between variables, developmental researchers need specialized research designs to study how people change and remain the same as they get older (Creasey, 2006; Schaie, 2000). To describe development, researchers have relied extensively on two types of research designs: the cross-sectional design and the longitudinal design. A third type of design, the sequential study, has come into use in an attempt to overcome the limitations of the other two techniques. We will consider these three designs and their strengths and weaknesses in turn.

Cross-Sectional Designs

In a **cross-sectional design**, the performances of people of different age groups, or cohorts, are compared. A **cohort** is a group of individuals born at the same time, either in the same year or within a specified span of years (for example, a generation is a cohort). A researcher interested in the development of vocabulary might gather samples of speech from several 2-, 3-, and 4-year-olds; calculate the mean (or average) number of distinct words used per child for each age group; and compare these means to describe how the vocabulary sizes of children age 2, 3, and 4 differ. The cross-sectional study provides information about *age differences*. By seeing how age groups differ, researchers can attempt to draw conclusions about how performance changes with age.

Suppose we are interested in learning about how people's use of computers, the Internet, and other communication technologies changes as they get older. Psychologists Patricia Tun and Margie Lachman (2010) conducted a cross-sectional study of computer use and its relationship to cognitive functioning in adulthood. They surveyed a national sample of adults ranging in age from 32 to 84 about how often they used computers. They then compared computer use across age groups. ■ **Figure 1.4** shows the percentage of each age group using computers to some extent. Clearly computer use was more common among younger adults

■ **Figure 1.4** Percentage of American adults of different ages who used computers to some extent in 2005–2006.

SOURCE: Adapted from Tun, P. A. & Lachman, M. E. (2010). The association between computer use and cognition across adulthood: Use it so you won't lose it? *Psychology and Aging*, 25, 560–568.

than among elderly adults. But can we conclude that computer use normally declines with age as people get older? Not really.

People who are in their 70s not only are older than people in their 50s and 30s but they also belong to a different cohort or generation and have had different formative experiences. The 70-year-olds in Tun and Lachman's study did not have computers when they were youth whereas the 30-year-olds may have. Do 70-year-olds use computers less because people lose interest in computers as they age, or is it that 70-year-olds were never as heavily into computers even when they were younger? Tun and Lachman's study does not tell us.

In cross-sectional studies, such as Tun and Lachman's, *age effects and cohort effects are confounded, or entangled.* **Age effects** are the relationship between age (a rough proxy for changes brought about by nature and nurture) and a particular aspect of development. **Cohort effects** are the effects of being born as a member of a particular cohort or generation in a particular historical context. Cross-sectional studies tell how people of different ages (cohorts) differ (cohort effect), but they do not necessarily tell how people normally *change* as they get older (age effect). In Tun and Lachman's study, for example, what initially looked like a developmental trend toward declining computer use in later life (an age effect) could actually be no more than a cohort effect resulting from differences in the formative experiences of the different generations studied. Do you expect you will still be using computers in your old age? We bet so. (By the way, Tun and Lachman's more interesting finding was that computer use was positively correlated with performance on cognitive tests among both younger and older adults. Because they used a correlational design, they could not determine whether computer use sharpens cognitive skills or whether sharp people use computers more, however.)

Cohort differences can tell us about the influence of the sociocultural environment on development and about the implications for development of being part of one generation or another (see **Exploration Box 1.3** on the millennial and baby boom generations). However, the presence of cohort effects poses a problem in cross-sectional research whenever the growing-up experiences of the cohorts studied differ. As you will see in Chapter 9, it was once believed, based on cross-sectional studies of performance on intelligence tests, that people experience significant declines in intellectual functioning starting in middle age. However, later longitudinal studies suggested that intellectual declines were much less steep and came later in life (Schaie, 2000). Why the discrepancy? The elderly adults in cross-sectional studies probably performed less well than younger cohorts not because they experienced steep losses of intellectual abilities during adulthood (a true developmental or age effect) but because they had received less education in their youth (a cohort effect). They probably always had lower intellectual abilities than younger cohorts as a result.

The second major limitation of the cross-sectional design besides the entanglement of age effects and cohorts is this: Because each person is observed at only one point, researchers learn nothing about how people change with age. Returning to our computer-use example, researchers cannot see whether different people show similar or different patterns of change in computer use as they get older or whether individuals who are heavy computer users as 30-year-olds are also heavy computer users at 70. To address issues like these, researchers need to do longitudinal research.

Despite the limitations of the cross-sectional design, it is a very important approach and developmentalists rely heavily on it. It has the great advantage of being quick and easy: researchers can go out this year, sample individuals of different ages, and be done with it. Moreover, cross-sectional studies should yield valid conclusions about age effects if the cohorts studied are likely to have had similar growing-up experiences—as when 3- and 4-year-olds rather than 30- and 40-year-olds are compared. It is when researchers attempt to make inferences about development over the span of many years that cohort effects in cross-sectional studies can yield a misleading picture of development.

Longitudinal Designs

In a **longitudinal design**, one cohort of individuals is assessed repeatedly over time. A study of the development of vocabulary would be longitudinal rather than cross-sectional if a researcher identified a group of 2-year-olds and measured their vocabulary sizes, then measured their vocabularies again at age 3 and then again at age 4, and compared the children's mean scores at ages 2, 3, and 4. In any longitudinal study, whether it covers only a few months in infancy or 50 years, the same individuals are studied as they develop. Thus, the longitudinal design provides information about *age changes* rather than age differences.

Imagine that we had had the foresight to design a longitudinal study of computer use back in 1970 and had surveyed 30-year-olds about their computer use in 1970 and every 20 years since until 2010 (when they would have been 70). The study would have shown that very few adults used computers in 1970 but that rates of computer use increased with age as more and more people gained access to computers. ■ **Figure 1.5** compares a cross-sectional and a longitudinal design for studying 30-, 50-, and 70-year-olds.

Because the longitudinal design traces changes in individuals as they age, it can tell whether most people change in the same direction or whether different individuals travel different

Exploration **1.3**

Cohort Effects: Millennials and Boomers

Does it make a difference what generation you belong to? Whether you are part of the Silent Generation (the World War II and Korean War generation born between 1925 and 1946), the **baby boom generation** (the huge cohort born after World War II between 1946 and 1964), Generation X (the small generation born between 1964 and 1982), or the **millennials** (also called Generation Y or the "baby boom-let" generation born from 1982 to 2004)?

Baby boomers and millennials have received more than their share of attention. We seem to believe that different cohorts or generations not only have different formative experiences but develop different characters. Popular writing on the subject often presents overgeneralized portraits of different generations—call it stereo-typing—based on little solid data. The first wave of baby boomers turned 65 in 2011: George W. and Laura Bush, Bill Clinton, Dolly Parton, Donald Trump, and Cher. They were a year old when Howdy Doody first appeared on the first home TVs and 17 when John F. Kennedy was assassinated; they grew up fearing nuclear bombs and Russians and listening to rock and roll; and many of them protested the Vietnam War or

fought in it (Adler, 2005). In the 1960s, boomers were stereotyped as antiestablishment, antiwar rebels who were into drugs and sexual freedom.

Members of Generation X (born between 1964 and 1981) grew up with MTV, personal computers, Watergate, and the AIDS epidemic and became a highly educated generation. Meanwhile millennials (born starting in 1982) grew up in a digital world, are close to their parents, and have been characterized as a self-absorbed, narcissistic, "pampered, over-praised, relentlessly self-confident generation" (Matchar, 2012, p. B1; and see Twenge, 2006; Twenge, Konrath, Foster, Campbell, & Bushman, 2008). There are undoubtedly more psychological differences within than between generations, but surveys reveal a few differences between the generations too. For example, some surveys suggest that younger generations such as the millennials are less committed to work and more interested in freedom and personal fulfillment than baby boomers (Fogg, 2008; Matchar, 2012). But are these generational (cohort) differences or are they developmental differences (age effects)? Maybe millennials appear to be more self-absorbed and interested

For baby boomers growing up in the 1950s, gender roles were more traditional than they are now. Fewer women worked outside the home, and more parents dressed and treated girls and boys differently.

in personal fulfillment than older adults because they do not yet have children and other adult responsibilities whereas baby boomers do. This could be another example of how, in cross-sectional studies comparing different age groups, we cannot easily separate cohort effects and age effects. Understanding how people change with age and understanding how they are affected by the historical–cultural context in which they develop are both important goals of the science of life-span development.

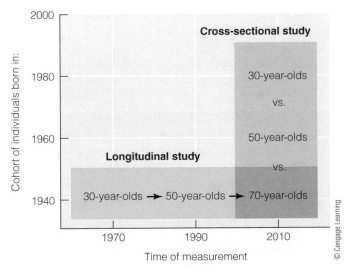

■ **Figure 1.5** Cross-sectional and longitudinal studies of development from age 30 to age 70. The longitudinal study involves repeated assessment every 20 years starting in 1970, whereas in the cross-sectional study, the three age groups of interest are compared in 2010.

developmental paths. It can indicate whether the characteristics and behaviors measured remain consistent over time—for example, whether people who used computers a lot at age 30 were still among the heaviest users at age 70. And it can tell whether experiences earlier in life predict traits and behaviors later in life. The cross-sectional design can do none of these.

What, then, are the limitations of the longitudinal design? Our hypothetical longitudinal study of computer use centered on *one cohort* of individuals: members of the 1940 birth cohort. These people were raised in an historical context in which computers were scarce and lived through a time when they became a fixture in almost every American home (Cotten, McCullough, & Adams, 2011). Their computer use probably increased over time as from 1970 to 2010 as a result—a developmental trend precisely the opposite of the "decline" with age in computer use in Tun and Lachman's (2010) cross-sectional study. However, such a longitudinal trend toward greater computer use with age does not necessarily mean that computer use *typically* increases with age. The technological advances that occurred from one time of measurement to the next during the time frame of this particular study could be responsible for the observed increase. **Time-of-measurement effects** in developmental research are the effects of historical events and trends occurring when the data are collected (for example, effects of an economic recession, a traumatic event like 9/11, advances in health care, or, here, the invention of personal computers and the Internet). In a longitudinal study, then, *age effects and time-of-measurement effects are confounded.*

Because of time-of-measurement effects, we may not be able to tell for sure whether the age-related changes observed in a longitudinal study are generalizable to people developing in other sociohistorical contexts. Perhaps we would obtain different "developmental" trends if we were to conduct a longitudinal study about computer use starting today rather than in 1970. Our research example was chosen to highlight problems in both cross-sectional studies (where cohort effects are tangled with age effects) and longitudinal studies (where time-of-measurement effects are tangled with age effects). Moral: It can be challenging to identify true developmental or age effects.

The longitudinal design has other disadvantages (Pulkkinen & Kokko, 2012):

- First, this approach is costly and time-consuming, particularly if it is used to trace development over a long span and at many points in time.
- Second, because knowledge is constantly changing, measurement methods that seemed good at the start of the study may seem dated or incomplete by the end.
- Third, participants drop out of long-term studies; they may move, lose interest, or, especially in studies of aging, die during the course of the study. The result is a smaller and often less representative sample on which to base conclusions.
- Finally, there may be effects of repeated testing; sometimes simply taking a test improves performance on that test the next time around.

Are both the cross-sectional and the longitudinal designs hopelessly flawed, then? Not at all. Cross-sectional studies are very efficient and informative, especially when the cohorts studied are not widely different in age or formative experiences. Longitudinal studies are extremely valuable for what they can reveal about how people change as they get older—even though it must be recognized that the cohort studied may not develop in precisely the same way that an earlier or later cohort does. Still, in an attempt to overcome the limitations of both cross-sectional and longitudinal designs, developmentalists have devised a more powerful method of describing developmental change: the sequential design.

Sequential Designs: The Best of Both Worlds

A **sequential design** combines the cross-sectional approach and the longitudinal approach in a single study (Schaie, 1994; Schaie & Caskie, 2005). In Chapter 9, you will read about an ambitious and important sequential study of changes in mental abilities during adulthood conducted by psychologist and gerontologist K. Warner Schaie (1996, 2005). Adults ranging in age from 22 to 70 and grouped into age groups (cohorts) were tested on a battery of mental ability tests (in a cross-sectional design), and then they were retested every 7 years (to create a longitudinal design). At each testing point new cohorts of adults in their 20s–70s was added to the study and those age groups were then retested. Some of the adults in the study were followed for as long as 45 years. This elaborate study has yielded many insights into intellectual aging. Not

only were systematic changes with age in mental abilities identified, but cohort and time-of-measurement effects were revealed, suggesting that intellectual functioning is indeed influenced by the times in which people develop (see also Alwin, 2009).

Sequential designs, by combining the cross-sectional and longitudinal approaches, improve on both. They can tell researchers

1. which age-related trends are truly developmental in nature and reflect how most people, *regardless of cohort*, can be expected to change over time (age effects);
2. which age trends differ from cohort to cohort and suggest that each generation is affected by its distinct growing-up experiences (cohort effects); and
3. which trends suggest that events during a specific period of history affect all cohorts alive at the time (time-of-measurement effects).

In short, sequential designs can begin to untangle the effects of age, cohort, and time of measurement. Yet they are extremely complex and expensive. Generally, the study of life-span human development has progressed from early (and sometimes misleading) cross-sectional studies to more long-term longitudinal studies and, increasingly, to more complex sequential studies, especially of adult development (Baltes, Lindenberger, & Staudinger, 2006). See ● **Table 1.4** for a summary of the three basic developmental designs.

Now that you have encountered examples of the various data collection methods and research designs used to study development, we challenge you to identify the research examples in **Engagement Box 1.1**

Checking Mastery

1. Design an experiment to determine whether test performance is better when students read a chapter all at once or when they read it section by section and have breaks between sections. Make it clear that your experiment has the three key features of an experiment and label the independent and dependent variables.

2. You conduct a longitudinal study of the development of self-esteem in college students from age 18 to age 22. What would you be able to learn that you could not learn by conducting a cross-sectional study of the same topic?

Making Connections

1. Explain how a cross-sectional study of age differences over the adult years in attitudes about gender roles could suggest that attitudes become more traditional with age, but a longitudinal study could suggest that gender attitudes become *less* traditional with age.

2. Professor Tunnelvision conducts a study that reveals a correlation of +.50 between self-esteem and academic achievement (grade point average) among college students. He then argues, based on this finding, that his college should launch a self-esteem–boosting program if it wants its students to gain more from their college experience. Convince the professor that there are at least two rival explanations for this correlation and suggest how he could do research to try to determine which explanation is most correct.

Recognizing Research Strategies

For each research example, identify the most appropriate descriptive term. Answers are printed upside down below.

1. A researcher creates a situation on a school playground in which children are excluded one by one from a group game by the teacher so that their emotional reactions can be studied.
   a. structured observation
   b. case study
   c. experiment
   d. correlational study

2. Every 5 years, a researcher assesses the job satisfaction of a group of managers who are age 30 in 2010, at the start of the study, and a similar group of managers who are age 30 in 2020.

   a. quasi-experimental
   b. correlational
   c. sequential
   d. cross-sectional

3. A new program to encourage teenage fathers to support their partners during labor and delivery is compared to a standard childbirth education program. The independent variable is:
   a. gender of parent
   b. type of program
   c. pain during labor and delivery
   d. support given by fathers

4. A researcher finds that adults who were college age when 9/11 occurred view the world as a scarier place than adults who were older at the time. This is:

   a. a cohort effect
   b. a time-of-measurement effect
   c. a sequential effect
   d. an age effect

5. A researcher finds a small or modest relationship indicating that the greater a child's weight, the fewer friends he or she has. The correlation coefficient calculated is probably around:
   a. +.70
   b. +.20
   c. –.70
   d –.20

Answers: 1. a 2. c 3. b 4. a 5. d

• **Table 1.4** Cross-sectional, Longitudinal, and Sequential Developmental Designs

	Cross-Sectional Design	**Longitudinal Design**	**Sequential Design**
Procedure	Observe people of different cohorts at one point in time	Observe people of one age group repeatedly over time	Combine cross-sectional and longitudinal approaches; observe different cohorts on multiple occasions
Information Gained	Describes age differences	Describes age changes	Describes age differences and age changes
Advantages	Demonstrates age differences in behavior and hints at developmental trends Takes little time to conduct and is inexpensive	Indicates how individuals are alike and different in the way they change over time Can reveal links between early behavior or experiences and later behavior	Helps separate the effects of age, cohort, and time of measurement Indicates whether developmental changes are similar in different cohorts
Disadvantages	Age trends may reflect cohort effects rather than true developmental change Provides no information about change in individuals over time	Age trends may reflect time of measurement effects during the study rather than true developmental change Relatively time-consuming and expensive Measures may later prove inadequate Participants drop out Participants can be affected by repeated testing	Complex, time-consuming, and expensive Despite being the strongest method, may still leave questions unresolved

© Cengage Learning

LEARNING OBJECTIVES:

- Discuss the challenges in conducting culturally sensitive research.

- Explain the four major ethical obligations of investigators to their research participants.

We hope we have convinced you that human development is worthy of study and requires serious and thoughtful research. We conclude this chapter by discussing two additional challenges in the study of human development: being sensitive to cultural and subcultural differences and protecting the rights of research participants.

Conducting Culturally Sensitive Research

Baltes's life-span perspective emphasizes that development is shaped by its cultural context. This implies that we need to study development in a variety of contexts using culturally sensitive research methods and measurements to understand both what is universal and what is culturally specific about human development (Cole & Packer, 2011). Easier said than done!

Developmentalists now appreciate the need to study samples of developing persons from a variety of ecological settings, not just white middle-class America. However, carrying out research in a variety of cultures and subcultures and ensuring that questionnaire, interview, and test questions and testing and observation procedures are meaningful in each culture and mean the same thing across different subcultural and cultural groups can be extremely challenging (Gardner et al., 2012; Rogoff, 2003). Example: When one organization translated a survey into 63 languages and then had the questions translated back into English, strange things happened: "married or living with a partner" was translated as "married but have a girlfriend," and "American ideas and customs" became "the ideology of America and border guards" (Morin, 2003). And when a team of researchers sought to conduct a cross-cultural study of caregiver–infant interactions, they faced a dilemma: Should they observe such interactions when the caregiver and infant were alone (typical in American homes) or when the caregiver and infant were in a group (typical in Micronesia)? They settled on observing in both social contexts to avoid findings that might be biased toward one cultural group or the other (Sostek et al., 1981). To make their research more culturally sensitive, many researchers now try to involve community members in the planning and design of their studies (Karlawish et al., 2009; Martin & Lantos, 2005).

In addition, researchers who study cultural influences on development or racial, ethnic, and socioeconomic differences in development must work hard to keep their own cultural values from biasing their perceptions of other groups. Too often, Western researchers have let **ethnocentrism**—the belief that one's own group and its culture are superior—creep into their research designs, procedures, and measures. And too often, researchers in the United States have judged minority group children and adults according to white middle-class standards, have labeled them "deficient" when they would better be described as "different," and have looked more at their vulnerabilities than at their strengths (Ogbu, 1981; Spencer, 2006). Also too often, researchers have assumed that all African Americans or Asian Americans or Hispanic Americans are alike psychologically, when in fact there is immense diversity within each racial or ethnic group (Helms, Jernigan, & Mascher, 2005). Today's developmentalists appreciate the importance of understanding human development in its ecological context, but actually doing so is a tremendous challenge.

Protecting the Rights of Research Participants

Developmental researchers must also be sensitive to **research ethics**—the standards of conduct that investigators are ethically bound to honor to protect their research participants from physical or psychological harm (see, for example, Buchanan, Fisher, & Gable, 2009; Kodish, 2005; Pimple, 2008).

Many ethical issues arise in developmental research. For example, is it ethical to tell children that they performed poorly on a test to create a temporary sense of failure? Is it an invasion of a family's privacy to ask adolescents questions about conversations they have had with their parents about sex? If a drug to treat memory loss in elderly adults with Alzheimer's disease appears

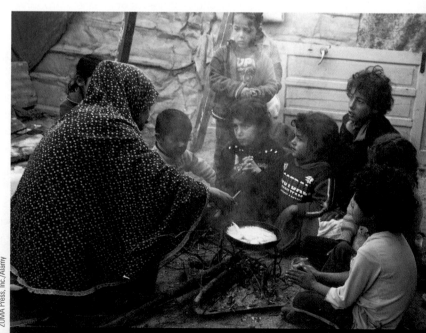

ZUMA Press, Inc./Alamy

Only cross-cultural research can tell us whether the findings of research conducted in our society hold true in societies very different from ours. Here a Bedouin woman in the Gaza Strip prepares food for her children inside the family's tent.

to be working, should it be withheld from the control group in the study?

Such issues have led the federal government (through the Office for Human Research Protections) and a variety of professional organizations such as the American Psychological Association to establish guidelines for ethical research with humans. Federal regulations require universities and other organizations that conduct research with humans to have institutional review boards (IRBs) that determine whether proposed research projects conform to ethical standards and to approve projects only if they comply.

Deciding whether a proposed study is on safe ethical ground involves weighing the possible benefits of the research (gains in knowledge and potential benefits to humanity or to the participants) against the potential risks to participants. If the potential benefits greatly outweigh the potential risks, and if there are no other less-risky procedures that could produce these same benefits, the investigation is likely to be viewed as ethical. The investigator's ethical responsibilities boil down to respecting the rights of research participants by (1) allowing them to freely give their informed consent, (2) debriefing them afterward if they are not told everything in advance or are deceived, (3) protecting them from harm, and (4) treating any information they provide as confidential.

Informed Consent

Researchers generally should inform potential participants of all aspects of the research that might affect their decision to participate so that they can make a voluntary decision based on full knowledge of what the research involves. But are young children or mentally impaired people such as older adults with Alzheimer's disease capable of understanding what they are being asked to do and of giving their *informed* consent? Often they are not or it can be challenging to tell if they are (for example, see Karlawish et al., 2009; Kim et al., 2004; Kodish, 2005). Therefore, researchers who study such "vulnerable" populations should obtain at least the "assent" or agreement of the individual (if possible) as well as the informed consent from someone who can decide on the individual's behalf—for example, the parent or guardian of a child or the legal representative of a cognitively impaired nursing home resident. Investigators also must take care not to pressure anyone to participate and must respect participants' right to refuse to participate, to drop out during the study, and to refuse to have their data used by the investigator.

Debriefing

Researchers generally tell participants about the purposes of the study in advance, but in some cases doing so would ruin the study. If you told college students in advance that you were studying moral development and then gave them an opportunity to cheat on a test, do you think anyone would cheat? Instead, you might set up a situation in which students believe they can cheat without being detected, see who cheats, and then debrief them afterward, explaining the true purpose of the study. You would also have an obligation to make sure that participants do not leave feeling upset about cheating.

Protection from Harm

Researchers are bound not to harm research participants either physically or psychologically. Infants may cry if they are left in a room with a stranger. Adolescents may become embarrassed if they are asked about their sex lives. Investigators must try to anticipate and prepare to deal with such consequences (for example, by having a counselor on call). If physical or psychological harm to participants seems likely, the researcher may need to find another way of answering the research question. Federal regulations provide extra protection from harm to children (Kodish, 2005).

Confidentiality

Researchers also have an ethical responsibility to keep confidential the information they collect. It would be unacceptable, for example, to tell a child's teacher that the child performed poorly on an intelligence test or to let an adult's employer know that he revealed a drinking problem in an interview. Only if participants give explicit permission to have information about them shared with someone else or, in rare cases, if the law requires disclosure of information (such as when a researcher learns that a child is being abused) can that information be passed on.

Clearly, developmental researchers have some serious issues to weigh if they want their research to be not only well designed but also culturally sensitive and ethically responsible. They must make many choices in designing their studies; as a result, all studies have limitations of one sort or another, and we are left to piece together the best picture of human development we can from the available (flawed) evidence. Understanding life-span human development would be downright impossible if researchers merely conducted study after study without guiding ideas, however. Theories of human development provide those guiding ideas and are the subject of Chapter 2.

▶ Checking Mastery

1. If researchers do not try to keep ethnocentrism out of their research, what can happen?
2. A researcher deceives research participants into thinking they are in a study of learning when the real purpose is to determine whether they are willing to inflict harm on people who make learning errors if told to do so by an authority figure. What ethical responsibilities does this researcher have?

▶ Making Connections

1. Now that you have your PhD in life-span developmental psychology, you want to interview elderly widows in Japan and in the United States about their emotional reactions to widowhood shortly after the deaths of their husbands. What ethical issues should you consider, and what steps should you take to make your study as ethical as possible?
2. What might you do to make this research as culturally sensitive as possible?

Chapter Summary

1.1 How Should We Think about Development?

- Development is systematic changes and continuities over the life span, involving gains, losses, and neutral changes in physical, cognitive, and psychosocial functioning; it is more than growth in childhood and biological aging in adulthood.
- Development takes place in an historical, cultural, and subcultural context and is influenced by age grades, age norms, and social clocks.
- Concepts of the life span and its distinctive periods have changed over history in Europe and North America and differ from culture to culture. Starting in the 17th century, children came to be seen as innocents; in the late 19th century, adolescence emerged as a distinct phase; and only in the 20th century did our society recognize emerging adulthood, a middle-aged "empty nest" period, and an old age characterized by retirement.
- Understanding the nature–nurture issue means understanding the interaction of biology and maturation with environment and learning.

1.2 What Is the Science of Life-Span Development?

- The study of life-span development, guided by the goals of description, prediction, explanation, and optimization, began with the baby biographies written by Charles Darwin and others.
- Through his use of questionnaires and attention to all phases of the life span, including the storm and stress of adolescence, American psychologist G. Stanley Hall came to be regarded as the founder of developmental psychology.
- The modern life-span perspective on human development set forth by Paul Baltes assumes that development (1) occurs throughout the life span, (2) can take many different directions, (3) involves gains and interlinked losses at every age, (4) is characterized by plasticity, (5) is affected by its historical and cultural context, (6) is influenced by multiple interacting causal factors, and (7) can best be understood if scholars from multiple disciplines join forces to study it.

1.3 How Is Development Studied?

- The scientific method involves formulating theories and testing hypotheses derived from them by conducting research with a sample (ideally a random sample) representative of a larger population of interest. Good theories should be internally consistent, falsifiable, and, ultimately, supported by the data.
- Common data collection methods include verbal reports, behavioral observations (naturalistic and structured), and physiological measures.
- The goal of explaining development is best achieved through experiments, which involve random assignments to conditions, manipulation of the independent variable, and experimental control. However, not all developmental issues can be studied with experiments. Case studies may have limited generalizability, and in correlational studies, one faces the directionality and third variable problems in interpreting findings. Developmentalists also use meta-analyses to synthesize the results of several studies of the same issue.
- Developmental research designs seek to describe age effects on development. Cross-sectional studies compare different age groups but confound age effects and cohort effects. Longitudinal studies study age change but confound age effects and time-of-measurement effects. Sequential studies combine the cross-sectional and longitudinal approaches.

1.4 What Special Challenges Do Developmental Scientists Face?

- To understand human development, researchers must study it in a variety of ecological contexts, develop culturally sensitive methods and measures, and keep their own cultural values and ethnocentrism from biasing their conclusions.
- Researchers must adhere to standards of ethical research practice, with attention to ensuring informed consent, debriefing individuals from whom information has been withheld, protecting research participants from harm, and maintaining confidentiality of data.

Checking Mastery Answers

For answers to Checking Mastery questions, please see Appendix B.

Key Terms

development **4**
growth **5**
biological aging **5**
depression **5**
aging **5**
emerging adulthood **5**
age grade **6**
rite of passage **6**
age norms **7**
social clock **7**
culture **7**
ethnicity **7**
socioeconomic status (SES) **7**
adolescence **8**
life expectancy **8**
nature–nurture issue **9**
maturation **9**
genes **9**
environment **9**
learning **9**

evidence-based practice **11**
baby biographies **11**
storm and stress **12**
gerontology **12**
life-span perspective **12**
plasticity **12**
neuroplasticity **12**
scientific method **14**
theory **14**
hypothesis **14**
sample **15**
population **15**
random sample **15**
naturalistic observation **15**
structured observation **16**
functional magnetic resonance
    imaging (fMRI) **16**
case study **17**
experiment **18**
independent variable **18**

dependent variable **18**
random assignment **18**
experimental control **19**
correlational method **19**
correlation coefficient **20**
directionality problem **20**
third variable problem **20**
meta-analysis **21**
cross-sectional design **21**
cohort **21**
age effects **22**
cohort effects **22**
longitudinal design **22**
baby boom generation **23**
millennials **23**
time-of-measurement effects **23**
sequential design **24**
ethnocentrism **26**
research ethics **26**

CENGAGE
brain.com   Get quizzes, flashcards, videos, and more at **www.cengagebrain.com**.

2 Theories of Human Development

Terrell, age 6, just started first grade last week, all decked out in his new blue shirt and khaki pants. Now he is begging his mother each morning to let him stay home. He cries and says that he has a terrible stomachache, and a headache and a sore foot besides, and is going to throw up any second so please, please, can he stay home. Because his symptoms clear up quickly if he is allowed to stay home, Terrell's problem does not appear to be a physical illness. But what *is* wrong?

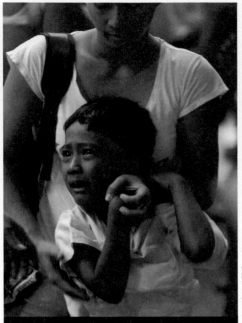

Noel Celis/AFP/Getty Images

Like many new first graders, this boy in the Philippines is not ready to leave his mother when he arrives at school for the first time.

School refusal is a reluctance or refusal to go to school or to remain there, sometimes called school phobia in the past because it often involves intense anxiety (C. A. Kearney, 2008; Thambirajah, De-Hayes, & Grandison, 2008). Did you seriously not want to go to school at some point in your educational career? School refusal affects as many as 5% of school-age children at any given time, and many more at some point in their development; it is most common among 5- to 7-year-olds like Terrell who are venturing off to school for the first time (Fremont, 2003; Heyne, King, & Tonge, 2004). School refusal can have a number of different causes, can involve considerable emotional distress for the child, and can have negative longer-term effects such as academic difficulty, dropping out, and even adjustment problems in adulthood (C. A. Kearney, 2008).

How might we explain a 6-year-old's refusal to go to school from a developmental perspective? What is your explanation? What explanations might the leading theories of human development offer? In this chapter we will illustrate that different theories of human development provide different lenses through which to view developmental phenomena such as school refusal.

2.1 Developmental Theories and the Issues They Raise

LEARNING OBJECTIVES:

• Explain why theories are needed in developmental science.

• Outline the four issues addressed by theories of human development.

As noted in Chapter 1, a theory is a set of ideas proposed to describe and explain certain phenomena—in this book, the phenomena of human development. In science, it is not enough simply to catalog facts without organizing this information around some set of concepts and propositions. Researchers would soon be overwhelmed by trivia and would lack "the big picture." A theory of human development provides needed organization, offering a lens through which researchers can interpret and explain any number of specific facts or observations. A theory also guides the collection of new facts or observations, making clear

• what is most important to study,
• what can be hypothesized or predicted about it, and
• how it should be studied.

Because different theorists often have different views on these critical matters, what is learned in any science greatly depends on which theoretical perspectives become dominant, which largely depends on how well they account for the facts.

In this chapter, we examine four major theoretical viewpoints, each with important messages about the nature of human development:

1. The *psychoanalytic* viewpoint developed by Sigmund Freud and revised by Erik Erikson and other neo-Freudians
2. The *learning* perspective developed by such pioneers as Ivan Pavlov, John Watson, B. F. Skinner, and Albert Bandura
3. The *cognitive developmental* viewpoint associated with Jean Piaget
4. The *systems theory* approach, exemplified by Urie Bronfenbrenner's bioecological model

We will be asking as we go whether these theoretical perspectives meet the criteria of good theories introduced in Chapter 1—that is, whether they are internally consistent (coherent), falsifiable (testable), and supported by data (confirmed by research). To further aid you in comparing the theories, we outline four key developmental issues on which theorists—and people in general—often disagree (Miller, 2011; Parke et al., 1994): nature–nurture, activity–passivity, continuity–discontinuity, and universality–context specificity. All of us hold some basic beliefs about human development—for example, about the importance of genes versus good parenting in healthy development. Reading this chapter will make you more aware of your own assumptions about human development and how they compare with those of

Where Do You Stand on Major Developmental Issues?

Choose one option for each statement, and write down the corresponding letter or fill it in at the end of the box. See Table 2.5 to compare your results with how the theorists described in this chapter view development.

1. Biological influences (heredity and maturational forces) and environmental influences (culture, parenting styles, and learning experiences) are thought to contribute to development. Overall,
   a. biological factors contribute far more than environmental factors.
   b. biological factors contribute somewhat more than environmental factors.
   c. biological and environmental factors are equally important.
   d. environmental factors contribute somewhat more than biological factors.
   e. environmental factors contribute far more than biological factors.

2. People are basically
   a. active beings who are the prime determiners of their own abilities and traits.
   b. passive beings whose characteristics are molded either by social influences (parents, other significant people, and outside events) or by biological changes beyond their control.

3. Development proceeds
   a. through stages so that the individual changes rather abruptly into a different kind of person than she was in an earlier stage.
   b. in a variety of ways—some stage-like and some gradual or continuous.
   c. continuously—in small increments without abrupt changes or distinct stages.

4. When you compare the development of different individuals, you see
   a. many similarities; children and adults develop along universal paths and experience similar changes at similar ages.
   b. many differences; different people often undergo different sequences of change and have widely different timetables of development.

Statement			
1	2	3	4
Your pattern of choices:			
__	__	__	__

---

the major theorists. We therefore invite you to clarify your stands on these issues by completing the questionnaire in **Engagement Box 2.1**. Table 2.5 at the end of the chapter indicates how the major developmental theorists might answer the questions, so you can compare your assumptions with theirs.

In Exploration boxes throughout this chapter, we imagine some major points each theorist might make about the causes of school refusal. We suggest that you predict what each theorist would say before you read each of these boxes to see whether you can successfully apply each theory. At the end of the chapter **(Application Box 2.1)**, we'll invite you to apply the different theories to understanding and preventing risky sexual behavior and unwanted teenage pregnancy. It is our hope that when you master the major theories of human development, you will be able to draw on their concepts and propositions to make better sense of—and perhaps to guide in more positive directions—your own and other people's development. Now to the four major issues addressed by theories of human development.

Nature–Nurture

Is development primarily the product of nature (biological forces) or nurture (environmental forces)? As you saw in Chapter 1, the nature–nurture issue is the most important and most complex issue in the study of human development (Goldhaber, 2012). Strong believers in nature stress the importance of individual genetic makeup, universal maturational processes guided by genes, biologically based predispositions built into genes over the course of evolution, and other biological

influences. They are likely to claim that all normal children achieve the same developmental milestones at similar times because of maturational forces, that major changes in functioning in late adulthood are biologically based, and that differences among children or adults are largely because of differences in genetic makeup and physiology.

By contrast, strong believers in nurture emphasize environment—influences outside the person. Nurture includes influences of the physical environment (crowding, pollution, and the like) as well as the social environment (for example, learning experiences, child-rearing methods, peer influence, societal trends, and the cultural context in which the person develops). A strong believer in nurture would argue that human development can take many paths depending on the individual's experiences over a lifetime.

Activity–Passivity

The **activity–passivity issue** focuses on the extent to which human beings are active in creating and influencing their own environments and, in the process, in producing their own development, or are passively shaped by forces beyond their control. Some theorists believe that humans are curious, active creatures who orchestrate their own development by exploring the world around them and shaping their environments. The girl who asks for dolls at the toy store and the boy who clamors instead for a toy machine gun are actively contributing to their own gender-role development. Both the budding scientist who experiments with chemicals in the basement and the sociable adolescent who spends hours text messaging are seeking out and creating a niche that suits their emerging traits and abilities—and that further develops those traits in the process (Harris, 2006).

Other theorists view humans as passive beings shaped largely by forces beyond their control—usually environmental influences but possibly strong biological forces. From this vantage point, children's academic failings might be blamed on the failure of their parents and teachers to provide them with the right learning experiences, and the problems of socially isolated older adults might be attributed to societal neglect of the elderly rather than to deficiencies within the individual.

Continuity–Discontinuity

Do you believe that humans change gradually, in ways that leave them not so different from the way they were before, or do you believe humans change abruptly and dramatically? One aspect of the **continuity–discontinuity issue** focuses on whether the changes people undergo over the life span are gradual or abrupt. Continuity theorists view human development as a process that occurs in small steps, without sudden changes, as when grade school children gradually gain weight from year to year. In contrast, discontinuity theorists tend to picture the course of development as more like a series of stair steps, each of which elevates the individual to a new (and often more advanced) level of functioning. When an adolescent boy rapidly shoots up 6 inches in height, gains a bass voice, and grows a beard, the change seems discontinuous.

The continuity–discontinuity issue also concerns whether changes are quantitative or qualitative in nature. Quantitative changes are changes in *degree* and indicate continuity: a person grows taller, knows more vocabulary words, gains more wrinkles, or interacts with friends less frequently. Or there may be continuity in the sense that people stay much the same. By contrast, qualitative changes are changes in *kind* and suggest discontinuity. They are changes that make the individual fundamentally different in some way (■ **Figure 2.1**). The transformations of a caterpillar into a butterfly rather than just a bigger caterpillar, of a nonverbal infant into a toddler who uses language, or of a prepubertal child into a sexually mature adolescent are examples of qualitative changes.

So continuity theorists typically hold that developmental changes are gradual and quantitative, whereas discontinuity theorists hold that they are more abrupt and qualitative. Discontinuity theorists often propose that people progress through **developmental stages**. A stage is a distinct phase of development characterized by a particular set of abilities, motives, emotions, or behaviors that form a coherent pattern. Development is said to involve fairly rapid transitions from one stage to another, each stage being qualitatively different from the stage before or the stage after. Thus, the preschool child may be said to have a fundamentally different way of thinking than the school-aged child—one that is more influenced by perceptions and less influenced by logic—or the adolescent may be able to grasp abstract concepts like human rights in a way that the school-aged child cannot. Or the middle-aged adult may be said to be concerned with fundamentally different life issues or conflicts than the young adult or older adult.

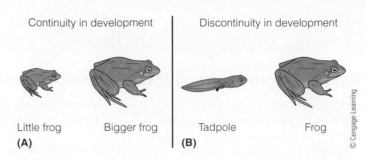

Continuity in development   Discontinuity in development

Little frog   Bigger frog   Tadpole   Frog
(A)   (B)

© Cengage Learning

■ **Figure 2.1** Is development continuous (A) or discontinuous (B)? That is, do people change quantitatively, becoming different in degree (as shown in Panel A with a size increase), or do they change qualitatively, becoming different in kind (as shown in Panel B, where a tadpole becomes a frog)?

Universality–Context Specificity

Finally, developmental theorists often disagree on the **universality–context-specificity issue**—or the extent to which developmental changes are common to all humans (universal) or are different across cultures, subcultures, task contexts, and individuals (context specific). Stage theorists typically believe that the stages they propose are universal. For example, a stage theorist might claim that virtually all children enter a new stage in their intellectual development as they enter adolescence or that most adults, sometime around age 40, experience a midlife crisis in which they raise major questions about their lives. From this perspective, development proceeds in certain universal directions.

But other theorists believe that human development is far more varied. Paths of development followed in one culture may be quite different from paths followed in another culture

To what extent is human development universal and to what extent is it culture specific? Only cross-cultural research can tell us.

• **Table 2.1** Issues in Human Development

Issue	Description
1. Nature–Nurture	Is development primarily the product of genes, biology, and maturation—or of experience, learning, and social influences?
2. Activity–Passivity	Do humans actively shape their own environments and contribute to their own development—or are they passively shaped by forces beyond their control?
3. Continuity–Discontinuity	Do humans change gradually and in quantitative ways—or do they progress through qualitatively different stages and change dramatically into different beings?
4. Universality–Context Specificity	Is development similar from person to person and from culture to culture—or do pathways of development vary considerably depending on the social context?

© Cengage Learning

(or subculture, neighborhood, or even performance context). For example, preschool children in the United States sometimes believe that dreams are real but give up this belief as they get older. By contrast, children raised in the Atayal culture of Taiwan have been observed to become more and more convinced as they get older that dreams are real, most likely because that is what adults in their culture believe (Kohlberg, 1966b). Within a particular culture, developmental change may also differ from subcultural group to subcultural group, from family to family, and from individual to individual. There seems to be both universality and context specificity in human development. So how alike—or how diverse—are the developmental paths we travel?

As we survey the major theories of human development, starting with Freud's well-known psychoanalytic perspective, look to see what stands each theory takes on these four key issues (● **Table 2.1**).

Checking Mastery

1. What are the two related meanings of discontinuity in development?

2. Stage theorists can disagree about a lot, but they are all likely to take certain stands on the issues of nature–nurture, continuity–discontinuity, and universality–context specificity. What stands?

Making Connections

1. Professor Whitehead has developed a theory of positive aging emphasizing that older adults all over the world are basically similar to younger adults in their psychological needs, that they have great potential to shape their own aging experience by selecting who they want to interact with and how, and that, unless they are thwarted by society, they will generally want to contribute positively to their communities rather than be dependent. What stands on the major issues in human development does Professor Whitehead seem to be taking? Explain why you think so.

2. What stands on the four major issues in human development do you feel your parents took in raising you? Why?

2.2 Freud: Psychoanalytic Theory

LEARNING OBJECTIVES:

- Summarize the three parts of the personality and the five psychosexual stages in Freud's psychoanalytic theory.

- Evaluate the strengths or contributions and the weaknesses of Freud's theory.

It is difficult to think of a theorist who has had a greater effect on Western thought than Sigmund Freud, the Viennese physician who lived from 1856 to 1939. This revolutionary thinker's **psychoanalytic theory**, which focused on the development and dynamics of the personality, challenged prevailing notions of human nature and human development. It proposed that people are driven by motives and emotional conflicts of which they are largely unaware and that they are shaped by their earliest experiences in the family (Hall, 1954; Westen, Gabbard, & Ortigo, 2008). Freud's ideas continue to influence thinking about human development, even though they are far less influential today than they once were. We introduce this historically important theorist briefly to set the stage for his influential follower, Erik Erikson.

Instincts and Unconscious Motivation

Central to Freudian psychoanalytic theory is the notion that humans have basic biological urges or drives that must be satisfied. Freud viewed the newborn as an inherently selfish and

Sigmund Freud's psychoanalytic theory was one of the first, and one of the most influential, theories of how the personality develops from childhood to adulthood. Here, Freud poses with his grandsons, Heinz and Ernst (and a lighted cigar).

aggressive creature driven by **instincts**—inborn biological forces that motivate behavior. These biological instincts are the source of the psychic (or mental) energy that fuels human behavior and that is channeled in new directions over the course of human development.

Freud strongly believed in **unconscious motivation**—the power of instincts and other inner forces to influence our behavior without our awareness. A preadolescent girl, for example, may not realize that she is acting in babyish ways in order to regain the security of her mother's love; a teenage boy may not realize that his devotion to body building is a way of channeling his sexual and aggressive urges. You immediately see that Freud's theory tilts toward the nature side of the nature–nurture issue: Development is shaped by biological forces that provide an unconscious motivation for behavior. Nevertheless, his theory also includes environmental influences on development, mostly in the form of experiences in the family during the first 5 years of life.

Id, Ego, and Superego

According to Freud (1933), the child's psychic energy is divided among three components of the personality as she develops: the id, the ego, and the superego. At birth, there is only the **id**—the impulsive, irrational, and selfish part of the personality whose mission is to satisfy the instincts. The id seeks immediate gratification, even when biological needs cannot be realistically or appropriately met. If you think about it, young infants do seem to be "all id" in many ways. When they are hungry or wet, they fuss and cry until their needs are met. They are not known for their patience.

The second component of the personality is the **ego**, the rational side of the individual that tries to find realistic ways of gratifying the instincts. According to Freud (1933), the ego begins to emerge during infancy and takes the form of cognitive processes such as perception, learning, and problem solving. The hungry toddler may be able to do more than merely cry when she is hungry; she may be able to draw on the resources of the ego to hunt down Dad, lead him to the kitchen, and say "cookie." As the ego matures further, children become more capable of postponing pleasures until a more appropriate time and of devising logical and realistic strategies for meeting their needs.

The third part of the Freudian personality is the **superego**, the individual's internalized moral standards. The superego develops from the ego as 3- to 6-year-old children internalize (take on as their own) the moral standards and values of their parents. Once the superego emerges, children have a parental voice in their heads that keeps them from violating society's rules and makes them feel guilty or ashamed if they do. The superego insists that people find socially acceptable or ethical outlets for the id's undesirable impulses.

Conflict among the id, ego, and superego is inevitable, Freud said. In the mature, healthy personality, a dynamic balance operates: the id communicates its basic needs, the ego restrains the impulsive id long enough to find realistic ways to satisfy these needs, and the superego decides whether the ego's problem-solving strategies are morally acceptable (Freud, 1940/1964). The ego has a tough job: It must strike a balance between the opposing demands of the id and the superego while accommodating the realities of the environment. Psychological problems often arise if there is imbalance among the three parts of the personality. For example, a salesman with an antisocial personality who routinely lies and cheats may have a strong id but a weak superego, whereas a married woman who cannot undress in front of her husband may have an overly strong superego that makes it difficult for her to fulfill her sexual needs. Through analysis of the dynamics operating among the id, ego, and superego, Freud and his followers attempted to describe and understand individual differences in personality and the origins of psychological disorders.

Psychosexual Stages

Freud (1940/1964) maintained that as the child matures biologically, the psychic energy of the sex instinct, which he called **libido**, shifts from one part of the body to another, seeking to gratify different biological needs. In the process, as outlined in ● **Table 2.2**, the child moves through five **psychosexual stages**: oral, anal, phallic, latency, and genital. Harsh child-rearing methods—punishing babies for mouthing paychecks and other interesting objects around the house, or toddlers for their toileting accidents, or preschoolers for taking interest in their genitals—can heighten these biologically based psychic conflicts and the child's anxiety.

The baby in the *oral stage* of psychosexual development focuses on the mouth as a source of sexual pleasure and can, according to Freud, experience anxiety and need to defend against it if denied oral gratification—for example, by being weaned too early. Through **fixation**, arrested development in which part of the libido remains tied to an earlier stage of development, an infant deprived of oral gratification might become "stuck" in the oral stage. He might become a chronic thumb

● **Table 2.2** The Stage Theories of Freud and Erikson

Freud's Psychosexual Theory		Erikson's Psychosocial Theory	
Stage (Age Range)	Description	Stage (Age Range)	Description
Oral stage (birth–1 year)	Libido is focused on the mouth as a source of pleasure. Obtaining oral gratification from a mother figure is critical to later development.	Trust vs. mistrust (birth–1 year)	Infants must learn to trust their caregivers to meet their needs. Responsive parenting is critical.
Anal stage (1–3 years)	Libido is focused on the anus, and toilet training creates conflicts between the child's biological urges and the society's demands.	Autonomy vs. shame and doubt (1–3 years)	Children must learn to be autonomous—to assert their wills and do things for themselves—or they will doubt their abilities.
Phallic stage (3–6 years)	Libido centers on the genitals. Resolution of the Oedipus or the Electra complex results in identification with the same-sex parent and development of the superego.	Initiative vs. guilt (3–6 years)	Preschoolers develop initiative by devising and carrying out bold plans, but they must learn not to impinge on the rights of others.
Latent period (6–12 years)	Libido is quiet; psychic energy is invested in schoolwork and play with same-sex friends.	Industry vs. inferiority (6–12 years)	Children must master important social and academic skills and keep up with their peers; otherwise, they will feel inferior.
Genital stage (12 years and older)	Puberty reawakens the sexual instincts as youths seek to establish mature sexual relationships and pursue the biological goal of reproduction.	Identity vs. role confusion (12–20 years)	Adolescents ask who they are and must establish social and vocational identities; otherwise, they will remain confused about the roles they should play as adults.
		Intimacy vs. isolation (20–40 years)	Young adults seek to form a shared identity with another person, but may fear intimacy and experience loneliness and isolation.
		Generativity vs. stagnation (40–65 years)	Middle-aged adults must feel that they are producing something that will outlive them, either as parents or as workers; otherwise, they will become stagnant and self-centered.
		Integrity vs. despair (65 years and older)	Older adults must come to view their lives as meaningful to face death without worries and regrets.

© Cengage Learning

sucker and then an adult who chain smokes and is overdependent on other people. How the child copes with the challenges of a stage and what parents do to help or hurt can leave a lasting imprint on the personality.

Similarly, the toddler in the *anal stage* must cope with new demands when toilet training begins. Parents who are impatient and punitive as their children learn to delay the gratification of relieving themselves can create high levels of anxiety and a personality that resists demands from authority figures. The parent's goal should be to allow some (but not too much) gratification of impulses while helping the child achieve reasonable (but not too much) control over these impulses.

The *phallic* stage from age 3 to age 6 is an especially treacherous time, according to Freud. Children develop an incestuous desire for the parent of the other sex and must defend against it. A boy experiencing an **Oedipus complex** loves his mother, fears that his father will retaliate by castrating him, and resolves this conflict through **identification** with his father. Identification involves taking on or internalizing the attitudes and behaviors of another person. The Oedipal boy is said to defend against his forbidden desire for his mother and hostility toward his father by possessing his mother vicariously through his father, who, through identification, is now an admired and less fear-provoking figure. Meanwhile, a girl experiencing an

Freud: Notes on School Refusal

(We suggest you read this and subsequent boxes on school refusal after you read about each theorist's theory; it will make more sense and you'll be able to test your ability to apply the theory.)

Children who refuse to attend school are quite often suffering from psychological problems, especially anxiety or depression (C. A. Kearney, 2008; Richards & Hadwin, 2011). So are their parents (Bahali, Tahiroglu, Avci, & Seydaoglu, 2011). Possibly the source of Terrell's problem, of which he is probably unaware, is not fear of school as much as separation anxiety (Bernstein & Victor, 2010). He may suffer from a fear of leaving his mother, probably originating in an unresolved Oedipal conflict involving his incestuous desire for his mother in the phallic stage of psychosexual development.

I would analyze the mother–son relationship from birth to find the source of this boy's problems. Lack of gratification, or too much gratification, during the oral or anal stages may have contributed to his current difficulty resolving his Oedipal conflict.

Electra complex is said to desire her father (and envy the fact that he has a penis, whereas she does not), view her mother as a rival, and ultimately resolve her conflict by identifying with her mother. When boys and girls resolve their emotional conflicts by identifying with the same-sex parent, they incorporate their same-sex parent's values into their superego, so the preschool phallic period is critical in both moral development and gender-role development.

During the *latency period*, sexual urges are tame and 6- to 12-year-olds invest psychic energy in schoolwork and play. However, adolescents experience new psychic conflicts as they reach puberty and enter the final stage of psychosexual development, the *genital stage*. Adolescents may have difficulty accepting their new sexuality, may reexperience conflicting feelings toward their parents that they felt during the phallic stage, and may distance themselves from their parents to defend themselves against these anxiety-producing feelings. Freud believed that psychosexual development stops with adolescence and that the individual remains in the genital stage throughout adulthood.

To defend itself against all the anxiety that can arise as these psychic conflicts play out, the ego adopts unconscious coping devices called **defense mechanisms** (Freud, 1940/1964). One well-known example (besides identification, which we already discussed) is **repression**, or removing unacceptable thoughts or traumatic memories from consciousness. Through repression, a young woman who was raped may have no memory at all of it. Or through the defense mechanism of **regression**, or retreating to an earlier, less traumatic stage of development, a preschool girl, threatened by her new baby brother, may revert to infantile behavior and want to be rocked.

We learn these and other defense mechanisms to cope with inner conflicts of which we are largely unaware, deceiving ourselves in order to save ourselves. Defense mechanisms can be healthy in that they allow us to function despite anxiety, but they can also spell trouble for some people if they involve too much distortion of reality. Moreover, they usually do not resolve the underlying psychic conflicts, which is why Freud believed that the goal of psychotherapy should be to bring unconscious fantasies, desires, and beliefs to the level of consciousness.

In **Exploration Box 2.1**, we imagine the notes that Freud might have scribbled down to explain Terrell's school refusal, as described at the start of the chapter. What might you say if you were Freud?

Strengths and Weaknesses

Many developmentalists fault Freud for proposing a theory that is ambiguous, internally inconsistent, difficult to pin down and test, and therefore not easily falsifiable (Fonagy & Target, 2000). Testing hypotheses that require studying unconscious motivations and the workings of the unseen id, ego, and superego has been challenging. Moreover, when the theory has been tested, many of its specific ideas—for example, ideas about the Oedipus and Electra conflicts—have not been well supported (Crews, 1996; Fisher & Greenberg, 1977). One critic went so far as to call it "a theory in search of some facts" (Macmillan, 1991, p. 548).

Yet many of Freud's general insights have stood up well and have profoundly influenced theories of human development, personality, and psychotherapy (Fonagy & Target, 2000; Westen et al., 2008). First, Freud called attention to *unconscious processes* underlying human behavior. His fundamental insights in this area are supported by modern psychological and neuropsychological research (Bargh & Morsella, 2008; Westen et al., 2008), and they have profoundly influenced psychotherapy. Second, he was one of the first to highlight the importance for later development of *early experiences* in the family, which, as we will see throughout this book, can be tremendously important. Finally, he emphasized the importance of *emotions* and emotional conflicts in development and the workings of personality. Developmentalists since Freud have often slighted emotional development (but see Chapter 14), focusing instead on observable behavior or on rational thought processes.

1. Jaime believes that people have both a moral side and a selfish side that work against each other. According to Freud's psychoanalytic theory, what are these "sides" called and when do they arise in development?
2. According to Freud, how do girls relate to their mothers and fathers during the phallic stage of development?
3. What is one thing Freud got right and one thing Freud got wrong?

1. In 2012, former Penn State assistant football coach, Jerry Sandusky, was convicted of multiple counts of sexually abusing boys, some of them in the athletic building's showers. Decades earlier, Sandusky founded a charitable organization called the Second Mile Foundation that helped disadvantaged children. Unfortunately, Second Mile provided Sandusky with a pipeline of vulnerable boys that he groomed to be his victims. At his sentencing, Sandusky denied his guilt and portrayed himself as the victim. What might Freud hypothesize about Sandusky's personality?

2.3 Erikson: Neo-Freudian Psychoanalytic Theory

LEARNING OBJECTIVES:

* Analyze how Erikson's neo-Freudian psychoanalytic theory differs from and expands on Freud's theory.

* Evaluate the strengths and weaknesses of Erikson's theory.

A sign of Freud's immense influence is that he inspired so many disciples and descendants to make their own contributions to the understanding of human development (Bergen, 2008). Among these well-known neo-Freudians were Alfred Adler, who suggested that siblings (and rivalries among siblings) are significant in development; Carl Jung, a pioneer in the study of adult development who claimed that adults experience a midlife crisis and then become freer to express both the "masculine" and the "feminine" sides of their personalities; Karen Horney, who challenged Freud's ideas about gender differences; Harry Stack Sullivan, who argued that close friendships in childhood set the stage for intimate relationships later in life; and Freud's daughter Anna, who developed techniques of psychoanalysis appropriate for children.

Erik Erikson built on Freudian theory and proposed that people experience eight psychosexual crises over their life span.

© Bettmann/Corbis

But the neo-Freudian who most influenced thinking about life-span development was Erik Erikson (1902–1994), whom we will revisit in more detail in Chapter 11. Erikson studied with Anna Freud and emigrated from Germany to the United States when Hitler rose to power (Friedman, 1999). Like Sigmund Freud, Erikson (1963, 1968, 1982) concerned himself with the inner dynamics of personality and proposed that the personality evolves through systematic stages. However, compared with Freud, Erikson:

* Placed less emphasis on sexual urges as the drivers of development and more emphasis on social influences—not only parent but peers, teachers, schools, and the broader culture.
* Placed less emphasis on the unconscious, irrational, and selfish id and more on the rational ego and its adaptive powers.
* Held a more positive view of human nature, seeing people as active in their development, largely rational, and able to overcome the effects of harmful early experiences.
* Put more emphasis on development after adolescence.

As one scholar summed it up, Erikson shifted Freudian thought "upward in consciousness, outward to the social world, and forward throughout the complete life span" (Hoare, 2005, p. 19).

Psychosocial Stages

Erikson believed that humans everywhere experience eight major **psychosocial stages**, or conflicts, during their lives. (Erikson's psychosocial stages are matched up with Freud's psychosexual stages in Table 2.2.) Whether the conflict of a particular stage is successfully resolved or not, the individual is pushed by both biological maturation and social demands into the next stage. However, the unsuccessful resolution of a conflict will influence how subsequent stages play out.

Erikson: Notes on School Refusal

Like a good Freudian, I would check for un-resolved conflicts from earlier stages of development. For example, might Terrell have developed a sense of shame and doubt rather than autonomy owing to negative reactions from his parents when he tried to assert himself as a toddler?

I would also focus on his current psychosocial stage, most likely industry versus inferiority. Might Terrell have performed poorly on school tasks during the first week of school and concluded that he is inferior to the other children?

Like Freud, I would also focus on the parent–child relationship, but I would recognize that other relationships count too. Something going on in Terrell's relationships with his classmates or teacher, or even something happening in his school or in the wider culture, may be upsetting him.

For example, the first conflict, *trust versus mistrust*, revolves around whether or not infants become able to rely on other people to be responsive to their needs. To develop a sense of trust, infants must be able to count on their primary caregivers to feed them, relieve their discomfort, come when beckoned, and return their smiles and babbles. Whereas Freud focused on the significance of the caregiver's feeding practices, Erikson believed that the caregiver's general responsiveness was critical to later development. If caregivers neglect, reject, or respond inconsistently to infants, infants will mistrust others. A healthy balance between the terms of the conflict must be struck for development to proceed optimally. Trust should outweigh mistrust, but an element of skepticism is also needed: an overindulged infant may become too trusting (a gullible "sucker").

So it goes for the remaining stages of childhood. If all goes well as children confront and resolve each conflict, they will gain a sense of self and develop *autonomy* (rather than shame and doubt about their ability to act independently), develop the *initiative* (as opposed to guilt) that allows them to plan and tackle big projects, and acquire the sense of *industry* (rather than inferiority) that will enable them to master important academic and social skills in school. This growth will position adolescents to successfully resolve the conflict for which Erikson (1968) is best known, *identity versus role confusion*. Erikson characterized adolescence as a time of "identity crisis" in which youth attempt to define who they are (in terms of career, religion, sexual identity, and so on), where they are heading, and how they fit into society. As part of their search, they often change their minds and experiment with new looks, new majors, new relationships, and new group memberships. Erikson should know: He was the tall, blond stepson of a Jewish doctor and wandered all over Europe after high school, trying out a career as an artist and other possibilities before he ended up studying child psychoanalysis under Anna Freud and finally found his calling in his mid-20s (Friedman, 1999).

Whereas Freud's stages stopped with adolescence, Erikson believed that psychosocial growth continues during the adult years. Successfully resolving the adolescent conflict of identity versus role confusion paves the way for resolving the early adulthood conflict of *intimacy versus isolation* and for becoming ready to form a shared identity with someone else in a committed, long-term relationship. Successful resolution of the middle-age conflict of *generativity versus stagnation* involves adults gaining a sense that they have produced something that will outlive them, whether by successfully raising children or by contributing something meaningful to the world through work or volunteer activities. Finally, elderly adults who resolve the psychosocial conflict of *integrity versus despair* find a sense of meaning in their lives that will help them face death.

Erikson clearly did not agree with Freud that the personality is essentially "set in stone" during the first 5 years of life. Yet he, like Freud and other psychoanalytic theorists, believed that people progress through systematic stages of development, undergoing similar personality changes at similar ages. Individual differences in personality presumably reflect the different experiences individuals have, not only in the family but beyond, as they struggle to cope with the challenges of each life stage. Both biological maturation and demands of the social and cultural environment influence the individual's progress through Erikson's sequence of psychosocial stages. As an illustration, **Exploration Box 2.2** shows what Erikson might have said about Terrell's school refusal.

Strengths and Weaknesses

Many people find Erikson's emphasis on our rational, adaptive nature and on an interaction of biological and social influences easier to accept than Freud's emphasis on unconscious, irrational motivations based in biological needs. Erikson also seems to have captured some important developmental issues in his eight stages. He has had an especially great impact on thinking about and research on adolescent identity formation and adult intimacy, generativity, and integrity (see Berzoff, 2008, and Chapter 11). Still, Erikson's theory has many of the same shortcomings as Freud's. It is sometimes vague and difficult to test. And although it provides a useful *description* of human personality development, it does not provide an adequate *explanation* of how this development comes about. Important psychoanalytic theorists such as Erikson continue to shape understanding of human development (Austrian, 2008), but many developmentalists have rejected the psychoanalytic perspective in favor of theories that are more precise and testable.

► **Checking Mastery**

1. What are four major ways in which Erikson's ideas differ from Freud's?
2. Wanda, at age 40, is depressed. She seems to doubt her ability to assert herself and take charge of situations, and she thinks other people will let her down. What Eriksonian stages might have been problematic for her in childhood, and how might her parents have contributed to her current problems?

► **Making Connections**

1. How might Erikson analyze Jerry Sandusky, the sexual abuser described in Section 2.2 Making Connections, and how would his analysis differ from Freud's?
2. Thinking about yourself, your parents, and your grandparents, can you see any evidence that Erikson's conflicts of adolescence and adulthood are relevant in your family?

2.4 Learning Theories

LEARNING OBJECTIVES:

- Explain how the learning theory perspective on development differs from stage theory perspectives like Freud's and Erikson's.

- Using examples, differentiate between Watson's classical conditioning, Skinner's operant conditioning, and Bandura's observational learning with regard to what learning involves and what can be learned.

- Evaluate the strengths and weaknesses of learning theories in general and discuss how Bandura overcame some of the weaknesses of earlier learning theories.

Give me a dozen healthy infants, well formed, and my own specified world to bring them up in, and I'll guarantee to take any one at random and train him to become any type of specialist I might select—doctor, lawyer, artist, merchant, chief, and yes, even beggar-man and thief, regardless of his talents, penchants, tendencies, abilities, vocations, and race of his ancestors. (Watson, 1925, p. 82)

This bold statement—that nurture is everything and that nature, or genetic endowment, counts for nothing—was made by John B. Watson, a pioneer of learning theory perspectives on human development. The English philosopher John Locke (1632–1704) had maintained that an infant is a **tabula rasa**, or "blank slate," waiting to be written on by life experiences. Watson and other learning theorists agreed: Children have no inborn tendencies, so how they turn out depends entirely on the environment in which they grow up and the ways in which their parents and other people in their lives treat them.

Early learning theorists such as Watson (1878–1958) and B. F. Skinner (1905–1990) emphasized that human behavior changes in direct response to environmental stimuli. Later learning theorists such as Albert Bandura (born in 1925) grant humans a more active and cognitive role in their own development but still believe that their development can take very different directions depending on their learning experiences. All learning theorists have provided us with important and practical tools for understanding how human behavior changes through learning and how learning principles can be applied to optimize development. We will lay out the basics of learning theory here and illustrate its significance throughout this book.

Watson: Classical Conditioning

Watson's (1913) **behaviorism** rested on his belief that conclusions about human development and functioning should be based on observations of overt behavior rather than on speculations about unobservable cognitive and emotional processes. Watson rejected psychoanalytic theory and demonstrated that some of Freud's fascinating discoveries about human behavior could be explained as learned associations between stimuli and responses (Rilling, 2000).

In his most famous study, Watson and colleague Rosalie Raynor (1920) set out to demonstrate that fears can be learned—that fears are not necessarily inborn, as was commonly thought. They used the principles of **classical conditioning**, a simple form of learning in which a stimulus that initially had no effect on the individual comes to elicit a response through its association with a stimulus that already elicits the response. The Russian physiologist Ivan Pavlov first discovered classical conditioning quite accidentally while studying the digestive systems of dogs. In a famous experiment, Pavlov demonstrated how dogs, who have an innate (unlearned) tendency to salivate at the sight of food, could learn to salivate at the sound of a bell if, during a training period, the bell was sounded each time a dog was given meat powder.

In their demonstration of classical conditioning, Watson and Raynor presented a gentle white rat to a now-famous infant named Albert, who showed no fear of it. However, every time the rat was presented, Watson would slip behind Albert and bang a steel rod with a hammer. Babies are naturally scared by loud noises and, through conditioning—through the pairing of the white rat and the loud noise—Albert learned to whimper and cry in response to the white rat alone. Through learning, an initially neutral stimulus, the white rat, had become a stimulus for fear. This conditioned or learned fear response generalized to other furry items such as a rabbit and a Santa Claus mask. By today's standards, Watson's experiment would be viewed as unethical (see Beck, Levinson, & Irons, 2009, for a fascinating investigation of just how unethical). However, he had made his point: *emotional responses can be learned*. Fortunately, fears learned through classical conditioning can be unlearned if the feared stimulus is paired with a stimulus for happy emotions (Jones, 1924).

Many emotional associations and attitudes, both positive and negative, are acquired through classical conditioning. Classical conditioning is undoubtedly involved when infants learn to love their parents, who become associated with the positive sensations of drinking milk, being rocked, and being comforted. And classical conditioning helps explain why adults find that certain songs, scents, or articles of clothing "turn them on." It also explains why so many of us have odd phobias (in the case of one of the authors, an aversion to antiseptic cotton, which started with the pain of having a skinned knee daubed with cotton and iodine, a disinfectant that burns when it hits a fresh wound). When a humor columnist polled his colleagues about their phobias, he found not only one who, like the author, "collapses on the ground in a fetal position" in response to someone tearing a cotton ball but also one whose arm hair stands up if he touches peach fuzz and another who feels "daggers shooting up my spine" when someone rubs pieces of Styrofoam together (Weingarten, 2011, p. 29). If you have your own unusual phobia, perhaps you can trace it to classical conditioning.

According to the learning theory perspective, it is a mistake to assume that children advance through a series of distinct stages guided by biological maturation, as Freud, Erikson, and other stage theorists have argued. Instead, learning theorists view development as nothing more than learning. For them, development is a continuous process of behavior change that is context specific and can differ enormously from person to person. Watson's basic view was further advanced by B. F. Skinner.

Skinner: Operant Conditioning

B. F. Skinner, probably the most famous American psychologist, had a long, distinguished career at Harvard University and a huge impact on approaches to behavior change (Rutherford, 2009). Through his research with animals, Skinner (1953) gained understanding of another important form of learning, **operant conditioning**, in which a learner's behavior becomes either more or less probable depending on the consequences it produces. In operant conditioning, a learner first behaves in some way (rather than reacting automatically to a stimulus, as in classical conditioning) and then comes to associate this action with the positive or negative consequences that follow it. The basic principle behind operant conditioning makes sense: People tend to repeat behaviors that have desirable consequences and cut down on behaviors that have undesirable consequences. Through operant conditioning, individuals can learn new skills and all kinds of habits, good and bad.

In the language of operant conditioning, *reinforcement* occurs when a consequence strengthens a response, or makes it more likely to occur. If a preschool child cleans his room, receives a hug, and then cleans his room more frequently thereafter, the hug provided **positive reinforcement** for room cleaning. *Positive* here means that something pleasant or desirable has been added to the situation, and *reinforcement* means that the behavior is strengthened. Thus, a positive reinforcer is a desirable

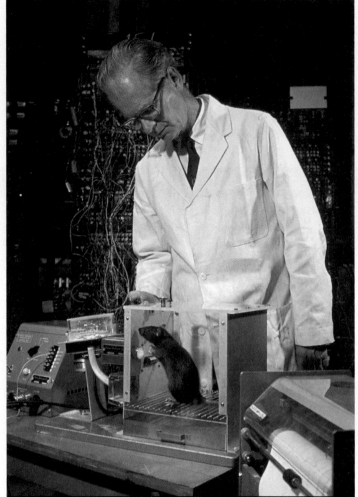

B. F. Skinner's operant conditioning theory emphasized the role of environment in controlling behavior. Here he delivers food pellets to a rat each time the rat presses a bar in what we now know as a "Skinner box."

Nina Leen/Time Life Pictures/Getty Images

event that, when introduced following a behavior, makes that behavior more probable. (Note that the effect on the child's behavior, not the parent's belief about what might be reinforcing, defines what is reinforcing.)

Negative reinforcement (which is *not*, we repeat *not*, a fancy term for punishment, as so many people believe) occurs when a behavioral tendency is strengthened because something unpleasant or undesirable is removed from the situation or is escaped or avoided after the behavior occurs. An example is the annoying sound that goes off in the car until you fasten your seat belt. The idea is that your buckling-up behavior will become a habit through negative reinforcement: Buckling your seat belt allows you to escape the unpleasant sound.

Bad habits can also develop because they allow people to avoid or escape unpleasant events. Teenagers may learn to lie to avoid lectures from their parents or to drink alcohol because it allows them to escape their feelings of social anxiety at parties. In each case, a behavior is strengthened through negative reinforcement—through the removal or elimination of something undesirable like a lecture or anxiety.

Contrast reinforcement, whether it is positive or negative, with punishment: Whereas reinforcement increases the strength of the behavior that preceded it, *punishment* decreases the strength of the behavior or weakens it. Two forms of punishment parallel the two forms of reinforcement. **Positive punishment** occurs when an unpleasant stimulus is the consequence of a behavior (for example, a child is spanked for misbehaving, or a cashier is criticized for coming up short of cash at the end of the day). **Negative punishment** occurs when a desirable stimulus is removed following the behavior (a misbehaving child loses the privilege of watching TV, or the amount the cashier was short is deducted from her pay). By definition, both positive and negative punishments decrease the likelihood that the punished behavior will be repeated.

The four possible consequences of a behavior are summarized in ■ **Figure 2.2**. In addition, some behavior has no consequence. Behavior that is ignored, or no longer reinforced, tends to become less frequent through the process of **extinction**. Indeed, a good alternative to punishing a child's misbehavior is ignoring it and instead reinforcing desirable behavior that is incompatible with it. Too often, the well-behaved child is ignored and the misbehaving child gets the attention—attention that can backfire because it serves as positive reinforcement for the misbehavior.

Skinnerian learning theorists have emphasized the power of positive reinforcement; their main child-rearing advice is, "Catch them being good." They have generally discouraged the use of physical punishment in child rearing. Yet, despite trends suggesting less acceptance of physical punishment today than in the past, most parents of young children in the United States believe that physical punishment of bad behavior is sometimes necessary and spank their children on occasion (Gershoff, 2008). What have researchers found?

Although it is generally best to use more positive approaches before resorting to punishment, physical punishment can be effective in changing behavior in the longer run if it (1) is administered immediately after the act (not hours later, when the child is being an angel), (2) is administered consistently after each offense, (3) is not overly harsh, (4) is accompanied by explanations, (5) is administered by an otherwise affectionate person, and (6) is used sparingly and combined with efforts to reinforce more acceptable behavior (Benjet & Kazdin, 2003; Domjan, 1993; Gershoff, 2002; Perry & Parke, 1975).

However, carefully designed studies conducted over many years indicate that physical punishment, especially if it is harsh, can have a number of undesirable effects, increasing aggression and mental health problems such as anxiety, depression, and substance use and even impairing children's intellectual and moral functioning (Durrant & Ensom, 2012; Gershoff, 2002; Taylor et al., 2010). For example, Lisa Berlin and her colleagues (2009) studied low-income African American, Mexican American, and white toddlers longitudinally when they were ages 1, 2, and 3. Spanking, but not verbal punishment, at age 1 was associated with more aggressive behavior at age 2 and lower mental development scores at age 3. Moreover, the researchers showed that physical punishment led to later aggressive behavior and intellectual delay even with early behavior and mental development controlled (see also Maguire-Jack, Gromoske, & Berger, 2012, where the negative effects of punishment were clear for behavior problems but not for cognitive development).

Especially worrisome is evidence that episodes of physical punishment sometimes turn into child abuse and that physical punishment can breed aggression in children (Benjet & Kazdin, 2003; Gershoff, 2002). Especially encouraging is evidence that parent training based on Skinnerian principles of reinforcement can have long-lasting, positive effects on both child behavior and parent adjustment (Patterson, Forgatch, & DeGarmo, 2010). Perhaps this is why more and more countries and states are banning spanking and other forms of physical punishment, not only in schools and child care settings but at home (Durrant & Ensom, 2012; Gershoff, 2008).

In sum, Skinner, like Watson, believed that the course of human development depends on the individual's learning experiences. One boy's aggressive behavior may be reinforced over time because he gets his way with other children or because his parents reinforce his "tough" behavior. Another boy may quickly learn that aggression is prohibited and punished. The two may develop in different directions based on their different histories of reinforcement and punishment.

	PLEASANT STIMULUS	UNPLEASANT STIMULUS
ADMINISTERED	**Positive reinforcement, adding a pleasant stimulus** (strengthens the behavior) Dad gives in to the whining and lets Moosie play Nintendo, making whining more likely in the future.	**Positive punishment, adding an unpleasant stimulus** (weakens the behavior) Dad calls Moosie a "baby." Moosie does not like this at all and is less likely to whine in the future.
WITHDRAWN	**Negative punishment, withdrawing a pleasant stimulus** (weakens the behavior) Dad confiscates Moosie's favorite Nintendo game to discourage whining in the future.	**Negative reinforcement, withdrawing an unpleasant stimulus** (strengthens the behavior) Dad stops joking with Lulu. Moosie gets very jealous when Dad pays attention to Lulu, so his whining enables him to bring this unpleasant state of affairs to an end.

© Cengage Learning

■ **Figure 2.2** Possible consequences of whining behavior. Moosie comes into the TV room and sees his father talking and joking with his sister, Lulu, as the two watch a football game. Soon Moosie begins to whine, louder and louder, that he wants them to turn off the television so he can play Nintendo. If you were Moosie's father, how would you react? Above are four possible consequences of Moosie's behavior. Consider both the type of consequence—whether it is a pleasant or aversive stimulus—and whether it is administered ("added to" the situation) or withdrawn (taken away). Notice that reinforcement, by definition, always strengthens whining behavior, or makes it more likely in the future, whereas punishment weakens it.

Skinner's operant conditioning principles can help explain many aspects of human development. And they are still widely applied in behavioral and, more recently, cognitive behavioral interventions in educational and therapeutic settings (A. J. Kearney, 2008; Mayer et al., 2009). Indeed, there are now smartphone apps based on Skinnerian principles to help people lose weight, exercise more, overcome addictions, and otherwise improve their health and well-being (Freedman, 2012). Yet many developmentalists believe that Skinner erred by not considering the role of cognitive processes in learning. Therefore, today's developmental scholars are more attracted to Albert Bandura's cognitive brand of learning theory than to Skinner's operant conditioning approach.

Bandura: Social Cognitive Theory

In his **social cognitive theory** (also called **social learning theory**), Stanford psychologist Albert Bandura (1977, 1986, 1989, 2000, 2006) claims that humans are cognitive beings whose active processing of information plays a critical role in their learning, behavior, and development. Bandura argues that human learning is very different from rat learning because humans have far more sophisticated cognitive capabilities. He agrees with Skinner that operant conditioning is an important type of learning, but he notes that people think about the connections between their behavior and its consequences, anticipate the consequences likely to follow from their behavior, and often are more affected by what they believe will happen than by the consequences they actually encounter. Individuals also reinforce or punish themselves with mental pats on the back and self-criticism, and these cognitions also affect behavior. Bandura prefers to call his position social cognitive theory rather than social learning theory for a reason: to distance himself from behavioral learning theories like Watson's and Skinner's and to emphasize that his theory is about the motivating and self-regulating role of cognition in human behavior (Bandura, 1986).

By highlighting observational learning as the most important mechanism through which human behavior changes, Bandura made his cognitive emphasis clear. **Observational learning** is simply learning by observing the behavior of other people (called *models*). By learning from and imitating other people, children can master computer skills and math problems, as well as how to swear and smoke. Observational learning is regarded as a more cognitive form of learning than conditioning because learners must pay attention, construct and remember mental representations (images and verbal summaries) of what they saw, retrieve these representations from memory later, and use them to guide behavior.

In a classic experiment, Bandura (1965) set out to demonstrate that children could learn a response neither elicited by a conditioned stimulus (as in classical conditioning) nor performed and then strengthened by a reinforcer (as in operant conditioning). He had nursery school children watch a short film in which an adult model attacked an inflatable "Bobo" doll: hitting the doll with a mallet while shouting "Sockeroo," throwing rubber balls at the doll while shouting "Bang, bang, bang," and so on. Some children saw the model praised, others saw the model punished, and still others saw no consequences follow the

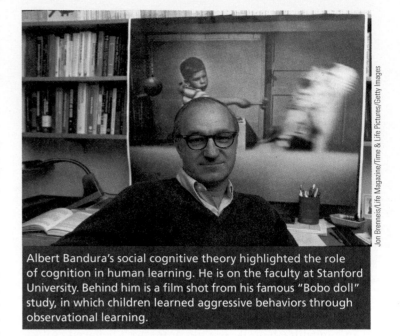

Albert Bandura's social cognitive theory highlighted the role of cognition in human learning. He is on the faculty at Stanford University. Behind him is a film shot from his famous "Bobo doll" study, in which children learned aggressive behaviors through observational learning.

model's violent attack. After the film ended, children were observed in a playroom with the Bobo doll and many of the props the model had used to work Bobo over.

What did the children learn? The children who saw the model rewarded and the children in the no-consequences condition imitated more of the model's aggressive acts than did the children who had seen the model punished. But interestingly, when the children who had seen the model punished were asked to reproduce all of the model's behavior they could remember, it turned out that they had learned just as much as the other children about how to treat a Bobo doll. Apparently, then, through a process termed **latent learning** in which learning occurs but is not evident in behavior, children can learn from observation even though they do not imitate (perform) the learned responses. Whether they will perform what they learn depends partly on **vicarious reinforcement** (or punishment), a process in which learners become more or less likely to perform a behavior based on whether consequences experienced by the model they observe are reinforcing or punishing. You are more likely to imitate someone who is rewarded for their behavior than someone who is punished.

So important is observational learning in human development that children everywhere show a tendency to *overimitate* what they see, even when it is pretty useless. In a study demonstrating this (Nielsen & Tomaselli, 2010), children in both urban Australia and the Kalahari bush of Africa watched an adult demonstrate how to open a box. Children in both cultures readily imitated the adult model's action of pushing a stick down on a knob on the front of the box, even though a more direct and effective way to open the box was to simply pull the knob with one's hand. More surprisingly, children also imitated completely irrelevant actions such as waving the stick three times over the box like a magic wand before opening the box. Such overimitation is not as evident among chimpanzees, who imitate only actions that directly help them reach their goals (Horner & Whiten, 2005).

Humans can learn almost anything through observational learning.

Why do humans overimitate, then? Possibly, Nielsen and Tomaselli (2010) suggest, because it has proven adaptive and helps them learn the many—and often arbitrary—rituals and rules of their culture.

Observational learning may be even more important in traditional societies than it is in modern ones (Rogoff et al., 2003). There, children learn not in schools where they are segregated from adults and given formal instruction, but through participation in everyday activities in which they actively observe and listen to their elders, learning skills such as weaving and hunting without the adults intentionally teaching them (Rogoff et al., 2003). In an interesting cross-cultural study (Correa-Chavez & Rogoff, 2009), Mayan children living in Guatemala, especially those whose mothers had had little Western schooling, were much more attentive while their siblings were taught to use a new toy than European American children from the United States were—and they learned more as a result. The Mayan children were used to learning by watching what was going on around them; the European American children seemed to wait for adults to arrange learning experiences directed toward them personally.

In his later work, Bandura (2000, 2006) moved beyond the study of observational learning to emphasize ways in which people deliberately exercise cognitive control over themselves, their environments, and their lives. From the time they are infants recognizing that they can make things happen in their worlds, people form intentions, foresee what will happen, evaluate and regulate their actions as they pursue plans, and reflect on their functioning. These cognitions play a real causal role in influencing their behavior. For example, individuals develop a high or low sense of **self-efficacy**, or belief that they can effectively produce a particular desired outcome. Whether you try to lose 10 pounds or get an A on a test, your success depends greatly on whether you have a sense of self-efficacy concerning your ability to achieve your goal.

Watson and Skinner may have believed that people are passively shaped by environment to become whatever those around them groom them to be, but Bandura does not. Because he views humans as active, cognitive beings, he holds that human development occurs through a continuous reciprocal interaction among the person (the individual's biological and psychological characteristics and cognitions), his or her behavior, and his or her environment—a perspective he calls **reciprocal determinism** (■ **Figure 2.3**). As Bandura sees it, environment does not rule, as it did in Skinner's thinking: people choose, build, and change their environments; they are not just shaped by them. And people's personal characteristics and behaviors affect the people around them, just as other people are influencing their personal characteristics and future behaviors.

Like Watson and Skinner, however, Bandura doubts that there are universal stages of human development. He maintains that development is context specific and can proceed along many paths. It is also continuous, occurring gradually through a lifetime of learning. Bandura acknowledges that children's cognitive capacities mature, so they can remember more about what they have seen and can imitate a greater variety of novel behaviors. Yet he also believes that children of the same age will be dissimilar if their learning experiences have differed considerably.

Obviously there is a fundamental disagreement between stage theorists such as Freud and Erikson and learning theorists such as Watson, Skinner, and Bandura (see ● **Table 2.3** for a summary of the three men's distinct contributions to the learning perspective on development). Learning theorists do not provide a general description of the typical course of human development because they insist that there is no such description to give. Instead, they offer a rich account of the mechanisms through which behavior can change, using principles of learning that are universal in their applicability to explain how each individual changes with age in unique ways (Goldhaber, 2000). We imagine what Watson, Skinner, and Bandura would say about school refusal in **Exploration Box 2.3**.

Strengths and Weaknesses

Pavlov's and Watson's demonstrations of classical conditioning, Skinner's work on operant conditioning, and Bandura's modern social cognitive theory with its highlighting of observational learning have contributed immensely to the understanding of

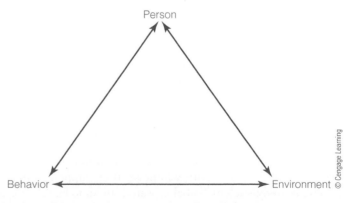

■ **Figure 2.3** Bandura's reciprocal determinism involves mutual influence of the person, the person's behavior, and the environment.

Learning Theorists: Notes on School Refusal

Anxiety disorders and phobias can be learned in a variety of ways.

John Watson might hypothesize that Terrell had a traumatic experience at school—maybe a fire drill alarm scared him or he became sick and threw up in class. Through classical conditioning, his classroom might have become a stimulus for anxious, fearful responses.

F. Skinner would insist that we should analyze the consequences of going to school versus staying at home for Terrell to see whether those consequences can explain his behavior (C. A. Kearney, 2008). If going to school results in punishing consequences (punches from a bully,

criticism from a teacher, embarrassment in the gym), the frequency of going to school will decline. If acting sick is negatively reinforcing because it helps Terrell avoid the anxiety of going to school, "sick" behavior will become more frequent. Terrell's mother could also be positively reinforcing stay-at-home behavior by giving Terrell extra attention and love when he is "sick" or letting him play video games in his bedroom all day. Research suggests that school refusal is more often about gaining reinforcers like parent attention or the chance to have fun than it is about avoiding or escaping anxiety-producing situations at school (Dube & Orpinas, 2009).

Through observational learning, Albert Bandura would add, a child who merely witnesses another child's anxious behavior at school may learn to behave anxiously. It is also important to understand what punishing consequences Terrell believes will occur if he attends school; beliefs about reinforcement or punishment can matter more than realities. And Bandura would ask whether Terrell may have lost his sense of self-efficacy for reading and writing when faced with the new challenges of first grade; even 6-year-olds have developed self-efficacy beliefs about schoolwork (Wilson & Trainin, 2007).

● **Table 2.3** A Summary of the Three Major Types of Learning

Learning Theorist	Type of Learning	What It Involves	What Is Learned
John Watson	Classical conditioning	A stimulus comes to elicit a response through its association with an unconditioned stimulus.	Emotional reactions (e.g., pleasant associations, phobias)
B. F. Skinner	Operant conditioning	Learning involves reacting to the consequences of one's behavior (reinforcement and punishment).	Skills; good and bad habits
Albert Bandura	Observational learning	Learning involves watching a model and, through vicarious reinforcement or punishment, the consequences of the model's behavior.	Skills, cognitions, and behaviors, including ones that the learner has not been directly reinforced for displaying

© Cengage Learning

development and continue to be influential. Learning theories are precise and testable. Carefully controlled experiments have shown how people might learn everything from altruism to alcoholism. Moreover, learning principles operate across the life span and can be used to understand behavior at any age. Finally, learning theories have incredibly important applications; they have been the basis for many highly effective behavioral and cognitive behavioral techniques for optimizing development and treating developmental problems.

Still, behavioral learning theories, and even Bandura's more recent social cognitive theory, leave something to be desired as explanations of human development. For instance, it has been demonstrated that reinforcing 3-month-old infants with smiles and gentle rubs on the chin whenever they happen to make babbling sounds, such as "bababa," causes them to babble more often than infants who receive the same social stimulation randomly, rather than only after each babbling sound they make (Weisberg, 1963). But does this mean that infants normally begin

to babble *because* babbling is reinforced by their caregivers? Not necessarily. All normal infants, even deaf ones, babble around 4 months of age. Moreover, no matter what learning experiences are provided to newborns, they will not be maturationally ready to babble. We must suspect, then, that the maturation of the neural and muscular control required for babbling has more than a little to do with the onset of babbling during infancy.

This example highlights two criticisms of learning theories as theories of human development. First, learning theorists rarely demonstrate that learning is responsible for commonly observed developmental changes; they show through their experiments only that learning *might* have resulted in developmental change, as in the case of reinforcement increasing the frequency of babbling. Some critics wish that learning theorists would provide a fuller account of normal changes across the life span. Second, learning theorists, even Bandura, probably put too little emphasis on biological influences on development, such as genetic endowment and maturational processes. We may well learn to fear snakes, for example. However, probably because snakes were a threat to our ancestors, we have evolved so that we are biologically prepared to be wary of these critters. Thus, we learn to fear snakes far more easily than we learn to fear bunnies or flowers (Ohman & Mineka, 2003). Today's learning theorists appreciate more than Watson and Skinner did that factors such as genetic endowment, previous learning, personality, and social context all affect how humans react to their learning experiences (Mineka & Zinbarg, 2006).

▶ Checking Mastery

1. The Foxes try to control their teenage daughter's behavior by (a) giving her an allowance only if she does her weekly chores, (b) setting her weekend curfew earlier if she stayed out later than she was supposed to the

weekend before, and (c) allowing her to get out of the distasteful task of cleaning the bathroom if she spends time with her grandmother. What specific consequences, using operant conditioning language, are illustrated by these three parenting tactics, and in each case, what effect do the parents hope to have on their daughter's behavior?

2. What are two main criticisms Albert Bandura might make of earlier behavioral learning theories?

▶ Making Connections

1. Marge, age 78, fell and broke her hip a year ago and has become overly dependent on her daughter for help ever since she left the rehabilitation hospital, even though she can get around quite well now. How might learning theorists explain her old-age dependency?

2.5 Piaget: Cognitive Developmental Theory

LEARNING OBJECTIVES:

* Explain the concept of constructivism and the differences in modes of thinking captured in the four stages in Piaget's cognitive-developmental theory.

* Evaluate the strengths and weaknesses of Piaget's theory, noting how the sociocultural and information-processing approaches have attempted to correct for its weaknesses.

After behavioral learning theories dominated the study of development in the 1950s and 1960s, many developmentalists began to look for a theory that was both more cognitive and more clearly developmental. They found what they wanted in the groundbreaking work of Jean Piaget. No theorist has contributed more to the understanding of children's minds than Piaget (1896–1980), a Swiss scholar who began to study children's intellectual development during the 1920s. This remarkable man developed quickly himself, publishing his first scientific work (a letter to the editor about an albino sparrow) at age 11. Eventually, Piaget blended his interest in zoology and animals' adaptation to their environments with his interest in philosophy. He then devoted his career to the study of how humans acquire knowledge and use it to adapt to their world.

Piaget's lifelong interest in cognitive development emerged while he worked at the Alfred Binet laboratories in Paris on the first standardized IQ test. IQ tests estimate individuals' intelligence based on the number of questions they answer correctly. Piaget soon became interested in children's wrong answers and noticed that children of about the same age gave the same kinds of wrong answers. By questioning them to find out how they were thinking about the problems presented to them, he began to realize that young children do not simply know less than older children; instead, they think in a qualitatively different way. Eventually Piaget developed a stage theory to account for changes in thinking from infancy to adolescence, a theory we will explore more thoroughly in Chapter 7.

Constructivism

Influenced by his background in biology, Piaget (1950) viewed intelligence as a process that helps an organism adapt to its environment. The infant who grasps a cookie and brings it to her mouth is behaving adaptively, as is the adolescent who solves algebra problems or the mechanic who fixes cars. As humans mature, they acquire ever more complex cognitive structures, or organized patterns of thought or action, that aid them in adapting to their environments.

Piaget insisted that children are not born with innate ideas about reality, as some philosophers have claimed. Nor did he think children are simply filled with information by adults, as learning theorists believe. Piaget's position, called **constructivism**, was that children actively construct their own understandings of the world based on their experiences. Thus preschool children may invent ideas that were not taught to them by adults, saying that the sun is alive because it moves across the sky, that children get diseases if they tell lies or otherwise misbehave, or that babies are bought at the baby store and then put in their mommies' tummies.

How do children construct more accurate understandings of the world? By being curious and active explorers: watching what is going on around them, seeing what happens when they experiment on the objects they encounter, and recognizing instances in which their current understandings are inadequate to explain events. Children use their current understandings of the world to help them solve problems, but they also revise their understandings to make them better fit reality (Piaget, 1952).

Stages of Cognitive Development

Piaget proposed four major periods of cognitive development: the sensorimotor stage (birth to age 2), the preoperational stage (ages 2–7), the concrete operations stage (ages 7–11), and the formal operations stage (ages 11–12 or older). These stages form what Piaget called an *invariant sequence*; that is, all children progress through the stages in the order they are listed without skipping stages or regressing to earlier stages. The ages given are only average ages; different children progress at different rates. The key features of each stage are summarized in ● **Table 2.4**. The core message is that humans of different ages think in qualitatively different ways (Inhelder & Piaget, 1958).

Infants in the **sensorimotor stage** deal with the world directly through their perceptions (senses) and actions (motor skills). They are unable to use symbols (gestures, images, or words representing real objects and events) to help them solve problems mentally. However, they learn a great deal about the world by exploring it, and they acquire tools for solving problems through their sensory and motor experiences.

The preschooler who has entered the **preoperational stage** of cognitive development has now developed the capacity for symbolic thought but is not yet capable of logical problem solving. The 4- or 5-year-old can use words as symbols to talk about a problem and can mentally imagine doing something before actually doing it. However, according to Piaget, preschool children are egocentric thinkers who have difficulty adopting perspectives other than their own and who may cling to incorrect ideas simply because they want them to be true. Lacking the tools of logical thought, preoperational children must also rely on their perceptions and as a result are easily fooled by appearances. Piaget demonstrated this by administering his famous conservation of liquid quantity task, in which a child is shown two short, wide glasses filled with equal amounts of water; sees the water poured from one of the squat glasses into a taller, thinner glass; and is then asked which glass has more water, the squat glass or

Swiss psychologist Jean Piaget revolutionized the field of human development with his cognitive developmental theory of intellectual growth.

© Farrell Grehan/Corbis

The *interaction* between biological maturation (most importantly, a developing brain) and experience (especially discrepancies between the child's understanding and reality) is responsible for the child's progress from one stage of cognitive development to a new, qualitatively different stage.

● **Table 2.4** Jean Piaget's Four Stages of Cognitive Development

Stage (Age Range)	Description
Sensorimotor (birth–2 years)	Infants use their senses and motor actions to explore and understand the world. At the start they have only innate reflexes, but they develop increasingly "intelligent" actions. By the end, they are capable of symbolic thought using images or words and can therefore plan solutions to problems mentally.
Preoperational (2–7 years)	Preschoolers use their capacity for symbolic thought to develop language, engage in pretend play, and solve problems. But their thinking is not yet logical; they are egocentric (unable to take others' perspectives) and are easily fooled by perceptions, failing conservation problems because they cannot rely on logical operations.
Concrete operations (7–11 years)	School-age children acquire concrete logical operations that allow them to mentally classify, add, and otherwise act on concrete objects in their heads. They can solve practical, real-world problems through a trial-and-error approach but have difficulty with hypothetical and abstract problems.
Formal operations (11–12 years and older)	Adolescents can think about abstract concepts and purely hypothetical possibilities and can trace the long-range consequences of possible actions. With age and experience, they can form hypotheses and systematically test them using the scientific method.

© Cengage Learning

Note: Piaget's theory is elaborated upon in Chapter 7.

Exploration **2.4**

Piaget: Notes on School Refusal

Cognition is an important influence on behavior. I agree with Bandura that we need to understand how Terrell is thinking about both his home life and school, but I would go at this by interviewing him and assessing his stage of cognitive development. If Terrell has not yet made the transition from the preoperational stage to the concrete-operational stage and

has therefore not yet mastered logical operations, his anxiety may be rooted in a faulty cause–effect analysis or a misunderstanding. He may, for example, believe the serial murderer or terrorist he saw on TV will kill his mother next or that the school shooting that happened in another state will happen at his school. His egocentrism could make it even

more likely that he would come to believe that these scary events will affect him. Children who show school refusal problems have lots of negative thoughts and make lots of cognitive errors, such as concluding from one failure that they can't do anything right (Maric, Heyne, de Heus, van Widenfelt, & Westenberg, 2012).

the taller glass. Preschool children fail to demonstrate **conservation**, the recognition that certain properties of an object or substance do not change when its appearance is altered. Tricked by the greater height of the water in the tall, thin glass, young children ignore the width of the glass and conclude that the amount of water had magically increased.

School-age children who have advanced to the **concrete operations stage** are more logical than preschoolers. They use a trial-and-error approach to problem solving and do well on problems that involve thinking about concrete objects. These children can perform many important logical actions, or operations, on concrete objects in their heads (hence, the term *concrete operations*, and Piaget's description of the preschool child

Jean Piaget believed that children are naturally curious explorers who try to make sense of their environment and learn through their actions on it—a good thing for parents to remember when they encounter still another toddler-created disaster area! After he has had breakfast, for example, Benjamin likes to pull books out of his favorite bookshelf and rearrange them on the floor.

as *preoperational*). For example, they can mentally categorize or mentally add and subtract objects, and they can mentally coordinate the height and width of glasses in order to solve conservation problems correctly. They can also draw sound, general conclusions based on their concrete or specific observations. However, they have difficulty dealing with abstract and hypothetical problems.

Adolescents who reach the **formal operations stage** are able to think more abstractly and hypothetically than school-age children. They can define *justice* abstractly, in terms of fairness, rather than concretely, in terms of the cop on the corner or the judge in the courtroom. They can formulate hypotheses or predictions in their heads, plan how to systematically test their ideas experimentally, and imagine the results of their experiments. It often takes some years before adolescents can adopt a thoroughly systematic and scientific method of solving problems and can think logically about the implications of purely hypothetical ideas. Then they may be able to devise grand theories about what is wrong with their parents or the federal government or analyze the long-term consequences of choosing a particular career or using drugs.

Obviously, children's cognitive capacities change dramatically between infancy and adolescence as they progress through Piaget's four stages of cognitive development. Infants, young children, school-age children, and adolescents and adults simply do not think the same way. What, then, do you suppose Piaget would have said about school refusal? **Exploration Box 2.4** sketches his possible thoughts.

Strengths and Weaknesses

Like Freud, Piaget was a true pioneer whose work has left a deep and lasting imprint on thinking about human development. You will see his influence throughout this text, for the mind that "constructs" understanding of the physical world also comes, with age, to understand sex differences, moral values, emotions, death, and a range of other important aspects of the human experience. Piaget's cognitive developmental perspective dominated the study of child development for about three decades, until the 1980s. Most developmentalists today continue to accept Piaget's basic beliefs that thinking changes in qualitative ways during childhood, that children are active in their own development, and that development occurs through an interaction of nature and nurture. Piaget's description of intellectual development has been tested and has been largely, although not wholly, supported. Finally, Piaget's ideas have influenced education and child rearing by encouraging teachers and parents to pitch their educational programs to children's levels of understanding and to stimulate children to discover new concepts through their own direct grappling with problems.

Still, Piaget has had his share of criticism (Lourenco & Machado, 1996; also see Chapter 7). For example, critics question whether Piaget's stages really hang together as general modes of thinking that are applied to a variety of types of problems. Research suggests that cognitive development proceeds at different rates for different types of problems. Critics also conclude that Piaget underestimated the cognitive abilities of young children. Recent studies suggest that some of Piaget's cognitive tasks put too many demands on children and that, if tasks are simplified, children master them earlier than Piaget believed they did (Desrochers, 2008). Piaget is also charged with putting too little emphasis on social and cultural influences on cognitive development. He said little about the role of parents and other more knowledgeable people in nurturing cognitive development and did not appreciate enough that it can go differently in different cultures (see Chapter 7). As a result, developmentalists began to seek theoretical perspectives that allowed more diversity in the pathways that cognitive development could take.

Other Perspectives on Cognitive Development

Two important approaches to cognitive development that challenged some of Piaget's thinking are Vygotsky's *sociocultural perspective* (discussed in Chapter 7) and the *information-processing approach* (discussed in Chapter 8). We will briefly discuss them here to elaborate on weaknesses in Piaget's cognitive developmental theory.

The **sociocultural perspective** on cognitive development offered by a contemporary of Piaget, Russian psychologist Lev Vygotsky (1896–1934), has become quite influential in recent years. Disagreeing with Piaget's notion of universal stages of cognitive development, Vygotsky maintained that cognitive development is shaped by the sociocultural context in which it occurs and grows out of children's interactions with members of their culture (Vygotsky, 1962, 1978). Each culture provides its members with certain tools of thought—most notably a language, but also tools such as pencils, art media, mathematical systems, and computers. The ways in which people in a particular culture approach and solve problems are passed from generation to generation through oral and written communication. Hence culture, especially as it is embodied in language, shapes thought. As a result, cognitive development is not the same universally; it varies across social and historical contexts. Whereas Piaget tended to see children as independent explorers, Vygotsky saw them as social beings who develop their minds through their interactions with more knowledgeable members of their culture.

Other challenges to Piaget came from scholars who saw a need to look more closely at the processes involved in thinking and factors affecting those processes. Factors like failing to

Lev Vygotsky believed that each culture provides children with certain tools of thought, most notably, a language, and that children develop their minds through their social interactions with knowledgeable members of the culture. Here, through the Vygotskian process now called guided participation, a father helps his son learn to play the guitar.

notice or pay attention to key aspects of the problem or being unable to keep in mind two dimensions at once (like the height *and* width of a glass) can help explain why young children fail Piagetian problems like conservation tasks. The **information-processing approach** to cognitive development, which became the dominant perspective starting in the 1980s, likens the human mind to a computer with hardware and software and examines the fundamental mental processes, such as attention, memory, decision making, and the like, involved in performing cognitive tasks. Development involves changes in the capacity and speed of the information-processing machine we call the brain, in the strategies used to process information, and in the information stored in memory. This approach is the focus of Chapter 8.

Checking Mastery

1. Distinguish between concrete operational thinking and formal operational thinking in terms of what is operated upon mentally, using a specific example if you can.

2. What one major criticism would advocates of (a) the sociocultural perspective on cognitive development and (b) the information-processing approach to cognition make of Piaget's cognitive developmental theory?

Making Connections

1. Although we will look at the implications of Piaget's theory for education more closely in Chapter 7, based on what you know so far, what recommendations might Piaget make to teachers of (a) 4-year-olds, (b) 9-year-olds, and (c) 14-year-olds to help them recognize the strengths and weaknesses of children of these ages?

LEARNING OBJECTIVES:

• Explain how systems theorists such as Uri Bronfenbrenner have changed the way developmentalists think about the roles of biological and environmental forces in development.

• Define and give an example of the five environmental systems in Bronfenbrenner's bioecological theory.

• Evaluate the strengths and weaknesses of Bronfenbrenner's theory.

Systems theories of development, sometimes called contextual theories, claim that changes over the life span arise from ongoing transactions in which a changing organism and a changing environment affect one another (see, for example, Fogel, King, & Shanker, 2008; Gottlieb, Wahlsten, & Lickliter, 2006; Lerner, 2006). The individual and the physical and social contexts with which he interacts are inseparable parts of a larger system in which everything affects everything else. Development can take a variety of paths depending on the complex interplay of multiple influences.

Bronfenbrenner's Bioecological Model

To help you think about a changing person in a changing environment, consider an influential conceptual model formulated by Russian-born American psychologist Urie Bronfenbrenner (1917–2005). Bronfenbrenner became disturbed that many early developmental scientists were studying human development out of context, expecting it to be universal and failing to appreciate how much it could vary from culture to culture, from neighborhood to neighborhood, and from home to home. Bronfenbrenner formulated an ecological model to describe how the environment is organized and how it affects development. He later renamed his framework a **bioecological model** of development to get the "person" back into the picture and stress how biology and environment interact to produce development (Bronfenbrenner, 1979, 1989; Bronfenbrenner & Morris, 2006).

In Bronfenbrenner's view, the developing person, with his or her genetic makeup and biological and psychological characteristics, is embedded in a series of environmental systems. These systems interact with one another and with the individual over time to influence development. The four environmental systems that influence and are influenced by the developing person are shown in ■ **Figure 2.4**.

1. A **microsystem** is an immediate physical and social environment in which the person interacts face-to-face with other people and influences and is affected by them. The primary microsystem for a firstborn infant is likely to be the family—perhaps infant, mother, and father, all reciprocally influencing one another. The developing child may also experience other microsystems such as a day care center or grandmother's house. We have much evidence that the family environment is an important influence on child development and have also come to appreciate the importance of other

microsystems such as peer groups, schools, workplaces, and the like.

2. The **mesosystem** consists of the interrelationships between two or more microsystems. For example, teenagers from Mexican, Chinese, and European American backgrounds who experience stressful events such as arguments in the family (one microsystem) report increased problems of poor attendance and difficulty learning at school (a second microsystem) for a couple of days afterward, as well as 4 years later (Flook & Fuligni, 2008). Similarly, problems at school spill over to the family, possibly because adolescents take their bad moods home with them, and have both short- and long-term effects on functioning. For any developing person, what happens in one microsystem can have implications, good or bad, for what happens in another microsystem—and for development.

3. The **exosystem** consists of linkages involving social settings that individuals do not experience directly but that can still influence their development. For example, children can be affected by how their parents' day at work went or by a decision by the local school board to focus instruction almost entirely on getting more children to pass the state reading examination or by a police department's decision not to enforce underage drinking laws very aggressively.

Uri Bronfenbrenner sought to understand how a person and the environmental systems in which the person is embedded interact over time to produce development.

Cornell University

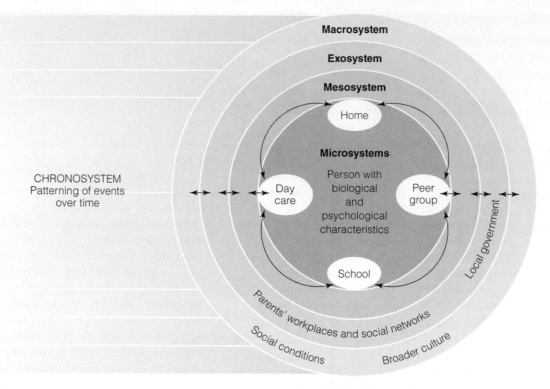

■ **Figure 2.4** Urie Bronfenbrenner's bioecological model of development pictures environment as a series of nested structures. The microsystem refers to relations between the developing person and her immediate environment, the mesosystem to connections among microsystems, the exosystem to settings that affect but do not contain the individual, the macrosystem to the broader cultural context of development, and the chronosystem to the patterning over time of historical and life events. All these systems influence and are influenced by the developing person.

SOURCE: Adapted from Kopp & Krakow (1982).

4. The **macrosystem** is the larger cultural context in which the microsystem, mesosystem, and exosystem are embedded. **Culture** is often defined as the shared understandings and way of life of a people, including beliefs and practices concerning the nature of humans in different phases of the life span, what children need to be taught to function in society, and how people should lead their lives as adults. Although the United States has a high standard of living, it is not a very family-friendly cultural environment in many ways, as Bronfenbrenner himself often lamented (Bronfenbrenner & Morris, 2006). For example, in one analysis, the United States was one of only 4 countries out of 168 studied that did not provide paid maternity leave to female employees (Heymann, Penrose, & Earle, 2006). The Family and Medical Leave Act of 1993, still in effect today, provides for 12 weeks of leave, but it is *unpaid* leave and it is not available to workers in small companies. Nor does the United States do as much as many other nations to ensure that workers can take leave to care for sick children or ailing elders or that children of all income levels have appropriate preschool and after-school programs.

In addition to the microsystem, mesosystem, exosystem, and macrosystem levels, Bronfenbrenner introduced the concept of

the **chronosystem** ("chrono" means time) to capture the idea that people and their environments and the relations between the two change over time and unfold in particular patterns or sequences over a person's lifetime. We cannot study development by taking still photos; we need video to understand how one event leads to another and how societal changes intertwine with changes in people's lives. Thus an economic crisis like the one of 2008 may precipitate a chain of events: a husband's job loss, marital conflict, divorce, and multiple changes in family relationships and children's lives and development. Each of us functions in particular microsystems linked through the mesosystem and embedded in the larger contexts of the exosystem and the macrosystem, all in continual flux.

Bronfenbrenner's bioecological model suggests that answers to questions about how child abuse, marriage, retirement, or other life experiences affect development will often be complex because outcomes depend on so many factors. Contextual effects on development can occur at any of the levels. To illustrate, Ann Crouter and her colleagues (2007) conducted a longitudinal study of changes in gender-role attitudes from age 7 to age 19 during a period of major changes in women's roles in society. They found that most children adopted less traditional attitudes as they got older. However, the attitudes of boys (but not girls) who grew up with traditional parents and brothers became

Exploration **2.5**

Bronfenbrenner: Notes on School Refusal

I would consider characteristics of both the child and the environmental systems in which he is developing and how they all interact with each other over time (C. A. Kearney, 2008; Lyon & Cotler, 2009; Thambirajah et al., 2008). Terrell could have a genetic predisposition to be anxious or could be lacking the academic skills it takes to succeed in first grade. The *microsystem* of his family (a helicopter parent, perhaps?) or the microsystem of the school (a bully or a gruff teacher?) may be a source of his difficulties. Perhaps the problem has been aggravated by poor communication between the school and Terrell's parents (the *mesosystem*). Stressors Terrell's parents are facing at work or in their social relationships (in the *exosystem*) may be undermining their ability to focus on Terrell and his emotional needs. I would also consider cultural influences (the *macrosystem*) such as the intense pressure on many children in our society today to excel academically from an early age. In Japan, school refusal has been increasing as mothers and teachers increase pressure on children to succeed in school (Kameguchi, 2004; Kameguchi & Murphy-Shigematsu, 2001). Finally, I would analyze changes in and interactions between person and environment over time (in the *chronosystem*). I would expect reciprocal influences among multiple factors to affect school refusal—not one simple cause.

---

more traditional over the years. In other words, both the child's personal characteristics (here, the child's gender) and the child's social context (parent and sibling characteristics) made for differences in developmental paths. According to Bronfenbrenner and Morris (2006), researchers who want to understand development need to consider key characteristics of the *person*, the *context*, the *time* dimension, and the *processes* through which an active person and his or her environment interact (for example, parent–child interactions about gender issues). Nature and nurture cannot be separated easily because they are part of a dynamic system, continually influencing one another.

More and more developmental scientists are adopting a systems or contextual perspective on development. In Chapter 3, you will learn that modern developmental psychobiologists maintain that genes do not dictate how development will go. Rather, both over the course of evolution and during the individual's development, genes and environment influence one another and "co-act" to make certain developmental outcomes more probable than others. In Chapter 5, you will encounter Esther Thelen's dynamic systems theory of motor development. In Chapter 7, you will see that Vygotsky's sociocultural perspective on cognitive development has the features of a systems or contextual theory, and in Chapter 15 you will come to appreciate the value of a family systems perspective on parenting and family life.

In **Exploration Box 2.5**, we imagine what Bronfenbrenner might have thought about contributors to school refusal.

Strengths and Weaknesses

Systems theories of development are complex, but that is because life-span human development is complex. We can applaud Bronfenbrenner and like-minded theorists for conceptualizing development as the often unpredictable product of biological and environmental forces interacting within a complex system and challenging us to look closely at ongoing transactions between the individual and his or her environment.

Yet systems theories can be faulted for not yet providing a clear picture of the course of human development and for being only partially formulated and tested at this point. Indeed, an even more serious criticism can be made: Systems perspectives may never provide a coherent picture of development. Why? If we take seriously the idea that development can take a range of paths depending on a range of interacting influences both within and outside the person, how can we ever state generalizations about development that will hold up for most people? If change over a lifetime depends on the ongoing transactions between a unique person and a unique environment, is each life span unique? The problem is this: "For the contextual or systems theorist, often the only generalization that holds is, 'It depends' " (Goldhaber, 2000, p. 33).

Human development may be more predictable than Bronfenbrenner's bioecological model implies, though. When children with normal human biological endowments develop in normal human environments, they may change in similar directions at similar ages, much as stage theorists like Piaget and Erikson maintain (Hoare, 2009; MacDonald & Hershberger, 2005). Perhaps it is still possible to see humans as moving in orderly directions in many aspects of their development while also appreciating the tremendous diversity and individuality in development and the many contextual influences on it (Goldhaber, 2012).

> ### Checking Mastery
>
> **1.** Describe how being given a big raise at work might affect a mother's parenting and which of Bronfenbrenner's systems would be involved if it did.
>
> **2.** Describe the relationship between nature and nurture in Bronfenbrenner's bioecological model.

2.7 Theories in Perspective

LEARNING OBJECTIVE:

- Compare and contrast the major theories in this chapter in terms of their stands on the four major issues in human development.

Just as developmental scientists need theories such as the ones we have surveyed in this chapter to guide their work, every parent, teacher, human services professional, and observer of humans is guided by some set of basic assumptions about how humans develop and why they develop as they do. We hope that you will think about your own assumptions about human development by comparing the answers you gave to the questions in Engagement Box 2.1 at the start of the chapter with the summary information in • **Table 2.5** and seeing which theorists' views are most compatible with your own.

Theories of human development can be grouped into categories based on the broad assumptions they make (Goldhaber, 2000; P. H. Miller, 2011; Pepper, 1942; Reese & Overton, 1970). Stage theorists such as Freud, Erikson, and Piaget form one broad group and have much in common. They believe that development is guided in certain universal directions by biological–maturational forces within the individual. Humans unfold—much as a rose unfolds from its beginnings as a seed—according to a master plan carried in their genes, assuming that they also grow up in a reasonably normal and stimulating environment. They evolve through distinct or discontinuous stages that are universal and lead to the same final state of maturity. Parents who subscribe to the stage theory perspective on development, especially Piaget's version, are likely to see themselves as *supporters* of development. They tend to trust their children's biologically based tendencies to seek the learning opportunities they most need in order to develop their own minds. They respond to their children's changing needs and interests, but they do not feel compelled to structure all their children's learning experiences. This position is like the philosophy of education incorporated in Montessori schools (Lillard, 2005).

By contrast, learning theorists such as Watson, Skinner, and Bandura emphasize the role of environment more than the role of biology in development. Parents who subscribe to a learning theory model of human development are not likely to trust genetically guided maturational forces to ensure that their children develop in healthy directions. Such parents are likely to act as *trainers*, assuming that their children will not develop properly (or at least will never be Harvard material) unless they are systematically exposed to particular learning experiences and shaped in positive directions.

Finally, systems and contextual theorists view biology and environment as inseparable components of a larger system. Children contribute actively to the developmental process (as stage theorists such as Piaget maintain), but the environment is also an active participant in the developmental drama (as learning theorists maintain). The potential exists for both qualitative (stagelike) change and quantitative change. Development can proceed along many paths depending on the intricate interplay of nature and nurture. Parents who adopt a systems theory of development are likely to appreciate that their children are influencing them just as much as they are influencing their children. They are likely to view themselves as *partners* with their children in the developmental process.

Our understanding of human development has changed, and will continue to change, as one prevailing view gives way to another. From the beginning of the study of human development at the beginning of the 20th century through the heyday of Freud's psychoanalytic theory, a stage theory perspective prevailed, emphasizing biological forces in development (Parke et al., 1994). In the 1950s and 1960s, learning theories came to the fore, and attention shifted from biology toward environment and toward the view that children are blank tablets to be written on. Then, with the rising influence of cognitive psychology and Piaget's theory of cognitive development in the late 1960s and 1970s, a stage theory model emphasizing the interaction of nature and nurture gained prominence. Finally, in the 1980s and 1990s, we gained a fuller appreciation of both biological–genetic and cultural–historical influences on development.

Where are we today? The broad perspective on key developmental issues taken by systems theorists such as Bronfenbrenner is the perspective that most 21st-century developmentalists have adopted. The field has moved beyond the extreme, black-or-white positions taken by many of its pioneers. We now appreciate that human development is always the product of nature and nurture interacting; that both humans and their environments are active in the developmental process; that development is both continuous and discontinuous in form; and that development has both universal aspects and aspects particular to certain cultures, times, and individuals. In short, the assumptions and theories that guide the study

● **Table 2.5** Compare Yourself with the Theorists

In Engagement Box 2.1, you were asked to indicate your position on basic issues in human development by answering four questions. If you transcribe your answers (a, b, c, d, or e) in the appropriate boxes at the bottom of the table below, you can compare your stands with those of the theorists described in this chapter—and review the theories. With whom do you seem to agree the most?

Theory : Theorist	Message	Nature–Nurture	Activity–Passivity	Continuity–Discontinuity	Universality–Context Specificity
Psychoanalytic Theory: Freud's Psychosexual Theory	Biologically based sexual instincts motivate behavior and steer development through five psychosexual stages, oral to genital.	b. More nature (biology drives development; early experience in the family influences it, too)	b. Passive (humans are influenced by forces beyond their control)	a. Discontinuous (stagelike)	a. Universal
Psychoanalytic Theory: Erikson's Psychosocial Theory	Humans progress through eight psychosocial conflicts, from trust vs. mistrust to integrity vs. despair.	c. Nature and nurture equally	a. Active	a. Discontinuous (stagelike)	a. Universal (although stages may be expressed differently in different cultures)
Learning Theory: Skinner's Behavioral Theory	Development is the product of learning from the consequences of one's behavior through operant conditioning.	e. Mostly nurture	b. Passive (humans are shaped by environment)	c. Continuous (habits gradually increase or decrease in strength)	b. Context specific (direction of development depends on experiences)
Learning Theory: Bandura's Social Cognitive Theory	Development is the product of cognition, as illustrated by observational learning and human agency	d. More nurture	a. Active (humans influence their environments)	c. Continuous	b. Context specific
Cognitive Developmental Theory: Piaget's Constructivism	Development proceeds through four stages of cognitive development, from sensorimotor to formal operations	b. More nature (maturation interacting with experience guides all through the same stages)	a. Active	a. Discontinuous (stagelike)	a. Universal
Systems Theories: Bronfenbrenner's Bioecological Model	Development takes many directions depending on transactions between a changing person and a changing environment	c. Nature and nurture equally	a. Active	b. Both continuous and discontinuous	b. Context specific
Your Answers: (From ENGAGEMENT BOX 2.1)	Question 1		Question 2	Question 3	Question 4

Application 2.1

Using Developmental Theories to Prevent Sexual Risk Behavior and Unwanted Pregnancy among Teens

Having sex at an early age, having many sexual partners, and having unprotected sex are common examples of sexual risk behaviors. Based on national statistics for 2006–2008, 42% of never-married females and 43% of never-married males in the 15–19 age range had had sexual intercourse at least once; moreover, teenagers had higher rates of sexually transmitted infections than adults (Abma, Martinez, & Copen, 2010; and see Chapter 12). Although teenage birth rates have decreased considerably since a mid-1950s peak (Ventura & Hamilton, 2011), the current birth rate of 39 per 1,000 teens in the United States is still higher than that in most other Western nations (Abma et al., 2010). Why is there so much sexual risk taking and unplanned pregnancy among American teens, and what might we as a society do to prevent them?

Psychoanalytic Theory

Freud would likely argue that teenagers get pregnant because they experience intense emotional conflicts during the genital stage of psychosexual development—that their new sexual urges are anxiety-provoking. From a psychoanalytic perspective, teenagers who engage in risky sex may not have developed strong enough egos or superegos to keep their selfish ids in check. Psychological problems arising in early childhood have been linked to having sex at an early age (see Schofield, Bierman, & Heinrichs, 2008).

Erikson might also wonder about unresolved conflicts from earlier stages of development but most likely would attribute unwanted teen pregnancy primarily to the adolescent psychosocial conflict of identity versus role confusion. In Erikson's view, adolescents seek a sense of identity by experimenting with different roles and behaviors to see what suits them; they try drugs, dye their hair orange, join radical groups, change majors every semester, and yes, have sex. Some adolescents may also try to find an easy resolution to their role confusion by prematurely latching onto an identity as someone's boyfriend or girlfriend rather than doing the hard work of experimenting to find out who they are (Erikson, 1968).

Psychoanalytic theorists tend to locate the causes of problems within the person. They would want to identify high-risk teenagers who are experiencing especially difficult psychic conflicts and treat them through psychoanalysis aimed at helping them resolve their conflicts. Although the psychoanalytic approach might work with teenagers who are indeed psychologically disturbed, most teenagers who become pregnant are not (Farber, 2003).

Piaget's Cognitive Developmental Theory

Cognitive limitations, failure to anticipate consequences, and lack of knowledge may all influence sexual decision making, Jean Piaget would say. Adolescents who are not yet solidly into the stage of formal operations may not be able to think through the long-range consequences of their sexual behavior. And misconceptions (pun intended!) about sex and contraception are rampant among adolescents (Aarons & Jenkins, 2002). In one study of 13- to 15-year-olds, more than 60% did not know that urinating after sex will not prevent pregnancy (Carrera et al., 2000).

According to Piaget's cognitive developmental perspective, the solution is improved sex education programs—programs that correct teens' misconceptions, provide them with accurate information and strategies for avoiding unwanted and unprotected sex, and help them think through the long-range consequences of their sexual decisions. A variety

What approaches might you consider to reduce the rate of unwanted pregnancy at the high school you attended?

Catchlight Visual Services / Alamy

of human development have become increasingly complex as the incredible complexity of human development has become more apparent.

As we have emphasized, a main function of theories in any science is to guide research. Thus, Freud stimulated researchers to study inner personality conflicts, Skinner inspired them to analyze how behavior changes when its consequences change, and Piaget inspired them to explore children's modes of thinking. Different theories make different assumptions, stimulate different kinds of research, and yield different kinds of facts about development and explanations of them, as you will see throughout this book. Theorists who view the world through different lenses not only study different things in different ways but are likely to disagree even when the same "facts" are set before them, because they will interpret those facts differently (Miller, 2011). This is the nature of science.

Theories also guide practice. As you have seen, each theory of human development represents a particular way of defining of carefully designed sex education programs can indeed delay initiation of sex, decrease number of sexual partners, and increase contraception use (Franklin & Corcoran, 2000; Jemmott, Jemmott, & Fong, 2010; Kirby & Laris, 2009). However, education alone is often not enough, so perhaps we need to consider solutions that locate the causes of teenage pregnancy in the environment rather than in the individual's psychological weaknesses or cognitive limitations.

Learning Theories

Through classical conditioning, John Watson might argue, teenagers may learn to associate the very presence of a partner with the pleasurable sensations associated with sexual activity. And, as B. F. Skinner might observe, teenagers probably have unprotected sex because having sex is reinforcing, whereas using contraceptives is not. Finally, Albert Bandura might emphasize observational learning, noting that teens who are exposed to lots of sexually explicit material on television and through other media begin having sex earlier in life and engage in more risky sexual behavior than other teens (Bleakley, Hennessy, & Fishbein, 2011; Brown et al., 2006; Chandra et al., 2008; O'Hara et al., 2012).

Learning theorists believe that changing the environment will change the person. In support of this belief, it appears that one effective approach to teenage pregnancy prevention is to make contraceptives readily available to teens and to teach them how to use them (Franklin & Corcoran, 2000). This approach reflects a Skinnerian philosophy of encouraging desired behavior by making it more reinforcing and less punishing. Albert Bandura's social cognitive theory

suggests that it would also help to provide teenagers with more role models of responsible sexual behavior and fewer examples of irresponsible sexual behavior (Unger, Molina, & Teran, 2000).

Bronfenbrenner's Bioecological Theory

Finally, Uri Bronfenbrenner would look for multiple, interacting causes of adolescent sexual risk behavior, analyzing the ongoing interactions between developing adolescents and the environmental systems in which they are developing. He might look at characteristics of the individual such as early puberty or the presence of depression and other mental health problems (Pilgrim & Blum, 2012). He would also analyze adolescents' microsystems and would not be surprised to learn that factors such as poor relationships with parents, involvement with peers who are having sex, and lack of connectedness to school can all increase the likelihood of risky sexual behavior (Henrich et al., 2006; Lansford et al., 2010; Pilgrim & Blum, 2012). He would suspect that relationships between the microsystems of home, peer group, and school— that is, the mesosystem—may be important. He would consider the exosystem—for example, the possibility that a shortage of local government funds for vocational training programs and a shortage of jobs in an area could contribute to a sense among youth that it is pointless to postpone parenthood in order to pursue an education (Cowan, 2011; Farber, 2003).

Bronfenbrenner might also wonder whether the broader cultural environment is one that considers teenage pregnancy a normal developmental milestone or a social problem. In some cultures, including some lower-income

subcultures in the United States, early parenthood is viewed as adaptive and teen pregnancy is common (Davies et al., 2003). The fact is that not all American teens view pregnancy as undesirable (Abma et al., 2010). Bronfenbrenner might also ask whether having sex at an early age is viewed in a particular cultural context as an important step in becoming a "man" and whether the culture's gender norms call for females to defer to the wishes of their partners (Pilgrim & Blum, 2012). Mainly, Bronfenbrenner would recognize that there is not *one* cause of teenage pregnancy; there is a whole system of interacting causes.

Systems theorists such as Bronfenbrenner would recommend comprehensive programs that attempt to change *both* the person and the environment—or really, the whole system of interacting influences on development (Pilgrim & Blum, 2012). The solution may need to address teenagers' socio-emotional needs (Allen, Seitz, & Apfel, 2007). The solution may also require changing the social context—for example, changing how adolescents and their parents, peers, and partners interact, addressing problems associated with poverty and family instability, and enabling youth in all segments of society to perceive opportunities to succeed in life if they focus on education and vocational preparation (Cowan, 2011; Farber, 2003; Jordahl & Lohman, 2009).

You can see, then, that the theoretical position one takes has a profound effect on how one attempts to optimize development. In all likelihood, multiple approaches will be needed to address complex problems such as sexual risk taking and unwanted pregnancy among teens—and to achieve the larger goal of understanding human development.

developmental issues and problems. Often, how you define a problem determines how you attempt to solve it. To illustrate, consider sexual risk taking and unwanted teenage pregnancy. How do you think major developmental theorists would explain them, and how do you think each would go about trying to reduce the rate of unwanted teenage pregnancy and other undesirable outcomes such as sexually transmitted infections? **Application Box 2.1** offers some ideas and will serve, too, as a review of the theories. You might think the problem through yourself before you read the box.

You need not choose one favored developmental theory and reject others. Because different theories often highlight different aspects of development, one may be more relevant to a particular issue or to a particular age group than another. Many developmentalists today are theoretical **eclectics** who rely on many theories, recognizing that no major theory of human development can explain everything but that each has something to contribute to our understanding.

1. How have stands on the nature–nurture issue changed during the 20th century from (a) Freud to (b) Skinner to (c) Bronfenbrenner?
2. Of the theorists discussed in this chapter, who is the only one with something specific to say about development during adulthood?

1. You have decided to become an eclectic. What would you identify as the one greatest insight from each of the four major perspectives in this chapter (psychoanalytic, learning, cognitive developmental, and systems theory)—and why?
2. Think about the development of cats and the development of humans. Which of the theories in this chapter are most and least applicable to both species—and why?

Chapter Summary

2.1 Developmental Theories and the Issues They Raise

- Theories organize and explain the facts of human development and should be internally consistent, falsifiable, and supported by data.
- The four major issues in the study of human development are nature and nurture, activity and passivity, continuity and discontinuity, and universality and context specificity.

2.2 Freud: Psychoanalytic Theory

- In Freud's psychoanalytic theory, humans are irrational beings primarily driven by inborn biological instincts of which they are largely unconscious. The personality is partitioned into the id, ego, and superego (which emerge in that order).
- Libido is rechanneled across five psychosexual stages—oral, anal, phallic, latent, and genital. Each stage involves psychic conflicts that can result in fixation at a stage, create the need for defense mechanisms, and have lasting effects on personality.
- Biological needs drive development, but parents affect a child's success in dealing with conflicts and can contribute to emotional problems, especially if they are overly restrictive or punitive.
- Although Freud made huge contributions by calling attention to the unconscious, to early experiences in the family, and to emotional aspects of development, his theory is not easily falsifiable and many of its specifics lack support.

2.3 Erikson: Neo-Freudian Psychoanalytic Theory

- Compared with Freud, neo-Freudian Erik Erikson emphasized biological urges less and social influences more; emphasized id less and ego more; held a more optimistic view of human nature and people's ability to overcome early problems; and theorized about the whole life span.
- According to Erikson, development proceeds through eight psychosocial stages involving issues of trust, autonomy, initiative, industry, identity, intimacy, generativity, and integrity. Parents, peers, and the larger culture influence how conflicts are resolved.
- The theories of both Freud and Erikson have been influential but are difficult to test and tend to describe development better than they explain it.

2.4 Learning Theories

- Learning theorists maintain that humans change gradually and can develop in many directions depending on environmental influences.
- Behaviorist Watson focused on the role of Pavlov's classical conditioning in the learning of emotional responses to stimuli, and Skinner highlighted operant conditioning and the roles of reinforcement in strengthening behavior and punishment in weakening it.
- Bandura's social cognitive theory emphasizes the importance of cognitive processes in learning, observational learning, and self-efficacy; reciprocal determinism among person, behavior, and environment shapes development.
- Learning theories are well supported and applicable across the life span, but they do not necessarily explain normal developmental changes and they underemphasize biological influences on development.

2.5 Piaget: Cognitive Developmental Theory

- Piaget's cognitive developmental perspective holds that humans adapt to and create new understandings of the world through their active interactions with it (constructivism).
- The interaction of biological maturation and experience causes children to progress through four universal, invariant, and qualitatively different stages of thinking: sensorimotor, preoperational, concrete operational, and formal operational.
- Despite Piaget's immense influence, critics think his concept of broad stages is flawed, that he underestimated young children, and that he put too little emphasis on social and cultural influences on development (according to Vygotsky's sociocultural perspective) and on cognitive processes such as attention and memory (according to the information-processing approach).

2.6 Systems Theories

- Systems and contextual theories view development as the product of ongoing transactions and mutual influence between the individual and the environment.
- Bronfenbrenner's bioecological model portrays person and environment (at the microsystem, mesosystem, exosystem,

and macrosystem levels) as mutually influencing each other over time (chronosystem).

- Systems theories are incomplete, however, and do not provide a coherent picture of human development.

2.7 Theories in Perspective

- During the 20th century, stage theories such as Freud's emphasizing biological forces gave way to learning theories emphasizing environmental influences and then to Piaget's cognitive developmental theory, which emphasizes the interaction of nature and nurture.

- Piaget's concept of universal stages has given way to more complex systems theories such as those of Bronfenbrenner, who expects developmental outcomes to be more or less probable depending on multiple factors in the ongoing interaction between person and the environment.

- Theories influence both research and practice, and many developmentalists are theoretical eclectics.

Checking Mastery Answers

For answers to Checking Mastery questions, please see Appendix B.

Key Terms

school refusal **32**
activity–passivity issue **33**
continuity–discontinuity issue **34**
developmental stage **34**
universality–context-specificity issue **34**
psychoanalytic theory **35**
instinct **36**
unconscious motivation **36**
id **36**
ego **36**
superego **36**
libido **36**
psychosexual stages **36**
fixation **36**
Oedipus complex **37**
identification **37**
Electra complex **38**
defense mechanisms **38**

repression **38**
regression **38**
psychosocial stages **39**
tabula rasa **41**
behaviorism **41**
classical conditioning **41**
operant conditioning **42**
positive reinforcement **42**
negative reinforcement **42**
positive punishment **43**
negative punishment **43**
extinction **43**
social learning theory **44**
social cognitive theory **44**
observational learning **44**
latent learning **44**
vicarious reinforcement **44**
self-efficacy **45**

reciprocal determinism **45**
constructivism **47**
sensorimotor stage **48**
preoperational stage **48**
conservation **49**
concrete operations stage **49**
formal operations stage **49**
sociocultural perspective **50**
information-processing approach **50**
systems theories **51**
bioecological model **51**
microsystem **51**
mesosystem **51**
exosystem **51**
macrosystem **52**
chronosystem **52**
eclectic **57**

CENGAGE Get quizzes, flashcards, videos, and more at **www.cengagebrain.com**.
brain.com

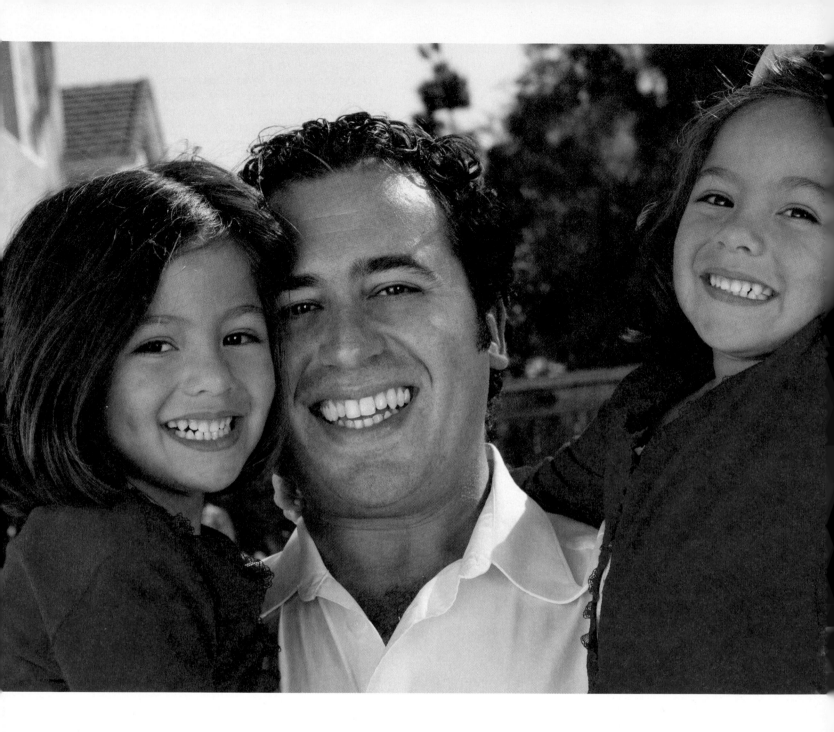

3 Genes, Environment, and Development

A newspaper story about Jim Lewis and Jim Springer inspired Thomas Bouchard Jr. and his associates at the University of Minnesota to undertake a study in which they reunited identical twins who had been separated soon after birth and asked them to complete a 50-hour battery of tests (Bouchard, 1984; Bouchard et al., 1990; and see Segal, 2012, for a summary of this study's many findings). Together after spending all but the first 4 weeks of their 39 years apart, Jim and Jim discovered that they had both married women named Linda—and then women named Betty. They named their first sons James Alan and James Allan, had dogs named Toy, and liked Miller Lite beer and Salem cigarettes. They liked math and hated spelling and enjoyed the same vacation spot in Florida.

Barbara Herbert and Daphne Goodship, also reunited after 39 years apart, both wore a beige dress and a brown velvet jacket when they met for the first time in London. They shared a habit of "squidging" (pushing up their noses), had fallen down the stairs at age 15, laughed more than anyone they knew, and never voted.

Identical twins Jessica and Rachel Wessell, despite having the same genes, growing up together, and being close, are far from identical. One excels in math, the other in English. One has cerebral palsy and is in a wheelchair, possibly because of lack of oxygen to her brain at birth; the other was in the marching band in high school (Helderman, 2003).

Identical but not identical. "We think the same. We've even bought each other the same birthday cards," says Geraldine (right) about herself and her identical twin, Christine. Yet Christine has arthritis and Geraldine does not, and this raises important questions about how environmental influences make identical twins different.

Do similarities between identical twins arise mainly because identical twins have identical genes, or is it because people treat individuals who look so alike the same way? How can we explain differences between individuals who have identical genes and grow up in the same environment?

The influence of genes on development must be taken seriously—but so must the influence of environment. How do nature and nurture, heredity and environment, contribute to the shaping of our physical and psychological characteristics? That is the complex puzzle we grapple with in this chapter—and throughout the book. Reading this chapter should increase your appreciation of genetic contributions to development, give you new insights into the importance of environmental influences, and most importantly, reveal how nature and nurture work together to guide development. We invite you to take the short quiz in **Engagement Box 3.1** to find out whether you come to this chapter with any misconceptions about genetic influence; the correct answers will become clear as you read, and they are also provided in the box.

We begin with a brief look at evolution and ways in which genes make humans similar. Then the chapter turns to what each individual inherits at conception and how this genetic endowment, in combination with environmental factors, influences the individual's traits. Then it explores research findings on how genes and environment contribute to differences among people in intelligence, personality, and other important characteristics. Finally, we examine key ways in which genes and environment work together—and influence one another—over the life span.

3.1 Evolution and Species Heredity

LEARNING OBJECTIVES:

- Summarize the basic argument of Darwin's theory of evolution and the significance of the theory for the study of development.
- Compare and contrast biological evolution and cultural evolution.

Most descriptions of heredity focus on its role in creating differences among people. Some individuals inherit genes for blue eyes, others genes for brown eyes; some inherit genes for blood type O, others genes for blood type A or B. But isn't it remarkable that almost every one of us has two eyes and that we all have blood coursing through our veins? Virtually all of us also develop in similar ways at similar ages—walking and talking around 1 year, maturing sexually from 12 to 14, watching our skin wrinkle in our 40s and 50s. Such similarities in development and aging are a product of **species heredity**—the genetic endowment that members of a species have in common, including genes that influence biological maturation and aging processes. Humans can feel guilty but cannot fly; birds can fly but cannot feel guilty. Each species has a distinct heredity. Species heredity is one reason certain patterns of development and aging are universal.

To understand where we got our species heredity, we must turn to evolutionary theory—to the path-blazing work of Charles Darwin (1809–1882; see Dewsbury, 2009). Darwin's theory of evolution sought to explain how the characteristics of a species change over time and how new species evolve from earlier ones (Darwin, 1859). The theory has been and continues to be controversial, but it is strongly supported by a wealth of evidence and guides scientific research not only in biology but in psychology and other fields (D. M. Buss, 2012). Darwin's theory makes these main arguments:

1. *There is genetic variation in a species.* Some members of the species have different genes than other members of the species do. If all members of the species were genetically identical, there would be no way for the genetic makeup of the species to change over time in response to changes in the environment.

2. *Some genes aid adaptation more than others do.* Suppose that some genes contribute to strength and intelligence whereas other genes tend to make people weak and dull. People with the genes for strength and intelligence would likely be better able to adapt to their environment—for example, to win fights for survival or to figure out how to obtain food.

Genetic Influence: What Is Myth, What Is Reality?

Answer each of the following questions True or False to identify before reading this chapter any misconceptions about genetic influences you may have. Then watch for the correct answers and their explanations throughout the chapter and return to review the answers (printed upside down in this box).

1. The most important reason that identical twins are similar psychologically is that they are treated similarly.

2. The father, not the mother, determines the sex of a child.

3. If a trait is highly influenced by genes, it is generally extremely hard for environmental forces to change it.

4. Most important psychological traits like intelligence and extraversion are influenced by a single pair of genes.

5. Environmental influences such as stress and a poor diet can cause certain genes to become inactive.

6. Homosexuality is genetically influenced, although environment plays an important role in its development too.

7. Most childhood psychological disorders are caused by dysfunctional parenting rather than by genes.

8. The contribution of genes to differences in intelligence typically decreases with age during childhood and adolescence as the effects of learning experiences become more evident.

9. Biological siblings turn out about as similar in personality if they grow up apart as if they grow up in the same home.

10. People's social attitudes and interests are influenced by environment rather than heredity.

Answers: 1. F (twins are treated similarly because they are so similar) 2. T (because sperm have either an X or a Y chromosome) 3. F (for example, genetically influenced IQ scores can be raised by enriched environments) 4. F (most are influenced by multiple genes) 5. T (environment influences gene expression) 6. T (genes and environment both contribute to homosexuality) 7. F (genes and unique or nonshared environment both play a role in psychological disorder; shared environmental influences are not as important) 8. F (heritability, a measure of the magnitude of genetic influence on individual differences, often increases from childhood to adulthood as intellectually inclined children seek out more intellectual stimulation than their less intellectually inclined peers) 9. T (shared environment has little effect on personality) 10. T (attitudes and interests are modestly influenced by genetic makeup)

---

3. *Genes that aid their bearers in adapting to their environment will be passed to future generations more frequently than genes that do not.* This is the key principle of **natural selection**—the idea that nature "selects," or allows to survive and reproduce, those members of a species whose genes permit them to adapt to their environment. Genes that reduce the chances that an individual will survive and reproduce will become rarer over time because they will not be passed to many offspring. Through natural selection, then, the genetic makeup of a species slowly changes—and will continue to change as long as individuals with certain genetic makeups reproduce more frequently than individuals with other genetic makeups. Change can eventually be sufficient to produce a new species. The result is what Darwin marveled at when he conducted observations in the Galapagos Islands: the incredible diversity of species on earth, each well adapted to its environment.

Now consider a classic example of evolution in action. H. B. D. Kettlewell (1959) carefully studied moths in England. There is genetic variation among moths that makes some dark and others light. By placing light and dark moths in several sites, Kettlewell found that in rural areas light-colored moths were more likely to survive but that in industrial areas dark moths were more likely to survive. The explanation? In rural areas, light-colored moths blend in well with light-colored trees and are therefore better protected from predators. Natural selection favors them. However, in sooty industrial areas, light-colored moths are easy pickings against the darkened trees, whereas dark moths are well disguised. When industry came to England, the proportion of dark moths increased; as pollution was brought under control in some highly industrialized areas, light-colored moths became more common again (Bishop & Cooke, 1975).

Notice, then, that evolution is not just about genes. It is about the *interaction between genes and environment*. A particular genetic makeup may enhance survival in one kind of environment but prove maladaptive in another. Which genes are advantageous, and therefore which become more common in future generations, depends on what environment a group experiences and what traits that environment demands. Genes that helped our ancestors hunt prey may not be as important in today's world as genes that help people master iPhone apps.

According to evolutionary theory, then, humans, like any other species, are as they are and develop as they do partly because they have a shared species heredity that evolved through natural selection. Modern **evolutionary psychology** is the application of evolutionary theory to understanding why humans think and behave as they do. Evolutionary psychologists ask important questions about how the characteristics and behaviors we observe in humans today may have helped our ancestors adapt to their environments and consequently may have become part of the shared genetic endowment of our species (Bjorklund & Pellegrini, 2002;

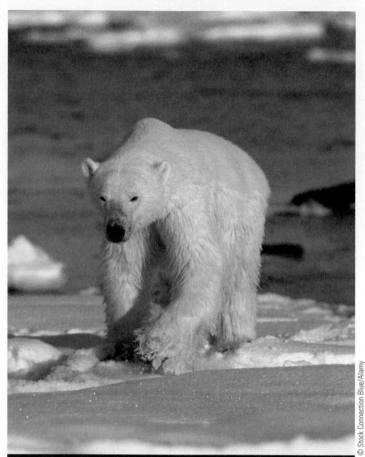
Each species has evolved through natural selection to be adapted to its environment.

previous generations a characteristically human environment and tried and true ways of adapting to it, learn to adjust to changing conditions, and pass on what we learn to the next generation (Bjorklund & Pellegrini, 2002). This cultural evolution of the human species through learning and socialization of the young works much more quickly than biological evolution, especially in our age of globalization and instant messaging. In the end, the most significant legacy of biological evolution may be a powerful and very flexible brain that allows humans to learn from their experiences, to devise better ways of adapting to their environments and even changing their environments to suit them better, and, with the help of language, to share what they have learned (Bjorklund & Pellegrini, 2002).

Checking Mastery

1. Biological evolution will not necessarily make humans better and better over time, but it *will* make them
_____.

2. For natural selection to work and for a species to evolve, what must be true of the genetic makeup of a species?

3. How would cultural evolution be involved in the fact that most of us have central heating and air conditioning?

Making Connections

1. Think of two human behaviors that you believe are so universal that they are probably built into the heredity of our species. Now, why might genes underlying these behaviors have been selected for in the course of evolution?

2. Think about people with a slow metabolism. Can you imagine an environment in which it would be beneficial to have a slow metabolism and another environment in which it could be harmful? What does this tell you about the "adaptiveness" of this human trait?

D. M. Buss, 2012). They ask, for example, whether humans are basically cooperative and helpful or selfish and aggressive, how males and females differ, why humans mate and raise children as they do, and why human children develop as they do.

Not all human similarity is because of genes, however. Through the process of **cultural evolution**, we "inherit" from

3.2 Individual Heredity

LEARNING OBJECTIVES:

- Describe the basics of the genetic code and what we inherit from our parents.

- Distinguish and give examples of the major mechanisms of inheritance (single gene-pair, sex-linked, and polygenic inheritance), mutations, and chromosome abnormalities.

- Summarize what a genetic counselor would say about the nature, inheritance, and management of selected genetic diseases (such as sickle-cell disease, Huntington's disease, and phenylketonuria [PKU]).

To begin to understand how genes contribute to *differences* among humans, we must start at **conception**—the moment when an egg is fertilized by a sperm—look at the workings of genes, and then consider the mechanisms through which genes can influence traits.

The Genetic Code

A sperm cell and an ovum each contribute 23 chromosomes to the **zygote**, or fertilized egg, to give it 46 chromosomes total, organized into 23 pairs. **Chromosomes** are threadlike bodies

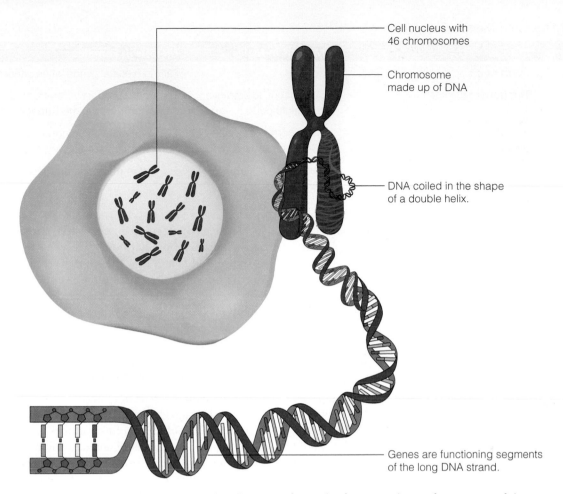

Cell nucleus with
46 chromosomes

Chromosome
made up of DNA

DNA coiled in the shape
of a double helix.

Genes are functioning segments
of the long DNA strand.

■ **Figure 3.1** The chromosomes in each cell consist of strands of DNA made up of sequences of the base chemicals A, T, C, and G. Some sequences are functional units called genes.

SOURCE: National Institute of General Medical Sciences, found at: http://publications.nigms.nih.gov/insidelifescience/genetics-numbers.html

in the nucleus of each cell and are made up of genes, the basic units of heredity (■ **Figure 3.1**). Thus, of each chromosome pair—and of each pair of genes located on corresponding sites on a chromosome pair—one member came from the father and one member came from the mother.

Sperm and ova, unlike other cells, have only 23 chromosomes because they are produced through the specialized process of cell division called **meiosis**. At the start of this process, a reproductive cell in the ovary of a female or the testis of a male that contains the usual 46 chromosomes splits to form two 46-chromosome cells, and then these two cells each split again to form a total of four cells. In this last step, though, each resulting cell receives only 23 chromosomes. The end product is one egg (and three nonfunctional cells that play no role in reproduction) in a female or four sperm in a male. Each resulting sperm cell or ovum thus has only one member of each of the parent's 23 pairs of chromosomes. Ova are formed prenatally and later ripen one by one during menstrual cycles; sperm are created starting in puberty and throughout adulthood.

A few hours after a sperm cell penetrates an ovum, the sperm cell begins to disintegrate, releasing its genetic material. The nucleus of the ovum releases its own genetic material, and a new cell

nucleus is created from the genetic material provided by mother and father. This new cell, called a zygote and only the size of a pinhead, is the beginning of a human. Conception has occurred.

The single-celled zygote formed at conception becomes a multiple-celled organism through the more usual process of cell division, **mitosis**. During mitosis, a cell (and each of its 46 chromosomes) divides to produce two identical cells, each containing the same 46 chromosomes. As the zygote moves through the fallopian tube toward its prenatal home in the uterus, it first divides into two cells; the two then become four, the four become eight, and so on, all through mitosis. Except for sperm and ova, all normal human cells contain copies of the 46 chromosomes provided at conception. Mitosis continues throughout life, creating new cells that enable us to grow and replacing old cells that are damaged. (● **Table 3.1 compares mitosis and meiosis**.)

Both members of a chromosome pair—one from the mother and one from the father—influence the same characteristics. Each chromosome consists of strands of deoxyribonucleic acid (**DNA**), the double helix molecule whose chemical code is our genetic endowment. DNA is made up of sequences of four chemicals known by the letters A (adenine), C (cytosine), G (guanine), and

● Table 3.1 Mitosis and Meiosis Compared

	Mitosis	Meiosis in Males	Meiosis in Females
Begins	Conception	Puberty	Early in prenatal period when unripened ova form
Continues	Throughout life span	Throughout adolescence and adulthood	Through reproductive years; an ovum ripens each month of the menstrual cycle
Produces	Two identical daughter cells, each with 46 chromosomes like its parent	Four sperm, each with 23 chromosomes	One ovum and three nonfunctional polar bodies, each with 23 chromosomes
Accomplishes	Growth of human from fertilized egg, renewal of the body's cells	Formation of male reproductive cells	Formation of female reproductive cells

T (thymine). Some of these sequences are functional units called genes. Geneticists used to think humans had about 100,000 genes, but the actual number is more like 20,000–25,000 (International Human Genome Sequencing Consortium, 2004). Each gene, of which there can be two or more different versions or variants, provides instructions that lead to the production of particular proteins, the building blocks of all bodily tissues and of essential substances such as hormones, neurotransmitters, and enzymes.

The Human Genome Project

Through the federally funded **Human Genome Project**, completed in 2003, researchers mapped the sequence of the chemical units or "letters" that make up the strands of DNA in a full set of 46 human chromosomes (Weiss, 2003). The human genome has about 3.1 billion of the chemical constituents A, C, G, and T. However, it turns out that only about 3% of the human genome consists of what has traditionally been defined as genes: Stretches of DNA that are transcribed into RNA (ribonucleic acid), which then serves as a template for the production of particular proteins (Brown & Boytchev, 2012; Plomin & Davis, 2009). The remaining stretches of DNA were at first called "junk DNA," but it soon became clear that they are not junk at all. These segments of DNA play critical roles in regulating the activity of the protein-producing genes, choreographing how they turn on and off in different types of cells at different times. It is now believed that genetic researchers got it wrong by focusing so much on the 3% of DNA (the protein-building genes) and need to pay much more attention to the 97% and its regulatory functions (Brown & Boytchev, 2012).

The Human Genome Project and the massive genome analysis projects that have followed it are yielding astounding new discoveries like this every year. The International HapMap Project, for example, described the genetic similarities and differences among 270 people from a variety of racial and ethnic groups around the world (Turnpenny & Ellard, 2011). It turns out that about 999 of 1,000 base chemicals are identical in all humans; it is the remaining 1 of 1,000 that makes us each unique. Analysis of DNA samples is also shedding light on evolution. For example, it has revealed gene variants that have evolved in response to changes in the environments of modern human populations. A classic example is gene variants that make people tolerate lactose in milk; these gene variants spread quite rapidly among Europeans as dairy farming became common, presumably because tolerating milk enhanced survival (McCabe & McCabe, 2008; Voight et al., 2006).

Through such studies, researchers are able to test in new ways some of the predictions of Darwin's theory and are gaining new insights into how the human species evolved and how humans are similar to and different from one another. As James Watson, codiscoverer of the double helix structure of DNA, said about the Human Genome Project, "We have the book, and now we've got to learn how to read it" (Weiss & Gillis, 2000, p. A12).

Genetic Uniqueness and Relatedness

People are both different from and like their relatives genetically because when a pair of parental chromosomes separates during meiosis, which of the two chromosomes ends up in a particular sperm or ovum is a matter of chance. And because each chromosome pair separates independently of all other pairs and each sperm or ovum contains 23 pairs of chromosomes, a single parent can produce 2^{23}—more than 8 million—genetically different sperm or ova. Any couple could theoretically have at least 64 trillion babies without producing 2 children with identical genes.

The genetic uniqueness of children of the same parents is even greater than this because of a quirk of meiosis known as **crossing over**. When pairs of chromosomes line up before they separate, they cross each other and parts of them are exchanged, much as if you were to exchange a couple of fingers with a friend at the end of a handshake. Crossing over increases even more the number of distinct sperm or ova that an individual can produce. In short, it is incredibly unlikely that there ever was or ever will be another human exactly like you genetically. The one exception is **identical twins** (or identical triplets, and so on), also called monozygotic twins because they result when one fertilized ovum divides to form two or more genetically identical individuals. This happens in about 1 of every 250 births (Segal, 2005).

How genetically alike are parent and child or brother and sister? You have 50% of your genes in common with your mother and 50% in common with your father because you received half of your chromosomes (and genes) from each parent. But if you have followed our mathematics, you will see that siblings may have many genes in common or few depending on the luck of the draw during meiosis. Because siblings receive half of their genes from the same mother and half from the same father, their average genetic resemblance to each other is 50%, the same genetic resemblance as that of parent and child. The critical difference is that they share half of their genes *on average*; some siblings share more and others fewer. Indeed, we have all known some siblings who are almost like twins and others who could not be more different if they tried.

Fraternal twins (also called dizygotic twins because two eggs are involved) result when two ova are released at approximately the same time and each is fertilized by a different sperm, as happens in about 1 of every 125 births (Plomin, 1990). Fraternal twins are no more alike genetically than brothers and sisters born at different times and can be of different sexes. Fraternal twins tend to run in families and have become more common in recent years because more couples are taking fertility drugs and undergoing in vitro fertilization (Segal, 2005).

Grandparent and grandchild, aunt or uncle and niece or nephew, and half brothers and half sisters share 25% of their genes in common on average. Thus, everyone except an identical twin is genetically unique, but each person also shares genes with kin that contribute to family resemblances.

Determination of Sex

Of the 23 pairs of chromosomes that each individual inherits, 22 are similar in males and females. The chromosomes of the 23rd pair are the sex chromosomes. A male child has one long chromosome called an **X chromosome** and a shorter companion with far fewer genes called a **Y chromosome**. Females have two X chromosomes. It is now understood that most of the genes on one or the other of a female's X chromosomes are normally inactivated early in the prenatal period and remain inactive in cells subsequently produced through mitosis (Ross et al., 2005). The photos on this page show male and female chromosomes that have been photographed through a powerful microscope, then arranged in pairs and rephotographed in a pattern called a **karyotype** that allows their number and form to be studied.

Because a mother's egg has only X chromosomes and a father's sperm cell has either an X chromosome or a Y chromosome (depending on which sex chromosome a sperm receives during meiosis), it is the father who determines a child's gender. If an ovum with its one X chromosome is fertilized by a sperm bearing a Y chromosome, the product is an XY zygote—a genetic male. A gene on the Y chromosome then sets in motion the biological events that result in male sexual development (Hawley & Mori, 1999; and see Chapter 12). If a sperm carrying an X chromosome reaches the ovum first, the result is an XX zygote—a genetic female. Perhaps if these facts had been known in earlier eras, women would not have been criticized, tortured, divorced, and even beheaded for failing to bear male heirs.

So a genetically unique boy or girl has a genome with 20,000–25,000 protein-building genes and a lot of regulatory DNA on 46 chromosomes arranged in 23 pairs. How do these genes, along with environmental factors, influence the individual's characteristics and development? The mystery is far from solved, but knowledge is expanding by leaps and bounds.

From Genotype to Phenotype

One does not have to understand cell biology to appreciate that environmental factors help determine which genetic potentials are translated into physical and psychological realities and which are not. Consider this: Some people inherit genes calling for exceptional height, and others inherit genes calling for a short stature. But **genotype**, the genetic makeup a person inherits, is different from **phenotype**, the characteristic or trait the person eventually has (for example, a height of 5 feet 8 inches). An individual whose genotype calls for exceptional height may or may not be tall. Indeed, a child who is severely malnourished from the prenatal period onward may have the genetic potential to be a basketball center but may end up too short to make the team. Environmental influences combine with genetic influences to determine how a particular genotype is translated into a particular phenotype—the way a person looks, thinks, feels, or behaves.

As you have seen, genes provide instructions for development by calling for the production of proteins. For example, genes set in motion a process that lays a pigment called *melanin* in the iris of the

CNRI/Science Source

The male karyotype (*left*) shows the 22 pairs of autosomal chromosomes and the 2 sex chromosomes—an elongated X and a shorter Y chromosome. The photographic arrangement of a female's chromosomes (*right*) shows 2 X chromosomes.

eye. Some people's genes call for much of this pigment, and the result is brown eyes; other people's genes call for less of it, and the result is blue eyes. Genetically coded proteins also guide the formation of cells that become neurons in the brain, influencing potential intelligence and personality. But genes both influence and are influenced by the biochemical environment surrounding them (Gottlieb, 2002; Meaney, 2010). During embryonic development, a particular cell can become part of an eyeball or part of a kneecap depending on what cells are next to it and what they are doing. Because all of a person's cells have the same genes on the same chromosomes, what makes brain, blood, and other cells different from each other is not what genes they contain but which of those genes are *expressed*.

A multitude of environmental factors—not only in the womb but throughout the life span—influence which genes go into action when (Champagne, 2010; Gottesman & Hanson, 2005). **Gene expression** is the activation of particular genes in particular cells of the body at particular times; only if a gene is "turned on" is it influential. Gene expression, then, is what ultimately influences our traits and therefore converts genotypes into phenotypes. Gene expression is guided in part by genetic influences such as the action of regulatory DNA. However, as we will see at the end of the chapter, great excitement now surrounds the discovery that gene expression can also be affected, starting prenatally but throughout the life span, and sometimes in lasting ways, by environmental factors such as diet, stress, drugs, toxins, and even early parenting (Champagne & Mashoodh, 2009; Zhang & Meaney, 2010). You should therefore think of the genetic "code" as written in erasable pencil rather than in indelible ink. Genes do not determine anything; rather, genes and environment interact and coact to influence development and behavior throughout the life span.

Mechanisms of Inheritance

Let us now consider the major mechanisms of inheritance—how parents' genes influence their children's genotypes and phenotypes. There are three main mechanisms of inheritance: single gene-pair inheritance, sex-linked inheritance, and polygenic (or multiple gene) inheritance.

Single Gene-Pair Inheritance

Through **single gene-pair inheritance**, each of thousands of human characteristics are influenced by only one pair of genes—one from the mother, one from the father (Turnpenny & Ellard, 2011). Although he knew nothing of genes, the 19th-century monk Gregor Mendel contributed greatly to our knowledge of single gene-pair inheritance and earned his place as the father of genetics by cross-breeding different strains of peas and carefully observing the outcomes (Henig, 2000). As an illustration of the principles of Mendelian inheritance, consider the remarkable fact that about three-fourths of us can curl our tongues upward into a tubelike shape, whereas one-fourth of us cannot. (We have no idea why.) It happens that there is a gene associated with tongue curling; it is a **dominant gene**, meaning that it will be expressed when paired with a **recessive gene**, a weaker gene that can be dominated (like one associated with the absence of tongue-curling ability).

The person who inherits one "tongue-curl" gene (label it U) and one "no-curl" gene (call it -) would be able to curl his tongue (that is, would have a tongue-curling phenotype) because the dominant tongue-curl gene overpowers the recessive no-curl gene. Using ■ **Figure 3.2** as a guide, you can calculate the odds that parents with various genotypes for tongue curling will have children who can or cannot curl their tongues. Each of the nine cells of the figure shows the four possible types of children that can result when a father contributes one of his two genes to a sperm and a mother contributes one of her two genes to an ovum and a child is conceived.

If a father with the genotype UU (a tongue curler) and a mother with the genotype - - (a non–tongue curler) have children, each child they produce will have one dominant gene for tongue curling and one recessive gene for a lack of tongue curling (genotype U-) and each will be a tongue curler because the tongue-curl gene will rule. You can say that this couple has a 100% chance of having a tongue-curling child. Notice that two different genotypes, UU and U-, both produce the same phenotype: an acrobatic tongue.

A tongue-curling man and a tongue-curling woman can surprise everyone and have a child who lacks this amazing talent. These two parents both must have the U- genotype. If the father's recessive gene and the mother's recessive gene happen to unite in the zygote, they will have a non–tongue-curling child (with the genotype - -). The chances are 25%—one out of four—that this couple will have such a child. Of course, the laws of conception are much like the laws of cards. This couple could beat the odds and have a whole family of non–tongue-curling children, or they could have none. Because people who cannot curl their tongues must have the - - genotype, two non–tongue-curling parents will have only non–tongue-curling (- -) children.

● **Table 3.2** lists a few examples of dominant and recessive traits associated with single gene-pair inheritance. In some cases, a dominant gene incompletely dominates a recessive partner gene and the result is a new trait that blends the parents' traits—as

● **Table 3.2** Examples of Traits Influenced by Dominant and Recessive Genes

Dominant Trait	Recessive Trait
Brown eyes	Gray, green, hazel, or blue eyes
Dark hair	Blond hair
Nonred hair	Red hair
Curly hair	Straight hair
Normal vision	Nearsightedness
Farsightedness	Normal vision
Broad lips	Thin lips
Double jointed	Normal joints
Pigmented skin	Albinism
Type A blood	Type O blood
Type B blood	Type O blood

Sources: Burns & Bottino, 1989; McKusick, 1990.

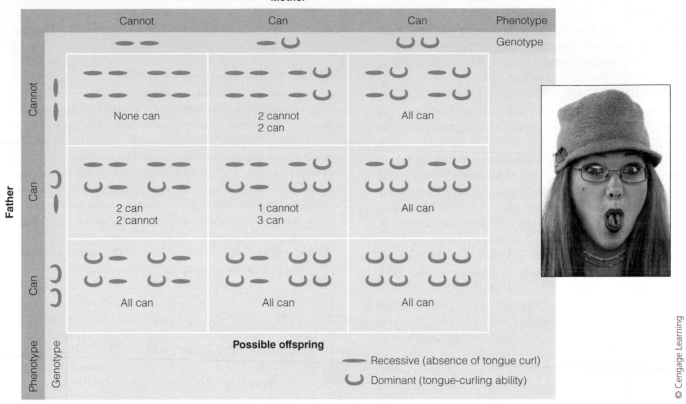

Mother

■ **Figure 3.2** Can you curl your tongue as shown? Tongue-curling ability is determined by a dominant gene; if you can curl your tongue, then either your mother or your father can, because one of them must have the dominant gene. All possibilities are shown in the figure; each of the nine boxes shows the gene combinations of the four possible children a particular mother and a particular father can have.

when crossing red and white flowers produces pink ones or when dark-skinned and light-skinned parents have a child with light brown skin. This phenomenon is called **incomplete dominance**. In other cases, two genes influence a trait but each is expressed in the product, as when crossing red and white flowers produces flowers with red and white streaks—a phenomenon called **codominance**. For example, an AB blood type is a mix of A and B blood types. So, Gregor Mendel got it mostly right, but single gene-pair inheritance is a bit more complex than he realized.

Sex-Linked Inheritance

Sex-linked characteristics are influenced by single genes located on the sex chromosomes rather than on the other 22 pairs of chromosomes. Indeed, you could say *X-linked* rather than *sex-linked* because most of these attributes are associated with genes located on X but not Y chromosomes.

Why do far more males than females display red–green color blindness? The inability to distinguish red from green is caused by a recessive gene that appears only on X chromosomes. Recall that Y chromosomes are shorter than X chromosomes and have fewer genes. If a boy inherits the recessive color-blindness gene on the X chromosome his mother provides to him, there is no color-vision gene on his Y chromosome that could dominate the color-blindness gene. He will be

■ **Figure 3.3** The workings of sex-linked inheritance in red–green color blindness.

color blind. By contrast, a girl who inherits the gene usually has a normal color-vision gene on her other X chromosome that can dominate the color-blindness gene (■ **Figure 3.3**). She would have to inherit two of the recessive color-blindness genes (one from each parent) to be color blind. **Hemophilia**, a deficiency in the blood's ability to clot, is also far more common among males than females because it is a sex-linked disorder associated with a recessive gene on X chromosomes.

Polygenic Inheritance

So far we have considered only the influence of single genes or gene pairs on human traits. Every week, it seems, we read in the newspaper that researchers have identified "the gene" for high blood pressure, happiness, or some other human trait. However, most important human characteristics are **polygenic traits**; they are influenced by multiple pairs of genes, interacting with multiple environmental factors, rather than by a single pair of genes. Examples of polygenic traits include height, weight, intelligence, personality, susceptibility to cancer and depression, and much more.

When a trait like intelligence is influenced by multiple genes, many degrees of it are possible, depending on how many of the genes associated with high levels of the trait individuals inherit. Most people will get some "high IQ" genes and some "low IQ" genes, so will have pretty average IQs. A few at the extremes will inherit only low intelligence genes or only high intelligence genes. The trait will therefore tend to be distributed in the population according to the familiar bell-shaped or normal curve: Many people are near the average of the distribution; fewer are at the extremes. This is in fact the way intelligence and most other measurable human traits are distributed. At this point, we do not know how many gene pairs influence intelligence or other polygenic traits. What we can say is that unknown and probably large numbers of genes, interacting with environmental forces, create a range of individual differences in most important human traits (Plomin & Davis, 2009).

Mutations

So far, we have described the three major mechanisms by which the genes inherited at conception influence traits: single gene-pair, sex-linked, and polygenic inheritance. Occasionally, however, a new gene appears as if out of nowhere; neither parent has it. A **mutation** is a change in the structure or arrangement of one or more genes that produces a new phenotype. Mutations can be either beneficial or harmful, depending on their nature and on the environment in which their bearers live (see later discussion of the gene for sickle-cell disease).

Experts believe that the recessive gene for the sex-linked disorder hemophilia was a mutation first introduced into the royal families of Europe by Queen Victoria and then passed on to some of her descendants. New cases of hemophilia, then, can be caused by either sex-linked inheritance or spontaneous mutations. The odds that mutations will occur are increased by environmental hazards such as radiation and toxic industrial waste, but most mutations are just spontaneous errors during cell division (Turnpenny & Ellard, 2011). Recently it has been discovered that fathers contribute about four times the number of new mutations as mothers do overall and that the odds of mutations increase steadily as fathers get older because more errors are made during sperm production (Kong et al., 2012). Mutations

associated with **autism** (O'Roak et al., 2012), schizophrenia (Frans et al., 2011), and other disorders become more likely as a father's age increases.

Chromosome Abnormalities

Genetic endowment can also influence human development through **chromosome abnormalities**, in which a child receives too many or too few chromosomes (or abnormal chromosomes) at conception (Gardner, Sutherland, & Shaffer, 2012). Most such abnormalities are caused by errors in chromosome division during meiosis. Through an accident of nature, an ovum or sperm cell may be produced with more or fewer than the usual 23 chromosomes. In most cases, a zygote with the wrong number of chromosomes is spontaneously aborted; chromosome abnormalities are the main cause of pregnancy loss.

One familiar chromosome abnormality is **Down syndrome**, also known as *trisomy 21* because it is associated with three rather than two 21st chromosomes. Children with Down syndrome have distinctive eyelid folds, short stubby limbs, and thick tongues. Their levels of intellectual functioning vary widely, but most have some degree of intellectual disability (formerly called **mental retardation** and associated with an IQ of below 70). They therefore develop and learn at a slower pace than most children, but they can benefit greatly from early stimulation programs,

Children with Down syndrome have distinctive eyelid folds, short limbs, and thick tongues.

special education, and vocational training (Hazlett, Hammer, Hooper, & Kamphaus, 2011; Roizen & Patterson, 2003). Witness Lauren Potter, the young woman with Down syndrome who plays a cheerleader on the TV program *Glee*; witness others of her generation who are working and even attending college (Rochman, 2012). In some parts of the world, over half of children with Down syndrome die in infancy, most often because of heart defects (Christianson, Howson, & Modell, 2006). However, in the United States and other wealthy nations, many people with Down syndrome are now living into middle age, when many of them develop signs of premature aging, including Alzheimer's disease (Berney, 2009; and see Chapter 16).

What determines who has a child with Down syndrome and who does not? Chance, partly. The errors in meiosis responsible for Down syndrome can occur in any mother—or father. However, the chances of chromosome abnormalities and other birth defects increase as a parent's age increases (Cleary-Goldman et al., 2005). The chances of having a baby with Down syndrome are about 13 births in 10,000, or 1 birth in 733, in the United States (Centers for Disease Control and Prevention, 2006a). The odds increase with the mother's age, especially from about age 35 on (■ **Figure 3.4**). A father's age also affects the odds of having a child with Down syndrome. Indeed, couples older than 40 have about six times the risk of having a child with Down syndrome as couples younger than 35(Fisch et al., 2003). The fact that many adults today are delaying parenthood until

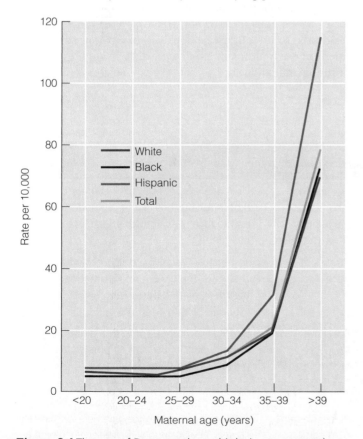

■ **Figure 3.4** The rate of Down syndrome births increases steeply as the mother's age increases. (Father's age is also a factor.)

Source: "Down Syndrome Prevalence at Birth" —United States, 1983–1990 (1994, August 26). *Mortality and Morbidity Weekly Reports, 43*, 617–622.

their 30s or 40s is likely to translate into increased numbers of chromosome abnormalities.

Most other chromosome abnormalities involve a child's receiving either too many or too few sex chromosomes. Like Down syndrome, these sex chromosome abnormalities can be attributed mainly to errors in meiosis, errors that become increasingly likely in older parents and parents whose chromosomes have been damaged by environmental hazards such as radiation (Wodrich, 2006). One example is **Turner syndrome**, in which a female (about 1 in 2,000 to 3,000) is born with a single X chromosome rather than two. These girls remain small and often have stubby fingers and toes, a "webbed" neck, and underdeveloped breasts. They are unable to reproduce, typically favor traditionally feminine activities, are socially immature, and often have lower-than-average spatial and mathematical abilities (Downey et al., 1991; Powell & Schulte, 2011).

Another example is **Klinefelter syndrome**, in which a male (1 in 500–1,000) is born with one or more extra X chromosomes (XXY). Klinefelter males tend to have long limbs and sometimes big ears, long faces, and other physical signs; they are sterile and at puberty develop feminine sex characteristics such as enlarged breasts. Most have normal intelligence test scores, but many have language learning disabilities and below-average school achievement (Hazlett, De Alba, & Hooper, 2011; Mandoki et al., 1991).

Finally, **fragile X syndrome** is also worth noting (Gropman & Batshaw, 2010; Hagerman, 2011; McConkie-Rosell et al., 2005). In this condition, all 46 chromosomes are present, but one arm of the X chromosome is only barely connected to the rest of the chromosome and looks as if it is about to break off—hence the term *fragile*. Fragile X syndrome causes intellectual disability or milder cognitive impairment in most affected persons and autism in many as well. The condition is usually not diagnosable until around age 3 unless parents know that fragile X runs in the family and ask for genetic testing so that their child can begin to receive early intervention (Roberts et al., 2009).

The abnormal X chromosome in fragile X syndrome is caused by sex-linked inheritance of a gene on the X chromosome (Hagerman, 2011). It is therefore more common among males than females. The affected individual has too many repeats or duplications of a sequence of three letters in the genetic code (over 200 such repeats), and the result is lack of a protein important in keeping the proliferation of synapses, or connections between neurons of the brain, from spinning out of control (Wallis, 2008; O'Donnell & Warren, 2002). The number of repeats of the DNA segment responsible for fragile X syndrome can increase from generation to generation in a family with the sex-linked gene responsible for fragile X syndrome, causing more serious intellectual disability in later generations of the family. **Copy number variations** like this—instances in which a person receives too many or too few copies of a stretch of DNA—turn out to be quite common; like mutations of whole genes, they can either be inherited from a parent or arise spontaneously. Increasingly, researchers are finding that some contribute to diseases and disorders, among them autism, schizophrenia, and attention deficit hyperactivity disorder (ADHD) (Rucker & McGuffin, 2012).

Genetic Diseases, Diagnosis, and Counseling

Diseases and disorders associated with a single gene or pair of genes, polygene disorders, and chromosome abnormalities, although rare, can profoundly affect human development. **Genetic counseling** is a service that provides information about and guidance regarding the nature, likelihood, effects, and treatment of genetically based diseases and disorders to people who suspect or learn that they or their unborn children are at risk (Resta et al., 2006; Turnpenny & Ellard, 2011). Thanks to the Human Genome Project and related research, today's genetic counselors have more information than ever about genetic defects and can quickly and quite inexpensively collect and analyze DNA samples by swabbing the inside of people's cheeks or drawing small samples of their blood. To illustrate issues in genetic diagnosis and counseling and the workings of some important genetic disorders, we focus on sickle-cell disease, Huntington's disease, and PKU. These diseases, along with another discussed earlier, hemophilia, are summarized in ● **Table 3.3**.

Sickle-Cell Disease

Suppose an African American couple visits a genetic counselor, has a genetic test done, and learns that they both are carriers of the recessive gene for **sickle-cell disease**. This is a blood disease, common among African Americans, in which red blood cells take on a sickle shape, become entangled, and distribute less oxygen through the circulatory system than round blood cells do (Serjeant, 2010; Smith & Baker, 2011). Individuals with sickle-cell disease have great difficulty breathing and exerting themselves, experience painful swelling of their joints, and often die early as a result of blood clots, strokes, and heart or kidney failure. Interestingly, the gene responsible probably started as a mutation which, because it protected people from malaria, became more common over many generations in Africa, Central America, and other tropical areas through natural selection. People with one of the recessive sickle-cell genes lived longer and produced more children than people without the protective gene—another example of an interaction between genes and environment. Unfortunately, the sickle-cell gene does more harm than good in environments where malaria is no longer a problem.

The genetic counselor might tell the couple that about 9% of African Americans in the United States have the genotype we will call Ss; they carry one dominant gene (S) that calls for round blood cells and one recessive gene (s) that calls for sickle-shaped blood cells (Thompson, 1975). Such people are called **carriers** because, although they do not have the disease, they can transmit the gene for it to their children. The child who inherits two recessive sickle-cell genes (ss) will have sickle-cell disease. The genetic counselor would therefore explain that an Ss father and an Ss mother (two carriers) have a one-in-four, or 25%, chance of having a child with sickle-cell disease (ss).

This couple also has a two-in-four, or 50%, chance of having a child who will be a carrier like themselves. This is significant because the dominant gene associated with round blood cells shows incomplete dominance. As a result, carriers of the sickle-cell gene have many round blood cells and some sickle-shaped cells. When they are at high altitudes, are given anesthesia, or are otherwise deprived of oxygen, carriers may experience symptoms of sickle-cell disease such as difficulty breathing and fatigue.

● Table 3.3 Some Genetic Disorders

Disease	Description	Genetic Mechanism	Diagnosis and Treatment
Hemophilia	Deficiency in blood's ability to clot; more common in males than females	Sex-linked inheritance (gene on X chromosome)	DNA analysis of fetal cells can detect it. Blood transfusions can improve clotting and reduce the negative effects of internal bleeding
Huntington's disease	Deterioration of the nervous system in middle age, associated with dementia, jerky movements, personality changes	Dominant gene	Test enables relatives to find out whether they have the gene. Preimplantation genetic diagnosis of embryonic cells may be used to ensure a healthy child
Phenylketonuria (PKU)	Lack of enzyme needed to metabolize phenylalanine in milk and other foods results in acid that attacks the nervous system and causes intellectual disability. Common in people of European descent.	Recessive gene pair	Routinely screened for with a blood test at birth; special diet low in phenylalanine prevents brain damage
Sickle-cell disease	Blood cells are sickle shaped, stick together, make breathing hard, and cause painful swelling of joints and blood clots; common in African Americans	Recessive gene pair; carriers were protected from malaria	Blood test can determine whether parents are carriers; newborns in U. S. are screened with a blood test. Antibiotics and blood transfusions prevent infections and relieve symptoms

Sources: Goldstein & Reynolds, 2011; Kingston, 2008; Pritchard & Korf, 2008; Turnpenny & Ellard, 2011.

Sickle-shaped (elongated) and normal (round) blood cells from a carrier of the sickle-cell gene.

A blood test is used to screen all newborns in the United States for sickle-cell disease. Affected children begin a life of treatment with blood transfusions, antibiotics to prevent infections, and sometimes early interventions to optimize their intellectual development (Smith & Baker, 2011). Such screening of newborns is lacking in areas like sub-Saharan Africa and central India, where the rate of sickle-cell disease is high, but could do much good in promoting the healthy development of affected children (Serjeant, 2010).

Huntington's Disease

Now consider **Huntington's disease**, a famous (and terrifying) example of a genetic defect associated with a single dominant gene. This disease typically strikes in middle age and disrupts the expression of genes in the nervous system (Anderson et al., 2008). Among the effects are motor disturbances such as slurred speech, an erratic and seemingly drunken walk, grimaces, and jerky movements; personality changes such as increased moodiness and irritability; and dementia or loss of cognitive abilities (Bishop & Waldholz, 1990; Sutton-Brown & Suchowersky, 2003). Any child of a parent with Huntington's disease is almost certain to develop the disease if she receives the dominant (but fortunately rare) Huntington's gene rather than its normal counterpart gene at conception. The risk for an individual who has a parent with Huntington's disease is therefore one out of two, or 50%.

A genetic counselor talking with the child of a Huntington's victim would note that there is a test to enable the relatives of Huntington's victims to find out whether or not they inherited the gene. Would you want to know? Some do, but many do not, partly because they fear discrimination by insurance companies or employers based on their genetic makeup, partly because they do not want to live with the knowledge that they will develop this awful disease (Bombard, 2009; Sutton-Brown & Suchowersky, 2003).

If it turns out that a prospective parent has the gene and wishes to have children, the genetic counselor might discuss prenatal diagnosis procedures that can detect many genetic abnormalities prenatally. Three widely used techniques—amniocentesis, chorionic villus sampling, and ultrasound—as well as the newer methods of preimplantation genetic diagnosis and maternal blood sampling, are described in **Application Box 3.1**.

For a video of an ultrasound test, see **Exploring Development Box 3.1**. For the parents whose tests reveal a normal embryo or fetus, there is relief. For parents who learn that their fetus has a serious defect, the choice between abortion and bearing a child with a serious disorder can be agonizing. For a would-be parent with the Huntington's gene who has an aversion to abortion and the necessary funds, preimplantation genetic diagnosis (see Application Box 3.1) might be appealing. Fertilized eggs can be tested for the presence of the Huntington's gene, and the doctor can then implant only eggs without the gene in the mother's uterus.

Phenylketonuria

Finally, a more upbeat story: the story of **phenylketonuria (PKU)**, a metabolic disorder caused by a single pair of recessive genes that results in brain damage and intellectual disability (Waisbren, 2011; Widaman, 2009). About 1 in 50 people in the United States are carriers of the PKU gene (Waisbren, 2011). Two carriers have a one in four chance of having a child with the condition. Affected children lack a critical enzyme needed to metabolize phenylalanine, a component of many foods, including milk. As phenylalanine accumulates in the body, it is converted to a harmful acid that attacks the nervous system and causes intellectual disability and **hyperactivity**.

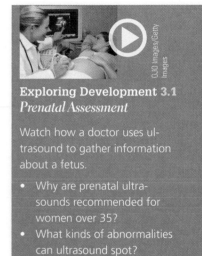

Exploring Development 3.1
Prenatal Assessment

Watch how a doctor uses ultrasound to gather information about a fetus.

- Why are prenatal ultrasounds recommended for women over 35?
- What kinds of abnormalities can ultrasound spot?

A simple blood test can detect PKU soon after birth, before damage is done. Today, newborn infants are routinely screened for PKU, and affected children are immediately placed on a special (and, unfortunately, distasteful) diet low in phenylalanine (J. A. Miller, 1995). It was once thought they could get off the diet after early childhood, but they are now advised to stay on it, at least to some extent, for the rest of their lives or risk deterioration in their cognitive functioning (Waisbren, 2011). It is especially important for a mother with PKU to stay on the special diet during pregnancy so that high levels of phenylalanine in her blood cannot harm her fetus (Widaman, 2009).

Here, then, genetic research led to the prevention of one cause of intellectual disability. And here is a beautiful example of the interaction between genes and environment: A child will develop the condition and become mentally retarded if he inherits two PKU genes *and* eats a normal (high-phenylalanine) diet but not if he eats the special (low-phenylalanine) diet.

Genetic counselors must keep up with breakthroughs in prevention, diagnosis, and treatment of genetically related diseases and disorders. For the many conditions that are polygenic in origin, it is usually not possible to do a definitive test or even give solid odds, but genetic counselors can educate families and

Prenatal Detection of Abnormalities

Pregnant women, especially those over 35 or 40, turn to a variety of medical techniques to tell them in advance whether their babies are likely to be normal (Simpson & Elias, 2003; Turnpenny & Ellard, 2011; Wilfond & Ross, 2009). What are the pros and cons of various prenatal diagnostic techniques?

Ultrasound

The easiest and most commonly used method is **ultrasound**, the use of sound waves to scan the womb and create a visual image of the fetus on a monitor screen. Ultrasound can indicate how many fetuses are in the uterus, their sex, and whether they are alive, and it can detect genetic defects that produce visible physical abnormalities. Ultrasound is widely used even when abnormalities are not suspected because it is considered very safe (Simpson & Elias, 2003).

Amniocentesis

To detect chromosome abnormalities such as Down syndrome and to determine, through DNA analysis, whether the genes for particular single gene-pair disorders are present, **amniocentesis** is used. A needle is inserted into the abdomen, a sample of amniotic fluid is withdrawn, and fetal cells that have been shed are analyzed. A risk of miscarriage exists but it is low, as few as 1 in 1,600 cases, making the procedure relatively safe and advisable for pregnant women over age 35 (Bornstein et al., 2009; Eddleman et al., 2006). Its main disadvantage is that it is not considered safe until the 15th week of pregnancy.

Chorionic Villus Sampling

Chorionic villus sampling (CVS) involves inserting a catheter through the mother's vagina and cervix (or, less commonly, through her abdomen) into the membrane called the *chorion* that surrounds the fetus, and then extracting tiny hair cells from the chorion that contain genetic material from the fetus. Sample cells are then analyzed for the same genetic defects that can be detected using amniocentesis. The difference is that chorionic villus sampling can be performed as early as the 10th week of pregnancy, allowing parents more time to weigh the pros and cons of continuing the pregnancy if an abnormality is detected (Simpson & Elias, 2003). The risks of CVS are only slightly greater than those of amniocentesis.

Maternal Blood Sampling

Maternal blood sampling has been used for a number of years to test the mother's blood for various chemicals that can indicate abnormalities in the fetus. However, now it can also be used to obtain loose embryonic DNA that has slipped through the placenta into the mother's blood—DNA that can then be analyzed *with no risk at all to the fetus* (Benn & Chapman, 2009). This method of prenatal diagnosis has not been reliable until recently, but now methods for detecting Down syndrome with high accuracy at around 10 weeks after conception have become available (Rubin, 2012; Verweij et al., 2012), and researchers can assess the fetus's entire genome by identifying and testing fetal DNA floating in the mother's blood (Fan et al., 2012). Maternal blood sampling of fetal DNA has the tremendous advantages of being noninvasive and usable early in the pregnancy. If it indeed becomes accurate enough, it may replace amniocentesis and CVS entirely.

Preimplantation Genetic Diagnosis

Finally, parents who know they are at high risk to have a baby with a serious condition can minimize their risk through **preimplantation genetic diagnosis**. This involves fertilizing a mother's eggs with a father's sperm in the laboratory using *in vitro fertilization (IVF) techniques* (see Chapter 4), conducting DNA tests on the first cells that result from mitosis of each fertilized egg, and implanting in the mother's uterus only eggs that do not have chromosome abnormalities or genes associated with disorders (Bick & Lau, 2006; Braude, 2006). Although costly, this option may appeal to couples who would not consider abortion but do not want to have a child with a serious defect.

Pros and Cons

Advances in prenatal diagnosis such as maternal blood sampling and preimplantation genetic diagnosis have the potential to prevent serious disorders and diseases. They also open the door to early interventions that might save the lives of babies with problems or set them on a healthier developmental path. Indeed, sequencing of the genomes of newborns is starting to be used to help pinpoint what is wrong with babies in neonatal intensive care units in order to treat them appropriately and prevent their death (Saunders et al., 2012).

Do you see any problems in knowing everything there is to know about the contents of a fetus's genome? The prospect that all pregnant women may soon have their blood analyzed for evidence of genetic abnormalities is raising ethical red flags, especially about the possibility that abortion rates will soar if more parents decide that they do not want babies with Down syndrome or other "undesirable" characteristics or if parents try to create "designer" babies who are healthy, smart, and of the desired gender (Benn & Chapman, 2009; Wilfond & Ross, 2009). Already data suggest that, due to high rates of termination of pregnancies that would produce a child with Down syndrome, the incidence of Down syndrome is lower than would be expected based on the growing number of older mothers (Skotko, 2009; Rochman, 2012).

So, prenatal diagnostic techniques such as ultrasound, amniocentesis, CVS, maternal blood sampling, and preimplantation genetic diagnosis can provide tremendously important information when there is reason to suspect a problem. Yet they clearly raise issues for society to grapple with as well.

attempt to correct their misunderstandings. It makes sense for all of us to become educated about any genetic conditions in our family trees.

▶ Checking Mastery

1. Ted and Ned, fraternal twins, are not very alike at all. Give both a "nature" explanation and a "nurture" explanation of their differences.

2. Hairy forehead syndrome (we made it up) is caused by a single dominant gene, *H*. Using diagrams such as those in Figure 3.2, figure out the odds that Herb (who has the genotype *Hh*) and Harriet (who also has the genotype *Hh*) will have a child with hairy forehead syndrome. Now repeat the exercise, but assume that hairy forehead syndrome is caused by a recessive gene, *h*, and that both parents again have an *Hh* genotype.

3. Juan has red–green color blindness. Knowing that he is color blind, what can you infer about his parents?

▶ Making Connections

1. A DNA sample taken by swabbing a person's cheek can now reveal the person's entire genome. What do you think will be the positive and negative consequences of this scientific breakthrough for society? On balance, should we be pleased or concerned about this development?

2. As it becomes possible for parents to obtain genetic analyses of embryonic cells early in pregnancy and elect to continue or terminate the pregnancy based on the results, do you think parents should have the right to terminate any pregnancy they wish to terminate? Should they, for example, be able to terminate a female fetus if they want a boy, a fetus with a likely learning disability if they want a genius? Why or why not?

3. Are you aware of any genetically influenced diseases that run in your family? If so, what are they and what do you know (or what can you learn) about the mechanism involved?

3.3 Studying Genetic and Environmental Influences

LEARNING OBJECTIVES: ▶

- Define the main goal and research methods of behavioral genetics and the meaning of *heritability*.

- Distinguish among the effects of genes, shared environmental influences, and nonshared environmental influences, and explain how a study of identical and fraternal twin pairs raised together versus raised apart can shed light on the importance of each of these influences.

- Explain what molecular genetics studies tell us that behavioral genetics studies cannot.

How do researchers study the contributions of genes and environment to variation among us in physical and psychological traits? **Behavioral genetics** is the scientific study of the extent to which genetic and environmental differences among people or animals are responsible for differences in their physical and psychological traits (Plomin et al., 2008; Rutter, 2006). It is impossible to say that a given person's intelligence test score is the result of, say, 80%, 50%, or 20% heredity and the rest environment. The individual would have no intelligence without both genetic makeup and experiences. It is, however, possible for behavioral geneticists to estimate the **heritability** of measured IQ and of other traits or behaviors. Heritability is the proportion of all the variability in the trait within a large sample of people that can be linked to genetic differences among those individuals. To say that measured intelligence is *heritable*, then, is to say that differences in tested IQ among the individuals studied are to some degree attributable to the different genetic endowments of these individuals (Plomin et al., 2008).

It may seem from their name that *behavioral geneticists* would tell us only about genetic contributions to development, but in fact their work tells us about the contributions of both genetic and environmental factors to differences among people. The variability in a trait that is not associated with genetic differences is associated with differences in environment.

Behavioral geneticists who study animals can gather evidence through experimental breeding studies. For example, if a trait like learning ability is genetically influenced, breeding animals with high learning ability with each other should produce more offspring with high learning ability over several generations than breeding animals with low learning ability together does (Plomin et al., 2008). Experimental breeding studies have shown that genes contribute to learning ability, activity level, emotionality, aggressiveness, sex drive, and many other attributes in rats, mice, and chickens (Plomin et al., 2008).

But people do not take kindly to the idea of being selectively bred. So how can researchers try to separate the contributions of genes and environment to human differences? How can they tell whether family resemblances are due to common genes or common experiences? Behavioral genetics research in humans has relied primarily on determining whether the degree of genetic similarity between pairs of people is associated with the degree of physical or psychological similarity between them. Twin, adoption, and other family studies provide this information. More recently, molecular genetics techniques that allow studying the effects of specific genes have expanded our knowledge (see Plomin et al., 2008).

Twin, Adoption, and Family Studies

Twins have long been recognized as important sources of evidence about the effects of heredity. A simple type of **twin study** to untangle genetic and environmental influences involves determining whether identical twins reared together are more similar to each other in the traits of interest than fraternal twins reared together. If genes matter, identical twins should be more similar because they have 100% of their genes in common, whereas fraternal twins share only 50% on average.

More complex twin studies include not only identical and fraternal twin pairs raised together but also identical and fraternal twins reared apart—four groups in all, differing in both whether they share 100% or 50% of their genes and whether they shared the same home environment. Identical twins separated near birth and raised in different environments—like the twins introduced at the beginning of the chapter—are particularly informative because any similarities between them cannot be attributed to common family experiences.

Although it is basically sound and widely used, the twin method has some limitations (Brendgen, Vitaro, & Girard, 2012). First, one can question whether findings based on twins will generalize to singleton children. Second, identical twins could be more psychologically similar than fraternal twins, even if they are separated at birth, because they shared a more similar **prenatal environment** than fraternal twins or other siblings did (Devlin, Daniels, & Roeder, 1997). Finally, the fact that identical twins are often treated more similarly than fraternal twins could explain their greater psychological similarity. As it turns out, though, there appears to be little relationship between how similarly twins are treated and how similar they turn out to be psychologically; more likely, twins' similarities result in their being treated similarly (Loehlin, 1992; Brendgen et al., 2012).

A second commonly used method of studying the effects of heredity is the **adoption study**. Are children adopted early in life psychologically similar to their biological parents, whose genes they share, or are they similar to their adoptive parents, whose environment they share? If adopted children resemble their biological parents in intelligence or personality, even though those parents did not raise them, genes must be influential. If they resemble their adoptive parents, even though they are genetically unrelated to them, a good case can be made for environmental influence. Like the twin method, the adoption method has proved useful but has its limitations. Researchers must appreciate that not only the genes of a biological mother but also the prenatal environment she provided could influence how an adopted child turns out (Gottlieb, Wahlsten, & Lickliter, 2006). Researchers must also be careful to correct for the tendency of adoption agencies to place children in homes similar to those they were adopted from. Finally, researchers must recognize that because adoptive homes are generally above-average environments, adoption studies may underestimate the effects of the full range of environments children can experience (Stoolmiller, 1999; but see McGue et al., 2007).

Finally, today's researchers are conducting complex **family studies** that include pairs of siblings who have a variety of different degrees of genetic similarity—for example, identical twins, fraternal twins, full biological siblings, half siblings, and unrelated stepsiblings who live together in stepfamilies (Plomin et al., 2008; Reiss et al., 2000). They are also measuring qualities of these family members' experiences to determine how similar or different the environments of siblings are. Behavioral geneticists are even looking at twins and other pairs of relatives longitudinally so that they can assess the contributions of genes and environment to continuity and change in traits as individuals develop.

Estimating Influences

Having conducted a twin, adoption, or family study, behavioral geneticists use statistical calculations to estimate the degree to which heredity and environment account for individual differences in a trait of interest. When they study traits that a person either has or does not have (for example, a smoking habit or diabetes), researchers calculate and compare **concordance rates**—the percentage of pairs of people studied (for example, pairs of identical twins or adoptive parents and children) in which if one member of a pair displays the trait, the other does too. If concordance rates are higher for more genetically related than for less genetically related pairs of people, the trait is heritable.

Suppose researchers are interested in whether homosexuality is genetically influenced. They might locate men who are gay and who have twins, either identical or fraternal, locate their twin siblings, and find out whether they, too, are gay. In one study of this type (Bailey & Pillard, 1991), the concordance rate for identical twins was 52% (29 of the 56 twins of gay men were also gay), whereas the concordance rate for fraternal twins was lower, 22% (12 of 54 twins of gay men were also gay). This finding and others suggest that genetic makeup contributes to both men's and women's sexual orientation (Bailey, Dunne, & Martin, 2000; Dawood, Bailey, & Martin, 2009; Kendler et al., 2000). Importantly, though, identical twins are *not* perfectly concordant, so environmental factors must also affect sexual orientation. After all, Bailey and Pillard found that in 48% of the identical twin pairs, one twin was gay but the other was not, despite their identical genes.

When a trait can be present in varying degrees, as is true of height or intelligence, correlation coefficients rather than concordance rates are calculated (see Chapter 1). In a behavioral genetics study of IQ scores, a correlation would indicate whether the IQ score of one twin is systematically related to the IQ score of the other, such that if one twin is bright, the other is bright, and if one is not so bright, the other is not so bright. The larger the correlation for a group of twins, the closer the resemblance between members of twin pairs.

To better appreciate what can be learned from behavioral genetics studies, consider what Robert Plomin and his colleagues (1988) found when they assessed aspects of personality among twins in Sweden whose ages averaged 59. One of their measures assessed an aspect of emotionality—the tendency to be angry or quick tempered. The scale was given to many pairs of identical twins and fraternal twins—some pairs raised together, others separated near birth and raised apart. Correlations reflecting the

Twins are concordant if they both display a trait of interest such as smoking.

Anna Peisl/Corbis

degree of similarity between twins are presented in ● **Table 3.4**. From such data, behavioral geneticists—and you too—can estimate the contributions of three factors to individual differences in angry emotionality: genes, shared environmental influences, and nonshared environmental influences.

1. *Genes.* In the example in Table 3.4, genetic influences are clearly evident, for identical twins are consistently more similar in angry emotionality than fraternal twins are. (Keep in mind that these correlations tell us how similar twin pairs are—not how high or low they score in angry emotionality.) The greater-than-zero correlation of 0.33 for identical twins reared apart also testifies to the role of genetic makeup. These data suggest that angry emotionality is heritable; specifically, Plomin et al. (1988) estimated that about a third of the variation in emotionality in the sample they studied can be linked to variations in genetic endowment.

2. *Shared environmental influences.* Individuals growing up in the same environment experience **shared environmental**

influences, common experiences that work to make them similar—for example, a common parenting style or exposure to the same toys, peers, schools, and neighborhood. In Table 3.4, notice that both identical and fraternal twins are slightly more similar in angry emotionality if they are raised together than if they are raised apart. These correlations tell us that shared environmental influences are evident but very weak: Twins are almost as similar when they grew up in different homes as when they grew up in the same home.

3. *Nonshared environmental influences.* Experiences unique to the individual—those that are not shared by other members of the family and that work to make individuals different from each other—are referred to as **nonshared environmental influences**. Whether they involve being treated differently by parents, having different friends or teachers, undergoing different life crises, or even being affected differently by the same life events, nonshared environmental influences make members of the same family different (Rowe, 1994). Where is evidence of this in Table 3.4? Notice that identical twins raised together are not identical in angry emotionality, even though they share 100% of their genes *and* the same family environment. The fact that the correlation of 0.37 for identical twins raised together is much lower than a perfect correlation of 1.00 tells us that nonshared environmental influences are at work—making identical twins raised together different from each other.

Anyone who has a brother or sister can attest that different children in the same family are not always treated identically by their parents. Researchers have indeed discovered that differences between identical twins in their prenatal and postnatal experiences are linked to differences in such characteristics as their levels of anxiety, aggression, and academic achievement (Asbury, Dunn, & Plomin, 2006; Vitaro et al., 2011). This is important: Failing to find strong shared environmental influences on a trait does *not* mean that family influences on development are unimportant. There are often strong nonshared environmental influences, both within and outside the home, working to make children in the same family different rather than similar.

Molecular Genetics

Behavioral genetics studies do not tell us which genes are responsible when they find that a trait is heritable. The Human Genome Project, by providing a map of the human genome, has opened the door to exciting new approaches to studying genetic and environmental influence. **Molecular genetics** is the analysis of particular genes and their effects. It involves identification of specific variants of genes that influence particular traits and comparisons of animals or humans who have these genes with those who do not. Thus, it can help determine which specific genes contribute to making a trait heritable in behavioral genetics studies and allow researchers to study the effects of those genes in combination with the effects of specific environmental influences.

● **Table 3.4** Correlations from a Twin Study of the Heritability of Angry Emotionality

	Raised Together	Raised Apart
Identical twin pairs	0.37	0.33
Fraternal twin pairs	0.17	0.09

Pointing to specific correlations in this table, can you find evidence that genes, shared environment, and nonshared environment all contribute to individual differences in angry emotionality?

Source: From Plomin, R. et al. (1988). EAS temperaments during the last half of the life span: Twins reared apart and twins reared together. *Psychology and Aging, 3.*

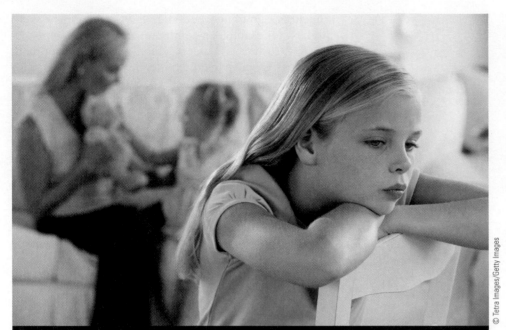

If you have brothers and sisters, do you think your parents treated you and your siblings differently? If so, what might have been the effects of these nonshared environmental influences on your development?

Schiepers et al., 2012). Moreover, having the *APOE4* gene *and* experiencing an environmental risk factor such as a head injury increases the odds of Alzheimer's disease still further—something college football and soccer players and boxers might want to note (Williams, 2003). Such research can help make possible early identification and help for people likely to develop Alzheimer's disease and other conditions that are genetically influenced.

Despite its limitations, behavioral genetics research involving experimental breeding studies of animals and twin, adoption, and family studies of humans has taught us a great deal about the contributions of genes (heritability), shared environment, and nonshared environment to similarities and differences among humans. Molecular genetics research is now leading to important discoveries about which specific genes, interacting with which environmental factors, are responsible.

If researchers are not sure which genes contribute to a trait, they can analyze research participants' entire genomes to identify which genes distinguish individuals who do or do not have the trait (Butcher et al., 2008; Plomin & Davis, 2009). Molecular genetics can therefore help identify the multiple genes that contribute to polygenic traits—the genes behind evidence from twin and adoption studies that traits are heritable (Plomin et al., 2008; Rende & Waldman, 2006). The goal is to be able to say, for instance, "This gene accounts for 20% of the variation, and these two other genes each account for 10% of the variation" in a phenotype or trait of interest. So far, molecular genetics studies have failed to identify genes that account for large percentages of the variation in traits like intelligence. Rather, these analyses suggest that many genes contribute to each polygenic trait or disorder and that each gene's contribution is very small (Chabris et al., 2012; Davis et al., 2010).

If a specific gene's location and role are already known, researchers may test people's DNA for the presence of the gene and determine how people who have a particular variant of a gene differ from those who have other variants of it. Consider Alzheimer's disease, the most common cause of dementia in later life (see Chapter 16). Twin studies indicate that it is heritable (Gatz et al., 2006), but what genes are behind it? One variant of a gene called *Apolipoprotein E (APOE4)* has been linked to a higher-than-average risk of Alzheimer's. Although *APOE4* is only one contributor to Alzheimer's disease and many Alzheimer's patients do not have the gene, researchers have been busily studying differences between individuals with the gene and individuals without it. For example, they find that elderly adults with the *APOE4* gene show greater deterioration in memory and reasoning over the years than do individuals without it, even though they do not have diagnosable Alzheimer's disease—at least not yet (Hofer et al., 2002;

▶ Checking Mastery

1. What does the following (hypothetical) table of correlations tell you about the contributions of genes, shared environment, and nonshared environment to frequency of use of marijuana?

	Raised together	Raised apart
Identical twins	+0.70	+0.40
Fraternal twins	+0.40	+0.10

2. What are two problems in adoption studies of genetic influence?

3. If twin studies show that genes strongly influence a psychological disorder, what good would it do to conduct molecular genetics studies of the disorder?

▶ Making Connections

1. Design both a twin study and an adoption study to examine the contributions of genes and environment to creativity. Explain what patterns of results would provide evidence of genetic or environmental influence.

2. Drawing on information about your family and friends, illustrate how genes, shared environmental influences, and nonshared environmental influences could each help explain why some teenagers are bigger risk takers behind the wheel of a car than others. Then design a study to find out which of these factors are most important.

LEARNING OBJECTIVES:

* Summarize the main themes in behavioral genetics research on intelligence, personality, and psychological disorder about the roles of genes, shared environment, and nonshared environment.

* Compare the heritabilities of physical traits, intelligence, personality, psychological disorder, and attitudes and interests.

Findings from behavioral genetics studies have challenged and changed understandings of human development, as you will see throughout this book. We give a few examples here to illustrate major themes in this research, drawing from studies of intellectual abilities, temperament and personality, and psychological disorders (see Kim, 2009; Plomin et al., 2008). Expect some surprises.

Intellectual Abilities

How do genes and environment contribute to individual differences in intellectual functioning, and how do their relative contributions change over the life span? Consider the average correlations between the IQ scores of different pairs of relatives presented in ● **Table 3.5**. These averages are primarily from a review by Thomas Bouchard Jr. and Matthew McGue (1981) of studies involving 526 correlations based on 113,942 pairs of children, adolescents, and adults. Clearly, correlations are higher when pairs of people are closely related genetically than when they are not and are highest when they are identical twins. Overall, the heritability of IQ scores is about 0.50, meaning that genetic differences account for about 50% of the variation in IQ scores and environmental differences account for the other half of the variation in the samples studied (Plomin, 1990; and see Segal & Johnson, 2009).

● **Table 3.5** Average Correlations between the IQ Scores of Pairs of Individuals

Family Pairs	Raised Together	Raised Apart
Identical twins	0.86	0.72
Fraternal twins	0.60	0.52
Biological siblings	0.47	0.24
Biological parent and child	0.42	0.22
Half siblings	0.31	—
Adopted siblings	0.34	—
Adoptive parent and adopted child	0.19	—
Unrelated siblings (same age, same home)	0.26	—

SOURCE: All but two of these averages were calculated by Bouchard and McGue (1981) from studies of both children and adults. The correlation for fraternal twins reared apart is based on data reported by Pedersen et al. (1985); that for unrelated children in the same home is based on data reported by Segal (2000).

Can you detect the workings of environment in the table? Notice that (1) pairs of family members reared together are somewhat more similar in IQ than pairs reared apart; (2) fraternal twins, who should have especially similar family experiences because they grow up at the same time, tend to be more alike than siblings born at different times; and (3) the IQs of adopted individuals are related to those of their adoptive parents (that is, the correlation is greater than 0). All these findings suggest that *shared* environmental influences tend to make individuals more alike if they live together than if they lived separately. Notice, however, that genetically identical twins reared together are not perfectly similar. This is evidence that their unique or *nonshared* experiences have made them different.

Do the contributions of genes and environment to differences in intellectual ability change over the life span? You might guess that genetic influences would decrease as children accumulate learning experiences, but you would be wrong. Genetic endowment appears to *gain* rather than lose importance from infancy to adulthood as a source of individual differences in intellectual performance (McCartney, Harris, & Bernieri, 1990; Plomin & Spinath, 2004). In a longitudinal study of identical and fraternal twins conducted by Ronald Wilson (1978, 1983), for example, identical twins scored no more similarly than fraternal twins did on a measure of infant mental development. Both types of twins scored similarly. Identical twins then stayed highly similar throughout childhood and into adolescence, the correlation between their IQ scores averaging about 0.85. Meanwhile, fraternal twins became *less* similar over the years; the correlation between their IQ scores dropped from around 0.80 to only 0.54 by adolescence. Because the difference between the correlations for identical and fraternal twins increased with age from infancy to adolescence, so did the heritability of IQ scores. Overall, genes explain only about 20% of the variation in IQ in infancy but about 50% in adolescence and adulthood (Davis, Haworth, & Plomin, 2009).

Whereas the heritability of intelligence test performance increases with age, shared environmental influences tends to become less significant with age, explaining about 30% of the variation in IQ in childhood but less in adulthood (Davis et al., 2009; Kaplan, 2012; Kirkpatrick, McGue, & Iacono, 2009; Plomin & Spinath, 2004). Siblings are probably exposed to similar (shared) learning experiences when they are young and spend a good deal of time with their parents. As they age, they probably seek and have different (nonshared) life experiences. Partly because of their different genetic makeups, they may elicit different reactions from their parents, join different peer groups, encounter different teachers, develop different hobbies, go to

Low SES   High SES

■ Genes   □ Shared environment   ■ Nonshared environment

■ **Figure 3.5** The proportions of variance in child IQ scores explained by genes, shared environment, and nonshared environment differ for children from low versus high socioeconomic status (SES) environments.

Source: From Turkheimer, E., Haley, M., D'Onofrio, B., & Gottesman, I. I. (2003). Socioeconomic status modifies heritability of IQ in young children, Psychological Science, 14(6), 623–628. Reprinted by permission of Sage Publications.

different colleges or universities and vocations, and so on. Even in old age, genetic influences on individual differences in intellectual functioning are still evident (Finkel & Reynolds, 2010). However, heritability may decrease some in very old age as diseases and other nonshared environmental influences make even identical twins more dissimilar than they were earlier in life (McGue & Johnson, 2008; Vogler, 2006).

Now a warning: Heritability estimates can differ quite dramatically depending on the environmental background of the individuals studied. Eric Turkheimer and his colleagues (2003) studied the heritability of IQ among children from very low-income families and children from affluent homes. As shown in ■ **Figure 3.5**, among children from wealthy (high SES) families, genes accounted for 72% of the variation in IQ, whereas shared environment was not very important—as in most previous studies. By contrast, genes explained only about 10% of the variation in IQ among children from poor (low SES) families, whereas shared environmental influences accounted for almost 60% of the variation (see also Harden, Turkheimer, & Loehlin, 2007; Tucker-Drob et al., 2011).

These findings hint that a deprived and unstimulating environment drags many poor children down, regardless of whether their genetic potential is high or low, but that some families living in poverty are able to offer a home environment that helps their children thrive despite their economic disadvantage. In addition, Elliot Tucker-Drob (2012) found that the large effect of shared family environment on IQ differences among twins from low-income homes decreases among children who attend preschool. Possibly the intellectual stimulation poor children receive in preschool helps many overcome the limiting effects of their home environments. In more affluent environments, children

have plenty of opportunities to build niches that allow them to develop whatever genetically based potentials and interests they have, intellectual or otherwise (Tucker-Drob et al., 2011). In any case, the fact that the heritability of IQ is higher for wealthy children than for poor ones illustrates that the heritability of a trait is not one number. It is a range of numbers that can be affected by the age, socioeconomic status, and other characteristics of the sample studied (Rutter, Moffitt, & Caspi, 2006).

Does evidence of the heritability of IQ scores imply that we cannot improve children's intellectual development by enriching their environment? Not at all. True, the IQs of adopted children are, by adolescence, correlated more strongly with the IQs of their biological parents than with the IQs of their adoptive parents. However, the *level* of intellectual performance that adopted children reach can increase dramatically (by 20 points on an IQ test) if they are adopted into more intellectually stimulating homes than those provided by their biological parents (Scarr & Weinberg, 1978, 1983; van IJzendoorn & Juffer, 2005). It is critical for parents, teachers, and others concerned with optimizing development to understand that they can make a difference—that genetically influenced qualities can very often be altered.

Temperament and Personality

As parents know well, different babies have different personalities. In trying to describe infant personality, researchers have focused on aspects of **temperament**—tendencies to respond in predictable ways, such as sociability and emotional reactivity, that serve as the building blocks of later personality (see Chapter 11). Genes contribute to individual differences in both early temperament and later personality (Gagne, Vendlinski, & Goldsmith, 2009; Krueger & Johnson, 2008).

Arnold Buss and Robert Plomin (1984) reported average correlations of around 0.50 to 0.60 between the temperament scores of identical twins. The corresponding correlations for fraternal

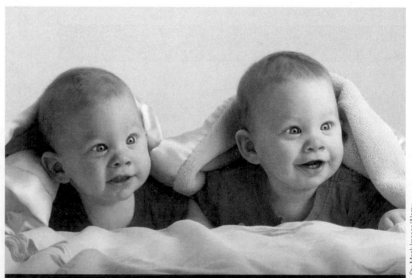

The temperament of infants is genetically influenced. These identical twins seem like easy babies, eager to socialize.

twins were not much greater than zero. Think about that: A zero correlation is what you would expect if fraternal twins were strangers living in different homes rather than siblings who, on average, share half their genes, the same home, and often the same bedroom! It does not seem to matter whether researchers look at fraternal twin pairs, ordinary siblings, or unrelated children adopted into the same family, *living in the same home generally does not make children more similar in personality* (Dunn & Plomin, 1990). This does not mean that the family is unimportant; it means that family influences do more to make children different from each other than to make them alike—that nonshared environment is more influential than shared environment.

Similar conclusions have been reached about the contributions of genes and environment to adult personality (Krueger, Johnson, & Kling, 2006; Loehlin et al., 1998; see also Chapter 11). By one estimate (Loehlin, 1985), about 40% of the variation among adults in personality is attributable to genetic differences (Loehlin, 1985). Only 5% of the variation reflects the effects of shared family environment. The remaining 55% of the variability in adult personalities is associated with nonshared environmental influences that make siblings different from each other.

Shared environmental influences can be important at times. For example, parents appear to influence their children to adopt attitudes and interests similar to their own, at least while the children are living at home (Eaves et al., 1997; Plomin et al., 2008). Shared environment also helps make adolescent siblings similar in the extent to which they engage in delinquent behavior and substance use, partly because siblings influence one another (Hopfer, Crowley, & Hewitt, 2003; Rowe, 1994). Shared environmental influences also show up sometimes in studies of child and adolescent disorders. Factors such as poor parent–child relationships and parent–child conflict sometimes cause multiple children in the same home to develop psychological problems (Burt, 2009).

Yet behavioral geneticists have discovered repeatedly that for many aspects of temperament and personality, unique, nonshared environmental influences rather than shared ones, along with genes, seem to be most significant (Plomin et al., 2008; Reiss et al., 2000). There is little evidence that parents mold all their children's personalities in similar directions. Increasingly, it seems more useful to ask how nonshared experiences inside and outside the home steer brothers and sisters along *different* developmental paths: Nonshared environmental influences are idiosyncratic and hard to pin down, but progress is being made (Krueger & Johnson, 2008).

Psychological Disorders

As you will see in this book, both genes and environment contribute to psychological disorders across the life span—to alcohol and drug abuse, autism, depression, attention deficit hyperactivity disorder, eating disorders, aggressive and criminal behavior, Alzheimer's disease, and every other psychological disorder that has been studied (Plomin et al., 2008; Rende & Waldman, 2006; Rutter, 2006; and see Chapter 16). Usually it's a matter of multiple genes, along with multiple environmental factors, each making a small contribution to the development of a disorder.

Consider just one example. **Schizophrenia** is a serious mental illness that involves disturbances in logical thinking, emotional expression, and social behavior. It typically emerges in late adolescence or early adulthood. Genes contribute substantially to this disorder (Gottesman & Hanson, 2005). The average concordance rate for schizophrenia in identical twin pairs is 48%; that is, if one twin has the disorder, in 48% of the cases the other has it too (Gottesman, 1991; Owen & O'Donovan, 2003). By comparison, the concordance rate for fraternal twins is only 17%. In addition, children who have at least one biological parent who is schizophrenic have an increased risk of schizophrenia—*even if they are adopted away early in life* (Heston, 1970). Thus, the increased risk these children face has more to do with their genes than with being brought up by a schizophrenic adult.

It is easy to conclude, mistakenly, that any child of a person with schizophrenia is doomed to become schizophrenic. But here are the facts: Whereas about 1% of people in the general population develop schizophrenia, about 10% of children who have a schizophrenic parent become schizophrenic (Gottesman, 1991; Plomin et al., 2008). For either the child of two parents with schizophrenia or an identical twin whose twin develops the disorder, the odds of developing schizophrenia rise to about one in two.

Clearly, then, environmental factors also contribute significantly to this mental illness. People do not inherit psychological disorders; they inherit *predispositions* to develop disorders. Genes and environment then interact so that a person who has inherited a genetic susceptibility to schizophrenia will likely not develop the disorder unless damaging environmental influences also come into play (King, St. Hilaire, & Heidkamp, 2010). For example, genetically at-risk children are more likely to develop schizophrenia if their mothers come down with an infectious disease like the flu during pregnancy (Patterson, 2007), they are deprived of oxygen during delivery (Cannon et al., 2003), or they are adopted into a dysfunctional adoptive home rather than a supportive one after birth (Tienari et al., 2004).

In short, children may inherit predispositions to develop problems and disorders; their experiences will interact with their genetic makeup to determine how well adjusted they turn out to be. Such research also shows that it is overly simple and often wrong to assume that any behavioral problem a child displays must be the result of bad parenting. Positive prenatal and postnatal experiences protect some at-risk children from some disorders for which they have a predisposition.

The Heritability of Different Traits

By now you may be wondering if there are any human characteristics that are not heritable. Although genes contribute to variation in virtually all human traits that have been studied, some traits are more heritable than others (Bouchard, 2004; Segal, 2012). ■ **Figure 3.6** presents, by way of summary, correlations obtained in the Minnesota Study of Twins Reared Apart between the traits of identical twins raised apart and reunited as adults.

Observable physical characteristics, from eye color to height, are strongly associated with individual genetic endowment. Even weight is heritable; adopted children resemble their biological parents but not their adoptive parents in weight, even

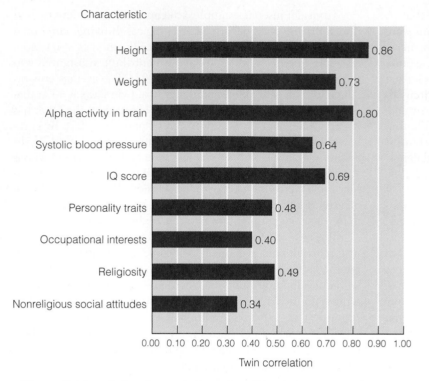

Characteristic

Height	0.86
Weight	0.73
Alpha activity in brain	0.80
Systolic blood pressure	0.64
IQ score	0.69
Personality traits	0.48
Occupational interests	0.40
Religiosity	0.49
Nonreligious social attitudes	0.34

0.00 0.10 0.20 0.30 0.40 0.50 0.60 0.70 0.80 0.90 1.00

Twin correlation

■ **Figure 3.6** Correlations between the traits of identical twins raised apart in the Minnesota Twin Study.

Source: From Bouchard, T. J., Jr., Lykken, D. T., McGue, M., Segal, N. L., & Tellegen, A. Sources of psychological differences: The Minnesota Study of Twins Reared Apart, Science, 250, 223–228. Copyright © 1990, The American Association for the Advancement of Science. Reprinted with permission.

though their adoptive parents feed them (Grilo & Pogue-Geile, 1991). Certain aspects of physiology, such as measured brain activity and reactions to alcohol, are highly heritable, too (Lykken, Tellegen, & Iacono, 1982; Neale & Martin, 1989), as is level of physical activity (Eriksson, Rasmussen, & Tynelius, 2006). In addition, genetic differences among older adults contribute to differences in their functioning and changes in markers of aging such as decreased lung capacity (Finkel et al., 2003; Finkel & Reynolds, 2010; Vogler, 2006). Genes also contribute to susceptibilities to many chronic diseases associated with aging, and genetic differences account for about one-third of the variation in longevity (Arking, 2006).

If physical and physiological characteristics are strongly heritable, general intelligence is moderately heritable: 50% or more of the variation among people is attributable to genes. Somewhat less influenced by genes are temperament and personality, for which about 40% of the variation can be traced to genes, and susceptibility to many psychological disorders, for which heritability varies from condition to condition. Finally, genetic endowment even contributes modestly to differences in attitudes and interests—for example, political conservatism or liberalism and vocational interests (Alford, Funk, & Hibbing, 2005; Olson et al., 2001; Segal, 2012). It has proven difficult to find a human characteristic that is *not* to some degree heritable. For most psychological traits, genes often account for somewhere up to half the variation in a group, and environmental factors (especially nonshared rather than shared ones) account for the other half or more (Plomin et al., 2008).

Checking Mastery

1. Professor Gene Ohm is studying genetic and environmental influences on individual differences in extraversion/introversion. Based on previous behavioral genetics studies, what should he expect?

2. Alan's biological parents both had schizophrenia, so he was placed in an adoptive home when he was only 2 months old. He grew up with his adoptive parents (neither of whom had psychological disorders) in a stable, loving family. What would you tell Alan, now age 18, about his chances of developing schizophrenia if you were a genetic counselor?

Making Connections

1. There's surely no single gene that directly makes people politically liberal or politically conservative, yet political liberalism/conservatism is heritable (Alford, Funk, & Hibbing, 2005). Develop an explanation of how genes could influence it. While you're at it, how might shared environment and nonshared environment influence it?

2. Sherrita believes that if intelligence is heritable, genes explain everything and nothing can be done to boost the intelligence of children who have low levels of it. Drawing on key evidence, convince Sherrita that she is wrong.

3.5 Genes and Environment Conspiring

LEARNING OBJECTIVES:

• Distinguish between a gene–environment interaction and a gene–environment correlation and between passive, evocative, and active types of gene–environment correlations.

• Explain what epigenetic effects are and what they say about the relationship between genes and environment.

• Explain why genetic research and behavioral genetic research are controversial.

Genes do not orchestrate our growth before birth and then leave us alone. Instead, they are "turning on" and "turning off" in patterned ways throughout the life span, helping shape our characteristics and behavior. No less important are ever-changing environmental influences, from conception to death. But genes and environment do not operate independently; they are interrelated in interesting and important ways.

As you have seen throughout this chapter, behavioral geneticists try to establish how much of the variation in human traits such as intelligence can be attributed to individual differences in genetic makeup and how much can be attributed to individual differences in experience. Useful as that research is, it does not take us far in understanding the complex interplay between genes and environment over the life span (Meaney, 2010; Turkheimer, 2000). As Ann Anastasi (1958) asserted many years ago, instead of asking *how much* is because of genes and how much is because of environment, researchers should be asking *how* heredity and environment work together to make us what we are. With that in mind, let's examine the workings of three tremendously important developmental mechanisms: gene–environment interactions, gene–environment correlations, and epigenetic effects on gene expression (Brendgen et al., 2012; Plomin et al., 2008).

Gene–Environment Interactions

Genes provide us with potentials that are or are not realized depending on our experiences. You have encountered some examples already but consider another one. Using molecular genetics techniques, Avshalom Caspi and his colleagues (2003) sought to understand why stressful life experiences cause some people but not others to become depressed. They performed DNA analysis on a large sample of New Zealanders to determine which variants of a gene (called *5-HTTLPR*) each person had. They knew that this gene affects stress reactivity by affecting levels of the neurotransmitter serotonin in the brain, and they knew that a low serotonin level is linked to depression. Caspi and colleagues also administered surveys to measure the stressful events each person had experienced between ages 21 and 26, and whether at age 26 each person had experienced a diagnosable episode of depression in the past year.

In ■ **Figure 3.7**, you can see the results, which illustrate wonderfully the concept of **gene–environment interaction**: The effects of our genes depend on what kind of environment we experience, and how we respond to the environment depends on what genes we have. In Figure 3.7, you see that individuals with two of the high-risk variants of the *5-HTTLPR* gene are more vulnerable to depression than people with two of the protective variants of the gene *only* if they experience multiple stressful events. By comparison, even multiple stressful events will not easily cause people with the protective variants of the gene to become depressed. Thus, the genes people have make a difference only when their environment is stressful, and a stressful environment has an effect only on individuals with a genotype that predisposes them to depression. Genes and environment interact.

Both human and animal studies indicate that the *5-HTTLPR* gene affects stress reactivity and can put individuals at risk

■ **Figure 3.7** The odds of a depressive episode at age 26 are highest for individuals who: (1) inherit two 5-HTTLPR gene variants known to increase the risk of depression rather than a pair known to protect against depression, and (2) experience four or more stressful life events between ages 21 and 26. This is an example of gene–environment interaction: the effects of genetic makeup on depression depend on how stressful a person's environment is, and the effects of stressful life events depend on the person's genotype.

Source: From Caspi et al., Influences of Life Stress on Depression, Science, July 18, 2003, Fig. 1B. Copyright © 2003. Reprinted by permission of AAAS.

for—or protect them from—a number of psychological disorders (Caspi et al., 2011; Karg et al., 2011). To cite but one example, bullying is more likely to result in emotional problems in children with the risky variants of *5-HTTLPR* than in children with the protective variants (Sugden et al., 2010). More generally, we now know that it often takes a combination of high-risk genes and a high-risk environment or stressful experiences to trigger psychological problems (Dick et al., 2011; Dodge & Rutter, 2011; Rutter, 2006). Meanwhile, other gene variants seem to protect children who experience traumatic events from developing disorders, helping to explain why some children are resilient despite terrible childhood experiences (Polanczyk et al., 2009).

From an applied standpoint, such research suggests that psychological problems might be prevented more effectively if we could identify and help those individuals whose genes predispose them to problems. For example, Gene Brody and his colleagues (2009) showed that 11-year-olds with the high-risk *5-HTTLPR* genes studied by Caspi and his colleagues could be spared from high rates of problem behaviors such as substance use and early sexual intercourse if their families participated in a prevention program that stressed good parenting skills and parent–child communication. Control group youth who had the high-risk genes but did not receive the prevention program engaged in problem behaviors at twice the rate of peers with the high-risk genes who participated in the prevention program and peers who did not have high-risk genes. More and more evidence of gene–environment interactions involving the *5-HTTLPR* gene and number of other important genes is emerging as researchers use molecular genetics to study interactions between specific genes and specific experiences (Dodge & Rutter, 2011; Lenroot & Giedd, 2011).

Gene–Environment Correlations

Not only do genes and environment interact, but each person's genetic makeup influences the kinds of experiences she seeks and has. Sandra Scarr and Kathleen McCartney (1983), drawing on the theorizing of Robert Plomin, John DeFries, and John Loehlin (1977), have proposed three kinds of **gene–environment correlations**, or ways in which a person's genes and his environment or experiences are systematically interrelated: passive, evocative, and active. The concept of gene–environment *interactions* tells us that people with different genes react differently to the experiences they have. By contrast, the concept of gene–environment *correlations* says that people with different genes have different experiences (Loehlin, 1992). As an illustration, imagine children with a genetic potential to be highly sociable and other children whose genes are likely to make them shy.

Passive Gene–Environment Correlations

The kind of home environment that parents provide for their children is influenced partly by the parents' genotypes. **Passive gene–environment correlations** work like this: Because parents provide children with both their genes and a home environment compatible with those genes, the home environments to which children are exposed are correlated with (and are typically likely to reinforce) their genotypes.

For instance, sociable parents not only transmit their "sociable" genes to their children but also, because they have "sociable" genes themselves, create a highly social home environment—inviting their friends over frequently, taking their children to social events, and so on. The combination of genes for sociability and a social environment may make their children more sociable than they would otherwise be. By contrast, the child with shy parents may receive genes for shyness *and* a correlated environment without much social stimulation.

Evocative Gene–Environment Correlations

In **evocative gene–environment correlations**, a child's genotype also *evokes* certain kinds of reactions from other people. The smiley, sociable baby is likely to get more smiles, hugs, and social stimulation—and more opportunities to build social skills—than the wary, shy baby who makes you fear he will howl if you try anything. Similarly, the sociable child may be chosen more often as a playmate by other children, the sociable adolescent may be invited to more parties, and the sociable adult may be given more job assignments involving public relations. In short, genetic makeup may affect the reactions of other people to an individual and, hence, the kind of environment the individual will experience through life. There is a message here for parents: It has been said that having a second child converts many parents from environmentalists who think they control their child's behavior and development to geneticists who appreciate that different children evoke different reactions from them (Goldman, 2012).

Active Gene–Environment Correlations

Finally, through **active gene–environment correlations**, children's genotypes influence the kinds of environments they *seek*. The individual with a genetic predisposition to be extraverted is likely to go to every party in sight, invite friends over, join organizations, have a multitude of Facebook friends, and otherwise build a "niche" that is highly socially stimulating and that strengthens social skills. The child with genes for shyness may actively avoid large group activities and instead develop solitary interests.

Passive, evocative, and active genotype–environment correlations can all operate throughout the life span (Rutter et al., 2006). However, Scarr and McCartney suggest that the balance of the three types of genotype–environment correlations shifts during development. Because infants are at home a good deal and are dependent on their caregivers, their environment is largely influenced by their parents through passive influences. Evocative influences operate throughout life; our characteristic, genetically influenced traits consistently evoke certain reactions from other people. Finally, as humans develop, they become increasingly able to build their own niches, so active gene–environment correlations become increasingly important.

Sorting Out Genetic Influences on the Environment

How much evidence supports Scarr and McCartney's claim that people's genes are correlated with, and possibly influence, their experiences in life? A good deal. Behavioral geneticists are discovering that measures of environment—especially the family environments of children—are themselves heritable (Butcher & Plomin, 2008)! What this means is that identical twins are more similar than fraternal twins, and biological siblings are more similar than adoptive siblings, in the environments they experience and in their perceptions of their environments. For example, genes are related to the following environmental factors:

- Both objective and perceived aspects of parenting, such as warmth and the quality of the parent–child relationship (Plomin & Bergeman, 1991; Reiss, 2005)
- Time spent watching television (Plomin et al., 1990)
- Number of stressful life events experienced, especially events like divorcing one's spouse that the person could have helped to cause, as opposed to uncontrollable events like death of a parent (Kendler et al., 1993)

If our genetically influenced personality traits affect how others treat us and what experiences we seek and have, these findings make sense. For example, identical twins who are irritable and difficult could help create a conflict-ridden family environment, whereas calm and controlled twins could help create a cohesive family environment (Krueger, Markon, & Bouchard, 2003).

Such findings challenge some of our most fundamental assumptions about human development. After all, they say that what we regard as purely environmental influences on development partly reflect the workings of heredity (Reiss et al., 2000; Rowe, 1994). As leading behavioral geneticist Robert Plomin

(1990) suggests, we must constantly question our assumptions about nature and nurture. Suppose, he says, we find that parents who read to their children have brighter children than parents who do not read to their children. In the not-so-distant past, most developmentalists would have interpreted this finding rather uncritically as evidence that parents make important contributions to their children's intellectual development by reading to them. Without denying the importance of parents, suppose we offer this alternative interpretation: Parents and children whose genes predispose them to be highly intelligent are more likely to seek opportunities to read than parents and children who are less intellectually inclined. If this is the case, can we be so sure that reading to children *causes* them to be brighter? Would we be able to show that reading to children is beneficial even when the parents and children involved are genetically unrelated?

Some of the most convincing evidence of the importance of gene–environment correlations comes from an ambitious family study by David Reiss, Jenae Neiderhiser, E. Mavis Hetherington, and Robert Plomin, summarized in their book *The Relationship Code* (2000). These researchers studied 720 pairs of same-sex adolescents who differed in their degree of biological relationship, from identical twins to biological siblings to unrelated stepsiblings. They measured environmental variables such as quality of parent–child interaction and adolescent adjustment variables such as self-esteem, sociability, depression, and antisocial behavior.

Repeatedly, genes shared by parents and adolescents partly or even largely accounted for relationships between children's experiences in the family and their developmental outcomes—for example, between negative parenting and antisocial behavior on the part of adolescents. In 44 of 52 instances in which significant relationships between measures of the family environment and adolescent adjustment were detected, genes influenced both family environment and adolescent adjustment and accounted for most of the relationship between the two (Reiss & Neiderhiser, 2000). Judging from most research of this sort, there are probably *reciprocal influences* at work in parent–child relationships. For example, harsh, negative parenting contributes to the development of antisocial behavior in children, but children genetically predisposed to be antisocial also bring out the worst in their parents (Larsson et al., 2008; O'Connor et al., 1998).

In short, simple correlational studies showing a relationship between some aspect of experience and some aspect of development cannot establish that experience really affects development. More and more, researchers are conducting "genetically informed" studies like the Reiss et al. (2000) study just described, to determine whether there are genetic explanations for environmental effects and establish more firmly whether environment alone matters (Johnson, Turkheimer, Gottesman, & Bouchard, 2009).

One approach they use is to establish that the effects of environment are just as evident among adoptive children, with genetic resemblance between parent and child out of the picture, as among biological children. Thus Amato and Cheadle (2008) showed that relationships between marital conflict and child behavior problems were equally strong in biological and adoptive families, suggesting a truly environmental effect.

Another genetically informed research tactic is to study identical twins to see if differences in their development are systematically related to differences in their experiences. Since they have identical genes and grow up in the same prenatal and postnatal environment, any differences in their behavior or development can be credited to differences in their experiences—to nonshared environmental influences. So, for example, Isabelle Ouellet-Morin and her colleagues (2011) studied 30 pairs of 12-year-old identical twin boys in which one twin had been bullied and the other had not. They found reduced levels of the stress hormone cortisol in reaction to stressful experiences in the twins who had been bullied, something also found in studies of maltreated children and of adults with post-traumatic stress disorder. The bullied twin was also more likely to develop emotional problems than the non-bullied twin (Sugden et al., 2010). In another study, identical twins who received more negative discipline from their parents at age 7 than their co-twins did turned out to have more conduct problems at age 12 (Viding et al., 2009).

These kinds of genetically informed studies offer convincing evidence that environment truly matters, even when

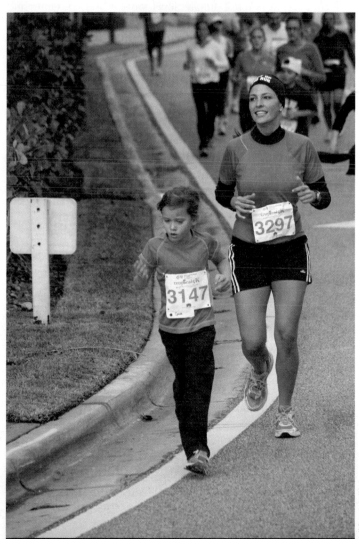

Jeff Greenberg/Alamy

If the daughter of a runner turns out to be a good runner, is it because of genetic endowment or experience? We cannot say because genes and environment are correlated. How might passive, evocative, and active gene–environment correlation influence this child's development as an athlete?

gene–environment correlations suggesting genetic influences on environment are controlled. And we end up appreciating that genes and environment conspire to shape development. Genes influence how parents, peers, and others treat children. These environmental influences then contribute to the individual's development, often reinforcing genetically based predispositions.

Epigenetic Effects on Gene Expression

Having seen that genes can influence one's environment through gene–environment correlations, let's look at how environment can influence genes. **Epigenesis** (*epi-* = "over and above" + *genesis* = "birth or origin") is a term for the general process through which nature and nurture co-act to bring forth particular developmental outcomes (see Carey, 2012; Roth, 2012). Think of it as what happens as genotypes are converted into phenotypes, or as one fertilized egg becomes a human being. According to psychobiologists like Gilbert Gottlieb (1992, Gottlieb et al., 2006; Gottlieb & Halpern, 2008), genes do not dictate development. Rather, genes and environment interact with and influence each other from conception on to shape development, to the point that their influences cannot be separated. Through what are now called **epigenetic effects**, environmental factors (diet, stress, alcohol and drugs, environmental toxins, and even early parental care) affect whether or not particular genes in particular cells are expressed (Champagne, 2010; Champagne & Mashoodh, 2009; Meaney, 2010). Through epigenetic effects, experience leaves records, chemical codings on top of certain genes in certain cells, that affect whether those genes are turned on or off. So, on top of our complex genome, we also have an "epigenome" consisting of all kinds of these epigenetic markings. The genes themselves are not altered when epigenetic effects occur; rather, their expression is altered—in ways that can affect health and mental health, cognition, and behavior.

Epigenetic effects are especially important during prenatal development, when both regulatory genes and environmental influences orchestrate early development. However, epigenetic effects can occur throughout the life span. Moreover, epigenetic codings etched on top of genes during a parent's life can sometimes be transmitted through sperm or eggs to offspring (Champagne, 2010). Quite possibly, then, a parent's good or bad habits today can affect his or her children or possibly even grandchildren tomorrow.

So why, despite their identical genes, are identical twins sometimes quite different? Mario Fraga and his colleagues (2005) suspected that the answer might lie partly in epigenetic effects on gene expression. They conducted analyses of the DNA and RNA of 40 pairs of identical twins ranging in age from 3 to 74. They found that older twin pairs were more different from each other than younger twin pairs in the patterns of activation of their genes. For example, close analysis of the RNA of 3-year-old twins showed that the genes of these young children had almost identical patterns of expression. If a gene was turned on in one twin, it was turned on in the other; if it was turned off in one twin, it was turned off in the other. By contrast, the genes of 50-year-old twins were expressed very differently; many genes that were activated in one twin were deactivated in the other. What's more, those adult twins who had spent less of their lives together and had led different lifestyles (as indicated, for example, by their

eating habits, levels of physical activity, and use of tobacco, alcohol, drugs) showed greater differences in their patterns of gene activation than did twins who had led similar lives.

Epigenetic research, which has been exploding in recent years, clearly indicates that environment influences gene expression and, in turn, traits and behavior (Zhang & Meaney, 2010). It is opening up new avenues for understanding why one twin develops a disorder like schizophrenia but the other does not. **Exploration Box 3.1** describes the groundbreaking work on the epigenetic effects of early parenting on development by Michael Meaney, Frances Champagne, and their colleagues (and see Chapter 4 on how epigenetic effects contribute to fetal programming that may affect health and mental health much later in life).

By altering gene expression, Meaney (2010) suggests, epigenetic effects may help organisms and their offspring adapt flexibly to whatever environmental conditions they encounter rather than wait generations for biological evolution to do its work. For example, growing up in poverty appears to result in epigenetic effects that make both the immune system and the stress response system highly reactive to threats (Evans & Kim, 2013; G. E. Miller et al., 2009). This would seem to be an adaptive response in an unsafe, threatening environment. Unfortunately, in the long run it also seems to take a toll on the body and makes individuals born into poverty more susceptible to chronic diseases and mental health problems later in life, even if they later become wealthier (G. E. Miller et al., 2009).

In the end, no one completely understands the remarkable epigenetic process that transforms a single cell with its genetic endowment into millions of diverse cells—blood cells, nerve cells, skin cells, and so on—all organized into a living, behaving human. Nor do we fully understand how genes and environment acting together help bring about certain developments at certain points in the life span. Yet it is becoming clearer that both genes and environment are active players in the developmental process at every step and that having this gene or that gene is less important than which genes are expressed and when.

Controversies Surrounding Genetic Research

Our society is grappling with the complex and troubling public policy and ethical issues that have arisen as geneticists have gained the capacity to identify the carriers and potential victims of diseases and disorders, to give parents information that might prompt them to abort a fetus that is not of the desired health status or intellect, and to experiment with techniques for altering the genetic code through gene therapy and possibly engineer new and improved humans (see McCabe & McCabe, 2008). **Gene therapy** involves substituting normal genes for the genes associated with a disease or disorder or otherwise altering a person's genetic makeup (Lewis, 2012; Turnpenny & Ellard, 2011). Gene therapy to treat such genetic disorders as hemophilia (through infusions of normal genes into the blood), the lung disease cystic fibrosis (using aerosol sprays to deliver normal genes to the lungs), and other diseases have had some success. However, progress in gene therapy has been slow because of a host of problems such as rejection of therapeutic genes by the immune system (McCabe & McCabe, 2008).

Early Experience and Gene Expression

Today there is tremendous excitement about new evidence that experience affects gene expression and, in turn, development. Michael Meaney, Francis Champagne, and their colleagues are in the forefront of research on such epigenetic effects. They have shown through a series of elegant studies how the early experience of rat pups can affect the activity of their genes and, in turn, not only their development but that of their offspring (see Champagne & Mashoodh, 2009; Francis et al., 1999; Kaffman & Meaney, 2007).

Here's how it goes. If the mothers of rat pups are nurturant—if they regularly lick and groom their pups and nurse them with an arched back in the first week of life—the pups grow up able to handle stress well. If rat moms are neglectful and do not provide this tender tactile care, rat pups become timid and easily stressed adults. But why? The differences in pups' reactivity to stress were not due to heredity. Raising the pups of nurturant mothers with neglectful mothers and the pups of neglectful mothers with nurturant mothers demonstrated that it was rearing that mattered, not heredity. Rats turned out to be stress resistant if raised by nurturant mothers and stress reactive if raised by neglectful mothers, regardless of their biological parentage.

But these styles of responding to stress also were not acquired through learning (for example, by watching a stress-reactive mother). Rather, Meaney and his colleagues found that early licking and grooming affect the develop-ment of the stress response system through epigenetic effects—effects of environment on gene expression. In nurtured pups, genes in cells in the hippocampus of the brain that influence the regulation of stress hormones stay turned on, whereas in neglected pups these genes turn off, making the hippocampus less able to tone down stress hormone responses. Early care therefore has a lasting effect on development by altering gene expression.

Too little licking and grooming in infancy also turns off genes that affect sensitivity to female hormones and later maternal behavior. As a result, daughters of neglectful mothers turn into neglectful mothers themselves. Here, then, we see epigenetic (rather than genetic) transmission of parenting styles across generations. The DNA sequence itself is not altered; rather, the early experience of neglected pups results epigenetic codings on certain genes in their brains that interfere with the expression of these genes. These epigenetic tags are replicated when cells divide—and, remarkably, can be passed on to offspring at conception.

Epigenetic effects like this represent no less than a whole new way in which parents influence their children besides genetic inheritance and social learning: *environmental influence on gene expression*. And there's now suggestive evidence that epigenetic effects similar to those observed in rat pups may help explain the transmission from mother to daughter of abu-sive and neglectful parenting among both monkeys (Maestripieri, Lindell, & Higley, 2007) and humans (McGowan et al., 2009). But the cycle of neglect and abuse can be broken: Meaney and his colleagues find that epigenetic effects of neglectful parenting on stress response and parenting style can be reversed if young animals are raised by sensitive, nurturing mothers or if drugs that affect gene expression in critical parts of the brain are administered (McGowan, Meaney, & Szyf, 2008; Zhang & Meaney, 2010).

So the race is on to understand the role of epigenetic effects in explaining how early life experiences affect us (Carey, 2012; Roth, 2012). It appears, for example, that some diseases and disorders arise not because a normal gene is missing but because it is not expressed normally, sometimes as a result of a poor diet, alcohol or drug use, toxins, or stressful experiences (Isles & Wilkinson, 2008). Consider this intriguing example of how epigenetic effects might help explain obesity and diabetes: Feeding a *father* rat (but not the mother rat) a high fat diet and making him overweight changes epigenetic codings in his sperm, which changes his female daughter's physiology so that she becomes more prone to obesity and diabetes—even though both she and her mother ate healthy diets (Ng et al., 2010; and see Chapter 4's discussion of fetal programming). It's not yet clear where epigenetic research will lead but you will certainly hear more about it.

If you think about it, it may also be simpleminded to think that gene therapies will ever prevent or cure most diseases and disorders. Why? Because, as you now understand, most conditions are the product of the interaction of multiple genetic and environmental factors. Researchers not only must deliver the right genes to the body in sufficient number to have the desired effect but also must get them to turn on and off when they should to produce normal functioning and control important environmental influences as well. No "quick fixes" such as the PKU diet are likely for most conditions, especially those that are polygenic in origin. Still, genetic (and most likely, epigenetic) diagnostic and therapy techniques will improve, and we as a society will have to decide how and how not to use them.

Likewise, behavioral genetics research is controversial among developmental scientists. On the one hand, it has provided truly important insights into human development: that genes influence most psychological differences, that the unique experiences of siblings are often more influential than those

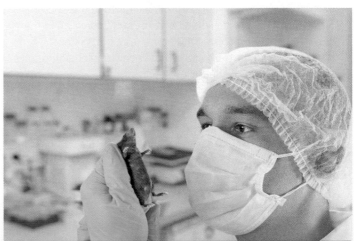

Research with mice and other laboratory animals paves the way for tests of gene therapies with humans.

anyaivanova/Shutterstock.com

they share, that children influence parents just as parents influence children. Behavioral genetics research sometimes provides more convincing evidence of the effects of the environment on development than studies that do not take genes and gene–environment correlations into account (Johnson et al., 2009).

Nonetheless, techniques for calculating heritability may attribute too much importance to genes by giving genes credit for some variation that is likely associated with both genes and environment (Brendgen et al., 2012; Rutter, 2006). Most importantly, some developmentalists question the whole idea of trying to separate the influences of genes and environment on differences between individuals when the two are so intertwined in the individual's development. They insist that behavioral genetics research will never tell us about what we should really want to understand: *epigenesis*, that long and complex process through which the interplay of genes and environment brings about development (Gottlieb et al., 2006; Meaney, 2010). From an epigenetic perspective, the nature–nurture issue is just not an issue, so inseparable are genes and environment.

Partly in response to criticism, behavioral geneticists are continually improving their methods of study and continue to offer new insights into genetic and environmental influences, as you will see throughout this book. If parents and helping professionals are sensitive to children's genetically based predispositions, they will be better able to strengthen each child's adaptive tendencies and weaken or work around the maladaptive ones. Providing children with optimal experiences, of course, depends on knowing which environments stimulate healthy development and which do not. It is fitting, then, that the next chapter takes a closer look at early environmental influences on development.

Checking Mastery

Label each example below as an example of (a) gene–environment interaction, (b) passive gene–environment correlation, (c) evocative gene–environment correlation, (d) active gene–environment correlation, or (e) epigenetic effects.

1. Roger inherited genes for artistic creativity from his parents and grew up watching them sketch and paint.
2. Tamara was abused as a child and this seems to have made her stress response system overly reactive.
3. Kayla inherited genes for mathematical ability and has been taking extra math and science courses in college.
4. Sydney inherited a gene that can cause intellectual disability but only in children who do not receive enough folic acid in their diet.
5. Jorge got genes for anxiety, and his anxious behavior makes his parents overprotective of him.

Making Connections

1. Assume that genes predispose some people to be highly religious and some people to be unreligious and that some environments nurture religiosity and others do not. Explain how a gene–environment interaction and a gene–environment correlation could each help make Peter more religious than Paul.
2. What information in this chapter makes you think you will turn out very much like your parents—and what information suggests that this may not be the case at all?

Chapter Summary

3.1 Evolution and Species Heredity

- As humans, we develop similarly in part because we share a species heredity, the product of evolution.
- According to Darwin's theory of biological evolution, if there is genetic variation in a species—and if some genes aid members of the species in adapting to their environment and reproducing—those genes will become more common in the population over time through natural selection.
- Humans also adapt to changes in their environments through the faster process of cultural evolution.

3.2 Individual Heredity

- Each human has an individual heredity provided at conception, when sperm and ovum, each with 23 chromosomes (thanks to meiosis), unite to form a single-cell zygote with 46 chromosomes. Parent and child share 50% of their genes in common; siblings share 50% on average.
- The chromosomes contain some 20,000–25,000 protein-building genes, along with regulatory DNA; the Human Genome Project and related studies have mapped these genes and revealed similarities and differences between the genes of different human groups and species.

- Environmental factors influence how a genotype (genetic makeup) is translated into a phenotype (actual traits); regulatory DNA and environmental factors influence the important process of gene expression.
- The three main mechanisms of inheritance are single gene-pair inheritance, sex-linked inheritance, and polygenic (multiple gene) inheritance. Some children are also affected by new or inherited changes in gene structure (mutations, copy number variations); others, because of errors in meiosis, have chromosome abnormalities such as Down, Turner, Klinefelter, and fragile X syndromes.
- Couples can obtain information about genetic diseases such as sickle-cell disease, Huntington's disease, and PKU from genetic counselors, and many genetic abnormalities can be detected prenatally through ultrasound, amniocentesis, chorionic villus sampling, maternal blood sampling, and preimplantation genetic diagnosis.

3.3 Studying Genetic and Environmental Influences

- Behavioral geneticists conduct twin, adoption, and other family studies that describe resemblances between pairs of people using concordance rates and correlation coefficients. They then estimate the heritability of traits and the contributions of shared (with siblings) and nonshared (unique) environmental influences.

- Techniques of molecular genetics are used to identify and study particular gene variants and to compare people who do and do not have them.

3.4 Selected Findings

- Performance on measures of intelligence is a heritable trait. From infancy to adulthood, individual differences in mental ability more strongly reflect both individual genetic makeup and non-shared environmental influences, whereas shared environmental influences wane.
- Aspects of temperament and personality are also genetically influenced, and nonshared environmental influences are significant whereas shared environmental influences are typically not.
- Similarly, psychological disorders such as schizophrenia have a genetic basis, but it often takes an interaction of genes and environmental stressors to produce disorder.
- Overall, physical and physiological characteristics are more strongly influenced by genetic endowment than are intellectual abilities and, in turn, temperament, personality traits, and psychological disorders, and finally, attitudes and interests.

3.5 Genes and Environment Conspiring

- Gene–environment interactions mean that environment influences the effects of genes and that genes influence how people react to the environment.
- Passive, evocative, and active gene–environment correlations suggest that people experience and seek out environments that often match and reinforce their genetic predispositions. Measures of environmental influence therefore partly reflect genetic makeup.
- Epigenetic effects, effects of environmental influences on gene expression, further illustrate how intertwined nature and nurture are in development.
- Genetic research is controversial, as illustrated by genetic diagnosis and gene therapy and by criticisms of behavioral genetics among some developmentalists, but genetically informed studies are important if we are to understand influences on development.

Checking Mastery Answers

For answers to Checking Mastery questions, please see Appendix B.

Key Terms

species heredity **62**
natural selection **63**
evolutionary psychology **63**
cultural evolution **64**
conception **64**
zygote **64**
chromosome **64**
meiosis **65**
mitosis **65**
DNA **65**
Human Genome Project **66**
crossing over **66**
identical twins **66**
fraternal twins **67**
X chromosome **67**
Y chromosome **67**
karyotype **67**
genotype **67**
phenotype **67**
gene expression **68**
single gene-pair inheritance **68**
dominant gene **68**
recessive gene **68**

incomplete dominance **69**
codominance **69**
sex-linked characteristic **69**
hemophilia **69**
polygenic trait **69**
mutation **70**
autism **70**
chromosome abnormalities **70**
Down syndrome **70**
mental retardation **70**
Turner syndrome **71**
Klinefelter syndrome **71**
fragile X syndrome **71**
copy number variations **71**
genetic counseling **72**
sickle-cell disease **72**
carrier **72**
Huntington's disease **73**
phenylketonuria (PKU) **73**
hyperactivity **73**
ultrasound **74**
amniocentesis **74**
chorionic villus sampling (CVS) **74**

maternal blood sampling **74**
preimplantation genetic diagnosis **74**
behavioral genetics **75**
heritability **75**
twin study **76**
prenatal environment **76**
adoption study **76**
family study **76**
concordance rate **76**
shared environmental influences **77**
nonshared environmental influences **77**
molecular genetics **77**
temperament **80**
schizophrenia **81**
gene–environment interaction **83**
gene–environment correlation **84**
passive gene–environment correlation **84**
evocative gene–environment correlation **84**
active gene–environment correlation **84**
epigenesis **86**
epigenetic effects **86**
gene therapy **86**

4 Prenatal Development and Birth

At age 26, Serena was not thinking about getting pregnant. She and her boyfriend, Tony, were both getting adjusted to new jobs and working long hours. Serena tried to keep up with her regular exercise routine and struggled through a nasty sinus infection requiring treatment with antibiotics. She wasn't too concerned when she gained a few pounds but began to worry when she missed several menstrual periods. A visit to her doctor revealed that she was nearly 5 months pregnant, probably a result of the antibiotics decreasing the effectiveness of her birth control. Serena's mind raced as she considered all the things she had—or had not—done during recent months that might have influenced her unborn baby. Did she drink too much alcohol? Had she eaten a healthy diet? These thoughts were quickly followed by concerns about what the childbirth experience would be like and how she and Tony would adjust to this rather unexpected change in their lives.

We will answer these questions and more in this chapter on prenatal development, the birth experience, and the first hours and days of life. You will learn why the environment of the womb is so important and how it can set the stage for healthy development across the entire life span. The material in this chapter is a good illustration of how developmentalists seek to optimize development by using research to guide practices before, during, and after pregnancy.

4.1 Prenatal Development

LEARNING OBJECTIVES:

• Summarize the main events and three phases of the prenatal period.

• Explain the major changes in brain development during the prenatal period.

Perhaps at no time in the life span does development occur faster, or is environment more important, than between conception and birth. What maturational milestones normally occur during this period?

Conception

Midway through the menstrual cycle, every 28 days or so, females ovulate: An ovum (egg cell) ripens, leaves the ovary, and begins its journey through the fallopian tube to the uterus.

Usually the egg disintegrates and leaves the body as part of the menstrual flow. However, if the woman has intercourse with a fertile man around the time of ovulation, the 300 million or so sperm cells in his seminal fluid swim, tadpole style, in all directions. Of the approximately 300 sperm that survive the 6-hour journey into the fallopian tubes, one may meet and penetrate the ovum on its descent from the ovary (Sadler, 2012; see also ■ Figure 4.1). Once this one sperm penetrates the egg cell, a biochemical reaction occurs that repels other sperm and keeps them from entering the already fertilized egg. As explained in

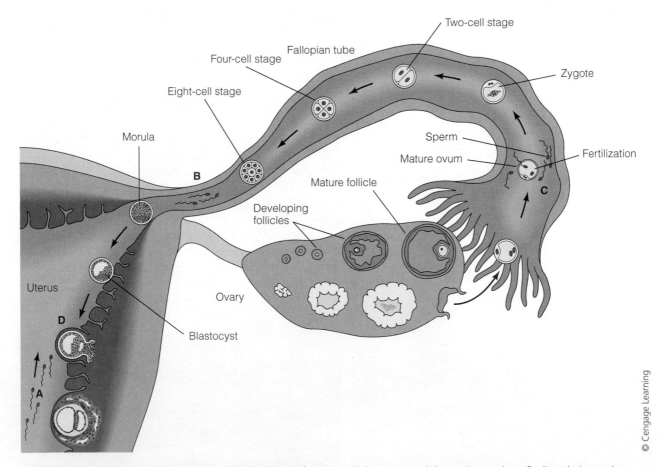

■ **Figure 4.1** Fertilization and implantation. (A) Millions of sperm cells have entered the vagina and are finding their way into the uterus. (B) Some sperm are moving up the fallopian tube (there is a similar tube on the other side) toward the ovum. (C) Fertilization occurs. The fertilized ovum drifts down the tube, dividing and forming new cells as it goes, until it implants itself in the wall of the uterus (D) by the seventh or eighth day after fertilization.

© Cengage Learning

Chapter 3, conception, the beginning of life, occurs when the genetic material of the sperm and egg unite to form a single-celled zygote.

The process may sound simple, but as many as one in four couples experience difficulties conceiving despite their strong desire to have a child. **Infertility**—not being able to get pregnant after a year of trying—is equally likely to be traced to the man as the woman and stems from a variety of causes. For example, adolescents and adults—both male and female—who have contracted sexually transmitted infections (STIs) may become infertile. Some men have a condition called *varicocele* in which enlarged veins on their testicles raise the temperature in the testes, interfering with sperm production (Centers for Disease Control, 2012a). Infertility traced to women is often related to problems with ovulation. Depending on the suspected cause of infertility, couples may be helped to conceive with simple solutions. A man may be advised to wear loose boxer shorts rather than tighter briefs that might elevate testicular temperature. A woman may be able to track her morning body temperature to determine when she ovulates and is therefore most likely to become pregnant.

When simpler methods fail, some couples move on to more elaborate (and expensive) assisted reproductive technologies (ARTs), medical techniques used to increase fertility. ART techniques typically start with or include prescription drugs for the woman to stimulate her ovaries to ripen and release several eggs. If this is unsuccessful, couples and their doctors may proceed to **artificial insemination** (also called intrauterine insemination), which involves injecting sperm, either from a woman's partner or from a donor, into her uterus. Or they may use **in vitro fertilization (IVF)**, in which several eggs are removed from a woman's ovary and manually combined with sperm in a laboratory dish before being returned to a woman's uterus in hopes that one egg will implant on the wall of the uterus. We should note that there are many variations of IVF, depending on who provides the eggs and the sperm. A couple wanting to have a child could donate both eggs and sperm and have the biological mother carry the baby to term. At the other end of the spectrum, an infant conceived through IVF could wind up with five "parents": a sperm donor, an egg donor, a surrogate mother in whom the fertilized egg is implanted, and a caregiving mother and father.

Infertility is costly, both economically and emotionally. Worldwide, the cost of IVF is highest in the United States, where each attempt is about $12,400 (Connolly, Hoorens, & Chambers, 2010). The success rate for women who use their own fresh (rather than frozen) eggs is about 1 in 4 overall, but decreases as mothers get older. IVF results in a live birth in 42% of women under 35 years but in only 5% of women 43–44 years of age (CDC, 2012a). Couples report that infertility is stressful, and unsuccessful treatment can have long-term psychosocial effects (Verhaak et al., 2005). For instance, women experiencing infertility report less satisfaction with their sex lives than other women (Millheiser et al., 2010). And those who perceive less control over their circumstances report greater emotional distress (Gourounti et al., 2012). Couples experiencing infertility who ultimately have children, either through ART or through adoption, have greater psychological well-being than couples who undergo IVF treatment and do not end up having children

(Hogström et al., 2012). Still, even couples who have not successfully conceived following infertility treatment are usually found to be well adjusted and stable, and looking back on the experience, they report positive growth in their lives as a result of this experience (Daniluk, 2001). Although their attempts to conceive were unsuccessful, they may feel satisfied that they actively pursued available options, consistent with findings that a sense of control is important to well-being.

Prenatal Stages

The zygote contains the 46 chromosomes that are the genetic blueprint for the individual's development. It takes about 266 days, or roughly 9 months, for the zygote to become a fetus of billions of cells that is ready to be born. Experts called **embryologists** who study early growth and development divide prenatal development into three stages or periods: the germinal period, the embryonic period, and the fetal period. More commonly, parents-to-be and their obstetricians organize pregnancy into trimesters corresponding to the first 3 months, the middle 3 months, and the last 3 months of the prenatal period.

The Germinal Period

The first trimester begins with the **germinal period**, which lasts approximately 2 weeks; the important events of this period are outlined in ● **Table 4.1**. For the first week or two, the zygote divides many times through mitosis, forming the **blastocyst**, a hollow ball of about 150 cells that is the size of the head of a pin. When the blastocyst reaches the uterus around day 6, it implants tendrils from its outer layer into the blood vessels of the uterine wall. This is quite an accomplishment; only about half of all fertilized ova are successfully implanted in the uterus. In addition, not all implanted embryos survive the early phases of prenatal development. Although estimates vary widely, somewhere between 8% and 30% of recognized pregnancies are short-lived, ending in **miscarriage** (also called spontaneous abortion) before survival outside the womb is possible, and as many as one-third of *unrecognized* pregnancies are believed to end in miscarriage (Hure et al., 2012; Tulandi & Al-Fozan, 2011). Many of these early losses are because of genetic defects.

● **Table 4.1** Events of the Germinal Period

Day	Event
1	Fertilization usually occurs within 24 hours of ovulation.
2	The single-celled zygote begins to divide 24–36 hours after fertilization.
3–4	The mass has 16 cells and is called a morula; it is traveling down the fallopian tube to the uterus.
5	An inner cell mass forms; the entire mass is called a blastocyst and is the size of a pinhead.
6–7	The blastocyst attaches to the wall of the uterus.
8–14	The blastocyst becomes fully embedded in the wall of the uterus. It now has about 250 cells.

© Cengage Learning

The Embryonic Period

The first trimester continues with the **embryonic period**, which occurs from the third to the eighth week after conception (● **Table 4.2**). During this short time, every major organ takes shape, in at least a primitive form, in a process called **organogenesis**. The layers of the blastocyst differentiate, forming structures that sustain development. The outer layer becomes both the **amnion**, a watertight membrane that fills with fluid that cushions and protects the embryo, and the **chorion**, a membrane that surrounds the amnion and attaches root-like extensions called *villi* to the uterine lining to gather nourishment for the embryo. The chorion eventually becomes the lining of the **placenta**, a tissue fed by blood vessels from the mother and connected to the embryo by the umbilical cord. Through the placenta and umbilical cord, the embryo receives oxygen and nutrients from the mother and eliminates carbon dioxide and metabolic wastes into the mother's bloodstream. A membrane called the *placental barrier* allows these small molecules to pass through, but it prevents the large blood cells of embryo and mother from mingling. It also protects the developing child from many harmful substances, but as you will see shortly, it is not infallible; some dangerous substances slip through.

Meanwhile, the cells in the interior of the blastocyst give rise to the ectoderm, mesoderm, and endoderm. These will eventually evolve into specific tissues and organ systems, including the central nervous system (brain and spinal cord) from the ectoderm; muscles, bones, cartilage, heart, arteries, kidneys, and gonads from the mesoderm; and gastrointestinal tract, lungs, and bladder from the endoderm (Sadler, 2012).

Development proceeds at a breathtaking pace. The beginnings of a brain are apparent after only 3–4 weeks, when the

About a month after conception, this embryo is shown up against a cross-section of the placenta. The umbilical cord is shown at the bottom of the photo, connecting the embryo to its vital source of life in the womb. The eyes are clearly visible, as are the arms, legs, and ear buds. The fingers are just beginning to differentiate, and the mouth is formed.

Mark Albertasky/RGB Ventures LLC dba SuperStock/Alamy

neural plate folds up to form the neural tube (■ **Figure 4.2**). The bottom of the tube becomes the spinal cord. "Lumps" emerge at the top of the tube and form the forebrain, midbrain, and hindbrain (■ **Figure 4.3**). The so-called primitive or lower portions of the brain develop earliest. They regulate such biological functions as digestion, respiration, and elimination; they also control sleep–wake states and permit simple motor reactions. These are the parts of the brain that make life possible.

In approximately 1 out of 2,000 pregnancies, the neural tube fails to fully close (Liptak, 2013). When this happens at the bottom of the tube, it can lead to **spina bifida**, in which part of the spinal cord is not fully encased in the protective covering of the spinal column (■ **Figure 4.4**). Children with spina bifida typically

● **Table 4.2** Events of the Embryonic Period

Week	Event
3	Now an embryo, the person-to-be is just 1/10 of an inch (2 mm) long. It has become elongated, and three layers emerge—the ectoderm, mesoderm, and endoderm.
4	The embryo is so curved that the two ends almost touch. The outer layer (ectoderm) folds into the neural tube. From the mesoderm, a tiny heart forms and begins to beat. The endoderm differentiates into a gastrointestinal tract and lungs. Between days 21 and 28, eyes develop.
5	Ears, mouth, and throat take shape. Arm and leg buds appear. The handplate from which fingers will emerge appears. The heart divides into two regions, and the brain differentiates into forebrain, midbrain, and hindbrain.
6–7	The embryo is almost 1 inch long. The heart divides into four chambers. Fingers emerge from the handplate, and primitive facial features are evident. The important process of sexual differentiation begins.
8	Most structures and organs are present. Ovaries and testes are evident. The embryo begins to straighten and assumes a more human appearance.

© Cengage Learning

Neural plate
Neural fold
Neural groove
Future brain
Developing heart bulge
Neural tube

© Cengage Learning

■ **Figure 4.2** The nervous system emerges from the neural plate, which thickens and folds to form the neural groove. When the edges of the groove meet, the neural tube is formed. All this takes place between 18 and 26 days after conception.

3 weeks after conception

7 weeks after conception

11 weeks after conception

At birth

© Cengage Learning

■ **Figure 4.3** The brain at four stages of development, showing hindbrain, midbrain, and forebrain.

Normal Spine

Spina Bifida

© Cengage Learning

■ **Figure 4.4** Unlike the normal spine, spina bifida is characterized by an opening in the spinal cord that may be relatively small and invisible, or as illustrated here, may be large enough to allow part of the spinal cord and nerves to bulge out of the protective spinal column.

have neurological problems ranging from very mild to severe depending on the location and size of the opening. Failure to close at the top of the neural tube can lead to **anencephaly**, a lethal defect in which the main portion of the brain above the brain stem fails to develop. Neural tube defects occur by 26 days after conception and are more common when the mother is deficient in folate, a type of B vitamin that is critical for normal gene function (Liptak, 2013). There are various reasons why folate levels might become diminished, including use of birth control pills and poor nutrition (deRegnier & Desai, 2010). Folate deficiency has helped highlight the importance of good maternal nutrition for development, about which we will have more to say in a later section.

Other critical organs are also taking shape. Just 4 weeks after conception, a tiny heart not only has formed but also has begun to beat. The eyes, ears, nose, and mouth rapidly take shape in the second month, and buds appear that will become arms and legs. During the second month, a primitive nervous system also makes newly formed muscles contract. Only 60 days after conception, at the close of the embryonic period, the organism is a little over an inch long and has a distinctly human appearance.

The important process of sexual differentiation begins during the seventh and eighth prenatal weeks. First, undifferentiated tissue becomes either male testes or female ovaries: If the embryo inherited a Y chromosome at conception, a gene on it calls for the construction of testes; in a genetic female with two X chromosomes, ovaries form instead. The testes of a male embryo secrete **testosterone**, the primary male sex hormone that stimulates the development of a male internal reproductive system, and another hormone that inhibits the development of a female internal reproductive system. In the absence of these hormones, the embryo develops the internal reproductive system of a female.

Clearly the embryonic period is dramatic and highly important because it is when the structures that

Here we see what the developing fetus looks like in the womb at 10 weeks after conception. Right, we see how things look at this same time on the outside: a "baby bump" is just barely visible on the mother, despite the amazing changes that have been taking place inside.

make us human evolve. Yet many pregnant women, either because they do not yet know they are pregnant—like Serena from the chapter opening story—or because they do not appreciate the value of early prenatal care, do not go to a doctor until *after* the eighth week of prenatal development. By this time, it may be too late to prevent the damage that can be caused by an unhealthy lifestyle.

The Fetal Period

The **fetal period** lasts from the ninth week of pregnancy until birth, which means it encompasses part of the first trimester and all of the middle and last trimesters (● **Table 4.3**). It is a critical period for brain development, which involves three processes: proliferation, migration, and differentiation. **Proliferation** of neurons involves their multiplying at a staggering rate during this period; by one estimate, the number of neurons increases by hundreds of thousands every minute throughout all of pregnancy, with a concentrated period of proliferation occurring between 6 and 17 weeks after conception (du Plessis, 2013;

McDonald, 2007). As a result of this rapid proliferation, the young infant has around 100 billion neurons. Another period of proliferation takes place after birth, but this produces an increase in glial cells, not nerve cells. Glial cells function primarily as support cells for neurons. In **migration**, the neurons move from their place of origin in the center of the brain to particular locations throughout the brain where they will become part of specialized functioning units. Migration is influenced by genetic instructions and by the biochemical environment in which brain cells find themselves. Some neurons migrate passively by getting pushed out of the way to make room for other neurons being born (Johnson, 2011). This form of migration is typical for neurons that will end up in the brain stem and thalamus. Other neurons, such as those that will form the cerebral cortex, take a more active role: They travel along the surface of glial cells and detach at programmed destinations in the developing brain (■ **Figure 4.5**). The first neurons to migrate stop at the closest or innermost layer of what will be the cerebral cortex. Other groups of neurons follow suit but need to travel further until all six layers of

Week	Event
9	Bone tissue emerges, and the embryo becomes a fetus. The head of the fetus looks huge relative to the rest of the body—it takes up about half the total length of the fetus. The fetus can open and close its mouth and turn its head.
10–12	Fingers and toes are clearly formed. External genitalia have developed. Movements have increased substantially—arms and legs kick vigorously, but the fetus is still too small for the mother to feel all these movements. The fetus also shows "breathing" movements with its chest and some reflexes.
13–16	The heartbeat should be audible with a stethoscope. Fetal movements may become apparent to the mother. The fetus is about 4½ inches long, and the skeleton is becoming harder.
17–22	Fingernails and toenails, hair, teeth buds, and eyelashes grow. Brain development is phenomenal, and brainwaves are detectable.
23–25	These weeks mark the age of viability, when the fetus has a *chance* of survival outside the womb. It is about 12 inches long and weighs about 1 pound.
26–32	The fetus gains weight, and its brain grows. The nervous system becomes better organized.
33–38	The last 6 weeks of a full-term pregnancy bring further weight gain and brain activity. The lungs mature and begin to expand and contract.

© Cengage Learning

Outer surface

Migrating zone

Migrating neuron

Glial fiber

Inner surface

© Cengage Learning

■ **Figure 4.5** Neurons move to their final destinations in the brain by attaching themselves to strands of glial fiber and then slowly progressing along the surface of the glial fiber.

the cerebral cortex have been formed. Although this process occurs throughout the prenatal period, much of this occurs between 8 and 15 weeks after conception (McDonald, 2007). Once a neuron reaches its "home," it begins to communicate with the surrounding neurons.

Along with proliferation and migration of cells, a third process, **differentiation**, is occurring (● **Table 4.4** summarizes these events). Early in development, every neuron starts with the potential to become any specific type of neuron; what it becomes—how it differentiates—depends on where it migrates.

Thus, if a neuron that would normally migrate to the visual cortex of an animal's brain is transplanted into the area of the cortex that controls hearing, it will differentiate as an auditory neuron instead of a visual neuron (Johnson, 2011). Under normal circumstances, this proliferation-migration-differentiation process proceeds smoothly and everything ends up where it should be. In some cases, though, as we'll see later in this chapter, cells get slowed down or sidetracked along their migratory path or they do not properly differentiate at their endpoint. This can lead to a nervous system that does not function as well as it could (McDonald, 2007).

Organ systems that formed during the embryonic period continue to grow and begin to function. Harmful agents will no longer cause major malformations because organs have already formed, but they can stunt the growth of the fetus and interfere with the wiring of its rapidly developing nervous system.

● **Table 4.4** Processes of Prenatal Brain Development

Process	Explanation
Proliferation	An intense period of cell growth, originating from stem cells undergoing rapid cell division.
Migration	Cells move or travel to their intended location in the nervous system. Chemical signals may serve as a neural GPS, guiding cells to their destination.
Differentiation	Cells change or transform into a particular type based on where they land following their migration. They set up camp and begin to communicate with surrounding neurons.

© Cengage Learning

In the third month of pregnancy, distinguishable external sex organs appear, the bones and muscles develop, and the fetus becomes frisky: By the end of the first trimester of pregnancy, it moves its arms, kicks its legs, makes fists, and even turns somersaults. The mother probably does not yet feel all this activity because the fetus is still only about 3 inches long. Nonetheless, this tiny being can swallow, digest food, and urinate. All this "behaving" contributes to the proper development of the nervous system, digestive system, and other systems of the body, and it is consistent with the behaviors that we observe *after* birth (Kurjak et al., 2004; du Plessis, 2013).

During the second trimester, more refined activities appear (including thumb sucking), and by the end of this period the sensory organs are functioning: Premature infants as young as 25 weeks respond to loud noises and bright lights (Allen & Capute, 1986; Sadler, 2012). At about 23 weeks after conception, midway through the fifth month, the fetus reaches the **age of viability**, when survival outside the uterus is possible *if* the brain and respiratory system are sufficiently developed. The age of viability is earlier today than at any time in the past because medical techniques for keeping fragile babies alive have improved considerably over the past few decades. Although there are cases of "miracle babies" who survive severely premature birth, many infants born at 22–25 weeks do not survive, and of those who do, many experience chronic health or neurological problems. Among infants born at the cusp of survivability—22–23 weeks— 92% do not survive beyond a few hours or days despite the use of aggressive medical therapies (Swamy et al., 2010). At 23 weeks, 25% of preemies survive, and with just one more week in the womb, the survival rate jumps to 55% (Berger et al., 2012). Thus, the age of viability is an indicator of when survival *may be possible*, but it is by no means a guarantee of life or health. Further, as ■ **Figure 4.6** shows, the odds of survival may also depend on the country where you live and even the birthing location within countries. Such differences likely reflect variations in how aggressively premature infants are resuscitated and treated (Berger et al., 2012).

During the *third trimester*, the fetus gains weight rapidly. This time is also critical in the development of the brain, as is the entire prenatal period (more on this in Chapter 5). Early in pregnancy, the basic architecture of the nervous system is developed. During the second half of pregnancy, neurons not only multiply at an astonishing rate (proliferation) but they also increase in size and develop an insulating cover, **myelin**, that improves their ability to transmit signals rapidly. Most importantly, guided by both a genetic blueprint and early sensory experiences, neurons connect with one another and organize into working groups that control vision, memory,

At 24 weeks of gestation, this fetus has reached the age of viability when it might have a chance to survive outside the womb if born early.

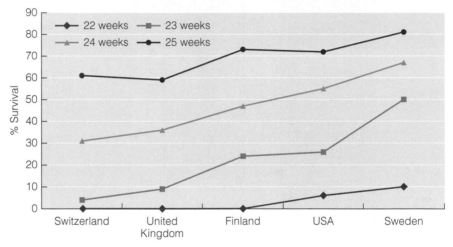

■ **Figure 4.6** Percentage survival at 22, 23, 24, and 25 weeks gestation. At 22 weeks gestational age, the chances of survival are very bleak. But with each additional week in the womb, the odds of survival improve. There are also cross-national variations: babies born very prematurely in Sweden have the best chances of survival relative to similarly premature babies born in one of the other countries shown here.

Source: Berger, T. M., Steurer, M. A., Woerner, A., Meyer-Schiffer, P., & Adams, M. (2012). Trends and centre-to-centre variability in survival rates of very preterm infants (<32 weeks) over a 10-year-period in Switzerland. *Archives of Disease in Childhood-Fetal and Neonatal Edition, 97, F323–F328. doi:10.1136/fetalneonatal-2011-301008*

motor behavior, and other functions. For good reason, parents should be concerned about damage to the developing human during the first trimester, when the brain and other organs are forming. However, they should not overlook the significance of the second and third trimesters, which are critical to normal brain functioning and therefore to normal development.

As the brain develops, the behavior of the fetus becomes more like the organized and adaptive behavior seen in the newborn. For example, Janet DiPietro and her colleagues (2006, 2007) assessed heart rates and activity levels at various points prenatally and post-natally. Heart rate was relatively stable from the prenatal period into early childhood. By 36 weeks of gestation, heart rate activity and movement become increasingly organized into coherent patterns of waking and sleeping known as *infant states*. Fetuses whose heart rates and movements were concordant (that is, matched) at 36 weeks showed better regulation of their behavioral states at 2 weeks old. They were more alert, less irritable, better able to sustain their attention, and more likely to main-tain control even during stressful parts of a postnatal exami-nation. Beyond this, fetal heart rate variability was associated with mental development at age 2 and language development at age 2½. In particular, fetuses with slower and more variable heart rates had higher levels of mental and language develop-ment in early childhood compared with those who had faster and less variable heart rates. The researchers speculate that slow and variable heart rates may reflect optimal regulation of the nervous system.

DiPietro and her colleagues (1996b) also found that, with age, fetal heart rates become increasingly responsive to such stimuli as a vibrator placed on the mother's abdomen. Fetuses moved, on average, about once a minute and were active 20–30% of the time. At 20 weeks, fetuses spent only about 17% of their time in an organized infant state such as quiet sleep, active sleep, or active waking. By the end of the prenatal period, though, they were in one distinct state or another at least 85% of the time. They spent most of their time snooz-ing, especially in active sleep. Whereas in the 20th week of pregnancy they were almost never active and awake, by the 32nd week they spent 11–16% of their time in an active, wak-ing state. Such findings are important because they point to greater organization of the nervous system around 28–32 weeks after conception, which corresponds to when premature infants are typically well equipped to survive. As the nervous system becomes more organized, so does behavior.

Interestingly, different fetuses display consistent differences in their patterns of heart rate and movement, and researchers have detected correlations between measures of fetal physiology and behavior and measures of infant temperament (DiPietro et al., 1996a, 2007; Werner et al., 2007). For example, active fetuses turned out to be active, difficult, and unpredictable ba-bies, and fetuses whose states were better organized were also better regulated at 3 months old, as indicated by their waking

The behaviors of the fetus (left, from 3D ultrasound) are remarkably similar to those exhibited by the infant after birth (right).

Thierry Berrod/Mona Lisa Production/Photo researchers

fewer times during the night. The message is clear: Newborn behavior does not spring from nowhere; it emerges long before birth. There is a good deal of continuity between prenatal be-havior and postnatal behavior.

By the middle of the ninth month, the fetus is so large that its most comfortable position in cramped quarters is head down with limbs curled in (the "fetal position"). The mother's uterus contracts at irregular intervals during the last month of preg-nancy. When these contractions are strong, frequent, and regular, the mother is in the first stage of labor and the prenatal period is drawing to a close. Under normal circumstances, birth will occur within hours.

Checking Mastery

1. What is conception, and what techniques can be used to assist conception?
2. How does the development of the brain and nervous system unfold during the embryonic and fetal periods?
3. When is survival outside the womb possible?

Making Connections

1. What ethical concerns should be considered with the use of artificial reproductive technologies? As technologies become more advanced in the future, what additional concerns may arise?
2. Based on what you know about the developments during the prenatal period, where would you focus attempts to optimize prenatal care and why?

LEARNING OBJECTIVES:

- Discuss the concept of fetal programming, and evaluate its usefulness in understanding connections between prenatal events and postnatal outcomes.

- Organize teratogens according to the seriousness of their impact on development (that is, from major structural abnormalities to those with small or undetermined effects).

- Summarize characteristics of the parents-to-be that may influence pregnancy and its outcomes.

The mother's womb is the prenatal environment for the unborn child. Just as children are influenced by their physical and social environments, so too is the fetus affected by its surroundings. The physical environment includes everything from the molecules that reach the fetus's bloodstream before birth to the architecture of a home to the climate outside it. The social environment includes all the people who can influence and be influenced by the developing person and the broader culture. Although early theorists tended to view environment as a set of forces that shaped the individual, as though a person were just a lump of clay to be molded, we now know this is not the case. Recall the concept in Chapter 2's discussion of the bioecological model of *reciprocal influences*: People shape their physical and social environments and are, in turn, affected by the environments they have helped create. For example, if a woman uses cocaine during pregnancy, her newborn may be extraordinarily fussy: Environment has affected development. But a fussy baby is likely to affect his environment by irritating his mother, who then expresses her tenseness in her interactions with him; this makes him fussier, which aggravates his mother even more, and her aggravation, in turn, makes him even crankier. Such transactions between person and environment begin at the moment of conception. When all is right, the prenatal environment provides just the stimulation and support needed for the fetus to mature physically and to develop a repertoire of behaviors that allow it to seek more stimulation, which in turn contributes to the development of more sophisticated behavior.

The developing embryo-then-fetus is a vulnerable little creature. Where it was once believed that the placenta served as a screen to protect the fetus from harmful substances, we now know that this is not the case. Research increasingly shows that events of the prenatal period can have lifelong effects on physical health and mental development (see, for example, Coe & Lubach, 2008; Hellemans et al., 2009). In Chapter 3, we introduced the idea of *epigenetic effects* whereby gene expression may be modified by environmental factors. The period of greatest environmental influence is during the prenatal period when growth and changes are occurring at an astonishingly fast rate. During this time, factors originating inside the mother such as her hormone levels or immune system functioning, as well as factors originating outside the mother such as exposure to pollution can alter the expression of genes throughout life (Perera & Herbstman, 2011). As we explained in Chapter 3, experience leaves its "fingerprint" on top of certain genes in certain cells, which influences whether those genes are turned on or not.

A growing body of research indicates that developmental outcomes may be influenced by **fetal programming** brought about by such epigenetic effects of the environment (DeRegnier & Desai, 2010; Sandman, Davis, & Glynn, 2012). The general idea of fetal programming is that environmental events during pregnancy may alter the expected genetic unfolding of the embryo/fetus or reset its physiologic functions. As a result of these alterations, prenatal experience can change a person's physiology and the wiring of the brain and influence how the individual responds to postnatal events. Conditions of the prenatal period, then, might set the stage for susceptibility to later health and mental health problems, perhaps decades down the road. But that's not all.

As ■ **Figure 4.7** illustrates, it is not only the unborn child who may be affected by prenatal environmental factors: The offspring of the unborn child may also be affected. Through epigenetic codings carried on the DNA of the reproductive

Mother - 1st generation

Fetus - 2nd generation

Reproductive cells - 3rd generation

© Cengage Learning

■ **Figure 4.7** A woman's experiences during pregnancy can impact not only her own health, but that of her unborn baby *and* future grandchildren.

cells of the developing fetus, a pregnant woman's health, diet, and environment may adversely affect her future grandchildren (Shrivastava et al., 2012). Epigenetics is a critical component in understanding fetal programming (Barouki et al., 2012; Wadhwa et al., 2009; and see Grandjean, 2008). According to research with animals and increasingly humans, prenatal imbalances in nutrition and exposure to environmental toxins may alter molecular pathways in ways leading to disease and health challenges later in life. Adult health and mental health conditions such as obesity, heart disease, and schizophrenia may have their origins in the prenatal environment and fetal programming (Kirkbride et al., 2012). Importantly, though, *good* health may also have its origins in the prenatal period, suggesting that this is a period of opportunity, not just a period of vulnerability.

How then can development during this period be optimized? What hazards does the fetus face? In the next sections, your main mission is to discover the extent to which early environmental influences, interacting with genetic influences, make or break later development. The nature–nurture issue, then, is the central question to consider when thinking about prenatal development and its influence on the developing person. Early exposure to certain environmental factors may help explain health and mental health trajectories later in life (Barouki et al., 2012). Such influences interact with genetic makeup throughout the life span to make us who we are. If a common genetic heritage (species heredity) can make different human beings alike in some respects, so can similar environments. If unique genes make one person different from another, so do unique experiences.

Teratogens

A **teratogen** is any disease, drug, or other environmental agent that can harm a developing fetus (for example, by causing deformities, blindness, brain damage, or even death). The list of teratogens has grown frighteningly long, and the environment contains many potential teratogens whose effects on development have not yet been assessed. Before considering the effects of some major teratogens, however, let us emphasize that *only 15% of newborns have minor problems, and even fewer—perhaps 5%—have more significant anomalies due to teratogens* (Sadler, 2012). We will start with a few generalizations about the effects of teratogens, which we will then illustrate with examples:

- *Critical period.* The effects of a teratogenic agent are worst during the critical period when an organ system grows most rapidly.
- *Dosage and duration.* The greater the level of exposure and the longer the exposure to a teratogen, the more likely it is that serious damage will occur.
- *Genetic makeup.* Susceptibility to harm is influenced by the unborn child's and by the mother's genetic makeup. Some fetuses are more (or less) resistant to teratogens and some mothers are more (or less) able to detoxify teratogens (Cassina et al., 2012). Therefore, not all embryos

and fetuses are affected, nor are they affected equally, by a teratogen.

- *Environment.* The effects of a teratogen depend on the quality of both the prenatal and the postnatal environments.

Look more closely at the first generalization, which is particularly important. A period of rapid growth is a **critical period** for an organ system—a time during which the developing organism is especially sensitive to environmental influences, positive or negative. As you will recall, organogenesis takes place during the embryonic period (weeks 3–8 of prenatal development). As ▪ **Figure 4.8** shows, it is during this time—before many women even realize they are pregnant—that most organ systems are most vulnerable to damage. Moreover, each organ has a critical period that corresponds to its own time of most rapid development (for example, weeks 3–6 for the heart and weeks 4–7 for the arms and fingers). Once an organ or body part is fully formed, it is usually less susceptible to damage. However, because some organ systems—above all, the nervous system—can be damaged throughout pregnancy, *sensitive periods* might be a better term than *critical periods*.

Drugs

The principles of teratology can be illustrated by surveying just a few of the many drugs—prescription, over-the-counter, and social—that can disrupt prenatal development. More than half of pregnant women take at least one prescription drug and as many as 75% take either a prescription or over-the-counter medication during pregnancy (Mitchell et al., 2011). Under a doctor's close supervision, medications used to treat ailments and medical conditions are usually safe for mother and fetus. However, certain individuals exposed to certain drugs in certain doses at certain times during the prenatal period are damaged for life.

Thalidomide. There is perhaps no more striking example of drug effects on prenatal development than **thalidomide** (Martinez-Frias, 2012). Approximately 50 years ago, this mild tranquilizer was widely used in Europe to relieve morning sickness (the periodic nausea and vomiting many women experience during pregnancy). Presumably, the drug was safe; it had no ill effects in tests on pregnant rats. Tragically, however, the drug had adverse effects on humans.

Thousands of women who used thalidomide during the first 2 months of pregnancy gave birth to babies with all or parts of their limbs missing, with the feet or hands attached directly to the torso like flippers, or with deformed eyes, ears, noses, and hearts. It soon became clear that there were critical periods for different deformities. If the mother had taken thalidomide 20–22 days after conception (34–36 days after the first day of a woman's last menstrual period), her baby was likely to be born without ears. If she had taken it 22–27 days after conception, the baby often had missing or small thumbs; if thalidomide was taken between 27 and 33 days after conception, the child was likely to have stunted legs or no legs. And if the mother waited until 35 or 36 days after conception before using thalidomide, her baby was usually not affected. Thus, thalidomide had specific effects on development, depending on which structures were developing when the drug was taken.

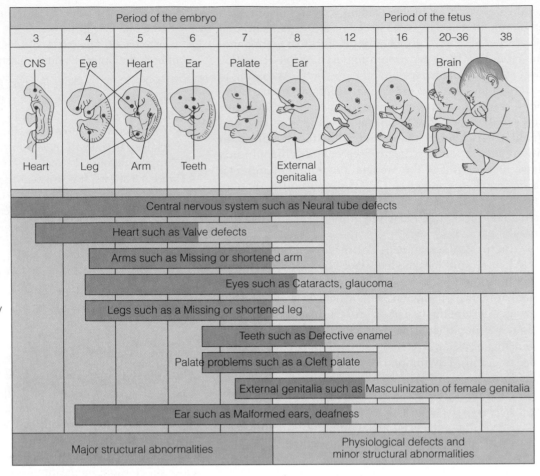

Figure 4.8 Sensitive periods of prenatal development. Teratogens are more likely to produce major structural abnormalities during the third through the eighth prenatal week. Note, however, that many organs and body parts remain sensitive to teratogenic agents throughout the 9-month prenatal period.

Source: Adapted from Moore, K. L. (2013). The developing human. Clinically oriented embryology. Philadelphia: W. B. Saunders.

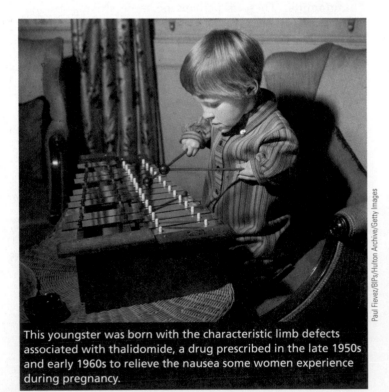

This youngster was born with the characteristic limb defects associated with thalidomide, a drug prescribed in the late 1950s and early 1960s to relieve the nausea some women experience during pregnancy.

Paul Fievez/BIPs/Hulton Archive/Getty Images

Thalidomide, banned for years, is again being prescribed by physicians, this time for treatment of conditions associated with leprosy, acquired immunodeficiency syndrome (AIDS), tuberculosis, and some forms of cancer. Given its tragic past association with birth defects, the manufacturers of thalidomide have taken significant steps to ensure it is used safely, including stamping each pill with a drawing of a pregnant woman inside a circle with a diagonal line through it (the universal "no" symbol) and including a picture of a baby with the characteristic stunted limbs on the packaging accompanying the pills. In addition, the prescribing physician and the patient must both abide by guidelines developed specifically for this drug (Celgene Corporation, 2012).

Tobacco. Warning labels on cigarette packages that smoking may damage fetuses have resulted in a decline, but not an absence, of smoking during pregnancy. About 17% of women (1 in 6) smoke during pregnancy, compared to about 25% among nonpregnant women (Substance Abuse, 2012). As ▪ **Figure 4.9** shows, rates vary by age and the race or Hispanic origin of the mother. The effects of smoking during pregnancy are varied and may include:

- increased risk of miscarriage
- prematurity, growth retardation, and small size
- respiratory problems

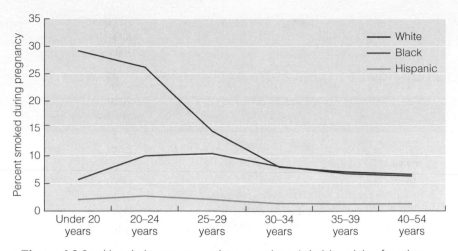

■ Figure 4.9 Smoking during pregnancy, by age and race/ethnicity origin of mother. Note that young white women are most likely to smoke during pregnancy and Hispanic women of any age are least likely to smoke during pregnancy.

Source: Adapted from Table 2 of Osterman, M. J. K., Martin, J. A., Mathews, T. J., & Hamilton, B. E. (2011). Expanded data from the new birth certificate, 2008. *National Vital Statistics Reports, 59(7).* Hyattsville, MD: National Center for Health Statistics.

- cleft lips (an opening in the top lip) and cleft palates (an opening in the roof of the mouth)
- central nervous system (CNS) impairment
- later health problems such as inflammatory bowel disease

Whether, and to what extent, infants experience ill effects from prenatal exposure to smoking depends, as our teratogenic principles would predict, on the length of exposure and the "dose." For example, more than half of infants born to heavy smokers (20 or more cigarettes a day) end up in neonatal intensive care and experience some degree of CNS impairment. Infants born to lighter smokers (5 cigarettes a day) may not have the same degree of CNS impairment, but they are more irritable and score lower on standard assessments of behavioral functioning than infants born to nonsmokers (Mansi et al., 2007). The more a woman smokes during pregnancy, the more likely it is that her infant will experience growth retardation and neurological problems (Law et al., 2003; Romo, Carceller, & Tobajas, 2009). Heavier smoking also raises the risk of **sudden infant death syndrome (SIDS)**, in which a sleeping baby suddenly stops breathing and dies. Further, the odds that problems from prenatal cigarette exposure will persist into childhood are greater when the mother was a heavier smoker (Burstyn et al., 2012; Campos, Bravo, & Eugenin, 2009; Duijts et al., 2012; Kanellopoulos et al., 2007).

Smoking causes these effects by restricting blood flow to the fetus, which in turn reduces the levels of growth factors, oxygen, and nutrients that reach the fetus, leading to a variety of negative outcomes (Huijbregts et al., 2006; Meyer et al., 2009). It's not just the nicotine in cigarettes that contributes to the poorer outcomes for exposed infants. Cigarettes contain more than 4,000 other chemicals and smoking cigarettes produces carbon monoxide, which reduces the flow of blood and oxygen to the fetus.

A rather alarming conclusion from some researchers is that chronic prenatal exposure to nicotine—a legal substance—may have more negative effects on CNS development than sporadic exposure to the illegal drug cocaine (Bada et al., 2005; Slotkin, 1998). But there is good news: Even women who start their pregnancies as smokers can improve the outcome for their babies by quitting smoking during their pregnancy (Polakowski, Akinbami, & Mendola, 2009). The benefits are greatest for those women who quit during their first trimester but are also apparent for the babies of mothers who quit during their second trimester. Thus, women should be encouraged and supported to stop or reduce smoking during pregnancy.

Finally, we must consider that women who smoke during pregnancy are likely to be white, young, low-income, and less educated than women who do not smoke during pregnancy (Whalen et al., 2006). It may be that some of these other factors act independently or in conjunction with cigarette smoking to create the less-than-ideal outcomes seen among these exposed infants (Huijbregts et al., 2006). **Exploration Box 4.1** describes a clever research design that helps clarify the connection between maternal smoking and the outcomes observed in infants.

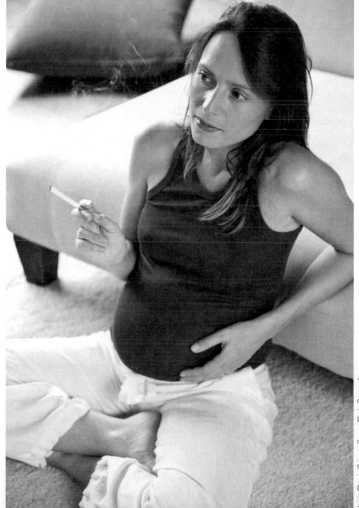

Smoking during pregnancy is associated with low birth weight, premature birth, and other birth complications. But the consequences do not stop with birth: these children are at greater risk of asthma and obesity as they get older.

The Prenatal Effects of Smoking: Do They Result from Nature or Nurture?

As we have noted, smoking during pregnancy is associated with several negative consequences for the babies who were exposed in utero. But how do we know that the ill effects seen in these offspring are due to the prenatal exposure to smoke and not to other connections between mother and child, namely the genes that the mother has passed along? Until recently, we didn't know the answer to this. But thanks to a clever study by British researchers, we are now able to uncouple the influences of the prenatal environment from inherited influences. Frances Rice, Anita Thapar, and their colleagues (2007, 2009) realized that the key to untangling these influences would be to study two groups of children conceived through in vitro fertilization: Children who were the biological offspring of the mother (that is, the mother's own eggs were retrieved, fertilized, and then implanted in her womb) and children who were not biologically related to the mother (that is, a donor egg was fertilized and then implanted in her womb). The researchers looked at two dependent variables: Birth weight and antisocial behavior at around

	Low Birth Weight Due to Smoking	Elevated Antisocial Behaviors
Own Egg Used for IVF	Yes	Yes
Donor (Unrelated) Egg Used for IVF	Yes	No

age 6, and the rather striking findings are summarized in the table above.

Polluting the environment of the womb with the by-products of cigarette smoke results in lower birth weights. Lower birth weights were observed in the babies of mothers who smoked regardless of the genetic connection between mother and child. As for antisocial behaviors, these were observed in the offspring of smokers only when there was a genetic connection between mother and child. The children who were conceived with donor eggs and whose mothers smoked during pregnancy did not show elevated rates of antisocial behavior. Thus, a prenatal environment of smoke by-products does not increase antisocial

behavior, but the mother's genetic contribution to her child does. There may be, for example, certain personality characteristics that make it more likely that a woman will smoke and that also contribute to antisocial behaviors that are passed along to offspring.

This research design, made possible by the advent of new reproductive technologies, is an innovative way to study the effects of nature versus early nurture. Other issues are now being tackled with this methodology. For instance, as we'll see later in the chapter, maternal stress during pregnancy affects later child reactivity to stress beyond what might also be contributed by shared genes (Rice et al., 2010).

Alcohol. Alcohol consumed by the mother readily crosses the placenta, where it can directly affect fetal development in various ways. For one, prenatal alcohol exposure disrupts the normal process of neuronal migration, leading to cells that do not end up at their proper final destination in the nervous system. Prenatal alcohol exposure can also lead to neuronal death and impair the function of the glial cells—those nonneuronal cells that are needed to support and nourish neurons (Goodlett & Horn, 2001). The outcomes of fetal alcohol exposure depend on the severity of the effects. The most severe is a cluster of symptoms dubbed **fetal alcohol syndrome (FAS)**, with noticeable physical symptoms such as a small head and distinctive facial abnormalities (■ **Figure 4.10**). Children with FAS are smaller and lighter than normal, and their physical growth lags behind that of their age-mates.

Most importantly, children with FAS also show signs of CNS damage. As newborns, they are likely to display excessive irritability, hyperactivity, seizures, or tremors. Most children with FAS score well below average on IQ tests throughout childhood and adolescence, and many are intellectually disabled (formerly called mentally retarded), with IQ scores below 70 (Howell et al., 2006; Nulman et al., 2007). Hyperactive behavior

and attention deficits are also common among these children (Bhatara, Loudenberg, & Ellis, 2006). Longitudinal research indicates that more than 90% of children born with FAS have mental health problems later in life, including attention deficit hyperactivity disorder (ADHD) and conduct disorders (Fryer et al., 2007). They are also likely to get into trouble at school, break the law, and experience job-related problems (Autti-Rämö, 2000; Merrick et al., 2006). These problems may arise because children with FAS are less skilled at interpreting and processing social information in group situations, leading to interpersonal difficulties (McGee et al., 2009).

Although estimates vary widely, most surveys indicate that, in the United States, approximately 10% of pregnant women drink some alcohol during pregnancy, about 3% admit to binge drinking, and less than 1% report heavy drinking (Substance Abuse, 2012). As a result, as many as 3 in 1,000 babies in the United States are born with FAS and suffer its symptoms all their lives. In Italy, where many people indulge in daily alcohol consumption with meals, the incidence of FAS and its milder forms may be as high as 37–47 out of 1,000 children (May et al., 2011). The World Health Organization (WHO) reports that South Africa's Western Cape province region has the highest

Small eye openings

Flat midface

Short nose

Indistinct groove between
nose and mouth

Epicanthal folds

Low nasal bridge

Minor ear anomalies

Thin upper lip

■ **Figure 4.10** Characteristic features of a child with fetal alcohol syndrome (FAS).

Source: From Sadler, T. W. (2004). Characteristics features of a child with fetal alcohol syndrome. In *Langman's medical embryology* (9th ed.). Copyright © 2004, Lippincott, Williams, & Wilkins. Reprinted with permission.

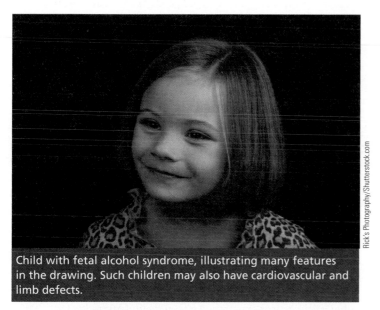

Child with fetal alcohol syndrome, illustrating many features in the drawing. Such children may also have cardiovascular and limb defects.

Rick's Photography/Shutterstock.com

FAS rates in the world, with 70–80 per 1,000 babies (Fetal Alcohol Syndrome, 2011). Children who were exposed prenatally to alcohol but do not have FAS experience milder alcohol-related effects labeled either *fetal alcohol effects* or *alcohol-related neurodevelopmental disorder* (Nulman et al., 2007). These individuals do not have all the features of FAS but have physical, behavioral, or cognitive problems or a combination of these.

How much drinking does it take to harm an unborn baby? In keeping with the dosage principle of teratology, mothers who consume larger quantities of alcohol are at greater risk for having children with alcohol-related complications (Roccella & Testa, 2003; Streissguth et al., 1999). The pattern of drinking is also important. Binge drinking (for women, consuming four or more drinks during a single session) has more negative effects on fetal development than consuming the same number of drinks across multiple sessions (Fraser et al., 2012; Jacobson & Jacobson, 1999). This makes sense when you consider that consuming four drinks in one evening results in higher blood alcohol levels for both mother and fetus than consuming one drink on each of four evenings. Finally, in keeping with the critical-period principle of teratogens, the effects of alcohol depend on which systems are developing at the time of exposure. The facial abnormalities associated with FAS result from consumption during the first trimester, more precisely the second half of the first trimester, when the face and skull bones are forming (Feldman et al., 2012). During the second and third trimesters, there is much fetal growth as well as rapid brain development; thus, alcohol consumption during this latter part of pregnancy is likely to stunt growth and brain development.

No amount of drinking seems to be entirely safe (O'Leary & Bower, 2012). Even a mother who drinks less than an ounce a day is at risk to have a sluggish or placid newborn whose mental development is slightly below average (Jacobson et al., 1993). One study found that exposure to less than one drink per week during pregnancy may be associated with mental health problems during childhood, at least among girls (Sayal et al., 2007). What is more, there is no well-defined critical period before or after which fetal alcohol effects cannot occur; drinking late in pregnancy can be as risky as drinking soon after conception.

Why do some babies of drinking mothers suffer ill effects but others do not? To answer this, you need to consider the nature–nurture issue again. First, the chances of damage depend partly on the mother's physiology—for example, on how efficiently she metabolizes alcohol and therefore how much is passed to the fetus (Shepard & Lemire, 2004). Complicating the situation, problem drinkers often have other issues that can aggravate the effects of alcohol on the fetus or cause independent damage that can be difficult to untangle from the effects of alcohol alone (Rodriguez et al., 2009). Women who consume unsafe levels of alcohol during pregnancy are also more likely to use drugs other than alcohol, smoke cigarettes, have inadequate prenatal care, and be young and single. Combining alcohol use with other risky behaviors increases the odds of pregnancy complications

(Odendaal et al., 2009). In addition, consistent with the third principle of teratogenic effects, the embryo's genetic makeup and physical condition influence its ability to resist and recover from damage. So, for example, one fraternal twin may show all the physical abnormalities associated with FAS, but the other twin, although exposed to the same prenatal environment, may show almost none; by contrast, identical twins respond similarly when exposed to alcohol prenatally (Streissguth & Dehaene, 1993). As the third principle of teratology states, then, both the child's and the mother's characteristics influence the extent to which a given teratogen proves damaging. Thus, the genetic makeup of both the mother and the child interact with environmental forces to determine the effects of alcohol on development.

Finally, note that it is not just the mother's use of alcohol that can adversely affect development. Some research suggests that a father's use of alcohol can influence fetal development through transmission of the father's genes to his offspring (Knopik et al., 2009). How might this occur? There are two possibilities. One is that a man's use of alcohol, as well as other substances, may cause mutations of some DNA that is then passed to the offspring. A second possibility is that epigenetic effects are the culprit. That is, a father's alcohol use may alter the epigenome that "sits" on top of the genome, altering the expression of genes, which may then be transmitted to the offspring through the father's sperm (Champagne, 2010; Curley, Mashoodh, & Champagne, 2011). We should also note, however, that some research shows that paternal drinking does not affect fetal development directly through genetic or epigenetic factors, but affects development indirectly through poor parenting (Knopik et al., 2009; Leonard & Das Eiden, 2002). Fathers who use or abuse alcohol may have parenting styles that differ from those of fathers who do not use or abuse alcohol. Thus, further research needs to be done to determine the pathways by which a father's alcohol use relates to his offspring's development.

Cocaine. Although there is no "cocaine syndrome" with characteristic physical abnormalities such as those associated with FAS, cocaine use can damage the fetus. It can cause spontaneous abortion in the first trimester of pregnancy and premature detachment of the placenta or fetal strokes later in pregnancy (Diaz, 1997). Cocaine also contributes to fetal malnourishment, retarded growth, and low birth weight (Bada et al., 2005). At birth, a small proportion of babies born to cocaine users experience withdrawal-like symptoms such as tremors and extreme irritability and have respiratory difficulties (Diaz, 1997).

Cocaine-exposed infants show deficits on several measures of information processing (Singer et al., 1999) and sensory motor skills during their first year (Arendt et al., 1998). Not all problems caused by prenatal cocaine exposure persist into childhood. For problems that persist, it is unclear whether they are caused by the prenatal exposure to cocaine or by other prenatal or postnatal risk factors that affected infants may experience as the children of substance-abusing parents (Bandstra et al., 2010). For instance, as noted earlier for women who consume alcohol during pregnancy, women who use cocaine during pregnancy also tend to engage in more than one risky behavior. In addition, cocaine-using mothers are less attentive to their babies and engage in fewer interactions with them during the first year than non–drug-using mothers or mothers who use drugs other than cocaine (Minnes et al., 2005). Mother–child interactions continue to be lower quality throughout early childhood (Mansoor et al., 2012). Children exposed to prenatal cocaine who are raised by adoptive or foster parents display fewer language problems at age 10 than those raised by their biological mother suggesting that the quality of the postnatal environment matters (Lewis et al., 2011).

● **Table 4.5** catalogs several substances and their known or suspected effects on the child. What should you make of these findings? You now understand that drugs do not damage all fetuses exposed to them in a simple, direct way. Instead, complex transactions between an individual with a certain genetic makeup and the prenatal, perinatal, and postnatal environments influence whether or not prenatal drug exposure does lasting damage. Still, women who are planning to become pregnant or who are pregnant should avoid all drugs unless they are prescribed by a physician and essential to health. Fortunately, most women have gotten the message and significantly alter their behavior during pregnancy to eliminate or reduce such unhealthy practices as drinking alcohol and smoking cigarettes and to increase healthy behaviors such as eating nutritious foods and getting regular prenatal care (Crozier et al., 2009; Tong et al., 2009).

Diseases

Just as drugs can jeopardize the prenatal environment, so can diseases. Here we take a look at four diseases—rubella, diabetes, syphilis, and AIDS—that illustrate principles of teratogens. ● **Table 4.6** summarizes these and other maternal conditions that may affect prenatal development.

Rubella. In the early 1940s, a doctor discovered that many infants born to women affected by **rubella** (German measles) during pregnancy had one or more of a variety of defects, including blindness, deafness, heart defects, and intellectual disability. Because rubella was fairly common, there were enough cases for doctors to see that the environment of the womb leaves the fetus vulnerable to outside influences. Rubella is most dangerous during the first trimester, a critical period in which the eyes, ears, heart, and brain are rapidly forming. Nearly 15% of pregnant women with rubella miscarry or experience a fetal death (Andrade et al., 2006). Yet not all babies whose mothers had rubella, even during the most critical period of prenatal development, will have problems. Birth defects occur in 60–85% of babies whose mothers had the disease in the first 2 months of pregnancy, in about 50% of those infected in the third month, and in only 16% of those infected in the fourth or fifth months (Kelley-Buchanan, 1988). Consistent with the critical-period principle, damage to the nervous system, eyes, and heart is most likely during that part of the first 8 weeks of pregnancy (the period of the embryo) when each of these organs is forming; deafness is more likely when the mother contracts rubella in weeks 6–13 of the pregnancy. Today, doctors stress that a woman should not try to become pregnant unless she has been immunized against rubella or has already had it. As a result of successful immunization programs, many women are now immune to this previously common infection. Nevertheless, recent outbreaks of rubella have been reported in several countries, including Poland and Romania (Measles and Rubella Monitoring, 2012).

- **Table 4.5** Some Drugs Taken by the Mother that Affect the Fetus or Newborn

Drug	Effects
Alcohol	Effects of prenatal exposure can include a small head, facial abnormalities, heart defects, low birth weight, and intellectual retardation (see main text).
Antiepileptic drugs	Drugs such as phenytoin (Dilantin), phenobarbital (Luminal), and carbamazepine (Tegretol), used to treat seizures, increase the incidence of cleft lip and palate, neural tube defects, kidney disease, and restricted growth (Kothare & Kaleyias, 2007). Approximately 1 in 12 infants exposed prenatally to antiepileptic drugs will develop a birth defect.
Antidepressant drugs	Treating pregnant women with antidepressant drugs such as Prozac may place their infants at greater risk for low-birth weight and respiratory distress (Oberlander et al., 2007b). Research findings on safety of these drugs have not always been conclusive or consistent because women who take antidepressants throughout pregnancy often have more severe depression than women who do not. What appear to be drug effects, then, may be due to the severity of the illness.
Over-the-counter pain/fever reducers (acetaminophen, aspirin, and ibuprofen)	An occasional low dose is okay, but used in large quantities, such drugs may cause neonatal bleeding and gastrointestinal discomfort. Large amounts of these over-the-counter pain relievers (e.g., Advil) have been associated with low birth weight, prematurity, and increased risk of miscarriage (Li, Liu, & Odouli, 2003; Rebordosa et al., 2009).
Chemotherapy drugs	Such drugs cross the placenta and attack rapidly dividing cells. They can increase malformations and lead to miscarriage, particularly when administered to the mother during the first trimester.
Marijuana	Heavy use of marijuana has been linked to premature birth, low birth weight, and mild behavioral abnormalities such as irritability at birth. It may lead to small deficits in general intelligence as well as in some of the skills that contribute to higher-level problem solving, including sustained attention and cognitive flexibility (Goldschmidt et al., 2004). Prenatal marijuana exposure also predicts the child's own likelihood of later marijuana use (Day et al., 2006).
Narcotics	Addiction to heroin, codeine, methadone, or morphine increases the risk of premature delivery and low birth weight. The newborn is often addicted and experiences potentially fatal withdrawal symptoms (e.g., vomiting and convulsions). Longer-term cognitive deficits are sometimes evident.
Sex hormones	Birth control pills containing female hormones have been known to produce heart defects and cardiovascular problems, but today's pill formulas are safer. Progesterone in drugs used to prevent miscarriage may masculinize the fetus. Diethylstilbestrol, once prescribed to prevent miscarriage, increased the risk of cervical cancer and created infertility and pregnancy problems in exposed daughters (DESAction, 2013).
Stimulants	Caffeine, found in coffees, teas, and many sodas, is a stimulant and diuretic. As such, it can increase blood pressure, heart rate, and urination. Heavy caffeine use has been linked to miscarriages, higher heart rates, growth restriction, and irritability at birth, but it does not seem to have long-lasting effects on development (Loomans et al., 2012). Cocaine is an illegal stimulate that can cause premature delivery, spontaneous abortion, and low birth weight, and it may result in later learning and behavioral problems (see main text).
Tobacco	Babies of smokers tend to be small and premature, have respiratory problems, and sometimes show intellectual deficits or behavioral problems later in development (see main text). Sons whose mothers smoked during their pregnancy may later have fertility problems (Storgaard et al., 2003). Secondhand smoke in the pregnant woman's environment can increase her risk of miscarriage (George et al., 2006).

Sources: Modified from Creasy et al., 2009; Paulson, 2013; Friedman & Polifka, 2000; Liptak, 2007; Sadler, 2012; Shepard & Lemire, 2010.

Diabetes. Diabetes is a fairly common pregnancy complication, with most cases arising during pregnancy (gestational diabetes) rather than from preexisting diabetes. Diabetes results from elevated blood glucose levels. When glucose levels are well controlled with diet, there are few ill effects on the developing fetus. But in poorly controlled maternal diabetes, there is increased risk of premature delivery, stillbirth or miscarriage, immature lung development, and large fetal size. Large size continues to be an issue among children born to women with

diabetes (Khoury et al., 2012). Not surprisingly, diabetes combined with other maternal conditions such as hypertension or obesity is especially risky to the unborn child (Catalano et al., 2012; Potti et al., 2012).

Syphilis. Now consider another teratogen, the sexually transmitted infection **syphilis**. Syphilis during pregnancy can cause miscarriage or stillbirth in approximately 6% of cases where the mother is infected with syphilis (CDC, 2012c). Babies born alive to mothers

• **Table 4.6** Maternal Diseases and Conditions that may Affect an Embryo, Fetus, or Newborn

Disease or Condition	Effects
Sexually Transmitted Infections (STIs)	
Acquired immunodeficiency syndrome (AIDS)	If transmitted from mother to child, AIDS destroys defenses against disease and may lead to death. Mothers can acquire it through sexual contact or contact with contaminated blood (see main text).
Chlamydia	Chlamydia can lead to premature birth, low birth weight, eye inflammation, or pneumonia in newborns. This most common STI is easily treatable.
Gonorrhea	This STI attacks the eyes of the child during birth; blindness is prevented by administering silver nitrate eyedrops to newborns.
Herpes simplex (genital herpes)	This disease may cause eye and brain damage or death in the first trimester. Mothers with active herpes are advised to undergo cesarean deliveries to avoid infecting their babies during delivery, because 85% of infants born with herpes acquire the virus during birth through the birth canal.
Syphilis	Untreated, it can cause miscarriage or serious birth defects such as blindness and mental retardation (see main text).
Other Maternal Conditions or Diseases	
Chickenpox	Chickenpox can cause spontaneous abortion, premature delivery, and slow growth, although fewer than 2% of exposed fetuses develop limb, facial, or skeletal malformations.
Cytomegalovirus (CMV)	This common infection shows mild flulike symptoms in adults. About 25% of infected newborns develop hearing or vision loss, mental retardation, or other impairments, and 10% develop severe neurological problems or even die.
Diabetes	Well-controlled diabetes typically poses few, if any, prenatal complications. However, poorly-controlled diabetes can lead to premature delivery or even fetal loss. In addition, maternal diabetes is associated with large-for-date fetuses, which can complicate delivery.
Influenza (flu)	The more powerful strains can cause spontaneous abortions or neural abnormalities early in pregnancy that may lead to decreased intelligence scores in adulthood (Eriksen, Sundet, & Tambs, 2009).
Rubella	Rubella may cause vision and hearing loss, mental retardation, heart defects, cerebral palsy, and microcephaly (see main text).
Toxemia	Affecting about 5% of mothers in the third trimester, its mildest form, preeclampsia, causes high blood pressure and rapid weight gain in the mother. Untreated, preeclampsia may become eclampsia and cause maternal convulsions, coma, and death of the mother, the unborn child, or both. Surviving infants may be brain damaged.
Toxoplasmosis	This illness, caused by a parasite in raw meat and cat feces, leads to blindness, deafness, and mental retardation in approximately 40% of infants born to infected mothers.

Sources: Modified from Bell, 2007; Winn & Hobbins, 2000.

who have syphilis and who do not receive treatment in a timely manner can end up suffering blindness, deafness, heart problems or brain damage, like those babies born to mothers who have rubella. This shows that different teratogens—here, syphilis and rubella—can be responsible for the same problem. However, whereas rubella is most damaging in the early stage of pregnancy, syphilis is most damaging in the middle and later stages of pregnancy. This is because syphilitic organisms cannot cross the placental barrier until the 18th prenatal week, providing a window of opportunity for treating the mother-to-be who finds out she has the disease. Even with appropriate treatment—penicillin—some infants are infected or die, although treatment substantially lowers this risk (Blencowe et al., 2011).

AIDS. The sexually transmitted infection of greatest concern in recent decades is **acquired immunodeficiency syndrome (AIDS)**, the life-threatening illness caused by the human immunodeficiency virus (HIV). AIDS destroys the immune system and makes victims susceptible to "opportunistic" infections that eventually kill them unless they are treated with multiple drugs. HIV-infected mothers can transmit the virus to their babies (1) prenatally, if the virus passes through the placenta; (2) perinatally, when blood may be exchanged between mother and child as the umbilical cord separates from the placenta; or (3) postnatally, if the virus is transmitted during breast-feeding. Without treatment, somewhere between 15% and 35% of babies born to HIV-infected mothers will become infected (Avert, 2012).

An infant of an HIV-infected mother receives nevirapine syrup to help protect this little one from mother-to-infant transmission of HIV.

ANNA ZIEMINSKI/AFP/Getty Images

The rate is much lower if these mothers are treated with anti-retroviral drugs, or if they and their newborns are given a drug called nevirapine, which helps block transmission of HIV at birth (Avert, 2012; Stringer et al., 2004). Bottle-feeding further reduces the rate of HIV transmission from affected mothers to their infants but breast-feeding can be safe if managed effectively with treatment (Becquet et al., 2012). Infected infants now live longer than they did at the outset of the AIDS epidemic because of the development of appropriate treatments—50–75% in the United States are alive at age 5, and some survive into adolescence (Greenfield, 2012).

Although mother-to-child transmission of HIV in the United States has decreased significantly since peaking in 1992, it continues to be a tremendous problem in Africa and other parts of the world with AIDS epidemics. In 2010, for example, an estimated 390,000 infants worldwide became infected with HIV from their mothers, most in sub-Saharan Africa (Avert, 2012).

Environmental Hazards

A mother can control what she ingests, but sometimes she cannot avoid a hazardous external environment. Next we discuss two environmental conditions—radiation and pollutants—that may endanger the unborn child.

Radiation. After atomic bombs were dropped on Hiroshima and Nagasaki in 1945, not one pregnant woman who was within one-half mile of the blasts gave birth to a live child, and 75% of those who were within a mile and a quarter of the blasts had stillborn infants or seriously handicapped children who died soon after birth (Apgar & Beck, 1974). Surviving children of these mothers had a higher-than-normal rate of intellectual disability and greater incidence of leukemia and cancers later in life (CDC, 2012b; Kodama, Mabuchi, & Shigematsu, 1996). Autopsies of these individuals would later reveal thinner than normal layers of cerebral cortex, an indication that neuronal

migration had been disrupted (McDonald, 2007). The aftermath of these atomic bombs provides striking evidence of the devastating effects that can occur from prenatal exposure to radiation. But it doesn't take a Hiroshima-sized bomb to cause damage. Even clinical doses of radiation, such as those used in X-rays and cancer treatment, are capable of causing mutations, spontaneous abortions, and a variety of birth defects, especially if the mother is exposed between weeks 8 and 15 (Hill & Haffner, 2002). Therefore, expectant mothers are routinely advised to avoid X-rays or radiation unless they are essential to their own survival, as might be the case with women undergoing certain cancer treatments.

Pollutants. Following the 9/11 attacks and collapse of the World Trade Centers (WTC) in New York City, the air quality was extremely poor and those living in the vicinity were exposed to large amounts of potentially toxic pollutants. In the months after 9/11, researchers enrolled pregnant women in a longitudinal study to track effects of prenatal exposure to pollution on a variety of infant outcomes. They measured by-products of pollution evident in umbilical cord blood at birth. From this, they were able to conclude that the fetuses of women who were closer to the WTC did indeed have greater exposure to pollution. These infants were born lighter, shorter, and slightly earlier than a control group of babies whose mothers were not living near the WTC (Lederman et al., 2004). And 3 years later, some of the children showed decreased cognitive abilities (Perera et al., 2007). Was it the pollution alone or pollution in combination with the inevitable stress that was experienced by these women? Other research has found that 9/11 stress did not adversely affect birth outcomes, so pollution is the more probable explanation (Endara et al., 2009). Research conducted in other locations confirms that pollution exposure is associated with lower birth weight (van den Hooven et al., 2012). But, importantly, there is another variable that the researchers considered as they were examining pollution: prenatal exposure to cigarette smoke (Lederman et al., 2004; Perera et al., 2007). It turns out that prenatal exposure to pollution *in combination with* cigarette smoke led to further complications that were not present in the children who were exposed to just one of these prenatal risk factors. As we'll see later in this chapter, the more hazards that a child faces, the more likely it is that she will struggle to get back on track. Thus, with good postnatal care, children might overcome negative consequences of prenatal exposure to pollution or to cigarette smoke, but overcoming multiple risk factors is more of a challenge.

Exposure to heavy metals, such as lead in the air we breathe and the water we drink, is an ongoing concern. Children exposed prenatally to lead are smaller at birth and may be born preterm (Jelliffe-Pawlowski et al., 2006; Schell et al., 2006). They also show impaired intellectual functioning as children in proportion to the amount of lead in their umbilical cords (Canfield et al., 2003; Yorifuji et al., 2011). This finding holds true even after controlling for other differences among children, such as socioeconomic status. Postnatal lead exposure is also dangerous. It is estimated that one in four children under age 6 in the United States lives in a home with lead dust from old paint or old lead water pipes (Rogan & Ware, 2003). Exposure to even very low levels of lead—lower than previously thought to be safe—is associated with lowered mental function during childhood (Jedrychowski et al., 2009).

Mercury exposure typically results from eating fish or receiving a vaccination containing thimerosal as a preservative, although most vaccines today are thimerosal-free, particularly those recommended for children under the age of 6. Studies looking at prenatal exposure to mercury from maternal consumption of fish suggest adverse consequences, including delayed development and memory, attention, and language problems, with the effects related to the amount of mercury exposure (Paulson, 2013). As for whether mercury from older vaccines had toxic effects on development, the vast majority of the research concludes that it did not (Paulson, 2013; Waterhouse, 2013). Some parents whose children developed autism around the time of a vaccination continue to question whether there might be a link between the two events, but there is no credible evidence of this (see Chapter 16).

Finally, prenatal exposure to pesticides, dioxins, and polychlorinated biphenyls (PCBs) has also been associated with perinatal and postnatal problems (see Govarts et al., 2012). For example, prenatal exposure to PCBs from maternal consumption of contaminated foods is associated with poor reflexes in infants and later learning difficulties, including lower IQ scores at age 9 (Paulson, 2013; Stewart et al., 2008). Children whose mothers were exposed to pesticides during pregnancy have greater body fat relative to children not exposed (Wohlfahrt-Veje et al., 2011). Boys exposed in utero to pesticides have smaller genitals than nonexposed boys and, consistent with the dose principle, the greater the exposure the smaller the genitals (Wohlfahrt-Veje et al., 2012a). And in girls, in utero exposure to pesticides is associated with earlier breast development, suggesting changes in hormone levels (Wohlfahrt-Veje et al., 2012b).

Clearly there is a critical need for more research aimed at identifying a huge number of chemicals, wastes, and other environmental hazards that may affect unborn children. There are more than 80,000 chemicals "out there" to which children may be exposed, but fewer than 3% of these have been evaluated for toxicity (Grandjean & Landigan, 2006; Paulson, 2013).

The message is unmistakable: The chemistry of the prenatal environment often determines whether an embryo or fetus survives and how it looks and functions after birth. A variety of teratogens can affect development, although as you have learned, the influence of teratogens varies. Effects are worst in critical periods when organ systems are growing most rapidly, and effects are more serious with greater exposure to teratogens. Not all embryos or fetuses are equally affected by the same teratogen; the genetic makeup of both the mother and her unborn child and the quality of the prenatal and postnatal environments all play a role in determining the effects (Cassina et al., 2012). By becoming familiar with the information

here and by keeping up with new knowledge, parents-to-be can do much to increase the already high odds that their unborn child will be normal as it approaches its next challenge: the birth process.

The Mother's State

What can parents, especially the mother-to-be, do to sustain a healthy pregnancy? **Application Box 4.1** explores how parents can set the stage for a healthy pregnancy. Here we describe several characteristics of the mother—her age and race/ethnicity, emotional state, and nutritional status—that can affect the quality of the prenatal environment.

Age and Race/Ethnicity

At one end of the age spectrum, 11- and 12-year-old girls have given birth; at the other end of the spectrum, a 70-year-old woman from rural India made it to the record book by giving birth to twins after IVF. These are, however, unusual cases. The safest, and more typical, time to bear a child appears to be from about age 20 to age 40, as shown by the fetal mortality rates in ■ **Figure 4.11**.

Very young mothers have higher-than-normal rates of birth complications, including premature deliveries and **stillbirths**—fetal deaths late in pregnancy (20 or more weeks gestational age). The reproductive system of the teenager (19 years or younger) may not be physically mature enough to sustain a fetus to full term, making this group more vulnerable to having a low-birth-weight baby. However, the greater problem appears to be that teenagers often do not seek prenatal care and they are more likely to live in poverty and drink alcohol than mothers in their 20s and older (Substance Abuse and Mental Health Services Administration, 2012). Unfortunately, these conditions are likely to persist after the birth, leading to increased death rates before their first birthday among infants born to mothers 15 years or younger (Phipps, Blume, & DeMonner, 2002).

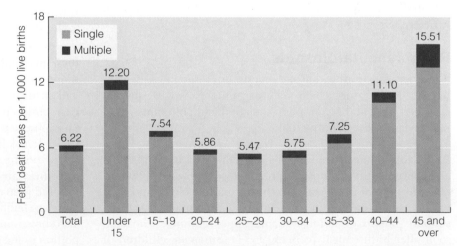

■ **Figure 4.11** Fetal mortality varies with the mother's age: Very young and very old mothers are at greater risk for fetal mortality. The best time to have a baby, if all other variables are the same, is when a woman is in her 20s or early 30s.

Source: CDC/NCHS, National Vital Statistics System, fetal mortality data, 2005.

Application 4.1

Growing Healthier Babies

The more we learn about important environmental influences on human development, the better able we are to optimize environment and therefore to optimize development. Although the quality of an individual's environment matters throughout the life span, it seems sensible to do as much as possible to get a baby's life off to a good start because events of the prenatal period may set the stage for a lifetime of good (or poor) health. Ideally, pregnancies are planned rather than "discovered" after the fact, when it may be too late to make certain lifestyle changes. All women of childbearing age, for example, should eat a diet that contains the recommended amount of folic acid and should try to quit or reduce their smoking. Women who are thinking about getting pregnant should talk to their doctor about any prescription drugs they may be taking for ongoing medical conditions such as depression, high blood pressure, or diabetes. Doctors and mothers-to-be can develop a plan for how best to manage any preexisting conditions during a pregnancy. Having these discussions and making these lifestyle changes before pregnancy help ensure that the cards are stacked in favor of having a healthy baby.

Once a woman is pregnant, she should seek good prenatal care as quickly as possible so that she will learn how to optimize the well-being of both herself and her unborn child and so that any problems during the pregnancy can be managed appropriately. Although the recommendations for pregnant women are not complicated, they are not always followed. They boil down to such practices as eating a good diet, taking prenatal vitamins, protecting oneself against diseases, and avoiding drugs and alcohol. Women who become ill during pregnancy should always check with their doctor before taking even seemingly safe over-the-counter drugs. Women should avoid eating undercooked meat because of the risks of toxoplasmosis and *Escherichia coli* (*E. coli*) contamination, and they should be cautious of eating some fish, namely those larger fish that consume lots of little fish. These tend to have higher concentrations of mercury.

Most women can continue to engage in all their regular activities, including exercise, during pregnancy unless advised against it by their health-care provider. Exercise can help keep muscles toned for the rigors of childbirth and also provides a sense of positive well-being. Exercise and a healthy diet during pregnancy may also influence the baby's metabolism and could set the stage for adult weight. In addition, researchers are beginning to find that prenatal exposure to certain environmental toxins may "program" the endocrine system in ways that lead to obesity across all stages of the life span (see, for example, Newbold et al., 2009).

Women who want to do some home renovations in preparation for the baby's arrival should be beware of lead paint that may be present in older homes and avoid inhaling paint fumes in poorly ventilated rooms. They may also want to have someone else clean the cat's litter box, because cat feces is another source of the parasite that causes toxoplasmosis. For women who can't avoid litter box duty, having cats tested and treated before pregnancy can eliminate potential exposure to parasites.

Finally, many couples today also enroll in classes that prepare them for childbirth. These classes started in the 1940s to help reduce the fear and pain experienced by many women during labor and delivery. The **Lamaze method** of prepared childbirth teaches women to associate childbirth with pleasant feelings and to ready themselves for the process by learning exercises, breathing and pushing methods, and relaxation techniques that make childbirth easier (Lamaze, 1958). Couples who participate in childbirth preparation classes report a greater sense of control during labor and delivery, and this sense of control is associated with higher levels of satisfaction with the childbirth experience (Hart & Foster, 1997). Unfortunately, after delivery many women say that their prenatal classes did not go as far as they could have in providing practice with the coping strategies useful for a smooth delivery (Spiby et al., 1999).

AMELIE-BENOIST/BSIP SA/Alamy

As for older women, they are more likely to experience trouble getting pregnant. For those who do conceive, there is an increased risk of miscarriage, stillbirth, and low-birth-weight babies (Arck et al., 2008; Borders et al., 2007). In the past, many fetal deaths in older women were caused by genetic abnormalities or defects arising during the first weeks after conception, when the major organs are forming. With today's extensive prenatal testing of women older than 35, however, fewer babies are dying from genetic problems, partly because many such fetuses are identified early and aborted. Still, as Figure 4.11 shows, fetal death rates remain higher for older women, particularly for those over age 45 (MacDorman & Kirmeyer, 2009). Compared with younger women, women over age 35 are more likely to release more than a single egg during ovulation, which increases their chances of conceiving fraternal twins (Beemsterboer et al., 2006). Though some women may be thrilled to learn that they are carrying twins, any multiple pregnancy and delivery carries additional health risks for the mother and the babies. Fetal mortality for higher-order pregnancies (three or more fetuses) is more than four times the rate for single pregnancies (MacDorman & Kirmeyer, 2009). Finally, keep in mind that despite the increased risks older women face in childbearing, most have normal pregnancies and healthy babies.

Does the mother's race/ethnicity impact pregnancy success? As ■ Figure 4.12 shows, fetal mortality rates do vary with the race/ethnicity of the mother. Most notable is that non-Hispanic black women have fetal mortality rates that are more than twice the rates experienced by other women. The reasons for this disparity are not completely understood but include poorer preconception health of the mother and less prenatal care. In addition, non-Hispanic black mothers are more susceptible to premature labor, which creates numerous health concerns that we will discuss in a later section.

Emotional Condition

Is the prenatal environment affected by how the mother feels about being pregnant or how her life is going while she is pregnant? Life is filled with many stressors—both chronic (poverty, for example, or ongoing job stress) and acute (experiencing a

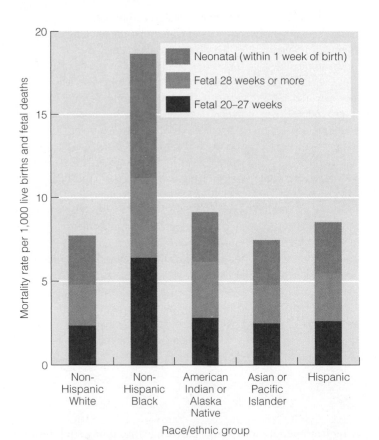

■ **Figure 4.12** Fetal and neonatal mortality rates by race/ethnicity of mother. What factors might contribute to the markedly higher mortality rates for black infants (and fetuses)?

SOURCE: Adapted from Figures 5 and 6 (p. 6) in MacDorman, M. F., Kirmeyer, S. E., & Wilson, E. C. (2012). Fetal and perinatal mortality, United States, 2006. *National Vital Statistics Reports*, 60(8).

serious car accident, for example, or the unexpected death of a loved one). Being pregnant does not make stress disappear; indeed, for some women with unintended or mistimed pregnancies, pregnancy may increase stress levels. How might the fetus be affected by the mother's experience of stress?

When a woman becomes emotionally aroused, her glands secrete powerful hormones such as adrenaline (also called epinephrine) that may cross the placental barrier and enter the fetus's bloodstream. At the least, these hormones temporarily increase the fetus's motor activity. A temporarily stressful experience such as falling or receiving a scare will generally not damage mother or fetus. Typically, it is only when a mother experiences *prolonged and severe* emotional stress and anxiety during her pregnancy (as a result, for example, of the death of her husband, chronic illness of another child, or unemployment) that long-lasting damage may be done (Borders et al., 2007; Hansen, Lou, & Olsen, 2001). The most immediate effects on the fetus are a faster and more irregular heart rate and stunted prenatal growth, which can lower birth weight, cause premature birth, and lead to birth complications (Berkowitz et al., 2003). Following birth, babies whose mothers had been highly stressed during pregnancy tend to be smaller, more active, more irritable, and more prone to crying than other babies (de Weerth, van Hees, & Buitelaar, 2003; Wurmser et al., 2006). They may experience delays in cognitive development and exhibit greater fearfulness as young children (Bergman et al., 2007; Laplante et al., 2008). Finally, severe maternal stress during the first trimester has been linked to the increased likelihood of developing *schizophrenia*, a serious mental disorder whose symptoms typically emerge in adolescence or early adulthood (Barouki et al., 2012; Susser et al., 2008). Still, it is clear that not all stressed mothers have babies who are small and arrive early. The outcomes may depend on the effect that the stressful event has on the woman's daily life. If the event significantly disrupts daily life, child outcomes may be worse than if the mother's daily life is affected very little by the event.

How might maternal stress stunt fetal growth and contribute to the offspring's irritability and anxiety? Likely through fetal programming involving epigenetic effects of the environment on gene expression, as discussed earlier (Gudsnuk & Champagne, 2011). Prenatal exposure to maternal stress hormones may program the developing fetal nervous system in such a way as to alter the postnatal stress response (Davis et al., 2011). Stress elevates levels of maternal cortisol, which crosses the placenta and influences, or sensitizes, developing fetal "stress" receptors in the brain. After birth, when the infant is exposed to stressful events, their prenatally sensitized nervous system is more reactive, leading to poor stress regulation. This prenatal environmental influence does not rule out that there might also be a genetic component to infant stress response. But children who are conceived through IVF and genetically unrelated to the mother also show this connection between prenatal stress and their stress response (Rice et al., 2010). Stress and anxiety are not the only maternal emotional states to consider. Maternal depression during pregnancy may contribute to motor delays in newborns and influence their temperament (Davis et al., 2007; Lundy et al., 1999). Depression affects levels of neurotransmitters (brain chemicals) in both mothers and their newborns.

Nutritional Condition

At the turn of the last century, doctors advised mothers to gain a mere 10–15 pounds while pregnant. With better understanding of nutrition and pregnancy, most doctors now recommend a well-balanced diet with about 300 additional calories per day, and a total weight gain of 25–35 pounds for normal-weight women. Healthy eating, including consuming lots of milk and leafy green vegetables, during pregnancy reduces the risk of having low-birth-weight babies (McCowan & Horgan, 2009). Doctors know that inadequate prenatal nutrition and lack of weight gain can be harmful. It is perhaps surprising, then, that fewer than half of pregnant women report that their practitioner talked to them about weight guidelines (Phelan et al., 2011). Just over half of women receive advice about diet and exercise during pregnancy (Brown & Avery, 2012). Clearly, then, there is room for improvement here as the consequences can be significant.

Severe maternal malnutrition, which occurs during famine, stunts prenatal growth and produces small, underweight babies (Barouki et al., 2012). The effects of malnutrition depend on when it occurs. During the first trimester, malnutrition can disrupt the formation of the spinal cord, result in fewer brain cells, and even cause stillbirth. Restrictive dieting, use of diuretics, and disordered eating behaviors during the first trimester can also cause serious problems, such as neural tube defects (Carmichael et al., 2003). During the third trimester, malnutrition is most likely to result in smaller neurons, a smaller brain, and a smaller child overall.

The offspring of malnourished mothers sometimes show cognitive deficits as infants and children. Through fetal programming, poor prenatal nutrition may also put some children at risk for certain diseases in adulthood, including hypertension, coronary heart disease, diabetes, and even the serious mental disorder schizophrenia (Barouki et al., 2012; Susser, St. Clair, & He, 2008). But let's be clear: There may be latent effects of prenatal malnutrition on some children and adults, but because of the complicated interplay of genetics, epigenetics, and environment, other children and adults will show no apparent ill effects.

Among women who are adequately nourished, it is even more difficult to establish a connection between specific nutrients and birth outcome or later behaviors (Langley-Evans & Langley-Evans, 2003; Mathews, Youngman, & Neil, 2004). One exception to this is a deficiency of folate, which, as mentioned earlier, has been linked to neural tube defects. In the mid-1990's, the United States and Canada initiated mandatory folate enrichment of cereal products in an effort to increase folate levels of women of childbearing age. These fortification programs have been associated with a decrease in the incidence of neural tube defects such as spina bifida. Although such fortification programs help, it may still be difficult to consume the "perfect" combination of foods to provide the full measure of recommended vitamins and minerals. Consequently, most health-care professionals prescribe prenatal vitamins for their pregnant patients.

Just as maternal malnutrition can lead to developmental issues, so too can maternal conditions leading to overnutrition.

Maternal obesity, as well as excessive weight gain during pregnancy, is associated with offspring obesity and diabetes (Barouki et al., 2012). And we now have evidence from research with animals that paternal obesity is also associated with offspring obesity and diabetes. In Chapter 3, we described some research with male rats that became overweight from being fed a high fat diet. This caused epigenetic changes in their sperm, which led to increased rates of obesity and diabetes when passed on to female offspring, even when the daughters—and their mothers—ate healthy diets (Ng et al., 2010). Prenatal environmental conditions as well as preconception conditions of the parents help to build the architecture of the developing fetus and set the stage for how its body will react and respond to events postnatally. Still, much depends on whether a child receives an adequate diet and good care after birth. Best, of course, is appropriate nourishment before conception for the parents, as well as good nutrition before *and* after birth for the offspring.

Now that we have had a chance to review the major teratogens that affect development during the prenatal period, go to **Engagement Box 4.1** to check your understanding of this material.

The Father's State

Does the father's state have any influence on the quality of the prenatal environment or the outcome of a pregnancy? Unfortunately, there is not a lot of research on the father's contributions to prenatal development beyond his genetic contribution. But researchers know that the father's age, just like the mother's age, can influence development. We noted earlier that teenagers and women older than 35 are at greater risk of miscarriage than women in their 20s and 30s. Similarly, the odds of miscarriage increase with paternal age and are approximately twice the rate when fathers are in their 40s or 50s than when they are in their 20s or 30s (Belloc et al., 2008; Frattarelli et al., 2008). The risk of birth complications is greater for teenage fathers, independent of any risk contributed by the mother's age (Chen et al., 2008). In addition, there is an elevated risk of congenital heart defects, neural tube defects, and kidney problems among children born to older fathers (McIntosh, Olshan, & Baird, 1995; Olshan, Schnitzer, & Baird, 1994). Like the risk of miscarriage, the odds of Down syndrome and genetic conditions caused by mutations are greater when both mother and father are older (Fisch et al., 2003; and see Chapter 3). Finally, researchers have consistently identified advanced paternal age (that is, 50 and older) as a risk factor for schizophrenia (see Chapter 3; Crystal et al., 2011).

A father's exposure to environmental toxins can also affect a couple's children. A father's prolonged exposure to radiation, anesthetic gases used in operating rooms, pesticides, or other environmental toxins can damage the genetic material in his sperm and cause genetic defects in his children (Stone, 1992; Strigini et al., 1990). We pointed out the adverse effects of maternal smoking. Paternal smoking also has an adverse effect that is independent of mother's smoking (Langley et al., 2012). In short, fathers, like mothers, should assess and, if need be, change their lifestyles and exposure to risk factors to optimize their chances of a healthy child.

Engagement 4.1

Understanding Effects of Teratogens

Check your understanding of how teratogens can influence the health and development of an unborn child by answering the following true–false questions.

___ 1.	Most teratogens have their most devastating effects during the third trimester.

___ 2.	Women should monitor their fish consumption during pregnancy.

___ 3.	The fetus is protected from most environmental insults once it has fully implanted in the uterus and the umbilical cord has been completely established.

___ 4.	Women who drink alcohol at any time during pregnancy will give birth to a baby with fetal alcohol syndrome.

___ 5.	A woman's age and race/ethnicity affect the odds of a healthy pregnancy.

Answers: 1. F (The most serious problems occur during the first trimester when most major organs are forming.) 2. T (Some fish, such as swordfish, can contain high levels of the heavy metal mercury and should be avoided or eaten in small quantities.) 3. F (The umbilical cord is not a very good filter for many harmful substances. Carbon monoxide from cigarette smoke, for example, is actually "allowed" to cross the placenta before oxygen.) 4. F (Although FAS is a possibility, there are many variables that determine how an individual child will fare if exposed prenatally to alcohol. Certainly, the dosage generalization is important here: The more alcohol a woman drinks during pregnancy, the more likely it is that her child will have FAS or precursors to full-blown FAS.) 5. T (Women between the ages of 20 and 35 have the lowest rates of fetal mortality. Non-Hispanic black women have some of the highest rates of fetal mortality and premature labor.)

▶ Checking Mastery

1.	What principles can help us understand the effects of teratogens?

2.	What have researchers learned about the effects on the child of alcohol consumption during pregnancy?

3.	What effects are likely to be seen among babies born to mothers who smoked throughout their pregnancies?

▶ Making Connections

1.	Consider Serena, whose story was summarized at the start of the chapter. What disadvantages might her child face, given Serena's lack of awareness of her pregnancy for the first 4–5 months?

2.	A close friend of yours has just gotten a positive reading on a home pregnancy test. What information would you give her about her activities during pregnancy and the potential impact of these on the development and health of her child?

4.3 The Perinatal Environment

LEARNING OBJECTIVES:

• Examine current childbirth practices and analyze the effects of various interventions on neonatal outcomes.

• Compare cultural practices surrounding labor, delivery, and neonatal life and predict how these differences might affect later child development.

The **perinatal environment** is the environment surrounding birth; it includes influences such as drugs given to the mother during labor, delivery practices, and the social environment shortly after birth. Like the prenatal environment, the perinatal environment can greatly affect human development.

In most Western cultures, a dramatic shift in birthing practices occurred during the 20th century. In 1930, 8 out of 10 births took place at home; by 1990, this figure had plummeted to just 1 out of 100 births before creeping back up in the past decade to 1 in 90 births (MacDorman, Mathews, & Declercq, 2012). This change in birth setting was accompanied by a shift from thinking about birth as a natural family event that occurred at home to thinking about it as a medical problem to be solved with high technology (Cassidy, 2006). In most cases, doctors assumed full authority for decisions regarding delivery.

Despite the continued medical setting of most births today, many couples want to give birth in a situation that combines the security of modern technology with a comfortable homelike feeling. Many hospitals have responded by restructuring their labor and delivery rooms and practices to give parents greater flexibility and control when it comes time to deliver. Today's parents are also pushing for greater voice in their delivery experiences

(Carmichael, 2004). Mothers-to-be have several choices when it comes to who will assist with their delivery, including family physicians, obstetricians, specialists in maternal–fetal medicine, and midwives. For high-risk pregnancies associated with delivery complications, a maternal–fetal specialist, or **perinatologist**, is recommended. However, for the majority of women, personal preference can determine the best caregiver for pregnancy and delivery. In many countries, such as England and France, midwives have been the traditional pregnancy caregivers. For the past century, most (around 90%) women in the United States have relied on physicians or obstetricians for pregnancy care, but the use of midwives is slowly increasing, from 4% in 1990 to 8% more recently (Declercq, 2012). In general, midwives view pregnancy and delivery as natural life events rather than as medical events requiring medical intervention. They partner with the laboring mother-to-be to assist her with delivery but do not dictate the conditions of labor and delivery.

Another change in the delivery room is the presence of a spouse, partner, mother, sister, and/or friend to provide support and share in the miracle of birth. Most women find the support provided by this familiar person helpful and reassuring. Some women have the support of a *doula*—an individual trained to provide continuous physical and emotional support throughout the childbirth process. Such support tends to shorten labor by as much as half and to reduce the need for pain medication and assisted delivery such as use of forceps or vacuum (Hodnett et al., 2012). The rate of cesarean sections is lower among women continuously supported by a doula or midwife (Dickinson et al., 2002). Mothers with continuous labor support also report more positive feelings about the birth experience, fewer symptoms of postnatal depression, and greater likelihood of breastfeeding than nonsupported mothers (Scott, Klaus, & Klaus, 1999). Clearly, then, the social context surrounding labor and delivery is important: Women who receive more support during childbirth have more positive experiences.

Childbirth is a three-stage process (■ **Figure 4.13**). The first stage of labor begins as the mother experiences regular contractions of the uterus and ends when her cervix has fully dilated (widened) so that the fetus's head can pass through. This stage of labor lasts an average of 9 hours for firstborn children and 4–6 hours for later-born children, but it may last longer (or shorter) depending on the individual and her circumstances (Albers, 1999; Jones & Larson, 2003). It ends when the cervix has dilated to 10 centimeters. The second stage of labor is delivery, which begins as the fetus's head passes through the cervix into the vagina and ends when the baby emerges from the mother's body. This is when the mother is often told to "bear down" (push) with each contraction to assist her baby through the birth canal. For first deliveries, this stage takes about 1 hour; for later deliveries, it can be 15–20 minutes (Albers, 1999; Jones &

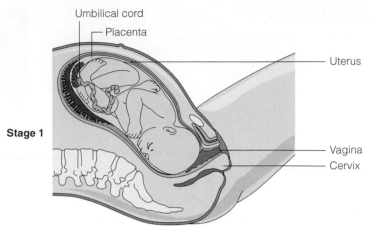

Stage 1

(A) Contractions occur and the cervix opens (dilates)

Stage 2

(B) After the head appears (crowns), the baby passes through the vagina

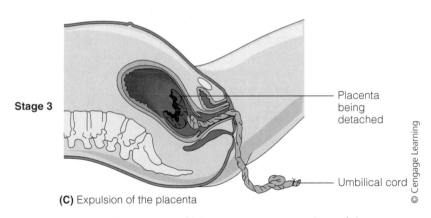

Stage 3

(C) Expulsion of the placenta

© Cengage Learning

■ **Figure 4.13** The three stages of labor. Stage 1: Contractions of the uterus cause dilation of the cervix. Stage 2: The mother pushes with each contraction, forcing the baby down the birth canal, and the head appears, followed by the shoulders and then the rest of the baby's body. Stage 3: With a few final pushes, the placenta is delivered.

Larson, 2003). Finally, the third stage of the birth process is the delivery of the placenta, which lasts only a few minutes.

When the birth process is completed, the mother (and often the father, if he is present) is typically physically exhausted, relieved to be through the ordeal of giving birth, and exhilarated all at once. Meanwhile, the fetus has been thrust from its carefree but cramped existence into a strange new world.

Possible Hazards

In most births the entire process goes smoothly, and parents and newborn quickly begin their relationship. Occasionally, however, problems arise.

Anoxia

One clear hazard during the birth process is **anoxia**, or oxygen shortage (also called *asphyxia*). Anoxia can occur for any number of reasons—for example, because the umbilical cord becomes pinched or tangled during birth, because sedatives given to the mother reach the fetus and interfere with the baby's breathing, because mucus lodged in the baby's throat prevents normal breathing, or because the baby is in a **breech presentation** (feet or buttocks first) during a vaginal delivery. If identified in advance, fetuses in breech position can be safely delivered by cesarean section to avoid possible anoxia that may occur with a vaginal delivery. Anoxia is dangerous primarily because brain cells die if they are starved of oxygen for more than a few minutes. Severe anoxia can initially cause poor reflexes, seizures, heart rate irregularities, and breathing difficulties. In the long run, severe anoxia can lead to memory impairment or **cerebral palsy**, a neurological disability primarily associated with difficulty controlling muscle movements; it also increases the risk of learning or intellectual disabilities and speech difficulties (Fehlings, Hunt, & Rosenbaum, 2007). Milder anoxia makes some infants irritable at birth or delays their motor and cognitive development but usually does not lead to permanent problems.

Fetal monitoring procedures during labor and delivery can alert caregivers to the possibility of anoxia and allow them to take preventive measures. For example, a vaginal delivery is nearly impossible for the 1 fetus in 100 that is found lying sideways in the uterus. The fetus must be turned to assume a head-down position or be delivered by **Cesarean section**, a surgical procedure in which an incision is made in the mother's abdomen and uterus so that the baby can be removed. Now, consider the potential hazards associated with delivery procedures and technologies.

Complicated Delivery

In some cases, mothers may need assistance with delivery, possibly because labor has proceeded too long with too little to show for it or because of concern about the well-being of the baby or mother. For years, doctors frequently used forceps (an instrument resembling an oversized pair of salad tongs) to assist with a vaginal delivery (see ■ **Figure 4.14**). However, forceps on the soft skull of the newborn occasionally caused serious problems, including cranial bleeding and brain damage. Alternatively, doctors may use vacuum extraction ("suction") to assist difficult deliveries. This procedure has fewer risks associated with it, although it is not risk free. In a vacuum extraction, a cup is inserted through the opening of the birth canal and attached to the baby's head. Suction is applied to make the cup adhere to the baby's scalp; during each contraction and with the mother bearing down, the doctor uses the traction created by the suction to help deliver the baby.

From the mother's point of view, vacuum extraction is less painful than forceps because the vacuum extractor takes up less space in the birth canal (and therefore is felt less) than forceps (Shekhar, Rana, & Jaswal, 2012). For the baby, however, there is likely to be

■ **Figure 4.14** Sometimes, a vaginal delivery needs to be assisted by either a vacuum extractor (top) or forceps (bottom).

swelling of the scalp and some marking where the vacuum cup was attached. Bleeding under the scalp is also possible, which may lead to a condition called jaundice. More serious injuries are possible if the vacuum is not properly used (Schot et al., 2012). Thus, relative to forceps, vacuum extraction may be less traumatic for the mother but more traumatic for the infant. This illustrates the complexity of perinatal issues that need to be considered to ensure a safe outcome for both mother and infant.

Cesarean sections, too, have been controversial. Use of this alternative to normal vaginal delivery has prevented the death of many babies—for example, when the baby is too large or the mother is too small to permit normal delivery, when a fetus out of position cannot be repositioned, when the placenta prematurely separates from the uterus, or when fetal monitoring reveals that a birth complication is likely. Still, overall rates of fetal/neonatal death have not improved with all these Cesareans (Blanchette, 2011). Medical advances have made Cesarean sections about as safe as vaginal deliveries, and few ill effects on mothers and infants have been observed. But mothers who have "C-sections" do take longer to recover from the birth process, are sometimes less positive toward and involved with their babies, and less often breast-feed their newborns (DiMatteo et al., 1996; Prior et al., 2012; Swain et al., 2008). Nonetheless, the development of babies born by cesarean appears to be perfectly normal and early observed differences in mother–infant interaction disappear by 6 months (Durik, Hyde, & Clark, 2000).

Many observers have questioned why cesarean deliveries have become so much more common—to the point that they accounted for 32% of births in the United States in 2008 (Hamilton et al., 2011). By one estimate, 11% of first-time cesarean sections are unnecessary and 65% of second-time cesareans are unnecessary (Kabir et al., 2005). Some obstetricians readily opt for C-section deliveries because it protects them from the costly malpractice suits that might arise from complications in vaginal deliveries (Childbirth Connection, 2012). C-sections also generate more revenue for physicians and medical practices than vaginal deliveries (Grant, 2009). Contributing to the high rate of C-sections is the strong likelihood (90%) for women who have had one C-section to deliver subsequent babies by C-section rather than attempting a vaginal delivery (Menacker, MacDorman, & Declercq, 2010). Although there is a very small risk of complications with a vaginal delivery following a C-section, it is safe for the large majority of women and having multiple C-sections carries its own set of risks (Blanchette, 2011). Finally, the high rate of C-section deliveries also reflects the fact that some mothers—and their doctors—prefer having a scheduled birth rather than contending with an unscheduled vaginal delivery (Fuglenes et al., 2012). In one study, 55% of repeat C-sections were elective, not medically necessary (Tita et al., 2009). In some instances, anxiety about a vaginal delivery may lead mothers-to-be to lobby for a C-section delivery (Ramvi & Tangerud, 2011). But mothers and their doctors need to be careful of the timing of elective C-sections. When nonemergency C-sections are performed at 38 weeks rather than 39 weeks, infants can experience greater respiratory complications (Blanchette, 2011; Tita et al., 2009). On the other side of this picture, C-sections performed at 41 or more weeks are also associated with complications, including risk of stillbirth. Thus, there is a fairly narrow window at 39–40 weeks when elective C-sections should be performed to optimize outcomes. Interestingly, mothers who undergo planned (as opposed to emergency) C-sections rate the birth experience more positively than any other group, including those who deliver vaginally (Blomquist et al., 2011).

Medications

Some of us were delivered in an era when mothers were routinely drugged into unconsciousness during delivery so that they would not experience any pain, or if they did, they wouldn't remember it. Not surprisingly, concerns have been raised about medications given to mothers during the birth process—analgesics and anesthetics to reduce their pain, sedatives to relax them, and stimulants to induce or intensify uterine contractions. Sedative drugs that act on the entire body cross the placenta and can affect the baby. Babies whose mothers receive large doses of sedative medications during delivery are generally sluggish and irritable, are difficult to feed or cuddle during the first few days of life, and smile infrequently (Elbourne & Wiseman, 2000). In short, they act as though they are drugged. Think about it: Doses of medication large enough to affect mothers can have much greater effects on newborns who weigh only 7 pounds and have immature circulatory and excretory systems that cannot get rid of drugs for days.

Regional analgesics, such as epidurals and spinal blocks, reduce sensation in specific parts of the body. Because they do not cross the placenta, they have fewer ill effects on babies and are preferred by many physicians over sedative drugs that *do* cross the placenta. Epidurals are also rated by mothers as more effective for pain control than other forms of analgesics (Anim-Soumuah, Smyth, & Jones, 2011). But with these advantages, mothers and physicians must weigh disadvantages: Women who have an epidural may obtain some pain relief but in doing so, they tend to lengthen their labor, and this leads to increased likelihood of needing instrumental assistance—forceps or vacuum extraction (Anim-Soumuah et al., 2011; Hasegawa et al., 2012). Alternative methods for controlling pain, such as systematic relaxation techniques, can be successful, but are not regularly offered and require more time from someone trained in these techniques than administering medication for pain control (Smith et al., 2011).

One of the most commonly used drugs is **oxytocin** (brand name Pitocin), a hormone released by the pituitary gland that can initiate and speed up contractions—moving labor along more quickly. Oxytocin may be administered if a woman's labor seems to have stalled or if she is beyond her due date or the amniotic sac has broken without contractions. The body naturally produces low levels of oxytocin throughout pregnancy, and administering synthetic oxytocin to assist delivery is considered very safe. In Chapter 14, we'll examine some of the other functions of oxytocin, which some have dubbed the "love hormone."

In sum, taking obstetric medications is not as risky a business today as it once was, but it is still a decision that requires the pros and cons to be weighed carefully. The effects depend on which drug is used, how much is taken, when it is taken, and by which mother.

Possible hazards during birth, then, include anoxia; breech presentation; the need for assisted delivery through forceps, vacuum extraction, or cesarean section; and the use of medications for pain relief or to speed up labor. Fortunately, most deliveries, although unique from the parents' perspective, are routine from a clinical perspective. In the next section, we consider the birth experience from a family perspective.

This woman chose to give birth in water, an experience that has been associated with increased feelings of relaxation and decreased pain. Water births can occur at home or in a birth center and even a hospital. While embraced by some, others express concerns about whether this is as safe as a non-water birth for the baby.

The Mother's Experience

What is it really like to give birth to a child? For every woman who has given birth, you are likely to hear a unique birth story. Most mothers admit that they experienced severe pain and a good deal of anxiety, including feelings of outright panic (Waldenström et al., 1996). Yet most also emerged from the delivery room feeling good about their achievement and their ability to cope ("I did it!"). Overall, 77% felt the experience was positive and only 10% said it was negative. And, despite longer labors and more medication, first-time mothers did not perceive labor and delivery much differently than experienced mothers did.

What factors influence a mother's experience of birth? Psychological factors such as the mother's attitude toward her pregnancy, her knowledge and expectations about the birth process, her sense of control over childbirth, and the social support she receives from her partner or someone else are important determinants of her experience of delivery and of her new baby (Waldenström et al., 1996; Wilcock, Kobayashi, & Murray, 1997). Social support can be especially important. When the father, or another supportive person whose main role is to comfort the mother, is continuously present during labor and delivery, women experience less pain, use less medication, are less likely to have cesarean sections, and are more likely to feel good about the birth process (Hodnett & Osborn, 1989; Kennell et al., 1991).

Cultural Factors

The experience of childbearing is shaped by the cultural context in which it occurs. For example, different cultures have different views of the desirability of having children. Many Islamic cultures favor large families, believing that children are a gift and blessing. In contrast, the People's Republic of China promotes a "one-child policy" to discourage multiple childbearing in hopes of slowing population growth and raising the standard of living. As a result of this policy, the average number of children a Chinese woman bears dropped from nearly five children in 1970 to fewer than two in recent years. The ratio of boys to girls has also changed; many parents want their one child to be a boy who can support them in old age and therefore abort female fetuses identified through ultrasound tests or abandon their female babies after they are born (Fitzpatrick, 2009). China's one-child policy has been harshly criticized, but although some recent news reports suggest that the government may transition to a two-child policy, there is no solid evidence of when, or whether, this will happen (see, for example, Wong, 2012).

Practices surrounding birth also differ widely. Consider three different birth scenarios that reflect different cultural beliefs about pregnancy and delivery. Among the Pokot people of Kenya, there is strong social support of the mother-to-be (O'Dempsey, 1988). The community celebrates the coming birth, and the father-to-be stops hunting lest he be killed by animals. As a result, he is available to support his wife. A midwife, aided by female relatives, delivers the baby. The placenta is buried in the goat enclosure, and the baby is washed in cold water and given a mixture of hot ash and boiled herbs so that it will vomit the amniotic fluid it has swallowed. Mothers are given plenty of time to recover. They go into seclusion for 1 month and devote themselves entirely to their babies for 3 months.

By contrast, in Uttar Pradesh in northern India, the blood associated with childbirth is viewed as polluting, and the whole event as shameful (Jeffery & Jeffery, 1993). A *dai*, a poorly paid attendant hired by the woman's mother-in-law, delivers the baby. The *dai* typically hates her menial, disgusting job, provides no pain relievers, discourages the mother from crying out in pain, and offers little emotional support. The mother is kept in the house for several days and in the family compound for weeks so that she will not pollute others. Because the baby is also believed to be polluted, its hair is shaved off.

Finally, among the !Kung San of Namibia, women typically labor by themselves (Cassidy, 2006). Giving birth alone is considered to be a strength. When labor begins, the !Kung woman goes off on her own and is expected to labor quietly. To do otherwise is considered a sign of weakness and possibly shows indifference toward the baby.

In contrast to these examples, childbirth in highly industrialized Western societies is highly "medicalized," with women hospitalized, hooked up to monitors, and separated from most friends and family members. Should we return to more traditional ways of birthing that view delivery less like a major medical event and more like a natural life event? As the Indian example illustrates, not all "traditional" practices would be viewed as in the best interests of parents and babies. Also, Western societies do a far better job than developing countries of preventing mother and infant mortality. In some areas of sub-Saharan Africa, for example, 10–12% of babies die during childbirth or in the first year of life (CIA, 2012). In Western, industrial societies, infant mortality rates have dropped over the past 50 years from 3% (30 infants out of 1,000) to less than 0.5% (4–5 infants out of 1,000) (CIA, 2012). Unfortunately, infant mortality is more than twice as high for black infants as

This Peruvian woman gives birth in an upright position, which reduces labor and delivery time by allowing gravity to assist with moving the baby down the birth canal. In societies that have medicalized childbirth, women are more likely to be lying horizontal on a bed, which may sound comfortable but is not the optimal laboring or birthing position.

© Mariana Bazo/Reuters/Corbis

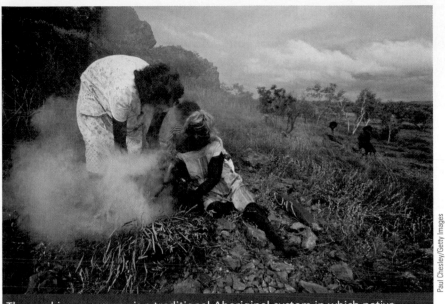

Paul Chesley/Getty Images

The smoking ceremony is a traditional Aboriginal custom in which native leaves are lit and the mother and newborn passed through the smoke as a way of promoting physical and spiritual health.

for white infants (MacDorman & Mathews, 2008). The secret to a more optimal birth experience may be to blend beneficial traditional practices such as offering emotional support to new mothers with modern medical know-how.

In addition to different cultural influences on childbirth practices, cultural beliefs influence behaviors during the postpartum period. In some cultures, women's activities and interactions with others are restricted for a period of time following childbirth (Eberhard-Gran et al., 2010). Depending on the culture, this practice may be to protect a mother and her newborn from "evil forces" or from the wind and cold, or it may be associated with fears that childbirth and the new mother are somehow unclean. Many postnatal differences across cultures have shrunk over the past several decades, although they have not entirely disappeared. In Western countries such as the United States and Canada, new mothers and their newborns might get a few days to a week respite from the hustle and bustle of daily living, but probably do not spend 40 days in isolation while other family or community members cover the chores needed to run a household (Eberhard-Gran et al., 2010).

Postpartum Depression

Some new mothers suffer from depression following the birth of their baby. Many new mothers report feeling tearful, irritable, moody, anxious, and depressed within the first few days after birth. This condition—the baby blues—is relatively mild, passes quickly, and is probably linked to the steep drops in levels of female hormones that normally occur after delivery and to the stresses associated with delivering a child and taking on the responsibilities of parenthood (not to mention coping with the lack of sleep experienced by many new mothers). Indeed, it may be difficult to find a new mother who does not experience at least some degree of moodiness or baby blues in the week following delivery.

A second, and far more serious, condition is **postpartum depression**—an episode of clinical depression lasting 2 or more weeks (rather than days) in a woman who has just given birth. It affects approximately 15% of new mothers according to a review of 28 studies (Gavin et al., 2005). Only rarely does a woman who has never had significant emotional problems become clinically depressed for the first time after giving birth. Most affected women have histories of depression, and many were depressed during pregnancy. Also, women vulnerable to depression are more likely to become depressed if they are experiencing other life stresses on top of the stresses of becoming a mother (Honey, Bennett, & Morgan, 2003). Lack of social support—especially a poor relationship with a partner—also increases the odds (Webster et al., 2011).

Postpartum depression has significant implications for the parent–infant relationship. One study compared the children of 58 mothers who experienced postpartum depression with the children of 42 nondepressed mothers over a 5-year period (Murray et al., 1999). The children of the depressed mothers were less securely attached to their mothers during infancy and were less responsive during interactions with their mothers at age 5. They also tended to respond negatively when another child approached them in a friendly manner. And they were more likely to have experienced depression by age 16 (Murray et al., 2011).

Mothers who had been postnatally depressed report more behavioral problems in their children. At age 11, children of postnatally depressed mothers show more violent behavior even when researchers control for family characteristics and later episodes of maternal depression (Hay et al., 2003). The violence exhibited by these children is associated with anger management problems, attention problems, and hyperactive behavior. Adolescents whose mothers had been postnatally depressed also show elevated levels of cortisol, which is associated with major depression (Halligan et al., 2004). The implication of these results is that early experiences with a depressed mother, prenatally or postnatally, might predispose these children to later depression.

How exactly might maternal depression in the weeks and months following delivery affect children's behavior and increase their odds of developing depression? Mothers who are depressed tend to be relatively unresponsive to their babies and may even feel hostility toward them. They are tired, distracted, and often lack the energy needed to be fully engaged with their infants. Even though mothers typically recover from postnatal depression, research suggests that their early attitudes about their babies and the resulting pattern of early mother–child interactions set the stage for ongoing interaction problems that affect the child's behavior (Murray, Halligan, & Cooper, 2010; Weinberg et al., 2006). The contributions of genes inherited from their depression-prone mothers, fetal programming from exposure to the prenatal chemistry of their mothers, and poor quality of the postnatal mother–child relationship can combine to precipitate depression or other problems in the child (Field, 2011). Thus, for their own sakes and for the sakes of their infants, mothers experiencing more than a mild case of the baby blues should seek professional help in overcoming their depression.

The Father's Experience

When birthing moved into hospitals, the medical establishment aggressively prohibited fathers from participating in their children's birth on the grounds that they would contaminate the sterile environment needed for a safe birth (Cassidy, 2006). It would take many decades, many lawsuits, and more progressive views about birth support before men were routinely accepted—and expected—in the delivery room. Today, many men prepare for fatherhood before delivery, attend prenatal classes with their partner, and are present for their child's birth. Fathers report that they want to be involved with their partner's pregnancy, although they don't always know how to make this happen (Draper, 2002).

Like mothers, fathers experience the process of becoming a parent as a significant event in their lives that involves a mix of positive and negative emotions. Also like mothers, fathers tend to be anxious during pregnancy and birth and some even experience some of the same physiological symptoms as their pregnant partner. These symptoms, called **couvade** (from the French word meaning "to hatch"), include bloating, weight gain, fatigue, insomnia, and nausea (Cassidy, 2006). And before you conclude that these symptoms must be "all in their heads," consider that some research shows hormonal shifts among expectant fathers that are similar to the hormonal shifts experienced by pregnant women (Cassidy, 2006).

As for the labor and delivery period, new fathers report feeling scared, unprepared, helpless, and frustrated (Chandler & Field, 1997; Chapman, 2000; Hallgren et al., 1999). They find labor to be more work than they had expected and sometimes

feel excluded as the medical professionals take over. For most men, attending prenatal classes with their partner improves their experience of childbirth, although for a few men the added knowledge that comes with these classes increases their anxiety (Greenhalgh, Slade, & Spiby, 2000). Stress levels among men tend to be highest during their partner's pregnancy and then decrease after the birth of the baby. Despite the stresses, negative emotions usually give way to relief, pride, and joy when the baby finally arrives (Chandler & Field, 1997). Those fathers present for delivery who cut their newborns umbilical cord are found to have greater emotional connection to their infants at 1 month (Brandão & Figueiredo, 2011). This doesn't mean that all fathers-to-be need to reach for the scissors and cut the umbilical cord, though; there are many other opportunities to develop a strong emotional connection between father and infant.

Checking Mastery

1. What steps occur during the process of childbirth?
2. What risks does the baby potentially face during the birth process?

Making Connections

1. Considering the research on birth and the perinatal environment, arrange the perfect birth experience for you and your baby and justify its features. Where would you be, who would be with you, and what would be done?
2. Some experts worry that cesarean sections are overused. What do you think? Should a woman be able to choose whether she delivers vaginally or by cesarean section? Should hospitals be permitted to force a woman to deliver by cesarean if they believe the fetus is in danger?

4.4 The Neonatal Environment

LEARNING OBJECTIVES:

* Compare and contrast breast- and bottle-feeding, offering pros and cons of both practices.
* Explain how we can optimize the development of at-risk newborns.

So now that parents have a baby, what do they do? Here we will look at the **neonatal** environment—the events of the first month and how parents might optimize the development of young infants.

There are marked differences in how parents interact with their newborns. As Meredith Small (1999) characterizes it, "Our ideas about parenting and infant care are as culturally constructed as what we wear, what we eat, or how we dance" (p. 41). For example, in societies where infant mortality is high, babies may not even be named or viewed as people until they seem likely to survive (Nsamenang, 1992). The Beng, who are concentrated in small farming towns along the Ivory Coast, believe that newborns are not entirely in this world but exist in the world the babies will eventually inhabit after death (Gottlieb, 2000). Once their umbilical cord

stump falls off on the fourth or fifth day of life, they begin to inhabit this world but still vacillate between the two worlds for another 4–5 years. During this time, the Beng regard their children as vulnerable. Spiritual beliefs influence their child care practices, leading, for example, to twice-daily enemas for infants using a chili pepper solution.

In Central Africa, babies born to forager families are carried upright in slings during the day and sleep in the same bed with their mothers at night. They are touched more than 70% of daytime hours, are breast-fed whenever they want (usually 20–40 times per day), and may not be weaned until the age of 4 (Fouts, Hewlett, & Lamb, 2012). Infants in such societies are indulged considerably, at least until their survival is assured. In contrast, babies born to farming

Welcome to the world, little one! Your journey over the past 9 months has been astonishing. At conception, you received all the genetic material necessary to develop into the baby that we now see. You have already taken your first breaths and the umbilical cord that sustained you in the womb will soon be cut. After being cleaned and wrapped up, you will begin to interact with your family and explore the world around you.

Breast or Bottle?

Over time and across cultures, feeding practices vary considerably. Without question, breast-feeding is the most natural form of nutrition for newborns. And until modern times, it was the sole source of nourishment until solid foods were introduced. For a variety of reasons, breast-feeding in the United States reached an all-time low in the early 1970s, when only 1 in 4 mothers attempted to nurse their newborn infants. Bottle-feeding with formula had become the norm (Eiger and Olds, 1999). Since then, research has shown numerous advantages of breast milk over formula and all major health organizations (for example, the American Academy of Family Physicians, Canadian Paediatric Society, National Health Service of Great Britain, WHO, and more) have advocated for exclusive breast-feeding in the first 6 months of life. As a result of public awareness campaigns regarding the advantages of breast-feeding, a majority of mothers—roughly 75%—now attempt to nurse their newborns. But only 50% are still breast-feeding after a month, and fewer than 20% are still at it by 6 months (Jones et al., 2011).

The health benefits of breast-feeding are numerous and include fewer ear infections and respiratory tract problems for children and lower risks of ovarian cancer and early breast cancer for mothers (Ip et al., 2007). In homes where a caregiver smokes cigarettes, breast-feeding offers some protection against the respiratory infections that frequently plague infants exposed to secondhand (passive) smoke (Yilmaz et al., 2009). Children who breast-feed for at least 4 months have stronger lung function, almost certainly because breast-feeding requires infants to suck stronger and longer to obtain the same amount of milk as when bottle-feeding (Ogbuanu et al., 2008). As well, breast-feeding for the first 4–6 months is associated with a handful of cognitive advances during infancy, especially among preterm babies (Quigley et al., 2012). Breast milk contains several substances that protect nursing infants from infections, and it has the perfect blend of nutrients for a quickly developing little person. For premature babies, breast milk has been referred to as "more of a medicine than a food" because of its positive effects on their immune systems and weight gain (Gross-Loh, 2006, p. 38). And mothers who breast-feed lose the weight gained during pregnancy more quickly than those who do not breast-feed following childbirth.

Given the health benefits of breast-feeding, why don't more women breast-feed? Women cite a number of reasons for not continuing with breast-feeding, ranging from their own discomfort to concerns that the infant is not getting adequate nutrition. Young women, those from low socioeconomic backgrounds, and those with less education are less likely to breast-feed than other women (Ryan & Zhou, 2006). In one survey, 95% of the mothers with the highest education started breast-feeding compared with 73% of the mothers with the least education; by 6 months of age, 39% of the more educated mothers were still breast-feeding compared with just 15% of the less educated mothers (Van Rossem et al., 2009). Being employed outside the home is also associated with lower breast-feeding rates, presumably because of the logistical problems of breast-feeding while at work (Ryan & Zhou, 2006). Finally, fewer black mothers breast-feed than white mothers (Ip et al., 2007). Interestingly, Hispanic mothers have a fairly high rate of breast-feeding until they immigrate to the United States, and then the rate decreases with the amount of

families in Central Africa are touched less often, breast-fed less often, and weaned at an earlier age than the babies in foraging families.

Infant care practices are considerably different in modern, industrialized societies where infant mortality is lower. Infants in industrialized nations like the United States are touched only 12–20% of daytime hours, and they are often trained to breast-feed or bottle-feed on a schedule, usually five to seven times a day (Hewlett, 1995). Babies may sleep in the same bed or room as their parents for just a few weeks before being settled into a crib in their own room, a practice that mothers in many other cultures, who sleep in the same bed with their babies until they are toddlers, find quite bizarre. Parents who do sleep with their babies should be mindful that babies are at increased risk of suffocation when they sleep in adult beds. Adults are obviously much larger and heavier, posing a hazard if they roll onto a baby while sleeping. Adult beds also have more bedding and pillows than an infant crib, and these can suffocate a tiny infant.

Regardless of where they live, new parents are often uncertain about how to relate to their babies and may find the period after birth stressful. Many seek information on what is "normal" behavior from their infant as well as feedback on their own behaviors as parents. To help parents appreciate their baby's competencies and feel competent themselves as parents, the Neonatal Behavioral Assessment Scale (NBAS), intended for practitioners such as pediatricians, and the Newborn Behavioral Observations (NBO) system, geared toward parents, were developed out of the pioneering work of T. Berry Brazelton (see Brazelton & Nugent, 2011; Nugent et al., 2007). Both instruments are intended to reveal infants' capabilities and readiness for the tasks they will need to navigate to survive and thrive. For instance, the NBO evaluates infants' ability to self-regulate or calm themselves as well as infants' ability to "tune out" lights and sounds so that they can sleep. The NBO is focused on helping parents form relationships with their infants by revealing the individual characteristics of their infant and profiling areas of strength and areas where greater attention might be needed.

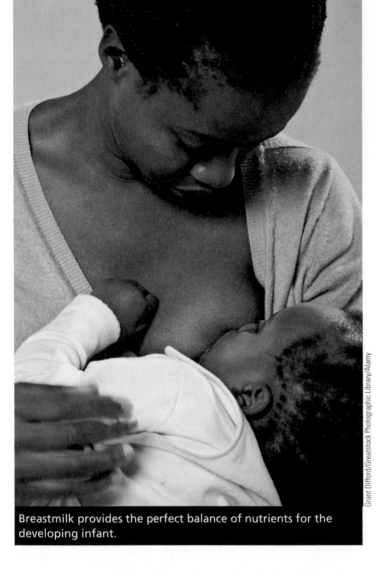
Breastmilk provides the perfect balance of nutrients for the developing infant.

However, one study found that hospitals may also inadvertently support bottle-feeding when they send new mothers home with gift packs containing formula samples (Rosenberg et al., 2008). The researchers found that mothers who went home with a gift pack containing formula were more likely to be using formula at 10 weeks postpartum than mothers who did not receive the formula in a gift pack. Despite the emphasis on breast-feeding while in the hospital, the formula in the gift pack may send the message that the hospital supports bottle-feeding and expects bottle-feeding at some point.

Identifying At-Risk Newborns

A few infants will be considered **at risk** for either short-term or long-term problems because of genetic defects, prenatal hazards, or perinatal damage. It is essential to these infants' survival and well-being that they be identified as early as possible. Newborns are routinely screened using the **Apgar test**, which provides a quick assessment of the newborn's heart rate, respiration, color, muscle tone, and reflexes (● **Table 4.7**; **Exploring Development Box 4.1**). The test has been used for more than 60 years and, despite its low-tech nature, is still considered a valuable diagnostic tool. The simple test is given immediately and 5 minutes after birth. It yields scores of 0, 1, or 2 for each of the five factors, which are then added to yield a total score that can range from 0 to 10. Infants who score 7 or higher are in good shape. Infants scoring 4 or lower are at risk—their heartbeats are sluggish or nonexistent, their muscles are limp, and their breathing is shallow and irregular, if they are breathing at all. These babies will immediately experience a different postnatal environment than the normal baby experiences because they require medical intervention in intensive care units to survive, as you will see at the end of the chapter.

Exploring Development 4.1
Birth and Apgar Assessment

Right after birth, a baby's condition is assessed according to the five-point Apgar scale.

- What characteristics does the Apgar test evaluate?
- What characteristic did this baby score poorly on?

time in the United States (Ahluwalia et al., 2012). This likely reflects U.S. cultural values toward breast-feeding, which are more ambivalent than those in many other countries. To improve breast-feeding rates, ambivalent (and in some cases, downright negative) views of breast-feeding need to be addressed so that women view breast-feeding as *the* option, not just *an* option.

Most hospitals promote breast-feeding and take time to teach new mothers successful breast-feeding techniques.

One particular group of at-risk babies that should be examined more closely are those with **low birth weight (LBW)**.

● **Table 4.7** The Apgar Test

Factors	Score		
	0	1	2
Heart Rate	Absent	Slow (<100 beats per minute)	Moderate (>100 beats per minute)
Respiratory Effort	Absent	Slow or irregular	Good; baby is crying
Muscle Tone	Flaccid; limp	Weak; some flexion	Strong; active motion
Color	Blue or pale	Body pink, extremities blue	Completely pink
Reflex Irritability	No response	Frown, grimace, or weak cry	Vigorous cry

© Cengage Learning

- **Table 4.8** Survival and Health of Premature Babies by Gestational Age

Factor	Results (in Weeks and %)			
Number of completed weeks since last menstruation	<23 weeks	23 weeks	24 weeks	25 weeks
Percentage of babies who survive	0–15%	2–35%	17–58%	35–85%
Percentage of survivors with chronic lung disease	89%	57–70%	33–89%	17–71%
Percentage of survivors with a severe neurodevelopmental disability*	69%	30%	17–45%	12–35%

*Includes cerebral palsy, mental retardation, blindness or severe myopia, and deafness.
Source: Based on data from Hack & Fanaroff, 1999.

As • **Table 4.8** illustrates, the younger (and smaller) the babies are at birth, the lower their chances of survival. Approximately 8% of babies born in the United States have LBW (less than 2,500 grams, or 5½ pounds). Some of these babies are born at term and are called "small for gestational age," but many are born preterm (less than 37 weeks of gestation) and are more at risk as a result. The survival and health of these small infants is a concern, particularly for infants who are very small (less than 1,500 grams or no more than 3.3 pounds). Prematurity is the leading cause of infant mortality. Although LBW infants account for about 8% of all births, they account for 65% of all infant deaths and nearly 60% of the money spent on pregnancies and deliveries (Callaghan et al., 2006; Schmitt, Sneed, & Phibbs, 2006). Very LBW infants are even more costly: They account for less than 1% of all births but 36% of the total hospital costs. Most fragile are the micropreemies—those weighing less than 800 grams or 1.75 pounds at birth. The high emotional and economic costs of LBW have made this an important medical and societal issue.

We don't always know what causes LBW, but research has identified a number of factors regularly associated with it. For starters, LBW is strongly linked to low socioeconomic status, probably because poor women are more likely to have poor nutrition and inadequate prenatal care (Goldenberg & Culhane, 2007; Hughes & Simpson, 1995). African American mothers are twice as likely as non-Hispanic white mothers to experience premature delivery and LBW. In addition, many other risk factors that we have already described, such as smoking and stress, are linked to LBW. And not surprisingly, the more risk factors experienced during pregnancy, the greater the likelihood of delivering a small baby (Rosenberg, 2001).

LBW is also associated with multiple births, which have increased substantially over the past several decades largely because of increased use of ovulation-stimulating drugs to treat infertility. In 1980, there were 37 higher-order multiple births (triplets or more) in every 100,000 births; by 1998, this figure had jumped to 194 higher-order multiples in every 100,000 births (Martin et al., 2005). Among single-birth infants, approximately 5% are LBW, but among twins, nearly half are LBW. Among higher-order multiples, 86% are LBW (Cohen et al., 1999). Higher-order multiples spend eight times as long in the hospital as singleton infants and cost more than six times as much in hospital costs (Henderson et al., 2004).

The good news is that most LBW babies born since the advent of neonatal intensive care in the 1960s function within the normal range of development and experience significant catch-up growth during their first months and years of life (Chyi et al., 2008; Wilson-Costello et al., 2007). However, compared with normal-birth-weight children, LBW children, especially those with extremely LBW are at greater risk for numerous neurobehavioral problems, including blindness, deafness, cerebral palsy, poor academic achievement, autism, and health problems. Many of these problems persist into childhood and adulthood for the smallest and earliest preterm babies (Aarnoudse-Moens et al., 2009; Johnson et al., 2009). Respiratory difficulties are likely because premature babies have not yet produced enough **surfactant**, a substance that prevents the air sacs of the lungs from sticking together and therefore aids breathing. Surfactant therapy for LBW infants became common practice around 1990 and seems to improve the survival rate among the sickest infants. However, it has not entirely improved health or long-term achievement scores of LBW babies in general, perhaps because small, earlier-born babies, who have the most complications, are now surviving to be among the school-age population of LBW survivors (Hagen et al., 2006; Paul et al., 2006; see also Bode et al., 2009).

In addition to the advances made thanks to the high-tech interventions now available in most neonatal intensive care units (NICUs), research has shown that several low-tech interventions can go far in improving the developmental outcomes of LBW, premature infants. For starters, these vulnerable infants benefit from their mother's breast milk even if they can't effectively nurse when they are hooked up to tubes and machines in the NICU. Mothers can pump their breast milk to provide nutrient-rich nourishment that helps boost their infant's fledgling immune system. Babies with extremely LBW who receive breast milk later score about 5 points higher on the Bayley Scale of Mental Development than similar babies who receive no breast milk (Vohr et al., 2006). And among babies receiving breast milk, there are measurable differences between those who consumed the largest quantities and those who consumed the least.

There is also evidence that skin-to-skin contact is therapeutic for these infants. Sometimes called **kangaroo care**, resting on a parent's chest helps maintain body temperature, heart rate, and oxygen levels in the blood (Conde-Agudelo, Belizán, & Diaz-Rossello, 2011) and the rhythmic sound of the parent's heartbeat calms the infant and may help simulate the environment of the womb. Premature infants who experience kangaroo care settle into more mature patterns of quiet sleep and alert wakefulness than premature infants who do not receive this treatment. And it is not only the infant who benefits: Mothers who participate in kangaroo care of their infants while in neonatal intensive care report positive feelings about the experience as long as they receive adequate education and support of the practice (Blomqvist & Nyqvist, 2010). One of the nice things about kangaroo care is that both mothers and fathers can participate. Doing so improves parents' sensitivity to their infant and makes the dynamics among the trio more positive (Feldman et al., 2003; Tessier et al., 2009).

Although modern technology permits the survival of younger and smaller babies, like this one, many experts believe we have reached the lowest limits of viability between 23 and 24 weeks of gestation. What is the long-term prognosis for premature babies?

© Annie Griffiths Belt/Corbis

In addition to skin-to-skin contact, Tiffany Field and her colleagues (Diego, Field, & Hernandez-Reif, 2005; Field, Diego, & Hernandez-Reif, 2010) have shown that premature infants benefit from massage therapy. For example, in one study, premature babies received either light or moderate massage three times per day for 5 days (Field et al., 2006). Those who received moderate-pressure massage gained significantly more weight on each of the days of the therapy than the premature babies in the light-massage group. Babies receiving moderate massage seemed to be more relaxed and less aroused, which may have facilitated greater weight gain (Field et al., 2006). In addition, the massage increased the efficiency of the digestive system, which is also associated with greater weight gain (Diego, Field, & Hernandez-Reif, 2005).

Although the long-term health prognosis for LBW babies is now good, many children born with an extremely LBW continue to experience neurosensory impairments and academic problems throughout their childhood and teen years (Doyle & Anderson, 2005; Saigal et al., 2007). These cognitive deficits in childhood can be traced to deficits in attention, speed, and memory evident in preterm infants during their first year (Rose et al., 2005). The fate of premature and LBW babies depends considerably on two factors. The first is their biological condition—their health and neurological status in particular. The second is the quality of the postnatal environment they experience. For instance, in a study of more than 8,000 infants, Dennis Hogan and Jennifer Park (2000) found that the disadvantages of LBW were amplified for children of minority status growing up in poverty with a single parent. In contrast, LBW babies who live with two parents and whose mother is well educated, although they start out with delays, improve and may even catch up to the average child by age 8 (Ment et al., 2003). And children born with very LBW whose mothers are consistently responsive to them throughout infancy and toddlerhood attain higher levels of cognitive achievement than similar children with less responsive mothers (Landry, Smith, & Swank, 2006). In contrast, premature infants whose mothers are "out of sync" with them exhibit less mature outcomes at age 2 (Feldman & Eidelman, 2006).

Other research shows that at-risk infants can benefit from programs that teach their parents how to provide responsive care and appropriate intellectual stimulation to them once they are home. Home visits to advise parents, combined with a stimulating day care program for LBW toddlers, can teach mothers how to be better teachers of their young children and stimulate these children's cognitive development. In an ambitious project called the Infant Health and Development Program, premature and LBW infants at eight sites have benefited from such early intervention (McCormick et al., 2006). The program involves weekly home visits during the first year of life and then biweekly home visits and attendance by the infant at a special day care center for half a day every day from age 1 to age 3. Mothers are given child care education and support.

The program appears to help parents provide a more growth-enhancing home environment—for example, to give their babies appropriate toys and learning materials and to interact with them in stimulating ways. The intervention also helped these at-risk babies, especially the heavier ones, achieve more cognitive growth by age 3 than they would otherwise have achieved. An impressive 14-point boost in IQ scores at age 3 for heavier LBW children who received the intervention had dropped to a 4-point advantage over control group children at age 8, but this small advantage was still evident at age 18 (McCarton et al., 1997; McCormick et al., 2006). Children who weighed 2,000 grams (4 pounds 6 ounces) or less at birth did not get much benefit from the program. Other research similarly shows that early intervention effects on premature infants fade over time (Johnson et al., 2005). Researchers have more to learn, then, about what it takes to keep the development of at-risk children on a

This 2 pound 10 ounce bundle is enjoying skin-to-skin contact with his mother. Such "kangaroo care" helps babies regulate body temperature and maintain a regular heart rate and oxygen levels in the blood.

Indeed it is, and researchers now have the results of major longitudinal studies that say so. For 40 years, Emmy Werner and her colleague Ruth Smith studied a group of babies born in 1955 on the island of Kauai in Hawaii (Werner, 1989a, 1989b; Werner & Smith, 1982, 1992, 2001). This was a monumental undertaking. All women of Kauai who were to give birth in 1955 were interviewed in each trimester of pregnancy, and physicians noted any prenatal, perinatal, or postnatal complications. On the basis of this information, each baby was categorized as having been exposed to severe, moderate, mild, or no prenatal or perinatal stress. At ages 1, 2, 10, 18, 32, and 40 years, researchers diligently tracked down their participants and conducted interviews (initially with the mothers and later with the children), administered psychological and cognitive tests, rated the quality of the family environment, and conducted medical examinations. Remarkably, at the 40-year follow-up, 70% (489 of 698) of the original group of babies born in 1955 still participated in the study.

One-third of the children classified as at risk showed considerable resilience, getting themselves back on a normal course of development. Through this self-righting capacity, they were able to mature into competent, successful adults with no evident learning, social, or vocational problems despite being at risk for poor outcomes. Two major findings emerge from this research:

- The effects of prenatal and perinatal complications decrease over time.
- The outcomes of early risk depend on the quality of the postnatal environment.

The postnatal environments of these successful at-risk children included two types of **protective factors**, influences that prevent the damaging effects of risk factors or help children overcome disadvantages. These are:

- *Personal resources.* Possibly because of their genetic makeup, some children have qualities such as intelligence, sociability, and communication skills that help them choose or create more nurturing and stimulating environments and cope with challenges. For example, parents and other observers noted that these children were agreeable, cheerful, and self-confident as infants, which elicited positive caregiving responses. They also believed that they were in control of their own fates—that through their actions, they could bring about positive outcomes.
- *Supportive postnatal environment.* Some at-risk children receive the social support they need within or outside the family. Most importantly, they are able to find at least one person who loves them unconditionally and with whom they feel secure.

Clearly, hazards during the important prenatal and perinatal periods can leave lasting scars, and yet many children show remarkable resilience. There seem to be some points in the life span, especially early on, in which both positive and negative environmental forces

positive track after the perinatal period comes to a close. However, everything we know about life-span environmental forces suggests that supportive parents and programs can do a great deal to optimize every child's development. It seems that premature, LBW babies can achieve normal levels of intellectual functioning during childhood when they live in middle-class homes, when their mothers are relatively educated, and most importantly, when their mothers, rich or poor, are consistently attentive and responsive when interacting with them (Landry et al., 2006).

Studies such as these raise a larger issue about the importance of early experience. Some developmentalists take seriously the concept of critical (or sensitive) periods in early development. Others stress the **resilience** of human beings, their ability to rebound from early disadvantages and to respond to environmental influences throughout their lives rather than only during so-called critical periods. Which is it?

Risk and Resilience

To what extent does harm done in the prenatal or perinatal period last, and to what extent can postnatal experiences make up for it? You have encountered many examples in this chapter of what can go wrong before or during birth. Some damaging effects are clearly irreversible: The thalidomide baby will never grow normal arms or legs, and the child with FAS will always be intellectually disabled. Yet throughout history, many children turned out fine even though their mothers—unaware of many risk factors—smoked and drank during their pregnancies, received heavy doses of medication during delivery, or experienced serious illness. So, although many factors place a fetus at risk and increase the likelihood of problems after birth, not all at-risk infants end up with problems (Fraser, 2004). Is it also possible that some babies exposed to and clearly affected by risks recover from their deficiencies later in life?

have especially strong effects. Yet *environment matters throughout life*. It would be a mistake to assume that all children who have problems at birth are doomed. In short, early experience by itself can, but rarely does, make or break development; later experience counts, too, sometimes enough to turn around a negative course of development.

Checking Mastery

1. What are two things you can do during your baby's first weeks and months of life to ensure a healthy start to life?
2. What are two factors that allow some babies to show resilience to negative events of the prenatal or perinatal periods?

Making Connections

1. Find out if your mother and grandmothers breast-fed their children, including you, and for how long. What are your thoughts on the breast-versus-bottle choice? What factors might make it more or less likely that you or your partner will breast-feed (or have breast-fed if you are already a parent)?
2. Given the high costs of low birth weight, what programs would you make part of a national effort to reduce the number of LBW babies born each year?

Chapter Summary

4.1 Prenatal Development

- Prenatal development begins with conception and proceeds through the germinal, embryonic, and fetal periods.
- Some couples experience difficulties conceiving and turn to assisted reproduction technologies to assist them with having a baby. These include drugs to stimulate the ovaries to release eggs, artificial insemination to inject sperm into a woman's uterus, and in vitro fertilization to fertilize an egg outside the womb and then insert it into a woman's uterus or fallopian tube.
- The germinal period lasts about 2 weeks. During this time, the single-celled zygote created when a sperm penetrates an egg repeatedly multiplies and travels to the uterus where it implants itself.
- The embryonic period lasts through the eighth week after conception. Every major organ takes shape during this time in a process called organogenesis. The placenta forms and connects the embryo to its mother through the umbilical cord. Major developments occur during this time, including formation and beating of the heart and the start of sexual differentiation.
- The fetal period lasts from the ninth week after conception until the end of pregnancy. The body and brain undergo much growth during this time. Neurons multiply, migrate, and differentiate into what they will finally become. The age of viability is reached at around 23–24 weeks' gestation.
- Growth during the prenatal period is faster than during any other period of the life span.

4.2 The Prenatal Environment and Fetal Programming

- The womb is an environment and can affect the embryo/fetus in positive as well as negative ways.
- Through fetal programming, prenatal conditions can alter the architecture of the fetal brain and its physiology, setting the stage for later vulnerabilities or for later resilience.
- Teratogens include diseases, drugs, or other environmental agents that can harm the developing fetus. Teratogens are most damaging to an organ during the time when the organ is developing most rapidly. In addition, the longer and stronger the exposure to a teratogen, the more likely that damage will occur

to the developing child. The genetic makeup of both mother and unborn baby influence the effect of a teratogen, as does the quality of the prenatal and postnatal environments.
- Numerous drugs—prescription, over-the-counter, and recreational—have been found to have teratogenic effects. One of the most widely used drugs—alcohol—results in a cluster of symptoms that have lifelong effects on the children who are exposed prenatally.
- Diseases such as rubella (German measles), syphilis, and AIDS can adversely affect the developing baby, as can environmental hazards such as radiation and pollution.
- Characteristics of the mother can influence the quality of the prenatal environment, including her age, emotional state, and nutritional status. Women in their 20s have the lowest rates of pregnancy and birth complications. Women who experience prolonged and severe emotional stress during pregnancy may give birth to smaller babies. Good nutrition is important throughout pregnancy and is often supplemented with vitamins and fortified foods.
- Characteristics of the father, such as his age, may also affect the baby.

4.3 The Perinatal Environment

- The perinatal environment includes delivery practices and drugs used to assist with delivery. Many births today take place in the medical setting of a hospital or birthing center.
- Childbirth is a three-stage process that begins with regular contractions of the uterus and dilation of the cervix. The second stage of labor is the actual delivery of the baby out of the woman's body. The third stage is the delivery of the placenta.
- Among the possible birth complications is anoxia, or an oxygen shortage, which may occur for a variety of reasons. Anoxia can lead to brain damage or cerebral palsy if the brain is deprived of oxygen for more than a few minutes.
- Some babies must be assisted through the birth canal with vacuum extraction or forceps. Some women undergo a cesarean section, or surgical removal of the baby. Many women in Western cultures are given medications to assist with delivery. Most common are epidural or spinal blocks to reduce pain and oxytocin to promote contractions.

- The experience of pregnancy and childbirth vary widely, across cultures as well as across women within a culture. Some women experience mild to moderate depression following childbirth. Fathers, too, often need time to adjust to the life changes that accompany becoming a parent, as do older siblings.

4.4 The Neonatal Environment

- The neonatal environment refers to the events of the first month or so after delivery. Caring for a newborn varies across cultures. Nearly all cultures promote breast-feeding as the ideal way to nourish the young infant. For a variety of reasons, some mothers bottle-feed their newborns or switch to bottle-feeding after a trial run with breast-feeding.
- Some infants are considered to be at risk for short-term or long-term problems and must receive extra care during the neonatal period. Babies born prematurely and who have low birth weight are at risk for a number of complications.
- Many at-risk babies show remarkable resilience and outgrow their problems, especially if they have personal resources, such as sociability and intelligence, and grow up in stimulating and supportive postnatal environments where someone loves them.

Checking Mastery Answers

For answers to Checking Mastery questions, please see Appendix B.

Key Terms

Infertility **93**

artificial insemination **93**

in vitro fertilization (IVF) **93**

embryologist **93**

germinal period **93**

blastocyst **93**

miscarriage **93**

embryonic period **94**

organogenesis **94**

amnion **94**

chorion **94**

placenta **94**

spina bifida **94**

anencephaly **95**

testosterone **95**

fetal period **96**

proliferation **96**

migration **96**

differentiation **97**

age of viability **98**

myelin **98**

fetal programming **100**

teratogen **101**

critical period **101**

thalidomide **101**

sudden infant death syndrome (SIDS) **103**

fetal alcohol syndrome (FAS) **104**

rubella **106**

syphilis **107**

acquired immunodeficiency syndrome (AIDS) **108**

stillbirth **110**

lamaze method **111**

perinatal environment **114**

perinatologist **115**

anoxia **116**

breech presentation **116**

cerebral palsy **116**

cesarean section **116**

oxytocin **117**

postpartum depression **119**

couvade **120**

neonatal **120**

at risk **122**

apgar test **122**

low birth weight (LBW) **122**

surfactant **123**

kangaroo care **123**

resilience **125**

protective factors **125**

CENGAGE   Get quizzes, flashcards, videos, and more at **www.cengagebrain.com**.
brain
.com

5 Body, Brain, and Health

Gary Goldfield and his colleagues from the Healthy Active Living & Obesity Research Group in Canada had 30 obese teenagers engage in light to moderate exercise on stationary bikes (Goldfield et al., 2012). After 10 weeks, perhaps the most important finding was *not* the expected change in weight or fitness levels. Instead, the intriguing outcome was that the teens showed improved psychosocial functioning; in particular, they experienced a boost in body image, social competence, and even perceived academic performance. Interviewed about the research for *Science Daily*, Goldfield noted, "If you can improve your physical activity and fitness even minimally, it can help improve your mental health. By teaching kids to focus on healthy active lifestyle behaviours, they are focusing on something they can control.... This new study is proof positive that even a modest dose of exercise is prescriptive for a mental health boost" (Children's Hospital of Eastern Ontario Research Institute, 2012).

This is just one of many examples illustrating the connections among our physical, cognitive, and socioemotional selves. In this chapter, we consider changes across the life span in body and brain and how these changes influence our physical and mental health. We begin with an overview of the major physical systems, most notably the brain and nervous system, that underlie human functioning. We also look at the reproductive system as it matures during adolescence and then changes during adulthood. Throughout, we consider factors that can interfere with health as well as those that might optimize health.

5.1 Building Blocks of Growth and Lifelong Health

LEARNING OBJECTIVES:

- Associate key processes of the endocrine and nervous systems with important aspects of growth and development.
- Describe and provide an example of each of the three major principles of growth.
- Articulate the main components of the life-span developmental model of health and the value of adopting this sort of approach to understanding health.

Our physical selves—brain, body, and all the behaviors that emerge from these—are fundamental to what we are able to do in life. A 5-year-old child is physically able to experience the world in ways markedly different from those available to a 5-month-old infant. Five-year-old Mariah, for example, can throw a ball with her mom, run with her dog, play hopscotch with her friends, feed and dress herself, and enjoy many of the rides at the amusement park. Changes in her brain have increased her memory abilities and capacity to think, and her language skills are astounding compared with those of the 5-month-old. Yet Mariah and other 5-year-olds are also limited by their physical selves. It will be years before their brains are fully developed, allowing greater concentration and more sophisticated thought processes. Their physical skills will continue to improve, and their bodies will grow taller and heavier and will mature sexually.

Human growth and development is an incredibly complex process, influenced by both genetic and environmental factors. At certain times and for certain developments, genetic influences dominate, whereas at other times, environmental influences are more powerful. But as we have explained in previous chapters, genetic and environmental forces are always working together. Consider height. The average female in the United States is just over 5 feet 4 inches (164 cm) and the average male is about 5 feet 10 inches (178 cm), but there is considerable variability. At 7 feet 8 inches, Yao Defen from China is likely the tallest woman in the world, her atypical height a stark contrast to women with Turner syndrome (see Chapter 3) who are typically 3 feet shorter than this—4 feet 8 inches on average. These are dramatic examples of variability in height, but even among those considered within the average range of height, there is variability. Genes account for some of this: Tall people tend to have tall parents, whereas short people often have "short genes" hanging on their family tree. Heritability studies confirm that, after infancy, there is a strong genetic influence in height (Dubois et al., 2012; Lettre, 2012).

But as noted in Chapter 3, even if you inherit the genetic propensity to be tall (or short), environment can influence the expression of those genes. If you lack adequate nutrition, for example, you may not realize your full growth potential. And consider the case of children with **celiac disease**, an inherited digestive problem in which gluten (the proteins found in all wheat products) triggers an immune response that leads to inflammation and damages the small intestine (see ■ **Figure 5.1**). This leaves affected children unable to absorb nutrients from food despite adequate consumption. Their disease, if untreated, can lead to malnutrition, which stunts growth and delays puberty. Early diagnosis for the estimated 3 million Americans with celiac disease is key to long-term health. Unfortunately, it often takes 10 years before the vague symptoms of bloating, diarrhea, fatigue, and upset stomach are properly diagnosed. As ■ **Figure 5.2** shows, treatment in the form of a gluten-free diet restores absorption of nutrients and can lead to dramatic **catch-up growth**. This catch-up growth after a period of malnutrition or illness reflects the body's struggle to get back on the growth course it is genetically programmed to follow.

To understand more fully how growth can be influenced by genes and environments, we need to consider the workings of the endocrine and nervous systems.

The physical capabilities of this young girl have advanced tremendously since she was an infant, yet those of her teenage brother are far more developed. He is able to do things with his physical skills that will remain out of reach to his young sister for at least a few more years.

PhotoAlto/Michel Bussy/PhotoAlto Agency RF Collections/Getty Images

Normal small intestine   **Celiac disease**

The Endocrine System

The endocrine, or hormonal, system consists of a group of **endocrine glands**, illustrated in ■ **Figure 5.3**, that secrete chemicals called *hormones* directly into the bloodstream. Perhaps the most critical of the endocrine glands is the **pituitary gland**, the so-called master gland located at the base of the brain. Directly controlled by the hypothalamus of the brain, it triggers the release of hormones from all other endocrine glands by sending

hormonal messages to those glands. Moreover, the pituitary produces **growth hormone**, which triggers the production of specialized hormones that directly regulate growth. Yao Defen's unusual height of 7 feet 8 inches resulted from unchecked release of growth hormone due to a tumor on her pituitary gland. In contrast, children who lack adequate growth hormone are unlikely to exceed 4 feet (or 130 cm) in height as adults if left untreated. Treatment with synthetic growth hormones can lead to near-expected adult height if administered early—well before the start of puberty (Bajpai et al., 2006; Reiter et al., 2006).

Children born small for their gestational age are often shorter as adults. Some of these children may also benefit from growth hormone therapy, but results with this group have been variable and controversial. The physical gains from taking the medication are around 2 inches of height and it is not clear whether these small gains add significantly to quality of life (Brütt et al., 2009; Sandberg et al., 2004). Adults who use human growth hormone in an attempt to enhance their athletic performance are at risk for a variety of health conditions, including cardiac problems and insulin resistance (Holt & Sönksen, 2008). Despite widespread beliefs about its potential performance-enhancing benefits, there are no clinically documented benefits to athletes who inject human growth hormone (O'Mathúna, 2006).

The thyroid gland also plays a key role in physical growth and development and in the development of the nervous system. Children whose mothers had a thyroid deficiency during pregnancy can experience intellectual problems (LaFranchi, Haddow, & Hollowell, 2005). Thyroid deficiency during infancy can also lead to intellectual disability and slow growth if unnoticed and untreated (see Zimmerman, 2007). Children who develop a thyroid deficiency later in life will not suffer brain damage, because most of their brain growth will have already occurred, but their physical growth will slow drastically.

In Chapter 4 you learned about another critical role of the endocrine system. A male fetus will not develop male reproductive organs unless (1) a gene on his Y chromosome triggers the development of the testes (which are endocrine glands), and (2) the testes secrete the most important of the male hormones, testosterone. Male sex hormones become highly important again during adolescence. When people speak of adolescence as a time

■ **Figure 5.2** This shows the rather dramatic catch-up growth that has occurred in a girl following treatment at around age 11 for her celiac disease.

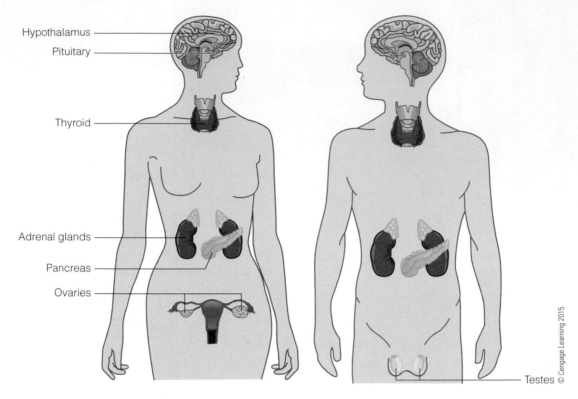

Hypothalamus
Pituitary
Thyroid
Adrenal glands
Pancreas
Ovaries
Testes

© Cengage Learning 2015

■ **Figure 5.3** The glands of the endocrine system secrete their chemicals, called hormones, directly into the bloodstream.

of "raging hormones," they are quite right. The testes of a male secrete large quantities of testosterone and other male hormones (called **androgens**). These hormones stimulate the production of growth hormone, which in turn triggers the adolescent growth spurt. Androgens are also responsible for the development of the male sex organs and contribute to sexual motivation during adulthood.

Meanwhile, in adolescent girls, the ovaries (also endocrine glands) produce larger quantities of the primary female hormone, **estrogen**, and of progesterone. Estrogen increases dramatically at puberty, stimulating the production of growth hormone and the adolescent growth spurt, much as testosterone does in males. It is also responsible for the development of the breasts, pubic hair, and female sex organs and for the control of menstrual cycles throughout a woman's reproductive years. Progesterone is sometimes called the "pregnancy hormone" because it orchestrates bodily changes that allow conception and then support a pregnancy. Finally, the adrenal glands secrete androgenlike hormones that contribute to the maturation of the bones and muscles in both sexes. The maturation of the adrenal glands during middle childhood results in sexual attraction well before puberty in both boys and girls and relates to sexual orientation in adulthood (Del Giudice, 2009; McClintock & Herdt, 1996). The roles of different endocrine glands in physical growth and development are summarized in ● **Table 5.1**.

In adulthood, endocrine glands continue to secrete hormones, under the direction of the hypothalamus and the pituitary gland, to regulate bodily processes. For example, thyroid hormones help the body's cells metabolize (break down) foods into usable nutrients, and the adrenal glands help the body cope with stress. Throughout the life span, then, the endocrine system works with the nervous system to keep the body on an even keel. Yet changes occur; for example, declines in levels of sex hormones are associated with menopause. And, as you will see later in this chapter, some theorists believe that changes in the functioning of the endocrine glands late in life help bring about aging and death.

In short, the endocrine system, in collaboration with the nervous system, is centrally involved in growth during childhood, physical and sexual maturation during adolescence, functioning over the life span, and aging later in life.

The Brain and Nervous System

None of the physical or mental achievements that we regard as human would be possible without a functioning nervous system. Briefly, the nervous system consists of the brain and spinal cord (central nervous system) and the neural tissue that extends into all parts of the body (peripheral nervous system). Its basic unit is a **neuron** (■ **Figure 5.4**). Although neurons come in many shapes and sizes, they have some common features. Branching, bushy dendrites receive signals from other neurons, and the long axon of a neuron transmits electrical signals to other neurons or, in some cases, directly to a muscle cell. The axon of one neuron makes a

Endocrine Gland	Hormones Produced	Effects on Growth and Development
Pituitary	Growth hormone	Regulates growth from birth through adolescence; triggers adolescent growth spurt
	Activating hormones	Signal other endocrine glands (such as ovaries and testes) to secrete their hormones
Thyroid	Thyroxine	Affects growth and development of the brain and helps regulate growth of the body during childhood
Testes	Testosterone	Is responsible for development of the male reproductive system during the prenatal period; directs male sexual development during adolescence
Ovaries	Estrogen and progesterone	Are responsible for regulating the menstrual cycle; estrogen directs female sexual development during adolescence
Adrenal glands	Adrenal androgens	Play a supportive role in the development of muscle and bones; contribute to sexual motivation

© Cengage Learning

connection with another neuron at a tiny gap called a **synapse**. By releasing neurotransmitters stored at the ends of its axons, one neuron can either stimulate or inhibit the action of another neuron.

The axons of many neurons become covered by a fatty sheath called *myelin*, which acts like insulation to speed the transmission of neural impulses. The process of **myelination**—neurons becoming encased in this protective substance that speeds transmission—begins prenatally but continues for many years after birth, proceeding from the spinal cord to the hindbrain, midbrain, and forebrain. Myelination has numerous implications for developmental changes observed across the life span. For instance, toddlers experience a vocabulary spurt following a period of rapid myelination of those parts of the brain involved in language development (Pujol et al., 2006). And teenagers are more likely than children to ask hypothetical "what if" questions and to reason about weighty abstractions such as truth and justice owing to myelination within the prefrontal lobes during adolescence. Progressive myelination of the pathways involved in attention and concentration helps explain why infants, toddlers, school-age children, and even young adolescents have shorter attention spans than do older adolescents and adults (Tanner, 1990). Finally, continued myelination into adulthood may account for adults being more able than teenagers to integrate thoughts and emotions (Benes, 1998; Nelson, Thomas, & de Haan, 2006). We will further explore these changes as we move through the life span in the following sections of this chapter.

■ Figure 5.4 Although neurons differ in size and function, they all contain three main parts: the dendrites, which receive messages from adjacent neurons; the cell body; and the axon, which sends messages across the synapse to other neurons.

© Cengage Learning 2015

These nerve fibers are covered with myelin, shown here in pink. What role does myelin play in neural activity?

Principles of Growth

Now that you know something about the endocrine and nervous systems, and how they contribute to growth early in life, is it possible to make general predictions about growth patterns? To do so, researchers often apply three general principles that underlie growth. It is easiest to see these principles in action during infancy when growth is fast. For instance, you have probably noticed that young infants seem to be all head compared with older children and adults. That is because growth follows the **cephalocaudal principle**, according to which growth occurs in a head-to-tail direction. This pattern is clear in ■ **Figure 5.5**: The head is far ahead of the rest of the body during the prenatal period and accounts for about 25% of the newborn's length and 13% of total body weight. But the head accounts for only 12% of an adult's height and 2% of an adult's weight (Zemel, 2002). During the first year after birth, the trunk grows the fastest; in the second year, the legs are the fastest growing part of the body.

While infants are growing from the head downward, they are also growing and developing muscles from the center outward to the extremities. This **proximodistal principle** of growth can be seen during the prenatal period, when the chest and internal organs form before the arms, hands, and fingers. During the first year of life, the trunk is rapidly filling out but the arms remain short and stubby until they undergo their own period of rapid development.

A third important principle of growth and development is the **orthogenetic principle**. This means that development starts globally and undifferentiated and moves toward increasing differentiation and hierarchical integration (Werner, 1957). Consider a human who starts as a single, undifferentiated cell at conception. As growth proceeds, that single cell becomes billions of highly specialized cells (neurons, blood cells, liver cells, and so on). These differentiated cells become organized, or integrated, into functioning systems such as the brain or the digestive system.

Having looked at the building blocks of body and brain, you are ready to examine the development, health, and aging of the physical self. We concentrate on changes in the body and brain that will help us understand the contributions of each to many other areas of development that will be covered in subsequent chapters. We also consider factors that are important to health at different ages. In doing so, we turn once again to a life-span model.

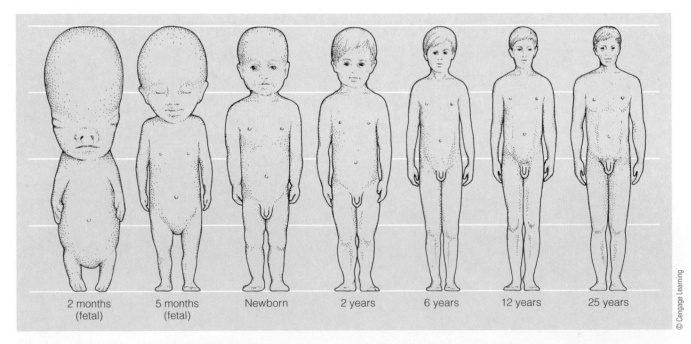

| 2 months (fetal) | 5 months (fetal) | Newborn | 2 years | 6 years | 12 years | 25 years |

■ **Figure 5.5** The cephalocaudal ("head-to-tail") principle of growth is illustrated in our body proportions from the fetal period through adulthood. At 2 months after conception, your head made up *half* of your total body length, but now, as an adult, your head is a mere 12–13% of your adult height. By contrast, during this same time frame, your legs have gone from being only about 12–13% of your early prenatal length to about half of your adult height.

A Life-Span Developmental Model of Health

The life-span developmental perspective introduced in Chapter 1 can be applied to our consideration of health and wellness as follows:

- Health is a lifelong process. It is influenced by personal choices over the life span and is constantly changing in response to these choices. For instance, whether you are 18, 48, or 78 years old when you begin an exercise program or stop smoking, these sorts of changes to your lifestyle can alter the path of your health.
- Health is determined by both genetic and environmental influences. According to the biodevelopmental framework from Harvard's Center on the Developing Child (see Shonkoff, 2010), a person's genetic predispositions interact with their environmental experiences to create adaptive (healthy) outcomes or disruptive (unhealthy) ones. As we learned in Chapter 4, by the time we are old enough to make our own choices, we have already been influenced by choices made by our parents and even our grandparents. As a result of fetal programming, an individual whose mother smoked or drank alcohol during pregnancy, for example, may have different health predispositions than one whose mother did not smoke or drink while pregnant.
- Health—and its study—is multidimensional. As we saw in the chapter opener, physical, mental, and social functioning are intertwined with one another and changes in one area influence other aspects of self.

- Changes in health involve both gains and losses; health both improves and declines over the life span in response to many factors.
- Health occurs in a sociohistorical context and can be enhanced or constrained by the social and historical factors that contribute to it. Especially important is socioeconomic status. Lower socioeconomic status is associated with poorer health and well-being and shorter life expectancy (Aldwin, Spiro, & Park, 2006).

Thus, an individual's health is determined by genetic factors, personal choice, and environmental influences working in concert across the life span. The importance of a life-span model of health will be clear as we view health in each of the following sections.

Checking Mastery

1. How does the endocrine system support development?
2. How does myelination contribute to developmental changes that we can observe?
3. What is one example each of cephalocaudal and proximodistal development?

Making Connections

1. Why is it important to view health from a life-span developmental perspective? Can you illustrate three aspects or components of this perspective as they apply to you or members of your family?

5.2 The Infant

LEARNING OBJECTIVES:

- Discuss typical changes in the brain during infancy.
- Summarize newborn capabilities that promote healthy adaptation to the world outside the womb.

Infancy is characterized by continued brain development, rapid growth, and impressive sensory and reflexive capabilities. Understanding the newborn's capacities and limitations brings a fuller appreciation of the dramatic changes that take place between birth and adulthood.

In Chapter 4 we traced the amazing evolution of the brain during the prenatal period. Here we pick up the story by looking at what goes on in the brain after birth. Although the brain is proportionately the largest and most developed part of the body at birth, much of its development takes place after birth. Postnatally, though, development is not so much about generating new neurons as about connecting existing neurons. Recall our discussion in Chapter 4 of how a new neuron migrates to its home in the nervous system and, like a good neighbor, begins reaching out and communicating with other neurons in the same region. Much of brain development in infancy and childhood consists of forging more and more connections between neurons (Johnson, 2011). ■ **Figure 5.6** shows how the complexity of the communication network—the dendrites extending from each neuron—increases over childhood. As we

Synaptic Density

At birth | 7 years | 15 years

© Cengage Learning 2015

■ **Figure 5.6** Between birth and 7 years of age, there is a tremendous amount of *synaptogenesis*, or the development of connections between neurons. But between 7 and 15 years of age, there is another process at work: *synaptic pruning* or elimination of unnecessary or unused connections.

go about our daily business of behaving and thinking, some of the connections among neurons become more numerous. But other connections, seldom used, seem to shrivel up and disappear. In Figure 5.6, the network of connections in the far right panel from a teenager is less dense than the network in the middle panel from a child. This illustrates the **synaptogenesis**, or growth of synapses, during childhood as well as the **synaptic pruning** or removal of unnecessary synapses that is also an important component of brain development.

The development of the brain early in life is heavily influenced by the unfolding of a genetic program that has evolved over many generations. But genes are not the only influence—an individual's experiences are also crucial to brain development. As Charles Nelson and colleagues (2006) describe it, "The brain's circuitry must rely on experience to customize connections to serve the needs of the individual" (p. 3). Assuming that the infant has normal opportunities to explore and experience the world, the result will be a normal brain and normal development. During the early brain spurt that begins before birth and continues during infancy, the brain is fine-tuned by experience through the dual processes of synaptogenesis and synaptic pruning.

Thus, the brain, especially early in its formation, has great **plasticity**; that is, it is responsive to the individual's experiences and can develop in a variety of ways (Kolb & Whishaw, 2013). On the negative side, the developing brain is highly vulnerable to damage if it is exposed to drugs or diseases (recall the description of teratogens in Chapter 4) or if it is deprived of sensory and motor experiences. On the positive side, this highly adaptable brain can often recover successfully from injuries. Neurons that are not yet fully committed to their specialized functions can often take over the functions of damaged neurons. Moreover, the immature brain is especially able to benefit from stimulating experiences. Rats that grow up in enriched environments with plenty of sensory stimulation develop larger, better-functioning brains with more synapses than rats that grow up in barren cages (Greenough, Black, & Wallace, 1987; Nilsson et al., 1999). Brain plasticity is greatest early in development. However, the organization of synapses within the nervous system continues to change in response to experience throughout the life span. Animals put through their paces in mazes grow bushier dendrites, whereas their brains lose some of their complexity if the animals are then moved to less stimulating quarters (Thompson, 2000).

In short, the *critical*, or *sensitive*, *period* for brain development— the time when it proceeds most rapidly—is during the late prenatal period and early infancy. The developing brain is characterized by a good deal of plasticity: Normal genes may provide rough guidelines about how the brain should be configured, but early experience determines the architecture of the brain.

Rapid Growth

Newborns are typically about 20 inches long and weigh 7–7½ pounds. However, weight and length at birth can mislead about eventual weight and height because the growth of some fetuses is stunted by a poor prenatal environment (Lejarraga, 2002). Size

during the first few months of life is related more to prenatal experiences (environment) than to size of parent (genes). This is easy to see in twins and other multiple births, because their prenatal growth is significantly restricted by siblings competing for the limited space in the mother's womb.

In the first few months of life, infants grow rapidly, gaining nearly an ounce of weight a day and an inch in length each month. By age 2, they have already attained about half of their eventual adult height and weigh 27–30 pounds on average. Although we usually think of growth as a slow and steady process, daily measurements of infant length show that babies grow in fits and starts (Lampl & Thompson, 2007). They may go weeks with no growth and then shoot up half an inch in 24 hours! Not surprisingly, these growth spurts are often accompanied by irritability that many parents, unaware of the phenomenal growth taking place, find puzzling. In the end, 90–95% of an infant's days are growth free, but their occasional bursts of physical growth add up to substantial increases in size. Infants whose overall weight gain outpaces gains in length (height) are at risk of childhood obesity (Taveras et al., 2009). We'll have more to say about obesity in subsequent sections of this chapter.

Bones and muscles are also developing quickly during infancy. At birth, most bones are soft, pliable, and difficult to break. They are too small and flexible to allow newborns to sit up or balance themselves when pulled to a standing position. The soft cartilagelike tissues of the young infant gradually ossify (harden) into bony material as calcium and other minerals are deposited into them. In addition, more bones develop, and they become more closely interconnected. As for muscles, young infants are relative weaklings. Although they have all the muscle cells they will ever have, their strength will increase only as their muscles grow.

Newborn Capabilities

Newborns used to be viewed as helpless little organisms, ill prepared to cope with the world outside the womb. We now know that they are quite well equipped to begin life. Just what can a newborn do? Among the most important capabilities are reflexes, functioning senses, a capacity to learn, and organized, individualized patterns of waking and sleeping. In this chapter, we'll examine their reflexes and brain development; in subsequent chapters, we address their sensory abilities (Chapter 6) and their potential to learn from experience (Chapters 7 and 8).

Reflexes

One of the newborn's greatest resources is a set of useful reflexes. A **reflex** is an unlearned and involuntary response to a stimulus, such as when the eye automatically blinks in response to a puff of air. ● **Table 5.2** lists some reflexes that can be readily observed in all normal newborns. These seemingly simple reactions are actually quite varied and complex patterns of behavior that provide infants with a way to begin interacting with their world (von Hofsten, 2007). The presence of these reflexes is important because it lets us know that the infant's nervous system is working.

Some reflexes are called *survival reflexes* because they have clear adaptive value. Examples include the breathing reflex

• **Table 5.2** Major Reflexes of Full-Term Newborns

Reflexes	Developmental Course	Significance
Survival Reflexes		
Breathing reflex	Permanent	Provides oxygen; expels carbon dioxide
Eye-blink reflex	Permanent	Protects eyes from bright light or foreign objects
Pupillary reflex: Constriction of pupils to bright light; dilation to dark or dimly lit surroundings	Permanent	Protects against bright light; adapts visual system to low illumination
Rooting reflex: Turning a cheek toward a tactile (touch) stimulus	Weakens by 2 months; disappears by 5 months	Orients child to breast or bottle
Sucking reflex: Sucking on objects placed (or taken) into mouth	Is gradually modified by experience over the first few months after birth; disappears by 7 months	Allows child to take in nutrients
Swallowing reflex	Is permanent but modified by experience	Allows child to take in nutrients; protects against choking
Primitive Reflexes		
Babinski reflex: Fanning then curling toes when bottom of foot is stroked	Disappears by 12–18 months of age	Presence at birth and disappearance in first year indicate normal neurological development
Grasping reflex: Curling fingers around objects (such as a finger) that touch the baby's palm	Disappears in first 3–4 months; is replaced by a voluntary grasp	Presence at birth and later disappearance indicate normal neurological development
Moro reflex: Loud noise or sudden change in position of baby's head will cause baby to throw arms outward, arch back, then bring arms toward each other	Disappears by 4 months; however, child continues to react to unexpected noises or a loss of bodily support by showing startle reflex	Presence at birth and later disappearance (or evolution into startle reflex) indicate normal neurological development (which does not disappear)
Swimming reflex: Infant immersed in water will display active movements of arms and legs and will involuntarily hold breath (thus staying afloat for some time)	Disappears in first 4–6 months	Presence at birth and later disappearance indicate normal neurological development
Stepping reflex: Infants held upright so that their feet touch a flat surface will step as if to walk	Disappears in first 8 weeks unless infant has regular opportunities to practice it	Presence at birth and later disappearance indicate normal neurological development

© Cengage Learning

Preterm infants may show little to no evidence of primitive reflexes at birth, and their survival reflexes are likely to be irregular or immature. However, the missing reflexes will typically appear soon after birth and will disappear a little later than they do among full-term infants.

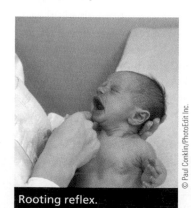
Rooting reflex.
© Paul Conklin/PhotoEdit Inc.

Grasping reflex.
© Ocean/Corbis

Stepping reflex.
© Jennie Woodcock; Reflections Photolibrary/Corbis

(useful for obvious reasons), the eye-blink reflex (which protects against bright lights or foreign particles), and the sucking reflex (needed to obtain food). Those called *primitive reflexes* are not clearly useful; many are believed to be remnants of evolutionary history that have outlived their purpose (but see Schott & Rossor, 2003, for another perspective). The Babinski reflex is a good example. Why would it be adaptive for infants to fan their toes when the bottoms of their feet are stroked? Frankly, we don't know. Other primitive reflexes may have some adaptive value, at least in some cultures. For example, the grasping reflex may help infants carried in slings or on their mothers' hips to hang on. Finally, some primitive reflexes—for example, the stepping reflex—are forerunners of useful voluntary behaviors that develop later in infancy. The expression of primitive reflexes at age 6 weeks, however, is not related to the expression of later motor behaviors (Bartlett, 1997). Thus, infants who demonstrate a strong primitive grasping reflex at 6 weeks are not necessarily the infants who demonstrate a strong voluntary grasp later in infancy.

Primitive reflexes typically disappear during the early months of infancy. For instance, the grasping reflex becomes weak by 4 months and is replaced by voluntary grasping. These primitive reflexes are controlled by the lower, subcortical areas of the brain and are lost as the higher centers of the cerebral cortex develop and make voluntary motor behaviors possible. Even though many primitive reflexes are not very useful to infants, they have proven to be useful in diagnosing infants' neurological problems. If such reflexes are not present at birth—or if they last too long in infancy—physicians know that something is wrong with a baby's nervous system. The existence of reflexes at birth tells them that infants are ready to respond to stimulation in adaptive ways. The disappearance of certain reflexes tells them that the nervous system is developing normally and that experience is affecting both brain and behavior. Thus, we see that the presence and then the absence of reflexes can serve as a general indicator of neurological health.

Behavioral States

Another sign that newborns are healthy and equipped for life is their ability to establish organized and individualized patterns of daily activity. Settling into an organized sleep–wake pattern is an indication that the baby is integrating biological, physiological, and psychosocial information (Sadeh, 1994, 1996). Infants must move from short sleep–wake cycles distributed throughout the day and night to a pattern that includes longer sleep periods at night with longer wake periods during the day. Much to their tired parents' dismay, newborns have no clear sense of night or day and may wake every 1–4 hours. By 3 months, infants begin to establish a predictable sleep–wake cycle, which becomes fairly stable by 6 months of age. Among premature infants, those who transition smoothly from one state to another exhibit more mature neurocognitive outcomes than other premature infants (Weisman et al., 2011). Infants who get more sleep at night tend to be more easygoing during the day (Spruyt et al., 2008). Are they more easygoing because they are well rested from a good night's sleep, or do they sleep well at night because

they are easygoing? We don't know the answer to this in infants, but we do know that adults who are normally easygoing can be irritable when deprived of sleep, so perhaps this is true for infants as well. Newborns spend half of their sleeping hours in active sleep, also called **REM sleep** (for the rapid eye movements that occur during it). Infants older than 6 months spend only 25–30% of their total sleep in REM sleep, which more closely resembles the 20% that adults spend in REM sleep.

Why do young infants sleep so much and spend so much more time in REM sleep than adults? Sleep patterns in infancy are associated with brain maturation and plasticity (Tarullo, Balsam, & Fifer, 2011). REM sleep in particular may be important for learning and memory processes (Diekelmann, Wilhelm, & Born, 2009). This may help explain why infants, who have so much to learn, spend more time in this sleep. Think about it: Infants are taking in vast amounts of new information during the times they are awake. These periods are invariably followed by sleep, which may help their brains learn and remember the new information. If deprived of sleep, infants may become "overloaded" with too much new information that their immature nervous systems cannot fully process. This may explain why infants are notoriously fussy at the end of a busy day—often at dinnertime when parents are tired and hoping for some peace. The infant's nervous system can be overstimulated by the flood of stimulation received during the day. Somehow, the arousal needs to be reduced—perhaps by crying and then sleeping. Adults sometimes marvel at how infants can sleep through the loudest noises and the brightest lights, but being able to do so may serve a valuable function.

Health and Wellness

What health issues must infants—and their parents—navigate? As noted in the previous chapter, modern medicine has made it possible for smaller and smaller babies to survive premature delivery, but sadly, most babies born weighing less than 1 pound 10½ ounces (750 grams) die within the first year (MacDorman & Matthews, 2008). The health problems associated with premature delivery and low birth weight often continue to challenge infants throughout their first year and beyond, illustrating one of the principles of the life-span model of health: Some events can have lifelong effects on health. Only about 12% of babies in the United States are premature, but as many as one-third of infant deaths are caused by complications of premature birth, making this the second leading cause of infant death (MacDorman & Matthews, 2008). **Congenital malformations**—defects that are present at birth, either from genetic factors or prenatal events—are the leading cause of death during the first year. Such malformations include heart defects, spina bifida, Down syndrome, cleft palates, and more.

Infant health has been dramatically improved in recent decades by administering vaccinations aimed at protecting infants from a variety of diseases (such as diphtheria, pertussis, polio, and measles). The approximately 20% of infants who do *not* receive the recommended immunizations are more likely than immunized babies to contract illnesses that can compromise their health (CDC, 2013b). Unfortunately, socioeconomic status in the United States often determines who has access to health care services that cover immunizations. As the life-span model maintains, one's sociohistorical context influences health.

Thus, health during infancy starts well before birth with prenatal care that helps prevent and/or treat potential congenital anomalies and preterm birth. Health after birth is enhanced by well-baby visits to the doctor to ensure that development is proceeding normally and by following recommendations for prevention of illness.

Checking Mastery

1. What are the most significant brain changes that occur during infancy?
2. What are two infant reflexes that may help ensure survival in the early months of life?
3. What can an infant's sleep–wake cycle indicate about her development?

Making Connections

1. In what ways is brain plasticity an advantage and in what ways might it be a disadvantage to the developing human?

5.3 The Child

LEARNING OBJECTIVES:

- Discuss the implications of brain lateralization for behavior and functioning.
- Outline the major physical accomplishments and health challenges of childhood.

Slow and steady is probably the best way to describe the growth that occurs throughout much of childhood. From age 2 until puberty, children gain about 2–3 inches and 5–6 pounds every year. This growth is often tracked on a chart that plots an individual's height and weight against normative data. This allows physicians and families to see how a particular child is progressing relative to other children of the same age and gender and to graph the pattern of growth over time. Children who are markedly different—higher, lower, or more erratic in their growth rate—may warrant additional investigation.

During middle childhood (ages 6–11), children may seem to grow little, probably because the gains are small in proportion to the child's size (4–4½ feet and 60–80 pounds on average) and therefore harder to detect. The cephalocaudal and proximodistal principles of growth continue to operate. As the lower parts of the body and the extremities fill out, the child takes on more adultlike body proportions. The bones continue to grow and harden, and the muscles strengthen.

As we'll see in the next section, there are also steady changes going on within the brain. The brain becomes further organized to support the behaviors, both mental and physical, in which its "owner" is regularly engaged.

Brain Lateralization

One important feature of the developing organization of the brain is the **lateralization**, or asymmetry and specialization of functions, of the two hemispheres of the cerebral cortex. Instead of developing identically, the functions controlled by the two hemispheres diverge (see ■ **Figure 5.7**). In most people, the left cerebral hemisphere controls the right side of the body and is adept at the *sequential* (that

is, step-by-step) processing needed for analytic reasoning and language processing. The right hemisphere generally controls the left side of the body and is skilled at the *simultaneous* processing of information needed for understanding spatial information and processing visual–motor information as well as the emotional content of information (Kensinger & Choi, 2009). Although it is an oversimplification, the left hemisphere is often called the *thinking* side of the brain, whereas the right hemisphere is called the *emotional* brain.

Having two hemispheres of the brain is not the same as having two brains. The hemispheres "communicate" and work together through the corpus callosum, "the super-highway of neurons connecting the halves of the brain" (Gazzaniga, 1998,

Left-hemisphere functions	Right-hemisphere functions
Sequential processing	Simultaneous processing
Analytic thought	Holistic thought
Logic	Intuition
Language	Creativity
Science and math	Art and music

© Cengage Learning 2015

■ **Figure 5.7** The brain consists of two hemispheres that specialize in different functions. Functions such as logic, analytic reasoning, and language are typically associated with the left hemisphere, whereas such functions as creativity, intuition, and holistic thinking are associated with the right hemisphere.

p. 50). Even though one hemisphere might be more active than the other during certain tasks, they both play a role in all activities. For example, the left hemisphere is considered the seat of language because it controls word content, grammar, and syntax, but the right hemisphere processes melody, pitch, sound intensity, and the affective content of language.

If one hemisphere is damaged, it may be possible for the other hemisphere to "take over" the functions lost. For example, most children who have one hemisphere removed to try to reduce or eliminate severe seizures regain normal language function (Liégeois et al., 2008; Vining et al., 1997). It does not matter whether the remaining hemisphere is the left or the right. Thus, although the left hemisphere processes language in most people (perhaps 92%), the right hemisphere may also be able to fill this function, although it is not yet known how this possibility might be limited—or enhanced—by age or other characteristics of the individual (Gazzaniga, 1998; Knecht et al., 2000).

When does the brain become lateralized? Signs of brain lateralization are clearly evident at birth. Newborns are more likely to turn their heads to the right than to the left (Thompson & Smart, 1993), and one-quarter clearly prefer the right hand in their grasp reflex (Tan & Tan, 1999). Newborns may also show more left hemispheric response to speech sounds (Kotilahti et al., 2009), although this response becomes stronger and more reliable in the second half of the first year (Holowka & Petitto, 2002).

Signs of lateralization so early in life suggest that it has a genetic basis. Further support for the role of genes comes from family studies of handedness. Overall, about 9 in 10 people rely on their right hands (or left hemispheres) to write and perform other motor activities. Males are somewhat more likely to be left-handed than females (Vuoksimaa et al., 2009). In families where both parents are right-handed, the odds of having a left-handed child are only 2 in 100. These odds increase to 17 in 100 when one parent is left-handed and to 46 in 100 when both parents are left-handed (Springer & Deutsch, 2001). Although this suggests a genetic basis to handedness, it could also indicate that children become left-handed because of experiences provided by left-handed parents. However, experience would not account for head-turning preferences in young infants or for the differential activation of the left and right hemispheres observed in newborns when listening to speech sounds.

Overall, then, the brain appears to be structured very early so that the two hemispheres of the cortex will be capable of specialized functioning. As we develop, most of us come to rely more on the left hemisphere to carry out language processing and more on the right hemisphere to do such things as perceive spatial relationships and emotions. We also come to rely more consistently on one hemisphere, usually the left, to control many of our physical activities.

Physical Behavior

Children's physical behaviors are noticeably advanced compared to those of infants and toddlers. For instance, although toddlers are capable of controlling their movements in relation to a *stationary* world, children master the ability to move capably in a *changing* environment (Sayre & Gallagher, 2001).

They must learn to modify their movements to adapt to changes in environment. This allows them to bring their hands together at just the right time to catch a ball and to avoid bumping into moving people when walking through a crowded mall. They also refine many motor skills. For example, young children throw a ball only with the arm, but older children learn to step forward as they throw. Their accuracy throwing a ball increases around age 7, as does their speed of throwing (Favilla, 2006). Thus, older children can throw a ball farther than younger ones can, not just because they are bigger and stronger but also because they can integrate multiple body movements—raising their arm, turning their body, stepping forward with one foot, and pushing their body forward with the other foot (Sayre & Gallagher, 2001).

As a child, one of your textbook authors was teased by an older brother for apparent lack of skill on the ball field. A regular taunt was "you throw like a girl!" It turns out there is a well-established gender difference in both throwing speed and distance: Girls do, indeed, throw like girls and not like boys (Thomas et al., 2010). A typical 13-year-old girl can throw a ball an average of 38.5 miles per hour, which sounds fast until you learn that the typical 13-year-old boy averages 53.5 miles per hour. Some of this difference seems to be nurture: Boys are given more things to throw, start earlier in sports that involve throwing, and spend more time practicing throwing. But practice and the environment do not explain all of the gender difference in throwing.

Apparently, even Olympic gold medal winner in gymnastics Gabby Douglas throws like a girl.

Boys may also be able to throw faster and farther because of their greater upper body muscle mass and their shoulder width.

We should note that girls are somewhat ahead of boys in hopping and tasks that require manual dexterity (Junaid & Fellowes, 2006; Van Beurden et al., 2002). But again, these differences seem to arise, at least in part, from practice and different expectations for males and females.

Health and Wellness

Children's health is influenced by a multitude of factors, some of which are beyond their control. For instance, parents' education and socioeconomic status affect their children's health (Matthews & Gallo, 2011). Children whose parents are less educated are more likely to experience poor or fair health than children with more educated parents. This is particularly true for black children and white children, but less true for Hispanic children and Asian children, whose health outcomes may be buffered by strong social networks that cut across educational and socioeconomic levels (■ **Figure 5.8**). This is another example of how the sociohistorical context of development plays a role in children's health and well-being.

Accidents constitute a major category of negative influences on children's health and well-being. Childhood is unfortunately marked by numerous unintentional injuries, making accidents the leading cause of death throughout the childhood years (CDC, 2013a). Crashes involving motor vehicles cause the largest number of fatal injuries during childhood. Parents can reduce the possibility of motor vehicle injuries by properly strapping their infants and young children into car seats, or as they get older, insisting that they sit in the backseat with a shoulder-strap seat belt.

Nutrition continues to be an important contributor to health throughout childhood, as it was during infancy. Much to parents' dismay, though, the toddler who sampled all sorts of new foods may turn into a picky eater during childhood. One reason for this is that the rate of growth has slowed down, diminishing children's appetites. Still, they need to have a well-balanced diet that addresses their nutritional needs. Unfortunately, societal influences often inadvertently encourage poor eating habits rather than good ones. Many children eat fast foods, which are often fried, and snack on foods high in carbohydrates and low on nutritional value. A determined group of researchers staked out local convenience stores that were located near urban schools (Borradaile et al., 2009). These were small stores within four blocks of the schools that were frequented by children on their way to and from school. For months, the researchers tracked everything the children purchased, briefly surveyed them regarding their purchases, and later analyzed the nutritional content of the food and beverages purchased. The most frequently purchased item was chips, followed by candy, and then sugar-sweetened artificially flavored drinks. In other words, the children were buying fatty, sugary foods and beverages with little nutritional value but high caloric value. Amazingly, these children spent an average of just $1 dollar to ingest an average of 356 empty calories. What a bargain!

Parents can help children to become healthy eaters by regularly offering a variety of healthy foods and beverages and by modeling healthy eating habits. Education level of mothers is a good predictor of whether children adopt healthy eating patterns (Northstone, Smith, Newby, & Emmett, 2012). More education may translate into greater awareness of healthy habits. These parents, for example, may be more aware of the recommendations for healthy eating and steer children away from the sugary sodas and other sugar-sweetened beverages that have become so very popular. A survey of fluid intake across childhood indicates that sodas and artificially flavored drinks make up a large portion of the fluids that children consume (Borradaile et al., 2009; He, Marrero, & MacGregor, 2008). Sodas not only contribute to weight gain and obesity, they are also associated with lower consumption of milk and intake of calcium, an important nutrient for bone health (Keller et al., 2009; Lim et al., 2009). Preschoolers who consume sugary sodas between meals are more than twice as likely to be overweight by the time they start school than preschoolers who do not (Dubois et al., 2007). Finally, there is also evidence that children may eat more at home and gain more weight if they are living in a stressful home situation. Craig Gundersen and his colleagues (2008) found that young children eat more "comfort foods" when their mothers are stressed, but only if these foods are available to them.

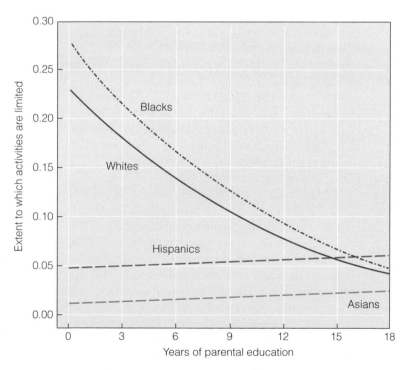

■ **Figure 5.8** Among white families and black families, parents' education levels influence the extent to which children's activities are limited by poor or fair health: children have more limitations when their parents are less educated. This is not true among Hispanic families and Asian families.

Source: From Chen, E., Martin, A. D., & Matthews, K. A. (2006). Understanding health disparities: The role of race and socioeconomic status in children's health. *American Journal of Public Health*, 96, 702–705. Reprinted by permission of the American Public Health Association.

ChooseMyPlate.gov

USDA

The U.S. Department of Agriculture introduced its new recommendations for healthy eating in 2011 with a food plate replacing the food pyramid that reigned for several decades. According to the new recommendations, fruits and vegetables should each make up 25% of your meal.

This illustrates Bronfenbrenner's exosystem (see Chapter 2): A child is influenced by things going on in the mother's life that may relate to her work, finances, and other factors that do not directly involve the child but still affect the child.

Also important is the larger environment—the neighborhood and school—of the child. Neighborhoods with higher levels of poverty and lower education levels are associated with higher rates of obesity (Kimbro & Denney, 2012). And when fast foods and junk foods are available in the neighborhood, in the form of fast food restaurants and convenience stores, children and their parents are more likely to partake of these often unhealthy eating options (He et al., 2012). Children and their families who do not live within easy access of junk food consume less of it. Thus, where you live can influence how you eat. But that's not all.

Children who live in neighborhoods that provide opportunities for safe outdoor activities are less likely to be overweight than their peers who live in settings that offer few such opportunities (Committee on Environmental Health, 2009). Particularly for families in urban neighborhoods, if parents do not believe that it is safe for their children to play outdoors, children tend to replace outdoor activity with sedentary indoor activity such as watching television (Cecil-Karb & Grogan-Kaylor, 2009). But indoor activity does not have to be completely sedentary. Children who play *active* sports or fitness video games—those that require fairly rigorous movement—benefit in comparison to children who play only the traditional, inactive video games, although they do not benefit as much as they would from physically participating in the actual sport (Daley, 2009; Graf et al., 2009; Graves et al., 2008). Further, children who attend preschools with more portable equipment (for example, balls and bikes) engage in more physical activity over the course of the day than children who attend preschools with more fixed equipment (such as swing sets)

(Dowda et al., 2009). But even the environments that encourage the most activity cannot turn every couch potato into an athletic powerhouse. Some children are predisposed by temperament to lead more sedentary lifestyles and resist even the most engaging playground equipment and incentives to be physically engaged (Saudino & Zapfe, 2008). Thus, characteristics of the environment in combination with characteristics of the child affect activity levels.

The schools that children attend are also important influences on children's eating habits and health. Students who attend schools with breakfast programs have healthier weights than students in schools without breakfast programs, as indicated by **body mass index (BMI)**, a marker of body fat calculated from a person's height and weight (Gleason & Dodd, 2009). Children who participate in their school's meal programs consume more milk, vegetables, and 100% fruit juice than children not participating (Condon, Crepinsek, & Fox, 2009). Further, children who eat a regular breakfast, either at home or at school, are less likely to snack or lunch on high-fat foods.

School lunches may pose special risks to health, though, which may come as a surprise to many parents. A survey of school meals shows that lunches offered to students contain more fat than the breakfasts (Crepinsek et al., 2009). Elementary school children who have French fries as a school lunch option are heavier than children whose schools do not offer French fries (Fox et al., 2009). In addition to being above recommended levels of fat, school lunches tend to have higher than recommended levels of sodium and lower amounts of fiber (Clark & Fox, 2009; Crepinsek et al., 2009). Schools are taking action to improve the nutrition of the foods offered to students for lunch and are reducing the availability of unhealthy snack items, such as French fries as a regular a la carte item and vending machines that offer fatty snacks and sugary sodas (Briefel et al., 2009). Perhaps because they have a more vocal student body, secondary schools lag behind elementary schools in eliminating the unhealthy options that contribute to higher BMIs (Story, Nanney, & Schwartz, 2009).

Health during childhood can be fostered not only by a good diet but also by regular physical activity. Children should do at least 60 minutes of moderate or vigorous physical activity everyday (CDC, 2012). Do they get this much activity? One group of researchers tracked older elementary school children with electronic monitors for a week to determine their activity levels (Trost et al., 2012). The children were sedentary, on average, for 63% of the time, somewhat active for 31%, and moderately to vigorously active just 6% of the time. Unfortunately, our contemporary lifestyles may inadvertently promote physical inactivity, which may explain why the fitness levels of children have shown a measurable decline in recent years. The average child spends 5–6 hours every day watching television or videos, playing video games, and working or playing on the computer (Roberts & Foehr, 2004). Children who watch more than 5 hours of television a day are about five times more likely to be overweight than children who watch 2 hours a day or less, perhaps because they get little exercise and eat the junk foods they see advertised on TV (see Council on Communications and Media, 2011). At the same time, some schools have reduced recess time and physical education requirements. Most kids get chauffeured everywhere they need to go in the family car, further decreasing their opportunities for walking and physical activity.

Children who achieve the recommended level of physical activity are, not surprisingly, more physically fit than children who lead a more sedentary lifestyle. What is especially important to consider, though, is that the benefits of exercise go beyond physical fitness: Physical activity enhances cognitive and psychological functioning. One researcher has referred to exercise as "brain food" (Ploughman, 2008). In a review of studies on children's participation in physical activity and their academic performance, Roy Shepard (1997) concluded that increased physical activity was associated with improved academic skills. But these data are largely correlational, and many factors may explain the connection between physical activity and academic performance. For instance, Mark Tremblay and colleagues (Tremblay, Inman, & Willms, 2000) found that although regular participation in physical activity did not strongly influence 12-year-olds' academic performance, it did positively affect their self-esteem. Students who are healthier and feel better about themselves may perform better in the classroom. Other research suggests that children's physical activity must be sustained and vigorous before academic benefits will be realized (Tomporowski et al., 2008). We'll consider this issue again in the next section on The Adolescent.

Checking Mastery

1. How are brain functions of the two hemispheres typically organized?
2. What are two major factors that contribute to health during childhood?
3. What are two things that schools or parents can do to influence children's eating behaviors in order to help them maintain or achieve a healthy weight?

Making Connections

1. Design an intervention to increase children's fitness levels and indicate how you will assess the effectiveness of your intervention.

5.4 The Adolescent

LEARNING OBJECTIVES:

- Explain how brain changes during adolescence influence teens' behavior.
- Compare and contrast the experience of puberty for males and females, including both physical and psychological correlates of puberty.

Adolescents are intensely focused on their physical self, and rightly so—dramatic physical changes are taking place during this period, both inside and out. Consider your own transformation from child to adult. You rapidly grew taller and took on the body size and proportions of an adult during your growth spurt. Moreover, you experienced **puberty**—the processes of biological change that result in an individual's attaining sexual maturity and becoming capable of producing a child. And although you could not see them, there were changes taking place in your brain that would contribute to your transition from child to adult. We look at all these processes, starting with the brain.

The Adolescent Brain: What's Going On in There?

The brain undergoes much change during adolescence. Magnetic Resonance Imaging (MRI) studies show that the brain's "gray matter," made up primarily of cell bodies and dendrites, undergoes change in an inverted-U pattern across adolescence. That is, the volume of gray matter increases, peaks, and then decreases throughout the teen years (Blakemore, Burnett, & Dahl, 2010). This pattern is believed to be associated with increased synaptogenesis just before puberty followed by a period of heightened pruning of synapses (Johnson & de Haan, 2011). In contrast to this inverted U-pattern, the brain's "white matter" consisting of clusters of axons, increases in linear fashion throughout adolescence, a likely result of the steady progression of myelination of axons (Blakemore et al., 2010). Can these changes in the brain explain why adolescents take more risks than adults? Adolescents are notorious for taking chances that most adults would not take. They often display poor judgment and decision making when it comes to alcohol, drug, and cigarette use; sexual activities; and driving (see ● **Table 5.3**).

● **Table 5.3** Risky Behaviors During Adolescence

- Smoking cigarettes (reported by 20% of adolescents)
- Drinking alcohol (45%)
- Drinking and driving (10%)
- Riding with a driver who has been drinking (29%)
- Using marijuana (20%)
- Carrying weapons (18% overall but 30% among males)
- Having sex without a condom (39%)
- Using alcohol or drugs before sexual intercourse (23%)
- Getting into a physical fight (35%)

SOURCE: Department of Health and Human Services, Youth Risk Behavior Survey, 2009.

There are two contrasting theories of how brain changes during adolescence might relate to risky behavior (Galvan, 2010). One theory is that the reward system of the brain is hyporesponsive to rewards, that is, it is *less* responsive. This underactivity may mean that teens need more stimulation to achieve the same level of satisfaction from reward that adults achieve with less stimulation, leading them to engage in more risky behaviors (Galvan, 2010). There is some support for this theory, although it is rather weak and indirect. For instance, adolescents rate some experiences as less exciting than do adults, perhaps indicating a higher threshold for excitement (Spear, 2010).

The competing theory is that the reward system of the brain is hyper-responsive: The adolescent brain has greater need for reward, which leads to more reward-seeking behaviors. Adriana Galvan and her colleagues (2007) measured activity in a part of the brain called the *accumbens* (thought to be associated with reward, pleasure, and addiction) as participants worked on a task with varying rewards for correct answers. They found that adolescents, relative to children and adults, exhibited higher levels of activity—hyper-responsiveness—in the accumbens in anticipation of both negative and positive consequences of risk taking. Importantly, though, the researchers found individual differences across all ages, showing that although adolescents as a group may be more prone to risk-taking behaviors, this is not true of all adolescents.

In terms of timing, teens experience this higher threshold for reward prior to attaining adult levels of decision making. In particular, the neurons serving the frontal lobes are among the last areas of the brain to become myelinated. The frontal lobes are essential to many higher-order mental activities of thinking, planning, and decision making. Thus, brain changes may leave adolescents in a vulnerable position: Their desire for reward increases before their ability to think through all the consequences of their actions (Steinberg, 2010). The area of the brain involved in inhibiting risky behavior is not fully developed until around age 25 (Giedd, 2004).

The connection between brain activity and risk-taking behavior during the teen years may be driven, in part, by neurotransmitters (brain chemicals). Animal research reveals that one chemical, dopamine, reaches peak levels during adolescence in the prefrontal cortex and limbic system before dropping and then leveling off (Lewis et al., 1998). This chemical is involved in novelty seeking and in determining the motivational value of activities (Jetha & Segalowitz, 2012). If this holds true for human adolescents, and many scientists believe it does, then their risky behaviors may reflect a combination of seeking new experiences and finding certain stimuli more attractive or motivating—both influenced by changes in brain chemistry and incomplete development of the prefrontal cortex during adolescence. The adolescent brain, then, is still a work in progress, and some risk taking by teenagers may be par for the course until further brain developments, such as maturation of the prefrontal cortex, refine their good judgment and decision making (Steinberg, 2007).

The Growth Spurt

As noted earlier in the chapter, the **adolescent growth spurt** is triggered by an increase in the level of growth hormones circulating through the body during adolescence. Boys and girls grow at different rates, as do different body parts. Girls' peak rate of growth for height is just under 12 years; for boys it is 13.4 years (Geithner et al., 1999). The peak rate of growth for weight is 12.5 years for girls and 13.9 years for boys. Thus, boys lag behind girls by 1–2 years. Both sexes return to a slower rate of growth after the peak of their growth spurts. Like infants, adolescents may grow in spurts rather than continuously. Girls achieve their adult height by around 16 years; boys are still growing at 18, 19, or even 20 years (Fryar, Gu, & Ogden, 2012).

Muscles also develop rapidly in both sexes, with boys normally gaining a greater proportion of muscle mass than girls do. Total body weight increases in both sexes, but it is distributed differently: Girls gain extra fat, primarily in the breasts, hips, and buttocks; boys develop broader shoulders.

Sexual Maturation

Long before the physical signs of puberty are evident, the body is changing to prepare for sexual maturity. The adrenal glands increase production of adrenal androgens sometime between the ages of 6 and 8 in both boys and girls. Known as **adrenarche**, this circulation of adrenal hormones contributes partly to such secondary sex characteristics as pubic and axillary (underarm) hair. But the more obvious signs of sexual maturity emerge with increased production of gonadal hormones (those produced by the testes or ovaries): androgens in males and estrogen and progesterone in females. The gonadal hormones are primarily responsible for the development of secondary sexual characteristics and sexual maturity. This increased hormone production will also trigger sexual thoughts, feelings, and maturation. Yes, teenagers think a lot about sex and, as we will discuss in Chapter 12, some teens begin to act on these thoughts. Here, we focus on the physical changes of puberty and the psychological implications of these changes.

Progression through puberty and attainment of sexual maturity is often measured using the "Tanner Scale," named for the British pediatrician who developed it (see Marshall & Tanner, 1969, 1970). The Tanner Scale includes five stages ranging from prepubertal—no evidence of secondary sexual characteristics— to adult secondary sexual characteristics (● **Table 5.4**). For girls, the most dramatic event in the sexual maturation process is **menarche**—the first menstruation—normally between ages 11 and 15, with an average of about 12.5 years. Menstruation is the process of shedding the lining of a uterus prepared to support a fertilized egg. However, some girls begin to menstruate before they have begun to ovulate, so they may not be capable of reproducing for a year or more after menarche (Spear, 2000a). But other girls *do* ovulate—release a mature egg capable of being fertilized—when they begin to menstruate and should know that sexual activity can lead to a pregnancy.

There is a great deal of variability in when secondary sex characteristics (such as breast buds and pubic hair) appear. Sexual maturation also proceeds at different rates in different ethnic groups. Several studies have found that African American and Mexican American girls begin to experience pubertal changes earlier than European American girls (Chumlea et al., 2003; Jean et al., 2011). At age 9, for example, 49% of African American

● **Table 5.4** Tanner's Stages of Secondary Sexual Characteristics and Annual Growth (in inches) for Boys and Girls

Stage	Boys	Girls
I	Prepubertal AG: 2–2.5 inches	Prepubertal AG: 2–2.5 inches
II Boys: ages 12.5–14.5 Girls: ages 10–12	Testes: a bit larger (first sign in boys) Scrotum: red Penis: still childlike but erections common AG: 2.75–3.25 inches	Breast: small bud, widened areola AG: 2.8–3.2 inches
III Boys: ages 13–15 Girls: ages 11–13	Testes: larger Scrotum: darker Penis: increases in length AG: 3.25 inches	Breasts: larger and more elevated AG: 3.2 inches
IV Boys: ages 13.5–15.5 Girls: ages 12–14	Testes: more enlargement Scrotum: more darkening Penis: becomes thicker AG: 4 inches	Breasts: secondary mound of areola from body AG: 2.8 inches
V Boys: ages 14–18 Girls: ages 14–18	Testes, scrotum, and penis all adult Final height by 18–19 years	Breasts: adult shape and size Final height by 16 years

AG=annual growth.

Adapted from Pediatrics Now (2013) *Puberty resource page.* Available at: http://www.pediatricsnow.com/2009/12/puberty-resource-page/.

girls have begun to develop breasts compared with only 16% of European American girls and 25% of Mexican American girls (Wu, Mendola, & Buck, 2002). A few girls (1% of European Americans and 3% of African Americans) show signs of breast or pubic hair development at age 3, and a few have not begun to mature even at age 12 (Herman-Giddens et al., 1997).

For the average boy, the sexual maturation process begins around age 11 to age 11½ with an initial enlargement of the testes and scrotum (the saclike structure that encloses the testes). Unpigmented, straight pubic hair appears soon thereafter, and about 6 months later, the penis grows rapidly about the same time that the adolescent growth spurt begins (refer again to Table 5.4). The marker of sexual maturation most like menarche in girls is **semenarche**, or a boy's first ejaculation—the emission of seminal fluid in a "wet dream" or while masturbating. It typically occurs around age 13. Just as girls often do not ovulate until sometime after menarche, boys often do not produce viable sperm until sometime after their first ejaculation.

Somewhat later, boys begin to sprout facial hair, first at the corners of the upper lip and finally on the chin and jawline. As the voice lowers, many boys have the embarrassing experience of hearing their voices "crack" uncontrollably up and down between a squeaky soprano and a deep baritone, sometimes within a single sentence. Boys may not see the first signs of a hairy chest until their late teens or early 20s, if at all.

What determines an adolescent's rate of development? Genes are part of the answer: Identical twins typically begin and end their growth spurts at very similar times, and early or late maturation tends to run in families (Silventoinen et al., 2008). In both sexes, the changes involved in physical and sexual maturation are

triggered when the hypothalamus of the brain stimulates activity in the endocrine system (see the description at the beginning of this chapter). Boys and girls have similar levels of both male and female sex hormones during childhood. By the time sexual maturation is complete, however, males have larger quantities of male hormones (androgens, including testosterone) circulating in their blood than females do, whereas females have larger quantities of female hormones (estrogen, progesterone, and others).

Physical and sexual maturation, then, are processes set in motion by the genes and executed by hormones. But environment also plays its part in the timing of maturation. This is dramatically illustrated by the **secular trend**—the historical trend in industrialized societies toward earlier maturation and greater body size. In 1840, for example, the average age of menarche was 16½ years, a full 4 years later than it is today (Rees, 1993).

What explains the secular trend? Better nutrition and advances in medical care seem to be the major factors (Gluckman & Hanson, 2006). As ● **Table 5.5** shows, the age of menarche varies across countries and tends to be earlier in countries with good nutrition, long life expectancies, and high literacy rates, reflecting the effect of both biological and environmental factors (Thomas et al., 2001). In industrialized nations, today's children are more likely than their parents or grandparents to reach their genetic potential for maturation and growth because they are better fed and less likely to experience growth-retarding illnesses. Even within the relatively affluent U.S. society, poorly nourished adolescents—both boys and girls—mature later than well-nourished ones do. Girls who are taller and heavier as children tend to mature earlier than other girls (Lee et al., 2007). In particular, being overweight during early childhood (birth to

• Table 5.5 Median Age of Menarche & Emergence of Secondary Sexual Characteristics (if available) in Select Countries

	Stage 2 Breast	Stage 2 Pubic Hair	Menarche
Mexico			12
China	9.2	10.4	12.3
U.S.	10.0	10.5	12.4
Iran	10.15	10.78	12.65
Canada			12.9
U.K.	10.14	10.92	12.9
Denmark	9.86		13.13
Tanzania			14.3
Bangladesh			15.1
North Korea (refugees)			16

SOURCES: Aksglaede et al. (2009); Bau et al., 2009; Bosch et al., 2008; Gohlke & Woelfle, 2009; Harris, Prior, & Koehoorn, 2008; Juul et al., 2006; Kashani et al., 2009; Ku et al., 2006; Ma et al., 2009; McDowell, Brody, & Hughes, 2007; Rabbani et al., 2008; Rebacz, 2009; Rubin et al., 2009; Torres-Mejía et al., 2005.

2 years) is associated with early puberty among girls (Wan, Deng, Archer, & Sun, 2012). By contrast, girls who engage regularly in strenuous physical activity and girls who suffer from anorexia nervosa (the life-threatening eating disorder that involves dieting to the point of starvation, discussed in Chapter 16) may begin menstruating late or stop menstruating after they have begun. These variations seem to be tied not to overall weight but to skeletal development, particularly maturation of the pelvic bones necessary for delivering a baby (Ellison, 2002).

Family situations can also affect the timing of puberty, at least for girls. For instance, girls whose mothers are depressed are likely to experience early puberty, as are girls who have a stepfather or mother's boyfriend present in the home (Ellis & Garber, 2000). In particular, girls who are relatively young when an unrelated male moves into the house and whose mothers and stepfathers or boyfriends have a more conflicted, stressful relationship are likely to experience early sexual maturity. Even without a stepfather or boyfriend present in the home, girls experience earlier puberty when their family is disrupted by a separation or divorce that removes their biological father from the home at an early age (Allison & Hyde, 2011; Tither & Ellis, 2008). This is especially true if the father, prior to leaving, displayed dysfunctional behaviors, at least in the eyes of his daughters. Living with an unemployed father or experiencing harsh mothering at a young age also seems to precipitate earlier puberty and menarche (Arim et al., 2011; Belsky et al., 2007). The common thread in all this research is stress in the girls' lives, starting at a relatively young age (James, Ellis, Schlomer & Garber, 2012; Simpson et al., 2012). Over time, stress can affect many bodily systems and functions and early menarche may be one by-product of these changes. Truly, then, physical and sexual maturation are the products of an interaction between heredity and environment, with some environments delaying maturation and others hastening it.

Psychological Implications

As noted previously, there are large individual differences in the timing of physical and sexual maturation. An early-maturing girl may develop breast buds at age 8 and reach menarche at age 10, whereas a late-developing boy may not begin to experience a growth of his penis until age 14½ or a height spurt until age 16. Within a middle school, then, there is a wide assortment of bodies, ranging from entirely childlike to fully adultlike. It is no wonder adolescents are self-conscious about their appearance!

What psychological effects do the many changes associated with puberty have on adolescents? Girls approaching or experiencing puberty tend to become self-conscious about their appearance and worry about how others will respond to them. One adolescent girl may think she is too tall, another that she is too short (Oldehinkel, Verhulst, & Ormel, 2011). One may try to pad her breasts; another may hunch her shoulders to hide hers. Some girls develop poor body images, possibly because they are bothered by the weight gains that typically accompany menarche (McCabe & Ricciardelli, 2004). These weight gains, though, are not driven solely by pubertal changes. Girls going through puberty report lack of energy and lower levels of activity, perhaps as a result of the hormonal changes but possibly also a result of their increased feelings of self-consciousness (Oldehinkel et al., 2011). Many girls exhibit mood changes, which seem to escalate as they proceed through puberty.

What about boys? Their body images are more positive than those of girls, and they are more likely to welcome their weight gain and voice changes. But they hope to be tall, hairy, and handsome, and they may become preoccupied with their physical and athletic prowess. Boys who experience slow growth and/or short stature can experience a rocky emotional road during adolescence as the smallest kid in the class, the last picked for sports, and the one least likely to be noticed in a romantic way by peers who are more developed. Their smaller size often means that others perceive them as younger and less mature. As they proceed through puberty, though, boys show a decrease in anxiousness and feelings of worthlessness (Oldehinkel et al., 2011).

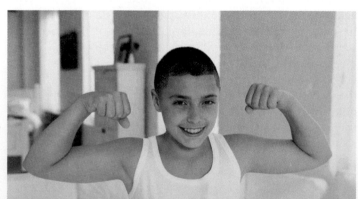

Why are boys generally more positive than girls about the physical changes in their bodies during adolescence?

Whereas menarche is a memorable event for girls, boys are often unaware of some of the physical changes they are experiencing. They notice their first ejaculation, but they rarely tell anyone about it and often were not prepared for it (Stein & Reiser, 1994). Although males express a mix of positive and negative reactions to becoming sexually mature, they generally react more positively to semenarche than girls do to menarche; 62% of boys regard semenarche positively, whereas only 23% of girls view menarche positively (Oldehinkel et al., 2011; Seiffge-Krenke, 1998).

Pubertal changes may prompt changes in family relations. Adolescents physically distance themselves from their parents by engaging in less body contact, especially with fathers, and they go to great lengths to avoid being seen naked by their parents (Schulz, 1991, in Seiffge-Krenke, 1998). Likewise, parents seem to restructure the parent–child relationship, placing greater distance between themselves and their children. Perhaps as a result of the barriers erected between adolescents and their parents, teens become more independent and less close to their parents (Steinberg, 1989). They are also more likely to experience conflicts with their parents, especially with their mothers—mostly about minor issues such as unmade beds, late hours, and loud music rather than about core values. Hormone changes in early adolescence may contribute to this increased conflict with parents and to moodiness, bouts of depression, lower or more variable energy levels, and restlessness (Buchanan, Eccles, & Becker, 1992). However, cultural beliefs about family relations and about the significance of becoming an adult also influence parent–child interactions during adolescence. For example, many Mexican American boys and their parents appear to become closer rather than more distant during the peak of pubertal changes (Molina & Chassin, 1996).

Even when parent–child relationships are disrupted during early adolescence, they become warmer once the pubertal transition is completed. Parents—mothers and fathers alike—can help adolescents adjust successfully to puberty by maintaining close relationships and helping adolescents accept themselves (Swarr & Richards, 1996). Overall, you should not imagine that the physical and hormonal changes of puberty cause direct and straightforward psychological changes in the individual. Instead, biological changes interact with psychological characteristics of the person and with changes in the social environment to influence how adolescence is experienced (Graber, Nichols, & Brooks-Gunn, 2010).

Early versus Late Development

If "timely" maturation has psychological implications, what is it like to be out of synch with your peers—to be an early or late developer? The answer depends on whether we are talking about males or females and also on whether we examine their adjustment during adolescence or later on.

Consider the short-term effects of being an early-developing or late-developing boy. Early-developing boys are judged to be socially competent, attractive, and self-assured, and they enjoy greater social acceptance by their peers (Mendle et al., 2010; Mensa et al., 2013). There are some negative aspects of being an early-maturing boy, namely increased risk of earlier involvement in substance use and other problem behaviors such as bullying, aggression, and delinquency (Kaltiala-Heino et al., 2003; Lynne

et al., 2007). By comparison, late maturation in boys has more negative effects. Late-maturing boys tend to be more anxious and less sure of themselves, and they experience more behavior and adjustment problems (Dorn, Susman, & Ponirakis, 2003; Graber et al., 2004). As a group, they even score lower than other students do, at least in early adolescence, on school achievement tests (Dubas, Graber, & Petersen, 1991). However, on the positive side, late-maturing boys are less likely to drink alcohol during adolescence (Bratberg et al., 2005).

Now consider early-maturing and late-maturing girls. Traditionally, physical prowess has not been as important in girls' peer groups as in boys', so an early-developing girl may not gain much status from being larger and more muscled. In addition, because girls develop about 2 years earlier than boys do, an early-developing girl may be subjected to teasing or bullying for being the only one in her grade who is developed. Perhaps for some of these reasons, early maturation appears to be more of a disadvantage than an advantage for girls. The early-maturing girl expresses higher levels of body dissatisfaction than her prepubertal classmates and may engage in unsafe dieting and exercising as a result of this discomfort. In addition, early maturity seems to alter girls' social environments, thrusting them into socializing with older peers (Allison & Hyde, 2011). As a result, they are likely to become involved in dating, smoking, drinking, having sex, and engaging in minor troublemaking at an early age. Girls who experience puberty earlier than their peers report higher levels of depression at least for the period of time that they are out of synch (Reynolds & Juvonen, 2012). It is not yet clear, though, which comes first: Does being depressed ignite biochemical changes in the body, triggering early puberty and sexual activity? Or does experiencing early puberty and sexual activity lead to being depressed? Researchers are still working to untangle these issues but some recent evidence links depressive symptoms among pubertal girls to environmental, not genetic, factors (Marceau et al., 2012).

Some research suggests that early puberty may be a form of stress, which may or may not lead to psychopathology, depending on the individual's coping mechanisms and family context (see Graber et al., 2010). Early puberty and its possible ill effects are intertwined with family processes. Poor quality family interactions may elevate stress levels, contributing to early puberty, and then these same poor family situations are unable to provide the supportive context needed to successfully navigate the potential pitfalls of early puberty. Ideally, family context would be positive prior to, as well as throughout, puberty to provide the optimal structure for teenage girls to manage the changes associated with puberty.

Late-maturing girls (like late-maturing boys) may experience some anxiety as they wait to mature, but they do not seem to be as disadvantaged as late-maturing boys. Indeed, whereas later-developing boys tend to perform poorly on school achievement tests, later-developing girls outperform other students (Dubas et al., 1991). Perhaps late-developing girls focus on academic skills when other girls have shifted some of their focus to extracurricular activities.

Do differences between early and late developers persist into later adolescence and adulthood? Typically, the effects of being out of synch are greatest during the time when the adolescent is most noticeably different from others. In other words, early-maturing girls experience negative feelings during early adolescence when their early maturation is most noticeable relative to peers. Late-maturing girls are more likely to experience negative feelings in mid- to late-adolescence, again when their late maturation is most noticeable (Reynolds & Juvonen, 2012). By the end of high school, though, most of the negative effects of being out of synch have disappeared because there are few observable differences by this time. Still, when tracked into adulthood, early-maturing girls have not always attained as much education as girls who were not early maturing (Johansson & Ritzén, 2005). And there may be lasting effects of some of the risky behaviors engaged in by early-maturing girls (such as sex and drinking). Early-maturing girls have a greater likelihood than all other groups of experiencing long-term adjustment problems, including anxiety and depression (Graber et al., 1997, 2004). Some of the advantages of being an early-maturing boy may carry over into adulthood, but early-maturing boys also seem to experience greater anxiety than late-maturing ones, who may learn some lessons about coping in creative ways from their struggles as adolescents (Zehr et al., 2007).

Overall, then, late-maturing boys and early-maturing girls are especially likely to find the adolescent period disruptive (Phillips & Edwards, 2013). However, psychological differences between early-maturing and late-maturing adolescents become smaller and more mixed in quality by adulthood. It is also important to note that differences between early and late maturers are relatively small and that many factors besides the timing of maturation influence whether this period goes smoothly or not. For example, girls who make the transition from elementary to middle school at the same time they experience puberty exhibit greater adjustment problems than girls who do not experience a school transition and pubertal changes simultaneously (Simmons & Blyth, 1987).

Finally, and perhaps most important, the effects of the timing of puberty depend on the adolescent's perception of whether pubertal events are experienced early, on time, or late (Seiffge-Krenke, 1998). Thus, one girl may believe she is a "late bloomer" when she does not menstruate until age 14. But another girl who exercises strenuously may believe that menarche at age 14 is normal because delayed menarche is typical of serious athletes. Peer and family-member reactions to an adolescent's pubertal changes are also instrumental in determining the adolescent's adjustment. This may help explain the difference in adjustment between early-maturing boys and early-maturing girls. Parents may be more concerned and negative about their daughter's emerging sexuality than they are about their son's. These attitudes may be inadvertently conveyed to teens, affecting their experience of puberty and their self-concept.

Health and Wellness

Adolescents should be reaching their peak of physical fitness and health and, indeed, many adolescents are strong, fit, and energetic. Unfortunately, the sedentary lifestyle of modern society may be undermining the health and fitness of an increasing number of teens. Fitness tests of American teenagers show that an alarming number of them have poor physical fitness. Fewer than one in five teenagers do the recommended 60 minutes of daily physical activity (CDCP, 2011). Barely 15% of students walk or bicycle to school and, once at school, only 2% of high schools have daily physical activity factored into the school day (CDCP, 2011). Girls tend to become less active than boys in adolescence, although this gender gap has certainly narrowed in recent years with federally mandated gender equality in athletics (Yan et al., 2009). Teens may be doing well in school, but they are flunking treadmill tests that measure heart and lung function (Pribis, 2010). Today's teens are showing up with high blood pressure, high cholesterol, and high blood sugar, putting them at risk for heart disease at earlier ages than previous generations.

Weight

As with children, the number of teens who meet the criteria for **obesity**—being 20% or more above the "ideal" weight for height, age, and sex—is increasing. As ■ **Figure 5.9** shows, obesity rates have increased from 10% to 15% over just a 12-year period. They are especially higher among certain ethnic minority groups, with, for example, 35% of non-Hispanic blacks meeting the definition for obesity compared to 24% of non-Hispanic whites (Flegal et al., 2012). Some of the same issues that we discussed earlier regarding children's weight also apply to adolescents. Adolescents have more sedentary lifestyles and consume more empty calories than they need, often in the form of beverages. Adolescents who drink more calorie-dense, nutrient-poor beverages not only gain weight, they have higher systolic blood pressure (Nguyen et al., 2009). The weight and the blood pressure put them at risk for later health problems, including heart and kidney disease, diabetes, liver problems,

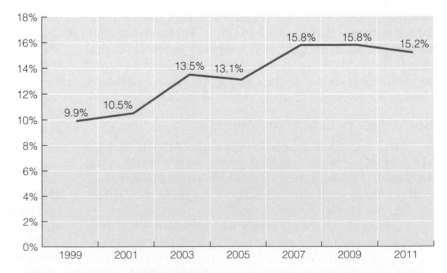

■ **Figure 5.9** Percentage of overweight high school students over a 12-year period, from 1999 to 2011.

Source: Centers for Disease Control and Prevention, National Center for Chronic Disease Prevention and Health Promotion, Youth Risk Behavior Surveillance System (YRBSS), various years, 1999–2011.

and arthritis. Rates of **diabetes**—high levels of sugar in the blood leading to various health problems—have significantly increased in recent years among adolescents, with more and more teens now taking antidiabetic drugs (Hsia et al., 2009).

Obesity is usually the product of both nature and nurture: Heredity is certainly important, but poor eating habits, inactivity, and parent behaviors contribute (Steffen et al., 2009). ● **Table 5.6** summarizes some of the environmental factors that contribute to obesity, in particular, the rise in rates of obesity in recent decades.

● **Table 5.6** Environmental Factors Contributing to the Obesity Epidemic

Inactive Lifestyles	Among adults, occupations have become more sedentary (think, sitting at computer all day) and, as a result, adults burn 100–150 fewer calories every day than they used to. Over a person's work life, this would add nearly 30 pounds of weight.
Portion Sizes	In just 20 years, the average soda size has increased from 6.5 to 20 ounces. Burgers at fast food restaurants increased from 4.5 to 8 ounces. The original McDonald's hamburger, in 1955, weighed just 1.6 ounces.
Fat Content	In 2000, average fat consumption was 75 pounds per year, up nearly 30 pounds from 1950.
Sugar	In 1822, each person consumed approximately 6 pounds per year; today, each person consumes nearly 108 pounds per year. This figure rises even higher—as much as 150 pounds per year—if all forms of sweeteners are combined. The American Heart Association recommends no more than 9.5 teaspoons per day.
Stress	Prenatal exposure to a mother's stress can craft a neural architecture that is associated with later obesity. And stress in one's own life is associated with accumulation of belly fat. Unhealthy snacking is a common response to stress. Although research has uncovered these connections between stress and obesity, it does not address whether stress has contributed to the rise in obesity.
Poverty	A large proportion of children who live in poverty are obese or overweight relative to children in households not affected by poverty. The number of households meeting the U.S. criteria for poverty has increased in recent years. Among adults, *higher* income tends to be associated with higher obesity rates for men, but with lower obesity rates for women.

SOURCES: CDC, NCCDPHP, 2012b; CDC, 2012a; Church et al., 2011; Guyenet & Landen, 2012; Molteni et al., 2002; *USDA Factbook*, 2012; Young & Nestle, 2002.

Children and adolescents whose parents are overweight have twin risk factors for becoming overweight themselves: the genes that their parents have passed along to them that may predispose them to be overweight and the environment that is created for them by overweight parents (Steffen et al., 2009; Thibault et al., 2009). For instance, overweight parents are less likely to engage their children in vigorous physical activity and they are more likely to model sedentary behaviors such as watching television. Overweight parents are also more likely to be economically disadvantaged, so they purchase less expensive foods that are often high in calories and low in nutritional value. Adolescents who are overweight tend to gravitate toward other overweight teens (Valente et al., 2009). Being friends with other teens who are overweight may be comfortable in that it reduces the stigma of being overweight. Further, it establishes an unhealthy pattern of behavior—inactivity coupled with poor eating habits—as normative and acceptable. There is little incentive to be different from the peers with whom you spend your time, so if they are sitting around eating junk food and drinking sugary drinks, then it is easy to do the same. **Exploration Box 5.1** considers recent concerns that obesity may be causing a "brain drain."

Risky Behaviors

Health risks that often originate during adolescence include alcohol and drug use and cigarette smoking. Lifestyle choices made by adolescents and young adults have important implications for their health, both in the short term and in the long term (VanKim et al., 2010). Consider the 22% of high school students who report occasional heavy or binge drinking (Eaton et al., 2012). Teens under the influence of alcohol are more likely to make additional risky choices:

1. They are more likely to smoke cigarettes and the more they smoke, the more likely they are to become addicted to nicotine.
2. They are more likely to engage in risky sexual behaviors including sex with multiple partners and unprotected sex. In turn, these behaviors are associated with unintended pregnancies and sexually transmitted diseases.
3. They are more likely to get into a car where the driver has been drinking, which greatly increases the risk of an accident.
4. They are more likely to get into physical fights, experience academic problems, and engage in illegal behaviors.

These behaviors, or the predisposition to these behaviors, may have been present before the alcohol use, but alcohol use can still exacerbate the problems. By some analyses, making the decision not to drink during adolescence may be one of the teen's most important health decisions.

Sleep

Another health issue that seems to plague many teenagers is insufficient sleep. Puberty ushers in changes in the sleep–wake cycle, melatonin production, and circadian rhythms, which can shift the "natural" time for falling asleep later and later. Research shows that the level of melatonin (a sleep-promoting hormone)

Could Obesity Trigger a "Brain Drain"?

Children and teens who are overweight or obese experience a number of challenges. The additional weight puts them at risk for such physical problems as diabetes and heart problems. There is an emotional toll as well, with obese youth reporting significantly lower levels of emotional, social, and psychosocial functioning relative to their average-weight peers (Zeller & Medi, 2006). They also report poorer self-concepts and lower levels of self-esteem, which is not surprising as 44% of adolescent girls and 31% of adolescent boys report being teased about their weight, either by peers, family members, or both (Eisenberg, Neumark-Sztainer, & Story, 2003; Wallander et al., 2009).

If these reasons are not compelling enough to be concerned about obesity rates among our youth, then consider some research that examined the brain function of obese youth with metabolic syndrome. **Metabolic syndrome (MeTS)** is a combination of risk factors that can lead to cardiovascular (that is, heart) disease. At the center of the risk factors is obesity and its associated factors of high blood pressure, unhealthy cholesterol levels, and insulin resistance, which can lead to diabetes (see Kassi, Pervanidou, Kaltsas, & Chrousos, 2011).

Researchers from New York University compared 49 adolescents with MeTS with 62 adolescents without MeTS (Yau et al., 2012).

The two groups were matched on multiple factors that might otherwise influence the results: age, gender, ethnicity, and socioeconomic status. The adolescents underwent endocrine testing, were evaluated with MRIs, and were assessed for cognitive and intellectual functioning.

The findings showed that adolescents with MeTS scored slightly lower—4 points—on overall IQ, but nearly 10 points lower on measures of math achievement. They also demonstrated some issues with attention and mental flexibility. While all scores were in the normal or average ranges, it is concerning that adolescents with MeTS are not operating at the same level of cognitive functioning as their non-MeTS peers. The MRIs revealed some structural differences between the two groups of adolescents. This suggests that MeTS, a condition typically found only among individuals who are obese, is associated with a different brain architecture. And the more MeTS risk factors that these teens had, the lower their cognitive functioning. Let's be careful, though, not to jump to the conclusion that obesity or MeTS caused brain damage. As the authors point out, there could be other factors in play, such as a delay in brain maturation. Nonetheless, the cognitive deficits, whether they are permanent or temporary, add to the larger picture of childhood and adolescent obesity, and collectively, the findings indi-

cate this is a serious health concern that cannot be ignored.

The incidence of MeTS and its associated health hazards can be reduced among teens as well as adults. An analysis of more than half a million adults showed that adhering to the so-called Mediterranean diet reduced the risk of MeTS (Kastorini et al., 2011). The Mediterranean diet has numerous components, including use of olive oil rather than butter, consumption of daily fruits and vegetables, weekly fish and poultry, and very little red meat. Not only does the Mediterranean diet help with the body weight that contributes to MeTS, but it may also provide healthy antioxidants.

But diet alone may not be sufficient. In other research, relatively inactive adults were twice as likely to have MeTS as their active peers (Ford et al., 2005). It turns out that sitting for long periods of time, whether it is in front of the TV or the computer, can affect your body's ability to process fats and is linked to increased risk of death (Dunstan et al., 2010). Amazingly, *just one day* of inactivity decreases your "good" cholesterol, which is considered "good" because it helps clear the "bad" cholesterol from your blood (Hamilton et al., 2008). Thus, reiterating a common theme in this chapter, we need to pay attention to both our eating habits and our levels of physical activity to optimize our health.

rises later at night for teens than for children or adults (National Sleep Foundation, 2013). Teens report later bedtimes from age 12 to age 18, and only 20% of them get the optimal amount of sleep on school nights. Although psychosocial factors may also contribute to later bedtimes than in childhood (for example, doing homework or text messaging with friends late into the night), biological factors—puberty in particular—seem primarily responsible. Teens who go to bed at 11 PM should not wake up until around 8 AM if they are to get the recommended 8–9 hours of sleep. However, most teens find themselves getting out of bed around 6:30 AM to get to school on time. High schools typically start earlier than elementary schools, often by 7:30 AM to accommodate bus schedules. Thus, just when their biological clocks are pushing back sleep times at night, schools are getting teens up earlier in the morning.

What are the consequences for teens who do not get enough sleep? Teens report greater sleepiness during the day,

which is associated with decreased motivation, especially for "boring" tasks (Carskadon, 2011b). Tired teens may be able to successfully navigate a favorite class or read a particularly good book, but these same teens may have trouble completing an assignment in their least favorite subject or studying for an exam. Teens who have had their sleep restricted display increased sleepiness in proportion to the number of nights that their sleep is reduced. But surprisingly—at least to many adults—these same teens "perk up" in the evenings and show high levels of energy that discourage them from going to bed early (Carskadon, 2011a).

Teens who sleep less at night or who stay up later on the weekends than their peers report higher levels of depression, irritability, and lack of tolerance for frustration (Carskadon, 2011b; Wolfson & Carskadon, 1998). They may also have difficulty controlling their emotional responses, which leads to greater expression of aggression or anger. As with younger children, teens who do not get enough sleep have trouble concentrating in school,

Adolescents seem to be especially likely to doze off during the day as puberty alters their sleep–wake cycles and leaves them short on sleep.

experience short-term memory problems, and may doze off in class (National Sleep Foundation, 2013).

Some teens report that, with their busy schedules, cutting back on sleep is unavoidable. Consider teens who have a big test scheduled for the next day but also have after-school obligations that will push back the start of their study time. Should they stay up late and study or should they go to bed with less study time? If you answered that they should go to bed and get a good night's sleep instead of studying, then you are correct according to recent research by Cari Gillen-O'Neel, Virginia Huynh, and Andrew Fuligni (2013). The researchers had students keep diaries of their sleep and study times for blocks of time in ninth, tenth, and twelfth grades. They found that amount of study time throughout the week did not matter if students ended up cutting short their sleep time. Students who got a good night's sleep the night before a test did better than students who sacrificed a good night's sleep to get in more study time. There is an important message here for you: Manage your time so that you get all the

study time you need *without sacrificing your sleep time*. Maintaining a consistent sleep–wake cycle with sufficient sleep time is an essential part of optimizing cognitive skills, not to mention physical health.

For all ages, learning more about sleep needs and the effects of sleep deprivation can lead to healthy lifestyle changes. Adhering to a regular bedtime and wake time on the weekends and on school and work days can help maintain healthy sleep habits. Unfortunately, "sleeping in" on the weekends alters the sleep–wake cycle and makes it more difficult to get up early for work or school Monday morning. So, next time you find yourself dozing off in class or at work, do not jump to the conclusion that the work you are doing is boring. It may be that your sleep–wake cycle is out of sync with the schedule imposed on you by school or work.

Checking Mastery

1. How do the typical brain changes throughout adolescence correlate with teen behavior?
2. Which group of teens is likely to have the "best" experience of puberty and which group is likely to experience more problems with the process of puberty?
3. What factors affect timing of menarche in girls?

Making Connections

1. What are the most significant health concerns during adolescence? If you could get adolescents to change two behaviors to improve their health, what would they be and why?
2. How would you counsel the parents of an early-maturing girl so that they understand the risks she may face and what they can do to help her adjust successfully?

5.5 The Adult

LEARNING OBJECTIVES:

• Integrate the findings of both gains and losses in the adult brain.

• Summarize changes in the reproductive system throughout adulthood, with attention to how the physical changes may influence psychological well-being.

• Classify the typical changes of adulthood according to their likely impact on daily functioning.

• Compare the major theories of aging and evaluate their contributions to our understanding of why we age and die.

The body of the young adult is at its prime in many ways. It is strong and fit; its organs are functioning efficiently; it is considered to be in peak health. But it is aging, as it has been all along. Physical aging occurs slowly and steadily over the life span. Physical and health changes begin to have noticeable effects on appearance and functioning in middle age and have an even more

significant effect by the time old age is reached, although more so in some people than in others.

But don't equate aging with only loss and decline: There are also gains and increases in some areas. This will be evident when we look at the brain in this chapter and then follow up in greater depth in Chapter 8 with the cognitive abilities of adults.

In the next sections, we discuss typical changes that occur as we progress through middle adulthood and old age. We also look at health issues that can challenge us and consider what it takes to age successfully. You will learn that lifestyle choices play a key role in your overall health and longevity.

The Changing Brain

When does the brain complete its development? In the past, we might have answered that the brain is fully developed by the end of infancy, or even by the end of pregnancy. Today, however, the answer is that *brain development is never truly complete*. The brain is responsive to experience and is capable of **neurogenesis**, the process of generating new neurons, across the life span. Consider first some research with mice. Mice that regularly work out on their treadmills (that is, running wheels) learn more quickly to navigate through a maze than their couch potato counterparts (mice without running wheels) (Pereira et al., 2007). By examining the brain tissue of the active mice, researchers found evidence of neurogenesis—new neurons were being created in response to the mouse's activity. And it turns out that adult songbirds can learn new songs with the help of new neurons (Goldman, 2008).

Neurogenesis in adult humans was once considered impossible, but there is now evidence suggesting it may be possible (see Gage, Song, & Kempermann, 2008a). Consider Terry Wallis who, injured at age 19 in a serious car accident, suffered severe brain damage and existed in a minimally conscious state for nearly 20 years (Hopkins, 2006). Doctors had assumed that recovery was not possible, but one day Terry "woke up" and began to talk. Although he remains disabled from injuries sustained during the accident, he has regained some functions and can communicate. Doctors attribute his miracle awakening to generation of new neurons and connections in the brain. But does what happened with this one individual hold true for other adults?

Fred Gage and his colleagues studied the effects of exercise on brain activity in a small group of adults (Pereira et al., 2007; and see Gage, Song, & Kempermann, 2008b). The adults were given a learning task, completed a 3-month aerobic exercise program, and were then given another learning task. Learning improved following the exercise program. The researchers could not examine actual brain tissue after exercise as they do with mice. However, they did study blood volume in the brain and found that it was almost twice as high after the exercise program in the hippocampus, a part of the brain involved in learning and memory. This increased blood volume seems to be associated with production of new neurons.

Denise Park and Chih-Mao Huang (2010) reviewed whether culture—growing up surrounded by Eastern Asian versus Western cultural values and experiences—has an effect on the organization of the brain. When asked to view pictures of an individual object, a background, and the object embedded in the background, East Asians and Westerners demonstrated different patterns of brain activity with each type of picture, as illustrated by images of blood flow captured by functional Magnetic Resonance Imaging (fMRI) (see Goh et al., 2007). Over various studies like this one, the findings suggest that different patterns of brain activity are associated with different cultural experiences reflecting the collectivist focus of East Asian and the

Pre-exercise   Post-exercise

Your brain on exercise. Using magnetic resonance imaging (MRI) technology that maps cerebral blood volume, researchers have found evidence of increased blood volume in a region of the hippocampus after exercise. This suggests the brain is capable of neurogenesis and could pave the way for developing new treatments for various conditions.

Proceedings of the National Academy of Sciences of the United States of America. vol. 104 no. 13 Copyright (2007) National Academy of Sciences, U.S.A.

individualistic focus of Western cultures. In other words, your cultural experiences shape your brain function and possibly also brain structure (Park & Huang, 2010). Your brain continues to be responsive to the environment; it is not "done" or set in stone at birth or even in infancy or childhood.

Thus, the brain displays plasticity early in life and signs of neurogenesis and synaptogenesis throughout life. It can change in response to physical and mental exercise. It may be able to regenerate some functions following injury, which holds great promise for future therapies for patients with a wide range of conditions such as stroke (Lindvall & Kokaia, 2008), epilepsy (Jessberger & Parent, 2008), and degenerative diseases such as Parkinson's and Alzheimer's (Brundin, Winkler, & Masliah, 2008). But although the adult brain can generate new neurons, it does so at a much lower rate than the young brain (Lee, Clemenson, & Gage, 2012). What does this mean for the average person? What happens to the typical brain as it ages?

Many people fear that aging means losing brain cells and ultimately becoming "senile." As you will see in Chapter 16, Alzheimer's disease and other conditions that cause serious brain damage and dementia are *not* part of normal aging; they do not affect most older people. Normal aging is associated with gradual and relatively mild degeneration within the nervous system—some loss of neurons, diminished functioning of many remaining neurons, and potentially harmful changes in the tissues surrounding and supporting the neurons, such as the protective myelin covering (Hof & Mobbs, 2001; Peters, 2002). Just as brain weight and volume increase over the childhood years, they decrease over the adult years, especially after age 50 (Courchesne et al., 2000; Resnick, 2000). As people age, more of their neurons atrophy or shrivel, transmit signals less effectively, and ultimately die (Hof & Mobbs, 2001). Elderly adults may end up with 5–30% fewer neurons, depending on the brain site studied, than they had in early adulthood. Neuron loss is greater in the areas of the brain that control sensory and motor activities than in either the association areas of the cortex (involved in thought) or the brain stem and lower brain (involved in basic life functions such as breathing).

Other signs of brain degeneration besides neuron loss include declines in the levels of important neurotransmitters; the formation of "senile plaques," hard areas in the tissue surrounding neurons that may interfere with neuronal functioning and are seen in abundance in people with Alzheimer's disease; and reduced blood flow to the brain, which may starve neurons of the oxygen and nutrients they need to function (Hof & Mobbs, 2001). One of the main implications of such degeneration, as you will see later, is that older brains typically process information more slowly than younger brains do.

On the positive side, research shows that middle age brings greater integration of the left and right hemispheres, which may help increase creativity and cognitive functioning. And the brain can remain healthy with exercise—both mental puzzles and physical aerobic workouts. Older adults who engage in high levels of aerobic activity show enhanced mental performance and corresponding increases in activity in certain regions of the brain (Bugg & Head, 2011; Voss, Nagamatsu, Liu-Ambrose, & Kramer, 2011). Some intriguing new research suggests that physical aerobic activity may be responsible for the number of new neurons generated in the brain, whereas mental activity influences the number of these new neurons that survive (Curlik & Shors, 2013).

What does it mean for older adults that both degeneration and plasticity—both losses and gains—characterize the aging brain? In some people, degeneration may win and declines in intellectual performance will occur. In other people, plasticity may prevail; their brains may form new and adaptive neural connections faster than they are lost so that performance on some tasks may actually improve with age (at least until very old age). Denise Park and Patricia Reuter-Lorenz (2009) make a compelling case that the aging brain may compensate for losses by increased activity in the prefrontal cortex. In particular, they propose the scaffolding theory of aging and compensation (STAC) to explain how the brain may adapt to losses by revving up in other areas. Thus, where a young adult's brain would use only the area that specializes in a particular kind of task to perform it, an older adult's brain might recruit other brain areas to help out. This kind of compensation may not always be possible due to health issues or genetic predispositions or adverse life experiences, but when it is, older adults may be able to maintain useful cognitive functioning for a longer period of time. Thus, you can reject the view that aging involves nothing but a slow death of neural tissue. Old brains *can* learn new tricks.

The Changing Reproductive System

During most of adulthood, the sex hormones that start to be secreted during adolescence help ensure interest in sexual behavior and the ability to have children, but they also have psychological implications and affect the experience of aging. In men, testosterone levels fluctuate annually, with peak levels detected in spring and lower levels in fall, and daily, with peak levels in the morning (Moskovic, Eisenberg, & Lipshultz, 2012; van Anders, 2012). Men with high levels of testosterone tend to be more sexually active and aggressive than other men, although this relationship is influenced by other factors (see Trainor & Nelson, 2012). Otherwise, it is not clear that changes in men's hormone levels are tied to changes in their moods and behavior.

By contrast, hormone levels in women shift drastically each month as they progress through their menstrual cycles. These shifts have psychological implications for some women. Estrogen and progesterone levels rise to a peak at midcycle, when a woman is ovulating, and decline as she approaches her menstrual period. The cyclic changes in hormones may lead to such symptoms as bloating, moodiness, breast tenderness, and headaches during the days just before the menstrual flow, symptoms collectively referred to as **premenstrual syndrome (PMS)**. Estimates of how many women experience PMS vary substantially. Roughly half of teenagers report that they experience PMS and a majority—as high as 90%—report at least some symptoms before menstruation and usually regard these as a normal accompaniment to the menstrual cycle (Delara et al., 2012; Wong, 2011). As many as 10% of women experience symptoms severe enough to interfere with their ability to perform daily activities and a few of these, perhaps 2–3%, may be diagnosed with a severe form of PMS called **premenstrual dysphoric disorder (PDD)**. PDD differs from PMS in that it includes affective symptoms in addition to physical symptoms associated with the menstrual cycle and it can be disabling—disrupting work and relationships (American Psychiatric Association, 2000). Women with PDD report poorer health-related quality of life than those without PDD (Delara et al., 2012).

In recent decades, there has been some debate about the validity of PMS. In research where women are simply asked to complete mood surveys every day and do not know that their menstrual cycles are being studied, most report little premenstrual mood change. This suggests that expectations and not hormones play a role in many cases of PMS. Still, symptoms consistent with PMS are reported across many cultures, including those that generally do not label or acknowledge the syndrome (see Yonkers & Casper, 2012). Changes in estrogen and progesterone levels are the likely causes of the symptoms associated with PMS. Various treatments are available for PMS, depending on the severity and type of symptoms experiences. For instance, some women with severe PMS may find relief when treated with antidepressant drugs such as Prozac (Dimmock et al., 2000). For women with milder forms of PMS, treatment with calcium and vitamin D may alleviate symptoms because the low estrogen levels experienced prior to menstruation can interfere with the absorption of these substances by the body (Thys-Jacobs, 2000). Clearly, individuals vary in how they experience menstrual cycles.

Female Menopause

Like other systems of the body, the reproductive system ages. The ending of a woman's menstrual periods in midlife is called **menopause**. Levels of estrogen and other female hormones decline so that the woman who has been through menopause has a hormone mix that is less "feminine" and more "masculine" than that of the premenopausal woman. When menopause is completed, a woman is no longer ovulating, no longer menstruating, and no longer capable of conceiving a child.

The average woman experiences menopause at age 51, and the usual age range is from 45 to 54 (National Institute on Aging, 2013). The process takes place gradually over 5–10 years as periods become either more or less frequent and less regular. Although life expectancy has increased and the age of menarche has decreased over history as part of the secular trend, the age of menopause does not appear to have changed much and is similar from culture to culture (Brody et al., 2000). What has changed is that women are now living long enough to experience a considerable period of postmenopausal life. The age at which a woman reaches menopause is somewhat related to both the age at which she reached menarche and the age at which her mother reached menopause (Varea et al., 2000). Researchers have discovered that menopause can be predicted by a hormone called anti-Müllerian hormone (Mishra & Dobson, 2012; Mishra & Kuh, 2012). Anti-Müllerian hormone peaks around age 16, remains stable until about age 25, and then begins a slow decline (Fong et al., 2012).

Society holds rather stereotypic views of menopausal women. They are regarded as irritable, emotional, depressed, and unstable. How much truth is there to this stereotype? Not much. About two-thirds of women in U.S. society experience **hot flashes**—sudden experiences of warmth and sweating, usually centered around the face and upper body, that occur at unpredictable times, last for a few seconds or minutes, and are often followed by a cold shiver (Whitbourne & Whitbourne, 2011). Many also experience vaginal dryness and irritation or pain during intercourse. Still other women experience no symptoms.

For years, **hormone replacement therapy (HRT)** (taking estrogen and progestin to compensate for hormone loss at menopause), was considered an effective cure for the symptoms that some women experience with menopause. HRT relieves physical symptoms of menopause, such as hot flashes and vaginal dryness, and prevents or slows osteoporosis. Unfortunately, trust in HRT was shattered in 2002 by a large government study that found that HRT increases women's chances of developing breast cancer and experiencing heart attacks and strokes (Women's Health Initiative, 2004). For most women, these risks outweigh the benefits of HRT, particularly if the hormones estrogen and progestin are taken over a long period. For women with severe menopausal symptoms associated with decreasing production of hormones, short-term HRT (for example, up to 2 years) may be warranted. Lifestyle changes such as exercising and getting adequate sleep may be the best options for menopausal women because they alleviate some complaints and are safe.

What about the psychological symptoms—irritability and depression? Again, researchers have discovered wide variation among menopausal women—and not much truth to the negative stereotypes. In a particularly well-designed study, Karen Matthews and her associates (Matthews, 1992; Matthews et al., 1990) studied 541 initially premenopausal women over a 3-year period, comparing those who subsequently experienced menopause with women of similar ages who did not become menopausal. The typical woman entering menopause initially experienced some physical symptoms such as hot flashes. Some women also reported mild depression and temporary emotional distress, probably in reaction to their physical symptoms, but only about 10% could be said to have become seriously depressed in response to menopause. Typically, menopause had no effect on the women's levels of anxiety, anger, perceived stress, or job dissatisfaction. When women do experience severe psychological problems during the menopausal transition, they often had those problems well before the age of menopause (Greene, 1984).

Women who have been through menopause generally say it had little effect on them or that it even improved their lives; they are usually more positive about it than women who have not been through it yet (Gannon & Ekstrom, 1993; Wilbur, Miller, & Montgomery, 1995). For most women, menopause brings no changes in sexual interest and activity, although sexual activity gradually declines in both women and men over the adult years (Laumann, Paik, & Rosen, 1999). In short, despite all the negative stereotypes, menopause seems to be "no big deal" for most women. Indeed, many women find the end of monthly periods to be quite liberating.

Why do some women experience more severe menopausal symptoms than others do? Again, part of the answer may lie with biology. Women who have a history of menstrual problems (such as PMS) report more menopausal symptoms, both physical and psychological (Morse et al., 1998). Thus, some women may experience greater biological changes or be more sensitive to them. But psychological and social factors of the sort that influence women's reactions to sexual maturation and to their menstrual cycles also influence the severity of menopausal symptoms. For example, women who expect menopause to be a negative experience are likely to get what they expect (Matthews, 1992). There is also a good deal of variation across cultures in how menopause is experienced. It appears that the effect of menopause is colored by the meaning it has for the woman, as influenced by her society's prevailing views of menopause and by her own personal characteristics.

Male Andropause

Obviously, men cannot experience menopause because they do not menstruate. They also do not experience the sharp drop in hormones that accompanies menopause in women. But over the past decade, some research has pointed to the possibility that men experience andropause as they age. **Andropause**, also called *age-associated hypogonadism*, is characterized by slowly decreasing levels of testosterone and a variety of symptoms including low libido, fatigue and lack of energy, erection problems, memory problems, and loss of pubic hair (Tan & Pu, 2004). By age 80, men have between 20% and 50% of the testosterone that they had at age 20. The sperm produced by older men may not be as active as those produced by younger men. Still, men can father children long after women become incapable of bearing children.

Some research reports that testosterone levels are markedly lower among men over age 50 with symptoms of andropause than among men without symptoms (Wu, Yu, & Chen, 2000). But other research does not show a clear connection between andropause symptoms and testosterone levels (see, for example, Vermeulen, 2000). In one study, for example, half of 50- to 70-year-old men complained of **erectile dysfunction**—inability to achieve or sustain an erection for intercourse—despite having sufficient levels of testosterone (Gould, Petty, & Jacobs, 2000). Most cases of erectile dysfunction are caused by medical conditions such as diabetes and not by lower hormone production. Erectile dysfunction among older men is often treatable with *sildenafil*, no doubt more familiar to you by the name Viagra.

In sum, the changes associated with andropause in men are more gradual, more variable, and less complete than those associated with menopause in women. As a result, men experience fewer psychological effects. Frequency of sexual activity does decline as men age. However, this trend cannot be blamed entirely on decreased hormone levels, because sexual activity often declines even when testosterone levels remain high (Gould et al., 2000; see also Chapter 12 on sexuality).

Other Typical Changes

What other changes can we expect across adulthood and old age? There are usually some changes in physical appearance and functioning, the reproductive system, and a slowing down when it comes to many physical activities. We'll look at these changes before turning our attention to their psychological implications and whether they arise from disease, disuse or abuse.

Appearance and Physical Functioning

Only minor changes in physical appearance occur in the 20s and 30s, but, as the interviews in **Exploring Development Box 5.1** illustrate, many people notice signs that they are aging as they reach their 40s. Skin becomes wrinkled, dry, and loose, especially among people who have spent more time in the sun. Hair thins and often turns gray from loss of pigment-producing cells. And to most people's dismay, they put on extra weight throughout much of adulthood as their metabolism rate slows but their eating and exercise habits do not adjust accordingly. The weight gain may be largely unnoticeable during our 20s but then seems to pick up speed after we pass the 30 mark with even greater acceleration after age 40. This "middle-aged spread" could be controlled by regular exercise but it occurs when many adults feel they have little time to exercise because family and work responsibilities demand a great deal of their time. Just 30% of adults engage in regular physical activity during their leisure time, less than 20% do strength training, and few engage in the level of aerobic exercise needed to maintain, let alone improve, their fitness (Schoenborn & Adams, 2010). Consequently, many middle-aged adults are overweight or even obese.

We discussed many of the health concerns associated with obesity in an earlier section. To impress upon you the magnitude of this issue, consider that obesity is a multi-billion dollar "business," accounting for 20% of the total health care costs in the United States (Cawley & Meyerhoefer, 2012). The U.S. Department of Health and Human Services has identified obesity as one of the most significant health care concerns facing Americans and has issued a number of recommended strategies for combating obesity. Many of these are the same ones recommended for children and adolescents: promoting healthy foods and beverages, discouraging consumption of those foods and beverages that add calories but not nutrition, and increasing physical activity through a variety of community programs. The upward trend in obesity rates must be curbed or future generations will face the unsettling prospect of shorter life spans than their parents or grandparents.

As people move into their 60s and beyond, they may begin to lose some weight, although this may not be evident until their 80s (Whitbourne & Whitbourne, 2011). Unfortunately, this loss of weight in old age is not from losing the fat gained in middle age but from losing valuable muscle and bone. Importantly, it is not age per se that reduces muscle mass but rather the sedentary lifestyle adopted by many older adults. When Abby King and colleagues (2000) surveyed nearly 3,000 women in middle and later adulthood, they found that only 9% met the criteria for being regularly active. And as age increased, level of activity decreased. Age is not the only culprit, however, in making adults less active; low level of education, poor neighborhood characteristics, and personal factors (such as caregiving responsibilities and lack of energy) also influence whether or not adults exercise (King et al., 2000).

Aging also involves a gradual decline in the efficiency of most bodily systems from the 20s on. Most systems increase to a peak sometime between childhood and early adulthood and decline slowly thereafter. No matter what physical function you look at—the capacity of the heart or lungs to meet the demands of exercise, the ability of the body to control its temperature, the ability of the immune system to fight disease, or strength—the gradual effects of aging are evident. For example, we lose nearly 10% of our strength capacity with each passing decade (Katzel & Steinbrenner, 2012). In terms of handgrip strength, both men and women show declines from early to late adulthood, with men's losses fairly evenly distributed over adulthood and women's losses starting out slow but then escalating after age 55 (Samson et al., 2000). Why consider handgrip strength? It turns out that handgrip strength in middle age is a good predictor of disability and ability to function in later life: Those with weaker handgrip in middle age are more likely to report greater difficulty with such everyday activities as housework, walking, dressing, and bathing 25 years later (Rantanen et al., 1999). Those with stronger handgrip at midlife are more likely to beat the odds and live to age 100 (Rantanen et al., 2012). Why would handgrip be associated with health and longevity? Likely because it is an external indication of internal health and wellness. Someone with a strong handgrip is likely more active and healthy than someone with a weak handgrip.

It should be noted that individual differences in physiological functioning increase with age (Harris et al., 1992). That is, aerobic capacity and other physiological measurements vary more widely among 70-year-olds than among 20-year-olds. Even though the *average* old person is less physiologically fit than the

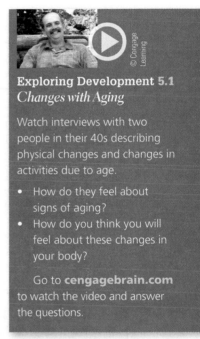

Exploring Development 5.1
Changes with Aging

Watch interviews with two people in their 40s describing physical changes and changes in activities due to age.

- How do they feel about signs of aging?
- How do you think you will feel about these changes in your body?

Go to **cengagebrain.com** to watch the video and answer the questions.

average young person, *not all older people have poor physiological functioning.* Older adults who remain physically active retain greater strength and faster reaction times than their less active peers (Katzel & Steinbrenner, 2012).

Another fact of physical aging is a decline in the **reserve capacity** of many organ systems—that is, their ability to respond to demands for extraordinary output, such as in emergencies (Goldberg & Hagberg, 1990). For example, old and young people do not differ much in resting heart rates, but older adults, even if they are disease-free, will have lower maximal heart rates (Lakatta, 1990). This means that older adults who do not feel very old as they go about their normal routines may feel very old indeed if they try to run up mountains.

Older adults are often less fit than younger ones because they decrease their involvement in vigorous physical activity as they get older—females earlier than males (Katzel & Steinbrenner, 2012). Older adults who are socially isolated and lonely reduce their physical activity even more than those who maintain strong social connections (Hawkley, Thisted, & Caciappo, 2009). By late adulthood, older adults may find that they get tired just climbing stairs or carrying groceries; running a marathon is out of the question. The average older person tires more quickly and needs more time to recover after vigorous activity than the average younger person.

Finally, if you have ever taken a walk with a grandparent or another older adult, you likely found yourself slowing down so as to not leave your older companion behind. Older adults walk more slowly than the average of 4 feet per second clocked by most of their younger counterparts. In many situations, the older adult may simply need to allow additional time for getting places. In other situations, though, their slow speed may pose a safety concern, such as crossing a busy street where stoplights are programmed for the average adult's walking speed and not the average *older* adult's walking speed (Lobjois & Cavallo, 2009). In addition, research has revealed that walking speed can be a useful predictor of survival among older adults. Stephanie Studenski and her colleagues (2011) examined the relationship between the walking speed of more than 34,000 adults over the age of 65 and their 5-year and 10-year survival rates. The findings showed that an older adult's walking speed can effectively predict survival, especially among those 75 years and older. Thus, the fast-walking 75-year-old is more likely to be alive 5 and 10 years later than her slow-walking companions. This makes sense when you consider that walking speed, like handgrip strength, gives us a window into the functioning of multiple internal organ systems. When one or more of the organ systems that contribute to walking (for example, lungs, heart, musculature, nervous system, and so on) is damaged or begins to deteriorate, this will be reflected externally in a slower gait.

Psychological Implications

How do these changes in appearance, functioning, and pace influence older adults? Do they maintain a positive or unchanged outlook on life, or are the physical changes accompanied by some psychological angst? Some people, influenced by societal stereotypes to equate "old" with "unattractive," find the physical changes in their appearance and functioning that occur with age difficult to accept. American society values youth and devalues old age and the physical changes that often accompany it. What are the psychological implications of growing older under these conditions? Negative stereotypes about older adults abound—they are sickly, frail, forgetful, unattractive, dependent, or otherwise incompetent. Such stereotypes can lead to **ageism**, or prejudice against elderly people (see also Chapter 11). Most elderly adults have internalized these negative views but believe they apply to other older adults and not to themselves—at least until they finally admit that they are "old" (Levy, 2009).

How do older adults feel about themselves and the changes in their physical appearance and functioning? Some adults are bothered by their physical appearance, women more so than men and white women somewhat more so than women of color (Frederick, Peplau, & Lever, 2006; Grabe & Shibley Hyde, 2006). Women often focus their clothes shopping on finding the best camouflage for their perceived body flaws (Tiggemann & Lacey, 2009). But the larger concern seems to be the ability to continue functioning at a desirable level. Laura Hurd (1999) interviewed women between ages 50 and 90 who attended programs at a "senior center." She found that the women actively worked to distance themselves from the "old" category and to remain in the "not old" category. These categories were defined not by age but by what individuals can and cannot do. Generally, the women believed that they were not old because they had the physical and mental abilities to avoid nursing home care. In particular, they believed that remaining active—both physically and socially—was the key to avoiding becoming old. Women who considered themselves "not old" believed that men and women who were old had given in to the stereotypes of aging by being inactive and solitary.

As you have seen, many older adults, even those who consider themselves "not old," have chronic diseases and impairments. Still, the majority of people 65 and older say they are in excellent, very good, or good health (Federal Interagency Forum, 2012). Whites are more likely to report they are in good health than blacks or Hispanics (78% compared to 63% and 63%). Relatively few older adults say they need assistance with daily activities, although the figure climbs with age—from 9% of those age 65 to

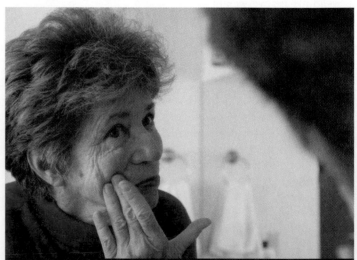

Older adults, like adolescents, often struggle to come to terms with the physical changes they experience as they age.

age 69 to 50% of those age 85 and older (Hobbs, 1996). Although having a chronic disease or disability tends to lower an older person's sense of well-being, many people with arthritis, diabetes, and other difficulties are no less content with their lives than anyone else (Kempen et al., 1997). Clearly, most older people are able to retain their sense of well-being and their ability to function independently despite an increased likelihood of impairments.

Disease, Disuse, or Abuse?

Many aspects of physical functioning seem to decline over the adult years in many individuals. But an important question arises: When researchers look at the performance of older people, are they seeing the effects of aging alone or the effects of something else? The "something else" could be disease, disuse of the body, abuse of the body—or all three.

Most older people have at least some chronic *disease* or impairment, such as arthritis or heart disease. How would an elderly person function if she could manage to stay disease-free? Birren and his colleagues (1963) addressed this question in a classic study of men aged 65–91. Extensive medical examinations were conducted to identify two groups of elderly men: (1) those who were almost perfectly healthy and had no signs of disease and (2) those who had slight traces of some disease in the making but no clinically diagnosable diseases. Several aspects of physical and intellectual functioning were assessed in these men, and the participants were compared with young men.

The most remarkable finding was that the healthier group of older men hardly differed from the younger men. They were equal in their capacity for physical exercise, and they beat the younger men on measures of intelligence requiring general information or knowledge of vocabulary words. Their main limitations were the slower brain activity and reaction times that seem to be so basic to the aging process. Overall, aging in the absence of disease had little effect on physical and psychological functioning. However, the men with slight traces of impending disease were deficient on several measures. Diseases that have progressed to the point of symptoms have even more serious consequences for performance.

So it is possible that disease, rather than aging, accounts for many declines in functioning in later life. We must note, however, that Birren and his colleagues had a tough time finding the perfectly healthy older people they studied. Most older people experience both aging and disease, and it is difficult to separate the effects of the two. Although aging and disease are distinct, increased vulnerability to disease is one part—and an important part—of normal aging.

Disuse of the body also contributes to steeper declines in physical functioning in some adults than in others. John Masters and Virginia Johnson (1966) proposed a "use it or lose it" maxim to describe how sexual functioning deteriorates if a person engages in little or no sexual activity. The same maxim can be applied to other systems of the body. Muscles atrophy if they are not used, and the heart functions less well if a person leads a sedentary life (Rosenbloom & Bahns, 2006). Changes such as these in some aging adults are much like the changes observed in people of any age confined to bed for a long time (Goldberg & Hagberg, 1990). The brain also needs "mental exercise" to display plasticity and to continue to function effectively in old age (Black, Isaacs, & Greenough, 1991). In short, most systems of the body seem to thrive on use, but too many people become inactive as they age.

Finally, *abuse* of the body contributes to declines in functioning in some people. Excessive alcohol consumption, a high-fat diet, and smoking are all clear examples. In addition, some older adults abuse drugs, either illicit or prescription, intentionally or unintentionally (Dowling, Weiss, & Condon, 2008; Martin, 2008). Experts believe that we may see an increase in recreational use of drugs among the elderly as the baby boomers who came of age during the drug culture of the 1960s retire (White et al., 2011). Drugs typically affect older adults more powerfully than they do younger adults; they can also interact with one another and with the aging body's chemistry to impair functioning.

Overall, then, poor functioning in old age may represent any combination of the effects of aging, disease, disuse, and abuse. We may not be able to do much to change basic aging processes but as you will see in the next section, we can change our lifestyles to optimize the odds of a long and healthy old age.

Health and Wellness

By the time people are 65 or older, it is hard to find many who do not have something wrong with their bodies. Acute illnesses such as colds and infections become less frequent from childhood on, but chronic diseases and disorders become more common. National health surveys indicate that many of the 70-and-older age group have at least one chronic impairment—whether a sensory loss, arthritis, hypertension, or a degenerative disease (Federal Interagency Forum, 2012). Arthritis alone affects 43% of elderly men and 54% of elderly women; in addition, about half have hypertension (high blood pressure), and about one-third have heart disease (Federal Interagency Forum, 2012). Among older adults who live in poverty, many of whom are members of a minority group, health problems and difficulties in day-to-day functioning are even more common and more severe (Clark & Maddox, 1992; Hobbs, 1996). Still, as ■ **Figure 5.10** suggests, only a minority of adults report physical limitations in daily life; most adults maintain the physical capabilities that allow them to function successfully.

It is clear that there is tremendous variability in the health, wellness, and functioning of older adults. Some are limited by health problems, but others enjoy active, healthy lives. A highly fit 75-year-old can outperform a sedentary 40-year-old couch potato. Indeed, some older adults are far more active than younger ones! For instance, Michael Stones and Albert Kozma (1985) cite the example of a 98-year-old man who could run a marathon (26.2 miles) in 7½ hours! What factors might account for such differences and what do we know about staying healthy in older adulthood? For one, older adults who exercise reap many benefits.

Exercise

Exercise can improve cardiovascular and respiratory functioning, slow bone loss, and strengthen muscles. In one study, older athletes (average age 69 years) were compared with older nonathletes on several physiological measures following exercise. The athletes showed better oxygen uptake capacity and greater cardiovascular

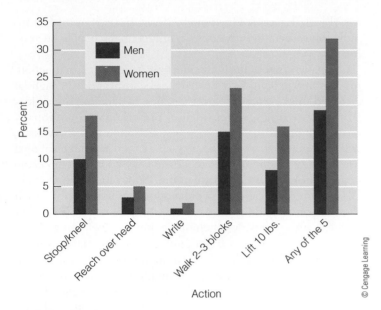

Percent

Action

■ **Figure 5.10** Percentage of older adults (65+ years) who report limitations in some basic physical functions. More women than men report functional limitations.

stamina than the nonathletes (Jungblut et al., 2000). In another study, elderly adults who did low-intensity exercise and weight lifting for 1 year became stronger and more flexible and experienced less pain as a result (Sharpe et al., 1997). Exercise can make aging adults feel less stressed and happier, and it can enhance their cognitive functioning (Barnes et al., 2003; Rowe & Kahn, 1998; Yaffe et al., 2001). Physical activity is also associated with a lower incidence of depression among older adults (Lampinen, Heikkinen, & Ruoppila, 2000). Overall, it is estimated that regular exercise by older adults can delay the onset of physical disabilities by up to 7 years (Vita et al., 1998). Indeed, it would be nearly impossible to overestimate the value of exercising and remaining physically fit.

Exercise is clearly beneficial to physical and mental health over the life span. What exercise cannot do is halt the inevitable aging process. Even frequent joggers gain weight and add inches to their waists as they enter middle age (Williams, 1997). True, people who exercise generally weigh less and have slimmer waists than those who do not, but a 30-year-old man who runs 20–30 miles a week until he is 50 would add almost 2 inches to his waist anyway; he would have to run farther each year to avoid it. To try to beat aging, then, it is not enough to remain active; a person must become *more* active over the years (Williams, 1997).

Bone Loss and Arthritis

Another factor that contributes to health and wellness is the presence or absence of disease. There are a number of diseases that become more prominent with age. Among the most common diseases of old age are osteoporosis and osteoarthritis. Extreme bone loss in later life results from **osteoporosis** (meaning "porous bone"), a disease in which a serious loss of minerals leaves the bones fragile and easily fractured. It involves pain and can result in death if the victim falls and fractures a hip. Nearly one-third of elderly adults who fracture a hip die within 1 year; hip fractures

are also a leading cause of nursing home admissions (Whitbourne & Whitbourne, 2011). One fall can change an older person's entire lifestyle, requiring a shift from independent living to assisted living. Not surprisingly, adults who have experienced a fall often begin to restrict their activities out of fear of falling again. Unfortunately, less activity can make them more vulnerable because it can lead to further decreases of muscle and bone mass (Whitbourne & Whitbourne, 2011). Osteoporosis is a special problem for older women, who never had as much bone mass as men and whose bones tend to thin rapidly after menopause. European and Asian women with light frames, those who smoke, and those with a family history of osteoporosis are especially at risk.

What can be done to prevent osteoporosis? For starters, dietary habits can influence a person's risk for osteoporosis. Many individuals do not get enough calcium to develop strong bones when they are young or to maintain bone health as they age (National Osteoporosis Foundation, 2013). Weight-bearing exercises such as walking or jogging can help prevent osteoporosis, as can the HRT that some women take following menopause (but see this chapter's earlier section, "Female Menopause," for a discussion of concerns about HRT). It is increasingly evident that good bone health starts in childhood and adolescence (Krucoff, 2000). Girls and young women who are physically active and eat a healthy diet develop higher bone density that protects them from bone loss in later life.

The joints also age over the adult years. The cushioning between bones wears out, and the joints stiffen. Many older adults experience pain or discomfort from arthritis, or joint inflammation. The most common joint problem among older adults is **osteoarthritis**, which results from gradual deterioration of the cartilage that cushions the bones from rubbing against one another. For some older adults, joint disease is deforming and painful and limits their activities. The older person who can no longer fasten buttons, stoop to pick up dropped items, or even get into and out of the bathtub may easily feel incompetent and dependent (Whitbourne & Whitbourne, 2011).

Theories of Aging: Why Do We Age and Die?

No matter what we do to stay fit and healthy and avoid the diseases associated with aging, we all eventually die. There is no simple answer to the question of why we age and die. However, several theories have been proposed, and each of them says something important about the aging process. These theories can be divided into two main categories: **Programmed theories of aging** emphasize the systematic genetic control of aging processes; **random error theories of aging** call attention to more haphazard processes that cause errors in cells to accumulate and organ systems to deteriorate (Arking, 2006; Hayflick, 2004). The question, really, is whether aging and death are the result of a biological master plan or of random insults to the body while we live.

Programmed Theories

Programmed theories assume that aging will unfold according to a species-specific genetic program. There is no doubt that **maximum life span**—a ceiling on the number of years that

Centenarian Secrets

A growing number of people around the world are **centenarians**—people who live to be 100 or older. In the United States alone, experts believe that there will be half a million people over the age of 100 by mid-century (U.S. Census Bureau, 2012). What can we learn from them about the secrets to a long, healthy life? A study of centenarians living in Okinawa, Japan, is instructive (Willcox et al., 2009). Take Tsuru, a 110-year-old woman who does not take any medications. Standing about 5 feet tall and weighing less than 70 pounds, she was at 104 energetic as she walked through her neighborhood, tended her garden, and served as head of her family. Remarkably, she had never had a major illness until she developed pneumonia at age 105, which slowed her down and left her dependent on relatives for help.

Like most other centenarians and supercentenarians (those age 110 or over) in Okinawa, Tsuru is female. She was a teacher, has an extraverted and optimistic personality, and eats small amounts of nutritious food (mainly sweet potatoes, vegetables, fruits, and a little fish and pork). She has led an active lifestyle that includes meaningful and valued activities (weaving, for example, brings status

to older women) and plenty of social interaction. Little smoking (although Tsuru got away with smoking for 40 years—until her 70s!) and little drinking round out what we in the United States would recognize as a healthy lifestyle. The small number of calories long-lived people like Tsuru consume amounts to caloric restriction, a demonstrated life extender.

So the key to the fountain of youth may simply be a healthy lifestyle. Moreover, when Japanese people move to countries in which meat, sugar, and other unhealthy food choices are popular, their life expectancies drop and they develop the diseases of their new country (Willcox et al., 2009). Such evidence suggests that the secret to long life lies in nurture rather than nature. However, other evidence suggests that genes account for about one-third of the variation in longevity, so as usual we must see both nature and nurture as important (Willcox et al., 2009). Or perhaps genetic and environ-

mental factors vary in their contributions to longevity at different points of the life span. Integrating several models of longevity, Peter Martin and colleagues (Martin, Hagberg, & Poon, 2012) suggest that psychosocial factors may get you to age 80, but good biology may be needed to take you from age 80 to 100.

If you would like to calculate how long you can be expected to live based on information about your lifestyle, stress level, eating habits, and health status, try completing The Living to 100 Life Expectancy Calculator developed by Dr. Thomas Perls and available at www.livingto100.com. You do not have to live in Okinawa or have super-centenarian genes to add years to your life.

© David McLain/Aurora

---

anyone lives—varies by species. The fruit fly is lucky to live for 2–3 months, whereas the mighty Galapagos tortoise can reach an astonishing 190 years. Among mammals, humans have the longest maximum life span, estimated at around 125 years (Weon & Je, 2009). To date, the longest documented and verified human life is that of Jeanne Louise Calment, a French woman who died in 1997 at age 122 (Willcox et al., 2009). She lived on her own until age 110 when she could no longer see well enough to safely cook or light her daily cigarette (Cruikshank, 2009). Nearly blind and deaf and confined to a wheelchair, she maintained her sense of humor to the end, attributing her longevity to everything from having a stomach "like an ostrich's" to being forgotten by God (Trueheart, 1997). Calment and others who live almost as long are the basis for setting the maximum human life span around 125 years. Despite the fact that the *average* life expectancy increased 30 plus years during the 20th century and that more and more people today are living to be 100, the *maximum* life span has changed very little (Kinsella, 2005). **Exploration Box 5.2** explores what it might take to live to be 100 or more.

Beyond the species-specific maximum life span, an individual's genetic makeup, combined with environmental factors, influences how rapidly he ages and how long he lives compared

with other humans. For example, genetic differences among us account for more than 50% of differences in the ability to stay free of major chronic diseases at age 70 or older (Reed & Dick, 2003) and for up to about a third of the variation in longevity (Melzer, Hurst, & Frayling, 2007). Among the oldest of the old, genetic factors may play an even greater role (Sebastiani et al., 2012). Perhaps, then, it is not surprising that a fairly good way to estimate how long you will live is to average the longevity of your parents and grandparents.

It is not clear yet exactly how genes influence aging and longevity, though. The most promising programmed aging theory is based on the work of Leonard Hayflick (1976, 1994), who discovered that cells from human embryos could divide only a certain number of times—50 times, plus or minus 10—an estimate referred to as the **Hayflick limit**. Hayflick also demonstrated that cells taken from human adults divide even fewer times, presumably because they have already used up some of their capacity for reproducing themselves. Moreover, the maximum life span of a species is related to the Hayflick limit for that species: The long-lived Galapagos tortoise's cells can divide 90–125 times whereas the cells of the short-lived fruit fly can divide far less than this.

Chromosome

Telomeres, end caps that
protect the chromosome

Cell

Cell

Cell

■ **Figure 5.11** As cells divide over time, telomeres shorten until, eventually, cells can no longer divide.

The mechanism behind the cellular aging clock suggested by Hayflick's limit on cell division has turned out to be **telomeres**—stretches of DNA that form the tips of chromosomes and that shorten with every cell division (see ■ **Figure 5.11**). This progressive shortening of telomeres eventually makes cells unable to replicate and causes them to malfunction and die. Thus telomere length is a yardstick of biological aging (Zhu, Belcher, & van der Harst, 2011).

But what determines how fast telomeres shorten? Fascinating research is revealing that chronic stress, such as that involved in caring for an ill child or a parent with dementia, is linked to shorter than normal white blood cell telomeres, which in turn are associated with heightened risk for cardiovascular disease and death (Epel, 2009; Epel et al., 2004, 2006). Many of us believe that stress ages people; now there is concrete evidence that stress speeds cellular aging. Moreover, lack of exercise, smoking, obesity, and low socioeconomic status—all risk factors for age-related diseases—are also associated with short telomeres (Cherkas et al., 2006, 2008). Research on telomeres was honored with a Nobel Prize in 2010 (to Carol Greider, Jack Szostak, and Elizabeth Blackburn) and is mushrooming.

According to programmed theories of aging, what might we do to extend life? It is possible that researchers might devise ways of manipulating genes to increase longevity or even the maximum life span (Arking, 2006). Life spans of 200–600 years are probably not possible, but some think researchers could raise the average age of death to around 112 years and enable 112-year-olds to function more like 78-year-olds (Miller, 2004). For example, researchers have established that the enzyme telomerase can be used to prevent the telomeres from shortening and thus keep cells replicating and working longer; telomerase treatments could backfire, however, if they also make cancerous cells multiply more rapidly (Wang, 2010; Wright & Shay, 2005).

Random Error Theories

In contrast to programmed theories of aging, random error theories generally propose that wear and tear—an accumulation of haphazard or random damage to cells and organs over the years—ultimately causes death (Hayflick, 2004). Like cars, we may have a limited warranty and simply give out after a certain number of years of use and abuse (Olshansky & Carnes, 2004). Early in life, DNA strands and cells replicate themselves faithfully; later in life this fidelity is lost and cells become increasingly damaged. Random error theorists believe that biological aging is about random damage rather than genetically programmed change.

According to one leading random error theory, damage to cells that compromises their functioning is done by **free radicals**, which are toxic and chemically unstable by-products of metabolism, or the everyday chemical reactions in cells such as those involved in the breakdown of food (Harman, 2001; Shringarpure & Davies, 2009). Free radicals are produced when oxygen reacts with certain molecules in the cells. They have an unpaired, or "free," electron and are highly reactive with and damaging to other molecules in the body, including DNA. Over time the genetic code contained in the DNA of more and more cells becomes scrambled, and the body's mechanisms for repairing such genetic damage simply cannot keep up with the chaos. More cells then function improperly or cease to function, and the organism eventually dies.

"Age spots" on the skin of older people are a visible sign of the damage free radicals can cause. Free radicals have also been implicated in some of the major diseases that become more common with age—most notably, cardiovascular diseases, cancer, and Alzheimer's disease (Harman, 2001). Moreover, they are implicated in the aging of the brain (Poon et al., 2004). However, the damage of most concern is damage to DNA because the result is more defective cells replicating themselves. Unfortunately, we cannot live and breathe without manufacturing free radicals.

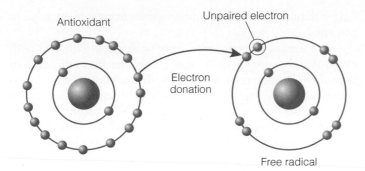

Antioxidant

Unpaired electron

Electron donation

Free radical

■ **Figure 5.12** Free radicals have an unpaired electron, which can cause damage as these free radicals can indiscriminately absorb or steal electrons from other cells throughout the body. Antioxidants are molecules that can safely donate an electron to free radicals, thereby neutralizing their potential for damage.

Many researchers adopting a random error perspective have focused on preventing the damage caused by free radicals. **Antioxidants** such as vitamins E and C (or foods high in them such as raisins, spinach, and blueberries) can donate one of their electrons to unstable free radicals, thereby neutralizing their damage to your body (see ■ **Figure 5.12**). At least when they are produced by the body or consumed in foods rather than taken in pill form, antioxidants may increase longevity, although not for long, by inhibiting free radical activity and in turn helping prevent age-related diseases (Meydani, 2001). One potential antioxidant receiving a great deal of interest in recent years is resveratrol, a natural substance in grapes, red wine, and peanuts (Ferro & DeSouza, 2011; Ungvari et al., 2011). More research is needed to fully understand how resveratrol works and the conditions under which it might be effective in ameliorating age-related damage.

One theory is that resveratrol's effects are similar to those that result from **caloric restriction**—a highly nutritious but severely restricted diet representing a 30–40% or more cut in normal total caloric intake (Anderson & Weindruch, 2012; Omodei & Fontana, 2011). Laboratory studies involving rats and primates suggest that caloric restriction extends both the average longevity and the maximum life span of a species and that it delays or slows the progression of many age-related diseases (Bodkin et al., 2003; Lane et al., 2001). By one estimate, a 40% reduction in daily calories results in a 40% decrease in body weight, a 40% increase in average longevity, and a 49% increase in the maximum life span of diet-restricted rats (Harman, 2001).

How does caloric restriction achieve these results? It clearly reduces the number of free radicals and other toxic products of metabolism. A restricted diet appears to alter gene activity and trigger the release of hormones that slow metabolism and protect cells against oxidative damage (Antebi, 2007; Arking, 2006). These changes help the half-starved organism hang on to life as long as possible. However, we do not know whether caloric restriction works as well for humans as it apparently has for rats, what calorie counts and combinations of nutrients are optimal, or whether humans who have a choice would put up with being half-starved for most of their lives. We do know that exceptionally long-lived people are rarely obese (Willcox et al., 2009).

Nature and Nurture Conspiring

The theories just described are some of the most promising explanations of why we age and die. Programmed theories of aging generally say that aging and dying are as much a part of nature's plan as sprouting teeth or uttering first words and may be the by-products of a genetic makeup that also contributed to early growth, development, and reproduction. Evidence for the genetic control of aging and dying comes from various sources: the maximum life span, the role of individual genetic makeup in longevity, the Hayflick limit on cell replication timed by telomeres, changes in the activity of certain genes as we age, and systematic changes in several bodily systems. By contrast, random error theories of aging hold that we eventually succumb to haphazard destructive processes, such as those caused by free radicals—processes that result in increasingly faulty DNA and abnormal cell functioning and ultimately a breakdown in bodily functioning.

Neither of these broad theories of aging has proved to be *the* explanation; instead, many interacting mechanisms involving both aging processes and disease processes are at work (Arking, 2006; Knight, 2000). For example, genes influence the capacity of cells to repair environmentally caused damage, and the random damage caused by free radicals alters genetic material. John Medina (1996) put it this way: "Toxic waste products accumulate because genes shut off. Genes shut off because toxic waste products accumulate" (p. 291). In short, nature and nurture, biological and environmental factors, interact to bring about aging and dying—just as they interact to produce development.

Successful Aging

Everyone wants to age "successfully," although we may differ in how we define successful aging. To some, this may mean maintaining good health and being free of diseases that might limit physical and mental skills and the ability to actively participate in desired daily activities (Rowe & Kahn, 1998). This definition emphasizes *optimal* aging—being free of diseases. Kristin Lowry and her colleagues (2012) offer a more generous definition of successful aging that considers the extent to which diseases or impairments limit an individual's daily activities and ability to participate in life activities. Whether they have diseases or do not, older adults age successfully if they are as independent as possible and pursue a lifestyle that makes them feel satisfied. Researchers are beginning to learn some of the secrets to successful aging.

In 1986, David Snowdon (2002) began the Nun Study with 678 nuns ranging in age from 75 to 106 years. Snowdon, an epidemiologist, chose to study the nuns because they were very similar with respect to socioeconomic status, housing, health care, and diet. In this remarkable longitudinal study, participants underwent annual mental and physical testing, provided complete access to a lifetime of health records, and agreed to donate their brains for examination following their deaths.

The first finding to emerge from the Nun Study was that level of education affected longevity and health. Those with a college degree lived longer and were more likely to remain independent. The risk of death among the college-educated nuns was lower at every age. Another major finding was that the nuns who were active, both physically and mentally, lived longer and healthier than nuns who were not as active.

Sister Esther, shown here at age 106, enjoys interacting with Nun Study researcher Dr. David Snowdon. What have we learned from the Nun Study?

A unique aspect of the Nun Study was that each nun had written an autobiography prior to taking her vows (average age of 22 years) and, decades later, these autobiographies became part of the data analyzed for the study. This analysis revealed that older nuns who were healthy had used more complex vocabulary in their autobiographies decades earlier (on average, 60 years earlier). They used words such as "particularly, privileged, and quarantined" as opposed to simple words such as "girls, boys, and sick" that were used by nuns who later developed symptoms of Alzheimer's disease (Snowdon, 2002, p. 107). In particular, idea density, a measure of language-processing ability, measured in early adulthood predicted mental functioning in later adulthood. In addition, nuns whose autobiographies expressed more positive emotions lived longer than nuns whose autobiographies expressed fewer positive emotions.

The message to take away from such research is that both physical and mental activity, along with a positive attitude, can help slow the effects of aging on both the body and brain. As noted earlier, we can't avoid the biological reality of aging, but we can make choices across the life span that will increase the odds of living a long life and aging successfully, as have the centenarians described in Exploration Box 5.2. Clearly, then, our health and well-being are influenced by an interaction of environmental and genetic factors.

Checking Mastery

1. What physical changes, including those in the brain, can we expect as we age?
2. What is the major difference between a programmed theory of aging and a random error theory of aging?
3. What have we learned about successful aging from the "Nun Study" and research on centenarians?

Making Connections

1. Many (indeed, most) stereotypes of the physical aging process are negative and depressing. What in this chapter gives you reason to be more optimistic about aging, and why? Cite specific concepts and research findings.
2. Suppose you set as your goal reaching age 100 in superb physical condition. Describe and justify a plan for achieving your goal, then indicate why you might not make it despite your best efforts.

Chapter Summary

5.1 Building Blocks of Growth and Lifelong Health

- Growth is influenced by genes and environments, through the working of the endocrine and nervous systems. The nervous system consists of the brain, the spinal cord, and peripheral neurons. Endocrine glands such as the pituitary, thyroid, testes, and ovaries regulate behavior by secreting hormones directly into the bloodstream. The workings of the endocrine and nervous systems can be hindered or enhanced by environmental forces.
- Physical growth proceeds according to the cephalocaudal (head-to-tail), proximodistal (center outward), and orthogenetic (global and undifferentiated to differentiated and integrated) principles.
- Health is best viewed from a life-span developmental perspective emphasizing genes, personal choice, and environmental factors in interaction.

5.2 The Infant

- The infant's brain undergoes synaptogenesis (growth of synapses) as well as synaptic pruning (loss of unused synapses). It is capable of responding to experiences, both positive and negative.
- Infants come into the world equipped with reflexes and organized states that allow them to adapt to their environments.
- Congenital malformations and complications of preterm birth are the leading causes of infant mortality. Preventative medicine such as well-baby visits to the doctor and vaccinations can improve infant health.

5.3 The Child

- During childhood, neural transmission speeds up and lateralization of various brain functions, although present at birth, becomes more evident in behavior.
- There is steady and marked improvement in all aspects of physical growth over the childhood years.
- Physical activity is an important component of health during childhood. Children's health is also influenced by their parents' socioeconomic status and lifestyle choices.
- Health is enhanced with proper nutrition and regular physical activity. Current lifestyles have decreased physical activity and increased sedentary media time, resulting in increased weight among today's children.

Steve Liss//Time Life Pictures/Getty Images

5.4 The Adolescent

- During adolescence, the brain (especially the prefrontal cortex) continues to develop, permitting sustained attention and strategic planning. Brain changes may place adolescents at greater risk for making unsafe decisions.

- The adolescent period is marked by physical growth—the adolescent growth spurt—and attainment of puberty or sexual maturity. Girls experience their growth spurt at a younger age than do boys. The major milestone of sexual maturity for girls is menarche—their first menstruation. For boys, it is the less-noted experience of semenarche, or first ejaculation. A combination of genes, hormones, and environmental factors determine the timing and rate of growth and puberty.

- The physical changes of adolescence are significant and have psychological implications. Girls' experience is often on the negative side, whereas boys tend to report a more positive reaction to growth and puberty. Boys who mature early experience largely positive benefits whereas late-maturing boys have a more negative experience. In contrast, girls who mature early are sometimes disadvantaged by teasing from their peers and the influence of the older peers with whom they often socialize. Late-maturing girls seem to benefit academically, possibly because they continue to spend more time on schoolwork than their early-maturing peers.

- Adolescents are a relatively healthy bunch, but the fitness level of some teens is poor because of a lack of physical activity and insufficient sleep.

5.5 The Adult

- The adult brain is capable of some degree of neurogenesis, or generating new neurons.

- The aging brain exhibits both degeneration and plasticity. Neurons atrophy and die, and blood flow to the brain decreases; but the aging brain forms new synapses to compensate for neural loss and reorganizes itself in response to learning experiences.

- Changes in appearance and functioning start to become evident during middle adulthood, and declines are noticeable in most older adults. There are large individual differences in physical functioning of older adults. Negative stereotypes about aging may lead many older adults to negatively interpret the natural changes that accompany aging.

- For both sexes, changes in the reproductive system are a normal part of aging. Women experience menopause, a cessation of menstruation, and an end of child-bearing years. Men experience andropause, a more gradual change in their reproductive system. The experience of menopause is variable and a variety of treatments are available to treat the symptoms.

- Aging, disease, disuse, and abuse of the body all affect performance in later life. Healthy older people function much like younger people except for their slower reactions, but the development of chronic diseases is a fact of aging for most people.

- Health and well-being during adulthood are influenced by genetic predispositions acting in concert with the environment and lifestyle choices. Exercise can enhance both physical and mental functioning. Common diseases among older adults include osteoporosis, which leads to fragile bones, and osteoarthritis, or joint inflammation.

- Two theories of aging and death include those that emphasize the genetic control of aging—the programmed theories—and those that emphasize haphazard loss—the random error theories.

- Physical and mental activity, as well as a positive attitude, improve the odds of successful aging.

Checking Mastery Answers

For answers to Checking Mastery questions, please see Appendix B.

Key Terms

celiac disease **130**

catch-up growth **130**

endocrine gland **131**

pituitary gland **131**

growth hormone **131**

androgens **132**

estrogen **132**

neuron **132**

synapse **133**

myelination **133**

cephalocaudal principle **134**

proximodistal principle **134**

orthogenetic principle **134**

synaptogenesis **136**

synaptic pruning **136**

plasticity **136**

reflex **136**

REM sleep **138**

congenital malformations **138**

lateralization **139**

body mass index (BMI) **142**

puberty **143**

adolescent growth spurt **144**

adrenarche **144**

menarche **144**

semenarche **145**

secular trend **145**

obesity **148**

diabetes **149**

metabolic syndrome (MeTS) **150**

neurogenesis **152**

premenstrual syndrome (PMS) **153**

premenstrual dysphoric disorder (PDD) **153**

menopause **153**

hot flashes **154**

hormone replacement therapy (HRT) **154**

andropause **154**

erectile dysfunction **154**

reserve capacity **156**

ageism **156**

osteoporosis **158**

osteoarthritis **158**

programmed theories of aging **158**

random error theories of aging **158**

maximum life span **158**

centenarians **159**

Hayflick limit **159**

telomere **160**

free radicals **160**

antioxidants **161**

caloric restriction **161**

6 Sensation, Perception, and Action

When asked to speculate on which of their senses would be most problematic to lose, many students indicate vision or hearing, as these senses seem to take center stage in so many daily activities. Some believe their visual sense would be a devastating loss as they would need to give up such activities as driving, a major source of independence. Others, though, conclude that losing their auditory sense would be most challenging, perhaps because social relationships hinge on hearing what others have to say. Gabriel Robles-De-La-Torre (2006) of the International Society for Haptics (an organization devoted to the study of how touch interfaces with humans and machines) suggests a third answer to the question of which sense would be most problematic to lose. She notes that sense of touch is often underappreciated because it is typically effortless and few people suffer a total loss of their sense of touch, leaving us with little idea how such loss might affect us.

(For a fascinating case study of near-total loss of sense of touch, refer to Jonathan Cole's [1995] book *Pride and a Daily Marathon*.) If you have ever received Novocain (a local anesthetic designed to cause numbness or loss of feeling) for a dental procedure, you have a tiny glimpse of what losing your sense of touch might be like. And as we consider the importance of our senses, let's not forget the enjoyment of our favorite meals, so dependent on our senses of smell and taste as well as our perceptions of what we are consuming. Gary Beauchamp and Julie Mennella (2011) of the Monell Chemical Senses Center make a case for the vital role of these senses to our health. Clearly, then, all the senses make important contributions to our experience of the world around us.

In this chapter, we examine how our senses provide us with the building blocks for understanding the world around us. We discuss the tremendous flood of sensations bombarding the infant and how infants come to "make sense" of this information. We trace major changes in sensation and perception through childhood, adolescence, and early adulthood, and then look at some of the inevitable declines that occur in middle and later adulthood. We also examine how perception is coupled with action in a *synergistic* fashion. As you changed from a largely immobile infant to an on-the-move toddler, for example, you coupled your burgeoning perceptual skills with advances in your nervous system and your body's growing physical capabilities to engage in goal-oriented actions. Finally, we look at the important role that attention plays in our awareness of the world around us and why some information is noticed and other information seems to drop off our "radar screens."

What do we mean by these terms *sensation*, *perception*, and *action*? Psychologists have long distinguished between sensation and perception. **Sensation** is the process by which sensory receptor neurons detect information and transmit it to the brain. From birth, infants sense their environment. They detect light, sound, odor-bearing molecules in the air, and other stimuli. But do they *understand* the patterns of stimulation coming in from the various sense organs? This is where **perception**, or the interpretation of sensory input, comes into play: recognizing what you see, understanding what is said to you, knowing that the odor you have detected is a sizzling steak, and so on. But let's be clear about something: The sense organs are not passive receptacles that detect and merely pass along information to the brain. Your eyes, nose, tongue, ears, and skin actually help shape the brain (Brynie, 2009). Sensation and perception are at the heart of human functioning. *Everything you do—all of your physical and mental actions—depends on your ability to sense and perceive the world around you.* To begin our journey, we consider perspectives on how we perceive the world and gain knowledge of reality, exploring again the nature–nurture issue.

6.1 Perspectives on Perception

LEARNING OBJECTIVES:

- Distinguish between the nativist and constructivist positions on perception.
- Summarize Gibson's ecological approach to perception and how it differs from approaches that are primarily constructivist or nativist.

Does the ability to perceive the world around us depend solely on innate biological factors, or is this ability acquired through experience and learning? **Constructivists**, including Jean Piaget who was introduced in Chapter 2 and will be further discussed in Chapter 7, come down on the side of nurture (Kellman & Arterberry, 2006). They argue that perceptions of the world are constructed over time through learning. Yes, we come equipped at birth with functioning sensory systems, but understanding the input coming in through our senses requires interacting with the environment and "learning to infer the meanings of our sensations" (Kellman & Arterberry, 2006, p. 112). For instance, the retinal image of an object located 50 feet from an observer is different from the retinal image of the same object located just 10 feet from the observer. According to the constructivists, we need experience with viewing objects at various distances to learn how to interpret the different retinal images that they project. With experience, we create an association between the retinal image (for example, small) and its meaning (for example, distant object).

Although the constructivist view of perception has long been very popular, more sophisticated methods of assessing infants' capabilities have yielded new findings about their perceptual abilities. As a result, some researchers have shifted toward a more nativist perspective on the origins of some aspects of perception. The **nativists** argue that perception is *not* created by interpreting external input; instead, innate capabilities and maturational programs are the driving forces in perceptual development (Kellman & Arterberry, 2006). Infants come equipped with basic sensory capabilities, which are further refined according to an innate plan. Nativists would argue that the infant does not need experience to learn how to interpret different retinal images cast by the same object at different distances. The brain automatically understands the meaning of different retinal images created as we move about our world (for example, a small image is automatically "read" by the brain as distant object). Thus, from the nativist perspective, perception is direct—it does not require interpretation based on previous experience (Kellman & Arterberry, 2006).

Falling somewhere in the middle of the nurture-based constructivists and the nature-focused nativists is Gibson's ecological theory of perception developed by Eleanor Gibson (2001) and her husband James Gibson (1966, 1979). In Chapter 2, we

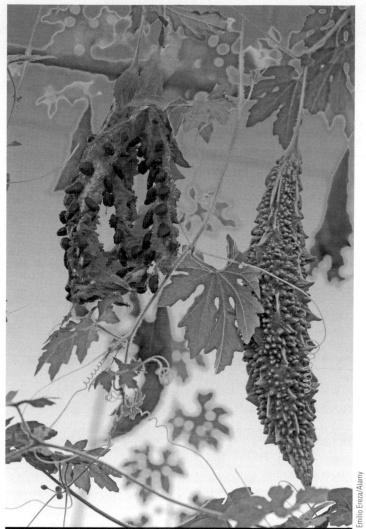

What do you see when you look at this orange object? According to the constructivist theory of perception, you use past experiences to construct an understanding of what this object might be.

Emilio Ereza/Alamy

approach argues that we do not need to construct how we might interact with this object. Instead, features of the object directly reveal its **affordances**: what it has to offer us and how it might be used by us. Thus, as the round object moves toward us, the pattern of light reaching our eyes provides all the information we need to know what this object *affords*: the prospect of getting hit in the face if we do not take some action.

In the ecological view, perception drives action. Perception provides us with valuable information on what objects in the environment can afford, or offer us: surfaces to sit on, pots and pans that can serve as musical instruments, sticks that can poke things, and so on. As James Gibson (1979) noted, "we must perceive in order to move, but we must also move in order to perceive" (p. 223). This is an important difference between how the Gibson ecologists and the constructivists view the role of the environment and past experience: The constructivists would argue that past learning experiences are needed to interpret the current perceptual situation, whereas the Gibson ecologists would say that all the information needed to interpret the current perceptual situation is available in the current situation.

Note that what an object or the environment affords depends on each individual's capabilities, including their genetic predispositions and current goals and motivations (Miller, 2011). A pencil may offer an 8-year-old the possibility of writing something on a piece of paper because the 8-year-old has the capacity to write and therefore perceives this affordance of this object. For a 12-month-old infant who has not yet developed this capability, the pencil may afford something quite different, such as a stick for poking or something else to chew. Thus, Gibson ecologists view nature and nurture as inseparable (Miller, 2011).

In this chapter, we will use the constructivist, nativist, and ecological perspectives to help us gain a better understanding of perception and action across the life span. As we begin our journey in infancy, we will look closely at sensation and perception because most fundamental capacities emerge and quickly develop during the first months of life. Later, you will see how much more "intelligent" perceptual abilities become during childhood and adolescence and will question the image of old age as a time of little more than sensory and perceptual decline.

introduced Bronfenbrenner's ecological (later, bioecological) theory that described how the environment is organized and affects development. Similarly, Gibson's ecological approach also considers the organization of the environment. In particular, Gibson's theory proposes that information important for perception is readily and directly available in the environment: in the to-be-perceived objects. As we move around in our world, our position relative to all other objects in the environment is constantly changing and altering the flow of information and the images projected to our retina. For example, suppose we look at a round object that gradually projects a larger image on our retina; how do we know what this is and how we might interact with it? The constructivists might say that we need to take all the pieces of information coming in from our senses and construct an understanding of what this object is and what it can do. It may take multiple interactions with the object before we put together all the pieces of the puzzle and learn its properties and figure out that a ball is moving toward us. In contrast, the ecological

Checking Mastery

1. How is perception different from sensation?
2. What is the difference in how constructivists and nativists view sensation and perception?
3. In what way is Gibson's ecological theory of perception distinct from the constructivist and the nativist views of perception?

Making Connections

1. How could you demonstrate that perception of an object's distance is innate rather than constructed through experience?

LEARNING OBJECTIVES:

- Describe the changes in visual capabilities from birth through the first year, and note the visual preferences exhibited by infants.

- Explain how infants come to "make sense" of the visual world.

- Outline the auditory capabilities of the pre- and early postnatal period, including a description of how researchers evaluate these capabilities.

- Summarize the infant's chemical senses as well as the functioning of their somaesthetic senses.

- Explain the early experiences needed for development of normal perceptual skills and the influence of early experience on the brain.

The pioneering American psychologist William James (1890) claimed that sights, sounds, and other sensory inputs formed a "blooming, buzzing confusion" to the young infant. James was actually noting that impressions from the several senses are fused rather than separable, but his statement has since been quoted to represent the view that the world of the young infant is hopelessly confusing.

Today the accepted view is that young infants have far greater perceptual abilities than anyone suspected. Their senses are functioning even before birth, and in the first few months of life they show many signs that they are perceiving a coherent rather than a chaotic world. Why the change in views? It is not that babies have become smarter. It is that researchers have become smarter. They have developed more sophisticated methods of studying what infants can and cannot do. Infants, after all, cannot tell researchers directly what they perceive, so the trick has been to develop ways to let their behavior speak for them. The main methods used to study infant perception are summarized in ● Table 6.1 and include habituation, preferential looking, evoked potentials, and operant conditioning techniques. These techniques have revealed a good deal about what infants perceive and what they do not, as you will now see.

Vision

As noted in the chapter opener, many of us tend to think of vision as our most indispensable sense. Because vision is indeed important, we examine its early development in some detail before turning to the other major senses.

Basic Capacities

How does something as complicated as vision work? The eye functions by taking in stimulation in the form of light and converting it to electrochemical signals to the brain. From the first minutes of life, the newborn can detect changes in brightness and can visually track a slow-moving picture or object (Slater et al., 2010b). Failure to follow an object when the object is presented within normal viewing range is often an early indicator of a visual problem. Even among sighted newborns, though, visual capabilities are lacking compared with those of a child or an adult. At birth, newborns' **visual acuity**, or the ability to perceive detail, is 40 times worse than an adult's, but improves across the first month of life to roughly the equivalent of 20/120 vision on the standard eye chart—being able to see only the big E

● **Table 6.1** Methods for Assessing Infant Perception

Habituation	The same stimulus is repeatedly presented until the infant grows bored with what has become familiar and disengages (e.g., looks away). Researchers can measure how long (e.g., how many trials) until an infant becomes bored. They can also measure how distinct a second, new stimulus needs to be in order to recapture the infant's attention.
Preferential looking	Two stimuli are simultaneously shown to an infant to determine which one they prefer, which is inferred to be the one they look at longer. Recent research has precisely measured preferential looking using head-mounted eye-tracking cameras (e.g., Franchak, Kretch, Soska, & Adolph, 2011).
Evoked potentials	Electrical activity in different parts of the brain is measured while the infant watches, listens to, or is otherwise exposed to stimulation. Electrodes are attached to the surface of the skull and a computer records the pattern of electrical activity corresponding to various stimuli.
Operant conditioning	Infants are conditioned to reliably respond a certain way to a certain stimulus (e.g., they are rewarded for turning their head every time they hear a sound). Once this response is well-established, the researcher can examine the conditions under which the infants will, or will not, continue to produce the behavior. Presumably, continued head turning suggests that infants do not detect a noticeable difference between the original and new stimuli, whereas lack of the conditioned response is evidence that they *do* distinguish between the two stimuli.

© Cengage Learning 2015

at the top of the chart (Hamer, 2009). Objects are blurry to young infants unless they are within about 12 inches (30 cm) from the face or are bold patterns with sharp light–dark contrasts—the face of a parent, for example. The young infant's world is also blurred because of limitations in **visual accommodation**—the ability of the lens of the eye to change shape to bring objects at different distances into focus. It is likely to take 6 months to 1 year before the infant can see as well as an adult (Slater et al., 2010b).

Very young infants also see the world in color, not in black and white as some early observers thought (Zemach, Chang, & Teller, 2006). How do researchers know this? Suppose they accustom an infant to a blue disk using the habituation technique described in Table 6.1. What will happen if they then present either a blue disk of a different shade or a green disk? Infants 4 months old will show little interest in a disk of a different blue but will be attentive to a green disk—even when the light reflected from these two stimuli differs in wavelength from the original blue stimulus by the same amount (Schiffman, 2000). Thus, 4-month-olds appear to discriminate colors and categorize portions of the continuum of wavelengths of light into the same basic color categories (red, blue, green, and yellow) that adults do. Color vision is present at birth, but newborns cannot discriminate some color differences well because their receptors are not yet mature. By 2–3 months, however, color vision is mature (Goldstein, 2007). Like adults, 4-month-old infants can detect a colored stimulus on a background that is a different shade of the same color (Franklin, Pilling, & Davies, 2005). However, also like adults, they are *faster* at detecting the stimulus on a background of a different color.

In short, the eyes of the young infant are not working at peak levels, but they are working. As one researcher (Hainline, 1998) summarizes it: Infants are able to see what they need to see, a conclusion consistent with Gibson's ecological approach. Even newborns can perceive light and dark, focus on nearby objects, distinguish colors, and see simple patterns. But does all this visual stimulation make any sense?

A physician checks a young infant's vision. What is this infant likely to be able to see?

Organizing the World of Objects

Alan Slater and his colleagues (2010b) note that, above all else, perception is organized. In what ways do infants organize their perceptions? One of the first challenges for the infant is to separate the visual field into distinct objects, even when parts of objects are hidden behind other objects or are adjacent to one another. In other words, where does one object end and another object begin? From an early age, infants show remarkable abilities to organize and impose order on visual scenes in much the same way that adults do. Research suggests an important breakthrough in **form perception**, or recognition of the patterns that constitute an object, starting around 2 or 3 months (see Colombo, 2001; Courage, Reynolds, & Richards, 2006). One-month-olds focus on the outer contours of forms such as faces, as if they are finding the boundaries of the object; see ■**Figure 6.1** (Johnson, 1997).

1-month-old　　　　2-month-old

Visual scanning of a geometric figure by 1- and 2-month-old infants

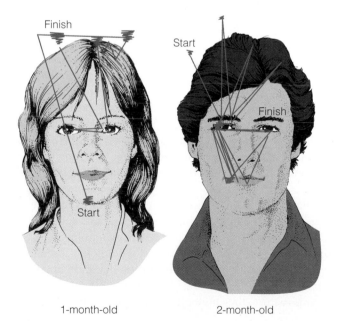

1-month-old　　　　2-month-old

Visual scanning of the human face by 1- and 2-month-old infants

■**Figure 6.1** Visual scanning in early infancy. The 1-month-old seems to be trying to locate where an object begins and ends, whereas the 2-month-old seems to be on the way to figuring out what an object is by exploring it inside and out.

Source: Adapted from Salapatek, 1975.

But starting around 2 months, infants no longer focus on some external boundary or contour; instead, they explore the interiors of figures thoroughly (for example, looking at a person's facial features rather than just at the chin, hairline, and top of the head). It is as though they are no longer content to locate where an object starts and where it ends, as 1-month-olds tend to do; they seem to want to know what it is. During this time, infants also become better at shifting their attention or disengaging from a stimulus (Colombo, 2001; Courage et al., 2006). Initially, their gaze seems to become "stuck" on the fixated object, and they have difficulty shifting it to another object. As you might imagine, this difficulty with shifting gaze limits what young infants can take in from their environment.

How exactly do infants determine where one object ends and another begins? Elizabeth Spelke and her colleagues (Kellman & Spelke, 1983; Spelke, 1990) have concluded that young infants are sensitive to several cues about the wholeness of objects, especially cues available when an object moves. For example, 4-month-olds seem to expect all parts of an object to move in the same direction at the same time, and they therefore use *common motion* as an important cue in determining what is or is not part of the same object (Kellman & Spelke, 1983). It takes infants longer, until about 6 months of age, to determine the boundaries or edges of *stationary* objects (Gibson & Pick, 2000). Thus, babies appear to have an innate ability to organize a visual scene into distinct objects, and they are better able to make sense of a world in motion—a world like the one they live in—than to make sense of a stationary world.

It's clear that infants try to impose order on the complex world of objects. In doing so, they demonstrate preferences for certain patterns over others. What are the properties of patterns that capture the young infant's attention?

- Young infants pay attention to patterns that have a large amount of light–dark transition, or **contour**; they are responsive to sharp boundaries between light and dark areas (Banks & Shannon, 1993; Farroni et al., 2005). Unfortunately, the pastel colors often presented to young infants may not have enough contrast to be detected (Brown & Lindsey, 2009).
- Infants are interested in displays that are dynamic (as opposed to static) or contain *movement* (Courage et al., 2006; Kavsek & Yonas, 2006). Newborns can and do track a moving target with their eyes, although their tracking at first is imprecise and likely to falter unless the target is moving slowly (Slater et al., 2010b).
- Young infants seem to be attracted to patterns that are *moderately complex*: not too simple, which would be boring, and not too complex, which would be overwhelming. Thus, they prefer a clear pattern (for example, a bold checkerboard pattern) to either a blank stimulus or an elaborate one such as a page from the *New York Times* (Fantz & Fagan, 1975). As infants mature, they prefer more complex stimuli.

To recap, researchers know that infants younger than 2 months have visual preferences, and they also know something about the physical properties of stimuli that attract infants' attention. Martin Banks and his colleagues have offered a simple explanation for these early visual preferences: *Young infants prefer to look at whatever they can see well* (Banks & Ginsburg, 1985). Because the young infant's eye is small and its neural receptors are immature, it has poor visual acuity and sees a highly complex visual

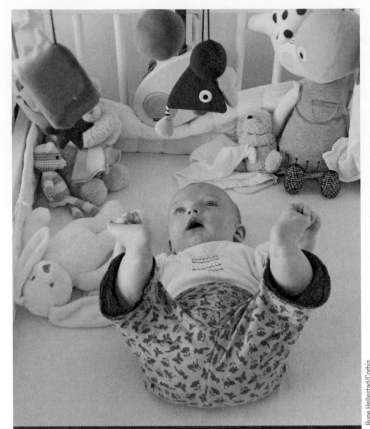

This young infant is attracted to the mobile's well-defined contours (or light-dark contrasts) and bold patterns (which are neither too simple nor too complex).

display as a big, dark blob. However, the pattern in a moderately complex display can be seen. Less-than-perfect vision would therefore explain why young infants prefer moderate complexity to high complexity. Indeed, limited vision can account for several of the infant's visual preferences. Young infants seem to actively seek the visual input they can see well—input that will stimulate the development of the visual centers of their brains (Banks & Shannon, 1993; Hainline, 1998).

Face Perception

One special pattern that has garnered much attention from researchers is the human face. Detecting faces from nonfaces and discriminating familiar from nonfamiliar faces are critical skills in successfully navigating the social world. Imagine the possible consequences, for example, if an infant was unable to detect the difference between a face and a balloon, or was unable to identify his mother's face from among the many faces that appear in his visual field each day.

Soon after birth, young infants prefer to look at schematic drawings of faces rather than other patterned stimuli and faces elicit more visual tracking by young infants than other targets (Gamé, Carchon, & Vital-Durand, 2003). Newborns can distinguish a human face from a monkey face, although they don't show a preference for the human face (Di Giorgio et al., 2012). They can also distinguish their mother's face from that of a stranger's, at least in static and simplified displays (for example,

Pascalis et al., 1995). Such findings seem to suggest an inborn tendency to discriminate faces from nonfaces. More challenging is being able to discriminate among faces in real settings where the faces are dynamic (moving) and embedded in an ever-changing environment. Lorraine Bahrick and her colleagues (for example, Bahrick, Gogate, & Ruiz, 2002; Bahrick & Newell, 2008) presented 5-month-olds with displays of women's faces as the women engaged in such tasks as brushing their teeth and blowing bubbles. Weeks later, they tested the infants for recognition of the action as well as the faces. The infants remembered the actions but did not remember or discriminate among the faces until the researchers either increased the infant's exposure time to the faces or removed the action and made the faces static. Bahrick, Lickliter, and Castellanos (2012) conclude that "actions are more salient than faces" (p. 2). Infants do not yet have sufficient attention resources: They can attend to the action or to the face, but not to both, and the action is more salient to their young attentional system.

Much remains to be learned about early perception of faces, including whether this is an innate ability or something that emerges only after having some experience looking at faces (Cassia et al., 2006; Johnson & de Haan, 2001; Slater et al., 2010a). Some scholars believe there is an innate preference for faces. But as we have learned, infants prefer contour, movement, and moderate complexity. Human faces have all of these physical properties. In addition, research shows that newborns have a preference for patterns that have more information in their upper visual field—that is, patterns that are "top heavy" (Cassia, Turati, & Simion, 2004; Cassia et al., 2006; Turati, 2004). Again, faces fit the bill: they are top heavy. Thus, what appears to be a preference for faces may be a preference for the features that happen to be connected with faces.

Nonetheless, we can conclude that infants truly perceive a meaningful face, not merely an appealing pattern, by 2–3 months of age. At this time, infants smile when they see faces as though they recognize them as familiar and appreciate their significance. So it goes with form perception more generally: As infants gain experience with different objects, their attention is drawn to certain objects not only because they have certain physical

Is face perception innate or does it emerge with experience? This infant is likely attracted to what features of mother's face?

Ashley Gill/Alamy

properties, but also because their forms are recognized as familiar. With experience comes greater expertise. One final note about face perception: Although infants "have" face recognition, there are further refinements in both accuracy and speed of face recognition throughout childhood (de Heering, Rossion, & Maurer, 2012).

Depth Perception

Another very important aspect of visual perception involves perceiving depth and knowing when objects are near or far. Although it can take years to learn to judge the size of objects in the distance, very young infants have some intriguing abilities to interpret spatial cues involving nearby objects. For example, they react defensively when objects move toward their faces; blinking in response to looming objects first appears around 1 month and becomes more consistent over the next few months (Kayed & van der Meer, 2007; Nanez & Yonas, 1994). By 4 months of age, infants demonstrate understanding of **size constancy**: They recognize that an object is of the same size despite changes in its distance from the eyes, which would project different images on the retina. Carl Granrud (2006) came to this conclusion using the habituation technique. Infants were initially habituated to either a small- or a medium-sized disk presented at different distances. They were then tested to see whether they preferred to look at a disk that was the same physical size but cast a different retinal image or one that was a different (that is, novel) physical size but cast the same retinal image. Keep in mind that once habituated to a stimulus, infants are bored with it and no longer attend to it. To recapture their attention, they need to be presented with a new stimulus that they can recognize as different—novel—from the original. Granrud found that the infants responded on the basis of actual object size, not size of the retinal image cast by the object. They preferred to look at the disk that was a novel physical size even though it cast the same retinal image as during the habituation phase. This indicates that infants recognize the size of an object even when the object is presented at different distances and thus produces different images on the retina.

Does this evidence of early spatial perception mean that infants who have begun to crawl know enough about space to avoid crawling off the edges of beds or staircases? The first attempt to examine depth perception in infants was carried out in classic research by Eleanor Gibson and Richard Walk (1960) using an apparatus called the **visual cliff**. This cliff consists of an elevated glass platform divided into two sections by a center board. On the "shallow" side a checkerboard pattern is placed directly under the glass. On the "deep" side the pattern is several feet below the glass, creating the illusion of a drop-off or "cliff." Infants are placed on the center board and coaxed by their mothers to cross both the shallow and the deep sides. Testing infants 6½ months of age and older, Gibson and Walk found that 27 of 36 infants would cross the shallow side to reach Mom, but only 3 of 36 would cross the deep side. Most infants of crawling age (typically 7 months or older) clearly perceive depth and are afraid of drop-offs. For a video of infants on the visual cliff, see **Exploring Development Box 6.1**.

But the testing procedure used by Gibson and Walk depended on the ability of infants to crawl. Would younger infants who cannot yet crawl be able to perceive a drop-off? Joseph Campos and his colleagues (Campos, Langer, & Krowitz, 1970) found that when they slowly lowered babies over the shallow and deep sides of the visual cliff, babies as young as 2 months had a slower heart rate on the deep side than on the shallow side. Why slower? When we are afraid, our hearts beat faster, not slower. A slow heart rate is a sign of interest. So, 2-month-old infants *perceive a difference* between the deep and the shallow sides of the visual cliff, but they have not yet learned to *fear* drop-offs.

Fear of drop-offs appears to be learned through crawling—and falling now and then, or at least coming close to it (Campos, Bertenthal, & Kermoian, 1992). Some beginning crawlers will shuffle right off the ends of beds or the tops of stairwells if they are not watched carefully. However, avoidance and fear of drop-offs is stronger in infants who have logged a few weeks of crawling than in infants of the same age who do not yet crawl. Alas, infants who have learned the lesson that crawling over drop-offs is risky do not transfer it to similarly risky situations they encounter once they begin walking. They must again learn what they can and cannot do when faced with, for example, a stair step or an open space in the floor that a foot could fall through (Adolph, Berger, & Leo, 2011; Kretch & Adolph, 2013). Both maturation and normal experiences moving about contribute to the perception and interpretation of depth, it seems.

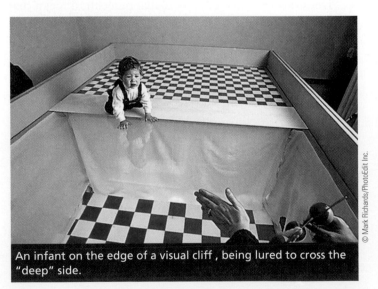

An infant on the edge of a visual cliff, being lured to cross the "deep" side.

The Infant as an Intuitive Theorist

The infant's visual perceptual abilities are impressive. But that's not all that is remarkable about the infant's growing perception and knowledge of the world. Researchers have been exploring infants' understandings of the physical laws that govern objects. For example, Elizabeth Spelke and her colleagues have been testing infants to determine what they know of Newtonian physics and the basic laws of object motion (Spelke & Hermer, 1996). Do babies know that a falling object will move downward along a continuous path until it encounters an obstruction? Spelke's studies suggest that infants only 4 months of age seem surprised when a ball dropped behind a screen is later revealed below a shelf rather than resting on it. They look longer at this "impossible" event than at the comparison event in which the ball's motion stops when it reaches a barrier. By 6 months, infants also seem surprised when a ball drops behind a screen and then, when the screen is lifted, appears to be suspended in midair rather than lying at the bottom of the display unit (Kim & Spelke, 1992; Spelke et al., 1992). This hints that they know something about the laws of gravity.

Do infants understand any other simple principles of physics? Yes; 4-month-olds watching a moving object disappear behind the left side of a screen seem to expect to see the object reappear from the right side of the screen (Bremner et al., 2005). And 4-month-olds are also surprised when a wide object disappears into a narrow container (Wang, Baillargeon, & Brueckner, 2004). By 6 months of age, infants understand that a person must be able to perceive an object before that person can show a preference for that object or act upon that object (Luo & Johnson, 2009).

Such findings have led some developmentalists to conclude that young infants do more than just sense the world—they come equipped with organized systems of knowledge, called **intuitive theories**, which allow them to make sense of the world (Gelman, 1996; Wellman & Gelman, 1992). From an early age, children distinguish between the domains of knowledge adults know as physics, biology, and psychology. They organize their knowledge in each domain around causal principles and seem to understand that different causal forces operate in different domains (for example, that desires influence the behavior of humans but not of rocks). According to this intuitive theories perspective, young infants have innate knowledge of the world, and they perceive and even reason about it much as adults do. Coming to know the physical world is then a matter of fleshing out understandings they have had all along rather than constructing entirely new ones as they age (Spelke, 1994). All in all, it is clear that young infants know a good deal more about the world around them than anyone imagined, although they learn more as they get older.

Hearing

Hearing is at least as important to us as vision, especially because we depend on it to communicate with others through spoken language. As Anne Fernald (2004) notes, "while vision may be primary in enabling infants to learn about the physical world, audition plays a powerful role in initiating infants into a social world" (p. 37).

The process of hearing begins when moving air molecules enter the ear and vibrate the eardrum. These vibrations are transmitted to the cochlea in the inner ear and are converted to signals that the brain interprets as sounds.

Basic Capacities

Newborns can hear well—better than they can see. They can also localize sounds: They are startled by loud noises and will turn from them, but they will turn toward softer sounds (see Burnham & Mattock, 2010). Even fetuses can hear some of what is going on in the world outside the womb as early as 19 weeks after conception. Researchers have detected changes in fetal heart rates that correspond to changes in sounds they are exposed to while in their mother's womb (Fifer, Monk, & Grose-Fifer, 2004; Saffran, Werker, & Werner, 2006). Infants seem to prefer listening to auditory stimuli that are relatively complex, a finding that is consistent with the preference for moderate complexity that we saw with visual stimuli (Richard et al., 2004).

Although the auditory sense is working before birth, infants appear to be a little less sensitive to very soft sounds than adults are (Saffran et al., 2006). As a result, a soft whisper may not be heard. Still, newborns can discriminate among sounds within their range of hearing that differ in loudness, duration, direction, and frequency or pitch, and these basic capacities improve rapidly during the first months of life (Fernald, 2009). In general, the sounds that penetrate the womb before birth are the ones that are the easiest for the infant to hear after birth.

Speech Perception

Young infants seem to be especially responsive to human speech and show a preference for speech over nonspeech sounds (Vouloumanos & Werker, 2007). In many ways, it seems as though the human brain was designed to produce and understand language (Fernald, 2009). We can discriminate basic speech sounds—called **phonemes**—very early in life. Peter Eimas (1975b, 1985) pioneered research in this area by demonstrating that infants 2–3 months old could discriminate between similar consonant sounds (for example, *ba* and *pa*). And newborns just hours old, recognize vowel sounds from their native language that they were exposed to in the womb. Researchers determined this by measuring how much newborns sucked on a special pacifier when exposed to a variety of vowels sounds from their native language as well as those from a nonnative language that they would not have been exposed to in the womb. The difference in their sucking rates showed that these newborns could discriminate between the native and nonnative sounds. Such results demonstrate that infants are not a blank slate at birth: They have already been learning in their prenatal environments (Moon, Lagercrantz, & Kuhl, 2013).

Infants can actually make some speech sound discriminations better than adults (Werker & Desjardins, 1995). They begin life biologically prepared to learn any language humans anywhere speak. As they mature, they become especially sensitive to the sound differences significant in their own language and less sensitive to sound differences irrelevant to that language. For example, young infants can easily discriminate the consonants *r* and *l* (Eimas, 1975a). So can adults who speak English, French, Spanish, or German. However, the Chinese and Japanese languages make no distinction between *r* and *l*, and adult native speakers of those languages cannot make this particular auditory discrimination as well as young infants can (Miyawaki et al., 1975). Similarly, infants raised in English-speaking homes can make discriminations

important in Hindi but nonexistent in English, but English-speaking adults have trouble doing so (Werker et al., 1981).

By 1 year of age, when infants are just beginning to utter their first words, they have already become largely insensitive to contrasts of sounds that are not made in their native language (see, for example, Werker, Yeung, & Yoshida, 2012). Further, over the first year, they show *increased* sensitivity to native language sounds (Kuhl et al., 2006). Their early auditory experiences have shaped the formation of neural connections, or synapses, in the auditory areas of their brains so that they are optimally sensitive to the sound contrasts that they have been listening to and that are important in the language they are acquiring (see Chapter 10). In short, experience shapes the brain.

Newborns are especially attentive to female voices (Ecklund-Flores & Turkewitz, 1996), but can they recognize their mother's voice? Indeed they can. Even unborn fetuses can distinguish their mother's voice from a stranger's voice. How do we know this? Canadian researchers measured fetal heart rate in response to a tape recording (played over the mother's stomach) of either their mother's voice or a stranger's voice (Kisilevsky et al., 2003). Heart rates increased in response to their mother's voice and decreased in response to the stranger's voice, indicating that fetuses detected a difference between the two. Newborns will learn to suck faster on a special pacifier when it activates a recording of the mother's voice (DeCasper & Fifer, 1980).

Does this early recognition extend to fathers' voices? Sorry, men, apparently not. Even by 4 months, infants show no preference for their father's voice over the voice of a strange man (Ward & Cooper, 1999). They can detect differences between various male voices, however, indicating that the lack of preference for the father's voice is not because of a failure to distinguish it.

Why would infants prefer their mother's but not their father's voice? Again, we need to look at what is happening before birth to answer this. In a now-classic study, Anthony DeCasper and Melanie Spence (1986) had mothers recite a portion of Dr. Seuss's *The Cat in the Hat* many times during the last 6 weeks of their pregnancies. At birth, the infants were tested to see if

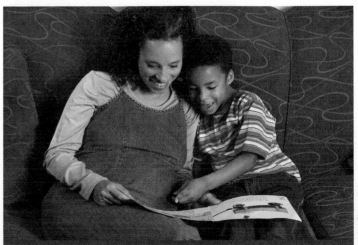

This mother is doing more than reading to her son. She is also exposing her unborn child to the sound of her voice and the rhythm of the story.

they would suck more to hear the story they had heard before birth or to hear a different story. Remarkably, they preferred the familiar story. Somehow these infants were able to recognize the distinctive sound pattern of the story they had heard in the womb. Auditory learning before birth could also explain why newborns prefer to hear their mother's voice to those of unfamiliar women but do not show a preference for their father's voice. They are literally bombarded with their mother's voice for months before birth, giving them ample opportunity to learn its auditory qualities.

So hearing is more developed than vision at birth. Infants can distinguish among speech sounds and recognize familiar sound patterns such as their mother's voice soon after birth. Within the first year, they lose sensitivity to sound contrasts insignificant in the language they are starting to learn, and they further refine their auditory perception skills. Unfortunately, some infants experience hearing problems, placing them at risk for language and communication problems. **Application Box 6.1** examines the importance of early identification and treatment of hearing problems.

The Chemical Senses: Taste and Smell

Can newborns detect different tastes and smells? Both of these senses rely on the detection of chemical molecules; thus, the characterization of them as the "chemical senses." The sensory receptors for taste—taste buds—are located mainly on the tongue. In ways not fully understood, taste buds respond to chemical molecules and produce perceptions of sweet, salty, bitter, or sour tastes. At birth, babies can clearly distinguish sweet, bitter, and sour tastes and show a preference for sweets. Indeed, sugar water—but not plain water—may help calm babies who are experiencing mildly stressful events. Some research had even suggested that sugar water may help alleviate pain experienced by infants during routine tests, but more recent research disputes this (Marceau, Murray, & Nanan, 2009).

Different taste sensations also produce distinct facial expressions in the newborn. Newborns lick their lips and sometimes smile when they are tasting a sugar solution but purse their lips and even drool to get rid of the foul taste when they are given a bitter solution (Mennella et al., 2009; Steiner, 1979). Their facial expressions become increasingly pronounced as a solution becomes sweeter or more bitter, suggesting that newborns can discriminate different concentrations of a substance. Even before birth, babies show a preference for sweets when they swallow more amniotic fluid that contains higher concentrations of sugar than amniotic fluid with lower concentrations of sugar (Fifer, Monk, & Grose-Fifer, 2004).

Although we may have a general—and innate—preference for sweets and avoidance of bitters, flavor preferences are highly responsive to learning. Research by Julie Mennella, Gary Beauchamp, and their colleagues suggests that food preferences may be influenced by early tastes that we are exposed to during infancy (Beauchamp & Mennella, 2009, 2011; Mennella & Beauchamp, 2002; Mennella et al., 2009). In one study, for example, infants were fed one of two formulas for 7 months, starting at 2 weeks of age. One formula was bland, and the other was bitter and tasted sour, at least to most

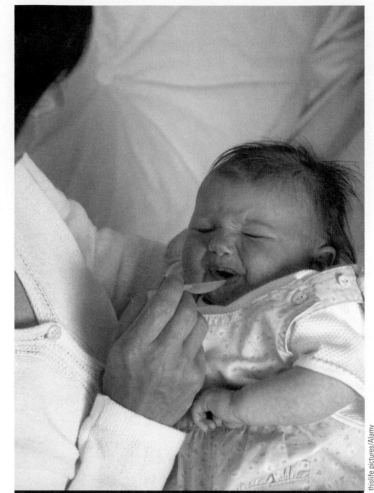

thislife pictures/Alamy

From birth, infants respond to tastes. In response to a sugar solution, newborns part their lips, lick their upper lips, make sucking movements, and sometimes smile. From this infant's expression, we might infer that she is not getting a spoonful of something sweet.

adults. After this period, the babies who had been fed the sour formula continued to consume it, but the other infants refused when it was offered to them. By 4–5 years, children fed the unpleasant-tasting formula were more likely to consume other sour-tasting foods (for example, a sour-flavored apple juice) than children exposed to only bland-tasting formula.

Such research may be key to helping researchers understand why some people are picky eaters, whereas others are open to a wide variety of tastes. Greater exposure to a variety of flavors during infancy—what a breast-fed baby with a mother who eats many different foods might experience—may lead to a more adventuresome eater later on. These early experiences with different flavors also extend to the prenatal period and exposure to different chemicals in the amniotic fluid. The foods eaten by pregnant women flavor the amniotic fluid that fetuses live in for 9 months (Mennella, Jagnow, & Beauchamp, 2001). Although learning plays a role in taste preferences, we cannot discount genetic predispositions. Discovery of several "taste genes" has shown that genetic variation can account for a lot of the variation

Aiding Infants and Children with Hearing Impairments

Although sensory impairments can change the course of normal life-span development, much can be done to help even those individuals born totally deaf or blind develop in positive directions and function effectively in everyday life. Here, we examine interventions for infants and children who have hearing impairments; in a later box, we examine interventions for hearing loss at the other end of the age spectrum.

For the 2 to 3 in 1,000 infants born deaf or hearing impaired, early identification and treatment are essential if they are to master spoken language. We know that children who receive no special intervention before age 2 usually have lasting difficulties with speech and language (for example, Vohr et al., 2011). As a result, most states have now mandated that all newborns be screened for hearing loss before they leave the hospital. How do you test the hearing of newborns? By using auditory evoked potentials (see again Table 6.1) to determine whether sounds trigger normal activity in the brain. Infants' behaviors also give physicians clues about their hearing. Does she turn her head when spoken to? Does he react to loud noises? Is she soothed by your voice? If the answers to these questions are no, a more thorough examination is warranted.

Once hearing-impaired infants are identified, interventions can be planned. Many programs attempt to capitalize on whatever residual hearing these children have by equipping them with hearing aids. Today, even profoundly deaf children can be helped to hear through an advanced amplification device called the **cochlear implant** (see the photo in this box). The device is implanted in the inner ear through surgery and connected to a microphone worn outside the ear. It works by bypassing damaged hair cells (sensory receptors located in the inner ear) and directly stimulating the auditory nerve with electrical impulses.

The younger children are when they receive the implant, the better the outcome. For example, deaf children provided with cochlear implants by age 4 recognize more spoken words and speak more intelligibly than do children who receive them later in childhood (Harrison, Gordon, & Mount, 2005). And those who received implants in their first year of life perform better on a variety of vocabulary and speech measures compared to those who received implants in their second or third years

Three-year-old Mustafa Ghazwan has just had his cochlear implant activated and will begin auditory training to learn how to interpret the impulses that it transmits to his auditory nerve.

© Kim Komenich/San Francisco Chronicle/Corbis

(Colletti et al., 2011). In addition, speech production and speech perception are improved in deaf children who have cochlear implants compared with deaf children who have traditional hearing aids, although performance still falls short of that of children with normal hearing (Houston et al., 2005; Schery & Peters, 2003). Children with two cochlear implants—one in each ear—show additional benefits, particularly for localizing sounds (Godar, Grieco, & Litovsky, 2007). For some, cochlear implants have truly opened up new horizons that they thought were not possible before the implant (see, for example, Denworth, 2006; Mishori, 2006).

Why, then, are not all hearing-impaired children provided with cochlear implants? First, they require surgery and are expensive—although the expense of cochlear implants may be offset by educational savings down the road (Cheng et al., 2000). Also, despite their benefits, cochlear implants do not have the full support of the deaf community (see, for example, Lee, 2012; Sparrow, 2010). Deaf children who use them, some say, will be given the message that they should be ashamed of being deaf. They will be deprived of participation in the unique culture that has developed in communities of deaf people who share a common language and identity. Because

their hearing will still be far from normal, they may feel they do not belong to either the deaf or the hearing world.

The correct amplification device and auditory training have proven effective in improving the ability of hearing-impaired infants and preschoolers to hear speech and learn to speak. Yet for other deaf and severely hearing-impaired children, the most important thing may be early exposure to sign language. Early intervention programs for parents of deaf infants can teach them strategies for getting their infants' attention and involving them in conversations using sign language (Chen, 1996). The earlier in life deaf children acquire some language system, whether spoken or signed, the better their command of language is likely to be later in life (Mayberry & Eichen, 1991). Using MRIs, researchers have found that delay in acquiring a language leads to structural changes in the organization of the brain (Pénicaud et al., 2013). Deaf children whose parents are deaf and use sign language with them, as well as deaf children of hearing parents who participate in early intervention programs, generally show normal patterns of development, whereas children who are not exposed to any language system early in life suffer for it (Marschark, 1993).

in children and adults' perception of bitterness and some of the variation in children's perception of sweetness (Knaapila et al., 2012; Mennella, Pepino, & Reed, 2005).

The sensory receptors for smell, or **olfaction**, are located in the nasal passage. Like taste, the sense of smell is working well at birth. Newborns react vigorously to unpleasant smells such as vinegar or ammonia and turn their heads away (Rieser, Yonas, & Wilkner, 1976). Even premature babies (born at 28 weeks of gestation) are capable of detecting various odors. Newborns also reliably prefer the scent of their own amniotic fluid over that of other amniotic fluid, suggesting that olfactory cues are detectable prenatally (Schaal, Barlier, & Soussignan, 1998). Exposure to a familiar odor—their own amniotic fluid or their mother's breast milk—can also calm newborns, resulting in less crying when their mothers are absent or when they undergo a painful procedure (Nishitani et al., 2009; Rattaz, Goubet, & Bullinger, 2005). All babies also show a preference for the smell of human milk over formula, even if they have consumed only formula (Delaunay-El Allam, Marlier, & Schaal, 2006; Marlier & Schaal, 2005). Furthermore, babies who are breast-fed can recognize their mothers solely by the smell of their breasts or underarms within 1 or 2 weeks of birth (Cernoch & Porter, 1985; Porter et al., 1992; Vaglio, 2009). Babies who are bottle-fed cannot, probably because they have less contact with their mothers' skin. On the flip side, mothers can identify their newborns by smell, and they are less repulsed by the odor of their own infant's dirty diaper than by one from an unfamiliar infant (Case, Repacholi, & Stevenson, 2006; Porter, 1999). Thus, the sense of smell we often take for granted may help babies and their parents get to know each other.

The Somaesthetic Senses

The **somaesthetic senses** are your "body" senses including your sense of touch, temperature, and pain, as well as your *kinesthetic sense* of knowing where your body is in relation to other body parts and to the environment. Whether you realize it or not, you use your kinesthetic sense throughout your waking hours. For example, you know when you are upright as opposed to laying down. And when walking along a crowded sidewalk, you constantly make adjustments to your body to avoid bumping into others. At what point are these somaesthetic senses operational?

The sense of touch seems to be operating nicely before birth and, with the body senses that detect motion, may be among the first senses to develop (Hollins, 2010). You saw in Chapter 5 that newborns respond with reflexes if they are touched in appropriate areas. For example, when touched on the cheek, a newborn will turn her head and open her mouth. Even in their sleep, newborns will habituate to strokes of the same spot on the skin but respond again if the tactile stimulation is shifted to a new spot—from the ear to the lips, for example (Kisilevsky & Muir, 1984). Sensitivity to tactile stimulation develops in the cephalocaudal (head-to-toe) direction described in Chapter 5, so the face and mouth are more sensitive than lower parts of the body. No wonder babies like to put everything in their mouths—the tactile sensors in and around the mouth allow babies to collect a great deal of information about the world. Most parents quickly recognize the power of touch for soothing a fussy baby. Touch has even greater benefits:

Premature babies who are systematically stroked over their entire body gain more weight and exhibit more relaxed behavior and more regular sleep patterns than premature babies who are not massaged (Field et al., 2006; Scafidi, Field, & Schanberg, 1993).

Newborns are also sensitive to warmth and cold; they can tell the difference between something cold and something warm placed on their cheeks. Finally, young babies clearly respond to painful stimuli such as needle pricks. For obvious ethical reasons, researchers have not exposed infants to severely painful stimuli. However, analyses of babies' cries and facial movements as they receive injections and have blood drawn leave no doubt that these procedures are painful. Even premature babies show cortical responses to pain (Slater et al., 2006). And pain is responsive to learning. For example, researchers have compared infants born to diabetic mothers, who have their heels pricked every few hours after birth to test their blood sugar levels, with infants born to nondiabetic mothers (Taddio, 2002). Both groups of infants have blood drawn from the back of their hands before they leave the hospital so several routine tests can be conducted. The infants who have already had their heels pricked show a larger response to having blood drawn than the infants who have never experienced presumably painful needle pricks in their feet. Indeed, some infants who had already experienced the heel pricks began to grimace when the nurse prepared their skin for the needle prick, indicating that they had learned from their prior experiences that a painful moment was coming.

Such research challenges the medical wisdom of giving babies who must undergo major surgery little or no anesthesia. It turns out that infants are more likely to survive heart surgery if they receive deep anesthesia that keeps them unconscious during the operation and for a day afterward than if they receive light anesthesia that does not entirely protect them from the stressful experience of pain (Anand & Hickey, 1992). And the American Academy of Pediatrics (2000) recommends that local anesthesia be given to newborn males undergoing circumcision. Finally, breastfeeding during painful events such as getting a vaccination or having blood drawn has been shown to reduce the behavioral signs that infants are experiencing pain (Codipietro, Ceccarelli, & Ponzone, 2008).

You have now seen that each of the major senses is operating in some form at birth and that perceptual abilities improve dramatically during infancy. Are any special experiences necessary to develop normal perceptual abilities?

Influences on Early Perceptual Development

The perceptual competencies of even very young infants are remarkable, as is the progress made within the first few months of life. All major senses begin working before birth and are clearly functioning at birth; parents would be making a huge mistake to assume that their newborn is not taking in the sensory world. Many perceptual abilities—for example, the ability to perceive depth or to distinguish melodies—emerge within just a few months of birth. Gradually, basic perceptual capacities are fine-tuned, and infants become more able to interpret their sensory experiences—to recognize a pattern of light as a face, for example. By the end of the second year, the most important aspects of perceptual development are complete. The senses and the mind are working to create a meaningful world of recognized objects, sounds, tastes, smells, and bodily sensations.

The fact that perceptual development takes place so quickly can be viewed as support for the "nature" side of the nature–nurture debate. Many basic perceptual capacities appear to be innate or to develop rapidly in all normal infants. What, then, is the role of early sensory experience in perceptual development?

Early Experience and the Brain

Classic studies that would ultimately lead to a Nobel Prize for David Hubel and Torsten Wiesel showed that depriving newborn kittens of normal visual experience by suturing one eye closed for 8 weeks resulted in a lack of normal connections between that eye and the visual cortex—and blindness even after the eye had been reopened (Hubel & Wiesel, 1970). Even as little as 1 week of deprivation during the critical period of the first 8 weeks of life can lead to permanent vision loss in the kitten (Kandel & Jessell, 1991). By contrast, depriving an adult cat's eye of light does not lead to permanent damage.

From other classic research with kittens, we know that kittens need to actively experience their environments to develop normal visual perception (Held & Hein, 1963). In an ingenious study, kittens were able to see their environment but from the vantage point of a passive rider in a cart pulled by another cat (picture a horse pulling a wagon with a passenger in it and then substitute kittens for the horse and passenger). Despite being able to see the world pass by, the passenger kittens did not have the opportunity to learn how their own movement influenced the incoming flow of visual images. They needed to have this active feedback loop between their actions, the visual stimulation, and their perception of this information. For cats, anyway, there seems to be a critical period of time when normal visual experiences are needed in order to develop normal visual perception.

In humans, it is probably more accurate to characterize the effects of early experience on vision in terms of **sensitive periods** rather than critical periods (Armstrong et al., 2006). A sensitive period is "a window of time during which an individual is *more* affected by experience, and thus has a higher level of plasticity than at other times throughout life" (p. 326). Terri Lewis and Daphne Maurer (2005, 2009) provide evidence for multiple sensitive periods during which vision can be influenced by experience. First, there is the period they call visually driven normal development. This is when expected developmental changes in vision will occur with exposure to "normal" visual input; these changes will not occur if visual input is absent. Second, there is a sensitive period for damage; that is, there is a period when abnormal or absent visual input is likely to lead to permanent deficits in some aspect of vision. Third, there is a sensitive period for recovery when the visual system has the potential to recover from damage (Lewis & Maurer, 2005, p. 164).

Sensory experience is vital in determining the organization of the developing brain. Imagine what visual perception would be like in an infant who was blind at birth but later had surgery to permit vision. This is the scenario for perhaps 3 of every 5,000 infants with congenital **cataracts**, a clouding of the lens that leaves these infants nearly blind from birth if it is not corrected. In the past, surgery to remove cataracts was often delayed until infants were older. But such delays meant that infants had weeks, months, or even years with little or no visual input. Consequently, some never developed normal vision even after the lens defect was removed.

It turns out that the visual system requires stimulation early in life, including patterned stimulation, to develop normally. Although the visual system has some plasticity throughout childhood, the first 3 months of life are considered critical (Lambert & Drack, 1996). During this time, the brain must receive clear visual information from both eyes. Unfortunately, not all infants with cataracts are identified early enough to benefit from surgery. One recent study found that even with visual screening programs for newborns before they leave the hospital, the vast majority of congenital cataracts are still not identified during the neonatal (first month) period (Sotomi et al., 2007). Early identification is essential. Identification and removal of cataracts by 10 weeks of age is associated with better long-term outcomes than identification and removal after this age (Lambert et al., 2006). Even after surgery restores their sight, these infants have difficulty, at least initially, perceiving their visual world clearly (Maurer, Mondloch, & Lewis, 2007). Although acuity immediately after surgery is what you might find in a newborn without cataracts—in other words, rather poor—it improves significantly during the month following surgery (Maurer et al., 1999).

Years after corrective surgery, individuals who missed out on early visual experience because of congenital cataracts show normal visual abilities in some areas, such as sensitivity to low spatial frequencies (for example, wide stripes) and recognition of faces based on the *shape* of facial features. However, they struggle with certain other visual tasks, including the ability to distinguish between mid- and high-spatial frequencies (for example, medium and narrow strips) as well as holistic face processing and recognizing faces based on *spacing* of facial features. What might account for this pattern?

Daphne Maurer and her colleagues (2007) argue that the lingering deficits reflect **sleeper effects**—delayed outcomes—of early visual deficits. Thus, patterned visual input early in life is critical to developing later sensitivity to detail and holistic face processing. Even though these abilities do not normally develop until after early infancy—and after corrective surgery has been done—early visual deprivation likely affects the brain in a way that prevents infants from developing these abilities even when normal visual input is restored (Maurer et al., 2007). Clearly, then, early visual experiences influence later visual perception.

The same message about the importance of early experience applies to the sense of hearing: Exposure to auditory stimulation early in life affects the architecture of the developing brain, which in turn influences auditory perception skills (Finitzo, Gunnarson, & Clark, 1990). Children with hearing impairments who undergo a cochlear implant, which bypasses damaged nerve cells in their inner ear, may struggle for months to understand the meaning of signals reaching their brain through the implant before they derive benefits (Allum et al., 2000; see also Application Box 6.1). Although the brain is being fed information, it must learn how to interpret these signals. Otherwise, the signals are a crashing jumble of nonsense that can be worse than not hearing (Colburn, 2000). The conclusion is clear: Maturation alone is not enough; normal perceptual development also requires normal perceptual experience.

The practical implication is also clear: Visual and hearing problems in children should be detected and corrected as early in life as possible (Joint Committee on Infant Hearing, 2000).

Fortunately, parents need not worry about arranging the right sensory environment for their children because young humans actively seek the stimulation they need to develop properly. Infants are active explorers and stimulus seekers; they orchestrate their own perceptual, motor, and cognitive development by exploring their environment and learning what it will *afford*, or allow, them to do (Gibson, 1988; Gibson & Pick, 2000).

According to Eleanor Gibson (1988), infants proceed through three phases of exploratory behavior:

1. From birth to 4 months, infants explore their immediate surroundings, especially their caregivers, by looking and listening, and they learn a bit about objects by mouthing them and watching them move.
2. From 5 to 7 months, once the ability to voluntarily grasp objects has developed, babies pay far closer attention to objects, exploring objects with their eyes as well as with their hands.
3. By 8 or 9 months, after most have begun to crawl, infants extend their explorations into the larger environment and carefully examine the objects they encounter on their journeys, learning all about their properties.

By combining perception and action in their exploratory behavior, infants actively create sensory environments that meet their needs and contribute to their own development (Eppler, 1995). As children become more able to attend selectively to the world around them, they become even more able to choose the forms and levels of stimulation that suit them best. Again, we see a coupling of perception and action.

Cultural Variation

Do infants who grow up in different cultural environments encounter different sensory stimulation and perceive the world in different ways? Perceptual preferences obviously differ from culture to culture. In some cultures, people think heavier women are more beautiful than slim ones or relish eating sheep's eyeballs or chicken heads. Are more basic perceptual competencies also affected by socialization?

People from different cultures differ little in basic sensory capacities, such as the ability to discriminate degrees of brightness or loudness (Berry et al., 1992). However, their perceptions and interpretations of sensory input can vary considerably. For example, you have already seen that

children become insensitive, starting at the end of the first year of life, to speech sound contrasts that they do not hear regularly because they are not important in their primary language. Michael Lynch and his associates (1990) have shown that the same is true for perceptions of music. Infants from the United States, they found, noticed equally notes that violated either Western musical scales or the Javanese pelog scale. This suggests that humans are born with the potential to perceive music from a variety of cultures. However, American adults were less sensitive to bad notes in the unfamiliar Javanese musical system than to mistuned notes in their native Western scale, suggesting that their years of experience with Western music had shaped their perceptual skills.

Another example of cultural influence concerns the ability to translate perceptions of the human form into a drawing. In Papua New Guinea, where there is no cultural tradition of drawing and painting, children aged 10–15 who have had no schooling do not have much luck drawing the human body; they draw scribbles or tadpolelike forms far more often than children in the same society who have attended school and have been exposed many times to drawings of people (Martlew & Connolly, 1996; ■ Figure 6.2). We all have the capacity to create two-dimensional representations, but we apparently develop that capacity more rapidly if our culture

■ **Figure 6.2** These human figures were drawn by children between the ages of 10 and 15. On the left, the drawings were made by children in Papua New Guinea, who often lack experience with drawing the human form and produce figures much like those done by far younger children (such as 4-year-olds) in the United States. The drawing on the right was made by a 12-year-old child in the United States. The contrast between the drawings on the left and the one on the right illustrates how cultural experience influences the ability to translate visual perceptions into representations on the page.

SOURCE: M. Martlew & K. J. Connolly, 1996, Human figure drawings by schooled and unschooled children in Papua New Guinea. *Child Development*, 6, p. 2743–2762. Reprinted by permission of John Wiley & Sons, Inc.

provides us with relevant experiences. Many other examples of the effects of cultural learning experiences on visual and auditory perception can be cited (Berry et al., 1992).

Checking Mastery

1. Describe two procedures used by researchers to assess perceptual abilities of infants.
2. During their first few months of life, what can infants see best?
3. What sorts of experiences are necessary to develop normal visual perception?

Making Connections

1. Drawing on your knowledge of the sensory and perceptual capacities of newborns, put yourself in the place of a newborn just emerging from the womb and describe your perceptual experiences. What do you see, feel, hear, and so on? What, if anything, do you make of all this information?
2. How would you design a nursery for an infant to make the best use of his sensory and perceptual abilities?

6.3 The Child

LEARNING OBJECTIVES:

- Explain how perception and action work together in the development and refinement of locomotor skills.

- Provide an example of both fine motor and gross motor skills and note the typical order in which these skills develop.

- Discuss the dynamic systems theory of motor development and summarize the research findings supporting this theory.

- Describe and provide two examples of cross-modal perception. Explain how researchers demonstrate that someone has cross-modal perception.

There are some refinements of the sensory systems during childhood. For example, visual acuity improves to adult levels sometime between 4 and 6 years, and sensitivity to visual contrasts develops completely by about 7 years of age (Maurer et al., 2007). Recognition of odors improves between ages 6 and 11, at which point it reaches adult levels (Stevenson, Mahmut, & Sundqvist, 2007). For the most part, though, sensory and perceptual development is largely complete by the end of infancy. Does anything remain to be accomplished during childhood? Yes, indeed. We will cover two important accomplishments with the transition from infancy to childhood: (1) the coupling of perception and action leading to purposeful movement; and (2) integration of multiple sources of sensory information.

Locomotion: The Coupling of Perception and Action

Locomotion, or movement from one place to another, is a vital aspect of development. One of young children's most impressive accomplishments is getting up off of their bellies, backs, or bottoms and moving with purpose throughout their environment on two legs. This shift from crawling to walking offers toddlers the opportunity to engage differently with their environments. They are no longer restricted to objects that are close by and close to the ground. They can now cross the room to get objects, access higher objects, and use their hands to share and interact with objects in new ways (Karasik, Tamis-LeMonda, & Adolph, 2011). In Gibson's ecological framework, walking opens up new environments and new affordances, or ways of interacting with objects in the environment. To make this transition, the young child must learn to integrate perception with action (Smitsman & Corbetta, 2010). This coupling occurs gradually and becomes more refined with experience.

The groundwork for walking occurs during infancy. Infants generally acquire **gross motor skills** (skills such as kicking the legs or drawing large circles that involve large muscles and whole-body or limb movements) before mastering **fine motor skills** (skills such as picking Cheerios off the breakfast table or writing letters of the alphabet that involve precise movements of the hands and fingers or feet and toes). If you examine the progression of these motor skills, you will notice the workings of the cephalocaudal and proximodistal principles of development (see Chapter 5). Early motor development follows the *cephalocaudal principle* because the neurons between the brain and the muscles acquire myelin sheaths in a head-to-tail manner. Thus, infants can lift their heads before they can control their trunks enough to sit, and they can sit before they can control their legs to walk. The *proximodistal principle* of development is also evident in early motor development. Activities involving the trunk are mastered before activities involving the arms and legs, and activities involving the arms and legs are mastered before activities involving the hands and fingers or feet and toes. Therefore, infants can roll over before they can walk or bring their arms together to grasp a bottle. As the nerves and muscles mature downward and outward, infants gradually gain control over the lower and the peripheral parts of their bodies. When this happens, infants are ready for the next step, literally. For examples of gross motor development during the first year, see **Exploring Development Box 6.2**.

Exploring Development 6.2
Gross Motor Development in the First Year

Observe how infants develop gross motor skills during their first year.

- What are some of the gross motor skills developed during the first 9 months?
- Does the order of developing these skills matter?

Although parents must be on their toes when their toddlers begin walking, they take great delight in witnessing this new milestone in motor development, which occurs around age 1. By collecting an enormous number of observations of infants' and toddlers' daily movements, Karen Adolph and her colleagues (2008, 2013) have found that it takes an average of 13 starts and stops over a period of days and sometimes weeks before toddlers show consistent performance of a motor skill. During the transition period of acquiring a new motor skill, they are truly taking "one step forward, two steps backward." They may appear to have started walking, only to revert to crawling, much to the chagrin of their proud parents. From the toddler's perspective, the apparent regression in skills is quite logical. They have mastered crawling and are quite fast at it, whereas walking on two legs is hard work and can slow them down (Adolph & Berger, 2006). So if they have important things to do, they might find it more efficient to use their reliable crawling skills than to labor at walking. With a little bit of practice, walking will soon become routine. Indeed, by 14 months of age, toddlers are taking 2,000 steps an hour, which is equivalent to traveling a distance of nearly seven football fields (see Adolph & Robinson, 2013). No wonder parents feel as though they can barely keep up with their toddlers at times. And there's more: Not only are toddlers traveling all over the house, but walking frees up their arms and hands. **Exploration Box 6.1** considers the remarkable changes taking place with the use of hands and fingers.

Motor Skills as Dynamic Action Systems

How do motor skills emerge? Esther Thelen (1995, 1996) observed infants throughout their first year and discovered that they spent a great deal of time engaged in **rhythmic stereotypies**. That is, they moved their bodies in repetitive ways—rocking, swaying, bouncing, mouthing objects, and banging their arms up and down. Thelen found that infants and toddlers performed these rhythmic stereotypies shortly before a new skill emerged but not after the skill had become established. Thus, infants might rock back and forth while on their hands and knees, but once they were crawling, they no longer rocked.

Esther Thelen's work has culminated in the development of the **dynamic systems theory** to explain such motor developments (Thelen & Smith, 1994; see also Spencer et al., 2006). According to dynamic systems theory, developments take place over time through a "self-organizing" process in which children use the sensory feedback they receive when they try different movements to modify their motor behavior in adaptive ways (Smith & Thelen, 1993; von Hofsten, 2007). Behaviors that seem to emerge in a moment of time are actually the cumulative effects of motor decisions that the infant

makes over a longer time (Spencer et al., 2006). In this view, motor milestones such as crawling and walking are the learned outcomes of a process of interaction with the environment in which infants do the best they can with what they have in order to achieve their goals (Thelen, 1995). Thus, development is highly individualistic: "infants must explore a wide range of behaviors to discover and select their own unique solutions in the context of their intrinsic dynamics and movement history" (Spencer et al., 2006, p. 1528). Neural maturation, physical growth, muscle strength, balance, and other characteristics of the child interact with gravity, floor surfaces, and characteristics of the specific task to influence what children can and cannot learn to do with their bodies.

Consistent with the dynamic systems approach, Karen Adolph and Anthony Avolio (2000) found that young toddlers could adjust their walking to changes in both their body dimensions and the slope of a walkway. The researchers had toddlers walk on slopes of different degrees while wearing a vest with removable "saddlebags" that could be weighted to simulate changes in their body dimensions (■**Figure 6.3**). The weights added mass and shifted the toddlers' center of gravity, akin to what happens when toddlers grow. Would toddlers be able to compensate for the changes in their body and

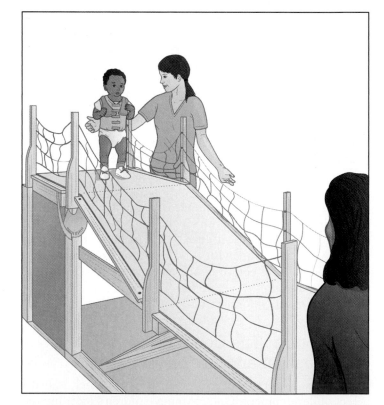

■ **Figure 6.3** Adolph and Avolio's walkway with adjustable slope. Infants are outfitted with weighted saddlebags to alter their body mass and center of gravity. While an experimenter stays beside infants to ensure safety, parents stand at the end of the walkway and encourage their child to walk toward them.

Grasping and Reaching

If you look at what children can do with their hands, you will find it progresses from reflexive activity of early infancy to more voluntary, coordinated behavior. By the middle of the first year, infants grasp objects well, although they use a rather clumsy, clamplike grasp in which they press the palm and outer fingers together—the **ulnar grasp**. Initially, they reach for objects using jerky movements and a locked elbow (Berthier & Keen, 2006). Over the next few months, their reaching movements become increasingly smooth and they anticipate how they need to adjust their hand so that it can effectively grasp an approaching object (Barrett & Needham, 2008; von Hofsten, 2007). We can again see the workings of the proximodistal principle of development as we watch infants progress from controlling their arms, then their hands, and finally their individual fingers enough to use a **pincer grasp**, involving only the thumb and the forefinger (or another finger). The pincer grasp appears as early as 5 months and is reliable by the child's first birthday (Wallace & Whishaw, 2003).

By 16 months, toddlers can scribble with a crayon, and by the end of the second year they can copy a simple horizontal or vertical line and even build towers of five or more blocks. They are rapidly gaining control of specific, *differentiated* movements, then *integrating* those movements into whole, coordinated actions. They use their new locomotor and manipulation skills to learn about and adapt to the world around them. By cornering bugs and stacking Cheerios, they develop their minds.

This toddler uses the pincer grasp to pick up a crayon for coloring.

Mark Wallis/Alamy

their environment? Yes—they adjusted their motor skills to adapt to rapid "growth" of their bodies and to changes in their environment (Adolph & Berger, 2006). Like adults carrying a heavy load on their shoulders, toddlers bent their knees and kept their upper bodies stiffly upright to maintain their balance with heavier loads. Toddlers with greater walking experience did better than those with less experience (Garciaguirre, Adolph, & Shrout, 2007). Toddlers also seemed to recognize when the walkway was too steep for safe travel—they either avoided it or scooted down on their bottoms or on their hands and knees. Young walkers (16 months) are also clever enough to figure out that they can use handrails to help maintain their balance while walking across bridges (Berger & Adolph, 2003). Further, they quickly discover that a sturdy handrail offers more support than a "wobbly" handrail and they are more adventuresome when they can use a sturdy handrail for support (Berger, Adolph, & Lobo, 2005). If they are not sure how to proceed across a potentially unstable surface, they look to their mothers for advice. With mother's encouragement, 75% of infants will try to navigate a questionable slope; only 25% of infants are brave enough to give it a shot when mothers express discouragement (Karasik et al., 2008; Tamis-LeMonda et al., 2008).

As every parent knows, toddlers do not become proficient walkers without experiencing more than a few falls—as many as 15 per hour by one estimate (see Adolph, 2008). As it turns out, these tumbles may help walkers learn which surfaces are safe and which

ones may be problematic (Joh & Adolph, 2006). With age, toddlers become increasingly adept at figuring out how to avoid falls, but they still appear awkward compared with the older child, who takes steps in more fluid and rhythmic strides and is better able to avoid obstacles. And children quickly become able to do more than just walk. By age 3, they can walk or run in a straight line, although they cannot easily turn or stop while running. Kindergarten children can integrate two motor skills—hopping on one foot with walking or running—into mature skipping (Loovis & Butterfield, 2000). With each passing year, school-age children can run a little faster, jump a little higher, and throw a ball a little farther.

What does the dynamic systems perspective say about the contribution of nature and nurture to development? According to Thelen (1995), toddlers walk not because their genetic code programs them to do so but because they learn that walking works well given their biomechanical properties and the characteristics of the environments they must navigate. In the dynamic systems approach, nature (that is, maturation of the central nervous system) and nurture (sensory and motor experience) are both essential and largely inseparable. Feedback from the senses and from motor actions is integrated with the ever-changing abilities of the infant. Having learned how to adjust one motor skill (such as crawling) to successfully navigate environmental conditions, however, does not mean that toddlers will generalize this knowledge to other motor skills (such as walking; see Adolph & Berger, 2006). Different motor

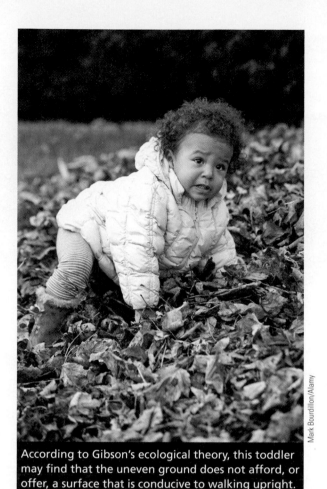

According to Gibson's ecological theory, this toddler may find that the uneven ground does not afford, or offer, a surface that is conducive to walking upright.

Mark Bourdillon/Alamy

skills present different challenges. Crawling toddlers, for instance, must learn to avoid such dangers as bumping their head on table legs. Walking toddlers face other challenges, such as not toppling over when turning around. To master these challenges, children need opportunities to gather feedback from each motor activity.

Finally, an important contribution of the dynamic systems approach to motor development is its integration of action with thought (von Hofsten, 2007). The motor behaviors we have been describing are not separate and distinct from the child's knowledge. Children have to think about how to organize their movements to optimize what they are able to get from their ever-changing environment. Thus, there is far more to motor development than implied by norms indicating when we might expect infants to sit up, stand alone, or walk independently. The emergence of motor skills is complex and is closely connected to perceptual–cognitive developments.

Integrating Sensory Information

Moving around the world opens up the floodgates of sensory information. In most situations, multiple senses provide the brain with different information and, ideally, the brain integrates these pieces of information into a single coherent understanding. If not, then our understanding of the world would be fragmented and rather chaotic. At what point are we able to put together information gained from viewing, fingering, sniffing, and otherwise exploring objects?

To some extent, the senses function in an integrated way at birth. For instance, newborns will look in the direction of a sound they hear, suggesting that vision and hearing are linked. They also expect to feel objects that they can see and are frustrated by a visual illusion that looks like a graspable object but proves to be nothing but air when they reach for it (Bower, Broughton, & Moore, 1970). Thus, vision and touch, as well as vision and hearing, seem to be interrelated early in life. This integration of the senses helps babies perceive and respond appropriately to the objects and people they encounter (Hainline & Abramov, 1992; Walker-Andrews, 1997). Although present in a rudimentary form in early infancy, fully and meaningfully integrating the senses develops fairly late relative to development of individual senses (Burr & Gori, 2012). Thus, it is not enough for each individual sense to be operational for multisensory integration to occur. This more advanced skill requires ongoing "conversation" among the various sensory systems and the brain. As the brain develops, so does the ability to consider multiple pieces of information and draw on memory of past experiences to better understand the meaning of multiple sources of input (Burr & Gori, 2012). With each new encounter of the nearly continuous flow of multisensory information, children refine their understanding of the rich sensory world.

An even more difficult task is to recognize through one sense an object familiar through another, a type of multisensory integration called **cross-modal perception**. This capacity is required in children's games that involve feeling objects hidden in a bag and identifying what they are by touch alone. Although some researchers (for example, Streri, 2003; Streri & Gentaz, 2004) report that newborns can recognize an object by sight that they had previously touched with their hand, others have had trouble demonstrating cross-modal perception in such young infants (for example, Maurer, Stager, & Mondloch, 1999). Apparently, early cross-modal perception is a fragile ability dependent on various task variables such as which hand is used to manipulate the object (Streri & Gentaz, 2004). Performance on complex cross-modal perception tasks that require matching patterns of sounds with patterns of visual stimuli continues to improve throughout childhood and even adolescence (Bushnell & Baxt, 1999).

Researchers now conclude that impressions from the different senses are "fused" or integrated early in life, making it easier for infants to perceive and use information that comes to them through multiple channels simultaneously (Walker-Andrews, 1997). Then, as the separate senses continue to develop and each becomes a more effective means of exploring objects, toddlers become more skilled at cross-modal perception and are able to coordinate information gained through one sense with information gained through another.

Advances in Attention

We have talked about perception without much focus on an important costar: attention. At least some of the advances in perceptual development across childhood and adolescence reflect the development of **attention**—the focusing of perception and cognition on something in particular. Youngsters become better able to use their senses deliberately and strategically to gather the information most relevant to a task at hand.

Intersensory perception. The ability to recognize through one sense (here, touch) what has been learned through another (vision) increases with age during infancy and childhood. Here, the birthday girl must identify prizes in the bag by touch alone.

© Mary Kate Denny/PhotoEdit Inc.

Infants actively use their senses to explore their environment, and they prefer some sensory stimuli to others. Selective as they are, though, young infants do not deliberately choose to attend to faces and other engaging stimuli. Instead, a novel stimulus attracts their attention and, once their attention is "caught," they sometimes seem unable to turn away (Butcher, Kalverboer, & Geuze, 2000; Ruff & Rothbart, 1996). Thus, there is some truth to the idea that the attention of the infant or very young child is "captured by" something and that of the older child is "directed toward" something. This difference has been described as the difference between having an **orienting system**, one that reacts to events in the environment, versus having a **focusing system**, one that deliberately seeks out and maintains attention to events (Ruff & Rothbart, 1996). As children get older, three things change: their attention spans become longer, they become more selective in what they attend to, and they are better able to plan and carry out systematic strategies for using their senses to achieve goals.

Longer Attention Span

If you have spent any time in the company of young children, then you are probably aware that they have short attention spans. Researchers know that they should limit their experimental sessions with young children to a few minutes, and nursery-school teachers often switch classroom activities every 15–20 minutes. Even when they are doing things they like, such as watching a television program or playing with a toy, 2- and 3-year-olds spend far less time concentrating on the program or the toy than older children do (Ruff & Capozzoli, 2003; Ruff & Lawson, 1990). In one study of sustained attention, children were asked to put strips of colored paper in appropriately colored boxes (Yendovitskaya, 1971). Children aged 2–3 worked for an average of 18 minutes and were easily distracted, whereas children aged 5–6 often persisted for 1 hour or more. Further improvements in sustained attention occur from ages 5–6 to ages 8–9 as those parts of the brain involved with attention become further myelinated (Betts et al., 2006). Beyond ages 8–9 there is not much increase in length of sustained attention, but children do become more accurate on tasks requiring sustained attention over the next few years (Betts et al., 2006).

More Selective Attention

Although infants clearly deploy their senses in a selective manner, they are not good at controlling their attention—deliberately concentrating on one thing while ignoring something else, or what is known as **selective attention**. With age, attention becomes more selective and less susceptible to distraction. As infants approach 2 years, they become able to form plans of action, which then guide what they focus on and what they ignore (Ruff & Rothbart, 1996).

Research suggests that preschool children have an adultlike orienting system but an immature focusing system of attention (Ristic & Kingstone, 2009). Between approximately 3½ and 4 years, there is a significant increase in focused attention. Kathleen Kannass and John Colombo (2007) tested 3½- and 4-year-olds while they worked on a task under one of three conditions: no distraction, constant distraction (a TV program in an unfamiliar language played continuously in the background), or intermittent distraction (the same TV program played in the background but was frequently turned on and off as the children worked). Among the 3½-year-olds, the two groups working with any distraction had more trouble completing their task than the group working without distraction. Among the 4-year-olds, only the group working with constant distraction had trouble finishing the task. Those working with intermittent distraction were able to stay as focused on the task as children working without distraction. Finally, the researchers found that when a distractor was present, looking away from the task led to worse performance, whereas looking away when there was no distraction did not impair performance. These findings should suggest to parents and teachers of young children that performance will be better if distractions in task materials and in the room are kept to a minimum. In particular, the presence of a continuous distractor will lead to trouble completing tasks (Kannass & Colombo, 2007).

More Systematic Attention

Finally, as they age, children become more able to plan and carry out systematic perceptual searches. You have already seen that older infants are more likely than younger ones to thoroughly explore a pattern. Research with children in the former Soviet Union reveals that visual scanning becomes considerably more detailed and exhaustive over the first 6 years of life (Zaporozhets, 1965). But the most revealing findings come from studies of how children go about a visual search. In general, children search more slowly than adults (Donnelly et al., 2007) but they are also less efficient. Elaine Vurpillot (1968) recorded the eye movements of 4- to 10-year-olds trying to decide whether two houses, each with several windows containing various objects, were identical or different. As ■ Figure 6.4 illustrates, children ages 4 and 5 were not systematic. They often looked at only a few windows and, as a result, came to wrong conclusions.

5-year-old: "The same"

8-year-old: "Not the same"

■ **Figure 6.4** Are the houses in each pair identical or different? As indicated by the lines, 8-year-olds are more likely than 5-year-olds to answer correctly because they systematically scan the visual features of the two pictures.

SOURCE: Adapted from Vurpillot, 1968, The development of scanning strategies and their relation to visual differentiation. *Journal of Experimental Child Psychology, 632–650.*

In contrast, most children older than 6 were very systematic; they typically checked each window in one house with the corresponding window in the other house, pair by pair. For most, improvements in visual search continue to be made throughout childhood and into early adulthood (Burack et al., 2000).

Checking Mastery

1. How do children master the important skill of walking and once they do so, how does this new skill affect their development in general?
2. Why is cross-modal perception important?
3. What are three ways that attention improves during childhood?

Making Connections

1. You have an unlimited budget for redesigning a local child care center that serves children 6 weeks to 6 years old. Given what you know about sensory and perceptual capabilities of infants and young children, what equipment and toys will you purchase, and how will you remodel and redecorate the rooms?
2. You are commissioned by a local pediatrician to write a brochure on "locomotor skills of the infant and young child." Begin this assignment by developing a bulleted list of the skills that support the development of walking and order these by when or what order they typically emerge.

6.4 The Adolescent

LEARNING OBJECTIVES:

- Document the changes in attention during the adolescent period and discuss the implications of today's multitasking lifestyle of many teens.

- Discuss the challenges to the auditory system during adolescence.

- Outline changes in the chemical senses of adolescents and indicate the likely contributing factors to these changes.

There is little news to report about sensation, attention, and perception during adolescence, except that some developments of childhood are not completed until then. Several issues during this time, though, warrant discussion: refinements in attention, potential insults to hearing from exposure to loud noise, and expanding taste horizons.

Attention

It is fairly clear that adolescents have longer attention spans than children. They can, for example, sit through longer classes, work on papers or study for lengthier periods of time, and take tests that last as long as 3–4 hours (for example, the SAT). This improved ability to sustain attention seems to be tied to increased myelination of those portions of the brain that help regulate attention (Tanner, 1990). As we noted in Chapter 5, a myelin coating on neurons helps insulate them to speed up transmission of neural impulses.

In addition, adolescents become still more efficient at ignoring irrelevant information so that they can concentrate on the task at hand. Not only do they learn more than children do about material they are supposed to master, but they also learn *less* about distracting information that could potentially interfere with their performance (Miller & Weiss, 1981). Children have the rudimentary skills to adapt to distractions, but compared with adolescents and adults, they are slowed down and more likely to be thrown off track by distractors.

Similarly, adolescents can divide their attention more systematically between two tasks. For instance, Andrew Schiff and Irwin Knopf (1985) watched the eye movements of 9-year-olds and 13-year-olds during a two-part visual search task. Children were to push a response key when particular symbols appeared at the center of a screen and to remember letters flashed at the corners of the screen. The adolescents developed efficient strategies for switching their eyes from the center to the corners and back at the right times. The 9-year-olds had an unfortunate tendency to look at blank areas of the screen or to focus too much attention on the letters in the corners of the screen, thereby failing to detect the symbols in the center.

But longer attention spans and being able to shift attention between two tasks does not mean that adolescents' attention spans are unlimited. Today's teens are flooded with information from multiple sources and are increasingly found juggling multiple tasks: They don't simply talk with a friend on the phone; they talk with one friend on their cell phone while watching YouTube videos and messaging local friends about what happened at school that day as well as messaging online acquaintances about the latest changes in their shared Internet game world. Meanwhile, they occasionally check on the younger sibling they are "supervising" after school until a parent arrives home. What are the consequences of such **multitasking**, attending to two or more tasks at the same time?

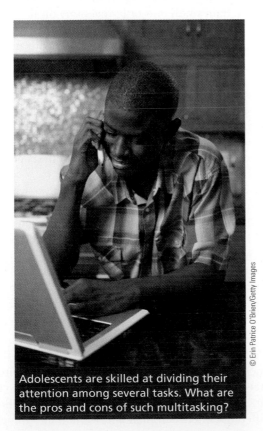

Adolescents are skilled at dividing their attention among several tasks. What are the pros and cons of such multitasking?

© Erin Patrice O'Brien/Getty Images

Among college students, at least 50% and as much as 55% of their time on the Internet is spent multitasking (Judd, 2013; Moreno et al., 2012). Terry Judd (2013) monitored computer sessions of students in an open computer laboratory and found that only 10% of the sessions were focused on a single task. When students are required to bring a laptop to class, presumably for course-related educational reasons, the majority of students use email and access unrelated material through the browser, and some spend time instant messaging (Kraushaar & Novak, 2010). Students surveyed about their multitasking during class report engaging in a wide range of additional behaviors, including texting (50% of students), working on other course work (18%), eating (26%), posting to Facebook (25%), instant messaging (13%), and listening to music (7%). These percentages are significantly higher when students are asked to report on their multitasking during an online class (Burak, 2012). And we suspect that if students report this much multitasking during class time, they are likely engaged in at least as much multitasking when studying outside of the class.

When college students text during a class lecture, they don't perform as well when tested on the lecture material as students who did not text (Ellis, Daniels, & Jauregui, 2010). The relationship here is fairly clear: As multitasking increases, students' grade point averages decrease (Burak, 2012). Students who multitask while reading or studying for a class take longer to complete their assignments. Their perceived study time, therefore, may be longer than their actual study time, deceiving them into thinking they have spent a sufficient amount of time studying. Dividing up our attentional resources can be risky to the learning enterprise. While we may be able to multitask two activities that are familiar and well-learned, our success at multitasking quickly disappears when the tasks are less familiar and relatively new to us (Schumacker et al., 2001). When faced with multiple pieces of information coming in for processing, our brains are forced to make some decisions about what to attend to first and what to "put on the back burner" (Dux et al., 2006). So next time you set aside time to study for a test, consider whether it would be more beneficial to spend time on this one task rather than allowing yourself to be interrupted and distracted by texting, tweeting, messaging, and more. You may find that focused attention to one task at a time is more efficient than attending to multiple tasks, but not effectively mastering any of them.

Hearing

Adolescence should be a period of optimal acuity of all the senses, but in today's world of concerts, iPods, power equipment, and so on, auditory acuity can become compromised in some adolescents. As ● **Table 6.2** shows, loud sounds—those above 75 decibels—may leave the listener with a loss of hearing. Fans of loud music, beware: The noise at rock concerts and nightclubs is often in the 120–130–decibel range, well above the level where damage may occur. And if you can hear the music coming from the earbuds or headphones connected to your friend's iPod, your friend may be damaging her hearing.

The most common outcome of noise exposure is **tinnitus**, or ringing sounds in one or both ears that can last for days, weeks, or

• Table 6.2 Noise Levels

The healthy ear can detect sounds starting at 0 decibels. Damage to hearing can start between 75 and 80 decibels and is more likely with long-term exposure to loud sounds. Using in-ear earphones to listen to music from an iPod at full volume can begin to cause damage after just 5 minutes.

Noise	Number of Decibels
Whisper	30
Normal speech	60
City traffic	80
Lawnmower	90
Rock concerts	110–140
iPod at full volume	110
Jet plane takeoff	120
Jackhammer	130
Firearm discharge	140

Source: *It's a Noisy Planet*, 2013. The National Institute on Deafness and Other Communication Disorders (NIDCD). http://www.noisyplanet.nidcd.nih.gov/Pages/Default.aspx

indefinitely. A majority—as many as 85%—of concert attendees report experiencing tinnitus (Bogoch, House, & Kudla, 2005; Chung et al., 2005). Hearing problems associated with short periods of exposure to loud sounds may be temporary, but damage from regular exposure to these same sounds can accumulate over time, leading to moderate or even severe hearing loss by adulthood.

Many teens report that they are aware of the potential for hearing loss from exposure to loud sounds, but they do not believe that hearing loss is a serious health concern for them (Chung et al., 2005). Thus, despite their awareness that noise exposure can lead to hearing loss and warnings from parents and health officials that noise can be hazardous, teens do little to protect their hearing because hearing loss is not perceived as an important issue. Few wear earplugs at concerts or ear protectors when operating power equipment (Bogoch et al., 2005; Chung et al., 2005). Part of the problem is the perception that ear protection is not "cool." Teens who are more open to behavioral change and those who are less concerned about appearance are more willing to use ear protection (Bogoch et al., 2005). In addition, teens from higher socioeconomic backgrounds tend to rate noise exposure as more negative, and therefore are more open to ear protection, than teens from lower socioeconomic backgrounds (Widén & Erlandsson, 2004; Widén et al., 2009).

Educational programs to improve hearing protection among teens need to focus on several issues to be effective. They need to help teens recognize that there may be long-term consequences of noise exposure; damage to the auditory system can accumulate over time. Second, they need to address teens' perception that hearing loss is not an important health issue. Until hearing is perceived as a priority, teens and others will have little motivation to protect this sensory system. And finally, education programs need to reduce the stigma associated with wearing hearing protection so teens feel comfortable making the decision to protect their hearing when they are in settings with loud noise.

Another Look at the Chemical Senses

Taste

Earlier, we introduced four basic tastes (sweet, sour, bitter, and salty) and discussed how smell contributes to the taste of foods. Are there any noticeable changes in taste during adolescence? There is a slight decline in preference for sweets and an increased sensitivity to—and liking of—sour tastes (University of Copenhagen, 2008). A preference for sour tastes, or at least a tolerance for sour tastes, is associated with willingness to try new foods and expand food horizons. This slight shift in an adolescent's taste palette leads to another difference between the child and adolescent: Adolescents are more likely to have developed an *acquired taste* for previously disliked or avoided foods. Most children may not enjoy, for example, eating snails (escargot) or fried squid (calamari), but many adolescents and adults have learned that these items can be quite tasty! Teenagers are more likely to enjoy foods with strong or strange tastes because they have had more opportunity to "acquire" these tastes through multiple exposures. Teenagers loosen up on the childhood tendency to reject new foods, and they are more open to experimenting with foods that may have odd textures or odors (Segovia et al., 2002). Of course, there are large individual differences in taste, with some teenagers enjoying very hot, spicy foods and others rejecting anything that has just a tiny amount of spice. Take the test in **Engagement Box 6.1** to see if you might be a supertaster who is more sensitive to low levels of chemicals hitting your taste receptors.

In addition, it turns out that your sense of taste is mediated by more than smell and taste receptors on the tongue. It is also determined by something called "chemosensory irritation," which is the reaction of your skin—in your mouth and nose—to certain chemical compounds of foods (Beauchamp & Mennella, 2009). When you feel the burn from hot peppers, the cooling sensation from menthol, or the tingle from a carbonated beverage, you are experiencing chemosensory irritation. This irritation of your skin contributes to your experience of a food, with, for example, some people reporting that they love to "feel the burn" of hot peppers and others completely turned off by it.

Taste is also influenced by cognition: You taste what you expect to taste. From past experience, we learn to associate certain features of food with certain tastes. For instance, brightly colored juices are thought to be tastier than their pale counterparts, even when the juices are identical other than the addition of a few drops of artificial coloring to some (Hoegg & Alba, 2007). Thus, we see a bright orange liquid in a cup and we believe that this will be more flavorful than a pale orange liquid.

Smell

Interestingly, gender plays a role in the sense of smell during adolescence and adulthood, with women generally demonstrating greater sensitivity than men to a variety of odors (Doty & Cameron, 2009; Ferdenzi et al., 2013). This may reflect hormonal differences between men and women and the effect of

Engagement 6.1

Are You a Supertaster?

Approximately 25% of the adult population has substantially more taste receptors than the other 75%, making them super sensitive to tastes (see Taste Science, 2010). The definitive super-taster test consists of a small paper filter that is infused with a special chemical. When placed on the tongue of a supertaster, it is perceived as incredibly bitter, but tastes bland or mildly bitter to those without the supertaster gene. Your answers to the following questions will give you an estimate of whether you might be a supertaster.

1. Do you enjoy or despise grapefruit juice?
2. Do you like milk chocolate or dark chocolate?
3. Do you hate raw broccoli or Brussels sprouts or think these veggies are okay or even good?
4. As a child, did you eat lots of vegetables?
5. Do you often think that desserts or cookies are too sweet while others report that the same foods taste just right?

Supertasters are likely to have a strong dislike for the bitter tastes of grapefruit juice, dark chocolate, or raw broccoli/Brussel sprouts. As children, supertasters avoided vegetables because they tasted "too strong." Supertasters are likely to think that too much sweetener has been used in foods and would prefer less sugar. To follow up, you can perform this relatively simple test using a drop of blue food coloring and a small piece of wax paper that you have punched with a single hole–puncher. Place a few drops of the blue food coloring on your tongue. Place the wax paper that has the hole punched in it over the blue patch on your tongue. Now carefully count the little pink circles that are within the circle. If you have a lot (25 or more) of little pink circles, then you have more than the average number of papillae and are a supertaster (each papillae contains 6–15 taste buds). If you have very few pink circles (less than 6), then you are a nontaster and are probably insensitive to bitter and other strong tastes. Anything between these two extremes is where most of us (50%) fall. With our average number of papillae, we enjoy most foods and don't find them too bitter or too sweet, but also don't find them bland.

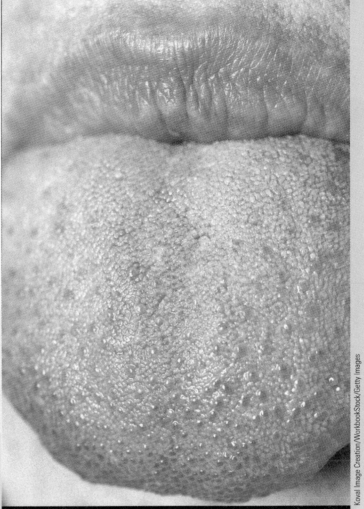

This tongue has an average number of papillae, or bumps containing taste buds. The tongue of a "supertaster" would have as many as twice the papillae seen here.

Koval Image Creation/WorkbookStock/Getty Images

different hormonal patterns on detection and interpretation of the chemicals that comprise odors. Among women, hormonal changes influence sensitivity—both discrimination and identification—to different smells (Derntl et al., 2013). Women who are fertile may use odor as part of their criteria for selecting a desirable mate, judging the body odor of some men—those who have symmetrical or balanced physical features—as more desirable than the body odor of other men during the time they are ovulating (Foster, 2008; Yamazaki & Beauchamp, 2007). Symmetry (having balanced features) may be a biological marker of better health.

Men, too, may use differences in women's body odors as a component of mate selection; they rate odor during ovulation as more pleasant than odor at other times of women's menstrual cycles (Singh & Bronstad, 2001). Evolutionary theory would predict that men and women want to select a mate who is healthy and capable of reproduction, and odor may provide some clues in this regard. Both men and women report that odor is an important consideration in choosing romantic partners, even though most cannot clearly articulate what constitutes a "good" or a "bad" smelling person (Sergeant et al., 2005). But be forewarned: Women are more sensitive to body odor than men, and it is more difficult to cover up body odor so that women do not detect it, whereas perfumes and other cover-ups often fool men (Wysocki et al., 2009). We learned earlier that babies and their mothers can recognize one another through smell. Now we see that odor is also important in later relationships, perhaps serving as a filter to allow some people to get close and discourage others.

6.5 The Adult

LEARNING OBJECTIVES:

* Describe typical changes in vision and hearing that occur over adulthood and indicate how these changes may affect daily activities.

* Summarize changes of the chemical and somaesthetic sensory systems that occur in the aging individual.

* Provide a balanced summary of the gains and losses that are typical of older adulthood.

What becomes of sensory and perceptual capacities during adulthood? There is good news and bad news, and we might as well dispense with the bad news first: Sensory and perceptual capacities decline gradually with age in the normal person. Whispers become harder to hear, seeing in the dark becomes difficult, food may not taste as good, and so on. Often these declines begin in early adulthood and become noticeable in the 40s, sometimes giving middle-aged people a feeling that they are getting old. Further declines take place in later life, to the point that you would have a hard time finding a person age 65 or older who does not have at least a mild sensory or perceptual impairment. The good news is that these changes are gradual and usually minor. As a result, we can usually compensate for them, making small adjustments such as turning up the volume on the TV set or adding a little extra seasoning to food. Because the losses are usually not severe and because of the process of compensation, only a minority of old people develop serious problems such as blindness and deafness.

The losses we are describing take two general forms. First, sensation is affected, as indicated by raised **sensory thresholds**. The threshold for a sense is the point at which low levels of stimulation can be detected—a dim light can be seen, a faint tone can be heard, a slight odor can be detected, and so on. Stimulation below the threshold cannot be detected, so the rise of the threshold with age means that sensitivity to very low levels of stimulation is lost. (You saw that the very young infant is also insensitive to some very low levels of stimulation.)

Second, perceptual abilities decline in some aging adults. Even when stimulation is intense enough to be well above the detection threshold, older people sometimes have difficulty processing or interpreting sensory information. As you will see, they may have trouble searching a visual scene, understanding rapid speech in a noisy room, or recognizing the foods they are tasting.

So, sensory and perceptual declines are typical during adulthood, although they are far steeper in some individuals than in others and can often be compensated for. These declines involve both a rise of thresholds for detecting stimulation and a weakening of some perceptual abilities.

Vision

Fortunately, few adults experience complete loss of vision, but many adults face some sort of vision problems as they get older. Why do these changes in the visual system occur, and is there anything you can do to prevent losses? Before we answer these questions, we need to briefly review the basic workings of the visual system.

As ■ **Figure 6.5** shows, light enters the eye through the cornea and passes through the pupil and lens before being projected (upside down) on the retina. From here, images are relayed to the brain by the optic nerve at the back of each eye. The pupil of the eye automatically becomes larger or smaller depending on the lighting conditions, and the lens changes shape, or accommodates, to keep images focused on the retina. In adolescents and young adults, the visual system is normally at peak performance. Aging brings changes to all components of the visual system and we summarize the most common vision problems in ● **Table 6.3**.

Some of these changes have important implications for everyday functioning. For example, changes in the pupil lead to difficulty with reading in dim lighting conditions, such as those found in many restaurants. Approximately one in three adults over the age of 85 years exhibits a tenfold loss of the ability to

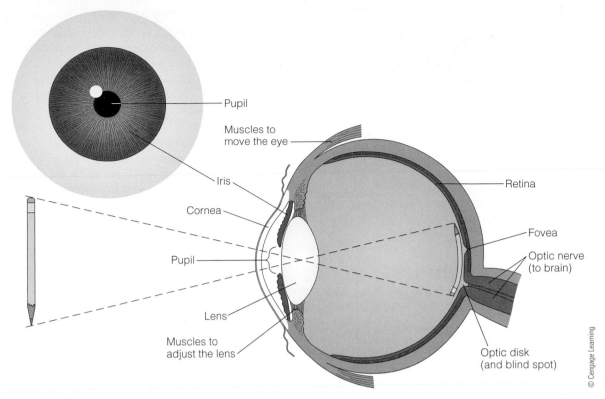

Labels on figure:
- Pupil
- Muscles to move the eye
- Iris
- Cornea
- Pupil
- Lens
- Muscles to adjust the lens
- Retina
- Fovea
- Optic nerve (to brain)
- Optic disk (and blind spot)

© Cengage Learning

■ **Figure 6.5** The human eye and retina. Light passes through the cornea, pupil, and lens and falls on the light-sensitive surface of the retina, where images of objects are projected upside down. The information is relayed to the brain by the optic nerve.

● **Table 6.3** Age-Related Changes in Visual System

Part of Eye	Age-Related Changes or Disease	Resulting Limitation(s)
Pupil	Less responsive to changes in lighting conditions and to dim light	Difficulty reading menus in dimly lit restaurants; trouble with night driving; unable to adjust quickly enough to oncoming lights at night or exiting a movie theatre into daylight
Lens	**Cataract**: Cloudiness of the lens	Blurred or distorted vision
	Presbyopia: Thickening or hardening of the lens	Decreased ability to see close objects; need for "reading" glasses
Retina	**Age-related macular degeneration (AMD)**: Photoreceptors in the middle of the retina, the *macula*, deteriorate	Loss of central vision, an important contributor to reading, driving, watching TV, and other daily activities
	Retinitis pigmentosa (RP): Deterioration of light-sensitive cells outside the macula	Loss of peripheral vision
Eyeball	**Glaucoma**: Increased fluid pressure in the eyeball	Loss of peripheral vision and eventual loss of all vision

© Cengage Learning 2015

read low-contrast words in dim lighting (Brabyn, 2000). But as ■ **Figure 6.6** shows, older adults may continue to read under ideal conditions of high contrast and bright light. Older adults may also struggle with night driving, as the pupil of the eye requires more time to adapt to the bright lights of oncoming cars and trucks, and then back again to the dark road.

The thickening and increasing rigidity of the lens of the eye make it difficult to focus on close objects. You may notice that many middle-aged and older adults use reading glasses or they may gradually move newspapers and books farther from their eyes to make them clearer—both methods of compensating for the decline of near vision that is associated with hardening of the eye's lens and is the most noticeable feature of presbyopia, or aging of the eye. As for distance vision, visual acuity as measured by standard eye charts increases in childhood, peaks in the 20s, remains steady through middle age, and steadily declines in old age (Evans et al., 2002; Klein et al., 2001). The implications for the average adult are fairly minor. For example, in one major study, three out of four older adults (75 years and older) had good corrected vision (Evans et al., 2002). At worst, most of them

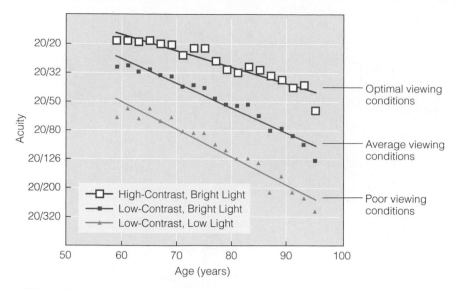

■ Figure 6.6 Visual acuity of older adults under optimal (high contrast and bright light), average (low contrast and bright light), and poor (low contrast and low light) stimulus conditions

SOURCE: Adapted from Haegerstrom-Portnoy, G., Schneck, M. E., & Brabyn, J. A. (2000). Seeing into old age: Vision function beyond acuity. *Optometry and Vision Science*, 76, 141–158. Reprinted by permission of Lippincott, Williams, and Wilkins.

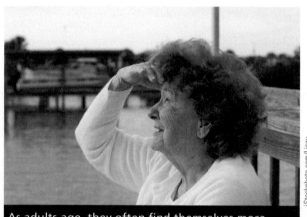

As adults age, they often find themselves more bothered by glare from bright lights or sun. What is the likely cause of this increased sensitivity?

could see at 20 feet what a person with standard acuity can see at 25 feet—not a big problem. Among the oldest adults—those in their 90s—37% are visually impaired, but only 7% have lost all functional vision. Several studies show that women experience greater declines in visual acuity than men (see, for example, Bailey et al., 2006). Older women with declining vision are more susceptible to falling and fracturing a bone, which is a serious threat to their independence (Pedula et al., 2006). Fracturing a hip often triggers a shift from independent to assisted living and can even be fatal. And poor vision that is not correctable can seriously decrease older adults' quality of life. According to one estimate, older adults with poor visual acuity (20/40 or worse) were as impaired as those with a major medical problem such as stroke (Chia et al., 2004).

With the serious retinal problem age-related macular degeneration (AMD), vision becomes blurry and begins to fade from the center of the visual field, leading to blank or dark space in the center of the image. Because cataracts are now often successfully corrected with surgery, AMD has become the leading cause of blindness in older adults. The causes of macular degeneration are largely unknown, but some research points to a genetic contribution; other research shows a connection with cigarette smoking (Evans, 2001; Khan et al., 2006). Currently, there is no cure for AMD, but several researchers are working to develop retinal implants that would stimulate the remaining cells of the retina and restore some useful vision (Boston Retinal Implant Project, 2013). In addition, some doctors prescribe vitamin and mineral supplements that have had some success in slowing the progression of AMD, preserving useful vision for as long as possible.

Changes in the retina also lead to decreased visual field, or a loss of peripheral (side) vision. Looking straight ahead, an older adult may see only half of what a young adult sees to the left and the right of center. Can you think of activities that might be hindered by a decreased visual field? Driving a car comes to mind. For example, when approaching an intersection, you need to be able to see what is coming toward you as well as what is coming from the side roads. **Exploration Box 6.2** describes some other sensory changes that might make driving more hazardous for older people.

To recap, you can expect some changes in vision as you age. (See **■ Figure 6.7** for a view of how the world looks through aging eyes affected by the conditions discussed here.) Sensory thresholds increase with age so that you need higher levels of stimulation than when you were young. Acuity, or sharpness of vision, decreases, near vision is negatively affected by hardening of the lens (presbyopia), and it takes longer for eyes to adapt to changes. Fortunately, it is possible to correct or compensate for most of these "normal" changes. And older adults who have good family support systems and personal coping mechanisms that focus on acceptance rather than wishful thinking adapt more successfully to visual impairment (Reinhardt, Boerner, & Horowitz, 2009). Some older adults will experience serious visual problems, such as those caused by changes in the retina, but early detection and treatment can preserve vision in most adults.

Attention and Visual Search

As you learned earlier in this chapter, perception is more than just seeing. It is using the senses intelligently and allocating attention efficiently. Some stimuli are more likely to capture attention than others. In a carefully designed series of studies, Greg West and his colleagues (West, Anderson, & Pratt, 2009) demonstrated that adults attend first to visual displays that signal a

Aging Drivers

Older drivers are perceived by many as more accident prone and slower than other drivers. Perhaps you have had the experience of zipping down the interstate when a slow-moving car driven by an elderly adult pulls into your path, forcing you to brake quickly. Is this experience representative, and is the stereotype of older drivers accurate? This is an important question, because 20% of all drivers will be older than 65 years by 2030 (Braver & Trempel, 2004; Lyman et al., 2002).

It is true that older adults (70 years and older) are involved in more automobile fatalities than middle-aged adults (see the graph in this box). But the most accident-prone group is young drivers between ages 16 and 24 (Insurance Institute for Highway Safety, 2013). When you take into account that young people drive more than elderly people, it turns out that both elderly drivers and young drivers have more accidents per mile driven than middle-aged drivers (Insurance Institute for Highway Safety, 2013).

Why is driving hazardous for elderly adults? Clearly, vision is essential to driving; vision accounts for approximately 90% of the information necessary to operate and navigate a car (Messinger-Rapport, 2003). Limited visual acuity or clarity is one component of problematic driving, but as noted in the main text, poor acuity is fairly easy to correct and is, therefore, unlikely to account for all the problems older drivers have.

Diminished peripheral vision may be an issue because good drivers must be able to see vehicles and pedestrians approaching from the side. Half the fatal automobile accidents involving older drivers occur at intersections, and older drivers are more than twice as likely as young drivers to have problems making left turns (Uchida, Fujita, & Katayama, 1999).

Another issue is being able to simultaneously process multiple pieces of information. Thus, older drivers have trouble reading street signs while driving (Dewar, Kline, & Swanson, 1995), and they are less able than younger adults to quickly change their focus

from the dashboard to the rearview mirror to the road ahead. When another vehicle is approaching, they must be able to evaluate the speed and trajectory of this vehicle and integrate this information with their own speed and trajectory to determine a course of action. For example, is the car approaching from the left going to hit my car, or will I be through the intersection before it reaches me? Finally, after understanding the dynamics of a potentially dangerous situation, the driver must be able to react quickly to threats (for example, a child chasing a ball into the street). As you learned in Chapter 5, older adults typically have slower response times than younger adults; thus, they need more time to react to the same stimulus (Horswill et al., 2008).

But the driving records of older adults are not as bad as might be expected, because many of them compensate for visual and other perceptual difficulties and slower reactions by driving less frequently, especially in conditions believed to be more hazardous—at night, during rush hour, and when the weather is poor (Messinger-Rapport, 2003). Older adults with visual

problems such as cataracts and those with cognitive problems are more likely to limit their driving than older adults without these problems (Messinger-Rapport, 2003). Some states have responded to concerns about elderly drivers with mandatory road retesting for license renewal, but most states have no distinct policies about license renewal for older adults. It is not that states do not care; rather, they face strong opposition from groups such as the American Association of Retired Persons and individual older adults (Cobb & Coughlin, 1998). To give up driving is to give up a big chunk of independence, something anyone would be loath to do. Most people want to find ways to drive safely as long as possible.

There is good news: Older drivers who return to the classroom for a refresher course on safe driving and get behind-the-wheel training can improve their driving (Marottoli, 2007). By understanding the strengths and limitations of their sensory–perceptual abilities, older adults will be in a good position to keep driving safely. Remember that the next time you are stuck behind a slow driver.

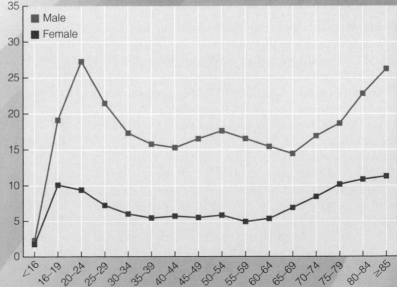

Source: Insurance Institute for Highway Safety, 2013, http://www.iihs.org/research/fatality.aspx?topicName=Olderpeople&year=2011

(A) Cataract

(B) Glaucoma

(C) Diabetic Retinopathy

(D) Age-related Macular Degeneration

(E) Retinitis Pigmentosa

■ **Figure 6.7** These photos illustrate how a scene might be viewed by someone with various eye conditions: (A) cataracts; (B) glaucoma; (C) diabetic retinopathy; (D) age-related macular degeneration; (E) retinitis pigmentosa.

elderly adults to locate a target (for example, a blue horizontal line) in a display where the distractor items were clearly different (for example, red vertical lines) or in a more difficult display where the distractors shared a common feature with the target (for example, blue vertical and red horizontal lines). Older adults were slower and less accurate on the more challenging search task. They were also more distracted by irrelevant information; they were especially slow compared with young adults when the number of distractor items in the display was high. In some situations, elderly people appear to have difficulty inhibiting responses to irrelevant stimuli so that they can focus their attention more squarely on relevant stimuli. Yet older adults can improve their visual search performance with practice, and they are more successful when they strategically use a feature of the display (for example, color) to help guide their search (Madden, Gottlob, & Allen, 1999).

In short, older adults have their greatest difficulties in processing visual information when the situation is *novel* (when they are not sure exactly what to look for or where to look) and when it is *complex* (when there is a great deal of distracting information to search through or when two tasks must be performed at once). By contrast, they have fewer problems when they have clear expectations about what they are to do and when the task is not overly complicated (Madden, 2007). Thus, an older factory worker who has inspected televisions for years may be just as speedy and accurate as a younger worker at this well-practiced, familiar task, but he might perform relatively poorly if suddenly asked to inspect pocket calculators and look for a much larger number of possible defects—a novel and complex task.

threat; for example, an angry face is attended to before a neutral face. Even among images that are not threatening, some are more likely to capture attention than others. Adults are typically able to control their attention to a greater extent than are children, deliberately focusing on the most relevant information and ignoring irrelevant information. What happens as we get older? Do we retain this ability to focus and sustain our attention on relevant information?

Several studies show that older adults do worse than younger ones on tests that require dividing attention between two tasks (divided attention) or selectively attending to certain stimuli while ignoring others (selective attention; see Juola et al., 2000; Madden & Langley, 2003). The more distractors a task involves, the more the performance of elderly adults falls short of the performance of young adults. In everyday life, this may translate into difficulty carrying on a conversation while driving or problems locating the asparagus amid all the frozen vegetables at the supermarket.

In one test of visual search skills, Charles Scialfa and his colleagues (Scialfa, Esau, & Joffe, 1998) asked young adults and

Hearing

There is some truth to the stereotype of the hard-of-hearing older person. Hearing impairment is approximately three times as prevalent as visual impairment among older adults (Davila et al., 2009). A majority of individuals older than 65 have at least mildly impaired hearing, and hearing becomes progressively worse with age (Cruickshanks et al., 2010; Punnoose, Lynm, & Golub, 2012). Most older people experience mild to moderate hearing impairments, some experience severe hearing loss, but only a few are deaf (Dalton et al., 2003).

These older adults are unlikely to experience problems locating items at their usual supermarket. But in an unfamiliar context, the same visual search of shelves for items may prove challenging.

LdF/Netta /Getty images

Basic Capacities

Sources of hearing problems range from excess wax buildup in the ears to infections to a sluggish nervous system. Most age-related hearing problems seem to originate in the inner ear, however (Fozard & Gordon-Salant, 2001). The cochlear hair cells that serve as auditory receptors, their surrounding structures, and the neurons leading from them to the brain degenerate gradually over the adult years. The most noticeable result is a loss of sensitivity to high-frequency or high-pitched sounds, the most common form of **presbycusis**, or problems of the aging ear. Thus, an older person may have difficulty hearing a child's high voice, the flutes in an orchestra, and high-frequency consonant sounds such as *s, z,* and *ch* (Whitbourne & Whitbourne, 2011) but may have less trouble with deep voices, tubas, and sounds such as *b.* After age 50, lower-frequency sounds also become increasingly difficult to hear (Kline & Scialfa, 1996). Thus, to be heard by the average older adult, a sound—especially a high-pitched sound but ultimately any sound—must be louder than it needs to be to exceed the auditory threshold of a younger adult.

Is this loss of hearing with age the inevitable result of basic aging processes, or is it caused by other factors? Researchers know that the loss is more noticeable among men than among women, that men are more likely to work in noisy industrial jobs, and that those who hold such jobs experience more hearing loss than other men (Martin & Clark, 2002; Reuben et al., 1998). But even when adults who have held relatively quiet jobs are studied, men show detectable hearing losses earlier in life (in their 30s) and lose hearing sensitivity at a faster rate than women do (Pearson et al., 1995). It seems, then, that most people, men more than women, will experience some loss of sensitivity to high-frequency sounds as part of the basic aging process, but that certain people will experience more severe losses because of their experiences.

Speech Perception

Perhaps the most important thing we do with our ears in everyday life is listen to other people during conversations. The ability to hear is one requisite for understanding speech, but this complex auditory perception task also depends on cognitive processes such as attention and memory. How well do aging adults do?

Older adults typically have more difficulty understanding conversation than younger adults do, even under ideal listening conditions. This age difference becomes smaller when differences in hearing are controlled but it does not entirely disappear. Under poor listening conditions—for example, loud background noise—group differences between older and young adults are larger, even when individual differences in hearing are accounted for (Schneider, Roth, & Ennemoser, 2000). Thus, older adults may recall fewer details of a conversation that takes place in a crowded, noisy restaurant.

Age-related declines in auditory sensitivity (that is, acuity) are partly responsible, but cognitive declines also seem to contribute to the observed declines in speech perception among older adults (Cervera et al., 2009; Murphy, Daneman, & Schneider, 2006). Patricia Tun and her colleagues (Tun, McCoy, & Wingfield, 2009) compared two groups of older and younger adults: those with good and poor hearing. Participants listened to words and then recalled as many of these words as possible. On half the trials, they did this while also performing a simple visual tracking task. Older adults with good hearing performed significantly worse than young adults with good hearing, so there is more to the recall of spoken words than having good auditory acuity. Moreover, the additional attentional demands of the second task had no significant effect on the younger adults, regardless of whether they had good or poor hearing, but older adults were disadvantaged by increased attentional demands and recalled few spoken words when they had to divide their attention.

In addition, auditory perception tasks, like visual perception tasks, are more difficult for older people when they are novel and complex. In familiar, everyday situations, older adults are able to use contextual cues to interpret what they hear (Fozard & Gordon-Salant, 2001). In one study, for example, elderly adults were about as able as young adults to recall meaningful sentences they had just heard (Wingfield et al., 1985). However, they had serious difficulty repeating back grammatical sentences that made no sense or random strings of words, especially when these meaningless stimuli were spoken rapidly. So an older

Application 6.2

Aiding Adults with Hearing Impairments

In Application 6.1, we examined ways to help infants and children who have hearing impairments, often from birth. Here we consider the other end of the life span. What can be done to assist hearing-impaired adults, most of whom were born with normal hearing? Unfortunately, many older adults are reluctant to admit that they have a hearing problem and do not seek assistance, or they may not even realize they have hearing loss as it occurs gradually and they have learned to compensate. Among those who acknowledge having a hearing problem, many refuse to wear a hearing aid because they feel it stigmatizes them as old, or they report that hearing aids do not work or do not help them to hear better (Lupsakko, Kautiainen, & Sulkava, 2005).

Those who do not have their hearing corrected may suffer depression, decreased independence, and strained relationships (Appollonio et al., 1996). Imagine how hard social interaction can become if you cannot understand what is being said, misinterpret what is said, or have to keep asking people to repeat what they said. One 89-year-old woman became extremely depressed and isolated: "There

is an *awfulness* about silence.... I am days without speaking a word. It is affecting my voice. I fear for my mind. I cannot hear the alarm clock, telephone ring, door bell, radio, television—or the human voice" (Meadows-Orlans & Orlans, 1990, pp. 424–425). In contrast, among those older adults who do use hearing aids, quality of life improves (Vuorialho, Karinen, & Sorri, 2006). We tend to think of vision as our most important sense, but hearing impairments may be more disruptive than visual impairments to cognitive and social functioning.

Hearing aids, although beneficial, cannot restore normal hearing; they tend to distort sounds and to magnify background noise as well as what the wearer is trying to hear. In addition, many older people are ill served by hearing aids that are of poor quality or that are poorly matched to their specific hearing problems. Because cochlear implants work best for individuals exposed to spoken language before they lost their hearing, elderly people are ideal candidates for them. They tolerate the surgical procedure required for implantation well, and their hearing-test scores increase significantly (Kelsall, Shallop, & Burnelli, 1995). In addition, adults who

receive cochlear implants report that their quality of life improves significantly (Faber & Grontved, 2000). Cochlear implants, however, cannot work overnight miracles; it can take months, even years, to learn how to interpret the messages relayed by the implant to the brain (Colburn, 2000).

Finally, the physical and social environment can be modified to help people of all ages with hearing losses. For example, furniture can be arranged to permit face-to-face contact; lights can be turned on to permit use of visual cues such as gestures and lip movements. Then there are the simple guidelines we can follow to make ourselves understood by hearing-impaired people. One of the most important is to avoid shouting. Shouting not only distorts speech but also raises the pitch of the voice (therefore making it more difficult for elderly people to hear); it also makes it harder for the individual to read lips. It is best to speak at a normal rate, clearly but without overarticulating, with your face fully visible at a distance of about 3–6 feet.

With modern technology, appropriate education, effective coping strategies, and help from those who hear, hearing-impaired and deaf individuals of all ages can thrive.

person may be able to follow an ordinary conversation but not a technical presentation on an unfamiliar topic—especially if the speaker makes the task harder by talking too fast.

Overall, then, most older adults have only mild hearing losses, especially for high-frequency sounds, and only minor problems understanding everyday speech, at least under good listening conditions. In addition, they can compensate for their difficulties successfully—for example, by reading lips and relying on contextual cues. Novel and complex speech heard under poor listening conditions is likely to cause more trouble. Fortunately, there are ways older people can improve their hearing or compensate for its loss, as **Application Box 6.2** describes.

Aging of the Chemical Senses

Does the aging of sensory systems also mean that older people become less able to appreciate tastes and aromas? On average, yes: there is a general decline in sensitivity to taste, with older men showing somewhat greater decline than older women (Schubert et al., 2012). But keep in mind that there is great variability: Some older adults will continue to have keen senses of smell and taste, while others experience sharp declines in these chemical

senses. Thus, some older adults may report that food tastes bland and use larger amounts of salt, sugar, and other seasonings than they used when they were younger. In addition, both middle-aged and older adults sometimes have difficulty discriminating among tastes that differ in intensity (Nordin et al., 2003). In one study, adults over 70 were less able than young adults to reliably judge one solution to be saltier, more bitter, or more acidic than another (Weiffenbach, Cowart, & Baum, 1986). In part, this may occur because older adults are more likely than younger adults to take medications that interfere with the taste receptors (Schiffman, 2009). In addition, older adults tend to produce less saliva than younger adults, and saliva facilitates distribution of the chemical molecules carrying information about taste around the mouth (Brynie, 2009). Interestingly, though, older adults do not have difficulty distinguishing degrees of sweetness; people apparently do not lose the sweet tooth they are born with!

The ability to perceive odors also typically declines with age. Sensitivity to odors increases from childhood to early adulthood then declines during adulthood, more so with increasing age (Finkelstein & Schiffman, 1999; Ship et al., 1996). However, differences among age groups are usually small, and many older people retain their sensitivity to odors. The age decline depends on the type of odor: Older adults can identify and remember unpleasant odors just as well as younger adults, although they show some decline in their ability to detect and remember pleasant odors (Larsson, Öberg-Blåvarg, & Jönsson, 2009). Women are more likely than men to maintain their ability to label odors in scratch-and-sniff tests, partly because they are less likely than men to have worked in factories and been exposed to chemicals that could damage the chemical receptors involved in odor perception (Corwin, Loury, & Gilbert, 1995; Ship & Weiffenbach, 1993). Also, healthy adults of both sexes retain their sense of smell better than do those who have diseases, smoke, or take medications (Wilson et al., 2006). Again, then, perceptual losses in later life are part of the basic aging process but vary from person to person depending on environmental factors.

How do declines in the senses of taste and smell affect the older person's experience of the foods they eat? Susan Schiffman (1977) blindfolded young adults and elderly adults and asked them to identify blended foods by taste and smell alone. As ● **Table 6.4** reveals, the older people were correct less often than the college students were. But was this because of a loss of taste sensitivity or smell sensitivity? Or was it a cognitive problem—difficulty coming up with the name of a food that was sensed?

Claire Murphy (1985) attempted to shed light on these questions by presenting young and elderly adults with 12 of the blended foods used by Schiffman. She observed that older people often came up with the wrong specific label but the right idea (identifying sugar as fruit or salt as peanuts, for example). Thus, at least some of their difficulty may have been cognitive. Murphy also tested women whose nostrils were blocked and found that both young and elderly women did miserably when they could not smell and had to rely on taste alone. These findings suggest that a reduced ability to identify foods in old age is less because of losses in the sense of taste than because of the small losses in the sense of smell as well as declines in the cognitive skills

● **Table 6.4** Age Differences in Recognition of Fruits and Veggies

Elderly adults have more difficulty than young college students in identifying most blended foods by taste and smell alone. Percentages of those recognizing food include reasonable guesses such as "orange" in response to "apple."

Percentage Recognizing Food		
Pureed Food Substance	**College Students (ages 18–22)**	**Elderly People (ages 67–93)**
Fruits		
Apple	93	79
Banana	93	59
Pineapple	93	86
Vegetables		
Broccoli	81	62
Carrot	79	55
Cucumber	44	28

SOURCE: Schiffman, 1977, Food recognition by the elderly. *Journal of Gerontology,* 586–592. Reprinted by permission of Oxford University Press.

required to remember and name what has been tasted (Murphy, Nordin, & Acosta, 1997).

If foods do not have much taste, an older person may lose interest in eating and may not get proper nourishment (Rolls, 1999). Alternatively, an older person may overuse seasonings such as salt or may eat spoiled food, which can threaten health in other ways. Yet these problems can be remedied. For example, when flavor enhancers were added to the food in one nursing home, elders ate more, gained muscle strength, and had healthier immune system functioning than they did when they ate the usual institutional fare (Schiffman & Warwick, 1993).

Conclusions about changes in taste and smell must be considered in perspective. These sensory and perceptual abilities are highly variable across the entire life span, not just in older adulthood. Taste and smell receptors are replaced throughout the life span and are influenced by such environmental factors as smoke, medications, and extreme temperatures. This means that, under optimal environmental conditions, many older adults will not experience deficits: They can continue to smell the roses and enjoy their food.

Changes in the Somaesthetic Senses

By now you have seen numerous indications that older adults are often less able than younger adults to detect weak sensory stimulation. This holds true for the sense of touch. The detection threshold for touch increases and sensitivity is gradually lost from middle childhood on. It is not clear that minor losses in touch sensitivity have many implications for daily life, however.

Similarly, older people may be less sensitive to changes in temperature than younger adults are (Frank et al., 2000). Some keep their homes too cool because they are unaware of being cold; others may fail to notice that it is too hot. Because older bodies are less able than younger ones to maintain an even temperature, elderly people face an increased risk of death in heat waves or cold spells (Worfolk, 2000).

It seems only fair that older people should also be less sensitive to painful stimulation, but are they? They are indeed less likely than younger adults to report *weak* levels of stimulation as painful, although the age differences in pain thresholds are not large or consistent (Verrillo & Verrillo, 1985). Yet older people seem to be no less sensitive to stronger pain stimuli. Unfortunately, older adults are more likely to experience chronic pain than younger adults but are less likely to obtain adequate pain relief (Gloth, 2000). Adults with arthritis, osteoporosis, cancer, and other diseases who also experience depression and anxiety are especially likely to perceive pain. Treating these secondary conditions and administering effective pain relief can improve the daily functioning and psychological well-being of older adults.

The Adult in Perspective

Of all the changes in sensation and perception during adulthood that we have considered, those involving vision and hearing appear to be the most important and the most universal. Not only do these senses become less keen, but older people also use them

● **Table 6.5** Percentage of Older Adults with Various Impairments Who Report Limits on Activities

Activity	With Visual Impairments	With Hearing Impairments	With Both Visual and Hearing Impairments	Without Visual or Hearing Impairments
Difficulty walking	43.3	30.7	48.3	22.2
Difficulty getting outside	28.6	17.3	32.8	11.9
Difficulty getting in or out of a bed or chair	22.1	15.1	25.0	10.4
Difficulty taking medicines	11.8	7.7	13.4	5.0
Difficulty preparing meals	18.7	11.6	20.7	7.8

SOURCE: Adapted from Campbell et al., 1999, Surveillance for sensory impairment, activity limitation, and health-related quality of life among older adults: United States, 1993–1997. *CDC MMWR Surveillance Summaries, 48 (SS08)*.

less effectively in such complex perceptual tasks as searching a cluttered room for a missing book or following rapid conversation in a noisy room. Declines in the other senses are less serious and do not affect as many people.

Although people compensate for many sensory declines, their effects cannot be entirely eliminated. At some point, aging adults find that changes in sensory abilities affect their activities. As ● **Table 6.5** shows, older adults with one or two sensory impairments are more likely to experience difficulty with basic tasks of living—walking, getting outside, getting in or out of bed or a chair, taking medicines, or preparing meals. Notice, however, that even older adults without sensory impairments report some difficulty with these tasks. People who are limited by sensory impairments usually have physical or intellectual impairments as well, most likely because of general declines in neural functioning that affect both perception and cognition (Baltes & Lindenberger, 1997; Salthouse et al., 1996). Most older adults, even those with sensory impairments, are engaged in a range of activities and are living full lives. Thus, although most adults will experience some declines in sensory abilities with age, these changes do not need to detract from their quality of life.

Checking Mastery

1. What are the most common eye problems experienced by older adults?
2. What is the greatest functional difficulty with hearing loss among older adults?
3. Which taste is best perceived across the life span (that is, there is little loss of acuity)?

Making Connections

1. You have been hired to teach a cooking course to elderly adults. First, analyze the perceptual strengths and weaknesses of your students: What perceptual tasks might be easy for them, and what tasks might be difficult? Second, considering at least three senses, think of five strategies you can use to help your students compensate for the declines in perceptual capacities that some of them may be experiencing.
2. You are the coordinator for social and educational activities at your community center, which means you work with people of all ages, ranging from the youngest infants to the oldest adults. In planning activities, what should you consider in trying to capture and hold the attention of different age groups?

Chapter Summary

6.1 Perspectives on Perception

- Sensation is the detection of sensory stimulation, and perception is the interpretation of what is sensed.
- Constructivists argue that the newborn is a "blank slate" and must acquire an understanding of the world through experience with sensory inputs. Thus, according to the constructivist perspective, nurture drives the development of perception.
- Nativists believe that each person is born with some innate understanding of how to interpret sensory information. Thus, according to the nativists, the origin of perception is largely nature.
- Gibson's ecological theory proposes that everything we need to understand the world around us is available in the environment itself. We are able to directly detect the affordances of objects—what they offer us in terms of how we might interact with them. In the ecological view, nature and nurture are integrally related.

6.2 The Infant

- Methods of studying infant perception include habituation, evoked potentials, preferential looking, and operant conditioning techniques.
- The visual system is fairly well developed at birth. Infants younger than 2 months old discriminate brightness and colors and are attracted to contour, moderate complexity, and movement. Starting at 2 or 3 months, infants more clearly perceive whole patterns such as faces and seem to understand a good deal about objects and their properties, guided by intuitive theories of the physical world.
- Spatial perception develops rapidly, and by about 7 months infants not only perceive drop-offs but also fear them.
- The auditory sense is well developed at birth. Young infants can recognize their mother's voice and distinguish speech sounds that adults cannot discriminate.

- The senses of taste and smell are also well developed at birth. In addition, newborns are sensitive to touch, temperature, and pain.
- The early presence of sensory and perceptual abilities suggests that they are innate, but they are also clearly influenced by early experiences. Certain experiences may be necessary for normal visual perception to develop, suggesting a sensitive period for the visual system.
- Infants actively seek out stimulation by exploring their environments, which typically provides them with the stimulation they need to develop normal sensory and perceptual skills.

6.3 The Child

- Sensory skills undergo little change during childhood, although children learn better how to use the information coming in through their senses.
- Coupling perception with action to develop locomotion skills—the ability to navigate one's body around the environment—is a major accomplishment of childhood made understandable by dynamic systems theory.
- Cross-modal perception, the ability to recognize through one sense what was learned by a different sense, originates in infancy but becomes more fully developed in childhood.
- Learning to control attention is an important part of perceptual development during childhood. Infants and young children are selectively attentive to the world around them, but they have not fully taken charge of their attentional processes.
- With age, children become more able to concentrate on a task for a long period, to focus on relevant information and ignore distractions, and to use their senses in purposeful and systematic ways to achieve goals.

6.4 The Adolescent

- Basic perceptual and attentional skills are perfected during adolescence. Adolescents are better than children at sustaining

their attention and using it selectively and strategically to solve the problem at hand.
- Teens often multitask, which can lead to less efficient learning of new information.
- Exposure to loud noise can cause tinnitus or ringing sounds in the ear that can be temporary or permanent. Damage to the auditory system from exposure to loud noise can accumulate over time, leading eventually to hearing impairment.
- The chemical senses operate at adult levels and may contribute to mate selection.

6.5 The Adult

- During adulthood, sensory and perceptual capacities gradually decline in most individuals, although many changes are minor and can be compensated for. Sensory thresholds—the amount of stimulation required for detection—rise, and perceptual processing of sensory information often declines. Moderate to severe declines that are not corrected can lead to declines in activities and quality of life among older adults.
- Visual changes include cataracts (clouding of the lens), reduced ability of the pupil to change in response to changes in light, thickening of the lens leading to decreased acuity (presbyopia), and retinal changes such as age-related macular degeneration and retinitis pigmentosa. Glaucoma, increased fluid pressure in the eye, becomes more common with age and can lead to blindness if untreated.
- Presbycusis—changes in hearing associated with aging—affects many older adults and most commonly leads to trouble detecting high-pitched sounds. Older adults have more difficulty with speech perception, especially under noisy conditions, than younger adults. Hearing aids can significantly improve older adults' abilities to detect sounds.
- Many older people have difficulty recognizing or enjoying foods, largely because of declines in the sense of smell and memory; touch, temperature, and pain sensitivity also decrease slightly, but intense pain stimuli still hurt.

Checking Mastery Answers

For answers to Checking Mastery questions, please see Appendix B.

Key Terms

CENGAGE brain .com   Get quizzes, flashcards, videos, and more at **www.cengagebrain.com.**

7 Cognition

"**Consider what would happen** if children of various ages were given a metal magnet for the first time. Six-month-olds might accommodate to the unfamiliar metallic taste, the peculiar (horseshoe) shape, and the sound of the magnet being dropped.... Three-year-olds, if given an assortment of objects, might accommodate to the fact that some of the objects cling to the magnet and might entertain explanations such as 'stickiness' and 'wanting to stay together'. Nine-year-old children might hypothesize that only objects with certain characteristics are attracted to the magnet and might test out the conditions in which magnetism occurs—through glass, water, and certain distances. Only in adolescence could children accommodate by formulating an abstract theory of magnetism and simultaneously consider all of the variables involved, such as the size and shape of the magnet and the distance from the object" (Miller, 2002, pp. 65–66).

In this example, four children—an infant, a 3-year-old, a 9-year-old, and an adolescent—interact with the same object, a magnet, but their interactions are influenced by their current level of development and lead to very different understandings. The infant is competent at getting objects into her mouth and so goes the magnet. The 3-year-old is probably amused by how some objects stick to the magnet without having any clue why this occurs. The 9-year-old may do some trial-and-error testing to see which objects stick to the magnet, and from this develops a fairly logical understanding of magnetism. The adolescent may generate hypotheses about magnetism, systematically test these hypotheses, and create an abstract understanding of the properties of magnetism.

At least this is how one prominent theory of cognitive development would interpret the situation. This theory developed by Jean Piaget after painstakingly observing and testing children of different ages, was introduced in Chapter 2. Psychology was significantly altered by Piaget's curiosity and desire to figure out what children were thinking and why their responses changed with age. The theory dominated the field for many decades and generated a tremendous amount of useful research. Some findings emerging from this research support Piaget's general description of the development of **cognition**—the activity of knowing and the processes through which knowledge is acquired and problems are solved. Other findings, though, have led to the emergence of alternative theories. Perhaps the most influential of these is Lev Vygotsky's sociocultural perspective on cognitive development. After gaining an understanding of these two theories, we consider a contemporary theory that incorporates some ideas from both Piaget and Vygotsky before turning our attention to changes in cognitive development across the life span.

7.1 Piaget's Constructivist Approach

LEARNING OBJECTIVES:

- Describe the processes of developmental change in Piaget's theory and give an example of each process.

- Discuss the strengths of Piaget's theory, noting features that remain fairly well supported by the research in this field.

- Explain the challenges to Piaget's theory that have emerged as scientists have conducted research to test hypotheses generated from the theory.

Piaget was an exceptional person. As you learned in Chapter 2, he became intrigued by children's mistakes because he noticed that children of the same age often made similar kinds of mental mistakes—errors typically different than those made by younger or older children. Could these age-related differences in error patterns reflect developmental steps, or stages, in intellectual growth? Piaget thought so, and he

Charles Gullung/Photonica/Getty Images

According to Piaget's theory, by actively exploring the physical world and seeing how their actions bring about changes, children like these two construct cognitive structures that help them organize and understand their world.

devoted his life to studying *how* children think, not just *what* they know (Flavell, 1963).

Piaget began his studies with close observation of his own three children as infants: how they explored new toys, solved simple problems that he arranged for them, and generally came to understand themselves and their world. Later, Piaget studied larger samples of children through what has become known as his **clinical method**, a flexible question-and-answer technique used to discover how children think about problems. Consider the following exchange between Piaget and 6-year-old Van (Piaget, 1926, p. 293):

Piaget: Why is it dark at night?
Van: Because we sleep better, and so that it shall be dark in the rooms.
Piaget: Where does the darkness come from?
Van: Because the sky becomes grey.
Piaget: What makes the sky become grey?
Van: The clouds become dark.
Piaget: How is that?
Van: God makes the clouds become dark.

Many contemporary researchers consider this method imprecise because it does not involve asking standardized questions of all children tested, but Piaget (1926) believed that the investigator should have the flexibility to pursue an individual child's line of reasoning to fully understand that child's mind. Using his naturalistic observations of his own children and the clinical method to explore how children understand everything from the rules of games to the concepts of space and time, Piaget formulated his view of the development of intelligence.

Using Piaget's clinical method, this interviewer might present a simple problem to solve or ask a question and see where the child's answer leads their conversation.

© Shannon Fagan/The Image Bank/Getty Images

What Is Intelligence?

Piaget's definition of intelligence reflects his background in biology: *intelligence is a basic life function that helps an organism adapt to its environment.* You can see adaptation when you watch a toddler attempting to get chunks of food from plate to mouth, a school-age child figuring out how to divide treats among friends, or an adult figuring out how to operate a new digital camera. The newborn enters an unfamiliar world with few means of adapting to it other than working senses and reflexes. But Piaget viewed infants as active agents in their own development, learning about the world of people and things by observing, investigating, and experimenting.

As infants and children explore their world, their brains respond by creating schemes (sometimes called *schema* in the singular and *schemata* in the plural). **Schemes** are cognitive structures—organized patterns of action or thought that people construct to interpret their experiences (Piaget, 1952, 1977). Schemes are like having a set of rules or procedures that can be repeated and generalized across various situations (Miller, 2011). For example, the infant's grasping actions and sucking responses are early behavioral schemes, patterns of action used to adapt to different objects. During their second year, children develop symbolic schemes, or concepts. They use internal mental symbols such as images and words to represent or stand for aspects of experience, such as when a young child sees a funny dance and carries away a mental model of how it was done. Older children become able to manipulate symbols in their heads to help them solve problems, such as when they add two numbers together mentally rather than on paper or with the aid of their fingers.

As children develop more sophisticated schemes, or cognitive structures, they become increasingly able to adapt to their environments. Because they gain new schemes as they develop, children of different ages will respond to the same stimuli differently. The infant may get to know a shoe mainly as something to chew, the preschooler may decide to let the shoe symbolize or represent a telephone and put it to her ear, and the school-age child may mentally count its shoelace eyelets.

How Does Intelligence Develop?

Recall from Chapter 2 that Piaget took an interactionist position on the nature–nurture issue: children actively create knowledge by building schemes from their experiences (nurture), using two inborn (nature) intellectual functions, which he called organization and adaptation. These processes operate throughout the life span. Through **organization**, children systematically combine existing schemes into new and more complex ones. Thus, their minds are not cluttered with an endless number of independent facts; they contain instead logically ordered and interrelated actions and ideas. For example, the infant who gazes, reaches, and grasps will organize these simple schemes into the complex structure of visually directed reaching. Complex cognitive structures in older children grow out of reorganizations of simpler structures.

Adaptation is the process of adjusting to the demands of environment (Piaget, 1971). It occurs through two complementary processes, assimilation and accommodation. Imagine that you are a 2-year-old, that the world is still new, and that you see your first horse. What will you make of it? You likely will try to relate it to something familiar. **Assimilation** is the process by which we interpret new experiences in terms of existing schemes or cognitive structures. Thus, if you already have a scheme that mentally represents your knowledge of dogs, you may label this new beast "doggie." Through assimilation, we deal with our environment in our own terms, sometimes bending the world to squeeze it into our existing categories. Throughout the life span, we rely on our existing cognitive structures to understand new events.

But if you notice that this "doggie" is bigger than most dogs and that it has a mane and an awfully strange "bark," you may be prompted to change your understanding of the world of four-legged animals. **Accommodation** is the process of modifying existing schemes to better fit new experiences. Perhaps you will need to invent a new name for this animal or ask what it is and revise your concept of four-legged animals accordingly.

If we always assimilated new experiences, our understandings would never advance. Piaget believed that all new experiences are greeted with a mix of assimilation and accommodation. Once we have schemes, we apply them to make sense of the world, but we also encounter puzzles that force us to modify our understandings through accommodation. According to Piaget, when new events seriously challenge old schemes, or prove our existing understandings to be inadequate, we experience cognitive conflict. This cognitive conflict, or disequilibrium, then stimulates cognitive growth and the formation of more adequate understandings (Piaget, 1985; ■ **Figure 7.1**). This occurs because mental conflict is not pleasant; we are motivated to reduce conflict through what Piaget called **equilibration**, the process of achieving mental stability where our internal thoughts are consistent with the evidence we are receiving from the external world (Piaget, 1978).

Intelligence, then, in Piaget's view, develops through the interaction of the individual with the environment. Nature provides the complementary processes of assimilation and accommodation that make adaptation to environments possible. The processes of adaptation and organization are driven by an innate tendency to maintain equilibration. As a result of the interaction

Equilibrium

Current understanding of the world (internal data) is consistent with external data.

Small furry animals with fluffy tails are called cats. They meow and smell nice.

Disequilibrium

Along comes a new piece of information that does not fit with current understanding of the world, leading to disequilibrium—an uncomfortable state of mind that the child seeks to resolve.

That's strange—this small furry creature has a fluffy tail but it doesn't meow and it certainly doesn't smell nice!

Assimilation and accommodation

This unbalanced (confused) state can be resolved through the processes of organization and adaptation (assimilation and accommodation).

This can't be a cat. Mommy called it a skunk, which must be a different kind of animal.

Equilibrium

These lead to a new way of understanding the world— a new state of equilibrium.

I'll have to remember that skunks and cats are different types of animals.

■ **Figure 7.1** Process of change in Jean Piaget's theory.

of biological maturation and experience, humans progress through four distinct stages of cognitive development:

1. The sensorimotor stage (birth to roughly 2 years)
2. The preoperational stage (roughly 2–7 years)
3. The concrete operations stage (roughly 7–11 years)
4. The formal operations stage (roughly 11 years and beyond)

These stages represent qualitatively different ways of thinking and occur in an invariant sequence—that is, in the same order in all children. However, depending on their experiences, children may progress through the stages at different rates, with some moving more rapidly or more slowly than others. Thus, the age ranges associated with the stages are only averages. A child's stage of development is determined by his reasoning processes, not his age. We'll describe each of the stages more fully as we move through this chapter.

Piaget's Contributions

Piaget is a giant in the field of human development. As one scholar quoted by Harry Beilin (1992) put it, "assessing the impact of Piaget on developmental psychology is like assessing

the impact of Shakespeare on English literature or Aristotle on philosophy—impossible" (p. 191). It is hard to imagine that researchers would know even a fraction of what they know about intellectual development without Piaget's groundbreaking work.

One sign of a good theory is that it stimulates research. Piaget asked fundamentally important questions about how humans come to know the world and showed that we can answer them "by paying attention to the small details of the daily lives of our children" (Gopnik, 1996, p. 225). His cognitive developmental perspective has been applied to almost every aspect of human development, and the important questions he raised continue to guide the study of cognitive development. Thus, his theory has undoubtedly stimulated much research in the decades following its creation.

We can credit Piaget with some lasting insights, including ones that have become so deeply entrenched in our way of thinking as to be taken for granted (Flavell, 1996). For example, Piaget showed us that infants and children are active in their own development—that from the start they seek to master problems and to understand the incomprehensible by using the processes of assimilation and accommodation to resolve their cognitive disequilibrium. And as you will see as you proceed through this

Piaget's theory makes the claim that this toddler and his teenage cousin think differently. They have different cognitive structures for guiding their actions and interpreting the world around them.

Septemberlegs/Alamy

chapter, Piaget taught us that young people think differently than older people do—and often in ways we never would have suspected.

In addition, many scholars today agree that Piaget was largely right in his basic *description* of cognitive development. The sequence he proposed—sensorimotor to preoperational to concrete operations to formal operations—seems to describe the course and content of intellectual development for children and adolescents from the hundreds of cultures and subcultures that have been studied (Flavell, Miller, & Miller, 1993). Although cultural factors influence the rate of cognitive growth, the direction of development is always from sensorimotor thinking to preoperational thinking to concrete operations to, for many, formal operations (or even postformal operations).

Challenges to Piaget

Partly because Piaget's theory has been so enormously influential, it has had more than its share of criticism: some of this has been mild—suggesting the need for minor tweaking of the theory—whereas other criticism has been more severe. John Broughton (1984), for example, concluded that Piaget's theory is fundamentally flawed and should be thrown out. Despite Broughton's self-proclaimed revolutionary position on Piaget, most challenges have used the decades of accumulated research on Piaget's theory to offer targeted refinements to specific areas of the theory. Here, we focus on four common criticisms (see Lourenco & Machado, 1996; Miller, 2011):

1. *Underestimating young minds.* Piaget seems to have underestimated the cognitive abilities of infants and young children, although he emphasized that he was more interested in understanding the sequences of changes than the specific ages at which they occur (Lourenco & Machado, 1996). When researchers use more familiar problems than Piaget's and simplify the tasks to their essentials, hidden competencies of young children—and of adolescents and adults—are sometimes revealed. What should we make of these earlier competencies when task demands are

reduced? It may be that Piaget failed to *distinguish between competence and performance.* There is an important difference between understanding a concept (competence) and passing a test designed to measure it (performance). Piaget may have been too quick to assume that children who failed one of his tests lacked competence; they may only have failed to demonstrate their competence in a particular situation. Perhaps more importantly, Piaget may have overemphasized the idea that knowledge is an all-or-nothing concept (Schwitzgebel, 1999). Instead of having or not having a particular competence, children probably gain competence gradually and experience long periods between not understanding and understanding. Indeed, many of the seemingly contradictory results of studies using Piagetian tasks can be accounted for with this idea of gradual change in understanding (Miller, 2011).

2. *Wrongly claiming that broad stages of development exist.* According to Piaget, each new stage of cognitive development is a coherent mode of thinking applied across a range of problems. Piaget emphasized the consistency of thinking *within* a stage and the difference *between* stages (Meadows, 2006). Yet individuals are often inconsistent in their performance on different tasks that presumably measure the abilities defining a given stage. This may occur because cognitive development is domain specific—that is, it is a matter of building skills in particular content areas—and growth in one domain may proceed much faster than growth in another (Fischer, Kenny, & Pipp, 1990). In addition, the transitions between stages are not swift and abrupt, as most of Piaget's writings suggest, but are often lengthy (over several years) and subtle (see Meadows, 2006). It is not always clear when a child has made the shift from one set of cognitive structures to a more advanced set of structures.

3. *Failing to adequately explain development.* Several critics suggest that Piaget did a better job of describing development than of explaining how it comes about (Bruner, 1997; Meadows, 2006). To be sure, Piaget wrote extensively about his interactionist position on the nature–nurture issue and did as much as any developmental theorist to tackle the question of how development comes about. Presumably, humans are always assimilating new experiences in ways that their level of maturation allows, accommodating their thinking to those experiences, and reorganizing their cognitive structures into increasingly complex modes of thought. Yet this explanation is vague. Researchers need to know far more about how specific maturational changes in the brain and specific kinds of experiences contribute to important cognitive advances.

4. *Giving limited attention to social influences on cognitive development.* Some critics say Piaget paid too little attention to how children's minds develop through their social interactions with more competent individuals and how they develop differently in different cultures (Karpov, 2005). Piaget's child often resembles an isolated scientist exploring the world alone, but children develop their minds through interactions with parents, teachers, peers, and siblings.

True, Piaget had interesting ideas about the role of *peers* in helping children adopt other perspectives and reach new conclusions (see Chapter 13 on moral development). But he did not believe that children learned much from their interactions with *adults*. This may seem counterintuitive, but Piaget believed that children see other children, but not adults, as "like themselves." Hearing a different perspective from someone like oneself can trigger internal conflict, but hearing a perspective from someone different from oneself may not be viewed as a challenge to one's current way of thinking because the person—and their views—are simply too different. Thus, in Piaget's model, no notable cognitive disequilibrium, and therefore little cognitive growth, occurs from children interacting with adults. As you will see shortly, the significance of social interaction and culture for cognitive development is the basis of the perspective on cognitive development offered by one of Piaget's early critics, Lev Vygotsky.

A Modern Take on Constructivism

By now, you should know that Piaget adopted a position called *constructivism*, maintaining that children actively create or build their own understandings of the world based on their experiences. Some scholars have attempted to be more precise on the specific mechanisms of *how* development occurs, that is, just how do children construct knowledge? One promising approach to this issue comes from work by Denis Mareschal and his colleagues (Mareschal, 2011; Mareschal et al., 2007) and Gert Westermann and colleagues (for example, Westermann, Thomas, & Karmiloff-Smith, 2010). They propose a model of cognitive development that builds on this central tenet of Piaget's theory, namely, that we construct increasingly complex mental representations of the world.

According to the **neuro-constructivism theory**, new knowledge is constructed through changes in the neural structures of the brain in response to experiences (Westermann et al., 2011). Piaget had a background in biology and certainly believed that biological factors played a role in cognitive development. Consider, though, that Piaget developed his theory in an era devoid of modern tests for measuring electrical activity and blood flow in the brain, before precise **reaction time** and eye tracking measures, and before genetic analyses could be performed. Thus, theories such as neuroconstructivism are not necessarily

an indication that Piaget was incorrect. Instead, they are taking our understanding of cognitive development to a level not possible when Piaget developed his theory. Where Piaget noted that cognitive structures become more sophisticated and others have argued that mental representations become more complex (for example, Karmiloff-Smith, 1992), the neuroconstructivists believe that the neural structures in the brain underlying these cognitive phenomenon develop and change in response to experience (Sirois et al., 2008).

Consider some research by Olivier Houdé and colleagues (2011). Children aged 5 to 10 years were given a classic Piagetian cognitive task in which they need to compare two rows of objects and determine whether the rows contain the same number of objects. As they were solving the task, researchers used functional magnetic resonance imaging (fMRI) to monitor brain activity. Children who successfully solved the task showed increased activity in parts of their brains that were not activated in children who did not solve the task. Both groups of children, solvers and nonsolvers, showed activity in a part of the brain associated with processing numbers; thus both groups understood the task to be about numbers. Obviously, though, this is not enough for success on the task. Those who were successful also showed activity in an area of their prefrontal lobes associated with working memory control.

We leave this section by concluding that, although there have been challenges to Piaget's theory, it continues to offer a useful framework for any discussion of cognitive development. Throughout this chapter, we describe advances in cognitive development using research from Piaget and other like-minded scholars in the field. First, though, we consider another influential theorist, Lev Vygotsky, who drew our attention to the role of culture in cognition.

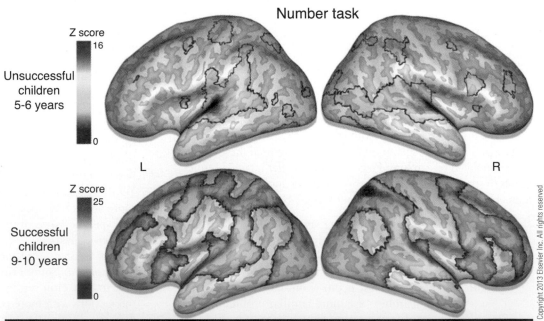

Images from functional magnetic resonance imaging (fMRI) reveal a big difference between children who successfully solve a number conservation task (the bottom images) and children who are not successful (the top images).

► **Checking Mastery**

1. What is a scheme in Piaget's theory?
2. How do assimilation and accommodation operate to bring about cognitive change?
3. What are two of Piaget's major contributions to our understanding of cognitive development?
4. What are three problems with, or challenges to, Piaget's theory of cognitive development?

► **Making Connections**

1. How might Piaget's theory be updated to accommodate some of the major criticisms and research findings that have emerged since he constructed his theory?
2. Using your own experiences, provide an example of how the inborn processes of organization and adaptation operate.

7.2 Vygotsky's Sociocultural Perspective

LEARNING OBJECTIVES:

• Indicate how culture and social interaction affect thought in Vygotsky's theory.

• Explain how tools, especially language, influence thought.

Lev Vygotsky was born in 1896, the same year as Piaget, and was an active scholar in the 1920s and 1930s when Piaget was formulating his theory. For many years, Vygotsky's work was banned for political reasons in his homeland, the former Soviet Union, and North American scholars lacked English translations of his work, which limited consideration of Vygotsky's ideas until recent decades. In addition, Vygotsky died of tuberculosis at age 38, before his theory was fully developed. However, his main theme is clear: cognitive growth occurs in a sociocultural context and evolves out of the child's social interactions.

Culture and Thought

Culture and society play a pivotal role in Vygotsky's theory. Indeed, intelligence in the Vygotskian model is held by the group, not the individual, and is closely tied to the language system and other tools of thinking the group has developed over time (Case, 1998). Culture and social experiences affect how we think, not just what we think.

Consider some research by Vygotsky's colleague, Alexander Luria, who tested groups of 9- to 12-year-old children growing up in different social environments. Children were given target words and asked to name the first thing that came to mind when they heard each word. Luria found that children growing up in a remote rural village with limited social experiences gave remarkably similar responses, whereas children growing up in a large city gave more distinctly individual answers. Vygotsky and Luria believed that this difference reflected the city children's broader exposure to various aspects of culture. On their own, the rural children were unable to develop certain types of knowledge. Knowledge, then, depends on social experiences.

Vygotsky would not be surprised to learn that adolescent formal-operational thought is rarely used in some cultures; he expected cognitive development to vary from society to society depending on the mental tools such as the language that the culture values and makes available. How do children acquire their society's mental tools? They acquire them

by interacting with parents and other more experienced members of the culture and by adopting their language and knowledge (Frawley, 1997).

Martin Harvey/Peter Arnold/Getty Images

According to Lev Vygotsky's theory, cognitive development is shaped by the culture in which children live and the kinds of problem-solving strategies that adults and other knowledgeable guides pass on to them.

Social Interaction and Thought

Consider this scenario: Annie, a 4-year-old, receives a jigsaw puzzle, her first, for her birthday. She attempts to work the puzzle but gets nowhere until her father sits down beside her and gives her some tips. He suggests that it would be a good idea to put the corners together first. He points to the pink area at the edge of one corner piece and says, "Let's look for another pink piece." When Annie seems frustrated, he places two interlocking pieces near each other so that she will notice them. And when she succeeds, he offers words of encouragement. As Annie gets the hang of it, he steps back and lets her work more independently. This kind of social interaction, said Vygotsky, fosters cognitive growth.

How? First, Annie and her father are operating in what Vygotsky called the **zone of proximal development**—the gap between what a learner can accomplish independently and what she can accomplish with the guidance and encouragement of a more-skilled partner. Skills within the zone are ripe for development and are the skills at which instruction should be aimed. Skills outside the zone are either well mastered already or still too difficult. In this example, Annie obviously becomes a more competent puzzle-solver with her father's help than without it. More importantly, she will internalize the problem-solving techniques that she discovered in collaboration with her father, working together in her zone of proximal development, and will use them on her own, rising to a new level of independent mastery. What began as a social process involving two people becomes a cognitive process within one.

An important implication of the zone of proximal development is that knowledge is not a fixed state and no single test or score can adequately reflect the range of a person's knowledge. The mind has potential for unlimited growth. Development consists of moving toward the upper range of the zone using the tools of society such as the language and the inventions it has created. The upper limit continues to move upward in response to cultural changes (Smagorinsky, 1995). Support for Vygotsky's idea of the zone of proximal development comes from various sources, including research showing that children's performance on assisted learning tasks is a good predictor of their future achievement (Meijer & Elshout, 2001). And research on pairing less-skilled readers with more-skilled ones shows that reading fluency increases substantially when the less-skilled readers are provided with a model of good reading and encouragement (Nes, 2003).

In many cultures, children do not go to school with other children to learn from teachers, nor do their parents explicitly teach them tasks such as weaving and hunting. Instead, they learn through **guided participation**—by actively participating in culturally relevant activities with the aid and support of their parents and other knowledgeable guides (Rogoff, 1998). Jerome Bruner (1983) had a similar concept in mind when he wrote of the many ways in which parents provide **scaffolding** for their children's development; that is, the more-skilled person gives structured help to a less-skilled learner but gradually reduces the help as the less-skilled learner becomes more

By working with a more knowledgeable partner, this child is able to accomplish more than would be possible on her own. According to Lev Vygotsky, the difference between what a child can accomplish alone and with a partner is the zone of proximal development.

competent. By calling attention to guided participation processes, in the zone of proximal development, Vygotsky was rejecting Piaget's view of children as independent explorers in favor of the view that they learn more sophisticated cognitive strategies through their interactions with more mature thinkers. To Piaget, the child's level of cognitive development determines what he can learn; to Vygotsky, learning in collaboration with more knowledgeable companions drives cognitive development.

Tools of Thought

Vygotsky believed that mental activity, like physical activity, is mediated by tools (Daniels, 2011). If a child wants to start a garden, we wouldn't send her outside empty handed and say, "Go ahead and make a garden." We would, instead, equip her with an array of tools—shovel, rake, gloves, fertilizer, seeds, and so on—that have already been proven useful for accomplishing this task. Further, we would probably show her how to best use these tools to accomplish the desired task. We might show the child how to poke holes in the soil and drop seeds inside, watch while the child attempted this, and perhaps correct her if she pushed the seeds in too deep. As the child practices and masters the use of the tools presented by the adult, the child adopts the tools as her own. The same process is involved in passing along cultural tools for mental activity.

In Vygotsky's view, adults use a variety of tools to pass culturally valued modes of thinking and problem solving to their children. Spoken language is the most important tool, but writing, using numbers, and applying problem-solving and memory strategies also convey information and enable thinking (Vygotsky, 1978). The type of tool used to perform a task influences performance on the task. Consider a study by Dorothy Faulkner and her colleagues (2000) with 9- and 10-year-old children. Children worked in pairs on a science project (a task developed by

Inhelder and Piaget that involves figuring out which chemicals to combine to make a colored liquid), using either a computer simulation of the task or the actual physical materials. The children who worked with the computerized version talked more, tested more possible chemical combinations, and completed the task more quickly than children who worked with the physical materials. The computer, then, was a tool that changed the nature of the problem-solving activity and influenced performance, as Vygotsky would have predicted.

Look more closely at Vygotsky's notion of how tools—especially language—influence thought. Whereas Piaget maintained that cognitive development influences language development, Vygotsky argued that language shapes thought in important ways and that thought changes fundamentally once we begin to think in words (Bodrova & Leong, 1996). Piaget and Vygotsky both noticed that preschool children often talk to themselves as they go about their daily activities, almost as if they were play-by-play sports announcers. ("I'm putting the big piece in the corner. I need a pink one. Not that one—this one.") Two preschool children playing next to each other sometimes carry on separate monologues rather than conversing. Piaget (1926) regarded such speech as egocentric—further evidence that preoperational thinkers cannot yet take the perspectives of other people (in this case, their conversation partners) and therefore have not mastered the art of social speech. He did not believe that egocentric speech played a useful role in cognitive development.

In contrast, Vygotsky called children's recitations **private speech**—speech to oneself that guides one's thought and behavior. Rather than viewing it as a sign of cognitive immaturity, he saw it as a critical step in the development of mature thought and as the forerunner of the silent thinking-in-words that adults engage in every day. Adults guide children's behavior with speech, a tool that children adopt and initially use externally, just as adults did with them. Gradually, this regulatory speech is internalized.

Studies conducted by Vygotsky and other researchers support his claim. For example, in one set of studies, Vygotsky (1934/1962) measured children's private speech first as they worked unimpeded on a task, then as they worked to overcome an obstacle placed in their path. Their use of private speech increased dramatically when they confronted an interruption of their work—a problem to solve. Thus, young children rely most heavily on private speech when they are struggling to solve difficult problems (Berk, 1992). Even adults sometimes revert to thinking aloud when they are stumped by a problem (John-Steiner, 1992).

The incidence of private speech varies with age and task demands. Both 3- and 4-year-olds use private speech, but 4-year-olds are more likely to use it systematically when engaged in a sustained activity. Four-year-olds are presumably more goal oriented than 3-year-olds and use private speech to regulate their behavior and achieve their goals (Winsler, Carlton, & Barry, 2000). As the task becomes familiar and children gain competence, the use of private speech decreases (Duncan & Pratt, 1997). Private speech is also more frequent during open-ended activities (such as pretend play) that have several possible outcomes than during closed-ended tasks that have a single outcome (Krafft & Berk, 1998). Open-ended activities tend to be directed more by the child than by an adult; they allow children to alter the difficulty level of the task so that it is appropriately challenging. In contrast, adult-directed activities provide fewer opportunities for children to regulate their own behavior.

Intellectually capable children rely more heavily on private speech in the preschool years and make the transition to inner speech earlier in the elementary school years than their less academically capable peers do (Berk & Landau, 1993). This suggests that the preschool child's self-talk is indeed a sign of cognitive maturity, as Vygotsky claimed, rather than a sign of immature egocentrism, as Piaget claimed.

In addition, heavy use of private speech contributes to effective problem-solving performance—if not immediately, then when children encounter similar problems in the future (Behrend, Rosengren, & Perlmutter, 1989; Bivens & Berk, 1990). The amount of private speech and the nature of what the child says are both related to performance (Chiu & Alexander, 2000). In particular, children who use private speech to talk themselves through a problem ("No, I need to change this. Try it over here. Yes, that's good.") show greater motivation toward mastery; that is, they are more likely to persist on a task even without adult prodding (Chiu & Alexander, 2000). Thus, private speech not only helps children think their way through challenging problems but also allows them to incorporate into their own thinking the problem-solving strategies they learned during their collaborations with adults. Notice that, as in guided participation, what is at first a social process becomes an individual psychological process. In other words, social speech (for example, the conversation between Annie and her father as they jointly worked a puzzle) gives rise to private speech (Annie talking aloud, much as her father talked to her, as she then tries to work the puzzle on her own), which in turn goes "underground" to become first mutterings and lip movements and then inner speech (Annie's silent verbal thought).

Evaluation of Vygotsky

Although many scholars find Vygotsky's ideas a refreshing addition to Piaget's, some concerns should be noted. Vygotsky died young (age 38), leaving us with many intriguing ideas but without a complete theory of cognitive development. It is, of course, impossible to know how the theory might have evolved had Vygotsky continued to work on it for as long as Piaget worked on his theory. Whereas Piaget has been criticized for placing too much emphasis on the individual and not enough on the social environment, Vygotsky has been criticized for doing the opposite: placing too much emphasis on social interaction (Feldman & Fowler, 1997). Vygotsky seemed to assume that all knowledge and understanding of the world is transmitted through social interaction. But at least some understanding is individually constructed, as Piaget proposed. Vygotsky and Piaget are often presented as opposites on a continuum

Improving Cognitive Functioning

What do the theories of Piaget and Vygotsky have to contribute to the goal of optimizing cognition? Studies suggest that many Piagetian concepts can be taught to children who are slightly younger than the age at which the concepts would naturally emerge. Training is sometimes difficult, and it does not always generalize well to new problems, but progress can be achieved. Dorothy Field (1981), for example, demonstrated that 4-year-olds could be trained to recognize the identity of a substance such as a ball of clay before and after its appearance is altered in Piaget's famous conservation task—that is, to understand that although the clay looks different, it is still the same clay and has to be the same amount of clay. Field found that nearly 75% of the children given this identity training could solve at least three of five conservation problems 2–5 months after training.

Similar training studies have demonstrated that children who function at the late concrete operations stage can be taught formal operations (Adey & Shayer, 1992). Researchers have had even more luck improving the cognitive performance of older adults, sometimes with simple interventions (Blackburn & Papalia, 1992). Make no mistake: No one has demonstrated that 2-year-olds can be taught formal operations. But at least these studies establish that specific training experiences can somewhat speed a child's progress through Piaget's stages or bring out more advanced capacities in an adult performing at a less advanced level.

In truth, Piaget disapproved of attempts by Americans to speed children's progress through his stages (Piaget, 1970). He believed parents should provide young children with opportunities to explore their world and teachers should use a discovery approach in the classroom that allows children to learn by doing. Given their natural curiosity and normal opportunities to try their hand at solving problems, children would construct ever more complex understandings on their own. Many educators have incorporated Piaget's ideas about discovery-based education into their lesson plans, especially in science classes. Teachers have also taken seriously Piaget's notion that children understand material best if they can assimilate it into their existing understandings. Finding out what the learner already knows or can do and providing instruction matched to the child's level of development are in the spirit of Piaget.

What would Vygotsky recommend to teachers who want to stimulate cognitive growth? As you might guess, Vygotsky's theoretical orientation leads to a different approach to education than Piaget's does— a more social one. Whereas students in Piaget's classroom would most likely be engaged in independent exploration, students in Vygotsky's classroom would be involved in guided participation, "co-constructing" knowledge during interactions with teachers and more knowledgeable peers. The roles of teachers and other more skillful collaborators would be to organize the learning activity, break it into steps, provide hints and suggestions carefully tailored to the student's abilities, and gradually turn over more of the mental work to the student. According to Vygotsky's sociocultural perspective, the guidance provided by a skilled partner will then be internalized by the learner, first as private speech and eventually as silent inner speech. Education ends up being a matter of providing children with tools of the mind important in their culture, whether hunting strategies or computer skills (Berk & Winsler, 1995; Bodrova & Leong, 1996).

Is there evidence that one of these theoretical approaches might be superior to the other? Consider what Lisa Freund (1990) found when she had 3- to 5-year-old children help a puppet with a sorting task: deciding which furnishings (sofas, beds, bathtubs, stoves, and so on) should be placed in each of six rooms of a dollhouse that the puppet was moving into. First the children were tested to determine what they already knew about proper furniture placement. Then each child worked at a similar task, either alone (as might be the case in Piaget's discovery-based education, although here children were provided with corrective feedback by the experimenter) or with his or her mother (Vygotsky's guided learning). Finally, to assess what they had learned, Freund asked the children to perform a final, rather complex furniture-sorting task. The results were clear: Children who had sorted furniture with help from their mothers showed dramatic improvements in sorting ability, whereas those who had practiced on their own showed little improvement. Moreover, the children who gained the most from guided participation with their mothers were those whose mothers talked the most about how to tackle the task. Collaborating with a competent peer can also produce cognitive gains that a child might not achieve working alone (Azmitia, 1992; Gauvain & Rogoff, 1989).

So children do not always learn the most when they function as solitary scientists, seeking discoveries on their own; often, conceptual growth springs more readily from children's interactions with other people— particularly with competent people who provide an optimal amount of guidance. Yet it would seem that many children might benefit most from the best of both worlds: opportunities to explore on their own and supportive companions to offer help when needed.

representing the extent to which cognitive development derives from social experience. However, a careful reading of the two theorists reveals that they are not as dissimilar as they are often presented to be (DeVries, 2000; Matusov & Hayes, 2000). Both Piaget and Vygotsky acknowledge the importance of the social context of development. Still, there are differences in their emphasis. ● **Table 7.1** summarizes some of the differences between Vygotsky's sociocultural perspective and Piaget's cognitive

● Table 7.1 A Comparison of Vygotsky and Piaget

Vygotsky's Sociocultural View	Piaget's Cognitive Developmental View
Processes of animal and human development are fundamentally different.	Processes of animal and human development are fundamentally the same.
Cognitive development is different in different social and historical contexts.	Cognitive development is mostly the same universally.
Appropriate unit of analysis is the social, cultural, and historical context in which the individual develops.	Appropriate unit of analysis is the individual.
Cognitive growth results from social interactions (guided participation in the zone of proximal development).	Cognitive growth results from the child's independent explorations of the world.
Children and their partners co-construct knowledge.	Children construct knowledge on their own.
Social processes become individual psychological ones (e.g., social speech becomes inner speech).	Individual, egocentric processes become more social (e.g., egocentric speech becomes social speech).
Adults are especially important because they know the culture's tools of thinking.	Peers are especially important because the cognitive conflict triggered by different perspectives of other children is not so overwhelming that it cannot be resolved.
Learning precedes development (tools learned with adult help become internalized).	Development precedes learning (children cannot master certain things until they have the requisite cognitive structures).
Training can help mediate development.	Training is largely ineffective in "speeding up" development.

developmental view. **Application Box 7.1** explains their views on improving cognitive functioning.

7.3 Fischer's Dynamic Skill Framework

LEARNING OBJECTIVES:

- Describe Fischer's perspective on context and performance.
- Explain what changes or develops in Fischer's dynamic skill framework.
- Compare Fischer's model of cognitive development to Piaget's theory.
- Indicate where Fischer's concepts of developmental change are similar to Vygotsky's concepts.

Beginning with his doctoral dissertation in 1970, Kurt Fischer has devoted his professional career to developing, testing, and revising a dynamic skill framework for understanding cognitive development (1980; Fischer & Bidell, 1998; Fischer & Pipp, 1984). According to this perspective, "it is not possible to analyze behavior outside the context in which it occurs. Behavior is not something that a person "has"; it emerges from interactions between person and context" (Rose & Fischer, 2011, p. 146). Consider the experience of studying for an exam and having your friend test your understanding with questions the day before the exam as you relax in a coffee shop. You answer the questions successfully and go into the exam feeling confident. But now, in the context of the exam room with the palpable stress in the room, you don't seem to "know" nearly as much as you did the day before. Or perhaps you can relate to the example of the basketball player who can make shots all day long when practicing in the gym, but then "chokes" and misses the hoop in the context of a game. In contrast, maybe you perform well under pressure and need the increased stress that comes with a testing or game situation to really focus and demonstrate your best performance. Fischer believes that such differences in performance across different contexts are perfectly normal. Indeed, when someone consistently performs at the same level over and over, we often say "he's like a machine." Such consistency across different contexts seems more typical of a machine than of a human. Unlike machines, human performance is **dynamic**, that is, it changes in response to changes in context.

Comparison to Piaget and Vygotsky

Fischer's dynamic system view is different from Piaget's view that the cognitive structures underlying each stage are inherent in the person. Piaget, and much of the research sprouting from Piaget's theory, tested children in rather artificial settings with carefully constructed tasks that may not be typical of tasks encountered in everyday life. Fischer and others, including Bronfenbrenner whom we discussed in Chapter 2, firmly believe that developmental psychologists need to put development back into its natural context and not study it in isolation.

Another difference between Piaget and Fischer is their view of *what* develops. According to Piaget, cognitive structures develop, whereas Fischer proposes that skill levels change and develop. A **skill** is a person's ability to perform on a particular task in a specific context (Fischer & Bidell, 1998). Someone who wins spelling bee contests is demonstrating skill to perform this task—spelling words—in the context of a competition. This person may or may not exhibit skill on a related task, such as defining words based on how they are used in sentences. A surgeon who has a 99% success rate of repairing retinal tears on eyeballs has a skill for this type of surgical procedure in the context provided by this type of surgical arena. The same surgeon may not be the one you want to have repairing your damaged heart valve. Thus, a skill is both task-specific and context-specific.

Similar to Piaget, Fischer proposes a series of four tiers, not stages, although they roughly correspond to Piaget's four stages. According to Fischer, thinking at each tier uses a different type of representation, as follows:

- Reflexive—basic reflexes operating during the first month or so of life that need to be prompted with stimulation
- Sensorimotor action—actions on observable objects
- Representations—symbolic operations on concrete objects
- Abstractions—operations integrate earlier representations into abstractions that involve mental juggling of concepts

In addition to these four main tiers, Fischer proposes several levels within each tier, where the highest level of one tier is also the lowest level of the next tier. Where Piaget believed that thinking underwent fairly dramatic qualitative—abrupt—change from one stage to the next, change in Fischer's model may or may not seem "stage-like." Under conditions with little support, children's development may appear to be gradual and linear as they slowly work themselves through the levels of acquiring a skill. But under conditions of high support, change

may occur swiftly and more closely resemble stages, as children master several levels within a short period of time.

Drawing directly from Vygotsky, Fischer uses the concept of *zone of proximal development* to explain how cognition advances from one level to another. The "zone" represents the opportunity for growth that exists between a person's potential ability and their actual performance on a given task in a particular context, that is, their current skill level. With research and further refinement of dynamic skill theory, Fischer and others have adopted the term **developmental range** to better capture their findings that people's abilities vary with context. With a supportive context, people can perform at an optimal level of skill. Most of the time, though, we perform below our optimal level because the support structure needed to perform optimally is not in place (Rose & Fischer, 1998). Thus, high levels of support can lead to larger jumps in skill acquisition, whereas low levels of support can result in slow linear acquisition of skills.

In sum, the dynamic skill theory that has taken shape over the past 40 years uses some ideas from Piaget and Vygotsky and proposes new concepts to account for the variability observed in actual performance. Piaget was interested in uncovering universal stages of cognitive development. Fischer and other dynamic theorists are especially interested in the variability of performance as research has repeatedly shown that people demonstrate inconsistent skills. Once a person "has" a skill, why wouldn't they always demonstrate optimal use of this skill? As we've seen, the dynamic skill theorists believe that skills do not exist in isolation from the task and the context. Seen from this perspective, many seemingly inconsistent performances begin to make much more sense.

We have now examined three major perspectives on cognitive development. In the following sections, we will look at specific aspects of cognitive development in infancy, childhood, adolescence, and adulthood, guided largely by Piaget's theory. We will also see how Vygotsky's and Fischer's perspectives enrich our understanding of cognitive development.

Checking Mastery

1. What is the meaning of the terms dynamic and skill in the dynamic skill framework?
2. How is the dynamic skill framework similar to Vygotsky's sociocultural theory?
3. In what ways is dynamic skill framework different from Piaget's theory of cognitive development?

Making Connections

1. How might a classroom teacher use the concept of Fischer's developmental range to optimize students' performance?
2. If you are preparing a team for a competition, whether this is an athletic, academic, musical, or other type of competition, what features of dynamic skill theory could you apply to your coaching to enhance your team's performance?

- Explain the importance of object permanence and describe the path from lack of object permanence to full understanding of object permanence.
- Note the major cognitive achievements emerging from the period of infancy.

What sort of cognitive activity is possible during infancy? One of the strengths of Piaget's approach to cognitive development is that he provided a rich description of what he observed infants and young children *doing*. From this, he inferred what they were *thinking* and how their minds were working. Piaget proposed that the groundwork for cognitive development occurred during the first 2 years of life as infants learn about the world through their senses and their motoric actions, which is how he arrived at naming this first stage of his theory the *sensorimotor stage*. The dominant cognitive structures of this stage are behavioral schemes—patterns of action that evolve as infants begin to coordinate sensory input (seeing an object) and motor responses (grasping an object). Because infants solve problems through their actions rather than with their minds, their mode of thought is qualitatively different from that of older children.

The six substages of the sensorimotor stage are outlined in
● **Table 7.2**. At the start of the sensorimotor period, infants may not seem highly intelligent, but they are already active explorers of the world around them. Researchers see increasing signs of intelligent behavior as infants pass through the substages, because they are gradually learning about the world and about cause and effect by observing the effects of their actions. They are transformed from reflexive creatures who adapt to their environment using their innate reflexes to reflective ones who can solve simple problems in their heads. The advances in problem-solving ability captured in the six substages of the sensorimotor period bring many important changes. We can illustrate the impressive advances in thinking across infancy by closely examining the acquisition of one of Piaget's most notable concepts—object permanence.

The Development of Object Permanence

According to Piaget, newborns lack an understanding of **object permanence** (also called *object concept*). This is the fundamental understanding that objects continue to exist—they are permanent—when they are no longer visible or otherwise detectable to the senses. It probably does not occur to you to wonder whether your coat is still in the closet after you shut the closet door (unless perhaps you have taken a philosophy course). But very young infants, because they rely so heavily on their senses, seem to operate as though objects exist only when they are perceived or acted on. According to Piaget and others, infants must construct the notion that reality exists apart from their experience of it.

Piaget believed that the concept of object permanence develops gradually over the sensorimotor period. Up through roughly 4–8 months, it is "out of sight, out of mind"; infants will not search for a toy if it is covered with a cloth or screen. By the end of the first year (substage 4), they master that trick but still rely on their perceptions and actions to "know" an object (Piaget, 1952). After his 10-month-old daughter, Jacqueline, had repeatedly retrieved a toy parrot from one hiding place, Piaget put it in a new spot while she watched him. Amazingly, she looked in the original hiding place. She seemed to assume that her behavior determined where the object would appear; she did not treat the object as if it existed apart from her actions or from its initial location. The surprising tendency of

● **Table 7.2** The Substages and Intellectual Accomplishments of the Sensorimotor Period

Substage	Description
1. Reflex activity (birth–1 month)	Active exercise and refinement of inborn reflexes (e.g., change sucking patterns to fit the shapes of different objects).
2. Primary circular reactions (1–4 months)	Repetition of interesting acts centered on the child's own body (e.g., repeatedly suck a thumb, kick legs, or blow bubbles). These typically begin as random acts but are then repeated for pleasure.
3. Secondary circular reactions (4–8 months)	Repetition of interesting acts on objects (e.g., repeatedly shake a rattle to make an interesting noise or bat a mobile to make it wiggle). Thus, circular actions extend beyond one's self (primary) to objects in the environment (secondary to self).
4. Coordination of secondary schemes (8–12 months)	Combination of actions to solve simple problems or achieve goals (e.g., push aside a barrier to grasp an object, using the scheme as a means to an end); first evidence of intentionality.
5. Tertiary circular reactions (12–18 months)	Experimentation to find new ways to solve problems or produce interesting outcomes (e.g., explore bathwater by gently patting it, then hitting it vigorously and watching the results; or stroke, pinch, squeeze, and pat a cat to see how it responds to varied actions).
6. Beginning of thought (18–24 months)	First evidence of insight; able to solve problems mentally and use symbols to stand for objects and actions; visualize how a stick could be used (e.g., move an out-of-reach toy closer).

© Cengage Learning

Until an infant masters the concept of object permanence, objects that are outside of his visual sight are "out of mind."

8- to 12-month-olds to search for an object in the place where they last found it (A) rather than in its new hiding place (B) is called the **A-not-B error**. The likelihood of infants making the A-not-B error increases with lengthier delays between hiding and searching and with the number of trials in which the object is found in spot A (Marcovitch & Zelazo, 1999).

As we suggested earlier in this chapter, task demands and physical limitations of infants may influence performance on the A-not-B task (Lew et al., 2007). To evaluate this, Ted Ruffman and his colleagues (2005) conducted a series of studies and concluded that multiple factors do influence performance, but infants do indeed have a conceptual problem when it comes to understanding that the object is located at B and not at A.

By 12–18 months of age (substage 5), the infant overcomes the A-not-B error but continues to have trouble with invisible displacements—as when you hide a toy in your hand, move your hand under a pillow, and then remove your hand, leaving the toy under the pillow. The infant will search where the object was last seen, seeming confused when it is not in your hand and failing to look under the pillow, where it was deposited. Finally, by the end of the second year (18–24 months), the infant is capable of mentally representing such invisible moves and conceiving of the object in its final location. According to Piaget, the concept of object permanence is fully mastered at this point.

This is one of those areas where simplifying the task leads to finding that infants develop at least some understanding of object permanence far earlier than Piaget claimed (Baillargeon, 2002; Ruffman, Slade, & Redman, 2005). For example, Renee Baillargeon and her colleagues have used a method of testing for object concept that does not require reaching for a hidden object, only looking toward where it should be. In one study, infants as young as 2½ months seemed surprised (as demonstrated by looking longer) when a toy that had disappeared behind one screen (left side of ■ **Figure 7.2**) reappeared from behind a second screen (right side of Figure 7.2) *without* appearing in the open space between the two screens (Aguiar & Baillargeon, 1999).

At this young age, however, understanding of hidden objects is still limited. Consider the scenario shown in ■ **Figure 7.3**. In the high-window condition, a toy is hidden as it moves along a track behind a block that has a window located at its top. There is nothing odd about this condition. In the low-window condition, a toy *should* be visible as it moves along a track behind a block that has a window located at its bottom, but it is not. To someone who understands the properties of object permanence, this should strike them as odd. At 2½ months, infants do not show signs that they detect a difference between an object moving along a track under the high-window and low-window conditions. But just 2 weeks later, 3-month-olds look longer at the low-window event compared with the high-window event, as if surprised (Aguiar & Baillargeon, 2002). Thus, by 3 months, infants have gained an understanding that objects have qualities that should permit them to be visible when nothing is obstructing them.

In general, then, it seems that babies sometimes know a good deal more about object permanence than they reveal through their actions when they are given the kinds of search tasks originally devised by Piaget (Baillargeon, 2002). This illustrates Fischer's notion that skill depends on the task demands and the context. When tested using the task demands specified by Piaget, infants demonstrate less skill. But changing the task demands, by peeling away some of the complexity and providing a supportive context, gives infants the opportunity to demonstrate optimal skill levels (Fischer & Bidell, 1991).

To be fair to Piaget, we should note that he contended that looking behaviors were developmental precursors to the reaching behaviors that he assessed. He did not believe, however, that looking represented complete understanding of object permanence. An analysis of infants' looking behaviors by Carolyn Rovee-Collier (2001) suggests that Piaget was wise to distinguish between infants' looking and reaching. In some situations, looking may developmentally precede reaching for an object, as Piaget suggested. In other situations, however, infants' looking behavior does not predict their subsequent action on an object. Regardless of the specific measure researchers use, infants gradually become more skilled at acting on their knowledge by searching in the right spot.

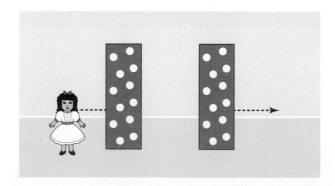

■ **Figure 7.2** Test stimuli used by Aguiar and Baillargeon (1999, 2002). The doll moves behind the screen on the left and reappears on the right side of the second screen without appearing in the space between screens.

Source: From Aguiar, A. & Baillargeon, R. (2002). Developments in young infants' reasoning about occluded objects, *Cognitive Psychology*, 45, pp. 267–336, Figure 1. Reprinted by permission of Elsevier.

High-window event

Low-window event

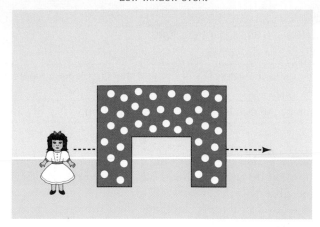

■ **Figure 7.3** There is nothing to be surprised about in the high-window event, but in the low-window event, the doll should (but does not) appear in the middle space as it moves along the track.

SOURCE: From Aguiar, A. & Baillargeon, R. (2002). Developments in young infants' reasoning about occluded objects, *Cognitive Psychology, 45*, p. 267–336, Figure 2. Reprinted by permission of Elsevier.

They improve their looking and reaching skills between 8 and 12 months, and by the end of the sensorimotor period, they have fully mastered object permanence and are masters of even very complex hide-and-seek games (Moore & Meltzoff, 2008).

The Emergence of Symbols

Perhaps the most important cognitive achievement of infancy is the emergence of the **symbolic capacity**—the ability to use images, words, or gestures to represent or stand for objects and experiences. This allows infants and young children to manipulate ideas mentally, not just motorically, opening the door to more sophisticated thinking based on manipulating ideas in their heads. Consider how the emergence of symbolic capacity changes the quality of infants' play activities. During the first month, young infants react reflexively to internal and external stimulation. In the primary circular reactions substage (1–4 months), they are more interested in their own bodies than in manipulating toys. Moving their tongues or fingers around is entertainment enough at this age. Piaget named this substage **primary circular reactions** because he observed infants repeating (hence, the term *circular*) actions relating to their own bodies (that is, primary to themselves) that had initially happened by chance. Piaget reports the example of his son, Laurent, at just over 1 month accidentally getting his thumb in his mouth. It falls out. This happens again on another day. Indeed, since the first accidental occurrence, Piaget observes it happening over and over again. Increasingly, a finger or thumb successfully makes it into the mouth, which pleases Laurent. He seeks opportunities to repeat this pleasant action involving his body (alas, Laurent was not to be a thumb-sucker for very long—by 2 or 3 months of age, Piaget had bandaged his son's hands to bring this pleasing activity to an end).

By the third substage of secondary circular reactions (4–8 months), infants derive pleasure from repeatedly performing an action, such as sucking or banging a toy. Now the repetitive actions are called **secondary circular reactions** because they involve something in the infant's external environment (that is, secondary to the self). In the fourth substage (8–12 months), called **coordination of secondary schemes**, infants combine (that is, coordinate) secondary actions to achieve simple goals such as when they *push* an obstacle out of the way in order to *grasp* a desired object.

Later, when they reach the substage of **tertiary circular reactions** (12–18 months), infants experiment in varied ways with toys, exploring them thoroughly and learning all about their properties. In this stage, a true sense of curiosity and interest in novel actions appears. Now it is interesting to the infant to repeat an action with variations, such as the infant who experiments with all the many ways that oatmeal can land on the floor and walls when launched from a highchair in different directions and at different velocities.

With the final substage, the beginning of thought (about 18 months), we see solid evidence of symbolic capacity, where one object can be used to represent another. For example, a cooking pot becomes a hat or a shoe becomes a telephone—simple forms of pretend play. It is also in this stage, according to Piaget, that infants can imitate models no longer present, because they can now create and later recall mental representations of what they have seen. Perhaps most importantly, with symbolic capacity, infants and toddlers understand that a word can be used to represent something else, such as an object, which leads to the language explosion associated with toddlerhood, which we will have more to say about in Chapter 10.

Checking Mastery

1. Why does the name "sensorimotor" stage seem to capture the essence of Piaget's first stage of development?
2. What must infants master or acquire in order to understand object permanence?

Making Connections

1. Suppose an infant fails to develop an understanding of object permanence. How would this deficit influence his behavior and knowledge of the world?
2. Trace the emergence of a behavior, such as opening a cabinet door to get to a box of animal crackers, from the beginning to the end of Piaget's sensorimotor period.

LEARNING OBJECTIVES:

• Describe the typical preschool-age child's pattern of thinking.

• Outline the characteristics of thought that enable (or inhibit) a child's ability to solve conservation tasks.

• Compare the elementary school child's thinking to that of a preschool child.

As with the period of infancy, our understanding of cognitive development during childhood has benefitted from Piaget's detailed observations of how children solve problems and what aspects of problems challenge their thinking. Here, we discuss how the largely symbolic thinking of preschoolers progresses to the logical thinking of elementary school-aged children.

Preschoolers: Symbolic Thinking

The *symbolic capacity* that emerged at the end of the sensorimotor stage runs wild in the preschool years and is the greatest cognitive strength of the preschooler. Imagine the possibilities: The child can now use words to refer to things, people, and events that are not physically present. Instead of being trapped in the immediate present, the child can refer to past and future. Pretend or fantasy play flourishes at this age: blocks can stand for telephones, cardboard boxes for trains. Some children—especially firstborns and only children who do not have ready access to play companions—even invent **imaginary companions** (Hoff, 2005a). Some of these imaginary companions are humans, and some are animals; they come with names like Zippy, Simply, Fake Rachel, and Sargeant Savage (Taylor et al., 2004). Their inventors know their companions are not real. Although parents may worry about such flights of fancy, they are normal. In fact, imaginative uses of

the symbolic capacity are associated with advanced cognitive and social development, as well as higher levels of creativity and imagery (Bouldin, 2006; Hoff, 2005b).

From his studies of children, Piaget concluded that the young child's mind is limited compared with that of an older child. Piaget called the preschool-age child's thinking *preoperational*, that is, not yet having (pre-) logical mental operations. Although less so than infants, preschoolers are highly influenced by their immediate perceptions. They often respond as if they have been captured by, or cannot go beyond, the most perceptually salient aspects of a situation. This focus on **perceptual salience**, or the most obvious features of an object or situation, means that preschoolers can be fooled by appearances. They have difficulty with tasks that require them to use logic to arrive at the right answer. Their "logic," if we can indeed refer to it as logic at all, is based on their intuitions. We can best illustrate this reliance on perceptions and lack of logical thought by considering Piaget's classic tests of conservation (also see **Exploration Box 7.1**).

Lack of Conservation

As we noted in Chapter 2, one of the many lessons about the physical world that children must master is the concept of **conservation**—the idea that certain properties of an object or substance do not change when its appearance is altered in

At the start of the conservation of liquid task, children confirm that the two glasses contain equal amounts of liquid.

As the child watches, liquid from one of the original containers is poured into a new container that is a different size.

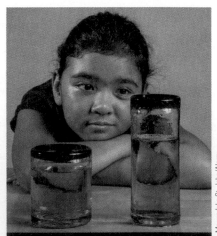

Now for the test: Does the new glass contain more, less, or the same amount of liquid as the glass next to it?

Exploration 7.1

Can There Really Be a Santa Claus?

© Creasource/Corbis

Many young children around the world believe in Santa Claus, St. Nicholas, the Tooth Fairy, or a similar magical being. Children whose parents endorse and promote Santa or another mythical being are more likely to believe than children whose parents do not (Harris et al., 2006; Woolley, Boerger, & Markman, 2004).

After all, children normally trust their parents and accept their statements about Santa at face value. Children also tend to accept supporting evidence of Santa (for example, there are presents under the tree) without questioning whether this evidence is conclusive proof of Santa's existence (Tullos & Woolley, 2009).

At what point, and why, do their beliefs in these figures begin to waiver? Research with 5- and 6-year-old children shows that they are already somewhat less confident about the existence of Santa and the Tooth Fairy than they are about two invisible but scientifically proven entities—germs and oxygen (Harris et al., 2006). According to Piaget's theory, children would begin to seriously question the existence of Santa Claus when they acquire concrete-operational thought. With their ability to reason logically, they may begin to ask questions such as, "How can Santa Claus get around to all those houses in one night?" "How can one sleigh hold all those gifts?" "Why haven't I ever seen a reindeer fly?" and "How does Santa get into houses without chimneys?"

What made sense to the preoperational child no longer adds up to the logical, concrete-operational thinker. With their focus on static endpoints, preschool-age children may not have a problem imagining presents for all the children in the world (or at least those on the "nice" list) sitting at the North Pole waiting to be delivered and then sitting under decorated trees Christmas morning. But once children understand transformations, they are confronted with the problem of how all those presents get from the North Pole to the individual houses in record time. The logical thinker notes that the gifts under the tree are wrapped in the same paper that Mom has in her closet. Some children question why gifts sport certain brand labels if Santa and his elves spent the year making gifts in their workshop. Thus, children begin using evidence to build a case against Santa (Tullos & Woolley, 2009).

As adults, we can resolve some of these inconsistencies for children to help maintain children's beliefs in Santa Claus. We can, for example, point out that Santa has many helpers and that reindeer native to the North Pole are unlike those ever seen in the wild or in a zoo. Some parents who want to perpetuate the Santa myth get tough and simply tell their children that non-believers will not get any presents. So the level of cognitive development and the surrounding culture play roles in whether or not children believe in Santa Claus and for how long.

---

some superficial way. Find a 4- or 5-year-old and try Piaget's conservation-of-liquid-quantity task. Pour equal amounts of water into two identical glasses, and get the child to agree that she has the same amount of water. Then, as the child watches, pour the water from one glass into a shorter, wider glass. Now ask whether the two containers—the tall, narrow glass and the shorter, broader one—have the same amount of water to drink or whether one has more water. Children younger than 6 or 7 will usually say that the taller glass has more water than the shorter one. They lack the understanding that the volume of liquid is conserved despite the change in the shape it takes in different containers.

How can young children be so easily fooled by their perceptions? According to Piaget, the preschooler is limited because they lack certain mental operations, outlined in ● **Table 7.3**. For starters, they are unable to engage in **decentration**—the ability to focus on two or more dimensions of a problem at once. Consider the conservation task: the child must focus on height and width simultaneously and recognize that the increased width of the short, broad container compensates for its lesser height. Preoperational thinkers engage in **centration**—the tendency to center attention on a single aspect of the problem. They focus on height alone and conclude that the taller glass has more liquid; or, alternatively, they focus on width and conclude that the short, wide glass has more. In this and other ways, preschoolers seem to have one-track minds.

A second contributor to success on conservation tasks is **reversibility**—the process of mentally undoing or reversing an action. Older children often display mastery of reversibility by suggesting that the water be poured back into its original container to prove that it is still the same amount. The young child shows irreversibility of thinking and may insist that the water would overflow the glass if it were poured back. Indeed, one young child tested by a college student shrieked, "Do it again!" as though pouring the water back without causing the glass to overflow were some unparalleled feat of magic.

● **Table 7.3** Comparison of Preoperational and Concrete-Operational Thinking

Preoperational Thinkers	Concrete-Operational Thinkers
Fail conservation tasks because they have:	Solve conservation tasks because they have:
• *Irreversible thought*—Cannot mentally undo an action.	• *Reversibility of thought*—Can mentally reverse or undo an action.
• *Centration*—Center on a single aspect of a problem rather than two or more dimensions at once.	• *Decentration*—Can focus on two or more dimensions of a problem at once.
• *Static thought*—Fail to understand transformations or processes of change from one state to another.	• *Transformational thought*—Can understand the process of change from one state to another.
Perceptual salience. Understanding is driven by how things look rather than derived from logical reasoning.	*Logical reasoning.* Children acquire a set of internal operations that can be applied to a variety of problems.
Transductive reasoning. Children combine unrelated facts, often leading them to draw faulty cause–effect conclusions simply because two events occur close together in time or space.	*Inductive reasoning.* Children draw cause–effect conclusions logically, based on factual information presented to them.
Egocentrism. Children have difficulty seeing things from other perspectives and assume that what is in their mind is also what others are thinking.	*Less egocentrism.* Children understand that other people may have thoughts different from their own.
Single classification. Children classify objects by a single dimension at one time.	*Multiple classification.* Children can classify objects by multiple dimensions and can grasp class inclusion.

© Cengage Learning

Finally, preoperational thinkers fail to demonstrate conservation because of limitations in **transformational thought**—the ability to conceptualize transformations, or processes of change from one state to another, as when water is poured from one glass to another. Preoperational thinkers engage in **static thought**, or thought that is fixed on end states rather than the changes that transform one state into another, as when the water is sitting in the two glasses, not being poured or manipulated.

In Piagetian theory, then, preoperational children do not understand the concept of conservation because they engage in centration, irreversible thought, and static thought. The older child, in the stage of concrete operations, has mastered decentration, reversibility, and transformational thought. The correct answer to the conservation task is a matter of logic to the older child; there is no longer a need to rely on perception as a guide. Another interpretation, though, has been offered by the "neuroconstructivists," who report that success on logic tasks such as conservation is supported by increased activity in parts of the frontal cortex associated with greater cognitive control that inhibits responding on the basis of perceptual salience (Houdé et al., 2010, 2011).

Egocentrism

Another characteristic of preschool-age children in Piaget's theory is their tendency to view the world solely from their own perspective and to have difficulty recognizing other points of view, what Piaget termed **egocentrism**. ■ **Figure 7.4** illustrates the task Piaget used to assess children's understanding of perspective. Piaget asked children to choose a drawing that shows what the display of three mountains would look like from a particular vantage point. Young children often chose the view that corresponded to their own position (Piaget & Inhelder, 1956). Similarly, young children often assume that if they know something, other people do, too (Ruffman & Olson, 1989). The same holds for desires: the 4-year-old who wants to go to McDonald's for dinner may say that Mom and Dad want to go to McDonald's, too, even if Mom does not like burgers or chicken nuggets and Dad would rather order Chinese takeout.

© Cengage Learning 2015

■ **Figure 7.4** Piaget's "Three Mountains" task to evaluate egocentrism. When the child is seated on the left and a doll is "seated" on the right, can the child correctly identify how the scene looks from the doll's perspective?

Difficulty with Classification

The limitations of relying on perceptions and intuitions are also apparent when young children are asked to classify objects and think about classification systems. When 2- or 3-year-old children are asked to sort objects on the basis of similarities, they make interesting designs or change their sorting criteria from moment to moment. Older preoperational children can group objects systematically on the basis of shape, color, function, or some other dimension of similarity (Inhelder & Piaget, 1964). However, even children ages 4–7 have trouble thinking about relations between classes and subclasses or between wholes and parts (Siegler & Svetina, 2006). For instance, given a set of furry animals, most of which are dogs but some of which are cats, preoperational children do fine when they are asked whether all the animals are furry and whether there are more dogs than cats. That is, they can conceive of the whole class (furry animals) or of the two subclasses (dogs and cats). However, when the question is, "Which group would have more—the dogs or the animals?" many 5-year-olds say, "Dogs." They cannot simultaneously relate the whole class to its parts; they lack the concept of **class inclusion**—the logical understanding that the parts are included within the whole. Notice that the child centers on the most striking perceptual feature of the problem—dogs are more numerous than cats—and is again fooled by appearances. Performance on class inclusion tasks increases steadily throughout childhood.

A Dynamic Approach

What if we examine children's performance through the lens of dynamic skill theory? Are preschool children really as bound to perceptions and as egocentric as Piaget believed? Many developmentalists believe that Piaget underestimated the competencies of preschool children by giving them very complex tasks to perform (Bjorklund, 1995). Consider a few examples of the strengths uncovered by researchers using simpler tasks.

Rochel Gelman (1972) simplified Piaget's conservation-of-number task and discovered that children as young as 3 years have some grasp of the concept that number remains the same even when items are rearranged spatially. She first got children to focus their attention on number by playing a game in which two plates, one holding two toy mice and one with three toy mice, were presented; and the plate with the larger number was always declared the winner. Then Gelman started introducing changes, sometimes adding or subtracting mice but sometimes just bunching

Are there more dogs or more animals in this picture? Children who understand class inclusion would correctly answer that there are more animals than dogs.

up or spreading out the mice. Young children were not fooled by spatial rearrangements; they seemed to understand that number remained the same. However, they showed their limitations when given larger sets of numbers they could not count.

Similarly, by reducing tasks to the bare essentials, several researchers have demonstrated that preschool children are not as egocentric as Piaget claimed. In one study, 3-year-olds were shown a card with a dog on one side and a cat on the other (Flavell et al., 1981). The card was held vertically between the child (who could see the dog) and the experimenter (who could see the cat). When children were asked what the experimenter could see, these 3-year-olds performed flawlessly.

Finally, preschool children seem to have a good deal more understanding of classification systems than Piaget believed. Sandra Waxman and Thomas Hatch (1992) asked 3- and 4-year-olds to teach a puppet all the different names they could think of for certain animals, plants, articles of clothing, and pieces of furniture. The goal was to see whether children knew terms associated with familiar classification hierarchies—for example, if they knew that a rose is a type of flower and is a member of the larger category of plants. Children performed well, largely because a clever method of prompting responses was used. Depending on which term or terms the children forgot to mention (rose, flower, or plant), they were asked about the rose: "Is this a dandelion?" "Is this a tree?" "Is this an animal?" Often, children came up with the correct terms in response (for example, "No, silly, [it's not an animal] it's a plant!"). Even though young children typically fail the tests of class inclusion that Piaget devised, then, they appear to have a fairly good grasp of familiar classification hierarchies.

Studies such as these are consistent with the dynamic skill framework and its notion of a developmental range of skills dependent on task demands and context. Simplified tasks that focus children's attention on relevant aspects of the task and do not place heavy demands on their memories or verbal skills tend to reveal that young children develop sound understandings of the physical world earlier than Piaget thought. These simplified tasks allow children to perform near the top of their developmental range. Yet Piaget was right in arguing that preschool children, although they have several sound intuitions about the world, are more perception-bound and egocentric thinkers than are elementary school children. Preschool children still depend on their perceptions to guide their thinking, and they fail to grasp the logic behind concepts such as conservation. They also have difficulty applying their emerging understanding to complex tasks that involve coordinating two or more dimensions.

Elementary-Aged Children: Logical Thinking

About the time children start elementary school, their minds undergo another transformation. According to Piaget, this transformation corresponded to the concrete-operational stage of development, extending from roughly 7 to 11 years of age. The concrete operations stage involves mastering the logical operations missing in the preoperational stage—becoming able to perform mental actions on objects, such as adding and subtracting Halloween candies, classifying dinosaurs, or arranging objects from largest to smallest. This allows school-age children to think effectively about the objects and events they experience in everyday life. For every limitation of the preoperational child, there is a corresponding strength of the concrete-operational child. These contrasts are summarized in Table 7.3

Conservation

Given the conservation-of-liquid task, the preoperational child centers on either the height or the width of the glasses, ignoring the other dimension. The concrete-operational child can decenter and juggle two dimensions at once. Reversibility allows the child to mentally reverse the pouring process and imagine the water in its original container. Transformational thought allows the child to better understand the process of change involved in pouring the water. Overall, armed with logical operations, the child now knows that there must be the same amount of water after it is poured into a different container; the child has logic, not just appearance, as a guide.

Seriation and Transitivity

To appreciate the nature and power of logical operations, consider the child's ability to think about relative size. A preoperational child given a set of sticks of different lengths and asked to arrange them from biggest to smallest is likely to struggle, awkwardly comparing one pair of sticks at a time. Concrete-operational children are capable of the logical operation of **seriation**, which enables them to arrange items mentally along a quantifiable dimension such as length or weight. Thus, they perform this seriating task quickly and correctly.

Concrete-operational thinkers also master the related concept of **transitivity**, which describes the necessary relations among elements in a series. If, for example, John is taller than Mark, and Mark is taller than Sam, who is taller—John or Sam? It follows logically that John must be taller than Sam, and the concrete operator grasps the transitivity of these size relationships. Lacking the concept of transitivity, the preoperational child will need to rely on perceptions to answer the question; she may insist that John and Sam stand next to each other to determine who is taller. Preoperational children probably have a better understanding of

such transitive relations than Piaget gave them credit for (Gelman, 1978; Trabasso, 1975), but they still have difficulty grasping the logical necessity of transitivity (Chapman & Lindenberger, 1988).

Other Advances

The school-age child overcomes much of the egocentrism of the preschool-age child, becoming increasingly better at recognizing other people's perspectives. Classification abilities improve as the child comes to grasp the concept of class inclusion and can bear in mind that subclasses (brown beads and white beads) are included in a whole class (wooden beads). Mastery of mathematical operations improves the child's ability to solve arithmetic problems and results in an interest in measuring and counting things precisely (and sometimes in fury if companions do not keep accurate score in games). Overall, school-age children appear more logical than preschoolers because they possess a powerful arsenal of "actions in the head."

But surely, if Piaget proposed a fourth stage of cognitive development, there must be some limitations to concrete operations. Indeed, there are. This mode of thought is applied to objects, situations, and events that are real or readily imaginable (thus the term *concrete operations*). As you will see in the next section, concrete operators have difficulty thinking about abstract ideas and unrealistic hypothetical propositions.

Checking Mastery

1. Name three ways that preoperational thought is limited relative to concrete-operational thought.
2. What is the defining feature of concrete-operational thought?

Making Connections

1. As a substitute teacher, you sometimes find yourself teaching young children who are mostly preoperational thinkers, while at other times you are teaching children who are concrete-operational thinkers. How would you adjust your lesson plan on stream ecology or global warming to best address these different levels of thought?

7.6 The Adolescent

LEARNING OBJECTIVES:

- Explain how adolescent thinking differs from the child's typical pattern of thinking.
- Describe the sorts of tasks that adolescents might be able to solve with their newly emerged reasoning skills.
- Assess Piaget's description of the adolescent as a formal-operational thinker who systematically considers hypothetical and abstract concepts.

Although tremendous advances in cognition occur from infancy to the end of childhood, other transformations of the mind are in store for the adolescent. If teenagers become introspective, question their parents' authority, dream of perfect worlds, and contemplate their futures, cognitive development may help explain why.

Emergence of Abstract Thought

Piaget set the beginning of the formal operations stage of cognitive development around age 11 or 12 and possibly later. If concrete operations are mental actions on objects (tangible things and events), formal operations are mental actions on ideas. Thus, the adolescent who acquires formal operations can mentally juggle and think logically about ideas, which cannot be seen, heard, tasted, smelled, or touched. In other words, formal-operational thought is more hypothetical and abstract than concrete-operational thought; it also involves adopting a more systematic and scientific approach to problem solving (Inhelder & Piaget, 1964). The video in **Exploring Development Box 7.1** compares how preadolescents and adolescents answer the question, "What if people had no thumbs?"

Hypothetical and Abstract Thinking

If you could have a third eye and put it anywhere on your body, where would you put it, and why? That question was posed to 9-year-old fourth-graders (concrete operators) and to 11- to 12-year-old sixth-graders (the age when the first signs of formal operations often appear). In their drawings, all the 9-year-olds placed the third eye on their foreheads between their existing eyes; many thought the exercise was stupid. The 11- and 12-year-olds were not as bound by the realities of eye location. They could invent ideas contrary to fact (for example, the idea of an

eye in a palm) and think logically about the implications of such ideas (■ **Figure 7.5**). Thus, concrete operators deal with realities, whereas formal operators can deal with possibilities, including those that contradict known reality.

Formal-operational thought is also more abstract than concrete-operational thought. The school-age child may define the justice system in terms of police and judges; the adolescent may define it more abstractly as a branch of government concerned with balancing the rights of different interests in society. Also, the school-age child may be able to think logically about concrete and factually true statements, as in this syllogism: If you drink poison, you will die. Fred drank poison. Therefore, Fred will die. The adolescent can do this but also engage in such if–then thinking about contrary-to-fact statements ("If you drink milk, you will die") or symbols (If P, then Q. P, therefore Q).

Scientific Reasoning

Formal operations also permit systematic and scientific thinking about problems. One of Piaget's famous tests for formal-operational thinking is the pendulum task (■ **Figure 7.6**). The child is given several weights that can be tied to a string to make a pendulum and is told that he may vary the length of the string, the amount of weight attached to it, and the height from which the weight is released to find out which of these factors, alone or in combination, determines how quickly the pendulum makes its arc. How would you go about solving this problem?

The concrete operator is likely to jump right in without much advanced planning, using a trial-and-error approach. That

Tanya's response   Ken's response   John's response

■ **Figure 7.5** Where would you put a third eye? Tanya (age 9) did not show much inventiveness in drawing her "third eye." But Ken (age 11) said of his eye on top of a tuft of hair, "I could revolve the eye to look in all directions." John (also 11) wanted a third eye in his palm: "I could see around corners and see what kind of cookie I'd get out of the cookie jar." Ken and John show early signs of formal-operational thought.

The child is shown how four factors can be varied.

| A pendulum is made by hanging a weight at the end of a string fixed at the other end. If released from A, it swings at a regular rate. | Length of string | Weight | Point of release | Amount of impetus |

Find out which of these factors makes the pendulum go faster or slower.

■ **Figure 7.6** The pendulum problem.

SOURCE: E. Labinowicz. *The Piaget primer*, p. 83. Copyright ©1980. Reprinted with permission.

is, the child may try a variety of things but fail to test different hypotheses systematically—for example, the hypothesis that the shorter the string is, the faster the pendulum swings, all other factors remaining constant. Concrete operators are therefore unlikely to solve the problem. They can draw proper conclusions from their observations—for example, from watching as someone else demonstrates what happens if a pendulum with a short string is compared with a pendulum with a long string.

What will the formal-operational individual do? In all likelihood, the teenager will first sit and think, planning an overall strategy for solving the problem. All the possible hypotheses should be generated; after all, the one overlooked may be the right one. Then it must be determined how each hypothesis can be tested. This is a matter of **hypothetical-deductive reasoning**, or reasoning from general ideas or rules to their specific implications. In the pendulum problem, it means starting with a hypothesis and tracing the specific implications of this idea in an if–then fashion: "If the length of the string matters, then I should see a difference when I compare a long string with a short string while holding other factors constant." The trick in hypothesis testing is to vary each factor (for example, the length of the string) while holding all others constant (the weight, the height from which the weight is dropped, and so on). (It is, by the way, the length of the string that matters; the shorter the string, the faster the swing.)

In sum, formal-operational thought involves being able to think systematically about hypothetical ideas and abstract concepts. It also involves mastering the hypothetical-deductive approach that scientists use—forming many hypotheses and systematically testing them through an experimental method. Before continuing, take a few minutes to assess your understanding of Piaget's stages of cognitive development with the questions in **Engagement Box 7.1**.

Progress toward Mastery of Formal Operations

Are 11- and 12-year-olds really capable of all these sophisticated mental activities? Anyone who has had dealings with this age group will know that the answer to this question is usually not. Piaget (1970) described the transition from concrete operations to formal operations as taking place gradually over years. Many

researchers have found it useful to distinguish between early and late formal operations. For example, 11- to 13-year-olds just entering the formal operations stage are able to consider simple hypothetical propositions such as the three-eye problem. But most are not yet able to devise an overall game plan for solving a problem or to systematically generate and test hypotheses. On a battery of Piagetian tasks designed to evaluate scientific reasoning, 11- to 14-year-old girls correctly solved only 20–30% of the problems (Martorano, 1977). By ages 16–17 this had improved, but only to 50–60% correct. Even with training, 11- to 12-year-olds continue to struggle to systematically coordinate multiple variables, although they may do fine on single-variable tasks (Kuhn, Pease, & Wirkala, 2009). Throughout adolescence, responses to scientific reasoning tasks reflect biases indicating that students more readily accept evidence consistent with their preexisting beliefs than evidence inconsistent with these beliefs (Klaczynski & Gordon, 1996a, 1996b; Kuhn, 1993).

Consider the findings from the Munich Longitudinal Study on the Ontogenesis of Individual Competencies (LOGIC) study (see Bullock, Sodian, & Koerber, 2009; Schneider & Bullock, 2009; Weinert & Schneider, 1999). LOGIC began in the 1980s with 200 school-aged children who were observed and tested on multiple dimensions over a 20-year period. One

Adolescents are more likely than children to benefit from some types of science instruction because formal-operational thought opens the door for reasoning about abstract and hypothetical material.

Engagement 7.1

How Well Do You Understand Piaget's Stages of Cognitive Development?

1. Baby Joel seems to be fascinated with the dog's tail: He repeatedly kicks at it with his foot, which makes the dog wag his big tail. Joel finds this highly amusing. This suggests that Joel is in which substage of the sensorimotor period?
   a. Primary circular reactions
   b. Secondary circular reactions
   c. Coordination of secondary schemes
   d. Tertiary circular reactions

2. Bill is playing with his infant daughter, Skylar, showing her a stuffed bear and then dropping it behind the sofa. Skylar seems interested in the toy when it is in front of her, but as soon as Bill drops it behind the sofa, she stops "playing" the game and looks at other things. This illustrates that Sklyar:
   a. Has not yet developed object permanence
   b. Is not really interested in the toy
   c. Is mentally trying to figure out where the toy has gone after it is dropped
   d. Is still operating with secondary circular reactions but has not yet learned to combine them to solve the problem

3. Which of the following statements is TRUE regarding Piaget's first stage of cognitive development?
   a. Piaget may have overestimated infants' abilities by allowing them multiple attempts to solve problems.
   b. Infants progress through the substages in an individualized order that does not permit researchers to make any generalizations about developments of this stage.
   c. Piaget underestimated infants' abilities because he placed many task demands on them in assessing their knowledge.
   d. Piaget was right on the mark with his description of the ages when infants typically acquire symbolic logic.

4. Jeremy used to just bang his shoe on the coffee table, but now he has started holding it up to his ear and "talking" to it as if he is using a telephone. Jeremy has acquired:
   a. Decentration
   b. Transformational thought
   c. Symbolic capacity
   d. Object permanence

5. Mira emphatically tells her older brother that "there *is* a Santa Claus because I see lots of presents under the tree!" Mira's thinking reflects:
   a. The "A-not-B error"
   b. Conservation

   c. Transformational thought
   d. The influence of perceptual salience

6. When Mom presents the kids with some cookies, big sister Kim immediately grabs for the unbroken cookie, saying she doesn't want the broken one. Little sister Sal happily takes the cookie broken in half, saying, "Ha-ha! I got more than you!" Sal seems to lack an understanding of:
   a. Egocentrism
   b. Conservation
   c. Class inclusion
   d. Object permanence

7. Ramon understands that if A is bigger than B, and B is bigger than C, then A must also be bigger than C. This shows that he has mastered:
   a. Transitivity
   b. Conservation
   c. Seriation tasks
   d. Reversibility of thought

8. Kira is furious that her father won't let her go out with a friend on a school night. She screams, "You have no idea what I'm feeling! You just want me to be miserable." Kira's response indicates that she:
   a. Has not yet acquired conservation of thought
   b. Is spoiled or has unreasonable parents
   c. Shows centration of thought
   d. Shows adolescent egocentrism

9. An important distinction between concrete-operational thought and preoperational thought is:
   a. The acquisition of logical reasoning skills in the concrete stage
   b. The acquisition of symbolic logic in the concrete stage
   c. The acquisition of hypothetical thinking in the concrete stage
   d. The use of deductive reasoning in the concrete stage

10. The defining difference between concrete-operational thought and formal-operational thought is:
    a. The use of logical reasoning
    b. The ability to reason about abstract and hypothetical problems
    c. The ability to imagine performing before an audience
    d. The ability to use relativistic thinking

Answers: 1. b 2. a 3. c 4. c 5. d 6. b 7. a 8. d 9. a 10. b

---

of the areas of study was scientific reasoning, and in particular, whether participants understood a crucial component of scientific reasoning—control of variables. Did they understand that scientific testing requires identifying and holding constant all relevant variables while systematically testing the effects of varying the variable of interest? The LOGIC participants were given a group of experiments to evaluate; each experiment contained a design error, such as not keeping all variables but one constant or not having a comparison group for an intervention study. In addition to evaluating experimental designs, participants were also tested to determine if they could produce their own experiments.

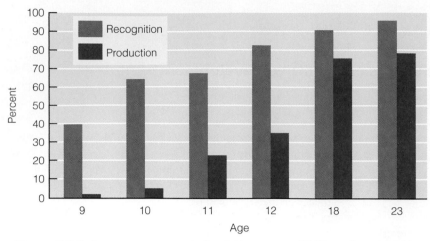

■ **Figure 7.7** Performance on control of variables strategy (CVS) use for recognition and production tasks (percent correct).

Source: From Bullock, M., Sodian, B., & Koerber, S. (2009). Doing experiments and understanding science: Development of scientific reasoning from childhood to adulthood. In Schneider, W. & Bullock, M. (Eds.) (2009). *Human development from early childhood to early adulthood: Findings from a 20 year longitudinal study*, pp. 173–197. Reprinted by permission of Taylor & Francis Group.

As ■ **Figure 7.7** shows, most participants, even those as young as 10, showed an understanding of this important principle of scientific thinking. However, there was a marked difference between their ability to recognize good scientific reasoning and their ability to produce it. For example, among 12-year-olds, more than 80% could recognize good and bad examples of experiments, but only 35% could create a good experiment themselves. By age 18, though, the ability to create a good experiment was catching up to the ability to recognize a good experiment (91% versus 85%). Thus, adolescents show an awareness of scientific reasoning ("I know it when I see it"), but they may not be able to produce logical scientific reasoning skills until they are older.

Piaget claimed that the perceptual reasoning of children reasoning is *replaced* by scientific reasoning as children age, but it turns out that the two forms of reasoning—intuitive and scientific—*coexist* in older thinkers (Klaczynski, 2000, 2001, 2009). Being able to shift between intuitive and scientific reasoning provides flexibility in problem-solving situations as long as the thinker can effectively select the appropriate strategy. However, like children (and adults), adolescents often seem to adopt an intuitive strategy, leading them to conclusions inconsistent with scientific judgment (Amsel et al., 2008; Klaczynski, 2001). With age, however, adolescents are increasingly able to **decontextualize**, or separate prior knowledge and beliefs from the demands of the task at hand (Kuhn & Franklin, 2006; Stanovich & West, 1997). For example, someone who believes that males are better at math than females may find it difficult to accept new evidence that girls attain higher classroom math grades than boys if intuitions based on their prior experiences do not allow them to scientifically process the new information. Decontextualizing increases the likelihood of using reasoning to analyze a problem logically rather than relying on intuition or faulty existing knowledge.

There is some evidence that recent cohorts of teens (ages 13–15) are better able than earlier cohorts to solve formal-operational tasks. For example, 66% of teens tested in 1996 showed formal-operational thought on a probability test, whereas 49% of teens tested in 1967 showed such skills (Flieller, 1999). Why might formal-operational skills improve over time? Changes in

school curricula are the likely explanation. Notably, science curricula were revised in the 1960s and have increasingly incorporated more hands-on discovery learning activities (Bybee, 1995). The achievement of formal-operational thinking depends on opportunities to learn scientific reasoning, as through exposure to math and science education (Babai & Levit-Dori, 2009; Karpov, 2005). The more hands-on the learning, the greater the benefit to performance on hands-on formal-operational tasks.

Several cross-cultural studies have tried to clarify the role of educational experience in cognitive development by studying naturally occurring groups that differ in whether or not adults have had structured schooling. The results of such research show that both age and education level influence performance on formal-operational tasks. For instance, adults with some formal education are able to solve logic problems, whereas adults in the same culture with no formal education are not able to do so (Luria, 1974/1976). Similarly, college and university students outperform adults with no advanced education in solving certain types of formal logic problems, and adults without advanced education in turn outperform adolescents who have not yet acquired as much education (Mwamwenda, 1999; Mwamwenda & Mwamwenda, 1989).

Progress toward the mastery of formal operations is slow, at least as measured by Piaget's scientific tasks. These findings have major implications for secondary-school teachers, who are often trying to teach abstract material to students with a range of thinking patterns. Teachers may need to give concrete thinkers extra assistance by using specific examples and demonstrations to help clarify general principles.

Implications of Formal Thought

Formal-operational thought contributes to other changes in adolescence—some good, some not so good. First, the good news: As you will see in upcoming chapters, formal-operational thought may prepare the individual to gain a sense of identity, think in more complex ways about moral issues, and understand other people better. Advances in cognitive development help lay the groundwork for advances in many other areas of development, including the appreciation of humor.

Now, the bad news: Hypothetical thinking may also be related to some of the more painful aspects of the adolescent experience. Children tend to accept the world as it is and to heed the words of authority figures. The adolescent armed with hypothetical and scientific reasoning abilities can think more independently, imagine alternatives to present realities, and raise questions about everything from why parents set certain rules to why there is injustice in the world. Questioning can lead to confusion and sometimes to rebellion against ideas that do not seem logical enough. Some adolescents become idealists, inventing perfect worlds and envisioning logical solutions to problems they detect in the imperfect world around them, sometimes losing sight of practical considerations and real barriers to social change. Just as infants flaunt the new schemes they develop, adolescents may go overboard

A teenage boy may feel that everyone is as preoccupied with his appearance as he is, a form of adolescent egocentrism known as the imaginary audience phenomenon.

with their new cognitive skills, irritate their parents, and become frustrated when the world does not respond to their flawless logic.

Some years ago, David Elkind (1967) proposed that formal-operational thought also leads to **adolescent egocentrism**—difficulty differentiating one's own thoughts and feelings from those of other people. The young child's egocentrism is rooted in ignorance that different people have different perspectives, but the adolescent's reflects an enhanced ability to reflect about one's own and others' thoughts. Elkind identified two types of adolescent egocentrism: the imaginary audience and the personal fable.

The **imaginary audience** phenomenon involves confusing your own thoughts with those of a hypothesized audience for your behavior. Thus, the teenage girl who ends up with pizza sauce on the front of her shirt at a party may feel extremely self-conscious: "They're all thinking what a slob I am! I wish I could crawl into a hole." She assumes that everyone in the room is as preoccupied with the blunder as she is. Or a teenage boy may spend hours in front of the mirror getting ready for a date, then may be so concerned with how he imagines his date is reacting to him that he hardly notices her: "Why did I say that? She looks bored. Did she notice my pimple?" (She, of course, is equally preoccupied with how she is playing to her audience. No wonder teenagers are often awkward and painfully aware of their every slip on first dates.)

The second form of adolescent egocentrism is the **personal fable**—a tendency to think that you and your thoughts and feelings are unique (Elkind, 1967). If the imaginary audience is a product of the inability to differentiate between self and other, the personal fable is a product of differentiating too much. Thus, the adolescent in love for the first time imagines that no one in the history of the human race has ever felt such heights of emotion. When the relationship breaks up, no one—least of all a parent—could possibly understand the crushing agony. The personal fable may also lead adolescents to feel that rules that apply to others do not apply to them. Thus, they will not be hurt if they speed down the highway without wearing a seat belt or drive under the influence of alcohol. And they will not become pregnant if they engage in sex without contraception, so they do not need to bother with contraception. As it turns out, high scores on measures of adolescent egocentrism are associated with behaving in risky ways (Greene et al., 1996; Holmbeck et al., 1994).

Elkind hypothesized that the imaginary audience and personal fable phenomena should increase when formal operations are first being acquired and then decrease as adolescents get older, gain fuller control of formal operations, and assume adult roles that require fuller consideration of others' perspectives. Indeed, both the self-consciousness associated with the imaginary audience and the sense of specialness associated with the personal fable are most evident in early adolescence and decline by late high school (Elkind & Bowen, 1979; Enright, Lapsley, & Shukla, 1979). Adolescent egocentrism may persist, however, when adolescents have insecure relationships with their parents—when they do not feel that their parents are supportive of them or reliable sources of security (see Chapter 14). Such parent–adolescent relationships may make teens self-conscious and may make them appear to lack self-confidence even as older adolescents (Ryan & Kuczkowski, 1994).

Contrary to what Piaget and Elkind hypothesized, however, researchers have been unable to link the onset of the formal operations stage to the rise of adolescent egocentrism (Gray & Hudson, 1984; O'Connor & Nikolic, 1990). It seems that adolescent egocentrism may arise when adolescents acquire advanced social perspective–taking abilities and contemplate how other people might perceive them and react to their behavior (Lapsley et al., 1986; Vartanian & Powlishta, 1996).

Furthermore, research by Joanna Bell and Rachel Bromnick (2003) suggests that adolescents are preoccupied with how they present themselves in public not because of an imaginary audience but because of a *real audience*. That is, research indicates that adolescents are aware that there are real consequences to how they present themselves. Their popularity and peer approval, as well as their self-confidence and self-esteem, are often influenced by how others (the real audience) perceive them. Adults, too, are aware that their actions and appearance are often judged by others, but although these adult concerns are usually assumed to be realistic, similar concerns by adolescents are sometimes viewed, perhaps unfairly, as trivial (Bell & Bromnick, 2003).

Checking Mastery

1. What change in thinking marks the shift from concrete to formal-operational thinking?
2. What is the hypothetical-deductive approach to problem solving?

Making Connections

1. Consider one or more assignments or tests that you recently completed for one (or more) of your courses. Conduct an analysis to determine whether your responses reflect primarily a concrete or a formal level of thinking. If they were primarily concrete, was this appropriate to the task demands? What distinguished the assignments that elicited concrete-operational answers from those that elicited formal-operational answers?
2. Design an educational plan or program that you think would help foster formal-operational thought in students who have not yet mastered it.

LEARNING OBJECTIVES:

- Outline the characteristic features of adult cognition.
- Discuss ways that adult thought is the most advanced level of thinking and ways that adult thought is limited.
- Evaluate whether a stage beyond Piaget's formal operations is warranted and outline what this stage might look like.
- Describe changes to cognitive skills in later adulthood.

Do adults think differently than adolescents do? Does cognition change over the adult years? Until fairly recently, developmentalists have not asked such questions. Piaget indicated that the highest stage of cognitive development, formal operations, was fully mastered by most people between age 15 and age 18. Why bother studying cognitive development in adulthood? As it turns out, it has been worth the effort. Research has revealed limitations in adult performance that must be explained, and it suggests that at least some adults progress beyond formal operations to more advanced forms of thought (Jacobs & Klaczynski, 2002).

Limitations in Adult Cognitive Performance

If many high school students are shaky in their command of formal operations, do most of them gain fuller mastery after the high school years? Gains are indeed made between adolescence and adulthood (Blackburn & Papalia, 1992). However, only about half of all college students show firm and consistent mastery of formal operations on Piaget's scientific reasoning tasks (Neimark, 1975). Similarly, sizable percentages of American adults do not solve scientific problems at the formal level, and there are some societies in which no adults solve formal-operational problems (Neimark, 1975).

Why do more adults not do well on Piagetian tasks? An average level of performance on standardized intelligence tests seems to be necessary for a person to achieve formal-operational thought (Inhelder, 1966). What seems more important than basic intelligence, however, is formal education (Neimark, 1979). In cultures in which virtually no one solves Piaget's problems, people do not receive advanced schooling. If achieving formal-operational thought requires education or specific experiences, Piaget's theory may be culturally biased, and his stages may not be as universal as he believed.

But neither lack of intelligence nor lack of formal education is a problem for most college students. Instead, they have difficulty with tests of formal operations when they lack expertise in a domain of knowledge. Piaget (1972) suggested that adults are likely to use formal operations in a field of expertise but to use concrete operations in less familiar areas. This is

precisely what seems to happen. For example, Richard De Lisi and Joanne Staudt (1980) gave three kinds of formal-operational tasks—the pendulum problem, a political problem, and a literary criticism problem—to college students majoring in physics, political science, and English. As ■ **Figure 7.8** illustrates, each group of students did well on the problem relevant to that group's field of expertise. On problems outside their fields, however, about half the students failed. Consistent with this, other research shows that task relevancy affects performance on reasoning tasks (Sebby & Papini, 1994). Possibly, then, many adolescents and adults fail to use formal reasoning on Piaget's scientific problems simply because these problems are unfamiliar to them and they lack relevant expertise.

As noted earlier, Fischer maintains that each person has an optimal level of cognitive performance that will show itself in familiar and well-trained content domains (Fischer, 1980; Fischer, Kenny, & Pipp, 1990). However performance is likely to be highly inconsistent across content areas unless the person has had a chance to build knowledge and skills in all these domains.

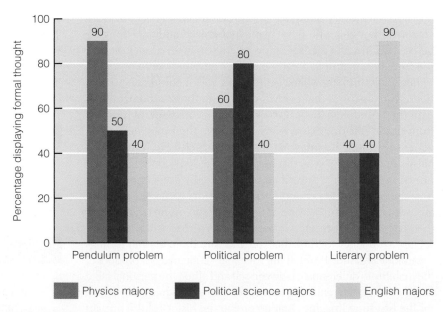

■ **Figure 7.8** Expertise and formal operations. College students show the greatest command of formal-operational thought in the subject area most related to their major.

Source: From De Lisi, R. Staudt, J. Individual differences in college students' performance on formal operations task, *Journal of Applied Developmental Psychology*, 1, pp. 206–208. Copyright © 1980 by permission of Elsevier.

More often, adults may use and strengthen formal modes of thinking only in their areas of expertise. By adopting a contextual perspective on cognitive development, you can appreciate that the individual's experience and the nature of the tasks she is asked to perform influence cognitive performance across the life span (Salthouse, 1990).

Growth beyond Formal Operations?

While some researchers have been asking why adults sometimes perform so poorly on cognitive tasks, others have been asking why they sometimes perform so well. Take Piaget. Was his ability to generate a complex theory of development no more than the application of formal-operational thought? This seems unlikely and, indeed, Fernando Vidal (1994) uses Piaget's own writings as a teen and young man to show how his thinking shifted over time from largely formal operational to something beyond formal operations. Others have argued that formal operations involves applying logic to a *closed* set of ideas and not to the *open* sets of ideas that characterize most adult issues (Broughton, 1984; Ricco, 1990). To illustrate this, consider again the pendulum problem. A defined or closed set of variables is associated with this problem; solving the problem is possible by systematically applying logic to this closed set of variables. You do not need to go beyond the problem set. But how do adults make decisions about complex dilemmas and problems that have no well-defined set of variables or that have variables that are constantly changing rather than static?

Several intriguing ideas have been proposed about stages of cognitive development that may lie beyond formal operations—that is, about **postformal thought**, ways of thinking that are more complex than those of the formal-operational stage (see Commons & Richards, 2003; Commons & Ross, 2008; Gurba, 2005). How might thought be qualitatively different in adulthood than it is in adolescence? Several theorists have taken a shot at exploring postformal thinking, and here we consider two of the possibilities: relativistic thinking and dialectical thinking.

As noted earlier, adolescents who have attained formal operations sometimes get carried away with their new powers of logical thinking. They insist that there is a logically correct answer for every question—that if you simply apply logic, you will arrive at the right answer, at some absolute truth. In contrast, adults often think flexibly and recognize that there is not a single right or wrong answer; there are shades of gray to many problems and flexible or creative thinking may be required to successfully navigate many of the complex issues of the adult world. Thus, adults are more likely to engage in **relativistic thinking**, or understanding that knowledge depends on its context and the subjective perspective of the knower (Marchand, 2002; Sinnott, 1984, 1996). Whereas an absolutist assumes that truth lies in the nature of reality and that there is only one truth, a relativist assumes that his starting assumptions influence the "truth" discovered and that a problem can be viewed in multiple ways.

Consider this logic problem: "A grows 1 cm per month. B grows 2 cm per month. Who is taller?" (Yan & Arlin, 1995, p. 230). The absolutist might say, "B," based on the information given, but the relativist would be more likely to say, "It depends." It depends on how tall A and B were to begin with and on how much time passes before their heights are measured. The

relativistic thinker will recognize that the problem is ill defined and that further information is needed, and he will be able to think flexibly about what the answer would be if he made certain assumptions rather than others.

Or consider this problem, given to preadolescents, adolescents, and adults by Gisela Labouvie-Vief and her colleagues (1983, p. 5):

> John is known to be a heavy drinker, especially when he goes to parties. Mary, John's wife, warns him that if he gets drunk one more time she will leave him and take the children. Tonight John is out late at an office party. John comes home drunk.

Does Mary leave John? Most preadolescents and many adolescents quickly and confidently said, "Yes." They did not question the assumption that Mary would stand by her word; they simply applied logic to the information they were given. Adults were more likely to realize that different starting assumptions were possible and that the answer depended on which assumptions were chosen. One woman, for example, noted that if Mary had stayed with John for years, she would be unlikely to leave him now. This same woman said, "There was no right or wrong answer. You could get logically to both answers" (p. 12). Postformal thinkers seem able to devise more than one logical solution to a problem (Sinnott, 1996).

In a fascinating study of cognitive growth over the college years, William Perry (1970) found that beginning college students often assumed that there were absolute, objective truths to be found by consulting their textbooks or their professors. They looked to what they believed were authoritative sources for *the* answer to a question, as if all problems have a single, correct answer. As their college careers progressed, they often became frustrated in their search for absolute truths. They saw that many questions seemed to have several answers, depending on the perspective of the respondent. Taking the extremely relativistic view that any opinion was as good as any other, several of these students said they were not sure how they could ever decide what to believe. Eventually, many understood that some opinions can be better supported than others; they were then able to commit themselves to specific positions, fully aware that they were choosing among relative perspectives.

Between adolescence and adulthood, then, many people start as absolutists, become relativists, and finally make commitments to positions despite their more sophisticated awareness of the nature and limits of knowledge (Sinnott, 1996). Not surprisingly, students at the absolute level of thinking use fewer thinking styles; they stick mainly with traditional or conventional modes of thinking (Zhang, 2002). Students who are relativistic thinkers use a greater variety of thinking styles, including ones that promote creativity and greater cognitive complexity (see Wu & Chiou, 2008). Some refer to this as "thinking outside the box," or thinking unconventionally. Try the 9-dot problem in ■ **Figure 7.9** to see if you can think outside the box. (You can find the answer online.)

Another possibility for advanced thought beyond formal operations is **dialectical thinking**, or detecting paradoxes and inconsistencies among ideas and trying to reconcile them (Basseches, 1984, 2005; Kramer, 1989; Riegel, 1973). For example, you engage in dialectical thinking when you recognize that the problem facing

■ **Figure 7.9** Your task is to connect all nine dots using four straight lines or less, without lifting your pen or pencil from the paper. Hint: To be successful, you need to think outside the box! For the solution, try typing "Solution for Nine Dot Problem" into an Internet search engine.

© Cengage Learning

you is multifaceted and will be difficult to solve; you "wrestle" with it mentally, considering the various possibilities and trying to reconcile the pieces that do not immediately make sense to you. You may solicit input from several trusted friends and then consider the pros and cons of each possible solution. Finally, you make a decision on the best way to address the problem, knowing that it is not necessarily a perfect solution, but it is the best option under the current conditions. By engaging in dialectical thinking, advanced thinkers repeatedly challenge and change their understanding of what constitutes "truth." For example, they may arrive at one conclusion, then think of an idea that contradicts their conclusion, and then synthesize the two ideas into a more complete understanding. They realize that the search for truth is an ongoing process and can take them down many different paths.

In an attempt to integrate various postformal ideas, Helena Marchand (2002) suggests these common features:

1. Understanding that knowledge is relative, not absolute; there are far more shades of gray than there are clear dichotomies of knowledge.
2. Accepting that the world (physical and mental) is filled with contradictions: inconsistent information can exist side by side.
3. Attempting to integrate the contradictions into some larger understanding.

Environments that expose us to a wider range of ideas, roles, and experiences seem to foster this higher level of thinking. College students who have greater diversity among their friends tend to exhibit more of these postformal characteristics than those whose friends are very similar (Galupo, Cartwright, & Savage, 2009). Among high school and college students, females report greater gender role conflict than males and also a more relativistic perspective on relationships (Kramer & Melchior, 1990).

It is not yet clear whether relativistic, dialectical, or other forms of advanced thinking might qualify as a new, postformal stage of cognitive development. Marchand (2002) concludes that a fifth stage of postformal thought may not be warranted. Adult thought may indeed be different or more advanced than the formal-operational thought of adolescence, though. Much

research confirms that cognitive growth does not end in adolescence. Yet growth during adulthood may not reflect a new Piagetian stage—a qualitatively different, structural change in thinking that is universal and irreversible (Lerner, 2006).

Aging and Cognitive Skills

What becomes of cognitive capacities in later adulthood? Some mental abilities decline as the average person ages, and it appears that older adults often have trouble solving Piagetian tests of formal-operational thinking (Blackburn & Papalia, 1992). Indeed, elderly adults sometimes perform poorly relative to young and middle-aged adults even on concrete-operational tasks assessing conservation and classification skills.

This does not mean that elderly adults regress to immature modes of thought. For one thing, these studies have involved cross-sectional comparisons of different age groups. The poorer performance of older groups does not necessarily mean that cognitive abilities are lost as people age. It could be caused by a cohort effect, because the average older adult today has had less formal schooling than the average younger adult has had. Older adults attending college tend to perform as well as younger college students on tests of formal operations (Blackburn, 1984; Hooper, Hooper, & Colbert, 1985). Moreover, brief training can quickly improve the performance of older adults long out of school, which suggests that the necessary cognitive abilities are there but merely need to be reactivated (Blackburn & Papalia, 1992).

Questions have also been raised about the relevance of the skills assessed in Piagetian tasks to the lives of older adults (Labouvie-Vief, 1985). Not only are these problems unfamiliar to many older adults, but they also resemble the intellectual challenges that children confront in school, not those that most adults encounter in everyday contexts. Thus, older people may not be motivated to solve them. Also, older adults may rely on modes of cognition that have proved useful to them in daily life but that make them look cognitively deficient in the laboratory (Salthouse, 1990).

Consider this example: Kathy Pearce and Nancy Denney (1984) found that elderly adults, like young children but unlike other age groups, often group two objects on the basis of some functional relationship between them (for example, putting a pipe and matches together because matches are used to light pipes) rather than on the basis of similarity (for example, putting a pipe and a cigar together because they are both ways of smoking tobacco). In school and in some job situations, Pearce and Denney suggest, people are asked to group objects on the basis of similarity, but in everyday life it may make more sense to associate objects commonly used together.

Such findings suggest that what appear to be deficits in older people may merely be differences in style. Similar stylistic differences in classification skills have been observed cross-culturally and can, if researchers are not careful, lead to the incorrect conclusion that uneducated adults from non-Western cultures lack basic cognitive skills. A case in point: Kpelle adults in Africa, when asked to sort foods, clothing, tools, and cooking utensils into groups, sorted them into pairs based on functional relationships. "When an exasperated experimenter finally asked, 'How would a fool do it?' he was given sorts of the type that were initially expected—four neat piles with foods in one, tools in another, and so on" (Glick, 1975, p. 636).

So today's older adults appear not to perform concrete-operational and formal-operational tasks as well as their younger contemporaries do. Planners of adult education for senior citizens might bear in mind that some (although by no means all) of their students may benefit from more concrete forms of instruction. However, these differences may be related to factors other than age, such as education and motivation; an age-related decline in operational abilities has not been firmly established. Most importantly, older adults who perform poorly on unfamiliar problems in laboratory situations often perform far more capably on the sorts of problems that they encounter in everyday contexts (Cornelius & Caspi, 1987; Salthouse, 1990). This is precisely the message from Fischer's skill theory: abilities vary with context. By providing older adults with a supportive context, we can optimize their level of performance.

Chapter Summary

7.1 Piaget's Constructivist Approach

- Jean Piaget developed a theory of how children come to know their world by constructing their own schemes or cognitive structures through active exploration.
- Studying children using the clinical method, a flexible question-and-answer technique, Piaget formulated four stages of cognitive development in which children construct increasingly complex schemes through an interaction of maturation and experience.
- Intelligence is a basic life function that allows organisms (including humans) to adapt to the demands of their environment.
- Children adapt to the world through the processes of organization and adaptation (assimilating new experiences to existing understandings and accommodating existing understandings to new experiences).
- Piaget's theory has stimulated much research over the years, which has added considerably to our understanding of cognitive development. Piaget showed us that infants are active, not passive, in their own development. He argued that children think differently during different phases of their development, as reflected in his four qualitatively different stages.
- Piaget has been criticized for underestimating the capacities of infants and young children, not considering factors besides competence that influence performance, failing to demonstrate that his stages have coherence, offering vague explanations of development, and underestimating the role of language and social interaction in cognitive development.
- Modern constructivist theories such as neuroconstructivism propose that observed differences in cognitive skills result from experience-induced changes in the underlying neural structures supporting these skills.

7.2 Vygotsky's Sociocultural Perspective

- Lev Vygotsky's sociocultural perspective emphasizes cultural and social influences on cognitive development more than Piaget's theory does.
- Through guided participation in culturally important activities, children learn problem-solving techniques from knowledgeable partners sensitive to their zone of proximal development.
- Language is the most important tool that adults use to pass culturally valued thinking and problem solving to their children. Language shapes their thought and moves from social speech to private speech and later to inner speech.

7.3 Fischer's Dynamic Skill Framework

- Development results from changes in skill levels. Skills reflect what a person can do on a particular task in a specific context.
- People operate within a developmental range, with higher levels of performance demonstrated within a supportive context and after more experience with a task.

7.4 The Infant

- Infants progress through six substages of the sensorimotor period by perceiving and acting on the world; they progress from using their reflexes to adapt to their environment to using symbolic or representational thought to solve problems in their heads.
- Major accomplishments of the sensorimotor stage include the development of object permanence, or the realization that objects continue to exist even when they are not directly experienced, and the symbolic capacity, or the ability to allow one thing to represent something else. The emergence of the symbolic capacity paves the way for language and pretend play.

7.5 The Child

- Preschool-age children are in Piaget's preoperational stage and do not yet reason logically; instead they rely on perceptually salient features of a task or object. Their prelogical set of cognitive structures leads them to have trouble with conservation and classification tasks. In particular, preoperational children lack the abilities to decenter, reverse thought, and understand transformations. In addition, they tend to be egocentric—viewing the world from their own perspective and not recognizing others' points of views.
- School-age children are in Piaget's concrete-operational stage and can reason logically about concrete information, which allows them to solve conservation and classification tasks. Concrete-operational children have acquired the abilities of decentration, reversibility of thought, and transformational thought. They can think about relations, grasping seriation and transitivity, and they understand the concept of class inclusion.

7.6 The Adolescent

- Adolescents may advance to Piaget's last stage of cognitive development—formal-operational thought, in which they can think about abstract concepts and apply their logical reasoning to hypothetical problems. Formal-operational thinkers can simultaneously consider multiple task components.
- Formal-operational thought may give rise to special forms of egocentrism, namely, the imaginary audience and personal fable.

7.7 The Adult

- Many adults seem to function at the concrete-operational level, rather than at Piaget's highest level of formal-operational thought. Formal-operational thought appears to be highly dependent on formal education. It is also influenced by culture and area of expertise.
- Some adults may acquire advanced levels of thought not considered by Piaget, such as relativistic thinking, or understanding that knowledge is dependent on the knower's subjective perspective, and dialectical thinking, or detecting and reconciling contradictory ideas.

Checking Mastery Answers

For answers to Checking Mastery questions, please see Appendix B.

Key Terms

cognition **200**
clinical method **200**
scheme (or schema; plural: schemes or schemata) **201**
organization **201**
adaptation **201**
assimilation **201**
accommodation **201**
equilibration **201**
neuroconstructivism theory **204**
reaction time **204**
zone of proximal development **206**
guided participation **206**
scaffolding **206**
private speech **207**

dynamic **210**
skill **210**
developmental range **210**
object permanence **211**
A-not-B error **212**
symbolic capacity **213**
primary circular reactions **213**
secondary circular reactions **213**
coordination of secondary schemes **213**
tertiary circular reactions **213**
imaginary companions **214**
perceptual salience **214**
conservation **214**
decentration **215**
centration **215**

reversibility **215**
transformational thought **216**
static thought **216**
egocentrism **216**
class inclusion **217**
seriation **218**
transitivity **218**
hypothetical-deductive reasoning **220**
decontextualize **223**
adolescent egocentrism **223**
imaginary audience **223**
personal fable **223**
postformal thought **225**
relativistic thinking **225**
dialectical thinking **225**

CENGAGE brain.com Get quizzes, flashcards, videos, and more at **www.cengagebrain.com**.

8 Memory and Information Processing

Think about everything you have learned and experienced up to this point in your life. Like most people, you probably have a rich and varied set of memories relating to your family, friends, school, work, and life. You rely on these memories every day: They provide you with a solid grounding in who you are, where you have been, and where you hope to go. Now imagine that every one of these memories is gone. It's hard to imagine, but this is what happened to Su Meck at the age of 22. One minute, she was making macaroni and cheese in the kitchen and lifting her young son up in the air, and in the next minute, the ceiling fan had dislodged and struck Su in the head (de Vise, 2011). She awoke a week later with no memories of her past. None. She did not know herself, let alone her husband and two young children. She had to start over. According to her husband, "She was Su 2.0. She had rebooted.... It was literally like she had died. Her personality was gone" (McGrory, 2013).

Su Meck started over at the age of 22 when a freak accident wiped out every memory up to that point. Su 2.0, as her husband dubbed her, completed a college degree 23 years after her brain "rebooted."

Over the next 25 years, Su would need to relearn everything and begin to form new memories. As her children were learning new things in school, Su would often be learning the same things alongside them. She eventually went to college (for the second time, as she had been in college prior to her freak accident) and earned a degree in music. To date, she has not recovered any memories from the first 22 years of her life.

This is an astonishing case of true **retrograde amnesia**, or loss of memory for information and events occurring prior to the incident that caused the amnesia. Such cases illustrate just how vital memory is to who we are and what we do; it allows us to learn from the past, function in the present, and plan for the future. It would be nearly impossible to overemphasize the importance of our memory system.

In this chapter, we consider how **memory**, our ability to store and later retrieve information about past events, develops and changes over the life span. We begin our journey down memory lane by examining the components of memory and the models that attempt to organize some of the findings that have emerged in the field of memory.

8.1 Conceptualizing Memory

LEARNING OBJECTIVES:

- Explain the workings of the memory system, from first exposure to information or an event to eventual retrieval of this information from memory.
- List and define the different forms of memory.
- Describe the neural underpinnings of memory.
- Discuss how stored information is processed to solve problems.

Modern models of memory have their origins in a 1958 book by Donald Broadbent, *Perception and Communication*, which speculated on how humans process information. At about this same time, the modern computer, with its capacity to systematically convert input to output, was emerging and garnering much interest. The computer seemed to provide a good analogy to the human mind, and indeed, efforts to program computers to play chess and solve other problems as well as human experts helped scientists understand a great deal about the strengths and limitations of human cognition (Newell & Simon, 1961; Simon, 1995). The computer, then, was the model for the **information-processing approach** to human cognition, which emphasizes the basic mental processes involved in attention, perception, memory, and decision making. And just as today's more highly developed computers have greater capacity than those of the past, maturation of the nervous system plus experience presumably enable adults to remember more than young children can and to perform more complex cognitive feats with greater accuracy (Kail & Bisanz, 1992).

Richard Atkinson and Richard Shiffrin (1968) proposed a simple information-processing framework with three memory stores, organized primarily by their duration:

- **Sensory register**, which ever-so-briefly (seconds, at most) holds the abundant sensory information that swirls around us
- **Short-term memory**, which holds a limited amount of information, perhaps five to seven items, for a short period of time

- **Long-term memory**, believed to be a relatively permanent and seemingly unlimited store of information

To illustrate the memory stores, imagine you are listening to a history lecture and among the many facts presented, your professor notes that the U.S. Constitution was ratified in 1789. This statement is an environmental stimulus "hitting" your sensory register. Assuming that you are not lost in a daydream, your sensory register will log it, holding it for a fraction of a second as a kind of afterimage (or, in this example, a kind of echo). Much that strikes the sensory register quickly disappears without further processing. Attentional processes (see Chapter 6) have a good deal to do with what information enters the sensory register and may be processed further. If you think you may need to remember 1789, it will be moved into short-term memory. To be remembered for any length of time, information must be moved from short-term memory into long-term memory, which represents what most people mean by memory. More than likely, you will hold the professor's statement in short-term memory just long enough to record it in your notes. Later, as you study your notes, you will rehearse the information in working memory to move it into long-term memory so that you can retrieve it the next day or week when you are taking the test.

This simplified model shows what you must do to learn and remember something. The first step is to **encode** the information: get it into the system. If it never gets in, it cannot be remembered. Second, information undergoes **consolidation**, during which it is processed and organized in a form suitable for long-term storage. Consolidation transforms the immediate sensory-perceptual experience of an event into a long-lasting memory trace, a process that is facilitated by sleep (Diekelmann & Born, 2010; Kopasz et al., 2010). In the absence of consolidation, the information would not make the leap from the first step of encoding to the third step of storage (Banai et al., 2010). **Storage**, of course, refers to holding information in a long-term memory store. Memories fade over time unless they are appropriately stored in long-term memory. Research has also made it clear that storing memories is a constructive process and not a static recording of what was encoded. As Mary Courage and Nelson Cowan (2009) describe it, "human memory does not record experience as a video camera would, but rather as an historian would: as a dynamic and inferential process with reconstructions that depend on a variety of sources of information" (p. 2).

Finally, for the memory process to be complete, there must be **retrieval**—the process of getting information out when it is needed. People say they have successfully remembered something when they can retrieve it from long-term memory. Retrieval can be accomplished in several ways. If you are asked a multiple-choice question about when the Constitution was ratified, you need not actively retrieve the correct date; you merely need to recognize it among the options. This is an example of **recognition memory**. If, instead, you are asked, "When was the

Constitution ratified?" this is a test of **recall memory**; it requires active retrieval without the aid of cues. Between recognition and recall memory is **cued recall memory**, in which you would be given a hint or cue to facilitate retrieval (for example, "When was the Constitution ratified? It is the year the French Revolution began and rhymes with *wine*."). Most people find questions requiring recognition memory easier to answer than those requiring cued recall, and those requiring cued recall easier than those requiring pure recall. This holds true across the life span, which suggests that many things people have apparently encoded or learned are "in there someplace" even though they may be difficult to retrieve without cues. Breakdowns in remembering may involve difficulties in initial encoding, storage, or retrieval.

Useful as this model has been, modifications and alternative models have been proposed as research has uncovered more and more about memory processes. A more comprehensive model is illustrated in ■ **Figure 8.1**. It shows, for example, that short-term memory is more complex than originally conceived. For one, most cognitive researchers distinguish between passive and active forms of short-term memory and use the term **working memory** to refer to a mental "scratch pad" that temporarily stores information while actively operating on it (Baddeley, 1986, 1992). It is what is "on one's mind," or in one's consciousness, at any moment. As you know, people can juggle only so much information at once without some of it slipping away or "falling out"

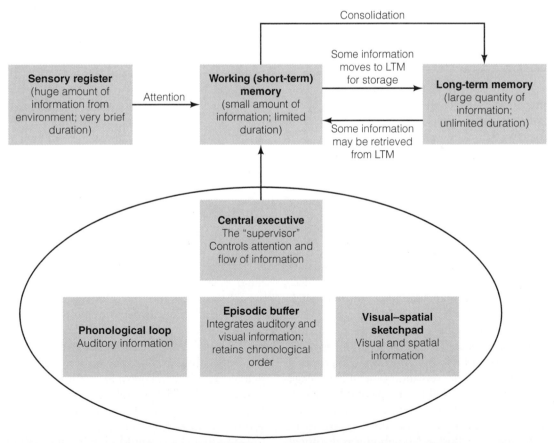

■ **Figure 8.1** A comprehensive model of memory. The central executive manages the important business of the short-term memory store. The bottom three boxes show the three types of short-term memory: phonological, visual-spatial, and the episodic buffer, which integrates the other two types of short-term memory.

of working memory. To illustrate working memory, look at the following seven numbers. Then look away and add the numbers in your head while trying to remember them:

7 2 5 6 1 4 7

Most likely, having to actively manipulate the numbers in working memory to add them disrupted your ability to rehearse them to remember them. People who are fast at adding numbers would have better luck than most people, because they would have more working-memory space left for remembering the items (Byrnes, 1996).

Alan Baddeley (1986, 2001) has proposed a four-component model of working memory to try to address the limitations in this area in the Atkinson and Shiffrin model. In particular, research showed that a single short-term memory store just was not sufficient as verbal and visual memories seem to be stored separately (Baddeley & Hitch, 1974). As illustrated in Figure 8.1, this expanded view of short-term memory consists of a **central executive**, which directs attention and controls the flow of information; it is the supervisor of the working-memory system. In addition, there are three types of short-term memory storage:

- Phonological, which briefly holds auditory information such as words or music
- Visual–Spatial, which holds visual information such as colors and shapes
- Episodic buffer, which links auditory and visual information

The episodic buffer was added to this model when research showed that some memories are not visual or verbal per se, but instead serve to connect visual and verbal information and facilitate long-term storage of episodic memories. In the next section, we'll explore these episodic memories in greater detail.

Implicit and Explicit Memory

Memory researchers have concluded that the long-term memory store responds differently depending on the nature of the task. They distinguish between **implicit memory** (including what is called procedural memory), which occurs unintentionally, automatically, and without awareness, and **explicit memory** (also called declarative memory), which involves deliberate, effortful recollection of events (see ■ **Figure 8.2**). Explicit memory is tested through traditional recognition and recall tests (such as a course's final exam with multiple-choice and essay questions) and can be further divided into **semantic memory** for general facts and **episodic memory** for specific experiences. Most memory experts agree that explicit memories, whether they are semantic general knowledge or the specific personal memories that make up episodic memories, are deeply entwined with language. To further clarify the two types of explicit memory, an example of episodic memory might be remembering that the 2013 Boston Marathon was disrupted when two bombs exploded near the finish line. Semantic memory might be knowing that Boston is the capital of Massachusetts. The first example illustrates memory for a specific event, whereas the second example reflects general knowledge about the world.

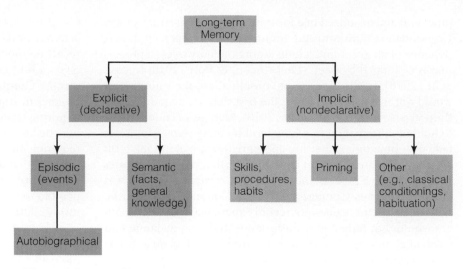

■ **Figure 8.2** Types of long-term memory.
SOURCE: Based on Squire (2004)

Implicit memory is a different beast. Learners are typically unaware that their memory is being assessed with implicit "tests." Consider an example: Individuals are exposed to a list of words (*orange, tablet, forest,* and so on) to be rated for likeability, not to be memorized. In a second task, they are given word stems such as *tab* and asked to complete them with the first word that comes to mind. People who are exposed to the word *tablet* in the initial task are more likely than people who are not exposed to the word to come up with *tablet* rather than *table* or *tabby* to complete the word stem, demonstrating that they learned something from their earlier exposure to the words even though they were not trying to learn. Adults with amnesia do poorly on tests of explicit memory in which they study words and then are asked to finish word stems such as *tab* with a word they studied earlier. Amazingly, however, if they are merely exposed to a list of words and then given an implicit memory test that asks them to write the first word that comes to mind, they do fine (Graf, Squire, & Mandler, 1984). Many forms of amnesia destroy explicit memory but leave implicit memory undamaged (Schacter, 1996). As Patricia Bauer (2007) describes it, explicit memory is fallible—subject to forgetting—whereas implicit memory is largely infallible—it remains intact.

Neural Bases of Memory

Until recently, the neural underpinnings of memory were largely a mystery, with only small glimpses into the inner workings of the brain afforded by occasional case studies of patients who had sustained brain damage and with this, specific memory problems. Su Meck, described in this chapter's opening, is one such case study. Perhaps the most famous case study has been that of an individual known for many years by his initials, "H.M." At the age of 27, Henry Molaison had the hippocampus removed from both sides of his brain as part of an effort to control his severe seizures. What his neurosurgeon did not realize at the time was that Henry would suffer from catastrophic memory loss for the remaining 55 years of his life (Henry died in 2008 at the age of 82). In particular, Henry experienced **anterograde amnesia**: He was no longer able to form new memories. He could not remember what he had eaten for dinner or watched on television just minutes earlier, nor could he learn new words or remember new people. What he could do was remember everything from his childhood, at least about as well as the rest of us can recall our childhoods.

Henry's unfortunate case provided the first solid evidence that memory has a neural basis. Advances in technology—positron emission tomography (PET) scans and functional Magnetic Resonance Imaging (fMRI)—have allowed researchers to make inferences about memory processes by observing brain activity taking place as subjects perform various types of memory tasks. From such studies, we have learned that different parts of the brain are involved in the different forms of memory (see ■ Figure 8.3). Procedural memory (such as memory of how to ride a bike), which is a type of implicit memory, is mediated by an area of the forebrain called the striatum. Explicit memory is largely localized in the medial temporal lobe of the brain (*medial* refers to the middle of the brain and the temporal lobe is located at the base of the brain). In particular, the medial temporal structures are thought to be crucial to consolidating information into a memory trace for long-term storage (Bauer, 2009). Damage to a specific region of the medial temporal lobe—the **hippocampus**—leads to significant impairments in creating new episodic memories, such as recalling that you went to the dentist on Monday morning (Vargha-Khadem et al., 1997). **Exploring Development Box 8.1** shows an amnesic trying to perform two different memory tasks.

The actual storage and retrieval of new information take place in whichever area of the cortex originally encoded or was activated by the information. For example, vocabulary seems to be stored in the limbic-temporal cortex, as evidenced by the vocabulary impairment experienced by individuals with damage to this part of the brain (Bauer, 2009). Thus, sensory information initially activates one of the cortical association areas distributed throughout the brain.

This information then passes to the medial temporal lobe for consolidation. If and when this consolidation occurs, the resulting memory trace is stored in the cortical association area of the brain that first registered the information, and it is from this area that the information must be retrieved.

Research suggests that implicit memory develops earlier in infancy than explicit memory (Bauer, 2008; Schneider, 2011). Explicit memory improves as the hippocampus becomes more mature during the second half of the first year (Nelson, Thomas, & de Haan, 2006). Further, the two types of memory follow different developmental paths. Explicit memory capacity increases from infancy to adulthood, then declines in later adulthood. By contrast, implicit memory capacity changes little; young children often do no worse than older children and elderly adults often do no worse than younger adults on tests of implicit memory (Schneider, 2011; Schneider & Bjorklund, 1998). Research on implicit memory shows that young and old alike learn and retain a tremendous amount of information from their everyday experiences without any effort.

Exploring Development 8.1
The Brain and Memory

Neuroscientists Larry Squire shows research findings about declarative (explicit) and nondeclarative (implicit) memory.

- What brain structure is most responsible for declarative memory?
- Why can a person with amnesia be trained to remember single pairs?
- Why is a person with amnesia unable to pair objects when they are all on the table at once?

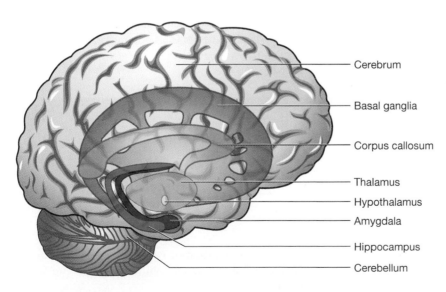

- Cerebrum
- Basal ganglia
- Corpus callosum
- Thalamus
- Hypothalamus
- Amygdala
- Hippocampus
- Cerebellum

■ **Figure 8.3** The hippocampus is part of the limbic system, located in the medial ("middle") temporal lobe of the brain. Scientists believe that the hippocampus is responsible for consolidation and formation of explicit memories. Just next to the hippocampus is the amygdala, which is involved in forming emotionally charged memories. Other parts of the brain, namely the basal ganglia and cerebellum, are important in the formation of procedural memories.

Advances in brain imaging have allowed researchers to "see" memory and problem solving by looking at patterns of blood flow in different regions of the brain. The yellow portions in this image show increased areas of blood flow as the person was remembering the image of a face.

Problem Solving

Think back to our example of the history professor who seems to want you to remember when the U.S. Constitution was ratified (1789, in case this did not get into your long-term memory store). Now imagine that you are asked how many years passed between this event and the signing of the Declaration of Independence (1776, remember?). This is a simple example of **problem solving**, or use of the information-processing system to achieve a goal or arrive at a decision (in this case, to answer the question). Here, too, the information-processing model describes what happens between stimulus and response. The question will move through the memory system. You will need to draw on your long-term memory to understand the question, then you will have to search long-term memory for the two relevant dates. Moreover, you will need to locate your stored knowledge of the mathematical operation of subtraction. You will then transfer this stored information to working memory so that you can use your subtraction "program" (1789 minus 1776) to derive the correct answer.

Notice that processing information successfully requires both knowing what you are doing and making decisions. This is why researchers have added **executive control processes** to the memory model. These control processes run the show, guiding the selection, organization, manipulation, and interpretation of information throughout. Stored knowledge about the world and about information processing guides what is done with new information.

Cognitive psychologists now recognize that information processing is more complex than this model or similar models suggest (Bjorklund, 1997). For example, they appreciate that people, like computers, engage in **parallel processing**, carrying out multiple cognitive activities simultaneously (for example, listening to a lecture and taking notes at the same time) rather than performing operations in a sequence (such as solving a math problem by carrying out a series of ordered steps). They also appreciate that different processing approaches are used in different domains of knowledge. Still, the information-processing approach to cognition has the advantage of focusing attention on how people remember things or solve problems, not just on what they recall or what answer they give. A young child's performance on a problem could break down in any number of ways: The child might not be paying attention to the relevant aspects of the problem, might be unable to hold all the relevant pieces of information in working memory long enough to do anything with them, might lack the strategies for transferring new information into long-term memory or retrieving information from long-term memory as needed, might simply not have enough stored knowledge to understand the problem, or might not have the executive control processes needed to manage the steps for solving problems. If researchers can identify how information processes in the younger individual differ from those in the older person, they will gain much insight into cognitive development.

Many processes involved in memory and problem solving improve between infancy and adulthood and then decline somewhat in old age, although this pattern is not uniform for all processes or all people. Our task in this chapter is to describe these age trends and, of greater interest, to try to determine why they occur.

Checking Mastery

1. What steps are required in order to learn, remember, and recall material?
2. What is the difference between implicit and explicit memory?
3. Why are recognition tasks generally easier than recall tasks?

Making Connections

1. Consider your own memory profile. On what types of memory tasks and under what conditions is your memory good, and conversely, which types of tasks and conditions challenge your memory?
2. In creating a memory assessment, how would you tap into someone's implicit memories as opposed to their explicit memories?

8.2 The Infant

LEARNING OBJECTIVES:

- Explain how researchers are able to assess the memory capabilities of infants.
- Outline the characteristics of infant memory.
- Describe the types of information that infants are likely to remember.

You have already seen that infants explore the world thoroughly through their senses. But are they remembering anything of their experiences?

Memory

Assessing infant memory requires some ingenuity because infants cannot tell researchers what they remember (Bauer, Larkina, & Deocampo, 2011; Courage & Cowan, 2009). Several methods have been used to uncover infants' memory capabilities. Here we consider imitation, habituation, and operant conditioning techniques before examining infants' abilities to recall previously presented information.

Imitation

Researchers can learn something about memory by noting whether or not infants can imitate an action performed by a model. Some studies suggest that young infants, even newborns, can imitate certain actions, such as sticking out the tongue or opening the mouth (see Meltzoff, 2004). These findings are exciting because they challenge Piaget's claim that infants cannot imitate actions until about 1 year, when they have some ability to represent mentally what they have seen.

Such findings have been viewed with skepticism by some, who believe that early tongue protrusions do not demonstrate true imitation but instead reflect reflexive responses to specific stimuli or attempts to "explore" interesting sights (see, for example, Bjorklund, 1995; Jones, 1996). However, observations of infants sticking out their tongues and moving their mouths in ways consistent with a model have now been replicated with different populations (Meltzoff & Moore, 1997). More importantly, though, infants as young as 6 months display **deferred imitation**, the ability to imitate a novel act after a delay, which clearly requires memory ability (see Bauer et al., 2011; Rovee-Collier & Cuevas, 2009b). Deferred imitation seems to represent an early form of explicit or declarative memory (Bauer et al., 2011).

Habituation

Another method to assess memory uses habituation, a simple and often overlooked form of learning introduced in Chapter 6. Habituation—learning *not* to respond to a repeated stimulus—might be thought of as learning to be bored by the familiar (for example, eventually not hearing the continual ticking of a clock or the drip of a leaky faucet) and is evidence that a stimulus is recognized as familiar. From birth, humans habituate to repeatedly presented lights, sounds, and smells; such stimuli are recognized as "old hat" (Rovee-Collier & Barr, 2010). Indeed, as we noted in Chapter 5, fetuses demonstrate through habituation that they can learn and remember prior to birth (Dirix et al., 2009). It is clear that newborns are capable of recognition memory and prefer a new sight to something they have seen many times. As they age, infants need less "study time" before a stimulus becomes old hat, and they can retain what they have learned for days or even weeks (Rovee-Collier & Cuevas, 2009b).

Operant Conditioning

To test long-term memory of young infants, Carolyn Rovee-Collier and her colleagues devised a clever task that relies on the operant conditioning techniques introduced in Chapter 2 (see Rovee-Collier & Cuevas, 2009b). When a ribbon is tied to a baby's ankle and connected to an attractive mobile, the infant will shake a leg now and then and learn very quickly (in minutes) that leg kicking brings about a positively reinforcing consequence: the jiggling of the mobile.

To test infant memory, the mobile is presented at a later time to see whether the infant will kick again. To succeed at this task, the infant must not only recognize the mobile but also recall that the thing to do is to kick. Before we review the research findings, what type of memory do you believe this task assesses? Consider whether infants are deliberately and effortfully remembering something or are unintentionally and automatically learning and remembering a connection between their kicking and the movement of the mobile. This task is tapping into implicit or procedural memory (Rovee-Collier & Cuevas, 2009a). When given two 9-minute training sessions, 2-month-olds remember how to make the mobile move for up to 2 days, 3-month-olds for about 1 week, and 6-month-olds for about 2 weeks (Rovee-Collier & Cuevas, 2009b). Using a modification

of this task for older infants, Rovee-Collier and her colleagues (see Hartshorn et al., 1998) have shown that by 18 months, infants can remember for at least 3 months—rather impressive! Further, the researchers could enhance young infants' memory by giving them three 6-minute learning sessions rather than two 9-minute sessions. Although the total training time is the same in the two conditions, the distributed, or spread out, training is more effective. As it turns out, distributed practice is beneficial across the life span—a good thing to keep in mind when you are studying for tests (Son, 2004).

What if stronger cues to aid recall are provided? Three-month-old infants who were reminded of their previous learning, by seeing the mobile move 2–4 weeks after their original learning experience, kicked up a storm as soon as the ribbon was attached to their ankles, whereas infants who were not reminded showed no sign of remembering to kick (Rovee-Collier & Barr, 2004). It seems, then, that cued recall (in this case, memory cued by the presence of the mobile or, better yet, its rotation by the experimenter) emerges during the first couple of months of life and that infants remember best when they are reminded of what they have learned. Other research shows

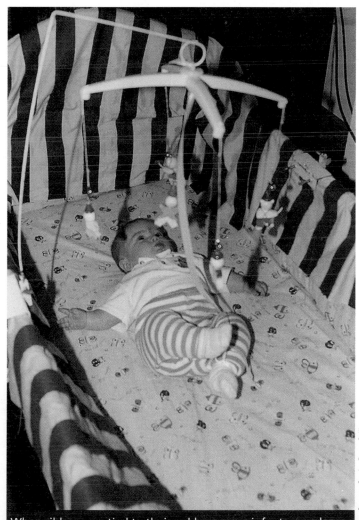

When ribbons are tied to their ankles, young infants soon learn to make a mobile move by kicking their legs. Carolyn Rovee-Collier has made use of this operant conditioning paradigm to find out how long infants will remember the trick for making the mobile move.

Courtesy Carolyn Rovee-Collier

that verbal reminders are also effective with 15-month-olds and can help them remember an event after a month as well as they did after a week (Hayne & Simcock, 2009).

However, this research also suggests that young infants have difficulty recalling what they have learned if cues are insufficient or different. They have trouble remembering when the mobile (for example, the specific animals hanging from it) or the context in which they encountered it (for example, the design on the playpen liner) is even slightly different from the context in which they learned. In short, early memories are *cue-dependent* and *context-specific*.

Recall

When are infants capable of pure recall—of actively retrieving information from memory when no cues are available? As noted earlier, infants as young as 6 months, given repeated exposure to a model's actions, can imitate novel behaviors (for example, pushing a button on a box to produce a beep) after a 24-hour delay (Barr, Dowden, & Hayne, 1996). As infants age, they demonstrate recall or deferred imitation over longer periods. By 6 months, infants can defer their imitation of an action over a longer delay and can recall the order of a simple sequence of events (Bauer, 2007). By age 2, events can be recalled for months, and recall is more flexible—less bound by the specific cues present at the time of learning (Hayne & Simcock, 2009; Klein & Meltzoff, 1999).

Patricia Bauer (1996; Bauer et al., 2000) and her colleagues have shown sequences of actions to infants of different ages and then asked them to imitate what they saw—for example, putting a teddy bear in bed, covering him with a blanket, and reading him a story. Infants as young as 13 months can reconstruct a sequence of actions for as long as 3 months afterward. Older infants (16 and 20 months) can store and retrieve events for 12 months after exposure (Bauer et al., 2000, 2011). Much like children and adults, infants remember best when they have repeated exposures to what they are to remember, when they are given plenty of cues to help them remember, and when the events they must remember occur in a meaningful or logical order.

By age 2, infants have become verbal and can use words to reconstruct events that happened months earlier. In one study, for example, researchers interviewed young children about emergency room visits for accidents the children had between about 1 and 3 years of age (Peterson & Rideout, 1998). Interviews were conducted soon after the ER visits and 6, 12, 18, or 24 months later. Children who were 18 months or younger at the time of their ER visit were unable to verbally recall aspects of their visits after a 6-month delay, but children 20 months or older were able to do so. Children who were at least 26 months old at the time of their ER visit could retain information and answer verbal questions about their experiences for at least 2 years following the event. It's clear that language helps memory performance (Hayne & Simcock, 2009).

Problem Solving

Infants, like children and adults, face problem-solving tasks every day. For example, they may want to obtain an object beyond their reach or to make a toy repeat the interesting sound it produced earlier. Can infants overcome obstacles to achieve desired goals? It appears they can. In one study, infants were presented with an object out of their reach; however, by pulling on a cloth, they could drag the object to within reach (Willats, 1990). Although 6-month-olds did not retrieve the object, 9-month-olds solved this problem. Even the younger infants were successful when given hints about how they might retrieve the object (Kolstad & Aguiar, 1995). By 14 months of age, infants have figured out that adults are often useful sources of information in problem-solving situations (Goubet et al., 2006). As they get older, infants increasingly pay attention to the cues provided by adults and they increasingly solicit help by pointing, reaching, or otherwise letting the adult know that assistance is needed. Simple problem-solving behaviors improve considerably over the first 2 years of life and then, as you will see shortly, flourish during childhood.

▶ Checking Mastery

1. How does the habituation task allow researchers to assess an infant's memory abilities?
2. At what age do infants begin to show reliable recall for events?

▶ Making Connections

1. Uncle Jed says there is no way a baby can learn or remember anything. His position is that babies just eat, sleep, cry, and poop. What three key pieces of evidence might you use to convince Uncle Jed that there is something going on inside the infant's head in terms of learning and memory?
2. Would you characterize infants' memory as robust or fragile? What factors influence the robustness of infants' memory?

8.3 The Child

LEARNING OBJECTIVES:

- Discuss and evaluate the four major reasons why memory improves over childhood.
- Describe autobiographical memory, provide an example, and list contributing factors.
- Use evidence to evaluate the accuracy of children's eyewitness memory.
- Explain changes in problem-solving ability throughout childhood.

The 2-year-old is already a highly capable information processor, as evidenced by the rapid language learning that takes place at this age. But dramatic improvements in learning, memory, and problem solving occur throughout the childhood years as children learn everything from how to flush toilets to how to work advanced math problems.

Memory Development

In countless situations, older children learn faster and remember more than younger children do. For example, 2-year-olds can repeat back about two digits immediately after hearing them, 5-year-olds about four digits, and 10-year-olds about six digits. And second-graders not only are faster learners than kindergartners but also retain information longer (Howe, 2000). Why is this? Here are four major hypotheses about why learning and memory improve (see Schneider, 2011):

1. *Changes in basic capacities.* Older children have higher-powered "hardware" than younger children do; neural advances in their brains have contributed to more working-memory space for manipulating information and an ability to process information faster.
2. *Changes in memory strategies.* Older children have better "software"; they have learned and consistently use effective methods for putting information into long-term memory and retrieving it when they need it.
3. *Increased knowledge about memory.* Older children know more about memory (for example, how long they must study to learn things thoroughly, which kinds of memory tasks take more effort, and which strategies best fit each task).
4. *Increased knowledge about the world.* Older children know more than younger children about the world in general. This knowledge, or expertise, makes material to be learned more familiar, and familiar material is easier to learn and remember than unfamiliar material.

Do Basic Capacities Change?

Because the nervous system continues to develop in the years after birth, it seems plausible that older children remember more than younger children do because they have a better "computer"—a larger or more efficient information-processing system. We can quickly rule out the idea that the storage capacity of long-term memory impairs memory performance in infants and young children. There is no consistent evidence that the capacity changes after the first month of life (Perlmutter, 1986). In fact, young and old alike have more room for storage than they could ever use. If long-term storage capacity does not contribute to developmental differences in memory, then what about the encoding and consolidation processes needed to move information into long-term storage?

Encoding begins with the sensory registration of stimuli from the environment. As we learned in Chapter 6, the sensory systems are working fairly well from a very early age and undergo only slight improvements during the first year. But although the senses themselves are functioning well, there is evidence that the *encoding* of this information improves over the first several years of life as the prefrontal cortex matures (see Bauer et al., 2011). It is also clear that the memory consolidation process undergoes developmental change. Of course, information that is not encoded in the first place is not going to be consolidated and stored. But separate from the changes in encoding, consolidation and storage of memories show improvement over infancy and childhood that seem to correspond to maturation of the hippocampus and other parts of the brain believed to be centrally involved in consolidation of memories. We also know that the

speed of mental processes improves with age, as neurons become myelinated, and this allows older children and adults to simultaneously perform more mental operations in working memory than young children can (Cowan et al., 2010). As basic mental processes become automatic, they can also be performed with little mental effort. This, in turn, frees space in working memory for other purposes, such as storing the information needed to solve a problem.

This focus on changes in working memory has been featured in revisions of Piaget's theory of cognitive development proposed by neo-Piagetian theorists who retain Piaget's original emphasis on stages and qualitative change, but try to articulate the processes of change more concretely. For example, Robbie Case (Case, 1985; Marini & Case, 1994) proposed that more advanced stages of cognitive development are made possible because children make better use of the available space in their working memory. Recall from Chapter 7 Piaget's finding that preschoolers tend to *center* on one aspect of a problem and lose sight of another (for example, to attend to the height of a glass but ignore its width, or vice versa). Perhaps, say the neo-Piagetians, this is not a matter of lacking certain cognitive structures; perhaps young children simply do not have enough working-memory capacity to keep both pieces of information in mind at once and to coordinate them. Similarly, young children may do poorly on memory tasks because they cannot keep the first items on a list in mind while processing later ones. And they may fail to solve mathematical problems correctly because they cannot keep the facts of the problem in mind while they are performing the calculations.

Some research suggests that the degree of improvement in short-term memory capacity that is evident as children age depends on what is tested or how it is tested. That is, short-term memory capacity is domain-specific—it varies with background knowledge and type of task (Conklin et al., 2007; Schneider, 2011). Greater knowledge in a domain or area of study increases the speed with which new, related information can be processed. In other words, the more you know about a subject, the faster you can process information related to this subject.

In sum, the basic capacities of the sensory register and long-term memory do not change much with age. There are, however, improvements with age in operating speed and efficiency of working memory, which includes improvements in the encoding and consolidation processes through which memories are processed for long-term storage. These changes correspond to maturational changes in the brain. During infancy, brain activity during working-memory tasks is scattered and general (Bell & Wolfe, 2007). By age 4 or 5, working memory has found its "home" in the frontal lobes of the brain. Maturation of the frontal lobes continues throughout childhood and adolescence, bringing further improvements in working memory and consolidation of memories (Bauer, 2009).

Do Memory Strategies Change?

If shown the 12 items in ■ **Figure 8.4**, 4-year-olds might recall only 2–4 of them, 8-year-olds would recall 7–9 items, and adults might recall 10–11 of the items after a delay of several minutes. Are there specific memory strategies that evolve during childhood to permit this dramatic improvement in performance?

■ **Figure 8.4** A memory task. Imagine that you have 120 seconds to learn the 12 objects pictured here. What tricks or strategies might you devise to make your task easier?

Children as young as 2 years can deliberately remember to do such "important" things as reminding Mom to buy candy at the grocery store. They are more likely to use external memory aids (for example, pointing at or holding a toy pig when asked to remember where it was hidden) if they are instructed to remember than if they are not (Fletcher & Bray, 1996). However, children younger than 4 show little flexibility in switching from an ineffective strategy to an effective one, and they typically do not generate new strategies even as they gain experience with a task (Chen, 2007). In contrast, many 4- and 5-year-olds will flexibly switch strategies and generate new strategies, making them more effective on memory tasks than younger children. Four-year-olds can also selectively focus on relevant information and ignore irrelevant information, although this ability will become more robust with age and experience (Schwenck, Bjorklund, & Schneider, 2009). Younger children have a tendency to make **perseveration errors**: they continue to use the same strategy that was successful in the *past* despite the strategy's *current* lack of success. Thus, if they previously found their favorite toy under the sofa, they search this location on future occasions when the toy is lost (Chen, 2007). They seem to be unable to get the old strategy—ineffective in the new situation—out of their mind and move on to a different strategy that could potentially be successful. By age 4, we see a decline in these perseveration errors.

Yet even 4-year-olds have not mastered many of the effective strategies for moving information into long-term memory. For example, when instructed to remember toys they have been shown, 3- and 4-year-olds will look carefully at the objects and will often label them once, but they only rarely use the memory strategy called **rehearsal**—the repeating of items they are trying to learn and remember (Baker-Ward, Ornstein, & Holden, 1984). To rehearse the objects in Figure 8.4, you might simply say, "apple, truck, grapes …" repeatedly. John Flavell and his associates found that only 10% of 5-year-olds repeated the names of pictures they were asked to recall, but more than half of 7-year-olds and 85% of 10-year-olds used this strategy (Flavell, Beach, & Chinsky, 1966).

Another important memory strategy is **organization**, or classifying items into meaningful groups. You might cluster the apple, the grapes, and the hamburger in Figure 8.4 into a category of foods and form other categories for animals, vehicles, and baseball equipment. You would then rehearse each category and recall it as a cluster. Another organizational strategy, *chunking*, is used to break a long number (6065551843) into manageable subunits (606-555-1843, a phone number). Organization is mastered later in childhood than rehearsal. Until about age 9 or 10, children are not much better at recalling lists of items that lend themselves readily to grouping than they are at recalling lists of unrelated words (Bjorklund, Dukes, & Brown, 2009).

Finally, the strategy of **elaboration** involves actively creating meaningful links between items to be remembered. Elaboration is achieved by adding something to the items, in the form of either words or images. Creating and using a sentence such as "the apple fell on the horse's nose" could help you remember two of the items in Figure 8.4. Elaboration is especially helpful in learning foreign languages. For example, you might link the Spanish word *pato* (pronounced pot-o) to the English equivalent *duck* by imagining a duck with a pot on its head. Children who can elaborate on the relationship between two items (for example, generating similar and different features of the items) have improved retention of these items (Howe, 2006).

Memory or encoding strategies develop in a fairly predictable order, with rehearsal emerging first, followed by organization, and then by elaboration. Children do not suddenly start using strategies, however. According to Patricia Miller (Miller, 1990, 1994; Miller & Seier, 1994), they typically progress through four phases on their way to successful strategy use. Initially, children have a **mediation deficiency**, which means they cannot spontaneously use or benefit from strategies, even if they are taught how to use them. Children with mediation deficiencies seem qualitatively unable to grasp the concept of the strategy. This gives way to a different kind of problem, a **production deficiency**, in which children can use strategies they are taught but do not produce them on their own. The third phase is a **utilization deficiency**, in which children spontaneously produce a strategy but their task performance does not yet benefit from using the strategy. This seems to be a precursor to the final stage in which children exhibit effective strategy use by both producing and benefiting from a memory strategy.

There is ample evidence of utilization deficiencies across various age groups and for different types of strategies (see Pressley & Hilden, 2006; Schwenck, Bjorklund, & Schneider, 2007). Why would children who use a strategy fail to benefit from it? One possibility is that using a new strategy is mentally taxing and leaves no free cognitive resources for other aspects of the task (Pressley & Hilden, 2006). Once using the strategy becomes routine, then other components of the task can be addressed simultaneously. Whatever the reason for utilization deficiencies, they reflect a child–task interaction; that is, it is not task difficulty per se, but how difficult a task is for a particular child, that matters (Bjorklund et al., 2009).

What memory strategies could this girl use to help her remember where she hid her birthday treasures?

Using effective storage strategies to learn material is only half the battle; retrieval strategies can also influence how much is recalled. Indeed, retrieving something from memory can often be a complex adventure when solving problems, such as when you try to remember when you went on a trip by searching for cues that might trigger your memory ("Well, I still had long hair then, but it was after Muffy's wedding, and …"). In general, young children rely more on external cues for both encoding and retrieving information than do older children (Schneider & Pressley, 1997). Thus, young children may need to put their toothbrushes next to their pajamas so that they have a physical reminder to brush their teeth before they go to bed. Older children are less likely to need such external cues but may continue to use them throughout elementary school (Eskritt & Lee, 2002). In many ways, then, command of memory strategies increases over the childhood years, but the path to effective strategy use is characterized more by noticeable jumps than by steady increases (Bjorklund et al., 2009; Schneider, Kron-Sperl, & Hünnerkopf, 2009). **Application Box 8.1** looks at whether children can be taught strategies to improve their memory.

Does Knowledge about Memory Change?

The term **metamemory** refers to knowledge of memory and to monitoring and regulating memory processes. It is knowing, for example, what your memory limits are, which memory strategies are more or less effective, and which memory tasks are more or less difficult. It is also noting that your efforts to remember something are not working and that you need to try something different. Metamemory is one aspect of **metacognition**, or knowledge of the human mind and of the range of cognitive processes. Your store of metacognitive knowledge might include an understanding that you are better at learning a new language than at learning algebra, that it is harder to pay attention to a task when there is distracting noise in the background than when it is quiet, and that it is wise to check a proposed solution to a problem before concluding that it is correct.

When do children first show evidence of metacognition? If instructed to remember where the *Sesame Street* character Big Bird has been hidden so that they can later wake him up, even 2- and 3-year-olds will go stand near the hiding spot, or at least look or point at that spot; they do not do these things as often if Big Bird is visible and they do not need to remember where he is (DeLoache, Cassidy, & Brown, 1985). By age 2, then, children understand that to remember something, you have to work at it. Researchers have found that 3-year-olds understand the difference between thinking about an object in their heads and experiencing it in reality and that 4-year-olds realize behavior is guided by beliefs (Flavell, 1999). These findings indicate that metacognitive awareness is present at least in a rudimentary form at a young age but there continue to be significant improvements throughout childhood (Ghetti, Lyons, & Cornoldi, 2008; MacKinlay et al., 2009).

Are increases in metamemory a major contributor to improved memory performance over the childhood years? Children with greater metamemory awareness demonstrate better memory ability, but several factors influence the strength of this relationship (Bjork & Bjork, 1998; Schneider, 2011). Researchers are most likely to see a connection between metamemory and memory performance among older children and among all children who have been specifically asked to remember something (DeMarie & Ferron, 2003; Schneider & Bjorklund, 1998). Not only is task experience important, but the nature of the task is also relevant. Awareness of memory processes benefits even young children on tasks that are simple and familiar and where connections between metamemory knowledge and memory performance are fairly obvious (Schneider & Sodian, 1988). Yet children who know what to do may not always do it, so good metamemory is no guarantee of good recall (Schneider & Pressley, 1997). It seems that children not only must know that a strategy is useful but also must know why it is useful in order to be motivated to use it and to benefit from its use (Justice et al., 1997). Metamemory is also influenced by children's language skills and by their general knowledge about mental states and their roles in behavior—what is known as theory of mind (Lockl & Schneider, 2007; see Chapter 13 for definition and discussion). The links between metamemory and memory performance, although not perfect, are strong enough to suggest the merits of teaching children more about how memory works and how they can make it work more effectively for them.

Does Knowledge of the World Change?

Ten-year-olds have greater semantic memory than 2-year-olds do. That is, they know considerably more about the world in general. The individual's knowledge of a content area to be learned, or **knowledge base**, as it has come to be called, clearly affects learning and memory performance. Think about the difference between reading about a topic that you already know well and reading about a new topic. In the first case, you can read quickly because you are able to link the information to the knowledge you have already stored. All you really need to do is check for any new information or information that contradicts what you already know. Learning about a highly unfamiliar topic is more difficult ("It's Greek to me").

Application 8.1

Improving Children's Memory and Study Skills

Have you noticed that the material in this chapter has great potential value to teachers? The information-processing perspective has yielded improved methods for diagnosing learning problems and improving instruction. Here we focus on interventions aimed at boosting the memory skills of young children. Just how much can be achieved through training?

Garrett Lange and Sarah Pierce (1992) took on the challenge of teaching the memory strategy of organization (grouping) to 4- and 5-year-olds. Using pictures of objects and animals as the stimuli, they taught these preschoolers a "group-and-name trick" that involved sorting items to be learned into groups based on similarity, naming the group, naming the items within the group, and, at recall, naming the group before calling out the items within that group. Because

such memory-training programs have not always been successful, these researchers attempted to increase motivation through encouragement and praise. They even included training in metamemory: They made sure children understood the rationale for the sorting strategy, knew when it could be used, and could see firsthand that it could improve their performance.

How successful was the training? These children did virtually no sorting of items to be learned before they were trained, but they did a good deal of it after training, even 7 days later. They clearly learned to use the organization strategy they were taught. They also outperformed untrained control children on measures of recall, but the gains in recall were fairly small compared with the much larger gains in strategy use. This discrepancy between gains in strategy use and gains in recall performance

shows that these young children experienced utilization deficiencies: They could not derive full benefit from the memory strategy they were taught, possibly because they did not have the working-memory capacity to carry out the strategy.

Other programs that teach memory strategies and metacognitive skills to elementary-school children often work much better, especially with children who are underachievers and who may be capable of executing strategies but fail to do so on their own (Hattie, Biggs, & Purdie, 1996). Still, the benefits of training are often domain specific: They do not generalize to learning tasks different from those that were the focus of training. Perhaps this makes sense if you realize that the strategies that work best in learning math skills may be different from the strategies that work best in learning historical facts or basketball skills.

Perhaps the most dramatic illustration of the powerful influence of knowledge base on memory was provided by Michelene Chi (1978). She demonstrated that even though adults typically outperform children on tests of memory, this age difference could be reversed if children have more expertise than adults. Chi recruited children who were expert chess players and compared their memory skills with those of adults who were familiar with the game but lacked expertise. On a test of memory for sequences of digits, the children recalled fewer than the adults did, demonstrating their usual deficiencies. But on a test of memory for the locations of chess pieces, the children clearly beat the adults (■ **Figure 8.5**). Because they were experts, these children were able to form more and larger mental chunks, or meaningful groups, of chess pieces, which allowed them to remember more. When child experts were compared with adult experts, there were no differences in performance (Schneider et al., 1993).

Pause to consider the implications: On most tasks, young children are the novices and older children or adults are the experts. Perhaps older children and adults recall longer strings of digits because they are more familiar with numbers than young children are, not because they have better basic learning capacities. Perhaps they recall more words in word lists simply because they have more familiarity with language. Perhaps

memory improves over childhood simply because older children know more about all kinds of things than younger children do (Bjorklund, 1995).

In their areas of expertise—whether baseball, dinosaurs, Pokémon cards, or *Harry Potter* trivia—children appear to develop highly specialized and effective strategies of information processing, just as the young chess players studied by Chi apparently had. Indeed, children with low general intellectual ability but high expertise sometimes understand and remember more about stories in their area of expertise than do children with higher intellectual ability but less expertise

■ **Figure 8.5** Effects of expertise on memory. Michelene Chi found that child chess experts outperformed adult chess novices on a test of recall for the location of chess pieces (although, in keeping with the usual developmental trend, these children could not recall strings of numbers as well as adults could).

(Schneider, Bjorklund, & Maier-Bruckner, 1996). Knowledge in a content area probably allows you to make better use of the limited capacity of working memory. It seems that the more you know, the more you *can* know.

Revisiting the Explanations

We can now draw four conclusions about the development of learning and memory:

1. Older children are faster information processors and can juggle more information in working memory. Maturation of the nervous system leads to improvements in consolidation of memories. Older and younger children, however, do not differ in terms of sensory register or long-term memory capacity.
2. Older children use more effective *memory strategies* in encoding and retrieving information. Acquisition of memory strategies reflects qualitative rather than quantitative changes.
3. Older children know more about memory, and good *metamemory* may help children choose more appropriate strategies and control and monitor their learning more effectively.
4. Older children know more in general, and their larger *knowledge base* improves their ability to learn and remember. A richer knowledge base allows faster and more efficient processing of information related to the domain of knowledge.

Is one of these explanations of memory development better than the others? Darlene DeMarie and John Ferron (2003) tested whether a model that includes three of these factors—basic capacities, strategies, and metamemory—could explain recall memory better than a single factor. For both younger (5–8 years) and older (8–11 years) children, the three-factor model predicted memory performance better than a single-factor model. Use of memory strategies was an especially strong predictor of recall. Importantly, there were also correlations among factors. Having good basic capacities, for example, was related to advanced metamemory and to command of strategies and had its own influence on recall as well. So all these phenomena may contribute something to the dramatic improvements in learning and memory that occur over the childhood years. We return to these four hypotheses when we consider changes in learning and memory in adulthood.

Autobiographical Memory

Children effortlessly remember all sorts of things: a birthday party last week, where they left their favorite toy, what to do when they go to a fast-food restaurant. Much of what children remember and talk about consists of personal experiences or events that have happened to them at a particular time and place. These **autobiographical memories**, episodic memories of personal events, are essential ingredients of present and future experiences as well as our understanding of who we are (see Berntsen & Rubin, 2012). Su Meck, introduced at the beginning of this chapter, lost all autobiographical memories

from before her accident and with them, she lost herself, or at least the self she had been. Here we look at how autobiographical memories are stored and organized and at factors that influence their accuracy.

When Do Autobiographical Memories Begin?

You learned earlier in this chapter that infants and toddlers are able to store memories. You also know that children and adults have many specific autobiographical events stored in long-term memory. Yet research shows that older children and adults exhibit **childhood** (or infantile) **amnesia**; that is, they have few autobiographical memories of events that occurred during the first few years of life (Hayne & Simcock, 2009). As Patricia Bauer (2007) notes, memories for the first few years of life seem to fall into a large black hole from which there is no return.

To determine how old we have to be when we experience significant life events to remember them, researchers typically ask adults to answer questions about early life experiences such as the birth of a younger sibling, a hospitalization, the death of a family member, or a family move early in life. In one study using this method, college students were able to recall some information from events that happened as early as age 2 (Usher & Neisser, 1993). But age 2 seems to be the lowest age limit for recall of early life events as an adult. Other research shows that most adults do not remember much until they were 4 or 5 years old (Davis, Gross, & Hayne, 2008; Jack & Hayne, 2007). For example, Nicola Davis and her colleagues (2008) asked college students who had experienced the birth of a younger sibling by the age of 5 to recall as much as they could about this early event. As ■**Figure 8.6** shows, college students who had been

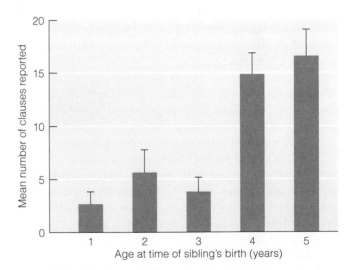

■ **Figure 8.6** College students' recall of the birth of a younger sibling increases as a function of how old they were at the time of the event. Those who were at least 4 years of age when their sibling was born recall much more than those who were younger than 4.

Source: Davis, N., Gross, J., & Hayne, H. (2008). Defining the boundary of childhood amnesia, *Memory*, 16(5), 465–474, Figure 2. Reprinted by permission of Taylor & Francis Group.

1, 2, or 3 years old at the time recalled very little of the event, but those who were 4 or 5 when their sibling was born recalled significantly more. Why do we remember little about our early years? As you have seen, infants and toddlers are certainly capable of encoding their experiences (Cleveland & Reese, 2008). Also, young preschool children seem able to remember a good deal about events that occurred when they were infants even though older children and adults cannot (Bauer, 1996; Fivush, Gray, & Fromhoff, 1987). One explanation of childhood amnesia is that infants and toddlers may not have enough space in working memory to hold the multiple pieces of information about actor, action, and setting needed to encode and consolidate a coherent memory of an event. As you learned earlier in this chapter, functional working-memory capacity increases with age as the brain, particularly the frontal lobe, matures. But this explanation is unsatisfactory because, as we have just noted, toddlers can remember these events, indicating that they were encoded to some degree.

Perhaps infants' lack of language is the answer. Because autobiographical memory seems to rely heavily on language skills, we would expect such memories to increase with increased language skills. Gabrielle Simcock and Harlene Hayne (Hayne & Simcock, 2009; Simcock & Hayne, 2002, 2003) assessed the verbal skills of young children (27, 33, and 39 months old) who participated in a unique event involving a "magic shrinking machine" that seemingly made items smaller in a matter of seconds. After a 6- or 12-month delay, children were tested for both verbal recall (answers to open-ended questions) and nonverbal recall (identification of photos of the items used in the activity) of the unique event. Their nonverbal recall improved across the age groups but was good at all ages. Verbal recall was poor and depended on the simpler verbal skills present at the time of encoding rather than the more developed verbal skills present at the time of recall. In other words, "children's verbal reports of the event were frozen in time" (p. 229). So a relative lack of verbal skills during the first few years of life may limit what we are able to recall from this period.

Although toddlers may have limited verbal skills, their parents presumably do not. There are large individual differences in toddler–parent "conversations" about past events (Fivush, 2009). An examination of mother–toddler conversations about past events shows that some mothers provide rich elaborations of these events, whereas others do not, in the course of conversing with their toddlers (Fivush, 2009). Years later, adolescents whose mothers had been more elaborative during their early mother–toddler conversations have stronger autobiographical memories than adolescents whose mothers were less elaborative (Jack et al., 2009; see also Reese, Hayne, & MacDonald, 2008).

Although language is an important component of autobiographical memories, the language explanation, like the encoding explanation, does not entirely account for why children cannot remember nonverbal information such as the faces of preschool classmates (Lie & Newcombe, 1999). We need to consider that toddlers lack a strong sense of self and as a result may not have the necessary pages on which they can write memories of personally experienced events (Howe, Courage, &

Rooksby, 2009). Without a sense of self, it is difficult to organize events as "things that happened to *me*." Indeed, young children's ability to recognize themselves in a mirror is a good predictor of children's ability to talk about their past (see Howe et al., 2009).

Finally, some researchers have also tried to explain childhood amnesia in terms of **fuzzy-trace theory** (Reyna & Brainerd, 1995). According to this explanation, children store verbatim and general accounts of an event separately. Verbatim information (such as word-for-word recall of a biology class lecture) is unstable and likely to be lost over long periods (Leichtman & Ceci, 1993); it is easier to remember the gist of an event (for example, recall of the general points covered in a biology lecture) than the details (Brainerd & Reyna, 1993; Koriat, Goldsmith, & Pansky, 2000). With age, we are increasingly likely to rely on gist memory traces, which are less likely to be forgotten and are more efficient than verbatim memory traces in the sense that they take less space in memory (Brainerd & Gordon, 1994; Klaczynski, 2001). Children pass through a transition period from storing largely verbatim memories to storing more gist memories, and the earlier verbatim memories are unlikely to be retained over time (Howe, 2000).

As you can see, there are plenty of ideas about the causes of childhood amnesia but still no firm explanation of why a period of life that is highly important to later development is a blank for most of us. Young children certainly encode many experiences and demonstrate recall during early childhood for these events. But due to a lack of sufficient working memory to encode events, language skills, a sense of self, or encoding only the verbatim details of what happened rather than a "fuzzy trace," the events of our early childhood do not seem to undergo the *consolidation* needed to store robust memories of this time (Bauer et al., 2007).

Scripts

As children engage in routine daily activities such as getting ready for bed or eating at a fast-food restaurant, they construct **scripts** or **general event representations (GERs)** of these activities (Nelson, 1986; Schank & Abelson, 1977). Scripts or GERs represent the typical sequence of actions related to an event and guide future behaviors in similar settings (Hudson & Mayhew, 2009). For instance, children who have been to a fast-food restaurant might have a script like this: You wait in line, tell the person behind the counter what you want, pay for the food, carry the tray of food to a table, open the packages and eat the food, gather the trash, and throw it away before leaving. With this script in mind, children can act effectively in similar settings. Children as young as 3 years use scripts when reporting familiar events (Hudson & Mayhew, 2009; Nelson, 1997). When asked about their visit to a fast-food restaurant the day before, children usually report what happens *in general* when they go to the restaurant rather than what specifically happened during yesterday's visit (Kuebli & Fivush, 1994). As children age, their scripts become more detailed. Perhaps more important than age, however, is experience: Children with greater experience of an event develop richer scripts than children with less experience (DeMarie, Norman, & Abshier, 2000).

Children develop scripts in memory for routine activities, such as visiting a fast-food restaurant, that guide their behavior in these situations.

Eyewitness Memory

Children's scripts affect how they form memories of new experiences as well as how they recall past events. For example, when presented with information inconsistent with their scripts, preschoolers may misremember the information so that it better fits their script (Nelson & Hudson, 1988). Four-year-old Damian may have a script for birthdays that includes blowing out candles, eating cake, and opening presents. Although his brother is sick on his birthday and eats applesauce instead of cake, Damian later recalls that they all ate cake before opening presents. This demonstrates that memory is a reconstruction, not an exact replication (Hudson & Mayhew, 2009). This, in turn, has significant implications for **eyewitness memory** (or testimony), or the reporting of events witnessed or experienced—for example, a child's reporting that she saw her little brother snitch some candy before dinner. Children are increasingly asked to report events that have happened in the context of abuse cases or custody hearings. To what extent can you "trust" a child's memory in these situations? What factors influence the accuracy of children's episodic memory when providing testimony?

When asked generally about events ("Tell me what happened at Uncle Joe's house"), preschoolers recall less information than older children, but the recall of both groups is accurate (Pipe & Salmon, 2009; Pipe, Thierry, & Lamb, 2007). General prompts (such as "What happened next?" or "Tell me more about that…") can elicit additional recall of information (Pipe & Salmon, 2009). Specific questions ("Was Uncle Joe wearing a red shirt?") can also elicit more information, but accuracy of recall begins to slip (Hilgard & Loftus, 1979). This is especially true as the questions become more directed or leading ("Uncle Joe touched you here, didn't he?"). Preschool-age children, more so than older children and adults, are suggestible; they can be influenced by information implied in direct questioning and by relevant information introduced after the event (Bjorklund, Brown, & Bjorklund, 2002).

Perhaps it is unfortunate, then, that preschoolers, because they initially offer less information in response to open-ended questions, are asked a larger number of directed questions than older children (Baker-Ward et al., 1993; Price & Goodman, 1990). They are also frequently subjected to repeated questioning, which increases errors in reporting among children (Bjorklund et al., 2002). Although repeated questioning with general, open-ended questions can increase accuracy, repeated questioning with directed or closed questions can decrease accuracy (Memon & Vartoukian, 1996). For example, in a study with 5- and 6-year-olds, researchers "cross-examined" children about events that occurred on a field trip to a police station during which the children saw a jail cell and police car and were fingerprinted and photographed (Zajac & Hayne, 2003). After a delay of 8 months, children's memories were probed using irrelevant, leading, and ambiguous questions like those you might hear in a courtroom. Many children "cracked" under the pressure as evidenced by backing down and changing their answers in response to the questioning. Fully one out of three children changed *all* their answers, and most changed at least one answer. So although children can demonstrate accurate recall when asked clear and unbiased questions, this study shows that young children's memory for past events can quickly become muddied when the questioning becomes tough.

Problem Solving

Memories are vital to problem-solving skills. To solve any problem, a person must process information about the task, as well as use stored information, to achieve a goal. Thus, working memory is a critical component of problem solving (Lee, Ng, & Ng, 2009). How do problem-solving capacities change during childhood? Piaget provided one answer to this question by proposing that children progress through broad stages of cognitive growth, but information-processing theorists were not satisfied with this explanation. They sought to pinpoint more specific reasons why problem-solving prowess improves so dramatically as children age.

Consider the problem of predicting what will happen to the balance beam in ■ **Figure 8.7** when weights are put on each side of the fulcrum, or balancing point. The goal is to decide which way the balance beam will tip when it is released. To judge correctly, you must take into account both the number of weights and their distances from the fulcrum. Piaget believed that concrete operational thinkers can appreciate the significance of either the amount of weight or its distance

■ **Figure 8.7** The balance beam apparatus used by Robert Siegler to study children's problem-solving abilities. Which way will the balance beam tip?

Source: Siegler, R.S. (1981). Developmental sequences within and between concepts, *Monographs of the Society for Research in Child Development*, 46, (2, Serial No. 189). Copyright © 1981. Reprinted with permission of John Wiley & Sons, Inc.

from the center but will not grasp the inverse relationship between the two factors. Only when they reach the stage of formal operations will new cognitive structures allow them to understand that balance can be maintained by decreasing a weight *and* moving it farther from the fulcrum or by increasing a weight *and* moving it closer to the fulcrum (Piaget & Inhelder, 1969).

Robert Siegler (1981, 2000) proposed that the information-processing perspective could provide a fuller analysis. His **rule assessment approach** determines what information about a problem children take in and what rules they then formulate to account for this information. This approach assumes that children's problem-solving attempts are not hit or miss but are governed by rules; it also assumes that children fail to solve problems because they fail to encode all the critical aspects of the problem and are guided by faulty rules.

Siegler (1981) administered balance beam problems to individuals ages 3–20. He detected clear age differences in the extent to which both weight and distance from the fulcrum were taken into account in the rules that guided decisions about which end of the balance beam would drop. Few 3-year-olds used a rule; they guessed. By contrast, 4- and 5-year-olds were governed by rules. More than 80% of these children used a simple rule that said the side of the balance beam with greater weight would drop; they ignored distance from the fulcrum. By age 8, most children had begun to consider distance from the fulcrum and weight under some conditions: When the weight on the two sides was equal, they appreciated that the side of the balance beam with the weights farthest from the fulcrum would drop. By age 12, most children considered both weight and distance on a range of problems, although they still became confused on complex problems in which one side had more weights but the other had its weights farther from the fulcrum. Finally, 30% of 20-year-olds discovered the correct rule—that the pull on each arm is a function of weight times distance. For example, if there are three weights on the second peg to the left and two weights on the fourth peg to the right, the left torque is $3 \times 2 = 6$ and the right torque is $2 \times 4 = 8$, so the right arm will drop.

The increased accuracy of young adults comes with a price—increased time to solve the problem (van der Maas & Jansen, 2003). Although, in general, information-processing time gets faster with age, the complex rules needed to successfully solve all the variations of the balance beam problem demand more time. So on some problems, adults are slower than children because they are using a more sophisticated strategy.

In most important areas of problem solving, Siegler (1996) concluded, children do not simply progress from one way of thinking to another as they age, as his balance beam research suggested. Instead, in working problems in arithmetic, spelling, science, and other school subjects, most children in any age group use multiple rules or problem-solving strategies rather than just one. In working a subtraction problem such as $12 - 3 = 9$, for example, children sometimes count down from 12 until they have counted off 3 and arrive at 9 but

other times count from 3 until they reach 12. In one study of second- and fourth-graders, more than 90% of the children used three or more strategies in working subtraction problems (Siegler, 1989).

Similarly, Michael Cohen (1996) found that most preschoolers used all possible strategies when attempting to solve a practical mathematical problem in the context of playing store. He also found that children's selection and use of strategies became more efficient over multiple task trials; that is, they increasingly selected strategies that would allow them to solve the task in fewer steps.

Such results suggest that cognitive development works much as evolution does, through a process of natural selection in which many ways of thinking are available and the most adaptive survive (DeLoache, Miller, & Pierroutsakos, 1998; Siegler, 1996, 2000). Rather than picturing development as a series of stages resembling stairsteps, Siegler argues, we should picture it as overlapping waves, as shown in ■ **Figure 8.8**. Siegler (2006) summarizes the **overlapping waves theory** as a "process of variability, choice, and change" (p. 478). Thus, the development of problem-solving skills is a matter of knowing and using a variety of strategies, becoming increasingly selective with experience about which strategy to use, and changing or adding strategies as needed. At each age, children have multiple problem-solving strategies available to them. As children gain more experience, which typically occurs as they age, they decrease their use of less-adaptive strategies and increase their use of more-adaptive strategies; occasionally, new strategies may appear. Strategies evolve from their initial acquisition in a particular context to their generalization to other contexts, which helps strengthen the fledgling strategies (Siegler, 2006). Gradually, children not only learn to choose the most useful strategy for a problem but also become increasingly effective at executing new strategies. Familiarity

■ **Figure 8.8** Cognitive development may resemble overlapping waves more than a staircase leading from one stage to another. Children of a particular age typically use multiple thinking strategies rather than just one.

SOURCE: Siegler, R.S. (1996). *Emerging minds: The process of change children's thinking* by Siegler. Copyright © 1996 by Oxford University Press, Inc. Used by permission of Oxford University Press, Inc.

with a task and with strategies frees processing space, allowing children to engage in more metacognitive analysis of the strategies at their disposal (Whitebread, 1999). Throughout, there is significant variability—both between children and within the same child across time and tasks.

Notice the difference between this information-processing explanation and Piaget's explanation of cognitive change. Piaget argued that change is qualitative, with new, more effective strategies replacing older, less effective strategies all at once as children move from one stage to another. Siegler argues that strategies emerge gradually and become more effective over time, with multiple strategies available any time.

Imagine how effective teachers might be if they, like Siegler, could accurately diagnose the information-processing strategies of their learners to know what each child is noticing (or failing to notice) about a problem and what rules or strategies each child is using when. Like a good car mechanic, the teacher would be able to pinpoint the problem and encourage less use of faulty strategies and rules and more use of adaptive ones. Much remains to be learned about how problem-solving strategies evolve as children age, and why. However, the rule assessment approach and overlapping waves theory give a fairly specific idea of what children are doing (or doing wrong) as they attack problems and illustrate how the information-processing approach to cognitive development provides a different view of development than Piaget's account does.

8.4 The Adolescent

LEARNING OBJECTIVES:

- Compare the typical adolescent's memory capabilities to those of the typical child.

- Explain why adolescents demonstrate stronger memory abilities than children.

Although parents in the midst of reminding their adolescent sons and daughters to do household chores or homework may wonder whether teenagers process any information at all, learning, memory, and problem solving continue to improve considerably during the adolescent years. Research on episodic memory shows that the performance of young teens (11–12 years) is quite similar to that of children, and both groups do markedly worse than young adults (Brehmer et al., 2007). Clearly, then, there is room for improvement during adolescence. How does this improvement occur?

Strategies

First, new learning and memory strategies emerge. It is during adolescence that the memory strategy of elaboration is mastered (Schneider & Pressley, 1997). Adolescents also develop and refine advanced learning and memory strategies highly relevant to school learning—for example, note-taking and underlining skills. Ann Brown and Sandra Smiley (1978)

asked students from 5th to 12th grade (approximately 11–18 years) to read and recall a story. Some learners were asked to recall the story immediately; others were given an additional 5 minutes to study it before they were tested. Amazingly, fifth-graders gained almost nothing from the extra study period except for those few who used the time to underline or take notes. The older middle school students benefited to an extent, but only senior high school students used underlining and note-taking methods effectively to improve their recall. When some groups of students were told specifically that they could underline or take notes if they wished, fifth-graders still did not improve, largely because they tended to underline everything rather than to highlight the most important points.

Adolescents also make more deliberate use of strategies that younger children use unconsciously (Bjorklund, 1985). For example, they may deliberately organize a list of words instead of simply using the organization or grouping that happens to be there already. And they use existing strategies more selectively. For example, they are adept at using their strategies to memorize the material on which they know they will be tested and at letting go of irrelevant information (Bray, Hersh, & Turner, 1985; Lorsbach & Reimer, 1997). To illustrate, Patricia Miller and Michael Weiss (1981) asked children to remember the locations of animals that had been hidden behind small doors and to ignore the household objects hidden behind other doors. As ■ Figure 8.9 shows, 13-year-olds recalled more than 7- and 10-year-olds about where the animals had been hidden, but they remembered less about task-irrelevant information (the locations of the household objects). Apparently, they are better able to push irrelevant information out of working memory so that it does not interfere with task performance (Lorsbach & Reimer, 1997). So, during elementary school, children get better at distinguishing between what is relevant and what is irrelevant, but during adolescence they advance further by selectively using their memory strategies only on the relevant material. If it is not going to be on the test, forget it!

Basic Capacities

Adolescents make other strides besides these changes in memory strategies. Basic capacities continue to increase; for example, adolescents perform any number of cognitive operations faster than children do (Kail, 1991). As discussed earlier in this chapter, adolescents have greater functional use of their working memory because maturational changes in the brain allow them to process information more quickly and to simultaneously process more chunks of information. Older teens (16–20 years) perform better than younger ones (less than 15 years) on highly complex cognitive tasks that require them to use recalled information to

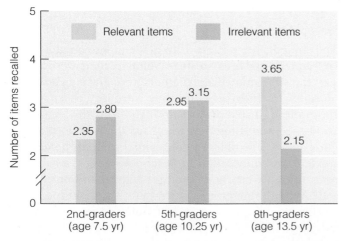

■ **Figure 8.9** Adolescents are better able than children to concentrate on learning relevant material and to ignore irrelevant material.

Source: Miller, P.H. & Weiss, M.G. (1981). Children's attention allocation, understanding of attention and performance on the incidental learning task, *Child Development*, 52, 1183–1190. Reprinted with permission of John Wiley & Sons, Inc.

strategically direct their search behavior (Luciana et al., 2005). There is no difference, though, on tasks of low complexity such as face recognition.

Metamemory and Knowledge Base

There is little to say about knowledge base other than that it continues to expand during adolescence. Therefore, adolescents may do better than children on some tasks simply because they know more about the topic.

Metamemory and metacognition also improve. In general, adolescents become better able to tailor their reading strategies to different purposes (studying versus skimming) and better able to realize when they do not understand something (Baker & Brown, 1984). About 80% of 12th graders report that they monitor their memory and learning strategies. But only 50–60% report that they think in advance to develop an effective plan for a difficult task or think back after completing a task to evaluate what worked or did not work (Leutwyler, 2009). Clearly, this leaves room for improvements beyond adolescence.

Successful metacognition can be seen in adolescents choosing the strategy of elaboration over rote repetition when they realize that the former is more effective (Pressley, Levin, & Ghatala, 1984). Adolescents are also fairly accurate at monitoring whether or not they have allocated adequate study time to learn new material (Kelemen, 2000). Teens typically allocate more study time to information judged to be difficult, indicating that they understand this material needs additional processing to be retained (Thiede & Dunlosky, 1999). Interestingly, when pressed for time, college students devote more study time to easy items (Son & Metcalfe, 2000). Apparently, they decide it is futile to work on the difficult material when they do not have adequate time, so they spend their time on what seems most likely to pay off. Hopefully, you can see the implication of this for your own studying: Set aside enough time to study all the material; otherwise, you may end up in a time crunch reviewing only the easy material. And take comfort in knowing that the better you learn something now, the more likely you will remember this material 20, 30, even 50 years from now (Bahrick, 1984; Conway, Cohen, & Stanhope, 2006). For more tips on how to improve your memory, visit **Engagement Box 8.1**.

It is interesting to note that the extent to which metacognition is employed during cognitive tasks varies by gender and socioeconomic background (Leutwyler, 2009). Adolescent girls consistently report using more metacognitive strategies than adolescent boys. This may help explain why girls earn higher grades in school than boys, a finding that we will explore in greater detail in Chapter 10. And students from higher socioeconomic backgrounds report more use of metacognitive strategies than their lower socioeconomic peers. Families with higher socioeconomic status may have more resources such as books in the home and may talk more explicitly about effective learning strategies.

Growth in strategies, basic capacities, knowledge base, and metacognition probably also helps explain the growth in everyday

Improve Your Memory!

What are some practical steps you can use to improve your memory? First, keep in mind that your brain, which is absolutely essential for memory, does not operate in isolation from the rest of you. Your brain, and therefore your memory, is affected by such factors as the amount of sleep you get, your nutrition, and your physical activity.

Consider sleep. The process of consolidation of memories is critical to moving them into long-term storage and is improved with sleep. Try reviewing to-be-remembered information right before you go to sleep at night and then get the recommended hours of sleep for your age (see Chapter 5). Studying in the afternoon and then taking a nap has also been shown to help consolidate memories. And before you start to study, plan to do some aerobic exercise. This increases oxygen to your brain and also helps you stay alert and focused once you settle down to study. As for nutrition, a growing body of research suggests that omega-3 fatty acids contribute to brain function, as do B vitamins and antioxidants. A good meal for your brain might be salmon, spinach salad, and a strawberry–blueberry smoothie.

So you have adopted healthy eating, exercise, and sleep habits. What can you do to improve your memory when actually studying course material for that upcoming test? We'll focus on a few things that will assist with encoding and consolidation of memories, as well as some helpful hints for retrieval.

1. PAY ATTENTION! If you are daydreaming in class or thinking of something else while reading, you will not encode the information to be learned. If you don't encode it, you will be out of luck when it comes time to retrieve the memory—it simply won't be there. To increase your attention, reduce the distractions that may be present in your environment.

2. ORGANIZE AND MAKE CONNECTIONS to existing knowledge. Organizing to-be-learned material into logical groups can aid in consolidation and storage of the information. What is logical depends on each individual and each task. The organizational scheme must make sense to the learner in the context that it needs to be learned. Consolidation is also more likely to occur when the new material can be related to existing knowledge. Think of how you might use familiar ideas to help you remember new ideas.

3. USE STRATEGIES THAT ENRICH AND ELABORATE the new material. Repeating items over and over is a simplistic strategy that helps store fairly simple facts. You need to dig deeper into your toolbox of strategies and choose those that will create richer connections to existing material or will allow you to elaborate the new material. Examples of these strategies might be to associate each new word to an existing concept; this could be taken a step further—elaborated—by thinking of the similarities and differences between the new and old material. Or think of an acronym using the first letter of each to-be-learned word. You could create a story that ties together a new set of concepts that you want to recall later; by retelling the story, you recall the concepts.

4. CUSTOMIZE YOUR LEARNING STRATEGIES to optimize your learning style. Some research suggests that students who use the strategy of verbal elaboration (that is, creating sentences about the material) have better recall than students who use mental imagery or another visual strategy (Kirchhoff & Buckner, 2006). But this same research also showed that individuals choose different strategies to learn the same material. Some learners tend to be more visual, whereas others excel with more verbal material and strategies.

5. OVERLEARN new material. If you study new material just enough to recognize or recall it for a short period, chances are good you will forget a considerable amount of this material. To prevent this from happening, you need to overlearn the material. Don't stop studying when you reach that point where you think you might be able to remember the material if you take the test very soon. Keep studying until retrieval of the information becomes quick and effortless. There is evidence that overlearning strengthens the neural connections involved in storing information and makes it more likely that you will be able to retrace these neural paths when it comes time to retrieve it.

---

problem-solving ability that occurs during the adolescent years. Teenagers perfect several information-processing skills and become able to apply them deliberately and spontaneously across a variety of tasks.

▶ Checking Mastery

1. What are the differences in basic memory capacities of children and adolescents?
2. What memory improvements are we likely to notice when a child becomes an adolescent?

▶ Making Connections

1. Using the information-processing model presented earlier in the chapter (see Figure 8.1), explain why 17-year-old Nathaniel outperforms his 7-year-old sibling when asked to recall a TV program on the Civil War both watched last week.
2. Abigail has a big exam coming up—the results could determine whether or not she earns a scholarship for college. How should she prepare for the exam and what characteristics of the test itself or the testing conditions might affect her performance?

LEARNING OBJECTIVES:

- Distinguish characteristics of someone with expertise in a field relative to someone who is a novice.
- Describe the characteristics of adult autobiographical memory.
- Discuss age-related changes in memory across adulthood, noting factors that enhance and factors that impede memory.
- Explain how older adults may compensate for declines in memory and problem-solving ability.

If you are about age 20, you will be pleased to know that the young adult college student has served as the standard of effective information processing against which all other age groups are compared. In other words, information processing is thought to be most efficient—at its peak—in emerging and young adults. Still, improvements in cognitive performance continue during the adult years before aging begins to take its toll on some memory and problem-solving capacities.

Developing Expertise

Comparing people new to their chosen fields of study with those more experienced tells researchers that experience pays off in more effective memory and problem-solving skills. In Chapter 7, you saw that people in Piaget's highest stage of cognitive development, formal operations, often perform better in their areas of specialization than in unfamiliar areas. Similarly, information-processing research shows that adults often function best cognitively in domains in which they have achieved expertise (Byrnes, 1996; Ericsson, 1996; Glaser & Chi, 1988). It seems to take about 10 years of training and experience to become a true expert in a field and to build a rich and well-organized knowledge base (Ericsson, 1996). But once this base is achieved, the expert not only knows and remembers more but also thinks more effectively than individuals who lack expertise.

Consider first the effects of semantic memory, or knowledge base, on performance. How might adults who are baseball experts and adults who care little for baseball perceive and remember the same game? George Spilich and his associates (1979) had baseball experts and novices listen to a tape of a half inning of play. Experts recalled more of the information central to the game—the important plays and the fate of each batter, in proper order—whereas novices were thrown off by irrelevant facts such as the threatening weather conditions and the number of people attending the game. Experts also recalled more details—for example, noting that a double was a line drive down the left-field line rather than just a double. At any age, experts in a field are likely to remember new information in that content domain more fully than novices do (Morrow et al., 1994).

In addition, experts are able to use their elaborately organized and complete knowledge bases to solve problems effectively and efficiently (Proffitt, Coley, & Medin, 2000). They are able to size up a situation quickly, see what the problem really is, and recognize how the new problem is similar to and different from problems encountered in the past (Glaser & Chi, 1988).

They can quickly, surely, and almost automatically call up the right information from their extensive knowledge base to devise effective solutions to problems and to carry them out efficiently.

Are the benefits of expertise content-specific, or does gaining expertise in one domain carry over into other domains and make a person a more generally effective learner or problem solver? This is an interesting and important question. One research team (Ericsson, Chase, & Faloon, 1980) put an average college student to work improving the number of digits he could recall. He practiced for about 1 hour a day, 3–5 days a week, for more than 1½ years—more than 200 hours in all. His improvement? He went from a memory span of 7 digits to one of 79 digits! His method involved forming meaningful associations between strings of digits and running times—for example, seeing 3492 as "3 minutes and 49 point 2 seconds, near world-record mile time" (p. 1181). It also involved chunking numbers into groups of three or four, then organizing the chunks into large units.

Did all this work pay off in a better memory for information other than numbers? Not really. When he was given letters of the alphabet to recall, this young man's memory span was unexceptional (about six letters). Clearly the memory ability he developed was based on strategies of use only in the subject

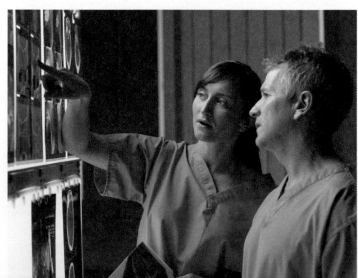

Phil Boorman/Cultura/Getty Images

Adults who have gained proficiency in their chosen fields can draw from their well-organized knowledge bases to find just the right information to fit the problem at hand. Solving problems is automatic and effortless for experts.

matter he was trying to remember. Similarly, Bob Petrella, a man with an exceptional memory for anything and everything related to sports, turns out to have ordinary prospective memory, or remembering things that need to be done in the future (ABCNews, 2010). Each expert apparently relies on domain-specific knowledge and domain-specific information-processing strategies to achieve cognitive feats (Ericsson & Kintsch, 1995; Schunn & Anderson, 1999).

Overall, experts know more than novices do, their knowledge base is more organized, and they are able to use their knowledge and the specialized strategies they have devised to learn, remember, and solve problems efficiently in their areas of expertise—but not in other domains. In effect, experts do not need to think much; they are like experienced drivers who can put themselves on "auto-pilot" and carry out well-learned routines quickly and accurately. By gaining expertise over the years, adults can often compensate to some extent for age-related losses in information-processing capacities (Jastrzembski, Charness, & Vasyukova, 2006).

Autobiographical Memory

Earlier in this chapter, we examined the emergence of autobiographical memories and you learned that most adults do not remember much about their first few years of life. Yet we also noted that the long-term memory store seems limitless in terms of space and longevity. Is everything we have ever experienced "in there" somewhere? Likely not, as most adults report difficulties recalling past events. So what determines whether an event is likely to be recalled at a later point in time? We will consider four factors identified by Patricia Bauer (2007) that may influence autobiographical memories: personal significance, distinctiveness, emotional intensity, and life phase of the event.

To begin, most people believe that the personal significance of an event affects our memory for the event—that events of great importance to the self will be remembered better than less important events. As it turns out, the personal significance of an event, as rated at the time the event occurs, has almost no effect on one's ability to later recall the event. It may be that what was once considered important becomes less so with the passage of time and with the broader perspective gained over the years. For example, imagine that at age 19, you break up with your boyfriend of 2 years. This is traumatic and of great importance to you as a 19-year-old. You expect you'll never get over it and that the details of the event will be forever etched into your memory. But over the next 10, 20, 30 years, or more, so many other events occur that the importance of this youthful breakup fades as you date others, marry, work, raise children, and so on. Thus, personal significance of events may influence memory for these events as long as they remain important to us. But as some events become less important and others become more important over time, there is an associated shift in memory for these events.

In contrast, the distinctiveness or uniqueness of an event has been consistently associated with better recall (Bauer, 2007). The more unique an event is, the more likely it is to be recalled later on, and to be recalled as a distinct event with relevant details. Common events and experiences are often recalled, if at all, as multiple events lumped together as one (Burt, Kemp, & Conway, 2003). Thus, if you attended the same camp every summer throughout your childhood, you may retain fond memories of your experiences at the camp. But the chances are good that you have integrated in your memory many of the common and similar camp experiences: You remember singing songs around the campfire, but because you did this every year of the camp, you don't recall the experience of one year as separate from your experience of all the other years. On the other hand, if one year a camper did something highly unusual during one of these campfire sing-alongs (for example, streaked through the fire), you may indeed remember this particular event for many years to come because of its uniqueness.

Bauer (2007) notes that the affective or emotional intensity of an event also influences later recall. Events associated with either highly negative or highly positive emotions are recalled better than events that were experienced in the context of more neutral emotions. This enhanced memory for emotion-arousing events occurs even though the emotion associated with the event tends to dissipate with time, especially if it is a negative emotion (Paz-Alonso et al., 2009). It is likely that strong emotions activate the body's arousal system and the neural components associated with arousal enhance encoding and consolidation of events. This can be seen with fMRI scans of the brain as participants are cued to retrieve an autobiographical memory. The brain scans show activation of the amygdala, an area of the brain associated with emotions, when participants retrieve an emotionally charged memory but not when they retrieve a neutral memory (see Rubin, 2012; St. Jacques, 2012).

Finally, research on autobiographical memory has revealed that people recall more information from their teens and 20s than from any other time except the near present (Fitzgerald, 1999; Rubin, 2002). ■ **Figure 8.10** shows the number of memories

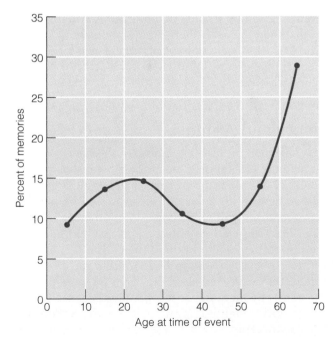

■ **Figure 8.10** Seventy-year-olds recall the times of their lives: What does this graph illustrate about the recall of autobiographical memories by older adults?

SOURCE: Rubin, D. C., Wetzler, S.E. & Nebes, R. D. (1986). Autobiographical memory across the adult lifespan. In D. C. Rubin (ed.), *Autobiographical memory*. Copyright © 1986 Cambridge University Press. Reprinted with permission.

recalled by 70-year-old adults. Not surprisingly, they recalled a lot from their recent past (for example, age 65). But the number of memories recalled from about ages 15–25 was higher than the number recalled from other points of the life span. Why? Possibly, this phase of life is more memorable because it is instrumental in shaping who people are as adults—their identity—and is often full of significant life changes (Fitzgerald, 1999). David Rubin (2002) suggests that this memory *bump*, as he calls it, occurs because memories from adolescence and early adulthood are more easily accessible than memories from other periods of the life span. They are more accessible because of their distinctiveness and the effort applied by adolescents and young adults to understanding the meaning of the events. Notably, this time of life typically coincides with the major life events of leaving home, acquiring education or training for a job or career, forming romantic relationships, starting a family, and having other experiences signifying adulthood (Berntsen & Rubin, 2002; Conway, 2005). These events form one's **life script**, those stories of our lives that we tell over and over again (Berntsen & Rubin, 2002; and see Chapter 11 on narrative identities). A typical life script might go something like this: "After high school, I traveled half-way across the country to go to college where I met my future spouse. Upon graduation from college, we both managed to get jobs in the same large city, close to his family but far from where I had grown up. We ended up staying there for 5 years, establishing our careers while helping out his ailing parents. Once they passed away, though, we saw an opportunity to move to a more ideal setting and settle down to have a family." Such life scripts are repeated over time and contexts, becoming further consolidated with each retelling, ensuring that these major life events are solidly secured in our memory system. Research shows that there may be other "bumps" in memory across the life span that are influenced by what particular cultures prescribe as important life events (Berntsen & Rubin, 2004; Fitzgerald & Broadbridge, 2012).

Memory and Aging

No less an expert on learning than B. F. Skinner complained about memory problems: "One of the more disheartening experiences of old age is discovering that a point you have just made—so significant, so beautifully expressed—was made by you in something you published a long time ago" (Skinner, 1983, p. 242). Most elderly adults report that they have at least minor difficulties remembering things (Smith et al., 1996). They are especially likely to have trouble recalling names and items they will need later; they are also more upset than young adults by memory lapses, perhaps because they view them as signs of aging (Cavanaugh, Grady, & Perlmutter, 1983). **Exploration Box 8.1** describes when forgetfulness is normal and when it is indicative of a more serious problem.

Areas of Strength and Weakness

Much research indicates that, on average, older adults learn new material more slowly and sometimes learn it less well than young and middle-aged adults do and that they

remember what they have learned less well. However, the following qualifications are important and will be expanded on in the following sections:

- Most of the research is based on cross-sectional studies that compare age groups, which suggests that the age differences detected could be related to factors other than age. (If needed, you can refresh your memory of the strengths and weaknesses of cross-sectional designs by referring back to Chapter 1.)
- Declines, when observed, typically do not become noticeable until we hit our 70s.
- Difficulties in remembering affect elderly people more noticeably as they continue to age and are most severe among the oldest elderly people.
- Not all older people experience these difficulties.
- Not all kinds of memory tasks cause older people difficulty.

Studies of memory skills in adulthood suggest that the aspects of learning and memory in which older adults look most deficient in comparison with young and middle-aged adults are some of the same areas in which young children compare unfavorably with older children (see Bauer, 2007). The following sections describe some of the major weaknesses—and, by implication, strengths—of older adults' memory skills.

Timed Tasks. On average, older adults are slower than younger adults to learn and retrieve information; they may need to go through the material more times to learn it equally well and may need more time to respond when their memory is tested. Thus, they are hurt by time limits (Finkel et al., 2003).

Unfamiliar or Artificial Content. Older adults fare especially poorly compared with younger adults when the material to be learned is unfamiliar or meaningless—when they cannot tie it to their existing knowledge. In a convincing demonstration of how familiarity influences memory, researchers had young and elderly adults examine words likely to be more familiar to the young adults at the time of the testing (for example, *dude*, *disco*, and *bummer*) and words from the past likely to be more familiar to the older adults (for example, *pompadour*, *gramophone*, and *vamp*). Young adults outperformed older adults on the "new" words, but older adults outperformed young adults on the "old" words (Barrett & Wright, 1981). Many memory tasks involve learning unfamiliar material and thus do not allow older adults to use their knowledge base.

Similarly, older adults perform significantly worse in laboratory contexts but can often outperform younger adults in real-world contexts (Henry et al., 2004). So when the task is meaningful—such as remembering to take several pills every morning—older adults may be able to draw on their greater experience or knowledge bases to enhance their memory performance.

Unexercised Skills. Older adults are also likely to be at a disadvantage when they are required to use learning and memory skills that they rarely use in daily life; they hold their own when they can rely on well-practiced skills that have become effortless and automatic with practice. For example, Lynne Reder, Cynthia Wible, and John Martin (1986) found that elderly adults were just as good as young adults at judging whether sentences presented

Forgetting: What Is Normal and What Is Not?

As we age, or watch parents and grandparents age, how can we distinguish between normal forgetfulness and abnormal memory changes? Many older adults worry that forgetting an appointment or where they put their reading glasses is a precursor to the devastating memory loss associated with AD (see Chapter 16). Fortunately, most of us will not develop AD and the atypical memory changes that accompany it. Most will, however, exhibit some changes in memory and information-processing skills. So how can we discriminate between normal memory changes and those associated with disease?

Cynthia Green (2001) suggests three criteria that can be used to alert us to atypical memory problems:

- Has memory gotten noticeably worse over the past 6 months?
- Do memory problems interfere with everyday activities at home or work?
- Are family and friends concerned about an individual's memory problems?

Answering "yes" to these questions may indicate unusual memory loss that should be evaluated by a professional.

In practical terms, it is normal to forget where you put something but abnormal to forget how to use it (Cherry & Smith, 1998). Thus, do not worry when Grandpa cannot find his car keys, but be alert if he cannot remember how to use them when they are in his hand. Similarly, it is normal to forget a new phone number you recently looked up in the phone book but abnormal to forget phone numbers you have known and used for years.

Researchers who study memory have identified a step between normal memory loss with age and severe, disease-related loss (Brandt et al., 2009; Petersen et al., 1997, 2001). Individuals with **mild cognitive impairment** experience significant memory problems—forgetting important appointments, having trouble learning new names, and repeating themselves to the same person—but otherwise do not appear to be suffering from dementia. At least not yet. Some research suggests that a majority of those with mild cognitive impairment will eventually develop forms of dementia such as AD (Lopez, 2013). Research also suggests that patients with mild cognitive impairment display deficits on other cognitive tasks as well, which could mean their problem is more general than memory impairment (Ribeiro, de Mendonca, & Guerreiro, 2006). This is a serious concern because 22% of older adults may have mild cognitive impairment and will require increased assistance as they continue to age (Plassman et al., 2008).

The good news is that age-related memory loss may be preventable, and some losses may be reversible. Reducing stress, for example, is one way to improve memory performance (Bremner & Narayan, 1998). Chronic stress elevates levels of cortisol in the brain, which impedes memory. Studies by the Mayo Clinic and the MacArthur Foundation found that three things predicted good memory over time: physical fitness and activity, mental activity, and a sense of control over life events (Geda et al., 2012; Rowe & Kahn, 1998). Mental activity—working crossword puzzles, reading, using a computer—increases connections among neurons. Physical activity increased blood flow to the brain and seems to release chemicals that protect neurons involved in cognitive function. Older adults who engage in moderate to high levels of physical activity are less likely to develop cognitive impairment than those who are not active (Etgen et al., 2010). Thus, remaining physically and mentally active can help protect against memory loss associated with aging. Having a sense of control over memory can boost both confidence and memory performance.

In sum, significant memory loss is not likely among healthy older adults. It is true that, relative to young adults, older adults exhibit poorer memory performance in some situations. But these changes are minor and can often be avoided or minimized by remaining physically and mentally active. Families and professionals should be on the lookout for older adults who show marked declines in their memory performance. They may be experiencing mild cognitive impairment and may eventually develop AD and impaired memory. The earlier they are identified and receive treatment, the better (see Chapter 16).

to them were plausible based on a story they had read. Judging whether something makes sense in the context of what has been read is a well-exercised ability. However, older adults were deficient when it came to judging whether specific sentences had or had not appeared in the story—a skill seldom used outside school. It seems that older adults read to get the gist or significance of a story and do not bother with the details, a strategy that may be adaptive if they have no need to memorize details and if their ability to do so has fallen off with age (Adams, 1991; Stine-Morrow, Loveless, & Soederberg, 1996). In other ways, age differences are smaller when well-practiced skills are assessed than when less-practiced skills are assessed (Denney, 1982).

Recall versus Recognition. Older adults are likely to be more deficient on tasks requiring recall memory than on tasks requiring only recognition of what was learned (Charles, Mather, &

Carstensen, 2003). In one study of memory for high school classmates (Bahrick, Bahrick, & Wittlinger, 1975), even adults who were almost 35 years past graduation could recognize which of five names matched a picture in their yearbook about 90% of the time. However, the ability to actively recall names of classmates when given only their photos as cues dropped considerably as the age of the rememberer increased. A large gap between recognition and recall shows that older people have encoded and stored the information but cannot retrieve it without the help of cues. Sometimes older adults fail to retrieve information because they never thoroughly encoded or learned it, but at other times they simply cannot retrieve information that is "in there."

Explicit Memory Tasks. Finally, older adults seem to have more trouble with explicit memory tasks that require mental effort than with implicit memory tasks that involve more automatic mental processes (Hoyer & Verhaeghen, 2006). Older adults, then, have little trouble with skills and procedures that have been routinized over the years—established as habits. But even though explicit memory declines, the magnitude of the decline varies with the type of explicit memory. Older adults retain fairly good semantic memory (general factual knowledge accumulated over time) but show steady declines in episodic memory (recall of specific events that are tied to a specific time and place) (see, for example, Spaniol, Madden, & Voss, 2006).

Overall, these findings suggest that older adults, like young children, have difficulty with tasks that are cognitively demanding—that require speed, the learning of unfamiliar material, the use of unexercised abilities, recall rather than recognition, or explicit and effortful rather than implicit and automatic memory. Yet older adults and young children have difficulty for different reasons, as you will now see.

Explaining Declines in Old Age

In asking why some older adults struggle with some learning and memory tasks, we will first return to the hypotheses used to explain childhood improvements in performance: knowledge base, metamemory, strategy use, and basic processing capacities. Then we will consider some additional possibilities.

Knowledge Base. If you start with the hypothesis that differences in knowledge base explain memory differences between older and younger adults, you immediately encounter a problem: Young children may lack knowledge, but elderly adults do not. Indeed, older adults are generally at least as knowledgeable as young adults: Semantic memory for vocabulary *increases* until about age 65 (Rönnlund et al., 2005). Verbal knowledge shows no decrease throughout mid- and older adulthood and may not decline until we are pushing 90 (Park et al., 2002; Rönnlund et al., 2005; Singer et al., 2003)! Older adults also know more than younger adults about real-world categories of information such as U.S. presidents, countries, international cities, and bodies of water (Foos & Sarno, 1998). In an important study, Harry Bahrick (1984) tested adults of various ages on their retention of Spanish vocabulary from high school or college classes. Amazingly, as much as 50% of the vocabulary

learned was retained nearly *50 years* later! And it may be worth your time and effort to learn as much as you can in your classes now: Bahrick also found that the more classes taken in a subject and the higher the grades in those courses, the better the retention of this material in the years to come. Adults who took several Spanish classes and earned "A" grades remembered more Spanish vocabulary 50 years later than adults who took one Spanish class and earned "C" grades remembered after a delay of just 1 year. Information that undergoes meaningful consolidation can clearly be retained in long-term memory for many years to come. So deficiencies in knowledge base are probably not the source of most memory problems that many older adults display. On the contrary, gains in knowledge probably help older adults compensate for losses in information-processing efficiency (Salthouse, 1993). Thus, older pilots are as adept as younger pilots and better than nonpilots at repeating back flight commands, but they show the usual effects of aging if they are given tasks less relevant to their work (Morrow et al., 1994). Older adults also perform better than younger adults on memory tasks in which they can spontaneously use analogies, another indication that a rich knowledge base can aid memory (Caplan & Schooler, 2001). Knowledge enhances learning. Indeed, as Paul Baltes has put it, "Knowledge is power!" (Baltes, Smith, & Staudinger, 1992, p. 143).

Metamemory. Could elderly adults, like young children, be deficient in the specific knowledge called metamemory? Is their knowledge of some of the strategies that prove useful in school learning—and in laboratory memory tasks—rusty? This theory sounds plausible, but research shows that older adults seem to know as much as younger adults about such things as which memory strategies are best and which memory tasks are hardest (Light, 1991). They can also monitor their memory to assist their learning (Hines, Touron, & Herzog, 2009). Still, older adults are more likely than younger ones to misjudge the accuracy of some aspects of their memory, such as the source of the memories (Dodson, Bawa, & Krueger, 2007).

Yvette Kelly uses a memory program to exercise her information-processing skills. Research suggests that both physical and mental workouts can aid memory across the life span.

So whereas metamemory seems largely intact across the life span, there may be some isolated areas of weakness. Moreover, although older adults know a lot about memory, they express more negative beliefs about their memory skills than do younger adults (Cavanaugh, 1996). Memory loss may contribute to a drop in confidence in memory skills, but negative beliefs about one's memory skills also appear to hurt memory performance (Hess, 2006). Therefore, it's not clear whether declines in actual memory performance lead to the development of negative beliefs about memory or whether negative beliefs—either your own or those of the surrounding culture—undermine memory performance (Hess, 2006; Hess, Hinson, & Hodges, 2009).

To understand the connection between memory performance and negative stereotypes, Becca Levy and Ellen Langer (1994) tested the memory of young and elderly adults (ages 59–91) in three groups: hearing Americans, deaf Americans, and hearing Chinese. In both the American deaf and Chinese cultures, elders are respected and negative stereotypes of intellectual aging are not as prevalent as they are among hearing Americans. As **Figure 8.11** shows, young adults in the three groups performed about equally well on a set of recall tasks, but Chinese elders clearly outperformed both deaf American elders (who were second best) and hearing American elders. Elderly Chinese adults scored only a little lower than young Chinese adults despite having less education. In

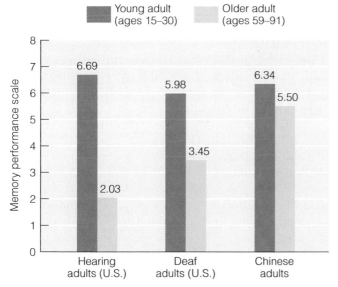

■ **Figure 8.11** Declines in memory skills in old age are not universal. In deaf culture and in Chinese culture, elderly people are not stereotyped as forgetful or senile. Perhaps as a result, Chinese elders perform almost as well as young Chinese adults on memory tasks, whereas in the United States, elders, especially in the hearing population, perform poorly.

SOURCE: Adapted from Levy, B., & Langer, E. (1994) Aging free from negative stereotypes: Successful memory in China and among the American deaf, *Journal of Personality and Social Psychology*, 66, 989–997. Copyright © 1994 by the American Psychological Association. Reprinted with permission.

addition, those older people in the study who believed that aging brings about memory loss performed more poorly than those who did not hold this belief. Levy (1996) has also shown that activating negative stereotypes in the minds of elderly adults (through rapid, subliminal presentation of words such as *Alzheimer's* and *senile* on a computer screen) causes them to perform worse on memory tests and to express less confidence in their memory skills than when positive stereotypes of old age are planted in their minds (through words such as *wise* and *sage*). Findings such as these clearly call into question the idea of a universal decline in memory skills in later life and point to the influence of culture and its views of aging on performance.

Memory Strategies. What about the hypothesis that failure to use effective memory strategies accounts for deficits in old age? Many older adults do not spontaneously use strategies such as organization and elaboration even though they know them and are capable of using them (Light, 1991; Smith & Earles, 1996). This may be an important part of the problem when older adults are asked to deliberately memorize something. Older adults' biggest problem, though, seems to be with effective *retrieval* of details of an event and not with the original *encoding* of the event (Thomas & Bulevich, 2006). This can be seen in the increased incidence of *tip-of-the-tongue* episodes, where individuals have the feeling that they know something such as a person's name but cannot retrieve it (Bucur et al., 2008). Although most of us experience at least an occasional episode of the tip-of-the-tongue phenomenon, older adults have more frequent episodes as they attempt to retrieve stored information. Thus, retrieval strategies may be more susceptible to aging than encoding strategies. But why do many older adults fail to use effective memory and retrieval strategies?

Basic Processing Capacities. The answer may lie in the fourth hypothesis—the notion that basic processing capacities change with age. Which capacities? Much attention has focused on declines in the capacity to use working memory to operate actively on a lot of information simultaneously. Working-memory capacity increases during childhood and adolescence, peaks around age 45, then begins to decline (Swanson, 1999). Moreover, working-memory capacity predicts how well adults will perform on a range of cognitive tasks (Hoyer & Verhaeghen, 2006). Older adults do fine on short-term memory tasks that require them to juggle just a few pieces of information in working memory. However, when the amount of information that they are to "operate on" increases, they begin to show deficits. Older adults may have more trouble than younger ones ignoring irrelevant task information. For instance, trying to memorize a list of words while walking is more problematic for older adults than for middle-aged or younger adults (Li et al., 2001; Lindenberger, Marsiske, & Baltes, 2000). Brain research confirms that older adults show increased activity in parts of the brain associated with inhibition of task-irrelevant information (Stevens et al., 2008).

Thus, their working-memory space may become cluttered with unnecessary information, limiting the space available for the task at hand (Hoyer & Verhaeghen, 2006).

Limitations in working-memory capacity are most likely rooted in slower functioning of the nervous system both early and late in life (see Hartley, 2006; also see Chapter 5). Much research shows that speed of processing increases during childhood and adolescence, peaks in early adulthood, then declines slowly over the adult years (Baudouin et al., 2009). The age differences in performance on cognitive tasks often shrink when age differences in speed of information processing are taken into account and controlled. Experience in a domain of learning can certainly enhance performance, but if children and older adults generally have sluggish "computers," they simply may not be able to keep up with the processing demands of complex learning and memory tasks (Hartley, 2006).

Using brain imaging techniques, researchers have also begun to identify different patterns of activity during memory tasks in the prefrontal cortex of younger and older adults (see, for example, Galdo-Alvarez, Lindin, & Diaz, 2009; Rypma et al., 2001). Although some studies show underactivity in older adults' brains, others show overactivity. Underactivity in the older brain is assumed to result from a deficiency of either the hardware of the brain or of the software it uses, such as the strategies that could be employed on a task (Reuter-Lorenz & Cappell, 2008). Overactivity, on the other hand, may indicate that the older brain is trying to compensate for age-related losses. By compensating, or working harder and drawing on more brain areas, the older brain may be able to perform as well as its younger counterpart, at least until this overactivity can no longer overcome steeper age-related declines (Meulenbroek et al., 2010).

Slow neural transmission, then, may be behind limitations in working memory in both childhood and old age (Bailey, Dunlosky, & Hertzog, 2009). Limitations in working memory, in turn, may contribute not only to limitations in long-term memory but also to difficulties performing a range of cognitive tasks, including problem-solving tasks and tests of intelligence, even those that have no time limits (Hartley, 2006; Salthouse, 2000).

To this point, then, you might conclude that many older adults, although they have a vast knowledge base and a good deal of knowledge about learning and memory, experience declines in basic processing capacity that make it difficult for them to carry out memory strategies that will drain their limited working-memory capacity. But the basic processing capacity hypothesis cannot explain everything about age differences in memory. You must consider some additional hypotheses, including sensory changes and a variety of contextual factors.

Sensory Changes. As you learned in Chapter 6, older adults experience declines in sensory abilities. Might these affect memory performance? Yes indeed. Research shows that visual and auditory skills are often better predictors than processing speed of cognitive performance among older adults (Anstey, Hofer, & Luszcz,

2003; Baltes & Lindenberger, 1997). As noted in Chapter 6, many older adults experience some hearing loss. Even young adults, when tested under moderately noisy conditions, show short-term memory performance decreases (Murphy et al., 2000). Sensory loss at any age may tax available processing resources, leading to memory deficits.

Contextual Contributors. Many researchers have adopted a contextual perspective on learning and memory, emphasizing both biological and genetic factors along with environmental and situational factors (Blanchard-Fields, Chen, & Norris, 1997; Dixon, 1992). They emphasize that performance on learning and memory tasks is the product of an interaction among (1) characteristics of the learner, such as goals, motivations, abilities, and health; (2) characteristics of the task or situation; and (3) characteristics of the broader environment, including the cultural context in which a task is performed. They are not convinced that there is a universal biological decline in basic learning and memory capacities because older individuals often perform capably in certain contexts.

First, cohort differences in education and IQ can explain age differences in some learning and memory skills. Elderly people today are less educated, on average, than younger adults are, and they are further removed from their school days. When education level is controlled for, age differences shrink, although they do not disappear (Nilsson et al., 2002; Rönnlund et al., 2005). Thus, to some extent, education can compensate for aging. Older adults who are highly educated or who have high levels of intellectual ability often perform as well as younger adults (Cherry & LeCompte, 1999; Haught et al., 2000).

Similarly, health and lifestyle differences between cohorts may contribute to age differences in learning and memory. Older adults are more likely than younger adults to have chronic or degenerative diseases, and even mild diseases can impair memory performance (Houx, Vreeling, & Jolles, 1991; Hultsch, Hammer, & Small, 1993). Older adults also lead less active lifestyles and perform fewer cognitively demanding activities than younger adults do, on average. These age group differences in lifestyle also contribute to age differences in cognitive performance. Older adults who engage in fitness training show enhanced cognitive ability, possibly because physical activity increases blood flow to the brain (Colcombe et al., 2004; Etgen et al., 2010). Increased blood flow to the hippocampus is associated with improved memory performance (Heo et al., 2010). Similarly, older adults who remain *mentally* active or take on challenging mental activities outperform other older adults on working memory and other cognitive tasks (Stine-Morrow et al., 2008).

The implications of such research are clear: Declines in information-processing skills are not inevitable or universal. Nature may place some boundaries on the information-processing system, but nurture plays a significant role in sustaining memory and problem-solving skills. Older adults may be able to maintain their memory skills if they are relatively well educated, stay healthy, and exercise their minds. Simply

Exploration 8.2

Can You Teach an "Old Dog" New Tricks?

In an important study of cognitive training effects, Sherry Willis and her colleagues in the ACTIVE Study Group (2006) followed four groups of older adults (average age of 74 years) over a period of 5 years. The groups differed in the type of cognitive training they received at the beginning of the study:

- Memory training—participants were taught strategies of organization, visualization, and association to remember verbal material.
- Reasoning training—participants were taught strategies for detecting a pattern in a series of letters or words.
- Speed training—participants learned to complete visual search tasks in increasingly less time, and they were trained to divide their attention between two tasks.
- No training—these participants served as a control group.

How did the groups fare after 5 years? Compared with the control group, the adults who received memory training still did better on memory tasks; those who received reasoning training performed better on reasoning tasks; and those who received speed training were much faster. Importantly, the benefits of training were evident not just on laboratory tasks but on activities important to daily living such as driving or understanding the interactions and side effects of prescription drugs.

This study and others (see Hertzog et al., 2009) show that older adults can profit from mental exercise that increasingly challenges them. Just as physical exercise contributes to overall physical well-being, mental exercise contributes to overall mental well-being. And just as your physical workouts need to increasingly challenge you (if you start out walking a half-mile at a slow pace, you need to increase your distance and/or your pace to reap the most benefits), your mental workouts must become more rigorous. If you start out solving easy Sudoku puzzles, you need to push yourself to move on to more difficult ones.

Consider the real-world memory problem of understanding and remembering information about drug prescriptions, which older adults often struggle more with compared with younger adults. By writing clear, organized instructions and spending time explaining to older patients what they are to do, health-care professionals can simplify the learning task (Morrell, Park, & Poon, 1989). Alternatively, older adults can be given external memory aids. Denise Park and her colleagues (1992) explored the benefits of two such aids: an organization chart (a poster or pocket-sized table giving an hour-by-hour account of when drugs should be taken) and a medication organizer (a dispenser with columns for different days of the week and pill compartments for times of the day). Adults older than 70 more often took their pills correctly when they were given both the chart and the organizer than when they were given one or neither. Because researchers know that poor health is one contributor to poor memory functioning, it makes especially good sense to reduce the cognitive demands on old and ailing patients by letting external memory aids do the mental work for them. Surely the best of all possible worlds for the aging learner would be one in which materials and teaching techniques are tailored to the learner's information-processing capacities and in which training is offered in how to stretch those capacities.

---

reviewing material after its presentation can help them improve their memory performance (Koutstaal et al., 1998; see **Exploration Box 8.2** for more ways to improve memory of older adults). Still, factors such as education and health cannot account completely for age differences in cognitive performance.

Perhaps the truth lies somewhere between the basic processing capacity view, which emphasizes nature by pointing to a universal decline in cognitive resources such as speed and working memory that affect performance on many cognitive tasks, and the contextual view, which emphasizes nurture. Contextual theorists stress variability from person to person and situation to situation based on cohort differences, motivational factors, and task demands. Most adults, at least if they live to an advanced old age, may experience some loss of basic processing resources. However, they may also have developed specialized knowledge and strategies that allow them to compensate for these losses as they carry out the everyday cognitive activities most important to them (Baltes et al., 1992).

Problem Solving and Aging

You know that problem-solving skills improve steadily from early childhood through adolescence, but what becomes of them in adulthood? On the one hand, you might expect to see a decline in problem-solving prowess paralleling declines in learning and memory performance. On the other hand, if adults increase their knowledge bases and develop expertise as they age, might not older adults outwit younger novices on many problem-solving tasks?

Familiar versus Unfamiliar Tasks

When given traditional problem-solving tasks to perform in the laboratory, young adults typically perform better than middle-aged adults, who in turn outperform older adults (Denney, 1989). However, consider research using the Twenty Questions task in which participants are shown an array of items and asked to find out, using as few questions as possible, which item the experimenter has in mind. The best problem-solving strategy is to ask **constraint-seeking questions**—ones that rule out more than one item (for example, "Is it an animal?"). Young children and older adults tend to pursue specific hypotheses instead ("Is it a pig?" "Is it a pencil?"). Consequently, they must ask more questions to identify the right object. However, if the task is altered to make it more familiar (for example, through the use of playing cards as stimuli), then older adults do far better. The familiarity of the material allows them to draw on their knowledge base to solve the problem. Thus, older adults are capable of using effective problem-solving strategies but do not use them in some contexts, especially when given unfamiliar tasks in a laboratory.

What if adults are asked to deal with real-life problems such as grease fires in the kitchen, family squabbles, or refrigerators that break down in the middle of the night? Nancy Denney and Kathy Pearce (1989) asked elderly adults to help them devise everyday problems that would be meaningful and familiar to older individuals. One problem was to generate ideas about how a 65-year-old recently widowed woman could improve her social life; another was to advise an elderly couple living on Social Security what to do when they were unable to pay their heating bill one winter. On these everyday problems, performance increased from early adulthood to middle age and declined in old age.

Other findings echo this one: When given everyday problems to which they can apply the expertise they have gained through experience, middle-aged adults often outperform young adults. Elderly adults sometimes equal and sometimes do worse than young and middle-aged adults; either way, they show smaller deficits on the everyday problems than they do on unfamiliar problems in the laboratory (Berg & Klaczynski, 1996; Marsiske & Willis, 1995). Ultimately, declines in basic capacities may limit the problem-solving skills of many elderly adults, not only in the laboratory but also in real life (Denney, 1989; Kasworm & Medina, 1990). You should bear in mind, however, the contextual view that cognitive competence among older adults varies widely because of differences in health, education, experience, and so on.

Exploring Development 8.2
Decision Making and Aging

See how a research study compares the speed and accuracy of older and younger adults' decisions and their memory for single words and pairs of words.

- Can older adults benefit from training in the task?
- What did the study demonstrate about associative recognition at different ages?

Selection, Optimization, and Compensation

Some cognitive researchers believe that older adults may approach problem solving differently than younger adults. It's true that younger adults generate more possible solutions to a problem than do older adults. But the solutions generated by older adults tend to be more goal-focused and selective, emphasizing quality over quantity (Marsiske & Margrett, 2006). **Exploring Development Box 8.2** shows this difference in a research project comparing decision making by older and younger adults. When faced with a broken water pipe in the middle of the night, an older couple may generate one solution—call their grown son who lives down the street. Although this may not seem like an ideal solution to the son, the older adults may realize that this is the easiest and fastest solution.

In addition, researchers have proposed a framework called **selective optimization with compensation (SOC)**, to understand how older adults may cope with and compensate for their diminishing cognitive resources (Baltes & Baltes, 1990; Baltes & Rudolph, 2013; Riediger, Li, & Lindenberger, 2006; and see Chapter 11). Three processes are involved: *selection* (focus on a limited set of goals and the skills most needed to achieve them), *optimization* (practice those skills to keep them sharp), and *compensation* (develop ways around the need for other skills). If cognitive resources are limited or unstable, then you can't take on everything; you need to be selective. Choose those tasks that are most important or have to be done. For example, prepare dinner (after all, you have to eat), but don't worry about getting every surface of the house dusted. Focus on what you do well—optimize your strengths and minimize weaknesses. If you still have the skills to balance a checkbook and this is something your partner struggles with, then you should take over managing the checkbook. If your vision is so bad that you cannot tell that your "clean" dishes have chunks of food remaining on them, then offload this task to a dishwasher or partner.

Researchers have investigated whether this selection, optimization, and compensation model can be applied to help older adults overcome weaknesses in explicit memory by taking advantage of their relative strength of implicit memory. For instance, Cameron Camp and his colleagues (Camp et al., 1996; Camp & McKitrick, 1992) have tried to help patients with dementia caused by Alzheimer's disease (AD) use the implicit memory capacities that they, like people with amnesia, retain even though they have serious deficits in explicit memory. For example, they have taught patients with AD to remember the names of staff members by having the patients name photos of staff members repeatedly and at ever longer intervals between trials. People who could not retain names for more than a minute were able to recall the names weeks later after training. The technique appears to work because it uses implicit memory processes; adults learn effortlessly when they repeatedly encounter the material to be learned. By selecting and optimizing, older adults can often compensate for their diminishing explicit memory, allowing them to maintain independence for a longer period of time (Riediger et al., 2006).

Checking Mastery

1. On what types of tasks are older adults most likely to experience memory problems?
2. How can adults minimize the effects of aging on memory and problem-solving tasks?

1. As a teacher in an Elderhostel program for older adults, you want to base your teaching methods on knowledge of the information-processing capacities of elderly adults. What practical recommendations would you derive from (a) the view that there is a universal decline with age in basic processing capacities and (b) the contextual perspective on cognitive aging?

2. Revisit Figure 8.10 showing the distribution of autobiographical memories over the life span. What factors might account for the rise and fall of autobiographical memories at different phases of the life span?

3. Every time your mother and grandmother forget something, they express concerns about "losing it" and "getting senile." Knowing that you have taken a course in life-span human development, they seek you out for reassurance. What can you tell them about memory and aging that might alleviate their concerns?

Chapter Summary

8.1 Conceptualizing Memory

- The information-processing approach uses a computer analogy to illustrate how the mind processes information. The human "computer" takes in information through the sensory registers, which hold the information for a very brief period. Information attended to may be further processed in short-term, or working, memory.

- Eventually, information may be stored in long-term memory, which seems to be unlimited in terms of size and permanency. In order for something to move into the long-term memory store, it must undergo a process of consolidation in which a memory trace of the event is created.

- Encoding and retrieval strategies influence memory performance. Types of retrieval include recognition, recall, and cued recall.

- Explicit memory is deliberate and effortful and changes over the life span, whereas implicit memory is automatic and relatively stable over the life span. Explicit and implicit memories are separate components of long-term memory and are localized in different parts of the brain.

- Memory has neurological underpinnings that influence memory effectiveness and contribute to developmental changes across the life span.

- Stored memories are instrumental to success at problem solving; stored information is used to achieve a goal. Executive control processes select, organize, manipulate, and interpret what is going on in the context of problem solving.

8.2 The Infant

- Using imitation, habituation, and operant conditioning techniques, researchers have gone from believing that infants have no memory beyond a few seconds to appreciating that even young 1-year-olds can recall experiences for weeks and even months under certain conditions.

- Infants clearly show recognition memory for familiar stimuli at birth and cued recall memory by about 2 months. More explicit memory, which requires actively retrieving an image of an object or event no longer present, appears to emerge toward the end of the first year. By age 2, it is even clearer that infants can recall events that happened long ago, for they, like adults, use language to represent and describe what happened.

- Simple problem solving improves throughout infancy, and infants realize that they can get adults to help them solve problems.

8.3 The Child

- Basic information-processing capacity increases as the brain matures and fundamental processes are automated to free working-memory space.

- Memory strategies such as rehearsal, organization, and elaboration improve. Metamemory improves and the general knowledge base grows. All these changes improve the processing of new information in areas of expertise.

- According to Robert Siegler, even young children use systematic rules to solve problems, but their problem-solving skills improve as they replace faulty rules with ones that incorporate all the relevant aspects of the problem. Multiple strategies are used at any age so that development proceeds through a natural selection process and resembles overlapping waves more than a set of stairsteps leading from one way of thinking to the next.

- Memory improves during childhood with increased efficiency of basic information-processing capacities, greater use of memory strategies, improvement in metamemory, and growth of general knowledge base.
- By age 3, children store routine daily events as scripts that they can draw on in similar situations. Our scripts influence what we remember about an event, which is also influenced by information related to but coming after the event.
- Much of what we remember is autobiographical. Even though infants and toddlers show evidence of memory, older children and adults often experience childhood amnesia, or lack of memory for events that happened during infancy and early childhood.

8.4 The Adolescent

- Adolescents master advanced learning strategies such as elaboration, note taking, and underlining, and they use their strategies more deliberately and selectively.
- Adolescents have larger knowledge bases, and their metamemory skills also improve and contribute to increased memory performance and problem-solving ability.

8.5 The Adult

- As adults gain expertise in a domain, they develop large and organized knowledge bases and highly effective, specialized, and automated ways of retrieving and using their knowledge.
- Many older adults perform less well than young adults on memory tasks that require speed, the learning of unfamiliar or meaningless material, the use of unexercised abilities, recall rather than recognition memory, and explicit rather than implicit memory.
- Declines in basic processing capacity and difficulty using strategies, plus contextual factors such as cohort differences and the irrelevance of many laboratory tasks to everyday life, contribute to age differences in memory.
- On average, older adults also perform less well than younger adults on laboratory problem-solving tasks, but everyday problem-solving skills are likely to improve from early adulthood to middle adulthood and to be maintained in old age.

Checking Mastery Answers

For answers to Checking Mastery questions, please see Appendix B.

Key Terms

CENGAGE brain.com Get quizzes, flashcards, videos, and more at **www.cengagebrain.com**.

9 Intelligence and Creativity

Sho Yano was born in Oregon, USA, and started writing at age 2, reading at age 3, and playing and composing music at age 4. By age 7, when most children are starting first grade, Sho was doing high school work under the tutelage of his mother because the gifted school he attended seemed unable to keep pace with his learning needs. He started college at age 9, and at age 12 he became the youngest person to enter the University of Chicago's joint MD/PhD program. He completed a PhD in molecular genetics and cell biology before getting too deeply into the MD portion of his program; after all, he needed to be 18 years of age before he could work with patients. At age 21, he became the youngest student to attain a medical degree from University of Chicago. He purportedly has an IQ of over 200 (Francis, 2012).

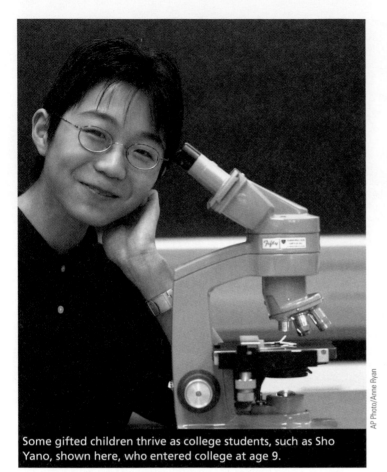

Some gifted children thrive as college students, such as Sho Yano, shown here, who entered college at age 9.

AP Photo/Anne Ryan

for shipping, going through the same set of steps for each package. They have a supervisor with them at all times as any changes in routine can be challenging for them. In the afternoons, Steven spends most of his time watching television before he is reminded to wash up and eat dinner. Evenings are filled with more television before Steven is prompted to shower and go to bed.

As these examples indicate, the range of human intellectual abilities is immense. So far, much of the material on cognitive development in this book has focused on what human minds have in common, not on how they differ. Piaget, after all, was interested in identifying universal stages of cognitive development. And the information-processing approach has been used mainly to understand the basic cognitive processes all people rely on to learn, remember, and solve problems.

This chapter continues the exploration of how the human mind normally changes over the life span. Here we introduce still another approach to the study of the mind: the psychometric, or testing, approach to intelligence, which led to the creation of intelligence tests. Many people find it hard to say anything nice about IQ tests. These measures have their limitations, and they have been misused. Yet they have also provided researchers with a good deal of information about intellectual development and about variations in intellectual performance. Further, since their inception they have been used for the practical purpose of identifying different levels of intelligence among school children, military recruits, and even potential employees.

This chapter examines how performance on intelligence tests typically changes and stays the same over the life span, what IQ tests reveal about a person, and why people's IQ scores differ. It also looks at both gifted and intellectually disabled individuals from a life-span perspective. We will also discuss creativity, a type of intellectual ability not measured by traditional intelligence tests. Before going further, take the quiz in **Engagement Box 9.1** to see if you have any misconceptions about intelligence and intelligence tests; this chapter will clarify why the correct answers are correct.

At age 35, Steven lives in a group home for individuals like himself who have IQ scores that classify them as intellectually disabled. Steven needs assistance to do most tasks of daily living, such as preparing meals and maintaining good personal hygiene. Along with several other housemates, Steven is taken to a local packaging plant where they work for several hours every day in a room specifically set aside for them. There, they prepare items

9.1 Defining Intelligence and Creativity

LEARNING OBJECTIVES:

- State how intelligence and creativity are typically defined.
- Analyze the accuracy and usefulness of traditional IQ tests.
- Explain the most prominent theories of intelligence.
- Evaluate the strengths and weaknesses of the theories of intelligence.

Let's begin by trying to understand intelligence, as defined by some of the most prominent scholars in this field. As noted in Chapter 7, Piaget defined intelligence as thinking or behavior that is adaptive. Other experts have offered different definitions, many of them centering on the ability to think abstractly or to solve problems effectively (for example, Sternberg, 2010a, 2010b). Early definitions of intelligence tended to reflect the

assumption that intelligence reflects innate ability—that it is genetically determined and fixed at conception. But it has become clear that intelligence is not fixed, that it is changeable and subject to environmental influence (see Nisbett et al., 2012). As a result, an individual's intelligence test scores sometimes vary considerably over a lifetime. Bear in mind that understanding of this complex human quality has changed since the first intelligence

What Do You Know about Intelligence and Creativity?

Answer each question true or false:

__ 1. On the leading tests of intelligence, a score of 100 is average.

__ 2. Most scholars now conclude that there is no such thing as general intelligence; there are only separate mental abilities.

__ 3. Individuals who are intellectually gifted are typically gifted in all mental abilities.

__ 4. Intellectually gifted children do well in school but are more likely than most children to have social and emotional problems.

__ 5. IQ predicts both a person's occupational status and his success compared with others in the same occupation.

__ 6. On average, performance on IQ tests declines for people in their 70s and 80s.

__ 7. Qualities associated with wisdom are as common among young and middle-aged adults as among elderly adults.

__ 8. It has been established that children's IQs are far more influenced by their environments than by their genes.

__ 9. How well a child does on a test of creativity cannot be predicted well from her IQ score.

__ 10. Creative achievers (great musicians, mathematicians, writers, and so on) typically do all their great works before about age 40 or 45 and produce only lesser works from then on.

Answers: 1-T, 2-F, 3-F, 4-F, 5-T, 6-T, 7-T, 8-F, 9-T, 10-F

---

tests were created at the turn of the last century—and that there is still no single, universally accepted definition of intelligence. Some researchers, such as Linda Gottfredson and Donald Saklofske (2009), have concluded that the field has shifted away from trying to answer the question of "what is intelligence?" to discussing the research findings that have emerged from using intelligence tests, whatever it is these tests might be measuring.

The Psychometric Approach

The research tradition that spawned the development of standardized tests of intelligence is the **psychometric approach**. According to psychometric theorists, intelligence is a trait or a set of traits that characterizes some people to a greater extent than others. The goals, then, are to identify these traits precisely and to measure them so that differences among individuals can be described. But from the start, experts could not agree on whether intelligence is one general cognitive ability or many specific abilities.

Early on, Charles Spearman (1927) proposed a two-factor theory of intelligence involving, first, a general mental ability (called g) that contributes to performance on many different kinds of tasks. This g factor is what accounts for Spearman's observation that people were often consistent across a range of tasks. For example, general intelligence has been found to correlate with performance on exams in 25 different academic subjects (Deary et al., 2007). However, Spearman also noticed that a student who excelled at most tasks might score low on a particular measure (for example, memory for words). So he proposed a second aspect of intelligence: s, or special abilities, each of which is specific to a particular kind of task. Some research suggests that g may play a greater role in IQ test performance during childhood than adolescence (Kane & Brand, 2006). By adolescence, many effortful processes that underlie the expression of g have become automated, freeing up cognitive resources to hone certain specific abilities.

Raymond Cattell and John Horn have greatly influenced current thinking concerning intelligence by distinguishing between two broad dimensions of intellect: fluid intelligence and crystallized intelligence (Cattell, 1963; Horn & Cattell, 1967; Horn & Noll, 1997). **Fluid intelligence** is the ability to use your mind actively to solve novel problems—for example, to solve verbal analogies, remember unrelated pairs of words, or recognize relationships among geometric figures (■ **Figure 9.1**). The skills involved—reasoning, seeing relationships among stimuli, and drawing inferences— are usually not taught and are believed to represent a person's

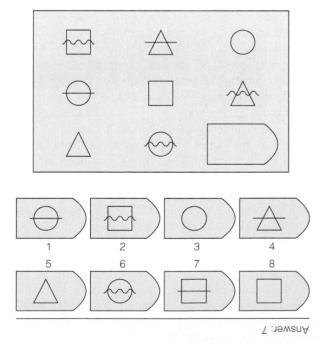

Answer: 7

■ **Figure 9.1** An item assessing fluid intelligence (similar to those in a test called the Raven Progressive Matrices Test). Which of the numbered pieces completes the design?

"raw information processing power" (Gottfred & Saklofske, 2009). **Crystallized intelligence**, in contrast, is the use of knowledge acquired through schooling and other life experiences. Tests of general information (At what temperature does water boil?), word comprehension (What is the meaning of *duplicate*?), and numerical abilities (What is 23 × 3?) are all measures of crystallized intelligence. Thus, fluid intelligence involves using your mind in new and flexible ways, whereas crystallized intelligence involves using what you have already learned through experience.

Obviously, there is no single answer to the question *What is intelligence?* Nonetheless, some consensus has emerged from the vast amount of research conducted over the years on this construct. Intelligence is most often viewed as a hierarchy that includes (1) a general ability factor at the top that influences how well people do on a range of cognitive tasks; (2) a few broad dimensions of ability that are distinguishable in factor analyses (for example, fluid intelligence, crystallized intelligence, memory capacity, and processing speed); and (3) at the bottom, many specific abilities such as numerical reasoning, spatial discrimination, and word comprehension that also influence how well a person performs cognitive tasks that tap these specific abilities (Carroll, 1993; Horn & Noll, 1997).

One of the most significant contributions to the psychometric approach to intelligence occurred in 1904 when Alfred Binet and Theodore Simon were commissioned by the French government to devise a test that would identify "dull" children who might need special instruction. Binet and Simon devised a large battery of tasks measuring the skills believed to be necessary for classroom learning: attention, perception, memory, reasoning, verbal comprehension, and so on. Items that discriminated between normal children and those described by their teachers as slow were kept in the final test.

This forerunner of the modern IQ test was soon revised so that the items were age-graded. For example, a set of "6-year-old" items could be passed by most 6-year-olds but by few 5-year-olds; "12-year-old" items could be handled by most 12-year-olds but not by younger children. This approach permitted the testers to describe a child's **mental age (MA)**—the level of age-graded problems that the child is able to solve. Thus, a child who passes all items at the 5-year-old level but does poorly on more advanced items—regardless of the child's actual age—is said to have a MA of 5.

Binet's test became known as the **Stanford-Binet Intelligence Scale** after Lewis Terman of Stanford University translated and published a revised version of the test for use with American children. Terman developed a procedure for comparing a child's MA with his chronological age (CA) by calculating an **intelligence quotient (IQ)**, which consisted of MA divided by CA and then multiplied by 100 ($IQ = MA/CA \times 100$). An IQ score of 100 indicates average intelligence, regardless of a child's age: The average child passes just the items that age-mates typically pass; MA increases each year, but so does CA. The child of 8 with a MA of 10 has experienced rapid intellectual growth and has a high IQ (specifically, 125); if she still has a MA of 10 when she is 15 years old, then she has an IQ of only 67 and is clearly below average compared with children of the same age.

The Stanford-Binet, now in its fifth edition, is still in use (Roid, 2003). Its **test norms**—standards of normal performance

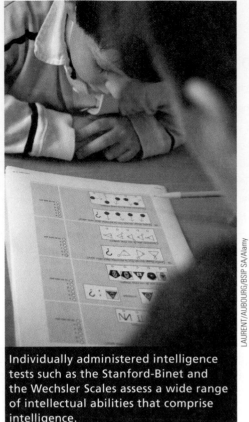

Individually administered intelligence tests such as the Stanford-Binet and the Wechsler Scales assess a wide range of intellectual abilities that comprise intelligence.

LAURENT/AUBOURG/BSIP SA/Alamy

expressed as average scores and the range of scores around the average—are based on the performance of a large, representative sample of people (2-year-olds through adults) from many socioeconomic and racial backgrounds. The concept of MA is no longer used to calculate IQ; instead, individuals receive scores that reflect how well or how poorly they do compared with others of the same age. An IQ of 100 is still average, and the higher the IQ score an individual attains, the better the performance is in comparison with that of age-mates.

David Wechsler constructed a set of intelligence tests, collectively referred to as the **Wechsler Scales**, also in wide use. The Wechsler Preschool and Primary Scale of Intelligence (WPPSI-III) is for children between ages 3 and 8 (Wechsler, 2002). The Wechsler Intelligence Scale for Children (WISC-IV) is appropriate for schoolchildren ages 6–16 (Wechsler, 2003), and the Wechsler Adult Intelligence Scale (WAIS-IV) is used with adults (Wechsler, 2008). The Wechsler tests yield a verbal IQ score based on items measuring vocabulary, general knowledge, arithmetic reasoning, and the like and a performance IQ based on such nonverbal skills as the ability to assemble puzzles, solve mazes, reproduce geometric designs with colored blocks, and rearrange pictures to tell a meaningful story. As with the Stanford-Binet, a score of 100 is defined as average performance for the person's age. A person's full-scale IQ is a combination of the verbal and performance scores.

Scores on both the Stanford-Binet and Wechsler Scales form a **normal distribution**, or a symmetrical, bell-shaped spread around the average score of 100 (■ **Figure 9.2**). Scores around

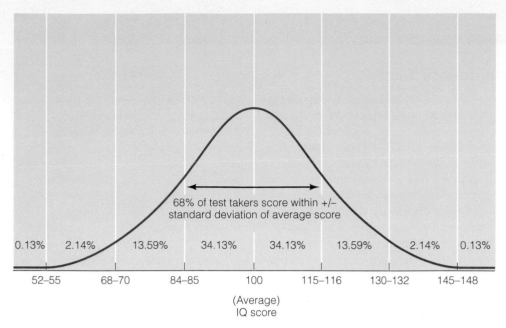

68% of test takers score within +/− standard deviation of average score

| 0.13% | 2.14% | 13.59% | 34.13% | 34.13% | 13.59% | 2.14% | 0.13% |

| 52–55 | 68–70 | 84–85 | 100 | 115–116 | 130–132 | 145–148 |

(Average)
IQ score

■ **Figure 9.2** A normal distribution curve showing traditional intelligence testing scores in the classic bell shape around the average score of 100.

the average are common; very high and very low scores are rare. We also know that the standard deviation is 16 points for the Stanford-Binet and 15 points for the Wechsler Scales. The **standard deviation** is a measure of how tightly the scores are clustered around the mean score. As Figure 9.2 shows, about two-thirds of people taking the Wechsler test have scores between 85 and 115 (one standard deviation unit above and below the mean) and nearly 95% have scores between 70 and 130 (two standard deviation units above and below the mean). Fewer than 3% have scores of 130 or above, a score often used as one criterion of giftedness. Similarly, fewer than 3% have IQs below 70, a cutoff commonly used to define intellectual disability.

In the end, the intelligence tests guided by psychometric theories have emphasized general intellectual ability by summarizing performance in a single IQ score, and they have assessed only some of the specialized abilities humans possess. Critics believe traditional psychometric tests have not fully described what it means to be an intelligent person, and some have offered alternative ways of thinking about intelligence that represent challenges to the traditional view. Reading about these approaches in the following sections will help you capture the nature of intelligence and appreciate the limitations of the tests used to measure it. In addition, **Exploration Box 9.1** examines two modern alternatives to the assessment of intelligence.

Gardner's Theory of Multiple Intelligences

As noted, not everyone agrees that the psychometric approach is the best way to understand intelligence. Howard Gardner (1999/2000; Chen & Gardner, 1997) rejects the idea that a single IQ score is a meaningful measure of human intelligence. He argues that there are many intelligences, most of which have been ignored by the

developers of standardized intelligence tests. Instead of asking, "How smart are you?" researchers should be asking, "How are you smart?" and identifying people's strengths and weaknesses across the full range of human mental faculties (Chen & Gardner, 1997). Gardner (2000) argues that there are at least eight distinct intellectual abilities:

1. *Linguistic intelligence.* Language skills, such as those seen in the poet's facility with words.
2. *Logical–mathematical intelligence.* The abstract thinking and problem solving shown by mathematicians and computer scientists and emphasized by Piaget.
3. *Musical intelligence.* Based on an acute sensitivity to sound patterns.
4. *Spatial intelligence.* Most obvious in great artists who can perceive things accurately and transform what they see.
5. *Bodily-kinesthetic intelligence.* The skillful use of the body to create crafts, perform, or fix things; shown, for example, by dancers, athletes, and surgeons.
6. *Interpersonal intelligence.* Social intelligence, social skill, exceptional sensitivity to other people's motivations and moods; demonstrated by salespeople and psychologists.
7. *Intrapersonal intelligence.* Understanding of one's own feelings and inner life.
8. *Naturalist intelligence.* Expertise in the natural world of plants and animals.

Traditional IQ tests emphasize linguistic and logical–mathematical intelligence, and to some extent they test spatial intelligence, perhaps because those are the forms of intelligence Western societies value most highly and work the hardest to nurture in school. But IQ tests can be faulted for ignoring most of the other forms of intelligence. Although Gardner does not claim that his is the definitive list of intelligences, he presents evidence suggesting that each of these eight abilities is distinct. For example, it is clear that a person can be exceptional in one ability but poor in others—witness **savant syndrome**, the phenomenon in which extraordinary talent in a particular area is displayed by a person otherwise intellectually disabled (Treffert, 2000). Leslie Lemke, one such individual, is affected by cerebral palsy, blindness, and intellectual disability, and could not talk until he was an adult (Treffert, 2000). Yet he can hear a musical piece once and play it flawlessly on the piano or imitate songs in perfect German or Italian even though his own speech is still primitive. He apparently has a high level of musical intelligence. Other savants, despite IQs below 70, can draw well enough to gain admittance to art school or can calculate on the spot what day of the week it was January 16, 1909 (Hermelin & Rutter, 2001). Some scholars think that the skills shown by savants are so specific and depend so much on

Alternatives to Traditional Intelligence Tests

Although the Stanford-Binet Intelligence Scale and the Wechsler Scales continue to dominate the assessment field, concerns about what these scales truly measure has led to the creation of several alternatives (see Urbina, 2011). Alan Kaufman and Nadeen Kaufman, for example, designed the Kaufman Assessment Battery for Children (K-ABC-II; Kaufman & Kaufman, 2003). This test, based on information-processing theory, focuses on *how* children solve problems rather than on *what* problems they solve (Kaufman, 2001; Sparrow & Davis, 2000). The K-ABC-II, which is appropriate for children ages 3–18, has two subscales. One measures a child's ability to process information sequentially; the other measures the ability to integrate several pieces of information. The test also has a separate section of questions to assess children's achievement or acquired knowledge.

Another promising approach is **Sternberg's Triarchic Abilities Test (STAT)**, driven by his theory (discussed in the chapter) that intelligence is a convergence of practical, creative, and analytical components. The test uses a variety of question formats, combining those found on traditional IQ tests with those designed to tap into the other components of intelligence. For instance, students write an essay on how they would reform their school system, offer solutions to everyday dilemmas such as how to plan a route around an obstacle, infer the meanings of "fake words" from the sentence context, and figure out analogies based on counterfactual information. Some studies suggest that the STAT is a valid measure of the three components of intelligence that it is intended to assess (Sternberg, 2011). In

addition, there is evidence that the STAT can augment other standardized tests to improve the prediction of school performance from the elementary and secondary levels to the college level (Stemler et al., 2006; Sternberg, 2009). By tapping into different types of intelligence not assessed by traditional tests, the STAT can uncover exceptional intelligence among individuals who might otherwise be overlooked.

Whether we use a traditional intelligence test or one of the alternatives, trying to boil down a person's intelligence to a single score is a formidable task. Human mental functioning is truly complex. Intelligence tests can provide us with only a snapshot in time—an estimate that is not always a good indicator of the person's underlying intellectual competence.

---

memory that they do not qualify as separate "intelligences" (Nettelbeck & Young, 1996). However, Gardner insists that savant syndrome simply cannot be explained by theories that emphasize a general intelligence factor, *g*.

Gardner also marshals evidence to show that each type of intelligence has its own distinctive developmental course. Many great musical composers and athletes, for example, revealed their genius in childhood, whereas exceptional logical–mathematical intelligence typically shows up later, after the individual has gained the capacity for abstract thought and has mastered an area of science. Finally, Gardner links his distinct intelligences to distinct structures in the brain, arguing that the eight intelligences are neurologically distinct.

Sternberg's Triarchic Theory and Successful Intelligence

Agreeing with Gardner that the traditional psychometric approach does not capture all that it means to be an intelligent person, Robert Sternberg (1985, 1988a, 2003, 2009b, 2011) has proposed a **triarchic theory of intelligence** that emphasizes three components that jointly contribute to intelligent behavior: practical, creative, and analytic components (■ **Figure 9.3**).

The Practical Component

First, according to the **practical component**, what is defined as intelligent behavior varies from one sociocultural context to another. What might be intelligent in one context may be quite illogical in another. People who are high in this practical

component of intelligence can adapt to the environment that they find themselves in, and they can shape the environment to optimize their strengths and minimize their weaknesses. These people have "street smarts," or common sense.

Just as intelligent behavior varies from one context to another, it also changes over time. Numerical abilities may not play as important a role in intelligent behavior now that calculators and computers are widely used, for example, whereas analytical skills may be more important than ever in a complex, urban world. And certainly the infant learning how to master new toys shows a different kind of intelligence than the adult mastering a college curriculum. Thus, the definition of intelligence in the context of infancy must differ from the definition of intelligence in the context of adulthood.

The practical component of Sternberg's triarchic theory, then, defines intelligent behavior differently depending on the sociocultural context in which it is displayed. Intelligent people adapt to the environment they are in (for example, a job setting), shape that environment to make it suit them better, or find a better environment. They can walk into a new situation, quickly evaluate it, and adapt their behavior to be successful in this new context. Although recognized by many people as an important form of intelligence, this real-world adaptability is not assessed by traditional intelligence tests.

The Creative Component

According to the **creative component** of the triarchic theory, what is intelligent when a person first encounters a new task is not the same as what is intelligent after extensive experience

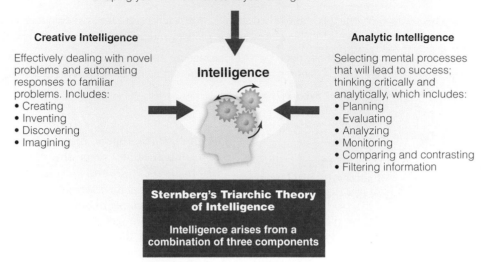

Practical Intelligence

Practical intelligence, or "street smarts," means successfully solving problems that arise in your everyday life. This includes:
• Adapting to the environment you are in
• Selecting environments in which you can succeed
• Shaping your environment to fit your strengths

Creative Intelligence

Effectively dealing with novel problems and automating responses to familiar problems. Includes:
• Creating
• Inventing
• Discovering
• Imagining

Intelligence

Analytic Intelligence

Selecting mental processes that will lead to success; thinking critically and analytically, which includes:
• Planning
• Evaluating
• Analyzing
• Monitoring
• Comparing and contrasting
• Filtering information

Sternberg's Triarchic Theory of Intelligence

Intelligence arises from a combination of three components

■ **Figure 9.3** Sternberg's triarchic theory of intelligence includes three components: analytic, practical, and creative intelligences.

with that task. The first kind of intelligence, *response to novelty*, requires active and conscious information processing. Sternberg believes that relatively novel tasks provide the best measures of intelligence because they tap the individual's ability to come up with creative ideas or fresh insights.

In daily life, however, people also perform more or less intelligently on familiar and repetitive tasks (driving a car, for example). This second kind of intelligence reflects **automatization**, or an increased efficiency of information processing with practice. It is intelligent to develop little "programs in the mind" for performing common, everyday activities efficiently and unthinkingly. Thus, according to Sternberg, it is crucial to know how familiar a task is to a person before assessing that person's behavior. For example, giving people of two different cultural groups an intelligence test whose items are familiar to one group and novel to the other introduces **culture bias** into the testing process, making it difficult to obtain a fair assessment of the groups' relative abilities.

The Analytic Component

The third aspect of the triarchic theory, the **analytic component**, focuses on the information-processing skills that produce answers to questions in traditional intelligence tests. These include thinking critically and analytically. Specifically, people who are high on this component can plan what to do, monitor progress, filter out irrelevant information and focus on the relevant, compare new information to existing knowledge, and evaluate outcomes.

As an information-processing theorist, Sternberg believes that the theories of intelligence underlying the development of traditional IQ tests ignore *how* people produce intelligent answers. He argues that a full picture of intelligence includes

not only the number of answers people get right but also the processes they use to arrive at their answers and the efficiency with which they use those processes. So, to fully assess how intelligent people are, researchers must consider the practical *context* in which they perform (their age, culture, and historical period), their ability to respond *creatively* to new tasks, and their *analytic* strategies. Individuals who are intelligent, according to this triarchic model, are able to carry out logical thought processes efficiently and effectively to solve both novel and familiar problems and to adapt to their environment. Before moving on, review Sternberg's three components of intelligence with the examples provided in ● **Table 9.1**.

What has Robert Sternberg contributed to our understanding of intelligence?

• Table 9.1 Sternberg's Triarchic Theory of Intelligence: Examples of Three Hypothetical Students, Each Excelling at One of the Three Components

Component	Description of Hypothetical Student
Practical	Practical Patty is not terribly creative, nor does she get the best grades in the classroom. However, if you want to get something done, enlist Patty's help; she can figure out a way to get a job done or get from point A to point B efficiently.
Analytic	Many people rate Analytic Alice as a gifted student, and teachers love having her in their classrooms. Although not very imaginative, she is able to analyze a collection of ideas and provide a logical critique of them.
Creative	Creative Cathy does not get as "deep" into understanding the material as her classmate Alice. But she generates lots of new ideas and can be counted on to offer a different perspective in class discussions.

SOURCE: Adapted from Sternberg, R. J. (1985). *Beyond IQ: A triarchic theory of intelligence.* Cambridge: Cambridge University Press.

Successful Intelligence

Sternberg (1999b, 2003, 2011) expanded his triarchic theory to include what he calls the theory of **successful intelligence**. According to the most recent version of this theory, successful intelligence consists of being able to:

- establish and achieve reasonable goals consistent with your skills and circumstances
- optimize your strengths and minimize weaknesses
- adapt to the environment through a combination of selecting a good environment and making modifications to self or the environment to increase fit
- use all three components of intelligence—analytic, creative, and practical.

The path to successful intelligence, then, is figuring out a reasonable goal given your skills and circumstances, and positioning yourself to allow your strengths to blossom and weaknesses to fade. It also means that when circumstances or skills change, you can adapt or alter the environment or move on to something that is a better fit. Consider Bob's story. After struggling with academics throughout middle and high school, Bob decided that college was not his best option. Instead, he found himself "in the right place at the right time" as his grandfather was getter older and looking for some help with his landscaping business. Bob had always loved working outdoors and had an eye for how to arrange plantings to their best advantage, something for which his grandfather never had much patience. After a few years, when his grandfather was ready to retire, Bob knew he had most of the skills needed to take over the business. He realized, though, that the business had not really been modernized and that he himself lacked the bookkeeping skills that would be needed to maintain and grow the business. He took a few courses at the local college and talked to some of the customers about their needs. From this, he developed a marketing and growth plan for the business. The business thrived, but after a few years, Bob recognized that his customers increasingly asked about water gardens, something he had not previously offered. After considering the pros and cons of branching out, Bob decided he could handle it. After all, he didn't want to lose customers to his competitors just because water gardens had not been "his thing" in the past. He figured he knew enough to incorporate this alternative type of garden into the business.

Bob does not necessarily exhibit the type of intelligence that many people may think of when they consider the meaning of intelligence, that is, intelligence for academic tasks. However, Bob illustrates successful intelligence: establishing a goal that made sense for him given his situation, being aware of his strengths and weaknesses, and adapting to changes over time. Take a few minutes to consider your own goals, your circumstances, and your pattern of strengths and weaknesses. What path might be an intelligent option for you?

Creativity

According to Sternberg, creativity is one of the three main components of intelligence. Most scholars define **creativity** as the ability to produce novel responses appropriate in context and valued by others—products both original and meaningful (Simon, 2001; Simonton, 1999; Sternberg, 2003). Thus, someone who comes up with a novel and useful idea is considered creative, whereas someone who comes up with a novel idea that has no apparent value may not be considered creative. Some researchers who study creativity, however, have concerns about defining as creative only those ideas that are deemed useful (see Smith, 2005). After all, who decides what is useful, and who is to say whether something will be valued by someone at some time? Consequently, some researchers examine all novel outputs and not just those that are deemed useful or valuable.

Research shows some connection between creativity and intelligence, although not a particularly strong connection (see Kaufman & Plucker, 2011). It turns out that IQ scores and creativity scores do not correlate very well because they measure two different types of thinking. IQ tests measure **convergent thinking**, which involves "converging" on the best answer to a problem. If we could typecast someone as a *convergent thinker*, it would be the person who wants to know *the* correct answer to a problem. In contrast, creativity involves **divergent thinking**, or coming up with a variety of ideas or solutions to a problem when there is no single correct answer. Responses on divergent thinking tasks can be analyzed along three dimensions: the originality or uniqueness of the generated ideas, the flexibility of thinking or how many different categories are expressed by the ideas, and the fluency of the ideas (Runco, 2010). This last one—**ideational fluency**, or the sheer number of different (including novel) ideas that a person can generate—is most often used to assess creativity because it is easy to score. Quick—list all the uses you can think of for a pencil. An uncreative person might say you could write letters, notes, postcards, and so forth; by contrast, one creative person envisioned a pencil as "a backscratcher, a potting stake, kindling for a fire, a rolling pin for baking, a toy for a woodpecker, or a small boat for a cricket" (Richards, 1996, p. 73).

This use of divergent thinking tasks to assess creativity reflects a psychometric, or testing, approach. That is, it assumes that creativity is a trait that is held to a greater or lesser degree by individuals and can be measured. While the psychometric approach can be useful, it may not consider the multitude of factors that constitute creativity. This is where Sternberg's **investment theory** of creativity is valuable (Sternberg, 2012). According to studies of creative achievement, creativity emerges from a *confluence*, or coming together, of these six factors:

- intellectual skills that include the trio of abilities comprising Sternberg's triarchic theory of intelligence discussed earlier
- enough knowledge of a field to have an understanding of the current state and what might be missing or needed in the field
- a thinking style that "enjoys" mentally toying with ideas
- a personality style that is open to some risk and is comfortable stepping outside the norm
- motivation to stay focused on the task and not give up when faced with obstacles
- an environment that supports and rewards creative output

Thus, according to the investment theory, creativity is a *confluence* of many factors, each added in appropriate concentrations at the proper time. We might think of creativity as analogous to making a good soufflé: It requires certain ingredients—including intelligence—in specific amounts, combined in a particular order, baked at the proper temperature, and for the right amount of time. All these things must come together or your soufflé will be a flop. And so it is with creativity.

As you can see, although the two constructs are related, intelligence, with its focus on convergent thinking, and creativity,

with its focus on divergent thinking, are distinct. In subsequent sections, as we discuss the intellectual profiles of children, adolescents, and adults, we will also consider the development of their creative selves. Note, however, that the infant is not included in our discussion of creativity because, to date, researchers have not developed a method for uncovering signs of creativity at this young age.

9.2 The Infant

LEARNING OBJECTIVES:

- Name and describe methods of assessing infant intelligence.
- Indicate the infant behaviors that are best connected to later intelligent behaviors and explain the reason for this connection.

As you saw in Chapters 7 and 8, the mind develops rapidly in infancy. But how can an infant's intellectual growth be measured? Is it possible to identify infants who are more or less intelligent than their age-mates? And how well does high (or low) intelligence in infancy predict high (or low) intelligence in childhood and adulthood?

Developmental Quotients

None of the standard intelligence tests can be used with children much younger than 3, because the test items require verbal skills and attention spans that infants and toddlers do not have. Some developmentalists have tried to measure infant intelligence by

assessing the rate at which infants achieve important developmental milestones. Perhaps the best known and most widely used infant test is the **Bayley Scales of Infant Development** (Bayley, 1993). This test, designed for infants and toddlers ages 1 month to 42 months, has three parts:

- The *motor scale*, which measures the infant's ability to do such things as grasp a cube and throw a ball
- The *mental scale*, which includes adaptive behaviors such as reaching for a desirable object, searching for a hidden toy, and following directions
- The *behavior rating scale*, a rating of the child's behavior on dimensions such as goal-directedness, emotional regulation, and social responsivity

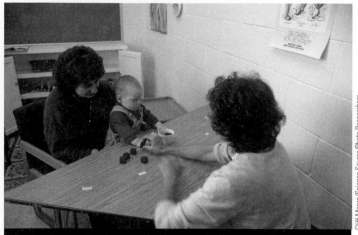

The Bayley Scales of Infant Development allow practitioners to evaluate an infant's performance relative to their peers on important developmental milestones.

On the basis of the first two scores, the infant is given a **developmental quotient (DQ)** rather than an IQ. The DQ summarizes how well or how poorly the infant performs in comparison with a large norm group of infants and toddlers the same age.

Infant Intelligence as a Predictor of Later Intelligence

As they age, infants progress through many developmental milestones of the kind assessed by the Bayley scales, so such scales are useful in charting infants' developmental progress. They are also useful in diagnosing neurological problems and intellectual disability— even when these conditions are mild and difficult to detect through standard pediatric or neurological examinations (Escalona, 1968; Honzik, 1983). But developmentalists have also been interested in the larger issue of continuity versus discontinuity in intellectual development: Is it possible to predict which infants are likely to be gifted, average, or intellectually disabled during the school years?

Not from their DQ Scores. Correlations between infant DQ and child IQ are low, sometimes close to zero. The infant who does well on the Bayley scales or other infant tests may or may not obtain a high IQ score later in life (Honzik, 1983; Rose et al., 1989). True, the infant who scores low on an infant test often turns out to be intellectually disabled, but otherwise there seems to be a good deal of discontinuity between early and later scores—at least until a child is 4 or older.

What might explain the poor connection between scores on infant development scales and children's later IQs? Perhaps the main reason is that infant tests and IQ tests tap qualitatively different kinds of abilities (Columbo, 1993). Piaget would undoubtedly approve of this argument. Infant scales focus heavily on the sensory and motor skills that Piaget believed are so important in infancy; IQ tests such as the Stanford-Binet and WISC-IV emphasize more abstract abilities, such as verbal reasoning, concept formation, and problem solving.

Robert McCall (1981, 1983) offers a second explanation, arguing that the growth of intelligence during infancy is highly influenced by powerful and universal maturational processes. Maturational forces (such as the unfolding of the genetic blueprint for intelligence) pull infants back on course if environmental influences (such as growing up in an impoverished home and neighborhood) cause them to stray. For this reason, higher or lower infant test scores are likely to be nothing more than temporary deviations from a universal developmental path. As the child nears age 2, McCall argues, maturational forces become less strong, so individual differences become larger and more stable over time. Consistent differences, related to both individual genetic makeup and environment, begin to emerge.

Should researchers give up on trying to predict later IQ on the basis of behaviors in infancy? At least one, Joseph Fagan, did not give up, but drew upon the information-processing approach discussed in Chapter 8 to give new life to the idea that there is continuity in intelligence from infancy to childhood. Fagan and other researchers have found that certain measures of infant attention predict later IQ better than do the rather misnamed infant intelligence tests (Fagan, 2011). For example, speed of habituation (how fast the infant loses interest in a repeatedly presented stimulus) and preference for novelty (the degree to which an infant prefers a novel stimulus to a familiar one), assessed in the first year of life, have an average correlation of about 0.45 with IQ in childhood, particularly with verbal IQ and memory skills (McCall & Carriger, 1993; Rose & Feldman, 1997; Rose, Feldman, & Jankowski, 2003). Thus, the infant who quickly becomes bored and likes novelty over familiarity is likely to be brighter in childhood than the infant who is slow to habituate and does not like novelty. In addition, fast reaction time in infancy (time taken to look in the direction of a visual stimulus as soon as it appears) predicts later IQ about as well as speed of habituation and novelty preferences scores (Dougherty & Haith, 1997).

From this, we can characterize the "smart" infant as the speedy information processor—the infant who quickly becomes bored by the same old thing, seeks novel experiences, and soaks up information rapidly. There seems to be some continuity between infant intelligence and childhood intelligence after all (Fagan, 2011). Such Bayley scale accomplishments as throwing a ball are unlikely to carry over into vocabulary-learning or problem-solving skills in childhood. However, the extent to which the young infant processes information quickly can predict the extent to which he will learn quickly and solve problems efficiently later in childhood.

Checking Mastery

1. What does a developmental quotient (DQ) assess?
2. What characteristics or behaviors of infants are associated with later intelligence?

Making Connections

1. Are there specific activities that parents should be doing with their infants to ensure that they develop to their intellectual potential? What might some of these activities be?

LEARNING OBJECTIVES:

- Summarize the research on stability of IQ scores over the course of childhood and indicate reasons why IQ scores might change or remain the same.

- Discuss the effects of poverty on children's intellectual abilities.

- Chart the path of creative abilities across childhood.

Over the childhood years, children generally become able to answer more questions, and more difficult questions, on IQ tests. That is, their MAs increase. But what happens to the IQ scores of individual children, which reflect how they compare with peers?

The Stability of IQ Scores during Childhood

It was once assumed that a person's IQ reflected her genetically determined intellectual capacity and therefore would remain stable over time. In other words, a child with an IQ of 120 at age 5 was expected to obtain a similar IQ at age 10, 15, or 20. Is this idea supported by research? As you have seen, infant DQs do not predict later IQs well. However, starting around age 4 there is a fairly strong relationship between early and later IQ, and the relationship grows even stronger by middle childhood.

- **Table 9.2** summarizes the results of a longitudinal study of 220 children ages 4–12 (Weinert & Hany, 2003; Weinert & Schneider, 1999). The shorter the interval between two testings, the higher the correlation between children's IQ scores on the two occasions. Even when several years have passed, however, IQ seems to be a stable attribute: The scores that children obtain at age 7 are clearly related to those they obtain 5 years later, at age 12.

These correlations do not reveal everything, however. They are based on a large group of children, and they do not necessarily mean that the IQs of individual children will remain stable over the years. As it turns out, many children show sizable ups and downs in their IQ scores over the course of childhood. Patterns of change differ considerably from child to child, as though each were on a private developmental trajectory (Gottfried et al., 1994). In one recent study, stability of scores was examined over a 2- to 3-year period (Watkins & Smith, 2013). For most of these children—three out of four—scores from one time to the next were relatively stable, with variations of just a few points. Indeed, the average difference in scores for the entire group of children was less than one-quarter of one point, indicating remarkable stability for the group as a whole. However, for the remaining one out of four children, the test-retest scores varied by 10 or more points. One child's score changed by a whopping 28 points (Watkins & Smith, 2013).

How do researchers reconcile the conclusion that IQ is relatively stable with this clear evidence of instability, at least for some children? They can still conclude that, within a group, children's standings (high or low) in comparison with peers stay stable from one point to another during the childhood years (Sternberg, Grigorenko, & Bundy, 2001). But many individual children experience drops or gains in IQ scores over the years. Remember, however, that this relates to performance on IQ tests rather than underlying intellectual competence. IQ scores are influenced not only by people's intelligence but also by their motivation, testing procedures and conditions, and many other factors that we will discuss in this chapter. As a result, IQ may be more changeable over the years than intellectual ability.

- **Table 9.2** Correlations of IQs Measured at Various Ages

Age of Child at Initial IQ Test	Correlation of IQ Scores When Retested at Age 9	Correlation of IQ Scores When Retested at Age 12
4	0.46	0.42
5	0.47	0.49
7	0.81	0.69
9	—	0.80

SOURCE: Weinert, F. E. & Hany, E. A. (2003). The stability of individual differences in intellectual development: Empirical evidence, theoretical problems, and new research questions, in Sternberg R. J., Lautrey J., & Lubart T. I. (Eds.), *Models of intelligence: International perspectives.* Copyright © 2003 by the American Psychological Association. Reprinted with permission.

Causes of Gain and Loss

Some wandering of IQ scores upward or downward over time is just random fluctuation—a good day at one testing, a bad day at the next. Yet there are patterns. Children whose scores fluctuate the most tend to live in unstable home environments; their life experiences fluctuate between periods of happiness and turmoil.

In addition, some children gain IQ points over childhood and others lose them. Who are the gainers, and who are the losers? Gainers seem to have parents who converse more with them, exposing them to a wide vocabulary, and offer more encouragement relative to the inevitable reprimands (Hart & Rissley, 1995). Noticeable drops in IQ with age often occur among children who live in poverty. Poverty is often defined by low family income, but **child poverty** involves more than low parent income: It also involves low levels of meeting children's basic needs (see Lipina & Colombo, 2009). Thus, children who live in poverty often have inadequate health and dental care and nutrition; they live in overcrowded and unsafe neighborhoods; their families experience chronic stress; their relationships with parents are not as affectionate or supportive; and they lack opportunities for cognitive stimulation that are commonplace in other homes. Numerous studies with animals demonstrate that being raised in an impoverished environment has a direct impact on brain development (see, for example, Markham & Greenough, 2004; Rosenzweig & Bennett, 1996). For example, rats raised in a large cage with a few other rats for company, wheels for exercising, and blocks to play with develop more neurons, more connections between neurons, and more glial cells supporting neurons than rats raised in isolation (Greenough, Black, & Wallace, 1987; Mohammed et al., 2002). The message is clear: The brain is influenced by the environment. So what happens when children are raised in impoverished environments?

Children who live in poverty average some 10–20 points below their middle-class age-mates on IQ tests (see Nisbett et al., 2012). This is true in all racial and ethnic groups (Helms, 1997). Socioeconomic status affects IQ scores as well as children's rate of intellectual growth (Espy, Molfese, & DiLalla, 2001). Thus, their cognitive development is slower and their endpoint is lower—on average, they end up a full standard deviation below their age peers. Otto Klineberg (1963) proposed a **cumulative-deficit hypothesis** to describe how impoverished environments inhibit intellectual growth, and these negative effects accumulate over time. There is some support for the cumulative-deficit hypothesis, especially when a child's parents are not only poor but also low in intellectual functioning themselves (Jensen, 1977; Ramey & Ramey, 1992). What if socioeconomic conditions were to improve?

The brain is responsive to environmental change—it has *neuroplasticity*. So improving the economic conditions of children's homes can improve their IQs. For example, Sandra Scarr and Richard Weinberg charted the intellectual growth of African American and European American children adopted before their first birthday (Scarr & Weinberg, 1983; Weinberg, Scarr, & Waldman, 1992). Many of these children came from disadvantaged family backgrounds and had biological parents who were poorly educated and somewhat below average in IQ. They were placed in middle-class homes with adoptive parents who were highly educated and above average in intelligence. Throughout childhood and adolescence, these adoptees posted average or above-average scores on standardized IQ tests—higher scores than they would have obtained if they had stayed in the disadvantaged environments offered by their natural parents. Research with French children who were adopted later—around age 5—indicates that increases in IQ are much larger among children adopted into affluent homes with highly educated parents than among those adopted into disadvantaged homes (Duyme, Dumaret, & Tomkiewicz, 1999). **Exploration Box 9.1** examines research on the effectiveness of various early intervention programs designed to raise the IQ scores and academic success of children living in poverty.

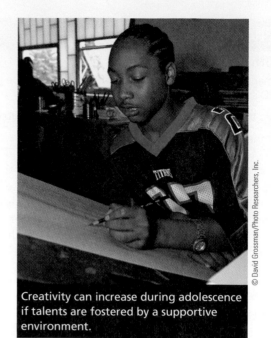

Creativity can increase during adolescence if talents are fostered by a supportive environment.

The Emergence of Creativity

We often hear young children's play activities and artwork described as "creative." When does creativity emerge, and what is the child who scores high on tests of creativity like? To answer the first question, researchers have measured divergent thinking at different ages throughout childhood. Early on, it became apparent that preschool-aged children display fairly high levels of divergent thought—generating many original ideas. As ■ **Figure 9.4** shows, creativity scores, as measured by *ideational fluency*, how many different ideas can be produced, increase until about third grade, level off during fourth and fifth grade, and then begin to decline rather significantly (Kim, 2011). Another measure of creativity, *originality*, the ability to produce original ideas, shows a sharp drop-off starting in sixth grade (see again Figure 9.4). Such declines may reflect pressures in middle school to conform to the group rather than be a "free spirit." Traditional classrooms tend to emphasize and reinforce convergent thinking, with tests constructed to assess whether students know *the* answer to a problem.

To address the second question, what the creative child is like, one group of researchers compared children who had high creativity scores but normal-range IQ scores with children who scored high in IQ but not in creativity (Getzels & Jackson, 1962). Personality measures suggested that the creative children showed more freedom, originality, humor, aggression, and playfulness than the high-IQ children. Perhaps as a result, the high-IQ children were more success oriented and received more approval from teachers. The unconventional responses of highly creative children are not always appreciated in the conventional classroom (Runco, 2007). Compared with their less creative peers, creative children also engage in more fantasy or pretend play, often inventing new uses for familiar objects and new roles for

Exploration **9.2**

Early Intervention

During the 1960s, several programs were launched to enrich the early learning experiences of disadvantaged preschoolers. Project Head Start is perhaps the best known of these interventions. The idea was to provide a variety of social and intellectual experiences that might better prepare these children for school. High-quality Head Start programs provide the nutrition, health care, parent training, and intellectual stimulation that can get disadvantaged children off to a good start. At first, Head Start and similar programs seemed to be a smashing success; children in the programs were posting average gains of about 10 points on IQ tests. But then discouragement set in: By the time children reached the middle years of grade school, their IQs were no higher than those of control-group children (Gray, Ramsey, & Klaus, 1982). Such findings led Arthur Jensen (1969) to conclude that "compensatory education has been tried and it apparently has failed" (p. 2).

But that was not the end of the story. Children in some of these programs have been followed into their teens, 20s, and beyond. It turns out that Project Head Start and other early intervention programs do in fact offer some long-term benefits (for example, Ludwig & Phillips, 2008). This is what we have learned:

- Children who participate in early intervention programs show immediate gains on IQ and school achievement tests, whereas nonparticipants do not. Although these gains rarely last more than 3 or 4 years after the program has ended, effects on measures other than IQ are more encouraging. In one first-grade intervention program, students attained higher scores on standardized achievement tests when they reached 12th grade (Bradshaw et al., 2009).
- Compensatory education improves both children's and mothers' attitudes about achievement. When asked to describe something that has made them feel proud of themselves, program participants are more likely than nonparticipants to mention scholastic achievements or (in the case of 15- to 18-year-olds) job-related successes. Mothers of program participants tend to be more satisfied with their children's school performance and to hold higher occupational aspirations for their children.

- Program participants are more likely than nonparticipants to complete high school and to attend some college (Garces, Thomas, & Currie, 2002; Schweinhart et al., 2005). They are less likely to be assigned to special education classes, to be retained in a grade, or to drop out of high school (Bradshaw et al., 2009).
- There is even some evidence that teenagers who have participated in early compensatory education are less likely to experience such negative life events as teen pregnancy and delinquency than nonparticipants. By age 40, they are less likely to have had multiple arrests (Schweinhart et al., 2005).

In sum, longitudinal evaluations suggest that compensatory education does work. Programs seem most effective if they start early, last long, and involve several components. For example, research has demonstrated good success with the Carolina Abecedarian Project, an early intervention for extremely disadvantaged, primarily African American children that involved an intellectually stimulating day care program, home visits and efforts to involve parents in their children's development, and medical and nutritional care from early infancy to kindergarten entry (Campbell & Ramey, 1995; Campbell, Shirley, & Caygill, 2002; Campbell et al., 2001). Program participants outperformed nonparticipants throughout childhood and into adolescence. By age 15, the impressive IQ advantage they had shown as young children had narrowed to less than 5 points, but they continued to perform better on math and reading achievement tests, were less likely to have been held back a grade, and were less in need of special education services. Some

children in the study were randomly assigned to a group whose intervention did not begin until school age, when a teacher worked with their regular teachers and their parents over a 3-year period. These children did not show as many gains as those who received the preschool intervention, suggesting that it is best to intervene early in children's lives (Campbell & Ramey, 1995). An early start is the premise behind the Born to Learn curriculum, which starts during the first year of life and shows benefits by age 3 (Drotar et al., 2008).

The success of early compensatory education for at-risk preschoolers has led some experts in the field to call for mandatory preschool education for all children (Barnett et al., 2007). Although many young children do attend some sort of program prior to entering kindergarten, the programs are quite varied in their quality and focus. A universal preschool system would aim to reduce these inequalities. Not all experts, though, agree that universal preschool should be the goal (Stipek & Hakuta, 2007). Instead, they believe that improving the existing preschool programs that target at-risk children, such as Head Start, Carolina Abecedarian Project, and Born to Learn, will help ensure that "no child starts from behind," struggling to catch up to peers on cognitive and social skills that they did not have the opportunity to develop at home (Stipek & Kahuta, 2007, p. 129).

High-quality Head Start programs provide the nutrition, health care, parent training, and intellectual stimulation that can get disadvantaged children off to a good start.

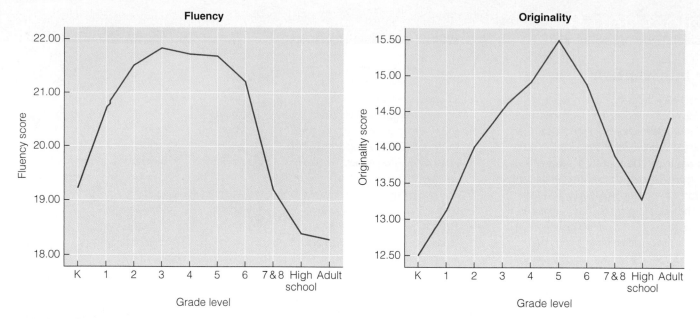

Fluency

Originality

■ **Figure 9.4** Two measures of creativity. On the left, fluency scores increase from kindergarten to 3rd grade, but then plateau and begin a marked decline from 5th grade on. On the right, originality scores peak in 5th grade, drop dramatically, and then increase from high school to adulthood. What factors might explain these patterns of creativity?

SOURCE: Adapted from Figure 1 (p 288) of Kim, K.H. (2011). The creativity crisis: The decrease in creative thinking scores on the Torrance Tests of Creative Thinking. *Creativity Research Journal*, 23, 285–295.

themselves (Kogan, 1983). They have active imaginations, and their parents are often tolerant of their sometimes unconventional ideas (Runco, 2007). Finally, creative children are more likely to be open to new experiences and ideas, as are their parents (Simonton, 1999).

As you will see later in this chapter, average IQ scores differ across racial and socioeconomic groups, but scores on creativity tests usually do not, nor do self-perceptions of one's creativity (Kaufman, 2006; Kogan, 1983). Moreover, genetic influences (a source of individual differences in IQ) have little to do with performance on tests of creativity; twins are similar in the degree of creativity they display, but identical twins are typically no more similar than fraternal twins (Plomin, 1990; Reznikoff et al., 1973). This suggests that certain qualities of the home environment tend to make brothers and sisters alike in their degree of creativity. What qualities? Although there is little research to go on, parents of creative children and adolescents tend to value nonconformity and independence, accept their children as they are, encourage their curiosity and playfulness, and grant them a good deal of freedom to explore new possibilities on their own (Harrington, Block, & Block, 1987). In some cases, the parent–child relationship is even distant; a surprising number of eminent creators seem to have experienced rather lonely, insecure, and unhappy childhoods (Ochse, 1990; Simonton, 1999). Out of their adversity may have come an active imagination and a strong desire to develop their talents. Although this may be true for some creative individuals, it is certainly not true for all of them. Overall, then,

creative abilities are influenced by factors distinct from those that influence the cognitive abilities measured on IQ tests.

Checking Mastery

1. Once children reach elementary school, how stable are their IQ scores as a group?
2. What is one reason for an individual's IQ score to increase and what is one reason for an individual's IQ score to decrease during childhood?

Making Connections

1. Would you want to know your IQ or your child's IQ? How might this knowledge affect you? Would you think or act any differently if you learned that you (or your child) had an IQ of 105 versus an IQ of 135? You might also consider whether teachers should know their students' IQ scores. What are some potential pros and cons of teachers having access to this information?
2. What are 2 or 3 things that society--schools, local governments, and parents—can do to ensure that children born into poverty are not intellectually disadvantaged by this circumstance?
3. Would you rather have a child who has average intelligence but is highly creative or one who has high intelligence but average creativity? What are the pros and cons of each?

LEARNING OBJECTIVES:

* Describe the Flynn Effect and what factors might account for this finding.

* Explain how IQ scores relate to school achievement.

* Discuss how schools and parents can foster creativity during adolescence.

Intellectual growth continues its rapid pace in early adolescence, then slows and levels off in later adolescence (Thorndike, 1997). As noted in Chapter 5, a spurt in brain development occurs around age 11 or age 12, when children are believed to enter Piaget's formal operational stage. Brain development may give children the information-processing speed and working-memory capacity they need to perform at adultlike levels on IQ tests (Kail & Salthouse, 1994). Thus, basic changes in the brain in early adolescence may underlie a variety of cognitive advances—the achievement of formal operations, improved memory and information-processing skills, and better performance on tests of intelligence.

Although adolescence is a time of impressive mental growth, it is also a time of increased stability of individual differences in intellectual performance. During the teen years, IQ scores become even more stable than they were in childhood and strongly predict IQ in middle age (Deary et al., 2004). Even while adolescents as a group are experiencing cognitive growth, then, each individual is establishing a characteristic level of intellectual performance that will most likely be carried into adult life unless the individual's environment changes dramatically.

Flynn Effect

Some evidence suggests that today's teens are smarter than their parents and grandparents were as teenagers. Indeed, over the 20th century, average IQ scores have increased in all countries studied, a phenomenon called the **Flynn effect** after James Flynn (1987, 1998, 1999, 2007, 2011), who focused our attention on this phenomenon. In the United States, the increase has amounted to 3–4 IQ points per decade. So a group of adults born in, say, 1980, will score on average 3–4 points higher than a similar group of adults born in 1970 and 6–8 points higher than those born in 1960. ■ **Figure 9.5** illustrates the gains in intelligence over a period of more than 50 years. Full-scale IQ scores have increased 18 points over this time, with scores on some subscales increasing as much as 24 points (for example, similarities and Raven's Progressive Matrices), others increasing 10 points (such as comprehension), and some increasing a slight 2–3 points (for example, information, arithmetic, and vocabulary). Further, Flynn (2007) presents data that suggest these trends extend back more than 100 years, leading him to ask, "How can our recent ancestors have been so unintelligent compared to ourselves?" (p. 9). How indeed?

Most researchers argue that increases of this size cannot be caused by genetic evolution and therefore must have environmental causes (but see Mingroni, 2004). For one thing, children today are better educated than earlier generations; 85% today complete high school, compared with just 5% in 1895 (Greve, 2006). But Flynn and others have suggested that improved nutrition and living conditions over the course of the 20th century have also contributed to the rise in intellectual functioning (for example, Lynn, 2009).

Researchers have examined average IQ scores by country and found that they are associated with the country's incidence and prevalence of infectious disease (Eppig, Fincher, & Thornhill, 2010). Thus, people in countries where rates of infectious diseases are high have, on average, lower IQ scores relative to those in countries where rates of infectious diseases are low. The authors believe that infectious diseases, especially parasitic diseases that cause diarrhea in infants and children, divert energy from the brain and rob the brain of needed nutrients. As countries reduce airborne and

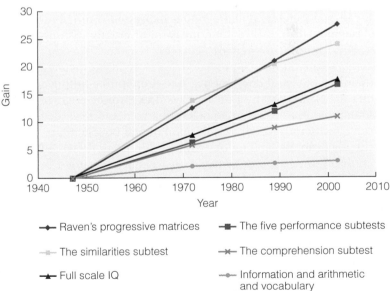

■ **Figure 9.5** Over a 50-year period, test scores on several measures of intelligence have risen substantially, illustrating the "Flynn effect." Are people really getting smarter? What factors might explain such a rise in intelligence test scores?

Source: Flynn, J. R. (2007), *What is intelligence: Beyond the Flynn* effect, Figure 1, p. 8. Reprinted by permission of Cambridge University Press.

water-borne diseases through vaccinations, clean water, and sewers, we can expect to see a rise in the average IQ scores of those countries.

IQ and School Achievement

The original purpose of IQ tests was to estimate how well children would do in school, and they do this fairly well. Correlations between children's and adolescents' IQ scores and their grades range from 0.50 to 0.86, making general intellectual ability one of the best predictors of school achievement available (Deary et al., 2007; Neisser et al., 1996). Adolescents with high IQs are also less likely to drop out of high school and more likely to go on to college than their peers with lower IQs; the correlation between IQ and years of education obtained averages 0.55 (Neisser et al., 1996). However, IQ scores do not predict college grades as well as they predict high school grades (Brody & Brody, 1976). Most college students probably have at least the average intellectual ability needed to succeed in college; success is therefore more influenced by personal qualities such as motivation. Overall, an IQ score is a good predictor of academic achievement, but it does not reveal everything about a student. Factors such as work habits, interests, and motivation to succeed also affect academic achievement.

Fostering Creativity

We noted earlier that there is a drop in creativity as children enter middle school. What happens during adolescence? In general, creativity, as measured by traditional divergent tasks or ideational fluency, remains rather depressed throughout adolescence (Kim, 2011). One measure of creativity, however, does continue to increase across adolescence. The ability to elaborate on ideas—provide details—tends to increase in middle school and does not begin to drop until adulthood (Kim, 2011). Elaborating on ideas is one form of creative thinking that may continue to be emphasized and rewarded in the classroom. Overall, the developmental course of creativity may vary depending on when children are pressured to conform and whether unusual answers are rewarded in school. But whether or not we are *observing* creativity among our adolescents, research suggests that teens are *feeling* creative (Claxton et al., 2005). Creative feelings include curiosity, imagination, and willingness to take calculated risks. And, importantly, there is continuity between childhood scores on creativity tasks and adulthood creative output (Cramond et al., 2005). So adolescents may put their creativity "on hold," perhaps to focus on other pressing issues of this important developmental period, but their creativity is not lost.

Is it possible to foster creativity? Training studies indicate that people can learn techniques to improve their creativeness (Ma, 2006; Scott et al., 2004). But training may only be effective if the person's environment supports and rewards creativity. Researchers have looked at individuals who demonstrate creativity in a particular field to try to identify the factors that contribute to their accomplishments. David Feldman (1982, 1986), for example, has studied children and adolescents who are prodigies in such areas as chess, music, and mathematics. These individuals were generally similar to their peers in areas outside their fields of expertise. What contributed to their special achievements? On the nature side, they had *talent* as well as a powerful *motivation* to develop their special talents—a real passion for what they were doing. Olympic gymnast Olga Korbut put it well: "If gymnastics did not exist, I would have invented it" (Feldman, 1982, p. 35). Other research confirms that internal motivation and a thirst for challenge are crucial elements of creative productivity (Sternberg, 2010; Yeh & Wu, 2006). Individuals with a positive outlook also seem more likely to display creativity, perhaps because they are more open to challenges and derive more pleasure from challenges (see Yeh & Wu, 2006). Creative thinkers have other personal qualities as well—they display a willingness to take risks and are able to put up with some ambiguity without becoming frustrated (Proctor & Burnett, 2004; Sternberg, 2010).

On the nurture side, creative individuals seem to be blessed with *environments* that recognize, value, and nurture their creative endeavors (Sternberg, 2010). Their environments allow them a certain degree of independence to explore different fields and acquire knowledge of their chosen field. According to Feldman (1982), the child with creative potential in a specific field must become intimately familiar with the state of the field if he is to advance or transform it, as the groundbreaking artist or musician does. Thus, building a knowledge base is a necessary, although not sufficient, component of creativity (Sternberg, 2006b). So parents can help foster creativity by giving their children freedom to explore and opportunities to experiment with ideas and activities. Likewise, schools can assist by encouraging idea generation, multiple correct answers, or multiple pathways to arrive at an answer, and elaboration of ideas.

Checking Mastery

1. Is creativity or intelligence more stable during adolescence?
2. What might explain the rise in IQ scores over the past century?
3. What is one environmental factor that could help enhance creativity?

Making Connections

1. To what extent have your schools fostered creativity? Is this something that *can* be fostered in schools and *should* it be fostered in schools?
2. IQ scores stabilize in adolescence and are highly correlated with adult IQ scores. Given this stability, should greater use be made of IQ scores? If so, what would be one or two meaningful uses of IQ scores during adolescence?

LEARNING OBJECTIVES:

- Evaluate whether IQ scores are a useful predictor of occupational status and health status of adults.

- Explain how intelligence might be expected to change over adulthood.

- Analyze the connection between wisdom and intelligence and determine who might be most likely to develop wisdom.

- Summarize the research on creative endeavors during adulthood.

We turn our attention now to intelligence during adulthood. Do IQ scores predict achievement and success after people have left school? Does performance on IQ tests change during the adult years? And do IQ scores decline in old age, as performance on Piagetian cognitive tasks and some memory tasks does?

IQ and Occupational Success

What is the relationship between IQ and occupational status? Professional and technical workers (such as scientists and engineers) score higher on IQ tests than white-collar workers (such as bank managers), who in turn score higher than blue-collar, or manual, workers (such as construction workers) (Nyborg & Jensen, 2001; Schmidt & Hunter, 2004). The connection among intelligence, income, and occupational prestige is striking when we look at findings from a longitudinal study using a large U.S. sample (Judge, Klinger, & Simon, 2010). ■ **Figure 9.6** shows that over the nearly 30-year period of the study, general intelligence was significantly related to both income and occupational prestige. Further, the gap between those with higher intelligence and

those with lower intelligence widened considerably over time. Those with higher intelligence started with a slight advantage for income and occupational prestige but quickly began rising at a faster rate than those with lower intelligence. Also, income did not plateau and occupational prestige did not drop among those with higher intelligence as they did for those with lower intelligence.

The reason for the relationship between IQ and occupational success is clear: It undoubtedly takes more intellectual ability to complete law school and become a lawyer, a high-status and higher paying occupation, than it does to be a farmhand, a low-status and lower-paying occupation. However, the prestige or status of the occupation is not as important as the complexity of the work (Gottfredson, 1997; Kuncel, Hezlett, & Ones, 2004). Greater intelligence is required to handle more complex or cognitively challenging work. Those with higher intelligence obtain more education and training and they use this to tackle more demanding jobs, which leads to a faster and steeper rise to the top of the occupational ladder (Judge et al., 2010). Still, IQs vary considerably in every occupational group, so many people in low-status jobs have high IQs.

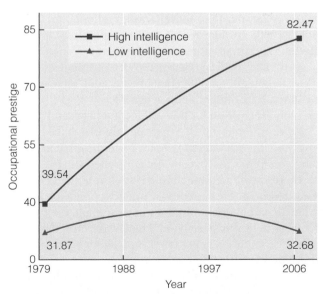

■ **Figure 9.6** The two graphs show income (*left*) and occupational prestige (*right*) of participants over nearly 30 years in relation to their intelligence test performance: Those with high intelligence start with a slight advantage over their less intelligent peers but quickly leave them behind. Why don't those with lower intelligence keep rising at the same rate over the years?

SOURCE: Judge T. A., Klinger, R. L., & Simon, L. S. (2010). Time is on my side: Time, general mental ability, human capital, and extrinsic career success. *Journal of Applied Psychology*, 95, (1), 92–107. Figure 2. Copyright © 2010 American Psychological Association. Reprinted by permission.

Now a second question: Are bright lawyers, electricians, or farmhands more successful or productive than their less intelligent colleagues? The answer here is also yes. The correlation between scores on tests of intellectual ability and such measures of job performance as supervisor ratings averages 0.30 to 0.50 (Neisser et al., 1996). General intellectual ability seems to predict job performance in a range of occupations better than any other indicator, and it predicts likelihood of success as accurately for members of racial and ethnic minority groups as for whites (Gottfredson, 2002; Schmidt & Hunter, 1998, 2004). More intellectually capable adults are better able to learn what they need to know about their occupations and to solve the problems that arise. This literally pays off (see again Figure 9.6): Individuals with greater cognitive ability earn more money than those with lower cognitive ability (Judge et al., 2010).

IQ and Health

People who score higher on measures of intelligence tend to be healthier and live longer than those who score lower on these tests (see, for example, Gottfredson, 2004; and Leon et al., 2009). This connection between intelligence and health and longevity has now been confirmed with research conducted in multiple countries. For instance, researchers in Scotland tracked nearly everyone born in that country in 1921 and 1936 who had taken an intelligence test during childhood (Deary, Whalley, & Starr, 2009). Following up on health and death records of these participants decades later, researchers found that individuals who scored one standard deviation (15 points) below the average were less likely to be alive at age 76 and more likely to have experienced stomach or lung cancers and cardiovascular or coronary heart disease. Stated another way, those children who scored in the top 25% on intelligence at age 11 were 2–3 times more likely to be alive 65 years later than those scoring in the bottom 25% (Deary et al., 2009). Similar results are emerging from a study in the United States that has tracked participants from adolescence to age 40 (Der, Batty, & Deary, 2009). Consistent with the Scotland research, higher intelligence in early adolescence is associated with fewer health problems at age 40.

A common explanation for this connection between IQ and health is socioeconomic status: Smart people may have better jobs, giving them the resources to obtain better health care. But when living conditions are statistically controlled (that is, held constant), there is still a connection between intelligence and health (Gottfredson & Deary, 2004). Similarly, providing equal access to health care reduces but does not eliminate the social-class differences in health (Steenland, Henley, & Thun, 2002).

So what else could be going on? Linda Gottfredson (2004) argues that good health takes more than access to material resources. It requires some of the abilities measured by intelligence tests, such as efficient learning and problem solving. In other words, successfully monitoring health and properly applying treatment protocols require a certain amount of intelligence. Consider the chronic illness diabetes. Successful management requires acquiring knowledge of the disease symptoms and course, identifying signs of inappropriate blood sugar levels, and making judgments about how to respond to blood sugar

fluctuations. A patient's IQ predicts how much knowledge of diabetes she acquires during the year following diagnosis (Taylor et al., 2003). Other research shows that many people with diabetes who have limited literacy, which correlates with intelligence, do not know the signs of high or low blood sugar and do not know how to correct unhealthy levels (Williams et al., 1998).

A study of nearly 10,000 adults examined the relationship between their IQ scores at age 11 and one marker of health collected from blood samples at age 45 (Calvin et al., 2011). Blood samples were examined for two inflammatory markers associated with cardiovascular disease. Higher IQ scores at age 11 were associated with lower levels of these cardiovascular disease markers in adulthood. The connection between these two is partly explained by differences in parental socioeconomic status. Research on relationships between IQ and health is still relatively new. But it suggests that IQ influences socioeconomic status, which in turn influences health, and that IQ also influences health directly. Smarter people are able to apply their intellectual skills to understanding and managing their health.

Changes in IQ with Age

Perhaps no question about adult development has been studied as thoroughly as that of how intellectual abilities change with age. We know that an individual's IQ score remains relatively stable from preadolescence (age 11) until well into older adulthood (Deary et al., 2004, 2009; Gow et al., 2011). Alan Gow, Ian Deary, and their colleagues (2011) have examined stability of intelligence over a lifetime by following up with individuals born in either 1921 or 1936 who had completed an intelligence test at age 11. These individuals were retested at ages 70 or 79, and those tested at age 79 were tested for a third time at age 87. This allowed researchers to examine stability of IQ over a lifetime (age 11 to ages 70, 79, or 87) as well as examine changes in IQ during late adulthood (ages 79–87).

In general, the findings of this remarkable longitudinal study show a high level of stability over many decades of life. The strongest predictor of intelligence in old age was intelligence at age 11. Such factors as education and socioeconomic status contributed only slightly to changes in IQ scores. Thus, where a person's IQ score falls within the spread of scores in a group is a good predictor of where this person's score will fall if retested with the same group later in life: High scorers tend to remain high scorers and low scorers tend to remain low scorers.

As we learned earlier from the research on IQ scores in childhood, even when there is high group stability, there are still bound to be some changes in IQ. This is true for adults as well. What might account for changes in IQ scores in adulthood? A comprehensive sequential study directed by K. Warner Schaie (2012) provides some evidence regarding the pattern of changes in IQ. Schaie's study began in 1956 with a sample of members of a health maintenance organization ranging in age from 22 to 70. They were given a revised test of primary mental abilities that yielded scores for five separate mental abilities: verbal meaning, spatial ability, reasoning, numerical ability, and word fluency. Seven years later, as many of them as could be found were retested. In addition, a new sample of adults ranging from their 20s to their 70s was tested. This design made it possible to determine how the performance of the same individuals changed over 7 years and to compare the performance of people who were 20 years old in 1956 with that of people who were 20 years old in 1963. This same strategy was repeated at regular intervals, giving the researchers a wealth of information about different cohorts, including longitudinal data on some people over a 45-year period.

Several findings have emerged from this important study. First, it seems that *when a person was born* has at least as much influence on intellectual functioning as age does. In other words, cohort or generational effects on performance exist. This evidence confirms the suspicion that cross-sectional comparisons of different age groups have usually yielded too grim a picture of declines in intellectual abilities during adulthood. Specifically, recently born cohorts (the youngest people in the study were born in 1973) tended to outperform earlier generations (the oldest were born in 1889) on most tests. Yet on the test of numerical ability, people born between 1903 and 1924 performed better than both earlier and later generations. Inductive reasoning scores have increased with every cohort tested since 1889. Scores on verbal meanings increased until 1952 but dropped off in the three most recently born cohorts (Schaie & Zanjani, 2006). So different generations may have a special edge in different areas of intellectual performance. Overall, though, judging from Schaie's findings, young and middle-aged adults today can look forward to better intellectual functioning in old age than their grandparents experienced.

Another important message of Schaie's study, and of other research, is that patterns of aging differ for different abilities (■ **Figure 9.7**). Fluid intelligence (those abilities requiring active thinking and reasoning applied to novel problems, as measured by tests such as the primary mental abilities tests of reasoning and space) usually declines earlier and more steeply than crystallized intelligence (those abilities involving the use of knowledge acquired through experience, such as in answering the verbal meaning test used by Schaie). Consistently, adults lose some of their ability to grapple with new problems starting in middle age, but their crystallized general knowledge and vocabulary stay steady throughout middle and older adulthood (Rabbitt, Chetwynd, & McInnes, 2003; Singer et al., 2003). Some research even shows that knowledge, such

as vocabulary, is greater among older adults than among younger adults (Field & Gueldner, 2001; Verhaeghen, 2003).

Why is this? Tests of performance and fluid IQ are often timed, and, as noted in Chapter 8, performance on timed tests declines more in old age than performance on untimed tests does. This may be linked to the slowing of central nervous system functioning that most people experience as they age (Salthouse, 1996; Sliwinski & Buschke, 1999; Zimprich & Martin, 2002). Indeed, we have seen that speed of information processing is related to intellectual functioning across the life span. Not only is rapid information processing in infancy associated with high IQ scores in childhood, but young adults with quick reaction times also outperform their more sluggish age-mates on IQ tests, and adults who lose information-processing speed in later life lose some of their ability to think through complex and novel problems (Jensen, 1993). It is not just that older adults cannot finish tests that have time limits; declines in performance intelligence occur in later life even on untimed tests (Kaufman & Kaufman, 1997). The problem is that the slower information processor cannot keep in mind and process simultaneously all relevant aspects of a complex problem.

You now have an overall picture of intellectual functioning in adulthood. Age group differences in performance suggest that older adults today are at a disadvantage on many tests compared with younger adults, partly because of deficiencies in the amount and quality of education they received early in life. But actual declines in intellectual abilities associated with aging are generally minor until people reach their late 60s or 70s. Even in old age, declines in fluid intelligence, performance intelligence, and performance on timed tests are more apparent than declines in crystallized intelligence, verbal intelligence, and performance on untimed tests. As you will soon see, declines in fluid intelligence can be reduced when adults remain cognitively stimulated through work or other activities (Weinert & Hany, 2003).

One last message of this research is worth special emphasis: Declines in intellectual abilities are not universal. Even among the 81-year-olds in Schaie's study, only about 30–40% had experienced a significant decline in intellectual ability in the previous 7 years (Schaie, 2012). Moreover, although few 81-year-olds maintained all five mental abilities, almost all retained at least one ability from testing to testing and about half retained four out of five (Schaie & Zanjani, 2006). The range of differences in intellectual functioning in a group of older adults is extremely large (Dixon, 2003). Anyone who stereotypes all elderly adults as intellectually limited is likely to be wrong most of the time.

Predictors of Decline

What is most likely to affect whether or not a person experiences declines in intellectual performance in old age? *Poor health*, not surprisingly, is one risk factor. People who have cardiovascular diseases or other chronic illnesses show steeper declines in mental abilities than their healthier peers (Schaie, 2012). Diseases (and most likely the drugs used to treat them) also contribute to a rapid decline in intellectual abilities within a few years of death (Johansson, Zarit, & Berg, 1992; Singer et al., 2003). This phenomenon has been given the depressing label **terminal drop**. Perhaps there is something, then, to the saying "Sound body, sound mind."

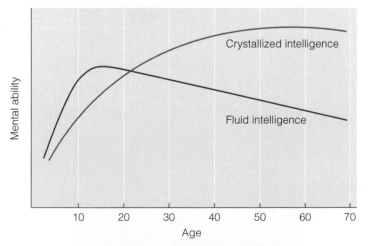

■ **Figure 9.7** What can you conclude about intelligence from reading this graph?

Source: Cattell, R., *Intelligence: Its structure, growth, and action*, p. 206. Copyright © 1986. Reprinted by permission of Elsevier.

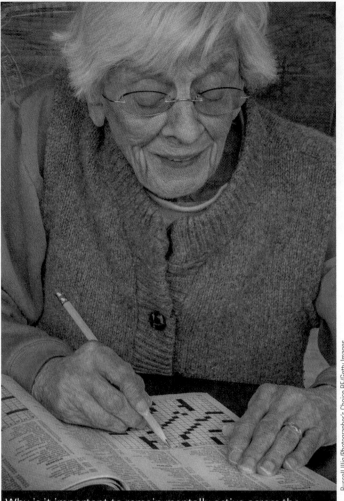
Why is it important to remain mentally active across the life span, as this older woman is by working on a crossword puzzle?

health, lifestyle, and other factors shape the individual's intellectual growth and decline. What is certain is that most people can look forward to many years of optimal intellectual functioning before some of them experience losses of some mental abilities in later life.

Potential for Wisdom

Many people believe—incorrectly, as you have seen—that intellectual decline is an inevitable part of aging. Yet many people also believe that old people are wise. Indeed, this belief has been expressed in many cultures throughout history. It is also featured in Erik Erikson's influential theory of life-span development. Erikson says that older adults often gain wisdom as they face the prospect of death and attempt to find meaning in their lives (see Chapter 11). Notice, too, that the word *wise* is rarely used to describe children, adolescents, or even young adults (unless perhaps it is to call one of them a *wise guy*). Is the association between wisdom and old age just a stereotype, or is there some truth to it?

People tend to believe that age brings wisdom. It can—but wisdom is rare even in later life. But first, what is wisdom, and how can researchers assess it? There is no consensus on these questions and, until fairly recently, little research (Sternberg, 2003). Researchers do know that wisdom is not the same as high intelligence: There are many highly intelligent people who are not wise. Paul Baltes and his colleagues define **wisdom** as a constellation of rich factual knowledge about life combined with procedural knowledge such as strategies for giving advice and handling conflicts (Pasupathi, Staudinger, & Baltes, 2001). Similarly, Robert Sternberg (2003) defines a wise person as someone who can combine successful intelligence with creativity to solve problems that require balancing multiple interests or perspectives.

A second factor in decline is an *unstimulating lifestyle*. Schaie and his colleagues found that the biggest intellectual declines were shown by elderly widows who had low social status, engaged in few activities, and were dissatisfied with their lives (Schaie, 2012). These women lived alone and seemed disengaged from life. Individuals who maintain their performance or even show gains tend to have above-average socioeconomic status, advanced education, intact marriages, intellectually capable spouses, and physically and mentally active lifestyles. Interestingly, married adults are affected by the intellectual environment they provide for each other. Their IQ test scores become more similar over the years, largely because the lower-functioning partner's scores rise closer to those of the higher-functioning partner (Gruber-Baldini, Schaie, & Willis, 1995; Weinert & Hany, 2003).

The moral is "Use it or lose it." This rule, applicable to muscular strength and sexual functioning, also pertains to intellectual functioning in later life. The plasticity of the nervous system throughout the life span enables elderly individuals to benefit from intellectual stimulation and training, to maintain the intellectual skills most relevant to their activities, and to compensate for the loss of less-exercised abilities (Dixon, 2003; Weinert & Hany, 2003; see also **Application Box 9.1**). There is still much to learn about how

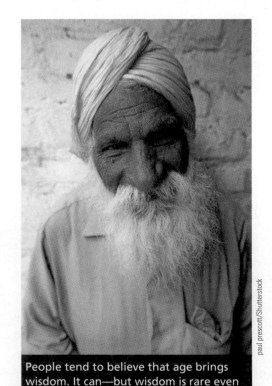
People tend to believe that age brings wisdom. It can—but wisdom is rare even in later life. Why is it difficult to attain wisdom?

Application **9.1**

IQ Training for Aging Adults

Can you teach old dogs new tricks? And can you reteach old dogs who have suffered declines in mental abilities the old tricks they have lost? K. Warner Schaie and Sherry Willis (1986; Willis & Schaie, 1986) sought to find out by training elderly adults in spatial ability and reasoning, two of the fluid mental abilities most likely to decline in old age. Within a group of older people ranging in age from 64 to 95 who participated in Schaie's longitudinal study of intelligence, they first identified individuals whose scores on one of the two abilities had declined over a 14-year period and individuals who had remained stable over the same period. The goal with the decliners would be to restore lost ability; the goal with those who had maintained their ability would be to improve it. Participants took pretests measuring both abilities, received 5 hours of training in either spatial ability or reasoning, and then were given posttests on both abilities. The spatial training involved learning how to rotate objects in space, at first physically and then mentally. Training in reasoning involved learning how to detect a recurring pattern in a series of stimuli (for example, musical notes) and to identify what the next stimulus in the sequence should be.

The training worked. Both those who had suffered ability declines and those who had maintained their abilities before the study improved, although decliners showed significantly more improvement in spatial ability than non-decliners did. Schaie and Willis estimated that 40% of the decliners gained enough through training to bring them back to the level of performance they had achieved 14 years earlier, before decline set in. What is more, effects of the training among those who had experienced declines in performance were still evident 7 years later (Schaie, 1996). And, as noted in Chapter 8, the benefits of cognitive training with older adults extends beyond improving their performance on laboratory-type tests; their daily functioning improved as well (Willis et al., 2006).

Other research shows similar evidence of *neuroplasticity*, or restructuring of the brain in response to training or experience, among older adults. Michelle Carlson and her colleagues (2009) conducted a pilot study with older women who were either trained for and then served as volunteers in the Experience Corps program or were on a waitlist for future participation and served as the control group. Experience Corps volunteers spend 15 hours per week for 6 months in classrooms assisting kindergarten through third-graders with their learning. Their activities draw upon memory, literacy, and problem-solving skills. The researchers took a look inside their brains using functional magnetic resonance imaging (fMRI). The results, seen in the figure in this box, are striking: Women who volunteered in the classroom as part of the Experience Corps program showed significant gains in brain activity relative to the women who had not yet volunteered. Their activity changed the workings of their brains. Similar findings are emerging from similar programs, such as Senior Odyssey, that get older adults actively thinking (Stine-Morrow et al., 2007).

The larger messages? You can teach old dogs new tricks—and reteach them old tricks—in a short amount of time. This research does not mean that cognitive abilities can be restored in elderly people who have Alzheimer's disease or other brain disorders and have experienced significant neural loss. Instead, it suggests that many intellectual skills decline in later life because they are not used—and that these skills can be revived with a little coaching and practice. This research, combined with research on children, provides convincing evidence of the neuroplasticity of cognitive abilities over the entire life span (see Hertzog et al., 2009).

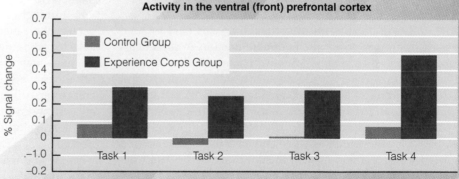

Carlson, M. C., et al., Evidence for neurocognitive plasticity in at-risk older adults: The Experience Corps program. *Journal of Gerontology A: Biological Sciences and Medical Sciences,* 64, 12, 1275–1282. Figure 3. Copyright © 2009. Reprinted by permission of Oxford University Press.

Does wisdom typically increase with age, or are life experiences more important than age in determining whether or not a person is wise? Ursula Staudinger, Jacqui Smith, and Paul Baltes (1992) attempted to find out by interviewing young (ages 25–35) and elderly (ages 65–82) women who were clinical psychologists or similarly well-educated professionals in other fields. The goal was to assess the relative contributions of age and specialized experience to wisdom, based on the assumption that clinical psychologists gain special sensitivity to human problems from their professional training and practice.

These women were interviewed about a person named Martha, who had chosen to have a family but no career and who met an old friend who had chosen to have a career but no family. The women were asked to talk about how Martha might review and evaluate her life after this encounter. Answers were scored for qualities judged to be indicators of wisdom.

What was found? First, wisdom proved to be rare; it seems that only about 5% of the answers given by adults to problems such as these qualify as wise (Smith & Baltes, 1990). Second, expertise proved to be more relevant than age to the development of wisdom. That is, clinical psychologists, whether young or old, displayed more signs of wisdom than other women did. Older women were generally no wiser—or less wise—than younger women.

Age, then, does not predict wisdom well. Yet the knowledge base that contributes to wisdom, like other crystallized intellectual abilities, holds up well later in life (Baltes et al., 1995). Older adults, like younger adults, are more likely to display wisdom if they have life experiences (such as work as a clinical psychologist) that sharpen their insights into the human condition. The immediate social context also influences the degree to which wisdom is expressed; wiser solutions to problems are generated when adults have an opportunity to discuss problems with someone whose judgment they value and when they are encouraged to reflect after such discussions (Staudinger & Baltes, 1996). Thus, consulting with your fellow students and work colleagues and thinking about their advice may be the beginning of wisdom.

Finally, wisdom seems to reflect a particular combination of intelligence, personality, and cognitive style (Baltes & Staudinger, 2000). For example, individuals who have a cognitive style of comparing and evaluating relevant issues and who show tolerance of ambiguity are more likely to demonstrate wisdom than individuals without these characteristics. In addition, external factors influence the development of wisdom. Monika Ardelt (2000) found that a supportive social environment (loving family, good friends) during early adulthood was positively associated with wisdom 40 years later.

At this early stage in the study of wisdom, there is much disagreement about what it is, how it develops, and how it is related to other mental abilities. However, research on wisdom provides further evidence that different mental faculties develop and age differently over the adult years.

Creative Endeavors

Many studies of creativity during the adult years have focused on a small number of so-called eminent creators in such fields as art, music, science, and philosophy. A major question of interest has been this: When in adulthood are such individuals most productive and most likely to create their best works? Is it early in adulthood, when they can benefit from youth's enthusiasm and freshness of approach? Or is it later in adulthood, when they have fully mastered their field and have the experience and knowledge necessary to make a breakthrough in it? And what becomes of the careers of eminent creators in old age?

Early studies by Harvey Lehman (1953) and Wayne Dennis (1966) provided a fairly clear picture of how creative careers unfold (see also Runco, 2007 and Sternberg, 1999a). In most fields, creative production increases steeply from the 20s to the late 30s and early 40s, then gradually declines thereafter, although not to the same low levels that characterized early adulthood. Peak times of creative achievement also vary from field to field (Csikszentmihalyi & Nakamura, 2006). As ■ **Figure 9.8** shows, the productivity of scholars in the humanities (for example, historians and philosophers) continues well into old age and peaks in the 60s, possibly because creative work in these fields often involves integrating knowledge that has crystallized over years. By contrast, productivity in the arts (for example, music or drama) peaks in the 30s and 40s and declines steeply thereafter, perhaps because artistic creativity depends on a more fluid or innovative kind of thinking. Scientists seem to be intermediate, peaking in their 40s and declining only in their 70s.

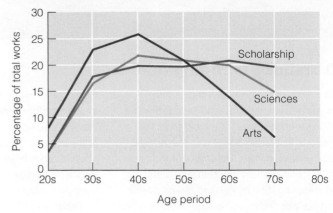

■ **Figure 9.8** Percentage of total works produced in each decade of the lives of eminent creators. The "scholarship" group includes historians and philosophers; the "sciences" category includes natural and physical scientists, inventors, and mathematicians; the "arts" creators include architects, musicians, dramatists, poets, and the like.

SOURCE: Data from Dennis, W. (1966). Creative productivity between the ages of 20 and 80 years. *Journal of Gerontology*, 21, 1–8. Reprinted by permission.

Even within the same general field, differences in peak times have been noted. For example, poets reach their peak before novelists do, and mathematicians peak before other scientists do (Dennis, 1966; Lehman, 1953).

Still, in many fields (including psychology), creative production rises to a peak in the late 30s or early 40s, and both the total number of works and the number of high-quality works decline thereafter (Simonton, 1990). This same pattern can be detected across different cultures and historical periods. Even so, the percentage of a creator's works that are significant changes little over the years (Simonton, 1999). This means that many creators are still producing outstanding works—sometimes their greatest works—in old age, not just rehashes of earlier triumphs. Michelangelo, for instance, was in his 70s and 80s when he worked on St. Peter's Cathedral, and Frank Lloyd Wright was 91 when he finished the blueprint for the Guggenheim Museum in New York City. Indeed, the most eminent among the eminent seem to start early and finish late (Simonton, 1999).

How can researchers account for changes in creative production over the adult years? One explanation, proposed long ago (Beard, 1874, in Simonton, 1984), is that creative achievement requires both enthusiasm and experience. In early adulthood, the enthusiasm is there, but the experience is not; in later adulthood, the experience is there, but the enthusiasm or vigor has fallen off. People in their 30s and 40s have it all.

Dean Simonton (1999) has offered another theory: Each creator may have a certain potential to create that is realized over the adult years; as the potential is realized, less is left to express. According to Simonton, creative activity involves two processes: ideation (generating creative ideas) and elaboration (executing ideas to produce poems, paintings, or scientific publications). After a career is launched, some time elapses before any ideas are generated or any works are completed. This would explain the rise in creative achievement between the 20s and 30s. Also, some kinds of work take longer to formulate or complete than others, which helps explain why a poet (who can generate and carry out ideas quickly) might reach a creative peak earlier in life than, say, a historian (who may need to devote years to the research and writing necessary to complete a book once the idea for it is hatched).

Why does creative production begin to taper off? Simonton (1999) suggests that older creators may simply have used up much of their stock of potential ideas. They never exhaust their creative potential, but they have less of it left to realize. Simonton argues, then, that changes in creative production over the adult years have more to do with the nature of the creative process than with a loss of mental ability in later life. Creators who start their careers late are likely to experience the same rise and fall of creative output that others do, only later in life. And those lucky creators with immense creative potential to realize will not burn out; they will keep producing great works until they die.

What about mere mortals? Here, researchers have fallen back on tests designed to measure creativity. In one study, scores on a test of divergent thinking abilities decreased at least modestly after about age 40 and decreased more steeply starting around 70 (McCrae, Arenberg, & Costa, 1987). It seems that elderly adults do not differ much from younger adults in the

originality of their ideas; the main difference is that they generate fewer of them (Jaquish & Ripple, 1981). Generally, then, these studies agree with the studies of eminent achievers: Creative behavior becomes less frequent in later life, but it remains possible throughout the adult years.

Checking Mastery

1. What do IQ scores predict during adulthood?
2. What are two factors that contribute to a decline in IQ scores among older adults?
3. How is wisdom different from intelligence?

Making Connections

1. As the administrator of a large health maintenance organization, would it be useful to collect information on intelligence from your clients? Why or why not?
2. In what ways are you smarter than your parents and grandparents and in what ways are these two older generations smarter or wiser than you? What are some factors that contribute to generational differences in intelligence and age differences in wisdom?

9.6 Factors that Influence IQ Scores over the Life Span

LEARNING OBJECTIVES:

- Analyze the research on genetic and environmental contributions to intelligence and formulate a conclusion about how these factors contribute to our intellectual abilities.

- Critique the research on race and intelligence to reach a balanced conclusion about whether these two constructs are connected in meaningful ways.

Now that we have surveyed changes in intellectual functioning over the life span, we will address a different question: Why do children or adults who are the same age differ in IQ? Part of the answer is that they differ in the kinds of motivational and situational factors that can affect performance on a given day. Yet there are real differences in underlying intellectual ability that need to be explained. As usual, the best explanation is that genetic and environmental factors interact to make us what we are.

Genes and Environments

The pioneers of the IQ testing movement believed that individual differences in IQ exist simply because some people inherit better genes at conception than others do. This position is still held by hereditarians (for example, Herrnstein & Murray, 1994; and Jensen, 1998) who draw upon twin studies and other family research to demonstrate a genetic contribution to intelligence. As you saw in Chapter 3, identical twins obtain more similar IQ scores than fraternal twins do even when they have been raised apart. Moreover, the IQs of adopted children, once they reach adolescence, are more strongly correlated with those of their biological parents than with those of their adoptive parents. Overall,

most researchers find that about half of the variation in IQ scores within a group of individuals is associated with genetic differences among them (Plomin & Spinath, 2004; van Leeuwen et al., 2008).

What exactly does it mean to conclude that there is a genetic influence on intelligence? First, we must make clear what it does *not* mean: Genetic influence, even if it is strong, does not mean that a trait, in this case intelligence, is "set in stone" or unresponsive to the environment (see Nisbett et al., 2012). Genetic factors may provide some upper and lower limits on what is possible, but environment can play a significant role in determining what and where, within these broad limits, behaviors fall. Genes need environments for expression. There are likely many genetic influences on intelligence. For example, one child might be predisposed to have a strong curiosity or openness to new experiences. As a result of this, the child asks more questions, picks up more books, works on more puzzles, accepts invitations to a variety of activities, goes on more trips, and so on. This creates an environment that may allow intelligence to bloom. So genetic factors are important, but they do not tell the entire story.

How, then, does the environment influence intelligence? Research by Arnold Sameroff and his colleagues (1993) provides a broad overview of some of the environmental factors that put children at risk for having low IQ scores—and, by implication, some of the factors associated with higher IQs. These researchers assessed the 10 risk factors shown in ● **Table 9.3** at age 4 and again at age 13. Every factor was related to IQ at age 4, and most predicted IQ at age 13. In addition, the greater the number of these risk factors affecting a child, the lower his IQ, a finding confirmed by other research (Lipina & Colombo, 2009). Which risk factors the child experienced was less important than how many he experienced. Clearly, it is not good for intellectual development to grow up in a disadvantaged home with an adult unable to provide much intellectual nurturance.

In what ways do parents and the home influence children's intellectual development? A widely used assessment of the intellectual stimulation of the home environment is the **Home Observation for Measurement of the Environment (HOME) inventory** (Bradley et al., 2001). Sample items from the preschool version of a HOME inventory are shown in ● **Table 9.4**. Bradley and his colleagues (1989) have found that scores on the HOME can predict the IQs of African American and European American children at age 3, with correlations of about 0.50 (see also Cleveland et al., 2000). HOME scores continue to predict IQ scores between ages 3 and 6 (Espy, Molfese, & DiLalla, 2001). Gains in intellectual performance from age 1 to age 3, as measured by habituation and speed of processing, are likely to occur among children from stimulating homes, whereas children from families with low HOME scores often experience drops in performance over the same period. These findings are consistent across numerous countries and racial/ethnic groups, with a few exceptions (Farah et al., 2008; Lipina & Colombo, 2009).

What aspects of the home environment best predict high IQs? Studies using the HOME inventory indicate that the most important factors are parental involvement with the child and opportunities for stimulation (Gottfried et al., 1994). However, the amount of stimulation parents provide to their young children may not be as important as whether that stimulation is responsive to the child's behavior (a smile in return for a smile) and matched to the child's competencies so that it is neither too simple nor too challenging (Miller, 1986; Smith, Landry, & Swank, 2000). In short, an intellectually stimulating home is one in which parents are eager to be involved with their children and are responsive to their developmental needs and behavior. This may help explain why some research on intelligence finds a connection to family size and birth order, with firstborns and children from small families scoring just slightly higher (about two points) on IQ tests than later-borns and children from large families (see, for example, Zajonc, 2001a, 2001b; see also Sulloway, 2007).

Do differences in stimulation in the home really cause individual differences in IQ? Parents with greater intelligence are more likely than less intelligent parents to provide intellectually stimulating home environments for their children and to pass on to their children genes that contribute to high intelligence; that is, there is evidence of the gene–environment correlations described in Chapter 3. Maternal IQ, for example, is correlated with a child's IQ at 3 years and is also correlated with family income and quality of the home environment (Bacharach & Baumeister, 1998). Although a mother's IQ is reliably associated with her children's IQ, a father's IQ is a less reliable predictor of his children's IQ.

So bright children are bright, not because of the genes they inherited *or* because of the home environment their bright parents provided. Instead, they are bright because genes and environments get combined in ways that allow children with particular genetic makeups to display high intelligence under some environmental conditions. Overall, intellectual development seems to go best when a motivated, intellectually capable child begging for intellectual nourishment is fortunate enough to get it from involved and responsive parents.

● **Table 9.3** How 10 Environmental Risk Factors Affect IQ of Children at Age 4

Risk Factor	Average IQ for Children Who *Experienced* Risk Factor	Average IQ for Children Who *Did Not Experience* Risk Factor
Child is member of minority group	90	110
Head of household is unemployed or low-skilled worker	90	108
Mother did not complete high school	92	109
Family has four or more children	94	105
Father is absent from family	95	106
Family experienced many stressful life events	97	105
Parents have rigid child-rearing values	92	107
Mother is highly anxious or distressed	97	105
Mother has poor mental health or diagnosed disorder	99	107
Mother shows little positive affect toward child	88	107

SOURCE: Adapted from Sameroff, A. J., Seifer, R., Baldwin, A., & Baldwin, C. (1993). Stability of intelligence from pre-school to adolescence: The influence of social and family risk factors. *Child Development, 64,* 80–97. Copyright © 1993 Blackwell Publishing. Reprinted with permission.

● **Table 9.4** Subscales and Sample Items from the HOME Inventory

Subscale 1: Emotional and Verbal Responsivity of Parent (11 Items)	
Sample Items	Parent responds verbally to child's vocalization or verbalizations.
	Parent's speech is distinct, clear, and audible.
	Parent caresses or kisses child at least once.
Subscale 2: Avoidance of Restriction and Punishment (8 Items)	
Sample Items	Parent neither slaps nor spanks child during visit.
	Parent does not scold or criticize child during visit.
	Parent does not interfere with or restrict child more than three times during visit.
Subscale 3: Organization of Physical and Temporal Environment (6 Items)	
Sample Items	Child gets out of house at least four times a week.
	Child's play environment is safe.
Subscale 4: Provision of Appropriate Play Materials (9 Items)	
Sample Items	Child has a push or pull toy.
	Parent provides learning facilitators appropriate to age—mobile, table and chairs, highchair, playpen, and so on.
	Parent provides toys for child to play with during visit.
Subscale 5: Parental Involvement with Child (6 Items)	
Sample Items	Parent talks to child while doing household work.
	Parent structures child's play periods.
Subscale 6: Opportunities for Variety in Daily Stimulation (5 Items)	
Sample Items	Father provides some care daily.
	Child has three or more books of his or her own.

SOURCE: Adapted from Caldwell & Bradley, 1984.

Race and Ethnicity

Most studies, using samples from numerous countries, find racial and ethnic differences in IQ scores, which has sparked much controversy (see Daley & Onwuegbuzie, 2011). In the United States, for example, Asian American and European American children tend to score higher, on average, on IQ tests than African American, Native American, and Hispanic American children (Lynn, 2008b). Although some research suggests that racial differences on IQ tests have been shrinking in recent decades, other research shows little narrowing of the gap between, for example, black and white children on IQ tests (Dickens & Flynn, 2006; Murray, 2006; Yeung & Pfeiffer, 2009). Different subcultural groups sometimes show distinctive profiles of mental abilities; for example, black children often do well on verbal tasks, whereas Hispanic children, perhaps because of language differences, tend to excel on nonverbal items (Lynn, 2009; Taylor & Richards, 1991). It is essential to keep in mind that we are talking about *group averages*. Like the IQ scores of white children, those of minority children run the range from intellectually disabled to gifted. Researchers certainly cannot predict an individual's IQ merely on the basis of racial or ethnic identity. Indeed, lumping people together based on some notion of a common racial background makes little sense to many scientists who find that the variability within groups and the overlap between groups renders the group concept meaningless (Daley & Onwuegbuzie, 2011). Having said that, why do these average group differences exist? Consider the following hypotheses: bias in the tests, motivational factors, genetic differences among groups, and environmental differences among groups.

Biased Tests?

Racial differences in IQ tests may be attributable to culture bias in testing; that is, IQ tests may be more appropriate for children from white middle-class backgrounds than for those from other subcultural groups (Helms, 1992; Lopez, 1997). Low-income African American children who speak a dialect of English (such as Ebonics or Black English) different from that spoken by middle-class European American children, as well as Hispanic children who hear Spanish rather than English at home, may not understand some test instructions or items. What is more, their experiences may not allow them to become familiar with some of the information called for on the tests (for example, What is a 747? Who wrote *Hamlet?*).

Minority-group children often do not have as much exposure to the culture reflected in the tests as nonminority children do. If IQ tests assess "proficiency in European American culture," minority children are bound to look deficient (Helms, 1992). Using IQ tests designed to be fair to all ethnic groups and introducing procedures to help minority children feel more comfortable and motivated can cut the usual IQ gap between African American and European American children in half (Kaufman, Kamphaus, & Kaufman, 1985). But even though standardized IQ test items sometimes have a white middle-class flavor, group differences in IQ probably cannot be traced solely to test bias. Culture-fair IQ tests include items that should be equally unfamiliar (or familiar) to people from all ethnic groups and social classes—for example, items that require completing a geometric design with a piece that matches the rest of the design. Still, racial and ethnic differences emerge on such tests (Jensen, 1980). In addition, IQ tests predict future school achievement as well for African Americans and other minorities as they do for European Americans (Neisser et al., 1996).

Motivational Differences?

Another possibility is that minority individuals are not motivated to do their best in testing situations because they are anxious or resist being judged by an examiner who is often of a different racial/ethnic background (Huang, 2009; Ogbu, 1994; Steele, 1997). Disadvantaged children score some 7–10 points higher when they are given time to get to know a friendly examiner or are given a mix of easy and hard items so that they do not become discouraged by a long string of difficult items (Zigler et al., 1982). Even though most children do better with a friendly examiner, it seems that African American children, even those from middle-class homes, are often less comfortable in testing situations than white middle-class children are (Moore, 1986). Minority children may be less likely to see value to themselves for performing well on a test (Okagaki, 2001). And their peers may accuse (or tease) them of "acting white" if they place too much emphasis on academic success and strong test scores, values that they may associate with white culture.

Claude Steele and his colleagues have argued that the performance of African Americans is especially likely to suffer whenever negative stereotypes of their group come into play (Steele, 1997, 1999; Steele & Aronson, 1995; see also Sackett, Hardison, & Cullen, 2004). In one study, female students at Stanford University were given difficult test items. Some students were told that they were taking a test of verbal abilities and would get feedback about their strengths and weaknesses; others were told that they were going to do some verbal problems but that their ability would not be evaluated. As ■ **Figure 9.9** shows, African American students performed poorly when they were led to believe that the test would reveal their level of intellectual ability, but performed more like European American students when they did not think their ability would be judged. Even being asked to identify their race in a personal information section at the start of a test of intellectual ability can undermine the performance of African American college students (Steele & Aronson, 1995).

Why? Steele concluded that African Americans perform poorly on IQ tests partly because of **stereotype threat** —fear that they will

■ **Figure 9.9** African American students perform poorly on tests of mental abilities when they think they are taking a test that may result in their being stereotyped as unintelligent.

Source: Steele, C. M., & Aronson, J. (1995). Stereotype threat and the intellectual test performance of African Americans. *Journal of Personality and Social Psychology*, 69, 797–811. Copyright © 1995 by the American Psychological Association. Reprinted by permission.

be judged to have the qualities associated with negative stereotypes of African Americans (see also Aronson et al., 1999). It is not that African Americans have internalized stereotypes and believe they are intellectually inferior, according to Steele. Instead, they become anxious and unable to perform well in testing situations that arouse concerns about being negatively stereotyped.

Gregory Walton and Steven Spencer (2009) conducted two meta-analyses of the effects of stereotype threat on test performance of thousands of students. They found substantial effects on SAT scores, the standardized test taken by many college-bound high school students. Stereotype threat seems to account for 40 points of the score gap between majority (white) and nonmajority (black and Hispanic) students. Thus, minority student performance is underestimated as a result of pervasive negative stereotypes.

On the positive side, other research has demonstrated that positive stereotypes about a group can increase the performance of members of that group. Margaret Shih and her colleagues

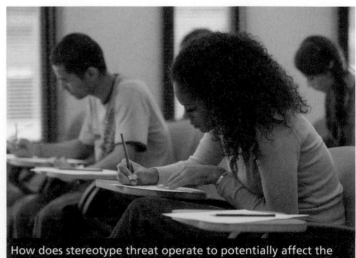

How does stereotype threat operate to potentially affect the test performance of this young African American woman?

(Shih, Pittinsky, & Ambady, 1999) gave Asian American women a math test under one of three conditions. In one, their identity as women was made noticeable; in another, their Asian American identity was made evident; and in a third condition, no identity was emphasized. Consistent with stereotypes, these women performed worse when their gender was emphasized and better when their ethnic background was emphasized, relative to the group that was not primed to think about either identity. So stereotypes can either hinder or enhance performance, depending on whether a person identifies with a group that is viewed negatively or positively on the dimension measured.

The effects of stereotype threat can be reduced by providing students with a mentor. Catherine Good, Joshua Aronson, and Michael Inzlicht (2003) had college students serve as mentors to seventh-graders likely to experience stereotype threat as a result of being female, impoverished, and a member of a minority group. The mentors encouraged students to interpret their academic troubles as a result of the transition to a new school for seventh grade. In addition, they talked about intelligence being flexible and responsive to new learning. Following such mentoring, the students performed better on standardized tests than students who did not receive mentoring. These findings provide a practical means for eliminating or reducing the negative influence of stereotype threat. Of course, eliminating the negative stereotypes that create the threat should also be a goal.

Genetic Factors?

We discussed the overall influence of genetic factors on intelligence, but is there any evidence that genetic differences *between* racial or ethnic groups account for different levels of performance? This is perhaps one of the most controversial ideas in psychology, and it has sparked much heated debate. Scholars such as Arthur Jensen (1969) and Herrnstein and Murray (1994) have suggested that IQ differences between European Americans and African Americans may be because of genetic differences between the races, and they have written books to present their positions.

However, most psychologists do not think the evidence that heredity contributes to *within-group* differences says much about the reasons for *between-group* differences. Consider this analogy from Richard Lewontin (1976): Suppose that corn seeds with different genetic makeups are randomly drawn from a bag and planted in two fields—one that has terrible soil with no nutrients and one that has rich, fertile soil. Because all the plants *within* each field were grown in the same soil, their differences in height would have to be because of differences in genetic makeup. A genetic explanation of differences would fit. But if the plants in the fertile field are generally taller than those in the nonfertile field, this *between-field* variation must be entirely because of environment. Similarly, even though genes partially explain individual differences in IQ *within* African American and European American groups, the average difference *between* the racial groups may still reflect nothing more than differences in the environments they typically experience. There is no direct evidence that differences in genetic makeup between the races account for average group differences in IQ (Neisser et al., 1996).

Environmental Influences?

It is time, then, to return to an environmental hypothesis about racial and ethnic differences in IQ. Many of the intellectual and academic differences attributed to race or ethnicity probably reflect racial and ethnic differences in socioeconomic status instead (Patterson, Kupersmidt, & Vaden, 1990). As noted earlier, placement in more advantaged homes has allowed lower-income African American children to equal or exceed the average IQ in the general population and to exceed the IQs of comparable African American children raised in more disadvantaged environments by 20 points (Moore, 1986; Scarr & Weinberg, 1983; Weinberg et al., 1992). This could not have happened if African American children were genetically deficient.

The major message of this research is that children, whatever their racial background, perform better on IQ tests when they grow up in intellectually stimulating environments with involved, responsive parents and are exposed to the "culture of the tests and the schools" (Scarr & Weinberg, 1983, p. 261). How much of the racial gap in IQ can be explained by racial differences in neighborhood and family socioeconomic conditions, mother's education, and qualities of the home environment? Jeanne Brooks-Gunn, Pamela Klebanov, and Greg Duncan (1996) used statistical procedures to correct for these environmental differences between African American and European American children so that they could estimate what the IQ difference would be if the two racial groups had been raised in similar environments. Without any controls for environmental differences, there was an IQ gap of 18 points. The gap narrowed to 8 points when family and neighborhood income levels were controlled and was reduced to 3 points, a trivial difference, when racial differences in the provision of a stimulating home environment (HOME scores) were also controlled. In short, that more African American than European American children live in poverty and have limited learning opportunities at home has a lot to do with racial difference in average IQ scores. Reducing poverty and offering more early developmental programs to offset the costs of impoverished home environments would go a long way toward eliminating racial differences in intellectual performance.

Checking Mastery

1. How does home environment, as measured with the HOME inventory, influence IQ scores?
2. What are two hypotheses about why IQ tests yield racial/ethnic differences in scores?

Making Connections

1. The Maori are a socioeconomically disadvantaged group in New Zealand, a country colonized by the British long ago. Maori children typically score lower on IQ tests than children of British background. Knowing what you know about minorities in the United States, what are your top two hypotheses about why Maori children perform relatively poorly, and how might you test these hypotheses?
2. Considering material from this chapter as well as material from Chapter 3 on genetic influences, evaluate the relative contributions of nature and nurture to intelligence. Does one or the other have a greater contribution to intelligence? How do their effects combine? What evidence supports your position?

LEARNING OBJECTIVES:

- Distinguish among different levels of intellectual disability.

- Summarize the likely causes of intellectual disability and what efforts might help reduce rates of intellectual disability.

- Explain the criteria used to identify someone as gifted.

- Trace the likely developmental path of a gifted individual through the life span.

- Compare and contrast, integrating where possible, the various theoretical perspectives on cognitive development covered in Chapters 7, 8, and now 9.

Although we have identified some of the factors that contribute to individual differences in intellectual performance, you cannot fully appreciate the magnitude of these differences without considering people at the extremes of the IQ continuum. Think back to Sho and Steven, introduced at the beginning of this chapter. Just how different are intellectually disabled individuals such as Steven and gifted individuals such as Sho? And how different are their lives?

Intellectual Disability

Intellectual disability, or mental retardation as it was called for many decades, is defined as significantly below-average intellectual functioning with limitations in areas of adaptive behavior such as self-care and social skills, originating before age 18 (see AAIDD, 2010; Schalock et al., 2010). An IQ score of 70–75 or lower suggests a limitation in intellectual functioning. This, along with difficulties meeting age-appropriate expectations in important areas of everyday functioning, is indicative of intellectually disability. Thus, intellectual disability is not merely a deficiency within the person; rather, it is the product of the interaction between person and environment, strongly influenced by the type and level of supportive help the individual receives. If this sounds familiar to you, perhaps you are thinking of Fischer's dynamic skill theory, discussed in Chapter 8, which proposed that skills can be optimized with a high level of support. A person with an IQ score of 65 in a supportive environment that is structured in ways that allow the individual to fit in and flourish

may not be considered disabled in this environment. However, in an environment with different expectations and support, this same individual may be viewed as disabled.

Individuals with intellectual disability differ greatly in their levels of functioning (● **Table 9.5**). An adult with an IQ in the range of about 55–70 is likely to have a MA comparable to that of an 8- to 12-year-old child. Individuals with mild intellectual disability can learn both academic and practical skills in school, and they can potentially work and live independently as adults. Many of these individuals are integrated into regular classrooms, where they excel academically and socially relative to comparable individuals who are segregated into special classrooms (Freeman, 2000). At the other end of the continuum, individuals with IQs below 20–25 and MAs below 3 years ("profoundly disabled") show major delays in all areas of development and require basic care, sometimes in institutional settings. However, they, too, can benefit considerably from training.

Intellectual disability has many causes. Those who are severely and profoundly disabled are often affected by "organic" conditions, meaning that their disability is because of some identifiable biological cause associated with hereditary factors, diseases, or injuries. Down syndrome, the condition associated with an extra 21st chromosome, and phenylketonuria (PKU) are familiar examples of conditions causing intellectual disability that are associated with genetic factors (Roizen, 2013; see also Chapter 3). Less common is the genetic condition that leads to Williams Syndrome, associated with IQ scores in the range of mild intellectual disability (Hodapp et al.,

● **Table 9.5** Levels and Characteristics of Intellectual Disability

	Level			
	Mild	**Moderate**	**Severe**	**Profound**
Approximate Range of IQ Scores	52–70	35–51	20–34	Below 19
Degree of Independence	Usually independent	Some independence; needs some supervision	May be semi-independent with close supervision	Dependent; needs constant supervision
Educational Achievement	Can do some academic work—usually to sixth-grade level; focus is on career	Focus is on daily living skills rather than academics; some career training	Focus is on self-care (toileting, dressing, eating) and communication skills	Focus is on self-care, mobility, and basic communication education

Source: Barack, J. A., Hodapp, R. M., & Zigler E. (Eds.). (1998). *Handbook of mental retardation and development.* Copyright © 1998 Cambridge University Press. Reprinted with permission.

2011). Other forms of organic disability are associated with prenatal risk factors—an alcoholic mother, exposure to rubella, and so on (Paulson, 2013; see also Chapter 4). Because many such children are seriously delayed or have physical defects, they can often be identified at birth or during infancy and come from all socioeconomic levels. However, most cases of intellectual disability have no identifiable organic cause; they are characterized by milder symptoms and appear to result from some combination of genetic endowment and environmental factors (Batshaw, Gropman, & Lanpher, 2013). Not surprisingly, then, these children often come from poor areas, have neglectful or abusive families, and frequently have a parent or sibling who is also disabled (Batshaw et al., 2013; Zigler, 1995).

Historically, about 3% of school-age children have been classified with intellectual disability, although this rate has decreased as fewer children today are diagnosed with mild disability (Patton, 2000). Oftentimes, these children have associated impairments, such as cerebral palsy, behavioral problems, physical impairments, or sensory disorders. As for children not diagnosed at birth, those with milder disabilities are typically diagnosed when as toddlers they fail to meet developmental milestones at a typical age. Once children are diagnosed, their parents experience complex reactions to their child and the disability itself (Boström, Broberg, & Hwang, 2010). Parents—mothers more so than fathers—of intellectually disabled children report higher levels of stress than parents of nondisabled children, but this stress is reduced where there are higher levels of marital and parenting satisfaction (Gerstein et al., 2009; Hill & Rose, 2009).

What becomes of these children as they grow up? Generally, they proceed along the same paths and through the same sequences of developmental milestones as other children do, although often at a slower rate (Hodapp et al., 2011). Their IQs remain low because they do not achieve the same level of growth that others do. They, like nondisabled people, show signs of intellectual aging in later life, especially on tests that require speed (Devenny et al., 1996). Individuals with Down syndrome may experience even greater intellectual deterioration later in life because they are at risk for premature Alzheimer's disease (Roizen, 2013).

As for their outcomes in life, consider a series of follow-up studies with a group of individuals with intellectual disabilities known as the "Camberwell Cohort" for the region of England from where they were originally recruited (Beadle-Brown, Murphy, & DiTerlizzi, 2009; Beadle-Brown, Murphy, & Wing, 2005, 2006). In their 40s, about 50% lived in community group homes, 25% lived with their family, and 20% lived in a larger residential facility. Social skills, important to daily interactions with others, remained largely unchanged over the 25-year period of study. But for those who as children started out more socially impaired than others in the sample, social impairments tended to worsen with age, possibly because social demands increased in adulthood or because support in social situations was diminished. The combination of intellectual disability and social impairment led to a poor or fair overall outcome for most of the individuals in the cohort. Not surprisingly, those who were not as intellectually disabled and did not have associated impairments had more favorable outcomes.

The results from the Camberwell Cohort suggest that overall quality of life is lower for adults diagnosed with intellectual disability early in life. However, outcomes varied and were related to severity of the disability. Despite the relatively lackluster outcomes for these individuals, the findings also provide grounds for optimism. Only a minority of the group lived in what might be considered an institutional setting; most lived in the community, either in small group homes or with their family, and participated in typical community activities. This is a marked improvement from previous decades, when nearly everyone with any level of disability lived segregated from the mainstream of society.

Giftedness

The gifted child used to be identified solely by an IQ score—one that was at least 130. Programs for gifted children still focus mainly on those with very high IQs, but there is increased recognition that some children are gifted because they have special abilities—think again of Gardner's eight intelligences discussed at the beginning of this chapter—rather than because they have high general intelligence. Even high-IQ children are usually not equally talented in all areas; contrary to myth, they cannot just become anything they choose (Winner, 1996). More often, high-IQ children have exceptional talent in an area or two and otherwise are good, but not exceptional, performers (Achter, Benbow, & Lubinski, 1997). So today's definitions emphasize that **giftedness** involves having a high IQ or showing special abilities in areas valued in society, such as mathematics, the performing and visual arts, or even leadership.

Joseph Renzulli (1998; Reis & Renzulli, 2011; Renzulli & Delcourt, 2013) has long argued that giftedness emerges from a combination of above-average ability, creativity, and task commitment. According to this view, someone might have a high IQ and even creative ability, but Renzulli questions whether they are truly gifted if they are not motivated to use this intelligence. Here we focus on individuals with exceptional IQs.

How early can intellectually gifted children be identified? Giftedness is usually apparent by toddlerhood, according to the Fullerton Longitudinal study by Allen Gottfried and his colleagues (1994). They tracked a large sample of children from age 1–8, determined which children had IQs of 130 or above

Gifted children have either high IQ scores or special abilities. This young girl is performing with the Pacific Symphony of Orange County, California.

at age 8, and then looked for differences between these gifted children and other children earlier in life. The gifted children turned out to be identifiable as early as 18 months, primarily by their advanced language skills. Other recent research confirms that early language ability is a good, although not perfect, clue to later intellectual giftedness (Colombo et al., 2009). Gifted children were also highly curious and motivated to learn; they even enjoyed the challenge of taking IQ tests more than most children.

Linda Silverman and her colleagues at the Gifted Development Center have used the Characteristics of Giftedness Scale to identify gifted children (see Gifted Development Center, 2013). They have found that gifted children can be distinguished from average children by the following attributes:

- Rapid learning
- Extensive vocabulary
- Good memory
- Long attention span
- Perfectionism
- Preference for older companions
- Excellent sense of humor
- Early interest in reading
- Strong ability with puzzles and mazes
- Maturity
- Perseverance on tasks

The early emergence of giftedness is consistent with research showing a strong genetic influence on high intellect (see Brant et al., 2009; and Haworth et al., 2009). Still, prediction of giftedness is not perfect, although the prediction of *non*giftedness is nearly so (Colombo et al., 2009). That is, experts are nearly always correct when they identify a child as not gifted; but among children identified early as gifted, some of these children drift out of this category as they get older (Colombo et al., 2009).

We get a richer understanding of the development of high-IQ children from a major longitudinal study launched in 1921 by Lewis Terman, developer of the Stanford-Binet test (Holahan & Sears, 1995; Oden, 1968; Terman, 1954). The participants were more than 1,500 California schoolchildren who were nominated by their teachers as gifted and who had IQs of 140 or higher. It soon became apparent that these high-IQ children (who came to be called *Termites*) were exceptional in many other ways. For example, they had weighed more at birth and had learned to walk and talk sooner than most toddlers. They reached puberty somewhat earlier than average and had better-than-average health. Their teachers rated them as better adjusted and more morally mature than their less intelligent peers. And, although they were no more popular than their classmates, they were quick to take on leadership responsibilities. Taken together, these findings destroy the stereotype that most gifted children are frail, sickly youngsters who are socially inadequate and emotionally immature.

Another demonstration of the personal and social maturity of most gifted children comes from a study of high-IQ children who skipped high school and entered the University of Washington as part of a special program to accelerate their education (see Robinson Center, 2013). Contrary to the common wisdom that gifted children will suffer socially and emotionally if they skip grades and are forced to fit in with much older students, these youngsters showed no signs of maladjustment (see Noble & Childers, 2009). On several measures of psychological and social maturity and adjustment, they equaled their much older college classmates and similarly gifted students who attended high school. Many of them thrived in college, for the first time finding friends like themselves—friends who were like-minded rather than like-aged (Noble, Childers, & Vaughan, 2008). Other research similarly shows that acceleration through school is associated with higher academic achievement and more positive social-emotional outcomes for gifted children than lack of acceleration (Steenbergen-Hu & Moon, 2011).

What happens as gifted children move into adulthood? Most of Terman's gifted children remained as remarkable in adulthood as they had been in childhood. Fewer than 5% were rated as seriously maladjusted. Their rates of such problems as ill health, mental illness, alcoholism, and delinquent behavior were but a fraction of those observed in the general population (Terman, 1954), although they were no less likely to divorce (Holahan & Sears, 1995).

The occupational achievements of the men in the sample were impressive. In middle age, 88% were employed in professional or high-level business jobs, compared with 20% of men in the general population (Oden, 1968). As a group, they had taken out more than 200 patents and written some 2,000 scientific reports, 100 books, 375 plays or short stories, and more than 300 essays, sketches, magazine articles, and critiques. These findings of notable accomplishment are echoed in recent follow-ups of other adults identified as gifted by age 13 (see Park, Lubinski, & Benbow, 2007). What about the gifted women in Terman's study? Because of the influence of gender-role expectations during the period covered by the study, gifted women achieved less than gifted men vocationally, often interrupting their careers or sacrificing their career goals to raise families. Still, they were more likely to have careers, and distinguished ones, than most women of their generation.

Finally, the Termites aged well. In their 60s and 70s, most of the men and women in the Terman study were highly active, involved, healthy, and happy people (Holahan & Sears, 1995). The men kept working longer than most men do and stayed involved in work even after they retired. The women too led exceptionally active lives. Contrary to the stereotype that gifted individuals burn out early, the Termites continued to burn bright throughout their lives.

Yet just as it is wrong to view intellectually gifted children as emotionally disturbed misfits, it is inaccurate to conclude that intellectually gifted children are models of good adjustment, perfect in every way. Some research suggests that children with IQs closer to 180 than 130 are often unhappy and socially isolated, perhaps because they are so out of step with their peers, and sometimes even have serious problems (Winner, 1996). Not all research on the profoundly gifted, as those with IQ's of 180 and higher are often called, finds an unusual level of social maladjustment, however (Lubinski et al., 2001). Even within this elite group, the quality of

• **Table 9.6** Comparison of Approaches to Intelligence

	Piagetian Cognitive-Developmental Theory	Fischer's Dynamic Skill Theory	Vygotskian Sociocultural Theory	Information-Processing Approach	Psychometric Approach	Sternberg's Triarchic Model
What Is Intelligence?	Cognitive structures that help people adapt	Refining skills to optimize performance given the task and context	Tools of culture	Attention, memory, and other mental processes	Mental abilities and scores on IQ tests	Components that allow people to succeed in their lives
What Changes with Age?	Stage of cognitive development	Skill levels change	Ability to solve problems without assistance of others and with use of inner speech	Hardware (speed) and software (strategies) of the mind	Mental age (difficulty of problems solved)	Ability to respond to novel problems and automate familiar ones, adapt to current environmental demands, and select appropriate "mental tools" for solving problems
What Is of Most Interest?	Universal changes	Variability in performance	Culturally influenced changes and processes	Universal processes	Individual differences	Adapting behavior to environmental challenges

the individual's home environment was important. The most well-adjusted and successful adults had highly educated parents who offered them both love and intellectual stimulation (Tomlinson-Keasey & Little, 1990).

Integrating Cognitive Perspectives

Our account of cognitive development over the life span is now complete. We hope you appreciate that each of the major approaches to the mind that we have considered—the Piagetian cognitive-developmental approach, Fischer's dynamic skill theory, and Vygotsky's sociocultural theory described in Chapter 7; the information-processing approach explained in Chapter 8; and the psychometric, or testing, approach, and Sternberg's triarchic model covered here—offers something of value. • **Table 9.6** lists how these approaches compare on their views of intelligence.

We can summarize the different approaches to cognitive development this way: Piaget has shown that comparing the thought of a preschooler with the thought of an adult is like comparing a caterpillar with a butterfly. Modes of thought change qualitatively with age. Fischer emphasized the concept of a developmental range of skills that might result depending on level of support provided. Vygotsky has highlighted the importance of culturally transmitted modes of thinking and interactions with others. The information-processing approach has helped researchers understand thinking processes and explain why the young child cannot remember as much information or solve problems as effectively as the adult can. The psychometric approach has told researchers that, if they look at the range of tasks to which the mind can be applied, they can recognize

distinct mental abilities that each person consistently displays in greater or lesser amounts. Finally, Sternberg has pushed us to look beyond traditional psychometric tests of intelligence that emphasize analytic skills valued in the classroom to consider creative and practical intelligence alongside the analytical.

You need not choose one approach and reject the others. Your understanding of the mind is likely to be richer if all six approaches continue to thrive. There are truly many intelligences, and it is foolish to think that a single IQ score can describe the complexities of human cognitive development.

Checking Mastery

1. How is intellectual disability defined?
2. What characterizes the typical gifted person?
3. How does the definition of intelligence vary across the various approaches presented in Chapters 7, 8, and 9?

Making Connections

1. Should gifted, "regular," and intellectually disabled children be educated in the same classroom? What are some of the pros and cons of such integrated education for each of the three groups of children?
2. Putting together material from Chapters 7, 8, and 9, how would you describe the cognitive functioning of a typical 70-year-old person? What are the greatest cognitive strengths of older adults, what are their greatest limitations, and how much can an individual do to optimize her functioning?

Chapter Summary

9.1 Defining Intelligence and Creativity

- The psychometric, or testing, approach to cognition defines intelligence as a set of traits that allows some people to think and solve problems more effectively than others. It can be viewed as a hierarchy consisting of a general factor (g), broad abilities such as fluid and crystallized intelligence, and many specific abilities. The Stanford-Binet and Wechsler Scales are the most common intelligence tests and compare an individual's performance on a variety of cognitive tasks with the average performance of age-mates.

- Gardner's theory of multiple intelligences, with its focus on eight distinct forms of intelligence, offers an alternative view. His theory includes these types of intelligence: linguistic, logical–mathematical, musical, spatial, bodily kinesthetic, interpersonal, intrapersonal, and naturalist.

- Sternberg's triarchic theory of intelligence proposes three components to intelligence. The practical component predicts that intelligent behavior will vary across different sociocultural contexts. According to the creative component, intelligent responses will vary depending on whether problems are novel or routine (automated). Finally, the analytical aspect of intelligence includes the thinking skills that a person brings to a problem-solving situation. This theory has been extended to the theory of successful intelligence, which identifies the additional factors needed to maximize your intelligence.

- Creativity is the ability to produce novel and socially valuable work. It involves divergent rather than convergent thinking and is often measured in terms of ideational fluency, the sheer number of different (including novel) ideas that a person can generate.

9.2 The Infant

- The Bayley scales include motor, mental, and behavior ratings to assess infant development. Although traditionally used as a measure of infant intelligence, they do not correlate well with later IQ scores.

- Infant measures that capture speed of information processing and preference for novelty are better at predicting later intelligence. Infants who can quickly process information are able to take in more information than those who are slower.

9.3 The Child

- During childhood, IQ scores become more stable so that scores at one point in time are generally consistent with scores obtained at a second point.

- Despite group stability, many individuals show wide variations in their IQ scores over time. Those who gain IQ points often have favorable home environments, whereas disadvantaged children often show a cumulative deficit.

- Social class impacts IQ scores, raising the issue of middle-class testing bias. Children who are moved from low to higher socioeconomic status homes show an increase in IQ scores.

- Creativity increases throughout early childhood but dips during later elementary school, possibly in response to societal expectations to conform. Creativity is associated with playfulness, openness to new experiences, and originality.

9.3 The Adolescent

- The Flynn effect describes a global increase in IQ scores over the past century that is likely the result of better nutrition, living conditions, and education.

- During adolescence, IQ scores are relatively stable and intellectual performance reaches near-adult level. IQ scores are useful for predicting the academic achievement of adolescents.

- Levels of creativity vary considerably from one individual to another. Some adolescents conform to societal norms and express little creativity, while others show a great deal of innovation.

- Adolescents with exceptional talents or creativity have both talent and motivation on the nature side and environments that foster their talents and value independence on the nurture side.

9.5 The Adult

- IQ scores are correlated with occupational status as well as health in adulthood.

- Both cross-sectional studies and longitudinal studies tend to show age-related decreases in IQ. Schaie's sequential study suggests that (1) date of birth (cohort) influences test performance, (2) no major declines in mental abilities occur until the late 60s or 70s, (3) some abilities (especially fluid ones) decline more than others (especially crystallized ones), and (4) not all people's abilities decline.

- A few adults display wisdom, or exceptional insight into complex life problems, which requires a rich knowledge base along with particular personality traits and cognitive styles and is influenced more by experience than age.

- Creative output increases sharply from early to middle adulthood, and although it then drops somewhat, it remains above the level where it started in young adulthood. The peak period of creativity varies from one field to another. Creative output may drop-off in older adulthood because people have already generated and expressed their creative potential.

9.6 Factors That Influence IQ Scores over the Life Span

- Individual differences in IQ at a given age are linked to genetic factors and to differences in intellectually stimulating qualities of the home environment such as parental involvement and responsive stimulation.

- Racial and ethnic differences in IQ also exist, with African American and Hispanic children typically scoring, on average, lower than European American children. Motivational differences, stereotype threat, genetic factors, and environment have all been considered as contributors.

9.7 The Extremes of Intelligence

- The extremes of intelligence are represented by intellectual disability at one end of the continuum and giftedness at the other end.
- Intellectual disability is defined by deficits in adaptive behavior combined with low IQ scores. Functioning varies by level of disability and is worse when accompanied by other conditions. Most intellectually disabled adults live in the community, either in group homes or with their families.
- Giftedness has most often been defined by high IQ scores, although more recent definitions recognize special talents not measured by traditional IQ tests. Life outcomes for gifted people are generally above average.

- Six major approaches to cognitive development have been presented in Chapters 7, 8, and 9. These include Piaget's focus on qualitatively different stages of thought, Fischer's dynamic skills, and Vygotsky's emphasis on culturally transmitted modes of thought. The information-processing approach reveals how memory and problem solving are influenced by characteristics of the person such as age and task factors such as complexity. The psychometric approach defines cognitive abilities in measurable ways, illustrating that people have more or less of distinct mental abilities. Sternberg's triarchic theory adds creative and practical intelligence to the more traditional analytic intelligence.

Checking Mastery Answers

For answers to Checking Mastery questions, please see Appendix B.

Key Terms

psychometric approach **265**
fluid intelligence **265**
crystallized intelligence **266**
mental age (MA) **266**
Stanford-Binet Intelligence Scale **266**
intelligence quotient (IQ) **266**
test norms **266**
Wechsler scales **266**
normal distribution **266**
standard deviation **267**
savant syndrome **267**
Sternberg's triarchic abilities test (STAT) **268**

triarchic theory of intelligence **268**
practical component **268**
creative component **268**
automatization **269**
culture bias **269**
analytic component **269**
successful intelligence **270**
creativity **270**
convergent thinking **270**
divergent thinking **270**
ideational fluency **270**
investment theory **271**

Bayley Scales of Infant Development **271**
developmental quotient (DQ) **272**
child poverty **273**
cumulative-deficit hypothesis **274**
Flynn effect **277**
terminal drop **281**
wisdom **282**
Home Observation for Measurement
    of the Environment (HOME) inventory **286**
stereotype threat **288**
intellectual disability **290**
giftedness **291**

CENGAGE
brain.com   Get quizzes, flashcards, videos, and more at **www.cengagebrain.com.**

10 Language and Education

"**As the cool stream** gushed over one hand, she [Annie] spelled into the other the word water, first slowly, then rapidly. I stood still, my whole attention fixed upon the motions of her fingers. Suddenly I felt a misty consciousness as of something forgotten—a thrill of returning thought; and somehow the mystery of language was revealed to me. I knew then that W-A-T-E-R meant the wonderful cool something that was flowing over my hand. . . . I left the well-house eager to learn. Everything had a name, and each name gave birth to a new thought. As we returned to the house every object which I touched seemed to quiver with life" (Keller, 1954, p. 15).

One of the most important milestones in development is mastering some type of language. Consider how the world changed for Helen Keller, deaf and blind from a young age, when she finally realized that every object, every person, every concept could be represented with a symbol. From this point on, she was able to communicate with the people around her and participate in the world in ways that were not available without a tool such as sign or spoken language. As you learned in Chapter 7, psychologist Lev Vygotsky argued that language is the primary vehicle through which adults pass culturally valued modes of thinking and problem solving to their children. He also believed that language is our most important tool of thinking.

In this chapter, we examine language skills, which become established largely through an informal education system consisting of parents, other grownups, peers, and even the media. We also consider formal education, which uses basic language skills to cultivate the reading, writing, thinking, and problem-solving skills that allow individuals to become fully functioning members of society. However, getting the most out of education requires more than acquiring language and literacy skills. As Terrel Bell, former secretary of education, asserted: "There are three things to remember about education. The first one is motivation. The second one is motivation. The third one is motivation" (quoted in Maehr & Meyer, 1997, p. 372). Thus, we also examine achievement motivation and its relationship to education and educational outcomes.

10.1 The System of Language

LEARNING OBJECTIVES:

- Describe the function of each component of a spoken language system.

- Articulate how the brain is organized to support language.

- Explain the major theoretical approaches to understanding how language develops.

Although language is one of the most intricate forms of knowledge we will ever acquire, all typically developing children master a language early in life. Indeed, many infants are talking before they can walk. Can language be complex, then? It certainly can be. Linguists (scholars who study language) define **language** as a communication system in which a limited number of signals—sounds or letters (or gestures, in the case of the sign language used by deaf people)—can be combined according to agreed-upon rules to produce an infinite number of messages. Linguists have yet to fully describe the rules of English or of any of the other 6,000 or so languages that exist throughout the world. To master a spoken language such as English, a child must learn basic sounds, how sounds are combined to form words, how words are combined to form meaningful statements, what words and sentences mean, and how to use language effectively in social interactions. How is this accomplished? To address this, we are guided, once again, by the nature–nurture framework. But first, we need to understand the basic components of language.

Close-up of a chalk board

clawan/Shutterstock.com

Basic Components

Every human language must have words (symbols) that represent the objects, people, ideas, and so on that are relevant to the community. In addition, there must be a system of rules to organize how the words are used and combined to facilitate communication among members of the community. Perhaps the most fundamental system involves **phonemes**, which are the basic units of *sound* that can change the meaning of a word. Substituting the phoneme /p/ for /b/ in the word *bit* changes the meaning of the word. Although there are 26 letters in the English alphabet, there are more phonemes than this because letters can be pronounced different ways. Trying to identify the precise number of phonemes in a language, though, is like trying to identify

the exact number of colors that exist in a rainbow; there are numerous subtleties and interpretations. In addition to individual phonemes, languages also specify how phonemes can be combined. In English, for example, we can combine /b/ and /r/ to say "brat" but we cannot combine /b/ with /m/ to produce "bmat."

Languages also have a system for organizing the **morphemes**, the basic units of *meaning* that exist in a word. Some words consist of just one morpheme: *view*. But we can add another morpheme, *re*, and the meaning of the word changes (*review*). Add a different morpheme, *pre*, and the meaning changes again (*preview*). Morphemes are not the same as syllables: a word with multiple syllables, such as the three-syllable *crocodile*, can still consist of one morpheme if it cannot be further broken down into a smaller meaningful unit. To convey the meaning of what we intend when we say "crocodile," we have to include all three syllables.

An important step in language acquisition is mastering its **syntax**, the systematic rules for forming sentences. Consider these three sentences: (1) Fang Fred bit. (2) Fang bit Fred. (3) Fred bit Fang. The first violates the rules of English sentence structure or syntax, although this word order would be acceptable in German. The second and third are both grammatical English sentences, but their different word orders—determined by rules of syntax—convey different meanings. Understanding the meanings of sentences also requires knowing the **semantics** of language. To understand the sentence "Sherry was green with jealousy," we must move beyond the literal meaning of each word, which would suggest that Sherry was the color green, to the meaning that is created when we combine these words into this particular sentence.

Finally, we must understand something of the **pragmatics** of language—rules for specifying how language is used appropriately in different social contexts. That is, children (and adults) have to learn when to say what to whom. They must learn to communicate effectively by taking into account who the listener is, what the listener already knows, and what the listener needs or wants to hear. "Give me that cookie!" may be grammatical English, but the child is far more likely to win Grandma's heart (not to mention a cookie) with a polite "May I please try one of your yummy cookies, Grandma?"

In addition to these features of language, producing meaningful speech also involves **prosody**, or *how* the sounds are produced (Patel & Brayton, 2009). Prosody has been called the "melody" of speech because it includes pitch or intonation, the stress or accentuation of certain syllables in a word or certain words in a sentence, and the duration or timing of speech. A child may say "dog" with little change in pitch, perhaps to make a statement meaning, *"There is a dog."* By raising his voice at the end of the word, though, the meaning is changed to a question, "Dog?" A parent may produce a loud, short, "NO!" to stop a child from running into the street, but produce a long "nooo" to perhaps sarcastically make a point with their teenager. Even young infants are sensitive to the prosody of speech and can distinguish between two languages based on their rhythms (Saffran, Werker, & Werner, 2006).

Thus, mastering a language includes knowing the phonemes and morphemes and how these can be combined, the syntax for turning words into sentences, the semantics for understanding the meaning of words and sentences, the pragmatics for how to best use language to suit the context and our conversational partner, and the prosody or sound features of speech. These basics of language are supported by a brain that is uniquely structured for language.

Until recently, our understanding of the brain's role in language came from observations of individuals who had the misfortune to sustain brain damage and an associated loss of some aspect of language (see Shafer & Garrido-Nag, 2009). From this, scientists concluded that language was largely a product of left hemisphere activity, with a region called Broca's area associated with speech production and another region called Wernicke's area associated with comprehension of language (see ■**Figure 10.1**). Thanks to improved methodologies such as functional magnetic resonance imaging (fMRI) and event-related potentials (ERPs), we are beginning to craft a more precise picture of how neural activity relates to and supports language.

We have learned that human brains show remarkably consistent organization for language across the life span, with the left hemisphere showing increased activity when listening to speech and the right hemisphere showing more activity when processing

■ **Figure 10.1** Brain regions associated with language.

the melody or rhythm of speech (Gervain & Mehler, 2010). Adults attempting to learn new words show different patterns of brain activity depending on whether they are successful or not: those who are successful show more connectivity between the left and right supramarginal gyrus, located in the parietal lobe, one of four main brain regions (Veroude et al., 2010). Studies using fMRI show that areas in both the left and right hemispheres are active in women's brains when processing language, whereas activity in men's brains is more typically localized in the left hemisphere (Shaywitz et al., 1995). We have also learned that Wernicke's area and Broca's area are connected with a band of fibers. Typically, incoming language is processed—comprehended—in Wernicke's area and then sent to Broca's area via these fibers (called the arcuate fasciculus) to be turned into speech. Damage to this band of fibers can cause a type of **aphasia**, or language disorder, in which the person might hear and understand linguistic input but be unable to vocally repeat the information. Finally, there is evidence that neurons in Broca's area are activated not only when a person produces speech but also when a person sees or hears another person speaking (Fogassi & Ferrari, 2007). This may facilitate language learning and suggests the presence of a mirror neuron system, which we discuss in more detail in Chapter 13.

Explaining Language: Nature and Nurture

To understand how children manage to master the remarkable skills of language, we revisit the nature–nurture issue to frame the theoretical explanations of language development.

Nature: The Contributions of Biology

On the nature side, the nativists minimize the role of the language environment and focus instead on the role of the child's biologically programmed capacities to acquire language. Noted linguist Noam Chomsky (2000) proposed that humans have a unique genetic capacity to learn language. According to this view, humans are equipped with knowledge of a **universal grammar**, a system of common rules and properties for learning any of the world's languages. Universal grammar offers a limited number of possibilities for forming language. As many as 75% of the world's languages have the basic word order of subject-verb-object (SVO; English, for example) or subject-object-verb (SOV; Japanese, for example). Another 15% have a word order that begins with a verb, whereas word order that begins with an object is quite unusual (Goodluck, 2009). Thus, most of the world's languages are based on a grammatical system that starts with a subject, followed by a verb and then an object or by an object and then a verb.

Universal grammar provides the framework for acquiring a language, but it is not language specific. Exposure to language activates the areas of the brain collectively called the **language acquisition device (LAD)**, which sifts through language, applies the universal rules, and begins tailoring the system to the specifics of the language spoken in the young child's environment (■ **Figure 10.2**). Infants listening to English determine that SVO is the typical grammatical sequence, whereas infants listening to Japanese detect that SOV is typical.

What evidence supports a nativist perspective on language development? First, there is what Chomsky and others have called the **poverty of the stimulus (POTS)**: children could not possibly acquire such an incredibly complex communication system with the limited linguistic input they receive (Clark & Lappin, 2011). That is, the environmental stimulus of language input is just too impoverished to support the linguistic output that we see emerge. For example, 18-month-olds show an understanding of syntax that they could not have acquired solely from information provided to them by others; they must have inferred rules of syntax on their own (Lidz, Waxman, & Freedman, 2003). Second, children all progress through the same sequences at roughly similar ages, and they even make the same kinds of errors, which suggests that language development is guided by a species-wide maturational plan. Third, these universal aspects of early language development occur despite cultural differences in the styles of speech that adults use in talking to young children. In some cultures, for example, parents believe that babies are incapable of understanding speech and do not even talk directly to them (Crago, Allen, & Hough-Eyamir, 1997).

Other evidence for the nativist position comes from studies of second-language learning. Much research shows that young children learn their native language with ease but often struggle later to learn a second language to the same level of proficiency. Does this mean that there is a critical period for language acquisition and that the brain becomes less responsive to language learning? As noted in Chapter 6, by the time infants begin to speak at around age one, they have already become largely insensitive to sounds that are not made in their native language

(see, for example, Werker, Yeung, & Yoshida, 2012). This may make it more difficult to hear the nuances of speech needed to fully develop native-like mastery of another language. Consider also research with deaf children, some of whom (especially those with hearing parents) do not have an opportunity to learn any language, oral or signed, in their early years. Rachel Mayberry (1994) studied language mastery in deaf college students exposed to American Sign Language (ASL) at different ages and found that the rule "the earlier, the better" applies (see also Mayberry, Lock, & Kazmi, 2002). Mastery of the syntax and semantics of sign language was greatest among students exposed to it in infancy or early childhood. Those who learned sign later in their development (ages 9–16) mastered it better if they had had some exposure to English early in life than if they had not been exposed to any language system before they encountered sign language. **Exploration Box 10.1** provides more details on what we can learn about language in general by studying language acquisition among deaf children. And in a later section of this chapter, we will consider lessons from studying individuals who acquire more than one language, either as infants or when older.

It is possible that the language-processing areas of the brain are shaped for a lifetime by early experience with language in ways that limit later learning of other languages. But it seems unlikely that there is a hard-and-fast critical period for language acquisition. Janet Werker and Richard Tees (2005) suggest that it is more accurate to say there is an "optimal period" during which languages are most easily and flawlessly acquired. And studies of brain architecture confirm that it is more appropriate to conclude that there may be a *sensitive* period for language acquisition (Fox, Levitt, & Nelson, 2010). Perhaps the main message is that young children are supremely capable of learning languages and advancing their cognitive development in the process.

Finally, there is evidence that the capacity for acquiring language has a genetic basis. Some of our linguistic competencies, including the ability to combine symbols to form short sentences, are shared with chimpanzees and other primates, suggesting that they arose during the course of evolution and are part of our genetic endowment as humans (Greenfield & Savage-Rumbaugh, 1993; Pinker, 1994). Many genes are implicated in language abilities, one of which, *FOXP2*, is associated with the motor skills necessary for speech (Tomblin, 2009; Vargha-Khadem et al., 1995). Individuals whose *FOXP2* gene is damaged are unable to speak, although they may have no other limitations. Some intriguing new research suggests that girls, who demonstrate advanced language skills relative to boys, have higher concentrations of *FOXP2* protein (Bowers et al., 2013).

■ **Figure 10.2** The language acquisition device (LAD).

Source: Chomsky, 1965.

Language Acquisition among Deaf Children

Many deaf children gain their first exposure to language by learning a sign language such as American Sign Language (ASL). These are true languages: The signs are arbitrary symbols, not attempts to mimic objects and events, and they are used according to a system of grammatical rules that determines their ordering. You ought to be able to learn some interesting lessons about language acquisition in general, then, by studying language acquisition among deaf children.

On average, deaf children growing up in homes where sign is the native language (that is, one or both parents use sign as their primary means of communication) acquire sign language in much the same sequence and at much the same rate as hearing children acquire their native spoken language (Lederberg, Schick, & Spencer, 2013). They also make many of the same kinds of errors along the way (Bellugi, 1988; Masataka, 2000). Interestingly, deaf infants whose parents are deaf "babble" in sign language. They experiment with gestures in much the same way that hearing infants experiment with sounds in preparation for their first meaningful communications (Petitto & Marentette, 1991). They then sign their first meaningful single words around 12 months, use their first syntax (combinations of two signs) between 18 and 24 months, and master many rules of language, such as past tense formation, between 2 and 3 years (Meier, 1991). Just as hearing children have difficulty with the pronunciation of certain words and overgeneralize certain rules, deaf children make predictable errors in their signing (Meier, 1991). Moreover, for both deaf and hearing children, advances in language development are linked closely to advances in cognitive development; for example, putting signs or words together in sentences happens around the same age that children put sequences of actions together in their play (Spencer, 1996).

The language environment experienced by deaf infants is also far more similar to that of hearing infants than you would imagine. For example, deaf mothers communicate using "child-directed signs." They present signs at a slower pace, repeat signs more, and exaggerate their signing motions more when they talk to their infants than when they talk to their deaf friends (Holzrichter & Meier, 2000). Moreover, just as hearing babies prefer the exaggerated intonations of child-directed speech, deaf infants pay more attention and give more emotional response when they are shown videos of infant-directed signing than tapes of adult-directed signing.

Finally, it turns out that language areas of the brain develop much the same in deaf children exposed to sign as in hearing children exposed to speech. In particular, reliance on areas of the left hemisphere of the cortex to process sentences was as evident among those who acquired ASL early in life (that is, native signers) as among hearing individuals who acquired English early in life (native speakers). And consider some research by Aaron Newman and his colleagues (2002). They examined brain activity during the processing of English and ASL sentences by native signers and those who acquired sign later, as a second language. Parts of the left hemisphere were activated in both groups when viewing the English sentences. A part of the right hemisphere was activated in both groups when viewing the ASL sentences. But only the native signers showed activation in a part of the right hemisphere called the angular gyrus when viewing the ASL sentences (refer again to Figure 10.1 in the chapter). The authors believe these findings may be evidence of a sensitive period for learning sign, similar to the sensitive period for learning a native spoken language. Early exposure to sign changes the way the brain responds when later exposed to sign language (see also Campbell, MacSweeney, & Water, 2008).

As you have seen, language development is sometimes delayed among deaf children of hearing parents if they cannot hear well enough to understand spoken language but are not exposed to sign language (Mayberry, 1994). Overall, then, studies of language acquisition among deaf children suggest that young humans are biologically prepared to master language and will do so if given the opportunity, whether that language is signed or spoken and whether it involves visual–spatial skills or auditory ones (see Goldin-Meadow, 2009).

© Stephen McBrady/PhotoEdit Inc.

Nurture: The Contributions of the Environment and Learning

How does the environment influence language development? It is no accident that children learn the language their parents speak, down to the regional accent. Children learn the words they hear spoken by others—even when the words are not spoken directly to them (Floor & Akhtar, 2006). For example, 18-month-olds can learn object labels and verbs by "eavesdropping" on a conversation between two adults (so be careful about what you say within earshot of toddlers). In addition, young children are more likely to start using new words if they are reinforced for doing so than if they are not (Whitehurst & Valdez-Menchaca, 1988). Finally, children whose caregivers frequently encourage them to converse by asking questions, making requests, and the like are more advanced in early language development than those whose parents are less conversational (Bohannon & Bonvillian, 2013).

However, learning theorists, with their focus on environment, have had an easier time explaining the development of phonology and semantics than accounting for how rules of syntax are acquired. For example, after analyzing conversations between mothers and young children, Roger Brown, Courtney Cazden, and Ursula Bellugi (1969) discovered that a mother's approval or disapproval depended on the truth value or semantics of what was said, not on the grammatical correctness of the statement. Thus, when a child looking at a cow says, "Her cow" (accurate but grammatically incorrect), Mom is likely to provide reinforcement ("That's right, darling"), whereas if the child were to say, "There's a dog, Mommy" (grammatically correct but inaccurate), Mom would probably correct the child ("No, sweetie—that's a cow"). Similarly, parents seem just as likely to reward a grammatically primitive request ("Want milk") as a well-formed version of the same idea (Brown & Hanlon, 1970). Such evidence casts doubt on the idea that the major mechanism behind syntactic development is reinforcement.

How would the learning theorists explain what is going on as this toddler imitates her mother's words? What aspects of language are most likely being acquired through such experiences?

John Wilkes/Corbis

Could imitation of adults account for the acquisition of syntax? The problem here is that young children produce many sentences they are unlikely to have heard adults using ("All gone cookie," "It swimmed," and so on). These kinds of sentences are not imitations. Also, an adult is likely to get nowhere in teaching syntax by saying, "Repeat after me," unless the child already has at least some knowledge of the grammatical form to be learned (Baron, 1992; McNeill, 1970). Young children frequently imitate other people's speech, and this may help them get to the point of producing new structures. But it is hard to see how imitation and reinforcement alone can account for the learning of grammatical rules.

Nature and Nurture Working Together

It's now time to merge the two sides of the nature–nurture issue and construct an interactionist account of language development. Consider what Steven Pinker (1995) concludes about importance of considering both the nature and nurture of language acquisition:

> All humans talk but no house pets or house plants do, no matter how pampered, so heredity must be involved in language. But a child growing up in Japan speaks Japanese whereas the same child brought up in California would speak English, so the environment is also crucial. Thus, there is no question about whether heredity or environment is involved in language, or even whether one or the other is "more important." Instead, language acquisition might be our best hope of finding out how heredity and environment interact. (p. 136)

Interactionists believe that both learning theorists (nurture) and nativists (nature) are correct: Children's biologically based competencies and their language environment interact to shape the course of language development (Bloom, 1998; Bohannon & Bonvillian, 2013). They emphasize that acquisition of language skills depends on and is related to the acquisition of many other capacities: perceptual, cognitive, motor, social, and emotional. They point out that the capacity for acquiring language is not unique, as nativists who speak of universal grammar and the LAD claim (Bates, O'Connell, & Shore, 1987). It is, instead, interrelated to other developments that are taking place concurrently with language acquisition. For example, young children first begin to use words as meaningful symbols when they begin to display nonlinguistic symbolic capacities, such as the ability to use gestures (waving bye-bye), and begin to engage in pretend play (treating a bowl as if it were a hat).

The interactionists' position is not unlike that taken by Piaget (1970). He believed that milestones in cognitive development pave the way for progress in language development and that maturation and environment interact to guide both cognitive development and language development. Like Piaget (but unlike learning theorists), many interactionists argue that language development depends on the maturation of cognitive abilities such as the capacity for symbolic thought. However, the interactionist position also emphasizes—as Vygotsky did but Piaget did not—ways in which social interactions with adults contribute to cognitive and linguistic development. Language is primarily a means of communicating—one that develops in the context of social interactions as children and their companions strive to get their messages across (Tomasello, 2009).

Long before infants use words, Jerome Bruner (1983) says, their caregivers show them how to take turns in conversations—even if the most these young infants can contribute when their turn comes is a laugh or a bit of babbling. As adults converse with young children, they create a supportive learning environment—a *scaffold*, in Bruner's terms, a *zone of proximal development* in Vygotsky's—that helps the children grasp the regularities of language (Bruner, 1983; Harris, 1992). For example, parents may go through their children's favorite picture books at bedtime and ask "What's this?" and "What's that?" This gives their children repeated opportunities to learn that conversing involves taking turns, that things have names, and that there are proper ways to pose questions and give answers. Soon the children are asking "What's this?" and "What's that?"

On a daily basis, toddlers in English-speaking homes hear between 5,000 and 7,000 utterances (Tomasello, 2006). As they gain new language skills, adults adjust their styles of communication accordingly. Language researchers use the term **child-directed speech** to describe the speech adults use with young children: short, simple sentences spoken slowly, in a high-pitched voice, often with much repetition, and with exaggerated emphasis on key words (Hills, 2013). For example, the mother trying to get her son to eat his peas might say, "Eat your *peas* now. Not the cracker. See those *peas*? Yes, eat the *peas*. Oh, such a good boy for eating your *peas*." Mothers also convey more exaggerated emotions (positive and negative) when speaking to their infants than when speaking to other adults (Kitamura & Burnham, 2003). From the earliest days of life, toddlers seem to pay more attention to the high-pitched sounds and varied intonational patterns of child-directed speech than to the speech adults use when communicating with one another (Ma et al., 2011). Importantly, caregivers' child-directed speech is dynamic—constantly changing in response to the child's utterances (Gros-Louis et al., 2006). For instance, when toddlers use an unfamiliar word, mothers may respond by repeating the word or perhaps giving another example, as if they want to help the toddler fully understand it (Olson & Masur, 2012). In contrast, when toddlers use a familiar word or phrase ("that plane"), mothers often respond with an **expansion**—a more grammatically complete expression of what the toddler stated ("Yes, that's a loud airplane"). Adults use conversational techniques such as expansions mainly to improve communication, not to teach grammar (Penner, 1987).

Would children learn language just as well if adults talked to them in an adultlike style? Perhaps not. The nativists seem to have underestimated the contributions of environment to language development. Mere exposure to speech is not enough; children must be actively involved in using language (Locke, 1997). Catherine Snow and her associates, for example, found that a group of Dutch-speaking children, although they watched a great deal of German television, did not acquire German words or grammar (Snow et al., 1976). True, there are cultural groups (the Kaluli of New Guinea, the natives of American Samoa, and the Trackton people of the Piedmont Carolinas) in which child-directed speech does not seem to be used. Children in these societies still seem to acquire their native language without noticeable delays (Ochs, 1982; Schieffelin, 1986). Yet even these children overhear speech and participate in social interactions

in which language is used, and that is what seems to be required to master a human language (Shneidman & Goldin-Meadow, 2012). As many a parent has learned, toddlers often pick up some of the colorful vocabulary that adults toss around thinking that sweet Suzy will not notice. She did, and it will slip out at some inopportune moment. How can adults best facilitate young children's language learning? What cognitive capacities enable children to learn how language works? Much remains to be learned about language development, but it does seem to require the interaction of a biologically prepared child with at least one conversational partner, ideally one who tailors her own speech to the child's level of understanding.

Developing language competence may be our earliest and greatest learning challenge, but it is only the beginning. There is much more to be mastered during the school years and beyond. Language lays the foundation for acquiring reading, writing, and countless other skills. But unlike language, which seems to develop effortlessly in the absence of formal education, these other skills typically require directed education. In the following sections, we look not only at language development but at education across the life span, examining changes in motivation for learning and changes in educational environments as learners get older.

Adults are not the only ones who use child-directed speech. Children also adjust their speech to their listener. How could this girl alter her speech to make it appealing and appropriate for her baby sister?

Checking Mastery

1. What are the basic components of language that children must master in order to communicate effectively?
2. How is the brain structured to support language skills?
3. What are the main features of the nativist and learning theories of language acquisition?

Making Connections

1. How should adults interact and talk with infants to ensure they have the best opportunities to develop a strong start with their language development?
2. What is the most compelling evidence that language is influenced by nature? And what evidence shows that it is not nature alone that determines language acquisition?

10.2 The Infant

LEARNING OBJECTIVES:

* Describe the typical path of language acquisition during the first 2 years.
* Identify factors that facilitate language development.
* Explain the course of early mastery motivation.
* Evaluate the components of a quality early education program.

Infants have a great deal to learn in the informal educational system of their family and neighborhoods before they enter the formal education system. In particular, they must master a language system, and most do so quickly and with little deliberate effort. Indeed, the speed with which most infants and children master language is astonishing. We trace the path to mastering language skills and then turn our attention to how infants take on mastering their environments.

Mastering Language

As you learned in Chapter 6, newborns seem to tune in to human speech immediately and show a preference for speech over nonspeech sounds and for their native language, which they listened to in the womb, over other languages (Gervain & Mehler, 2010; Moon, Lagercrantz, & Kuhl, 2013). Very young infants can distinguish between phonemes such as /b/ and /p/ or /d/ and /t/ (Eimas, 1975a). Before they ever speak a word, infants are also becoming sensitive to the fact that pauses in speech fall between clauses, phrases, and words rather than in the middle of these important language units. By 7½ months, infants demonstrate **word segmentation** ability when they detect a target word in a stream of speech (see Jusczyk, Houston, & Newsome, 1999). Thus, when they hear the sentence "The cat scratched the dog's nose," they understand that this is not one long word but a string of six words. Word segmentation is a formidable task, but infants seem to be sensitive to a number of cues marking the boundaries between words and this skill improves throughout the first 2 years of life (Saffran et al., 2006). One thing that helps infants with this task is the repetition of many common words throughout the days, weeks, and months leading to language acquisition. By repeatedly hearing "cat" embedded in many different sentences, infants come to understand that "cat" must represent a unit that is separate from other spoken units. They are also sensitive to the stress placed on certain syllables

(see Hollich, 2010). In English, for example, the first syllable of nouns is typically stressed, and infants exposed to English language learn that when they hear a stressed syllable, it probably signals the start of a word.

What about producing sounds? From birth, infants produce sounds—cries, burps, grunts, and sneezes. These sounds help exercise the vocal cords and give infants an opportunity to learn how airflow and different mouth and tongue positions affect sounds. By 5 months, infants realize that their sounds have an effect on their caregivers' behavior (Goldstein, Schwade, & Bornstein, 2009). Parents respond to as many as 50% of prelinguistic sounds as if they were genuine efforts to communicate (Goldstein et al., 2009; McCune et al., 1996). For instance, in response to her infant's hiccup sound, a mother replies, "My goodness! What's going on in there? Huh? Tell Mommy." The mother draws her infant into a sort of dialogue. Such prelinguistic sounds, and the feedback infants receive, eventually pave the way for meaningful speech sounds (Hoff, 2014).

The next milestone in vocalization, around 6–8 weeks of age, is **cooing**—repeating vowel-like sounds such as "ooooooh" and "aaaaah." Babies coo when they are content and often in response to being spoken to in a happy voice. Do infants this age understand the words spoken to them? Not likely—they primarily respond to the intonation or "melody" of speech (Hirsh-Pasek, Golinkoff, & Hollich, 1999). Parents can say some rather nasty things to their young infants ("You're driving me nuts today!") as long as they say them with a happy voice, illustrating the importance of prosody.

Around 3–4 months, infants expand their vocal range considerably as they begin to produce consonant sounds. They enter a period of **babbling** between about 4 and 6 months, repeating consonant–vowel combinations such as "baba" or "dadadada," in what Jean Piaget would call a primary circular reaction—the repeating of an interesting noise for the pleasure of making it.

Up to about 6 months, infants all over the world, even deaf ones, sound pretty much alike, but the effects of experience soon become apparent. Without auditory feedback, deaf infants fall behind hearing infants in their ability to produce well-formed syllables (Oller & Eilers, 1988). By the time infants are about 8 months old, they babble with something of an accent; adults can often tell which language infants have been listening to from the sound of their babbling (Poulin-Dubois & Goodz, 2001). These advanced babblers increasingly restrict their sounds to phonemes in the language they are hearing, and they pick up the intonation patterns of that language (Hoff, 2014; Snow, 2006). Once these intonation patterns are added to an infant's babbles, the utterances sound a great deal like real speech until you listen closely and realize you have no idea what the infant is saying! (Hollich, 2010). We shouldn't assume, though, that infants are as clueless as we are: what they are "saying" may make complete sense to them. **Exploring Development Box 10.1** links to a video with examples of various stages of language development in the first couple of years.

As they attempt to master the semantics of language, infants come to understand many words before they can produce them. That is, *comprehension* (or reception) is ahead of *production* (or expression) in language development. Ten-month-olds can comprehend, on average, about 50 words but do not yet produce any of these (Golinkoff & Hirsh-Pasek, 2006). This gap between comprehension and production persists and may reflect the relative importance of understanding speech over producing speech (Bornstein & Hendricks, 2012). Research shows that early understanding of words is related to academic achievement in elementary school: the 10-month-olds who understand more words are later the children who get better grades (Hohm et al., 2007).

Shortly before speaking their first true words, as they approach 1 year, infants really seem to understand familiar words. How do they figure out what words mean? When Mom points to a small, four-legged furry animal and says, "There's Furrball," how do infants learn that "Furrball" refers to this particular cat and not to its movement or to its tail or to a general category of furry animals? It turns out that infants and toddlers use a variety of cues in learning to connect words with their referents—the objects, people, or ideas represented by a name. At first, 10-month-old infants rely on attentional cues such as how important an object seems to be from their perspective (Pruden et al., 2006). Thus, if their attention is captured by the ball in front of them, they may assume that mom's verbalizations refer to this ball. By 12 months of age, though, their reliance on personal relevance is decreasing and infants begin to use social and linguistic cues to learn words. One important social cue is **joint attention**, or social eye gaze—two people looking at the same thing (Carpenter, Nagell, & Tomasello, 1998; Woodward & Markman, 1998). Infants listen to parents repeatedly labeling and pointing at objects, directing their gaze, and otherwise making clear the connection between words and their referents (Hollich, Hirsh-Pasek, & Golinkoff, 2000). If Mom says "cat" when both she and her child are looking at the furry animal, then this likely is the referent for the label. Importantly, early development of joint attention skills seems to pave the way for early vocabulary development (Beuker et al., 2013).

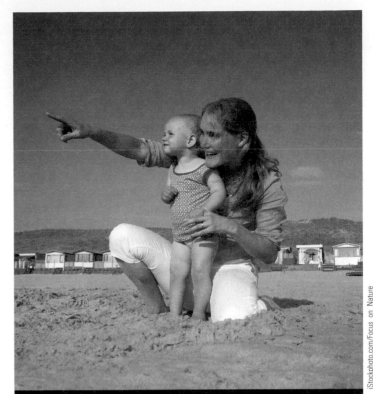

Like many parents, this mother uses pointing and eye gaze to direct her daughter's attention. Coupling this with words helps toddlers acquire the meaning of words.

iStockphoto.com/Focus_on_Nature

Finally, children use the process of **syntactic bootstrapping** when they use the syntax of a sentence—that is, where a word is placed in a sentence—to determine the meaning of the word (Naigles & Swensen, 2007). In the earlier example, if mom had said, "There's *a* furball" or "The cat is hacking up a furball" instead of the original "There's Furrball," the syntactic placement—how *furball* was used in the sentence—would have changed the meaning of the word.

Exploring Development 10.1
Development of Language in Infants and Toddlers

© Cengage Learning

Observe speech interactions between infants and toddlers and adults.

- How are cooing and babbling different?
- What is the purpose of parentese, or child-directed speech?
- How can you tell that a child has a larger receptive than expressive vocabulary?

The First Words

An infant's first meaningful word, spoken around 1 year, is a special event for parents. First words have been called **holophrases** because a single word often conveys an entire sentence's worth of meaning. These single-word "sentences" can serve different communication functions depending on the way they are said and the context in which they are said (Tomasello, 2009). For example, 17-month-old Shelley used the word *ghetti* (spaghetti) in three different ways over a 5-minute period. First, she pointed to the pan on the stove and seemed to be asking, "Is that spaghetti?" Later, the function of her holophrase was to name the spaghetti when shown the contents of the pan, as in "It's spaghetti." Finally, there was little question that she was requesting spaghetti when she tugged at her companion's sleeve as he was eating and used the word in a whining tone.

Although there are limits to the meaning that can be packed into a single word and its accompanying intonation pattern and gestures, 1-year-olds in the holophrastic stage of language development seem to have mastered such basic language functions as naming, questioning, requesting, and demanding. When they begin to use words as symbols, they also begin to use nonverbal symbols—gestures such as pointing, raising their arms to signal "up," or panting heavily to say "dog" (Goldin-Meadow, 2009).

What do 1-year-olds talk about? They talk mainly about familiar objects and actions—those things that they encounter every day and are important to them (●Table 10.1). Most research shows that the first fifty words typically consist of common nouns representing objects and people (Waxman et al., 2013). It may be easier for young children to decipher nouns and their referents in the language around them, and adults tend to use more nouns in their conversations with children (Uccelli & Pan, 2013). Another possibility, though, is that it is easy to create an image of the things represented by nouns and images give us something tangible to remember (McDonough et al., 2011). Verbs, though, pose more of a challenge because it can be difficult to create an image for an action.

Initial language acquisition proceeds literally at one word at a time. Three or four months may pass before the child has a vocabulary of 10 words, slowly acquired one by one. There is a great deal of variability in early language acquisition: While one child may be speaking her fiftieth word as she celebrates her first birthday, another child may be reaching this milestone around the time of his second birthday (Newman & Sachs, 2012).

Then, in what is called the **vocabulary spurt**, around 18 months of age, when the child has mastered about 30–50 words, the pace of word learning quickens dramatically (Bloom, 1998; Carroll, 2008). Steven Pinker (1995), an experimental psychologist who has studied and written extensively on all aspects of language development, estimates that a new word is acquired every 2 hours during this time (see also Tomasello, 2003)! At 20 months, children are producing an average of 150 words, and just 4 months later, this has doubled to 300 words (Camaioni, 2004). What makes this possible? Something called **fast mapping**, which allows children to determine the object or other referent of a word and then remember this for future encounters with the word (for example, Spiegel & Halberda, 2011). Of course, this is a simplification of what is, undoubtedly, a very complex process. Contributing to fast mapping is the greater memory capabilities of the toddler and the growing ability to use a word's context to decipher its meaning. Like Helen Keller with her "aha" realization that the letters being tapped on her one hand were related to the object (water) in her other hand, toddlers seem to arrive at the critical realization that everything has a name and that by learning the names of things they can share what they are thinking with someone else and vice versa (Bloom & Tinker, 2001).

With such a rapidly increasing vocabulary, it should come as no surprise that children sometimes make mistakes. Although they rarely get the meaning entirely wrong, they often use a word too broadly or too narrowly (Uccelli & Pan, 2013). One error is **overextension**, or using a word to refer to too wide a range of objects or events, as when a 2-year-old calls all furry, four-legged animals "doggie." The second, and opposite, error is **underextension**, as when a child initially uses the word *doggie* to refer only to basset hounds like the family pet. Notice that both overextension and underextension are examples of Piaget's concept of assimilation, using existing concepts to interpret new experiences. Getting semantics right seems to be mainly a matter of discriminating similarities and differences—for example, categorizing animals on the basis of size, shape, the sounds they make, and other perceptual features (Clark & Clark, 1977). By 2½–3 years of age, these sorts of semantic errors begin to disappear from children's conversations.

But might children know more about the world than their semantic errors suggest? Yes. Two-year-olds who say "doggie" when they see a cow will point to the cow rather than the dog when asked to find the cow (Naigles & Gelman, 1995; Thompson & Chapman, 1977). Children may overextend the meaning of certain words such as *doggie* not because they misunderstand word meanings but because they want to communicate, have only a small vocabulary with which to do so, and have not yet learned to call something a "whatchamacallit" when they cannot come up with the word for it (Naigles & Gelman, 1995).

You must be careful about applying these generalizations about early language acquisition to all children because they mask large individual differences in speaking style (Nelson, 2007). As ■ **Figure 10.3** shows, one 24-month-old may have a vocabulary of approximately 50 words, and another may be able to produce

● **Table 10.1** Examples of Words Used by Children Younger than 20 Months

Category	Words
Sound effects	*baa baa, meow, moo, ouch, uh-oh, woof, yum-yum*
Food and drink	*apple, banana, cookie, cheese, cracker, juice, milk, water*
Animals	*bear, bird, bunny, dog, cat, cow, duck, fish, kitty, horse, pig, puppy*
Body parts and clothing	*diaper, ear, eye, foot, hair, hand, hat, mouth, nose, toe, tooth, shoe*
House and outdoors	*blanket, chair, cup, door, flower, keys, outside, spoon, tree, TV*
People	*baby, daddy, gramma, grampa, mommy, [child's own name]*
Toys and vehicles	*ball, balloon, bike, boat, book, bubbles, plane, truck, toy*
Actions	*down, eat, go, sit, up*
Games and routines	*bath, bye, hi, night-night, no, peek-a-boo, please, shhh, thank you, yes*
Adjectives and descriptors	*all gone, cold, dirty, hot*

SOURCE: Jean Berko Gleason, *The development of language*, 6th ed., Table 4.1, p. 122. Copyright © 2005. Reprinted by permission of Pearson Education, Inc.

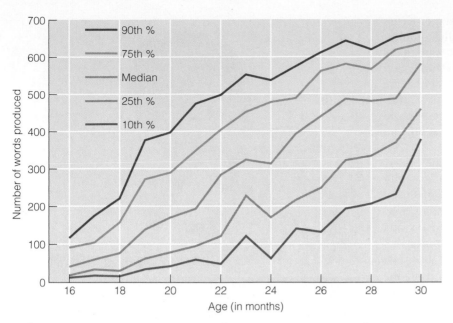

■ **Figure 10.3** The range of individual differences in vocabulary size from 16 to 30 months.

SOURCE: Fenson, L., et al. (1994) Variability in early communicative development. *Monographs of the Society for Research in Child Development*, 59 (Serial No. 242). Copyright © 1994. Reprinted with permission of John Wiley & Sons, Inc.

more than 500 words (Fenson et al., 1994). Some children use a referential style—lots of nouns referring to objects, such as "ball" and "truck." Others seem to treat language as a social tool; they use an expressive style of speaking with more personal pronouns and memorized social routines such as "bye-bye" and "I want it" (Nelson, 2007). Culture exerts some influence: infants learning English use many nouns and few verbs in their early speech, whereas infants learning Korean use more verbs (Gopnik & Choi, 1995). More important, differences in the daily language experiences of children contribute to the differences in their speech. Both quantity of speech (how many words the child hears in the home) and quality of speech (how sophisticated the speech is) affect young children's vocabularies (Hoff, 2014; Weizman & Snow, 2001). So there are many differences across children, making it difficult to make generalizations about language development. Yet when we look at individual children over time, we see stability (Bornstein & Putnick, 2012). That is, relative to other children in a group, each individual child maintains her relative position in the group over time: The children who score high on measures of language at one age also tend to be the ones who score high at other ages.

Telegraphic Speech

The next step in language development, normally occurring at 18–24 months of age, is combining two words into a simple sentence. Toddlers all over the world use two-word sentences to express the same basic ideas (● **Table 10.2**). Early combinations of two, three, or more words are sometimes called **telegraphic speech** because, like telegrams of the past where costs were minimized by eliminating unnecessary words, these sentences contain critical content words and omit frills such as articles, prepositions, and auxiliary verbs.

It is ungrammatical in adult English to say "No want" or "Where ball." However, these two-word sentences are not just random word combinations or mistakes; they reflect children's developing understanding of syntax. Psycholinguists such as Lois Bloom (1998) believe it is appropriate to describe children's early sentences in terms of a **functional grammar**—one that emphasizes the semantic relationships among words, the meanings being expressed, and the functions served by sentences (such as naming, questioning, or commanding). For example, young children often use the same word order to convey different meanings. "Mommy nose" might mean "That's Mommy's nose" in one context, but for one 22-month-old girl one afternoon it meant "Mommy, I've just wiped my runny nose the length of the living room couch." Word order sometimes does matter: "Billy hit" and "Hit Billy" may mean different things. Body language and tone of voice also communicate meanings, such as when a child points and whines to request ice cream, not merely to note its existence.

Between ages 2 and 5, children experience a dramatic increase in the number and type of sentences they produce. Consider 3-year-old Kyle's reply to his mother after she suggests that he release a bug:

> After I hold him, then I'll take the bug back to his friends. Mommy, where did the bug go? Mommy, I didn't know where the bug go. Find it. Maybe Winston's on it [the family dog]. Winston, get off the bug! [Kyle spots the bug and picks it up. His mother again asks him to "let the bug go back to his friends."] He does not want to go to his friends. [Kyle drops the bug and squashes it, much to his mother's horror.] I stepped on it and it will not go to his friends.

● **Table 10.2** Two-Word Sentences Serve Similar Functions in Different Languages

Function of Sentence	Language	
	English	German
To locate or name	There book	Buch da (book there)
To demand	More milk	Mehrmilch (more milk)
To negate	No wet	Nichtblasen (not blow)
To indicate possession	My shoe	Mein ball (my ball)
To modify or qualify	Pretty dress	Armerwauwau (poor doggie)
To question	Where ball	Wo ball (where ball)

SOURCE: Adapted from Slobin, 1979.

Compared with a child in the telegraphic stage, Kyle's sentences are much longer and more grammatically complex, although not free of errors, and he is better able to participate in the give-and-take of conversation. Kyle has also begun to add the little function words such as articles and prepositions that are often missing in the earlier telegraphic sentences (Hoff, 2014). For another example of preschoolers' language, see 4-year-old Caroline's description of bowling and miniature golf at the end of the video in **Exploring Development Box 10.2**.

How do people know when children are mastering new rules? Oddly enough, their progress sometimes reveals itself in new "mis-takes." A child who has been saying "feet" and "went" may suddenly start to say "foots" and "goed." Does this represent a step backward? Not at all. The child was probably using the correct irregular forms at first by imitating adult speech without understanding the meaning of plurality or verb tense. The use of "foots" and "goed" is a breakthrough: the child has inferred the morphological rules of adding -s to pluralize nouns and adding -ed to signal past tense. At first, however, the youngster engages in **over-regularization**, overapplying the rules to cases in which the proper form is irregular. When the child masters exceptions to the rules, she will say "feet" and "went" once more.

Children must also master rules for creating variations of the basic declarative sentence; that is, they must learn the syntactic rules for converting a basic idea such as "I am eating pizza" into such forms as questions ("Am I eating pizza?"), negative sentences ("I am not eating pizza"), and imperatives ("Eat the pizza!"). The prominent linguist Noam Chomsky (1968, 1975) drew attention to the child's learning of these rules by proposing that language be described in terms of a **transformational grammar**, or rules of syntax for transforming basic underlying thoughts into a variety of sentence forms.

How do young children learn to phrase the questions that they so frequently ask to fuel their cognitive growth? The earliest questions often consist of nothing more than two- or three-word sentences with rising intonation ("See kitty?"). Sometimes *wh-* words such as *what* or *where* appear ("Where kitty?"). During the second stage of question asking, children begin to use auxiliary, or helping, verbs, but their questions are of this form: "What Daddy is eating?" "Where the kitty is going?" Their understanding of transformation rules is still incomplete (Tager-Flusberg & Zukowski, 2013). Finally, they learn the transformation rule that calls for moving the auxiliary verb ahead of the subject (as in the adultlike sentence "What is Daddy eating?").

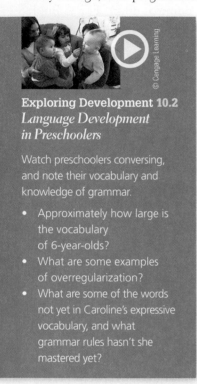

Exploring Development 10.2
Language Development in Preschoolers

Watch preschoolers conversing, and note their vocabulary and knowledge of grammar.

- Approximately how large is the vocabulary of 6-year-olds?
- What are some examples of overregularization?
- What are some of the words not yet in Caroline's expressive vocabulary, and what grammar rules hasn't she mastered yet?

Every day, infants and young children display their innate mastery motive.

Mastery Motivation

As they are mastering language, infants are also mastering many other important tasks to prepare them for success in life. Much evidence supports the claim that infants are curious, active explorers constantly striving to understand and to exert control over the world around them. This, you should recall, was one of Piaget's major themes. **Mastery motivation**, a striving for mastery or competence, appears to be inborn and universal and will display itself in the behavior of all typical infants without prompting from parents. We can clearly see this desire for mastery when infants struggle to open kitchen cabinets, take their first steps, or figure out how new toys work—and derive great pleasure from their efforts (Jennings & Dietz, 2003; Masten & Reed, 2002). Even so, some infants appear to be more mastery oriented than others. Given a new push toy, one baby may simply look at it, but another may mouth it, bang it, and push it across the floor (Jennings & Dietz, 2003). Why might some infants have a stronger mastery motive than others?

One possibility is that the goal itself may hold greater value to some infants: If that red ball looks highly appealing to Joanie, she may expend more time and energy to retrieve it than Naomi, who just doesn't judge it worthy of her attention (Kenward et al., 2009). Mastery motivation also seems higher when parents frequently provide sensory stimulation designed to arouse and amuse their babies—tickling them, bouncing them, playing games of pat-a-cake, giving them stimulating toys, and so on (Busch-Rossnagel, 1997). Mastery motivation flourishes when infants grow up in a responsive environment that provides plenty of opportunities to see for themselves that they can control their environments and experience successes (Maddux, 2002; Masten & Reed, 2002). Consider the toddler who, faced with the challenge of retrieving a cookie from the kitchen counter, struggles to maneuver a chair across the room and to climb up without tipping the chair or falling off. When Mom offers to help him, he shrieks, "Me do it!" And when he does it, he feels a sense of accomplishment that increases the likelihood he will tackle future challenges. Parents who return smiles and coos or respond promptly to cries show infants they can affect people around them. By contrast, the children of parents who are depressed show less interest in and persistence on challenging tasks, perhaps because their parents are not responsive to them (Redding, Harmon, & Morgan, 1990). As well, children who are raised by parents who constantly stifle their initiatives ("you will *not* move the chair across the room!") may be less likely to take on new tasks.

An infant's level of mastery motivation affects her later achievement behavior. Babies who actively attempt to master challenges at 6 and 12 months score higher on tests of mental development at 2 and 3 years than their less mastery-oriented peers (Jennings & Dietz, 2003; Messer et al., 1986). There is even some continued influence of early mastery motivation, measured at age 1, into adulthood, as measured at age 32, at least for males (Jennings, Yarrow, & Martin, 1984). In short, infants are intrinsically motivated to master challenges, but parents may help strengthen this inborn motive by stimulating their infants appropriately and responding to their actions. What about infants and toddlers who spend considerable amounts of time away from their parents? Is their motivation influenced by time spent in preschool?

Early Education

As you have seen in previous chapters, babies learn a great deal in the first few years of life. But do infants and toddlers need specific educational experiences? Despite the popular appeal of products such as *Baby Einstein* and *Baby Mozart*, many experts dispute the idea that typically developing children need direct instruction during

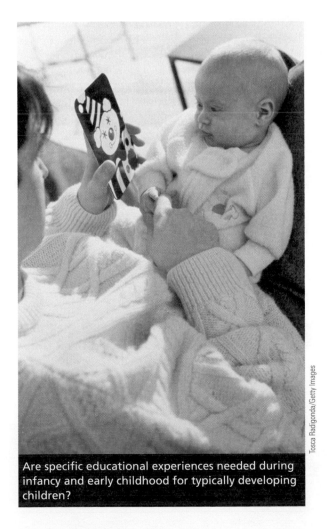

Are specific educational experiences needed during infancy and early childhood for typically developing children?

Tosca Radigonda/Getty Images

their first 3 years (for example, Carlsson-Paige, 2008). And some, such as David Elkind (1987), author of *Miseducation: Preschoolers at Risk*, fear that the push for earlier education may be going too far and that young children today are not given enough time simply to be children—to play and socialize as they choose. Elkind even worries that children may lose their self-initiative and intrinsic motivation to learn when their lives are orchestrated by parents who pressure them to achieve at early ages. Is there anything to these concerns?

Some research seems to confirm Elkind's fears. Frederick Zimmerman, Dimitri Christakis, and Andrew Meltzoff (2007; see also Christakis, 2008) studied infants who watched *Baby Einstein* or *Brainy Baby* videos. They found, rather alarmingly, that for each hour spent watching videos, babies understood 6–8 fewer words than babies who did not watch videos. The research did not follow infants into childhood to determine if the video-watching babies later caught up to the other babies, but the findings do raise a red flag, at least with respect to language abilities. Other research on the effects of these programs shows a similarly dismal outcome. Infants who spent 6 weeks watching "Baby Wordsmith" videos, which focus on vocabulary, demonstrated absolutely no differences in vocabulary knowledge or language development from infants who did not view this program (Richert et al., 2010; and recall Chapter 1's discussion of baby videos and language development, for example, DeLoache et al., 2010). If educational videos are not valuable, and may even be detrimental, what about educational infant and preschool programs?

In one study, 4-year-olds in preschools with strong academic thrusts gained an initial advantage in basic academic skills such as knowledge of letters and numbers but lost it by the end of kindergarten (Hyson, Hirsh-Pasek, & Rescorla, 1989). What is more, they proved to be less creative, more anxious in testing situations, and more negative toward school than children who attended preschool programs with a social rather than academic emphasis. Similarly, Deborah Stipek and her colleagues (1995) have found that highly academic preschool programs raise children's academic achievement test scores but decrease their expectancies of success and pride in accomplishment. So it may be possible to undermine achievement motivation by overemphasizing academics in the preschool years.

However, preschool programs that offer a healthy mix of play and academic activities in the form of guided play can be beneficial to young children (Weisberg, Hirsh-Pasek, & Golinkoff, 2013). This sort of academic skill-building may be especially helpful to disadvantaged children. This was the premise for the federally funded Head Start Program, started in 1965 as part of the "War on Poverty." Roughly 50 years later, experts are still debating whether or not the program has been worth its cost. Over the decades, most of the research on Head Start has found that it produces at least initial gains in skills associated with school success. For example, a recent study of nearly 7,000 children found that those who attended Head Start had higher reading and math scores upon entering kindergarten (Lee et al., 2013). Unfortunately, though, such early benefits seem short-lived. The Head Start Impact Study found that any advantages Head Start children had while in the program quickly disappeared and were not evident by third grade (Puma et al., 2012). So if Head Start has not always proven effective, are there any early childhood education programs that show promise?

Consider the Abecedarian Project, a full-time educational program from infancy (starting around 4–5 months) to age 5 for

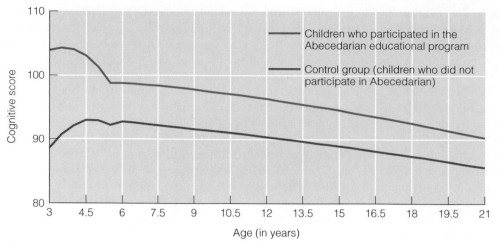

■ **Figure 10.4** Cognitive growth curves as a function of preschool treatment.

SOURCE: Campbell, F. A, et al. The development of cognitive and academic abilities: Growth curves from an early childhood educational experience, *Developmental Psychology*, 37, 231–242. Copyright © (2001), American Psychological Association. Reprinted with permission.

children from low-income families (Campbell et al., 2001; and see Chapter 9). Compared with children who did not participate, Abecedarian children showed impressive cognitive gains during and immediately after the program (■ **Figure 10.4**). But are the effects of good early educational programs truly life changing? To find out, the researchers followed-up on the Abecedarian participants at age 30 (Campbell et al., 2012). Remarkably, they were able to examine outcomes for a majority of the original participants. Those who had participated in the Abecedarian program had completed more years of education than those in the comparison group. In particular, 23% of the children who had been in the program had earned a college degree compared to only 6% in the comparison group. About 75% of the Abecedarian adults worked full-time compared to 50% of the nonparticipant adults. Despite these advantages of a high quality preschool program, such early intervention did not "fix" everything. There were no differences, for example, between the two groups in criminal activity at age 30: In both the Abecedarian and the comparison adults, just over 25% had been convicted of a crime. So what can be done?

An alternative type of program focuses on educating parents about the importance of the early environment and the types of experiences that can be beneficial to their children. It turns out that parent training pays off. In one such program, *Born to Learn*, children displayed higher levels of mastery motivation than nonparticipants by 36 months of age, or even earlier— 24 months—if they were from disadvantaged families (Drotar et al., 2008). In another program, the *Milwaukee Project* (Garber, 1988), full-time child care was provided for youngsters along with job and academic training for mothers. Following up on these participants in the eighth grade showed that they remained intellectually ahead of their peers who had not participated.

Thus, positive effects on later school achievement are especially likely if the preschool experience not only stimulates children's cognitive growth but also provides some sort of programming for parents and includes follow-up during elementary school (Nelson, Westhaus & MacLeod, 2003). In addition, the more successful programs are full day and long-lasting, unlike Head Start, which began as a part-time, short-term program. More generally, preschool programs that build school readiness skills but also allow plenty of time for play and social interaction can help all children make a smooth transition to kindergarten and elementary school.

What should preschools do to optimize development and maintain high levels of motivation among children?

© Yellow Dog Productions/Getty Images

Checking Mastery

1. Through what stages does early language acquisition progress?
2. Give an example of an overregularization of language.
3. What is mastery motivation?
4. What is one advantage and one potential disadvantage of early education programs for infants and toddlers?

Making Connections

1. What should parents and early childhood educators look for (or listen for) to confirm that infants and toddlers are progressing typically with regard to their language acquisition at ages 1, 2, and 3?
2. Should preschool education be mandatory? At what age should formal education begin? Provide some evidence to support your answer.
3. How can parents and early childhood teachers foster mastery motivation in their children?

LEARNING OBJECTIVES:

* Indicate the changes in language development that occur in childhood.
* Demonstrate understanding of different types of motivational styles by describing and giving an example of each.
* Analyze the outcomes typically associated with each motivational style.

With infancy behind them, children begin to expand their language skills and show true achievement motivation. As you'll now see, formal education uses these building blocks to develop lifelong skills and knowledge.

Expanding Language Skills

School-age children improve their pronunciation skills, produce longer and more complex sentences, and continue to expand their vocabularies. The average first-grader starts school with a vocabulary of about 10,000 words and adds somewhere between 5 and 13 new words a day throughout the elementary-school years (Hoff, 2014). School-age children also begin to think about and manipulate language in ways previously impossible (Melzi & Schick, 2013). They can, for example, interpret passive sentences such as "Goofy was liked by Donald" and conditional sentences such as "If Goofy had come, Donald would have been delighted" (Boloh & Champaud, 1993; Sudhalter & Braine, 1985).

Throughout childhood, advances in cognitive development are accompanied by advances in language and communication skills. For example, as children become less cognitively egocentric, they are more able to take the perspective of their listeners (Hoff, 2014). Middle childhood also brings increased **metalinguistic awareness**, or knowledge of language as a system (Melzi & Schick, 2013). Children with metalinguistic awareness understand the concept of words and can define words (semantics). Development of metalinguistic awareness also means that children can distinguish between grammatically correct and grammatically incorrect sentences (syntax) and can understand how language can be altered to fit the needs of the specific social context in which it is used (pragmatics). Children who are **bilingual**, knowing two or more languages, have better metalinguistic skills than nonbilingual (that is, monolingual) children (Schwartz et al., 2008). In **Exploration Box 10.2**, we explore some of the other effects of bilingualism.

Achievement Motivation

All children occasionally experience failure in their efforts to master challenges and meet achievement standards. What are the differences between children who persist and triumph in the face of failure and those who give up? Carol Dweck and her colleagues (for example, Dweck, 2006; Dweck & Elliott, 1983; Blackwell, Trzesniewski, & Dweck, 2007) have spent over 30 years searching for the answers. From this, Dweck has concluded that it is not so much what you have—your ability, talent, or intelligence—but *how you think about* what you have (Dweck, 2006). In particular, those who have a **fixed mindset** tend to believe that "what they have" is fixed or static. Thus, they either "have" a talent or do not; they either "are" intelligent or they are not. With this sort of mindset, there is little reason to put forth great effort on a task because it cannot change a fixed trait. Students with a fixed mindset, even those who are highly talented, typically select tasks that they know will showcase their talents with little effort. They tend to avoid challenging tasks as they do not believe they can be successful on these.

In contrast, those who have a **growth mindset** believe that abilities and talent are not fixed but are malleable: They can be fostered through hard work and effort. With this sort of mindset, students are motivated to put forth effort as this will lead to learning and advancement. A growth mindset can be fostered by praising students' efforts, not just the end products of their work (Dweck, 2007). In contrast, praising students for their intelligence ("you did well on that test because you are so intelligent") may lead students to think that their performance is driven by intelligence alone and is not related to effort. What about the inevitable feedback about mistakes? Students with a fixed mindset interpret such feedback as an indication that they lack ability. Thus, upon receiving low grades or a paper filled with lots of comments from their teacher, the student with a fixed mindset is more likely to feel defeated by their sense of lack of ability rather than energized to work harder and improve. Students with a growth mindset are more likely to interpret feedback about mistakes as useful information that can be used to improve for the future (Moser et al., 2011). How do some children end up with more successful mindsets? Characteristics of children, parents, and schools all contribute to motivation style and level.

Child Contributions

Several characteristics of the child contribute to achievement levels and motivation or mindset to succeed. First is the child's age or developmental level. Before age 7 or so, children tend to be unrealistic optimists who think they can succeed on almost any task (Stipek & Mac Iver, 1989). With age, children's perceptions of their academic abilities become more accurate (Wigfield et al., 1997). Even after repeated poor performances, young children often continue to think they have high ability and will do well, whereas older children tend to give up (Miller, 1985; Ruble, Eisenberg, & Higgins, 1994). Young children may also give up if their failures are clear-cut and they conclude they have been bad (Burhans & Dweck, 1995), but they are clearly more confident of their abilities than older children.

Why is this? Young children are protected from damaging self-perceptions partly because they believe that ability is

Bilingualism

An increasing number of children and adults are bilingual. There are, after all, more than 6,000 languages throughout the world and people move with relative ease from one language region to another. It has been estimated that more than half of the world's children grow up learning more than one language (Grosjean, 2010). What effects might bilingualism have on these children relative to their mono- (single) language peers?

For starters, ongoing exposure to multiple languages alters the neural connections in the brain (Petitto et al., 2012). As monolingual infants begin to lose some sensitivity to sounds produced in other languages, bilingual and multilingual infants retain sensitivity to the wider range of sounds used in the languages they hear. This may help explain why infants and young children who are regularly exposed to multiple languages seem to acquire the multiple languages with just about as much ease as those learning a single language. There may be times when children learning two languages struggle to find the correct vocabulary word or may take slightly longer on some linguistic tasks. But, for the most part, children who are bilingual end up with more advantages than disadvantages (Bialystok, Craik, & Luk, 2012).

It turns out that if you are bilingual, using one of your languages activates the other one at the same time (Marian & Shook, 2012). Although you may not realize that both languages are active, studies of eye movements and neuroimages of the brain indicate that both are indeed activated. Perhaps as a result of this, bilingual children and adults demonstrate enhanced abilities to switch back and forth between different tasks (Barac & Bialystok,

2012; Prior & MacWhinney, 2010). Their working memory is more robust than monolinguals (Morales, Calvo, & Bialystok, 2013; Rubio-Fernández & Glucksberg, 2012). They are also more skilled at ignoring irrelevant information and focusing on the relevant features of a task (Prior & MacWhinney, 2010).

Such evidence tells us that the constant juggling of two languages that bilinguals must perform strengthens the higher level executive control components of the cognitive system. Just as physical exercise affects your body structure as well as its functioning, the early and regular mental exercise required to become bilingual affects the brain's neural wiring as well as the brain's functioning (Marian & Shook, 2012).

What's more, bilingualism seems to bolster a person's cognitive reserve (Bialystok et al., 2012). As we get older, cognitive reserve may allow us to retain our mental capabilities longer by increasing our mental processing efficiency (Stern, 2002). In one study, bilingual adults developed symptoms and were diagnosed with Alzheimer's disease 4–5 years later than monolingual adults (Craik, Bialystok, & Freedman, 2010).

What if we acquire a second language later in life? The outcomes are not the same for later second language learners relative to those who are exposed to a second language from birth and acquire the two languages simultaneously. As with single language acquisition, there seems to be a sensitive period for second-language learning (Newport, 1991). In one study (Johnson & Newport, 1989), native speakers of Korean or Chinese who had come to the United States between age 3

and age 39 were tested for mastery of English grammar. Among those who began learning English before puberty, those who learned it earliest knew it best. Among those who arrived in the United States after puberty, performance was generally poor regardless of age of arrival or number of years using English. Such findings have been used to argue that there is a sensitive period for language acquisition that ends around puberty. But other research shows that, even beyond puberty, age of arrival in the United States is related to proficiency in English as a second language (Birdsong, 1999, 2005). Thus, adults relocating at age 25 develop greater proficiency than adults relocating at age 30, an advantage related more to age than to length of residence in the United States (Stevens, 1999). And although adults are generally less likely than children to ever attain native-like proficiency in a second language—suggesting a sensitive period—some adults achieve such proficiency, usually through massive effort and exposure to the second language (Birdsong, 1999).

So it seems as though it is easier to learn a second language when learning a first language during infancy, that is, to be bilingual rather than to acquire a second language later. Bilingualism also imposes some benefits that do not seem to come with later second language learning. In particular, bilinguals experience enhanced executive control and cognitive reserve. Given the benefits of bilingualism, perhaps more parents-to-be should be encouraged to brush up on their multilanguage skills in order to raise their children bilingual. When their children are old, they might appreciate having that extra cognitive reserve.

---

a changeable quality and that they can become smarter and improve their ability if they work hard. This view of ability encourages them to adopt **mastery goals** (also called learning goals) in achievement situations, aiming to learn new things so that they can improve their abilities (Brophy, 2010). A focus on mastery goals tends to dominate throughout the lower elementary grades (Bong, 2009).

As children age, in our society at least, they begin to see ability as a fixed trait that does not change much with effort. As

a result, by late elementary and middle school, more of them adopt **performance goals** in school; they aim to *prove* their ability rather than to *improve* it and seek to be judged smart rather than dumb (Bong, 2009; Dweck & Leggett, 1988; Erdley et al., 1997; and see ● **Table 10.3**). These changes in the understanding of ability are probably caused both by cognitive development—especially an increased ability to analyze the causes of successes and failures and to infer enduring traits from behavior—and by an accumulation of feedback in school (Stipek, 1984).

• **Table 10.3** Comparison of Mastery and Performance Goals

Mastery Goals	Performance Goals
• Ability as a changeable trait	• Ability as a fixed trait
• Focus on increasing competence or knowledge ("I understand this material better than I did before")	• Focus on increasing status relative to others ("I did better on this than the other students did")
• Self-regulated learning; ability to monitor understanding of material and adjust behavior (for example, effort) accordingly	• Other-regulated learning; ability to monitor performance relative to peers and increase effort (approach) to outperform them or decrease effort (avoidance) to save face (to say that failures are because of a lack of effort, not incompetence)
• Deep-level processing of material (for example, learning to understand)	• Superficial-level processing of material (for example, memorizing for a test)
• Feelings of pride and satisfaction associated with success, with failures indicating a need for more effort or different learning strategies	• Feelings of anxiety and shame associated with failure; boastful feelings associated with success

SOURCE: Adapted from Covington, 2000; Elliot & Church, 1997.

Importantly, children with growth mindsets who continue to focus on mastery or learning goals tend to do better in school than those who adopt fixed mindsets and switch to performance goals (Butler, 1999; Covington, 2000; Stipek & Gralinski, 1996). Children focused on mastery goals do not become as disheartened by a low grade if they have nonetheless progressed in their understanding of the material. For these children, the *process* of learning is enjoyable; it helps quench their curiosity (Fisher, Marshal, & Nanayakkara, 2009). Their ability to enjoy the learning process may help explain why these children exhibit higher levels of achievement (Von Stumm, Hell, & Chamorro-Premuzic, 2011). In contrast, children with a focus on performance goals are more discouraged because for them the *outcome*—the grade—was the goal, not the process of learning. These children are more likely to report anxiety and boredom, factors that are negatively associated with achievement (Daniels et al., 2009; Pekrun, Elliot, & Maier, 2009). The two groups of children—those with mastery or learning goals and those with performance goals—even display different patterns of neurological activity in response to their performance outcomes, further evidence that these two groups are truly experiencing their successes and failures differently (Fisher et al., 2009). Importantly, the two types of goals are not mutually exclusive; that is, it is possible to be motivated by both mastery goals and performance goals (Darnon et al., 2010). What is important, though, is the predominant focus that students hold as they work to achieve their goals. As Table 10.3 illustrates, when students believe that ability is primarily a fixed entity that they either have or do not have and conclude that they lack it, they set performance goals rather than learning goals; figuring that hard work will not payoff, they run the risk of giving up in the classroom (Dweck & Leggett, 1988). Even gifted students can fall into this trap (Ablard & Mills, 1996). Evaluate your own motivation style with the exercise in **Engagement Box 10.1**.

In addition to their age, children's level of intelligence, not surprisingly, contributes to their success in academics (Spinath et al., 2006). But clearly level of intelligence is just one piece of the puzzle because some students with above average intelligence do not do particularly well in school and others exceed expectations based solely on their IQ scores. It turns out that both motivation and achievement levels are higher when children value a subject—when they believe that it is important (Spinath et al., 2006). Think of this in relation to your own learning and motivation and you will likely recognize that you try harder and perform better when something is important to you.

Parent Contributions

As you saw earlier, parents can foster mastery motivation in infancy by providing their babies with appropriate sensory stimulation, being responsive, and (as you will see in Chapter 14) building a secure attachment relationship. Parents can then strengthen their children's achievement motivation by stressing and reinforcing the *process* of learning rather than emphasizing the product (Moser et al., 2011). They can also emphasize the learning opportunities provided by making mistakes. Individuals who believe intelligence is influenced by effort—how hard they work—are more likely to show improvement following mistakes than individuals who believe that intelligence is a fixed trait (Moser et al., 2011). As children begin formal schooling, parents can help foster high levels of achievement motivation by getting involved with their child's education and emphasizing practices that stimulate curiosity and engagement in learning (Gottfried et al., 2009).

Finally, parents can provide a cognitively stimulating home environment (Gottfried, Fleming, & Gottfried, 1998). This includes having reading material in the home, engaging in intellectual discussions, attending lectures or cultural events, visiting museums, and holding high expectations for children's education. By doing these things, parents stimulate intellectual curiosity and a desire to learn. Children who are encouraged and supported in a positive manner are likely to enjoy new challenges and feel confident about mastering them. They are also unlikely to make

What's Your Motivation Style?

Indicate whether you agree (A) or disagree (D) with each of the following statements, as they pertain to your typical approach or thoughts about learning and coursework.

___ 1. I read the chapter because the material was interesting to me.

___ 2. I read the chapter because the instructor said there would be a quiz on the material.

___ 3. I often look up some additional information related to the course material so that I can better understand what is discussed in class or presented in the textbook.

___ 4. I feel good when I am able to convey my understanding of the material on the exam.

___ 5. I need to earn a B+ or higher in this class to maintain my scholarship.

___ 6. I want to get an A on this test to show the professor that I'm good.

___ 7. I want to get an A on all the quizzes this semester because then I will be exempt from taking the final exam.

___ 8. As long as I pass this class, I'll be happy because I know I've learned something new from a really difficult professor.

___ 9. I like to see how others in the class score on the assignments so I can get an idea of how well I'm doing.

___ 10. I don't really care how other people in the class score because their performance is unrelated to my learning.

___ 11. I get bored and frustrated when the instructor spends time on easy material and quizzes us on stuff that seems obvious.

___ 12. I get frustrated when the instructor goes over difficult material that is going to be hard to study to earn a good grade.

___ 13. There is nothing I like more than a good challenging homework assignment that makes me think harder or differently.

___ 14. I like getting a homework assignment that is easy and fairly mindless to complete. I know I can get it done and the instructor will be happy with my answers.

___ 15. I usually find that I can master a task or material by working really hard on it.

___ 16. If I cannot solve a task right away, I usually stop working on it because I'm not going to be able to solve it.

Scoring: Count the number of "Agree" answers to these questions: 1, 3, 4, 8, 10, 11, 13, 15. Count the number of "Agree" answers to these questions: 2, 5, 6, 7, 9, 12, 14, 16. If the number of "Agree" answers to the first set (1, 3, 4, 8, 10, 11, 13, 15) is higher than the number of "Agree" answers to the second set (2, 5, 6, 7, 9, 12, 14, 16), then you focus more on learning or mastery goals. You are more interested in mastering material for the sake of learning and not for the sake of grades. If, on the other hand, the number of your "Agree" answers to the second set of questions is higher than the number of "Agree" answers to the first set, then you focus more on performance goals. You are motivated to perform well and earn good grades. According to the text, which of these motivation styles—mastery versus performance—ultimately leads to a deeper and richer understanding of material? What could you do to shift from one style to the other?

the kinds of counterproductive attributions ("I'm dumb") that can cause them to lose interest in schoolwork (Glasgow et al., 1997). Children typically feel competent when their parents are satisfied with their performance (McGrath & Repetti, 2000). By contrast, parents can undermine a child's school performance and intrinsic motivation to learn if they are uninvolved and offer little guidance or if they are highly controlling, nag continually about homework, offer bribes for good grades, and criticize bad grades (Ginsburg & Bronstein, 1993; Gottfried et al., 2009). Over an 8-year interval from age 9 to 17, children maintain higher levels of motivation when their parents initially focus on intrinsic goals (learning for the sake of learning) rather than extrinsic goals (learning to earn high grades or money; Gottfried et al., 2009).

In a fascinating study, Harvard economist Roland Fryer, Jr. (see Ripley, 2010) spent millions of dollars to learn whether students could be bribed into earning higher standardized test scores. He enlisted school districts in four major cities and used a different set of incentives in each location. For example, in Chicago, ninth-graders could earn up to $2,000 per year (!) by getting paid $50 for each A test grade, $35 for each B grade, and $20 for each C grade. A similar scheme was used in New York City with younger students—fourth- and seventh-graders. In Washington, D.C., students were paid for such things as

attendance and staying out of trouble. The Dallas program enlisted the youngest students in the study—second-graders—and paid them the least, $2 every time they read a book and completed a quiz on their reading.

What factors will determine whether this student remains motivated and focused on mastery goals or shifts to performance goals and possibly becomes disinterested with school?

The results may surprise you. The program was a bust in Chicago and New York City: students earned lots of money for getting good grades on tests throughout the year but showed no improvement on standardized tests given at the end of the school year. In Washington, the results were somewhat mixed, although promising in that standardized reading scores improved among children who were rewarded not for grades but for behaviors such as attendance throughout the school year. The program that proved to have the biggest bang for the bucks was the one that paid the least and targeted not grades but a behavior that all children could already perform and could control—their reading. Young students who were paid for reading books and answering quiz questions significantly improved their standardized reading comprehension scores. We still need to see how students in the various groups perform over time—and ensure that rewarding activities such as reading books does not eventually undermine intrinsic motivation for reading. But the results suggest that rewarding children not for the final products of their work (that is, the grades) but for the steps that contribute to the final product (such as reading and attendance) can have a positive effect on their performance. Fryer and others involved in the study found that students who had the opportunity to earn the most money for high test scores were very excited by this prospect but did not know how to go about achieving it. Instead of bribing students for the grades they earn, it might be better to encourage students to involve themselves in behaviors they can control that contribute to greater engagement with the course material. Ultimately, this is what will lead to greater achievement gains.

School Contributions

How do schools affect achievement? Nearly every school asserts that the major goal of classroom instruction is improvement of children's learning. Many of these same schools, however, are structured in ways that focus on the external rewards that students can earn (such as grades or stickers). As a result, they may encourage children, either deliberately or inadvertently, to set performance goals rather than mastery or learning goals (Covington, 2000). Many classrooms are competitive places where students try to outdo each other to earn the best grades and gain teacher recognition. Students receive a grade (good or bad), indicating their performance on a test or project, and that is the end of it. If they did not fully learn the material, they are given no opportunity to do so: They learn that the grade, not learning, is the goal.

Martin Covington (1998, 2000) believes that schools can foster children's academic motivation by downplaying the competitive race for the best grades in class. How might this work? Consider some research by Elaine Elliott and Carol Dweck (1988). They asked fifth-graders to perform a novel task. The students were led to believe that they had either low or high ability and were warned that they would soon be performing similar tasks that would prove difficult. Half the children worked under a performance goal (not unlike the goals emphasized in many classrooms): They were told that their performance would be compared with that of other children and evaluated by an expert. The remaining children were induced to adopt a learning or mastery goal: Although they would make some mistakes, they

were told, working at the tasks would "sharpen the mind" and help them at school.

As expected, the only children who became frustrated and gave up were those who believed they had low ability and were pursuing a performance goal. For them, continuing to work on the difficult task meant demonstrating again that they were stupid. By contrast, even "low ability" students who pursued a mastery goal persisted despite their failures and showed remarkably little frustration, probably because they believed they could grow from their experience. Perhaps, then, teachers undermine achievement motivation by distributing gold stars and grades and frequently calling attention to how students compare with one another (Brophy, 2010). Children might be better off if teachers nurtured their intrinsic motivation to master challenges and structured their classrooms to emphasize mastery rather than performance goals (Murayama & Elliot, 2009). Then, slower learners could view their mistakes as a sign that they should change strategies to improve their competencies rather than as further proof that they lack ability.

Finally, the school climate can influence achievement. In situations where a student does not do well, teachers who offer comfort by saying something such as, "Don't worry, not everyone is good at this subject" may do more harm than good (Rattan, Good, & Dweck, 2012). Although well-intended, such statements can send that message that the student does not have the ability and cannot develop the ability. Students hearing this message tend to lower their personal expectations for success in this area and they display lower levels of motivation for the subject (Rattan et al., 2012). Students might be better served by hearing that, although the subject matter is challenging for them, they can change their level of performance by using a different learning strategy or working harder.

To recap what you have learned so far, children approach achievement tasks with either a fixed or growth mindset, based on how they view their abilities: unchangeable or malleable. As they age, children are more likely to believe that ability is a stable trait and shift from focusing on mastery goals to focusing on performance goals. These changes, brought about by both cognitive development and feedback in school, may make them more vulnerable to "failure syndrome," a tendency to give up at the first obstacle they encounter (Brophy, 2010). Yet some children remain far more motivated to succeed in school than others, and parents and schools have a lot to do with that.

Learning to Read

Perhaps the most important achievement in school is acquiring the ability to read. Mastery of reading paves the way for mastering other academic skills. Skilled readers consume more printed material than unskilled readers, giving them an advantage in other academic areas that increasingly rely on reading skills over the school years (Sparks, Patton, & Murdoch, 2013; Stanovich, 1986). Unlike language acquisition, a natural learning task that typically requires no formal education, reading acquisition usually requires direct instruction. Fortunately, the brain seems to be structured to support the acquisition of reading skills (Dehaene, 2009). How, though, do children master this complex and important skill?

Mastering the Alphabetic Principle

Before children can read, they must understand the **alphabetic principle**—the idea that the letters in printed words represent the sounds in spoken words in a systematic way (O'Connor, 2011). According to Linnea Ehri (1999), this is a four-step process, as follows.

- Prealphabetic phase: Children memorize selected visual cues to remember words. They can "read" text that they have memorized during previous readings. A picture on a page in a favorite book, for instance, triggers a child to recall the words she has often heard her mother read when they turned to this page.
- Partial alphabetic phase: Children learn the shapes and sounds of letters. They begin to connect at least one letter in a word—usually the first—to its corresponding sound. For example, they recognize the curved shape of the letter C and begin to associate this with a particular sound. Not surprisingly, children typically recognize the initial letter of their first name before other letters (Treiman & Broderick, 1998).
- Full alphabetic phase: Children make complete connections between written letters and their corresponding sounds. They use **phonological awareness**—the sensitivity to the sound system of language that enables them to segment spoken words into sounds or phonemes (Carroll et al., 2003). Children who have phonological awareness can recognize that *cat* and *trouble* both have the phoneme /t/ in them, can tell you how many distinct sounds there are in the word *bark*, and can tell you what will be left if you take the /f/ sound out of *fat*. Children can decode words never before seen by applying their knowledge of phonetics.
- Consolidated alphabetic phase: Children are able to group letters that regularly occur together into a unit. For instance, the letter sequence *ing*, which frequently appears at the end of verbs, is perceived as a single unit rather than as three separate letters. This grouping speeds the processing of the multisyllabic words that older children are increasingly exposed to in their books.

Thus, the basic components of literacy include mastering a language system, understanding connections between sounds and their printed symbols (the alphabetic principle), and discriminating phonemes that make up words (phonological awareness). How does the child pull all this together into reading?

Emergent Literacy

Several factors influence **emergent literacy**—the developmental precursors of reading skills in young children (Whitehurst & Lonigan, 1998). Emergent literacy includes knowledge, skills, and attitudes that will facilitate the acquisition of reading ability. Children with greater working memory and attention control demonstrate a higher degree of reading readiness than other children, suggesting that activities strengthening these skills can help foster reading achievement (Welsh et al., 2010). One way to do this is through reading storybooks to preschoolers (Evans & Shaw, 2008). Repetitious storybook reading enhances children's vocabulary and allows them to see the connection between printed and spoken words. Importantly, parents should read *with* their child rather than *to* their child, meaning they should actively involve their child in the activity rather than having the

How is pointing at an image in a picture book contributing to emergent literacy?

child remain the passive recipient (Phillips, Norris, & Anderson, 2008). With each successive reading, parents who ask increasingly complex questions about the text can move their child from a superficial to a deeper understanding (van Kleeck et al., 1997). Even older children benefit from reading the same book on multiple occasions (Faust & Glenzer, 2000) and from shared reading with a parent (Clarke-Stewart, 1998). Parents, with their greater mastery of reading, can help their fledgling readers develop an understanding of printed words. If you think of this in Vygotsky's framework, it is an example of parent and child operating in the zone of proximal development.

Rhyming stories and games can help foster phonological awareness. For this reason, listening to books with a rhyming structure (for example, Dr. Seuss's *The Cat in the Hat*) can benefit children. Young children's sensitivity to rhyme (for example, *cat–sat*) helps predict their later reading success (Bryant, 1998; Goswami, 1999).

By assessing preschool children's emergent literacy skills, parents and early childhood educators can develop a fairly accurate idea of what children's later reading skills will be. In particular, differences among children in knowledge of letters (for example, knowing the alphabet), phonological awareness, and word segmentation skills predict later differences in their reading ability (Carroll et al., 2003; Kendeou et al., 2009). In addition, semantic knowledge as reflected in children's ability to retrieve words, provide word definitions, and assign meaning to the printed symbols that represent words predicts later reading ability (Kendeou et al., 2009; Roth, Speece, & Cooper, 2002). This suggests that parents can help children get a head start on reading by encouraging activities such as rhyming, repeating the ABCs, and defining words.

Skilled and Unskilled Readers

After children have received reading instruction, why are some children quick, advanced readers but others struggle to master the most basic reading material? For starters, skilled readers have a solid understanding of the alphabetic principle—the notion that letters must be associated with phonemes. Thus, when they see the letter *b*, they know the sound that it represents. A large body of research also confirms that reading ability is influenced by a child's level of phonological awareness (Adams, Treiman, & Pressley, 1998; Bus & van IJzendoorn, 1999). Children with higher levels of phonological awareness usually become better readers than children with lower levels of phonological awareness (Schneider, Roth, & Ennemoser, 2000).

But there is more to being a skilled reader than connecting letters with sounds. Analyses of eye movement patterns show that unskilled readers skip words or parts of words, whereas skilled readers' eyes hit all the words (Perfetti, 1999). Skilled readers do not use context to help them identify words, although they may use context to help with comprehension. As noted previously, they rely on phonology to identify words, something most unskilled readers have trouble with.

Some children have serious difficulties learning to read, even though they have normal intellectual ability and no sensory impairments or emotional difficulties that could account for their problems. These children have **dyslexia**, or a reading disability. A minority have the kind of visual perception problem that used to be seen as the heart of dyslexia; they cannot distinguish between letters with similar appearances, or they

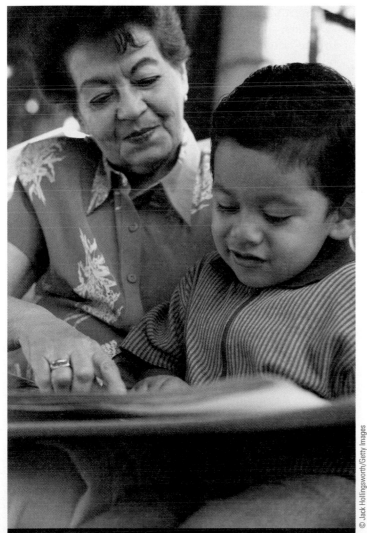

Repeatedly reading the same story fosters vocabulary and deepens children's understanding of the story content.

© Jack Hollingsworth/Getty Images

read words backward (*top* might become *pot*). However, it is now clear that the difficulties of most dyslexic children involve auditory perception more than visual perception (see, for example, Temple et al., 2000).

Specifically, children who become dyslexic readers often show deficiencies in phonological awareness well before they enter school (Bruck, 1992; Vellutino et al., 1996). There is even evidence that the brains of dyslexic children respond differently than those of other children to speech sounds soon after birth, and functional imaging of the brain shows that distinctive patterns of neural activity persist in children with dyslexia (see, for example, Caylak, 2009; Shaywitz et al., 2001). This suggests that a perceptual deficit may develop during the prenatal period of brain development. Because dyslexic children have difficulty analyzing the sounds in speech, they also have trouble detecting sound–letter correspondences, which in turn impairs their ability to recognize printed words automatically and effortlessly (Bruck, 1990). They must then devote so much effort to decoding the words on the page that they have little attention to spare for interpreting and remembering what they have read. Dyslexic children continue to perform poorly on tests of phonological awareness and tests of word recognition as adolescents and adults, even if they have become decent readers (Bruck, 1990, 1992; Shaywitz et al., 1999). It is now clear that dyslexia is a lifelong disability, not just a developmental delay that is eventually overcome (Shaywitz et al., 1999).

How Should Reading Be Taught?

What does all this suggest about teaching children to read? For years a debate has raged over the merits of two broad approaches to reading instruction: the phonics approach and the whole-language approach. The phonics (or code-oriented) approach teaches children to analyze words into their component sounds; that is, it systematically teaches them letter–sound correspondence rules. By contrast, the whole-language (or look–say) approach emphasizes reading for meaning and teaches children to recognize specific words by sight or to figure out what they mean using clues in the surrounding context (Donat, 2006). It assumes that the parts of printed words (the letters) are not as meaningful as the whole words and that by focusing on whole words children can learn to read as effortlessly and naturally as they learn to understand speech.

Research strongly supports the phonics approach. To read well, children must somehow learn that spoken words are made up of sounds and that the letters of the alphabet correspond to these sounds (Foorman, 1995). Teaching phonological awareness skills can pay off in better reading skills (National Reading Panel, 1999). ● **Table 10.4** shows what happened when a third-grade boy with poor phonological awareness tried to read the sentence, "A boy said, 'run, little girl' " by the look–say method. He ended up with an incorrect interpretation ("A baby is running little go") and lost the intended meaning of the sentence. Better decoding skills (phonics) might have enabled him to read the sentence accurately. Once children have begun to master phonics, they can be encouraged to attend to meaning and context.

Given the importance of phonics, several programs have been developed for at-risk and dyslexic children who have

• Table 10.4 One Boy's Misreading of the Sentence "A Boy Said, 'Run, Little Girl'."

Words in Target Sentence	Strategies Employed by Reader	Words "Read"
A	Sight word known to reader	A
boy	Unknown; uses beginning *b* to guess *baby*	baby
said, "Run,	*Said* unknown; jumps to the next word *(run)*, which he recognizes, then uses the *s* in *said* and his knowledge of syntax to generate *is running*	is running
little	Sight word known to reader	little
girl."	Unknown; uses beginning *g* to guess *go*	go

SOURCE: Adapted from Ely, 2001.

special difficulty discriminating speech sounds that are made rapidly, such as /b/, /d/, and /t/. By playing an entertaining computer game, children are able to practice discriminating pairs of these hard-to-distinguish sounds, which are altered so that they are stretched in time and thereby made easier to perceive (Merzenich et al., 1996; Tallal et al., 1996). After only a month of such game playing, children's ability to recognize fast sequences of speech sounds and to understand language improves dramatically. These gains eventually pay off in improved reading performance as children become more able to sound out words on the page (Foorman et al., 1998).

The debate over reading instruction and its effectiveness raises a broader question about just how well schools are doing at educating children. What factors contribute to effective schools, and in doing so, presumably contribute to more effective learning by children?

Effective Schools, Effective Learning

Some schools seem to do a better job than others—they graduate a higher percentage of students or have a higher percentage of students at or above the proficient level in one or more subjects. Why? To understand why some schools seem more effective than others, we must consider characteristics of the students, characteristics of the teachers and school settings, and the interaction between student and environment.

Student Characteristics

First, a school's effectiveness depends in part on what it has to work with—the students it takes in. With respect to the children, genetic differences among children contribute to differences in aptitude among them. As you learned in Chapters 3 and 9, IQ scores have a genetic component, and children with higher IQs attain higher grades throughout their 12 years of school (Gutman, Sameroff, & Cole, 2003). Schools cannot eliminate these genetic differences among children, but they can influence (that is, raise) overall levels of academic achievement (Zvoch & Stevens, 2006). In addition, academic achievement, on average, tends to be higher in schools with a preponderance of economically advantaged students; children are better able to make academic progress in school when they come from homes that are stocked with computers, books, and intellectually stimulating toys (Portes & MacLeod, 1996). However, this does not mean that schools are only as good as the students they serve. Many schools that serve disadvantaged populations are highly effective at motivating students and preparing them for jobs or further education. To really determine a school's effectiveness, researchers need to look at how students change from before to after they receive instruction (Zvoch & Stevens, 2006). This is, in large part, the goal of the federally mandated *No Child Left Behind* (NCLB) in the United States—to ensure that children, regardless of how high or low they score at the start, improve their performance after each year of instruction.

Studies of effective learning environments provide another illustration of the interaction of nature and nurture. High-achieving parents pass their genes to their children, providing genetic potential for high achievement to their children (Rutter & Maughan, 2002). These same high-achieving parents are likely to select schools that have strong academic reputations, often by choosing to live in a neighborhood served by a "good" school district (Rutter & Maughan, 2002). This is an example of a passive gene–environment correlation, described in Chapter 3, in which children are influenced by their parent's genes directly through genetic transmission and indirectly through the environments their parents create for them.

Teacher and School Characteristics

Andrew Wayne and Peter Youngs (2003) reviewed research on the relationship between teacher characteristics and student achievement. They found that student achievement scores rose with increases in the quality of their teachers' undergraduate institutions and their teachers' licensure examination scores. Perhaps the most intriguing findings about teacher effectiveness come from statistical analyses conducted by William Sanders, who concludes that "the answer to why children learn well or not isn't race, it isn't poverty, it isn't even per-pupil expenditure at the elementary level. It's teachers, teachers, teachers" (Sanders, 1999). He draws this conclusion after finding that students who are lucky enough to get the best teachers 3 years in a row achieve as much as 50 points higher on standardized tests than students who are unfortunate enough to get the worst teachers 3 years in a row (Sanders & Horn, 1995; Sanders & Rivers, 1996). What is an effective teacher? According to Sanders, effectiveness

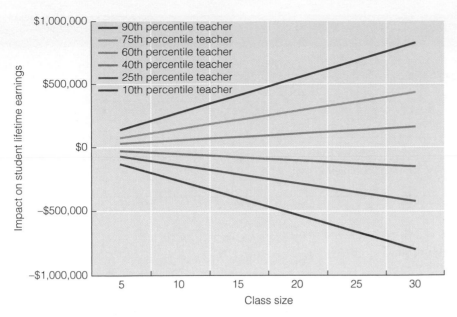

■ Figure 10.5 As this striking analysis by economist Eric Hanushek shows, having an effective teacher can make a big difference, especially in larger classes.

SOURCE: Hanushek, E. A. (2011). The economic value of higher teacher quality. *Economics of Education Review*, 30, 466–479.

can be defined by how far teachers can advance their students each year. Eric Hanushek reached a similar conclusion after finding that students with the best teachers advance 1.5 years in 1 school year, whereas students with the worst teachers advance only half a year over the course of the school year (see Hanushek, Rivkin, & Kain, 2005). These effects are cumulative and long-lasting: a student with the best teachers 2 years in a row progresses the equivalent of 3 years, whereas the student with the worst teachers 2 years in a row progresses just 1 year and will be 2 years behind the other student in achievement level. Ultimately, a person's earnings over their lifetime may be impacted by whether they had teachers who were highly effective, average, or below average (see **■ Figure 10.5**).

What might be going on in the classrooms of the students who show the most progress each year? Basically, the effective school environment is a comfortable but businesslike setting in which teachers are involved with students, students are motivated to learn, and serious teaching takes place (Mac Iver, Reuman, & Main, 1995; Phillips, 1997; Rutter, 1983). More specifically, in effective schools and classrooms, teachers:

- Strongly emphasize academics. They demand a lot from their students, expect them to succeed, regularly assign homework, and work hard to achieve their objectives in the classroom.
- Create a task-oriented but comfortable atmosphere. For example, they waste little time starting activities or dealing with distracting discipline problems, provide clear instructions and feedback, and encourage and reward good work.
- Manage discipline problems effectively. For example, they enforce the rules on the spot rather than sending offenders to the principal's office, and they avoid the use of physical punishment.

Student-Environment Interaction

Finally, characteristics of the student and characteristics of the learning environment often interact to affect student outcome. This is an example of the concept of goodness of fit—an appropriate match between the person's characteristics and her environment (see Chapter 11). Much educational research has been based on the assumption that one teaching method, organizational system, or philosophy of education will prove superior for all students, regardless of their ability levels, learning styles, personalities, and cultural backgrounds. This assumption is often wrong. Instead, many educational practices are highly effective with some kinds of students but ineffective with other students. The secret is to find an appropriate match between the learner and the teaching method.

In a good illustration of goodness of fit between learners and environments, highly achievement-oriented students adapt well to unstructured classrooms in which they have a good deal of choice, whereas less achievement-oriented students often do better with more structure (Peterson, 1977). Sometimes an alternative teaching method works as well as a traditional one for highly capable students but only one of these methods suits less capable students. In one study, for example, highly distractible students got more from computer-assisted instruction than from a teacher's presentation of the same material, whereas more attentive students benefited equally from both methods (Orth & Martin, 1994). Finally, students tend to have more positive outcomes when they and their teacher share similar backgrounds (Goldwater & Nutt, 1999). Evidence of the importance of the fit between student and classroom environment implies that educational programs are likely to be most effective when they are highly individualized—tailored to suit each student's developmental competencies and needs.

Checking Mastery

1. What is the difference between a mastery (or learning) goal and a performance goal?
2. What is one characteristic that differentiates a skilled reader from a less-skilled reader?
3. What are three factors that characterize an effective learning environment?

Making Connections

1. Using the material on effective learning environments, evaluate your high school and indicate ways it could improve to become a highly effective learning environment.
2. Unlike most of his peers, Johnny, age 7, is not yet reading despite having the usual classroom instruction. What might account for Johnny's trouble with reading?

LEARNING OBJECTIVES:

- Explain why levels of academic achievement decline in adolescence and provide two methods to stop this decline.

- Describe the main findings of cross-cultural research on math performance and delineate steps to improve math scores in countries near or below average relative to other countries.

- Analyze the pros and cons of employment during high school.

- Indicate conditions that contribute to a smooth transition for teens completing high school and moving on to college or work.

Adolescents make critical decisions about such matters as how much time to devote to studying, whether to work part-time after school, whether to go to college, and what to be when they grow up. They become more capable of making these educational and vocational choices as their cognitive and social skills expand; in turn, the choices they make shape their development. But many of them lose interest in school when they leave elementary school.

Declining Levels of Achievement

You might think that adolescents would become more dedicated to academic success once they begin to realize that they need a good education to succeed in life. But consider what Deborah Stipek (1984) concluded after reviewing studies on the development of achievement motivation from early childhood to adolescence:

> On the average, children value academic achievement more as they progress through school, but their expectations for success and self-perceptions of competence decline, and their affect toward school becomes more negative. Children also become increasingly concerned about achievement outcomes and reinforcement (for example, high grades) associated with positive outcomes and less concerned about intrinsic satisfaction in achieving greater competence. (p. 153)

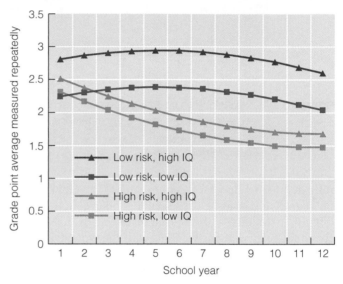

■ **Figure 10.6** Grade point average from 1st grade to 12th grade for students with high and low risk and IQ.

Source: Gutman, L. M., Samereroff, A. J., & Cole, R. Academic growth curve trajectories from 1st grade to 12th grade: Effects of multiple social risk factors and preschool child factors, *Developmental Psychology*, 39, 777–790. Copyright © 2003 by the American Psychological Association. Reprinted with permission.

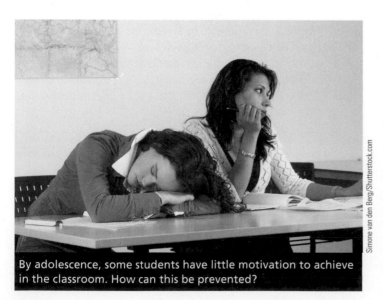

By adolescence, some students have little motivation to achieve in the classroom. How can this be prevented?

Simone van den Berg/Shutterstock.com

Many of the negative trends Stipek describes become especially apparent as young adolescents make the transition from elementary school to middle school (typically grades 6–8) or junior high school (grades 7–9). At this critical juncture, achievement motivation, self-esteem, and grades may all decline. ■ **Figure 10.6** shows the academic trajectories for four groups of students studied by Leslie Gutman and his colleagues: those with high and low IQ scores who had either many or few risk factors (Gutman, Sameroff, & Cole, 2003). Risk factors included minority group status, low maternal education and mental health, stressful life events, family size, and father absence. Students with more risk factors showed a steady decline in academic achievement throughout their schooling, regardless of whether they had high or low IQ scores to begin with. Students with few risk factors showed a slight increase in achievement until around grade 6 or 7, at which time achievement began to drop slowly. Boys show greater declines in motivation and school interest than girls (Dotterer, McHale, & Crouter, 2009).

What might explain these discouraging trends? To answer this question, we'll first examine what is going on at the individual level, and then consider family and peer influences before ending with a look at the wider context of school and society.

At the individual level, children become increasingly capable of analyzing the causes of events, interpreting feedback from teachers, and inferring enduring traits such as high or low ability from their behavior (Stipek & Mac Iver, 1989). The result is that they view their strengths and weaknesses more realistically—and lose some of their high academic self-esteem and high expectancies of success (Stipek & Mac Iver, 1989; Wigfield et al., 1997). Those who manage to maintain an emphasis on mastery or learning goals attain higher grades in high school than those who do not (Gutman, 2006). Students who believe that success is a matter of luck have lower grades than students without this attributional style (House, 2006).

At the family level, several characteristics are associated with lower achievement and more absences from school. Being a member of a minority group, growing up in a single-parent family, and having a mother with less education or with mental health problems are potential academic risk factors (Gutman, Sameroff, & Cole, 2003; Gutman, Sameroff, & Eccles, 2002). In contrast, living in a small, caring family with at least one stable parent who uses consistent discipline can bolster school performance (Gutman, Sameroff, & Eccles, 2002). Mothers who talk to their middle-school children about assuming responsibility and making decisions have teens who are more likely to complete high school and continue their education (Tenenbaum et al., 2007). Adolescents who believe their parents are more involved in their schooling are generally more academically motivated than adolescents who believe their parents are less involved (Spera, 2006). Importantly, it is the students' *perceptions* of parental involvement and not actual involvement that is related to motivation levels.

The adolescent's achievement motivation is also affected by the increasing importance of the peer group, which at times can undermine parents' and teachers' efforts to encourage school achievement. Many years ago, when James Coleman (1961) asked high school students how they would like to be remembered, only 31% of the boys and 28% of the girls wanted to be remembered as bright students. They were more concerned with having the athletic and social skills that lead to popularity. Not much has changed in 50 years: Tim Urdan and Miranda Mestas (2006) interviewed high school seniors about their reasons for pursuing performance goals. Many of the responses indicated that teens were motivated by a desire to avoid looking dumb or to look competent and make their parents proud. But some of the students specifically noted that they wanted to be average and not appear to be too smart. As one student said, "I just want to be normal, not the best. I don't want to be the worst but I just want to be normal" (p. 361).

Peer pressures that undermine achievement motivation tend to be especially strong for many lower-income males and for minority students (Véronneau et al., 2008). In particular, African American and Hispanic peer cultures in many low-income areas actively discourage academic achievement, whereas European American and especially Asian American peer groups tend to value and encourage it (Steinberg, Dornbusch, & Brown, 1992). High-achieving African American students in some inner-city schools risk being rejected by their African American peers if their academic accomplishments cause them to be perceived as "acting white" (Fordham & Ogbu, 1986). They may feel that they have to abandon their cultural group and racial identity to succeed in school, and this takes a psychological toll (Arroyo & Zigler, 1995; Ogbu, 2003). Some students may disengage from academics to preserve their cultural identity with a group that has historically not always been treated fairly by the educational system (Ogbu, 2003). Although African American parents are as likely as European American parents to value education and to provide the kind of authoritative parenting that encourages school achievement, their positive influences are sometimes canceled out by negative peer influences (Steinberg et al., 1992).

For those African American teens who belong to a supportive peer group, academic achievement is strengthened (Gutman et al., 2002). In addition, African American teens who strongly value their ethnic group membership and have positive beliefs about how society views African Americans tend to have more positive beliefs about education (Chavous et al., 2003). But even a strong ethnic identity may not be able to overcome the subtle and negative effects of the discrimination still experienced by many minority students in the classroom that erodes their self-confidence and lowers their motivation (Thomas et al., 2009).

Finally, we must consider that some of the decline in the achievement motivation of adolescents may reflect a poor fit between person and environment. Adopting a goodness-of-fit explanation, Jacquelynne Eccles and her colleagues (Eccles, Lord, & Midgley, 1991; Eccles et al., 1993) argue that the transition to middle school or junior high school is likely to be especially difficult because young adolescents are often experiencing major physical and psychological changes at the time they are switching schools (see also Hill & Tyson, 2009). For example, girls who were reaching puberty when they were moving from sixth grade in an elementary school to seventh grade in a junior high school were more likely to experience drops in self-esteem and other negative changes than girls who remained in a K–8 school during this vulnerable period (Simmons & Blyth, 1987).

Could it be that more adolescents would remain interested in school if they did not have to change schools when they are experiencing pubertal changes? This idea became an important part of the rationale for shifting from junior high schools, in which students transitioned between the sixth and seventh grades, to middle schools where the transition occurs between the fifth and sixth grades. Research conducted in Germany, where the transition to a new school happens even earlier—after fourth grade, prior to pubertal changes for most students—helps answer this question (Arens et al., 2013). Students, both boys and girls, experienced lowered self-perceptions, including perceptions of their academic competence, following the school transition. This suggests that the school transition itself can be challenging, apart from whether pubertal changes are occurring at the same time.

The transition to middle or junior high school often involves going from a small school with close student–teacher relationships, a good deal of choice regarding learning activities, and reasonable discipline to a larger, more bureaucratized environment in which student–teacher relationships are impersonal, good grades are more emphasized but harder to come by, opportunities for choice are limited, assignments are not as intellectually stimulating, and discipline is rigid—all when adolescents are seeking more rather than less autonomy and are becoming more rather than less intellectually capable (Hill & Tyson, 2009). Giving students a sense of ownership and some degree of control in their learning helps maintain their interest and motivation (Tsai et al., 2008; Valiente et al., 2008).

Eccles and her colleagues have demonstrated that the fit between developmental needs and school environment is an important influence on adolescent adjustment to school. In one study (Mac Iver & Reuman, 1988), the transition to junior high school brought about a decline in intrinsic motivation to learn mainly among students who wanted more involvement in classroom decisions but ended up with fewer such opportunities than they had in elementary school. In another study (Midgley, Feldlaufer, & Eccles, 1989), students experienced negative changes in their attitudes toward mathematics only when their move from elementary school to junior high resulted in less personal and supportive relationships with math teachers. For those few students whose junior high school teachers were more supportive than those they had in elementary school, interest in academics increased. Similarly, other research has shown that training staff members to understand and respond appropriately to the developmental needs of this age group helps students maintain a positive outlook on learning and perform better in school (Martin, 2008). Moreover, the middle-school slump is largely avoided among students whose mothers display a high interest in academics and hold high expectations (Dotterer et al., 2009). Thus, here is something tangible that parents can do to help their children experience continued success in school.

The message? Declines in academic motivation and performance are not inevitable during early adolescence. Students may indeed form more realistic expectancies of success as their growing cognitive abilities allow them to use the increasingly informative feedback they receive from teachers. Experiencing pubertal changes at the same time as other stressful changes and needing to downplay academics to gain popularity may also hurt school achievement. However, educators can help keep adolescents engaged in school by creating school environments that provide a better fit to the developmental needs and interests of adolescents. Whether they are called middle schools or junior high schools, such schools should provide warm, supportive relationships with teachers, intellectual challenges, and increased opportunities for self-direction (Eccles et al., 1993). Parents can also help by remaining supportive and involved in their child's education throughout the middle-school years rather than pulling back (Hill & Tyson, 2009).

Mathematics and the Cross-Cultural Divide

More advanced cognitive skills of concrete-operational and then formal-operational thought enable children to tackle more challenging academic tasks. Much attention has been focused on mathematics, which, along with reading and writing, is considered one of the basic skills important for success in many industrialized nations. How well do secondary-school students perform in math and how might achievement in this area be optimized?

■ **Figure 10.7** shows average mathematics achievement test scores of eighth-grade students in various countries. Students in the United States score above the international average but significantly below achievement levels in nations such as Singapore, Japan, and Korea. When researchers looked at the best students—those in the top 10% of all eighth-graders surveyed in the 48 nations—only 7% of U.S. students met the criteria in math compared to nearly half of eighth-graders in

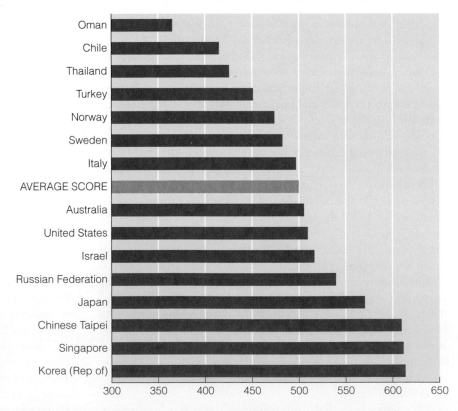

■ **Figure 10.7** International comparison of eighth-grade mathematics performance.

SOURCE: Adapted from Table 4 (p. 11) of Kastberg, D., Ferraro, D., Lemanski, N., Roey, S., & Jenkins, F. (2012). Highlights from TIMSS 2011: Mathematics and science achievement of U.S. fourth- and eighth-grade students in an international context. National Center for Education Statistics.

Chinese Taipei, Singapore, and the Republic of Korea. What might account for these international differences in math achievement? Are students in some nations simply more intelligent than students in other nations?

Cross-cultural research conducted by Harold Stevenson and his colleagues (Chen & Stevenson, 1995; Stevenson, Chen, & Lee, 1993; Stevenson & Stigler, 1992) shows that American schoolchildren perform about as well on IQ tests as their Asian counterparts when they enter school (Stevenson et al., 1985). They score at least as well as Japanese and Chinese students on tests of general information not typically covered in school (Stevenson et al., 1993). Instead, the achievement gap between American and Asian students seems to be rooted in cultural differences in attitudes concerning education and educational practices. Here is what some of this cross-cultural research on education and achievement shows:

- Asian students spend more time being educated. They attend school more days of the year and their school day is often longer than the comparable American school experience (Stevenson, Lee, & Stigler, 1986). When they are in school, they spend more time on-task: Asian students spend about 95% of their time engaged in activities such as listening to the teacher and completing assignments, whereas American students spend only about 80% of their time on-task. This additional time on academics extends outside the classroom and regular school hours as well. Asian students, especially Japanese students, are assigned and complete considerably more homework than American students (Verma & Larson, 2003).
- Asian parents are strongly committed to the educational process. About 40% think their children should have 3 hours or more of homework each day (Ebbeck, 1996). Asian parents are rarely satisfied with how their children are doing in school or with the quality of education their children are receiving; American parents seem to settle for less (Mathews, 2003). Asian parents also receive frequent communications from their children's teachers in notebooks children carry to and from school each day. They find out how their children are progressing and follow teachers' suggestions for encouraging and assisting their children at home (Stevenson & Lee, 1990).
- Asian parents, teachers, and students all share a strong belief that hard work or effort will pay off in better academic performance (that is, they have a growth mindset and set what Dweck calls learning goals), whereas Americans tend to put more emphasis on ability as a cause of good or poor performance. The result may be that Americans give up too quickly on a child who appears to have low intellectual ability. In doing so, they may help create a case of learned helplessness. In contrast, Asian teachers will continue to question a student following both correct and incorrect answers to a problem (Schleppenbach et al., 2007).

This cross-cultural research carries an important message: The secret of effective learning is to get teachers, students, and parents working together to make education the top priority for youth, to set high achievement goals, and to invest the day-by-day effort required to attain those goals. Many states and local school districts have begun to respond to evidence that American schools are being outclassed by schools in other countries by strengthening curricula, tightening standards for teacher certification, and raising standards for graduation and promotion from grade to grade.

Integrating Work and School

A sizable number of teens in the United States work part-time during their high school careers. In tenth grade, about one-third of students have a part-time job, with most working less than 15 hours per week (Bachman et al., 2013). By twelfth grade, approximately 60% of students are working with at least some of these, perhaps 15%, working 26 or more hours per week (Bachman et al., 2013). How do these early work experiences affect their development and, in particular, their school achievement?

Laurence Steinberg and his associates have compared working and nonworking high school students in terms of such outcomes as autonomy from parents, self-reliance, self-esteem, sense of investment in school, academic performance, delinquency, and drug and alcohol use (Greenberger & Steinberg, 1986; Steinberg & Dornbusch, 1991; Steinberg, Fegley, & Dornbusch, 1993). Overall, this research offers more bad news than good. The good news is that working students seem to gain knowledge about work, consumer issues, and financial management and sometimes about greater self-reliance. However, high school students who worked 20 or more hours a week had lower grade-point averages than students who did not work or who worked only 10 or fewer hours per week (Steinberg & Dornbusch, 1991). Working students were also more likely than nonworkers to be disengaged from school—bored and uninvolved in class, and prone to cut class and spend little time on homework. A recent Canadian study with over 3,000 students found that those who worked more than just 7 hours per week were more likely than peers working few or no hours to report that they intended to drop out of school (Taylor et al., 2012).

In addition, the more adolescents worked, the more independent they were of parental control, the more likely they were to be experiencing psychological distress (anxiety, depression, and physical symptoms such as headaches), and the more frequently they used alcohol and drugs and engaged in delinquent acts. These negative effects of work generally increased as the number of hours a student worked increased.

Jerald Bachman and his colleagues (2003, 2011) have found that not-yet-employed students who want to work long hours tend to be disenchanted with school, have low grades, and are more likely to use alcohol and cigarettes. Once they start working, the disenchantment and problem behaviors are exacerbated (Bachman et al., 2003, 2011). Similarly, longitudinal research on adolescents and work confirms that academically struggling students are the ones likely to work more hours (Warren, LePore, & Mare, 2000). But the negative outcomes associated with working in high school are not entirely attributable to preexisting characteristics of these teens. Bachman and his colleagues (2011) found some negatives of work even when they attempted to control for a variety of preexisting problem behaviors among the teens who worked the most hours during high school. Notably, teens who worked the most were less likely to have completed college when the researchers followed up with them when they were 29–30 years of age.

Somewhat surprising, the teens who were most disadvantaged by working long hours during high school were Whites, especially Whites from high socioeconomic backgrounds, and Asian Americans, relative to Hispanic and African Americans. The latter two groups tend to have more trouble finding employment during high school, so perhaps those who managed to find work are a unique group, for example, more hard working. And Whites from higher socioeconomic homes who work long hours while in high school are probably also an unusual group.

When all the research is examined as a package, the findings suggest that working while attending high school is often more damaging than beneficial. Much depends on the nature of the work adolescents do (Taylor et al., 2012). Many teenagers work in food service jobs (pouring soft drinks behind the counter at fast-food restaurants, scooping ice cream, and the like) or perform manual labor (especially cleaning or janitorial work). These routine and repetitive jobs offer few opportunities for self-direction or decision making and only rarely call on academic skills such as reading and mathematics (Greenberger & Steinberg, 1986). They are not the kinds of jobs that build character or teach new skills. Adolescents experience gains in mastery motivation and become less depressed over time when the work they do provides opportunities for advancement and teaches useful skills, but they lose mastery motivation and become more depressed when they hold menial jobs that interfere with their schooling

(Call, Mortimer, & Shanahan, 1995; Shanahan et al., 1991). Thus, many adolescents who are flipping hamburgers might be better off postponing work or working only a limited number of hours, less than 7 per week, so that they can concentrate on obtaining a solid education and exploring their career options (Taylor et al., 2012).

Pathways to Adulthood

The educational paths and attainments of adolescents are partially set long before they enter adolescence. Because many individuals' IQ test scores remain stable from childhood on, some children enter adolescence with more aptitude for schoolwork than others do (see Chapter 9). Moreover, some students have more achievement motivation than others. Clearly, a bright and achievement-oriented student is more likely to obtain good grades and go on to college and is less likely to drop out of school than a student with less ability and less need to achieve. By early elementary school, and sometimes even before they enter school, future dropouts are often identifiable by such warning signs as low IQ and achievement test scores, poor grades, aggressive behavior, low socioeconomic status, and troubled homes (Bierman et al., 2013; Ensminger & Slusarcick, 1992). Among middle school students, those who regularly smoke cigarettes, drink alcohol, and engage in sexual activity are more likely to drop out of high school than their peers who do not engage in such problem behaviors (Hawkins, Jaccard, & Needle, 2013). Perhaps not surprisingly, students who are victims of bullying also have higher dropout rates (Cornell et al., 2013). But it is often not just a single factor that leads students to drop out or fail out of school. Instead, there is often a combination of two or more factors that place students at risk for failure (Lucio, Hunt & Bornovalova, 2012).

The stakes are high. Students who achieve good grades are more likely to complete high school; recently, 94% of White students, 88% of African American students, 95% of Asian Americans, and an alarmingly low 71% of Hispanic students achieved this milestone (National Center for Education Statistics, 2013). They then stand a chance of being among the 39% of Whites, 20% of African Americans, 56% of Asian Americans, and 13% of Hispanics who complete 4 years of college or more (National Center for Education Statistics, 2013). These youth, in turn, are likely to have higher career aspirations and to end up in higher status occupations than their peers who do not attend college or do not even finish high school (McCaul et al., 1992). If their grades are good, they are likely to perform well in those jobs and advance far in their careers (Roth et al., 1996). In a real sense, then, individuals are steered along "high success" or "low success" routes starting in childhood. Depending on their own decisions and family, peer, and school influences, adolescents are more distinctly "sorted" in ways that will affect their adult lifestyles, income levels, and adjustment. Meanwhile, high school dropouts not only have less successful careers but also miss out on the beneficial effects that every year of schooling has on intellectual functioning (Ceci & Williams, 1997).

Working in fast-food restaurants is not usually the kind of intellectually challenging job that can contribute positively to adolescent development. If a high school student does work during the school year, what guidelines would help ensure a healthy blend of work and academics?

© Jeff Greenberg/PhotoEdit Inc.

In addition, they experience more psychological problems than those who stay in school (Kaplan, Damphousse, & Kaplan, 1994).

Checking Mastery

1. What are two reasons why achievement motivation may decline during adolescence?
2. Why might students in Asian schools outperform many other students in science and math?
3. What is one advantage and one disadvantage of working while in high school?

Making Connections

1. Research shows that achievement motivation and grades often drop as students move through middle school and high school. Develop a program to combat this trend, keeping in mind that students of different backgrounds may lose motivation for different reasons.
2. After finishing up ninth grade, your teenager says he wants to work for the next 3 years while in high school. What advice will you give him?

10.5 The Adult

LEARNING OBJECTIVES:

* Describe language changes in adulthood.
* Explore the achievement motivations of adults.
* Explain the challenges for adults who struggle with literacy.
* Outline pros and cons of continuing education for adults.

The lives of adults are dominated by work—paid or unpaid, outside the home or within the home. We consider, first, how language and achievement motivation change during this period of life. We also examine the educational options available to adults and the benefits of lifelong education.

Language

What happens to language skills during adulthood? Adults simply hold onto the knowledge of phonology they gained as children, although elders can have difficulty distinguishing speech sounds (such as /b/ from /p/) if they have hearing impairments or deficits in the cognitive abilities required to make out what they hear (Thornton & Light, 2006). Adults also retain their knowledge of grammar or syntax. Older adults tend to use less complex sentences than younger adults do, however. Also, those with memory difficulties may have trouble understanding sentences that are highly complex syntactically (for example, "The children warned about road hazards refused to fix the bicycle of the boy who crashed"); they may not be able to remember the beginning of the sentence by the time they get to the end (Kemtes & Kemper, 1997; Stine, Soederberg, & Morrow, 1996).

Meanwhile, knowledge of the semantics of language, of word meanings, often expands during adulthood, at least until people are in their 70s or 80s (Obler, 2013; Schaie, 1996). After all, adults gain experience with the world from year to year, so it is not surprising that their vocabularies continue to grow and that they enrich their understandings of the meanings of words. However, older adults more often have the "tip-of-the-tongue" experience of not being able to recall the name of an object (or especially a person's name) when they need it (Thornton & Light, 2006). This problem is a matter of not being able to retrieve information stored in memory rather than a matter of no longer knowing the words. In order to maintain fluency in the face of these retrieval problems, older adults speak a little more slowly and plan their choice of words further in advance than when they were younger (Spieler & Griffin, 2006).

Adults also refine their pragmatic use of language—adjusting it to different social and professional contexts (Obler, 2013). Physicians, for example, must develop a communication style that is effective with their patients. Partners who have been together for years often develop a unique way of communicating with one another that is distinctly different from how they communicate with others. Overall, command of language holds up well in later life unless the individual experiences major declines in cognitive functioning (Kemper & Mitzner, 2001; Stine et al., 1996).

Achievement Motivation

The level of achievement motivation that we acquire in childhood and adolescence carries into adulthood to influence our decisions and life outcomes (Wlodkowski, 1999). For instance, women who have a strong need to achieve are more likely than less achievement-oriented women to work outside the home (Krogh, 1985). Adults with strong achievement needs are also likely to be more competent workers than adults who have little concern with mastering challenges (Helmreich, Sawin, & Carsrud, 1986; Spence, 1985).

What happens to achievement motivation in later life? Is there any support for the common belief that older adults lose some of their drive to excel? Joseph Veroff, David Reuman, and Sheila Feld (1984) explored this question by analyzing motivational themes in stories that American adults told in response to pictures. Older men displayed only slightly lower levels of achievement motivation than young or middle-aged men did. Here, then, there is no support for the stereotyped idea that older adults are "unmotivated" or have ceased to pursue goals (Filipp, 1996; McAdams, de St. Aubin, & Logan, 1993).

Veroff and his associates (1984) did find that women's achievement motivation declined fairly steeply with age (see also Mellinger & Erdwins, 1985). However, this age trend pertained mainly to career-related motivation and an interest in striving for success in competitive situations. Women's motivation in other areas remained high. Many women have traditionally set aside career-achievement goals after they have children and make nurturing those children their priority (Krogh, 1985). However, highly educated women often regain a strong motive to achieve outside the home once their children are older and they can invest more energy in outside work. Apparently, then, women are especially likely to be motivated to achieve career success when they have the educational background that would allow them to pursue attractive career goals and when they are not pursuing family-related goals.

Overall, adults' achievement-related motives are far more affected by changes in work and family contexts than by the aging process (Filipp, 1996). Adults of different ages are often more alike than they are different, and different people tend to retain their characteristic levels of achievement motivation over the years, much as they retain many personality traits (Stevens & Truss, 1985). There is little evidence that elderly adults inevitably lose their motivation to pursue important goals. Moreover, those elders who have a strong sense of purpose and direction and feel they are achieving their goals enjoy greater physical and psychological well-being than those who do not (Hooker & Siegler, 1993; Rapkin & Fischer, 1992; Reker, Peacock, & Wong, 1987). Throughout the life span, then, setting and achieving goals are important.

Many older adults remain motivated to learn and seek challenging experiences.

© Ian Shaw/Alamy

Literacy

Literacy is the ability to use printed information to function in society, achieve goals, and develop one's potential. Few adults are completely illiterate, but many adults do not have functional literacy skills despite years of formal education. The National Adult Literacy Survey found that about 22% of adults in the United States demonstrate the lowest level of literacy skills, which is roughly equivalent to a third-grade or lower reading ability (Kirsch et al., 2002). Such an adult could probably find an expiration date on a driver's license and sign a form but would have trouble filling out an application or reading a simple book to a child. Although one-quarter of this group consists of immigrants learning English as a second language, most individuals in this group are U.S.-born citizens and nearly two-thirds did not finish high school.

Another 25% of adults have just rudimentary, or basic, literacy skills, allowing them to perform simple literacy tasks such as using a television guide or comparing prices on two receipts, but limiting their abilities to consult reference information online or in texts. Approximately half of the adults demonstrated proficient, or higher, levels of literacy. Literacy contributes to economic security through occupational advancement. Nearly half of the adults with the lowest literacy scores live in poverty, whereas few adults with the highest literacy scores do (Bowen, 1999). Improving the literacy skills of impoverished adults, however, does not automatically raise them out of poverty. For many low-income and functionally illiterate adults, other obstacles must be overcome, including addiction, discrimination, and disabilities (Bowen, 1999).

Programs to raise the literacy level of adults are rarely successful. Several factors limit the success of such programs. For one thing, despite having limited literacy skills, many of these adults (75%) reported that they could read or write "well" or "very well"—attitudes that must make it difficult to motivate them to improve their literacy skills. Second, adults do not stay in literacy programs long enough to make improvements (Amstutz & Sheared, 2000). The dropout rate is as high as 70–80%, and many leave in the first weeks of the program (Quigley & Uhland, 2000). Adults who do not persist report that the programs are boring and do not meet their needs (Imel, 1996; Kerka, 1995; Quigley, 1997). Materials, for example, are often geared toward children, not adults who have families, jobs, and different interests than children do.

Continuing Education

Increasingly, adults are seeking education beyond basic literacy skills. In 2011, 33% of all college students were 25 years or older, and a full 50% of students attending college part-time were over the age of 25 (National Center for Education Statistics, 2013). The number of "older" adults attending college is expected to increase as the overall population ages. Whether we call them adult learners, nontraditionals, returning students, mature students, or lifelong learners, these adults represent a diverse group. They bring different work and life experiences to the classroom, and they report a variety of reasons for enrolling in postsecondary education (Ross-Gordon, 2011).

Many "traditional" students (17- to 24-year-olds) are motivated to attend college by external expectations, but older students are often motivated by internal factors (Ross-Gordon, 2011). Women are more likely to return to the classroom for personal enrichment

Application 10.1

What Can Theory and Research Contribute to Education?

To help you appreciate the practical implications for school reform and school achievement of the material in Chapters 6 through 9, we provide the following recommendations based on the research and theories discussed in these chapters:

Piaget

- Provide opportunities for independent, hands-on interaction with the physical environment, especially for younger children.
- With the child's current level of understanding in mind, create some disequilibrium by presenting new information slightly above the child's current level. Children who experience disequilibrium—cognitive discomfort with their understanding (or lack of understanding)—will work to resolve it, achieving a higher level of mastery of the material.
- Encourage interaction with peers, which will expose children to other perspectives and give them an opportunity to reevaluate and revise their own view.

Vygotsky

- Provide opportunities for children to interact with others who have greater mastery of the material—an older peer, teacher, or parent. These more advanced thinkers can help "pull" children to a level of understanding they would be unable to achieve on their own.

- Encourage students, especially young ones, to talk to themselves as they work on difficult tasks. Such private speech can guide behavior and facilitate thought.
- Present challenging tasks, but do not expect students to complete such tasks successfully without guidance. With support, students can accomplish more difficult tasks than those they would be able to achieve independently.

Research on Information Processing

- Provide opportunities for rehearsal and other memory strategies to move information into long-term memory. Realize that young children do not spontaneously use memory strategies but often can use them when prompted.
- Structure assignments so that retrieval cues are consistent with cues present at acquisition to facilitate retrieval of information from long-term memory.
- Enable learners to develop a knowledge base and expertise in domains of study. When beginning a new lesson, start with and build on what students already know.
- Assess the knowledge and strategies required to solve assigned problems; then determine which aspects of a task pose difficulties for learners and target these for further instruction.

- Be aware that well-learned and frequently repeated tasks become automatized over time, freeing information-processing capacity for other tasks.

Research on Intelligence

- Realize that individual differences in intelligence have implications for the classroom. Students at both ends of the continuum may need special educational services to optimize their learning.
- Recognize that although IQ scores do a reasonably good job of predicting achievement in the classroom, such tests have weaknesses that limit their usefulness, especially in assessing members of minority groups.

Research on Sensory and Perceptual Abilities

- Test all children early and regularly for sensory and perceptual problems that might limit their ability to benefit from regular classroom instruction.
- Be aware of developmental differences in attention span. Clearly, a young child will not be able to attend to a task for as long as a teenager.
- Minimize distractions in the learning environment. Younger students have trouble "tuning out" background noise and focusing on the task at hand.

---

or interest, whereas men are more likely to take classes required or recommended for their work (Sargant et al., 1997). Both men and women today sometimes find that they need further education in order to become employable as the job market changes. The internal motivation of adult students often leads to deeper levels of processing information (Harper & Kember, 1986). In other words, returning students may put forth greater effort to truly understand material because they want to learn and want (or need) to use the material. Traditional students who do not have the benefit of experience may learn the material necessary to do well on an examination but may not process the material in ways that will lead to long-term retention.

Continued or lifelong education has its drawbacks. Mainly, it is often difficult for adults already busy with jobs and family to find the time to take classes. Successful continuing education programs

must devise ways to schedule classes at convenient times and must be responsive to the lifestyles of their adult learners (Parnham, 2001). Yet the benefits of lifelong education typically outweigh drawbacks. For instance, continued education allows adults to remain knowledgeable and competitive in fields that change rapidly. Adults who return to school for bachelor's or master's degrees can also advance their careers, particularly if their education and work are closely related (Senter & Senter, 1997). Finally, you learned in Chapter 5 that higher education is associated with maintaining or improving physical and mental health.

In this and previous chapters, you have examined a great deal of material on thinking and learning across the life span. How can principles of cognitive development be used to improve education for all ages? Before closing this chapter, we summarize, in **Application Box 10.1**, what theorists Piaget and

Vygotsky contribute to education and what research on information processing, intelligence, and perception suggests about optimal learning environments.

Checking Mastery

1. How might men's and women's achievement motivation change during adulthood?
2. Why is literacy important to adults and are literacy programs successful?

Making Connections

1. If you find that one of your parents (or spouse) is going through a midlife "career slump," what might you do to foster a higher level of achievement motivation during this stage of their life?
2. Based on what you have learned in this and previous chapters about memory, thinking, problem solving, and language skills, how would you teach older adult students versus students of traditional high school or college age?

Chapter Summary

10.1 The System of Language

- The complex process of language acquisition appears to occur effortlessly through an interaction of inborn readiness and a normal language environment.
- To acquire language, children must master phonology (sound), semantics (meaning), and syntax (sentence structure). They must also learn how to use language appropriately (pragmatics) and how to understand prosody.
- Theories of language development include learning theories, nativist theories, and interactionist theories. The interactionist view emphasizes the child's biologically based capacities and experience conversing with adults who use child-directed speech and strategies such as expansion that simplify the language-learning task.

10.2 The Infant

- Infants are able to discriminate speech sounds and progress from crying, cooing, and babbling to one-word holophrases (at 12 months) and then to telegraphic speech (at 18 months).
- During the preschool years, language abilities improve dramatically, as illustrated by overregularizations and new transformation rules.
- Precursors of achievement motivation can be seen among infants who strive to master their environments. Mastery motivation is fostered by a responsive environment that provides plenty of opportunities for infants to learn that they can control their environments and experience successes.
- Early education can help prepare disadvantaged children for formal schooling, but an overemphasis on academics at the expense of exploration and play may hinder young children's development.

10.3 The Child

- School-age children and adolescents refine their language skills and become less egocentric communicators.
- During childhood, some children develop higher levels of achievement motivation than others; they tend to have a growth mindset rather than a fixed mindset regarding abilities, and they set learning goals rather than performance goals in the classroom.
- To read, children must master the alphabetic principle and develop phonological awareness so that they can grasp

letter–sound correspondence rules. Emergent literacy activities such as listening to storybooks facilitate later reading. Compared with unskilled readers, skilled readers have better understanding of the alphabetic principle and greater phonological awareness.
- Learning is influenced by characteristics of students and their teachers. Students perform best when (1) they are intellectually capable and motivated; (2) their teachers create a motivating, comfortable, and task-oriented setting and involve parents in their children's schooling; and (3) there is a good fit between children's characteristics and the kind of instruction they receive.

10.4 The Adolescent

- Achievement motivation and grades tend to drop during adolescence for a variety of reasons, including cognitive growth, family characteristics, peer pressure, and a poor fit between the student and the school.
- Middle school and high school include a greater focus on mathematics education. U.S. students score close to the international average but below several other countries in math. Cross-cultural research suggests that the success of Asian schools is rooted in more class time spent on academics, more homework, more parent involvement, more peer support, and a stronger belief that hard work pays off.

10.5 The Adult

- Language skills remain fairly stable throughout adulthood, unless there are substantial sensory impairments or cognitive declines.
- Level of achievement carries over from adolescence into adulthood. There may be some decline in achievement motivation among women who set aside career goals to raise children, but career goals reemerge as their children age, especially among women with higher levels of education.
- Some adults, despite years of education, have not acquired the skills of functional literacy. Literacy programs have had minimal success in improving literacy rates.
- Adults increasingly are seeking continued educational opportunities for both personal and work-related reasons.

Checking Mastery Answers

For answers to Checking Mastery questions, please see Appendix B.

Key Terms

CENGAGE brain.com Get quizzes, flashcards, videos, and more at **www.cengagebrain.com.**

11 Self and Personality

In her memoir *My Beloved World* *(2013)*, Supreme Court Justice Sonia Sotomayor describes her humble beginnings: growing up in a poor, Puerto Rican section of New York City as a child with diabetes, an alcoholic father who died when she was only 9, and an overworked and emotionally distant mother (see Barnes, 2013). Not being sure she could count on her parents and fearing that she would die young, she learned to give herself insulin injections at age 7 and developed a strong independent streak and a drive to succeed that contributed to her later success in law. She had doubts about whether she was as capable as her classmates at Princeton but concluded that some of her deficiencies in knowledge were the product of her background and that she could overcome them through hard work. She also says this about herself: "I think my life approach is never to look at the negative of what I'm experiencing but also always trying to see its positive" (Barnes, 2013, p. C3).

Sonia Sotomayor's life story involved turning experiences of poverty, childhood diabetes, and an alcoholic father into an independence and drive that propelled her to the Supreme Court of the United States.

Sonia Sotomayor, by writing her autobiography, created a life story that defines her as a unique person who overcame challenges and self-doubts and rose to a position of prominence. How would you tell your life story? Who are you and what is unique about you?

This chapter is about the self and the personality and the ways in which personalities, and our perceptions of those personalities, change—and remain the same—over the life span. It is, in other words, about the issue of continuity (consistency or stability) and discontinuity (change) in human development (see Chapter 2). It is also about influences on and implications of our self-concepts and personalities.

11.1 Conceptualizing the Self and Personality

LEARNING OBJECTIVES:

- Define and give examples of the aspects of personality called dispositional traits, characteristic adaptations, and narrative identity.

- Distinguish among self-concept, self-esteem, and identity.

- Compare how psychoanalytic, trait, and social learning theorists view personality and its development.

We begin our inquiry by clarifying some terms used in describing the personality and the self and then consider some very different theoretical perspectives on the self and personality.

Basic Concepts

Personality is often defined as an organized combination of attributes, motives, values, and behaviors unique to each individual. Most people describe personalities in terms of relatively enduring **dispositional traits** such as extraversion or introversion, independence or dependence, and the like. As Dan McAdams and Jennifer Pals (2006) note, though, at least two other aspects of personality besides traits deserve attention. People also differ in **characteristic adaptations**, more situation-specific and changeable ways in which people adapt to their roles and environments. Characteristic adaptations include motives, goals, plans, schemas, self-conceptions, developmental issues and concerns, and coping mechanisms. We differ too in **narrative identities**, unique and integrative life stories that we construct about our pasts and futures to give ourselves an identity and our lives meaning (as Sonia Sotomayor seems to have done). McAdams and Pals believe that both biological factors, including a "human nature" we share with our fellow humans and our individual genetic makeup, and cultural and situational influences help shape these three aspects of personality.

When you describe yourself, you may not be describing your personality so much as revealing your **self-concept**—your perceptions, positive or negative, of your unique attributes and traits as a person. We all know people who seem to have unrealistic self-conceptions—the fellow who thinks he is "God's gift to women" (who do not agree) or the woman who believes she is a dull plodder (but is actually brilliant). A closely related aspect of self-perception is **self-esteem**—your overall evaluation of your worth as a person, high or low, based on all the positive and negative self-perceptions that make up your self-concept. Self-concept is about "what I am," whereas self-esteem concerns "how good I am" (Harter, 1999, 2012). We will examine both, as well as how adolescents pull together their various self-perceptions to form an **identity**—an overall sense of who they are, where they are heading, and where they fit into society.

Theories of Personality

Although these concepts give us a vocabulary for talking about the self and the personality, we also gain perspective on the nature of personality development and how to study it by considering these three major theoretical perspectives: psychoanalytic theory, trait theory, and social learning theory.

Psychoanalytic Theory

Psychoanalytic theorists generally use in-depth interviews and similar techniques to get below the surface of the person and her behavior and to understand the inner dynamics of personality. As you will recall from Chapter 2, Sigmund Freud believed that children progressed through universal stages of psychosexual development, ending with the genital stage of adolescence. Freud did not see psychosexual growth continuing during adulthood. Indeed he believed that the personality was formed during the first 5 years of life and showed considerable continuity thereafter. Anxieties arising from harsh parenting or other unfavorable early experiences in the family, he said, would leave a permanent mark on the personality and reveal themselves in adult personality traits.

The psychosocial theory of personality development formulated by neo-Freudian Erik Erikson, also introduced in Chapter 2, took quite different positions and will be highlighted in this chapter. Like Freud, Erikson concerned himself with the inner dynamics of personality and proposed that people undergo similar personality changes at similar ages as they confront the challenges associated with different stages of development (Erikson, 1963, 1968, 1982). Compared with Freud, however, Erikson placed more emphasis on social influences such as peers, teachers, and cultures; the rational ego and its adaptive powers; and possibilities for overcoming the effects of harmful early experiences. Most importantly, he saw the potential for personal growth and change throughout the life span.

Trait Theory

The approach to personality that has most strongly influenced efforts to study it is trait theory, based on the psychometric approach that guided the development of intelligence tests (see Chapter 9). According to trait theorists, personality is a set of dispositional trait dimensions or continua along which people can differ. (You may want to complete the brief personality scale in **Engagement Box 11.1** before reading further.) To identify distinct trait dimensions, researchers administer personality scales to people and use the statistical technique of factor analysis to identify groupings of personality scale items that are correlated with each other but not with other groupings of items. Trait theorists assume that personality traits are quite consistent across situations and relatively enduring. Like psychoanalytic theorists, then, they expect to see carryover in personality over the years; unlike psychoanalytic theorists,

however, they do not believe that the personality unfolds in a series of stages.

How many personality trait dimensions are there? Many scholars now agree that human personalities can best be described in terms of a five-factor model—with five major dimensions of personality that have come to be known as the **Big Five** (Digman, 1990; McCrae & Costa, 2003, 2008). These five personality dimensions—openness to experience, conscientiousness, extraversion, agreeableness, and neuroticism—are described in ● **Table 11.1**. If you take and score the short personality scale in Engagement Box 11.1, you will get a rough sense of where you fall on these Big Five trait dimensions.

All five trait dimensions in the five-factor model of personality appear to be genetically (but also environmentally) influenced and emerge fairly early in life (Krueger, Johnson, & Kling, 2006; McCrae & Costa, 2008; Yamagata et al., 2006). The Big Five also seem to be universal; they capture the ways in which people all over the world describe themselves and other people (Heine & Buchtel, 2009; McCrae, 2004). This is true even though levels of Big Five traits differ from culture to culture (for example, Europeans appear to be more extroverted on average than Asians or Africans) and even though traits may be expressed differently in different cultures (as when a Chinese extravert smiles warmly at seeing an old friend but an American extravert grins and gives the friend a big bear hug). You will soon learn more about these trait dimensions.

Social Learning Theory

Finally, social learning (or social cognitive) theorists such as Albert Bandura (1986; and see Chapter 2) and Walter Mischel (1973; Mischel & Shoda, 2008) not only reject the notion of universal stages of personality development but also question the existence of enduring personality traits that show themselves in a variety of situations and over long

● **Table 11.1** The Big Five Personality Dimensions

Dimension	Basic Definition	Key Characteristics
Openness to experience	Curiosity and interest in variety vs. preference for sameness	Openness to fantasy, esthetics, feelings, actions, ideas, values
Conscientiousness	Discipline and organization vs. lack of seriousness	Competence, order, dutifulness, striving for achievement, self-discipline, deliberation
Extraversion	Sociability and outgoingness vs. introversion	Warmth, gregariousness, assertiveness, activity, excitement seeking, positive emotions
Agreeableness	Compliance and cooperativeness vs. suspiciousness	Trust, straightforwardness, altruism, compliance, modesty, tender-mindedness
Neuroticism	Emotional instability vs. stability	Anxiety, hostility, depression, self-consciousness, impulsiveness, vulnerability

As a mnemonic device, notice that the first letters of the five dimensions spell *ocean*.
SOURCE: Adapted from Costa & McCrae, 1992.

Engagement 11.1

A Brief Personality Scale

Here are several personality traits that may or may not apply to you. Write a number from 1 to 7 next to each statement to indicate the extent to which you agree or disagree with that statement. You should rate the extent to which the pair of traits applies to you, even if one characteristic applies more strongly than the other.

1 = Disagree strongly   5 = Agree a little
2 = Disagree moderately   6 = Agree moderately
3 = Disagree moderately   7 = Agree strongly
4 = Neither agree nor disagree

I see myself as:

1. _____ Extraverted, enthusiastic
2. _____ Critical, quarrelsome
3. _____ Dependable, self-disciplined
4. _____ Anxious, easily upset
5. _____ Open to new experiences, complex
6. _____ Reserved, quiet
7. _____ Sympathetic, warm
8. _____ Disorganized, careless
9. _____ Calm, emotionally stable
10. _____ Conventional, uncreative

To score yourself, reverse the scoring of items marked below with R so that a score of 1 becomes 7, 2 becomes 6, 3 becomes 5, 4 stays 4, 5 becomes 3, 6 becomes 2, and 7 becomes 1. Then add the pair of scores listed here for each of the Big Five personality dimensions:

Extraversion	Item 1 + item 6R =
Agreeableness	Item 2R + item 7 =
Conscientiousness	Item 3 + item 8R =
Low neuroticism (high emotional stability)	Item 4R + item 9 =
Openness to experience	Item 5 + item 10R =

To help you see roughly where you stand on the Big Five personality dimensions, the average sums for each pair of two items for a sample of 1813 college students tested by Samuel Gosling and colleagues (2003) were 8.88 for extraversion, 10.46 for agreeableness, 10.80 for conscientiousness, 9.66 for low neuroticism (high emotional stability), and 10.76 for openness to experience. Bear in mind that this scale is much shorter than standard measures of the Big Five.

SOURCE: Reprinted from Gosling, S. D., Rentfrow, P. J., & Swann, W. B. (2003). A very brief personality scale. *Journal of Research in Personality, 37*, 525, with permission from Elsevier, © 2003.

stretches of the life span. Instead, they emphasize that people's behavior is influenced by the situations they are in and changes if their environments change and different behaviors are reinforced.

From the social learning perspective, personality boils down to a set of behavioral tendencies shaped by interactions with other people in specific social situations. Because social context is so powerful, consistency in personality over time is most likely if the person's social environment remains the same. Thus, if Rick the rancher continues to run the same ranch in the same small town for a lifetime, he might stay the "same old Rick." However, most of us experience new social environments as we grow older. Just as we behave differently when we are in a library than when we are in a bar, we become "different people" as we take on new roles, develop new relationships, or move to new locations. A great example: Firstborns are often thought to be bossy, and they may well be when they tend younger siblings, but this trait does not necessarily carry over into situations in which they interact with peers who are similar in age and competence and cannot be pushed around as easily as younger brothers and sisters (Harris, 2000, 2006). Different situation, different personality.

Armed with basic concepts and a sense of the strikingly different perspectives psychoanalytic, trait, and social learning theorists take on personality, we will now explore continuity and discontinuity in self-conceptions and personality traits across the life span.

Checking Mastery

1. What is the difference between a dispositional trait and a characteristic adaptation?
2. What is the difference between self-esteem and self-concept?
3. Why do social learning theorists think trait theorists are wrong about personality?

Making Connections

1. Using the concepts of dispositional traits, characteristic adaptations, and narrative identities, the three aspects of personality highlighted by McAdams and Pals, do an analysis of the main features of your own personality. What are your prominent dispositional traits and characteristic adaptations, and what is the plot of your narrative identity or life story?
2. Think about two people you know well and list for each of them five dispositional traits that you believe capture their personalities well. Now look at the Big Five dimensions in Table 11.1 and see if you can match the traits you see in these individuals to the Big Five dimensions and their key characteristics. Based on this analysis, do you agree that the Big Five dimensions capture the main ways in which humans differ—or do you believe that something is missing from the Big Five? Why?

LEARNING OBJECTIVES:

- Explain how we come to know ourselves in the first 2 years of life.

- Summarize three different approaches to describing infants' temperaments and the roles of genes and environment in their development.

When do infants display a sense of themselves as distinct individuals? Do they have unique personalities?

The Emerging Self

Infants may be born without a sense of self, but they quickly develop an implicit, if not conscious, sense of self. It is based in their perceptions of their bodies and actions and grows out of their interactions with caregivers (Rochat, 2010; Rochat & Striano, 2000; Thompson, 2006; Trevarthen, 2011). The capacity to differentiate self from world becomes more apparent by around 2 or 3 months of age as infants display a sense of agency—a sense that they can cause things to happen in the world. For example, 2-month-old infants whose arms are connected by strings to audiovisual equipment delight in producing the sight of a smiling infant's face and the theme from *Sesame Street* by pulling the strings (Lewis, Alessandri, & Sullivan, 1990). When the strings are disconnected and the infants can no longer produce such effects, they pull harder and become frustrated and angry. Over the first 6 months of life, then, infants discover properties of their physical selves, distinguish between the self and the rest of the world, and come to appreciate that they can act upon other people and objects.

In the second half of their first year, infants realize that they and their companions are separate beings with different perspectives, perspectives that can be shared (Thompson, 2006). This is illustrated by the phenomenon of *joint attention*, in which infants about 9 months of age or older and their caregivers share perceptual experiences by looking at the same object at the same time (Mitchell, 1997; Mundy & Acra, 2006; and see Chapter 7). When an infant points at an object and looks toward her companions in an effort to focus their attention on the object, she shows awareness that self and other do not always share the same perceptions.

Around 18 months, infants recognize themselves visually as distinct individuals. To establish this, Michael Lewis and Jeanne Brooks-Gunn (1979) used an ingenious technique first used with chimpanzees to study **self-recognition**—the ability to recognize oneself in a mirror or photograph. Mother daubs a spot of rouge or lipstick on an infant's nose and then places the infant in front of a mirror. If the infant has some mental image of his own face and recognizes his mirror image as himself, he should soon notice the red spot and reach for or wipe his own nose or turn to a companion and point to his own nose rather than touch the nose of the mirror image or look behind the mirror for this interesting new playmate.

When infants 9–24 months old were given this mirror test, the youngest infants showed no self-recognition: they seemed to treat the image in the mirror as if it were "some other baby" and sometimes touched the mirror. Some 15-month-olds recognized themselves, but only starting at 18 months of age did most infants pass the test, showing clear evidence of self-recognition.

Does this boy know that he is the fascinating tot in the mirror? Probably not. Most infants do not master self-recognition until they are 18 months old.

© Joseph Pobereskin/Getty Images

As babies develop, they also form a **categorical self**; that is, they classify themselves into social categories based on age, sex, and other visible characteristics, figuring out what is "like me" and what is "not like me." Before they are 18 months old, toddlers can tell themselves apart from toddlers of the other sex or from older individuals; as they approach age 2, they also become able to distinguish between photos of themselves and photos of other infants of the same sex (Brooks-Gunn & Lewis, 1981; Lewis & Brooks-Gunn, 1979). By 18–24 months, then, most infants have an awareness of who they are—at least as a physical self with a unique appearance and as a categorical self belonging to specific age and gender categories. They now begin to use their emerging language skills to talk about themselves and to construct stories about events in their life, past and present (Thompson, Winer, & Goodvin, 2011).

What contributes to self-awareness in infancy? First, self-recognition depends on *cognitive development* and requires the maturation of certain areas of the brain (Bertenthal & Fischer, 1978; Lewis & Carmody, 2008). Intellectually disabled children are slow to recognize themselves in a mirror but can do so once they have attained a mental age of at least 18 months (Hill & Tomlin, 1981). Second, self-awareness depends on *social interaction*. Chimpanzees who have been raised without contact with other chimps fail to recognize themselves in a mirror as normal chimps do (Gallup, 1979). And human toddlers who have formed secure attachments to their parents are better able to recognize themselves in a mirror and know more about their names and genders than do toddlers whose relationships are less secure (Pipp, Easterbrooks, & Harmon, 1992). Finally, as **Exploration Box 11.1** reveals, how much a child's culture emphasizes individuality and autonomy can make a difference. Throughout life, we forge new self-concepts from the information and feedback we receive from other people (Harter, 2012).

Achieving conscious self-awareness at around 18 months of age, thanks to both cognitive development and social interaction, is an exciting breakthrough that paves the way for other critical emotional and social developments. Toddlers who recognize themselves in the mirror are more able than those who do not to:

- Talk about themselves and to assert their wills (DesRosiers et al., 1999)
- Experience self-conscious emotions such as pride upon mastering a new toy or embarrassment if asked to show off by dancing in front of strangers (Lewis et al., 1989; and see Chapter 14)
- Coordinate their own perspectives with those of other individuals—for example, communicate with playmates by imitating their actions (Asendorpf, Warkentin, & Baudonnière, 1996); cooperate with peers to achieve common goals such as retrieving toys from containers (Brownell & Carriger, 1990); and empathize with peers in distress (Eisenberg, Spinrad, & Sadovsky, 2006)

Temperament

Although it takes infants some time to become aware of themselves as individuals, they have distinctive personalities from the first weeks of life. The study of infant personality has centered on dimensions of **temperament**—early, genetically based but also environmentally influenced tendencies to respond in predictable ways to events that serve as the building blocks of later personality (see Rothbart, 2011; Rothbart & Bates, 2006; Shiner et al., 2012). Learning theorists have tended to view babies as "blank slates" who can be shaped in any number of directions by their experiences. However, it is now clear that babies are not blank slates—that they differ from the start in basic response tendencies. Temperament has been defined and measured in several ways, each of which gives us insights into baby personality (Zentner & Shiner, 2012).

Easy, Difficult, and Slow-to-Warm-Up Temperaments

One of the first attempts to characterize infant temperaments was the influential work of Alexander Thomas, Stella Chess, and their colleagues (Chess & Thomas, 1999; Thomas & Chess, 1986). These researchers gathered information about nine dimensions of infant behavior, including typical mood, regularity or predictability of biological functions such as feeding and sleeping habits, tendency to approach or withdraw from new stimuli, intensity of emotional reactions, and adaptability to new experiences and changes in routine. Based on the overall patterning of these temperamental qualities, most infants could be placed into one of three categories:

- **Easy temperament.** Easy infants are even tempered, typically content or happy, and open and adaptable to new experiences such as the approach of a stranger or their first taste of strained plums. They have regular feeding and sleeping habits, and they tolerate frustrations and discomforts.
- **Difficult temperament.** Difficult infants are active, irritable, and irregular in their habits. They often react negatively (and vigorously) to changes in routine and are slow to adapt to new people or situations. They cry frequently and loudly and often have tantrums when they are frustrated by such events as being restrained or having to live with a dirty diaper.
- **Slow-to-warm-up temperament.** Slow-to-warm-up infants are relatively inactive, somewhat moody, and only moderately regular in their daily schedules. Like difficult infants, they are slow to adapt to new people and situations, but they typically respond in mildly, rather than intensely, negative ways. For example, they may resist cuddling by looking away from the cuddler rather than by kicking or screaming. They eventually adjust, showing a quiet interest in new foods, people, or places.

Of the infants in Thomas and Chess's longitudinal study of temperament, 40% were easy infants, 10% were difficult infants, and 15% were slow-to-warm-up infants. The remaining third could not be clearly placed in one category because they shared qualities of two or more categories. Thomas and Chess went on to study the extent of continuity and discontinuity in temperament from infancy to early adulthood (Chess & Thomas, 1984; Thomas & Chess, 1986). Difficult infants who had fussed when they could not have more milk often became children who fell apart if they could not work mathematics problems correctly. By adulthood, however, an individual's adjustment had little to do with her temperament during infancy, suggesting a good deal of discontinuity over this long time span (Guerin et al., 2003).

Behavioral Inhibition

Jerome Kagan and his colleagues identified another aspect of early temperament that they believe is highly significant—**behavioral inhibition**, or the tendency to be extremely shy, restrained, and distressed in response to unfamiliar people and situations (Kagan, 1994, 2010; Kagan et al., 2007; Kagan & Snidman, 2004). In the language of the Big Five personality dimensions, inhibited children could be considered low in extraversion with some

Exploration **11.1**

Self-Recognition around the World

Does mirror self-recognition develop universally at 18 months of age, or is there cultural variation in this milestone? Joscha Kärtner and colleagues (2012) expected that self-awareness might develop more rapidly in **individualistic cultures**—cultures that emphasize autonomy and encourage children to pursue their own goals as individuals—than in **collectivist cultures**—cultures that emphasize relatedness to others and subordinating individual goals to the goals of the group (see Triandis, 1989, 1995). Parents in individualistic cultures would be likely to help children get to know themselves and their preferences and assert themselves, whereas parents in collectivist cultures would not call attention to the child as an individual and would instead socialize their children to be sensitive to others and respectful of their elders.

The researchers compared the development of mirror self-recognition in two individualistic, or autonomous, cultures (urban Germany and urban India) and two collectivist, or relational, cultures (rural India and the Nso culture in rural Cameroon, Africa). Sure enough, almost all toddlers in the individualistic/urban cultures recognized themselves in a mirror by 18 or 19 months (for example, touched the lipstick mark that had been placed on their face) whereas only a minority of those in the collectivist/rural cultures did.

How can we explain these cultural differences? In case you are wondering, it was not just that rural children had no experience with mirrors. Rural toddlers did have less access to mirrors than urban children, but their performance did not quickly improve over six weekly assessments as would be expected if they just had to get more familiar with mirrors to succeed. Although differences in cognitive development were not ruled out as a reason for cultural differences, the researchers attributed the findings to the cultural differences in mothers' socialization goals. Mothers in the individualistic cultures emphasized goals like getting their children to express their preferences and develop their own interests; mothers in the collectivist cultures focused on goals like sharing and obeying elders. In earlier work (Keller et al., 2005), these researchers had found that urban German mothers engaged in more face-to-face interaction and were more responsive to their 3-month-old babies' actions than rural Nso mothers. Moreover, this maternal responsiveness to the infant as an individual was correlated with later self-recognition. These findings reinforce the broader theme that babies get to know themselves through their social interactions.

Kärtner et al. (2012) concluded that the mirror self-recognition task is culturally valid because, in all four cultural groups studied, accomplishing the task was associated with more use by toddlers of their own names and personal pronouns (Me do it! Mine!). However, Tanya Broesch and her colleagues (2011), after testing children in several different cultures, are not so sure. In Kenya, for example, only 2 of 82 children ranging in age from 18 to 72 months touched the mark that had been put on their face during the mirror self-recognition task; instead, they froze and stared at the mirror. The researchers were convinced that they knew who they were but simply did not know how to react in this situation or perhaps did not think they had permission to remove the mark. If so, this would render the test invalid in this cultural context. So, can cultural differences in self-recognition be traced to differences in socialization goals in individualistic and collectivist cultures or to the use of a test of self-awareness that may be more valid in some cultures than in others? That is a question in need of further research.

---

neuroticism or anxiety thrown in (Muris et al., 2009). Kagan (1989) estimates that about 15% of toddlers have this inhibited temperament, whereas 10% are extremely uninhibited, exceptionally eager to jump into new situations.

At 4 months, behaviorally inhibited infants wriggle, kick their legs, and fuss and fret more than most infants in response to a novel stimulus such as a moving mobile (Fox et al., 2001; Moehler et al., 2008). They become overaroused by things that other babies take in stride. At 21 months, they take a long time to warm up to a strange examiner, retreat from a large robot, and fret and cling to their mothers, whereas uninhibited toddlers readily and enthusiastically engage with strangers, robots, and all manner of new experiences (Kagan, 1994). As children, inhibited youngsters are shy in a group of strange peers and afraid to try a balance beam. And as adolescents, they continue to be wary and cautious in new social situations and worry a lot (Kagan, 2010; Kagan et al., 2007).

Behavioral inhibition is biologically rooted. Individuals with inhibited temperaments display strong brain responses and high heart rates in reaction to unfamiliar stimuli (Kagan et al., 2007; Schwartz et al., 2003), and twin studies suggest that their temperament is genetically influenced (DiLalla, Kagan, & Reznick, 1994).

When this temperament becomes ingrained, behavioral inhibition puts individuals at risk for later anxiety disorders (Fox et al., 2005).

Surgency/Extraversion, Negative Affect, and Effortful Control

Finally, Mary Rothbart and her colleagues (Putnam, Gartstein, & Rothbart, 2006; Rothbart, 2007, 2011; Rothbart, Ahadi, & Evans, 2000; Rothbart & Derryberry, 2002) have gone in a different direction and defined infant temperament not only in terms of reactivity, as Thomas and Chess and Kagan have done, but also in terms of self-regulation. That is, they have focused on how easily we become emotionally aroused and how able we are to control or regulate our arousal. Rothbart became interested in temperament in part because her two boys were so different. The first liked to be rocked or handed a pacifier when he was distressed, but the second son was upset rather than soothed by these things; he preferred low levels of stimulation and wanted to lie quietly by himself to calm himself down (Rothbart, 2011).

Rothbart and her colleagues have identified at least three dimensions of temperament, each with more specific aspects.

The first two are evident from infancy on; effortful control emerges more clearly in toddlerhood and early childhood and continues to develop into adulthood:

- **Surgency/extraversion**—the tendency to actively, confidently, and energetically approach new experiences in an emotionally positive way (rather than to be inhibited and withdrawn).
- **Negative affectivity**—the tendency to be sad, fearful, easily frustrated, and irritable (as opposed to laid back and adaptable).
- **Effortful control**—the ability to focus and shift attention when desired, inhibit responses, and appreciate low-intensity activities such as sitting on a parent's lap. Perhaps you remember the children's game, "Simon Says." Effortful control is illustrated by being able to inhibit an action like hand clapping when the command is "Clap your hands" rather than "*Simon says* clap your hands." At age 3, only 22% can inhibit forbidden actions like this; by age 4, 90% can (Rothbart, 2011).

• **Table 11.2** summarizes the ways in which Thomas and Chess, Kagan, and Rothbart characterize infant temperaments. Today, Rothbart's dimensions of temperament have become especially influential, probably because they share similarities with the Big Five dimensions used to describe adult personality (Rothbart, 2011). Surgency/extraversion clearly matches up well with the Big Five's extraversion, negative affectivity with neuroticism, and effortful control with conscientiousness. In some of her work, Rothbart has also examined an affiliativeness dimension that matches up with agreeableness in the Big Five, and an orienting sensitivity dimension that has to do with curiosity and interest in stimuli and aligns well with openness to experience (Rothbart, 2011). Accumulating evidence suggests that Rothbart and her colleagues are on the right track and that there are meaningful connections between temperament in infancy and early childhood and personality later in life (Saucier & Simonds, 2006; Shiner & Caspi, 2012).

Goodness of Fit

Differences in temperament appear to be rooted in part in genetically based differences in levels of certain neurotransmitters and in the functioning of the brain (Saudino & Wang, 2012). However, prenatal factors such as maternal stress and substance use also help shape it (Huizink, 2012; see Chapter 4). The postnatal environment then helps determine how adaptive particular temperamental qualities are and whether they persist or change (Bates, Schermerhorn, & Petersen, 2012; Rothbart, 2011). Much may depend on what Thomas and Chess call the **goodness of fit**

• **Table 11.2** Summary of Temperament Dimensions

Researchers	Dimensions of Temperament
Thomas and Chess	Easy temperament Difficult temperament Slow-to-warm-up temperament
Kagan	Behaviorally inhibited Uninhibited
Rothbart	Surgency/extraversion Negative affectivity Effortful control

© Cengage Learning

between child and environment—the extent to which the child's temperament is compatible with the demands and expectations of the social world to which she must adapt.

The case of Carl, one of the children studied by Thomas and Chess, illustrates the significance for later personality development of the match between a child's temperament and his social environment. Early in life, Carl was clearly a difficult child: "Whether it was the first bath or the first solid foods in infancy, the beginning of nursery and elementary school, or the first birthday parties or shopping trips, each experience evoked stormy responses, with loud crying and struggling to get away" (Chess & Thomas, 1984, p. 188). Carl's mother became convinced that she was a bad parent, but his father accepted and even delighted in Carl's "lusty" behavior. He patiently and supportively waited for Carl to adapt to new situations. As a result, Carl did not develop serious behavioral problems as a child and became a well-adjusted adult after weathering some adjustment problems when he started college.

If the fit between his difficult temperament and his parents' demands and expectations had been poor—for example, if his parents had been impatient, angry, and overly demanding instead of sensitive—research suggests Carl might have been headed for serious behavioral problems and poor adjustment

Loisjoy Thurstun/Bubbles/Photolibrary/Alamy

Difficult or behaviorally inhibited children may remain so if there is a "bad fit" between them and an impatient parent.

(Guerin et al., 2003; Leerkes, Blankson, & O'Brien, 2009). Similarly, behaviorally inhibited children are likely to remain inhibited if their parents are either overprotective or angry and impatient, but can overcome their inhibition if their parents create a good fit by preparing them for potentially upsetting experiences and making reasonable but firm demands that they cope (Kagan, 1994).

The moral for parents is clear: Get to know your baby as an individual, and allow for his personality quirks. Infants' temperaments and their parents' parenting reciprocally influence one another and interact over time to steer the direction of later personality development (Bates et al., 2012). Training parents of irritable, difficult babies in how to interpret their infants' cues and respond sensitively and appropriately to them can produce calmer infants who cry less and become less irritable preschoolers (van den Boom, 1995; Crockenberg & Leerkes, 2003). Interventions can also help parents of school-aged children and their teachers understand and interact effectively with children who have difficult temperaments and prevent emotional and behavioral problems (McClowry & Collins, 2012).

▶ Checking Mastery

1. What important development in the self happens at around 18 months of age, and what makes it possible?
2. In Rothbart's terms, Serena is low in surgency/extraversion, high in negative affectivity, and low in effortful control. How would (a) Thomas and Chess and (b) Kagan likely describe Serena?

▶ Making Connections

1. The mirror test has become the main way of assessing self-awareness in infants. What do you see as the strengths and limitations of this approach? Can you think of other ways to assess infant self-awareness?
2. Gracie the toddler throws fits when her routines are changed, a stranger comes to visit, or she is asked to try something she has never tried before. Using two different systems for analyzing temperament, help her parents understand her temperament and, more importantly, what they can do to help her become as well adjusted as possible.

11.3 The Child

LEARNING OBJECTIVES:

- Summarize how children's self-concepts typically change as they get older.
- Explain the multidimensional and hierarchical nature of self-esteem and the factors that contribute to its being high or low.
- Assess the implications of personality in early childhood for later personality and adjustment.

Children's personalities continue to form, and children acquire much richer understandings of themselves as individuals, as they continue to experience cognitive growth and interact with other people during the preschool and school years.

Elaborating on a Sense of Self

Once toddlers begin to talk, they can and do tell us about their emerging self-concepts. By age 2, many toddlers are already using the personal pronouns *I*, *me*, *my*, and *mine* (or their names) when referring to the self and *you* when addressing a companion (Lewis & Brooks-Gunn, 1979; Stipek, Gralinski, & Kopp, 1990). Toddlers also reveal their emerging categorical selves when they describe themselves in terms of age and sex ("Katie big girl"). Parent–child conversations that focus on the children's experiences and the emotions associated with them help young children pull together what they know of themselves into a consistent self-concept (Bird & Reese, 2006; Thompson et al., 2011).

The preschool child's emerging self-concept is concrete and physical (Damon & Hart, 1988; Harter, 2012). Asked to describe themselves, preschoolers note their physical characteristics, possessions, physical activities and accomplishments, and preferences. One exuberant 3-year-old described herself this way:

> I'm 3 years old and I live in a big house with my mother and father and my brother, Jason, and my sister, Lisa. I have blue eyes and a kitty that is orange and a television in my own room. I know all of my ABC's, listen: A, B, C, D, E, F, G, H, J, L, K, O, M, P, Q, X, Z. I can run real fast. I like pizza and I have a nice teacher at preschool. I can count up to 100, want to hear me? I love my dog Skipper. (Harter, 2012, p. 29)

Few young children mention their psychological traits or inner qualities. At most, young children use global terms such as *nice* or *mean* and *good* or *bad* to describe themselves and others (Livesley & Bromley, 1973). However, their descriptions of their characteristic behaviors and preferences ("I like to play by myself at school") may provide the foundation for later personality trait descriptions ("I'm shy"; Eder, 1989).

Self-conceptions emphasize psychological and social qualities more by around age 8, thanks in part to cognitive growth (Harter, 2012). First, children begin to describe their enduring qualities using personality trait terms such as *funny* and *smart* (Harter, 2012; Livesley & Bromley, 1973). Second, children form social identities, defining themselves as part of social groups ("I'm a Kimball, a second-grader at Brookside School, a Brownie Scout"; Damon & Hart, 1988). Third, they become more capable of **social comparison**—of using information about how they compare with other individuals to characterize and evaluate themselves (Frey & Ruble, 1985; Pomerantz et al., 1995). The preschooler who said she could hit a baseball becomes the elementary school child who says she is a better batter than her teammates.

Young children typically think they are quite wonderful, even in the face of compelling evidence that they have been outclassed by other kids (Butler, 1990; Diehl et al., 2011; but see Rhodes and Brickman, 2008, for evidence that even 4- and 5-year-olds can be crushed by failure experiences on occasion—such as when they are outdone by a member of the other sex!). By first grade, children are very interested in social comparisons and more aware of their implications. They glance at each other's papers, ask "How many did you miss?" and say things like "I got more right than you did" (Frey & Ruble, 1985; Pomerantz et al., 1995). As they get older, children learn to be more diplomatic about what they say when they outdo others, but they increasingly use social comparisons to evaluate their strengths and weaknesses (Diehl et al., 2011).

Self-Esteem

As children amass a range of perceptions of themselves and engage in social comparisons, they begin to evaluate their worth. Susan Harter (2003, 2012) has developed self-perception scales for use with different age groups and has found that self-esteem becomes more differentiated or *multidimensional* with age. Preschool children distinguish only two broad aspects of self-esteem: their competence (both physical and cognitive) and their personal and social adequacy (for example, their social acceptance). By mid–elementary school, children differentiate among five aspects of self-worth:

- scholastic competence (feeling smart or doing well in school)
- social acceptance (being popular or feeling liked)
- behavioral conduct (staying out of trouble)
- athletic competence (being good at sports)
- physical appearance (feeling good-looking)

When Harter's scale was given to third- through ninth-graders, even third-graders showed that they had well-defined senses of where they stood, high or low, in each of these five areas. As children get older, they also integrate their self-perceptions in these distinct domains to form an overall, abstract sense of self-worth (Harter, 2012; Marsh & Ayotte, 2003). Now self-esteem is not only *multidimensional* but *hierarchical* in nature. Picture global self-worth at the top of the hierarchy and the five specific dimensions of self-concept below it.

The accuracy of children's self-evaluations increases steadily over the elementary school years (Harter, 2012; Marsh, Craven, & Debus, 1999). Children as young as 5 years already have some sense of whether they are worthy and lovable (Verschueren, Buyck, & Marcoen, 2001). However, the self-esteem scores of young children sometimes reflect their desires to be liked or to be good at various activities more than their true competencies (Harter, 2012). Around age 8, children's self-evaluations become more accurate—more consistent with objective indicators. For example, those with high scholastic self-esteem are more likely than those with low scholastic self-esteem to be rated as intellectually competent by their teachers, and those with high athletic self-esteem are frequently chosen by peers to be on sports teams (Harter, 2012).

At the same time, children are forming an ever grander sense of what they "should" be like—an **ideal self**. With age, the gap between the real self and the ideal self increases; older children therefore run a greater risk than younger children do of thinking that they fall short of what they should be (Glick & Zigler, 1985; Oosterwegel & Oppenheimer, 1993). Social comparisons that do not always come out well, a widening gap between the real self and the ideal self, and a tendency for parents and teachers to "raise the bar" and give older children more critical feedback than they give younger children all contribute to a decrease in average self-esteem from early to middle childhood (Harter, 2012).

Influences on Self-Esteem

Why do some children develop higher self-esteem than others? Part of the answer lies in genes; this may surprise you but self-esteem, like most human characteristics, is heritable (Kamakura, Ando, & Ono, 2007). Experiences are also important: Some children discover that they are more competent than other children, and, apart from their competence, some children receive more positive social feedback (Harter, 2012).

Children who are more capable than other children experience more success in areas important to them and come out better in social comparisons. Thus, for example, achievement in school has a positive effect on academic self-concept (Guay, Marsh, & Boivin, 2003; Marsh & Craven, 2006). However, even when two children are equally competent and do equally well in social comparisons, social feedback from parents, teachers, and peers can make a big difference in their self-perceptions. Most notably, children with high self-esteem tend to be securely attached to parents who are warm and democratic (Arbona & Power, 2003; Coopersmith, 1967). Loving parents frequently communicate approval and acceptance rather than saying, through words, looks, or actions, "Why can't you be better?" (Doyle, Markiewicz, et al., 2000). Democratic parents who establish and enforce clear rules of behavior but allow their children to participate in decisions give children a basis for evaluating their behavior and tell them that their opinions count. The relationship between high self-esteem and a warm, democratic parenting style holds up in a variety of ethnic groups in the United States as well as in a variety of countries (Scott, Scott, & McCabe, 1991; Steinberg, Dornbusch, & Brown, 1992).

Once a child's level of self-esteem has been established, it tends to remain surprisingly stable over the elementary school years. Moreover, high self-esteem is positively correlated with a variety of measures of good adjustment (Coopersmith, 1967; Harter, 2012). Yet interventions can sometimes boost the self-esteem of children who are low in it in specific areas such as mathematics (Harter, 2012; O'Mara et al., 2006). So, self-esteem is both important and modifiable.

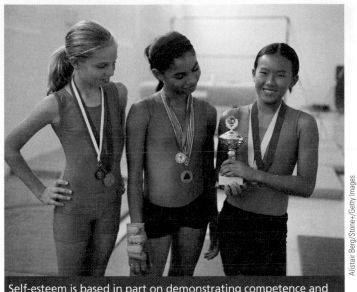
Self-esteem is based in part on demonstrating competence and coming out well in social comparisons.

Nonetheless, William Damon (1994), Susan Harter (2012), and other observers believe that American parents and educators go overboard in trying to make all children feel good about themselves, giving them stickers, stars, and well-meaning shouts of "Good job!" at every turn. These critics note the failure of California's self-esteem movement in the 1990s to improve school achievement and reduce problems like drug abuse (Harter, 2012). They emphasize that self-esteem means little unless it grows out of a child's real achievements. Moreover, they say, children need opportunities to learn about their limitations and develop a realistic sense of self as they progress through school. Giving children an inflated and unrealistic sense of their worth is likely to do more harm than good in the end—for example, by undermining their motivation to improve. What we need to appreciate is that self-esteem and outcomes like school performance often influence one another reciprocally (Marsh & Craven, 2006). From this perspective, it will not work in the long run to tell children they are the greatest when they can see for themselves that they are not. However, helping children succeed at important tasks can boost their self-esteem, and higher self-esteem can then help fuel future achievements.

The Developing Personality

For many years, research on infant temperament and research on adult personality went their separate ways. Now they are coming together. The early response tendencies called temperament are elaborated into a predictable personality during childhood, which then predicts later personality and adjustment (Shiner & Caspi, 2012). For example, in a longitudinal study of 1,000 children in New Zealand, Avshalom Caspi and his colleagues (Caspi, 2000; Caspi et al., 2003) found that inhibited, overcontrolled 3-year-olds who are shy and fearful tend to become teenagers who are cautious and unassertive and later become young adults who have little social support, tend to be depressed, and

are not very engaged in life. By contrast, 3-year-olds who are irritable, highly emotional, and lacking in self-control tend to be difficult to manage later in childhood and end up as impulsive adolescents and adults who do not get along well with other people at home and on the job, are easily upset, get into scrapes with the law, and abuse alcohol. Finally, well-adjusted ("easy") 3-year-olds tend to remain well adjusted.

As noted already, dimensions of early temperament, especially Rothbart's, are related to Big Five personality traits later in life (Hagekull & Bohlin, 1998; Rothbart, 2011; Shiner & Caspi, 2012). Self-control in childhood, an outgrowth of Rothbart's effortful-control dimension of temperament, seems to be especially predictive of good developmental outcomes. Self-controlled children do well in school, are socially and morally mature, and have fewer adjustment problems than their less self-controlled peers (Rueda, 2012). They even go on to be healthier, more financially stable, and less likely to get into trouble with substance use and crime in their 30s (Moffitt et al., 2011; and see Mischel et al., 2011, and Chapter 13). Highly self-regulated individuals have willpower; they are able to focus on their long-term goals, act responsibly to pursue them, and resist temptations that might distract them.

Despite such evidence of continuity between early temperament and later personality, however, we cannot accept Freud's view that the personality is mostly formed by age 5. Personalities change in response to parenting, cultural pressures, and other environmental influences. As a result, correlations between early childhood traits and adult traits are usually quite small. Moreover, some dimensions of personality do not seem to "gel" until the elementary school years, when children's traits begin to predict their adolescent and adult personality and adjustment much better (Tackett et al., 2008). Indeed, some aspects of personality do not seem to stabilize until adolescence or even adulthood, as we will see later (Caspi & Roberts, 2001; McCrae & Costa, 2003). Overall, then, the older the individual, the more accurately personality traits predict later personality and adjustment.

The goodness-of-fit concept can help explain continuity and change in children's personalities. One key finding is that traits are more likely to persist if they are valued by a culture than if they are not (Rothbart, 2011). This may be because culture can affect whether certain personality traits are viewed as adaptive or maladaptive. A wonderful illustration is research by Xinyin Chen and his colleagues on the implications of shyness for children in Eastern and Western cultures (see Chen, Cen, Li, & He, 2005; Chen, Wang, & Wang, 2009; Chen, Yang, & Fu, 2012). In North America's individualistic culture, where autonomy and initiative are valued, shyness can be a liability, sometimes predicting poor functioning at school and in social relationships, low self-esteem, and even depression. In China's collectivist culture, by contrast, the self-effacing personality of the shy child is prized and predicts good social adjustment, success in school, and psychological well-being. Interestingly, shyness continues to be an asset in rural China today, but it has become correlated with poor adjustment in urban areas of China where Western capitalism is rapidly taking hold and a more forceful, outgoing personality is now valued (Chen et al., 2005, 2009). In this and other ways, the historical and cultural environment shapes personality development (Chen et al., 2012).

▶ Checking Mastery

1. What are three major ways in which the self-description of 9-year-old Alonzo might differ from that of his brother, 4-year-old Jamal?

2. What are three main reasons that Lisa may have developed high self-esteem?

3. How does the adaptiveness of shyness differ in individualistic versus collectivist cultures?

▶ Making Connections

1. Some educators believe that nurturing high self-esteem in all children is critical; they favor giving all children lots of positive feedback and sparing them from failure experiences so that they will feel competent. What are the pros and cons of doing this, and what does research say about it?

2. Revisit the Big Five personality dimensions in Table 11.1. If you wanted to determine whether these trait dimensions are evident at age 2, how would you go about doing so?

11.4 The Adolescent

LEARNING OBJECTIVES:

• Discuss how self-descriptions and self-esteem typically change between childhood and adolescence.

• Explain how identity formation in adolescence has been studied and what has been learned about progress in such key areas as ethnic identity and vocational identity.

• Identify and illustrate the major influences on the achievement of identity.

Perhaps no period of the life span is more important to the development of the self than adolescence. Adolescence is truly a time for "finding oneself," as research on adolescent self-conceptions, self-esteem, and identity formation illustrates.

Self-Concept

Raymond Montemayor and Marvin Eisen (1977) learned a great deal about the self-concepts of children and adolescents in grades 4–12 by asking students to write 20 different answers to the question "Who am I?" How would you answer that question? And, looking at **Engagement Box 11.2**, how would you describe the developmental trends evident there in the answers given by a 9-year-old, an 11½-year-old, and a 17-year-old?

Self-descriptions change considerably between childhood and adolescence (Damon & Hart, 1988; Harter, 2012). Self-conceptions:

• become *less physical and more psychological* (contrast "I have brown eyes" with "I am lonely" in Engagement 11.2).

• become *less concrete and more abstract*, thanks to cognitive development (contrast "I love! sports" with "I am a truthful person" or the even more abstract "I am a pseudoliberal").

• become *more differentiated*; for example, the child's "social self," which reflects perceived acceptance by peers, splits into three distinct aspects: acceptance by the larger peer group, acceptance by close friends, and acceptance by romantic partners (Harter, 2012), and adolescents appreciate that they are different "selves" in different social contexts—for example, with family versus with friends (Diehl et al., 2011; Harter & Monsour, 1992).

• become *more integrated and coherent; thus, children and young a*dolescents who do not recognize inconsistencies in their behavior—for example, that they are happy in some situations, grumpy in others—start to notice and be bothered by such inconsistencies in their mid-teens and then, in their late teens, can integrate such discrepant self-perceptions, perhaps explaining that they are moody or that they are happier around people who accept them than around people who are critical of them (Harter & Monsour, 1992).

• reflect *greater self-awareness* as adolescents think more about the self and sometimes become painfully self-conscious (Harter, 2012).

In sum, from childhood to adolescence and over the course of adolescence, self-understandings become more psychological, abstract, differentiated, and integrated, while self-awareness increases. Many adolescents even become sophisticated personality theorists who reflect for hours upon the workings of their own personalities and those of their companions.

Self-Esteem

Self-esteem tends to decrease from childhood to early adolescence for a number of reasons. Adolescents become more knowledgeable and realistic about their strengths and weaknesses (Jacobs et al., 2002; Robins et al., 2002), can become temporarily unsure of themselves when they move from elementary school to middle school or junior high school (Cole et al., 2001), and often become unhappy with their changing bodies (Paxton et al., 2006). This early adolescent dip in self-esteem affects only some teens, though. It is most common among white females, especially those facing multiple stressors at once—for example, entering middle school, coping with pubertal changes, beginning to date, and so on (Gray-Little & Hafdahl, 2000; Simmons et al., 1987). Experiencing a change in the peers available for

How Do Self-Conceptions Change with Age?

What do these three answers to the question, "Who am I?" say about how self-conceptions change with age? Come to your own conclusions and then compare them to those in Section 11.4.

9-year-old: My name is Bruce C. I have brown eyes. I have brown hair . . . I have great! eye sight. I have lots! of friends. I live at . . . I have an uncle who is almost 7 feet tall. My teacher is Mrs. V. I play hockey! I'm almost the smartest boy in the class. I love! food . . . I love! school.

11½-year-old: My name is A. I'm a human being . . . a girl . . . a truthful person. I'm not pretty. I do so-so in my studies. I'm a very good cellist. I'm a little tall for my age. I like several boys . . . I'm old fashioned. I am a very good swimmer . . . I try to be helpful . . . Mostly I'm good, but I lose my temper.

17-year-old: I am a human being . . . a girl. . . an individual . . . I am a Pisces. I am a moody person . . . an indecisive person . . . an ambitious person. I am a big curious person . . . I am lonely. I am an American (God help me). I am a Democrat. I am a liberal person. I am a radical. I am conservative. I am a pseudoliberal. I am an Atheist. I am not a classifiable person (i.e., I don't want to be). (Montemayor & Eisen, 1977, pp. 317–318)

social comparison—for example, moving from a regular class to a gifted or advanced class—can also depress self-esteem (Marsh et al., 1995).

In the end, though, adolescence is not as hazardous to self-esteem as most people believe. Although some adolescents do experience drops in self-esteem in early adolescence, most emerge from this developmental period with higher self-esteem than they had at the start (Donnellan, Trzesniewski, & Robins, 2006; Erol & Orth, 2011). Assuming that adolescents have opportunities to feel competent in areas important to them and to experience the approval and support of parents, peers, and other important people in their lives, they are likely to feel good about themselves (Harter, 2012). It matters: As adults, adolescents with high self-esteem tend to have better physical and mental health, better career and financial prospects, and lower involvement in criminal behavior than adolescents with low self-esteem (Trzesniewski et al., 2006).

Forging a Sense of Identity

Erik Erikson (1968) characterized adolescence as a critical period in the lifelong process of forming an identity as a person and proposed that adolescents experience the psychosocial conflict of **identity versus role confusion**. The concept of *identity*, as noted at the start of the chapter, refers to a definition of who you are, where you are going, and where you fit into society. To achieve a sense of identity, the adolescent must integrate the varied perceptions that are part of the self-concept into a coherent sense of self. The search for identity involves grappling with many important questions: What kind of career do I want? What religious, moral, and political values can I really call my own? Who am I as a man or woman and as a sexual being? Where do I fit in?

If you have struggled with such issues, you can appreciate the uncomfortable feelings that adolescents may experience when they cannot seem to work out a clear sense of who they are. Erikson believed that many young people in complex societies such as the United States experience a full-blown and painful "identity crisis." There are many reasons they might do so. First, their bodies are changing and they must revise their body images (an important part of their self-concepts) and adjust to being sexual beings. Second, cognitive growth allows adolescents to think systematically about hypothetical possibilities, including ideal selves and possible future selves. Third, social demands are placed on them to "grow up"—to decide what they want to do in life and to get on with it. According to Erikson (1968), our society supports youths by allowing them a **moratorium period**— a time during the high school and college years when they are relatively free of responsibilities and can experiment with different roles to find themselves. But complex societies like ours also make establishing an identity hard by giving youths a huge number of options and encouraging them to believe they can be anything they want to be.

Adolescents sometimes experiment with a variety of looks in their search for a sense of identity.

Developmental Trends

James Marcia (1966) expanded on Erikson's theory and stimulated much research on identity formation by developing an interview procedure to assess where an adolescent is in the process of identity formation. Adolescents are classified into one of four identity statuses based on their progress toward an identity in each of several domains (for example, occupational, religious, and political–ideological). The key questions are whether an individual has experienced a *crisis* (or has seriously grappled with identity issues and explored alternatives) and whether he has achieved a *commitment* (that is, resolved the questions raised and settled on an identity). On the basis of crisis and commitment, the individual is classified into one of the four identity statuses shown in ■ **Figure 11.1**.

How long does it take to achieve a sense of identity? Philip Meilman's (1979) study of college-bound boys between 12 and 18, 21-year-old college males, and 24-year-old young men provides interesting answers (■ **Figure 11.2**). Most of the 12- and 15-year-olds were in either the identity diffusion status or the identity foreclosure status. At these ages, many adolescents simply have not yet thought about who they are—either they have no idea or they know that any ideas they do have could change next month (the **diffusion status**, with no crisis and no commitment). Other adolescents have made commitments, may say things like "I'm going to be a doctor like my dad," and appear to have their acts together. However, it becomes apparent that they have never thought through on their own what suits them best or investigated alternatives; they have simply accepted identities suggested to them by their parents or other people (the **foreclosure status**, involving a commitment without a crisis).

As Figure 11.2 indicates, progress toward identity achievement becomes more evident starting at age 18. Notice that diffusion drops off steeply and more individuals begin to fall into the **moratorium status**. Now they are experiencing a crisis or actively exploring identity issues; now they may be questioning their religious upbringing, experimenting with drugs, changing majors or relationships, or putting outrageous postings in Facebook, all to find themselves. Presumably, entering the moratorium status is a good sign; if the individual can not only raise questions but answer them, he will move to the **identity achievement status**. About 20% of the 18-year-olds, 40% of the college students, and slightly more than half of the 24-year-olds in Meilman's study had achieved a firm identity based on a careful weighing of alternatives.

Females progress toward achieving a clear sense of identity at about the same rate as males do (Kroger, 2007). However, one reliable sex difference has been observed: Although college women are just as concerned about establishing a career identity as men are, they attach greater importance to and think more about the aspects of identity that center on sexuality, interpersonal relations, and balancing career and family goals (Archer, 1992; Kroger, 2007). These concerns probably reflect the influence of traditional gender roles.

Judging from such research, identity formation *takes a long time*. Still, many young men and women move from the diffusion or the foreclosure status to the moratorium status and achievement status in their late teens or early 20s, during the period of emerging adulthood (Kroger, 2007; Waterman, 1982). But this is by no means the end of the identity formation process. Some adults continue in a moratorium status for years; others reopen the question of who they are and recycle through the identity statuses after thinking they had all the answers earlier in life (Anthis & LaVoie, 2006; Kroger, 2007). Even in late adulthood, some adults are reworking and strengthening their sense of identity (Zucker, Ostrove, & Stewart, 2002).

Identity formation not only takes a long time but *occurs at different rates in different domains of identity*. For example, Sally Archer (1982) assessed the identity statuses of 6th- to 12th-graders in four domains: occupational choice, gender-role attitudes, religious beliefs, and political ideologies. Only 5% of the adolescents were in the same identity status in all four areas, and more than 90% were in two or three statuses across the four areas. Finally, identity formation is messy; rather than proceeding along one standard path, it takes a variety of paths (Reis & Youniss, 2004). Some adolescents undergo a number of changes in Marcia's identity statuses—some in the direction of identity achievement, but others reflecting reconsideration of earlier

Commitment?

	No Commitment Made	Commitment Made
No Crisis Experienced	**Diffusion Status** The individual has not yet thought about or resolved identity issues and has failed to chart directions in life. Example: "I haven't really thought much about religion, and I guess I don't know what I believe exactly."	**Foreclosure Status** The individual seems to know who he or she is but has latched onto an identity prematurely with little thought. Example: "My parents are Baptists, and I'm a Baptist; it's just the way I grew up."
Crisis Experienced	**Moratorium Status** The individual is experiencing an identity crisis, actively raising questions, and seeking answers. Example: "I'm in the middle of evaluating my beliefs and hope that I'll be able to figure out what's right for me. I've become skeptical about some of what I have been taught and am looking into other faiths for answers."	**Identity Achievement Status** The individual has resolved his/her identity crisis and made commitments to particular goals, beliefs, and values. Example: "I really did some soul-searching about my religion and other religions, too, and finally know what I believe and what I don't."

*(left axis label: **Crisis?**)*

© Cengage Learning

■ **Figure 11.1** The four identity statuses as they apply to religious identity.

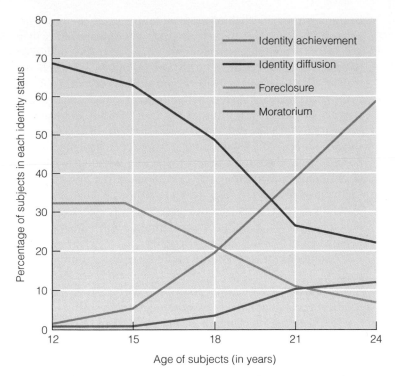

■ **Figure 11.2** Percentage of subjects in each of James Marcia's four identity statuses as a function of age. Note that only 4% of the 15-year-olds and 20% of the 18-year-olds had achieved a stable identity.

Source: From Meilman, P. W. Cross-sectional age changes in ego identity status during adolescence. *Developmental Psychology, 15*, 230–231.

identities and backsliding; many other adolescents remain in the same identity status for years, as though their identity status were part of their personality (Meeus et al., 2010). In short, identity formation takes a long time, occurs at different rates in different domains, and plays out in a variety of ways.

Other researchers have looked at identity formation by studying adolescents' *narrative identities*, those life stories that tell our personal histories, imagine our futures, and give our lives meaning and purpose (McAdams, 2008, 2011; McAdams & Pals, 2006). In a study of narrative identity, you might be asked to picture your life as a book, outline the major scenes and turning points that have defined who you are, and lay out your dreams and fears for the future. A life story, much like an identity in Erikson's sense, says "who I am, how I came to be, and where my life is going in the future" (McAdams, 2005, p. 241). And indeed, constructing a meaningful life story during late adolescence or emerging adulthood and making progress through Marcia's identity statuses toward identity achievement are correlated (McLean & Pratt, 2006). Life stories then become an important element of our adult personalities and are revised over the years and reflected upon in old age (Birren & Schroots, 2006). Watch three adolescents in **Exploring Development Box 11.1** talk about their future.

Developing a Positive Ethnic Identity

An important aspect of identity development is forging an **ethnic identity**—a sense of personal identification with an ethnic group and its values and cultural traditions (Phinney, 1996, 2006;

Umaña-Taylor & Alfaro, 2006). Although everyone has an ethnic and racial background, members of minority groups tend to put more emphasis than majority group adolescents on defining who they are ethnically or racially. White adolescents in the United States may not even think of themselves as having an ethnicity (Bracey, Bamaca, & Umaña-Taylor, 2004; Laursen & Williams, 2002).

The process of forming an ethnic identity begins in infancy as babies notice differences among people. Three-month-old Caucasian infants already show a preference for looking at other Caucasian babies rather than at babies from other ethnic backgrounds (Kelly et al., 2005). African babies show a similar preference for African faces, though not if they grow up among Caucasians, suggesting that babies form these preferences based on the faces they see most often (Bar-Haim et al., 2006).

During the preschool years, children learn about different racial and ethnic categories and gradually become able to classify themselves correctly into one (Spencer & Markstrom-Adams, 1990). For example, Mexican American preschool children may learn behaviors associated with their culture, such as how to give a Chicano handshake, but may not learn until about age 8 what ethnic labels apply to them or that their ethnicity will last a lifetime (Bernal & Knight, 1997). During elementary school, children learn a lot more about their ethnic group and can talk about it in terms of qualities such as language, physical appearance, heritage, and status in society (Rogers et al., 2012).

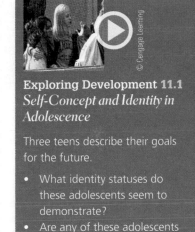

Exploring Development 11.1
Self-Concept and Identity in Adolescence

Three teens describe their goals for the future.

- What identity statuses do these adolescents seem to demonstrate?
- Are any of these adolescents likely to achieve their goals?

In forming a positive ethnic identity, adolescents seem to proceed through the same identity statuses as they do in forming a vocational or religious identity (Phinney, 1993; Seaton, Scottham, & Sellers, 2006). School-age children and young adolescents say either that they identify with their racial or ethnic group because their parents and others in their ethnic group influenced them to do so (foreclosure status) or that they have not given the matter much thought (diffusion status). In their mid- to late teens, many minority youths move into the moratorium and achievement statuses with respect to ethnic identity (Seaton et al., 2006). Others do not reflect on their ethnic identity until their 20s, especially if they have grown up in a homogenous environment and have had little interaction with other ethnic and racial groups (Phinney, 2006).

What are the ingredients of a positive ethnic identity? Youth are most likely to explore ethnic identity issues, establish a positive ethnic identity, and enjoy high self-esteem when their parents socialize them regarding their ethnicity by teaching them about their group's cultural traditions, preparing them to live in a culturally diverse society, and even preparing them to deal with prejudice, at least as long as it is done in a way that does not breed anger

Establishing a positive ethnic identity is more central for minority adolescents than for white ones.

and mistrust (Hughes et al., 2006; Neblett et al., 2008; Umaña-Taylor, Bhanot, & Shin, 2006; Umaña-Taylor & Guimond, 2010).

Once formed, a positive ethnic identity can protect adolescents from the damaging effects of racial or ethnic discrimination (Neblett, Rivas-Drake, & Umaña-Taylor, 2012; Wong, Eccles, & Sameroff, 2003), contribute to high overall self-esteem (Bracey et al., 2004; Umaña-Taylor, Gonzales-Backen, & Guimond, 2009), help promote academic achievement and good adjustment (Laursen & Williams, 2002; Rodriguez et al., 2009), and reduce depression symptoms (Mandara et al., 2009). For immigrant youth, both identifying as a member of an ethnic group and identifying as an American can be beneficial (Kiang, Witkow, & Champagne, 2012). Overall, most minority adolescents cope well with the special challenges they face in identity formation. They settle their questions of ethnic identity, resolve other identity issues around the same ages that European American youth do (Markstrom-Adams & Adams, 1995), and wind up feeling at least as good about themselves (Gray-Little & Hafdahl, 2000).

Vocational Identity and Choice

I wanted to be a firefighter, then I touched a spark. I'm too afraid. I wanted to be a teacher, then I babysat for a 4-year-old. I'm too impatient. I wanted to be a model, then I looked in the mirror. I'm too short.

I know, I know—I can be anything I want when I am all grown up. But I am rapidly approaching all grown up and I see less of what I can be and more of what I cannot be. (Kelly Witte, *The Washington Post*, April 2, 2006, p. D1)

Vocational identity is a central aspect of identity with major implications for adult career development. How do adolescents choose career paths? Children younger than about age 10 actively explore vocational possibilities but their choices often reflect fantasy rather than reality; they may want to be zookeepers, professional basketball players, firefighters, rock stars, or whatever else strikes them as glamorous and exciting (Ginzberg, 1972, 1984; Hartung, Porfeli, & Vondracek, 2005). Children make important progress, though,

beginning to narrow their ideas about future careers to those consistent with their emerging self-concepts—as humans rather than as lions or ninja turtles, as males rather than as females, and so on (Gottfredson, 1996). From an early age, for instance, boys choose traditionally masculine occupations, and girls choose traditionally female occupations, setting themselves on paths to traditional gender-stereotyped careers (Hartung et al., 2005; Porfeli, Hartung, & Vondracek, 2008; Schuette, Ponton, & Charlton, 2012; Weisgram, Bigler, & Liben, 2010). Girls today are more open than they used to be to thinking about masculine-stereotyped jobs, though, whereas boys remain as determined as ever to avoid feminine choices (Schuette et al., 2012; Weisgram et al., 2010). Children also learn about the prestige or social status associated with different careers; they may begin to prefer the idea of being a surgeon to the idea of being a car mechanic (Gottfredson, 1996).

Like teenager Kelly Witte, quoted in the beginning of this section, adolescents age 11 to age 18 become more realistic, begin to weigh factors other than their wishes, and make preliminary vocational choices. According to theorist Eli Ginzberg (1972, 1984), they consider their *interests* ("Would I enjoy counseling people?"), their *capacities* ("Am I skilled at relating to people?"), and their *values* ("Is it really important to me to help people, or do I value power or money more?").

As they get still older, adolescents begin to take into account the realities of the job market and the physical and intellectual requirements for different occupations, and they begin serious preparation for their chosen occupations (Ginzberg, 1984; Hirschi & Vondracek, 2009; Walls, 2000). By late adolescence or emerging adulthood, they are in a good position to consider the availability of job openings in a field such as school counseling, the years of education required, the work conditions, and other relevant factors.

The main developmental trend evident in vocational choice, then, is *increasing realism with age*—a shift from fantasy to informed choice based on knowledge of both the self and the world of work. As adolescents narrow career choices in terms of both personal factors (their own interests, capacities, and values) and environmental factors (the realities of the job market), they seek the vocation that best suits them. According to influential vocational theorist John Holland (1985, 1996), vocational choice is just this: a search for an optimal fit between one's self-concept and personality and an occupation (see also Ozer & Benet-Martinez, 2006; Super, Savickas, & Super, 1996). You may well have taken a vocational interest inventory guided by Holland's person-environment fit theory of vocational development. Holland identified six personality types that lead people to different vocational choices:

- *investigative* types who enjoy learning, solving problems, and working creatively with ideas (for example, scientists)
- *social* types who like interacting with and helping other people (for example, teachers and counselors)
- *realistic* types who favor practical work with concrete objects (for example, car mechanics, construction workers)
- *artistic* types who are nonconforming and want to express themselves creatively (for example, artists, musicians)
- *conventional* types who prefer order, structure, and predictability (for example, librarians, accountants)
- *enterprising* types who seek to influence others and attain status (for example, sales people, entrepreneurs, leaders of organizations)

High career aspirations in adolescence are related to career choices and achievements later in life (Ashby & Schoon, 2012). Unfortunately, youth from lower-income families, especially minority group members face limited opportunities, discrimination, and stress. They may aim high at first but, as they become more aware of constraints on their success, lower their career aspirations and aim toward the jobs they think they are likely to get rather than the jobs that interest them most or fit best with their personalities (Armstrong & Crombie, 2000; Hartung et al., 2005; Phillips & Pittman, 2003).

Similarly, the vocational choices of females have been and continue to be constrained by traditional gender norms. Young women who have adopted traditional gender-role attitudes and expect to marry and start families early in adulthood sometimes set their educational and vocational sights low, choosing careers they think will make it easier for them to combine work and family (Bleske-Rechek et al., 2011; Mahaffy & Ward, 2002). Males and females also emphasize different values, which can lead them in different career directions. Thus, for example, males tend to emphasize money and power more than females, leading them to prefer traditionally male-stereotyped jobs that satisfy these values; females tend to emphasize family values and helping others more, leading them to traditionally female-stereotyped choices (Weisgram et al., 2010). Although more young women today than ever aspire toward high-status and male-dominated occupations, many, influenced by traditional gender norms, aim instead toward feminine-stereotyped, and often lower-status and lower-paying, occupations (Armstrong & Crombie, 2000; Hartung et al., 2005).

Moreover, many teenagers, male and female, simply do not do as Erikson and vocational theorists would advise—explore a range of possible occupations, then make informed choices (Bright, Pryor, & Harpham, 2005). Those adolescents who *do* investigate a range of options are more likely than those who do not to choose careers that fit their personalities (Grotevant & Cooper, 1986). In turn, a good person-environment fit between vocational interests or personality and type of vocation

or job predicts greater job satisfaction, better performance, and a higher likelihood of staying in the job, supporting Holland's theory of vocational development (Nye, Su, Rounds, & Drasgow, 2012; Spokane, Meir, & Catalano, 2000). The saving grace is that those who do not explore thoroughly as adolescents have time to change their minds as adults.

Influences on Identity Formation

Taking everything into consideration, an adolescent's progress toward achieving identity in various domains is a product of at least five factors:

- **Cognitive development.** Adolescents who have achieved solid mastery of formal-operational thought, who think in complex and abstract ways, and who are self-directed and actively seek relevant information when they face decisions are more likely than other adolescents to raise and resolve identity issues (Berzonsky & Kuk, 2000; Waterman, 1992).
- **Personality.** Adolescents who explore and achieve identity tend to score low in neuroticism and high in openness to experience and conscientiousness (Ozer & Benet-Martinez, 2006). That is, they are emotionally stable, curious, and responsible.
- **Quality of relationship with parents.** Youths who get stuck in the diffusion status of identity formation and drift for years are sometimes neglected or rejected by their parents and emotionally distant from them. Adolescents in the foreclosure status are often extremely close to parents who are loving but overly protective and controlling; these adolescents have few opportunities to make decisions and may never question their parents' ideas about what they should be. Adolescents in the moratorium and identity achievement statuses generally have warm and democratic parents, the same kind of parents who foster high self-esteem (Emmanuelle, 2009; Kroger, 2007; Waterman, 1982). In family discussions, these adolescents experience a sense of closeness and mutual respect but also feel free to disagree with their parents (Grotevant & Cooper, 1986).
- **Opportunities for exploration.** Adolescents who attend college are exposed to diverse ideas and are encouraged to think through issues independently and explore different possibilities. College provides the kind of moratorium period with freedom to explore that Erikson felt was essential to identity formation (Kroger, 2007).
- **Cultural context.** The notion that adolescents should forge a personal identity after carefully exploring many options may well be most relevant in modern industrialized Western societies (Côté & Levine, 1988; Flum & Blustein, 2000). Teens in more traditional societies centered around activities like farming, fishing, or herding may simply adopt the adult roles most adults adopt in their culture, without much soul-searching or experimentation; that is, identity foreclosure may be the most adaptive path to adulthood in such cultures (Côté & Levine, 1988).

In Western industrialized societies, anyway, the adolescent who is able to raise serious questions about the self and

In traditional societies, teens do not explore a variety of careers in order to choose the best fit. Instead, they start at an early age to do whatever adults in their society do.

Sidney Bahrt / Photo Researchers, Inc.

answer them—that is, the individual who achieves identity—is likely to be better off for it. Identity achievement is associated with psychological well-being and high self-esteem, complex thinking about moral and social issues, a willingness to accept and cooperate with other people, and a variety of other psychological strengths (Kroger, 2007; Waterman, 1992).

▶ Checking Mastery

1. How are 17-year-old Kwan's self-descriptions likely to differ from those of her 9-year-old sister Min?
2. College student Jack is in the foreclosure status with respect to vocational identity, whereas his roommate Tim is in the diffusion status. What does each status mean, and what kind of parenting is associated with it?
3. What besides warm, democratic parenting is likely to foster identity achievement?

▶ Making Connections

1. Write three brief descriptions of yourself to show how you might have answered the question "Who am I?" at age 4, age 8, and age 18. What developmental changes in self-conceptions do your self-descriptions illustrate?
2. In our culture, we assume that giving youth a long moratorium period in which to explore possible vocational identities is a good thing, so we send them to college and give them lots of time to experiment before they must take on adult responsibilities. More traditional societies simply ask youth to assume the adult roles specified for them in their culture at an early age. What do you see as the pros and cons of these two approaches?
3. Analyze your own, current identity statuses in the areas of vocational, ethnic, religious, and sexual identity and what you perceive as the major influences on them.

11.5 The Adult

LEARNING OBJECTIVES:

• Discuss age differences in self-esteem across the life span and strategies that aging adults use to maintain self-esteem, as well as how self-conceptions differ in individualistic and collectivist cultures.

• Referring to the two different senses in which there can be continuity or discontinuity in personality, describe what we know about continuity and discontinuity in the Big Five trait dimensions over the adult years.

• Discuss the extent to which research supports Erikson's stages of adult development and Levinson's concept of midlife crisis.

• Summarize the typical course of career development and the factors that would enable older workers to adjust well to retirement and have a successful aging experience.

We enter adulthood having gained a great deal of understanding of what we are like as individuals—but we are far from done developing. Both self-conceptions and personalities change, and both can affect and be affected by the careers that adults establish and end.

Self-Concepts and Self-Esteem

Adults differ greatly in their self-perceptions and levels of self-esteem. To what extent do age and cultural context contribute to this variation?

Age Differences

It is commonly believed that adults gain self-esteem as they cope successfully with the challenges of adult life but then lose it as aging, disease, and losses of roles and relationships take their toll in later life. Is there truth to this view? A large Internet survey of more than 300,000 people ages 9–90 conducted by Richard Robins and his colleagues (2002) suggests there is. Self-esteem tends to be relatively high in childhood, to drop in adolescence, to rise gradually through the adult years until the mid-60s, then to drop in late old age, as shown in ■ **Figure 11.3**. The same pattern is evident when longitudinal assessments are done: self-esteem

increases in early adulthood, peaks in people's 50s and 60s, and declines in late old age (Orth, Robins, & Widaman, 2012; Orth, Trzesniewski, & Robins, 2010). In parallel, people's sense of clarity about who they are rises through middle age and declines in old age, especially if poor health forces them to leave work and family roles (Lodi-Smith & Roberts, 2010).

As in Figure 11.3, males often display higher self-esteem than females in early adulthood but gender differences disappear in old age. Black and white adults have similar levels of self-esteem but blacks often show more decline in late adulthood, possibly because they experience steeper declines in financial well-being and health (Orth et al., 2010). Meanwhile, high self-esteem matters: It contributes to later relationship and job satisfaction, health, and happiness (Orth et al., 2012).

How, then, can older adults maintain positive self-images as long as possible, even as they experience the health problems, drops in income, and other losses that may come with aging? Reducing the gap between the ideal and real self, changing one's goals and standards of self-evaluation, making social comparisons to other old people, and avoiding negative self-stereotyping can all help.

Reducing the Gap between Ideal and Real Self Comparing young, middle-aged, and elderly adults, Carol Ryff (1991) found

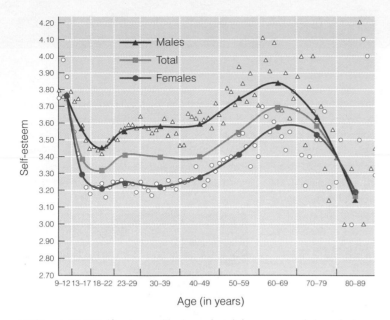

■ Figure 11.3 Self-esteem dips in early adolescence and rises during the adult years until it declines in very old age. Males have higher scores than females except in childhood and late old age. The lines graph mean or average self-esteem for the various age groups shown; the triangles (for males) and circles (for females) plot mean self-esteem at particular ages in the various studies summarized in this meta-analysis.

Source: From Robins, R. W., et al., J. Global self-esteem across the life span, *Psychology and Aging, 17*, 423–434.

that self-ratings of the present self changed little across the adult years, but that older adults scaled down their visions of what they could ideally be. As a result, their ideal and present selves converged. Notice, then, that the gap between the ideal self and the real self that opens up during childhood, widens during adolescence, and gives us a sense of falling short, apparently closes again in later life, helping us maintain self-esteem.

Adjusting Goals and Standards of Self-Evaluation People's goals and standards often change with age so that what seem like losses or failures to a younger person may not be perceived as such by an older adult (Carstensen & Freund, 1994). A 40-year-old may be devastated at being passed over for a promotion, whereas a 60-year-old nearing retirement may not be bothered at all (Carstensen & Freund, 1994). And, for the older adult with a disability, walking a mile may be as much a triumph as running a mile might have been earlier in life (Rothermund & Brandtstädter, 2003b). As our goals and standards change over the life span, we apply different measuring sticks in evaluating ourselves and do not mind failing to achieve goals that are no longer realistic or important.

Comparing to Other Older Adults Older adults are able to maintain self-esteem by making social comparisons primarily to other older adults who have the same kinds of chronic diseases and impairments they have rather than to younger adults (Brandtstädter & Greve, 1994; Helgeson & Mickelson, 2000).

Indeed, if they really want to feel good about themselves, they can strategically select worse-off peers to judge themselves against, making what are called downward social comparisons (Bauer, Wrosch, & Jobin, 2008; Frieswijk et al., 2004), as in, "My mind's a lot sharper than poor Bessie's is."

Not Internalizing Ageist Stereotypes Finally, older adults are likely to maintain self-esteem better if they can resist **self-stereotyping**—applying negative stereotypes of aging people to themselves. Becca Levy (2003, 2009) argues that stereotypes of old people, which we usually learn in childhood, can become damaging self-stereotypes when people reach old age. Although we hold some positive stereotypes of older people (they are wise, agreeable, and kindly), negative stereotypes of older adults (they are sick, fragile, forgetful, incompetent, and so on) outnumber positive ones and show up in a variety of cultures (see Chan et al., 2012; Hess, 2006; Hummert, 2011). These negative stereotypes are reinforced over the years and are available to be applied to the self once people begin to think of themselves as "old." This may be why so many aging adults go to great lengths to deny that they are old! If they can avoid identifying with their age group, they are likely to feel younger than they actually are, perceive more time ahead of them, and enjoy higher self-esteem (Weiss & Lang, 2012; Weiss & Freund, 2012; Westerhof, Whitbourne, & Freeman, 2012). But eventually, when aging adults can deny their years no longer, they apply the "old" label to themselves and run the risk of negatively stereotyping themselves and losing self-esteem (Levy, 2009; Rothermund & Brandtstädter, 2003a).

To demonstrate that negative self-stereotyping can hurt the performance of elderly adults, Levy and her associates (Hausdorff, Levy, & Wei, 1999) used a priming technique. Words reflecting either negative stereotypes of aging or positive stereotypes of aging were flashed rapidly on a computer screen to elderly participants in the study so that the words were perceived but below the level of awareness. After this priming experience, these adults were asked to walk down a hall wearing measuring devices on their feet that registered how rapidly they walked and how lightly they stepped (how long their feet were off the ground). Older adults primed with positive stereotypes of aging clocked faster speeds and more sprightly foot-off-the-floor time than older adults who were exposed to negative stereotypes and shuffled along like old people. As Chapter 8 revealed, Levy (1996) has also found that priming older adults with words such as *senile* results in poorer memory performance than priming them with words such as *wise*.

Levy, Slade, and Kasl (2002) have even found that middle-aged adults who have positive perceptions of their own aging (for example, who disagree with statements such as "Things keep getting worse as I get older") end up not only in better health in old age but live more than 7 years longer than adults who have less positive self-perceptions of aging. This was the case even when age, health, socioeconomic status, and other variables related to longevity were controlled (and see Levy et al., 2009). These studies and others suggest that ageist stereotypes are indeed harmful to performance, health, and self-esteem, especially among people who have come to identify themselves as "old" and apply old-age stereotypes to themselves (Hess, 2006; O'Brien & Hummert, 2006). **Application Box 11.1** asks what we can do to combat ageist stereotypes.

Combating Negative Stereotypes of Aging

Frail, forgetful, lonely, depressed? What other negative stereotypes pop into your head when you think about "old people." We have so many ageist stereotypes—and so many jokes based on them. As we have seen, negative stereotypes of older adults can have negative effects on self-perceptions, behavior, and even health and longevity if they are internalized and applied to the self through self-stereotyping. So how might we as a society combat these ageist stereotypes and the harm they do?

Intervention might need to begin in childhood, as that is when we first learn ageist stereotypes (Hess, 2006). For example, intergenerational programs in which elderly adults work with children in the schools not only help children learn but also improve their attitudes toward older people (Cummings, Williams, & Ellis, 2003).

Efforts to combat ageism need to be aimed at seniors too, though. For example, Levy's (2003) work suggests that activating positive stereotypes of aging before older people perform cognitive tasks can boost their performance, at least temporarily. Other research suggests that older adults may feel younger and even live longer if they minimize cues to their own aging—for example, by dying their hair or socializing or even living with people younger than themselves (Hsu, Chung, & Langer, 2010). Our society's overvaluing of youth may be part of what needs changing, however (Cruikshank, 2009).

In a now classic study, Judith Rodin and Ellen Langer (1980) demonstrated that changing the attributions aging adults make for problems they experience can make a difference. They discovered that 80% of elderly nursing home residents blamed physical aging for many of their difficulties in functioning and did not consider that the nursing home environment could be a source of their problems. In an experiment, Rodin and Langer exposed one group of nursing home residents to a new theory highlighting environmental causes of their limitations in functioning: That they had difficulty walking, for example, was attributed to the nursing home floors, which were tiled and therefore slippery for people of any age. Compared with an untreated control group and a group that received medical information that physical aging was not the major source of their difficulties, the group that learned to attribute everyday problems in functioning to the nursing home environment rather than to old age became more active, sociable, and even healthy.

Ultimately, societal-level change is needed. Some countries (China, for example) clearly have more positive views of old age than the United States does and grant elders more respect (Levy & Langer, 1994). Possibly more positive views of aging can be promoted through new social policies, media campaigns, and education and training programs (Braithwaite, 2002). It is especially important that training for nurses and other helping professionals incorporate messages about positive aspects of aging, not just messages that reinforce negative stereotypes (Ferrario et al., 2008). Yet programs could backfire if they present too rosy a picture of aging, for then many seniors might feel deficient when they compare themselves to the vibrant, active elders they see in the media. At this point, older adults may be best off if they become more aware of negative stereotypes of old people and their potentially damaging effects, resist taking them personally, and avoid blaming any difficulties they encounter on the ravages of old age.

What stereotypes do we have of elderly women—and to what extent do they believe the stereotypes apply to them?

In sum, self-esteem appears to rise in early and middle adulthood and to drop off in old age. Older adults can maintain self-esteem, however, by bringing their ideal selves into line with their real selves, adjusting their goals and standards of self-evaluation, making social comparisons with other older people, and not applying negative stereotypes of old people to themselves.

Cultural Differences

Self-conceptions in adulthood show the imprint not only of age and individual experiences but also of culture. Recall that in an *individualistic culture*, individuals are socialized to put their own goals as autonomous beings ahead of their social group's goals, whereas in a *collectivist culture*, people give group goals and relationships higher priority than personal goals (Triandis, 1989, 1995). North American and Western European societies typically have an individualistic orientation, whereas many societies in Latin America, Africa, and East Asia are primarily collectivist.

Hazel Markus and her colleagues have carefully studied the meanings of self in the United States and Japan (Cross, 2000; Markus, 2004; Markus, Mullally, & Kitayama, 1997; and see Heine & Buchtel, 2009). They have found that being a person in the United States (an individualistic culture) means being your own person—independent and different from other people—whereas being a person in Japan (a collectivist culture) means being interdependent with others, embedded in society. Thus, when asked to describe themselves, American adults talk about their unique personal qualities but Japanese adults more often refer to their social roles and social identities and mention other people (for example, "I try to make my parents happy").

In addition, Americans describe their generalizable personality traits—traits they believe they display in most situations and relationships. By contrast, Japanese adults describe their behavior in specific contexts such as home, school, or work and often describe themselves differently depending on the social situation or context they are talking about. Interestingly, the Japanese language has no word to refer to *I* apart from social context (Cross, 2000). In short, Americans think like trait theorists and feel they have an inner self that is consistent across situations and over time, whereas Japanese people seem to adopt a social learning theory perspective on personality and see situational influences on behavior as powerful (Heine & Buchtel, 2009; Tafarodi et al., 2004).

Finally, Americans are more obsessed with self-esteem and show self-enhancing biases when they evaluate themselves, believing they live in Lake Wobegon and are all above average (Harter, 2012). Japanese and other East Asian adults are more modest and self-effacing. They readily note their inadequacies and a desire to overcome them, seem reluctant to call attention to ways in which they are better than other people or even to make social comparisons, and do not seem as concerned with protecting and bolstering their self-esteem (Harter, 2012; Heine & Buchtel, 2009; also see
● **Table 11.3** for a summary of these differences).

Differences in self-descriptions between individuals in individualistic and collectivist cultures can be detected as early as age 3 or 4 by asking children to talk about themselves and their experiences (Wang, 2004, 2006). American children talk about their preferences, characteristics, and feelings, whereas Chinese children describe themselves in terms of social roles and social

● **Table 11.3** Views of the Self in Individualistic and Collectivist Cultures

Individualistic (e.g., United States)	Collectivist (e.g., Japan)
Separate	Connected
Independent	Interdependent
Traitlike (personal qualities transcend specific situations and relationships)	Flexible (different in different social contexts)
Self-enhancing: Need for self-esteem results in seeing self as above average	Self-effacing: Self-critical, aware of inadequacies
Emphasis on uniqueness	Emphasis on group memberships and similarities to others

SOURCE: Adapted from Markus, H. R., Mullally, P. R., & Kitayama, S. Self-ways: Diversity in modes of cultural participation. In U. Neisser & D. A. Jopling (Eds.), *The conceptual self in context, culture, experience, self-understanding.* Copyright © 1997 Cambridge University Press. Reprinted with permission.

routines such as family dinners. They are a good deal more modest, too, saying things like "I sometimes forget my manners." How might parents help create these cultural differences? Possibly through everyday conversations; for example, American mothers tell stories in which their children are the stars, whereas Chinese mothers talk about the experiences of the family as a group (Wang, 2004). Perhaps as a result, as American children become adolescents, they put less emphasis on their relationships with their parents in their self-definitions, whereas Chinese students continue to keep their parents in a prominent role, as indicated by their responses to items like, "My relationships with my parents are an important part of who I am" (Pomerantz, Qin, Wang, & Chen, 2009).

Cross-cultural studies of individualistic and collectivist cultures challenge the Western assumption that a person cannot develop normally without individuating himself from others and coming to know his identity as an individual. In much of the world, it's about "self-in-relation-to-others," not about individuals with their own unique identities (Shweder et al., 2006). These studies also suggest that our methods for studying the self—asking people who they are, having them respond to global self-esteem scales, and giving them personality scales about how they *generally* behave across social contexts—may be culturally biased. It is wise to remind ourselves, then, that the self is culturally defined.

Continuity and Discontinuity in Personality

How much continuity and how much change is there in personality over the adult years? Actually, we must ask two questions:

- Do *individual* adults retain their rankings on trait dimensions compared with others in a group over the years?
- Do *average* scores on personality trait measures increase, decrease, or remain the same as age increases?

Do People Retain Their Rankings?

Paul Costa, Robert McCrae, and their colleagues have closely studied personality change and continuity by giving adults from their 20s to their 90s Big Five personality tests and administering these tests repeatedly over the years (McCrae & Costa, 2003, 2008). They have found a good deal of *consistency in rankings within a group*, as indicated by high correlations between scores on the same trait dimensions at different ages. In other words, the person who tends to be extraverted as a young adult is likely to be extraverted as an elderly adult, and the introvert is likely to remain introverted over the years. Similarly, the adult who shows high or low levels of neuroticism, conscientiousness, agreeableness, or openness to new experiences is likely to retain that ranking when compared with peers years later. Correlations between personality trait scores on two occasions 20–30 years apart average about 0.60 across Big Five personality dimensions, suggesting consistency in personality over time but also room for change (McCrae & Costa, 2003; Morizot & Le Blanc, 2003).

The tendency to be consistent increases with age. In a meta-analysis of 152 studies in which personality was assessed on two

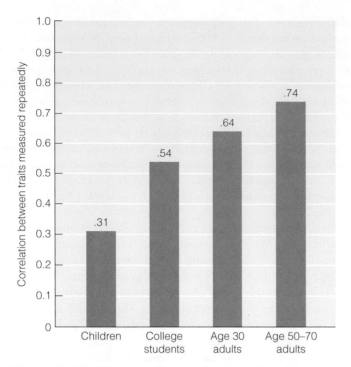

■ **Figure 11.4** Rank-order consistency of personality trait measures at different ages. Consistency, as indicated by strong correlations between scores obtained 6–7 years apart, increases with age.

SOURCE: Data from Roberts, B. W., & DelVecchio, W. F. (2000). The rank-order consistency of personality traits from childhood to old age: A quantitative review of longitudinal studies. *Psychological Bulletin, 126*, 3–25.

or more occasions, Brent Roberts and Wendy DelVecchio (2000) found that the average correlation between scores at two testings an average of 6–7 years apart increased quite steadily from infancy and early childhood to late adulthood, as shown in ■ **Figure 11.4**. Personalities are still forming in childhood and even adolescence and young adulthood; after around age 50, they are quite consistent (Lodi-Smith, Turiano, & Mroczek, 2011; Roberts & DelVecchio, 2000).

Do Mean Personality Scores Change?

Do most people change systematically in common directions over the years? You may be consistently more extraverted than your best friend over the years, and yet both of you could, along with others, become less extraverted at age 70 than you were at age 20. This second major type of continuity in personality, *stability in the mean level of a trait*, is relevant when we ask whether there is truth to stereotypes of older adults—for example, that they are more rigid, grumpy, depressed, or passive than younger adults.

McCrae, Costa, and their colleagues (2000) have examined age-group differences in scores on the Big Five personality dimensions in countries as diverse as Turkey, the Czech Republic, and Japan. From adolescence to middle age, they find, extraversion (especially excitement-seeking) and openness

to experience decline modestly, whereas emotional stability (the opposite of neuroticism), agreeableness, and conscientiousness increase. From adolescence to middle adulthood, then, we become less in need of stimulation and less open to new experiences but a lot more psychologically mature—more emotionally stable, more cooperative and easy to get along with, and more disciplined and responsible (see also Lodi-Smith et al., 2011; Roberts, Walton, & Viechtbauer, 2006; Roberts, Donnellan, & Hill, 2013).

What personality changes can people expect later—from middle age to old age? Not as many. Activity level—the tendency to be energetic and action oriented, an aspect of extraversion—begins to decline in people's 50s and continues declining through the 80s and 90s (McCrae & Costa, 2003). Openness to experience may keep decreasing, whereas agreeableness and conscientiousness often continue increasing (Lodi-Smith et al., 2011; Roberts et al., 2006). Otherwise, most of us will not undergo similar personality changes as part of the aging experience. Either we will remain much the same or we will change in response to life experiences in our own ways and at our own times (Helson, Jones, & Kwan, 2002).

Overall, most evidence points to (1) a good deal of cross-age consistency, more with age, in people's rankings compared with other people on Big Five personality trait dimensions; (2) personality growth from adolescence to middle adulthood highlighted by greater emotional stability, conscientiousness, and agreeableness; and (3) relatively little personality change from middle adulthood to later adulthood except decreased activity level. In short, there is both continuity and discontinuity in personality during adulthood.

Why Do People Change or Remain the Same?

What makes a personality remain stable over the years? Here are a few ideas (see Roberts, Wood, & Caspi, 2008). First, *genetic makeup* contributes to continuity (Borkenau et al., 2001; Krueger &

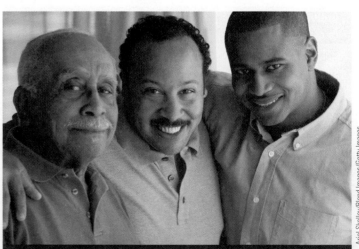

Research on changes in personality during adulthood suggests that the grandfather in this family may be less open to experience and lower in activity level but more mature [agreeable, conscientious, and emotionally stable] than his grandson.

Johnson, 2008). Second, *lasting effects of childhood experiences* may contribute; you have seen, for example, that parents can either help a child overcome a difficult temperament or contribute to its becoming an enduring pattern of response. Third, traits may remain stable because people's *environments remain stable*; playing consistent social roles like mother or engineer may be especially important in creating consistency in personality (Roberts, Wood, & Caspi, 2008. Fourth, *gene–environment correlations* can promote continuity. That is, genetic endowment may influence the kinds of experiences we have, and those experiences, in turn, may strengthen our genetically based predispositions through a kind of snowball effect (Caspi, 1998; Roberts & Caspi, 2003; also see Chapter 3). Thus, an extravert's early sociability will elicit friendly responses from others, cause her to seek out social activities, and in the process strengthen her initial tendency to be extraverted—while the introvert seeks and experiences an environment that reinforces introversion.

What, then, might cause the significant changes in personality that some adults experience? *Biological factors* such as disease and dementia can contribute. The nervous system deterioration associated with Huntington's disease or Alzheimer's disease, for example, can cause affected individuals to become moody, irritable, and irresponsible (McCrae & Costa, 2003). Adult personalities also change in response to *changes in the environment*, including major life events, changes in social and vocational roles, and psychotherapy (Roberts et al., 2008; Lüdtke, Roberts, Trautwein, & Nagy, 2011; Maiden et al., 2003; Sutin et al., 2010).

Finally, change is more likely when there is *a poor person–environment fit* (Roberts & Robins, 2004). For example, Florine Livson (1976) discovered that independent women who did not have traditionally feminine traits experienced more personality change during midlife than traditional women who fit the stereotypically feminine roles of wife and mother better. Bothered by the mismatch between their personalities and their traditionally feminine roles, the nontraditional women redirected their lives in their 40s, expressed their masculine sides, and experienced better psychological health by their 50s (see also Weiss, Freund, & Wiese, 2012). Similarly, Livson (1981) found that men who fit the traditional male role changed less over the years than nontraditional men who felt cramped by this role and who, after a

crisis in their 40s, began to express their more feminine, emotional sides. For both men and women, then, a poor person–environment fit prompted personality change.

Thus, genes, lasting effects of early childhood experiences, stable environments, and gene–environment correlations all contribute to the continuity seen in adult personality. Change in personality becomes more likely if people's biologies or environments change or if there is a poor fit between their personalities and their lifestyles. All things considered, the forces for continuity are often stronger than the forces for change, perhaps in part because we want to retain our identities as individuals and keep building the same niches for ourselves even when we move, change jobs, or make other life changes (Roberts et al., 2008).

When all is said and done, personality has a tremendous impact on life-span development. Personal strengths such as emotional stability and conscientiousness are correlated with both good physical health and good mental health (Kern & Friedman, 2010; Hampson & Friedman, 2008; Lucas & Diener, 2008). Moreover, personality affects how we react to and cope with life events. For example, highly agreeable people are able to adjust better than most people to becoming disabled (Boyce & Wood, 2011), and people high in emotional stability (low in neuroticism) handle the death of loved ones better (Robinson & Marwit, 2006). We will encounter more examples of the role of personality in adjustment later in this book.

Eriksonian Psychosocial Growth

Researchers who conclude that adults change in only a few ways over the years typically study personality by administering standardized personality scales. These tests were designed to assess enduring dispositional traits and probably reveal the most stable aspects of personality. Researchers who interview people in depth about their lives often detect considerably more change and growth (McCrae & Costa, 2003).

This is evident in research on Erikson's theory of psychosocial development through the life span. Erikson's stages of psychosocial development, listed in ● **Table 11.4**, will be reviewed briefly here in relation to changes in the self, mainly as a preface to looking at psychosocial development during adulthood (see also Chapter 2). Both maturational forces and social demands,

● **Table 11.4** The Eight Stages of Erikson's Psychosocial Theory

Stage	Age Range	Central Issue	Virtue or Strength
1. Trust vs. mistrust	Birth–1 year	Can I trust others?	Hope
2. Autonomy vs. shame and doubt	1–3 years	Can I act on my own?	Will
3. Initiative vs. guilt	3–6 years	Can I carry out my plans successfully?	Purpose
4. Industry vs. inferiority	6–12 years	Am I competent compared with others?	Competence
5. Identity vs. role confusion	12–20 years	Who am I and where am I going?	Fidelity
6. Intimacy vs. isolation	20–40 years	Am I ready for a committed relationship?	Love
7. Generativity vs. stagnation	40–65 years	Have I given something to future generations?	Care
8. Integrity vs. despair	65 years and older	Has my life been meaningful?	Wisdom

© Cengage Learning

Erikson believed, push humans everywhere through these eight psychosocial crises. Later conflicts may prove difficult to resolve if early conflicts were not resolved successfully. For development to proceed optimally, a healthy balance between the terms of each conflict must be struck; if this happens, the individual gains a particular "virtue," or psychosocial strength.

The Path to Adulthood

During Erikson's first psychosocial conflict **trust versus mistrust**, infants learn to trust other people if their caregivers are responsive to their needs; otherwise, the balance of trust versus mistrust will tip in the direction of mistrust. Erikson believed that infants come to recognize that they are separate from their caregivers. Indeed, as you saw earlier in this chapter, infants begin to distinguish self from other (typically the mother) as early as the first 2 or 3 months of life.

Toddlers acquire an even clearer sense of themselves as individuals as they struggle with the psychosocial conflict of **autonomy versus shame and doubt**. According to Erikson, they assert that they have wills of their own. Consistent with this view, toddlers recognize themselves in a mirror and lace their speech with "me" and "no" around 18–24 months of age. Four- and five-year-olds who have achieved a sense of autonomy then enter Erikson's stage of **initiative versus guilt**. They develop a sense of purpose by devising bold plans and taking great pride in accomplishing the goals they set. As you have seen, preschoolers define themselves in terms of their physical activities and accomplishments.

A sense of initiative, Erikson believed, paves the way for success when elementary school children face the conflict of **industry versus inferiority** and focus on mastering important cognitive and social skills. As you have seen, elementary school children engage in more social comparison than younger children and are likely to acquire a sense of industry rather than inferiority if those comparisons turn out favorably.

According to Erikson, children who successfully master each of these childhood psychosocial conflicts gain new ego strengths. Moreover, they learn a good deal about themselves and position themselves to resolve the adolescent crisis of *identity versus role confusion*, Erikson's fifth stage, which was discussed in some detail earlier in this chapter.

What happens to adolescents with newfound identities during the adult years? Erikson thought that stagelike changes in personality—and exciting possibilities for personal growth—continue during adulthood through psychosocial crises focused on intimacy versus isolation, generativity versus stagnation, and integrity versus despair. In a longitudinal study of college students from their college years to their 40s and 50s, Susan Whitbourne and her colleagues (Whitbourne, Sneed, & Saver, 2009) assessed progress in resolving all eight of Erikson's issues. They found steady growth even in qualities like trust and autonomy that are associated with the childhood stages, along with especially rapid growth with respect to the adult issues centered on intimacy, generativity, and integrity. So, as Erikson himself recognized, psychosocial development is not quite as stagelike as his stages imply because people can go back and work on issues associated with earlier stages. However, there is most certainly psychosocial growth throughout the life span.

Early Adult Intimacy

As Erikson saw it, early adulthood is a time for dealing with the psychosocial conflict of **intimacy versus isolation**. A person must achieve a sense of individual identity before becoming able to commit himself to a shared identity with another person. The young adult who has no clear sense of self may be threatened by the idea of entering a committed, long-term relationship and being "tied down," or he may become overdependent on a romantic partner (or possibly a close friend) as a source of identity.

Does identity indeed pave the way for genuine intimacy? To find out, Susan Whitbourne and Stephanie Tesch (1985) measured identity status and intimacy status among college seniors and 24- to 27-year-old alumni from the same university. The researchers interviewed people about their closest relationships and placed each person in one of six "intimacy statuses." These included being a social isolate with no close relationships, being in a shallow relationship with little communication or involvement, being in a deep relationship but not yet being ready to make a long-term commitment to one's partner, and being in a genuinely intimate relationship that has it all—close involvement in each other's lives, open communication about one's true feelings, and a long-term commitment to one another. College graduates had progressed farther than college seniors in resolving intimacy issues; more of them were also in long-term, committed relationships. In addition, the college graduates who had well-formed identities were more likely than those who did not to be capable of genuine and lasting intimacy.

As Erikson theorized, then, we must know ourselves before we can truly love another person (see also Beyers &

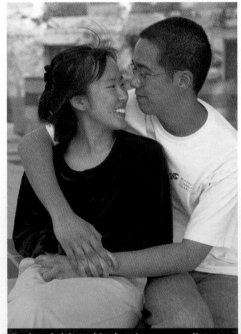

Cassy Muronaka/PhotoEdit

Early adulthood is the time, according to Erik Erikson, for deciding whether to commit to a shared identity with another person—for resolving the conflict of intimacy versus isolation.

Seiffge-Krenke, 2010; Montgomery, 2005). Yet Erikson believed that women resolve identity questions when they choose a mate and fashion an identity around their roles as wife and mother-to-be. Is this old-fashioned view correct? Only for some women, especially those who developed in a sociocultural context with traditional gender-role expectations and defined themselves primarily as wives and mothers (Dyk & Adams, 1990; George, Helson, & John, 2011; Kroger, 2007). Also influenced by traditional sex-role expectations, other women resolved intimacy issues before identity issues: They married and had children and, only after the children were older, asked who they were as individuals and pursued careers that suited their personalities (George et al., 2011). Still other women, especially those with more masculine gender-role orientations, have followed the identity-before-intimacy route that characterizes men, settling on a career first, thinking about a serious relationship later (Dyk & Adams, 1990). Today, more and more women are following this identity-before-intimacy path (Beyers & Seiffge-Krenke, 2010). As Erikson himself would appreciate, then, development is influenced by its historical and cultural context.

Midlife Generativity

What does psychosocial development look like in middle age? George Vaillant (1977), a psychoanalytic theorist, conducted an in-depth longitudinal study of mentally healthy Harvard men from college to middle age and a similar longitudinal study of blue-collar workers (Vaillant, 1983; Vaillant & Milofsky, 1980). Vaillant found support for Erikson's view that the 20s are a time for intimacy issues. He found that in their 30s, men shifted their energies to advancing or consolidating their careers and were seldom reflective or concerned about others. In their 40s, though, many men became concerned with Erikson's issue of **generativity versus stagnation**. This psychosocial conflict involves gaining the capacity to generate or produce something that outlives you and to care about the welfare of future generations through such activities as parenting, teaching, mentoring, and leading (de St. Aubin, McAdams, & Kim, 2004; Slater, 2003).

Vaillant's 40-something men expressed more interest in passing on something of value, to their own children, to younger people at work, or to their communities. They were growing as individuals, often becoming more caring and self-aware as they entered their 50s. One of these men expressed the developmental progression Vaillant detected perfectly: "At 20 to 30, I think I learned how to get along with my wife. From 30 to 40, I learned how to be a success in my job. And at 40 to 50, I worried less about myself and more about the children" (1977, p. 195).

Middle-aged men and women are more likely than young adults to have achieved a sense of generativity (de St. Aubin et al., 2004; McAdams, Hart, & Maruna, 1998; Timmer, Bode, & Dittmann-Kohli, 2003). Moreover, those adults who have attained identity and intimacy are more likely than other adults to achieve generativity as well, as Erikson predicted (Christiansen & Palkovitz, 1998). Adults who have good self-regulatory capacities (conscientiousness in Big Five language) seem to be more successful than those low in self-control at resolving this and earlier Eriksonian crises (Busch & Hofer, 2011). Extraversion and openness to experience also help (Cox, Wilt,

Olson, & McAdams, 2010). Overall, research on generativity supports Erikson's view that both women and men are capable of impressive psychosocial growth during middle adulthood.

Old-Age Integrity

Elderly adults, according to Erikson, confront the psychosocial issue of **integrity versus despair**. They try to find a sense of meaning in their lives that will help them face the inevitability of death. If they constructed a life story or narrative identity during their early adult years, they may work on accepting it in old age as the only life they could have led (McAdams, 2011; McAdams & Adler, 2006). Progress toward integrity can be charted through "integrity statuses" much like the identity and intimacy statuses developed to study other Erikson stages (Hearn et al., 2012). Those older adults who achieve integrity have dealt successfully with previous stages (Hearn et al., 2012; James & Zarrett, 2005; Torges, Stewart, & Duncan, 2008). They are generally well-adjusted people who think in mature and complex ways, have a strong sense of well-being, and are not depressed (Hearn et al., 2012; James & Zarrett, 2005).

Noted gerontologist Robert Butler (1963) proposed that elderly adults engage in a process called **life review**, in which they reflect on unresolved conflicts of the past to come to terms with themselves, find new meaning and coherence in their lives, and prepare for death (see also Haber, 2006; Webster & Haight, 2002). Elders who engage in life review display a stronger sense of integrity and better overall adjustment and well-being than those who do not reminisce much or who mainly stew about unresolved regrets (Bohlmeijer, Roemer, Cuijpers, Smit, 2007; Wong & Watt, 1991; Wrosch, Bauer, & Scheier, 2005). Finding that life review can be beneficial, Butler and other gerontologists have turned it into a therapy approach in which elderly adults reconstruct and reflect on their life stories, sometimes with the help of photo albums and other memorabilia (Haight & Haight, 2007; Kunz & Soltys, 2007).

On balance, Erikson's view that humans experience psychosocial growth throughout the life span is supported by research. Erikson's childhood stages have inspired little research, but his

Reminiscence and life review can help older adults achieve a sense of integrity.

Cardinal/Corbis

theorizing about the adolescent stage of identity versus role confusion has been tested extensively and is well supported. In addition, achieving a sense of identity in adolescence paves the way for forming a truly intimate relationship in early adulthood, gaining a sense of generativity in middle adulthood, and resolving the issue of integrity versus despair through life review in later adulthood.

Midlife Crisis?

> Midlife is when you reach the top of the ladder and find that it was against the wrong wall. (Joseph Campbell, cited in S. Weiss, 2008)

This quotation captures the essence of midlife crisis. But where in all the evidence of stability and change in personality traits over the adult years and of psychosocial growth through Erikson's stages is the midlife crisis that many people believe is a standard feature of personality development in middle age? Although Erikson, and Vaillant after him, saw few signs of a midlife crisis, another psychoanalytic theorist, Daniel Levinson (1986, 1996; Levinson et al., 1978) did. He proposed a stage theory of adult development based on intensive interviews with 40 men and later reported that it applied to a sample of women he interviewed as well (Levinson, 1996).

Levinson claimed that adults go through a repeated process of first building a "life structure," or pattern of living, and then questioning and altering it during a transition period every 7 years or so. He believed that the transition period from age 40 to age 45 is an especially significant transition, a time of **midlife crisis** in which a person questions his life structure and raises unsettling issues about where he has been and where he is heading. Most middle-aged adults Levinson interviewed did not seek divorces, quit their jobs, buy red sports cars, or behave like lovesick adolescents, as popular images of the midlife crisis would have it, but most did seem to experience a psychological crisis in their early 40s.

Many researchers agree that middle age is often a time when people confront important issues like aging, evaluate their lives, and revise their goals (Freund & Ritter, 2009; Hermans & Oles, 1999; McAdams & Adler, 2006). Some also experience midlife changes in personality in response to life events such as divorce, a job change, or the death of a parent. However, there is little support for Levinson's claim that most adults experience a genuine crisis in their early 40s (Freund & Ritter, 2009; Hedlund & Ebersole, 1983; Vaillant, 1977). It seems sounder to call what many middle-aged adults experience midlife *questioning*, to recognize that it can occur in response to life events at a variety of ages, and to appreciate that it is usually not a true psychological crisis.

Vocational Development and Adjustment

Although Levinson's concept of midlife crisis is not well supported, he was right to emphasize that adults revise important life decisions as they develop. To illustrate, consider the important area of vocational development, an outgrowth and expression of an individual's self-concept and personality (George et al., 2011; Judge & Bono, 2001). After much experimenting in early adulthood, people settle into chosen occupations in their 30s and strive for success. Ultimately, they prepare for the end of their careers, make the transition into retirement, and attempt to establish a satisfying lifestyle during their "golden years."

Establishing a Career

Early adulthood is a time for exploring vocational possibilities, launching careers, making tentative commitments, revising them if necessary, seeking advancement, and establishing yourself firmly in what you hope is a suitable occupation. Mentors can be of great help in getting young adults' careers launched (Kammeyer-Mueller & Judge, 2008; McDonald et al., 2007), but it often takes time and involves lots of false starts and job changes.

To illustrate, Susan Phillips (1982), using data from a longitudinal study of males tracked from adolescence to age 36, examined whether men's decisions about jobs at different ages were tentative and exploratory (for example, "to see if I really liked that kind of work") or more final (for example, "to get started in a field I wanted [to enter]"). The proportions of decisions that were predominantly exploratory were 80% at age 21, 50% at age 25, and 37% at age 36. From age 21 to age 36, then, young adults progressed from wide-open exploration of different career possibilities to tentative or trial commitments to a stabilization of their choices. Even in their mid-30s, however, about a third of adults were still exploring what they wanted to be when they grew up! The average man held *seven* full-time jobs or training positions between age 18 and age 36 (Phillips, 1982). The picture for women is similar (Fuller, 2008; Jenkins, 1989). In a bad economy, avoiding unemployment and making progress toward a real career seem to hinge on maintaining high aspirations and clear career goals, even if they are different from goals established earlier (Vuolo, Staff, & Mortimer, 2012).

After their relatively unsettled 20s and decision-making 30s, adults often reach the peaks of their careers in their 40s (Simonton, 1990). They often have major responsibilities and define themselves in terms of their work. The days of one employer or even one career for life are disappearing, though (Porfeli & Vondracek, 2009). Many workers, even in their 40s and beyond, find themselves recycling through the process of career exploration and choice, retraining, and changing jobs.

Personality is an important influence on how careers go. Job success is consistently correlated with the Big Five qualities of conscientiousness, extraversion, and emotional stability (Ozer & Benet-Martinez, 2006). Person–environment fit can be critical, too: people tend to perform poorly and become open to changing jobs when the fit between their personality and aptitudes and the demands of their job or workplace is poor (Hoffman & Woehr, 2006; Nye et al., 2012). Gender is another significant influence on vocational development, as we will now see.

Gender and Career

Although women are entering a much wider range of fields today than they were a few decades ago, most administrative assistants, teachers, and nurses are still women. What's more, U.S. women who work full time and year round earn about 77 cents for every dollar men earn (DeNavas-Walt, Proctor, & Smith, 2012). Why the continuing gap? It is probably caused by both the influence of gender-role norms on the choices women make and by discrimination in the workplace.

Traditional gender-role norms have prompted many women to subordinate career goals to family goals. Women are more likely than men to interrupt their careers, drop down to part-time work, take less demanding jobs, and turn down promotions that would require transferring to a new location so that they can have and raise children (Biemann, Zacher, & Feldman, 2012; Kirchmeyer, 2006; Moen, 1992). Giving birth results in a drop in women's earnings for several years (Cooke et al., 2009). The hours mothers spend on homemaking and childcare tasks when their children are young often reduce their productivity at work; meanwhile, young fathers may become more productive at work in order to provide for their new families (Wallace & Young, 2008). In the process, women end up with lower odds of rising to higher paid, more responsible positions. The women who *do* make it to the top of the career ladder, especially in male-dominated fields, sometimes achieve this success by remaining single, divorcing, or limiting their childbearing (Jenkins, 1989). On average, women without children achieve more in their careers than women with children (Carr et al., 1998; Wilson, 2003).

But women's vocational and family choices cannot explain everything. Discrimination also plays a role. Traditionally "female" jobs pay less than traditionally "male" jobs even when the intellectual demands of the work are similar (England, Reid, & Kilbourne, 1996). And consider this: A gender pay gap is evident even among college graduates only a year after graduation, and it cannot be explained away entirely by gender differences in majors or career choices (Corbett & Hill, 2012). Even when women enter jobs with the same management degrees and salaries as men, and receive equal performance ratings, they still may not rise as far in the organization or earn as much as their male peers (Cox & Harquail, 1991). Perhaps this explains why only 15% of senior executives in Fortune 100 companies are women (Spar, 2012).

In sum, although we make preliminary vocational choices as adolescents, we remain open to making new choices as young adults and take some time to settle on careers that fit our personalities and gender roles. Meanwhile, our vocational experiences affect our personalities (Wille, Beyers, & De Fruyt, 2012). For instance, people whose work is complex and intellectually challenging become more able to handle intellectual problems adeptly and are more self-confident (Kohn & Schooler, 1982; Schooler, Mulatu, & Oates, 1999). Attaining a responsible position at work can also result in increased social dominance (an aspect of extraversion), conscientiousness, and emotional stability (Roberts et al., 2008). In the end, person-environment fit and the dynamic, reciprocal influences of personality on career and of career on personality shape adult vocational development (Hesketh, Griffin, & Loh, 2011; Wille et al., 2012).

Unemployment

In the wake of the economic recession that began in 2008, it seems important to ask how adults are affected when they suddenly lose their jobs. Because work is such a central part of an adult life, unemployment can threaten a man's or woman's sense of identity (Price, Friedland, & Vinokur, 1998). Moreover, it is likely to be accompanied by a cascade of other stressors such as the need to apply for unemployment benefits, alter routines, or move to cheaper housing. It can, as a result, have negative effects on both physical and mental health (Burgard, Brand, & House, 2007; Feldman & Ng, 2013; Howe et al., 2012; Paul & Moser, 2009). It can even increase an individual's risk of death (Garcy & Vågerö, 2012). In the long run, one instance of unemployment may not have much lasting effect. However, after they have retired, adults who had repeated periods of unemployment experience more depression and anxiety symptoms and have lower life satisfaction than those who managed to stay employed during their adult years (Zenger, Brähler, Berth, & Stöbel-Richter, 2011).

Unemployment also affects the individual's whole family. Not only may job losers become angry and depressed, but their partners may too; they can be harmed by new stressors, their partner's difficult behavior, or an erosion in the quality of their relationship with their partner (Howe, Levy, & Caplan, 2004). We also know that when economic hardship causes parents to be depressed and to fight with one another, parenting deteriorates and child behavior problems tend to increase (Conger et al., 1992; and see Chapter 15). In sum, the whole family may need help coping with job loss.

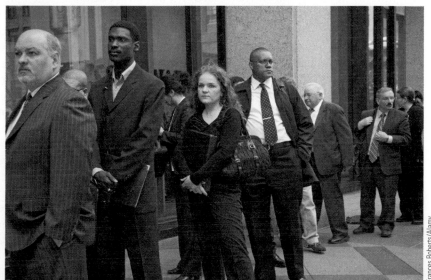

Since the recession of 2008, many adults have experienced the stress that accompanies unemployment.

Frances Roberts/Alamy

The Aging Worker

Many people believe that adults become less able or less motivated to perform well on the job as they approach retirement. As it turns out, the job performance of workers in their 50s and 60s is largely similar overall to that of younger workers (Ng & Feldman, 2008; Rhodes, 1983). Judging from a meta-analysis of multiple studies (Ng & Feldman, 2008), age is largely unrelated to quality of task performance and creativity on the job. Older workers actually outperform younger workers in areas such as good citizenship and safety and have fewer problems with counterproductive behavior such as aggression, substance use, tardiness, and absenteeism. The one place where older workers do not perform as well is in training programs, possibly because many of them involve new computer technologies. However, most negative stereotypes of older workers—for example, that they are unmotivated and unwilling to change—are baseless (Ng & Feldman, 2012).

Why is the performance of older workers not hurt by some of the age-related physical and cognitive declines described earlier in this book? First, these declines typically do not become significant until people are in their 70s and 80s, long after they have retired, and even then they do not affect everyone. The "older" workers in most studies are mainly middle-aged adults in their 40s, 50s, and 60s. Second, older workers have often accumulated a good deal of on-the-job expertise that helps them continue to perform well (Hansson et al., 1997).

Third and finally, the answer may lie in the strategies that aging adults use to cope with aging. Gerontologists Paul and Margaret Baltes (1990) have theorized that older people can best cope with aging through the strategy of *selective optimization with compensation (SOC)* (Baltes & Baltes, 1990; Baltes & Freund, 2003; Freund & Riediger, 2006; Lang, Rohr, & Williger, 2011; and see Chapter 8). Using SOC, an overworked 60-year-old lawyer might, for example, avoid spreading herself too thin by focusing on her strongest specialty area and delegating other types of assignments to younger workers (selection); put a lot of time into staying up-to-date in her main area of specialization (optimization); and make up for her failing memory by taking more notes at meetings (compensation). For pianist Arthur Rubenstein, maintaining excellence in old age meant playing fewer different pieces (selection), practicing them more (optimization), and compensating for loss of speed by increasing the contrast between the slower and faster parts of a piece to make the faster parts sound faster (Baltes, Lindenberger, & Staudinger, 2006). SOC works for a variety of aging workers (Abraham & Hansson, 1995; Freund & Riediger, 2006).

The federal government may have recognized that older workers are generally effective workers when it raised or eliminated mandatory retirement ages, increased the age of eligibility for receiving Social Security, and, through the Age Discrimination in Employment Act, protected older workers from age discrimination in hiring and retention (Hansson et al., 1997). But much remains to be done to accommodate the strengths and limitations of older workers and to meet the needs of those who have the desire and ability to continue working well into old age (see Hedge, Borman, & Lammlein, 2006).

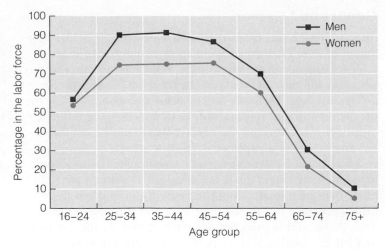

■ **Figure 11.5** Male and female labor force participation by age group in the United States in 2010. Labor force participation increases in people's 20s, peaks in their late 20s through 40s, and declines steeply starting at age 55. Most adults are out of the labor force by age 65–69. Men's participation is higher than women's, especially during the child-rearing years, but the gender gap is much narrower than it used to be.

SOURCE: U.S. Department of Labor, U.S. Bureau of Labor Statistics; Table 3.3, Civilian labor force participation rates by age, sex, race, and ethnicity. http://www.bls.gov/emp/ep_table_303.htm

Retirement

A century ago in North America, most working adults continued working as long as they were able, as people in many traditional societies today do. As late as 1930, more than half of all men age 65 or older in the United States were still working (Palmore et al., 1985). The introduction of Social Security in 1934, affluence, and increased availability of private pension plans changed that, making it financially possible for more men and women to retire and to do so earlier. And they have! As shown in ■ Figure 11.5, the labor force participation of men and women increases in early adulthood, plateaus, and then starts decreasing steeply in people's late 50s. Around half of adults are out of the labor force by age 62–64, around two-thirds are out by age 65–69, and over 90% are out by age 75 and older.

Men are still more involved in work than women, but the labor force participation rates of older men and women have become more similar since the 1960s as more women have spent more years in the work force and more men have retired earlier (Federal Interagency Forum on Aging Related Statistics, 2008). Since the 1960s, the average age of retirement dropped from over 67 to 62, but it has been inching up again since the mid-1990s. Why the recent rise in retirement age? Older workers are healthier, mandatory retirement policies are gone, economic uncertainty and rising health care costs make people feel they need to continue working for financial reasons, and the age of eligibility for full Social Security benefits has increased (Song & Manchester, 2009; Toossi, 2012).

Retirement is not a single event; it is a process that often plays out over a number of years. While some workers do retire "cold turkey" all at once, many others retire gradually, cutting back their work hours, becoming self-employed, taking part-time "bridge" jobs between full-time work and retirement, and sometimes cycling in and out of retirement multiple times before they settle into full retirement (Calvo, Haverstick, & Sass, 2009; Zissimopoulos & Karoly, 2009).

How do people adjust to the final chapter of the work life cycle? They face two main challenges: adjusting to the loss of their work role and developing a satisfying and meaningful lifestyle in retirement (van Solinge & Henkens, 2008). Robert Atchley (1976) proposed that adults progress through phases as they make the transition from worker to retiree. The process of adjustment begins with a *preretirement phase* in which workers nearing retirement gather information and plan for the future (Ekerdt, Kosloski, & DeViney, 2000). Discussing retirement with one's spouse and working out a financial plan during the preretirement phase are likely to pay off in greater well-being after retirement (Noone, Stephens, & Alpass, 2009).

Deciding when to retire is an important part of the process; people can become worried in the preretirement phase about whether they will be able to retire when they want to and still be financially secure (van Solinge & Henkens, 2008). Some workers retire early because they have the means to live comfortably and want to pursue new goals; others are forced to retire early because of poor health or mental health or because they are pushed out of their jobs (Beehr et al., 2000; Hansson et al., 1997; Olesen, Butterworth, & Rodgers, 2012). Similarly, some workers postpone retirement because they love their work (witness Supreme Court justice Ruth Bader Ginsburg and billionaire investor Warren Buffett), while others do so because they need the money.

Just after they retire, according to Atchley, workers often experience a *honeymoon phase* in which they relish their newfound freedom; they head for the beach, golf course, or camp grounds and do all the projects they never had time to do while they worked. Then, according to Atchley, many enter a *disenchantment phase* as the novelty wears off; they feel aimless and sometimes unhappy. Finally, they move to a *reorientation phase* in which they begin to put together a realistic and satisfying lifestyle.

Consider Don, who retired early at age 58. In the first weeks, he took trips and renovated his house: "That was great—I loved it." But after some months of this fun and of taking on more volunteer consulting jobs than he intended, he was reassessing how he wanted to spend his time and worrying that his money might not last: "Here I am over a year down the road and I don't like where I am. I don't think I've got my life coursed out correctly." A few more months and he felt he'd worked out a lifestyle he liked.

Research offers some support for Atchley's view of the adjustment process. For example, David Ekerdt and his colleagues (Ekerdt, Bossé, & Levkoff, 1985) found that (1) men who had been retired only a few months were in a honeymoon period, highly satisfied with life and optimistic about the future, (2) men who had been retired 13–18 months were rather disenchanted, and (3) men who had been retired for longer periods were relatively satisfied. Yet not everyone follows this pattern; for example, almost half of retirees in one study adjusted easily and within a month to retirement, whereas one in five found it took much longer and was challenging (van Solinge & Henkens, 2008).

After retirees have adjusted to retirement, are they better or worse off than they were before they retired? Negative images of the retired person abound in our society; the retiree supposedly ends up feeling old, useless, bored, sickly, and dissatisfied with life. Yet research shows that retirement has surprisingly few effects on adults (Hansson et al., 1997; Palmore et al., 1985). Retirement's most consistent effect is to reduce the individual's income (Palmore et al., 1985). Because women typically outlive their husbands and, because they move in and out of the work force more and do not earn as much as men, they more than men can find inadequate income in retirement a problem (Cruikshank, 2009).

Otherwise, retired people generally do not experience a decline in health simply because they retire. Poor health more often causes retirement than retirement causes poor health. Similarly, retirement does not diminish cognitive functioning (Coe et al., 2012). Retirees' social lives do not deteriorate either (Palmore et al., 1985). Retirement typically has no noticeable effect on the size of people's social networks, the frequency of their social contacts, or their satisfaction with the social support they receive. Finally, retirement generally does not reduce life satisfaction or damage mental health.

Overall, then, retirees are likely to experience an initial adjustment process, sometimes involving preretirement and then honeymoon, disenchantment, and reorientation phases. They then usually adapt successfully to retirement and to the drop in income that it typically involves. Yet there are huge differences in how it goes. What makes for a favorable adjustment? According to research (Bender, 2012; Fouquereau et al., 2005; Palmore et al., 1985; Robinson, Demetre, & Corney, 2010; Wang, Henkens, & van Solinge, 2011; Wong & Earl, 2009), good long-term adjustment is most likely among adults who

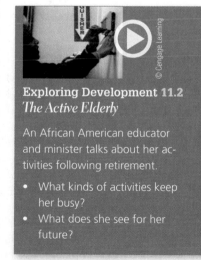

Exploring Development 11.2
The Active Elderly

An African American educator and minister talks about her activities following retirement.

- What kinds of activities keep her busy?
- What does she see for her future?

- retire voluntarily rather than involuntarily and feel in control of their retirement decision
- enjoy good physical and mental health
- have positive personality traits such as agreeableness and emotional stability
- have the financial resources to live comfortably
- are married or otherwise have strong social support

Some seniors subscribe to activity theory and want to maintain a highly active lifestyle in their later years.

Oote Boe Ph/Alamy

The retired educator interviewed in **Exploring Development Box 11.2** exemplifies many of these characteristics.

Personality and Successful Aging

What lifestyle decisions make not only for a successful transition to retirement but also for a happy and fulfilling old age? Theories of successful aging have been offered for years to answer that question and help us all enjoy a satisfying old age.

Activity theory holds that aging adults will find their lives satisfying to the extent that they can maintain their previous lifestyles and activity levels, either by continuing old activities or by finding substitutes—for example, by replacing work with hobbies, volunteer work, or other stimulating pursuits (Fry, 1992; Havighurst, Neugarten, & Tobin, 1968). According to this view, psychological needs do not really change as people enter old age: most aging individuals continue to want an active lifestyle. Retirement communities with plenty of recreational opportunities are based on activity theory. This view is also promoted in our society by communications that youthfulness is valued and "that *defying* aging is the primary way to *go about* aging" (Settersten & Trauten, 2009, p. 464).

By contrast, **disengagement theory** says that successful aging involves a withdrawal of the aging individual from society that is satisfying to both (Achenbaum & Bengtson, 1994; Cumming & Henry, 1961). The aging individual is said to have needs different from those she once had and seeks to leave old roles behind and reduce activity. Meanwhile, society both encourages and benefits from the older person's disengagement, which makes room for the younger generation.

Which is it? Throughout this text, you have seen evidence that individuals who remain active in old age benefit from their activity. Those who are physically active maintain their health longer (see Chapter 5), those who are physically and intellectually active maintain their cognitive functions longer (see Chapter 9), and those who remain involved in meaningful social relationships are more satisfied with their lives (see Chapter 14). In other words, there is more support for activity theory than for disengagement theory.

But before you conclude that activity theory explains all you need to know about successful aging, add three qualifications. First, the relationship between level of activity and life satisfaction or well-being is surprisingly weak (Fry, 1992). Apparently, many inactive seniors are nonetheless happy with their lives, and many busy seniors are nonetheless miserable. This suggests that quality of activity is probably more important than its quantity (Pinquart & Sorensen, 2000).

Second, we do see signs of disengagement among older adults (Achenbaum & Bengtson, 1994). As our review of personality changes in later life revealed, for example, older adults often become less active and energetic than they were earlier in life. Moreover, most seniors today do indeed withdraw voluntarily from certain roles and activities. Most notably, most choose to retire from work in their 60s, and society generally supports their doing so.

But third, neither activity theory nor disengagement theory says enough about the role of personality in influencing well-being in old age. Generally, people who are extraverted, conscientious, and emotionally stable have a greater sense of well-being than other adults (Siegler & Brummett, 2000). Even more important, a good fit between the individual's lifestyle and the individual's needs, preferences, and personality seems to be the real secret to successful aging (Fry, 1992; Seleen, 1982). Energetic and outgoing Linda may want to maintain her active lifestyle in old age by being highly involved in church activities and family affairs, whereas Albert, who always found work to be stressful and annoying, may like nothing better than to disengage by fishing the day away. Linda might be happy but Albert might be miserable if made to participate in a retirement community's sing-alongs, dances, and skits.

Rather than remaining highly active or disengaging entirely, many older adults find satisfaction by focusing on a few highly important roles, relationships, and personally meaningful projects, optimizing their competencies in those areas, and compensating for performance declines in other areas (Lawton et al., 2002; Turk-Charles & Carstensen, 1999). That is, they engage in SOC, which not only helps aging workers maintain good job performance but also works as a strategy for successful aging (Baltes & Carstensen, 2003; Freund & Riediger, 2006). In short, you cannot assume, as both activity theory and disengagement theory do, that what suits one suits all. Rather, you should again adopt an interactionist model of development that emphasizes the goodness of fit between person and environment and their influence on one another. In the next chapter, we explore some fascinating interactions between biology and environment that contribute to differences between males and females in cognition, personality, and behavior.

1. Identify two different senses in which there could be continuity in the Big Five dimension of conscientiousness from age 40 to age 50?
2. According to Erikson, when and how might an adult gain a sense of generativity?
3. Who theorizes that adults experience a midlife crisis in their early 40s, and what does research say about that?
4. What are three factors likely to make retirement a negative experience?

1. Costa and McCrae have argued that people's personalities are very stable by age 30 and hardly change thereafter. What evidence would you cite to refute them?
2. Aunt Rosalia is about to retire and wants to establish a satisfying lifestyle in old age. What would an activity theorist, a disengagement theorist, and an SOC theorist advise that she should do and why?

Chapter Summary

11.1 Conceptualizing the Self and Personality

- Personality is an organized combination of attributes unique to the individual. McAdams and Pals describe personality in terms of three aspects: dispositional traits, more changeable characteristic adaptations, and unique narrative identities. Self-concept is an individual's perceptions of those attributes; self-esteem one's overall evaluation of self-worth; and identity a coherent self-definition.
- Psychoanalytic theorists such as Erikson maintain that we all experience stagelike personality changes at similar ages; trait theorists believe that aspects of personality such as the Big Five trait dimensions are expressed across situations and are enduring, and social learning theorists maintain that people can change in any number of directions at any time if their social environments change.

11.2 The Infant

- Early in their first year, infants sense that they are separate from the world around them and develop a sense of agency; at around 18 months, at least in individualistic rather than collectivist cultures, they display self-recognition and form a categorical self based on age and sex.
- Infants differ in temperament: in easy, difficult, or slow-to-warm-up temperament (Thomas and Chess); behavioral inhibition (Kagan); and surgency/extraversion, negative affectivity, and effortful control (Rothbart). Temperament is influenced by

genes and goodness of fit with the environment, and some dimensions of temperament match up with Big Five personality dimensions.

11.3 The Child

- Whereas the self-concepts of preschool children are focused on physical characteristics and activities, 8-year-olds describe their inner psychological traits and social ties and evaluate their competencies through social comparison.
- Children are most likely to develop high self-esteem when they are competent, receive positive feedback in social comparisons, and have warm, democratic parents.
- Links between temperament in early childhood and later personality and adjustment are detectable, but some personality traits gel only in childhood and become even more consistent in adolescence and adulthood. Culture affects the adaptiveness of certain traits.

11.4 The Adolescent

- During adolescence, self-concepts become more psychological, abstract, differentiated, and integrated, and self-awareness increases; self-esteem dips for some but mainly increases over the adolescence.
- In resolving Erikson's conflict of identity versus role confusion, many college-age youths progress from the diffusion or foreclosure to the moratorium and identity achievement statuses, at different rates in different domains. Analyzing life stories, or narrative identities, is another approach to studying identity.

- Developing a positive ethnic identity is more central to minority than to majority group adolescents. Adolescents' vocational choices become increasingly realistic with age; the choices made by low-income youth and females are sometimes constrained, but as John Holland theorized, a good fit between personality and vocation predicts good vocational outcomes.
- Cognitive development, personality, parenting, opportunities for exploration, and culture, all influence identity development.

11.5 The Adult

- Although self-esteem typically rises into middle age and declines in late old age, older adults can maintain self-esteem by converging their ideal and real selves, changing their goals and standards of self-evaluation, comparing themselves with other aging adults, and not self-stereotyping. Self-conceptions differ in individualistic cultures and collectivist cultures.
- Individuals' rankings on Big Five dimensions of personality become more stable with age; excitement seeking, openness to experience, and, later, activity level typically decline, while maturity (emotional stability, conscientiousness, and agreeableness) increases over the adult years.

- Stability of personality may be caused by genes, early experience, stable environments, and gene–environment correlations; personality change may result from biological or environmental changes or a poor person–environment fit.
- Consistent with Erikson's psychosocial theory, resolution of conflicts centering on trust, autonomy, initiative, and industry paves the way for achieving a sense of identity in adolescence, intimacy in early adulthood, generativity in middle age, and integrity through life review in old age.
- Daniel Levinson's theory that adults experience a midlife crisis in their early 40s is not well supported, but young adults do engage in much career exploration and questioning before they settle down in their 30s and achieve peak success in their 40s. Older workers are generally as effective as younger workers, possibly because they use selective optimization with compensation (SOC) to cope with aging.
- Retiring workers may experience preretirement, honeymoon, disenchantment, and reorientation phases, and a drop in income, but little change in health, social involvement, or psychological well-being.
- In accounting for successful aging, neither activity theory nor disengagement theory places enough emphasis on personality, person–environment fit, or selective optimization with compensation.

Checking Mastery Answers

For answers to Checking Mastery questions, please see Appendix B.

Key Terms

CENGAGE   Get quizzes, flashcards, videos, and more at **www.cengagebrain.com**
brain.com

12 Gender Roles and Sexuality

Many of us have grown up taking our sex and gender for granted and living comfortably in our assigned category: male-female, boy-girl, man-woman. But are sex and gender really so simple that they can be captured with two distinct categories? Consider Kathryn who, at age 2, told her parents that she was a boy (see Dvorak, 2012). She was so determined that she was a boy and so unhappy about being viewed as a girl that her parents took her to a psychologist for advice. After much thought, they allowed their child to begin living as a boy, changed his name, shopped for "boy" clothes and toys, and referred to their child with masculine pronouns. The family's decision to allow their child to make this change was influenced, in part, by another family whose son, "Will," struggled throughout childhood with his male sex and gender, firmly believing that he was a girl (Dvorak, 2012). He threatened suicide at age 6 and was taken to therapists who concluded that the child "was probably just gay." It wasn't until their child was a teenager that the family finally capitulated and allowed "him" to live as "her," but then felt great remorse at forcing the male gender on their child for so long, leading to a childhood of misery.

Which of These Sex Differences Is Real?

Which of the following do you think are consistent sex differences that have been demonstrated in studies comparing males and females? Mark each statement true or false. Answers are printed upside down; they will be clarified in the main text.

_____ 1. Males are more aggressive than females.

_____ 2. Males are more active than females.

_____ 3. Females are more social than males.

_____ 4. Females have stronger verbal abilities than males.

_____ 5. Males have greater achievement motivation than females.

_____ 6. Males are more analytical than females.

_____ 7. Females are more suggestible and prone to conform than males.

_____ 8. Females are more emotionally unstable than males.

_____ 9. Males are more rational and logical than females.

_____ 10. Males have greater spatial and mathematical abilities than females.

Answers: 1-T, 2-T, 3-F, 4-T, 5-F, 6-F, 7-F, 8-F, 9-F, 10-T.

As illustrated by these two examples of **transgender** children—individuals who identify with a gender other than their biological one—sex and gender may not be as simple as we try to make them. These are not new issues. Among many Native American cultures, there has long been a third gender category ("two spirits") for those individuals who do not neatly fit into the male or the female category (Bonvillain, 2010). Similarly, in India, the term *hijras* is used to describe third-sex individuals, often individuals with biologically male or ambiguous genitalia who dress in ways that appear feminine but do not view themselves as either male or female. And in Sulawesi, an island in Indonesia, as many as five gender categories are recognized to capture the diversity of this characteristic (Davies, 2006). Clearly, there is much more complexity than the dichotomy of male-female, man-woman, suggests.

Gender matters. It used to be that the first question asked following a birth was whether the baby was a boy or girl. With today's technology, this question is often posed as soon as a pregnancy is announced. In most cases, as children develop, girls discover that they are girls and many acquire a taste for wearing pink clothes and playing with dolls, while boys discover that they are boys and often wrestle each other on the lawn. As an adult, you are probably keenly aware of being either a man or a woman and may define yourself partly in terms of roles or activities that highlight gender, such as mother, boyfriend, husband, wife, and so on. In short, being female or male is a highly important aspect of the self throughout the life span. Before you read any further, try the quiz in **Engagement Box 12.1** to see if you know which of the many beliefs we hold about males and females have some truth to them.

12.1 Sex and Gender

LEARNING OBJECTIVES:

* Distinguish between the concepts of sex and gender.

* Explore the emergence of gender stereotypes and explain the two main gender roles.

* Evaluate whether it makes more sense to talk about gender differences or gender similarities.

To what extent are you influenced by being a male or a female? Chances are good that sex and gender have influenced several characteristics that make you the unique person that you are, from your physical characteristics and abilities, to some of the roles you play in society, to some of your psychological characteristics. When we talk about your **biological sex**, we mean those physical characteristics that define male and female, whereas **gender** incorporates all those features that a society associates with or considers appropriate for men and women. For example, women menstruate as a result of their hormonal and physiologic makeup, making this a component of their biological sex. Men typically have larger bones and muscle mass than women,

another biological sex difference. Consider, though, that women as a group earn less money than men (Bureau of Labor Statistics, U.S. Department of Labor, 2013). This is not a sex difference but a gender difference because it arises from societal forces that have created different expectations and outcomes for males and females in the workforce. To understand how sex and gender might influence your life, let us consider some of the obvious physical differences before examining the psychological correlates of gender.

The physical differences between males and females are undeniable. A zygote that receives an X chromosome from each parent is a genetic (XX) female, whereas a zygote that receives a Y chromosome from the father is a genetic (XY) male. In rare cases of sex chromosome abnormalities (see Chapter 3), this is not the case; a girl may have only one X chromosome or a boy may have three sex chromosomes (XYY or XXY). Chromosomal differences result in different prenatal hormone balances in males and females, and hormone balances before and after birth are responsible for the facts that the genitals of males and females differ and that only females can bear children. Moreover, males typically grow to be taller, heavier, and more muscular than females, although females may be the hardier sex in that they live longer and are less susceptible to many physical disorders (but see Van Oyen et al., 2013 for a discussion of how longer life span may come at the cost of living with greater infirmities). As you will see later in the chapter, some theorists argue that biological differences between males and females are responsible for psychological and social differences.

There is, however, much more to being a man or woman than the biological features that define one's sex. Virtually all societies expect the two sexes to take on different **gender roles**— the patterns of behavior that females and males should adopt in a particular society (for example, the roles of wife, mother, and woman for females and of husband, father, and man for males). Characteristics and behaviors viewed as desirable for males or females are specified in *gender-role norms*—society's expectations or standards concerning what males and females *should be* like. Each society's norms generate **gender stereotypes**, overgeneralized and largely inaccurate beliefs about the characteristics of all males and all females (Halim & Ruble, 2010). For example, when trying to decide who should drive to a friend's house in an unfamiliar location, John may say to his new girlfriend, "I'll drive because you women always get lost," to which she replies, "Well, unlike you guys, at least women stop to ask for directions." They have both applied stereotypes about a group to an individual member of the group. The reality is that this particular woman may be a superb navigator and John may be highly likely to stop and ask directions. Where did such gender stereotypes come from and is there any truth behind them?

Gender Roles and Stereotypes

Many stereotypes originate with a grain of truth, and in the case of gender stereotypes, the grain may be the physical makeup of males and females. One clear physical difference between the sexes is women's ability to bear and nurse children. As a result, women have adopted the role of childbearer and nurturer and this role has shaped the gender-role norms that prevail in many societies, including our own. At the heart of the nurturer gender role is **communality** (or communion), an orientation that emphasizes connectedness to others and includes traits of emotionality and sensitivity to others (Best & Williams, 1993; Rosenkrantz et al, 1968). Girls who adopt communal traits will presumably be prepared to play the roles of wife and mother—to keep the family functioning and to raise children successfully. By contrast, the central aspect of the masculine gender role is **agency**, an orientation toward individual action and achievement that emphasizes traits of dominance, independence, assertiveness, and competitiveness. Boys have been encouraged

to adopt agentic traits to fulfill the traditionally defined roles of husband and father, which involve providing for the family and protecting it from harm. Taking this one step further, Baron-Cohen (2003) claims that men's focus on work, achievement, and independence stems from the male brain's tendency to **systemize**, or analyze and explore how things work. Communion and agency have long been viewed as two fundamental psychological dimensions of human nature that are widespread across a variety of cultures (Abele, 2003; Abele et al., 2008; Bakan, 1966; Williams & Best, 1990).

With gender-role norms in many cultures mandating that females play a communal role and males play an agentic role, stereotypes have arisen saying that females possess communal traits and males possess agentic traits (Williams & Best, 1990). If you are thinking that these stereotypes have disappeared as attention to women's rights has increased and as more women have entered the labor force, think again. Although some changes have occurred, children, adolescents, and adults still endorse many traditional stereotypes about men and women (see Sczesny et al., 2008). Boys are more likely than girls to endorse traditional stereotypes, perhaps because stereotypes about males (such as "independent") tend to be more positive than the stereotypes about females (for example, "dependent") (Rowley et al., 2007).

Moreover, males and females continued to describe themselves differently after gender roles changed dramatically during the 20th century. When Jean Twenge (1997) analyzed studies conducted from 1970 to 1995 in which standard scales assessing

Gelpi/Shutterstock.com

Take a look at this baby boy and write down a few adjectives describing what you think he might have been feeling or thinking at the time this photo was taken. Now suppose you learn that this "boy" is actually a girl. Do the adjectives still seem to fit? Do any of them reflect gender stereotyping?

gender-relevant traits had been administered, she found that men and women in the mid-1990s described themselves more similarly than men and women did 20 years previously, largely because modern women saw themselves as having more agentic traits. However, male and female personality profiles continued to differ in ways consistent with gender stereotypes.

Gender Differences or Similarities?

Much research has attempted to answer the question of whether there are meaningful gender differences in behavior. Although differences in some areas have been identified, other areas show no gender differences. Early research on gender seemed focused on trying to reveal differences of any size or value, and psychological differences between men and women were emphasized (see, for example, Tannen, 1991). More recently, Janet Hyde (2005, 2007) and others have proposed that it is more appropriate to focus on gender similarities. They advance a **gender similarities hypothesis**, which states that "males and females are similar on most, but not all, psychological variables. That is, men and women, as well as boys and girls, are more alike than they are different" (Hyde, 2005, p. 581). As you review the following research on gender, try to evaluate for yourself whether there are more gender similarities or differences, and where there are differences, decide whether they are large and meaningful or negligible and unimportant. Also keep in mind that these are *group differences*, and even when research shows that women score higher (or lower) than men on average, there will be individual women who score lower (or higher) than individual men. With this in mind, here is what the research shows:

- *Females sometimes display greater verbal abilities than males, but on most verbal tasks the difference is small.* One verbal task where females consistently outperform males is reading (Organization for Economic Co-operation and Development [OECD], 2012). This difference is observed in many different countries, and the size of the difference is often quite large.

- *Males outperform females on many tests of spatial ability* (for example, arranging blocks in patterns or identifying the same figure from different angles). Although some research suggests that these differences emerge only in adolescence, differences on some tests—especially mental rotations—can be detected in childhood and persist across the life span (for example, Choi & Silverman, 2003; Kaufman, 2007). It should be noted that on a few tests of spatial ability, namely remembering object locations, females outperform males (Voyer et al., 2007). Further, training in the form of playing action video games can reduce or eliminate the gender difference on most spatial tasks (Feng, Spence, & Pratt, 2007). Even the seemingly robust gender difference in favor of males on mental rotation tasks can be reduced or eliminated if individual differences in confidence to perform the task are eliminated (Estes & Felker, 2012). It may also be the case that it is having a masculine gender identity, something males have more than females, that leads to the apparent gender difference on mental rotation tasks (Reilly & Neumann, 2013).

Suppose you are asked to imagine how this cheese board would appear from a different perspective. How quickly and accurately can you mentally rotate the image in your mind and determine the appearance of the cheese from another viewpoint? Historically, males have demonstrated greater mental rotation skills than females.

Tetra Images/Getty Images

- Historically, males outperformed females on standardized tests of mathematical ability, but this male advantage has been shrinking in the United States and many other countries: *females and males perform similarly on most but not all standardized math tests, and females obtain slightly higher math grades in the classroom than males* (Else-Quest, Hyde, & Linn, 2010; Lachance & Mazzocco, 2006). In some countries (such as Austria, Chile, Germany, and Japan), there is a male advantage in math, perhaps reflecting different educational opportunities for males and females in these countries (OECD, 2012). In a handful of countries, females score higher than males (for example, Qatar and Jordan). Thus, in most cases there are not significant gender differences in math performance, but in those cases where there is a difference, it typically is in favor of males. Interestingly, males express more positive attitudes about math than do females, and this more positive outlook may create more opportunities for males to gain experience and comfort with math; for example, they may be more likely to sign up for higher level math classes than females (Else-Quest et al., 2010). A notable exception to the disappearing gender differences in this area is the College Board SAT Mathematics test, on which males continue to score approximately 30 points higher than females (College Board, 2012). Among the top scorers on the SAT-Math test, males outnumber females by a ratio of 2 to 1.

- *Girls display greater memory ability than boys.* Some studies show that this is a general or overall advantage (Johnson & Bouchard, 2007), whereas other research suggests that female's memory advantage is in specific areas. As noted earlier, there is a female advantage when it comes to remembering object locations, and other research shows females excel at recalling verbal information, as well as faces, particularly female faces (see Herlitz & Rehnman,

2008). Finally, listen to your female friends if they tell you something smells bad because women also show an advantage over men when it comes to recognizing familiar odors (Herlitz & Rehnman, 2008).

- *Males engage in more physical and verbal aggression than females, starting as early as 17 months* (Baillargeon et al., 2007; Burton, Hafetz, & Henninger, 2007; Buss & Perry, 1992). Across 21 diverse countries, teachers in nearly all the countries report that boys are more aggressive than girls (Rescorla et al., 2007; but see Kim, Kim, & Kamphaus, 2010). Sex differences are more obvious for physical aggression than for other forms of aggression. For example, at 17 months, for every girl who is physically aggressive there are five boys who display frequent physical aggression (Baillargeon et al., 2007). Males also commit more serious and more physically violent crimes (Barash, 2002). Some research shows that females tend to specialize in subtle, indirect, and relational forms of aggression such as gossiping about and excluding others (Crick & Bigbee, 1998; Murray-Close, Ostrov, & Crick, 2007; Ostrov & Godleski, 2010).
- Even before birth and throughout childhood, *boys are more physically active* than girls (Almli, Ball, & Wheeler, 2001); they fidget and squirm more as infants and run around more as children. In 19 out of 21 countries studied by Leslie Rescorla and colleagues (2007), teachers report that boys are more hyperactive than girls.
- *Boys are more developmentally vulnerable*, not only to prenatal and perinatal (birth-related) stress (for example, they die more often before birth) but also to several diseases and to disorders such as reading disabilities, speech defects, hyperactivity, emotional problems, and mental retardation (Henker & Whalen, 1989; Jacklin, 1989; Raz et al., 1994).
- *Girls are more tactful and cooperative, as opposed to being forceful and demanding, and are more compliant with requests from adults*, although they are no more likely than boys to give in to peers (Baron-Cohen, 2003; Maccoby, 1998).
- *Both males and females report that females are more nurturant and empathic.* Sex differences in behaviors are small but show females empathizing more than males (Baron-Cohen, 2003; Deutsch, 1999; Feingold, 1994).
- *Females are more prone to develop anxiety disorders, depression, and phobias* (Pigott, 2002). In contrast, *males are more likely to display antisocial behaviors and drug and alcohol abuse* (Hicks et al., 2007).
- *Males use computers more than females and express greater confidence in their computer abilities* (Li & Kurkup, 2007; Misa, 2010). These findings do not tell us, though, whether there are gender differences in computer ability.

What have you concluded from this collection of research on gender? Are males and females different in meaningful ways or are any differences trivial, as would be predicted by the gender similarities hypothesis? To help answer this, consider that if we ordered people based on degree of aggressiveness from most aggressive to the least aggressive person in a group, only 5% of the observed differences could be attributed to whether a person is male or female (Hyde, 1984). It is worth repeating the point we made earlier: *Average* levels of a behavior such as aggression may be noticeably different for males and females, but within each sex there are both extremely aggressive and extremely non-aggressive individuals. Therefore it is impossible to predict accurately how aggressive a person is simply by knowing that person's biological sex. Gender differences in most other abilities and personality traits are similarly small.

If, as we have just seen, females and males are more psychologically similar than different, then why do unfounded stereotypes persist? Partly because we, as the holders of male–female stereotypes, are biased in our perceptions. We are more likely to notice and remember behaviors that confirm our beliefs than to notice and remember exceptions, such as independent behavior in a woman or emotional sensitivity in a man (Martin & Halverson, 1981).

In addition, Alice Eagly's (2012) **social-role theory** suggests that differences in the roles that women and men play in society do a lot to create and maintain gender stereotypes. For example, men have traditionally occupied powerful roles in business and industry that require them to be dominant and forceful. Women have more often filled the role of homemaker and therefore have been called upon to be nurturant and sensitive to their children's needs. As a result, we begin to see men as dominant or agentic by nature and women as nurturant or communal by nature. We lose sight of the fact that the differences in the social roles they play cause men and women to behave differently; it is not all "by nature." Individuals even perceive themselves differently

According to Alice Eagly's social-role theory, this man would be perceived as nurturant, warm, and caring because he has assumed the role of caregiver.

depending on which of their roles they are considering: more agentic when thinking of their work role and more communal when thinking of their family role (Uchronski, 2008). Might gender differences in behavior be minimized or reversed if women ran companies and men raised children?

Some research suggests that this may be the case. Both men and women rate male and female homemakers as equally communal (Bosak, Sczesny, & Eagly, 2008). Thus, men who are in the role of homemaker are perceived as being just as caring and affectionate as women in this role. Still, women presented in employee roles are not always judged as equally agentic as men in employee roles. This may be a result of continued gender segregation of the workforce, with far more women in such occupations as nurse and teacher and far more men in occupations such as plumber, corporate executive, and construction worker. Thus, conjuring up the role of employee for men and women may lead not to a single image of what this role involves but to multiple images based on existing gender differences in types of work (Bosak et al., 2008).

Although psychological gender differences are often small, it still makes a difference in society whether a person is male or female. First, gender norms and stereotypes, even when they are unfounded, affect how we perceive ourselves and other people. As long as people expect females to be less competent in math than males, for example, females may lack confidence in their abilities and perform less competently (Eccles, Jacobs, & Harold, 1990). This was the conclusion reached by Zachary Estes and Sydney Felker (2012) in their research on mental rotation ability: Gender differences on this task were eliminated when males and females had the same confidence levels.

In addition, even though males and females are similar psychologically, they are steered toward different roles in society. In childhood, girls and boys conform to their gender roles by segregating themselves by biological sex and developing different interests and play activities (Maccoby, 1998). As adolescents and adults, males and females pursue different vocations and lifestyles. Although more women are entering male-dominated fields today than in the past, they are underrepresented in many traditionally male-dominated fields, and men rarely enter female-dominated fields (Bureau of Labor Statistics, U.S. Department of Labor, 2013). Occupations therefore remain highly gender segregated. For instance, the top five occupations held by U.S. women continue to be secretary, nurse, teacher, cashier, and nursing or health aide (U.S. Department of Labor, 2012). More men are sharing child-rearing and household responsibilities with their partners, but many couples still divide the labor along traditional lines, so that the woman is primarily responsible for child care and housework and the man is primarily responsible for income and money management (Perkins & DeMeis, 1996; Poortman & Van Der Lippe, 2009; Sayer, 2005). When we think about who asks whom out on a date, who stays home from work when a child has an ear infection, or who sews the buttons back on shirts, we must conclude that, despite significant social change, traditional gender roles are alive and well.

▶ Checking Mastery

1. What is the central feature of agency and of communion?
2. What are four differences between males and females, two that favor females and two that favor males, and how large or meaningful are these differences?
3. How does Eagly's social-role theory explain gender differences?

▶ Making Connections

1. What roles do you play as a result of your biological sex? For example, are you a son or a daughter? How do these roles influence your behavior? Would you, for instance, behave any differently if you were a son rather than a daughter (or vice versa)?
2. Your grandmother strongly believes that boys and girls (and men and women) are quite different. Sometimes, she is even bothered by some of your behaviors because she doesn't believe you are behaving like a "proper" young woman or man. How did her thinking about gender become so entrenched, and what could be done to soften her views?

12.2 The Infant

LEARNING OBJECTIVES:

- Describe how infants may be treated differently based on their biological sex and indicate how this may lead to gender differences.
- Explain what infants know about gender as a social category.

At birth there are few differences, other than the obvious anatomical ones, between males and females. Male newborns tend to be somewhat more irritable than females, and female newborns are more alert than males (Boatella-Costa et al., 2007). But overall, differences between males and females at birth are small and inconsistent. Nonetheless, it does not take long after newborns are labeled as girls or boys for gender stereotypes to affect how they are perceived and treated—and for infants to notice that males and females are different.

Differential Treatment

When the baby is still in the hospital delivery room or nursery, parents tend to use masculine terms when talking to or about their infant son (such as "big guy" or "tiger") and to comment on the strength of his cries, kicks, and grasps. Girl infants are more likely to be labeled "sugar" or "sweetie" and to be described as soft, cuddly, and adorable (see Eliot, 2009). Even when objective examinations reveal no such differences between boys and girls at birth, adults perceive boys as strong, large featured, and coordinated and view girls as weaker, finer featured, and more awkward (Rubin, Provenzano, & Luria, 1974). Soon boys and girls are decked out in either blue or pink and provided with "sex-appropriate" hairstyles, toys, and room furnishings (Pomerleau et al., 1990).

In an early study of the effects of gender stereotyping, college students watched a videotape of a 9-month-old infant who was introduced as either "Dana," a girl, or as "David," a boy (Condry & Condry, 1976). Students who saw "David" interpreted his strong reaction to a jack-in-the-box as anger, whereas students who watched "Dana" concluded that the same behavior was fear. A similar study found that college students rated babies introduced as males as stronger and more "masculine" than babies introduced as females (Burnham & Harris, 1992). Although stereotyping of boys and girls from birth could be partly the effect of differences between the sexes (Benenson, Philippoussis, & Leeb, 1999), it may also be a cause of such differences.

Early Learning

Yet infants are not merely the passive targets of other people's reactions to them; they are actively trying to get to know the social world around them and to get to know themselves. In a study that measured visual tracking of objects by 3- to 8-month-old infants, males spent more time looking at a truck whereas females spent more time looking at a doll (Alexander, Wilcox, & Woods, 2009). This suggests a rudimentary recognition of gender-stereotypic information. At around 3–4 months of age, infants can distinguish between male and female faces (Quinn et al., 2002). By the end of the first year, babies look longer at a male (or female) face when they hear a male (or female) voice than when they hear a voice that does not match the gender of the face, demonstrating cross-modal association of gender-related information (Fagot & Leinbach, 1993; Poulin-Dubois & Serbin, 2006). By 24 months, they look longer at males and females performing gender-inconsistent activities (such as a man putting on makeup) than those performing activities consistent with gender stereotypes (such as a man mowing the grass; Hill & Flom, 2007). Their response shows that they recognize something incongruent or odd about males and females engaged in activities inconsistent with gender stereotypes.

As they begin to categorize other people as males and females, they also figure out which of these two significant social categories they belong to. By 18 months, most toddlers seem to have an emerging understanding that they are either like other males or like other females, even if they cannot verbalize it (Martin, Ruble, & Szkrybalo, 2002). Girls as young as 24 months understand which activities are associated with males and which ones are more typical of females (Poulin-Dubois et al., 2002; see also Serbin, Poulin-Dubois, & Eichstedt, 2002). Boys, however, do not show the same understanding until at least 6 months later.

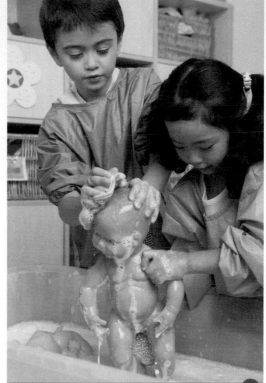

blue jean images/Getty Images

Which of these siblings, the brother or the sister, is likely to feel greater pressure to conform to gender stereotypes and play with toys that are thought to be gender-congruent? Why?

Almost all children give verbal proof that they have acquired a basic sense of **gender identity**, or an awareness that they are either a boy or a girl, by age 2½ to age 3 (Halim & Ruble, 2010; Zosuls et al., 2009).

As they acquire their gender identities, boys and girls also begin to behave differently. At an early age, boys usually prefer trucks and cars to other playthings, whereas girls of this age would rather play with dolls and soft toys (Berenbaum et al., 2008). Many 18- to 24-month-old toddlers are not interested in playing with toys regarded as appropriate for the opposite sex—even when there are no other toys to play with (Caldera, Huston, & O'Brien, 1989). As they approach age 2, then, infants are already beginning to behave in ways considered gender appropriate in our society.

The Beginnings of a Sexual Self

Sigmund Freud (see Chapter 2) made the seemingly outrageous claim that humans are sexual beings from birth onward. We are born, he said, with a reserve of sexual energy redirected toward different parts of the body as we develop. Freud may have been wrong about some things, but he was right that infants are sexual beings.

Babies are biologically equipped at birth with male or female chromosomes, hormones, and genitals. Moreover, young infants in Freud's oral stage of development appear to derive pleasure from sucking, mouthing, biting, and other oral activities. But the

Young children tend to be comfortable with their bodies and are curious about how they work and how they compare to other bodies. Most societies, though, impose restrictions on nakedness and discourage children from expressing too much curiosity about the body, which adults interpret as sexual expressions.

What should you make of these infant behaviors? Infants feel body sensations, but they are hardly aware that their behavior is "sexual" (Crooks & Baur, 2014). Infants are sexual beings primarily in the sense that their genitals are sensitive and their nervous systems allow sexual responses. They are also as curious about their bodies as they are about the rest of the world. They enjoy touching all parts of their body, especially those that produce pleasurable sensations, and are likely to continue touching themselves unless reprimands from parents or other grownups discourage this behavior, at least in public (Thigpen, 2009). From these early experiences, children begin to learn what human sexuality is about and how the members of their society regard it.

Checking Mastery

1. What is gender identity, and what evidence shows understanding of this concept during infancy?

Making Connections

1. Think of someone who recently became a new parent. In what ways has this person's thinking, and the thinking of his or her surrounding social network, already been shaped by knowing the biological sex of the baby? What is the baby's world like—can you tell by looking at its room or clothes whether it is a boy or girl?

clincher is this: Both male babies and female babies have been observed to touch and manipulate their genital areas, to experience physical arousal, and to undergo what appear to be orgasms (Hyde & DeLamater, 2014; Leung & Robson, 1993).

12.3 The Child

LEARNING OBJECTIVES:

- Analyze how children acquire gender stereotypes and how they are influenced by these stereotypes.
- Explain how children acquire a solid understanding of gender identity.
- Describe typical gendered behaviors that we can expect to see throughout childhood.
- Summarize and evaluate the usefulness of each theory of gender-role development.
- Outline children's understanding of sex and reproduction.

Much of the action in gender-role development takes place during the toddler and preschool years. Having already come to understand their basic gender identity, young children rapidly acquire gender stereotypes, or beliefs about what groups of males and females are supposedly like, and gender-typed behavioral patterns, or tendencies to favor "gender-appropriate" activities and behaviors over those typically associated with the other sex. Through the process of **gender typing**, children not only become aware that they are biological males or females but also acquire the motives, values, and patterns of behavior that their culture considers appropriate for members of their biological sex. Through the gender-typing process, for example, Susie may learn a gender-role norm stating that women should strive to be good mothers and gender-role stereotypes indicating that women are more skilled at nurturing children than men are. As an adult, Susan may then adopt the traditional communal role by switching from full-time to part-time work when her first child is born and devoting herself to the task of mothering.

It would be a mistake, then, to attribute any differences that we observe between girls and boys (or women and men) solely to biological causes. They could just as easily be caused by differences in the ways males and females are perceived and raised.

Acquiring Gender Stereotypes

As early as 2–3 years of age, children seem to understand society's gender stereotypes and act in gendered ways. Judith Blakemore (2003) showed pictures of toys to 3- to 11-year-olds and asked them whether boys or girls would usually play with each toy. Toys included masculine-stereotyped ones (for example, GI Joe dolls) and feminine-stereotyped ones (for example, Barbie dolls). Even the youngest children (3 years) knew that girls, but not boys, play with Barbie dolls and vice versa for GI Joes. They also recognized that boys and girls differ in clothes and hairstyles. Preschoolers are interviewed about gender stereotypes in the video in **Exploring Development Box 12.1**, "Gender in Early

Childhood." By age 5, boys hold more gender-stereotypical toy preferences than girls (Cherney, Harper, & Winter, 2006).

Over the next several years, children acquire considerably more "knowledge" about the toys and activities considered appropriate for girls or boys (Blakemore, 2003; Serbin, Powlishta, & Gulko, 1993). In one study, for instance, researchers (Levy, Sadovsky, & Troseth, 2000) asked 4- and 6-year-olds whether men or women would be better in two masculine-stereotyped occupations (car mechanic and airplane pilot) and two feminine-stereotyped occupations (clothes designer and secretary). Children believed that men would be more competent than women as mechanics and pilots, whereas women would make better designers and secretaries. Boys and girls also expressed positive emotions at the thought of growing up and holding gender-stereotypic occupations. They reacted negatively, however, when asked to consider holding gender-counterstereotypic occupations.

How seriously do children take the gender-role norms and stereotypes that they are rapidly learning? It depends on how old they are. Robin Banerjee and Vicki Lintern (2000) tested the rigidity of 4- to 9-year-olds' gender-stereotypic beliefs with four brief stories in which characters had either gender-stereotypic interests (for example, a boy named Tom who was best friends with another boy and liked playing with airplanes) or gender-counterstereotypic interests (for example, a boy named John who was best friends with a girl and liked playing with doll carriages). Children were then asked whether the target child would like to play with dolls, play football, skip, or play with toy guns. Younger children (4- and 6-year-olds) were considerably more rigid in their beliefs than older children; they did not believe boys would want to play with dolls or skip (stereotypic girl activities) or girls would want to play with footballs or toy guns (stereotypic boy activities). Some children seem particularly offended when peers step outside of traditional gender-stereotypic behaviors and will act as "enforcers" of gender-stereotyped behaviors, telling boys, "You shouldn't be playing with that doll" or telling girls, "That game is for boys" (see Martin & Ruble, 2010). Consistent with earlier research (Damon, 1977), rigidity about gender stereotypes is especially high during the preschool years (around ages 4–7), but then decreases over the elementary school years (Ruble et al., 2007). Research with children of different ethnic backgrounds also shows strong adherence to gender-typed behavior in the preschool-age group (Halim et al., 2013). Similar findings emerged from a longitudinal study of gender stereotypes. Hanns Trautner and his colleagues (2005) followed the same group of children from age 5 through age 10 to see if children who held rigid beliefs about gender stereotypes at age 5 remained unshakable in these beliefs over the next 5 years. As ■ Figure 12.1 shows, peak levels of rigidity occurred between ages 5 and 7, followed by significant relaxation of beliefs from age 7 to 10.

Why? The younger children are in the process of acquiring a clear understanding that their biological sex will remain constant, making them intolerant of anyone who violates traditional gender-role standards. These norms now have the force of absolute moral laws and must be obeyed: Boys must not play with dolls. Eleanor Maccoby (1998) suggests that young

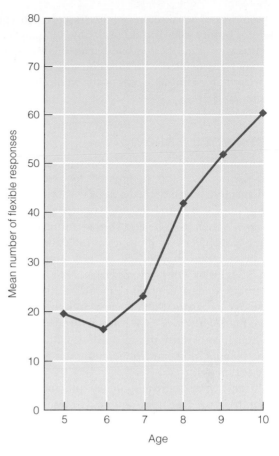

■ **Figure 12.1** Once gender identities are clearly established, usually by age 7, children become much more open about gender behaviors, as illustrated by the sharp increase in number of flexible responses to questions about what is "acceptable" behavior for boys and girls.

SOURCE: From Trautner, H. M., et al., Rigidity and flexibility of gender stereotypes in childhood: Developmental or differential? *Infant and Child Development*, 14, 370. Copyright © 2005. Reprinted with permission of John Wiley & Sons, Inc.

children may exaggerate gender roles to cognitively clarify these roles. However, once their gender identities are more firmly established, children can afford to be more flexible in their thinking about what is "for boys" and what is "for girls." They still know the stereotypes but no longer believe the stereotypes are "written in stone" (Martin et al., 2002). Other research suggests that children's rigidity about gender-role violations depends on how essential a behavior is to children's understanding of gender identity (Blakemore, 2003). Thus, children believe it would be bad for

Exploring Development 12.1
Gender in Early Childhood

Preschoolers are asked about their gender identity and about their perceptions of gender stereotypes.

- What characteristics do preschoolers understand as defining the difference between boys and girls?
- What behaviors do these preschoolers see as female and what behaviors as male?

boys to wear dresses because dresses are strongly associated with the feminine gender role. But if boys wanted to play with a toy kitchen, this would not be too bad because, although the toy kitchen may be associated with the feminine gender role, it is not considered an essential aspect of the feminine gender role (Blakemore, 2003).

Gender-Typed Behavior

Finally, children rapidly come to behave in "gender-appropriate" ways. As you have seen, preferences for gender-appropriate toys are detectable in infancy. Apparently, babies establish preferences for "boys' toys" (such as action figures and building toys) or "girls' toys" (such as dolls and stuffed animals) even before they have established clear identities as males or females or can correctly label toys as "boy things" or "girl things" (Cherney & London, 2006; Fagot, Leinbach, & Hagan, 1986). In childhood, preference for gender-congruent toys and activities is still evident, although occasionally both boys and girls choose "boys' toys" more than "girls' toys" (Cherney, 2005; Martin & Dinella, 2012). Their leisure activities also differ, with boys spending more time playing sports and video/computer games than girls (Cherney & London, 2006).

Children begin to favor same-sex playmates as early as 30–36 months of age (see, for example, Howes, 1988; Martin & Fabes, 2001). During the elementary school years, boys and girls develop even stronger preferences for peers of their own sex and show increased **gender segregation**, separating themselves into boys' and girls' peer groups and interacting far more often with their own sex than with the other sex (Halim & Ruble, 2010). Gender segregation occurs in a variety of cultures, including Botswana, Kenya, India, and the Philippines, and it increases with age (Bock, 2005; Leaper, 1994; Whiting & Edwards, 1988). At age 4½, children in the United States spend three times more time with same-sex peers than with peers of the other sex; by age 6½, they spend 11 times more time (**■ Figure 12.2**; Maccoby & Jacklin, 1987). This is partly because of incompatibilities between boys' and girls' play styles. Boys are too rowdy, domineering, and unresponsive to suit the tastes of many girls, so girls gravitate toward other girls and develop a style of interacting among themselves different from the rather timid style they adopt in the company of boys (Maccoby, 1998; Pellegrini et al., 2007).

But there is more to gender segregation than different activity levels of boys and girls (Martin et al., 2013). Preschool girls who are just as active as boys often start the school year playing with boys but end up in gender-segregated groups as they progress through the year in preschool (Pellegrini et al., 2007). Socialization pressures seem to encourage these active girls to drift away from the boys and create their own playgroup, separate from the active boys and the less-active girls. In a recent analysis of gender segregation, Carol Martin and her colleagues (2013) found that gender of potential playmates, and not the activity of the playmates, is the primary criterion for selecting playmates.

Some research suggests that children who insist most strongly on clear boundaries between the sexes and avoid consorting with the opposite sex tend to be socially competent and

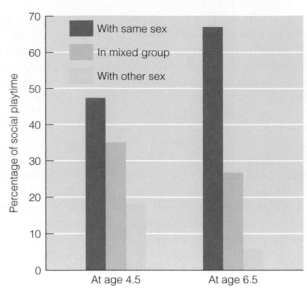

■ **Figure 12.2** Do children prefer playmates of their own sex? Apparently so. Both boys and girls spend more time playing with same-sex peers, especially at age 6.

Source: Reprinted from Maccoby, E. E., & Jacklin, C. N., Gender segregation in childhood, in *Advances in child development and behavior*, Volume 20, edited by H. Reese. Copyright © 1987 with permission from Elsevier.

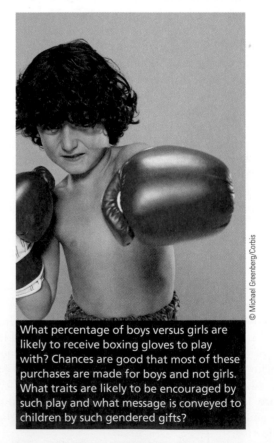

What percentage of boys versus girls are likely to receive boxing gloves to play with? Chances are good that most of these purchases are made for boys and not girls. What traits are likely to be encouraged by such play and what message is conveyed to children by such gendered gifts?

popular, whereas children who violate gender segregation rules tend to be less well adjusted and run the risk of being rejected by their peers (Rieger & Savin-Williams, 2012). But other research challenges these findings (Martin et al., 2012). Nonconforming children do seem to have fewer peer interactions, which means they have fewer socialization opportunities. Importantly, though, their more limited socialization does not seem to lead to problem behavior as earlier research suggested (Martin et al., 2012).

Boys face stronger pressures to adhere to gender-role expectations than girls do. This may be why they develop stronger gender-typed preferences at earlier ages (Banerjee & Lintern, 2000; O'Brien et al., 2000). Just ask your female classmates if they were tomboys when they were young; you are likely to find that somewhere between one-third and one-half readily acknowledge that they were "tomboys" or had masculine interests (Bailey, Bechtold, & Berenbaum, 2002; Martin & Dinella, 2012). But we challenge you to find many male classmates who willingly admit they were "sissies" or had feminine interests in their youth. Finally, it is important to note that gender-typed behavior in childhood—as early as age 3—is consistent with later gender-typed behavior (Golombok et al., 2012). Thus, boys and girls who display feminine or masculine behaviors at age 3 continue to have feminine or masculine preferences in adolescence.

We have now surveyed some major milestones in gender-role development. Now comes the most intriguing question about gender-role development in childhood and adolescence: How can it be explained?

Explaining Gender-Role Development

Several theories about the development of gender roles have been proposed. Some theories emphasize the role of biological differences between the sexes, whereas others emphasize social influences on children. Some emphasize what society does to children; others focus on what children do to themselves as they try to understand gender and all its implications. In Chapter 2, we learned that Freud believed that gender-role behaviors are shaped early, during the phallic stage, when children harbor a strong, biologically based love for the parent of the other sex; experience internal conflict and anxiety as a result of this incestuous desire; and resolve the conflict through a process of identification with the same-sex parent. Although Freud's views on gender sparked controversy and research, there is little support for this theory of gender-typing. Here, we will examine a biologically oriented theory and then consider the more "social" approaches offered by social learning theory, cognitive-developmental theory, and gender schema theory.

Biosocial Theory

The **biosocial theory** of gender-role development proposed by John Money and Anke Ehrhardt (1972) calls attention to the ways in which biological events influence the development of boys and girls. But it also focuses on ways in which early biological developments influence how people react to a child and suggests that these social reactions have much to do with children's assuming gender roles.

Chromosomes, Hormones, and Social Labeling Money and Ehrhardt stress that the male (XY) or female (XX) chromosomes most of us receive at conception are merely a starting point in biological differentiation of the sexes. Several critical events

affect a person's eventual preference for the masculine or feminine role (see also Breedlove, 1994):

1. If certain genes on the Y chromosome are present, a previously undifferentiated tissue develops into testes as the embryo develops; otherwise, it develops into ovaries.
2. The testes of a male embryo normally secrete more of the male hormone testosterone, which stimulates the development of a male internal reproductive system, and another hormone that inhibits the development of female organs. Without these hormones, the internal reproductive system of a female will develop from the same tissues.
3. Three to four months after conception, secretion of additional testosterone by the testes normally leads to the growth of a penis and scrotum. If testosterone is absent (as in normal females), or if a male fetus's cells are insensitive to the male sex hormones he produces, female external genitalia (labia and clitoris) will form.
4. The relative amount of testosterone alters the development of the brain and nervous system. For example, it signals the male brain to stop secreting hormones in a cyclical pattern so that males do not experience menstrual cycles at puberty.

Thus, fertilized eggs have the potential to acquire the anatomical and physiological features of either sex. Events at each critical step in the sexual differentiation process determine the outcome.

Once a biological male or female is born, social labeling and differential treatment of girls and boys interact with biological factors to steer development. Parents and other people label and begin to react to children on the basis of the appearance of their genitalia. If children's genitals are abnormal and they are mislabeled as members of the other sex, this incorrect label will affect their future development. For example, if a biological male were consistently labeled and treated as a girl, he would, by about age 3, acquire the gender identity of a girl. Finally, biological factors reenter the scene at puberty when large quantities of hormones are released, stimulating the growth of the reproductive system and the appearance of secondary sex characteristics. These events, combined with a person's earlier self-concept as a male or female, provide the basis for adult gender identity and role behavior. The complex series of critical points in biological maturation and social reactions to biological changes that Money and Ehrhardt (1972) propose is diagrammed in ■ **Figure 12.3**. But how much is nature, and how much is nurture?

Evidence of Biological Influences Much evidence suggests that biological factors influence the development of males and females in many species of animals (Breedlove, 1994). Evolutionary psychologists notice that most societies socialize males to have agentic traits and females to have communal ones; they conclude that traditional gender roles may be a reflection of species heredity (Archer, 1996; Buss, 1995). In addition, individual differences in agency and communality may be partly genetic. Twin studies suggest that individual heredity accounts for 20–50% of the variation in the extent to which people describe themselves as having masculine and feminine psychological

■ **Figure 12.3** Critical events in John Money and Anke Ehrhardt's biosocial theory of gender typing.

SOURCE: From *Man and woman, boy and girl*, by J. Money and A. Ehrhardt, 1972, Johns Hopkins University Press. Reprinted by permission.

traits (Iervolino et al., 2005; Loehlin, 1992). In other words, experience does not explain everything.

Biological influences on development are also evident in studies of children exposed to the "wrong" hormones prenatally. For instance, consider the consequences to offspring of mothers who, in past decades, were given drugs containing progestins to help prevent miscarriages (Brunskill, 1992). The drugs were converted by the mother's body into the male hormone testosterone and, depending on the dose and timing, ended up masculinizing female fetuses so that, despite their XX genetic endowment and female internal organs, they were born with external organs that resembled those of a boy (for example, a large clitoris that looked like a penis and fused labia that resembled a scrotum). Several of these **androgenized females**—girls prenatally exposed to excess androgens—were recognized as genetic females, underwent surgery to alter their genitals, and were then raised as girls. When compared with their sisters and other girls, it became apparent that many more androgenized girls were tomboys and preferred boys' toys and vigorous activities to traditionally feminine pursuits (Money & Ehrhardt, 1972; see also Meyer-Bahlburg et al., 2006). As adolescents, they began dating somewhat later than other girls and felt that marriage should be delayed until they had established their careers. A high proportion (37%) described themselves as homosexual or bisexual (Money, 1985; see also Dittman, Kappes, & Kappes, 1992). Androgenized females may also perform better than most other females on tests of spatial ability, further evidence that early exposure to male hormones has "masculinizing" effects on a female fetus (Kimura, 1992; Resnick et al., 1986; but see Malouf et al., 2006).

In addition, male exposure to testosterone and other male hormones may be part of the reason males are more likely than females to commit violent acts (Rubinow & Schmidt, 1996). Evidence from experiments conducted with animals is quite convincing. For example, female rhesus monkeys exposed prenatally to the male hormone testosterone often threaten other monkeys, engage in rough-and-tumble play, and try to "mount" a partner as males do at the beginning of a sexual encounter (Young, Goy, & Phoenix, 1964; Wallen, 1996). Men with high testosterone levels tend to have high rates of delinquency, drug abuse, abusiveness, and violence, although nature interacts with nurture so that these links between testosterone and antisocial behavior are not nearly as evident among men high in socioeconomic status as among men low in socioeconomic status (Dabbs & Morris, 1990). Note, however, that these are correlational studies showing an association between testosterone and aggression; they do not show us the direction of the relationship. In addition, we need to consider how levels of testosterone operate in conjunction with other hormones, particularly cortisol and serotonin, which might mediate the effects of testosterone (see Montoya et al., 2012).

Biologist Robert Sapolsky (1998) has argued that being in an aggressive situation may raise testosterone levels. Because testosterone levels rise as a result of aggressive and competitive activities, it has been difficult to establish unambiguously that high concentrations of male hormones cause aggressive behavior in humans (Archer, 1991). Still, animal experiments show that early experiences can alter the developing nervous systems of males and females and, in turn, their behavior (Breedlove,

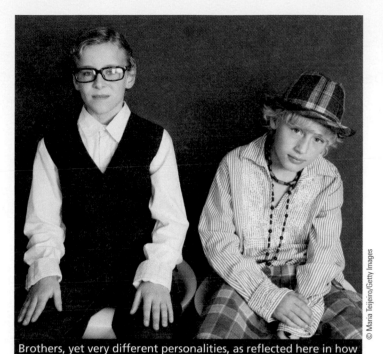

Brothers, yet very different personalities, as reflected here in how they are dressed. According to the biosocial theory, what factors influence children's acquisition of gender-typed behaviors?

1994). Much evidence suggests that prenatal exposure to male or female hormones has lasting effects on the organization of the brain and, in turn, on sexual behavior, aggression, cognitive skills such as spatial abilities, and other aspects of development (Auyeung et al., 2012; Rubinow & Schmidt, 1996). Yet biology does not dictate gender-role development. Instead, gender-role development evolves from the complex interaction of biology, social experience, and the individual's behavior.

Evidence of Social-Labeling Influences We must also take seriously the social aspect of Money and Ehrhardt's biosocial theory. How a child is labeled and treated can considerably affect gender development. For instance, some androgenized females were labeled as boys at birth and raised as such until their abnormalities were detected. Money and Ehrhardt (1972) report that the discovery and correction of this condition (by surgery and relabeling as a girl) caused few adjustment problems if the sex change took place before 18 months. After age 3, sexual reassignment was exceedingly difficult because these genetic females had experienced prolonged masculine gender typing and had already labeled themselves as boys. These findings led Money and Ehrhardt to conclude that there is a critical period between 18 months and 3 years for the establishment of gender identity when the label society attaches to the child is likely to stick. Yet some studies in which infants are presented to some people as boys but to others as girls indicate that labeling has little effect on how people perceive and treat these infants (Stern & Karraker, 1989). And, as **Exploration Box 12.1** on social labeling and biological destiny shows, biological males who are labeled as girls during the so-called critical period sometimes adopt a male gender identity later in life despite their early labeling and socialization, suggesting that we should refer to a sensitive rather than a

critical period. Once again, then, we see both nature and nurture at work in development.

Social Learning Theory

According to social learning theorists, children learn masculine or feminine identities, preferences, and behaviors through two processes. First, through *differential reinforcement*, children are rewarded for sex-appropriate behaviors and are punished for behaviors considered more appropriate for members of the other sex. Second, through *observational learning*, children adopt the attitudes and behaviors of same-sex models. In this view, children's gender-role development depends on which of their behaviors people reinforce or punish and on what sorts of social models are available. Change the social environment and you change the course of gender-role development.

Differential Reinforcement Parents use differential reinforcement to teach boys how to be boys and girls how to be girls (Lytton & Romney, 1991). By the second year of life, parents are already encouraging sex-appropriate play and discouraging cross-sex play, before children have acquired their basic gender identities or display clear preferences for male or female activities (Fagot & Leinbach, 1989). By 20–24 months, daughters are reinforced for dancing, dressing up (as women), following their parents around, asking for help, and playing with dolls; they are discouraged from manipulating objects, running, jumping, and climbing. By contrast, sons are not encouraged to pursue such "feminine" behavior as playing with dolls or seeking help and they receive more positive responses from their parents when they play with "masculine" toys such as blocks, trucks, and push-and-pull toys (Blakemore, 2003; Fagot, 1978; Fagot, Leinbach, & O'Boyle, 1992). Mothers and fathers may also discipline their sons and daughters differently, with fathers more likely to use physical forms of discipline (such as spanking) than mothers and mothers more likely to use reasoning to explain rules and consequences (Conrade & Ho, 2001; Russell et al., 1998). In addition, boys end up on the receiving end of a spanking more often than girls do (Day & Peterson, 1998). Some of this differential treatment is influenced by multiple factors, including children's birth order and gender composition of siblings (Crouter, Whiteman, & Osgood, 2007). For instance, being the youngest daughter with only brothers as siblings leads to a different set of experiences in the family than being the youngest brother with only sisters as siblings.

In research by Barbara Morrongiello and Kerri Hogg (2004), mothers were asked to imagine how they would react if their 6- to 10-year-old son or daughter misbehaved in some way that might be dangerous (for example, bicycling fast down a hill they had been told to avoid). Mothers reported that they would be angry with their sons but disappointed and concerned with their daughters for misbehaving and putting themselves in harm's way. Boys will be boys, they reasoned, but girls should know better. To prevent future risky behaviors, mothers said they would be more rule-bound with their daughters but would not do anything different with their sons. After all, they reasoned, there is no point in trying to prevent these risky behaviors in boys because it is "in their nature." Girls' behavior, on the other

Is the Social Label Everything, or Is Biology Destiny?

When biological sex and social labeling conflict, which wins out? Consider the tragic case of a male identical twin, named Bruce at birth, whose penis was damaged beyond repair during a botched circumcision (Money & Tucker, 1975). On the advice of John Money, who at the time was considered the world's leading authority on gender identity, the parents agreed to a surgical procedure that removed what was left of the damaged penis and altered their 21-month-old boy's external genitals to appear feminine. From then on, they treated him like a girl. By age 5, Money reported that this boy-turned-girl, now named Brenda, was different from her genetically identical brother. According to Money and the team in charge of her treatment, Brenda clearly knew she was a girl; had developed strong preferences for feminine toys, activities, and apparel; and was far neater and daintier than her brother. This, then, was supposedly a vivid demonstration that the most decisive influence on gender-role development is how a child is labeled and treated during the critical period for such development. But there is much more to the story.

Milton Diamond and H. Keith Sigmundson (1997) followed up on this twin and found that the story had a very different and ultimately disastrous ending from what Money reported (see also Colapinto, 1997, 2000, 2004). It turns out that Brenda was never comfortable with doll play and other traditionally feminine pursuits; she preferred to dress up in men's clothing, play with her twin brother's toys, and take things apart to see how they worked. She used the jumping rope she was given to whip people and tie them up; she was miserable when she was forced to make daisy chains and become a Girl Scout rather than a Boy Scout (Colapinto, 1997). Somewhere around age 10, she had the distinct feeling that she was not a girl: "I began to see how different I felt and was . . . . I thought I was a freak or something . . . but I didn't want to admit it. I figured I didn't want to wind up opening a can of worms" (Colapinto, 2000, pp. 299–300). Being rejected by other children because of her masculine looks and feminine dress and being

called "cavewoman" and "gorilla" also took their toll, as did continued pressure from psychiatrists to behave in a more feminine manner. Finally, at age 14 and after years of inner turmoil and suicidal thinking, Brenda had had it and simply refused to take the female hormones prescribed for her and pretend to be a girl any longer. When finally told that she was a chromosomal male and had started life as a normal baby boy, Brenda was relieved: "Suddenly it all made sense why I felt the way I did. I *wasn't* some sort of weirdo" (Colapinto, 1997, p. 92). She then received male hormone shots, a double mastectomy, and surgery to construct a penis and emerged as a nice young man who eventually dated girls, married at age 25, and for a time, seemed to settle into his hard-won identity as an adult male named David.

When he realized that his case was being used to justify sex change operations on other infants with injured or ambiguous genitals, he went public with his story and spoke out against this practice. David and his family struggled for years with the aftermath of the attempt to change his sex. His twin brother died of a drug overdose at age 36, and 2 years later David committed suicide.

This disturbing case study shows that we must back off from the conclusion that social learning is all that matters. Clearly, for Bruce/Brenda/David, gender identity was not as pliable as Money believed. And this is not the only case that illustrates that biology, along with social environment, matters when it comes to gender identity. Researchers studied a group of 18 biological males in the Dominican Republic who had a genetic condition that made their cells insensitive to the effects of male hormones (Imperato-McGinley et al., 1979, 1991; see also Herdt & Davidson, 1988). They had begun life with ambiguous genitals, were mistaken for girls, and so were labeled and raised as girls. However, under the influence of male hormones produced at puberty, they sprouted beards and became entirely masculine in appearance. How, in light of Money and Ehrhardt's critical-period hypothesis, could a person possibly adjust to becoming a man after leading an entire childhood as a girl?

Amazingly, 16 of these 18 individuals seemed able to accept their late conversion

David, shown here as an adult, after spending his childhood as Brenda.

from female to male and to adopt masculine lifestyles, including the establishment of heterosexual relationships. One retained a female identity and gender role, and the remaining individual switched to a male gender identity but still dressed as a female. This study also casts doubt on the notion that socialization during the first 3 years is critical to later gender-role development. Instead, it suggests that hormonal influences may be more important than social influences. It is possible, however, that Dominican adults, knowing that this genetic disorder was relatively common in their society, treated these girls-turned-boys differently from other girls when they were young or that these youngsters recognized on their own that their genitals were not normal (Ehrhardt, 1985). As a result, we cannot rule out the possibility that the socialization of these children may have been different from that of other children (Saucier & Ehresman, 2010).

What studies such as these of individuals with genital abnormalities appear to teach us is this: We are predisposed by our biology to develop as males or females; the first 3 years of life are a sensitive period perhaps, but not a critical period, for gender-role development; and both biology and social labeling contribute to gender-role development.

hand, can be influenced, so mothers may believe that it is worth enforcing an existing rule or instituting a new one. It's not just mothers: Other research shows that fathers are more protective of their preschool-aged daughters than their preschool-aged sons (Hagan & Kuebli, 2007).

Remember those androgenized females who were exposed to masculinizing hormones prenatally? You learned that these girls often exhibited a more masculine profile of play preferences and abilities and that this may result from the biological influence of prenatal hormones. But consider also that parents seem to treat girls who were prenatally exposed to masculine hormones differently than other girls (Wong et al., 2013). For instance, parents are more likely to encourage counter-stereotypical play in their daughters with ambiguous or masculinized genitalia. This differential socialization may be in response to behavioral differences detected in these girls and may function to further reinforce their male gender-typed behavior.

Does the "gender curriculum" in the home influence children? It certainly does. Parents who show the clearest patterns of differential reinforcement have children who are relatively quick to label themselves as girls or boys and to develop strongly sex-typed toy and activity preferences (Fagot & Leinbach, 1989; Fagot et al., 1992). Fathers play a central role in gender socialization; they are more likely than mothers to reward children's gender-appropriate behavior and to discourage behavior considered more appropriate for the other sex (Leve & Fagot, 1997; Lytton & Romney, 1991). This may reflect fathers' use of more explicit—directly stated—gender stereotypes about how boys and girls should act, whereas mothers are less likely to explicitly express gender stereotypes (Endendijk et al., 2013). Thus, fathers may overtly state their gender stereotypes (for example, "guys shouldn't wear jewelry"), whereas mothers may be unconsciously influenced by implicit stereotypes without directly stating these stereotypes (for example, throwing away a brochure for a math camp, assuming a daughter will not be interested in this). Fathers, then, may be an especially important influence on the gender-role development of both sons and daughters.

Could differential treatment of boys and girls by parents also contribute to gender differences in ability? Possibly so. Jacquelynne Eccles and her colleagues (1990) have conducted several studies to determine why girls tend to shy away from math and science courses and are underrepresented in occupations that involve math and science (see also Benbow & Arjmand, 1990). They suggest that parental expectations about gender differences in mathematical ability become self-fulfilling prophecies. The plot goes something like this:

1. Parents, influenced by societal stereotypes about gender differences in ability, expect their sons to outperform their daughters in math and expect their sons will be more interested in math and science than their daughters (Tenenbaum & Leaper, 2003).
2. Parents attribute their sons' successes in math to ability but credit their daughters' successes to hard work. Perhaps as a result of this, fathers talk differently to their sons and daughters when discussing science with them (Tenenbaum &

Leaper, 2003). With their sons, they use more scientific terms, provide more detailed explanations, and ask more abstract questions than with their daughters. These differences reinforce the belief that girls lack mathematical talent and turn in respectable performances only through plodding effort.
3. Children begin to internalize their parents' views, so girls come to believe that they are "no good" in math. Girls report that they are less competent and more anxious about their performance than boys (Pomerantz, Altermatt, & Saxon, 2002).
4. Thinking they lack ability, girls become less interested in math, are less likely to take math courses, and are less likely to pursue career possibilities that involve math after high school.

In short, parents who expect their daughters to have trouble with numbers may get what they expect. The negative effects of low parental expectancies on girls' self-perceptions are evident regardless of their performance. Indeed, girls feel less competent than do boys about math and science even when they outperform the boys (Pomerantz et al., 2002). Girls whose parents are nontraditional in their gender-role attitudes and behaviors do not show the declines in math and science achievement in early adolescence that girls from more traditional families display, so apparently the chain of events Eccles describes can be broken (Updegraff, McHale, & Crouter, 1996).

Observational Learning Social learning theorists call attention to differential treatment of girls and boys by parents, peers, and teachers; they also emphasize that observational learning contributes in important ways to gender typing. Children see which toys and activities are "for girls" and which are "for boys" and imitate individuals of their own sex. Around age 6 or 7, children begin to pay much closer attention to same-sex models than to other-sex models; for example, they will choose toys that members of their own sex prefer even if it means passing up more attractive toys (Frey & Ruble, 1992). Children who see their mothers perform agentic tasks and their fathers perform household and child care tasks tend to be less aware of gender stereotypes and less gender typed than children exposed to traditional gender-role models at home (Sabattini & Leaper, 2004; Turner & Gervai, 1995). Similarly, boys with sisters and girls with brothers have less gender-typed activity preferences than children who grow up with same-sex siblings perhaps, as you learned earlier, because the socialization within the family varies according to both the gender composition and the age of siblings (Colley et al., 1996; Endendijk et al., 2013; Rust et al., 2000).

Not only do children learn by watching the children and adults with whom they interact, but they also learn from the media—radio, television, movies, video games—and even from their picture books and elementary school texts. Although sexism in children's books has decreased over the past 50 years, male characters are still more likely than female characters to engage in active, independent activities such as climbing, riding bikes, and making things, whereas female characters are more often depicted as passive, dependent, and helpless, spending their time picking flowers, playing quietly indoors, and "creating problems that require masculine solutions" (Crabb & Marciano, 2011; Diekman & Murnen, 2004). Several analyses of children's books show continued gender-stereotypic representations of men and women in these books (Adams, Walker, & O'Connell, 2011; Anderson & Hamilton, 2007; DeWitt, Cready, & Seward, 2013). Although discouraging, the reality is that these gender-stereotypic portrayals in children's book largely mirror the continued gender-stereotypic roles in real life.

In recent decades, blatant gender stereotyping of television characters has decreased but not disappeared. Male characters still dominate on many children's programs, prime-time programs, and advertisements (Ganahl, Prinsen, & Netzley, 2003; Glascock, 2001; Smith et al., 2010). Even on shows with an equal number of male and female characters, the male characters assume more prominent roles (Ogletree et al., 2004). Typically, men are influential individuals who work at a profession, whereas many women—especially those portrayed as married—are passive, emotional creatures who manage a home or work at "feminine" occupations such as nursing (Signorielli & Kahlenberg, 2001). Women portrayed as single are often cast in traditionally male occupations. The message children receive is that men work regardless of their marital status and they do important business, but women only work at important jobs if they are single (Signorielli & Kahlenberg, 2001). Children who watch a large amount of television are more likely to choose gender-appropriate toys and to hold stereotyped views of males and females than their classmates who watch little television (Signorielli & Lears, 1992).

Perhaps the strongest traditional gender stereotypes are found in today's video games, which males play at a much higher rate than females (Ogletree & Drake, 2007). College students, both male and female, report that female video game characters are portrayed as helpless and sexually provocative, in contrast to male characters who are portrayed as strong and aggressive (Ogletree & Drake, 2007). Men do not find these stereotypes as offensive as do women, perhaps because men already hold more traditional gender stereotypes than women (Brenick et al., 2007).

Males of all ages play video games more than do females.

To recap, there is much evidence that both differential reinforcement and observational learning contribute to gender-role development. However, social learning theorists often portray children as the passive recipients of external influences: Parents, peers, television and video game characters, and others show them what to do and reinforce them for doing it. Perhaps this perspective does not put enough emphasis on what children contribute to their own gender socialization. Youngsters do not receive gender-stereotyped birthday presents simply because their parents choose these toys for them. Instead, parents tend to select gender-neutral and often educational toys for their children, but their boys ask for trucks and their girls request tea sets (Alexander, 2003; Robinson & Morris, 1986; Servin, Bohlin, & Berlin, 1999).

Cognitive Theories

Some theorists have emphasized cognitive aspects of gender-role development, noting that as children acquire understanding of gender, they actively teach themselves to be girls or boys. Lawrence Kohlberg based his cognitive theory on Jean Piaget's cognitive-developmental theory, whereas Carol Martin and Charles Halverson, Jr., based their theory on an information-processing approach to cognitive development.

Cognitive-Developmental Theory Kohlberg (1966a) proposed a cognitive theory of gender typing that is different from the other theories you have considered and that helps explain why boys and girls adopt traditional gender roles even when their parents do not want them to do so. Among the major themes of this cognitive-developmental perspective are the following:

- Gender-role development depends on stage-like changes in cognitive development; children must acquire certain understandings about gender before they will be influenced by their social experiences.
- Children engage in self-socialization; instead of being the passive targets of social influence, they actively socialize themselves.

According to both psychoanalytic theory and social learning theory, children are influenced by their companions to adopt male or female roles before they view themselves as girls or boys and identify with (or habitually imitate) same-sex models. Kohlberg suggests that children first understand that they are girls or boys and then actively seek same-sex models and a range of information about how to act like a girl or a boy. To Kohlberg, it is not "I'm treated like a boy; therefore, I must be a boy." It is more like "I'm a boy, so now I'll do everything I can to find out how to behave like one." Or, as May Ling Halim and Diane Ruble (2010) explain, the theory "views children as internally, self-initiated 'gender detectives'—agents who actively construct the meaning of gender categories, rather than as passive recipients of external gender socialization agents" (p. 495).

What understandings are necessary before children will teach themselves to behave like boys or girls? Kohlberg believes that children everywhere progress through the following three steps as they acquire **gender constancy**, or understanding that our genders remain the same throughout our lives and despite superficial changes in appearance.

1. Basic gender identity is established by age 2 or 2½, when children can recognize and label themselves as males or females (Campbell, Shirley, & Caygill, 2002; Zosuls et al., 2009).

2. Somewhat later—around age 3—children acquire **gender stability**—that is, they come to understand that gender identity is stable over time. They know that boys invariably become men and girls grow up to be women.

3. The gender concept is complete, somewhere between age 5 and age 7, when children achieve **gender consistency** and realize that their sex is also stable across situations. Now children know that their sex cannot be altered by superficial changes such as dressing up as a member of the other sex or engaging in cross-sex activities.

Research shows that children 3–5 years of age often do lack the concepts of gender stability and gender consistency; they often say that a boy could become a mommy if he really wanted to or that a girl could become a boy if she cut her hair and wore a football uniform (Warin, 2000). It is at this point that many girls succumb to "PFD syndrome," the strong desire to wear pink, frilly dresses and embrace all that is pink (see Halim and Ruble, 2010; Ruble, Lurye, & Zosuls, 2007). Doing so may help these young 'gender detectives' solidify their new understanding of themselves as girls. Boys may also go through a similar stage where they adhere to all things boy-like (for example, clothing with action figures or camouflage) and, just as importantly for boys, avoidance of all things girl-like such as pink, frilly dresses (Halim & Ruble, 2010).

As children enter Piaget's concrete-operational stage of cognitive development and come to grasp concepts such as conservation of liquids, they also realize that gender is conserved—remains constant—despite changes in appearance. Gender constancy is demonstrated by very few 3- to 5-year-olds, about half of 6- to 7-year-olds, and a majority of 8- to 9-year-olds (Trautner, Gervai, & Nemeth, 2003). In support of Kohlberg's theory, Jo Warin (2000) found that children who have achieved the third level of understanding display more gender-stereotypic play preferences than children who have not yet grasped gender consistency.

But not all research supports this view of gender-role development. In one study, children who had acquired only the first step in the process—applying gender labels to themselves— began to engage in more gender-typed play, which, according to Kohlberg's model, shouldn't occur until after the third step (Zosuls et al., 2009). Other research similarly shows that children need not reach the concrete operations stage to understand gender stability and consistency if they have sufficient knowledge of male and female anatomy to realize that people's genitals make them male or female (Bem, 1989). Children who have younger siblings often arrive at this understanding earlier than children with only older siblings or those without siblings (Karniol, 2009). The most controversial aspect of Kohlberg's cognitive-developmental theory, however, has been his claim that only when children fully grasp that their biological sex is

unchangeable, around age 5 to age 7, do they actively seek same-sex models and attempt to acquire values, interests, and behaviors consistent with their cognitive judgments about themselves. Although some evidence supports some aspects of Kohlberg's version of cognitive-developmental theory, this chapter shows that children learn many gender-role stereotypes and develop clear preferences for same-sex activities and playmates long before they master the concepts of gender stability and gender consistency and then, according to Kohlberg, attend more selectively to same-sex models (Halim & Ruble, 2010). It seems that only a rudimentary understanding of gender is required before children learn gender stereotypes and preferences.

Gender Schema Theory Martin and Halverson (1981, 1987) have proposed a somewhat different cognitive theory, an information-processing one that overcomes the key weakness of Kohlberg's theory. Like Kohlberg, they believe that children are intrinsically motivated to acquire values, interests, and behaviors consistent with their cognitive judgments about the self. However, Martin and Halverson argue that self-socialization begins as soon as children acquire a basic gender identity, around age 2 or age 3. According to their schematic-processing model, children acquire **gender schemata** (plural of **schema**)— organized sets of beliefs and expectations about males and females that influence the kinds of information they will attend to and remember.

First, children acquire a simple in-group–out-group schema that allows them to classify some objects, behaviors, and roles as appropriate for males and others as appropriate for females (cars are for boys, girls can cry but boys should not, and so on). Then they seek more elaborate information about the role of their own sex, constructing an own-sex schema. Thus, a young girl who knows her basic gender identity might first learn that sewing is for girls and building model airplanes is for boys. Then, because she is a girl and wants to act consistently with her own self-concept, she gathers a great deal of information about sewing to add to her own-sex schema, largely ignoring any information that comes her way about how to build model airplanes (**■ Figure 12.4**).

Consistent with this schema-processing theory, children appear to be especially interested in learning about objects or activities that fit their own-sex schemata. For instance, in one study, elementary school aged children who perceived themselves as gender typical showed greater interest in gender-typical activities than in gender atypical ones (Patterson, 2012). In another study, 4- to 9-year-olds were given boxes of gender-neutral objects (hole punches, burglar alarms, and so on) and were told that some objects were "girl" items and some were "boy" items (Bradbard et al., 1986). Boys explored boy items more than girls did, and girls explored girl items more than boys did. A week later, the children easily recalled which items were for boys and which were for girls; they had apparently sorted the objects according to their in-group–out-group schemata. In addition, boys recalled more in-depth information about boy items than did girls, whereas girls recalled more than boys about these same objects if they had been labeled girl items. If children's information-gathering efforts are guided by their own-sex

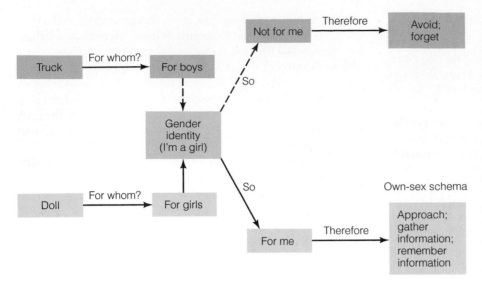

■ **Figure 12.4** Gender schema theory in action. A young girl classifies new information according to an in-group-out-group schema as either "for boys" or "for girls." Information about boys' toys and activities is ignored, but information about toys and activities for girls is relevant to the self and is added to an even-larger own-sex schema.

Source: Adapted from Martin & Halverson, 1987.

gender-consistent activities (for example, a boy playing with a truck) and pictures of children performing gender-inconsistent activities (for example, a girl sawing wood). A week later, the children easily recalled the sex of the actor performing gender-consistent activities; when an actor expressed gender-inconsistent behavior, however, children often distorted the scene to reveal gender-consistent behavior (for example, by saying that it was a boy, not a girl, who had sawed wood). This research gives some insight into why inaccurate gender stereotypes persist. The child who believes that women cannot be doctors may be introduced to a female doctor but may remember meeting a nurse instead and continue to state that women cannot be doctors. Even adults have trouble suppressing gender stereotypes and are influenced by their gender stereotypes when reading and interpreting text (Oakhill, Garnham, & Reynolds, 2005). To learn whether researchers have had any success in changing gender-role attitudes and behavior, check out the material in **Application Box 12.1**.

schemata in this way, you can easily see how boys and girls might acquire different stores of knowledge as they develop.

Once gender schemata are in place, children will distort new information in memory so that it is consistent with their schemata (Liben & Signorella, 1993; Martin & Halverson, 1983). For example, Martin and Halverson (1983) showed 5- and 6-year-olds pictures of children performing

An Attempt at Integration

The biosocial, social learning, and cognitive perspectives all contribute to our understanding of sex differences and gender-role development (● **Table 12.1**). The biosocial model offered by Money and Ehrhardt notes the importance of biological developments that influence how people label and treat a child. Yet

● **Table 12.1** An Integrative Overview of the Gender-Typing Process

Developmental Period	Events and Outcomes	Pertinent Theory or Theories
Prenatal period	The fetus develops male or female genitalia, which others will react to once the child is born.	Biosocial
Birth to 3 years	Parents and other companions label the child as a boy or a girl; they begin to encourage gender-consistent behavior and discourage cross-sex activities. As a result of these social experiences and the development of basic classification skills, the young child acquires some gender-typed behavioral preferences and the knowledge that he or she is a boy or a girl (basic gender identity).	Social learning
3–6 years	Once children acquire a basic gender identity, they begin to seek information about sex differences, form gender schemata, and actively try to behave in ways viewed as appropriate for their own sex.	Gender schema
7 to puberty	Children finally acquire the concepts of gender stability and consistency, recognizing that they will be males or females all their lives and in all situations. They begin to look closely at the behavior of same sex models to acquire attributes consistent with their firm self-categorization as male or female.	Cognitive developmental
Puberty and beyond	The biological changes of adolescence, with social pressures, intensify gender differences and stimulate formation of an adult gender identity.	Biosocial, Social learning, Gender schema, Cognitive developmental

Changing Gender-Role Attitudes and Behavior

Some people believe that the world would be a better place if boys and girls were no longer socialized to adopt traditional masculine or feminine roles, interests, and behaviors. Children of both sexes would then have the freedom to be androgynous; women would no longer suffer from a lack of assertiveness in the world of work, and men would no longer be forced to suppress their emotions. Just how successful are efforts to encourage more flexible gender roles?

In several projects designed to change gender-role behavior, children have been exposed to nonsexist films, encouraged to imitate models of cross-sex behavior, reinforced by teachers for trying cross-sex activities, and provided with nonsexist educational materials (Katz, 1986; Katz & Walsh, 1991). For example, Rebecca Bigler and Lynn Liben (1990) reasoned that if they could alter children's gender stereotypes, they could head off the biased information processing that stereotypes promote. They exposed 6- to 11-year-olds to a series of problem-solving discussions emphasizing that (1) the most important considerations in deciding who could perform well in such traditionally masculine or feminine occupations as construction worker

and beautician are the person's interests and willingness to learn and (2) the person's gender is irrelevant. Compared with children who received no such training, program participants showed a clear decline in occupational stereotyping, especially if they had entered the study with firm ideas about which jobs are for women and which are for men. Moreover, this reduction in stereotyping brought about the predicted decrease in biased information processing: Participants were more likely than nonparticipants to remember counterstereotypic information presented to them in stories (for example, recalling that the garbage collector in a story was a woman).

Yet many efforts at change that work in the short run fail to have lasting effects. Children encouraged to interact in mixed-sex groups revert to their preference for same-sex friends as soon as the program ends (Lockheed, 1986; Serbin, Tonick, & Sternglanz, 1977). Why is it so difficult to change children's thinking? Perhaps because children are groomed for their traditional gender roles from birth and are bombarded with traditional gender-role messages every day. A short-term intervention project may have little chance of succeeding in this larger context.

Other research shows that it is often difficult to change the gender schemata we have constructed. Farah Hughes and Catherine Seta (2003) gave fifth-graders descriptions of men and women behaving in ways inconsistent with traditional gender stereotypes. The children were then asked to rate the likelihood that another man or woman would behave in gender-inconsistent ways. Despite being exposed to a model of gender-stereotype inconsistent behavior, children believed that the other man (although not the other woman) would behave in a gender-consistent manner. The authors interpret this in terms of gender schema theory and children's desire to maintain their stereotypic gender schemata by countering an inconsistent piece of information with a highly consistent one. It also illustrates that simply exposing children to models of people who defy gender stereotypes is not going to miraculously lead to changes in the way children think about gender-stereotypic behavior: Men should still behave in masculine ways, women in feminine ways, although, consistent with other research presented in this chapter, Hughes and Seta found that women were given more flexibility than men to express both their feminine and masculine sides.

socialization agents are teaching children how to be girls or boys well before they understand that they are girls or boys. Differences in social learning experiences may also help explain why, even though virtually all children form gender concepts and schemata, some children are far more gender typed than others in their preferences and activities (Serbin et al., 1993).

Kohlberg's cognitive-developmental theory and Martin and Halverson's gender schema approach convince us that cognitive growth and self-socialization processes also contribute to gender-role development. Once children acquire a basic gender identity as a boy or a girl and form gender schemata, they become highly motivated to learn their appropriate roles. When they finally grasp, from age 5 to age 7, that their sex will never change, they become even more determined to learn their gender roles and pay special attention to same-sex models. Parents who want to avoid socializing their children into traditional gender roles are often amazed to see their children turn into traditional girls and boys on their own.

In short, children have a male or female biological endowment that helps guide their development, are influenced by other people from birth on to become "real boys" or "real girls," and

actively socialize themselves to behave in ways that seem consistent with their understandings that they are either boys or girls. Most developmentalists today would agree that what children learn regarding how to be male or female depends on an interaction between biological factors and social influences. Thus, we must respect the role of genes and hormones in gender-role development but also view this process from a contextual perspective and appreciate that the patterns of male and female development that we observe in society today are not inevitable. In another era, in another culture, the process of gender-role socialization could produce different kinds of boys and girls.

Childhood Sexuality

Although boys and girls spend much of their time in gender-segregated groups, most are nonetheless preparing for the day they will participate in sexual relationships with the other sex. They learn a great deal about sexuality and reproduction, continue to be curious about their bodies, and begin to interact with the other sex in ways that will prepare them for dating in adolescence.

Understanding Sex and Reproduction

With age, children learn that sexual anatomy is the key differentiator between males and females, and they acquire a more correct and explicit vocabulary for discussing sexual organs (Gordon, Schroeder, & Abrams, 1990). Children's understandings of where babies come from proceeds through a sequence consistent with Piaget's cognitive-developmental stages (Bernstein & Cowan, 1975; see Chapter 7). Accordingly, young children with their preoperational reasoning seem to assume either that babies are just there all along or that they are somehow manufactured, much as toys might be. According to Jane, age 3½, "You find [the baby] at a store that makes it . . . . Well, they get it and then they put it in the tummy and then it goes quickly out" (p. 81). Another preschooler, interpreting what he could of an explanation about reproduction from his mom, created this scenario (author's files):

> The woman has a seed in her tummy that is fertilized by something in the man's penis. (*How does this happen?*) The fertilizer has to travel down through the man's body into the ground. Then it goes underground to get to the woman's body. It's like in our garden. (*Does the fertilizer come out of his penis?*) Oh no. Only pee-pee comes out of the penis. It's not big enough for fertilizer.

As these examples illustrate, young children construct their own understandings of reproduction well before they are told the "facts of life." Consistent with Piaget's theory of cognitive development, children construct their understanding of sex by assimilating and accommodating information into their existing cognitive structures. Some children as young as age 6 know that sexual intercourse plays a role in the making of babies, but their understanding of just how this works is limited (Caron & Ahlgrim, 2012). By age 12, most children have integrated information about sexual intercourse with information about the biological union of egg and sperm and can provide an accurate description of intercourse and its possible outcomes. Thus, as children mature cognitively and as they gain access to information, they are able to construct ever more accurate understandings of sexuality and reproduction.

Sexual Behavior

According to Freudian theory, preschoolers in the phallic stage of psychosexual development are actively interested in their genitals and seek bodily pleasure through masturbation, but school-age children enter a latency period during which they repress their sexuality and turn their attention instead to schoolwork and friendships with same-sex peers. It turns out that Freud was half right and half wrong.

Freud was correct that preschoolers are highly curious about their bodies, masturbate, and engage in both same-sex and cross-sex sexual play (see Kellogg, 2009). Between ages 2 and 5, interest increases and at least half of all children engage in sexual play (playing doctor or house), and sexual exploration such as looking at and touching genitals—their own, a peer's, or a younger sibling's (Kellogg, 2009; Larsson & Svedin, 2002). Freud was wrong, though, to believe that such activities occur infrequently among school-age children. Elementary school age children in Freud's latency period may be more discreet

about their sexual experimentation than preschoolers, but they have by no means lost their sexual curiosity. Surveys show, for example, that about two-thirds of boys and half of girls have masturbated by age 13 (Janus & Janus, 1993; Larsson & Svedin, 2002) and are beginning to engage in "light" sexual activities (holding hands, kissing) with other young teens (Williams, Connolly, & Cribbie, 2008).

Gilbert Herdt and Martha McClintock (2000) have gathered evidence that age 10 is an important point in sexual development, a time when many boys and girls experience their first sexual attraction (often to a member of the other sex if they later become heterosexual or to a member of their own sex if they later become gay or lesbian). This milestone in development appears to be influenced by the maturation of the adrenal glands (which produce male androgens). It comes well before the maturation of the sex organs during puberty and therefore challenges the view of Freud (and many of the rest of us) that puberty is the critical time in sexual development. As Herdt and McClintock note, our society does little to encourage fourth-graders to have sexual thoughts, especially about members of their own sex, so perhaps a hormonal explanation of early sexual attraction makes more sense than an environmental one (see also Halpern, 2006).

► Checking Mastery

1. At what age are children likely to be most concerned about adhering to traditional gender-role behaviors? Why?

2. What are two factors that contribute to gender segregation during childhood?

3. What are the main components of the biosocial theory of gender?

4. How do cognitive-developmental theorists explain gender typing?

5. What are gender schemas, and what role do they play in gender typing?

► Making Connections

1. Jen and Ben are fraternal twins whose parents are determined that they should grow up having no gender-stereotypic attitudes or behaviors. Nonetheless, when the twins are only 4, Jen wants frilly dresses and loves to play with her Barbie doll, and Ben wants a machine gun and loves to pretend he's a football player and tackle people. Each seems headed for a traditional gender role. Which of the theories in this chapter do you think explains this best, which has the most difficulty explaining it, and why did you reach these conclusions?

2. Boys and girls have sometimes been characterized as living in two different worlds. Thinking about your own childhood, how was your world similar or different from that of your other-sexed siblings (if any) and friends?

3. After reviewing the theories of gender-role development, where do you stand on the relative contributions of biology and environment to one's gender-role identity?

LEARNING OBJECTIVES:

- Describe the typical path of gender-role development in adolescence.
- Discuss the emergence of sexual identity and indicate where paths may diverge for those with heterosexual, homosexual, and/or bisexual identities.
- Analyze the evolution of sexual morality that has led to the current perspectives on sexual morality among adolescents.
- Outline the typical pattern of adolescent sexual behaviors and note factors that influence sexual behaviors of males and females.

After going their separate ways in childhood, boys and girls come together in the most intimate ways during adolescence. How do they prepare for the gender roles that will likely characterize their adulthood?

Adhering to Gender Roles

As you learned in the prior section, young elementary school children are highly rigid in their thinking about gender roles, whereas older children think more flexibly, recognizing that gender norms are not absolute, inviolable laws. Curiously, adolescents again seem to become highly intolerant of certain role violations and stereotyped in their thinking about the proper roles of males and females in adolescence. They are more likely than somewhat younger children to make negative judgments about peers who violate expectations by engaging in cross-sex behavior or expressing cross-sex interests (Alfieri, Ruble, & Higgins, 1996; Sigelman, Carr, & Begley, 1986).

Consider what Trish Stoddart and Elliot Turiel (1985) found when they asked children ages 5–13 questions about boys who wear a barrette in their hair or put on nail polish and about girls who sport a crew haircut or wear a boy's suit. Both the kindergartners and the adolescents judged these behaviors to be wrong, whereas third-graders and fifth-graders viewed them far more tolerantly. Like the elementary school children, eighth-graders clearly understood that gender-role expectations are just social conventions that can easily be changed and do not necessarily apply in all societies. However, these adolescents had also begun to conceptualize gender-role violations as a sign of psychological abnormality and could not tolerate them.

Increased intolerance of deviance from gender-role expectations is tied to a larger process of **gender intensification**, in which gender differences may be magnified by hormonal changes associated with puberty and increased pressure to conform to gender roles (Boldizar, 1991; Galambos, Almeida, & Petersen, 1990). According to this process, boys begin to see themselves as more masculine and girls emphasize their feminine side. There is some support for this, at least in terms of higher levels of "femininity" reported by teen girls than by boys (Priess, Lindberg, & Hyde, 2009). When it comes to "masculinity," though, teen boys and girls report roughly the same levels. When gender intensification does occur, it is largely related to peer influence and the growing importance of dating. Adolescents increasingly find that they must conform to traditional gender norms to appeal to the other sex. A girl who was a tomboy and thought nothing of it may find that, as a teenager, she must dress and behave in more "feminine" ways to attract boys and must give up her tomboyish ways (Burn, O'Neil, & Nederend, 1996; Carr, 2007). A boy may find that he is more popular if he projects a more sharply "masculine" image. Social pressures on adolescents to conform to traditional roles may even help explain why sex differences in cognitive abilities sometimes become more noticeable as children enter adolescence (Hill & Lynch, 1983; Roberts et al., 1990). It should be noted that the social pressure to conform to gender stereotypes does not need to be real—adolescents' *perceptions* of their peers' thoughts and expectations can affect their behaviors and lead to gender intensification (Pettitt, 2004). Later in adolescence, teenagers again become more comfortable with their identities as men and women and more flexible in their thinking.

Attaining Sexual Maturity

Although infants and children are sexual beings, sexuality assumes far greater importance once sexual maturity is achieved. Adolescents must incorporate into their identities as males or females concepts of themselves as sexual males or females. Moreover, they must figure out how to express their sexuality in relationships. As part of their search for identity, teenagers raise questions about their sexual attractiveness, their sexual values, and their goals in close relationships. They also experiment with sexual behavior—sometimes with good outcomes, sometimes with bad ones. And what do the teens' parents think of this burgeoning sexuality? As Sinikka Elliott (2012) describes in her book, *Not My Kid*, parents believe that other teenagers are sexual beings and may be trying to lure their innocent child into sexual exploits, but their child is not yet sexual or is far too young for such matters. As you will see, however, it is not the case that only *other* adolescents are interested in sexual activity.

Sexual Orientation

Part of establishing a sexual identity, part of an individual's larger task of resolving Erikson's conflict of identity versus role confusion, is becoming aware of one's **sexual orientation**—that is, preference for sexual partners of the same or other sex, or both. Sexual orientation exists on a continuum, with many experts now recognizing five classifications of sexual identity: heterosexual, mostly heterosexual, mostly homosexual, homosexual, or bisexual (Vrangalova & Savin-Williams, 2012). Most adolescents establish a heterosexual sexual orientation without much soul-searching, what Elizabeth Morgan (2012) refers to as "commitment with passive exploration." For youths attracted to members of their own sex, however, the process of accepting that they have a homosexual, mostly homosexual, or bisexual orientation and establishing a positive identity in the face of negative societal attitudes can be a long and torturous one. Many have an initial awareness of their sexual preference before reaching puberty but do not accept being gay or lesbian, or gather the courage to "come out," until their mid-20s (Savin-Williams, 2001). Among 17- to 25-year-olds with same-sex attractions, fewer than half have told both their parents and about one-third have not told either parent about their sexual orientation (Savin-Williams & Ream, 2003). Those who have disclosed to one or both parents did so around age 19. By this age, most are out of high school and have achieved some independence from their parents, which may give them the confidence to share this information.

Experimentation with homosexual activity is fairly common during adolescence, but few adolescents become part of the estimated 5–6% of adults who establish an enduring homosexual or bisexual sexual orientation (Savin-Williams & Ream, 2007). Contrary to societal stereotypes of gay men as effeminate and lesbian women as masculine, gay and lesbian individuals have the same range of psychological and social attributes that heterosexual adults do. Knowing that someone prefers same-sex romantic partners reveals no more about his or her personality than knowing that someone is heterosexual.

For the most part, sexual orientation is stable across the life span, at least for those individuals who identify themselves as 100% heterosexual or 100% homosexual (Mock & Eibach, 2012; Savin-Williams, Joyner, & Rieger, 2012). For individuals who identify as bisexual, there is less stability over time, with only one in four remaining in this category over time. Ritch Savin-Williams and colleagues (2012) report that females who initially identified as bisexual are most likely to later identify as

According to a 2013 Gallup poll, 3.5% of the U.S. population self-identifies as lesbian, gay, bisexual, or transgender.

Jari Hindstroem/Shutterstock.com

● **Table 12.2** Percentage of Twins Who Are Concordant (Alike) for Nonheterosexual Sexual Orientation

Identical twins	32%
Same-sex fraternal twins	13%
All fraternal twins (same and other sex)	8%

SOURCE: Adapted from Kendler, K. S., Thornton, L. M., Gilman, S. E., & Kessler, R. C. (2000). Sexual orientation in a U.S. national sample of twin and nontwin sibling pairs. *American Journal of Psychiatry, 157*, 1843–1846, Figure 2.
Note: Nonheterosexual is any sexual orientation other than heterosexual (that is, includes homosexual and bisexual). Higher rates of similarity for identical twin pairs than for fraternal twin pairs provide evidence of genetic influence on nonheterosexuality.

"mostly heterosexual," whereas males who initially identify as bisexual are much more variable in their identity at later points in time. In longitudinal research with women, Lisa Diamond (2008) found that orientation as lesbian or bisexual was relatively enduring over a 10-year period, although women often defied attempts to be defined exclusively by a single sexual orientation. Many preferred to be unlabeled, perhaps reflecting an openness to changes in sexual orientation or an attraction to the person without regard to that person's biological sex (see Diamond, 2008).

What influences the development of sexual orientation? Part of the answer lies in the genetic code. Twin studies have established that identical twins are more alike in sexual orientation than fraternal twins (Bailey & Pillard, 1991; Bailey et al., 1993; Kendler et al., 2000). As ● **Table 12.2** reveals, however, in as many as two-thirds of identical twin pairs, one twin is homosexual or bisexual but the other is heterosexual. Thus, although more identical twins than fraternal twins are concordant (alike) for sexual orientation, the majority of identical twins are still not concordant—they are dissimilar—for sexual orientation. This means that environment contributes at least as much as genes to the development of sexual orientation (Bailey, Dunne, & Martin, 2000; Kendler et al., 2000).

Looking at childhood behaviors, research shows that many gay men and lesbian women expressed strong cross-sex interests when they were young, despite being subjected to the usual pressures to adopt a traditional gender role (Bailey et al., 2000; Golombok et al., 2012; Lippa, 2008). For example, as ■ **Figure 12.5** shows, Richard Lippa (2008) found that homosexual adults—both male and female—were significantly more likely than heterosexual adults to recall **childhood gender nonconformity (CGN)**. CGN, or not adhering to the typical gender-role norms expected for members of one's assigned gender group, is also more common for females than males.

Still, it is important to note that sexual orientation is every bit as heritable among gay men who were typically masculine boys and lesbian women who were typically feminine girls as among those who showed early gender nonconformity (Bailey & Pillard, 1991; Bailey et al., 1993). Although it might be tempting to infer sexual orientation from early childhood behaviors, all we really know is that *some* gay and lesbian adults knew from an early age that traditional gender-role expectations did not suit them, but others did not.

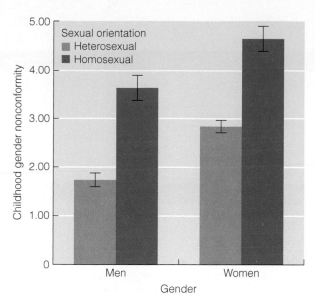

■ Figure 12.5 Childhood gender nonconformity as a function of gender and sexual orientation (bars represent 95% confidence intervals).

What environmental factors may help determine whether a genetic predisposition toward homosexuality is actualized? We do not know yet, although we can reject the old psychoanalytic view that male homosexuality stems from having a domineering mother and a weak father (LeVay, 1996). Growing up with a gay or lesbian parent also seems to have little effect on later sexual orientation (Patterson, 2004). Nor is there any support for the idea that homosexuals were seduced into a homosexual lifestyle by older individuals.

A more promising hypothesis is that hormonal influences during the prenatal period influence sexual orientation (Ellis et al., 1988; Meyer-Bahlburg et al., 1995). For example, androgenized females are more likely than other women to adopt a lesbian or bisexual orientation, suggesting that high prenatal doses of male hormones may predispose at least some females to homosexuality (Dittman et al., 1992; Money, 1988). Later-born males with older brothers may be more prone to a homosexual orientation because, according to one theory, their mother produces anti-male antibodies that accumulate over the course of each pregnancy with a male (see Blanchard & Lippa, 2007). However, this does not explain why some firstborn males or males without older brothers develop a homosexual orientation (see Gooren, 2006). Another possibility is that nature and nurture interact: Biological factors may predispose an individual to have certain traits, which in turn influence the kinds of social experiences the person has, which in turn shape her sexual orientation (Byne, 1994). However, even the experts cannot yet clearly define which factors in the prenatal or postnatal environment contribute, with genes, to a homosexual orientation.

Sexual Morality

Whatever their sexual orientation, adolescents establish attitudes regarding what is and is not appropriate sexual behavior. The sexual attitudes of adolescents changed dramatically during the 20th century, especially during the 1960s and 1970s, yet at least some of the old values have endured (Caron & Moskey, 2002). Three generalizations emerge from the research on sexual attitudes.

First, many adolescents—approximately three out of four—have come to believe that sex with affection in the context of a committed relationship is acceptable (Caron & Moskey, 2002). They no longer buy the traditional view that premarital intercourse is always morally wrong (● **Table 12.3**). Brooke Wells and Jean Twenge (2005) analyzed 530 studies of sexual behavior and attitudes, spanning a period of over 50 years. They found that the percentage of men who approved of premarital sex jumped from 40% to 79%, but the change in women's attitudes was even more dramatic, going from 12% to 73% who approved of premarital sex. However, adolescents do not all go so far as to approve of casual or "nonromantic" sex, although males have somewhat more permissive attitudes about this than females (see Olmstead et al., 2013). Consistent with this, most adolescents believe that partners should be in a long-term romantic relationship or feel a close emotional involvement with each other (Caron & Moskey, 2002). Most adolescents—both male and female—report that their first sexual relationship was with someone with whom they were romantically, not casually, involved (Ryan, Manlove, & Franzetta, 2003; Williams & Russell, 2013). On average, teens wait about 5 months before having sex with a romantic partner. Even adolescents who have sex with a nonromantic partner report that there were emotional and social components to the relationship (Williams & Russell, 2013). Thus, casual sex is not the norm among young teenagers.

Teens who go off to college may find casual sexual encounters somewhat more normative in this context. The typical **hookup** is a brief sexual encounter between two people who have often just met at a party and have little expectation of forming a romantic relationship (Garcia, Reiber, Massey, & Merriwether, 2012; Paul, McManus, & Hayes, 2000). Males and females are similar in their descriptions of what transpires during a typical hookup, but women express a wider range of mostly negative emotional reactions to hooking up (Paul & Hayes, 2002). Women with higher rates of casual sex—hookups—are more likely to experience depression relative to those having no or little casual sex (Welsh, Grello & Harper, 2006). In contrast, men with higher rates of casual sex have some of the lowest levels of depression. Women are also more likely than men to experience guilt and remorse following casual sex (Fielder & Carey, 2010; Owen et al., 2010). These differences may be explained, at least in part, by the next finding.

A second finding is that the **double standard** has declined but not disappeared over the years (Crawford & Popp, 2003; Peterson & Hyde, 2010). According to the double standard, sexual behavior that is viewed as appropriate for males is considered inappropriate for females; there is one standard for males, another for females. In the "old days," a young man was expected to sow some wild oats and obtain some sexual experience, and gained respect from peers for his sexual exploits ("he's a stud"). In contrast, a young woman was expected to remain a virgin until she married and was viewed negatively for engaging in sexual behaviors ("she's a slut"). College students still tend to believe that a woman who has many sexual partners is more

- **Table 12.3** Changes in Sexual Beliefs and Behaviors over 50 Years: Percentage of Respondents from the Classes of 1950, 1975, and 2000 Who Agreed with the Following Statements

	1950	1975	2000
Having sex as a teenager would go against my beliefs, even if in a serious relationship.	65%	27%	20%
I believe it is OK to have sex as a teenager.	24%	60%	70%
If I had sex as a teenager, it would have been OK with my parents.	6%	8%	33%
If I had sex as a teenager, it would have been OK with my friends.	15%	75%	81%
If I had sex with boyfriend/girlfriend, it would have made our relationship stronger.	14%	21%	37%
Based on Your Beliefs While in High School, When Was It Acceptable to Have Sex?			
Within the first month of dating	8%	18%	15%
After the relationship became serious	19%	72%	76%
Only after becoming married	73%	10%	9%
Respondents Who Had Sex in High School			
	24%	65%	69%
Of Those Respondents Who Had Sex by the End of High School, Their Age at First Sex			
12–14 years	21%	15%	22%
15 years old	32%	10%	9%
16 years old	32%	30%	45%
17 years or older	15%	45%	24%

SOURCE: Adapted from Caron, Sandra L. & Moskey, Eilean G. (2002). Changes over time in teenage sexual relationships: Comparing the high school class of 1950, 1975, and 2000. *Adolescence, 37*, 515–526, Tables 1 and 4.

immoral than an equally promiscuous man (Blumberg, 2003; Crawford & Popp, 2003). In part, the double standard for male–female sexuality may persist because it fits entrenched societal expectations, even though actual sexual behaviors of males and females are more similar than different. Males are more likely than females to retain the double standard, although both males and females believe women should be more careful with casual sexual encounters out of fear that women may experience social stigma or be subjected to various rape myths (Conley, Ziegler, & Moors, 2013; Rudman, Fetterolf, & Sanchez, 2013). The persistence of the double standard may help explain why males report primarily positive feelings from casual hookups, whereas females report mostly negative feelings from these encounters.

A third generalization that emerges from research on sexual attitudes is that adolescents are confused about sexual norms. Adolescents continually receive mixed messages about sexuality (Ponton, 2001). They are encouraged to be popular and attractive to the other sex, and they watch countless television programs and movies that glamorize sexual behavior. Yet they are told to value virginity and to fear and avoid pregnancy, bad reputations, and AIDS and other sexually transmitted infections (STIs). Adults often tell teens that they are too young to engage in sexual activity, yet they make teens feel ashamed or embarrassed about masturbating (Halpern et al., 2000; Ponton, 2001). The standards for males and females are now more similar, and adolescents tend to agree that sexual intercourse in the context of emotional involvement is acceptable; but teenagers still must forge their own codes of behavior, and they differ widely in what they decide.

Sexual Behavior

If attitudes about sexual behavior have changed over the years, has sexual behavior itself changed? Yes, it has. Today's teenagers are involved in more intimate forms of sexual behavior at earlier ages than adolescents of the past were. Several themes emerge from the research on teens' sexual behavior:

- Rates of sexual activity climbed in the 1960s and continued to climb through the 1980s before leveling off and then declining somewhat from the mid-1990s on (CDCP, 2012).
- The percentages of both males and females who have had intercourse increased steadily over the past century.
- Perhaps reflecting the decline of the double standard, the sexual behavior of females has changed more than that of males, and the difference in experience between the sexes has largely disappeared (CDC, 2012; Peterson & Hyde, 2010). As noted earlier, today's male and female teenagers begin having sex at about the same age.

The percentage of adolescents with sexual experience increases steadily over the adolescent years, although as
- **Table 12.4** shows, this varies by the students' gender and race/ethnicity. By age 21 to age 24, 85% of young adults report having had sexual intercourse (Meschke et al., 2000). Of course, rates of sexual activity depend greatly on how sexual activity is defined. What constitutes "having sex"? Virtually all college students—both male and female—agree that penile–vaginal intercourse is having sex, but by 2007 only 20% of college students agreed that they had "had sex" when they engaged in oral–genital

Table 12.4 Percentage of High School Students Who Have Ever Had Sexual Intercourse

	White	Black	Hispanic
Female	44%	61%	44%
Male	42%	75%	58%

Source: Eaton et al., 2006.

stimulation (Hans, Gillen, & Akande, 2010). Perhaps this is why there are higher rates of **oral sex** than intercourse among today's high school students (Prinstein, Meade, & Cohen, 2003). If their cognitive schema of having sex does not include oral sex (or anal sex for some teens), they can engage in oral sex without feeling they are really having sex. Consequently, as many as 40% of college students who label themselves virgins report giving or receiving oral sex, and some of these have had three or more oral sex partners (Chambers, 2007).

Interestingly, today's teens rate oral sex as less intimate than intercourse, the opposite of what many from their parent's generation believe (Chambers, 2007). This may help explain the rise in oral sex among teenagers. Another reason is teens' inaccurate perception that oral sex is safer than vaginal penetration. Although oral sex without intercourse may sharply reduce pregnancy rates, it does not prevent transmission of STIs unless partners consistently use protection. Unfortunately, many teens lack knowledge about how to protect themselves during oral sex (Brady & Halpern-Fisher, 2007; Chambers, 2007). In addition to possible health consequences, there may be emotional consequences for teens who engage in oral sex. Teens who engage only in oral sex (without intercourse) report less positive feelings about themselves and their relationship than other sexually active teens (Brady & Halpern-Fisher, 2007).

Becoming sexually active is a normal part of development, but parents and society often express concerns about teens becoming sexually active when they are too young because early sexual activity is associated with risky behaviors that can lead to unwanted pregnancies and STIs. Jessica Siebenbruner and her colleagues (Zimmer-Gembeck & Egeland; 2007) studied the antecedents of early sexual behavior among three groups of 16-year-olds who had previously been evaluated on a variety of measures at ages 6, 9, 12, and 13. The researchers distinguished among three groups on the basis of self-reported sexual behaviors at age 16: sexual abstainers who had not yet had sexual intercourse, low risk-takers who reported having five or fewer sexual partners and always using contraception, and high risk-takers who reported having six or more sexual partners and inconsistently using contraception. The researchers wanted to know whether they could predict which of these three groups a teen would end up in at age 16 based on information collected at the earlier ages.

Several findings emerged from this research. High-risk sexual behavior at age 16 seemed to be part of a general pattern of problem behavior that started at birth with a mother who was unmarried (Siebenbruner et al., 2007). Unwed mothers tend to be younger, less educated, and more likely to experience economic hardships. High-risk teens grew up in homes that were characterized as less emotionally responsive and they were rated

by teachers as engaging in more externalizing behaviors at ages 9 and 12. In these respects, the high-risk teens were different from both the low-risk teens and the abstainers throughout childhood. In contrast, the low-risk teens and the abstainers were similar throughout childhood, yet began to diverge in early adolescence. At age 13, low-risk teens *looked* more mature than abstainers and were more involved in romantic relationships. They were also somewhat more likely to drink alcohol at age 16 than the abstainers. Their mature appearance may have led others to respond to them differently, leading them to romantic relationships, sexual involvement, and alcohol use at an earlier age than their peers who appeared less mature. These findings suggest that parents who are concerned about early involvement in sex should be on the alert for problem behaviors during childhood, provide an emotionally responsive home environment, and talk to their teens about how their appearance may influence how others perceive and treat them.

Some teens seem headed for engaging in riskier sexual behaviors than other teens. Lynne Cooper (2010) evaluated the sexual behaviors of nearly 2,000 young adults and found that numerous factors, including within-person factors, situational factors, and interactions of the two, contribute to the chances of engaging in risky sex. Within-person factors associated with more risky sexual behaviors included low levels of impulse control and communality and high levels of adventuresomeness and negative emotionality (a tendency to feel anxious and depressed and react poorly to stressful situations). Situations involving sex with a new partner were associated with drinking more alcohol and choosing a riskier partner but also with a greater likelihood of using a condom. Research consistently shows that alcohol use is associated with riskier sexual behaviors (see Cooper, 2002; Testa, Hoffman, & Livingston, 2010). Compared with adults, teens and young adults from minority groups, especially males, are more likely to engage in risky sex practices (see Espinosa-Hernandez & Lefkowitz, 2009; Lee & Hahm, 2010). The consequences can be long-lasting and devastating. And as **Exploration Box 12.2** explains, experiencing abusive sexual encounters can have lifelong consequences.

Although most adolescents seem to adjust successfully to becoming sexually active, there have also been some casualties among those who are psychologically unready for sex or who end up with an unintended pregnancy or an STI. Sexually active adolescent couples often fail to use contraception, partly because they are cognitively immature and do not take seriously the possibility that their behavior could have unwanted long-term consequences (Loewenstein & Furstenberg, 1991). Although condom use has increased over past decades, it is still lower than health-care professionals would like to see. Overall, 40% of sexually active teens did not use a condom during their last sexual intercourse (Centers for Disease Control and Prevention, 2012). Adolescent females report less frequent condom use than males, possibly because their sexual partners are often several years older and because condom use among males declines from mid to late adolescence (Eaton et al., 2006). In addition, adolescent couples who are in long-term, monogamous relationships often stop using condoms because they no longer fear transmission of human immunodeficiency virus (HIV) or other STIs.

Exploration 12.2

Childhood Sexual Abuse

Every day in this country, children, adolescents, and even infants are sexually abused by the adults closest to them. A typical scenario would be this: A girl aged 12 or 13—although it happens to boys, too—is abused repeatedly by her father, stepfather, or another male relative or family friend (Freyd et al., 2005; Putnam, 2003). Estimates of the percentages of girls and boys who are sexually abused vary wildly, perhaps because so many cases go unreported and because definitions vary substantially. The Centers for Disease Control and Prevention (2010) surveyed nearly 10,000 women and 8,000 men as part of the Adverse Childhood Experiences (ACE) Study, revealing that 25% of the women and 16% of the men reported having been sexually molested at some time (Centers for Disease Control and Prevention, 2010). Clearly, childhood sexual abuse is a serious and widespread social problem. Unfortunately, only one out of every four abused children tells someone about the abuse within the first 24 hours and one in four remains silent, never telling anyone about their painful experience (Kogan, 2004).

What is the effect of sexual abuse on the survivor? Kathleen Kendall-Tackett, Linda Williams, and David Finkelhor (1993) offer a useful account, based on their review of 45 studies. No single distinctive "syndrome" of psychological problems characterizes abuse survivors. Instead, they may experience any number of problems commonly seen in emotionally disturbed individuals, including anxiety, depression, low self-esteem, aggression, acting out, withdrawal, and school learning problems. Roughly 20–30% experience each of these problems, and boys seem to experience the same types and degrees of disturbance as girls do.

Many of these aftereffects boil down to lack of self-worth and difficulty trusting others (Freyd et al., 2005; Putnam, 2003). A college student who had been abused repeatedly by her father and other relatives wrote this about her experience (author's files):

> It was very painful, emotionally, physically, and psychologically. I wanted to die to escape it. I wanted to escape from my body . . . . I developed a "good" self and a "bad" self. This was the only way I could cope with the experiences . . . . I discovered people I trusted caused me harm . . . . It is difficult for me to accept the fact that people can care for me and expect nothing in return . . . . I dislike closeness and despise people touching me.

Two problems seem to be especially linked to being sexually abused. First, about a third of survivors engage in sexualized behavior, acting out sexually by putting objects in their vaginas, masturbating in public, behaving seductively, or if they are older, behaving promiscuously (Kendall-Tackett et al., 1993). One theory is that this sexualized behavior helps survivors master or control the traumatic events they experienced (Tharinger, 1990). Second, about a third of survivors display the symptoms of **posttraumatic stress disorder**. This clinical disorder, involving nightmares, flashbacks to the traumatizing events, and feelings of helplessness and anxiety in the face of danger, affects some soldiers who have experienced combat and other survivors of extreme trauma (Kendall-Tackett et al., 1993).

In a few children, sexual abuse may contribute to severe psychological disorders, yet about a third of children seem to experience no psychological symptoms (Kendall-Tackett et al., 1993; Putnam, 2003). Some of these symptomless children may experience problems in later years. Nevertheless, some children are less severely damaged and more able to cope than others are.

Which children have the most difficulty? The effects of abuse are likely to be most severe when the abuse involved penetration and force and occurred frequently over a long period, when the perpetrator was a close relative such as the father, and when the child's mother did not serve as a reliable source of emotional support (Beitchman et al., 1991; Kendall-Tackett et al., 1993; Trickett & Putnam, 1993). Children are likely to recover better if they have high-quality relationships with their mother and friends (Adams & Bukowski, 2007; Aspelmeier, Elliott, & Smith, 2007). Psychotherapy aimed at treating the anxiety and depression many survivors experience and teaching them coping and problem-solving skills so that they will not be revictimized can also contribute to the healing process (Cuevas et al., 2010; Finkelhor & Berliner, 1995).

Finally, not all sex abuse offenders fit the stereotype of an adult who is an obvious pervert. Some offenders are themselves juveniles taking advantage of peers or somewhat younger children (Finkelhor, 2009). With appropriate and timely intervention and education, they can learn acceptable behaviors that reduce the likelihood of continued offending. Education can also prepare children to respond to inappropriate advances in ways that derail the possibility of an offense occurring. This three-pronged approach—working with the survivors, the offenders, and all children on prevention of sexual abuse—may be behind a recent decline in reports of childhood abuse (Finkelhor et al., 2010).

Sexual behaviors are also shaped by the social and cultural contexts in which children develop. For example, research shows that teens are less likely to use condoms if their friends report engaging in sex without condoms (Henry et al., 2007). Conversely, teens are more likely to use condoms if they believe their friends are using condoms. Examining the larger cultural context, Eric Widmer and his colleagues (Widmer, Treas, & Newcomb, 1998) found wide variations in sexual beliefs across the 24 countries that they studied. These prevailing cultural beliefs, whether conservative, permissive, or somewhere in the middle, influence how teens construct their individual sexual identities. Teens growing up in cultures that have more permissive attitudes about sexuality are likely to interpret their own behaviors differently than teens growing up in cultures with largely conservative beliefs. And importantly, parents can influence their teens to delay sex and to engage in responsible sex. In particular, parents who have clear household routines, monitor their teens, and establish strong relationships with their sons and daughters tend to have adolescents who delay sex or avoid casual sex (Manlove et al., 2012). Thus, sexual behavior is not driven

There are numerous contraceptives available in most developed countries. Which one helps protect against STIs as well as unwanted pregnancies?

© Charles Thatcher/Getty Images

simply by the surge in hormones that accompanies puberty; it is mediated by social context and by the personal beliefs that are constructed in response to physical changes and cultural beliefs.

For the adolescent who gives birth, the consequences of teenage sexuality can include an interrupted education, a low income, and a difficult start for both her and her child (see Hoffman & Maynard, 2008). This young mother's life situation and her child's developmental status are likely to improve later, especially if she goes back to school and limits her family size, but she is likely to remain economically disadvantaged compared with her peers who postpone parenthood until their 20s or later (Hoffman & Maynard, 2008). Fortunately, after increasing for many years, rates of teenage pregnancy have begun to decline in recent years (Kost, Henshaw, & Carlin, 2010).

In addition to unplanned pregnancy, poorly planned sexual activity can have health consequences, namely STIs. ● **Table 12.5** provides an overview of STIs that can result from inconsistent or inadequate safe sex practices. Sadly, few adolescents are doing

● **Table 12.5** Sexually Transmitted Infections (STIs) with their Cause, Symptoms, and Treatment

STI	Cause and Treatment	Symptoms and Side Effects
Chlamydia: Highest rates among 15- to 19-year-olds, followed by 20- to 24-year-olds	Caused by a bacteria; can be treated and cured with antibiotics	Few or no symptoms; when present, symptoms include slight discharge from vagina or penis, burning with urination, and lower abdominal pain. If left untreated, it can result in pelvic inflammatory disease, which is associated with infertility.
Trichomoniasis: Highest rates among women aged 30 and older	Caused by a parasite; can be treated and cured with antibiotics	Few or no symptoms; when present, symptoms include irritation or itching of the genital area, painful urination and intercourse, and possibly lower abdominal pain.
Gonorrhea: Highest rates among adolescents and young adults	Caused by bacteria; can be treated and usually cured with antibiotics although some strains have become resistant	Few or no symptoms; when present, symptoms include genital discharge and painful urination. Gonorrheal infections can also invade the mouth and throat through oral sex with an infected partner, or the anus and rectum through anal sex with an infected partner. Can lead to infertility if untreated.
Genital Herpes: Incidence increases across age groups, peaking in middle adulthood	Caused by herpes simplex virus; can be treated but not cured	Symptoms include genital discharge, itching or burning, and painful blisters in the genital and anal regions. Although blisters may disappear in 2–3 weeks, the underlying virus that causes genital herpes remains and can cause symptom recurrence at any time. On average, infected persons have four occurrences per year.
Genital Warts: Highest rates among those in their early 20s	Caused by human papillomavirus (HPV); can be treated with surgery or cauterization of warts but may recur if immune system does not completely eliminate virus	Symptoms include small painless bumps on the vagina, cervix, or vulva (females) and penis (males); the anus and mouth may also be affected. If left untreated, the growths can grow into a larger clump of warts resembling cauliflower. Some strains of HPV are associated with cervical cancer and a vaccine has been developed to prevent HPV.
Syphilis: Highest rates among 20-somethings	Caused by *Treponema pallidum* bacteria, which is highly contagious; can be treated in early stages with antibiotics	Symptoms emerge in stages: The first symptom is typically one or more ulcerlike sores around the genitals, although these sores, called chancres, can also appear in the mouth or anal area depending on point of contact with an infected person. This is followed by a body rash and flulike symptoms, which may last for several weeks. The underlying bacteria can remain dormant for years, or it can resurface in the lungs, heart, or brain. Can cause brain disease, dementia, or blindness if left untreated.

SOURCES: Adapted from Centers for Disease Control and Prevention (2012, December). *Sexually transmitted disease surveillance, 2011.* Atlanta: U.S. Department of Health and Human Services; Dunne, E. F., Unger, E. R., Sternberg, M., McQuillan, G., Swan, D. C., Patel, S. S., & Markowitz, L. E. (2007). Prevalence of HPV infection among females in the United States. *JAMA, 297,* 813–819; Guttmacher Institute (2009, June). *Facts on sexually transmitted infections in the United States.* Available at: www.guttmacher.org/pubs /FIB_STI_US.html. Accessed June 22, 2013.

what they would need to do to protect themselves from STIs: abstaining from sex or using a condom *every* time. No wonder many educators are calling for stronger programs of sex education and distribution of free condoms at school. There is little chance of preventing the unwanted consequences of teenage sexuality unless more adolescents either postpone sex or practice safer sex.

One encouraging finding is that teens who feel close to their parents, especially their mothers, and who report having closer parental supervision are more likely to delay initiating sexual activity (L'Engle & Jackson, 2008). In addition to delaying initiation of any sexual activity, parent–teen communication about sexuality can also delay the age of first intercourse, particularly when mothers point out the negative consequences of having sex at an early age (Usher-Seriki, Bynum, & Callands, 2008). Unfortunately, many parents do not communicate clearly or regularly with their teens about matters of sexuality (Guilamo-Ramos et al., 2008). In a survey of mothers of at-risk urban middle-school students, those who thought that a conversation about sex would embarrass their teen or felt unsure of what to say or how to initiate such a conversation tended not to talk to their teen about sex. In contrast, mothers who thought that talking about sex would encourage their teen to think more maturely, believed it wouldn't be too embarrassing, thought they would be able to answer their teen's questions, and felt comfortable with themselves and with the idea of talking about sex were more likely to have such conversations (Guilamo-Ramos et al., 2008; Pluhar, DiIorio, & McCarty, 2008). This suggests that successful

sex education programs need to reach out to parents and help educate parents as well as their teens.

Another encouraging finding is that educational programs that emphasize abstinence have proven to be effective (Jemmott, Jemmott, & Fong, 2010). Such programs can encourage young adolescents to delay sexual intercourse. Importantly, when teens who participate in abstinence-only programs have intercourse, they are just as likely to use a condom as teens who participate in alternative educational programs focusing on safe sex (Jemmott et al., 2010). This is good news for those who worry that focusing on abstinence may not provide teens with sufficient knowledge about safe sex.

Checking Mastery

1. What do we know about the sexual beliefs of many of today's teens?
2. Are there differences in sexual behavior of males and females?
3. What factors likely contribute to one's sexual orientation?

Making Connections

1. What factors are likely to influence the age at which young people today become sexually active? If you wanted to delay the age of first intercourse, what would be two ways to do this?

12.5 The Adult

LEARNING OBJECTIVES:

- Explore changes in gender roles across adulthood.
- Evaluate the pros and cons of androgyny.
- Indicate how women and men have managed to integrate the various roles of adulthood: career, relationships, and parenting.
- Discuss changes in sexual behaviors and sexuality throughout adulthood.

You might think that once children and adolescents have learned their gender roles, they simply play them out during adulthood. Instead, as people face the challenges of adult life and enter new social contexts, their gender roles and their concepts of themselves as men and women change. So, too, do their sexual behaviors and their perceptions of their own sexuality.

Changes in Gender Roles

Although males and females fill their agentic or communal roles throughout their lives, the specific content of those roles changes considerably over the life span. The young boy may act out his agentic role by playing with trucks or wrestling with his buddies; the grown man may play his role by holding down a job. Moreover, the degree of difference between male and female roles also changes. Children and adolescents adopt behaviors consistent with their "boy" or "girl" roles, but the two sexes otherwise

adopt similar roles in society—namely, those of children and students. Even as they enter adulthood, male and female roles differ little because members of both sexes are often single and in school or working.

However, the roles of men and women become more distinct when they marry or settle into a stable romantic relationship and especially when (and if) they become parents. David Gutmann (1987, 1997) has offered the intriguing hypothesis that gender roles and gender-related traits in adulthood are shaped by what he calls the **parental imperative**—the requirement that mothers and fathers adopt different roles to raise children successfully. Drawing on his own cross-cultural research and that of others, he suggests that in many cultures, young and middle-aged men must emphasize their "masculine" qualities to feed and protect their families, whereas young and middle-aged women must express their "feminine" qualities to nurture the young and meet the emotional needs of their families.

The birth of a child tends to make even egalitarian couples divide their labors in more traditional ways than they did before the birth and migrate toward more traditional gender-role attitudes: Mothers become primarily responsible for child care and household tasks and fathers tend to emphasize their role as breadwinner for the family (Katz-Wise, Priess, & Hyde, 2010). The American Time Use Survey shows that, in most heterosexual couples with children, the mother typically does about 18 hours of housework and 14 hours of childcare, whereas the father does about 10 hours of housework and 7 hours of childcare (Pew Research Center, 2013). In contrast, fathers spend more hours working outside the home (37 hours per week) compared to mothers (21 hours). Thus, there may be something to the concept of the parental imperative, although perhaps not to the extent suggested by Gutmann.

Women have less leisure time than men, perhaps as a result of their desire to "have it all." Michelle Hoffnung (2004; Hoffnung and Williams, 2013) interviewed women in their senior year of college and found that these young women wanted marriage, career, and motherhood. Following graduation, the women planned to focus first on establishing their careers. When Hoffnung (2004) checked up on the women 7 years after graduation, she found that some of the women were now married, but marital status was not related to educational attainment or career status. In contrast, motherhood was related to both educational attainment and career status: those women who had children had not gone as far with their education or career as those women without children. Thus, as they neared the age of 30, women seemed to be able to have marriage and a career, or marriage and a baby, but having all three led to some compromises, namely less progress in their careers.

Sixteen years after college graduation, when they were in their mid- to late-30s, Hoffnung and Williams (2013) again interviewed the women. At this point, about 90% had married and about 75% had children. Only 57% of those with children were employed full time. Most women indicated that they still "wanted to have it all," but not necessarily all at the same time. Women with children who were not employed full time indicated that they looked forward to working full time sometime in the future. And some childfree working women indicated that they had not ruled out becoming mothers. Thus, women may have it all by juggling the various roles and adjusting their expectations to the realities of fitting all the pieces together.

What happens after the children are grown? Gutmann suggests that, freed from the demands of the parental imperative, men become less active and more passive, take less interest in community affairs, and focus more on religious contemplation and family relationships. They also become more sensitive and emotionally expressive. Women, meanwhile, are changing in the opposite direction. After being relatively passive and nurturing in their younger years, they become more active, domineering, and assertive in later life. In many cultures, they take charge of the household after being the underlings of their mothers-in-law and become stronger forces in their communities. In short, then, the roles of men and women are fairly similar before marriage, maximally different during the child-rearing years, and similar again later (Gutmann, 1997).

What traits might we associate with this woman based on her agentic role in the workplace?

© Rainer Elstermann/Getty Images

Androgyny?

Do the shifts in the roles played by men and women during adulthood affect them psychologically? For years, psychologists assumed that "being masculine" or having agentic traits and "being feminine" or having communal traits were at opposite ends of a single continuum and mutually exclusive. If a person possessed agentic traits, then that person must be noncommunal, whereas being highly communal implied being nonagentic. This bipolar view was challenged with evidence that at least some individuals can be characterized by psychological **androgyny**—that is, by a balancing or blending of both agentic traits and communal traits (Spence, Helmreich, & Stapp, 1973). According to this perspective, then, agency and communion are two separate dimensions of personality. A male or female who has many agentic traits and few communal ones is considered to have a stereotypic "masculine" gender type. A person who has many communal traits and few agentic traits is said to have a "feminine" gender type. The androgynous person possesses both agentic and communal traits, whereas the undifferentiated individual lacks both kinds of attributes.

Most college students—both males and females—believe that the ideal person is androgynous (Slavkin & Stright, 2000). However, being well-adjusted psychologically is generally associated with gender-congruent personality traits (that is, males displaying agentic traits and females expressing communal traits), agentic traits in general, and having flexible attitudes about gender (Didonato & Berenbaum, 2010). In addition, you may need to distinguish between the androgynous individual who possesses *positive* agentic and communal traits and the one who possesses *negative* agentic and communal traits (Woodhill & Samuels, 2003, 2004). People with positive androgyny score higher on measures of mental health and well-being than those with negative androgyny (Woodhill & Samuels, 2003). It may be premature, then, to conclude that it is better in all respects to be androgynous rather than either agentic or communal in orientation. Still, you can at least conclude that it is unlikely to be damaging for men to become a little more communal or for women to become a little more agentic than they have traditionally been.

Changes in Sexuality

Adults' sexual lifestyles are as varied as their personalities and intellects. Some adults remain single—some of them actively seeking a range of partners, others having one partner at a time, and still others leading celibate lives. Almost 9 of 10 Americans marry, and most adults are married at any given time. Men have more sexual partners and report more sexual activity than women during their adult lives, but most members of both sexes have just one sexual partner at a time (Cherlin, 2009; Peterson & Hyde, 2010).

Among married couples, there is a small decline in quality of sex over the course of marriage, as well as a drop in the quantity of sex (Liu, 2003). There are also some gender differences, with married women reporting somewhat less satisfaction with their sex lives than married men (Liu, 2003). Middle-aged women report more positive moods and lower stress levels on days following sexual behavior with a partner (Burleson, Trevathan, & Todd, 2007). This benefit may be due to sexual activity alone or in combination with the affection that many women reported with the sexual activity. Tim Wadsworth (2013) analyzed survey results on frequency of sex and happiness levels of over 15,000 men and women. He found that as one went up, so did the other: Adults are happier when they are having more frequent sex. What's more, adults who believe they are having sex more frequently than their peers are even happier (Wadsworth, 2013).

What becomes of people's sex lives as they age? Just as parents may be uncomfortable thinking of their teens as sexual beings, many young people struggle to conceive of their parents or—heaven forbid—their grandparents as sexual beings. We tend to stereotype older adults as sexless or asexual. But we are wrong: People continue to be sexual beings throughout the life span. For example, in a survey of more than 6,000 adults ranging in age from 25 to 85, most adults reported being interested in sex and being sexually active (Lindau & Gavrilova, 2010). Gender differences were small among younger adults but became larger with age, leading to relatively large differences among the oldest adults: 75- to 85-year-old men were twice as likely to be sexually

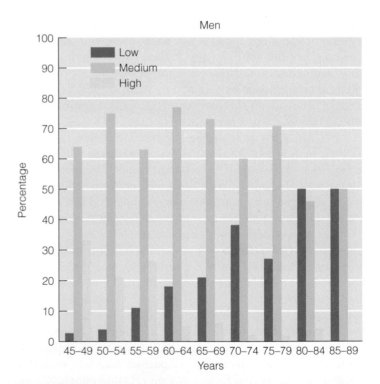

■ **Figure 12.6** Percentage of women (top graph) and men (bottom graph), by age, reporting low, moderate, and high levels of sexual desire.

SOURCE: From DeLamater, J. S.. & Sill, M., (2005). Sexual desire in later life, *Journal of Sex Research*, 42, 138–149.

active and four times as likely to express interest in sex as women the same age. Other research shows a decline in sexual desire with age, although as ■ **Figure 12.6** illustrates, desire can remain moderate or high well into old age.

Most adults continue to be interested in sex and engage in sexual behaviors on a regular basis. For those older adults who experience a decline in sexual desire or behavior, what factors might be behind the change?

© A. Green/Corbis

a refractory, or recovery, period of only minutes before he is capable of sexual activity again. The older man is likely to be slower—slower to arouse, slower to ejaculate after being aroused, and slower to recover afterward. In addition, levels of male sex hormones decline gradually with age in many men. This may contribute to diminished sexual functioning among older men (Schiavi et al., 1991), although most researchers do not believe that hormonal factors fully explain the changes in sexual behavior that most men experience (Kaye, 1993).

Physiological changes in women are less dramatic. Females reach their peak of sexual responsiveness later than men do, often not until their mid-30s. Women are capable of more orgasms in a given time span than men are because they have little or no refractory period after orgasm, and this capacity is retained into old age. As noted in Chapter 5, menopause does not seem to reduce sexual activity or interest for most women. However, like older men, older women typically are slower to become sexually excited. Moreover, some experience discomfort associated with decreased lubrication that occurs as estrogen levels drop with menopause.

The physiological changes that men and women experience do not explain why many of them become less sexually active in middle and old age. Masters and Johnson concluded that both men and women are physiologically capable of sexual behavior well into old age. Women retain this physiological capacity even longer than men, yet they are less sexually active in old age.

Apparently, we must turn to factors other than biological aging to explain changes in sexual behavior. In summarizing these factors, Pauline Robinson (1983) quotes Alex Comfort (1974): "In our experience, old folks stop having sex for the same reason they stop riding a bicycle—general infirmity, thinking it looks ridiculous, and no bicycle" (p. 440; and see DeLamater, 2012).

Under the category of infirmity, diseases and disabilities, as well as the drugs prescribed for them, can limit sexual functioning (DeLamater & Sill, 2005). Older adults in good or excellent health not only report engaging in more frequent sex than their peers in poor or fair health, they also report more interest in sex and greater satisfaction with their sexual activity (Lindau & Gavrilova, 2010). Poor health may be especially problematic for men, who may become impotent if they have high blood pressure, coronary disease, diabetes, or other health problems. Mental health problems are also important: Many cases of impotence among middle-aged and elderly men are attributable to psychological causes such as stress at work and depression rather than to physiological causes (Persson & Svanborg, 1992).

The second source of problems is social attitudes that view sexual activity in old age as ridiculous, or at least inappropriate. Old people are stereotyped as sexually unappealing and sexless (or as "dirty old men") and are discouraged from expressing sexual interests. These negative attitudes may be internalized by elderly people, causing them to suppress their sexual desires (Kaye, 1993; Purifoy, Grodsky, & Giambra, 1992). Older females

With longer and healthier life spans and greater recognition and acceptance of middle and older adults' sexual activity, there have been some unexpected consequences. Perhaps most alarming has been the doubling of STIs among those 45 and older (Bodley-Tickell et al., 2008). Many postmenopausal women assume that there is no need to practice "safe sex" because the threat of an unintended pregnancy is no longer present. They may be uninformed about STIs and too embarrassed to ask for information. Even more disturbing, many older adults do not get tested for STIs, including HIV, and may not get the treatment to save their life or improve the quality of their life (Jacobs & Kane, 2010). Consider Jane Fowler's story (Evans & Goldman, 2010): Divorced at age 47 after 23 years of marriage and monogamous sex, Jane dated a few men whom she knew from her larger circle of friends. She didn't worry about using condoms because she knew pregnancy wouldn't be an issue and, after all, she *knew* these men; they weren't strangers. But a routine blood test for an insurance company revealed that Jane was infected with HIV. In the aftermath of her shocking diagnosis, Jane withdrew from many activities and retired from her career as a journalist. Fortunately, she eventually overcame her embarrassment and fears over contracting an STI in midlife and founded an organization, *HIV Wisdom for Older Women*, to educate other women on the importance of safe sex practices at all ages (Evans & Goldman, 2010). Such cases illustrate that we need to do much more to improve sex education across the entire life span.

For older adults who experience declines in sexual interest and activity, what might explain this change? Consider first the physiological changes in sexual capacity that occur with age, as revealed by the pioneering research of William Masters and Virginia Johnson (1966, 1970). Males are at their peak of sexual responsiveness in their late teens and early 20s and gradually become less responsive thereafter. A young man is easily and quickly aroused; his orgasm is intense; and he may have may be even further inhibited by the double standard of aging, which regards aging in women more negatively than aging in men (Arber & Ginn, 1991).

Third, there is the "no bicycle" part of Comfort's analogy—the lack of a partner, or at least of a willing and desirable partner. Most older women are widowed, divorced, or single and face the reality that there just are not enough older men to go around. Lack of a partner, then, is the major problem for elderly women, many of whom continue to be interested in sex, physiologically capable of sexual behavior, and desirous of love and affection (DeLamater & Sill, 2005; Karraker, DeLamater, & Schwartz, 2011).

Perhaps we should add one more element to Comfort's bicycle analogy: lack of cycling experience. Masters and Johnson (1966, 1970) proposed a "use it or lose it" principle of sexual behavior to reflect two findings. First, an individual's level of sexual activity early in adulthood predicts his level of sexual activity in later life. The relationship is not necessarily causal, by the way; it could simply be that some people are more sexually motivated than others throughout adulthood. A second aspect of the use it or lose it rule may be causal, however: Middle-aged and elderly adults who experience a long period of sexual abstinence often have difficulty regaining their sexual capacity.

Checking Mastery

1. How do gender roles shift during adulthood?
2. What is androgyny? Is it beneficial to be androgynous?
3. How do sexual behaviors change across adulthood?

Making Connections

1. The extent to which males and females differ changes from infancy to old age. When are gender differences in psychological characteristics and roles played in society most evident, and when are they least evident? How would you account for this pattern?
2. Fewer women than men become architects. Drawing on the material in this chapter, explain the extent to which nature and nurture may be responsible for this, citing evidence.

Chapter Summary

12.1 Sex and Gender

- Differences between males and females can be detected in the physical, psychological, and social realms; gender differences arise from an interaction of biological influences and socialization into gender roles (including the learning of gender-role norms and stereotypes).
- Research comparing males and females indicates that the two sexes are far more similar than different psychologically. The average male is more aggressive and better at spatial tasks and some mathematical problem-solving tasks, but less adept at verbal tasks, than the average female. Males also tend to be more active, assertive, and developmentally vulnerable than females, who tend to be more compliant with adults' requests, tactful, nurturant, and anxious. Most sex differences are small, however, and some are becoming smaller.

12.2 The Infant

- During infancy, boys and girls are similar but adults treat them differently.
- Because their sex is important to those around them, and because they see that males and females differ, infants begin to form categories of "male" and "female."
- By age 2, infants have often gained knowledge of their basic gender identity and display "gender-appropriate" play preferences.

12.3 The Child

- Gender-role development proceeds with remarkable speed. By the time they enter school, children have long been aware of their basic gender identities, have acquired many stereotypes about how the sexes differ, and have come to prefer gender-appropriate activities and same-sex playmates.
- During middle childhood, their knowledge continues to expand as they learn more about gender-stereotyped psychological traits, but they also become more flexible in their thinking about gender roles. Their behavior, especially if they are boys, becomes even more gender typed, and they segregate themselves even more from the other sex.
- Theories of gender-role development include the biosocial theory proposed by Money and Ehrhardt, which emphasizes prenatal biological developments and stresses the importance of how a child is labeled and treated during a critical period for gender identity information.
- Social learning theorists focus on differential reinforcement and observational learning.
- Kohlberg's cognitive-developmental theory emphasizes that children master gender roles once they master the concepts of gender identity, gender stability, and gender consistency.
- Martin and Halverson's gender schema theory holds that children socialize themselves as soon as they have a basic gender identity and can construct gender schemata. Each theory has some support, but none is completely right.
- School-age children engage in sex play and appear to experience their first sexual attractions around age 10.

12.4 The Adolescent

- Adolescents become intolerant in their thinking about gender-role deviations and, through gender intensification, show increased concern with conforming to gender norms.
- In adolescence, forming a positive sexual identity is an important task, one that can be difficult for those with a gay or lesbian sexual orientation.
- During the past century, we have witnessed increased endorsement of the view that sex with affection is acceptable, a weakening of the double standard, and increased confusion about sexual norms.

12.5 The Adult

- Gender roles become more distinct when adults marry and have children, as men and women fulfill their roles as husband/wife and father/mother. Once children are grown, however, older adults often display greater flexibility in their behavior.
- Some adults display androgyny, a combination of both masculine-stereotypic and feminine-stereotypic traits. Some evidence suggests that androgyny is beneficial, but not at all ages or in all situations.
- Many older adults continue having sexual intercourse, and many of those who cease having it or have it less frequently continue to be sexually motivated. Elderly people can continue to enjoy an active sex life if they retain their physical and mental health, do not allow negative attitudes surrounding sexuality in later life to stand in their way, have a willing and able partner, and continue to "use" their capacity for sex.

Checking Mastery Answers

For answers to Checking Mastery questions, please see Appendix B.

Key Terms

transgender **366**	gender identity **371**	sexual orientation **385**
biological sex **366**	gender typing **372**	childhood gender nonconformity (CGN) **386**
gender **366**	gender segregation **374**	hookup **387**
gender roles **367**	biosocial theory **375**	double standard **387**
gender stereotypes **367**	androgenized females **376**	oral sex **389**
communality **367**	gender constancy **380**	posttraumatic stress disorder **390**
agency **367**	gender stability **381**	parental imperative **392**
systemize **367**	gender consistency **381**	androgyny **393**
gender similarities hypothesis **368**	gender schema (schemata) **381**	
social-role theory **369**	gender intensification **385**	

CENGAGE brain.com Get quizzes, flashcards, videos, and more at **www.cengagebrain.com.**

13 Social Cognition and Moral Development

Certain campers one summer repeatedly pulled a prank on Edward. Edward was a small, uneven-legged, mildly retarded adult who was the basic maintenance staffer for the camp. He was kind, conscientious in his duties, and proud that he was earning his way in life. There was just one thing: At a point of frustration or moment of embarrassment, Ed would invariably unleash a torrent of profanities that was surprising and, to some campers, entertaining. Several campers had devised a way to set off this "entertainment." Ed worked hard mowing and doing other chores on the camp grounds and would sometimes take a nap during the day.... Seeing Ed asleep, the plotters would move in. They would gently sink one of Ed's hands into a pail of water. Ed would wet his pants in bed and awaken, swearing madly and running frantically after the hysterically laughing campers (Gibbs, 2010, p. 1).

John Gibbs (2010), author of the book *Moral Development and Reality*, attended the camp just described, watched the torment of Edward play out again and again, and feels guilty to this day that he did nothing to stop it, fearful of his fellow campers' reactions if he did. Many of you, we wager, can recall episodes like this when you and/or your peers did something hurtful to a nerdy, overweight, or otherwise different individual who did not deserve it, when you failed to take the perspective of and empathize with an innocent victim. What might have stopped you from mistreating someone like Edward or prompted you to intervene to save him from abuse by others? What does it take to optimize the helpful and cooperative tendencies of human beings and reduce the antisocial ones?

In this chapter, we continue our examination of the development of the self by exploring how we come to understand the social world and make decisions about issues of right and wrong like those raised by the campers' treatment of Edward. We begin with a look at the development of thinking about people and their behavior, which includes learning to take the perspectives of other people, including victims like Edward. We then look closely at moral development and positive and negative social behavior. We ask how humans acquire moral standards, how they decide what to do when faced with moral dilemmas, how empathy, guilt, and other emotions influence what they do, and why some individuals behave more morally than others.

13.1 Social Cognition

LEARNING OBJECTIVES:

- Define social cognition and explain the meaning and significance of having a theory of mind.

- Summarize key steps in the development of a theory of mind and the contributions of nature and nurture to this development.

- Describe developments in trait perception and perspective taking and explain why social cognitive skills hold up well in later life.

Social cognition is thinking about the perceptions, thoughts, emotions, motives, and behaviors of self, other people, groups, and even whole social systems (Flavell, 1985; and see Harris, 2006). We have already touched on some important aspects of social cognitive development in this book, seeing, for example, that older children think differently than younger children about what they are like as individuals and about how males and females differ. Here we focus on developmental changes in the ability to understand human psychology, describe other people, and adopt other people's perspectives.

Developing a Theory of Mind

Imagine that you are a young child, are brought to the laboratory, and are led through the research scenario portrayed in ■ **Figure 13.1**. A girl named Sally, you are told, puts her marble in her basket and leaves the room. While she is gone, Anne moves the marble to her box. Sally returns to the room. Where will Sally look for her marble?

This task, called a **false belief task**, assesses the understanding that people can hold incorrect beliefs and that these beliefs, even though incorrect, can influence their behavior. The task was used in a pioneering study by Simon Baron-Cohen, Alan Leslie, and Uta Frith (1985) to determine whether young children, children with Down syndrome, and children with autism have a theory of mind. A **theory of mind** is the understanding that people have mental states such as desires, beliefs, and intentions and that these mental states guide (or cause, if you like) their behavior. We all rely on a theory of mind, also called mind-reading skills, to predict and explain human behavior. We refer to mental states every day, saying, for example, that people did what they did because they wanted to, intended to, or believed that doing so would have a desired effect.

Sally places her marble in a basket.

Sally leaves the room.

The child being tested watches as Anne transfers Sally's marble to the box.

Sally returns.

The child being tested is asked the critical question: Where will Sally look for her marble?

■ **Figure 13.1** The false belief task involving Sally and Anne. The child who has developed a theory of mind should say that Sally will look in the basket based on her *false belief* that the marble is there. The child who has not yet developed a theory of mind fails this false belief task, saying that Sally will look in the box (where the child knows the marble has been moved).

SOURCE: From Baron-Cohen, S., Leslie, A. M., & Frith, U. Does the Autistic Child Have a "Theory of Mind"? *Cognition, 21*, 37–46. Copyright © 1985. Reprinted with permission from Elsevier.

Children who pass the false belief task in Figure 13.1, and therefore show evidence of having a theory of mind to explain human behavior, say that Sally will look for her marble in the basket (where she falsely believes it to be) rather than in the box (where it was moved without her knowledge). Children who have a theory of mind believe that Sally's behavior will be guided by her false belief about the marble's location. They are able to set aside their own knowledge of where the marble ended up after Anne moved it.

In the study by Baron-Cohen and his colleagues, about 85% of 4-year-olds of normal intelligence and older children with Down syndrome passed the false belief task about Sally and her marble. Yet despite mental ages greater than those of the children with Down syndrome, 80% of the children with autism failed. They incorrectly said Sally would look where they knew the marble to be (in the box) rather than where Sally had every reason to believe it was (in the basket).

This study aroused much excitement because it suggested that children with autism display the social deficits they display because they lack a theory of mind and suffer from a kind of "mind blindness" (Baron-Cohen, 1995; and see Chapter 16). Imagine trying to understand and interact with people if you were unable to appreciate such fundamentals of human psychology as that people look for objects where they believe the objects are located, choose things that they want and reject things that they dislike, and sometimes attempt to plant false beliefs in others (that is, lie).

Temple Grandin, a woman with autism who is intelligent enough to be a professor of animal sciences, describes what it is like to lack a theory of mind: She must create a memory bank of how people behave and what emotions they express in various situations and then "compute" how people might be expected to behave in similar situations (Sacks, 1993). Although she can grasp simple emotions like happiness, she confesses that she could never quite get what *Romeo and Juliet* was all about. She feels awkward trying to carry on everyday conversations with people but relates well to animals and has used that talent to develop more humane ways of handling livestock. Just as we cannot understand falling objects without employing the concept of gravity, we cannot understand humans without invoking the concept of mental states and our theory of mind.

First Steps in Infancy

Although children normally do not pass the false belief task (Figure 13.1) until about age 4, a theory of mind begins to form in infancy. Indeed, infants have far more sophisticated social cognitive skills than we ever suspected. Several abilities are considered important early steps in developing a theory of mind; intriguingly, most of these skills are deficient in children with autism (see, for example, Charman, 2000; and Doherty, 2009):

- *Joint attention.* Starting around 9 months, infants and their caregivers engage in joint attention, both looking at the same object at the same time (see Chapter 10). At this age, infants sometimes point to toys and then look toward their companions, encouraging others to look at what they are looking at. By doing so, infants show awareness that other people have different perceptual experiences than they do—and that two people can share a perceptual experience. It turns out that an infant's ability to get involved in bouts of joint attention is a good predictor of later social competence (Van Hecke et al., 2007).
- *Understanding intentions.* In their first months of life, infants seem to understand that other people have *intentions*, set goals, and act to achieve them (Woodward, 2009). For example, by 6 months of age, if not earlier, infants much prefer a "helper" who helps an actor achieve a goal to a "hinderer" who blocks goal achievement, showing that they understand good and bad intentions when they see them (Hamlin & Wynn, 2011; Hamlin, Wynn, & Bloom, 2007).
- *Pretend play.* When infants engage in their first simple *pretend play*, between 1 and 2 years, they show at least a primitive understanding of the difference between pretense (a kind of false belief) and reality (see Chapter 14). They show that they know the difference between a pretend tea party and a real one, for example, when they make exaggerated lip-smacking noises as they drink from a cup at a pretend tea party.
- *Imitation.* Imitation of other people in the first year of life reveals an ability to mentally represent their actions—and very likely the goals or intentions behind them.
- *Emotional understanding.* As we will see when we look at infant empathy and helping, comforting a playmate who is crying or teasing a sibling in the second year of life reflects an understanding that other people have emotions and that these emotions can be influenced for good or bad (Flavell, 1999).

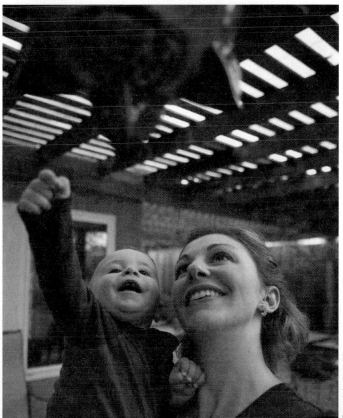

Even 1-year-olds show awareness that other people can have mental states (perceptions) different from their own when they point at objects so that their companions and they can jointly attend to the same object.

Some researchers even claim that infants as young as 15 months understand that people can hold false beliefs. By simplifying the false belief task, Kristine Onishi and Renée Baillargeon (2005) found that infants this age are surprised (as indicated by looking longer) when an actor does not look for a toy where she should believe it was hidden (and see Scott & Baillargeon, 2009). This intuitive surprise is probably not the same as the more explicit, conscious understanding of how false beliefs can lead people astray that children normally achieve by age 4 (Doherty, 2009; Sodian, 2011), but it certainly adds to our picture of an infant who is very ready to understand and participate in the social world.

Desire and Belief–Desire Psychologies

We have even more solid evidence that preschool children, starting at age 2, are developing theories of mind when they begin to talk about mental states (Bretherton & Beeghly, 1982). For example, Ross (at 2 years, 7 months) was asked why he kept asking why and replied, "I want to say 'why,' " explaining his behavior in terms of his desire; Adam (at 3 years, 3 months) commented about a bus, "I thought it was a taxi," showing awareness that he held a false belief about the bus (Wellman & Bartsch, 1994, p. 345). Children as young as 2½ years of age (and certainly older preschool children) will even attempt to deceive other people; they will try to plant a false belief in an experimenter if they are shown how to erase telltale footprints leading toward the spot where a bag of gold coins and jewels is hidden and to lay new footprints heading in the wrong direction (Chandler, Fritz, & Hala, 1989).

Based on studies like these, Henry Wellman (1990) has theorized that children's theories of mind unfold in two phases. Around age 2 children develop a **desire psychology**. Toddlers talk about what they want and explain their own behavior and that of others in terms of wants or desires. This early desire psychology could be seen even among 18-month-olds in a clever study by Betty Repacholi and Alison Gopnik (1997). An experimenter tried two foods—Goldfish crackers and broccoli florets—and expressed happiness in response to one but disgust in response to the other. Because the toddlers almost universally preferred the crackers to the broccoli, the acid test was a scenario in which toddlers saw the experimenter express her liking for broccoli but her disgust at the crackers ("Eww! Crackers! I tasted crackers! Eww!"). When confronted with the two bowls of food and asked to give the experimenter some, would these toddlers give her broccoli or crackers? The 14-month-olds in the study either did not comply with the request or gave the experimenter crackers, despite her distaste for them. However, the 18-month-olds gave her broccoli (undoubtedly against their better judgment!), showing that they were able to infer and honor her desire based on her previous emotional reactions to the two foods.

By age 4, children normally progress to a **belief–desire psychology**. They appreciate that people do what they do because they *desire* certain things and because they *believe* that certain actions will help them fulfill their desires. They now pass false belief tasks like the one about Sally and her

marble, demonstrating an explicit understanding that beliefs, true or false, guide people's behavior just as desires do (Wellman, Cross, & Watson, 2001; Wellman & Liu, 2004).

Notice that the 4-year-olds described by theory-of-mind researchers are more sophisticated students of psychology than the egocentric preschoolers described by Jean Piaget (see Chapter 7). However, it is better to think of a theory of mind as a set of understandings that children begin to develop well before age 4, and continue to refine and learn to use long afterward, than to view it as something children "have" at 4 years (Miller, 2012; Wellman & Liu, 2004). Even much older children can be challenged when they are asked to understand sarcasm, where the intended meaning of a statement is different from the literal meaning, as in the sample task in **Engagement Box 13.1** (Peterson, Wellman, & Slaughter, 2012). In late elementary school, children are also still mastering complex second-order belief statements such as, "Mary thinks that Jeff thinks that she hates him," in which people have beliefs about other people's beliefs (Harris, 2006; Miller, 2012). Moreover, it is not until late elementary school that children grasp that different minds construct different views of reality and that their interpretations of events are influenced by these views (Flavell, 1999).

Nature and Nurture

How do nature and nurture contribute to the development of theory-of-mind skills? We seem to need both the brain for it and the right kinds of social experience.

An Evolved Brain On the nature side of the nature–nurture issue, evolutionary theorists argue that having a theory of mind proved adaptive to our ancestors and became part of our biological endowment as a species through natural selection (Buss, 2012; Tomasello & Herrmann, 2010). You can easily appreciate that theory-of-mind skills would help humans function as members of a social group, gain or protect resources, and therefore survive. Figuring out other people's intentions would be useful in deciding whether to trust them or be wary of them. Social behaviors such as bargaining, conflict resolution, cooperation, and competition all depend on understanding other people and predicting their behavior accurately.

Some support for an evolutionary perspective on theory-of-mind skills comes from studies of other primates. As it turns out, chimpanzees, gorillas, and other great apes share with humans some basic theory-of-mind skills. They can, for example, deceive others to get what they want (Hare, Call, & Tomasello, 2006; Tomasello, Call, & Hare, 2003). Yet human children have more advanced theory-of-mind skills and are more able than chimps to cooperate with others to achieve a goal (Tomasello & Herrmann, 2010).

In further support of the nature side of the nature–nurture issue, developing a theory of mind requires a certain level of neurological and cognitive maturation. This may be why children everywhere develop a theory of mind and progress from a desire psychology to a belief–desire psychology in the same manner at about the same age. Abnormal brain development in chil-

Engagement 13.1

Do You Have a Theory of Mind?

Try this example of a higher-level theory-of-mind problem suitable for elementary school-aged children (from Peterson et al., 2012, pp. 474 and 485; based on Happé,1994):

The girl and boy [shown in a picture] are going on a picnic. It is the boy's idea. He says it will be a lovely sunny day.

But when they get the food out, big storm clouds come. It rains and the food gets all wet. The girl says: "It's a lovely day for a picnic."

1. Is it true, what the girl said?
2. Why did the girl say 'it's a lovely day for a picnic?
3. Was the girl happy about the rain?

In the Peterson et al. (2012) study, only 4% of children ages 3 to 5 passed the key item, question 2, compared to 41% of children 7½ to 11½. Thus even the older children tested found this theory of mind task challenging. How did you do? (See the scoring guide below.)

This task assesses a child's ability to recognize sarcasm. The critical test question is the second question, "Why did the girl say 'it's a lovely day for a picnic'?"

Passing Answers
(reflecting understanding that the girl's intended meaning is different from the literal meaning of what she said):
She's being sarcastic/sarcasm; she doesn't mean it; because it's an idiom; she tricked him; it's her way of telling him she is upset; just to make up a little joke; she is saying politely that she is not happy; because she is a smart aleck; because she is meaning "Why tell me it was nice?"

Failing Answers:
Because it is sunny [raining]; it's lovely outside; she likes rain [picnics]/we need rain; she wants to play in the puddles; because she [the cake] got wet; because he lied to her; she thought it was sunny/did not see clouds; she's cross; to tell him off; because it's not sunny; so he doesn't feel bad; because he said it first; because her Dad likes the rain but she doesn't.

---

dren with autism is suspected to be behind their great difficulty passing theory-of-mind tasks.

Neuropsychologists have identified areas in the prefrontal cortex and the temporoparietal junction of the brain that are uniquely involved in thinking about people's beliefs (Sabbagh, 2006; Saxe, Carey, & Kanwisher, 2004; Saxe & Powell, 2006). Using *functional magnetic resonance imaging (fMRI)* to determine which areas of the brain are active while a person completes a task, for example, Rebecca Saxe and Nancy Kanwisher (2003) found that the areas of adults' brains that respond strongly during false belief tasks do not respond to similar tasks that do not involve thinking about mental states. Moreover, 4- to 6-year-old children who pass false belief tasks rely on the same brain areas to think about others' beliefs as adults do, whereas children who fail these tasks use different brain areas (Liu, Meltzoff, & Wellman, 2009; and see Saxe et al., 2009). As children develop, then, their brains increasingly behave like adult brains in responding to information about mental states (Gweon, Dodell-Feder, Bedney, & Saxe, 2012).

Neuropsychologists also believe social cognition involves **mirror neurons**, neurons that are activated both when we perform an action and when we observe someone else perform the same action (Iacoboni, 2009; Oberman & Ramachandran, 2007; Pineda, 2009; Rizzolatti & Sinigaglia, 2008). Thus, observing someone grasp a ball activates the same neurons that fire when we grasp a ball ourselves. Mirror neuron systems may therefore facilitate learning and imitation of what we see and hear, including language development. These neurons, evident in multiple areas of the brain, may also be critical in allowing us to quickly infer another person's mental

state based on our own experiences of the same visible actions and facial expressions and corresponding internal states. For example, by watching a person reach for a Coke on a hot day, we readily infer that she's thirsty and wants a drink, and when she takes a sip, we readily infer from her facial expression, which we are likely to unconsciously and subtly imitate, that she's happy. Through mirror neuron systems, we make sense of other people by drawing on what we know of ourselves (Oberman & Ramachandran, 2007).

Mirror neuron systems appear to be involved in imitation, theory-of-mind understandings, language, and empathy (Iacoboni & Dapretto, 2006; Oberman & Ramachandran, 2007), and mirror neuron deficits may help explain the difficulty individuals with autism have in these areas (Gallese, Rochat, & Berchio, 2013; Glenberg, 2011). For example, as the **Exploring Development Box 13.1** video discusses, the mirror neurons of individuals with autism are not as active as those of typically developing individuals when they are asked to observe or imitate others' actions (Dapretto et al., 2006; Williams et al., 2006). In addition, individuals with autism do not automatically and subtly mimic other

Exploring Development 13.1
Mirror Neurons

Some cognitive neuroscientists are calling mirror neurons another sensory system, like vision, hearing, and taste.

- How do mirror neurons affect empathy?
- How are mu waves being used in the treatment of autism?

This mother signs "You" to her deaf son on his fifth birthday. Deaf children who can communicate with their companions through sign language develop theory-of-mind skills on schedule.

people's facial expressions of emotion the way the rest of us do—as when we cringe while watching someone else in pain (McIntosh et al., 2006). Ultimately, social cognition depends on both automatic neural processes like mirror neuron firings and more conscious reasoning supported by the higher centers of the brain. Our human brains seem to be magnificently designed for social cognition.

Talk of Mental States On the nurture side of the nature–nurture issue is evidence that acquiring a theory of mind and other social cognitive skills, much like acquiring language, requires not only a normal human brain but also experience interacting with other humans—participating in a "community of minds" (Nelson et al., 2003). Children do not construct their theories of mind on their own; instead, they construct them jointly with others during conversations about mental states (Doherty, 2009; Thompson, 2006).

The evidence? Social interaction involving language seems to be critical to the development of a theory of mind. Deaf children of deaf parents, who can communicate with their companions using sign language, develop theory-of-mind skills right on schedule. However, deaf children of hearing parents, who usually do not have an opportunity to converse in sign language from an early age, achieve milestones in social cognitive development slowly, sometimes struggling with false belief tasks even at ages 8–10 (Peterson & Siegal, 1999; Peterson & Wellman, 2009; Peterson et al., 2012).

Parents contribute to the development of theory-of-mind skills in several ways. They do so by forming secure attachments with their children and being sensitive to their needs and perspectives (Symons & Clark, 2000; Thompson, 2012). Even more important may be a parent's "mind-mindedness." Mothers who talk in elaborated ways about their children's mental states ("You were probably sad because you thought Grandma would stay with us longer") tend to have children with advanced theory-of-mind skills (Meins et al., 2002; Peterson & Slaughter, 2003). So do mothers

who encourage their children to imagine what others may have thought or felt after the child misbehaved (Pears & Moses, 2003).

Conversations with siblings may also contribute to mind-reading skills. Children with siblings seem to grasp the elements of a theory of mind earlier than children without siblings (McAlister & Peterson, 2006, 2007). Pretend play sessions with siblings involve sharing beliefs about a pretend world (Youngblade & Dunn, 1995). Sibling conflicts may also generate lots of talk about mental states ("I thought you were done with your ice cream," "I didn't mean to step on your head").

Finally, cultural influences are evident: Although most children worldwide master false belief tasks around age 4 and develop theory-of-mind skills in much the same order (Wellman et al., 2001), children are slow to develop theory-of-mind skills in cultures where there is not much talk about mental states. This is the case in Samoa; others' minds are considered largely unknowable so mental states are not discussed much. Perhaps as a result, it was not until age 8 that a majority of Samoan children in one study tested passed false belief tasks (Mayer & Träuble, 2013; and see Vinden & Astington, 2000).

In sum, acquiring a theory of mind—the foundation for all later social cognitive development—begins in infancy and toddlerhood with first steps such as joint attention, understanding of intentions, pretend play, imitation, and emotional understanding and advances from a desire psychology to a belief–desire psychology and beyond universally (see ● **Table 13.1** for a timetable). It is the product of both nature and nurture; that is, it is an evolved set of skills that relies on specialized areas of the brain and mirror neurons and that will not emerge without normal neurological and cognitive growth but that also will not develop normally without social experiences that involve talking about mental states with parents, siblings, and other companions.

It is fundamentally important to master theory-of-mind skills if we want to participate in the social world. Beyond that, children who have mastered these skills generally can think more maturely about moral issues and other social problems, and they tend to have more advanced social skills and better social adjustment than those who have not (Doherty, 2009; Miller, 2012; Repacholi et al., 2003). However, theory-of-mind skills can be used for good or bad ends. Bullies and good liars often prove to be very adept at "mind reading" too (Repacholi et al., 2003; Talwar & Lee, 2008), so there is no guarantee that good "mind readers" will be socially well adjusted or behave in moral ways.

● **Table 13.1** Milestones in the Development of Theory of Mind

Age	Achievements
Birth to 2	Joint attention, understanding of intentions, pretend play, imitation, emotional understanding
Age 2	Desire psychology
Age 4	Belief–desire psychology
Age 5 and beyond	Understanding of second-order beliefs, sarcasm, different views of reality

© Cengage Learning 2015

Trait Perception

Although research on theory of mind shows that even infants and preschool children are budding psychologists, they still have a way to go to understand people in terms of their enduring personality traits and to predict how people will react and behave. Consider first how children of different ages describe people they know—parents, friends, disliked classmates, and so on.

As you discovered in Chapter 11, children younger than 7 or 8 describe themselves primarily in physical rather than psychological terms. They describe other people that way, too (Livesley & Bromley, 1973; Yuill, 1993). Thus, 4-year-old Evan says of his father, "He has one nose, one Mom, two eyes, brown hair." And 5-year-old Keisha says, "My daddy is big. He has hairy legs and eats mustard. Yuck! My daddy likes dogs—do you?" Not much of a personality profile there.

Young children perceive others primarily in terms of their physical appearance, possessions, and activities. When they use psychological terms, the terms are often global, evaluative ones such as "nice" or "mean," "good" or "bad," rather than specific personality-trait labels (Ruble & Dweck, 1995). Moreover, preschool children do not yet seem to understand traits as enduring qualities that predict how a person will behave in the future and explain why a person behaves as he does. The 5-year-old who describes a friend as "dumb" may be using this trait label only to describe that friend's recent "dumb" behavior; she may expect "smart" behavior tomorrow. As happens so often, though, recent research tells us that young children understand more than we used to appreciate. For example, 4- and 5-year-olds seem to be able to infer from a few examples of selfish behavior that a person has the trait of selfishness, and they can predict that a person who has the trait of selfishness will behave selfishly in the future; they just can't quite put these two insights together to predict future behavior from past behavior via inferring the person's trait (Liu, Gelman, & Wellman, 2007).

Around age 7 or 8, children's descriptions of people show that they think about others in terms of their enduring psychological traits. Thus, 10-year-old Juanita describes her friend Tonya: "She's funny and friendly to everyone, and she's in the gifted program because she's smart, but sometimes she's too bossy." As children reach age 11 or 12, they make more use of psychological traits to explain why people behave as they do, saying, for instance, that Mike pulled the dog's tail *because* he is cruel (Gnepp & Chilamkurti, 1988). Clearly, then, children become more psychologically minded as their emerging social cognitive abilities permit them to make inferences about enduring inner qualities from the behavior they observe in the people around them.

When asked to describe people they know, adolescents offer personality profiles that are even more psychological than those provided by children (Livesley & Bromley, 1973). They see people as unique individuals with distinctive personality traits, interests, values, and feelings. Moreover, they are able to create more integrated, or organized, person descriptions, analyzing how an individual's often inconsistent traits fit together and make sense as a whole personality. Dan, for example, may notice that Noriko brags about her abilities at times but seems unsure of herself at other times, and he may integrate these seemingly discrepant impressions by concluding that Noriko is basically insecure and boasts to hide her insecurity. Some adolescents spend hours "psychoanalyzing" people, trying to figure out what makes them tick.

As was the case for self-descriptions, then, you can detect a progression in perceptions of other people from (1) physical descriptions and global evaluations of other people as good or bad during the preschool years to (2) more differentiated descriptions that refer to specific, enduring personality traits starting at age 7 or 8 and, finally, to (3) more integrated personality profiles during adolescence that show how even seemingly inconsistent traits fit together.

Perspective Taking

Another important aspect of social cognitive development involves outgrowing the egocentrism that characterizes young children and developing **perspective-taking skills**, also called **role-taking skills**: the ability to adopt another person's perspective and understand her thoughts and feelings. Perspective-taking skills are essential in thinking about moral issues from different points of view, predicting the consequences of a person's actions for others, and empathizing with others (Gibbs, 2010). If the campers at the start of the chapter had taken Edward's perspective, perhaps they would have laid off him.

Robert Selman (1976, 1980; Yeates & Selman, 1989) contributed greatly to our understanding of role-taking abilities by asking children questions about interpersonal dilemmas like this one (Selman, 1976, p. 302):

> Holly is an 8-year-old girl who likes to climb trees. She is the best tree climber in the neighborhood. One day while climbing down from a tall tree, she falls . . . but does not hurt herself. Her father sees her fall. He is upset and asks her to promise not to climb trees anymore. Holly promises.
>
> Later that day, Holly and her friends meet Shawn. Shawn's kitten is caught in a tree and can't get down. Something has to be done right away or the kitten may fall. Holly is the only one who climbs trees well enough to reach the kitten and get it down but she remembers her promise to her father.

To assess how well a child understands the perspectives of Holly, her father, and Shawn, Selman asks: "Does Holly know how Shawn feels about the kitten? How will Holly's father feel if he finds out she climbed the tree? What does Holly think her father will do if he finds out she climbed the tree? What would you do in this situation?" Children's responses to these questions led Selman (1976) to conclude that perspective-taking abilities develop in a stagelike manner as children progress through Piaget's stages of cognitive development. Here are highlights of this progression:

- Children 3–6 years old tend to respond egocentrically to stories like this, assuming that others share their point of view. If young children like kittens, for example, they assume that Holly's father does, too, and therefore will be delighted if Holly saves the kitten. They have difficulty taking the perspectives of both Holly and her father.

Adolescents who have advanced role-taking, or social perspective-taking, skills are better able than those who do not to resolve conflicts with their parents (Selman et al., 1986). They are better able to adopt the perspectives of their parents (and parents in general) and to identify mutually acceptable solutions.

- By age 8–10, children appreciate that two people can have different points of view even if they have access to the same information. Children are able to think about their own thoughts and about the thoughts of another person, and they realize that their companions can do the same. Thus, they can appreciate that Holly may think about her father's concern for her safety but may also believe that he will understand her reasons for climbing the tree.
- Adolescents, at roughly age 12, become capable of mentally juggling multiple perspectives, including the perspective of the "generalized other," or the broader social group. The adolescent might consider how fathers in general react when children disobey them and consider whether Holly's father is similar to or different from the typical father. Adolescents thus become even better mental jugglers, keeping in the air their own perspective, that of another person, and that of an abstract "generalized other" representing a larger social group.

These advances in social cognition are more likely if parents are good models of perspective taking, consider their children's feelings and thoughts, and rely on explanation rather than punishment in disciplining them. Perspective-taking skills are also sharpened through peer interactions. In turn, children with advanced perspective-taking skills are likely to be sociable and popular and enjoy good relationships with peers (Kurdek & Krile, 1982; LeMare & Rubin, 1987). This may be because their social behavior is more positive than negative (Fitzgerald & White, 2003). Meanwhile, coaching in perspective taking can help improve the social behavior of disruptive children (Grizenko et al., 2000).

Social Cognition in Adulthood

As you saw in earlier chapters, nonsocial cognitive abilities, such as those used in remembering what you have read and solving scientific problems, tend to improve during early and middle adulthood and decline in later life. Do social cognitive skills also increase to a peak in middle age and decline later?

Social cognitive development during adulthood appears to involve more gains than losses (Blanchard-Fields, 1996; Hess, 1999). For example, Fredda Blanchard-Fields (1986) presented adolescents, young adults, and middle-aged adults with dilemmas that required them to engage in role taking and to integrate discrepant perspectives—for example, between a teenage boy and his parents regarding whether he must visit his grandparents with the family. Adults, especially middle-aged ones, were better able than adolescents to see both sides of the issues and to integrate the perspectives of both parties into a workable solution. Here, then, is evidence that social cognitive skills continue to improve after adolescence.

Do elderly people continue to display the sophisticated social cognitive skills that middle-aged adults display? The evidence here is mixed but, overall, social cognitive skills hold up quite well late in life. Igor Grossmann and his colleagues (2010) asked young, middle-aged, and elderly American adults from diverse socioeconomic backgrounds to reason about both interpersonal and intergroup conflicts—conflicts between individuals that appeared in letters to advice columns and conflicts between ethnic or national groups as described in newspaper articles. In one of the interpersonal conflicts, for example, the single friend of both members of a married couple was being pressured by her female friend to take the friend's side when she and her husband quarreled. Social cognitive performance improved across the three age groups, as indicated by such criteria as taking multiple perspectives, seeing possibilities for compromise, and recognizing the limits of one's knowledge. This improvement in social cognition with age occurred despite a decline in fluid intelligence with age. Interestingly, these age differences were not as evident in a sample of Japanese adults (Grossmann et al., 2012); Japanese young and middle-aged adults outperformed their American counterparts and achieved about the same level of performance as both Japanese and American elders. Possibly in Japan's collectivist society, then, people learn earlier in adulthood sophisticated ways to resolve social conflicts.

When elderly adults do perform more poorly than middle-aged or young adults on social cognitive tasks, it may be because their basic mental capacities are overloaded (see Chapters 8 and 9). In one study of 50- to 90-year-olds who were given adult versions of theory-of-mind tasks, a decrease with age in theory-of-mind performance could be explained by declines with age in fluid intelligence, executive control processes, and information-processing speed (Charlton et al., 2009; and see Sullivan and Ruffman, 2004). In other studies, memory limitations have been found to hurt the performance of older adults on some social cognition tasks (Happé, Winner, & Brownell, 1998; Keightley et al., 2006). So, declines in basic cognitive functions such as memory capacity and processing speed sometimes take a toll on their social cognitive performance (Hess, 1999).

Overall, though, social cognitive skills hold up well—better than nonsocial cognitive abilities—in later life (Blanchard-Fields & Kalinauskas, 2009; Hess, Osowski, & Leclerc, 2005; Keightley et al., 2006). Why? One possible explanation is that the areas of the cortex that support social cognition and emotional

Social cognitive skills hold up well when older adults remain socially active like Gwendolyn Connally, age 93, on the right, who is enjoying the beat of the disco song "Freak Out" during a dance competition at her senior center.

psychology at age 4, thanks to both nature and nurture. Children's descriptions of other people progress from a focus on physical features and activities to a focus on inner psychological traits to the integration of trait descriptions, and perspective-taking skills improve with age. Social cognitive skills then often improve during early and middle adulthood and hold up well in old age if adults remain socially active.

Having examined some important and dramatic changes in social cognition over the life span, we are well positioned to focus on an important area of development in which social cognitive skills play a crucial role: moral development. Along the way, we will see how theory-of-mind and perspective-taking skills help shape thinking about right and wrong.

Checking Mastery

1. Sharon wonders if Baby Ben, age 18 months, is on his way to developing a theory of mind. What four developments in infancy can you point to as early signs of a developing theory of mind?

2. If you were trying to make sure a deaf child, Luis, develops a theory of mind, what kinds of experiences would you try to provide him?

3. What breakthrough in perspective-taking skills is achieved at about age 8–10 according to Robert Selman?

Making Connections

1. Eavesdrop on a conversation in which your friends gossip or talk about other people, and write down any statements in which they refer to people's beliefs, desires, intentions, emotions, and the like in attempting to account for someone's behavior. What evidence do you see that your friends have and use a theory of mind?

2. Picture two adults with advanced social cognitive skills: one who wants to do good, one who wants to do evil. How would each use his skills?

understanding age more slowly than the areas that support nonsocial cognition (MacPherson, Phillips, & Della Sala, 2002). Another is that people use social cognitive abilities every day and accumulate expertise about the world of people (Charlton et al., 2009). Their experience and expertise may allow them to come to sound conclusions without needing to use mentally taxing cognitive processes (Blanchard-Fields & Kalinauskas, 2009). Social skills vary, though. Those seniors who have the sharpest social cognitive skills tend to be socially active and involved in meaningful social roles such as spouse, grandparent, church member, and worker (Dolen & Bearison, 1982; Hess et al., 2005). It is mainly when elderly people become socially isolated or inactive that their social cognitive skills become rusty.

In sum, social cognition takes shape in infancy through precursors of a theory of mind such as joint attention and pretend play; a desire psychology at age 2; and then a belief–desire

13.2 Perspectives on Moral Development

LEARNING OBJECTIVES:

- Define and illustrate the three main components of morality.

- Compare and contrast the main messages about moral development of psychoanalytic, cognitive-developmental, social learning, and evolutionary theorists.

- Distinguish between Kohlberg's preconventional, conventional, and postconventional levels of moral reasoning.

Although we could debate endlessly what **morality** is (see Gibbs, 2010; Turiel, 2006), most of us might agree that it involves the ability to distinguish right from wrong, to act on this distinction, and to experience emotions like pride when we do the right things and guilt or shame when we do not. Accordingly, three basic components of morality have been of interest to developmental scientists:

1. The *emotional* component consists of the feelings (guilt, concern for others' feelings, and so on) that surround right or wrong actions and that motivate moral thoughts and actions.

2. The *cognitive* component centers on how we think about right and wrong and make decisions about how to behave, drawing on social cognitive skills such as role taking.

3. The *behavioral* component reflects how we behave when, for example, we experience the temptation to cheat or are called upon to help a needy person.

Major theoretical perspectives on moral development focus on different aspects of morality. So in this section we look at what psychoanalytic theory and more recent perspectives emphasizing emotions say about moral emotion, what cognitive-developmental theory says about moral cognition or reasoning, and what social learning (or social cognitive) theory reveals about moral behavior. Then we view morality from a broad, evolutionary perspective.

Moral Emotion: Psychoanalytic Theory and Beyond

What kind of moral emotions do you experience if you contemplate cheating or lying? Chances are you experience such negative feelings as shame, guilt, anxiety, and fear of being detected—feelings that keep you from doing what you know is wrong. You may also experience disgust or righteous anger when witnessing harmful acts and injustices (Tangney, Stuewig, & Mashek, 2007). Positive emotions, such as pride and self-satisfaction when you have done the right thing and admiration or gratitude when you witness moral acts, are also an important part of morality (Turiel, 2006). Moral emotions, both positive and negative, require being able to evaluate whether you or others have exceeded or fallen short of standards of behavior (Tangney et al., 2007). We are generally motivated to avoid negative moral emotions and to experience positive ones by acting in moral ways.

Empathy is the vicarious experiencing of another person's feelings (for example, smiling at another person's good fortune or experiencing another person's distress). Although it is not a specific emotion, it is an emotional process believed to be especially important in moral development by theorists such as Martin Hoffman (2000, 2008), whom we will encounter later. Empathizing with individuals who are suffering—not only taking their perspective but also feeling their pain—can motivate

prosocial behavior—positive social acts, such as helping or sharing, that reflect concern for the welfare of others. Empathy can also keep us from engaging in **antisocial behavior**—behavior that violates social norms, rules, or laws and often involves harming other people or society (for example, lying, stealing, behaving aggressively). If the campers in the chapter opener had really empathized with Edward's distress, they might have refrained from picking on him.

When do children begin to experience moral emotions? Sigmund Freud's (1960) psychoanalytic theory offered an answer (see Chapter 2). As you will recall, Freud believed that the *superego*, or conscience, has the important task of ensuring that any plans formed by the rational ego to gratify the id's selfish urges are morally acceptable. The superego is formed during the phallic stage (ages 3–6), when children are presumed to experience an emotional conflict over their love for the other-sex parent and resolve it by identifying with the same-sex parent, taking on the parent's moral standards as his or her own. Having a superego, then, is like having a parent inside your head—there, even when your parent is not, to tell you what is right or wrong and to arouse emotions such as shame and guilt if you so much as think about doing wrong.

Although the particulars of Freud's theory of moral development lack support (Hoffman, 2000; Silverman, 2003), his main themes are taken very seriously today, as you will see shortly. Research has shown that: (1) moral emotions are an important part of morality and motivate of moral behavior, (2) early relationships with parents contribute in important ways to moral development, and (3) children must somehow internalize moral standards if they are to behave morally even when no authority figure is present to detect and punish their misbehavior (Kochanska & Aksan, 2006; Turiel, 2006). As we will see later, modern theorists such as Martin Hoffman (2000) and Grazyna Kochanska (1993, 2002) place a great deal of emphasis on the importance of the emotional side of morality and on the motivating role of moral emotions such as empathy and guilt, starting early in childhood.

Moral Reasoning: Cognitive-Developmental Theory

Cognitive-developmental theorists study morality by looking at the development of **moral reasoning**—the thinking process involved in deciding whether an act is right or wrong. These theorists assume that moral development depends on social cognitive development, particularly perspective-taking skills that allow us to picture how our victims might react to our misdeeds or how people in distress must feel. Moral reasoning is said to progress through universal stages, each of which represents a consistent way of thinking about moral issues. To cognitive-developmental theorists, what is of interest is *how* we decide what to do, not what we decide or what we actually do. A young child and an adult may both decide not to steal a pen, but the reasons they give for their decision may be entirely different.

Jean Piaget paved the way for the influential cognitive-developmental theory of moral development put forth by Lawrence Kohlberg. Piaget (1965) studied children's concepts of rules by

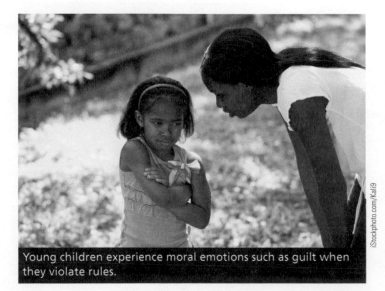

Young children experience moral emotions such as guilt when they violate rules.

iStockphoto.com/Kali9

asking Swiss children about their games of marbles and explored children's concepts of right and wrong by presenting them with moral dilemmas to ponder. He concluded that preschool children do not truly understand rules and are best thought of as "premoral." Children ages 6–10, he observed:

- Emphasize the consequences of more than the intentions behind acts in judging their wrongness (for example, they judge a boy who accidentally broke 15 cups while obeying his mother naughtier than a boy who broke only one cup while trying to sneak jam from the kitchen)
- Believe that rules are handed down by parents and other authorities and are unalterable (as when elementary school children remind their parents to buckle their seat belts and stick to the speed limit).

At age 10 or 11, Piaget found, children weigh more heavily whether a person's intentions were good or bad in judging his actions. They also begin to appreciate that rules are agreements between individuals—agreements that can be changed through a consensus of those individuals.

Inspired by Piaget's pioneering work, Lawrence Kohlberg (1963, 1981, 1984; Colby & Kohlberg, 1987) formulated his own cognitive-developmental theory of moral development by asking 10-, 13-, and 16-year-old boys questions about various moral dilemmas to assess how they thought about these issues. Careful analysis of the responses led Kohlberg to conclude that moral growth progresses through a universal and invariant sequence of three broad moral levels, each of which is composed of two distinct stages. Each stage grows out of the preceding stage and represents a more complex way of thinking about moral issues.

Kohlberg's Stages of Moral Reasoning

Think about how you would respond to the following moral dilemma posed by Kohlberg and his colleagues (Colby et al., 1983, p. 79):

> There was a woman who had very bad cancer, and there was no treatment known to medicine that would save her. Her doctor, Dr. Jefferson, knew that she had only about 6 months to live. She was in terrible pain, but she was so weak that a good dose of a pain killer like ether or morphine would make her die sooner. She was delirious and almost crazy with pain, and in her calm periods she would ask Dr. Jefferson to give her enough ether to kill her. She said she couldn't stand the pain and she was going to die in a few months anyway. Although he knows that mercy killing is against the law, the doctor thinks about granting her request.

Should Dr. Jefferson give her the drug that would make her die? Why or why not? Should the woman have the right to make the final decision? Why or why not? These are among the questions that people are asked after hearing the dilemma. You may want to answer them for yourself before reading further so that you can then analyze your own moral thinking.

Remember, Kohlberg's goal is to understand the complexity of a person's reasoning, not whether she is for or against providing the woman with the drug. Individuals at each stage of moral reasoning might endorse either of the alternative courses of

Moral dilemma: Do you think a doctor should give a pain-ridden and terminal patient a drug that would hasten her death if she asks for it? Amelie Van Esbeen, pictured in her bed in a home for the elderly in Belgium, thought so. The 93-year-old went on a hunger strike when her request for mercy killing was denied. She had already tried to commit suicide.

action, but for different reasons. Following are Kohlberg's three levels of moral reasoning, and the two stages within each level.

Level 1: Preconventional Morality At the level of **preconventional morality**, rules are external to the self rather than internalized. The child conforms to rules imposed by authority figures to avoid punishment or to obtain personal rewards. The perspective of the self dominates: What is right is what one can get away with or what is personally satisfying.

- *Stage 1: Punishment-and-Obedience Orientation.* The goodness or badness of an act depends on its consequences. The child will obey authorities to avoid punishment but may not consider an act wrong if it will not be punished. The greater the harm done or the more severe the punishment, the more "bad" the act is.
- *Stage 2: Instrumental Hedonism.* A person at the second stage of moral development conforms to rules to gain rewards or satisfy personal needs. There is some concern for the perspectives of others, but it is motivated by the hope of benefit in return. "You scratch my back and I'll scratch yours" and "an eye for an eye" are the guiding philosophies.

Level 2: Conventional Morality At the level of **conventional morality**, the individual has internalized many moral values. He strives to obey the rules set by others (parents, peers, the government), at first to win their approval, later to maintain social order. The perspectives of other people are clearly recognized and given serious consideration.

- *Stage 3: "Good Boy" or "Good Girl" Morality.* What is right is now what pleases, helps, or is approved by others. People are often judged by their intentions; "meaning well" is valued, and being "nice" is important. Other people's feelings, not just one's own, should be considered. At its best, Stage 3 thinking involves **reciprocity**, consideration of not only your perspective but others' perspectives—a simple Golden Rule morality of doing unto someone else what you would want done unto you.

- *Stage 4: Authority and Social Order–Maintaining Morality.* Now what is right is what conforms to the rules of legitimate authorities and is good for society as a whole. The principle of reciprocity becomes more abstract and is applied on a broader societal level. The reason for conforming is not so much a fear of punishment as a belief that rules and laws maintain a social order worth preserving. Doing one's duty and respecting law and order are valued.

Level 3: Postconventional Morality At the final level of moral reasoning, **postconventional morality**, the individual defines what is right in terms of broad principles of justice that have validity apart from the views of particular authority figures. The individual may distinguish between what is morally right and what is legal, recognizing that some laws—for example, the racial segregation laws that Dr. Martin Luther King, Jr., challenged—violate basic moral principles or human rights. Thus, the person transcends the perspective of a particular social group or authority and begins to take the perspective of *all* individuals.

- *Stage 5: Morality of Contract, Individual Rights, and Democratically Accepted Law.* At this "social contract" stage, there is an understanding of the underlying purposes served by laws and a concern that rules should be arrived at through a democratic consensus so that they express the will of the majority and maximize social welfare. Whereas the person at stage 4 is unlikely to challenge an established law, the moral reasoner at stage 5 might call for democratic change in a law that compromises basic rights.
- *Stage 6: Morality of Individual Principles of Conscience.* At this "highest" stage of moral reasoning, the individual defines right and wrong on the basis of self-generated principles that are broad and universal in application. The stage 6 thinker does not just make up whatever principles she chooses. She discovers, through reflection, abstract principles of respect for all individuals and for their rights—principles that all religions or moral authorities would view as moral. Kohlberg (1981) described stage 6 thinking as a kind of "moral musical chairs" in which the person facing a moral dilemma is able to take the "chair," or perspective, of each person and group and social system, present or future, that could potentially be affected by a decision and to arrive at a solution that would be regarded as just from every chair. Stage 6 is Kohlberg's vision of ideal moral reasoning, but it is so rarely observed that Kohlberg stopped attempting to measure its existence.

In ● **Table 13.2**, we present examples of how people at the preconventional, conventional, and postconventional levels might reason about the mercy-killing dilemma. As you can see, progress through Kohlberg's stages of moral reasoning depends partly on the development of perspective-taking abilities. Specifically, as individuals become more able to consider perspectives other than their own, moral reasoning progresses from an egocentric focus on personal welfare at the preconventional level, to

a concern with the perspectives of other people (parents, friends, and other members of society) at the conventional level, and to an ability to coordinate multiple perspectives and determine what is right from the perspective of all people at the postconventional level (Carpendale, 2000).

Influences on Moral Thinking

Whereas Freud emphasized the role of parents in moral development, Kohlberg, like Piaget before him, believed that the two main influences on moral development are cognitive growth and social interactions with peers. Regarding cognitive growth, reaching the conventional level of moral reasoning and becoming concerned about living up to the moral standards of parents and society requires perspective-taking skills, and gaining the capacity for postconventional moral reasoning requires still more cognitive growth—namely, a solid command of formal-operational thinking (Tomlinson-Keasey & Keasey, 1974; Walker, 1980).

The social interactions that count involve taking the perspectives of others and experiencing growth-promoting cognitive disequilibrium when one's own ideas conflict with those of other people. Piaget and Kohlberg both maintained that interactions with peers or equals, in which we must work out differences between our own and others' perspectives through negotiation, contribute more to moral growth than one-sided interactions with adult authority figures in which children are expected to bow to the adult's power. Discussions of moral issues with peers *do* contribute to moral growth, especially when peers challenge our ideas. However, Piaget and Kohlberg probably underestimated the importance of parents in moral development, as we will see (Walker, Hennig, & Krettenauer, 2000).

Growth-promoting social interaction also comes through advanced schooling. Going to college contributes to cognitive growth and exposes students to diverse perspectives (Pratt et al., 1991). Finally, participating in a complex, diverse, and democratic society can stimulate moral development by encouraging people to weigh the opinions of many groups and appreciate that laws reflect a consensus of the citizens.

So Kohlberg maintained that progress from preconventional to conventional to postconventional moral reasoning is most likely to occur if the individual has acquired the necessary cognitive skills (perspective-taking skills and, later, formal-operational thinking) and has growth-inducing social interactions, especially discussions with peers, advanced education, and participation in democratic governance.

Moral Behavior: Social Learning Theory

Social learning theorists such as Albert Bandura (1991, 2002; Bandura et al., 2001), whose social cognitive theory was introduced in Chapter 2, have been primarily interested in the behavioral component of morality—in what we actually do when faced with temptation or with an opportunity to behave prosocially. These theorists say that moral behavior is learned in the same way that other social behaviors are learned: through observational learning and reinforcement and punishment principles. They also consider moral behavior to be strongly influenced by situational factors—for example, by how closely

Give the Drug	Do Not Give the Drug
Preconventional Morality	**Preconventional Morality**
Stage 1: The doctor should give the terminally ill woman a drug that will kill her because there is little chance that he will be found out and punished.	**Stage 1:** The doctor runs a big risk of losing his license and being thrown in prison if he gives her the drug.
Stage 2: He should give her the drug; he might benefit from the gratitude of her family if he does what she wants. He should think of it as the right thing to do if it serves his purposes to be for mercy killing.	**Stage 2:** He has little to gain by taking such a big chance. If the woman wants to kill herself, that is her business, but why should he help her if he stands to gain little in return?
Conventional Morality	**Conventional Morality**
Stage 3: Most people would understand that the doctor was motivated by concern for the woman's welfare rather than by self-interest. They would be able to forgive him for what was essentially an act of kindness.	**Stage 3:** Most people are likely to disapprove of mercy killing. The doctor would clearly lose the respect of his colleagues if he administered the drug. A good person simply would not do this.
Stage 4: The doctor should give the woman the drug because of the Hippocratic oath, which spells out a doctor's duty to relieve suffering. This oath is binding and should be taken seriously by all doctors.	**Stage 4:** Mercy killing like this is against the laws that doctors are obligated to uphold. The Bible is another compelling authority, and it says, "Thou shalt not kill." The doctor simply cannot take the law into his own hands; rather, he has a duty to uphold the law.
Postconventional Morality	**Postconventional Morality**
Stage 5: Although most of our laws have a sound basis in moral principle, laws against mercy killing do not. The doctor's act is morally justified because it relieves the suffering of an agonized human without harming other people. Yet if he breaks the law in the service of a greater good, he should still be willing to be held legally accountable because society would be damaged if everyone simply ignored laws they do not agree with.	**Stage 5:** The laws against mercy killing protect citizens from harm at the hands of unscrupulous doctors and selfish relatives and should be upheld because they serve a positive function for society. If the laws were to be changed through the democratic process, that might be another thing. But right now the doctor can do the most good for society by adhering to them.
Stage 6: We must consider the effects of this act on everyone concerned—the doctor, the dying woman, other terminally ill people, and all people everywhere. Basic moral principle dictates that all people have a right to dignity and self-determination as long as others are not harmed by their decisions. Assuming that no one else will be hurt, then, the dying woman has a right to live and die as she chooses. The doctor may be doing right if he respects her integrity as a person and saves her, her family, and all of society from needless suffering.	**Stage 6:** If we truly adhere to the principle that human life should be valued above all else and all lives should be valued equally, it is morally wrong to "play God" and decide that some lives are worth living and others are not. Before long, we would have a world in which no life has value.

© Cengage Learning

a professor watches exam takers, by whether jewelry items are on the counter or behind glass in a department store. Due to situational influences, what we do (moral performance) is not always reflective of our internalized values and standards (moral competence).

Applying his social cognitive perspective, Bandura went on to emphasize that moral cognition is linked to moral action through *self-regulatory mechanisms* that involve monitoring and evaluating our own actions (or anticipated actions), disapproving of ourselves when we contemplate doing wrong, and approving of ourselves when we behave responsibly or humanely. By applying consequences to ourselves in this way, we become able to exert self-control, inhibit urges to misbehave, and keep our behavior in line with internalized standards of moral behavior.

Sometimes this system of moral self-regulation can triumph over strong situational influences pushing us to do wrong. However, according to Bandura we have also devised mechanisms of **moral disengagement** that allow us to avoid condemning ourselves when we engage in immoral behavior, even though we know the difference between right and wrong. For example, a store clerk who feels underpaid and mistreated by his employer may convince himself that he is justified in pilfering items from the store, or people may disengage morally from the use of military force by their country by dehumanizing their foes (McAlister, Bandura, & Owen, 2006). Many of us learn the right moral standards, but some people hold themselves strictly to those standards while others find ways to disengage morally and slither out from under guilt. Those individuals who have perfected

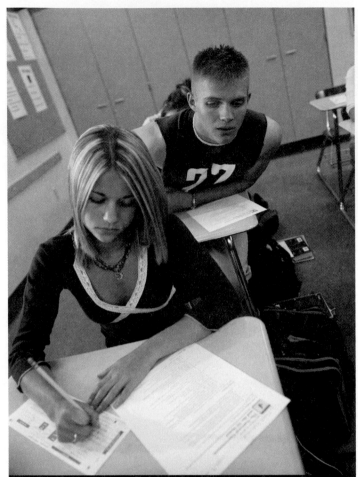

How many students in your class would admit to having cheated in high school? Fifty years ago, only about one in five college students admitted to it, but in more recent surveys at least three in five, and often more, admit to having cheated in high school (Crary, 2008; Kleiner & Lord, 1999). Cheating is also rampant in college and graduate school; in one survey, 56% of MBA students admitted to cheating or plagiarizing in the past year (McCabe, Butterfield, & Trevino, 2006). Why do you think cheating is so rampant today?

techniques of moral disengagement engage in more antisocial and unethical behavior than other people (Detert, Treviño, & Sweitzer, 2008; Paciello et al., 2008).

The Functions of Morality: Evolutionary Theory

Finally, evolutionary theorists such as Dennis Krebs, Michael Tomasello, and others have given us still other insights into moral development and prosocial and antisocial behavior (Buss, 2012; Krebs, 2008, 2011; Tomasello, 2009; Tomasello & Vaish, 2013). Their focus is on morality and human nature—on how all three aspects of morality (moral emotion, thought, and behavior) may have helped humans adapt to their environments over the course of evolution. Just as having a theory of mind helps humans get along with others and adapt to living in groups, Krebs argues, prosocial behaviors such as cooperation and altruism may have

evolved because our ancestors were better able to obtain food and protect themselves from harm if they worked together than if they went it alone and pursued their selfish interests. Similarly, mechanisms for controlling and inhibiting antisocial behavior such as rules and laws may have evolved because they enhanced survival. To evolutionary theorists, then, humans are not blank slates. Morality and prosocial behavior are rooted in human nature. Unfortunately, so are immorality and antisocial behavior (Krebs, 2011).

How can humans have evolved to have altruistic tendencies when altruists who sacrifice their lives for others die rather than pass on their genes? Evolutionary theorists have argued that it can be in our genetic self-interest to act altruistically toward kin because they will pass on the family's genes if we help them survive (Verbeek, 2006). Even helping nonrelatives may be adaptive if we have reason to believe that the help we give will be reciprocated. Cooperating with other people to obtain resources that the individual could not obtain alone also makes good genetic sense, as do abiding by society's rules in order to avoid punishment and punishing people who *do* violate society's rules (Krebs, 2008). So, whereas Freud emphasized the dark, selfish and aggressive side of human nature, Krebs (2008) and other evolutionary theorists argue that humans have an evolved genetic makeup that predisposes them not only to behave antisocially in some situations but also to empathize with their fellow humans and to behave prosocially and morally.

Indeed, humans may be a uniquely prosocial species. Michael Tomasello has concluded that what makes humans different from chimpanzees and other great apes and provides a basis for morality is our readiness to participate in groups and to collaborate and cooperate with others (Tomasello, 2009; Tomasello & Herrmann, 2010; Tomasello & Vaish, 2013). Primates are capable of some pretty impressive social cognitive feats such as figuring out others' goals and intentions but their skills likely evolved in competitive situations where they could get food, mates, and other resources, or protect those they had, if they could outwit rivals. Compared to chimps and orangutans, toddlers and young children excel at theory-of-mind tasks, social learning and imitation, and communication. To not only understand others' intentions but to be able to *share* intentions with others in order to pursue common goals, Tomasello believes, is what distinguishes the human species. You will learn more about Tomasello's fascinating research later.

To highlight differences among the four theoretical perspectives on moral development we have discussed, ● **Table 13.3** compares them and shows how different theorists might try to predict whether a college student (call him Bart) will cheat on his upcoming math test.

We are now ready to trace the development of morality, and aspects of prosocial and antisocial behavior, from infancy to old age, considering moral emotion, cognition, and behavior as we go.

Checking Mastery

1. What are the three components of morality, and what is a theory of moral development that emphasizes each?

- **Table 13.3** Comparison of Theoretical Perspectives on Moral Development

Perspective/ Theorists	Focus	Message	Predicting Behavior (Will Bart cheat on his math test?)
Psychoanalytic theory (Freud)	Moral emotion	Early parenting and emotional conflicts forge the superego and guilt.	Did Bart develop a strong superego (conscience) and sense of guilt in his preschool years?
Cognitive-developmental theory (Piaget, Kohlberg)	Moral reasoning	Cognitive maturation and interaction with peers bring stagelike changes in thinking about moral issues.	At what stage is Bart's reasoning about moral dilemmas?
Social learning theory (Bandura)	Moral behavior	Observational learning, reinforcement, self-regulation processes, and situational influences affect what we do.	Did Bart's parents model and reinforce moral behavior and punish misbehavior? Do well-developed self-regulatory mechanisms cause Bart to take responsibility for his actions rather than disengage morally? Do situational forces in the class discourage or encourage cheating?
Evolutionary theory (Krebs, Tomasello)	Moral emotion, reasoning, and behavior	Humans have evolved not only to be aggressive on occasion but to have moral and prosocial tendencies that equip them to live cooperatively in groups.	Does cheating, or refraining from cheating, serve adaptive functions for Bart and his social group? Does the classroom environment encourage or discourage cheating?

© Cengage Learning

2. What is the main difference between conventional and preconventional moral reasoning about why stealing is wrong?
3. How do evolutionary theorists differ from Freud regarding the nature of human beings?

Making Connections

1. A preconventional thinker, a conventional thinker, and a postconventional thinker all face a moral dilemma the night before the final exam: A friend has offered them a key to the test. Should they use it? Provide examples of the reasoning you might expect at each of Kohlberg's three main levels of moral development—one argument in favor of cheating and one against it at each level. Are any of these arguments especially easy or difficult to make? Why?

2. Jamal decides to become a kidney donor and live the rest of his life with only one kidney so that his brother Malcolm can live. How do you think Freud, Kohlberg, Bandura, and Krebs would explain his altruistic action?

13.3 The Infant

LEARNING OBJECTIVES:

- Summarize evidence that infants are capable of empathy and prosocial behavior.
- Describe antisocial behavior in infancy and how it differs from that of older children.
- Explain how parents can help their infants develop a conscience.

Do infants have a sense of right or wrong? If a baby takes a teddy bear that belongs to another child, would you label the act stealing? If an infant bashes another child on the head with a sippy cup, would you insist that the infant be put on trial for assault? Of course not. We tend to view infants as **amoral**—that is, lacking any sense of morality. We do not believe that infants are capable of evaluating their behavior in relation to moral standards, and so we do not hold them responsible for wrongs they commit (although we certainly attempt to prevent them from harming others). Nor do we expect them to be "good" when we are not around to watch them. Yet we learn a lot about human nature from infant behavior. It is now clear that infants are predisposed to be empathic, prosocial beings, just as they are predisposed to engage in aggression. They also learn many important moral lessons during their first 2 years of life and develop a conscience.

Empathy and Prosocial Behavior

Infants are not as selfish, egocentric, and unconcerned about other people as Freud, Piaget, Kohlberg, and many other theorists have assumed. Rather, some of their behavior supports the view of evolutionary theorists that empathy and prosocial behavior are part of our evolutionary heritage (Tomasello, 2009). As Dale Hay (2009) puts it, "Infants don't have to learn to care about other people, but they learn *how* to care for them" (p. 476).

Start at birth: even newborns display a primitive form of empathy, becoming distressed by the cries of other newborns (Hastings, Zahn-Waxler, & McShane, 2006; Hoffman, 2000; Martin & Clark, 1982). It is unlikely that young infants distinguish between another infant's distress and their own, however. From age 1 to age 2, according to Martin Hoffman (2000, 2008), infants become capable of a truer form of empathy that motivates helping and other forms of moral behavior. Toddlers begin to understand that someone else's distress is different from their own, and they try to comfort the person in distress. So, for example, a 10-month-old watching a peer cry, looked sad and buried her head in her mother's lap, as she often did when she herself was distressed. A 2-year-old, though, brought his own teddy bear to comfort a distressed friend and, when that failed, offered the friend's teddy instead, showing an ability to take the perspective of the friend (Hoffman, 2000).

As children get older, according to Hoffman, empathy becomes less egocentric and more sophisticated as cognitive processes, including the child's developing perspective-taking skills, shape it into a variety of moral emotions such as guilt, sympathy, and eventually a sense of injustice (see also Eisenberg, Spinrad, & Sadovsky, 2006; Gibbs, 2010). Both genetic and environmental influences then make some children more empathic than others (Knafo et al., 2008).

How prosocial are infants? Some years ago, Carolyn Zahn-Waxler and her colleagues (1992) reported that more than half of the 13- to 15-month-old infants they observed engaged in at least one act of prosocial behavior—helping, sharing, expressing concern, comforting, and so on. These behaviors became increasing common from age 1 to age 2, when all but one child in the study acted prosocially. More recently, Michael Tomasello (the evolutionary theorist you met earlier) and other researchers have been documenting impressive prosocial acts by toddlers in their laboratories:

- *Helping.* As early as 14 months, infants will spontaneously—without being asked—help an adult who drops a clothes pin on the floor while trying to hang items on a line, who is carrying an armful of papers and cannot open a cabinet door, or who otherwise needs help to achieve a goal (Warneken & Tomasello, 2007). This spontaneous helping by 1-year-olds has been observed to be common in cultures as diverse as Canada, India, and Peru (Callaghan et al., 2011).
- *Cooperation.* As early as 14 months, infants can also participate in simple cooperative games and will even try to get their adult partner reengaged if she stops playing, suggesting that they understand that they and their partner had a shared goal (Warneken & Tomasello, 2007).
- *Altruistic rather than selfish motivations.* Before they are 2, children show greater happiness when they give treats like Goldfish crackers to an appreciative puppet than when they receive them, especially when they altruistically give up their own treats (Aknin, Hamlin, & Dunn, 2012). By 2, toddlers' patterns of arousal suggest that they react the same way physiologically when someone else helps a person in need as when they

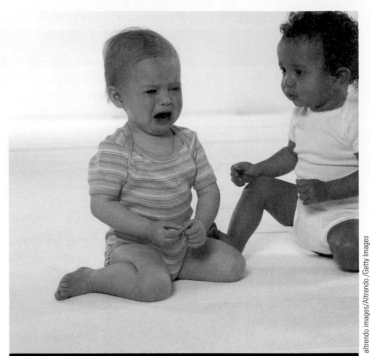

altrendo images/Altrendo /Getty Images

Before they are age 2, toddlers show evidence of early moral sensibilities when they attempt to comfort distressed peers.

help the person themselves, suggesting genuine concern for the individual in need rather than merely a desire for personal reward or credit for being a good helper (Hepach, Vaish, & Tomasello, 2012). Such studies hint that humans may have evolved to find prosocial behavior intrinsically rewarding.

Antisocial Behavior

If prosocial tendencies are so evident by a year or so of age, when do antisocial tendencies first show themselves? According to Richard Tremblay (2011), humans do not need to learn to be aggressive; they mainly need to learn how not to be aggressive. Physical aggression, behavior that harms another person physically, comes naturally to humans, starting as soon as babies are able to hit, bite, push, or otherwise harm others. Verbal aggression begins almost as soon as infants utter their first words. Antisocial behavior therefore seems to be as much a part of human nature as empathy and prosocial behavior are. Infants are less likely than older children to intend to cause harm, however. Often their goal is to get a toy they want or to defend a toy they had played with and put down (Hay, Hurst, et al., 2011; Tremblay, 2011). As they develop better self-control, they will become more able to delay gratification and wait for the toy.

As early as 1½ years of age, some toddlers engage in more physical aggression than others, though (Tremblay, 2011). Their high rates of aggressive behavior can be traced to both their genetic makeup and environmental factors such as harsh, coercive parenting or a depressed, emotionally unavailable parent (Dionne et al., 2003; Hay, Mundy, et al., 2011; Tremblay, 2011). Their peers, meanwhile, are learning to control their aggressive urges better. The frequency of aggression normally rises from infancy to a peak around age 4 or 5 and then decreases (Tremblay, 2011).

Exploration 13.1

Marshmallows and the Life-Span Significance of Self-Control

Whether you call it the aspect of temperament called effortful control, the dimension of personality called conscientiousness, self-control, executive control, or even willpower, it is a good thing to have. Nowhere is this better illustrated than in the famous marshmallow study conducted by social learning theorist Walter Mischel starting in the 1960s (Mischel, Shoda, & Peake, 1988). The experimenter gave 4- to 5-year-olds a choice: Eat the marshmallow I am giving you now, or get a second marshmallow if you wait until I return (in 15–20 minutes). Apparently marshmallows are irresistible to 4-year-olds: Only about 30% of the children passed this **delay of gratification** task and were able to wait for the more desirable two-marshmallow reward later. Most children gave in to their desire to eat the marshmallow in less than 3 minutes. (You can find videos of this task

on the Internet, by the way; if you search for "marshmallow test.")

Mischel was primarily interested in the strategies children used to exert self-control and delay gratification in this situation—strategies like distracting themselves by singing songs or covering their eyes. But the most fascinating finding of the research was revealed when the children were followed up as adolescents and then as adults. As adolescents, the children who delayed gratification were judged by their parents to be more academically and socially competent, more responsible, and more able to cope with stress; they even scored significantly higher on the SAT exam than their peers who gave in to temptation (Mischel et al., 1988; Shoda, Mischel, & Peake, 1990). As adults, the more self-controlled individuals also had fewer drug problems and lower body mass indexes (Casey et al., 2011; Mischel et al., 2011).

In a similar longitudinal study, Terri Moffitt and her colleagues (2011) controlled for factors such as intelligence and socioeconomic status that are correlated with self-control in examining relationships between self-control in childhood and adult outcomes. Children's self-control was measured this time not with marshmallows but through behavioral observations and parent-, teacher-, and child-reports of behavior). Childhood self-control predicted becoming an adolescent who stayed in school and avoided delinquent behavior and a 30-year-old with good physical health and financial stability who avoided substance dependence and criminal activity. So, whether self-control shows itself in being able to wait for that second yummy marshmallow, keeping at your studies while your friends party, or resisting the temptation to do wrong, it is a very useful skill to develop.

Early Moral Training

Part of the reason for increased prosocial and decreased antisocial tendencies as infants become children may be moral socialization. Roger Burton (1984) relates how his daughter Ursula, age 1, was so taken by the candy that she and her sisters had gathered on Halloween that she snatched some from her sisters' bags. The sisters immediately said, "No, that's mine," and conveyed their outrage in the strongest terms. A week later, the sisters again found some of their candy in Ursula's bag and raised a fuss, and it was their mother's turn to explain the rules to Ursula. The problem continued until finally Burton came upon Ursula looking at some forbidden candy. Ursula looked up and said, "No, this is Maria's, not Ursula's" (p. 199).

It is partly through such social learning experiences, accumulated over years, that children come to understand and internalize moral rules and standards. Infants begin to learn that their actions have consequences, some good, some bad; they learn a lot from how their companions react to their missteps (Thompson, Meyer, & McGinley, 2006). Thus parents can foster early moral development by discussing their toddlers' behavior and its good or bad effects on others (Laible & Thompson, 2000; Thompson, 2012).

Grazyna Kochanska has studied the development of a conscience in toddlerhood and believes it involves mastering two components of conscience: (1) moral emotions—learning to associate negative emotions like guilt with violating rules and learning to empathize with people who are in distress, and (2) self-control—being able to inhibit one's impulses when tempted to violate internalized rules (Kochanska, 1993, 2002).

By 18–24 months, children are already beginning to show visible signs of distress such as anticipating disapproval when they break things, spill their drinks, or otherwise violate standards of behavior (Cole, Barrett, & Zahn-Waxler, 1992; Kagan, 1981). Made to think that they have caused a doll's head to fall off, some toddlers even show signs of guilt, as opposed to mere distress, as evidenced by frantic attempts to repair the doll or otherwise make amends (Kochanska, Casey, & Fukumoto, 1995). Self-control also becomes evident in infancy—for example, when toddlers are able to comply with a parent's rule not to play with certain toys even after the parent leaves the room (Aksan & Kochanska, 2005). It then improves into early adulthood (Berkman, Graham & Fisher, 2012). In **Exploration Box 13.1**, we see just how important **self-control**—the ability to control or regulate one's desires, impulses, and behavior—is in many aspects of development.

How can parents help children develop moral emotions, self-control, and thus a strong conscience? Kochanska and her colleagues have found that forming a secure parent–infant attachment is the best way to get moral socialization off to a good start (Kochanska, Barry, Stellern, & O'Bleness, 2009). Then it is important for caregiver and child to establish a **mutually responsive orientation**—a close, emotionally positive, and cooperative relationship in which child and caregiver care about each other and are sensitive to each other's needs (Kochanska & Aksan, 2006). Parents who are responsive to their infants are likely to raise children who are responsive to them. A mutually responsive orientation between parent and child makes children trust their caregivers and want to comply with their rules and adopt their values and standards. These children then learn moral emotions such as guilt and empathy, develop the capacity for advanced moral reasoning, and become able to resist temptation even when no one is around to catch them.

By establishing a secure attachment and a mutually responsive orientation, working toward mutual understandings of what is and is not acceptable, and discussing the emotional consequences of the child's behavior, parents help infants and toddlers develop a conscience (Emde et al., 1991; Thompson et al., 2006).

Checking Mastery

1. According to Martin Hoffman, when is empathy first evident in infancy and how does it change thereafter?
2. When one infant pushes another, what is usually the motive?

3. What is Grazyna Kochanska's main message to parents who want their infants to develop a conscience?

Making Connections

1. Suppose you want to study how toddlers in a day care center react when their peers are upset. How might you distinguish between true empathy for a classmate and personal distress in reaction to the classmate's crying?
2. Philosopher John Locke and learning theorists like B. F. Skinner have viewed human beings as "blank slates" (tabulae rasae) who have no biologically based predispositions to be either antisocial or prosocial. Thinking about evolutionary theory and research on infant social behavior, what arguments can you give against the blank slate position?

13.4 The Child

LEARNING OBJECTIVES:

- Discuss ways in which children are more morally sophisticated than Piaget and Kohlberg believed.

- Summarize an optimal approach to socializing morality in childhood.

Research on moral development during childhood has explored how children of different ages think about moral issues and how parents can raise moral children. This research shows that children's moral thinking is far more sophisticated than Piaget and Kohlberg believed and that parents can have a big impact on their children's moral development.

Moral Understandings

The hypothetical moral dilemmas that Lawrence Kohlberg devised to assess stages of moral reasoning (for example, the mercy-killing dilemma presented in Section 13.2) were intended primarily for adolescents and adults; the youngest individuals Kohlberg studied were age 10. As a result, Kohlberg did not have much to say about children except that they are mostly preconventional moral reasoners. They take an egocentric perspective on morality and define as right those acts that are rewarded and as wrong those acts that are punished (Colby et al., 1983). At best, older school-age children are beginning to make the transition to conventional moral reasoning by internalizing authorities' rules and displaying a stage 3 concern with being a good boy or a good girl who takes others' perspectives and is concerned with others' approval. However, both Piaget and Kohlberg seriously underestimated children. Having already seen that infants are well on their way to being moral beings, you will not be surprised to learn that even preschool-aged children engage in some very sophisticated thinking about right and wrong.

Weighing Intentions

Both Piaget and Kohlberg believed that young children (indeed, children under 10) were primarily focused on the consequences of acts rather than the intentions behind them. However, it turns out that even 3-year-olds can take both intentions and consequences into account if presented with simple stories portrayed in drawings (Nelson, 1980). They judge a ball thrower less favorably when he hits his playmate in the head than when the playmate catches the ball, but they also judge a well-intentioned boy who had wanted to play ball more favorably than a boy who intended to hurt his friend, even when the friend caught the ball and was not harmed. Apparently, then, even young children can base their moral judgments on both a person's intentions and the consequences of his act. Sensitivity to the intentions behind actions does increase as children get older, however (Lapsley, 2006).

Applying Theory of Mind

Intentions are mental states, of course, and are therefore part of what children come to understand better as they develop a theory of mind. Indeed, children's moral thinking becomes more sophisticated once they have the basics of a theory of mind down at about age 4 (Killen et al., 2011; Lane et al., 2010). Showing that they appreciate that intentions matter, 4-year-old children who have a theory of mind and pass false belief tasks may cry, "I didn't mean it! I didn't mean it!" when they stand to be punished. Moreover, their understandings of a wrongdoer's beliefs at the time he committed a harmful act ("Spencer didn't know Lauren was in the box when he pushed it down the stairs!") influence their judgments about whether the act was intentional and therefore how bad it was.

Children who pass theory-of-mind tasks are more forgiving when a wrong is committed accidentally than when it is committed intentionally (Chandler, Sokol, & Wainryb, 2000; Killen et al., 2011). They are also better able than children who fail theory-of-mind tasks to distinguish between lying (deliberately promoting false beliefs) and simply having one's facts wrong

(Peterson & Siegal, 2002). Children who have mastered theory-of-mind skills are also more attuned to other people's feelings and welfare when they think about the morality of snatching a friend's toy or calling a friend a bad name (Dunn, Cutting, & Demetriou, 2000). In short, mastering the basics of a theory of mind at age 4 and refining those skills later put children in better position to interpret the motives behind and the consequences of people's actions when judging right and wrong.

Distinguishing among Rules

Piaget claimed that 6- to 10-year-old children view all rules as sacred prescriptions laid down by respected authority figures that cannot be questioned or changed. However, Elliot Turiel (1978, 1983, 2006) has discovered that children distinguish between different kinds of rules. Most importantly, they distinguish between **moral rules**, or standards that focus on the welfare and basic rights of individuals, and **social-conventional rules**, standards determined by social consensus that tell us what is appropriate in particular social settings. Moral rules include rules against hitting, stealing, lying, and otherwise harming others or violating their rights. Social-conventional rules are more like rules of social etiquette; they include the rules of games, school rules that forbid eating snacks in class or going to the restroom without permission, and parent rules that require saying "Please" and "Thank you."

From their preschool years, children understand that moral rules are more compelling and unalterable than social-conventional rules (Smetana, 2006; Turiel, 2006). Judith Smetana (1981; Smetana et al., 2012), for example, has discovered that children as young as age 3 regard moral transgressions such as hitting, stealing, or refusing to share as more serious and deserving of punishment than social-conventional violations. Similarly, young children appreciate that hitting is wrong even if the teacher did not see it; even if the rules say hitting is okay; and whether it is done at home, at school, or in a faraway land with different laws. They also give the right reasons for their views, emphasizing the harm done by hitting (Killen & Smetana, 2008). Three-year-olds also seem to have a genuine respect for rules; they follow them not just to avoid punishment but because they are becoming members of a social group and view it as important to respect the group's rules (Schmidt & Tomasello, 2012). Thus, if a puppet plays a new game incorrectly, a 3-year-old is likely to enforce the rules, saying, "No, you have to do it like this."

Piaget also claimed that 6- to 10-year-old children view any rule or law laid down by adults as sacred. Instead, children appear to be quite capable of questioning adult authority (Tisak & Tisak, 1990). School-age children say, for example, that it is inappropriate and unjustifiable for parents to arbitrarily restrict their children's friendship choices, which children view as a matter of personal choice. And they maintain that not even God can proclaim that stealing is morally right and make it so (Nucci & Turiel, 1993). In other words, school-age children will not blindly accept any dictate offered by an authority figure as legitimate.

Overall, then, both Piaget and Kohlberg seriously underestimated how sensitive even toddlers are to moral issues and how much moral growth takes place during infancy and early childhood. We now know that even young children judge acts as right or wrong according to whether the actor's intentions were good or bad; use their theories of mind to analyze the motives behind and the emotional consequences of actions; distinguish between moral rules and social-conventional rules and view only moral rules as absolute, sacred, and unchangeable; and challenge adult authority when they believe it is illegitimate.

Moral Socialization

How can parents best raise a child who can be counted on to behave morally in most situations? You have already seen that a secure attachment and a mutually responsive orientation between parent and child starting in infancy help. Social learning theorists like Bandura would also advise parents to reinforce moral behavior, punish immoral behavior (but mildly and with caution, as discussed in Chapter 2), and serve as models of moral behavior.

The important work of Martin Hoffman (2000) has provided additional insights into how to foster not only moral behavior but also moral thought and emotion. As you saw earlier, Hoffman (2000) believes that empathy is a key motivator of moral behavior and that a key task in moral socialization, therefore, is to foster empathy. Many years ago, Hoffman (1970) reviewed the child-rearing literature to determine which approaches to discipline were associated with high levels of moral development. Three major discipline approaches were compared:

1. **Love withdrawal**. Withholding attention, affection, or approval after a child misbehaves—in other words, creating anxiety by threatening a loss of reinforcement from parents.
2. **Power assertion**. Using power to threaten, chastise, administer spankings, take away privileges, and so on—in other words, using punishment.
3. **Induction**. Explaining to a child why the behavior is wrong and should be changed by emphasizing how it affects other people.

Suppose that little Angel has just put the beloved family cat through a cycle in the clothes dryer. Using love withdrawal, a parent might say, "How could you do something like that? I can't stand to look at you!" Using power assertion, a parent might say, "Get to your room this minute; you're going to get it." Using induction, a parent might say, "Angel, look how scared Fluffball is. You could have killed her, and you know how sad we'd be if she died." Induction, then, is a matter of providing rationales or explanations that focus attention on the consequences of wrongdoing for other people (or cats).

Which approach best fosters moral development? Induction is more often positively associated with children's moral maturity than either love withdrawal or power assertion, and power assertion is the least effective approach (Brody & Shaffer, 1982). In Hoffman's (2000) view, induction works well because it breeds empathy. Anticipating empathic distress if we contemplate harming someone keeps us from doing harm; empathizing with individuals in distress motivates us to help them.

A Case Study in Raising a Moral Child

It takes only a few observations at the day care center to see that Doug, father of 3-year-old Trina, has mastered everything developmental psychologists know about how to foster moral development and prosocial behavior. He is sensitive to his daughter's emotional needs, often staying when he drops her off in the morning until he is sure she is ready for him to leave. He asks her to look after the new teacher because it's her first day and she might need help. As they hug and kiss, he tells Trina how happy it makes him to get hugs and kisses.

One day, Doug witnessed a little boy grab an 18-month-old girl, causing her to cry. He separated the two children, comforted the girl, and explained to the boy that grabbing hurts and that the girl was crying because she was hurt. He asked the boy to say he was sorry and to give the girl a hug because it might make her feel better.

Trina's father has developed what Kochanska calls a mutually responsive orientation with her. He models and reinforces prosocial behavior, perspective-taking skills, and empathy, talking about his feelings and those of other people and pointing out that antisocial behavior makes other people feel bad, whereas prosocial behavior makes them feel good. Using the discipline technique that Martin Hoffman finds to be most effective, induction, he explains why hurtful behaviors are wrong by emphasizing their consequences for other people and fosters empathy in the process. And using proactive parenting strategies, he teaches his daughter about prosocial values.

As you might predict, Trina is following in her father's footsteps. She frequently comforts children who cry when their mothers drop them off in the morning; regularly offers toys to children who are upset; often hugs and pats and holds the hand of a smaller, more timid girl; and cheerfully cleans up all the toys when play time is over. What might the world be like if it were full of model parents like Doug?

Martin Hoffman's formula for raising a moral child involves lots of induction and affection and only occasional power assertion.

Although expressing disappointment in a child's behavior can be effective on occasion, making a child worry that their parents' love can be snatched away at any time usually is not effective (Patrick & Gibbs, 2007). Frequent use of power assertion is more often associated with moral immaturity than with moral maturity. At the extreme, children whose parents are physically abusive feel less guilt and engage in more immoral behaviors such as stealing than other children (Koenig, Cicchetti, & Rogosch, 2004). But even frequent use of milder power tactics such as physical restraint and prohibitions is generally ineffective (Kochanska, Aksan, & Nichols, 2003). Power assertion does not foster empathy, the internalization of moral rules, or the development of self-control, and physical punishment in particular can produce unwanted consequences such as anxiety and aggression (see Section 2.4).

Despite this evidence, Hoffman (2000) concludes that mild power assertion tactics such as a forceful "No," a reprimand, or the taking away of privileges can be useful occasionally if they arouse some but not too much fear and motivate a child to pay close attention to the inductions that follow. Such careful uses of power assertion work best in the context of a loving and mutually responsive parent–child relationship. All in all, Hoffman's work provides a fairly clear roadmap of how parents can best contribute to the moral growth of their children. As he puts it, the winning formula is "a blend of frequent inductions, occasional power assertions, and a lot of affection" (Hoffman, 2000, p. 23).

Let's add that effective parents also use **proactive parenting strategies**, tactics designed to prevent misbehavior and therefore reduce the need for any of Hoffman's types of discipline—techniques such as distracting young children from temptations and explicitly teaching older children values (Thompson et al., 2006). In **Exploration Box 13.2**, you can see in action a parent who illustrates several effective strategies for fostering moral growth.

Yet parents do not settle on one best approach and use it all the time. Both the moral socialization technique chosen and its effectiveness depend on a host of factors such as the particular misdeed, child, parent, situation, and cultural context (Critchley & Sanson, 2006; Grusec, 2006; Grusec, Goodnow, & Kuczynski, 2000). Consider the child's temperament. It turns out to be an important influence on how morally trainable she is and what motivates her to comply with parents' rules and requests (Thompson et al., 2006). Grazyna Kochanska and her colleagues have found that children are likely to be easiest to socialize if (1) they are by temperament fearful or inhibited (see Section 11.2), and therefore are likely to experience guilt when they do wrong, become appropriately distressed when they are disciplined, and want to avoid such distress in the future; and

(2) they are capable of effortful control, and therefore are able to inhibit their urges to engage in wrongdoing (Kochanska, Barry, Jimenez, et al., 2009; and see Eisenberg, Smith, & Spinrad, 2011).

Children with different temperaments may require different socialization approaches. Fearful, inhibited children can be socialized through a gentle approach that capitalizes on their anxiety but does not terrorize them (Fowles & Kochanska, 2000). Children who are fearless or uninhibited do not respond to this gentle approach—but they do not respond to being treated harshly, either. These fearless children are most likely to learn to comply with rules and requests when there is a mutually responsive orientation between parent and child, and the child is therefore motivated to please the parent and maintain a good relationship (Fowles & Kochanska, 2000; and see Kochanska, Aksan, & Joy, 2007). Here, then, is another example of the importance of the goodness of fit between a child's temperament and her social environment. Socialized in a way that suits their temperament, most children will internalize rules of conduct, experience appropriate moral emotions, learn to regulate their behavior, and behave more prosocially than antisocially.

Checking Mastery

1. How is a moral rule different from a social-conventional rule and at what age can children tell the difference?
2. What capacities shown by preschool children contradict Piaget's and Kohlberg's views that they are limited moral thinkers?
3. Create an example of induction and explain why Martin Hoffman concludes that it is the best approach to discipline.

Making Connections

1. Ben, age 6, lies and steals frequently, bullies other children, and rarely complies with rules at home or at school. Using what you have learned about moral socialization and referring to appropriate concepts and research, describe how ineffective parenting might have contributed to the development of this apparently immoral child.
2. What approaches to moral socialization did your parents use with you? If you have siblings, can you see any signs that your parents adopted different approaches to moral socialization with different children? Finally, do your parents' strategies seem sound in retrospect?

13.5 The Adolescent

LEARNING OBJECTIVES:

• Describe how moral reasoning changes during adolescence and the significance of developing a moral identity.

• Compare how Kenneth Dodge and Gerald Patterson account for the behavior of aggressive youth.

• Explain the roles of nature and nurture in aggression and the approaches that have been used to prevent it.

As adolescents gain the capacity to think about abstract and hypothetical ideas, and as they begin to chart their future identities, many of them reflect on their values and moral standards and some make morality a central part of their identities. At the other extreme are the adolescents who end up engaging in serious antisocial behavior.

Moral Identity

Some teens come to view being a moral person who is caring, fair, and honest as a central part of who they are—that is, they develop a **moral identity**. Those adolescents who develop a sense of moral identity tend to be more capable than other adolescents of advanced moral reasoning (Hart, 2005). Especially if something in the situation reminds them of their moral values, they are also more likely to act morally than adolescents who do not define themselves in moral terms (Aquino & Reed, 2002; Aquino et al., 2009). Thus developing a moral identity may be critical when it comes to translating one's moral values into moral action (Hardy & Carlo, 2011). If you have a strong moral identity, you cannot live with yourself if you do wrong.

A moral identity may start to take shape during childhood. In her work on the development of conscience, Grazyna Kochanska and her colleagues (2010) found that conscience in toddlerhood (following parent's rules even when they are out of the room and showing empathy for a parent's distress) predicts the development at age 5 or 6 of a "moral self," a sense of being a good boy or girl who tries to follow rules, avoids misbehaving, and cares about other people. Children with a strong moral self agreed with statements like, "When I break something, I tell someone about it right away," not statements like, "When I break something, I try to hide it so no one finds out." A strong moral self at age 5 was, in turn, related to parent and teacher perceptions at age 6 to 7 that the child was prosocial and well-adjusted rather than antisocial. A moral self in childhood, then, appears to lay a good foundation for both later moral behavior and possibly a full-fledged sense of moral identity in adolescence.

Development of a moral identity in adolescence can be fostered by parents who use induction and on occasion express disappointment in their teen's behavior rather than relying on power assertion and love withdrawal (Patrick & Gibbs, 2012). It can also be fostered through involvement in community service and other prosocial activities (Hardy & Carlo, 2011; Pratt et al., 2003).

Changes in Moral Reasoning

Adolescence is a period of significant moral growth. Consider the results of Lawrence Kohlberg's 20-year longitudinal study that involved repeatedly asking the 10-, 13-, and 16-year-old boys he originally studied to respond to moral dilemmas (Colby et al., 1983). ■ **Figure 13.2** shows the percentage of judgments offered at each age that reflected each of Kohlberg's six stages.

Several interesting developmental trends can be seen here. Notice that the preconventional reasoning (stage 1 and 2 thinking) that dominates among 10-year-olds decreases considerably during the teen years. During adolescence, conventional reasoning (stages 3 and 4) becomes the dominant mode of moral thinking. So, among 13- to 14-year-olds, most moral judgments reflect either a stage 2 (instrumental hedonism) approach—"You scratch my back and I'll scratch yours"—or a stage 3 (good boy or good girl) concern with being nice and earning approval. More than half the judgments offered by 16- to 18-year-olds embody stage 3 reasoning, and about a fifth were scored as stage 4 (authority and social order–maintaining morality) arguments. These older adolescents were beginning to take a broad societal perspective on justice and were concerned about acting in ways that would help maintain the social system.

In short, the main developmental trend in moral reasoning during adolescence is a shift from preconventional to conventional reasoning. During this period, most individuals begin to express a genuine concern with living up to the moral standards

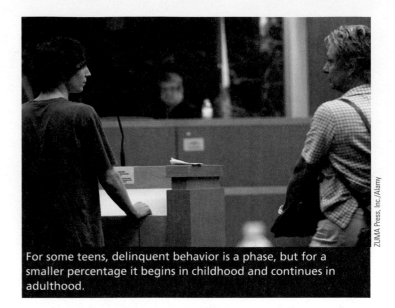

For some teens, delinquent behavior is a phase, but for a smaller percentage it begins in childhood and continues in adulthood.

that parents and other authorities have taught them and ensuring that laws designed to make human relations just and fair are taken seriously and maintained. Postconventional reasoning does not emerge until adulthood—if at all.

Antisocial Behavior

Although most adolescents internalize society's moral standards and behave morally, a few youths are involved in serious antisocial conduct—muggings, rapes, armed robberies, knifings, drive-by shootings. School shootings by adolescent and young adult males—from Columbine to Virginia Tech to Newtown and beyond—have only heightened concern about what causes serious antisocial behavior and how to prevent it. Is it guns, video games, mental illness, a violent culture, or what? As you can guess, the answer is complex.

Most severely antisocial adults start their antisocial careers in childhood and continue them in adolescence. The consequences of their early misbehavior cumulate, and they engage in **juvenile delinquency**, law breaking by a minor. They find themselves leaving school early, participating in troubled and sometimes abusive relationships, having difficulty keeping jobs, and engaging in lawbreaking as adults (Huesmann, Dubow, & Boxer, 2009; Maughan & Rutter, 2001). Some of these individuals qualify as youth for psychiatric diagnoses such as **conduct disorder**—a persistent pattern of violating the rights of others or age-appropriate societal norms through such behaviors as fighting, bullying, and cruelty; as adults, they may qualify for a diagnosis of antisocial personality disorder (see Dodge, Coie, & Lynam, 2006).

Yet most adolescents who engage in aggressive behavior and other antisocial acts do not grow up to be antisocial adults. There seem to be at least two subgroups of antisocial youths, then (Moffitt & Caspi, 2001; Monahan, Steinberg, & Cauffman, 2009; Odgers et al., 2008; Quinsey et al., 2004):

- a small, early-onset, seriously disturbed group that is recognizable in childhood through acts such as hurting animals and other children and is persistently antisocial across the life span,

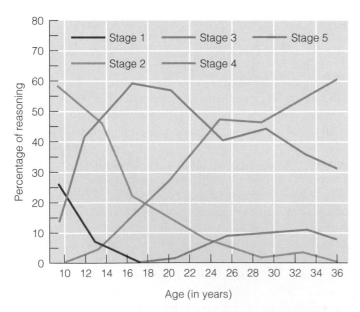

■ **Figure 13.2** Average percentage of moral reasoning at each of Lawrence Kohlberg's stages for males from age 10 to age 36.

SOURCE: From Colby, A., Kohlberg, L., Gibbs, J., & Lieberman, M. A longitudinal study of moral judgment. *Monographs of the Society for Research in Child Development, 48* (1–2, Serial No. 200). Copyright © 1983 Blackwell Publishing. Reprinted with permission.

- a larger, later-onset, less seriously antisocial group that behaves more antisocially during adolescence, partly in response to peer influences, and outgrows this behavior in early adulthood.

The decline of antisocial behavior after adolescence may reflect increased autonomy and increased ability to resist peer pressures, or it may result from entry into adult roles. It may also reflect brain development—the maturation of the prefrontal cortex of the brain that continues into the mid-20s and results in better control of impulses and a greater ability to think through long-term consequences (Giedd et al., 2013). Crime rates rise to peak during adolescence and then fall in most societies, especially for "hell-raising" crimes such as vandalism (Agnew, 2003; Tremblay, 2010). This developmental trend is reflected in the official statistics on arrests for violent crime in the United States shown in ■ **Figure 13.3**, which also makes clear that males are far more involved in violent crime than females.

What causes some youths to become menaces to society? Might adolescents who engage repeatedly in aggressive, antisocial acts be cases of arrested moral development who have not internalized conventional moral values? Juvenile delinquents are indeed more likely than nondelinquents to rely on preconventional moral reasoning (Raaijmakers, Engels, & Van Hoof, 2005; Stams et al., 2006). Yet many delinquents are capable of conventional moral reasoning but commit illegal acts anyway. So to understand the origins of antisocial conduct, we must consider more than stage of moral reasoning (see Gibbs, 2010; Quinsey et al., 2004).

What about the moral emotions of antisocial youth? Highly aggressive, antisocial adolescents are less likely than other adolescents to show empathy and concern for others in distress, and they often feel little guilt and remorse about their acts (Gibbs, 2010; Lovett & Sheffield, 2007). Apparently their moral emotions have not been socialized in ways that would promote moral behavior. Children who show such "callous-unemotional traits" over the years are of special concern; they are especially likely to engage in severe forms of antisocial behavior in adolescence

and beyond (Fontaine et al., 2011; Marsee & Frick, 2010). So lack of appropriate moral emotions is important, but as will now become clear, highly antisocial adolescents also process social information differently than other adolescents do.

Dodge's Social Information-Processing Model

Kenneth Dodge and his colleagues have advanced our understanding by offering a social information-processing model of aggressive behavior (Crick & Dodge, 1994; Dodge, 1986). Imagine that you are walking down the aisle in a classroom, trip over a classmate's leg, and end up in a heap on the floor. As you fall, you are not sure what happened. Dodge believes that our reactions to frustration, anger, or provocation depend on the ways in which we process and interpret cues in situations like this. An individual who is provoked (as by being tripped) progresses through the six steps in information processing shown in ● **Table 13.4**, according to Dodge. Look for these steps in the **Exploring Development Box 13.2** video about relational aggression.

People do not necessarily go through these steps in precise order; we can cycle among them or work on two or more simultaneously (Crick & Dodge, 1994). And at any step, we may draw not only on

Exploring Development 13.2
Relational Aggression

For boys, aggression is likely to be physical, but for girls, aggression is often relational (see also Chapter 14). The late Dr. Nicki Crick was one of the psychologists studying this type of aggression.

- What have been found to be causes of relational aggression?
- What are some consequences of relational aggression?

information available in the immediate situation but also on a stored database that includes memories of previous social experiences. The skills involved in carrying out the six steps in social information processing improve with age (Dodge & Price, 1994; Mayeux & Cillessen, 2003). Why, then, are some children more aggressive than other children the same age?

Highly aggressive youths, including adolescents incarcerated for violent crimes, show deficient or biased information processing at every step (Dodge, 1993; Slaby & Guerra, 1988), as illustrated in Table 13.4. Many aggressive youths act impulsively, "without thinking"; they respond automatically based on their database of past experiences. These youths have often developed a **hostile attribution bias**; they tend to see the world as a hostile place and quickly assume that any harm to them was deliberate rather than accidental (Crick & Dodge, 1994; Orobio de Castro et al., 2002). Severely violent youths have often experienced abandonment, neglect,

■ **Figure 13.3** Arrests for violent crimes by males and females of different ages in the United States, 2010. Violent crimes include murder, manslaughter, rape, robbery, and aggravated assault.

Source: U.S. Department of Justice, Federal Bureau of Investigation, Crime in the United States 2010. Figures retrieved and calculated from Tables 39 and 40, http://www.fbi.gov/about-us/cjis/ucr/crime-in-the-u.s/2010/crime-in-the-u.s.-2010/persons-arrested

Step	Behavior	Likely Response of Aggressive Youth
1. Encoding of cues	Search for, attend to, and register cues in the situation	Focus on cues suggesting hostile intent; ignore other relevant information
2. Interpretation of cues	Interpret situation; infer other's motive	Show hostile attribution bias, assuming other person meant to do harm
3. Clarification of goals	Formulate goal in situation	Make goal to retaliate rather than smooth relations
4. Response search	Generate possible responses	Generate few options, most of them aggressive
5. Response decision	Assess likely consequences of responses generated; choose the best	See advantages in responding aggressively rather than nonaggressively (or fail to evaluate consequences)
6. Behavioral enactment	Carry out chosen response	Behave aggressively

Social information processors use a database of information about past social experiences, social rules, and social behavior at each step of the process and may skip or repeat steps. Based on material in Dodge (1993) and Crick & Dodge (1994).

abuse, bullying, and other insults that may have given them cause to view the world as a hostile place and to feel little concern for others (Lansford et al., 2007; Margolin & Gordis, 2000). They can even feel morally justified in taking antisocial action because they believe they are only retaliating against individuals who are "out to get them" (Gibbs, 2010; Smithmyer, Hubbard, & Simons, 2000). And, of course, the responses that pop to mind when they are provoked are mostly aggressive ones.

Dodge's social information-processing model is helpful in understanding why children and adolescents might behave aggressively in particular situations. However, it leaves somewhat unclear the extent to which the underlying problem is *how one thinks* (how skilled the person is at processing social information), *what one thinks* (for example, whether the individual believes that other people are hostile), or *whether one thinks* (how impulsively the person acts). Moreover, we have to look further to understand why only some children develop the social information-processing styles associated with aggressive behavior.

Patterson's Coercive Family Environments

Gerald Patterson and his colleagues have found that highly antisocial children and adolescents often grow up in **coercive family environments** in which family members are locked in power struggles,

each trying to control the others through negative, coercive tactics (Kiesner, Dishion, & Poulin, 2001; Patterson, 2008; Patterson, DeBaryshe, & Ramsey, 1989). Parents learn (through negative reinforcement) that they can stop their children's misbehavior, temporarily at least, by threatening, yelling, and hitting. Meanwhile, children learn (also through negative reinforcement) that they can get their parents to lay off them by ignoring requests, whining, throwing full-blown temper tantrums, and otherwise being difficult. As both parents and children learn to rely on coercive tactics to avoid or escape unpleasant encounters, parents increasingly lose control over their children's behavior until even the loudest lectures and hardest spankings have little effect and the child's conduct problems spiral out of control. It is easy to see how a child who has grown up in a coercive family environment might attribute hostile intent to other people and rely on aggressive tactics to resolve disputes.

Growing up in a coercive family environment sets in motion the next steps in the making of an antisocial adolescent, according to Patterson and his colleagues (see ■ **Figure 13.4**): The child, already aggressive and unpleasant to be around, ends up performing poorly in school and being rejected by other children. Having no better options, he becomes involved in a peer group made up of other low-achieving, antisocial, and unpopular youths, who positively reinforce one another's delinquency. There is much support for Patterson's

■ **Figure 13.4** Gerald Patterson's model of the development of antisocial behavior starts with poor discipline and coercive cycles of family influence.

Source: Adapted from Patterson, G. R., DeBaryshe, B. D., & Ramsey, E., VA Developmental perspective on antisocial behavior, *American Psychologist, 44*, 329–335.

view that ineffective parenting in childhood contributes to behavior problems, peer rejection, involvement with antisocial peers, and, in turn, antisocial behavior in adolescence (Dodge et al., 2008).

Nature and Nurture

In the final analysis, severe antisocial behavior is the product of a complex interplay between genetic predisposition and environmental influences. We can start by putting aggression in an evolutionary context. For example, males are more physically aggressive overall than females and engage in three or four times as much crime (as shown in Figure 13.3). The male edge in aggression is evident in many cultures and in many species (Barash, 2002; Lansford et al., 2012), and it shows up as early as infancy (Baillargeon et al., 2007). It has been argued that aggression may have evolved in males in part because becoming dominant in the male peer group enables adolescent males to compete successfully for mates and pass their genes to future generations (Buss, 2012).

In addition, some individuals, male or female, are more genetically predisposed than others to have difficult, irritable temperaments; impulsive tendencies; and other response tendencies and personality traits that contribute to aggressive, delinquent, and criminal behavior (Niv & Baker, 2013; Rhee & Waldman, 2002). Genetic differences among us are estimated to account for about 40% of individual differences in antisocial behavior and environmental influences for the remaining 60% of the variation (Rhee & Waldman, 2002). A number of specific genes that affect neurotransmitters and hormones have been identified as contributors to antisocial behavior; researchers are also now exploring *epigenetic effects* of harsh and stressful early experiences on the expression of certain genes that play a role in aggressive behavior (Niv & Baker, 2013; Tremblay, 2010).

Through the mechanism of *gene–environment interaction*, children with certain genetic predispositions may become antisocial if they also grow up in a dysfunctional family and receive poor parenting or, worse, are physically abused (Button et al., 2005; Dodge, 2009; Kuny-Slock & Hudziak, 2013). For example, Kenneth Dodge (2009) has summarized research on the monoamine oxidase A (MAO-A) gene, a gene on the X chromosome that affects our ability to control our tempers when we are threatened or provoked. If children have a variant of this gene that results in low MAO-A activity *and* if they are abused or mistreated, they readily attribute hostile intentions to others if provoked, cannot control their anger, lash out impulsively, and show higher levels of antisocial behavior as adults (Caspi et al., 2002; and see Kim-Cohen et al., 2006). Meanwhile, positive environmental influences such as living in a two-parent home or having nondelinquent friends can mute the effects of risky variants of genes like MAO-A (Guo, 2011).

Through the mechanism of *gene–environment correlation*, children who inherit a genetic predisposition to become aggressive may actually evoke the coercive parenting that Patterson and his colleagues find breeds aggression. This *evocative gene–environment correlation* effect is evident when aggression-prone children grow up with adoptive parents rather than with their biological parents and bring out negativity even in their adoptive parents. In the end, child antisocial behavior and negative parenting influence one another reciprocally over time: aggressive children evoke negative and coercive parenting, and negative, coercive parenting further strengthens their aggressive tendencies (Larsson et al., 2008; O'Connor et al., 1998).

Finally, many other environmental risk and protective factors can help determine whether or not a child develops a pattern of antisocial behavior (Guerra & Williams, 2006). The prenatal environment—for example, exposure to alcohol, opiate drugs, and lead poisoning—has been linked to conduct problems (Dodge & Pettit, 2003). Complications during delivery may also contribute, especially if the child later grows up in a deprived home (Arseneault et al., 2002).

Some cultural contexts are more likely to breed aggression than others (Lansford et al., 2012). In Japan, a collectivist culture in which children are taught early to value social harmony, children are less angered by interpersonal conflicts and less likely to react to them aggressively than American children are (Zahn-Waxler et al., 1996). Similarly, Hispanic American youths who have been brought up with traditional Hispanic cultural values such as the importance of family are less likely than those who are more acculturated into American society to engage in antisocial behavior (Cota-Robles, 2003; Soriano et al., 2004). The United States is a relatively violent country: Guns are numerous, homicide rates are high, and corporal punishment of children is common (Lansford & Dodge, 2008; Lim, Bond, & Bond, 2005). Moreover, violence pervades television, movies, video games, and other media. Effects of violent television and video games on aggressive behavior have been observed in a number of studies (Anderson et al., 2010; Bushman & Anderson, 2001; Willoughby, Adachi, & Good, 2012). Yet the studies are sometimes flawed and inconclusive, and one cannot necessarily conclude based on short-term effects of exposure to violence on mild forms of aggression that violence in the media is a major cause of violent crime and mass shootings (Ferguson, 2013; Ferguson & Savage, 2012).

Subcultural and neighborhood factors can contribute to youth aggression and violence (Barry et al., 2012; Guerra & Williams, 2006). Rates of aggression and violent crime are two to three times higher in lower socioeconomic neighborhoods and communities, especially transient and unstable ones, than in middle-class ones (Elliott & Ageton, 1980; Maughan, 2001). Exposure to community violence is associated with high rates of aggressive behavior and low rates of prosocial behavior among urban teens (McMahon et al., 2012). Finally, certain schools have higher rates of delinquency and aggression than others, even when socioeconomic factors are controlled (Barboza et al., 2009; Maughan, 2001).

In sum, we must recognize the contributions of biology and genetic predisposition, individual psychological factors such as information-processing styles and personality traits, and sociocultural and contextual factors to aggression (Dodge & Pettit, 2003). A number of influences such as harsh parenting and association with antisocial peers, playing out over childhood and adolescence in something like the model displayed in Figure 13.4, can result in chronic and serious violence in adolescence and beyond (Dodge et al., 2008). The more risk factors at work and interacting with each other over the years, the greater the odds of an aggressive adult. Then, unfortunately, this antisocial adult stands a good chance of contributing to the intergenerational transmission of aggression—of becoming the kind of harsh, coercive parent who helps raise another generation of aggressive children, who then use the same coercive style with their own children (Conger et al., 2003; Dogan et al., 2007).

Stopping the Bullies

Phoebe Prince, a 15-year-old in Massachusetts who was believed to be moving in on other girls' boyfriends, was taunted mercilessly—jokes about an "Irish slut" on Facebook (she had recently moved to the United States from Ireland), a humiliating accusation in the school cafeteria, kids cruising up next to her in a car as she walked home, throwing an empty soda can at her, and calling her "whore" (Bennett, 2010). Phoebe killed herself; some of her tormentors were charged with criminal offenses, pled guilty to reduced charges, and were placed on probation and required to do community service.

Bullying is repeatedly inflicting harm through words or actions on peers who often have difficulty defending themselves. It is aggression directed at a particular target, and although it was once written off as just a normal part of growing up, it is now a major societal concern (Hwang, Kim, & Leventhal, 2013; Olweus, 1993; Salmivalli & Peets, 2009). The victims can be almost anyone but recent immigrants, gay and lesbian youth, and youth with disabilities or emotional problems get more than their fair share of bullying (Blake et al., 2012; Burton et al., 2013). Bullying takes many forms, from physical aggression to more indirect or covert forms of aggression such as excluding or gossiping about someone (see the Exploring Development Box 13.2 video). These days it includes cyberbullying, which enables bullies to spread rumors, insults, embarrassing photographs, and threats quickly and widely via computer or digital device (Hinduja & Patchin, 2013; Smith et al., 2008).

We can divide the world of youth into bullies, victims, bully-victims, and neither. By one estimate, 15–20% of elementary school and younger secondary school students in the United States are involved in bullying as repeat victims and/or perpetrators (Hwang et al., 2013). Bullying is universal: A survey in 40 Western countries revealed that, overall, about 26% of 11- to 15-year-olds report repeatedly bullying and/or being bullied by peers at least two to three times a month (Craig et al., 2009). Rates vary considerably, though, from under 10% in Scandinavian countries like Sweden to around 40% in Baltic countries like Lithuania, with the United States in the middle. Bullying is also a life-span phenomenon; for example, adult bullying in the workplace is a matter of societal concern too (Samnani & Singh, 2012).

Bullying is done for many reasons, not just to hurt others (Guerra, 2012; Rigby, 2012). Bullies may be seeking enjoyment (like the campers who tormented Edward for fun, in the opening scenario of the chapter), peer acceptance and status, resources like money, or a sense of control or power, for example. For some children and adolescents, being hounded by bullies can lead to becoming a bully and to aggression and delinquency, as well as to depression, health issues such as stress-related headaches and pains, and self-harmful behavior, including suicide (Barker et al., 2008; Burton et al., 2013; Espinoza, Gonzales, & Fuligni, 2012; Hwang et al., 2013; Perren, Ettekal & Ladd, 2013; Ttofi, Farrington, & Lösel, 2012). Academic performance suffers too: Schools where bullying is rampant have higher dropout rates than schools with less bullying, even controlling for factors like school size, socioeconomic status, and racial and ethnic makeup (Cornell et al., 2012; and see Strøm et al., 2013).

So what is being done about it? Virtually all states in the United States now have antibullying laws that mandate antibullying programs in the schools and sometimes establish criminal penalties for bullying (Bennett, 2010). Schools now take active steps to combat bullying and to encourage students to report or intervene in bullying incidents (Beane, 2009).

One of the most widely used and well-known interventions is the Olweus Bullying Prevention Program (Olweus, 1993; Olweus & Limber, 2010). Launched in Norway in the wake of three teen suicides attributed to bullying, it is a comprehensive program with several components. It focuses on the school as a whole (for example, through a school coordinating group with staff and student representatives and teacher training), the class (for example, through posting of rules against bullying and regular class discussions of bullying), the individual (through talks with bullies, victims, and their parents and development of individual action plans for those involved in bullying), and the broader community (through school-community partnerships).

So far, although effects have been more consistent in Norway than in the United States, this multifaceted program has had some success reducing bullying and changing attitudes toward it (Olweus & Limber, 2010; Schroeder et al., 2012). If we analyze bullying using Bronfenbrenner's bioecological model (Hong & Espelage, 2012; Chapter 2), we quickly appreciate that a host of problems within the person, family, school, community, and broader culture must be addressed to stop the bullies once and for all.

Prevention

Prevention of antisocial behavior should clearly be a national priority, but how do we go about it? Many approaches have been tried. For example, **Application Box 13.1** describes the special problem of bullying and a prevention program that has been used in many schools to combat it. Other researchers, drawing on Kohlberg's theory of moral development, have involved youth, including juvenile offenders, in discussion of moral dilemmas and democratic decision making in the schools in order to improve their moral reasoning (Gibbs, 2010; Nucci, 2006; Power & Higgins-D'Alessandro, 2008; Snarey & Samuelson, 2008). Dodge's model has been applied to improve the social information-processing skills of juvenile delinquents (Guerra & Slaby, 1990). And Patterson's coercive cycles model has been used to train parents in positive behavior management techniques (Bank et al., 1991; Patterson, 2005). All these approaches have had some positive effects, but none has been able to completely turn around the lives of serious juvenile offenders.

A more comprehensive strategy that starts earlier in life and aims at prevention seems to be needed. Many experts believe that prevention should start in infancy or toddlerhood with a strong emphasis on positive parenting (Dodge, Coie, et al., 2006; Tremblay, 2010). Since risk factors like harsh parenting and disruptive child behavior reciprocally influence each other, it also makes sense to try to change both the child and the environment (Jaffee, Strait, & Odgers, 2012). For instance, the Fast Track Program, designed by Kenneth Dodge and other members of the Conduct Problems Prevention Research Group (2007), began in first grade, extended over 10 years, and used a multipronged approach involving the teaching of social information processing and social skills, efforts to improve academic skills, and behavior management training for parents. It has proven effective in reducing antisocial behavior and preventing diagnoses of conduct disorder and related psychiatric disorders. The program worked best with those children who were at highest risk initially. It was very costly, however, suggesting the need to aim prevention programs more squarely at the children most in need of them.

Finally, still other researchers have decided that there has been too much emphasis on reducing adolescent problem behavior and too little on helping more youth develop in positive directions. **Positive youth development (PYD)** is an approach that emphasizes developing the strengths of youth. In one formulation (Lerner et al., 2005; Lerner, Phelps, Forman, & Bowers, 2009), "five Cs" serve as the goals:

- Competence (academic, vocational, and so on)
- Confidence (self-esteem and self-efficacy)
- Character (moral development, respect for rules)
- Connection (bonds to family, friends, and institutions like schools and churches)
- Caring (empathy, prosocial behavior)

PYD programs can help youths develop more positive identities, build "five C" strengths, increase their positive contributions to their communities, and yes, reduce their problem behaviors (Eichas et al., 2010; Jelicic et al., 2007; Lerner et al., 2005; Mueller et al.,

2011). For racial and ethnic minority youth, who too often have been viewed more in terms of their vulnerabilities to problems than in terms of their strengths, this "emphasize the positive" approach may be especially welcomed. Indeed, the strengths of different racial and ethnic groups—racial pride, family values, spirituality—can be incorporated in PYD programs (Evans et al., 2012; Kenyon & Hanson, 2012; Knight & Carlo, 2012). In short, we would do well to recognize and nurture the positive potentials of youth.

Checking Mastery

1. What is the main change in moral reasoning during adolescence?

2. What are the main contributions of (1) Kenneth Dodge and (2) Gerald Patterson to understanding why some adolescents are highly aggressive?

3. What is an example of the contribution of a gene–environment interaction to the development of aggression?

Making Connections

1. To demonstrate to yourself that Dodge's social information-processing model can be applied not only to antisocial behavior but to prosocial behavior, picture a situation in which you are one of the campers in the story at the beginning of this chapter and witness two other campers put the hand of Edward, the camp employee, in a bucket of water while he naps. Show how considerations at each of the six steps of Dodge's model (see Table 13.4) might contribute to your intervening to help Edward—and then how they might keep you from helping.

2. You hear that still another teenage boy has gone on a shooting rampage at his school. Drawing on material in this section, what main hypotheses would you have about why he might have done what he did?

3. The Supreme Court has had to rule on the question of whether minors who commit capital offenses like murder should face the death penalty. What is your view on this issue, and what theory and research in this chapter would you cite to support it?

13.6 The Adult

LEARNING OBJECTIVES:

- Summarize changes in moral reasoning over the adult years.

- Analyze the limitations of Kohlberg's theory of moral development with reference to cultural differences in moral thinking and dual-process models of moral decision making.

- Distinguish between religiousness and spirituality and discuss their development and relationships to adjustment.

How does moral thinking change during adulthood, and what becomes of moral emotion and moral behavior? And does moral development intersect with religiousness and spirituality in people's lives?

Changes in Moral Reasoning

Much research on moral development in adulthood has been guided by Kohlberg's theory. As you have discovered (see Figure 13.2), Kohlberg's postconventional moral reasoning appears to emerge only during the adult years (if it emerges). In Kohlberg's 20-year longitudinal study (Colby et al., 1983), most adults in their 30s still reasoned at the conventional level, although many of them had shifted from stage 3 to stage 4. A minority of individuals—one out of six at most—had begun to use stage 5 postconventional reasoning, showing a deeper understanding of the basis for laws and distinguishing between just and unjust laws. Clearly there is opportunity for moral growth in early adulthood.

Do these growth trends continue into later adulthood? Most studies find no major age differences in complexity of moral reasoning, at least when relatively educated adults are studied and when the age groups compared have similar levels of education (Pratt & Norris, 1999; Pratt et al., 1991, 1996). Older adults are also more likely than younger adults to feel that they have learned important lessons from moral dilemmas they have faced during their lives (Pratt & Norris, 1999). This, then, is further evidence that social cognitive skills hold up well across the life span.

Overall, research based on Kohlberg's influential theory of moral development shows that children think about hypothetical moral dilemmas primarily in a preconventional manner, that adolescents adopt a conventional mode of moral reasoning, and that a minority of adults shift to a postconventional perspective. Kohlberg claimed that his stages form an invariant and universal sequence of moral growth, and longitudinal studies of moral growth in several countries support his view that at least the first three or four stages form an invariant sequence (Colby & Kohlberg, 1987; Gibbs, 2010; Rest et al., 1999).

However, despite Kohlberg's major contributions to the study of moral development, his theory has its limitations. You have already seen that young children are more sophisticated moral thinkers than either Piaget or Kohlberg appreciated. Let us now consider concerns about whether Kohlberg's focus on deliberative reasoning about rights and justice captures the nature of moral thinking in non-Western cultures, whether it neglects a much more intuitive or emotional way of responding to moral issues, and whether Kohlberg said enough about influences on how people actually behave when they face moral dilemmas.

Culture and Morality

Questions have been raised about whether Kohlberg's theory is culture biased. Although support for the theory has been obtained in more than 20 countries (Gibbs et al., 2007), critics charge that Kohlberg's highest stages reflect a Western ideal of justice centered on individual rights and the rule of law and does not recognize that people in non-Western societies often think differently about moral issues (Sachdeva, Singh, & Medin, 2011; Shweder, Mahapatra, & Miller, 1990; Turiel, 2006). In fact, cross-cultural studies suggest that postconventional moral reasoning emerges primarily in Western democracies (Snarey, 1985). People in *collectivist cultures*, which emphasize social harmony and place the good of the group ahead of the good of the individual, often look like stage 3 conventional moral thinkers in Kohlberg's system, yet may have sophisticated concepts of justice that focus on the individual's duty to the group and responsibility for others' welfare (Snarey, 1985; Tietjen & Walker, 1985).

photosindia/Getty Images

Ideas about right and wrong can differ widely from culture to culture, as research comparing American and Indian children and adults has demonstrated.

Richard Shweder et al. (1990), studying the moral judgments of children and adults in India and the United States, identified even more striking cultural differences in thinking about right and wrong. For example, Hindu children and adults rated a son's getting a haircut and eating chicken the day after his father's death as one of the most morally offensive of the 39 acts they were asked to rate, whereas Americans dismissed it as only a matter of breaking seemingly arbitrary social-conventional rules about appropriate mourning behavior. Meanwhile, Americans viewed a husband's beating of his "disobedient" wife for going to the movies without his permission as a serious moral violation, whereas Hindus viewed it as appropriate behavior. To orthodox Hindus, not showing proper respect for the dead violates a moral rule required by natural law, not an arbitrary social-conventional rule, and it is morally necessary for a man to beat his disobedient wife to uphold his obligations as head of the family.

Cross-cultural findings like this challenge the cognitive-developmental position that important aspects of moral development are universal. Instead, they support a social learning perspective on moral development, suggesting that our moral judgments are shaped by the social context in which we develop. Possibly the resolution is this: Individuals all over the world think in more complex ways about moral issues as they get older, as Kohlberg claimed, but they also adopt different notions about what is right and what is wrong depending on what they are taught (Miller, 2006).

Moral Intuition and Emotion

(Before you read this section, we invite you to read and respond to **Engagement Box 13.2**.) Developmentalists today are trying to correct for Kohlberg's overemphasis on moral reasoning by exploring the emotional component of morality more fully. As you have seen already, Martin Hoffman, Grazyna Kochanska, and others have long highlighted the critical role of emotions

Runaway Trolleys

Read and respond to these two moral dilemmas (Greene et al., 2001, p. 2105) and then return to the section Moral Intuition and Emotion.

Switch Dilemma. A runaway trolley is headed for five people who will be killed if it proceeds on its present course. The only way to save them is to hit a switch that will turn the trolley onto an alternate set of tracks where it will kill one person instead of five. Ought you to turn the trolley in order to save five people at the expense of one?

Footbridge Dilemma. As before, a trolley threatens to kill five people. You are standing next to a large stranger on a footbridge that spans the tracks, in between the oncoming trolley and the five people. ... The only way to save the five people is to push this stranger off the bridge, onto the tracks below. He will die if you do this, but his body will stop the trolley from reaching the others. Ought you to save the five others by pushing this stranger to his death?

like empathy and guilt in motivating moral action. Now a number of scholars are converging on the idea that gut emotional reactions and intuitions play a critical role in moral decision making (Gibbs, 2010; Greene, 2008; Haidt, 2008).

Think about whether you would eat your fellow passengers after a plane crash in the mountains if there were nothing else to eat. Most of us say, "Ewww," finding the idea morally repugnant. We immediately know in our gut, without a need for contemplation, that cannibalism is wrong. Jonathan Haidt (2001, 2008, 2011) argues that we have evolved as a species to have many such quick moral intuitions, which are often based in emotions like disgust. He believes that these intuitions are more important than deliberative reasoning in shaping moral decisions. If deliberate thought of the sort emphasized by Kohlberg plays a role at all, Haidt suggests, it is mainly to rationalize after the fact what we have already decided intuitively. Often, we cannot even come up with reasons for our gut reactions.

Like Haidt, Joshua Greene has proposed a **dual-process model of morality** in which *both* deliberate thought and intuition/emotion play distinct roles (see ● **Table 13.5**; and Gibbs, 2010). Greene has tried to explain why we sometimes make judgments based on quick, emotion-based intuitions and other times make judgments using more deliberative cognitive processes. Look again at the Engagement Box 13.2. Despite the similarities between the two trolley car scenarios there, most people would hit the switch in the switch scenario but would not push the stranger off the bridge in the footbridge scenario. Was that your response? Why do you think you reacted that way?

Greene and his colleagues (2001) have proposed that it is because the footbridge dilemma evokes a strong emotional response that the first scenario does not: we are appalled at the idea of directly killing a person with our own hands, possibly because we have evolved to feel such revulsion. Using fMRI techniques, Greene and his colleagues demonstrated that areas of the brain associated with emotion are more active when people think about killing the large man in the footbridge scenario, whereas areas of the brain associated with rational cognition are more active when people consider sacrificing the one for the many in the switch problem. Thus the findings were consistent with Greene's (2008) concept of a dual-process model of morality involving: (1) an emotion-based intuitive process that prompts us, quickly and without awareness, to focus on (and abhor) the harm that would be done if we violated moral principle (as by pushing a stranger to his death); and (2) a more deliberative, cognitive approach in which we weigh the costs and benefits of an action in a cool and calculating manner (and conclude that it is more rational to sacrifice one life than to lose five).

Other evidence supports Greene's dual-process model, suggesting that we use different parts of the brain to make intuitive and deliberative moral decisions (Greene, 2009; Greene et al., 2008; Moore, Lee, Clark, & Conway, 2011). Much remains to be learned, though. When do we go with our gut reactions and when do we rely on conscious deliberation? What happens when the two processes in the dual-process model of morality pull in different directions? And why is it that some people rely more on their "heart," while others rely more on their "head" in making moral judgments (Paxton & Greene, 2010; Paxton, Ungar, & Greene, 2012)? Both Haidt and Greene raise new and interesting questions about the distinct roles of quick, emotion-based intuition and deliberate reasoning in morality.

● **Table 13.5** Dual-Process Models of Morality

Moral Cognition/ Reasoning (Emphasized by Kohlberg)	Moral Emotion/Intuition (Emphasized by Haidt, Greene)
Rational thought	Intuition
Cold logic	Hot emotion
Controlled processes	Automatic processes
Impartiality	Empathy
Careful deliberation	Quick gut reaction

© Cengage Learning

Predicting Moral Action

Kohlberg looked primarily at moral reasoning, but does how one reasons have anything to do with how one behaves? Although a person may decide to uphold or to break a law at any of Kohlberg's stages of moral reasoning, Kohlberg argued that more advanced moral reasoners are more likely to behave morally than less advanced moral reasoners are. For example, where the preconventional thinker might readily decide to cheat if the chances of being detected were small and the potential rewards were large, the postconventional thinker would be more likely to appreciate that cheating is wrong in principle, regardless of the chances of punishment or reward, because it infringes on the rights of others and undermines social order.

What does research tell us? Individuals determined to be at higher stages of moral reasoning are more likely than individuals at lower stages to behave prosocially (Gibbs, 2010; Walker, 2004). For example, they are more likely to do good through their involvement in social organizations (Matsuba & Walker, 2004) and to be helpful in everyday life (Midlarsky et al., 1999). They are also less likely to behave immorally—to cheat or to engage in delinquent and criminal activity (Judy & Nelson, 2000; Rest et al., 1999). Yet relationships between stage of moral reasoning and moral behavior are usually weak. We now appreciate that a variety of other factors are important in motivating and explaining moral and immoral behavior—the situational factors social learning theorists like Bandura emphasize, the gut emotional reactions Haidt and Greene call attention to, the moral rules that operate in certain cultures, and so on.

In sum, Kohlberg's stage theory has a good deal of support, but it

- underestimates children's moral sophistication
- fails to recognize cultural differences in thinking about morality
- neglects intuition/emotion, as pointed out by dual-process theorists such as Haidt and Greene
- says too little about the many influences besides moral reasoning on moral behavior

In the end, we do best recognizing that the moral reasoning of interest to Piaget and Kohlberg, the moral emotions and intuitions of interest to Freud and Hoffman and more recently Haidt and Greene, and the self-regulatory and moral disengagement processes highlighted by Albert Bandura—together with many other personal and situational factors—all help predict whether a person will behave morally or immorally when faced with an important moral choice.

Religion and Spirituality

Lawrence Kohlberg viewed moral development and religious development as distinct, but they are clearly interrelated for the many people whose religious or spiritual values and beliefs guide their moral thinking and behavior (Nelson, 2009). Indeed, James Fowler (1981; Fowler & Dell, 2006) proposed stages in the development of religious faith from infancy to adulthood that parallel quite closely Kohlberg's stages of moral development. Fowler's stages lead from concrete images of God in childhood, to internalization of conventional beliefs in adolescence, to soul searching in emerging or early adulthood, and, for a few, progression to a more universal perspective on faith in middle age and beyond. This concept of universal stages of religious development, like Kohlberg's theory of moral development, has come into question. However, researchers are more interested than ever in the roles religion and spirituality play in development across the life span (Ai, Wink, & Ardelt, 2010; Nelson, 2009; Pargament, Exline, & Jones, 2013).

Religiousness has generally been defined as sharing the beliefs and participating in the practices of an organized religion. **Spirituality** is harder to define but involves a quest for ultimate meaning and for a connection with something greater than oneself, whether God, love, nature, or some other cosmic force (see Nelson, 2009). Spiritual seeking may be carried out within the context of a religion (some people are both religious and spiritual) or outside it (some people say they are spiritual but not religious).

Children often adopt the beliefs of their parents, especially if their parents are religious and are warm and supportive (Power & McKinney, 2013). Children also think on their own about religious and spiritual matters, though, and do so in increasingly complex ways as they get older (Boyatzis, 2013). Adolescence or emerging adulthood can become an important time for raising religious and spiritual questions as part of identity formation (Alisat & Pratt, 2012; Good & Willoughby, 2008; Nelson, 2009). For most, the result is staying in the religious tradition in which one was raised but sometimes with a deeper and more personalized understanding. For others, questioning results in rejecting the religious beliefs one was taught as a child, undergoing a spiritual conversion, or developing one's own belief system. Religious commitment, if it translates into a strong moral identity, encourages empathy for others and works against antisocial tendencies (Hardy, Walker, Rackham, & Olsen, 2012). Adolescents who are highly religious may also gain a sense of social connection and shared vision that fosters moral behavior and positive development (Ebstyne King & Furrow, 2004).

What happens during adulthood? Is old age a special time for religious and spiritual growth? Most studies suggest that while formal participation in religious activities may decline in late adulthood owing to poor health and disability, the importance attached to religion and involvement in more personal forms of participation like prayer remain steady or even increase (Ai et al., 2010). Using data from a longitudinal study of California adults born in the 1920s, Michelle Dillon and Paul Wink sought to understand changes over the years in both religiousness and spirituality, as well as the relationships of both to psychosocial functioning in old age (Dillon & Wink, 2007; Wink & Dillon, 2002, 2003). The researchers coded interviews for degree of religiousness (defined as participating in traditional forms of religion practice) and degree of spirituality (seeking, in a more personal way, a relationship with a higher power). One finding was that individuals are highly consistent over the years in their degrees of religiousness and spirituality (Wink & Dillon, 2003). That is, some are consistently high and others consistently low in religiousness and spirituality over the years, with correlations of around +.70 between earlier and later assessments.

As shown in ■ **Figure 13.5**, Part A, average levels of religiousness proved to be high in adolescence; decreased somewhat in middle age, possibly because people had many responsibilities and little time; and rose back to its earlier levels in people's late 60s and 70s. By comparison, spirituality (see Figure 13.5, Part B) was at lower levels than religiousness throughout adulthood and changed more dramatically with age, increasing significantly from middle age to later adulthood (Dillon & Wink, 2007). This was especially true among women, who are generally both more

Religiousness

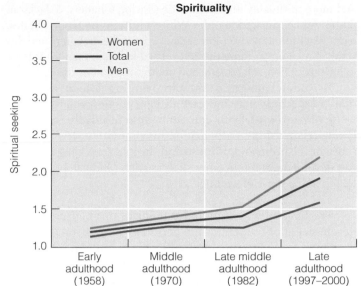

Spirituality

■ **Figure 13.5** Changes over time in religiousness and spirituality among adults born in the 1920s. Levels of rated spirituality are lower than levels of religiousness but increase more dramatically in old age, especially among women.

Source: Dillon, M.& Wink, P. (2007). *In the course of a lifetime: Tracing religious belief, practice, and change,* Figures 1 and 4. Reprinted by permission of the University of California Press.

religious and more spiritual than men (see also Brown, Chen, Gehlert, & Piedmont, 2012). These findings and others confirm Erik Erikson's view that old age can be a time for reflecting on larger questions and finding meaning in life (Atchley, 2009; Nelson, 2009; but see Brown et al., 2012).

We must as usual recognize that development can be affected by the times in which people grow up and live. In 2012, for example, almost 20% of Americans, up from 8% in 1990, said that they are not affiliated with a traditional religious group, although many of them indicated that they believe in God and follow certain spiritual practices (Pew Forum on Religion and Public Life, 2012). Approximately one-third of adults under 30 fell into this "no affiliation" group, whereas only 1 in 10 seniors did, suggesting a trend over time away from organized religion, although not from religious or spiritual belief.

Does it benefit adults to be highly religious or spiritual? Correlation is not necessarily causation, but both religiousness and spirituality are positively associated with health, mental health, and well-being (Ai et al., 2010; Greenfield, Vaillant, & Marks, 2009; Wink & Dillon, 2008). For example, highly religious adults not only socialize their adolescents into their religious beliefs but are more likely than less religious adults to model a happy marital relationship and to use positive parenting techniques, with the result that their adolescents later become not only more religious but better spouses and parents (Spilman et al., 2013). Thus, religious commitment may help people develop and maintain good family relationships.

Religiousness and spirituality may be especially beneficial in late adulthood, when Wink and Dillon found both to be correlated with a sense of well-being (Wink & Dillon, 2003). Highly religious adults, they observed, are often very involved in their religious communities and act on their religious beliefs by serving others, and highly spiritual adults seem to gain

The church is at the center of the African American community and can have both health and mental health benefits for those elderly people who are highly involved in it.

well-being from their active quest for meaning. Religiousness and spirituality are linked to having a sense of meaning and purpose in life and well as to being part of a caring community; perhaps for both reasons, they are also correlated with good health, good mental health, and prosocial behavior in later life (Ai et al., 2010; Krause, 2013; Nelson, 2009). Moreover, religiousness and spirituality may help people cope with crises in their lives (Chan, Rhodes, & Pérez, 2012).

Religion and spirituality appear to be especially important in certain racial and ethnic groups (Krause, 2013; Mattis & Grayman-Simpson, 2013). For example, both African American and Caribbean Blacks age 55 and older report more religious participation of various types, more use of prayer to cope with stress, and more spirituality than Whites do (Taylor, Chatters, & Jackson, 2007). And compared to older White adults in the United States, older Black adults derive more meaning from their religion, and this sense of meaning is more strongly related for them than for Whites to life satisfaction, self-esteem, and optimism (Krause, 2003).

In sum, religiousness and spirituality are distinct, and spirituality especially may increase in later life, especially among women. Moreover, both can contribute positively to healthy family relationships, participation in community service, and a sense of meaning and purpose and, in turn, to a range of positive developmental outcomes such as good physical and mental health and a sense of well-being.

We have now completed our series of chapters on the development of the self, or the person as an individual, having examined the development of self-conceptions and personality (Chapter 11), identities as males or females (Chapter 12), and now social cognition and morality. But individual development does not occur in a vacuum. Repeatedly, you have seen that an individual's development may take different paths depending on the social and cultural context in which it occurs. Our task in upcoming chapters will be to put the individual even more squarely in social context. It should become clear that throughout our lives we are both independent and interdependent—separate from and connected to other developing persons.

Chapter Summary

13.1 Social Cognition

- Social cognition (thinking about self and others) is involved in all social behavior, including moral behavior. Starting in infancy with milestones such as joint attention, understanding of intentions, and pretend play, children develop a theory of mind—a desire psychology at age 2 and a belief–desire psychology at age 4 as evidenced by passing false belief tasks. Developing a theory of mind requires a normal brain (including mirror neuron systems) and appropriate communication experience.
- In characterizing other people, preschool children focus on physical features and activities, children 8 years and older on inner psychological traits, and adolescents on integrating trait descriptions to create personality profiles. With age, children also become more adept at perspective taking. Social cognitive skills often improve during adulthood and hold up well but may decline late in life if a person is socially isolated.

13.2 Perspectives on Moral Development

- Morality has emotional, cognitive, and behavioral components. Sigmund Freud's psychoanalytic theory emphasized the superego and moral emotions, and Martin Hoffman has emphasized empathy as a motivator of moral behavior.
- Building on the work of cognitive-developmental theorist Jean Piaget, Lawrence Kohlberg proposed three levels of moral reasoning—preconventional, conventional, and postconventional—each with two stages.

- Social cognitive theorist Albert Bandura focused on how moral behavior is influenced by learning, situational forces, self-regulatory processes, and moral disengagement.
- Evolutionary theorists (Krebs, Tomasello) consider emotion, cognition, and behavior and maintain that humans have evolved to be moral beings because morality and prosocial behavior have proven adaptive for the human species.

13.3 The Infant

- Although infants are amoral in some respects, they begin learning about right and wrong through their early disciplinary encounters, internalize rules, and display empathy and prosocial behavior early in life, just as they show antisocial behavior on occasion. Their moral growth is facilitated by a secure attachment and what Grazyna Kochanska calls a mutually responsive orientation between parent and child.

13.4 The Child

- Kohlberg and Piaget underestimated the moral sophistication of young children (for example, their ability to consider intentions, to distinguish between moral and social-conventional rules, and to question adult authority); still, most children display preconventional moral reasoning.
- Reinforcement, modeling, Hoffman's disciplinary approach of induction, and proactive parenting can foster moral growth, and a child's temperament interacts with the approach to moral training parents adopt to influence outcomes.

13.5 The Adolescent

- During adolescence, a shift from preconventional to conventional moral reasoning is evident, and some adolescents forge a moral identity.
- Antisocial behavior can be understood in terms of Kenneth Dodge's social information-processing model, Gerald Patterson's coercive family environments and the negative peer influences they set in motion, and, more generally, the interaction of genetic predisposition with a variety of psychological and social–environmental influences. Attempts to reduce antisocial behavior, including bullying, have taken a variety of directions, including the positive youth development movement.

13.6 The Adult

- A minority of adults progress from the conventional to the postconventional level of moral reasoning; elderly adults typically reason as complexly as younger adults.
- Kohlberg's early stages of moral reasoning form an invariant sequence, but he underestimated children, failed to recognize cultural differences, and slighted moral emotion and the many other influences on moral behavior.
- Researchers like Haidt and Greene have proposed dual-process models of morality that include both deliberative reasoning and emotion-based intuitions.
- Religiousness and especially spirituality become stronger in later life and are associated with good physical and mental health and well-being.

Checking Mastery Answers

For answers to Checking Mastery questions, please see Appendix B.

Key Terms

social cognition **400**
false belief task **400**
theory of mind **400**
desire psychology **402**
belief–desire psychology **402**
mirror neurons **403**
perspective-taking skills **405**
role-taking skills **405**
morality **407**
empathy **408**
prosocial behavior **408**
antisocial behavior **408**
moral reasoning **408**

preconventional morality **409**
conventional morality **409**
reciprocity **410**
postconventional morality **410**
moral disengagement **411**
amoral **413**
delay of gratification **415**
self-control **415**
mutually responsive orientation **415**
moral rules **417**
social-conventional rules **417**
love withdrawal **417**
power assertion **417**

induction **417**
proactive parenting strategies **418**
moral identity **419**
juvenile delinquency **420**
conduct disorder **420**
hostile attribution bias **421**
coercive family environment **422**
bullying **424**
positive youth development (PYD) **425**
dual-process model of morality **427**
religiousness **428**
spirituality **428**

CENGAGE Get quizzes, flashcards, videos, and more at **www.cengagebrain.com.**
brain.com

14

Emotions, Attachment, and Social Relationships

Mike Pohle was about to graduate and wanted to find a job close to his fiancée, Marcy Crevonis (Jones, 2007). He slept every night in a Phillies jersey she gave him, filled her dorm room with chocolate kisses on Valentine's Day, and had already named the five children they hoped to have. They were soul mates. As Marcy put it, "We were the same person. We shared the same thoughts. We finished each other's sentences" (Jones, 2007, p. C1).

Mike Pohle was one of the 32 victims of the mass murders at Virginia Tech University, April 16, 2007. Marcy had walked him part of the way to his German class that morning and raced to find him when his class was to end but was blocked by the police. Told of Mike's death, she went back to his apartment, put on the Phillies jersey, and wept.

The shooter, Seung Hui Cho, had no soul mates. He was an unusually quiet child who did not respond to greetings; one high school classmate recalled the jokes about him: "We would just say, 'Did you see Seung say nothing again today?' " (Cho & Gardner, 2007, p. A8). Cho spent his lonely days writing stories of violence and death. He had been diagnosed and treated for social anxiety disorder and selective mutism as a child, but he never made this known to Virginia Tech and deteriorated in college (Schulte & Craig, 2007). As a result, he was almost completely isolated from the human community.

How did their developmental experiences prepare Mike and Marcy to fall in love? What kept Seung from developing close human relationships, and what made him so angry at his fellow humans? Think about Mike Pohle and Seung Hui Cho as you read this chapter. It concerns our emotional lives and closest social relationships and their interrelationships across the life span.

We explore how we develop the emotional security and social competence it takes to interact positively with other people and to enter into intimate relationships with them, and we examine the developmental implications of being deprived of close relationships. We begin by examining the emotions that are so much a part of our close relationships.

14.1 Emotional Development

LEARNING OBJECTIVES:

- Distinguish between primary and secondary or self-conscious emotions, giving examples and indicating when they emerge.

- Discuss age-related changes in mastery of emotion regulation skills, the concept of mixed emotions, and display rules for emotion.

- Using socioemotional selectivity theory, explain why older adults typically have greater emotional well-being than adolescents.

What is an emotion? It is a complex phenomenon that involves a subjective feeling ("I'm mad"), physiological changes (a pounding heart), behavior (an enraged face, a door slammed), and often a cognitive appraisal as well ("No wonder I'm mad—He embarrassed me in front of everyone.") (see Thompson, Winer, & Goodvin, 2011). Emotions are detectable in the first days of life, but their character changes as we develop cognitively and as we learn to express and regulate or control them. Parent–child relationships involve strong emotions, and caregivers are critical in shaping the course of emotional development.

First Emotions and Emotion Regulation

Carroll Izard (1982; Izard & Ackerman, 2000) and his colleagues maintain that basic emotions are biologically based, develop early in life, and play critical roles in motivating and organizing behavior. By videotaping infants' responses to such events as having a toy taken away or seeing their mothers return after a separation, analyzing specific facial movements (such as the raising of the brows and the wrinkling of the nose), and asking raters to judge what emotion a baby's face reveals, Izard has established that very young infants express distinct emotions in response to different experiences and that adults can interpret which emotions they are expressing (see also Saarni et al., 2006). The work of Izard and others allows us to piece together an account of the early development of a number of so-called **primary emotions**, distinct basic emotions that emerge within the first 6 months of life (Lewis, 2008; and see ■ Figure 14.1).

At birth, babies show contentment (by smiling), interest (by staring intently at objects), and distress (grimaces in response to pain or discomfort). Within the first 6 months, six

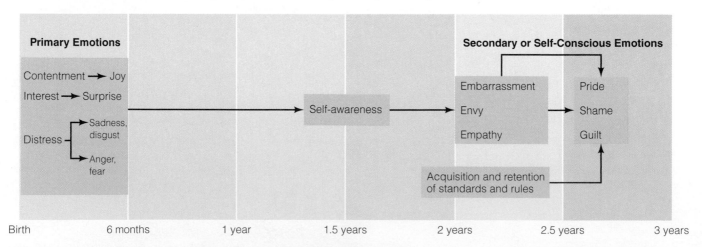

■ **Figure 14.1** The emergence of different emotions. Primary emotions (joy, surprise, fear, anger, sadness, and disgust) emerge in the first 6 months of life and evolve from there. Once self-awareness or mirror self-recognition is achieved, the first secondary or self-conscious emotions emerge starting from about 18 months to 2 years. Later in the second year, self-conscious emotions that require evaluating the self against standards (pride, for example) emerge.

SOURCE: From Lewis, M. The emergence of human emotions. In M. Lewis, J. M. Haviland-Jones, & L. Feldman Barrett (Eds.), *Handbook of Emotions* (3rd ed.). Copyright © 2008. Reprinted with permission of Guilford Publications, Inc.

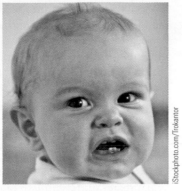

(a)   (b)

What emotions do you see in Baby A and Baby B? Your choices are the six primary emotions: anger, disgust, fear, surprise, joy, and sadness.

(a) sadness; (b) anger

specific primary emotions evolve from these three. By 3 months of age or so, contentment becomes joy—pleasure at the sight of something familiar such as a big smile in response to Mom's face. Interest becomes surprise, such as when expectations are violated in games of peekaboo. Distress soon evolves into four familiar negative emotions, starting with disgust (in response to foul-tasting foods) and sadness. Angry expressions appear as early as 4 months—about the time infants acquire enough control of their limbs to push unpleasant stimuli away. Now instead of just being distressed when they are physically restrained, they look angrily at the person who is restraining them. Finally, fear is the last to appear.

Next, as Figure 14.1 also shows, come the so-called secondary or **self-conscious emotions**. These emotions require self-awareness and begin to emerge after 18 months of age, the age when infants become able to recognize themselves in a mirror and may start using words like "I" and "me" (see Chapter 11 on self-recognition). By around this age, infants may show embarrassment when they are asked to dance or sing for guests (Lewis, 2008). Then, later in the second year, when toddlers become able to judge their behavior against standards of performance, they may display the self-conscious emotions that involve evaluating the self: pride, shame, and guilt (Lewis, 2008). They can feel proud if they catch a ball because they know that's what you're supposed to do when a ball is tossed your way—or guilty if they spill their milk because they know you are not supposed to make messes. By age 2 or 3, toddlers also appreciate that other people's emotions can be manipulated and are ready to tease and torment a sibling (Thompson et al., 2011).

Nature, Nurture, and Emotions

Primary or basic emotions such as interest and fear seem to be biologically programmed. They emerge in all normal infants at roughly the same ages and are displayed and interpreted similarly in all cultures (Izard, 1982; Malatesta et al., 1989). The timing of their emergence is linked to cognitive maturation (Lewis,

2008). As Charles Darwin recognized long ago, basic emotions probably evolved in humans because they helped our ancestors appraise and respond appropriately to new stimuli and situations (Cole, Martin, & Dennis, 2004). As John Bowlby, a theorist you will soon meet, emphasized, infants' emotional signals—whether expressions of joy or distress—also prompt their caregivers to respond to them and have adaptive value for that reason as well (Kopp & Neufield, 2003).

Whether an infant tends to be predominantly happy and eager to approach new stimuli or irritable and easily upset depends in part on his genetically based temperament (Goldsmith, 2003; Rothbart, 2011). However, caregivers also help shape infants' predominant patterns of emotional expression (Fitness, 2013; Thompson et al., 2011). Observational studies of face-to-face interactions between mothers and infants suggest that young infants display a range of positive and negative emotions, changing their expressions with lightning speed (once every 7 seconds) while their mothers do the same (Malatesta et al., 1986, 1989). Mothers mainly display interest, surprise, and joy, thus serving as models of positive emotions and eliciting positive emotions from their babies. Mothers also respond selectively to their babies' expressions; over the early months, they become increasingly responsive to their babies' expressions of happiness, interest, and surprise and less responsive to their negative emotions. Through basic learning processes, then, infants are trained to show happy faces more often than grumpy or sad ones—and they do just that over time.

At around 9 months of age, infants also begin to monitor their companions' emotional reactions to stimuli and use this information to decide how they should feel and behave—a phenomenon called **social referencing** (Feinman, 1992). If their mothers are wary when a stranger approaches, they too may be wary and back away; if their mothers smile at the stranger, they may approach the stranger eagerly. It is not just that 1-year-olds are imitating their parents' emotions, then; they are using their parents' emotional reactions to decide how to behave in a situation. Indeed, infants are more attentive to and affected by adults' reactions in ambiguous situations than their reactions in situations where it is clear how to react (Kim & Kwak, 2011). Infants are also especially attentive to negative emotional reactions such as fear or anger in their caregivers, as if they know that these emotions are warning signals (Carver & Vaccaro, 2007). Unfortunately, this means that social referencing may be one way in which parents who are socially anxious train their babies to be socially anxious too (Murray et al., 2008).

Parents also socialize their infants' and young children's emotions by talking about emotions in daily life (Fitness, 2013; Thompson & Meyer, 2007). For example, parents educate their infants about emotions by saying things like, "What a happy baby you are now!" and "You're mad that you can't have more, aren't you?" Sensitive parents also help children express their feelings so that the parents can respond to their emotional needs. Gradually, in the context of a secure parent–child relationship in which there is plenty of emotional communication, infants and young children learn to understand emotions and express them appropriately (Thompson et al., 2011).

Emotion Regulation

To conform to their culture's and caregivers' rules about when and how different emotions should be expressed, and, perhaps most importantly, to keep themselves from being overwhelmed by their emotions, infants must develop strategies for **emotion regulation**—the processes involved in initiating, maintaining, and altering emotional responses (Bridges & Grolnick, 1995; and see Calkins & Mackler, 2011; Gross, 2007; Schulz & Lazarus, 2011). Emotion regulation can be accomplished through such tactics as not putting oneself in, or thinking about, situations likely to arouse unwanted emotions (by avoiding monster movies and thoughts of monsters), reappraising or reinterpreting events or one's reactions to them (saying it wasn't really a monster or I wasn't really afraid—I was just surprised), or altering one's emotional responses to events (putting on a brave face to replace a scared face). Emotion regulation often involves suppressing or otherwise controlling negative emotions like anger and fear, but it also includes trying to heighten or prolong positive emotional experiences. You can think of it as an aspect of self-control (refer to Chapter 13).

Infants are active from the start in regulating their emotions, but at first they have only a few simple emotion regulation strategies. Very young infants are able to reduce their negative arousal by turning from unpleasant stimuli or by sucking vigorously on a pacifier (Mangelsdorf, Shapiro, & Marzolf, 1995). By the end of the first year, infants can move away from upsetting events or rock themselves. They also actively seek their caregivers when they are upset because these individuals have a calming effect.

By 18–24 months, toddlers will try to control whatever is upsetting them—for example, by pushing a bothersome peer or a noisy mechanical toy away (Mangelsdorf et al., 1995). They may be able to cope with the frustration of waiting for snacks and gifts by playing with toys and otherwise distracting themselves (Grolnick, Bridges, & Connell, 1996), and they may knit their brows or compress their lips in an attempt to suppress their anger or sadness (Malatesta et al., 1989). Finally, as children gain the capacity for symbolic thought and language, they become able to regulate their distress cognitively—for example, by repeating the words, "Mommy home soon, Mommy home soon," after Mom goes out the door (Thompson, 1994).

The development of emotion regulation skills is influenced by both an infant's temperament and a caregiver's behavior (Grolnick, McMenamy, & Kurowski, 2006). Recall from Chapter 11 that babies differ temperamentally in both how emotionally reactive they are to events and how able they are to exert effortful control over their reactions (Rothbart, 2011). These aspects of temperament matter, but so does parenting. Very young infants who have few emotion regulation strategies of their own rely heavily on caregivers to help them—for example, by stroking them gently or rocking them when they are distressed, by calming them down after a joyful bout of play (Calkins & Hill, 2007; Cole, Michel, & Teti, 1994). As infants age, they gain control of emotion regulation strategies first learned in the context of the parent–child relationship and can regulate their emotions on their own (for example, by rocking themselves rather than looking to be rocked). By being sensitive, responsive caregivers, parents can help keep fear, anger, and other negative emotions to a minimum (Pauli-Pott, Mertesacker, & Beckmann,

2004). Children who are not able to get a grip on their negative emotions, either because of their temperamental characteristics or because their caregivers do not help them master emotion regulation skills, tend to experience stormy relationships with both caregivers and peers and are at risk to develop behavior problems later in childhood (Rothbart, 2011; Saarni et al., 2006).

Emotional Learning in Childhood

As children get older, they gain still more **emotional competence**; that is, they develop characteristic patterns of emotional expression, greater understanding of emotion, and better emotion regulation skills (Denham, Bassett, & Wyatt, 2007; Denham et al., 2003; Thompson et al., 2011). Children who express emotions appropriate to the situation and have a good balance of positive to negative emotions, who understand their own and others' feelings and the situations that trigger them, and who manage their emotions well make sensitive and enjoyable companions. As a result, early emotional competence is a good predictor of social competence—for example, peer acceptance and teachers' ratings of social adjustment (Denham et al., 2003).

Consider this example of advances in the understanding of emotions during childhood. It apparently takes children some time to recognize that a person can have mixed emotions about the same object at the same time—for example, that a child in therapy can both love and hate her mother. Susan Harter and Bonnie Buddin (1987) showed children aged 4–12 photographs of two different facial expressions of emotion at a time and asked them to explain how someone could have both emotions at once. Preschool children could not think of how to put two emotions together. As one put it, "It's hard to think of two feelings at the same time because you only have one mind" (Harter & Buddin, 1987). At age 8–9, children were better able to explain how two positive or two negative emotions could co-occur—for example, how you could be both sad and mad when a toy is broken. Only by age 11–12, though, were most children able to explain how you could have both a positive and a negative emotion about something simultaneously—for example, how you could be happy you made it to the finals but afraid you would do poorly. Overall, then, as children get older they learn more about different emotions and the situations that arouse them and become more able to integrate distinct emotions into the same emotional experience. A similar study of children ages 5–12 showed that older children are also more likely than younger children to report experiencing mixed emotions themselves in response to a bittersweet film scene (Larsen, To, & Fireman, 2007).

As children get older, they also learn about **display rules for emotion**—cultural rules specifying what emotions should and should not be expressed under what circumstances (Harris, 1989; Saarni, 1984; Thompson et al., 2011). Rules such as "Don't laugh when someone falls down," "Look sad at a funeral," and "Act pleased when you receive a lousy gift" are examples. As children learn display rules, the gap between what they are experiencing inside and what they express to the world widens (a nice way of saying that they become more skilled in the art of deceit!), and they become more aware of this gap between inner and expressed emotions.

Emotion Coaching or Emotion Dismissing?

How emotionally expressive were your parents when you were growing up, and how did they react to your emotional outbursts? Parents differ a good deal in their beliefs about emotions, and these emotional philosophies guide how they express and regulate their own emotions, react to their children's emotions, and teach their children about emotions (Bariola, Gullone, & Hughes, 2011; Halberstadt, 1991; Katz, Maliken, & Stettler, 2012). John Gottman and his colleagues (Gottman, Katz, & Hooven, 1996) have identified two quite different approaches parents take to emotions. *Emotion coaching* involves:

- being aware of even low-intensity emotions
- viewing children's expressions of emotion as opportunities for closeness and teaching
- accepting and empathizing with children's emotional experiences

- helping children understand and express their feelings
- helping children deal with whatever triggered their emotions

The following example of a mother comforting her 5-year-old son after a frustrating game-playing session with other boys captures the spirit of emotion coaching:

You didn't like that he was bouncing your guy off the game, and that made you really mad. It's hard when you feel so angry. You're going "AAAH, he's bouncing my guy off there!" right? It makes you sad thinking about it, doesn't it? You know, after you stopped the game, the other guys said, "You know, Joey wasn't really doing so bad." You thought you were losing, but you weren't (Thompson et al., 2011, p. 238).

Emotion dismissing, by contrast, involves ignoring, denying, or even criticizing or punishing negative emotions or trying to convert them as quickly as possible into positive emotions.

If a child is not allowed to express frustration and anger, even by a well-meaning parent who tries to cheer her out of her bad mood, she misses opportunities to learn about anger and how to deal with it and does not get the sense that someone understands and empathizes with her and will help her cope with whatever prompted her emotional reaction.

In studies comparing emotion coaching and emotion dismissing, the emotion coaching approach wins hands down. It is associated with healthy emotional development and fewer emotional and behavioral problems (Katz et al., 2012). An intervention called Tuning in to Kids teaches emotion coaching skills to parents of preschool children and appears to be effective in increasing children's emotional knowledge and reducing their behavior problems (Havighurst et al., 2009, 2010). Research on emotion coaching provides still more evidence of the power of parents to foster healthy emotional development.

Carolyn Saarni (1984) conducted an interesting study of display-rule learning. Children aged 7, 9, and 11 were rewarded for their labors in a first research session with a nice gift—a can of juice, a candy bar, and 50 cents. After a second research session, when they were expecting a nice gift, they got a boring baby toy. Here, then, was a situation (not unlike that faced by children who are given underwear or weird gifts from distant aunts on their birthdays) in which our culture's display rule is, "Look pleased about a gift, even if it's a disappointing one."

Children's reactions were coded as positive (an enthusiastic "thank you," a big smile), negative (an "ugh," shrug, wrinkled nose, and so on), and transitional (a lame attempt to follow the display rule such as a mumbled "thank you" or distressed smile). The 7-year-olds in the study, especially the boys, were not skilled at all at masking their disappointment; they just said "ugh" a lot. Older children, especially girls, were more able to conform to the display rule by pretending to be delighted. It may not seem good that children become increasingly able to hide and alter their true feelings as they grow older, but life might be unbearable if adults were as open about their feelings as most young children are!

Display rules and how parents react to and socialize their children's emotions differ from culture to culture (see Friedlmeier, Corapci, & Cole, 2011). For example, parents in individualistic cultures like the United States are more likely than parents in collectivist cultures like China to encourage open expression of emotion; they want their children to assert themselves and feel proud when they do well and even express negative emotions like anger when appropriate. Chinese and other East Asian parents are likely to view such self-centered emotional displays as disruptive to smooth social relationships and to want their children to suppress self-focused emotions like anger. They do more to encourage the expression of other-focused emotions—for example, empathy for someone in distress or shame after letting people down. **Exploration Box 14.1** examines more closely how the philosophies parents have about emotional expression can affect their children's development, and the video in **Exploring Development Box 14.1** profiles a research study of emotional expression by Asian American and nonimmigrant college students.

Adolescent Moods

Ever since the founder of developmental psychology, G. Stanley Hall, characterized adolescence as a time of *storm and stress*, adolescents

Exploring Development 14.1
Culture and Emotion

Watch how researchers explore emotional reactions of first- or second-generation Asian American and nonimmigrant college students.

- Does intensity of emotions differ among these students?
- How is flat affect sometimes interpreted in the United States?

have been viewed as moody and emotionally volatile. When children and adolescents have been asked to report their emotional experiences at random times during the day, adolescents do not appear to be more subject than children are to extreme mood swings, so the storm and stress view of adolescents' emotional lives does not have much support (Larson & Lampman-Petraitis, 1989). However, adolescents do appear to experience mildly negative moods more often than children. Why might this be?

Adolescents experience more negative life events than children do and so may simply have more to be depressed, anxious, or moody about (Larson & Ham, 1993; Schulz & Lazarus, 2011). But another possibility is suggested by an interesting study comparing the emotional experiences of adolescents to those of adults of different ages by Michaela Riediger and her colleagues (Riediger, Schmiedek, Wagner, & Lindenberger, 2009). They called participants ranging in age from 14 to 86 at random times on mobile phones and had them report their emotional experience—specifically, whether they were currently experiencing joyful, contented, interested, angry, nervous, and downhearted feelings. Participants were also asked about their emotion regulation goals—specifically, whether they were trying to enhance, maintain, or dampen their positive or negative emotions.

As ■ **Figure 14.2** shows, the teens showed more "contra-hedonic" behavior than adults: rather than wanting to optimize good moods, they often wanted to maintain or enhance bad moods or dampen good ones. At the other extreme, elderly adults were the most "prohedonic" of all age groups, reporting that they were trying to maintain positive affect and dampen negative affect. As a result, the adolescents had the most mixed emotional lives, and everyday emotional well-being—the difference between positive and negative affect—increased with age from adolescence to old age.

Why did the teens seem to want to be miserable? A closer look revealed that they often reported positive and negative emotions simultaneously and seemed to crave being able to combine the two, as in being afraid at a horror movie while enjoying the scary experience or being mad at a classmate but enjoying plotting revenge. Research also tells us that adolescents may not be as able as adults to regulate negative emotions once they arise (Lougheed & Hollenstein, 2012; Silvers et al., 2012). Teens may have somewhat more negative emotional lives than children or adults, then, because they lead stressful lives, because they have difficulty regulating their emotions at times, or because they actively choose to savor negative or mixed emotions at times, much as they sometimes choose to engage in risk-taking behavior as they attempt to establish their identities and autonomy (Riediger et al., 2009).

Emotions and Aging

What happens to our emotional lives as we age? Many think there is a blunting of both emotional expression and inner emotional experience in old age—that elderly adults do not react to events with as much emotional intensity as younger and middle-aged adults do or do not show as much emotion. Others believe that older adults, because of the losses and health problems that often come with aging, experience more negative emotions than younger adults. It is now clear that both these views are wrong.

In an early study (Malatesta & Kalnok, 1984), young, middle-aged, and older adults were questioned about their emotional experiences and expressions. There was no sign that older adults experienced more negative emotions, that emotions were any less important to them, or that they experienced emotions any less intensely. What's more, their faces were equally expressive when they recalled events that had made them feel various emotions (see also Levenson et al., 1991). We would be making a mistake, then, to assume that most elderly people no longer experience strong emotions or experience mostly negative ones.

As it turns out, the emotional experiences of younger and older adults are far more similar than different—but when they differ, older adults seem to live more positive emotional lives, as the Riediger et al. (2009) study results in Figure 14.2 illustrate. Older adults appear to be quite skilled at emotion regulation—especially at maximizing their positive emotions and minimizing their negative ones (Carstensen et al., 2011; Labouvie-Vief et al., 2007; Magai et al., 2006; Mroczek, 2004). The main exception is this: On occasion, older adults may be overwhelmed by multifaceted negative life events that overtax their resources (Wrzus, Muller, et al., 2013).

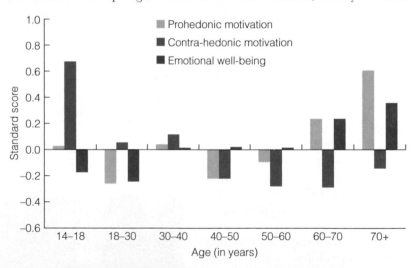

■ **Figure 14.2** Age differences in use of emotion regulation strategies aimed at optimizing positive emotions and minimizing negative ones (prohedonic motivation) versus optimizing negative emotions and minimizing positive ones (contra-hedonic motivation), as well as everyday emotional well-being (balance of positive to negative emotions). Adolescents seem to seek—and experience—lots of negative and mixed emotions, whereas elderly adults have the strongest pro-hedonic motivation and—and indeed experience greater emotional well-being than any other age group.

SOURCE: Riediger, M., Schmiedek, F., Wagner, G. G., & Lindenberger, U. (2009). Seeking pleasure and seeking pain. Differences in prohedonic and contra-hedonic motivation from adolescence to old age, *Psychological Science*, 20(12), 1529–1535, Figure 1, p. 1531.

In an especially ambitious and revealing study, Laura Carstensen and her colleagues (2000, 2011) sampled the emotional experiences of African American and European American adults between age 18 and age 94 by paging them at random times over a 1-week period as they went about their lives and asking them to report their emotional state. They reassessed these people's daily emotional experiences 5 and 10 years later. In this study, younger and older adults differed little in the frequency with which they experienced positive emotions but negative emotions became less frequent with age. As a result, overall emotional well-being—the balance of positive to negative emotions—increased with age, until leveling off in very old age.

Older adults also experienced longer-lasting positive emotions and more fleeting negative moods and fewer emotional ups and downs in a day, suggesting that they are more able than younger adults to savor happy emotions while cutting short the sad and angry ones (see also Kliegel, Jager, & Phillips, 2007). As Carstensen et al. (2011), concluded, "Contrary to the popular view that youth is the 'best time in life,' . . . the peak of emotional life may not occur until well into the 7th decade (p. 29)." Finally, this study revealed that everyday emotional experience may matter: A positive ratio of positive to negative emotional experiences was related to survival over a 13-year period.

Based on these kinds of findings, Carstensen (1992) has put forth **socioemotional selectivity theory** to help explain both the positive emotional lives and the changing social relationships of aging adults (see also Charles & Carstensen, 2007, 2010; Lang & Carstensen, 2002). According to this view, the perception that one has little time left to live prompts aging adults to put less emphasis on the goal of acquiring information for future use and more emphasis on the goal of fulfilling current emotional needs. As a result, older adults narrow their range of social partners to those who bring them emotional pleasure, usually family members and close friends, and let other social relationships fall by the wayside. Whereas younger adults, seeing all kinds of time ahead of them, want the social stimulation and new information that contacts with strangers and acquaintances provide—and are even willing to sacrifice some emotional well-being to have many social contacts—older adults put their emotional well-being first.

Carstensen has discovered that older adults achieve their goal of emotional fulfillment in part through what she calls a **positivity effect**: a tendency for older adults to pay more attention to, better remember, and place more priority on positive information than on negative information (Kennedy, Mather, & Carstensen, 2004; Reed & Carstensen, 2012). The positivity effect could spell trouble if it means ignoring or avoiding important negative information, but older adults seem able to attend to negative information when they really need to (Reed & Carstensen, 2012). Meanwhile, the positivity effect allows older adults to optimize positive emotions and maintain well-being despite some of the challenges associated with aging.

In sum, older adults lead rich and rewarding emotional lives. They are able to experience and express emotions fully but also regulate them effectively to optimize positive feelings and minimize negative ones. Many factors could be involved, but Carstensen's socioemotional selectivity theory and the positivity effect suggest that emphasis on emotional fulfillment goals and a

Contrary to stereotype, elderly adults lead rich and generally positive emotional lives, possibly because they see little time left to them and seek emotional gratification in close relationships.

bias toward positive input contribute to older adults' rich and fulfilling emotional lives. You will encounter socioemotional selectivity theory again (in Section 14.6) as we now turn to the social relationships that have so much to do with our emotional lives.

Checking Mastery

1. What milestone in development must be achieved before an infant will show an emotion like embarrassment?
2. What is an example of an emotional display rule?
3. According to Carstensen's socioemotional selectivity theory, why do older adults typically have good emotional well-being?

Making Connections

1. Based on what we know about the emotional lives of adolescents, argue for and against G. Stanley Hall's view of adolescence as a time of emotional "storm and stress."
2. Much research suggests that good emotion regulation in childhood is associated with good developmental outcomes. Argue that there could be such a thing as too much emotion regulation and illustrate the negative effects it could have.

LEARNING OBJECTIVES:

- Outline the main argument of Bowlby and Ainsworth's attachment theory, with emphasis on the role of nature and nurture in attachment and the mechanism through which early attachments have lasting effects on development.

- Discuss two theorists who claim that peers are more important than parents in development.

Developmental theorists agree that social relationships are critical in human development but they have disagreed about which relationships are most critical. Many noted theorists have argued that no social relationship is more important than the first: the one between parent and child. Sigmund Freud (1930) left no doubt about his opinion: a warm and stable mother–child relationship is essential for normal personality development. His follower Erik Erikson tended to agree, emphasizing the importance of responsive parenting to the development of trust in the parent–infant relationship. These theorists, in turn, influenced the architects of today's most influential theory of close human relationships, attachment theory, to emphasize the lasting significance of the parent–infant relationship. As you will see later, though, other theorists believe that peers are at least as significant as parents in the developmental process.

Attachment Theory

Attachment theory was formulated by British psychiatrist John Bowlby (1969, 1973, 1980, 1988), and it was elaborated on by his colleague Mary Ainsworth, an American developmental psychologist (1989; Ainsworth et al., 1978). The theory was based primarily on **ethology**, the study of the behavior of various species in their natural environments and the evolution of that behavior (Archer, 1992). Attachment theory therefore asked how attachment might have helped our ancestors adapt to their environment. Bowlby also drew on concepts from psychoanalytic theory (he was a therapist trained in psychoanalytic thinking about the contribution of mother–child relationships to psychopathology and studied war orphans separated from their mothers) and cognitive theory (Bowlby called attention to expectations about self and other, as you will see).

According to Bowlby (1969), an **attachment** is a strong affectional tie that binds a person to an intimate companion. It is also a behavioral system through which humans regulate their emotional distress when under threat and achieve security by seeking proximity to another person. For most of us, the first attachment we form, around 6 or 7 months of age, is to a parent. How do we know when baby Alberto becomes attached to his mother? He will try to maintain proximity to her—crying, clinging, approaching, following, doing whatever it takes to maintain the desired closeness to her and expressing his displeasure when he cannot. He will prefer her to other people, reserving his biggest smiles for her and seeking her when he is upset, discomforted, or afraid; she is irreplaceable in his eyes. He will also be confident about exploring his environment as long as he knows that his mother is there to provide the security he needs.

Notice that an infant attached to a parent is rather like an adult "in love" (like Mike or Marcy at the start of the chapter). True, close emotional ties are expressed in different ways, and serve different functions, at different points in the life span. Adults, for example, do not usually feel compelled to follow their mates around the house, and they look to their loved ones for more than comforting hugs and smiles. Nonetheless, there are basic similarities among the infant attached to a caregiver, the child attached to a best friend, and the adolescent or adult attached to a romantic partner. Throughout the life span, the objects of our attachments are special, irreplaceable people to whom we want to be close and from whom we derive a sense of security (Ainsworth, 1989).

Nature, Nurture, and Attachment

Drawing on ethological theory and research, Bowlby argued that both infants and parents are biologically predisposed to form attachments. Ethologists and other evolutionary theorists assume that all species, including humans, are born with behavioral tendencies that have been built into their species over the course of evolution because they have contributed to survival. It makes sense to think, for example, that young birds tended to survive if they stayed close to their mothers so that they could be fed and protected from predators—but that they starved or were gobbled up, and therefore failed to pass their genes to future generations, if they strayed. Thus, chicks, ducks, and goslings may have evolved so that they engage in **imprinting**, an innate form of learning in which the young will follow and become attached to a moving object (usually the mother) during a critical period early in life.

Ethologist Konrad Lorenz demonstrated that goslings would become imprinted to him rather than to their mother if he was the first moving object they encountered during their critical period for imprinting. Human attachment is more complex.

Noted ethologist Konrad Lorenz (1937) observed imprinting in young goslings and found that it is automatic and unlearned, that it occurs only within a critical period shortly after the bird has hatched, and that it is irreversible—once the gosling begins to follow a particular object, whether its mother or Lorenz, it will remain attached to that object. The imprinting response is considered a prime example of a species-specific and largely innate behavior that has evolved because it has survival value. However, subsequent research has shown that it is not quite as automatic and different from other learning as originally claimed, that the "critical" period is more like a "sensitive" period, that imprinting can be reversed, and that imprinting does not happen without the right interplay of biological and environmental factors (Spencer et al., 2009).

What about human infants? Babies may not become imprinted to their mothers, but they certainly form attachments in infancy and follow their love objects around. Bowlby argued that they come equipped with several other behaviors besides proximity seeking that help ensure adults will love them, stay with them, and meet their needs. Among these behaviors are sucking and clinging, smiling and vocalizing (crying, cooing, and babbling), and expressions of negative emotion (fretting and crying).

Moreover, Bowlby argued, just as infants are programmed to respond to their caregivers, adults are biologically programmed to respond to an infant's signals. Just see if you can ignore a baby's cry or fail to smile when a baby grins at you. Adults are even hormonally prepared for caregiving. **Oxytocin** is a hormone produced primarily in the hypothalamus that plays roles in facilitating parent–infant attachment, romance, and other trusting social relationships (Hart, 2008; Schneiderman, Zagoory-Sharon, Leckman, & Feldman, 2012; Taylor, Saphire-Bernstein, & Seeman, 2010). It affects the muscles that facilitate contractions during labor and the release of milk during breastfeeding. Moreover, mothers with high levels of oxytocin before birth engage in higher levels of positive attachment behavior after the birth, think more about their relationships with their infants, and check more often on their infants than mothers with lower levels of the hormone (Feldman et al., 2007). Oxytocin seems to prime parents to form attachments to their babies, then.

Just as the imprinting of goslings occurs during a critical period, human attachments form during what Bowlby viewed as a sensitive period for attachment, the first 3 years of life. But attachments do not form automatically. According to Bowlby, a responsive social environment is critical: an infant's preprogrammed signals to other people may eventually wane if caregivers are unresponsive to them. Ultimately, the security of an attachment relationship depends on both nature and nurture—on the interaction over time between a biologically prepared infant and a biologically prepared caregiver and on the sensitivity of each partner to the other's signals.

Attachment and Later Development

Bowlby maintained that the quality of the early parent–infant attachment has lasting impacts on development, especially on later relationships. He proposed that, based on their interactions with caregivers, infants construct expectations about relationships called **internal working models**—cognitive representations of themselves and other people that guide their processing of social information and behavior in relationships (Bowlby, 1973; see also Bretherton, 1996). Securely attached infants who have received responsive care will form internal working models suggesting that they are lovable and that other people can be trusted to care for them. By contrast, insecurely attached infants subjected to insensitive, neglectful, or abusive care may conclude that they are difficult to love, that other people are unreliable, or both. These insecure infants would be expected to have difficulty participating in close relationships later in life. They may, for example, be wary of getting too close to anyone or become jealous and overly dependent if they do.

In sum, attachment theory, as developed by John Bowlby and elaborated with Mary Ainsworth, claims that:

- the capacity to form attachments is part of our evolutionary heritage
- attachments unfold through an interaction of biological and environmental forces during a sensitive period early in life
- the quality of the attachment between infant and caregiver shapes later development and the quality of later relationships
- internal working models of self and other are the mechanism through which early experience affects later development.

Peers and the Two Worlds of Childhood

A **peer** is a social equal, someone who functions at a similar level of behavioral complexity—often someone of similar age (Lewis & Rosenblum, 1975). Although the parent–infant relationship is undoubtedly important in development, some theorists argue that relationships with peers are at least as significant. In effect, they argue, there are "two social worlds of childhood"—one involving adult–child relationships, the other involving peer relationships—and these two worlds contribute differently to development (Harris, 1998, 2006; Youniss, 1980).

From an evolutionary perspective, it makes sense to think that humans evolved to live as members of groups, just as they evolved to form close one-on-one attachments to parents. And as you saw in Chapter 13, Jean Piaget believed that because peers are equals rather than powerful authority figures, they help children learn that relationships are reciprocal, force them to hone their perspective-taking skills, and contribute to their social cognitive and moral development in ways that parents cannot.

Another theorist who believed in the power of peer relationships, especially friendships, was neo-Freudian theorist Harry Stack Sullivan (1953; see also Buhrmester & Furman, 1986). Sullivan stressed that social needs change as we get older and are gratified through different kinds of social relationships at different ages. The parent–child relationship is central up to about age 6 in providing tender care and nurturance, but then peers become increasingly important. At first children need playmates; then they need acceptance by the peer group; and then around age 9 to age 12 they begin to need intimacy in the form of a close friendship. Sullivan stressed the developmental significance of these **chumships**, or close childhood friendships. Having a close friend or chum not only teaches children to take others' perspectives but validates and supports children and can protect them from the otherwise harmful effects of a poor parent–child relationship or rejection by the larger peer group. Chumships also teach children how to participate in emotionally intimate relationships and pave the way for romantic relationships during adolescence. Research bears Sullivan out, as we will see as we now examine the roles of both parents and peers in our changing social worlds (Bukowski, Motzoi, & Mayer, 2009).

3. Which two theorists argued that peers are at least as important as parents as contributors to development?

► **Checking Mastery**

1. How do ethological theorists explain why imprinting occurs in young goslings?
2. According to attachment theory, what is the mechanism through which early experience affects later social development?

► **Making Connections**

1. Ethological theory, psychoanalytic theory, and cognitive psychology all influenced John Bowlby as he formulated attachment theory. Which elements of attachment theory do you think most reflect each of these three theoretical perspectives, and why?
2. Return to the chapter opener and analyze Marcy's and Mike's thoughts and behavior from the perspective of the Bowlby–Ainsworth attachment theory, using their language.
3. Who do you believe you are attached to currently, and what evidence would you cite that each such relationship is a true attachment?

14.3 The Infant

LEARNING OBJECTIVES:

• Discuss how both the caregiver's attachment and the infant's attachment grow during the first year of life.

• Distinguish among the four types of parent–infant attachments and explain how a parent's behavior, an infant's temperament, and the cultural context can influence which type of attachment develops.

• Summarize the main lessons learned about attachment and later development from studies of infants in deprived institutions, infants separated from parents, infants attending day care, and infants with secure versus insecure attachments.

• Characterize the ability of infants to participate in relationships with peers.

Human infants are social beings from the start, but their social relationships change dramatically once they form close attachments to caregivers and develop the social skills that allow them to coordinate their own activities with those of other infants.

An Attachment Forms

Like any relationship, the parent–infant attachment is reciprocal. Parents become attached to their infants, and infants become attached to their parents.

The Caregiver's Attachment to the Infant

Parents often begin to form emotional attachments to their babies even before they are born. Moreover, parents who have an opportunity for skin-to-skin contact with their babies during the first few hours after birth often feel a special bond forming, although such **bonding** is neither crucial nor sufficient for the development of strong parent–infant attachments (Goldberg, 1983). Not only are newborns cute, but their early reflexive behaviors, such as sucking, rooting, and grasping, help endear them to their parents (Bowlby, 1969). Smiling is an especially important social signal. Although it is initially a reflexive response to almost any stimulus, it is triggered by

Smiling is one of the biologically based behaviors that help ensure adults will fall in love with babies.

voices at 3 weeks of age and by faces at 5 or 6 weeks (Bowlby, 1969; Wolff, 1963).

Babies are also endearing because they are responsive. Over the weeks and months, caregivers and infants develop **synchronized routines** much like dances, in which the partners take turns responding to each other's leads (Stern, 1977; Tronick,

1989). Note the synchrony as this mother plays peekaboo with her infant (Tronick, 1989, p. 112):

> The infant abruptly turns away from his mother as the game reaches its "peak" of intensity and begins to suck on his thumb and stare into space with a dull facial expression. The mother stops playing and sits back watching. . . . After a few seconds the infant turns back to her with an inviting expression. The mother moves closer, smiles, and says in a high-pitched, exaggerated voice, "Oh, now you're back!" He smiles in response and vocalizes. As they finish crowing together, the infant reinserts his thumb and looks away. The mother again waits. [Soon] the infant turns. . . . to her and they greet each other with big smiles.

Synchronized routines are likely to develop when caregivers are sensitive, providing social stimulation when a baby is alert and receptive but not pushing their luck when the infant's message is "Cool it—I need a break from all this stimulation." When parent–infant synchrony can be achieved, it contributes to a secure attachment relationship (Jaffe et al., 2001) as well as to the development of emotion regulation (Feldman, 2007).

The Infant's Attachment to the Caregiver

Infants progress through four phases in forming attachments (Ainsworth, 1973; Bowlby, 1969):

1. *Undiscriminating social responsiveness (birth to 2 or 3 months).* Very young infants are responsive to voices, faces, and other social stimuli, but any human interests them. They do not yet show a clear preference for one person over another.
2. *Discriminating social responsiveness (2 or 3 months to 6 or 7 months).* Infants begin to express preferences for familiar companions. They direct their biggest grins and most enthusiastic babbles toward those companions, although they are still friendly toward strangers.
3. *Active proximity seeking or true attachment (6 or 7 months to about 3 years).* Around 6 or 7 months, infants form their first clear attachments, most often to their mothers. Now an infant will follow her mother, protest when her mother leaves, and greet her mother warmly when she returns. Soon most infants become attached to other people as well—fathers, siblings, grandparents, and regular babysitters (Schaffer & Emerson, 1964).
4. *Goal-corrected partnership (3 years and older).* By about age 3, partly because they have more advanced social cognitive abilities, children can participate in a **goal-corrected partnership**, taking a parent's goals and plans into consideration and adjusting their behavior to achieve the goal of maintaining optimal closeness to the attachment figure—or simply knowing that the parent is available if needed. Thus, a 1-year-old cries and tries to follow when Dad leaves the house to talk to a neighbor, whereas a 4-year-old can understand where Dad is going and wait for his return. This final, goal-corrected partnership phase lasts a lifetime.

Attachment-Related Fears

Infants no sooner experience the pleasures of love than they discover the agonies of fear. One form of fear is **separation anxiety**: once attached to a parent, a baby often becomes wary or fretful when separated from that parent. Separation anxiety normally appears after the first attachment forms, peaks between 14 and 18 months, and gradually becomes less frequent and less intense (Weinraub & Lewis, 1977). Still, even children and adolescents may become homesick and distressed when separated from their parents for a long time (Thurber, 1995).

A second fearful response that often emerges shortly after an infant becomes attached to someone is **stranger anxiety**—a wary or fretful reaction to the approach of an unfamiliar person (Schaffer & Emerson, 1964). Anxious reactions to strangers—often mixed with signs of interest—become common late in the first year and then decline (Sroufe, 1996). **Application Box 14.1** suggests how babysitters and health-care professionals can head off outbreaks of fear and trembling.

Exploratory Behavior

The formation of a strong attachment to a caregiver also facilitates exploratory behavior. Ainsworth and her colleagues (1978) emphasized that an attachment figure serves as a **secure base** for exploration—a point of safety from which an infant can feel free to venture—as well as a **safe haven** to which the infant can return for comfort if frightened. Thus Isabelle, a securely attached infant visiting a neighbor's home with Mom, may be comfortable cruising the living room as long as she can check occasionally to see that Mom is still on the sofa but may freeze and fret and stop exploring if Mom disappears into the bathroom. Isabelle may also beat a quick retreat to the safe haven Mom provides if stressed by the doorbell or some other unexpected event. Secure attachments allow us to explore the world but they also protect us from it when it becomes too scary.

Quality of Attachment

Ainsworth's most important contribution to attachment theory was to devise a way to assess differences in the quality of parent–infant attachments. She and her associates created the **Strange Situation**, a now-famous procedure for measuring the quality of an attachment (Ainsworth et al., 1978). It consists of eight episodes that gradually escalate the amount of stress infants experience as they react to the approach of an adult stranger and two departures and returns of their caregiver. On the basis of an infant's pattern of behavior across the episodes, the quality of his attachment to a parent can be characterized as one of four types, one secure and three insecure (resistant, avoidant, and disorganized–disoriented).

1. **Secure attachment**. About 60–65% of 1-year-olds in our society, and 55% or more in the many other societies that have been studied, are securely attached to their mothers or primary caregivers (Colin, 1996; Howe, 2011). The securely attached infant actively explores the room when alone with his mother because she serves as a secure base. The infant is upset by separation but greets his mother warmly and is quickly comforted by her presence when she returns. The securely attached child is outgoing with a stranger when his mother is present. In the Bowlby–Ainsworth view, the securely attached infant "stays close and continuously monitors [the caregiver's] whereabouts (*proximity maintenance*), retreats to her for comfort if needed (*safe haven*), resists and

Preventing Stranger Anxiety

It is not unusual for 1- or 2-year-olds meeting a new babysitter or being approached by a nurse or doctor at the doctor's office to break into tears. Stranger-wary infants often stare at the stranger for a moment, then turn away, whimper or cry, and seek the comfort of their parents. Occasionally, infants become terrified. Obviously it is in the interests of babysitters, health-care professionals, and other "strangers" to prevent such negative reactions. What might we suggest?

- *Keep familiar companions available.* Stranger anxiety is less likely to occur if an attachment figure is nearby to serve as a secure base and safe haven. In one study, less than one-third of 6- to 12-month-olds were wary of an approaching stranger when they were seated on their mothers' laps, but two-thirds were visibly upset if their mothers were 4 feet away (Morgan & Ricciuti, 1969). A security blanket or beloved stuffed animal can have much the same calming effect as a parent's presence for some infants (Passman, 1977).

- *Arrange for the infant's companions to respond positively to the stranger.* As you have seen, infants about 9 months or older engage in social referencing, using other people's emotional reactions to guide their own responses. Infants are likely to respond favorably to a stranger's approach if their mothers or fathers greet the stranger warmly.

- *Make the setting more "familiar."* Stranger anxiety is less likely to occur in familiar settings than in unfamiliar ones—for example, if the babysitter comes to the child's home rather than if the child is taken to the babysitter's home or some other unfamiliar place (Sroufe, Waters, & Matas, 1974). Yet an unfamiliar environment can become a familiar one if infants are given the time to get used to it. In one study (Sroufe et al., Waters, & Matas, 1974), more than 90% of 10-month-olds became upset if a stranger approached within 1 minute after they had been placed in an unfamiliar room, but only 50% did so when they were given 10 minutes to become used to the room.

- *Be a sensitive, unobtrusive stranger.* Encounters with a stranger go best if the stranger initially keeps her distance and then approaches slowly while smiling, talking, and offering a familiar toy or suggesting a familiar activity (Bretherton, Stolberg, & Kreye, 1981; Sroufe, 1977). It also helps if the stranger, like any sensitive caregiver, takes her cues from the infant (Mangelsdorf, 1992). Babies prefer strangers they can control!

- *Try not to look any stranger than need be.* Finally, infants are most likely to be afraid of people who violate their mental schemas or expectations (Kagan, 1972). Babysitters who favor unusual hairstyles or clothes and health-care professionals who don surgical masks or stethoscopes, beware!

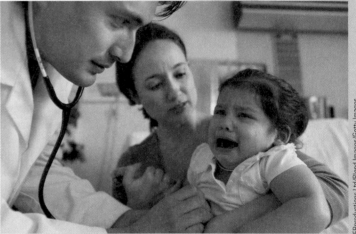
ERproductions Ltd/Blend Images/Getty Images

---

is distressed by separations from her (*separation distress*), and explores happily as long as she is present and attentive (*secure base*)" (Hazan, Campa, & Gur-Yaish, 2006, p. 190).

2. **Resistant attachment**. About 10% of 1-year-olds show a resistant attachment, an insecure attachment characterized by anxious, ambivalent reactions (and also called anxious/ambivalent attachment). The resistant infant does not dare venture off to play even when her mother is present; her mother does not seem to serve as a secure base for exploration. Yet this infant becomes distressed when her mother departs, often showing stronger separation anxiety than the securely attached infant. When her mother returns, the infant is ambivalent: she may try to remain near her but does not calm down; she seems to resent the mother for having left, may resist if she tries to make physical contact, and may even hit and kick her in anger (Ainsworth et al., 1978).

Resistant infants are also wary of strangers, even when their mothers are present. It seems, then, that resistant or ambivalent infants do all they can to get affection and comfort but never quite succeed.

3. **Avoidant attachment**. Infants with avoidant attachments (up to 15% of 1-year-olds) may play alone but are not very adventuresome, show little apparent distress when separated from their mothers, and avoid contact or seem indifferent when their mothers return. These insecurely attached infants are not particularly wary of strangers but sometimes avoid or ignore them, much as these babies avoid or ignore their mothers. In contrast to resistant infants, avoidant infants seem to have shut down their emotions and distanced themselves from their parents, almost as if they were denying their need for affection or had learned not to express their emotional needs.

4. **Disorganized–disoriented attachment**. Ainsworth's work initially focused on secure, resistant, and avoidant attachment styles, but some infants do not develop any of these consistent ways of coping with their need for proximity to their caregiver when they are stressed. They seem confused. Up to 15% of infants—more in high-risk families—display what is now recognized as a fourth attachment classification, one that is associated with later emotional problems (van IJzendoorn, Schuengel, & Bakermans-Kranenburg, 1999).

Reunited with their mothers after a separation, these infants may act dazed and freeze or lie on the floor immobilized—or they may seek contact but then abruptly move away as their mothers approach them, only to seek contact again (Main & Solomon, 1990). Infants with a disorganized–disoriented attachment have not been able to devise a consistent strategy for regulating their negative emotions; they seem frightened of their parent and stuck between approaching and avoiding this frightening figure (Hesse & Main, 2006). She is clearly not a source of comfort for them.

• **Table 14.1** summarizes the features of these four patterns of attachment, which have been the subject of considerable research. What determines which of these attachment patterns will characterize a parent–infant relationship? The caregiver, the infant, and the context all contribute.

The Caregiver's Contributions

According to Freud, infants in the oral stage of psychosexual development become attached to the individual who provides them with oral pleasure, and the attachment bond will be most secure if a mother is relaxed and generous in her feeding practices. Early learning theorists put it differently but also believed that infants learn positive emotional responses to their mother by associating her with food. In a classic study conducted by Harry Harlow and Robert Zimmerman (1959), the psychoanalytic and learning theory views dominant at the time were put to the test—and failed. Monkeys were reared with two surrogate mothers: a wire "mother" and a cloth "mother" wrapped in foam rubber and covered with terrycloth (see the photo on next page). Half the infants were fed by the cloth mother, and the remaining infants were fed by the wire mother. To which mother did these infants become attached? There was no contest: Infants strongly preferred the cuddly cloth mother, regardless of which mother had fed them. Even if their food came from the wire mother, they spent most of their time clinging to the cloth mother, ran to her when they were upset or afraid, and showed every sign of being attached to her.

Harlow's research demonstrated that **contact comfort**, the pleasurable tactile sensations provided by a soft and cuddly "parent," is a more powerful contributor to attachment in monkeys than feeding or hunger reduction. Contact comfort also promotes human attachments (Anisfeld et al., 1990). Moreover, many infants become attached to someone other than the adult who feeds them, and variations in feeding schedules and the age at which infants are weaned have little effect on the quality of infants' attachments (Schaffer & Emerson, 1964).

Styles of parenting strongly influence the infant attachment styles described in Table 14.1, however. Infants who enjoy *secure* attachments to their parents have parents who are sensitive and responsive to their needs and emotional signals, as Bowlby and Ainsworth proposed (Ainsworth et al., 1978; De Wolff & van IJzendoorn, 1997). The importance of sensitive, responsive parenting in creating a secure attachment is one of the best established findings in developmental science.

• **Table 14.1** Child Behaviors in the Strange Situation Associated with Attachment Types and Related Parenting Styles

| Behavior | Type of Attachment | | | |
	Secure	Resistant	Avoidant	Disorganized–Disoriented
Child explores when caregiver is present to provide a secure base for exploration?	Yes, actively	No, clings	Yes, but play is not as constructive as that of secure infant	No
Child responds positively to stranger?	Yes, comfortable if caregiver is present	No, fearful even when caregiver is present	No, often indifferent, as with caregiver	No, confused responses
Child protests when separated from caregiver?	Yes, at least mildly distressed	Yes, extremely upset	No, seemingly unfazed	Sometimes; unpredictable
Child responds positively to caregiver at reunion?	Yes, happy to be reunited, quickly calmed	Yes and no, seeks contact, but resents being left; ambivalent, sometimes angry	No, ignores or avoids caregiver	Confused; may approach or avoid caregiver or do both
Parenting style	Sensitive, responsive	Inconsistent, often unresponsive (e.g., depressed)	Rejecting–unresponsive or intrusive–overly stimulating	Frightened (e.g., overwhelmed) and frightening (e.g., abusive)

The wire and cloth surrogate "mothers" used in Harlow's classic research. This infant monkey has formed an attachment to the cloth mother that provides "contact comfort," even though it must stretch to the wire mother in order to feed.

Finally, a *disorganized–disoriented* style of attachment is evident in as many as 80% of infants who have been physically abused or maltreated (Carlson et al., 1989; and see Baer & Martinez, 2006). It is also common among infants whose mothers are severely depressed or abuse alcohol and drugs (Beckwith, Rozga, & Sigman, 2002). The parents of infants with a disorganized attachment pattern have been described as frightening and frightened—as fearful adults who are not up to the challenge of caring for an infant and create an unpredictable, scary environment for their babies (Hesse & Main, 2006). Infants with a disorganized attachment are understandably confused about whether to approach or avoid a parent who can be loving one minute but angry and abusive or indifferent the next. Each of the four types of attachment, then, reflects a reasonable way of coping with a particular brand of parenting.

The Infant's Contributions

An infant's temperament can also influence quality of attachment. Attachments tend to be insecure when infants are by temperament fearful, irritable, or unresponsive (Beckwith et al., 2002). The caregiver's style of parenting and the infant's temperament can also interact to determine the outcome. To illustrate, ■ **Figure 14.3** shows the percentages of 12-month-olds who tested as securely attached as a function of whether they were difficult-to-read infants born prematurely and whether their mothers were depressed (Poehlmann & Fiese, 2001). Only when a depressed mother was paired with a difficult-to-read, premature infant did the odds of a secure attachment become low (and see Stifter, 2003). A sensitive parent can do a lot to convert a difficult,

Babies who show a *resistant* pattern of attachment often have parents who are inconsistent in their caregiving; they react enthusiastically or indifferently, depending on their moods, and are frequently unresponsive (Isabella, 1993; Isabella & Belsky, 1991). Mothers who are depressed, for example, often have difficulty responding sensitively to their babies' signals and do not provide the comforting that helps babies regulate their negative emotions (Dawson & Ashman, 2000). The infant copes with such unreliable caregiving by trying desperately—through clinging, crying, and other attachment behaviors—to obtain emotional support and comfort, and then becomes sad and resentful when these efforts fail.

The parents of infants with an *avoidant* attachment may deserve to be avoided. Some are rejecting; they are impatient, unresponsive, and resentful when the infant interferes with their plans (Ainsworth, 1979; Isabella, 1993). Some of these parents find an infant's crying extremely aversive and are unresponsive as a result (Mills-Koonce et al., 2007). Others have been called "intrusive"; they are overzealous and provide high levels of stimulation even when their babies become uncomfortably aroused and need a break so that they can regain control of their emotions (Isabella & Belsky, 1991). Infants with an avoidant attachment style may learn to avoid and make few emotional demands on adults who either seem to dislike their company or bombard them with stimulation they cannot handle.

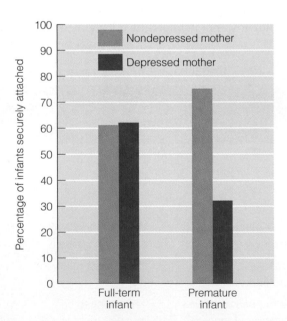

■ **Figure 14.3** The combination of a depressed mother and a premature infant means low odds that a secure attachment will form.

Source: Data from Poehlmann, J. & Fiese, B. H. The interaction of maternal and infant vulnerabilities on developing attachment relationships, *Development and Psychopathology, 13,* 1–11. Copyright © 2001 Guilford. Reprinted by permission from Cambridge University Press.

distressed baby into a baby who has learned to regulate his emotions and is socially competent (Leerkes, Blankson, & O'Brien, 2009).

So who affects the quality of parent–infant attachment more, the parent or the infant? The parent is clearly more influential. We know the infant's temperament is not the main influence on security of attachment because:

- Relationships between infant temperament and quality of attachment are often quite weak (Roisman & Groh, 2011). Apparently difficult infants can become securely attached and easy babies can become insecurely attached.
- Many infants are securely attached to one parent but insecurely attached to the other (Kochanska & Kim, 2013; van IJzendoorn & De Wolff, 1997).
- An infant's genes, although they influence the infant's temperament, have little influence on quality of attachment, which is influenced most by whether a parent is responsive or unresponsive (Fearon et al., 2006; Raby et al., 2012; Roisman & Fraley, 2008).
- Caregivers who are responsive and adjust to their baby's temperamental quirks are able to establish secure relationships even with temperamentally difficult babies (Mangelsdorf et al., 1990).
- Infant temperament seems to be more related to amount of emotional distress infants display during stress tests like the Strange Situation than with whether or not their attachment is secure and reunion with the caregiver is comforting (Raby et al., 2012).

Contextual Contributors

Finally, the broader social context surrounding caregiver and infant can affect how they react to each other. For example, the stresses associated with living in poverty or experiencing marital problems may make it difficult for parents to provide sensitive care and may contribute to insecure attachments (Howes & Markman, 1989; Murray et al., 1996). The cultural context in which caregiver and baby interact also colors their relationship (see Erdman & Ng, 2010). For instance, German parents strongly encourage independence and discourage clingy behavior, fearing that if they are too responsive to cries they will spoil their infants. This may explain why many German infants make few emotional demands on their parents and are often classified as avoidantly attached in the Strange Situation (Grossmann, Grossmann, & Keppler, 2005). By contrast, Japanese babies, who are rarely separated from their mothers early in life and are encouraged to be dependent on their mothers, become highly distressed by separations such as those they must endure in the Strange Situation. As a result, they are more likely than American babies to be classified as resistantly attached (Takahashi, 1990; van IJzendoorn & Sagi, 1999).

Could findings like this mean that research on infant attachment is culturally biased? Fred Rothbaum and his colleagues (Rothbaum & Morelli, 2005; Rothbaum, Weisz et al., 2000) suggest that secure attachment may indeed mean something different in *individualistic cultures* such as Germany, where the primary goal is to become autonomous, and in *collectivist*

Compared with American babies, Japanese infants become more anxious in the Strange Situation because they are rarely separated from their mothers.

© Jose Luis Pelaez, Inc./Corbis

cultures such as Japan, where the goal is to become integrated into the group. Nonetheless, the main predictions of attachment theory—especially the critical importance of parent sensitivity and responsiveness in fostering a secure attachment—are well supported across cultures (see van IJzendoorn & Sagi-Schwartz, 2008). Overall, then, sensitivity and responsiveness of the caregiver (or in many cultures, caregivers) is the primary influence, but characteristics of the baby and the surrounding social environment also affect the quality of the emerging attachment.

Implications of Early Attachment

From Freud on, almost everyone has assumed that the parent–child relationship is critical in human development. Just how important is it? Several lines of research offer answers: studies of socially deprived infants; studies of infants who experience separations from their caregivers, including those who attend day care; and studies of the later development of securely and insecurely attached infants.

Social Deprivation

What happens to infants who never have an opportunity to form an attachment? It is better to have loved and lost than never to have loved at all, say studies of infants who grow up in deprived institutional settings and are never able to form attachments (Leiden Conference, 2012; MacLean, 2003). In the 1990s, children from deprived institutions in Romania were adopted into homes in the United States, the United Kingdom, and Canada after the fall of the Romanian government (Gunnar, Bruce, & Grotevant, 2000). These adoptees reportedly spent their infancies in orphanages with 20–30 children in a room and only one caregiver for every 10–20 children; they spent most of their time rocking in their cribs with little human contact, much less hugs, bouts of play, and synchronous routines (Fisher et al., 1997). How have they turned out?

Infants who spent their first 6 months or more in deprived orphanages displayed a host of negative effects—poor growth, medical problems, brain abnormalities, and delays in physical, cognitive, and social-emotional development (Gunnar et al., 2000; Leiden Conference, 2012; MacLean, 2003; Rutter et al., 2010). They recovered rapidly once they were adopted, and some children overcame their developmental problems entirely, especially if they had sensitive adoptive parents, but others had long-term problems (Judge, 2003; van den Dries et al., 2012).

What of their attachments? High proportions of children in deprived institutions show disorganized attachments to their favorite caregivers and then abnormal patterns of attachment to their adoptive parents after they leave (Bakermans-Kranenburg et al., 2011; Smyke, Dumitrescu, & Zeanah, 2002). Some are diagnosed with **reactive attachment disorder**, a psychiatric diagnosis applied to socially deprived and maltreated children who display either emotionally withdrawn behavior or a disinhibited attachment pattern involving indiscriminate friendliness, lack of normal wariness of strangers, and an inability to sustain give-and-take social interactions (O'Connor et al., 2003; Zeanah, Bertin, & Boris, 2011).

A meta-analysis of many studies of institutionalized and otherwise maltreated and neglected children concluded that those who are adopted before 1 year of age have a good chance of becoming as securely attached to their caregivers as other children, but that high rates of insecure and disturbed attachment are observed in children adopted after their first birthday (van den Dries et al., 2009). Even institutionalized children who are provided with good physical care and sensory and intellectual stimulation but lack a stable team of caregivers are likely to be developmentally delayed and have long-lasting social and emotional difficulties (Hodges & Tizard, 1989). Nor is the problem lack of a single "mother figure." In adequately staffed institutions and communes, infants cared for by a few responsive caregivers turn out fine (Groark et al., 2005; Smyke et al., 2002). Indeed, organizing children in an institution that provides good medical and physical care into small groups with a few, consistent caregivers who interact with the children caringly can prevent most of the negative effects of living in a large residential institution (St. Petersburg–USA Orphanage Research Team, 2008).

Apparently, then, normal development requires sustained interactions with responsive caregivers—whether one or a few. Apparently too, children are resilient, provided that they are given reasonable opportunities to socialize and to find someone to love. However, as Bowlby claimed, early social experiences can sometimes leave lasting marks on development.

Separations

Now consider babies who form an attachment but are separated from their caregivers as a result of illness, war, death, divorce, or other circumstances. Bowlby (1960, 1980) discovered that these infants go through a grieving process in which they first protest and search frantically for their loved one, then become sad and listless once they give up, and sometimes then ignore or avoid their caregiver if she returns, only gradually warming up to her again.

Long-term separation of young children from a parent is an issue for military families when a family member is deployed to a war zone, or deployed and redeployed repeatedly as happened in

For military families, deployment means separation anxiety on the part of all concerned.

the Iraq and Afghanistan wars. This can be a Strange Situation–like stress test not only for children but for their parents, whose attachments to their partners are disrupted and who both face many challenges. Although most families cope well, some infants and children develop emotional and behavioral problems (Maholmes, 2012; Riggs & Riggs, 2011). The most important influence on whether children adapt well is whether the at-home parent can continue providing sensitive and responsive care, which is most likely if she has good social support and is able to maintain good mental health (Posada, Longoria, Cocker, & Lu, 2011). Programs specially designed for military families can help reduce the negative effects of deployment on all concerned (Lester et al., 2012).

What about infants who are permanently separated from a caregiver due to death, divorce, or other reasons? They have adjustment difficulties but normally recover if they have the security of an existing attachment or can form a new one (Bowlby, 1960, 1980; van IJzendoorn & Juffer, 2006; and see Chapter 17). It is children who experience a series of permanent separations from caregivers, as happens to some infants and children moving from foster care placement to foster care placement, that we should worry more about. They may have long-lasting attachment-related problems and psychological disorders as a result of their repeated experiences of loving and losing (Tarren-Sweeney, 2013; Ward, Munro, & Dearden, 2006).

Day Care

What of the daily separations from their parents that infants experience when they are placed in day care centers or in family care homes (in which caregivers take children into their homes)? Day care is unlikely to keep infants from forming or maintaining close relationships with their parents. It can have positive or negative effects, depending on several factors, but it normally does not damage child development (Friedman & Boyle, 2008). This is good news for the more than 60% of mothers in the United States who work outside the home at least part-time.

A major national longitudinal study supported by the National Institute of Child Health and Human Development that tracked infants through adolescence is our best source of evidence (NICHD, 2006; NICHD Early Child Care Research Network [ECCRN], 1997, 2003, 2005, 2006; Vandell, 2010). Overall, infants who experienced routine care by someone other than their mothers were not much different than infants cared for almost exclusively by their mothers in the many aspects of development studied. Most notably for our purposes, infants who received alternative care were no less securely attached to their mothers overall than infants who were tended by their mothers (Friedman & Boyle, 2008; NICHD ECCRN, 1997).

Quality of parenting was a much stronger influence on these infants' attachments and development than whether they had day care experience. Quality of day care, defined in terms of sensitive caregiving and cognitive and language stimulation, also had impacts (Belsky et al., 2007; NICHD ECCRN, 2006; Vandell et al., 2010). And the quality of the home environment interacted with the quality of the day care environment to influence outcomes. Infants fared especially poorly if their mothers were insensitive and unresponsive *and* they were subjected to poor-quality day care on top of it (NICHD ECCRN, 1997). Under these circumstances, about half the infants were insecurely attached to their mothers. Infants fared better if they received quality care either at home or in day care. In sum, infants and young children who spend time in day care are not less securely attached to their parents than infants and young children cared for at home, on average. However, they are most likely to thrive when they interact with both sensitive and stimulating parents and sensitive and stimulating substitute caregivers.

Later Development of Securely and Insecurely Attached Infants

Finally, we can assess the importance of early attachment experiences by asking this: How much difference does having a secure rather than insecure attachment in infancy make later in life? According to Bowlby and Ainsworth's attachment theory, a secure attachment should contribute positively to intellectual, social, and emotional development—and it does. Three main qualities distinguish children who were securely attached infants from those who were insecurely attached:

- *Intellectual curiosity.* Children who were securely attached as infants are described by teachers as more curious, self-directed, and eager to learn than insecurely attached children (Waters, Wippman, & Sroufe, 1979). They have benefitted from having a secure base for exploration.
- *Social competence.* Children who had been securely attached as infants are more able to initiate play activities, more sensitive to the needs and feelings of other children, more popular, and generally more socially competent (Booth-LaForce & Kerns, 2009;

Waters et al., 1979). Their positive interactions with caregivers have allowed them to develop positive internal working models of self and other and social skills.
- *Emotion regulation.* Secure attachment in infancy is linked to positive emotional development, especially the capacity to cope with stress and regulate emotions (Gunnar, 1998; Kochanska, 2001). The comforting and help with emotion regulation securely attached babies receive from their sensitive parents appear to make their stress response systems less reactive to stress than those of children who had insecure attachments, whether resistant or avoidant (Diamond & Fagundes, 2010). Good emotion regulation, as you saw earlier, is in turn associated with fewer emotional and behavioral problems in childhood.

In late childhood and adolescence, children who have enjoyed secure relationships with their parents early in life continue to be well adjusted (Elicker, Englund, & Sroufe, 1992; Simpson et al., 2007). In a revealing longitudinal study, Jeffrey Simpson and his colleagues (2007) studied 78 individuals from infancy to their early 20s. Secure attachment in the Strange Situation at 12 months of age was linked to the quality of a child's peer relations in elementary school, which in turn predicted quality of friendships in adolescence, which in turn predicted the emotional quality of romantic relationships in early adulthood. Although quality of attachment during infancy and quality of romantic relationship in adulthood were not directly linked, they were indirectly associated through a chain of influence in which the quality of relationships in each developmental period affects the quality of relationships in the next period, as shown in ■ Figure 14.4. Similarly, maternal caregiving sensitivity, social competence, and the quality of a best friend relationship at earlier points in life predict a secure style of attachment at age 18 (Fraley et al., 2013).

In sum, children are unlikely to develop normally if they never have the opportunity to form an attachment or if their relationships with adults are repeatedly severed. By contrast, a secure attachment during infancy has many positive implications for later intellectual, social, and emotional development. Yet you must avoid concluding that infants who are securely attached to their mothers are forever blessed—or that infants who are insecurely attached to their mothers are doomed.

First, affectionate ties to fathers (or siblings or grandparents) can compensate for insecure mother–infant relationships (Kochanska & Kim, 2013; Main & Weston, 1981). Second, early

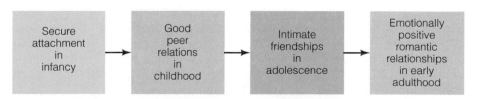

■ **Figure 14.4** Simpson et al. (2007) found that relationship quality at each step in development affects relationship quality at the next step.

Source: From Simpson, J. A., Collins, W. A., Tran, S., & Haydon, K. C. Attachment and the experience and expression of emotions in romantic relationships: A developmental perspective, *Journal of Personality and Social Psychology, 92,* 355–367. Copyright © 2007 American Psychological Association. Reprinted with permission.

attachments may have no long-term consequences if they change later—if stressful life events such as divorce, financial woes, and illness convert sensitive parents into insensitive ones and, in turn, secure attachments into insecure ones, or if positive life changes make parents more sensitive and insecure attachments more secure (Beijersbergen et al., 2012; Weinfield, Sroufe, & Egeland, 2000). As Bowlby appreciated, internal working models are just that: *working* models, subject to revision based on later social experiences (Sroufe et al., 2005).

All things considered, the Bowlby–Ainsworth attachment theory is well supported. Studies of the long-term consequences of early attachment support Bowlby's claim that internal working models formed early in life shape later relationships and development. Still, many of us learn new social skills and different attitudes toward relationships in our later interactions not only with parents but also with peers, friends, lovers, and spouses. It is time, then, to supplement this description of parent–child relations with a look at the "second world of childhood"—the world of peer relations.

First Peer Relations

Evolution seems to have equipped human infants not only with a capacity for forming attachments to caregivers but also with a capacity for establishing social relationships with peers and living in groups (Hay, Caplan, & Nash, 2009; Rubin, Bukowski, & Parker, 2006). Infants show an interest in other babies from an early age and show capacities for sharing, cooperation, and empathy as early as their first year (see Chapter 13).

Infants begin to interact with peers in earnest in about the middle of the first year; by then, infants will often smile or babble at their tiny companions, vocalize, offer toys, and gesture to one another, although many of their friendly gestures go unnoticed and unreciprocated (Hay, Nash, & Pedersen, 1983; Vandell, Wilson, & Buchanan, 1980). During their first year, they may share toys nicely at times but also get into squabbles over them, though they only rarely hit each other (Hay et al., 2009).

By about 18 months, infants are able to engage in simple forms of reciprocal, complementary play with peers (Mueller & Lucas, 1975). They turn rounds of imitation into social games (Howes & Matheson, 1992). They can also adopt and reverse roles in their play. Thus, the toddler who receives a toy may immediately offer a toy in return, or the one who has been the chaser will become the chasee. Toward the end of the second year, infants have become proficient at this kind of turn-taking and reciprocal exchange, especially if they are securely attached to their parents (Fagot, 1997).

Some infants even form special, distinctive relationships with certain preferred playmates—friendships (Hay et al., 2009; Rubin et al., 2006). On Israeli kibbutzim, where children are cared for in groups, Martha Zaslow (1980) discovered that many pairs of infants as young as 1 year became truly attached to each other. Hadara and Rivka, for instance, consistently sought each other as playmates, mourned each other's absence, and disturbed everyone with their loud babbling "conversations" when they were confined to their cribs. Clearly the

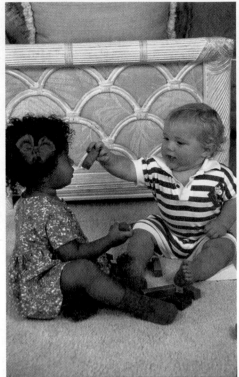
Even at a year of age, infants seem ready to engage in social interactions.

Myrleen Pearson/PhotoEdit

caregiver–infant relationship is not the only important social relationship that develops during infancy; peer relations are well under way, too.

Checking Mastery

1. What are two important developments that result soon after infants form their first attachments?
2. Compare how infants with a resistant attachment and infants with an avoidant attachment react to separations from their caregivers and the reunions that follow.
3. What does research on infants from deprived institutions suggest infants most need in order to develop normally?

Making Connections

1. Some years ago, a 2-year-old named Baby Jessica made news because she was taken suddenly from the parents who thought they had adopted her and awarded by the court to her biological parents because her biological father had not consented to the adoption. What would attachment theory and research on attachment predict about Jessica's reactions and later development? Once you answer, speculate about why Jessica reportedly turned into a happy, well-adjusted child instead (Ingrassia & Springen, 1994).
2. Explain how infants with resistant attachments, avoidant attachments, and disorganized attachments are each trying to regulate their emotions as best they can, given the parenting they receive.

LEARNING OBJECTIVES:

- Describe how parent–child attachments and peer networks change during childhood.

- Explain how play becomes more social, more imaginative, and more rule-governed over the childhood years and what we can conclude about its contributions to development.

- Describe what we learn from sociometric studies of peer acceptance about children who are popular, rejected, or neglected.

- Explain the unique contributions of friendships to child development.

Relationships with parents and peers change from infancy to childhood as children become more involved in play activities and seek acceptance by their peers. These social relationships contribute to development in a variety of ways.

Parent–Child Attachments

Starting at about age 3, Bowlby (1969) believed, the parent–child attachment becomes a *goal-corrected partnership* in which parent and child accommodate to each other's needs and the child becomes a more sensitive partner and grows more independent of the parent. Young preschool children want separations to be predictable and controllable and will negotiate with their parents to make sure that certain rituals such as the reading of a favorite book occur before bedtime or before parents go out for the evening (Mercer, 2006). Children continue to seek attention and approval from their parents, and they rush to their parents for safe haven when they are frightened or hurt. However, they also look more to peers for social and emotional support (Furman & Buhrmester, 1992). The result during the elementary school years is that children continue to perceive their parents as available to them, and turn to them when they really need comfort, but rely on their parents less and their peers more as they get older (Kerns, Tomich, & Kim, 2006).

Peer Networks

From age 2 to age 12, children spend more time with peers and less time with adults; about 10% of social interactions in toddlerhood but 30% of those in middle childhood are with peers (Rubin et al., 2006). This trend was evident in a study by Sharri Ellis and her colleagues (Ellis, Rogoff, & Cromer, 1981) of 436 children playing in their homes and around the neighborhood. In this study, youngsters of all ages spent less time with age-mates (defined as children whose ages were within 1 year of their own) than with children who were more than 1 year older or younger. However, American children spend much of their time in day care, preschool, and school classes in which they are segregated by age. Cross-cultural research tells us that, overall, children in the United States consort more with same-age children and less with different-age children and adults than children in more traditional cultures do.

As shown in ■ **Figure 14.5**, for instance, Barbara Rogoff and her colleagues found that 2- and 3-year-old Efe children in the Democratic Republic of the Congo and Mayan children in

Guatemala spend more time with older children and less with age-mates than children in two U.S. cities do (Rogoff, Morelli, & Chavajay, 2010). Children in traditional cultures are often involved in the day-to-day life of the community and mingle with people of all ages. The implications for development are not entirely clear, but possibly American children miss out on opportunities to learn from older and wiser children and adults because they grow up in a relatively age-segregated world.

American children also live in a gender-segregated world. Ellis and her colleagues (1981) found that even 1- to 2-year-olds in the United States played more often with same-sex companions than with other-sex companions. This gender segregation became increasingly strong with age (see Chapter 12), as it does in most other cultures (Munroe & Romney, 2006). Once in their sex-segregated worlds, boys and girls experience different kinds of social relationships and interactions. For example, there seems

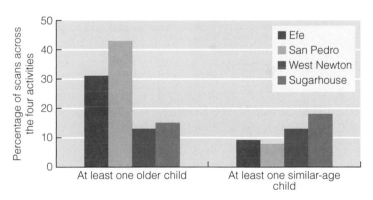

■ **Figure 14.5** Involvement of 2- and 3-year-old children with older children versus similar-age children in four cultural settings: Efe children in a nomadic community of foragers in the Democratic Republic of Congo; Mayan children in San Pedro, Guatemala; and middle-class American children in West Newton, Massachusetts and Sugarhouse, Utah. Children were observed in naturally occurring activities (lessons, work, play, and conversations). Young children interacted less with older children and more with similar-age children in the United States than in the other two cultures, suggesting that American children live in a relatively age-segregated social world.

SOURCE: Rogoff, B., Morelli, G. A., & Chavajay, P. (2010). Children's integration in communities and segregation from people of differing ages, *Perspectives on Psychological Science*, 5, 431–440, Figure 1, p. 435.

to be truth to the saying that boys travel in packs, girls in pairs: boys spend more time than girls in groups (on sports teams, for example), and girls spend more time than boys in dyads (Fabes, Martin, & Hanish, 2003). Overall, then, children in our society spend an increasing amount of time with peers as they get older, typically same-sex children roughly similar in age who enjoy similar, gender-typed activities.

Play

Children spend a lot of time playing and play in a variety of ways (Pellegrini, 2009): through locomotor play (as in games of tag or ball), object play (stacking blocks, making crafts), social play (as in mutual imitation or playing board games), and pretend play (enacting roles). So important is play in the life of the child from age 2 to age 5 that these years are sometimes called *the play years.* This is when children hop about the room shrieking with delight, don capes and go off on dragon hunts, and whip up cakes and cookies made of clay, sand, or air. We can detect two major changes in play between infancy and age 5: it becomes more social, and it becomes more imaginative; for examples of the development of social play between 2 and 5, see the video in **Exploring Development Box 14.2**. After age 5 or so, the exuberant and fanciful play of the preschool years gives way to somewhat more serious, skill-building play (Smith, 2005).

Exploring Development 14.2
Play in Early Childhood

Observe different types of play by children from 2 to 5 years old.

- How does children's play evolve?
- What social relationships do you observe in the last example of play?

Play Becomes More Social

Years ago, Mildred Parten (1932) classified the types of play engaged in by preschool children of different ages. Her six categories of activity, arranged from least to most social, are as follows:

1. *Unoccupied play.* Children stand idly, look around, or engage in apparently aimless activities such as pacing.
2. *Solitary play.* Children play alone, typically with objects, and appear to be highly involved in what they are doing.
3. *Onlooker play.* Children watch others play, taking an active interest in and perhaps even talking to the players but not directly participating.
4. *Parallel play.* Children play next to one another, doing much the same thing, but they interact little (for example, two girls might sit near each other, both drawing pictures, without talking to each other to any extent).
5. *Associative play.* Children interact by swapping materials, conversing, or following each other's

lead, but they are not united by the same goal (for example, the two girls may swap crayons and comment on each other's drawings as they draw).
6. *Cooperative play.* Children join forces to achieve a common goal; they act as a pair or group, dividing their labor and coordinating their activities in a meaningful way (for example, the two girls collaborate to draw a mural for their teacher).

The major message of Parten's study (and of others like it) is that play becomes increasingly social and socially skilled from age 2 to age 5 (Barnes, 1971; Smith, 1978). Unoccupied and onlooker activities are evident at all ages; solitary and parallel play become less frequent with age; and associative and cooperative play, the most social and complex of the types of play, become more frequent with age (see ■ Figure 14.6).

The picture is actually more complex than Parten's work suggests, though (Coplan & Abreau, 2009; Rubin et al., 2011). Older children continue to engage in solitary play, often to build skills. They also often work their way into play groups by first being onlookers and then playing in parallel with the other children before trying to join the ongoing activity (Rubin et al., 2006). Thus, although there is an age trend toward more associative and cooperative play as social skills improve, all of Parten's forms of play can serve useful functions for children young and old depending on the occasion.

Play Becomes More Imaginative

The first **pretend play**—play in which one actor, object, or action symbolizes or stands for another—occurs around age 1, when an infant may raise an empty cup, or perhaps a forbidden treat, to her lips, smile, give a parent a knowing glance, and make loud lip-smacking sounds (Nicolich, 1977). The earliest pretend play is just like this: The infant performs actions that

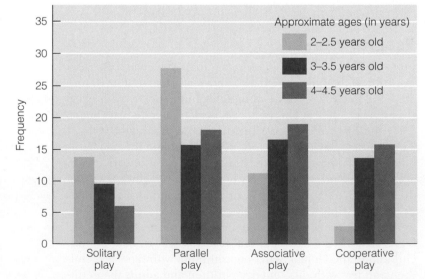

■ **Figure 14.6** Frequency of activities engaged in by preschool children of different ages. With age, solitary and parallel play occur less frequently, whereas associative and cooperative play occur more frequently.

Source: Adapted from Barnes, 1971.

symbolize familiar activities such as eating, sleeping, and washing. By age 2, toddlers readily join in pretense; if you hand them a towel and suggest that they wipe up the imaginary tea you just spilled, they will (Harris & Kavanaugh, 1993)! Because there is no tea in sight, this willingness to clean it up is remarkable. It means that toddlers can use their new symbolic capacity to construct a mental representation of a pretend event and act according to this representation.

Pretend play fully blossoms from age 2 to age 5, increasing in both frequency and sophistication (Howes & Matheson, 1992; Rubin et al., 2006). As children age, they can depict heroes and heroines more different from themselves and can enact their dramas using fewer props. Most important, children combine their capacity for increasingly social play and their capacity for pretense to create **social pretend play**, play in which children cooperate with others to enact dramas (Howes & Matheson, 1992). Social pretend play episodes can become quite sophisticated and require a good deal of social competence, including the theory-of-mind or people-reading skills discussed in Chapter 13 (Doherty, 2009). Consider the following example, in which a 5-year-old (M) wants her partner (E), playing the role of a mother, to leave her babies and come to M's house. The two girls negotiate what will happen next, managing to stay in role and keep in mind the other's role as they do so (Garvey, 1990, p. 137):

M: You come here. The babies are sleeping now and . . . (interrupted).
E: No, they'll cry when I leave 'cause they'll hear the car.
M: Nooo. The car's broken. I have the car.
E: All right, but one baby will have to take care of these little babies.

Although social pretend play is universal, the quality and content of preschoolers' play are influenced by the culture in which they live (Haight et al., 1999). For example, U.S. children like to play superheroes and act out themes of danger and fantasy, whereas Korean children take on family roles and enact everyday activities (Farver & Lee-Shin, 1997). American children also talk a lot about their own actions, reject other children's ideas, and boss others around, whereas Korean children are more prone to focus on their partners' activities, make polite

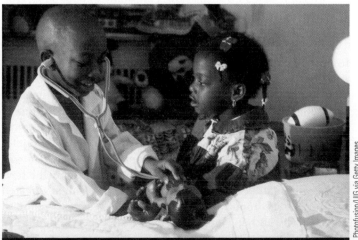

Social pretend play during the preschool years contributes to intellectual, social, and emotional development.

Photofusion/UIG via Getty Images

requests, and agree with one another. Through their play, then, children in the United States (an individualistic culture) learn to assert their identities as individuals, whereas children in Korea (a collectivist culture) learn how to keep their egos and emotions under control to achieve group harmony.

Play Becomes More Rule-Governed

After they enter school, children engage less frequently in pretend play. Now they spend more of their time playing organized games with rules—board and computer games, games of tag or hide-and-seek, organized sports, and so on (Smith, 2005). They also develop individual hobbies, such as building model cars, collecting coins, or making scrapbooks, that help them acquire skills and knowledge.

Although we now know that Jean Piaget (1965) probably underestimated young children and that they are capable of learning, respecting, and even enforcing social norms or rules (Schmidt & Tomasello, 2012), he was probably right that once children reach the stage of concrete operations, around age 6 or 7, they become more capable of cooperating with other children to follow the rules of games. Older children—11- and 12-year-olds who are entering the stage of formal operations—gain a more mature understanding of rules, appreciating that they are arbitrary agreements that can be changed as long as the players agree. Partly because of cognitive advances, then, the play of the school-age child is more organized and rule-governed—and less fanciful—than that of the preschool child.

What Good Is Play?

In 19th-century America, child's play was discouraged because it was viewed as a frivolous waste of time (Athey, 1984). Today's parents who program their children's lives in hopes of molding little Einsteins, like preschool teachers who emphasize learning one's ABCs over playing, may also have lost sight of the importance of play in child development (Bartlett, 2011; Hirsh-Pasek et al., 2009; Singer, Golinkoff, & Hirsh-Pasek, 2006). The fact that playful activity occurs among the young of so many species strongly suggests that play is an evolved behavior that helps the young adapt during childhood and prepare for adulthood (Coplan & Abreau, 2009; Pellegrini, 2009). It is easy to see how girls playing with dolls might be grooming themselves for traditional roles as mothers or how the rough-and-tumble play of boys, like the playful fighting observed in young males of many species, prepares them to compete with other males later in life.

Play allows children to exercise and develop many skills. Leading developmental theorists Jean Piaget and Lev Vygotsky (see Chapter 7) both highlighted the significance of pretend play, although Piaget saw it more as an expression of cognitive development, whereas Vygotsky viewed it as a uniquely important producer of cognitive growth (Lillard et al., 2013). Vygotsky (1978) believed that play was crucial in learning to separate thought from reality (for example, to act on a block as though it were an imagined smart phone rather than a block). He thought play allows children to operate at the high end of their *zone of proximal development* and thus paves the way for new development.

Play is indeed associated with the development of motor, cognitive, language, social, and emotional skills (Coplan & Abreau, 2009; Lillard et al., 2013; Smith, 2005). Physical or locomotor play, from the leg kicking of infants to the soccer playing of children, is associated with neural maturation, increased bone density, and the development of motor skills (Pelligrini, 2009; Smith, 2005). Engaging in lots of pretend play has been linked to better performance on tests of cognitive development, language skills, executive function, and creativity (Fisher, 1992; Lillard et al., 2013). Social pretend play has been linked to children's theory-of-mind development and understanding of others' perspectives, as well as to their social skills and popularity (Connolly & Doyle, 1984; Coplan & Abreau, 2009; Lillard et al., 2013).

Finally, play may contribute to healthy emotional development by providing opportunities to express bothersome feelings, regulate emotions, resolve emotional conflicts, and master challenges (Coplan & Abreau, 2009; Landreth & Homeyer, 1998). If Yoko, for example, has recently been scolded by her mother for drawing on the dining room wall, she may gain control of the situation by scolding her "child" for doing the same thing. And Jackie, an abused 5-year-old, coped with his abuse by having an alligator puppet swallow a small child doll and then smashing the alligator with a mallet and burying it in the sandbox (Landreth & Homeyer, 1998).

But a warning: Angeline Lillard and her colleagues (2013) conducted a careful review of research on pretend play—the type of play many experts view as the most developmentally valuable. They concluded that the scientific evidence is often not solid enough to say that pretend play truly causes positive developmental outcomes; most of the research is correlational or has other weaknesses, and it could be that other factors—for example, how parents interact with and stimulate their children—account for the correlation between engaging in lots of pretend play and being developmentally advanced. Nonetheless, they agree with other experts that young children often learn best when they can do so in self-chosen, hands-on, and playful ways (and see Hirsh-Pasek et al., 2009).

So, although children play because it is fun, not because it sharpens their skills, they can contribute to their own development—or at least exercise the skills they have developed—by playing. And parents can support that development by participating in the social give-and-take of play with their children (Lindsey & Mize, 2000).

Peer Acceptance

Being accepted by peers means having the opportunity to play and interact with other children and in the process to develop normally. Researchers study peer-group acceptance through **sociometric techniques**—methods for determining who is liked and who is disliked in a group (Cillessen, 2009; Cillessen, Schwartz, & Mayeux, 2011). In a sociometric survey, children in a classroom may be asked to nominate several classmates whom they like and several whom they dislike or to rate all their classmates in terms of their desirability or undesirability as companions. It is important to find out both who is liked and who is disliked; this allows children to be classified into the following distinct categories of social status (Coie, Dodge, & Coppotelli, 1982):

1. *Popular.* Well liked by most and rarely disliked.
2. *Rejected.* Rarely liked and often disliked.
3. *Neglected.* Neither liked nor disliked; these children seem to be invisible to their classmates.
4. *Controversial.* Liked by many but also disliked by many.
5. *Average.* In the middle on both the liked and disliked scales.

Influences on Sociometric Status

Why are some children more popular than others, and why are some children rejected by their peers? Popularity or peer acceptance is affected by some personal characteristics that a child can do little to change. For instance, physically attractive children are usually more liked than physically unattractive children, and children who are relatively intelligent tend to be more socially accepted than those who are not (Bellanti, Bierman, & Conduct Problems Prevention Research Group, 2000). Social competence—the successful use of social cognitive skills in initiating social interactions, responding positively to peers, resolving interpersonal conflicts smoothly, and so on—strongly predicts popularity (Coie, Dodge, & Kupersmidt, 1990; Rubin et al., 2006). Finally, well-liked children are able to regulate their emotions well (Graziano, Keane, & Calkins, 2007).

What does it take to be rejected or highly disliked by peers? "Rejected" children are often highly aggressive, although some are socially isolated, submissive children who are overly sensitive to teasing and are seen by others as "easy to push around" (Parkhurst & Asher, 1992; Rubin et al., 2006). Children who fall into the neglected category of sociometric status often have reasonably good social skills; they are usually nonaggressive and tend to be shy and unassertive (Coie et al., 1990). As a result, no one really notices them. Controversial children are interesting: They often have good social skills and leadership qualities, like popular children, but they are also viewed as aggressive bullies, like many rejected children (DeRosier & Thomas, 2003; Miller-Johnson et al., 2003).

To appreciate how social skills contribute to popularity, consider what happens when children try to enter and gain acceptance in play groups (Dodge et al., 1990; Putallaz & Wasserman, 1989). When children who ultimately become popular want to join a group's activity, they first hold back and assess what is going on, then smoothly blend into the group, commenting pleasantly about whatever the other children are discussing and doing as they do. By contrast, children who are eventually rejected by their peers tend to be pushy and disruptive. Jimmy, for example, may sit beside two boys who are playing a computer game and distract them by talking about a TV program he saw the night before. Even worse, he may criticize the way the boys are playing, start pecking computer keys at random, or threaten to turn off the computer if he is not allowed to play. By contrast, children who end up being neglected by their peers often hover around the edges of a group without taking positive steps to initiate contact, and they may shy away from peers who attempt to make contact with them.

In sum, popularity or peer acceptance is affected by many factors. It helps to have an attractive face and cognitive skills, but it is probably more important to behave in socially competent ways and to be able to regulate one's emotions. As you have seen, children who enjoy secure relationships with their parents as infants tend to become popular children because they have learned social and emotion regulation skills that make for positive relationships with peers.

Implications of Peer Acceptance

Do the outcomes of childhood popularity polls matter? Very much so, especially for the 10 to 15% of children who are rejected by their peers (Rubin et al., 2006). Children who are neglected by peers often gain greater acceptance later, maybe because they often have reasonably good social skills (Bierman, 2004; Cillessen et al., 1992). An exception would be extremely socially withdrawn children like Seung Hui Cho, the Virginia Tech killer—children whose social anxiety keeps them from interacting with peers and exposes them to victimization by peers. Such socially withdrawn children are at risk for a variety of negative outcomes (Rubin, Coplan, & Bowker, 2009). Meanwhile, children who are rejected because of aggressive behavior are likely to maintain their rejected status from grade to grade (Bierman, 2004; Cillessen et al., 1992). More significantly, these rejected children may end up even more poorly adjusted as a result of the experience of being rejected. Their self-esteem suffers, they lose opportunities to learn social skills, they develop negative attitudes toward others, they are negatively influenced by the other antisocial children they end up hanging out with, and their academic performance suffers (Coie, 2004; Prinstein et al., 2009; Wentzel, 2003). There is even new evidence that experiencing social rejection is associated with inflammatory processes in the body that potentially can contribute to health problems later in life (Murphy, Slavich, Rohleder, & Miller, 2012).

However, we can take heart from the fact that some students who do poorly in sociometric polls manage to feel good about their social acceptance and end up well adjusted nonetheless, possibly because they develop a niche where they feel they fit in and are accepted (McElhaney, Antonishak, & Allen, 2008). Moreover, children who are neglected or rejected by peers can benefit greatly from social skills training and coaching programs that aim to improve their interaction skills and, in turn, their acceptance by peers (Bierman & Powers, 2009).

Friendships

Being accepted by the wider peer group and having close friends are distinct and serve different functions for children. True, popular children are more likely than unpopular children to have friends, but many unpopular children have at least one reciprocated friendship and many popular children do not. In a study of 7- and 8-year-olds, for example, 39% of children rejected by peers had at least one mutual or reciprocated friendship, whereas 31% of popular children lacked such a friendship (Gest, Graham-Bermann, & Hartup, 2001).

Chumships in late elementary school, said Harry Stack Sullivan, are a training ground for later intimate relationships.

Having at least one friend increases the odds that a child will be happy and socially competent and reduces the odds that a child will be lonely and depressed (Bukowski, Motzoi, & Meyer, 2009; Rubin et al., 2011). This is especially true if the friendships are with peers who are well adjusted and supportive rather than antisocial or depressed (Vaughn et al., 2000; Vitario, Boivin, & Bukowski, 2009). As you learned in Section 14.1, psychoanalytic theorist Harry Stack Sullivan (1953) theorized that having a close friend or chum has many developmental benefits, and research bears him out (Bukowski et al., 2009). Research supports Sullivan's view that chumships teach us how to be emotionally intimate with someone and, as we will see shortly, pave the way for romantic relationships in adolescence. Friends also provide social support and comfort that can help children weather stressful events, from the first day of kindergarten to a divorce (Bukowski et al., 2009; Ladd, 1999). True friendships are true attachments.

Checking Mastery

1. Which two of Parten's six types of play are the most socially complex?
2. What are the two main trends in the development of play over the preschool years?
3. What are three important influences on popularity or sociometric status in childhood?

Making Connections

1. Addi's parents would like to help advance her physical, cognitive, and social development through play activities, but they do not know how to go about it. Give them some ideas of what they can do with a 1-, 4-, and 8-year-old to provide age-appropriate play experiences.
2. Darren's sociometric status is neglected, whereas Alonzo's is rejected. What training program might you design for each boy to help him become more popular and why?

LEARNING OBJECTIVES:

* Describe the significance of attachments to parents and friendships in adolescence.

* Distinguish between cliques and crowds and describe their evolution and functions during adolescence.

* Describe four phases in the development of adolescent romantic relationships and the typical effects of dating on adolescent development.

Although children are already highly involved in peer activities, adolescents spend even more time with peers and less time with parents. The quality of the individual's attachment to parents continues to be highly important throughout adolescence, but peers, including romantic partners, begin to rival or surpass parents as sources of intimacy and support (Furman & Buhrmester, 1992). Moreover, the quality of peer relations changes. Not only do adolescents begin to form boy–girl friendships and go on dates, but they also become more capable of forming deep and intimate attachments.

Attachments to Parents

Just as infants must have a secure base if they are to explore, adolescents need the security, as well as the encouragement to explore, provided by supportive parents to become independent and autonomous individuals (Markiewicz et al., 2006; Scharf, Mayseless, & Kivenson-Baron, 2004). Adolescents may feel conflicted as they seek greater autonomy from their parents yet continue to need their support, but a balance of exploration and attachment is the key to successful development at this age (Allen, 2008). Adolescents who enjoy secure attachment relationships with their parents generally have a stronger sense of identity, higher self-esteem, greater social competence, better emotional adjustment, and fewer behavioral problems than their less securely attached peers (Allen, 2008; Arbona & Power, 2003; Kenny & Rice, 1995).

For many youths in our society, going off to college qualifies as a "naturally occurring Strange Situation"—a potentially stressful separation that activates the attachment system (Kenny, 1987). Students who go home on weekends or talk to Mom or Dad on their cell phones every day during their first semester are engaging in attachment behavior just as surely as the infant who whimpers for his mommy. From an attachment theory perspective, experiencing separation anxiety in this situation is normal and adaptive. Preoccupation with parents typically decreases over the first semester and predicts adjustment problems only when it is extreme and prolonged (Berman & Sperling, 1991). In the end, college students who are securely attached to their parents display better psychological and social adjustment and academic performance during the potentially difficult transition to college than students who are insecurely attached (Larose, Bernier, & Tarabulsy, 2005; Mayseless, Danieli, & Sharabany, 1996).

David Burch/Media Bakery

Going to college is a "Strange Situation" that activates attachment behaviors, such as hugging, phoning, and e-mailing or texting, designed to maintain contact with attachment figures.

Friendships

Friendships change qualitatively with age. They are based largely on (1) enjoyment of common activities in early childhood, (2) mutual loyalty and caring in late childhood, and (3) intimacy and self-disclosure in adolescence (Collins & Madsen, 2006; Rubin et al., 2011). Like children, teenagers form friendships with peers who are similar to themselves in physical characteristics (age and gender, for example), as well as in behavior (for example, academic motivation, hobbies). In this spirit, most high school students choose friends of the same ethnic background (Hamm, 2000; Graham, Taylor, & Ho, 2009). However, adolescents increasingly choose friends whose *psychological* qualities—interests, attitudes, values, and personalities—match their own. In adolescence—and this applies to both males and females and across racial and ethnic groups—friends become like-minded individuals who understand you and whom you can tell anything, people you can trust with your secrets and count on to be there when you need them (Way & Silverman, 2011).

Although same-sex friendships remain important throughout adolescence, teenagers increasingly form close cross-sex friendships too. Ruth Sharabany and her colleagues (Sharabany, Gershoni, & Hofman, 1981), asking 5th- to 11th-graders about their friendships, found that same-sex friendships were emotionally intimate throughout this age range, whereas cross-sex friendships did not attain a high level of emotional intimacy until 11th grade. These findings support Harry Stack Sullivan's view that children learn lessons about intimate attachments in their same-sex chumships that they later apply in their heterosexual relationships (Buhrmester & Furman, 1986). In addition, girls tended to report higher degrees of intimacy in their friendships than boys did, and they achieved emotional intimacy in their cross-sex relationships at earlier ages.

Emotionally intimate friendships seem like a plus, but they can almost become too close sometimes. Girls are more likely than boys to disclose their problems to friends, expecting they will feel better and strengthen their friendships (Rose et al., 2012). In a study of third-, fifth-, seventh-, and ninth-graders followed over a 6-month period, however, Amanda Rose and her colleagues (Rose, Carlson, & Waller, 2007) found that when girlfriends spend a lot of time engaging in **co-rumination**—excessive discussion of personal problems with a friend—they strengthen their friendships but also worsen rather than relieve their symptoms of depression and anxiety (see also Schwartz-Mette & Rose, 2012). This can snowball: Co-rumination increases symptoms of distress, which in turn leads to more co-rumination and in turn more distress. For boys, co-ruminating about problems had a positive effect on friendship without the negative effects of increased depression and anxiety.

Changing Social Networks

Most elementary school children take interest in members of the other sex, talk at length about who likes whom, develop crushes, and in the process prepare themselves for heterosexual relationships (Thorne, 1993). Still, how do boys and girls who live in their own gender-segregated worlds and often seem to hate each other eventually come to date each other?

Some time ago, Dexter Dunphy (1963) offered a plausible account of how peer-group structures change during adolescence to pave the way for dating relationships. His five steps are still helpful today in understanding how peer relations lay the foundation for romantic attachments (see also Brown, 2011; Collins & Madsen, 2006; and Furman & Collins, 2009):

1. In late childhood, boys and girls become members of same-sex **cliques**, or small friendship groups, and have little to do with the other sex.

2. Boy cliques and girl cliques then begin to interact. Just as parents provide a secure base for peer relationships, same-sex cliques provide a secure base for romantic relationships. For an adolescent boy, talking to a girl at the mall with his friends and her friends there is far less threatening than doing so on his own.

3. Around age 11 or 12 and entry into middle school or junior high school, the most popular boys and girls form a heterosexual clique.

4. As less popular teens also form mixed-sex cliques, a new peer-group structure, the **crowd**, completes its evolution. The crowd, a collection of several heterosexual cliques, provides a vehicle for socializing with the other sex through organized social gatherings such as parties. In larger schools, there are likely to be multiple crowds, each with its own distinctive identity and lifestyle. Those adolescents who become members of a mixed-sex clique and a crowd (not all do) have many opportunities to get to know members of the other sex as both friends and romantic partners.

5. More and more couples form and the crowd disintegrates in late high school, having served its purpose of bringing boys and girls together.

Notice that the most popular teens initiate the transition from same-sex cliques to mixed-sex cliques, crowds, and dating. Who are these individuals? In childhood, popular kids have many likable characteristics, but, starting in late childhood and adolescence, it is important to distinguish between **sociometric popularity**, or being liked by many peers, and **perceived popularity**, or being viewed as someone who is popular in the sense of having status, power, and visibility in the peer group (Mayeux, Houser, & Dyches, 2011; Parkhurst & Hopmeyer, 1998). If you conjure up an image of the "popular" kids in high school, you quickly realize that they had lots of power but were not all so well liked.

Teens with high perceived popularity have good social and leadership skills and are often attractive and well dressed, but they also may be aggressive and can do a lot of damage by snubbing, excluding, bullying, and otherwise being mean to others kids. They often excel at **relational aggression**—subtle and indirect aggression that involves gossiping about and ignoring or excluding others, as explored in **Exploration Box 14.2**. Their aggression, both physical and relational, helps them climb the social status ladder and maintain their position there. They then become the ones who establish norms of behavior for everyone else and lead the way toward mixed-sex cliques and dating. As they gain perceived popularity, they often lose sociometric popularity—they become less well liked (Mayeux, Sandstrom, & Cillessen, 2008).

Implication of Crowd Membership

High school crowds not only bring boys and girls together but give adolescents a social identity and a place in the social order. The names may vary, but most schools have their crowds of, for example, elites ("populars"), academics ("brains'), athletes ("jocks"), and deviants ("druggies," "goths," and so on), each consisting of adolescents who are similar in some way (Brown & Dietz, 2009; Brown, Mory, & Kinney, 1994). Everyone in high school seems to recognize these differences: "[The brains] all wear glasses and 'kiss up' to teachers and after school they all tromp uptown to the library" (Brown et al., 1994,

Exploration **14.2**

Relational Aggression

The 2004 film *Mean Girls* painted a vivid picture of the treacherous world of teenage peer relations. The film concerns the tribulations of Cady, a newcomer to North Shore High School who was homeschooled in Africa and has much to learn about her new school's social world. The center of this world is Regina George, the "queen bee" of a clique called the Plastics, described by another girl this way: "And evil takes a human form in Regina George. Don't be fooled, because she may seem like your typical selfish, back-stabbing slut-faced ho-bag, but in reality she's so much more than that." No one escapes the insults, vicious rumors, and betrayals that permeate this society of "mean girls."

Although appreciative of the many positive contributions of peer acceptance and friendship to child and adolescent development, developmentalists also understand that peer relationships have a dark side (Hartup, 2006; Rubin et al., Bukowski, & Parker, 2006). We examined bullying in Chapter 13 but did not focus in on the relational aggression at which Regina George excelled—indirect aggression such as gossiping about and ignoring and excluding others, even presumed friends. Although boys engage in more direct aggression than girls, girls tend to engage in more relational aggression, at least in adolescence (Smith, Rose, & Schwartz-Mette, 2010).

Amanda Rose and her colleagues believe that it will be hard to stamp out relational aggression because it works for girls (though not boys) during adolescence (though not in middle childhood) to enhance their perceived popularity (Rose, Swenson, & Waller, 2004). Worse, it makes boys like them more (Smith et al., 2010). High perceived popularity also predicts more use of relational aggression later on—for both males and females. Thus, adolescents may climb the social ladder by engaging in relational aggression and then discover that they can use their social power and status to engage in even more of it. Moreover, they seem to get away with it without the negative consequences for their own adjustment that befall teens who are overtly aggressive, perhaps because they can seem so nice while doing it (Rose & Swenson, 2009). Meanwhile, the victims of their relational aggression suffer the negative consequences of social rejection.

Is there anything good to be said about relational aggression? It may serve positive functions by helping to hold the peer-group culture together and encouraging adherence to its social norms (Killen, Rutland, & Jampol, 2009). And although being stabbed in the back by someone you thought was your friend is no fun, it is still the case that peer relations, painful though they can be at times, are an essential—and, in the end, mostly positive—force in human development.

p. 128), "The partiers goof off a lot more than the jocks do, but they don't come to school stoned like the burnouts do" (p. 133). Sometimes in large, diverse high schools, racial or ethnic groups function as crowds for minority teens (Brown et al., 2008).

Which crowd or crowds an adolescent belongs to has important implications for her social identity and self-esteem; it is easier to feel good about yourself if you are a "popular" or a "jock" than if you are a "dweeb," a "burnout," or a social isolate (like Seung Hui Cho of Virginia Tech) who does not belong to any crowd (Brown & Lohr, 1987). Indeed, self-perceived crowd membership in high school predicts adjustment in adulthood. In one study (Barber, Eccles, & Stone, 2001), "brains" tended to graduate from college and have high self-esteem at age 24; "basket cases" were more likely than their peers to have seen a psychologist and attempted suicide; "jocks" achieved financial success but shared with "criminals" a tendency to drink too much; and "criminals" were the least well adjusted.

Crowd membership partly reflects personality traits, abilities, and values that existed before the adolescent ever got involved with a particular crowd; teens often select or are selected into the crowds that suit them. However, experiences in a crowd also socialize behavior and shape future development (Burk, van der Vorst, Kerr, & Stattin, 2012; Giordano, 2003). That is, both selection and socialization contribute to similarity among members of the same crowd. Thus, for example, adolescents who drink select friends who drink but then become more similar in their drinking patterns as a result of socializing with each other (Burk et al., 2012). Later in adolescence, as adolescents forge their individual identities and become more resistant to peer influences, crowds and the group identities they provide become less important (Brown, 2011; Monahan, Steinberg, & Cauffman, 2009).

Peer Influence

A common misconception in our society is that peers are a bad influence on adolescents. As it turns out, peers typically do more to foster social learning and positive behavior than to encourage antisocial behavior (Berndt & Murphy, 2002; Rubin et al., 2006). True, much depends on the crowd to which an adolescent belongs: "brains" discourage drug use, for example, while "druggies" encourage it (Sussman et al., 2007). Moreover, at around

MACIEJ NOSKOWSKI/E+/Getty Images

The self-esteem and social identity of adolescents, as well as their development, often hinge on which cliques and crowds they belong to. Conformity in dress and behavior helps adolescents fit in and avoid being excluded.

age 14 or 15 adolescents are especially dependent on their peers and may conform to peers or "go along with the crowd" and take risks that they would not take when alone (Berndt & Murphy, 2002; Gardner & Steinberg, 2005).

However, parents have considerable influence on whether peer influences are good or bad. Getting in trouble by conforming to peers is much less likely among adolescents who have secure attachments to warm and authoritative parents who are neither too lax nor too strict (Brown et al., 1993; Goldstein, Davis-Kean, & Eccles, 2005). These parents are likely to ask where their kids are going and with whom rather than to forbid their teens to see certain friends—a technique that may backfire and increase the odds of contact with deviant peers and delinquent behavior (Keijsers et al., 2012). In sum, the influences of peers and friends on development are usually healthy but can be destructive, depending on what cliques and crowds adolescents belong to, how good their relationships with their parents are, and how much they need the security of peer acceptance.

Dating

As Dunphy's model of change in the structure of the peer network tells us, the transition to dating takes place in the context of the larger peer group (Collins & Laursen, 2004; Rubin et al., 2006). These days, many high school students (and most college students) participate not only in dating relationships but in "hookups," uncommitted sexual encounters between individuals who are not dating or in a romantic relationship with each other (Garcia, Reiber, Massey, & Merriwether, 2012). Although hookups are supposed to have no strings attached, many participants hope that the relationship will evolve into dating and, all things considered, would prefer to be in a romantic relationship. Most adolescents seem to get their wish by the end of high school: About 25% of 12-year-olds, 50% of 15-year-olds, and 70% of 18-year-olds claim that they have been involved in a "special romantic relationship" in the past 18 months (Carver, Joyner, & Udry, 2003).

Dating relationships in early adolescence are more superficial and short lived than dating relationships in later adolescence and emerging adulthood (Brown, Feiring, & Furman, 1999; Connolly & McIsaac, 2011). In B. Bradford Brown's (1999) view, adolescent romantic relationships evolve through the following four phases:

1. *Initiation phase.* In early adolescence, the focus is on the self—specifically, on coming to see oneself as a person capable of relating to potential dating partners in a romantic way. This is a time of crushes, posturing, and awkward beginnings.
2. *Status phase.* In mid-adolescence, peer approval is what counts; having a romantic relationship, and having it with the "right kind" of partner, is important for the status it brings in the larger peer group.
3. *Affection phase.* In late adolescence, the focus is finally on the relationship rather than on self-concept or peer status. Romantic relationships become more personal and caring; they are often set in the context of a mixed-sex clique of friends who provide advice and emotional support.
4. *Bonding phase.* In the transition to early adulthood, the emotional intimacy achieved in the affection phase is coupled with a long-term commitment to create a lasting attachment.

Brown's phases were quite evident in an 8-year longitudinal study of German adolescents who were age 13 at the start of the study (Seiffge-Krenke, 2003). The 13-year-olds who had romantic relationships tended to have relatively low-quality and unstable, although emotionally intense, relationships that lasted an average of only about 3 months. With age, relationships lasted longer (an average of 21 months by age 21) and became more emotionally intimate and supportive. Moreover, having a committed romantic relationship at age 21 was associated with having a positive self-concept at age 13, supportive peer relationships at age 15, and a supportive romantic relationship at age 17 (see also Madsen & Collins, 2011). Parents contributed to romantic success too: Supportive relationships with both mother and father proved to be at least as important as supportive relationships with peers in predicting involvement in a love relationship in early adulthood (see also Connolly & McIsaac, 2011; Furman & Collins, 2009).

How does the development of romantic relationships go for sexual minority youth—gay, lesbian, and bisexual teens, as well as teens who are not yet sure of their sexual orientation or are open to different possibilities? These teens often participate in a variety of relationships: sexual experimentation with both same-sex and other-sex partners, passionate friendships that are about emotional intimacy rather than about sex, and dating and romantic relationships can all be part of the mix (Diamond, Savin-Williams, & Dubé, 1999). Although sexual minority teens, like straight teens, ultimately seek intimate romantic relationships, they face obstacles to finding them and cannot rely on support from the larger, heterosexually oriented peer culture as they try. In fact, they are at risk to be the victims of peer bullying, sexual harassment, and dating violence (Burton et al., 2013; William, Connolly, Pepler, & Craig, 2003). The challenges may be especially great for sexual minority youth in rural areas owing to social isolation and lack of support (Poon & Saewyc, 2009; and see Glover, Galliher, & Lamere, 2009).

How does dating affect development and adjustment? For any teen, dating at an early age may have more negative than positive implications for social and emotional adjustment, either because troubled adolescents start dating early or because early daters get hurt or become involved in problem behavior such as sex, drinking, and drug use before their time (Collins, 2003; Compian, Gowen, & Hayward, 2004; Mendle et al., 2013). Overall, though, dating typically has more positive than negative effects on development and can even compensate for a poor relationship with parents, as Sullivan theorized. Involvement in a steady relationship is good for self-esteem and well-being (although breakups hurt and can trigger depression), and adolescents who date tend to be better adjusted than those who do not (Connolly & McIsaac, 2011; Furman & Collins, 2009). Quality is more important than quantity: a large number of dating partners in adolescence is associated with lower-quality romantic relationships in early adulthood, whereas high-quality dating experience in adolescence is associated with high-quality romantic relationships later on (Madsen & Collins, 2011).

Adolescence is clearly a tremendously important time of change in attachment relationships. As adolescents get older, they look more to peers, both friends and romantic partners, to fulfill some of the attachment needs that parents fulfilled when they were younger—needs for closeness, a secure base for exploration, and a safe haven in times of stress (Markiewicz et al., 2006). Even so, parents, especially mothers, remain a critical source of security and support throughout the adolescent years. Moreover, the quality of the parent–adolescent relationship and the parent's parenting style have a lot to do with the quality of an adolescent's relationships with peers and romantic partners (Brown & Bakken, 2011; Gorrese & Ruggieri, 2012)

Checking Mastery

1. According to Dunphy, what is the difference between a clique and a crowd?
2. Before they are capable of truly caring romantic relationships, what two things do young teens seek from dating

relationships, according to B. Bradford Brown's four phases of dating?

Making Connections

1. Analyze the clique and crowd structure in your high school, where you fit in it, and how you might have been affected by your experience. [Hint: Think hard. Many of us deny that we were part of any particular crowd.]
2. How well does Brown's account of four phases in adolescent dating relationships fit you? Where does your dating history differ, and why might that be?

14.6 The Adult

LEARNING OBJECTIVES:

* Explain how social networks change over the adult years and how socioemotional selectivity theory accounts for this change.

* Characterize romantic relationships in terms of the primary basis for partner choice, the triangular theory of love, and the four adult attachment styles.

* Describe the positive effects on adult development of a secure adult attachment style and of having at least one close friend or confidant.

Relationships with family and friends are no less important during adulthood than they are earlier in life, but they take on different qualities. How do people's social networks change over the adult years and why, and what is the character of their romantic relationships and friendships?

Social Networks

Some years ago, Robert Kahn and Toni Antonucci (1980; and see Antonucci, Birditt, & Akiyama, 2009) proposed that each of us has a **social convoy**, a social network and support system that accompanies us during our life's journey, changing as we go. The social convoy provides social support in the form of aid, affection, and affirmation (validation of our values and goals). An infant's social convoy may consist only of parents. The convoy enlarges over the years as others (relatives, friends, supportive teachers, romantic partners, colleagues, and so on) join it, then typically shrinks after early adulthood and especially in later life (Levitt, Weber, & Guacci, 1993; Wrzus, Hänel, et al., 2013). As new members are added, some members drift away. Others remain in the convoy, but our relationships with them change, as when the infant son thoroughly dependent on his mother becomes the adolescent son clamoring for his independence—and later the middle-aged son on whom his aging mother depends for help when she needs it.

With whom do adults of different ages interact, and how socially active are they? Young adults are busily forming romantic relationships and friendships. The trend toward greater intimacy in cross-gender relationships that began in adolescence continues (Reis et al., 1993), and young women also continue to form closer friendship ties than men do (Antonucci et al., 2009). Because of all their social network building, young adults typically have more friends than middle-aged and older adults do.

As adults have children, take on increasing job responsibilities, and age, their social networks of friends and acquaintances shrink, although their family networks stay about the same size (Antonucci et al., 2009; Fischer et al., 1989; Wrzus, Hänel, et al., 2013). The trend toward smaller social networks with age after early adulthood can be seen in many ethnic groups, but ethnic group differences are also evident. For example, from early adulthood on, African American adults' networks tend to be smaller, to be more dominated by kin, and to involve more frequent contact than those of European Americans (Ajrouch, Antonucci, & Janevic, 2001). Cultural differences are evident too; for example, although their family network sizes are similar, adults in individualistic cultures have larger networks of friends and acquaintances than adults in collectivist cultures do (Wrzus, Hänel, et al., 2013).

Shrinking social networks in later life may be forced in part by chronic illness and disability. Life events and changes in roles also affect network size; for example, getting married or starting a new job increases social network size, the death of a spouse decreases it (Wrzus, Hänel, et al., 2013). But as you saw in Section 14.1, Laura Carstensen's *socioemotional selectivity theory* suggests that older adults actively choose to shrink their social networks to better meet their emotional needs as they realize that little time is left to them. Consistent with socioemotional selectivity theory, older adults narrow their social networks to close family and friends and feel very emotionally close to these intimate companions (Carstensen, 1992; Lang & Carstensen, 1994). Socioemotional selectivity, loss of roles, and failing health may all lead to shrinking social networks shrink with age, then. However, older adults are at least as satisfied as young adults with their relationships (Lansford, Sherman, & Antonucci, 1998) and are less likely to find them emotionally unpleasant (Akiyama et al., 2003; Windsor & Anstey, 2010).

Romantic Relationships

An important developmental task for young adults is to resolve Erikson's issue of intimacy versus isolation by finding a romantic partner and entering into a committed relationship. How do we choose partners, what does love involve, and how do the internal working models of self and others that we form starting in infancy affect our romantic attachments?

Partner Choice

Many models and schemes have been developed to answer the question of how people choose romantic partners (see Regan, 2008; Strong, DeVault, & Cohen, 2011). Filter theories of mate selection or partner choice have envisioned it as a process in which we progress through a series of filters leading us from all possible partners to one partner in particular (see Regan, 2008; Strong et al., 2011). Assuming two people have an opportunity to meet, similarities in physical appearance, race or ethnicity, education, socioeconomic status, religion, and the like serve as the first filters and provides a basis for dating. Then partners may disclose more about themselves and look for similarity in inner qualities such as values, attitudes, beliefs, and personality traits. If they continue to find themselves compatible, their relationship may survive; if not, it may end. There is little agreement, though, on how many such filters there might be. More importantly, mate selection does not appear to unfold in a stagelike manner as filter theories imply (Regan, 2008).

Researchers agree, however, that the greatest influence on mate selection is similarity, or **homogamy** (Finkel et al., 2012; Strong et al., 2011). Once homogamy is assured, people may also look for **complementarity**—for partners who are different from them but who have strengths that compensate for their own weaknesses or otherwise complement their own characteristics. However, the saying "birds of a feather flock together" has far more validity than the saying "opposites attract" when it comes to mate selection. Partner choice works much the same in gay and lesbian relationships as in heterosexual relationships (Diamond & Butterworth, 2009).

According to filter theories, we choose romantic partners mainly on the basis of homogamy or similarity—at first surface similarities such as belonging to the same ethnic group may attract us to someone, but we look for psychological similarities as well.

Some online dating sites use algorithms to match partners for similarity and sometimes complementarity as well based on responses to questionnaires. However, research to date suggests that this kind of mechanical matching can go only so far. Why? It ignores the important fact that relationships grow out of partners' interactions over time, that aspects of personality like emotional stability and agreeableness influence success in relationships, and that it is hard to predict which relationships will turn into lasting "true love" (Finkel et al., 2012).

Love

Philosophers and poets have struggled for centuries to define love, but it is an elusive concept and there are many kinds of it (Berscheid, 2010). The concept of romantic love is not just a Western phenomenon or a modern phenomenon, as some people incorrectly believe (Hatfield & Rapson, 2006); it has been documented in at least 88% of the world's cultures (Jankowiak & Fischer, 1992). Robert Sternberg (1988b, 2006a) gives us a way to think about romantic love with his **triangular theory of love**, which identifies different types of love based on the strength of three components of love. As shown in ■ **Figure 14.7**, the three components are passion, intimacy, and commitment:

- *Passion* involves sexual attraction, romantic feelings, and excitement. A 24-year-old woman in love expressed it well: "I get so excited when I know that I'm going to see him, and then when I do see him, I can't breathe I'm so full of want" (Regan, 2008, p. 142).

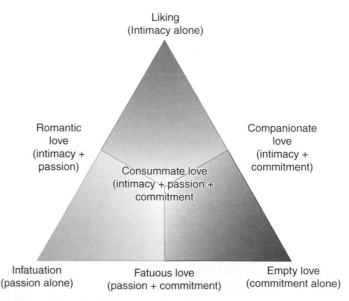

■ **Figure 14.7** The three components of love in Sternberg's triarchic theory of love. Think about each component being high or low and what the resulting quality of a relationship would be. For example, companionate love has high intimacy and commitment but low passion; infatuation has high passion but low intimacy and commitment.

SOURCE: Adapted from Sternberg, R. J. (1988b). Triangulating love. In R. J. Sternberg & M. L. Barnes (Eds.), *The psychology of love*. New Haven, CT: Yale University Press, p. 122.

- *Intimacy* involves feelings of warmth, caring, closeness, trust, and respect in the relationship. It is about emotional togetherness, communication, and happiness.
- *Commitment* involves first deciding that one loves the other person and then committing to a long-term relationship.

Sternberg identified seven types of love that can result depending on whether each of the three dimensions of love is high or low, making the point that love can take a variety of forms. In our culture, couples often experience passion early in a dating relationship and then move on to greater intimacy and finally to commitment as their relationship evolves. In cultures with arranged marriages, commitment may come first, with the parents who arranged the marriage hoping that passion and intimacy will bloom later (Regan, 2008).

If couples are lucky, they will enjoy high levels of passion, intimacy, and commitment—or what is called **consummate love**—all of their days. Passion, that intense feeling of "being in love," may have evolved because it lures partners into relationships that will lead to mating and childbearing (Reis & Aron, 2008). However, it often wanes with time in a relationship, whereas commitment often grows (Ahmetoglu, Swami, & Chamorro-Premuzic, 2010). Thus romantic relationships involving passion in their early stages sometimes evolve into relationships characterized by **companionate love**, friendshiplike, affectionate love defined by high intimacy and commitment but not much passion (Regan, 2008; Reis & Aron, 2008). Sternberg's work suggests that relationships are likely to fare best if two people have similar balances of passion, intimacy, and commitment; it can spell trouble if one partner is passionate or committed and the other is not, for example.

Adult Attachment Styles

Intrigued by parallels between an infant's attachment to a parent figure and a young adult's love for a romantic partner, researchers like Phillip Shaver and his colleagues began studying adult romantic relationships from the perspective of attachment theory (Fraley & Shaver, 2008; Mikulincer & Shaver, 2007; Shaver & Mikulincer, 2012). Many, though not all, love relationships qualify as attachment relationships. The intimacy component of Sternberg's triangular theory of love does suggest a caring attachment between romantic partners, however. And signs of attachment anxiety early in a dating relationship are at least as important as passion or sexual desire in predicting whether a serious relationship will evolve (Eastwick & Finkel, 2008). Like the infant who is attached to a parent, the adult who is in love experiences a strong emotional bond to her partner, wants to be close, takes comfort from the bond, is upset by separations, and finds the partner irreplaceable, as illustrated by the story of star-crossed lovers Mike and Marcy at the start of the chapter.

■ **Figure 14.8** shows how the internal working models that Bowlby theorized we start to construct early in life may affect the quality of romantic relationships (Bartholomew & Horowitz, 1991; Crowell, Fraley, & Shaver, 1999). It describes the four adult attachment styles that result when view of the self is either positive

or negative and view of other people is either positive or negative. These four adult attachment styles can also be described in terms of two dimensions of attachment (Roisman, 2009): anxiety (extent of concern about whether partners will be emotionally available and responsive) and avoidance (extent of discomfort being intimate with and depending on a partner).

Adults with a *secure* working model and adult attachment style feel good about both themselves and others; they are not afraid of entering intimate relationships or of being abandoned once they do. People with a *preoccupied* internal working model have a positive view of other people but feel unlovable. Resembling resistantly attached infants, they crave closeness to others as a means of validating their self-worth, tend to become overly dependent on their partners, and are highly fearful of abandonment; thus, they are high in attachment anxiety but low in avoidance.

Adults with a *dismissing* style of attachment often have a positive view of self but do not trust other people and dismiss the importance of close relationships. Like avoidantly attached infants, they defend themselves against hurt by not expressing their need for love. They downplay the importance of relationships, find it hard to trust or depend upon partners, feel that others want them to be more intimate than they wish to be, and keep partners at a distance. That is, they are low in attachment anxiety but high in avoidance. Bowlby (1973) described dismissing or avoidant individuals as "compulsively self-reliant." Finally, adults with a *fearful* internal working model

MODEL OF SELF		
	POSITIVE	**NEGATIVE**
POSITIVE	**SECURE** *Secure attachment history* Healthy balance of attachment and autonomy; freedom to explore Low anxiety, low avoidance	**PREOCCUPIED** *Resistant attachment history* Desperate for love to feel worthy as a person; worry about abandonment; express anxiety and danger openly High anxiety, low avoidance
NEGATIVE	**DISMISSING** *Avoidant attachment history* Shut out emotions; defend against hurt by avoiding intimacy, dismissing the importance of relationships, and being "compulsively self-reliant" Low anxiety, high avoidance	**FEARFUL** *Disorganized–disoriented attachment history* Need relationships but doubt own worth and fear intimacy; lack a coherent strategy for meeting attachment needs High anxiety, high avoidance

(MODEL OF OTHER along the left axis: POSITIVE / NEGATIVE)

■ **Figure 14.8** Adult attachment styles based on internal working models of self and other people arising from early experiences in relationships. These four types of attachment also differ in terms of attachment anxiety (fear of abandonment) and avoidance (discomfort being intimate and dependent) dimensions (Gallo, Smith, & Ruiz, 2003; Mikulincer & Shaver, 2003).

Source: Adapted with permission from Bartholomew, K., & Horowitz, L. M. Attachment styles among young adults: A test of a four-category model, *Journal of Personality and Social Psychology, 61*, 226–244. Copyright © 1991 American Psychological Association.

Internal Working Models of Attachment

Which of the internal working models of attachment or attachment styles in Figure 14.8—secure, dismissing, preoccupied, or fearful—is expressed in each of the following statements? And which working model best describes you (Bartholomew & Horowitz, 1991, p. 244; adapted from Hazan & Shaver, 1987)?

___ 1. "I want to be completely emotionally intimate with others, but I often find that others are reluctant to get as close as I would like. I am uncomfortable being without close relationships, but I sometimes worry that others don't value me as much as I value them."

___ 2. "I am somewhat uncomfortable getting close to others. I want emotionally close relationships, but I find it difficult to trust others completely or to depend on them. I sometimes worry that I will be hurt if I allow myself to become too close to others."

___ 3. "It is relatively easy for me to become emotionally close to others. I am comfortable depending on others and having others depend on me. I don't worry about being alone or having others not accept me."

___ 4. "I am comfortable without close emotional relationships. It is very important to me to feel independent and self-sufficient, and I prefer not to depend on others or have others depend on me."

Answers: 1. Preoccupied 2. Fearful 3. Secure 4. Dismissing

show both high anxiety and high avoidance, resembling infants with disorganized attachments. They take a dim view of both themselves and other people and display a confusing, unpredictable mix of neediness and fear of closeness.

To give you a sense of how many adults display each attachment style, an analysis of multiple samples of mothers suggests that 58% can be classified as secure, 19% as preoccupied (resistant), and 23% as dismissing (avoidant); 18% were also coded as having an unresolved loss or trauma, which is sometimes associated with a fearful or disorganized–disoriented attachment style (Bakermans-Kranenburg & van IJzendoorn, 2009). Distributions for men were similar. You may wish to see if you can identify the adult attachment styles expressed by the statements in **Engagement Box 14.1**.

In a pioneering study, Cindy Hazan and Phillip Shaver (1987) demonstrated that adults' styles of attachment are related to the quality of their romantic relationships (see also Creasey & Jarvis, 2009). For example, adults with a secure attachment style experience a good deal of trust and many positive emotions in their current love relationships, and their relationships tend to last longer than those of adults with insecure attachment styles. Avoidant lovers fear intimacy, whereas resistant individuals tend to be obsessed with their partners and jealous. When engaged and married partners discuss problems in their relationships, those with a secure attachment style calmly share their feelings and thoughts; avoidant-style adults show physiological signs of shutting down or inhibiting their true feelings; and resistant-style adults become highly emotionally aroused, as indicated by high heart rates (Roisman, 2007; see also Creasey & Jarvis, 2009).

The quality of the parent–child relationship that an adult experienced earlier in life predicts both adult attachment style and romantic relationship quality (Fraley et al., 2013; Grossmann et al., 2002a; Howe, 2011). So, as Bowlby theorized, internal working models of self and other formed on the basis of parent–child interactions are associated with the quality of later relationships.

Adults' attachment styles predict a lot more than romantic relationship quality, though. A secure internal working model provides a secure base for exploration, predicting the extent to which adults have the confidence and curiosity to explore and master their environments (Elliot & Reis, 2003; Mikulincer & Shaver, 2003). Merely thinking about a close relationship can give people the sense of security and energy they need to contemplate adventures like foreign travel (Luke, Sedikides, & Carnelley, 2012). Securely attached adults enjoy their work and are good at it, whereas preoccupied (resistantly attached) adults want approval and grumble about not being valued enough, and dismissing (avoidantly attached) adults bury themselves in their work and do little socializing with coworkers (Hazan & Shaver, 1990).

Internal working models and attachment styles are also related to an adult's capacity for caregiving—most importantly, for being a sensitive and responsive parent (Mikulincer & Shaver, 2003). Mothers and fathers who had secure relations with their parents tend to interact more sensitively with their children and form more secure attachment relationships with them than parents whose early attachments were insecure (Howe, 2011; Roisman & Groh, 2011; van IJzendoorn, 1995). Mothers with a preoccupied style tend to be anxious parents, whereas mothers with a dismissing attachment style seem to derive little pleasure from their babies (Adam, Gunnar, & Tanaka, 2004). Attachment styles can even be transmitted across three generations in a family—from grandparent to parent to child (Benoit & Parker, 1994). They also predict the quality of caregiving adults provide for aging family members (Morse et al., 2011).

Finally, attachment styles are even related to well-being and both physical and mental health in later life (Howe, 2011). Victor Cicirelli (2010) attempted to find out who elderly adults view as attachment figures and would turn to when they need proximity, a secure base, or a safe haven—for example, when they are stressed and need someone to help them relax. Compared to younger adults in other studies, the 60- to 99-year-olds in Cicirelli's study had fewer attachment figures per person but a greater variety of kinds of them. Whereas younger adults often name romantic partners or spouses, parents, friends, and siblings, older adults often named some of these but also often named adult children, deceased loved ones, and God. Based on an adult attachment scale, 50% of the older adults studied were categorized as secure, most of the rest (38%) dismissing-avoidant, and only 12% preoccupied or fearful. The proportion of dismissing attachment styles was especially high (60%) among people who were widowed. Carol Magai and her colleagues (2001; Magai, 2008), who likewise found that most of the European American and African American elderly adults they studied fell in either the dismissing–avoidant or the secure attachment category, also found that adults with either of these two styles were happier than those with preoccupied or fearful styles.

These studies suggest, then, that older adults are less anxious but more avoidant (dismissing) when it comes to relationships than younger adults. Either to cope with the loss of attachment figures or to avoid dependency on others, many older adults seem to become quite self-reliant and independent in their old age and are happy that way. As we will see in Chapter 17, attachment styles also affect how older adults—people of any age for that matter—cope with the loss of an attachment figure (Shaver & Fraley, 2008).

Overall, internal working models and secure, preoccupied, dismissing, and fearful adult attachment styles have significant implications adult development—for quality of romantic relationships, exploratory and mastery behavior at work, parenting and caregiving, and adjustment in later life.

Adult Relationships and Adult Development

As you are learning, adults are better off in many ways when they enjoy close social relationships. Research tells us this: The quality rather than the quantity of an individual's social relationships is most closely related to that person's sense of well-being and life satisfaction (Litwin & Shiovitz-Ezra, 2011; O'Connor, 1995; Pinquart & Sorensen, 2000). Similarly, perceived social support is more important than the social support actually received (Uchino, 2009). Just as people can feel lonely despite being surrounded by other people, or deprived of social support even though they receive a lot of it, they can have restricted social networks and receive little social support yet be quite satisfied.

The size of an adult's social network is not nearly as important as whether it includes at least one **confidant**—a spouse, relative, or friend to whom the individual feels especially attached and with whom thoughts and feelings can be shared (de Jong-Gierveld, 1986; Levitt, 1991). For most married adults, spouses are the most important confidants, and the quality of an adult's marriage is one of the strongest influences on overall satisfaction with life (Fleeson, 2004). Men are particularly dependent on their spouses; women rely more than men on friends, siblings, and children for emotional support (Gurung, Taylor, & Seeman, 2003). Even in very old age, most adults have at least one close friend and are in frequent contact with them (Ueno & Adams, 2006).

Adults benefit not only from having at least one confidant but also from having interactions with others that are rewarding rather than stressful (Krause, 1995). Probably because of their personality traits, people who have positive (or negative) interactions in one relationship tend to have similar experiences in other relationships, creating a constellation of supportive (or stressful) relationships (Krause & Rook, 2003). Relationships with spouses, children, or other significant companions can undermine rather than bolster emotional well-being if they involve mostly negative exchanges (Newsom et al., 2003).

So a small number of close, harmonious, and supportive relationships can improve the quality of an adult's life, whereas negative relationships (or none) can make life unpleasant. It is more than that, however: Social support, especially that provided by close family attachments, has positive effects on the cardiovascular, endocrine, and immune systems; improves the body's ability to cope with stress; and contributes to better physical and cognitive functioning and even a longer life, especially in old age (Cohen & Janicki-Deverts, 2009; Pietromonaco, DeBuse, & Powers, 2013; Uchino, 2009). John Cacioppo concludes that humans have evolved to be with other people and that isolation and loneliness wear the body down, affecting genes, stress hormones, and the brain in ways that speed the aging process and death (Cacioppo & Patrick, 2008; Luo et al., 2012). Special programs can help reduce the loneliness of socially isolated older adults—for example, home visitors who befriend them, senior centers that allow them to meet and form friendships with other elders, and cognitive behavioral treatments to change maladaptive thoughts that make them feel lonely (Aday, Kehoe, & Farney, 2006; Andrews et al., 2003; Masi et al., 2011).

Whatever our ages, our well-being and development hinge considerably on the quality of our ties to our fellow humans—particularly on having a close and gratifying emotional bond with at least one person. It is fitting, then, that we conclude this chapter by illustrating, in **Application Box 14.2**, how attachment theory has been applied to improve our most important relationships.

Gaby Gerster/laif/Redux

Most older adults have at least one close friend or confidant—and it is good they do.

Attachment Therapies

How might attachment theory be applied to help humans develop closer and more developmentally beneficial relationships across the life span? As you have seen, stressed parents who are likely to be insensitive caregivers and infants who have difficult temperaments are at risk for forming insecure attachments. In one study grounded in attachment theory (van den Boom, 1995), low-income mothers in Holland with irritable babies were given a series of three 2-hour training sessions designed to help them recognize, interpret, and respond appropriately to their infants' signals. Trained mothers became more sensitive caregivers, and their infants were more likely than those of mothers who received no training to be able to soothe themselves when upset, to be securely attached at age 1, to remain securely attached at age 3 and to have more positive relationships with peers. Similarly, parents who are depressed can be trained in only a few sessions to be more sensitive caregivers and, as a result, to build more secure attachments with even difficult infants (Berlin, Zeanah, & Lieberman, 2008; Van Doesum et al., 2008; Velderman et al., 2006).

Perhaps most impressively, Kristin Bernard and her colleagues (2012) showed that it is possible to increase secure attachments and decrease disorganized attachments among children ages 1–3 whose parents had been identified by child protective services as at high risk for maltreating them. Disorganized attachments, as you have learned, are very common among abused and neglected infants and young children. The 10-session program these researchers tested emphasized "providing nurturing care when children are distressed, following children's lead and expressing delight when children are not distressed, and not behaving in frightening ways" (Bernard et al., 2012, p. 623). Compared to children whose parents received a control treatment, children in the special program had significantly higher rates of secure attachment (52% vs. 33%) and lower rates of disorganized attachments (32% vs. 57%).

Attachment theory has also inspired therapy for couples experiencing relationship problems. The **emotionally focused therapy** developed by Susan Johnson (2004, 2008; Johnson & Wittenborn, 2012) is a good example. This psychotherapy approach helps partners understand their attachment-related emotions (for example, to appreciate that it is okay to need one another or to be fearful of separation); to communicate their emotions, including painful ones about experiences of betrayal or unresponsiveness; and to collaborate to better meet one another's emotional needs and heal old wounds. Basically, it helps couples either build or rebuild a secure attachment in which there is love, trust, and sensitivity and responsiveness to one another's emotional needs (Johnson, 2012). Multiple studies suggest that emotionally focused therapy is effective (Johnson, 2012). This and other research suggests that insecure and troubled relationships can be converted into secure ones that serve as secure bases for exploration, safe havens in times of stress, and foundations for healthy development across the life span.

▶ Checking Mastery

1. What qualities does a companionate love relationship have, according to Sternberg's triangular theory of love?
2. How would you characterize people with a preoccupied internal working model in terms of their (1) views of self and others and (2) position on the dimensions of attachment anxiety and avoidance?
3. What kinds of relationships contribute most to adult well-being?

▶ Making Connections

1. Laura Carstensen's socioemotional selectivity theory suggests that adults narrow their social networks with age to better meet their emotional needs. Develop some alternative hypotheses about why elderly adults have smaller social networks than young adults.
2. Analyze the internal working models that guide you and your partner in your current (or if you are not in a current relationship, most recent) romantic relationship. What are (were) the implications?

Chapter Summary

14.1 Emotional Development

- Biologically based primary emotions such as anger and fear appear in the first year of life, secondary or self-conscious emotions in the second year after self-awareness is achieved. Attachment figures socialize emotions and help infants regulate their emotions until they can develop better emotion regulation strategies of their own.
- Children gain emotional competence (emotional expression, understanding, and regulation) with age; they come to understand that it is possible to have mixed emotions and they learn to follow display rules for emotion.
- Adolescents have more negative moods than children or adults, sometimes because they seek them.
- Carstensen's socioemotional selectivity theory and the positivity effect suggest that older adults achieve high emotional well-being by emphasizing emotional fulfillment rather than information seeking and positive rather than negative information as time runs short.

14.2 Perspectives on Relationships

- The developmental significance of early parent–child relationships is emphasized in the Bowlby–Ainsworth attachment theory, which argues that attachments are built into the human species, develop through an interaction of nature and nurture during a sensitive period, and affect later development by shaping internal working models of self and other.
- The second world of childhood, the peer world, was believed to be especially important by Jean Piaget, who emphasized the reciprocal nature of relations with peers or equals, and by Harry Stack Sullivan, who emphasized chumships as a source of social support and training ground for later intimate relationships.

14.3 The Infant

- Parents typically become attached to infants before or shortly after birth, and parent and child quickly establish synchronized routines. Infants progress through phases of undiscriminating social responsiveness, discriminating social responsiveness, active proximity seeking, and goal-corrected partnership. The formation of a first attachment around 6 or 7 months is accompanied by separation anxiety and stranger anxiety, as well as by exploration from a secure base and retreat to the safe haven the caregiver provides.
- Research using Mary Ainsworth's Strange Situation classifies the quality of parent–infant attachment as secure, resistant, avoidant, or disorganized–disoriented. Harry Harlow demonstrated that contact comfort is more important than feeding in attachment; secure attachment is associated more with sensitive, responsive parenting than with infant temperament.
- Repeated long-term separations and social deprivation can make it difficult for an infant to form normal attachments, although recovery is evident. Attending day care normally does not disrupt parent–child attachments, although quality of care matters.

Secure attachments contribute to later cognitive, social, and emotional competence, but attachment quality often changes over time, and insecurely attached infants are not doomed to a lifetime of poor relationships.
- Infants are interested in peers and become increasingly able to coordinate their own activity with that of their small companions; by 18 months, they participate in reciprocal complementary play and may form friendships.

14.4 The Child

- From ages 2 to 12, children participate in goal-corrected partnerships with their parents and spend increasing amounts of time with peers, especially same-sex ones, engaging in increasingly social and imaginative play, including social pretend play, and later in rule-governed games and hobbies.
- Physical attractiveness, cognitive ability, social competence, and emotion regulation skills contribute to popular—rather than rejected, neglected, or controversial—sociometric status. Children who are rejected by their peers or who have no friends are especially at risk for future problems.

14.5 The Adolescent

- During adolescence, same-sex, and later cross-sex, friendships increasingly involve emotional intimacy and self-disclosure, and a transition is made from same-sex cliques, to mixed-sex cliques and larger crowds, and finally to dating relationships, which at first meet self-esteem and status needs and later become more truly affectionate and committed.
- Although susceptibility to negative peer pressure peaks around age 14 or 15, peers are more often a positive than a negative force in development, unless poor relationships with parents lead to association with the wrong crowd.

14.6 The Adult

- Adult social networks, except for family networks, shrink with age, possibly in part because of increased socioemotional selectivity.
- Various filters may be involved in partner choice or mate selection and choices are based mainly on homogamy, with complementarity a lesser consideration. According to Sternberg's triangular theory, love involves passion, intimacy, and commitment and different types of love differ in the amounts of each component.
- Adults have secure, preoccupied, dismissing, or fearful internal working models and adult attachment styles that appear to be rooted in their early attachment experiences and that affect their romantic relationships, approaches to work, caregiving skills, and adjustment in old age.
- At least one close confidant and supportive rather than stressful relationships benefit life satisfaction, physical health, cognitive functioning, and even longevity in adulthood.

Checking Mastery Answers

For answers to Checking Mastery questions, please see Appendix B.

Key Terms

primary emotions **434**

self-conscious emotions **435**

social referencing **435**

emotion regulation **436**

emotional competence **436**

display rules for emotion **436**

socioemotional selectivity theory **439**

positivity effect **439**

attachment theory **440**

ethology **440**

attachment **440**

imprinting **440**

oxytocin **441**

internal working model **441**

peer **441**

chumship **441**

bonding **442**

synchronized routines **442**

goal-corrected partnership **443**

separation anxiety **443**

stranger anxiety **443**

secure base **443**

safe haven **443**

strange situation **443**

secure attachment **443**

resistant attachment **444**

avoidant attachment **444**

disorganized–disoriented attachment **445**

contact comfort **445**

reactive attachment disorder **448**

pretend play **452**

social pretend play **453**

sociometric techniques **454**

co-rumination **457**

clique **457**

crowd **457**

sociometric popularity **457**

perceived popularity **457**

relational aggression **457**

social convoy **460**

homogamy **461**

complementarity **461**

triangular theory of love **461**

consummate love **462**

companionate love **462**

confidant **464**

emotionally focused therapy **465**

15 The Family

Listen to the words of Susan Klebold, mother of one of two students who, in 1999, killed 12 students and a teacher and injured 24 more students before taking their own lives in a now-infamous massacre at Columbine High School in Colorado (Klebold, 2009, p. 5):

"I was widely viewed as a perpetrator or at least an accomplice since I was the person who had raised a 'monster.' In one newspaper survey, 83 percent of respondents said that the parents' failure to teach Dylan and Eric proper values played a major part in the Columbine killings. If I turned on the radio, I heard angry voices condemning us for Dylan's actions. Our elected officials stated publicly that bad parenting was the cause of the massacre… I tried to identify a pivotal event in his upbringing that could account for his anger. Had I been too strict? Not strict enough? Had I pushed too hard, or not hard enough?"

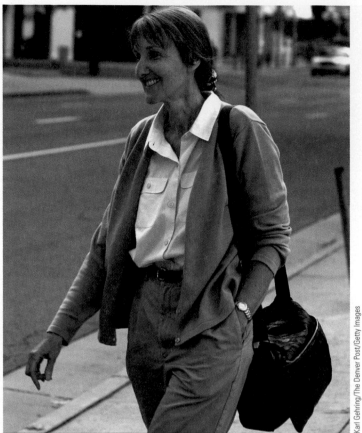

Susan Klebold, mother of Columbine High School shooter Dylan Klebold. Does she look like the producer of a mass murderer?

asked to help around the house, and he and Eric Harris were arrested after they broke into a van, but he was not that different from other teens, was looking into where to attend college, and certainly did not seem deranged. His mother had no idea that Dylan was severely depressed and suicidal and certainly had no idea that he was capable of murder.

Undoubtedly the parents of other mass murderers have experienced anguish similar to Susan Klebold's; we *do* tend to blame parents when their children do horrible things. But are we justified in doing so? One of the big issues we address in this chapter concerns parenting and the extent to which parents influence how children turn out. You will learn that it's more complex than "blame the parent" thinking would suggest. The Klebold family's story also illustrates the important concept, put forward by Glen Elder and his colleagues (Elder & Johnson, 2003; Elder & Shanahan, 2006), that we lead **linked lives**—that our lives and development are intertwined with those of other members of our families. Susan Klebold's life, and that of her husband and other son, were changed forever the day of the Columbine massacre. Despite hours of therapy, she is still in anguish over not seeing her son's problem coming so that she could have helped him and prevented the tragedy of Columbine. It seems, then, that just as parents influence their children, children influence their parents, for good or bad.

This chapter examines the family and its central roles in human development throughout the life span. How should we think about families and how have they changed in recent years? How do infants, children, and adolescents experience family life, and how are they affected by their relationships with parents and siblings and the parenting they receive? How is adult development affected by such family transitions as marrying, becoming a parent, watching children leave the nest, and becoming a grandparent? Finally, what are the implications of the immense diversity that characterizes today's families—and of such decisions as remaining childless or divorcing?

Susan Klebold has lived every mother's nightmare. From her telling, Dylan was an easy toddler who loved origami and Legos and was a gifted elementary school student. In adolescence, he lost interest in school and became quiet and a little resistant when

15.1 Understanding the Family

LEARNING OBJECTIVES:

- Discuss the concept of the family as a changing system within a changing world, using the concepts of family systems theory, Bronfenbrenner's bioecological model, and the family life cycle to do so.

- Describe some of the major changes in the family since the 1950s and evaluate which are most positive and most negative.

The family is a system—and a system within other systems. It is also a changing system—and a changing system in a changing world. We invite you to see how much you know about American family life by making the estimates called for in **Engagement Box 15.1** before reading on.

The Family as a System within Systems

Debate rages in the United States today about whether marriage, the basis for most families, must be between a husband and wife or can be between two men or two women. This controversy

illustrates that it may not be possible to define *family* in a way that applies across all cultures and eras; many forms of family life have worked and continue to work for humans (Coontz, 2000; Leeder, 2004). However we define it, proponents of **family systems theory** conceptualize a family as a system. This means that the family, like the human body, is truly a whole consisting of interrelated parts, each of which affects and is affected by every other part, and each of which contributes to the functioning of the whole (Bornstein & Sawyer, 2006; Bowen, 1978). Moreover, the family is a dynamic system—a self-organizing system that adapts itself to changes in its members and to changes in its environment (Maccoby, 2007). In the past, developmentalists did

Do You Know Today's American Family?

The family has changed dramatically over the past century: Do you have a good feel for characteristics of American family life today? Fill in the blanks below with a number you would guess is close to the correct percentage and then compare your answers with the statistics in A Changing System in a Changing World, on pages 472–473. Read that section a bit more closely if your guesses are wildly different from the real percentages.

_____ 1. What percentage of adults can be expected to marry at some point in their lives?

_____ 2. What percentage of births are now to unmarried rather than married women?

_____ 3. What percentage of women with children younger than age 6 work outside the home?

_____ 4. What percentage of newly married couples can expect to divorce?

_____ 5. What percentage of children live with two parents (whether biological, adoptive, or stepparents)?

_____ 6. What percentage of women age 65 and older live alone?

---

not adopt this family systems perspective. They typically focused almost entirely on the mother–child relationship, assuming that the only process of interest within the family was the mother's influence on the child's development.

The traditional **nuclear family** consists of father, mother, and at least one child. Some scholars think it makes more sense to talk of the "immediate family" consisting of children and whoever cares for them to embrace single-parent families, gay and lesbian families, and so on (McGoldrick, Carter, & Garcia Preto, 2011). In any case, even a simple man, woman, and infant "family system" can be complex. An infant interacting with her mother is already involved in a process of reciprocal influence: The baby's smile is greeted by a smile from Mom, and Mom's smile is reciprocated by the infant's grin. However, the presence of both parents means that we must consider husband–wife, mother–infant, and father–infant relationships (Belsky, 1981). Every individual and every relationship within the family affects every other individual and relationship through reciprocal influence.

Now think about how complex the family system becomes if we add another child (or two or six) to it. We must then understand the husband–wife relationship, the relationships between each parent and each of their children, and the relationships between siblings. The family now becomes a system with subsystems—in this case, marital, parent–child, and sibling subsystems (Parke & Buriel, 2006). In addition, researchers have identified another subsystem, **coparenting**, or the ways in which two parents coordinate their parenting and function well (or poorly) as a team in relation to their children (McHale & Lindahl, 2011; McHale et al., 2002). Do they talk to each other about the children, are they consistent in the rules they set, do they back one another up—or do they contradict one another, compete for their children's affection, and undermine each other's parenting? Mutually supportive coparenting can make a big difference in child development, beyond the impact of a close marital relationship.

Now consider the complexity of an **extended family household**, in which parents and their children live with other kin—some combination of grandparents, siblings, aunts, uncles, nieces, and nephews. Extended family households are common in many cultures (Ruggles, 1994). Indeed, it has been suggested that humans evolved to involve the whole "village," or at least many members of the extended family rather than just a mother and father, in raising children (Hrdy, 2005). In the United States, African Americans, Hispanic Americans, and other ethnic minorities tend to place more emphasis on extended family bonds than European Americans do (Parke & Buriel, 2006). For example, African American single mothers often obtain needed help with child care and social support by living with their mothers (Burton, 1990; Oberlander, Black, & Starr, 2007). Even when members of the extended family live in their own households, they often interact frequently and share responsibility for raising children, often to the benefit of the children.

The family is also a *system within other systems*; whether it is of the nuclear or the extended type, it does not exist in a vacuum. Urie Bronfenbrenner's *bioecological model*, a systems theory introduced in Chapter 2, emphasizes nicely that the family is a system that is embedded in and interacts with larger social systems such as a neighborhood, a community, a subculture, and a broader culture (Bronfenbrenner & Morris, 2006). The family experience in our culture is different from that in cultures where new brides become underlings in the households of their mothers-in-law or where men can have several wives (Strong, DeVault, & Cohen, 2011). There is an almost infinite variety of family forms and family contexts in the world and so a wide range of developmental experiences within the family.

The Family as a Changing System

It would be difficult enough to study the family as a system if it kept the same members and continued to perform the same activities for as long as it existed. However, family membership changes as new children are born and as grown children leave the nest, as parents separate or die. Moreover, each family member is a developing individual, and the relationships between husband and wife, parent and child, and sibling and sibling change in systematic ways over the years. Changes in family membership and changes in any person or relationship within the family affect the dynamics of the whole system.

The earliest theories of family development featured the concept of a **family life cycle**—a sequence of changes in family composition, roles, relationships, and developmental tasks from the time people marry until they die (Duvall, 1977; Hill & Rodgers, 1964). Family theorist Evelyn Duvall (1977), for example, outlined eight stages of the family life cycle, from the married couple without children through the family with children to the aging family, as shown in ● **Table 15.1**. Each stage has a particular set of family members, and family members play distinctive roles—husband, wife, daughter, and so on. They also carry out distinctive developmental tasks—for example, establishing a satisfying relationship in the newlywed phase, adjusting to the demands of new parenthood in the childbearing phase, and adapting to the departure of children in the "launching" phase.

In this chapter, we look at some of these common family transitions, but you will see that an increasing number of people do not experience this traditional family life cycle. Many adults enter into romantic relationships but remain single or childless, marry multiple times, or otherwise follow a different path than the one in which a man and woman form a nuclear family, raise children, and grow old together (Cherlin, 2009; Patterson & Hastings, 2007). As a result, many family researchers today find fault with early models of the family life cycle like Duvall's. They have embraced Duvall's concept that family systems, like the individuals in them, develop and change over the life span. However, they are expanding on the traditional family life cycle concept to describe the tremendous variety in family life cycle experiences today (see, for example, McGoldrick, Carter, & Garcia Preto, 2011).

A Changing System in a Changing World

Not only is the family a system embedded within systems, and not only is it a developing system, but the world in which it is embedded is ever changing. Since the 1950s, several dramatic social changes have altered the makeup of the typical family and the quality of family experience. Here are some of the trends in the United States (see Cherlin, 2009; Federal Interagency Forum on Child and Family Statistics, 2012; Silverstein & Giarrusso, 2010; Wilmoth & Longino, 2006):

1. *More single adults.* More adults are living as singles (never-married, divorced, and widowed adults) today than in the past. The "never married" portion of the U.S. population has grown to 28% (Cohn et al., 2011). Often single adults are living with a partner or a partner and children but are unmarried. The percentage of the population that is married at any given time has been dropping, especially among lower-income and less educated adults, and is down to only 51% of the adult population (Cohn et al., 2011).

2. *More postponed marriages.* Do not conclude that marriage is completely out of style, though; almost 90% of adults can still be expected to marry at some time in their lives (Cherlin, 2009). It is just that marriage is being postponed in the late 20th and early 21st centuries—a worldwide trend. In 1960, the average age at first marriage was 20 for women and 23 for men; by 2011, it was 26 for women and 29 for men (Cohn et al., 2011).

3. *More unmarried parents.* With marriage being postponed, more and more females, especially less educated ones, are giving birth without being married to their child's father. About 18% of births in 1980 but a whopping 41% of births in 2010 were to unmarried women (Federal Interagency Forum on Child and Family Statistics, 2012). About half of these women are living with the fathers of their children, but many others are parenting children single-handedly (Kennedy & Bumpass, 2008).

4. *Fewer children.* Today's adults are also having fewer children than women in the mid-20th century did and therefore spend fewer years of their lives raising children. Increasing numbers of young women are also remaining childless: The percentage has climbed from 10% in the 1970s to almost 20% (Livingston & Cohn, 2010).

5. *More working mothers.* In 1950, 12% of married women with children younger than 6 years worked outside the home; by 2011 the figure had climbed to about 64%, a

● **Table 15.1** Stages of the Family Life Cycle

Stage	Available Roles
1. Married couple without children	Wife Husband
2. Childbearing family (oldest child from birth to 30 months)	Wife–mother Husband–father Infant daughter or son
3. Family with preschool children (oldest child from 30 months to 6 years)	Wife–mother Husband–father Daughter–sister Son–brother
4. Family with school-age children (oldest child up to 12 years)	Wife–mother Husband–father Daughter–sister Son–brother
5. Family with teenagers (oldest child from 13 to 20 years)	Wife–mother Husband–father Daughter–sister Son–brother
6. Family launching young adults (First child gone to last child gone)	Wife–mother–grandmother Husband–father–grandfather Daughter–sister–aunt Son–brother–uncle
7. Family without children (empty nest to retirement)	Wife–mother–grandmother Husband–father–grandfather
8. Aging family (retirement to death)	Wife–mother–grandmother Husband–father–grandfather Widow or widower

Source: Adapted from Duvall, 1977.

truly remarkable social change (Bureau of Labor Statistics, 2012). Over 70% of all mothers of children under age 18 are in the labor force.

6. *More divorce.* The divorce rate increased substantially over the 20th century. Between 40% and 50% of newly married couples can expect to divorce (Cherlin, 2010), and up to half of children can expect to experience a divorce at some point in their development (Lansford, 2009).

7. *More single-parent families.* Because of more births to unmarried women and more divorce, more children live in single-parent families. In 1960, only 9% of children lived with one parent, usually a widowed one (Whitehead & Popenoe, 2003). In 2012, 69% of children younger than 18 years lived with two parents, 23% lived with their mothers only, and the rest lived with fathers only or with grandparents or other nonparents (Federal Interagency Forum on Child and Family Statistics, 2012; and see ■ **Figure 15.1**).

8. *More children living in poverty.* The larger number of single-parent families has increased the proportion of children living in poverty. About 22% of children in the United States live in poverty today (Federal Interagency Forum on Child and Family Statistics, 2012). Those affected are disproportionately children under 6, children in female-headed homes (where 47% are poor), and minority children.

9. *More remarriages.* As more married couples have divorced, more adults have been remarrying. Often they form new, **reconstituted families**, also called blended families, that include at least a parent, a stepparent, and a child; sometimes they blend multiple children from two families into a new family.

10. *More years without children.* Because modern couples are compressing their childbearing into a shorter time span, because some divorced adults do not remarry, and mainly

because people are living longer, adults today spend more of their later years as couples—or, especially if they are women, as single adults—without children in their homes. Men 65 and over are more likely than women 65 and over to live with spouses (72% vs. 42%); meanwhile, older women are more likely than older men to live alone (37% vs. 19%), largely because more women are widowed (Federal Interagency Forum on Aging Related Statistics, 2012).

11. *More multigenerational families.* As a result of these same trends, three- and even four-generation families became more common over the 20th century. More children today than in the past know their grandparents and even their great-grandparents, parent–child and grandparent–child relationships are lasting longer, and multigenerational bonds are becoming more important (Bengtson, 2001). Usually the different generations of a family do not live together. However, the economic woes of the early 21st century have forced an increasing number of Americans to live in multigenerational households out of economic necessity (St. George, 2010).

12. *Fewer caregivers for aging adults.* Smaller families with fewer children, increases in the numbers of adults living alone, increased longevity, increased geographic mobility, and the large Baby Boom generation now entering old age mean that more and more aging adults need care from relatives but have fewer children to provide it, some of whom (stepchildren?) may not feel much obligation to provide it (Brody, 2004; Silverstein & Giarrusso, 2010).

Clearly, many incredibly significant changes in the family have been occurring. Some observers view these changes as evidence of a "decline of the family." They emphasize the often negative effects on children of increased births to unmarried parents, divorce, single-parent families, and poverty, and the problem of more elderly adults having fewer children to support them. Some observers also worry because most Americans now view marriage as an institution whose purpose is more to meet the emotional needs of adults than to nurture children (Cohn et al., 2011; Whitehead & Popenoe, 2003).

Family scholar Andrew Cherlin (2009) adds that American children today experience a dizzying "merry-go-round" of changes as their parents switch from one partner to another and from singlehood to cohabitation or marriage and back. He argues that Americans very much want to be married but also want the freedom to end relationships that are not fulfilling enough. The instability in family life that results from these conflicting desires, he feels, is not good for child development. It means that more children are not living with both of their parents, that more parents are not living with their children, and that "the family" is harder to find these days because it is not all living under one roof any more (Cherlin, 2010).

Can you see any positives in this list of trends in life family? Some scholars can (Connidis, 2010; White & Rogers, 2000). For example, postponing marriage improves its chances of success because partners are more mature and financially stable, men's and women's roles in the family are more equal than they used

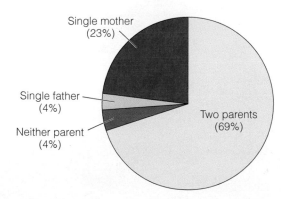

■ **Figure 15.1** Percentage of children from birth to age 17 in various living arrangements. In all, 31% of children today do not live with two parents; 23% live with their mother, 4% with their father, and 4% with someone else, most often grandparents.

Source: Data from Federal Interagency Forum on Child and Family Statistics. (2012). *America's children: Key national indicators of well-being, 2012.* Washington, DC: U.S. Government Printing Office. Available at: http://childstats.gov.

to be, and families are better off financially with two wage earners than with only one. Moreover, more children have relationships with their grandparents and great-grandparents. From this perspective, the family is not dying; it is just different. It can even be characterized as a highly "adaptable institution" in that it has survived despite many social changes that could have done it in (Amato et al., 2003).

Whether it is in decline or not, the American family is more diverse than ever before. Our stereotyped image of the family—the nuclear family with a married couple consisting of a breadwinner–husband/father, a full-time housewife/mother, plus children—has become just that: a stereotype. Clearly, we must broaden our image of the family to include the many dual-career, single-parent, reconstituted, childless, and other types of families that exist today. We must also avoid assuming that families that do not fit the stereotypical family pattern are deficient.

Checking Mastery

1. According to Duvall, what changes in a family as it moves through the phases of the family life cycle?
2. What are three changes over the 20th century that have resulted in fewer children living their childhoods in a stereotypical nuclear family with a married breadwinner father and homemaker mother?

Making Connections

1. What does it really mean to be a family? Bearing in mind the diversity of families today, offer a definition of "family" and justify it.
2. In what ways are your family's experiences traditional and in what ways are they modern and reflective of the trends in family life over the past few decades?

15.2 The Infant

LEARNING OBJECTIVES:

- Compare and contrast the traditional roles of mothers and fathers in childrearing and describe how these roles have been changing.
- Define and give an example of good coparenting and of a positive indirect effect of one parent on the other parent's interaction with their infant.

We begin this look at family development by exploring relationships between parenting and the child's development in the family from infancy to adolescence. Later, we will adopt the perspective of this child's parents and see how the family life cycle looks to them. The main caregiving role for parents of infants is to nurture them and form secure attachments with them. We can see clearly that the family consisting of mother, father, and infant is a system.

Mother–Infant and Father–Infant Relationships

Once developmentalists took seriously the idea that the family is a system, they discovered the existence of fathers and began to look more carefully at how both mothers and fathers interact with their children. Gender stereotypes would suggest that fathers are not cut out to care for infants and young children; however, the evidence says they are (Lamb, 2013; Lamb & Tamis-Lemonda, 2004; Parke, 1996). Researchers repeatedly find that fathers and mothers are more similar than different in the ways they interact with infants and young children. For example, fathers prove to be no less able than mothers to feed their babies effectively (Parke & Sawin, 1976). And fathers, like mothers, provide sensitive parenting, become objects of attachment, and serve as secure bases for their infants' explorations (Cox et al., 1992; Schoppe-Sullivan et al., 2006). We have no basis for thinking that mothers are uniquely qualified to parent or that men are hopelessly inept around babies.

However, that fathers are capable of sensitive parenting does not mean that they play the same roles as mothers in their

children's lives. Fathers used to be viewed primarily as husbands and breadwinners rather than parents; developmental theorists like Freud believed that mothers were all-important in child development. Now, however, a new father role is emerging and more attention is being paid to fathers as parents (Lamb, 2013).

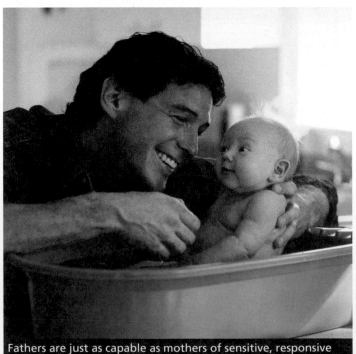

Fathers are just as capable as mothers of sensitive, responsive parenting.

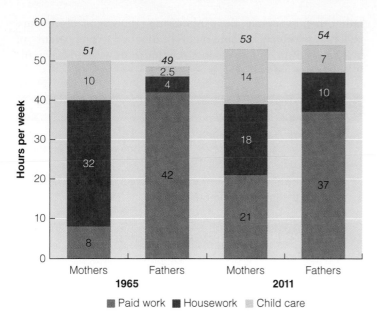

■ Figure 15.2 Changes in time use of mothers and fathers between 1965 and 2011.

Source: Parker, K.& Wang, W. (2013). Modern parenthood. Roles of Moms and Dads converge as they balance work and family. Pew Research Center Social and Demographic Trends.Available at: http://www.pewsocialtrends.org/2013/03/14/modern-parenthood-roles-of-moms-and-dads-converge-as-they-balance-work-and-family/. Data for 1965 from Bianchi, Robinson, and Milkie, 2006; data for 2011 from Pew Research analysis of the American Time Use Survey.

Fathers today are more involved with their children than ever (Bianchi, 2011; Pleck & Masciadrelli, 2004). **■ Figure 15.2** shows just how much the daily lives of mothers and fathers have changed from 1965 to 2011. Women have increased their involvement in paid work, decreased their involvement in housework, and managed somehow (by not sleeping?) to spend more time in child care than mothers in 1965 did. Fathers have helped make this possible by increasing their involvement in childcare from 2.5 to 7 hours a week and their housework time from 4 to 10 hours a week. Some fathers are even sharing responsibility for child care equally with their spouses rather than just "helping," especially if they hold egalitarian views about gender roles (Bulanda, 2004; Deutsch, 2001). Thus, the roles of mothers and fathers are converging. Yet mothers still spend more overall time with children, and more time directly caring for them and interacting with them, than fathers do (Bianchi, 2011). This gender difference is common across cultures, causing some to argue that it has been built into the biology of males and females during the course of evolution.

Mothers and fathers also have been found to differ in their styles of interacting with young children. When mothers interact with their babies, a large proportion of their time is devoted to caregiving: offering food, changing diapers, wiping noses, and so on. Fathers spend much of their time with children playing (Lamb, 2013). They specialize in tickling, poking, bouncing, and surprising infants, whereas mothers hold, talk to, and play quietly with them (Laflamme, Pomerleau, & Malcuit, 2002;

Neville & Parke, 1997). Yet fathers are able to adopt a "mother-like" caregiver role if they have primary responsibility for their children, so their playful parenting may be more about being in the role of the "backup" parent than about being male rather than female (Phares, 1999). The rowdy play style shown by many fathers in our culture does not show up in all cultures, either (Lamb, 2013). It seems, then, that both nature (evolution) and nurture (societal gender-role norms) contribute to mother–father differences in parental involvement and styles of interacting with young children.

In the end, fathers contribute best to development when they, like mothers, are sensitive and responsive caregivers and form secure attachments with their infants. Children do fare better cognitively, socially, and emotionally if they have a supportive father in their lives than if they do not (Holden, 2010; Lamb, 2013). However, much the same can be said for any second parent figure, male or female (Biblarz & Stacey, 2010). So fathers are important, but their contribution may not be as unique as once thought (Lamb, 2013).

Although more fathers are involved in child care than ever before, more fathers also live apart from their children than ever before. As Livingston and Parker (2011) put it, we have "a tale of two fathers," the engaged kind and the absent kind. What does the fact that 41% of babies are now born to unmarried mothers mean for father involvement? Generally, unmarried fathers who do not live with their child's mother are not very involved parents. However, they can be under some conditions. Studies of low-income, urban fathers over the first 3 years of their child's life suggest that much hinges on the quality of the relationship between mother and father (Cabrera, Fagan, & Farrie, 2008; Fagan & Palkovitz, 2011; Fagan et al., 2009). If they have a good relationship, even if it is no longer a romantic one, and if the father feels supported in his coparenting, he is likely to be more involved with his child.

Unmarried mothers and their children clearly benefit when unmarried fathers become partners in child rearing; meanwhile, becoming an involved father seems to help some young men mature and make positive changes in their lives (Fagan et al., 2009). Couples groups emphasizing parenting skills, couple communication, and effective coping strategies can help increase a father's engagement with his child, improve his relationship with his partner, and positively affect child development, whether he lives with his children or not (Cowan et al., 2009).

Mothers, Fathers, and Infants: The System at Work

Now let's view the new family as a three-person system. The mother–child relationship cannot be understood without considering the father; nor can the father–child relationship be understood without taking the mother into account. This is because parents have **indirect effects** on their children by influencing on the behavior of their spouses. More generally, indirect effects within the family are instances in which the relationship or interaction between two individuals in the family is modified by the behavior or attitudes of a third family member.

Fathers indirectly influence the mother–infant relationship in many ways. For example, mothers who have close, supportive relationships with their husbands tend to interact more patiently and sensitively with their babies than do mothers who are experiencing marital tension and who feel that they are raising their children largely without help (Cox et al., 1992; Lamb & Tamis-Lemonda, 2004). By affecting his wife, then, a father can indirectly affect how well she parents their child. Meanwhile, mothers indirectly affect the father–infant relationship. For example, fathers who have just had pleasant conversations with their wives are more supportive and engaged when they interact with their children than fathers who have just had arguments with their wives (Kitzmann, 2000). And a crying baby could have a negative indirect effect on the marital relationship by causing a stressed father to blow up at his wife.

As you can imagine, infant development goes best when parents get along well. A strong relationship between partners helps both parents engage with their infants (Carlson, Pilkauskas, McLanahan, & Brooks-Gunn, 2011). When the relationship is good, couples not only support each other but are likely to coparent effectively (Parke & Buriel, 2006). When parents compete rather than cooperate, their infants may show signs of insecure attachment or may become securely attached to one parent but be blocked from enjoying close relationships with both parents (Caldera & Lindsey, 2006).

> ### Checking Mastery
>
> 1. In terms of their parenting roles, what is one way in which fathers are similar to mothers and one way in which they are different?
> 2. Give an example of a negative indirect effect of a father on the mother–infant relationship.
>
> ### Making Connections
>
> 1. Because of his wife's death during childbirth, Alex suddenly finds himself the sole parent of his infant son, Aaron. Given the material in this section, how do you think this will affect Aaron's welfare and development compared with what would have happened if Alex had been the one who died and his wife had to raise Aaron on her own?

15.3 The Child

LEARNING OBJECTIVES:

- Compare and contrast the authoritarian, authoritative, permissive, and neglectful parenting styles in terms of where they fall on the acceptance-responsiveness and demandingness-control dimensions of parenting and how they are likely to affect development.

- Discuss three explanations of why high- and low-SES parents use different parenting styles.

- Define and illustrate with examples the parent effects, child effects, interactional, and transactional models of family influence.

- Summarize the nature of the sibling relationship and its contributions to development.

As children reach age 2 or age 3, parents continue to be caregivers and playmates, but they also become socialization agents. They teach their offspring how (and how not) to behave and how to become contributing members of society using child rearing and discipline techniques, teaching, and other means (Grusec & Davidov, 2010). Siblings also serve as socialization agents and become an important part of the child's developmental experience.

Parenting Styles

How can I be a good parent? Certainly this question is uppermost in most parents' minds. You can go far in understanding which parenting styles are effective by considering just two dimensions of parenting: acceptance–responsiveness and demandingness–control (Darling & Steinberg, 1993; Holden, 2010; Maccoby & Martin, 1983; Schaefer, 1959).

Parental **acceptance–responsiveness** refers to the extent to which parents are warm, supportive, sensitive to their children's needs, and willing to provide affection and praise when their children meet their expectations. Accepting, responsive parents are affectionate and often smile at, praise, and encourage their children, although they also let children know when they misbehave. Less accepting and responsive parents are often quick to criticize, belittle, punish, or ignore their children and rarely communicate to children that they are loved and valued.

Demandingness–control (sometimes called *permissiveness–restrictiveness*) refers to how much control over decisions lies with the parent as opposed to with the child. Controlling and demanding parents set rules, expect their children to follow them, and monitor their children closely to ensure that the rules are followed. Less controlling and demanding parents make fewer demands and allow their children a great deal of autonomy in exploring the environment, expressing their opinions and emotions, and making decisions about their activities.

By crossing the acceptance and demandingness dimensions, we have four basic patterns of child rearing to consider, as shown in ■ **Figure 15.3**:

1. **Authoritarian parenting**. This is a restrictive parenting style combining high demandingness–control and low acceptance–responsiveness. Parents impose many rules, expect strict obedience, rarely explain why the child should comply

Parental acceptance–responsiveness

■ **Figure 15.3** The acceptance–responsiveness and demandingness–control dimensions of parenting. Which combination best describes your parents' approach?

Source: From Maccoby, E. E. & Martin, J. A. Socialization in the context of the family: Parent–child interaction. In E. M. Hetherington (Ed.), P. H. Mussen (Ed. in Chief), *Handbook of child psychology: Vol.4, Socialization, personality, and social development* (4th ed.). Copyright © 1983 by Wiley. Reprinted with permission.

with rules, and often rely on power-assertion tactics such as physical punishment to gain compliance.

2. **Authoritative parenting**. Authoritative parents are more flexible; they are demanding and exert control, but they are also sensitive to their children. They set clear rules and consistently enforce them, but they have rationales for their rules and explain them, are responsive to their children's needs and points of view, and involve their children in family decision making. They are reasonable and democratic in their approach; although it is clear that they are in charge, they communicate respect for their children.

3. **Permissive parenting** (sometimes called indulgent parenting). This style is high in acceptance–responsiveness but low in demandingness–control. Permissive parents are child-centered; they have relatively few rules and make relatively few demands, encourage children to express their feelings and impulses, and rarely exert control over their behavior.

4. **Neglectful parenting** (sometimes called disengaged or uninvolved parenting). Finally, parents who combine low demandingness–control and low acceptance–responsiveness are relatively uninvolved in their children's upbringing. They seem not to care much about their children. They may be hostile and rejecting or indifferent—or they may be so overwhelmed by their own problems that they cannot devote sufficient energy to expressing love and setting and enforcing rules (Maccoby & Martin, 1983).

We assume that you have no difficulty deciding that parental acceptance and responsiveness are preferable to parental rejection, neglect, or insensitivity. As you have seen in this book,

warm, responsive parenting is associated with secure attachments to parents, academic competence, high self-esteem, good social skills, peer acceptance, a strong sense of morality, good mental health, and many other virtues, whereas neglect or rejection are associated with a host of developmental problems. The benefits of perceived parent acceptance are clear across the life span (Holden, 2010; Khaleque & Rohner, 2012).

The degree of demandingness and control shown by parents is also important. The authoritarian, authoritative, and permissive parenting styles were originally identified and defined by Diana Baumrind (1967, 1977, 1991, 2013). In a pioneering longitudinal study, Baumrind found that children raised by authoritative parents were the best adjusted: They were cheerful, socially responsible, self-reliant, achievement oriented, and cooperative with adults and peers.

Children of authoritarian parents tended to be moody and seemingly unhappy, relatively aimless, and unpleasant to be around. Children of permissive parents were often impulsive, aggressive, self-centered, rebellious, aimless, and low in independence and achievement. Note, however, that a warm, permissive style can be effective with older children and adolescents who have developed more self-control and need less guidance.

Subsequent research has shown that the worst developmental outcomes are associated with the neglectful, uninvolved style of parenting. Children of neglectful parents display behavioral problems such as aggression and frequent temper tantrums as early as age 3 (Miller et al., 1993). They tend to become hostile and antisocial adolescents who abuse alcohol and drugs and get in trouble (Lamborn et al., 1991; Weiss & Schwarz, 1996). Parents who provide little guidance and communicate that they do not care breed children who are resentful and prone to strike back at their uncaring parents and other authority figures.

In short, children develop best when they have both love and limits. If they are indulged or neglected and given little guidance, they will not learn self-control and may become selfish and lacking in direction. If they receive lots of guidance but little sensitivity to their needs and perspectives, as the children of authoritarian parents do, they will have few opportunities to learn self-reliance and may lack confidence in their own decision-making abilities. The link between authoritative parenting and positive developmental outcomes is evident in most ethnic groups and socioeconomic groups studied to date in the United States (Sorkhabi & Mandara, 2013; Steinberg, 2001) and in a variety of other cultures (Sorkhabi & Mandara, 2013; Vazsonyi, Hibbert, & Snider, 2003).

Nonetheless, the effectiveness of different parenting approaches can differ depending on the cultural or subcultural context in which they are used. Much seems to hinge on how common a parenting style is in a culture and whether children view it as normal and acceptable (see also Grolnick & Pomerantz, 2009; Lansford et al., 2005; Rothbaum & Trommsdorff, 2007; Sorkhabi & Mandara, 2013). In a cross-cultural study of several countries, Jennifer Lansford and her colleagues (2005), for example, found a strong relationship between frequent use of physical discipline and high levels of child aggression and anxiety in

Culture and the Tiger Mother

Sophia and Lulu could never attend sleepovers or have playdates, watch television or play computer games, get a grade less than A, or choose their own extracurricular activities or musical instruments. Their mother rejected the birthday cards they made her one year because they were poorly done. Their mother, once called "garbage" by her father, called Sophia "garbage" once for disrespecting her. And poor 7-year-old Lulu: After she tore her musical score for "Little White Donkey" to bits during a long battle over playing the difficult piano piece, her mother put her doll-house in the car and said she'd donate it to the Salvation Army, threatened no dinner and no birthday parties for years, and called her lazy and pathetic.

Not exactly our image of the perfect parent. Amy Chua, a law professor at Yale, caused a firestorm when an excerpt from her book, *Battle Hymn of the Tiger Mother*, was published in *The Wall Street Journal* (Chua, 2011a, 2011b). This "Tiger Mother" described raising her daughters, Sophia and Lulu, in what struck most American parents as an almost abusively demanding, controlling, and unresponsive manner: Authoritarian parenting to the max. As Chua sees it, American parents (including her husband) are too child-centered and spineless. They worry too much about their children's self-esteem and protect them from struggling with difficult challenges rather than having confidence that children can handle and will benefit from failure and criticism. They don't view children as obligated to obey their parents and make them proud, as Chinese parents do, and they bow to their children's desires rather than relying on their own judgment about what is best for children.

Lulu did finally play the piano piece correctly after hours more work on it, beamed at her hard-won accomplishment, and celebrated with her mother. As far as we can tell, both daughters have turned out exceptionally well. Meanwhile, Chua admits that she made mistakes and went too far at times in trying to implement a traditional, strict Chinese parenting style and describes later in her book moving toward a more moderate parenting style, partly in response to Lulu's rebellion. Still, how do we square the generally positive outcomes of a traditional Chinese upbringing with mounds of research suggesting that the warmer and more reasonable authoritative parenting style is the best way to raise children? Why aren't Chinese children stressed, moody, and incapable of making their own decisions rather than achievement oriented and accomplished?

Developmentalist Ruth Chao (1994, 2000) wondered why too. She concluded from her research that Chinese parents are not really authoritarian in our Western sense of the term. In Chinese culture, training children entails parent involvement and self-sacrifice, along with an emphasis on hard work, discipline, and doing well to uphold the family's honor. Parents are demanding, true; they offer clear and specific guidelines for behavior, believing that this is the best way to express their love and train their children properly. Children understand that their parent's strictness is an expression of love and that their responsibility is to obey. Parents do not explain their rules or involve their children in decision making—but children do not expect them to. Although the Chinese style seems overly controlling to European American eyes, Chinese parents and children view it as warm, caring parenting (and thus more like authoritative parenting than like the colder, more arbitrary authoritarian style) and children respond well to it as a result. Perhaps this is why Sophia Chua-Rubenfeld (2011), an accomplished pianist and Harvard student, wrote of how grateful she was to her Tiger Mom.

Abundant evidence says that the authoritative parenting style works well, not only for European Americans but for children from a variety of cultural and ethnic backgrounds, including Chinese American children like Tiger Mother's daughters (Sorkhabi & Mandara, 2013). Yet parents in many cultures around the world adopt a more traditional, authoritarian approach to parenting and get good results with it. The moral of the Tiger Mother story, then, is that we must always be careful to interpret parenting in its cultural and subcultural context and understand that styles that do not seem acceptable to us may be acceptable and effective in other sociocultural settings.

---

cultures where the use of physical discipline was rare. However, physical discipline was not as strongly associated with these child behavior problems in cultures where physical punishment is widely accepted and frequently used and children know that. Similarly, African American parents living in high-crime poverty areas in the United States sometimes rely on authoritarian and even harsh parenting in an effort to protect their children from harm. Their children tend to view this as a sign that their parents care rather than as a sign of hostility and rejection. As a result, this authoritarian parenting style does not have the same negative effects it tends to have in middle-class communities (Deater-Deckard, Dodge, & Sorbring, 2005; Laird et al., 2009; McElhaney & Allen, 2012). We explore the importance of cultural context in influencing the effectiveness of parenting styles further in **Exploration Box 15.1**.

Social Class, Economic Hardship, and Parenting

Middle-class and lower-class parents as groups have been found to pursue different socialization goals, emphasize different values, and rely on different parenting styles in raising children—with some important implications. Compared with middle-class and upper-class parents, lower-class and working-class parents tend to stress obedience and respect for authority more. They are often more restrictive and authoritarian, reason with their children less frequently, and show less warmth and affection (Conger & Dogan, 2007; McLoyd, 1990). Although you will find a range of parenting styles in any social group, of course, these average social-class differences in parenting help explain social-class differences in developmental outcomes such as school achievement, adjustment, and life success (Conger & Dogan, 2007).

Why do these socioeconomic differences in parenting styles and child outcomes exist? Let's consider three explanations: socioeconomic status (SES) differences in financial stresses, resources invested in children, and socialization goals.

Financial Stress

One well-established explanation, developed by Rand Conger and his colleagues and called the **family stress model**, centers on the negative effects of financial stresses on parent mental health, parenting, and, in turn, child development (Conger & Dogan, 2007; Donnellan, Martin, Conger, & Conger, 2013). As shown in ▪ **Figure 15.4**, Conger and his associates (1992, 2002; Conger, Patterson, & Ge, 1995) have found that parents experiencing financial problems experience economic pressure, which tend to make them depressed, which increases conflict between them. Like depression, marital conflict disrupts each partner's ability to be a supportive, involved, and effective parent—another example of indirect effects within the family. This breakdown in parenting then contributes to negative child outcomes such as low self-esteem, poor school performance, poor peer relations, and adjustment problems such as aggression and depression. The family stress model seems to apply across ethnic groups and cultures (Donnellan et al., 2013). It is also useful in explaining the effects of other stressors on parents and, in turn, children—for example, the effects of living in a dangerous neighborhood or being an immigrant parent who does not speak English or understand the culture well (White et al., 2009).

Now consider poor families. Stresses are magnified for families living below the poverty line or moving in and out of poverty as a result of job loss and other economic crises. Both parenting and child development may suffer due to the stresses of coping with a physical environment characterized by pollution, noise, and crowded, unsafe living conditions and a social environment characterized by family instability and violence (Evans, 2004). Parents dealing with poverty tend to be especially restrictive, punitive, and inconsistent, sometimes to the point of being abusive and neglectful (Brooks-Gunn, Britto, & Brady, 1999; Seccombe, 2000). Partly owing to its effects on parenting, poverty is associated with child health problems, emotional and behavioral problems, and school failure (Bradley & Corwyn, 2002; Evans, 2004; Evans & Kim, 2013).

Resource Investment

A second explanation of social-class differences in parenting and child outcomes is that low-SES parents have fewer resources to invest in their children's development than high-SES parents do (Conger & Dogan, 2007; Donnellan et al., 2013). Wealthier parents can invest more money and time in getting their children good child care and a good education; providing books, computers, and other learning materials in the home; taking their children to educational events; and otherwise stimulating their children's minds (Conger & Dogan, 2007). They can also spend more on good nutrition and health care and devote more time to interacting with and supervising their children.

Socialization Goals

Third and finally, high- and low-SES parents have different socialization goals in preparing their children for the world of work because they have had different work experiences (Conger & Dogan, 2007). Wealthier parents may reason with their children and foster initiative and creativity more because these are the attributes that count for business executives, professionals, and other white-collar workers. Parents from lower socioeconomic groups tend to be authoritarian and emphasize obedience to authority figures in part because that is what is required in jobs like their own (Kohn, 1969).

To summarize, then, low family SES and economic hardship may be associated with poor developmental outcomes because of (1) economic stresses that result in less nurturant, more authoritarian, and less consistent parenting; (2) limited investment of resources, financial and otherwise, in children's development; and (3) an orientation toward preparing children to obey a boss rather than be the boss. **Exploration Box 15.2** examines the implications of the economic recession of 2008 not only for parenting and child development but other aspects of family life.

Models of Influence in the Family

In thinking about influences within the family, we will bet that you, like most developmental scientists, think first about parents affecting children. But consider four different models of influence in the family: the parent effects, child effects, interactional, and transactional models.

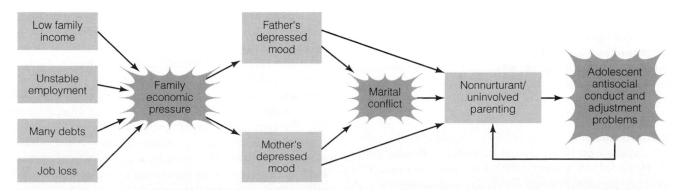

▪ **Figure 15.4** A model of the relationship among family economic stress, patterns of parenting, and adolescent adjustment.

SOURCE: Adapted from Conger, R. D., Conger, K. J., Elder, G. H., Jr., Lorenz, F. O., Simons, R. L., & Whitbeck, L. B. (1992). A family process model of economic hardship and adjustment of early adolescent boys. *Child Development*, *63*, 526–541.

The Great Recession and Family Life

Nothing makes the point that the family is a changing system in a changing world like a global economic crisis. The economic downturn of around 2008 that has come to be known as the Great Recession is likely to have effects on family life and human development for years to come. Valerie Adrian and Stephanie Coontz (2010; see also Donnellan et al., 2013) highlight a number of likely consequences when unemployment rises, family incomes drop, and families are evicted from their homes and thrown into poverty:

- Marriage rates decrease because people postpone marriage, especially if they have little income or financial stability.
- Childbearing is delayed for similar reasons: not enough money to support a child.
- As Rand Conger's family stress model predicts, economic pressure on the family increases marital conflict.
- Divorce filings decrease but this is not the good news it appears to be: Couples do not divorce because they cannot afford to divide their assets and create separate households so they continue to live unhappily—and expose their children to the damaging effects of marital conflict.
- Parenting deteriorates; stressed parents have difficulty being warm and responsive and are sometimes irritable and harsh.
- Deteriorated parenting and decreased investment of money and time in children negatively affects children's cognitive and social and emotional development, their physical health and mental health, and their longer-term development, especially if they are thrown into poverty.
- Family violence, both partner violence and child maltreatment, increases.
- Young adults who struggle to afford an education and find jobs either do not leave the nest or refill the nest, moving back in with their parents. Their longer-term vocational success and earnings, as well as their mental health, can suffer (see Chapter 11 on unemployment).
- Middle-aged parents are increasingly "sandwiched" between generations, being called upon to provide more financial support for longer to their young adult children and to help their aging parents as well (Parker & Patten, 2013).
- Older adults, who may seem protected by Social Security and Medicare, see their retirement funds dwindle and their families less able to help support them; some want or need to work but cannot get jobs.

These interacting changes in the family system can have long-lasting ripple effects. We know from Glen Elder's classic research on the Great Depression of the 1930s (Elder, Liker, & Cross, 1984; and see Chapter 1) that the negative effects of being unemployed and tossed into poverty can trickle down to the next generation. When stressed parents became less affectionate and less consistent in their discipline, their children ended up with behavior problems and poor academic records and grew up to be men with erratic careers and unstable marriages and women who were viewed by their children as irritable parents (see also Donnellan et al., 2013). We have here, then, another good illustration of how development is shaped by its historical-cultural context.

Parent Effects Model

The study of human development has been guided through most of its history by a simple **parent effects model** of family influence (Holden, 2010; Maccoby, 2007). This model assumes that influences run one way, from parent (particularly mother) to child. This is the "blame the parents" model that Susan Klebold encountered after her son became a mass murderer. You have just reviewed research demonstrating positive and negative effects of parenting styles on child development. But what if you turn things around: Could it be that a child's behavior influences the style of parenting his parents adopt and that what appear to be parent effects are instead child effects?

Child Effects Model

A **child effects model** of family influence highlights the influences of children on their parents (Crouter & Booth, 2003; Sanson, Hemphill, & Smart, 2004). One good example of a child effect is the influence of a child's age and competence on the style of parenting used with that child. For example, infants in their first year of life require and elicit sensitive care, whereas older infants who are asserting their wills and toddling here and there force parents to set limits (Fagot & Kavanaugh, 1993). Normally parents then become less restrictive as their children mature and gradually, with parental guidance, become capable of making their own decisions. As children develop, then, parenting shifts from parent regulation of the child, to parent and child coregulation of the child, to self-regulation by a now more capable child (Holden, 2010).

Now consider the possibility that a child's genetic makeup and personality influence the parenting she receives. Is it not possible that easygoing, manageable children cause their parents to be warm and authoritative? Could not difficult, stubborn, and aggressive children help mold parents who are rejecting rather than accepting—and who either rule with an authoritarian iron hand or throw up their hands in defeat and become neglectful? The *gene–environment correlations* discussed in Chapter 3, especially evocative ones in which children evoke certain kinds of treatment from other people, are examples of child effects. Indeed, evidence is accumulating that children's genetically influenced characteristics can influence not only parenting styles but marital relationships and sibling behavior—the whole family system (Reiss & Neiderhiser, 2011).

In a clever and convincing experimental demonstration of child effects, Barbara Keller and Richard Bell (1979) had female college students attempt to convince 9-year-old girls to behave altruistically (for example, to spend more time sewing a pillow for a handicapped child than sewing a pillow for themselves). The girls had been coached to respond either attentively or inattentively. As expected, college students confronted with an attentive child used what Chapter 13 called induction, explaining how other children might feel if the child behaved selfishly. By contrast, college students who interacted with an inattentive child relied on power-assertion techniques such as promising rewards for altruism and threatening penalties for selfishness (see also Kerr & Stattin, 2003).

Interactional Model

The **interactional model** improves on the parent effects and child effects models by recognizing that parent and child characteristics may combine in certain ways to influence development. The concept of *gene–environment interaction* (see Chapter 3) illustrates the interactional model; for example, aggressive behavior may result if a child has a certain variant of the MAO-A gene associated with temper control problems *and* is raised by an abusive parent (Caspi et al., 2002; Dodge, 2009). It takes the combination of an at-risk child and a negative environment. There appear to be many examples of such interactions between child characteristics and characteristics of the child-rearing environment (Dodge & Rutter, 2011). They tell us that the effect of a particular parenting approach depends on the child with whom it is used, and that the effect of a particular child characteristic depends on how children with that characteristic are parented.

Transactional Model

The interactional model is a step forward, but it focuses on what characteristics child and parent bring to a relationship rather than how their characteristics change over time as they interact with each other. In the **transactional model** of family influence, parent and child are seen as influencing one another reciprocally over time, sometimes in unpredictable ways (Sameroff, 1975, 2009). Child problems may develop when *the relationship* between parent and child somehow goes bad as the two interact over time. We could imagine a pretty normal child and a pretty normal parent somehow getting off on the wrong foot and developing a toxic relationship that has negative effects on child development. By the same token, healthy child development could result when, whatever characteristics each brings to the relationship, the transactions between parent and child evolve in more positive directions over time.

As Chapter 13 revealed, we now understand that antisocial behavior most likely results when a child who behaves aggressively elicits negative, coercive parenting and when that parenting contributes further to the child's aggression—that is, when there is reciprocal influence over time between parent and child and an escalating *coercive cycle* develops (Ge et al., 1996; O'Connor et al., 1998; Williams & Steinberg, 2011). When such a destructive family process evolves, it becomes impossible to say who is more influential, parent or child.

● **Table 15.2** Models of Family Influence.

Model of Family Influence	Pattern of Influence
Parent effects model	Parent influences child
Child effects model	Child influences parent
Interactional model	The combination of a particular kind of child with a particular kind of parent determines developmental outcomes
Transactional model	The reciprocal influence of parent and child on one another over time determines how the parent–child relationship and the child's development unfold

Demonstrations of child effects, interactional effects, and transactional effects within the family are tremendously important. They mean that parents are not solely responsible for whether their children turn out "good" or "bad," even though they probably have somewhat more influence overall than children do on how the parent–child relationship unfolds (Holden, 2010; Kuczynski & Parkin, 2007). We must remind ourselves repeatedly that the family is a system in which family members lead linked lives and are influenced in reciprocal ways by both their genes and the environments they create for one another. ● **Table 15.2** compares the models of family influence discussed in this section.

Sibling Relationships

A family system consisting of mother, father, and child is changed by the arrival of a new baby and becomes a new—and considerably more complex—family system. How do children adapt to a new baby in the house, how does the sibling relationship change as children age, and what do brothers and sisters contribute to each other's development in the final analysis?

A New Baby Arrives

When Judy Dunn and Carol Kendrick (1982; see also Dunn, 1993, 2007) carefully studied young children's reactions to a new sibling, they found that mothers typically pay less attention to their firstborns after the new baby arrives than before. Partly for this reason, firstborns often find being "dethroned" an unpleasant experience. They sometimes become more difficult and demanding, or more dependent and clingy, and they may develop problems with their sleeping, eating, and toileting routines. Most of their battles are with their mothers, but a few firstborns are not above hitting, poking, and pinching their younger brothers or sisters. Secure attachments can even become insecure, especially if firstborns are 2 years old or older and can fully appreciate how much they have lost (Teti et al., 1996). Although positive effects such as an increased insistence on doing things independently are also common, it is clear that many firstborns resent losing their parents' attention, and that their difficult behavior may alienate their parents further.

A careful analysis of this and other research by Brenda Volling (2012) suggests that we should apply Bronfenbrenner's bioecological perspective and recognize that the entry of a new family member perturbs the family system and that what happens depends on transactions between the children, parents, and larger social context. Volling concludes the entry of a new sibling is not usually the developmental crisis for firstborns that many of us believe. Some older siblings grow from the experience, some have difficulties, and most adjust quite smoothly. Among the most commonly observed effects are temporary decreases in children's affection for and responsiveness to their mothers.

So what makes for a smooth transition and how can adjustment problems be minimized? It helps if both parents maintain good mental health and a sense of self-efficacy as parents and if they have good social support to help them cope with the challenges of parenting (Volling, 2012). Adjustment to a new sibling is also easier if the marital relationship is good and remains good after the birth and if the firstborn had secure relationships with both parents before the younger sibling arrived—and continues to enjoy close relationships with them afterward (Dunn, 2007; Teti et al., 1996). If parents continue providing love and attention to their firstborn and maintain the child's routines as much as possible—a cause helped greatly if the father increases his involvement in child care—things are likely to go well (Volling, 2005).

Ambivalence in Sibling Relationships

Fortunately, most older siblings adjust fairly quickly to having a new brother or sister. Yet even in the best of sibling relationships, **sibling rivalry**—the spirit of competition, jealousy, and resentment between brothers and sisters—is normal. It may be rooted in an evolutionary fact: Although siblings share half their genes on average and are therefore more motivated to help one another than to help genetically unrelated individuals, siblings also compete with one another for their parents' time and resources to ensure their own survival and welfare (Bjorklund & Pellegrini, 2002). Siblings may also be at odds because they live in close proximity but lack the mature social skills needed to resolve conflicts and because they often feel they are treated differently by their parents (Holden, 2010). For all these reasons, perhaps, sibling relationships typically involve both closeness and conflict and are best described as ambivalent.

The number of skirmishes between very young siblings can be as high as 56 per hour (Dunn, 1993). Jealousies, bouts of teasing, shouting matches, and occasional kicks and punches continue to be part of the sibling relationship throughout childhood; squabbles are most often about possessions (McGuire et al., 2000). Each combatant, of course, feels that he is blameless and has been terribly wronged (Wilson et al., 2004). Thankfully, levels of conflict normally decrease after early adolescence as teenagers spend more time away from the family (Furman & Buhrmester, 1992; Larson et al., 1996).

Sibling relationships are friendlier and less conflicted if mothers and fathers get along well as a couple and if they respond warmly and sensitively to all their children rather than unfairly favoring one over another (Dunn, 2007). Children are able to accept that differences in treatment can be fair, and therefore

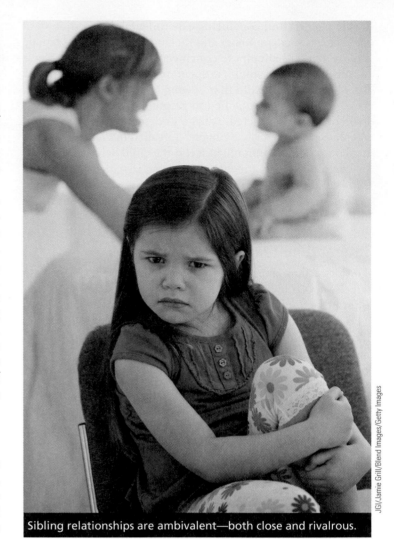

Sibling relationships are ambivalent—both close and rivalrous.

JGI/Jamie Grill/Blend Images/Getty Images

not objectionable, if they are based on differences in the ages, competencies, and personalities of the siblings, but they resent seemingly unfair differences in treatment (Kowal et al., 2002).

Sibling Influences on Development

Despite sibling rivalry, the sibling relationship is generally close, interactions with siblings are mostly positive, and siblings play mostly positive roles in one another's development (McHale, Updegraff, & Whiteman, 2012). Four important function of siblings stand out:

- *Emotional support.* Brothers and sisters confide in one another, often more than they confide in their parents (Howe et al., 2000). They protect and comfort one another in rough times. Even preschoolers jump in to comfort their infant siblings when their mothers leave or when strangers approach (Stewart & Marvin, 1984).
- *Caregiving.* Siblings babysit and tend young children. Indeed, in a study of 186 societies, older children were the principal caregivers for infants and toddlers in 57% of the cultures studied (Weisner & Gallimore, 1977; and see Rogoff, 2003).
- *Teaching.* Although older brothers and sisters are not always as skilled at teaching as parents are (Perez-Granados & Callanan, 1997), they clearly feel a special responsibility to

discovered that if an older sibling is competent, this contributes positively to his mother's psychological functioning, which makes her more likely to provide supportive parenting to a younger sibling, which in turn increases the odds that the younger sibling will also be competent. By contrast, an incompetent older sibling can set in motion a negative chain of events leading to less supportive parenting and less positive outcomes for the younger sibling.

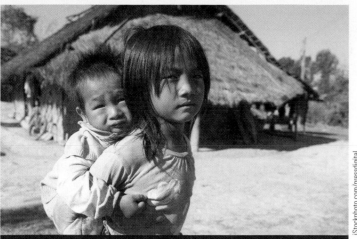

In many societies, older siblings are major caregivers for young children. This girl in Laos looks after her brother every day.

teach, and younger siblings actively seek their guidance on any number of things.

- *Social experience.* Having at least one sibling to interact with can have positive effects on a child's social cognitive skills and social competence (Dunn, 2007; McHale, Kim, & Whiteman, 2006; and see Chapter 13). In their interactions with siblings, especially all those skirmishes, children learn how to take others' perspectives, read others' minds, express their feelings, negotiate, and resolve conflicts.

So siblings provide emotional support, caregiving, teaching, and social experience. Interestingly, siblings can affect each other not only directly but also through the indirect effects they have on their parents. In an excellent illustration, Gene Brody (2003, 2004)

Checking Mastery

1. What does an authoritative parenting style involve?
2. What are two reasons that low-SES parents might use a more authoritarian and less warm and nurturing parenting style than high-SES parents do?
3. What is the main difference between the interactional model and the transactional model of family influence?
4. How would you characterize the typical sibling relationship?

Making Connections

1. Alison, a 16-year-old teenager who was drunk at the time, plowed the family car into a Dairy Queen and is being held at the police station for driving under the influence. Her father must pick her up. What would you expect an authoritarian, authoritative, permissive, and neglectful father to say and do in this situation? What implications might these contrasting approaches to parenting have for this young woman's development?
2. If only the child effects model of family influence were at work, what behavior by children do you think would be most likely to push parents to use each of the main parenting styles: authoritarian, authoritative, permissive, and neglectful?

15.4 The Adolescent

LEARNING OBJECTIVES:

- Describe how the parent–child relationship both changes and remains the same in early adolescence.

- Discuss how parents can best foster autonomy and how the process may differ in individualistic versus collectivist cultures.

When you picture the typical relationship between a teenager and her parents, do you envision a teenager who is out all the time with friends, resents every rule and restriction, and talks back at every opportunity? Do you imagine parents wringing their hands in despair and wondering if they will survive their children's adolescent years? Many people believe that the period of the family life cycle during which parents have adolescents in the house is a particularly stressful time, with close parent–child relationships deteriorating into bitter tugs-of-war. How much truth is there to these characterizations?

Ripples in the Parent–Child Relationship

Contrary to belief, most parent–adolescent relationships are close, and most retain whatever quality they had in childhood (Collins & Laursen, 2006). It is rare for a parent–child relationship to suddenly turn bad at adolescence; more likely, a troubled parent–adolescent relationship has grown out of a troubled parent–child relationship and has been shaped by both the parent's parenting and the child's personality (Eisenberg et al., 2008).

Yet the parent–child relationship does change during adolescence. Time spent together decreases as adolescents become more involved with peers, and this can make adolescents feel less involved with and supported by their parents (Collins & Laursen, 2006; De Goede, Branje, & Meeus, 2009). Parent–child conflict also increases temporarily in early adolescence, around the onset of puberty (McGue et al., 2005; Shanahan et al., 2004). Young adolescents assert themselves, and they and their parents squabble more. The bickering is mainly about minor matters such as disobedience, homework, household chores, and access to

Parent–child conflict escalates in early adolescence, but it is generally about minor issues.

privileges (Collins & Laursen, 2006). These skirmishes in early adolescence alter the parent–child relationship—not so much its closeness as the balance of power between parents and adolescents, as we will now see.

Achieving Autonomy

A key developmental task of adolescence is achieving **autonomy**, or the capacity to make decisions independently and manage life tasks without being overly dependent on other people. If adolescents are to "make it" as adults, they cannot be rushing home for reassuring hugs after every little setback or depending on parents to get them to work on time or manage their checkbooks. Achieving autonomy is about establishing an identity separate from one's parents and preparing to leave the nest and fly on one's own.

As children reach puberty and become more physically and cognitively mature and more capable of acting autonomously, they assert themselves more. As they do so, their parents give up some of their power, adolescents assume more control of their lives, and the parent–child relationship becomes more equal (De Goede et al., 2009; Steinberg, 2011). It is usually best for the development of autonomy if adolescents maintain close attachments with their parents and parents maintain authoritative control but also give adolescents more responsibility for decision making (Lamborn & Steinberg, 1993; Longmore, Manning, & Giordano, 2013). Gaining some separation from parents is healthy; becoming detached from them is not (Beyers et al., 2003). A blend of autonomy and attachment, or independence and interdependence, is most desirable.

How much autonomy adolescents want and parents grant differs from culture to culture. In individualistic cultures like ours autonomy is clearly prized, whereas in collectivist cultures maintaining respect for parents and family harmony are valued more (McElhaney & Allen, 2012). Studying different ethnic groups in the United States, Andrew Fuligni (1998) discovered that Filipino and Mexican American adolescents are more likely than European American adolescents to believe that they should not disagree with their parents, and Chinese American adolescents are less likely to expect the freedom to go to parties and to date at a young age. Chinese adolescents also maintain a strong sense of responsibility to their parents during the years when American teens are losing some of theirs (Pomerantz et al., 2011). Similarly, adolescents in Japan remain closer to their mothers and fathers than American adolescents do through the adolescent years. They do not feel as much need to distance themselves from their parents, and they spend less time with peers (Rothbaum et al., 2000). In collectivist Asian cultures, then, parents continue to be in command, the balance of power does not shift as much, and the quest for autonomy is less evident, at least during early and middle adolescence, than in the United States. Yet most adolescents in both individualistic and collectivist cultures strive for—and will eventually achieve—autonomy.

Across cultures, adolescents are most likely to become autonomous, achievement oriented, and well adjusted if their parents consistently enforce a reasonable set of rules, involve their teenagers in decision making, recognize their need for greater autonomy, monitor their comings and goings, gradually loosen the reins, and continue to be warm, supportive, and involved throughout adolescence (Holden, 2010; Lamborn et al., 1991; Longmore et al., 2013). In short, the winning approach is usually authoritative parenting. However, we must again recognize that in some cultures and subcultures a more authoritarian style or a more permissive style may have a different meaning and may also produce good outcomes (Garcia & Gracia, 2009; McElhaney & Allen, 2012; Steinberg, Dornbusch, & Brown, 1992).

An authoritative parenting style gives adolescents opportunities to strengthen their independent decision-making skills while retaining the benefit of their parents' guidance and advice. When parents are extremely strict and stifle autonomy, or when they are extremely lax and fail to guide and monitor their adolescents, teens are likely to become psychologically distressed, socialize with the wrong crowds, and get into trouble (Goldstein, Davis-Kean, & Eccles, 2005; Lamborn et al., 1991).

▶ Checking Mastery

1. What do the parent–adolescent conflicts of early adolescence generally concern?
2. What parenting style is most likely to foster autonomy, and why?

▶ Making Connections

1. At age 13, Miki moved from Japan to the United States with her family and now finds her relationship with her parents strained. Drawing on the material in this section, how would you analyze what is going on?
2. Analyze how your parents (or those of one of your high school friends) handled (or mishandled) the parenting challenge of maintaining a close relationship with their teen, maintaining reasonable authoritative control, and allowing for greater autonomy.

LEARNING OBJECTIVES:

• Characterize the major effects on couples of the first year of marriage, new parenthood, raising two or more children, entering the empty nest phase of family life, and grandparenting.

• Summarize how marital, sibling, and parent–child relationships are likely to change during adulthood.

So far we have offered a child's-eye view of family life. How does it look to adults? We will follow a couple through the establishment, new-parenthood, child-rearing, empty nest, and grandparenthood phases of the family life cycle.

Establishing a Marriage

In U.S. society, almost 90% of adults choose to marry at some point in their lives (Cherlin, 2009). Although love and marriage go together in most modern societies today, in many traditional societies marriages are not formed on the basis of love. They are arranged by leaders of kin groups who are concerned with acquiring property, allies, and the rights to any children the marriage produces (Ingoldsby & Smith, 1995; Regan, 2008). So in reading what follows, remember that the modern, Western way of establishing families is not the only way.

Marriage is a significant life transition for most adults: it involves taking on a new role (as husband or wife) and adjusting to life as a couple. We rejoice at weddings and view newlyweds as supremely happy beings. Indeed, they feel on top of the world, their self-esteem rises, and some develop a more secure attachment style as a result of marrying (Crowell, Treboux, & Waters, 2002; Giarrusso et al., 2000).

However, Ted Huston and his colleagues have found that the honeymoon is short, on average (Huston, McHale, & Crouter, 1986; Huston & Melz, 2004; Huston et al., 2001; also

The honeymoon is great, but for many couples marital satisfaction declines somewhat during the first year of marriage.

Tom Grill/Spirit/Corbis

see Kurdek, 1999). In a longitudinal study of newlywed couples, these researchers discovered that perceptions of the marital relationship became less favorable and marital satisfaction declined during the first year after the wedding. Behavior changed as well: "One year into marriage, the average spouse says, 'I love you,' hugs and kisses their partner, makes their partner laugh, and has sexual intercourse about half as often as when they were newly wed" (Huston & Melz, 2004, p. 951). Although partners spend only slightly less time together, more of that time is devoted to getting tasks done and less to having fun or just talking.

Most couples are far more satisfied than dissatisfied with their relationships after the "honeymoon" is over. Moreover, marital satisfaction holds steady for some couples while it is declining for others (Lavner & Bradbury, 2010). Still, adapting to marriage clearly involves some strains. Blissfully happy relationships sometimes evolve into still happy but more realistic ones (Huston et al., 2001; Lavner & Bradbury, 2010). Whether this happens because couples begin to see "warts" that they did not notice before marriage, stop trying to be on their best behavior, have run-ins as an inevitable part of living together, or start taking each other for granted, it is normal.

Does the quality of a couple's relationship early in their marriage have any implications for their later marital adjustment? It does. Huston and his colleagues (2001) assessed couples 2 months, 1 year, and 2 years into their marriages and again 13–14 years after the wedding. Compared with couples who were happily married after 13 years, couples who remained married but were unhappy had had relatively poor relationships all along. Even as newlyweds—and probably even before they married—these couples were less blissfully in love and acted more negatively toward each other than couples who stayed married and remained happy in their marriages. Couples who divorced did not usually experience escalating conflict; rather, they lost their positive feelings for each other.

So the establishment phase of the family life cycle involves a modest loss of enthusiasm on average but there is much variety in how it goes. Couples seem most likely to survive when they can maintain a high level of positive and supportive interaction to help them weather the conflicts that inevitably arise in any relationship (Fincham, 2003; Gottman, 2011). Participating in a premarital education program can help (Stanley et al., 2006).

New Parenthood

By age 40, 85% of women have given birth to a child and 76% of men have fathered one (Martinez, Daniels, & Chandra, 2012). How does the arrival of a new baby affect a mother, a father, and their relationship? (Gay and lesbian families are discussed in

Section 15.6.) Some people believe that having children draws a couple closer together; others believe that children strain a relationship. Which is it?

On average, new parenthood is best described as a stressful life transition that involves both positive and negative changes (Cowan & Cowan, 2000; Nomaguchi & Milkie, 2003). On the positive side, parents claim that having a child brings them joy and fulfillment and contributes to their own growth as individuals (Emery & Tuer, 1993; Palkovitz, 2002). But couples have added new roles (as mothers and fathers) to their existing roles (as spouses, workers, and so on), and new parents often find juggling work and family responsibilities challenging. They not only have a lot of new work to do as caregivers, but they also lose sleep, worry about their baby, find that they have less time to themselves, and sometimes face financial difficulties.

In addition, even egalitarian couples who previously shared household tasks often adopt more traditional gender-role attitudes and divide their labors along more traditional lines. She specializes in the "feminine" role by becoming the primary caregiver and housekeeper, often reducing her involvement in work outside the home and increasing her hours of labor inside the home, while he emphasizes his "masculine" role as provider and works harder in his job (Cowan & Cowan, 2000; Katz-Wise, Priess, & Hyde, 2010; Noller, 2006). This pattern is slowly changing, though (Dribe & Stanfors, 2009; and see our discussion in Section 15.2 of the convergence of mothers' and fathers' roles).

What are the effects of increased stress and of sharper gender-role differentiation? Marital satisfaction typically declines somewhat in the first year after a baby is born and continues to decline thereafter (Doss et al., 2009; Gottman & Notarius, 2000; Mitnick, Heyman, & Smith Slep, 2009). This decline is often steeper for women than for men, primarily because child care responsibilities typically fall more heavily on mothers (Levy-Shiff, 1994; Noller, 2006). Happiness and satisfaction with life in general are not as affected as marital satisfaction and may even increase temporarily (Dyrdal & Lucas, 2013; Galatzer-Levy, Mazursky, Mancini, & Bonnano, 2011; Nelson et al., 2013).

However, individuals vary widely in their adjustment to new parenthood. Some new parents experience the transition as a bowl of cherries, others as the pits—as a full-blown crisis in their lives. What might make this life event easier or harder to manage? Characteristics of the baby, the parent, and the social context all count.

A baby who is difficult (for example, cries endlessly because of colic) creates more stresses and anxieties for parents than an infant who is quiet, sociable, responsive, and otherwise easy to love (Levy-Shiff, 1994; Meredith & Noller, 2003). Parent characteristics matter too. Parents who have good problem-solving and communication skills, are in good mental health, and find adaptive ways to restructure and organize their lives to accommodate a new baby adjust well (Cox et al., 1999; Levy-Shiff, 1994). Similarly, parents who have realistic expectations about parenthood and about infants and children tend to adjust more easily than those who have an unrealistically rosy view (Kalmuss, Davidson, & Cushman, 1992; Mylod, Whitman, & Borkowski, 1997).

Finally, the social context can make a great deal of difference to the new parent. Most important is partner support: things go considerably better for a new mother when she has a good relationship with the father, and when he shares the burden of child care and housework, than when she has no partner or an unsupportive one (Demo & Cox, 2000; Levy-Shiff, 1994). When a mother feels that she has less quality time with her partner and thinks that the division of labor is unfair, her marital satisfaction drops (Dew & Wilcox, 2011). Social support from friends and relatives can also help new parents cope (Stemp, Turner, & Noh, 1986), as can interventions designed to help expecting mothers and fathers prepare realistically for the challenges ahead and support each other as they deal with these challenges (Doherty, Erickson, & LaRossa, 2006; Schulz, Cowan, & Cowan, 2006).

In sum, parents who have an easy baby to contend with; who possess positive personal qualities and coping skills; and who receive reliable support from their partners and other people are in the best position to cope adaptively with new parenthood, a transition that is normally both satisfying and stressful and that can undermine marital satisfaction.

The Child-Rearing Family

The child-rearing family is the family with children in it. What can parents look forward to as they have additional children and as their children age? A heavier workload! The stresses and strains of caring for a toddler are greater than those of caring for an infant, and the arrival of a second child means additional stress (O'Brien, 1996). Parents must not only devote time to the new baby but also deal with their firstborn child's normal anxieties

New parenthood brings joy, but it is also a stressful transition involving new challenges.

Photodisc/GettyImages

about this intruder. Parents complain of the hassles of cleaning up food and toys, constantly keeping an eye on their children, and dealing with their perfectly normal but irritating demands for attention, failures to comply with requests, and bouts of whining (O'Brien, 1996). Because the workload increases, fathers often become more involved in child care after a second child is born (Dunn, 2007). However, the mother who is raising multiple children as a single parent or the mother whose partner is not very involved may find herself without a moment's rest as she tries to keep up with two or more active, curious, mobile, and dependent youngsters.

Additional challenges sometimes arise for parents when their children enter adolescence. As you saw earlier, parent–child conflicts become more frequent for a while as children enter adolescence. Moreover, parents' conflicts with each other over how to raise their adolescent children can stress their marriage and undermine their marital satisfaction (Cui & Donnellan, 2009). When the firstborn child in the family reaches puberty, marital love and satisfaction often dip a bit (Whiteman, McHale, & Crouter, 2007).

Middle-aged parents are affected by how well adjusted their children are. They may have difficulty maintaining a sense of well-being if their children are experiencing problems or having trouble launching themselves successfully into adulthood (Greenfield & Marks, 2006). The negative effects on parents' mental health of a child's problems as a teenager are sometimes still evident in old age (Milkie, Norris, & Bierman, 2011). Here, then, is another example of child effects within the family system. But it works the other way, too: When parents are unhappy or are experiencing marital problems, the parent–child relationship and parenting can deteriorate and teens can be placed at greater risk for problems such as delinquency, alcohol and drug use, anxiety, depression, and emotional distress (Chung, Flook, & Fuligni, 2009; Cui, Conger, & Lorenz, 2005).

Children clearly complicate their parents' lives by demanding everything from fresh diapers and close monitoring to college tuition. By claiming time and energy that might otherwise go into nourishing the marital relationship and by adding stresses to their parents' lives, children seem to have a negative—although typically only slightly negative—effect on marital satisfaction through the child-rearing years (Gorchoff, John, & Helson, 2008; Kurdek, 1999; Rollins & Feldman, 1970). Yet when parents are interviewed about the costs and benefits of parenthood, they generally emphasize the positives and feel that parenthood has contributed a great deal to their personal development, making them more responsible and caring people (Palkovitz, 2002).

The Empty Nest

As children reach maturity, the family becomes a "launching pad" that fires adolescents and young adults into the world to work and start their own families. The term **empty nest** describes the family after the departure of the last child—a phase of the family life cycle that became common only starting in the 20th century as people began to live longer but have fewer children. Clearly, the emptying of the nest involves changes in roles and

lifestyle for parents. There can be moments of deep sadness but also moments of celebration:

> Pamela automatically started to toss Doritos and yucky dip into her cart—and then remembered. "I almost burst into tears," she recalls. "I wanted to stop some complete stranger and say, 'My son's gone away to college.' I had such a sense of loss" (Span, 2000, p. 15)

> We can find the TV remote. The only dirty dishes are in the dishwasher. No doors slam at 2 a.m. The floors are clothes-free zones. We always know where the car keys are. Grocery bills are mere double-digits (Kelly, 2013, p. B2).

On balance, parents react more positively than negatively to the emptying of the nest. Whereas the entry of children into the family causes modest decreases in marital satisfaction, the departure of the last child seems to be associated with increases, or at least no decline, in marital satisfaction (Gorchoff et al., 2008; Silverstein & Giarrusso, 2010; White & Edwards, 1990). After the nest empties, women often feel that their marriages are more equitable and that their spouses are more accommodating to their needs (Mackey & O'Brien, 1995; Suitor, 1991). Only a minority of parents find this transition disturbing or depressing (Mitchell & Lovegreen, 2009).

Why are parents generally not upset by the empty nest? First, they have fewer roles and responsibilities and therefore experience less stress and strain. Second, they have more opportunity to focus on their marital relationship; for women, increased enjoyment of time with their partners is a key reason for increased marital satisfaction (Gorchoff et al., 2008). Third, parents are likely to view the emptying of the nest as evidence that they have done their job of raising children well and have earned what Erik Erikson called a sense of generativity (Mitchell & Lovegreen, 2009). One 44-year-old mother put it well: "I have five terrific daughters who didn't just happen. It took lots of time to mold, correct, love, and challenge them. It's nice to see such rewarding results." Finally, most parents continue to enjoy a good deal of contact with their children after the nest empties, so it is not as if they are really losing the parent–child relationship (White & Edwards, 1990).

In recent years, an increasing number of adult children have been remaining in the nest, or leaving and then refilling it in a kind of "boomerang effect." Indeed, the generation of young adults affected by the Great Recession of 2008 has been called the boomerang generation (Parker, 2012). Almost 22% of adults ages 25–34 live in a multigenerational household, compared to only 11% in 1980 (Parker, 2012).

Boomerang children are often unemployed, have limited finances, are divorced or separated, or have experienced other difficulties or delays getting their adult lives on track (Ward & Spitze, 1992; White & Rogers, 1997). Although some empty nesters have difficulty adapting, most adapt well, especially if their children are responsible young adults who are attending school, working, or otherwise making progress toward flying on their own rather than freeloading (Aquilino, 2006; Parker, 2012; Ward & Spitze, 2004). The fact that most of these adult children pay rent to their parents or help with household finances suggests that this arrangement can benefit both generations (Parker, 2012).

Grandparenthood

Although we tend to picture grandparents as white-haired, jovial elders who knit mittens and bake cookies, most adults become grandparents when they are middle-aged, not elderly, and when they are likely to be highly involved in work and community activities (Conner, 2000; Connidis, 2010). Grandparenting styles are diverse, as illustrated by the results of a national survey of grandparents of teenagers that identified three major styles of grandparenting (Cherlin & Furstenberg, 1986):

1. *Remote.* Remote grandparents (29% of the sample) were symbolic figures seen only occasionally by their grandchildren. Primarily because they were geographically distant, they were emotionally distant as well.

2. *Companionate.* This was the most common style of grandparenting (55% of the sample). Companionate grandparents saw their grandchildren frequently and enjoyed sharing activities with them. They only rarely played a parental role and liked it that way. As companionate grandparents put it, "I'm happy to see them when they come and I'm happy to see them go" (Bates & Taylor, 2013, p. 59).

3. *Involved.* Finally, 16% of the grandparents took on a parent-like role. Like companionate grandparents, they saw their grandchildren frequently and were playful with them, but unlike companionate grandparents, they often helped with child care, gave advice, and played other practical roles in their grandchildren's lives. Indeed, some involved grandparents lived with and served as substitute parents for their grandchildren because their daughters or sons could not care for the children themselves. More and more grandparents today, especially in African American and Hispanic families, have custody of and are the primary parent figures for their grandchildren (Hayslip, 2009).

You can see, then, that grandparenting takes many forms but that most grandparents see at least some of their grandchildren frequently and prefer a companionate role that is high in enjoyment and affection but low in responsibility. Most grandparents find the role gratifying, especially if they *do* see their

grandchildren frequently (Connidis, 2010; Reitzes & Mutran, 2004). Yet parents control grandparents' access to their grandchildren, and grandparents may suffer if they suddenly lose all contact with their grandchildren because their child loses a custody battle or they fall out of favor with a son- or daughter-in-law (Ahrons, 2007; Bates & Taylor, 2013).

Grandparents have been called "the family national guard" because they must be ever ready to come to the rescue when there is a crisis in the family and they never know when they will be called (Hagestad, 1985). Grandmothers often help their daughters adjust to new parenthood and aid with child care when their grandchildren are very young or step in to raise grandchildren when an unmarried teenage daughter gives birth or a son or daughter divorces, develops a drug problem, or dies (Dunn, Fergusson, & Maughan, 2006).

Grandparents who do get "called to duty" sometimes contribute greatly to their grandchildren's development. Indeed, maternal grandmothers have probably been the most important helpers of mothers throughout history and continue to be important today (Coall & Hertwig, 2011). A grandmother who mentors a teen mother and coparents with her can help her gain competence as a parent (Oberlander et al., 2007). A close grandparent–grandchild relationship can protect the child of a depressed mother from becoming depressed (Silverstein & Ruiz, 2006). And although teenagers raised by single mothers tend to have low educational attainment and high rates of problem behavior on average, they resemble children raised by two parents if they are raised by a single mother and a grandparent (DeLeire & Kalil, 2002; and see Attar-Schwartz et al., 2009; Ruiz & Silverstein, 2007).

Involved grandparenting can take a toll on grandparents, however: They sometimes suffer from stress, depression, and deteriorating health when grandchildren move in with them and they must become the primary parents (Musil et al., 2011; Patrick & Goedereis, 2009). In one study of African American grandparents raising grandchildren, 94% reported significant levels of stress (Ross & Aday, 2006). Although grandparents may also benefit from the intellectual challenges and emotional rewards that parenting brings (Ehrle, 2001), their development and well-being can suffer if they become overwhelmed by their responsibilities.

Changing Family Relationships

What becomes of relationships between spouses, siblings, and parents and children during the adult years? All family relationships develop and change with time.

Marital Relationships

As you have seen, marital satisfaction dips somewhat after the honeymoon period is over, dips still lower in the new-parenthood phase, continues to drop as new children are added to the family, and may recover only when the children leave the nest, especially for women. The character of marital relationships also changes over the years. Frequency of sexual intercourse decreases (see Chapter 12), but psychological intimacy often increases. The love relationship often changes from one that is passionate to

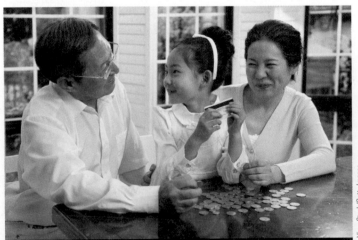

Most grandparents prefer and adopt a companionate style of grandparenting in which the idea is to have fun.

View Stock/Getty Images

one that is companionate, more like a best-friends relationship (Bierhoff & Schmohr, 2003; Reis & Aron, 2008). Elderly couples are often even more affectionate than middle-aged couples, have fewer conflicts, and are able to resolve their conflicts without as much negative emotion (Carstensen, Levenson, & Gottman, 1995; Gagnon et al., 1999; Smith et al., 2009).

Overall, however, knowing what stage of the family life cycle an adult is in does not tell us much about how satisfied that person is with his marriage. Personality is far more important. Happily married people have more agreeable personalities than unhappily married people; for example, they are more emotionally stable and vent negative feelings less often (Robins, Caspi, & Moffitt, 2000). Moreover, in happy marriages, the personalities of marriage partners are similar and are likely to remain similar or even become more similar over the years, as each partner reinforces in the other the traits that brought them together (Caspi, Herbener, & Ozer, 1992; Gonzaga, Campos, & Bradbury, 2007).

In the end, partners affect each other's development. For example, Denis Gerstorf and his colleagues (2009) studied older married couples averaging 75 years of age over a 10-year period. If a husband had good memory skills, his wife was less likely to suffer a decline in memory performance over the next 2 years. If a wife was depressed, her husband was likely to experience increased symptoms of depression and decreased memory performance. This and other studies show that we really do lead linked lives and that, as suggested by the transactional model of family influence, we influence and are influenced by our partners in close relationships.

The family life cycle ends with widowhood. By the time they reach age 65 or older, about 72% of men are married and live with their wives but only 42% of women are married and live with their husbands (Federal Interagency Forum on Aging Related Statistics, 2012). Marriages face new challenges when one of the partners becomes seriously ill or impaired and needs care. As our upcoming discussion of caregiver burden will suggest, wives may suffer poor physical and mental health and feel socially isolated when they must care for a dying husband. However, they generally manage to cope with their spouse's death and rebuild their lives, often feeling afterward that they have grown (Connidis, 2010; Seltzer & Li, 2000; and see Chapter 17).

Without question, the marital relationship is centrally important in the lives and development of most adults. Overall, married adults tend to be "happier, healthier, and better off financially" than other adults and are likely to remain so if they can weather bad times in their marriages (Waite & Gallagher, 2000).

Sibling Relationships

The sibling relationship is typically the longest-lasting relationship we have, linking us to individuals who share many of our genes and experiences (Cicirelli, 1991; Connidis, 2010). Today, of course, sibling relationships involve not only biological siblings but often half siblings, stepsiblings, and adoptive siblings (Connidis, 2010). These relationships can be close, conflicted, or, for most of us, ambivalent.

Relationships between siblings often change for the better once they no longer live together in the same home. Conflict

and rivalry diminish and relationships often become warmer and more equal in adulthood (Connidis, 2010; Scharf, Shulman, & Avigad-Spitz, 2005). Siblings often grow even closer in old age (Cicirelli, 1995; Connidis, 2010). Most adult siblings are in frequent contact and have positive feelings toward one another (Spitze & Trent, 2006). They may not often discuss intimate problems or help one another, but they usually feel that they can count on one another in a crisis (Cicirelli, 1982, 1995).

Some of the ambivalence that characterizes sibling relationships during childhood carries over into adulthood, however (Cicirelli, 1995; Connidis, 2010). Siblings may compete with one another as they build their lives. And whereas siblings who enjoyed a close relationship during childhood are likely to be drawn closer after significant life events such as a parent's illness or death, siblings who had poor relationships during childhood may clash in response to the same life events—for example, bickering about who is doing more to help an ailing parent or how a deceased parent's estate should be divided (Lerner et al., 1991; Ross & Milgram, 1982). Adult siblings who perceive that their parents played favorites when they were children or play favorites currently do not get along as well as those who believe their parents have treated them equitably (Suitor et al., 2009).

Parent–Child Relationships

Parent and child generations in most families are in close contact and enjoy affectionate give-and-take relationships throughout the adult years. When aging parents eventually need support, children are there to help.

Evolving Relationships Like sibling relationships, parent–child relationships are ambivalent (Birditt & Fingerman, 2013). Even after emerging adults have left the nest, there are likely to be tensions in most parent–adult child relationships along with the love. Parents can become stressed when their children have problems or when they are asked to help solve those problems; children can become irritated when their parents try to meddle in their lives or demand more of them than they want to give (Birditt et al., 2009; Blieszner, 2006; Connidis, 2010). Parents and children are at different points in the life cycle, and parents may be more invested in the parent–child relationship than children who are building their own families are. As a result, the well-being of parents can be positively affected when their children marry or become parents, but negatively affected when their children experience divorce or other negative events (Kalmijn & De Graaf, 2012).

Yet adults have an opportunity to negotiate a new phase of their relationship with their parents in which they move beyond playing out roles as child and parent, see their parents as "real people" with flaws, understand them better, and become more like friends (Birditt & Fingerman, 2013; Birditt et al., 2008). A more mutual, friendlike relationship is especially likely to evolve if parents were supportive, authoritative parents earlier in the child's life (Belsky et al., 2001).

When children are middle-aged and their parents are elderly, the two generations typically continue to care about, socialize with, and help each other (Umberson & Slaten, 2000). Aging mothers enjoy closer relations and more contact with

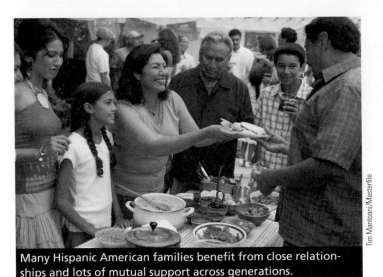

Many Hispanic American families benefit from close relationships and lots of mutual support across generations.

their children, especially their daughters, than aging fathers do (Umberson & Slaten, 2000). And Hispanic American, African American, and other minority group elders often enjoy more supportive relationships with their families than European Americans typically do, especially when it comes to living together or near one another and providing mutual help (Bengtson, Rosenthal, & Burton, 1996; Sarkisian, Gerena, & Gerstel, 2007).

Typically, relationships between the generations are not only close and affectionate but equitable: Each generation gives something, and each generation gets something in return (Conner, 2000; Markides, Boldt, & Ray, 1986). If anything, aging parents give more (Brody, 2004; Fingerman & Birditt, 2011). Aging families do *not* typically experience a **role reversal** in which the parent becomes the child and the child becomes the caregiver. Only when parents reach advanced ages and develop serious physical or mental problems does the parent–child relationship sometimes become lopsided like this and usually it is only for a short time (Connidis, 2010; Fingerman & Birditt, 2011). However it goes, parents and children clearly affect one another's well-being for life (Fingerman & Birditt, 2011).

Caring for Aging Parents Elaine Brody (1985, 2004) uses the term **middle generation squeeze** (others call it the *sandwich generation* phenomenon) to describe the situation of middle-aged adults pressured by demands from both the younger and the older generations simultaneously (see also Grundy & Henretta, 2006; Zarit & Talley, 2013). Imagine a 55-year-old woman caring for her daughter's children (and maybe even her granddaughter's children) as well as for her own ailing parents (and possibly her grandparents). That's middle generation squeeze!

Adults with children who still depend on them increasingly find themselves caring for their aging parents; about one-third of women ages 55–69 report helping members of both the older and younger generations (Grundy & Henretta, 2006). Although spouses or partners are the first in line to care for frail elders, they often are not available or up to the challenge, so today caregiving responsibility most often falls on adult children (Silverstein & Giarrusso, 2010). Daughters spend more time than sons providing emotional support to aging parents and in-laws and carry more of the burden overall, although sons are about as involved as daughters in providing help with practical tasks and financial assistance (Chesley & Poppie, 2009). The greater involvement of women in caregiving is partly because traditional gender-role norms call for women to be the **kinkeepers** of the family—the ones who keep family members in touch with each other and handle family problems when they arise (Brody, 2004).

In many collectivist Asian societies, daughters-in-law have been the first choice as caregivers. Aging parents have often been taken in by a son, usually the oldest, and cared for by his wife (Youn et al., 1999). But this pattern of living with a son and his wife is changing as societies modernize. In China, for example, the government's former policy of only one child per family and rapid industrialization have meant that elders, especially those in rural areas whose children have moved to the cities, sometimes have no one to care for them (Zhang, 2009). Urban elders in China are faring better; although they do not as often live with children as they used to, most have pensions, medical care, and housing and more and more live together and provide one another with support.

In our individualistic society, most aging parents strongly resist having to live with and be dependent on their children. They prefer to live close to but not with their children; they enjoy their independence and do not want to burden their children when their health fails (Connidis, 2010; Brody, 2004). However, families remain the major providers of care for the frail elderly today. We see little support for the view that today's families have abandoned or failed to meet their responsibilities to their oldest members. However, concerns are now being expressed about whether children whose parents divorced or stepchildren will be as supportive of older adults, especially fathers and stepfathers, in future years (Connidis, 2010; Silverstein & Giarrusso, 2010; Stein, 2009).

Middle-aged adults who must foster their children's development while tending to their own development and caring for aging parents sometimes find their situation overwhelming. They may experience **caregiver burden**—psychological distress associated with the demands of providing care for someone with physical or cognitive impairments (Knight & Losada, 2011; Zarit & Talley, 2013). Caring for an ailing loved one can be rewarding and can even have beneficial effects on health and well-being (Brown et al., 2009). Yet many adult children providing such care experience emotional, physical, and financial strains and suffer for it (Pinquart & Sorensen, 2006). A woman who is almost wholly responsible for a dependent elder may feel angry and resentful because she has no time for herself. She may experience role conflict between her caregiver role and her roles as wife, mother, and employee (Stephens et al., 2001, 2009). This can undermine her sense of well-being and put her at risk for depression.

Caregiver burden is likely to be lighter if the elderly parent has physical health problems rather than Alzheimer's disease or another form of dementia and the disruptive and socially inappropriate behaviors that often go along with dementia (Pinquart & Sorensen, 2003). The caregiver's motivations can also matter: daughters who help out of love experience helping as less stressful and burdensome than those who help mainly out of a sense of duty or who are not very motivated by either love or duty (Cicirelli, 1993; Lyonette & Yardley, 2003). And those who are secure rather than anxious or avoidant in their attachments seem to provide the best care and experience the least caregiver burden and depression (Karantzas, Evans, & Foddy, 2010; Morse et al., 2011).

Cultural and contextual factors may enter in: for example, African American caregivers devote more hours but feel less burdened than white caregivers do, possibly because of differences in norms regarding family responsibility for elder care (Kosberg et al., 2007). Finally, strains are likely to be less if a caregiving daughter has a supportive marriage (Brody et al., 1992; Scharlach, Li, & Dalvi, 2006; Stephens et al., 2009).

In short, the caregivers most likely to experience caregiver burden are those who must care for parents or spouses with behavioral problems, who do not want to help or help out of duty rather than love, who lack personal resources such as a secure attachment style, and who lack social and cultural support for caregiving. What can be done for burdened caregivers? Behavior management training, anger management training, and cognitive behavioral therapy can help caregivers sharpen their caregiving skills, teach their aging parents self-care skills, learn to react less negatively to the difficult behavior often shown by elderly adults with dementia, and cope with the stress associated with their role and the conflicts that may arise between it and their other roles (Gallagher-Thompson & Coon, 2007; Zarit, 2009;

Zarit & Talley, 2013). Respite services that give caregivers a break now and then can also be tremendously important.

Checking Mastery

1. If you were drawing a graph line to show changes in marital satisfaction over the family life cycle, what would it look like?
2. What are three factors that can make new parenthood a stressful transition?
3. Which of the three main grandparental roles do grandparents prefer, and what does it involve?
4. What are two factors that might increase the caregiver burden on a middle-aged woman taking care of her mother with Alzheimer's disease?

Making Connections

1. Martha has just married George and wonders how her experience of the events in the traditional family life cycle is likely to differ from his. Can you enlighten her?
2. You may want to ask your mother, but to what extent does the research on changes in the marital relationship and in parent–child relationships (relationships with parents and with children) apply to your mother? If there are differences, why do you think they arose?

15.6 Diverse Family Experiences

LEARNING OBJECTIVES:

- Describe the "typical" implications of never marrying, cohabiting with a partner, remaining childless, living in a dual-career family, and living in a gay or lesbian family.

- Discuss the "typical" effects of divorce on parents and children and what factors are likely to make for good adjustment.

Useful as it is, the traditional family life cycle concept does not capture the tremendous diversity of family experiences today—the diversity so evident in the popular television program *Modern Family*. Many adults do not progress in an orderly way through the phases of the traditional family life cycle. Some never marry, and some of those live alone, whereas others cohabit with a romantic partner, heterosexual or homosexual, sometimes raising children together. Some, married or not, never have children. Some continue working when their children are young, others stop or cut back. And an increasing number of adults change their family circumstances with some frequency—for example, marrying, divorcing, and cohabiting or remarrying. Let us examine some of these variations in family life.

Singles

It is nearly impossible to describe the "typical" single adult. This category includes not only young adults who have not yet married but also middle-aged and elderly people who experienced divorce or the death of a spouse or who never married. It is

typical to start adulthood as a single person, though; the large majority of adults ages 18–29 are unmarried (Cohn et al., 2011). As ■ Figure 15.5 shows, the percentage of adults who are married has dropped considerably since 1960, whereas the percentages of never-married and divorced or separated adults have grown. Because adults have been postponing marriage, the number of young, single adults has grown considerably.

Cohabitation, living with a romantic partner without being married, is also on the rise, to the point that most marriages are now preceded by cohabitation (Cohan, 2013). Many cohabiters have children; by one estimate, 4 out of 10 children will live in a family headed by a cohabiting couple sometime during childhood (Whitehead & Popenoe, 2003). Never-married people live together for a variety of reasons (Cohan, 2013; Connidis, 2010):

- *Convenience*: They are in a romantic relationship and want an affordable living arrangement or get tired of commuting to be together.
- *Trial marriage*: They live together to find out whether they are compatible enough to marry.

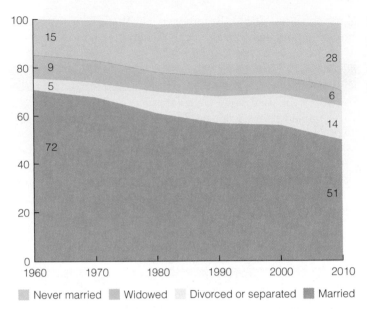

■ **Figure 15.5** The percentage of U.S. adults who are married fell between 1960 and 2010, while the percentages of never married and divorced or separated adults rose. Postponement of marriage accounts for much, but not all, of the drop in the percentage of adults who are married.

SOURCE: Cohn, D., Passel, J. S., Wang, W., & Livingston, G. (2011). *Barely half of U. S. adults are married—A record low*. Washington, DC: Pew Research Center Social & Demographic Trends. Retrieved from www.pewsocialtrends.org.

- *Alternative to marriage*: They have no intention to marry. Some reject the concept of marriage. Some are older adults who want companionship but do not want to jeopardize their financial situation or upset their children by remarrying (Brown, Bulanda, & Lee, 2012; Connidis, 2010). Some of these older adults decide instead to "live apart together," maintaining their own households but staying at each other's places with some frequency (Cherlin, 2010; Connidis, 2010).

Exploring Development 15.1
The Decision to Have Children

Jennifer and Darrin agreed they wanted kids some day, but Katie came sooner than they'd planned. Pam and Ed, in contrast, decided they did not want children.

- Which couple do you think will be happier? Why?
- What are reasons not to have children?

It makes sense to think that couples who live together before marrying would have more opportunity than those who do not to determine whether they are truly compatible before they tie the knot. Yet couples who live together and then marry are, on average, more dissatisfied with their marriages and more likely to divorce than couples who do not live together before marrying (Cohan, 2013). Why?

One explanation is that cohabiters are different from people who marry without cohabiting; for example, they tend to be younger and lower in income and they may have less conventional family attitudes and less commitment to marriage as an institution (Booth & Johnson, 1988; Cohan, 2013). This is less likely to be the reason, though, as more and more couples cohabit. Indeed, in European countries where cohabitation is widespread and well-accepted and gender attitudes are more egalitarian, cohabiting women are no less happy than married women—the happiness gap disappears (Lee & Ono, 2012).

A second explanation is that many adults who cohabitate do not go into it with an intention to marry but end up marrying anyway, largely out of inertia (Stanley et al., 2010). That is, some couples whose relationship is not very strong may slide into more nights in the same bed without a commitment to each other and marry only because their lives and assets have become entangled and it has become difficult to leave (Cohan, 2013; Stanley et al., 2010).

If partners are engaged before they decide to live together, if they have not cohabited with other partners before, and if they do not have a child before they marry, their odds of marital success improve (Cohan, 2013; Tach & Halpern-Meekin, 2009). But if couples who live together have characteristics that make them poor bets for marital success or if they marry out of inertia rather than true love, their marriages are more likely to fail.

What of the 10% or so of adults who never marry? Stereotypes suggest that they are miserably lonely and maladjusted. However, single adults often make up for their lack of spouse and children by forming close bonds with siblings, friends, or younger adults who become like sons or daughters to them (Connidis, 2010; Rubinstein et al., 1991). It is divorced or widowed rather than never-married single adults who tend to be least happy with their singlehood in old age (Pudrovska, Schieman, & Carr, 2006).

Childless Married Couples

Many married couples who remain childless want children but cannot have them. However, a growing number of adults voluntarily decide to delay having children or not have them at all, for a host of different reasons (Abma & Martinez, 2006; Allen & Wiles, 2013; Keizer, Dykstra, & Jansen, 2008). The video in **Exploring Development Box 15.1** interviews two couples; one couple had a child without deciding to, and the other talks about why they decided not to have a child.

Although trying and failing to conceive a child is a difficult and demoralizing experience (Schwerdtfeger & Shreffler, 2009), childlessness generally does not diminish the well-being of adults and sometimes boosts it (Umberson, Pudrovska, & Reczek, 2010). The marital satisfaction of childless couples tends to be higher than that of couples with children during the child-rearing years (Kurdek, 1999). And middle-aged and elderly childless couples are no less satisfied with their lives than parents whose children have left the nest (Allen, Blieszner, & Roberto, 2000; Rempel, 1985) and in some studies are less depressed (Bures, Koropeckyj-Cox, & Loree, 2009). Children apparently do not guarantee happiness; nor does not having children doom people to an unhappy old age (Connidis, 2010). However, elderly women who find themselves without children and without a partner may have no one to help them when they develop health problems (Gray, 2009).

Dual-Career Families

Because of the huge increase over several decades in the numbers of mothers who work outside the home, developmental scientists have wondered how family life and child development are affected when a mother works outside the home rather than being a stay-at-home mother. For one thing, half or more of working moms—and working dads too—now say they find it difficult to balance work and family (Parker & Wang, 2013). In other words, work-family conflict has become an issue for both men and women, especially when children are young (Erickson, Martinengo, & Hill, 2010). Working parents are subject to **spillover effects**—ways in which events at work affect home life and events at home carry over into the workplace, for good or bad. Most research has focused on negative spillover effects from work to home (Barnett, 1994; Crouter, 2006). After parents have a stressful day at work, for example, they tend to be withdrawn from their spouse and children and angry and irritable if provoked (Repetti, Wang, & Saxbe, 2009). By contrast, a rewarding, stimulating job can have positive effects on a person's interactions within the family (Greenberger, O'Neil, & Nagel, 1994).

Despite the potential for work-family conflict and negative spillover effects, dual-career families generally fare well (Gottfried & Gottfried, 2006). There is no indication that a mother's working, in itself, has damaging effects on child development. Children, especially girls, can even benefit from the positive role model a working mother provides; they may adopt less stereotyped views of men's and women's family and work roles and set higher educational and vocational goals for themselves (Hoffman, 1989; Riggio & Desrochers, 2005).

The decision to work can have positive or negative effects, however, depending on the age of the child, its effects on parenting, and the family's circumstances (Gottfried & Gottfried, 2006; Holden, 2010). Living in a dual-career family is likely to be good for children when it means an increase in family income, when mothers are happy with the choice they have made and remain good parents, when fathers become more involved, and when children receive high quality day care or after-school care (Hoffman, 2000; Lerner & Noh, 2000). Having two working parents can be a negative experience, however, if the parents are unable to remain warm and involved and share "quality time" with their children (Moorehouse, 1991).

Fortunately, most dual-career couples are able to stay involved with their children and enjoy the personal and financial benefits of working without compromising their children's development. They might be able to do so even more successfully if the United States, like other nations, provided paid leave for parents and other family caregivers and did more to support families through flexible work hours, day care and preschool programs, after-school programs, and other support systems (Heymann & Earle, 2009; Heymann, Penrose, & Earle, 2006). In a survey of 190 countries, Heymann and Earle (2009) found that 178 of them guaranteed paid maternal leave by law and over 50 offered paid paternal leave as well. The United States was in the company of Papua New Guinea, Swaziland, and Australia as the countries without a national policy of paid parental leave—and Australia now has one (Human Rights Watch, 2011).

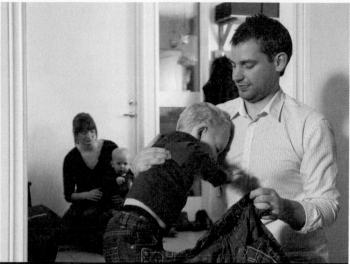

Dual-career families work best when partners share the workload.

Gay and Lesbian Families

What are the family experiences of gay men, lesbian women, and other sexual minority adults like? They are most notable for their diversity (Goldberg, 2009; Peplau & Fingerhut, 2007; Rith & Diamond, 2013). Generally, gay and lesbian relationships evolve through the same stages of development, are satisfying or dissatisfying for the same reasons, and are typically as rewarding as those of married or cohabiting heterosexuals (Kurdek, 1995, 2006; Peplau & Fingerhut, 2007). Sexual minority couples end their relationships more than married heterosexual couples do but at about the same rate as cohabiting heterosexual couples (Rith & Diamond, 2013).

In the United States, several million gay men and lesbian women are parents, most through previous heterosexual relationships, others through adoption, artificial insemination, or surrogate parents. Some no longer live with their children, but others raise them as single parents and still others raise them in families that have two mothers or two fathers. Other gay men and lesbian women live as singles or as couples without children throughout their lives, some forming families that consist of a group of friends (Diamond & Butterworth, 2009).

Gay and lesbian families face special challenges, as evidenced by our continuing national controversy over whether gay and lesbian couples should be allowed to marry. These families are not fully recognized as families by society and are sometimes victims of discrimination (Peplau & Fingerhut, 2007; Rith & Diamond, 2013). For example, a gay or lesbian person's life partner may not be embraced as a full member of the family, allowed to make life-and-death decisions if their partner becomes ill, or given custody of the partner's children if the partner dies (Connidis, 2010). Social attitudes have consequences: In one study, lesbian mothers in the United States were more worried about their legal status and possible discrimination and showed more symptoms of depression than lesbian mothers in Canada, a country that offers more protections to gays and lesbians (Shapiro, Peterson, & Stewart, 2009). In another study, the well-being of the children of sexual minority individuals was affected by whether the social climate of the area in which they lived was supportive of sexual minorities (Lick et al., 2012).

Contrary to myth, gay and lesbian couples usually do not have one adopt the traditional "husband" role and the other the "wife" role (Rith & Diamond, 2013). Instead, relationships are usually egalitarian; partners share responsibilities equally and tend to work out a division of labor based on who is especially talented at or does not mind doing certain tasks (Huston & Schwartz, 1995). Even after the transition to parenthood, most couples report that their child has two involved parents, although the biological parent usually takes the lead role (Goldberg & Perry-Jenkins, 2007; Rith & Diamond, 2013).

What are the implications for children of being raised by gay or lesbian parents? Comparing lesbian mothers with heterosexual mothers in two-parent and single-parent homes, Susan Golombok and her colleagues (2003) found that lesbian mothers tend to hit children less and to engage in imaginative and domestic play more but are otherwise similar to heterosexual mothers. Moreover, children who lived with two parents of the same sex had better developmental outcomes than children living with a single mother, and they were no different than children living with two heterosexual parents. This study and others suggest that gay and lesbian adults who raise children are as likely as heterosexual parents to parent effectively and to produce competent and well-adjusted children (Farr, Forssell, & Patterson, 2010; Goldberg, 2009; Rith & Diamond, 2013). Moreover, contrary to what many people believe, their children are no more likely than the children of heterosexual parents to develop a homosexual or bisexual orientation. After reviewing such research, the American Academy of Pediatrics has concluded that it is best for children of sexual minority adults to be raised by parents who have made a long-term commitment to each other and have the legal status as parents that comes with marriage (Perrin, Siegel, & the Committee on Psychosocial Aspects of Child and Family Health, 2013).

This lesbian couple has twins, thanks to a sperm donation. Research tells us that the children of gay and lesbian parents generally turn out no different than the children of heterosexual couples on average. The secret to success in any family is good parenting.

67photo/Alamy

Divorcing Families

Progress through the family life cycle is disrupted when a married couple divorces. Divorce is not just one life event. Rather, divorce—and the same can be said of the separation of a cohabiting couple—is a series of stressful experiences for the entire family that begins with difficulties before the divorce and includes a complex series of life changes as the relationship unravels and family members reorganize their lives (Amato, 2000, 2010; Demo & Fine, 2010; Hetherington & Kelly, 2002). Why do people divorce (or separate)? What effects does divorce typically have on family members? And how can we explain why some adults and children thrive after a divorce whereas others experience persisting problems?

Before the Divorce

Scholars have pieced together a profile of the couples at highest risk for divorce (Amato, 2010; Demo & Fine, 2010; Kitson, 1992; Teachman, 2002). Generally they are young adults, in their 20s and 30s, who have been married for an average of only about 7 years (hence the term "seven year itch"?) and who often have young children. Couples are especially likely to divorce if they married as teenagers, had a short courtship, conceived a child before marrying, and are low in SES—all factors that might suggest an unreadiness for marriage and unusually high financial and psychological stress accompanying new parenthood. Personality problems and problem behaviors such as alcohol or drug abuse often play a role as well.

Couples typically divorce because they feel their marriages lack communication, emotional fulfillment, or compatibility. Wives tend to have longer lists of complaints than their husbands do and often have more to do with initiating the breakup (Hewitt, Western, & Baxter, 2006; Thompson & Amato, 1999). Whereas historically divorce was considered a drastic step taken only when adultery, desertion, abuse, or a similar crisis was involved, starting in the late 20th century it came to be viewed as more like a right—an action to be taken when people do not feel personally fulfilled in their relationship. Under no-fault divorce laws in most states, either partner can cite irreconcilable differences and end the marriage simply because they want to (Cherlin, 2009). Still, most divorcing couples experience a few years of marital distress and often try separations before they make the final decision to divorce (Demo & Fine, 2010; Kitson, 1992).

After the Divorce

Most families going through a divorce experience it as a genuine crisis—a period of considerable disruption that often lasts at least 1–2 years—although there is tremendous variation in how it goes (Amato, 2000; Demo & Fine, 2010; Hetherington, 2006). The wife, who usually ends up as the primary caregiver for any children, is likely to be angry, depressed, and otherwise distressed, although often she is relieved as well. The husband is also likely to be distressed, particularly if he did not want the divorce and feels shut off from his children. Both individuals must revise their identities and their relationship. Both may feel isolated from former friends and unsure of themselves in new romantic relationships. Divorced women with children are likely to face the added problem of getting by with considerably less money (Amato, 2000).

Because of these stressors, divorced adults are at higher risk than married adults for depression and psychological distress, physical health problems, and even death (Amato, 2000; Sbarra, Law, & Portley, 2011; and see Kamp Dush, 2011, 2013, on similar mental health problems among cohabiting couples who separate). Adjustment is especially likely to be poor among those who have little income, do not find a new relationship, take a dim view of divorce, and did not initiate the divorce (Wang & Amato, 2000).

As you might suspect, psychologically distressed adults do not make the best parents. Moreover, children going through a divorce do not make the best children because they too are suffering. They are often angry, fearful, depressed, and guilty, especially if they fear that they were somehow responsible for their parents' breakup (Buehler, Lange, & Franck, 2007; Hetherington, 1981). They are also likely to be whiny, dependent, disobedient, and disrespectful.

Mavis Hetherington and her associates (Hetherington, Cox, & Cox, 1982; Hetherington & Kelly, 2002) have found that stressed custodial mothers often become impatient and insensitive to their children's needs. In terms of the major dimensions of child rearing, they become less accepting and responsive and less in control. Less authoritative and less consistent in their discipline, they occasionally try to seize control of their children with a heavy-handed, authoritarian approach, but more often they fail to carry through in enforcing rules and make few demands that their children behave maturely (see also Demo & Buehler, 2013). Noncustodial fathers, meanwhile, are likely to be overly permissive, indulging their children during visitations (Amato & Sobolewski, 2004), and good coparenting becomes difficult.

This is not the formula for producing well-adjusted, competent children. A vicious circle of the sort described by the transactional model of family influence can result: Children's behavioral problems make effective parenting more difficult, and deterioration in parenting aggravates children's behavioral problems. When this breakdown in family functioning occurs, children are likely to display not only behavioral problems at home but also strained relations with peers, low self-esteem, academic problems, and adjustment difficulties at school (Hetherington, 2006; Lansford, 2009).

Families typically begin to pull themselves back together about 2 years after the divorce, and by the 6-year mark most differences between children of divorce and children of intact families have disappeared (Hetherington & Kelly, 2002). Yet even after the crisis phase has passed, divorce can leave a residue of negative effects on at least some individuals that lasts years (Amato, 2006; Hetherington & Kelly, 2002). For example, as adolescents, children of divorce are less likely than other youth to perceive their relationships with their parents, especially their fathers, as close and caring, and many are still unhappy about what divorce has done to their lives (Amato, 2010; Woodward, Fergusson, & Belsky, 2000). About 20 to 25% of children of divorce still have emotional scars and psychological problems as young adults (Demo & Buehler, 2013; Hetherington & Kelly, 2002). Adults whose parents divorced are also less likely than adults from intact families to marry and more likely to experience marital conflict and divorce if they do (Afifi & Denes, 2013; Amato, 2006; Maier & Lachman, 2000).

On a more positive note, not all families experience divorce as a major crisis, and of those that do, most parents and children rebound from their crisis period and adapt well in the long run, some even undergoing impressive growth as a result of their experience (Demo & Fine, 2010; Hetherington & Kelly, 2002). Some adults feel better about themselves and their lives after extracting themselves from a bad marriage. And a conflict-ridden two-parent family is usually more detrimental to a child's development than a cohesive single-parent family (Afifi & Demes, 2013; Amato, 2006), so it is not always wise to "stay together for the good of the children." Moreover, some of the problems in children that we attribute to divorce appear to emerge before the divorce and are the result of parent conflict, not divorce (Demo & Buehler, 2013; Lansford, 2009).

Influences on Adjustment

Perhaps the most important message of research on divorce is that the outcomes of this stressful experience vary widely (Demo & Fine, 2010; Lansford, 2009). Several factors can help facilitate a positive adjustment to divorce and prevent lasting damage:

1. *Adequate financial support.* Families fare better after a divorce if the noncustodial parent, usually the father, pays child support and the family has adequate finances (Amato & Sobolewski, 2004; Marsiglio et al., 2000). Adjustment is likely to be more difficult for mother-headed families that fall into poverty and must struggle to survive.

2. *Good parenting by the custodial parent.* If the custodial parent can manage to remain warm, authoritative, and consistent, children are far less likely to experience problems (Hetherington, 2006). Interventions for divorced parents can improve their parenting skills and, in turn, their children's adjustment (Forgatch & DeGarmo, 1999; see also Wolchik et al., 2000).

3. *Good parenting by the noncustodial parent.* Children may suffer when they lose contact with their noncustodial parent over time, as a quarter or so of children living with their mothers do (Cheadle, Amato, & King, 2010; Demo & Cox, 2000). More important than amount of contact, however, is the quality of parenting provided (Amato & Sobolewski, 2004; King & Sobolewski, 2006). Adolescents who have a good relationship with their noncustodial father are better adjusted than adolescents who live with their fathers but do not feel close to them (Booth, Scott, & King, 2010). At the same time, if a nonresident father engages in high levels of antisocial behavior and harsh parenting, children may be better off without their dad in their lives (Coley, Carrano, & Lewin-Bizan, 2011).

4. *Minimal conflict between parents.* Children should be protected from continuing marital conflict after the divorce and efforts by parents to undermine each other in their children's eyes (Amato, 1993; Lansford, 2009). When parents can agree on joint custody, children's adjustment tends to be better (Bauserman, 2002). When the mother has custody, positive coparenting in which parents coordinate and cooperate can help keep fathers close to and involved with their

children and reduce behavior problems (Amato, Kane, & James, 2011; Sobolewski & King, 2005).

5. *Additional social support.* Divorcing adults are less depressed if they have close confidants than if they do not (Menaghan & Lieberman, 1986). Children also benefit from support from close friends (Lustig, Wolchik, & Braver, 1992) and from participating in peer-support programs in which they and other children of divorce can share their feelings and learn positive coping skills (Grych & Fincham, 1992).

6. *Minimal other changes.* Generally families do best if additional changes are kept to a minimum—for example, if parents do not have to move, get new jobs, cope with the loss of their children, and so on (Buehler et al., 1985–1986). It is easier to deal with a couple of stressors than a mountain of them.

7. *Personal resources.* Finally, personal resources such as intelligence, emotional stability, and good coping skills often put some individuals—even some members of the same family—on a more positive trajectory than others after a divorce (Demo & Fine, 2010; Lansford, 2009).

As Paul Amato (1993) concludes, adjustment to divorce will depend on the "total configuration" of stressors the individual faces and on the resources he has available to aid in coping, including both personal strengths and social supports.

Reconstituted Families

Within 3–5 years of a divorce, about 75% of single-parent families experience yet another major transition when a parent remarries and the children acquire a stepparent—and sometimes new siblings (Hetherington & Stanley-Hagan, 2000; and see McGoldrick & Carter, 2011; Teachman & Tedrow, 2008). Because about 60% of remarried couples divorce, an increasing number of adults and children today find themselves in recurring cycles of singlehood, cohabitation or marriage, conflict, and separation or divorce (Cherlin, 2009).

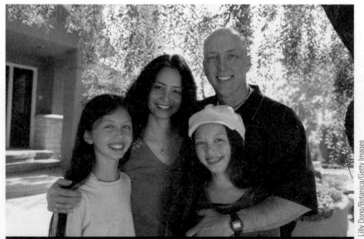

Most children adjust to being part of a reconstituted family, but it can be hard when both partners bring children to remarriage.

How do children fare when their custodial parent remarries? The first few years are a time of conflict and disruption as a new family system takes shape and new family roles and relationships are ironed out (Hetherington & Stanley-Hagan, 2000). Interviewed 20 years after their parents divorced, about one-third of the adults in one study recalled the remarriage as more stressful than the divorce (Ahrons, 2007).

The difficulties are likely to be worse if both parents bring children to the family than if only one parent does (Hetherington, 2006). Girls may have more trouble than boys, too; they are often so closely allied with their mothers that they may resent either a stepfather competing for their mother's attention or a stepmother attempting to play a substitute-mother role. Most adapt with time, but on average adolescents in reconstituted or blended families with children from more than one marriage, like children in single-parent families after a divorce, are less well adjusted and show more problems such as depression and antisocial behavior than adolescents who live in intact two-parent families (Hetherington, 2006). There is hope, though: One team of researchers showed that a parent training program for parents in newly reconstituted families not only improved parenting skills, strengthened coparenting, and reduced child behavior problems at school but also enhanced the relationship between parents, thus improving the whole family system (Bullard et al., 2010).

What should we conclude overall about the implications of today's diverse families for child development? As Mavis Hetherington (2006) concludes, "It is family process rather than family structure that is critical to the well-being of children" (p. 232). That is, children and adolescents can thrive in any type of family as long as they receive good parenting.

Checking Mastery

1. What are two main reasons that cohabitation before marriage is associated with later marital problems?
2. Is growing up in a dual-career family typically damaging to child development? Why or why not?
3. What is the typical effect of a custodial parent's remarriage after a divorce, and what kind of reconstituted family seems to have the most difficulty adjusting?

Making Connections

1. Three months after her divorce from Alex, Blanca has become depressed and increasingly withdrawn. Her son Carlos, age 7, has become a terror around the house and a discipline problem at school. How might (a) the parent effects model, (b) the child effects model, (c) the interactional model, and (d) the transactional model of family influence explain what is going on in this single-parent family?
2. Suppose you are a counseling psychologist and Blanca comes to you for advice on how she and her family can deal most effectively with their divorce. What would you tell her based on research on factors affecting adjustment to divorce?

LEARNING OBJECTIVES:

- Describe the various forms that family violence can take.

- Illustrate how characteristics of the abuser, child, and social context can all contribute to child abuse.

- Summarize the effects of child abuse on victims and two approaches to preventing abuse.

As this chapter makes clear, family relationships normally contribute positively to human development at every point in the life span. At the same time, families can be the cause of much anguish and of development gone astray. Nowhere is this more obvious than in cases of family violence (St. George, 2001, p. A20):

> From a young age, I have had to grow up fast. I see families that are loving and fathers who care for their children, and I find myself hating them. . . . I have nightmares pertaining to my father. I get angry and frustrated when family is around.

These sobering words were written by Sonyé Herrera, an abused adolescent who for years had been hit, threatened with guns, choked, and otherwise victimized—and had witnessed her mother abused—by an alcoholic father. The abuse continued even after the couple divorced. At age 15, unable to stand any more, Herrera had her father charged with assault, but he returned one afternoon, hit her, and shot and killed both her and her mother before turning his gun on himself (St. George, 2001, p. A21).

Child abuse, mistreating or harming a child physically, emotionally, or sexually, is perhaps the most visible form of family violence. Every day, infants, children, and adolescents are burned, bruised, beaten, starved, suffocated, sexually abused, or otherwise mistreated by their caretakers (Del Vecchio, Eckardt Erlanger, & Smith Slep, 2013; Miller & Knudsen, 2007). Accurate statistics are hard to come by because much abuse goes unreported, but official statistics for the United States suggest that, in 2010, 1 of every 100 children under age 18 was the victim of substantiated **child maltreatment**, a broad term that includes both abuse and neglect of the child's basic needs (Federal Interagency Forum on

Child and Family Statistics, 2012). Of these victims, 75% were neglected, 16% physically abused, 9% sexually abused, 7% emotionally or psychologically abused, and 8% experienced other types of maltreatment. Many children experienced more than one of the preceding types; therefore the percentages add up to more than 100%.

Child abuse commands a good deal of attention and tugs at our heartstrings, but the potential for abuse exists in all possible relationships within the family (Tolan, Gorman-Smith, & Henry, 2006). Children and adolescents batter, and in rare cases kill, their parents (Agnew & Huguley, 1989). Siblings, especially brothers, abuse one another in countless ways, especially if there is violence elsewhere in the family (Hoffman, Kiecolt, & Edwards, 2005). And spousal or intimate partner abuse appears to be the most common form of family violence worldwide. Globally it has been estimated that about one-third of women are beaten, coerced into sex, or emotionally abused by their partners (Murphy, 2003). In the United States, surveys suggest that about 15% of couples experience physical violence in a year, ranging from pushing to use of weapons (Heyman, Foran, & Wilkinson, 2013; Straus & Gelles, 1990). Much "mild" partner abuse is mutual. In more serious (and rarer) cases where there is not only violent behavior but injury, the violence is one-sided: Men batter their female partners, often in an attempt to control them (Heyman et al., 2013; Tolan, Gorman-Smith, & Henry, 2006). Worse, millions of children witness domestic violence and are harmed by what they see (Grych, Oxtoby, & Lynn, 2013; McDonald et al., 2006). Some also get hurt themselves, intentionally or accidentally—sometimes while trying to protect their mothers (Mbilinyi et al., 2007).

Elderly adults are also targets of family violence. Frail or impaired older people are physically or psychologically mistreated, neglected, financially exploited, and stripped of their rights—most often by stressed adult children or spouses serving as their caregivers (Jayawardena & Liao, 2006; Nerenberg, 2008). Around 5% of elderly adults are probably neglected or abused in various ways (Tolan et al., 2006); many cases probably go unreported (Nerenberg, 2008).

Family violence is not a pretty picture. Here is a social problem of major dimensions that causes untold suffering and harms the development of family members of all ages. What can be done to prevent it, or to stop it once it has started? To answer this question, we must understand why family violence occurs.

Why Does Child Abuse Occur?

Various forms of family violence have many similarities, and the contributors are often similar (Tolan et al., 2006). Because child

Child abuse occurs in all ethnic and racial groups, often when a vulnerable parent is overwhelmed by stress.

The Intergenerational Transmission of Abusive Parenting

Do you think the way your parents raised you was influenced by the way your grandparents raised them, and that you will use the same parenting approach your parents used with you? We now know that both harsh, abusive parenting and positive parenting can be transmitted across generations (Conger, Belsky, & Capaldi, 2009). But how? Consider some possible contributions of nature and nurture to the intergenerational transmission of abusive parenting.

On the nature side of the nature–nurture issue, parents could affect the next generation's parenting styles through the direct effects of genes they pass to their children—or through gene–environment interactions and gene–environment correlations involving these genes. We saw plenty of evidence in Chapter 13, for example, that aggressive behavior is influenced in part by genetic makeup.

On the nurture side of the issue, one possibility is that abusive parenting causes children to develop traits that then make them abuse-prone. Tricia Neppl and her colleagues (2009), for example, studied 187 young adults, their mothers, and their preschool-age children. They found correlations between the harshness of grandmothers' parenting styles (for example, their hostility and coerciveness) and the harshness of their daughters' parenting styles with their preschoolers. Harsh parenting, their analysis revealed, contributed to the development of conduct problems like aggressiveness in children, and these conduct problems then contribute to a harsh parenting style when these children become parents. Alternatively, we could draw on social learning theory and the concept of observational learning to suggest that children learn harsh parenting tactics by watching their abusive parents.

Finally, we now suspect that epigenetic transmission of parenting across generations is possible. That is, nurture—being treated harshly—could, through *epigenetic effects*, alter the expression of genes that affect parenting later in life. As discussed in Chapter 3, research with rats reveals that early experience with a neglectful mother affects gene expression in ways that make offspring unable to cope effectively with stress and neglectful of their own offspring. Epigenetic effects on gene expression also help explain the transmission from mother to daughter of abusive parenting among monkeys (Maestripieri, Lindell, & Higley, 2007). And analysis of suicide victims who were abused as children reveals patterns of gene expression similar to those observed in neglected and abused animals—but not evident in suicide victims who were not abused as children (McGowan et al., 2009).

So genetic makeup (and its interplay with environmental factors), socialization of traits like aggressiveness that are associated with abusive behavior, observational learning of harsh parenting, and epigenetic effects of early experiences of abuse or neglect on gene expression could all help explain why harsh, abusive parenting runs in families. The moral is that abusive and neglectful parents who seek help now in improving their parenting skills could well benefit not only their children but their grandchildren and perhaps even their great-grandchildren.

---

abuse has been studied the longest, we will look at what has been learned about how characteristics of the abuser, the abused, and the social context contribute to it.

The Abuser

Hard as it may be to believe, only about 1 child abuser in 10 appears to have a severe psychological disorder, although mental illness is one risk factor for abuse (Jaffe, 2013; Kempe & Kempe, 1978). Rather, the abusive parent is most often a young mother who tends to have many children, to live in poverty, to be unemployed, and to have no partner to share her load (U.S. Department of Health and Human Services, 2007; Wolfner & Gelles, 1993). Yet child abusers come from all races, ethnic groups, and social classes. Many of them appear to be fairly typical, loving parents—except for their tendency to become extremely irritated with their children and to do things they will later regret.

A few reliable differences between parents who abuse their children and those who do not have been identified. First, child abusers tend to have been abused as children. Although most maltreated children do not abuse their own children when they become parents, a relatively high percentage, 30%, do (Kaufman & Zigler, 1989). Abuse victims are prone to engage in other forms of family violence as well (Delsol & Margolin, 2004; Kwong et al., 2003). This cycle of abuse is not inevitable; it can be broken if abused individuals receive emotional support from parent substitutes, therapists, or spouses and are spared from severe stress as adults (Egeland, Jacobvitz, & Sroufe, 1988; Vondra & Belsky, 1993). Yet it happens and is an example of a broader phenomenon, the **intergenerational transmission of parenting**, or the passing down from generation to generation of parenting styles, abusive or otherwise. As **Exploration Box 15.3** illustrates, we are beginning to get a clearer picture of how the intergenerational transmission of abusive parenting works.

Second, abusive mothers are often battered by their partners (Coohey & Braun, 1997; McCloskey, Figueredo, & Koss, 1995). Adults are more likely to end up in an abusive romantic relationship or marriage if they were abused or witnessed abuse as a child (Stith et al., 2000). Thus, many abusive mothers may have learned through their experiences both as children and as romantic partners that violence is the way to solve problems, or they may take out some of their frustrations about being abused on their children.

Third, abusers are often insecure individuals with low self-esteem. Their unhappy experiences in insecure attachment relationships with their parents, reinforced by their negative experiences in romantic relationships, may lead them to formulate negative internal working models of themselves and others

(Pianta, Egeland, & Erickson, 1989; and see Chapter 14). These adults often see themselves as victims, feel powerless as parents, and find the normal challenges of parenting stressful and threatening (Bugental, 2009; Bugental & Beaulieu, 2003).

Fourth, abusive parents often have unrealistic expectations about what children can do at different ages and have twisted perceptions of the normal behavior of infants and young children (Haskett, Johnson, & Miller, 1994). For example, when infants cry to communicate needs such as hunger, nonabusive mothers correctly interpret infants' cries as signs of hunger or discomfort, but abusive mothers often infer that the baby is somehow criticizing or rejecting them (Egeland, 1979; Egeland, Sroufe, & Erickson, 1983). Similarly, one mother interpreted her 3-month-old's babbling as "talking back" (Bugental, 2009). (See why the study of human development is useful?)

In short, abusive parents tend to have been exposed to harsh parenting and abusive relationships themselves, to be insecure, and to find caregiving more stressful and ego threatening than other parents do. Still, it has been difficult to identify a particular kind of person who is highly likely to turn into a child abuser. Could some children bring out the worst in parents?

The Abused

An abusive parent sometimes singles out only one child in the family as a target; this offers a hint that child characteristics might matter (Gil, 1970). No one is suggesting that children are to blame for being abused, but some children appear to be more at risk than others. For example, children who have medical problems or who have difficult temperaments are more likely to be abused than quiet, healthy, and responsive infants who are easier to care for (Bugental & Beaulieu, 2003). Yet many difficult children are not mistreated, and many seemingly cheerful and easygoing children are.

Just as characteristics of the caregiver cannot fully explain why abuse occurs, then, neither can characteristics of children. There is now intriguing evidence supporting the interactional model of family influence and indicating that it is the combination of a high-risk parent and a challenging child that spells trouble. For example, a mother who feels powerless to deal with children, and who must raise a child who has a disability or illness or is otherwise difficult, is prone to overreact emotionally when the child cannot be controlled and to use harsh discipline (Bugental, 2009). Such powerless parents experience higher levels of stress than most parents, as indicated by high cortisol levels and fast heart rates, when interacting with children who are unresponsive. Through a more transactional process, their uneasiness can make such children even less responsive, provoking even more use of power tactics by the parent (Bugental, 2009; Martorell & Bugental, 2006). So, the match between child and caregiver may not be enough to explain abuse; as the transactional model suggests, relationships between parents and children sometimes just evolve in bad directions over time as each influences the other. We must also, as always, consider the ecological context surrounding the family system (Cicchetti & Valentino, 2006).

The Context

Consistently, abuse is most likely to occur when a parent is under great stress and has little social support (Cano & Vivian, 2003; Egeland et al., 1983). Life changes such as the loss of a job or a move can disrupt family functioning and contribute to abuse or neglect (Berger et al., 2011; Wolfner & Gelles, 1993). Abuse rates are also highest in deteriorating neighborhoods where families are poor, transient, socially isolated, and lacking in community services and informal social support—neighborhoods in which parents do not look after each other's children and the motto "It takes a village to raise a child" has little meaning (Korbin, 2001).

Finally, the larger macroenvironment is important. Ours is a violent society in which the use of physical punishment is common and the line between physical punishment and child abuse can be difficult to draw (Lansford & Dodge, 2008). Parents who believe strongly in the value of physical punishment are more at risk than those who do not to become abusive if they are under stress (Crouch & Behl, 2001). Child abuse is less common in societies that discourage or outlaw physical punishment and advocate nonviolent ways of resolving interpersonal conflicts (Holden, Vittrup, & Rosen, 2011; Levinson, 1989).

As you can see, child abuse is a complex phenomenon with many causes and contributing factors. It is not easy to predict who will become a child abuser and who will not, but abuse seems most likely when a vulnerable individual faces overwhelming stress with insufficient social support. Much the same is true of intimate partner abuse, elder abuse, and other forms of family violence.

What Problems Do Abused Children Display?

Physically abused and otherwise maltreated children tend to have many problems, ranging from physical injuries, health problems, impaired brain development, and cognitive deficits to social, emotional, and behavioral problems and psychological disorders (Cicchetti & Valentino, 2006; Del Vecchio et al., 2013; Margolin & Gordis, 2000). Our information on the effects of abuse all comes from correlational studies, of course; experiments in which some children are deliberately abused would be unethical. So, although researchers attempt to control for differences between abused and nonabused children in their studies, they cannot firmly establish cause-effect relationships between abuse and development.

Intellectual deficits and academic difficulties are common among mistreated children (Malinosky-Rummell & Hansen, 1993; Shonk & Cicchetti, 2001). A revealing study focused on 5-year-old identical and fraternal twins to rule out possible genetic influences on the association between exposure to domestic violence and intellectual development (Koenen et al., 2003). Children exposed to high levels of domestic violence had IQ scores 8 points lower, on average, than those of children who were not exposed to domestic violence, even taking genetic influences on IQ into account.

Preventing Child Abuse by Empowering Parents

Daphne Bugental and her colleagues (Bugental, 2009; Bugental & Beaulieu, 2003; Bugental et al., 2002) have found that abuse results when parents who feel powerless face the challenge of raising a child who is unresponsive and difficult. To evaluate a child abuse prevention program based on this research (see Bugental & Beaulieu, 2003), they targeted high-risk mothers who had recently emigrated from Mexico to California and who scored high on a measure of family stress. Some had infants who were high risk (who were born prematurely or scored low on the Apgar examination at birth and were therefore at risk for future health problems), and others had infants who were low risk. Bugental's experimental home visitation program aimed at empowering these mothers by teaching them to analyze the causes of caregiving problems without blaming either themselves or their children and to devise, try out, and evaluate the effectiveness of solutions to these caregiving problems. Families were randomly assigned to the empowerment program, another home visitation program without empowerment training, or a control condition in which families were referred to regular community services.

After the intervention period, mothers who received empowerment training had a greater sense of power in the family than mothers in the other conditions did, and they reported fewer postpartum depression symptoms. Their rate of physical abuse, including spanking and slapping, was only 4%, compared with 23% in the other home visitation group and 26% in the community referral group. Moreover, the children in the empowerment group were in better health and were better able to manage stress.

Importantly, the benefits of the program were greatest for families with high-risk children. As the graph here shows, after empowerment training, harsh parenting was unlikely whether the child was at risk for health problems or not, whereas in the control conditions, children at risk were treated far more harshly than low-risk children, suggesting that they were headed for trouble developmentally. A similar program implemented by Bugental and her colleagues resulted in mothers being more emotional available to their children and less likely to physically punish them, with the result that their children behaved less aggressively at age 3 than control children (Bugental, Corpuz, & Schwartz, 2012; Bugental & Schwartz, 2009). Judging from this work, a good deal of damage can be prevented if more parents are helped to develop confidence in their power to be effective parents.

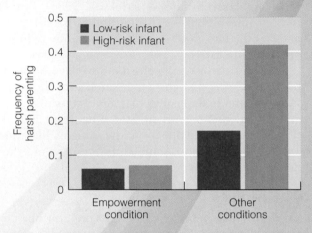

Empowerment training for low-income mothers under stress reduces harsh parenting, especially among the mothers who are most at risk of being abusive because their babies had medical problems or were born prematurely.

Source: From Bugental and Beaulieu (2003) in *Advances in child development and behavior*, Vol. 31, R. V. Kail (Ed.), page 252. Copyright 2003, with permission from Elsevier.

Social, emotional, and behavioral problems are also common among physically abused and other maltreated children (Flores, Cicchetti, & Rogosch, 2005). Some tend to be explosively aggressive youngsters, rejected by their peers for that reason (Bolger & Patterson, 2001). Even as adults, individuals who were abused as children also tend to have higher-than-average rates of depression, anxiety, and other psychological problems (Draper et al., 2008; Margolin & Gordis, 2000). One of the most disturbing links is between being physically abused and lacking normal empathy in response to the distress of others. Whereas toddlers typically show concern and offer comfort when a peer cries, abused toddlers are likely to become angry and attack the crying child, reacting to the distress of peers much as their abusive parents react to their distress (Main & George, 1985).

Remarkable as it may seem, though, many maltreated children are resilient and turn out fine. What distinguishes these children from the ones who have long-term problems? First, they may have genes that protect them from the negative psychological effects of abuse and possibly other negative life events—that make them stress resistant or equip them to cope effectively (Caspi et al., 2002; Kim-Cohen & Gold, 2009). Second, environmental factors, especially an attachment to at least one nonabusive adult, contribute to resilience too (Egeland et al., 1988; Houshyar, Gold, & DeVries, 2013).

How Do We Stop the Violence?

Knowing what we know about the causes and effects of child abuse, what can be done to prevent it, stop it, and undo the damage? What would you propose? Despite the complexity of the problem, progress is being made (see Dodge & Coleman, 2009).

Consider the task of preventing violence before it starts. One effective approach is to teach positive parenting skills to parents who use harsh parenting techniques that can easily cross the line into abuse (Dodge & Coleman, 2009; Knerr, Gardner, & Cluver, 2013). This kind of training can have positive effects on both children and parents (Patterson, Forgatch, & DeGarmo, 2010). **Application Box 15.1** explores another approach: empowering parents who might be at risk for abuse to manage child-rearing challenges more confidently and effectively.

What can be done for families in which abuse has already occurred? Here the challenge is more difficult. In cases of serious abuse, it may be necessary to prosecute the abuser and protect the children from injury and death by removing them from the home, although courts are reluctant to take this step (Emery & Laumann-Billings, 1998). In most cases a comprehensive, ecological approach designed to convert a pathological family system into a healthy one is likely to be most effective. Abusive parents need emotional support and the opportunity to learn more effective parenting, problem-solving, and coping skills. Victims of abuse need day care programs, developmental training, and psychotherapy to help them overcome cognitive, social, and emotional deficits caused by abuse (Leenarts et al., 2013; Malley-Morrison & Hines, 2004). Change is needed in families' neighborhoods and communities as well to ensure that families have the services and supports they need (Dodge et al., 2009).

Clearly family life can make us or break us. We hope this examination of diverse family experiences has convinced you that we do indeed live linked lives throughout the life span and that the family is centrally important in human development. Our next chapter looks more closely at some of the many ways in which development can go awry.

Checking Mastery

1. Identify one characteristic of the parent, one characteristic of the child, and one contextual factor that could contribute to child abuse.
2. What does Bugental's intervention to prevent child abuse involve?

Making Connections

1. Given what you now know about the roles of the abuser, the abused, and the context in child abuse, how do you think these three sets of factors enter into intimate partner violence?
2. Given the societal problems that stem from abuse and neglect of children, what do you think about the idea of licensing parents, much as we license drivers, to ensure that they have appropriate knowledge and skills? Licensing could involve pledging to support children financially and to refrain from maltreating them; it could even involve being of a certain age or passing a parenting skills course (see Holden, 2010). What do you see as the pros and cons of this?

Chapter Summary

15.1 Understanding the Family

- The family, whether nuclear or extended, is best viewed, as suggested by Bronfenbrenner's bioecological perspective, the family life cycle concept, and family systems theory, as a changing social system embedded in larger social systems that are also changing. Social changes in the past half century or more have resulted in more single adults, later marriage, more unmarried parents, fewer children, more women working, more divorce, more single-parent families, more children in poverty, more reconstituted families, more years without children, more multigenerational families, and fewer caregivers for aging adults.

15.2 The Infant

- Infants affect and are affected by their parents. Fathers are capable parents but have been less involved in caregiving than mothers and more likely to specialize in rowdy play, although the roles of mothers and fathers have been converging.
- Developmental outcomes are likely to be positive when parents coparent and have positive indirect effects on development because of their positive influences on each other.

15.3 The Child

- Parenting styles can be described in terms of the dimensions of acceptance–responsiveness and demandingness–control; children are generally more competent when their parents adopt an authoritative style. Socioeconomic status, economic hardship, and culture all affect parenting styles.
- Research on the parent effects, child effects, interactional, and transactional models of family influence tells us that children's problem behaviors are not always solely caused by ineffective parenting.
- When a second child enters the family system, firstborns may find the experience stressful; sibling relationships are characterized by ambivalence, and siblings play important roles as providers of emotional support, caregiving, teaching, and social experience.

15.4 The Adolescent

- Parent–child relationships typically remain close in adolescence but involve increased conflict around puberty.
- Parent–child relationships are renegotiated to become more equal as adolescents strive for autonomy; the goal of autonomy is best supported by authoritative parenting.

15.5 The Adult

- Marital satisfaction declines somewhat on average as newlyweds adjust to each other and become parents and raise children, whereas the empty nest transition and a companionate style of grandparenthood are generally positive experiences. Marital satisfaction is more affected by personality than phase of the family life cycle, though.
- In adulthood, siblings have less contact but normally continue to feel both emotionally close and rivalrous. Young adults often establish more mutual relationships with their parents, and most middle-aged adults continue to experience mutually supportive relationships with their elderly parents until some experience middle generation squeeze, caregiver burden, and possibly a short period of role reversal.

15.6 Diverse Family Experiences

- Inadequately described by the traditional family life cycle concept are single adults (some of whom cohabit with partners), childless married couples, dual-career families, and gay and lesbian families.
- Divorce creates a crisis in the family for 1 or 2 years; most adjust, but some children of divorce living in single-parent and reconstituted families experience not only short-term but longer-term adjustment problems, although many factors can make the experience better.

15.7 The Problem of Family Violence

- Parent characteristics such as being abused, child characteristics such as a difficult temperament, and contextual factors such as lack of social support all contribute to child abuse and must be considered in formulating prevention and treatment programs.

Checking Mastery Answers

For answers to Checking Mastery questions, please see Appendix B.

Key Terms

linked lives **470**
family systems theory **470**
nuclear family **471**
coparenting **471**
extended family household **471**
family life cycle **472**
reconstituted families **473**
indirect effects **475**
acceptance–responsiveness **476**
demandingness–control **476**
authoritarian parenting **476**

authoritative parenting **477**
permissive parenting **477**
neglectful parenting **477**
family stress model **479**
parent effects model **480**
child effects model **480**
interactional model **481**
transactional model **481**
sibling rivalry **482**
autonomy **484**
empty nest **487**

role reversal **490**
middle generation squeeze **490**
kinkeeper **490**
caregiver burden **490**
cohabitation **491**
spillover effects **493**
child abuse **497**
child maltreatment **497**
intergenerational transmission
of parenting **498**

16 Developmental Psychopathology

Peggy, a 17-year-old female, was referred by her pediatrician to a child psychiatry clinic for evaluation of an eating disorder. She had lost 10 pounds in 2 months and her mother was concerned. . . . At the clinic she stated that she was not trying to lose weight, had begun to sleep poorly about 2 months ago unless she had several beers, and that she and friends "got trashed" on weekends. Her relationship with her parents was poor; she had attempted suicide a year previously with aspirin and was briefly hospitalized. The day before this evaluation she had taken a razor to school to try to cut her wrists, but it was taken away by a friend. She admitted being depressed and wanting to commit suicide and finally told of discovering that she was pregnant 4 months earlier. Her boyfriend wanted her to abort, she was ambivalent, and then she miscarried spontaneously about 2 months after her discovery. After that, "It didn't really matter how I felt about anything" (Committee on Adolescence, 1996, pp. 71–72).

Does Peggy have any diagnosable psychological disorders? It would seem from this description that she may have diagnosable problems with substance abuse and depression and possibly even an eating disorder. However, her pregnancy and miscarriage may have provoked her symptoms: How do we differentiate between psychological disorders and normal responses to negative life events? How did Peggy's problems unfold and where might they lead?

We do not all have as many problems as Peggy, but it is the rare person who makes it through the life span without having at least some difficulty adapting to the challenges of living. Each phase of life poses unique challenges, and some of us inevitably run into trouble mastering them. This chapter is about psychological disorder—about some of the ways in which human development can go awry. It is about how development influences psychopathology and how psychopathology influences development. By applying a life-span development perspective to the study of psychological disorders, we understand them better. And by learning more about abnormal patterns of development, we gain new perspectives on the forces that guide and channel—or block and distort—human development more generally.

16.1 What Makes Development Abnormal?

LEARNING OBJECTIVES:

- Describe three broad criteria of abnormal behavior and the approach taken by DSM-5 in diagnosing disorders such as major depressive disorder.

- Define developmental psychopathology and contrast the developmental psychopathology perspective to a medical or disease perspective.

- Explain and illustrate the diathesis–stress model of psychopathology.

Clinical psychologists, psychiatrists, and other mental health professionals struggle to define the line between normal and abnormal behavior and diagnose psychological disorders, often thinking about three broad criteria in doing so:

1. *Statistical deviance.* Does the person's behavior fall outside the normal range of behavior? By this criterion, a mild case of the "blahs" or "blues" would not be diagnosed as clinical depression because it is so statistically common, but a more enduring, severe, and persistent case might be.
2. *Maladaptiveness.* Does the person's behavior interfere with adaptation or pose a danger to self or others? Psychological disorders disrupt functioning and create problems for the individual, other people, or both.
3. *Personal distress.* Does the behavior cause personal anguish or discomfort? Many psychological disorders involve personal suffering and are of concern for that reason alone.

Although these general guidelines provide a start at defining abnormal behavior, and we can see how each applies to Peggy at the start of the chapter, they are vague. We must identify specific forms of statistical deviation, maladaptiveness, and personal distress.

DSM Diagnostic Criteria

Professionals who diagnose and treat psychological disorders use the more specific diagnostic criteria in the *Diagnostic and Statistical Manual of Mental Disorders*. The newest version, **DSM-5**, was published in 2013 (American Psychiatric Association, 2013). It spells out defining features and symptoms for numerous psychological disorders. Many hope that advances in genetics, brain imaging, blood testing, and other diagnostic approaches will allow better identification of the biological state or disease behind a disorder's symptoms, much as doctors can test for the HIV virus when someone appears to have symptoms of AIDS, but that hope is not yet realized (Addington & Rapoport, 2012). As you'll see, rather than having one clear cause, most psychological disorders have many variations and many contributors.

The 2013 publication of DSM-5 ushered in several important changes in diagnostic practice, some of which have stirred controversy:

- Use of a single category of "autism spectrum disorder" for not only autism but related conditions like Asperger's syndrome (see later discussion)
- Use of the term *intellectual disability* in place of *mental retardation*
- Addition of a new diagnosis, "disruptive mood dysregulation disorder," for abnormally intense and frequent temper tantrums in children
- Greater latitude to diagnose depression in individuals who are grieving a loss
- Reorganization of dementia diagnoses to create mild and severe versions of what are now called "neurocognitive disorders" (for example, Alzheimer's disease)
- Increased attention to how age, gender, and race or ethnicity may affect diagnoses.

Because depression is so common across the life span, we will highlight it in this chapter and use it here as an example of how DSM-5 defines disorders. Depression is a family of several affective or mood disorders, some relatively mild and some severe. One of the most important is **major depressive disorder**, defined in DSM-5 as at least one episode of feeling profoundly depressed, sad, and hopeless, and/or losing interest in and the ability to derive pleasure from almost all activities, for at least 2 weeks (American Psychiatric Association, 2013). To qualify as having a major depressive episode, the individual must experience at least five of the following types of symptoms (described more fully in the manual), including one of the first two, persistently during a 2-week period:

1. Depressed mood (or irritable mood in children and adolescents) nearly every day
2. Greatly decreased interest or pleasure in activities most of the day
3. Significant weight loss when not dieting or weight gain (or for children, failure to achieve expected weight gains)
4. Insomnia or sleeping too much
5. Agitation or restlessness, or sluggishness and slowing, of behavior
6. Fatigue and loss of energy
7. Feelings of worthlessness or extreme guilt
8. Decreased ability to think or concentrate or indecisiveness
9. Recurring thoughts of death, recurring suicidal ideas, or a suicide attempt or plan to commit suicide

In addition, the manual calls for distinguishing major depressive disorder from certain other disorders and requires that the symptoms cause significant distress or impaired functioning and are not due to the direct effects of a substance (an abused drug or a medication) or a general medical condition. Whereas the previous edition allowed major depression to be diagnosed in bereaved individuals only if symptoms were present at least 2 months after the death, DSM-5 allow the diagnosis to be made even sooner after a death or other painful loss. Now the issue in diagnosis is the nature, frequency, and severity of the person's symptoms, even if normal life events like a loved one's death precipitated them.

By DSM-5 criteria, a man suffering from major depression might feel extremely discouraged, no longer seem to care about his job or even about sexual relations with his wife, lose weight or have difficulty sleeping, speak and move slowly as though lacking the energy to perform even the simplest actions, have trouble getting his work done, dwell on how guilty he feels about his many failings, and begin to think he would be better off dead. Major depressive disorder would not be diagnosed if the individual is merely a little "down"; many more people experience depressive symptoms than qualify as having a clinically defined depressive disorder.

DSM-5 recognizes that both cultural and developmental considerations should be taken into account in diagnosing major depressive disorder. For example, some studies find that Asians who are depressed are likely to complain of **somatic symptoms** (body symptoms such as tiredness and aches) more than psychological symptoms such as guilt and may be underdiagnosed if this cultural difference is not taken into account (Sue et al., 2012). And although DSM-5 takes the position that depression in a child is fundamentally similar to depression in an adult, it points out that some depressed children express their depression by being irritable rather than sad. An interesting question we'll examine in this chapter is how the flavor of depression changes over the life span.

Developmental Psychopathology

Psychologists and psychiatrists have long brought major theories of human development to bear in attempting to understand and treat psychological disorders. Freudian psychoanalytic theory once guided most thinking about psychopathology and clinical practice; behavioral theorists have applied learning principles to the understanding and treatment of behavioral problems; and cognitive psychologists have called attention to how individuals interpret their experiences and perceive themselves.

More recently, evolutionary psychologists have begun asking interesting questions about whether psychological disorders may have served adaptive functions for our ancestors (Keller, 2008). For example, depression may be an adaptive response to loss, helping people conserve energy and avoid further stress (Mealey, 2005). And attention deficit hyperactivity disorder (ADHD) may be associated with a sometimes adaptive tendency to be alert to dangers that others would tune out as distracting and to act quickly in response (Pearson, 2011). Some scholars even suggest that the fetuses of stressed mothers are programmed to develop characteristics associated with ADHD to prepare them to live in a stressful and unpredictable environment (Glover, 2011; and see Chapter 4 on fetal programming).

There is now an entire field devoted to the study of abnormal behavior from a developmental perspective—**developmental psychopathology** (Cicchetti, 2006; Cicchetti & Toth, 2009; Rutter & Sroufe, 2000; Sroufe, 2009). As defined by pioneers L. Alan Sroufe and Michael Rutter (1984), developmental psychopathology is the study of the origins and course of maladaptive behavior. Developmental psychopathologists appreciate the need to evaluate abnormal development in relation to normal development and to study the two in tandem. They want to know how disorders arise and how their expression changes as the individual develops, and they search for causal pathways and mechanisms involving genes, the nervous system, the person, and the social environment that lead to normal or abnormal adjustment (Rutter & Sroufe, 2000). In doing so, they bring life span, interdisciplinary, and systems perspectives to the study of abnormal behavior, looking at the interplay among biological, psychological, and social factors over the course of development.

Psychopathology as Development, Not Disease

Some developmental psychopathologists fault DSM-5 and similar diagnostic systems for being rooted in a medical or disease model of psychopathology that views psychological problems as diseaselike entities that people either have or do not have. Alan Sroufe (2009, p. 181) puts it this way:

> Psychopathology is not a condition that some individuals simply have or are born to have; rather, it is the outcome of a developmental process. It derives from the successive adaptations of individuals in their environment across time, each adaptation providing a foundation for the next.

■ **Figure 16.1** illustrates the concept of psychopathology as development. It portrays progressive branchings that lead development on either an optimal or a less-than-optimal course. Start with the assumption that typical human genes and typical human environments normally work to push development along a normal course and pull it back on course if it strays (Grossman et al., 2003). Some individuals—even some whose genes or experiences put them at risk to develop a disorder—manage to stay on a route to competence and good adjustment. Some start out poorly but get

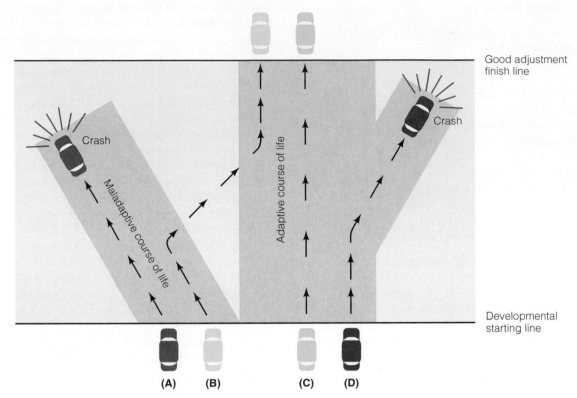

Course of Life

Good adjustment finish line

Crash

Maladaptive course of life

Adaptive course of life

Crash

Developmental starting line

(A)   (B)   (C)   (D)

■ **Figure 16.1** Developmental pathways leading to normal and abnormal outcomes. Some individuals start on a maladaptive course and deviate further from developmental norms as they age (route A); some start poorly but return to a more adaptive course later (route B); others stay on a route to competence and good adjustment all along (route C); and still others start off well but deviate later in life (route D).

SOURCE: Patterned after: Sroufe, L. A. (1997). Psychopathology as an outcome of development, *Development and Psychopathology, 9,* 251–268. Copyright © Cambridge University Press. Reprinted with permission.

back on a more adaptive course later; others start off well but deviate later. Still others start on a maladaptive course due to genes and early experience and deviate further from developmental norms as they age because their early problems make it harder and harder for them to master later developmental tasks and challenges (Kendler, Gardner, & Prescott, 2002).

Now picture Figure 16.1 with many more roadways. In this developmental pathways model, change is possible at many points, and the lines between normal and abnormal development are blurred. A number of different pathways can lead to the same disorder, and the same risk factors can lead to a variety of different outcomes (Cicchetti & Toth, 2009). A model of this sort may seem complex, but it fits the facts of development.

More is being learned every day about relationships among genes, the brain, and behavior and about the role of the brain and its neurotransmitters in psychological disorders. As a result, many experts believe that psychological disorders should be viewed as life-span *neurodevelopmental* disorders (Davis, 2012; March, 2009). This neurodevelopmental perspective requires looking at normal and abnormal pathways of brain development and their implications for functioning. It involves using genetic and brain imaging techniques in diagnosing disorders in hopes of intervening early with individuals

who are at risk for various disorders to put them on healthier developmental trajectories.

Social Norms and Age Norms

Developmental psychopathologists appreciate that behaviors are abnormal or normal only within particular social and developmental contexts (Lopez & Guarnaccia, 2000). **Social norms** are expectations about how to behave in a particular social context—whether a culture, a subculture, or an everyday setting. What is normal in one social context may be abnormal in another. For example, John Weisz and his colleagues (1997) have discovered that Thai children are more likely than American children to report (or to be reported by parents to have) symptoms of inner distress such as anxiety and depression and are less likely to engage in aggression and other forms of "acting out." One reason for the difference may be that the Thai culture places high value on emotional control and socializes children to control rather than vent their negative emotions (see also Weiss et al., 2009).

Another example of the need to consider cultural norms concerns one of the behaviors used in diagnosing autism (see later section): lack of normal eye contact. But what is normal eye contact? In China and certain other East Asian cultures, it is viewed

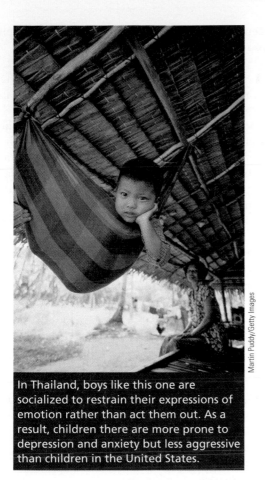

In Thailand, boys like this one are socialized to restrain their expressions of emotion rather than act them out. As a result, children there are more prone to depression and anxiety but less aggressive than children in the United States.

as rude to look directly into someone's eyes; looking at the nose area is more culturally appropriate (Norbury & Sparks, 2013). If an evaluator is not attentive to such cultural differences, an incorrect diagnosis could be made. As such examples hint, the definitions, meanings, symptoms, rates, and developmental courses and correlates of abnormal behavior are likely to vary from culture to culture, from subculture to subculture, and from historical period to historical period (Norbury & Sparks, 2013; Serafica & Vargas, 2006). Although there are universal aspects of psychopathology too, it is shaped by its social context.

In addition, developmental psychopathologists are very aware that abnormal behavior must be defined in relation to age norms—societal expectations about what behavior is appropriate or normal at various ages. The 4-year-old boy who frequently cries, acts impulsively, wets his bed, is afraid of the dark, and talks to his imaginary friend may be perceived as—and may be—normal. The 40-year-old who does the same things needs help! You simply cannot define abnormal behavior and development without having a solid grasp of normal behavior and development.

Developmental Issues

As they attempt to understand developmental pathways to adaptive or maladaptive functioning, developmental psychopathologists grapple with the same developmental issues that have concerned us throughout this book—most notably, the nature–nurture issue (Rutter, Moffitt, & Caspi, 2006) and the issue of continuity and discontinuity in development (Rutter,

Kim-Cohen, & Maughan, 2006; and see Chapter 2). Addressing the nature–nurture issue involves asking important questions such as these:

- How do biological, psychological, and social factors interact over time to give rise to psychological disorders?
- What are the important risk factors for psychological disorders—and what are the protective factors that keep some individuals who are at risk from developing disorders?

Addressing the continuity–discontinuity issue means asking these sorts of questions:

- Are most childhood problems passing phases that have no bearing on adjustment in adulthood, or does poor functioning in childhood predict poor functioning later in life?
- How do expressions of psychopathology change as the developmental status of the individual changes?

The Diathesis–Stress Model

In their efforts to understand how nature and nurture contribute to psychopathology, developmental psychopathologists have long found a **diathesis–stress model** of psychopathology useful (Coyne & Whiffen, 1995; Ingram & Price, 2001). This model proposes that psychopathology results from the interaction over time of a predisposition or vulnerability to psychological disorder (called a *diathesis*, which can involve a particular genetic makeup, physiology, set of cognitions, personality, or a combination of these) and the experience of stressful events. The diathesis–stress concept should remind you of the concept of gene–environment interaction.

Consider depression. We know that certain people are genetically predisposed to become depressed (Rice & Thapar, 2009). Genetic factors account for about 40–60% of the variation in a group of people in symptoms of major depressive disorder (Garber, 2010; Glowinski et al., 2003). A genetic vulnerability to depression manifests itself as imbalances in serotonin and other key neurotransmitters that affect mood and in such characteristics as high emotional reactivity to stress, including high production of the stress hormone cortisol, and self-defeating patterns of thinking in the face of negative events (Garber & Flynn, 2001; Gotlib et al., 2006).

According to the diathesis–stress model, however, individuals predisposed to become depressed are not likely to do so unless they experience significant losses or other stressful events, as illustrated in ■ **Figure 16.2**. One stressful life event is usually not enough to trigger major depression, but when negative events pile up or become chronic, a vulnerable person may succumb. Meanwhile, individuals who do not have a diathesis—a vulnerability to depression—may be able to withstand high levels of stress without becoming depressed.

Researchers can now pinpoint some specific diathesis–stress interactions. For example, inheriting a particular variant of a gene involved in controlling levels of the neurotransmitter serotonin and experiencing multiple stressful events results in an especially high probability of major depression (Caspi, Sugden, Moffitt, et al., 2003; and see Petersen et al., 2012). Among people with one or two of the high-risk genes, about 10% became depressed if they experienced no negative life events between ages 21 and 26, but 33% became depressed if they experienced four or more such events.

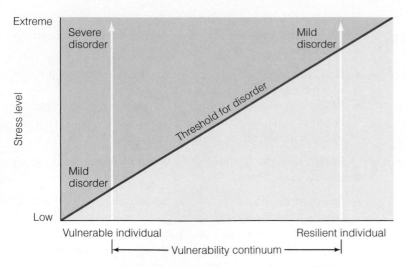

Stress level — Extreme / Low

Severe disorder

Mild disorder

Threshold for disorder

Mild disorder

Vulnerable individual

Resilient individual

|← Vulnerability continuum →|

■ **Figure 16.2** The diathesis-stress model. For a vulnerable individual, even mild stress can result in disorder. For an individual who is resilient and does not have a vulnerability or diathesis to disorder, it would take extremely high levels of stress to cause disorder; even then, the disorder might be only mild and temporary.

SOURCE: Adapted from Ingram & Price, 2001.

By comparison, even when exposed to many stressful events, only 17% of individuals with two low-risk versions of the gene became depressed.

Depressive disorders (and many other psychological disorders) often evolve from an interaction of diathesis and stress—or, to use familiar developmental terms, from an interaction between genes and environment. It is messier than Figure 16.2 suggests, though. For example, genes not only predispose some people to depression but also influence the extent to which they experience stressful life events (Rice, Harold, & Thapar, 2003). Moreover, the relationship between stress and disorder is reciprocal: Life stress aggravates disorder, but disorder also makes life more stressful (Garber, 2010; Grant et al., 2004). Finally, in a person genetically predisposed to depression, a depressive episode early in life in response to intense stress may bring about changes in gene activity and in the neurobiology of the stress-response system (the hypothalamic–pituitary–adrenal [HPA] axis). These changes may lower the threshold for a future depressive episode (the diagonal line in Figure 16.2) so that later in life depression may reoccur even without major stressful events precipitating it (Grossman et al., 2003; Monroe & Reid, 2009).

For some disorders we examine in this chapter, the diathesis for disorder is strong, probably more important than environmental influences in causing disorder. Environment may still play an important role, however, by shaping the course of the disorder and its effects on functioning and later development (Steinberg & Avenevoli, 2000). A depressed adolescent like Peggy growing up in a hostile, disturbed family context, for example, is likely to fare worse than a depressed adolescent who receives parental support and appropriate professional treatment.

This chapter will now illustrate the concepts of developmental psychopathology in action by examining a few developmental problems associated with different phases of the life span—for example, autism to illustrate disorders arising in infancy; ADHD to illustrate childhood disorders; anorexia nervosa and substance abuse to illustrate disorders arising in adolescence; and Alzheimer's disease to illustrate disorders of old age. In addition, we look at depression in every developmental period to see how its symptoms and significance change over the life span.

Checking Mastery

1. What are two of the three broad criteria useful in defining when a psychological disorder is present?
2. Jake says psychological disorders are diseases that some people have and other people don't. What might a developmental psychopathologist tell Jake?
3. What is a diathesis?

Making Connections

1. Dr. Blinderson is used to diagnosing depression in American college students. Think through what this psychologist might want to consider if he began to diagnose major depression in an Asian culture and among both preschool children as well as elderly adults.
2. Revisit the case of Peggy at the start of the chapter and hypothesize about how the diathesis–stress model might apply to her.

16.2 The Infant

LEARNING OBJECTIVES:

- Describe the two defining features and main characteristics, including brain functioning, associated with autism spectrum disorder.
- Explain why rates of autism spectrum disorder are increasing, how nature and nurture may contribute to it, and what can be done to treat it.
- Explain why there is controversy about whether infants can have true depressive disorders and what factors contribute to depression symptoms in infancy.

Adults worry about infants who do not eat properly, who cry endlessly, or who seem overly withdrawn and timid. Because infant development is strongly channeled by biological maturation, few infants develop severe psychological problems. Yet psychological disorder exists in infancy, and its effects can be profound.

Autism Spectrum Disorder

Jeremy, 3½ years old, has big brown eyes and a sturdy body. His mother carries him down the corridor toward the examiner, who greets them. Jeremy glances at the examiner's face but does not smile or say hello. They walk together into a playroom. Jeremy's mother puts him down, and he sits on the carpet in front of some toys. He picks up two blocks, bangs them together, and begins to stack the blocks, one on top of the other, not stopping until he has used the entire set. Jeremy does not look at the examiner or his mother while he works, nor when he finishes. And he does not make a sound. The examiner asks him to give her a red block. He does not respond. On their way out, Jeremy and his mother stop to look at a poster of a waterfall surrounded by redwood trees. "Yosemite Valley," Jeremy reads out—the name beneath the picture. His voice sounds automated, almost robotic. (Sigman & Capps, 1997, p. 1)

Autism was first identified and described by Leo Kanner in 1943. Now diagnosed as **autism spectrum disorder (ASD)**, it usually begins in infancy and is characterized by abnormal social and communication development and restricted interests and repetitive behavior. Picture the typical infant that we have described in this book: a social being who responds to others and forms close attachments starting at 6 or 7 months of age, a linguistic being who babbles and later uses one- and two-word sentences to converse with companions, and a curious explorer who is fascinated by new objects and experiences. Now consider the two defining features of autism highlighted in DSM-5 (and see Waterhouse, 2013):

1. *Social and communication deficits.* Autistic children have difficulty forming social relationships, responding appropriately to social cues, sharing experiences with other people, and participating in normal social interactions. Some autistic children are mute and quite asocial; others acquire language skills with varying degrees of success but are socially awkward and have difficulty carrying on true, back-and-forth conversations (Tager-Flusberg, 2000; Waterhouse, 2013).

2. *Restricted and repetitive interests and behavior.* Autistic children seek sameness and repetition. They may become obsessed with particular objects and interests—bug collecting, for example—and may repeat phrases over and over. They may engage in stereotyped behaviors such as rocking, flapping their hands in front of their faces, or spinning toys. If they are more intellectually able, they may carry out elaborate rituals and routines such as a particular sequence of getting-dressed activities. They resist change and can become highly distressed when their physical environment is even slightly altered (as when a chair in the living room is moved a few feet).

The social impairments associated with ASD strike us most. Like Jeremy, some children with ASD seem to live in a world of their own, as though they find social contact aversive rather than pleasurable. They are far less likely than other infants to make eye contact, jointly attend to something with a social partner, seek other people for comfort, snuggle when held, and make friends. They also have great difficulty reading other people's minds and emotions, responding with empathy when others are distressed, and demonstrating self-awareness and self-conscious emotions such as embarrassment and guilt. Although over half of autistic children form secure attachments to their parents (Rutgers et al., 2004), a higher than average number display what Chapter 14 described as disorganized–disoriented attachments (Sigman & Capps, 1997).

It is critical to recognize that individuals with ASD vary greatly in the degree and nature, as well as the causes, of their deficits. As a result, some experts talk of "autisms" rather than autism, believing that ASD is actually a number of different underlying disorders (Hu, 2013; Jones & Klin, 2009). Others conclude that even the "autisms" perspective is flawed because the symptoms, brain deficits, and causes of ASD are so unique to the individual (Waterhouse, 2013).

The concept of ASDs was devised to reflect this diversity. In DSM-5, though, previously distinct disorders are all diagnosed as one ASD syndrome that can vary from mild to severe. As a result, ASD is now the diagnosis given to individuals who show classic autism, "pervasive developmental disorders—not otherwise specified," child disintegrative disorder, and the now familiar Asperger syndrome. In **Asperger syndrome**, a mild form of ASD, the child has normal or above-average intelligence, good verbal skills, and a clear desire to establish social relationships but has deficient social cognitive and social-communication skills. Affected children are sometimes called "little professors" because they talk rather stiffly and formally, and sometimes at mind-numbing length, about the particular subjects that obsess them. Many have been largely invisible until recently; rather than being diagnosed with a disorder, they were simply viewed as odd and socially awkward. Some experts are concerned that some of these individuals will be missed by the DSM-5 diagnostic criteria.

Many individuals with autism continue to function poorly as adolescents and adults, but some improve with age. One "improver," Jerry, described his childhood as a reign of "confusion and terror" in which "nothing seemed constant; everything was unpredictable and strange" (Bemporad, 1979, p. 192).

Jan Sonnenmair/AuroraPhotos

Is There an Epidemic?

Rates of autism appear to be rising. DSM-III-R, published in 1987, indicated that autism affected about 4 or 5 of every 10,000 children (American Psychiatric Association, 1987). In a 2006 survey by the U.S. Centers for Disease Control and Prevention, autism in the broader sense of a spectrum of disorders was estimated to affect 1 in 110, or almost 1%, of children aged 8 in the United States (Autism and Developmental Disabilities Monitoring Network, 2009). Only 2 years later, the estimate jumped to 1 per 88 children, over 1% (Autism and Developmental Disabilities Monitoring Network, 2012). There are four or five affected boys for every girl.

Why have rates of autism been increasing so steeply over the past few decades? A debate has raged (Chakrabarti & Fombonne, 2005; Gillberg et al., 2006). You may have heard that the vaccine infants receive for measles, mumps, and rubella is the culprit. The evidence is clear: There is no support for this charge, which unfortunately has made some parents fear having their children immunized and has bumped up rates of childhood diseases (Waterhouse, 2013). The main research study linking this vaccine or a preservative in it to autism, authored by Andrew Wakefield and others, was retracted by the medical journal that published it after it was found to be fraudulent and incorrect (Editors of *The Lancet*, 2010; Waterhouse, 2013). Still, because some celebrities have spread this myth, and perhaps because the vaccination is normally given to infants at about 15 months of age when children with autism often begin to display their autistic symptoms, the vaccine myth has persisted.

But why are rates of ASD increasing, then? Most researchers believe that increased rates are mainly a result of increased awareness, a broader definition that includes the entire autistic spectrum (including more mild cases), and increased diagnosis of children who might previously have been diagnosed with language impairments or learning disabilities or simply considered to be odd children (Benaron, 2009; Gillberg et al., 2006; Waterhouse, 2013). Consider that autism was not added to a U.S. government list of disabilities eligible for special education services until 1991, and Asperger syndrome was not added to DSM-IV until 1994. Rates also differ considerably from state to state, as might happen if some states used more liberal standards for diagnosis than others.

In sum, the recent rise in the prevalence of ASDs seems to be more about detection of cases that were there all along than about new cases and causes. Variations in diagnostic practices probably also contribute to large differences in rates of ASD across cultures—from as low as 1 or 2 per 10,000 in Oman to as high as 260 in 10,000 in South Korea (Norbury & Sparks, 2013). Still, it is not quite time to rule out the possibility that there has been a true increase in the prevalence of ASD associated with some as yet unknown cause (Autism and Developmental Disabilities Monitoring Network, 2012; Waterhouse, 2013).

Characteristics

Most children with ASD are probably autistic from birth. However, because at first they often seem to be normal and exceptionally good babies, or because physicians are slow to make the diagnosis even when parents express concerns about their child's development, many autistic children have traditionally not been diagnosed until they are 5 or older and even now are usually not diagnosed until they are 2 or 3 (Benaron, 2009; Klin et al., 2004). Researchers are working feverishly to improve early screening and detection because the earlier these children receive treatment, the more likely it is that they can be steered onto a more typical developmental pathway.

Autistic infants may be given away by their lack of normal interest in and responsiveness to social stimuli—for example, by failure to display normal infant behaviors such as orienting to someone calling their name, preference for human over nonhuman stimuli, eye contact, visual focus on faces in a scene (autistic babies tend to focus on objects in the background), joint attention (a key precursor of theory-of-mind skills), imitation, and turn taking, as in mutual smiling and peekaboo games (Ingersoll, 2011; Klin et al., 2004; Zwaigenbaum et al., 2005). Some researchers are using checklists of such abilities to screen 1-year-olds for ASD (Pierce et al., 2011). Others believe that they can identify infants with ASD from their tendency to take longer than most infants to disengage from one visual stimulus and orient toward a new stimulus (Elison et al., 2013; Elsabbagh et al., 2013). Still others are using brain imaging techniques to try to identify these babies (Wolff et al., 2012) or are looking for diagnostically useful biomarkers in the blood (Glatt et al., 2012).

Complicating efforts to understand ASD is the fact that it is often **comorbid** with—that is, co-occurs with—a number of other disorders such as intellectual disability, language disorders, ADHD, epilepsy, anxiety disorders, and more (Waterhouse, 2013). Consider intellectual functioning. Some children with ASD have average or above-average IQs, but many—half or more—have intellectual disabilities and IQ scores of 70 or lower (Autism and Developmental Disabilities Monitoring Network, 2009; Ingersoll, 2011). Meanwhile, some autistic individuals, whether their IQs are high or low, show *savant abilities*–that is, special talents such as the ability to quickly calculate days of the week corresponding to dates on the calendar or to memorize incredible amounts of information about train schedules (see Heaton & Wallace, 2004; and the description of *savant syndrome* in Chapter 9). Consider Ezra, age 15. Obsessed with animated films (he memorized the release dates of hundreds of them), animals, and breakfast cereals, he would greet people he knew with unusual conversation openers like, "Hi, Bonnie! You had Post Honeycombs in your kitchen in August of 2004!" (Fields-Meyer, 2011). Yet he could not seem to remember the names of the seven children in his classroom at school.

Autism used to be viewed as a prime example of development that is qualitatively different from normal development. No more. Because we know more about the milder end of the autism spectrum, the social impairment that defines autism is now viewed as the extreme end of a continuum of social responsiveness, quantitatively rather than qualitatively different from typical social behavior (Baron-Cohen, 2010; Robinson et al., 2011). In other words, many of us have some of the traits associated with autism to some degree; the dividing line between normality and abnormality is arbitrary.

Brain Functioning

Many autistic children display neurological abnormalities (Volkmar et al., 2004; Waterhouse, 2013). However, the neurological abnormalities are varied, and it is not yet clear which are most central in explaining the characteristics of individuals with ASD. We'll highlight a few focuses of neuroscience research: abnormal brain growth and connectivity, mirror neuron deficits, executive function impairments, and an extreme male brain.

Abnormal Brain Growth and Connectivity. One hypothesis is that in children who later develop ASD, neurons in the frontal cortex and certain other areas of the brain proliferate wildly during the early sensitive period for brain development in infancy but do not become interconnected with other areas of the brain and pruned in a normal way (Benaron, 2009; Courchesne, Carper, & Akshoomoff, 2003; Schumann et al., 2009). Poor connectivity among brain areas would explain social impairments, as many brain areas are called into action when we interact with other people. It may also explain why individuals with ASD often excel on detail-oriented tasks that require only a particular brain area rather than many. Like most hypotheses, though, this abnormal brain growth and connectivity hypothesis seems to fit only some children with ASD (Waterhouse, 2013).

Mirror Neuron Deficits. Deficits in mirror neuron systems located in a number of brain areas might account for the difficulties many individuals with autism have with theory-of-mind tasks in which they must understand people's behavior by reading their mental states, as well as their difficulties with imitation, empathy, and language tasks (Gallese, Rochat, & Berchio, 2013; Oberman & Ramachandran, 2007). As we saw in Chapter 13, mirror neuron systems allow us to make sense of other people's feelings and thoughts. In one study (McIntosh et al., 2006), autistic and nonautistic adults watched pictures of happy and angry facial expressions so that the researchers could see if their faces automatically and subtly mimicked the expressions they saw—a sign of mirror neurons at work allowing us to relate other people's emotions to our own. Although people with autistic disorders could mimic the faces they saw if asked to do so, they did not do so spontaneously—one example of accumulating evidence suggesting that their mirror neuron systems do not function normally (Gallese et al., 2013; Oberman & Ramachandran, 2007).

Executive Function Impairments. Autistic individuals have difficulty with certain **executive functions**, higher level control functions based in the prefrontal cortex of the brain that allow us to plan, organize our thoughts, change flexibly from one course of action to another, and inhibit actions. Impairments in executive function may explain the repetitive behavior of individuals with ASD; they may become fixated on doing an activity again and again and be unable to switch to another activity. Individuals with ASD also tend to focus well on details (for example, finding Waldo in a complex scene) but sometimes have difficulty integrating pieces of information to get "the big picture," or overall meaning (see Pellicano, 2010).

Extreme Male Brain. To make the mystery of autism even more intriguing, Simon Baron-Cohen (2003, 2010; yes, he is the cousin of comedian Sasha Baron-Cohen) has put forth an extreme male brain hypothesis regarding autistic spectrum disorders. In this view, exposure to high levels of the male hormone testosterone prenatally results in a brain extremely strong in the masculine-stereotyped ability to *systemize* (analyze things to figure out how they work, extract rules that determine what leads to what) and extremely weak in the feminine-stereotyped ability to empathize (read people's thoughts and emotions and respond appropriately). This hypothesis helps us understand why Asperger's syndrome is common among "male-brained" scientists and engineers and highlights that people with ASD have cognitive strengths, not just deficits (Baron-Cohen, 2003). It may also help explain why ASD is so much more common among males than females. However, the evidence for it is not consistent and it probably applies to only some cases of ASD (Hu, 2013; Waterhouse, 2013).

It is hard to say whether abnormal brain growth and connectedness, lack of normally functioning mirror neuron systems, poor executive functions, an extreme male brain, and/or other neural impairments that are being investigated will prove to be at the heart of the problems children with ASDs display. So far no one "core deficit" behind ASD has been identified. Given the diversity of ASD, one may never be identified (Waterhouse, 2013). Perhaps it is not surprising that a number of cognitive and social deficits have been identified and a number of aspects of brain functioning are believed to be impaired. ASD is, after all, a *pervasive* neurodevelopmental disorder that disrupts brain development in a global way and affects multiple areas of functioning.

Suspected Causes

Interest in solving the mysteries of autism is intense, and some fascinating hypotheses have been put forward in recent years to explain why individuals with ASDs show the characteristics they do. Early theorists suggested that rigid and cold parenting by "refrigerator moms" caused autism, but this harmful myth has long been put to rest (Achenbach, 1982). It is now understood that interacting with an autistic child can easily cause parents to be tense and frustrated. Moreover, the parents of autistic children, because ASD is genetically influenced, sometimes have mild autistic spectrum traits themselves. Bad parenting is not responsible for autism.

Genes do contribute strongly to autism (Curran & Bolton, 2009; Veenstra-Vanderweele & Cook, 2003). Almost 19% of 3-year-olds who have an older sibling with ASD have it too; 32% have it if more than one older sibling has it (Ozonoff et al., 2011). Moreover, a twin study indicated that if one identical twin was autistic, the other was autistic in 60% of the twin pairs studied; by comparison, the concordance rate for fraternal twin pairs was 0% (Bailey et al., 1995). When the broader autistic spectrum was considered, 92% of the identical twins but only 10% of the fraternal twins were alike (see also Ronald & Hoekstra, 2011). Yet the nature–nurture issue is not settled.

A recent twin study (Hallmayer et al., 2011) suggests that the genetic contribution, while still evident, may be smaller than this and that shared environmental influences—prenatal or postnatal experiences that make even fraternal twins similar—may be more important than previously believed. Since one identical twin can have ASD when the other does not, non-shared environmental factors must also be at work (Ronald & Hoekstra, 2011).

Hundreds of genes on several chromosomes, each with small effects, have been implicated (Waterhouse, 2013). Most likely, individuals with autism inherit from their parents, or acquire through new mutations, several genes that put them at risk. In some cases too, segments of DNA that affect neural communication appear to have been copied too many times or, more often, too few times during cell division. These *copy number variations* can be present in the parent and then inherited by the child or can arise as new errors (Autism Genome Project Consortium, 2007; Waterhouse, 2013). Autism occurs more often when parents, especially fathers, are older; this is because as we age, mutations and copy number variations become more common, especially in the formation of sperm (Hultman et al., 2011; O'Roak et al., 2012). When these genetic errors occur, the normal process through which genes and experience guide the development of the brain and its neural connections can be disrupted.

Early environmental influences also contribute (Hu, 2013; Waterhouse, 2013). An environmental trigger such as a virus or chemicals in the environment could interact with a genetic predisposition to cause autism. Prenatal exposure to teratogens such as rubella, alcohol, and thalidomide are known to contribute to ASD. Epigenetic effects in which early experience turns off genes that guide normal brain development are also being investigated. Researchers are also noticing links between obesity and diabetes in mothers and ASD and other neurodevelopmental problems in children (Krakowiak et al., 2012), raising the interesting question of whether the autism epidemic could be related in some way to the obesity epidemic. Autism also occurs more frequently when there is maternal bleeding or other complications during pregnancy (Gardener, Spiegelman, & Buka, 2009). In short, there are almost as many possible environmental contributors to ASD as genetic ones.

Developmental Outcomes and Treatment

What becomes of children with autism as they get older? A small minority seem to outgrow their autism and function like typically developing children (Fein et al., 2013). However, although most individuals with ASD improve in functioning, they are usually autistic for life. Fewer than half are totally independent as adults in the sense of living away from their parents and having a job; few marry and many have physical and mental health problems. Positive outcomes are most likely among those who have IQ scores above 70 and reasonably good communication skills by age 5. We know almost nothing about what happens to adults with ASD in old age (Howlin & Moss, 2012).

Can treatment help autistic children overcome their problems? Some autistic children are given drugs to control behavioral problems such as hyperactivity or obsessive–compulsive behavior or drugs such as antipsychotics and antidepressants that help them benefit from educational programs but these do not cure autism (Benaron, 2009; Volkmar, 2001). Researchers continue to search for drugs that will correct the suspected brain dysfunctions of these individuals, but there is probably no one "magic pill."

The most effective approach to treating ASD is intensive and highly structured behavioral and educational programming, beginning as early as possible, continuing throughout childhood, and involving the family (Koegel, Koegel, & McNerney, 2001; Simpson & Otten, 2005). The goal is to make the most of the plasticity of the young brain during its sensitive period for development. O. Ivar Lovaas and his colleagues pioneered the use of **applied behavior analysis (ABA)**, the application of reinforcement principles to teach skills and change behavior, to shape social and language skills in children with autism (Lovaas & Smith, 2003). In an early study, Lovaas (1987) compared a group that received very intensive treatment—more than 40 hours a week of one-on-one training for 2 or more years during their preschool years—with a control group of similarly disturbed children who, because of staff shortages or transportation problems, received treatment for only 10 or fewer hours a week.

Trained student therapists worked with the children using reinforcement principles to reduce their aggressive and self-stimulatory behavior and to teach them developmentally appropriate skills such as how to imitate others, play with toys and with peers, and use language. Parents were taught to use the same behavioral techniques at home. Lovaas reported astounding results—for example, IQ scores about 30 points higher in the treatment group than in the control group. Other researchers have criticized this study's design, however, because it was not a true experiment with random assignment of children to treatment and control groups (Reichow & Wolery, 2009).

Subsequent research indicates that early behavioral interventions usually do not convert children with autism into typically functioning children. Nonetheless, many children with autism, especially those who are young and do not have severe intellectual disabilities, make significant gains if they receive intensive cognitive and behavioral training and comprehensive family services starting early in life (Dawson et al., 2010; Klinger & Williams, 2009; Reichow & Wolery, 2009).

In an especially well-conducted study with random assignment to treatment and control groups, an intensive ABA program focused on social interaction not only increased IQ, language, and social skills but also changed brain functioning (Dawson et al., 2012). It made ASD children's neural responses to faces like those of typically developing children. We know that the young brain is very plastic so there is a good chance that such early intervention programs, by increasing social interaction, change the course of brain development. The impacts may not be as great later in life, but training programs for the growing number of adults with autism and support services for their families are also advised.

Depression

Does it seem possible to you that an infant could experience major depressive disorder as defined in DSM-5? Infants are not capable of the negative cognitions common among depressed adults—the low self-esteem, guilt, worthlessness, hopelessness, and so on. After all, until late infancy, they have not yet acquired the capacity for symbolic thought or self-awareness that would allow them to reflect on their experience. Yet infants *can* exhibit some of depression's behavioral symptoms (such as loss of interest in activities or psychomotor slowing) and somatic, or physical, symptoms such as weight loss (Garber, 2010; Luby & Belden, 2012).

At present, DSM-5 allows diagnosis of major depressive disorder in childhood but is silent about infancy. While psychologists and psychiatrists debate whether true depression can occur in infancy, a small number of babies are clearly experiencing serious depressive states and symptoms (Garber, 2010; Luby, 2009). Moreover, young children who receive diagnoses of major depressive disorder are often said by their parents to have shown symptoms such as tearfulness, irritability, and a lack of joy even as infants (Luby & Belden, 2012). Indeed, babies can experience a whole range of mental health problems—problems involving feeding, sleeping, anxiety, attachment, and more (Keren et al., 2010; Zeanah, 2009). A special adaptation of DSM has been developed by the Zero to Three Project to help infant mental health specialists better identify depression and other psychological disorders in infants so that they can be treated (Zero to Three, 2005). The developers of this system believe that major depressive disorder does occur in infancy, contrary to earlier thinking.

Why would a baby become depressed? Depressive symptoms are most likely to be observed in infants who are abused or neglected or otherwise lack a secure attachment relationship, have an all-important attachment severed, or have a depressed caregiver (Boris & Zeanah, 1999). Infants who display a disorganized pattern of attachment, in which they do not seem to know whether to approach or avoid their caregiver (see Chapter 14)—an attachment style common among abused children—are especially likely to show symptoms of depression (Egeland & Carlson, 2004). And infants who are permanently separated from their mothers between 6 and 12 months of age have long been known to be at risk to become sad, weepy, listless, unresponsive, and withdrawn and to show delays in virtually all aspects of development (Spitz, 1946).

Infants whose mothers—or fathers—are depressed are also at risk (Gotlib et al., 2006). These babies adopt an interaction style that resembles that of their depressed caregivers; they vocalize little and look sad, even when interacting with women other than their mothers, and they show developmental delays (Field, 1995). They are at increased risk of becoming clinically depressed themselves later in life and of developing other psychological disorders. This may be because of a combination of genes and stressful experiences with their unpredictable mothers (that is, because of diathesis–stress). Stress early in life, it turns out, can produce children with an overactive stress-response system who are easily

What are the implications for this baby of growing up with a depressed mother? Infants whose mothers are depressed may show heightened reactivity to stress and develop depression symptoms of their own.

distressed, cannot regulate their negative emotions, are more reactive to stress later in life, and are more likely to develop psychological disorders (Bruce, Gunnar, Pears, & Fisher, 2013; Gotlib et al., 2006; Gunnar & Quevedo, 2007; Wismer Fries, Shirtcliff, & Pollak, 2008).

Mental health problems in infants can often be traced to a dysfunctional family environment in which parent–infant attachment and interaction are unhealthy (Keren et al., 2010). Intervening to change family systems—for example, to treat stressed, depressed, or abusive parents and help them parent more effectively—is therefore critical. As we saw in Chapter 14, for example, depressed parents can be trained to interact more sensitively with their babies.

Checking Mastery

1. What two major groups of symptoms would you expect to see in a child with autism spectrum disorder?
2. If you were told that your son has an "extreme male brain," what would that suggest?
3. What are two early experiences that could contribute to depressive symptoms in an infant?

Making Connections

1. How do you think the now discredited view that autism is caused by cold, "refrigerator" mothers arose, and how would you now characterize the parents of children with autism?
2. Why do you think the idea that autism can be caused by vaccinations, or a preservative that used to be put in vaccinations, has persisted so long despite a lack of solid evidence?

- Distinguish between externalizing and internalizing problems and discuss nature/nurture and continuity/discontinuity issues pertaining to childhood problems.
- Characterize ADHD in terms of its symptoms, developmental course, suspected causes, and treatment.
- Discuss the importance and challenges of recognizing depression in children.

Many children experience developmental problems—fears, recurring stomachaches, temper tantrums, and so on. A smaller proportion qualify as having a psychological disorder and a smaller proportion still are diagnosed as having a psychological disorder and treated for it. It is estimated that about 10% of children have a diagnosable psychological disorder at a given time (Ford, Goodman, & Meltzer, 2003).

Externalizing and Internalizing Problems

Many developmental problems of childhood can be placed in one of two broad categories that reflect whether the child's behavior is out of control or overly controlled (Achenbach & Edelbrock, 1978). When children have **externalizing problems**, they lack self-control and act out in ways that disturb other people and violate social expectations. They may be aggressive, disobedient, difficult to control, or disruptive. We discussed conduct disorder and aggressive behavior in Chapter 13 and will discuss ADHD here as an example. In **internalizing problems**, negative emotions are internalized, or bottled up, rather than externalized, or expressed. Internalizing problems include anxiety disorders (such as persistent worrying about separation from loved ones), phobias, severe shyness and withdrawal, and depression.

Externalizing behaviors decrease from age 4 to age 18, whereas internalizing difficulties increase (Bongers et al., 2003). Externalizing problems are typically more common among boys, whereas internalizing problems are more prevalent among girls. This gender difference is evident across cultures (Crijnen, Achenbach, & Verhulst, 1997). Children from low socioeconomic status (SES) families show more externalizing and internalizing problems than children from higher-SES families, partly because their environments are more stressful (Amone-P'Olak et al., 2009).

How do externalizing and internalizing problems arise, and to what extent do such problems in childhood spell trouble later in life? These questions concern the issues of nature–nurture and continuity–discontinuity in development.

Nature and Nurture

Most of us have a strong belief in the power of the social environment, particularly the family, to shape child development. This belief in a *parent effects model* of family influence (see Chapter 15) often leads us to blame parents—especially mothers—if their children are sad and withdrawn, uncontrollable and "bratty," or otherwise different from most children. Parents whose children develop problems often draw the same conclusion, feeling guilty because they assume they are at fault. If instead we view developmental disorders from a family systems perspective and apply a *transactional model* of family influence, we appreciate how emerging problems both affect and are affected by family interactions. We understand that parents are important but that they both influence and are influenced by their children (Cowan & Cowan, 2006).

It is true that youngsters with depression, conduct disorder, and many other psychological disorders tend to come from problem-ridden families in which there is often a history of psychological disorder (Connell & Goodman, 2002). However, a child in such a family may have a genetically based predisposition to disorder that would be expressed even if the child were adopted into another home early in life (Plomin et al., 2008). In addition, "poor parenting" can be the effect of a child's disorder rather than its cause. Children's problem behaviors can negatively affect their parents' moods, marital relationships, and parenting behaviors (Cowan & Cowan, 2006).

Unquestionably, stress on a family and the ineffective parenting that sometimes results from it contribute to and aggravate many childhood problems. Early abuse and neglect have even worse consequences—for example, contributing to chronic depression extending into adulthood (Uher, 2011). In addition, children who are at risk because their parents have psychological disorders or their temperaments predispose them to problems may or may not develop disorders themselves depending on whether they are parented effectively (Johnson et al., 2001; Sentse et al., 2009). As the diathesis–stress model suggests, then, disorders often arise from the toxic interaction of a genetically based vulnerability and stressful experiences, both early in life and leading up to the emergence of a disorder (Uher, 2011). Abnormal development, like normal development, is the product of both nature and nurture and of a history of complex transactions between person and environment in which each influences the other (Rutter et al., 2006).

Continuity and Discontinuity

The parents of children who develop psychological problems often want to know this: Will my child outgrow these problems, or will they persist? These parents are understandably concerned with the issue of continuity versus discontinuity in development. You have already seen that ASD persists beyond childhood in most individuals, but what about the broader range of childhood problems? A number of studies point to some *continuity* in susceptibility to problems over the years and suggest that early problems tend to have significance for later development (Jokela, Ferrie, & Kivimäki, 2009; Mesman, Bongers, & Koot, 2001). Relationships between early behavioral problems and later psychopathology tend to be weak, however, so there is also *discontinuity* in development; some children outgrow their problems. For example, in a 14-year follow-up of children and adolescents with behavioral and emotional problems, about 40% still had significant problems in adulthood, but most did not (Hofstra, Van der Ende, & Verhulst, 2000). In short, having psychological problems as a child does not doom most individuals to a life of maladjustment.

Why might we see continuity of problem behavior in some children but discontinuity in others? If children have mild rather than severe psychological problems and if they receive help, their difficulties are more likely to disappear (Essex et al., 2009). Some children also show remarkable **resilience**, functioning well despite exposure to risk factors for disorder or overcoming even severe early problems to become well adjusted (Garmezy, 1994; Masten & Tellegen, 2012). Resilient children appear to benefit from protective factors such as their own competencies (especially intellectual ability and social skills) and strong social support (especially a stable family situation with at least one caring parent figure). For an example of such children and researchers studying resilience, see the video in **Exploring Development Box 16.1**.

With the nature–nurture and continuity-discontinuity issues in mind, let us focus on two illustrative childhood problems: attention deficit hyperactivity disorder, an externalizing disorder, and depression, an internalizing disorder.

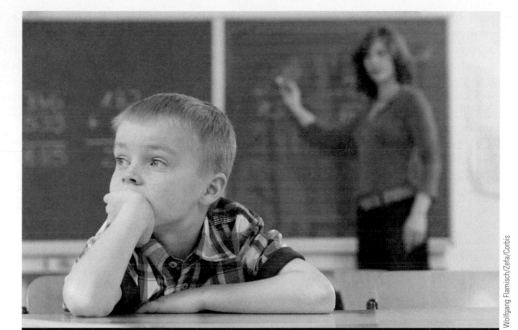

Most children with attention deficit hyperactivity disorder show inattention but not hyperactivity; they often seem "spaced out" in the classroom.

Attention Deficit Hyperactivity Disorder

Upon entering high school I was determined to make high honor roll every quarter. It didn't quite work out that way though. . . . I was completely lost. I couldn't focus on work, I couldn't pay attention in class, and I couldn't concentrate on homework, rarely completing it as a result. Emotionally, I didn't really know how to handle it. I was completely frustrated because I didn't understand why I was having such trouble. . . . My teachers knew I had the potential to do well, but they just figured I was lazy and not motivated. My parents were angry with me because my teachers told them I never did my homework. . . . I would try to sit down and write a paper, but there were too many thoughts in my head and too many things going on around me to even get a paragraph down. I would sit in the front row of my math class, with my notebook open and ready to take notes, but then something would catch my eye out the window and I'd miss the whole lesson (Stone, 2009).

In this story, Rachel Stone describes her struggles with sustaining and focusing her attention, illustrating a key feature of **attention deficit hyperactivity disorder (ADHD)**. ADHD is diagnosed if either one of the following two sets of symptoms, or a combination of the two, is present (DSM-5; see also Selikowitz, 2009; Weyandt, 2007):

1. *Inattention.* The individual does not seem to listen, is easily distracted, makes careless errors, has trouble following instructions, misses details, is distractible, does not stick to activities and finish tasks, and tends to be forgetful and unorganized.
2. *Hyperactivity and Impulsivity.* The individual is restless, perpetually fidgeting, finger tapping, or chattering, and has trouble remaining seated; he or she acts impulsively before thinking, cannot wait to have a turn in an activity, and may talk too much, blurt things out, and interrupt others.

ADHD is common. According to parents, 9% of children aged 5 to 17 in the United States have been diagnosed as ADHD at some point in their lives (Akinbami et al., 2011). And almost 9% of school-age children meet the diagnostic criteria for ADHD at a given time, even though only about half have been diagnosed as such (Froehlich et al., 2007). At least two boys for every girl have the disorder, although girls may be under-diagnosed because they often show inattention rather than the more easily observable hyperactive behavior that boys more often show (Weyandt, 2007). The primarily inattentive form of ADHD is roughly twice as common as the primarily hyperactive-impulsive form (Froehlich et al., 2007).

Developmental Course

ADHD expresses itself differently at different ages. When the predominant symptom is hyperactivity/impulsivity, the condition often reveals itself in infancy. As infants, children with ADHD are typically very active, have difficult temperaments, and show irregular feeding and sleeping patterns (Teeter, 1998). As preschool children, they are in perpetual motion, quickly moving from one activity to another. Because most young children are energetic and have short attention

Exploring Development 16.1
Resilient Children

A mother living in a homeless shelter with her three sons, ages 6, 11, and 14, illustrates some of the findings of resilience research at the University of Minnesota's Institute of Child Development into children's ability to recover from serious disruptions in their lives.

- What characteristics can help children cope with adversity?
- Who can help children gain these characteristics?

spans, behavior must be evaluated in relation to developmental norms; otherwise, we might mistake most average 3- and 4-year-olds for hyperactive children. Finally, by the grade-school years, overactive behavior is less of a problem, but children with ADHD are fidgety, restless, and inattentive to schoolwork (American Psychiatric Association, 2013).

What becomes of hyperactive children later in life? It used to be thought that they outgrew their problems. Most children with ADHD do outgrow their overactive behavior (DuPaul & Stoner, 2003). However, as illustrated by Rachel's story, adolescents with ADHD continue to be restless, to have difficulty concentrating on their academic work, and to behave impulsively; on average, they perform poorly in school and are prone to committing reckless delinquent acts without thinking about the consequences (Brassett-Harknett & Butler, 2007). Those able to go on to college can often benefit from services to help them make the transition successfully (Weyandt & DuPaul, 2013).

The picture is somewhat more positive by early adulthood; yet many individuals with ADHD get in trouble because they have lapses of concentration, make impulsive decisions, and procrastinate (Brassett-Harknett & Butler, 2007; Schmidt & Petermann, 2009). In one study following hyperactive and control children from about age 7 to age 21, the hyperactive adults had lower educational attainment and achievement, had been fired more and received lower performance ratings from their employers, had fewer close friends and more problems in social relations, and had become involved in sexual activity and parenthood earlier (Barkley et al., 2006; and see Schmidt & Petermann, 2009; Selikowitz, 2009). In a national study, almost half of children diagnosed with ADHD continued to meet the diagnostic criteria for ADHD as adults; inattention problems persisted more than hyperactivity/impulsivity problems (Kessler et al., 2010). This evidence of continuity in ADHD across the life span is consistent with findings that over 4% of adults in the United States have diagnosable ADHD (Kessler et al., 2006). ADHD is evident even in old age (Brod et al., 2012); it is clearly not "kid stuff." If you complete the short assessment in **Engagement Box 16.1**, you can see whether you show some of the behaviors characteristic of adult ADHD.

Suspected Causes

What causes this disorder? No consistent evidence of brain damage or of structural defects in the brain is found in most individuals with ADHD. It is widely agreed, though, that their brains work differently than the brains of other individuals and that the cause is most likely differences in brain chemistry rather than physical brain damage. Russell Barkley (1997, 2000) has put forth the view that the frontal lobes of individuals with ADHD do not function as they do in typically developing children; this results in deficiencies in executive functions—most importantly, difficulty inhibiting responses and otherwise organizing and regulating one's behavior. Low levels of the neurotransmitters dopamine and norepinephrine, which are involved in communication among neurons in the frontal lobes, may be at the root of the executive function impairments and other differences in cognitive functioning individuals with ADHD show (Selikowitz, 2009; Weyandt, 2007).

Genes predispose some individuals to develop ADHD and probably underlie the differences in brain functioning associated with it. Genes account for as much as 60–90% of the variation among individuals in whether they have ADHD (Franke, Neale, & Faraone, 2009; Waldman & Gizer, 2006). First-degree relatives of someone with ADHD have 4 to 5 times the usual risk (Thapar, 2003). There is not one ADHD gene, however. Researchers have now identified around 200 gene variants common in individuals with ADHD that influence levels of dopamine and other relevant neurotransmitters in their brains (Smith, Mick, & Faraone, 2009; Waldman & Gizer, 2006).

Environmental influences are also important, not so much as the main cause of ADHD but as forces that help determine whether a genetic potential turns into a reality and whether the individual adapts well or poorly as she develops (Brassett-Harknett & Butler, 2007). The misconception that ADHD is due to consuming sugar has long been put to rest (Weyandt, 2007). There is still some uncertainty about whether food colorings or dyes contribute. It seems clear that food dyes are not a major cause of ADHD, but they may have small negative effects on some children, ADHD or not, and more research may be in order (Arnold, Lofthouse, & Hurt, 2012; Kleinman et al., 2011). Low birth weight and maternal smoking and alcohol use during pregnancy, both associated with a shortage of oxygen prenatally, appear to contribute to some cases of ADHD (Banerjee, Middleton, & Faraone, 2007; Lehn et al., 2007). And genes and environment interact: individuals who inherit genes that adversely affect dopamine levels and who also experience family adversity show more ADHD symptoms than children who do not have both genes and environment working against them (Laucht et al., 2007).

Treatment

Many children with ADHD are given stimulant drugs such as methylphenidate (Ritalin), and most are helped by these drugs. Although it may seem odd to give overactive children stimulants, the brains of individuals with ADHD are actually underaroused. These drugs increase levels of dopamine and other neurotransmitters in the frontal lobes of the brain to normal levels and, by doing so, allow these children to concentrate (Selikowitz, 2009). Listen to Rachel Stone again:

> I was put on the medication Adderall [another stimulant drug] one month before sophomore year concluded. I was able to pull up all my grades and end up with an eighty-five for my fourth quarter average, making the honor roll for the first time in my high school career. . . . Things only got better with junior year. I almost didn't pass math sophomore year, and almost didn't take it junior year because I didn't think it would be worth it. With the Adderall, I was able to focus in class and remember how much I liked math! I ended up with the highest average in the pre-calculus classes. . . (Stone, 2009).

Why, then, does controversy surround the use of stimulants with ADHD children? Some critics feel that these drugs are prescribed to too many children, including some who do not have ADHD (Mayes, Bagwell, & Erkulwater, 2009).

Engagement Box 16.1

Could You Have ADHD?

Check the box that best describes how you have felt and conducted yourself over the past 6 months.

	Never	Rarely	Sometimes	Often	Very Often
1. How often do you have trouble wrapping up the final details of a project once the challenging parts have been done?					
2. How often do you have difficulty getting things in order when you have to do a task that requires organization?					
3. How often do you have problems remembering appointments or obligations?					
4. When you have a task that requires a lot of thought, how often do you avoid or delay getting started?					
5. How often do you fidget or squirm with your hands or feet when you have to sit down for a long time?					
6. How often do you feel overly active and compelled to do things, like you were driven by a motor?					

Add up the number of check marks in the shaded boxes. If you have four or more checks in the shaded boxes, then you may want to talk to a professional about your behaviors and feelings to determine if you might have ADHD. Remember that this self-assessment is not a definitive diagnosis and needs follow-up if your answers are suggestive of ADHD.

Source: Adapted from the World Health Organization's 18-question Adult ADHD Self-Report Scale, Version 1.1 (Adult ASRS-V1.1), Symptom Checklist. ASRS-V1.1 Screener Copyright © 2003 World Health Organization (WHO). Reprinted by permission.

Although it is probably true that Ritalin and other stimulants are overprescribed in some communities, it is also true that many children with ADHD who could benefit from drug treatment go untreated. Others are concerned that stimulant drugs have undesirable side effects such as loss of appetite and headaches (see Mayes et al., 2009). Moreover, the drugs do not cure ADHD; they improve functioning only until their effects wear off.

Behavioral treatment is also used to treat ADHD. The Multimodal Treatment Study of Attention Deficit Hyperactivity Disorder (MTA), a carefully conducted national study of 579 children with ADHD ranging in age from 7 to 9, pitted medication and behavioral treatment against each other (Jensen et al., 2001; Molina et al., 2009). The study randomly assigned children to receive optimally delivered medication, state-of-the-art behavioral treatment (a combination of parent training, child training through a summer program, and school intervention), a combination of the two approaches, or routine care in the community over 14 months. The findings were clear: Medication alone was more effective than behavioral treatment alone or routine care in reducing ADHD symptoms (see also Scheffler et al., 2009). However, a

combination of medication and behavioral treatment was superior to medication alone when the goal was defined as not only reducing ADHD symptoms but also improving academic performance, social adjustment, and parent–child relations. A multipronged approach is generally recommended now: not only medication but

- behavioral programs designed to teach children with ADHD to stay focused on tasks, control their impulsiveness, and interact socially;
- parent training designed to help parents understand and manage the behavior of these often-difficult youngsters; and
- interventions at school to structure the learning environment (Chronis, Jones, & Raggi, 2006; Weyandt, 2007).

A caveat, though: An 8-year follow-up of children in the Multimodal Treatment Study revealed that differences among the treatment groups had faded by the time these children were adolescents and that, regardless of which treatment they received, the participants with ADHD had more academic and social problems than comparison children who did not have ADHD (Molina et al., 2009). Most children who had received medication during the study had since stopped using it but were doing as well as those who continued their medication. Outcomes were best for children who responded well initially to treatment. Overall, however, the study suggests that, while medication or medication combined with behavior treatment can significantly improve functioning in the short term, achieving long-term improvement is more challenging.

Depression

As you saw earlier, the depressive symptoms displayed by some infants may or may not qualify as major depressive disorder. When, then, can children experience true clinical depression? For years many psychologists and psychiatrists, especially those influenced by psychoanalytic theory, argued that young children simply could not be depressed. Feelings of worthlessness, hopelessness, and self-blame were not believed to be possible until the child was older (Garber, 1984). Besides, childhood is supposedly a happy, carefree time, right?

It is now clear that even young children can meet the same DSM criteria for major depressive disorder used in diagnosing adults (Garber, 2010). Depression in children is rarer than depression in adolescents and adults, but an estimated 2% of children have diagnosable depressive disorders (Gotlib & Hammen, 1992). It used to be thought that depression in children was expressed in a "masked" manner as other problems. Instead, it is often comorbid with other disorders. Depressed children are especially prone to anxiety and anxiety disorders (Garber, 2010; Moffitt et al., 2007). Many depressed children also have a conduct disorder or ADHD. Comorbidity of two or more psychiatric conditions in the same individual is very common, especially in childhood but also throughout the life span. Disorders that are comorbid with depression in childhood are distinct diagnoses, though, not masked or disguised symptoms of depression.

Even young children can experience a major depressive episode.

Depression expresses itself somewhat differently in a young child than in an adult, however (Garber, 2010; Weiss & Garber, 2003). Like depressed infants, depressed preschool children are more likely to display the behavioral and somatic symptoms of depression (losing interest in activities, eating poorly, and so on) than to talk about feeling depressed or hopeless (American Psychiatric Association, 2000; Kaslow et al., 2000). Yet as early as age 3 some children who are depressed express excessive shame or guilt—claiming, for example, that they are bad (Luby et al., 2009). Some act out themes of death and suicide in their play (Luby, 2004). All things considered, the main characteristics to look for are either sadness or irritability (children may express their depression either way) along with the lack of interest in usually enjoyable activities that depressed adults display (Garber, 2010; Luby et al., 2006).

What may not have occurred to you is that children as young as age 2 or 3 are also capable of attempting suicide (Rosenthal & Rosenthal, 1984; Shaffer & Pfeffer, 2001):

- At age 3, Jeffrey repeatedly hurled himself down a flight of stairs and banged his head on the floor; upset by the arrival of a new brother, he was heard to say, "Jeff is bad, and bad boys have to die" (Cytryn & McKnew, 1996, p. 72).
- An 8-year-old, after writing her will, approached her father with a large rock and asked in all seriousness, "Daddy, would you crush my head, please?" (Cytryn & McKnew, 1996, pp. 69–70).
- Other children have jumped from high places, run into traffic, and stabbed themselves, often in response to abuse, rejection, or neglect.

Moreover, children who attempt suicide once often try again (Shaffer & Pfeffer, 2001). Very few children actually commit suicide (Westefeld et al., 2010), but the moral is clear: Parents, teachers, and human service professionals need to appreciate that childhood is not always a happy, carefree time and that children can develop serious depressive disorders and suicidal tendencies. Children's claims that they want to die should be taken dead seriously.

Do depressed children tend to have recurring bouts of depression, becoming depressed adolescents and adults? Most children make it through mild episodes of sadness, and carryover of depression problems from childhood to adulthood is not as strong as carryover from adolescence to adulthood (Rutter et al., 2006). However, 5- and 6-year-olds who report many symptoms of depression are more likely than their peers to be depressed as adolescents, to think suicidal thoughts, to struggle academically, and to be perceived as in need of mental health services (Ialongo, Edelsohn, & Kellam, 2001). It is estimated that half of children and adolescents diagnosed as having major depressive disorder have recurrences in adulthood (Kessler, Avenevoli, & Merikangas, 2001).

Fortunately, most depressed children—and children with other psychological disorders too—respond well to psychotherapy (Carr, 2009; Kazdin, 2003. **Cognitive behavioral therapy**, a well-established psychotherapy approach that identifies and changes distorted thinking and the maladaptive emotions and behavior that stem from it, has proved

Challenges in Treating Children

The first challenge in treating children with psychological problems is getting them to treatment. According to the Surgeon General of the United States, fewer than one in five U.S. children with psychological disorders receives treatment (Shute, 2001). Sometimes the child does not think she has a problem and resists; sometimes parents do not recognize the problem or cannot face reality. Other times, parents are dismissed by doctors or other professionals who say that that they are worrying too much or that their child is only going through "a phase" (Carter, Briggs-Gowan, & Davis, 2004). Cost factors also enter in, especially for families without health insurance.

Assuming children do enter treatment, the next challenge is to recognize that they are not adults and cannot be treated as such (Kazdin, 2003; Koocher & Daniel, 2012). Because children are usually referred for treatment by parents who are disturbed by their behavior and because children do not have the same legal rights as adults, therapists must view both the child and his parents as the "client." Children's therapeutic outcomes often depend greatly on the cooperation and involvement of their parents, but not all parents cooperate (Bailey, 2000; Heru, 2006).

Finally, children function at different levels of cognitive and emotional development than adults do, and this must be taken into consideration in both diagnosing and treating their problems—a point appreciated by students of human development. For example, young children cannot easily participate in therapies that require them to verbalize their problems and gain insight into the causes of their behavior. A more developmentally appropriate approach for young children used by some therapists is play therapy, in which disturbed children are encouraged to act out concerns that they cannot easily express in words (see Schaefer, 2010; Wethington et al., 2008).

Behavioral approaches, which apply observational learning and reinforcement principles and do not require insight and verbal skills, are effective with young children. Children can also benefit from an approach that has proven highly effective in treating adult psychological problems, cognitive behavioral therapy, even though it requires more cognitive and verbal skill than behavioral therapy (Brent & Maalouf, 2009; Hofmann et al., 2012). Still other approaches especially designed for young children and their parents have been developed. For example, one intervention for depressed preschool children works with both the children and their parents to build a more nurturing parent–child relationship in which the parent helps the child learn to better recognize and regulate her emotions (Luby, Lenze, & Tillman, 2012).

Mainly, if children get to mental health professionals and if their parents cooperate with a therapist, many childhood disorders, both externalizing and internalizing, can be treated successfully.

Play therapy can help young children who lack verbal skills to express their feelings. Here it is used to help Ashwin Balaji, age 4, deal with his anxieties about his upcoming surgery.

especially effective (Brent & Maalouf, 2009; Weisz, McCarty, & Valeri, 2006). Because children are not adults, though, treating children with depression and other psychological disorders poses several special challenges, as **Application Box 16.1** reveals.

Depressed children have also been treated with antidepressant drugs called selective serotonin reuptake inhibitors, such as Prozac (fluoxetine), that correct for low levels of the neurotransmitter serotonin in the brains of depressed individuals. However, these drugs do not appear to be as effective with children as with adults, and some research has suggested that they may increase the risk of suicidal thoughts and behavior among young users. A warning regarding the possibility of increased suicidality in child and adolescent patients was issued by the U.S. Food and Drug Administration in 2004 (Vedantam, 2006; Vitiello, Zuvekas, & Norquist, 2006). Antidepressants are still prescribed in some cases for seriously depressed youth who are likely to be at even greater risk of suicide if they are not treated with medication. However, these drugs are prescribed less often and with more careful monitoring of the child's reactions (Nemeroff et al., 2007).

Checking Mastery

1. What is the main difference between an externalizing and an internalizing disorder in childhood?
2. What two major sets of symptoms characterize ADHD?
3. What is the agreed-upon best way to treat ADHD and how is it limited?
4. How is major depression in a preschool child similar to and different from depression in an adult?

Making Connections

1. Focusing on depression in childhood and citing evidence, what do you conclude about the nature/nurture and continuity/discontinuity issues as they pertain to depression?
2. Some experts believe that ADHD is overdiagnosed and overtreated with medications. Others, however, believe that not enough cases of ADHD are being identified and treated with medications. What is your position on diagnosis and treatment of ADHD and how does the material in this chapter support—and fail to support—your view?

LEARNING OBJECTIVES:

- Evaluate the "storm and stress" view of adolescence.
- Summarize the nature, causes, and preferred treatment of anorexia nervosa.
- Describe normal substance use in adolescence and how the cascade model accounts for the development of substance use problems.
- Explain why depression rates climb in adolescence, especially among females.
- Describe gender differences in adolescent suicidal behavior and explain why some adolescents attempt or commit suicide.

If any age group has a reputation for having problems, it is adolescents. This is supposedly the time when angelic children are transformed into emotionally unstable, unruly, problem-ridden delinquents. The view that adolescence is a time of emotional storm and stress was set forth by the founder of developmental psychology, G. Stanley Hall (1904). It has been with us ever since.

Storm and Stress?

Are adolescents really more likely than either children or adults to experience psychological problems? On one hand, adolescents have a worse reputation than they deserve. Most adolescents are not emotionally disturbed and do not engage in serious problem behaviors such as drug abuse and chronic delinquency. Instead, significant mental health problems—real signs of storm and stress in the form of diagnosable disorders—characterize 20%, possibly as many as 25%, of adolescents, adolescents like Peggy, described at the beginning of the chapter (Ford, Goodman, & Meltzer, 2003; Merikangas et al., 2010). Moreover, many of these adolescents were maladjusted before they reached puberty and continue to be maladjusted during adulthood (Reinherz et al., 1999).

Yet there is some truth in the storm-and-stress view. Adolescence is a period of risk taking, of problem behaviors such as substance abuse and delinquency, and of heightened vulnerability to some forms of psychological disorder (Cicchetti & Rogosch, 2002; Steinberg, 2011). The 20% plus rate of diagnosable psychological disorders at a given time among adolescents is higher than the estimated rate of about 10% among children (Ford, Goodman, & Meltzer, 2003), but it is no higher than the rate for adults (Kessler et al., 2005). Teenagers face greater stress than children; they must cope with physical maturation, changing brains and cognitive abilities, tribulations of dating, changes in family dynamics, moves to new and more complex school settings, societal demands to become more responsible and to assume adult roles, and more (Cicchetti & Rogosch, 2002). Most adolescents cope with these challenges remarkably well, maintain the level of adjustment they had when they entered adolescence, and undergo impressive psychological growth. Many feel depressed, anxious, and irritable occasionally, though, and a minority experience a buildup of stressors that precipitate serious psychopathology. These adolescents' problems should not be dismissed as adolescent moodiness and irritability.

Many adolescents get themselves into trouble by overusing alcohol and drugs, having risky sex, engaging in delinquent behavior, and displaying other so-called adolescent problem behaviors. These behaviors, although common and often correlated with each other, usually do not reach the level of seriousness to qualify as psychological disorders (Boles, Biglan, & Smolkowski, 2006; Jessor, 1998). Indeed, they are often normal outgrowths of adolescents' efforts to define who they are and gain acceptance by their peers.

Problem behaviors may also peak in adolescence because the normal timetable for brain development endows adolescents with strong sensation-seeking and reward-seeking tendencies but immature self-regulatory capabilities (Albert, Chein, & Steinberg, 2013; Spear, 2010; and see Chapter 5's discussion of risk taking and brain development). The result is sometimes impulsive risk taking in pursuit of excitement and enjoyment without much self-control or thought of the likely consequences. This risky behavior is most likely when adolescents are with friends and their emotions are aroused.

Here we focus on some diagnosable disorders that become more prevalent in adolescence. Having discussed adolescent externalizing problems like aggression, delinquency, and conduct disorder in Chapter 13, we look here at eating disorders such as anorexia nervosa that can make the adolescent period treacherous and even fatal; experimentation with alcohol and drugs that can turn into substance abuse; and depression, whose rate increases dramatically from childhood to adolescence. These problems interfere with normal adolescent development; yet they become far more understandable when viewed in the context of adolescence.

Eating Disorders

Perhaps no psychological disorders are more closely associated with adolescence than the eating disorders that disproportionately strike adolescent females, especially during the transition from childhood to adolescence at around age 14 and again during the transition from adolescence to emerging adulthood at around age 18 (Bryant-Waugh, 2007; Eddy, Keel, & Leon, 2010). Eating disorders—anorexia nervosa, bulimia nervosa, binge eating disorder (a new distinct disorder starting in DSM-5), and related conditions—have become more common in industrialized countries in recent decades (Eddy et al., 2010; Milos et al., 2004).

They are serious—indeed, potentially fatal—conditions that are difficult to cure.

Anorexia nervosa, which literally means "nervous loss of appetite," is characterized by:

- body weight that is less than minimally normal for the person's gender, height, and age;
- a strong fear of becoming overweight or behavior that interferes with gaining weight; and
- a tendency to feel fat despite being emaciated, to be overly influenced by weight or shape in evaluating the self, and to fail to appreciate the seriousness of one's low body weight (American Psychiatric Association, 2013).

Bulimia nervosa, the so-called binge–purge syndrome, involves recurrent episodes of consuming huge quantities of food followed by purging activities such as self-induced vomiting, use of laxatives, rigid dieting and fasting, or obsessive exercising (Pinhas et al., 2007). **Binge eating disorder** involves binge eating without the purging.

A recent study of adolescent females involving annual diagnostic interviews administered from age 13 to age 21 revealed that by age 20 over 5% of these young women had experienced at least one of these three disorders (less than 1% anorexia, 2.6% bulimia, and 3% binge eating disorder (Stice, Marti, & Rohde, 2012). A total of 13% had experienced either one of these eating disorders or a milder, "subthreshold" form of eating disorder. We will focus here on anorexia, the least common but most life threatening of the three disorders.

The typical individual with anorexia may begin dieting soon after reaching puberty and simply continue, insisting, even when she weighs only 60 or 70 pounds, that she needs to lose a few more pounds (Hsu, 1990). Praised at first for losing weight, she becomes increasingly obsessed with dieting and exercising and gains a sense of control by resisting the urgings of parents and friends to eat more (Levenkron, 2000).

There are about 11 affected females for every 1 affected male (van Hoeken, Seidell, & Hoek, 2003), a huge gender difference that has aroused the curiosity of researchers. You may think the reason for the difference is that females are under more social pressure to be thin, but **Exploration Box 16.1** suggests that biological factors may also be involved. Individuals with anorexia are getting younger; one third-grader was so severely affected that she considered five Cheerios a meal (Tyre, 2005). It is a myth that anorexia nervosa is restricted to European American females from upper-middle-class backgrounds. It occurs at all socioeconomic levels and in all racial and ethnic groups. African American females are less affected, however, probably because they are more satisfied with their bodies and less concerned than European American and Asian American females with dieting and being thin (Franko & George, 2009).

Suspected Causes

Both nature and nurture contribute to eating disorders. On the nurture side, cultural factors are significant and rates of eating disorders vary widely around the world, being highest in Western or Westernized countries and in urban areas within countries (Anderson-Fye, 2009). We live in a society obsessed with thinness

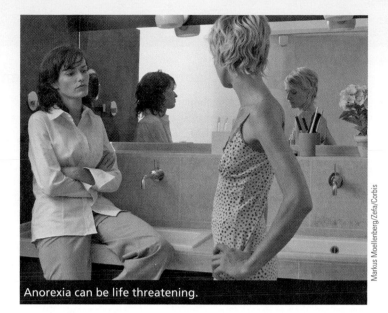

Anorexia can be life threatening.

Markus Moellenberg/Zefa/Corbis

as the standard of physical attractiveness—a society that makes it hard for young women to feel good about themselves (Eddy et al., 2010; Keel & Klump, 2003). As the Western ideal of thinness has spread to other countries, rates of eating disorders in those countries have risen. Interestingly, exposure to television on the island of Fiji converted girls raised to view plump bodies as a status symbol associated with the generous sharing of food into girls who feel too fat and try to lose weight (Becker et al., 2002).

Well before they reach puberty, starting as early as preschool, girls in our society begin to associate being thin with being attractive, fear becoming fat, and wish they were thinner (Hill, 2007; Ricciardelli & McCabe, 2001). Their desire to be thin and their feelings about themselves and their bodies are influenced by how much emphasis they think their peers place on thinness and how much television they watch focused on appearance (Dohnt & Tiggemann, 2006). Ultrathin Barbie dolls with unattainable body proportions also contribute to young girls' poor body images (Dittmar, Halliwell, & Ive, 2006). Perhaps all these cultural messages explain why about a fourth of second-grade girls in one study dieted (Thelen et al., 1992; and see Hill, 2007).

As girls experience normal pubertal changes, they naturally gain fat and become, in their minds, less attractive; they have more reason than ever to be obsessed with controlling their weight (Murnen & Smolak, 1997). This may help explain why adolescence is prime time for the emergence of eating disorders (but take the information in Exploration Box 16.1 into consideration too). But why do relatively few adolescent females in our society develop anorexia, even though almost all of them experience social pressure to be thin?

Genes, though we are not sure which ones, serve as a diathesis, predisposing certain individuals to develop eating disorders (Eddy et al., 2010; Keel & Klump, 2003). Twin and adoption studies suggest that more than half of the variation in risk for eating disorders is attributable to genes (Bulik et al., 2006; Klump et al., 2009). In a longitudinal study aimed at identifying early risk factors for the development of anorexia by age 30, feeding

Explaining Eating Disorders among Adolescent Girls

Why are eating disorders so much more prevalent among females than males, and why do they become more common at puberty? Some interesting answers have come from research by Kelly Klump and her colleagues. In an early study, these researchers gave an eating behavior survey used to identify individuals at risk for eating disorders to female twins who were age 11 and prepubertal, age 11 and pubertal, and age 17 and pubertal (Klump, McGue, & Iacono, 2003). The survey covered areas like body dissatisfaction, weight preoccupation, binge eating, and purging behaviors. The researchers then compared how similarly identical and fraternal twin pairs responded. In prepubertal girls, genes did not matter. Heritability was 0% because identical twins were no more similar in their eating attitudes and behaviors than fraternal twins. Shared environmental factors made both types of twins similar to each other. Among girls who had reached puberty, however, identical twins were far more similar than fraternal twins, and genes explained 54% of the variation in

survey responses. This study hinted that genes involved in triggering eating disorders in adolescence may be activated by biochemical changes associated with puberty and may not be expressed until adolescence.

Does this same increase in the heritability of disordered eating behaviors from pre- to post-puberty apply to boys? Apparently not. In another study that included both male and female twins, genes accounted for 51% of the variations in boys' responses to an eating behavior survey whether the survey was taken before puberty, during puberty, or in early adulthood (Klump et al., 2012). In girls, the earlier finding held true: heritability was 0% before puberty but rose to 51% during and after puberty.

What accounts for this increase in the heritability of eating-disordered behavior among girls starting at puberty, then? Klump and her colleagues suspect that increases in female hormones during puberty activate a genetically based risk for eating disorders in certain girls. One sign is that their basic finding applies not only to humans but to rats.

They have shown that differences in eating behavior between female rats that are or are not genetically predisposed to one form of eating disorder, binge eating, do not show up until puberty (Klump et al., 2011). They point to evidence that female hormones not only orchestrate pubertal development but influence neurotransmitters like serotonin that are implicated in eating disorders (Klump et al., 2012). Finally, they have found that the heritability of eating disorders is high in adolescent twin girls who have high levels of the female hormone estradiol but low in twins with low levels of this female hormone (Klump et al., 2010).

Often we think first of social and cultural influences when we try to explain eating disorders among adolescent females—factors like social pressure to conform to the thin ideal. Klump's research suggests the need to consider biology too--genetic makeup and hormonal influences at puberty—in explaining why some girls are so susceptible to eating disorders when they reach adolescence.

---

problems in infancy and a history of undereating were among the predictive factors, suggesting a biologically based and early-developing problem (Nicholls & Viner, 2009).

Indeed, biochemical abnormalities have been found in individuals with anorexia that may underlie their symptoms (Klump & Culbert, 2007; Wilson, Becker, & Hefferman, 2003). For example, their genes may call for low levels of the neurotransmitter serotonin, which is involved in both appetite and mood and has been linked to both eating disorders and mood disorders (Keel & Fulkerson, 2001; Klump & Culbert, 2007). The neurotransmitter dopamine, involved in the brain's reward system, has also been implicated; eating disorders, like alcohol and drug addiction, may involve compulsive behavior that becomes reinforcing (Halmi, 2009; and see Klump & Culbert, 2007). Genes may also contribute to a personality profile that puts certain individuals at risk; females with anorexia tend to be highly anxious and obsessive perfectionists who are driven to control their eating (Halmi, 2009; Lilenfeld et al., 2006).

Yet anorexia still may not emerge unless a genetically predisposed girl living in a weight-conscious culture also experiences a family environment that fosters eating problems and a buildup of stressful events (Eddy et al., 2010). Girls who are overly concerned about their weight tend to come from families preoccupied with weight where mothers may model and reinforce disordered eating (Eddy et al., 2010; Sim et al., 2009;

Strober et al., 2000). Some are insecurely attached to their parents and show extreme anxiety about separation from loved ones (O'Shaughnessy & Dallos, 2009; Sharpe et al., 1998). Ultimately, it often takes stressors or traumatic events to push a vulnerable young woman over the edge (Reyes-Rodríguez et al., 2011).

In anorexia nervosa, then, we have another clear example of the diathesis–stress model at work. A young woman who is at risk for it partly because of her genetic makeup may not develop anorexia unless she also grows up in a culture that overvalues thinness and in a family that makes it hard to forge a positive identity—and also faces overwhelming stress.

Prevention and Treatment

Can eating disorders be prevented before they start? Eric Stice and his colleagues have been testing the effectiveness of a dissonance-producing intervention that can be administered either on the Internet or in groups (Stice & Presnell, 2007; Stice et al., 2009). It attempts to get adolescent girls and college women who have body image concerns to stop viewing a thin body as ideal by having them critique the thin ideal in essays, role plays, and the like. The cognitive dissonance created by coming out against the thin ideal is expected to motivate these young women to stop pursuing thinness as their goal. In an intervention study with 306 adolescent girls who had body image concerns, the researchers compared a school-based cognitive dissonance program with an educational brochure on eating disorders. The program proved effective in reducing internalization of the thin body ideal and in turn reducing body dissatisfaction, dieting efforts, and eating disorder symptoms. An Internet-based version of the program and group sessions led by peer leaders have also proven effective with both high school and college students (Stice et al., 2012, 2013). Here, then, an ounce of prevention may be worth at least a pound of cure, although we cannot yet be sure that prevention programs like this truly prevent disorder.

Effective therapies for individuals who have developed anorexia start with behavior modification programs designed to bring their eating behavior under control, help them gain weight, and deal with any medical problems they may have, in a hospital or treatment facility if necessary (Patel, Pratt, & Greydanus, 2003). Then it is possible to move on to such options as individual psychotherapy designed to help them understand and gain control of their problem, family therapy designed to change parent–child relationships, and medication for depression and related psychological problems (see Grilo & Mitchell, 2010; Jaffa & McDermott, 2007).

Research suggests that family therapy approaches may have more lasting effects than individual treatment (Couturier, Kimber, & Szatmari, 2013). The Maudsley approach to family therapy, named after the hospital in London where it originated, appears to be an especially effective approach to treating eating disorders (Hurst, Read, & Wallis, 2012; Loeb et al., 2007; Sperry, Roehrig, & Thompson, 2009). Among its elements are

- focusing on weight gain initially;
- viewing the family as part of the treatment team rather than the cause of the patient's problems;
- temporarily putting parents in charge of getting their daughter to eat, until she is ready to take over that responsibility herself;
- gaining the cooperation of all family members and helping them to see the problem as serious but stop blaming themselves;
- assessing family interactions surrounding eating and the patient's symptoms, and helping the family respond more constructively to the patient's eating behavior in order to facilitate weight gain;
- once sufficient weight is gained and control of eating is returned to the adolescent, focusing on any broader family or individual issues such as the adolescent's need for more autonomy.

Individuals with anorexia are difficult to treat because they so strongly resist admitting that they have a problem and may go to great lengths to hide the fact that they are not eating. More success can be achieved if the problem is diagnosed and treated before age 18 than if it becomes chronic (Halmi, 2009).

Substance Use Disorders

She lost count of the vodka shots. It was New Year's Eve. . ., and for this high school freshman, it was time to party. She figured she'd be able to sleep it off—she'd done it before. But by the time she got home the next day, her head was still pounding, her mouth was dry,

and she couldn't focus. This time, the symptoms were obvious even to her parents. After that night, she realized the weekend buzzes had gone from being a maybe to a must. (Aratani, 2008, p. C1)

One of the ways in which some adolescents explore their identities, strive for peer acceptance, and reach toward adulthood is by experimenting with smoking, drinking, and drug use. For some, like this high school freshman (and Peggy at the start of the chapter), substance use moves beyond experimentation to abuse. In DSM-5 language, *substance use disorders* occur when a person continues to use a substance, whether alcohol, marijuana, or something else, despite adverse consequences such as putting the individual in physically dangerous situations, interfering with performance in school or at work, or contributing to interpersonal problems. People with substance use disorders may crave a substance or substances, be unable to control their use of substances or quit, develop an increased tolerance for a substance, and experience withdrawal symptoms if use is terminated. Substance use disorders increase over the adolescent years, especially starting at around age 15, and then decrease in early adulthood (Chassin et al., 2010).

The tolls of substance use disorders on development can be heavy. As noted in Chapter 5, for example, teens under the influence of alcohol are likely to make additional risky choices that can have negative consequences for themselves or others: smoking, engaging in risky sex, driving under the influence, riding in cars with drivers who have been drinking, getting into fights, engaging in illegal behavior, and so on. Concerns also include possible toxic effects of drinking, especially binge drinking, on the nervous system during a time of important brain development and neural pruning. Then there are the negative impacts on academic achievement, occupational success, and interpersonal relationships (Chassin et al., 2010; Colder et al., 2010). Moreover, use of alcohol or other substances in childhood or early adolescence predicts later problems with substance abuse (Dodge, Malone, et al., 2009).

Substance Use Rates

What do we know about substance use in adolescence? For years, the Monitoring the Future study based at the University of Michigan has tracked it (Johnston et al., 2013). The percentages of adolescents at various grade levels who reported in 2012 that they had used different substances are shown in ■ Figure 16.3. These percentages are not as high as those reported in the 1970s and early 1980s, but they are higher than those in the early 1990s. They indicate that some experimentation with alcohol and other substances is normal. For most substances, use increases with age. The exception is inhalants (glue, nail polish remover, solvents, and so on), which are used more by young teens than by older teens, probably because they are cheap and readily obtainable around the house and at stores. If inhalants are counted, almost half of 12th-graders (17- to 18-year-olds) have tried an illicit drug, most often marijuana.

Alcohol has long been the most widely used substance. By 12th grade, almost 70% have had a drink, and 24% report binge drinking in the past 2 weeks—drinking five or more drinks on one occasion (Johnston et al., 2013). Binge drinking is an even more

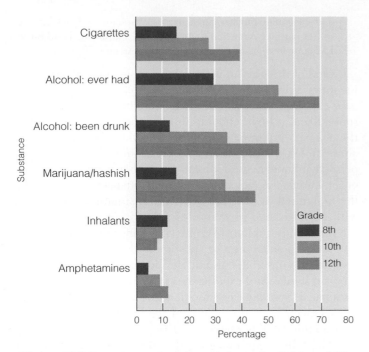

■ **Figure 16.3** Percentages of adolescents in grades 8, 10, and 12 who report ever using various substances. Other substances studied, such as cocaine and heroin, have been tried by very few.

SOURCE: Johnston, L. D., O'Malley, P. M., Bachman, J. G., & Schulenberg, J. E. (2013). *Monitoring the future. National results on drug use: 2012 overview, Key findings on adolescent drug use.* Ann Arbor: Institute for Social Research, The University of Michigan. Retrieved from: http://www.monitoringthefuture.org/; data are from Table 5, pp. 56–58.

Binge drinking is common among both high school and college students; for some, it leads to substance use disorder.

serious problem among college students (Grucza, Norberg, & Bierut, 2009). The potential for brain damage and even death from this kind of drinking to get drunk is real. One emergency room physician put it this way: "We're seeing kids coming in with blood alcohol levels in the mid-.3s, even .4, which is four to five times the legal limit for driving. That's the level at which 50% of people die" (Listfield, 2011, p. 7).

Ethnic differences in substance use are evident: Native American youth have high rates of use, Hispanic white and non-Hispanic white youth have medium rates, and Asian American and African American youth have the lowest rates (Johnston et al., 2013; Woo & Keatinge, 2008). Males have traditionally had higher rates of substance use and abuse than females, but the gap has narrowed (Aratani, 2008; Woo & Keatinge, 2008).

A Cascade Model of Contributors

It is now evident that the developmental pathway to adolescent substance use and abuse begins in childhood. A major study by Kenneth Dodge, Patrick Malone, and others (2009) attempted to integrate what is known about contributors to the use of illicit drugs in adolescence in a **cascade model of substance use**. Similar cascade models have been formulated to help account for the development of a variety of problems (Dodge et al., 2008; Masten et al., 2005; and see Chapter 13 on aggression). A cascade model is a transactional, multifactor model that envisions development as a flow of water over a series of waterfalls, gaining momentum as it goes as each influence along the way helps realize the previous factors and contributes to the next influence in the chain of influence. Dodge's cascade of substance use begins with

(1) a child who is at risk due to a difficult temperament, born into

(2) an adverse family environment characterized by such problems as poverty, stress, and substance use, who is

(3) exposed to harsh parenting and family conflict, and therefore develops

(4) behavior problems, especially aggression and conduct problems, and therefore is

(5) rejected by peers and gets into more trouble at school, so that

(6) parents, perhaps in frustration, give up trying to monitor and supervise their now difficult-to-control adolescent, which contributes to

(7) involvement in a deviant peer group, where the adolescent is exposed to and reinforced for drug taking and other deviant behavior.

The cascade model was tested in a longitudinal study that entailed annual assessments of 585 children from prekindergarten through 12th grade. Substance use was measured in grade 7 to grade 12 as any use of marijuana, inhalants, cocaine, heroin, or another illicit drug. Use clearly increased with age, from 5% in grade 7 to 22% in grade 10 to 51% in grade 12. The seven groups of factors in the cascade model each predicted both the next step in the cascade and involvement in substance use. All in all, the model captures well the developmental concept that adolescent problem behaviors and psychological disorders do not spring out of nowhere. Instead, they grow out of the

Exploration 16.2

Peer Socialization or Peer Selection?

If we don't blame adolescent problem behavior on bad parenting, we tend to blame it on negative peer influences. We say, for example, that someone got into trouble with alcohol and drugs because she got in with the "wrong crowd." In an interesting behavioral genetics study of twins, regular siblings, and their best friends, Jennifer Hill and her colleagues (2008) tried to determine whether similarities between adolescents and their friends in alcohol use are the result of *socialization* (peer influence on adolescents) or *selection* (the tendency of adolescents to choose friends who are like themselves, whether they are heavy drinkers or teetotalers). As it turned out, adolescents' predispositions to drink alcohol, which were influenced by both their genetic makeup and shared family envi-

ronmental influences, led them over time to associate with friends whose predispositions to drink matched their own. Thus, the study supported the selection hypothesis over the socialization hypothesis: friends' drinking did not influence adolescent behavior so much as reflect it.

Other studies suggest that both socialization and selection shape adolescent substance use (Cruz, Emery, & Turkheimer, 2012; Simons-Morton & Farhat, 2010). Jennifer Cruz and her colleagues (2012), for example, established that the level of alcohol use in an adolescent's peer network predicted changes over time in the adolescent's drinking, even with genetic factors controlled. In fact, when identical twins differed in their drinking habits, the twin whose peer group drank a lot drank more than

the twin whose peer group drank less—solid evidence of a true peer socialization effect. At the same time, there was evidence that certain teens, due to a genetic predisposition to drink, chose drinking friends—support for the selection hypothesis.

Here, then, is another illustration of the importance of taking genes into account before jumping to conclusions about parent or peer influence on development. It appears that adolescent substance use can indeed be influenced by peer use of substances—but it is also partly the product of genetic makeup and its influence on which crowds adolescents choose to associate with. To fully understand peer influences on development, we must grapple repeatedly with the issue of peer socialization versus peer selection.

---

accumulating effects of transactions among an individual and parents, peers, and other aspects of the social environment over many years. The model points to the possible value of substance abuse prevention programs targeting at-risk children long before adolescence. Although it becomes harder to stop the cascade toward substance use as the years go by, there are new opportunities to intervene at each step, and we know that preventive interventions to delay drinking and drug use in adolescence can head off problematic substance use in adulthood (Spoth et al., 2009; and see Sloboda, 2009).

What is missing from the cascade model? Some explanations of substance use and abuse put more emphasis on genetic contributors. Because of their genes, some individuals are more vulnerable to substance abuse as well as to the effects of the sorts of environmental influences described in the cascade model (Dick, Prescott, & McGue, 2009; Sartor et al., 2010; Woo & Keatinge, 2008). Moreover, what we think are socialization effects of peer drinking (effects of peers' substance use on an adolescent's use) could instead be selection effects (effects of genes on whether an adolescent hangs out with drinking or nondrinking friends), as **Exploration Box 16.2** illustrates. In the end, alcohol and drug abuse are the developmental outcomes of interactions among many genes and a cascade of many environmental factors.

Depression and Suicidal Behavior

Before puberty, boys and girls have similarly low rates of depression; after puberty, rates climb, and we end up with twice the rate of depression for females as for males in adolescence and adulthood, in our society and in others (Garber, 2010). In one study of female adolescents, the rate of major depressive disorder at some

time in the individual's life was 1% among girls younger than age 12 but 17% among young women age 19 and older—about 1 in 6 (Glowinski et al., 2003). Adolescent depression looks much like adult depression. However, depressed adolescents sometimes act out and look more like delinquents than like victims of depression. They also may show more "vegetative" symptoms such as lacking energy and sleeping all the time (Garber, 2010).

Factors in Depression

Why is adolescence a depressing period for some? For one thing, genetic influences on symptoms of depression seem to become stronger in adolescence than they were in childhood (Rutter et al., 2006; Scourfield et al., 2003). Pubertal changes may be responsible (Conley & Rudolph, 2009; Ge et al., 2003). In addition, teenagers, especially females, who have experienced family disruption and loss in childhood seem to be vulnerable to interpersonal stress after they reach puberty (Flook, 2011; Rudolph & Flynn, 2007).

Girls are more likely than boys to experience an accumulation of stressful events in early adolescence (Ge et al., 1994; Mezulis et al., 2011). Experiencing such events—especially interpersonal ones such as relationship breakups—predicts increases in depressive symptoms (Ge, Natsuaki, & Conger, 2006). To make matters worse, girls are also more likely than boys to rely on **ruminative coping**, dwelling unproductively on their problems (Nolen-Hoeksema, 1990; Nolen-Hoeksema, Wisco, & Lyubomirsky, 2008). As we saw in Chapter 14, girls also engage in more *co-rumination* with their friends. Compared to coping tactics favored by boys such as distraction and active problem solving, ruminative coping and co-rumination may make problems worse. Indeed, heavy reliance on ruminative coping is now viewed as a risk factor not only for depression but for anxiety, substance use, and eating disorders (Nolen-Hoeksema & Watkins, 2011; Nolen-Hoeksema et al., 2007).

Suicidal Behavior

As depression becomes more common from childhood to adolescence, so do suicidal thoughts, suicide attempts, and actual suicides. Individuals with major depression are more likely to make suicide attempts during adolescence than before or after (Rohde et al., 2013). Indeed, suicide is the third leading cause of death for 15- to 24-year-olds, far behind accidental injuries and just behind homicides; the yearly rate is about 10 per 100,000 for this age group (National Center for Health Statistics, 2010). For every adolescent suicide, there are many unsuccessful attempts; suicidal thoughts are even more common (Shaffer & Pfeffer, 2001). Almost 12% of male and 19% of female high school students in the United States seriously considered suicide in the past year; 6% of males and almost 10% of females attempted it (Eaton et al., 2012).

Before you conclude that adolescence is the peak time for suicidal behavior, however, consider the suicide rates for different age groups shown in ■ **Figure 16.4**. It is clear that adults are more likely to commit suicide than adolescents are. The suicide rate for women peaks in middle age, and the suicide rate for white men climbs throughout adulthood, making white men 65 and older the group most likely to commit suicide. Rates for minority group members, especially minority females, are very low by comparison.

Overall, males are more likely to commit suicide than females, by a ratio of at least three to one—a difference that holds up across most cultures studied (Girard, 1993; Shaffer & Pfeffer, 2001). When we look at suicide attempts, this ratio is reversed,

with females leading males by a ratio of about three to one. Apparently, then, females attempt suicide more often than males do, but males more often commit suicide when they try. This is probably because men use more lethal techniques (especially guns).

If suicide rates are higher in adulthood than in adolescence, why do we hear so much about teenage suicide? Probably because adolescents attempt suicide more frequently than adults do. The typical adolescent suicide attempt has been characterized as a "cry for help"—a desperate effort to get others to notice and help resolve problems that have become unbearable (Berman & Jobes, 1991; Lester, 1994). The adolescent who attempts suicide often wants a better life rather than death. This by no means suggests that adolescent suicide attempts should be taken lightly. Their message is clear: "I've got serious problems; wake up and help me!" Indeed, even suicidal thoughts during adolescence should be taken seriously; adolescents who have such thoughts are more likely than those who do not to attempt suicide, to have psychological disorders, and to display difficulties in functioning at age 30 (Reinherz et al., 2006).

You will not be surprised to learn that suicidal behavior in adolescence is the product of diathesis–stress. Four key risk factors are youth psychological disorder, family pathology and psychopathology, stressful life events, and access to firearms (Gould et al., 2003; and see Beautrais, 2003):

- More than 90% of adolescent suicide victims, partly because of genetic predisposition, suffered from depression, a substance-use disorder, an anxiety disorder, or another diagnosable psychological problem at the time of their deaths (Shaffer & Pfeffer, 2001). The more problem behaviors an adolescent displays (binge drinking, risky sexual behavior, eating disorders, aggression, and so on), the more likely she is to go from thinking suicidally to taking action (Miller & Taylor, 2005).
- Many suicide attempters also have histories of troubled family relationships, and often psychopathology and even suicide run in the family.
- In the period leading up to a suicide attempt, the adolescent has often experienced a buildup of stressful life events that breeds a sense of helplessness—deteriorating relationships with parents and peers, academic and social failures, run-ins with the law (Berman & Jobes, 1991; Woo & Keatinge, 2008).
- The availability of firearms makes it easy to act on suicidal impulses.

Engagement Box 16.2 shows some of the behavioral warning signs that can help you recognize that someone you know may be planning to commit suicide and needs help. The adolescent who attempts suicide once may try again if he receives little help and continues to feel incapable of coping with problems; as a result, professional help is appropriate after an unsuccessful suicide attempt (Rotheram-Borus et al.,

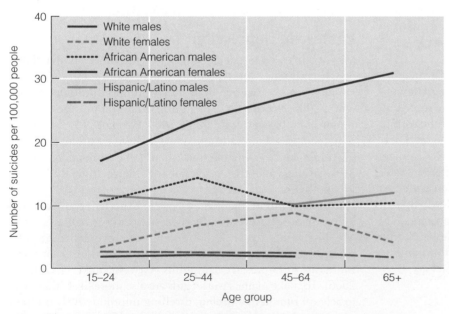

■ **Figure 16.4** Number of suicides per 100,000 people by age and sex among European Americans, African Americans, and Hispanic Americans in the United States.

SOURCE: National Center for Health Statistics (2012). *Health, United States, 2011.* Hyattsville, MD: U.S. Department of Health and Human Services, Centers for Disease Control and Prevention, National Center for Health Statistics. Retrieved from: http://www.cdc.gov/nchs/hus.htm.

Is Anyone You Know Suicidal? Know the Warning Signs

Do you have any friends, relatives, or acquaintances who you think might be suicidal? If so, see if they show the following warning signs of suicidality in young people, compiled by a committee of suicide experts (Rudd et al., 2006) and disseminated by the U.S. government's Substance Abuse and Mental Health Services Administration (SAMHSA, 2012):

Call 9-1-1 or seek immediate help from a mental health provider when you hear, say, or see any one of these behaviors:

- Someone threatening to hurt or kill themselves

- Someone looking for ways to kill themselves: seeking access to pills, weapons, or other means
- Someone talking or writing about death, dying, or suicide

Seek help by contacting a mental health professional or calling 1-800-273-TALK for a referral should you witness, hear, or see anyone exhibiting any one or more of these behaviors:

- Hopelessness
- Rage, anger, seeking revenge
- Acting reckless or engaging in risky activities, seemingly without thinking

- Feeling trapped—like there's no way out
- Increasing alcohol or drug use
- Withdrawing from friends, family, or society
- Anxiety, agitation, unable to sleep, or sleeping all the time
- Dramatic changes in mood
- No reason for living; no sense of purpose in life

Source: Rudd, M. D., Berman, A. L., Joiner, T. E. Jr., Nock, M. K., Silverman, M. M., Mandrusiak, M., . . . Witte, T. (2006). Warning signs for suicide: Theory, research, and clinical applications. *Suicide and Life-Threatening Behavior*, 36(3), Table 2, p. 259.

2000). Although, as we have seen, adolescence is not a time of "storm and stress" for most, it is a period in which biological, psychological, and social influences can conspire to make several mental health problems more likely.

Checking Mastery

1. What does the fact that 20% or more of adolescents have diagnosable psychological disorders say for and against the notion that adolescence is a period of storm and stress?
2. What are three main factors that contribute to anorexia nervosa?
3. Judging from the cascade model of substance use, what are three factors you might look for if you wanted to

identify children who are at risk for illicit drug use when they become adolescents?

4. How do males and females differ with respect to (a) suicide attempts and (b) completed suicides?

Making Connections

1. How would you characterize your own mental health during adolescence? Consider whether the concept of "storm and stress," as well as the specific diagnoses we have discussed in this section, apply to you in any way.
2. Peggy, the young woman described at the beginning of the chapter, attempted suicide. Using the material on suicide in this section, develop a theory of why she might have done so, showing how both diathesis and stress may have contributed.

16.5 The Adult

LEARNING OBJECTIVES:

- Explain how depression is related to age, gender, and ethnicity in adulthood.
- Describe the major characteristics of dementia and Alzheimer's disease in particular.
- Summarize what we know about the biology and causes and contributors of Alzheimer's disease.
- Explain how one can distinguish between irreversible dementias like Alzheimer's disease and reversible dementias, delirium, depression, and normal aging.

By the time we reach adulthood, it appears that most of us have already had at least one diagnosable psychological disorder, whether it was recognized and treated or not. This surprising finding comes from studies that administer diagnostic interviews repeatedly over the years rather than asking retrospectively about previous disorders. One such study involved interviews conducted nine times between age 9 and age 21 with a sample of children and their parents in the southeastern United States (Copeland et al., 2011). Over 60% of participants had met the criteria for a

psychological disorder at some point in their lives—and another 20% had what DSM calls a "subthreshold" or less clear-cut case of disorder at some point. Although the percentage of youth with a disorder at any particular point in time is much lower (the 20% plus we discussed earlier), apparently abnormal behavior is very normal! While community surveys like this may overestimate rates of disorder, they make the point that most of us move back and forth between "normal" and "abnormal" developmental pathways over our lives.

Most adult psychological disorders originate in childhood or adolescence. And, as is true of psychological problems in childhood and adolescence, psychological problems in adulthood usually emerge when a vulnerable individual faces overwhelming stress. As it turns out, adults typically experience the greatest number of life strains and stressors in early adulthood (Almeida et al., 2011; McLanahan & Sorensen, 1985; Pearlin, 1980). Life strains decrease from early to middle adulthood, perhaps as many adults settle into more stable lifestyles and stop changing residences, jobs, and relationships so much. And older adults? Despite increased health problems, elderly adults report fewer hassles and strains overall than middle-aged adults do (Almeida & Horn, 2004; Martin, Grunendahl, & Martin, 2001). This may be because they have fewer roles and responsibilities to juggle or because they have learned to take many problems in stride.

Age differences in stressful experiences help explain age differences in rates of psychological disorder. Diagnostic interviews with adults age 18 or older in the United States reveal that rates of affective disorders (major depression and related mood disorders), alcohol abuse and dependence, schizophrenia, anxiety disorders, and antisocial personality all decrease from early adulthood to late adulthood (Myers et al., 1984; Robins & Regier, 1991). The only category of disorder that increases with age is cognitive impairment, as increasing numbers of older adults develop Alzheimer's disease and other forms of dementia (to be described shortly). Overall, about 25% (one in four) American adults experienced a psychological disorder in the past year (Kessler & Wang, 2008; Kessler, Chiu, et al., 2005).

With that as background, we can look more closely at one of the disorders to which young adults are especially susceptible, depression, and then turn to an examination of Alzheimer's disease and related cognitive impairments in later life.

Depression

Major depression and other affective disorders are among the most common psychological problems experienced by adults. Who gets depressed, and what does this reveal?

Age, Gender, and Ethnic Differences

The average age of onset of major depression is in the early 20s (Woo & Keatinge, 2008). Contrary to stereotypes of elderly people, older adults tend to be less vulnerable to major depression and other severe affective disorders than young or middle-aged adults are (Hybels, Blazer, & Hays, 2009, Kessler et al., 2010). Still, there are good reasons to be concerned about depression in old age. First, we know that depressed elderly adults are more likely than depressed adolescents to take their own lives. Second, reports of depression symptoms, if not diagnosable disorders, increase when people reach their 70s and beyond (Nguyen & Zonderman, 2006; Teachman, 2006). Although only about 1–2% of elderly adults have major depressive disorder at a given time, somewhere between 15% and 25% experience symptoms of depression (Hybels et al., 2009; Knight et al., 2006). These individuals are most likely to be very old women who are physically ill, poor, and socially isolated, and many could benefit from treatment (Blazer, 1993; Falcon & Tucker, 2000).

Might some of these mildly depressed and demoralized elders have a more serious but undiagnosed depressive disorder? It's possible. Depression can be difficult to diagnose in later life

Although few elderly adults have diagnosed depression, a sizable minority experiences at least some symptoms of depression.

(Charney et al., 2003). Think about it: Symptoms of depression include fatigue and lack of energy, sleeping difficulties, cognitive deficits, and somatic (body) complaints. What if an 80-year-old woman and/or her doctor note these symptoms but interpret them as nothing more than aging, as the result of the chronic illnesses so common in old age or medications for them, or as signs of dementia? A case of depression could be missed. To complicate diagnosis, elderly adults sometimes deny that they are sad, guilty, or suicidal and may instead report slowing, weight loss, and other somatic symptoms that could be interpreted as signs of physical disease (Edelstein & Segal, 2011; Nguyen & Zonderman, 2006). So clinicians working with older adults need to be sensitive to the differences between normal aging, physical disease, and psychopathology. For the most part, they are, and depression is diagnosed appropriately (Whitbourne & Meeks, 2011).

As noted already, women are twice as likely as men to be diagnosed as depressed. This gender difference probably results from a variety of factors (Kuehner, 2003; Nolen-Hoeksema, 2002): hormones and biological reactions to stress; levels of stress (including more exposure to interpersonal stressors among women); ways of expressing distress (women being more likely to express classic depression symptoms, men being more likely to become angry or overindulge in alcohol and drugs); and styles of coping with distress (especially the tendency for women to engage in more counterproductive ruminative coping). Interestingly, male and female rates of depression become more similar in old age (Wasserman, 2006).

Ethnic differences in depression are also evident. In a national study of adults age 55 and older (Woodward et al., 2012), the percentages of adults who had been affected by mood disorders, including major depressive disorder, during their lifetime were quite high for Latinos (13.9%) and non-Hispanic Whites (13.8%), and much lower for African Americans (5.4%) and Asian Americans (6.4%). It is not clear why, but Jimenez et al. (2010) suggest some hypotheses. Although other studies indicate that younger Latinos have lower rates of depression than non-Hispanic whites, it is possible that elderly Latino adults who are recent immigrants to the United States feel socially isolated and stressed as younger members of their families become acculturated. Older African Americans who are religious may be protected from depression by their religious faith and the social support they receive through their churches. Older Asian Americans may be underdiagnosed; for example, they tend to view mental illness in terms of physical symptoms and may be hesitant to admit that they have psychological problems or seek help for them (Jimenez et al., 2012; Sue et al., 2012). Whatever the many reasons, we can expect rates of depression to be highest among young adults, females, and both Hispanic and non-Hispanic whites.

Treatment

One of the biggest challenges in treating adults with major depression and other psychological disorders is getting them to seek treatment; many eventually do but often after going years without help (Wang et al., 2005). Older adults are especially likely to go undiagnosed and untreated, particularly if they are minority group members (Karel, Gatz, & Smyer, 2012; Neighbors et al., 2007). Older adults and members of their families may believe, wrongly, that problems such as depression and anxiety are just part of getting old or becoming ill or that it is somehow shameful to have psychological problems or need help. Mental health professionals, meanwhile, may underdiagnose or misdiagnose the problems of elderly individuals and may view elderly adults as less treatable than younger adults (Graham et al., 2003; Meeks et al., 2009). Few psychologists and psychiatrists are specially trained to treat a growing global population of older adults (Karel et al., 2012).

Despite these barriers, depressed elderly adults who seek psychotherapy benefit from it (Scogin et al., 2005). Moreover, those treated with antidepressant drugs not only overcome their depression in most cases but also show improved cognitive functioning (Blazer, 2003; Butters et al., 2000). As with many psychological problems, the most effective approach is often a combination of drug treatment and psychotherapy, especially cognitive behavioral therapy aimed at addressing carefully identified problems (Hollon, Thase, & Markowitz, 2002; March, 2009).

Aging and Dementia

Perhaps nothing scares us more about aging than the thought that we will become "senile." **Dementia** is a progressive deterioration of neural functioning associated with cognitive decline—for example, memory impairment, declines in tested intellectual ability, poor judgment, difficulty thinking abstractly, and often personality changes as well (see Lyketsos, 2009). The term dementia has been dropped from DSM-5 in favor of the less stigmatizing term "neurocognitive disorder" but we will continue to use it here. Different causes of neurocognitive disorder such as Alzheimer's disease are distinguished as subtypes, and each has "major" and "minor," or more and less severe, forms (American Psychiatric Association, 2013; Bajenaru et al., 2012).

Developing dementia is not part of normal aging. Yet rates of dementia increase steadily with age. Overall, dementia affects up to 10% of adults age 65 and older (Karel et al., 2012). Rates climb steeply with age, as shown in ■ Figure 16.5—from less than 2% at age 65–69 to over 35% at age 90 and older.

Dementia is not a single disorder. Much damage can be done by labeling any older person with cognitive impairments as senile—or even as having Alzheimer's disease—and then

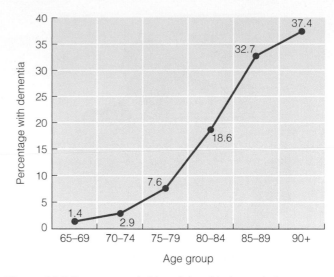

■ **Figure 16.5** Percentage of older adults with dementia by age group.
SOURCE: Data compiled by Karel, M. J., Gatz, M., & Smyer, M. A. (2012). Aging and mental health in the decade ahead. What psychologists need to know, *American Psychologist, 67*, 184–198, Table 1, p. 186.

assuming that he is a lost cause. Many different conditions can produce symptoms we associate with senility, and some of them are curable or reversible. Let us look at the leading cause of dementia, Alzheimer's disease, and then at related conditions.

Alzheimer's Disease

With Alzheimer's disease, you just know you're going to forget things, and it's impossible to put things where you can't forget them because people like me can always find a place to lose things and we have to flurry all over the house to figure where in the heck I left whatever it was…. It's usually my glasses…. You've got to have a sense of humor in this kind of business, and I think it's interesting how many places I can find to lose things…. [People with Alzheimer's] want things like they used to be. And we just hate the fact that we cannot be what we used to be. It hurts like hell. (Cary Henderson, age 64, former history professor diagnosed with Alzheimer's disease at age 55; Rovner, 1994, pp. 12–13)

Alzheimer's disease is the most common subtype of dementia, or major neurocognitive disorder, accounting for 50–70% of all cases, including those of former president Ronald Reagan and more recently famed women's basketball coach Pat Summitt (Geldmacher, 2009; Qui & Fratiglioni, 2009; Tanzi & Parson, 2000). The disease can strike in middle age but becomes increasingly likely with advancing age. Because more people are living into advanced old age, more will end up with Alzheimer's disease unless ways of preventing it or slowing its progression are found.

Alzheimer's disease leaves two telltale signs in the brain: *senile plaques* (masses of dying neural material outside neurons with a toxic protein called **beta-amyloid** at their core), and *neurofibrillary tangles* (twisted strands made of neural fibers and the protein **tau** within the bodies of neural cells). The effects of these physical changes—loss of connections between neurons, deterioration and death of neurons, increasingly impaired mental functioning, and personality changes—are progressive and irreversible or incurable. The disease begins to affect the brain in early and middle adulthood, maybe even earlier, long before cognitive functioning is affected

Pat Summitt, winner of 1,098 women's basketball games in 38 years of coaching at the University of Tennessee, receives the Medal of Freedom Award from President Obama in 2012. In 2011, she was diagnosed with early-onset Alzheimer's dementia. It began with losing her keys three times a day instead of just once, forgetting when team meetings were scheduled, and sometimes drawing blanks about what to call during games (Jenkins, 2011). When one of the doctors advised her to retire immediately, she said, "Do you have any idea who you're dealing with?" (Jenkins, 2011, p. A1). She continued to help her team as head coach emeritus. "I've forgotten I have it," she cracked (Jenkins, 2011, A14).

being able to retrace one's steps to find them. As the disorder progresses, people with Alzheimer's may have trouble remembering not only recently acquired but old information, have more trouble coming up with the words they want during conversations, and forget what to do next midway through making a sandwich or getting ready for bed. If tested, they may be unable to answer simple questions about where they are, what the date is, and who the president of the United States is. Eventually they become incapable of caring for themselves; no longer recognize loved ones; lose all verbal abilities; and die, some earlier and some later, but on average about 8–10 years after onset (National Institute on Aging, 2012).

Not only do patients with Alzheimer's disease become increasingly unable to function, but they also often test the patience of caregivers by forgetting they have left something cooking on the stove, wandering away and getting lost, accusing people of stealing the items they have misplaced, or taking off their clothes in public. Many become highly agitated and uncontrollable; large numbers suffer from depression and become apathetic; and some experience psychotic symptoms such as hallucinations (Geldmacher, 2009).

Causes and Contributors What causes Alzheimer's disease? It has a genetic basis, but there is no single "Alzheimer's gene" (Gatz, 2007; Tanzi & Parson, 2000). Alzheimer's disease strikes repeatedly and early in some families. By analyzing blood samples from families with many Alzheimer's victims, genetic researchers were able to identify genetic mutations on three chromosomes that cause early-onset (before age 60) Alzheimer's disease. Anyone who inherits just one of these dominant genes will develop the disease. However, these genes account for less than 5% of all cases of Alzheimer's disease (Gatz, 2007).

Genetic contributors to late-onset Alzheimer's disease, by far more common than the early-onset variety, are not as clear-cut. Rather than making Alzheimer's disease inevitable, a number of genes increase a person's risk slightly (Gatz, 2007; National Institute on Aging, 2012). APOE4 is the most famous; having two of the risk-inducing APOE4 variants of the APOE gene means having up to 15 times the normal risk of Alzheimer's disease (Lyketsos, 2009). It is believed that the APOE4 gene increases the buildup of beta-amyloid—the damaging substance in senile plaques—and speeds the progression of Alzheimer's disease (National Institute on Aging, 2012). Yet not everyone with the APOE4 gene, or even a pair of them, develops Alzheimer's disease, and many people with Alzheimer's disease lack the gene. Overall, genes account for about 60% of the variation in Alzheimer's, which means that environmental factors are also involved (Qui & Fratiglioni, 2009).

It has not been easy to pinpoint environmental contributors, however (Gatz, 2007). Epigenetic effects—influences of the environment on gene expression—are

Exploring Development 16.2
The Progression of Alzheimer's

As this woman attests, Alzheimer's takes away much more than memory.

- What behaviors signaled that her mother was suffering from more than age-related forgetfulness?
- What capacities does Alzheimer's impair?

and even longer before the disease is diagnosed. The first noticeable symptoms of the disease, detectable 2–3 years before dementia can be diagnosed, are usually difficulties remembering recently encountered material such as names and phone numbers (Geldmacher, 2009; Howieson et al., 1997).

The individual on a path to Alzheimer's may be recognized as having *mild cognitive impairment (MCI)*, discussed in Chapter 8. MCI is often—though not always—an early warning that dementia will follow (Lyketsos, 2009; Tabert et al., 2006). Similar to what is now called minor neurocognitive disorder in DSM-5, it is more serious than the slower cognitive functioning and minor memory problems common among aging adults. If all it took to warrant a diagnosis of MCI or dementia were occasional episodes of misplacing keys or being unable to remember someone's name, many young and middle-aged adults, not to mention textbook writers, would qualify! In the **Exploring Development Box 16.2** video, a woman describes her mother's progression into Alzheimer's.

In the early stages of Alzheimer's disease, warning signs include getting lost, having trouble managing money and paying bills, telling and retelling the same stories to the same people or repeatedly asking the same questions, and losing items but not

Positron emission tomography (PET scanning) shows metabolic activity in the brain and reveals areas of high brain activity (in red and yellow) and low brain activity (in blue or black). Here we see more activity in a normally functioning brain (left) than in the brain of a person with Alzheimer's disease (right).

being investigated, for example by comparing twin pairs in which one twin has Alzheimer's disease but the other does not (Chouliaras et al., 2010; Zawia, Lahiri, & Cardozo-Pelaez, 2009). Head injuries, such as those suffered by some boxers and football or soccer players, increase the risk of Alzheimer's disease (DeKosky, Ikonomovic, & Gandy, 2010; Plassman et al., 2000) Obesity and a diet that increases the odds of high blood pressure, high cholesterol, and cardiovascular disease also contribute (Nourhashemi et al., 2000; Savva & Brayne, 2009).

Researchers are also becoming more aware of the importance of **cognitive reserve**—extra brain power or cognitive capacity that some people can fall back on as aging and disease begin to take a toll on brain functioning (Gatz et al., 2001). People who have advanced education and high intelligence and have been mentally, physically, and socially active over the years have more cognitive reserve than less active people. As a result, if they do develop Alzheimer's disease, their more elaborate neural connections may allow them to continue functioning well even as the disease begins to damage their brains (Andel et al., 2008; Savva & Brayne, 2009; Sharp & Gatz, 2011).

Prevention and Treatment What can be done to treat, or possibly even prevent, Alzheimer's disease? Drugs aimed at increasing levels of neurotransmitters involved in memory are regularly prescribed (for example, Aricept [donepezil] and Namenda [memantine]). They modestly improve cognitive functioning, reduce behavioral problems, and slow the progression of the disease in some patients (Farlow & Boustani, 2009; Grossberg & Desai, 2003). However, they are not very effective and are certainly not a cure. So the search is on for drugs to reduce levels of beta-amyloid and tau in the brain (Gandy & DeKosky, 2013; National Institute on Aging, 2012).

Some also believe in the value of combating oxidation with antioxidants such as vitamins E and C and statin drugs prescribed to treat high cholesterol. This is based on evidence that beta-amyloid contributes to the production of damaging free radicals in the brain (National Institute on Aging, 2012; Wilkinson, 2009). And since the same lifestyle factors that contribute to cardiovascular disease and to metabolic disorders such as diabetes and obesity contribute to dementia as well, the same healthy eating recommendations are appropriate. Finally, both physical and mental exercise, including cognitive training programs, have been shown to delay cognitive decline in later life and may slow the progression of dementia as well (Hertzog et al., 2009; Larson et al., 2006).

Today researchers are looking hard for ways to diagnose Alzheimer's disease earlier, through brain imaging and biomarkers in the blood, in hopes of intervening to slow or even halt the disease's progression before much damage is done (National Institute on Aging, 2012; Weiner, Garrett, & Bret, 2009). However, even though deterioration leading to death must be expected in today's Alzheimer's patients, a great deal can be done to make the disease more bearable. Memory training and memory aids (for example, reminder notes around the house), the use of behavioral management techniques and medications to deal with behavioral problems, and educational programs and psychological interventions for both patients and their caregivers to help them understand and cope with dementia and function better can all contribute (Grossberg & Desai, 2003; Kasl-Godley & Gatz, 2000).

Other Causes of Cognitive Impairment

Many other conditions can result in cognitive impairment in aging adults. The second most common type of neurocognitive disorder, often occurring in combination with Alzheimer's disease, is **vascular dementia** (Szoeke et al., 2009; Thompson, 2006). Also called multi-infarct dementia, most cases are caused by a series of minor strokes that cut off the blood supply to areas of the brain. Whereas Alzheimer's disease usually progresses slowly and steadily, vascular dementia often progresses in a steplike manner, with further deterioration after each small stroke. Whereas Alzheimer's disease impairs memory most, vascular dementia often does its greatest damage to executive functions (Román, 2003; Szoeke et al., 2009). And whereas Alzheimer's disease is more strongly influenced by genes, vascular dementia is more closely associated with environmental risk factors for cerebrovascular diseases that affect blood flow in the brain—smoking, eating a fatty diet, and so on (Thompson, 2006). Some other causes of neurocognitive disorder are described in ● **Table 16.1**.

Careful diagnosis is critical because certain conditions can be mistaken for irreversible dementia. First, some individuals—perhaps 10%—have **reversible dementias**, cases of significant cognitive decline that can be treated and cured (Gurland, 1991; Lipton & Weiner, 2003). Reversible dementias can be caused by alcoholism, toxic reactions to medication, infections, metabolic disorders, vitamin deficiencies, and malnutrition. If these problems are corrected—for example, if the individual is taken off a recently prescribed medicine or is placed on a nutritious diet—a once "senile" person can be restored to normal mental functioning. By contrast, if that same person is written off as a case of Alzheimer's disease, a potentially curable condition may become a progressively worse and irreversible one.

Second, some elderly adults are mistakenly diagnosed as suffering from dementia when they are actually experiencing **delirium**. This treatable neurocognitive disorder, which emerges more rapidly than dementia and comes and goes over the course of the day, is a disturbance of consciousness characterized by periods of disorientation, wandering attention, confusion, and hallucinations (American Psychiatric Association, 2013; Weiner et al., 2009). One 66-year-old woman with a history of seizures, for example, called 911 repeatedly because she believed burglars were in her home; in her agitated state, she even threatened her housemate with a knife (Weiner et al., 2009). After she was taken to the hospital, she continued to be highly

- **Table 16.1** Some Common Forms and Causes of Dementia, or Neurocognitive Disorder, Besides Alzheimer's Disease

Name	Description
Vascular dementia	Also called multi-infarct dementia. Caused by minor strokes that cut off blood supply to areas of brain; results in steplike deterioration after each stroke.
Lewy body dementia	May be as common as vascular dementia. Caused by protein deposits called Lewy bodies in neurons. Motor problems, as in Parkinson's disease, plus visual hallucinations, attention and alertness problems, unpredictable cognitive functioning.
Frontotemporal dementia	Early-onset dementia associated with shrinking of the frontal and temporal lobes. Executive function problems (e.g., impulsive behavior) are more common than memory problems. The best known type is Pick's disease.
Parkinson's disease	Lewy bodies in subcortical areas of the brain contribute to motor problems (tremors, slowing/freezing while walking); treatment with the drug L-dopa to make up for dopamine deficiency is effective, but some patients develop dementia in the later stages.
Huntington's disease	Caused by single dominant gene (see Chapter 3). Subcortical brain damage results in involuntary flicking movement of the arms and legs; hallucinations, paranoia, depression, personality changes.
Alcohol-related dementia	Caused by alcohol abuse; memory problems are the primary symptom in what is called Wernicke–Korsakoff's syndrome.
AIDS dementia complex or ADC	Caused by HIV virus infection. Encephalitis, behavioral changes, decline in cognitive function, progressive slowing of motor functions.

Note: The first four conditions in the table are the most common causes of dementia besides Alzheimer's disease; the rest are rarer.

SOURCES: The following websites were consulted: http://www.alz.org/dementia/types-of-dementia.asp; http://www.dementiacarecentral.com/node/576; http://www.ninds.nih.gov/disorders/dementias/detail_dementia.htm#2300219213

agitated, moving and talking constantly, not trusting the staff. Her episode of delirium appeared to be the result of a urinary infection combined with early Alzheimer's disease, and she was able to return home after 5 days in the hospital.

Many hospital patients experience delirium in reaction to any number of stressors—illness, surgery, drug overdoses, interactions of different drugs, or malnutrition. It is essential to watch for signs of delirium, identify possible causes, and intervene to change them quickly (Flaherty & Morley, 2004). Unfortunately the condition often goes undetected or misdiagnosed. When elderly patients experience delirium but are not identified and are sent home from the hospital without treatment for it, they are at high risk of death (Kakuma et al., 2003; Moraga & Rodriguez-Pascual, 2007).

Third, elderly adults who are depressed are sometimes misdiagnosed as suffering from dementia. After all, depression's symptoms include cognitive impairments such as being forgetful and mentally slow (Butters et al., 2004). Treatment of depression with antidepressant drugs and psychotherapy can significantly improve the functioning of such individuals. However, if their depression goes undetected and they are written off as senile, they may deteriorate further.

Fourth, relatives who do not understand dementia may mistake the cognitive declines that many people experience as part of normal aging for incurable dementia. The moral is clear: It is critical to distinguish among irreversible dementias (most notably, Alzheimer's and vascular dementia), reversible dementias, delirium, depression, and other conditions that may be mistaken for irreversible dementias—including aging itself. This requires a thorough assessment, including a medical history, physical and neurological examinations, and assessments of cognitive functioning (Thompson, 2006). Only after all other causes, especially potentially treatable ones, have been ruled out should a diagnosis of Alzheimer's disease be made.

So ends our tour of psychopathology across the life span. It can be discouraging to read about the countless ways in which genes and environment can conspire to make human development go awry and about the high odds that most of us will experience a psychological disorder sometime during our lives. Yet research provides an increasingly solid basis for attempting to prevent developmental psychopathology through a two-pronged strategy of eliminating risk factors (such as abusive parenting and stress) and strengthening protective factors (such as effective parenting and social support). If prevention proves impossible, most psychological disorders and developmental problems can be treated successfully, enabling the individual to move onto a healthier developmental pathway.

Checking Mastery

1. In which adult age group, gender, and ethnic groups would you expect the highest rates of major depressive disorder?
2. How does Alzheimer's disease progress with regard to the timing of plaques and tangles in the brain, cognitive deficits, diagnosable dementia, and death?
3. What are two approaches used to treat Alzheimer's disease?
4. What are two key differences between delirium and dementia?

Making Connections

1. So now that you have read this whole chapter, what do you think of the DSM-5's position that major depressive disorder is basically the same from early childhood to old age? Argue for the DSM-5 position and then argue against it.
2. Grandpa Fred is starting to display memory problems: sometimes he asks questions that he just asked, forgets where he left his glasses, and cannot come up with the names of visiting grandchildren. Fred's son Will is convinced that his father has Alzheimer's disease and is a lost cause. What possibilities would you like to rule out before accepting that conclusion—and why?

Chapter Summary

16.1 What Makes Development Abnormal?

- To diagnose psychological disorders, clinicians may consider broad criteria such as statistical deviance, maladaptiveness, and personal distress and apply DSM-5 criteria for specific disorders.
- Developmental psychopathology is concerned with the origins and course of maladaptive behavior and contrasts with a medical or disease model.
- A diathesis–stress model has proved useful in understanding how nature and nurture contribute to psychological disorders.

16.2 The Infant

- Autism spectrum disorder is characterized by social and communication impairments and by restricted and repetitive interests and behavior. It is genetically influenced, involves abnormalities in brain growth and connectivity, mirror neuron systems, and executive functions, and responds to early and intensive behavioral training.
- Infants who have been maltreated, separated from their attachment figure, or raised by a depressed caregiver may display symptoms of depression.

16.3 The Child

- Many childhood disorders can be categorized as externalizing (acting out) or internalizing (bottling up) problems; they are often a product of diathesis–stress, or gene–environment interaction, and they often persist, although mild problems tend to be more passing.
- Attention deficit hyperactivity disorder (ADHD) involves inattention and/or hyperactivity/impulsivity, often continues into adulthood, and can be treated most effectively through a combination of stimulant drugs and behavioral treatment.
- Major depressive disorder and suicidal behavior can occur during early childhood; depression manifests itself somewhat differently in childhood, tends to recur, and can be treated.

16.4 The Adolescent

- Adolescents are more vulnerable than children but no more vulnerable than adults to psychological disorders; 20% plus at any given time experience the "storm and stress" of a psychological disorder.
- Anorexia nervosa arises when a genetically predisposed female who lives in a society that strongly encourages dieting experiences family pressures and stress.
- Substance use disorders can grow out of normal and widespread adolescent experimentation with substances; according to the cascade model, the developmental pathway toward illicit drug use begins in childhood.
- Risks of depression rise during adolescence, especially among females. Adolescents, in a cry for help, are more likely to attempt but less likely to commit suicide than adults, older white men being the group most likely to commit suicide.

16.5 The Adult

- Young adults experience both more life strains and more psychological disorders, including depression, than older adults.
- Diagnosing depression among older adults can be tricky if their symptoms are attributed to aging, chronic disease, or dementia; older adults have low rates of diagnosable depression but 15–25% suffer some symptoms of depression.
- Dementia, now called major neurocognitive disorder, is a progressive deterioration in neural functioning associated with significant cognitive decline that increases with age. Alzheimer's disease, the most common cause of dementia, and vascular dementia, another irreversible dementia, must be carefully distinguished from correctible conditions such as reversible dementia, delirium, and depression.

Checking Mastery Answers

For answers to Checking Mastery questions, please see Appendix B.

Key Terms

DSM-5 **506**

major depressive disorder **506**

somatic symptoms **507**

developmental psychopathology **507**

social norms **508**

diathesis-stress model **509**

autism spectrum disorder (ASD) **511**

Asperger syndrome **511**

comorbid **512**

executive functions **513**

applied behavior analysis (ABA) **514**

externalizing problem **516**

internalizing problem **516**

resilience **517**

attention deficit hyperactivity disorder (ADHD) **517**

cognitive behavioral therapy **520**

anorexia nervosa **523**

bulimia nervosa **523**

binge eating disorder **523**

cascade model of substance use **526**

ruminative coping **527**

dementia **531**

Alzheimer's disease **531**

beta-amyloid **531**

tau **531**

cognitive reserve **533**

vascular dementia **533**

reversible dementias **533**

delirium **533**

17 The Final Challenge: Death and Dying

December 14, 2012, Sandy Hook Elementary School, Newtown, Connecticut: Another day of national mourning. The killer snuffed the lives of 27 people, including 20 6- and 7-year-old children. The victims included the other children in school that day. One of their teachers sought to comfort her charges as they hid in their darkened and locked classroom: "I'm thinking, as a 6-year-old, 7-year-old, what are their thoughts? So I said to them, 'I need you to know that I love you all very much and that it is going to be okay.' Because I thought it was the last thing they were ever going to hear" (Vogel, Horwitz, & Fahrenthold, 2012, p. A15).

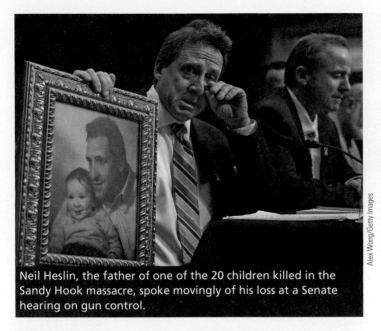

Neil Heslin, the father of one of the 20 children killed in the Sandy Hook massacre, spoke movingly of his loss at a Senate hearing on gun control.

The victims also included the family and friends of the slain. One of the slain children, Ana, loved singing, dancing, and the Bible. Her mother, Nelba Marquez-Greene, said this about life since that day: "Some days I want to get up and go outside and get groceries, and some days I can't brush my teeth. Some days I feel I can be a good parent to my son, and some days I just want to stay in bed and sleep" (Applebome & Maker, 2013). A father, Neil Heslin, wept as he testified at a Senate hearing on gun control about his last moments with his son Jesse: "I can still feel that hug, and that pat on the back. He said, 'everything's going to be ok, Dad, it's all going to be ok.' And it wasn't ok" (Wilkie, 2013).

Images of 9/11, Virginia Tech, Aurora, Sandy Hook, the Boston Marathon bombing, and other national tragedies have come to symbolize for many of us the horror of death. Whether we are 4, 24, or 84 when death strikes a loved one, death hurts. By adulthood, most of us have experienced a significant loss, even if it was "only" the death of a beloved pet. Even when death is not striking so closely, it is there, lurking somewhere in the background as we go about the tasks of living—in the newspaper, on television, and the internet, fleeting through our minds. Some psychologists argue that much of human behavior and culture is an effort to defend against the terror of death (Greenberg, Solomon, & Arndt, 2008; Pyszczynski, Solomon, & Greenberg, 2003). Yet sooner or later we all face the ultimate developmental task: the task of dying.

This chapter explores death and its place in life-span human development, starting with a discussion of the meanings and causes of death. You will discover that death is part of the human experience throughout the life span, but that each person's experience of it depends on his level of development, personality, life circumstances, and sociocultural context.

17.1 Matters of Life and Death

LEARNING OBJECTIVES:

- Discuss the Harvard Medical School definition of brain death and the issues it raises.
- Distinguish between forms of active and passive euthanasia and attitudes toward them.
- Illustrate how reactions to death differ in different cultures and racial/ethnic groups.
- Analyze trends in the likelihood of death and causes of death across the life span.

What is death, biologically and socially? When are we most vulnerable to it, and what kills us?

What Is Death?

There is a good deal of confusion and controversy in our society today about when life begins and when it ends. Proponents and opponents of legalized abortion argue vehemently about when life really begins. And we hear similarly heated debates about whether a person in an irreversible coma is truly alive and whether a terminally ill patient who is in agonizing pain should be kept alive with the help of life-support machines or allowed to die naturally. Definitions of death as a biological phenomenon change; so do the social meanings attached to death.

Biological Death

Biological death is hard to define because it is not a single event but a complex process. Different systems of the body die at different rates, and some individuals who have stopped breathing or who lack a heartbeat or pulse, and who would have been declared dead in earlier times, can now be revived before their brains cease to function. Moreover, basic body processes such as respiration and blood circulation can be maintained by life-support machines in patients who have fallen into a coma and whose brains have ceased to function.

In 1968 a special committee of the Harvard Medical School offered a definition of biological death that has shaped modern legal definitions of death (Berger, 1993; Kastenbaum, 2012). The Harvard group defined biological death in terms of brain functioning and insisted that, in cases where there is doubt, death has not occurred until there is **total brain death**. This means an irreversible loss of functioning in the entire brain, both the higher centers of the cerebral cortex that are involved in conscious awareness and thought and the lower centers of the brain that control basic life processes such as breathing. Specifically, to be judged dead a person must meet the following criteria:

1. Be totally unresponsive to stimuli, including painful ones
2. Fail to move for 1 hour and fail to breathe for 3 minutes after being removed from a ventilator

3. Have no reflexes (for example, no eye blink and no constriction of the eye's pupil in response to light)
4. Register a flat electroencephalogram, indicating an absence of electrical activity in the cortex of the brain

As an added precaution, the testing procedure is repeated 24 hours later. Moreover, because a coma is sometimes reversible if the cause is either a drug overdose or an abnormally low body temperature, these conditions must be ruled out before a person in a coma is pronounced dead. This definition means that a coma patient whose heart and lungs are kept going only through artificial means such as a mechanical ventilator but who has no sign of functioning in the brain stem is dead.

Since the Harvard committee's declaration, there has been continued debate about people in comas. In the mid-2000s, one young woman in a coma, Terri Schiavo, spurred a ferocious national debate (Cerminara, 2006; Foley, 2011; Kastenbaum, 2012). In 1990 Ms. Schiavo had suffered a cardiac arrest, possibly as a result of an eating disorder, that caused irreversible and massive brain damage. She was not dead by the Harvard criteria; her brain stem allowed her to breathe, swallow, and undergo sleep–wake cycles. After losing hope of a recovery as the years passed, her husband wanted to remove her feeding tube as he believed she would have wanted. However, her parents believed that she retained some awareness of her environment and wanted to keep her alive. After receiving medical testimony, a Florida court ruled that her feeding tube should be withdrawn. Finally, after the issue was debated at length in legislative bodies (including Congress), courts (including the Supreme Court), and the media, the tube was removed when appeals of the court's decision failed. Ms. Schiavo died at the age of 41 in 2005.

Famous right-to-die cases like the Terri Schiavo case highlight the different positions people can take on the issue of when a person is dead. The position laid out in the Harvard definition of total brain death (and in the laws of the states of the United States and many nations) is quite conservative. By the Harvard criteria, Ms. Schiavo was not dead, even though she was in an irreversible coma, because her brain stem was still functioning enough to support breathing and other basic body functions. Shouldn't we keep such seemingly hopeless patients alive in case we discover ways to revive them? A more liberal position is that a person should be declared dead when the cerebral cortex is irreversibly dead, even if some body functions are still maintained by the more primitive portions of the brain. After all, is a person really a person if she lacks any awareness and if there is no hope that conscious mental activity will be restored? But are we sure there is no awareness? As **Exploration Box 17.1** shows, defining the line between life and death has become even more complicated now that it has been demonstrated that some people determined to be in "vegetative states" have more cognitive function than suspected.

Life and Death Choices

Cases such as Schiavo's raise issues concerning **euthanasia**—a term meaning "happy" or "good" death that usually refers to hastening the death of someone suffering from an incurable illness or injury. *Active euthanasia*, or "mercy killing," is deliberately and directly causing a person's death—for example, by administering a lethal dose of drugs to a pain-racked patient in the late stages of cancer or smothering a spouse with advanced Alzheimer's disease. *Passive euthanasia*, by contrast, means allowing a terminally ill person to die of natural causes—for example, by withholding extraordinary life-saving treatments (as happened when Terri Schiavo's feeding tube was removed). Between active euthanasia and passive euthanasia is **assisted suicide**—not directly killing someone, as in active euthanasia, but making available to a person who wishes to die the means by which she may do so. This includes physician-assisted suicide—for example, a doctor's writing a prescription for sleeping pills at the request of a terminally ill patient who has made known his desire to die, in full knowledge that he will probably take an overdose (Foley, 2011; Quill, 1993).

How do we as a society view these options? We invite you to explore your own views in **Engagement Box 17.1**. There is overwhelming support among medical personnel and members of the general public for passive euthanasia (Shannon, 2006; Stillion & McDowell, 1996). And, surprisingly, more than 70% of U.S. adults appear to support a doctor's ending the life of a patient with a terminal illness if the patient and family request it (Givens & Mitchell, 2009). African Americans and other minority group members are generally less accepting of actions to hasten death than European Americans, possibly because they do not trust the medical establishment or possibly for religious or philosophical reasons (Kwak & Haley, 2005; Werth et al., 2002).

An interesting study of attitudes toward end-of-life options conducted in South Korea compared support among cancer patients, family caregivers, oncologists, and the general public for several different forms of end-of-life interventions (Yun et al., 2011). As shown in ■ **Figure 17.1**, support for the withdrawal of futile life-sustaining treatment (without the intention to end the person's life), active pain control, and even the withholding of drugs, life-support, and other life-prolonging

Do you believe Terri Schiavo, who could breathe on her own but suffered massive brain damage, should or should not have been taken off her feeding tube? Her husband Michael thought she should be taken off it but her parents fought him.

Getty Images

Are You in There? Communicating with Patients in Vegetative States

Defining the line between life and death has become more complicated now that Adrian Owen and his colleagues (2006) have demonstrated that at least some people who are in "vegetative states" and are believed to lack consciousness and cognitive functions may have more awareness than suspected. Unlike coma patients, who lack both awareness and wakefulness, people in vegetative states (a dehumanizing term if there ever was one) lack awareness but experience sleep-wake cycles, may open their eyes, and move now and then. Determining that a patient is in a vegetative state has depended in part on observing that they do not respond behaviorally to commands. Owen and his colleagues have broken new ground by assessing their brains' responses to commands.

In their first demonstration, these researchers asked a young woman who had been in a vegetative state for 5 months as a result of a car accident to imagine playing tennis or visiting the rooms of her house. Brain imaging with functional MRI techniques showed that her brain responded exactly as healthy adults' brains respond to these tasks, suggesting that she could understand and respond intentionally to instructions and implying that she had some degree of consciousness. A subsequent study found brain responses of this sort in 5 of 54 patients who were classified as in either a "vegetative" or "minimally conscious" state; one was even able to answer yes–no questions by willfully controlling his brain (Monti et al., 2010).

Owen's team has now shown that a less expensive and more portable brain assessment procedure using EEG rather than fMRI can also identify patients who are not truly in a vegetative state lacking consciousness (Cruse et al., 2011). The procedure involves a series of trials in which the patient is asked, upon hearing a beep, to imagine squeezing her right hand into a fist or, on other trials, to imagine wiggling her toes. No fingers or toes actually moved but 3 of 16 patients showed EEG responses similar to those of normal control participants imagining these two acts. As the authors note, showing these brain responses consistently implies that patients were able to attend, understand the instructions, remember which action to imagine over multiple trials, and select which response to make—all cognitive functions we associate with normal consciousness and a functioning cerebral cortex.

What does it all mean? Although most of the patients studied did not respond and therefore do indeed seem to lack consciousness, and although questions have been raised about the analysis of the data (Goldfine et al., 2013; but see Cruse et al., 2013), this research appears to open up a new methodology for communicating with those individuals in vegetative states who do show some level of consciousness. For example, they could be told to imagine a tight fist to say Yes or to imagine wiggling their toes to say No and then be asked to respond to questions (Are you hungry? Are you in pain?).

Yet this research also has troubling implications: Just how many patients in vegetative states are treated as though they are dead when in fact they are mentally alive and waiting for someone to recognize it? People in vegetative states, like people in comas, are alive according to the total brain death definition of death because their lower brain centers still function. However, determining that a person in a vegetative state has higher cognitive capacities might argue against a decision to stop providing food and other life support. Terri Schiavo's mother was convinced that her daughter showed some awareness of her surroundings, and her brother, upon learning of the Cruse et al. (2011) study, said he regretted that Terri did not have a chance to have her brain's responsiveness tested before the court decided to remove her feeding tube (Stein, 2011).

treatments with the intention of ending the patient's life were all highly supported by all four groups. Active euthanasia and physician-assisted suicide were less widely supported, but about half of the cancer patients and members of the general public approved of them. Doctors in Korea, like doctors in the United States and Europe, were less supportive than other groups of these options, possibly because these actions violate their oath and they would be held accountable. The authors note that these results are quite similar to those in the United States and other countries overall; they speculate that Koreans' lower support for euthanasia and physician-assisted suicide may be because Koreans place less emphasis on individual autonomy than Westerners do.

What does the law say of end-of-life interventions? Although active euthanasia is still treated as murder in the United States and most countries, it is legal in most states to withhold extraordinary life-extending treatments from terminally ill patients and to "pull the plug" on life-support equipment when that is the wish of the dying person or when the immediate family can show that the individual expressed, when she was able to do so, a desire to reject life-support measures (Cantor, 2001). A **living will**, a type of advance directive, allows people to state that they do not want extraordinary medical procedures applied to them if they become hopelessly ill. Advance directives can also specify who should make decisions if the dying person becomes unable to make them, whether organs should be donated, and what other instructions should be carried out after the person's death. (You can download state-specific advance directives and obtain other relevant information on death and dying at Caring Connections, http://www.caringinfo.org.)

In 1997, Oregon became the first state to legalize physician-assisted suicide. Following strict guidelines, terminally ill adults in Oregon with 6 or fewer months to live can request lethal medication from a physician, as patients in the European countries of Netherlands, Belgium, and Luxembourg can do. The few people in Oregon who have taken this option have usually had terminal cancer and believed that they faced only hopeless pain and suffering and a loss of dignity with no chance of

Engagement 17.1

Life and Death Attitudes

Imagine that you have terminal cancer and are told that there is no more that can be done for you and no hope of recovery. What would be your answers to the following questions? There are no right or wrong answers.

1. Who would you want with you and what would you want to do with your last days or weeks?
2. Would you want to spend your last days or weeks in a hospital, in a hospice facility for terminally ill people, or at home?
3. Would you want the doctors to do all that is possible to keep you alive as long as possible, in case a new treatment is discovered?
4. Would you choose to take large doses of pain medicine even though it might limit your ability to think clearly and interact with people?
5. Would you want the following applied to you to keep you alive: (a) resuscitation if your heart stops, (b) a respirator to keep you breathing if you stop breathing on your own, (c) a feeding tube inserted in your nose or abdomen to provide nourishment if you can no longer take food through your mouth?
6. Would you want to be able to ask for and receive a drug with which you could end your own life if you desired?
7. Would you want to be able to ask your doctor to give you a drug to end your life?

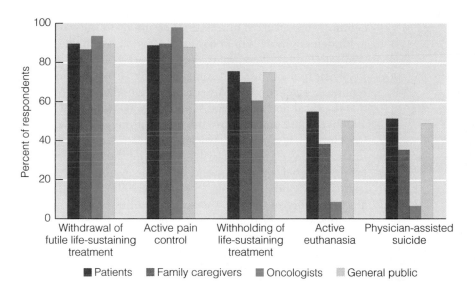

■ **Figure 17.1** Percentages of Korean respondents in four groups expressing support for different end-of-life interventions with terminally ill patients. As in the United States, withdrawing or withholding life-extending treatment is more acceptable than active euthanasia or physician-assisted suicide. Doctors are the least supportive of these more active interventions, cancer patients the most supportive.

SOURCE: Yun, Y. H., Han, K. H., Park, S., Park, B. W., Cho, C., Kim, S., . . . Chun, M. (2011). Attitudes of cancer patients, family caregivers, oncologists and members of the general public toward critical interventions at the end of life of terminally ill patients, *Canadian Medical Association Journal*, *183*(10), E673–E679, Figure 1, p. E677.

recovery (Georges et al., 2007; Wineberg & Werth, 2003). Only Washington State has since gone the way of Oregon; in fact, 40 states have enacted laws *against* assisted suicide (Glascock, 2009). As a result, there is a gap between more and more supportive public attitudes and the law (Allen et al., 2006; Cohen et al., 2013).

On such life-or-death issues, right-to-die advocates, who maintain that people should have a say in how they die, fight right-to-life advocates, who say that everything possible should be done to maintain life and that nothing should be done to cut it short. It makes sense to think through these issues now in case you must someday decide whether you or a loved one should live or die (see Shannon, 2006).

Social Meanings of Death

Death is not only a biological process but also a psychological and social one. The social meanings attached to death vary widely from historical era to historical era and from culture to culture (Rosenblatt, 2008, 2013). True, people everywhere die, and people everywhere grieve deaths. Moreover, all societies have evolved some manner of reacting to this universal experience—of interpreting its meaning, disposing of corpses, and expressing grief. Beyond these universals, however, the similarities end.

Historical Change. As Philippe Ariès (1981) has shown, the social meanings of death have changed over the course of history. In Europe during the Middle Ages, people were expected to recognize that their deaths were approaching so that they could bid their farewells and die with dignity surrounded by loved ones. Since the late 19th century, Ariès argues, Western societies have engaged in a "denial of death." We have taken death out of the home and put it in the hospital and funeral parlor to be managed by physicians and funeral directors; as a result, we have less direct experience with it than our ancestors did (Röcke & Cherry, 2002; Taylor, 2003).

Right-to-die and death-with-dignity advocates have been arguing that we should return to the old ways, bringing death into the open, allowing it to occur more naturally, and making it again a normal life experience to be shared with family rather than a medical failure. As you will see later, this is just what the hospice movement has aimed to achieve. We are also witnessing a trend away from traditional funerals with caskets; the percentage of deaths involving cremation rather than burial has increased from 4% in the mid-1960s to more than a third (Phillips, 2009).

Cultural Variation The experience of dying also differs from culture to culture. Societies take different stands, for example, on whether to support frail elders or speed their deaths. Anthony Glascock (2009) found that in 21 of 41 cultures he examined, practices that hastened the death of frail elderly people existed, whereas only 12 of the societies were entirely supportive of frail elders and had no death-hastening practices—practices such as depriving frail elders of food, driving them from their homes, or stabbing them upon their request.

The dama funeral ceremony practiced by the Dogon people of Mali in western Africa involves a masquerade that leads the souls of the deceased to their final resting places in the next world. Mourning rituals differ considerably from culture to culture.

David Sutherland/Photographer's Choice/Getty Images

If we look at how people in other cultures grieve and mourn a death, we quickly realize that there are many alternatives to our Western ways and no single, biologically mandated grieving process (Klass, 2001; Rosenblatt, 2008, 2013). Depending on the society, "funerals are the occasion for avoiding people or holding parties, for fighting or having sexual orgies, for weeping or laughing, in a thousand different combinations" (Metcalf & Huntington, 1991, p. 24). In most societies, there is some concept of spiritual immortality. Yet here, too, there is much variety, from concepts of heaven and hell to the idea of reincarnation to a belief in ancestral ghosts who meddle in the lives of the living (Rosenblatt, 1993).

We need not look beyond North America to find considerable variation in the social meanings of death. Different ethnic and racial groups clearly have different rules for expressing grief (Rosenblatt, 2013). For example, it is customary among Puerto Ricans, especially women, to display intense emotions after a death (Cook & Dworkin, 1992), and Mexican American mourners do more viewing, touching, and kissing of the deceased than European Americans (Bonanno, 2009). Japanese Americans, by contrast, are socialized to restrain their grief—to smile so as not to burden others with their pain and to avoid the shame associated with losing self-control (Cook & Dworkin, 1992).

Different ethnic and racial groups also have different mourning practices. Irish Americans have traditionally believed that the dead deserve a good sendoff, a wake with food, drink, and jokes—the kind of party the deceased might have enjoyed (McGoldrick et al., 1991). African Americans tend to regard the funeral not as a time for rowdy celebration but as a forum for expressing grief, in some congregations by wailing and singing spirituals (McGoldrick et al., 1991; Perry, 1993). Jewish families are even more restrained; they quietly withdraw from normal activities for a week of mourning, called *shivah*, then honor the dead again at the 1-month and 1-year marks (Cytron, 1993).

In short, the experiences of dying individuals and of their survivors are shaped by the historical and cultural contexts in which death occurs. Death may be universal, and the human tendency to mourn a loss may be too (Parkes, 2000). Otherwise, death is truly what we humans make of it; there is no one "right" way to die or to grieve a death.

What Kills Us and When?

As Chapter 5's discussion of basic theories of aging and death revealed, genes and environment conspire to ensure that all humans not only develop but age and die. How long are we likely to live, and what is likely to kill us?

Life Expectancy

In the United States the life expectancy at birth—the average number of years a newborn can be expected to live—is almost 79 years (Miniño & Murphy, 2012). This average life expectancy disguises important differences between males and females, among racial and ethnic groups, and among social classes. As shown in ■ **Figure 17.2**, the life expectancy for males is generally lower than that for females: 76 years versus 81 years overall. Female hormones seem to protect women from high blood

■ **Figure 17.2** Life expectancy at birth for males and females of different racial and ethnic groups in the United States in 2010. Females outlive males; Hispanics have the longest, African Americans the shortest life expectancy.

Source: Miniño, A. M. & Murphy, S. L. (2012, July). Death in the United States, 2010. NCHS Data Brief, No. 99. U.S. Department of Health and Human Services, Centers for Disease Control and Prevention, National Center for Health Statistics. Retrieved from: http://www.cdc.gov/nchs/data/databriefs/db99.htm

Across racial and ethnic groups, life expectancies are lower in poor areas than in affluent areas (Malmstrom et al., 1999).

Life expectancies have increased steadily over the centuries, from 30 years in ancient Rome to around 80 years in modern affluent societies (Harman, 2001). Despite improvements in all regions of the world, however, life expectancies in some parts of the world lag behind life expectancies in others. In some less developed countries plagued by malaria, famine, AIDS, and other such killers, many of them in Africa, the life expectancy is under 50 (Central Intelligence Agency, 2013). Among these countries are South Africa, Chad, Swaziland, and Afghanistan. By contrast, the life expectancy at birth is over 80 now in many highly developed and affluent countries such as Japan, Hong Kong, and Singapore in Asia and France, Italy, Spain, Sweden, and Switzerland in Europe (Central Intelligence Agency, 2013).

Death across the Life Span

Death rates change over the life span, as illustrated by the "Total Deaths" statistics for different age groups in ● **Table 17.1**. Infants are relatively vulnerable; infant mortality in the United States has dropped considerably in recent years, however, and now stands at a bit over 6 out of 1,000 live births (Miniño & Murphy, 2012). Assuming that we survive infancy, we have a relatively small chance of dying during childhood or adolescence. Death rates then climb steeply and steadily throughout adulthood.

What kills us? The leading causes of death change dramatically over the life span, as also shown in Table 17.1. Infant deaths are mainly associated with complications in the period surrounding birth and congenital abnormalities that infants bring with them to life. The leading cause of death among preschool and school-age children is unintentional injuries or accidents (especially car accidents but also poisonings, falls, fires, drownings, and so on). Adolescence and early adulthood are generally periods of good health. Accidents (especially car accidents), homicides, and suicides are the leading killers of adolescents.

Accidents and cancers kill young adults, and heart diseases also begin to take a toll. Starting in the 45–64 age group, cancers are the leading cause of death, followed by heart diseases, probably because certain individuals' genetic endowments, unhealthy lifestyles, or both put them at risk to develop these and other

pressure and heart problems, and they are less exposed than men to violent deaths and accidents and to health hazards such as smoking and drinking (Kajantie, 2008; Kaplan & Erickson, 2000). Women live longer than men in most other countries as well (United Nations, 2007). Ethnic differences are evident as well: life expectancy is highest for Hispanics, medium for non-Hispanic whites, and lowest for African Americans, more of whom experience the health hazards associated with poverty.

● **Table 17.1** Leading Causes of Death for Different Age Groups in the United States

Age Group	Total Deaths, 2006	No. 1 Cause	No. 2 Cause	No. 3 Cause
Younger than 1 year	28,527	Congenital abnormalities	Short gestation, low birth weight	Sudden infant death syndrome
1–4 years	4,631	Unintentional injuries	Congenital abnormalities	Cancers
5–14 years	6,149	Unintentional injuries	Cancers	Homicide
15–24 years	34,887	Unintentional injuries	Homicide	Suicide
25–44 years	125,995	Unintentional injuries	Cancers	Heart diseases
45–64 years	466,432	Cancers	Heart diseases	Unintentional injuries
65 years and older	1,759,423	Heart diseases	Cancers	Cerebrovascular diseases

Source: Based on data from National Center for Health Statistics, 2010.

diseases prematurely (Horiuchi et al., 2003). The incidence of chronic diseases climbs steadily with age. Among adults 65 and older, heart diseases lead the list by far, accounting for more than a third of all deaths, followed by cancers and cerebrovascular diseases (strokes), with chronic respiratory diseases close behind. By this age, general aging processes that affect all of us increase the odds that one disease or another will strike (Horiuchi et al., 2003).

In sum, life expectancies are higher than ever. After we make it through the vulnerable period of infancy, we are at low risk of death through adolescence and are most likely to die suddenly because of an accident if we do die. As we age, we become more vulnerable to chronic diseases—and the often slower and more expected deaths associated with them.

Checking Mastery

1. Why was Terry Schiavo not dead according to the Harvard definition of death?
2. What would be most likely to kill a 10-year-old? A 70-year-old?

Making Connections

1. What would you have decided about whether Terri Schiavo should have been taken off her feeding tube and why—and what does your answer imply about how you think death should be defined?
2. An 85-year-old British man and his 74-year-old wife, who was dying of terminal liver and pancreatic cancer, paid an organization in Switzerland to help them achieve an assisted suicide in which they both drank poison and lay down to die together (Gibbs, 2009). The husband had weak vision and hearing but no major health problems; he mainly did not want to go on living without his beloved wife. Do you believe that (1) the wife and (2) the husband should be able to choose death in circumstances like these? Why or why not? And how would you characterize your reasoning in terms of Kohlberg's preconventional, conventional, and postconventional levels of moral development, as described in Chapter 13?

17.2 The Experience of Death

LEARNING OBJECTIVES:

- Assess Elisabeth Kübler-Ross's stages of dying and what her view misses about the dying person's experience.

- Assess the Parkes/Bowlby attachment model of bereavement and compare how it is similar to and different from Kübler-Ross's model.

- Compare the dual-process model of bereavement to the Parkes/Bowlby model.

People who die suddenly may be blessed, because those who develop life-threatening illnesses face the challenge of coping with the knowledge that they are seriously ill and are likely to die. What is it like to be dying, and how does the experience compare to the experience of losing a loved one to death?

Perspectives on Dying

Perhaps no one has done more to focus attention on the emotional needs and reactions of dying patients than psychiatrist Elisabeth Kübler-Ross, whose "stages of dying" are widely known and whose 1969 book *On Death and Dying* revolutionized the care of dying people. In interviews with terminally ill patients, Kübler-Ross (1969, 1974) detected a common set of emotional responses to the knowledge that one has a serious, and probably fatal, illness. She believed that similar reactions might occur in response to any major loss, so bear in mind that the family and friends of the dying person may experience similar emotional reactions during the loved one's illness and after the death.

Kübler Ross's Stages of Dying

Kübler-Ross's five "stages of dying" are as follows:

1. *Denial.* A common first response to dreadful news is to say, "No! It can't be!" **Denial** is a defense mechanism in

Psychiatrist Elisabeth Kübler-Ross called on physicians to emphasize caring rather than curing.

Duane Howell/Denver Post/Getty Images

which anxiety-provoking thoughts are kept out of conscious awareness. A woman who has just been diagnosed as having lung cancer may insist that the diagnosis is wrong—or accept that she is ill but be convinced that she will beat the odds and recover. Denial can be a marvelous coping device: It can get us through a time of acute crisis until we are ready to cope more constructively. Yet even after dying patients face the facts and become ready to talk about dying, care providers and family members often engage in their own denial.

2. *Anger.* As the bad news begins to register, the dying person asks, "Why me?" Feelings of rage or resentment may be directed at anyone who is handy—doctors, nurses, or family members. Kübler-Ross advises those close to the dying person to be sensitive to this reaction so that they will not avoid this irritable person or become angry in return.

3. *Bargaining.* When the dying person bargains, he says, "Okay, me, but please. . . ." The bargainer begs for some concession from God, the medical staff, or family members—if not for a cure, perhaps for a little more time, a little less pain, or provision for his children.

4. *Depression.* As the dying person becomes even more aware of the reality of the situation, depression, despair, and a sense of hopelessness become the predominant emotional responses. Grief focuses on the losses that have already occurred (for example, the loss of functional abilities) and the losses to come (separation from loved ones, the inability to achieve dreams, and so on).

5. *Acceptance.* If the dying person is able to work through the emotional reactions of the preceding stages, she may accept the inevitability of death in a calm and peaceful manner. Kübler-Ross (1969) described the acceptance stage this way: "It is almost void of feelings. It is as if the pain had gone, the struggle is over, and there comes a time for 'the final rest before the long journey,' as one patient phrased it" (p. 100).

In addition to these five stages of dying, Kübler-Ross emphasized a sixth response that runs throughout the stages: *hope.* She believed that it is essential for terminally ill patients to retain some sense of hope, even if it is only the hope that they can die with dignity. Sadly, Kübler-Ross spent her own dying days mostly alone, a prisoner in her armchair with the television for company (O'Rourke, 2010).

Problems with Kübler-Ross's Stages

Kübler-Ross deserves immense credit for sensitizing our society to the emotional needs of dying people. She convinced medical professionals to emphasize caring rather than curing in working with terminally ill people. At the same time, there are flaws in her account of the dying person's experience (Kastenbaum, 2012; Walter & McCoyd, 2009). Among the points critics make are these: emotional responses to dying are not stagelike; the nature and course of an illness affects reactions to it; individuals differ widely in their responses; and dying people focus on living, not just dying.

The first and most important problem with Kübler-Ross's stages is that *the dying process is simply not stagelike.* Although

dying patients often display symptoms of depression as death nears, the other emotional reactions Kübler-Ross describes seem to affect only minorities of dying people (Schulz & Aderman, 1974). Moreover, when these responses occur, they do not unfold in a standard order. It might have been better if Kübler-Ross had, from the start, described her stages simply as emotional reactions to dying. Unfortunately, some overzealous medical professionals have tried to push dying patients through the "stages" in order, believing incorrectly that their patients would never accept death unless they experienced the "right" emotions at the "right" times (Kastenbaum, 2012).

Edwin Shneidman (1973, 1980) offered an alternate view, arguing that dying patients experience a complex and ever-changing interplay of emotions, alternating between denial and acceptance of death. One day a patient may seem to understand that death is near; the next day she may talk of getting better and going home. Along the way many reactions—disbelief, hope, terror, bewilderment, rage, apathy, calm, anxiety, and others—come and go and are even experienced simultaneously. According to Shneidman, then, dying people experience many unpredictable emotional swings rather than distinct stages. Research tends to support him (Chochinov & Schwartz, 2002).

Second, Kübler-Ross's theory *does not take into account the disease a person has and its course or trajectory* (Glaser & Strauss, 1968; Kastenbaum, 2012). When a patient is slowly and gradually worsening over time, the patient, family members, and staff can all become accustomed to the death that lies ahead, whereas when the path toward death is more erratic, perhaps involving remissions and relapses and surgeries along the way, emotional ups or downs are likely each time the patient's condition takes a turn for better or worse.

Third, Kübler-Ross's approach *overlooks the influence of personality on how a person experiences dying.* People cope with dying much as they have coped with life (Schulz & Schlarb, 1987–1988). For example, cancer patients who previously faced life's problems directly and effectively, were satisfied with their lives, and maintained good interpersonal relationships before they became ill display less anger and are less depressed and withdrawn during their illnesses than patients who were not so well adjusted before their illnesses (Hinton, 1975). Depending on their predominant personality traits, coping styles, and social competencies, some dying people may deny until the bitter end, some may "rage against the dying of the light," some may quickly be crushed by despair, and still others may display incredible strength.

Fourth and finally, Kübler-Ross focused on emotional responses to the news that one is dying but *gave little attention to how dying people approach living.* An interesting study by Rinat Nissim and colleagues (2012) identified themes in interviews with Canadian patients who had advanced cancer and less than 2 years to live. An important discovery was that these patients continued to set and work toward goals. Their goals centered on

- *controlling dying* (primarily by focusing on their chemotherapy and other treatments but also, for some, by holding in the back of their mind the possibility of suicide if necessary)

- *valuing life in the present* (getting the most out of their remaining time, even if they could no longer make long-range plans)
- *creating a living legacy* (for example, getting their affairs in order, creating good memories in their children, touching others' lives)

In short, these patients were not just coping with difficult emotions and they were certainly not just lying back waiting to die. As the researchers put it, they were "striving to grow in the land of the living/dying (Nissim et al., 2012, p. 368). In sum, Kübler-Ross highlighted five relevant emotional responses to dying but we should not think of them as stages, or as applicable to all diseases or all personalities, or as all that is going on in people who are not only coping with dying but trying to live.

Perspectives on Bereavement

Most of us are more familiar with the process of grieving a death than the process of dying. To describe responses to the death of a loved one, we must distinguish among three terms: **Bereavement** is a state of loss, **grief** is an emotional response to loss, and **mourning** is a culturally prescribed way of displaying reactions to death. Thus, we can describe a bereaved person who grieves by experiencing such emotions as sadness, anger, and guilt and who mourns by attending the funeral and laying flowers on the grave each year.

Unless a death is sudden, relatives and friends, like the dying person, will experience many painful emotions before the death, from the initial diagnosis through the last breath (Grbich, Parker, & Maddocks, 2001). They, too, may alternate between acceptance and denial. They also may experience what has been termed **anticipatory grief**—grieving before death occurs for what is happening and for what lies ahead (Rando, 1986). Anticipatory grief can lessen later distress and improve outcomes of bereavement if it involves accepting the coming loss (Metzger & Gray, 2008). Yet no amount of preparation and anticipatory grief can entirely eliminate the need to grieve after the death occurs. How, then, do we grieve?

The Parkes/Bowlby Attachment Model

Pioneering research on the grieving process was conducted by Colin Murray Parkes and his colleagues in Great Britain (Parkes, 1991, 2006; Parkes & Prigerson, 2010; Parkes & Weiss, 1983). John Bowlby (1980), whose influential theory of attachment was outlined in Chapter 14, and Parkes conceptualized grieving in the context of attachment theory as a reaction to separation from a loved one. As Parkes (2006) notes, "love and loss are two sides of the same coin. We cannot have one without risking the other" (p. 1). The grieving adult is very much like the infant who experiences separation anxiety when her mother disappears from view and tries to retrieve her. As humans, we have evolved not only to form attachments but also to protest their loss.

The **Parkes/Bowlby attachment model of bereavement** describes four predominant reactions. They overlap considerably and therefore should be viewed as phases, not as sequential stages. These reactions are numbness, yearning, disorganization and despair, and reorganization (see also Jacobs et al.,

- **Table 17.2** Models of Dying and Bereavement

Kübler-Ross's Stages of Dying	The Parkes/Bowlby Attachment Model of Bereavement
1. Denial	1. Numbness
2. Anger	2. Yearning (including anger and guilt)
3. Bargaining	
4. Depression	3. Disorganization and despair
5. Acceptance	4. Reorganization

1987–1988, and see ● **Table 17.2** to view this phase model of bereavement side by side with Kübler-Ross's stages of dying and appreciate their similarities and differences):

1. *Numbness.* In the first few hours or days after the death, the bereaved person is often in a daze—gripped by a sense of unreality and disbelief and almost empty of feelings. Underneath this state of numbness and shock is a sense of being on the verge of bursting, and, occasionally, painful emotions break through. The bereaved person is struggling to defend himself against the full weight of the loss; the bad news has not fully registered.

2. *Yearning.* As the numbing sense of shock and disbelief diminishes, the bereaved person experiences more agony. This is the time of acute separation anxiety and efforts to reunite with the lost loved one. Grief comes in pangs or waves that typically are most severe from 5 to 14 days after the death. The grieving person has feelings of panic, bouts of uncontrollable weeping, and physical aches and pains. She is likely to be extremely restless, unable to concentrate or to sleep, and preoccupied with thoughts of the loved one and of the events leading to the death. Most importantly, the bereaved person pines and yearns and searches for the loved one, longing to be reunited.

   According to Parkes and Bowlby, it is these signs of separation anxiety—the distress of being parted from the object of attachment—that most clearly make grieving different from other kinds of emotional distress. A widow may think she heard her husband's voice or saw him in a crowd; she may sense his presence in the house and draw comfort from it; she may be drawn to his favorite chair—or may try to recover him by smelling his bathrobe. Ultimately the quest to be reunited, driven by separation anxiety, fails.

   Both anger and guilt are common during the early weeks and months of bereavement. Frustrated in their quest for reunion, bereaved people often feel irritable and sometimes experience intense rage—at the loved one for dying, at the doctors for not doing a better job, at almost anyone. They seem to need to pin blame somewhere. Unfortunately, they often find reason to blame themselves—to feel guilty. A father may moan that he should have spent more time teaching his son gun safety; the friend of a young man who dies of AIDS may feel that he was not a good enough friend. One of the London widows studied by Parkes felt guilty because she never made her husband bread pudding.

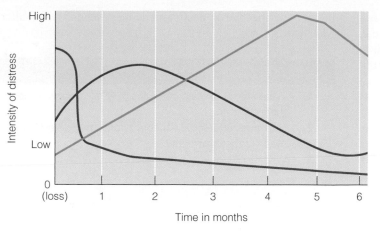

— Numbness and disbelief   — Separation anxiety   — Despair and depression

■ **Figure 17.3** The overlapping phases of grief in the Parkes-Bowlby attachment model of bereavement. Numbness and disbelief quickly give way to yearning and pining (signs of separation anxiety) and then to despair or depression (and, although not shown here, growing acceptance and reorganization).

SOURCE: Jacobs, S. C., et al. (1987–1988). Attachment theory and multiple dimensions of grief, *Omega: Journal of Death and Dying, 18*, 41–52, Figure 1. Reprinted by permission of Baywood Publishing Co., Inc.

3. *Disorganization and despair.* As time passes, pangs of intense grief and yearning become less frequent, although they still occur. As it sinks in that a reunion with the loved one is impossible, depression, despair, and apathy increasingly predominate. During most of the first year after the death, and longer in many cases, bereaved individuals often feel apathetic and may have difficulty managing and taking interest in their lives.

4. *Reorganization.* Eventually, bereaved people begin to pull themselves together again as their pangs of grief and periods of apathy become less frequent. They invest less emotional energy in their attachment to the deceased and more in their attachments to the living. If they have lost a spouse, they begin to make the transition from being a wife or husband to being a widow or widower, revising their identities. They begin to feel readier for new activities and possibly for new relationships or attachments.

■ **Figure 17.3** shows the changing mix of overlapping reactions predicted by this attachment model of grief (Jacobs et al., 1987–1988). To test the Parkes-Bowlby model, Paul Maciejewski and his colleagues (2007) assessed disbelief, yearning, anger, depression, and acceptance in 233 bereaved individuals from 1 to 24 months after their loss of a loved one to death from natural causes. The different emotional reactions peaked in the predicted order (disbelief, yearning, anger, and despair/depression), while acceptance steadily gained strength over time. Although the worst of the grieving process for widows and widowers is during the first 6 months after the loss, the process normally takes a year or more and can take much longer (Parkes & Prigerson, 2010).

The Dual-Process Model of Bereavement

Like responses to dying, responses to bereavement have proven to be messy—messier than the Parkes/Bowlby phase model suggests (Röcke & Cherry, 2002). Margaret Stroebe and Henk Schut have put forth a **dual-process model of bereavement** in which the bereaved oscillate, often unpredictably, between coping with the emotional blow of the loss and coping with the practical challenges of living, as illustrated in ■ **Figure 17.4** (Stroebe & Schut, 1999; and see Hansson & Stroebe, 2007; Stroebe & Schut, 2010). **Loss-oriented coping** involves dealing with one's emotions and reconciling oneself to the loss, whereas **restoration-oriented coping** is focused on managing daily living, rethinking one's life, and mastering new roles and challenges. The bereaved need to grieve, but they also need to figure out their finances, take over household tasks that the loved one used to do, get reinvolved in life, revise their identities, and manage other challenges.

Both loss- and restoration-oriented issues need to be confronted, but they also need to be avoided at times or they would exhaust us. We therefore have to strike a balance between confrontation and avoidance of coping challenges and between loss-oriented and restoration-oriented coping. So, for example, working on practical tasks like preparing taxes—or just watching a movie—may give a widow relief from dealing with painful emotions so that she can reenergize for a while before shifting back to a focus on her loss. Both processes in the dual-process model involve both positive and negative thoughts and emotions (for example, happy memories of good times with the loved one, painful memories of days in the hospital). Bereaved people ideally oscillate between the two types of coping rather than focusing on only one; otherwise, they would either fail to deal with their loss or fail to take steps toward recovery. Over time, though, emphasis shifts from loss-oriented to restoration-oriented coping and from negative to positive thoughts and emotions.

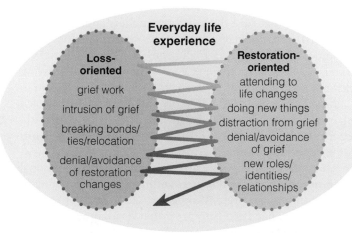

■ **Figure 17.4** The dual-process model of coping with bereavement. The bereaved oscillate between loss-oriented and restoration-oriented coping, both of which involve both positive and negative emotions and thoughts.

SOURCE: From Stroebe, M. S. & Schut, H. A. W. (1999). The dual process model of coping with bereavement, *Death Studies, 23*, 197–224, Figure 1. Reprinted by permission of Taylor & Francis Group.

The dual-process model may remind you of Shneidman's view that dying patients oscillate between acceptance and denial. It suggests that adjustment to bereavement, like adjustment to dying, is not very stagelike or even phaselike. Most researchers agree that bereavement is a complex and multidimensional process that involves many ever-shifting emotions, varies greatly from person to person, and often takes a long time.

Meanwhile, the rest of us are sympathetic toward the bereaved immediately after a death—eager to help in any way we can—but we quickly grow weary of someone who is depressed, irritable, or preoccupied. We begin to think, sometimes after only a few days or weeks, that it is time for the bereaved person to cheer up and get on with life. We are wrong. To be of help to bereaved people, we must understand that their reactions of numbness and disbelief, yearning, and despair, and their needs to engage in both loss-oriented and restoration-oriented coping, may linger a long time.

We have now considered some major perspectives on how people experience dying and bereavement. However, these perspectives have been based primarily on the responses of adults. How do infants, children, and adolescents respond to death? What does death even mean to infants and young children? A life-span perspective on death and dying is needed (see Walter & McCoyd, 2009).

Checking Mastery

1. What are three main criticisms of Kübler-Ross's stage theory of dying?
2. How does attachment theory inform the Parkes/Bowlby model of bereavement?
3. What oscillates in the dual-process model of bereavement?

Making Connections

1. Look carefully at the five stages of dying that Elisabeth Kübler-Ross believes terminally ill patients experience and at the four phases of adjustment bereaved people experience according to Colin Murray Parkes and John Bowlby (see Table 17.2). What common themes do you see? How do these models differ?
2. If you worked in a hospital wing with terminally ill adults, how might you use Kübler-Ross's perspective to improve care? And how might you avoid misusing it?

17.3 The Infant

LEARNING OBJECTIVES:

- Explain how infants might first come to understand death.
- Describe how John Bowlby characterized infants' responses to separation from an attachment figure and how these responses resemble grief.

Looking at bereavement from an attachment theory perspective makes us wonder how infants understand and cope with the death of an attachment figure. Infants surely do not comprehend death as the cessation of life, but they do gain an understanding of concepts that pave the way for an understanding of death (Corr, 2010). Infants may, for example, grasp the concepts of being and nonbeing, here and "all gone," from such experiences as watching objects and people appear and disappear, playing peekaboo, and even going to sleep and "coming alive" again in the morning (Maurer, 1961). Possibly, infants first form a global category of things that are "all gone" and later divide it into subcategories, one of which is "dead" (Kastenbaum, 2000). Infants lack the concept of death as permanent separation and loss, however. And, although they may notice changes in the emotional climate in their home when their companions are grieving or may miss a no longer present caregiver (Corr, 2010), they lack the cognitive capacity to interpret what has happened when someone in the family dies.

The experience most directly relevant to the infant's emerging concept of death is separation from a loved one, and it is here that Bowlby's theory of attachment and research are helpful. Only after infants form their first attachments around 6 or 7 months do they begin to display separation anxiety when their beloved caregivers leave them. According to Bowlby, they are biologically programmed to protest separations by crying, searching for their loved one, and attempting to follow, thereby increasing the chances that they will be reunited with the caregiver and protected from harm.

Games of peekaboo help infants understand the concept of "all gone" and pave the way for an understanding of death.

Bowlby (1980) observed that infants separated from their attachment figures first engage in vigorous *protest*—yearning and searching for the loved one and expressing outrage when they fail. One 17-month-old girl said only, "Mum, Mum, Mum" for 3 days after her mother died. She was willing to sit on a nurse's lap but would turn her back, as if she did not want to see that the nurse was not "Mum" (Freud & Burlingham, cited in Bowlby, 1980).

If, after some hours or days of protest, an infant has not succeeded in finding the loved one, he begins to *despair*, displaying depression-like symptoms. The baby loses hope, ends the search, and becomes apathetic and sad. Grief may be reflected in a poor appetite, a change in sleeping patterns, excessive clinginess, or regression to less mature behavior (Furman, 1984; Walter & McCoyd, 2009; and see the description of infant depression in Chapter 16). After some days—longer in some cases—the bereaved infant may enter a *detachment* phase, in which he takes renewed interest in toys and companions and may begin to seek new relationships. Infants will recover from their protest, despair, and detachment most completely if they can rely on an existing attachment figure (for example, the surviving parent) or have

the opportunity to attach themselves to someone else who will be sensitive and responsive to them (Walter & McCoyd, 2009). Notice the similarities between these reactions and the yearning, disorganization and despair, and reorganization phases of the Parkes/Bowlby attachment model of adult bereavement.

17.4 The Child

LEARNING OBJECTIVES:

- Summarize the four key components of an understanding of biological death and when they develop in childhood.
- Characterize the reactions of terminally ill children to their situation.
- Describe children's common reactions to bereavement and what is most critical in helping them to adjust.

Much as parents would like to shelter their children from unpleasant life experiences, children encounter death in their early years, whether only of bugs and birds or, in the case of Sandy Hook Elementary School students, of their siblings, classmates, and teachers. How do they come to understand and cope with their experiences of death?

Grasping the Concept of Death

Contrary to what many adults assume, young children are highly curious about death, think about it with some frequency, build it into their play, and can talk about it (Kastenbaum, 2012). Yet their beliefs about death often differ considerably from those of adults. In Western societies, a "mature" understanding of death has several components (Brent et al., 1996; Hoffman & Strauss, 1985; Kenyon, 2001; Slaughter, Jaakkola, & Carey, 1999). We see death as characterized by the following:

- *Finality*. It is the cessation of life and of all life processes, such as movement, sensation, and thought.
- *Irreversibility*. It cannot be undone.
- *Universality*. It is inevitable and happens to all living beings.
- *Biological causality*. It is the result of natural processes internal to the organism, even if external causes set off these internal changes.

Researchers have studied children's conceptions of death by asking them the sorts of questions contained in ● **Table 17.3**. Children between age 3 and age 5 have some understanding of death, especially of its universality (Brent et al., 1996). Rather than viewing death as a final cessation of life functions, however, many of them picture the dead as living under altered

● **Table 17.3** Western Children's Concepts of Death and Questions Pertaining to Them

Concept	Questions
Finality	Can a dead person move? Get hungry? Speak? Think? Dream? Do dead people know that they are dead?
Irreversibility	Can a dead person become a live person again? Is there anything that could make a dead animal come back to life?
Universality	Does everyone die at some time? Will your parents die someday? Your friends? Will you die?
Biological causality	What makes a person die? Why do animals die?

Sources: Adapted from Hoffman & Strauss, 1985; Florian & Kravetz, 1985; and other sources.

circumstances and retaining at least some of their capacities (Slaughter et al., 1999). According to these preschoolers, the dead may have hunger pangs, wishes, and beliefs and may continue to love their moms (Bering & Bjorklund, 2004).

Some preschool-age children also view death as reversible rather than irreversible. They may liken it to sleep (from which a person can awaken) or to a trip (from which a person can return). With the right medical care, the right chicken soup, or a bit of magic, a dead person might be brought back to life (Speece & Brent, 1984). Finally, young children think death is caused by one external agent or another; one may say that people die because they eat aluminum foil; another may say the cause is eating a dirty bug or a Styrofoam cup (Koocher, 1974). They do not grasp the ultimate biological cause of death.

Children ages 5–7 (the age range of the classmates of the children slain at Sandy Hook) make considerable progress in acquiring a mature concept of death. Most children this age understand that death is characterized by finality (cessation of life functions), irreversibility, and universality (Grollman, 1995; Speece & Brent, 1992). Understanding the biological causality of death is the hardest concept of death for children to master but it is typically mastered by about age 10 (Bonoti, Leondari, & Mastora, 2013; Kenyon, 2001). Paula, age 12, had clearly mastered the concept that all deaths ultimately involve a failure of internal biological processes: "When the heart stops, blood stops circulating, you stop breathing and that's it. . . . there's lots of ways it can get started, but that's what really happens" (Koocher, 1974, pp. 407–408).

Children's understanding of death is influenced by both their level of cognitive development and their cultural and life experiences. Major breakthroughs in the understanding of death occur in the 5–7 age range—when, according to Piaget's theory, children progress from the preoperational stage of cognitive development to the concrete-operational stage. A mature understanding of death is also correlated with a high IQ (Kenyon, 2001).

In addition, children's concepts of death are influenced by the cultural context in which they live and the specific cultural and religious beliefs to which they are exposed (Sagara-Rosemeyer & Davies, 2007; Stambrook & Parker, 1987). For example, Jewish and Christian children in Israel, who are taught our Western concept of death, provide more "mature" answers to questions about death than Druze children, who are taught to believe in reincarnation (Florian & Kravetz, 1985). Understandably, a child who is taught that dead people are reincarnated may not view death as an irreversible cessation of life processes.

Within any society, children's unique life experiences also affect their understanding of death. Children who have had personal experience with a death in their immediate or extended family have more mature understandings of death than similar children who have not yet experienced the loss of a family member (Bonoti et al., 2013). And children who have life-threatening illnesses or who have personally encountered violence and death sometimes grasp death sooner than other children (O'Halloran & Altmaier, 1996). How parents and others communicate with children about death can also make a difference. How is a young child to overcome the belief that death is temporary, for example, if parents and other adults claim that relatives who have died are "asleep"? And if a child is told that "Grandma has gone away," is it not logical to ask why she cannot hop a bus and return?

Experts on death insist that adults only make death more confusing and frightening to young children when they use such euphemisms. They point out that children often understand more than we think, as illustrated by the 3-year-old who, after her father explained that her long-ill and just deceased grandfather had "gone to live on a star in the sky," looked at him quizzically and said, "You mean he is dead?" (Silverman, 2000, pp. 2–3). Experts recommend that parents give children simple but honest answers to the many questions they naturally ask about death and capitalize on events such as the death of a pet to teach children about death and help them understand and express their emotions (Kastenbaum, 2012; Silverman, 2000). Developmentally appropriate educational programs can also help familiarize children with the concepts of life and death (Schonfeld & Kappelman, 1990; Slaughter & Lyons, 2003).

Sion Touhig/Getty Images

After the September 11, 2001, attack on the World Trade Center, the Sesame Workshop asked school-age children to draw pictures of their fears and worries. As one child wrote, "My worries is that terrist [sic] will harm my family, and I will be left with no family like the kids in New York" (Stepp, 2001, p. C4). Similarly, while Syria's bloody internal war rages, children's drawings portray bombs, guns, flames, and tanks and use extraordinary amounts of the color red (Morello, 2013). Children's views of death and concerns about it are clearly affected by their sociocultural context and the historical events they experience.

The Dying Child

Parents and doctors often assume that terminally ill children are unaware that they will die and are better off remaining so. Yet research shows that dying children are far more aware of what is happening to them than adults realize (Essa & Murray, 1994; Stevens et al., 2010). Consider what Myra Bluebond-Langner (1977) found when she observed children ranging in age from 2 to 14 who had leukemia. Even many preschool children arrived, over time, at an understanding that they were going to die and that death is irreversible. Despite the secretiveness of adults, these children noticed changes in their treatments and subtle changes in the way adults interacted with them, and they paid close attention to what happened to other children who had the same disease and were receiving the same treatments. Over time, many of these ill children stopped talking about the long-term future and wanted to celebrate holidays such as Christmas early. A doctor trying to get one boy to cooperate with a procedure said, "I thought you would understand, Sandy. You told me once you wanted to be a doctor." Sandy threw an empty syringe at the doctor and screamed, "I'm not going to be anything!" (p. 59). Yet it may be difficult for parents to figure out what their dying child knows because, just as parents try to protect children, children sometimes keep their knowledge that they are dying from their parents (Stevens et al., 2010).

How do terminally ill children cope with the knowledge that they are dying? They experience many of the emotions that dying adults experience (Waechter, 1984). Preschool children may not talk about dying, but they may reveal their anxiety by having temper tantrums or portraying violent acts in their pretend play. School-age children understand more about their situation and can talk about their feelings if given an opportunity to do so. They want to participate in normal school and sports activities so that they will not feel inadequate compared with their peers, and they want to maintain a sense of control or mastery, even if the best they can do is take charge of deciding which finger should be pricked for a blood sample.

Yarelis, a five-year-old with leukemia, is comforted by her mother as she awaits a bone marrow donation from her older sister. Children who are dying need to know they are loved and need opportunities to express their concerns and fears.

Children with terminal illnesses need the love and support of parents, siblings, and other significant individuals in their lives. Most of all they need a strong sense that their parents are there to care for them (Worchel, Copeland, & Barker, 1987). In one study of Swedish families (Kreicbergs et al., 2004), about a third of parents of terminally ill children talked to their children about dying, and none regretted it. By comparison, 27% of the parents who did not talk with their children regretted not having done so, especially if they sensed their child was aware of dying (as over half the parents did). Perhaps the best advice to parents is to follow the child's lead, enabling children to talk about their feelings if they wish (Faulkner, 1997).

The Bereaved Child

Children's coping capacities are also tested when a parent, sibling, pet, or other loved one dies. Four major messages have emerged from studies of bereaved children: children grieve, they express their grief differently than adults do, they lack some of the coping resources that adults command, and some are vulnerable to long-term negative effects of bereavement (Lieberman et al., 2003; Osterweis, Solomon, & Green, 1984; Silverman, 2000).

Consider first some of the reactions that have been observed in young children whose parents have died (Christ, 2010; Lewis & Lippman, 2004; Lieberman et al., 2003; Silverman, 2000). These children often misbehave or strike out in rage at their surviving parent; they can become unglued when favorite routines are not honored (Lieberman et al., 2003). They ask endless questions: Where is Daddy? When is he coming back? Will I get a new Daddy? Anxiety about attachment and separation are common; more than half the bereaved children in one study reported being scared that other family members might die (Sanchez et al., 1994). Yet at other times bereaved children go about their activities as if nothing had happened, denying the loss or distracting themselves from it by immersing themselves in play. You can see how caregivers might be disturbed by some of these behaviors (although, as you may also have noticed, they are not unlike the emotional swings and oscillations that bereaved adults' experience).

Because they lack the cognitive abilities and coping skills that older individuals command, young children may have trouble grasping what has happened and attempt to deny and avoid emotions too overwhelming to face. Young children also have mainly behavioral or action coping strategies at their disposal (Skinner & Zimmer-Gembeck, 2007). So, for example, 2-year-old Reed found comfort by taking out a picture of his mother and putting it on his pillow at night, then returning it carefully to the photo album in the morning (Lieberman et al., 2003). Older children are able to use cognitive coping strategies such as conjuring up mental representations of their lost parents (Compas et al., 2001; Skinner & Zimmer-Gembeck, 2007).

Grief reactions differ greatly from child to child, but the preschooler's grief is likely to manifest itself in problems with sleeping, eating, toileting, and other daily routines (Oltjenbruns, 2001; Osterweis et al., 1984). Negative moods, dependency, and temper tantrums are also common. Older children express their sadness, anger, and fear more directly, although somatic symptoms such as headaches and other physical ailments are also common (Worden & Silverman, 1996).

Well beyond the first year after the death, some bereaved children continue to display problems such as unhappiness, low self-esteem, social withdrawal, difficulty in school, and problem behavior (Osterweis et al., 1984; Worden & Silverman, 1996). In a longitudinal study of school-age children, one in five children who had lost a parent had serious adjustment problems 2 years after the death (Worden & Silverman, 1996; see also Dowdney, 2000). Some children, though a minority, even develop psychological problems that carry into adulthood—for example, over-reactivity to stress and stress-related health problems, depression and other psychological disorders, or insecurity in later attachment relationships (Harris & Bifulco, 1991; Luecken, 2008; Miralt, Bearor, & Thomas, 2001–2002).

However, most bereaved children—especially those who have effective coping skills and solid social support—are resilient and adapt quite well. They are especially likely to fare well if their caregiver maintains her own mental health, has a secure relationship with the child, and provides good parenting (Little et al., 2011). Bereavement with the help of a caring and supportive caregiver is associated with adaptive responses to stress in adulthood, whereas a perceived lack of caring support after a death can translate into difficulty handling stress later in life (Luecken et al., 2009).

Peers can also make a difference in adjustment (Dopp & Cain, 2012). Supportive friends can help a child who has lost a parent adjust, especially if the child's remaining parent has difficulty being supportive. Yet relationships with peers can become strained if the child develops behavior problems or withdraws socially. Peers can also do damage through insensitive remarks. Some bereaved children are told by other kids that they are making up the death (Dopp & Cain, 2012). One 7-year-old girl was distraught when told, "You can't go to the father-daughter dance because your daddy is dead," and was calmed only when her mother assured her uncles very much wanted to take her (Christ, 2010, p. 172).

Checking Mastery

1. What are two factors that might lead Jared develop a fuller understanding of death concepts than Jeremy at age 5?

2. What three concepts of death are children likely to master by ages 5–7 and what concept would they still be missing?

3. What reactions on the part of bereaved children might irritate their caregivers?

Making Connections

1. How might you as a parent help or hinder your children from developing a mature concept of death?

2. If your child had untreatable cancer, would you talk to her about dying? Why or why not? Would the child's age affect your decision? How?

17.5 The Adolescent

LEARNING OBJECTIVES:

- Explain how understandings of death change in adolescence.

- Analyze how features of the adolescent period are reflected in the dying and bereavement experiences of adolescents.

Adolescents expand their understandings of death and show some of the characteristics we associate with the adolescent period when they encounter death.

Advanced Understandings of Death

Adolescents typically understand death as the irreversible cessation of biological processes. They also are able to think in more abstract ways about death as they progress from Piaget's concrete-operational stage to his formal-operational stage (Corr, 1995; Koocher, 1973). They use their new cognitive capacities to ponder the meaning of deaths they encounter and such hypotheticals as an afterlife (McCarthy, 2009; Noppe & Noppe, 1997). Yet, although they clearly know that biological processes cease at death, adolescents (and adults too) share with young children a belief that psychological functions such as knowing, believing, and feeling continue even after bodily functions have ceased (Bering & Bjorklund, 2004; Bonoti et al., 2013). Why is this?

Adolescents often acquire a belief in an afterlife—a belief common across cultures (Bering & Bjorklund, 2004). Many people end up, then, with both a biological view of death and a supernatural or religious view of it. Developing a belief that the soul or spirit lives on after death does not mean giving up a biological understanding of death as a cessation of bodily functions—nor does learning about biology replace beliefs about the supernatural based on cultural and religious teachings. Rather, the two views live side by side in adolescents' thinking and can be called upon as needed, depending on the situation and what they are trying to explain (Legare et al., 2012).

Experiences with Death

Themes of the adolescent period are reflected in how adolescents deal with having a terminal illness, losing a parent, and losing a friend.

Dying

Just as children's reactions to death and dying reflect their developmental capacities and needs, adolescents' reactions to becoming terminally ill are likely to reflect the themes of adolescence

(Balk & Corr, 2009; Knapp et al., 2010; Stevens & Dunsmore, 1996). Concerned about their body images as they experience physical and sexual maturation, adolescents may be acutely disturbed if their illness brings hair loss, weight gain, amputation, loss of sexual attractiveness and responsiveness, or other such physical changes. Wanting to be accepted by peers, they may feel like "freaks" or become upset when friends who do not know what to say or do abandon them. Eager to become more autonomous, they may be distressed by having to depend on parents and medical personnel and may struggle to assert their will and maintain a sense of control. Wanting to establish their own identities and chart future goals, adolescents may be angry and bitter at having their dreams snatched from them.

Losing a Parent

"When my mother died I thought my heart would break," recalled Geoffrey, age 14. "Yet I couldn't cry. It was locked inside. It was private and tender and sensitive like the way I loved her. They said to me, 'You're cool man, real cool, the way you've taken it,' but I wasn't cool at all. I was hot—hot and raging. All my anger, all my sadness was building up inside me. But I just didn't know any way to let it out." (Raphael, 1983, p. 176)

The reactions of adolescents to the deaths of family members also reflect the themes of the adolescent period (Balk & Corr, 2001; Tyson-Rawson, 1996). As in Geoffrey's case, adolescents are sometimes reluctant to express their grief for fear of seeming abnormal, losing control, or seeming overdependent; they may express their anguish instead through delinquent behavior and somatic ailments (Osterweis et al., 1984; Walter & McCoyd, 2009). Still being dependent on their parents for emotional support and guidance, adolescents who lose a parent to death may carry on an internal dialogue with the dead parent for years (Silverman & Worden, 1993). They may weave the death of the parent into their emerging identity and life story (Christ, 2010).

As is true of children, adolescents may experience mental health problems and have difficulty functioning after a loss. Adolescent responses to the sudden loss of a parent through suicide, accident, or sudden natural causes like heart attacks have been studied in depth by David Brent and his colleagues (Brent et al., 2009, 2012; Dietz et al., 2013; Melhem et al., 2011). Participants ranged from age 7 to age 18 at the time of the death and were assessed periodically until 5 years after the death. Among the important findings were these:

- About 30% experienced significant grief reactions in the first year that then gradually diminished, while another 10% continued to experience significant grief reactions even 3 years later and were at higher risk to develop diagnosable depression (Melhem et al., 2011). The remainder (almost 60%) had milder grief reactions.
- Bereaved youth were more likely than nonbereaved comparison youth to suffer from major depression and alcohol and substance abuse; posttraumatic stress disorder (PTSD) was also more common among bereaved youth, but only in the first year after the death (Brent et al., 2009).
- Cortisol measurements suggested that the stress response systems of bereaved youth were affected; their cortisol levels were

higher than those of nonbereaved youth and did not increase normally in response to a social stress task (Dietz et al., 2013).
- Bereavement also disrupted the completion of key developmental tasks of adolescence. Compared to nonbereaved youths, bereaved youth had less close attachments to peers, more difficulties at work, lower educational aspirations, and less well-developed career plans (Brent et al., 2012).
- Overall, outcomes were poorest for those who lost their mothers, blamed others for the death, had low self-esteem, used negative coping strategies, had earlier bouts of depression, and had a surviving parent or caregiver who was suffering from severe grief reactions or depression (Brent et al., 2009; Melhem et al., 2011).

Losing a Friend

Given the importance of peers in adolescence, it is not surprising that some adolescents also experience psychological problems when a close friend dies (Servaty-Seib, 2009). As Table 17.1 revealed, the leading causes of death in adolescence are unintentional injuries (especially car accidents), homicides, and suicides, so a friend's death is often sudden, violent, and potentially traumatic. A national survey of adolescents revealed that one in five adolescents ages 12–17 experienced the death of a close friend in the past year; they were especially likely to lose a friend if they were minority group members (except Asian/Pacific Islanders) and were from lower-income families (Rheingold et al., 2004). Moreover, experiencing such a death was associated with higher rates of substance abuse (although it could also be that substance-using teens run a greater risk of death). In another study, 32% of teenagers who lost a friend to suicide experienced clinical levels of depression after the suicide (Bridge et al., 2003).

So, the death of a friend can have serious implications for the mental health of some teens. Yet grief over the loss of a friend is often not taken as seriously as grief over the loss of a family member. Parents, teachers, and friends may not appreciate how much the bereaved adolescent is hurting and provide needed support (Ringler & Hayden, 2000; Servaty-Seib, 2009).

The death of a friend can be a deeply affecting and transformational experience for adolescents.

1. Why might we say that adolescents seem to "regress" to a less mature concept of death, and why would this be incorrect?

2. In David Brent's study of bereavement after a parent's death, what were three differences between bereaved and nonbereaved youth?

3. Why might some bereaved adolescents be unable to express their grief?

1. Miki (age 3), Rosario (age 9), and Jasmine (age 16) have all been diagnosed with cancer. They have been given chemotherapy and radiation treatments for several months but seem to be getting worse rather than better. Write a short monologue for each child conveying how she understands death.

2. Think about Miki (3), Rosario (9), and Jasmine (16) again but this time write about each girl's major concerns and wishes based on what you know of normal development at each age.

17.6 The Adult

LEARNING OBJECTIVES:

• Summarize what research tells us about the effects of widowhood on adults, including the different patterns of reaction uncovered by George Bonanno and his colleagues.

• Compare the impacts of the death of a child and the death of a parent.

• Outline and critique the grief work perspective on bereavement, citing relevant evidence.

• Analyze key factors that can contribute to complicated or prolonged grief after a death—or to posttraumatic growth.

For adults, dealing with the loss of a spouse or partner and accepting their own mortality can be considered normal developmental tasks (Röcke & Cherry, 2002). We have already introduced models describing adults' experiences of dying and bereavement. Here we will elaborate by examining bereavement from a family systems perspective, then trying to define the line between normal and abnormal grief reactions and identify factors that make coping easier or harder.

Death in the Family Context

To better understand bereavement, it is useful to adopt a family systems perspective and examine how a death alters relationships, roles, and patterns of interaction within the family, as well as interactions between the family and its environment (Kissane et al., 2013; Silverman, 2000; Traylor et al., 2003). Consider the challenges associated with three kinds of death in the family: the loss of a spouse or partner, the loss of a child, and the loss of a parent.

Loss of a Spouse or Partner

> How odd to smile during Richard's funeral. He was dead and I was smiling to myself. Grief does that. Laughter lies close in with despair, numbness nearby acuity, and memory with forgetfulness. I would have to get used to it, but I didn't know this at the time. All I knew, as I sat in Thomas Jefferson's church next to Richard's coffin, was that memory had given pleasure first, and then cracking pain. (Jamison, 2009, pp. 126–127)

Most of what we know about bereavement is based on studies of widows and widowers. Experiencing the death of a spouse or partner becomes increasingly likely as we age; in heterosexual relationships, it is something most women can expect to endure because women tend both to live longer than men and to marry men who are older than they are. The marital relationship is a central one for most adults, and the loss of a marriage partner or other romantic

attachment figure can mean the loss of a great deal. Moreover, the death of a partner often precipitates a cascade of other stressors—the need to move, enter the labor force or change jobs, assume responsibilities that the partner formerly performed, parent single-handedly, cope with less money, and so on. Finally, bereaved partners must often redefine their identities and assumptions about life in fundamental ways (Lopata, 1996; Parkes & Prigerson, 2010). Consider Rachel after her husband died of a heart attack: "I was Frank's wife, that was it mostly. He's gone. And I am basically, I am, now—I am nobody" (Bonanno, 2009, p. 97).

As noted earlier in this chapter, Colin Murray Parkes, in extensive research on widows and widowers younger than age 45, concluded that bereaved adults progress through overlapping phases of numbness, yearning, disorganization and despair, and reorganization. What tolls does this grieving process take on physical, emotional, and cognitive functioning? Parkes (2006) found that widows and widowers are at risk for illness and physical symptoms such as loss of appetite and sleep disruption, and they tend to overindulge in alcohol, tranquilizers, and cigarettes. Cognitive functions such as memory and decision making are often impaired, and emotional problems such as loneliness and anxiety are common. Most bereaved partners do not become clinically depressed, but many display increased symptoms of depression in the year after the death (Wilcox et al., 2003). Widows and widowers as a group have higher-than-average risks of death as well, especially when their loss is unexpected rather than the result of chronic disease (Shah et al., 2013).

Modest disruptions in cognitive, emotional, physical, and interpersonal functioning are common, usually lasting for a year; less severe, recurring grief reactions may then continue for several years (Bonanno & Kaltman, 2000). Although not captured in the Parkes/Bowlby attachment model, positive thoughts about the deceased, expressions of love, and feelings of gaining from the loss are also part of the typical picture, as in the quote at the beginning of this section.

Importantly, though, George Bonanno and his colleagues have found much diversity in patterns of response to loss (Boerner, Mancini, & Bonanno, 2013; Bonanno, Boerner, & Wortman, 2008). Bonanno studied adults who lost a partner from an average of 3 years before the death to 6 and 18 months afterward (Boerner, Wortman, & Bonanno, 2005; Bonanno, Wortman, & Nesse, 2004; Bonanno et al., 2002; and see Galatzer-Levy & Bonanno, 2012). The sample was assessed again 4 years after their loss to examine the long-term implications of different patterns of grieving. Gathering data both before and after the death of a partner revealed patterns of adjustment over time that had not been evident in studies focused only on adjustment after a loss.

■ **Figure 17.5** shows the average depression symptom scores over time associated with the five most prevalent patterns of adjustment shown by widows and widowers:

- A resilient pattern in which distress is at low levels all along
- Common grief, with heightened and then diminishing distress after the loss
- Chronic grief in which loss brings distress and the distress lingers
- Chronic depression in which individuals were depressed before the loss and remained so after it
- A depressed–improved pattern in which individuals who were depressed before the loss become less depressed after the death

Chronic depression (7.8% of sample)
Depressed–improved (10.2%)
Common grief (10.7%)
Resilience (45.9%)
Chronic grief (15.6%)

■ **Figure 17.5** Depression symptom scores of five subgroups of elderly widows and widowers an average of 3 years before, 6 months after, and 18 months after the death of their spouse. In parentheses are the percentages of the sample showing each pattern. Notice that resilience—a low level of depression all along—is the most common response, characterizing almost half. This runs counter to our belief that all bereaved people must go through a period of significant distress.

SOURCE: From Bonanno, G. A., Wortman, C. B., & Neese, R. M., Prospective patterns of resilience and maladjustment during widowhood, *Psychology and Aging, 19,* 260–271. Copyright © 2004 American Psychological Association. Reprinted with permission.

Resilience. The biggest surprise in this study was that the resilient pattern of adjustment involving low levels of distress all along turned out to be the most common pattern of response, characterizing almost half the sample. The resilient grievers were not just cold, unfeeling people who did not really love their partners. Rather, as indicated by data collected before their partners died, they seemed to be well-adjusted and happily married people with good coping resources (Bonanno et al., 2002). Nor was there any sign that they were defensively denying or avoiding painful feelings initially and would pay for it by having delayed grief reactions later (Boerner et al., 2005). Rather, although they experienced emotional pangs in the first months after the death, they were more comforted than most by positive thoughts of their partners and simply coped effectively with their loss. Other studies confirm that a surprisingly high proportion of bereaved people, around half, can be described as resilient (Bonanno, 2009).

Patterns of Depression. This study also helps us understand that some bereaved people who display symptoms of depression after a loss were depressed even before the death, whereas others become depressed in response to their loss. Those who are depressed before the loss tend to remain depressed even 4 years later. Those who become depressed in response to the loss often recover from their depression within a year or two; they show the "common grief" pattern that most of us believe is typical (Boerner et al., 2005; Bonanno et al., 2004). Another 15%, the chronic grief group, become depressed after the loss and stay depressed for a long time.

The "depressed–improved" individuals in Bonanno's study who were depressed before the death but recovered quickly afterward are intriguing. Most likely many were experiencing

Most widows adjust to their loss and show resilience, but about 15% experience complicated grief, showing significant distress even 2 years or more after their loss. Adjustment can be especially hard for a young widow whose husband is killed violently in war.

caregiver burden (see Chapter 15) before the death and were relieved of stress after it. Richard Schulz and his colleagues (2003) have found that it is common among those who bear the burden of caring for family members with Alzheimer's disease and other forms of dementia to experience more depression before their partner's death than after. More than 70% admit that the death came as a relief to both themselves and their loved one.

Gay and Lesbian Partners. Bonanno and his colleagues (2005) wondered whether resilience would also be common among the partners of gay men who die of AIDS. Many of these men not only experienced the burden of caring for their dying partners but were HIV infected themselves and therefore stressed by their own illness and likely death, as well as by the stigma surrounding both AIDS and homosexuality. About half of the partners of gay men who died of AIDS showed resilience—the same proportion as among heterosexual widows and widowers. This finding is all the more surprising because gay and lesbian partners sometimes experience what Kenneth Doka (1989, 2008) calls **disenfranchised grief**, grief that is not fully recognized or appreciated by other people and therefore may not receive much sympathy and support. Losses of ex-spouses, extramarital lovers, foster children, pets, and fetuses can also occasion disenfranchised grief, which is generally likely to be harder to cope with than socially recognized grief.

Complicated Grief. Overall, most adults who lose spouses or partners are either resilient and show low levels of distress or, if they experience significant grief, begin to show signs of recovery a year or so after the death. Even 20 years after their loss, though, it is normal for widowed men and women to think about their spouses once every week or two and to continue to talk about and feel sad about the spouse now and then, especially on special dates such as the anniversary of the death (Carnelley et al., 2006).

For a minority, up to about 15%, significant grieving and psychological distress continue for years (Bonanno, 2009). In such cases psychologists speak of **complicated grief** to refer to grief that is unusually prolonged or intense and that impairs functioning (Parkes, 2006). People who have difficulty coping with loss are often diagnosed as having a depressive disorder or, if the death was traumatic, PTSD. However, some experts have concluded that complicated or prolonged grief, because it has unique symptoms such as intense yearning for the deceased, is distinct from these other conditions and should be considered a distinct psychological disorder (Boelen & Prigerson, 2013; Prigerson, Vanderwerker, & Maciejewski, 2008).

The 2013 Diagnostic and Statistical Manual of Mental Disorders, DSM-5, now discusses a condition called "persistent complex bereavement-related disorder" as worthy of further study as a distinct disorder (American Psychiatric Association, 2013). Others think that absent, inhibited, and delayed grief reactions should also be viewed as psychological disorders (Rando et al., 2012). Meanwhile, critics warn that what is viewed as complicated grief will vary from society to society (Rosenblatt, 2013) or question the whole idea of treating certain responses to the normal human experience of bereavement as psychological disorders (Wakefield, 2013).

In sum, the loss of a spouse or partner is a painful and sometimes damaging experience that carries risks of developing physical or mental health problems or even dying. Some widows and widowers experience emotional aftereffects for years. Yet around half of those who lose spouses or romantic partners show resilience and manage to cope without becoming highly distressed.

Loss of a Child

> My child has died! My heart is torn to shreds. My body is screaming. My mind is crazed. The question is always present on my mind. Why? How could this possibly have happened? The anger is ever so deep, so strong, so frightening. (Bertman, 1991, p. 323, citing a mother's reflections on how she reacted to her 16-year-old daughter's death in a car accident after the initial numbness wore off.)

As the parents whose children were killed in the Sandy Hook school shooting can testify, no loss seems more difficult for an adult than the death of a child (Murphy, 2008; Parkes, 2006). Even when there is forewarning, the loss of a child seems unexpected, untimely, and unfair. In one study, only 12% of parents whose adolescent or young adult child died of an accident, suicide, or homicide had found meaning in the death 1 year later, and only 57% had found it 5 years later (Murphy, Johnson, & Lohan, 2003b). Being unable to make sense of a child's death is associated with more intense grief (Keesee, Currier, & Neimeyer, 2008). The age of the child who dies has little effect on the severity of the grief: parents, especially mothers, can experience severe grief reactions after a miscarriage, the loss of a premature baby, or the loss of a young infant to sudden infant death syndrome, as well as to the death of an adult child (Broen et al., 2004; Buchi et al., 2007; Walter & McCoyd, 2009).

The death of a child alters the family system, affecting the marital relationship, parenting, and the well-being of surviving siblings and grandparents. The marital relationship is likely

The death of a child can be devastating for parents.

Oleg Popov/Reuters/Corbis

to be strained because each partner grieves in a unique way and is not always able to provide emotional support for the other (Bohannon, 1990–1991). Strains are likely to be especially severe if the marriage was shaky before the death. The odds of marital problems and divorce tend to increase after the death of a child, although most couples stay together and some feel closer than ever (Dijkstra & Stroebe, 1998; Najman et al., 1993).

Typically, mothers focus more on loss-oriented coping and grieve more openly while throwing themselves into caring for the surviving children, whereas fathers take a more restoration-oriented approach, focusing on work and rebuilding the family's life (Alam et al., 2012). A study guided by the dual-process model of bereavement found that parents who lost a child fared better if they focused more on restoration-oriented coping and less on loss-oriented coping (Wijngaards-de Meij et al., 2008). Men whose wives were restoration oriented were better adjusted than those whose wives dwelled on the loss.

What of the brothers and sisters of the child who dies? Children are deeply affected when a brother or sister dies, but their grief is often not fully appreciated and their distraught parents may not be able to support them effectively (Koehler, 2010; Lohan & Murphy, 2001–2002). Siblings of children battling cancer, for example, may resent it if they are neglected by their parents, may be anxious about their own health, may feel guilty about some of the unsavory feelings of rivalry they have, and may feel pressure to be perfect or to replace the lost child in their parents' eyes (Adams & Deveau, 1987; Koehler, 2010). One 12-year-old boy whose brother died described his experience this way: "My dad can't talk about it, and my mom cries a lot. It's really hard on them. I pretend I'm O.K. I usually just stay in my room" (Wass, 1991, p. 29).

Finally, grandparents also grieve after the death of a child, both for their grandchild and for their child, the bereaved parent. As one grandparent said, "It's like a double whammy!" (DeFrain, Jakub, & Mendoza, 1991–1992, p. 178). Grandparents are likely to feel guilty about surviving their grandchildren and helpless to protect their adult children from pain (Fry, 1997). They may also experience disenfranchised grief, ignored while all the supportive attention focuses on the parents (Hayslip & White, 2008). Clearly, then, those who are attempting to help bereaved families need to include the whole family in their efforts.

Loss of a Parent

Even if we escape the death of a child or spouse, the death of a parent is a normative life transition that most of us will experience. As noted already, some children experience long-lasting problems after the death of a parent. Fortunately, most of us do not have to face this event until we are in middle age. We are typically less dependent on our parents by then. Moreover, we expect that our parents will die someday and have prepared ourselves, at least to some degree.

Perhaps for these reasons, adjusting to the death of a parent is usually not as difficult as adjusting to the death of a romantic partner or child (Parkes, 2006). Yet it can be a turning point in an adult's life, with effects on his identity and his relationships with his partner, children (who are grieving the loss of their grandparent), surviving parent, and siblings (Umberson, 2003). Adult children may feel vulnerable and alone in the world when their parents no longer stand between them and death (Walter & McCoyd, 2009). Guilt about not doing enough for the deceased parent is also common (Moss et al., 1993).

The Grief Work Perspective and Challenges to It

It's time to step back and reflect. The view that has guided much research on bereavement has come to be called the **grief work perspective**—the view that to cope adaptively with death, bereaved people must:

- confront their loss
- experience painful emotions and work through those emotions
- move toward a detachment from the deceased

This view, which grew out of Freudian psychoanalytic theory, is widely held in our society, not only among therapists but among people in general, and it influences what we view as an abnormal reaction to death (Stroebe, 2001; Wortman & Silver, 2001). From the grief work perspective, either complicated, prolonged grief that lasts longer and is more intense than usual, or both, or an absence, inhibition, or delay of grief, in which the bereaved never seems to confront and express painful feelings, is viewed as pathological.

In Mexico, dating back to the Aztecs but now integrated with Catholic days of remembrance, the Day of the Dead (Dia de los Muertos) on November 2 is a time to remember deceased loved ones and to encourage their souls to visit (Bonanno, 2009). Costumes are worn, skulls and skeletons are everywhere, and the festivities are lighthearted, making this yearly event somewhat like American's Halloween. Altars in the home with sugar skulls, marigolds, and the deceased's favorite foods are assembled, and gifts are taken to the grave. What is appropriate "grief work" when grieving and mourning take different forms in different cultures?

This grief work perspective has come under serious attack, however. Questions have been raised about its assumptions that there is a right way to grieve, that bereaved people must experience and work through intense grief to recover, and that they must sever their bonds with the deceased to move on with their lives (Bonanno, 2004; Wortman & Boerner, 2007).

One Right Way?

Cross-cultural studies reveal that there are many ways to grieve and suggest that the grief work model of bereavement may be culturally biased (Rosenblatt, 2008, 2013). An Egyptian mother may be conforming to her culture's norms of mourning if she sits alone, withdrawn and mute, for months or even years after a child's death. Likewise, a Balinese mother is following the rules of her culture if she is calm, composed, and even seemingly cheerful soon after a child's death (Wikan, 1988, 1991). We would be wrong to conclude, based on our own society's norms, that the Egyptian mother is suffering from prolonged grief or the Balinese mother from absent or inhibited grief.

Working Through Grief?

There is also surprisingly little support for the grief work perspective's assumption that bereaved individuals must confront their loss and experience painful emotions to cope successfully (Boerner et al., 2013; Wortman & Silver, 2001). As you saw earlier, the many bereaved individuals who fail to show much emotional distress during the early months after the loss do not seem to pay for their lack of grief with delayed grief later, as the grief work model says they should. Delayed grief is extremely rare, and the individuals who adjust best to death are those very resilient ones who display relatively little distress at any point in their bereavement, experience many positive emotions and thoughts, and manage to carry on with life despite their loss (Boerner et al., 2013). In fact, there is growing evidence that too much "grief work," like ruminative coping that involves overanalyzing one's problems, may backfire and *prolong* psychological distress rather than relieve it (Bonanno et al., 2005).

Breaking Bonds?

Finally, the grief work view that we must break our bonds to the deceased to overcome our grief is flawed. Freud believed that bereaved people had to let go in order to invest their psychic energy elsewhere. However, John Bowlby (1980) noticed that many bereaved individuals revise their internal working models of self and others and continue their relationships with their deceased loved ones on new terms (Bonanno & Kaltman, 1999). Recent research supports Bowlby, suggesting that many bereaved individuals maintain their attachments to the deceased indefinitely through **continuing bonds**. They reminisce and share memories of the deceased, derive comfort from the deceased's possessions, consult with the deceased and feel his or her presence, seek to make the deceased proud of them, and so on. Bereavement rituals in some cultures (in Japan and China, for instance) are actually designed to ensure a continued bond between the living and the dead (Klass, 2001).

Is it pathological to maintain a relationship with a deceased parent for many years? It is common practice in Japan to remember each morning during worship ancestors who have died, to leave them food and otherwise care for them, and to tell them about one's triumphs and disasters (Klass, 2001). A continuing bond with, rather than detachment from, the deceased is common in many cultural contexts and is sometimes associated with good rather than poor bereavement outcomes. This 53-year-old mourns his wife, mother-in-law, and father-in-law, all lost in the tsunami and earthquake that struck Japan in 2011.

Jeremy Sutton-Hibbert/Getty Images News/Getty Images

Individuals who continue their bonds rather than severing them do not necessarily show poorer adjustment than those who do not. In fact, many benefit from the continuing, but redefined, attachment (Field et al., 1999; Stroebe, Schut, & Boerner, 2010). Nigel Field and his colleagues (1999) tried to determine when continuing bonds are healthy and when they may not be. They investigated whether continuing attachment to a deceased spouse was positively or negatively related to grief symptoms among widows and widowers at 6 months, 14 months, and 25 months after their loss. Those who expressed their continuing attachment by having and sharing fond memories of the deceased and by sensing that their loved one was watching over and guiding them experienced relatively low levels of distress. By contrast, those who used their spouse's possessions to comfort themselves at the 6-month mark showed high levels of distress and little decrease in grief over the coming months. Similarly, Field and Filanosky (2010) found that carrying an internal image of the loved one that provides a secure base for becoming more independent can facilitate growth after bereavement, whereas intrusive visions of the deceased may reflect continued efforts to reunite and difficulty coping, especially when the death was violent or the bereaved person feels responsible for it.

Apparently, then, maintaining continuing bonds is adaptive for some people but a sign of continued yearning and prolonged or complicated grief for others (Field, 2008). Cultural context can make a big difference. In one study, for example, maintaining continuing bonds was associated with distress soon after the death in both China and the United States. By 18 months after the death, though, it was related to better adjustment in China but to poorer adjustment in the United States, possibly because continuing a relationship with the deceased is viewed as more appropriate in China (Lalande & Bonanno, 2006).

Overall, then, the traditional grief work perspective is flawed:

- Norms for expressing grief vary widely across cultures, so there is no one "right" way to grieve.
- There is little evidence that bereaved people must do intense "grief work" or that those who do not do it will pay later with a delayed grief reaction.
- People do not need to sever their attachment to the deceased to adjust to a loss and sometimes benefit from continuing bonds.

More fundamentally, researchers are now questioning the grief work model's assumption that grief is a pathological process—like a disease that we catch, suffer from, and eventually get over (Bonanno, 2001). As you saw earlier, only about 15% of bereaved individuals experience complications of grief so severe that they can be described as pathological. Moreover, it is common to experience positive emotions along with the negative ones and to feel in the end that one has benefited or grown from one's loss (Bonanno, 2009; Davis & Nolen-Hoeksema, 2001; Joseph, 2012). We must conclude that grief is more complex and less pathological than the grief work model implies.

Who Copes and Who Succumbs?

Even if it is difficult to find the line between normal grief and complicated grief, we can still ask what risk and protective factors distinguish people who cope well with loss from people who cope poorly. Coping with bereavement is influenced by the individual's personal resources, the nature of the loss, and the surrounding context of support and stressors (Burke & Neimeyer, 2013; Dyregrov & Dyregrov, 2013; Piper et al., 2011).

Personal Resources

Just as some individuals are better able to cope with their own dying than others are, some are better equipped to handle the stresses of bereavement due to their *personal resources*. *Attachment style* is one important resource (or liability). Bowlby's attachment theory emphasizes that early experiences in attachment relationships influence the internal working models we form of self and other, how we later relate to romantic partners, and how we handle losses of relationships. If infants and young children receive loving and responsive care, they form internal working models of self and others that tell them that they are lovable and that other people can be trusted, and they develop a secure attachment style (see Chapter 14). Otherwise, they may develop one of the insecure attachment styles.

Attachment styles are systematically related to reactions to death (Fraley et al., 2006; Mikulincer & Shaver, 2013; Parkes, 2006):

- A secure attachment style is associated with coping relatively well with the death of a loved one.
- A resistant (or preoccupied) style of attachment, which involves being anxious about being abandoned, is linked to being overly dependent and displaying extreme and prolonged grief and anxiety after a loss, ruminating about the

death, and clinging to the loved one rather than revising the attachment bond.

- An avoidant (or dismissing) attachment style is associated with difficulty expressing emotions or seeking comfort; such individuals may do little grieving and may disengage from or even devalue the person lost.
- A disorganized (or fearful) attachment style, which is rooted in unpredictable and anxiety-arousing parenting, is associated with being especially unequipped to cope with loss; these individuals may turn inward, harm themselves, or abuse alcohol or drugs.

In the language of the dual-process model of bereavement, securely attached individuals are able to oscillate appropriately between loss-oriented and restoration-oriented coping and are likely to emphasize positive memories of the deceased; resistant/preoccupied individuals focus on their loss and dwell on negative thoughts and emotions; avoidant/dismissing individuals focus on restoration and avoid dealing with their emotions; and disorganized/fearful individuals have difficulty developing a coherent way of coping (Stroebe et al., 2010).

Personality and coping style also influence how successfully people cope with death. For example, individuals who have difficulty coping tend to score high on measures of the Big Five personality dimension of neuroticism (Robinson & Marwit, 2006; Wijngaards-de-Meij et al., 2007). They may have had chronic psychological problems such as depression before they were bereaved (Bonanno et al., 2004; Piper et al., 2011). Many also rely on ineffective coping strategies such as denial or avoidance, escape through alcohol and drugs, or unproductive rumination about their loss (Morina, 2011; Murphy, Johnson, & Lohan, 2003a). By contrast, people who are optimistic, look for and find positive ways of interpreting their loss, and use active coping strategies, experience less intense grief reactions and are more likely to report personal growth after their losses than other bereaved adults (Riley et al., 2007).

Nature of the Loss

Bereavement outcomes are also influenced by the nature of the loss. The closeness of the person's relationship to the deceased is a key factor. For example, we grieve more for members of our immediate family than for distant relatives (Armstrong & Shakespeare-Finch, 2011), and spouses grieve especially hard if their relationship to the deceased was very close and if they were highly dependent on their partners (Carr, 2008; Johnson et al., 2007; Piper et al., 2011).

The cause of death can also influence bereavement outcomes. Surprisingly, sudden deaths are not necessarily harder to cope with in the long run than expected deaths from illnesses, although the initial grief reaction may be more intense (Piper et al., 2011). The advantages of being forewarned of death may be offset by the strains of caregiver burden during a long illness (Schulz, Boerner, & Hebert, 2008). Sudden deaths that are violent or traumatic, such as suicides and homicides, can be especially difficult to bear, however (Piper et al., 2011). One reason the death of a child is so painful is that children's deaths are often the result of "senseless" and violent events (Parkes & Prigerson, 2010).

The Bright Side of Bereavement: Posttraumatic Growth

Think about your greatest loss, crisis, or trauma, whether a death or another difficult experience. Now respond to the following items on a scale from 0 to 5, where 0 means "I did not experience this change as a result of my crisis," and 5 means, "I experienced this change to a very great degree as a result of my crisis."

_____ 1. I changed my priorities about what is important in life.

_____ 2. I have a greater appreciation for the value of my own life.

_____ 3. I am able to do better things with my life.

_____ 4. I have a better understanding of spiritual matters.

_____ 5. I have a greater sense of closeness with others.

_____ 6. I established a new path for my life.

_____ 7. I know better that I can handle difficulties.

_____ 8. I have a stronger religious faith.

_____ 9. I discovered that I'm stronger than I thought I was.

_____ 10. I learned a great deal about how wonderful people are.

To the extent that you agreed with these statements, you show signs of posttraumatic growth.

SOURCE: Cann, A., Calhoun, L. G., Tedeschi, R. G., Taku, K., Vishnevsky, T., Triplett, K. N., & Danhauer, S. C. (2010). A short form of the Posttraumatic Growth Inventory, *Anxiety, Stress & Coping, 23*(2), 127–137, Table 1, p. 130.

Supports and Stressors

Finally, grief reactions are influenced positively by the presence of social support and negatively by additional life stressors (Hansson & Stroebe, 2007; Parkes, 2006). Social support is crucial at all ages. It is especially important for the child or adolescent whose parent dies to have good parenting (Haine et al., 2006). Brothers and sisters can help each other cope (Hurd, 2002). Adult children can ease the adjustment of their widowed parents (Ha, 2010). Indeed, family members of all ages recover best when the family is cohesive and family members can share their emotions (Traylor et al., 2003).

There are also simple things that friends and colleagues can do to be supportive. Many of us are clueless about what to say or do that will be helpful, but it is not sage advice that bereaved individuals want and appreciate. Rather, they report that they are helped most by family and friends who say they are sorry to hear of the loss, make themselves available to serve as confidants, ask how things are going, and allow bereaved individuals to express painful feelings freely if and when they choose rather than trying to cheer them up and talk them out of their grief (Herkert, 2000; Hinds, 2007; Lehman, Ellard, & Wortman, 1986).

Sensitive social support can make all the difference to the bereaved.

Monkey Business Images/Shutterstock.com

Just as social support helps the bereaved, additional stressors hurt. For example, outcomes tend to be poor for widows who must cope with financial problems after bereavement and for widowers who must manage household tasks without their wives (Lopata, 1996). Widows and widowers may have more than the usual difficulty adjusting if they must also single-handedly care for young children, find a new job, or move (Parkes, 1996; Worden & Silverman, 1993). These kinds of stressors all demand what the dual-process model of bereavement calls restoration-oriented coping; they take energy and resources that elderly widows in poor health, especially those living in poverty with little social support, may not have (Hansson & Stroebe, 2007).

By taking into account the person who has experienced a death, the nature of the death, and the context of supports and stressor surrounding it, we can put together a profile of the individuals who are most likely to have long-term problems after bereavement. These individuals have had an unfortunate history of interpersonal relationships, perhaps suffering the death of a parent when they were young or experiencing insecurity in their early attachments. They have had previous psychological problems and generally have difficulty coping effectively with adversity. The person who died is someone whom they loved deeply and on whom they depended greatly, and the death was untimely and seemingly senseless. Finally, these high-risk individuals lack the kinds of social support that can aid them in overcoming their loss, and they are burdened by multiple stressors.

Posttraumatic Growth

The grief work perspective on bereavement put the focus on the negative side of bereavement, but psychologists have come to appreciate that bereavement and other life crises also have positive consequences and sometimes even foster personal growth (Joseph, 2012; Tedeschi & Calhoun, 2004). Granted, it can be a painful way to grow, and we could hardly recommend it as a plan for optimizing human development. Still, the literature on death and dying is filled with testimonials about the lessons that can be learned. We invite you to consider the statements in **Engagement Box 17.2** and whether they apply to you.

Posttraumatic growth refers to positive psychological change resulting from highly challenging experiences such as being diagnosed with a life-threatening illness or losing a loved one (Tedeschi & Calhoun, 1995). A focus within what has come to be known as positive psychology, research on posttraumatic growth has involved asking people whether they perceive that they have changed in positive ways as a result of losses—strengthened their relationships, seen new possibilities for their lives, gained or recognized that they had personal strengths, undergone spiritual change, or come to appreciate life more.

So far this research suggests that posttraumatic stress and posttraumatic growth go hand in hand. Growth is unlikely where there is little psychological distress and it is unlikely where the distress is overwhelming, as when a diagnosable disorder such as PTSD is suffered (Joseph, 2012). Instead, growth seems most likely when distress is significant but not crushing (Armstrong & Shakespeare-Finch, 2011; Currier, Holland, & Neimeyer, 2012). Positive outcomes are also more likely if the individual tends to be good at finding the positives in any situation (Ong, Fuller-Rowell, & Bonanno, 2010).

Although we need more studies demonstrating growth on objective measures of psychological functioning, many bereaved individuals believe that they have become stronger, wiser, more loving, and more religious people with a greater appreciation of life (Tedeschi & Calhoun, 2004). Many widows master new skills, become more independent, and emerge with new identities and higher self-esteem, especially those who depended heavily on their spouses and then discover that they can manage life on their own (Carr, 2004; Lopata, 1996). A mother whose infant died said it all: "Now I can survive anything" (DeFrain, Taylor, & Ernst, 1982, p. 57). So perhaps by encountering tragedy we learn to cope with tragedy, and perhaps by struggling to find meaning in death we come to find meaning in life.

Checking Mastery

1. What is the single most common pattern of adjustment observed in studies of widows and widowers?
2. What are two elements of the grief work perspective that are not well supported by evidence?
3. How would individuals with a resistant (preoccupied) attachment style or orientation and those with an avoidant (or dismissing) style be expected to differ in their grief reactions?

Making Connections

1. Using the section "Who Copes and Who Succumbs," analyze your capacity to cope with death. If you have experienced a significant loss, analyze your actual success in coping and the factors that may have influenced it; if you have not experienced a significant loss, predict how you will respond to your first significant loss and why you think so.
2. Many people have misconceptions about what is normal and what is abnormal when it comes to grieving, as this chapter has illustrated. Identify two such misconceptions and, using relevant research, show why they are just that—misconceptions.

17.7 Taking the Sting Out of Death

LEARNING OBJECTIVES:

- Assess how the hospice/palliative care approach differs from the standard medical approach to dying patients and how it affects patients and their families.

- Illustrate how individual therapy, family interventions, and mutual support groups can benefit bereaved individuals.

What can be done to help children and adults who are dying or who are bereaved grapple with death and their feelings about it? Here is a sampling of strategies.

For the Dying

Dramatic changes in the care of dying people have occurred in the past few decades, thanks partly to the efforts of Elisabeth Kübler-Ross and others. The hospice movement is a prime example. A **hospice** is a program that supports dying people and their families through a philosophy of "caring" rather than "curing" (Connor, 2000; Knee, 2010; Saunders, 2002). One of the founders of the hospice movement and of St. Christopher's Hospice in London, Dr. Cicely Saunders (2002), put it this way: "I remain committed to helping people find meaning in the end of life and not to helping them to a hastened death" (p. 289).

The hospice concept spread quickly to North America, where hospices have been established in most communities to serve individuals with cancer, AIDS, and other life-threatening diseases. In many hospice programs today, however, dying patients stay at home and are visited by hospice workers. Hospice care is part of a larger movement to provide **palliative care**, care aimed primarily at bringing comfort to and meeting the physical, psychological, and spiritual needs of patients with serious illnesses (Shannon, 2006).

What makes hospice care different from hospital care? Whether hospice care is provided in a facility or at home, it entails these key features (Connor, 2000; Corr & Corr, 1992; Siebold, 1992):

- The dying person and his family—not the "experts"—decide what support they need and want.
- Attempts to cure the patient or prolong his life are deemphasized (but death is not hastened either).

While in hospice care, Nancy Mathre, age 77, got a visit from two representatives of the famed New York dancing group, the Rockettes. She wanted to be a Rockette when she was 13 but was told she was too short. Dancing with the Rockettes was on her "bucket list."

- Pain control is emphasized.
- The setting for care is as normal as possible (preferably the patient's own home or a homelike facility that does not have the sterile atmosphere of many hospital wards).
- Bereavement counseling is provided to the family before and after the death.

Do dying patients and their families fare better when they receive hospice care? There is suggestive evidence that patients have less interest in physician-assisted suicide when they have access to hospice care and their pain is better controlled (Foley & Hendin, 2002). In one study, a third of individuals cared for by a home healthcare agency, nursing home, or hospital felt they received too little emotional support, whereas only about 20% of those receiving home hospice services felt this way (Teno et al., 2004). And an evaluation of hospice facility care, at-home hospice care, and conventional hospital care in Great Britain found that hospice patients spent more of their last days without pain, underwent fewer medical interventions and operations, and received nursing care that was more oriented to their emotional needs (Seale, 1991). Moreover, spouses and partners, parents, and other relatives of dying people who received hospice care appear to display fewer symptoms of grief and have a greater sense of well-being 1 to 2 years after the death than similar relatives who coped with a death without benefit of hospice care (Ragow-O'Brien, Hayslip, & Guarnaccia, 2000). **Exploring Development Box 17.1**

Exploring Development 17.1
Hospice Care

A hospice worker talks about her feeling that it is a gift to be with a person when they die.

- What physical changes indicate that a person is nearing death?

takes you to an interview with a hospice director who describes the role of hospice care.

In the United States, at least, hospice care is usually restricted to individuals who are judged to be within 6 months of dying but palliative care, a broader concept, can be provided throughout a patient's medical care by a hospital or other treatment facility. Jennifer Temel and her colleagues (2010) randomly assigned patients with lung cancer who had less than a year to live to receive either palliative care while they were receiving chemotherapy and other medical treatment or just the standard medical treatments. Palliative care here involved visits from a clinician who assessed the patients' physical and psychological issues, established goals of care with them, helped them make decisions about their treatment, and helped ensure that their individual needs were met. The results were quite remarkable. Patients in palliative care reported a better quality of life and were half as likely as those receiving standard care to have clinically significant depression symptoms. More surprisingly, they survived almost 3 months longer, despite having received less aggressive and costly medical treatment.

The palliative care approach and hospice services may not work for all, but for some it means an opportunity to die with dignity, free of pain and surrounded by loved ones. The next challenge may be to extend this philosophy of caring rather than curing to more children (Davies et al., 2007; Orloff & Huff, 2010). Many children who die of cancer and other terminal illnesses die in hospitals rather than at home, without palliative care, possibly because their doctors and parents cannot accept that the child is dying. Parents of dying children who do participate in palliative care are highly satisfied with it (Sheetz & Bowman, 2013).

For the Bereaved

Most bereaved individuals do not need psychological interventions to help them cope with death. They deal with this normal life transition on their own and with support from significant others and do not benefit much from therapy if they receive it (Mancini, Griffin, & Bonanno, 2012). More good can be done by aiming therapy at those bereaved children, adolescents, and adults who are experiencing or are likely to experience severe and persistent distress—complicated grief. Bereaved individuals at risk for complicated grief clearly benefit from cognitive behavioral therapy and other approaches aimed at preventing or treating debilitating grief (Boelen, van den Hout, & van Den Bout, 2013; Neimeyer & Currier, 2009; Rosner, Kruse, & Hagl, 2010).

Because death takes place in a family context, family therapy often makes good sense (Kissane et al., 2013). Interventions designed for the whole family can help bereaved parents and children communicate more openly and support one another. Family interventions can also help parents deal with their own emotional issues so that they can provide the warm and supportive parenting that can be so critical to their children's adjustment. This is well illustrated by a major study of the Family Bereavement Program, described in **Application Box 17.1**.

Mutual support or self-help groups are another option (Lieberman & Videka-Sherman, 1986; Murphy et al., 2003a).

Application 17.1

The Family Bereavement Program

The Family Bereavement Program is a successful intervention for families in which a parent has died (Sandler et al., 2003; Sandler, Ayers, et al., 2010; Sandler, Ma, et al., 2010). Children and adolescents ages 8 to 16 who had lost a parent and the surviving parent were randomly assigned to either the program or a control condition that involved self-study of books about grief. Program participants met for 14 sessions (2 individual and 12 group sessions for either parents, children, or adolescents). The aims of the program for children and adolescents included helping them interpret stressful events, use positive coping strategies, and find adaptive ways to express their grief. The aims for surviving parents were to help them deal with their mental health problems and maintain close parent–child relationships and effective discipline at home. A behavioral approach involving modeling and role-playing of target skills and homework assignments to apply skills was used.

A follow-up of child participants indicated that they showed a greater reduction in problematic grief symptoms 6 years later than control youth did (Sandler, Ma, et al., 2010). The program also decreased children's internalizing problems (depression, anxiety) and externalizing problems (acting out, aggression) and improved their self-esteem (Sandler, Ayers, et al., 2010). The program even had positive effects on children's stress response systems, as measured by their cortisol levels, 6 years later (Luecken et al., 2013).

The Family Bereavement Program was effective in part because it focused on the whole family. It reduced surviving parents' depression symptoms (Sandler, Ayers, et al., 2010). Moreover, it increased their warmth toward their children and use of effective discipline, effects on parenting that were still evident at the 6-year mark (Hagan et al., 2012). Overall, then, the program enabled surviving parents to do a better job of helping their children cope with their loss while strengthening the ability of children and adolescents to help themselves.

These days, of course, bereavement self-help groups are available online (Wagner, 2013). Examples of well-established self-help organizations with local chapters around the country are: The Compassionate Friends for parents whose children have died; the Widowed Persons Service for widows and widowers; and the National Alliance for Grieving Children. Support groups may offer everything from practical advice to emotional support and friendship. Sometimes other bereaved people are in the best position to understand what a bereaved person is going through and to offer effective social support. One widow summed it up this way: "What's helpful? Why, people who are in the 'same boat' " (Bankoff, 1983, p. 230).

Taking Our Leave

We have reached the end not only of the life span but of this book and want to leave you with a few parting words. Notice that the book's inside back cover provides a chart summarizing key developments in different periods of the life span; it will help you put the "whole person" back together again and see at a glance relationships among the domains of physical, cognitive, personal, and social development. Also notice the appendix on Careers in Human Development—a resource for those of you who think you may want to make a life of studying development or intervening to optimize it.

Finally, we leave you with a reminder of some of the themes echoed throughout this book, many of them part of the life-span perspective on development formulated by Paul Baltes (1987; see Chapter 1). We hope you can now think of many illustrations of each:

1. **Nature and Nurture Truly Interact in Development:** It's clear that both biology and environment, reciprocally influencing each other all the way, steer development.

2. **We Are Whole People throughout the Life Span:** Advances in one area of development (motor development, for example) have implications for other areas of development (cognitive development through exploration, for example); we must understand interrelationships among domains of development to understand whole human beings.

3. **Development Proceeds in Multiple Directions:** We experience gains and losses, along with changes that simply make us different than we were, at every age. We must reject the view that childhood is only gain—and old age only loss.

4. **There Is Both Continuity and Discontinuity in Development:** Each of us is at once "the same old person" and a new person, qualitatively different from the person who came before; development is also both gradual and stagelike.

5. **There Is Much Plasticity in Development:** We can change in response to experience at any age, getting off one developmental pathway and onto another. True, plasticity, both neural and behavioral, is greatest among infants and young children. However, aging adults also respond positively to interventions designed to improve their lives and their functioning.

6. **We Are Individuals, Becoming Even More Diverse with Age:** Developing humans are diverse from the start—and become even more diverse with age.

7. **We Develop in a Cultural and Historical Context:** Human development takes different forms in different times and cultures, in different socioeconomic and racial/ethnic groups, and in different social niches.

8. **We Are Active in Our Own Development:** We help create our environments, influence those around us, and, by doing so, contribute to our own development.

9. **Development Is a Lifelong Process:** We never stop developing, and our development during any one phase of life is

best understood in relation to what came before and what is to come.

10. **Development Is Best Viewed from Multiple Perspectives:** Many disciplines have something to contribute to a comprehensive understanding of human development—and we need them all.

We hope that you are intrigued enough by the mysteries of life-span human development to observe more closely your own development and that of those around you—or even to seek further course work and practical experience in the field. And we sincerely hope that you will use what you learn to steer your own and others' development in positive directions.

Checking Mastery

1. What are three key features of hospice care?
2. What are two approaches used to help bereaved individuals cope?

Making Connections

1. If you were in charge of developing policies and programs to help families deal with death and dying, what would you propose and why?
2. Which of the life-span development themes illustrated throughout this book can you detect in this chapter on death and dying?

Chapter Summary

17.1 Matters of Life and Death

- In defining death as a biological process, the Harvard definition of total brain death has been influential. Many controversies surround issues of active and passive euthanasia and assisted suicide, complicated by findings of higher brain functioning in some people who are supposedly in "vegetative states"; meanwhile, the social meanings of death vary widely.
- The average life expectancy for a newborn in the United States has risen to almost 79 years, higher than that in less developed countries; it varies by gender, race/ethnicity, and socioeconomic status. Death rates decline after infancy but rise in adulthood as accidents give way to chronic diseases as the primary causes of death.

17.2 The Experience of Death

- Elisabeth Kübler-Ross stimulated much concern for dying patients by describing five stages of dying, but, as Edwin Shneidman emphasized, dying people experience ever-changing emotions; their reactions also depend on the course of their disease and on their personality, and they include setting goals for living rather than just coping with dying.
- Bereavement precipitates grief and mourning; grief is expressed, according to the Parkes/Bowlby attachment model, in overlapping phases of numbness, yearning, disorganization and despair, and reorganization.
- The dual-process model describes oscillation between loss-oriented coping and restoration-oriented coping, each involving a mix of positive and negative emotions.

17.3 The Infant

- Infants may not comprehend death except as a form of "all gone," but, as John Bowlby noticed, they clearly grieve—protesting, despairing, and then detaching after separations from attachment figures.

17.4 The Child

- Children are curious about death and usually understand by age 5 to 7 that it is a final cessation of life functions that is irreversible and universal, later realizing that it is ultimately caused by internal biological changes.
- Terminally ill children often become very aware of their plight, and bereaved children may experience bodily symptoms, academic difficulties, and behavioral problems, especially if they lack a secure attachment and good parenting.

17.5 The Adolescent

- Adolescents understand death more abstractly than children do and typically develop a supernatural view of death that includes an afterlife but do not abandon their understanding of death's biological finality.
- They cope with dying and bereavement in ways that reflect the developmental themes of adolescence, and some develop psychological disorders after a significant loss.

17.6 The Adult

- Although George Bonanno's research suggests that around half of widows and widowers show resilience and the rest show different trajectories of grief reactions, on average widows and widowers experience physical, emotional, and cognitive symptoms for a year or more and are at increased risk of dying.
- The death of a child is often even more difficult for an adult to bear, whereas the death of a parent is often easier because it is more expected.

- The grief work perspective has been challenged. What is normal depends on the cultural context; many people display resilience, never doing "grief work" or paying with delayed grief because they did not; and many people benefit from continuing rather than severing their attachment bonds.
- Complicated grief is especially likely among individuals who have insecure attachment styles, who have neurotic personalities and limited coping skills, who had close and dependent relationships with individuals who died violently and senselessly, and who lack social support or face additional stressors.
- When grief is significant but not crushing, bereaved individuals often report postraumatic growth.

17.7 Taking the Sting Out of Death

- Successful efforts to take the sting out of death have included hospices and other forms of palliative care for dying patients and their families and individual therapy, family therapy, and mutual support groups for the bereaved.
- Themes of this book include many themes that are part of the life-span perspective on development formulated by Paul Baltes and introduced in Chapter 1.

Checking Mastery Answers

For answers to Checking Mastery questions, please see Appendix B.

Key Terms

total brain death **538**	mourning **546**	disenfranchised grief **556**
euthanasia **539**	anticipatory grief **546**	complicated grief **556**
assisted suicide **539**	Parkes/Bowlby attachment model of	grief work perspective **557**
living will **540**	bereavement **546**	continuing bonds **558**
denial **544**	dual-process model of bereavement **547**	posttraumatic growth **561**
bereavement **546**	loss-oriented coping **547**	hospice **561**
grief **546**	restoration-oriented coping **547**	palliative care **561**

Appendix: A Careers in Human Development

What career possibilities exist for students interested in understanding or optimizing human development? Being developmentalists ourselves, we would argue that anyone who works with people can benefit from an understanding of life-span human development. We are not alone in our belief: Preparation for many "people" professions—teaching, counseling, and nursing and other allied health professions—includes coursework in human development. Indeed, some of you are taking this course because it is required for your chosen career.

If you think you are interested in a career in human development, you might first ask yourself some basic questions:

- What *level of education* do you seek—bachelor's, master's, or doctoral?
- Are you interested in a particular *age group*—infants, children, adolescents, adults, elderly people?
- Are you interested in a particular *aspect of development*—physical, cognitive, or social development, normal or abnormal development?
- Are you most interested in *research, teaching,* or *practice* (work as a helping professional of some kind)?

We will sketch out some career possibilities within the broad areas of research, teaching, and professional practice, illustrating as we go how the level of education you seek and the age groups and aspects of development of interest to you come into play. Much information is drawn from the U.S. Bureau of Labor Statistics's *Occupational Outlook Handbook* (see Resources list at end of this appendix), available online; you may want to consult it to learn more about the employment outlook and average salaries in some of the professions discussed.

Research

Depending on what level of authority and responsibility you seek, you can conduct research on human development with a bachelor's degree, master's degree (typically 2 years of coursework and either a comprehensive examination or completion of a thesis), or doctoral degree (typically 5–7 years of work, including courses, a qualifying or comprehensive exam, and completion of a doctoral dissertation research project). Research on normal life-span development and aging, abnormal development, and genetic and environmental influences on development is conducted in a variety of settings:

- colleges and universities
- medical schools, hospitals, and other healthcare facilities
- government institutes and agencies (for example, the National Institutes of Health, including the National Institute of Child Health and Human Development and the National Institute on Aging, and state and local health and human services agencies)

- social research organizations (some of the larger ones that conduct research on children, families, aging, and social policy are Abt Associates, SRI International, Mathematica, MDRC, RAND, and Westat)
- other for-profit and nonprofit organizations

With a bachelor's degree, you could be hired as a research assistant, interviewer, or other member of a research team and might work on research tasks such as reviewing literature, conducting telephone surveys, testing children, observing and coding behavior, analyzing physiological data, and compiling tables and graphs. With additional work experience—or with a master's degree in a relevant field such as developmental psychology, including coursework in research methods and statistics—you would become eligible for positions of greater responsibility. For example, you might be hired as the project coordinator for an investigator's study, responsible for implementing the data collection plan and supervising the work of research assistants, or you might become a specialist in testing infants, administering tasks to elderly adults, or analyzing data.

Finally, with a doctor of philosophy (PhD) degree in developmental psychology or a related field, you would qualify to be a principal investigator and head a research team—to be the one who designs research projects, submits research proposals to the federal government or foundations to obtain funding, guides implementation of the study, supervises the research staff, analyzes data, writes up findings, and submits papers for publication in professional journals (publications that are then cited in textbooks like this one). Because research is conducted in so many settings, your options as a PhD include many besides becoming a college or university professor who combines teaching and research. And the topics you can study are as wide ranging as those in this book.

How can you get a start on a career in human development research now? You might ask professors at your college or university about graduate programs and job opportunities in areas of development that interest you. Seek as much research experience as you can get, too:

- Ask your professors whether they need help with their research and be on the lookout for notices about research projects that need student assistants on either a voluntary or paid basis.
- Sign up for an independent study course that would allow you to conduct a literature review or do a research project with guidance from a professor.
- Seek undergraduate research fellowships that might allow you to do a research project with financial support, possibly a summer living stipend; some colleges and universities offer such research fellowships not only to their own students but also to students from other universities (for example, through the National Science Foundation's Research Experiences for Undergraduates program).

- Do a senior thesis or capstone project if it is an option in your major.
- If you are seeking work, look for jobs that involve research, program evaluation, or policy analysis; even if the research is not directly related to human development, you may learn useful research skills.
- Attend campus lectures and professional conferences to gain exposure to researchers in your area of interest and hear about the latest research they are conducting.
- Use PsycInfo and other online databases to find out who is doing good research of interest to you and at what universities.

These sorts of activities will help you find out whether you like research and what aspects of it you like (or don't). They will also help you acquire research skills, get to know professors who can write reference letters for you and otherwise help you pursue your career plans, and demonstrate to graduate programs or employers that you are interested in research and have some experience with it. Increasingly, admission to doctoral programs requires experience assisting with research, presenting papers at professional conferences, or even publishing articles with professors.

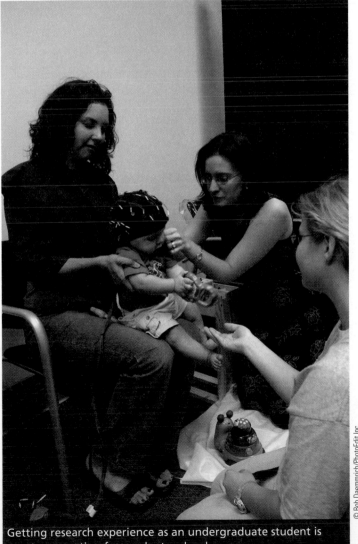

Getting research experience as an undergraduate student is great preparation for graduate school.

© Bob Daemmrich/PhotoEdit Inc.

Some students seek paid research staff positions after completing their bachelor's degree, do well, and work their way up to more responsible positions. Others work for a while and go on for an advanced degree after they have gained some experience. Others enter master's programs, and still others who are certain they want a research career apply directly to doctoral programs as college seniors. In most graduate programs, students gain hands-on experience by serving as research assistants for professors while they are taking courses; they then draw on this apprenticeship experience in designing and conducting a master's thesis or doctoral dissertation project of their own.

Teaching

Teachers clearly need to understand the developmental characteristics and learning capacities of their students to teach effectively and make a difference in their students' lives. As a result, coursework in human development is a required part of teacher training at the bachelor's and master's levels. Colleges of education offer teacher preparation programs in preschool or early childhood, kindergarten, elementary school, middle school, secondary school, and adult education; in the teaching of specific subjects such as English or science; and in special education (the teaching of students with developmental disabilities, behavior disorders, and other special learning needs). Teachers normally need to complete a teacher education program leading to a bachelor's or master's degree and then obtain certification from the state in which they will teach by demonstrating that they have taken the required coursework and passing a standardized teacher exam.

To teach at the college or university level, a doctoral degree, usually a doctor of philosophy (PhD) degree, is normally required. Much of what we said earlier about doctoral education for researchers applies to doctoral education for professors. Most PhD programs are highly research-oriented and involve learning both about the field through coursework and how to contribute to the field through research. Some community colleges hire professors with master's degrees in certain areas but more and more hire only PhDs. In schools of education, either a PhD or an EdD (doctor of education) can qualify an individual for a faculty position; the PsyD degree, discussed later, prepares people to be practicing psychologists and is not the right choice for those interested primarily in research and teaching positions.

Students may get the impression that their professors do nothing but teach, but the job description of a faculty member often includes not only teaching and advising students but also conducting research and providing service to the college or university (for example, through committee work or administrative positions such as department chair or program director) as well as to the local community and profession (for example, by consulting with local nonprofit organizations or schools, by serving as a reviewer for a journal that publishes research in one's field, or as an officer in a professional organization). Specific responsibilities vary considerably depending on the type of institution. Generally, teaching responsibilities are heavy and research responsibilities are light at a community college, whereas research may be the first and foremost responsibility of a professor at a large research university, who may teach only a course or two a semester. Large universities also appoint some PhDs as "research professors," who typically support their salaries by getting grants from the federal government and other sources and spend virtually all their time doing research.

If you are considering applying to doctoral programs, we strongly recommend that you do serious research to identify programs that are a good fit to your interests and qualifications. Doctoral-level training in human development can be found in a bewildering array of departments, schools, centers, and institutes within universities. The American Psychological Association's (2012) publication *Graduate Study in Psychology* is an excellent resource for students seeking a graduate program in developmental psychology (typically located in a psychology department), human development (typically an interdisciplinary program located in its own department or even school), family studies (also interdisciplinary, sometimes part of a larger "human development and family studies" or "family and consumer sciences" program), educational psychology (in either schools of education or psychology departments), or gerontology (also often interdisciplinary and sometimes based in a center or institute).

Most professors who teach human development or aging did their doctoral work in either psychology or education, but some departments of sociology and anthropology around the country also have strength in the study of families or aging. Moreover, graduate programs in biology often have faculty who specialize in developmental biology, and neuroscience and cognitive neuroscience programs often have specialists in developmental neuroscience, developmental disabilities, dementia, and other topics relevant to development and aging. The more you know about your own research and teaching interests, the better; you will then be able to seek programs in the right field that have scholars whose interests match yours and can apply to particular programs because you want to work with specific professors there. Professors in research-oriented doctoral programs typically select students who share their research interests and want to work with them. Doctoral programs are highly competitive, but many doctoral students have their education paid for by fellowships and teaching and research assistantships.

Professional Practice

By *professional practice* we mean the use of knowledge of human development to optimize development and functioning. Opportunities for professional practice are even more varied than those for research and teaching.

Pre-Bachelor's- or Bachelor's-Level Positions

If you decide you want to enter one of the many helping professions, it makes sense to seek applied experience while you are completing your bachelor's degree or afterward—for example, through unpaid or paid internships or jobs in counseling centers, hospitals, human services agencies, treatment facilities for children or adolescents, or senior centers or nursing homes, depending on your interests (Landrum, 2009). This is a great way to gauge your interests and abilities and develop skills. Some

relevant jobs available to individuals with a bachelor's degree or less include:

- **Child care worker:** The pay is not good, but individuals who love working with children can, with a bachelor's degree or less, work in day care and preschool facilities, before- and after-school programs, camps and recreation programs, and residential programs for disturbed children (U.S. Bureau of Labor Statistics, 2013).
- **Social and human service assistant:** Countless entry-level positions in human services, mental health, and health care are available, carrying diverse titles such as case management aide, community outreach worker, residential counselor, life skills counselor, and gerontology aide. Social and human service assistants assist psychologists, nurses, social workers, and other professionals in hospitals, mental health centers and facilities, and government agencies, performing such tasks as assessing client needs, conducting intake interviews, keeping case records, processing paperwork, teaching life skills, supervising clients in residential facilities, and leading group or family sessions.

Some human service workers organize and lead activities at senior day care centers and residential facilities for elderly adults. Here an aide helps an elderly woman at the On Lok Senior Health Service in San Francisco.

© Ronnie Kaufman/Corbis

- **Social and community service manager:** A bachelor's degree, especially if combined with work experience, may qualify an individual to manage a social service program or community outreach organization, setting policies and practices, overseeing the budget, supervising staff, and so on (U.S. Bureau of Labor Statistics, 2013). Fundraising is often part of the job description in nonprofit organizations that depend on grants and donations for their survival.

Most of the following career options require graduate coursework in areas such as assessment and treatment approaches; supervised practicum and internship experiences in which learning is put to practice; and the passing of an examination after completion of studies in order to be licensed or certified by a state to practice.

Applied Developmental Psychologist

If you want to be squarely in the field of human development and have a positive impact on development but do not want to become a therapist or a counselor, you might look into master's or doctoral programs in applied developmental psychology, a fairly new subfield of psychology, or in the broader, multidisciplinary field of applied developmental science. Although many graduate programs in developmental psychology, human development, and family studies engage in real-world, policy-relevant research, applied developmental psychology programs make a point of it. Applied developmental psychologists may be trained to conduct research on practical problems such as improving early childhood education, supporting at-risk families, or reducing childhood injuries; assess the developmental status of infants and children; design, implement, and evaluate interventions aimed at preventing or treating problems such as alcohol and drug abuse, aggression, or abusive parenting; and consult or serve as expert witnesses in juvenile court proceedings, custody hearings, and the like. After earning a doctorate, applied developmental psychologists may seek a license to practice psychology as a scientist-practitioner; they must obtain the required supervised field experience and pass a licensure examination (Kuther & Morgan, 2013).

Counselor, Psychologist, or Therapist

Now consider some options if you want to provide counseling or psychotherapy to individuals or families as a state-licensed or certified psychologist. Wearing the title "psychologist" generally requires doctoral-level training in the United States. Individuals with master's degrees in fields such as clinical or counseling psychology are needed in mental health centers and facilities, but they are hired as "psychological assistants" or "psychological associates" and must be supervised by doctoral-level psychologists or psychiatrists (see U.S. Bureau of Labor Statistics, 2013). There are three types of doctoral-level, practicing psychologists.

Clinical Psychologist

Clinical psychologists are trained to diagnose and treat individuals with psychological disorders. Child clinical psychologists focus their practice and research on infants, children, and adolescents. Pediatric psychologists, who sometimes obtain their degrees in health psychology programs, focus on child health care, often working in medical schools, hospitals, and other health-care facilities. Still other clinical psychologists, now called clinical geropsychologists, specialize in treatment of elderly people.

Becoming a clinical psychologist normally requires earning either a PhD or a PsyD (the doctor of psychology degree, a more practice-oriented and less research-oriented degree than the PhD). You should decide whether you want to be primarily a scientist, primarily a practitioner, or a scientist-practitioner who integrates the two roles and then look closely at the extent to which a program of interest is practice-oriented versus research-oriented. You should also understand that clinical psychology programs are extremely selective, requiring high grades, high scores on the Graduate Record Examinations (GREs), relevant experience, and excellent recommendations.

Counseling Psychologist

Counseling psychologists may earn a PhD, EdD, or PsyD. Like clinical psychologists they qualify to be licensed as psychologists. Compared with clinical psychologists, though, they tend to emphasize optimizing mental health and more often work with everyday problems of adjustment (for example, as a counselor in a college or university, company, or community mental health center).

School Psychologist

After completing either an education specialist (EdS) degree (which requires about 3 years of study and a yearlong internship) or a PhD, EdD, or PsyD in school psychology, a school psychologist is prepared to use IQ tests and other assessment instruments to evaluate students believed to have learning disabilities or other special educational needs, consult with teachers and parents on how best to educate them, and provide other supportive psychological services in schools.

Now consider some additional possibilities for careers in counseling and therapy, some of which do not require doctoral-level education.

Psychiatrist

Becoming a psychiatrist involves earning a doctor of medicine (MD) degree and choosing psychiatry as one's specialty; job descriptions and employment opportunities are much like those of clinical psychologists, but psychiatrists can prescribe medications for psychological disorders.

Counselor

A wide range of counseling programs exist in psychology departments, schools of education, and human development and family studies programs. Many provide opportunities for independent practice after earning a master's degree and passing a state licensing examination. Subareas of counseling

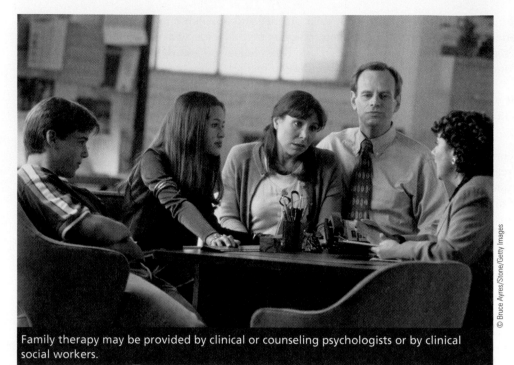
Family therapy may be provided by clinical or counseling psychologists or by clinical social workers.

© Bruce Ayres/Stone/Getty Images

bachelor's, master's, and even doctoral programs in gerontology (see Association for Gerontology in Higher Education under Resources). Services for older adults are varied and are expanding, providing plenty of opportunities for individuals with bachelor's and master's degrees. Our society clearly needs more individuals in a variety of disciplines and professions who care about and have expertise in aging.

Health Professionals

Let's briefly note that a wide range of careers in medicine and allied health professions offer opportunities to apply knowledge of human development and aging to practice. Physicians can focus their careers on newborns, children, adolescents, or elderly adults, as they choose, selecting specialties such as pediatrics or geriatrics in medical school and seeking positions that allow them to work with the age groups and health problems of greatest interest to them. Similarly, nurses can become hospice or palliative care nurses who work with terminally ill patients, developmental disabilities nurses, or psychiatric nurses—or can specialize in the care of a particular age group. Other allied health professions such as speech therapy, physical therapy, and occupational therapy also allow for specialization in particular age groups and type of problems.

include school counseling (which may involve helping students who have academic or personal problems or, at the secondary school level, helping high school students plan their futures), career counseling, rehabilitation counseling (work in the vocational rehabilitation field helping adults with disabilities adapt to their disabilities and find appropriate jobs), substance abuse or addiction counseling, mental health or community counseling, marriage and family therapy, genetic counseling, gerontological counseling, and more (see U.S. Bureau of Labor Statistics, 2013, on Counselors).

Social Worker

Careers in social work normally require at least a master's degree in social work (MSW). Specialties include child, family, and school social work; medical and public health social work; and mental health or clinical social work (U.S. Bureau of Labor Statistics, 2013). Some social workers are employed by human services agencies as caseworkers who work with families on welfare, neglected or abused children and their families, or aging adults and their families; medical social workers are based in healthcare facilities and support patients and their families. Clinical social workers are trained in diagnosing personal and family problems and in providing counseling and therapy. Clinical social workers with an MSW can practice independently, whereas psychologists must have a doctoral degree to do so.

Given the steady growth of the aging population, career opportunities for psychologists, counselors, and social workers with training in gerontology are likely to expand. A number of universities offer certificates or minors in gerontology that students can combine with any number of academic majors to position themselves to work with elderly people; other universities offer

Other Options

Finally, we need an "Other" category to say that individuals with training in developmental psychology, counseling, and other human development fields land in surprising places. Many people who enter the occupations we have discussed here advance to become administrators; for example, a teacher may become a principal, a psychologist, counselor, or social worker may become the director of a treatment facility or human service agency. Some of these helping professionals seek further education relevant to their administrative roles (for example, a master's degree in business administration, public administration, or heath care management); others simply take on higher administrative roles and learn on the job.

People with training in human development also find their way into business and industry. One may become a book editor in a company that publishes books on psychology; another may test toys or other products for children; another may advise a company's employees on retirement issues. Many also work as self-employed consultants, offering help to agencies, organizations, and businesses in areas in which they have expertise. ● **Table A.1** summarizes some of the career options we have discussed.

• **Table A.1** Some Career Options in Human Development

Degree Required	Research	Teaching	Professional Practice
Bachelor's or master's degree	Research assistant Research staff member Project coordinator	Teacher's aide Teacher in preschool, elementary, secondary, or adult education	Child care worker Social and human services worker Psychological assistant or associate Social worker* School psychologist*
Doctoral degree	Professor or research professor Principal investigator in university, hospital, health or mental health facility, research organization	Professor (e.g., of developmental psychology, human development, family studies, clinical or counseling psychology, or social work)	Applied developmental psychologist Clinical psychologist Counseling psychologist Psychiatrist Counselor Health professional (medicine, allied health)

* Master's degree required.

We hope this is enough to get you thinking and dreaming—and, better yet, taking concrete steps now to gain the knowledge, skills, and experience that will help you formulate and realize your dream. We are confident that the need for individuals who understand the complexities and marvels of life-span human development and can steer it in healthy directions will remain strong as long as humans develop and age.

Resources

American Psychological Association. The APA website, www.apa.org, has information and publications about careers in psychology, including a short overview of the different types of jobs psychologists hold at: www.apa.org/careers/resources/guides/careers.aspx.

American Psychological Association. (2012). *Graduate study in psychology: 2013 Edition.* Washington, DC: American Psychological Association. This invaluable guide for students looking for appropriate graduate programs profiles more than 600 graduate programs in the United States and Canada, noting program emphases, admission standards, information about the employment of graduates, and the like.

Association for Gerontology in Higher Education. This organization's website, www.aghe.org, lists member universities and provides other resources on educational programs and job opportunities in gerontology and geriatrics. It published a *Directory of educational programs in gerontology and geriatrics* in 2009.

Careers in Aging. This website, http://www.careersinaging.com/careersinaging/job_career.html, although dated, orients students to career opportunities in gerontology and geriatrics.

GradSchools.com. This website allows you to search for graduate programs at the master's and doctoral levels in various fields and link to the web pages of those programs efficiently. The web address is http://GradSchools.com.

JobWeb.com. This site of the National Association of Colleges and Employers is aimed at new college graduates and provides useful guidance on resume preparation and job search strategies, as well as job listings. The web address is www.JobWeb.com.

Kuther, T. L. (2012). *The psychology major's handbook* (3rd ed.). Belmont, CA: Cengage Learning. A good general guide to succeeding as a psychology major and preparing for graduate school and careers available with a bachelor's degree. (It can be read online but not reproduced.)

Kuther, T. L., & Morgan, R. D. (2013). *Careers in psychology: Opportunities in a changing world* (4th ed.). Belmont, CA: Cengage Learning. A survey of opportunities in the various subfields of psychology, along with advice on applying to graduate school and seeking jobs.

Landrum, R. R. (2009). *Finding jobs with a psychology bachelor's degree: Expert advice for launching your career.* Washington, DC: American Psychological Association. Professionals in a wide range of careers describe their jobs, how a bachelor's degree in psychology helped them in their careers, and how to search for jobs.

U. S. Bureau of Labor Statistics. (2013). *Occupational outlook handbook, 2012–13.* A huge but wonderful government resource describing, for all major occupational fields, the nature of the work involved, working conditions, training and other qualifications, employment data, job prospects, and average earnings; includes sections on Psychologists and Counselors. It is updated yearly and available free at www.bls.gov/ooh.

Wegenek, A. R., & Buskist, W. (2010). *The insider's guide to the psychology major: Everything you need to know about the degree and profession.* Washington, DC: American Psychological Association. This guide aims to help psychology majors get the most out of their education and position themselves for careers in psychology.

Appendix B: Checking Mastery Answers

Chapter 1

Section 1.1

1. Whereas biological aging refers to the biological deterioration of the organism leading to death, aging refers to positive as well as negative changes in a range of areas (physical, cognitive, psychosocial) in mature organisms.
2. An age grade is an age group with certain rights and responsibilities; an age norm is an expectation about how to behave if you are at a certain age.

Section 1.2

1. Description: How often do children behave in helpful ways? Prediction: What is the relationship between gender and helpfulness? Explanation: What causes gender differences in helpfulness? Optimization: Would modeling helpful behavior increase children's helpfulness?
2. Life-span perspective assumptions 4 (plasticity is about the effects of environmental influences), 5 (the historical-cultural context is an aspect of the environment), and 6 (development is influenced by multiple factors, both biological and environmental).

Section 1.3

1. In this experiment, students would be randomly assigned to two groups in order to manipulate the independent variable, study approach. One group would be required to read a chapter in one long session, the other group would be required to read each section of the chapter and then take a short break before reading the next section. All other differences in treatment of the two groups would be kept the same through experimental control. The effect of the independent variable, study approach, on the dependent variable, performance on a test covering the chapter, would be assessed.
2. In a longitudinal study as opposed to cross-sectional study, you would learn about age changes (not just age differences); you would be able to correlate self-esteem at age 18 with self-esteem at age 22 in a group to determine whether it is a consistent characteristic; you could look at differences between individuals in their trajectories of change over their college careers; and you could examine relationships between early experiences with parents or other factors (if you ask about them) and later self-esteem.

Section 1.4

1. If they do not try to overcome their ethnocentrism, researchers can make the mistake of viewing cultural and subcultural groups that are different as deficient and as all alike.

2. The researcher must debrief the participants afterward about the true purpose of the study and ensure that they do not leave feeling upset about how they behaved. In this study, the researcher might also need to be concerned about protection of participants from harm if some are stressed during the experience or upset afterward.

Chapter 2

Section 2.1

1. Discontinuity can mean changing abruptly rather than gradually or it can mean changing qualitatively (in kind) rather than quantitatively (in degree). Stage theorists are likely to believe that nature is important (nurture may be important too, but stages are generally guided by maturation), that development is discontinuous (stages are distinct from each other), and that development has at least some universal characteristics (all people progress through the same stages).

Section 2.2

1. The moral side of the personality is the superego and arises in the phallic stage at about age 3–6 when a child resolves the Oedipal or Electra complex by identifying with the same sex parent; the selfish side is the id and it is there from birth.
2. The girl experiencing an Electra complex is said to desire her father and be fearful of retaliation by her mother. She resolves her dilemma by identifying with her mother, developing a feminine gender role and a superego.
3. Freud's theory is recognized for calling attention to the importance of unconscious processes, early experience, and emotions in development (any of the three themes can be considered "right"), but there is little support for his ideas about the Oedipal/Electra conflict and children fantasizing about sexual seduction by their parents.

Section 2.3

1. Compared to Freud, Erikson placed more emphasis on (1) social influences, (2) the rational ego, (3) the potential for overcoming early problems, and (4) the whole life span.
2. If Wanda's parents were unreliable and unresponsive to her needs during infancy, she may not have resolved the trust vs. mistrust issue appropriately and may not trust other people to care about her. If her parents were punitive when she tried to assert herself and do things independently as a toddler, she may not have resolved the conflict of autonomy vs. shame and doubt satisfactorily, which would explain her self doubts.

Section 2.4

1. The consequences applied by these parents are (a) positive reinforcement intended to increase chore performance, (b) negative punishment intended to reduce staying out too late (by taking away hours allowed out on the weekend), and (c) negative reinforcement to increase spending time with grandma (which allows her to avoid unpleasant bathroom cleaning duty).
2. Bandura would charge that behavioral learning theories (a) ignore the important roles of cognition in human learning, (b) fail to appreciate the importance of observational learning, and (c) do not put enough emphasis on the person (and therefore biological influences), which is part of his concept of reciprocal determinism involving person, behavior, and environment.

Section 2.5

1. Concrete operations are mental actions on tangible objects (as in mentally adding and subtracting cookies); formal operations are mental actions on hypothetical ideas or abstract concepts (as in thinking about the general processes of addition and subtraction).
2. Vygotsky's sociocultural perspective claims that Piaget put too little emphasis on the role of the social environment (culture, mentors) in cognitive development; the information-processing approach to cognition emphasizes mental processes like attention and memory and influences on them more than Piaget, who emphasized knowledge or understanding.

Section 2.6

1. An event in the exosystem (here, the mother's workplace) could make her child's environment better by making the mother happier and more confident.
2. Bronfenbrenner saw nature (the person's biological and psychological characteristics) and environment (the various environmental systems) as having mutual or reciprocal influence on one another.

Section 2.7

1. Stands on nature–nurture have changed from (a) Freud's emphasis on biological forces to (b) Skinner's emphasis on environmental influences to (c) Bronfenbrenner's insistence that both are important and "co-act" to shape development.
2. Only Erikson proposes specific new developments during the adult years.

Chapter 3

Section 3.1

1. Biological evolution will make humans better adapted to the particular environment in which they live. (However, genes that are selected by natural selection because they enhance survival in one environment may prove maladaptive in another.)
2. For evolution to work, there must be genetic variation (some members of the species must have different genes than others) and some genes must aid in adaptation, and therefore be passed on to future generations, more than others.
3. Humans are able to learn how to solve problems they face (like keeping warm) and to communicate what they learn (for example, how to build furnaces) to future generations.

Section 3.2

1. Nature: By the luck of the draw (which parent chromosomes end up in a particular zygote), fraternal twins may inherit far less than 50% of the same genes. Nurture: Their prenatal or postnatal environments could have differed, and these differences in experience could have affected them either directly or through environmental effects on gene expression. Examples: One was positioned more favorable in the womb and got more nourishment, one was favored by parents.
2. If the gene is dominant (*H*), 75% or three of four of the couple's children would be expected to have Hairy Forehead Syndrome (only the child with an *hh* genotype will not). If the gene is recessive (*h*), the couple has only a 25% chance of having a child with the *hh* genotype and the syndrome.
3. Red–green color blindness is sex-linked and the recessive gene for it is on the X chromosome. A boy gets his X from his mother, so Juan's mother *must* be a carrier of the color-blindness gene (but would be color blind herself only if she has a second color blindness gene). Juan's father may or may not have the gene (and would be color blind like Juan if he did).

Section 3.3

1. In this example, genes are important because identical twins are more similar in frequency of marijuana use than fraternal twins; shared environment is important because both types of twins are more alike when raised together than when raised apart, and nonshared environment is somewhat important too because we see some dissimilarity between identical twins raised together (.70 is less than 1.00).
2. Adopted children can be affected not only by their biological parents' genes but also by the prenatal environment their biological mother provided before they were adopted away; they may be placed in homes similar to those they were adopted from; and they are typically placed in above-average environments (so adoption studies may underestimate the full effects of good and bad environments).
3. Molecular genetics research can help identify which genes are responsible for the findings of twin studies (for example, researchers can scan the genomes of people with and without a psychological disorder of interest to see which specific genes distinguish between them).

Section 3.4

1. Research suggests that about 40% of the variation among people in extraversion-introversion will be attributable to genetic differences, 55% to nonshared environmental influences, and only 5% to shared environmental influences.
2. The odds are about 50%, or one in two, that Alan will develop schizophrenia since both biological parents have it—but the quality of the home environment his adoptive parents provide may increase or decrease his odds.

Section 3.5

1. passive gene—environment correlation
2. epigenetic effects
3. active gene—environment correlation
4. gene—environment interaction
5. evocative gene—environment correlation

Chapter 4

Section 4.1

1. Conception occurs when a single sperm penetrates an ovum (or egg cell), quickly creating a zygote containing the 46 chromosomes that are the blueprint for that individual's life. There are several Assisted Reproductive Technologies (ARTs) that are used to assist conception. These include drugs to stimulate the release of eggs, artificial insemination, and in vitro fertilization.
2. The brain and nervous system undergo dramatic change during the embryonic and fetal periods. From the interior of the primitive blastocyst, the ectoderm layer of cells gives rise to the brain and nervous system. The ectoderm folds into the neural tube and buds emerge at the top of this tube that will become the brain and the spinal cord emerges from the bottom of the tube. During the fetal period, neurons proliferate (multiply), migrate, and differentiate into what they will finally become.
3. The age of viability is reached at around 23–24 weeks of gestation and is influenced by many factors. Those infants surviving such early arrivals may experience serious health complications.

Section 4.2

1. Teratogens have their greatest impact during the critical period when an organ is emerging or rapidly developing; the effects depend on how much and for how long the fetus is exposed; the genetic makeup of both the unborn baby and the mother influence susceptibility to harmful effects of teratogens; and the quality of the prenatal and postnatal environments can influence the outcome of teratogens.
2. Alcohol consumption during pregnancy, particularly if heavy and/or prolonged, can lead to fetal alcohol syndrome, a collection of physical and neurological problems with lifelong effects. Problems among children whose mothers drank during pregnancy include cognitive delays, attention deficit disorder, and conduct disorders.
3. Babies born to mothers who smoked throughout their pregnancies are more likely to be born premature and with low birth weight. They may experience respiratory problems as infants and behavioral problems as children. Some research shows that they are at greater risk for neurological problems that impede cognitive development.

Section 4.3

1. Childbirth begins with regular contractions of the uterus that eventually cause the woman's cervix to dilate or widen so the baby's head can pass through. The second stage of childbirth is the actual delivery of the baby from the mother's body, and the final stage of childbirth is the expulsion of the placenta from the mother's body.
2. The birth process may pose risks for the baby if the flow of oxygen is cut off or if the baby is not in the head-down position that facilitates delivery. A prolonged labor can stress the unborn baby and lead to a cesarean section delivery. Some medications administered to the mother for pain may also affect the birth experience.

Section 4.4

1. Two important actions to ensure a good start to life include breastfeeding and identifying newborns who might be at risk for problems.
2. Some babies seem to have more personal resources, such as "good genes" for traits that allow them to surmount difficulties. In addition, at-risk infants who grow up in a supportive postnatal environment are more likely to overcome negative events of the prenatal or perinatal periods.

Chapter 5

Section 5.1

1. The endocrine system consists of a set of glands that secrete chemicals called hormones directly into the bloodstream. One of these is the pituitary gland, which produces growth hormone and is involved in triggering the release of hormones from other glands. Thus, the pituitary gland is involved in development both directly through its production of growth hormone and indirectly through its influence on the other glands of the endocrine system.
2. Myelination speeds up neural "communication" and proceeds in a predictable order from the spinal cord to hindbrain, midbrain, and then forebrain. Behaviors associated with activity in the forebrain (for example, attention) will emerge or mature later than behaviors associated with activity in areas of the brain that become myelinated earlier.
3. An example of cephalocaudal (head to tail) growth is that the head is proportionately the largest part of the body at birth. Proximodistal (center outward) development can be seen in the ability to control large muscle groups at the center of the body—the torso—earlier than small muscle groups at the extremities.

Section 5.2

1. The young brain undergoes synaptogenesis, or growth of synapses (connections between neurons), as well as synaptic pruning, the weeding out of unused or unnecessary synapses. In addition, the brain shows a great deal of plasticity early in life; that is, it is responsive to a person's experiences.
2. The sucking reflex allows infants to gain nourishment and the blinking reflex protects the eyes.
3. Establishing a regular sleep–wake cycle can show that infants are integrating external signals with internal brain function. Spending more time in REM sleep may help infants process the deluge of new information they are exposed to on a daily basis.

Section 5.3

1. Activity within the two hemispheres of the brain is typically complementary but specialized. For most people, the left hemisphere supports sequential processing, language, and logic, whereas the right hemisphere supports simultaneous processing, creativity, and intuitive reasoning.
2. Unintentional injuries are a major cause of death during childhood. Nutrition and physical activity are important components of health.
3. Schools and parents can provide a variety of healthy, tasty foods. It is also important that they model healthy eating habits.

Section 5.4

1. A heightened period of synaptogenesis and pruning seems to occur at the start of puberty, which may help explain the poor judgment and risk-taking that we may observe among teenagers.
2. Experience with the process of puberty will be influenced by many individual as well as cultural factors. But, in general, early-maturing boys are perceived as being more mature and competent, and are often admired by their peers. This can make them feel good about themselves, but can also lead to earlier involvement with risky behaviors. For girls, those maturing later often outperform their peers academically and stay focused on academics for a longer period of time. Early-maturing girls are at greater risk for hanging out with older peers and engaging in risky behaviors that can have far-reaching consequences.
3. Timing of menarche is influenced by genetic factors, body weight (in particular, how much body fat a girl has), nutrition, and strenuous physical activity. Girls tend to mature at about the same age as the other women in their family. They mature earlier if they are heavier, well nourished, and do not engage in strenuous physical activity. Lack of body fat and/or poor nutrition as well as regular hard physical workouts can delay menarche.

Section 5.5

1. With old age come some physical changes, including slowing down of neural transmissions, which may lead to slower reaction times. Still, the aging brain, if stimulated by regular mental activity, can remain agile.
2. Programmed theories of aging emphasize predictable, genetically-based sources of aging, whereas random error theories of aging emphasize haphazard damage to the body that accumulates over a person's life.
3. From the "Nun" Study, we know there is a connection between level of education and later health. Further, those nuns who were active both physically and mentally lived longer and were healthier than less active nuns. Further, nuns who had a more positive attitude had fewer ailments when they were old. Nuns who exhibited greater depth in their vocabulary at a young age tended to have higher mental functioning when they were old than nuns who stuck with relatively simple vocabulary.

Chapter 6

Section 6.1

1. Perception is the interpretation of the information that is detected by the sensory receptors. Sensation is the "raw material" and perception is the meaningful interpretation of this material.
2. Constructivists believe perception is constructed from our learning experiences, whereas nativists believe perception stems from innate capabilities and does not need to be created from our experiences. Thus, the constructivists represent the nurture side of the nature–nurture issue and the nativists represent the nature side of the issue.
3. Gibson's theory considers how the organization of the environment influences how we understand what we encounter in the world around us. In particular, Gibson's theory proposes that information important for perception is readily and directly available in the environment: in the to-be-perceived objects. Thus, we do not need to construct an understanding of these objects.

Section 6.2

1. Researchers may habituate an infant to a stimulus by repeatedly presenting it until the infant becomes bored and stops attending to it. They then present a different stimulus and the infant's response to this new stimulus provides information about whether the infant can perceive the difference. Alternatively, researchers can present two stimuli at the same time and infer preference by noting the amount of time the infant attends to each of the stimuli.
2. Infants see best those objects that are relatively close to their face (within 8–12 inches), have sharp contrast (for example, black and white or bold colors), and are moderately complex. They are also attracted to objects that move, as long as the movement is not too slow or too fast.
3. Normal visual perception requires opportunities for visual stimulation as well as experience regarding how visual input is influenced by one's actions, especially the relationship between moving about the environment and the visual stimulation that results.

Section 6.3

1. Children master walking by integrating perception with action. They use feedback from their bodies to figure out how they can efficiently and safely move through their environment. The shift to walking offers toddlers the opportunity to engage with their environments in new ways. They are no longer restricted to objects that are close by and close to the ground and their hands are freed up to interact with objects.
2. Cross-modal perception allows for more efficient and robust perceptual skills as children can coordinate information gained through one sense with information gained through another.
3. Attention during childhood becomes longer, more selective, and more systematic, allowing children to focus more deliberatively on chosen tasks.

Section 6.4

1. Adolescents are at risk for long-term hearing loss if they are regularly exposed to loud noises, as might occur when operating loud machinery or attending music concerts without ear protection, or regularly listening to music with in-ear headphones that deliver loud sound directly to the ears.
2. Adolescents are more likely than children to show acquired tastes, that is, to have learned that they like or dislike a particular taste. In addition, there is evidence of gender differences, with women, for example, somewhat better at detecting odors than men.

Section 6.5

1. Many older adults have trouble with changing light conditions as the pupil of the eye does not adapt as quickly to change. In addition, the lens of the eye often becomes cloudy with age, leading to cataracts. Problems with the retina can lead to age-related macular degeneration.
2. The greatest functional impairment related to hearing loss among older adults is trouble understanding speech in conversations, particularly under certain poor listening conditions such as loud background noise.
3. It turns out that we always have a "sweet tooth": Young infants (and even fetuses) as well as older adults have reliable perception of sweet tastes.

Chapter 7

Section 7.1

1. A scheme or schema is an organized pattern of thought that helps a person interpret his or her experiences.
2. Assimilation is using an existing scheme to make sense of a new experience, such as seeing a raccoon for the first time and calling it a cat. Accommodation is creating a new scheme, or changing the way you think, in order to understand new material. After having the differences between raccoons and cats pointed out on several occasions, a child may accommodate his or her thinking by creating a new schema or category of raccoons.
3. Piaget was instrumental in pointing out that we are active in our own development, even as infants. He also argued that our thinking does not just grow incrementally over time, but shifts qualitatively at several points over the life span.
4. Piaget probably underestimated what infants and young children know and are able to do. His idea of several qualitative shifts in thinking has been challenged by research suggesting more gradual changes over time and evidence of inconsistent levels of thinking across tasks at a given point in time. Although Piaget did a great job of describing children's cognitive abilities, he has been criticized for not fully explaining the changes.

Section 7.2

1. Vygotsky gave much more attention to social and cultural factors than Piaget. Vygotsky believed that children learn a great deal through social interaction with others and cultural transmission of knowledge
2. The zone of proximal development is the difference between what a learner can accomplish independently and what he or she can accomplish with the guidance or support of someone who is more skilled. For example, a boy may not be able to solve a new math problem on his own until he receives a few tips from his teacher.

Section 7.3

1. Fischer uses the term *dynamic* to convey the fluidity or change in performance that occurs with changes in context. *Skill* refers to a person's ability to perform a task in a particular context. Thus, a skill is not necessarily present across all situations but may be revealed under certain conditions.
2. Fischer's dynamic skill framework uses a concept similar to Vygotsky's zone of proximal development to convey his belief that there is an opportunity for growth from where a person currently performs to where he or she can potentially perform with support. Both also emphasize the importance of context, including support from others, in cognitive performance.
3. Dynamic skill framework emphasizes the environment or context in which a skill is performed, with some contexts conducive to the skill and others not. In contrast, Piaget's theory suggests that once a child has acquired a skill, it is available and can be used in any context.

Section 7.4

1. In the first stage of Piaget's theory, infants learn much about the world by taking in information through their senses and acting motorically on this information. Thus, the name "sensorimotor" captures the main focus of this stage.
2. In order to understand object permanence, infants must come to realize that objects continue to exist even if they are

not directly perceived, that is, an object or person still exists when it is in a different room and can't be seen or heard or otherwise detected.

Section 7.5

1. Preoperational thought is limited relative to concrete operational thought by its reliance on perceptual salience—what is most obvious about a problem—rather than on logical reasoning about a problem. It is also characterized by difficulties mentally reversing actions, grasping transformations from one state to another, and decentrating or decentering so as to focus on multiple aspects of a task.
2. The defining feature of concrete-operational thought is the ability to reason logically about concrete problems. This allows children to decentrate, mentally reverse actions, and think about transformations, which leads to success on conservation problems.

Section 7.6

1. The shift from concrete to formal-operational thinking comes when adolescents can apply their logical reasoning abilities to abstract or hypothetical issues and not just to concrete problems.
2. Hypothetical-deductive thinking is reasoning from general ideas or rules to specific examples of these rules. It allows an individual to take a theory and generate specific hypotheses that follow from the theory and then systematically test the hypotheses to determine their validity.

Section 7.7

1. Adults are most likely to use formal-operational thought in their area(s) of expertise, or those areas where they have the greatest experience.
2. Relativistic thinking is understanding that knowledge is subjective and depends on each individual's perspective on or assumptions about the information available to them.

Chapter 8

Section 8.1

1. Information must be encoded (gotten into the system by paying attention to it), consolidated (processed and organized to prepare it for storage), stored (retained in long-term memory), and finally recalled (retrieved from long-term memory) for use in working memory.
2. Implicit memories occur unintentionally, automatically, and without awareness, whereas explicit memories involve deliberate, effortful recollection of events.
3. Recognition tasks present the answer and require identifying whether this information is familiar or not. This is easier than a recall task in which the answer must be conjured up "from scratch," without it being in front of you.

Section 8.2

1. The habituation task allows researchers to measure how long it takes for infants to become "bored" seeing the stimulus repeatedly presented to them. After reaching this point of boredom and looking away, researchers can change the stimulus and determine if infants can detect the change, measured by whether the infant pays attention to the new stimulus.
2. Six-month-olds can recall simple events over a 24-hour period and 9-month-olds can recall these same events for up to 1 month. By 12 to 18 months of age, infants can recall events over several months. Memory is more robust and reliable, though, starting around 2 years of age, when we see more complicated events recalled for as long as a year.

Section 8.3

1. Older children know more, that is, they have larger knowledge bases than younger children; this provides a richer scaffold for remembering events. Older children also have a better understanding of their own memory strengths and weaknesses and of memory strategies—metamemory—which may be necessary in order to improve memory.
2. Scripts or general event representations (GERs) are created as we engage in routine activities; they influence what we recall about past events and what we attend to and store about future events.
3. The main point of the overlapping waves theory is that people have a "toolbox" of different strategies and, with experience, they become increasingly selective about which strategy to use and modify or add strategies to their toolbox as needed.

Section 8.4

1. Compared to children, adolescents are capable of more sophisticated memory strategies, although they do not always use them. Adolescents can also simultaneously juggle more information in working memory and can process information more quickly than they could during childhood.
2. Adolescents acquire new strategies, such as elaboration, and they become more deliberate in their use of strategies than children. They often demonstrate faster memory and problem-solving skills than children because familiar and frequently performed tasks have become automated. Finally, adolescents show greater awareness of their memory strengths and weaknesses compared to children and may be able to use these improved metamemory skills to improve performance.

Section 8.5

1. Some older adults may begin to experience problems on tasks that require speed or working with unfamiliar material or unexercised skills.

2. Older adults may be able to minimize the effects of shrinking resources by selecting, optimizing, and compensating so that they maximize their strengths and minimize their weaknesses.

Chapter 9

Section 9.1

1. Fluid intelligence involves using your mental skills to solve novel problems. Crystallized intelligence is using knowledge you have acquired through school or experience to answer questions.
2. Gardner's theory emphasizes that there are multiple—at least 8—types of intelligence and there are many possible intellectual profiles based on each individual's set of strengths and weaknesses.
3. Sternberg believes that three factors contribute to intelligence: creativity or ability to respond to novelty, practical skills that facilitate adaptation to one's sociocultural context, and analytic skills for solving problems.
4. Creativity is the ability to produce novel responses. It is typically measured with tasks that assess divergent thinking, or the ability to come up with a variety of ideas in response to a problem when there is no single correct answer. In contrast, measures of intelligence typically require coming up with a single correct answer.

Section 9.2

1. The DQ assesses how well (or poorly) an infant performs on motor skills, behaviors, and simple tasks relative to other infants of the same age.
2. The speed with which infants process information shows some relationship to later intelligence as intelligence across the life span seems related to being able to process information quickly.

Section 9.3

1. From elementary school on, IQ scores are fairly stable, at least in terms of a person's place within the group of individuals initially assessed. That is, a person's relative ranking within a group stays much the same over time unless something dramatic alters his or her circumstances and leads to a marked increase or decrease in performance.
2. IQ scores might decrease if children experience significant health problems that affect their ability to learn, process information, or perform well on tests. Scores might increase if children are moved from an impoverished environment to an enriched environment that promotes their physical and mental development.

Section 9.4

1. Intelligence is likely to be much more stable in adolescence than creativity. The basic elements of intelligence change very little throughout adolescence but creativity can be highly variable.
2. Fewer infectious diseases and improved educational opportunities seem to be associated with the Flynn effect—the rise in IQ scores over the past century.
3. Creativity can be fostered by providing an environment that provides some independence as well as opportunities to explore numerous activities and then opportunities to delve deeper into areas of interest.

Section 9.5

1. IQ scores of adults have been found to correlate with occupational prestige and income. Further, adults with higher IQs tend to live healthier and longer lives than those with lower IQs.
2. Poor health is likely to contribute to declining IQ scores among older adults, as is an unstimulating life style. Older adults who remain physically and mentally active are more likely to do well on tasks requiring intelligence than their peers who are inactive.
3. Someone can be intelligent, as measured by the questions on an IQ test, but not necessarily wise. With wisdom comes the ability to combine multiple perspectives with experience to solve problems.

Section 9.6

1. A home environment that has age-appropriate stimulating toys, books, and parents who are responsive to their children's need can boost IQ scores.
2. There may be racial/ethnic differences on IQ tests because of biases in the tests, motivational differences between groups, stereotypes that affect performance, or differences in environment (for example, wealth versus poverty).

Section 9.7

1. Intellectual disability is defined by two factors: an IQ score of 70–75 or lower and deficits in adaptive functioning (that is, problems with everyday tasks).
2. The typical gifted person usually scores high on an IQ test and does well in school, although some exceptionally gifted children are so bored in the regular classroom that they may actually perform poorly. As adults, most have above average outcomes.
3. The psychometric approach to intelligence assumes that intelligence is a mental trait that varies across people and is measurable. Piaget defined intelligence as a basic life function that helps a person adapt to his or her environment. Sternberg's triarchic theory echoes this emphasis on the ability to adapt well to one's environment. Vygotsky highlighted the importance of interacting with others who could convey important information and support learning. Fischer's dynamic framework shows that context is important for skills. The information processing approach focuses on mental processes and the speed with which information can be processed.

Chapter 10

Section 10.1

1. Children must learn which sounds are used in their language and how these sounds are used to produce meaningful words, and then how words are combined to form sentences based on agreed-upon rules.
2. The brain is structured to support language in various ways, with incoming language processed in a portion of the left hemisphere called Wernicke's area and speech production occurring in a portion of the brain called Broca's area. These two important parts of the brain are connected by a band of fibers that, if damaged, can lead to aphasia or language disorder.
3. Nativists believe that we are born with an innate ability to sift through the language we hear around us and from this generate rules of language that we use to guide our verbalizations. Learning theorists believe that we acquire language through the same learning mechanisms that guide other forms of learning: imitation of the speech around us and reinforcement (or not) for proper speech.

Section 10.2

1. Young infants begin making sounds and demonstrate sensitivity to intonation. They produce "coos," or repetitive vowel-like sounds before moving on to "babbling," which adds consonant sounds. Babbling gives way to single words or holophrases, which are then followed by simple sentences in the telegraphic stage of language development.
2. In overregularization, a child might learn that putting "ed" on the end of an action word or verb typically forms the past tense. She may then produce words that follow this rule, such as saying "I goed out," until she learns the exceptions to the rule.
3. Mastery motivation refers to the infant's desire to take control of—master—the objects in his or her environment, such as figuring out how to operate a new toy.
4. Early education programs can offer children from disadvantaged homes the opportunity to gain experience and knowledge that prepares them for formal schooling. But focusing exclusively on academic drills at an early age can detract from other equally important developmental tasks such as play and socializing.

Section 10.3

1. A mastery or learning goal emphasizes understanding something in order to improve knowledge or skills. A performance goal focuses on the outcome (showing intelligence by performing well). A student with a performance goal might ask, "What grade did I earn?" whereas one with a mastery goal might ask, "What did I learn?"
2. Skilled readers have mastered the alphabetic principle and quickly associate sounds with printed letters. In addition, skilled readers have higher levels of phonological awareness, which allows them to segment words into sounds and "sound out" printed words.

3. Effective schools maximize time on academics and minimize time on such incidentals as transitions from class to class; they hold students to high standards and clearly state their expectations; and they squash behavior problems on-the-spot, before they escalate.

Section 10.4

1. Adolescents are better able than younger children to realistically evaluate their strengths and weaknesses and may become discouraged if they focus on their weaknesses, leading to a decline in achievement motivation. Adolescents may also become frustrated by the emphasis on grades or abandon learning goals in favor of performance goals.
2. Asian schools typically spend more time on academics and they are backed up by parents who place a high priority on education, encouraging study time and homework. Peer groups also support studying and friends often get together to study, as opposed to getting together to "hang out."
3. Working during high school can foster independence from parents and knowledge of how work places operate. But students who work during high school are often disengaged from school and do not perform as well academically as those who do not work or work just a few hours.

Section 10.5

1. Achievement motivation is fairly consistent over the adult years: Those who entered adulthood with high achievement motivation tend to retain this high desire to achieve, whereas those who were always lackluster tend to remain lackluster. Achievement motivation is more influenced by work and family situations than by age.
2. Literacy is the ticket to many opportunities in adulthood and is required to compete in most workplace environments and to advance to higher-paying positions. Unfortunately, literacy programs are not very successful: Adults who could benefit from them often do not believe they need to improve and do not stay enrolled long enough to achieve success.

Chapter 11

Section 11.1

1. In McAdams and Pals's view, dispositional traits are broad and relatively stable personality dimensions such as the Big Five, whereas characteristic adaptations are more situation-specific and changeable ways of adapting to roles and life situations such as self-concepts, goals, and coping styles.
2. Self-esteem is an overall evaluation of your worth as a person (high or low); self-concept is all the varied perceptions you have of yourself (positive and negative).
3. Social learning theorists do not expect behavior to be consistent across different situations and over time as trait theorists do. They believe that situational influences are powerful and that people learn to behave differently when their environments change.

Section 11.2

1. At around 18 months, toddlers show self-recognition when placed in front of a mirror, an achievement that requires both cognitive development and social experience.
2. Thomas and Chess would likely say a child low in surgency/extraversion, high in negative affect, and low in effortful control has a difficult temperament; Kagan would say she is behaviorally inhibited.

Section 11.3

1. Nine-year-old Alonzo's self-description would likely say more than his 4-year-old brother's about psychological traits, say more about his social affiliations or group memberships, and contain more social comparisons.
2. High self-esteem is associated with being competent in important areas; coming out well in social comparisons; and receiving positive social feedback from warm, democratic parents. Genetic makeup also affects self-esteem.
3. According to Chen's research, shyness may have negative implications in individualistic cultures, predicting poor functioning academically and socially, low self-esteem, and depression. In collectivist cultures, the self-effacing personality of the shy child may be valued more and predicts good social adjustment, success in school, and psychological well-being.

Section 11.4

1. The self-descriptions of an older adolescent should be more psychological, abstract, differentiated, and yet integrated, and should reflect more self-awareness, than the self-descriptions of a child.
2. The adolescent in the foreclosure status knows what career he wants but latched on to the idea without any exploration or questioning (no crisis, commitment); his parents may be loving but overprotective. The adolescent in the diffusion status has done little exploration and has no idea what he wants to be (no crisis, no commitment); his parents may be unsupportive, either neglecting or rejecting.
3. Identity achievement is facilitated by cognitive development, personality traits such as openness to experience, opportunities to explore possible identities, and a culture that encourages identity exploration.

Section 11.5

1. Continuity in personality can mean that there is consistency of people's rankings within a group (as indicated by a high correlation between people's age 40 and age 50 scores) or it can mean that the group mean level of a trait does not change from age 40 to age 50.
2. Generativity, Erikson theorized, can develop in middle age if adults have a strong sense of caring for future generations expressed through parenting, mentoring, or otherwise producing something that will outlive them.

3. Daniel Levinson claimed that a midlife crisis in the early 40s is universal. His claim is not well supported, although adults do raise questions about their lives at various ages.
4. Retirement is not likely to go well if it is involuntary, if the person has poor health, if the person has inadequate financial resources, or if the person is unmarried or otherwise lacking in social support.

Chapter 12

Section 12.1

1. The main components of agency are an orientation toward independence, dominance, assertiveness, and competition. The main features of communality are connectedness and sensitivity to others.
2. On average, females may demonstrate greater verbal skills, particularly on reading tasks. They also display greater memory ability, although this may be limited to particular memory tasks such as object locations, verbal information, and faces. Males, on average, outperform females on most spatial tasks such as mental rotation and they engage in more aggressive behaviors than females.
3. According to Eagly's social-role hypothesis, most gender stereotypes arise from the different roles that women and men play in society. For example, women have typically stayed close to home to nurse and raise children, making it seem as though they are more nurturant (communal) than men. The social-role hypothesis would predict that men who stay home to raise children would be just as nurturant as required by this role.

Section 12.2

1. Gender identity is an awareness of self as boy or girl, man or woman. By 18–24 months, toddlers are categorizing the people around them as well as themselves as male or female. By 2½–3 years, children can clearly state that they are boys or girls and behave according to which gender category they believe they fit into.

Section 12.3

1. Children seemed most concerned about gender roles during the preschool period, which is soon after they have acquired a gender identity and are learning about societal expectations and stereotypes regarding gender. During elementary school, their rigidity with respect to gender roles eases up and children are OK with blurring the boundaries to some extent.
2. Gender segregation is obvious as children enter elementary school, with boys playing primarily with other boys and girls "hanging out" with other girls. This may occur because of different play styles; boys may be too active and physical in their play to suit girls. But socialization is also important in separating the boys from the girls. Peers tend to tease or belittle boys and girls who play with children of the opposite-sex,

which is a strong incentive to these children to stay within the gender boundaries established by their group.

3. According to biosocial theory, gendered behavior results from a combination of biological events and social reactions. Chromosomes and hormones set the stage with physical characteristics typical of males or females and society responds differently to these male-female characteristics, which serves to emphasize and reinforce them.

4. According to cognitive developmentalists, children socialize themselves into gendered behavior once they acquire the cognitive understanding of themselves as male or female. With this understanding, they are motivated to behave in ways that are consistent with their beliefs.

5. Gender schemas are organized beliefs about males and females that influence how we think: what we pay attention to and what we remember. A woman who has a gender schema that power tools are "for men" may ignore a commercial for a power drill because she does not believe this is relevant to her as a nonmember of the group in her schema.

Section 12.4

1. Most teens today believe that sex in the context of a committed romantic relationship is acceptable and do not believe that couples necessarily need to wait until marriage to have sex. Many teens report confusion about what is acceptable, though, because of mixed messages received from parents, media, schools, etc.

2. Males are more likely than females to engage in risky sex behaviors such as multiple sex partners. Females are more likely to want sex to be accompanied by an emotional commitment than males. Males engage in more masturbation than females.

3. Sexual orientation is probably determined, in part, by biological events that occur prenatally, including one's genetic makeup and hormone exposure. But these predispositions may require environmental triggers, as yet unidentified, to activate the predisposition.

Section 12.5

1. Gender roles seem to become more sharply defined after couples have children, with women displaying more communal traits and men more agentic traits. But after children are raised and out of the house, adults may shed these traditional roles and become more androgynous, displaying greater flexibility in their behaviors.

2. Androgyny refers to combining both agentic (masculine) and communal (feminine) traits. Androgyny itself doesn't seem to be especially beneficial; instead, it is having the agentic traits associated with androgyny that seems to be associated with some advantages.

3. Desire for sex declines in older adults, but certainly does not disappear. The amount of sexual activity declines over adulthood, often because of lack of opportunity or availability of a partner. Health conditions may also influence sexual desire and activity among older adults. Still, we remain sexual beings across our entire lifespan.

Chapter 13

Section 13.1

1. Joint attention, understanding of intentions, pretend play, imitation, and emotional understanding are all early signs of a theory of mind.

2. An opportunity to converse in sign language or *some* language is critical in developing a theory of mind. Also helpful are interactions with siblings or other children, and frequent parent talk about mental states (mind-mindedness).

3. Children 8–10 years of age can think about both their own thoughts and the thoughts of another person and understand that two people can have different views even when they have the same information.

Section 13.2

1. Morality has an affective component (Freudian psychoanalytic theory), a cognitive component (Piaget's or Kohlberg's cognitive developmental theory), and a behavioral component (Bandura's social cognitive theory).

2. Preconventional morality is concerned only with the perspective of the self and is about avoiding punishment and gaining rewards, so stealing would be wrong if it would have negative consequences for the stealer. Conventional morality reflects taking the perspective of others, internalizing the rules of authority figures, and being motivated to do the right thing as others define it, so stealing would be wrong because it is disapproved by other people and against the law and we should respect authorities and laws.

3. Freud saw humans as selfish and aggressive in nature, whereas evolutionary theorists, while recognizing that humans have evolved aggressive tendencies, maintain that humans have also evolved to be moral beings because cooperation and other forms of prosocial behavior enhance survival.

Section 13.3

1. According to Hoffman, a primitive form of empathy is evident at birth; as social perspective-taking skills develop, empathy becomes less egocentric and takes on more varied forms.

2. When one infant pushes another, the motive is usually to get a toy or other item rather than to harm the other infant.

3. Kochanska would tell parents who want their infants to become moral beings to form a secure attachment and develop a mutually responsive orientation in which child and parent are sensitive to each other's needs.

Section 13.4

1. Moral rules concern the welfare and rights of other people (as in rules against hitting), whereas social-conventional rules concern the social appropriateness of behavior (as in rules against belching in public). The distinction is recognized as early as age 3.

2. Contrary to Piaget's and Kohlberg's views, preschool children consider whether an actor's intentions were good or bad (they don't just judge acts wrong based on their consequences), view only some rules (moral ones) as sacred and unchangeable, are capable of challenging adult authority, and use their theories of mind to analyze people's motives and the emotional consequences of their acts.
3. An appropriate example of induction would explain to a child how his or her behavior harmed someone and therefore is wrong; induction fosters empathy, which can keep children from doing harm in the future.

Section 13.5

1. Adolescents normally progress from preconventional (stage 2) reasoning to conventional (mainly stage 3) reasoning.
2. Dodge's social information-processing model helps explain deficiencies and biases in the way aggressive youth process information and react in social situations. Patterson's coercive family environment model explains how coercive parenting creates coercive cycles in the family that breed aggression in children and set them on a path toward delinquency.
3. The combination of a gene for low MAOA activity in the brain (and hence poor anger control) plus abuse or maltreatment significantly increases the odds of aggressive behavior.

Section 13.6

1. Over the adult years, a minority of adults progress from conventional to postconventional moral reasoning; older adults retain their moral reasoning skills quite well.
2. The two processes in dual-process models of morality are rational, conscious deliberation and quick, emotion-based intuition.
3. Highly religious individuals adopt the views of a religious community and participate in it; highly spiritual individuals seek and hold more personalized beliefs about something larger than themselves that they develop through their own soul searching.

Chapter 14

Section 14.1

1. The milestone in development that must be achieved before an infant will show secondary or self-conscious emotions like embarrassment is self-awareness, or self-recognition in the mirror.
2. An example of an emotional display rule would be "look sad at a funeral" or "look pleased when you receive a gift."
3. According to Carstensen's socioemotional selectivity theory, older adults have good emotional well-being because, as they realize time is short, they choose emotional fulfillment goals over information-seeking goals and focus on their most emotionally fulfilling relationships.

Section 14.2

1. Imprinting is said to have been built into the species over the course of evolution because the young were more likely to survive if they stayed close to their mothers where they would be fed and protected from predators.
2. Early experience shapes later development through the internal working models of self and others that develop based on interactions with caregivers and that say how lovable you are and how trustworthy other people are.
3. Jean Piaget (with his emphasis on peers as equals) and Harry Stack Sullivan (with his emphasis on chumships as a source of intimacy and social support and preparation for later romantic relationships) both argued that relationships with peers are at least as significant as attachments to parents.

Section 14.3

1. Once an attachment to a caregiver forms, infants display separation anxiety, stranger anxiety, use of the attachment figure as a secure base for exploration, and use of the attachment figure as a safe haven.
2. Resistant infants cry long and hard to get the caregiver back but are ambivalent when they do get her back; avoidant infants deal with their anxiety by seeming unfazed when the caregiver leaves and ignoring or avoiding her when she returns.
3. Infants most need responsive and sustained care from someone, whether it is from one caregiver or a few consistent caregivers.

Section 14.4

1. The two most complex of Parten's six types of play are associative play and cooperative play.
2. Over the preschool years, play becomes more social (as associative and cooperative play become more common) and more imaginative (as pretend play and social pretend play become more common).
3. Physical attractiveness, cognitive ability, social competence, and emotion regulation skills all influence sociometric status.

Section 14.5

1. A clique is a small friendship group, either same sex or mixed sex; a crowd is a collection of mixed-sex cliques that organize social activities.
2. Young teens seek to establish in early dating relationships that they are desirable romantic partners (initiation phase) and they seek status in the peer group by dating desirable partners (status phase).

Section 14.6

1. Companionate love involves high levels of intimacy and commitment but a low level of passion.

2. People with a preoccupied attachment style view other people positively but do not believe they are lovable and worry about being abandoned.
3. Adult well-being is more strongly related to having at least one confidant than to having a large social network and also depends on whether social interactions are positive or stressful.

Chapter 15

Section 15.1

1. Over the family life cycle, there are changes in family membership, the roles played by family members, and the developmental tasks they must complete.
2. Changes away from the stereotypical breadwinner father/homemaker mother family include more unmarried parents, more women working, more divorce, more single-parent families, and more reconstituted families.

Section 15.2

1. Fathers are similar to mothers in that they are as capable of sensitive and responsive caregiving, but they spend less time than mothers with their children and they often adopt a playful rather than a caregiving role.
2. A father could negatively affect a mother's parenting and relationship with her child by being highly critical or even abusive in his interactions with her.

Section 15.3

1. Authoritative parenting is high on both the parental acceptance-responsiveness and demandingness-control dimensions.
2. Low-SES parents under economic stress could become depressed, experience marital conflict, and as a result become less nurturing toward their children; or they may have less time and other resources to invest in their children's care and supervision; or they may feel that teaching children to obey without question is the best way to prepare them for working class jobs in which they must follow orders. If they are poor and live in high-crime areas, parents may also become authoritarian to protect their children from harm.
3. The interaction effects model highlights how the combination of parent and child characteristics affects development (for example, a certain kind of parent with a certain kind of child may result in maladjustment). The transactional model emphasizes ongoing, reciprocal influences of the parent on the child and the child on the parent over time. In this model, it may not matter as much what characteristics each person brings to the relationship as how the relationship unfolds over time.
4. Sibling relationships typically involve both closeness and conflict or rivalry.

Section 15.4

1. Parent–adolescent conflicts are typically about quite minor issues such as disobedience, homework, household chores, and access to privileges.
2. Autonomy is fostered best by the authoritative parenting style because it gives adolescents opportunities to strengthen their independent decision-making skills without losing their parents' guidance and support and creates a climate in which teenagers confide in their parents.

Section 15.5

1. Marital satisfaction shows an inverted-U pattern over the family life cycle, declining soon after the honeymoon and often declining more in response to new parenthood and the oldest child's entrance into adolescence and rebounding when the nest empties.
2. New parenthood can be difficult if the baby is difficult, the parent lacks personal resources such as good coping skills and a secure orientation toward attachment, and the parent lacks social support from a partner or other people.
3. The companionate grandparent role is preferred because it involves spending enjoyable time with grandchildren without heavy child care responsibilities.
4. Caregiver burden is heaviest when the ailing parent displays behavioral problems, and when caregivers do not want to help or help out of duty rather than love, lack personal resources such as good coping skills, lack social support, and are members of a cultural or subcultural group that has a weak sense of responsibility for parent care.

Section 15.6

1. Cohabitation itself probably does not cause later marital problems, but (a) the kinds of people who cohabit may differ from those who do not (for example, be more prone to relationship problems and/or less traditional in their views of marriage) or (b) people who live together may marry out of inertia because it becomes hard to leave the cohabitation arrangement.
2. Overall, children from dual-career families turn out as well as children with stay-at-home mothers. That is most likely because most working couples manage to stay involved with their children and provide effective parenting.
3. Typically, remarriage after a divorce creates adjustment difficulties for children that last a few years but work themselves out in time. Adjusting to a reconstituted family is especially hard when both partners bring children to the remarriage.

Section 15.7

1. Parents who are at risk for being abusive have been abused as children, have been abused by their partners, are low in self-esteem, and are unrealistic in their expectations of children. Abused children sometimes have medical problems

or a difficult temperament. Contextual factors such as lack of social support and a culture that condones violence may also contribute.

2. Bugental's program attempts to empower high-risk parents to deal with their difficult and unresponsive children by teaching them how to more objectively analyze and devise solutions to caregiving problems.

Chapter 16

Section 16.1

1. Psychological disorders are assessed in terms of the broad criteria of statistical deviance, maladaptiveness, and personal distress, as well as more specific DSM-5 diagnostic criteria.

2. Developmental psychopathologists view psychological disorders as maladaptive development and emphasize that many people move on and off pathways leading to adaptive or maladaptive developmental outcomes over a lifetime.

3. A diathesis is a predisposition or vulnerability to a psychological disorder—for example, a particular genetic makeup, physiology, or personality that puts a person at risk.

Section 16.2

1. Autism is characterized by abnormal social and communication development and by restricted interests and repetitive behavior.

2. Saying that a child has an "extreme male brain" means that the child is very good at systemizing (for example, analyzing machines to figure out how they work) but not at all good at empathizing (understanding and responding appropriately to people's thoughts and emotions).

3. Depressive symptoms in an infant could result from separation from an important attachment figure or from interacting with a depressed, unresponsive, or rejecting caregiver.

Section 16.3

1. In internalizing problems like depression, the expression of negative emotions is controlled or internalized (bottled up), whereas in externalizing problems like conduct disorder those negative emotions are expressed (acted out).

2. ADHD is associated with either inattention or hyperactivity/impulsivity or both.

3. The best way to treat ADHD is a combination of medication and behavioral treatment (along with parent training and school interventions as well), but it is still not well established that the effects of such combined treatments last beyond childhood.

4. Although even young children can meet the same DSM-5 criteria for depression as adults meet, children who are depressed may show it by being irritable, may also be anxious, and tend to show more of the somatic and behavioral symptoms of depression than the cognitive symptoms.

Section 16.4

1. The 20% plus rate of significant mental health problems in adolescence is higher than the rate in childhood (about 10%), offering some support for the storm and stress view, and yet 20–25% is a minority of adolescents, not most adolescents, and the adolescent rate of disorder is no higher than the adult rate.

2. Anorexia nervosa has been associated with a genetic predisposition, a culture obsessed with thinness, a family concerned with weight and eating issues, and overwhelming stress.

3. Early contributors to illicit drug use in adolescence include a difficult temperament; an adverse environment (poverty, stress, substance use in the family); exposure to harsh, ineffective parenting and family conflict; early conduct problems; and early rejection by peers.

4. Females attempt suicide more than males do, but males commit suicide more than females do.

Section 16.5

1. Young adults have higher rates of depressive disorder than older adults, females have twice the rate of males, and Hispanic and non-Hispanic whites tend to have higher rates than other racial and ethnic groups.

2. Changes in the brain in people with Alzheimer's disease appear to begin in early adulthood, and possibly earlier; noticeable cognitive problems may not appear until years later; 2–3 years after that, Alzheimer's disease will be advanced enough that it can be diagnosed; and 8–10 years after diagnosis the person can be expected to die.

3. Approaches used to treat Alzheimer's disease range from efforts to improve cognitive functioning (drugs to improve memory, diets high in antioxidants, physical and mental exercise) to efforts to help families cope with cognitive and behavioral problems (for example, memory aids, behavioral management techniques, educational programs for both patients and caregivers).

4. Compared to dementia, delirium emerges more rapidly than dementia, comes and goes over the course of a day or week, and is reversible if its cause can be identified.

Chapter 17

Section 17.1

1. The Harvard definition of death requires total brain death, and Ms. Schiavo's lower brain (brain stem) was functioning to allow her to breathe, swallow, and maintain sleep–wake cycles.

2. Children are most often killed by unintentional injuries or accidents (especially car accidents), whereas elderly people are most often killed by chronic diseases (especially heart diseases, followed by cancers and cerebrovascular diseases).

Section 17.2

1. Kübler-Ross's theory has been criticized because emotional responses to dying are not stagelike; experiences differ depending on the nature and course of the individual's condition; and the individual's personality and coping style shape emotional responses.
2. Attachment theory, the basis for the Parkes/Bowlby model of bereavement, says that humans experience separation anxiety when they lose a loved one and therefore engage in yearning (until they give up their effort to retrieve the loved one and fall into a phase of disorganization and despair).
3. Two types of coping oscillate in the dual-process model of bereavement: loss-oriented coping focused on grieving the loss, and restoration-oriented coping focused on carrying on life activities.

Section 17.3

1. Experiences in which people disappear and are "all gone," as in peek-a-boo games, and experiences going to sleep and awakening may pave the way for later understanding of death as a permanent separation.
2. Grief reactions in infancy are not evident until an attachment forms at around 6–7 months; infants then display separation anxiety when separated from their attachment figure and appear to be grieving.

Section 17.4

1. An advanced understanding of death concepts (that is, of death as a biological phenomenon) is associated with an advanced level of cognitive development, living in a culture in which these death concepts are accepted by adults, and having personal experiences with death.
2. By age 5–7, children usually master the concepts that death is final, irreversible, and universal; they will later appreciate that death is ultimately caused by a failure of internal biological processes.
3. Bereaved children may upset adults by expressing anger and misbehaving, becoming upset if their routines are not honored, asking endless questions, and fearing that others in the family will die — or, at times, by going about their play as if nothing happened.

Section 17.5

1. Because adolescents often acquire a belief in an afterlife, they may understand death as a final cessation of biological functions but, like a younger child, may say that psychological functions such as thinking and feeling continue after death. They are not regressing to a less mature concept of death so much as they are being socialized into religious and societal concepts of death.
2. Differences between bereaved and nonbereaved youth in Brent's study included more major depression and alcohol and other substance abuse, more PTSD, higher cortisol levels and abnormal stress responses, and difficulty completing developmental tasks (for example, forming close peer relationships, developing educational aspirations and career goals).
3. Adolescents may bottle up their grief to avoid seeming abnormal, losing control, or reverting to childlike dependency.

Section 17.6

1. The most common pattern of adjustment observed in studies of widows and widowers is the resilient pattern in which distress is at a relatively low level from before the death to well after it.
2. The elements of the grief work perspective that lack research support say that there is a right way to grieve, that bereaved individuals must experience intense grief in order to recover or will suffer later, and that the bereaved must sever their bonds to the deceased to recover.
3. A resistant attachment style is associated with overdependence on others and intense and prolonged grief; an avoidant attachment is associated with difficulty expressing emotions or seeking support from other people.

Section 17.7

1. In hospice care, the dying person and family make decisions, efforts to cure or prolong life are deemphasized, pain control is emphasized, the care setting is as normal as possible, and counseling is offered to the family before and after the death.
2. Individual therapy, family therapy, and mutual support groups have all proven effective in helping bereaved individuals cope.

Glossary

A-not-B error The tendency of 8- to 12- month-old infants to search for a hidden object in the place they last found it (A) rather than in its new hiding place (B).

acceptance–responsiveness A dimension of parenting capturing the extent to which parents are supportive, sensitive to their children's needs, and willing to provide affection and praise when their children meet their expectations.

accommodation In Piaget's cognitive developmental theory, the process of modifying existing schemes to incorporate or adapt to new experiences. Contrast with *assimilation*. In vision, a change in the shape of the eye's lens to bring objects at differing distances into focus.

acquired immunodeficiency syndrome (AIDS) The life-threatening disease in which the human immunodeficiency virus (HIV) destroys the immune system and makes victims susceptible to rare, so-called opportunistic, infections that eventually kill them. AIDS is transmitted through sexual activity, drug needle sharing, and from mother to child before or during birth.

active gene-environment correlation Phenomenon in which children's genotypes influence the kinds of environments they seek out and therefore experience. Contrast with *evocative gene-environment correlation* and *passive gene-environment correlation*.

activity theory A perspective holding that aging adults will find satisfaction to the extent that they maintain an active lifestyle. Contrast with *disengagement theory*.

activity–passivity issue The issue in developmental theory centering on whether humans are active contributors to their own development or are passively shaped by forces beyond their control.

adaptation In Piaget's cognitive developmental theory, a person's inborn tendency to adjust to the demands of the environment, consisting of the complementary processes of *assimilation* and *accommodation*.

adolescence The transitional period between childhood and adulthood that begins with puberty and ends when the individual has acquired adult competencies and responsibilities; roughly ages 10 to 18 or later.

adolescent egocentrism A characteristic of adolescent thought that involves difficulty differentiating between the person's own thoughts and feelings and those of other people; evident in the *personal fable* and *imaginary audience* phenomena.

adolescent growth spurt The rapid increase in physical growth that occurs during adolescence.

adoption study Method of studying genetic and environmental influence that involves determining whether adopted children are more similar to their biological parents (whose genes they share) or adoptive parents (who shaped their environment).

adrenarche A period of increased production of adrenal hormones, starting around 6–8 years of age, that normally precedes increased production of gonadal hormones associated with puberty.

affordances In Eleanor and James Gibson's ecological theory of perception, characteristics of an object that reveal what it has to offer humans and how it might be used by them.

age effects In developmental research, the effects of getting older or of developing. Contrast with *cohort effects* and *time of measurement effects*.

age grades Socially defined age groups or strata, each with different statuses, roles, privileges, and responsibilities in society.

age norms Expectations about what people should be doing or how they should behave at different points in the life span.

age of viability A point (around the 24th prenatal week) when a fetus may survive outside the uterus if the brain and respiratory system are well enough developed and if excellent medical care is available.

ageism Prejudice and discrimination against elderly people.

agency An orientation toward individual action and achievement that emphasizes traits of dominance, independence, assertiveness, and competitiveness; considered masculine.

age-related macular degeneration Damage to cells in the retina responsible for central vision.

aging To most developmentalists, positive, negative, and neutral changes in the mature organism; different from *biological aging*.

alphabetic principle The idea that the letters in printed words represent the sounds in spoken words.

Alzheimer's disease A pathological condition of the nervous system that results in an irreversible loss of cognitive capacities; the leading cause of dementia, or neurocognitive disorder, in later life.

amniocentesis A method of extracting amniotic fluid from a pregnant woman so that fetal body cells within the fluid can be tested for chromosomal abnormalities and other genetic defects.

amnion A watertight membrane that surrounds the developing embryo, regulating its temperature and cushioning it against injuries.

amoral Lacking any sense of morality; without standards of right and wrong.

analytic component In Sternberg's triarchic theory of intelligence, the information-processing skills such as thinking critically and analytically.

androgenized female A genetic female who was exposed to male sex hormones during the prenatal period and therefore developed malelike external genitals and some masculine behaviors.

androgens Male hormones that help trigger the adolescent growth spurt and the development of the male sex organs, secondary sex characteristics, and sexual motivation.

androgyny A gender-role orientation in which the person blends both positive masculine-stereotyped and positive feminine-stereotyped personality traits.

androgyny shift A psychological change that begins in midlife, when parenting responsibilities are over, in which both men and women retain their gender-typed qualities but add to them qualities traditionally associated with the other sex, thus becoming more androgynous.

andropause The slower and less-dramatic male counterpart of *menopause*, characterized by decreasing levels of testosterone and symptoms that include low libido, fatigue and lack of energy, erection problems, memory problems, and loss of pubic hair.

anencephaly Condition in which the top of the neural tube fails to close and the main portion of the brain above the brain stem fails to develop properly.

anorexia nervosa A life-threatening eating disorder characterized by failure to maintain a normal weight, a strong fear of weight gain, and a distorted body image; literally, "nervous lack of appetite."

anoxia A lack of sufficient oxygen to the brain that may result in neurological damage or death.

anterograde amnesia The inability to form new memories of recent experiences. Contrast with *retrograde amnesia*.

anticipatory grief Grieving before death for what is happening and for what lies ahead.

antioxidant Vitamins C, E, and similar substances that may increase longevity, although not for long, by inhibiting the free radical activity associated with oxidation and in turn preventing age-related diseases.

Antisocial behavior Behavior that violates social norms, rules, or laws and harms others or society (for example, lying, stealing, behaving aggressively).

Apgar test A test routinely used to assess a newborn's heart rate, respiration, color, muscle tone, and reflexes immediately after birth and 5 minutes later; used to identify high-risk babies.

aphasia A language disorder.

applied behavior analysis (ABA) The application of reinforcement principles to teach skills and change behavior, for example to shape social and language skills in children with autism.

artificial insemination A method of conception that involves injecting sperm from a woman's partner or from a donor into the uterus.

Asperger syndrome A form of autistic spectrum disorder in which the individual has normal or above-average intelligence, has good verbal skills, and wants to establish social relationships but has seriously deficient mindreading and social skills. No longer a separate diagnosis in DSM 5.

assimilation Piaget's term for the process by which children interpret new experiences in terms of their existing schemata. Contrast with *accommodation*.

assisted suicide Making available to individuals who wish to commit suicide the means by which they may do so, such as when a physician provides a terminally ill patient who wants to die with enough medication to overdose.

at risk Children who have a higher than normal chance of either short-term or long-term problems because of genetic defects, prenatal hazards, or perinatal damage.

attachment A strong affectional tie that binds a person to an intimate companion and is characterized by affection and a desire to maintain proximity.

attachment theory The theory of close relationships developed by Bowlby and Ainsworth and grounded in ethological theory (with psychoanalytic theory and cognitive theory); it says that close emotional bonds such as parent–child attachments are biologically based and contribute to species survival.

attention Focusing perception and cognition on something in particular.

attention deficit hyperactivity disorder (ADHD) A disorder characterized by attentional difficulties, or overactive and impulsive behavior, or both.

authoritarian parenting A restrictive style of parenting combining high demandingness–control and low acceptance–responsiveness in which adults impose many rules, expect strict obedience, and often rely on power tactics rather than explanations to elicit compliance.

authoritative parenting A flexible style of parenting combining high demandingness–control and high acceptance–responsiveness in which adults lay down clear rules but also take their children's views into account and explain the rationale for their restrictions.

autism See autism spectrum disorder.

autism spectrum disorder (ASD) A category of pervasive developmental disorders that includes what was previously called autism, Asperger syndrome, and related conditions and that involves (1) social and communication problems and (2) restricted interests and repetitive behavior.

autobiographical memory Memory of everyday events that the individual has experienced.

automatization The process by which information processing becomes effortless and highly efficient as a result of continued practice or increased expertise.

autonomy The capacity to make decisions independently, serve as one's own source of emotional strength, and otherwise manage life tasks without being overdependent on other people; an important developmental task of adolescence.

autonomy versus shame and doubt The psychosocial conflict in which toddlers attempt to demonstrate their independence from and control over other people; second of Erikson's stages.

avoidant attachment An insecure infant caregiver bond or other intimate relationship characterized by little separation anxiety and a tendency to avoid or ignore the attachment object upon reunion.

babbling An early form of vocalization that appears between 4 and 6 months of age and involves repeating consonant–vowel combinations such as "baba" or "dadada."

baby biographies Carefully recorded observations of the growth and development of children by their parents over a period; the first scientific investigations of development.

baby boom generation The huge generation of people born between 1946 (the close of World War II) and 1964.

Bayley Scales of Infant Development Standardized test to measure the mental, motor, and behavioral progress of infants and young children.

behavioral genetics The scientific study of the extent to which genetic and environmental differences among individuals are responsible for differences among them in traits such as intelligence and personality.

behavioral inhibition A temperamental characteristic reflecting a person's tendency to withdraw from unfamiliar people and situations.

behaviorism A school of thinking in psychology that holds that conclusions about human development should be based on controlled observations of overt behavior rather than on speculation about unconscious motives or other unobservable phenomena; the philosophical underpinning of early theories of learning.

belief–desire psychology The theory of mind reflecting an understanding that people's desires and beliefs guide their behavior and that their beliefs are not always an accurate reflection of reality; evident by age 4. Contrast with *desire psychology*.

bereavement A state of loss that provides the occasion for grief and mourning.

beta-amyloid A toxic protein that injures neurons and is located in the senile plaques outside neural cells that are associated with Alzheimer's disease.

Big Five The five major dimensions used to characterize people's personalities: neuroticism, extraversion, openness to experience, agreeableness, and conscientiousness.

bilingual Knowing two or more languages.

binge eating disorder Eating disorder that, like bulimia, involves binge eating but, unlike bulimia, does not involve purging.

bioecological model Bronfenbrenner's model of development that emphasizes the roles of both nature and nurture as the developing person interacts with a series of environmental systems (microsystem, mesosystem, exosystem, and macrosystem) over time (chronosystem).

biological aging The deterioration of organisms that leads inevitably to their death.

biological sex The physical characteristics that define male and female.

biosocial theory Money and Ehrhardt's theory of gender-role development that focuses on how biological events influence the development of boys and girls and how early biological developments influence how society reacts to children.

blastocyst A hollow sphere of about 100 to 150 cells that the zygote forms by rapid cell division as it moves through the fallopian tube.

body mass index (BMI) An indicator of body fat calculated from a person's height and weight.

bonding As distinguished from attachment, a more biologically-based process in which parent and infant form a connection through contact in the first hours after birth when both are highly alert.

breech presentation A delivery in which the fetus emerges feet first or buttocks first rather than head first.

bulimia nervosa A life-threatening eating disorder characterized by recurrent eating binges followed by purging activities such as vomiting.

bullying Repeatedly inflicting harm through words or actions on weaker peers who cannot or do not defend themselves.

caloric restriction A technique demonstrated to extend the life span of laboratory animals involving a highly nutritious but severely calorie-restricted diet.

caregiver burden The psychological distress associated with providing care for someone with physical, cognitive, or both types of impairment.

carrier In genetics, individuals who possesses a recessive gene associated with a disease and who, although they do not have the disease, can transmit the gene for it to offspring.

cascade model of substance use Transactional, multifactor model of substance use that envisions a chain of influences starting with a child with a difficult temperament born into troubled family and ending with involvement in a deviant adolescent peer group.

case study An in-depth examination of an individual (or a small number of individuals), typically carried out by compiling and analyzing information from a variety of sources such as observing, testing, and interviewing the person or people who know the individual.

cataract A pathologic condition of the eye involving opacification (clouding) of the lens that can impair vision or cause blindness.

catch-up growth A phenomenon in which children who have experienced growth deficits will grow rapidly and catch up to the growth trajectory they are genetically programmed to follow.

categorical self A person's classification of the self along socially significant dimensions such as age and sex.

celiac disease An inherited digestive problem in which gluten (the proteins found in all wheat products) triggers an immune response that damages a person's small intestine.

centenarian An individual who lives to be 100 years of age.

central executive Mechanism that directs attention and controls the flow of information in the working memory system.

centration In Piaget's theory, the tendency to focus on only one aspect of a problem when two or more aspects are relevant.

cephalocaudal principle The principle that growth proceeds from the head (cephalic region) to the tail (caudal region).

cerebral palsy A neurological disability caused by anoxia that is associated with difficulty controlling muscle movements.

cesarean section A surgical procedure in which an incision is made in the mother's abdomen and uterus so that the baby can be removed through the abdomen.

characteristic adaptations Compared to traits, more situation-specific and changeable aspects of personality; ways in which people adapt to their roles and environments, including motives, goals, plans, schemas, self-conceptions, stage-specific concerns, and coping mechanisms.

child abuse Mistreating or harming a child physically, emotionally, or sexually, as distinguished from another form of child maltreatment, neglect of the child's basic needs.

child effects model A model of family influence in which children are believed to influence their parents rather than vice versa.

child maltreatment A broad term for inadequate care or harmful treatment of a child; encompasses both child abuse and child neglect.

child poverty A household climate that includes low income along with low levels of responsive to children's basic needs.

child-directed speech Speech used by adults speaking with young children, it involves short, simple sentences spoken slowly and in a high-pitched voice, often with much repetition and with exaggerated emphasis on key words.

childhood amnesia A lack of memory for the early years of a person's life.

childhood gender nonconformity (CGN) Lack of adherence as a child to the typical gender-role norms for members of one's assigned gender group.

chorion A membrane that surrounds the amnion and becomes attached to the uterine lining to gather nourishment for the embryo.

chorionic villus sampling (CVS) An alternative to amniocentesis in which a catheter is inserted through the cervix to withdraw fetal cells from the chorion for prenatal testing to detect genetic defects.

chromosome A threadlike structure made up of genes; in humans, there are 46 chromosomes in the nucleus of each cell.

chromosome abnormalities Conditions in which a child has too few, too many, or incomplete chromosomes because of errors in the formation of sperm or ova.

chronosystem In Bronfenbrenner's bioecological approach, the system that captures the way changes in environmental systems, such as social trends and life events, are patterned over a person's lifetime.

chumship According to neo-Freudian Harry Stack Sullivan, a close friendship in childhood that provides emotional support and teaches children how to participate in intimate relationships.

class inclusion The logical understanding that parts or subclasses are included in the whole class and that the whole is therefore greater than any of its parts.

classical conditioning A type of learning in which a stimulus that initially had no effect on the individual comes to elicit a response because of its association with a stimulus that already elicits the response.

clinical method An unstandardized interviewing procedure used by Piaget in which a child's response to each successive question (or problem) determines what the investigator will ask next.

clique A small friendship group that interacts frequently. See *crowd*.

cochlear implant A surgically implanted amplification device that stimulates the auditory nerve to provide the sensation of hearing to a deaf individual.

codominance In genetics, an instance in which two different but equally powerful genes produce a phenotype in which both genes are expressed.

coercive family environment A home in which family members are locked in power struggles, each trying to control the other through aggressive tactics such as threatening, yelling, and hitting.

cognition The activity of knowing and the processes through which knowledge is acquired (for example, attending, perceiving, remembering, and thinking).

cognitive behavioral therapy Well-established psychotherapy approach that involves identifying and changing distorted thinking and maladaptive emotions and behavior associated with it.

cognitive reserve The extra brain power or cognitive capacity that some people can fall back on as aging and diseases such as Alzheimer's begin to take a toll on brain functioning.

cohabitation The living together of two single adults as an unmarried couple.

cohort A group of people born at the same time; a particular generation of people.

cohort effects In cross-sectional research, the effects on findings that the different age groups (cohorts) being compared were born

at different times and had different formative experiences. Contrast with *age effects* and *time of measurement effects*.

collectivist culture A culture in which people define themselves in terms of group memberships, give group goals higher priority than personal goals, and socialize children to seek group harmony. Contrast with *individualistic culture*.

communality An orientation that emphasizes the well-being of others and includes traits of emotionality and sensitivity to others; considered feminine.

comorbid Co-occurring, as when two or more psychiatric conditions affect the same individual.

companionate love In Sternberg's triangular theory of love, affectionate love characterized by high intimacy and commitment but low passion.

complementarity Basis for mate selection in which people choose partners who are different from them but have strengths that compensate for their weaknesses or otherwise complement their own characteristics. Contrast with *homogamy*.

complicated grief An emotional response to a death that is unusually prolonged or intense and that impairs functioning; pathological grief.

conception The moment of fertilization, when a sperm penetrates an ovum, forming a zygote.

concordance rate The percentage of cases in which a particular attribute is present for both members of a pair of people (for example, twins) if it is present for one member.

concrete operations stage Piaget's third stage of cognitive development, lasting from about age 7 to age 11, when children are acquiring logical operations and can reason effectively about real objects and experiences.

conduct disorder A persistent pattern of behavior in which a child or adolescent violates the rights of others or age-appropriate societal norms, as through fighting, bullying, and cruelty.

confidant A spouse, relative, or friend to whom a person feels emotionally close and with whom that person can share thoughts and feelings.

congenital malformations Defects that are present at birth and are caused by genetic factors, prenatal events, or both.

conservation The recognition that certain properties of an object or substance do not change when its appearance is altered in some superficial way.

consolidation In information processing, the processing and organizing of information into a form suitable for long-term storage.

constraint-seeking questions In the Twenty Questions task and similar hypothesis-testing tasks, questions that rule out more than one answer to narrow the field of possible choices rather than asking about only one hypothesis at a time.

constructivism The position taken by Piaget and others that humans actively create their own understandings of the world from their experiences, as opposed to being born with innate ideas or being programmed by the environment.

consummate love In Sternberg's triangular theory of love, love with high levels of all three components of love: passion, intimacy, and decision/commitment.

contact comfort The pleasurable tactile sensations provided by a parent or a soft, terry cloth mother substitute; believed to foster attachments in infant monkeys and possibly humans.

continuing bond Maintenance of attachment to a loved one after the person's death through reminiscence, use of the person's possessions, consultation with the deceased, and the like.

continuity–discontinuity issue The debate among theorists about whether human development is best characterized as gradual and continuous or abrupt and stagelike.

contour The amount of light-dark transition or boundary area in a visual stimulus.

conventional morality Kohlberg's term for the third and fourth stages of moral reasoning in which societal values are internalized and judgments are based on a desire to gain approval or uphold law and social order.

convergent thinking Thinking that involves "converging" on the one best answer to a problem; what IQ tests measure. Contrast with *divergent thinking*.

cooing An early form of vocalization that involves repeating vowel-like sounds.

coordination of secondary schemes During Piaget's sensorimotor period, the infant's combining of actions to solve problems, using one scheme as a means to an end, as in batting aside a barrier in order to grasp a toy.

coparenting The extent and manner in which the two parents coordinate their parenting and function as a team in relation to their children.

copy number variations Instances in which a person receives too many or too few copies of a stretch of DNA; like gene mutations, they can either be inherited from a parent or arise spontaneously and can contribute to diseases and disorders.

correlation coefficient A measure, ranging from +1.00 to −1.00, of the extent to which two variables or attributes are systematically related to each other in either a positive or a negative way.

correlational method A research technique that involves determining whether two or more variables are related. It cannot indicate that one thing caused another, but it can suggest that a causal relationship exists or allow us to predict one characteristic from our knowledge of another.

co-rumination Excessive discussion and analysis of personal problems with a close friend.

couvade Sympathetic pregnancy, or the experiencing by fathers of some of the same physiological symptoms their pregnant partners experience (for example, bloating, weight gain, fatigue, insomnia, and nausea).

creative component In Sternberg's triarchic theory of intelligence, the aspect of intelligence that varies with experience on a task.

creativity The ability to produce novel responses or works; see also *divergent thinking*.

critical period A defined period in the development of an organism when it is particularly sensitive to certain environmental influences; outside this period, the same influences will have far less effect.

crossing over A process in which genetic material is exchanged between pairs of chromosomes during meiosis.

cross-modal perception The ability to use one sensory modality to identify a stimulus or a pattern of stimuli already familiar through another modality.

cross-sectional design A developmental research design in which different age groups are studied at the same point in time and compared.

crowd A network of heterosexual cliques that forms during adolescence and facilitates mixed-sex social activities. See *clique*.

crystallized intelligence Those aspects of intellectual functioning that involve using knowledge acquired through experience. Contrast with *fluid intelligence*.

cued recall memory Recollecting objects, events, or experiences in response to a hint or cue. Contrast with pure *recall memory* and *recognition memory*.

cultural evolution Change in a species achieved not through biological evolution but through learning and passing on from one generation to the next new ways of adapting to the environment.

culture A system of meanings shared by a population of people and transmitted from one generation to the next.

culture bias The situation that arises in testing when one cultural or subcultural group is more familiar with test items than another group and therefore has an unfair advantage.

cumulative-deficit hypothesis The notion that impoverished environments inhibit intellectual growth and that these inhibiting effects accumulate over time.

decentration The ability to focus on two or more dimensions of a problem at one time.

decontextualize To separate the demands of a task at hand from prior beliefs and knowledge.

defense mechanisms Mechanisms used by the ego to defend itself against anxiety caused by conflict between the id's impulses and social demands.

deferred imitation The ability to imitate a novel act after a delay.

delay of gratification The willingness to give up a reward now for a more desirable reward later; related to *self-control*.

delirium A clouding of consciousness characterized by alternating periods of disorientation and coherence.

demandingness–control A dimension of parenting reflecting the extent to which parents as opposed to children exert control over decisions and set and enforce rules; also called permissiveness-restrictiveness.

dementia A progressive loss of cognitive capacities such as memory and judgment that affects some aging individuals and that has a variety of causes; now called neurocognitive disorder.

denial A defense mechanism in which anxiety-provoking thoughts are kept out of, or isolated from, conscious awareness.

dependent variable The aspect of behavior measured in an experiment and assumed to be under the control of, or dependent on, the independent variable.

depression See *major depressive disorder*.

desire psychology The earliest theory of mind: an understanding that desires guide behavior (for example, that people seek things they like and avoid things they hate). Contrast with *belief–desire psychology*.

development Systematic changes in the individual occurring between conception and death; such changes can be positive, negative, or neutral.

developmental norm The age at which half of a large group of infants or children master a skill or display a behavior; the average age for achieving a milestone in development.

developmental psychopathology A field of study concerned with the origins and course of maladaptive or psychopathological behavior.

developmental quotient (DQ) A numerical measure of an infant's performance on a developmental test relative to the performance of other infants the same age.

developmental range In Fischer's dynamic skill framework, the concept that people's abilities vary depending on the context, from optimal levels in highly supportive contexts to lower levels in unsupportive situations.

developmental stage A distinct phase within a larger sequence of development; a period characterized by a particular set of abilities, motives, behaviors, or emotions that occur together and form a coherent pattern.

diabetes A metabolic disorder characterized by high levels of glucose or sugar in the blood leading to symptoms of thirst, excessive urination, fatigue, and problems involving eyes, kidneys, and other organs.

dialectical thinking An advanced form of thought that involves detecting paradoxes and inconsistencies among ideas and trying to reconcile them.

diathesis–stress model The view that psychopathology results from the interaction of a person's predisposition to psychological problems and the experience of stressful events.

differentiation In brain development, the progressive diversification of cells that results in their taking on different characteristics and functions.

difficult temperament Characteristic mode of response in which the individual is irregular in habits and adapts slowly, often with vigorous protest, to changes in routine or new experiences. Contrast with *easy temperament* and *slow-to-warm-up temperament*.

diffusion status Identity status characterizing individuals who have not questioned who they are and have not committed themselves to an identity.

directionality problem The problem in correlational studies of determining whether a presumed causal variable is the cause or the effect. See also *third variable problem*.

disenfranchised grief Grief that is not fully recognized or appreciated by other people and therefore may not receive much sympathy and support, as in the loss of a gay partner.

disengagement theory A perspective that holds that successful aging involves a mutually satisfying withdrawal of the aging individual and society from each other. Contrast with *activity theory*.

disorganized–disoriented attachment An insecure infant–caregiver bond, common among abused children, that combines features of the resistant and avoidant attachment styles and is characterized by the infant's dazed response to reunion and confusion about whether to approach or avoid the caregiver.

display rule for emotion A cultural rule specifying what emotions should and should not be expressed under what circumstances.

dispositional traits Relatively enduring dimensions or qualities of personality along which people differ (for example, extraversion, aloofness).

divergent thinking Thinking that requires coming up with a variety of ideas or solutions to a problem when there is no one right answer. Contrast with *convergent thinking*.

DNA Deoxyribonucleic acid, the double helix molecule whose chemical code makes up chromosomes and serves as our genetic endowment; it is made up of sequences of the chemicals (adenine), C (cytosine), G (guanine), and T (thymine).

dominant gene A relatively powerful gene that is expressed phenotypically and masks the effect of a less-powerful recessive gene.

double standard The view that sexual behavior appropriate for members of one gender is inappropriate for members of the other.

Down syndrome A chromosomal abnormality in which the child has inherited an extra 21st chromosome and is, as a result, mentally retarded; also called trisomy 21.

DSM-5 The fifth edition of the *Diagnostic and Statistical Manual of Mental Disorders* published by the American Psychiatric Association, which spells out defining features and symptoms for the range of psychological disorders.

dual-process model of bereavement A theory of coping with bereavement in which the bereaved oscillate between loss-oriented coping in which they deal with their emotions, restoration-oriented coping in which they try to manage practical tasks and reorganize their lives, and periods of respite from coping.

dual process model of morality The view that *both* deliberate thought and more automatic emotion-based intuitions can inform decisions about moral issues and motivate behavior.

dynamic In Fischer's dynamic skill framework, the idea that human performance changes in response to changes in context.

dynamic systems theory A perspective on development which, when applied to motor development, proposes that more sophisticated patterns of motor behavior emerge over time through a "self-organizing" process in which children modify their motor behavior in adaptive ways on the basis of the sensory feedback they receive when they try different movements.

dyslexia Serious difficulties learning to read in children who have normal intellectual ability and no sensory impairments or emotional difficulties that could account for their learning problems.

easy temperament Characteristic mode of response in which the individual is even-tempered, content, and open and adaptable to new experiences. Contrast with *difficult temperament* and *slow-to-warm-up temperament*.

eclectic In the context of science, an individual who recognizes that no single theory can explain everything but that each has something to contribute to our understanding.

effortful control Dimension of temperament pertaining to being able to sustain attention, control one's behavior, and regulate one's emotions (as opposed to unable to regulate one's arousal and stay calm and focused). See also *negative affectivity* and *surgency/extraversion*.

ego Psychoanalytic term for the rational component of the personality.

egocentrism The tendency to view the world from the person's own perspective and fail to recognize that others may have different points of view.

elaboration A strategy for remembering that involves adding something to or creating meaningful links between the bits of information the person is trying to retain.

Electra complex Female version of the *Oedipus complex*, in which a 4- to 6-year-old girl is said to envy her father for possessing a penis and would choose him as a sex object in the hope of sharing this valuable organ that she lacks.

embryologist Scientist who studies early growth and development during the prenatal period.

embryonic period Second phase of prenatal development, lasting from the third through the eighth prenatal week, during which the major organs and anatomical structures begin to develop.

emergent literacy The developmental precursors of reading skills in young children, including knowledge, skills, and attributes that will facilitate the acquisition of reading competence.

emerging adulthood Newly identified period of the life span extending from about age 18 to age 25 or even later, when young people are neither adolescents nor adults and are exploring their identities, careers, and relationships.

emotion regulation The processes involved in initiating, maintaining, and altering emotional responses.

emotional competence Mastery of emotions in terms of appropriate expression of emotions, understanding of emotions and what triggers them, and ability to regulate emotions.

empathy The vicarious experiencing of another person's feelings.

emotionally focused therapy Psychotherapy approach based on attachment theory that helps partners understand their attachment-related emotions, communicate their emotions, and collaborate to better meet one another's emotional needs.

empty nest The term used to describe the family after the last child departs the household.

encoding The first step in learning and remembering something, it is the process of getting information into the information-processing system, or learning it.

endocrine gland A type of gland that secretes chemicals called hormones directly into the bloodstream. Endocrine glands play critical roles in stimulating growth and regulating bodily functions.

environment Events or conditions outside the person that are presumed to influence and be influenced by the individual.

epigenesis The process through which nature and nurture, genes and environment, jointly bring forth development in ways that are difficult to predict at the outset.

epigenetic effects Ways in which environmental influences alter the expression of genes (whether genes are turned on or off) and therefore the influence of genes on traits.

episodic memory A type of explicit memory consisting of specific episodes that one has experienced.

equilibration In Piaget's theory, the process of seeking a state of mental stability in which our thoughts (schemes) are consistent with the information we receive from the external world.

erectile dysfunction A man's inability to achieve or sustain an erection for intercourse, despite having sufficient levels of testosterone.

estrogen The female hormone responsible for the development of the breasts, the female sex organs, and secondary sex characteristics and for the beginning of menstrual cycles.

ethnic identity A sense of personal identification with the individual's ethnic group and its values and cultural traditions.

ethnicity A person's classification in or affiliation with a group based on common heritage or traditions.

ethnocentrism The belief that one's own cultural or ethnic group is superior to others.

ethology A discipline and theoretical perspective that focuses on the evolved behavior of different species in their natural environments.

euthanasia Literally, "good death"; specifically, hastening, either actively or passively, the death of someone suffering from an incurable illness or injury.

evidence-based practice Grounding what professionals do in research and ensuring that the curricula and treatments provided to students or clients have been demonstrated to be effective.

evocative gene-environment correlation Phenomenon in which children's genotypes *evoke* certain kinds of reactions from other people so that their genetic makeup and experiences are correlated. Contrast with *active gene-environment correlation* and *passive gene-environment correlation*.

evoked potentials Electrical activity in the brain, as measured through electrodes attached to the surface of the skull, in response to various stimuli; used to study infant perception.

evolutionary psychology The application of evolutionary theory and its concept of natural selection to understanding why humans think and behave as they do.

executive control processes Processes that direct and monitor the selection, organization, manipulation, and interpretation of information in the information-processing system, including executive functions.

executive functions The planning, organizational, and inhibitory functions carried out in the prefrontal cortex of the brain.

exosystem In Bronfenbrenner's bioecological approach, settings not experienced directly by individuals that still influence their development (for example, effects of events at a parent's workplace on children's development).

expansion A conversational tactic used by adults in speaking to young children in which they respond to a child's utterance with a more grammatically complete expression of the same thought.

experiment A research strategy in which the investigator manipulates or alters some aspect of a person's environment to measure its effect on the individual's behavior or development.

experimental control The holding of all other factors besides the independent variable in an experiment constant so that any changes in the dependent variable can be said to be caused by the manipulation of the independent variable.

explicit memory Memory that involves consciously recollecting the past. Contrast with *implicit memory*.

extended family household A family unit composed of parents and children living with other kin such as grandparents, aunts and uncles, cousins, or a combination of these. Compare with *nuclear family*.

externalizing problem Childhood behavioral problem that involves "undercontrolled" behavior such as aggression or acting out difficulties that disturb other people. Contrast with *internalizing problem*.

extinction The gradual weakening and disappearance of a learned response when it is no longer reinforced.

eyewitness memory Remembering and reporting events the person has witnessed or experienced.

false belief task A research paradigm used to assess an important aspect of a theory of mind, mainly the understanding that people can hold incorrect beliefs and be influenced by them.

family life cycle The sequence of changes in family composition, roles, and relationships that occurs from the time people marry until they die.

family stress model Model of the effects of economic hardship in families that centers on the negative effects of financial stresses on parent mental health, parenting, and, in turn, child development.

family study Method of studying genetic and environmental influence that examines similarities in traits between pairs of siblings who have different degrees of genetic similarity—for example, identical twins, full biological siblings, half siblings, and unrelated stepsiblings who live together in stepfamilies.

family systems theory The conceptualization of the family as a whole consisting of interrelated parts, each of which affects and is affected by every other part, and each of which contributes to the functioning of the whole.

fast mapping The capacity of young language learners to readily determine the object or other referent of a word and then remember this for future encounters with the word.

fetal alcohol syndrome (FAS) A group of symptoms commonly observed in the offspring of mothers who use alcohol heavily during pregnancy, including a small head, widely spaced eyes, and mental retardation.

fetal period The third phase of prenatal development, lasting from the ninth prenatal week until birth; during this period, the major organ systems begin to function effectively and the fetus grows rapidly.

fetal programming Processes through which the prenatal environment affects the genetic unfolding of the embryo/fetus and its physiologic functions in ways that can influence health and mental health much later in life.

fine motor skills Skills that involve precise movements of the hands and fingers or feet and toes. Contrast with *gross motor skills*.

fixation In psychoanalytic theory, a defense mechanism in which development is arrested and part of the libido remains tied to an early stage of development.

fixed mindset The belief that intelligence and other traits are fixed or static; associated with the tendency to want to prove rather than improve one's ability. Contrast with *growth mindset*.

fluid intelligence Aspects of intelligence that involve actively thinking and reasoning to solve novel problems. Contrast with *crystallized intelligence*.

Flynn effect The rise in average IQ scores over the 20th century.

focusing system Attentional system that that deliberately seeks out and maintains attention to events. Contrast with *orienting system*, which is captured by stimuli.

foreclosure status An identity status characterizing individuals who appear to have committed themselves to a life direction but who have adopted an identity prematurely, without much thought.

form perception In visual perception, recognition of the patterns that constitute an object.

formal operations stage Piaget's fourth and final stage of cognitive development (from age 11 or 12), when the individual begins to think more rationally and systematically about abstract concepts and hypothetical ideas.

fragile X syndrome A chromosome abnormality in which one arm of the X chromosome is only barely connected to the rest of the chromosome; the most common hereditary cause of mental retardation.

fraternal twins Twins who are not identical and who result when a mother releases two ova at roughly the same time and each is fertilized by a different sperm.

free radicals Chemically unstable byproducts of metabolism that have an unpaired electron and react with other molecules to produce toxic substances that damage cells and contribute to aging.

functional grammar An analysis of the semantic relations (meanings such as naming and locating) that children express in their earliest sentences.

functional magnetic resonance imaging (fMRI) A brain-scanning technique that uses magnetic forces to measure the increase in blood flow to an area of the brain that occurs when that brain area is active. By having children and adults perform cognitive tasks while lying very still in an fMRI scanner, researchers can determine which parts of the brain are involved in particular cognitive activities.

fuzzy-trace theory The view that verbatim and general or gistlike accounts of an event are stored separately in memory.

gender A combination of all those features that a society associates with or considers appropriate for being a man and woman.

gender consistency The stage of gender typing in which children realize that their sex is stable across situations or despite changes in activities or appearance.

gender constancy A solid understanding of oneself as male-female, man-woman, over time and across situations.

gender identity Individuals' basic awareness that they are either a male or a female.

gender intensification A magnification of differences between males and females during adolescence associated with increased pressure to conform to traditional gender roles.

gender role A pattern of behaviors and traits that defines how to act the part of a female or a male in a particular society.

gender schema (plural: schemata) Organized sets of beliefs and expectations about males and females that guide information processing.

gender segregation The formation of separate boys' and girls' peer groups during childhood.

gender similarities hypothesis The hypothesis that males and females are similar on most, but not all, psychological variables.

gender stability The stage of gender typing in which children realize that their sex remains the same over time.

gender stereotypes Overgeneralized and largely inaccurate beliefs about what males and females are like.

gender typing The process by which children become aware of their gender and acquire the motives, values, and behaviors considered appropriate for members of their biological sex.

gene A functional unit of heredity made up of DNA and transmitted from generation to generation.

gene expression The activation of particular genes in particular cells of the body at particular times in life.

gene therapy Interventions that involve substituting normal genes for the genes associated with a disease or disorder; otherwise altering a person's genetic makeup.

gene–environment correlation A systematic interrelationship between an individual's genes and that individual's environment; ways in which genes influence the kind of home environment provided by parents (*passive gene–environment correlation*), the social reactions to the individual (*evocative gene–environment correlation*), and the types of experiences the individual seeks (*active gene–environment correlation*).

gene–environment interaction The phenomenon in which the effects of people's genes depend on the kind of environment they experience and in which the effects of the environment depend on their genetic endowment.

general event representation Representations that people create over time of the typical sequence of actions related to an event; also called "scripts."

generativity versus stagnation The psychosocial conflict in which middle-aged adults must gain the sense that they have produced something that will outlive them and genuinely care for younger generations to avoid self-preoccupation; seventh of Erikson's stages.

genetic counseling A service designed to inform people about genetic conditions they or their unborn children are at risk of inheriting.

genotype The genetic endowment that an individual inherits. Contrast with *phenotype*.

germinal period First phase of prenatal development, lasting about 2 weeks from conception until the developing organism becomes attached to the wall of the uterus.

gerontology The study of aging and old age.

giftedness The possession of unusually high general intellectual potential or of special abilities in such areas as creativity, mathematics, or the arts.

glaucoma A condition in which increased fluid pressure in the eye damages the optic nerve and causes progressive loss of peripheral vision and ultimately blindness.

goal-corrected partnership In Bowlby's attachment theory, the most mature phase of attachment in which parent and child accommodate to each other's needs and the child becomes more independent.

goodness of fit The extent to which the child's temperament and the demands of the child's social environment are compatible or mesh, according to Thomas and Chess; more generally, a good match between person and environment.

grief The emotional response to loss. Contrast with *mourning*.

grief work perspective The view commonly held, but now challenged, that to cope adaptively with death bereaved people must confront their loss, experience painful emotions, work through these emotions, and move toward a detachment from the deceased.

gross motor skills Skills that involve large muscles and whole body or limb movements (for example, kicking the legs or drawing large circles). Contrast with *fine motor skills*.

growth The physical changes that occur from conception to maturity.

growth hormone Hormone produced by the pituitary gland that stimulates childhood physical growth and the adolescent growth spurt.

growth mindset The belief that intelligence is not fixed but malleable and can therefore be improved through hard work and effort. Contrast with *fixed mindset*.

guided participation A process in which children learn by actively participating in culturally relevant activities with the aid and support of their parents and other knowledgeable individuals.

habituation A simple form of learning that involves learning not to respond to a repeated stimulus; learning to be bored by the familiar.

Hayflick limit The estimate that human cells can double only 50 times, plus or minus 10, and then will die.

hemophilia A deficiency in the blood's ability to clot. It is more common among males than females because it is associated with a sex-linked gene on the X chromosome.

heritability The amount of variability in a population on some trait dimension that is attributable to genetic differences among those individuals.

hippocampus Structure in the medial temporal lobe of the brain centrally involved in the formation of memories.

holophrase A single-word utterance used by an infant that represents an entire sentence's worth of meaning.

Home Observation for Measurement of the Environment (HOME) inventory A widely used instrument that allows an observer to determine how intellectually stimulating or impoverished a home environment is.

homogamy Basis for mate selection centered on similarity between partners in demographic and personal characteristics. Contrast with *complementarity*.

hookup A sexual encounter between two people who have often just met and have little expectation of forming a romantic relationship.

horizontal décalage A term used by Piaget to characterize that different cognitive skills related to the same stage of cognitive development emerge at different times.

hormone replacement therapy (HRT) Taking estrogen and progestin to compensate for hormone loss because of menopause in women.

hospice A program that supports dying persons and their families through a philosophy of caring rather than curing, either in a facility or at home.

hostile attribution bias The tendency of aggressive individuals to attribute hostile intentions to others, assuming that any harm to them was deliberate rather than accidental.

hot flash A sudden experience of warmth and sweating, often followed by a cold shiver, that occurs in a menopausal woman.

Human Genome Project The massive, government-sponsored effort to decipher the human genetic code.

Huntington's disease A genetic disease caused by a single, dominant gene that strikes in middle age to produce a deterioration of physical and mental abilities and premature death.

hyperactivity See *attention deficit hyperactivity disorder* (ADHD).

hypothesis A theory-based prediction about what will hold true if we observe a phenomenon.

hypothetical-deductive reasoning A form of problem solving in which a person starts with general or abstract ideas and deduces or traces their specific implications; "if–then" thinking.

id A psychoanalytic term for the inborn component of the personality that is driven by the instincts or selfish urges.

ideal self Idealized expectations of what one's attributes and personality should be like.

ideational fluency The sheer number of different (including novel) ideas that a person can generate; a measure of *creativity* or *divergent thinking*.

identical twins Monozygotic twins who develop from a single zygote that later divides to form two genetically identical individuals.

identification Freud's term for the individual's tendency to emulate, or adopt the attitudes and behaviors of, another person, particularly the same-sex parent.

identity A self-definition or sense of who one is, where one is going, and how one fits into society.

identity achievement status An identity status characterizing individuals who have carefully thought through identity issues and made commitments or resolved their identity issues.

identity versus role confusion The psychosocial conflict in which adolescents must form a coherent self-definition or remain confused about their life directions; fifth of Erikson's stages.

imaginary audience A form of adolescent egocentrism that involves confusing one's own thoughts with the thoughts of a hypothesized audience for behavior and concluding that others share these preoccupations.

imaginary companion A play companion invented by a child in the preoperational stage who has developed the capacity for symbolic thought.

implicit memory Memory that occurs unintentionally and without consciousness or awareness. Contrast with *explicit memory*.

imprinting An innate form of learning in which the young of certain species will follow and become attached to moving objects (usually their mothers) during a critical period early in life.

incomplete dominance A condition in which a stronger gene fails to mask all the effects of a weaker partner gene; a phenotype results that is similar but not identical to the effect of the stronger gene.

independent variable The aspect of the environment that a researcher deliberately changes or manipulates in an experiment to see its effect on behavior; a causal variable. Contrast with *dependent variable*.

indirect effect The instance in which the relationship between two individuals in a family is modified by the behavior or attitudes of a third family member.

individualistic culture A culture in which individuals define themselves as individuals and put their own goals ahead of their group's goals and in which children are socialized to be independent and self-reliant. Contrast with *collectivist culture*.

induction A form of discipline that involves explaining why a child's behavior is wrong and should be changed by emphasizing its effects on other people.

industry versus inferiority The psychosocial conflict in which school-aged children must master important cognitive and social skills or feel incompetent; fourth of Erikson's stages.

infertility A couple's inability to get pregnant after a year of trying to do so.

information-processing approach An approach to cognition that emphasizes the fundamental mental processes involved in attention, perception, memory, and decision making.

initiative versus guilt The psychosocial conflict in which preschool children must learn to initiate new activities and pursue bold plans or become self-critical; third of Erikson's stages.

instinct An inborn biological force assumed to motivate a particular response or class of responses.

integrity versus despair The psychosocial conflict in which elderly adults attempt to find a sense of meaning in their lives and to accept the inevitability of death; eighth of Erikson's stages.

intellectual disability Significantly below-average intellectual functioning with limitations in areas of adaptive behavior such as self-care and social skills, originating before age 18 (previously known as mental retardation).

intelligence quotient (IQ) A numerical measure of a person's performance on an intelligence test relative to the performance of other examinees of the same age, typically with a score of 100 defined as average.

interactional model A model of family influence in which it is the combination of a particular kind of child with a particular kind of parent that determines developmental outcomes.

intergenerational transmission of parenting The passing down from generation to generation of parenting styles, abusive or otherwise.

internal working model In attachment theory, cognitive representation of self and other that children construct from their interactions with caregivers and that shape their expectations about relationships.

internalizing problem Childhood behavioral problem that represents an "overcontrolled" pattern of coping with difficulties and is expressed in anxiety, depression, and other forms of inner distress. Contrast with *externalizing problem*.

intimacy versus isolation The psychosocial conflict in which young adults must commit themselves to a shared identity with another person or remain aloof and unconnected to others; sixth of Erikson's stages.

intuitive theories Organized systems of knowledge, believed to be innate, that allow children to make sense of the world in areas such as physics and psychology.

investment theory Sternberg's view that creativity emerges from a *confluence*, or coming together, of several ingredients, each in the right amounts and at the right times: intellectual abilities, knowledge, cognitive style, personality, motivation, and a supportive environment.

in vitro fertilization (IVF) Procedure in which several eggs are removed from a woman's ovary, fertilized by sperm in a petri dish in the laboratory, then transferred to the woman's uterus in hopes that one will implant on the wall of the uterus.

joint attention The act of looking at the same object at the same time with someone else; a way in which infants share perceptual experiences with their caregivers.

juvenile delinquency Law-breaking by a minor.

kangaroo care Holding a young infant skin-to-skin on a parent's chest; often used with premature babies to help maintain body temperature, heart rate, and oxygen levels in the blood.

karyotype A chromosomal portrait created by staining chromosomes, photographing them under a high-power microscope, and arranging them into a predetermined pattern.

kinkeeper An individual, typically a woman, who keep family members in touch with each other and handles family problems when they arise.

Klinefelter syndrome A sex chromosome abnormality in which males inherit two or more X chromosomes (XXY or XXXY); these males fail to develop secondary sex characteristics and often show deficiencies on tests of verbal abilities.

knowledge base A person's existing information about a content area, significant for its influence on how well that individual can learn and remember.

Lamaze method Prepared childbirth in which parents attend classes and learn mental exercises and relaxation techniques to ease delivery.

language A symbolic system in which a limited number of signals can be combined according to rules to produce an infinite number of messages.

language acquisition device (LAD) A set of linguistic processing skills that nativists believe to be innate; presumably the LAD enables a child to infer the rules governing others' speech and then use these rules to produce language.

latent learning Learning occurs but is not evident in behavior; children can learn from observation even though they do not imitate (perform) the learned responses.

lateralization The specialization of the two hemispheres of the cerebral cortex of the brain.

learning A relatively permanent change in behavior (or behavioral potential) that results from a person's experiences or practice.

learning goal A goal adopted by learners in which they seek to learn new things so that they can improve their abilities. Contrast with *performance goal*.

libido Freud's term for the biological energy of the sex instinct.

life expectancy The average number of years a newborn baby can be expected to live; now about 78 years in the United States.

life review Process in which elderly adults reflect on unresolved conflicts of the past and evaluate their lives; it may contribute to a sense of integrity and readiness for death.

life script The story a person constructs about his or her life story and tells over and over again.

life-span perspective A perspective that views development as a lifelong, multidirectional process that involves gain and loss, is characterized by considerable plasticity, is shaped by its historical-cultural context, has many causes, and is best viewed from a multidisciplinary perspective.

linked lives The concept that the development of the individual is intertwined with the development of other family members.

literacy The ability to use printed information to function in society, achieve goals, and develop potential.

living will A document, also called an advance directive, in which people state in advance that they do not wish to have extraordinary medical procedures applied if they are hopelessly ill.

locomotion The process of moving from one location to another.

longitudinal design A developmental research design in which one group of subjects is studied repeatedly over months or years.

long-term memory Memory store in which information that has been examined and interpreted is stored relatively permanently.

loss-oriented coping In the dual-process model of bereavement, coping focused on dealing with one's emotions and reconciling oneself to the loss. Contrast with *restoration-oriented coping*.

love withdrawal A form of discipline that involves withholding attention, affection, or approval after a child misbehaves.

low birth weight (LBW) A weight at birth of less than 2500 grams, or 5 ½ pounds, associated with increased risk of developmental problems.

macrosystem In Bronfenbrenner's bioecological approach, the larger cultural or subcultural context of development.

major depressive disorder An affective or mood disorder characterized by at least one episode of feeling profoundly sad and hopeless, losing interest in almost all activities, or both.

mastery (learning) goal In achievement situations, aiming to learn new things in order to learn or improve ability; contrast with *performance goal*.

mastery motivation An intrinsic motive to master and control the environment evident early in infancy.

maternal blood sampling A noninvasive method of prenatal diagnosis involving testing for substances in maternal blood; more recently, analysis of fetal cells that have slipped through the placenta into the mother's blood.

maturation Developmental changes that are biologically programmed by genes rather than caused primarily by learning, injury, illness, or some other life experience.

maximum life span A ceiling on the number of years that any member of a species lives; 120 years for humans.

mediation deficiency The initial stage of mastery of memory strategies in which children cannot spontaneously use or benefit from strategies even if they are taught to use them.

meiosis The process in which a germ cell divides, producing sperm or ova, each containing half of the parent cell's original complement of chromosomes; in humans, the products of meiosis normally contain 23 chromosomes.

memory The ability to store and later retrieve information about past events.

menarche A female's first menstrual period.

menopause The ending of a woman's menstrual periods and reproductive capacity around age 51.

mental age A measure of intellectual development that reflects the level of age-graded problems that a child is able to solve; the age at which a child functions intellectually.

mental retardation See *intellectual disability*.

mesosystem In Bronfenbrenner's bioecological approach, interrelationships between microsystems or immediate environments (for example, ways in which events in the family affect a child's interactions at a day care center).

meta-analysis A research method in which the results of multiple studies addressing the same question are synthesized to produce overall conclusions.

metabolic syndrome (MeTS) A combination of risk factors that can lead to heart disease, notably obesity, high blood pressure, unhealthy cholesterol levels, and insulin resistance (which can lead to diabetes).

metacognition Knowledge of the human mind and of the range of cognitive processes, including thinking about personal thought processes.

metalinguistic awareness Knowledge of language as a system.

metamemory A person's knowledge about memory and about monitoring and regulating memory processes.

microsystem In Bronfenbrenner's bioecological approach, the immediate settings in which the person functions (for example, the family).

middle generation squeeze The phenomenon in which middle-aged adults sometimes experience heavy responsibilities for both the younger and the older generations in the family.

midlife crisis A period of major questioning, inner struggle, and re-evaluation hypothesized to occur in an adult's early 40s.

migration Process in early brain development in which neurons move from their place of origin in the center of the brain to particular locations throughout the brain where they will become part of specialized functioning units.

mild cognitive impairment A level of memory loss between normal loss with age and pathological loss from disease.

millennials Also called Generation Y or the "baby boomlet" generation, the American generation born from 1982 to 2004.

mirror neurons Neural cells in several brain areas that are activated not only when we perform an action but also when we observe someone else performing it. Implicated in imitation, theory of mind skills, empathy, and language.

miscarriage Loss of a pregnancy before survival of the baby outside the womb is possible.

mitosis The process in which a cell duplicates its chromosomes and then divides into two genetically identical daughter cells.

molecular genetics The analysis of particular genes and their effects, including the identification of specific genes that influence particular traits and the comparison of animals or humans who have these specific genes and those who do not.

moral disengagement According to Bandura, the ability to avoid self condemnation when engaged in immoral behavior by justifying, minimizing, or blaming others for one's actions.

moral identity Viewing being caring, fair, honest, and otherwise moral as a central aspect of who you are.

moral reasoning The cognitive component of morality; the thinking that occurs when people decide whether acts are right or wrong.

moral rules Standards of conduct that focus on the basic rights and privileges of individuals. Contrast with *social-conventional rules*.

morality The ability to distinguish right from wrong, to act on this distinction, and to experience pride when doing something right and to experience guilt or shame when doing something wrong. Morality has emotional, cognitive, and behavioral components.

moratorium period A period of time in high school or college when young adults are relatively free of responsibilities and can experiment with different roles to find their identities.

moratorium status Identity status characterizing individuals who are experiencing an identity crisis or actively exploring identity issues but who have not yet achieved an identity.

morphemes The basic units of meaning that exist in a word.

mourning Culturally prescribed ways of displaying reactions to a loss. Contrast with *grief*.

multitasking Attending to and performing two or more tasks at the same time.

mutation A change in the structure or arrangement of one or more genes that produces a new phenotype.

mutually responsive orientation A close, affectively positive, and cooperative relationship in which child and parent are attached to each other and are sensitive to each other's needs; a contributor to moral development.

myelin A fatty sheath that insulates neural axons and thereby speeds the transmission of neural impulses.

myelination The depositing of a fatty sheath around neural axons that insulates them and thereby speeds the transmission of neural impulses.

narrative identities Unique and integrative "life stories" that we construct about our pasts and futures to give ourselves an identity and our lives meaning; an aspect of personality.

nativist An individual whose approach to human development emphasizes the contribution of genetic factors; specifically, a person who believes that infants enter the world equipped with knowledge that allows them to perceive a meaningful world from the start.

natural selection The evolutionary principle that individuals who have characteristics advantageous for survival in a particular environment are most likely to survive and reproduce. Over many generations, this process of "survival of the fittest" will lead to changes in a species and the development of new species.

naturalistic observation A research method in which the scientist observes people as they engage in common everyday activities in their natural habitats. Contrast with *structured observation*.

nature–nurture issue The debate over the relative roles of biological predispositions (nature) and environmental influences (nurture) as determinants of human development.

negative affectivity Dimension of temperament that concerns the tendency to be sad, fearful, easily frustrated, and irritable (as opposed to laid back and adaptable). See also *effortful control* and *surgency/extraversion*.

negative punishment The process in operant conditioning in which a response is weakened or made less probable when its consequence is the removal of a pleasant stimulus from the situation.

negative reinforcement The process in operant conditioning in which a response is strengthened or made more probable when its consequence is the removal of an unpleasant stimulus from the situation.

neglectful parenting A parenting style low in demandingness–control and low in acceptance–responsiveness; uninvolved parenting.

neonatal Pertaining to events or developments in the first month after birth.

neuro-constructivism theory Approach that explains the construction of new knowledge by the child in terms of changes in neural structures in response to experience.

neurogenesis The process of generating new neurons across the lifespan.

neuron The basic unit of the nervous system; a nerve cell.

neuroplasticity The brain's remarkable ability to change in response to experience throughout the life span, as when it recovers from injury or benefits from stimulating learning experiences.

nonshared environmental influences Experiences unique to the individual that are not shared by other members of the family and that tend to make members of the same family different. Contrast with *shared environmental influences*.

normal distribution A symmetrical (bell-shaped) curve that describes the variability of a characteristic within a population. Most people fall at or near the average score; there are relatively few high or low scores.

nuclear family A family unit consisting of husband–father, wife–mother, and at least one child. Compare with *extended family household*.

obesity Condition of being overweight; specifically, being 20% or more above the "ideal" weight for one's height, age, and sex.

object permanence The understanding that objects continue to exist when they are no longer visible or otherwise detectable to the senses; fully mastered by the end of infancy.

observational learning Learning that results from observing the behavior of other people; emphasized in Bandura's social cognitive theory.

Oedipus complex Freud's term for the conflict that 4- to 6-year-old boys experience when they develop an incestuous desire for their mothers and a jealous and hostile rivalry with their fathers.

olfaction The sense of smell, made possible by sensory receptors in the nasal passage that react to chemical molecules in the air.

operant conditioning Also called instrumental conditioning, a form of learning in which freely emitted acts (or operants) become more or less probable depending on the consequences they produce.

oral sex Sexual activity involving contact between the mouth and genitals.

organization In Piaget's cognitive developmental theory, a person's inborn tendency to combine and integrate available schemes into more coherent and complex systems or bodies of knowledge; as a memory strategy, a technique that involves grouping or classifying stimuli into meaningful clusters.

organogenesis The process, occurring during the period of the embryo, in which major organs take shape.

orienting system An attentional system that reacts to events in the environment; contrast with a *focusing system* that deliberately seeks out and maintains attention to events.

orthogenetic principle Werner's principle that development proceeds from global and undifferentiated states toward more differentiated and integrated patterns of response.

osteoarthritis A joint problem among older adults resulting from a gradual deterioration of the cartilage that cushions the bones and keeps them from rubbing together.

osteoporosis A disease affecting older adults in which bone tissue is lost, leaving bones fragile and easily fractured.

overextension The young child's tendency to use a word to refer to a wider set of objects, actions, or events than adults do (for example, using the word *car* to refer to all motor vehicles). Contrast with *underextension*.

overlapping waves theory Siegler's view that the development of problem-solving skills is not a matter of moving from one problem solving approach to a better one with age but of knowing and using a variety of strategies at each age, becoming increasingly selective with experience about which strategies to use in particular situations, and adding new strategies to one's collection.

overregularization The overgeneralization of observed grammatical rules to irregular cases to which the rules do not apply (for example, saying *mouses* rather than *mice*).

oxytocin A hormone that plays important roles in facilitating parent-infant attachment as well as reducing anxiety and encouraging affiliation in other social relationships.

palliative care Care aimed not at curing but at meeting the physical, psychological, and spiritual needs of dying patients.

parallel processing Carrying out multiple cognitive operations simultaneously rather than in a sequence.

parent effects model A model of family influence in which parents (particularly mothers) are believed to influence their children rather than vice versa.

parental imperative The notion that the demands of parenthood cause men and women to adopt distinct roles and psychological traits.

Parkes/Bowlby attachment model of bereavement Model of grieving describing four predominant reactions to loss of an attachment figure: numbness, yearning, disorganization and despair, and reorganization.

passive gene-environment correlation Phenomenon in which, because parents provide children with both their genes and a home environment compatible with those genes, the home environments to which children are exposed are correlated with (and typically reinforce) their genotypes. Contrast with *active gene-environment correlation* and *evocative gene-environment correlation*.

peer A social equal; a person who functions at a level of behavioral complexity similar to that of the self, often someone of similar age.

perception The interpretation of sensory input.

perceptual salience Phenomenon in which the most obvious features of an object or situation have disproportionate influence on the perceptions and thought of young children.

perceived popularity Perceived status, power, and visibility in the peer group, as distinct from likeability. Contrast with *sociometric popularity*.

performance goal A goal adopted by learners in which they attempt to prove their ability rather than to improve it. Contrast with *learning (or mastery) goal*.

perinatal environment The environment surrounding birth.

perinatologist A maternal-fetal specialist who focuses on high-risk pregnancies.

permissive parenting A lax style of parenting combining low demandingness–control and high acceptance–responsiveness in which adults love their children but make few demands on them and rarely attempt to control their behavior.

perseveration error Mistake made when an information processor continues to use the same strategy that was successful in the past over and over despite the strategy's lack of success in the current situation.

personal fable A form of adolescent egocentrism that involves thinking that oneself and one's thoughts and feelings are unique or special.

personality The organized combination of attributes, motives, values, and behaviors that is unique to each individual.

perspective-taking skills The ability to assume other people's perspectives and understand their thoughts, feelings, and behaviors; role-taking skills.

phenotype The way in which a person's genotype is expressed in observable or measurable characteristics.

phenylketonuria (PKU) A genetic disease in which the child is unable to metabolize phenylalanine; if left untreated, it soon causes hyperactivity and mental retardation.

phoneme One of the basic units of sound used in a particular spoken language.

phonological awareness The understanding that spoken words can be decomposed into some number of basic sound units, or phonemes; an important skill in learning to read.

pincer grasp A grasp in which the thumb is used in opposition to the fingers, enabling an infant to become more dexterous at lifting and manipulating objects.

pituitary gland The "master gland" located at the base of the brain that regulates the other endocrine glands and produces growth hormone.

placenta An organ, formed from the chorion and the lining of the uterus, that provides for the nourishment of the unborn child and the elimination of its metabolic wastes.

plasticity An openness of brain cells or of the organism as a whole to positive and negative environmental influence; a capacity to change in response to experience.

polygenic trait A characteristic influenced by the action of many gene pairs rather than a single pair.

population A well-defined group that a researcher who studies a sample of individuals is interested in drawing conclusions about.

positive punishment The process in operant conditioning whereby a response is weakened when its consequence is an unpleasant event.

positive reinforcement The process in operant conditioning whereby a response is strengthened when its consequence is a pleasant event.

positive youth development (PYD) An approach that emphasizes developing the strengths of youth rather than reducing their problem behaviors.

positivity effect The tendency of older adults to pay more attention to, better remember, and put more priority on positive information than on negative information; see also *socioemotional selectivity theory*.

postconventional morality Kohlberg's term for the fifth and sixth stages of moral reasoning, in which moral judgments are based on a more abstract understanding of democratic social contracts or on universal principles of justice that have validity apart from the views of particular authority figures.

postformal thought Proposed stages of cognitive development that lie beyond formal operations.

postpartum depression An episode of severe, clinical depression lasting for months in a woman who has just given birth; to be contrasted with milder cases of the "baby blues," in which a new mother is tearful and moody in the first days after birth.

posttraumatic growth Positive psychological change resulting from highly challenging experiences such as being diagnosed with a life-threatening illness or losing a loved one.

posttraumatic stress disorder A psychological disorder involving flashbacks to traumatizing events, nightmares, and feelings of helplessness and anxiety in the face of danger experienced by victims of extreme trauma such as soldiers in combat and sexually abused children.

poverty of the stimulus (POTS): Term for the notion that the language input to young children is so impoverished or limited that they could not possibly acquire language (without a powerful, innate *language acquisition device*).

power assertion A form of discipline that involves the use of superior power to administer spankings, withhold privileges, and so on.

practical component In Sternberg's triarchic theory of intelligence, the aspect of intelligence that varies from one sociocultural context to another.

pragmatics Rules specifying how language is to be used appropriately in different social contexts to achieve goals.

preconventional morality Kohlberg's term for the first two stages of moral reasoning, in which society's rules are not yet internalized and judgments are based on the punishing or rewarding consequences of an act.

preimplantation genetic diagnosis Prenatal diagnostic procedure in which a mother's eggs are fertilized in the laboratory using in vitro fertilization techniques, DNA tests are conducted on the first cells that result from mitosis of each fertilized egg, and only eggs that do not have chromosome abnormalities or genes associated with disorders are implanted in the uterus.

premenstrual dysphoric disorder (PDD) Severe form of premenstrual syndrome that includes affective symptoms in addition to physical symptoms associated with the menstrual cycle and that can be disabling or disruptive to work and relationships.

premenstrual syndrome (PMS) Several symptoms experienced shortly before each menstrual period that include having tender breasts, feeling bloated, and being irritable and moody.

prenatal environment The physical environment of the womb during the 9 months of pregnancy.

preoperational stage Piaget's second stage of cognitive development, lasting from about age 2 to age 7, when children think at a symbolic level but have not yet mastered logical operations.

presbycusis Problems of the aging ear, which commonly involve loss of sensitivity to high-frequency or high-pitched sounds.

presbyopia Problems of the aging eye, especially loss of near vision related to a decreased ability of the lens to accommodate to objects close to the eye.

pretend play Symbolic play in which one actor, object, or action symbolizes or stands for another.

primary circular reaction During Piaget's sensorimotor period, the infant's repetition of interacting acts centered on his or her own body (e.g., repeatedly kicking).

primary emotion One of the distinct basic emotions that emerges within the first six months of life universally (joy, surprise, sadness, disgust, anger, fear).

private speech Nonsocial speech, or speech for the self, commonly used by preschoolers to guide their activities and believed by Vygotsky to be the forerunner of inner speech, or silent thinking in words.

proactive parenting strategies Parenting tactics that prevent misbehavior and therefore reduce the need for discipline (for example, teaching values, removing temptations).

problem solving The use of the information processing system to achieve a goal or arrive at a decision.

production deficiency A phase in the mastery of memory strategies in which children can use strategies they are taught but cannot produce them on their own.

programmed theories of aging Theories that emphasize the systematic genetic control of aging processes. Contrast with *random error theories of aging*.

proliferation Process in early brain development in which neurons multiply at a staggering rate throughout the prenatal period

prosocial behavior Positive actions toward other people such as helping and cooperating.

prosody The melody or sound pattern of speech, including intonation, stress, and timing with which something is said.

protective factors Influences that prevent the damaging effects of risk factors or help children overcome disadvantages.

proximodistal principle In development, the principle that growth proceeds from the center of the body (or the proximal region) to the extremities (or the distal regions).

psychoanalytic theory The theoretical perspective associated with Freud and his followers that emphasizes unconscious motivations for behavior, conflicts within the personality, and stages of psychosexual development.

psychometric approach The research tradition that spawned standardized tests of intelligence and that views intelligence (or personality) as a set of traits that can be measured and that varies from person to person.

psychosexual stages Freud's five stages of development, associated with biological maturation and shifts in the libido: oral, anal, phallic, latency, and genital.

psychosocial stages Erikson's eight stages of development (trust, autonomy, initiative, industry, identity, intimacy, generativity, and integrity), emphasizing social influences more and biological urges less than Freud's psychosexual stages.

puberty The processes of biological change that result in an individual's attaining sexual maturity and becoming capable of producing a child.

random assignment A technique in which research participants are placed in experimental conditions in an unbiased or random way so that the resulting groups are not systematically different.

random error theories of aging Theories that emphasize several haphazard processes that cause cells and organ systems to deteriorate. Contrast with *programmed theories of aging*.

random sample A sample formed by identifying all members of the larger population of interest and then selecting a portion of them in an unbiased or random way to participate in the study; a technique to ensure that the sample studied is representative or typical of the larger population of interest.

reaction time The interval between the presentation of a stimulus and a response to it.

reactive attachment disorder A psychiatric diagnosis affecting socially deprived and maltreated children that involves either emotionally withdrawn behavior or "disinhibited" attachment in which the child shows indiscriminate interest in people but lack of appropriate wariness.

recall memory Recollecting or actively retrieving objects, events, and experiences when examples or cues are not provided. Contrast with *cued recall memory* and *recognition memory*.

recessive gene A less powerful gene that is not expressed phenotypically when paired with a *dominant gene*.

reciprocal determinism The notion in social cognitive theory that the flow of influence between people and their environments is a two-way street; the environment may affect the person, but the person's characteristics and behavior will also influence the environment.

reciprocity The mutual give and take by both parties in a human relationship that forms an important basis for morality.

recognition memory Identifying an object or event as one that has been experienced before, such as when a person must select the correct answer from several options. Contrast with *cued recall memory* and *recall memory*.

reconstituted family A new family that forms after the remarriage of a single parent, sometimes involving the blending of two families into a new one.

reflex An unlearned and automatic response to a stimulus.

regression A defense mechanism that involves retreating to an earlier, less traumatic stage of development.

rehearsal A strategy for remembering that involves repeating the items the person is trying to retain.

relational aggression Subtle and indirect aggression that involves gossiping about and ignoring or excluding others.

relativistic thinking A form of postformal operational thought in which it is understood that there are multiple ways of viewing a problem and that the solutions people arrive at will depend on their starting assumptions and perspective.

religiousness Sharing the beliefs and participating in the practices of an organized religion. Contrast with *spirituality*.

REM sleep A state of active, irregular sleep associated with dreaming; named for the rapid eye movements associated with it.

repression Removing unacceptable thoughts or traumatic memories from consciousness, as when a young woman who was raped has no memory at all of having been raped (or less drastically, engages in denial, knowing deep down that she was raped but not accepting the reality of it).

research ethics Standards of conduct that investigators are ethically bound to honor to protect their research participants from physical or psychological harm.

reserve capacity The ability of many organ systems to respond to demands for extraordinary output, such as when the heart and lungs work at maximal capacity.

resilience The ability to function well despite exposure to risk factors for maladaptive development or to overcome early developmental problems to become well adjusted.

resistant attachment An insecure infant-caregiver bond or other intimate relationship characterized by strong separation anxiety and a tendency to show ambivalent reactions to the attachment object upon reunion, seeking and yet resisting contact and not being comforted.

restoration-oriented coping In the dual-process model of bereavement, coping focused on managing daily living, rethinking one's life, and mastering new roles and challenges. Contrast with *loss-oriented coping*.

retinitis pigmentosa (RP) A group of hereditary disorders that involve gradual deterioration of the light-sensitive cells of the retina.

retrieval The process of retrieving information from long-term memory when it is needed.

retrograde amnesia Loss of memory for information and events occurring prior to the incident that caused the amnesia. Contrast with *anterograde amnesia*.

reversibility In Piaget's theory, the ability to reverse or negate an action by mentally performing the opposite action.

reversible dementia Significant cognitive decline that, unlike most dementia, can be cured or reversed; causes include alcoholism, toxic reactions to medication, infections, metabolic disorders, vitamin deficiencies, and malnutrition.

rhythmic stereotypies Repetitive movements observed in infants shortly before a new motor skill emerges.

rite of passage A ritual that marks a person's "passage" from one status to another, usually in reference to rituals marking the transition from childhood to adulthood.

role reversal Phenomenon in which the aging parent becomes the child and the child becomes the caregiver, not typical of most aging parent-child relationships.

role-taking skills The ability to assume other people's perspectives and understand their thoughts, feelings, and behaviors. See *perspective-taking skills*.

rubella A disease that has little effect on a pregnant woman but may cause several serious birth defects, such as blindness, deafness, and mental retardation, in unborn children exposed in the first 3 to 4 months of gestation; German measles.

rule assessment approach Siegler's approach to studying the development of problem solving that determines what information about a problem children take in and what rules they then formulate to account for this information.

ruminative coping Way of managing stress that involves dwelling on problems and attempting to analyze them; may help explain higher rates of depression in females than in males.

safe haven A point of safety, represented by an infant's attachment figure, to which the infant can return for comfort if frightened.

sample The group of individuals chosen to be the subjects of a study.

savant syndrome The phenomenon in which extraordinary talent in a particular area is displayed by a person who is otherwise mentally retarded.

scaffolding Jerome Bruner's term for providing structure to a less skilled learner to encourage advancement.

scheme (or schema; plural: schemes or schemata) A cognitive structure or organized pattern of action or thought used to deal with experiences.

schizophrenia A serious form of mental illness characterized by disturbances in logical thinking, emotional expression, and interpersonal behavior.

school refusal A reluctance or refusal to go to school or to remain there, sometimes called school phobia because it often involves intense anxiety.

scientific method An attitude or value about the pursuit of knowledge that dictates that investigators must be objective and must allow their data to decide the merits of their theorizing.

script A mental representation of a typical sequence of actions related to an event that is created in memory and that then guides future behaviors in similar settings.

secondary circular reaction During Piaget's sensorimotor period, the infant's repetition of interesting actions on objects (e.g., repeatedly shaking a rattle to make a noise).

secular trend A trend in industrialized societies toward earlier maturation and greater body size.

secure attachment An infant–caregiver bond or intimate relationship in which the individual welcomes close contact, uses the attachment object as a source of comfort, and dislikes but can manage separations.

secure base A point of safety, represented by an infant's attachment figure, that permits exploration of the environment.

selective attention Deliberately concentrating on one thing and ignoring something else.

selective optimization with compensation (SOC) The concept that older people cope with aging through a strategy that involves focusing on the skills most needed, practicing those skills, and developing ways to avoid the need for declining skills.

self-concept People's perceptions of their unique attributes or traits.

self-conscious emotion A "secondary emotion" such as embarrassment or pride that requires an awareness of self; unlikely to emerge until about 18 months of age.

self-control The ability to control or regulate one's desires, impulses, and behavior.

self-efficacy The belief that one can effectively produce desired outcomes in a particular area of life.

self-esteem People's overall evaluation of their worth as based on an assessment of the qualities that make up the self-concept.

self recognition The ability to recognize oneself in a mirror or photograph, which occurs in most infants by 18 to 24 months of age.

self-stereotyping Applying stereotypes of one's group (for example, negative stereotypes of older adults) to oneself.

semantic memory A type of explicit memory consisting of general facts.

semantics The aspect of language centering on meanings.

semenarche A boy's first ejaculation.

sensation The process by which information is detected by the sensory receptors and transmitted to the brain; the starting point in perception.

sensitive period As compared to a critical period, a period of life during which the developing individual is especially susceptible to the effects of experience or has an especially high level of plasticity.

sensorimotor stage Piaget's first stage of cognitive development, spanning the first 2 years of life, in which infants rely on their senses and motor behaviors in adapting to the world around them.

sensory register The first memory store in information processing in which stimuli are noticed and are briefly available for further processing.

sensory threshold The point at which low levels of stimulation can be detected.

separation anxiety A wary or fretful reaction that infants display when separated from their attachment objects.

sequential design A developmental research design that combines the cross-sectional approach and the longitudinal approach in a single study to compensate for the weaknesses of each.

seriation A logical operation that allows a person to mentally order a set of stimuli along a quantifiable dimension such as height or weight.

sex-linked characteristic An attribute determined by a gene that appears on one of the two types of sex chromosomes, usually the X chromosome.

sexual orientation A person's preference for sexual partners of the same or other sex, often characterized as primarily heterosexual, homosexual, or bisexual.

shared environmental influences Experiences that individuals living in the same home environment share and that work to make them similar. Contrast with *nonshared environmental influences*.

short-term memory The memory store in which limited amounts of information are temporarily held; called *working memory* when its active quality is being emphasized.

sibling rivalry A spirit of competition, jealousy, or resentment that may arise between two or more brothers or sisters.

sickle-cell disease A genetic blood disease in which red blood cells assume an unusual sickle shape and become inefficient at distributing oxygen throughout the body.

single gene-pair inheritance The genetic mechanism through which a characteristic is influenced by only one pair of genes, one gene from the mother and its partner from the father.

size constancy The tendency to perceive an object as the same size despite changes in its distance from the eyes.

skill In Fischer's dynamic skill framework, a person's ability to perform a particular task in a specific context.

sleeper effect The delayed effect of an earlier experience, for example of early deprivation of visual stimulation.

slow-to-warm-up temperament A characteristic mode of response in which the individual is relatively inactive and moody and displays mild resistance to new routines and experiences but gradually adapts. Contrast with *easy temperament* and *difficult temperament*.

social clock A personal sense of when things should be done in life and when the individual is ahead of or behind the schedule dictated by age norms.

social cognition Thinking about the thoughts, feelings, motives, and behavior of the self and other people.

social cognitive theory Bandura's social learning theory, which holds that children and adults can learn novel responses merely by observing the behavior of a model, making mental notes on what they have seen, and then using these mental representations to reproduce the model's behavior; more broadly, a theory emphasizing the importance of cognitive processing of social experiences.

social comparison The process of defining and evaluating the self through comparisons with other people.

social convoy The changing cadre of significant people who serve as sources of social support to the individual during the life span.

social learning theory See *social cognitive theory*.

social norm A socially defined expectation about how people should behave in particular social contexts.

social pretend play A form of play that involves both cooperation with playmates and pretend or symbolic activity.

social referencing Infants' monitoring of companions' emotional reactions in ambiguous situations and use of this information to decide how they should feel and behave.

social-conventional rules Standards of conduct determined by social consensus that indicate what is appropriate within a particular social setting. Contrast with *moral rules*.

social-role theory Eagly's view that gender-role stereotypes are created and maintained by differences in the roles that men and women play in society rather than being inherent in males and females.

sociocultural perspective Vygotsky's theory of development, which maintains that cognitive development is shaped by the sociocultural context in which it occurs and grows out of children's social interactions with members of their culture.

socioeconomic status (SES) The position people hold in society based on such factors as income, education, occupational status, and the prestige of their neighborhoods.

socioemotional selectivity theory Carstensen's notion that our needs change as we grow older and that we actively choose to narrow our range of social partners to those who can best meet our emotional needs.

sociometric popularity Being liked by many peers and disliked by few. Contrast with *perceived popularity*.

sociometric techniques Methods for determining who is well liked and popular and who is disliked or neglected in a group.

somaesthetic senses Body senses, including the senses of touch, temperature, and pain, as well as the *kinesthetic sense* of where one's body parts are in relation to other body parts and to the environment.

somatic symptoms Physical or bodily signs of emotional distress such as loss of appetite or disruption of normal sleep patterns.

species heredity The genetic endowment that members of a particular species have in common; a contributor to universal species traits and patterns of maturation.

spillover effects Instances in which events at work affect home life, and events at home carry over into the work place.

spina bifida Condition in which the bottom of the neural tube fails to fully close during prenatal development and part of the spinal cord is not fully encased in the protective covering of the spinal column.

spirituality A search for ultimate meaning in life that may or may not be carried out in the context of religion. Contrast with *religiousness*.

standard deviation A measure of the dispersion or spread around the mean of a distribution of scores; in the case of IQ tests with a mean score of 100, the standard deviation is 15, meaning that about two-thirds of people taking the test have scores between 85 and 115.

Stanford–Binet Intelligence Scale One of the most widely used, individually administered intelligence tests, which yields an IQ score.

static thought In Piaget's theory, the thought characteristic of the preoperational period that is fixed on end states rather than on the changes that transform one state into another. Contrast with *transformational thought*.

stem cell Undifferentiated, primitive cells that have the ability both to multiply and to differentiate into a variety of specific cells.

stereotype threat An individual's fear of being judged to have the qualities associated with negative stereotypes of his or her social group.

Sternberg's Triarchic Abilities Tests (STAT) An intelligence test based on Sternberg's triarchic theory that uses a variety of question formats to assess practical, creative, and analytical components of intelligence.

stillbirth Fetal death that occurs late in pregnancy when survival outside womb would normally have been possible.

storage In information processing, the holding of information in the long-term memory store.

storm and stress G. Stanley Hall's term for the emotional ups and downs and rapid changes that he believed characterize adolescence.

Strange Situation A series of mildly stressful experiences involving the departure of the parent and exposure to a stranger to which infants are exposed to determine the quality of their attachments; developed by Ainsworth.

stranger anxiety A wary or fretful reaction that infants often display when approached by an unfamiliar person.

structured observation A research method in which scientists create special conditions designed to elicit the behavior of interest to achieve greater control over the conditions under which they gather behavioral data. Contrast with *naturalistic observation*.

successful intelligence Sternberg's concept that people are intelligent to the extent that they are able to succeed in life in their sociocultural context.

sudden infant death syndrome (SIDS) The death of a sleeping baby because of a failure of the respiratory system; linked to maternal smoking.

superego The psychoanalytic term for the component of the personality that consists of the individual's internalized moral standards.

surfactant A substance that aids breathing by preventing the air sacs of the lungs from sticking together.

surgency/extraversion Dimension of temperament that involves the tendency to actively and energetically approach new experiences in an emotionally positive way (rather than to be inhibited and withdrawn). See *negative affectivity* and *effortful control*.

symbolic capacity The capacity to use symbols such as words, images, or actions to represent or stand for objects and experiences; representational thought.

synapse The point at which the axon or dendrite of one neuron makes a connection with another neuron.

synaptic pruning The removal of unnecessary synapses between neurons in response to experience.

synaptogenesis The growth of synapses, or connections between neurons.

synchronized routine Harmonious, dancelike interaction between infant and caregiver in which each adjusts behavior in response to that of the other.

syntactic bootstrapping Using the syntax of a sentence—that is, where a word is placed in a sentence—to determine the meaning of the word.

syntax Rules specifying how words can be combined to form meaningful sentences in a language.

syphilis A common sexually transmitted disease that may cross the placental barrier in the middle and later stages of pregnancy, causing miscarriage or serious birth defects.

systemize To analyze things and explore how they work; male brains (and the brains of autistic individuals) are hypothesized by Baron-Cohen to excel at systemizing, whereas females excel at empathizing.

systems theories Theories of development holding that changes over the life span arise from the ongoing interrelationships between a changing organism and a changing environment, both of which are part of a larger, dynamic system.

tabula rasa The idea that the mind of an infant is a "blank slate" and that all knowledge, abilities, behaviors, and motives are acquired through experience.

tau Protein in the neurofibrillary tangles in the bodies of neural cells of individuals with Alzheimer's disease.

telegraphic speech Early sentences that consist primarily of content words and omit the less meaningful parts of speech such as articles, prepositions, pronouns, and auxiliary verbs.

telomere A stretch of DNA that forms the tip of a chromosome and that shortens after each cell division, serving as an aging clock and timing the death of cells.

temperament A genetically based pattern of tendencies to respond in predictable ways; building blocks of personality.

teratogen Any disease, drug, or other environmental agent that can harm a developing fetus.

terminal drop A rapid decline in intellectual abilities that people within a few years of dying often experience.

tertiary circular reaction During Piaget's sensorimotor period, the infant's experimenting with actions to find new ways to solve problems or produce interesting effects.

test norms Standards of normal performance on psychometric instruments based on the average scores and range of scores obtained by a large, representative sample of test takers.

testosterone The most important of the male hormones, or androgens; essential for normal sexual development during the prenatal period and at puberty.

thalidomide A mild tranquilizer that, taken early in pregnancy, can produce a variety of malformations of the limbs, eyes, ears, and heart.

theory A set of concepts and propositions designed to organize, describe, and explain a set of observations.

theory of mind The understanding that people have mental states (feelings, desires, beliefs, intentions) and that these states underlie and help explain their behavior.

third variable problem In correlation studies, the problem posed by the fact that the association between the two variables of interest may be caused by some third variable; see also *directionality problem*.

time of measurement effects In developmental research, the effects on findings of historical events occurring when the data for a study are being collected (for example, psychological changes brought about by an economic depression rather than as a function of aging). Contrast with *age effects* and *cohort effects*.

tinnitus Condition caused by exposure to high noise levels that involves ringing sounds in one or both ears and that can last for days, weeks, or indefinitely.

total brain death An irreversible loss of functioning in the entire brain, both the higher centers of the cerebral cortex that are involved in thought and the lower centers of the brain that control basic life processes such as breathing.

transactional model A model of family influence in which parent and child are believed to influence each other reciprocally over time and development is influenced by how their relationship evolves.

transformational grammar Rules of syntax that allow a person to transform statements into questions, negatives, imperatives, and other kinds of sentences.

transformational thought In Piaget's theory, the ability to conceptualize transformations, or processes of change from one state to another, which appears in the stage of concrete operations. Contrast with *static thought*.

transgender Pertaining to individuals who identify with a gender other than their biological one.

transitivity The ability to recognize the necessary or logical relations among elements in a serial order (for example, that if A is taller than B, and B is taller than C, then A must be taller than C).

triangular theory of love Robert Sternberg's model describing types of love in terms of three components: passion, intimacy, and commitment.

triarchic theory of intelligence Sternberg's information-processing theory of intelligence that emphasizes three aspects of intelligent behavior: a practical component emphasizing the effect of context on what is intelligent; a creative component centering on coping with both novel and familiar problems; and an analytic component focused on the cognitive processes used to solve a problem.

trust versus mistrust The psychosocial conflict of infancy in which infants must learn to trust others to meet their needs in order to trust themselves; first stage in Erikson's theory.

Turner syndrome A sex chromosome abnormality in which females inherit only one X chromosome (XO); they remain small in stature, fail to develop secondary sex characteristics, and may show some mental deficiencies.

twin study Method of studying genetic and environmental influence in which the similarity of identical twins is compared to that of (less genetically similar) fraternal twins, often in studies involving both twins reared together and twins reared apart.

ulnar grasp Holding objects by clamping them between the palm of hand and the fingers.

ultrasound Method of examining physical organs by scanning them with sound waves—for example, scanning the womb and thereby producing a visual outline of the fetus to detect gross abnormalities.

unconscious motivation Freud's term for feelings, experiences, and conflicts that influence a person's thinking and behavior even though they cannot be recalled.

underextension The young child's tendency to use general words to refer to a smaller set of objects, actions, or events than adults do (for example, using *candy* to refer only to mints). Contrast with *overextension*.

universal grammar A system of common rules and properties of language that may allow infants to grow up learning any of the world's languages.

universality–context-specificity issue The debate over the extent to which developmental changes are common to everyone (universal, as in most stage theories) or different from person to person (particularistic).

utilization deficiency The third phase in mastery of memory strategies in which children fail to benefit from a memory strategy they are able to produce.

vascular dementia The deterioration of functioning and cognitive capacities caused by a series of minor strokes that cut off the blood supply to areas of the brain; also called multi-infarct dementia, it is one cause of neurocognitive disorder.

vicarious reinforcement In observational learning, the consequences experienced by models, because of their behavior, that affect the learner's likelihood of imitating the behavior.

visual accommodation The ability of the lens of the eye to change shape to bring objects at different distances into focus.

visual acuity The ability to perceive detail in a visual stimulus.

visual cliff An elevated glass platform that creates an illusion of depth and is used to test the depth perception of infants.

vocabulary spurt A phenomenon occurring around 18 months of age when the pace of word learning quickens dramatically.

Wechsler Scales A set of widely used, individually administered intelligence tests that yield verbal, performance, and overall IQ scores.

wisdom A combination of rich factual knowledge about life and procedural knowledge such as strategies for giving advice and handling conflicts.

word segmentation In language development, the ability to break the stream of speech sounds into distinct words.

working memory A memory store, often referred to as a mental "scratch pad," that temporarily holds information when it is being actively operated upon or in one's consciousness.

X chromosome The longer of the two sex chromosomes; normal females have two X chromosomes, whereas normal males have only one.

Y chromosome The shorter of the two sex chromosomes; normal males have one Y chromosome, whereas females have none.

zone of proximal development Vygotsky's term for the difference between what a learner can accomplish independently and what a learner can accomplish with the guidance and encouragement of a more skilled partner.

zygote A single cell formed at conception from the union of a sperm and an ovum.

References

ABC News. (2010). *He never forgets: Meet the super-memory man*. Retrieved from http://abcnews.go.com/Nightline/story?id=7075443&page=3

Abele, A. E. (2003). The dynamics of masculine-agentic and feminine-communal traits: Findings from a prospective study. *Journal of Personality and Social Psychology, 85*, 768–776.

Abele, A. E., Uchronski, M., Suitner, C., & Wojciszke, B. (2008). Towards an operationalization of the fundamental dimensions of agency and communion: Trait content ratings in five countries considering valence and frequency of word occurrence. *European Journal of Social Psychology, 38*, 1202–1217.

Aber, L., Morris, P., & Raver, C. (2012). Children, families and poverty. Definitions, trends, emerging science and implications for policy. SRCD *Social Policy Report, 26*, 1–19.

Ablard, K. E., & Mills, C. J. (1996). Implicit theories of intelligence and self-perceptions of academically talented adolescents and children. *Journal of Youth and Adolescence, 25*, 137–148.

Abma, J. C., & Martinez, G. M. (2006). Childlessness among older women in the United States: Trends and profiles. *Journal of Marriage and Family, 68*, 1045–1056.

Abma, J. C., Martinez, G. M., & Copen, C. E. (2010). *Teenagers in the United States: Sexual activity, contraceptive use, and childbearing, National Survey of Family Growth 2006–2008* (Series 23, Number 31). Hyattsville, MD: National Center for Health Statistics, Vital Health Statistics.

Abraham, J. D., & Hansson, R. O. (1995). Successful aging at work: An applied study of selection, optimization, and compensation through impression management. *Journals of Gerontology: Psychological Sciences, 50*, P94–P103.

Achenbach, T. M., & Edelbrock, C. S. (1978). The classification of child psychopathology: A review and analysis of empirical efforts. *Psychological Bulletin, 85*, 1275–1301.

Achenbaum, W. A., & Bengtson, V. L. (1994). Re-engaging the disengagement theory of aging: On the history and assessment of theory development in gerontology. *Gerontologist, 34*, 756–763.

Achter, J. A., Benbow, C. P., & Lubinski, D. (1997). Rethinking multipotentiality among the intellectually gifted: A critical review and recommendations. *Gifted Child Quarterly, 41*, 5–15.

Ackerman, S. J. (2007). The adolescent brain. In F. Bloom, M. F. Beal, & D. J. Kupfer (Eds.), *The DANA Guide to Brain Health: A Practical Family Reference from Medical Experts. Journal of Neurology Neurosurgery and Psychiatry, 78*, 779.

Adam, E. K., Gunnar, M. R., & Tanaka, A. (2004). Adult attachment, parent emotion, and observed parenting behavior: Mediator and moderator models. *Child Development, 75*, 110–122.

Adams, C. (1991). Qualitative age differences in memory for text: A life-span developmental perspective. *Psychology and Aging, 6*, 323–336.

Adams, D. W., & Deveau, E. J. (1987). When a brother or sister is dying of cancer: The vulnerability of the adolescent sibling. *Death Studies, 11*, 279–295.

Adams, M., Walker, C., & O'Connell, P. (2011). A content analysis of representations of parenting in young children's picture books in the UK. *Sex Roles, 65*, 259–270.

Adams, M. J., Treiman, R., & Pressley, M. (1998). Reading, writing, and literacy. In I. E. Sigel & K. A. Renninger (Vol. Eds.), W. Damon (Editor-in-Chief), *Handbook of child psychology: Vol. 4. Child psychology in practice* (5th ed., pp. 275–355). New York: Wiley.

Adams, R. E., & Bukowski, W. M. (2007). Relationships with mothers and peers moderate the association between childhood sexual abuse and anxiety disorders. *Child Abuse and Neglect, 31*, 645–656.

Aday, R. H., Kehoe, G. C., & Farney, L. A. (2006). Impact of senior center friendships on aging women who live alone. *Journal of Women & Aging, 18*, 57–73.

Addington, A. M., & Rapoport, J. L. (2012). Annual research review: Impact of advances in genetics in understanding developmental psychopathology. *Journal of Child Psychology and Psychiatry, 53*, 510–518.

Adey, P. S., & Shayer, M. (1992). Accelerating the development of formal thinking in middle and high school students: II. Postproject effects on science achievement. *Journal of Research in Science Teaching, 29*, 81–92.

Adolph, K. E. (2008). Learning to move. *Current Directions in Psychological Science, 17*, 213–218.

Adolph, K. E., & Avolio, A. M. (2000). Walking infants adapt locomotion to changing body dimensions. *Journal of Experimental Psychology: Human Perception and Performance, 26*, 1148–1166.

Adolph, K. E., & Berger, S. E. (2006). Motor development. In D. Kuhn & R. Siegler (Vol. Eds.), *Handbook of child psychology: Cognition, perception, and language* (6th ed.). Hoboken, NJ: Wiley and Sons.

Adolph, K. E., & Robinson, S. R. (2013). The road to walking: What learning to walk tells us about development. In P. Zelazo (Ed.), *Oxford handbook of developmental psychology* (pp. 17–34). New York: Oxford University Press.

Adolph, K. E., Berger, S. E., & Leo, A. J. (2011). Developmental continuity? Crawling, cruising, and walking. *Developmental Psychology, 14*, 306–318.

Adolph, K. E., Robinson, S. R., Young, J. W., & Gill-Alvarez, F. (2008). What is the shape of developmental change? *Psychological Review, 115*, 527–543.

Adrian, V., & Coontz, S. (2010). *The long-range impact of the recession on families.* A report for the 13th Annual Conference on Contemporary Families, Augustana College, April 16–17, 2010. Retrieved from http://www.contemporaryfamilies.org/economic-issues/the-long-range-impact-of-the-recession-on-families.html

Afifi, T. D., & Denes, A. (2013). Divorced and single-parent families. Risk, resiliency, and the role of communication. In A. L. Vangelisti (Ed.), *Routledge handbook of family communication.* New York: Routledge.

Agnew, R. (2003). An integrated theory of the adolescent peak in offending. *Youth & Society, 34*, 263–299.

Agnew, R., & Huguley, S. (1989). Adolescent violence toward parents. *Journal of Marriage and the Family, 51*, 699–711.

Aguiar, A., & Baillargeon, R. (1999). 2.5-month-old infants' reasoning about when objects should and should not be occluded. *Cognitive Psychology, 39*, 116–157.

Aguiar, A., & Baillargeon, R. (2002). Developments in young infants' reasoning about occluded objects. *Cognitive Psychology, 45*, 267–336.

Ahluwalia, I. B., D'Angelo, D., Morrow, B., & McDonald, J. A. (2012). Association between acculturation and breastfeeding among Hispanic women: Data from the pregnancy risk assessment and monitoring system. *Journal of Human Lactation, 28*, 167–173.

Ahmetoglu, G., Swami, V., & Chamorro-Premuzic, T. (2010). The relationship between dimensions of love, personality, and relationship length. *Archives of Sexual Behavior, 39*, 1181–1190.

Ahrons, C. R. (2007). Family ties after divorce: Long-term implications for children. *Family Process, 46*, 53–65.

Ai, A. L., Wink, P., & Ardelt, M. (2010). Spirituality and aging: A journey. In J. C. Cavanaugh & C. K. Cavanaugh (Eds.), *Aging in America: Vol. 3. Societal issues.* Santa Barbara, CA: Praeger/ABC-CLIO.

Ainsworth, M. D. S. (1973). The development of infant–mother attachment. In B. M. Caldwell & H. N. Ricciuti (Eds.), *Review of child development research* (Vol. 3). Chicago: University of Chicago Press.

Ainsworth, M. D. S. (1979). Attachment as related to mother–infant interaction. In J. G. Rosenblatt, R. A. Hinde, C. Beer, & M. Busnel (Eds.), *Advances in the study of behavior* (Vol. 9). New York: Academic Press.

Ainsworth, M. D. S. (1989). Attachments beyond infancy. *American Psychologist, 44,* 709–716.

Ainsworth, M. D. S., Blehar, M., Waters, E., & Wall, S. (1978). *Patterns of attachment.* Hillsdale, NJ: Erlbaum.

Ajrouch, K. J., Antonucci, T. C., & Janevic, M. R. (2001). Social networks among blacks and whites: The interaction between race and age. *Journals of Gerontology: Psychological Sciences and Social Sciences, 56,* S112–S118.

Akinbami, L. J., Liu, X., Pastor, P. N., & Reuben, C. A. (2011). Attention deficit hyperactivity disorder among children aged 5–17 in the United States, 1998–2009. NCHS Data Brief, No. 70. Hyattsville, MD: National Center for Health Statistics. Retrieved from http://www.cdc.gov/nchs/fastats/adhd.htm

Akiyama, H., Antonucci, T., Takahashi, K., & Langfahl, E. S. (2003). Negative interactions in close relationships across the life span. *Journals of Gerontology: Psychological Sciences and Social Sciences, 58,* P70–P79.

Aknin, L. B., Hamlin, J. K., & Dunn, E. W. (2012). Giving leads to happiness in young children. *Plos One, 7,* e39211.

Alam, R., Barrera, M., D'Agostino, N., Nicholas, D. B., & Schneiderman, G. (2012). Bereavement experiences of mothers and fathers over time after the death of a child due to cancer. *Death Studies, 36,* 1–22.

Albert, D., Chein, J., & Steinberg, L. (2013). The teenage brain: Peer influences on adolescent decision making. *Current Directions in Psychological Science, 22,* 114–120.

Aldwin, C. M., Spiro, A., & Park, C. L. (2006). Health, behavior, and optimal aging. In J. E. Birren & K. W. Schaie (Eds.), *Handbook of the psychology of aging.* Boston: Elsevier Academic Press.

Alexander, G. M. (2003). An evolutionary perspective of sex-typed toy preferences: Pink, blue, and the brain. *Archives of Sexual Behavior, 32,* 7–14.

Alexander, G. M., Wilcox, T., & Woods, R. (2009). Sex differences in infants' visual interest in toys. *Archives of Sexual Behavior, 38,* 427–433.

Alfieri, T., Ruble, D. N., & Higgins, E. T. (1996). Gender stereotypes during adolescence: Developmental changes and the transition to junior high school. *Developmental Psychology, 32,* 1129–1137.

Alisat, S., & Pratt, M. W. (2012). Characteristics of young adults' personal religious narratives and their relation with the identity status model: A longitudinal, mixed methods study. *Identity: An International Journal of Theory and Research, 12,* 29–52.

Allen, J., Chavez, S., DeSimone, S., Howard, D., Johnson, K., LaPierre, L., et al. (2006). Americans' attitudes toward euthanasia and physician-assisted suicide, 1936–2002. *Journal of Sociology and Social Welfare, 33,* 5–23.

Allen, K. R., Blieszner, R., & Roberto, K. A. (2000). Families in the middle and later years: A review and critique of research in the 1990s. *Journal of Marriage and the Family, 62,* 911–926.

Allen, R. E. S., & Wiles, J. L. (2013). How older people position their late-life childlessness: A qualitative study. *Journal of Marriage and Family, 75,* 206–220.

Allison, C. M., & Hyde, J. S. (2011). Early menarche: Confluence of biological and contextual factors. *Sex Roles, 68,* 55–64.

Allum, J. H., Greisiger, R., Straubhaar, S., & Carpenter, M. G. (2000). Auditory perception and speech identification in children with cochlear implants tested with the EARS protocol. *British Journal of Audiology, 34,* 293–303.

Almeida, D. M., & Horn, M. C. (2004). Is daily life more stressful during middle adulthood? In O. G. Brim, C. D. Ryff, & R. C. Kessler (Eds.), *How healthy are we? A national study of well-being at midlife.* Chicago: University of Chicago Press.

Almeida, D. M., Piazza, J. R., Stawski, R. S., & Klein, L. C. (2011). The speedometer of life: Stress, health and aging. In K. W. Schaie & S. L. Willis (Eds.), B. G. Knight, B. Levy, & D. C. Park (Assoc. Eds.), *Handbook of the psychology of aging.* Burlington, MA: Academic Press/Elsevier.

Almli, C. R., Ball, R. H., & Wheeler, M. E. (2001). Human fetal and neonatal movement patterns: Gender differences and fetal-to-neonatal continuity. *Developmental Psychobiology, 38,* 252–273.

Amato, P. R. (1993). Children's adjustment to divorce: Theories, hypotheses, and empirical support. *Journal of Marriage and the Family, 55,* 23–38.

Amato, P. R. (2000). The consequences of divorce for adults and children. *Journal of Marriage and the Family, 62,* 1269–1287.

Amato, P. R. (2006). Marital discord, divorce, and children's well-being: Results from a 20-year longitudinal study of two generations. In A. Clarke-Stewart & J. Dunn (Eds.), *Families count: Effects on child and adolescent development.* New York: Cambridge University Press.

Amato, P. R. (2010). Research on divorce: Continuing trends and new developments. *Journal of Marriage and Family, 72,* 650–666.

Amato, P. R., & Cheadle, J. E. (2008). Parental divorce, marital conflict and children's behavior problems: A comparison of adopted and biological children. *Social Forces, 86,* 1139–1161.

Amato, P. R., & Sobolewski, J. M. (2004). The effects of divorce on fathers and children: Nonresidential fathers and stepfathers. In M. E. Lamb (Ed.), *The role of the father in child development* (4th ed.). Hoboken, NJ: John Wiley & Sons.

Amato, P. R., Johnson, D. R., Booth, A., & Rogers, S. J. (2003). Continuity and change in marital quality between 1980 and 2000. *Journal of Marriage and the Family, 65,* 1–22.

Amato, P. R., Kane, J. B., & James, S. (2011). Reconsidering the "good divorce". *Family Relations: An Interdisciplinary Journal of Applied Family Studies, 60,* 511–524.

American Academy of Pediatrics. (2000). Prevention and management of pain and stress in the neonate (RE9945). *Pediatrics, 105,* 454–461.

American Association on Intellectual and Developmental Disabilities. (2010). *Definition of intellectual disability.* Retrieved from www.aaidd.org

American Psychiatric Association. (2000). *Diagnostic and statistical manual of mental disorders DSM–IV–TR* (4th ed., text revision). Arlington, VA: American Psychiatric Association.

American Psychiatric Association. (2013). *Diagnostic and statistical manual of mental disorders (5th ed.) DSM-5.* Washington, DC: American Psychiatric Publishing.

Amone-P'Olak, K., Ormel, J., Huisman, M., Verhulst, F. C., Oldehinkel, A. J., & Burger, H. (2009). Life stressors as mediators of the relation between socioeconomic position and mental health problems in early adolescence: The TRAILS study. Journal of the *American Academy of Child & Adolescent Psychiatry, 48,* 1031–1038.

Amsel, E., Klaczynski, P. A., Johnston, A., Bench, S., Close, J., Sadler, E., et al. (2008). A dual-process account of the development of scientific reasoning: The nature and development of metacognitive intercession skills. *Cognitive Development, 23,* 452–471.

Amstutz, D. D., & Sheared, V. (2000). The crisis in adult basic education. *Education and Urban Society, 32,* 155–166.

Anand, K. J., & Hickey, P. R. (1992). Halothane-morphine compared with high-dose sufentanil for anesthesia and postoperative analgesia in neonatal cardiac surgery. *New England Journal of Medicine, 326,* 1–9.

Andel, R., Crowe, M., Pedersen, N. L., Fratiglioni, L., Johansson, B., & Gatz, M. (2008). Physical exercise at midlife and risk of dementia three decades later: A population-based study of swedish twins. *The Journals of Gerontology: Series A: Biological Sciences and Medical Sciences, 63A*(1), 62–66.

Anderson, C. A., Shibuya, A., Ihori, N., Swing, E. L., Bushman, B. J., Sakamoto, A., et al. (2010). Violent video game effects on aggression, empathy, and prosocial behavior in Eastern and Western countries: A meta-analytic review. *Psychological Bulletin, 136,* 151–173.

Anderson, D. A., & Hamilton, M. (2007). Gender role stereotyping of parents in children's picture books: The invisible father. *Sex Roles, 52,* 145–151.

Anderson, D. R., & Pempek, T. A. (2005). Television and very young children. *American Behavioral Scientist, 48,* 505–522.

Anderson, R. M., & Weindruch, R. (2012). The caloric restriction paradigm: Implications for healthy human aging. *American Journal of Human Biology, 24,* 101–106.

Anderson-Fye, E. (2009). Cross-cultural issues in body image among children and adolescents. In L. Smolak & J. K. Thompson (Eds.), *Body image, eating disorders, and obesity in youth.* Washington, DC: American Psychological Association.

Andrews, G. J., Gavin, N., Begley, S., & Brodie, D. (2003). Assisting friendships, combating loneliness: Users' views on a "befriending" scheme. *Ageing & Society, 23,* 349–362.

Anim-Soumuah, M., Smyth, R. M., & Jones, L. (2011, December 7). Epidural versus non-epidural or no analgesia in labour. *Cochrane Database of Systematic Reviews.* doi:10.1002/14651858.CD000331.pub3

Anisfeld, E., Casper, V., Nozyce, M., & Cunningham, N. (1990). Does infant carrying promote attachment? An experimental study of the effects of increased physical contact on the development of attachment. *Child Development, 61,* 1617–1627.

Anstey, K. J., Hofer, S. M., & Luszcz, M. A. (2003). A latent growth curve analysis of late-life sensory and cognitive function over 8 years: Evidence for specific and common factors underlying change. *Psychology and Aging, 18,* 714–726.

Antebi, A. (2007). Ageing: When loss is more. *Nature, 447,* 536–537.

Anthis, K., & LaVoie, J. C. (2006). Readiness to change: A longitudinal study of changes in adult identity. *Journal of Research in Personality, 40,* 209–219.

Antonucci, T. C., Birditt, K. S., & Akiyama, H. (2009). Convoys of social relations: An interdisciplinary approach. In V. L. Bengtson, M. Silverstein, N. M. Putney, & D. Gans (Eds.), *Handbook of theories of aging* (2nd ed.). New York: Springer.

Applebome, P., & Maker, E. (2013, January 20). Private pain and public debate take toll on Newtown parents. *The New York Times.* Retrieved from http://www.nytimes.com/2013/01/21/nyregion/newtown-families-negotiate-private-pain-amid-public-debate.html?_r=0

Appollonio, I., Carabellese, C., Frattola, L., & Trabucchi, M. (1996). Effects of sensory aids on the quality of life and mortality of elderly people: A multivariate analysis. *Age and Ageing, 25,* 89–96.

Aquilino, W. S. (2006). Family relationships and support systems in emerging adulthood. In J. J. Arnett & J. L. Tanner (Eds.), *Coming of age in the 21st century.* Washington, DC: American Psychological Association.

Aquino, K., & Reed, A. (2002). The self-importance of moral identity. *Journal of Personality & Social Psychology, 83,* 1423–1440.

Aquino, K., Freeman, D., Reed, A., II, Felps, W., & Lim, V. K. G. (2009). Testing a social-cognitive model of moral behavior: The interactive influence of situations and moral identity centrality. *Journal of Personality and Social Psychology, 97,* 123–141.

Aratani, L. (2008, February 10). Catching up to the boys, in the good and the bad. *The Washington Post,* pp. C1, C14.

Arber, S., & Ginn, J. (1991). *Gender and later life: A sociological analysis of resources and constraints.* London: Sage.

Arbona, C., & Power, T. G. (2003). Parental attachment, self-esteem, and antisocial behaviors among African American, European American, and Mexican American adolescents. *Journal of Counseling Psychology, 50,* 40–51.

Archer, J. (1992). *Ethology and human development.* Hertfordshire, UK: Harvester Wheatsheaf.

Archer, J. (1996). Sex differences in social behavior: Are the social role and evolutionary explanations compatible? *American Psychologist, 51,* 909–917.

Archer, S. L. (1982). The lower age boundaries of identity development. *Child Development, 53,* 1551–1556.

Ardelt, M. (2000). Antecedents and effects of wisdom in old age. *Research on Aging, 22,* 360–394.

Arens, A. K., Yeung, A. S., Craven, R. G., Watermann, R., & Hasselhorn, M. (2013). Does timing of transition matter? Comparison of German students' self-perceptions before and after transition to secondary school. *International Journal of Educational Research, 57,* 1–11.

Ariès, P. (1981). *The hour of our death* (H. Weaver, Trans.). New York: Knopf. (Original work published 1977).

Arim, R., Tramonte, L., Shapka, J. D., Dahinten, V. S., & Willms, J. D. (2011). The family antecedents and the subsequent outcomes of early puberty. *Journal of Youth & Adolescence, 40,* 1423–1435.

Arking, R. (2006). *The biology of aging: Observations and principles* (3rd ed.). New York: Oxford University Press.

Armstrong, D., & Shakespeare-Finch, J. (2011). Relationship to the bereaved and perceptions of severity of trauma differentiate elements of posttraumatic growth. *Omega: Journal of Death and Dying, 63,* 125–140.

Armstrong, P. I., & Crombie, G. (2000). Compromises in adolescents' occupational aspirations and expectations from grades 8 to 10. *Journal of Vocational Behavior, 56,* 82–98.

Armstrong, V. L., Brunet, P. M., He, C., Nishimura, M., Poole, H. L., & Spector, F. (2006). What is so critical? A commentary on the reexamination of critical periods. *Developmental Psychobiology, 48,* 326–331.

Arnett, J. J. (2011). Emerging adulthoods(s): The cultural psychology of a new life stage. In L. A. Jensen (Ed.), *Bridging cultural and developmental approaches to psychology: New syntheses in theory, research, and policy* (pp. 255–275). New York: Oxford University Press.

Arnold, L. E., Lofthouse, N., & Hurt, E. (2012). Artificial food colors and attention-deficit/hyperactivity symptoms: Conclusions to dye for.*Neurotherapeutics, 9,* 599–609.

Aronson, J., Lustina, M. J., Good, C., Keough, K., Steele, C. M., & Brown, J. (1999). When white men can't do math: Necessary and sufficient factors in stereotype threat. *Journal of Experimental Social Psychology, 35,* 29–46.

Arroyo, C. G., & Zigler, E. (1995). Racial identity, academic achievement, and the psychological well-being of economically disadvantaged adolescents. *Journal of Personality and Social Psychology, 69,* 903–914.

Arseneault, L., Tremblay, R. E., Boulerice, B., & Saucier, J. (2002). Obstetrical complications and violent delinquency: Testing two developmental pathways. *Child Development, 73,* 496–508.

Asendorpf, J. B., Warkentin, V., & Baudonnière, P. M. (1996). Self-awareness and other-awareness: 2. Mirror self-recognition, social contingency awareness, and synchronic imitation. *Developmental Psychology, 32,* 313–321.

Ashby, J. S., & Schoon, I. (2012). Living the dream? A qualitative retrospective study exploring the role of adolescent aspirations across the life span. *Developmental Psychology, 48,* 1694–1706.

Aspelmeier, J. E., Elliott, A. N., & Smith, C. H. (2007). Childhood sexual abuse, attachment, and trauma symptoms in college females: The moderating role of attachment. *Child Abuse and Neglect, 31,* 549–566.

Atchley, R. C. (1976). *The sociology of retirement.* Cambridge, MA: Schenkman.

Atchley, R. C. (2009). *Spirituality and aging.* Baltimore: Johns Hopkins University Press.

Athey, I. (1984). Contributions of play to development. In T. D. Yawkey & A. D. Pellegrini (Eds.), *Child's play: Developmental and applied.* Hillsdale, NJ: Erlbaum.

Atkinson, R. C., & Shiffrin, R. M. (1968). Human memory: A proposed system and its control processes. In K. W. Spence & J. T. Spence (Eds.), *The psychology of learning and motivation: Advances in research and theory* (Vol. 2). New York: Academic Press.

Attar-Schwartz, S., Tan, J., Buchanan, A., Flouri, E., & Griggs, J. (2009). Grandparenting and adolescent adjustment in two-parent biological, lone-parent, and step-families. *Journal of Family Psychology, 23,* 67–75.

Autism and Developmental Disabilities Monitoring Network Surveillance Year 2006 Principal Investigators (2009, December 18). Prevalence of autism spectrum disorders—Autism and Developmental Disabilities Monitoring Network, United States, 2006. *MMWR Surveillance Summaries, 58*(SS10), 1–20. Retrieved from www.cdc.gov/mmwr/preview/mmwrhtml/ss5810a1.htm

Autism and Developmental Disabilities Monitoring Network Surveillance Year 2008 Principal Investigators. (2012, March 30). Prevalence of autism spectrum disorders—Autism and Developmental Disabilities Monitoring Network, 14 sites, United States, 2008. *Morbidity and Mortality Weekly Report, 61,* 1–19. Retrieved from http://www.cdc.gov/mmwr/preview/mmwrhtml/ss6103a1.htm

Autism Genome Project Consortium. (2007). Mapping autism risk loci using genetic linage and chromosomal rearrangements. *Nature Genetics, 39,* 319–328.

Auyeung, B., Knickneyer, R., Ashwin, E., Taylor, K., Hackett, G., & Baron-Cohen, S. (2012). Effects of fetal testosterone on visuospatial ability. *Archives of Sexual Behavior, 41,* 571–581.

Avert. (2012). *Preventing mother-to-child transmission of HIV (PMTCT).* Retrieved from http://www.avert.org/motherchild.htm

Azmitia, M. (1992). Expertise, private speech, and the development of self-regulation. In R. M. Diaz & L. E. Berk (Eds.), *Private speech: From social interaction to self-regulation.* Hillsdale, NJ: Erlbaum.

Babai, R., & Levit-Dori, T. (2009). Several CASE lessons can improve students' control of variables reasoning scheme ability. *Journal of Science Education and Technology, 18,* 429–446.

Bacharach, V. R., & Baumeister, A. A. (1998). Direct and indirect effects of maternal intelligence, maternal age, income, and home environment on intelligence of preterm, low-birth-weight children. *Journal of Applied Developmental Psychology, 19,* 361–375.

Bachman, J. G., Safron, D. J., Sy, S. R., & Schulenberg, J. E. (2003). Wishing to work: New perspectives on how adolescents' part-time work intensity is linked to educational disengagement, substance use, and other problem behaviors. *International Journal of Behavioral Development, 27,* 301–315.

Bachman, J. G., Staff, J., O'Malley, P. M., & Freedman-Doan, P. (2013). Adolescent work intensity, school performance, and substance use: Links vary by race/ethnicity and socioeconomic status. *Developmental Psychology, 49,* 2125–2134.

Bachman, J. G., Staff, J., O'Malley, P. M., Schulenberg, J. E., & Freedman-Doan, P. (2011). Twelfth-grade student work intensity linked to later educational attainment and substance use: New longitudinal evidence. *Developmental Psychology, 47,* 344–363.

Baddeley, A. (1986). *Working memory.* Oxford: Oxford University Press.

Baddeley, A. (1992). Working memory. *Science, 255,* 556–559.

Baddeley, A. (2000). The episodic buffer: a new component of working memory? *Trends in Cognitive Science, 4,* 417–423.

Baddeley, A. (2001). Is working memory still working? *American Psychologist, 56,* 851–864.

Baddeley, A., & Hitch, G. J. (1974). Working memory. In G. Bower (Ed.), *The psychology of learning and motivation: Advances in research and theory* (Vol. 8, pp. 47–89). New York: Academic Press.

Baer, J. C., & Martinez, C. D. (2006). Child maltreatment and insecure attachment: A meta-analysis. *Journal of Reproductive and Infant Psychology, 24,* 187–197.

Bahali, K., Tahiroglu, A. Y., Avci, A., & Seydaoglu, G. (2011). Parental psychological symptoms and familial risk factors of children and adolescents who exhibit school refusal. *East Asian Archives of Psychiatry, 21,* 164–169.

Bahrick, H. P. (1984). Semantic memory content in permastore: Fifty years of memory for Spanish learned in school. *Journal of Experimental Psychology: General, 113,* 1–29.

Bahrick, H. P., Bahrick, P. O., & Wittlinger, R. P. (1975). Fifty years of memory for names and faces: A cross-sectional approach. *Journal of Experimental Psychology: General, 104,* 54–75.

Bahrick, L. E. (2010). Intermodal perception and selective attention to intersensory redundancy: Implications for typical social development and autism. In J. G. Bremner & T. D. Wachs (Eds.), *The Wiley-Blackwell Handbook of Infant Development* (2nd ed., Vol 1: Basic Research, pp. 120–166). Malden, MA: John Wiley & Sons.

Bahrick, L. E., & Newell, L. (2008). Infant discrimination of faces in naturalistic events: Actions are more salient than faces. *Developmental Psychology, 44,* 983–996.

Bahrick, L. E., Gogate, L. J., & Ruiz, I. (2002). Attention and memory for faces and actions in infancy: The salience of actions over faces in dynamic events. *Child Development, 73,* 1629–1643.

Bahrick, L. E., Lickliter, R., & Castellanos, I. (2013). The development of face perception in infancy: Intersensory interference and unimodal visual facilitation. *Developmental Psychology, 49,* 1919–1930.

Bailey, A., Lecouteur, A., Gottesman, I., Bolton, P., Simonoff, E., Yuzda, E. et al. (1995). Autism as a strongly genetic disorder: Evidence from a British twin study. *Psychological Medicine, 25,* 63–77.

Bailey, C. E. (Ed.) (2000). *Children in therapy: Using the family as a resource.* New York: W. W. Norton.

Bailey, H., Dunlosky, J., & Hertzog, C. (2009). Does differential strategy use account for age-related deficits in working-memory performance? *Psychology and Aging, 24,* 82–92.

Bailey, J. M., & Pillard, R. C. (1991). A genetic study of male sexual orientation. *Archives of General Psychiatry, 48,* 1089–1096.

Bailey, J. M., Bechtold, K. T., & Berenbaum, S. A. (2002). Who are tomboys and why should we study them? *Archives of Sexual Behavior, 31,* 333–341.

Bailey, J. M., Dunne, M. P., & Martin, N. G. (2000). Genetic and environmental influences on sexual orientation and its correlates in an Australian twin sample. *Journal of Personality and Social Psychology, 78,* 524–536.

Bailey, J. M., Pillard, R. C., Neale, M. C., & Agyei, Y. (1993). Heritable factors influence sexual orientation in women. *Archives of General Psychiatry, 50,* 217–223.

Bailey, R. N., Indian, R. W., Zhang, X., Geiss, L. S., Duenas, M. R., & Saaddine, J. B. (2006). Visual impairment and eye care among older adults—five states. *Morbidity and Mortality Weekly Report, 55,* 1321–1325.

Baillargeon, R. (2002). The acquisition of physical knowledge in infancy: a summary in eight lessons. In U. Goswami (Ed.), *Blackwell handbook of child cognitive development* (pp. 47–83). Oxford: Blackwell.

Baillargeon, R. H., Zoccolillo, M., Keenan, K., Côté, S., Pérusse, D., Wu, H., Boivin, M., & Tremblay, R. E. (2007). Gender differences in physical aggression: A prospective population-based survey of children before and after 2 years of age. *Developmental Psychology, 43,* 13–26.

Bajenaru, O., Tiu, C., Antochi, F., & Roceanu, A. (2012). Neurocognitive disorders in DSM 5 project—Personal comments. *Journal of the Neurological Sciences, 322,* 17–19.

Bajpai, A., Kabra, M., Gupta, A. K., & Menon, P. S. (2006). Growth pattern and skeletal maturation following growth hormone therapy in growth hormone deficiency: Factors influencing outcome. *Indian Pediatrics, 43,* 593–599.

Bakan, D. (1966). *The duality of human existence: Isolation and communion in Western man.* Boston: Beacon Press.

Baker, L., & Brown, A. L. (1984). Metacognitive skills and reading. In P. D. Pearson (Ed.), *A handbook of reading research.* New York: Longman.

Bakermans-Kranenburg, M. J., & van IJzendoorn, M. H. (2009). The first 10,000 adult attachment interviews: Distributions of adult attachment representations in clinical and non-clinical groups. *Attachment and Human Development, 11,* 223–263.

Bakermans-Kranenburg, M. J., Sonuga-Barke, E. J. S., Bos, K. B., Kelley, M., Dobrova-Krol, N. A., Engle, P. L., et al (2011). Children without permanent parents: Research, practice, and policy. *Monographs of the Society for Research in Child Development, 76*(4, Serial No. 291).

Baker-Ward, L., Gordon, B. N., Ornstein, P. A., Larus, D. M., & Clubb, P. A. (1993). Young children's long-term retention of a pediatric examination. *Child Development, 64,* 1519–1533.

Baker-Ward, L., Ornstein, P. A., & Holden, D. J. (1984). The expression of memorization in early childhood. *Journal of Experimental Child Psychology, 37,* 555–575.

Balk, D. E., & Corr, C. A. (2001). Bereavement during adolescence: A review of research. In M. S. Stroebe, R. O. Hansson, W. Stroebe, & H. Schut (Eds.), *Handbook of bereavement research: Consequences, coping, and care.* Washington, DC: American Psychological Association.

Balk, D. E., & Corr, C. A. (Eds.) (2009). *Adolescent encounters with death, bereavement, and coping.* New York: Springer.

Baltes, P. B. (1987). Theoretical propositions of life-span developmental psychology: On the dynamics between growth and decline. *Developmental Psychology, 23,* 611–626.

Baltes, P. B., & Rudolph, C. W. (2013). The theory of selection, optimization, and compensation. In M. Wang (Ed.), *The Oxford handbook of retirement* (pp. 88–101). New York: Oxford University Press.

Baltes, P. B., & Baltes, M. M. (1990). Psychological perspectives on successful aging: The model of selective optimization with compensation. In P. B. Baltes & M. M. Baltes (Eds.), *Successful aging: Perspectives from the behavioral sciences.* New York: Cambridge University Press.

Baltes, P. B., & Carstensen, L. L. (2003). The process of successful aging: Selection, optimization and compensation. In U. M. Staudinger & U. Lindenberger (Eds.), *Understanding human development: Dialogues with life-span psychology.* Dordecht, Netherlands: Kluwer Academic Press.

Baltes, P. B., & Freund, A. M. (2003). Human strengths as the orchestration of wisdom and selective optimization with compensation. In L. G. Aspinwall & U. M. Staudinger (Eds.), *A psychology of human strengths: Fundamental questions and future directions for a positive psychology.* Washington, DC: American Psychological Association.

Baltes, P. B., & Lindenberger, U. (1997). Emergence of a powerful connection between sensory and cognitive functions across the adult life span: A new window to the study of cognitive aging? *Psychology and Aging, 12,* 12–21.

Baltes, P. B., & Staudinger, U. M. (2000). Wisdom: A metaheuristic (pragmatic) to orchestrate mind and virtue toward excellence. *American Psychologist, 55,* 122–136.

Baltes, P. B., Lindenberger, U., & Staudinger, U. M. (2006). Life span theory in developmental psychology. In W. Damon & R. M. Lerner (Eds. in Chief) & R. M. Lerner (Vol. Ed.), *Handbook of child psychology: Vol. 1. Theoretical models of human development* (6th ed.). Hoboken, NJ: Wiley.

Baltes, P. B., Smith, J., & Staudinger, U. M. (1992). Wisdom and successful aging. In T. B. Sonderegger (Ed.), *Nebraska symposium on motivation: Vol. 39. Psychology and aging.* Lincoln: University of Nebraska Press.

Baltes, P. B., Staudinger, U. M., Maercker, A., & Smith, J. (1995). People nominated as wise: A comparative study of wisdom-related knowledge. *Psychology and Aging, 10,* 155–166.

Banai, K., Ortiz, J. A., Oppenheimer, J. D., & Wright, B. A. (2010). Learning two things at once: Differential constraints on the acquisition and consolidation of perceptual learning. *Neuroscience, 165,* 436–444.

Bandstra, E. S., Morrow, C. E., Mansoor, E., & Accornero, V. H. (2010). Prenatal drug exposure: Infant and toddler outcomes. *Journal of Addictive Disorders, 29,* 245–258.

Bandura, A. (1986). *Social foundations of thought and action: A social cognitive theory.* Englewood Cliffs, NJ: Prentice Hall.

Bandura, A. (1991). Social cognitive theory of moral thought and action. In W. M. Kurtines & J. L. Gewirtz (Eds.), *Handbook of moral behavior and development: Vol. 1. Theory.* Hillsdale, NJ: Erlbaum.

Bandura, A. (2002). Selective moral disengagement in the exercise of moral agency. *Journal of Moral Education, 31,* 101–119.

Bandura, A., Caprara, G. V., Barbaranelli, C., Pastorelli, C., & Regalia, C. (2001). Sociocognitive self-regulatory mechanisms governing transgressive behavior. *Journal of Personality & Social Psychology, 80,* 125–135.

Banerjee, R., & Lintern, V. (2000). Boys will be boys: The effect of social evaluation concerns on gender-typing. *Social Development, 9,* 397–408.

Banerjee, T. D., Middleton, F., & Faraone, S. V. (2007). Environmental risk factors for attention-deficit hyperactivity disorder. *Acta Paediatrica, 96,* 1269–1274.

Bank, L., Marlowe, J., Reid, J., Patterson, G., & Weinrott, M. (1991). A comparative evaluation of parent-training interventions for families of chronic delinquents. *Journal of Abnormal Child Psychology, 19,* 15–33.

Bankoff, E. A. (1983). Aged parents and their widowed daughters: A support relationship. *Journal of Gerontology, 38,* 226–230.

Banks, M. S., & Ginsburg, A. P. (1985). Infant visual preferences: A review and new theoretical treatment. In H. W. Reese (Ed.), *Advances in child development and behavior* (Vol. 19). Orlando, FL: Academic Press.

Banks, M. S., & Shannon, E. (1993). Spatial and chromatic visual efficiency in human neonates. In C. E. Granrud (Ed.), *Visual perception and cognition in infancy.* Hillsdale, NJ: Erlbaum.

Banti, S., Mauri, M., Oppo, A., Borri, C., Rambelli, C., Ramacciotti, D., et al. (2011). From the third month of pregnancy to 1 year postpartum. Prevalence, incidence, recurrence, and new onset of depression. Results from the perinatal depression-research & screening unit study. *Comprehensive Psychiatry, 52,* 343–351.

Barac, R., & Bialystok, E. (2012). Bilingual effects on cognitive and linguistic development: Role of language, cultural background, and education. *Child Development, 83,* 413–422.

Barber, B. L., Eccles, J. S., & Stone, M. R. (2001). Whatever happened to the jock, the brain, and the princess? Young adult pathways linked to adolescent activity involvement and social identity. *Journal of Adolescent Research, 16,* 429–455.

Barboza, G. E., Schiamberg, L. B., Oehmke, J., Korzeniewski, S. J., Post, L. A., & Heraux, C. G. (2009). Individual characteristics and the multiple contexts of adolescent bullying: An ecological perspective. *Journal of Youth and Adolescence, 38,* 101–121.

Bar-Haim, Y., Ziv, T., Lamy, D., & Hodes, R. M. (2006). Nature and nurture in own-race face processing. *Psychological Science, 17,* 159–163.

Bariola, E., Gullone, E., & Hughes, E. K. (2011). Child and adolescent emotion regulation: The role of parental emotion regulation and expression. *Clinical Child and Family Psychology Review, 14,* 198–212.

Barker, E. D., Arseneault, L., Brendgen, M., Fontaine, N., & Maughan, B. (2008). Joint development of bullying and victimization in adolescence: Relations to delinquency and self-harm. *Journal of the American Academy of Child and Adolescent Psychiatry, 47,* 1030–1038.

Barkley, R. A. (1997). Behavioral inhibition, sustained attention, and executive functions: Constructing a unifying theory of ADHD. *Psychological Bulletin, 121,* 65–94.

Barkley, R. A. (2000). Genetics of childhood disorders: XVII. ADHD, Part 1: The executive functions and ADHD. *Journal of the American Academy of Child and Adolescent Psychiatry, 39,* 1064–1068.

Barkley, R. A., Fischer, M., Smallish, L., & Fletcher, K. (2006). Young adult outcome of hyperactive children: Adaptive functioning in major life activities. *Journal of the American Academy of Child and Adolescent Psychiatry, 45,* 192–202.

Barnes, D. E., Yaffe, K., Satariano, W. A., & Tager, I. B. (2003). A longitudinal study of cardiorespiratory fitness and cognitive function in healthy older adults. *Journal of the American Geriatrics Society, 51,* 459–465.

Barnes, K. E. (1971). Preschool play norms: A replication. *Developmental Psychology, 5,* 99–103.

Barnes, R. (2013, January 14). In memoir, Sotomayor lays bare a tough life. *The Washington Post,* pp. C1, C3.

Barnett, R. C. (1994). Home-to-work spillover revisited: A study of full-time employed women in dual-earner couples. *Journal of Marriage and the Family, 56,* 647–656.

Barnett, W. S., Brown, K. C., Finn-Stevenson, M., & Henrich, C. (2007). From visions to systems of universal prekindergarten. In J. L. Aber, S. J. Bishop-Josef, S. M. Jones, K. T. McLearn, & D. A. Phillips (Eds.), *Child development and social policy: Knowledge for action.* Washington, DC: American Psychology Association.

Baron, N. S. (1992). *Growing up with language: How children learn to talk.* Reading, MA: Addison-Wesley.

Baron-Cohen, S. (1995). *Mindblindness: An essay on autism and theory of mind.* Cambridge, MA: MIT Press.

Baron-Cohen, S. (2003). *The essential difference: The truth about the male and female brain.* New York: Basic Books.

Baron-Cohen, S. (2010). Autism and the empathizing-systemizing (E-S) theory. In P. D. Zelazo, M. Chandler, & E. Crone (Eds.), *Developmental social cognitive neuroscience.* New York: Psychology Press.

Baron-Cohen, S., Leslie, A. M., & Frith, U. (1985). Does the autistic child have a "theory of mind"? *Cognition, 21,* 37–46.

Barouki, R., Gluckman, P. D., Grandjean, P., Hanson, M., & Heindel, J. J. (2012). Developmental origins of non-communicable disease: Implications for research and public health. *Environmental Health, 11,* 3–9. Retrieved from http://www.ehjournal.net/content/11/1/42

Barr, R., Dowden, A., & Hayne, H. (1996). Developmental changes in deferred imitation by 6- to 24-month-old infants. *Infant Behavior & Development, 19,* 159–170.

Barrett, T. M., & Needham, A. (2008). Developmental differences in infants' use of an object's shape to grasp it securely. *Developmental Psychobiology, 50,* 97–106.

Barrett, T. R., & Wright, M. (1981). Age-related facilitation in recall following semantic processing. *Journal of Gerontology, 36,* 194–199.

Barry, T. D., Lochman, J. E., Fite, P. J., Wells, K. C., & Colder, C. R. (2012). The influence of neighborhood characteristics and parenting practices on academic problems and aggression outcomes among moderately to highly aggressive children. *Journal of Community Psychology, 40,* 372–379.

Bartholomew, K., & Horowitz, L. M. (1991). Attachment styles among young adults: A test of a four-category model. *Journal of Personality and Social Psychology, 61,* 226–244.

Bartlett, D. (1997). Primitive reflexes and early motor development. *Journal of Developmental and Behavioral Pediatrics, 18,* 151–157.

Bartlett, T. (2011, February 25). The case for play. How a handful of researchers are trying to save childhood. *Chronicle of Higher Education*, pp. B6–B10.

Basseches, M. (1984). *Dialectical thinking and adult development*. Norwood, NJ: Ablex.

Basseches, M. (2005). The development of dialectical thinking as an approach to integration. *Integral Review, 1*, 47–63.

Bates, E., O'Connell, B., & Shore, C. (1987). Language and communication in infancy. In J. D. Osofsky (Ed.), *Handbook of infant development* (2nd ed.). New York: Wiley.

Bates, J. E., Schermerhorn, A. C., & Petersen, I. T. (2012). Temperament and parenting in developmental perspective. In M. Z. Zentner & R. L. Shiner (Eds.), *Handbook of temperament*. New York: Guilford.

Bates, J. S., & Taylor, A. C. (2013). Taking stock of theory in grandparent studies. In M. A. Fine & F. D. Fincham (Eds.), *Handbook of family theories. A context-based approach*. New York: Routledge.

Batshaw, M. L., Gropman, A., & Lanpher, B. (2013). Genetics and developmental disabilities. In M. L. Batshaw, N. J. Roizen, & G. R. Lotrecchiano (Eds.), *Children with disabilities* (7th ed., pp. 3–24). Baltimore: Paul H. Brookes.

Baudouin, A., Clarys, D., Vanneste, S., & Isingrini, M. (2009). Executive functioning and processing speed in age-related differences in memory: Contribution of a coding task. *Brain and Cognition, 71*, 240–245.

Bauer, I., Wrosch, C., & Jobin, J. (2008). I'm better off than most other people: The role of social comparisons for coping with regret in young adulthood and old age. *Psychology and Aging, 23*, 800–811.

Bauer, P. J. (1996). What do infants recall of their lives? Memory for specific events by one- to two-year-olds. *American Psychologist, 51*, 29–41.

Bauer, P. J. (2007). *Remembering the times of our lives: Memory in infancy and beyond*. Mahwah, NJ: Lawrence Erlbaum.

Bauer, P. J. (2008). Toward a neuro-developmental account of the development of declarative memory. *Developmental Psychobiology, 50*, 19–31.

Bauer, P. J. (2009). The cognitive neuroscience of the development of memory. In M. L. Courage & N. Cowan (Eds.), *The development of memory in infancy and childhood* (pp. 115–144). New York: Psychology Press.

Bauer, P. J., Burch, M. M., Scholin, S. E., & Güler, O. E. (2007). Using cue words to investigate the distribution of autobiographical memories in childhood. *Psychological Science, 18*, 910–916.

Bauer, P. J., Larkina, M., & Deocampo, J. (2011). Early memory development. In U. Goswami (Ed.), *The Wiley-Blackwell handbook of childhood cognitive development* (2nd ed., pp. 153–179). Malden, MA: John Wiley & Sons.

Bauer, P. J., Wenner, J. A., Dropik, P. L., & Wewerka, S. S. (2000). Parameters of remembering and forgetting in the transition from infancy to early childhood. *Monographs of the Society for Research in Child Development, 65*(Serial No. 263).

Baumrind, D. (1967). Child care practices anteceding three patterns of preschool behavior. *Genetic Psychology Monographs, 75*, 43–88.

Baumrind, D. (1977, March). *Socialization determinants of personal agency*. Paper presented at the biennial meeting of the Society for Research in Child Development, New Orleans.

Baumrind, D. (1991). Effective parenting during the early adolescent transition. In P. A. Cowan & M. Hetherington (Eds.), *Family transitions*. Hillsdale, NJ: Erlbaum.

Baumrind, D. (2013). Authoritative parenting revisited: History and current status. In R. E. Larzelere, A. S. Sheffield, & A. W. Harrist (Eds.), *Authoritative parenting. Synthesizing nurturance and discipline for optimal child development*. Washington, DC: American Psychological Association.

Bauserman, R. (2002). Child adjustment in joint-custody versus sole-custody arrangements: A meta-analytic review. *Journal of Family Psychology, 16*, 91–102.

Bayley, N. (1993). *Bayley scales of infant development* (2nd ed.). San Antonio: Psychological Corporation.

Beadle-Brown, J., Murphy, G., & DiTerlizzi, M. (2009). Quality of life for the Camberwell cohort. *Journal of Applied Research in Intellectual Disabilities, 22*, 4, 380–438390.

Beadle-Brown, J., Murphy, G., & Wing, L. (2005). Long-term outcome for people with severe intellectual disabilities: Impact of social impairment. *American Journal on Mental Retardation, 110*, 1–12.

Beadle-Brown, J., Murphy, G., & Wing, L. (2006). The Camberwell cohort 25 years on: Characteristics and changes in skills over time. *Journal of Applied Research in Intellectual Disabilities, 19*, 317–329.

Beane, A. L. (2009). *Bullying prevention for schools: A step-by-step guide to implementing a successful anti-bullying program*. San Francisco: Jossey-Bass.

Beauchamp, G. K., & Mennella, J. A. (2009). Early flavor learning and its impact on later feeding behavior. *Journal of Pediatric Gastroenterology and Nutrition, 48*, S25–S30.

Beauchamp, G. K., & Mennella, J. A. (2011). Flavor perception in human infants: Development and functional significance. *Digestion, 83*, 1–6.

Beautrais, A. L. (2003). Life course factors associated with suicidal behaviors in young people. *American Behavioral Scientist, 46*, 1137–1156.

Beck, H. P., Levinson, S., & Irons, G. (2009). Finding Little Albert. A journey to John B. Watson's infant laboratory. *American Psychologist, 64*, 605–614.

Becker, A. E., Burwell, R. A., Herzog, D. B., Hamburg, P., & Gilman, S. E. (2002). Eating behaviours and attitudes following prolonged exposure to television among ethnic Fijian adolescent girls. *British Journal of Psychiatry, 180*, 509–514.

Beckwith, L., Rozga, A., & Sigman, M. (2002). Maternal sensitivity and attachment in atypical groups. In R. V. Kail (Ed.), *Advances in child development and behavior* (Vol. 30). San Diego: Academic Press.

Becquet, R., Marston, M., Dabis, F., Moulton, L. H., Gray, G., Coovadia, H. M., et al. (2012). Children who acquire HIV infection perinatally are at higher risk of early death than those acquiring infection through breastmilk: A meta-analysis. *PLoS ONE, 7*, e28510.

Beehr, T. A., Glazer, S., Nielson, N. L., & Farmer, S. J. (2000). Work and nonwork predictors of employee's retirement age. *Journal of Vocational Behavior, 57*, 206–225.

Behrend, D. A., Rosengren, K., & Perlmutter, M. (1989). A new look at children's private speech: The effects of age, task difficulty, and parent presence. *International Journal of Behavioral Development, 12*, 305–320.

Beijersbergen, M. D., Juffer, F., Bakermans-Kranenburg, M., & van IJzendoorn, M. H. (2012). Remaining or becoming secure: Parental sensitive support predicts attachment continuity from infancy to adolescence in a longitudinal adoption study. *Developmental Psychology, 48*, 1277–1282.

Beilin, H. (1992). Piaget's enduring contribution to developmental psychology. *Developmental Psychology, 28*, 191–204.

Beitchman, J. H., Zucker, K. J., Hood, J. E., daCosta, G. A., & Akman, D. (1991). A review of the short-term effects of child sexual abuse. *Child Abuse & Neglect, 15*, 537–556.

Bell, J. H., & Bromnick, R. D. (2003). The social reality of the imaginary audience: A grounded theory approach. *Adolescence, 38*, 205–219.

Bell, M. A., & Wolfe, C. D. (2007). Changes in brain functioning from infancy to early childhood: Evidence from EEG power and coherence working memory tasks. *Developmental Neuropsychology, 31*, 21–38.

Bellanti, C. J., Bierman, K. L., & Conduct Problems Prevention Research Group. (2000). Disentangling the impact of low cognitive ability and inattention on social behavior and peer relationships. *Journal of Clinical Child Psychology, 29*, 66–75.

Bellugi, U. (1988). The acquisition of a spatial language. In F. S. Kessel (Ed.), *The development of language and language researchers: Essays in honor of Roger Brown*. Hillsdale, NJ: Erlbaum.

Belsky, J. (1981). Early human experience: A family perspective. *Developmental Psychology, 17*, 3–23.

Belsky, J., Burchinal, M., McCartney, K., Vandell, D. L., Clarke-Stewart, K. A., Owen, M. T., et al. (2007). Are there long-term effects of early child care? *Child Development, 78*, 681–701.

Belsky, J., Jaffee, S., Hsieh, K., & Silva, P. A. (2001). Child-rearing antecedents of intergenerational relations in young adulthood: A prospective study. *Developmental Psychology, 37*, 801–813.

Bem, S. L. (1989). Genital knowledge and gender constancy in preschool children. *Child Development, 60*, 649–662.

Bemporad, J. R. (1979). Adult recollections of a formerly autistic child. *Journal of Autism and Developmental Disorders, 9*, 179–197.

Benaron, L. D. (2009). *Autism*. Westport, CT: Greenwood Press.

Benbow, C. P., & Arjmand, O. (1990). Predictors of high academic achievement in mathematics and science by mathematically talented students: A longitudinal study. *Journal of Educational Psychology, 82*, 430–441.

Bender, K. A. (2012). An analysis of well-being in retirement: The roles of pensions, health, and 'voluntariness' of retirement. *The Journal of Socio-Economics, 41*, 424–433.

Benenson, J. F., Philippoussis, M., & Leeb, R. (1999). Sex differences in neonates' cuddliness. *Journal of Genetic Psychology, 160*, 332–342.

Benes, F. M. (1998). Human brain growth spans decades. *American Journal of Psychiatry, 155*, 1489.

Bengtson, V. L. (2001). Beyond the nuclear family: The increasing importance of multigenerational bonds. *Journal of Marriage and Family, 63*, 1–16.

Bengtson, V., Rosenthal, C., & Burton, L. (1996). Paradoxes of families and aging. In R. H. Binstock, L. K. George, V. W. Marshall, G. C. Myers, & J. H. Schulz (Eds.), *Handbook of aging and the social sciences* (4th ed.). San Diego: Academic Press.

Bennett, J. (2010, October 11). From lockers to lockup. *Newsweek*, pp. 38–41.

Benoit, D., & Parker, K. C. (1994). Stability and transmission of attachment across three generations. *Child Development, 65*, 1444–1456.

Berenbaum, S. A., Martin, C. L., Hanish, L. D., Briggs, P. T., & Fabes, R. A. (2008). Sex differences in children's play. In J. B. Becker, K. J. Berkley, N. Geary, E. Hampson, J. Herman, & E. Young (Eds.), *Sex differences in the brain: From genes to behavior* (pp. 275–290). New York: Oxford University Press.

Berg, C. A., & Klaczynski, P. A. (1996). Practical intelligence and problem solving: Searching for perspectives. In F. Blanchard-Fields & T. M. Hess (Eds.), *Perspectives on cognitive change in adulthood and aging*. New York: McGraw-Hill.

Berger, A. S. (1993). *Dying and death in law and medicine: A forensic primer for health and legal professionals*. Westport, CT: Praeger.

Berger, R. P., Fromkin, J. B., Stutz, H., Makoroff, K., Scribano, P. V., Feldman, K., et al. (2011). Abusive head trauma during a time of increased unemployment: A multicenter analysis. *Pediatrics, 128*, 637–643.

Berger, S. E., & Adolph, K. E. (2003). Infants use handrails as tools in locomotor task. *Developmental Psychology, 39*, 594–605.

Berger, S. E., Adolph, K. E., & Lobo, S. A. (2005). Out of the toolbox: Toddlers differentiate wobbly and wooden handrails. *Child Development, 76*, 1294–1307.

Berger, T. M., Steurer, M. A., Woerner, A., Meyer-Schiffer, P., & Adams, M. (2012). Trends and centre-to-centre variability in survival rates of very preterm infants (<32 weeks) over a 10-year-period in Switzerland. *Archives of Disease in Childhood-Fetal and Neonatal Edition, 97*, F323–F328.

Bering, J. M., & Bjorklund, D. F. (2004). The natural emergence of reasoning about the afterlife as a developmental regularity. *Developmental Psychology, 40*, 217–233.

Berk, L. E. (1992). Children's private speech: An overview of theory and the status of research. In R. M. Diaz & L. E. Berk (Eds.), *Private speech: From social interaction to self-regulation*. Hillsdale, NJ: Erlbaum.

Berk, L. E., & Landau, S. (1993). Private speech of learning disabled and normally achieving children in classroom academic and laboratory contexts. *Child Development, 64*, 556–571.

Berk, L. E., & Winsler, A. (1995). *Scaffolding children's learning: Vygotsky and early childhood education*. Washington, DC: National Association for the Education of Young Children.

Berkman, E. T., Graham, A. M., & Fisher, P. A. (2012). Training self-control: A domain-general translational neuroscience approach. *Child Development Perspectives, 6*, 374–384.

Berlin, L. J., Zeanah, C. H., & Lieberman, A. F. (2008). Prevention and intervention programs for supporting early attachment security. In J. Cassidy & P. R. Shaver (Eds.), *Handbook of attachment: Theory, research, and clinical applications* (2nd ed.). New York: Guilford.

Berman, A. L., & Jobes, D. A. (1991). *Adolescent suicide: Assessment and intervention*. Washington, DC: American Psychological Association.

Berman, W. H., & Sperling, M. B. (1991). Parental attachment and emotional distress in the transition to college. *Journal of Youth and Adolescence, 20*, 427–440.

Bernal, M. E., & Knight, G. P. (1997). Ethnic identity of Latino children. In J. G. Garcia & M. C. Zea (Eds.), *Psychological interventions and research with Latino populations*. Boston: Allyn & Bacon.

Bernard, K., Dozier, M., Bick, J., Lewis-Morrarty, E., Lindhiem, O., & Carlson, E. (2012). Enhancing attachment organization among maltreated children: Results of a randomized clinical trial. *Child Development, 83*, 623–636.

Berndt, T. J., & Murphy, L. M. (2002). Influences of friends and friendships: Myths, truths, and research recommendations. In R. V. Kail (Ed.), *Advances in child development and behavior* (Vol. 30). San Diego: Academic Press.

Bernstein, A. C., & Cowan, P. A. (1975). Children's concepts of how people get babies. *Child Development, 46*, 77–91.

Bernstein, G. A., & Victor, A. M. (2010). Separation anxiety disorder and school refusal. In M. K. Dulcan (Ed.), *Dulcan's textbook of child and adolescent psychiatry* (pp. 325–338). Arlington, VA: American Psychiatric Publishing.

Berntsen, D., & Rubin, D. C. (2002). Emotionally charged autobiographical memories across the lifespan: The recall of happy, sad, traumatic, and involuntary memories. *Psychology and Aging, 17*, 636–652.

Berntsen, D., & Rubin, D. C. (2004). Cultural life scripts structure recall from autobiographical memory. *Memory & Cognition, 32*, 427–442.

Berntsen, D., & Rubin, D. C. (Eds.). (2012). *Understanding autobiographical memory: Theories and approaches*. New York: Cambridge University Press.

Berry, J. W., Poortinga, Y. H., Segall, M., & Dasen, P. R. (1992). *Cross-cultural psychology: Research and applications*. Cambridge, UK: Cambridge University Press.

Berscheid, E. (2010). Love in the fourth dimension. *Annual Review of Psychology, 61*, 1–25.

Bertenthal, B. I., & Fischer, K. W. (1978). Development of self-recognition in the infant. *Developmental Psychology, 14*, 44–50.

Berthier, N. E., & Keen, R. (2006). Development of reaching in infancy. *Experimental Brain Research, 169*, 507–518.

Bertman, S. L. (1991). Children and death: Insights, hindsights, and illuminations. In D. Papadatou & C. Papadatos (Eds.), *Children and death*. New York: Hemisphere.

Berzonsky, M. D., & Kuk, L. S. (2000). Identity status, identity processing style, and the transition to university. *Journal of Adolescent Research, 15*, 81–98.

Best, D. L., & Williams, J. E. (1993). A cross-cultural viewpoint. In A. E. Beall & R. J. Sternberg (Eds.), *The psychology of gender* (pp. 215–248). New York: Guilford Press.

Betts, J., McKay, J., Maruff, P., & Anderson, V. (2006). The development of sustained attention in children: The effect of age and task load. *Child Neuropsychology, 12*, 205–221.

Beuker, K. T., Rommelse, N. N. J., Donders, R., & Buitelaar, J. K. (2013). The development of early communication skills in the first two years of life. *Infant Behavior & Development, 36*, 71–83.

Beyers, J. M., Bates, J. E., Pettit, G. S., & Dodge, K. A. (2003). Neighborhood structure, parenting processes, and the development of youths' externalizing behaviors: A multilevel analysis. *American Journal of Community Psychology, 31*, 35–53.

Beyers, W., & Seiffge-Krenke, I. (2010). Does identity precede intimacy? Testing Erikson's theory on romantic development in emerging adults of the 21st century. *Journal of Adolescent Research, 25*, 387–415.

Bialystok, E., Craik, F. I. M., & Luk, G. (2012). Bilingualism: Consequences for mind and brain. *Trends in Cognitive Sciences, 16*, 240–250.

Bialystok, E., & Feng, X. (2011). Language proficiency and its implications for monolingual and bilingual children. In A. Y. Durgunoglu & C. Goldenberg (Eds.), *Language and literacy development in bilingual settings* (pp. 121–139). Guilford Press.

Bianchi, S. M. (2011). Family change and time allocation in american families. *Annals of the American Academy of Political and Social Science, 638*, 21–44.

Bianchi, S. M., Robinson, J. P., & Milkie, M. A. (2006). *Changing rhythms of American family life*. New York: Russell Sage.

Biblarz, T. J., & Stacey, J. (2010). How does the gender of parents matter? *Journal of Marriage and Family, 72*, 3–22.

Biemann, T., Zacher, H., & Feldman, D. C. (2012). Career patterns: A twenty-year panel study. *Journal of Vocational Behavior, 81*, 159–170.

Bierhoff, H., & Schmohr, M. (2003). Romantic and marital relationships. In F. R. Lang & K. L. Fingerman (Eds.), *Growing together. Personal relationships across the life span*. Cambridge, UK: Cambridge University Press.

Bierman, K. L. (2004). *Peer rejection: Developmental processes and intervention strategies*. New York: Guilford.

Bierman, K. L., & Powers, C. J. (2009). Social skills training to improve peer relations. In K. H. Rubin, W. M. Bukowski, & B. Laursen (Eds.), *Handbook of peer interactions, relationships, and groups*. New York: Guilford.

Bierman, K. L., Coie, J., Dodge, K., Greenberg, M., Lochman, J., McMohan, R., et al. (2013). School outcomes of aggressive-disruptive children: Prediction from kindergarten risk factors and impact of the Fast Track Prevention Program. *Aggressive Behavior, 39*, 114–130.

Bigler, R. S., & Liben, L. S. (1990). The role of attitudes and interventions in gender-schematic processing. *Child Development, 61*, 1440–1452.

Bihaqi, S. W., Schumacher, A., Maloney, B., Lahiri, D. K., & Zawia, N. H. (2012). Do epigenetic pathways initiate late onset Alzheimer disease (LOAD): Towards a new paradigm. *Current Alzheimer Research, 9*, 574–588.

Bird, A., & Reese, E. (2006). Emotional reminiscing and the development of an autobiographical self. *Developmental Psychology, 42*, 613–626.

Birditt, K. S., & Fingerman, K. L. (2013). Parent-child and intergenerational relationships in adulthood. In M. A. Fine & F. D. Fincham (Eds.), *Handbook of family theories. A context-based approach*. New York: Routledge.

Birditt, K. S., Fingerman, K. L., Lefkowitz, E. S., & Dush, C. M. K. (2008). Parents perceived as peers: Filial maturity in adulthood. *Journal of Adult Development, 15*, 1–12.

Birditt, K. S., Miller, L. M., Fingerman, K. L., & Lefkowitz, E. S. (2009). Tensions in the parent and adult child relationship: Links to solidarity and ambivalence. *Psychology and Aging, 24*, 287–295.

Birdsong, D. (1999). Introduction: Whys and why nots of the critical period hypothesis for second language acquisition. In D. Birdsong (Ed.), *Second language acquisition and the critical period hypothesis*. Mahwah, NJ: Erlbaum.

Birdsong, D. (2005). Interpreting age effects in second language acquisition. In J. Kroll & A. de Groot (Eds.), *Handbook of bilingualism: Psycholinguistic approaches*. New York: Oxford University Press.

Birren, J. E., & Schroots, J. J. F. (2006). Autobiographical memory and the narrative self over the life span. In J. E. Birren & K. W. Schaie (Eds.), *Handbook of the psychology of aging* (6th ed.). Burlington, MA: Elsevier Academic Press.

Birren, J. E., Butler, R. N., Greenhouse, S. W., Sokoloff, L., & Yarrow, M. R. (Eds.). (1963). *Human aging: A biological and behavioral study*. Washington, DC: U.S. Government Printing Office.

Bivens, J. A., & Berk, L. E. (1990). A longitudinal study of the development of elementary school children's private speech. *Merrill-Palmer Quarterly, 36*, 443–463.

Bjork J. M., Knutson B., Fong G. W., Caggiano D. M., Bennett S. M., Hommer D. W. (2004). Incentive-elicited brain activation in adolescents: similarities and differences from young adults. *Journal of Neuroscience, 24*, 1793–1802.

Bjork, R. A., & Bjork, E. L. (Eds.). (1998). *Memory*. New York: Academic Press.

Bjorklund, D. F. (1985). The role of conceptual knowledge in the development of organization in children's memory. In C. J. Brainerd & M. Pressley (Eds.), *Basic processes in memory development: Progress in cognitive development research*. New York: Springer-Verlag.

Bjorklund, D. F. (1995). *Children's thinking: Developmental function and individual differences*. Pacific Grove, CA: Brooks/Cole.

Bjorklund, D. F. (1997). In search of a metatheory for cognitive development (or, Piaget is dead and I don't feel so good myself). *Child Development, 68*, 144–148.

Bjorklund, D. F., & Pellegrini, A. D. (2002). *The origins of human nature*. Washington, DC: American Psychological Association.

Bjorklund, D. F., Brown, R. D., & Bjorklund, B. R. (2002). Children's eyewitness memory: Changing reports and changing representations. In P. Graf & N. Ohta (Eds.), *Life-span development of human memory* (pp. 101–126). Cambridge, MA: Massachusetts Institute of Technology.

Bjorklund, D. F., Dukes, C., & Brown, R. D. (2009). The development of memory strategies. In M. L. Courage & N. Cowan (Eds.), *The development of memory in infancy and childhood* (pp. 145–176). New York: Psychology Press.

Black, J. E., Isaacs, K. R., & Greenough, W. T. (1991). Usual vs. successful aging: Some notes on experiential factors. *Neurobiology of Aging, 12*, 325–328.

Blackburn, J. A. (1984). The influence of personality, curriculum, and memory correlates on formal reasoning in young adults and elderly persons. *Journal of Gerontology, 39*, 207–209.

Blackburn, J. A., & Papalia, D. E. (1992). The study of adult cognition from a Piagetian perspective. In R. J. Sternberg & C. A. Berg (Eds.), *Intellectual development*. New York: Cambridge University Press.

Blackwell, L. S., Trzesniewski, K. H., & Dweck, C. S. (2007). Implicit theories of intelligence predict achievement across an adolescent transition: A longitudinal study and an intervention. *Child Development, 78*, 246–263.

Blake, J. J., Lund, E. M., Zhou, Q., Kwok, O., & Benz, M. R. (2012). National prevalence rates of bully victimization among students with disabilities in the United States. *School Psychology Quarterly, 27*, 210–222.

Blakemore, J. E. O. (2003). Children's beliefs about violating gender norms: Boys shouldn't look like girls, and girls shouldn't act like boys. *Sex Roles, 49*, 411–420.

Blakemore, S, & Robbins, T. W. (2012). Decision-making in the adolescent brain. *Nature Neuroscience, 15*, 1184–1191.

Blanchard, R., & Lippa, R. A. (2007). Birth order, sibling sex ratio, handedness, and sexual orientation of male and female participants in a BBC internet research project. *Archives of Sexual Behavior, 36*, 163–176.

Blanchard-Fields, F. (1986). Reasoning on social dilemmas varying in emotional saliency: An adult developmental perspective. *Psychology and Aging, 1*, 325–333.

Blanchard-Fields, F. (1996). Social cognitive development in adulthood and aging. In F. Blanchard-Fields & T. M. Hess (Eds.), *Perspectives on cognitive change in adulthood and aging*. New York: McGraw-Hill.

Blanchard-Fields, F., & Kalinauskas, A. (2009). Theoretical perspectives on social context, cognition, and aging. In V. L. Bengtson, M. Silverstein, N. M. Putney, & D. Gans (Eds.), *Handbook of theories of aging* (2nd ed.). New York: Springer.

Blanchard-Fields, F., Chen, Y., & Norris, L. (1997). Everyday problem solving across the adult life span: Influence of domain specificity and cognitive appraisal. *Psychology and Aging, 12*, 684–693.

Blanchette, H. (2011). The rising cesarean delivery rate in America: What are the consequences? *Obstetrics and Gynecology, 118*, 687–690.

Blazer, D. G. (1993). *Depression in late life*. St. Louis: Mosby.

Blazer, D. G. (2003). Depression in late life: Review and commentary. *Journal of Gerontology: Medical Sciences, 58A*, 249–265.

Bleakley, A., Hennessy, M., Fishbein, M., & Jordan, A. (2011). Using the integrative model to explain how exposure to sexual media content influences adolescent sexual behavior. *Health Education & Behavior, 38*, 530–540.

Blencowe, H., Cousens, S., Kamb, M., Berman, S., & Lawn, J. E. (2011). Lives Saved Tool supplement detection and treatment of syphilis in pregnancy to reduce syphilis related stillbirths and neonatal mortality. *BMC Public Health, 11*(Suppl. 3), S9.

Bleske-Rechek, A., Fuerstenberg, E. A., Harris, H. D., & Ryan, D. E. (2011). Men and women, work and family: A test of competing perspectives. *Journal of Social, Evolutionary, and Cultural Psychology, 5*, 275–292.

Blieszner, R. (2006). A lifetime of caring: Dimensions and dynamics in late-life close relationships. *Personal Relationships, 13*, 1–18.

Blomquist, J. L., Quiroz, L. H., MacMillan, D., Mccullough, A., & Handa, V. L. (2011). Mothers' satisfaction with planned vaginal and planned cesarean birth. *American Journal of Perinatology, 28*, 383–388.

Blomqvist, Y. T., & Nyqvist, K. H. (2010). Swedish mothers' experience of continuous Kangaroo mother care. *Journal of Clinical Nursing, 20*, 1472–1480.

Bloom, L. (1998). Language acquisition in its developmental context. In D. Kuhn & R. S. Siegler (Vol. Eds.), W. Damon (Editor-in-Chief), *Handbook of child psychology: Vol. 2.*

Cognition, perception, and language (5th ed., pp. 309–370). New York: Wiley.

Bloom, L., & Tinker, E. (2001). The intentionality model and language acquisition: Engagement, effort, and the essential tension. *Monographs of the Society for Research in Child Development, 66*(Serial No. 267).

Bluebond-Langner, M. (1977). Meanings of death to children. In H. Feifel (Ed.), *New meanings of death*. New York: McGraw-Hill.

Blumberg, E. S. (2003). The lives and voices of highly sexual women. *The Journal of Sex Research, 40*, 146–157.

Boatella-Costa, E., Costas-Moragas, C., Botet-Mussons, F., Fornieles-Deu, A., & De Cáceres-Zurita, M. L. (2007). Behavioral gender differences in the neonatal period according to the Brazelton scale. *Early Human Development, 83*, 91–97.

Bock, J. (2005). Farming, foraging, and children's play in the Okavango Delta, Botswana. In A. D. Pellegrini & P. K. Smith (Eds.), *The nature of play: Great apes and humans*. New York: Guilford Press.

Bodkin, N. L., Alexander, T. M., Ortmeyer, H. K., Johnson, E., & Hansen, B. C. (2003). Morbidity and mortality in laboratory-maintained rhesus monkeys and effects of long-term dietary restriction. *Journal of Gerontology Series A: Biological Sciences, 58A*, 212–219.

Bodley-Tickell, A. T., Olowokure, B., Bhaduri, S., White, D. J., Ward, D., Ross, J. D., et al. (2008). Trends in sexually transmitted infections (other than HIV) in older people: Analysis of data from an enhanced surveillance system. *Sexually Transmitted Infections, 84*, 312–317.

Bodrova, E., & Leong, D. J. (1996). *Tools of the mind: The Vygotskian approach to early childhood education*. Englewood Cliffs, NJ: Prentice Hall.

Boelen, P. A., & Prigerson, H. G. (2013). Prolonged grief disorder as a new diagnostic category in DSM-5. In M. Stroebe, H. Schut & J. van den Bout (Eds.), *Complicated grief: Scientific foundations for health care professionals*. New York: Routledge/Taylor & Francis.

Boelen, P. A., van den Hout, M., & van den Bout, J. (2013). Prolonged grief disorder: Cognitive-behavioral theory and therapy. In M. Stroebe, H. Schut & J. van den Bout (Eds.), *Complicated grief: Scientific foundations for health care professionals*. New York: Routledge/Taylor & Francis.

Boerner, K., Mancini, A. D., & Bonanno, G. (2013). On the nature and prevalence of uncomplicated and complicated patterns of grief. In M. Stroebe, H. Schut & J. van den Bout (Eds.), *Complicated grief: Scientific foundations for health care professionals*. New York: Routledge/Taylor & Francis.

Boerner, K., Wortman, C. B., & Bonanno, G. A. (2005). Resilient or at risk? A 4-year study of older adults who initially showed high or low distress following conjugal loss. *Journal of Gerontology: Psychological Sciences, 60B*, P67–P73.

Bogoch, I. I., House, R. A., & Kudla, I. (2005). Perceptions about hearing protection and noise-induced hearing loss of attendees of rock concerts. *Canadian Journal of Public Health, 96*, 69–72.

Bohannon, J. N., & Bonvillian, J. D. (2013). Theoretical approaches to language acquisition. In J. Berko Gleason & N. B. Ratner (Eds.), *The development of language* (7th ed.). Boston: Allyn & Bacon.

Bohannon, J. R. (1990–1991). Grief responses of spouses following the death of a child: A longitudinal study. *Omega: Journal of Death and Dying, 22*, 109–121.

Bohlmeijer, E., Roemer, M., Cuijpers, P., & Smit, F. (2007). The effects of reminiscence on psychological well-being in order adults: A meta-analysis. *Aging & Mental Health, 11*, 291–300.

Boldizar, J. P. (1991). Assessing sex-typing and androgyny in children: The children's sex-role inventory. *Developmental Psychology, 27*, 505–515.

Boles, S., Biglan, A., & Smolkowski, K. (2006). Relationships among negative and positive behaviours in adolescence. *Journal of Adolescence, 29*, 33–52.

Bolger, K. E., & Patterson, C. J. (2001). Developmental pathways from child maltreatment to peer rejection. *Child Development, 72*, 549–568.

Boloh, Y., & Champaud, C. (1993). The past conditional verb form in French children: The role of semantics in late grammatical development. *Journal of Child Language, 20*, 169–189.

Bonanno, G. A. (2001). Introduction. New direction in bereavement research and theory. *American Behavioral Scientist, 44*, 718–725.

Bonanno, G. A. (2004). Loss, trauma, and human resilience: Have we underestimated the human capacity to thrive after extremely aversive events? *American Psychologist, 59*, 20–28.

Bonanno, G. A. (2009). *The other side of sadness. What the new science of bereavement tells us about life after loss*. New York: Basic Books.

Bonanno, G. A., & Kaltman, S. (1999). Toward an integrative perspective on bereavement. *Psychological Bulletin, 125*, 760–776.

Bonanno, G. A., & Kaltman, S. (2000). The varieties of grief experience. *Clinical Psychology Review, 21*, 705–734.

Bonanno, G. A., Boerner, K., & Wortman, C. B. (2008). Trajectories of grieving. In M. S. Stroebe, R. O. Hansson, H. Schut, & W. Stroebe (Eds.), *Handbook of bereavement research and practice. Advances in theory and intervention*. Washington, DC: American Psychological Association.

Bonanno, G. A., Papa, A., Lalande, K., Zhang, N., & Noll, J. G. (2005). Grief processing and deliberate grief avoidance: A prospective comparison of bereaved spouses and parents in the United States and the People's Republic of China. *Journal of Consulting and Clinical Psychology, 73*, 86–98.

Bonanno, G. A., Wortman, C. B., Lehman, D. R., Tweed, R. G., Haring, M., Sonnega, J., et al.

(2002). Resilience to loss and chronic grief: A prospective study from preloss to 18 months postloss. *Journal of Personality and Social Psychology, 83*, 1150–1164.

Bonanno, G. A., Wortman, C. B., & Nesse, R. M. (2004). Prospective patterns of resilience and maladjustment during widowhood. *Psychology and Aging, 19*, 260–271.

Bong, M. (2009). Age-related differences in achievement goal differentiation. *Journal of Educational Psychology, 101*, 879–896.

Bongers, I. L., Koot, H. M., van der Ende, J., & Verhulst, F. C. (2003). The normative development of child and adolescent problem behavior. *Journal of Abnormal Psychology, 112*, 179–192.

Bonoti, F., Leondari, A., & Mastora, A. (2013). Exploring children's understanding of death: Through drawings and the death concept questionnaire. *Death Studies, 37*, 47–60.

Bonvillain, N. (2010). *Cultural anthropology* (2nd ed.). New Jersey: Pearson.

Booth, A., & Johnson, D. (1988). Premarital cohabitation and marital success. *Journal of Family Issues, 9*, 255–272.

Booth, A., Scott, M. E., & King, V. (2010). Father residence and adolescent problem behavior: Are youth always better off in two-parent families? *Journal of Family Issues, 31*, 585–605.

Booth-LaForce, C., & Kerns, K. A. (2009). Child-parent attachment relationships, peer relationships, and peer-group functioning. In K. H. Rubin, W. M. Bukowski, & B. Laursen (Eds.), *Handbook of peer interactions, relationships, and groups*. New York: Guilford.

Boris, N. W., & Zeanah, C. H. (1999). Disturbances and disorders of attachment in infancy: An overview. *Infant Mental Health Journal, 20*, 1–9.

Borkenau, P., Riemann, R., Angleitner, A., & Spinath, F. M. (2001). Genetic and environmental influences on observed personality: Evidence from the German Observational Study of Adult Twins. *Journal of Personality and Social Psychology, 80*, 655–668.

Bornstein, M. H., & Hendricks, C. (2012). Basic language comprehension and production in >100,000 young children from sixteen developing nations. *Journal of Child Language, 39*, 899–918.

Bornstein, M. H., & Putnick, D. L. (2012). Stability of language in childhood: A multiage, multidomain, multimeasure, and multisource study. *Developmental Psychology, 48*, 477–491.

Bornstein, M. H., & Sawyer, J. (2006). Family systems. In K. McCartney & D. Phillips (Eds.), *Blackwell handbook of early childhood development*. Malden, MA: Blackwell.

Borradaile, K. E., Sherman, S., Vander Veur, S., McCoy, T., Sandoval, B., Nachmani, J., et al. (2009). Snacking in children: The role of urban corner stores. *Pediatrics, 124*, 1292–1297.

Bosak, J., Sczesny, S., & Eagly, A. H. (2008). Communion and agency judgments of women and men as a function of role information and response format. *European Journal of Social Psychology, 38*, 1148–1155.

Bosch, A. M., Willekens, F. J., Baqui, A. H., Van Ginneken, J. K., & Hutter, I. (2008). Association between age at menarche and early-life nutritional status in rural Bangladesh. *Journal of Biosocial Science, 40,* 223–237.

Boston Retinal Implant Project. (2013). Retrieved from http://www.bostonretinalimplant.org/index.php/blindness-and-disease/

Bouldin, P. (2006). An investigation of fantasy predisposition and fantasy style of children with imaginary companions. *The Journal of Genetic Psychology, 167,* 17–29.

Bowen, B. A. (1999). Four puzzles in adult literacy: Reflections on the National Adult Literacy Survey. *Journal of Adolescent & Adult Literacy, 42,* 314–323.

Bowen, M. (1978). *Family therapy in clinical practice.* New York: Aronson.

Bowen, M. W., & Firestone, M. H. (2011). Pathological use of electronic media: Case studies and commentary. *Psychiatric Quarterly, 82,* 229–238.

Bower, T. G. R., Broughton, J. M., & Moore, M. K. (1970). The coordination of vision and tactile input in infancy. *Perception and Psychophysics, 8,* 51–53.

Bowers, M., Perez-Pouchoulen, M., Edwards, N. S., & Mccarthy, M. M. (2013, February 20). Foxp2 mediates sex differences in ultrasonic vocalization by rat pups and directs order of maternal. *The Journal of Neuroscience, 33*(8), 3276. doi:10.1523/JNEUROSCI.0425-12.2013

Bowlby, J. (1960). Separation anxiety. *International Journal of Psychoanalysis, 41,* 89–113.

Bowlby, J. (1969). *Attachment and loss: Vol. 1. Attachment.* New York: Basic Books.

Bowlby, J. (1973). *Attachment and loss: Vol. 2. Separation.* New York: Basic Books.

Bowlby, J. (1980). *Attachment and loss: Vol. 3. Loss, sadness and depression.* New York: Basic Books.

Bowlby, J. (1988). *A secure base: Parent–child attachment and healthy human development.* New York: Basic Books.

Boyatzis, C. J. (2013). The nature and functions of religion and spirituality in children. In K. I. Pargament, J. J. Exline, & J. W. Jones (Eds.), *APA handbook of psychology, religion, and spirituality: Vol. 1. Context, theory, and research.* Washington, DC: American Psychological Association.

Boyce, C. J., & Wood, A. M. (2011). Personality prior to disability determines adaptation: Agreeable individuals recover lost life satisfaction faster and more completely. *Psychological Science, 22,* 1397–1402.

Bracey, J. R., Bamaca, M. Y., & Umaña-Taylor, A. J. (2004). Examining ethnic identity and self-esteem among biracial and monoracial adolescents. *Journal of Youth and Adolescence, 33,* 123–132.

Bradbard, M. R., Martin, C. L., Endsley, R. C., & Halverson, C. F. (1986). Influence of sex stereotypes on children's exploration and memory: A competence versus performance distinction. *Developmental Psychology, 22,* 481–486.

Bradley, R. H., & Corwyn, R. F. (2002). Socioeconomic status and child development. *Annual Review of Psychology, 53,* 371–399.

Bradley, R. H., Caldwell, B. M., Rock, S. L., Ramey, C. T., Barnard, K. E., Gray, C., et al. (1989). Home environment and cognitive development in the first 3 years of life: A collaborative study involving six sites and three ethnic groups in North America. *Developmental Psychology, 25,* 217–235.

Bradley, R. H., Convyn, R. F., Burchinal, M., McAdoo, H. P., & Coll, C. G. (2001). The home environments of children in the United States, part II: Relations with behavioral development through age thirteen. *Child Development, 72,* 1868–1886.

Bradshaw, C. P., Zmuda, J. K., Kellam, S. G., & Ialongo, N. S. (2009). Longitudinal impact of two universal preventive interventions in first grade on educational outcomes in high school. *Journal of Educational Psychology, 101,* 926–937.

Brady, S. S., & Halpern-Fisher, B. L. (2007). Adolescents' reported consequences of having oral sex versus vaginal sex. *Pediatrics, 119,* 229–236.

Brainerd, C. J., & Gordon, L. L. (1994). Development of verbatim and gist memory for numbers. *Developmental Psychology, 30,* 163–177.

Brainerd, C. J., & Reyna, V. F. (1993). Domains of fuzzy trace theory. In M. L. Howe & R. Pasnak (Eds.), *Emerging themes in cognitive development: Vol. 1. Foundations.* New York: Springer-Verlag.

Braithwaite, V. (2002). Reducing ageism. In T. D. Nelson (Ed.), *Ageism: Stereotyping and prejudice against older persons.* Cambridge, MA: The MIT Press.

Brandão, S., & Figueiredo, B. (2012). Fathers' emotional involvement with the neonate: Impact of the umbilical cord cutting experience. *Journal of Advanced Nursing, 68,* 2730–2739. doi:10.1111/j.1365-2648.2012.05978.x

Brandt, J., Aretouli, E., Neijstrom, E., Samek, J., Manning, K., Albert, M. S., et al. (2009). Selectivity of executive function deficits in mild cognitive deficit. *Neuropsychology, 23,* 607–618.

Brandtstädter, J., & Greve, W. (1994). The aging self: Stabilizing and protective processes. *Developmental Review, 14,* 52–80.

Brant, A. M., Haberstick, B. C., Corley, R. P., Wadsworth, S. J., DeFries, J. C., & Hewitt, J. K. (2009). The developmental etiology of high IQ. *Behavior Genetics, 39,* 393–405.

Brassett-Harknett, A., & Butler, N. (2007). Attention-deficit/hyperactivity disorder: An overview of the etiology and a review of the literature relating to the correlates and lifecourse outcomes for men and women. *Clinical Psychology Review, 27,* 188–210.

Braver, E. R., & Trempel, R. E. (2004). Are older drivers actually at higher risk of involvement in collisions resulting in deaths or non-fatal injuries among their passengers and other road users? *Injury Prevention, 10,* 27–32.

Bray, N. W., Hersh, R. E., & Turner, L. A. (1985). Selective remembering during adolescence. *Developmental Psychology, 21,* 290–294.

Brazelton, T. B., & Nugent, J. K. (2011). *Neonatal behavioral assessment scale* (4th ed.). London: Mac Keith Press.

Breedlove, S. M. (1994). Sexual differentiation of the human nervous system. *Annual Review of Psychology, 45,* 389–418.

Bremner, J. D., & Narayan, M. (1998). The effects of stress on memory and the hippocampus throughout the life cycle: Implications for childhood development and aging. *Development and Psychopathology, 10,* 871–886.

Bremner, J. G., Johnson, S. P., Slater, A., Mason, U., Foster, K., Cheshire, A., et al. (2005). Conditions for young infants' perception of object trajectories. *Child Development, 76,* 1029–1043.

Brendgen, M., Vitaro, F., & Girard, A. (2012). Evaluating gene-environment interplay. In B. Laursen, T. D. Little, & N. A. Card (Eds.), *Handbook of developmental research methods* (pp. 687–705). New York: Guilford.

Brenick, A., Henning, A., Killen, M., O'Connor, A., & Collins, M. (2007). Social evaluations of stereotypic images in video games: Unfair, legitimate, or 'just entertainment'? *Youth & Society, 38,* 395–419.

Brent, D. A., & Maalouf, F. T. (2009). Pediatric depression: Is there evidence to improve evidence-based treatments? *Journal of Child Psychology and Psychiatry, 50,* 143–152.

Brent, D., Melhem, N., Donohoe, M. B., & Walker, M. (2009). The incidence and course of depression in bereaved youth 21 months after the loss of a parent to suicide, accident, or sudden natural death. *American Journal of Psychiatry, 166,* 786–794.

Brent, D., Melhem, N., Masten, A., Porta, G., & Payne, M. (2012). Longitudinal effects of parental bereavement on adolescent developmental competence. *Journal of Clinical Child and Adolescent Psychology, 41,* 778–791.

Brent, S. B., Speece, M. W., Lin, C. G., Dong, Q., & Yang, C. M. (1996). The development of the concept of death among Chinese and U.S. children 3–17 years of age: From binary to "fuzzy" concepts? *Omega: Journal of Death and Dying, 33,* 67–83.

Bretherton, I. (1996). Internal working models of attachment relationships as related to resilient coping. In G. G. Noam, & K. W. Fischer (Eds.), *Development and vulnerability in close relationships.* Mahwah, NJ: Erlbaum.

Bretherton, I., & Beeghly, M. (1982). Talking about internal states: The acquisition of an explicit theory of mind. *Developmental Psychology, 18,* 906–921.

Bretherton, I., Stolberg, U., & Kreye, M. (1981). Engaging strangers in proximal interaction: Infants' social initiative. *Developmental Psychology, 17,* 746–755.

Bridge, J. A., Day, N. L., Day, R., Richardson, G. A., Birmaher, B., & Brent, D. A. (2003). Major depressive disorder in adolescents exposed to a friend's suicide. *Journal of the American Academy of Child and Adolescent Psychiatry, 42,* 1294–1300.

Bridges, L. J., & Grolnick, W. S. (1995). The development of emotional self-regulation in infancy and early childhood. In N. Eisenberg (Ed.), *Social development: Vol. 15. Review of personality and social psychology.* Thousand Oaks, CA: Sage.

Briefel, R. R., Crepinsek, M. K., Cabili, C., Wilson, A., & Gleason, P. M. (2009). School food environments and practices affect dietary behaviors of U.S. public school children. *Journal of the American Dietetic Association, 109,* S91–107.

Brod, M., Schmitt, E., Goodwin, M., Hodgkins, P., & Niebler, G. (2012). ADHD burden of illness in older adults: A life course perspective. *Quality of Life Research, 21,* 795–799.

Brody, E. B., & Brody, N. (1976). *Intelligence: Nature, determinants, and consequences.* New York: Academic Press.

Brody, E. M. (2004). *Women in the middle: Their parent care years* (2nd ed.). New York: Springer.

Brody, E. M., Litvin, S. J., Hoffman, C., & Kleban, M. H. (1992). Differential effects of daughters' marital status on their parent care experiences. *Gerontologist, 32,* 58–67.

Brody, G. H. (2003). Parental monitoring: Action and reaction. In A. C. Crouter, & A. Booth (Eds.), *Children's influence on family dynamics: The neglected side of family relationships.* Mahwah, NJ: Erlbaum.

Brody, G. H. (2004). Siblings' direct and indirect contributions to child development. *Current Directions in Psychological Science, 13,* 124–126.

Brody, G. H., Beach, S. R. H., Philibert, R. A., Chen, Y., & Murry, V. M. (2009). Prevention effects moderate the association of 5-HTTLPR and youth risk behavior initiation: Gene x environment hypotheses tested via a randomized prevention design. *Child Development, 80,* 645–661.

Brody, G. H. (2004). Siblings' direct and indirect contributions to child development. *Current Directions in Psychological Science, 13,* 124–126.

Brody, G. H., Beach, S. R. H., Philibert, R. A., Chen, Y., & Murry, V. M. (2009). Prevention effects moderate the association of 5-HTTLPR and youth risk behavior initiation: Gene x environment hypotheses tested via a randomized prevention design. *Child Development, 80,* 645–661.

Brody, G. H., & Shaffer, D. R. (1982). Contributions of parents and peers to children's moral socialization. *Developmental Review, 2,* 31–75.

Brody, J. A., Grant, M. D., Frateschi, L. J., Miller, S. C., & Zhang, H. (2000). Reproductive longevity and increased life expectancy. *Age and Ageing, 29,* 75–78.

Broen, A. N., Moum, T., Bodtker, A. S., & Ekeberg, O. (2004). Psychological impact on women of miscarriage versus induced abortion: A 2-year follow-up study. *Psychosomatic Medicine, 66,* 265–271.

Broesch, T., Callaghan, T., Henrich, J., Murphy, C., & Rochat, P. (2011). Cultural variations in children's mirror self-recognition. *Journal of Cross-Cultural Psychology, 42,* 1018–1029.

Bronfenbrenner, U., & Morris, P. A. (2006). The bioecological model of human development. In W. Damon & R. M. Lerner (Eds. in Chief) & R. M. Lerner (Vol. Ed.), *Handbook of child psychology: Vol. 1. Theoretical models of human development* (6th ed.). Hoboken, NJ: Wiley.

Brooks-Gunn, J., & Lewis, M. (1981). Infant social perception: Responses to pictures of parents and strangers. *Developmental Psychology, 17,* 647–649.

Brooks-Gunn, J., Britto, P. R., & Brady, C. (1999). Struggling to make ends meet: Poverty and child development. In M. E. Lamb (Ed.), *Parenting and child development in "nontraditional" families.* Mahwah, NJ: Erlbaum.

Brooks-Gunn, J., Klebanov, P. K., & Duncan, G. J. (1996). Ethnic differences in children's intelligence test scores: Role of economic deprivation, home environment, and maternal characteristics. *Child Development, 67,* 396–408.

Brophy, J. (2010). *Motivating students to learn* (3rd ed.). New York: Routledge.

Broughton, J. M. (1984). Not beyond formal operations, but beyond Piaget. In M. L. Commons, F. A. Richards, & C. Armon (Eds.), *Beyond formal operations: Late adolescent and adult cognitive development* (pp. 395–411). New York: Praeger.

Brown, A. L., & Smiley, S. S. (1978). The development of strategies for studying text. *Child Development, 49,* 1076–1088.

Brown, A. M., & Lindsey, D. T. (2009). Contrast insensitivity: The critical immaturity in infant visual performance. *Optometry and Vision Science, 86,* 572–576.

Brown, A., & Avery, A. (2012). Healthy weight management during pregnancy: What advice and information is being provided. *Journal of Human Nutrition & Diet, 25,* 378–388.

Brown, B. B. (1999). "You're going out with who?" Peer group influences on adolescent romantic relationships. In W. Furman, B. B. Brown, & C. Feiring (Eds.), *The development of romantic relationships in adolescence.* Cambridge, UK: Cambridge University Press.

Brown, B. B. (2011). Popularity in peer group perspective. The role of status in adolescent peer systems. In A. H. N. Cillessen, D. Schwartz, & L. Mayeux (Eds.), *Popularity in the peer system.* New York: Guilford.

Brown, B. B., & Bakken, J. P. (2011). Parenting and peer relationships: Reinvigorating research on family–peer linkages in adolescence. *Journal of Research on Adolescence, 21,* 153–165.

Brown, B. B., & Dietz, E. L. (2009). Informal peer groups in middle childhood and adolescence. In K. H. Rubin, W. M. Bukowski, & B. Laursen (Eds.), *Handbook of peer interactions, relationships, and groups.* New York: Guilford.

Brown, B. B., & Lohr, M. J. (1987). Peer-group affiliation and adolescent self-esteem: An integration of ego–identity and symbolic-interaction theories. *Journal of Personality and Social Psychology, 52,* 47–55.

Brown, B. B., Feiring, C., & Furman, W. (1999). Missing the love boat. Why researchers have shied away from adolescent romance. In W. Furman, B. B. Brown, & C. Feiring (Eds.), *The development of romantic relationships in adolescence.* Cambridge, UK: Cambridge University Press.

Brown, B. B., Herman, M., Hamm, J. V., & Heck, D. J. (2008). Ethnicity and image: Correlates of crowd affiliation among ethnic minority youth. *Child Development, 79,* 529–546.

Brown, B. B., Mory, M. S., & Kinney, D. (1994). Casting adolescent crowds in a relational perspective: Caricature, channel, and context. In R. Montemayor, G. R. Adams, & T. P. Gulotta (Eds.), *Personal relationships during adolescence.* Thousand Oaks, CA: Sage.

Brown, B. B., Mounts, N., Lamborn, S. D., & Steinberg, L. (1993). Parenting practices and peer group affiliation in adolescence. *Child Development, 64,* 467–482.

Brown, D., & Boytchev, H. (2012, September 6). Our 'junk DNA' not so useless after all. *The Washington Post,* pp. A1, A20.

Brown, I. T., Chen, T., Gehlert, N. C., & Piedmont, R. L. (2012). Age and gender effects on the Assessment of Spirituality and Religious Sentiments (ASPIRES) Scale: A cross-sectional analysis. *Psychology of Religion and Spirituality,* No Pagination Specified. doi:10.1037/a0030137

Brown, R., Cazden, C., & Bellugi, U. (1969). The child's grammar from I to III. In J. P. Hill (Ed.), *Minnesota Symposia on Child Psychology* (Vol. 2). Minneapolis: University of Minnesota Press.

Brown, S. L., Bulanda, J. R., & Lee, G. R. (2012). Transitions into and out of cohabitation in later life. *Journal of Marriage and Family, 74,* 774–793.

Brown, S. L., Smith, D. M., Schulz, R., Kabeto, M. U., Ubel, P. A., Poulin, M., Yi, J., Kim, C., & Langa, K. M. (2009). Caregiving behavior is associated with decreased mortality risk. *Psychological Science, 20,* 488–494.

Brownell, C. A., & Carriger, M. S. (1990). Changes in cooperation and self/other differentiation during the second year. *Child Development, 61,* 1164–1174.

Bruce, J., Gunnar, M. R., Pears, K. C., & Fisher, P. A. (2013). Early adverse care, stress neurobiology, and prevention science: Lessons learned. *Prevention Science.* doi:10.1007/s11121-012-0354-6

Bruck, M. (1990). Word recognition skills of adults with childhood diagnoses of dyslexia. *Developmental Psychology, 26,* 439–454.

Bruck, M. (1992). Persistence of dyslexics' phonological awareness deficits. *Developmental Psychology, 28,* 874–886.

Brundin, P., Winkler, J., & Masliah, E. (2008). Adult neurogenesis in neurodegenerative diseases. In F. H. Gage, G. Kempermann, & H. Song (Eds.), *Adult neurogenesis* (pp. 503–533). New York: Cold Spring Harbor Laboratory Press.

Bruner, J. S. (1983). *Child's talk: Learning to use language.* New York: Norton.

Bruner, J. S. (1997). Celebrating divergence: Piaget and Vygotsky. *Human Development, 40,* 63–73.

Brunskill, P. J. (1992). The effects of fetal exposure to danazol. *British Journal of Obstetrics & Gynaecology, 99,* 212–215.

Brütt, A. L., Sandberg, D. E., Chaplin, J., Wollmann, H., Noeker, M., Kołtowska-Häggström, M., & Bullinger, M. (2009). Assessment of health-related quality of life and patient satisfaction in children and adolescents with growth hormone deficiency or idiopathic short stature - part 1: A critical evaluation of available tools. *Hormone Research, 72,* 65–73.

Bryant, P. (1998). Sensitivity to onset and rhyme does predict young children's reading: A comment on Muter, Hulme, Snowling, and Taylor (1997). *Journal of Experimental Child Psychology, 71,* 39–44.

Bryant-Waugh, R. (2007). Anorexia nervosa in children and adolescents. In T. Jaffa & B. McDermott (Eds.), *Eating disorders in children and adolescents.* Cambridge, UK: Cambridge University Press.

Brynie, F. H. (2009). *Brain sense: The science of the senses and how we process the world around us.* New York: AMACOM.

Buchanan, C. M., Eccles, J. S., & Becker, J. B. (1992). Are adolescents the victims of raging hormones? Evidence for activational effects of hormones on moods and behavior at adolescence. *Psychological Bulletin, 111,* 62–107.

Buchi, S., Morgeli, H., Schnyder, U., Jenewein, J., Hepp, U., Jina, E., Neuhaus, R., Fauchere, J., Bucher, H. U., & Sensky, T. (2007). Grief and post-traumatic growth in parents 2–6 years after the death of their extremely premature baby. *Psychotherapy and Psychosomatics, 76,* 106–114.

Bucur, B., Madden, D. J., Spaniol, J., Provenzale, J. M., Cabeza, R., White, L. E., et al. (2008). Age-related slowing of memory retrieval: Contributions of perceptual speed and cerebral white matter integrity. *Neurobiological Aging, 29,* 1070–1079.

Buehler, C. A., Hogan, M. J., Robinson, B. E., & Levy, R. J. (1985–1986). The parental divorce transition: Divorce-related stressors and well-being. *Journal of Divorce, 9,* 61–81.

Buehler, C., Lange, G., & Franck, K. L. (2007). Adolescents' cognitive and emotional responses to marital hostility. *Child Development, 78,* 775–789.

Buerger, M. (2011, June 23). Two brothers make a splash: 'Age of Champions' highlights athletes in Senior Games [Local Living section]. *The Washington Post,* pp. 18–19.

Bugental, D. (2009). Predicting and preventing child maltreatment: A biocognitive transactional approach. In A. Sameroff (Ed.), *The transactional model of development. How children and contexts shape each other.* Washington, DC: American Psychological Association.

Bugental, D. B., & Beaulieu, D. A. (2003). A bio-social-cognitive approach to understanding and promoting the outcomes of children with medical and physical disorders. In R. V. Kail (Ed.), *Advances in child development and behavior* (Vol. 31). San Diego: Academic Press.

Bugental, D. B., Beaulieu, D. A., & Silbert-Geiger, A. (2010). Increases in parental investment and child health as a result of an early intervention. *Journal of Experimental Child Psychology, 106,* 30–40.

Bugental, D. B., Corpuz, R., & Schwartz, A. (2012). Preventing children's aggression: Outcomes of an early intervention. *Developmental Psychology, 48,* 1443–1449.

Bugental, D. B., Ellerson, P. C., Lin, E. K., Rainey, B., Kokotovic, A., & O'Hara, N. (2002). A cognitive approach to child abuse prevention. *Journal of Family Psychology, 16,* 243–258.

Bugental, D. B., & Schwartz, A. (2009). A cognitive approach to child mistreatment prevention among medically at-risk infants. *Developmental Psychology, 45,* 284–288.

Bugg, J. M., & Head, D. (2011). Exercise moderates age-related atrophy of the medial temporal lobe. *Neurobiology of Aging, 32,* 506–514.

Buhrmester, D., & Furman, W. (1986). The changing functions of friends in childhood: A neo-Sullivanian perspective. In V. J. Derlega & B. A. Winstead (Eds.), *Friendship and social interaction.* New York: Springer-Verlag.

Bukowski, W. M., Buhrmester, D., & Underwood, M. K. (2011). Peer relations as a developmental context. In M. K. Underwood & L. H. Rosen (Eds.), *Social development. Relationships in infancy, childhood, and adolescence.* New York: Guilford.

Bukowski, W. M., Motzoi, C., & Meyer, F. (2009). Friendship as process, function, and outcome. In K. H. Rubin, W. M. Bukowski, & B. Laursen (Eds.), *Handbook of peer interactions, relationships, and groups.* New York: Guilford.

Bulanda, R. E. (2004). Paternal involvement with children: The influence of gender ideologies. *Journal of Marriage and Family, 66,* 40–45.

Bulik, C. M., Sullivan, P. F., Tozzi, F., Furberg, H., Lichtenstein, P., & Pedersen, N. L. (2006). Prevalence, heritability, and prospective risk factors for anorexia nervosa. *Archives of General Psychiatry, 63,* 305–312.

Bullard, L., Wachlarowicz, M., DeLeeuw, J., Snyder, J., Low, S., Forgatch, M., & DeGarmo, D. (2010). Effects of the Oregon model of parent management training (PMTO) on marital adjustment in new stepfamilies: A randomized trial. *Journal of Family Psychology, 24,* 485–496.

Bullock, M., Sodian, B., & Koerber, S. (2009). Doing experiments and understanding science: Development of scientific reasoning from childhood to adulthood. In W. Schneider & M. Bullock (Eds.), *Human development from early childhood to early adulthood: Findings from a 20-year longitudinal study* (pp. 173–197). New York: Psychology Press.

Burack, J. A., Enns, J. T., Iarocci, G., & Randolph, B. (2000). Age differences in visual search for compound patterns: Long-versus short-range grouping. *Developmental Psychology, 36,* 731–740.

Burack, J. A., Hodapp, R. M., & Zigler, E. (Eds.). (1998). *Handbook of development and mental retardation.* New York: Cambridge University Press.

Burak, L. (2012). Multitasking in the university classroom. *International Journal for the Scholarship of Teaching and Learning, 6,* 1–12.

Bureau of Labor Statistics. (2012). *Employment characteristics of families summary.* Retrieved from http://www.bls.gov/news.release/famee.toc.htm

Bures, R. M., Koropeckyj-Cox, T., & Loree, M. (2009). Childlessness, parenthood, and depressive symptoms among middle-aged and older adults. *Journal of Family Issues, 30,* 670–687.

Burgard, S. A., Brand, J. E., & House, J. S., (2007). Toward a better estimation of the effect of job loss on health. *Journal of Health and Social Behavior, 48,* 369–384.

Burhans, K. K., & Dweck, C. S. (1995). Helplessness in early childhood: The role of contingent worth. *Child Development, 66,* 1719–1738.

Burk, W. J., van der Vorst, H., Kerr, M., & Stattin, H. (2012). Alcohol use and friendship dynamics: Selection and socialization in early-, middle-, and late-adolescent peer networks. *Journal of Studies on Alcohol and Drugs, 73,* 89–98.

Burke, L. A., & Neimeyer, R. A. (2013). Prospective risk factors for complicated grief: A review of the empirical literature. In M. Stroebe, H. Schut & J. van den Bout (Eds.), *Complicated grief: Scientific foundations for health care professionals.* New York: Routledge/Taylor & Francis.

Burleson, M. H., Trevathan, W. R., & Todd, M. (2007). In the mood for love or vice versa? Exploring the relations among sexual activity, physical affection, affect, and stress in the daily lives of mid-aged women. *Archives of Sexual Behavior, 36,* 357–368.

Burn, S., O'Neil, A. K., & Nederend, S. (1996). Childhood tomboyishness and adult androgyny. *Sex Roles, 34,* 419–428.

Burnham, D. K., & Harris, M. B. (1992). Effects of real gender and labeled gender on adults' perceptions of infants. *Journal of Genetic Psychology, 153,* 165–183.

Burnham, D., & Mattock, K. (2010). Auditory development. In J. G. Bremner & T. D. Wachs (Eds.), *The Wiley-Blackwell handbook of infant development, 2nd ed., Vol 1: Basic research* (pp. 81–119). Malden, MA: John Wiley & Sons.

Burr, D., & Gori, M. (2012). Multisensory integration develops late in humans. In M. M. Murray & M. T. Wallace (Eds.), *The neural bases of multisensory processes.* Boca Raton, FL: CRC Press.

Burstyn, I. I., Kuhle, S. S., Allen, A. C., & Veugelers, P. P. (2012). The role of maternal smoking in effect of fetal growth restriction on poor scholastic achievement in elementary school. *International Journal of Environmental Research on Public Health, 9,* 408–420.

Burt, C. D. B., Kemp, S., & Conway, M. A. (2003). Themes, events, and episodes in autobiographical memory. *Memory & Cognition, 31,* 317–325.

Burton, C. M., Marshal, M. P., Chisolm, D. J., Sucato, G. S., & Friedman, M. S. (2013). Sexual minority-related victimization as a mediator of mental health disparities in sexual minority youth: A longitudinal analysis. *Journal of Youth and Adolescence, 42,* 394–402.

Burton, L. A., Hafetz, J., & Henninger, D. (2007). Gender differences in relational and physical aggression. *Social Behavior and Personality, 35,* 41–50.

Burton, L. M. (1990). Teenage childrearing as an alternative life-course strategy in multigenerational black families. *Human Nature, 1,* 123–143.

Burton, L. M. (1996). Age norms, the timing of family role transitions, and intergenerational caregiving among aging African American women. *Gerontologist, 36,* 199–208.

Burton, R. V. (1984). A paradox in theories and research in moral development. In W. M. Kurtines & J. L. Gewirtz (Eds.), *Morality, moral behavior, and moral development.* New York: Wiley.

Bus, A. G., & van IJzendoorn, M. H. (1999). Phonological awareness and early reading: A meta-analysis of experimental training studies. *Journal of Educational Psychology, 91,* 403–414.

Busch, H., & Hofer, J. (2011). Self-regulation and milestones of adult development: Intimacy and generativity. *Developmental Psychology, 48,* 282–293.

Busch-Rossnagel, N. A. (1997). Mastery motivation in toddlers. *Infants and Young Children, 9,* 1–11.

Bushman, B. J., & Anderson, C. A. (2001). Media violence and the American public. Scientific facts versus media misinformation. *American Psychologist, 56,* 477–489.

Bushnell, E. W., & Baxt, C. (1999). Children's haptic and cross-modal recognition with familiar and unfamiliar objects. *Journal of Experimental Psychology: Human Perception and Performance, 25,* 1867–1881.

Buss, A. H., & Perry, M. (1992). The aggression question. *Journal of Personality and Social Psychology, 63,* 452–459.

Buss, D. M. (1995). Psychological sex differences: Origins through sexual selection. *American Psychologist, 50,* 164–168.

Buss, D. M. (2012). *Evolutionary psychology: The new science of the mind* (4th ed.). Boston: Allyn & Bacon.

Butcher, P. R., Kalverboer, A. F., & Geuze, R. H. (2000). Infants' shifts of gaze from a central to a peripheral stimulus: A longitudinal study of development between 6 and 26 weeks. *Infant Behavior & Development, 23,* 3–21.

Butler, R. (1990). The effects of mastery and competitive conditions on self-assessment at different ages. *Child Development, 61,* 201–210.

Butler, R. (1999). Information seeking and achievement motivation in middle childhood and adolescence: The role of conceptions of ability. *Developmental Psychology, 35,* 146–163.

Butler, R. N. (1963). The life review: An interpretation of reminiscence in the aged. *Psychiatry, 26,* 65–76.

Butters, M. A., Becker, J. L., Nebes, R. D., Zmuda, M. D., Mulsant, B. H., Pollock, B. G., et al. (2000). Changes in cognitive functioning following treatment of late-life depression. *American Journal of Psychiatry, 157,* 1949–1954.

Butters, M. A., Whyte, E. M., Nebes, R. D., Begley, A. E., Dew, M. A., Mulsant, B. H., et al. (2004). The nature and determinants of neuropsychological functioning in late-life depression. *Archives of General Psychiatry, 61,* 587–595.

Button, T. M. M., Scourfield, J., Martin, N., Purcell, S., & McGuffin, P. (2005). Family dysfunction interacts with genes in the causation of antisocial symptoms. *Behavior Genetics, 35,* 115–120.

Bybee, R. W. (1995). Science curriculum reform in the United States. In R. W. Bybee & J. D. McInerney (Eds.), *Redesigning the science curriculum.* Colorado Springs, CO: Biological Sciences Curriculum Study.

Byne, W. (1994). The biological evidence challenged. *Scientific American, 270,* 50–55.

Byrnes, J. P. (1996). *Cognitive development and learning in instructional contexts.* Boston: Allyn & Bacon.

Cabrera, N. J., Fagan, J., & Farrie, D. (2008). Explaining the long reach of fathers? Prenatal involvement on later paternal engagement. *Journal of Marriage and Family, 70,* 1094–1107.

Cacioppo, J. T., & Patrick, B. (2008). *Loneliness: Human nature and the need for social connection.* New York: W. W. Norton.

Caldera, Y. M., & Lindsey, E. W. (2006). Coparenting, mother–infant interaction, and infant–parent attachment relationships in two-parent families. *Journal of Family Psychology, 20,* 275–283.

Caldera, Y. M., Huston, A. C., & O'Brien, M. (1989). Social interactions and play patterns of parents and toddlers with feminine, masculine, and neutral toys. *Child Development, 60,* 70–76.

Caldwell, B. M., & Bradley, R. H. (1984). *Manual for the home observation for measurement of the environment.* Little Rock: University of Arkansas.

Calkins, S. D., & Hill, A. (2007). Caregiver influences on emerging emotion regulation: Biological and environmental transactions in early development. In J. J. Gross (Ed.), *Handbook of emotion regulation.* New York: Guilford.

Calkins, S. D., & Mackler, J. S. (2011). Temperament, emotion regulation, and social development. In M. K. Underwood & L. H. Rosen (Eds.), *Social development. Relationships in infancy, childhood, and adolescence.* New York: Guilford.

Call, K. T., Mortimer, J. T., & Shanahan, M. (1995). Helpfulness and the development of competence in adolescence. *Child Development, 66,* 129–138.

Callaghan, T., Moll, H., Rakoczy, H., Warneken, F., Liszkowski, U., Behne, T., & Tomasello, M. (2011). Early social cognition in three cultural contexts. *Monographs of the Society for Research in Child Development, 76* (2, Serial No. 299).

Calvin, C. M., Batty, G. D., Lowe, G. D. O., & Deary, I. J. (2011). Childhood intelligence and midlife inflammatory and hemostatic biomarkers: The National Child Development Study (1958) cohort. *Health Psychology, 30,* 710–718.

Calvo, E., Haverstick, K., & Sass, S. A. (2009). Gradual retirement, sense of control, and retirees' happiness. *Research on Aging, 31,* 112–135.

Camaioni, L. (2004). Early language. In G. Bremner & A. Fogel (Eds.), *Blackwell handbook of infant development* (pp. 404–426). Malden, MA: Blackwell Publishing.

Cameron, C. E., Brock, L. L., Murrah, W. M., Bell, L. H., Worzalla, S. L., Grissmer, D., & Morrison, F. J. (2012). Fine motor skills and executive function both contribute to kindergarten achievement. *Child Development, 83,* 1229–1244.

Camp, C. J., & McKitrick, L. A. (1992). Memory interventions in Alzheimer's-type dementia populations: Methodological and theoretical issues. In R. L. West & J. D. Sinnott (Eds.), *Everyday memory and aging: Current research and methodology* (pp. 155–172). New York: Springer-Verlag.

Camp, C. J., Foss, J. W., O'Hanlon, A. M., & Stevens, A. B. (1996). Memory interventions for persons with dementia. *Applied Cognitive Psychology, 10,* 193–210.

Campbell, A., Shirley, L., & Caygill, L. (2002). Sex-typed preferences in three domains: Do two-year-olds need cognitive variables? *British Journal of Psychology, 93,* 203–217.

Campbell, F. A., & Ramey, C. T. (1995). Cognitive and school outcomes for high-risk African-American students at middle adolescence: Positive effects of early intervention. *American Educational Research Journal, 32,* 743–772.

Campbell, F. A., Pungello, E. P., Burchinal, M., Kainz, K., Pan, Y., Wasik, B. H., Barbarin, O. A., Sparling, J. J., & Ramey, C. T. (2012). Adult outcomes as a function of an early childhood educational program: An Abecedarian Project follow-up. *Developmental Psychology, 48,* 1033–1043.

Campbell, F. A., Pungello, E. P., Miller-Johnson, S., Burchinal, M., & Ramey, C. T. (2001). The development of cognitive and academic abilities: Growth curves from an early childhood educational experiment. *Developmental Psychology, 37,* 231–242.

Campbell, R., MacSweeney, M., & Water, D. (2008). Sign language and the brain: A review. *Journal of Deaf Studies and Deaf Education, 13.*

Campbell, V. A., Crews, J. E., Moriarty, D. G., Zack, M. M., & Blackman, D. K. (1999). Surveillance for sensory impairment, activity limitation, and health-related quality of life among older adults: United States, 1993–1997. *CDC MMWR Surveillance Summaries, 48*(SS08), 131–156.

Campos, J. J., Bertenthal, B. I., & Kermoian, R. (1992). Early experience and emotional development: The emergence of wariness of heights. *Psychological Science, 3,* 61–64.

Campos, J. J., Langer, A., & Krowitz, A. (1970). Cardiac responses on the visual cliff in prelocomotor human infants. *Science, 170,* 196–197.

Cann, A., Calhoun, L. G., Tedeschi, R. G., Taku, K., Vishnevsky, T., Triplett, K. N., & Danhauer, S. C. (2010). A short form of the Posttraumatic Growth Inventory. *Anxiety, Stress & Coping, 23,* 127–137.

Cano, A., & Vivian, D. (2003). Are life stressors associated with marital violence? *Journal of Family Psychology, 17,* 302–314.

Cantor, N. L. (2001). Twenty-five years after Quinlan: A review of the jurisprudence of death and dying. *Journal of Law, Medicine, and Ethics, 29,* 182–196.

Caplan, L. J., & Schooler, C. (2001). Age effects on analogy-based memory for text. *Experimental Aging Research, 27,* 151–165.

Carey, N. (2012). *The epigenetics revolution: How modern biology is rewriting our understanding of genetics, disease, and inheritance.* New York: Columbia University Press.

Carlson, M. C., Erickson, K. I., Kramer, A. F., Voss, M. W., Bolea, N., Mielke, M., et al. (2009). Evidence for neurocognitive plasticity in at-risk older adults: The Experience Corps Program. *Journals of Gerontology A: Biological Sciences and Medical Sciences, 64,* 1275–1282.

Carlson, M. J., Pilkauskas, N. V., McLanahan, S. S., & Brooks-Gunn, J. (2011). Couples as partners and parents over children's early years. *Journal of Marriage and Family, 73,* 317–334.

Carlson, V., Cicchetti, D., Barnett, D., & Braunwald, K. (1989). Disorganized/disoriented attachment relationships in maltreated infants. *Developmental Psychology, 25,* 525–531.

Carlsson-Paige, N. (2008). *Taking back childhood.* London, Penguin.

Carnelley, K. B., Wortman, C. B., Bolger, N., & Burke, C. T. (2006). The time course of grief reactions to spousal loss: Evidence from a national probability sample. *Journal of Personality and Social Psychology, 91,* 476–492.

Caron, S., & Ahlgrim, C. J. (2012). Children's understanding and knowledge of conception and birth: Comparing children from England, the Netherlands, Sweden, and the United States. *American Journal of Sexuality Education, 7,* 16–36.

Caron, S. L., & Moskey, E. G. (2002). Changes over time in teenage sexual relationships: Comparing the high school class of 1950, 1975, and 2000. *Adolescence, 37,* 515–526.

Carpendale, J. I. M. (2000). Kohlberg and Piaget on stages and moral reasoning. *Developmental Review, 20,* 181–205.

Carpenter, M., Nagell, K., & Tomasello, M. (1998). Social cognition, joint attention, and communicative competence from 9 to 15 months of age. *Monographs of the Society for Research in Child Development, 63*(Serial No. 255).

Carr, A. (2009). *What works with children, adolescents and adults? A review of research on the effectiveness of psychotherapy.* New York: Routledge/Taylor & Francis Group.

Carr, C. L. (2007). Where have all the tomboys gone? Women's accounts of gender in adolescence. *Sex Roles, 56,* 439–448.

Carr, D. (2004). Gender, preloss marital dependence, and older adults' adjustment to widowhood. *Journal of Marriage and Family, 66,* 220–235.

Carr, D. (2008). Factors that influence late-life bereavement: Considering data from the Changing Lives of Older Couples Study. In M. S. Stroebe, R. O. Hansson, H. Schut, & W. Stroebe (Eds.), *Handbook of bereavement research and practice. Advances in theory and intervention.* Washington, DC: American Psychological Association.

Carr, P. L., Ash, A. S., Friedman, R. H., Scaramucci, A., Barnett, R. C., Szalacha, L., et al. (1998). Relation of family responsibilities and gender to the productivity and career satisfaction of medical faculty. *Annals of Internal Medicine, 129,* 532–538.

Carroll, D. W. (2008). *Psychology of language* (5th ed.). Belmont, CA: Wadsworth.

Carroll, J. B. (1993). *Human cognitive abilities: A survey of factor-analytic studies.* Cambridge, UK: Cambridge University Press.

Carroll, J. M., Snowling, M. J., Hulme, C., & Stevenson, J. (2003). The development of phonological awareness in preschool children. *Developmental Psychology, 39,* 913–925.

Carskadon, M. A. (2011a). Sleep in adolescents: The perfect storm. *Pediatric Clinics of North America, 58,* 637–647.

Carskadon, M. A. (2011b). Sleep's effects on cognition and learning in adolescence. *Progress in Brain Research, 190,* 137–143.

Carstensen, L. L. (1992). Social and emotional patterns in adulthood: Support for socio-emotional selectivity theory. *Psychology and Aging, 7,* 331–338.

Carstensen, L. L., & Freund, A. M. (1994). Commentary: The resilience of the aging self. *Developmental Review, 14,* 81–92.

Carstensen, L. L., Levenson, R. W., & Gottman, J. M. (1995). Emotional behavior in long-term marriages. *Psychology and Aging, 10,* 140–149.

Carstensen, L. L., Pasupathi, M., Mayr, U., & Nesselroade, J. R. (2000). Emotional experience in everyday life across the adult life span. *Journal of Personality and Social Psychology, 79,* 644–655.

Carstensen, L. L., Turan, B., Scheibe, S., Ram, N., Ersner-Hershfield, H., Samanez-Larkin, G., et al. (2011). Emotional experience improves with age: Evidence based on over 10 years of experience sampling. *Psychology and Aging, 26,* 21–33.

Carter, A. S., Briggs-Gowan, M. J., & Davis, N. O. (2004). Assessment of young children's social-emotional development and psychopathology: Recent advances and recommendations for practice. *Journal of Child Psychology and Psychiatry and Allied Disciplines, 45,* 109–134.

Carver, K., Joyner, K., & Udry, J. R. (2003). National estimates of adolescent romantic relationships. In P. Florsheim (Ed.), *Adolescent romantic relations and sexual behavior: Theory, research, and practical implications.* Mahwah, NJ: Erlbaum.

Carver, L. J., & Vaccaro, B. G. (2007). 12-month-old infants allocate increased neural resources to stimuli associated with negative adult emotion. *Developmental Psychology, 43,* 54–69.

Case, R. (1985). *Intellectual development: Birth to adulthood.* Orlando, FL: Academic Press.

Case, R. (1998). The development of conceptual structures. In D. Kuhn & R. S. Siegler (Vol. Eds.), W. Damon (Editor-in-Chief), *Handbook of child psychology: Vol. 2. Cognition, perception, and language* (5th ed., pp. 745–800). New York: Wiley.

Case, T. I., Repacholi, B. M., & Stevenson, R. J. (2006). My baby doesn't smell as bad as yours: The plasticity of disgust. *Evolution and Human Behavior, 27,* 357–365.

Casey, B. J., Somerville, L. H., Gotlib, I. H., Ayduk, O., Franklin, N. T., Askren, M. K., & Shoda, Y. (2011). Behavioral and neural correlates of delay of gratification 40 years later. *Proceedings of the National Academy of Sciences of the United States of America, 108,* 14998–15003.

Caspi, A. (1998). Personality development across the life course. In R. M. Lerner (Vol. Ed.), W. Damon (Editor-in-Chief), *Handbook of child psychology: Vol. 1. Theoretical models of human development* (5th ed.). New York: Wiley.

Caspi, A. (2000). The child is father of man: Personality continues from childhood to adulthood. *Journal of Personality and Social Psychology, 78,* 158–172.

Caspi, A., & Roberts, B. W. (2001). Personality development across the life course: The argument for change and continuity. *Psychological Inquiry, 12,* 49–66.

Caspi, A., Hariri, A. R., Holmes, A., Uher, R., & Moffitt, T. E. (2011). Genetic sensitivity to the environment: The case of the serotonin transporter gene and its implications for studying complex diseases and traits. In K. A. Dodge & M. Rutter (Eds.), *Gene-environment interactions in developmental psychopathology* (pp. 18–58). New York: Guilford.

Caspi, A., Harrington, H., Milne, B., Amell, J. W., Theodore, R. F., & Moffitt, T. E. (2003). Children's behavioral styles at age 3 are linked to their adult personality traits at age 26. *Journal of Personality, 71,* 495–513.

Caspi, A., Herbener, E. S., & Ozer, D. J. (1992). Shared experiences and the similarity of personalities: A longitudinal study of married couples. *Journal of Personality and Social Psychology, 62,* 281–291.

Caspi, A., McClay, J., Moffitt, T., Mill, J., Martin, J., Craig, I. W., Taylor, A., & Poulton, R. (2002). Role of genotype in the cycle of violence in maltreated children. *Science, 297,* 851–854.

Cassia, V. M., Kuefner, D., Westerlund, A., & Nelson, C. A. (2006). A behavioural and ERP investigation of 3-month-olds' face preferences. *Neuropsychologia, 44,* 2113–2125.

Cassia, V. M., Turati, C., & Simion, F. (2004). Can a nonspecific bias toward top-heavy patterns explain newborns' face preference? *Psychological Science, 15,* 379–383.

Cassina, M., Salviati, L., Di Gianantonio, E., & Clementi, M. (2012). Genetic susceptibility to teratogens: State of the art. *Reproductive Toxicology, 34,* 186–191.

Catalano, P. M., McIntyre, H. D., Cruickshank, J. K., McCance, D. R., Dyer, A. R., Metzger, B. E., et al. (2012). The hyperglycemia and adverse pregnancy outcome study: Associations of GDM and obesity with pregnancy outcomes. *Diabetes Care, 35,* 780–786.

Cattell, R. B. (1963). Theory of fluid and crystallized intelligence: A critical experiment. *Journal of Educational Psychology, 54,* 1–22.

Cattell, R. B. (1987). *Intelligence: Its structure, growth, and action* (p. 206). New York: Elsevier Science.

Cavanaugh, J. C. (1996). Memory self-efficacy as a moderation of memory change. In

F. Blanchard-Fields & T. M. Hess (Eds.), *Perspectives on cognitive change in adulthood and aging*. New York: McGraw-Hill.

Cavanaugh, J. C., Grady, J. G., & Perlmutter, M. (1983). Forgetting and use of memory aids in 20 to 70 year olds' everyday life. *International Journal of Aging and Human Development, 17*, 113–122.

Cawley, J., & Meyerhoefer, C. (2012). The medical care costs of obesity: An instrumental variables approach. *Journal of Health Economics, 31*, 219.

Caylak, E. (2009). Neurobiological approaches on brains of children with dyslexia: Review. *Academic Radiology, 16*, 1003–1024.

Ceci, S. J., & Williams, W. M. (1997). Schooling, intelligence, and income. *American Psychologist, 52*, 1051–1058.

Celgene Corporation. (2012). *System for Thalidomide Education and Prescribing Safety*. Retrieved from http://www.thalomid.com

Center on the Developing Child at Harvard University (2011). Building the Brain's "Air Traffic Control" System: HowEarly Experiences Shape the Development of Executive Function: Working Paper No. 11. Retrieved from http://www.developingchild.harvard.edu

Centers for Disease Control and Prevention. (2010). *Adverse childhood experiences study*. Retrieved from www.cdc.gov/nccdphp/ace/prevalence.htm

Centers for Disease Control and Prevention (2011). School health guidelines to promote healthy eating and physical activity. *MMWR, 60* (No. 5), 3–14.

Centers for Disease Control and Prevention. (2012a). *Assisted reproductive technology*. Retrieved from http://www.cdc.gov/art/

Centers for Disease Control and Prevention. (2012b). *Radiation and pregnancy: A fact sheet for the public*. Retrieved from http://www.bt.cdc.gov/radiation/prenatal.asp

Centers for Disease Control and Prevention. (2012c). *Sexually transmitted diseases*. Retrieved from http://www.cdc.gov/std/pregnancy/STDFact-Pregnancy.htm

Centers for Disease Control and Prevention. (2012d). *Sexually transmitted disease surveillance 2011*. Atlanta: U.S. Department of Health and Human Services. Retrieved from http://www.cdc.gov/std/stats11/default.htm

Centers for Disease Control and Prevention. (2012e). *Youth risk behavior surveillance—United States, 2011*. Morbidity and Mortality Weekly Report, 61, 1–268.

Centers for Disease Control and Prevention. (2013). What would happen if we stopped vaccinations? Retrieved from http://www.cdc.gov/vaccines/vac-gen/whatifstop.htm.

Central Intelligence Agency. (2013). *The world factbook. Country comparison: Life expectancy at birth*. Retrieved from https://www.cia.gov/library/publications/the-world-factbook/rankorder/2102rank.html

Cerminara, K. L. (2006). Theresa Marie Schiavo's long road to peace. *Death Studies, 30*, 101–112.

Cernoch, J. M., & Porter, R. H. (1985). Recognition of maternal axillary odors by infants. *Child Development, 56*, 1593–1598.

Cervera, T. C., Soler, M. J., Dasi, C., & Ruiz, J. C. (2009). Speech recognition and working memory capacity in young-elderly listeners: Effects of hearing sensitivity. *Canadian Journal of Experimental Psychology, 63*, 216–226.

Chabris, C. F., Hebert, B. M., Benjamin, D. J., Beauchamp, J., Cesarini, D., van der Loos, M., et al. (2012). Most reported genetic associations with general intelligence are probably false positives. *Psychological Science, 23*, 1314–1323.

Chakrabarti, S., & Fombonne, E. (2005). Pervasive developmental disorders in preschool children: Confirmation of high prevalence. *American Journal of Psychiatry, 162*, 1133–1141.

Chambers, W. C. (2007). Oral sex: Varied behaviors and perceptions in a college population. *Journal of Sex Research, 44*, 28–42.

Champagne, F. A. (2010). Epigenetic influence of social experiences across the lifespan. *Developmental Psychobiology, 52*, 299–311.

Chan, W., McCrae, R. R., Fruyt, F. D., Jussim, L., Lockenhoff, C. E., De Bolle, M., Costa, P. T., Jr. (2012). Stereotypes of age differences in personality traits: Universal and accurate? *Journal of Personality and Social Psychology, 103*, 1050–1066.

Chandler, M. J., Sokol, B. W., & Wainryb, C. (2000). Beliefs about truth and beliefs about rightness. *Child Development, 71*, 91–97.

Chandler, M., Fritz, A. S., & Hala, S. (1989). Small-scale deceit: Deception as a marker of two-, three-, and four-year-olds' early theories of mind. *Child Development, 60*, 1263–1277.

Chao, R. K. (1994). Beyond parental control and authoritarian parenting style: Understanding Chinese parenting through the cultural notion of training. *Child Development, 65*, 1111–1119.

Chao, R. K. (2000). Cultural explanations for the role of parenting in the school success of Asian American children. In R. D. Taylor & M. C. Wang (Eds.), *Resilience across contexts: Family, work, culture, and community*. Mahwah, NJ: Erlbaum.

Chapman, M., & Lindenberger, U. (1988). Functions, operations, and décalage in the development of transitivity. *Developmental Psychology, 24*, 542–551.

Charles, S. T., & Carstensen, L. L. (2007). Emotion regulation and aging. In J. J. Gross, J. J. (Ed.), *Handbook of emotion regulation*. New York: Guilford.

Charles, S. T., & Carstensen, L. L. (2010). Social and emotional aging. *Annual Review of Psychology, 61*, 383–409.

Charles, S. T., Mather, M., & Carstensen, L. L. (2003). Aging and emotional memory: The forgettable nature of negative images for older adults. *Journal of Experimental Psychology: General, 132*, 310–324.

Charlton, R. A., Barrick, T. R., Markus, H. S., & Morris, R. G. (2009). Theory of mind associations with other cognitive functions and brain imaging in normal aging. *Psychology and Aging, 24*, 338–348.

Charman, T. (2000). Theory of mind and the early diagnosis of autism. In S. Baron-Cohen, H. Tager-Flusberg, & D. J. Cohen (Eds.), *Understanding other minds: Perspectives from developmental cognitive neuroscience* (2nd ed.). Oxford: Oxford University Press.

Charney, D. S., Reynolds, C. F., Lewis, L., Lebowitz, B. D., Sunderland, T., Alexopoulos, G. S. et al. (2003). Depression and Bipolar Support Alliance consensus statement on the unmet needs in diagnosis and treatment of mood disorders in late life. *Archives of General Psychiatry, 60*, 664–672.

Chassin, L., Beltran, I., Lee, M., Haller, M., & Villalta, I. (2010). Vulnerability to substance use disorders in childhood and adolescence. In R. E. Ingram & J. M. Price (Eds.), *Vulnerability to psychopathology. Risk across the lifespan* (2nd ed.). New York: Guilford.

Chavous, T. M., Bernat, D. H., Schmeelk-Cone, K., Caldwell, C. H., Kohn-Wood, L., & Zimmerman, M. A. (2003). Racial identity and academic attainment among African American adolescents. *Child Development, 74*, 1076–1090.

Cheadle, J. E., Amato, P. R., & King, V. (2010). Patterns of nonresident father contact. *Demography, 47*, 205–225.

Chen, A. (2007). Learning to map: Strategy discovery and strategy change in young children. *Developmental Psychology, 43*, 386–403.

Chen, C., & Stevenson, H. W. (1995). Motivation and mathematics achievement: A comparative study of Asian-American, Caucasian-American, and East Asian high school students. *Child Development, 66*, 1214–1234.

Chen, D. (1996). Parent-infant communication: Early intervention for very young children with visual impairment or hearing loss. *Infants and Young Children, 9*, 1–12.

Chen, J. Q., & Gardner, H. (1997). Alternative assessment from a multiple intelligences theoretical perspective. In D. P. Flanagan, J. Genshaft, & P. L. Harrison (Eds.), *Contemporary intellectual assessment: Theories, tests, and issues*. New York: Guilford.

Chen, X., Cen, G., Li, D., & He, Y. (2005). Social functioning and adjustment in Chinese children: The imprint of historical time. *Child Development, 76*, 182–195.

Chen, X., Wang, L., & Wang, Z. (2009). Shyness-sensitivity and social, school, and psychological adjustment in rural migrant and urban children in China. *Child Development, 80*, 1499–1513.

Chen, X., Yang, F., & Fu, R. (2012). Culture and temperament. In M. Z. Zentner & R. L. Shiner (Eds.), *Handbook of temperament*. New York: Guilford.

Cheng, A. K., Rubin, H. R., Powe, N. R., Mellon, M. K., Francis, H. W., & Niparko, J. K. (2000). Cost-utility analysis of the cochlear implant in children. *Journal of the American Medical Association, 284*, 850–856.

Cherkas, L. F., Aviv, A., Valdes, A. M., Hunkin, J. L., Gardner, J. P., Surdulescu, G. L., et al. (2006). The effects of social status on biological aging as measured by white-blood-cell telomere length. *Aging Cell, 5,* 361–365.

Cherkas, L. F., Hunkin, J. L., Kato, B. S., Richards, J. B., Gardner, J. P., Surdulescu, G. L., et al. (2008). The association between physical activity in leisure time and leukocyte telomere length. *Archives of Internal Medicine, 168,* 154–158.

Cherlin, A. J. (2009). *The marriage-go-round. The state of marriage and the family in America today.* New York: Knopf Doubleday Publishing Group.

Cherlin, A. J. (2010). Demographic trends in the United States: A review of research in the 2000s. *Journal of Marriage and Family, 72,* 403–419.

Cherlin, A. J., & Furstenberg, F. F., Jr. (1986). *The new American grandparent: A place in the family, a life apart.* New York: Basic Books.

Cherney, I. D. (2005). Children's and adults' recall of sex-stereotyped toy pictures: Effects of presentation and memory task. *Infant and Child Development, 14,* 11–27.

Cherney, I. D., Harper, H. J., & Winter, J. A. (2006). Nouveaux jouets: Ce que les enfants identifient comme 'jouets de garçons' et 'jouets de filles.' *Enfance, 58,* 266–282.

Cherney, I. S., & London, K. (2006). Gender-linked differences in the toys, television shows, computer games, and outdoor activities of 5- to 13-year-old children. *Sex Roles, 54,* 717–726.

Cherry, K. E., & LeCompte, D. C. (1999). Age and individual differences influence prospective memory. *Psychology and Aging, 14,* 60–76.

Cherry, K. E., & Smith, A. D. (1998). Normal memory aging. In M. Hersen & V. B. Van Hasselt (Eds.), *Handbook of clinical geropsychology* (pp. 87–110). New York: Plenum.

Chesley, N., & Poppie, K. (2009). Assisting parents and in-laws: Gender, type of assistance, and couples' employment. *Journal of Marriage and Family, 71,* 247–262.

Chess, S., & Thomas, A. (1984). *Origins and evolution of behavior disorders: From infancy to early adult life.* New York: Brunner/Mazel.

Chess, S., & Thomas, A. (1999). *Goodness of fit: Clinical applications from infancy through adult life.* Ann Arbor, MI: Edwards Brothers.

Chi, M. T. H. (1978). Knowledge structures and memory development. In R. Siegler (Ed.), *Children's thinking: What develops?* Hillsdale, NJ: Erlbaum.

Chia, E. M., Wang, J. J., Rochtchina, E., Smith, W., Cumming, R. R., & Mitchell, P. (2004). Impact of bilateral visual impairment on health-related quality of life: The Blue Mountains Eye Study. *Investigations in Ophthalmology & Visual Science, 45,* 71–76.

Childbirth Connection. (2012). *Cesarean section.* Retrieved from http://www.childbirthconnection.org/article.asp?ck=10456&ClickedLink=274&area=27

Children's Hospital of Eastern Ontario Research Institute (2012, October 1). Overweight teens get mental health boost from even small amounts of exercise. *ScienceDaily.* Retrieved from http://www.sciencedaily.com

China One-Child Policy: Government Think Tank Urges Country's Leaders To Start Phasing Out Policy Immediately. (2012, October 31). Retrieved from http://www.huffingtonpost.com/2012/10/31/china-one-child-policy-think-tank-phase-out_n_2050149.html

Chiu, S., & Alexander, P. A. (2000). The motivational function of preschoolers' private speech. *Discourse Processes, 30,* 133–152.

Chochinov, H. M., & Schwartz., L. (2002). Depression and the will to live in the psychological landscape of terminally ill patients. In K. Foley, & H. Hendin (Eds.), *The case against assisted suicide: For the right to end-of-life care.* Baltimore: The Johns Hopkins Press.

Choi, J., & Silverman, I. (2003). Processes underlying sex differences in route-learning strategies in children and adolescents. *Personality and Individual Differences, 34,* 1153–1166.

Chomsky, N. (1965). *Aspects of the theory of syntax.* Cambridge: MIT Press.

Chomsky, N. (1968). *Language and mind.* New York: Harcourt Brace & World.

Chomsky, N. (1975). *Reflections on language.* New York: Pantheon Books.

Chomsky, N. (2000). *New horizons in the study of language and mind.* Cambridge: Cambridge University Press.

Chouliaras, L., Rutten, B. P. F., Kenis, G., Peerbooms, O., Visser, P. J., Verhey, F., et al. (2010). Epigenetic regulation in the pathophysiology of Alzheimer's disease. *Progress in Neurobiology, 90,* 498–510.

Christ, G. H. (2010). Children bereaved by the death of a parent. In C. A. Corr & D. E. Balk (Eds.), *Children's encounters with death, bereavement, and coping.* New York: Springer.

Christakis, D. (2008). The effects of infant media usage: What do we know and what should we learn? *Acta Paediatrica.* doi:10.1111/j.1651-2227.2008.01027.x

Christiansen, S. L., & Palkovitz, R. (1998). Exploring Erikson's psychosocial theory of development: Generativity and its relationship to parental identity, intimacy, and involvement with others. *Journal of Men's Studies, 7,* 133–156.

Chronis, A. M., Jones, H. A., & Raggi, V. L. (2006). Evidence-based psychosocial treatments for children and adolescents with attention-deficit/hyperactivity disorder. *Clinical Psychology Review, 26,* 486–502.

Chua, A. (2011a). *Battle hymn of the Tiger Mother.* New York: Penguin.

Chua, A. (2011b, January 8). Why Chinese mothers are superior. Can a regimen of no playdates, no TV, no computer games and hours of music practice create happy kids? And what happens when they fight back? *Wall Street Journal* (Online). Retrieved from http://online.wsj.com/article/SB10001424052748704111504576059713528698754.html

Chua-Rubenfeld, S. (2011, January 17). Why I love my strict Chinese mom. *New York Post.* Retrieved from http://www.nypost.com/p/entertainment/why_love_my_strict_chinese_mom_uUvfmLcA5eteY0u2KXt7hM/0

Chumlea, W. C., Schubert, C. M., Roche, A. F., Kulin, H. E., Lee, P. A., Himes, J. H., et al. (2003). Age at menarche and racial comparisons in US girls. *Pediatrics, 111,* 110–113.

Chung, G. H., Flook, L., & Fuligni, A. J. (2009). Daily family conflict and emotional distress among adolescents from Latin American, Asian, and European backgrounds. *Developmental Psychology, 45,* 1406–1415.

Chung, J. H., Des Roches, C. M., Meunier, J., & Eavey, R. D. (2005). Evaluation of noise-induced hearing loss in young people using a web-based survey technique. *Pediatrics, 115,* 861–867.

Church, T. S., Thomas, D. M., Tudor-Locke, C., Katzmarzyk, P. T., & Earnest, C. P., et al. (2011). Trends over 5 decades in U.S. occupation-related physical activity and their associations with obesity. *PLoS ONE, 6*(5), e19657.

CIA (2012). *World fact book.* Retrieved from https://www.cia.gov/library/publications/the-world-factbook/rankorder/2091rank.html

Cicchetti, D. (2006). Development and psychopathology. In D. Cicchetti & D. J. Cohen (Eds.). *Developmental psychopathology: Vol. 1. Theory and method* (2nd ed.). Hoboken, NJ: Wiley.

Cicchetti, D., & Rogosch, F. A. (2002). A developmental psychopathology perspective on adolescence. *Journal of Consulting and Clinical Psychology, 70,* 6–20.

Cicchetti, D., & Toth, S. L. (2009). The past achievements and future promises of developmental psychopathology: The coming of age of a discipline. *Journal of Child Psychology and Psychiatry, 50,* 16–25.

Cicchetti, D., & Valentino, K. (2006). An ecological–transactional perspective on child maltreatment: Failure of the average expectable environment and its influence on child development. In D. Cicchetti & D. J. Cohen (Eds.), *Developmental psychopathology: Vol. 3. Risk, disorder, and adaptation* (2nd ed.). Hoboken, NJ: Wiley.

Cicirelli, V. G. (1982). Sibling influence throughout the life span. In M. E. Lamb & B. Sutton-Smith (Eds.), *Sibling relationships: Their nature and significance across the life-span.* Hillsdale, NJ: Erlbaum.

Cicirelli, V. G. (1993). Attachment and obligation as daughters' motives for caregiving behavior and subsequent effect on subjective burden. *Psychology and Aging, 8,* 144–155.

Cicirelli, V. G. (1995). *Sibling relationships across the life span.* New York: Plenum.

Cicirelli, V. G. (2010). Attachment relationships in old age. *Journal of Social and Personal Relationships, 27,* 191–199.

Cillessen, A. H. N. (2009). Sociometric methods. In K. H. Rubin, W. M. Bukowski, & B.

Laursen (Eds.), *Handbook of peer interactions, relationships, and groups*. New York: Guilford.

Cillessen, A. H. N., Schwartz, D., & Mayeux, L. (Eds.) (2011). *Popularity in the peer system*. New York: Guilford.

Cillessen, A. H., Van IJzendoorn, H. W., Van Lieshout, C. F., & Hartup, W. W. (1992). Heterogeneity among peer-rejected boys: Subtypes and stabilities. *Child Development, 63*, 893–905.

Clark, A., & Lappin, S. (2011). *Linguistic nativism and the poverty of the stimulus*. Hoboken, NJ: Wiley-Blackwell.

Clark, D. O., & Maddox, G. L. (1992). Racial and social correlates of age-related changes in functioning. *Journal of Gerontology Series B: Social Sciences, 47*, S222–S232.

Clark, H. H., & Clark, E. V. (1977). *Psychology and language: An introduction to psycholinguistics*. New York: Harcourt Brace Jovanovich.

Clark, M. A., & Fox, M. K. (2009). National quality of the diets of U.S. public school children and the role of the school meal programs. *Journal of the American Dietetic Association, 109*, S44–56.

Clarke-Stewart, K. A. (1998). Reading with children. *Journal of Applied Developmental Psychology, 19*, 1–14.

Claxton, A. F., Pannells, T. C., & Rhoads, P. A. (2005). Developmental trends in the creativity of school-age children. *Creativity Research Journal, 17*, 327–335.

Cleveland, E. S., & Reese, E. (2008). Children remember early childhood: Long-term recall across the offset of childhood amnesia. *Applied Cognitive Psychology, 22*, 127–142.

Cleveland, H. H., Jacobson, K. C., Lipinski, J. J., & Rowe, D. C. (2000). Genetic and shared environmental contributions to the relationship between the home environment and child and adolescent achievement. *Intelligence, 28*, 69–86.

Coall, D. A., & Hertwig, R. (2011). Grandparental investment: A relic of the past or a resource for the future? *Current Directions in Psychological Science, 20*, 93–98.

Cobb, R. W., & Coughlin, J. F. (1998). Are elderly drivers a road hazard? Problem definition and political impact. *Journal of Aging Studies, 12*, 411–420.

Codipietro, L., Ceccarelli, M., & Ponzone, A. (2008). Breastfeeding or oral sucrose solution in term neonates receiving heel lance: A randomized, controlled trial. *Pediatrics, 122*, 716–721.

Coe, N. B., von Gaudecker, H., Lindeboom, M., & Maurer, J. (2012). The effect of retirement on cognitive functioning. *Health Economics, 21*, 913–927.

Cohan, C. L. (2013). The cohabitation conundrum. In M. A. Fine & F. D. Fincham (Eds.), *Handbook of family theories. A context-based approach*. New York: Routledge.

Cohen, J., Van Landeghem, P., Carpentier, N., & Deliens, L. (2013). Public acceptance of euthanasia in Europe: A survey study in 47 countries. *International Journal of Public Health*.

Cohen, M. (1996). Preschoolers' practical thinking and problem solving: The acquisition of an optimal solution strategy. *Cognitive Development, 11*, 357–373.

Cohen, S., & Janicki-Deverts, D. (2009). Can we improve our physical health by altering our social networks? *Perspectives on Psychological Science, 4*, 375–378.

Cohn, D., Passel, J. S., Wang, W., & Livingston, G. (2011). *Barely half of U. S. adults are married—A record low*. Washington, DC: Pew Research Center Social & Demographic Trends. Retrieved from http://www.pewsocialtrends.org/2011/12/14/barely-half-of-u-s-adults-are-married-a-record-low/

Coie, J. D. (2004). The impact of negative social experiences on the development of antisocial behavior. In J. B. Kupersmidt & K. A. Dodge (Eds.), *Children's peer relations: From development to intervention*. Washington, DC: American Psychological Association.

Coie, J. D., Dodge, K. A., & Coppotelli, H. (1982). Dimensions and types of social status: A cross-age perspective. *Developmental Psychology, 18*, 557–570.

Coie, J. D., Dodge, K. A., & Kupersmidt, J. B. (1990). Peer group behavior and social status. In S. R. Asher & J. D. Coie (Eds.), *Peer rejection in childhood*. Cambridge, UK: Cambridge University Press.

Colapinto J. (2004, June 3). *What were the real reasons behind David Reimer's suicide?* Retrieved from www.slate.com/id/2101678

Colapinto, J. (1997, December 11). The true story of John Joan. *Rolling Stone*, pp. 54–97.

Colapinto, J. (2000). *As nature made him: The boy who was raised as a girl*. New York: Harper Collins.

Colburn, D. (2000, October 3). Wired for sound. *The Washington Post—Health*, pp. 13–18.

Colby, A., & Kohlberg, L. (1987). *The measurement of moral judgment. Vol. 1: Theoretical foundations and research validation*. Cambridge, UK: Cambridge University Press.

Colby, A., Kohlberg, L., Gibbs, J., & Lieberman, M. (1983). A longitudinal study of moral judgment. *Monographs of the Society for Research in Child Development, 48* (1–2, Serial No. 200).

Colcombe, S. J., Kramer, A. F., Erickson, K. I., Scalf, P., McAuley, E., Cohen, N. J., et al. (2004). Cardiovascular fitness, cortical plasticity, and aging. *Proceedings of the National Academy of Sciences, 101*, 3316–3321.

Colder, C. R., Chassin, L., Lee, M. R., & Villatta, I. K. (2010). Developmental perspectives: Affect and adolescent substance use. In J. D. Kassel (Ed.), *Substance abuse and emotion*. Washington, DC: American Psychological Association.

Cole, D. A., Maxwell, S. E., Martin, J. M., Peeke, L. G., Seroczynski, A. D., Tram, J. M., et al. (2001). The development of multiple domains of child and adolescent self-concept: A cohort sequential longitudinal design. *Child Development, 72*, 1723–1746.

Cole, J. (1995). *Pride and a Daily Marathon*. MIT Press.

Cole, M., & Packer, M. (2011). Culture in development. In M. E. Lamb & M. H. Bornstein (Eds.), *Social and personality development: An advanced textbook* (pp. 67–123). New York: Psychology Press.

Cole, P. M., Barrett, K. C., & Zahn-Waxler, C. (1992). Emotion displays in two-year-olds during mishaps. *Child Development, 63*, 314–324.

Cole, P. M., Martin, S. E., & Dennis, T. A. (2004). Emotion regulation as a scientific construct: Methodological challenges and directions for child development research. *Child Development, 75*, 317–333.

Cole, P. M., Michel, M. K., & Teti, L. O. (1994). The development of emotion regulation and dysregulation: A clinical perspective. In N. Fox (Ed.), *The development of emotion regulation: Biological and behavioral considerations. Monographs of the Society for Research in Child Development, 59*(Nos. 2–3, Serial No. 240).

Coleman, J. (1961). *The adolescent society*. New York: Free Press.

Coley, R. L., Carrano, J., & Lewin-Bizan, S. (2011). Unpacking links between fathers' antisocial behaviors and children's behavior problems: Direct, indirect, and interactive effects. *Journal of Abnormal Child Psychology, 39*, 791–804.

Colin, V. (1996). *Human attachment*. New York: McGraw-Hill.

College Board. (2012). *Total group profile report*. Retrieved from http://media.collegeboard.com/digitalServices/pdf/research/TotalGroup-2012.pdf

Colletti, L., Mandalà, M., Zoccante, L., Shannon, R. V., & Colletti, V. (2011). Infants versus older children fitted with cochlear implants: Performance over 10 years. *International Journal of Pediatric Otorhinolaryngology, 75*, 504–509.

Colley, A., Griffiths, D., Hugh, M., Landers, K., & Jaggli, N. (1996). Childhood play and adolescent leisure preferences: Associations with gender typing and the presence of siblings. *Sex Roles, 35*, 233–245.

Collins, W. A. (2003). More than myth: The developmental significance of romantic relationships during adolescence. *Journal of Research on Adolescence, 13*, 1–24.

Collins, W. A., & Laursen, B. (2004). Changing relationships, changing youth: Interpersonal contexts of adolescent development. *Journal of Early Adolescence, 24*, 55–62.

Collins, W. A., & Laursen, B. (2006). Parent-adolescent relationships. In P. Noller, & J. A. Feeney (Eds.), *Close relationships: Functions, forms and processes*. Hove, England: Psychology Press/Taylor & Francis.

Collins, W. A., & Madsen, S. D. (2006). Personal relationships in adolescence and early adulthood. In A. L. Vangelisti & D. Perlman (Eds.), *The Cambridge handbook of personal relationships*. New York: Cambridge University Press.

Colombo, J. (2001). The development of visual attention in infancy. *Annual Review of Psychology, 52*, 337–367.

Colombo, J., Shaddy, D. J., Blaga, O. M., Anderson, C. J., & Kannass, K. N. (2009). High cognitive ability in infancy and early childhood. In F. D. Horowitz, R. F. Subotnik, & D. J. Matthews (Eds.), *The development of giftedness and talent across the life span*. Washington, DC: American Psychological Association.

Columbo, J. (1993). *Infant cognition: Predicting later intellectual functioning*. Newbury Park, CA: Sage.

Committee on Adolescence. (1996). *Adolescent suicide* (Group for the Advancement of Psychiatry, Report No. 140). Washington, DC: American Psychiatric Press.

Commons, M. L., & Richards, F. A. (2003). Four postformal stages. In J. Demick & C. Andreoletti (Eds.), *Handbook of adult development* (pp. 199–220). New York: Plenum.

Commons, M. L., & Ross, S. N. (2008). What postformal thought is, and why it matters. *World Futures, 64*, 321–329.

Compas, B. E., Connor-Smith, J. K., Saltzman, H., Thomsen, A. H., & Wadsworth, M. E. (2001). Coping with stress during childhood and adolescence: Problems, progress, and potential in theory and research. *Psychological Bulletin, 127*, 87–127.

Compian, L., Gowen, L. K., & Hayward, C. (2004). Peripubertal girls' romantic and platonic involvement with boys: Associations with body image and depression symptoms. *Journal of Research on Adolescence, 14*, 23–47.

Conde-Agudelo, A., Belizán, J. M., & Diaz-Rossello, J. (2011). Kangaroo mother care to reduce morbidity and mortality in low birthweight infants. *Cochrane Database of Systematic Reviews*, Issue 3. Art. No.: CD002771. doi:10.1002/14651858.CD002771.pub2

Condon, E. M., Crepinsek, M. K., & Fox, M. K. (2009). School meals: Types of foods offered to and consumed by children at lunch and breakfast. *Journal of the American Dietetic Association, 109*, S67–78.

Condry, J., & Condry, S. (1976). Sex differences: A study in the eye of the beholder. *Child Development, 47*, 812–819.

Conduct Problems Prevention Research Group. (2007). Fast Track randomized controlled trial to prevent externalizing psychiatric disorders: Findings from grades 3 to 9. *Journal of the American Academy of Child and Adolescent Psychiatry, 46*, 1250–1262.

Conger, K. J., Rueter, M. A., & Conger, R. D. (2000). The role of economic pressure in the lives of parents and their adolescents: The family stress model. In L. J. Crockett, & R. K. Silbereisen (Eds.), *Negotiating adolescence in times of social change*. New York: Cambridge University Press.

Conger, R. D., & Dogan, S. J. (2007). Social class and socialization in families. In J. E. Grusec & P. D. Hastings (Eds.), *Handbook of socialization theory and research*. New York: Guilford.

Conger, R. D., Belsky, J., & Capaldi, D. M. (2009). The intergenerational transmission of parenting: Closing comments for the special section. *Developmental Psychology, 45*, 1276–1283.

Conger, R. D., Conger, K. J., Elder, G. H., Jr., Lorenz, F. O., Simons, R. L., & Whitbeck, L. B. (1992). A family process model of economic hardship and adjustment of early adolescent boys. *Child Development, 63*, 526–541.

Conger, R. D., Neppl, T., Kim, K. J., & Scaramella, L. (2003). Angry and aggressive behavior across three generations: A prospective, longitudinal study of parents and children. *Journal of Abnormal Child Psychology, 31*, 143–160.

Conger, R. D., Patterson, G. R., & Ge, X. (1995). It takes two to replicate: A mediational model for the impact of parents' stress on adolescent adjustment. *Child Development, 66*, 80–97.

Conger, R. D., Wallace, L. E., Sun, Y., Simons, R. L., McLoyd, V. C., & Brody, G. H. (2002). Economic pressure in African American families: A replication and extension of the family stress model. *Developmental Psychology, 38*, 179–193.

Conklin, H. M., Luciana, M., Hooper, C. J., & Yarger, R. S. (2007). Working memory performance in typically developing children and adolescents: Behavioral evidence of protracted frontal lobe development. *Developmental Neuropsychology, 31*, 103–128.

Conley, C. S., & Rudolph, K. D. (2009). The emerging sex difference in adolescent depression: Interacting contributions of puberty and peer stress. *Development and Psychopathology, 21*, 593–620.

Conley, T. D., Ziegler, A., & Moors, A. C. (2013). Backlash from the bedroom: Stigma mediates gender differences in acceptance of casual sex offers. *Psychology of Women Quarterly, 37*, 392–407.

Connell, A. M., & Goodman, S. H. (2002). The association between psychopathology in fathers versus mothers and children's internalizing and externalizing behavior problems: A meta-analysis. *Psychological Bulletin, 128*, 746–773.

Conner, K. A. (2000). *Continuing to care. Older Americans and their families*. New York: Falmer Press.

Connidis, I. A. (2010). *Family ties and aging* (2nd ed.). Thousand Oaks, CA: Pine Forge Press.

Connolly, J. A., & Doyle, A. B. (1984). Relation of social fantasy play to social competence in preschoolers. *Developmental Psychology, 20*, 797–806.

Connolly, J., &McIsaac, C. (2011). Romantic relationships in adolescence. In M. K. Underwood & L. H. Rosen (Eds.), *Social development. Relationships in infancy, childhood, and adolescence*. New York: Guilford.

Connolly, M. P., Hoorens, S., & Chambers, G. M. (2010, June 8). The costs and consequences of assisted reproductive technology: An economic perspective. *Human Reproduction Update, 16*, 603–613.

Connor, S. R. (2000). Hospice care and the older person. In A. Tomer (Ed.), *Death attitudes and the older adult: Theories, concepts, and applications*. Philadelphia, PA: Brunner-Routledge.

Conrade, G., & Ho, R. (2001). Differential parenting styles for fathers and mothers: Differential treatment for sons and daughters. *Australian Journal of Psychology, 53*, 29–35.

Conway, M. A. (2005). Memory and the self. *Journal of Memory and Language, 53*, 594–628.

Conway, M. A., Cohen, G., & Stanhope, N. (2006). Very long-term memory for knowledge acquired at school and university. *Applied Cognitive Psychology, 6*, 467–482.

Coohey, C., & Braun, N. (1997). Toward an integrated framework for understanding child physical abuse. *Child Abuse and Neglect, 21*, 1081–1094.

Cook, A. S., & Dworkin, D. S. (1992). *Helping the bereaved. Therapeutic interventions for children, adolescents, and adults*. New York: Basic Books.

Cooke, T. J., Boyle, P., Couch, K., & Feijten, P. (2009). A longitudinal analysis of family migration and the gender gap in earnings in the United States and Great Britain. *Demography, 46*, 147–167.

Coontz, S. (2000). Historical perspectives on family diversity. In D. H. Demo, K. R. Allen, & M. A. Fine (Eds.), *Handbook of family diversity*. New York: Oxford University Press.

Cooper, M. L. (2002). Alcohol use and risky sexual behavior among college students and youth: Evaluating the evidence. *Journal of Studies on Alcohol, 14*(Suppl.), 101–117.

Cooper, M. L. (2010). Toward a person x situation model of sexual risk-taking behaviors: Illuminating the conditional effects of traits across sexual situations and relationship contexts. *Journal of Personality and Social Psychology, 98*, 319–341.

Coopersmith, S. (1967). *The antecedents of self-esteem*. San Francisco: W. H. Freeman.

Copeland, W., Shanahan, L., Costello, E. J., & Angold, A. (2011). Cumulative prevalence of psychiatric disorders by young adulthood: A prospective cohort analysis from the Great Smoky Mountains Study. *Journal of the American Academy of Child & Adolescent Psychiatry, 50*, 252–261.

Coplan, R. J., & Abreau, K. A. (2009). Peer interactions and play in early childhood. In K. H. Rubin, W. M. Bukowski, & B. Laursen (Eds.), *Handbook of peer interactions, relationships, and groups*. New York: Guilford.

Corbett, C., & Hill, C. (2012). *Graduating to a pay gap. The earnings of women and men one year after college graduation*. Washington, DC: AAUW. Retrieved from AAUW website http://www.aauw.org/GraduatetoaPayGap/index.cfm

Cornelius, S. W., & Caspi, A. (1987). Everyday problem solving in adulthood and old age. *Psychology and Aging, 2*, 144–153.

Cornell, D., Gregory, A., Huang, F., & Fan, X. (2012). Perceived prevalence of teasing and bullying predicts high school dropout rates. *Journal of Educational Psychology, 105*, 138–149.

Corr, C. A. (1995). Entering into adolescent understanding of death. In E. A. Grollman (Ed.), *Bereaved children and teens.* Boston: Beacon Press.

Corr, C. A. (2010). Children's emerging awareness and understandings of loss and death. In C. A. Corr & D. E. Balk (Eds.), *Children's encounters with death, bereavement, and coping.* New York: Springer.

Corr, C. A., & Corr, D. M. (1992). Children's hospice care. *Death Studies, 16,* 431–449.

Corwin, J., Loury, M., & Gilbert, A. N. (1995). Workplace, age, and sex as mediators of olfactory function: Data from the National Geographic Smell Survey. *Journals of Gerontology Series B: Psychological Sciences and Social Sciences, 50,* 179–186.

Costa, P. T., Jr., & McCrae, R. R. (1992). Trait psychology comes of age. In T. B. Sonderegger (Ed.), *Nebraska symposium on motivation: Vol 39. Psychology and aging.* Lincoln, NE: University of Nebraska Press.

Cota-Robles, S. (2003, April). *Traditional Mexican cultural values and the reduced risk for delinquency: Acculturation, familism and parent– adolescent process.* Poster presented at the biennial meeting of the Society for Research in Child Development, Tampa, FL.

Cote, J. E., & Levine, C. (1988). A critical examination of the ego identity status paradigm. *Developmental Review, 8,* 147–184.

Cotten, S. R., McCullough, B. M., & Adams, R. G. (2011). Technological influences on social ties. In K. L. Fingerman, C. A. Berg, J. Smith, & T. C. Antonucci (Eds.), *Handbook of lifespan development* (pp. 649–674). New York: Springer.

Council on Communications and Media. (2011). Children, adolescents, obesity, and the media. *Pediatrics, 128,* 201–209.

Courage, M. L., & Cowan, N. (Eds.). (2009). *The development of memory in infancy and childhood.* New York: Psychology Press.

Courage, M. L., Reynolds, G. D., & Richards, J. E. (2006). Infants' attention to patterned stimuli: Developmental change from 3 to 12 months of age. *Child Development, 77,* 680–695.

Courchesne, E., Carper, R., & Akshoomoff, N. (2003). Evidence of brain overgrowth in the first year of life in autism. *Journal of the American Medical Association, 290,* 337–344.

Courchesne, E., Chisum, H. J., Townsend, J., Cowles, A., Covington, J., Egaas, B., et al. (2000). Normal brain development and aging: Quantitative analysis at in vivo MR imaging in healthy volunteers. *Radiology, 216,* 672–682.

Couturier, J., Kimber, M., & Szatmari, P. (2013). Efficacy of family-based treatment for adolescents with eating disorders: A systematic review and meta-analysis. *International Journal of Eating Disorders, 46,* 3–11.

Covington, M. V. (1998). *The will to learn.* New York: Cambridge University Press.

Covington, M. V. (2000). Goal theory, motivation, and school achievement: An integrative review. *Annual Review of Psychology, 51,* 171–200.

Cowan, B. W. (2011). Forward-thinking teens: The effects of college costs on adolescent risky behavior. *Economics of Education Review, 30,* 813–825.

Cowan, C. P., & Cowan, P. A. (2000). *When partners become parents: The big life change for couples.* Mahwah, NJ: Erlbaum.

Cowan, N., Morey, C. C., AuBuchon, A. M., Zwilling, C. E., & Gilchrist, A. L. (2010). Seven-year-olds allocate attention like adults unless working memory is overloaded. *Developmental Science, 13,* 120–133.

Cowan, P. A., & Cowan, C. P. (2006). Developmental psychopathology from family systems and family risk factors perspectives: Implications for family research, practice, and policy. In D. Cicchetti & D. J. Cohen (Eds.), *Developmental psychopathology: Vol. 1. Theory and method* (2nd ed.). Hoboken, NJ: Wiley.

Cowan, P. A., Cowan, C. P., Pruett, M. K., Pruett, K., & Wong, J. J. (2009). Promoting fathers' engagement with children: Preventive interventions for low-income families. *Journal of Marriage and Family, 71,* 663–679.

Cox, K. S., Wilt, J., Olson, B., & McAdams, D. P. (2010). Generativity, the Big Five, and psychosocial adaptation in midlife adults. *Journal of Personality, 78,* 1185–1208.

Cox, M. J., Owen, M. T., Henderson, V. K., & Margand, N. A. (1992). Prediction of infant-father and infant-mother attachment. *Developmental Psychology, 28,* 474–483.

Cox, M. J., Paley, B., Burchinal, M., & Payne, C. C. (1999). Marital perceptions and interactions across the transition to parenthood. *Journal of Marriage and the Family, 61,* 611–625.

Cox, T. H., & Harquail, C. V. (1991). Career paths and career success in the early career stages of male and female MBAs. *Journal of Vocational Behavior, 39,* 54–75.

Coyne, J. C., & Whiffen, V. E. (1995). Issues in personality as diathesis for depression: The case of sociotropy dependency and autonomy self-criticism. *Psychological Bulletin, 118,* 358–378.

Crabb, P. B., & Marciano, D. L. (2011). Representations of material culture and gender in award-winning children's books: A 20-year follow-up. *Journal of Research in Childhood Education, 25,* 390–398.

Crago, M. B., Allen, S. E., & Hough-Eyamir, W. P. (1997). Exploring innateness through cultural and linguistic variation. In M. Gopnik (Ed.), *The inheritance and innateness of grammars* (pp. 70–90). New York: Oxford University Press.

Craik, F. I., Bialystok, E., & Freedman, M. (2010). Delaying the onset of Alzheimer disease: bilingualism as a form of cognitive reserve. *Neurology, 75,* 1726–9.

Cramond, B., Matthews-Morgan, Bandalos, D., & Zuo, L. (2005). A report on the 40-year follow-up of the Torrance Tests of Creative Thinking: Alive and well in the new millennium. *Gifted Child Quarterly, 49,* 283–291.

Crawford, M., & Popp, D. (2003). Sexual double standards: A review and methodological critique of two decades of research. *The Journal of Sex Research, 40,* 13–26.

Creasey, G., & Jarvis, P. (2009). Attachment and marriage. In M. C. Smith (Ed.) & N. DeFrates-Densch (Asst. Ed.), *Handbook of research on adult learning and development.* New York: Routledge.

Creasy, R., Resnik, R., & Iams, J. (2009). *Creasy and Resnik's Maternal-Fetal Medicine: Principles and Practice,* 6th ed. Elsevier Health Sciences.

Crepinsek, M. K., Gordon, A. R., McKinney, P. M., Condon, E. M., & Wilson, A. (2009). Meals offered and served in U.S. public schools: Do they meet nutrient standards? *Journal of the American Dietetic Association, 109,* S31–43.

Crick, N. R., & Bigbee, M. (1998). Relational and overt forms of peer victimization: A multiinformant approach. *Journal of Consulting and Clinical Psychology, 66,* 337–347.

Crick, N. R., & Dodge, K. A. (1994). A review and reformulation of social information-processing mechanisms in children's social adjustment. *Psychological Bulletin, 115,* 74–101.

Crijnen, A. A. M., Achenbach, T. M., & Verhulst, F. C. (1997). Comparisons of problems reported by parents of children in 12 cultures: Total problems, externalizing, and internalizing. *Journal of the American Academy of Child and Adolescent Psychiatry, 36,* 1269–1277.

Critchley, C. R., & Sanson, A. V. (2006). Is parent disciplinary behavior enduring or situational? A multilevel modeling investigation of individual and contextual influences on power assertive and inductive reasoning behaviors. *Journal of Applied Developmental Psychology, 27,* 370–388.

Crockenberg, S., & Leerkes, E. (2003). Infant negative emotionality, caregiving, and family relationships. In A. C. Crouter & A. Booth (Eds.), *Children's influence on family dynamics. The neglected side of family relationships.* Mahwah, NJ: Erlbaum.

Crooks, R. L., & Baur, K. (2014). *Our sexuality* (12th ed.). Cengage Learning.

Cross, S. E. (2000). What does it mean to "know thyself" in the United States and Japan? The cultural construction of the self. In T. J. Owens (Ed.), *Self and identity through the life course in cross-cultural perspective.* Stamford, CT: JAI Press.

Crouch, J. L., & Behl, L. E. (2001). Relationships among parental beliefs in corporal punishment, reported stress, and physical child abuse potential. *Child Abuse and Neglect, 25,* 413–419.

Crouter, A. C. (2006). Mothers and fathers at work: Implications for families and children. In A. Clarke-Stewart & J. Dunn (Eds.), *Families count: Effects on child and adolescent development.* New York: Cambridge University Press.

Crouter, A. C., & Booth, A. (Eds.) (2003). *Children's influence on family dynamics. The neglected side of family relationships.* Mahwah, NJ: Erlbaum.

Crouter, A. C., Whiteman, S. D., McHale, S. M., & Osgood, D. W. (2007). Development of gender attitude traditionality across middle childhood and adolescence. *Child Development, 78,* 911–926.

Crouter, A. C., Whiteman, S., & Osgood, D. W. (2007). Development of gender attitude traditionality across middle childhood and adolescence. *Child Development, 78,* 911–926.

Crowell, J. A., Fraley, R. C., & Shaver, P. R. (1999). Measurement of individual differences in adolescent and adult attachment. In J. Cassidy & P. R. Shaver (Eds.), *Handbook of attachment: Theory, research, and clinical applications.* New York: Guilford.

Crowell, J. A., Treboux, D., & Waters, E. (2002). Stability of attachment representations: The transition to marriage. *Developmental Psychology, 38,* 467–479.

Cruickshanks, K. J., Nondahl, D. M., Tweed, T. S., Wiley, T. L., Klein, B. E., Klein, R., et al. (2010). Education, occupation, noise exposure history and the 10-yr cumulative incidence of hearing impairment in older adults. *Hearing Research, 264,* 3–9, Epub ahead of print.

Cruikshank, M. (2009). *Learning to be old: Gender, culture, and aging* (2nd ed.). Lanham, MD: Rowman & Littlefield.

Cruse, D., Chennu, S., Chatelle, C., Bekinschtein, T. A., Fernández-Espejo, D., Pickard, J. D., & Owen, A. M. (2011). Bedside detection of awareness in the vegetative state: A cohort study. *Lancet, 378*(9809), 2088–2094.

Cruse, D., Chennu, S., Chatelle, C., Bekinschtein, T. A., Fernández-Espejo, D., Pickard, J. D., & Owen, A. M. (2013). Reanalysis of "bedside detection of awareness in the vegetative state: A cohort study" - authors' reply. *Lancet, 381*(9863), 291–292.

Cruz, J. E., Emery, R. E., & Turkheimer, E. (2012). Peer network drinking predicts increased alcohol use from adolescence to early adulthood after controlling for genetic and shared environmental selection. *Developmental Psychology, 48,* 1390–1402.

Crystal, S., Kleinhaus, K., Perrin, M., & Malaspina, D. (2011). Advancing paternal age and the risk for schizophrenia. In A. S. Brown & P. H. Patterson (Eds.), *The origins of schizophrenia* (pp. 140–155). New York: Columbia University Press.

Csikszentmihalyi, M., & Nakamura, J. (2006). Creativity through the life span from an evolutionary systems perspective. In C. Hoare (Ed.), *Handbook of adult development and learning.* New York: Oxford University Press.

Cuevas, C. A., Finkelhor, D., Clifford, C., Ormrod, R. K., & Turner, H. A. (2010). Psychological distress as a risk factor for re-victimization in children. *Child Abuse & Neglect, 34,* 235–243.

Cui, M., Conger, R. D., & Lorenz, F. O. (2005). Predicting change in adolescent adjustment from change in marital problems. *Developmental Psychology, 41,* 812–823.

Cui, M., & Donnellan, M. B. (2009). Trajectories of conflict over raising adolescent children and marital satisfaction. *Journal of Marriage and Family, 71,* 478–494.

Cumming, E., & Henry, W. E. (1961). *Growing old, the process of disengagement.* New York: Basic Books.

Cummings, S. M., Williams, M. M., & Ellis, R. A. (2003). Impact of an intergenerational program on 4th graders' attitudes toward elders and school behaviors. *Journal of Human Behavior in the Social Environment, 6,* 91–107.

Curlik, D. M., & Shors, T. J. (2013). Training your brain: Do mental and physical (MAP) training enhance cognition through the process of neurogenesis in the hippocampus? *Neuropharmacology, 64,* 506–514.

Curran, S., & Bolton, P. (2009). Genetics of autism. In Y. Kim (Ed.), *Handbook of behavior genetics.* New York: Springer.

Currier, J. M., Holland, J. M., & Neimeyer, R. A. (2012). Prolonged grief symptoms and growth in the first 2 years of bereavement: Evidence for a nonlinear association. *Traumatology, 18,* 65–71.

Cytron, B. D. (1993). To honor the dead and comfort the mourners: Traditions in Judaism. In D. P. Irish, K. F. Lundquist, & V. J. Nelson (Eds.), *Ethnic variations in dying, death, and grief: Diversity in universality.* Washington, DC: Taylor & Francis.

Cytryn, L., & McKnew, D. H., Jr. (1996). *Growing up sad: Childhood depression and its treatment.* New York: W. W. Norton.

Dabbs, J. M., & Morris, R. (1990). Testosterone, social class, and antisocial behavior in a sample of 4462 men. *Psychological Science, 1,* 209–211.

Dalton DS, Cruickshanks KJ, Klein BE, Klein R, Wiley TL, & Nonhdahl DM. (2003) The impact of hearingloss on quality of life in older adults. *Gerontologist 43,* 661–668.

Daley, C. E., & Onwuegbuzie, A. J. (2011). Race and intelligence. In R. Sternberg & S. B. Kaufman (Eds.), *The Cambridge handbook of intelligence* (pp. 293–306). New York: Cambridge University Press.

Damon, W. (1977). *The social world of the child.* San Francisco: Jossey-Bass.

Damon, W. (1994). *Greater expectations: Overcoming the culture of indulgence in America's homes and schools.* New York: Free Press.

Damon, W., & Hart, D. (1988). *Self-understanding in childhood and adolescence.* New York: Cambridge University Press.

Daniels, H. (2011). Vygotsky and psychology. In U. Goswami, (Ed.), *The Wiley-Blackwell handbook of childhood cognitive development,* 2nd ed. (pp. 673–696). Malden, MA: John Wiley.

Daniels, L. M., Stupnisky, R. H., Pekrun, R., Haynes, T. L., Perry, R. P., & Newall, N. E. (2009). A longitudinal analysis of achievement goals: From affective antecedents to emotional effects and achievement outcomes. *Journal of Educational Psychology, 101,* 948–963.

Dapretto, M., Davies, M. S., Pfeifer, J. H., Scott, A. A., Sigman, M., Bookheimer, S. Y., & Iacoboni, M. (2006). Understanding emotions in others: Mirror neuron dysfunction in children with autism spectrum disorders. *Nature Neuroscience, 9,* 28–30.

Darling, N., & Steinberg, L. (1993). Parenting style as context: An integrative model. *Psychological Bulletin, 113,* 487–496.

Darnon, C., Dompnier, B., Gilliéorn, O., & Butera, F. (2010). The interplay of mastery and performance goals in social comparison: A multiple-goal perspective. *Journal of Educational Psychology, 102,* 212–222.

Davies, B., Collins, J., Steele, R., Cook, K., Distler, V., & Brenner, A. (2007). Parents' and children's perspectives of a children's hospice bereavement program. *Journal of Palliative Care, 23,* 14–23.

Davies, S. G. (2006). Thinking of gender in a holistic sense: Understandings of gender in Sulawesi, Indonesia. In D. Vasilikie & M. T. Segal (Eds.), *Gender and the local-global nexus: Theory, research, and action* (Vol. 10, pp. 1–24). Emerald Group Publishing Limited.

Davila, E. P., Caban-Martinez, A. J., Muennig, P., Lee, D. J., Fleming, L. E., Ferraro, K. F., et al. (2009). Sensory impairment among older US workers. *American Journal of Public Health, 99,* 1378–1385.

Davis, A. S. (Ed.). (2012). *Psychopathology of childhood and adolescence.A neuropsychological approach.* New York: Springer.

Davis, C. G., & Nolen-Hoeksema, S. (2001). Loss and meaning: How do people make sense of loss? *American Behavioral Scientist, 44,* 726–741.

Davis, E. P., Glynn, L. M., Waffram, F., & Sandman, C. A. (2011). Prenatal maternal stress programs infant stress regulation. *Journal of Child Psychology and Psychiatry, 52,* 119–129.

Davis, K., Christodoulou, J., Seider, S., & Gardner, H. (2011). The theory of multiple intelligence. In R. J. Sternberg & S. B. Kaufman (Eds.), *The Cambridge handbook of intelligence* (pp. 485–503). New York: Cambridge University Press.

Davis, N., Gross, J., & Hayne, H. (2008). Defining the boundary of childhood amnesia. *Memory, 16,* 465–474.

Davis, O. S. P., Butcher, L. M., Docherty, S. J., Meaburn, E. L., Curtis, C. J. C., Simpson, M. A., et al. (2010). A three-stage genome-wide association study of general cognitive ability: Hunting the small effects. *Behavior Genetics, 40,* 759–767.

Davis, O., Haworth, C., & Plomin, R. (2009). Dramatic increase in heritability of cognitive development from early to middle childhood: An 8-year longitudinal study of 8,700 pairs of twins. *Psychological Science, 20,* 1301–1308.

Dawson, G., & Ashman, S. B. (2000). On the origins of a vulnerability to depression: The influence of the early social environment on the development of psychobiological systems related to risk for affective disorder. In C. A. Nelson (Ed.), *Minnesota Symposium on Child Psychology: Vol. 31. The effects of early adversity on neurobe-havioral development.* Mahwah, NJ: Erlbaum.

Dawson, G., Jones, E. J. H., Merkle, K., Venema, K., Lowy, R., Faja, S., et al. (2012). Early behavioral intervention is associated with normalized brain activity in young children with autism. *Journal of the American Academy of Child & Adolescent Psychiatry, 51,* 1150–1159.

Dawson, G., Rogers, S., Munson, J., Smith, M., Winter, J., Greenson, J., et al. (2010). Randomized, controlled trial of an intervention for toddlers with autism: The Early Start Denver Model. *Pediatrics, 125,* e17–e23.

Day, N. L., Goldschmidt, L., & Thomas, C. A. (2006). Prenatal marijuana exposure contributes to the prediction of marijuana use at age 14. *Addiction, 101,* 1313–1322.

Day, R. D., & Peterson, G. W. (1998). Predicting spanking of younger and older children by mothers and fathers. *Journal of Marriage & the Family, 60,* 79–92.

De Goede, I. H. A., Branje, S. J. T., & Meeus, W. H. J. (2009). Developmental changes in adolescents' perceptions of relationships with their parents. *Journal of Youth and Adolescence, 38,* 75–88.

De Heering, A., Rossion, B., & Maurer, D. (2012). Developmental changes in face recognition during childhood: Evidence from upright and inverted faces. *Cognitive Development, 27,* 17–27.

de Jong-Gierveld, J. (1986). Loneliness and the degree of intimacy in interpersonal relationships. In R. Gilmour & S. Duck (Eds.), *The emerging field of personal relationships.* Hillsdale, NJ: Erlbaum.

De Lisi, R., & Staudt, J. (1980). Individual differences in college students' performance on formal operations tasks. *Journal of Applied Psychology, 1,* 163–174.

de St. Aubin, E., McAdams, D. P., & Kim, T. (2004). The generative society: An introduction. In E. de St. Aubin, D. P. McAdams, & T. Kim (Eds.), *The generative society: Caring for future generations.* Washington, DC: American Psychological Association.

De Vise, D. (2011, May 21). Gaithersburg woman earns college degree two decades after complete memory loss. *The Washington Post, Education Section.* Retrieved from http://articles.washingtonpost.com/2011-05-21/local/35265255_1_amnesia-memory-husband

De Wolff, M. S., & van IJzendoorn, M. H. (1997). Sensitivity and attachment: A meta-analysis on parental antecedents of infant attachment. *Child Development, 68,* 571–591.

Deary, I. J., Strand, S., Smith, P., & Fernandes, C. (2007). Intelligence and educational achievement. *Intelligence, 35,* 13–21.

Deary, I. J., Whalley, L. J., & Starr, J. M. (2009). *A lifetime of intelligence: Follow-up studies of the Scottish mental surveys of 1932 and 1947.* Washington, DC: American Psychological Association.

Deary, I. J., Whiteman, M. C., Starr, J. M., Whalley, L. J., & Fox, H. C. (2004). The impact of childhood intelligence on later life: Following up the Scottish Mental Surveys of 1932 and 1947. *Journal of Personality and Social Psychology, 86,* 130–147.

Deater-Deckard, K., Dodge, K. A., & Sobring, E. (2005). Cultural differences in the effects of physical punishment. In M. Rutter & M. Tienda (Eds.), *Ethnicity and causal mechanisms.* New York: Cambridge University Press.

DeCasper, A. J., & Fifer, W. P. (1980). Of human bonding: Newborns prefer their mothers' voices. *Science, 208,* 1174–1176.

DeCasper, A. J., & Spence, M. J. (1986). Prenatal maternal speech influences newborns' perception of speech sounds. *Infant Behavior and Development, 9,* 133–150.

Declercq, E. (2012). Trends in midwife-attended births in the United States, 1989–2009. *Journal of Midwifery & Women's Health, 57,* 321–326.

DeFrain, J. D., Jakub, D. K., & Mendoza, B. L. (1991–1992). The psychological effects of sudden infant death on grandmothers and grandfathers. *Omega: Journal of Death and Dying, 24,* 165–182.

DeFrain, J., Taylor, J., & Ernst, L. (1982). *Coping with sudden infant death.* Lexington, MA: Lexington Books.

Dehaene, S. (2009). *Reading in the brain: The science and evolution of a human invention.* New York: Viking.

DeKosky, S. T., Ikonomovic, M. D., & Gandy, S. (2010). Traumatic brain injury: Football, warfare, and long-term effects. *The New England Journal of Medicine, 363,* 1293–1296.

Del Giudice, M. (2009). Sex, attachment, and the development of reproductive strategies. *Behavioral Brain Science, 32,* 1–67.

Del Vecchio, T., Eckardt Erlanger, A. C., & Smith Slep, A. M. (2013). Theories of child abuse. In M. A. Fine & F. D. Fincham (Eds.), *Handbook of family theories. A context-based approach.* New York: Routledge.

DeLamater, J. (2012). Sexual expression in later life: A review and synthesis. *Journal of Sex Research, 49,* 125–141.

DeLamater, J. D., & Sill, M. (2005). Sexual desire in later life. *Journal of Sex Research, 42,* 138–149.

Delara, M., Ghofranipour, F., Azadfallah, P. Tavafian, S. S., Kazemnejad, A., & Montazeri, A. (2012). Health related quality of life among adolescent with premenstrual disorders: A cross sectional study. *Health and Quality of Life Outcomes, 10,* 1–5.

Delaunay-El Allam, M., Marlier, L., & Schaal, B. (2006). Learning at the breast: Preference formation for an artificial scent and its attraction against the odor of material milk. *Infant Behavioral Development, 29,* 308–321.

DeLeire, T. C., & Kalil A. (2002). Good things come in threes: Single-parent multigenerational family structure and adolescent adjustment. *Demography, 39,* 393–413.

DeLoache, J. S., Chiong, C. S., Sherman, K., Islam, N., Vanderborght, M., Troseth, G. L., et al. (2010). Do babies learn from baby media? *Psychological Science, 21,* 1570–1574.

DeLoache, J. S., Miller, K. F., & Pierroutsakos, S. L. (1998). Reasoning and problem solving. In D. Kuhn & R. Siegler (Vol. Eds.), W. Damon (Editor-in-Chief), *Handbook of child psychology: Vol. 2. Cognition, perception, and language* (5th ed., pp. 801–850). New York: Wiley.

Delsol, C., & Margolin, G. (2004). The role of family-of-origin violence in men's marital-violence perpetration. *Clinical Psychology Review, 24,* 99–122.

DeMarie, D., & Ferron, J. (2003). Capacity, strategies, and metamemory: Tests of a three-factor model of memory development. *Journal of Experimental Child Psychology, 84,* 167–193.

DeMarie, D., Norman, A., & Abshier, D. W. (2000). Age and experience influence different verbal and nonverbal measures of children's scripts for the zoo. *Cognitive Development, 15,* 241–262.

Demo, D. H., & Buehler, C. (2013). Theoretical approaches to studying divorce. In M. A. Fine & F. D. Fincham (Eds.), *Handbook of family theories. A context-based approach.* New York: Routledge.

Demo, D. H., & Cox, M. J. (2000). Families with young children: A review of research in the 1990s. *Journal of Marriage and the Family, 62,* 876–895.

Demo, D. H., & Fine, M. A. (2010). *Beyond the average divorce.* Los Angeles: Sage.

DeNavas-Walt, C., Proctor, B. D., & Smith, J. C. (2012). *Income, poverty, and health insurance coverage in the United States: 2011.* U. S., Census Bureau, Current Population Reports, P60–243. Washington, DC: U.S. Government Printing Office. Retrieved from United States Census Bureau http://www.census.gov/newsroom/releases/archives/income_wealth/cb12-172.html

Denham, S. A., Bassett, H. H., & Wyatt, T. (2007). The socialization of emotional competence. In J. E. Grusec & P. D. Hastings (Eds.), *Handbook of socialization: Theory and research.* New York: Guilford Press.

Denham, S. A., Blair, K. A., DeMulder, E., Levitas, J., Sawyer, K., Auerbach-Major, S., & Queenan, P. (2003). Preschool emotional competence: Pathway to social competence? *Child Development, 74,* 238–256.

Denney, N. W. (1989). Everyday problem solving: Methodological issues, research findings, and a model. In L. W. Poon, D. C. Rubin, & B. A. Wilson (Eds.), *Everyday cognition in adulthood and late life.* Cambridge, UK: Cambridge University Press.

Denney, N. W., & Pearce, K. A. (1989). A developmental study of practical problem solving in adults. *Psychology and Aging, 4,* 438–442.

Dennis, W. (1966). Creative productivity between the ages of 20 and 80 years. *Journal of Gerontology, 21,* 1–8.

Denworth, L. (2006, April 10). The sun has finally come out for Alex. *Newsweek,* p. 26.

Der, G., Batty, G. D., & Deary, I. J. (2009). The association between IQ in adolescence and a range of health outcomes at 40 in the 1979 US National Longitudinal Study of Youth. *Intelligence, 37,* 573–580.

deRegnier, R., & Desai, S. (2010). Fetal development. In J. Gavin Bremner & T. D. Wachs (Eds.), *The Wiley-Blackwell handbook of infant development. Vol. 2: Applied and Policy Issues* (2nd ed., pp. 9–32). West Sussex, UK: Blackwell Publishing.

DeRosier, M. E., & Thomas, J. M. (2003). Strengthening sociometric prediction: Scientific advances in the assessment of children's peer relations. *Child Development, 74,* 1379–1392.

DES Action. (2010). *DES daughters*. Retrieved from http://www.desaction.org/desdaughters.htm

DesRosiers, F., Vrsalovic, W. T., Knauf, D. E., Vargas, M., & Busch-Rossnagel, N. A. (1999). Assessing the multiple dimensions of the self-concept of young children: A focus on Latinos. *Merrill-Palmer Quarterly, 45*, 543–566.

Detert, J. R., Treviño L. K., & Sweitzer, V. L. (2008). Moral disengagement in ethical decision making: A study of antecedents and outcome. *Journal of Applied Psychology, 93*, 374–391.

Deutsch, F. M. (1999). *Having it all: How equally shared parenting works*. Cambridge, MA: Harvard University Press.

Deutsch, F. M. (2001). Equally shared parenting. *Current Directions in Psychological Science, 10*, 25–28.

Devenny, D. A., Silverman, W. P., Hill, A. L., Jenkins, E., Sersen, E. A., & Wisniewski, K. E. (1996). Normal ageing in adults with Down's syndrome: A longitudinal study. *Journal of Intellectual Disability Research, 40*, 208–221.

DeVries, R. (2000). Vygotsky, Piaget, and education: A reciprocal assimilation of theories and educational practices. *New Ideas in Psychology, 18*, 187–213.

Dew, J., & Wilcox, W. B. (2011). If momma ain't happy: Explaining declines in marital satisfaction among new mothers. *Journal of Marriage and Family, 73*, 1–12.

Dewar, R. E., Kline, D. W., & Swanson, H. A. (1995). Age differences in the comprehension of traffic sign symbols. *Transportation Research Record, 1456*, 1–10.

DeWitt, A. L., Cready, C. M., & Seward, R. R. (2013). Parental role portrayals in twentieth century children's picture books: More egalitarian or ongoing stereotyping? *Sex Roles, 69*, 89–106.

Di Giorgio, E., Leo, I., Pascalis, O., & Simion, F. (2012). Is the face-perception system human-specific at birth? *Developmental Psychology, 48*, 1083–1090.

Diamond, L. (2008). Female bisexuality from adolescence to adulthood: Results from a 10-year longitudinal study. *Developmental Psychology, 44*, 5–14.

Diamond, L. M., & Butterworth, M. (2009). The close relationships of sexual minorities. Partners, friends, and family. In M. C. Smith (Ed.) & N. DeFrates-Densch (Asst. Ed.), *Handbook of research on adult learning and development*. New York: Routledge.

Diamond, L. M., & Fagundes, C. P. (2010). Psychobiological research on attachment. *Journal of Social and Personal Relationships, 27*, 218–225.

Diamond, L. M., Savin-Williams, R., & Dubé, E. M. (1999). Sex, dating, passionate friendships, and romance: Intimate peer relations among lesbian, gay, and bisexual adolescents. In W. Furman, B. B. Brown & C. Feiring (Eds.), *The Development of Romantic Relationships in Adolescents* (pp. 175–210). New York: Cambridge University Press.

Diamond, M., & Sigmundson, H. K. (1997). Sex reassignment at birth: Long-term review and

clinical implications. *Archives of Pediatric and Adolescent Medicine, 151*, 298–304.

Dick, D. M., Meyers, J. L., Latendresse, S. J., Creemers, H. E., Lansford, J. E., Pettit, G. S., et al. (2011). CHRM2, parental monitoring, and adolescent externalizing behavior: Evidence for gene-environment interaction. *Psychological Science, 22*, 481–899.

Dick, D. M., Prescott, C., & McGue, M. (2009). The genetics of substance use and substance use disorders. In Y. Kim (Ed.), *Handbook of behavior genetics*. New York: Springer.

Dickens, W. T., & Flynn, J. R. (2006). Black Americans reduce the racial IQ gap: Evidence from standardization samples. *Psychological Science, 17*, 913–920.

Didonato, M. D., & Berenbaum, S. A. (2010, April 3). The benefits and drawbacks of gender typing: How different dimensions are related to psychological adjustment. *Archives of Sexual Behavior, 40*, 457–463.

Diehl, M., Youngblade, L. M., Hay, E. L., & Chui, H. (2011). The development of self-representations across the life span. In K. L. Fingerman, C. A. Berg, J. Smith, & T. C. Antonucci (Eds.). *Handbook of life-span development*. New York: Springer.

Diekelmann, S., & Born, J. (2010). The memory function of sleep. *Nature Reviews, 11*, 114–126.

Diekelmann, S., Wilhelm, I., & Born, J. (2009). The whats and whens of sleep-dependent memory consolidation. *Sleep Medicine Reviews, 13*(5), 309–321.

Diekman, A. B., & Murnen, S. K. (2004). Learning to be little women and little men: The inequitable gender equality of nonsexist children's literature. *Sex Roles, 50*, 373–385.

Dietz, L. J., Stoyak, S., Melhem, N., Porta, G., Matthews, K. A., Walker Payne, M., & Brent, D. A. (2013). Cortisol response to social stress in parentally bereaved youth. *Biological Psychiatry, 73*, 379–387.

Digman, J. M. (1990). Personality structure: Emergence of the 5-factor model. *Annual Review of Psychology, 41*, 417–440.

Dijkstra, I. C., & Stroebe, M. S. (1998). The impact of a child's death on parents: A myth (not yet) disproved? *Journal of Family Studies, 4*, 159–185.

DiLalla, L. F., Kagan, J., & Reznick, S. J. (1994). Genetic etiology of behavioral inhibition among 2-year-old children. *Infant Behavior and Development, 17*, 405–412.

Dillon, M., & Wink, P. (2007). *In the course of a lifetime: Tracing religious belief, practice, and change*. Ewing, NJ: University of California Press.

Dimmock, P. W., Wyatt, K. M., Jones, P. W., & O'Brien, P. M. S. (2000). Efficacy of selective serotonin-reuptake inhibitors in premenstrual syndrome: A systematic review. *Lancet, 356*, 1131–1136.

Dionne, G., Tremblay, R., Boivin, M., Laplante, D., & Perusse, D. (2003). Physical aggression and expressive vocabulary in 19-month-old twins. *Developmental Psychology, 39*, 261–273.

Dirix, C. E. H., Nijhuis, J. G., Jongsma, H. W., & Hornstra, G. (2009). Aspects of fetal learning

and memory. *Child Development, 80*, 1251–1258.

Dittman, R. W., Kappes, M. E., & Kappes, M. H. (1992). Sexual behavior in adolescent and adult females with congenital adrenal hyperplasia. *Psychoneuroendocrinology, 17*, 153–170.

Dittmar, H., Halliwell, E., & Ive, S. (2006). Does Barbie make girls want to be thin? The effect of experimental exposure to images of dolls on the body image of 5- to 8-year-old girls. *Developmental Psychology, 42*, 283–292.

Dixon, R. A. (1992). Contextual approaches to adult intellectual development. In R. J. Sternberg & C. A. Berg (Eds.), *Intellectual development*. New York: Cambridge University Press.

Dixon, R. A. (2003). Themes in the aging of intelligence: Robust decline with intriguing possibilities. In R. J. Sternberg, J. Lautrey, & T. I. Lubart (Eds.), *Models of intelligence: International perspectives* (pp. 151–167). Washington, DC: American Psychological Association.

Dodge, K. A. (1986). A social information processing model of social competence in children. In M. Perlmutter (Ed.), *Minnesota Symposia on Child Psychology* (Vol. 18). Hillsdale, NJ: Erlbaum.

Dodge, K. A. (1993). Social-cognitive mechanisms in the development of conduct disorder and depression. *Annual Review of Psychology, 44*, 559–584.

Dodge, K. A. (2009). Mechanisms of gene-environment interaction effects in the development of conduct disorder. *Perspectives on Psychological Science, 4*, 408–414.

Dodge, K. A., & Coleman, D. L. (Eds.) (2009). *Preventing child maltreatment. Community approaches*. New York: Guilford.

Dodge, K. A., & Pettit, G. S. (2003). A bio-psychosocial model of the development of chronic conduct problems in adolescence. *Developmental Psychology, 39*, 349–371.

Dodge, K. A., & Price, J. M. (1994). On the relation between social information processing and socially competent behavior in early school-aged children. *Child Development, 65*, 1385–1397.

Dodge, K. A., & Rutter, M. (Eds.). (2011). *Gene-environment interactions in developmental psychopathology*. New York: Guilford.

Dodge, K. A., Coie, J. D., & Lynam, D. (2006). Aggression and antisocial behavior in youth. In N. Eisenberg (Vol. Ed.), & W. Damon & R. M. Lerner (Eds. in Chief), *Handbook of child psychology: Vol. 3. Social, emotional, and personality development* (6th ed.). Hoboken, NJ: Wiley.

Dodge, K. A., Coie, J. D., Pettit, G. S., & Price, J. M. (1990). Peer status and aggression in boys' groups: Developmental and contextual analysis. *Child Development, 61*, 1289–1309.

Dodge, K. A., Greenberg, M. T., Malone, P. S., & Conduct Problems Prevention Research Group. (2008). Testing an idealized dynamic cascade model of the development of serious violence in adolescence. *Child Development, 79*, 1907–1927.

Dodge, K. A., Malone, P. S., Lansford, J. E., Miller, S., Pettit, G. S., & Bates, J. E. (2009). A dynamic cascade model of the development of substance-use onset. *Monographs of the Society for Research in Child Development, 74*(3, Serial No. 294).

Dodson, C. S., Bawa, S., & Krueger, L. E. (2007). Aging, metamemory, and high-confidence errors: A misrecollection account. *Psychological Aging, 22,* 122–133.

Dogan, S. J., Conger, R. D., Kim, K. J., & Masyn, K. E. (2007). Cognitive and parenting pathways in the transmission of antisocial behavior from parents to adolescents. *Child Development, 78,* 335–349.

Doherty, M. J. (2009). *Theory of mind. How children understand others' thoughts and feelings.* New York: Psychology Press.

Doherty, W. J., Erickson, M. F., & LaRossa, R. (2006). An intervention to increase father involvement and skills with infants during the transition to parenthood. *Journal of Family Psychology, 20,* 438–447.

Dohnt, H., & Tiggemann, M. (2006). The contribution of peer and media influences to the development of body satisfaction and self-esteem in young girls: A prospective study. *Developmental Psychology, 42,* 929–936.

Doka, K. J. (1989). *Disenfranchised grief: Recognizing hidden sorrow.* Lexington, MA: Lexington Books.

Doka, K. J. (2008). Disenfranchised grief in historical and cultural perspective. In M. S. Stroebe, R. O. Hansson, H. Schut, & W. Stroebe (Eds.), *Handbook of bereavement research and practice. Advances in theory and intervention.* Washington, DC: American Psychological Association.

Dolen, L. S., & Bearison, D. J. (1982). Social interaction and social cognition in aging. *Human Development, 25,* 430–442.

Donat, D. J. (2006). Reading Their Way: A Balanced approach that increases achievement. *Reading and Writing Quarterly, 22,* 305–323.

Donnellan, M. B., Martin, M. J., Conger, K. J., & Conger, R. D. (2013). Economic distress and poverty in families. In M. A. Fine & F. D. Fincham (Eds.), *Handbook of family theories. A context-based approach.* New York: Routledge.

Donnellan, M. B., Trzesniewski, K. H., & Robins, R. W. (2006). Personality and self-esteem development in adolescence. In D. K. Mroczek & T. D. Little (Eds.), *Handbook of personality development.* Mahwah, NJ: Erlbaum.

Donnelly, N., Cave, K., Greenway, R., Hadwin, J. A., Stevenson, J., & Sonuga-Barke, E. (2007). Visual search in children and adults: Top-down and bottom-up mechanisms. *Quarterly Journal of Experimental Psychology, 60,* 120–136.

Dopp, A. R., & Cain, A. C. (2012). The role of peer relationships in parental bereavement during childhood and adolescence. *Death Studies, 36,* 41–60.

Dorn, L. D., Susman, E. J., & Ponirakis, A. (2003). Pubertal timing and adolescent adjustment and behavior: Conclusions vary by rater. *Journal of Youth and Adolescence, 32,* 157–167.

Dotterer, A. M., McHale, S. J., & Crouter, A. C. (2009). The development and correlates of academic interests from childhood through adolescence. *Journal of Educational Psychology, 101,* 509–519.

Doty, R. L., & Cameron, E. L. (2009). Sex differences and reproductive hormone influences on human odor perception. *Physiological Behavior, 97,* 213–228.

Dougherty, T. M., & Haith, M. M. (1997). Infant expectations and reaction time as predictors of childhood speed of processing and IQ. *Developmental Psychology, 33,* 146–155.

Dowdney, L. (2000). Annotation: Childhood bereavement following parental death. *Journal of Child Psychology and Psychiatry and Allied Disciplines, 41,* 819–830.

Dowling, G. J., Weiss, S. R., & Condon, T. P. (2008). Drugs of abuse and the aging brain. *Neuropsychopharmacology, 33,* 209–218.

Doyle, A. B., Markiewicz, D., Brendgen, M., Lieberman, M., & Voss, K. (2000). Child attachment security and self-concept: Associations with mother and father attachment style and marital quality. *Merrill-Palmer Quarterly, 46,* 514–539.

Draper, B., Pfaff, J. J., Pirkis, J., Snowdon, J., Lautenschlager, N. T., Wilson, I., & Almeida, O. P. (2008). Long-term effects of childhood abuse on the quality of life and health of older people: Results from the Depression and Early Prevention of Suicide in General Practice Project. *Journal of the American Geriatrics Society, 56,* 262–271.

Dribe, M., & Stanfors, M. (2009). Does parenthood strengthen a traditional household division of labor? *Journal of Marriage and Family, 71,* 33–45.

Drotar, D., Robinson, J., Jeavons, L., & Kirchner, H. L. (2008). A randomized, controlled evaluation of early intervention: The born to learn curriculum. *Child: Care, Health, and Development, 35,* 643–649.

du Plessis, A. (2013). Fetal Development. In M. L. Batshaw, N. J. Roizen, & G. R. Lotrecchiano (Eds.), *Children with disabilities* (7th ed., pp. 25–36). Baltimore: Paul H. Brookes.

Dube, S. R., & Orpinas, P. (2009). Understanding excessive school absenteeism as school refusal behavior. *Children & Schools, 31,* 87–95.

Dubois, L., Farmer, A., Girard, M., & Peterson, K. (2007). Regular sugar-sweetened beverage consumption between meals increases risk of overweight among preschool-aged children. *Journal of the American Dietetic Association, 107,* 924–934.

Dubois, L., Ohm Kyvik, K., Girard, M., Tatone-Tokuda, F., Perusse, D., et al. (2012) Genetic and Environmental Contributions to Weight, Height, and BMI from Birth to 19 Years of Age: An International Study of Over 12,000 Twin Pairs. PLoS ONE 7(2): e30153. doi:10.1371/journal.pone.0030153

Duijts, L., Jaddoe, V. W., van der Valk, R. J. P., Henderson, J. A., Hofman, A., Raat, H., et al. (2012). Fetal exposure to maternal and paternal smoking and the risks of wheezing in preschool children: The Generation R study. *Chest, 141,* 876–885.

Duncan, R. M., & Pratt, M. W. (1997). Microgenetic change in the quantity and quality of preschoolers' private speech. *International Journal of Behavioral Development, 20,* 367.

Dunn, J. (1993). *Young children's close relationships. Beyond attachment.* Newbury Park, CA: Sage.

Dunn, J. (2007). Siblings and socialization. In J. E. Grusec & P. D. Hastings (Eds.), *Handbook of socialization: Theory and research.* New York: Guilford.

Dunn, J., & Kendrick, C. (1982). *Siblings: Love, envy, and understanding.* Cambridge, MA: Harvard University Press.

Dunn, J., Cutting, A. L., & Demetriou, H. (2000). Moral sensibility, understanding others, and children's friendship interactions in the preschool period. *British Journal of Developmental Psychology, 18,* 159–177.

Dunn, J., Fergusson, E., & Maughan, B. (2006). Grandparents, grandchildren, and family change in contemporary Britain. In A. Clarke-Stewart & J. Dunn (Eds.), *Families count: Effects on child and adolescent development.* New York: Cambridge University Press.

Dunne, E. F., Unger, E. R., Sternberg, M., McQuillan, G., Swan, D. C., Patel, S. S., & Markowitz, L. E. (2007). Prevalence of HPV infection among females in the United States. *Journal of the American Medical Association, 297,* 813–819.

Dunphy, D. C. (1963). The social structure of urban adolescent peer groups. *Sociometry, 26,* 230–246.

Dunstan, D. W., Barr, E.L.M., Healy, G.N., Salmon, J., Shaw, J. E., Balkau, B., Magliano, D. J., Cameron, A.J., Zimmet, P.Z., & Owen, N. (2010). Television viewing time and mortality: The Australian Diabetes, Obesity and Lifestyle Study (AusDiab). *Circulation, 121,* 384–391.

DuPaul, G. J., & Stoner, G. (2003). *ADHD in the schools. Assessment and intervention strategies* (2nd ed.). New York: Guilford.

Durrant, J., & Ensom, R. (2012). Physical punishment of children: Lessons from 20 years of research. *Canadian Medical Association Journal, 184,* 1373–1377.

Duvall, E. M. (1977). *Marriage and family development* (5th ed.). Philadelphia: J. B. Lippincott.

Dux, P. E., Ivanoff, J. G., Asplund, C. L., & Marois, R. (2006). Isolation of a central bottleneck of information processing with time-resolved FMRI. *Neuron, 52*(6), 1109–1120.

Duyme, M., Dumaret, A., & Tomkiewicz, S. (1999). How can we boost IQs of "dull children"? A late adoption study. *Proceedings of the National Academy of Sciences of the United States of America, 96,* 8790–8794.

Dvorak, P. (2012, May 20). Transgender at five. *The Washington Post,* pp. A1, A14–15.

Dweck, C. S. (2006). *Mindset: The new psychology of success.* New York: Ballantine Books.

Dweck, C. S. (2007). The perils and promise of praise. *Educational Leadership, 65,* 34–39.

Dweck, C. S., & Elliott, E. S. (1983). Achievement motivation. In P. H. Mussen (Gen. Ed.), E. M. Hetherington (Vol Ed.), *Handbook of child psychology: Vol. IV. Social and personality development* (pp. 643–691). New York: Wiley.

Dweck, C. S., & Leggett, E. L. (1988). A social-cognitive approach to motivation and personality. *Psychological Review, 95,* 256–273.

Dyk, P. H., & Adams, G. R. (1990). Identity and intimacy: An initial investigation of three theoretical models using cross-lag panel correlations. *Journal of Youth and Adolescence, 19,* 91–110.

Dyrdal, G. M., & Lucas, R. E. (2013). Reaction and adaptation to the birth of a child: A couple-level analysis. *Developmental Psychology, 49,* 749–761.

Dyregrov, A., & Dyregrov, K. (2013). Complicated grief in children. In M. Stroebe, H. Schut & J. van den Bout (Eds.), *Complicated grief: Scientific foundations for health care professionals.* New York: Routledge/Taylor & Francis.

Eagly, A. H. (2012). Social role theory. In P. A. M. Van Lange, A. W. Kruglanski, & E. T. Higgins (Eds.), *Handbook of theory of social psychology* (Vol. 2, pp. 458–476). Thousand Oaks, CA: Sage Publications.

Eastwick, P. W., & Finkel, E. J. (2008). The attachment system in fledgling relationships: An activating role for attachment anxiety. *Journal of Personality and Social Psychology, 95,* 628–647.

Eaton, D. K., Kann, L., Kinchen, S., Ross, J., Hawkins, J., Harris, W. A., et al. (2006, June 9). Youth risk behavior surveillance—United States, 2005. *Morbidity and Mortality Weekly Report, 55,* 1–108.

Eaton, D. K., Kann, L., Kinchen, S., Shanklin, S., Flint, K. H., Hawkins, J., et al. (2012, June 8).Youth Risk Behavior Surveillance—United States, 2011. *Morbidity and Mortality Weekly Reports, 61.* Retrieved from http://www.cdc.gov/mmwr/pdf/ss/ss6104.pdf

Ebbeck, M. (1996). Parents' expectations and child rearing practices in Hong Kong. *Early Child Development and Care, 119,* 15–25.

Eberhard-Gran, M., Garthus-Niegel, S., Garthus-Niegel, K., & Eskild, A. (2010). Postnatal care: A cross-cultural and historical perspective. *Archives of Women's Mental Health, 13,* 459–466.

Ebstyne King, P., & Furrow, J. L. (2004). Religion as a resource for positive youth development: Religion, social capital, and moral outcomes. *Developmental Psychology, 40,* 703–713.

Eccles, J. S., Jacobs, J. E., & Harold, R. D. (1990). Gender role stereotypes, expectancy effects, and parents' socialization of gender differences. *Journal of Social Issues, 46,* 183–201.

Eccles, J. S., Lord, S., & Midgley, C. (1991). What are we doing to early adolescents? The impact of educational contexts on early adolescents. *American Journal of Education, 99,* 521–542.

Eccles, J. S., Midgley, C., Wigfield, A., Buchanan, C. M., Reuman, D., Flanagan, C., et al. (1993). Development during adolescence: The impact of stage-environment fit on young adolescents' experiences in schools and in families. *American Psychologist, 48,* 90–101.

Ecklund-Flores, L., & Turkewitz, G. (1996). Asymmetric headturning to speech and nonspeech in human newborns. *Developmental Psychobiology, 29,* 205–217.

Eddy, K. T., Keel, P. K., & Leon, G. R. (2010). Vulnerability to eating disorders in childhood and adolescence.In R. E. Ingram & J. M. Price (Eds.).*Vulnerability to psychopathology.Risk across the lifespan* (2nded.). New York: Guilford.

Edelstein, B. A., & Segal, D. L. (2011). Assessment of emotional and personality disorders in older adults. In K. W. Schaie & S. L. Willis (Eds.), B. G. Knight, B. Levy, & D. C. Park (Assoc. Eds.), *Handbook of the psychology of aging.* Burlington, MA: Academic Press/Elsevier.

Eder, R. A. (1989). The emergent personologist: The structure and content of 3½-, 5½-, and 7½-year-olds' concepts of themselves and other persons. *Child Development, 60,* 1218–1228.

Egeland, B. (1979). Preliminary results of a prospective study of the antecedents of child abuse. *International Journal of Child Abuse and Neglect, 3,* 269–278.

Egeland, B., & Carlson, E. A. (2004). Attachment and psychopathology. In L. Atkinson & S. Goldberg (Eds.), *Attachment issues in psychopathology and intervention.* Mahwah, NJ: Erlbaum.

Egeland, B., Jacobvitz, D., & Sroufe, L. A. (1988). Breaking the cycle of abuse. *Child Development, 59,* 1080–1088.

Egeland, B., Sroufe, L. A., & Erickson, M. (1983). The developmental consequences of different patterns of maltreatment. *International Journal of Child Abuse and Neglect, 7,* 459–469.

Ehrhardt, A. A. (1985). The psychobiology of gender. In A. S. Rossi (Ed.), *Gender and the life course.* New York: Aldine.

Ehri, L. C. (1999). Phases of development in learning to read words. In J. Oakhill & R. Beard (Eds.), *Reading development and the teaching of reading* (pp. 79–108). Oxford: Blackwell.

Ehrle, G. M. (2001). Grandchildren as moderator variables in the family, social, physiological, and intellectual development of grandparents who are raising them. In E. L. Grigorenko & R. J. Sternberg (Eds.), *Family environment and intellectual functioning: A life-span perspective.* Mahwah, NJ: Erlbaum.

Eimas, P. D. (1975a). Auditory and phonetic cues for speech: Discrimination of the (r-l) distinction by young infants. *Perception and Psychophysics, 18,* 341–347.

Eimas, P. D. (1975b). Speech perception in early infancy. In L. B. Cohen & P. Salapatek (Eds.), *Infant perception: From sensation to cognition.* New York: Academic Press.

Eimas, P. D. (1985). The perception of speech in early infancy. *Scientific American, 252,* 46–52.

Eisenberg, M., Neumark-Sztainer, D., & Story, M. (2003). Associations of weight-based teasing and emotional well-being among adolescents. *Archives of Pediatric Medicine, 157,* 733–738.

Eisenberg, N., Hofer, C., Spinrad, T. L., Gershoff, E. T., Valiente, C., Losoya, S., Zhou, Q., Cumberland, A., Liew, J., Reiser, M., & Maxon, E. (2008). Understanding mother-adolescent conflict discussions: Concurrent and across-time prediction from youths' dispositions and parenting. *Monographs of the Society for Research in Child Development, 73* (2, Serial No. 290).

Eisenberg, N., Smith, C. L., & Spinrad, T. L. (2011). Effortful control: Relations with emotion regulation, adjustment, and socialization in childhood. In K. D. Vohs, & R. F. Baumeister (Eds.), *Handbook of self-regulation: Research, theory, and applications* (2nd ed.). New York: Guilford Press.

Eisenberg, N., Spinrad, T. L., & Sadovsky, A. (2006). Empathy-related responding in children. In M. Killen & J. G. Smetana (Eds.), *Handbook of moral development.* Mahwah, NJ: Erlbaum.

Ekerdt, D. J., Bossé, R., & Levkoff, S. (1985). Empirical test for phases of retirement: Findings from the Normative Aging Study. *Journal of Gerontology, 40,* 95–101.

Ekerdt, D. J., Kosloski, K., & DeViney, S. (2000). The normative anticipation of retirement by older adults. *Research on Aging, 22,* 3–22.

Elder, G. H., Jr., & Shanahan, M. J. (2006). The life course and human development. In W. Damon & R. M. Lerner (Eds. in Chief) & R. M. Lerner (Vol. Ed.), *Handbook of child psychology: Vol. 1. Theoretical models of human development* (6th ed.). Hoboken, NJ: Wiley.

Elder, G. H., Jr., Liker, J. K., & Cross, C. E. (1984). Parent–child behavior in the Great Depression: Life course and intergenerational influences. In P. B. Baltes & O. G. Brim Jr. (Eds.), *Life-span development and behavior* (Vol. 6). Orlando, FL: Academic Press.

Elder, G., Jr., & Johnson, M. K. (2003). The life course and aging: Challenges, lessons and new directions. In R. Settersten, Jr. (Ed.), *Invitation to the life course: Toward new understandings of later life.* Amityville, NY: Baywood.

Elicker, J., Englund, M., & Sroufe, L. A. (1992). Predicting peer competence and peer relationships in childhood from early parent–child relationships. In R. D. Parke & G. W. Ladd (Eds.), *Family-peer relationships: Modes of linkage.* Hillsdale, NJ: Erlbaum.

Eliot, L. (2009). *Pink brain, blue brain: How small differences grow into troublesome gaps—and what we can do about it.* Boston: Houghton Mifflin Harcourt.

Elison, J. T., Paterson, S. J., Wolff, J. J., Reznick, J. S., Sasson, N. J., Gu, H., et al. (2013). White matter microstructure and atypical visual orienting in 7-month-olds at risk for autism.*American Journal of Psychiatry, 170,* 899–908.

Elkind, D. (1967). Egocentrism in adolescence. *Child Development, 38,* 1025–1034.

Elkind, D. (1987). *Miseducation: Preschoolers at risk.* New York: Knopf.

Elkind, D., & Bowen, R. (1979). Imaginary audience behavior in children and adolescents. *Developmental Psychology, 15,* 38–44.

Elliot, A. J., & Reis, H. T. (2003). Attachment and exploration in adulthood. *Journal of Personality & Social Psychology, 85,* 317–331.

Elliott, D. S., & Ageton, S. S. (1980). Reconciling race and class differences in self-reported and official estimates of delinquency. *American Sociological Review, 45,* 95–110.

Elliott, E. S., & Dweck, C. S. (1988). Goals: An approach to motivation and achievement. *Journal of Personality and Social Psychology, 54,* 5–12.

Elliott, S. (2012). *Not my kid: What parents believe about the sex lives of their teenagers*. New York: New York University Press.

Ellis, B. J., & Garber, J. (2000). Psychosocial antecedents of variation in girls' pubertal timing: Maternal depression, stepfather presence, and marital and family stress. *Child Development, 71*, 485–501.

Ellis, L., Ames, M. A., Peckham, W., & Burke, D. M. (1988). Sexual orientation in human offspring may be altered by severe emotional distress during pregnancy. *Journal of Sex Research, 25*, 152–157.

Ellis, S., Rogoff, B., & Cromer, C. C. (1981). Age segregation in children's social interactions. *Developmental Psychology, 17*, 399–407.

Ellis, Y., Daniels, W., & Jauregui, A. (2010). The effect of multitasking on the grade performance of business students. *Research in Higher Education Journal, 8*, 1–11.

Ellison, P. T. (2002). Puberty. In N. Cameron (Ed.), *Human growth and development* (pp. 65–84). New York: Academic Press.

Elsabbagh, M., Fernandes, J., Jane Webb, S., Dawson, G., Charman, T., & Johnson, M. H. (2013). Disengagement of visual attention in infancy is associated with emerging autism in toddlerhood. *Biological Psychiatry, 74*, 189–194.

Else-Quest, N. M., Hyde, J. S., & Linn, M. C. (2010). Cross-national patterns of gender differences in mathematics: A meta-analysis. *Psychological Bulletin, 136*, 103–127.

Emde, R. N., Biringen, Z., Clyman, R. B., & Oppenheim, D. (1991). The moral self of infancy: Affective core and procedural knowledge. *Developmental Review, 11*, 251–270.

Emery, R. E., & Laumann-Billings, L. (1998). An overview of the nature, causes, and consequences of abusive family relationships: Toward differentiating maltreatment and violence. *American Psychologist, 53*, 121–135.

Emery, R. E., & Tuer, M. (1993). Parenting and the marital relationship. In T. Luster & L. Okagaki (Eds.), *Parenting. An ecological perspective.* Hillsdale, NJ: Erlbaum.

Emmanuelle, V. (2009). Inter-relationships among attachment to mother and father, self-esteem, and career indecision. *Journal of Vocational Behavior, 75*, 91–99.

Endendijk, J. J., Groeneveld, M. G., van Berkel, S. R., Hallers-Haalboom, E. T., Mesman, J., & Bakermans-Kranenburg, M. J. (2013). Gender stereotypes in the family context: Mothers, fathers, and siblings. *Sex Roles, 68*, 577–590.

England, P., Reid, L. L., & Kilbourne, B. S. (1996). The effect of the sex composition of jobs on starting wages in an organization: Findings from the NLSY. *Demography, 33*, 511–521.

Enright, R., Lapsley, D., & Shukla, D. (1979). Adolescent egocentrism in early and late adolescence. *Adolescence, 14*, 687–695.

Ensminger, M. E., & Slusarcick, A. L. (1992). Paths to high school graduation or dropout: A longitudinal study of a first-grade cohort. *Sociology of Education, 65*, 95–113.

Epel, E. S., Blackburn, E. H., Lin, J., Dhabhar, F. S., Adler, N. E., Morrow, J. D., et al. (2004). Accelerated telomere shortening in response to life stress. *Proceedings of the National Academy of Sciences, 101*, 17312–17315.

Epel, E. S., Lin, J., Wilhelm, F. H., Wolkowitz, O. M., Cawthon, R., Adler, N. E., et al. (2006). Cell aging in relation to stress arousal and cardiovascular disease risk factors. *Psychoneuroendocrinology, 31*, 277–287.

Eppig, C., Fincher, C. L., & Thornhill, R. (2010). Parasite prevalence and the worldwide distribution of cognitive ability. *Proceedings of the Royal Society, 277*, 3801–3808.

Eppler, M. A. (1995). Development of manipulatory skills and the deployment of attention. *Infant Behavior & Development, 18*, 391–405.

Epstein, R. (2013, January/February). Yet another stage of life? *Scientific American Mind*, pp. 18–19.

Erdley, C. A., Loomis, C. C., Cain, K. M., & Dumas-Hines, F. (1997). Relations among children's social goals, implicit personality theories, and responses to social failure. *Developmental Psychology, 33*, 263–272.

Erdman, P., & Ng, K. (Eds.). (2010). *Attachment. Expanding the cultural connections*. New York: Routledge.

Ericsson, K. A. (1996). The acquisition of expert performance: An introduction to some of the issues. In K. A. Ericsson (Ed.), *The road to excellence: The acquisition of expert performance in the arts and sciences, sports, and games*. Mahwah, NJ: Erlbaum.

Ericsson, K. A., & Kintsch, W. (1995). Long-term working memory. *Psychological Review, 102*, 211–245.

Ericsson, K. A., Chase, W. G., & Faloon, S. (1980). Acquisition of a memory skill. *Science, 208*, 1181–1182.

Erikson, E. H. (1963). *Childhood and society* (2nd ed.). New York: Norton.

Erikson, E. H. (1968). *Identity: Youth and crisis*. New York: Norton.

Erikson, E. H. (1982). *The life cycle completed: A review*. New York: Norton.

Erickson, J. J., Martinengo, G., & Hill, E. J. (2010). Putting work and family experiences in context: Differences by family life stage. *Human Relations, 63*, 955–979.

Eriksen, W., Sundet, J. M., & Tambs, K. (2009). Register data suggest lower intelligence in men born the year after flu pandemic. *Annals of Neurology, 66*, 284–9.

Erol, R. Y., & Orth, U. (2011). Self-esteem development from age 14 to 30 years: A longitudinal study. *Journal of Personality and Social Psychology, 101*, 607–619.

Escalona, S. (1968). *The roots of individuality: Normal patterns of individuality*. Chicago: Aldine.

Eskritt, M., & Lee, K. (2002). "Remember where you last saw that card": Children's production of external symbols as a memory aid. *Developmental Psychology, 38*, 254–266.

Espinosa-Hernandez, G., & Lefkowitz, E. S. (2009). Sexual behaviors and attitudes and ethnic identity during college. *Journal of Sex Research, 46*, 471–482.

Espinoza, G., Gonzales, N. A., & Fuligni, A. J. (2012). Daily school peer victimization experiences among Mexican American adolescents: Associations with psychosocial, physical and school adjustment. *Journal of Youth and Adolescence, 42*, 1775–1788.

Espy, K. A., Molfese, V. J., & DiLalla, L. F. (2001). Effects of environmental measures on intelligence in young children: Growth curve modeling of longitudinal data. *Merrill-Palmer Quarterly, 47*, 42–73.

Essa, E. L., & Murray, C. I. (1994). Young children's understanding and experience with death. *Young Children, 49*, 74–81.

Essex, M. J., Kraemer, H. C., Slattery, M., Burk, L. R., Boyce, W. T., Woodward, H. R., & Kupfer, D. J. (2009). Screening for childhood mental health problems: Outcomes and early identification. *Journal of Child Psychology and Psychiatry, 50*, 562–570.

Estes, Z., & Felker, S. (2012). Confidence mediates the sex difference in mental rotation performance. *Archives of Sexual Behavior, 41*, 557–590.

Evans, D., & Goldman, B. (2010). First person: Jane Fowler. *The Body: The Complete HIV/AIDS Resource, HIV/AIDS Resource Center for Women*. Retrieved from http://www.thebody.com/content/art45791.html

Evans, G. W. (2004). The environment of childhood poverty. *American Psychologist, 59*, 77–92.

Evans, G. W., & Kim, P. (2012). Childhood poverty and young adults' allostatic load: The mediating role of childhood cumulative risk exposure. *Psychological Science, 23*, 979–983.

Evans, G. W., Kim, P. (2013). Childhood poverty, chronic stress, self-regulation, and coping. *Child Development Perspectives, 7*, 43–48.

Evans, J. R. (2001). Risk factors for age-related macular degeneration. *Progress in Retinal and Eye Research, 20*, 227.

Evans, J. R., Fletcher, A. E., Wormald, R. P., Ng, E. S., Stirling, S., Smeeth, L., et al. (2002). Prevalence of visual impairment in people aged 75 years and older in Britain: Results from the MRC Trial of assessment and management of older people in the community. *Ophthalmology*, 795–800.

Evans, M. A., & Shaw, D. (2008). Home grown for reading: Parental contributions to young children's emergent literacy and word recognition. *Canadian Psychology, 49*, 89–95.

Faber, C. E., & Grontved, A. M. (2000). Cochlear implantation and change in quality of life. *Acta Otolaryngology Supplement, 543*, 151–153.

Fabes, R. A., Martin, C. L., & Hanish, L. D. (2003). Young children's play qualities in same-, other-, and mixed-sex peer groups. *Child Development, 74*, 921–932.

Fagan, J. F. (2011). Intelligence in infancy. In R. J. Sternberg & S. B. Kaufman (Eds.), *The Cambridge handbook of intelligence* (pp. 130–143). New York: Cambridge University Press.

Fagan, J., & Palkovitz, R. (2011). Coparenting and relationship quality effects on father engagement: Variations by residence, romance. *Journal of Marriage and Family, 73*, 637–653.

Fagan, J., Palkovitz, R., Roy, K., & Farrie, D. (2009). Pathways to paternal engagement: Longitudinal effects of risk and resilience on nonresident fathers. *Developmental Psychology, 45*, 1389–1405.

Fagot, B. I. (1978). The influence of sex of child on parental reactions to toddler children. *Child Development, 49*, 459–465.

Fagot, B. I. (1997). Attachment, parenting, and peer interactions of toddler children. *Developmental Psychology, 33*, 489–499.

Fagot, B. I., & Kavanaugh, K. (1993). Parenting during the second year: Effects of children's age, sex, and attachment classification. *Child Development, 64*, 258–271.

Fagot, B. I., & Leinbach, M. D. (1989). The young child's gender schema: Environmental input, internal organization. *Child Development, 60*, 663–672.

Fagot, B. I., & Leinbach, M. D. (1993). Gender-role development in young children: From discrimination to labeling. *Developmental Review, 13*, 205–224.

Fagot, B. I., Leinbach, M. D., & Hagan, R. (1986). Gender labeling and the adoption of sex-typed behaviors. *Developmental Psychology, 22*, 440–443.

Fagot, B. I., Leinbach, M. D., & O'Boyle, C. (1992). Gender labeling, gender stereotyping, and parenting behaviors. *Developmental Psychology, 28*, 225–230.

Falcon, L. M., & Tucker, K. L. (2000). Prevalence and correlates of depressive symptoms among Hispanic elders in Massachusetts. *Journal of Gerontology: Social Sciences, 55*, S108–S116.

Fan, H. C., Gu, W., Wang, J., Blumenfeld, Y. J., El-Sayed, Y. Y., & Quake, S. R. (2012). Non-invasive prenatal measurement of the fetal genome. *Nature, 48*(7407), 320–326.

Fantz, R. L., & Fagan, J. F. (1975). Visual attention to size and number of pattern details by term and preterm infants during the first six months. *Child Development, 46*, 3–18.

Farah, M. J., Betancourt, L., Shera, D. M., Savage, J. H., Giannetta, J. M., Brodsky, N. L., et al. (2008). Environmental stimulation, parental nurturance and cognitive development in humans. *Developmental Science, 11*, 793–801.

Farlow, M. R., & Boustani, M. (2009). Pharmacological treatment of Alzheimer disease and mild cognitive impairment. In M. F. Weiner & A. M. Lipton (Eds.), *The American Psychiatric Publishing Textbook of Alzheimer disease and other dementias.* Washington, DC: American Psychiatric Publishing.

Farr, R. H., Forssell, S. L., & Patterson, C. J. (2010). Parenting and child development in adoptive families: Does parental sexual orientation matter? *Applied Developmental Science, 14*, 164–178.

Farroni, T., Johnson, M. H., Menon, E., Zulian, L., Faraguna, D., & Csibra, G. (2005). Newborns' preference for face-relevant stimuli: Effects of contrast polarity. *Proceedings of the National Academy of Sciences, 102*, 17245–17250.

Farver, J. A. M., & Lee-Shin, Y. (1997). Social pretend play in Korean and Anglo American preschoolers. *Child Development, 68*, 544–556.

Faulkner, D., Joiner, R., Littleton, K., Miell, D., & Thompson, L. (2000). The mediating effect of task presentation on collaboration and children's acquisition of scientific reasoning. *European Journal of Psychology of Education, 15*, 417–430.

Faulkner, K. W. (1997). Talking about death with a dying child. *American Journal of Nursing, 97*, 64, 66, 68–69.

Faust, M. A., & Glenzer, N. (2000). "I could read those parts over and over": Eighth graders rereading to enhance enjoyment and learning with literature. *Journal of Adolescent and Adult Literacy, 44*, 234–239.

Favilla, M. (2006). Reaching movements in children: Accuracy and reaction time development. *Journal of Experimental Brain Research, 169*, 122–125.

Fearon, R. M., P., van IJzendoorn, M. H., Fonagy, P., Bakermans-Kranenburg, M. J., Schuengel, C., & Bokhorst, C. L. (2006). In search of shared and nonshared environmental factors in security of attachment: A behavior-genetic study of the association between sensitivity and attachment security. *Developmental Psychology, 42*, 1026–1040.

Federal Interagency Forum on Aging Related Statistics. (2008). *Older Americans 2008: Key indicators of well-being.* Washington, DC: U. S. Government Printing Office. Retrieved from www.agingstats.gov

Federal Interagency Forum on Aging Related Statistics. (2012). *Older Americans 2012. Key indicators of well-being.* Washington, DC: U.S. Government Printing Office. Retrieved from http://www.agingstats.gov

Federal Interagency Forum on Child and Family Statistics. (2012). *America's children in brief: Key national indicators of well-being, 2012.* Washington, DC: U.S. Government Printing Office. Retrieved from http://www.childstats.gov/americaschildren

Fein, D., Barton, M., Eigsti, I., Kelley, E., Naigles, L., Schultz, R. T., et al. (2013). Optimal outcome in individuals with a history of autism. *Journal of Child Psychology and Psychiatry, 54*, 195–205.

Feingold, A. (1994). Gender differences in personality: A meta-analysis. *Psychological Bulletin, 116*, 429–456.

Feinman, S. (1992). *Social referencing and the social construction of reality in infancy.* New York: Plenum.

Feldman, D. C., & Ng, T. W. H. (2013). Theoretical approaches to the study of job transitions. In N. W. Schmitt, S. Highhouse, & I. B. Weiner (Eds.), *Handbook of psychology: Vol. 12. Industrial and organizational psychology.* Hoboken, NJ: Wiley.

Feldman, D. H. (1986). *Nature's gambit: Child prodigies and the development of human potential.* New York: Basic Books.

Feldman, D. H., & Fowler, R. C. (1997). The nature(s) of developmental change: Piaget, Vygotsky, and the transition process. *New Ideas in Psychology, 3*, 195–210.

Feldman, H., Jones, K., Lindsay, S., Slymen, D., Klonoff-Cohen, H., Kao, K., et al. (2012). Prenatal alcohol exposure patterns and alcohol-related birth defects and growth deficiencies: A prospective study. *Alcoholism: Clinical and Experimental Research, 36*(4), 670–676.

Feldman, R. (2007). Parent-infant synchrony. Biological foundations and developmental outcomes. *Current Directions in Psychological Science, 16*, 340–345.

Feldman, R. D. (1982). *Whatever happened to the quiz kids? Perils and profits of growing up gifted.* Chicago: Chicago Review Press.

Feldman, R., Weller, A., Zagoory-Sharon, O., & Levine, A. (2007). Evidence for a neuroendocrinological foundation of human affiliation. *Psychological Science, 18*, 965–970.

Feng, J., Spence, I., & Pratt, J. (2007). Playing an action video game reduces gender differences in spatial cognition. *Psychological Science, 18*, 850–855.

Fenson, L., Dale, P. S., Reznick, J. S., Bates, E., Thal, D. J., & Pethick, S. J. (1994). Variability in early communicative development. *Monographs of the Society for Research in Child Development, 59* (Serial No. 242).

Ferdenzi, C., Roberts, S. C., Schirmer, A., Delplanque, S., Cekic, S., Porcherot, C., et al. (2013). Variability of affective responses to odors: Culture, gender, and olfactory knowledge. *Chemical Senses, 38*, 175–186.

Ferguson, C. J. (2013). Violent video games and the Supreme Court. Lessons for the scientific community in the wake of Brown v. Entertainment Merchants Association. *American Psychologist, 68*, 57–74.

Ferguson, C. J., & Savage, J. (2012). Have recent studies addressed methodological issues raised by five decades of television violence research? A critical review. *Aggression and Violent Behavior, 17*, 129–139.

Fernald, A. (2009). Hearing, listening, and understanding: Auditory development in infancy. In J. G. Bremner & A. Fogel (Eds.), *Blackwell handbook of infant development* (pp. 35–70).Malden, MA: Blackwell publishing.

Ferrario, C. G., Freeman, F. J., Nellett, G., & Scheel, J. (2008). Changing nursing students' attitudes about aging: An argument for the successful aging paradigm. *Educational Gerontology, 34*, 51–66.

Fetal alcohol syndrome: Dashed hopes, damaged lives. (2011). *Bulletin World Health Organization* [online], 89, 398–399. Retrieved from http://www.scielosp.org/scielo php?script=sci_arttext&pid=S0042

Field, D. (1981). Can preschool children really learn to conserve? *Child Development, 52*, 326–334.

Field, D., & Gueldner, S. H. (2001). The oldest-old: How do they differ from the old-old? *Journal of Gerontological Nursing, 27*, 20–27.

Field, N. P. (2008). Whether to relinquish or maintain a bond with the deceased. In M. S. Stroebe, R. O. Hansson, H. Schut, & W. Stroebe (Eds.), *Handbook of bereavement research and practice. Advances in theory and intervention.* Washington, DC: American Psychological Association.

Field, N. P., & Filanosky, C. (2010). Continuing bonds, risk factors for complicated grief, and adjustment to bereavement. *Death Studies, 34,* 1–29.

Field, N. P., Nichols, C., Holen, A., & Horowitz, M. J. (1999). The relation of continuing attachment to adjustment in conjugal bereavement. *Journal of Consulting & Clinical Psychology, 67,* 212–218.

Field, T. (2011). Prenatal depression effects on early development: A review. *Infant Behavior and Development, 34,* 1–14.

Field, T. M. (1995). Infants of depressed mothers. *Infant Behavior and Development, 18,* 1–13.

Field, T., Diego, M. A., Hernandez-Reif, M., Deeds, O., & Figuereido, B. (2006). Moderate versus light pressure massage therapy leads to greater weight gain in preterm infants. *Infant Behavior and Development,* 574–578.

Field, T., Diego, M., & Hernandez-Reif, M. (2010). Preterm infant massage therapy research: A review. *Infant Behavior & Development, 33,* 115–124.

Fielder, R. L., & Carey, M. P. (2010). Predictors and consequences of sexual "hookups" among college students: A short-term prospective study. *Archives of Sexual Behavior, 39,* 1105–1119.

Fields-Meyer, T. (2011, December 13). Trivia is hardly trivial for my son. *The Washington Post,* pp. E1, E6.

Fifer, W. P., Monk, C. E., & Grose-Fifer, J. (2004). Prenatal development and risk. In G. Bremner & A. Fogel (Eds.), *Blackwell handbook of infant development* (pp. 505–542). Malden, MA: Blackwell Publishing.

Filipp, S. H. (1996). Motivation and emotion. In J. E. Birren, K. W. Schaie, R. P. Abeles, M. Gatz, & T. A. Salthouse (Eds.), *Handbook of the psychology of the aging* (4th ed.). San Diego: Academic Press.

Fincham, F. D. (2003). Marital conflict: Correlates, structure, and context. *Current Directions in Psychological Science, 12,* 23–27.

Fingerman, K. L., & Birditt, K. S. (2011). Relationships between adults and their aging parents. In K. W. Schaie & S. L. Willis (Eds.) B. G. Knight, B. Levy, & D. C. Park (Assoc. Eds.), *Handbook of the psychology of aging,* MA: Academic Press/Elsevier.

Finitzo, T., Gunnarson, A. D., & Clark, J. L. (1990). Auditory deprivation and early conductive hearing loss from otitis media. *Topics in Language Disorders, 11,* 29–42.

Finkel, D., & Reynolds, C. A. (2010). Cognitive and physical aging pathways: Contributions from behavioral genetics. In J. C. Cavanaugh & C. K. Cavanaugh (Eds.), *Aging in America: Vol. 2. Physical and mental health* (pp. 26–56). Santa Barbara, CA: ABC-CLIO.

Finkel, D., Pedersen, N. L., Reynolds, C. A., Berg, S., de Faire, U., & Svartengren, M. (2003). Genetic and environmental influences on decline in biobehavioral markers of aging. *Behavior Genetics, 33,* 107–123.

Finkel, E. J., Eastwick, P. W., Karney, B. R., Reis, H. T., & Sprecher, S. (2012). Online dating: A critical analysis from the perspective of psychological science. *Psychological Science in the Public Interest, 13,* 1–66.

Finkelhor, D. (2009). The prevention of childhood sexual abuse. *Future Children, 19,* 169–194.

Finkelhor, D., & Berliner, L. (1995). Research on the treatment of sexually abused children: A review and recommendations. *Journal of the American Academy of Child and Adolescent Psychiatry, 34,* 1408–1423.

Finkelhor, D., Turner, H., Ormrod, R., & Hamby, S. L. (2010). Trends in childhood violence and abuse exposure: Evidence from two national surveys. *Archives of Pediatric & Adolescent Medicine, 164,* 238–242.

Finkelstein, J. A., & Schiffman, S. S. (1999). Workshop on taste and smell in the elderly: An overview. *Physiological Behavior, 66,* 173–176.

Fischer, J. L., Sollie, D. L., Sorell, G. T., & Green, S. K. (1989). Marital status and career stage influences on social networks of young adults. *Journal of Marriage and the Family, 51,* 521–534.

Fischer, K. W. (1980). A theory of cognitive development: The control and construction of hierarchies of skills. *Psychological Review, 87,* 477–531.

Fischer, K. W., & Bidell, T. (1991). Constraining nativist inferences about cognitive capacities. In S. Carey & Gelman (Eds.), *The epigenesis of mind: Essays on biology and cognition.* Hillsdale, NJ: Erlbaum.

Fischer, K. W., & Bidell, T. R. (1998). Dynamic development of psychological structures in action and thought. In R. M. Lerner (Ed.), *Handbook of child psychology. Vol 1: Theoretical models of human development* (5th ed., pp. 467–561). New York: Wiley.

Fischer, K. W., & Pipp, S. L. (1984). Processes of cognitive development: Optimal level and skill acquisition. In R. J. Steinberg (Ed.), *Mechanisms of cognitive development* (pp. 45–80). San Francisco: Freeman.

Fischer, K. W., Kenny, S. L., & Pipp, S. L. (1990). How cognitive processes and environmental conditions organize discontinuities in the development of abstractions. In C. N. Alexander & E. J. Langer (Eds.), *Higher stages of human development: Perspectives on adult growth.* New York: Oxford University Press.

Fisher, E. P. (1992). The impact of play on development: A meta-analysis. *Play and Culture, 5,* 159–181.

Fisher, K. R., Marshall, P. J., & Nanayakkara, A. R. (2009). Motivational orientation, error monitoring, and academic performance in middle childhood: A behavioral and electrophysiological investigation. *Mind, Brain, and Education, 3,* 56–62.

Fischer, K. W., & Yan, Z. (2002). The Development of Dynamic Skill Theory. In R. Lickliter & D. Lewkowicz (Eds.), *Conceptions of development: Lessons from the laboratory.* Hove, UK: Psychology Press.

Fitness, J. (2013). The communication of emotion in families. In A. L. Vangelisti (Ed.), *The Routledge handbook of family communication.* New York: Routledge.

Fitzgerald, D.P. White, K. J. (2003). Linking children's social worlds: Perspective-taking in parent-child and peer contexts. *Social Behavior and Personality, 31,* 509–522.

Fitzgerald, J. M. (1999). Autobiographical memory and social cognition: Development of the remembered self in adulthood. In T. M. Hess & F. Blanchard-Fields (Eds.), *Social cognition and aging* (pp. 143–171). San Diego: Academic Press.

Fitzgerald, J. M., & Broadbridge, C. L. (2012). Theory and research in autobiographical memory: A life-span developmental perspective. In D. Berntsen & D. C. Rubin (Eds.), *Understanding autobiographical memory* (pp. 246–266). Cambridge, UK: Cambridge University Press.

Fitzpatrick, L. (2009, July 27). Brief history of China's One-Child Policy. *Time World.* http://www.time.com/time/world/article/0,8599,1912861,00.html

Fivush, R. (2009). Sociocultural perspectives on autobiographical memory. In M. L. Courage & N. Cowan (Eds.), *The development of memory in infancy and childhood* (pp. 283–302). New York: Psychology Press.

Fivush, R., Gray, J. T., & Fromhoff, F. A. (1987). Two-year-olds talk about the past. *Cognitive Development, 2,* 393–409.

Flaherty, J. H., & Morley, J. E. (2004). Delirium: A call to improve current standards of care. *Journal of Gerontology: Medical Sciences, 59A,* M341–M343.

Flavell, J. H. (1963). *The developmental psychology of Jean Piaget.* New York: Van Nostrand Reinhold.

Flavell, J. H. (1985). *Cognitive development* (2nd ed.). Englewood Cliffs, NJ: Prentice Hall.

Flavell, J. H. (1996). Piaget's legacy. *Psychological Science, 7,* 200–203.

Flavell, J. H. (1999). Cognitive development: Children's knowledge about the mind. *Annual Review of Psychology, 50,* 21–45.

Flavell, J. H., Beach, D. R., & Chinsky, J. M. (1966). Spontaneous verbal rehearsal in a memory task as a function of age. *Child Development, 37,* 283–299.

Flavell, J. H., Everett, B. H., Croft, K., & Flavell, E. R. (1981). Young children's knowledge about visual perception: Further evidence for the level 1– level 2 distinction. *Developmental Psychology, 17,* 99–103.

Flavell, J. H., Miller, P. H., & Miller, S. A. (1993). *Cognitive development.* Englewood Cliffs, NJ: Prentice Hall.

Fleeson, W. (2004). The quality of American life at the end of the century. In O. G. Brim, C. D. Ryff, & R. C. Kessler (Eds.), *How healthy are we? A national study of well-being at midlife.* Chicago: University of Chicago Press.

Fletcher, K. L., & Bray, N. W. (1996). External memory strategy use in preschool children. *Merrill-Palmer Quarterly, 42,* 379–396.

Flieller, A. (1999). Comparison of the development of formal thought in adolescent cohorts aged 10 to 15 years (1967–1996 and 1972–1993). *Developmental Psychology, 35,* 1048–1058.

Flook, L. (2011). Gender differences in adolescents' daily interpersonal events and well-being. *Child Development, 82,* 454–461.

Floor, P., & Akhtar, N. (2006). Can 18-month-old infants learn words by listening in on conversations? *Infancy, 9,* 327–339.

Flores, E., Cicchetti, D., & Rogosch, F. A. (2005). Predictors of resilience in maltreated and nonmaltreated Latino children. *Developmental Psychology, 41,* 338–351.

Florian, V., & Kravetz, S. (1985). Children's concepts of death. A cross-cultural comparison among Muslims, Druze, Christians, and Jews in Israel. *Journal of Cross-Cultural Psychology, 16,* 174–189.

Flum, H., & Blustein, D. L. (2000). Reinvigorating the study of vocational research. *Journal of Vocational Behavior, 56,* 380–404.

Flynn, J. R. (1987). Massive IQ gains in 14 nations: What IQ tests really measure. *Psychological Bulletin, 101,* 171–191.

Flynn, J. R. (1998). IQ gains over time: Toward finding the causes. In U. Neisser (Ed.), *The rising curve: Long-term gains in IQ and related measures.* Washington, DC: American Psychological Association.

Flynn, J. R. (1999). Search for justice: The discovery of IQ gains over time. *American Psychologist, 54,* 5–20.

Flynn, J. R. (2007). *What is intelligence?* New York: Cambridge University Press.

Flynn, J. R. (2011). Secular changes in intelligence. In R. J. Sternberg & S. B. Kaufman (Eds.), *The Cambridge handbook of intelligence* (pp. 647–665). New York: Cambridge University Press.

Flyvbjerg, B. (2011). Case study. In N. K. Denzin & Y. S. Lincoln (Eds.), *The sage handbook of qualitative research* (4th ed., pp. 301–316). Thousand Oaks, CA: Sage.

Fogassi, L., & Ferrari, P. F. (2007). Mirror neurons and the evolution of embodied language. *Current Directions in Psychological Science, 17,* 136–141.

Foley, E. P. (2011). *The law of life and death.* Cambridge, MA: Harvard University Press.

Foley, K., & Hendin, H. (2002). Conclusion: Changing the culture. In K. Foley, & H. Hendin (Eds.), *The case against assisted suicide: For the right to end-of-life care.* Baltimore: The Johns Hopkins Press.

Fong, L.S., Visser, J. A., Welt, C. K., de Rijke, Y. B., Eijkemans, M. J. C., Broekmans, F. J., Roes, E. M., Peters, W. H. M., Hokken-Koelega, A. C. S., Fauser, B. C. J. M., Themmen, A. P. N., de Jong, F. H., Schipper, I., Laven, J. S. E. (2012).Serum anti-Müllerian hormone levels in healthy females: A nomogram ranging from infancy to adulthood. *Journal of Clinical Endocrinology & Metabolism, 97,* 4650–4655.

Fontaine, N. M. G., McCrory, E. J. P., Boivin, M., Moffitt, T. E., & Viding, E. (2011). Predictors and outcomes of joint trajectories of callous–unemotional traits and conduct problems in childhood. *Journal of Abnormal Psychology, 120,* 730–742.

Foorman, B. R. (1995). Research on "The Great Debate": Code-oriented versus whole language approaches to reading instruction. *School Psychology Review, 24,* 376–392.

Foorman, B. R., Francis, D. J., Fletcher, J. M., Schatschneider, C., & Mehta, P. (1998). The role of instruction in learning to read: Preventing reading failure in at-risk children. *Journal of Educational Psychology, 90,* 37–55.

Foos, P. W., & Sarno, S. J. (1998). Adult age differences in semantic and episodic memory. *Journal of Genetic Psychology, 159,* 297–312.

Ford, E. S., Kohl, H. W., Mokdad, A. H., & Ajani, U. A. (2005). Sedentary behavior, physical activity, and the metabolic syndrome among U.S. adults. *Obesity Research, 13,* 608–614.

Ford, T., Goodman, R., & Meltzer, H. (2003). The British child and adolescent mental health survey 1999: The prevalence of DSM-IV disorders. *Journal of the American Academy of Child and Adolescent Psychiatry, 42,* 1203–1211.

Fordham, S., & Ogbu, J. U. (1986). Black students' school success: Coping with the "burden of 'acting white.'". *Urban Review, 18,* 176–206.

Forgatch, M. S., & DeGarmo, D. S. (1999). Parenting through change: An effective prevention program for single mothers. *Journal of Consulting and Clinical Psychology, 67,* 711–724.

Foster, J. D. (2008). Beauty is mostly in the eye of the beholder: Olfactory versus visual cues of attractiveness. *Journal of Social Psychology, 148,* 765–773.

Fouquereau, E., Fernandez, A., Fonseca, A. M., Paul, M. C., & Uotinen, V. (2005). Perceptions of and satisfaction with retirement: A comparison of six European Union countries. *Psychology and Aging, 20,* 524–528.

Fouts, H. N., Hewlett, B. S., & Lamb, M. E. (2012). A biocultural approach to breastfeeding interactions in Central Africa. *American Anthropologist, 114,* 123–136.

Fowler, J. W. (1981). *Stages of faith: The psychology of human development and the quest for meaning.* San Francisco: Harper & Row.

Fowler, J., & Dell, M. (2006). Stages of faith from infancy through adolescence: Reflections on three decades of faith development theory. In E. Roehlkepartain, P. King, L. Wagener, & P. Benson (Eds.), *The handbook of spiritual development in childhood and adolescence.* Thousand Oaks, CA: Sage.

Fowles, D. C., & Kochanska, G. (2000). Temperament as a moderator of pathways to conscience in children: The contribution of electrodermal activity. *Psychophysiology, 37,* 788–795.

Fox, M. K., Dodd, A. H., Wilson, A., & Gleason, P. M. (2009). Association between school food environment and practices and body mass index of U.S. public school children. *Journal of the American Dietetic Association, 109,* S108–117.

Fox, N. A., Henderson, H. A., Marshall, P. J., Nichols, K. E., & Ghera, M. M. (2005). Behavioral inhibition: Linking biology and behavior within a developmental framework. *Annual Review of Psychology, 56,* 235–262.

Fox, N. A., Henderson, H. A., Rubin, K. H., Calkins, S. D., & Schmidt, L. A. (2001). Continuity and discontinuity of behavioral inhibition and exuberance: Psychophysiological and behavioral influences across the first four years of life. *Child Development, 72,* 1–21.

Fox, S. E., Levitt, P., & Nelson, C. A. (2010). How the timing and quality of early experiences influence the development of brain architecture. *Child Development, 81,* 28–40.

Fozard, J. L., & Gordon-Salant, T. (2001). Changes in vision and hearing with aging. In J. E. Birren & K. W. Schaie (Eds.), *Handbook of the psychology of aging* (5th ed., pp. 241–266). San Diego: Academic Press.

Fraley, R. C., & Shaver, P. R. (2008). Attachment theory and its place in contemporary personality theory. In O. P. John, R. W. Robins, & L. A. Pervin (Eds.), *Handbook of personality theory and research* (3rd ed.). New York: Guilford.

Fraley, R. C., Fazzari, D. A., Bonanno, G. A., & Dekel, S. (2006). Attachment and psychological adaptation in high exposure survivors of the September 11th attack on the World Trade Center. *Personality and Social Psychology Bulletin, 32,* 538–551.

Fraley, R. C., Roisman, G. I., Booth-LaForce, C., Owen, M. T., & Holland, A. S. (2013). Interpersonal and genetic origins of adult attachment styles: A longitudinal study from infancy to early adulthood. *Journal of Personality and Social Psychology, 104,* 817–838.

Franchak, J. M., Kretch, K. S., Soska, K. C., & Adolph, K. E. (2011). Head-mounted eye tracking: A new method to describe infant looking. *Child Development, 82,* 1738–1750.

Francis, E. (2012, June 4). M.D. at 21, Sho Yano is real-life 'Doogie Howser.' *ABCNews.* Retrieved from http://abcnews.go.com/blogs/headlines/2012/06/m-d-at-21-sho-yano-is-real-life-doogie-howser/.

Frank, S. M., Raja, S. N., Bulcao, C., & Goldstein, D. S. (2000). Age-related thermoregulatory differences during core cooling in humans. *American Journal of Physiological Regulation, Integration, and Comparative Physiology, 279,* R349–354.

Franke, B., Neale, B. M., & Faraone, S. V. (2009). Genome-wide association studies in ADHD. *Human Genetics, 126,* 13–50.

Franklin, Z., Pilling, M., & Davies, I. (2005). The nature of infant color categorization: Evidence from eye movements on a target detection task. *Journal of Experimental Child Psychology, 91,* 227–248.

Franko, D. L., & Goerge, J. B. E. (2009). Overweight, eating behaviors, and body image in ethnically diverse youth. In L. Smolak & J. K. Thompson (Eds.), *Body image, eating disorders, and obesity in youth.* Washington, DC: American Psychological Association.

Frans, E. M., McGrath, J. J., Sandin, S., Lichtenstein, P., Reichenberg, A., Långström, N., et al. (2011). Advanced paternal and grandpaternal age and schizophrenia: A three-generation perspective. *Schizophrenia Research, 133,* 120–124.

Fraser, S. L., Muckle, G., Abdous, B. B., Jacobson, J. L., & Jacobson, S. W. (2012). Effects of binge drinking on infant growth and development in an Inuit sample. *Alcohol, 46,* 277–283.

Frawley, W. (1997). *Vygotsky and cognitive science: Language and the unification of the social and computational mind*. Cambridge, MA: Harvard University Press.

Frederick, D. A., Peplau, L. A., & Lever, J. (2006). The swimsuit issue: Correlates of body image in a sample of 52,677 heterosexual adults. *Body Image, 3*, 413–419.

Freedman, D. H. (2012, June). The perfected self. *The Atlantic, 309*, 42–52.

Freeman, S. F. N. (2000). Academic and social attainments of children with mental retardation in general education and special education settings. *Remedial and Special Education, 21*, 3–19.

Freud, S. (1930). *Three contributions to the theory of sex*. New York: Nervous and Mental Disease Publishing Company. (Original work published 1905).

Freud, S. (1960). *A general introduction to psychoanalysis*. New York: Washington Square Press. (Original work published 1935).

Freund, A., & Riediger, M. (2006). Goals as building blocks of personality and development in adulthood. In D. K. Mroczek & T. D. Little (Eds.), *Handbook of personality development*. Mahwah, NJ: Erlbaum.

Freund, A. M., & Ritter, J. O. (2009). Midlife crisis: A debate. *Gerontology, 55*, 582–591.

Freund, L. S. (1990). Maternal regulation of children's problem solving behavior and its impact on children's performance. *Child Development, 61*, 113–126.

Frey, K. S., & Ruble, D. N. (1985). What children say when the teacher is not around: Conflicting goals in social comparison and performance assessment in the classroom. *Journal of Personality and Social Psychology, 48*, 550–562.

Frey, K. S., & Ruble, D. N. (1992). Gender constancy and the cost of sex-typed behavior: A test of the conflict hypothesis. *Developmental Psychology, 28*, 714–721.

Freyd, J. J., Putnam, F. W., Lyon, T. D., Becker-Blease, K. A., Cheit, R. E., Siegel, N. B., et al. (2005). The science of child sexual abuse. *Science, 308*, 501.

Friedlmeier, W., Corapci, F., & Cole, P. M. (2011). Emotion socialization in cross-cultural perspective. *Social and Personality Psychology Compass, 5*, 410–427.

Friedman, J. M., & Polifka, J. E. (2000). *Teratogenic effects of drugs: A resource for clinicians (TERIS)*. Baltimore, MD: Johns Hopkins University Press.

Friedman, S. L., & Boyle, D. E. (2008). Attachment in US children experiencing nonmaternal care in the early 1990s. *Attachment and Human Development, 10*, 225–261.

Frieswijk, N., Buunk, B. P., Steverink, N., & Slaets, J. P. J. (2004). The effect of social comparison information on the life satisfaction of frail older persons. *Psychology and Aging, 19*, 183–190.

Froehlich, T. E., Lanphear, B. P., Epstein, J. N., Barbaresi, W. J., Katusic, S. K., & Kahn, R. S. (2007). Prevalence, recognition, and treatment of attention-deficit/hyperactivity disorder in a national sample of US children. *Archives of Pediatric & Adolescent Medicine, 161*, 857–864.

Fry, P. S. (1992). Major social theories of aging and their implications for counseling concepts and practice: A critical review. *Counseling Psychologist, 20*, 246–329.

Fry, P. S. (1997). Grandparents' reactions to the death of a grandchild: An exploratory factor analytic study. *Omega: Journal of Death and Dying, 35*, 119–140.

Fryar, C.D., Gu, Q., & Ogden, C,L. (2012). Anthropometric reference data for children and adults: United States, 2007–2010. National Center for Health Statistics. Vital Health Statistics, 11(252).

Fuglenes, D., Aas, E., Botten, G., Øian, P., & Kristiansen, I. S. (2012). Maternal preference for cesarean delivery: Do women get what they want? *Obstetrics and Gynecology, 120*, 252–260.

Fuligni, A. J. (1998). Authority, autonomy, and parent–adolescent conflict and cohesion: A study of adolescents from Mexican, Chinese, Filipino, and European backgrounds. *Developmental Psychology, 34*, 782–792.

Fuller, S. (2008). Job mobility and wage trajectories for men and women in the United States. *American Sociological Review, 73*, 158–183.

Furman, E. (1984). Children's patterns in mourning the death of a loved one. In H. Wass & C. A. Corr (Eds.), *Childhood and death*. Washington, DC: Hemisphere.

Furman, W., & Buhrmester, D. (1992). Age and sex differences in perceptions of networks of personal relationships. *Child Development, 63*, 103–115.

Furman, W., & Collins, W. A. (2009). Adolescent romantic relationships and experiences. In K. H. Rubin, W. M. Bukowski, & B. Laursen (Eds.), *Handbook of peer interactions, relationships, and groups*. New York: Guilford.

Gage, F. H., Song, H., & Kempermann, G. (2008). Adult neurogenesis: A prologue. In F. H. Gage, G. Kempermann, & H. Song (Eds.), *Adult neurogenesis* (pp. 1–6). New York: Cold Spring Harbor Laboratory Press.

Gagnon, M. D., Hersen, M., Kabacoff, R. I., & Vanhasselt, V. B. (1999). Interpersonal and psychological correlates of marital dissatisfaction in late life: A review. *Clinical Psychology Review, 19*, 359–378.

Galambos, N. L., Almeida, D. M., & Petersen, A. C. (1990). Masculinity, femininity, and sex role attitudes in early adolescence: Exploring gender intensification. *Child Development, 61*, 1905–1914.

Galatzer-Levy, I., & Bonanno, G. A. (2012). Beyond normality in the study of bereavement: Heterogeneity in depression outcomes following loss in older adults. *Social Science & Medicine, 74*, 1987–1994.

Galatzer-Levy, I., Mazursky, H., Mancini, A. D., & Bonanno, G. A. (2011). What we don't expect when expecting: Evidence for heterogeneity in subjective well-being in response to parenthood. *Journal of Family Psychology, 25*, 384–392.

Galdo-Alvarez, S., Lindin, M., & Diaz, F. (2009). Age-related prefrontal over-recruitment in semantic memory retrieval: Evidence from successful face naming and the tip-of-the-tongue state. *Biological Psychology, 82*, 89–96.

Gallagher-Thompson, D., & Coon, D. W. (2007). Evidence-based psychological treatments for distress in family caregivers of older adults. *Psychology and Aging, 22*, 37–51.

Gallese, V., Rochat, M. J., & Berchio, C. (2013). The mirror mechanism and its potential role in autism spectrum disorder. *Developmental Medicine & Child Neurology, 55*, 15–22.

Gallup, G. G., Jr. (1979). Self-recognition in chimpanzees and man: A developmental and comparative perspective. In M. Lewis & L. A. Rosenblum (Eds.), *Genesis of behavior: Vol. 2. The child and its family*. New York: Plenum.

Galupo, M. P., Cartwright, K. B., & Savage, L. S. (2009, December 16). Cross-category friendships and postformal thought among college students. *Journal of Adult Development*. Springer Netherlands: Published online.

Galvan, A. (2010). Adolescent development of the reward system. *Frontiers of Human Neuroscience, 4*, 6.

Galvan, A., Hare, T., Voss, H., Gover, G., & Casey, B. J. (2007). Risk-taking and the adolescent brain: Who is at risk? *Developmental Science, 10*, F8–F14.

Gamé, F., Carchon, I., & Vital-Durand, F. (2003). The effect of stimulus attractiveness on visual tracking in 2- to 6-month-old infants. *Infant Behavior & Development, 26*, 135–150.

Ganahl, D. J., Prinsen, T. J., & Netzley, S. B. (2003). A content analysis of prime time commercials: A contextual framework of gender representation. *Sex Roles, 49*, 545–551.

Gandy, S., & DeKosky, S. T. (2013). 2012: The year in dementia.*Lancet Neurology, 12*, 4–6.

Gannon, L., & Ekstrom, B. (1993). Attitudes toward menopause: The influence of sociocultural paradigms. *Psychology of Women Quarterly, 17*, 275–288.

Garber, H. L. (1988). *The Milwaukee Project: Preventing Mental Retardation in Children At Risk*. Washington, D.C.: American Association on Mental Retardation

Garber, J. (1984). The developmental progression of depression in female children. In D. Cicchetti & K. Schneider-Rosen (Eds.), *Childhood depression* (New Directions for Child Development, No. 26). San Francisco: Jossey-Bass.

Garber, J. (2010). Vulnerability to depression in childhood and adolescence.In R. E. Ingram & J. M. Price (2010). *Vulnerability to psychopathology. Risk across the lifespan* (2nded.). New York: Guilford.

Garber, J., & Flynn, C. (2001). Vulnerability to depression in childhood and adolescence. In R. E. Ingram & J. M. Price (Eds.), *Vulnerability to psychopathology. Risk across the life-span*. New York: Guilford.

Garces, E., Thomas, D., & Currie, J. (2002). Longer term effects of Head Start. *American Economic Review, 92*, 999–1102.

Garcia, F., & Gracia, E. (2009). Is always authoritative the optimum parenting style? Evidence from Spanish families. *Adolescence, 44*, 101–131.

Garcia, J. R., Reiber, C., Massey, S. G., & Merriwether, A. M. (2012). Sexual hookup culture: A review. *Review of General Psychology, 16*, 161–176.

Garciaguirre, J. S., Adolph, K. E., & Shrout, P. E. (2007). Baby carriage: Infants walking with loads. *Child Development, 78*, 664–680.

Garcy, A. M., & Vågerö, D. (2012). The length of unemployment predicts mortality, differently in men and women, and by cause of death: A six year mortality follow-up of the Swedish 1992–1996 recession. *Social Science & Medicine, 74*, 1911–1920.

Gardener, H., Spiegelman, D., & Buka, S. L. (2009). Prenatal risk factors for autism: Comprehensive meta-analysis. *British Journal of Psychiatry, 195*, 7–14.

Gardner, H. (1993a). *Creating minds: An anatomy of creativity as seen through the lives of Freud, Einstein, Picasso, Stravinsky, Eliot, Graham, and Gandhi*. New York: Basic Books.

Gardner, H. (1993b). *Frames of mind: The theory of multiple intelligences* (Tenth anniversary ed.). New York: Basic Books.

Gardner, H. (1999/2000). *Intelligence reframed: Multiple intelligences for the 21st century*. New York: Basic Books.

Gardner, M., & Steinberg, L. (2005). Peer influence on risk taking, risk preference, and risky decision making in adolescence and adulthood: An experimental study. *Developmental Psychology, 41*, 625–635.

Gardner, P., Katagiri, K., Parsons, J., Lee, J., & Thevannoor, R. (2012). "Not for the fainthearted": Engaging in cross-national comparative research. *Journal of Aging Studies, 26*, 253–261.

Gardner, R. J. M., Sutherland, G. R., & Shaffer, L. G. (Eds.). (2012). *Chromosome abnormalities and genetic counseling* (4th ed.). New York: Oxford University Press.

Garmezy, N. (1994). Reflections and commentary on risk, resilience, and development. In R. J. Haggerty, L. R. Sherrod, N. Garmezy, & M. Rutter (Eds.), *Stress, risk and resilience in children and adolescents: Processes, mechanisms, and interventions*. Cambridge, UK: Cambridge University Press.

Garvey, C. (1990). *Play* (enlarged ed.). Cambridge, MA: Harvard University Press.

Gatz, M. (2007). Genetics, dementia, and the elderly. *Current Directions in Psychological Science, 16*, 123–127.

Gatz, M., Svedberg, P., Pedersen, N. L., Mortimer, J. A., Berg, S., & Johansson, B. (2001). Education and the risk of Alzheimer's disease: Findings from the study of dementia in Swedish twins. *Journal of Gerontology: Psychological Sciences, 56B*, 292–300.

Gauvain, M., & Rogoff, B. (1989). Collaborative problem-solving and children's planning skills. *Developmental Psychology, 25*, 139–151.

Gavin, N., Gaynes, B., Lohr, K., Meltzer-Brody, S., Gartlehner, G., & Swinson, T. (2005). Perinatal depression: A systematic review of prevalence and incidence. *Obstetrics and Gynecology, 106*, 1071–1083.

Gazzaniga, M. S. (1998). The split brain revisited. *Scientific American, 279*, 50–55.

Ge, X., Best, K. M., Conger, R. D., & Simons, R. L. (1996). Parenting behaviors and the occurrence and co-occurrence of adolescent depressive symptoms and conduct problems. *Developmental Psychology, 32*, 717–731.

Ge, X., Kim, I. J., Brody, G. H., Conger, R. D., Simons, R. L., Gibbons, F. X., & Cutrona, C. E. (2003). It's about timing and change: Pubertal transition effects on symptoms of major depression among African American youths. *Developmental Psychology, 39*, 430–439.

Ge, X., Lorenz, F. O., Conger, R. D., Elder, G. H., Jr., & Simons, R. L. (1994). Trajectories of stressful life events and depressive symptoms during adolescence. *Developmental Psychology, 30*, 467–483.

Ge, X., Natsuki, M. N., & Conger, R. D. (2006). Trajectories of depressive symptoms and stressful life events among male and female adolescents in divorced and nondivorced families. *Development and Psychopathology, 18*, 253–273.

Geda, Y. E., Silber, T. C., Roberts, R. O., Knopman, D. S., Christianson, T. J. H., Pankratz, V. S., et al. (2012). Computer activities, physical exercise, aging, and mild cognitive impairment: A population-based study. *Mayo Clinic Proceedings, 87*, 437–442.

Geithner, C. A., Satake, T., Woynarowska, B., & Malina, R. M. (1999). Adolescent spurts in body dimensions: Average and modal sequences. *American Journal of Human Biology, 11*, 287–295.

Geldmacher, D. S. (2009). Alzheimer disease. In M. F. Weiner & A. M. Lipton (Eds.), *The American Psychiatric Publishing textbook of Alzheimer disease and other dementias*. Washington, DC: American Psychiatric Publishing.

Gelman, R. (1978). Cognitive development. *Annual Review of Psychology, 29*, 297–332.

Gelman, R. S. (1972). Logical capacity of very young children: Number invariance rules. *Child Development, 43*, 75–90.

Gelman, S. A. (1996). Concepts and theories. In R. Gelman & T. K. Au (Eds.), *Perceptual and cognitive development*. San Diego: Academic Press.

George, L. G., Helson, R., & John, O. P. (2011). The "CEO" of women's work lives: How Big Five conscientiousness, extraversion, and openness predict 50 years of work experiences in a changing sociocultural context. *Journal of Personality and Social Psychology, 101*, 812–830.

Georges, J., Onwuteaka-Philipsen, B. D., Muller, M. T., van der Wal, G., van der Heide, A., & van der Maas, P. J. (2007). Relatives' perspective on the terminally ill patients who died after euthanasia or physician-assisted suicide: A retrospective cross-sectional interview study in the Netherlands. *Death Studies, 31*, 1–15.

Gershoff, E. T. (2008). *Report on physical punishment in the United States: What research tells us about its effects on children*. Columbus, OH: Center for Effective Discipline. Retrieved from The Center for Effective Discipline website: http://www.phoenixchildrens.com/community/injury-prevention-center/effective-discipline.html

Gerstein, E. D., Crnic, K. A., Blacher, J., & Baker, B. L. (2009). Resilience and the course of daily parenting stress in families of young children with intellectual disabilities. *Journal of Intellectual Disability Research, 53*, 981–997.

Gerstorf, D., Hoppmann, C. A., Kadlec, K. M., & McArdle, J. J. (2009). Memory and depressive symptoms are dynamically linked among married couples: Longitudinal evidence from the AHEAD study. *Developmental Psychology, 45*, 1595–1610.

Gervain, J., & Mehler, J. (2010). Speech perception and language acquisition in the first year of life. *Annual Review of Psychology, 61*, 191–218.

Gest, S. D., Graham-Bermann, S. A., & Hartup, W. W. (2001). Peer experience: Common and unique features of number of friendships, social network centrality, and sociometric status. *Social Development, 10*, 23–40.

Getzels, J. W., & Jackson, P. W. (1962). *Creativity and intelligence: Explorations with gifted children*. New York: Wiley.

Ghetti, S., Lyons, K. E., & Cornoldi, C. (2008). The development of metamemory monitoring during retrieval: The case of memory strength and memory absence. *Journal of Experimental Child Psychology, 99*, 157–181.

Giarrusso, R., Feng, D., Silverstein, M., & Bengtson, V. L. (2000). Self in the context of the family. In K. W. Schaie & J. Hendrick (Eds.), *The evolution of the aging self. The societal impact on the aging process*. New York: Springer.

Gibbs, J. C. (2010). *Moral development and reality. Beyond the theories of Kohlberg and Hoffman* (2nd ed.). Boston, MA: Allyn & Bacon.

Gibbs, J. C., Basinger, K. S., Grime, R. L., & Snarey, J. R. (2007). Moral judgment development across cultures: Revisiting Kohlberg's universality claims. *Developmental Review, 27*, 443–500.

Gibbs, N. (2009, August 3). Dying together. An elderly British couple's suicide pact is a beautifully romantic act—and a troubling one. *Time, 64*.

Gibson, E. J. (1988). Exploratory behavior in the development of perceiving, acting, and the acquiring of knowledge. *Annual Review of Psychology, 39*, 1–41.

Gibson, E. J. (2001). *Perceiving the affordances: A portrait of two psychologists*. Mahwah, NJ: Lawrence Erlbaum Associates.

Gibson, E. J., & Pick, A. D. (2000). *An ecological approach to perceptual learning and development*. New York: Oxford University Press.

Gibson, E. J., & Walk, R. D. (1960). The "visual cliff." *Scientific American, 202*, 67–71.

Gibson, J. J. (1966). *The senses considered as perceptual systems*. Boston: Houghton Mifflin.

Gibson, J. J. (1979). *The ecological approach to visual perception*. Hillsdale: Lawrence Erlbaum Associates.

Giedd, J. N. (2004). Structural magnetic resonance imaging of the adolescent brain. *Annals of the New York Academic of Sciences, 1021*, 77–85.

Giedd, J. N., Adeyemi, E., Stockman, M., Alexander-Block, A., Lee, N. R., Raznahan, A., Lenroot, R. K., & Kruesi, M. J. P. (2013). Neuroanatomic maturation and aggression during adolescence. In C. R. Thomas & K. Pope (Eds.), *The origins of antisocial behavior: A developmental perspective*. New York: Oxford University Press.

Gifted Development Center. (2013). *Characteristics of giftedness*. Retrieved from http://www .gifteddevelopment.com/What_is_Gifted/ characgt.htm

Gil, D. G. (1970). *Violence against children*. Cambridge, MA: Harvard University Press.

Gillberg, C., Cederlund, M., Lamberg, K., & Zeijlon, L. (2006). "The autism epidemic." The registered prevalence of autism in a Swedish urban area. *Journal of Autism and Developmental Disorders, 36*, 429–435.

Gillen-O'Neel, C., Huynh, V. W., & Fuligni, A. J. (2013). To study or to sleep? The academic costs of extra studying at the expense of sleep. Child Development, 84, 133–142.

Ginsburg, G. S., & Bronstein, P. (1993). Family factors related to children's intrinsic/extrinsic motivational orientation and academic performance. *Child Development, 64*, 1461–1474.

Ginzberg, E. (1972). Toward a theory of occupational choice: A restatement. *Vocational Guidance Quarterly, 20*, 169–176.

Ginzberg, E. (1984). Career development. In D. Brown, L. Brooks, & Associates (Eds.), *Career choice and development*. San Francisco: Jossey-Bass.

Giordano, P. C. (2003). Relationships in adolescence. *Annual Review of Sociology, 29*, 257–281.

Girard, C. (1993). Age, gender, and suicide: A cross-national analysis. *American Sociological Review, 58*, 553–574.

Givens, J. L., & Mitchell, S. L. (2009). Concerns about end-of-life care and support for euthanasia. *Journal of Pain and Symptom Management, 38*, 167–173.

Glascock, A. (2009). Is killing necessarily murder? Moral questions surrounding assisted suicide and death. In J. Sokolovsky (Ed.), *The cultural context of aging* (3rd ed.). Westport, CT: Praeger.

Glascock, J. (2001). Gender roles on prime-time network television: Demographics and behaviors. *Journal of Broadcasting & Electronic Media, 45*, 656–669.

Glaser, B. G., & Strauss, A. L. (1968). *Time for dying*. Chicago: Aldine.

Glaser, R., & Chi, M. T. H. (1988). Overview. In M. T. H. Chi, R. Glaser, & M. Farr (Eds.), *The nature of expertise*. Hillsdale, NJ: Erlbaum.

Glasgow, K. L., Dornbusch, S. M., Troyer, L., Steinberg, L., & Ritter, P. L. (1997). Parenting styles, adolescents' attributions, and educational outcomes in nine heterogeneous high schools. *Child Development, 68*, 507–529.

Glatt, S. J., Tsuang, M. T., Winn, M., Chandler, S. D., Collins, M., Lopez, L., et al. (2012). Blood-based gene expression signatures of infants and toddlers with autism. *Journal of the American Academy of Child and Adolescent Psychiatry, 51*, 934–944.

Gleason, P. M., & Dodd, A. H. (2009). School breakfast program but not school lunch program participation is associated with lower body mass index. *Journal of the American Dietetic Association, 109*, S118–S128.

Glenberg, A. M. (2011). Positions in the mirror are closer than they appear. *Perspectives on Psychological Science, 6*, 408–410.

Glick, J. C. (1975). Cognitive development in cross-cultural perspective. In F. Horowitz (Ed.), *Review of child development research* (Vol. 1). Chicago: University of Chicago Press.

Glick, M., & Zigler, E. (1985). Self-image: A cognitive developmental approach. In R. L. Leahy (Ed.), *The Development of the self*. Orlando, FL: Academic Press.

Gloth, F. M. (2000). Geriatric pain: Factors that limit pain relief and increase complications. *Geriatrics, 55*, 51–54.

Glover, J. A., Galliher, R. V., &Lamere, T. G. (2009). Identity development and exploration among sexual minority adolescents: Examination of a multidimensional model. *Journal of Homosexuality, 56*, 77–101.

Glover, V. (2011). Prenatal stress and the origins of psychopathology: An evolutionary perspective. *Journal of Child Psychology and Psychiatry, 52*, 356–367.

Glowinski, A. L., Madden, P. A. F., Bucholz, K. K., Lynskey, M. T., & Heath, A. C. (2003). Genetic epidemiology of self-reported lifetime DSM-IV major depressive disorder in a population-based twin sample of female adolescents. *Journal of Child Psychology and Psychiatry and Allied Disciplines, 44*, 988–996.

Gluckman, P. D., & Hanson, M. A. (2006). Evolution, development and timing of puberty. *Trends in Endocrinology and Metabolism, 17*, 7–12.

Gnepp, J., & Chilamkurti, C. (1988). Children's use of personality attributions to predict other people's emotional and behavioral reactions. *Child Development, 59*, 743–754.

Godar, S. P., Grieco, T. M., & Litovsky, R. Y. (2007, April). *Emergence of bilateral abilities in children who transition from using one to two cochlear implants*. Presented at the 11th International Cochlear Implant Conference, Charlotte, NC.

Goh, J. O., Chee, M. W., Tan, J. C., Venkatraman, V., Hebrank, A., Leshikar, E. D., et al. (2007). Age and culture modulate object processing and object-scene binding in the ventral visual area. Cognitive, Affective, & Behavioral Neuroscience, 7, 44–52.

Gohlke, B., & Woelfle, J. (2009). Growth and puberty in German children: Is there still a positive secular trend? *Deutsches Ärzteblatt International, 106*, 377–382.

Goldberg, A. E. (2009). *Lesbian and gay parents and their children: Research on the family life cycle*. Washington, DC: American Psychological Association.

Goldberg, A. E., & Perry-Jenkins, M. (2007). The division of labor and perceptions of parental roles: Lesbian couples across the transition to parenthood. *Journal of Social and Personal Relationships, 24*, 297–318.

Goldberg, A. P., & Hagberg, J. M. (1990). Physical exercise in the elderly. In E. L. Schneider & J. W. Rowe (Eds.), *Handbook of the biology of aging* (3rd ed.). San Diego: Academic Press.

Goldberg, S. (1983). Parent-infant bonding: Another look. *Child Development, 54*, 1355–1382.

Goldfield, G. S., Adamo, K. B., Rutherford, J., & Murray, M. (2012). The effects of aerobic exerciese on psychosocial functioning of adolescents who are overweight or obese. *Journal of Pediatric Psychology, 37*, 1136–1147.

Goldfine, A. M., Bardin, J. C., Noirhomme, Q., Fins, J. J., Schiff, N. D., & Victor, J. D. (2013). Reanalysis of 'bedside detection of awareness in the vegetative state: A cohort study'. *The Lancet, 381*(9863), 289–291.

Goldhaber, D. (2012). *The nature-nurture debates: Bridging the gap*. New York: Cambridge University Press.

Goldin-Meadow, S. (2009). From gesture to word. In E. L. Bavin (Ed.), *The Cambridge handbook of child language* (pp. 145–160). New York: Cambridge University Press.

Goldman, D. (2012). *Our genes, our choices. How genotype and gene interactions affect behavior*. Waltham, MA: Academic Press.

Goldman, S. (2008). Neurogenesis in the adult songbird: A model for inducible striatal neuronal addition. In F. H. Gage, G. Kempermann, & H. Song (Eds.), *Adult neurogenesis* (pp. 593–617). New York: Cold Spring Harbor Laboratory Press.

Goldschmidt, L., Richardson, G. A., Cornelius, M. D., & Day, N. L. (2004). Prenatal marijuana and alcohol exposure and academic achievement at age 10. *Neurotoxicology& Teratology, 26*, 521–532.

Goldsmith, H. H. (2003). Genetics of emotional development. In R. J. Davidson, K. R. Scherer, & H. H. Goldsmith (Eds.), *Handbook of affective sciences*. New York: Oxford University Press.

Goldstein, E. B. (2007). *Sensation and perception* (7th ed.). Belmont, CA: Wadsworth.

Goldstein, M. H., Schwade, J. A., & Bornstein, M. H. (2009). The value of vocalizing: Five-month-old infants associate their own noncry vocalizations with responses from caregivers. *Child Development, 80*, 636–644.

Goldstein, S. E., Davis-Kean, P. E., & Eccles, J. S. (2005). Parents, peers, and problem behavior: A longitudinal investigation of the impact of relationship perceptions and characteristics on the development of adolescent problem behavior. *Developmental Psychology, 41*, 401–413.

Goldstein, S., & Reynolds, C. R. (Eds.). (2011). *Handbook of neurodevelopmental and genetic disorders in children* (2nd ed.). New York: Guilford.

Goldwater, O. D., & Nutt, R. L. (1999). Teachers' and students' work-culture variables associated with positive school outcome. *Adolescence, 34*, 653–664.

Golinkoff, R. M., & Hirsh-Pasek, K. (2006). Baby wordsmith: From associationist to social sophisticate. *Current Directions in Psychological Science, 15*, 30–33.

Golombok, S., Perry, B., Burston, A., Murray, C., Mooney-Somers, J., Stevens, M., & Golding, J. (2003). Children with lesbian parents: A community study. *Developmental Psychology, 39*, 20–33.

Golombok, S., Rust, J., Zervoulis, K., Golding, J., & Hines, M. (2012). Continuity in sex-typed behavior from preschool to adolescence: A longitudinal population study of boys and girls aged 3–13 years. *Archives of Sexual Behavior, 41*, 591–597.

Gonzaga, G. C., Campos, B., & Bradbury, T. (2007). Similarity, convergence, and relationship satisfaction in dating and married couples. *Journal of Personality and Social Psychology, 93*, 34–48.

Good, C., Aronson, J., & Inzlicht, M. (2003). Improving adolescents' standardized test performance: An intervention to reduce the effects of stereotype threat. *Journal of Applied Developmental Psychology, 24*, 645–662.

Good, M., & Willoughby, T. (2008). Adolescence as a sensitive period for spiritual development. *Child Development Perspectives, 2*, 32–37.

Goodlett, C. R., & Horn, K. H. (2001). Mechanisms of alcohol-induced damage to the developing nervous system. *Alcohol Research & Health, 25*, 175–184.

Goodluck, H. (2009). Formal and computational constraints on language development. In E. Hoff & M. Shatz (Eds.), *Blackwell handbook of language development* (pp. 46–67). Malden, MA: Wiley-Blackwell.

Gooren, L. (2006). The biology of human psychosexual differentiation. *Hormonal Behavior, 50*, 589–601.

Gopnik, A. (1996). The post-Piaget era. *Psychological Science, 7*, 221–225.

Gopnik, A., & Choi, S. (1995). Names, relational words, and cognitive development in English and Korean speakers: Nouns are not always learned before verbs. In M. Tomasello & W. E. Merriman (Eds.), *Beyond names for things: Young children's acquisition of verbs* (pp. 83–90). Hillsdale, NJ: Erlbaum.

Gorchoff, S. M., John, O. P., & Helson, R. (2008). Contextualizing change in marital satisfaction during middle age. *Psychological Science, 19*, 1194–1200.

Gordon, B. N., Schroeder, C. S., & Abrams, J. M. (1990). Children's knowledge of sexuality: A comparison of sexually abused and nonabused children. *American Journal of Orthopsychiatry, 60*, 250–257.

Gorrese, A., & Ruggieri, R. (2012). Peer attachment: A meta-analytic review of gender and age differences and associations with parent attachment. *Journal of Youth and Adolescence, 41*, 650–672.

Gosling, S. D., Rentfrow, P. J., & Swann, W. B. (2003). A very brief measure of the Big-Five personality domains. *Journal of Research in Personality, 37*, 504–528.

Goswami, U. (1999). Causal connections in beginning reading: The importance of rhyme. *Journal of Research in Reading, 22*, 217–241.

Gotlib, I. H., & Hammen, C. L. (1992). *Psychological aspects of depression. Toward a cognitive-interpersonal integration.* Chichester, UK: John Wiley & Sons.

Gotlib, I. H., Joormann, J., Minor, K. L., & Cooney, R. E. (2006). Cognitive and biological functioning in children at risk for depression. In T. Canli (Ed.), *Biology of personality and individual differences.* New York: Guilford.

Gottfredson, L. S. (1997). Why g matters: The complexity of everyday life. *Intelligence, 24*, 79–132.

Gottfredson, L. S. (2002). g: Highly general and highly practical. In R. J. Sternberg & E. L. Grigorenko (Eds.), *The general factor in intelligence: How general is it?* Mahwah, NJ: Erlbaum.

Gottfredson, L. S. (2004). Intelligence: Is it the epidemiologists' elusive "fundamental cause" of social class inequalities in health? *Journal of Personality and Social Psychology, 86*, 174–199.

Gottfredson, L. S., & Deary, I. (2004). Intelligence predicts health and longevity, but why? *Current Directions in Psychological Science, 13*, 1–4.

Gottfredson, L., & Saklofske, D. H. (2009). Intelligence: Foundations and issues in assessment. *Canadian Psychology, 50*, 183–195.

Gottfried, A. E., Fleming, J. S., & Gottfried, A. W. (1998). Role of cognitively stimulating home environment in children's academic intrinsic motivation: A longitudinal study. *Child Development, 69*, 1448–1460.

Gottfried, A. E., & Gottfried, A. W. (2006). A long-term investigation of the role of maternal and dual-earner employment in children's development: The Fullerton Longitudinal Study. *American Behavioral Scientist, 49*, 1310–1327.

Gottfried, A. E., Marcoulides, G. A., Gottfried, A. W., & Oliver, P. H. (2009). A latent curve model of parental motivational practices and developmental decline in math and science academic intrinsic motivation. *Journal of Educational Psychology, 101*, 729–739.

Gottfried, A. W., Gottfried, A. E., Bathurst, K., & Guerin, D. W. (1994). *Gifted IQ: Early developmental aspects: The Fullerton Longitudinal Study.* New York: Plenum.

Gottman, J. M. (2011). *The science of trust. Emotional attunement for couples.* New York: W. W. Norton.

Gottman, J. M., & Notarius, C. I. (2000). Decade review: Observing marital interaction. *Journal of Marriage and the Family, 62*, 927–947.

Gottman, J. M., Katz, L., & Hooven, C. (1996). Parental meta-emotion philosophy and the emotional life of families: Theoretical models and preliminary data. Journal of Family Psychology, 10, 243–268.

Goubet, N., Rochat, P., Maire-Leblond, C., & Poss, S. (2006). Learning from others in 9-18-month-old infants. *Infant and Child Development, 15*, 161–177.

Gould, D. C., Petty, R., & Jacobs, H. S. (2000). The male menopause—does it exist? *British Medical Journal, 320*, 858–861.

Gould, M. S., Greenberg, T., Velting, D. M., & Shaffer, D. (2003). Youth suicide risk and preventive interventions: A review of the past 10 years. *Journal of the American Academy of Child and Adolescent Psychiatry, 42*, 386–405.

Gourounti, K., Anagnostopoulos, F., Potamianos, G., Lykeridou, K., Schmidt, L., & Vaslamatzis, G. (2012). Perception of control, coping and psychological stress of infertile women undergoing IVF. *Reproductive BioMedicine Online, 24*, 670–679.

Govarts, E., Nieuwenhuijsen, M., Schoeters, G., Ballester, F., Bloemen, K., de Boer, M., et al. (2012). Birth weight and prenatal exposure to polychlorinated biphenyls (PCBs) and dichlorodiphenyldichloroethylene (DDE): A meta-analysis within 12 European birth cohorts. *Environmental Health Perspectives, 120*, 162–170.

Gow, A. J., Johnson, W., Pattie, A., Brett, C. E., Roberts, B., Starr, J. M., et al. (2011). Stability and change in intelligence from age 11 to ages 70, 79, and 87: The Lothian birth cohorts of 1921 and 1936. *Psychology and Aging, 26*, 232–240.

Grabe, S., & Shibley Hyde, J. (2006). Ethnicity and body dissatisfaction among women in the United States: A meta-analysis. *Psychological Bulletin, 132*, 622–640.

Graber, J. A., Lewinsohn, P. M., Seeley, J. R., & Brooks-Gunn, J. (1997). Is psychopathology associated with the timing of pubertal development? *Journal of the American Academy of Child and Adolescent Psychiatry, 36*, 1768–1776.

Graber, J. A., Nichols, T. R., & Brooks-Gunn, J. (2010). Putting pubertal timing in developmental context: Implications for prevention. *Developmental Psychobiology, 52*, 254–262.

Graber, J. A., Seeley, J. R., Brooks-Gunn, J., & Lewinsohn, P. M. (2004). Is pubertal timing associated with psychopathology in young adulthood? Journal of the American Academy of Child and Adolescent Psychiatry, 43, 718–726.

Graf, P., Squire, L. R., & Mandler, G. (1984). The information that amnesic patients do not forget. *Journal of Experimental Psychology: Learning, Memory, and Cognition, 10*, 164–178.

Graham, N., Lindesay, J., Katona, C., Bertolote, J. M., Camus, V., Copeland, J. R. M., de Mendonca Lima, C. A., Gaillard, M., Nargeot, M. C. G., Gray, J., Jacobsson, L., Kingma, M., Kuhne, N., O'Loughlin, A., Rutz, W., Saraceno, B., Taintor, Z., & Wancata, J. (2003). Reducing stigma and discrimination against older people with mental disorders: A technical consensus statement. *International Journal of Geriatric Psychiatry, 18*, 670–678.

Graham, S., Taylor, A. Z., & Ho, A. Y. (2009). Race and ethnicity in peer relations research. In K. H. Rubin, W. M. Bukowski, & B. Laursen (Eds.), *Handbook of peer interactions, relationships, and groups.* New York: Guilford.

Grandjean, P. (2008). Late insights into early origins of disease. *Basic Clinical Pharmacological Toxicology, 102,* 94–99.

Grandjean, P., & Landrigan, P. J. (2006). Developmental neurotoxicity of industrial chemicals. *The Lancet, 368,* 2167–2178.

Granrud, C. E. (2006). Size constancy in infants: 4-month-olds' responses to physical versus retinal image size. *Journal of Experimental Psychology: Human Perception and Performance, 32,* 1398–1404.

Grant, K. E., Compas, B. E., Thurm, A. E., McMahon, S. D., & Gipson, P. Y. (2004). Stressors and child and adolescent psychopathology: Measurement issues and prospective effects. *Journal of Clinical Child and Adolescent Psychology, 33,* 412–425.

Gray, A. (2009). The social capital of older people. *Ageing & Society, 29,* 5–31.

Gray, S. W., Ramsey, B. K., & Klaus, R. A. (1982). *From 3 to 20: The early training project.* Baltimore: University Park Press.

Gray, W. M., & Hudson, L. M. (1984). Formal operations and the imaginary audience. *Developmental Psychology, 20,* 619–627.

Gray-Little, B., & Hafdahl, A. R. (2000). Factors influencing racial comparisons of self-esteem: A quantitative review. *Psychological Bulletin, 126,* 26–54.

Graziano, P. A., Keane, S. P., & Calkins, S. D. (2007). Cardiac vagal regulation and early peer status. *Child Development, 78,* 264–278.

Grbich, C., Parker, D., & Maddocks, I. (2001). The emotions and coping strategies of caregivers of family members with a terminal cancer. *Journal of Palliative Care, 17,* 30–36.

Green, C. R. (2001). *Total memory workout: 8 easy steps to maximum memory fitness.* New York: Bantam Doubleday.

Greenberg, J., Solomon, S., & Arndt, J. (2008). A basic but uniquely human motivation: Terror management. In J. Y. Shah & W. L. Gardner (Eds.), *Handbook of motivation science.* New York: Guilford.

Greenberger, E., & Steinberg, L. (1986). *When teenagers work: The psychological and social costs of adolescent employment.* New York: Basic Books.

Greenberger, E., O'Neil, R., & Nagel, S. K. (1994). Linking workplace and homeplace: Relations between the nature of adults' work and their parenting behaviors. *Developmental Psychology, 30,* 990–1002.

Greene, J. D. (2008). The secret joke of Kant's soul. In W. Sinnott-Armstrong (Ed.), *Moral psychology: The neuroscience of morality: Emotion, brain disorders, and development.* Cambridge, MA: MIT Press.

Greene, J. D. (2009). Dual-process morality and the personal/impersonal distinction: A reply to McGuire, Langdon, Coltheart, and MacKenzie. *Journal of Experimental Social Psychology, 45,* 581–584.

Greene, J. D., Morelli, S. A., Lowenberg, K., Nystrom, L. E., & Cohen, J. D. (2008). Cognitive load selectively interferes with utilitarian moral judgment. *Cognition, 107,* 1144–1154.

Greene, J. D., Sommerville, R. B., Nystrom, L. E., Darley, J. M., & Cohen, J. D. (2001). An fMRI investigation of emotional engagement in moral judgment. *Science, 293,* 2105–2108.

Greene, J. G. (1984). *The social and psychological origins of the climacteric syndrome.* Hants, England & Brookfield, VT: Gower.

Greene, K., Rubin, D. L., Hale, J. L., & Walters, L. H. (1996). The utility of understanding adolescent egocentrism in designing health promotion messages. *Health Communication, 8,* 131–152.

Greenfield, E. A., & Marks, N. F. (2006). Linked lives: Adult children's problems and their parents' psychological and relational well-being. *Journal of Marriage and Family, 68,* 442–454.

Greenfield, E. A., Vaillant, G. E., & Marks, N. E. (2009). Do formal religious participation and spiritual perceptions have independent linkages with diverse dimensions of psychological well-being? *Journal of Health and Social Behavior, 50,* 196–212.

Greenfield, P. M., & Savage-Rumbaugh, E. S. (1993). Comparing communicative competence in child and chimp: The pragmatics of repetition. *Journal of Child Language, 20,* 1–26.

Greenfield, R. A. (2012). *Pediatric HIV infection.* Retrieved from http://emedicine.medscape.com/article/965086-overview

Greenough, W. T., Black, J. E., & Wallace, C. S. (1987). Experience and brain development. *Child Development, 58,* 539–559.

Greenough, W. T., Black, J. E., & Wallace, C. S. (1987). Experience and brain development. *Child Development, 58,* 539–559.

Greve, F. (2006, February 3). Rise in average IQ scores makes kids today exceptional by earlier standards. *Knight Ridder Washington Bureau.*

Grilo, C. M., & Mitchell, J. E. (Eds.). (2010). *The treatment of eating disorders: A clinical handbook.* New York: Guilford.

Grizenko, N., Zappitelli, M., Langevin, J. P., Hrychko, S., El-Messidi, A., Kaminester, D., Pawliuk, N., & Stepanian, M. T. (2000). Effectiveness of a social skills training program using self/other perspective-taking: A nine-month follow-up. *American Journal of Orthopsychiatry, 70,* 501–509.

Groark, C. J., Muhamedrahimov, R. J., Palmov, O. I., Nikiforova, N. V., & McCall, R. B. (2005). Improvements in early care in Russian orphanages and their relationship to observed behaviors. *Infant Mental Health Journal, 26,* 96–109.

Grollman, E. A. (1995). Explaining death to young children: Some questions and answers. In E. A. Grollman (Ed.), *Bereaved children and teens.* Boston: Beacon Press.

Grolnick, W. S., & Pomerantz, E. M. (2009). Issues and challenges in studying parental control: Toward a new conceptualization. *Child Development Perspectives, 3,* 165–170.

Grolnick, W. S., Bridges, L. J., & Connell, J. P. (1996). Emotion regulation in two-year-olds: Strategies and emotional expression in four contexts. *Child Development, 67,* 928–941.

Grolnick, W. S., McMenamy, J. M., & Kurowski, C. O. (2006). Emotional self-regulation in infancy and toddlerhood. In L. Balter & C. S. Tamis-LeMonda (Eds.), *Child psychology: A handbook of contemporary issues* (2nd ed.). New York: Psychology Press.

Gropman, A. L., & Batshaw, M. L. (2010). Epigenetics, copy number variation, and other molecular mechanisms underlying neurodevelopmental disabilities: New insights and diagnostic approaches. *Journal of Developmental and Behavioral Pediatrics, 31,* 582–591.

Grosjean, F. (2010). *Bilingual: Life and reality.* Cambridge, MA: Harvard University Press.

Gros-Louis, J., West, M. J., Goldstein, M. H., & King, A. P. (2006). Mothers provide differential feedback to infants' prelinguistic sounds. *International Journal of Behavioral Development, 30,* 509–516.

Gross, J. J. (Ed.) (2007). *Handbook of emotion regulation.* New York: Guilford.

Grossberg, G. T., & Desai, A. K. (2003). Management of Alzheimer's disease. *Journal of Gerontology: Medical Sciences, 58A,* 331–353.

Grossman, A. W., Churchill, J. D., McKinney, B. C., Kodish, I. M., Otte, S. L., & Greenough, W. T. (2003). Experience effects on brain development: Possible contributions to psychopathology. *Journal of Child Psychology and Psychiatry and Allied Disciplines, 44,* 33–63.

Grossmann, I., Karasawa, M., Izumi, S., Na, J., Varnum, M. E. W., Kitayama, S., Nisbett, R. E. (2012). Aging and wisdom: Culture matters. *Psychological Science, 23,* 1059–1066.

Grossmann, I., Na, J., Varnum, M. E. W., Park, D. C., Kitayama, S., & Nisbett, R. E. (2010). Reasoning about social conflicts improves into old age. *Proceedings of the National Academy of Sciences—PNAS, 107,* 7246–7250.

Grossmann, K. E., Grossmann, K., & Keppler, A. (2005). Universal and culture-specific aspects of human behavior: The case of attachment. In W. Friedlmeier, P. Chakkarath, & B. Schwarz (Eds.), *Culture and human development. The importance of cross-cultural research for the social sciences.* New York: Psychology Press.

Grossmann, K. E., Grossmann, K., Winter, M., & Zimmermann, P. (2002a). Attachment relationships and appraisal of partnership: From early experience of sensitive support to later relationship representation. In L. Pulkkinen & A. Caspi (Eds.), Paths to successful development: Personality in the life course. Cambridge, UK: Cambridge University Press.

Grotevant, H. D., & Cooper, C. R. (1986). Individuation in family relations. A perspective on individual differences in the development of identity and role-taking skills in adolescence. *Human Development, 29,* 82–100.

Gruber-Baldini, A. L., Schaie, K. W., & Willis, S. L. (1995). Similarity in married couples: A longitudinal study of mental abilities and rigidity-flexibility. *Journal of Personality and Social Psychology, 69,* 191–203.

Grucza, R. A., Norberg, K. E., & Bierut, L. J. (2009). Binge drinking among youths and young adults in the United States: 1979–2006. *Journal of the American Academy of Child & Adolescent Psychiatry, 48,* 692–702.

Grundy, E., & Henretta, J. C. (2006). Between elderly parents and adult children: A new look at the intergenerational care provided by the 'sandwich generation.' *Ageing and Society, 26,* 707–722.

Grusec, J. E. (2006). The development of moral behavior and conscience from a socialization perspective. In M. Killen & J. G. Smetana (Eds.), *Handbook of moral development.* Mahwah, NJ: Erlbaum.

Grusec, J. E., & Davidov, M. (2010). Integrating different perspectives on socialization theory and research: A domain-specific approach. *Child Development, 81,* 687–709.

Grusec, J. E., Goodnow, J. J., & Kuczynski, L. (2000). New directions in analyses of parenting contributions to children's acquisition of values. *Child Development, 71,* 205–211.

Grych, J. H., & Fincham, F. D. (1992). Interventions for children of divorce: Toward greater integration of research and action. *Psychological Bulletin, 111,* 434–454.

Grych, J., Oxtoby, C., & Lynn, M. (2013). The effects of interparental conflict on children. In M. A. Fine & F. D. Fincham (Eds.), *Handbook of family theories. A context-based approach.* New York: Routledge.

Gudsnuk, K. M. A., & Champagne, F. A. (2011). Epigenetic effects of early developmental experiences. *Clinical Perinatology, 38,* 703–717.

Guerra, N. G. (2012). Can we make violent behavior less adaptive for youth? *Human Development, 55,* 105–106.

Guerra, N. G., & Slaby, R. G. (1990). Cognitive mediators of aggression in adolescent offenders: 2. Intervention. *Developmental Psychology, 26,* 269–277.

Guerra, N. G., & Williams, K. R. (2006). Ethnicity, youth violence, and the ecology of development. In N. G. Guerra, & E. P. Smith (Eds.), *Preventing youth violence in a multicultural society.* Washington, DC: American Psychological Association.

Guilamo-Ramos, V., Jaccard, J., Dittus, P., & Collins, S. (2008). Parent-adolescent communication about sexual intercourse: An analysis of maternal reluctance to communicate. *Health Psychology, 27,* 760–769.

Gundersen, C., Lohman, B. J., Garasky, S., Stewart, S., & Eisenmann, J. (2008). Food security, maternal stressors, and overweight among low-income US children: Results from the National Health and Nutrition Examination Survey (1999–2002). *Pediatrics, 122,* e529–e540.

Gunnar, M. R., Bruce, J., & Grotevant, H. D. (2000). International adoption of institutionally reared children: Research and policy. *Development and Psychopathology, 12,* 677–693.

Gunnar, M., & Quevedo, K. (2007). The neurobiology of stress and development. *Annual Review of Psychology, 58,* 145–153.

Guo, G. (2011). Gene-environment interactions for delinquency: Promises and difficulties. In K. A. Dodge & M. Rutter (Eds.). *Gene-environment interactions in developmental psychopathology.* New York: Guilford.

Gurba, E. (2005). On the specific character of adult thought: Controversies over post-formal operations. *Polish Psychological Bulletin, 36,* 175–185.

Gurland, B. (1991). Epidemiology of psychiatric disorders. In J. Sadavoy, L. W. Lazarus, & L. F. Jarvik (Eds.), *Comprehensive review of geriatric psychiatry.* Washington, DC: American Psychiatric Press.

Gurung, R. A. R., Taylor, S. E., & Seeman, T. E. (2003). Accounting for changes in social support among married older adults: Insights from the MacArthur Studies of Successful Aging. *Psychology and Aging, 18,* 487–496.

Gutman, L. (2006). How student and parent goal orientations and classroom goal structures influence the math achievement of African Americans during the high school transition. *Contemporary Educational Psychology, 31,* 44–63.

Gutman, L. M., Sameroff, A. J., & Cole, R. (2003). Academic growth curve trajectories from 1st grade to 12th grade: Effects of multiple social risk factors and preschool child factors. *Developmental Psychology, 39,* 777–790.

Gutman, L. M., Sameroff, A. J., & Eccles, J. S. (2002). The academic achievement of African American students during early adolescence: An examination of multiple risk, promotive, and protective factors. *American Journal of Community Psychology, 39,* 367–399.

Gutmann, D. (1987). *Reclaimed powers: Toward a new psychology of men and women in later life.* New York: Basic Books.

Gutmann, D. (1997). *The human elder in nature, culture, and society.* Boulder, CO: Westview.

Guttmacher Institute. (2006). *Facts on American teens' sexual and reproductive health.* Retrieved from www.guttmacher.org/pubs/fb_ATSRH.html

Guttmacher Institute. (2009, June). *Facts on sexually transmitted infections in the United States.* Retrieved from www.guttmacher.org/pubs/FIB_STI_US.html

Guyenet, S., & Landen, J. (2012, Feb 19). American Per-Capita Sugar Consumption Hits 100 Pounds Per Year. *Whole health source.* Retrieved from http://articles.businessinsider.com/2012-02-19/news/31076374_1_chart-capita-american#ixzz2As44BTCt

Gweon, H., Dodell-Feder, D., Bedny, M., & Saxe, R. (2012). Theory of mind performance in children correlates with functional specialization of a brain region for thinking about thoughts. *Child Development, 83,* 1853–1868.

Ha, J. (2010). The effects of positive and negative support from children on widowed older adults' psychological adjustment: A longitudinal analysis. *The Gerontologist, 50,* 471–481.

Haber, D. (2006). Life review: Implementation, theory, research, and therapy. *International Journal of Aging & Human Development, 63,* 153–171.

Hagan, L. K., & Kuebli, J. (2007). Mothers' and fathers' socialization of preschoolers' physical risk taking. *Journal of Applied Developmental Psychology, 28,* 2–14.

Hagan, M. J., Tein, J., Sandler, I. N., Wolchik, S. A., Ayers, T. S., & Luecken, L. J. (2012). Strengthening effective parenting practices over the long term: Effects of a preventive intervention for parentally bereaved families. *Journal of Clinical Child and Adolescent Psychology, 41,* 177–188.

Hagekull, B., & Bohlin, G. (1998). Preschool temperament and environmental factors related to the five-factor model of personality in middle childhood. *Merrill-Palmer Quarterly, 44,* 194–215.

Hagerman, R. J. (2011). Fragile X syndrome and fragile X-associated disorders. In S. Goldstein & C. R. Reynolds (Eds.), *Handbook of neurodevelopmental and genetic disorders in children* (2nd ed., pp. 276–292). New York: Guilford.

Hagestad, G. O. (1985). Continuity and connectedness. In V. L. Bengtson & J. F. Robertson (Eds.), *Grandparenthood.* Beverly Hills, CA: Sage.

Haidt, J. (2001). The emotional dog and its rational tail: A social intuitionist approach to moral judgment. *Psychological Review, 108,* 814–834.

Haidt, J. (2008). Morality. *Perspectives on Psychological Science, 3,* 65–72.

Haidt, J. (2012). *The righteous mind: Why good people are divided by politics and religion.* New York: Pantheon/Random House.

Haight, B. K., & Haight, B. S. (2007). *The handbook of structured life review.* Baltimore: Health Professions Press.

Haight, W. L., Wong, X., Fung, H. H., Williams, K., & Mintz, J. (1999). Universal, developmental, and variable aspects of young children's play: A cross-cultural comparison of pretending at home. *Child Development, 70,* 1477–1488.

Haine, R. A., Wolchik, S. A., Sandler, I. N., & Milsap, R. E. (2006). Positive parenting as a protective resource for parentally bereaved children. *Death Studies, 30,* 1–28.

Hainline, L. (1998). The development of basic visual abilities. In A. Slater (Ed.), *Perceptual development: Visual, auditory and speech perception in infancy* (pp. 37–44). Hove, East Sussex, UK: Psychology Press.

Hainline, L., & Abramov, I. (1992). Assessing visual development: Is infant vision good enough? *Advances in Infancy Research, 7,* 39–102.

Halberstadt, A. G. (1991). Toward an ecology of expressiveness: Family socialization in particular and a model in general. In R. S. Feldman & B. Rime (Eds.), *Fundamentals of nonverbal behavior.* New York: Cambridge University Press.

Halim, M. L., & Ruble, D. (2010). Gender identity and stereotyping in early and middle childhood. In J. C. Chrisler & D. R. McCreary (Eds.), *Handbook of gender research in psychology* (pp. 495–525). New York: Springer Science+Business Media.

Halim, M. L., Ruble, D., Tamis-LeMonda, C., & Shrout, P. E. (2013). Rigidity in gender-typed behaviors in early childhood: A longitudinal study of ethnic minority children. *Child Development, 84,* 1269–1284.

Hall, G. S. (1904). *Adolescence* (2 vols.). New York: Appleton.

Hallmayer, J., Cleveland, S., Torres, A., Phillips, J., Cohen, B., Torigoe, T., et al. (2011). Genetic heritability and shared environmental factors among twin pairs with autism. *Archives of General Psychiatry, 68,* 1095–1102.

Halmi, K. A. (2009). Perplexities and provocations of eating disorders. *Journal of Child Psychology and Psychiatry, 50,* 163–169.

Halpern, C. J. T., Udry, J. R., Suchindran, C., & Campbell, B. (2000). Adolescent males' willingness to report masturbation [Special issue]. *Journal of Sex Research, 37,* 327–332.

Halpern, C. T. (2006). Integrating hormones and other biological factors into a developmental systems model of adolescent female sexuality. *New Directions for Child and Adolescent Development, 112,* 9–22.

Hamann, K., Warneken, F., & Tomasello, M. (2012). Children's developing commitments to joint goals. *Child Development, 83,* 137–145.

Hamer, R. D. (2009). *What can my baby see?* San Francisco: Smith-Kettlewell Eye Research Institute. Retrieved from www.ski.org/Vision/babyvision.html

Hamilton, M. T., Healy, G. N., Dunstan, D. W., Zderic, T. W., & Owen, N. (2008). Too little exercise and too much sitting: Inactivity physiology and the need for new recommendations on sedentary behavior. *Current Cardiovascular Risk Reports, 2,* 292–298.

Hamilton, B. E., Martin, J. A., & Ventura, S. J. (2011). Births: Preliminary data for 2010. *National Vital Statistics Report, 60,* 1–25. Retrieved from www.cdc.gov/nchs/data/nvsr/nvsr60/nvsr60_02.pdf

Hamlin, J. K., & Wynn, K. (2011). Young infants prefer prosocial to antisocial others. *Cognitive Development, 26,* 30–39.

Hamlin, J. K., Wynn, K., & Bloom, P. (2007). Social evaluation by preverbal infants. *Nature, 450,* 557–560.

Hamm, J. V. (2000). Do birds of a feather flock together? The variable bases for African American, Asian American, and European American adolescents' selection of similar friends. *Developmental Psychology, 36,* 209–219.

Hampson, S. E., & Friedman, H. S. (2008). Personality and health. A lifespan perspective. In O. P. John, R. W. Robins, & L. A. Pervin (Eds.), *Handbook of personality theory and research* (3rd ed.). New York: Guilford.

Hans, J. D., Gillen, M., & Akande, K. (2010, June). Sex redefined: The reclassification of oral-genital contact. *Perspectives on Sexual and Reproductive Health, 42,* 74–78.

Hansson, R. O., & Stroebe, M. S. (2007). *Bereavement in late life: Coping, adaptation,* *and developmental influences.* Washington, DC: American Psychological Association.

Hansson, R. O., DeKoekkoek, P. D., Neece, W. M., & Patterson, D. W. (1997). Successful aging at work: Annual review, 1992–1996: The older worker and transitions to retirement. *Journal of Vocational Behavior, 51,* 202–233.

Hanushek, E. A. (2011). The economic value of higher teacher quality. *Economics of Education Review, 30,* 466–479.

Hanushek, E., Rivkin, S., & Kain, J. (2005). Teachers, schools and academic achievement. *Econometrica, 73,* 417–458.

Happé, F. (1994). An advanced test of theory of mind. *Journal of Autism & Developmental Disorders, 24,* 129–154.

Hardy, S. A., & Carlo, G. (2011). Moral identity: What is it, how does it develop, and is it linked to moral action? *Child Development Perspectives, 5,* 212–218.

Hare, B., Call, J., & Tomasello, M. (2006). Chimpanzees deceive a human competitor by hiding. *Cognition, 101,* 495–514.

Harlow, H. F., & Zimmerman, R. R. (1959). Affectional responses in the infant monkey. *Science, 130,* 421–432.

Harman, D. (2001). Aging: An overview. In S. C. Park, E. S. Hwang, H. Kim, & W. Park (Eds.), *Annals of the New York Academy of Sciences: Vol. 928. Molecular and cellular interactions in senescence.* New York: The New York Academy of Sciences.

Harman, D. (2001). Aging: An overview. In S. C. Park, E. S. Hwang, H. Kim, & W. Park (Eds.), *Annals of the New York Academy of Sciences: Vol. 928. Molecular and cellular interactions in senescence.* New York: The New York Academy of Sciences.

Harper, G., & Kember, D. (1986). Approaches to study of distance education students. *British Journal of Educational Technology, 17,* 211–212.

Harrington, D. M., Block, J. H., & Block, J. (1987). Testing aspects of Carl Rogers's theory of creative environments: Child-rearing antecedents of creative potential in young adolescents. *Journal of Personality and Social Psychology, 52,* 851–856.

Harris, J. R. (1998). *The nurture assumption. Why children turn out the way they do.* New York: Free Press.

Harris, J. R. (2000). Context-specific learning, personality, and birth order. *Current Directions in Psychological Science, 9,* 174–177.

Harris, J. R. (2006). *No two alike: Human nature and human individuality.* New York: W. W. Norton.

Harris, J. R., Pedersen, N. L., McClearn, G. E., Plomin, R., & Nesselroade, J. R. (1992). Age differences in genetic and environmental influences for health from the Swedish Adoption/Twin Study of Aging. *Journal of Gerontology Series B: Psychological Sciences, 47,* 213–220.

Harris, M. (1992). *Language experience and early language development: From input to uptake.* Hove, UK: Erlbaum.

Harris, M. A., Prior, J. C., & Koehoorn, M. (2008). Age at menarche in the Canadian population: Secular trends and relationship to adulthood BMI. *Journal of Adolescent Health, 43,* 548–554.

Harris, P. L. (1989). *Children and emotion: The development of psychological understanding.* Oxford, UK: Basil Blackwell.

Harris, P. L., & Kavanaugh, R. D. (1993). Young children's understanding of pretense. *Monographs of the Society for Research in Child Development, 58* (1, Serial No. 181).

Harris, P. L., Pasquini, E. S., Duke, S., Asscher, J. J., & Pons, F. (2006). Germs and angels: The role of testimony in young children's ontology. *Developmental Science, 9,* 76–96.

Harris, T., & Bifulco, A. (1991). Loss of parent in childhood, attachment style, and depression in adulthood. In C. M. Parkes, J. Stevenson-Hinde, & P. Marris (Eds.), *Attachment across the life cycle.* London: Tavistock/Routledge.

Harrison, R. V., Gordon, K. A., & Mount, R. J. (2005). Is there a critical period for cochlear implantation in congenitally deaf children? Analyses of hearing and speech perception performance after implantation. *Developmental Psychobiology, 46,* 252–261.

Hart, B., & Rissley, T. (1995). *Meaningful differences in the everyday experience of young American children.* Baltimore: Paul H. Brookes Publishing.

Hart, D. (2005). The development of moral identity. *Nebraska Symposium on Motivation, 51,* 165–196.

Hart, S. (2008). *Brain, attachment, and personality. An introduction to neuroaffective development.* London: Karmac.

Hart, S. A., Logan, J. A. R., Soden-Hensler, B., Kershaw, S., Talor, J., & Schatschneider, C. (2013). Exploring how nature and nurture affect the development of reading: An analysis of the Florida Twin Project on reading. *Developmental Psychology, 49,* 1971–1981.

Harter, S. (1999). *The construction of the self. A developmental perspective.* New York: Guilford.

Harter, S. (2003). The development of self-representations during childhood and adolescence. In M. R. Leary & J. P. Tangney (Eds.), *Handbook of self and identity.* New York: Guilford.

Harter, S. (2012). *The construction of the self: Developmental and sociocultural foundations* (2nd ed.). New York: Guilford.

Harter, S., & Buddin, B. J. (1987). Children's understanding of the simultaneity of two emotions: A five stage developmental acquisition sequence. *Developmental Psychology, 23,* 388–399.

Harter, S., & Monsour, A. (1992). Development analysis of conflict caused by opposing attributes in the adolescent self-portrait. *Developmental Psychology, 28,* 251–260.

Hartley, A. (2006). Changing role of the speed of processing construct in the cognitive psychology of human aging. In J. E. Birren & K. W. Schaie (Eds.), *Handbook of the psychology of aging.* Boston: Elsevier Academic Press.

Hartshorn, K., Rovee-Collier, C., Gerhardstein, P., Bhatt, R. S., Wondoloski, T. L., Klein, P., et al. (1998). The ontogeny of long-term memory over the first year and a half of life. *Developmental Psychobiology, 32,* 69–89.

Hartung, P. J., Porfeli, E. J., & Vondracek, F. W. (2005). Child vocational development: A review and reconsideration. *Journal of Vocational Behavior, 66,* 385–419.

Hartup, W. W. (2006). Relationships in early and middle childhood. In A. L. Vangelisti & D. Perlman (Eds.), *The Cambridge handbook of personal relationships.* New York: Cambridge University Press.

Hasegawa, J., Farina, A., Turchi, G., Hasegawa, Y., Zanello, M., & Baroncini, S. (2013). Effects of epidural analgesia on labor length, instrumental delivery, and neonatal short-term outcome. *Journal of Anesthesia, 27,* 43–47.

Haskett, M. E., Johnson, C. A., & Miller, J. W. (1994). Individual differences in risk of child abuse by adolescent mothers: Assessment in the perinatal period. *Journal of Child Psychology and Psychiatry and Allied Disciplines, 35,* 461–476.

Hastings, P. D., Zahn-Waxler, C., & McShane, K. (2006). *Empathy, emotions, and aggression: Biological bases of concern for others.* Mahwah, NJ: Erlbaum.

Hatfield, E., & Rapson, R. L. (2006). Passionate love, sexual desire, and mate selection: Cross-cultural and historical perspectives. In P. Noller & J. A. Feeney (Eds.), *Close relationships: Functions, forms, and processes.* New York: Psychology Press.

Hattie, J., Biggs, J., & Purdie, N. (1996). Effects of learning skills interventions on student learning: A meta-analysis. *Review of Educational Research, 66,* 99–136.

Haught, P. A., Hill, L. A., Nardi, A. H., & Walls, R. T. (2000). Perceived ability and level of education as predictors of traditional and practical adult problem solving. *Experimental Aging Research, 26,* 89–101.

Havighurst, R. J., Neugarten, B. L., & Tobin, S. S. (1968). Disengagement and patterns of aging. In B. L. Neugarten (Ed.), *Middle age and aging.* Chicago: University of Chicago Press.

Havighurst, S. S., Wilson, K. R., Harley, A. E., & Prior, M. R. (2009). Tuning in to Kids: An emotion-focused parenting program—Initial findings from a community trial. *Journal of Community Psychology, 37,* 1008–1023.

Havighurst, S. S., Wilson, K. R., Harley, A. E., Prior, M. R., &Kehoe, C. (2010).Tuning in to Kids: Improving emotion socialization practices in parents of preschool children – findings from a community trial. *Journal of Child Psychology and Psychiatry, 51,* 1342–1350.

Hawkins, R. L., Jaccard, J., & Needle, E. (2013). Nonacademic factors associated with dropping out of high school: Adolescent problem behaviors. *Journal of the Society for Social Work and Research, 4,* 58–75.

Hawkley, L. C., Thisted, R. A., & Caciappo, J. T. (2009). Loneliness predicts reduced physical activity: Cross-sectional & longitudinal analyses. *Health Psychology, 28,* 354–363.

Haworth, C. M. A., Wright, M. J., Martin, N. W., Martin, N. G., Boomsma, D. I., Bartels, M., et al. (2009). A twin study of the genetics of high cognitive ability selected from 11,000 twin pairs in six studies from four countries. *Behavior Genetics, 39,* 359–370.

Hay, D. F. (2009). The roots and branches of human altruism. *British Journal of Psychology, 100,* 473–479.

Hay, D. F., Caplan, M., & Nash, A. (2009). The beginnings of peer relations. In K. H. Rubin, W. M. Bukowski, & B. Laursen (Eds.), *Handbook of peer interactions, relationships, and groups.* New York: Guilford.

Hay, D. F., Hurst, S., Waters, C. S., & Chadwick, A. (2011). Infants' use of force to defend toys: The origins of instrumental aggression. *Infancy, 16,* 471–489.

Hay, D. F., Mundy, L., Roberts, S., Carta, R., Waters, C. S., Perra, O., et al. (2011). Known risk factors for violence predict 12-month-old infants' aggressiveness with peers. *Psychological Science, 22,* 1205–1211.

Hay, D. F., Nash, A., & Pedersen, J. (1983). Interaction between six-month-old peers. *Child Development, 54,* 557–562.

Hayflick, L. (1976). The cell biology of human aging. *New England Journal of Medicine, 295,* 1302–1308.

Hayflick, L. (1994). *How and why we age.* New York: Ballantine.

Hayflick, L. (2004). "Anti-aging" is an oxymoron. *Journal of Gerontology Series A: Biological Sciences, 59A,* 573–578.

Hayne, H., & Simcock, G. (2009). Memory development in toddlers. In M. L. Courage & N. Cowan (Eds.), *The development of memory in infancy and childhood* (pp. 43–68). New York: Psychology Press.

Hayslip, B., Jr. (2009). Ethnic and cross-cultural perspectives on custodial grandparenting. In J. Sokolovsky (Ed.), *The cultural context of aging* (3rd ed.). Westport, CT: Praeger.

Hayslip, B., Jr., & White, D. L. (2008). The grief of grandparents. In M. S. Stroebe, R. O. Hansson, H. Schut, & W. Stroebe (Eds.), *Handbook of bereavement research and practice. Advances in theory and intervention.* Washington, DC: American Psychological Association.

Hazan, C., & Shaver, P. (1987). Romantic love conceptualized as an attachment process. *Journal of Personality and Social Psychology, 52,* 511–524.

Hazan, C., & Shaver, P. (1990). Love and work: An attachment-theoretical perspective. *Journal of Personality and Social Psychology, 59,* 270–280.

Hazan, C., Campa, M., & Gur-Yaish, N. (2006). Attachment across the lifespan. In P. Noller & J. A. Feeney (Eds.), *Close relationships: Functions, forms, and processes.* New York: Psychology Press.

Hazlett, H. C., De Alba, M. G., & Hooper, S. R. (2011). Klinefelter syndrome. In S. Goldstein & C. R. Reynolds (Eds.), *Handbook of neurodevelopmental and genetic disorders in children* (2nd ed., pp. 382–424). New York: Guilford.

Hazlett, H. C., Hammer, J., Hooper, S. R., & Kamphaus, R. W. (2011). Down syndrome. In S. Goldstein & C. R. Reynolds (Eds.), *Handbook of neurodevelopmental and genetic disorders in children* (2nd ed., pp. 362–381). New York: Guilford.

He, F. J., Marrero, N. M., & MacGregor, G. A. (2008). Salt intake is related to soft drink consumption in children and adolescents: A link to obesity? *Hypertension, 51,* 629–634.

He, M., Tucker, P., Gilliland, J., Irwin, J. D., Larsen, K., & Hess, P. (2012). The influence of local food environments on adolescents' food purchasing behaviors. *International Journal of Environmental Research and Public Health, 9,* 1458–1471.

Hearn, S., Saulnier, G., Strayer, J., Glenham, M., Koopman, R., & Marcia, J. E. (2012). Between integrity and despair: Toward construct validation of Erikson's eight stage. *Journal of Adult Development, 19,* 1–20.

Heaton, P., & Wallace, G. L. (2004). Annotation: The savant syndrome. *Journal of Child Psychology and Psychiatry, 45,* 899–911.

Hedge, J. W., Borman, W. C., & Lammlein, S. E. (Eds.) (2006). *The aging workforce: Realities, myths, and implications for organizations.* Washington, DC: American Psychological Association.

Hedlund, B., & Ebersole, P. (1983). A test of Levinson's midlife reevaluation. *Journal of Genetic Psychology, 143,* 189–192.

Heine, S. J., & Buchtel, E. E. (2009). Personality: The universal and the culturally specific. *Annual Review of Psychology, 60,* 369–394.

Held, R. and Hein A. (1963). Movement-produced stimulation in the development of visually guided behavior. *Journal of Comparative and Physiological Psychology, 56,* 872–876.

Helmreich, R. L., Sawin, L. L., & Carsrud, A. L. (1986). The honeymoon effect in job performance: Temporal increases in the predictive power of achievement motivation. *Journal of Applied Psychology, 71,* 185–188.

Helms, J. E. (1992). Why is there no study of cultural equivalence in standardized cognitive-ability testing? *American Psychologist, 47,* 1083–1101.

Helms, J. E. (1997). The triple quandary of race, culture, and social class in standardized cognitive ability testing. In D. P. Flanagan, J. Genshaft, & P. L. Harrison (Eds.), *Contemporary intellectual assessment: Theories, tests, and issues.* New York: Guilford.

Helson, R., Jones, C., & Kwan, V. S. Y. (2002). Personality change over 40 years of adulthood: Hierarchical linear modeling analyses of two longitudinal samples. *Journal of Personality and Social Psychology, 83,* 752–766.

Henker, B., & Whalen, C. K. (1989). Hyperactivity and attention deficits. *American Psychologist, 44,* 216–223.

Henry, D. B., Schoeny, M. E., Deptula, D. P., & Slavick, J. T. (2007). Peer selection and socialization effects on adolescent intercourse without a condom and attitudes about the costs of sex. *Child Development,* 78, 825–838.

Henry, J. D., MacLeod, M. S., Phillips, L. H., & Crawford, J. R. (2004). A meta-analytic review of prospective memory and aging. *Psychology and Aging,* 19, 27–39.

Heo, S., Prakash, R. S., Voss, M. W., Erickson, K. L., Ouyang, C., Sutton, B. P., et al. (2010). Resting hippocampal blood flow, spatial memory and aging. *Brain Research, 1315,* 119–127.

Hepach, R., Vaish, A., & Tomasello, M. (2012). Young children sympathize less in response to unjustified emotional distress. *Developmental Psychology,* 49, 1132–1138.

Herdt, G., & Davidson, J. (1988). The Sambia "turnim-man": Sociocultural and clinical aspects of gender formation in male pseudohermaphrodites with 5-alpha-reductase deficiency in Papua New Guinea. *Archives of Sexual Behavior, 17,* 33–56.

Herdt, G., & McClintock, M. (2000). The magical age of 10. *Archives of Sexual Behavior, 29,* 587–606.

Herkert, B. M. (2000). Communicating grief. *Omega: Journal of Death and Dying, 41,* 93–115.

Herlitz, A., & Rehnman, J. (2008). Sex differences in episodic memory. *Current Directions in Psychological Science, 17,* 52–56.

Herman-Giddens, M. E., Slora, E. J., Wasserman, R. C., Bourdony, C. J., Bhapkar, M. V., Koch, G. G., et al. (1997). Secondary sexual characteristics and menses in young girls seen in office practice: A study from the Pediatric Research in Office Settings network. *Pediatrics,* 99, 505–512.

Hermans, H. J., & Oles, P. K. (1999). Midlife crisis in men: Affective organization of personal meanings. *Human Relations, 52,* 1403–1426.

Hermelin, B. (with foreword by M. Rutter). (2001). *Bright splinters of the mind: A personal story of research with autistic savants.* London: Jessica Kingsley Publishers, Ltd.

Herrnstein, R. J., & Murray, C. (1994). *The bell curve: Intelligence and class structure in American life.* New York: Free Press.

Hertzog, C., Kramer, A. F., Wilson, R. S., & Lindenberger, U. (2009). Enrichment effects on adult cognitive development: Can the functional capacity of older adults be preserved and enhanced? *Psychological Science in the Public Interest,* 9, 1–65.

Heru, A. M. (2006). Family psychiatry: From research to practice. *American Journal of Psychiatry,* 163, 962–968.

Hesketh, B., Griffin, B., & Loh, V. (2011). A future-oriented retirement transition adjustment framework. *Journal of Vocational Behavior,* 79, 303–314.

Hess, T. M. (1999). Cognitive and knowledge-based influences on social representations. In T. M. Hess & F. Blanchard-Fields (Eds.), *Social cognition and aging.* San Diego: Academic Press.

Hess, T. M. (2006). Attitudes toward aging and their effects on behavior. In J. E. Birren & K. W. Schaie (Eds.), *Handbook of the psychology of aging* (6th ed.). Burlington, MA: Elsevier Academic Press.

Hess, T. M., Osowski, N. L., & Leclerc, C. M. (2005). Age and experience influences on the complexity of social inferences. *Psychology and Aging,* 20, 447–459.

Hess, T., Hinson, J. T., & Hodges, E. A. (2009). Moderators of and mechanisms underlying stereotype threat effects on older adults' memory performance. *Experimental Aging Research,* 35, 153–177.

Hesse, E., & Main, M. (2006). Frightened, threatening, and dissociative parental behavior in low-risk samples: Description, discussion, and interpretations. *Development and Psychopathology,* 18, 309–343

Hetherington, E. M. (1981). Children and divorce. In R. W. Henderson (Ed.), *Parent–Child Interaction: Theory, Research and Prospects.* New York: Academic Press.

Hetherington, E. M. (2006). The influence of conflict, marital problem solving and parenting on children's adjustment in nondivorced, divorced and remarried families. In A. Clarke-Stewart & J. Dunn (Eds.), *Families count: Effects on child and adolescent development.* New York: Cambridge University Press.

Hetherington, E. M., & Kelly, J. (2002). *For better or for worse: Divorce reconsidered.* New York: Norton.

Hetherington, E. M., & Stanley-Hagen, M. (2000). Diversity among stepfamilies. In D. H. Demo, K. R. Allen, & M. A. Fine (Eds.), *Handbook of family diversity.* New York: Oxford University Press.

Hetherington, E. M., Cox, M., & Cox, R. (1982). Effects of divorce on parents and children. In M. E. Lamb (Ed.), *Nontraditional families.* Hillsdale, NJ: Erlbaum.

Hewitt, B., Western, M., & Baxter, J. (2006). Who decides? The social characteristics of who initiates marital separation. *Journal of Marriage and Family,* 68, 1165–1177.

Heyman, R. E., Foran, H. M., & Wilkinson, J. L. (2013). Theories of intimate partner violence. In M. A. Fine & F. D. Fincham (Eds.), *Handbook of family theories. A context-based approach.* New York: Routledge.

Heymann, J., & Earle, A. (2009). *Raising the global floor: Dismantling the myth that we can't afford good working conditions for everyone.* Stanford, CA: Stanford University Press.

Heymann, S. J., Penrose, K., & Earle, A. (2006). Meeting children's needs: How does the United States measure up? *Merrill-Palmer Quarterly,* 52, 189–215.

Hicks, B. M., Blonigen, D. M., Kramer, M. D., Krueger, R. F., Patrick, C. J., Iacono, W. G., et al. (2007). Gender differences and developmental change in externalizing disorders from late adolescence to early adulthood: A longitudinal twin study. *Journal of Abnormal Psychology,* 116, 433–447.

Hilgard, E. R., & Loftus, E. F. (1979). Effective interrogation of the eyewitness. *International Journal of Clinical and Experimental Psychology,* 27, 342–357.

Hill, A. J. (2007). The development of children's shape and weight concerns. In T. Jaffa & B. McDermott (Eds.), *Eating disorders in children and adolescents.* Cambridge, UK: Cambridge University Press.

Hill, C., & Rose, J. (2009). Parenting stress in mothers of adults with an intellectual disability: Parental cognitions in relation to child characteristics and family support. *Journal of Intellectual Disability Research,* 53, 969–980.

Hill, J. P., & Lynch, M. E. (1983). The intensification of gender-related role expectations during early adolescence. In J. Brooks-Gunn & A. C. Petersen (Eds.), *Girls at puberty: Biological and psychosocial perspectives.* New York: Plenum.

Hill, J., Emery, R. E., Harden, K. P., Mendle, J., & Turkheimer, E. (2008). Alcohol use in adolescent twins and affiliation with substance using peers. *Journal of Abnormal Child Psychology,* 36, 81–94.

Hill, N. E., & Tyson, D. F. (2009). Parental involvement in middle school: A meta-analytic assessment of the strategies that promote achievement. *Developmental Psychology,* 45, 740–763.

Hill, R., & Rodgers, R. H. (1964). The developmental approach. In H. Christensen (Ed.), *Handbook of marriage and the family.* Chicago: Rand-McNally.

Hill, S. D., & Tomlin, C. (1981). Self-recognition in retarded children. *Child Development,* 52, 145–150.

Hill, S. E., & Flom, R. (2007). 18- and 24-month-olds' discrimination of gender-consistent and inconsistent activities. *Infant Behavior & Development,* 30, 168–173.

Hills, T. (2013). The company that words keep: Comparing the statistical structure of child-versus adult-directed language. *Journal of Child Language,* 40, 586–604.

Hinds, J. D. (2007, May 28). 'I'm sorry' shouldn't be the hardest words. *Newsweek,* 20.

Hinduja, S., & Patchin, J. W. (2013). Social influences on cyberbullying behaviors among middle and high school students. *Journal of Youth and Adolescence,* 42, 711–722.

Hines, J. C., Touron, D. R., & Hertzog, C. (2009). Metacognitive influences on study time allocation in an associative recognition task: An analysis of adult age differences. *Psychology and Aging,* 24, 462–275.

Hinton, J. (1975). The influence of previous personality on reactions to having terminal cancer. *Omega: Journal of Death and Dying,* 6, 95–111.

Hirschi, A., & Vondracek, F. W. (2009). Adaptation of career goals to self and opportunities in early adolescence. *Journal of Vocational Behavior,* 75, 120–128.

Hirsh-Pasek, K., Golinkoff, R. M, Berk, L. E, & Singer, D. G. (2009). *A mandate for playful learning in preschool: Presenting the evidence.* New York: Oxford University Press.

Hirsh-Pasek, K., Golinkoff, R. M., & Hollich, G. (1999). Trends and transitions in language development: Looking for the missing piece. *Developmental Neuropsychology, 16,* 139–162.

Hoare, C. (2009). Models of adult development in Bronfenbrenner's bioecological theory and Erikson's biopsychosocial life stage theory: Moving to a more complete three-model view. In M. C. Smith & N. DeFrates-Densch (Eds.), *Handbook of research on adult learning and development* (pp. 68–102). New York: Routledge.

Hobbs, F. B. (with B. L. Damon). (1996). *65 in the United States.* Washington, DC: U.S. Bureau of the Census.

Hodapp, R. M., Griffin, M. M., Burke, M. M., & Fisher, M. H. (2011). Intellectual disabilities. In R. J. Sternberg & S. B. Kaufman (Eds.), *The Cambridge handbook of intelligence* (pp. 193–209). New York: Cambridge University Press.

Hodges, J., & Tizard, B. (1989). IQ and behavioral adjustment of exinstitutional adolescents. *Journal of Child Psychology and Psychiatry, 30,* 53–75.

Hodnett, E. D., Simon, G., Hofmeyr, G. J., & Sakala, C. (2012). Continuous support for women during childbirth. *Cochrane Database of Systematic Reviews,* Issue 10. Art. No.: CD003766. doi:10.1002/14651858.CD003766. pub4

Hoegg, J., & Alba, J. W. (2007, March). Taste perception: More than meets the tongue. *Journal of Consumer Research, 33,* 490–498.

Hof, P., & Mobbs, C. (2001). *Functional neurobiology of aging.* San Diego, CA: Academic Press.

Hoff, E. (2014). *Language development* (5th ed.). Belmont, CA: Wadsworth.

Hoff, E. V. (2005a). A friend living inside me—The forms and functions of imaginary companions. *Imagination, Cognition, and Personality, 24,* 151–189.

Hoff, E. V. (2005b). Imaginary companions, creativity, and self-image in middle childhood. *Creativity Research Journal, 17,* 167–180.

Hoffman, K. L., Kiecolt, K. J., & Edwards, J. N. (2005). Physical violence between siblings: A theoretical and empirical analysis. *Journal of Family Issues, 26,* 1103–1130.

Hoffman, L. W. (1989). Effects of maternal employment in the two-parent family. *American Psychologist, 44,* 283–292.

Hoffman, L. W. (2000). Maternal employment: Effects of social context. In R. D. Taylor & M. C. Wang (Eds.), *Resilience across contexts: Family, work, culture, and community.* Mahwah, NJ: Erlbaum.

Hoffman, M. L. (1970). Moral development. In P. H. Mussen (Ed.), *Carmichael's manual of child psychology* (Vol. 2). New York: Wiley.

Hoffman, M. L. (2000). *Empathy and moral development: Implications for caring and justice.* Cambridge, UK: Cambridge University Press.

Hoffman, M. L. (2008). Empathy and prosocial behavior. In M. Lewis, J. M. Haviland-Jones, & L. F. Barrett (Eds.), *Handbook of emotions* (3rd ed.). New York: Guilford.

Hoffman, S., & Maynard, R. A. (2008). *Kids having kids: Economic costs and social consequences of teen pregnancy.* Washington, DC: The Urban Institute Press.

Hoffman, S. I., & Strauss, S. (1985). The development of children's concepts of death. *Death Studies, 9,* 469–482.

Hoffnung, M. (2004). Wanting it all: Career, marriage, and motherhood during college-educated women's 20s. *Sex Roles, 50,* 711–723.

Hoffnung, M., & Williams, M. A. (2013). Balancing act: Career and family during college-educated women's 30s. *Sex Roles, 68,* 321–334.

Hofmann, S. G., Asnaani, A., Vonk, I. J. J., Sawyer, A. T., & Fang, A. (2012). The efficacy of cognitive behavioral therapy: A review of meta-analyses. *Cognitive Therapy and Research, 36,* 427–440.

Hofstra, M. B., Van der Ende, J., & Verhulst, F. C. (2000). Continuity and change of psychopathology from childhood into adulthood. *Journal of the American Academy of Child & Adolescent Psychiatry, 39,* 850–858.

Hogström, L., Johansson, M., Janson, P. O., Berg, M., Francis, J., Sogn, J., et al. (2012). Quality of life after adopting compared with childbirth with or without assisted reproduction. *Actaobstetricia Et Gynecologicascandinavica, 91,* 1077–1085.

Hohm, E., Jennen-Steinmetz, C., Schmidt, M. H., & Laucht, M. (2007). Language development at ten months: Predictive of language outcome and school achievement ten years later? *European Child & Adolescent Psychiatry, 16,* 149–156.

Holahan, C., & Sears, R. (1995). *The gifted group in later maturity.* Stanford, CA: Stanford University Press.

Holden, G. W. (2010). *Parenting. A dynamic perspective.* Thousand Oaks, CA: Sage.

Holden, G. W., Vittrub, B., & Rosen, L. H. (2011). Families, parenting, and discipline. In M. K. Underwood & L. H. Rosen (Eds), *Social development: Relationships in infancy, childhood and adolescence.* New York: Guilford.

Holland, J. L. (1985). *Making vocational choices: A theory of vocational personalities and work environments* (2nd ed.). Englewood Cliffs, NJ: Prentice-Hall.

Holland, J. L. (1996). Exploring careers with a typology: What we have learned and some new directions. *American Psychologist, 51,* 397–406.

Hollich, G. (2010). Early language. In J. G. Bremner & T. D. Wachs (Eds.), *The Wiley-Blackwell handbook of infant development, 2nd ed., Vol. 1: Basic research* (pp. 426–449). Malden, MA: Blackwell.

Hollich, G. J., Hirsh-Pasek, K., & Golinkoff, R. M. (2000). Breaking the language barrier: An emergentist coalition model for the origins of word learning. *Monographs of the Society for Research in Child Development, 65*(No. 262).

Hollins, M. (2010). Somesthetic senses. *Annual Review of Psychology, 61,* 243–271.

Hollon, S. D., Thase, M. E., & Markowitz, J. C. (2002). Treatment and prevention of depression. *Psychological Science in the Public Interest, 3,* 39–77.

Holmbeck, G. N., Crossman, R. E., Wandrei, M. L., & Gasiewski, E. (1994). Cognitive development, egocentrism, self-esteem, and adolescent contraceptive knowledge, attitudes, and behavior. *Journal of Youth and Adolescence, 23,* 169–193.

Holowka, S., & Petitto, L. A. (2002). Left hemisphere cerebral specialization for babies while babbling. *Science, 297,* 1515.

Holzrichter, A. S., & Meier, R. P. (2000). Child-directed signing in American sign language. In C. Chamberlain, J. P. Morford, & R. Mayberry (Eds.), *Language acquisition by eye.* Mahwah, NJ: Lawrence Erlbaum.

Honey, K. L., Bennett, P., & Morgan, M. (2003). Predicting postnatal depression. *Journal of Affective Disorders, 76,* 201–10.

Hong, J. S., & Espelage, D. L. (2012). A review of research on bullying and peer victimization in school: An ecological system analysis. *Aggression and Violent Behavior, 17,* 311–322.

Honzik, M. P. (1983). Measuring mental abilities in infancy: The value and limitations. In M. Lewis (Ed.), *Origins of intelligence: Infancy and early childhood* (2nd ed.). New York: Plenum.

Hooker, K., & Siegler, I. C. (1993). Life goals, satisfaction, and self-rated health: Preliminary findings. *Experimental Aging Research, 19,* 97–110.

Hooper, F. H., Hooper, J. O., & Colbert, K. K. (1985). Personality and memory correlates of intellectual functioning in adulthood: Piagetian and psychometric assessments. *Human Development, 28,* 101–107.

Hopkins M. (2006, July 3). '*Miracle recovery' shows brain's resilience.* Retrieved from http://www.bioedonline.org/news/news. cfm?art=2630

Horiuchi, S., Finch, C. E., Mesle, F., & Vallin, J. (2003). Differential patterns of age-related mortality increase in middle age and old age. *Journal of Gerontology: Biological Sciences, 58A,* 495–507.

Horn, J. L., & Cattell, R. B. (1967). Age differences in fluid and crystallized intelligence. *Acta Psychologica, 26,* 107–129.

Horn, J. L., & Noll, J. (1997). Human cognitive capabilities: *Gf-Gc* theory. In D. P. Flanagan, J. Genshaft, & P. L. Harrison (Eds.), *Contemporary intellectual assessment: Theories, tests, and issues.* New York: Guilford.

Horner, V., & Whiten, A. (2005). Causal knowledge and imitation/emulation switching in chimpanzees (Pan troglodytes) and children (Homo sapiens). *Animal Cognition, 8,* 164–181.

Horswill, M. S., Marrington, S. A., McCullough, C. M., Wood, J., Pachana, N. A., McWilliam, J., et al. (2008). The hazard perception ability of older drivers. *Journals of Gerontology, Series B: Psychological Sciences and Social Sciences, 63,* P212–P218.

Houdé, O., Pineau, A., Leroux, G., Poirel, N., Perchey, G., Lanoë, C., et al. (2011). Functional magnetic resonance imaging study of Piaget's conservation-of-number task in preschool and school-age children: A neo-Piagetian approach. *Journal of Experimental Child Psychology*.

Houdé, O., Rossi, S., Lubin, A., & Joliot, M. (2010). Mapping numerical processing, reading, and executive functions in the developing brain: An fMRI meta-analysis on 52 studies including 842 children. *Developmental Science, 13*, 876–885.

House, J. D. (2006). Mathematics beliefs, instructional strategies, and algebra achievement of adolescent students in Japan: Results from the TIMSS 1999 assessment. *International Journal of Instructional Media, 33*, 443–462.

Houshyar, S., Gold, A., & DeVries, M. (2013). Resiliency in maltreated children. In S. Goldstein & R. B. Brooks (Eds.), *Handbook of resilience in children* (2nd ed.). New York: Springer Science+Business Media.

Houston, D. M., Pisoni, D. B., Kirk, K. I., Ying, E. A., & Miyamoto, R. T. (2005). Speech perception skills of deaf infants following cochlear implantation: A first report. *International Journal of Pediatric Otorhinolaryngology, 67*, 1479–495.

Houx, P. J., Vreeling, F. W., & Jolles, J. (1991). Rigorous health screening reduces age effect on memory scanning task. *Brain and Cognition, 15*, 246–260.

Howe, D. (2011). *Attachment across the lifecourse. A brief introduction*. New York: Palgrave Macmillan.

Howe, G. W., Hornberger, A. P., Weihs, K., Moreno, F., & Neiderhiser, J. M. (2012). Higher-order structure in the trajectories of depression and anxiety following sudden involuntary unemployment. *Journal of Abnormal Psychology, 121*, 325–338.

Howe, G. W., Levy, M. L., & Caplan, R. D. (2004). Job loss and depressive symptoms in couples: Common stressors, stress transmission, or relationship disruption? *Journal of Family Psychology, 18*, 639–650.

Howe, M. L. (2000). *The fate of early memories: Developmental science and the retention of childhood experiences*. Washington, DC: American Psychological Association.

Howe, M. L. (2006). Developmental invariance in distinctiveness effects in memory. *Developmental Psychology, 42*, 1193–1205.

Howe, M. L., Courage, M. L., & Rooksby, M. (2009). In M. L. Courage & N. Cowan (Eds.), *The development of memory in infancy and childhood* (pp. 177–196). New York: Psychology Press.

Howe, N., Aquan-Assee, J., Bukowski, W. M., Rinaldi, C. M., & Lehoux, P. M. (2000). Sibling self-disclosure in early adolescence. *Merrill-Palmer Quarterly, 46*, 653–671.

Howes, C. (1988). Same- and cross-sex friends: Implications for interaction and social skills. *Early Childhood Research Quarterly, 3*, 21–37.

Howes, C., & Matheson, C. C. (1992). Sequences in the development of competent play with peers: Social and social pretend play. *Developmental Psychology, 28*, 961–974.

Howes, P., & Markman, H. J. (1989). Marital quality and child functioning: A longitudinal investigation. *Child Development, 60*, 1044–1051.

Howieson, D. B., Dame, A., Camicioli, R., Sexton, G., Payami, H., & Kaye, J. A. (1997). Cognitive markers preceding Alzheimer's dementia in the healthy oldest old. *Journal of the American Geriatrics Society, 45*, 584–589.

Howlin, P., & Moss, P. (2012). Adults with autism spectrum disorders. *Canadian Journal of Psychiatry, 57*, 275–283.

Hoyer, W. J., & Verhaeghen, P. (2006). Memory aging. In J. E. Birren & K. W. Schaie (Eds.), *Handbook of the psychology of aging*. Boston: Elsevier Academic Press.

Hrdy, S. B. (2005). On why it takes a village. Cooperative breeders, infant needs, and the future. In R. L. Burgess & K. MacDonald (Eds.), *Evolutionary perspectives on human development*. Thousand Oaks, CA: Sage.

Hsia, Y., Neubert, A. C., Rani, F., Viner, R. M., Hindmarsh, P. C., & Wong, I. C. (2009). An increase in the prevalence of type 1 and 2 diabetes in children and adolescents: Results from prescription data from a UK general practice database. *British Journal of Clinical Pharmacology, 67*, 242–249.

Hsu, L. K. G. (1990). *Eating disorders*. New York: Guilford Press.

Hsu, L. M., Chung, J., & Langer, E. J. (2010). The influence of age-related cues on health and longevity. *Perspectives on Psychological Science, 5*, 632–648.

Hu, V. W. (2013). From genes to environment: Using integrative genomics to build a "systems-level" understanding of autism spectrum disorders. *Child Development, 84*, 89–103.

Huang, M. (2009). Race of the interviewer and the black-white test score gap. *Social Science Research, 38*, 29–38.

Hubel, D. H., & Wiesel, T. N. (1970). The period of susceptibility to the physiological effects of unilateral eye-closure in kittens. *Journal of Physiology, 206*, 419–436.

Hudson, J. A., & Mayhew, E. M. Y. (2009). The development of memory for recurring events. In M. L. Courage & N. Cowan (Eds.), *The development of memory in infancy and childhood* (pp. 69–92). New York: Psychology Press.

Huesmann, L. R., Dubow, E. F., & Boxer, P. (2009). Continuity of aggression from childhood to early adulthood as a predictor of life outcomes: Implications for the adolescent-limited and life-course-persistent models. *Aggressive Behavior, 35*, 136–149.

Hughes, D., Rodriguez, J., Smith, E. P., Johnson, D. J., Stevenson, H. C., & Spicer, P. (2006). Parents' ethnic socialization practices: A review of research and directions for future study. *Developmental Psychology, 42*, 747–770.

Hughes, F. M., & Seta, C. E. (2003). Gender stereotypes: Children's perceptions of future compensatory behavior following violations of gender roles. *Sex Roles, 49*, 685–691.

Huizink, A. C. (2012). Prenatal factors in temperament: The role of prenatal stress and substance use exposure. In M. Z. Zentner & R. L. Shiner (Eds.), *Handbook of temperament*. New York: Guilford.

Hultman, C. M., Sandin, S., Levine, S. Z., Lichtenstein, P., &Reichenberg, A. (2011). Advancing paternal age and risk of autism: New evidence from a population-based study and a meta-analysis of epidemiological studies. *Molecular Psychiatry, 16*, 1203–1212.

Hultsch, D. F., Hammer, M., & Small, B. J. (1993). Age differences in cognitive performance in later life: Relationships to self-reported health and activity life style. *Journal of Gerontology Series B: Psychological Sciences, 48*, 1–11.

Human Rights Watch. (2011). *United States failing its families.Lack of paid leave and work-family supports in the U.S.* New York: Human Rights Watch. Retrieved from http://www.hrw.org/node/96432e

Hummert, M. L. (2011). Age stereotypes and aging. In K. W. Schaie & S. L. Willis (Eds.), B. G. Knight, B. Levy, & D. C. Park (Assoc. Eds.), *Handbook of the psychology of aging*. Boston, MA: Elsevier.

Hurd, L. C. (1999). "We're not old!" Older women's negotiation of aging and oldness. *Journal of Aging Studies, 13*, 419–439.

Hurd, R. C. (2002). Sibling support systems in childhood after a parent dies. *Omega: Journal of Death and Dying, 45*, 299–320.

Hure, A. J., Powers, J. R., Mishra, G. D., Herbert, D. L., Byles, J. E., & Loxton, D. (2012). Miscarriage, preterm delivery, and stillbirth: Large variations in rates within a cohort of Australian women. *PLoS ONE, 7*, 1–8.

Hurst, K., Read, S., & Wallis, A. (2012). Anorexia nervosa in adolescence and Maudsley family-based treatment. *Journal of Counseling & Development, 90*, 339–345.

Huston, A. C., & Bentley, A. C. (2010). Human development in societal context. *Annual Review of Psychology, 61*, 411–437.

Huston, M., & Schwartz, P. (1995). The relationships of lesbians and gay men. In J. T. Wood & S. Duck (Eds.), *Under-studied relationships: Off the beaten track*. Thousand Oaks, CA: Sage.

Huston, T. L., & Melz, H. (2004). The case for (promoting) marriage: The devil is in the details. *Journal of Marriage and Family, 66*, 943–958.

Huston, T. L., Caughlin, J. P., Houts, R. M., Smith, S. E., & George, L. J. (2001). The connubial crucible: Newlywed years as predictors of marital delight, distress, and divorce. *Journal of Personality and Social Psychology, 80*, 237–252.

Huston, T. L., McHale, S. M., & Crouter, A. C. (1986). When the honeymoon's over: Changes in the marriage relationship over the first year. In R. Gilmour & S. Duck (Eds.), *The emerging field of personal relationships*. Hillsdale, NJ: Erlbaum.

Hwang, S., Kim, Y. S., & Leventhal, B. (2013). Bullying and the development of antisocial behavior. In C. R. Thomas & K. Pope (Eds.), *The origins of antisocial behavior. A developmental perspective*. New York: Oxford University Press.

Hybels, C. F., Blazer, D. G., & Hays, J. C. (2009). Demography and epidemiology of psychiatric disorders in late life. In D. G. Blazer & D. C. Steffens (Eds.), *The American Psychiatric Publishing textbook of geriatric psychiatry* (4th ed.). Washington, DC: American Psychiatric Publishing.

Hyde, J. S. (1984). How large are gender differences in aggression? A developmental meta-analysis. *Developmental Psychology, 20*, 722–736.

Hyde, J. S. (2005). The gender similarities hypothesis. *American Psychologist, 60*, 581–592.

Hyde, J. S. (2007). New directions in the study of gender similarities and differences. *Current Directions in Psychological Science, 16*, 259–263.

Hyde, J. S., & DeLamater, J. D. (2014). *Human sexuality* (12th ed.). McGraw-Hill.

Iacoboni, M. (2009). Imitation, empathy, and mirror neurons. *Annual Review of Psychology, 60*, 653–670.

Iacoboni, M., & Dapretto, M. (2006). The mirror neuron system and the consequences of its dysfunction. *Nature Reviews Neuroscience, 7*, 942–951.

Ialongo, N. S., Edelsohn, G., & Kellam, S. G. (2001). A further look at the prognostic power of young children's reports of depressed mood. *Child Development, 72*, 736–747.

Iervolino, A. C., Hines, M., Golombok, S. E., Rust, J., & Plomin, R. (2005). Genetic and environmental influences on sex-typed behavior during the preschool years. *Child Development, 76*, 826–840.

Torres-Mejía, G., Cupul-Uicab, L. A., Allen, B., Galal, O., Salazar-Martínez, E., & Lazcano-Ponce, E. C. (2005). Comparative study of correlates of early age at menarche among Mexican and Egyptian adolescents. *American Journal of Human Biology, 17*, 654–658.

Imel, S. (1996). *Adult literacy education: Emerging directions in program development. ERIC Digest No. 179*. Columbus, OH: ERIC Clearinghouse on Adult, Career and Vocational Education, Ohio State University.

Imperato-McGinley, J., Miller, M., Wilson, J. D., Peterson, R. E. Shackleton, C., Gajdusek, D. C. (1991. A cluster of male pseudohermaphrodites with 5α-reductase deficiency in Papua New Guinea *Clinical Embryology, 34*, 293–298.

Imperato-McGinley, J., Peterson, R. E., Gautier, T., & Sturla, E. (1979). Androgens and the evolution of male gender identity among male pseudohermaphrodites with 5a-reductase deficiency. *New England Journal of Medicine, 300*, 1233–1237.

Ingersoll, B. (2011). Recent advances in early identification and treatment of autism.*Current Directions in Psychological Science, 20*, 335–338.

Ingoldsby, B. B., & Smith, S. (1995). *Families in multicultural perspective*. New York: Guilford.

Ingram, R. E., & Price, J. M. (2001). The role of vulnerability in understanding psychopathology. In R. E. Ingram & J. M. Price (Eds.), *Vulnerability to psychopathology. Risk across the lifespan*. New York: Guilford.

Ingrassia, M., & Springen, K. (1994, March 21). She's not baby Jessica anymore. *Newsweek, 123*, 60–66.

Inhelder, B. (1966). Cognitive development and its contribution to the diagnosis of some phenomena of mental deficiency. *Merrill-Palmer Quarterly, 12*, 299–319.

Inhelder, B., & Piaget, J. (1964). *Early growth of logic in the child: Classification and seriation*. New York: Harper & Row.

Insurance Institute for Highway Safety. (2013). Retrieved from http://www.iihs.org/research/fatality.aspx?topicName=Older people&year=2011

Isabella, R. A. (1993). Origins of attachment: Maternal interactive behavior across the first year. *Child Development, 64*, 605–621.

Isabella, R. A., & Belsky, J. (1991). Interactional synchrony and the origins of infant-mother attachment: A replication study. *Child Development, 62*, 373–384.

Izard, C. E. (1982). *Measuring emotions in infants and children*. New York: Cambridge University Press.

Izard, C. E., & Ackerman, B. P. (2000). Motivational, organizational, and regulatory functions of discrete emotions. In M. Lewis & J. M. Haviland-Jones (Eds.), *Handbook of emotions* (2nd ed.). New York: Guilford.

Jack, F., & Hayne, H. (2007). Eliciting adults' earliest memories: Does it matter how we ask the question? *Memory, 15*, 647–663.

Jack, F., MacDonald, S., Reese, E., & Hayne, H. (2009). Maternal reminiscing style during early childhood predicts the age of adolescents' earliest memories. *Child Development, 80*, 496–505.

Jacklin, C. N. (1989). Male and female: Issues of gender. *American Psychologist, 44*, 127–133.

Jacobs, J. E., & Klaczynski, P. A. (2002). The development of judgment and decision making during childhood and adolescence. *Current Directions in Psychological Science, 11*, 145–149.

Jacobs, J. E., Lanza, S., Osgood, D. W., Eccles, J. S., & Wigfield, A. (2002). Changes in children's self-competence and values: Gender and domain differences across grades one through twelve. *Child Development, 73*, 509–527.

Jacobs, R. J., & Kane, M. N. (2010). HIV-related stigma in midlife and older women. *Social Work Health Care, 49*, 68–89.

Jacobs, S. C., Kosten, T. R., Kasl, S. V., Ostfeld, A. M., Berkman, L., & Charpentier, P. (1987–1988). Attachment theory and multiple dimensions of grief. *Omega: Journal of Death and Dying, 18*, 41–52.

Jaffa, T., & McDermott, B. (Eds.) (2007). *Eating disorders in children and adolescents*. Cambridge, UK: Cambridge University Press.

Jaffe, J., Beebe, B., Feldstein, S., Crown, C. L., & Jasnow, M. D. (2001). Rhythms of dialogue in infancy: Coordinated timing in development. *Monographs of the Society for Research in Child Development, 66* (2, Serial No. 265).

Jaffee, S. R. (2013). Family violence and parent psychopathology: Implications for children's socioemotional development and resilience. In S. Goldstein, & R. B. Brooks (Eds.), *Handbook of resilience in children* (2nd ed.). New York: Springer Science+Business Media.

Jaffee, S. R., Strait, L. B., & Odgers, C. L. (2012). From correlates to causes: Can quasi-experimental studies and statistical innovations bring us closer to identifying the causes of antisocial behavior? *Psychological Bulletin, 138*, 272–295.

James, J., Ellis, B. J., Schlomer, G. L., & Garber, J. (2012). Sex-specific pathways to early puberty, sexual debut, and sexual risk taking: Tests of an integrated evolutionary-developmental model. *Developmental Psychology, 48*, 687–702.

James, J. B., & Zarrett, N. (2005). Ego integrity in the lives of older women: A follow-up of mothers from the Sears, Maccoby, and Levin (1951) Patterns of Child Rearing Study. *Journal of Adult Development, 12*, 155–167.

James, W. (1890). The *Principles of Psychology*. London: Henry Holt & Co.

Jamison, K. R. (2009). *Nothing was the same*. New York: Alfred A. Knopf.

Jankowiak, W. R., & Fischer, E. F. (1992). A cross-cultural perspective on romantic love. *Ethnology,31*, 149–155.

Janus, J. S., & Janus, C. L. (1993). *The Janus report on sexual behavior*. New York: Wiley.

Jaquish, G. A., & Ripple, R. E. (1981). Cognitive creative abilities and self-esteem across the adult life-span. *Human Development, 24*, 110–119.

Jastrzembski, T. S., Charness, N., & Vasyukova, C. (2006). Expertise and age effects on knowledge activation in chess. *Psychology and Aging, 21*, 401–405.

Jayawardena, K. M., & Liao, S. (2006). Elder abuse at the end of life. *Journal of Palliative Medicine, 9*, 127–136.

Jean, R. T., Wilkinson, A. V., Spitz, M. R., Prokhorov, A., Bondy, M., & Forman, M. R. (2011). Psychosocial risk and correlates of early menarche in Mexican-American girls. *American Journal of Epidemiology, 173*, 1203–1210.

Jelicic, H., Bobek, D. L., Phelps, E., Lerner, R. M., & Lerner, J. V. (2007). Using positive youth development to predict contribution and risk behaviors in early adolescence: Findings from the first two waves of the 4-H study of positive youth development. *International Journal of Behavioral Development, 31*, 263–273.

Jemmott, J. B., III, Jemmott, L. S., & Fong, G. T. (2010). Efficacy of a theory-based abstinence-only intervention over 24 months: A randomized controlled trial with young adolescents. *Archives of Pediatric & Adolescent Medicine, 164*, 152–159.

Jenkins, S. R. (1989). Longitudinal prediction of women's careers: Psychological, behavioral, and social–structural influences. *Journal of Vocational Behavior, 34*, 204–235.

Jennings, K. D., & Dietz, L. J. (2003). Mastery motivation and goal persistence in young children. In M. H. Bornstein & L. Davidson (Eds.), *Well-being: Positive development across the life course* (pp. 295–309). Mahwah, NJ: Lawrence Erlbaum.

Jennings, K. D., Yarrow, L. J., & Martin, P. D. (1984). Mastery motivation and cognitive development: A longitudinal study from infancy to 3 and 1/2 years of age. *International Journal of Behavioral Development, 7,* 441–461.

Jensen, A. R. (1969). How much can we boost IQ and scholastic achievement? *Harvard Educational Review, 39,* 1–123.

Jensen, A. R. (1977). Cumulative deficit in the IQ of blacks in the rural South. *Developmental Psychology, 13,* 184–191.

Jensen, A. R. (1980). *Bias in mental testing.* New York: Free Press.

Jensen, A. R. (1993). Why is reaction time correlated with psychometric g? *Current Directions in Psychological Science, 2,* 53–56.

Jensen, A. R. (1998). *The g factor: The science of mental ability.* Westport, CN: Praeger.

Jensen, P. S., Hinshaw, S. P., Swanson, J. M., Greenhill, L. L., Conners, C. K., Arnold, L. E., Abikoff, H. B., Elliott, G., Hechtman, L., Hoza, B., March, J. S., Newcorn, J. H., Severe, J. B., Vitiello, B., Wells, K., & Wigal, T. (2001). Findings from the NIMH Multimodal Treatment Study of ADHD (MTA): Implications and applications for primary care providers. *Journal of Developmental and Behavioral Pediatrics, 22,* 60–73.

Jessberger, S., & Parent, J. M. (2008). Epilepsy and adult neurogenesis. In F. H. Gage, G. Kempermann, & H. Song (Eds.), *Adult neurogenesis* (pp. 535–547). New York: Cold Spring Harbor Laboratory Press.

Jessor, R. (Ed.) (1998). *New perspectives on adolescent risk behavior.* Cambridge, UK: Cambridge University Press.

Jetha, M. K., & Segalowitz, S. (2012). *Adolescent brain development: Implications for behavior.* Waltham, MA: Academic Press.

Jimenez, D. E., Alegría, M., Chen, C., Chan, D., & Laderman, M. (2010). Prevalence of psychiatric illnesses in older ethnic minority adults. *Journal of the American Geriatrics Society, 58,* 256–264.

Joh, A. S., & Adolph, K. E. (2006). Learning from falling. *Child Development, 77,* 89–102.

Johansson, B., Zarit, S. H., & Berg, S. (1992). Changes in cognitive functioning of the oldest old. *Journal of Gerontology Series B: Psychological Sciences, 47,* P75–P80.

Johansson, T., & Ritzén, E. M. (2005). Very long-term follow-up of girls with early and late menarche. *Endocrine Development, 8,* 126–136.

Johnson, J. G., Cohen, P., Kasen, S., Smailes, E., & Brook, J. (2001). Association of maladaptive parental behavior with psychiatric disorder among parents and their offspring. *Archives of General Psychology, 58,* 453–460.

Johnson, J. G., Zhang, B., Greer, J. A., & Prigerson, H. G. (2007). Parental control, partner dependency, and complicated grief among widowed adults in the community. *Journal of Nervous and Mental Disease, 195,* 26–30.

Johnson, J., & Newport, E. (1989). Critical period effects in second language learning: The influence of maturational state on the acquisition of English as a second language. *Cognitive Psychology, 21,* 60–99.

Johnson, M. H. (1997). *Developmental cognitive neuroscience.* Cambridge, MA: Blackwell.

Johnson, M. H., & de Haan, M. D. (2001). Developing cortical specialization for visual-cognitive function: The case of face recognition. In J. L. McClelland & R. S. Siegler (Eds.), *Mechanisms of cognitive development: Behavioral and neural perspectives* (pp. 253–270). Mahwah, NJ: U Sum Associates Publishers.

Johnson, M. H., & with de Haan, M. (2011). *Developmental cognitive neuroscience* (3rd ed.). Malden, MA: Wiley-Blackwell.

Johnson, S. M. (2004). *The practice of emotionally focused couple therapy: Creating connection.* New York: Brunner/Routledge.

Johnson, S. M. (2008). Couple and family therapy. An attachment perspective. In J. Cassidy & P. R. Shaver (Eds.), *Handbook of attachment: Theory, research, and clinical applications* (2nd ed.). New York: Guilford.

Johnson, S. M., & Wittenborn, A. K. (2012). New research findings on emotionally focused therapy: Introduction to special section. *Journal of Marital and Family Therapy, 38,* 18–22.

Johnson, W., & Bouchard, T. J. (2007). Sex differences in mental abilities: g masks the dimensions on which they lie. *Intelligence, 35,* 23–39.

John-Steiner, V. (1992). Private speech among adults. In R. M. Diaz & L. E. Berk (Eds.), *Private speech: From social interaction to self-regulation* (pp. 285–296). Hillsdale, NJ: Erlbaum.

Johnston, L. D., O'Malley, P. M., Bachman, J. G., & Schulenberg, J. E. (2009). *Monitoring the future. National Results on Adolescent Drug Use. Overview of key findings, 2008.* Bethesda, MD: National Institute on Drug Abuse, U.S. Department of Health and Human Services. Retrieved from http://monitoringthefuture.org/pubs/monographs/overview2008.pdf

Johnston, L. D., O'Malley, P. M., Bachman, J. G., & Schulenberg, J. E. (2013). *Monitoring the future. National results on drug use: 2012 overview, Key findings on adolescent drug use.* Ann Arbor: Institutefor Social Research, The University of Michigan. Retrieved from http://www.monitoringthefuture.org/

Joint Committee on Infant Hearing. (2000). Year 2000 position statement: Principles and guidelines for early hearing detection and intervention programs. *Pediatrics, 106,* 798–817.

Jokela, M., Ferrie, J., & Kivimäki, M. (2009). Childhood problem behaviors and death by midlife: The British National Child Development Study. *Journal of the American Academy of Child & Adolescent Psychiatry, 48,* 19–24.

Jones, H., Karuri, S., Cronin, C., Ohlsson, A., Peliowski, A., Synnes, A., et al. (2005). Actuarial survival of a large Canadian cohort of preterm infants. *BMC Pediatrics, 5,* 1–13.

Jones, J. R., Kogan, M. D., Singh, G. K., Dee, D. L., & Grummer-Strawn, L. M. (2011). Factors associated with exclusive breastfeeding in the United States. *Pediatrics, 128,* 1117–1125.

Jones, S. S. (1996). Imitation or exploration? Young infants' matching of adults' oral gestures. *Child Development, 67,* 1952–1969.

Jones, T. (2007, April 18). A tragedy beyond the imagination. *The Washington Post,* pp. C1, C4.

Jones, W., & Klin, A. (2009). Heterogeneity and homogeneity across the autism spectrum: The role of development. *Journal of the American Academy of Child & Adolescent Psychiatry, 48,* 471–473.

Jordahl, T., & Lohman, B. J. (2009). A bioecological analysis of risk and protective factors associated with early sexual intercourse of young adolescents. *Children and Youth Services Review, 31,* 1272–1282.

Joseph, S. (2012). What doesn't kill us.... *The Psychologist, 25,* 816–819.

Judd, T. (2013). Making sense of multitasking: Key behaviours. *Computers & Education, 63,* 358–367.

Judge, S. (2003). Developmental recovery and deficit in children adopted from Eastern European orphanages. *Child Psychiatry and Human Development, 34,* 49–62.

Judge, T. A., & Bono, J. E. (2001). Relationship of core self-evaluation traits—self-esteem, generalized self-efficacy, locus of control, and emotional stability—with job satisfaction and job performance: A meta-analysis. *Journal of Applied Psychology, 86,* 80–92.

Judge, T. A., Klinger, R. L., & Simon, L. W. (2010). Time is on my side: Time, general mental ability, human capital, and extrinsic career success. *Journal of Applied Psychology, 95,* 92–107.

Judy, B., & Nelson, E. S. (2000). Relationship between parents, peers, morality, and theft in an adolescent sample. *High School Journal, 83,* 31–42.

Junaid, K. A., & Fellowes, S. (2006). Gender differences in the attainment of motor skills on the Movement Assessment Battery for Children. *Physical and Occupational Therapy in Pediatrics, 26,* 5–11.

Jungblut, P. R., Ostorne, J. A., Quigg, R. J., McNeal, M. A., Clauser, J., Muster, A. J., et al. (2000). Echocardiographic Doppler evaluation of left ventricular diastolic filling in older, highly trained male endurance athletes. *Echocardiography, 17,* 7–16.

Juola, J. F., Koshino, H., Warner, C. B., McMickell, M., & Peterson, M. (2000). Automatic and voluntary control of attention in young and older adults. *American Journal of Psychology, 113,* 159–178.

Jusczyk, P. W., Houston, D. M., & Newsome, M. (1999). The beginnings of word segmentation in English-learning infants. *Cognitive Psychology, 39,* 159–207.

Justice, E. M., Bakerward, L., Gupta, S., & Jannings, L. R. (1997). Means to the goal of remembering: Developmental changes in awareness of strategy use-performance relations. *Journal of Experimental Child Psychology, 65,* 293–314.

Juul, A., Teilmann, G., Scheike, T., Hertel, N. T., Holm, K., Laursen, E. M., et al. (2006). Pubertal development in Danish children: Comparison of recent European and US data. *International Journal of Andrology, 29,* 247–255.

Kagan, J. (1972). Do infants think? *Scientific American,226,* 74–82.

Kagan, J. (1981). *The second year: The emergence of self-awareness.* Cambridge, MA: Harvard University Press.

Kagan, J. (1989). Temperamental contributions to social behavior. *American Psychologist, 44,* 668–674.

Kagan, J. (1994). *Galen's prophecy: Temperament in human nature.* New York: Basic Books.

Kagan, J. (2010). *The temperamental thread. How genes, culture, time, and luck make us what we are.* New York: Dana Press.

Kagan, J., & Snidman, N. (2004). *The long shadow of temperament.* Cambridge, MA: The Belknap Press of Harvard University Press.

Kagan, J., Snidman, N., Kahn, V., & Towsley, S. (2007).The preservation of two infant temperaments into adolescence. *Monographs of the Society for Research in Child Development, 72,* 1–75.

Kail, R. (1991). Developmental change in speed of processing during childhood and adolescence. *Psychological Bulletin, 109,* 490–501.

Kail, R., & Bisanz, J. (1992). The information-processing perspective on cognitive development in childhood and adolescence. In R. J. Sternberg & C. A. Berg (Eds.), *Intellectual development.* New York: Cambridge University Press.

Kail, R., & Salthouse, T. A. (1994). Processing speed as a mental capacity. *Acta Psychologica, 86,* 199–225.

Kajantie, E. (2008). Physiological stress response, estrogen, and the male-female mortality gap. *Current Directions in Psychological Science, 17,* 348–352.

Kakuma, R., duFort, G. G., Arsenault, L., Perrault, A., Platt, R. W., Monette, J., Moride, Y., & Wolfson, C. (2003). Delirium in older emergency department patients discharged home: Effect on survival. *Journal of the American Geriatrics Society, 51,* 443–450.

Kalmijn, M., & De Graaf, P. M. (2012). Life course changes of children and well being of parents. *Journal of Marriage and Family, 74,* 269–280.

Kalmuss, D., Davidson, A., & Cushman, L. (1992). Parenting expectancies, experiences, and adjustment to parenthood: A test of the violated expectations framework. *Journal of Marriage and the Family, 54,* 516–526.

Kamakura, T., Ando, J., & Ono, Y. (2007). Genetic and environmental effects on stability and change in self-esteem during adolescence. *Personality and Individual Differences, 42,* 181–190.

Kammeyer-Mueller, J. D., & Judge, T. A. (2008). A quantitative review of mentoring research: Test of a model. *Journal of Vocational Behavior, 72,* 269–283.

Kamp Dush, C. M. (2011). Relationship-specific investments, family chaos, and cohabitation dissolution following a nonmarital birth. *Family Relations, 60,* 586–601.

Kamp Dush, C. M. (2013). Marital and cohabitation dissolution and parental depressive symptoms in fragile families. *Journal of Marriage and Family, 75,* 91–109.

Kandel, E. R., & Jessell, T. (1991). Early experience and the fine tuning of synaptic connections. In E. R. Kandel, J. H. Schwartz, & T. Jessell (Eds.), *Principles of neural science* (3rd ed., pp. 945–958). Norwalk, CT: Appleton & Lange.

Kane, H. D., & Brand, C. R. (2006). The variable importance of general intelligence (g) in the cognitive abilities of children and adolescents. *Educational Psychology, 26,* 751–767.

Kannass, K. N., & Colombo, J. (2007). The effects of continuous and intermittent distractors on cognitive performance and attention in preschoolers. *Journal of Cognition and Development, 8,* 63–77.

Kaplan, D. S., Damphousse, K. R., & Kaplan, H. B. (1994). Mental health implications of not graduating from high school. *Journal of Experimental Education, 62,* 105–123.

Kaplan, J. S. (2012). The effects of shared environment on adult intelligence: A critical review of adoption, twin, and MZA studies. *Developmental Psychology, 48,* 1292–1298.

Kaplan, R. M., & Erickson, J. (2000). Quality adjusted life expectancy for men and women in the United States. In S. B. Manuck, R. Jennings, B. S. Rabin, & A. Baum (Eds.), *Behavior, health, and aging.* Mahwah, NJ: Erlbaum.

Karantzas, G. C., Evans, L., & Foddy, M. (2010). The role of attachment in current and future parent caregiving. *Journals of Gerontology: Series B: Psychological Sciences and Social Sciences, 65B,* 573–580.

Karasik, L. B., Tamis-LeMonda, C. S., & Adolph, K. E. (2011). Transition from crawling to walking and infants' actions with objects and people. *Child Development, 82,* 1199–1209.

Karasik, L. B., Tamis-LeMonda, C. S., Adolph, K. E., & Dimitropoulou, K. A. (2008). How mothers encourage and discourage infants' motor actions. *Infancy, 13,* 366–392.

Karel, M. J., Gatz, M., & Smyer, M. A. (2012). Aging and mental health in the decade ahead: What psychologists need to know. *American Psychologist, 67,* 184–198.

Karg, K., Burmeister, M., Shedden, K., & Sen, S. (2011). The serotonin transporter promoter variant (5-HTTLPR), stress, and depression meta-analysis revisited: Evidence of genetic moderation. *Archives of General Psychiatry, 68,* 444–454.

Karmiloff-Smith, A. (1992). Beyond modularity: A developmental perspective on cognitive science. Cambridge, MA: MIT Press.

Karniol, R. (2009). Israeli kindergarten children's gender constancy for others' counter-stereotypic toy play and appearance: The role of sibling gender and relative age. *Infant and Child Development, 18,* 73–94.

Karpov, Y. V. (2005). *The neo-Vygotskian approach to child development.* New York: Cambridge University Press.

Karraker, A., DeLamater, J., & Schwartz, C. R. (2011). Sexual frequency decline from midlife to later life. *Journals of Gerontology, Series B: Psychological Sciences and Social Sciences, 66,* 502–512.

Kart, C. S., Metress, E. K., & Metress, S. P. (1992). *Human aging and chronic disease.* Boston: Jones and Bartlett.

Kärtner, J., Keller, H., Chaudhary, N., & Yovsi, R. D. (2012). The development of mirror self-recognition in different sociocultural contexts. *Monographs of the Society for Research in Child Development, 77(4),* 4–101.

Kashani, H. H., Kavosh, M. S., Keshteli, A. H., Montaze, M., Rostampour, N., Kelishadi, R., et al. (2009). Age of puberty in a representative sample of Iranian girls. *World Journal of Pediatrics, 5,* 132–135.

Kasl-Godley, J., & Gatz, M. (2000). Psychosocial interventions for individuals with dementia: An integration of theory, therapy, and a clinical understanding of dementia. *Clinical Psychology Review, 20,* 755–782.

Kaslow, N., Mintzer, M. B., Meadows, L. A., & Grabill, C. M. (2000). A family perspective on assessing and treating childhood depression. In C. E. Bailey (Ed.), *Children in therapy. Using the family as a resource.* New York: W. W. Norton.

Kassi, E., Pervanidou, P., Kaltsas, G., & Chrousos, G. (2011). Metabolic syndrome: definitions and controversies. *BMC Medicine, 9* (48), 1–13.

Kastberg, D., Ferraro, D., Lemanski, N., Roey, S., & Jenkins, F. (2012). *Highlights from TIMSS 2011: Mathematics and science achievement of U.S. fourth- and eighth-grade students in an international context.* Washington, DC: National Center for Education Statistics.

Kastenbaum, R. (2000). *The psychology of death.* New York: Springer.

Kastenbaum, R. J. (2012). *Death, society, and human experience* (11th ed.). Boston: Pearson.

Kastorini, C., Milionis, H. J., Esposito, K., Giugliano, D., Goudevenos, J. A., & Panagiotakos, D. B. (2011). The effect of Mediterranean diet on metabolic syndrome and its components: A meta-analysis of 50 studies and 534,906 individuals. *Journal of the American College of Cardiology, 57,* 1299.

Kasworm, C. E., & Medina, R. A. (1990). Adult competence in everyday tasks: A cross-sectional secondary analysis. *Educational Gerontology, 16,* 27–48.

Katz, L. F., Maliken, A. C., & Stettler, N. M. (2012). Parental meta-emotion philosophy: A review of research and theoretical framework. *Child Development Perspectives, 6,* 417–422.

Katz, P. A. (1986). Modification of children's gender-stereotyped behavior: General issues and research considerations. *Sex Roles, 14,* 591–602.

Katz, P. A., & Walsh, P. V. (1991). Modification of children's gender-stereotyped behavior. *Child Development, 62,* 338–351.

Katzel, L. I., & Steinbrenner, G. M. (2012). Physical exercise and health. In S. K. Whitbourne & M. J. Sliwinski (Eds.) *The Wiley-Blackwell Handbook of Adulthood and Aging* (pp. 97–117). Malden, MA: Wiley-Blackwell.

Katz-Wise, S., Priess, H. A., & Hyde, J. S. (2010). Gender-role attitudes and behavior across the transition to parenthood. *Developmental Psychology, 46,* 18–28.

Kaufman, A. S., & Kaufman, N. L. (1997). The Kaufman Adolescent and Adult Intelligence Test. In D. P. Flanagan, J. L. Genshaft, & P. L. Harrison (Eds.), *Contemporary intellectual assessment: Theories, tests, and issues.* New York: Guilford.

Kaufman, A. S., & Kaufman, N. L. (2003). *Kaufman Assessment Battery for Children* (2nd ed.). San Antonio, TX: Pearson.

Kaufman, A. S., Kamphaus, R. W., & Kaufman, N. L. (1985). New directions in intelligence testing: The Kaufman Assessment Battery for Children (K-ABC). In B. B. Wolman (Ed.), *Handbook of intelligence.* New York: Wiley.

Kaufman, J., & Zigler, E. (1989). The intergenerational transmission of child abuse. In D. Cicchetti & V. Carlson (Eds.), *Child maltreatment. Theory and research on the causes and consequences of child abuse and neglect.* New York: Cambridge University Press.

Kaufman, J. C. (2006). Self-reported differences in creativity by ethnicity and gender. *Applied Cognitive Psychology, 20,* 1065–1082.

Kaufman, J. C., & Plucker, J. A. (2011). Intelligence and creativity. In R. J. Sternberg & S. B. Kaufman (Eds.), *The Cambridge handbook of intelligence* (pp. 771–783). New York: Cambridge University Press.

Kaufman, S. B. (2007). Sex differences in mental rotation and spatial visualization ability: Can they be accounted for by differences in working memory capacity? *Intelligence, 35,* 211–223.

Kavsek, M., & Yonas, A. (2006). The perception of moving subjective contours by 4-month-old infants. *Perception, 35,* 215–227.

Kaye, R. A. (1993). Sexuality in the later years. *Aging and Society, 13,* 415–426.

Kayed, N. S., & van der Meer, A. L. (2007). Infants' timing strategies to optical collisions: A longitudinal study. *Infant Behavior and Development, 30,* 50–59.

Kazdin, A. E. (2003). Psychotherapy for children and adolescents. *Annual Review of Psychology, 54,* 253–276.

Keel, P. K., & Fulkerson, J. A. (2001). Vulnerability to eating disorders in childhood and adolescence. In R. E. Ingram & J. M. Price (Eds.), *Vulnerability to psychopathology. Risk across the lifespan.* New York: Guilford.

Keel, P. K., & Klump, K. L. (2003). Are eating disorders culture-bound syndromes? Implications for conceptualizing their etiology. *Psychological Bulletin, 129,* 747–769.

Keesee, N. J., Currier, J. M., & Neimeyer, R. A. (2008). Predictors of grief following the death of one's child: The contribution of finding meaning. *Journal of Clinical Psychology, 64,* 1145–1163.

Keightley, M. L., Winocur, G., Burianova, H., Hongwanishkul, D., & Grady, C. L. (2006). Age effects on social cognition: Faces tell a different story. *Psychology and Aging, 21,* 558–572.

Keijsers, L., Branje, S., Hawk, S. T., Schwartz, S. J., Frijns, T., Koot, H. M., et al. (2012). Forbidden friends as forbidden fruit: Parental supervision of friendships, contact with deviant peers, and adolescent delinquency. *Child Development, 83,* 651–666.

Keizer, R., Dykstra, P. A., & Jansen, M. D. (2008). Pathways into childlessness: Evidence of gendered life course dynamics. *Journal of Biosocial Science, 40,* 863–878.

Kelemen, W. L. (2000). Metamemory cues and monitoring accuracy: Judging what you know and what you will know. *Journal of Educational Psychology, 92,* 800–810.

Keller, B. B., & Bell, R. Q. (1979). Child effects on adult's method of eliciting altruistic behavior. *Child Development, 50,* 1004–1009.

Keller, H. (1954). *The story of my life.* New York: Doubleday.

Keller, H., Kärtner, J., Borke, J., Yovsi, R., & Kleis, A. (2005). Parenting styles and the development of the categorical self: A longitudinal study on mirror self-recognition in Cameroonian Nso and German families. *International Journal of Behavioral Development, 29,* 496–504.

Keller, K. L., Kirzner, J., Pietrobelli, A., St-Onge, M. P., & Faith, M. S. (2009). Increased sweetened beverage intake is associated with reduced milk and calcium intake in 3- to 7-year-old children at multi-item laboratory lunches. *Journal of the American Dietetic Association, 109,* 497–501.

Keller, M. C. (2008). The evolutionary persistence of genes that increase mental disorders risk. *Current Directions in Psychological Science, 17,* 395–399.

Kellman, P. J., & Arterberry, M. E. (2006). Infant visual perception. In D. Kuhn & R. Siegler (Vol. Eds.), *Handbook of child psychology: Cognition, perception, and language.* Hoboken, NJ: Wiley.

Kellman, P. J., & Spelke, E. S. (1983). Perception of partly occluded objects in infancy. *Cognitive Psychology, 15,* 483–524.

Kellogg, N. D. (2009). Clinical report—The evaluation of sexual behaviors in children. *Pediatrics, 124,* 992–998.

Kelly, D. J., Quinn, P. C., Slater, A. M., Lee, K., Gibson, A., Smith, M., Ge, L. Z., & Pascalis, O. (2005). Three-month-olds, but not newborns, prefer own-race faces. *Developmental Science, 8,* F31–F36.

Kelly, J. (2013, March 20). An empty-nester sampler: What some parents do when the children have flown. *Washington Post,* p. B2.

Kelsall, D. C., Shallop, J. K., & Burnelli, T. (1995). Cochlear implantation in the elderly. *American Journal of Otology, 16,* 609–615.

Kempe, R. S., & Kempe, C. H. (1978). *Child abuse.* Cambridge, MA: Harvard University Press.

Kempen, G. I. J. M., Jelicic, M., & Ormel, J. (1997). Personality, chronic medical morbidity, and health-related quality of life among older persons. *Health Psychology, 16,* 539–546.

Kemper, S., & Mitzner, T. L. (2001). Production and comprehension. In J. E. Birren & K. W. Schaie (Eds.), *Handbook of the psychology of aging* (5th ed.). San Diego, CA: Academic Press.

Kemtes, K. A., & Kemper, S. (1997). Younger and older adults' on-line processing of syntactically ambiguous sentences. *Psychology and Aging, 12,* 362–371.

Kendall-Tackett, K. A., Williams, L. M., & Finkelhor, D. (1993). Impact of sexual abuse on children: A review and synthesis of recent empirical studies. *Psychological Bulletin, 113,* 164–180.

Kendeou, P., van den Broek, P., White, M. J., & Lynch, J. S. (2009). Predicting reading comprehension in early elementary school: The independent contributions of oral language and decoding skills. *Journal of Educational Psychology, 101,* 765–778.

Kendler, K. S., Gardner, C. O., & Prescott, C. A. (2002). Toward a comprehensive developmental model for major depression in women. *American Journal of Psychiatry, 159,* 1133–1145.

Kendler, K. S., Thornton, L. M., Gilman, S. E., & Kessler, R. C. (2000). Sexual orientation in a U.S. national sample of twin and nontwin sibling pairs. *American Journal of Psychiatry, 157,* 1843–1846.

Kennedy, Q., Mather, M., & Carstensen, L. L. (2004). The role of motivation in the age-related positivity effect in autobiographical memory. *Psychological Science, 15,* 208–214.

Kennedy, S., & Bumpass, L. (2008). Cohabitation and children's living arrangements: New estimates from the United States. *Demographic Research, 19,* 1663–1692.

Kenny, M. E. (1987). The extent and function of parental attachment among first-year college students. *Journal of Youth and Adolescence, 16,* 17–29.

Kenny, M. E., & Rice, K. G. (1995). Attachment to parents and adjustment in late adolescent college students: Current status, applications, and future considerations. *The Counseling Psychologist, 23,* 433–456.

Kensinger, E. A., & Choi, E. S. (2009). When side matters: Hemispheric processing and the visual specificity of emotional memories. *Journal of Experimental Psychology: Learning, Memory, and Cognition, 35,* 247–253.

Kenward, B., Folke, S., Holmberg, J., Johansson, A., & Gredebäck, G. (2009). Goal directedness and decision making in infants. *Developmental Psychology, 45,* 809–819.

Kenyon, B. L. (2001). Current research in children's conceptions of death: A critical review. *Omega: Journal of Death and Dying, 43,* 63–91.

Kenyon, D. B., & Hanson, J. D. (2012). Incorporating traditional culture into positive youth development programs with American Indian/Alaska native youth. *Child Development Perspectives, 6,* 272–279.

Keren, M., Dollberg, D., Koster, T., Danino, K., & Feldman, R. (2010). Family functioning and interactive patterns in the context of infant psychopathology. *Journal of Family Psychology, 24,* 597–604.

Kerka, S. (1995). *Adult learner retention revisited. ERIC Digest No. 166.* Columbus, OH: ERIC Clearinghouse on Adult, Career, and Vocational Education.

Kern, M. L., & Friedman, H. S. (2010). Why do some people thrive while others succumb to disease and stagnation? Personality, social relations, and resilience. In P. S. Fry & C. L. M. Keyes (Eds.), *New frontiers in resilient aging. Life-strengths and well-being in late life*. New York: Cambridge University Press.

Kerns, K. A., Tomich, P. L., & Kim, P. (2006). Normative trends in children's perceptions of availability and utilization of attachment figures in middle childhood. *Social Development, 15*, 1–22.

Kerr, M., & Stattin, H. (2003). Parenting of adolescents: Action or reaction? In A. C. Crouter, & A. Booth (Eds.), *Children's influence on family dynamics: The neglected side of family relationships*. Mahwah, NJ: Erlbaum.

Kessler, R. C., Avenevoli, S., & Merikangas, K. R. (2001). Mood disorders in children and adolescents: An epidemiologic perspective. *Biological Psychiatry, 49*, 1002–1014.

Kessler, R. C., Birnbaum, H. G., Shahly, V., Bromet, E., Hwang, I., McLaughlin, K. A., et al. (2010). Age differences in the prevalence and co-morbidity of DSM-IV major depressive episodes: Results from the WHO world mental health survey initiative. *Depression and Anxiety, 27*, 351–364.

Kessler, R., Galea, S., Jones, R., & Parker, H. (2006). Mental illness and suicidality after Hurricane Katrina. *Bulletin of the World Health Organization, 84*, 930–939.

Kessler, R. C., Green, J. G., Adler, L. A., Barkley, R. A., Chatterji, S., Faraone, S. V., et al. (2010). Structure and diagnosis of adult attention-deficit/hyperactivity disorder: Analysis of expanded symptom criteria from the adult ADHD clinical diagnostic scale. *Archives of General Psychiatry, 67*, 1168–1178.

Kessler, R. C., & Wang, P. S. (2008). The descriptive epidemiology of commonly occurring mental disorders in the United States. *Annual Review of Public Health, 29*, 115–129.

Khaleque, A., & Rohner, R. P. (2012). Pancultural associations between perceived parental acceptance and psychological adjustment of children and adults: A meta-analytic review of worldwide research. *Journal of Cross-Cultural Psychology, 43*, 784–800.

Khan, J. C., Thurlby, D. A., Shahid, H., Yates, J. R. W., Bradley, M., Moore, A. T., & Bird, A. C. (2006). Smoking and age related macular degeneration: the number of pack years of cigarette smoking is a major determinant of risk for both geographic atrophy and choroidal neovascularization. *British Journal of Ophthalmology, 90*, 75–80.

Khoury, J. C., Dolan, L. M., VanDyke, R., Rosenn, B., Feghali, M., & Miodovnik, M. (2012). Fetal development in women with diabetes: Imprinting for a life-time? *Journal of Maternal-Fetal & Neonatal Medicine, 25*, 11–14.

Kiang, L., Witkow, M. R., & Champagne, M. C. (2013). Normative changes in ethnic and American identities and links with adjustment among Asian American adolescents. *Developmental Psychology, 49*, 1713–1722.

Kiesner, J., Dishion, T. J., & Poulin, F. (2001). A reinforcement model of conduct problems in children and adolescents: Advances in theory and intervention. In J. Hill & B. Maughan (Eds.), *Conduct disorders in childhood and adolescence*. New York: Cambridge University Press.

Killen, M., Mulvey, K. L., Richardson, C., & Jampol, N. (2011). The accidental transgressor: Morally-relevant theory of mind. *Cognition, 119*, 197–215.

Killen, M., Rutland, A., & Jampol, N. S. (2009). Social exclusion in childhood and adolescence. In K. H. Rubin, W. M. Bukowski, & B. Laursen (Eds.), *Handbook of peer interactions, relationships, and groups*. New York: Guilford Press.

Killen, M., & Smetana, J. (2008). Moral judgment and moral neuroscience: Intersections, definitions, and issues. *Child Development Perspectives, 2*, 1–6.

Kim, K. H. (2011). The creativity crisis: The decrease in creative thinking scores on the Torrance Tests of Creative Thinking. *Creativity research journal, 23*, 285–295.

Kim, K. H., Cramond, B., & VanTassel-Baska, J. (2010). The relationship between creativity and intelligence. In J. C. Kaufman & R. J. Sternberg (Eds.), *The Cambridge Handbook of Creativity*, vol. 2 (pp. 395–412). New York: Cambridge University Press.

Kimbro, R. T., & Denney, J. T. (2013). Neighborhood context and racial/ethnic differences in young children's obesity: Structural barriers to interventions. *Social Science and Medicine, 95*, 97–105.

Kim, G., & Kwak, K. (2011). Uncertainty matters: Impact of stimulus ambiguity on infant social referencing. *Infant and Child Development, 20*, 449–463.

Kim, K., & Spelke, E. J. (1992). Infants' sensitivity to effects of gravity on visible object motion. *Journal of Experimental Psychology: Human Perception and Performance, 18*, 385–393.

Kim, S., Kim, S., & Kamphaus, R. W. (2010). Is aggression the same for boys and girls? Assessing measurement invariance with confirmatory factor analysis and item response theory. *School Psychology Quarterly, 25*, 45–61.

Kim-Cohen, J., & Gold, A. L. (2009). Measured gene—environment interactions and mechanisms promoting resilient development. *Current Directions in Psychological Science, 18*, 138–142.

Kim-Cohen, J., Caspi, A., Taylor, A., Williams, B., Newcombe, R., Craig, I. W., & Moffitt, T. E. (2006). MAOA, maltreatment, and gene-environment interaction predicting children's mental health: New evidence and a meta-analysis. *Molecular Psychiatry, 11*, 903–913.

Kimura, D. (1992). Sex differences in the brain. *Scientific American, 267*, 119–125.

King, A. C., Castro, C., Wilcox, S., Eyler, A. A., Sallis, J. F., & Brownson, R. C. (2000). Personal and environmental factors associated with physical inactivity among different racial-ethnic groups of U.S. middle-aged and older-aged women. *Health Psychology, 19*, 354–364.

King, S., St. Hilaire, A., & Heidkamp, D. (2010). Prenatal factors in schizophrenia. *Current Directions in Psychological Science, 19*, 209–213.

King, V., & Sobolewski, J. M. (2006). Nonresident fathers' contributions to adolescent well-being. *Journal of Marriage and Family, 68*, 537–557.

Kingston, H. M. (2008). *ABC of clinical genetics* (3rd ed.). Hoboken, NJ: Blackwell.

Kirchhoff, B. A., & Buckner, R. L. (2006). Functional-anatomic correlates of individual differences in memory. *Neuron, 51*, 263–274.

Kirchmeyer, C. (2006). The different effects of family on objective career success across gender: A test of alternative explanations. *Journal of Vocational Behavior, 68*, 323–346.

Kirkbride, J. B., Susser, E., Kundakovic, M., Kresovich, J. K., Smith, G. D., & Relton, C. L. (2012). Prenatal nutrition, epigenetics and schizophrenia risk: Can we test causal effects? *Epigenomics, 4*, 303–315.

Kirsch, I. S., Jungeblut, A., Jenkins, L., & Kolstad, A. (2002). *Adult literacy in America: A first look at the findings on the National Adult Literacy Survey* (3rd ed.). National Center for Education Statistics.

Kisilevsky, B. S., & Muir, D. W. (1984). Neonatal habituation and dishabituation to tactile stimulation during sleep. *Developmental Psychology, 20*, 367–373.

Kisilevsky, B. S., Hains, S. M., Lee, K., Xie, X., Huang, H., Ye, H. H., et al. (2003). Effects of experience on fetal voice recognition. *Psychological Science, 14*, 220–224.

Kissane, D. W., Zaider, T. I., Li, Y., & Del Gaudio, F. (2013). Family therapy for complicated grief. In M. Stroebe, H. Schut & J. van den Bout (Eds.), *Complicated grief: Scientific foundations for health care professionals*. New York: Routledge/Taylor & Francis.

Kitamura, C., & Burnham, D. (2003). Pitch and communicative intent in mother's speech: Adjustments for age and sex in the first year. *Infancy, 4*, 85–110.

Kitson, G. C. (1992). *Portrait of divorce: Adjustment to marital breakdown*. New York: Guilford.

Kitzmann, K. M. (2000). Effects of marital conflict on subsequent triadic family interactions and parenting. *Developmental Psychology, 36*, 3–13.

Klaczynski, P. A. (2000). Motivated scientific reasoning biases, epistemological beliefs, and theory polarization: A two-process approach to adolescent cognition. *Child Development, 71*, 1347–1366.

Klaczynski, P. A. (2001). Analytic and heuristic processing influences on adolescent reasoning and decision-making. *Child Development, 72*, 844–861.

Klaczynski, P. A. (2009). Cognitive and social cognitive development: Dual-process research and theory. In J. S. B. T. Evans & K. Frankish (Eds.), *In two minds: Dual processes and beyond* (pp. 265–292). New York: Oxford University Press.

Klaczynski, P. A., & Gordon, D. H. (1996a). Everyday statistical reasoning during adolescence and young adulthood: Motivational, general ability, and developmental influences. *Child Development, 67*, 2873–2892.

Klaczynski, P. A., & Gordon, D. H. (1996b). Self-serving influences on adolescents' evaluations of belief-relevant evidence. *Journal of Experimental Child Psychology, 62*, 317–339.

Klass, D. (2001). Continuing bonds in the resolution of grief in Japan and North America. *American Behavioral Scientist, 44*, 742–763.

Klebold, S. (2009, November). I will never know why. *O Magazine*. Retrieved from http://www.oprah.com/world/Susan-Klebolds-O-Magazine-Essay-I-Will-Never-Know-Why

Klein, P. J., & Meltzoff, A. N. (1999). Long-term memory, forgetting, and deferred imitation in 12-month-old infants. *Developmental Science, 2*, 102–113.

Klein, R., Klein, B. E., Lee, K. E., Cruickshanks, K. J., & Chappell, R. J. (2001). Changes in visual acuity in a population over a 10-year period: The Beaver Dam Eye Study. *Ophthalmology, 108*, 1757–1766.

Kleinman, R. E., Brown, R. T., Cutter, G. R., DuPaul, G. J., & Clydesdale, F. M. (2011). A research model for investigating the effects of artificial food colorings on children with ADHD. *Pediatrics, 127*, e1575-e1584.

Kliegel, M., Jager, T., & Phillips, L. H. (2007). Emotional development across adulthood: Differential age-related emotional reactivity and emotion regulation in a negative mood induction procedure. *International Journal of Aging and Human Development, 64*, 217–244.

Klin, A., Chawarska, K., Rubin, E., & Volkmar F. (2004). Clinical assessment of young children at risk for autism. In R. DelCarmen-Wiggins & A. Carter (Eds.), *Handbook of infant, toddler, and preschool mental health assessment*. New York: Oxford University Press.

Kline, D. W., & Scialfa, C. T. (1996). Visual and auditory aging. In J. E. Birren & K. W. Schaie (Eds.), *Handbook of the psychology of aging* (4th ed.). San Diego: Academic Press.

Klineberg, O. (1963). Negro-white differences in intelligence test performance: A new look at an old problem. *American Psychologist, 18*, 198–203.

Klinger, L. G., & Williams, A. (2009). Cognitive-behavioral interventions for students with autism spectrum disorders. In M. J. Mayer, R. Van Acker, J. E. Lochman, & F. M. Gresham (Eds.), *Cognitive-behavioral interventions for emotional and behavioral disorders*. New York: Guilford.

Klump, K. L., & Culbert, K. M. (2007). Molecular genetic studies of eating disorders. Current status and future directions. *Current Directions in Psychological Science, 16*, 37–41.

Klump, K. L., Culbert, K. M., Slane, J. D., Burt, S. A., Sisk, C. L., &Nigg, J. T. (2012). The effects of puberty on genetic risk for disordered eating: Evidence for a sex difference. *Psychological Medicine, 42*, 627–637.

Klump, K. L., Keel, P. K., Sisk, C., & Burt, S. A. (2010). Preliminary evidence that estradiol moderates genetic influences on disordered eating attitudes and behaviors during puberty. *Psychological Medicine, 40*, 1745–1753.

Klump, K. L., Suisman, J. L., Burt, S. A., McGue, M., & Iacono, W. G. (2009). Genetic and environmental influences on disordered eating: An adoption study. *Journal of Abnormal Psychology, 118*, 797–805.

Klump, K. L., Suisman, J. L., Culbert, K. M., Kashy, D. A., & Sisk, C. L. (2011). Binge eating proneness emerges during puberty in female rats: A longitudinal study. *Journal of Abnormal Psychology, 120*, 948–955.

Knaapila, A., Hwang, L., Lysenko, A., Duke, F. F., Fesi, B., Khoshnevisan, A., et al. (2012). Genetic analysis of chemosensory traits in human twins. *Chemical Senses, 37*, 869–881.

Knafo, A., Zahn-Waxler, C., Van Hulle, C., Robinson, J. L., & Rhee, S. H. (2008). The developmental origins of a disposition toward empathy: Genetic and environmental contributions. *Emotion, 8*, 737–752.

Knapp, C., Quinn, G. P., Murphy, D., Brown, R., & Madden, V. (2010). Adolescents with life-threatening illnesses. *American Journal of Hospice and Palliative Care, 27*, 139–144.

Knecht, S., Deppe, M., Drager, B., Bobe, L., Lohmann, H., Ringelstein, E., et al. (2000). Language lateralization in healthy right-handers. *Brain, 123*, 74–81.

Knee, D. O. (2010). Hospice care for the aging population in the United States. In J. C. Cavanaugh & C. K. Cavanaugh (Eds.), *Aging in America: Vol 3. Societal issues*. Santa Barbara, CA: Praeger/ABC-CLIO.

Knerr, W., Gardner, F., & Cluver, L. (2013). Improving positive parenting skills and reducing harsh and abusive parenting in low- and middle-income countries: A systematic review. *Prevention Science, 14*, 352–362.

Knight, B. G., & Losada, A. (2011). Family caregiving for cognitively or physically frail older adults: Theory, research, and practice. In K. W. Schaie & S. L. Willis (Eds.), B. G. Knight, B. Levy, & D. C. Park (Assoc. Eds.), *Handbook of the psychology of aging*. MA: Academic Press/Elsevier.

Knight, B. G., Kaskie, B., Shurgot, G. R., & Dave, J. (2006). Improving the mental health of older adults. In J. E. Birren & K. W. Schaie (Eds.), *Handbook of the psychology of aging* (6th ed.). Burlington, MA: Elsevier Academic Press.

Knight, G. P., & Carlo, G. (2012). Prosocial development among Mexican American youth. *Child Development Perspectives, 6*, 258–263.

Knight, J. A. (2000). The biochemistry of aging. *Advances in Clinical Chemistry, 35*, 1–62.

Kochanska, G. (1993). Toward a synthesis of parental socialization and child temperament in early development of conscience. *Child Development, 64*, 325–347.

Kochanska, G. (2001). Emotional development in children with different attachment histories: The first three years. *Child Development, 72*, 474–490.

Kochanska, G. (2002). Mutually responsive orientation between mothers and their young children: A context for the early development of conscience. *Current Directions in Psychological Science, 11*(6), 191–195.

Kochanska, G., & Aksan, N. (2006). Children's conscience and self-regulation. *Journal of Personality, 74*, 1587–1617.

Kochanska, G., & Kim, S. (2013). Early attachment organization with both parents and future behavior problems: From infancy to middle childhood. *Child Development, 84*, 283–296.

Kochanska, G., Aksan, N., & Joy, M. E. (2007). Children's fearfulness as a moderator of parenting in early socialization: Two longitudinal studies. *Developmental Psychology, 43*, 222–237.

Kochanska, G., Aksan, N., & Nichols, K. E. (2003). Maternal power assertion in discipline and moral discourse contexts: Commonalities, differences, and implications for children's moral conduct and cognition. *Developmental Psychology, 39*, 949–963.

Kochanska, G., Barry, R. A., Jimenez, N. B., Hollatz, A. L., & Woodard, J. (2009). Guilt and effortful control: Two mechanisms that prevent disruptive developmental trajectories. *Journal of Personality and Social Psychology, 97*, 322–333.

Kochanska, G., Barry, R. A., Stellern, S. A., & O'Bleness, J. J. (2009). Early attachment organization moderates the parent—child mutually coercive pathway to children's antisocial conduct. *Child Development, 80*, 1288–1300.

Kochanska, G., Casey, R. J., & Fukumoto, A. (1995). Toddlers' sensitivity to standard violations. *Child Development, 66*, 643–656.

Kochanska, G., Koenig, J. L., Barry, R. A., Kim, S., & Yoon, J. E. (2010). Children's conscience during toddler and preschool years, moral self, and a competent, adaptive developmental trajectory. *Developmental Psychology, 46*, 1320–1332.

Koegel, R. L., Koegel, L. K., & McNerney, E. K. (2001). Pivotal areas in intervention for autism. *Journal of Clinical Child Psychology, 30*, 19–32.

Koehler, K. (2010). Sibling bereavement in childhood. In C. A. Corr & D. E. Balk (Eds.), *Children's encounters with death, bereavement, and coping*. New York: Springer.

Koenen, K. C., Moffitt, T. E., Caspi, A., Taylor, A., & Purcell, S. (2003). Domestic violence is associated with environmental suppression of IQ in young children. *Development and Psychopathology, 15*, 297–311.

Koenig, A. L., Cicchetti, D., & Rogosch, F. A. (2004). Moral development: The association between maltreatment and young children's prosocial behaviors and moral transgressions. *Social Development, 13*, 97–106.

Kogan, N. (1983). Stylistic variation in childhood and adolescence: Creativity, metaphor, and cognitive styles. In J. H. Flavell & E. H. Markman (Eds.), *Handbook of child psychology: Vol. 3. Cognitive development* (4th ed.). New York: Wiley.

Kogan, S. M. (2004). Disclosing unwanted sexual experiences: Results from a national sample of adolescent women. *Child Abuse & Neglect, 28*, 147–165.

Kohlberg, L. (1963). The development of children's orientations toward a moral order: I. Sequence in the development of moral thought. *Vita Humana, 6*, 11–33.

Kohlberg, L. (1966). A cognitive-developmental analysis of children's sex-role concepts and attitudes. In E. E. Maccoby (Ed.), *The development of sex differences*. Stanford, CA: Stanford University Press.

Kohlberg, L. (1981). *Essays on moral development: Vol. 1. The philosophy of moral development*. San Francisco: Harper & Row.

Kohlberg, L. (1984). *Essays on moral development: Vol. 2. The psychology of moral development*. San Francisco: Harper & Row.

Kohn, M. L. (1969). *Class and conformity: A study of values*. Homewood, IL: Dorsey Press.

Kohn, M. L., & Schooler, C. (1982). Job conditions and personality: A longitudinal assessment of their reciprocal effects. *American Journal of Sociology, 87*, 1257–1286.

Kolb, B., & Whishaw, I.Q. (2013). An Introduction to Brain and Behavior, 4th ed. Worth Publishers.

Kolstad, V., & Aguiar, A. (1995, March). *Means–end sequences in young infants*. Paper presented at the biennial meeting of the Society for Research in Child Development, Indianapolis.

Kong, A., Frigge, M. L., Masson, G., Besenbacher, S., Sulem, P., Magnusson, G., et al. (2012). Rate of de novo mutations and the importance of father's age to disease risk. *Nature, 488*(7412), 471–475.

Koocher, G. P. (1973). Childhood, death, and cognitive development. *Developmental Psychology, 9*, 369–375.

Koocher, G. P. (1974). Talking with children about death. *American Journal of Orthopsychiatry,44*, 404–411.

Koocher, G. P., & Daniel, J. H. (2012). Treating children and adolescents. In S. J. Knapp, M. C. Gottlieb, M. M. Handelsman & L. D. VandeCreek (Eds.), *APA handbook of ethics in psychology, Vol 2: Practice, teaching, and research*. Washington, DC: American Psychological Association.

Kopasz, M., Loessi, H. M., Riemann, D., Nissen, C., Piosczyk, H., & Voderholzer, U. (2010). Sleep and memory in healthy children and adolescents—A critical review. *Sleep Medicine Reviews, 14*, 167–177.

Kopp, C. B., & Neufield, S. J. (2003). Emotional development during infancy. In R. J. Davidson, K. R. Scherer, & H. H. Goldsmith (Eds.), *Handbook of affective sciences*. New York: Oxford University Press.

Korbin, J. E. (2001). Context and meaning in neighborhood studies of children and families. In A. Booth, & A. C. Crouter (Eds.), *Does it take a village? Community effects on children, adolescents, and families*. Mahwah, NJ: Erlbaum.

Koriat, A., Goldsmith, M., & Pansky, A. (2000). Toward a psychology of memory accuracy. *Annual Review of Psychology, 51*, 481–538.

Kosberg, J. I., Kaufman, A. V., Burgio, L. D., Leeper, J. D., & Sun, F. (2007). Family caregiving to those with dementia in rural Alabama: Racial similarities and differences. *Journal of Aging and Health, 19*, 3–21.

Kost, K., Henshaw, S., & Carlin, L. (2010). U.S. teenage pregnancies, births and abortions: National and state trends and trends by race *and ethnicity*. Retrieved from www.guttmacher.org/pubs/USTPtrends.pdf.

Kotilahti, K., Nissilä, I., Näsi, T., Lipiäinen, L., Noponen, T., Meriläinen, P., et al. (2010). Hemodynamic responses to speech and music in newborn infants. *Human Brain Mapping, 31*, 595–603.

Koutstaal, W., Schacter, D. L., Johnson, M. K., Angell, K. E., & Gross, M. S. (1998). Post-event review in older and younger adults: Improving memory accessibility of complex everyday events. *Psychology and Aging, 13*, 277–296.

Kowal, A., Kramer, L., Krull, J. L., & Crick, N. R. (2002). Children's perceptions of the fairness of parental preferential treatment and their socioemotional well-being. *Journal of Family Psychology, 16*, 297–306.

Krafft, K. C., & Berk, L. E. (1998). Private speech in two preschools: Significance of open-ended activities and make-believe play for verbal self- regulation. *Early Childhood Research Quarterly, 13*, 637–658.

Krakowiak, P., Walker, C. K., Bremer, A. A., Baker, A. S., Ozonoff, S., Hansen, R. L., & Hertz-Picciotto, I. (2012). Maternal metabolic conditions and risk for autism and other neurodevelopmental disorders. *Pediatrics, 129*, e1121-e1128.

Kramer, D. A. (1989). A developmental framework for understanding conflict resolution processes. In J. D. Sinnott (Ed.), *Everyday problem solving in adulthood* (pp. 133–152). New York: Praeger.

Kramer, D. A., & Melchior, J. (1990). Gender, role conflict, and the development of relativistic and dialectical thinking. *Sex Roles, 23*, 553–575.

Krause, N. (1995). Negative interaction and satisfaction with social support among older adults. *Journal of Gerontology: Psychological Sciences, 50B*, 59–73.

Krause, N. (2003). Religious meaning and subjective well-being in late life. *Journals of Gerontology, 58*, S160–S170.

Krause, N. (2013). Religious involvement in the later years of life. In K. I. Pargament, J. J. Exline, & J. W. Jones (Eds.), *APA handbook of psychology, religion, and spirituality: Vol. 1. Context, theory, and research*. Washington, DC: American Psychological Association.

Krause, N., & Rook, K. S. (2003). Negative interaction in late life: Issues in the stability and generalizability of conflict across relationships. *Journals of Gerontology: Psychological Sciences and Social Sciences, 58*, 88–99.

Kraushaar, J. M., & Novak, D. C. (2010). Examining the effect of student multitasking with laptops during lecture. *Journal of Information Systems Education, 21*, 241–251.

Krebs, D. L. (2008). Morality. An evolutionary account. *Perspectives on Psychological Science, 3*, 149–172.

Krebs, D. L. (2011). *The origins of morality. An evolutionary account*. New York: Oxford University Press.

Kreicbergs, U., Valdimarsdottir, U., Onelov, E., Henter, J., & Steineck, G. (2004). Talking about death with children who have severe malignant disease. *New England Journal of Medicine, 351*, 1175–1186.

Kretch, K. S., & Adolph, K. E. (2013). Cliff or step? Posture-specific learning at the edge of a drop-off. *Child Development, 84*, 226–240.

Kroger, J. (2007). *Identity development. Adolescence through adulthood* (2nd ed.). Thousand Oaks, CA: Sage.

Krogh, K. M. (1985). Women's motives to achieve and to nurture in different life stages. *Sex Roles, 12*, 75–90.

Krucoff, C. (2000, May 16). Good to the bone. *The Washington Post—Health*, p. 8.

Krueger, R. F., & Johnson, W. (2008). Behavioral genetics and personality. A new look at the integration of nature and nurture. In O. P. John, R. W. Robins, & L. A. Pervin (Eds.), *Handbook of personality theory and research* (3rd ed.). New York: Guilford.

Krueger, R. F., Johnson, W., & Kling, K. C. (2006). Behavior genetics and personality development. In D. K. Mroczek & T. D. Little (Eds.), *Handbook of personality development*. Mahwah, NJ: Erlbaum.

Ku, S. Y., Kang, J. W., Kim, H., Kim, Y. D., Jee, B. C., Suh, C. S., et al. (2006). Age at menarche and its influencing factors in North Korean female refugees. *Human Reproduction, 21*, 833–836.

Kübler-Ross, E. (1969). *On death and dying*. New York: Macmillan.

Kübler-Ross, E. (1974). *Questions and answers on death and dying*. New York: Macmillan.

Kuczynski, L., & Parkin, C. M. (2007). Agency and bidirectionality in socialization. Interactions, transactions, and relational dialectics. In J. E. Grusec & P. D. Hastings (Eds.), *Handbook of socialization: Theory and research*. New York: Guilford.

Kuebli, J., & Fivush, R. (1994). Children's representation and recall of event alternatives. *Journal of Experimental Child Psychology, 58*, 25–45.

Kuehner, C. (2003). Gender differences in unipolar depression: An update of epidemiological findings and possible explanations. *Acta Psychiatrica Scandinavia,108*, 163–174.

Kuhl, P. K., Stevens, E., Hayashi, A., Deguchi, T., Kiritani, S., & Iverson, P. (2006). Infants show a facilitation effect for native language phonetic perception between 6 and 12 months. *Developmental Science, 9*, F13–F21.

Kuhn, D. (1993). Connecting scientific and informal reasoning. *Merrill-Palmer Quarterly, 39*, 74–103.

Kuhn, D., & Franklin, S. (2006). The second decade: What develops (and how)? In D. Kuhn & R. Siegler (Eds.), *Handbook of child psychology, Vol. 2: Cognitive, perception, and language* (6th ed., pp. 953–994). New York: Wiley.

Kuhn, D., Pease, M., & Wirkala, C. (2009). Coordinating the effects of multiple variables: A skill fundamental to scientific thinking. *Journal of Experimental Child Psychology, 103*, 268–284.

Kuncel, N. R., Hezlett, S. A., & Ones, D. S. (2004). Academic performance, career potential, creativity, and job performance: Can one construct predict them all? *Journal of Personality and Social Psychology, 86,* 148–161.

Kuny-Slock, A. V., & Hudziak, J. J. (2013). Genetic and environmental influences on aggression and deviant behavior. In C. R. Thomas & K. Pope (Eds.), *The origins of antisocial behavior. A developmental perspective.* New York: Oxford University Press.

Kunz, J. A., & Soltys, F. G. (Eds.). (2007). *Transformational reminiscence: Life story work.* New York: Springer.

Kurdek, L. A. (1995). Lesbian and gay couples. In A. R. Augelli & C. J. Patterson (Eds.), *Lesbian and gay identities over the life span: Psychological perspectives on personal, relational, and community processes.* New York: Oxford University Press.

Kurdek, L. A. (1999). The nature and predictors of the trajectory of change in marital quality for husbands and wives over the first 10 years of marriage. *Developmental Psychology, 35,* 1283–1296.

Kurdek, L. A. (2006). Differences between partners from heterosexual, gay, and lesbian cohabiting couples. *Journal of Marriage and Family, 68,* 509–528.

Kurdek, L. A., & Krile, D. (1982). A developmental analysis of the relation between peer acceptance and both interpersonal understanding and perceived social self-competence. *Child Development, 53,* 1485–1491.

Kvitvær, B. G., Miller, J., & Newell, D. (2012). Improving our understanding of the colicky infant: A prospective observational study. *Journal of Clinical Nursing, 21,* 63–69.

Kwak, J., & Haley, W. E. (2005). Current research findings on end-of-life decision making among racially and ethnically diverse groups. *Gerontologist, 45,* 634–641.

Kwong, M. J., Bartholomew, K., Henderson, A. J. Z., & Trinke, S. J. (2003). The inter-generational transmission of relationship violence. *Journal of Family Psychology, 17,* 288–301.

L'Engle, K. L., & Jackson, C. (2008). Socialization influences on early adolescents' cognitive susceptibility and transition to sexual intercourse. *Journal of Research on Adolescence, 18,* 353–378.

Labinowicz, E. (1980). *The Piaget Primer: Thinking, Learning, Teaching.* Menlo Park, CA: Addison-Wesley Longman, 83.

Labouvie-Vief, G. (1985). Intelligence and cognition. In J. E. Birren & K. W. Schaie (Eds.), *Handbook of the psychology of aging* (2nd ed.). New York: Van Nostrand Reinhold.

Labouvie-Vief, G., Diehl, M., Jain, E., & Zhang, F. (2007). Six-year change in affect optimization and affect complexity across the adult life span: A further examination. Psychology and Aging, 22, 738–751.

Lachance, J. A., & Mazzocco, M. M. (2006). A longitudinal analysis of sex differences in math and spatial skills in primary school age children. *Learning and Individual Differences, 16,* 195–216.

Ladd, G. W. (1999). Peer relationships and social competence during early and middle childhood. *Annual Review of Psychology, 50,* 333–359.

Laflamme, D., Pomerleau, A., & Malcuit, G. (2002). A comparison of fathers' and mothers' involvement in childcare and stimulation behaviors during free-play with their infants at 9 and 15 months. *Sex Roles, 47,* 507–518.

LaFranchi, S. H., Haddow, J. E., & Hollowell, J. G. (2005). Is thyroid inadequacy during gestation a risk factor for adverse pregnancy and developmental outcomes? *Thyroid, 15,* 60–71.

Laible, D. J., & Thompson, R. A. (2000). Mother–child discourse, attachment security, shared positive affect, and early conscience development. *Child Development, 71,* 1424–1440.

Laird, R. D., Criss, M. M., Pettit, G. S., Bates, J. E., & Dodge, K. A. (2009). Developmental trajectories and antecedents of distal parental supervision. *Journal of Early Adolescence, 29,* 258–284.

Lakatta, E. G. (1990). Heart and circulation. In E. L. Schneider & J. W. Rowe (Eds.), *Handbook of the biology of aging* (3rd ed.). San Diego: Academic Press.

Lalande, K. L., & Bonanno, G. A. (2006). Culture and continuing bonds: A prospective comparison of bereavement in the United States and the People's Republic of China. *Death Studies, 30,* 303–324.

Lamb, M. E. (2013). The changing faces of fatherhood and father-child relationships. From fatherhood as status to father as Dad. In M. A. Fine & F. D. Fincham (Eds.), *Handbook of family theories. A context-based approach.* New York: Routledge.

Lamb, M. E., & Tamis-Lemonda, C. S. (2004). The role of the father: An introduction. In M. E. Lamb (Ed.), *The role of the father in child development* (4th ed.). Hoboken, NJ: John Wiley & Sons.

Lambert, S. R., & Drack, A. V. (1996). Infantile cataracts. *Survey of Ophthalmology, 40,* 427–458.

Lambert, S. R., Lynn, M. J., Reeves, R., Plager, D. A., Buckley, E. G., & Wilson, M. E. (2006). Is there a latent period for the surgical treatment of children with dense bilateral congenital cataracts? *Journal of the American Association for Pediatric Ophthalmology and Strabismus, 10,* 30–36.

Lamborn, S. D., & Steinberg, L. (1993). Emotional autonomy redux: Revisiting Ryan and Lynch. *Child Development, 64,* 483–499.

Lamborn, S. D., Mounts, N. S., Steinberg, L., & Dornbusch, S. M. (1991). Patterns of competence and adjustment among adolescents from authoritative, authoritarian, indulgent, and neglectful families. *Child Development, 62,* 1049–1065.

Lampinen, P., Heikkinen, R., & Ruoppila, I. (2000). Changes in intensity of physical exercise as predictors of depressive symptoms among older adults: An eight-year follow-up. *Preventive Medicine, 30,* 371–380.

Lampl, M., & Thompson, A. L. (2007). Growth chart curves do not describe individual growth biology. *American Journal of Human Biology, 19,* 643–653.

Lancaster, S. M., Schick, U. M., Osman, M. M., & Enquobahrie, D. A. (2012). Risk factors associated with epidural use. *Journal of Clinical Medicine Research, 4,* 119–126.

Landreth, G., & Homeyer, L. (1998). Play as the language of children's feelings. In D. P. Fromberg & D. Bergen (Eds.), *Play from birth to twelve and beyond.* New York: Garland.

Landry, S. H., Smith, K. E., & Swank, P. R. (2006). Responsive parenting: Establishing early foundations for social, communication, and independent problem-solving skills. *Developmental Psychology, 42,* 627–642.

Lane, J. D., Wellman, H. M., Olson, S. L., LaBounty, J., & Kerr, D. C. R. (2010). Theory of mind and emotion understanding predict moral development in early childhood. *British Journal of Developmental Psychology, 28,* 871–889.

Lane, M. A., Black, A., Handy, A., Tilmont, E. M., Ingram, D. K., & Roth, G. S. (2001). Caloric restriction in primates. In S. C. Park, E. S. Hwang, H. Kim, & W. Park (Eds.), *Annals of the New York Academy of Sciences: Vol. 928. Molecular and cellular interactions in senescence.* New York: The New York Academy of Sciences.

Lang, F. R., & Carstensen, L. L. (1994). Close emotional relationships in late life: Further support for proactive aging in the social domain. *Psychology and Aging, 9,* 315–324.

Lang, F. R., & Carstensen, L. L. (2002). Time counts: Future time perspective, goals, and social relationships. *Psychology and Aging, 17,* 125–139.

Lang, F. R., Rohr, M. K., & Williger, B. (2011). Modeling success in life-span psychology: The principles of selection, optimization, and compensation. In K. L. Fingerman, C. A. Berg, J. Smith, & T. C. Antonucci (Eds.), *Handbook of life-span development.* New York: Springer.

Lange, G., & Pierce, S. H. (1992). Memory-strategy learning and maintenance in preschool children. *Developmental Psychology, 28,* 453–462.

Langley, K., Heron, J., Smith, G. D., & Thapar, A. (2012). Maternal and paternal smoking during pregnancy and risk of ADHD symptoms in offspring: Testing for intrauterine effects. *American Journal of Epidemiology, 176,* 261–268.

Lansford, J. E. (2009). Parental divorce and children's adjustment. *Perspectives on Psychological Science, 4,* 140–152.

Lansford, J. E., & Dodge, K. A. (2008). Cultural norms for adult corporal punishment of children and societal rates of endorsement and use of violence. *Parenting: Science and Practice, 8,* 257–270.

Lansford, J. E., & Dodge, K. A. (2008). Cultural norms for adult corporal punishment of children and societal rates of endorsement and use of violence. *Parenting: Science and Practice, 8,* 257–270.

Lansford, J. E., Chang, L., Dodge, K. A., Malone, P. S., Oburu, P., Palmerus, K., Bacchini, D., Pastorelli, C., Bombi, A. S., Zelli, A., Tapanya, S., Chaudhary, N., Deater-Deckard, K., Manke, B., & Quinn, N. (2005). Physical discipline and children's adjustment: Cultural normativeness as a moderator. *Child Development, 76,* 1234–1246.

Lansford, J. E., Miller-Johnson, S., Berlin, L. J., Dodge, K. A., Bates, J. E., & Pettit, G. S. (2007). Early physical abuse and later violent delinquency: A prospective longitudinal study. *Child Maltreatment, 12,* 233–245.

Lansford, J. E., Sherman, A. M., & Antonucci, T. C. (1998). Satisfaction with social networks: An examination of socioemotional selectivity theory across cohorts. *Psychology and Aging, 13,* 544–552.

Lansford, J. E., Skinner, A. T., Sorbring, E., Di Giunta, L. D., Deater-Deckard, K., Dodge, K. A., et al. (2012). Boys' and girls' relational and physical aggression in nine countries. *Aggressive Behavior, 38,* 298–308.

Lansford, J. E., Yu, T., Erath, S. A., Pettit, G. S., Bates, J. E., & Dodge, K. A. (2010). Developmental precursors of number of sexual partners from ages 16 to 22. *Journal of Research on Adolescence, 20,* 651–677.

Lapsley, D. K. (2006). Moral stage theory. In M. Killen & J. G. Smetana (Eds.), *Handbook of moral development.* Mahwah, NJ: Erlbaum.

Lapsley, D. K., Milstead, M., Quintana, S. M., Flannery, D., & Buss, R. R. (1986). Adolescent egocentrism and formal operations: Tests of a theoretical assumption. *Developmental Psychology, 22,* 800–807.

Larose, S., Bernier, A., & Tarabulsy, G. M. (2005). Attachment state of mind, learning dispositions, and academic performance during the college transition. *Developmental Psychology, 41,* 281–289.

Larsen, J. T., To, Y. M., & Fireman, G. (2007). Children's understanding and experience of mixed emotions. *Psychological Science, 18,* 186–191.

Larson, E. B., Wang, L., Bowen, J. D., McCormick, W. C., Teri, L., Crane, P., & Kukull, W. (2006). Exercise is associated with reduced risk for incident dementia among persons 65 years of age and older. *Annuals of Internal Medicine, 144,* 73–81.

Larson, R. W., Richards, M. H., Moneta, G., Holmbeck, G., & Duckett, E. (1996). Changes in adolescents' daily interactions with their families from ages 10 to 18: Disengagement and transformation. *Developmental Psychology, 32,* 744–753.

Larson, R., & Ham, M. (1993). Stress and "storm and stress" in early adolescence: The relationship of negative events with dysphoric affect. *Developmental Psychology, 29,* 130–140.

Larson, R., & Lampman-Petraitis, C. (1989). Daily emotional states as reported by children and adolescents. *Child Development, 60,* 1250–1260.

Larsson, M., Öberg-Blåvarg, C., & Jönsson, F. U. (2009). Bad odors stick better than good ones: Olfactory qualities and odor recognition. *Experimental Psychology, 56,* 375–380.

Larsson, H., Viding, E., Rijsdijk, F. V., & Plomin, R. (2008). Relationships between parental negativity and childhood antisocial behavior over time: A bidirectional effects model in a longitudinal genetically informative design. *Journal of Abnormal Child Psychology, 36,* 633–645.

Larsson, I., & Svedin, C. (2002). Sexual experiences in childhood: Young adults' recollections. *Archives of Sexual Behavior, 31,* 263–273.

Laucht, M., Skowronek, M. H., Becker, K., Schmidt M. H., Esser, G., Schulze, T. G., & Rietschel, M. (2007). Interacting effects of the dopamine transporter gene and psychosocial adversity on attention-deficit/hyperactivity disorder symptoms among 15-year-olds from a high-risk community sample. *Archives of General Psychiatry, 64,* 585–590.

Laumann, E. O., Paik, A., & Rosen, R. C. (1999). Sexual dysfunction in the United States: Prevalence and predictors. *Journal of the American Medical Association, 281,* 537–544.

Laursen, B., & Williams, V. (2002). The role of ethnic identity in personality development. In L. Pulkkinen & A. Caspi (Eds.), *Paths to successful development. Personality in the life course.* Cambridge, UK: Cambridge University Press.

Lavner, J. A., & Bradbury, T. N. (2010). Patterns of change in marital satisfaction over the newlywed years. *Journal of Marriage and Family, 72,* 1171–1187.

Lawton, M. P., Moss, M. S., Winter, L., & Hoffman, C. (2002). Motivation in later life: Personal projects and well-being. *Psychology and Aging, 17,* 539–547.

Leaper, C. (1994). *Childhood gender segregation: Causes and consequences (New directions for child development, Vol. 65).* San Francisco: Jossey-Bass.

Lederberg, A. R., Schick, B., & Spencer, P. E. (2013). Language and literacy development of deaf and hard-of-hearing children: Successes and challenges. *Developmental Psychology, 49,* 15–30.

Lee, C. (2012). Deafness and cochlear implants: A deaf scholar's perspective. *Journal of Child Neurology, 27,* 821–823.

Lee, J. M., Appugliese, D., Kaciroti, N., Corwyn, R. F., Bradley, R. H., & Lumeng, J. C. (2007). Weight status in young girls and the onset of puberty. *Pediatrics, 119,* E624–E630.

Lee, J., & Hahm, H. C. (2010). Acculturation and sexual risk behaviors among Latina adolescents transitioning to young adulthood. *Journal of Youth and Adolescence, 39,* 414–427.

Lee, K., Ng, E. L., & Ng, S. F. (2009). The contributions of working memory and executive functioning to problem representation and solution generation in algebraic word problems. *Journal of Educational Psychology, 101,* 373–387.

Lee, K. S., & Ono, H. (2012). Marriage, cohabitation, and happiness: A cross national analysis of 27 countries. *Journal of Marriage and Family, 74,* 953–972.

Lee, R., Zhai, F., Brooks-Gunn, J., Han, W., & Waldfogel, J. (2013, March 25). Head Start participation and school readiness: Evidence from the Early Childhood Longitudinal Study–Birth Cohort. *Developmental Psychology.*

Lee, S. W., Clemenson, G. D., Gage, F. H. (2012). New neurons in an aged brain. *Behavioural Brain Research, 227,* 497–507.

Leeder, E. J. (2004). *The family in global perspective. A gendered journey.* Thousand Oaks, CA: Sage.

Leenarts, L. E. W., Diehle, J., Doreleijers, T. A. H., Jansma, E. P., & Lindauer, R. J. L. (2013). Evidence-based treatments for children with trauma-related psychopathology as a result of childhood maltreatment: A systematic review. *European Child & Adolescent Psychiatry, 22,* 269–283.

Leerkes, E. M., Blankson, A. N., & O'Brien, M. (2009). Differential effects of maternal sensitivity to infant distress and nondistress on social-emotional functioning. *Child Development, 80,* 762–775.

Leerkes, E. M., Blankson, A. N., & O'Brien, M. (2009). Differential effects of maternal sensitivity to infant distress and nondistress on social-emotional functioning. *Child Development, 80,* 762–775.

Legare, C. H., Evans, E. M., Rosengren, K. S., & Harris, P. L. (2012). The coexistence of natural and supernatural explanations across cultures and development. *Child Development, 83,* 779–793.

Lehman, D. R., Ellard, J. H., & Wortman, C. B. (1986). Social support for the bereaved: Recipients' and providers' perspectives on what is helpful. *Journal of Consulting and Clinical Psychology, 54,* 438–446.

Lehman, H. C. (1953). *Age and achievement.* Princeton, NJ: Princeton University Press.

Lehn, H., Derks, E. M., Hudziak, J. J., Heutink, P., van Beijsterveldt, T. C. E. M., & Boomsma, D. I. (2007). Attention problems and attention-deficit/hyperactivity disorder in discordant and concordant monozygotic twins: Evidence of environmental mediators. *Journal of the American Academy of Child and Adolescent Psychiatry, 46,* 83–91.

Leichtman, M. D., & Ceci, S. J. (1993). The problem of infantile amnesia: Lessons from fuzzy-trace theory. In M. L. Howe & R. Pasnak (Eds.), *Emerging themes in cognitive development: Vol. 1. Foundations.* New York: Springer-Verlag.

Leiden Conference on the Development and Care of Children without Permanent Parents. (2012). The development and care of institutionally reared children. *Child Development Perspectives, 6,* 174–180.

Lejarraga, H. (2002). Growth in infancy and childhood: A pediatric approach. In N. Cameron (Ed.), *Human growth and development* (pp. 21–44). New York: Academic Press.

LeMare, L. J., & Rubin, K. H. (1987). Perspective taking and peer interaction: Structural and developmental analyses. *Child Development, 58,* 306–315.

Lenroot, R. K., & Giedd, J. N. (2011). Developmental considerations of gene by environment interactions. *Journal of Child Psychology and Psychiatry and Allied Disciplines, 52,* 429–441.

Leon, D. A., Lawlor, D. A., Clark, H., Batty, G. D., & Macintyre, S. (2009). The association of childhood intelligence with mortality risk from adolescence to middle age: Findings from the Aberdeen children of the 1950s cohort study. *Intelligence, 37,* 520–528.

Lepore, J. (2011, March). Twilight: Growing old and even older. *The New Yorker,* pp. 30–35.

Lerner, J. V., & Noh, E. R. (2000). Maternal employment influences on early adolescent development: A contextual view. In R. D. Taylor & M. C. Wang (Eds.), *Resilience across contexts: Family, work, culture, and community.* Mahwah, NJ: Erlbaum.

Lerner, M. J., Somers, D. G., Reid, D., Chiriboga, D., & Tierney, M. (1991). Adult children as caregivers: Egocentric biases in judgments of sibling contributions. *Gerontologist, 31,* 746–755.

Lerner, R. M. (2006). Developmental science, developmental systems, and contemporary theories of human development. In W. Damon & R. M. Lerner (Editor-in-Chief), R. M. Lerner (Vol. Ed.), *Handbook of child psychology: Vol. 1. Theoretical models of human development* (6th ed.). Hoboken, NJ: Wiley.

Lerner, R. M., Lerner, J. V., Almerigi, J. B., Theokas, C., Phelps, E., Gestsdottir, S., et al. (2005). Positive youth development, participation in community youth development programs, and community contributions of fifth-grade adolescents: Findings from the first wave of the 4-H study of positive youth development. *Journal of Early Adolescence, 25,* 17–71.

Lester, D. (1994). Are there unique features of suicide in adults of different ages and developmental stages. *Omega: Journal of Death and Dying, 29,* 337–348.

Lester, P., Saltzman, W. R., Woodward, K., Glover, D., Leskin, G. A., Bursch, B., et al. (2012). Evaluation of a family-centered prevention intervention for military children and families facing wartime deployments. *American Journal of Public Health, 102,* S48–S54.

Lettre, G. (2012). Using height association studies to gain insights into human idiopathic short and syndromic stature phenotypes. *Pediatric Nephrology,* 1–6.

Leung, A. K. C., & Robson, W. L. M. (1993). Childhood masturbation. *Clinical Pediatrics, 32,* 238–241.

Leutwyler, B. (2009). Metacognitive learning strategies: Differential development patterns in high school. *Metacognition Learning, 4,* 111–123.

LeVay, S. (1996). *Queer science: The use and abuse of research into homosexuality.* Cambridge, MA: MIT Press.

Leve, L. D., & Fagot, B. I. (1997). Gender-role socialization and discipline processes in one- and two-parent families. *Sex Roles, 36,* 1–21.

Levenkron, S. (2000). *Anatomy of anorexia.* New York: W. W. Norton.

Levenson, R. W., Carstensen, L. L., Friesen, W. V., & Ekman, P. (1991). Emotion, physiology, and expression in old age. *Psychology and Aging, 6,* 28–35.

Levinson, D. (1989). *Family violence in cross-cultural perspective.* Newbury Park, CA: Sage.

Levinson, D. J. (1986). A conception of adult development. *American Psychologist, 41,* 3–13.

Levinson, D. J. (in collaboration with J. D. Levinson) (1996). *The seasons of a woman's life.* New York: Alfred A. Knopf.

Levinson, D. J., Darrow, C. N., Klein, E. B., Levinson, M. H., & McKee, B. (1978). *The seasons of a man's life.* New York: Ballantine Books.

Levitt, M. J. (1991). Attachment and close relationships: A life-span perspective. In J. L. Gewirtz & W. M. Kurtines (Eds.), *Intersections with attachment.* Hillsdale, NJ: Erlbaum.

Levitt, M. J., Weber, R. A., & Guacci, N. (1993). Convoys of social support: An intergenerational analysis. *Psychology and Aging, 8,* 323–326.

Levy, B. (1996). Improving memory in old age through implicit self-stereotyping. *Journal of Personality and Social Psychology, 71,* 1092–1107.

Levy, B. (2009). Stereotype embodiment. A psychosocial approach to aging. *Current Directions in Psychological Science, 18,* 332–336.

Levy, B. R. (2003). Mind matters: Cognitive and physical effects of aging self-stereotypes. *Journals of Gerontology: Psychological Sciences & Social Sciences, 58,* 203–211.

Levy, B. R., Slade, M. D., & Kasl, S. V. (2002). Longitudinal benefit of positive self-perceptions of aging on functional health. *Journals of Gerontology: Psychological Sciences and Social Sciences, 57,* 409–417.

Levy, B. R., Zonderman, A. B., Slade, M. D., & Ferrucci, L. (2009). Age stereotypes held earlier in life predict cardiovascular events in later life. *Psychological Science, 20,* 296–298.

Levy, B., & Langer, E. (1994). Aging free from negative stereotypes: Successful memory in China and among the American deaf. *Journal of Personality and Social Psychology, 66,* 989–997.

Levy, G. D., Sadovsky, A. L., & Troseth, G. L. (2000). Aspects of young children's perceptions of gender-typed occupations. *Sex Roles, 42,* 993–1006.

Levy-Shiff, R. (1994). Individual and contextual correlates of marital change across the transition to parenthood. *Developmental Psychology, 30,* 591–601.

Lew, A. R., Hopkins, B., Owen, L. H., & Green, M. (2007, March 1). Postural change effects on infants' AB task performance: Visual, postural, or spatial? *Journal of Experimental Psychology, 97,* 1–13.

Lewis, B. A., Minnes, S., Short, E. J., Weishampel, P., Satayathum, S., Min, M. O., et al. (2011). The effects of prenatal cocaine on language development at 10 years of age. *Neurotoxicology and Teratology, 33,* 17–24.

Lewis, D. A., Sesack, S. R., Levey, A. I., & Rosenberg, D. R. (1998). Dopamine axons in primate prefrontal cortex: Specificity of distribution, synaptic targets, and development. *Advances in Pharmacology, 42,* 703–706.

Lewis, L. E., & Conway, J. M. (2010). Self-other awareness and peer relationship in toddlers: Gender comparisons. *Infant and Child Dvelopment, 19,* 455–464.

Lewis, M. (2008). The emergence of human emotions. In M. Lewis, J. M. Haviland-Jones, & L. Feldman Barrett (Eds.), *Handbook of emotions* (3rd ed.). New York: Guilford.

Lewis, M., & Brooks-Gunn, J. (1979). *Social cognition and the acquisition of self.* New York: Plenum.

Lewis, M., & Rosenblum, M. A. (1975). *Friendship and peer relations.* New York: Wiley.

Lewis, M., Sullivan, M. W., Stanger, C., & Weiss, M. (1989). Self-development and self-conscious emotions. *Child Development, 60,* 146–156.

Lewis, P. G., & Lippman, J. G. (2004). *Helping children cope with the death of a parent. A guide for the first year.* Westport, CT: Praeger.

Lewis, R. (2012). *Forever fix: Gene therapy and the boy who saved it.* New York: St. Martin's.

Lewis, T. L., & Maurer, D. (2005). Multiple sensitive periods in human visual development: Evidence from visually deprived children. *Developmental Psychobiology, 46,* 163–183.

Lewis, T. L., & Maurer, D. (2009). Effects of early pattern deprivation on visual development. *Optometry and Vision Science, 86,* 640–646.

Lewontin, R. C. (1976). Race and intelligence. In N. J. Block & G. Dworkin (Eds.), *The IQ controversy.* New York: Pantheon.

Li, D. K., Liu, L., & Odouli, R. (2003). Exposure to non-steroidal anti-inflammatory drugs during pregnancy and risk of miscarriage: population based cohort study. *British Medical Journal, 327,* 368.

Li, K. Z. H., Lindenberger, U., Freund, A. M., & Baltes, P. B. (2001). Walking while memorizing: Age-related differences in compensatory behavior. *Psychological Science, 12,* 230–237.

Li, N., & Kirkup, G. (2007). Gender and cultural differences in Internet use: A study of China and the UK. *Computers & Education, 48,* 301–317.

Liben, L. S., & Signorella, M. L. (1993). Gender-schematic processing in children: The role of initial interpretations of stimuli. *Developmental Psychology, 29,* 141–149.

Lidz, J., Waxman, S., & Freedman, J. (2003). What infants know about syntax but couldn't have learned: Experimental evidence for syntactic structure at 18 months. *Cognition, 89,* B65–B73.

Lie, E., & Newcombe, N. S. (1999). Elementary school children's explicit and implicit memory for faces of preschool classmates. *Developmental Psychology, 35*, 102–112.

Lieberman, A. F., Compton, N. C., Van Horn, P., & Ippen, C. G. (2003). *Losing a parent to death in the early years. Guidelines for the treatment of traumatic bereavement in infancy and early childhood.* Washington, DC: Zero to Three Press.

Lieberman, M. A., & Videka-Sherman, L. (1986). The impact of self-help groups on the mental health of widows and widowers. *American Journal of Orthopsychiatry,56*, 435–449.

Liégeois, F., Cross, J. H., Polkey, C., Harkness, W., & Vargha-Khadem, F. (2008). Language after hemispherectomy in childhood: Contributions from memory and intelligence. *Neuropsychologia, 46*, 3101–3107.

Light, L. L. (1991). Memory and aging: Four hypotheses in search of data. *Annual Review of Psychology, 42*, 333–376.

Lilenfeld, L. R. R., Wonderlich, S., Riso, L. P., Crosby, R., & Mitchell, J. (2006). Eating disorders and personality: A methodological and empirical review. *Clinical Psychology Review, 26*, 299–320.

Lillard, A. S., Lerner, M. D., Hopkins, E. J., Dore, R. A., Smith, E. D., &Palmquist, C. M. (2013). The impact of pretend play on children's development: A review of the evidence. *Psychological Bulletin, 139*, 1–34.

Lim, F., Bond, M. H., & Bond, M. K. (2005). Linking societal and psychological factors to homicide rates across nations. *Journal of Cross-Cultural Psychology, 36*, 515–536.

Lim, S., Zoellner, J. M., Lee, J. M., Burt, B. A., Sandretto, A. M., Sohn, W., et al. (2009). Obesity and sugar-sweetened beverages in African-American preschool children: A longitudinal study. *Obesity, 17*, 1262–1268.

Lindau, S. T., & Gavrilova, N. (2010). Sex, health, and years of sexually active life gained due to good health: Evidence from two US population based cross sectional surveys of ageing. *British Medical Journal, 340*, C810. Retrieved from www.bmj.com/cgi/content/full/340/mar09_2/c810

Lindenberger, U., Marsiske, M., & Baltes, P. B. (2000). Memorizing while walking: Increase in dual-task costs from young adulthood to old age. *Psychology and Aging, 15*, 417–436.

Lindsey, E. W., & Mize, J. (2000). Parent–child physical and pretense play: Links to children's social competence. *Merrill-Palmer Quarterly, 46*, 565–591.

Lindvall, O., & Kokaia, Z. (2008). Neurogenesis following stroke affecting the adult brain. In F. H. Gage, G. Kempermann, & H. Song (Eds.), *Adult neurogenesis* (pp. 549–570). New York: Cold Spring Harbor Laboratory Press.

Lippa, R. A. (2008). The relation between childhood gender nonconformity and adult masculinity-femininity and anxiety in heterosexual and homosexual men and women. *Sex Roles, 59*, 684–693.

Liptak, G. S. (2013). Neural tube defects. In M. L. Batshaw, N. J. Roizen, & G. R. Lotrecchiano (Eds.), *Children with disabilities* (7th ed., pp. 451–472). Baltimore: Paul H. Brookes.

Lipton, A. M., & Weiner, M. F. (2003). Differential diagnosis. In M. F. Weiner & A. M. Lipton (Eds.), *The dementias. Diagnosis, treatment, and research.* Washington, DC: American Psychiatric Publishing.

Listfield, E. (2011, June 12). The underage drinking epidemic. *Parade Magazine*, pp. 6–8, 12.

Little, M., Sandler, I. N., Schoenfelder, E., & Wolchik, S. A. (2011). A contextual model of gender differences in the development of depression after the death of a parent. In T. J. Strauman, P. R. Costanzo, & J. Garber (Eds.), *Depression in adolescent girls. Science and prevention.* New York: Guilford.

Litwin, H., & Shiovitz-Ezra, S. (2011). Social network type and subjective well-being in a national sample of older Americans. *The Gerontologist, 51*, 379–388.

Liu, C. (2003). Does quality of marital sex decline with duration? *Archives of Sexual Behavior, 32*, 55–60.

Liu, D., Gelman, S. A., & Wellman, H. M. (2007). Components of young children's trait understanding: Behavior-to-trait inferences and trait-to-behavior predictions. *Child Development, 78*, 1543–1558.

Liu, D., Meltzoff, A., & Wellman, H. M. (2009). Neural correlates of belief- and desire-reasoning. *Child Development, 80*, 1163–1171.

Livesley, W. J., & Bromley, D. B. (1973). *Person perception in childhood and adolescence.* London: Wiley.

Livesley, W. J., & Bromley, D. B. (1973). *Person perception in childhood and adolescence.* London: Wiley.

Livingston, G., & Cohn, D. (2010). *Childlessness up among all women; down among women with advanced degrees.* Pew Research Center Social and Demographic Trends. Retrieved from http://www.pewsocialtrends.org/2010/06/25/childlessness-up-among-all-women-down-among-women-with-advanced-degrees/

Livingston, G., & Parker, K. (2011). *A tale of two fathers. More are active, but more are absent.* Pew ResearchCenter Social and Demographic Trends. Retrieved from http://www.pewsocialtrendsorg/2011/06/15/a-tale-of-two-fathers/

Livson, F. B. (1976). Patterns of personality in middle-aged women: A longitudinal study. *International Journal of Aging and Human Development, 7*, 107–115.

Livson, F. B. (1981). Paths to psychological health in the middle years: Sex differences. In D. H. Eichorn, J. A. Clausen, N. Haan, M. P. Honzik, & P. H. Mussen (Eds.), *Present and past in middle life.* New York: Academic Press.

Lobjois R, & Cavallo V. (2009). The effects of aging on street-crossing behavior: From estimation to actual crossing. *Accident Analysis and Prevention, 41*, 259–267.

Lock, A., & Zukow-Goldring, P. (2010). Preverbal communcation. In J. G. Bremner & T. D. Wachs (Eds.), *The Wiley-Blackwell handbook of infant development, 2nd ed. vol. 1: basic research* (pp. 394–425). Malden, MA: Blackwell.

Locke, J. L. (1997). A theory of neurolinguistic development. *Brain and Language, 58*, 265–326.

Lockheed, M. E. (1986). Reshaping the social order: The case of gender segregation. *Sex Roles, 14*, 617–628.

Lockl, K., & Schneider, W. (2007). Knowledge about the mind: Links between theory of mind and later metamemory. *Child Development, 78*, 148–167.

Lodi-Smith, J., & Roberts, B. W. (2010). Getting to know me: Social role experiences and age differences in self-concept clarity during adulthood. *Journal of Personality, 78*, 1383–1410.

Lodi-Smith, J., Turiano, N., & Mroczek, D. (2011). Personality trait development across the life span. In K. L. Fingerman, C. A. Berg, J. Smith, & T. C. Antonucci (Eds.), *Handbook of life-span development.* New York: Springer.

Loeb, K. L., Walsh, B. T., Lock, J., leGrange, D., Jones, J., Marcus, S., Weaver, J., & Dobrow, I. (2007). Open trial of family-based treatment for full and partial anorexia nervosa in adolescence. *Journal of the American Academy of Child & Adolescent Psychiatry, 46*, 792–800.

Loehlin, J. C. (1992). *Genes and environment in personality development (Individual differences and development series, Vol. 2).* Newbury Park, CA: Sage.

Loewenstein, G., & Furstenberg, F. (1991). Is teenage sexual behavior rational? *Journal of Applied Social Psychology, 21*, 957–986.

Lohan, J. A., & Murphy, S. A. (2001–2002). Parents' perceptions of adolescent sibling grief responses after an adolescent or young adult child's sudden, violent death. *Omega: Journal of Death and Dying, 44*, 77–95.

Longmore, M. A., Manning, W. D., & Giordano, P. (2013). Parent-child relationships in adolescence. In M. A. Fine & F. D. Fincham (Eds.), *Handbook of family theories. A context-based approach.* New York: Routledge.

Loomans, E. M., Hofland, L., van der Stelt, O., van der Wal, M. F., Koot, H. M., Van den Bergh, B. R. H., et al. (2012). Caffeine intake during pregnancy and risk of problem behavior in 5- to 6-year-old children. *Pediatrics, 130*, e305–e313.

Loovis, E. M., & Butterfield, S. A. (2000). Influence of age, sex, and balance on mature skipping by children in grades K-8. *Perceptual and Motor Skills, 90*, 974–978.

Lopata, H. Z. (1996). *Current widowhood: Myths and realities.* Thousand Oaks, CA: Sage.

Lopez, E. C. (1997). The cognitive assessment of limited English proficient and bilingual children. In D. P. Flanagan, J. Genshaft, & P. L. Harrison (Eds.), *Contemporary intellectual assessment: Theories, tests, and issues.* New York: Guilford.

Lopez, O. L. (2013). Mild cognitive impairment. *CONTINUUM: Lifelong Learning in Neurology, 19*, 411–424.

Lopez, S. R., & Guarnaccia, P. J. J. (2000). Cultural psychopathology: Uncovering the social world of mental illness. *Annual Review of Psychology, 51*, 571–598.

Lorenz, K. Z. (1937). The companion in the bird's world. *Auk,54*, 245–273.

Lorsbach, T. C., & Reimer, J. F. (1997). Developmental changes in the inhibition of previously relevant information. *Journal of Experimental Child Psychology, 64*, 317–342.

Lougheed, J. P., &Hollenstein, T. (2012). A limited repertoire of emotion regulation strategies is associated with internalizing problems in adolescence. *Social Development, 21*, 704–721.

Lourenco, O., & Machado, A. (1996). In defense of Piaget's theory: A reply to 10 common criticisms. *Psychological Review, 103*, 143–164.

Lovaas, O. I. (1987). Behavioral treatment and normal educational and intellectual functioning in young autistic children. *Journal of Consulting and Clinical Psychology, 55*, 3–9.

Lovaas, O. I., & Smith, T. (2003). Early and intensive behavioral intervention in autism. In A. E. Kazdin & J. R. Weisz (Eds.), *Evidence-based psychotherapies for children and adolescents.* New York: Guilford.

Lovett, B. J., & Sheffield, R. A. (2007). Affective empathy in aggressive children and adolescents: A critical review. *Clinical Psychology Review, 27*, 1–13.

Lowry, K A., Vallejo, A. N., Studenski, S. A. (2012). Successful aging as a continuum of functional independence: Lessons from physical disability models of aging. *Aging and Disease, 3*, 5–15.

Lubinski, D., Webb, R. M., Morelock, M. J., & Benbow, C. P. (2001). Top 1 in 10,000: A 10-year follow-up of the profoundly gifted. *Journal of Applied Psychology, 86*, 718–729.

Luby, J. L. (2004). Affective disorders. In R. DelCarmen-Wiggins & A. Carter (Eds.), *Handbook of infant, toddler, and preschool mental health assessment.* New York: Oxford University Press.

Luby, J. L. (2009). Depression. In C. H. Zeanah (Ed.), *Handbook of infant mental health* (3rd ed.). New York: Guilford.

Luby, J. L., Sullivan, J., Belden, A., Stalets, M., Blankenship, S., & Spitznagel, E. (2006). An observational analysis of behavior in depressed preschoolers: Further validation of early-onset depression. *Journal of the American Academy of Child and Adolescent Psychiatry, 45*, 203–212.

Luby, J., & Belden, A. (2012). Depressivesymptom onset during toddlerhood in a sample of depressed preschoolers: Implications for future investigations of major depressive disorder in toddlers. *Infant Mental Health Journal, 33*, 139–147.

Luby, J., Belden, A., Sullivan, J., Hayen, R., McCadney, A., & Spitznagel, E. (2009). Shame and guilt in preschool depression: Evidence for elevations in self-conscious emotions in depression as early as age 3. *Journal of Child Psychology and Psychiatry, 50*, 1156–1166.

Luby, J., Lenze, S., & Tillman, R. (2012). A novel early intervention for preschool depression: Findings from a pilot randomized controlled trial. *Journal of Child Psychology and Psychiatry, 53*, 313–322.

Lucas, R. E., & Diener, E. (2008). Personality and subjective well-being. In O. P. John, R. W. Robins, & L. A. Pervin (Eds.), *Handbook of personality theory and research* (3rd ed.). New York: Guilford.

Luciana, M., Conklin, H. M., Hooper, C. J., & Yarger, R. S. (2005). The development of nonverbal working memory and executive control processes in adolescents. *Child Development, 76*, 697–712.

Lucio, R., Hunt, E., & Bornovalova, M. (2012). Identifying the necessary and sufficient number of risk factors for predicting academic failure. *Developmental Psychology, 48*, 422–428.

Lüdtke, O., Roberts, B. W., Trautwein, U., & Nagy, G. (2011). A random walk down university avenue: Life paths, life events, and personality trait change at the transition to university life. *Journal of Personality and Social Psychology, 101*, 620–637.

Ludwig, J., & Phillips, D. A. (2008). Long-term effects of Head Start on low-income children. *Annals of the New York Academy of Science, 1136*, 257–268.

Luecken, L. J. (2008). Long-term consequences of parental death in childhood: Psychological and physiological manifestations. In M. S. Stroebe, R. O. Hansson, H. Schut, & W. Stroebe (Eds.), *Handbook of bereavement research and practice: Advances in theory and intervention.* Washington, DC: American Psychological Association.

Luecken, L. J., Hagan, M. J., Sandler, I. N., Tein, J., Ayers, T. S., & Wolchik, S. A. (2013). Longitudinal mediators of a randomized prevention program effect on cortisol for youth from parentally bereaved families. *Prevention Science.* doi:10.1007/s11121-013-0385-7

Luecken, L. J., Kraft, A., Appelhans, B. M., & Enders, C. (2009). Emotional and cardiovascular sensitization to daily stress following childhood parental loss. *Developmental Psychology, 45*, 296–302.

Luke, M. A., Sedikides, C., & Carnelley, K. (2012). Your love lifts me higher! The energizing quality of secure relationships. *Personality and Social Psychology Bulletin, 38*, 721–733.

Luo, Y. L., Haworth, C. M., & Plomin, R. (2010). A novel approach to genetic and environmental analysis of cross-lagged associations over time: The cross-lagged relationship between self-perceived abilities and school achievement is mediated by genes as well as the environment. *Twin Research and Human Genetics, 13*, 426–436.

Luo, Y., & Johnson, S. C. (2009). Recognizing the role of perception in action at 6 months. *Developmental Science, 12*, 142–149.

Luo, Y., Hawkley, L. C., Waite, L. J., &Cacioppo, J. T. (2012). Loneliness, health, and mortality in old age: A national longitudinal study. *Social Science & Medicine, 74*, 907–914.

Lupsakko, T. A., Kautiainen, H. J., & Sulkava, R. (2005). The non-use of hearing aids in people aged 75 years and over in the city of Kuopio in Finland. *European Archives of Oto-Rhino-Laryngology, 262*, 165–169.

Luria, A. R. (1974/1976). *Cognitive development: Its cultural and social foundations.* Cambridge, MA: Harvard University Press.

Lustig, J. L., Wolchik, S. A., & Braver, S. L. (1992). Social support in chumships and adjustment in children of divorce. *American Journal of Community Psychology, 20*, 393–399.

Lyketsos, C. G. (2009). Dementia and milder cognitive syndromes. In D. G. Blazer & D. C. Steffens (Eds.), *The American Psychiatric Publishing textbook of geriatric psychiatry* (4th ed.). Washington, DC: American Psychiatric Publishing.

Lyman, S., Ferguson, S. A., Braver, E. R., & Williams, A. F. (2002). Older driver involvements in police reported crashes and fatal crashes: Trends and projections. *Injury Prevention, 8*, 116–120.

Lynch, M. P., Eilers, R. E., Oller, D. K., & Urbano, R. C. (1990). Innateness, experience, and music perception. *Psychological Science, 1*, 272–276.

Lynn, R. (2008). *The global bell curve: Race, IQ, and inequality worldwide.* Augusta, GA: Washington Summit Publishers.

Lynn, R. (2009). Fluid intelligence but not vocabulary has increased in Britain, 1979–2008. *Intelligence, 37*, 249–255.

Lynne, S. D., Graber, J. A., Nichols, T. R., Brooks-Gunn, J., & Botvin, G. J. (2007). Links between pubertal timing, peer influences, and externalizing behaviors among urban students followed through middle school. *Journal of Adolescent Health, 40*, 181.e7–181.e13.

Lyon, A. R., & Cotler, S. (2009). Multi-systemic intervention for school refusal behavior: Integrating approaches across disciplines. *Advances in School Mental Health Promotion, 2*, 20–34.

Lyonette, C., & Yardley, L. (2003). The influence on carer wellbeing of motivations to care for older people and the relationship with the care recipient. *Ageing & Society, 23*, 487–506.

Lytton, H., & Romney, D. M. (1991). Parents' differential socialization of boys and girls: A meta-analysis. *Psychological Bulletin, 109*, 267–296.

Ma, H. H. (2006). A synthetic analysis of the effectiveness of single components and packages in creativity training programs. *Creativity Research Journal, 18*, 435–446.

Ma, H. M., Du, M. L., Luo, X. P., Chen, S. K., Liu, L., Chen, R. M., et al. (2009). Onset of breast and pubic hair development and menses in urban Chinese girls. *Pediatrics, 124*, e269–77.

Ma, W., Golinkoff, R. M., Houston, D. M., & Hirsh-Pasek, K. (2011). Word learning in infant- and adult-directed speech. *Language Learning and Development, 7*, 185–201.

Mac Iver, D. J., & Reuman, D. A. (1988, April). *Decision-making in the classroom and early adolescents' valuing of mathematics.* Paper presented at the annual meeting of the American Educational Research Association, New Orleans.

Mac Iver, D. J., Reuman, D. A., and Main, S. R. (1995). Social structuring of school: Studying what is, illuminating what could be. In M. R. Rosenzweig and L. W. Porter (Eds.), *Annual review of psychology, 46*, 375–400.

Macartney, S. (2011). *Child poverty in the United States 2009 and 2010: Selected race groups and Hispanic origin* (American Community Survey Briefs 10–05). Washington, DC: U.S. Census Bureau.

Maccoby, E. E. (1998). *The two sexes: Growing up apart, coming together*. Cambridge, MA: Harvard University Press.

Maccoby, E. E. (2007). Historical overview of socialization research and theory. In J. E. Grusec & P. D. Hastings (Eds.), *Handbook of socialization theory and research*. New York: Guilford.

Maccoby, E. E., & Jacklin, C. N. (1987). Gender segregation in childhood. In H. W. Reese (Ed.), *Advances in child development and behavior* (Vol. 20). Orlando, FL: Academic Press.

Maccoby, E. E., & Martin, J. A. (1983). Socialization in the context of the family: Parent–child interaction. In E. M. Hetherington (Vol. Ed.), P. H. Mussen (Editor-in-Chief), *Handbook of child psychology: Vol. 4. Socialization, personality, and social development* (4th ed.). New York: Wiley.

MacDorman, M. F., & Mathews, T. J. (2008, October). *Recent trends in infant mortality in the United States* (NCHS Data Brief No. 9). Hyattsville, MD: National Center for Health Statistics.

MacDorman, M. F., Kirmeyer, S. E., & Wilson, E. C. (2012). Fetal and perinatal mortality, United States, 2006. National Vital Statistics Reports, 60 (8).

MacDorman, M. F., Mathews, T. J., & Declercq, E. (2012). Home births in the United States, 1990–2009. *NCHS Data Brief, 84*, 1–8.

MacDorman, M., & Kirmeyer, S. (2009). *The challenge of fetal mortality* (NCHS data brief, no 16). Hyattsville, MD: National Center for Health Statistics.

Maciejewski, P. K., Zhang, B., Block, S. D., & Prigerson, H. G. (2007). An empirical examination of the stage theory of grief. *JAMA, 297*, 716–723.

Mackey, R. A., & O'Brien, B. A. (1995). *Lasting marriages: Men and women growing together*. Westport, CT: Praeger.

Mackinlay, R. J., Kliegel, M., Mäntylä, T., & Kliegel, M. (2009). Predictors of time-based prospective memory in children. *Journal of Experimental Child Psychology, 102*, 251–264.

MacLean, K. (2003). The impact of institutionalization on child development. *Development and Psychopathology, 15*, 853–884.

MacPherson, S. E., Phillips, L. H., & Della Sala, S. (2002). Age, executive function and social decision making: A dorsolateral prefrontal theory of cognitive aging. *Psychology and Aging, 17*, 598–609.

Madden, D. J. (2007). Aging and visual attention. *Current Directions in Psychological Science, 16*, 70–74.

Madden, D. J., & Langley, L. K. (2003). Age-related changes in selective attention and perceptual load during visual search. *Psychology and Aging, 18*, 54–67.

Madden, D. J., Gottlob, L. R., & Allen, P. A. (1999). Adult age differences in visual search accuracy: Attentional guidance and target detectability. *Psychology and Aging, 14*, 683–694.

Maddux, J. E. (2002). Self-efficacy: The power of believing you can. In C. R. Snyder & S. J.

Lopez (Eds.), *Handbook of positive psychology* (pp. 277–287). New York: Oxford University Press.

Madsen, S. D., & Collins, W. A. (2011). The salience of adolescent romantic experiences for romantic relationship qualities in young adulthood. *Journal of Research on Adolescence, 21*, 789–801.

Maehr, M., & Meyer, H. (1997). Understanding motivation and schooling: Where we've been, where we are, and where we need to go. *Educational Psychology Review, 9*, 371–409.

Maestripieri, D., Lindell, S. G., & Higley, J. D. (2007). Intergenerational transmission of maternal behavior in rhesus macaques and its underlying mechanisms. *Developmental Psychobiology, 49*, 165–171.

Magai, C. (2008). Attachment in middle and later life. In J. Cassidy & P. R. Shaver (Eds.), *Handbook of attachment: Theory, research, and clinical applications* (2nd ed.). New York: Guilford.

Magai, C., Cohen, C., Milburn, N., Thorpe, B., McPherson, R., & Peralta, D. (2001). Attachment styles in older European American and African American adults. *Journals of Gerontology: Psychological Sciences and Social Sciences, 56*, S28–S35.

Magai, C., Consedine, N. S., Krivoshekova, Y. S., Kudadjie-Gyamfi, E., & McPherson, R. (2006). Emotion experience and expression across the adult life span: Insights from a multimodal assessment study. *Psychology and Aging, 21*, 303–317.

Maguire-Jack, K., Gromoske, A. N., & Berger, L. M. (2012). Spanking and child development during the first 5 years of life. *Child Development, 83*, 1960–1977.

Mahaffy, K. A., & Ward, S. K. (2002). The gendering of adolescents' childbearing and educational plans: Reciprocal effects and the influence of social context. *Sex Roles, 46*, 403–417.

Maholmes, V. (2012). Adjustment of children and youth in military families: Toward developmental understandings. *Child Development Perspectives, 6*, 430–435.

Maiden, R. J., Peterson, S. A., Caya, M., & Hayslip, B. (2003). Personality changes in the old-old: A longitudinal study. *Journal of Adult Development, 10*, 31–39.

Maier, E. H., & Lachman, M. E. (2000). Consequences of early parental loss and separation for health and well-being in midlife. *International Journal of Behavioral Development, 24*, 183–189.

Main, M., & George, C. (1985). Responses of abused and disadvantaged toddlers to distress in agemates: A study in the day-care setting. *Developmental Psychology, 21*, 407–412.

Main, M., & Solomon, J. (1990). Procedures for identifying infants as disorganized/disoriented during the Ainsworth Strange Situation. In M. T. Greenberg, D. Cicchetti, & E. M. Cummings (Eds.), *Attachment in the preschool years: Theory, research, and intervention*. Chicago: University of Chicago Press.

Main, M., & Weston, D. R. (1981). The quality of the toddler's relationship to mother

and to father: Related to conflict and the readiness to establish new relationships. *Child Development, 52*, 932–940.

Malatesta, C. Z., & Kalnok, M. (1984). Emotional experience in younger and older adults. *Journal of Gerontology, 39*, 301–308.

Malatesta, C. Z., Culver, C., Tesman, J. R., & Shepard, B. (1989). The development of emotion expression during the first two years of life. *Monographs of the Society for Research in Child Development, 54* (1–2, Serial No. 219).

Malatesta, C. Z., Grigoryev, P., Lamb, C., Albin, M., & Culver, C. (1986). Emotional socialization and expressive development in preterm and full-term infants. *Child Development, 57*, 316–330.

Malinosky-Rummell, R., & Hansen, D. J. (1993). Long-term consequences of childhood physical abuse. *Psychological Bulletin, 114*, 68–79.

Malley-Morrison, K., & Hines, D. A. (2004). *Family violence in a cultural perspective. Defining, understanding, and combating abuse*. Thousand Oaks, CA: Sage.

Malmstrom, M., Sundquist, J., Bajekal, M., & Johansson, S. E. (1999). Ten-year trends in all-cause mortality and coronary heart disease mortality in socioeconomically diverse neighbourhoods. *Public Health, 113*, 279–284.

Malouf, M. A., Migeon, C. J., Carson, K. A., Petrucci, L., & Wisniewski, A. B. (2006). Cognitive outcome in adult women affected by congenital adrenal hyperplasia due to 21-hydroxylase deficiency. *Hormone Research, 65*, 142–150.

Mancini, A. D., Griffin, P., & Bonanno, G. A. (2012). Recent trends in the treatment of prolonged grief. *Current Opinion in Psychiatry, 25*, 46–51.

Mandal, B., Ayyagari, P., & Gallo, W. T. (2011). Job loss and depression: The role of subjective expectations. *Social Science and Medicine, 72*, 576–583.

Mandara, J., Gaylord-Harden, N. K., Richards, M. H., & Ragsdale, B. L. (2009). The effects of changes in racial identity and self-esteem on changes in African-American adolescents' mental health. *Child Development, 80*, 1660–1675.

Mangelsdorf, S. C. (1992). Developmental changes in infant-stranger interaction. *Infant Behavior and Development, 15*, 191–208.

Mangelsdorf, S. C., Gunnar, M., Kestenbaum, R., Lang, S., & Andreas, D. (1990). Infant proneness-to-distress temperament, maternal personality, and mother–infant attachment: Associations and goodness of fit. *Child Development, 61*, 820–831.

Mangelsdorf, S. C., Shapiro, J. R., & Marzolf, D. (1995). Developmental and temperamental differences in emotion regulation in infancy. *Child Development, 66*, 1817–1828.

Manlove, J., Wildsmith, E., Ikramullah, E., Terry-Humen, E, & Schelar, E. (2012). Family environments and the relationship context of first adolescent sex: Correlates of first sex in a casual versus steady relationship. *Social Science Research, 41*, 861–875.

Mansoor, E., Morrow, C. E., Accornero, V. H., Xue, L., Johnson, A. L., Anthony, J. C., et al. (2012). Longitudinal effects of prenatal cocaine use on mother-child interactions at ages 3 and 5 years. *Journal of Developmental & Behavioral Pediatrics, 33,* 32–41.

Marceau, J. R., Murray, H., & Nanan, R. K. (2009). Efficacy of oral sucrose in infants of methadone-maintained mothers. *Neonatology, 97,* 67–70.

Marceau, K., Neiderhiser, J. M., Lichtenstein, P., & Reiss, D. (2012). Genetic and environmental influences on the association between pubertal maturation and internalizing symptoms. *Journal of Youth and Adolescence, 41,* 1111–1126.

March, J. S. (2009). The future of psychotherapy for mentally ill children and adolescents. *Journal of Child Psychology and Psychiatry, 50,* 170–179.

Marchand, H. (2002). Some reflections on postformal thought. *The Genetic Epistemologist, 29,* 2–9.

Marcia, J. E. (1966). Development and validation of ego identity status. *Journal of Personality and Social Psychology, 3,* 551–558.

Marcovitch, S., & Zelazo, D. (1999). The A-not-B error: Results from a logistic meta-analysis. *Child development, 70,* 1297–1313.

Mareschal, D. (2011). From NEOconstructivism to NEUROconstructivism. *Child Development Perspectives, 5,* 169–170.

Mareschal, D., Johnson, M. H., Sirois, S., Spratling, M., Thomas, M. S. C., & Westermann, G. (2007). *Neuroconstructivism: How the brain constructs cognition.* Cambridge University Press.

Margolin, G., & Gordis, E. B. (2000). The effects of family and community violence on children. *Annual Review of Psychology, 51,* 445–479.

Marian, V., & Shook, A. (2012, October 12). *The cognitive benefits of being bilingual.* The Dana Foundation. Retrieved from http://dana.org/news/cerebrum/detail.aspx?id=39638

Maric, M., Heyne, D. A., de Heus, P., van Widenfelt, B. M., & Westenberg, P. M. (2012). The role of cognition in school refusal: An investigation of automatic thoughts and cognitive errors. *Behavioural and Cognitive Psychotherapy, 40,* 255–269.

Marini, Z., & Case, R. (1994). The development of abstract reasoning about the physical and social world. *Child Development, 65,* 147–159.

Markham, J. A., & Greenough, W. T. (2004). Experience-driven brain plasticity: Beyond the synapse. *Neuron and Glia Biology, 1,* 351–363.

Markides, K. S., Boldt, J. S., & Ray, L. A. (1986). Sources of helping and intergenerational solidarity: A three-generations study of Mexican Americans. *Journal of Gerontology, 41,* 506–511.

Markiewicz, D., Lawford, H., Doyle, A. B., & Haggart, N. (2006). Developmental differences in adolescents' and young adults' use of mothers, fathers, best friends, and romantic partners to fulfill attachment needs. *Journal of Youth and Adolescence, 35,* 127–140.

Markstrom-Adams, C., & Adams, G. R. (1995). Gender, ethnic group, and grade differences in psychosocial functioning during middle adolescence. *Journal of Youth and Adolescence, 24,* 397–417.

Markus, H. R. (2004). Culture and personality: Brief for an arranged marriage. *Journal of Research in Personality, 38,* 75–83.

Markus, H. R., Mullally, P. R., & Kitayama, S. (1997). Self-ways: Diversity in modes of cultural participation. In U. Neisser & D. A. Jopling (Eds.), *The conceptual self in context. Culture, experience, self-understanding.* Cambridge, UK: Cambridge University Press.

Marlier, L., & Schaal, B. (2005). Human newborns prefer human milk: Conspecific milk odor is attractive without postnatal exposure. *Child Development, 76,* 155–168.

Marottoli, R. A. (2007). *Enhancement of driving performance among older drivers.* Washington, DC: AAA Foundation for Traffic Safety. Retrieved from www.aaafoundation.org/pdf/EnhancingSeniorDrivingPerfReport.pdf.

Marschark, M. (1993). *Psychological development of deaf children.* New York: Oxford University Press.

Marsee, M. A., & Frick, P. J. (2010). Callous-unemotional traits and aggression in youth. In W. F. Arsenio & E. A. Lemerise (Eds.), *Emotions, aggression, and morality in children. Bridging development and psychopathology.* Washington, DC: American Psychological Association.

Marsh, H. W., & Craven, R. G. (2006). Reciprocal effects of self-concept and performance from a multidimensional perspective: Beyond seductive pleasure and unidimensional perspectives. *Perspectives on Psychological Science, 1,* 133–163.

Marsh, H. W., Chessor, D., Craven, R., & Roche, L. (1995). The effect of gifted and talented programs on academic self-concept: The big fish strikes again. *American Educational Research Journal, 32,* 285–319.

Marsh, H. W., Craven, R., & Debus, R. (1999). Separation of competency and affect components of multiple dimensions of academic self-concept: A developmental perspective. *Merrill-Palmer Quarterly, 45,* 567–701.

Marshall, W. A., & Tanner, J. M. (1969). Variations in the pattern of pubertal changes in girls. *Archives of Disease in Childhood, 44,* 291–303.

Marshall, W. A., & Tanner, J. M. (1970). Variations in the pattern of pubertal changes in boys. *Archives of Disease in Childhood, 45,* 13–23.

Marsiglio, W., Amato, P., Day, R. D., & Lamb, M. E. (2000). Scholarship on fatherhood in the 1990s and beyond. *Journal of Marriage and the Family, 62,* 1173–1191.

Marsiske, M., & Margrett, J. A. (2006). Everyday problem solving and decision making. In J. E. Birren & K. W. Schaie (Eds.), *Handbook of the psychology of aging.* Boston: Elsevier Academic Press.

Marsiske, M., & Willis, S. L. (1995). Dimensionality of everyday problem solving in older adults. *Psychology and Aging, 10,* 269–283.

Martin, A. (2008). Enhancing student motivation and engagement: The effects of a multidimensional intervention. *Contemporary Educational Psychology, 33,* 239–269.

Martin, C. L., & Dinella, L. M. (2012). Congruence between gender stereotypes and activity preference in self-identified tomboys and non-tomboys. *Archives of Sexual Behavior, 41,* 599–610.

Martin, C. L., & Fabes, R. A. (2001). The stability and consequences of young children's same-sex peer interactions. *Developmental Psychology, 37,* 431–446.

Martin, C. L., & Halverson, C. F., Jr. (1981). A schematic processing model of sex typing and stereotyping in children. *Child Development, 52,* 1119–1134.

Martin, C. L., & Halverson, C. F., Jr. (1983). The effects of sex-typing schemas on young children's memory. *Child Development, 54,* 563–574.

Martin, C. L., & Halverson, C. F., Jr. (1987). The roles of cognition in sex-roles and sex-typing. In D. B. Carter (Ed.), *Current conceptions of sex roles and sex-typing: Theory and research.* New York: Preager.

Martin, C. L., & Ruble, D. N. (2010). Patterns of gender development. *Annual Review of Psychology, 61,* 353–381.

Martin, C. L., & Ruble, D. N. (2004). Children's search for gender cues: Cognitive perspectives on gender development. *Current Directions in Psychological Science, 13,* 67–70.

Martin, C. L, Ruble, D. N., & Szkrybalo, J. (2002). Cognitive Theories of Early Gender Development. *Psychological bulletin, 128,* 903–933.

Martin, C. L., DiDonato, M. D., Clary, L., Fabes, R. A., Kreiger, T., Palermo, F., & Hanish, L. et al. (2012). Preschool children with gender normative and gender non-normative peer preferences: Psychosocial and environmental correlates. *Archives of Sexual Behavior, 41,* 831–847.

Martin, C. L., Kornienko, O., Schaefer, D. R., Hanish, L. D., Fabes, R. A., & Goble, P. (2013). The role of sex of peers and gender-typed activities in young children's peer affiliative networks: A longitudinal analysis of selection and influence. *Child Development, 84,* 921–937.

Martin, F. N., & Clark, J. G. (2002). *Introduction to audiology* (8th ed.). New York: Allyn & Bacon.

Martin, G. B., & Clark, R. D., III. (1982). Distress crying in neonates: Species and peer specificity. *Developmental Psychology, 18,* 3–9.

Martin, M., Grunendahl, M., & Martin, P. (2001). Age differences in stress, social resources, and well-being in middle and old age. *Journal of Gerontology: Psychological Sciences, 56,* 214–222.

Martin, P., Hagberg, B., & Poon, L. W. (2012). Models for studying centenarians and healthy ageing. *Asian Journal of Gerontology & Geriatrics, 7,* 14–18.

Martinez, G., Daniels, K., & Chandra, A. (2012, April 12). Fertility of men and women aged 15–44 years in the United States: National survey of family growth, 2006–2010. *National Health Statistics Reports*, No. 51.

Martinez-Frias, M. L. (2012). The thalidomide experience: Review of its effects 50 years later. *MedicinaClinca*, 139, 25–32.

Martlew, M., & Connolly, K. J. (1996). Human figure drawings by schooled and unschooled children in Papua New Guinea. *Child Development*, 67, 2743–2762.

Martorano, S. C. (1977). A developmental analysis of performance on Piaget's formal operations tasks. *Developmental Psychology*, 13, 666–672.

Martorell, G. A., & Bugental, D. B. (2006). Maternal variations in stress reactivity: Implications for harsh parenting practices with very young children. *Journal of Family Psychology*, 20, 641–647.

Masataka, N. (2000). The role of modality and input in the earliest stage of language acquisition: Studies of Japanese sign language. In C. Chamberlain, J. Morford, & R. I. Mayberry (Eds.), *Language acquisition by eye* (pp. 3–24). Mahwah, NJ: Lawrence Erlbaum.

Masi, C. M., Chen, H., Hawkley, L. C., &Caccioppo, J. T. (2011). A meta-analysis of interventions to reduce loneliness. *Personality and Social Psychology Review*, 15, 219–266.

Masten, A. S., & Reed, M. J. (2002). Resilience in development. In C. R. Snyder & S. J. Lopez (Eds.), *Handbook of positive psychology* (pp. 74–88). New York: Oxford University Press.

Masten, A. S., & Tellegen, A. (2012). Resilience in developmental psychopathology: Contributions of the Project Competence Longitudinal Study. *Development and Psychopathology*, 24, 345–361.

Masten, A. S., Roisman, G. I., Long, J. D., Burt, K. B., Obradovic, J., Riley, J. R., Boelcke-Stennes, K., & Tellegen, A. (2005). Developmental cascades: Linking academic achievement and externalizing and internalizing symptoms over 20 years. *Developmental Psychology*, 41, 733–746.

Masters, W. H., & Johnson, V. E. (1966). *Human sexual response*. Boston: Little, Brown.

Masters, W. H., & Johnson, V. E. (1970). *Human sexual inadequacy*. Boston: Little, Brown.

Matchar, E. (2012, August 19). Why your office needs more bratty millennials. *The Washington Post*, pp. B1, B4.

Mathews, J. (2003, October 1). Not quite piling on the homework. *The Washington Post*, pp. A1, A4.

Matsuba, M. K., & Walker, L. J. (2004). Extraordinary moral commitment: Young adults involved in social organizations. *Journal of Personality*, 72, 413–436.

Matthews, K. A. (1992). Myths and realities of the menopause. *Psychosomatic Medicine*, 54, 1–9.

Matthews, K. A., & Gallo, L. C. (2011). Psychological Perspectives on Pathways Linking Socioeconomic Status and Physical Health. *Annual review of psychology*, 62, 501–530.

Matthews, K. A., Wing, R. R., Kuller, L. H., Meilahn, E. N., Kelsey, S. F., Costello, E. J., & Caggiula, A. W. (1990). Influences of natural menopause on psychological characteristics and symptoms of middle-aged healthy women. *Journal of Consulting and Clinical Psychology*, 58, 345–351.

Mattis, J. S., & Grayman-Simpson, N. (2013). Faith and the sacred in African American life. In K. I. Pargament, J. J. Exline, & J. W. Jones (Eds.), APA *handbook of psychology, religion, and spirituality: Vol. 1. Context, theory, and research*. Washington, DC: American Psychological Association.

Matusov, E., & Hayes, R. (2000). Sociocultural critique of Piaget and Vygotsky. *New Ideas in Psychology*, 18, 215–239.

Maughan, B. (2001). Conduct disorder in context. In J. Hill & B. Maughan (Eds.), *Conduct disorders in childhood and adolescence*. New York: Cambridge University Press.

Maughan, B., & Rutter, M. (2001). Antisocial children grown up. In J. Hill & B. Maughan (Eds.), *Conduct disorders in childhood and adolescence*. New York: Cambridge University Press.

Maurer, A. (1961). The child's knowledge of nonexistence. *Journal of Existential Psychiatry*, 2, 193–212.

Maurer, D., Lewis, T. L., Brent, H. P., & Levin, A. V. (1999). Rapid improvement in the acuity of infants after visual input. *Science*, 286, 108–110.

Maurer, D., Mondloch, C. J., & Lewis, T. L. (2007). Sleeper effects. *Developmental Science*, 10, 40–47.

Maurer, D., Stager, C. L., & Mondloch, C. J. (1999). Cross-modal transfer of shape is difficult to demonstrate in one-month-olds. *Child Development*, 70, 1047–1057.

May, P. A., Fiorentino, D., Coriale, G., Kalberg, W. O., Hoyme, H. E., Aragón, A. S., et al. (2011). Prevalence of children with severe fetal alcohol spectrum disorders in communities near Rome, Italy: New estimated rates are higher than previous estimates. *International Journal of Environmental Research and Public Health*, 8, 2331–2351.

Mayberry, R. I. (1994). The importance of childhood to language acquisition: Evidence from American sign language. In J. C. Goodman & H. C. Nusbaum (Eds.), *The development of speech perception: The transition from speech sounds to spoken words*. Cambridge, MA: MIT Press.

Mayberry, R. I., & Eichen, E. B. (1991). The long-lasting advantage of learning sign language in childhood: Another look at the critical period for language acquisition. *Journal of Memory and Language*, 30, 486–512.

Mayberry, R. I., Lock, E., & Kazmi, H. (2002). Linguistic ability and early language exposure. *Nature*, 417, 38.

Mayer, A., & Träuble, B. E. (2013). Synchrony in the onset of mental state understanding across cultures? A study among children in Samoa. *International Journal of Behavioral Development*, 37, 21–28.

Mayer, C. (2011, April). Amortality: Why acting your age is a thing of the past. *Time*, pp. 44–51.

Mayes, R., Bagwell, C., & Erkulwater, J. (2009). *Medicating children: ADHD and pediatric mental health*. Cambridge, MA: Harvard University Press.

Mayeux, L., & Cillessen, A. H. N. (2003). Development of social problem solving in early childhood: Stability, change, and associations with social competence. *Journal of Genetic Psychology*, 164, 153–173.

Mayeux, L., Houser, J. J., & Dyches, K. D. (2011). Social acceptance and popularity: Two distinct forms of peer status. In A. H. N. Cillessen, D. Schwartz, & L. Mayeux (Eds.), *Popularity in the peer system*. New York: Guilford.

Mayeux, L., Sandstrom, M. J., & Cillessen, A. H. N. (2008). Is being popular a risky proposition? *Journal of Research on Adolescence*, 18, 49–74.

Mayseless, O., Danieli, R., & Sharabany, R. (1996). Adults' attachment patterns: Coping with separations. *Journal of Youth and Adolescence*, 25, 667–690.

Mbilinyi, L. F., Edleson, J. L., Hagemeister, A. K., & Beeman, S. K. (2007). What happens to children when their mothers are battered? Results from a four city anonymous telephone survey. *Journal of Family Violence*, 22, 309–317.

McAdams, D. P. (2005). Studying lives in time: A narrative approach. In R. Levy, P. Ghisletta, J. Le Goff, D. Spini, & E. Widmer (Eds.), *Advances in life course research. Vol. 10: Towards an interdisciplinary perspective on the life course*. Amsterdam: Elsevier.

McAdams, D. P. (2008). Personal narratives and the life story. In O. P. John, R. W. Robins, & L. A. Pervin (Eds.), *Handbook of personality theory and research* (3rd ed.). New York: Guilford.

McAdams, D. P. (2011). Life narratives. In K. L. Fingerman, C. A. Berg, J. Smith, & T. C. Antonucci (Eds.), *Handbook of life-span development*. New York: Springer.

McAdams, D. P., & Adler, J. M. (2006). How does personality develop? In D. K. Mroczek & T. D. Little (Eds.), *Handbook of personality development*. Mahwah, NJ: Erlbaum.

McAdams, D. P., & Pals, J. L. (2006). A new Big Five: Fundamental principles for an integrative science of personality. *American Psychologist*, 61, 204–217.

McAdams, D. P., Hart, H. M., & Maruna, S. (1998). The anatomy of generativity. In D. P. McAdams & E. de St. Aubin (Eds.), *Generativity and adult development: How and why we care for the next generation*. Washington, DC: American Psychological Association.

McAdams, P. P., de St. Aubin, E., & Logan, R. L. (1993). Generativity among young, middle, and older adults. *Psychology and Aging*, 8, 221–230.

McAlister, A. L., Bandura, A., & Owen, S. V. (2006). Mechanisms of moral disengagement in support of military force: The impact of Sept. 11. *Journal of Social and Clinical Psychology*, 25, 141–165.

McAlister, A., & Peterson, C. C. (2006). Mental playmates: Siblings, executive functioning and theory of mind. *British Journal of Developmental Psychology, 24,* 733–751.

McAlister, A., Peterson, C. (2007). A longitudinal study of child siblings and theory of mind development. *Cognitive Development, 22,* 258–270.

McCall, R. B. (1981). Nature-nurture and the two realms of development: A proposed integration with respect to mental development. *Child Development, 52,* 1–12.

McCall, R. B. (1983). A conceptual approach to early mental development. In M. Lewis (Ed.), *Origins of intelligence: Infancy and early childhood* (2nd ed.). New York: Plenum.

McCall, R. B., & Carriger, M. S. (1993). A meta-analysis of infant habituation and recognition memory performance as predictors of later IQ. *Child Development, 64,* 57–79.

McCarthy, J. R. (2009). Young people making meaning in response to death and bereavement. In D. E. Balk & C. A. Corr (Eds.), *Adolescent encounters with death, bereavement, and coping.* New York: Springer.

McCaul, E. J., Donaldson, G. A., Coladarci, T., & Davis, W. E. (1992). Consequences of dropping out of school: Findings from high school and beyond. *Journal of Educational Research, 85,* 198–207.

McClintock, M. K., & Herdt, G. (1996). Rethinking puberty: The development of sexual attraction. *Current Directions in Psychological Science, 5,* 178–183.

McCloskey, L. A., Figueredo, A. J., & Koss, M. P. (1995). The effects of systematic family violence on children's mental health. *Child Development, 66,* 1239–1261.

McClowry, S. G., & Collins, A. (2012). Temperament-based intervention. Reconceptualized from a response-to-intervention framework. In M. Z. Zentner & R. L. Shiner (Eds.), *Handbook of temperament.* New York: Guilford.

McCrae, R. R. (2004). Human nature and culture: A trait perspective. *Journal of Research in Personality 38,* 3–14.

McCrae, R. R., & Costa, P. T., Jr. (2003). *Personality in adulthood: A five-factor theory perspective* (2nd ed.). New York: Guilford Press.

McCrae, R. R., & Costa, P. T., Jr. (2008). *The five-factor theory of personality.* In O. P. John, R. W. Robins, & L. A. Pervin (Eds.), *Handbook of personality theory and research* (3rd ed.). New York: Guilford.

McCrae, R. R., Arenberg, D., & Costa, P. T., Jr. (1987). Declines in divergent thinking with age: Cross-sectional, longitudinal, and cross-sequential analyses. *Psychology and Aging, 2,* 130–137.

McCrae, R. R., Costa, P. T., Jr., Ostendorf, F., Angleitner, A., Hrebickova, M., Avia, M. D., Sanz, J., Sanchez-Bernardos, M. L., Kusdil, M. E., Woodfield, R., Saunders, P. R., & Smith, P. B. (2000). Nature over nurture: Temperament, personality, and life span development. *Journal of Personalty and Social Psychology, 78,* 173–186.

McCune, L., Vihman, M. M., Roug-Hellichius, L., Delery, D. B., & Gogate, L. L. (1996). Grunt communication in human infants (*Homo sapiens*). *Journal of Comparative Psychology, 110,* 27–27.

McDonald, A. (2007). Prenatal development—the Dana guide. In F. E. Bloom, M. F. Beal, & D. J. Kupfer (Eds.), *The Dana Guide to Brain Health* (pp. 61–82). New York: The Dana Foundation.

McDonald, R., Jouriles, E. N., Ramisetty-Mikler, S., Caetano, R., & Green, C. E. (2006). Estimating the number of American children living in partner-violent families. *Journal of Family Psychology, 20,* 137–142.

McDonald, S., Erickson, L. D., Johnson, M. K., & Elder, G. H. (2007). Informal mentoring and young adult employment. *Social Science Research, 36,* 1328–1347.

McDonough, C., Song, L., Hirsh-Pasek, K., Golinkoff, R. M., & Lannon, R. (2011). An image is worth a thousand words: Why nouns tend to dominate verbs in early word learning. *Developmental Science, 14,* 181–189.

McDowell, M. A., Brody, D. J., & Hughes, J. P. (2007). Has age at menarche changed? Results from the National Health and Nutrition Examination Survey (NHANES) 1999–2004. *Journal of Adolescent Health, 40,* 227–231.

McElhaney, K. B., & Allen, J. P. (2012). Sociocultural perspectives on adolescent autonomy. In P. K. Kerig, M. S. Schulz, & S. T. Hauser (Eds.), *Adolescence and beyond. Family processes and development.* New York: Oxford University Press.

McGoldrick, M., Almeida, R., Hines, P. M., Garcia-Preto, N., Rosen, E., & Lee, E. (1991). Mourning in different cultures. In F. Walsh & M. McGoldrick (Eds.), *Living beyond loss: Death in the family.* New York: W. W. Norton.

McGoldrick, M., & Carter, B. (2011). Families transformed by the divorce cycle: Reconstituted, multinuclear, recoupled, and remarried families. In M. McGoldrick, B. Carter, & N. Garcia Preto, *The expanded family life cycle: Individual, family, and social perspectives* (4th ed.). Boston, MA: Allyn & Bacon.

McGoldrick, M., Carter, B., & Garcia Preto, N. (2011). *The expanded family life cycle: Individual, family, and social perspectives* (4th ed.). Boston, MA: Allyn & Bacon.

McGowan, P. O., Sasaki, A., D'Alessio, A.C., Dymov, S., Labonté, B., Szyf, M., Turecki, G., & Meaney, M. J. (2009). Epigenetic regulation of the glucocorticoid receptor in human brain associates with childhood abuse. *Nature Neuroscience, 12,* 342–348.

McGrath, E. P., & Repetti, R. L. (2000). Mothers' and fathers' attitudes toward their children's academic performance and children's perceptions of their academic competence. *Journal of Youth and Adolescence, 29,* 713–723.

McGrory, C. (2013). *Reboot and rebirth.* Retrieved from http://www.realitysandwich.com/reboot_and_rebirth

McGue, M., Elkins, I., Walden, B., & Iacono, W. G. (2005). Perceptions of the parent–adolescent relationship: A longitudinal investigation. *Developmental Psychology, 41,* 971–984.

McGuire, S., Manke, B., Eftekhari, A., & Dunn, J. (2000). Children's perceptions of sibling conflict during middle childhood: Issues and sibling (dis)similarity. *Social Development, 9,* 173–190.

McHale, J. P., & Lindahl, K. M. (Eds.). (2011). *Coparenting. A conceptual and clinical examination of family systems.* Washington, DC: American Psychological Association.

McHale, J., Khazan, I., Erera, P., Rotman, T., DeCourcey, W., & McConnell, M. (2002). Coparenting in diverse family systems. In M. H. Bornstein (Ed.), *Handbook of parenting: Vol. 3. Being and becoming a parent* (2nd ed.). Mahwah, NJ: Erlbaum.

McHale, S. M., Kim, J., & Whiteman, S. D. (2006). Sibling relationships in childhood and adolescence. In P. Noller & J. A. Feeney (Eds.), *Close relationships: Functions, forms, and processes.* New York: Psychology Press.

McHale, S. M., Updegraff, K. A., & Whiteman, S. D. (2012). Sibling relationships and influences in childhood and adolescence. *Journal of Marriage and Family, 74,* 913–930.

McIntosh, D. N., Reichmann-Decker, A., Winkielman, P., & Wilbarger, J. L. (2006). When the social mirror breaks: Deficits in automatic, but not voluntary, mimicry of emotional facial expressions in autism. *Developmental Science, 9,* 295–302.

McLanahan, S. S., & Sorensen, A. B. (1985). Life events and psychological well-being over the life course. In G. H. Elder Jr. (Ed.), *Life course dynamics: Trajectories and transitions, 1968–1980.* Ithaca, NY: Cornell University Press.

McLean, K. C., & Pratt, M. W. (2006). Life's little (and big) lessons: Identity statuses and meaning-making in the turning point narratives of emerging adults. *Developmental Psychology, 42,* 714–722.

McLoyd, V. C. (1990). The impact of economic hardship on black families and children: Psychological distress, parenting, and socio-emotional development. *Child Development, 61,* 311–346.

McMahon, S. D., Todd, N. R., Martinez, A., Coker, C., Sheu, C., Washburn, J., & Shah, S. (2012). Aggressive and prosocial behavior: Community violence, cognitive, and behavioral predictors among urban African American youth. *American Journal of Community Psychology, 51,* 407–421. Advanced online publication. Retrieved from http://link.springer.com/article/10.1007/s10464-012-9560-4/fulltext.html

McMullen, S., Langley-Evans, S. C., Gambling, L., Lang, C., Swali, A., & McArdle, H. J. (2012). A common cause for a common phenotype: The gatekeeper hypothesis in fetal programming. *Medical Hypotheses, 78,* 88–94.

McNeill, D. (1970). *The acquisition of language.* New York: Harper & Row.

Meadows, S. (2006). *The child as thinker: The development and acquisition of cognition in childhood* (2nd ed.). New York: Routledge.

Meadows-Orlans, K. P., & Orlans, H. (1990). Responses to loss of hearing in later life. In D. F. Moores & K. P. Meadows-Orlans (Eds.), *Educational and developmental aspects of deafness.* Washington, DC: Gallaudet University Press.

Mealey, L. (2005). Evolutionary psychopathology and abnormal development. In R. L. Burgess & K. MacDonald (Eds.), *Evolutionary perspectives on human development.* Thousand Oaks, CA: Sage.

Meaney, M. (2010). Epigenetics and the biological definition of gene x environment interactions. *Child Development, 81,* 41–79.

Measles and rubella monitoring. (2012, June). *Surveillance Report #12.* Stockholm: European Centre for Disease Prevention and Control.

Medina, J. J. (1996). *The clock of ages: Why we age—how we age—Winding back the clock.* Cambridge, UK: Cambridge University Press.

Meeks, T. W., Lanouette, N., Vahia, I., Dawes, S., Jeste, D. V., & Lebowitz, B. (2009). Psychiatric assessment and diagnosis in older adults. *Focus, 7,* 3–16.

Meeus, W., van de Schoot, R., Keijsers, L., Schwartz, S. J., & Branje, S. (2010). On the progression and stability of adolescent identity formation: A five-wave longitudinal study in early-to-middle and middle-to-late adolescent. *Child Development, 81,* 1565–1581.

Meier, R. P. (1991). Language acquisition by deaf children. *American Scientist, 79,* 69–70.

Meijer, J., & Elshout, J. J. (2001). The predictive and discriminant validity of the zone of proximal development. *British Journal of Educational Psychology, 71,* 93–113.

Meilman, P. W. (1979). Cross-sectional age changes in ego identity status during adolescence. *Developmental Psychology, 15,* 230–231.

Meins, E., Fernyhough, C., Wainwright, R., Gupta, M., Fradley, E., & Tuckey, M. (2002). Maternal mind-mindedness and attachment security as predictors of theory of mind understanding. *Child Development, 73,* 1715–1726.

Melhem, N. M., Porta, G., Shamseddeen, W., Payne, M. W., & Brent, D. A. (2011). Grief in children and adolescents bereaved by sudden parental death. *Archives of General Psychiatry, 68,* 911–919.

Mellinger, J. C., & Erdwins, C. J. (1985). Personality correlates of age and life roles in adult women. *Psychology of Women Quarterly, 9,* 503–514.

Meltzoff, A. N. (2004). Imitation as a mechanism of social cognition: Origins of empathy, theory of mind, and the representation of action. In U. Goswami (Ed.), *Blackwell handbook of childhood cognitive development* (pp. 6–25). Malden, MA: Blackwell Publishing.

Meltzoff, A. N., & Moore, M. K. (1997). Explaining facial imitation: Theoretical model. *Early Development and Parenting, 6,* 179–192.

Melzer, D., Hurst, A. J., & Frayling, T. (2007). Genetic variation and human aging: Progress and prospects. *Journal of Gerontology Series A: Medical Sciences, 62A,* 301–307.

Melzi, G., & Schick, A. (2013). Language and literacy in the school years. In J. Berko Gleason & N. B. Ratner (Eds.), *The development of language* (7th ed.). Boston: Allyn & Bacon.

Memon, A., & Vartoukian, R. (1996). The effects of repeated questioning on young children's eyewitness testimony. *British Journal of Psychology, 87,* 403–415.

Menacker, F., MacDorman, M. F., & Declercq, E. (2010). Neonatal mortality risk for repeat cesarean compared to vaginal birth after cesarean (VBAC) deliveries in the United States, 1998–2002 birth cohorts. *Maternal and Child Health Journal, 14,* 147–154.

Menaghan, E. G., & Lieberman, M. A. (1986). Changes in depression following divorce: A panel study. *Journal of Marriage and the Family, 48,* 319–328.

Mendle, J., Ferrero, J., Moore, S. R., & Harden, K. P. (2013). Depression and adolescent sexual activity in romantic and nonromantic relational contexts: A genetically-informative sibling comparison. *Journal of Abnormal Psychology, 122,* 51–63.

Mendle, J., Harden, K.P., Brooks-Gunn, J., & Graber, J.A. (2010). Development's tortoise and hare: Pubertal timing, pubertal tempo, and depressive symptoms in boys and girls. *Developmental Psychology, 46,* 1341–1353

Mennella, J.A. and Beauchamp, G.K. (2002) Flavor experiences during formula feeding are related to preferences during childhood. *Early Human Development, 68,* 71–82.

Mennella, J. A., Forestell, C. A., Morgan, L. K., & Beauchamp, G. K. (2009). Early milk feeding influences taste acceptance and liking during infancy. *American Journal of Clinical Nutrition, 90,* 780S–788S.

Mennella, J. A., Jagnow, C. P., & Beauchamp, G. K. (2001). Prenatal and postnatal flavor learning by human infants. *Pediatrics, 107,* E88.

Mennella, J. A., Pepino, M. Y., & Reed, D. R. (2005). Genetic and environmental determinants of bitter perception and sweet preferences. *Pediatrics, 115,* E216–222.

Mensa, F. K., Bayer, J. K., Wake, M., Carlin, J. B., Allen, N. B., & Patton, G. C. (2013). Early Puberty and Childhood Social and Behavioral Adjustment. *Journal of adolescent health, 53,* 118–124.

Mercer, J. (2006). *Understanding attachment: Parenting, child care, and emotional development.* Westport, CT: Praeger.

Meredith, P., & Noller, P. (2003). Attachment and infant difficultness in postnatal depression. *Journal of Family Issues, 24,* 668–686.

Merikangas, K. R., He, J., Burstein, M., Swanson, S. A., Avenevoli, S., Cui, L., et al. (2010). Lifetime prevalence of mental disorders in U.S. adolescents: Results from the National Comorbidity Survey Replication-Adolescent Supplement (NCS-A). *Journal of the American Academy of Child & Adolescent Psychiatry, 49,* 980–989.

Merzenich, M. M., Jenkins, W. M., Johnston, P., Schreiner, C., Miller, S. L., & Tallal, P. (1996). Temporal processing deficits of language-learning impaired children ameliorated by training. *Science, 271,* 77–81.

Meschke, L. L., Zweig, J. M., Barber, B. L., & Eccles, J. S. (2000). Demographic, biological, psychological, and social predictors of the timing of first intercourse. *Journal of Research on Adolescence, 10,* 315–338.

Mesman, J., Bongers, I. L., & Koot, H. M. (2001). Preschool developmental pathways to preadolescent internalizing and externalizing problems. *Journal of Child Psychology and Psychiatry and Allied Disciplines, 42,* 679–689.

Messer, D. J., McCarthy, M. E., McQuiston, S., MacTurk, R. H., Yarrow, L. J., & Vietze, P. M. (1986). Relation between mastery behavior in infancy and competence in early childhood. *Developmental Psychology, 22,* 366–372.

Messinger-Rapport, B. J. (2003). Assessment and counseling of older drivers: A guide for primary care physicians. *Geriatrics, 58,* 16.

Metcalf, P., & Huntington, R. (1991). *Celebrations of death. The anthropology of mortuary ritual* (2nd ed.). Cambridge, UK: Cambridge University Press.

Metzger, P. A., & Gray, M. J. (2008). End-of-life communication and adjustment: Pre-loss communication as a predictor of bereavement-related outcomes. *Death Studies, 32,* 301–325.

Meulenbroek, O., Kessels, R. P. C., de Rover, M., Petersson, M., Rikkert, M. G., Rijpkema, M., et al. (2010). Age-effects on associative object-location memory. *Brain Research, 22,* 100–110.

Meydani, M. (2001). Nutrition interventions in aging and age-associated disease. In S. C. Park, E. S. Hwang, H. Kim, & W. Park (Eds.), *Annals of the New York Academy of Sciences: Vol. 928. Molecular and cellular interactions in senescence.* New York: The New York Academy of Sciences.

Meyer-Bahlburg, H. F. L., Ehrhardt, A. A., Rosen, L. R., & Gruen, R. S. (1995). Prenatal estrogens and the development of homosexual orientation. *Developmental Psychology, 31,* 12–21.

Meyer-Bahlburg, H. F., Dolezal, C., Baker, S. W., Ehrhardt, A. A., & New, M. I. (2006). Gender development in women with congenital adrenal hyperplasia as a function of disorder severity. *Archives of Sexual Behavior, 35,* 667–684.

Mezulis, A. H., Hyde, J. S., Simonson, J., & Charbonneau, A. M. (2011). Integrating affective, biological, and cognitive vulnerability models to explain the gender difference in depression. The ABC model and its implications for intervention. In T. J. Strauman, P. R. Costanzo, & J. Garber (Eds.), *Depression in adolescent girls. Science and prevention.* New York: Guilford.

Midgley, C., Feldlaufer, H., & Eccles, J. S. (1989). Student/teacher relations and attitudes toward mathematics before and after the transition to junior high school. *Child Development, 60*, 981–992.

Midlarsky, E., Kahana, E., Corley, R., Nemeroff, R., & Schonbar, R. A. (1999). Altruistic moral judgment among older adults. *International Journal of Aging and Human Development, 49*, 27–41.

Mikulincer, M., & Shaver, P. R. (2003). The attachment behavioral system in adulthood: Activation, psychodynamics, and interpersonal processes. In M. P. Zanna (Eds.), *Advances in experimental social psychology* (Vol. 35). San Diego: Academic Press.

Mikulincer, M., & Shaver, P. R. (2007). *Attachment in adulthood. Structure, dynamics, and change.* New York: Guilford.

Mikulincer, M., & Shaver, P. R. (2013). Attachment insecurities and disordered patterns of grief. In M. Stroebe, H. Schut & J. van den Bout (Eds.), *Complicated grief: Scientific foundations for health care professionals.* New York: Routledge/Taylor & Francis.

Milkie, M. A., Norris, D. R., & Bierman, A. (2011). The long arm of offspring: adult children's troubles as teenagers and elderly parents' mental health. *Research and Aging, 33*, 327.

Miller, A. (1985). A developmental study of the cognitive basis of performance impairment after failure. *Journal of Personality and Social Psychology, 49*, 529–538.

Miller, G. E., Chen, E., Fok, A. K., Walker, H., Lim, A., Nicholls, E. F., et al. (2009). Low early-life social class leaves a biological residue manifested by decreased glucocorticoid and increased proinflammatory signaling. *Proceedings of the National Academy of Sciences of the United States of America, 106*, 14716–14721.

Miller, J. G. (2006). Insight into moral development from cultural psychology. In M. Killen & J. G. Smetana (Eds.), *Handbook of moral development.* Mahwah, NJ: Erlbaum.

Miller, J., & Knudsen, D. D. (2007). *Family abuse and violence: A social problems perspective.* Lanham, MD: AltaMira Press.

Miller, N. B., Cowan, P. A., Cowan, C. P., Hetherington, E. M., & Clingempeel, W. G. (1993). Externalizing in preschoolers and early adolescents: A cross-study replication of a family model. *Developmental Psychology, 29*, 3–18.

Miller, P. H. (1990). The development of strategies of selective attention. In D. F. Bjorklund (Ed.), *Children's strategies: Contemporary views of cognitive development.* Hillsdale, NJ: Erlbaum.

Miller, P. H. (1994). Individual differences in children's strategic behavior: Utilization deficiencies. *Learning and Individual Differences, 6*, 285–307.

Miller, P. H. (2002). *Theories of developmental psychology* (4th ed.). New York: Worth.

Miller, P. H. (2011). *Theories of developmental psychology* (5th ed.). New York: Worth.

Miller, P. H. (2011). Piaget's theory: past, present, and future. In U. Goswami, (Ed.), *The Wiley-Blackwell handbook of childhood cognitive development, 2nd ed.* (pp. 650–672). Malden, MA: John Wiley.

Miller, P. H., & Seier, W. S. (1994). Strategy utilization deficiencies in children: When, where and why. In H. W. Reese (Ed.), *Advances in child development and behavior* (Vol. 25, pp. 107–156). New York: Academic Press.

Miller, P. H., & Weiss, M. G. (1981). Children's attention allocation, understanding of attention, and performance on the incidental learning task. *Child Development, 52*, 1183–1190.

Miller, R. A. (2004). Extending life: Scientific prospects and political obstacles. In S. G. Post & R. H. Binstock (Eds.), *The Fountain of Youth: Cultural, scientific, and ethical perspectives on a biomedical goal.* New York: Oxford University Press.

Miller, S. A. (1986). Parents' beliefs about their children's cognitive abilities. *Developmental Psychology, 22*, 276–284.

Miller, S. A. (2013). *Developmental research methods* (4th ed.). Thousand Oaks, CA: Sage.

Miller, T. R., & Taylor, D. M. (2005). Adolescent suicidality: Who will ideate, who will act? *Suicide and Life-Threatening Behavior, 35*, 425–435.

Miller. S. A. (2012). *Theory of mind. Beyond the preschool years.* New York: Psychology Press/Taylor and Francis.

Miller-Johnson, S., Costanzo, P. R., Coie, J. D., Rose, M. R., Browne, D. C., & Johnson, C. (2003). Peer social structure and risk-taking behaviors among African American early adolescents. *Journal of Youth and Adolescence, 32*, 375–384.

Millheiser, L. S., Helmer, A. E., Quintero, R. B., Westphal, L. M., Milki, A. A., & Lathi, R. B. (2010). Is infertility a risk factor for female sexual dysfunction? A case-control study. *Fertility and Sterility, 94*, 2022–2025.

Mills-Koonce, W. R., Gariepy, J., Propper, C., Sutton, K., Calkins, S., Moore, G., & Cox, M. (2007). Infant and parent factors associated with early maternal sensitivity: A caregiver-attachment systems approach. *Infant Behavior and Development, 30*, 114–126.

Milos, G., Spindler, A., Schnyder, U., Martz, J., Hoek, H. W., & Willi, J. (2004). Incidence of severe anorexia nervosa in Switzerland: 40 years of development. *International Journal of Eating Disorders, 35*, 250–258.

Mingroni, M. A. (2004). The secular rise in IQ: Giving heterosis a closer look. *Intelligence, 32*, 65–83.

Miniño, A. M., & Murphy, S. L. (2012, July). Death in the United States, 2010. NCHS Data Brief, No. 99. U.S. Department of Health and Human Services, Centers for Disease Control and Prevention, National Center for Health Statistics. Retrieved from http//www.cdc.gov/nchs/data/databriefs/db99.htm

Miralt, G., Bearor, K., & Thomas, T. (2001–2002). Adult romantic attachment among women who experienced childhood maternal loss. *Omega: Journal of Death and Dying, 44*, 97–104.

Misa, T. J. (Ed.). (2010). *Gender codes: Why women are leaving computing.* Hoboken, NJ: John Wiley & Sons.

Mischel, W. (1973). Toward a cognitive social learning reconceptualization of personality. *Psychological Review, 80*, 252–283.

Mischel, W., & Shoda, Y. (2008). Toward a unified theory of personality: Integrating dispositions and processing dynamics within the cognitive–affective processing system. In O. P. John, R. W. Robins, & L. A. Pervin (Eds.), *Handbook of personality theory and research* (3rd ed.). New York: Guilford.

Mischel, W., Ayduk, O., Berman, M. G., Casey, B. J., Gotlib, I. H., Jonides, J., et al. (2011). 'Willpower' over the life span: Decomposing self-regulation. *Social Cognitive and Affective Neuroscience, 6*, 252–256.

Mishori, R. (2006, January 10). Increasingly, wired for sound. *The Washington Post*, pp. F1, F5.

Mishra, G. D., & Dobson, A. (2012). Using longitudinal profiles to characterize women's symptoms through midlife: Results from a large prospective study. *Menopause, 19*, 549–555.

Mishra, G. D., & Kuh, D. (2012). Health symptoms during midlife in relation to menopausal transition: British prospective cohort study. *British Medical Journal, 344*, e402.

Mitchell, A. A., Gilboa, S. M., Werler, M. M., Kelley, K. E., Louik, C., Hernandez-Diaz, S., et al. (2011). Medication use during pregnancy, with particular focus on prescription drugs: 1976–2008. *American Journal of Obstetrics & Gynecology, 205*, e1–e8.

Mitchell, B. A., & Lovegreen, L. D. (2009). The empty nest syndrome in midlife families: A multimethod exploration of parental gender differences and cultural dynamics. *Journal of Family Issues, 30*, 1651–1670.

Mitchell, P. (1997). *Introduction to theory of mind: Children, autism, and apes.* London: Arnold.

Mitnick, D. M., Heyman, R. E., & Smith Slep, A. M. (2009). Changes in relationship satisfaction across the transition to parenthood: A meta-analysis. *Journal of Family Psychology, 23*, 848–852.

Miyawaki, K., Strange, W., Verbrugge, R., Liberman, A. M., Jenkins, J. J., & Fujimura, D. (1975). An effect of linguistic experience: The discrimination of [r] and [l] by native speakers of Japanese and English. *Perception and Psychophysics, 18*, 331–340.

Mock, S. E., & Eibach, R. P. (2012). Stability and change in sexual orientation identity over a 10-year period in adulthood. *Archives of Sex Behavior, 41*, 641–648.

Moehler, E., Kagan, J., Oelkers-Ax, R., Brunner, R., Poustka, L., Haffner, J., & Resch, F. (2008). Infant predictors of behavioural inhibition. *British Journal of Developmental Psychology, 26*, 145–150.

Moen, P. (1992). *Women's two roles: A contemporary dilemma*. New York: Auburn House.

Moffitt, T. E., & Caspi, A. (2001). Childhood predictors differentiate life-course persistent and adolescence-limited antisocial pathways among males and females. *Development and Psychopathology, 13*, 355–375.

Moffitt, T. E., Arseneault, L., Belsky, D., Dickson, N., Hancox, R. J., Harrington, H., Houts, R., Poulton, R., Roberts, B. W., Ross, S., Sears, M. R., Thomson, W. M., & Caspi, A. (2011). A gradient of childhood self-control predicts health, wealth, and public safety. *Proceedings of the National Academy of Sciences, 108*, 2693–2698.

Moffitt, T. E., Harrington, H., Caspi, A., Kim-Cohen, J., Goldberg, D., Gregory, A. M., & Poulton, R. (2007). Depression and generalized anxiety disorder: Cumulative and sequential comorbidity in a birth cohort followed prospectively to age 32 years. *Archives of General Psychiatry, 64*, 651–660.

Mohammed, A. H., Zhu, S. W., Darmopil, S., Hjerling-Leffler, J., Ernfors, P., Winblad, B., et al. (2002). Environmental enrichment and the brain. *Progress in Brain Research, 138*, 109–133.

Molina, B. S. G., & Chassin, L. (1996). The parent-adolescent relationship at puberty: Hispanic ethnicity and parent alcoholism as moderators. *Developmental Psychology, 32*, 675–686.

Molina, B. S. G., Hinshaw, S. P., Swanson, J. M., Arnold, L. E., Vitiello, B., Jensen, P. S., et al. (2009). The MTA at 8 years: Prospective follow-up of children treated for combined-type ADHD in a multisite study. *Journal of the American Academy of Child & Adolescent Psychiatry, 48*, 484–500.

Mollborn, S. (2009). Norms about nonmarital pregnancy and willingness to provide resources to unwed parents. *Journal of Marriage and Family, 71*, 122–134.

Molteni, R., Barnard, R.J., Zing, Z., Roberts, C.K., & Gómez-Pinilla, F. (2002). A high-fat, refined sugar diet reduces hippocampal brain-derived neurotrophic factor, neuronal plasticity, and learning. *Neuroscience, 112*, 803–814.

Monahan, K. C., Steinberg, L., & Cauffman, E. (2009). Affiliation with antisocial peers, susceptibility to peer influence, and antisocial behavior during the transition to adulthood. *Developmental Psychology, 45*, 1520–1530.

Monahan, K. C., Steinberg, L., &Cauffman, E. (2009). Affiliation with antisocial peers, susceptibility to peer influence, and antisocial behavior during the transition to adulthood. *Developmental Psychology, 45*, 1520–1530.

Money, J. (1985). Pediatric sexology and hermaphroditism. *Journal of Sex and Marital Therapy, 11*, 139–156.

Money, J. (1988). *Gay, straight, and in-between: The sexology of erotic orientation*. New York: Oxford University Press.

Money, J., & Ehrhardt, A. (1972). *Man and woman, boy and girl*. Baltimore: Johns Hopkins University Press.

Money, J., & Tucker, P. (1975). *Sexual signatures: On being a man or a woman*. Boston: Little, Brown.

Montemayor, R., & Eisen, M. (1977). The development of self-conceptions from childhood to adolescence. *Developmental Psychology, 13*, 314–319.

Montgomery, M. J. (2005). Psychosocial intimacy and identity: From early adolescence to emerging adulthood. *Journal of Adolescent Research, 20*, 346–374.

Monti, M. M., Vanhaudenhuyse, A., Coleman, M. R., Boly, M., Pickard, J. D., Tshibanda, L., Owen, A. M., & Laureys, S. (2010). Willful modulation of brain activity in disorders of consciousness. *New England Journal of Medicine, 362*, 579–589.

Montoya, E. R., Terburg, D., Bos, P. A., & van Honk, J. (2012). Testosterone, cortisol, and serotonin as key regulators of social aggression: A review and theoretical perspective. *Motivation and Emotion, 36*, 65–73.

Moon, C., Lagercrantz, H., & Kuhl, P. (2013). Language experienced in utero affects vowel perception after birth: A two-country study. *Acta Paediatrica, 102*, 156–160.

Moon, S. M., & Steenbergen-Hu, S. (2011). The effects of acceleration on high-ability learners: A meta-analysis. *Gifted Child Quarterly, 55*, 39–53.

Moore, A. B., Lee, N. Y. L., Clark, B. A. M., & Conway, A. R. A. (2011). In defense of the personal/impersonal distinction in moral psychology research: Cross-cultural validation of the dual process model of moral judgment. *Judgment and Decision Making, 6*, 186–195.

Moore, E. G. J. (1986). Family socialization and the IQ test performance of traditionally and transracially adopted black children. *Developmental Psychology, 22*, 317–326.

Moore, K. L., Persaud, T. V. N., & Torchia, M. G. (2013). *The developing human: Clinically oriented embryology* (9th ed.). Philadelphia, PA: Saunders.

Moore, M. K., & Meltzoff, A. N. (2008). Factors affecting infants' manual search for occluded objects and the genesis of object permanence. *Infant Behavior and Development, 31*, 168–180.

Moorehouse, M. J. (1991). Linking maternal employment patterns to mother–child activities and children's school competence. *Developmental Psychology, 27*, 295–303.

Moreno, M. A., Jelenchick, L., Koff, R., Eikoff, J., Diermyer, C., & Christakis, D. A. (2012). Internet use and multitasking among older adolescents: An experience sampling approach. *Computers in Human Behavior, 28*, 1097–1102.

Moraga, A. V., & Rodriguez-Pascual, C. (2007). Accurate diagnosis of delirium in elderly patients. *Current Opinion in Psychiatry, 20*, 262–267.

Morales, J., Calvo, A., & Bialystok, E. (2013). Working memory development in monolingual and bilingual children. *Journal of Experimental Child Psychology, 114*, 187–202.

Morello, C. (2013, January 2). Conflict in Syria takes emotional toll on children. *The Washington Post*, pp. A1, A9.

Morgan, E. M. (2012). Not always a straight path: College students' narratives of heterosexual identity development. *Sex Roles, 66*, 79–93.

Morgan, G. A., & Ricciuti, H. N. (1969). Infants' responses to strangers during the first year. In B. M. Foss (Ed.), *Determinants of infant behavior* (Vol. 4). London: Methuen.

Morina, N. (2011). Rumination and avoidance as predictors of prolonged grief, depression, and posttraumatic stress in female widowed survivors of war. *Journal of Nervous and Mental Disease, 199*, 921–927.

Morizot, J., & Le Blanc, M. (2003). Continuity and change in personality traits from adolescence to midlife: A 25-year longitudinal study comparing representative and adjudicated men. *Journal of Personality, 71*, 705–755.

Morrell, R. W., Park, D. C., & Poon, L. W. (1989). Quality of instructions on prescription drug labels: Effects on memory and comprehension in young and old adults. *Gerontologist, 29*, 345–354.

Morrongiello, B. A., & Hogg, K. (2004). Mothers' reactions to children misbehaving in ways that can lead to injury: Implications for gender differences in children's risk taking and injuries. *Sex Roles, 50*, 1003–1118.

Morrow, D., Leirer, V., Altieri, P., & Fitzsimmons, C. (1994). When expertise reduces age differences in performance. *Psychology and Aging, 9*, 134–148.

Morse, C. A., Dudley, E., Guthrie, J., & Dennerstein, L. (1998). Relationships between premenstrual complaints and perimenopausal experiences. *Journal of Psychosomatic Obstetrics and Gynecology, 19*, 182–191.

Morse, J. Q., Shaffer, D. R., Williamson, G. M., Dooley, W. K., & Schulz, R. (2011). Models of self and others and their relation to positive and negative caregiving responses. *Psychology and Aging, 27*, 211–218.

Moser, J. S., Schroder, H. S., Heeter, C., Moran, T. P., & Lee, Y. (2011). Mind your errors: Evidence for a neural mechanism linking growth mind-set to adaptive post-error adjustments. *Psychological Science, 22*, 1484–1489.

Moskovic, D. J., Eisenberg, M. L., Lipshultz, L. I. (2012). Seasonal fluctuations in testosterone-estrogen ratio in men from the Southwest United States. *Journal of Andrology, 33*, 1298–1304.

Moss, M. S., Moss, S. Z., Rubinstein, R., & Resch, N. (1993). Impact of elderly mother's death on middle age daughters. *International Journal of Aging and Human Development, 37*, 1–22.

Mroczek, D. K. (2004). Positive and negative affect at midlife. In O. G. Brim, C. D. Ryff, & R. C. Kessler (Eds.), *How healthy are we? A national study of well-being at midlife*. Chicago: University of Chicago Press.

Mueller, E., & Lucas, T. (1975). A developmental analysis of peer interactions among toddlers. In M. Lewis & L. Rosenblum (Eds.), *Friendship and peer relations*. New York: Wiley.

Mundy, P. C., & Acra, C. F. (2006). Joint attention, social engagement, and the development of social competence. In P. J. Marshall & N. A. Fox (Eds.), *The development of social engagement: Neurobiological perspectives.* Oxford, NY: Oxford University Press.

Munroe, R. L., & Romney, A. K. (2006). Gender and age differences in same-sex aggregation and social behavior: A four-culture study. *Journal of Cross-Cultural Psychology, 37,* 3–19.

Murayama, K., & Elliot, A. J. (2009). The joint influence of personal achievement goals and classroom goal structures on achievement-relevant outcomes. *Journal of Educational Psychology, 101,* 432–447.

Muris, P., Bos, A. E. R., Mayer, B., Verkade, R., Thewissen, V., & Dell'Avvento, V. (2009). Relations among behavioral inhibition, Big Five personality factors, and anxiety disorder symptoms in non-clinical children. *Personality and Individual Differences, 46,* 525–529.

Murnen, S. K., & Smolak, L. (1997). Femininity, masculinity and disordered eating: A meta-analytic review. *International Journal of Eating Disorders, 22,* 231–242.

Murphy, C. (1985). Cognitive and chemosensory influences on age-related changes in the ability to identify blended foods. *Journal of Gerontology, 40,* 47–52.

Murphy, C., Nordin, S., & Acosta, L. (1997). Odor learning, recall, and recognition memory in young and elderly adults. *Neuropsychology, 11,* 126–137.

Murphy, D. R., Craik, F. I. M., Li, K. Z. H., & Schneider, B. A. (2000). Comparing the effects of aging and background noise on short-term memory performance. *Psychology and Aging, 15,* 323–334.

Murphy, D. R., Daneman, M., & Schneider, B. A. (2006). Why do older adults have difficulty following conversations? *Psychology and Aging, 21,* 49–61.

Murphy, E. M. (2003). Being born female is dangerous for your health. *American Psychologist, 58,* 205–210.

Murphy, M. L. M., Slavich, G. M., Rohleder, N., & Miller, G. E. (2012). Targeted rejection triggers differential pro- and anti-inflammatory gene expression in adolescents as a function of social status. *Clinical Psychological Science, 1,* 30–40.

Murphy, S. A. (2008). The loss of a child: Sudden death and extended illness perspectives. In M. S. Stroebe, R. O. Hansson, H. Schut, & W. Stroebe (Eds.), *Handbook of bereavement research and practice. Advances in theory and intervention.* Washington, DC: American Psychological Association.

Murphy, S. A., Johnson, C., & Lohan, J. (2003b). Finding meaning in a child's violent death: A five-year prospective analysis of parents' personal narratives and empirical data. *Death Studies, 27,* 381–404.

Murray, C. (2006). Changes over time in the black-white difference on mental tests: Evidence from the children of the 1979 cohort of the National Longitudinal Survey of Youth. *Intelligence, 34,* 527–540.

Murray, L., Arteche, A., Fearon, P., Halligan, S., Goodyer, I., & Cooper, P. (2011). Maternal postnatal depression and the development of depression in offspring up to 16 years of age. *Journal of the American Academy of Child and Adolescent Psychiatry, 50*(5), 460–470.

Murray, L., de Rosnay, M., Pearson, J., Bergeron, C., Schofield, E., Royal-Lawson, M., & Cooper, P. J. (2008). Intergenerational transmission of social anxiety: The role of social referencing processes in infancy. *Child Development, 79,* 1049–1064.

Murray, L., Fiori-Cowley, A., Hooper, R., & Cooper, P. (1996). The impact of postnatal depression and associated adversity on early mother–infant interactions and later infant outcome. *Child Development, 67,* 2512–2526.

Murray, L., Halligan, S., & Cooper, P. (2010). Effects of postnatal depression on mother-infant interactions, and child development. In T. Wachs & G. Bremner (Eds.), *Blackwell handbook of infant development* (pp. 192–220). New York: Wiley.

Murray-Close, D., Ostrov, J. M., & Crick, N. R. (2007). A short-term longitudinal study of growth of relational aggression during middle childhood: Associations with gender, friendship intimacy, and internalizing problems. *Development and Psychopathology, 19,* 187–203.

Musil, C. M., Gordon, N. L., Warner, C. B., Zauszniewski, J. A., & Standing, T., & Wykle, M. (2011). Grandmothers and caregiving to grandchildren: Continuity, change, and outcomes over 24 months. *The Gerontologist, 51,* 86–100.

Mwamwenda, T. S. (1999). Undergraduate and graduate students' combinatorial reasoning and formal operations. *Journal of Genetic Psychology, 160,* 503–506.

Mwamwenda, T. S., & Mwamwenda, B. A. (1989). Formal operational thought among African and Canadian college students. *Psychological Reports, 64,* 43–46.

Myers, J. K., Weissman, M. M., Tischler, G. L., Holzer, C. E., III, Leaf, P. J., & Orvaschel, H. (1984). Six-month prevalence of psychiatric disorders in three communities. *Archives of General Psychiatry, 41,* 959–967.

Mylod, D. E., Whitman, T. L., & Borkowski, J. G. (1997). Predicting adolescent mothers' transition to adulthood. *Journal of Research on Adolescence, 7,* 457–478.

Naigles, L. G., & Gelman, S. A. (1995). Overextensions in comprehension and production revisited: Preferential-looking in a study of dog, cat, and cow. *Journal of Child Language, 22,* 19–46.

Naigles, L. R., & Swensen, L. D. (2007). Syntactic supports for word learning. In E. Hoff & M. Shatz (Eds.), *Blackwell handbook of language development* (pp. 212–231). Malden Blackwell Publishing.

Najman, J. M., Vance, J. C., Boyle, F., Embleton, G., Foster, B., & Thearle, J. (1993). The impact of a child death on marital adjustment. *Social Science and Medicine, 37,* 1005–1010.

Nanez, J. E., & Yonas, A. (1994). Effects of luminance and texture motion on infant defensive reactions to optical collision. *Infant Behavior and Development, 17,* 165–174.

National Center for Education Statistics. (1998). National Household Education Survey (NHES), "Adult Education Interview," 1991, 1995, 1999.; *Projections of Education Statistics to 2008* (NCES 98–016).

National Center for Education Statistics. (2013). *The Condition of Education.* Table A-48-1. Percentage of 25- to 29-year-olds who attained the selected levels of education, by race/ethnicity and sex: Selected years, 1980–2011. Retrieved from http://nces.ed.gov/programs/coe/tables/table-eda-1.asp

National Center for Health Statistics. (2010). *Health, United States, 2009.* Hyattsville, MD: U.S. Department of Health and Human Services, Centers for Disease Control and Prevention, National Center for Health Statistics. Retrieved from www.cdc.gov.nchs/hus.htm

National Center for Health Statistics. (2011). *Health, United States, 2010: With special feature on death and dying* (DHHS Publication No. 2011–1232). Hyattsville, MD: Department of Health and Human Services.

National Institute on Aging, Alzheimer's Disease Education and Referral Center (2012). *2011–2012 Alzheimer's disease progress report. Intensifying the research effort.* Washington, DC: U. S. Department of Health and Human Services. Retrieved from http://www.nia.nih.gov/alzheimers/publication/2011-2012-alzheimers-disease-progress-report/

National Institute on Aging of the National Institutes of Health. (2013). *AgePage.* Retrieved from http://www.nia.nih.gov/health/publication/menopause

National Osteoporosis Foundation. (2013). Calcium and Vitamin D: What You Need to Know. Retrieved from http://www.nof.org/articles/10

National Reading Panel. (1999). *Teaching children to read: An evidence-based assessment of the scientific literature on reading and its implications for reading instruction.* Washington, DC: National Institute of Child Health & Human Development.

National Scientific Council on the Developing Child. (2007). *The timing and quality of early experiences combine to shape brain architecture: Working paper #5.* http://www.developingchild.net.

National Sleep Foundation. (2013). *Teens and Sleep.* Available: http://www.sleepfoundation.org/article/sleep-topics/teens-and-sleep

Neblett, E. W. J., Rivas-Drake, D., & Umaña-Taylor, A. J. (2012). The promise of racial and ethnic protective factors in promoting ethnic minority youth development. *Child Development Perspectives, 6,* 295–303.

Neblett, E. W. Jr., White, R. L., Ford, K. R., Philip, C. L., Nguyên, H. X., & Sellers, R. M.(2008). Patterns of racial socialization and psychological adjustment: Can parental communications about race reduce the impact of racial discrimination? *Journal of Research on Adolescence, 18,* 477–515.

Neighbors, H. W., Caldwell, C., Williams, D. R., Nesse, R., Taylor, R. J., Bullard, K. M., Torres, M., & Jackson, J. S. (2007). Race, ethnicity, and the use of services for mental disorders: Results from the National Survey of American Life. *Archives of General Psychiatry, 64,* 485–494.

Neimark, E. D. (1975). Longitudinal development of formal operations thought. *Genetic Psychology Monographs, 91,* 171–225.

Neimark, E. D. (1979). Current status of formal operations research. *Human Development, 22,* 60–67.

Neimeyer, R. A., & Currier, J. M. (2009). Grief therapy. Evidence of efficacy and emerging directions. *Current Directions in Psychological Science, 18,* 352–356.

Neisser, U., Boodoo, G., Bouchard, T. J., Jr., Boykin, A. W., Brody, N., Ceci, S. J., et al. (1996). Intelligence: Knowns and unknowns. *American Psychologist, 51,* 77–101.

Nelson, G., Westhues, A., & MacLeod, J. (2003). A meta-analysis of longitudinal research on preschool prevention programs for children. *Prevention & Treatment, 6.* Retrieved from http://journals.apa.org/prevention/volume6/toc-dec18-03.html

Nelson, J. M. (2009). *Psychology, religion, and spirituality.* New York: Springer Science+Business Media.

Nelson, K. (1986). *Event knowledge: Structure and function in development.* Hillsdale, NJ: Erlbaum.

Nelson, K. (1997). Event representations then, now, and next. In P. W. van den Broek & P. J. Bauer (Eds.), *Developmental spans in event comprehension and representation: Bridging fictional and actual events* (pp. 1–26). Mahwah, NJ: Erlbaum.

Nelson, K. (2007). *Young minds in social worlds: Experience, meaning, and memory.* Cambridge, MA: Harvard University Press.

Nelson, K., & Hudson, J. (1988). Scripts and memory: Functional relationship in development. In F. E. Weinert & M. Perlmutter (Eds.), *Memory development: Universal changes and individual differences.* Hillsdale, NJ: Erlbaum.

Nelson, S. K., Kushlev, K., English, T., Dunn, E. W., & Lyubomirsky, S. (2013). In defense of parenthood: Children are associated with more joy than misery. *Psychological Science, 24,* 3–10.

Nelson, K., Skwerer, D. P., Goldman, S., Henseler, S., Presler, N., & Walkenfeld, F. F. (2003). Entering a community of minds: An experiential approach to "theory of mind." *Human Development, 46,* 24–46.

Nelson, S. A. (1980). Factors influencing young children's use of motives and outcomes as moral criteria. *Child Development, 51,* 823–829.

Nemeroff, C. B., Kalai, A., Keller, M. B., Charney, D. S. Lenderts, S. E., Cascade, E. F., Stephenson, H., & Schatzberg, A. F. (2007). Impact of publicity concerning pediatric suicidality data on physician practice patterns in the United States. *Archives of General Psychiatry, 64,* 466–472.

Neppl, T. K., Conger, R. D., Scaramella, L. V., & Ontai, L. L. (2009). Intergenerational continuity in parenting behavior: Mediating pathways and child effects. *Developmental Psychology, 45,* 1241–1256.

Nerenberg, L. (2008). *Elder abuse prevention. Emerging trends and promising strategies.* New York: Springer.

Nes, S. L. (2003). Using paired reading to enhance the fluency skills of less-skilled readers. *Reading Improvement, 40,* 179–193.

Nettelbeck, T., & Young, R. (1996). Intelligence and savant syndrome: Is the whole greater than the sum of the fragments? *Intelligence, 22,* 49–68.

Neville, B., & Parke, R. D. (1997). Waiting for paternity: Interpersonal and contextual implications of the timing of fatherhood. *Sex Roles, 37,* 45–59.

Newell, A., & Simon, H. A. (1961). Computer simulation of human thinking. *Science, 134,* 2011–2017.

Newman, A. J., Bavelier, D., Corina, D., Jezzard, P., & Neville, H. J. (2002). A critical period for right hemisphere recruitment in American sign language processing. *Nature Neuroscience, 5,* 76–80.

Newman, R., & Sachs, J. (2012). Communication development in infancy. In J. Berko Gleason & N. Bernstein Ratner (Eds.), *The development of language* (8th ed.). Boston: Allyn & Bacon.

Newport, E. L. (1991). Contrasting conceptions of the critical period for language. In S. Carey & R. Gelman (Eds.), *The epigenesis of mind: Essays on biology and cognition.* Hillsdale, NJ: Erlbaum.

Newsom, J. T., Nishishiba, M., Morgan, D. L., & Rook, K. S. (2003). The relative importance of three domains of positive and negative social exchanges: A longitudinal model with comparable measures. *Psychology and Aging, 18,* 746–754.

Ng, S. F., Yin, R. C. Y., Laybutt, R., Barres, R., Owens, J. A., & Morris, M. J. (2010). Chronic high-fat diet in fathers programs beta-cell dysfunction in female rat offspring. *Nature, 467,* 963–967.

Ng, T. W. H., & Feldman, D. C. (2008). The relationship of age to ten dimensions of job performance. *Journal of Applied Psychology, 93,* 392–423.

Ng, T. W. H., & Feldman, D. C. (2012). Evaluating six common stereotypes about older workers with meta-analytical data. *Personnel Psychology, 65,* 821–858.

Nguyen, H. T., & Zonderman, A. B. (2006). Relationship between age and aspects of depression: Consistency and reliability across two longitudinal studies. *Psychology and Aging, 21,* 119–126.

Nguyen, S., Choi, H. K., Lustig, R. H., & Hsu, C. Y. (2009). Sugar-sweetened beverages, serum uric acid, and blood pressure in adolescents. *Journal of Pediatrics, 154,* 807–813.

NICHD. (2006). *The NICHD study of early child care and youth development: Findings for children up to age 4 ½ years.* Retrieved from www.nichd.nih.gov/publications/pubs.cfm

NICHD Early Child Care Research Network. (1997). The effects of infant child care on infant-mother attachment security: Results of the NICHD Study of Early Child Care. *Child Development, 68,* 860–879.

NICHD Early Child Care Research Network. (2003). Does quality of child care affect child outcomes at age 4 ½? *Developmental Psychology, 39,* 451–469.

NICHD Early Child Care Research Network. (2005). *Child care and child development: Results from the NICHD study of early child care and youth development.* New York: Guilford.

NICHD Early Child Care Research Network. (2006). Child-care effect sizes for the NICHD Study of Early Child Care and Youth Development. *American Psychologist, 61,* 99–116.

Nicholls, D. E., & Viner, R. M. (2009). Childhood risk factors for lifetime anorexia nervosa by age 30 in a national birth cohort. *Journal of the American Academy of Child and Adolescent Psychiatry, 48,* 791–799.

Nickerson, R. S. (2011). Developing intelligence through instruction. In R. J. Sternberg & S. B. Kaufman (Eds.), *The Cambridge Handbook of Intelligence* (pp. 107–129). New York: Cambridge University Press.

Nicolich, L. M. (1977). Beyond sensorimotor intelligence: Assessment of symbolic maturity through analysis of pretend play. *Merrill-Palmer Quarterly, 23,* 89–99.

Nielsen, M., & Tomaselli, K. (2010). Overimitation in Kalahari Bushman children and the origins of human cultural cognition. *Psychological Science, 21,* 729–736.

Nilsson, L., Adolfsson, R., Bäckman, L., Cruts, M., Edvardsson, H., Nyberg, L., et al. (2002). Memory development in adulthood and old age: The Betula prospective-cohort study. In P. Graf & N. Ohta (Eds.), *Lifespan development of human memory* (pp. 185–204). Cambridge, MA: Massachusetts Institute of Technology.

Nilsson, M., Perfilieva, E., Johansson, U., Orwar, O., & Eriksson, P. S. (1999). Enriched environment increases neurogenesis in the adult rat dentate gyrus and improves spatial memory. *Journal of Neurobiology, 39,* 569–578.

Nisbett, R. E., Aronson, J., Blair, C., Dickens, W., Flynn, J., Halpern, D. F., & Turkheimer, E. (2012). Intelligence: New findings and theoretical developments. *American Psychologist, 67,* 130–159.

Nishitani, S., Miyamura, T., Tagawa, M., Sumi, M., Takase, R., Doi, H., et al. (2009). The calming effect of a maternal breast milk odor on the human newborn infant. *Neuroscience Research, 63,* 66–71.

Nissim, R., Rennie, D., Fleming, S., Hales, S., Gagliese, L., & Rodin, G. (2012). Goals set in the land of the living/dying: A longitudinal study of patients living with advanced cancer. *Death Studies, 36,* 360–390.

Niv, S., & Baker, L. A. (2013). Genetic markers for antisocial behavior. In C. R. Thomas & K. Pope (Eds.), *The origins of antisocial behavior. A developmental perspective.* New York: Oxford University Press.

Noble, K. D., & Childers, S. A. (2009). Swimming in deep waters: 20 years of research about early university entrance at the university of washington. In L. V. Shavinina (Ed.), *The international handbook on giftedness* (pp. 1345–1364). New York: Springer Science+Business Media.

Noble, K. D., Childers, S. A., & Vaughan, R. C. (2008). A place to be celebrated and understood: The impact of early university entrance from parents' points of view. *Gifted Child Quarterly, 52,* 256–268.

Nolen-Hoeksema, S. (1990). *Sex differences in depression.* Stanford, CA: Stanford University Press.

Nolen-Hoeksema, S. (2002). Gender differences in depression. In I. H. Gotlib & C. L. Hammen (Eds.), *Handbook of depression.* New York: Guilford.

Nolen-Hoeksema, S., & Watkins, E. R. (2011). A heuristic for developing transdiagnostic models of psychopathology: Explaining multifinality and divergent trajectories. *Perspectives on Psychological Science, 6,* 589–609.

Nolen-Hoeksema, S., Stice, E., Wade, E., & Bohon, C. (2007). Reciprocal relations between rumination and bulimic, substance abuse, and depressive symptoms in female adolescents. *Journal of Abnormal Psychology, 116,* 198–207.

Nolen-Hoeksema, S., Wisco, B. E., & Lyubomirsky, S. (2008). Rethinking rumination. *Perspectives on Psychological Science, 3,* 400–424.

Noller, P. (2006). Marital relationships. In P. Noller & J. A. Feeney (Eds.), *Close relationships: Functions, forms, and processes.* New York: Psychology Press.

Nomaguchi, K. M., & Milkie, M. A. (2003). Costs and rewards of children: The effects of becoming a parent on adults' lives. *Journal of Marriage and the Family, 65,* 356–374.

Noone, J. H., Stephens, C., & Alpass, F. M. (2008). Preretirement planning and well-being in later life. A prospective study. *Research on Aging, 31,* 295–317.

Noppe, I. C., & Noppe, L. D. (1997). Evolving meanings of death during early, middle, and later adolescence. *Death Studies, 21,* 253–275.

Norbury, C. F., & Sparks, A. (2013). Difference or disorder? Cultural issues in understanding neurodevelopmental disorders. *Developmental Psychology, 49,* 45–58.

Nordin, S., Razani, L. J., Markison, S., & Murphy, C. (2003). Age-associated increases in intensity discrimination for taste. *Experimental Aging Research, 29,* 371–381.

North, M. S., & Fiske, S. T. (2012). An inconvenienced youth? Ageism and its potential intergenerational roots. *Psychological Bulletin, 138,* 982–997.

Northstone, K., Smith, A. D., Newby, P.K., Emmett, P. M. (2013). Longitudinal comparisons of dietary patterns derived by cluster analysis in 7- to 13-year-old children. *British Journal of Nutrition, 109,* 2050–2058.

Nourhashemi, F., Gillette-Guyonnet, S., Andrieu, S., Ghisolfi, A., Ousset, P. J., Grandjean, H., Grand, A., Pous, J., Vellas, B., & Albarede, J. L. (2000). Alzheimer disease: Protective factors. *American Journal of Clinical Nutrition, 71,* 643s–649s.

Nucci, L. (2006). Education for moral development. In M. Killen & J. G. Smetana (Eds.), *Handbook of moral development.* Mahwah, NJ: Erlbaum.

Nucci, L., & Turiel, E. (1993). God's word, religious rules, and their relation to Christian and Jewish children's concepts of morality. *Child Development, 64,* 1475–1491.

Nugent, J. K., Keefer, C. H., Minear, S., Johnson, L. C., & Blanchard, Y. (2007). *Understanding newborn behaviors and early relationships: The Newborn Behavioral Observation (NBO) system handbook.* Baltimore, MD: Brookes Publishing.

Nyborg, H., & Jensen, A. R. (2001). Occupation and income related to psychometric g. *Intelligence, 29,* 45–55.

Nye, C. D., Su, R., Rounds, J., & Dragsow, F. (2012). Vocational interests and performance: A quantitative summary of over 60 years of research. *Perspectives on Psychological Science, 7,* 384–403.

O'Brien, L. T., & Hummert, M. L. (2006). Memory performance of late middle-aged adults: Contrasting self-stereotyping and stereotype threat accounts of assimilation to age stereotypes. *Social Cognition, 24,* 338–358.

O'Brien, M. (1996). Child-rearing difficulties reported by parents of infants and toddlers. *Journal of Pediatric Psychology, 21,* 433–446.

O'Brien, M., Peyton, V., Mistry, R., Hruda, L., Jacobs, A., Caldera, Y., et al. (2000). Gender-role cognition in three-year-old boys and girls. *Sex Roles, 42,* 1007–1025.

O'Connor, B. P. (1995). Family and friend relationships among older and younger adults: Interaction motivation, mood, and quality. *International Journal of Aging and Human Development, 40,* 9–29.

O'Connor, B. P., & Nikolic, J. (1990). Identity development and formal operations as sources of adolescent egocentrism. *Journal of Youth and Adolescence, 19,* 149–158.

O'Connor, R. E. (2011). Phoneme awareness and the alphabetic principle. In R. E. O'Connor & P. F. Vadasy (Eds.), *Handbook of reading interventions* (pp. 9–26). New York: The Guilford Press.

O'Connor, T. G., Deater-Deckard, K., Fulker, D., Rutter, M., & Plomin, R. (1998). Genotype-environment correlations in late childhood and early adolescence: Antisocial behavioral problems and coercive parenting. *Developmental Psychology, 34,* 970–981.

O'Connor, T. G., Marvin, R. S., Rutter, M., Olrick, J. T., & Britner, P. A. (2003). Child–parent attachment following early institutional deprivation. *Development and Psychopathology, 15,* 19–38.

O'Halloran, C. M., & Altmaier, E. M. (1996). Awareness of death among children: Does a life-threatening illness alter the process of discovery? *Journal of Counseling and Development, 74,* 259–262.

O'Hara, R. E., Gibbons, F. X., Gerrard, M., Li, Z., & Sargent, J. D. (2012). Greater exposure to sexual content in popular movies predicts earlier sexual debut and increased sexual risk taking. *Psychological Science, 23,* 984–993.

O'Leary, C. M., & Bower, C. (2012). Guidelines for pregnancy: What's an acceptable risk, and how is the evidence (finally) shaping up? *Drug & Alcohol Review, 31,* 170–183.

O'Mara, A. J., Marsh, H. W., Craven, R. G., & Debus, R. L. (2006). Do self-concept interventions make a difference? A synergistic blend of construct validation and meta-analysis. *Educational Psychologist, 41,* 181–206.

O'Mathúna, D. P. (2006). Human growth hormone for improved strength and increased muscle mass in athletes. *Alternative Medicine Alert, 8,* 97–101.

O'Roak, B. J., Vives, L., Girirajan, S., Karakoc, E., Krumm, N., Coe, B. P., et al. (2012). Sporadic autism exomes reveal a highly interconnected protein network of de novo mutations. *Nature, 485(7397),* 246–250.

O'Rourke, M. (2010, February 1). Good grief. Is there a better way to be bereaved? *The New Yorker,* 66–72.

O'Shaughnessy, R., & Dallos, R. (2009). Attachment research and eating disorders: A review of the literature. *Clinical Child Psychology and Psychiatry, 14,* 559–574.

Oakhill, J., Garnham, A., & Reynolds, D. (2005). Immediate activation of stereotypical gender information. *Memory and Cognition, 33,* 972–983.

Oberlander, S. E., Black, M. M., & Starr, R. H., Jr. (2007). African American adolescent mothers and grandmothers: A multigenerational approach to parenting. *American Journal of Community Psychology, 39,* 37–46.

Oberlander, T. F., Reebye, P., Misri, S., Papsdorf, M., Kim, J., & Grunau, R. E. (2007). Externalizing and attentional behaviors in children of depressed mothers treated with a selective serotonin reuptake inhibitor antidepressant during pregnancy. Archives of Pediatric & Adolescent Medicine, 161, 22–29.

Oberlander, T. F., Warburton, W., Misri, S., Aghajanian, J., Hertzman, C. (2006). Neonatal outcomes after prenatal exposure to selective serotonin reuptake inhibitor antidepressants and maternal depression using population-based linked health data. *Journal of the american medical association, 63,* 898–906.

Oberman, L. M., & Ramachandran, V. S. (2007). The simulated social mind: The role of the mirror neuron system and simulation in the social and communicative deficits of autism spectrum disorders. *Psychological Bulletin, 133,* 310–327.

Obler, L. K. (2013). Developments in the adult years. In J. Berko Gleason & N. B. Ratner (Eds.), *The development of language* (7th ed.). Boston: Allyn & Bacon.

Boström, P. K., Broberg, M., & Hwang, P. (2010). Parents' descriptions and experiences of young children recently diagnosed with intellectual disability. *Child: Care, Health and Development*, 36, 93–100.

Ochs, E. (1982). Talking to children in Western Samoa. *Language in Society*, 11, 77–104.

Ochs, E., & Izquierdo, C. (2009). Responsibility in childhood: Three developmental trajectories. *Ethos*, 37, 391–413.

Ochse, R. (1990). *Before the gates of excellence: The determinants of creative genius.* Cambridge, UK: Cambridge University Press.

Oden, M. H. (1968). The fulfillment of promise: 40-year follow-up of the Terman gifted group. *Genetic Psychology Monographs*, 77, 3–93.

Derntl, B., Schöpf, V., Kollndorfer, K., & Lanzenberger, R. (2013). Menstrual cycle phase and duration of oral contraception intake affect olfactory perception. *Chemical Senses*, 38, 67–75.

Odgers, C. L., Moffitt, T. E., Broadbent, J. M., Dickson, N., Hancox, R. J., Harrington, H., Poulton, R., Sears, M. R., Thomson, W. M., & Caspi, A. (2008). Female and male antisocial trajectories: From childhood origins to adult outcomes. *Development and Psychopathology*, 20, 673–716.

OECD. (2012). *Factbook 2012, mean scores by gender in PISA.* OECD Publishing.

Etgen, T., Sander, D., Huntgeburth, U., Poppert, H., Förstl, H., & Bickel, H. (2010). Physical activity and incident cognitive impairment in elderly persons. *Archives of Internal Medicine*, 170, 186–193.

Ogbu, J. U. (1994). From cultural differences to differences in cultural frames of reference. In P. M. Greenfield & R. R. Cocking (Eds.), *Cross-cultural roots of minority child development.* Hillsdale, NJ: Erlbaum.

Ogbu, J. U. (2003). *Black American students in an affluent suburb: A study of academic disengagement.* Lawrence Erlbaum.

Ogletree, S. M., & Drake, R. (2007). College students' video game participation and perceptions: Gender differences and implications. *Sex Roles*, 56, 537–542.

Ogletree, S. M., Martinez, C. N., Turner, T. R., & Mason, B. (2004). Pokemon: Exploring the role of gender. *Sex Roles*, 50, 851–859.

Holt, R. I., & Sönksen, P. H. (2008). Growth hormone, IGF-I and insulin and their abuse in sport. *British Journal of Pharmacology*, 154, 542–556.

Okagaki, L. (2001). Triarchic model of minority children's school achievement. *Educational psychologist*, 36, 9–20.

Oldehinkel, A. J., Verhulst, F. C., & Ormel, J. (2011). Mental health problems during puberty: Tanner stage-related differences in specific symptoms: The TRAILS study. *Journal of Adolescence*, 34, 73–85.

Omodei, D., & Fontana, L. (2011). Calorie restriction and prevention of age-associated chronic disease. *Federation of European Biochemical Societies*, 585, 1537–1542.

Olesen, S. C., Butterworth, P., & Rodgers, B. (2012). Is poor mental health a risk factor for retirement? Findings from a longitudinal population survey. *Social Psychiatry and Psychiatric Epidemiology*, 47, 735–744.

Oller, D. K., & Eilers, R. E. (1988). The role of audition in infant babbling. *Child Development*, 59, 441–449.

Olmstead, S. B., Billen, R. M., Conrad, K. A., Pasley, K., & Fincham, F. D. (2013). Sex, commitment, and casual sex relationships among college men: A mixed-methods analysis. *Archives of Sexual Behavior*, 42, 561–571.

Olshansky, S. J., & Carnes, B. A. (2004). In search of the holy grail of senescence. In S. G. Post & R. H. Binstock (Eds.), *The fountain of youth: Cultural, scientific, and ethical perspectives on a biomedical goal.* New York: Oxford University Press.

Olshansky, S. J., Antonucci, T., Berkman, L., Binstock, R. H., Boersch-Supan, A., Cacioppo, J. T., et al. (2012). Differences in life expectancy due to race and educational differences are widening, and many may not catch up. *Health Affairs*, 31, 1803–1813.

Olson, J., & Masur, E. F. (2012). Mothers respond differently to infants' familiar versus non-familiar verbal imitations. *Journal of Child Language*, 39, 731–752.

Oltjenbruns, K. A. (2001). Developmental context of childhood: Grief and regrief phenomena. In M. S. Stroebe, R. O. Hansson, W. Stroebe, & H. Schut (Eds.), *Handbook of bereavement research. Consequences, coping, and care.* Washington, DC: American Psychological Association.

Olweus, D. (1993). *Bullying at school.* Oxford, UK: Blackwell.

Olweus, D., & Limber, S. P. (2010). Bullying in school: Evaluation and dissemination of the Olweus Bullying Prevention Program. *American Journal of Orthopsychiatry*, 80, 124–134.

Ong, A. D., Fuller-Rowell, T., & Bonanno, G. A. (2010). Prospective predictors of positive emotions following spousal loss. *Psychology and Aging*, 25, 653–660.

Onishi, K. H., & Baillargeon, R. (2005). Do 15-month-old infants understand false beliefs? *Science*, 308, 255–258.

Oosterwegel, A., & Oppenheimer, L. (1993). *The self-system: Developmental changes between and within self-concepts.* Hillsdale, NJ: Erlbaum.

Orloff, S. F., & Huff, S. M. (2010). Pediatric palliative and hospice care. In C. A. Corr & D. E. Balk (Eds.), *Children's encounters with death, bereavement, and coping.* New York: Springer.

O'Roak, B. J., Vives, L., Girirajan, S., Karakoc, E., Krumm, N., Coe, B. P., et al. (2012). Sporadic autism exomes reveal a highly interconnected protein network of de novo mutations. *Nature*, 485, 246–250.

Orobio de Castro, B., Veerman, J. W., Koops, W., Bosch, J. D., & Monshouwer, H. J. (2002). Hostile attribution of intent and aggressive behavior: A meta-analysis. *Child Development*, 73, 916–934.

Rönnlund, M., Nyberg, L., Bäckman, L., & Nillson, L.-G. (2005). Stability, growth, and decline in adult life span development of declarative memory: Cross-sectional and longitudinal data from a population-based study. *Psychology and Aging*, 20, 3–18.

Orth, L. C., & Martin, R. P. (1994). Interactive-effects of student temperament and instruction method on classroom behavior and achievement. *Journal of School Psychology*, 32, 149–166.

Orth, U., Robins, R. W., & Widaman, K. F. (2012). Life-span development of self-esteem and its effects on important life outcomes. *Journal of Personality and Social Psychology*, 102, 1271–1288.

Orth, U., Trzesniewski, K. H., & Robins, R. W. (2010). Self-esteem development from young adulthood to old age: A cohort-sequential longitudinal study. *Journal of Personality and Social Psychology*, 98, 645–658.

Osterman, M. J., & Martin, J. A. (2011, April 6). Epidural and spinal anesthesia use during labor: 27-state reporting area, 2008. *National Vital Statistics Reports: From the Centers for Disease Control and Prevention, National Center for Health Statistics*, 59, 1–13, 16.

Osterman, M.J.K., Martin, J.A., Mathews, T.J., & Hamilton, B.E. (2011). Expanded data from the new birth certificate, 2008. National Vital Statistics Reports; vol 59, no 7. Hyattsville, MD: National Center for Health Statistics.

Osterweis, M., Solomon, F., & Green, M. (Eds.). (1984). *Bereavement: Reactions, consequences, and care.* Washington, DC: National Academy Press.

Ostrov, J. M., & Godleski, S. A. (2010). Toward an integrated gender-linked model of aggression subtypes in early and middle childhood. *Psychological Review*, 117, 233–242.

Ouellet-Morin, I., Danese, A., Bowes, L., Shakoor, S., Ambler, A., Pariante, C. M., et al. (2011). A discordant monozygotic twin design shows blunted cortisol reactivity among bullied children. *Journal of the American Academy of Child & Adolescent Psychiatry*, 50, 574–582.

Overton, W. F. (2010). Life-span development: Concepts and issues. In W. F. Overton (Vol. ed.) & R. M. Lerner (Editor-in-Chief), *Handbook of life-span development: Vol. 1. Cognition, biology, and methods across the lifespan* (pp. 1–29). Hoboken, NJ: Wiley.

Owen, A. M., Coleman, M. R., Boly, M., Davis, M. H., Laureys, S., & Pickard, J. D. (2006). Detecting awareness in the vegetative state. *Science, 313*(5792), 1402.

Owen, J. J., Rhoades, G. K., Stanley, S. M., & Fincham, F. D. (2010). "Hooking up" among college students: Demographic and psychosocial correlates. *Archives of Sexual Behavior, 39,* 653–663.

Ozonoff, S. (2012). DSM-5 and autism spectrum disorders—two decades of perspectives from the JCPP. *Journal of Child Psychology and Psychiatry, and Allied Disciplines, 53,* e4–e6.

Ozonoff, S., Young, G.S., Carter, A, Messinger, D., Yirmiya, N., Zwaigenbaum, L., et al. (2011). Recurrence risk for autism spectrum disorders: a Baby Siblings Research Consortium study. *Pediatrics, 128,* 488–495.

Ozer, D. J., & Benet-Martinez, V. (2006). Personality and the prediction of consequential outcomes. *Annual Review of Psychology, 57,* 401–421.

Paciello, M., Fida, R., Tramontano, C., Lupinetti, C., & Caprara, G. V. (2008). Stability and change of moral disengagement and its impact on aggression and violence in late adolescence. *Child Development, 79,* 1288–1309.

Pakistani eunuchs to have distinct gender (2009, December 23). *BBC News.* Retrieved from *http://news.bbc.co.uk/2/hi/south_asia/ 8428819.stm*

Palkovitz, R. (2002). *Involved fathering and men's adult development: Provisional balances.* Mahwah, NJ: Erlbaum.

Palmore, E. B., Burchett, B. M., Fillenbaum, G. G., George, L. K., & Wallman, L. M. (1985). *Retirement. Causes and consequences.* New York: Springer.

Pargament, K. I., Exline, J. J., & Jones, J. W. (Eds.) (2013), *APA handbook of psychology, religion, and spirituality: Vol. 1. Context, theory, and research.* Washington, DC: American Psychological Association.

Park, D. C., & Huang, C-M. (2010). Culture wires the brain: A cognitive neuroscience perspective. *Perspectives on Psychological Science, 5,* 391–400.

Park, D.C., & Reuter-Lorenz, P. (2009). The adaptive brain: Aging and neurocogntive scaffolding. *Annual Review of Psychology, 60,* 173–196.

Park, D. C., Lautenschlager, G., Hedden, T., Davidson, N. S., Smith, A. D., & Smith, P. K. (2002). Models of visuospatial and verbal memory across the adult life span. *Psychological Aging, 17,* 299–320.

Park, D. C., Morrell, R. W., Frieske, D., & Kincaid, D. (1992). Medication adherence behaviors in older adults: Effects of external cognitive supports. *Psychology and Aging, 7,* 252–256.

Park, G., Lubinski, D., & Benbow, C. P. (2007). Contrasting intellectual patterns predict creativity in the arts and sciences. *Psychological Science, 18,* 948–952.

Parke, R. D. (1996). *Fatherhood.* Cambridge, MA: Harvard University Press.

Parke, R. D., & Buriel, R. (2006). Socialization in the family: Ethnic and ecological perspectives. In N. Eisenberg (Ed.), W. Damon & R. M. Learner (Eds. in Chief),

Handbook of child psychology: Vol. 3. Social, emotional, and personality development. Hoboken, NJ: Wiley.

Parke, R. D., & Sawin, D. B. (1976). The father's role in infancy: A reevaluation. *Family Coordinator,25,* 365–371.

Parker, K. (2012). The boomerang generation. Feeling OK about living with Mom and Dad. Pew Research Center Social and Demographic Trends. Retrieved from http:// www.pewsocialtrends.org/2012/03/15/ the-boomerang-generation/

Parker, K., & Patten, E. (2013). The sandwich generation. Rising financial burdens for middle-aged Americans. Pew Research Center Social and Demographic Trends. Retrieved from http://www.pewsocialtrends. org/2013/01/30/the-sandwich-generation/

Parker, K., & Wang, W. (2013). Modern parenthood. Roles of Moms and Dads converge as they balance work and family. Pew Research Center Social and Demographic Trends, http://www. pewsocialtrends.org/2013/03/14/modern- parenthood-roles-of-moms-and-dads-converge- as-they-balance-work-and-family/

Parkes, C. M. (1991). Attachment, bonding, and psychiatric problems after bereavement in adult life. In C. M. Parkes, J. Stevenson-Hinde, & P. Marris (Eds.), *Attachment across the life cycle.* London: Tavistock/Routledge.

Parkes, C. M. (1996). *Bereavement: Studies of grief in adult life* (3rd ed.). London: Routledge.

Parkes, C. M. (2000). Comments on Dennis Klass' article "Developing a cross-cultural model of grief." *Omega: Journal of Death and Dying, 41,* 323–326.

Parkes, C. M. (2006). *Love and loss. The roots of grief and its complications.* London: Routledge.

Parkes, C. M., & Prigerson, H. G. (2010). *Bereavement. Studies of grief in adult life* (4th ed.). New York: Routledge.

Parkes, C. M., & Weiss, R. S. (1983). *Recovery from bereavement.* New York: Basic Books.

Parkhurst, J. T., & Asher, S. R. (1992). Peer rejection in middle school: Subgroup differences in behavior, loneliness, and interpersonal concerns. *Developmental Psychology, 28,* 231–241.

Parkhurst, J. T., &Hopmeyer, A. (1998). Sociometric popularity and peer-perceived popularity: Two distinct dimensions of peer status. *Journal of Early Adolescence, 18,* 125–144.

Parnham, J. (2001). Lifelong learning: A model for increasing the participation of non-traditional adult learners. *Journal of Further and Higher Education, 25,* 57–65.

Parten, M. B. (1932). Social participation among preschool children. *Journal of Abnormal and Social Psychology, 27,* 243–269.

Pascalis, O., de Schonen, S., Morton, J., Deruelle, C., & Fabre-Grenet, M. (1995). Mother's face recognition by neonates: A replication and an extension. *Infant Behavior and Development, 16,* 79–85.

Passman, R. H. (1977). Providing attachment objects to facilitate learning and reduce distress: Effects of mothers and security blankets. *Developmental Psychology, 13,* 25–28.

Pasupathi, M., Staudinger, U. M., & Baltes, P. B. (2001). Seeds of wisdom: Adolescents' knowledge and judgment about difficult life problems. *Developmental Psychology, 37,* 351–361.

Patel, D. R., Pratt, H. D., & Greydanus, D. E. (2003). Treatment of adolescents with anorexia nervosa. *Journal of Adolescent Research, 18,* 244–260.

Patel, R., & Brayton, J. T. (2009). Identifying prosodic contrasts in utterances produced by 4-, 7-, and 11-year-old children. *Journal of Speech, Language, and Hearing Research, 52,* 790–801.

Patrick, J. H., & Goedereis, E. A. (2009). The importance of context and the gain-loss dynamic for understanding grandparent caregivers. In K. Shifren (Ed.), *How caregiving affects development. Psychological implications for child, adolescent, and adult caregivers.* Washington, DC: American Psychological Association.

Patrick, R. B., & Gibbs, J. C. (2007). Parental expression of disappointment: Should it be a factor in Hoffman's model of parental discipline? *Journal of Genetic Psychology, 168,* 131–145.

Patrick, R. B., & Gibbs, J. C. (2012). Inductive discipline, parental expression of disappointed expectations, and moral identity in adolescence. *Journal of Youth and Adolescence, 41,* 973–983.

Patterson, C. J. (2004). Gay fathers. In M. E. Lamb (Ed.), *The role of the father in child development* (4th ed.). Hoboken, NJ: John Wiley & Sons.

Patterson, C. J., & Hastings, P. D. (2007). Socialization in the context of family diversity. In J. E. Grusec & P. D. Hastings (Eds.), *Handbook of socialization: Theory and research.* New York: Guilford.

Patterson, C. J., Kupersmidt, J. B., & Vaden, N. A. (1990). Income level, gender, ethnicity, and household composition as predictors of children's school-based competence. *Child Development, 61,* 485–494.

Patterson, G. R. (2005). The next generation of PMTO models. *The Behavior Therapist, 28,* 27–33.

Patterson, G. R. (2008). A comparison of models for interstate wars and for individual violence. *Perspectives on Psychological Science, 3,* 203–223.

Patterson, G. R., DeBaryshe, B. D., & Ramsey, E. (1989). A developmental perspective on antisocial behavior. *American Psychologist, 44,* 329–335.

Patterson, G. R., Forgatch, M. S., & DeGarmo, D. S. (2010). Cascading effects following intervention. *Development and Psychopathology, 22,* 949–970.

Patterson, M. M. (2012). Self-perceived gender typicality, gender-typed attributes, and gender stereotype endorsement in elementary-school- aged children. *Sex Roles, 67,* 422–434.

Patton, J. R. (2000). Educating students with mild mental retardation. *Focus on Autism and Other Developmental Disabilities, 15,* 80–89.

Paul, A. M. (2010). *Origins: How the nine months before birth shape the rest of our lives*. New York: Free Press.

Paul, D. A., Lee, K. H., Locke, R. G., Bartoshesky, L., Walrath, J., & Stefano, J. L. (2006). Increasing illness severity in very low birth weight infants over a 9-year period. *BMC Pediatrics, 6*, Retrieved from http://www.biomedcentral.com/1471-2431/6/2

Paul, E. L., & Hayes, A. (2002). The casualties of 'casual' sex: A qualitative exploration of the phenomenology of college students' hookups. *Journal of Social and Personal Relationships, 19*, 639–661.

Paul, E. L., McManus, B., & Hayes, A. (2000). "Hookups": Characteristics and correlates of college students' spontaneous and anonymous sexual experiences. *Journal of Sex Research, 37*, 76–88.

Paul, K. I., & Moser, K. (2009). Unemployment impairs mental health: Meta-analyses. *Journal of Vocational Behavior, 74*, 264–282.

Pauli-Pott, U., Mertesacker, B., & Beckmann, D. (2004). Predicting the development of infant emotionality from maternal characteristics. *Development and Psychopathology, 16*, 19–42.

Paulson, J. (2013). Environmental toxicants and neurocognitive development. In M. L. Batshaw, N. J. Roizen, & G. R. Lotrecchiano (Eds.), *Children with disabilities* (7th ed., pp. 37–46). Baltimore: Paul H. Brookes.

Paxton, J. M., & Greene, J. D. (2010). Moral reasoning: Hints and allegations. *Topics in Cognitive Science, 2*, 511–527.

Paxton, J. M., Ungar, L., & Greene, J. D. (2012). Reflection and reasoning in moral judgment. *Cognitive Science, 36*, 163–177.

Paxton, S. J., Neumark-Sztainer, D., Hannan, P. J., Eisenberg, M. E. (2006). Body dissatisfaction prospectively predicts depressive mood and low self-esteem in adolescent girls and boys. *Journal of Clinical Child and Adolescent Psychology, 35*, 539–549.

Paz-Alonso, P. E., Larson, R. P., Castelli, P., Alley, D., & Goodman, G. (2009). In M. L. Courage & N. Cowan (Eds.), *The development of memory in infancy and childhood* (pp. 197–240). New York: Psychology Press.

Pea, R., Nass, C., Meheula, L., Rance, M., Kumar, A., Bamford, H., et al. (2012). Media use, face-to-face communication, media multitasking, and social well-being among 8- to 12-year-olds. *Developmental Psychology, 48*, 327–336.

Pearce, K. A., & Denney, N. W. (1984). A lifespan study of classification preference. *Journal of Gerontology, 39*, 458–464.

Pearlin, L. I. (1980). Life strains and psychological distress among adults. In N. J. Smelser & E. H. Erikson (Eds.), *Themes of work and love in adulthood*. Cambridge, MA: Harvard University Press.

Pears, K. C., & Moses, L. J. (2003). Demographics, parenting, and theory of mind in preschool children. *Social Development, 12*, 1–19.

Pearson, A. (2011, May 6). Out-of-Africa migration selected novelty-seeking genes. *NewScientist*, Issue 2811. Retrieved from http://www.newscientist.com/article/ mg21028114.400-outofafrica-migration-selected-noveltyseeking-genes.html

Pearson, J. D., Morell, C. H., Gordon-Salant, S., Brant, L. J., Metter, E. J., Klein, L., et al. (1995). Gender differences in a longitudinal study of age-associated hearing loss. *Journal of the Acoustical Society of America, 97*, 1196–1205.

Pedula, K. L., Coleman, A. L., Hillier, T. A., Ensrud, K. E., Nevitt, M. C., Hochberg, M. C., et al. (2006). Visual acuity, contrast sensitivity, and mortality in older women: Study of osteoporotic fractures. *Journal of American Geriatric Society, 54*, 1871–1877.

Pekrun, R., Elliot, A. J., & Maier, M. A. (2009). Achievement goals and achievement emotions: Testing a model of their joint relations with academic performance. *Journal of Educational Psychology, 101*, 115–135.

Pellegrini, A. D., Long, J. D., Roseth, C. J., Bohn, C. M., & Van Ryzin, M. (2007). A short-term longitudinal study of preschoolers' (*Homo sapiens*) sex segregation: The role of physical activity, sex, and time. *Journal of Comparative Psychology, 121*, 282–289.

Pellicano, E. (2010). Individual differences in executive function and central coherence predict developmental changes in theory of mind in autism. *Developmental Psychology, 46*, 530–544.

Pelligrini, A. D. (2009). Research and policy on children's play. *Child Development Perspectives, 3*, 131–136.

Pénicaud, S., Klein, D., Zatorre, R. J., Chen, J., Witcher, P., Hyde, K., et al. (2013). Structural brain changes linked to delayed first language acquisition in congenitally deaf individuals. *NeuroImage, 66*, 42–49.

Penner, S. G. (1987). Parental responses to grammatical and ungrammatical child utterances. *Child Development, 58*, 376–384.

Peplau, L. A., & Fingerhut, A. W. (2007). The close relationships of lesbians and gay men. *Annual Review of Psychology, 58*, 405–424.

Pereira, A. C., Huddleston, D. E., Brickman, A. M., Sosunov, A. A., Hen, R., McKhann, G. M., et al. (2007). An in vivo correlate of exercise-induced neurogenesis in the adult dentate gyrus. *Proceedings of the National Academy of Sciences, 104*, 5638–5643.

Perera, F., & Herbstman, J. (2011). Prenatal environmental exposures, epigenetics, and disease. *Reproductive Toxicology, 31*, 363–373.

Perez-Granados, D. R., & Callanan, M. A. (1997). Conversations with mothers and siblings: Young children's semantic and conceptual development. *Developmental Psychology, 33*, 120–134.

Perfetti, C. A. (1999). Cognitive research and the misconceptions of reading education. In J. Oakhill & R. Beard (Eds.), *Reading development and the teaching of reading* (pp. 42–58). Malden, MA: Blackwell.

Perkins, H. W., & DeMeis, D. K. (1996). Gender and family effects on the "second-shift" domestic activity of college educated young adults. *Gender & Society, 10*, 78–93.

Perlmutter, M. (1986). A life-span view of memory. In P. B. Baltes, D. L. Featherman, & R. M. Lerner (Eds.), *Life-span development and behavior* (Vol. 7). Hillsdale, NJ: Erlbaum.

Perren, S., Ettekal, I., & Ladd, G. (2013). The impact of peer victimization on later maladjustment: Mediating and moderating effects of hostile and self-blaming attributions. *Journal of Child Psychology and Psychiatry, 54*, 46–55.

Perrin, E. C., Siegel, B. S., & the Committee on Psychosocial Aspects of Child and Family Health (2013). Promoting the well-being of children whose parents are gay or lesbian. *Pediatrics, 131*, e1374–1383.

Perry, H. L. (1993). Mourning and funeral customs of African Americans. In D. P. Irish, K. F. Lundquist, & V. J. Nelson (Eds.), *Ethnic variations in dying, death, and grief: Diversity in universality*. Washington, DC: Taylor and Francis.

Perry, W. G., Jr. (1970). *Forms of intellectual and ethical development in the college years: A scheme*. New York: Holt, Rinehart & Winston.

Persson, G., & Svanborg, A. (1992). Marital coital activity in men at the age of 75: Relation to somatic, psychiatric, and social factors at the age of 70. *Journal of the American Geriatrics Society, 40*, 439–444.

Peters, A. (2002). The effects of normal aging on myelin and nerve fibers: A review. *Journal of Neurocytology, 31*, 581–593.

Petersen, I. T., Bates, J. E., Goodnight, J. A., Dodge, K. A., Lansford, J. E., Pettit, G. S., et al. (2012). Interaction between serotonin transporter polymorphism (5-HTTLPR) and stressful life events in adolescents' trajectories of anxious/depressed symptoms. *Developmental Psychology, 48*, 1463–1475.

Petersen, R. C., Smith, G. E., Waring, S. C., & Ivnik, R. J. (1997). Aging, memory, and mild cognitive impairment. *International Psycho-Geriatrics, 65*(Supplement).

Petersen, R. C., Stevens, J. C., Ganguli, M., Tangalos, E. G., Cummings, J. L., & DeKosky, S. T. (2001). Early detection of dementia: Mild cognitive impairment. *Neurology, 56*, 1133–1142.

Peterson, C. C., & Rideout, R. (1998). Memory for medical emergencies experienced by 1 and 2-year-olds. *Developmental Psychology, 34*, 1059–1072.

Peterson, C. C., & Siegal, M. (1999). Representing inner worlds: Theory of mind in autistic, deaf, and normal hearing children. *Psychological Science, 10*, 126–129.

Peterson, C. C., & Siegal, M. (2002). Mind reading and moral awareness in popular and rejected preschoolers. *British Journal of Developmental Psychology, 20*, 205–224.

Peterson, C. C., & Slaughter, V. (2003). Opening windows into the mind: Mothers' preferences for mental state explanations and children's theory of mind. *Cognitive Development, 18*, 399–429.

Peterson, C. C., & Wellman, H. M. (2009). From fancy to reason: Scaling deaf and hearing children's understanding of theory of mind and pretense. *British Journal of Developmental Psychology, 27,* 297–310.

Peterson, C. C., Wellman, H. M., & Slaughter, V. (2012). The mind behind the message: Advancing theory-of-mind scales for typically developing children, and those with deafness, autism, or Asperger syndrome. *Child Development, 83,* 469–485.

Peterson, J. L., & Hyde, J. S. (2010). A meta-analytic review of research on gender differences in sexuality, 1993–2007. *Psychological Bulletin, 136,* 21–38.

Peterson, P. L. (1977). Interactive effects of student anxiety, achievement orientation, and teacher behavior on student achievement and attitude. *Journal of Educational Psychology, 69,* 779–792.

Petitto, L. A., & Marentette, P. F. (1991). Babbling in the manual mode: Evidence for the ontogeny of language. *Science, 251,* 1493–1496.

Petitto, L. A., Berens, M. S., Kovelman, I., Dubins, M. H., Jasinska, K., & Shalinsky, M. (2012). The "Perceptual Wedge Hypothesis" as the basis for bilingual babies' phonetic processing advantage: New insights from fNIRS brain imaging. *Brain and Language, 121,* 130–143.

Pettitt, L. M. (2004). Gender intensification of peer socialization during puberty. *New Directions for Child and Adolescent Development, 106,* 23–34.

Pew Forum on Religion and Public Life. (2012). *"Nones" on the rise: One-in-five adults have no religious affiliation.* Retrieved from www.pewforum.org/Unaffiliated/nones-on-the-rise.aspx

Pew Research Center. (2013, March 14). *Modern parenthood: Roles of moms and dads converge as they balance work and family.* Retrieved from http://www.pewsocialtrends.org/files/2013/03/FINAL_modern_parenthood_03-2013.pdf

Phares, V. (1999). *"Poppa" psychology. The role of fathers in children's mental well-being.* Westport, CT: Praeger.

Phelan, S., Phipps, M. G., Abrams, B., Darroch, F., Schaffner, A., & Wing, R. R. (2011). Practitioner advice and gestational weight gain. *Journal of Women's Health, 20,* 585–591.

Phillips, L. M., Norris, S. P., & Anderson, J. (2008). Unlocking the door: Is parents' reading to children the key to early literacy development? *Canadian Psychology, 49,* 82–88.

Phillips, M. (1997). What makes schools effective? A comparison of the relationships of communitarian climate and academic climate to mathematics achievement and attendance during middle school. *American Educational Research Journal, 34,* 633–662.

Phillips, M. (2009, March 16). Where death comes cheap. *Newsweek,* 45–46.

Phillips, S. D. (1982). Career exploration in adulthood. *Journal of Vocational Behavior, 20,* 129–140.

Phillips, T. M., & Pittman, J. F. (2003). Identity processes in poor adolescents: Exploring the linkages between economic disadvantage and the primary task of adolescence. *Identity, 3,* 115–129.

Phinney, J. S. (1993). A three-stage model of ethnic identity development in adolescence. In M. E. Bernal, & G. P. Knight (Eds.), *Ethnic identity: Formation and transmission among Hispanics and other minorities.* Albany, NY: State University of New York Press.

Phinney, J. S. (1996). When we talk about American ethnic groups, what do we mean? *American Psychologist, 51,* 918–927.

Phinney, J. S. (2006). Ethnic identity exploration in emerging adulthood. In J. J. Arnett, & J. L. Tanner (Eds.), *Emerging adults in America: Coming of age in the 21st century.* Washington, DC: American Psychological Association.

Piaget, J. (1926). *The child's conception of the world.* New York: Harcourt, Brace & World.

Piaget, J. (1952). *The origins of intelligence in children.* New York: International Universities Press.

Piaget, J. (1965). *The moral judgment of the child.* New York: Free Press. (Original work published 1932).

Piaget, J. (1970). Piaget's theory. In P. H. Mussen (Ed.), *Carmichael's manual of child psychology* (Vol. 1). New York: Wiley.

Piaget, J. (1971). *Biology and knowledge.* Edinburgh, UK: Edinburgh University Press.

Piaget, J. (1972). Intellectual evolution from adolescence to adulthood. *Human Development, 15,* 1–12.

Piaget, J. (1977). The role of action in the development of thinking. In W. F. Overton & J. M. Gallagher (Eds.), *Knowledge and development* (Vol. 1). New York: Plenum.

Piaget, J. (1978). *The development of thought: Equilibration of cognitive structures.* Oxford, UK: Blackwell.

Piaget, J. (1985). *The equilibration of cognitive structures: The central problem of intellectual development* (T. Brown & K. J. Thampy, Trans.). Chicago: University of Chicago Press.

Piaget, J., & Inhelder, B. (1956). *The child's conception of space.* New York: Norton.

Piaget, J., & Inhelder, B. (1969). In H. Weaver (Ed.), *The psychology of the child* (H. Weaver, Trans.). New York: Basic Books. (Original work published 1966).

Pianta, R., Egeland, B., & Erickson, M. F. (1989). The antecedents of maltreatment: Results of the Mother–child Interaction Research Project. In D. Cicchetti & V. Carlson (Eds.), *Child maltreatment: Theory and research on the causes and consequences of child abuse and neglect.* Cambridge, UK: Cambridge University Press.

Pierce, K., Carter, C., Weinfeld, M., Desmond, J., Hazin, R., Bjork, R., & Gallagher, N. (2011). Detecting, studying, and treating autism early: The one-year well-baby check-up approach. *Journal of Pediatrics, 159,* 458–465.

Pietromonaco, P. R., DeBuse, C. J., & Powers, S. I. (2013). Does attachment get under the skin? adult romantic attachment and cortisol responses to stress. *Current Directions in Psychological Science, 22,* 63–68.

Pigott, T. A. (2002). Anxiety disorders. In S. G. Kornstein & A. H. Clayton (Eds.), *Women's mental health: A comprehensive textbook* (pp. 195–221). New York: The Guilford Press.

Pilgrim, N. A., & Blum, R. W. (2012). Protective and risk factors associated with adolescent sexual and reproductive health in the English-speaking Caribbean: A literature review. *Journal of Adolescent Health, 50,* 5–23.

Pineda, J. A. (Ed.). (2009). *Mirror neuron systems: The role of mirroring processes in social cognition.* Totowa, NJ: Humana Press.

Pinhas, L., Katzman, D. K., Dimitropoulos, G., & Woodside, D. B. (2007). Bingeing and bulimia nervosa in children and adolescents. In T. Jaffa & B. McDermott (Eds.), *Eating disorders in children and adolescents.* Cambridge, UK: Cambridge University Press.

Pinker, S. (1994). *The language instinct.* New York: Harper Collins.

Pinker, S. (1995). Language acquisition. In L. R. Gleitman, M. Liberman, & D. N. Osherson (Eds.), *An invitation to cognitive science: Vol. 1. Language* (2nd ed., pp. 135–182). Cambridge, MA: MIT Press.

Pinquart, M., & Sorenson, S. (2000). Influences of socioeconomic status, social network, competence, or subjective competence in later life: A meta-analysis. *Psychology and Aging, 15,* 187–224.

Pinquart, M., & Sorensen, S. (2003). Associations of stressors and uplifts of caregiving with caregiver burden and depressive mood: A meta-analysis. *Journal of Gerontology: Psychological Sciences, 58B,* 112–128.

Pinquart, M., & Sorensen, S. (2006). Gender differences in caregiver stressors, social resources, and health: An updated meta-analysis. *Journals of Gerontology: Psychological Sciences, 61B,* P33–P45.

Pipe, M. E., Thierry, K., & Lamb, M.-E. (2007). The development of event memory: Implications for child witness testimony. In M. P. Toglia, J. D. Read, D. F. Ross, & R. C. L. Lindsay (Eds.), *Handbook of eyewitness psychology. Volume 1: Memory for events.* Mahwah, NJ: Lawrence Erlbaum.

Pipe, M., & Salmon, K. (2009). Memory development in the forensic context. In M. L. Courage & N. Cowan (Eds.), *The development of memory in infancy and childhood* (pp. 241–282). New York: Psychology Press.

Piper, W. E., Ogrodniczuk, J. S., Joyce, A. S., & Weideman, R. (2011). *Short-term group therapies for complicated grief. Two research-based models.* Washington, DC: American Psychological Association.

Pipp, S., Easterbrooks, M. A., & Harmon, R. J. (1992). The relation between attachment and knowledge of self and mother in one-year-old infants to three-year-old infants. *Child Development, 63,* 738–750.

Plassman, B. L., Havlik, R. J., Steffens, D. C., Helms, M. J., Newman, T. N., Drosdick, D., Phillips, C., Gau, B. A., Welsh-Bohmer, K. A., Burke, J. R., Guralnik, J. M., & Breitner, J. C. (2000). Documented head injury in early childhood and risk of Alzheimer's disease and other dementias. *Neurology, 55,* 1158–1166.

Plassman, B. L., Langa, K. M., Fisher, G. G., Heeringa, S. G., Weir, D. R., Ofstedal, M. B., et al. (2008). Prevalence of cognitive impairment without dementia in the United States. *Annals of Internal Medicine, 148,* 427–434.

Pleck, J. H., & Masciadrelli, B. P. (2004). Paternal involvement by U.S. residential fathers: Levels, sources, and consequences. In M. E. Lamb (Ed.), *The role of the father in child development* (4th ed.). Hoboken, NJ: John Wiley & Sons.

Plomin, R. (1990). *Nature and nurture. An introduction to human behavioral genetics.* Pacific Grove, CA: Brooks/Cole.

Plomin, R., & Spinath, F. M. (2004). Intelligence, genetics, genes, and genomics. *Journal of Personality and Social Psychology, 86,* 112–129.

Plomin, R., DeFries, J. C., McClearn, G. E., & McGuffin, P. (2008). *Behavioral genetics* (5th ed.). New York: Worth.

Ploughman, M. (2008). Exercise is brain food: The effects of physical activity on cognitive function. *Developmental Neurorehabilitation, 11,* 236–240.

Pluhar, E. I., DiIorio, C. K., & McCarty, F. (2008). Correlates of sexuality communication among mothers and 6- to 12-year-old children. *Child: Care, Health and Development, 34,* 283–290.

Poehlmann, J., & Fiese, B. H. (2001). The interaction of maternal and infant vulnerabilities on developing attachment relationships. *Development and Psychopathology, 13,* 1–11.

Polanczyk, G., Caspi, A., Williams, B., Price, T. S., Danese, A., Sugden, K., et al. (2009). Protective effect of CRHR1 gene variants on the development of adult depression following childhood maltreatment: Replication and extension. *Archives of General Psychiatry, 66,* 978–985.

Pomerantz, E. M., Altermatt, E. R., & Saxon, J. L. (2002). Making the grade but feeling distressed: Gender differences in academic performance and internal distress. *Journal of Educational Psychology, 94,* 396–404.

Pomerantz, E. M., Qin, L., Wang, Q., & Chen, H. (2009). American and Chinese early adolescents' inclusion of their relationships with their parents in their self-construals. *Child Development, 80,* 792–807.

Pomerantz, E. M., Qin, L., Wang, Q., & Chen, H. (2011). Changes in early adolescents' sense of responsibility to their parents in the United States and China: Implications for academic functioning. *Child Development, 82,* 1136–1151.

Pomerantz, E. M., Ruble, D. N., Frey, K. S., & Grenlich, F. (1995). Meeting goals and confronting conflict: Children's changing perceptions of social comparison. *Child Development, 66,* 723–738.

Pomerleau, A., Bolduc, D., Malcuit, G., & Cossette, L. (1990). Pink or blue: Environmental gender stereotypes in the first two years of life. *Sex Roles, 22,* 359–367.

Ponton, L. (2001). *The sex lives of teenagers: Revealing the secret world of adolescent boys and girls.* New York: Plume.

Poon, C. S., & Saewyc, E. M. (2009). Out yonder: Sexual-minority adolescents in rural communities in British Columbia. *American Journal of Public Health, 99,* 118–124.

Poon, H. F., Calabrese, V., Scapagnini, G., & Butterfield, D. A. (2004). Free radicals: Key to brain aging and heme oxygenase as a cellular response to oxidative stress. *Journal of Gerontology Series A: Medical Science, 59A,* 478–493.

Poortman, A., & Van Der Lippe, T. (2009). Attitudes toward housework and child care and the gendered division of labor. *Journal of Marriage & Family, 71,* 526–541.

Porfeli, E. J., & Vondracek, F. W. (2009). Career development, work, and occupational success. In M. C. Smith (Ed.) & N. DeFrates-Densch (Asst. Ed.), *Handbook of research on adult learning and development.* New York: Routledge.

Porfeli, E. J., Hartung, P. J., & Vondracek, F. W. (2008). Children's vocational development: A research rationale. *Career Development Quarterly, 57,* 25–37.

Porter, R. H. (1999). Olfaction and human kin recognition. *Genetica, 104,* 259–263.

Porter, R. H., Makin, J. W., Davis, L. B., & Christensen, K. M. (1992). Breast-fed infants respond to olfactory clues from their own mother and unfamiliar lactating females. *Infant Behavior and Development, 15,* 85–93.

Portes, A., & MacLeod, D. (1996). Educational progress of children of immigrants: The roles of class, ethnicity, and school context. *Sociology of Education, 69,* 255–275.

Portion Distortion. (2012). Retrieved from http://hp2010.nhlbihin.net/portion/index.htm

Posada, G., Longoria, N., Cocker, C., & Lu, T. (2011). Attachment ties in military families: Mothers' perception of interactions with their children, stress, and social competence. In S. M. Wadsworth, & D. Riggs (Eds.), *Risk and resilience in U.S. military families.* New York: Springer Science+Business Media.

Potti, S., Jain, N. J., Mastrogiannis, D. S., & Dandolu, V. (2012). Obstetric outcomes in pregnant women with diabetes versus hypertensive disorders versus both. *Journal of Maternal-Fetal and Neonatal Medicine, 25,* 385–388.

Poulin-Dubois, D., & Serbin, L. A. (2006). Infants' knowledge about gender stereotypes and categories. *Enfance, 58,* 283–310.

Poulin-Dubois, D., Serbin, L. A., Eichstedt, J. A., Sen, M. G., & Beissel, C. F. (2002). Men don't put on make-up: Toddlers' knowledge of the gender stereotyping of household activities. *Social Development, 11,* 166–181.

Powell, M. P., & Schulte, T. (2011). Turner syndrome. In S. Goldstein & C. R. Reynolds (Eds.), *Handbook of neurodevelopmental and genetic disorders in children* (2nd ed., pp. 261–275). New York: Guilford.

Power, F. C., & Higgins-D'Alessandro, A. (2008). The Just Community approach to moral education and the moral atmosphere of the school. In L. P. Nucci & D. Narvaez (Eds.), *Handbook of moral and character education.* New York: Routledge.

Pratt, M. W., & Norris, J. E. (1999). Moral development in maturity. Life-span perspectives on the processes of successful aging. In T. M. Hess & F. Blanchard-Fields (Eds.), *Social cognition and aging.* San Diego: Academic Press.

Pratt, M. W., Diessner, R., Hunsberger, B., Pancer, S. M., & Savoy, K. (1991). Four pathways in the analysis of adult development and aging: Comparing analyses of reasoning about personal-life dilemmas. *Psychology and Aging, 4,* 666–675.

Pratt, M. W., Diessner, R., Pratt, A., Hunsberger, B., & Pancer, S. M. (1996). Moral and social reasoning and perspective taking in later life: A longitudinal study. *Psychology and Aging, 11,* 66–73.

Pratt, M. W., Hunsberger, B., Pancer, S. M., & Alisat, S. (2003). A longitudinal analysis of personal values socialization: Correlates of a moral self-ideal in late adolescence. *Social Development, 12,* 563–585.

Pressley, M., & Hilden, K. (2006). Cognitive strategies. In D. Kuhn & R. Siegler (Vol. Eds.), *Handbook of child psychology: Cognition, perception, and language: Vol. 2.* Hoboken, NJ: Wiley and Sons.

Pressley, M., Levin, J. R., & Ghatala, E. S. (1984). Memory strategy monitoring in adults and children. *Journal of Verbal Learning and Verbal Behavior, 23,* 270–288.

Pribis, P., Burtnack, C. A., McKenzie, S. O., & Thayer, J. (2010). Trends in body fat, body mass index and physical fitness among male and female college students. *Nutrients, 2,* 1075–1085.

Price, D. W. W., & Goodman, G. S. (1990). Visiting the wizard: Children's memory for a recurring event. *Child Development, 61,* 664–680.

Price, R. H., Friedland, D. S., & Vinokur, A. D. (1998). Job loss: Hard times and eroded identity. In J. H. Harvey (Ed.), *Perspectives on loss: A sourcebook.* Philadelphia: Brunner/Mazel.

Priess, H. A., Lindberg, S. M., & Hyde, J. S. (2009). Adolescent gender-role identity and mental health: Gender intensification revisited. *Child Development, 80,* 1531–1544.

Prigerson, H. G., Vanderwerker, L. C., & Maciejewski, P. K. (2008). A case for inclusion of Prolonged Grief Disorder in DSM-V. In M. Stroebe, R. Hansson, H. Schut, & W. Stroebe (Eds.), *Handbook of bereavement research and practice: Advances in theory and intervention.* Washington, DC: American Psychological Association.

Prinstein, M. J., Meade, C. S., & Cohen, G. L. (2003). Adolescent oral sex, peer popularity, and perceptions of best friends' sexual behavior. *Journal of Pediatric Psychology, 28*, 243–249.

Prinstein, M. J., Rancourt, D., Guerry, J. D., & Browne, C. R. (2009). Peer reputations and psychological adjustment. In K. H. Rubin, W. M. Bukowski, & B. Laursen (Eds.), *Handbook of peer interactions, relationships, and groups*. New York: Guilford.

Prior, A., & MacWhinney, B. (2010). A bilingual advantage in task switching. *Bilingualism: Language and Cognitive, 13*, 253–262.

Prior, E., Santhakumaran, S., Gale, C., Phillipps, L. H., Modi, N., & Hyde, M. J. (2012). Breastfeeding after cesarean delivery: A systematic review and meta-analysis of world literature. *American Journal of Clinical Nutrition, 95*, 1113–1135.

Proctor, R. M. J., & Burnett, P. C. (2004). Measuring cognitive and dispositional characteristics of creativity in elementary students. *Creativity Research Journal, 16*, 421–429.

Proffitt, J. B., Coley, J. D., & Medin, D. L. (2000). Expertise and category-based induction. *Journal of Experimental Psychology: Learning, Memory, and Cognition, 26*, 811–828.

Pruden, S. M., Hirsh-Pasek, K., Golinkoff, R. M., & Hennon, E. A. (2006). The birth of words: Ten-month-olds learn words through perceptual salience. *Child Development, 77*, 266–280.

Pudrovska, T., Schieman, S., & Carr, D. (2006). Strains of singlehood in later life: Do race and gender matter? *Journals of Gerontology: Social Sciences, 61B*, S315–S322.

Pujol, J., Soriano-Mas, C., Ortiz, H., Sebastián-Gallés, N., Losilla, J. M., & Deus, J. (2006). Myelination of language-related areas in the developing brain. *Neurology, 66*, 339–343.

Pulkkinen, L., & Kokko, K. (2012). Foundational issues in longitudinal data collection. In B. Laursen, T. D. Little, & N. A. Card (Eds.), *Handbook of developmental research methods* (pp. 129–147). New York: Guilford.

Puma, M., Bell, S., Cook, R., Heid, C., Broene, P., Jenkins, F., et al. (2012). *Third grade follow-up to the Head Start impact study final report, executive summary* (OPRE Report # 2012-45b). Washington, DC: Office of Planning, Research and Evaluation, Administration for Children and Families, U.S. Department of Health and Human Services.

Punnoose, A. R., Lynm, C., & Golub, R. M. (2012). Adult hearing loss. *Journal of the American Medical Association, 307*, 1215.

Purifoy, F. E., Grodsky, A., & Giambra, L. M. (1992). The relationship of sexual daydreaming to sexual activity, sexual drive, and sexual attitudes for women across the life-span. *Archives of Sexual Behavior, 21*, 369–385.

Putallaz, M., & Wasserman, A. (1989). Children's naturalistic entry behavior and sociometric status: A developmental perspective. *Developmental Psychology, 25*, 297–305.

Putnam, F. W. (2003). Ten-year research update review: Child sexual abuse. *Journal of the American Academy of Child and Adolescent Psychiatry, 42*, 269–278.

Putnam, S. P., Gartstein, M. A., & Rothbart, M. K. (2006). Measurement of fine-grained aspects of toddler temperament: The Early Childhood Behavior Questionnaire. *Infant Behavior and Development, 29*, 386–401.

Pyszczynski, T., Solomon, S., & Greenberg, J. (2003). *In the wake of 9/11: The psychology of terror*. Washington, DC: American Psychological Association.

Qui, C., & Fratiglioni, L. (2009). Epidemiology of Alzheimer's disease. In G. Waldemar & A. Burns (Eds.), *Alzheimer's disease*. Oxford: Oxford University Press.

Quigley, B. A. (1997). *Rethinking literacy education: The critical need for practice-based change*. San Francisco: Jossey-Bass.

Quigley, B. A., & Uhland, R. L. (2000). Retaining adult learners in the first three critical weeks: A quasi-experimental model for use in ABE programs. *Adult Basic Education, 10*, 55–68.

Quigley, M. A., Hockley, C., Carson, C., Kelly, Y., Renfrew, M. J., & Sacker, A. (2012). Breastfeeding is associated with improved child cognitive development: A population-based cohort study. *The Journal of Pediatrics, 160*, 25–32.

Quill, T. E. (1993). *Death and dignity: Making choices and taking charge*. New York: W. W. Norton.

Quinn, P. C., Yahr, J., Kuhn, A., Slater, A. M., & Pascalis, O. (2002). Representation of the gender of human faces by infants: A preference for female. *Perception, 31*, 1109–1121.

Raaijmakers, Q. A. W., Engels, R. C. M. E., & Van Hoof, A. (2005). Delinquency and moral reasoning in adolescence and young adulthood. *International Journal of Behavioral Development, 29*, 247–258.

Rabbani, A., Khodal, S., Mohammad, K., Sotoudeh, A., Karbakhsh, M., Nouri, K., et al. (2008). Pubertal development in a random sample of 4.020 urban Iranian girls. *Journal of Pediatric Endocrinology & Metabolism, 21*, 681–687.

Rabbitt, P., Chetwynd, A., & McInnes, L. (2003). Do clever brains age more slowly? Further exploration of a nun result. *British Journal of Psychology, 94*, 63–71.

Raby, K. L., Cicchetti, D., Carlson, E. A., Cutuli, J. J., Englund, M. M., & Egeland, B. (2012). Genetic and caregiving-based contributions to infant attachment: Unique associations with distress reactivity and attachment security. *Psychological Science, 23*, 1016–1023.

Ragow-O'Brien, D., Hayslip, B., & Guarnaccia, C. A. (2000). The impact of hospice on attitudes toward funerals and subsequent bereavement adjustment. *Omega: Journal of Death and Dying, 41*, 291–305.

Ramey, C. T., & Ramey, S. L. (1992). Effective early intervention. *Mental Retardation, 30*, 337–345.

Ramvi, E., & Tangerud, M. (2011). Experiences of women who have a vaginal birth after requesting a cesarean section due to fear of birth: A biographical, narrative, interpretative study. *Nursing and Health Sciences, 13*, 269–274.

Rando, T. A. (1986). A comprehensive analysis of anticipatory grief: Perspectives, processes, promises, and problems. In T. A. Rando (Ed.), *Loss and anticipatory grief*. Lexington, MA: Lexington Books.

Rando, T. A., Doka, K. J., Fleming, S., Franco, M. H., Lobb, E. A., Parkes, C. M., & Steele, R. (2012). A call to the field: Complicated grief in the DSM-5. *Omega, 65*, 251–255.

Rantanen, T., Guralnik, J. M., Foley, D., Masaki, K., Leveille, S., Curb, J. D., et al. (1999). Midlife hand grip strength as a predictor of old age disability. *Journal of the American Medical Association, 281*, 558–560.

Rantanen, T., Masaki, K., He, Q., Ross, G. W., Willcox, B. J., & White, L. (2012). Midlife muscle strength and human longevity up to age 100 years: a 44-year prospective study among a decedent cohort. *Age, 34*, 563–70.

Raphael, B. (1983). *The anatomy of bereavement*. New York: Basic Books.

Rapkin, B. D., & Fischer, K. (1992). Personal goals of older adults: Issues in assessment and prediction. *Psychology and Aging, 7*, 127–137.

Rattan, A., Good, C., & Dweck, C. S. (2012). "It's ok — Not everyone can be good at math": Instructors with an entity theory comfort (and demotivate) students. *Journal of Experimental Social Psychology, 48*, 731–737.

Rattaz, C., Goubet, N., & Bullinger, A. (2005). The calming effect of a familiar odor on full-term newborns. *Journal of Developmental and Behavioral Pediatrics, 26*, 86–92.

Raz, S., Goldstein, R., Hopkins, T. L., Lauterbach, M. D., Shah, F., Porter, C. L., et al. (1994). Sex differences in early vulnerability to cerebral injury and their neurodevelopmental implications. *Psychobiology, 22*, 244–253.

Rebacz, E. (2009). Age at menarche in schoolgirls from Tanzania in light of socioeconomic and sociodemographic conditioning. *Collegium Antropologicum, 33*, 23–29.

Redding, R. E., Harmon, R. J., & Morgan, G. A. (1990). Maternal depression and infants' mastery behaviors. *Infant Behavior and Development, 13*, 391–395.

Reder, L. M., Wible, C., & Martin, J. (1986). Differential memory changes with age: Exact retrieval versus plausible inference. *Journal of Experimental Psychology: Learning, Memory, and Cognition, 12*, 72–81.

Reed, A. E., & Carstensen, L. L. (2012). The theory behind the age-related positivity effect. *Frontiers in Psychology, 3*, Article 339.Published online September 27 2012, doi:10.3389/fpsyg.2012.00339

Reed, T., & Dick, D. M. (2003). Heritability and validity of healthy physical aging (wellness) in elderly male twins. *Twin Research, 6*, 227–234.

Rees, M. (1993). Menarche when and why? *Lancet, 342*, 1375–1376.

Reese, E., Hayne, H., & MacDonald, S. (2008). Looking back to the future: Mäori and Pakeha mother-child birth stories. *Child Development, 79*, 114–125.

Regan, P. C. (2008). *The mating game* (2nd ed.). Thousand Oaks, CA: Sage.

Regan, P. C. (2008). *The mating game* (2nd ed.). Thousand Oaks, CA: Sage.

Reichow, B., & Wolery, M. (2009).Comprehensive synthesis of early intensive behavioral interventions for young children with autism based on the UCLA Young Autism Project model.*Journal of Autism and Developmental Disorders, 39*, 23–41.

Reilly, D., & Neumann, D. (2013). Gender-role differences in spatial ability: A meta-analytic review. *Sex Roles, 68*, 521–535.

Reinhardt, J. P., Boerner, K., & Horowitz, A. (2009). Personal and social resources and adaptation to chronic vision impairment over time. *Aging & Mental Health, 13*, 367–375.

Reinherz, H. Z., Giaconia, R. M., Hauf, A. M. C., Wasserman, M. S., & Silverman, A. B. (1999). Major depression in the transition to adulthood: Risks and impairments. *Journal of Abnormal Psychology, 108*, 500–510.

Reinherz, H. Z., Tanner, J. L., Berger, S. R., Beardslee, W. R., & Fitzmaurice, G. M. (2006). Adolescent suicidal ideation as predictive of psychopathology, suicidal behavior, and compromised functioning at age 30. *American Journal of Psychiatry, 163*, 1226–1232.

Reis, H. T., & Aron, A. (2008). Love: What is it, why does it matter, and how does it operate? *Perspectives on Psychological Science, 3*, 80–86.

Reis, H. T., Lin, Y., Bennett, M. E., & Nezlek, J. B. (1993). Change and consistency in social participation during early adulthood. *Developmental Psychology, 29*, 633–645.

Reis, O., & Youniss, J. (2004). Patterns of identity change and development in relationships with mothers and friends. *Journal of Adolescent Research, 19*, 31–44.

Reis, S. M., & Renzulli, J. S. (2011). Intellectual giftedness. In R. J. Sternberg & S. B. Kaufman (Eds.), *The Cambridge handbook of intelligence* (pp. 235–252). New York: Cambridge University Press.

Reiss, D., & Neiderhiser, J. M. (2000). The interplay of genetic influences and social processes in developmental theory: Specific mechanisms are coming into view. *Development and Psychopathology, 12*, 357–374.

Reiss, D., & Neiderhiser, J. M. (2011). Marital dynamics and child proaction. Genetics takes a second look at developmental theory. In K. A. Dodge & M. Rutter (Eds.), *Gene-environment interactions in developmental psychopathology*. New York: Guilford.

Reiss, D., Neiderhiser, J. M., Hetherington, E. M., & Plomin, R. (2000). *The relationship code: Deciphering genetic and social influences on adolescent development*. Cambridge, MA: Harvard University Press.

Reiter, E. O., Price, D. A., Wilton, P., Albertsson-Wikland, K., & Ranke, M. B. (2006). Effect of growth hormone (GH) treatment on the near-final height of 1258 patients with idiopathic GH deficiency: Analysis of a large international database. *The Journal of Clinical Endocrinology and Metabolism, 91*, 2147–2054.

Reitzes, D. C., & Mutran, E. J. (2004). Grandparenthood: Factors influencing frequency of grandparent–grandchildren contact and grandparent role satisfaction. *Journal of Gerontology: Social Sciences, 59B*, S9–S16.

Reker, G. T., Peacock, E. J., & Wong, P. T. P. (1987). Meaning and purpose in life and well-being: A life-span perspective. *Journal of Gerontology, 42*, 44–49.

Rempel, J. (1985). Childless elderly: What are they missing? *Journal of Marriage and the Family, 47*, 343–348.

Renzulli, J., & Delcourt, M. A. B. (2013). Gifted behaviors versus gifted individuals. In C. Callahan & H. H. Davis (Eds.), *Fundamentals of gifted education: Considering multiple perspectives* (pp. 36–48). New York: Taylor & Francis.

Renzulli, J. S. (1998). The three-ring conception of giftedness. In S. M. Baum, S. M. Reis, & L. R. Maxfield (Eds.), *Nurturing the gifts and talents of primary grade students*. Mansfield Center, CT: Creative Learning Press.

Repacholi, B. M., & Gopnik, A. (1997). Early reasoning about desires: Evidence from 14- and 18-month-olds. *Developmental Psychology, 33*, 12–21.

Repacholi, B., Slaughter, V., Pritchard, M., & Gibbs, V. (2003). Theory of mind, Machiavellianism, and social functioning in childhood. In B. Repacholi & V. Slaughter (Eds.). *Individual differences in theory of mind: Implications for typical and atypical development*. New York: Psychology Press.

Repetti, R., Wang, S., & Saxbe, D. (2009). Bringing it all back home. How outside stressors shape families' everyday lives. *Current Directions in Psychological Science, 18*, 106–111.

Rescorla, L. A., Achenbach, T. M., Ginzburg, S., Ivanova, M., Dumenci, L., Almqvist, F., et al. (2007). Consistency of teacher-reported problems for students in 21 countries. *School Psychology Review, 36*, 91–110.

Resnick, S. M. (2000). One-year age changes in MRI brain volumes in older adults. *Cerebral Cortex, 10*, 464–472.

Resnick, S. M., Berenbaum, S. A., Gottesman, I. I., & Bouchard, T. J., Jr. (1986). Early hormonal influences on cognitive functioning in congenital adrenal hyperplasia. *Developmental Psychology, 22*, 191–198.

Rest, J., Narvaez, D., Bebeau, M. J., & Thoma, S. J. (1999). *Postconventional moral thinking. A neo-Kohlbergian approach*. Mahwah, NJ: Erlbaum.

Reuben, D. B., Walsh, K., Moore, A. A., Damesyn, M., & Greendale, G. A. (1998). Hearing loss in community-dwelling older persons: National prevalence data and identification using simple questions. *Journal of the American Geriatric Society, 46*, 1008–1011.

Reuter-Lorenz, P. A., & Cappell, K. A. (2008). Neurocognitive aging and the compensation hypothesis. *Current Directions in Psychological Science, 17*, 177–182.

Reyes-Rodríguez, M. L., Von Holle, A., Ulman, T. F., Thornton, L. M., Klump, K. L., Brandt, H., et al. (2011). Posttraumatic stress disorder in anorexia nervosa. *Psychosomatic Medicine, 73*, 491–497.

Reyna, V. F., & Brainerd, C. J. (1995). Fuzzy-trace theory: An interim synthesis. *Learning and Individual Differences, 7*, 1–75.

Reynolds, B. M., & Juvonen, J. (2012). Pubertal timing fluctuations across middle school: Implications for girls' psychological health. *Journal of Youth & Adolescence, 41*, 677–690.

Reznikoff, M., Domino, G., Bridges, C., & Honeyman, M. (1973). Creative abilities in identical and fraternal twins. *Behavior Genetics, 3*, 365–377.

Rhee, S. H., & Waldman, I. D. (2002). Genetic and environmental influences on antisocial behavior: A meta-analysis of twin and adoption studies. *Psychological Bulletin, 128*, 490–529.

Rheingold, A. A., Smith, D. W., Ruggiero, K. J., Saunders, B. E., Kilpatrick, D. G., & Resnick, H. S. (2004). Loss, trauma exposure, and mental health in a representative sample of 12-17-year-old youth: Data from the national survey of adolescents. *Journal of Loss and Trauma, 9*, 1–19.

Rhodes, M., & Brickman, D. (2008). Preschoolers' responses to social comparisons involving relative failure. *Psychological Science, 19*, 968–972.

Rhodes, S. R. (1983). Age-related differences in work attitudes and behavior: A review and conceptual analysis. *Psychological Bulletin, 93*, 328–367.

Ribeiro, F., de Mendonca, A., & Guerreiro, M. (2006). Mild cognitive impairment: Deficits in cognitive domains other than memory. *Dementia and Geriatric Cognitive Disorders, 21*, 284–290.

Ricciardelli, L. A., & McCabe, M. P. (2001). Children's body image concerns and eating disturbance: A review of the literature. *Clinical Psychology Review, 21*, 325–344.

Ricco, R. B. (1990). Necessity and the logic of entailment. In W. Overton (Ed.), *Reasoning, necessity, and logic: Developmental perspectives* (pp. 45–66). Hillsdale, NJ: Lawrence Earlbaum.

Rice, F., & Thapar, A. (2009). Depression and anxiety in childhood and adolescence: Developmental pathways, genes and environment. In Y. Kim (Ed.), *Handbook of behavior genetics*. New York: Springer.

Rice, F., Harold, G. T., & Thapar, A. (2003). Negative life events as an account of age-related differences in the genetic aetiology of depression in childhood and adolescence. *Journal of Child Psychology and Psychiatry and Allied Disciplines, 44*, 977–987.

Rice, F., Harold, G. T., Boivin, J., van den Bree, M., Hay, D. F., & Thapar, A. (2010). The links between prenatal stress and offspring development and psychopathology: Disentangling environmental and inherited influences. *Psychological Medicine, 40*, 335–345.

Richard, J. F., Normandeau, J., Brun, V., & Maillet, M. (2004). Attracting and maintaining infant attention during habituation: Further evidence of the importance of stimulus complexity. *Infant and Child Development, 13*, 277–286.

Richards, H. J., & Hadwin, J. A. (2011). An exploration of the relationship between trait anxiety and school attendance in young people. *School Mental Health, 3*, 236–244.

Richards, R. (1996). Beyond Piaget: Accepting divergent, chaotic, and creative thought. In M. A. Runco (Ed.), *Creativity from childhood through adulthood: The developmental issues*. San Francisco: Jossey-Bass.

Richert, R. A., Robb, M. B., Fender, J. G., & Wartella, E. (2010). Word learning from baby videos. *Archives of Pediatric and Adolescent Medicine, 164*, 432–437.

Riediger, M., Li, S., & Lindenberger, U. (2006). Selection, optimization, and compensation as developmental mechanisms of adaptive resource allocation: Review and preview. In J. E. Birren & K. W. Schaie (Eds.), *Handbook of the psychology of aging*. Boston: Elsevier Academic Press.

Riediger, M., Schmiedek, F., Wagner, G. G., & Lindenberger, U. (2009). Seeking pleasure and seeking pain. Differences in prohedonic and contra-hedonic motivation from adolescence to old age. *Psychological Science, 20*, 1529–1535.

Riegel, K. F. (1973). Dialectic operations: The final period of cognitive development. *Human Development, 16*, 346–370.

Rieger, G., & Savin-Williams, R. C. (2012). Gender nonconformity, sexual orientation, and psychological well-being. *Archives of Sexual Behavior, 41*, 611–621.

Rieser, J., Yonas, A., & Wilkner, K. (1976). Radial localization of odors by human newborns. *Child Development, 47*, 856–859.

Rigby, K. (2012). Bullying in schools: Addressing desires, not only behaviours. *Educational Psychology Review, 24*, 339–348.

Riggio, H. R., & Desrochers, S. (2005). The influence of maternal employment on the work and family expectations of offspring. In D. F. Halpern & S. E. Murphy (Eds.), *From work-family balance to work-family interaction: Changing the metaphor*. Mahwah, NJ: Erlbaum.

Riggs, S. A., & Riggs, D. S. (2011). Risk and resilience in military families experiencing deployment: The role of the family attachment network. *Journal of Family Psychology, 25*, 675–687.

Riley, L. P., LaMontagne, L. L., Hepworth, J. T., & Murphy, B. A. (2007). Parental grief responses and personal growth following the death of a child. *Death Studies, 31*, 277–299.

Ringler, L. L., & Hayden, D. C. (2000). Adolescent bereavement and social support: Peer loss compared to other losses. *Journal of Adolescent Research, 15*, 209–230.

Ripley, A. (2010, April 8). Should kids be bribed to do well in school? *Time*. Retrieved from www.time.com/time/printout/0,8816,1978589,00.html.

Ristic, J., & Kingstone, A. (2009). Rethinking attentional development: Reflexive and volitional orienting in children and adults. *Developmental Science, 12*, 289–296.

Rith, K. A., & Diamond, L. M. (2013). Same-sex relationships. In M. A. Fine & F. D. Fincham (Eds.), *Handbook of family theories. A context-based approach*. New York: Routledge.

Rizzolatti, G., & Sinigaglia, C. (2008). *Mirrors in the brain: How our minds share actions, emotions* (F. Anderson, Trans.). Oxford, NY: Oxford University Press. (Original work published 2006).

Robb, M. B., Richert, R. A., & Wartella, E. A. (2009). Just a talking book? Word learning from watching baby videos. *British Journal of Developmental Psychology, 27*, 27–45.

Roberts, B. W., & Caspi, A. (2003). The cumulative continuity model of personality development: Striking a balance between continuity and change in personality traits across the life course. In U. M. Staudinger & U. Lindenberger (Eds.), *Understanding human development: Dialogues with life-span psychology*. Dordrecht, Netherlands: Kluwer Academic.

Roberts, B. W., & Robins, R. W. (2004). Person–environment fit and its implications for personality development: A longitudinal study. *Journal of Personality, 72*, 89–110.

Roberts, B. W., Donnellan, M. B., & Hill, P. L. (2013). Personality trait development in adulthood. In H. Tennen, J. Suls & I. B Weiner (Eds.), *Handbook of psychology: Vol. 5. Personality and social psychology* (2nd ed.). Hoboken, NJ: John Wiley & Sons Inc.

Roberts, B. W., Walton, K. E., & Viechtbauer, W. (2006). Patterns of mean-level change in personality traits across the life course: A meta-analysis of longitudinal studies. *Psychological Bulletin, 132*, 1–25.

Roberts, B. W., Wood, D., & Caspi, A. (2008). The development of personality traits in adulthood. In O. P. John, R. W. Robins, & L. A. Pervin (Eds.), *Handbook of personality theory and research* (3rd ed.). New York: Guilford.

Roberts, L. R., Sarigiani, P. A., Petersen, A. C., & Newman, J. L. (1990). Gender differences in the relationship between achievement and self image during early adolescence. *Journal of Early Adolescence, 10*, 159–175.

Roberts, S. E., Wotton, C. J., Williams, J. G., Griffith, M., & Goldacre, M. J. (2011). Perinatal and early life risk factors for inflammatory bowel disease. *World Journal of Gastroenterology, 17*, 743–749.

Robins, L. N., & Regier, D. A. (Eds.). (1991). *Psychiatric disorders in America. The Epidemiologic Catchment Area Study*. New York: The Free Press.

Robins, R. W., Caspi, A., & Moffitt, T. E. (2000). Two personalities, one relationship: Both partners' personality traits shape the quality of their relationship. *Journal of Personality and Social Psychology, 79*, 251–259.

Robins, R. W., Trzesniewski, K. H., Tracy, J. L., Gosling, S. D., & Potter, J. (2002). Global self-esteem across the life span. *Psychology and Aging, 17*, 423–434.

Robinson Center. (2013). Retrieved from https://depts.washington.edu/cscy

Robinson, C. C., & Morris, J. T. (1986). The gender-stereotyped nature of Christmas toys received by 36-, 48-, and 60-month-old children: A comparison between nonrequested vs. requested toys. *Sex Roles, 15*, 21–32.

Robinson, E. B., Koenen, K. C., McCormick, M. C., Munir, K., Hallett, V., Happé, F., et al. (2011). Evidence that autistic traits show the same etiology in the general population and at the quantitative extremes (5%, 2.5%, and 1%). *Archives of General Psychiatry, 68*, 1113–1121.

Robinson, O. C., Demetre, J. D., & Corney, R. (2010). Personality and retirement: Exploring the links between the Big Five personality traits, reasons for retirement and the experience of being retired. *Personality and Individual Differences, 48*, 792–797.

Robinson, P. K. (1983). The sociological perspective. In R. B. Weg (Ed.), *Sexuality in the later years: Roles and behavior*. New York: Academic Press.

Robinson, T., & Marwit, S. J. (2006). An investigation of the relationship of personality, coping, and grief intensity among bereaved mothers. *Death Studies, 30*, 677–696.

Robles-De-La-Torre, G. (2006, July-September). The importance of the sense of touch in virtual and real environment. *IEEE MultiMedia*, 24–30.

Rochat, P. (2010). The innate sense of the body develops to become a public affair by 2-3 years. *Neuropsychologia, 48*, 738–745.

Rochat, P., & Striano, T. (2000). Perceived self in infancy. *Infant Behavior and Development, 23*, 513–530.

Rochat, P., Broesch, T., & Jayne, K. (2012). Social awareness and early self-recognition. *Consciousness and Cognition: An International Journal,21*, 1491–1497.

Rochman, B. (2012, February 27). Early decision: Will new advances in prenatal testing shrink the ranks of babies with Down syndrome? *Time*, pp. 35–40.

Röcke, C., & Cherry, K. E. (2002). Death at the end of the 20th century: Individual processes and developmental tasks in old age. *International Journal of Aging and Human Development, 54*, 315–333.

Rodin, J., & Langer, E. (1980). Aging labels: The decline of control and the fall of self-esteem. *Journal of Social Issues, 36*, 12–29.

Rodriguez, A., Olsen, J., Kotimaa, A. J., Kaakinen, M., Moilanen, I., Henriksen, T. B., Linnet, K. M., Miettunen, J., Obel, C., Taanila, A., Ebeling, H., & Järvelin, M. R. (2009). Is prenatal alcohol exposure related to inattention and hyperactivity symptoms in children? Disentangling the effects of social adversity. *Journal of Child Psychology and Psychiatry, 50*, 1073–1083.

Rogers, L. O., Zosuls, K. M., Halim, M. L., Ruble, D., Hughes, D., & Fuligni, A. (2012). Meaning making in middle childhood: An exploration of the meaning of ethnic identity. *Cultural Diversity and Ethnic Minority Psychology, 18*, 99–108.

Rogoff, B. (1998). Cognition as a collaborative process. In D. Kuhn & R. S. Siegler (Vol. Eds.), W. Damon (Editor-in-Chief), *Handbook of child psychology: Cognition, perception, and language* (5th ed.). New York: Wiley.

Rogoff, B. (2003). *The cultural nature of human development*. New York: Oxford University Press.

Rogoff, B., Morelli, G. A., & Chavajay, P. (2010). Children's integration in communities and segregation from people of differing ages. *Perspectives on Psychological Science, 5*, 431–440.

Rohde, P., Lewinsohn, P. M., Klein, D. N., Seeley, J. R., & Gau, J. M. (2013). Key characteristics of major depressive disorder occurring in childhood, adolescence, emerging adulthood, and adulthood. *Clinical Psychological Science, 1*, 41–53.

Roid, G. (2003). *Stanford-Binet Intelligence Scales* (5th ed.). Itasca, IL: Riverside Publishing.

Roisman, G. I. (2007). The psychopathology of adult attachment relationships: Autonomic reactivity in marital and premarital interactions. *Developmental Psychology, 43,* 39–53.

Roisman, G. I. (2009). Adult attachment. Toward a rapprochement of methodological cultures. *Current Directions in Psychological Science, 18,* 122–126.

Roisman, G. I., & Fraley, R. C. (2008). A behavior-genetic study of parenting quality, infant attachment security, and their covariation in a nationally representative sample. *Developmental Psychology, 44,* 831–839.

Roisman, G. I., & Groh, A. M. (2011). Attachment theory and research in developmental psychology: An overview and appreciative critique. In M. K. Underwood & L. H. Rosen (Eds.), *Social development. Relationships in infancy, childhood, and adolescence.* New York: Guilford.

Roizen, N. J. (2013). Down syndrome (Trisomy 21). In M. L. Batshaw, N. J. Roizen, & G. R. Lotrecchiano (Eds.), *Children with disabilities* (7th ed., pp. 307–318). Baltimore: Paul H. Brookes.

Rollins, B. C., & Feldman, H. (1970). Marital satisfaction over the family life cycle. *Journal of Marriage and the Family, 32,* 20–28.

Rolls, B. J. (1999). Do chemosensory changes influence food intake in the elderly? *Physiological Behavior, 66,* 193–197.

Román, G. C. (2003). Neurological aspects of vascular dementia: Basic concepts, diagnosis, and management. In P. A. Lichtenberg, D. L. Murman, & A. M. Mellow (Eds.), *Handbook of dementia. Psychological, neurological, and psychiatric perspectives.* Hoboken, NJ: John Wiley & Sons.

Ronald, A., & Hoekstra, R. A. (2011). Autism spectrum disorders and autistic traits: A decade of new twin studies. *American Journal of Medical Genetics, Part B, Neuropsychiatric Genetics, 156B,* 255–274.

Rose, A. J., Carlson, W., & Waller, E. M. (2007). Prospective associations of co-rumination with friendship and emotional adjustment: Considering the socioemotional trade-offs of co-rumination. *Developmental Psychology, 43,* 1019–1031.

Rose, A. J., Schwartz-Mette, R. A., Smith, R. L., Asher, S. R., Swenson, L. P., Carlson, W., & Waller, E. M. (2012). How girls and boys expect disclosure about problems will make them feel: Implications for friendships. *Child Development, 83,* 844–863.

Rose, A. J., Swenson, L. P., & Waller, E. M. (2004). Overt and relational aggression and perceived popularity: Developmental differences in concurrent and prospective relations. *Developmental Psychology, 40,* 378–387.

Rose, A. J., & Swenson, L. P. (2009). Do perceived popular adolescents who aggress against others experience emotional adjustment problems themselves? Developmental Psychology, 45, 868–872.

Rose, L. T., & Fischer, K. W. (2007). Dynamics systems theory. In R. A. Shweder (Ed.), *Chicago Companion to the Child.* Chicago: University of Chicago Press

Rose, L. T., & Fischer, K. W. (2011). Intelligence in childhood. In R. Sternberg & S. B. Kaufman (Eds.), *The Cambridge handbook of intelligence* (pp. 144–173). New York: Cambridge University Press.

Rose, S. A., & Feldman, J. F. (1997). Memory and speed: Their role in the relation of infant information processing to later IQ. *Child Development, 68,* 630–641.

Rose, S. A., Feldman, J. F., & Jankowski, J. J. (2003). Infant visual recognition memory: Independent contributions of speed and attention. *Developmental Psychology, 39,* 563–571.

Rose, S. A., Feldman, J. F., Wallace, I. F., & McCarton, C. (1989). Infant visual attention: Relation to birth status and developmental outcome during the first 5 years. *Developmental Psychology, 25,* 560–576.

Rose, S. P., & Fischer, K. W. (1998). Models and rulers in dynamical development. *British Journal of Developmental Psychology, 16,* 123–131.

Rosenblatt, P. C. (1993). Cross-cultural variation in the experience, expression, and understanding of grief. In D. P. Irish, K. F. Lundquist, & V. J. Nelson (Eds.), *Ethnic variations in dying, death, and grief: Diversity in universality.* Washington, DC: Taylor and Francis.

Rosenblatt, P. C. (2008). Grief across cultures: A review and research agenda. In M. S. Stroebe, R. O. Hansson, H. Schut, & W. Stroebe (Eds.), *Handbook of bereavement research and practice. Advances in theory and intervention.* Washington, DC: American Psychological Association.

Rosenblatt, P. C. (2013). The concept of complicated grief: Lessons from other cultures. In M. Stroebe, H. Schut & J. van den Bout (Eds.), *Complicated grief: Scientific foundations for health care professionals.* New York: Routledge/Taylor & Francis.

Rosenbloom, C., & Bahns, M. (2006). What can we learn about diet and physical activity from master athletes? *Holistic Nursing Practice, 20,* 161–167.

Rosenkrantz, P., Vogel, S., Bee, H., Broverman, I., & Broverman, D. M. (1968). Sex-role stereotypes and self-concepts in college students. *Journal of Consulting and Clinical Psychology, 32,* 287–295.

Rosenthal, P. A., & Rosenthal, S. (1984). Suicidal behavior by preschool children. *American Journal of Psychiatry, 141,* 520–525.

Rosenzweig, M. R., & Bennett, E. L. (1996). Psychobiology of plasticity: Effects of training and experience on brain and behavior. *Behavioral Brain Research, 78,* 57–65.

Rosner, R., Kruse, J., & Hagl, M. (2010). A meta-analysis of interventions for bereaved children and adolescents. *Death Studies, 34,* 99–136.

Ross, E. E. T., & Aday, L. A. (2006). Stress and coping in African American grandparents who are raising their grandchildren. *Journal of Family Issues, 27,* 912–932.

Ross, H. G., & Milgram, J. I. (1982). Important variables in adult sibling relationships: A qualitative study. In M. E. Lamb & B. Sutton-Smith (Eds.), *Sibling relationships: Their nature and significance across the lifespan.* Hillsdale, NJ: Erlbaum.

Ross-Gordon, J. M. (2011, Winter). Research on adult learners: Supporting the needs of a student population that is no longer nontraditional. *Peer Review, 13*(1). Retrieved from http://www.aacu.org/peerreview/pr-will/prwill_rossgordon.cfm

Roth, F. P., Speece, D. L., & Cooper, D. H. (2002). A longitudinal analysis of the connection between oral language and early reading. *Journal of Educational Research, 95,* 259–272.

Roth, P. L., Bevier, C. A., Switzer, F. S., & Schippmann, J. S. (1996). Meta-analyzing the relationship between grades and job performance. *Journal of Applied Psychology, 81,* 548–556.

Roth, T. L. (2012). Epigenetics of neurobiology and behavior during development and adulthood. *Developmental Psychobiology, 54,* 590–597.

Rothbart, M. K. (2007). Temperament, development, and personality. *Current Directions in Psychological Science, 16,* 207–212.

Rothbart, M. K. (2011). *Becoming who we are: Temperament and personality development.* New York: Guilford.

Rothbart, M. K., & Bates, J. E. (2006). Temperament. In N. Eisenberg (Vol. Ed.) & W. Damon & R. M. Lerner (Eds. in Chief), *Handbook of child psychology: Vol. 3. Social, emotional, and personality development* (6th ed.). Hoboken, NJ: Wiley.

Rothbart, M. K., & Derryberry, D. (2002). Temperament in children. In C. von Hofsten & L. Backman (Eds.), *Psychology at the turn of the millennium: Vol. 2. Social, developmental, and clinical perspectives.* New York: Taylor & Francis.

Rothbart, M. K., Ahadi, S. A., & Evans, D. E. (2000). Temperament and personality: Origins and outcomes. *Journal of Personality and Social Psychology, 78,* 122–135.

Rothbaum, F., & Morelli, G. (2005). Attachment and culture: Bridging relativism and universalism. In W. Friedlmeier, P. Chakkarath, & B. Schwarz (Eds.), *Culture and human development: The importance of cross-cultural research for the social sciences.* New York: Psychology Press.

Rothbaum, F., & Trommsdorff, G. (2007). Do roots and wings complement or oppose one another? The socialization of relatedness and autonomy in cultural context. In J. E. Grusec & P. D. Hastings (Eds.), *Handbook of socialization: Theory and research.* New York: Guilford.

Rothbaum, F., Weisz, J., Pott, M., Miyake, K., & Morelli, G. (2000). Attachment and culture: Security in the United States and Japan. *American Psychologist, 55,* 1093–1104.

Rothbaum, F., Weisz, J., Pott, M., Miyake, K., & Morelli, G. (2000). Attachment and culture: Security in the United States and Japan. *American Psychologist, 55,* 1093–1104.

Rotheram-Borus, M. J., Piacentini, J., Cantwell, C., Belin, T. R., & Song, J. W. (2000). The

18-month impact of an emergency room-intervention for adolescent female suicide-attempters. *Journal of Consulting and Clinical Psychology, 68,* 1081–1093.

Rothermund, K., & Brandtstädter, J. (2003a). Age stereotypes and self-views in later life: Evaluating rival assumptions. *International Journal of Behavioral Development, 27,* 549–554.

Rothermund, K., & Brandtstädter, J. (2003b). Coping with deficits and losses in later life: From compensatory action to accommodation. *Psychology and Aging, 18,* 896–905.

Rovee-Collier, C., & Barr, R. (2004). Infant learning and memory. In G. Bremner & A. Fogel (Eds.), *Blackwell handbook of infant development* (pp. 139–168). Malden, MA: Blackwell Publishing.

Rovee-Collier, C., & Barr, R. (2010). Infant learning and memory. In J. G. Bremner & T. D. Wachs (Eds.), *The handbook of infant development, Vol. 1* (2nd ed., pp. 271–294). Malden, MA: John Wiley & Sons.

Rovee-Collier, C., & Cuevas, K. (2009a). Multiple memory systems are unnecessary to account for infant memory development: An ecological model. *Developmental Psychology, 45,* 160–174.

Rovee-Collier, C., & Cuevas, K. (2009b). The development of infant memory. In M. L. Courage & N. Cowan (Eds.), *The development of memory in infancy and childhood* (pp. 11–42). New York: Psychology Press.

Rovner, S. (1994, March 29). An Alzheimer's journal. *The Washington Post—Health,* pp. 12–15.

Rowe, J. W., & Kahn, R. L. (1998). *Successful aging.* New York: Pantheon.

Rowley, S. J., Jurtz-Costes, B., Mistry, R., & Feagans, L. (2007). Social status as a predictor of race and gender stereotypes in late childhood and early adolescence. *Social Development, 16,* 150–156.

Rubin, C., Maisonet, M., Kieszak, S., Monteilh, C., Holmes, A., Flanders, D., et al. (2009). Timing of maturation and predictors of menarche in girls enrolled in a contemporary British cohort. *Paediatric and Perinatal Epidemiology, 23,* 492–504.

Rubin, D. C. (2002). Autobiographical memory across the lifespan. In P. Graf & N. Ohta (Eds.), *Lifespan development of human memory* (pp. 159–184). Cambridge, MA: Massachusetts Institute of Technology.

Rubin, D. C. (2012). The basic systems model of autobiographical memory. In D. Berntsen & D. C. Rubin (Eds.), *Understanding autobiographical memory: Theories and approaches* (pp. 11–32). New York: Cambridge University Press.

Rubin, D. C., Wetzler, S. E., & Nebes, R. D. (1986). Autobiographical memory across the adult lifespan. In D. C. Rubin (Ed.), *Autobiographical memory across the lifespan.* Cambridge University Press.

Rubin, J. Z., Provenzano, F. J., & Luria, Z. (1974). The eye of the beholder: Parents' views on sex of newborns. *American Journal of Orthopsychiatry, 44,* 512–519.

Rubin, K. H., Bukowski, W. M., & Parker, J. G. (2006). Peer interactions, relationships, and groups. In N. Eisenberg (Vol. Ed.), & W. Damon & R. M. Lerner (Eds. in Chief), *Handbook of child psychology: Vol. 3. Social, emotional, and personality development* (6th ed.). Hoboken, NJ: Wiley.

Rubin, K. H., Coplan, R. J., & Bowker, J. C. (2009). Social withdrawal in childhood. *Annual Review of Psychology, 60,* 141–171.

Rubin, K. H., Coplan, R., Chen, X., Bowker, J., & McDonald, K. L. (2011). Peer relationships in childhood. In M. E. Lamb & M. H. Bornstein (Eds.), *Social and personality development. An advanced textbook.* New York: Psychology Press.

Rubin, R. (2012, November 27). New fetal test creates dilemma for some women. *The Washington Post,* pp. E1, E6.

Rubinow, D. R., & Schmidt, P. J. (1996). Androgens, brain, and behavior. *American Journal of Psychiatry, 153,* 974–984.

Rubinstein, R. L., Alexander, R. B., Goodman, M., & Luborsky, M. (1991). Key relationships of never married, childless older women: A cultural analysis. *Journal of Gerontology: Social Sciences, 46,* S270–S277.

Rubio-Fernández, P., & Glucksberg, S. (2012). Reasoning about other people's beliefs: Bilinguals have an advantage. *Journal of Experimental Psychology: Learning, Memory, and Cognition, 38,* 211–217.

Ruble, D. N., & Dweck, C. S. (1995). Self-conceptions, person conceptions, and their development. In N. Eisenberg (Ed.), *Social development.* Thousand Oaks, CA: Sage.

Ruble, D. N., Eisenberg, R., & Higgins, E. T. (1994). Developmental changes in achievement evaluation: Motivational implications of self-other differences. *Child Development, 65,* 1095–1110.

Ruble, D. N., Lurye, L. E., & Zosuls, K. M. (2007). *Pink frilly dresses (PFD) and early gender identity. Princeton Report on Knowledge, vol 2.* Retrieved from http://www.princeton.edu/prok/issues/2-2/pink_frilly.xml

Ruble, D. N., Taylor, L. J., Cypers, L., Greulich, F. K., Lurye, L. E., & Shrout, P. E. (2007). The role of gender constancy in early gender development. *Child Development, 78,* 1121–1136.

Rucker, J. H., & McGuffin, P. (2012). Genomic structural variation in psychiatric disorders. *Development and Psychopathology, 24,* 1335–1344.

Rudd, M. D., Berman, A. L., Joiner, T. E. Jr., Nock, M. K., Silverman, M. M., Mandrusiak, M., et al. (2006). Warning signs for suicide: Theory, research, and clinical applications. *Suicide and Life-Threatening Behavior, 36,* 255–262.

Rudman, L. A., Fetterolf, J. C., & Sanchez, D. T. (2013). What motivates the sexual double standard? More support for male versus female control theory. *Social Psychology Bulletin, 39,* 250–263.

Rudolph, K. D., & Flynn, M. (2007). Childhood adversity and youth depression: Influence of gender and pubertal status. *Development and Psychopathology, 19,* 497–521.

Rueda, M. R. (2012). Effortful control. In M. Z. Zentner & R. L. Shiner (Eds.), *Handbook of temperament.* New York: Guilford.

Ruff, H. A., & Capozzoli, M. C. (2003). Development of attention and distractibility in the first 4 years of life. *Developmental Psychology, 39,* 877–890.

Ruff, H. A., & Lawson, K. R. (1990). Development of sustained, focused attention in young children during free play. *Developmental Psychology, 26,* 85–93.

Ruff, H. A., & Rothbart, M. K. (1996). *Attention in early development: Themes and variations.* New York: Oxford University Press.

Ruffman, T. K., & Olson, D. R. (1989). Children's ascriptions of knowledge to others. *Developmental Psychology, 25,* 601–606.

Ruffman, T., Slade, L., & Redman, J. (2005). Young infants' expectations about hidden objects. *Cognition, 97,* 835–843.

Ruffman, T., Slade, L., Sandino, J. C., & Fletcher, A. (2005). Are A-Not-B errors caused by a belief about object location? *Child Development, 76,* 122–136.

Ruggles, S. (1994). The origins of African-American family structure. *American Sociological Review, 59,* 136–151.

Ruiz, S. A., & Silverstein, M. (2007). Relationships with grandparents and the emotional well-being of late adolescence and young adult grandchildren. *Journal of Social Issues, 63,* 793–808.

Runco, M. A. (2007). *Creativity—Theories and themes: Research, development, and practice.* Burlington, MA: Elsevier Academic Press.

Runco, M. A. (2010). Divergent thinking, creativity, and ideation. In J. C. Kaufman & R. J. Sternberg (Eds.), *The Cambridge handbook of creativity, v Vol. 2* (pp. 413–446). New York: Cambridge University Press.

Russell, A., Aloa, V., Feder, T., Glover, A., Miller, H., & Palmer, G. (1998). Sex-based differences in parenting styles in a sample with preschool children. *Australian Journal of Psychology, 50,* 89–99.

Rust, J., Golombok, S., Hines, M., Johnston, K., & Golding, J. (2000). The role of brothers and sisters in the gender development of preschool children. *Journal of Experimental Child Psychology, 77,* 292–303.

Rutgers, A. H., Bakermans-Kranenburg, M., van IJzendoorn, M. H., & van Berckelaer-Onnes, I. A. (2004). Autism and attachment: A meta-analytic review. *Journal of Child Psychology and Psychiatry, 45,* 1123–1134.

Rutter, M. (1983). School effects on pupil progress: Research findings and policy implications. *Child Development, 54,* 1–29.

Rutter, M., & Maughan, B. (2002). School effectiveness findings 1979–2002. *Journal of School Psychology, 50,* 451–475.

Rutter, M., & Sroufe, L. A. (2000). Developmental psychopathology: Concepts and challenges. *Development and Psychopathology, 12,* 265–296.

Rutter, M., Kim-Cohen, J., & Maughan, B. (2006). Continuities and discontinuities in psychopathology between childhood and adult life. *Journal of Child Psychology and Psychiatry, 47*, 276–295.

Rutter, M., Moffitt, T. E., & Caspi, A. (2006). Gene–environment interplay and psychopathology: Multiple varieties but real effects. *Journal of Child Psychology and Psychiatry, 47*, 226–261.

Ryan, R. M., & Kuczkowski, R. (1994). The imaginary audience, self-consciousness, and public individuation in adolescence. *Journal of Personality, 62*, 219–238.

Ryan, S., Manlove, J., & Franzetta, K. (2003). *The first time: Characteristics of teens' first sexual relationships* (Pub. no. 2003–16). Washington, DC: Child Trends.

Ryff, C. D. (1991). Possible selves in adulthood and old age: A tale of shifting horizons. *Psychology and Aging, 6*, 286–295.

Rypma, B., Prabhakaran, V., Desmond, J. E., & Gabrieli, J. D. E. (2001). Age differences in prefrontal cortical activity in working memory. *Psychology and Aging, 16*, 371–384.

Saarni, C. (1984). An observational study of children's attempts to monitor their expressive behavior. *Child Development, 55*, 1504–1513.

Saarni, C., Campos, J. J., Camras, L. A., & Withington, D. (2006). Emotional development: Action, communication, and understanding. In N. Eisenberg (Vol. Ed.), & W. Damon & R. M. Lerner (Eds. in Chief), *Handbook of child psychology: Vol. 3. Social, emotional, and personality development* (6th ed.). Hoboken, NJ: Wiley.

Sabattini, L., & Leaper, C. (2004). The relation between mothers' and fathers' parenting styles and their division of labor in the home: Young adults' retrospective reports. *Sex Roles, 50*, 217–225.

Sabbagh, M. A. (2006). Neurocognitive bases of preschoolers' theory-of-mind development: Integrating cognitive neuroscience and cognitive development. In P. J. Marshall & N. A. Fox (Eds.), *The development of social engagement: Neurobiological perspectives.* New York: Oxford University Press.

Sachdeva, S., Singh, P., & Medin, D. (2011). Culture and the quest for universal principles in moral reasoning. *International Journal of Psychology, 46*, 161–176.

Sackett, P. R., Hardison, C. M., & Cullen, M. J. (2004). On interpreting stereotype threat as accounting for African American-White differences on cognitive tests. *American Psychologist, 59*, 7–13.

Sacks, O. (1993, December 27). A neurologist's notebook: An anthropologist on Mars. *The New Yorker*, 106–125.

Sadeh, A. (1994). Assessment of intervention for infant night waking: Parental reports and activity-based home monitoring. *Journal of Consulting and Clinical Psychology, 62*, 63–68.

Sadeh, A. (1996). Evaluating night wakings in sleep-disturbed infants: A methodological study of parental reports and actigraphy. *Sleep, 19*, 757–762.

Sadler, T. W. (2004). *Langman's Medical Embryology*, 9th ed. Baltimore: Lippincott Williams & Wilkins.

Sadler. (2012). *Langman's Medical Embryology* (12th ed.). Baltimore: Lippincott Williams & Wilkins.

Saffran, J. R., Werker, J. F., & Werner, L. A. (2006). The infant's auditory world: Hearing, speech, and the beginnings of language. In D. Kuhn & R. Siegler (Vol. Eds.), *Handbook of child psychology: Cognition, perception, and language: Vol. 2* (6th ed.). Hoboken, NJ: Wiley.

Sagara-Rosemeyer, M., & Davies, B. (2007). The integration of religious traditions in Japanese children's view of death and afterlife. *Death Studies, 31*, 223–247.

Şaahin, M. (2012). An investigation into the efficiency of empathy training program on preventing bullying in primary schools. *Children and Youth Services Review, 34*, 1325–1330.

Salapatek, P. (1975). Pattern perception in early infancy. In L. B. Cohen & P. Salapatek (Eds.), *Infant perception: From sensation to cognition, Vol 1.* New York: Academic Press.

Salmivalli, C., & Peets, K. (2009). Bullies, victims, and bully-victim relationships in middle childhood and early adolescence. In K. H. Rubin, W. M. Bukowski, & B. Laursen (Eds.), *Handbook of peer interactions, relationships, and groups.* New York: Guilford.

Salthouse, T. A. (1990). Cognitive competence and expertise in aging. In J. E. Birren & K. W. Schaie (Eds.), *The handbook of the psychology of aging* (3rd ed.). San Diego: Academic Press.

Salthouse, T. A. (1993). Speed and knowledge as determinants of adult age differences in verbal tasks. *Journal of Gerontology Series B: Psychological Sciences, 48*, 29–36.

Salthouse, T. A. (1996). General and specific speed mediation of adult age differences in memory. *Journals of Gerontology B: Psychological Sciences and Social Sciences, 51B*, 30–42.

Salthouse, T. A. (2000). Aging and measures of processing speed. *Biological Psychology, 54*, 35–54.

Salthouse, T. A., Hancock, H. E., Meinz, E. J., & Hambrick, D. Z. (1996). Interrelations of age, visual acuity, and cognitive functioning. *Journals of Gerontology: Psychological Sciences and Social Sciences, 51*, 317–330.

Sameroff, A. (1975). Early influences on development: Fact or fancy? *Merrill-Palmer Quarterly, 21*, 263–294.

Sameroff, A. J., Seifer, R., Baldwin, A., & Baldwin, C. (1993). Stability of intelligence from preschool to adolescence: The influence of social and family risk factors. *Child Development, 64*, 80–97.

Samnani, A., & Singh, P. (2012). 20 years of workplace bullying research: A review of the antecedents and consequences of bullying in the workplace. *Aggression and Violent Behavior, 17*, 581–589.

Samson, M. M., Meeuwsen, I. B. A. E., Crowe, A., Dessens, J. A. G., Duursma, S. A., & Verhaar, H. J. J. (2000). Relationships between physical performance measures, age, height and body weight in healthy adults. *Age and Ageing, 29*, 235–242.

Sanchez, L., Fristad, M., Weller, R. A., Weller, E. B., & Moye, J. (1994). Anxiety in acutely bereaved prepubertal children. *Annals of Clinical Psychiatry, 6*, 39–43.

Sandberg, D. E., Bukowski, W. M., Fung, C. M., Noll, R. B. (2004). Height and social adjustment: are extremes a cause for concern and action? *Pediatrics, 114*, 744–50.

Sanders, W. (1999, September 1). Teachers, teachers, teachers! *DLC: Blueprint Magazine*. Retrieved from www.dlc.org/ndol_ci.cfm?contentid=1199&kaid=110&subid=135

Sanders, W. L., & Horn, S. P. (1995). The Tennessee Value-Added Assessment System: (TVAAS): Mixed model methodology in educational assessment. In A. J. Shrinkfield & D. Stufflebeam (Eds.), *Teacher evaluation: Guide to effective practice* (pp. 337–350). Boston, MA: Kluwer.

Sanders, W. L., & Rivers, J. C. (1996, November). *Cumulative and residual effects of teachers on future student academic achievement* (Research Progress Report). Knoxville, TN: University of Tennessee Value-Added Research and Assessment Center.

Sandler, I. , Ayers, T. S., Tein, J., Wolchik, S., Millsap, R., Khoo, S. T., et al. (2010). Six-year follow-up of a preventive intervention for parentally bereaved youths. *Archives of Pediatric and Adolescent Medicine, 164*, 907–914.

Sandler, I. N., Ayers, T. S., Wolchik, S. A., Tein, J., Kwok, O., Haine, R. A., Twohey-Jacobs, J., Suter, J., Lin, K., Padgett-Jones, S., Weyer, J. L., Cole, E., Kriege, G., & Griffin, W. A. (2003). The Family Bereavement Program: Efficacy evaluation of a theory-based prevention program for parentally-bereaved children and adolescents. *Journal of Consulting and Clinical Psychology, 71*, 587–600.

Sandler, I. N., Ma, Y., Tein, J., Ayers, T. S., Wolchik, S., Kennedy, C., & Millsap, R. (2010). Long-term effects of the Family Bereavement Program on multiple indicators of grief in parentally bereaved children and adolescents. *Journal of Consulting and Clinical Psychology, 78*, 131–143.

Sandman, C. A., Davis, E. P., & Glynn, L. M. (2012). Prescient human fetuses thrive. *Psychological Science, 23*, 93–100.

Sapolsky, R. (1998). *The trouble with testosterone and other essays on the biology of the human predicament.* New York: Scribner.

Sargant, N., Field, J., Francis, H., Schuller, T., & Tuckett, A. (1997). *The learning divide.* Brighton, UK: National Organisation for Adult Learning.

Sarkisian, N., Gerena, M., & Gerstel, N. (2007). Extended family integration among Euro and Mexican Americans: Ethnicity, gender, and class. *Journal of Marriage and Family, 69*, 40–54.

Sartor, C. E., Grant, J. D., Bucholz, K. K., Madden, P. A. F., Heath, A. C., Agrawal, A., Whitfield, J. B., Statham, D. J., Martin, N. G., & Lynskey,

M. T. (2010). Common genetic contributions to alcohol and cannabis use and dependence symptomatology. *Alcoholism: Clinical and Experimental Research, 34,* 545–554.

Saucier, D., & Ehresman, C. (2010). The physiology of sex differences. In J. C. Chrisler & D. R. McCreary (Eds.), *Handbook of gender research in psychology* (pp. 215–233). New York: Spring Science+Business Media.

Saucier, G., & Simonds, J. (2006). The structure of personality and temperament. In D. K. Mroczek & T. D. Little (Eds.), *Handbook of personality development.* Mahwah, NJ: Erlbaum.

Saudino, K. J., & Wang, M. (2012). Quantitative and molecular genetic studies of temperament. In M. Z. Zentner & R. L. Shiner (Eds.), *Handbook of temperament.* New York: Guilford.

Saunders, C. (2002). A hospice perspective. In K. Foley, & H. Hendin (Eds.), *The case against assisted suicide: For the right to end-of-life care.* Baltimore: The Johns Hopkins Press.

Saunders, C. J., Miller, N. A., Soden, S. E., Dinwiddie, D. L., Noll, A., Alnadi, N. A., et al. (2012). Rapid whole-genome sequencing for genetic disease diagnosis in neonatal intensive care units. *Science Translational Medicine, 4*(154), 154ra135.

Savin-Williams, R. C. (2001). *Mom, Dad. I'm gay. How families negotiate coming out.* Washington DC: American Psychological Association.

Savin-Williams, R. C., & Ream, G. L. (2003). Sex variations in the disclosure to parents of same-sex attractions. *Journal of Family Psychology, 17,* 429–438.

Savin-Williams, R. C., & Ream, G. L. (2007). Prevalence and stability of sexual orientation components during adolescence and young adulthood. *Archives of Sexual Behavior, 36,* 385–394.

Savin-Williams, R. C., Joyner, K., & Rieger, G. (2012). Prevalence and stability of self-reported sexual orientation identity during young adulthood. *Archives of Sex Behavior, 41,* 103–110.

Savva, G. M., & Brayne, C. (2009). Epidemiology and impact of dementia. In M. F. Weiner & A. M. Lipton (Eds.), *The American Psychiatric Publishing textbook of Alzheimer disease and other dementias.* Washington, DC: American Psychiatric Publishing.

Saxe, R., Carey, S., & Kanwisher, N. (2004). Understanding other minds: Linking developmental psychology and functional neuroimaging. *Annual Review of Psychology, 55,* 87–124.

Saxe, R., & Kanwisher, N. (2003). People thinking about thinking people: The role of the temporo-parietal junction in "theory of mind." *NeuroImage, 19,* 1835–1842.

Saxe, R., & Powell, L. J. (2006). It's the thought that counts: Specific brain regions for one component of theory of mind. *Psychological Science, 17,* 692–699.

Saxe, R. R., Whitfield-Gabrieli, S., Scholz, J., & Pephrey, K. A. (2009). Brain regions for perceiving and reasoning about other people in

school-aged children. *Child Development, 80,* 1197–1209.

Sayer, L. C. (2005). Gender, time and inequality: Trends in women's and men's paid work, unpaid work and free time. *Social Forces, 84,* 285–303.

Sayre, N. E., & Gallagher, J. D. (2001). *The young child and the environment.* Boston: Allyn & Bacon.

Sbarra, D. A., Law, R. W., & Portley, R. M. (2011). Divorce and death: A meta-analysis and research agenda for clinical, social, and health psychology. *Perspectives on Psychological Science, 6,* 454–474.

Scafidi, F. A., Field, T., & Schanberg, S. M. (1993). Factors that predict which preterm infants benefit most from massage therapy. *Journal of Developmental and Behavioral Pediatrics, 14,* 176–180.

Scarr, S., & Weinberg, R. A. (1983). The Minnesota adoption studies: Genetic differences and malleability. *Child Development, 54,* 260–267.

Schaal, B., Barlier, L., & Soussignan, R. (1998). Olfactory function in the human fetus: Evidence from selective neonatal responsiveness to the odor of amniotic fluid. *Behavioral Neuroscience, 112,* 1438–1449.

Schacter, D. L. (1996). *Searching for memory: The brain, the mind, and the past.* New York: Basic Books.

Schaefer, C. E. (Ed.) (2010). *Play therapy for preschool children.* Washington, DC: American Psychological Association.

Schaefer, E. S. (1959). A circumplex model for maternal behavior. *Journal of Abnormal and Social Psychology, 59,* 226–235.

Schaffer, H. R., & Emerson, P. E. (1964). The development of social attachments in infancy. *Monographs of the Society for Research in Child Development, 29* (3, Serial No. 94).

Schaie, K. W. (1996). *Intellectual development in adulthood: The Seattle Longitudinal Study.* Cambridge, UK: Cambridge University Press.

Schaie, K. W. (2011). Historical influences on aging and behavior. In K. W. Schaie & S. L. Willis (Eds.), B. G. Knight, B. Levy, & D. C. Park (Assoc. Eds.), *Handbook of the psychology of aging* (pp. 41–55). Burlington, MA: Academic Press/Elsevier.

Schaie, K. W. (2012). *Developmental influences on adult intelligence: The Seattle longitudinal study (2nd ed).* Oxford University Press.

Schaie, K. W., & Willis, S. L. (1986). Can decline in adult intellectual functioning be reversed? *Developmental Psychology, 22,* 223–232.

Schaie, K. W., & Zanjani, F. A. K. (2006). Intellectual development across adulthood. In C. Hoare (Ed.), *Handbook of adult development and learning.* New York: Oxford University Press.

Schalock, R. L., Borthwick-Duffy, S. A., Bradley, V. J., Buntinx, W. H. E., Coulter, D. L., Craig, E. M., et al. (2010). *Intellectual disability: Definition, classification, and systems of supports* (11th ed.). Washington,

DC: American Association on Intellectual and Developmental Disabilities.

Schank, R. C., & Abelson, R. P. (1977). *Scripts, plans, goals, and understanding.* Hillsdale, NJ: Erlbaum.

Scharf, M., Mayseless, O., & Kivenson-Baron, I. (2004). Adolescents' attachment representations and developmental tasks in emerging adulthood. *Developmental Psychology, 40,* 430–444.

Scharf, M., Shulman, S., & Avigad-Spitz, L. (2005). Sibling relationships in emerging adulthood and in adolescence. *Journal of Adolescent Research, 20,* 64–90.

Scharlach, A., Li, W., & Dalvi, T. B. (2006). Family conflict as a mediator of caregiver strain. *Family Relations, 55,* 625–635.

Scheffler, R. M., Brown, T. T., Fulton, B. D., Hinshaw, S. P., Levine, P., Stone, S. (2009, May). Positive association between attention deficit/hyperactivity disorder medication use and academic achievement during elementary school. *Pediatrics, 123,* 1273–1279.

Schery, T. K., & Peters, M. L. (2003). Developing auditory learning in children with cochlear implants. *Topics in Language Disorders, 23,* 4–15.

Schiavi, R. C., Schreiner-Engel, P., White, D., & Mandeli, J. (1991). The relationship between pituitary-gonadal function and sexual behavior in healthy aging men. *Psychosomatic Medicine, 53,* 363–374.

Schieffelin, B. B. (1986). *How Kaluli children learn what to say, what to do, and how to feel.* New York: Cambridge University Press.

Schiepers, O. J. G., Harris, S. E., Gow, A. J., Pattie, A., Brett, C. E., Starr, J. M., et al. (2012). APOE E4 status predicts age-related cognitive decline in the ninth decade: Longitudinal follow-up of the Lothian birth cohort 1921. *Molecular Psychiatry, 17,* 315–324.

Schiff, A. R., & Knopf, I. J. (1985). The effect of task demands on attention allocation in children of different ages. *Child Development, 56,* 621–630.

Schiffman, H. R. (2000). *Sensation and perception* (5th ed.). New York: Wiley.

Schiffman, S. S. (1977). Food recognition by the elderly. *Journal of Gerontology, 32,* 586–592.

Schiffman, S. S. (2009). Effects of aging on the human taste system. *Annals of the New York Academy of Sciences, 1170,* 725–729.

Schiffman, S. S., & Warwick, Z. S. (1993). Effect of flavor enhancement of foods for the elderly on nutritional status: Food intake, biochemical indices, and anthropometric measures. *Physiological Behavior, 53,* 395–402.

Schleppenbach, M., Perry, M., Miller, K. F., Sims, L., & Fang, G. (2007). The answer is only the beginning: Extended discourse in Chinese and U.S. mathematics classrooms. *Journal of Educational Psychology, 99,* 380–396.

Schmidt, F. L., & Hunter, J. E. (1998). The validity and utility of selection methods in personnel psychology: Practical and theoretical implications of 85 years of research findings. *Psychological Bulletin, 124,* 262–274.

Schmidt, F. L., & Hunter, J. E. (2004). General mental ability in the world of work: Occupational attainment and job performance. *Journal of Personality and Social Psychology, 86,* 162–173.

Schmidt, M. F. H., & Tomasello, M. (2012). Young children enforce social norms. *Current Directions in Psychological Science, 21,* 232–236.

Schmidt, M. F. H., & Tomasello, M. (2012). Young children enforce social norms. *Current Directions in Psychological Science, 21,* 232–236.

Schmidt, S., & Petermann, F. (2009). Developmental psychopathology: Attention deficit hyperactivity disorder (ADHD). *BMC Psychiatry, 9,* 58.

Schneider, W. (2011). Memory development in childhood. In U. Goswami (Ed.), *The Wiley-Blackwell handbook of childhood cognitive development* (2nd ed., pp. 347–376). Malden, MA: John Wiley & Sons.

Schneider, W., & Bjorklund, D. F. (1998). Memory. In D. Kuhn & R. S. Siegler (Vol. Eds.), W. Damon (Editor-in-Chief), *Handbook of child psychology: Vol. 2. Cognition, perception, and language* (5th ed., pp. 467–522). New York: Wiley.

Schneider, W., & Bullock, M. (Eds.). (2009). *Human development from early childhood to early adulthood.* New York: Psychology Press.

Schneider, W., & Pressley, M. (1997). *Memory development between two and 20* (2nd ed.). Mahwah, NJ: Erlbaum.

Schneider, W., & Sodian, B. (1988). Metamemory-memory behavior relationships in young children: Evidence from a memory-for-location task. *Journal of Experimental Child Psychology, 45,* 209–233.

Schneider, W., Bjorklund, D. F., & Maier-Bruckner, W. (1996). The effects of expertise and IQ on children's memory: When knowledge is, and when it is not enough. *International Journal of Behavioral Development, 19,* 773–796.

Schneider, W., Gruber, H., Gold, A., & Opwis, K. (1993). Chess expertise and memory for chess positions in children and adults. *Journal of Experimental Child Psychology, 56,* 328–349.

Schneider, W., Roth, E., & Ennemoser, M. (2000). Training phonological skills and letter knowledge in children at risk for dyslexia: A comparison of three kindergarten intervention programs. *Journal of Educational Psychology, 92,* 284–295.

Schneiderman, I., Zagoory-Sharon, O., Leckman, J. F., & Feldman, R. (2012). Oxytocin during the initial stages of romantic attachment: Relations to couples' interactive reciprocity.*Psychoneuroendocrinology, 37,* 1277–1285.

Schoenborn, C. A., & Adams, P. F. (2010). Health behaviors of adults: United States, 2005–2007. National Center for Health Statistics. Vital Health Statistics, 10(245).

Schofield, H. T., Bierman, K. L., & Heinrichs, B. (2008). Predicting early sexual activity with behavior problems exhibited at school entry and in early adolescence. *Journal of Abnormal Child Psychology, 36,* 1175–1188.

Schonfeld, D. J., & Kappelman, M. (1990). The impact of school-based education on the young child's understanding of death. *Developmental and Behavioral Pediatrics, 11,* 247–252.

Schooler, C., Mulatu, M. S., & Oates, G. (1999). The continuing effects of substantively complex work on the intellectual functioning of older workers. *Psychology and Aging, 14,* 483–506.

Schoppe-Sullivan, S. J., Diener, M. L., Mangelsdorf, S. C., Brown, G. L., & McHale, J. L. (2006). Attachment and sensitivity in family context: The roles of parent and infant gender. *Infant and Child Development, 15,* 367–385.

Schot, M. J. C., Halbertsma, F. J. J., Katgert, T., & Bok, L. A. (2013). Development of children with symptomatic intracranial hemorrhage born after vacuum extraction. *Journal of Child Neurology, 28,* 520–523.

Schott, J. M., & Rossor, M. N. (2003). The grasp and other primitive reflexes. *Journal of Neurology and Neurosurgical Psychiatry, 74,* 558–560.

Schroeder, B. A., Messina, A., Schroeder, D., Good, K., Barto, S., Saylor, J., & Masiello, M. (2012). The implementation of a statewide bullying prevention program: Preliminary findings from the field and the importance of coalitions. *Health Promotion Practice, 13,* 489–495.

Schubert, C. R., Cruickshanks, K. J., Fischer, M. E., Huang, G., Klein, B. E. K., Klein, R., et al. (2012). Olfactory impairment in an adult population: The Beaver Dam Offspring Study. *Chemical Senses, 37,* 325–334.

Schuette, C. T., Ponton, M. K., & Charlton, M. L. (2012). Middle school children's career aspirations: Relationship to adult occupations and gender. *Career Development Quarterly, 60,* 35–46.

Schulte, B., & Craig, T. (2007, August 27). Unknown to Va. Tech, Cho had a disorder. Fairfax helped student cope with anxiety. *The Washington Post,* pp. A1, A8.

Schulz, M. S., & Lazarus, R. S. (2011). Regulating emotion in adolescence: A cognitive-mediational conceptualization. In P. K. Kerig, M. S. Schulz, & S. T. Hauser (Eds.), *Adolescence and beyond. Family processes and development.* New York: Oxford University Press.

Schulz, R., & Aderman, D. (1974). Clinical research and the stages of dying. *Omega: Journal of Death and Dying, 5,* 137–143.

Schulz, R., & Schlarb, J. (1987–1988). Two decades of research on dying: What do we know about the patient? *Omega: Journal of Death and Dying, 18,* 299–317.

Schulz, R., Belle, S. H., Czaja, S. J., Gitlin, L. N., Wisniewski, S. R., & Ory, M. G. (2003). Introduction to the special section on Resources for Enhancing Alzheimer's Caregiver Health (REACH). *Psychology and Aging, 18,* 357–360.

Schulz, R., Boerner, K., & Hebert, R. S. (2008). Caregiving and bereavement. In M. S. Stroebe, R. O. Hansson, H. Schut, & W. Stroebe (Eds.), *Handbook of bereavement research and practice. Advances in theory and intervention.* Washington, DC: American Psychological Association.

Schumacker, E. H., Seymour, T. L., Glass, J.M., Fencsik, D. E., Lauber, E. J., Kieras, D. E., & Meyer, D. E. (2001). Virtually perfect time sharing in dual-task performance: Uncorking the central cognitive bottleneck. *Psychological Science, 12,* 101–108.

Schumann, C. M., Barnes, C. C., Lord, C., & Courchesne, E. (2009). Amygdala enlargement in toddlers with autism related to severity of social and communication impairments. *Biological Psychiatry, 66,* 942–949.

Schunn, C. D., & Anderson, J. R. (1999). The generality/specificity of expertise in scientific reasoning. *Cognitive Science, 23,* 337–370.

Schwartz, M., Share, D. L., Leikin, M., & Kozminsky, E. (2008). On the benefits of bi-literacy: just a head start in reading or specific orthographic insights? *Reading and Writing, 21,* 905–927.

Schwartz, C. E., Wright, C. I., Shin, L. M., Kagan, J., & Rauch, S. L. (2003). Inhibited and uninhibited infants "grown up": Adult amygdalar response to novelty. *Science, 300,* 1952–1953.

Schwartz-Mette, R., & Rose, A. J. (2012). Co-rumination mediates contagion of internalizing symptoms within youths' friendships. *Developmental Psychology, 48,* 1355–1365.

Schweinhart, L. J., Montie, J., Xiang, Z., Barnett, W. S., Belfield, C. R., & Nores, M. (2005). *Lifetime effects: The High Scope Perry Preschool Study through age 40.* Ypsilanti, MI: High Scope Educational Research Foundation.

Schwenck, C., Bjorklund, D. F., & Schneider, W. (2007). Factors influencing the incidence of utilization deficiencies and other patterns of recall/strategy-use relations in a strategic memory task. *Child Development, 78,* 1771–1787.

Schwenck, C., Bjorklund, D. F., & Schneider, W. (2009). Developmental and individual differences in young children's use and maintenance of a selective memory strategy. *Developmental Psychology, 45,* 1034–1050.

Schwerdtfeger, K. L., & Shreffler, K. M. (2009). Trauma of pregnancy loss and infertility among mothers and involuntarily childless women in the United States. *Journal of Loss and Trauma, 14,* 211–227.

Schwitzgebel, E. (1999). Gradual belief change in children. *Human Development, 42,* 283–296.

Scialfa, C. T., Esau, S. P., & Joffe, K. M. (1998). Age, target-distracter similarity, and visual search. *Experimental Aging Research, 24,* 337–358.

Scogin, F., Walsh, D., Hanson, A., Stump, J., & Coates, A. (2005). Evidence-based psychotherapies for depression in older adults. *Clinical Psychology: Science and Practice, 12,* 222–237.

Scott, G., Leritz, L. E., & Mumford, M.D. (2004). The effectiveness of creativity training: A quantitative review. *Creativity Research Journal, 16*, 361–388.

Scott, R. M., & Baillargeon, R. (2009). Which penguin is this? Attributing false beliefs about object identity at 18 months. *Child Development, 80*, 1172–1196.

Scourfield, J., Rice, F., Thapar, A., Harold, G. T., Martin, N., & McGuffin, P. (2003). Depressive symptoms in children and adolescents: Changing etiological influences with development. *Journal of Child Psychology and Psychiatry and Allied Disciplines, 44*, 968–976.

Sczesny, S., Bosak, J., Diekman, A. B., & Twenge, J. M. (2008). Dynamics of sex-role stereotypes. In Y. Kashima, K. Fiedler, & P. Freytag (Eds.), *Stereotype dynamics: Language-based approaches to the formation, maintenance, and transformation of stereotypes* (pp. 135–163). New York: Taylor & Francis.

Seale, C. (1991). A comparison of hospice and conventional care. *Social Science and Medicine, 32*, 147–152.

Seaton, E. K., Scottham, K. M., & Sellers, R. M. (2006). The status model of racial identity development in African American adolescents: Evidence of structure, trajectories, and well-being. *Child Development, 77*, 1416–1426.

Sebastiani, P., Solovieff, N., DeWan, A. T., Walsh, K. M., Puca, A., et al. (2012). Genetic signatures of exceptional longevity in humans. PLoS ONE 7(1): e29848. doi:10.1371/journal.pone.0029848

Sebby, R., & Papini, D. (1994). Postformal reasoning during adolescence and young adulthood: The influence of problem relevancy. *Adolescence, 29*, 389–400.

Seccombe, K. (2000). Families in poverty in the 1990s: Trends, causes, consequences, and lessons learned. *Journal of Marriage and the Family, 62*, 1094–1113.

Segal, N. L. (2012). *Born together—reared apart. The landmark Minnesota Twin Study.* Cambridge, MA: Harvard University Press.

Segovia, C., Hutchinson, I., Laing, D. G., & Jinks, A. L. (2002). A quantitative study of fungiform papillae and taste pore density in adults and children. *Developmental Brain Research, 138*, 135–146.

Seiffge-Krenke, I. (1998). *Adolescents' health: A developmental perspective.* Mahwah, NJ: Erlbaum.

Seiffge-Krenke, I. (2003). Testing theories of romantic development from adolescence to young adulthood: Evidence of a developmental sequence. *International Journal of Behavioral Development, 27*, 519–531.

Seleen, D. R. (1982). The congruence between actual and desired use of time by older adults: A predictor of life satisfaction. *Gerontologist, 22*, 95–99.

Selikowitz, M. (2009). *ADHD: The facts*, 2nd ed. New York: Oxford.

Selman, R. L. (1976). Social cognitive understanding: A guide to educational and clinical experience. In T. Lickona (Ed.), *Moral development and behavior: Theory, research and social issues.* New York: Holt, Rinehart & Winston.

Selman, R. L. (1980). *The growth of interpersonal understanding.* New York: Academic Press.

Seltzer, M. M., & Li, L. W. (2000). The dynamics of caregiving: Transitions during a three-year prospective study, *Gerontologist, 40*, 165–178.

Senter, M. S., & Senter, R. (1997). Student outcomes and the adult learner. *Continuing Higher Education Review, 61*, 75–87.

Sentse, M., Veenstra, R., Lindenberg, S., Verhulst, F. C., & Ormel, J. (2009). Buffers and risks in temperament and family for early adolescent psychopathology: Generic, conditional, or domain-specific effects? The Trails Study. *Developmental Psychology, 45*, 419–435.

Serafica, F. C., & Vargas, L. A. (2006). Cultural diversity in the development of child psychopathology. In D. Cicchetti & D. J. Cohen (Eds.), *Developmental psychopathology: Vol. 1. Theory and method* (2nd ed.). Hoboken, NJ: Wiley.

Serbin, L. A., Poulin-Dubois, D., & Eichstedt, J. A. (2002). Infants' response to gender-inconsistent events. *Infancy, 3*, 531–542.

Serbin, L. A., Powlishta, K. K., & Gulko, J. (1993). The development of sex typing in middle childhood. *Monographs of the Society for Research in Child Development, 58*(2, Serial No. 232).

Serbin, L. A., Tonick, I. J., & Sternglanz, S. H. (1977). Shaping cooperative cross-sex play. *Child Development, 48*, 924–929.

Sergeant, M. J. T., Davies, M. N. O., Dickins, T. E., & Griffiths, M. D. (2005). The self-reported importance of olfaction during human mate choice. *Sexualities, Evolution, and Gender, 7*, 199–213.

Serjeant, G. R. (2010). One hundred years of sickle cell disease. *British Journal of Haematology, 151*, 425–429.

Servaty-Seib, H. L. (2009). Death of a friend during adolescence. In D. E. Balk & C. A. Corr (Eds.), *Adolescent encounters with death, bereavement, and coping.* New York: Springer.

Servin, A., Bohlin, G., & Berlin, L. (1999). Sex differences in 1-, 3-, and 5-year-olds' toy-choice in a structured play-session. *Scandinavian Journal of Psychology, 40*, 43–48.

Settersten, R. A., Jr., & Trauten, M. E. (2009). The new terrain of old age: Hallmarks, freedoms, and risks. In V. L. Bengtson, M. Silverstein, N. M. Putney, & D. Gans (Eds.), *Handbook of theories of aging* (2nd ed.). New York: Springer.

Shafer, V. L., & Garrido-Nag, K. (2009). The neurodevelopmental bases of language. In E. Hoff & M. Shatz (Eds.), *Blackwell handbook of language development* (pp. 21–45). Malden, MA: Wiley-Blackwell.

Shaffer, D., & Pfeffer, C. R. (2001). Practice parameters for the assessment and treatment of children and adolescents with suicidal behavior. *Journal of the American Academy of Child and Adolescent Psychiatry, 40*, 24S–51S.

Shah, S. M., Carey, I. M., Harris, T., Dewilde, S., Victor, C. R., & Cook, D. G. (2013). The effect of unexpected bereavement on mortality in older couples. *American Journal of Public Health, 103*, 1140–1145.

Shanahan, L., McHale, S. M., Osgood, D. W., & Crouter, A. C. (2004). Conflict frequency with mothers and fathers from middle childhood to late adolescence: Within- and between-families comparisons. *Developmental Psychology, 43*, 539–550.

Shanahan, M. J., Finch, M. D., Mortimer, J. T., & Ryu, S. (1991). Adolescent work experience and depressive affect. *Social Psychology Quarterly, 54*, 299–317.

Shannon, J. B. (2006). *Death and dying sourcebook* (2nd ed.). Detroit, MI: Omnigraphics.

Shapiro, D. N., Peterson, C., & Stewart, A. J. (2009). Legal and social contexts and mental health among lesbian and heterosexual mothers. *Journal of Family Psychology, 23*, 255–262.

Sharabany, R., Gershoni, R., & Hofman, J. E. (1981). Girlfriend, boyfriend: Age and sex differences in intimate friendship. *Developmental Psychology, 17*, 800–808.

Sharp, E. S., & Gatz, M. (2011). Relationship between education and dementia: An updated systematic review. *Alzheimer Disease and Associated Disorders, 25*, 289–304.

Sharpe, P. A., Jackson, K. L., White, C., Vaca, V. L., Hickey, T., Gu, J., et al. (1997). Effects of a one-year physical activity intervention for older adults at congregate nutrition sites. *Gerontologist, 37*, 208–215.

Sharpe, T. M., Killen, J. D., Bryson, S. W., Shisslak, C. M., Estes, L. S., Gray, N., Crago, M., & Taylor, C. G. (1998). Attachment style and weight concerns in preadolescent and adolescent girls. *International Journal of Eating Disorders, 23*, 39–44.

Shaver, P. R., & Fraley, R. C. (2008). Attachment, loss, and grief: Bowlby's views and current controversies. In J. Cassidy & P. R. Shaver (Eds.), *Handbook of attachment: Theory, research, and clinical applications* (2nd ed.). New York: Guilford.

Shaver, P. R., & Mikulincer, M. (2012). Attachment theory. In P. A. M. Van Lange, A. W. Kruglanski & E. T. Higgins (Eds.), *Handbook of theories of social psychology* (pp. 160–179). Thousand Oaks, CA: Sage.

Shaywitz, B. A., Shaywitz, S. E., Pugh, K. R., Constable, R. T., Skudlarski, P., & Fulbright, R. K. (1995). Sex differences in the functional organization of the brain for language. *Nature, 373*, 607–609.

Shaywitz, B. A., Shaywitz, S. E., Pugh, K. R., Fulbright, R. K., Mencl, E., Bonstable, R. T., et al. (2001). The neurobiology of dyslexia. *Clinical Neuroscience, 1*, 291–299.

Shaywitz, S. E., Fletcher, J. M., Holahan, J. M., Shneider, A. E., Marchione, K. E., Stuebing, K. K., et al. (1999). Persistence of dyslexia: The Connecticut Longitudinal Study at Adolescence. *Pediatrics, 104*, 1351–1359.

Sheetz, M. J., & Bowman, M. S. (2013). Parents' perceptions of a pediatric palliative program. *American Journal of Hospice & Palliative Care, 30*, 291–296.

Shekhar, S., Rana, N., & Jaswal, R. (2012, August 28). A prospective randomized study comparing maternal and fetal effects of forceps delivery and vacuum extraction. *The Journal of Obstetrics and Gynecology of India* [Epub ahead of print].

Shepard, R. J. (1997). Curricular physical activity and academic performance. *Pediatric Exercise Science, 9,* 113–126.

Shepard, T. H. (2010). *Catalog of teratogenic agents* (13th ed.). Baltimore, MD: Johns Hopkins University Press.

Shih, M., Pittinsky, T. L., & Ambady, N. (1999). Stereotype susceptibility: Identity salience and shifts in quantitative performance. *Psychological Science, 10,* 80–83.

Shiner, R. L., & Caspi, A. (2012). Temperament and the development of personality traits, adaptation, and narratives. In M. Z. Zentner & R. L. Shiner (Eds.), *Handbook of temperament.* New York: Guilford.

Shiner, R. L., Buss, K. A., McClowry, S. G., Putnam, S. P., Saudino, K. J., & Zentner, M. (2012). What is temperament now? Assessing progress in temperament research on the twenty-fifth anniversary of Goldsmith et al. (1987). *Child Development, 6,* 436–444.

Ship, J. A., Pearson, J. D., Cruise, L. J., Brant, L. J., & Metter, E. J. (1996). Longitudinal changes in smell identification. *Journals of Gerontology: Biological Sciences and Medical Sciences, 51,* M86–M91.

Ship, J. A., & Weiffenbach, J. M. (1993). Age, gender, medical treatment, and medication effects on smell identification. *Journal of Gerontology, 48,* M26–M32.

Shneidman, E. S. (1973). *Deaths of man.* New York: Quadrangle.

Shneidman, E. S. (1980). *Voices of death.* New York: Harper & Row.

Shneidman, L. A., & Goldin-Meadow, S. (2012). Language input and acquisition in a Mayan village: How important is directed speech? *Developmental Science, 15,* 659–673.

Shoda, Y., Mischel, W., & Peake, P. K. (1990). Predicting adolescent cognitive and self-regulatory competencies from preschool delay of gratification: Identifying diagnostic conditions. *Developmental Psychology, 26,* 978–986.

Shonk, S. M., & Cicchetti, D. (2001). Maltreatment, competency deficits, and risk for academic and behavioral maladjustment. *Developmental Psychology, 37,* 3–17.

Shonkoff, J. P. (2010). Building a new biodevelopmental framework to guide the future of early childhood policy. Child Development, 81, 357–367.

Shringarpure, R., & Davies, K. J. A. (2009). Free radicals and oxidative stress in aging. In V. L. Bengtson, M. Silverstein, N. M. Putney, & D. Gans (Eds.), *Handbook of theories of aging* (2nd ed.). New York: Springer.

Shrivastava, A., Murrin, C., O'Brien, J., Viljoen, K., Heavey, P., Grant, T., et al. (2012). Grandparental morbidity and mortality patterns are associated with infant birth weight in the Lifeways Cross-Generation Cohort Study

2001–2010. *Journal of Developmental Origins of Health and Disease,* 1–11.

Shute, N. (2001, January 15). Children in anguish. A call for better treatment of kids' mental ills. *U.S. News & World Report,* 42.

Shweder, R. A., Goodnow, J. J., Hatano, G., LeVine, R. A., Markus, H. R., & Miller, P. J. (2006). The cultural psychology of development: One mind, many mentalities. In W. Damon & R. M. Lerner (Eds. in Chief) & R. M. Lerner (Vol. Ed.), *Handbook of child psychology: Vol. 1. Theoretical models of human development* (6th ed.). Hoboken, NJ: Wiley.

Shweder, R. A., Mahapatra, M., & Miller, J. G. (1990). Culture and moral development. In J. W. Stigler, R. A. Shweder, & G. Herdt (Eds.), *Cultural psychology. Essays on comparative human development.* Cambridge, UK: Cambridge University Press.

Siebenbruner, J., Zimmer-Gembeck, M. J., & Egeland, B. (2007). Sexual partners and contraceptive use: A 16-year prospective study predicting abstinence and risk behavior. *Journal of Research on Adolescence, 17,* 179–206.

Siebold, C. (1992). *The hospice movement. Easing death's pains.* New York: Twayne Publishers.

Siegler, I. C., & Brummett, B. H. (2000). Associations among NEO personality assessments and well-being at mid-life: Facet-level analyses. *Psychology and Aging, 15,* 710–714.

Siegler, R. S. (1981). Developmental sequences within and between concepts. *Monographs of the Society for Research in Child Development, 46*(2, Serial No. 189).

Siegler, R. S. (1989). Hazards of mental chronometry: An example from children's subtraction. *Journal of Educational Psychology, 81,* 497–506.

Siegler, R. S. (1996). *Emerging minds: The process of change in children's thinking.* New York: Oxford University Press.

Siegler, R. S. (2000). The rebirth of children's learning. *Child Development, 71,* 26–35.

Siegler, R. S. (2006). Microgenetic analysis of learning. In D. Kuhn & R. Siegler (Vol. Eds.), *Handbook of child psychology: Cognition, perception, and language: Vol. 2* (pp. 464–510). Hoboken, NJ: Wiley and Sons.

Siegler, R. S., & Svetina, M. (2006). What leads children to adopt new strategies? A microgenetic/cross sectional study of class inclusion. *Child Development, 77,* 997–1015.

Sigelman, C. K., Carr, M. B., & Begley, N. L. (1986). Developmental changes in the influence of sex-role stereotypes on person perception. *Child Study Journal, 16,* 191–205.

Sigman, M., & Capps, L. (1997). *Children with autism. A developmental perspective.* Cambridge, MA: Harvard University Press.

Signorielli, N., & Kahlenberg, S. (2001). Television's world of work in the nineties. *Journal of Broadcasting and Electronic Media, 45,* 4–22.

Signorielli, N., & Lears, M. (1992). Children, television, and conceptions about chores: Attitudes and behaviors. *Sex Roles, 27,* 157–170.

Silventoinen, K., Haukka, J., Dunkel, L., Tynelius, P., & Rasmussen, F. (2008). Genetics of pubertal timing and its associations with relative weight in childhood and adult height: The Swedish young male twins study. *Pediatrics, 121,* e885–e891.

Silverman, I. W. (2003). Gender differences in resistance to temptation: Theories and evidence. *Developmental Review, 23,* 219–259.

Silverman, P. R. (2000). *Never too young to know. Death in children's lives.* New York: Oxford University Press.

Silverman, P. R., & Worden, J. W. (1993). Children's reactions to the death of a parent. In M. S. Stroebe, W. Stroebe, & R. O. Hansson (Eds.), *Handbook of bereavement. Theory, research, and intervention.* Cambridge, UK: Cambridge University Press.

Silvers, J. A., McRae, K., Gabrieli, J. D. E., Gross, J. J., Remy, K. A., & Ochsner, K. N. (2012). Age-related differences in emotional reactivity, regulation, and rejection sensitivity in adolescence. *Emotion, 12,* 1235–1247.

Silverstein, M., & Giarrusso, R. (2010). Aging and family life: A decade review. *Journal of Marriage and Family, 72,* 1039–1058.

Silverstein, M., & Ruiz, S. (2006). Breaking the chain: How grandparents moderate the transmission of maternal depression to their grandchildren. *Family Relations, 55,* 601–612.

Sim, L. A., Homme, J. H., Lteif, A. N., Vande Voort, J. L., Schak, K. M., & Ellingson, J. (2009). Family functioning and maternal distress in adolescent girls with anorexia nervosa. *International Journal of Eating Disorders, 42,* 531–539.

Simcock, G., & Hayne, H. (2002). Breaking the barrier? Children fail to translate their preverbal memories into language. *Psychological Science, 13,* 225–231.

Simcock, G., & Hayne, H. (2003). Age-related changes in verbal and nonverbal memory during early childhood. *Developmental Psychology, 39,* 805–814.

Simmons, R. G., & Blyth, D. A. (1987). *Moving into adolescence: The impact of pubertal change and school context.* New York: Hawthorne, Aldine de Gruyter.

Simmons, R. G., & Blyth, D. A. (1987). *Moving into adolescence: The impact of pubertal change and school context.* New York: Hawthorne, Aldine de Gruyter.

Simmons, R. G., & Blyth, D. A. (1987). *Moving into adolescence: The impact of pubertal change and school context.* New York: Hawthorne, Aldine de Gruyter.

Simon, H. A. (1995). The information-processing theory of mind. *American Psychologist, 50,* 507–508.

Simon, H. A. (2001). Creativity in the arts and sciences. *The Canyon Review and Stand, 23,* 203–220.

Simons-Morton, B. G., & Farhat, T. (2010). Recent findings on peer group influences on adolescent smoking. *Journal of Primary Prevention, 31,* 191–208.

Simonton, D. K. (1984). *Genius, creativity, and leadership: Historiometric inquiries.* Cambridge, MA: Harvard University Press.

Simonton, D. K. (1990). Creativity in the later years: Optimistic prospects for achievement. *Gerontologist, 30,* 626–631.

Simonton, D. K. (1990). Creativity in the later years: Optimistic prospects for achievement. *Gerontologist, 30,* 626–631.

Simonton, D. K. (1999). Creativity from a historiometric perspective. In R. J. Sternberg (Ed.), *Handbook of creativity.* New York: Cambridge University Press.

Simpson, J. A., Collins, W. A., Tran, S., & Haydon, K. C. (2007). Attachment and the experience and expression of emotions in romantic relationships: A developmental perspective. *Journal of Personality and Social Psychology, 92,* 355–367.

Simpson, J. A., Griskevicius, V., Kuo, S. I. Sung, S., & Collins, W. A. (2012). Evolution, stress, and sensitive periods: The influence of unpredictability in early versus late childhood on sex and risky behavior. *Developmental Psychology, 48,* 674–686.

Simpson, R., & Otten, K. (2005). Structuring behavior management strategies and building social competence. In D. Zager (Ed.), *Autism spectrum disorders. Identification, education, and treatment* (3rd ed.). Mahwah, NJ: Erlbaum.

Singer, D. G., Golinkoff, R. M., & Hirsh-Pasek, K. (Eds.) (2006). *Play = learning: How play motivates and enhances children's cognitive and social-emotional growth.* New York: Oxford University Press.

Singer, T., Verhaeghen, P., Ghisletta, P., Lindenberger, U., & Baltes, P. B. (2003). The fate of cognition in very old age: Six-year longitudinal findings in the Berlin Aging Study (BASE). *Psychology and Aging, 18,* 318–331.

Singer, T., Verhaeghen, P., Ghisletta, P., Lindenberger, U., & Baltes, P. B. (2003). The fate of cognition in very old age: Six-year longitudinal findings in the Berlin Aging Study (BASE). *Psychology and Aging, 18,* 318–331.

Singh, D., & Bronstad, P. M. (2001). Female body odour is a potential cue to ovulation. *Proceedings of Biological Science, 268,* 797–801.

Sinnott, J. (1996). The developmental approach: Postformal thought as adaptive intelligence. In F. Blanchard-Fields & T. M. Hess (Eds.), *Perspectives on cognitive change in adulthood and aging.* New York: McGraw-Hill.

Sinnott, J. D. (1984). Postformal reasoning: The relativistic stage. In M. L. Commons, F. A. Richards, & C. Armon (Eds.), *Beyond formal operations* (pp. 298–325). New York: Praeger.

Sirois, S., Spratling, M. W., Thomas, M. S. C., Westermann, G., Mareschal, D., & Johnson, M. H. (2008). Précis of neuroconstructivism: How the brain constructs cognition. *Behavioral and Brain Sciences, 31,* 321–331.

Skinner, B. F. (1983). Intellectual self-management in old age. *American Psychologist, 38,* 239–244.

Skinner, E. A., & Zimmer-Gembeck, M. J. (2007). The development of coping. *Annual Review of Psychology, 58,* 119–144.

Slaby, R. G., & Guerra, N. G. (1988). Cognitive mediators of aggression in adolescent offenders: 1. Assessment. *Developmental Psychology, 24,* 580–588.

Slater, A., Morison, V., Town, C., Rose, D. (1985). Movement perception and identity constancy in the newborn baby. *British Journal of Developmental Psychology, 3,* 211–220.

Slater, A., Quinn, P. C., Kelly, D. J., Longmore, C. A., McDonald, P. R., & Pascalis, O. (2010). The shaping of face space in early infancy: Becoming a native face processor. *Child Development Perspective, 4,* 205–211.

Slater, A., Riddell, P., Quinn, P. C., Pascalis, O., Lee, K., & Kelly, D. J. (2010). Visual perception. In J. G. Bremner & T. D. Wachs (Eds.), *The Wiley-Blackwell handbook of infant development, 2nd ed., Vol 1: Basic research* (pp. 40–80). Malden, MA: John Wiley & Sons.

Slater, C. L. (2003). Generativity versus stagnation: An elaboration of Erikson's adult stage of human development. *Journal of Adult Development, 10,* 53–65.

Slater, R., Cantarella, A., Gallella, S., Worley, A., Boyd, S., Meek, J., et al. (2006). Cortical pain responses in human infants. *The Journal of Neuroscience, 26,* 3662–3666.

Slaughter, V., & Lyons, M. (2003). Learning about life and death in early childhood. *Cognitive Psychology, 46,* 1–30.

Slaughter, V., Jaakkola, R., & Carey, S. (1999). Constructing a coherent theory: Children's biological understanding of life and death. In M. Siegal & C. C. Peterson (Eds.), *Children's understanding of biology and health.* Cambridge, UK: Cambridge University Press.

Slavkin, M., & Stright, A. D. (2000). Gender role differences in college students from one- and two-parent families. *Sex Roles, 42,* 23–37.

Sliwinski, M., & Buschke, H. (1999). Cross-sectional and longitudinal relationships among age, cognition, and processing speed. *Psychology and Aging, 14,* 18–33.

Slobin, D. I. (1979). *Psycholinguistics* (2nd ed.). Glenview, IL: Scott, Foresman.

Sloboda, Z. (2009). School prevention. In C. G. Leukefeld, T. P. Gullotta, & M. Staton-Tindall (Eds.), *Adolescent substance abuse. Evidence-based approaches to prevention and treatment.* New York: Springer.

Smagorinsky, P. (1995). The social construction of data: Methodological problems of investigating learning in the zone of proximal development. *Review of Educational Research, 65,* 191–212.

Small, S., & Memmo, M. (2004). Contemporary models of youth development and problem prevention: Toward an integration of terms, concepts, and models. *Family Relations, 53,* 3–11.

Smetana, J. G. (1981). Preschool children's conceptions of moral and social rules. *Child Development, 52,* 1333–1336.

Smetana, J. G. (2006). Social-cognitive domain theory: Consistencies and variations in children's moral and social judgments. In M. Killen & J. G. Smetana (Eds.), *Handbook of moral development.* Mahwah, NJ: Erlbaum.

Smetana, J. G., Rote, W. M., Jambon, M., Tasopoulos-Chan, M., Villalobos, M., & Comer, J. (2012). Developmental changes and individual differences in young children's moral judgments. *Child Development, 83,* 683–696.

Smith, A. D., & Earles, J. L. K. (1996). Memory changes in normal aging. In F. Blanchard-Fields & T. M. Hess (Eds.), *Perspectives on cognitive change in adulthood and aging.* New York: McGraw-Hill.

Smith, A. K., Mick, E., & Raraone, S. V. (2009). Advances in genetic studies of attention-deficit/hyperactivity disorder. *Current Psychiatry Reports, 11,* 143–148.

Smith, C. A., Levett, K. M., Collins, C. T., & Crowther, C. A. (2011, December 7). Relaxation techniques for pain management in labour. *Cochrane Database of Systematic Reviews,* CD009514.

Smith, G. E., Petersen, R. C., Ivnik, R. J., Malec, J. F., & Tangalos, E. G. (1996). Subjective memory complaints, psychological distress, and longitudinal change in objective memory performance. *Psychology and Aging, 11,* 272–279.

Smith, G. J. W. (2005). How should creativity be defined? *Creativity Research Journal, 17,* 293–295.

Smith, J. T., & Baker, D. A. (2011). Sickle cell disease. In S. Goldstein & C. R. Reynolds (Eds.), *Handbook of neurodevelopmental and genetic disorders in children* (2nd ed., pp. 338–361). New York: Guilford.

Smith, J., & Baltes, P. B. (1990). Wisdom-related knowledge: Age/cohort differences in response to life-planning problems. *Developmental Psychology, 26,* 494–505.

Smith, K. E., Landry, S. H., & Swank, P. R. (2000). Does the content of mothers' verbal stimulation explain differences in children's development of verbal and nonverbal cognitive skills? *Journal of School Psychology, 38,* 27–49.

Smith, L. B., & Thelen, E. (1993). *A dynamic systems approach to development: Applications.* Cambridge, MA: MIT Press.

Smith, P. K. (1978). A longitudinal study of social participation in preschool children: Solitary and parallel play reexamined. *Developmental Psychology, 14,* 517–523.

Smith, P. K. (2005). Types and functions of play in human development. In B. J. Ellis & D. F. Bjorklund (Eds.), *Origins of the social mind.* New York: Guilford Press.

Smith, P. K., Mahdavi, J., Carvalho, M., Fisher, S., Russell, S., & Tippett, N. (2008). Cyberbullying: Its nature and impact in secondary school pupils. *Journal of Child Psychology and Psychiatry, 49,* 376–385.

Smith, R. L., Rose, A. J., & Schwartz-Mette, R. A. (2010). Relational and overt aggression in childhood and adolescence: Clarifying mean-level gender differences and associations with peer acceptance. *Social Development, 19,* 243–269.

Smith, S. L., Pieper, K. M., Granados, A., & Choueiti, M. (2010). Assessing gender-related portrayals in top-grossing G-rated films. *Sex Roles, 62,* 774–786.

Smith, T. W., Berg, C. A., Florsheim, P., Uchino, B. N., Pearce, G., Hawkins, M., Henry, N. J. M., Beveridge, R. M., Skinner, M. A., & Olsen-Cerny, C. (2009). Conflict and collaboration in middle-aged and older couples: I. Age differences in agency and communion during marital interaction. *Psychology and Aging, 24,* 259–273.

Smithmyer, C. M., Hubbard, J. A., & Simons, R. F. (2000). Proactive and reactive aggression in delinquent adolescents: Relations to aggression outcome expectancies. *Journal of Clinical Child Psychology, 29,* 86–93.

Smitsman, A. W., & Corbetta, D. (2010). Action in infancy—Perceptives, concepts, and challenges. In J. G. Bremner & T. D. Wachs (Eds.), *The Wiley-Blackwell handbook of infant development, 2nd ed., Vol 1: Basic research* (pp. 167–203). Malden, MA: John Wiley & Sons.

Smyke, A. T., Dumitrescu, A., & Zeanah, C. H. (2002). Attachment disturbances in young children. I: The continuum of caretaking casualty. *Journal of the American Academy of Child and Adolescent Psychiatry, 41,* 972–982.

Snarey, J. R. (1985). Cross-cultural universality of social–moral development: A critical review of Kohlbergian research. *Psychological Bulletin, 97,* 202–232.

Snarey, J., & Samuelson, P. (2008). Moral education in the cognitive developmental tradition: Lawrence Kohlberg's revolutionary ideas. In L. P. Nucci & D. Narvaez (Eds.), *Handbook of moral and character education.* New York: Routledge.

Snow, C. E., Arlman-Rupp, A., Hassing, Y., Jobse, J., Joosken, J., & Vorster, J. (1976). Mother's speech in three social classes. *Journal of Psycholinguistic Research, 5,* 1–20.

Snow, D. (2006). Regression and reorganization of intonation between 6 and 23 months. *Child Development, 77,* 281–296.

Snowdon, D. (2002). *Aging with grace: What the Nun Study teaches us about leading longer, healthier, and more meaningful lives.* New York: Bantam Books.

Sobolewski, J. M., & King, V. (2005). The importance of the coparental relationship for nonresident fathers' ties to children. *Journal of Marriage and Family, 67,* 1196–1212.

Son, L. K. (2004). Spacing one's study: Evidence for a metacognitive control strategy. *Journal of Experimental Psychology: Learning, Memory, and Cognition, 30,* 601–604.

Son, L. K., & Metcalfe, J. (2000). Metacognitive and control strategies in study-time allocation. *Journal of Experimental Psychology: Learning, Memory, and Cognition, 26,* 204–221.

Song, J., & Manchester, J. (2009). Revisiting the 1983 Social Security reforms, 25 years later. *Research on Aging, 31,* 233–260.

Soriano, F. I., Rivera, L. M., Williams, K. J., Daley, S. P., & Reznik, V. M. (2004). Navigating between cultures: The role of culture in youth violence. *Journal of Adolescent Health, 34,* 169–176.

Sorkhabi, N., & Mandara, J. (2013). Are the effects of Baumrind's parenting styles culturally specific or culturally equivalent? In R. E. Larzelere, A. S. Sheffield, & A. W. Harrist (Eds.), *Authoritative parenting. Synthesizing nurturance and discipline for optimal child development.* Washington, DC: American Psychological Association.

Sotomayor, S. (2013). *My beloved world.* New York: Knopf.

Sotomi, O., Ryan, C. A., O'Connor, G., & Murphy, B. P. (2007). Have we stopped looking for a red reflex in newborn screening? *Irish Medical Journal, 100,* 398–400.

Span, P. (2000, August 27). Home alone. *The Washington Post Magazine,* pp. 12–15, 24–25.

Spaniol, J., Madden, D. J., & Voss, A. (2006). A diffusion model analysis of adult age differences in episodic and semantic long-term memory retrieval. *Journal of Experimental Psychology: Learning, Memory, and Cognition, 32,* 101–117.

Spar, D. (2012, October 1 and 8). American women have it wrong. *Newsweek,* pp. 38–48.

Sparks, R. L., Patton, J., & Murdoch, A. (2013, March). Early reading success and its relationship to reading achievement and reading volume: Replication of '10 years later.' *Reading and Writing.* doi:10.1007/s11145-013-9439-2

Sparrow, R. (2010). Implants and ethnocide: Learning from the cochlear implant controversy. *Disability and Society, 25,* 455–466.

Sparrow, S. S., & Davis, S. M. (2000). Recent advances in the assessment of intelligence and cognition. *Journal of Child Psychology and Psychiatry, 41,* 117–131.

Spear, L. P. (2000a). The adolescent brain and age-related behavioral manifestations. *Neuroscience and Biobehavioral Reviews, 24,* 417–463.

Spear, L. P. (2010). *The behavioral neuroscience of adolescence.* New York: W. W. Norton.

Spearman, C. (1927). *The abilities of man.* New York: Macmillan.

Speece, M. W., & Brent, S. B. (1984). Children's understanding of death: A review of three components of a death concept. *Child Development, 55,* 1671–1686.

Speece, M. W., & Brent, S. B. (1992). The acquisition of a mature understanding of three components of the concept of death. *Death Studies, 16,* 211–229.

Spelke, E. S. (1990). Principles of object perception. *Cognitive Science, 14,* 29–56.

Spelke, E. S. (1994). Initial knowledge: Six suggestions. *Cognition, 50,* 431–445.

Spelke, E. S., & Hermer, L. (1996). Early cognitive development: Objects and space. In R. Gelman & T. Fong (Eds.), *Handbook of perception and cognition* (2nd ed.). New York: Academic Press.

Spelke, E. S., Breinlinger, K., Macomber, J., & Jacobson, K. (1992). Origins of knowledge. *Psychological Review, 99,* 605–632.

Spence, J. T. (1985). Achievement American style: The rewards and costs of individualism. *American Psychologist, 40,* 1285–1295.

Spence, J. T., Helmreich, R. L., & Stapp, J. (1973). The Personal Attributes Questionnaire: A measure of sex-role stereotypes and masculinity-femininity. *JSAS Catalog of Selected Documents in Psychology, 4,* 43–44 (Ms. 617).

Spencer, J. P., Blumberg, M. S., McMurray, B., Robinson, S. R., Samuelson, L. K., & Tomblin, J. B. (2009). Short arms and talking eggs: Why we should no longer abide the nativist-empiricist debate. *Child Development Perspectives, 3,* 79–87.

Spencer, J. P., Corbetta, D., Buchanan, P., Clearfield, M., Ulrich, B., & Schoner, G. (2006). Moving toward a grand theory of development: In memory of Esther Thelen. *Child Development, 77,* 1521–1538.

Spencer, M. B., & Markstrom-Adams, C. (1990). Identity processes among racial and ethnic minority children in America. *Child Development, 61,* 290–310.

Spencer, P. E. (1996). The association between language and symbolic play at two years: Evidence from deaf toddlers. *Child Development, 67,* 867–876.

Spengler, M., Gottschling, J., & Spinath, F. M. (2012). Personality in childhood. A longitudinal behavior genetic approach. *Personality and Individual Differences, 53,* 411–416.

Spera, C. (2006). Adolescents' perceptions of parental goals, practices, and styles in relation to the motivation and achievement. *Journal of Early Adolescence, 26,* 456–490.

Sperry, S., Roehrig, M., & Thompson, J. K. (2009). Treatment of eating disorders in childhood and adolescence. In L. Smolak & J. K. Thompson (Eds.), *Body image, eating disorders, and obesity in youth.* Washington, DC: American Psychological Association.

Spiegel, C., & Halberda, J. (2011). Rapid fast-mapping abilities in 2-year-olds. *Journal of Experimental Psychology, 109,* 132–140.

Spieler, D. H., & Griffin, Z. M. (2006). The influence of age on the time course of word preparation in multiword utterances. *Language and Cognitive Processes, 21,* 291–321.

Spilich, G. J., Vesonder, G. T., Chiesi, H. L., & Voss, J. F. (1979). Text processing of domain-related information for individuals with high and low domain knowledge. *Journal of Verbal Learning and Verbal Behavior, 18,* 275–290.

Spinath, B., Spinath, F. M., Harlaar, N., & Plomin, R. (2006). Predicting school achievement from general cognitive ability, self-perceived ability, and intrinsic value. *Intelligence, 34,* 363–374.

Spitz, R. A. (1946). Anaclitic depression: An inquiry into the genesis of psychiatric conditions in early childhood, II. *Psychoanalytic Study of the Child, 2,* 313–342.

Spitze, G., & Trent, K. (2006). Gender differences in adult sibling relations in two-child families. *Journal of Marriage and Family, 68,* 977–992.

Spokane, A. R., Meir, E. I., & Catalano, M. (2000). Person-environment congruence and Holland's theory: A review and reconsideration. *Journal of Vocational Behavior, 57,* 137–187.

Spoth, R., Trudeau, L., Guyll, M., Shin, C., & Redmond, C. (2009). Universal intervention effects on substance use among young adults mediated by delayed adolescent substance initiation. *Journal of Consulting and Clinical Psychology, 77,* 620–632.

Springer, S., & Deutsch, G. (2001). *Left brain, right brain: Perspectives from cognitive neuroscience* (5th ed.). New York: W. H. Freeman.

Spruyt, K., Aitken, R., So, K., Charlton, M., Adamson, T., & Horne, R. (2008). Relationship between sleep/wake patterns, temperament and overall development in term infants over the first year of life. *Early Human Development, 84*(5), 289–296.

Sroufe, L. A. (1977). Wariness of strangers and the study of infant development. *Child Development, 48,* 1184–1199.

Sroufe, L. A. (1996). *Emotional development: The organization of emotional life in the early years.* Cambridge, UK: University of Cambridge Press.

Sroufe, L. A. (1997). Psychopathology as an outcome of development. *Development and Psychopathology, 9,* 251–268.

Sroufe, L. A. (2009). The concept of development in developmental psychopathology. *Child Development Perspectives, 3,* 178–183.

Sroufe, L. A., Egeland, B., Carlson, E., & Collins, W. A. (2005). Placing early attachment experiences in developmental context: The Minnesota Longitudinal Study. In K. E. Grossmann, K. Grossmann, & E. Waters (Eds.), *Attachment from infancy to adulthood: The major longitudinal studies.* New York: Guilford Press.

Sroufe, L. A., & Rutter, M. (1984). The domain of developmental psychopathology. *Child Development, 55,* 17–29.

Sroufe, L. A., Waters, E., & Matas, L. (1974). Contextual determinants of infant affectional response. In M. Lewis & L. A. Rosenblum (Eds.), *The origins of fear.* New York: Wiley.

St. George, D. (2001, June 8). A child's unheeded cry for help. *The Washington Post,* pp. A1, A20–A21.

St. George, D. (2010, March 18). Households with little room for a generation gap. *The Washington Post,* p. B6.

St. Jacques, P. L. (2012). Functional neuroimaging of autobiographical memory. In D. Berntsen & D. C. Rubin (Eds.), *Understanding autobiographical memory: Theories and approaches* (pp. 114–138). New York: Cambridge University Press.

St. Petersburg–USA Orphanage Research Team. (2008). The effects of early social-emotional and relationship experience on the development of young orphanage children. *Monographs of the Society for Research in Child Development, 73* (3, Serial No. 291).

Stambrook, M., & Parker, K. C. H. (1987). The development of the concept of death in childhood: A review of the literature. *Merrill-Palmer Quarterly, 33,* 133–157.

Stams, G. J., Brugman, D., Dekovic, M., van Rosmalen, L., van der Laan, P., & Gibbs, J. C. (2006). The moral judgment of juvenile delinquents: A meta-analysis. *Journal of Abnormal Child Psychology, 34,* 692–708.

Stanley, S. M., Amato, P. R., Johnson, C. A., & Markman, H. J. (2006). Premarital education, marital quality, and marital stability: Findings from a large, random household survey. *Journal of Family Psychology, 20,* 117–126.

Stanley, S. M., Rhoades, G. K., Amato, P. R., Markman, H. J., & Johnson, C. A. (2010). The timing of cohabitation and engagement: Impact on first and second marriages. *Journal of Marriage and Family, 72,* 906–918.

Stanovich, K. E. (1986). Matthew effects in reading: Some consequences of individual differences in the acquisition of literacy. *Reading Research Quarterly, 21,* 360–407.

Stanovich, K. E., & West, R. F. (1997). Reasoning independently of prior belief and individual differences in actively open-minded thinking. *Journal of Educational Psychology, 89,* 342–357.

Staudinger, U. M., & Baltes, P. B. (1996). Interactive minds: A facilitative setting for wisdom-related performance? *Journal of Personality and Social Psychology, 71,* 746–762.

Staudinger, U. M., & Glück, J. (2011). Intelligence and wisdom. In R. J. Sternberg & S. B. Kaufman (Eds.), *The Cambridge Handbook of Intelligence* (pp. 827–846). New York: Cambridge University Press.

Staudinger, U. M., Smith, J., & Baltes, P. B. (1992). Wisdom-related knowledge in a life review task: Age differences and the role of professional specialization. *Psychology and Aging, 7,* 271–281.

Steele, C. M. (1997). A threat in the air: How stereotypes shape intellectual identity and performance. *American Psychologist, 52,* 613–629.

Steele, C. M. (1999). Thin ice: "Stereotype threat" and black college students. *Atlantic, 284,* 44–54.

Steele, C. M., & Aronson, J. (1995). Stereotype threat and the intellectual test performance of African Americans. *Journal of Personality and Social Psychology, 69,* 797–811.

Steenland, K., Henley, J., & Thun, M. (2002). All-cause and cause-specific death rates by educational status for two million people in two American Cancer Society cohorts, 1959–1999. *American Journal of Epidemiology, 156,* 11–21.

Steffen, L. M., Dai, S., Fulton, J. E., & Labarthe, D. R. (2009). Overweight in children and adolescents associated with TV viewing and parental weight: Project HeartBeat! *American Journal of Preventive Medicine, 37*(Suppl. 1), S50–S55.

Stein, C. H. (2009). "I owe it to them": Understanding felt obligation toward parents in adulthood. In K. Shifren (Ed.), *How caregiving affects development. Psychological implications for child, adolescent, and adult caregivers.* Washington, DC: American Psychological Association.

Stein, J. H., & Reiser, L. W. (1994). A study of white middle-class adolescent boys' responses to "semenarche" (the first ejaculation). *Journal of Youth and Adolescence, 23,* 373–384.

Stein, R. (2011, November 10). Scientists find new way to talk to 'vegetable state' patients. *The Washington Post,* p. A9.

Steinberg, L. (1989). Pubertal maturation and parent-adolescent distance: An evolutionary perspective. In G. R. Adams, R. Montemayor, & T. P. Gullotta (Eds.), *Advances in adolescent behavior and development* (pp. 71–97). Newbury Park, CA: Sage.

Steinberg, L. (2001). We know some things: Parent–adolescent relationships in retrospect and prospect. *Journal of Research on Adolescence, 11,* 1–19.

Steinberg, L. (2007). Risk taking in adolescence: New perspectives from brain and behavioural science. *Current Directions in Psychological Sciences, 16,* 55–59.

Steinberg, L. (2010). A dual systems model of adolescent risk-taking. *Developmental Psychobiology, 52,* 216–224

Steinberg, L. (2011). *Adolescence* (9thed.). New York: McGraw-Hill.

Steinberg, L., & Avenevoli, S. (2000). The role of context in the development of psychopathology: A conceptual framework and some speculative propositions. *Child Development, 71,* 66–74.

Steinberg, L., & Dornbusch, S. M. (1991). Negative correlates of part-time employment during adolescence: Replication and elaboration. *Developmental Psychology, 27,* 304–313.

Steinberg, L., Dornbusch, S. M., & Brown, B. B. (1992). Ethnic differences in adolescent achievement: An ecological perspective. *American Psychologist, 47,* 723–729.

Steinberg, L., Fegley, S., & Dornbusch, S. M. (1993). Negative impact of part-time work on adolescent adjustment: Evidence from a longitudinal study. *Developmental Psychology, 29,* 171–180.

Steiner, J. E. (1979). Human facial expressions in response to taste and smell stimulation. In H. W. Reese & L. P. Lipsitt (Eds.), *Advances in child development and behavior* (Vol. 13). New York: Academic Press.

Stemler, S. E., Grigorenko, E. L., Jarvin, L., & Sternberg, R. J. (2006). Using the theory of successful intelligence as a basis for augmenting AP exams in psychology and statistics. *Contemporary Educational Psychology, 31,* 344–376.

Stemp, P. S., Turner, J., & Noh, S. (1986). Psychological distress in the postpartum period: The significance of social support. *Journal of Marriage and the Family, 48,* 271–277.

Stephens, M. A. P., Franks, M. M., Martire, L. M., Norton, T. R., & Atienza, A. A. (2009). Women at midlife: Stress and rewards of balancing parent care with employment and other family roles. In K. Shifren (Ed.), *How caregiving affects development. Psychological implications for child, adolescent, and adult caregivers.* Washington, DC: American Psychological Association.

Stephens, M. A., Townsend, A. L., Martire, L. M., & Druley, J. A. (2001). Balancing parent care with other roles: Interrole conflict of adult daughter caregivers. *Journal of Gerontology: Psychological Sciences, 56B,* P24–34.

Stepp, L. S. (2001, November 2). Children's worries take new shape. *The Washington Post*, pp. C1, C4.

Stern, D. (1977). *The first relationship: Infant and mother*. Cambridge, MA: Harvard University Press.

Stern, M., & Karraker, K. H. (1989). Sex stereotyping of infants: A review of gender labeling studies. *Sex Roles, 20*, 501–522.

Stern, Y. (2002). What is cognitive reserve? Theory and research application of the reserve concept. *Journal of the International Neuropsychological Society, 8*, 448–460.

Sternberg, R. J. (1985). *Beyond IQ: A triarchic theory of human intelligence*. Cambridge, MA: Cambridge University Press.

Sternberg, R. J. (1988b). Triangulating love. In R. J. Sternberg and M. L. Barnes (Eds.), *The psychology of love*. New Haven, CT: Yale University Press.

Sternberg, R. J. (1999b). The theory of successful intelligence. *Review of General Psychology, 3*, 292–316.

Sternberg, R. J. (2003). *Wisdom, intelligence, and creativity synthesized*. Cambridge, UK: Cambridge University Press.

Sternberg, R. J. (2010a). Academic intelligence is not enough! WICS: An expanded model for effective practice in school and later life. In D. D. Preiss & R. J. Sternberg (Eds.), *Innovations in educational psychology: Perspectives on learning, teaching, and human development* (pp. 403–440). New York: Springer.

Sternberg, R. J. (2010b). WICS: A new model for cognitive education. *Journal of Cognitive Education and Psychology, 9*, 34–46.

Sternberg, R. J. (2011). The theory of successful intelligence. In R. J. Sternberg & S. B. Kaufman (Eds.), *The Cambridge handbook of intelligence* (pp. 504–527). New York: Cambridge University Press.

Sternberg, R. J. (2012). The assessment of creativity: An investment-based approach. *Creativity Research Journal, 24*, 3–12.

Sternberg, R. J. (Ed.). (1999a). *Handbook of creativity*. New York: Cambridge University Press.

Sternberg, R. J., Grigorenko, E. L., & Bundy, D. A. (2001). The predictive value of IQ. *Merrill-Palmer Quarterly, 47*, 1–41.

Stevens, D. P., & Truss, C. V. (1985). Stability and change in adult personality over 12 and 20 years. *Developmental Psychology, 21*, 568–584.

Stevens, G. (1999). Age at immigration and second language proficiency among foreign-born adults. *Language in Society, 28*, 555–578.

Stevens, M. M., & Dunsmore, J. C. (1996). Adolescents who are living with a life-threatening illness. In C. A. Corr & D. E. Balk (Eds.), *Handbook of adolescent death and bereavement*. New York: Springer.

Stevens, M. M., Rytmeister, R. J., Proctor, M., & Bolster, P. (2010). Children living with life-threatening or life-limiting illnesses: A dispatch from the front lines. In C. A. Corr & D. E. Balk (Eds.), *Children's encounters with death, bereavement, and coping*. New York: Springer.

Stevens, W. D., Hasher, L., Chiew, K. S., & Grady, C. L. (2008). A neural mechanism underlying memory failure in older adults. *Journal of Neuroscience, 28*, 12820–12824.

Stevenson, H. W., & Lee, S. Y. (1990). Contexts of achievement: A study of American, Chinese, and Japanese children. *Monographs of the Society for Research in Child Development, 55*(1–2, Serial No. 221).

Stevenson, H. W., Chen, C., & Lee, S. (1993). Mathematics achievement of Chinese, Japanese, and American children: Ten years later. *Science, 259*, 53–58.

Stevenson, H. W., Lee, S. Y., & Stigler, J. W. (1986). Mathematics achievement of Chinese, Japanese, and American children. *Science, 231*, 693–699.

Stevenson, H. W., & Stigler, J. (1992). *Learning gap: Why our schools are failing and what we can learn from Japanese and Chinese education*. New York: Simon & Schuster.

Stevenson, H. W., Stigler, J. W., Lee, S., Lucker, G. W., Kitamura, S., & Hsu, C. (1985). Cognitive performance and academic achievement of Japanese, Chinese, and American children. *Child Development, 56*, 718–734.

Stevenson, R. J., Mahmut, M., & Sundqvist, N. (2007). Age related changes in odor discrimination. *Developmental Psychology, 43*, 253–260.

Stewart, R. B., & Marvin, R. S. (1984). Sibling relations: The role of conceptual perspective-taking in the ontogeny of sibling caregiving. *Child Development, 55*, 1322–1332.

Stice, E., & Presnell, K. (2007). *The Body Project: Promoting body acceptance and preventing eating disorders: Facilitator guide*. New York: Oxford University Press.

Stice, E., Marti, C. N., & Rohde, P. (2012). Prevalence, incidence, impairment, and course of the proposed DSM-5 eating disorder diagnoses in an 8-year prospective community study of young women. *Journal of Abnormal Psychology*, doi:10.1037/a0030679

Stice, E., Rohde, P., Gau, J., & Shaw, H. (2009). An effectiveness trial of a dissonance-based eating disorder prevention program for high-risk adolescent girls. *Journal of Consulting and Clinical Psychology, 77*, 825–834.

Stice, E., Rohde, P., Shaw, H., & Marti, C. N. (2013). Efficacy trial of a selective prevention program targeting both eating disorders and obesity among female college students: 1- and 2-year follow-up effects. *Journal of Consulting and Clinical Psychology, 81*, 183–189.

Stifter, C. (2003). Child effects on the family: An example of the extreme case and a question of methodology. In A. C. Crouter & A. Booth (Eds.), *Children's influence on family dynamics. The neglected side of family relationships*. Mahwah, NJ: Erlbaum.

Stillion, J. M., & McDowell, E. E. (1996). *Suicide across the life span: Premature exits* (2nd ed.). Washington, DC: Taylor & Francis.

Stine, E. A. L., Soederberg, L. M., & Morrow, D. G. (1996). Language and discourse processing through adulthood. In F. Blanchard-Fields & T. M. Hess (Eds.), *Perspectives on cognitive change in adulthood and aging*. New York: McGraw-Hill.

Stine-Morrow, E. A. L., Loveless, M. K., & Soederberg, L. M. (1996). Resource allocation in online reading by younger and older adults. *Psychology and Aging, 11*, 475–486.

Stine-Morrow, E. A. L., Parisi, J. M., Morrow, D. G., Greene, J., & Park, D. C. (2007). An engagement model of cognitive optimization through adulthood. *Journals of Gerontology B: Psychological and Social Sciences, 62*, 62–69.

Stine-Morrow, E. A. L., Parisi, M. M., Morrow, D. G., & Park, D. C. (2008). The effects of an engaged lifestyle on cognitive vitality: A field experiment. *Psychology and Aging, 23*, 778–786.

Stipek, D., Gralinski, H., & Kopp, C. (1990). Self-concept development in the toddler years. *Developmental Psychology, 26*, 972–977.

Stipek, D., & Hakuta, K. (2007). Strategies to ensure that no child starts from behind. In J. L. Aber, S. J. Bishop-Josef, S. M. Jones, K. T. McLearn, & D. A. Phillips (Eds.), *Child development and social policy: Knowledge for action*. Washington, DC: American Psychology Association.

Stipek, D. J. (1984). The development of achievement motivation. In R. Ames & C. Ames (Eds.), *Research on motivation in education* (Vol. 1). Orlando, FL: Academic Press.

Stipek, D. J., & Gralinski, J. H. (1996). Children's beliefs about intelligence and school performance. *Journal of Educational Psychology, 88*, 397–407.

Stipek, D. J., & Mac Iver, D. J. (1989). Developmental change in children's assessment of intellectual competence. *Child Development, 60*, 521–538.

Stipek, D. J., Feiler, R., Daniels, D., & Milburn, S. (1995). Effects of different instructional approaches on young children's achievement and motivation. *Child Development, 66*, 209–223.

Stoddart, T., & Turiel, E. (1985). Children's concepts of cross-gender activities. *Child Development, 56*, 1241–1252.

Stone, R. (2009). *A teenager talks about growing up with ADHD*. NYU Child Study Center. Retrieved from www.aboutoutkids.org

Stones, M. J., & Kozma, A. (1985). Physical performance. In N. Charness (Ed.), *Aging and human performance*. Chichester, UK & NY: Wiley.

Story, M., Nanney, M. S., & Schwartz, M. B. (2009). Schools and obesity prevention: Creating school environments and policies to promote healthy eating and physical activity. *Milbank Quarterly, 87*, 71–100.

Strauch, B. (2010). *The secret life of the grown-up brain*. New York: Penguin.

Straus, M. A., & Gelles, R. J. (Edited with C. Smith) (1990). *Physical violence in American families. Risk factors and adaptations to violence in 8145 families*. New Brunswick, NJ: Transaction Publishers.

Streri, A., & Gentaz, E. (2004). Cross-modal recognition of shape from hand to eyes and handedness in human newborns. *Neuropsychologia, 42*, 1365–1369.

Strober, M., Freeman, R., Lampert, C., Diamond, J., & Kaye, W. (2000). Controlled family study of anorexia nervosa and bulimia nervosa: Evidence of shared liability and transmission of partial syndromes. *American Journal of Psychiatry, 157,* 393–401.

Stroebe, M. (2001). Bereavement research and theory: Retrospective and prospective. *American Behavioral Scientist, 44,* 854–865.

Stroebe, M. S., & Schut, H. A. W. (1999). The dual process model of coping with bereavement: Rationale and description. *Death Studies, 23,* 197–224.

Stroebe, M., & Schut, H. (2010). The dual process model of coping with bereavement: A decade on. *Omega: Journal of Death and Dying, 61,* 273–289.

Stroebe, M., Schut, H., & Boerner, K. (2010). Continuing bonds in adaptation to bereavement: Toward theoretical integration. *Clinical Psychology Review, 30,* 259–268.

Strøm, I. F., Thoresen, S., Wentzel-Larsen, T., & Dyb, G. (2013). Violence, bullying and academic achievement: A study of 15-year-old adolescents and their school environment. *Child Abuse & Neglect, 37,* 243–251.

Strong, B., DeVault, C., & Cohen, T. F. (2011). *The marriage and family experience: Intimate relationships in a changing society* (11th ed.). Belmont, CA: Wadsworth Cengage Learning.

Substance Abuse and Mental Health Services Administration (2011). *Results from the 2010 National Survey on Drug Use and Health: Summary of national findings,* NSDUH Series H-41, HHSPublication No. (SMA) 11-4658. Rockville, MD: Substance Abuse and Mental Health Services Administration, 2011.

Substance Abuse and Mental Health Services Administration (2012). *Preventing suicide: A toolkit for high schools.* HHS Publication No. SMA-12-4669. Rockville, MD: Center for Mental Health Services, Substance Abuse and Mental Health Services Administration

Substance Abuse and Mental Health Services Administration. (2012). *Results from the 2011 National Survey on Drug Use and Health: Summary of National Findings* (NSDUH Series H-44, HHS Publication No. (SMA) 12–4713). Rockville, MD: Author.

Sudhalter, V., & Braine, M. D. S. (1985). How does comprehension of passives develop? A comparison of actional and experiential verbs. *Journal of Child Language, 12,* 455–470.

Sue, S., Cheng, J. K. Y., Saad, C. S., & Chu, J. P. (2012). Asian American mental health. A call to action. *American Psychologist, 67,* 532–544.

Sugden, K., Arseneault, L., Harrington, H., Moffitt, T. E., Williams, B., & Caspi, A. (2010). Serotonin transporter gene moderates the development of emotional problems among children following bullying victimization.

Journal of the American Academy of Child & Adolescent Psychiatry, 49, 830–840.

Suitor, J. J. (1991). Marital quality and satisfaction with the division of household labor across the family life cycle. *Journal of Marriage and the Family, 53,* 221–230.

Suitor, J. J., Sechrist, J., Plikuhn, M., Pardo, S. T., Gilligan, M., & Pillemer, K. (2009). The role of perceived maternal favoritism in sibling relations in midlife. *Journal of Marriage and Family, 71,* 1026–1038.

Sullivan, H. S. (1953). *The interpersonal theory of psychiatry.* New York: Norton.

Sullivan, S., & Ruffman, T. (2004). Social understanding: How does it fare with advancing years? *British Journal of Psychology, 95,* 1–18.

Sulloway, F. J. (2007). Birth order and intelligence. *Science, 316,* 1711–1717.

Super, D. E., Savickas, M. L., & Super, C. M. (1996). The life-span, life-space approach to careers. In D. Brown, L. Brooks, & Associates (Eds.), *Career choice and development* (3rd ed.). San Francisco: Jossey-Bass.

Susser, E., St. Clair, D., & He, L. (2008). Latent effects of prenatal malnutrition on adult health: The example of schizophrenia. *Annual New York Academy of Sciences, 1136,* 185–192.

Sussman, S., Pokhrel, P., Ashmore, R. D., & Brown, B. B. (2007). Adolescent peer group identification and characteristics: A review of the literature. *Addictive Behaviors, 32,* 1602–1627.

Sutin, A. R., Costa, P. T. Jr., Wethington, E., & Eaton, W. (2010). Turning points and lessons learned: Stressful life events and personality trait development across middle adulthood. *Psychology and Aging, 25,* 524–533.

Sutter, C., Zöllig, J., Allemand, M., & Martin, M. (2012). Sleep quality and cognitive function in healthy old age: The moderating role of subclinical depression. *Neuropsychology, 26,* 768–775.

Swamy, R., Mohapatra, S., Bythell, M., & Embleton, N. D. (2010). Survival in infants live born at less than 24 weeks' gestation: The hidden morbidity of non-survivors. *Archives of Disease in Childhood-Fetal and Neonatal Edition, 95,* 293–294.

Swanson, H. L. (1999). What develops in working memory? A life span perspective. *Developmental Psychology, 35,* 986–1000.

Swarr, A. E., & Richards, M. H. (1996). Longitudinal effects of adolescent girls' pubertal development, perceptions of pubertal timing, and parental relations on eating problems. *Developmental Psychology, 32,* 636–646.

Symons, D. K., & Clark, S. E. (2000). A longitudinal study of mother–child relationships and theory of mind in the preschool period. *Social Development, 9,* 3–23.

Szoeke, C. E. I., Campbell, S., Chiu, E., & Ames, D. (2009). Vascular cognitive disorder. In M. F. Weiner & A. M. Lipton (Eds.), *The American Psychiatric Publishing Textbook of Alzheimer disease and other dementias.* Washington, DC: American Psychiatric Publishing.

Tabert, M. H., Manly, J. J., Liu, X., Pelton, G. H., Rosenblum, S., Jacobs, M., Zamora, D., Goodkind, M., Bell, K., Stern, Y., Devanand, D. P. (2006). Neuropsychological prediction of conversion to Alzheimer disease in patients with mild cognitive impairment. *Archives of General Psychiatry, 63,* 916–924.

Tach, L., & Halpern-Meekin, S. (2009). How does premarital cohabitation affect trajectories of marital quality? *Journal of Marriage and Family, 71,* 298–317.

Tackett, J. L., Krueger, R. F., Iacono, W. G., & McGue, M. (2008). Personality in middle childhood: A hierarchical structure and longitudinal connections with personality in late adolescence. *Journal of Research in Personality, 42,* 1456–1462.

Taddio, A. (2002). Conditioning and hyperalgesia in newborns exposed to repeated heel lances. *Journal of the American Medical Association, 288,* 857–861.

Tafarodi, R. W., Lo, C., Yamaguchi, S., Lee, W. W., & Katsura, H. (2004). The inner self in three countries. *Journal of Cross-Cultural Psychology, 35,* 97–117.

Tager-Flusberg, H. (2000). Language and understanding minds: Connections in autism. In S. Baron-Cohen, H. Tager-Flusberg, & D. J. Cohen (Eds.), *Understanding other minds. Perspectives from developmental cognitive neuroscience* (2nd ed.). Oxford: Oxford University Press.

Tager-Flusberg, H., & Zukowski, A. (2013). Putting words together: Morphology and syntax in the preschool years. In J. Berko Gleason & N. B. Ratner (Eds.), *The development of language* (7th ed.). Boston: Allyn & Bacon.

Takahashi, K. (1990). Are the key assumptions of the "Strange Situation" procedure universal? A view from Japanese research. *Human Development, 33,* 23–30.

Tallal, P., Miller, S. L., Bedi, G., Byma, G., Wang, X., Nagarajan, S. S., et al. (1996). Language comprehension in language-learning impaired children improved with acoustically modified speech. *Science, 271,* 81–84.

Talwar, V., & Lee, K. (2008). Social and cognitive correlates of children's lying behavior. *Child Development, 79,* 866–881.

Tamis-LeMonda, C. S., Adolph, K. E., Lobo, S. A., Karasik, L. B., Ishak, S., & Dimitropoulou, K. A. (2008). When infants take mothers' advice: 18-month-olds integrate perceptual and social information to guide motor action. *Developmental Psychology, 44,* 734–746.

Tan, R. S., & Pu, S. J. (2004). Is it andropause? Recognizing androgen deficiency in aging men. *Postgraduate Medicine, 115,* 62–66.

Tan, U., & Tan, M. (1999). Incidences of asymmetries for the palmar grasp reflex in neonates and hand preference in adults. *Neuroreport: For Rapid Communication of Neuroscience Research, 10,* 3254–3256.

Tannen, D. (1991). *You just don't understand: Women and men in conversation.* New York: Ballantine.

Tanner, J. M. (1990). *Foetus into man: Physical growth from conception to maturity* (2nd ed.). Cambridge, MA: Harvard University Press.

Tanzi, R. E., & Parson, A. B. (2000). *Decoding darkness. The search for the genetic causes of Alzheimer's disease*. Cambridge, MA: Perseus Publishing.

Tarren-Sweeney, M. (2013). An investigation of complex attachment- and trauma-related symptomatology among children in foster and kinship care. *Child Psychiatry and Human Development*, online doi:10.1007/s10578-013-0366-x

Tarullo, A. R., Balsam, P. D. and Fifer, W. P. (2011), Sleep and infant learning. *Infant and Child Development*, 20, 35–46.

Taste science. (2010). The Taste Science Laboratory. Retrieved from www.tastescience.com

Taveras, E. M., Rifas-Shiman, S. L., Belfort, M. B., Kleinman, K. P., Oken, E., & Gillman, M. W. (2009). Weight status in the first 6 months of life and obesity at 3 years of age. *Pediatrics, 123*, 1177–1183.

Taylor, C. A., Manganello, J. A., Lee, S. J., & Rice, J. C. (2010). Mothers' spanking of 3-year-old children and subsequent risk of children's aggressive behavior. *Pediatrics, 125*, 1057–1065.

Taylor, G., Lekes, N., Gagnon, H., Kwan, L., & Koestner, R. (2012). Need satisfaction, work–school interference and school dropout: An application of self-determination theory. *British Journal of Educational Psychology, 82*, 622–646.

Taylor, M. D., Frier, B. M., Gold, A. E., & Deary, I. J. (2003). Psychosocial factors and diabetes-related outcomes following diagnosis of Type 1 diabetes. *Diabetic Medicine, 20*, 135–146.

Taylor, M. R. (2003). Dealing with death: Western philosophical strategies. In C. D. Bryant (Ed.), *Handbook of death and dying*. Thousand Oaks, CA: Sage.

Taylor, M., Carlson, S. M., Maring, B. L., Gerow, L., & Charley, C. M. (2004). The characteristics and correlates of fantasy in school-age children: Imaginary companions, impersonation, and social understanding. *Developmental Psychology, 40*, 1173–1187.

Taylor, R. E., & Richards, S. B. (1991). Patterns of intellectual differences of black, Hispanic, and white children. *Psychology in the Schools, 28*, 5–9.

Taylor, R. J., Chatters, L. M., & Jackson, J. S. (2007). Religious and spiritual involvement among older African Americans, Caribbean black, and non-Hispanic whites: Findings from the National Survey of American Life. *Journal of Gerontology: Social Sciences, 62B*, S238–S250.

Taylor, S. E., Saphire-Bernstein, S., & Seeman, T. E. (2010). Are plasma oxytocin in women and plasma vasopressin in men biomarkers of distressed pair-bond relationships? *Psychological Science, 21*, 3–7.

Teachman, B. A. (2006). Aging and negative affect: The rise and fall and rise of anxiety and depression symptoms. *Psychology and Aging, 21*, 201–207.

Teachman, J. D. (2002). Stability across cohorts in divorce risk factors. *Demography, 39*, 331–351.

Teachman, J., & Tedrow, L. (2008). The demography of stepfamilies in the United States. In J. Pryor (Ed.), *The international handbook of stepfamilies: Policy and practice in legal, research, and clinical environments*. Hoboken, NJ: Wiley.

Tedeschi, R. G., & Calhoun, L. G. (1995). *Trauma and transformation: Growing in the aftermath of suffering*. Thousand Oaks, CA: Sage.

Tedeschi, R. G., & Calhoun, L. G. (2004). Posttraumatic growth: Conceptual foundations and empirical evidence. *Psychological Inquiry, 15*, 1–18.

Teeter, P. A. (1998). *Interventions for ADHD. Treatment in developmental context*. New York: Guilford.

Temel, J. S., Greer, J. A., Muzikansky, A., Gallagher, E. R., Admane, S., Jackson, V. A., et al. (2010). Early palliative care for patients with metastatic non-small-cell lung cancer. *The New England Journal of Medicine, 363*, 733–742.

Temple, E., Poldrack, R. A., Protopapas, A., Nagarajan, S., Salz, T., Tallal, P., et al. (2000). Disruption of the neural response to rapid acoustic stimuli in dyslexia: Evidence from functional MRI. *Proceedings of the National Academy of Science, 97*, 13907–13912.

Tenenbaum, H. R., & Leaper, C. (2003). Parent-child conversations about science: The socialization of gender inequities. *Developmental Psychology, 39*, 34–47.

Tenenbaum, H. R., Poe, M. V., Snow, C. E., Tabors, P., & Ross, S. (2007). Maternal and child predictors of low-income children's educational attainment. *Journal of Applied Development Psychology, 28*, 227–238.

Teno, J. M., Clarridge, B. R., Casey, V., Welch, L. C., Wetle, T., Shield, R., & Mor, V. (2004). Family perspectives on end-of-life care at the last place of care. *Journal of the American Medical Association, 291*, 88–93.

Terman, L. M. (1954). The discovery and encouragement of exceptional talent. *American Psychologist, 9*, 221–238.

Tessier, R., Charpak, N., Giron, M., Cristo, M., de Calume, Z. F., & Ruiz-Peláez, J. G. (2009). Kangaroo mother care, home environment and father involvement in the first year of life: A randomized controlled study. *Acta Paediatrica, 98*, 1444–1450.

Testa, M., Hoffman, J. H., & Livingston, J. A. (2010). Alcohol and sexual risk behaviors as mediators of the sexual victimization-revictimization relationship. *Journal of Consulting and Clinical Psychology, 78*, 249–259.

Thambirajah, M. S., De-Hayes, L., & Grandison, K. J. (2008). *Understanding school refusal: A handbook for professionals in education, health and social care*. Philadelphia, PA: Jessica Kingsley.

Thapar, A. (2003). Attention deficit hyperactivity disorder: New genetic findings, new directions. In R. Plomin, J. C. DeFries, I. W. Craig, & P. McGuffin (Eds.), *Behavioral genetics in the postgenomic era*. Washington, DC: American Psychological Association.

Tharinger, D. (1990). Impact of child sexual abuse on developing sexuality. *Professional Psychology: Research & Practice, 21*, 331–337.

Editors of *The Lancet*. (2010, February 2). Retraction—Ileal-lymphoid-nodular hyperplasia, non-specific colitis, and pervasive developmental disorder in children. Retrieved from www.thelancet.com

Thelen, E. (1995). Motor development: A new synthesis. *American Psychologist, 50*, 79–95.

Thelen, E. (1996). The improvising infant: Learning about learning to move. In M. R. Merrens & G. G. Brannigan (Eds.), *The developmental psychologists: Research adventures across the life span* (pp. 21–35). New York: McGraw-Hill.

Thelen, E., & Smith, L. B. (1994). *A dynamic systems approach to the development of cognition and action*. Cambridge, MA: MIT Press.

Thelen, M. H., Powell, A. L., Lawrence, C., & Kuhnert, M. E. (1992). Eating and body image concerns among children. *Journal of Clinical Child Psychology, 21*, 41–46.

Thibault, H., Contrand, B., Saubusse, E., Baine, M., & Maurice-Tison, S. (2010). Risk factors for overweight and obesity in French adolescents: Physical activity, sedentary behavior and parental characteristics. *Nutrition, 26*, 192–2000.

Thiede, K. W., & Dunlosky, J. (1999). Toward a general model of self-regulated study: An analysis of selection of items for study and self-paced study time. *Journal of Experimental Psychology: Learning, Memory, and Cognition, 25*, 1024–1037.

Thigpen, J. W. (2009). Early sexual behavior in a sample of low-income, African American children. *Journal of Sex Research, 46*, 67–79.

Thomas, A. K., & Bulevich, J. B. (2006). Effective cue utilization reduces memory errors in older adults. *Psychological Aging, 21*, 379–389.

Thomas, A., & Chess, S. (1986). The New York Longitudinal Study: From infancy to early adult life. In R. Plomin & J. Dunn (Eds.), *The study of temperament: Changes, continuities, and challenges*. Hillsdale, NJ: Erlbaum.

Thomas, F., Renaud, F., Benefice, E., de Meeus, T., & Guegan, J. (2001). International variability of ages at menarche and menopause: Patterns and main determinants. *Human Biology, 73*, 271.

Thomas, J. R., Alderson, J. A., Thomas, K. T., Campbell, A. C., & Elliott, B. C. (2010). Developmental gender differences for overhand throwing in Aboriginal Australian children. *Research Quarterly in Exercise Sport, 81*, 432–441.

Thomas, O. N., Caldwell, C. H., Faison, N., & Jackson, J. S. (2009). Promoting academic achievement: The role of racial identity in buffering perceptions of teacher discrimination on academic achievement among African American and Caribbean Black adolescents. *Journal of Educational Psychology, 101*, 420–431.

Thompson, A. M., & Smart, J. L. (1993). A prospective study of the development of laterality: Neonatal laterality in relation to perinatal factors and maternal behavior. *Cortex, 29,* 649–659.

Thompson, J. R., & Chapman, R. S. (1977). Who is "Daddy" revisited? The status of two-year-olds' overextended words in use and comprehension. *Journal of Child Language, 4,* 359–375.

Thompson, R. A. (1994). Emotion regulation: A theme in search of definition. In N. A. Fox (Ed.), The development of emotion regulation: Biological and behavioral considerations. *Monographs of the Society for Research in Child Development, 59* (Nos. 2–3, Serial No. 240).

Thompson, R. A. (2006). Conversation and developing understanding: Introduction to the special issue. *Merrill-Palmer Quarterly, 52,* 1–16.

Thompson, R. A. (2006). Conversation and developing understanding: Introduction to the special issue. *Merrill-Palmer Quarterly, 52,* 1–16.

Thompson, R. A. (2012). Whither the preconventional child? Toward a life-span moral development theory. *Child Development Perspectives, 6,* 423–429.

Thompson, R. A., & Amato, P. R. (1999). The post divorce family. An introduction to the issues. In R. A. Thompson & P. R. Amato (Eds.), *The post divorce family. Children, parenting, & society.* Thousand Oaks, CA: Sage.

Thompson, R. A., & Meyer, S. (2007). Socialization of emotion regulation in the family. In J. J. Gross (Ed.), *Handbook of emotion regulation.* New York: Guilford.

Thompson, R. A., Meyer, S., & McGinley, M. (2006). Understanding values in relationships: The development of conscience. In M. Killen & J. G. Smetana (Eds.), *Handbook of moral development.* Mahwah, NJ: Erlbaum.

Thompson, R. A., Winer, A. C., & Goodvin, R. (2011). The individual child: Temperament, emotion, self, and personality. In M. E. Lamb & M. H. Bornstein (Eds.), *Social and personality development. An advanced textbook.* New York: Psychology Press.

Thompson, R. F. (2000). *The brain: An introduction to neuroscience* (3rd ed.). New York: Worth.

Thompson, S. B. N. (2006). *Dementia and memory: A handbook for students and professionals.* Hampshire, UK: Ashgate Publishing.

Thorndike, R. L. (1997). The early history of intelligence testing. In D. P. Flanagan, J. L. Genshaft, & P. L. Harrison (Eds.), *Contemporary intellectual assessment: Theories, tests, and issues.* New York: Guilford.

Thorne, B. (1993). *Gender play: Girls and boys in school.* New Brunswick, NJ: Rutgers University Press.

Thornton, R., & Light, L. L. (2006). Language comprehension and production in normal aging. In J. E. Birren & K. W. Schaie (Eds.), *Handbook of the psychology of aging.* Boston: Elsevier Academic Press.

Thurber, C. A. (1995). The experience and expression of homesickness in preadolescent and adolescent boys. *Child Development, 66,* 1162–1178.

Thys-Jacobs, S. (2000). Micronutrients and the premenstrual syndrome: The case for calcium. *Journal of the American College of Nutrition, 19,* 220–227.

Tietjen, A. M., & Walker, L. J. (1985). Moral reasoning and leadership among men in a Papua New Guinea society. *Developmental Psychology, 21,* 982–992.

Tiggemann, M., & Lacey, C. (2009). Shopping for clothes: Body satisfaction, appearance investment, and functions of clothing among female shoppers. *Body Image, 6,* 285–291.

Timmer, E., Bode, C., & Dittmann-Kohli, F. (2003). Expectations of gains in the second half of life: A study of personal conceptions of enrichment in a lifespan perspective. *Ageing & Society,23,* 3–24.

Tisak, M. S., & Tisak, J. (1990). Children's conceptions of parental authority, friendship, and sibling relations. *Merrill-Palmer Quarterly, 36,* 347–368.

Tither, J. M., & Ellis, B. J. (2008). Impact of fathers on daughters' age at menarche: A genetically and environmentally controlled sibling study. *Developmental Psychology, 44,* 1409–1420.

Tolan, P., Gorman-Smith, D., & Henry, D. (2006). Family violence. *Annual Review of Psychology, 57,* 557–583.

Tomasello, M. (2003). *Constructing a language: A usage-based theory of language acquisition.* Cambridge, MA: Harvard University Press.

Tomasello, M. (2006). Acquiring linguistic constructions. In D. Kuhn & R. Siegler (Vol. Eds.), *Handbook of child psychology: Cognition, perception, and language: Vol. 2* (6th ed.). Hoboken, NJ: Wiley and Sons.

Tomasello, M. (2009). The usage-based theory of language acquisition. In E. L. Bavin (Ed.), *The Cambridge handbook of child language* (pp. 69–87). New York: Cambridge University Press.

Tomasello, M. (with C. Dweck, J. Silk, B. Skryms, & E. Spelke) (2009). *Why we cooperate.* Cambridge, MA: MIT Press.

Tomasello, M., & Herrmann, E. (2010). Ape and human cognition: What's the difference? *Current Directions in Psychological Science, 19,* 3–8.

Tomasello, M., & Vaish, A. (2013). Origins of human cooperation and morality. *Annual Review of Psychology, 64,* 231–255.

Tomasello, M., Call, J., & Hare, B. (2003). Chimpanzees understand psychological states: The question is which ones and to what extent. *Trends in Cognitive Sciences, 7,* 153–156.

Tomblin, J. B. (2009). Children with specific language impairment. In E. L. Bavin (Ed.), *The Cambridge handbook of child language* (pp. 418–431). New York: Cambridge University Press.

Tomlinson-Keasey, C., & Keasey, C. B. (1974). The mediating role of cognitive development in moral judgment. *Child Development, 45,* 291–298.

Tomlinson-Keasey, C., & Little, T. D. (1990). Predicting educational attainment, occupational achievement, intellectual skill, and personal adjustment among gifted men and women. *Journal of Educational Psychology, 82,* 442–455.

Tomporowski, P. D., Davis, C. L., Miller, P. H., & Naglieri, J. A. (2008). Exercise and children's intelligence, cognition, and academic achievement. *Educational Psychology Review, 20,* 111–131.

Toossi, M. (2012). Labor force projections to 2020: A more slowly growing workforce. *Monthly Labor Review, 135,* 43–64.

Torges, C. M., Stewart, A. J., & Duncan, L. E. (2008). Achieving ego integrity: Personality development in late midlife. *Journal of Research in Personality, 42,* 1004–1019.

Trabasso, T. (1975). Representation, memory, and reasoning: How do we make transitive inferences? In A. D. Pick (Ed.), *Minnesota Symposia on Child Psychology* (Vol. 9). Minneapolis: University of Minnesota.

Trainor, B.C., Nelson, R. J. (2012). Neuroendocrinology of Aggression. In G. Fink, D. W. Pfaff, & J. E. Levine (Eds.) *Handbook of Neuroendocrinology* (pp. 509–520). San Diego: Academic Press.

Trautner, H. M., Gervai, J., & Nemeth, R. (2003). Appearance-reality distinction and development of gender constancy understanding in children. *International Journal of Behavioral Development, 27,* 275–281.

Trautner, H. M., Ruble, D. N., Cyphers, L., Kirsten, B., Behrendt, R., & Hartmann, P. (2005). Rigidity and flexibility of gender stereotypes in childhood: Developmental or differential? *Infant and Child Development, 14,* 365–381.

Traylor, E. S., Hayslip, B. Jr., Kaminski, P. L., & York, C. (2003). Relationships between grief and family system characteristics: A cross lagged longitudinal analysis. *Death Studies, 27,* 575–601.

Treffert, D. A. (2000). *Extraordinary people: Understanding savant syndrome.* Lincoln, Nebraska: iUniverse.com.

Treiman, R., & Broderick, V. (1998). What's in a name? Children's knowledge about the letters in their own names. *Journal of Experimental Child Psychology, 70,* 97–116.

Tremblay, M. S., Inman, J. W., & Willms, J. D. (2000). The relationship between physical activity, self-esteem, and academic achievement in 12-year-old children. *Pediatric Exercise Science, 12,* 312–323.

Tremblay, R. E. (2010). Developmental origins of disruptive behaviour problems: The original sin hypothesis, epigenetics and their consequences for prevention. *Journal of Child Psychology and Psychiatry, 51,* 341–367.

Tremblay, R. E. (2011). Origins, development, and prevention of aggressive behavior. In D.

P. Keating (Ed.), *Nature and nurture in early child development*. New York: Cambridge University Press.

Trevarthen, C. (2011). What is it like to be a person who knows nothing? Defining the active intersubjective mind of a newborn human being. *Infant and Child Development, 20,* 119–135.

Triandis, H. C. (1989). Self and social behavior in differing cultural contexts. *Psychological Review, 96,* 269–289.

Triandis, H. C. (1995). *Individualism and collectivism.* Boulder, CO: Westview Press.

Trickett, P. K., & Putnam, F. W. (1993). Impact of child sexual abuse on females: Toward a developmental, psychobiological integration. *Psychological Science, 4,* 81–87.

Tronick, E. Z. (1989). Emotions and emotional communication in infants. *American Psychologist, 44,* 112–119.

Trost, S. G., McCoy, T. A., Vander Veur, S. S., Mallya, G., Duffy, M. L., & Foster, G. D. (2013). Physical activity patterns of inner-city elementary school children. *Medicine & Science in Sports and Exercise, 45,* 470–474.

Trueheart, C. (1997, August 5). Champion of longevity ends her reign at 122. *The Washington Post,* pp. A1, A12.

Trzesniewski, K. H., Donnellan, M. B., Moffitt, T. E., Robins, R. W., Poulton, R., & Caspi, A. (2006). Low self-esteem during adolescence predicts poor health, criminal behavior, and limited economic prospects during adulthood. *Developmental Psychology, 42,* 381–390.

Tsai, Y.-M., Kunter, M., Ludtke, O., Trautwein, U., & Ryan, R. M. (2008). What makes lessons interesting? The role of situational and individual factors in three school subjects. *Journal of Educational Psychology, 100,* 460–472.

Ttofi, M. M., Farrington, D. P., & Lösel, F. (2012). School bullying as a predictor of violence later in life: A systematic review and meta-analysis of prospective longitudinal studies. *Aggression and Violent Behavior, 17,* 405–418.

Tucker-Drob, E. M. (2012). Preschools reduce early academic-achievement gaps: A longitudinal twin approach. *Psychological Science, 23,* 310–319.

Tucker-Drob, E. M., & Harden, K. P. (2012). Intellectual interest mediates gene x socioeconomic status interaction on adolescent academic achievement. *Child Development, 83,* 743–757.

Tucker-Drob, E. M., Rhemtulla, M., Harden, K. P., Turkheimer, E., & Fask, D. (2011). Emergence of a gene x socioeconomic status interaction on infant mental ability between 10 months and 2 years. *Psychological Science, 22,* 125–133.

Tulandi, T., & Al-Fozan, H. M. (2011). Spontaneous abortion: Risk factors, etiology, clinical manifestations, and diagnostic evaluation. *Up to Date,* Wolters Kluwer. Retrieved from http://www.uptodate.com/contents/spontaneous-abortion-risk-factors-etiology-clinical-manifestations-and-diagnostic-evaluation

Tullos, A., & Woolley, J. D. (2009). The development of children's ability to use evidence to infer reality status. *Child Development, 80,* 101–114.

Tun, P. A., & Lachman, M. E. (2010). The association between computer use and cognition across adulthood: Use it so you won't lose it? *Psychology and Aging, 25,* 560–568.

Tun, P. A., McCoy, S., & Wingfield, A. (2009). Aging, hearing acuity, and the attentional costs of effortful listening. *Psychology and Aging, 24,* 761–766.

Turati, C. (2004). Why faces are not special to newborns: An alternative account of the face preference. *Current Directions in Psychological Science, 13,* 5–8.

Turiel, E. (1978). The development of concepts of social structure: Social convention. In J. Glick & A. Clarke-Stewart (Eds.), *The development of social understanding.* New York: Gardner Press.

Turiel, E. (1983). *The development of social knowledge. Morality and convention.* Cambridge, UK: Cambridge University Press.

Turiel, E. (2006). The development of morality. In N. Eisenberg (Vol. Ed.), & W. Damon & R. M. Lerner (Eds. in Chief), *Handbook of child psychology: Vol. 3. Social, emotional, and personality development* (6th ed.). Hoboken, NJ: Wiley.

Turk-Charles, S., & Carstensen, L. L. (1999). The role of time in the setting of social goals across the life span. In T. M. Hess & F. Blanchard-Fields (Eds.), *Social cognition and aging.* San Diego: Academic Press.

Turner, P. J., & Gervai, J. (1995). A multidimensional study of gender typing in preschool children and their parents: Personality, attitudes, preferences, behavior, and cultural differences. *Developmental Psychology, 31,* 759–772.

Turnpenny, P. D., & Ellard, S. (2011). *Emery's elements of medical genetics* (14th ed.). London: Elsevier.

Twenge, J. M. (1997). Changes in masculine and feminine traits over time: A meta-analysis. *Sex Roles, 36,* 305–325.

Twenge, J. M. (2006). *Generation me. Why today's young Americans are more confident, assertive, entitled—and more miserable than ever before.* New York: Free Press.

Twenge, J. M., Konrath, S., Foster, J. D., Campbell, W. K., & Bushman, B. J. (2008). Egos inflating over time: A cross-temporal meta-analysis of the Narcissistic Personality Inventory. *Journal of Personality, 76,* 875–902.

Tyre, P. (2005, December 5). No one to blame. *Newsweek,* 50–59.

Tyson-Rawson, K. J. (1996). Adolescent responses to the death of a parent. In C. A. Corr & D. E. Balk (Eds.), *Handbook of adolescent death and bereavement.* New York: Springer.

U. S. Department of Health and Human Services, Administration on Children, Youth, and Families. (2007). *Child maltreatment 2005.* Washington, DC: U. S. Government Printing Office. Retrieved from www.acf.hhs.gov/programs/cb/pubs/cm05/ index.htm

U.S. Census Bureau, Population Division. (2012, December). Table 2. Projections of the Population by Selected Age Groups and Sex for the United States: 2015 to 2060 (NP2012-T2).

U.S.D.A. Factbook. (2012). *Profiling food consumption in America. Retrieved from* http://www.usda.gov/factbook/chapter2.pdf. Accessed 10/28/2012

U.S. Department of Labor, Bureau of Labor Statistics. (2013). *Women as a percent of total employed in selected occupations, 2011.* Retrieved from http://www.bls.gov/opub/ted/2012/ted_20120501.htm

Bau, A. M., Ernert, A., Schenk, L., Wiegand, S., Martus, P., Grüters, A., et al. (2009). Is there a further acceleration in the age at onset of menarche? A cross-sectional study in 1840 school children focusing on age and bodyweight at the onset of menarche. *European Journal of Endocrinology, 160,* 107–113.

Brehmer, Y., Li, S., Müller, V., von Oertzen, T., & Lindenberger, U. (2007). Memory plasticity across the life-span: Uncovering children's latent potential. *Developmental Psychology, 43,* 465–478.

Uccelli, P., & Pan, B. A. (2013). Semantic development: Learning the meanings of words. In J. Berko Gleason & N. B. Ratner (Eds.), *The development of language* (7th ed.). Boston: Allyn & Bacon.

Uchida, N., Fujita, K., & Katayama, T. (1999). Detection of vehicles on the other crossing path at an intersection: Visual search performance of elderly drivers. *Japanese Society of Automotive Engineers Review, 20,* 381.

Uchino, B. N. (2009). Understanding the links between social support and physical health. A life-span perspective with emphasis on the separation of perceived and received support. *Perspectives on Psychological Science. 4,* 236–255.

Uchronski, M. (2008). Agency and communion in spontaneous self-descriptions: Occurrence and situational malleability. *European Journal of Social Psychology, 38,* 1093–1102.

Ueno, K., & Adams, R. G. (2006). Adult friendship: A decade review. In P. Noller & J. A. Feeney (Eds.), *Close relationships: Functions, forms, and processes.* New York: Psychology Press.

Uher, R. (2011). Genes, environment, and personalized treatment for depression. In K. A. Dodge & M. Rutter (Eds.), *Gene-environment interactions in developmental psychopathology.* New York: Guilford.

Umaña-Taylor, A. J., & Alfaro, E. C. (2006). Ethnic identity among U. S. Latino adolescents: Theory, measurement, and implications for well-being. In F. A. Villarruel & T. Luster (Eds.), *The crisis in youth mental health: Critical issues and effective programs: Vol 2. Disorders in adolescence.* Westport, CT: Praeger.

Umaña-Taylor, A. J., Bhanot, R., & Shin, N. (2006). Ethnic identity formation during adolescence:

The critical role of families. *Journal of Family Issues, 27,* 390–414.

Umaña-Taylor, A. J., Gonzales-Backen, M. A., & Guimond, A. B. (2009). Latino adolescents' ethnic identity: Is there a developmental progression and does growth in ethnic identity predict growth in self-esteem? *Child Development, 80,* 391–405.

Umaña-Taylor, A. J., & Guimond, A. B. (2012). A longitudinal examination of parenting behaviors and perceived discrimination predicting Latino adolescents' ethnic identity. *Journal of Latino Psychology, 1,* 14–35.

Umberson, D. (2003). *Death of a parent: Transition to a new adult identity.* Cambridge, UK: Cambridge University Press.

Umberson, D., & Slaten, E. (2000). Gender and intergenerational relationships. In D. H. Demo, K. R. Allen, & M. A. Fine (Eds.), *Handbook of family diversity.* New York: Oxford University Press.

Umberson, D., Pudrovska, T., & Reczek, C. (2010). Parenthood, childlessness, and well-being: A life course perspective. *Journal of Marriage and Family, 72,* 612–629.

Ungvari, Z. Sonntag, W. E., de Cabo, R., Baur J. A., & Csiszar, A. (2011). Mitochondrial protection by resveratrol. *Exercise and Sports Science Review, 39,* 128–132.

United Nations, Department of Economic and Social Affairs, Population Division. (2007). *World population prospects: The 2006 revision, highlights.* Retrieved from www.un.org/esa/population/ publications/wpp2006/WPP2006_Highlights_rev .pdf. Working Paper No. ESA/P/WP.202.

University of Copenhagen. (2008, December 18). Girls have superior sense of taste to boys. *Sciencedaily.* Retrieved from www.sciencedaily.com/releases/2008/12/081216104035.htm

Updegraff, K., McHale, S. M., & Crouter, A. C. (1996). Gender roles in marriage: What do they mean for girls' and boys' school achievement? *Journal of Youth and Adolescence, 25,* 73–88.

Urbina, S. (2011). Tests of intelligence. In R. J. Sternberg & S. B. Kaufman (Eds.), *The Cambridge handbook of intelligence* (pp. 20–38). New York: Cambridge University Press.

Urdan, T., & Mestas, M. (2006). The goals behind performance goals. *Journal of Educational Psychology, 98,* 354–365.

Schneider, W., Kron-Sperl, V., & Hünnerkopf, M. (2009). The development of young children's memory strategies: Evidence from the Wurzburg Longitudinal Memory Study. *European Journal of Developmental Psychology, 6,* 70–99.

Usher, J. A., & Neisser, U. (1993). Childhood amnesia and the beginnings of memory for four early life events. *Journal of Experimental Psychology: General, 122,* 155–165.

Usher-Seriki, K. K., Bynum, M. S., & Callands, T. A. (2008). Mother-daughter communication about sex and sexual intercourse among middle- to upper-class African American girls. *Journal of Family Issues, 29,* 901–917.

Vaglio, S. (2009). Chemical communication and mother-infant recognition. *Communicative and Integrative Biology, 2,* 279–281.

Vaillant, G. E. (1977). *Adaptation to life.* Boston: Little, Brown.

Vaillant, G. E. (1983). Childhood environment and maturity of defense mechanisms. In D. Magnusson & V. L. Allen (Eds.), *Human development. An interactional perspective.* New York: Academic Press.

Vaillant, G. E., & Milofsky, E. (1980). Natural history of male psychological health. IX: Empirical evidence for Erikson's model of the life cycle. *American Journal of Psychiatry, 137,* 1348–1359.

Valente, T. W., Fujimoto, K., Chou, C. P., & Spruijt-Metz, D. (2009). Adolescent affiliations and adiposity: A social network analysis of friendships and obesity. *Journal of Adolescent Health, 45,* 202–204.

Valiente, C., Lemery-Chalfant, K., Swanson, J., & Reiser, M. (2008). Prediction of children's academic competence from their effortful control, relationships, and classroom participation. *Journal of Educational Psychology, 100,* 67–77.

Valkenburg, P. M., & Peter, J. (2007). Preadolescents' and adolescents' online communication and their closeness to friends. *Developmental Psychology, 43,* 267–277.

Valkenberg, P. M., & Peter, J. (2009). Social consequences of the internet for adolescents. *Current Directions in Psychological Sciences, 18,* 1–5.

van Anders, S. (2012). Testosterone and sexual desire in healthy women and men. *Archives of Sexual Behavior, 41,* 1471–1484.

Van Beurden, E., Zask, A., Barnett, L. M., & Dietrich, U. C. (2002). Fundamental movement skills—How do primary school children perform? The "Move it, Groove it" program in rural Australia. *Journal of Science and Medicine on Sport, 5,* 244–252.

van den Boom, D. C. (1995). Do first-year intervention effects endure? Follow-up during toddlerhood of a sample of Dutch irritable infants. *Child Development, 66,* 1798–1816.

Van den Dries, L., Juffer, F., van IJzendoorn, M. H., & Bakermans-Kranenburg, M. J. (2009). Fostering security? A meta-analysis of attachment in adopted children. *Children and Youth Services Review, 31,* 410–421.

Van den Dries, L., Juffer, F., van IJzendoorn, M. H., Bakermans-Kranenburg, M., &Alink, L. R. A. (2012). Infants' responsiveness, attachment, and indiscriminate friendliness after international adoption from institutions or foster care in China: Application of emotional availability scales to adoptive families. *Development and Psychopathology, 24,* 49–64.

van den Hooven, E. H., Pierik, F. H., de Kluizenaar, Y., Willemsen, S. P., Hofman, A., van Ratingen, S. W., et al. (2012). Air pollution exposure during pregnancy, ultrasound measures of fetal growth, and adverse birth outcomes: A prospective cohort study. *Environmental Health Perspectives, 120,* 150–156.

van der Maas, H., & Jansen, B. R. J. (2003). What response times tell of children's behavior on the balance scale task. *Journal of Experimental Child Psychology, 85,* 141–177.

Van Doesum, K. T. M., Riksen-Walraven, J. M., Hosman, C. M. H., & Hoefnagels, C. (2008). A randomized controlled trial of a home-visiting intervention aimed at preventing relationship problems in depressed mothers and their infants. *Child Development, 79,* 547–561.

Van Hecke, A. V., Mundy, P. C., Acra, C. F., Block, J. J., Delgado, C. E. F., Parlade, M. V., Meyer, J. A., Neal, A. R., & Pomares, Y. B. (2007). Infant joint attention, temperament, and social competence in preschool children. *Child Development, 78,* 53–69.

van Hoeken, D., Seidell, J., & Hoek, H. (2003). Epidemiology. In J. Treasure, U. Schmidt, & E. Van Furth (Eds.), *Handbook of eating disorders* (2nd ed.). Chicester, UK: Wiley.

van IJzendoorn, M. H. (1995). Adult attachment representations, parental responsiveness, and infant attachment: A meta-analysis on the predictive validity of the Adult Attachment Interview. *Psychological Bulletin, 117,* 387–403.

van IJzendoorn, M. H., & DeWolff, M. S. (1997). In search of the absent father: Meta-analyses of infant-father attachment: A rejoinder to our discussants. *Child Development, 68,* 604–609.

van IJzendoorn, M. H., & Juffer, F. (2006). The Emanuel Miller Memorial Lecture 2006: Adoption as intervention: Meta-analytic evidence for massive catch-up and plasticity in physical, socio-emotional, and cognitive development. *Journal of Child Psychology and Psychiatry, 47,* 1228–1245.

van IJzendoorn, M. H., & Sagi, A. (1999). Cross-cultural patterns of attachment: Universal and contextual dimensions. In J. Cassidy & P. R. Shaver (Eds.), *Handbook of attachment.* New York: Guilford.

van IJzendoorn, M. H., & Sagi-Schwartz, A. (2008). Cross-cultural patterns of attachment. Universal and contextual dimensions. In J. Cassidy & P. R. Shaver (Eds.), *Handbook of attachment: Theory, research, and clinical applications* (2nd ed.). New York: Guilford.

van IJzendoorn, M. H., Bakermans-Kranenburg, M. J., & Alink, L. R. A. (2012). Meta-analysis in developmental science. In B. Laursen, T. D. Little, & N. A. Card (Eds.), *Handbook of developmental research methods* (pp. 667–686). New York: Guilford.

van IJzendoorn, M. H., Schuengel, C., & Bakermans-Kranenburg, M. J. (1999). Disorganized attachment in early childhood: Meta-analysis of precursors, concomitants, and sequelae. *Development and Psychopathology, 11,* 225–249.

VanKim, N. A., Laska, M. N., Ehlinger, E., Lust, K., & Story, M. (2010). Understanding young adult physical activity, alcohol and tobacco use in community colleges and 4-year post-secondary institutions: A cross-sectional analysis of epidemiological surveillance data. *British Medical Journal, 10,* 208.

van Kleeck, A., Gillam, R. B., Hamilton, L., & McGrath, C. (1997). The relationship between middle-class parents' book-sharing discussion and their preschooler's abstract language development. *Journal of Speech, Language, and Hearing Research, 40*, 1261–1271.

Van Leeuwen, M., Van den Berg, S. M., & Boomsma, D. I. (2008). A twin-family study of general IQ. *Learning and Individual Differences, 18*, 76–88.

Van Oyen, H., Nusselder, W., Jagger, C., Kolip, P., Cambois, E., & Robine, J. (2013). Gender differences in healthy life years within the EU: An exploration of the "health-survival" paradox. *International Journal of Public Health, 58*, 143–155.

Van Solinge, H., & Henkens, K. (2008). Adjustment to and satisfaction with retirement: Two of a kind? *Psychology and Aging, 23*, 422–434.

Vandell, D. L., Belsky, J., Burchinal, M., Steinberg, L., Vandergrift, N., & NICHD Early Child Care Research Network. (2010). Do effects of early child care extend to age 15 years? Results from the NICHD Study of Early Child Care and Youth Development. *Child Development, 81*, 737–756.

Vandell, D. L., Wilson, K. S., & Buchanan, N. R. (1980). Peer interaction in the first year of life: An examination of its structure, content, and sensitivity to toys. *Child Development, 51*, 481–488.

Varea, C., Bernis, C., Montero, P., Arias, S., Barroso, A., & Gonzalez, B. (2000). Secular trend and intrapopulational variation in age of menopause in Spanish women. *Journal of Biosocial Science, 32*, 383–393.

Vargha-Khadem, F., Gadian, D. G., Watkins, K. E., Connelly, A., Van Paesschen, W., & Mishkin, M. (1997). Differential effects of early hippocampal pathology on episodic and semantic memory. *Science, 277*, 376–380.

Vargha-Khadem, F., Watkins, K., Alcock, K., Fletcher, P., & Passingham, R. (1995). Praxic and nonverbal cognitive deficits in a large family with a genetically transmitted speech and language disorder. *Proceedings of the National Academy of Sciences of the United States of America, 92*, 930–933.

Vartanian, L. R., & Powlishta, K. K. (1996). A longitudinal examination of the social-cognitive foundations of adolescent egocentrism. *Journal of Early Adolescence, 16*, 157–178.

Vaughn, B. E., Azria, M. R., Krzysik, L., Caya, L. R., Bost, K. K., Newell, W., & Kazura, K. L. (2000). Friendship and social competence in a sample of preschool children attending head start. *Developmental Psychology, 36*, 326–338.

Vazsonyi, A. T., Hibbert, J. R., & Snider, J. B. (2003). Exotic enterprise no more? Adolescent reports of family and parenting processes from youth in four countries. *Journal of Research on Adolescence, 13*, 129–160.

Vedantam, S. (2006, December 14). Antidepressants a suicide risk for young adults. *The Washington Post*, p. A16.

Veenstra-Vanderweele, J., & Cook, E. H. (2003). Genetics of childhood disorders: XLVI. Autism, part 5: Genetics of autism. *Journal of the American Academy of Child and Adolescent Psychiatry, 42*, 116–118.

Velderman, M.K., Bakermans-Kranenburg, M. J., Juffer, F., & van IJzendoorn, M. H. (2006). Effects of attachment-based interventions on maternal sensitivity and infant attachment: Differential susceptibility of highly reactive infants. *Journal of Family Psychology, 20*, 266–274.

Vellutino, F. R., Scanlon, D. M., Sipay, E. R., & Small, S. G. (1996). Cognitive profiles of difficult-to-remediate and readily remediated poor readers: Early intervention as a vehicle for distinguishing between cognitive and experiential deficits as basic causes of specific reading disability. *Journal of Educational Psychology, 88*, 601–638.

Ventura, S. J., & Hamilton, B. E. (2011). *U. S. teenage birth rate resumes decline* (NCHS Data Brief No. 58). Hyattsville, MD: National Center for Health Statistics.

Verbeek, P. (2006). Everyone's monkey: Primate moral roots. In M. Killen & J. G. Smetana (Eds.), *Handbook of moral development.* Mahwah, NJ: Erlbaum.

Verhaeghen, P. (2003). Aging and vocabulary scores: A meta-analysis. *Psychology and Aging, 18*, 332–339.

Verma, S., & Larson, R. (Eds.). (2003). *Examining adolescent leisure time across cultures: New directions for child and adolescent development, No. 99.* San Francisco: Jossey-Bass.

Veroff, J., Reuman, D., & Feld, S. (1984). Motives in American men and women across the adult life span. *Developmental Psychology, 20*, 1142–1158.

Veroudea, K., Norrisa, D. G., Shumskayaa, E., Gullberg, M., & Indefrey, P. (2010). Functional connectivity between brain regions involved in learning words of a new language. *Brain and Language, 113*, 21–27.

Verrillo, R. T., & Verrillo, V. (1985). Sensory and perceptual performance. In N. Charness (Ed.), *Aging and human performance.* Chichester, UK: Wiley.

Verschueren, K., Buyck, P., & Marcoen, A. (2001). Self-representations and socioemotional competence in young children: A 3-year longitudinal study. *Developmental Psychology, 37*, 126–134.

Verweij, E. J., van den Oever, J. M., de Boer, M. A., Boon, E. M., & Oepkes, D. (2012). Diagnostic accuracy of noninvasive detection of fetal trisomy 21 in maternal blood: A systematic review. *Fetal Diagnosis and Therapy, 31*, 81–86.

Vidal, F. (1994). *Piaget before Piaget.* MA: Harvard University Press.

Viding, E., Fontaine, N. M. G., Oliver, B. R., & Plomin, R. (2009). Negative parental discipline, conduct problems and callous-unemotional traits: Monozygotic twin differences study. *British Journal of Psychiatry, 195*, 414–419.

Vinden, P. G., & Astington, J. W. (2000). Culture and understanding other minds. In S. Baron-Cohen, H. Tager-Flusberg, & D. J. Cohen (Eds.), *Understanding other minds. Perspectives from developmental cognitive neuroscience* (2nd ed.). Oxford: Oxford University Press.

Vining, E. P. G., Freeman, J. M., Pillas, D. J., Uematsu, S., Carson, B. S., Brandt, J., et al. (1997). Why would you remove half a brain? The outcome of 58 children after hemispherectomy—The Johns Hopkins experience: 1968 to 1996. *Pediatrics, 100*, 163–171.

Vita, A. J., Terry, R. B., Hubert, H. B., & Fries, J. F. (1998). Aging, health risks, and cumulative disability. *New England Journal of Medicine, 338*, 1035–1041.

Vitario, F., Boivin, M., & Bukowski, W. M. (2009). The role of friendship in child and adolescent psychosocial development. In K. H. Rubin, W. M. Bukowski, & B. Laursen (Eds.), *Handbook of peer interactions, relationships, and groups.* New York: Guilford.

Vitaro, F., Brendgen, M., Boivin, M., Cantin, S., Dionne, G., Tremblay, R. E., et al. (2011). A monozygotic twin difference study of friends' aggression and children's adjustment problems. *Child Development, 82*, 617–632.

Vitiello, B., Zuvekas, S. H., & Norquist, G. S. (2006). National estimates of antidepressant medication use among U.S. children. *Journal of the American Academy of Child and Adolescent Psychiatry, 45*, 271–279.

Vogel, S., Horwitz, S., & Fahrenthold, D. A. (2012, December 16). Wrenching details but few answers. *The Washington Post*, pp. A1, A12, 14–15.

Vohr, B., Jodoin-Krauzyk, J., Tucker, R., Topol, D., Johnson, M. J., Ahlgren, M., et al. (2011). Expressive vocabulary of children with hearing loss in the first 2 years of life: Impact of early intervention. *Journal of Perinatology, 31*, 274–280.

Volkmar, F. R. (2001). Pharmacological interventions in autism: Theoretical and practical issues. *Journal of Clinical Child Psychology, 30*, 80–87.

Volkmar, F. R., Lord, C., Bailey, A., Schultz, R. T., & Klin, A. (2004). Autism and pervasive developmental disorders. *Journal of Child Psychology and Psychiatry and Allied Disciplines, 45*, 135–170.

Volling, B. L. (2012). Family transitions following the birth of a sibling: An empirical review of changes in the firstborn's adjustment. *Psychological Bulletin, 138*, 497–528.

von Hofsten, C. (2007). Action in development. *Developmental Science, 10*, 54–60.

Vondra, J., & Belsky, J. (1993). Developmental origins of parenting: Personality and relationship factors. In T. Luster & L. Okagaki (Eds.), *Parenting. An ecological perspective.* Hillsdale, NJ: Erlbaum.

von Stumm, S., Hell, B., & Chamorro-Premuzic, T. (2011). The hungry mind: Intellectual curiosity as third pillar of academic performance. *Perspectives on Psychological Science, 6*, 574–588.

Voss M. W., Nagamatsu, L. S., Liu-Ambrose, T., Kramer, A. F. (2011). Exercise, brain, and cognition across the life span. *Journal of Applied Physiology, 111*, 1505–1513.

Vouloumanos, A., & Werker, J. F. (2007). Listening to language at birth: Evidence for a bias for speech in neonates. *Developmental Science, 10,* 159–171.

Voyer, D., Postma, A., Brake, B., & Imperato-McGinley, J. (2007). Gender differences in object location memory: A meta-analysis. *Psychonomic Bulletin and Review, 14,* 23–38.

Vrangalova, Z., & Savin-Williams, R. C. (2012). Mostly heterosexual and mostly gay/lesbian: Evidence for new sexual orientation identities. *Archives of Sex Behavior, 41,* 85–101.

Vuoksimaa, E., Koskenvuo, M., Rose, R. J., & Kaprio, J. (2009). Origins of handedness: A nationwide study of 30,161 adults. *Neuropsychologia, 47,* 1294–1301.

Vuolo, M., Staff, J., & Mortimer, J. T. (2012). Weathering the great recession: Psychological and behavioral trajectories in the transition from school to work. *Developmental Psychology, 48,* 1759–1773.

Vuorialho, A., Karinen, P., & Sorri, M. (2006). Effect of hearing aids on hearing disability and quality of life in the elderly. *International Journal of Audiology, 45,* 400–405.

Vurpillot, E. (1968). The development of scanning strategies and their relation to visual differentiation. *Journal of Experimental Child Psychology, 6,* 632–650.

Vygotsky, L. S. (1962). *Thought and language* (E. Hanfmann & G. Vakar, Eds.). Cambridge, MA: MIT Press.

Vygotsky, L. S. (1978). *Mind in society: The development of higher mental processes* (M. Cole, V. John-Steiner, S. Scribner, & E. Souberman, Eds.). Cambridge, MA: Harvard University Press.

Vygotsky, L. S. (1978). *Mind in society: The development of higher mental processes* (M. Cole, V. John-Steiner, S. Scribner, & E. Souberman, Eds.). Cambridge, MA: Harvard University Press. (Original work published 1930, 1933, 1935).

Wadhwa, P. D., Buss, C., Entringer, S., & Swanson, J. M. (2009). Developmental origins of health and disease: Brief history of the approach and current focus on epigenetic mechanisms. *Seminars in Reproductive Medicine, 27,* 358–368.

Wadsworth, T. (2013). Sex and the pursuit of happiness: How other people's sex lives are related to our sense of well-being. *Social Indicators Research.* Published online before print February 28, 2013, doi:10.1007/s11205-013-0267-1.

Waechter, E. H. (1984). Dying children. Patterns of coping. In H. Wass & C. A. Corr (Eds.), *Childhood and death.* Washington, DC: Hemisphere.

Wagner, B. (2013). Internet-based bereavement interventions and support: An overview. In M. Stroebe, H. Schut & J. van den Bout (Eds.), *Complicated grief: Scientific foundations for health care professionals.* New York: Routledge/Taylor & Francis.

Waisbren, S. E. (2011). Phenylketonuria. In S. Goldstein & C. R. Reynolds (Eds.), *Handbook of neurodevelopmental and genetic disorders*

in children (2nd ed., pp. 398–424). New York: Guilford.

Waite, L. J., & Gallagher, M. (2000). *The case for marriage. Why married people are happier, healthier, and better off financially.* New York: Doubleday.

Wakefield, J. C. (2013). Is complicated/prolonged grief a disorder? Why the proposal to add a category of complicated grief disorder to the DSM-5 is conceptually and empirically unsound. In M. Stroebe, H. Schut & J. van den Bout (Eds.), *Complicated grief: Scientific foundations for health care professionals.* New York: Routledge/Taylor & Francis.

Waldman, I. D., & Gizer, I. R. (2006). The genetics of attention deficit hyperactivity disorder. *Clinical Psychology Review, 26,* 396–432.

Walker, L. J. (1980). Cognitive and perspective-taking prerequisites of moral development. *Child Development, 51,* 131–139.

Walker, L. J. (2004). Gus in the gap: Bridging the judgment-action gap in moral reasoning. In D. K. Lapsley & D. Narvaez (Eds.), *Moral development, self, and identity.* Mahwah, NJ: Erlbaum.

Walker, L. J., & Frimer, J. A. (2011). The science of moral development. In M. K. Underwood, & L. H. Rosen (Eds.), *Social development: Relationships in infancy, childhood, and adolescence* (pp. 235–262). New York: Guilford Press.

Walker, L. J., Hennig, K. H., & Krettenauer, T. (2000). Parent and peer contexts for children's moral reasoning development. *Child Development, 71,* 1033–1048.

Walker-Andrews, A. S. (1997). Infants' perception of expressive behaviors: Differentiation of multimodal information. *Psychological Bulletin, 121,* 437–456.

Wallace, J. E., & Young, M. C. (2008). Parenthood and productivity: A study of demands, resources and family-friendly firms. *Journal of Vocational Behavior, 72,* 110–122.

Wallace, P. S., & Whishaw, I. Q. (2003). Independent digit movements and precision grip patterns in 1-5-month-old human infants: Hand-babbling, including vacuous then self-directed hand and digit movements, precedes targeted reaching. *Neuropsychologia, 41,* 1912–1918.

Wallander, J. L., Taylor, W. C., Grunbaum, J. A., Franklin, F.A., Harrison, G. G. , Kelder, S. H., & Schuster, M. A. (2009). Weight status, quality of life, and self-concept in African American, Hispanic, and white fifth-grade children. *Obesity, 17,* 1363–1368.

Wallen, K. (1996). Nature needs nurture: The interaction of hormonal and social influences on the development of behavioral sex differences in rhesus monkeys. *Hormones and Behavior, 30,* 364–378.

Walls, R. T. (2000). Vocational cognition: Accuracy of 3rd-, 6th-, 9th-, and 12th-grade students. *Journal of Vocational Behavior, 56,* 137–144.

Walter, C. A., & McCoyd, J. L. M. (2009). *Grief and loss across the lifespan. A biopsychosocial perspective.* New York: Springer.

Walton, G., & Spencer, S. (2009). Latent ability: Grades and test scores systematically

underestimate the intellectual ability of negatively stereotyped students. *Psychological Science, 20,* 1132–1139.

Wan, W., Deng, X., Archer, K. J., & Sun, S. S. (2012). Pubertal pathways and the relationship to anthropometric changes in childhood: The Fels longitudinal study. *Open Journal of Pediatrics, 2,* 1128–126.

Wang, H. Y., & Amato, P. R. (2000). Predictors of divorce adjustment: Stressors, resources, and definitions. *Journal of Marriage and the Family, 62,* 655–668.

Wang, M., Henkens, K., & van Solinge, H. (2011). Retirement adjustment: A review of theoretical and empirical advancements. *American Psychologist, 66,* 204–213.

Wang, P. S., Berglund, P., Olfson, M., Pincus, H. A., Wells, K. B., & Kessler, R. C. (2005). Failure and delay in initial treatment contact after first onset of mental disorders in the National Comorbidity Survey Replication. *Archives of General Psychiatry, 62,* 603–613.

Wang, Q. (2004). Cultural self-constructions: Autobiographical memory and self-description in European American and Chinese children. *Developmental Psychology, 40,* 3–15.

Wang, Q. (2006). Culture and the development of self-knowledge. *Current Directions in Psychological Science, 15,* 182–187.

Wang, S. H., Baillargeon, R., & Brueckner, L. (2004). Young infants' reasoning about hidden objects: Evidence from violation-of-expectation tasks with test trials only. *Cognition, 93,* 167–198.

Wang, S. S. (2010, March 30). Making cells live forever in quest for cures. *The Wall Street Journal,* p. D3.

Ward, C. D., & Cooper, R. P. (1999). A lack of evidence in 4-month-old human infants for paternal voice preference. *Developmental Psychobiology, 35,* 49–59.

Ward, H., Munro, E. R., & Dearden, C. (2006). *Babies and young children in care: Life pathways, decision-making and practice.* London: Jessica Kingsley.

Ward, R., & Spitze, G. (1992). Consequences of parent–adult child coresidence. *Journal of Family Issues, 13,* 533–572.

Ward, R., & Spitze, G. (2004). Marital implications of parent–adult child coresidence: A longitudinal view. *Journal of Gerontology: Social Sciences, 59B,* S2–S8.

Warin, J. (2000). The attainment of self-consistency through gender in young children. *Sex Roles, 42,* 209–231.

Warneken, F., & Tomasello, M. (2007). Helping and cooperation at 14 months of age. *Infancy, 11,* 271–294.

Warren, J. R., LePore, P. C., & Mare, R. D. (2000). Employment during high school: Consequences for students' grades in academic courses. *American Educational Research Journal, 37,* 943–970.

Washburn, L., Dillard, R., Goldstein, D., Klinepeter, K., deRegnier, R., & O'Shea, T. (2007). Survival and major neurodevelopmental impairment in extremely low gestational age newborns born 1990–2000: A retrospective cohort study. *BMC Pediatrics, 7,* 1–9.

Wass, H. (1991). Helping children cope with death. In D. Papadatou & C. Papadatos (Eds.), *Children and death*. New York: Hemisphere.

Wasserman, D. (2006). *Depression: The facts*. Oxford, UK: Oxford University Press.

Waterhouse, L. (2013). Environmental risk factors link autism to many other outcomes. In *Rethinking Autism* (pp. 223–279). San Diego, CA: Academic Press.

Waterhouse, L. (2013). *Rethinking autism. Variation and complexity*. Waltham, MA: Academic Press.

Waterman, A. S. (1982). Identity development from adolescence to adulthood: An extension of theory and a review of research. *Developmental Psychology, 18*, 341–358.

Waterman, A. S. (1992). Identity as an aspect of optimal psychological functioning. In G. R. Adams, T. P. Gullotta, & R. Montemayor (Eds.), *Adolescent identity formation* (Advances in Adolescent Development, Vol. 4). Newbury Park, CA: Sage.

Waters, E., Wippman, J., & Sroufe, L. A. (1979). Attachment, positive affect, and competence in the peer group: Two studies in construct validation. *Child Development, 50*, 821–829.

Watkins, M. W., & Smith, L. G. (2013). Long-term stability of the Wechsler Intelligence Scale for Children—Fourth Edition. *Psychological Assessment, 25*, 477–483.

Waxman, S., Fu, X., Arunachalam, S., Leddon, E., Geraghty, K., & Song, H. (2013). Are nouns learned before verbs? Infants provide insight into a long-standing debate. *Child Development Perspectives, 7*, 155–159.

Waxman, S. R., & Hatch, T. (1992). Beyond the basics: Preschool children label objects flexibly at multiple hierarchical levels. *Journal of Child Language, 19*, 153–166.

Waxman, S. R., & Lidz, J. (2006). Early word learning. In D. Kuhn & R. Siegler (Eds.), *Handbook of child psychology, 6th Edition*, Volume 2 (pp. 299–335). Hoboken NJ: Wiley.

Way, N., & Silverman, L. R. (2011). The quality of friendships during adolescence: Patterns across context, culture, and age. In P. K. Kerig, M. S. Schulz, & S. T. Hauser (Eds.), *Adolescence and beyond. Family processes and development*. New York: Oxford University Press.

Wayne, A. J., & Youngs, P. (2003). Teacher characteristics and student achievement gains: A review. *Review of Educational Research, 73*, 89–122.

Webster, J. D., & Haight, B. K. (Eds.) (2002). *Critical advances in reminiscence work: From theory to application*. New York: Springer.

Webster, J., Nicholas, C., Velacott, C., Cridland, N., & Fawcett, L. (2011). Quality of life and depression following childbirth: Impact of social support. *Midwifery, 27*, 745–749.

Wechsler, D. (2002). *Wechsler preschool and primary scale of intelligence* (3rd ed.). The Psychological Corporation.

Wechsler, D. (2003). *Wechsler intelligence scale for children* (4th ed.). San Antonio, TX: The Psychological Corporation.

Wechsler, D. (2008). *Wechsler adult intelligence scale* (4th ed.). Toronto: Pearson.

Weiffenbach, J. M., Cowart, B. J., & Baum, B. J. (1986). Taste intensity perception in aging. *Journal of Gerontology, 41*, 460–468.

Weinberg, R. A., Scarr, S., & Waldman, I. D. (1992). The Minnesota transracial adoption study: A follow-up of IQ test performance at adolescence. *Intelligence, 16*, 117–135.

Weiner, M. F., Garrett, R., & Bret, M. E. (2009). Neuropsychiatric assessment and diagnosis. In M. F. Weiner & A. M. Lipton (Eds.), *The American Psychiatric Publishing textbook of Alzheimer disease and other dementias*. Washington, DC: American Psychiatric Publishing.

Weinert, F. E., & Hany, E. A. (2003). The stability of individual differences in intellectual development: Empirical evidence, theoretical problems, and new research questions. In R. J. Sternberg, J. Lautrey, & T. I. Lubart (Eds.), *Models of intelligence: International perspectives* (pp. 169–181). Washington, DC: American Psychological Association.

Weinert, F. E., & Schneider, W. (1999). *Individual development from 3 to 12: Findings from the Munich Longitudinal Study*. Cambridge, UK: Cambridge University Press.

Weinert, F. E., & Schneider, W. (1999). *Individual development from 3 to 12: Findings from the Munich Longitudinal Study*. Cambridge, UK: Cambridge University Press.

Weinfield, N. S., Sroufe, L. A., & Egeland, B. (2000). Attachment from infancy to early adulthood in a high-risk sample: Continuity, discontinuity, and their correlates. *Child Development, 71*, 695–702.

Weingarten, G. (2011, July). Touchy subject: Warning—This may rub you the wrong way. *The Washington Post Magazine*, p. 29.

Weinraub, M., & Lewis, M. (1977). The determinants of children's responses to separation. *Monographs of the Society for Research in Child Development*, (4, Serial No. 172).

Weisberg, D. S., Hirsh-Pasek, K., & Golinkoff, R. M. (2013). Guided play: Where curricular goals meet a playful pedagogy. *Mind, Brain, and Education, 7*, 104–112.

Weisgram, E. S., Bigler, R. S., & Liben, L. S. (2010). Gender, values, and occupational interests among children, adolescents, and adults. *Child Development, 81*, 778–796.

Weisman, O., Magori-Cohen, R., Louzoun, Y., Eidelman, A. I., & Feldman, R. (2011). Sleep-wake transitions in premature neonates predict early development. *Pediatrics, 128*, 706-714.

Weisner, T. S., & Gallimore, R. (1977). My brother's keeper: Child and sibling caretaking. *Current Anthropology, 18*, 169–190.

Weiss, B., & Garber, J. (2003). Developmental differences in the phenomenology of depression. *Development and Psychopathology, 15*, 403–430.

Weiss, B., Tram, J. M., Weisz, J. R., Rescorla, L., & Achenbach, T. M. (2009). Differential symptom expression and somatization in Thai versus U. S. children. *Journal of Consulting and Clinical Psychology, 77*, 987–992.

Weiss, D., & Freund, A. M. (2012). Still young at heart: Negative age-related information motivates distancing from same-aged people. *Psychology and Aging, 27*, 173–180.

Weiss, D., & Lang, F. R. (2012). "They" are old but "I" feel younger: Age-group dissociation as a self-protective strategy in old age. *Psychology and Aging, 27*, 153–163.

Weiss, D., Freund, A. M., & Wiese, B. S. (2012). Mastering developmental transitions in young and middle adulthood: The interplay of openness to experience and traditional gender ideology on women's self-efficacy and subjective well-being. *Developmental Psychology, 48*, 1774–1784.

Weiss, L. H., & Schwarz, J. C. (1996). The relationship between parenting types and older adolescents' personality, academic achievement, adjustment, and substance use. *Child Development, 67*, 2101–2114.

Weiss, S. (2008, April 1). Midlife. What crisis? *The Washington Post*, pp. F1, F5.

Weisz, J. R., McCarty, C. A., & Valeri, S. M. (2006). Effects of psychotherapy for depression in children and adolescents: A meta-analysis. *Psychological Bulletin, 132*, 132–149.

Weisz, J. R., McCarty, C. A., Eastman, K. L., Chaiyasit, W., & Suwanlert, S. (1997). Developmental psychopathology and culture: Ten lessons from Thailand. In S. S. Luthar, J. A. Burack, D. Cicchetti, & J. R. Weisz (Eds.). *Developmental psychopathology: Perspectives on adjustment, risk and disorder*. Cambridge, UK: Cambridge University Press.

Weizman, A. O., & Snow, C. E. (2001). Lexical input as related to children's vocabulary acquisition: Effects of sophisticated exposure and support for meaning. *Developmental Psychology, 37*, 265–279.

Wellman, H. M. (1990). *The child's theory of mind*. Cambridge, MA: MIT Press.

Wellman, H. M., & Bartsch, K. (1994). Before belief: Children's early psychological theory. In C. Lewis & P. Mitchell (Eds.), *Children's early understanding of mind: Origins and development*. Hove, UK: Erlbaum.

Wellman, H. M., & Gelman, S. A. (1992). Cognitive development: Foundational theories of core domains. *Annual Review of Psychology, 43*, 337–375.

Wellman, H. M., & Liu, D. (2004). Scaling of theory-of-mind-tasks. *Child Development, 75*, 523–541.

Wellman, H. M., Cross, D., & Watson, J. (2001). Meta-analysis of theory-of-mind development: The truth about false-belief. *Child Development, 72*, 655–684.

Wells, B. E., & Twenge, J. M. (2005). Changes in young people's sexual behavior and attitudes, 1943–1999: A cross-temporal meta-analysis. *Review of General Psychology, 9*, 249–261.

Welsh, D. P., Grello, C. M., & Harper, M. S. (2006). No strings attached: The nature of casual sex in college students. *Journal of Sex Research, 43*, 255–267.

Welsh, J. A., Nix, R. L., Blair, C., Bierman, K. L., & Nelson, K. E. (2010). The development of cognitive skills and gains in academic school readiness for children from low-income families. *Journal of Educational Psychology, 102*, 43–53.

Wentzel, K. R. (2003). Sociometric status and adjustment in middle school: A longitudinal study. *Journal of Early Adolescence, 23*, 5–28.

Weon, B. M., & Je, J. H. (2009). Theoretical estimation of maximum human lifespan. *Biogerontology, 10*, 65–71.

Werker, J. F., & Tees, R. C. (2005). Speech perception as a window for understanding plasticity and commitment in language systems of the brain. *Developmental Psychobiology, 46*, 233–234.

Werker, J. F., Yeung, H. H., & Yoshida, K. A. (2012). How Do Infants Become Experts at Native-Speech Perception? *Current issues in psychological science, 21*, 221–226.

Werner, H. (1957). The concept of development from a comparative and organismic point of view. In D. B. Harris (Ed.), *The concept of development: An issue in the study of human behavior.* Minneapolis: University of Minnesota Press.

Werth, J. L., Jr., Blevins, D., Toussaint, K. L., & Durham, M. R. (2002). The influence of cultural diversity on end-of-life care and decisions. *American Behavioral Scientist, 46*, 204–219.

West, G. L., Anderson, A. A. K., & Pratt, J. (2009). Motivationally significant stimuli show visual prior entry: Evidence for attentional capture. *Journal of Experimental Psychology: Human Perception and Performance, 35*, 1032–1042.

Westefeld, J. S., Bell, A., Bermingham, C., Button, C., Shaw, K., Skow, C., et al. (2010). Suicide among preadolescents: A call to action. *Journal of Loss and Trauma, 15*, 381–407.

Westerhof, G. J., Whitbourne, S. K., & Freeman, G. P. (2012). The aging self in a cultural context: The relation of conceptions of aging to identity processes and self-esteem in the United States and the Netherlands. *Journals of Gerontology: Series B: Psychological Sciences and Social Sciences, 67*, 52–60.

Westermann, G., Mareschal, D., Johnson, M. H., Sirois, S., Spratling, M. W., & Thomas, M. S. C. (2007). Neuroconstructivism. *Developmental Science, 10*, 75–83.

Westermann, G., Thomas, M. S. C. and Karmiloff-Smith, A. (2010) Neuroconstructivism. In U. Goswami (Ed), *Wiley-Blackwell Handbook of Childhood Cognitive Development*, 2nd ed., Oxford, UK: Wiley-Blackwell.

Wethington, H. R., Hahn, R. A., Fuqua-Whitley, D. S., Crosby, A. E., Liberman, A. M., Price, L. N., Kalra, G., Chattopadhyay, S. K., Tuma, F. K., Moscicki, E., Johnson, R. L., & Sipe, T. A., Task Force on Community Preventive Services. (2008). The effectiveness of interventions to reduce psychological harm from traumatic events among children and adolescents: A systematic review. *American Journal of Preventive Medicine, 35*, 287–313.

Weyandt, L. L. (2007). *An ADHD primer* (2nd ed.). Mahwah, NJ: Erlbaum.

Weyandt, L. L., & DuPaul, G. J. (2013). *College students with ADHD: Current issues and future directions.* New York: Springer Science+Business Media.

Whitbourne, S. K. Sneed, J. R., & Sayer, A. (2009). Psychosocial development from college through midlife: A 34-year sequential study. *Developmental Psychology, 45*, 1328–1340.

Whitbourne, S. K., & Whitbourne, S. B. (2011). *Adult development and aging: Biopsychosocial Perspectives*, 4th Ed. John Wiley.

Whitbourne, S. K., & Meeks, S. (2011). Psychopathology, bereavement, and aging. In K. W. Schaie & S. L. Willis (Eds.), B. G. Knight, B. Levy, & D. C. Park (Assoc. Eds.), *Handbook of the psychology of aging.* Burlington, MA: Academic Press/Elsevier.

Whitbourne, S. K., & Tesch, S. A. (1985). A comparison of identity and intimacy statuses in college students and alumni. *Developmental Psychology, 21*, 1039–1044.

White, J. B., Duncan, D. F., Nicholson, T., Bradley, D., & Bonaguro, J. (2011). Generational shift and drug abuse in older Americans. *Journal of Social, Behavioral, and Health Sciences, 5*, 58–66.

White, L., & Edwards, J. N. (1990). Emptying the nest and parental well-being: An analysis of national panel data. *American Sociological Review, 55*, 235–242.

White, L., & Rogers, S. J. (1997). Strong support but uneasy relationships: Coresidence and adult children's relationships with their parents. *Journal of Marriage and the Family, 59*, 62–76.

White, L., & Rogers, S. J. (2000). Economic circumstances and family outcomes: A review of the 1990s. *Journal of Marriage and the Family, 62*, 1035–1051.

White, R. M. B., Roosa, M. W., Weaver, S. R., & Nair, R. L. (2009). Cultural and contextual influences on parenting in Mexican American families. *Journal of Marriage and Family, 71*, 61–79.

Whitebread, D. (1999). Interactions between children's metacognitive abilities, working memory capacity, strategies and performance during problem-solving. *European Journal of Psychology of Education, 14*, 489–507.

Whitehead, B. D., & Popenoe, D. (2003). *The state of the unions. The social health of marriage in America 2003. Essay: Marriage and children: Coming together again?* The National Marriage Project, Rutgers University. Retrieved from http://marriage.rutgers.edu/Publications/Print/PrintSOOU2003.htm

Whitehurst, G. J., & Lonigan, C. J. (1998). Child development and emergent literacy. *Child Development, 69*, 848–872.

Whitehurst, G. J., & Valdez-Menchaca, M. C. (1988). What is the role of reinforcement in early language acquisition? *Child Development, 59*, 430–440.

Whiteman, S. D., McHale, S. M., & Crouter, A. C. (2007). Longitudinal changes in marital relationships: The role of offspring's pubertal development. *Journal of Marriage and Family, 69*, 1005–1020.

Whiting, B. B., & Edwards, C. P. (1988). *Children of different worlds: The formation of social behavior.* Cambridge, MA: Harvard University Press.

Widén, S. E., & Erlandsson, S. I. (2004). The influence of socio-economic status on adolescent attitude to social noise and hearing protection. *Noise Health, 7*, 59–70.

Widén, S. E., Holmes, A. E., Johnson, T., Bohlin, M., & Erlandsson, S. I. (2009). Hearing, use of hearing protection, and attitudes towards noise among young American adults. *International Journal of Audiology, 48*, 537–545.

Widmer, E. D., Treas, J., & Newcomb, R. (1998). Attitudes toward nonmarital sex in 24 countries. *Journal of Sex Research, 35*, 349–358.

Wigfield, A., Eccles, J. S., Yoon, K. S., & Harold, R. D. (1997). Change in children's competence beliefs and subjective task values across the elementary school years: A 3-year study. *Journal of Educational Psychology, 89*, 451–469.

Wijngaards-de Meij, L., Stroebe, M., Schut, H., Stroebe, W., van den Bout, J., van der Heijden, P., & Dijkstra, I. (2008). Parents grieving the loss of their child: Interdependence in coping. *Journal of Clinical Psychology, 47*, 31–42.

Wijngaards-de-Meij, L., Stroebe, M., Schut, H., Stroebe, W., van den Bout, J., van der Heijden, P., & Dijkstra, I. (2007). Neuroticism and attachment insecurity as predictors of bereavement outcome. *Journal of Research in Personality, 41*, 498–505.

Wikan, U. (1988). Bereavement and loss in two Muslim communities: Egypt and Bali compared. *Social Science and Medicine, 27*, 451–460.

Wikan, U. (1991). *Managing turbulent hearts.* Chicago: University of Chicago Press.

Wilbur, J., Miller, A., & Montgomery, A. (1995). The influence of demographic characteristics, menopausal status, and symptoms on women's attitudes toward menopause. *Women and Health, 23*, 19–39.

Wilcox, A. J., Weinberg, C. R., O'Connor, J. F., Baird, D. D., Schlatterer, J. P., Canfield, R. E., et al. (1988). Incidence of early loss of pregnancy. *New England Journal of Medicine, 319*, 189.

Wilcox, S., Evenson, K. R., Aragaki, A., Wassertheil-Smoller, S., Mouton, C. P., & Loevinger, B. L. (2003). The effects of widowhood on physical and mental health, health behaviors, and health outcomes: The Women's Health Initiative. *Health Psychology, 22*, 513–522.

Wilkie, C. (2013, February 27). Neil Heslin, father of Newtown victim, testifies at Senate assault weapons ban hearing. *Huffington Post.* Retrieved from http://www.huffingtonpost.com/2013/02/27/neil-heslin-assault-weapons-ban-newtown_n_2774598.html

Wilkinson, D. (2009). Pharmacological treatment of Alzheimer's disease. In G. Waldemar & A. Burns (Eds.), *Alzheimer's disease.* Oxford: Oxford University Press.

Willats, P. (1990). Development of problem solving strategies in infancy. In D. F. Bjorklund (Ed.), *Children's strategies.* Hillsdale, NJ: Erlbaum.

Willcox, D. C., Willcox, B. J., Rosenbaum, M., Sokolovsky, J., & Suzuki, M. (2009). Exceptional longevity and the quest for healthy aging: Insights from the Okinawa Centenarian Study. In J. Sokolovsky (Ed.), *The cultural context of aging* (3rd ed.). Westport, CT: Praeger.

Wille, B., Beyers, W., & De Fruyt, F. (2012). A transactional approach to person-environment fit: Reciprocal relations between personality development and career role growth across young to middle adulthood. *Journal of Vocational Behavior, 81*, 307–321.

Williams, J. E., & Best, D. L. (1990). *Measuring sex stereotypes: A multination study* (rev. ed.). Newbury Park, CA: Sage.

Williams, J. H., Waiter, G. D., Gilchrist, A., Perrett, D. I., Murray, A. D., & Whiten, A. (2006). Neural mechanisms of imitation and 'mirror neuron' functioning in autistic spectrum disorder. *Neuropsychologia, 44*, 610–621.

Williams, L. R., & Russell, S. T. (2013). Shared social and emotional activities within adolescent romantic and non-romantic sexual relationships. *Archives of Sexual Behavior, 42*, 649–658.

Williams, L. R., & Steinberg, L. (2011). Reciprocal relations between parenting and adjustment in a sample of juvenile offenders. *Child Development, 82*, 633–645.

Williams, M. E., Rogers, K. C., Carson, M. C., Sherer, S., & Hudson, B. O. (2012). Opportunities arising from transformation from treatment as usual to evidence-based practice. *Professional Psychology: Research and Practice, 43*, 9–16.

Williams, M. V., Baker, D. W., Parker, R. M., & Nurss, J. R. (1998). Relationship of functional health literacy to patients' knowledge of their chronic disease. *Archives of Internal Medicine, 158*, 166–172.

Williams, P. T. (1997). Evidence for the incompatibility of age-neutral overweight and age-neutral physical activity standards from runners. *American Journal of Clinical Nutrition, 65*, 1391–1396.

Williams, T., Connolly, J., & Cribbie, R. (2008). Light and heavy heterosexual activities of young Canadian adolescents: Normative patterns and differential predictors. *Journal of Research on Adolescence, 18*, 145–172.

Williams, T., Connolly, J., Pepler, D., & Craig, W. (2003). Questioning and sexual minority adolescents: High school experiences of bullying, sexual harassment and physical abuse. *Canadian Journal of Community Mental Health, 22*, 47–58.

Willis, S. L., & Schaie, K. W. (1986). Training the elderly on the ability factors of spatial orientation and inductive reasoning. *Psychology and Aging, 1*, 239–247.

Willis, S. L., Tennstedt, S. L., Marsiske, M., Ball, K., Elias, J., Koepke, K. M., et al. (2006). Long-term effects of cognitive training on everyday functional outcomes in older adults. *Journal of the American Medical Association, 296*, 2805–2814.

Willis, S. L., Tennstedt, S. L., Marsiske, M., Ball, K., Elias, J., Koepke, K. M., et al. (2006). Long-term effects of cognitive training on everyday functional outcomes in older adults. *Journal of the American Medical Association, 296*, 2805–2814.

Willoughby, T., Adachi, P. J. C., & Good, M. (2012). A longitudinal study of the association between violent video game play and aggression among adolescents. *Developmental Psychology, 48*, 1044–1057.

Wilson, A. E., Smith, M. D., Ross, H. S., & Ross, M. (2004). Young children's personal accounts of their sibling disputes. *Merrill-Palmer Quarterly, 50*, 39–60.

Wilson, G. T., Becker, C. B., & Heffernan, K. (2003). Eating disorders. In E. J. Mash & R. A. Barkley (Eds.), *Child psychopathology* (2nd ed.). New York: Guilford Press.

Wilson, K. M., & Trainin, G. (2007). First-grade students' motivation and achievement for reading, writing, and spelling. *Reading Psychology, 28*, 257–282.

Wilson, R. (2003, December 5). How babies alter careers for academics. *The Chronicle of Higher Education*, A1, A6–A8.

Wilson, R. S., Arnold, S. E., Tang, Y., & Bennett, D. A. (2006). Odor identification and decline in different cognitive domains in old age. *Neuroepidemiology, 26*, 61–67.

Wilt, J., Condon, D. M., & Revelle, W. (2012). Telemetrics and online data collection: Collecting data at a distance. In B. Laursen, T. D. Little, & N. A. Card (Eds.), *Handbook of developmental research methods* (pp. 163–180). New York: Guilford.

Windsor, T. D., & Anstey, K. J. (2010). Age differences in psychosocial predictors of positive and negative affect: A longitudinal investigation of young, midlife, and older adults. *Psychology and Aging, 25*, 641–652.

Wineberg, H., & Werth, J. L. Jr. (2003). Physician-assisted suicide in Oregon: What are the key factors? *Death Studies, 27*, 501–518.

Wingfield, A., Poon, L. W., Lombardi, L., & Lowe, D. (1985). Speed of processing in normal aging: Effects of speech rate, linguistic structure, and processing time. *Journal of Gerontology, 40*, 579–595.

Wink, P., & Dillon, M. (2002). Spiritual development across the adult life course: Findings from a longitudinal study. *Journal of Adult Development, 9*, 79–94.

Wink, P., & Dillon, M. (2003). Religiousness, spirituality, and psychosocial functioning in late adulthood: findings from a longitudinal study. *Psychology and Aging, 18*, 916–924.

Wink, P., & Dillon, M. (2008). Religiousness, spirituality, and psychosocial functioning in late adulthood: Findings from a longitudinal study. *Psychology of Religion and Spirituality, S* (1), 102–115.

Winner, E. (1996). *Gifted children: Myths and realities*. New York: Basic Books.

Winsler, A., Carlton, M. P., & Barry, M. J. (2000). Age-related changes in preschool children's systematic use of private speech in a natural setting. *Journal of Child Language, 27*, 665–687.

Wismer Fries, A. B., Shirtcliff, E. A., & Pollak, S. D. (2008). Neuroendocrine dysregulation following early social deprivation in children. *Developmental Psychobiology, 50*, 588–599.

Witte, K. (2006, April 2). Untitled. *Washington Post*, p. D1.

Wittmann, B. C., & D'Esposito, M. (2012). Functional magnetic resonance imaging. In H. Cooper (Editor-in-Chief), P. M. Camic, D. L. Long, A. T. Panter, D. Rindskopf, & K. J. Sher (Assoc. Eds.), *APA handbook of research methods in psychology: Vol. 1. Foundations, planning, measures, and psychometrics* (pp. 547–566). Washington, DC: American Psychological Association.

Wlodkowski, R. J. (1999). *Enhancing adult motivation to learn: A comprehensive guide for teaching all adults*. San Francisco: Jossey-Bass Higher and Adult Education Series.

Wohlfahrt-Veje, C., Andersen, H. R., Jensen, T. K., Grandjean, P., Skakkebaek, N. E., & Main, K. M. (2012a). Smaller genitals at school age in boys whose mothers were exposed to non-persistent pesticides in early pregnancy. *International Journal of Andrology, 35*, 265–272.

Wohlfahrt-Veje, C., Andersen, H. R., Schmidt, I. M., Aksglaede, L., Sørensen, K., Juul, A., et al. (2012b). Early breast development in girls after prenatal exposure to non-persistent pesticides. *International Journal of Andrology, 35*, 273–282.

Wohlfahrt-Veje, C., Main, K. M., Schmidt, I. M., Boas, M., Jensen, T. K., Grandjean, P., et al. (2011). Lower birth weight and increased body fat at school age in children prenatally exposed to modern pesticides: A prospective study. *Environmental Health: A Global Access Science Source, 10*, 79.

Wolchik, S. A., West, S. G., Sandler, I. N., Tein, J. Y., Coatsworth, D., Lengua, L., Weiss, L., Anderson, E. R., Greene, S. M., & Griffin, W. A. (2000). An experimental evaluation of theory-based mother and mother–child programs for children of divorce. *Journal of Consulting and Clinical Psychology, 68*, 843–856.

Wolff, J. J., Gu, H., Gerig, G., Elison, J. T., Styner, M., Gouttard, S., et al. (2012). Differences in white matter fiber tract development present from 6 to 24 months in infants with autism. *American Journal of Psychiatry, 169*, 589–600.

Wolff, P. H. (1963). Observations on the early development of smiling. In B. M. Foss (Ed.), *Determinants of infant behavior* (Vol. 2). London: Methuen.

Wolfner, G. D., & Gelles, R. J. (1993). A profile of violence toward children: A national study. *Child Abuse and Neglect, 17*, 197–212.

Wolfson, A. R., & Carskadon, M. A. (1998). Sleep schedules and daytime functioning in adolescents. *Child Development, 69*, 875–998.

Women's Health Initiative. (2004). *The estrogen-plus-progestin study*. Retrieved from http://www.nhlbi.nih.gov/whi/estro_pro.htm

Wong, C. A., Eccles, J. S., & Sameroff, A. (2003). The influence of ethnic discrimination and ethnic identification on African American adolescents' school and socioemotional adjustment. *Journal of Personality, 71*, 1197–1232.

Wong, E. (2012, July 23). Pressure grows in China to end one-child law. *The New York Times*, p. A1.

Wong, J. Y., & Earl, J. K. (2009). Towards an integrated model of individual, psychosocial, and organizational predictors of retirement adjustment. *Journal of Vocational Behavior, 75*, 1–13.

Wong, L. P. (2011). Attitudes toward menstruation, menstrual-related symptoms, and premenstrual syndrome among adolescent girls: A rural school-based survey. *Women & Health, 51*, 340–364.

Wong, P. T. P., & Watt, L. M. (1991). What types of reminiscence are associated with successful aging? *Psychology and Aging, 6*, 272–279.

Wong, W. I., Pasterski, V., Hindmarsh, P. C., Geffner, M. E., & Hines, M. (2013). Are there parental socialization effects on the sex-typed behavior of individuals with congenital adrenal hyperplasia? *Archives of Sexual Behavior, 42*, 381–391.

Woo, S. M., & Keatinge, C. (2008). *Diagnosis and treatment of mental disorders across the lifespan.* New York: Wiley.

Woodhill, B. M., & Samuels, C. A. (2003). Positive and negative androgyny and their relationship with psychological health and well-being. *Sex Roles, 49*, 555–565.

Woodhill, B. M., & Samuels, C. A. (2004). Desirable and undesirable androgyny: A prescription for the twenty-first century. *Journal of Gender Studies, 13*, 15–28.

Woodward, A. L. (2009). Infants' grasp of others' intentions. *Current Directions in Psychological Science, 18*, 53–57.

Woodward, A. L., & Markman, E. M. (1998). Early word learning. In D. Kuhn & R. S. Siegler, (Vol. Eds.), W. Damon (Editor-in-Chief), *Handbook of child psychology: Vol. 2. Cognition, perception, and language* (5th ed., pp. 371–420). New York: Wiley.

Woodward, A. T., Taylor, R. J., Bullard, K. M., Aranda, M. P., Lincoln, K. D., & Chatters, L. M. (2012). Prevalence of lifetime DSM-IV affective disorders among older African Americans, black Caribbeans, Latinos, Asians and non-Hispanic white people. *International Journal of Geriatric Psychiatry, 27*, 816–827.

Woodward, L., Fergusson, D. M., & Belsky, J. (2000). Timing of parental separation and attachment to parents in adolescence: Results of a prospective study from birth to age 16. *Journal of Marriage and the Family, 62*, 162–174.

Woolley, J. D., Boerger, E. A., & Markman, A. B. (2004). A visit from the Candy Witch: Factors influencing young children's belief in a novel fantastical being. *Developmental Science, 7*, 456–468.

Worchel, F. F., Copeland, D. R., & Barker, D. G. (1987). Control-related coping strategies in pediatric oncology patients. *Journal of Pediatric Psychology, 12*, 25–38.

Worden, J. W., & Silverman, P. R. (1996). Parental death and the adjustment of school-age children. *Omega: Journal of Death and Dying, 33*, 91–102.

Worden, J. W., & Silverman, P. S. (1993). Grief and depression in newly widowed parents with school-age children. *Omega: Journal of Death and Dying, 27*, 251–261.

Worfolk, J. B. (2000). Heat waves: Their impact on the health of elders. *Geriatric Nursing, 21*, 70–77.

Wortman, C. B., & Boerner, K. (2007). Beyond the myths of coping with loss: Prevailing assumptions versus scientific evidence. In H. S. Friedman & R. C. Silver (Eds.), *Foundations of health psychology.* New York: Oxford University Press.

Wortman, C. B., & Silver, R. C. (2001). The myths of coping with loss revisited. In M. S. Stroebe, R. O. Hansson, W. Stroebe, & H. Schut (Eds.), *Handbook of bereavement research. Consequences, coping, and care.* Washington, DC: American Psychological Association.

Wrosch, C., Bauer, I., & Scheier, M. F. (2005). Regret and quality of life across the adult life span: The influence of disengagement and available future goals. *Psychology and Aging, 20*, 657–670.

Wrzus, C., Hänel, M., Wagner, J., & Neyer, F. J. (2013). Social network changes and life events across the life span: A meta-analysis. *Psychological Bulletin, 139*, 53–80.

Wrzus, C., Müller, V., Wagner, J., Lindenberger, U., & Riediger, M. (2013). Affective and cardiovascular responding to unpleasant events from adolescence to old age: Complexity of events matters. *Developmental Psychology, 49*, 384–397.

Wu, P., & Chiou, W. (2008). Postformal thinking and creativity among late adolescents: A post-Piagetian approach. *Adolescence, 43*, 237–251.

Wu, T., Mendola, P., & Buck, G. M. (2002). Ethnic differences in the presence of secondary sex characteristics and menarche among US girls: The third national health and nutrition examination survey, 1988–1994. *Pediatrics, 110*, 752–757.

Wysocki, C. J., Louie, J., Leyden, J. J., Blank, D., Gill, M., Smith, L., et al. (2009, April 7). Cross-adaptation of a model human stress-related odor with fragrance chemicals and ethyl esters of axillary odorants: Gender-specific effects. *Flavour and Fragrance Journal, 24*(5), 209–218.

Yaffe, K., Barnes, D., Nevitt, M., Lui, L., & Covinsky, K. (2001). A prospective study of physical activity and cognitive decline in elderly women. *Archives of Internal Medicine, 161*, 1703–1708.

Yamagata, S., Suzuki, A., Ando, J., Ono, Y., Kijima, N., Yoshimura, K., Ostendorf, F., Angleitner, A., Riemann, R., Spinath, F. M., Livesley, W. J., & Jang, K. L. (2006). Is the genetic structure of human personality universal? A cross-cultural twin study from North America, Europe, and Asia. *Journal of Personality and Social Psychology, 90*, 987–998.

Yamazaki, K., & Beauchamp, G. K. (2007). Genetic Basis for MHC Dependent Mate Choice. In D. Yamamoto (Ed.), *Advances in Genetics*, vol 59 (pp. 129–145). Academic Press.

Yan, A. F., Voorhees, C. C., Clifton, K., Burnier, C., Voorhees, C. C., Clifton, K., et al. (2009). "Do you see what I see?—correlates of multidimensional measures of neighborhood types and perceived physical activity-related neighborhood barriers and facilitators for urban youth. *Preventive Medicine*, Epub ahead of print.

Yan, B., & Arlin, P. K. (1995). Nonabsolute/relativistic thinking: A common factor underlying models of postformal reasoning? *Journal of Adult Development, 2*, 223–240.

Yao Defen as Tallest Women in The World. (2012). Retrieved from http://worldmostamazingrecords.org/yao-defen-as-tallest-women-in-the-world/

Yau, P. L., Castro, M. G., Tagani, A., Tsui, W. H., & Convit, A. (2012). Obesity and metabolic syndrome and functional and structural brain impairments in adolescence. *Pediatrics, 130*, 1–9.

Yeates, K. O., & Selman, R. L. (1989). Social competence in the schools: Toward an integrative developmental model for intervention. *Developmental Review, 9*, 64–100.

Yeh, Y., & Wu, J. (2006). The cognitive processes of pupils' technological creativity. *Creativity Research Journal, 18*, 213–227.

Yendovitskaya, T. V. (1971). Development of attention. In A. V. Zaporozhets & D. B. Elkonin (Eds.), *The psychology of preschool children.* Cambridge, MA: MIT Press.

Yeung, W. J., & Pfeiffer, K. M. (2009). The black-white test score gap and early home environment. *Social Science Research, 38*, 412–437.

Yonkers, K. A., & Casper, R. F. (2012). *Epidemiology and pathogenesis of premenstrual syndrome and premenstrual dysphoric disorder.* Retrieved from http://www.uptodate.com/contents/epideiology-and-pathogenesis-of-premenstrual-syndrome

Yorifuji, T., Debes, F., Weihe, P., & Grandjean, P. (2011). Prenatal exposure to lead and cognitive deficit in 7- and 14-year-old children in the presence of concomitant exposure to similar molar concentration of methylmercury. *Neurotoxicology & Teratology, 33*, 205–211.

Youn, G. Y., Knight, B. G., Jeong, H. S., & Benton, D. (1999). Differences in familism values and caregiving outcomes among Korean, Korean American, and White American dementia caregivers. *Psychology and Aging, 14*, 355–364.

Young, L. R., & Nestle, M. (2002). The contribution of expanding portion sizes to the US obesity epidemic. *American Journal of Public Health, 92*, 246–249.

Young, W. C., Goy, R. W., & Phoenix, C. H. (1964). Hormones and sexual behavior. *Science, 143*, 212–218.

Youniss, J. (1980). *Parents and peers in social development. A Sullivan–Piaget perspective.* Chicago: University of Chicago Press.

Youth Risk Behavior Survey. (2009). *National trends in risk behaviors.* Retrieved from http://www.cdc.gov/HealthyYouth/yrbs/trends.htm

Yuenyong, S., O'Brien, B., & Jirapeet, V. (2010). Effects of labor support from close female relative on labor and maternal satisfaction in a Thai setting. *Journal of Obstetrics, Gynecology & Neonatal Nursing, 41*, 45–56.

Yuill, N. (1993). Understanding of personality and dispositions. In M. Bennett (Ed.), *The development of social cognition: The child as psychologist.* New York: Guilford.

Yun, Y. H., Han, K. H., Park, S., Park, B. W., Cho, C., Kim, S., et al. (2011). Attitudes of cancer patients, family caregivers, oncologists and members of the general public toward critical interventions at the end of life of terminally ill patients. *Canadian Medical Association Journal, 183,* E673-E679.

Zahn-Waxler, C., Friedman, R. J., Cole, P. M., Mizuta, I., & Himura, N. (1996). Japanese and United States preschool children's responses to conflict and distress. *Child Development, 67,* 2462–2477.

Zahn-Waxler, C., Radke-Yarrow, M., Wagner, E., & Chapman, M. (1992). Development of concern for others. *Developmental Psychology, 28,* 126–136.

Zajac, R., & Hayne, H. (2003). I don't think that's what really happened: The effect of cross-examination on the accuracy of children's reports. *Journal of Experimental Psychology: Applied, 9,* 187–195.

Zajonc, R. B. (2001a). Birth order debate resolved? *American Psychologist, 56,* 522–523.

Zajonc, R. B. (2001b). The family dynamics of intellectual development. *American Psychologist, 56,* 490–496.

Zaporozhets, A. V. (1965). The development of perception in the preschool child. *Monographs of the Society for Research in Child Development, 30*(2, Serial No. 100), 82–101.

Zarit, S. H. (2009). Empirically supported treatment for family caregivers. In S. H. Qualls & S. H. Zarit (Eds.), *Aging families and caregiving.* Hoboken, NJ: John Wiley.

Zarit, S. H., & Talley, R. C. (Eds.). (2013). *Caregiving for Alzheimer's disease and related disorders: Research, practice, policy.* New York: Springer Science+Business Media.

Zaslow, M. (1980). Relationships among peers in kibbutz toddler groups. *Child Psychiatry and Human Development, 10,* 178–189.

Zawia, N. H., Lahiri, D. K., & Cardozo-Pelaez, F. (2009). Epigenetics, oxidative stress, and Alzheimer disease. *Free Radical Biology & Medicine, 46,* 1241–1249.

Zeanah, C. H. (Ed.). (2009). *Handbook of infant mental health* (3rd ed.). New York: Guilford.

Zeanah, C. H., Berlin, L. J., & Boris, N. W. (2011). Clinical applications of attachment theory and research for infants and young children. *Journal of Child Psychology and Psychiatry, 52,* 819–833.

Zehr, J. L., Culbert, K. M., Siska, C. L., & Klump, K. L. (2007). An association of early puberty with disordered eating and anxiety in a population of undergraduate women and men. *Hormones and Behavior, 52,* 427–435.

Zeller, M. H., & Modi, A. C. (2006). Predictors of health-related quality of life in obese youth. *Obesity, 14,* 122–130.

Zemach, I., Chang, S., & Teller, D. Y. (2006). Infant color vision: Prediction of infants' spontaneous color preferences. *Vision Research, 47,* 1368–1381.

Zemel, B. (2002). Body composition during growth and development. In N. Cameron (Ed.), *Human growth and development* (pp. 271–293). New York: Academic Press.

Zenger, M., Brahler, E., Berth, H., & Stobel-Richter, Y. (2011). Unemployment during working life and mental health of retirees: Results of a representative survey. *Aging & Mental Health, 15,* 178–185.

Zentner, M. Z., & Shiner, R. L. (Eds.) (2012). *Handbook of temperament.* New York: Guilford.

Zero to Three. (2005). *Diagnostic classification of mental health and developmental disorders of infancy and early childhood* (rev. ed.). Washington, DC: Zero to Three Press.

Zhang, H. (2009). The new realities of aging in contemporary China: Coping with the decline in family care. In J. Sokolovsky (Ed.), *The cultural context of aging* (3rd ed.). Westport, CT: Praeger.

Zhang, L. (2002). Thinking styles and cognitive development. *Journal of Genetic Psychology, 163,* 179–195.

Zhu, H., Belcher, M. and van der Harst, P. (2011) Healthy aging and disease: role for telomere biology? *Clinical Science, 120,* 427–440.

Zigler, E. (1995). Can we "cure" mild mental retardation among individuals in the lower socioeconomic stratum? *American Journal of Public Health, 85,* 302–304.

Zigler, E., Abelson, W. D., Trickett, P. K., & Seitz, V. (1982). Is an intervention program necessary to improve economically disadvantaged children's IQ scores? *Child Development, 53,* 340–348.

Zimmerman, F. J., Christakis, D. A., & Meltzoff, A. N. (2007). Associations between media viewing and language development in children under age 2 years. *Journal of Pediatrics, 151,* 364–368.

Zimmermann, M. B. (2007). The adverse effects of mild-to-moderate iodine deficiency during pregnancy and childhood: A review. *Thyroid, 17,* 829–835.

Zimprich, D., & Martin, M. (2002). Can longitudinal changes in processing speed explain longitudinal age changes in fluid intelligence? *Psychology and Aging, 17,* 690–695.

Zissimopoulos, J. M., & Karoly, L. A. (2009). Labor-force dynamics at older ages. Movements into self-employment for workers and nonworkers. *Research on Aging, 31,* 89–111.

Zosuls, K. M., Ruble, D. N., Bornstein, M. H., & Greulich, F. K. (2009). The acquisition of gender labels in infancy: Implications for gender-typed play. *Developmental Psychology, 45,* 688–701.

Zucker, A. N., Ostrove, J. M., & Stewart, A. J. (2002). College-educated women's personality development in adulthood: Perceptions and age differences. *Psychology and Aging, 17,* 236–244.

Zvoch, K., & Stevens, J. J. (2006). Longitudinal effects of school context and practice on middle school mathematics achievement. *Journal of Educational Research, 99,* 347–356.

Zwaigenbaum, L., Bryson, S., Rogers, T., Roberts, W., Brian, J., & Szatmari, P. (2005). Behavioral manifestations of autism in the first year of life. *International Journal of Developmental Neuroscience, 23,* 143–152.

Name Index

Braine, M. D. S., 311
Brainerd, C. J., 244
Braithwaite, V., 350
Brake, B., 368
Brand, C. R., 265
Brand, J. E., 357
Brandão, S., 120
Brandt, H., 524
Brandt, J., 253, 140
Brandtstädter, J., 349
Branje, S., 345, 459, 483
Brant, A. M., 292
Brant, L. J., 193–194
Brassett-Harknett, A., 518
Braude, P., 74
Braun, N., 498
Braunwald, K., 446
Braver, E. R., 191
Braver, S. L., 496
Bravo, E., 103
Bray, N. W., 240, 248
Brayne, C., 533
Brayton, J. T., 299
Brazelton, T. B., 121
Breedlove, S. M., 375–376
Brehmer, Y., 247
Breinlinger, K., 172
Breitner, J. C., 533
Bremner, J. D., 253
Bremner, J. G., 172
Brendgen, M., 76–77, 83, 88, 340, 424
Brenick, A., 380
Brenner, A., 562
Brent, D. A., 521, 553
Brent, H. P., 177
Brent, S. B., 549–550, 553
Bret, M. E., 533
Bretherton, I., 402, 441, 444
Brett, C. E., 78, 280
Brian, J., 512
Brickman, A. M., 13, 152
Brickman, D., 340
Bridge, J. A., 553
Bridges, C., 276
Bridges, L. J., 436
Briefel, R. R., 142
Briggs, P. T., 371
Briggs-Gowan, M. J., 521
Britner, P. A., 448
Britto, P. R., 479
Broadbent, J. M., 420
Broadbridge, C. L., 252
Broberg, M., 291
Brod, M., 518
Broderick, V., 316
Brodie, D., 464
Brodsky, N. L., 286
Brody, D. J., 146
Brody, E. B., 278
Brody, E. M., 473, 490–491
Brody, G. H., 417
Brody, J. A., 154
Brody, N., 278
Broen, A. N., 556
Broene, P., 309
Bromet, E., 518
Bromley, D. B., 339, 405
Bromnick, R. D., 223
Bronfenbrenner, U., 51–52, 471
Bronstad, P. M., 187
Bronstein, P., 314
Brook, J., 516
Brooks-Gunn, J., 147, 335, 339, 476, 479
Brophy, J., 312, 315
Broughton, J. M., 182, 225
Broverman, D. M., 367

Broverman, I., 367
Brown, A. L., 248
Brown, A., 66, 113
Brown, B. B., 321, 340, 457–460, 484
Brown, G. L., 57
Brown, I. T., 429
Brown, J., 288
Brown, K. C., 275
Brown, R. D., 240, 245
Brown, R. T., 518
Brown, S. L., 492
Browne, C. R., 455
Browne, D. C., 454
Brownell, C. A., 336
Brownell, H., 406
Brownson, R. C., 155
Bruce, J., 447, 515
Bruck, M., 317
Brueckner, L., 172
Brummett, B. H., 360
Brun, V., 173
Brundin, P., 152
Bruner, J. S., 203, 303
Brunet, P. M., 177
Brunner, R., 337
Brunskill, P. J., 376
Brütt, A. L., 131
Bryant, P., 316
Bryant-Waugh, R., 522
Brynie, F. H., 166, 194
Bryson, S. W., 512, 524
Buchanan, A., 488
Buchanan, C. M., 147
Buchanan, N. R., 450
Buchanan, P., 180
Bucher, H. U., 556
Buchi, S., 556
Bucholz, K. K., 509, 527
Buchtel, E. E., 333, 350–351
Buck, G. M., 145
Buckley, E. G., 177
Buckner, R. L., 249
Bucur, B., 255
Buddin, B. J., 436
Buehler, C. A., 495–496
Buerger, M., 3
Bugental, D. B., 499–500
Bugg, J. M., 153
Buhrmester, D., 441, 451, 456–457, 482
Buitelaar, J. K., 112
Buka, S. L., 514
Bukowski, W. M., 390, 442, 450, 455, 458
Bulanda, J. R., 492
Bulanda, R. E., 475
Bulcao, C., 195
Bulevich, J. B., 255
Bulik, C. M., 523
Bullard, K. M., 530, 531
Bullard, L., 496
Bullinger, A., 176
Bullinger, M., 131
Bullock, M., 220, 222
Bumpass, L., 472
Bundy, D. A., 273
Buntinx, W. H. E., 290
Burack, J. A., 184
Burak, L., 185
Burch, M. M., 244
Burchett, B. M., 358–359
Burchinal, M., 146, 275, 286, 310, 449, 486
Bureau of Labor Statistics, 358, 366, 370, 473
Bures, R. M., 492
Burgard, S. A., 357
Burger, H., 516
Burgio, L. D., 491
Burhans, K. K., 311

Burianova, H., 406
Buriel, R., 471, 476
Burk, L. R., 458
Burk, W. J., 458
Burke, C. T., 556
Burke, D. M., 387
Burke, J. R., 533
Burke, L. A., 559
Burke, M. M., 291
Burleson, M. H., 394
Burmeister, M., 83
Burn, S., 385
Burnelli, T., 194
Burnett, P. C., 278
Burnham, D., 173, 303, 371
Burnier, C., 148
Burr, D., 182
Bursch, B., 448
Burstein, M., 522
Burston, A., 494
Burstyn, I. I., 103
Burt, B. A., 141
Burt, C. D. B., 251
Burt, K. B., 526
Burt, S. A., 523
Burtnack, C. A., 148
Burton, C. M., 424, 459
Burton, L. A., 7, 369
Burton, L. M., 471
Burton, R. V., 415
Burwell, R. A., 523
Bus, A. G., 317
Busch, H., 355
Buschke, H., 281
Busch-Rossnagel, N. A., 308
Bushman, B. J., 21, 23, 423
Bushnell, E. W., 182
Buss, A. H., 369
Buss, C., 101
Buss, D. M., 62, 64, 375, 402, 412, 423
Buss, K. A., 336
Buss, R. R., 223
Butcher, L. M., 78
Butcher, P. R., 183
Butera, F., 313
Butler, N., 518
Butler, R., 313, 340
Butterfield, D. A., 160
Butterfield, S. A., 181
Butters, M. A., 531, 534
Butterworth, M., 461, 493
Butterworth, P., 359
Button, C., 520
Button, T. M. M., 423
Buunk, B. P., 349
Buyck, P., 340
Bybee, R. W., 222
Byles, J. E., 93
Byma, G., 318
Byne, W., 387
Bynum, M. S., 392
Byrnes, J. P., 234, 250
Bythell, M., 98

C

Caban-Martinez, A. J., 192
Cabeza, R., 16
Cabili, C., 142
Cabrera, N. J., 475
Cacioppo, J. T., 156, 464
Caetano, R., 497
Caggiula, A. W., 154
Cain, A. C., 552
Cain, K. M., 312
Calabrese, V., 160
Caldera, Y. M., 371, 375, 476

Caldwell, B. M., 287
Caldwell, C. H., 321, 531
Calhoun, L. G., 560–561
Calkins, S. D., 436, 446, 454
Call, J., 402
Call, K. T., 324
Callaghan, T., 337, 414
Callaghan, W. M., 123, 414
Callanan, M. A., 482
Callands, T. A., 392
Calume, Z. F., 123
Calvin, C. M., 280
Calvo, A., 312
Calvo, E., 359
Camaioni, L., 306
Cambois, E., 367
Cameron, A. J., 150
Cameron, E. L., 186
Camicioli, R., 532
Camp, C. J., 258
Campa, M., 444
Campbell, A., 140, 275, 381
Campbell, F. A., 275, 310
Campbell, R., 301
Campbell, V. A., 196
Campbell, W. K., 23
Campos, B., 489
Campos, J. J., 172
Camras, L. A., 434, 436
Camus, V., 531
Canfield, R. L., 109
Cann, A., 560
Cannon, M., 81
Cano, A., 499
Cantarella, A., 176
Cantin, S., 77
Cantor, N. L., 540
Cantwell, C., 528
Capaldi, D. M., 498
Caplan, L. J., 254
Caplan, M., 450
Caplan, R. D., 357
Capozzoli, M. C., 183
Cappell, K. A., 256
Capps, L., 511
Caprara, G. V., 410, 412
Capute, A. J., 98
Carabellese, C., 194
Carceller, R., 103
Carchon, I., 170
Cardozo-Pelaez, F., 533
Carey, I. M., 554
Carey, M. P., 387
Carey, N., 86–87
Carey, S., 403
Carlin, J. B., 147
Carlin, L., 391
Carlo, G., 419–420, 425
Carlson, E. A., 447, 450, 465, 515
Carlson, M. C., 283
Carlson, M. J., 476
Carlson, S. M., 214
Carlson, W., 457
Carlsson-Paige, N., 309
Carlton, M. P., 207
Carmichael, S. L., 113
Carnehon, M., 115
Carnelley, K. B., 463, 556
Carnes, B. A., 160
Caron, S. L., 384, 387–388
Carpendale, J. I. M., 410
Carpenter, M. G., 177, 305
Carpentier, N., 541
Carper, R., 513
Carr, A., 520
Carr, C. L., 385

Carr, D., 492, 559, 561
Carr, M. B., 385
Carr, P. L., 357
Carrano, J., 495
Carrera, M., 56
Carriger, M. S., 272, 336
Carroll, D. W., 306
Carroll, J. B., 266
Carroll, J. M., 316
Carskadon, M. A., 150
Carson, B. S., 140
Carson, C., 121
Carson, K. A., 376
Carsrud, A. L., 325
Carstensen, L. L., 254, 349, 360, 438–439, 460
Carta, R., 414
Carter, A. S., 513, 521
Carter, B., 471–472, 496
Carter, C., 512
Cartwright, K. B., 226
Carvalho, M. R., 424
Carver, K., 459
Carver, L. J., 435
Cascade, E. F., 521
Case, R., 205, 239
Case, T. I., 176
Casey, B. J., 144, 341, 415, 562
Casey, R. J., 415
Casey, V., 562
Caskie, G. I. L., 24
Casper, R. F., 153
Casper, V., 445
Caspi, A., 80, 83, 227, 338, 341, 352–353, 420, 423, 481, 489, 500, 509
Cassia, V. M., 171
Cassidy, T., 114, 118, 120
Cassina, M., 101, 110
Castellanos, I., 171
Castelli, P., 251
Castro, C., 155
Castro, M. G., 150
Catalano, M., 347
Catalano, P. M., 107
Cattell, R. B., 265
Cattell, R., 281
Cauffman, E., 420, 458
Caughlin, J. P., 485
Cavallo, V., 156
Cavanaugh, J. C., 252, 255
Cave, K., 183
Cawley, J., 155
Cawthon, R., 160
Caya, L. R., 455
Caya, M., 353
Caygill, L., 275, 381
Caylak, E., 317
Ceccarelli, M., 176
Ceci, S. J., 244, 324
Cecil-Karb, R., 142
Cederlund, M., 512
Celgene Corporation, 102
Cen, G., 341
Centers for Disease Control and Prevention, 71, 148, 389–391, 512, 528, 543
Central Intelligence Agency, 543
Cerminara, K. L., 539
Cernoch, J. M., 176
Cervera, T. C., 193
Cesarini, D., 78
Chabris, C. F., 78
Chadwick, A., 414
Chaiyasit, W., 508
Chakrabarti, S., 512
Chambers, G. M., 93
Chambers, W. C., 389
Chamorro-Premuzic, T., 313, 462

Champagne, F. A., 68, 86–87, 106, 112
Champagne, M. C., 346
Champaud, C., 311
Chan, D., 530
Chan, W., 349
Chandler, M. J., 402, 416
Chandler, S., 512
Chandra, A., 57, 485
Chang, L., 423, 477
Chang, S., 169
Chao, R. K., 478
Chaplin, J., 131
Chapman, A. R., 74
Chapman, M., 218
Chapman, R. S., 306
Chappell, R. J., 189
Charbonneau, A. M., 527
Charles, S. T., 253, 439
Charley, C. M., 214
Charlton, M. L., 138, 346
Charlton, R. A., 406–407
Charman, T., 401
Charness, N., 251
Charney, D. S., 521, 530
Charpentier, P., 547
Chase, W. G., 250
Chassin, L., 147, 525
Chatelle, C., 540
Chatters, L. M., 430, 530
Chattopadhyay, S. K., 521
Chaudhary, N., 337, 477
Chavajay, P., 451
Chavous, T. M., 321
Chawarska, K., 512
Cheadle, J. E., 85, 495
Chee, M. W., 152
Chein, J., 522
Cheit, R. E., 390
Chen, A., 240
Chen, C., 323
Chen, D., 175
Chen, E., 86
Chen, H., 359, 464
Chen, J. Q., 175, 267
Chen, R. M., 146
Chen, S. K., 146
Chen, T., 429
Chen, X., 341, 456
Chen, Y., 256
Cheng, A. K., 175
Cheng, J. K. Y., 507, 531
Chennu, S., 540
Cherkas, L. F., 160
Cherlin, A. J., 394, 472–473, 485, 488, 492, 494, 496
Cherney, I. D., 373–374
Cherney, I. S., 374
Cherry, K. E., 253, 256, 541, 547, 554
Cheshire, A., 172
Chesley, N., 490
Chess, S., 336, 338
Chessor, D., 343
Chetwynd, A., 281
Chi, M. T. H., 242, 250
Chia, E. M., 190
Chiesi, H. L., 250
Chiew, K. S., 255
Chilamkurti, C., 405
Childers, S. A., 292
Chinsky, J. M., 240
Chiong, C. S., 18
Chiou, W., 225
Chiriboga, D., 489
Chisolm, D. J., 424, 459
Chisum, H. J., 152
Chiu, E., 533

Chiu, S., 207
Chiu, W. T., 530
Cho, C., 541
Chochinov, H. M., 558
Choi, E. S., 139
Choi, H. K., 148
Choi, J., 368
Choi, S., 307
Chomsky, N., 299–300, 308
Chou, C. P., 149
Choueiti, M., 380
Chouliaras, L., 533
Christ, G. H., 551–553
Christakis, D. A., 19–20, 309
Christensen, K. M., 176
Christiansen, S. L., 355
Christianson, T. J. H., 253
Christodoulou, J., 112
Chronis, A. M., 519
Chrousos, G., 150
Chu, J. P., 507, 531
Chua, A., 478
Chua-Rubenfeld, S., 478
Chui, H., 340, 342
Chumlea, W. C., 144
Chun, M., 541
Chung, G. H., 487
Chung, J. H., 186, 350
Church, T. S., 149
Chyi, L. J., 123
Cicchetti, D., 418, 499–500, 507–508, 522
Cicirelli, V. G., 463, 489, 491
Cillessen, A. H. N., 421, 454–455, 457
Clark, A., 300
Clark, B. A. M., 427
Clark, D. O., 157
Clark, E. V., 306
Clark, H. H., 280, 306
Clark, J. G., 193
Clark, J. L., 177
Clark, M. A., 142
Clark, R. D., 414
Clark, S. E., 404
Clarke-Stewart, K. A., 146, 316, 449
Clarridge, B. R., 562
Clarys, D., 256
Clauser, J., 158
Claxton, A. F., 278
Clearfield, M., 180
Cleary-Goldman, J., 71
Clemenson, G. D., 152
Clementi, M., 101, 110
Cleveland, E. S., 244
Cleveland, H. H., 286
Cleveland, S., 514
Clifford, C., 390
Clifton, K., 148
Clingempeel, W. G., 477
Close, J., 222
Clubb, P. A., 245
Cluver, L., 500
Clydesdale, F. M., 518
Clyman, R. B., 416
Coall, D. A., 488
Coates, A., 531
Cobb, R. W., 191
Cocker, C., 448
Codipietro, L., 176
Coe, B. P., 359
Coe, C. L., 100
Coe, N. B., 359
Cohan, C. L., 491–492
Cohen, B., 514
Cohen, C., 463
Cohen, G. L., 248, 389
Cohen, J. D., 427, 520

Cohen, M., 246
Cohen, N. J., 256
Cohen, P., 516
Cohen, S., 464
Cohen, T. F., 461, 471
Cohn, D., 472–473, 491
Coie, J. D., 420, 425, 454–455
Coker, C., 423
Coladarci, T., 324
Colapinto, J., 378
Colbert, K. K., 226
Colburn, D., 177, 194
Colby, A., 409, 416, 420, 426
Colcombe, S. J., 256
Colder, C. R., 525
Cole, D. A., 342
Cole, E., 563
Cole, J., 166
Cole, M., 26
Cole, P. M., 436–437
Cole, R., 318, 320–321
Coleman, A. L., 190
Coleman, D. L., 500
Coleman, J., 321
Coleman, M. R., 540
Coley, J. D., 250
Coley, R. L., 495
Colin, V., 443
Coll, C. G., 286
Colletti, L., 175
Colletti, V., 175
Colley, A., 379
Collins, A., 339
Collins, C. T., 117
Collins, J., 562
Collins, M., 512
Collins, S., 392
Collins, W. A., 449, 456–457, 459, 483–484
Colombo, J., 169–170, 183, 272, 274, 286, 292
Comer, J., 417
Comfort, A., 395
Committee on Adolescence, 505
Committee on Environmental Health, 142
Commons, M. L., 225
Compas, B. E., 551
Compian, L., 459
Compton, N. C., 551
Conde-Agudelo, A., 123
Condon, D. M., 15
Condon, E. M., 142
Condon, T. P., 157
Condry, J., 371
Condry, S., 371
Conduct Problems Prevention Research Group, 423, 425, 454
Conger, K. J., 479–480
Conger, R. D., 8, 423, 478–479, 487, 498, 527
Conklin, H. M., 239, 248
Conley, C. S., 527
Conley, T. D., 388
Connell, A. M., 516
Connell, J. P., 436
Connelly, A., 235
Connelly, J. R., 235
Conner, K. A., 488, 490
Conners, C. K., 519
Connidis, I. A., 473, 488–493
Connolly, J. A., 454, 459
Connolly, K. J., 178
Connolly, M. P., 93
Connor, S. R., 561
Connor-Smith, J. K., 551
Conrad, K. A., 387
Conrade, G., 377
Consedine, N. S., 438

Constable, R. T., 299
Contrand, B., 149
Convit, A., 150
Convyn, R. F., 286
Conway, A. R. A., 427
Conway, M. A., 248, 251–252
Coohey, C., 498
Cook, A. S., 542
Cook, D. G., 554
Cook, E. H., 513
Cook, K., 562
Cook, R., 309
Cook, T. J., 357
Cooke, L. M., 63
Cooke, T. J., 357
Coon, D. W., 491
Cooney, R. E., 509, 515
Coontz, S., 470, 480
Cooper, C. R., 347
Cooper, D. H., 316, 389
Cooper, M. L., 389
Cooper, P. J., 119, 435
Cooper, R. P., 173
Coopersmith, S., 340
Coovadia, H. M., 109
Copeland, D. R., 551
Copeland, J. R. M., 531
Copeland, W., 529
Copen, C. E., 56
Coplan, R. J., 452–455
Coppotelli, H., 454
Corapci, F., 437
Corbett, C., 357
Corbetta, D., 179–180
Corcoran, J., 57
Corina, D., 301
Corley, R. P., 292, 428
Cornelius, S. W., 107, 227
Cornell, D., 424
Corney, R., 359
Cornoldi, C., 241
Corpuz, R., 500
Corr, C. A., 548, 552–553, 561
Corr, D. M., 561
Correa-Chavez, M., 45
Corwin, J., 195
Corwyn, R. F., 479
Cossette, L., 371
Costa, P. T. Jr., 285, 333, 341, 349, 351–353, 361
Costanzo, P. R., 454, 527, 552
Costas-Moragas, C., 370
Costello, E. J., 154, 529
Cota-Robles, S., 423
Côté, J. E., 347
Côté, S., 369
Cotler, S., 53
Cotten, S. R., 13
Coughlin, J. F., 191
Coulter, D. L., 290
Council on Communications and Media, 142
Courage, M. L., 19, 169–170, 236, 244
Courchesne, E., 152, 513
Cousens, S., 108
Couturier, J., 525
Covington, J., 152
Covington, M. V., 313
Covinsky, K., 158
Cowan, B. W., 57
Cowan, C. P., 486, 516
Cowan, N., 236
Cowan, P. A., 486
Cowart, B. J., 194
Cowles, A., 152
Cox, K. S., 355

Cox, M. J., 474, 476, 486, 495
Cox, R., 495
Cox, T. H., 357
Coxe, S., 563
Coyne, J. C., 509
Crabb, P. B., 380
Crago, M. B., 300, 524
Craig, E. M., 290
Craig, I. W., 423
Craig, T., 433
Craig, W., 459
Craik, F. I. M., 312
Cramond, B., 278
Crane, P., 533
Craven, R. G., 340–341
Crawford, J. R., 252
Crawford, M., 387–388
Cready, C. M., 380
Creasey, G. L., 14–15, 21, 463
Creasy, R., 107
Crepinsek, M. K., 142
Crews, F., 38
Crews, J. E., 196
Cribbie, R., 384
Crick, N. R., 369, 421–422
Cridland, N., 119
Crijnen, A. A. M., 516
Criss, M. M., 478
Critchley, C. R., 418
Crockenberg, S., 339
Croft, K., 217
Crombie, G., 347
Cromer, C. C., 451
Crooks, R. L., 372
Cross, C. E., 13, 480
Cross, D., 402
Cross, S. E., 350–351
Crouch, J. L., 499
Crouter, A. C., 52, 320, 377, 379,
    480, 485, 487, 493
Crowell, J. A., 462, 485
Crowley, T. J., 81
Crozier, S. R., 106
Cruickshank, J. K., 107
Cruickshanks, K. J., 189, 192, 194
Cruikshank, M., 5, 159, 350, 359
Cruse, D., 540
Cruz, J. E., 527
Crystal, S., 113
Csikszentmihalyi, M., 284
Cuevas, C. A., 390
Cuevas, K., 237
Cui, L., 522
Cui, M., 487
Cuijpers, P., 355
Culbert, K. M., 524
Culhane, J. F., 123
Cullen, M. J., 288
Cumberland, A., 483
Cumming, E., 360
Cumming, R. R., 190
Cummings, J. L., 253
Cummings, S. M., 350
Cunningham, H., 8
Curlik, D. M., 153
Curran, S., 513
Currie, J., 275
Currier, J. M., 556, 561–562
Cushman, L., 486
Cutrona, C. E., 527
Cutter, G. R., 518
Cutting, A. L., 417
Cutuli, J. J., 447
Cyphers, L., 373
Cytron, B. D., 542
Cytryn, L., 520

D
D'Alessio, A.C., 87, 498
D'Esposito, M., 16
D'Onofrio, B., 80
Dabbs, J. M., 376
Dabis, F., 109
Dahinten, V. S., 146
Dahl, R. E., 143
Daley, A. J., 142
Daley, C. E., 287
Dallos, R., 524
Dalton, D. S., 192
Dalvi, T. B., 491
Damon, W., 339, 341–342, 373
Damphousse, K. R., 325
Daneman, M., 193
Danhauer, S. C., 560
Daniel, J. H., 521
Danieli, R., 456
Daniels, H., 206
Daniels, K., 485
Daniels, L. M., 313
Daniels, M., 76
Daniels, W., 185
Daniluk, J. C., 93
Danino, K., 515
Dapretto, M., 403
Darling, N., 476
Darmopil, S., 274
Darnon, C., 313
Darroch, F., 113
Darwin, C., 11, 62
Das Eiden, R., 106
Dave, J., 530
Davidov, M., 476
Davidson, A., 486
Davidson, J., 378
Davies, B., 550, 562
Davies, I., 169
Davies, K. J. A., 160
Davies, M. N. O., 187
Davies, M. S., 403
Davies, S. G., 366
Davies, S. L., 57
Davila, E. P., 192
Davis, A. S., 508
Davis, C. G., 559
Davis, C. L., 143
Davis, E. P., 100, 112
Davis, L. B., 176
Davis, M. H., 540
Davis, N. O., 243, 521
Davis, O. S. P., 66, 70, 78–79
Davis, S. M., 268
Davis, W. E., 324
Davis-Kean, P. E., 459, 484
Dawes, S., 531
Dawood, K., 76
Dawson, G., 446, 514
Day, N. L., 107, 553
Day, R. D., 495, 553
De Alba, M. G., 71
de Boer, M. A., 74, 110
De Bolle, M., 349
de Cabo, R., 161
De Cáceres-Zurita, M. L., 370
de Faire, U., 82, 252
De Fruyt, F., 357
De Goede, I. H. A., 483–484
De Graaf, P. M., 489
de Haan, M. D., 133, 143, 171
De Heering, A., 171
de Jong-Gierveld, J., 464
De Lisi, R., 224
de Meeus, T., 145
de Mendonca Lima, C. A., 531

de Mendonca, A., 253
de Rosnay, M., 435
de Rover, M., 256
de Schonen, S., 171
de St, Aubin, E., 326, 355
De Vise, D., 231
de Weerth, C., 112
De Wolff, M. S., 445, 447
Dearden, C., 448
Deary, I. J., 265, 277–278, 280
Deater-Deckard, K., 85, 423, 477–478, 481
DeBaryshe, B. D., 422
Debes, F., 109
Debus, R. L., 340
DeBuse, C. J., 464
DeCasper, A. J., 173
Declercq, E., 114–115, 117
DeCourcey, W., 471
Deeds, O., 124, 176
DeFrain, J. D., 557, 561
DeFries, J. C., 81–84, 292, 516
DeGarmo, D. S., 43, 495–496, 500
Deguchi, T., 173
Dehaene, P., 106
Dehaene, S., 315
De Haan, M., 143
De-Hayes, L., 32
Dekel, S., 559
DeKoekkoek, P. D., 358
DeKosky, S. T., 253, 533
Del Gaudio, F., 554, 562
Del Giudice, M., 132
DeLamater, J. D., 372, 395–396
Delaunay-El Allam, M., 176
Delcourt, M. A. B., 291
DeLeeuw, J., 496
DeLeire, T. C., 488
Delery, D. B., 304
Delgado, C. E. F., 401
Dell, M., 428
Dell'Avvento, V., 337
Della Sala, S., 407
DeLoache, J. S., 18, 20, 241, 246, 309
Delsol, C., 498
DelVecchio, W. F., 352
DeMarie, D., 241, 243–244
DeMeis, D. K., 370
Demetre, J. D., 359
Demetriou, H., 417
Demo, D. H., 486, 494–496
DeMonner, S. M., 110
DeMulder, E., 436
den Hove, D.,L.A., 533
DeNavas-Walt, C., 357
Denes, A., 495
Deng, X., 146
Denham, S. A., 436
Dennerstein, L., 154
Denney, J. T., 142
Denney, N. W., 226, 257–258
Dennis, N. A., 16
Dennis, T. A., 435
Dennis, W., 284
Denworth, L., 175
Deocampo, J., 236–237
Deppe, M., 140
Deptula, D. P., 390
Der, G., 280
deRegnier, R., 95, 100
Derks, E. M., 518
Derntl, B., 187
DeRosier, M. E., 454
Derryberry, D., 337
Deruelle, C., 171
Des Roches, C. M., 186
Desai, A. K., 533

Eilers, R. E., 305
Eimas, P. D., 173, 304
Eisen, M., 342–343
Eisenberg, M. E., 150, 342
Eisenberg, M. L., 153
Eisenberg, N., 326., 336, 414, 419, 483
Eisenberg, R., 311
Eisenmann, J., 141
Ekeberg, O., 556
Ekerdt, D. J., 359
Ekman, P., 438
Ekstrom, B., 154
Elbourne, D., 117
Elder, G. H., Jr., 17, 13, 470, 479–480
Elias, J., 12, 283
Elias, S., 74
Elicker, J., 449
Eliot, L., 371
Elison, J. T., 512
Elkind, D., 223, 309
Elkins, I., 483
Ellard, J. H., 560
Ellard, S., 66, 68, 70, 72, 74, 86
Ellerson, P. C., 500
Ellingson, J., 524
Elliot, A. J., 313, 315, 463
Elliot, G., 519
Elliott, A. N., 390
Elliott, B. C., 140
Elliott, D. S., 423
Elliott, E. S., 311, 315
Elliott, G., 519
Elliott, S., 385
Ellis, B. J., 146
Ellis, L., 387
Ellis, R. A., 350
Ellis, S., 451
Ellis, Y., 185
Ellison, P. T., 146
El-Messidi, A., 406
Elsabbagh, M., 512
El-Sayed, Y. Y., 74
Else-Quest, N. M., 368
Elshout, J. J., 206
Ely, R., 318
Embleton, G., 557
Embleton, N. D., 98
Emde, R. N., 416
Emerson, P. E., 443, 445
Emery, R. E., 486, 501, 527
Emmanuelle, V., 347
Emmett, P. M., 141
Endara, S. M., 109
Enders, C., 552
Endsley, R. C., 381
Engels, R. C. M. E., 421
England, P., 357
Engle, P. L., 448
Englund, M., 449
Ennemoser, M., 193, 317
Enns, J. T., 184
Enright, R., 223
Ensminger, M. E., 324
Ensom, R., 43
Ensrud, K. E., 190
Entringer, S., 101
Epel, E. S., 160
Eppig, C., 277
Eppler, M. A., 178, 447
Epstein, J. N., 517
Epstein, R., 6
Erdley, C. A., 312
Erdman, P., 447
Erdwins, C. J., 326
Erera, P., 471
Erickson, J. J., 493. 543

Erickson, K. I., 256
Erickson, K. L., 256
Erickson, L. D., 12, 356
Erickson, M. F., 486, 499
Ericsson, K. A., 250–251
Eriksen, W., 108
Erikson, E. H., 39–40, 56, 333, 343, 487
Eriksson, M., 82
Eriksson, P. S., 136
Erkulwater, J., 518–519
Erlandsson, S. I., 186
Ernert, A., 146
Ernfors, P., 274
Ernst, L., 561
Erol, R. Y., 343
Ersner-Hershfield, H., 439
Esau, S. P., 192
Escalona, S., 272
Eskild, A., 119
Eskritt, M., 241
Espelage, D. L., 424
Espinosa-Hernandez, G., 389
Espinoza, G., 424
Esposito, K., 150
Espy, K. A., 274, 286
Essa, E. L., 551
Esser, G., 518
Essex, M. J., 517
Estes, L. S., 524
Estes, Z., 368, 370
Etgen, T., 253, 256
Ettekal, I., 424
Eugenin, J., 103
Evans, D., 395
Evans, E. M., 552
Evans, G. W., 7–9, 425, 479
Evans, J. R., 189–190, 337
Evans, L., 491
Evans, M. A., 316
Everett, B. H., 217
Exline, J. J., 428
Eyler, A. A., 155

F

Faber, C. E., 194
Fabes, R. A., 371, 374, 452
Fabio, A., 499
Fabre-Grenet, M., 171
Fagan, J. F., 170, 272, 475
Fagot, B. I., 374, 377, 379, 450
Fagundes, C. P., 449
Fahrenthold, D. A., 537
Faison, N., 321
Faith, M. S., 141
Faja, S., 514
Falcon, L. M., 530
Faloon, S., 250
Fan, H. C., 74
Fan, X., 424
Fang, A., 521
Fang, G., 323
Fantz, R. L., 170
Faraguna, D., 170
Farah, M. J., 286
Faraone, S. V., 518
Farber, N., 56–57
Farhat, T., 527
Farina, A., 117
Farlow, M. R., 533
Farmer, A., 141
Farmer, S. J., 359
Farney, L. A., 464
Farr, R. H., 494
Farrie, D., 475
Farrington, D. P., 424
Farroni, T., 170

Farver, J. A. M., 453
Fask, D., 80
Fauchere, J., 556
Faulkner, D., 206
Faulkner, K. W., 551
Faust, M. A., 316
Favilla, M., 140
Fawcett, L., 119
Fazzari, D. A., 559
Feagans, L., 367
Fearon, P., 119
Fearon, R. M. P., 447
Feder, T., 377
Federal Interagency Forum of Child and Family
    Statistics, 472–473, 497
Federal Interagency Forum on Aging, 156–157, 358,
    473, 489
Feghali, M., 107
Fegley, S., 323
Fehlings, D., 116
Feijten, P., 357
Feiler, R., 309
Fein, D., 514
Feingold, A., 369
Feinman, S., 435
Feiring, C., 459
Feld, S., 325–326
Feldlaufer, H., 322
Feldman, D. C., 357–358
Feldman, D. H., 207, 278
Feldman, H., 105, 487
Feldman, J. F., 123, 272
Feldman, K., 499
Feldman, R. D., 124, 278, 441, 443
Feldstein, S., 443 Felker, S., 368, 370
Fellowes, S., 141
Felps, W., 419
Fencsik, D. E., 185
Fender, J. G., 309
Feng, D., 485
Feng, J., 368
Fenson, L., 307
Ferguson, C. J., 21, 423
Ferguson, S. A., 191
Fergusson, D. M., 495
Fergusson, S. A., 191
Fernald, A., 172–173
Fernandes, C., 265, 278
Fernandes, J., 512
Fernandez, A., 359
Fernández-Espejo, D., 540
Fernyhough, C., 404
Ferrari, P. F., 299
Ferrario, C. G., 350
Ferraro, D., 322
Ferraro, K. F., 192
Ferrero, J., 459
Ferrie, J., 516
Ferron, J., 241, 243
Ferrucci, L., 349
Fesi, B., 176
Fetterolf, J. C., 388
Fida, R., 412
Field, D., 208, 281
Field, J., 327
Field, N. P., 558
Field, P. A., 120
Field, T. M., 120, 124, 176, 515
Fielder, R. L., 387
Fields-Meyer, T., 512
Fiese, B. H., 446
Fifer, W. P., 138
Fifer, W. P., 138, 173–174
Figueiredo, B., 120
Figueredo, A. J., 498
Figuereido, B., 124, 176

Filanosky, C., 558
Filipp, S. H., 326
Fillenbaum, G. G., 358–359
Finch, C. E., 544
Finch, M. D., 324
Fincham, F. D., 387, 485, 496
Fincher, C. L., 277
Fine, M. A., 494–496
Fingerhut, A. W., 493
Fingerman, K. L., 489–490
Finitzo, T., 177
Finkel, D., 80, 82, 252
Finkel, E. J., 461–462
Finkelhor, D., 390
Finkelstein, J. A., 194
Finn-Stevenson, M., 275
Fins, J. J., 540
Fiori-Cowley, A., 447
Fireman, G., 436
Firestone, M. H., 17
Fisch, H., 71, 113
Fischer, E. F., 461
Fischer, J. L., 460
Fischer, K. W., 203, 209–210, 212, 224, 326,
    336, 460
Fischer, M., 194, 518
Fishbein, M., 57
Fisher, C. B., 26
Fisher, E. P., 454
Fisher, G. G., 253
Fisher, K. R., 313
Fisher, M. H., 290–291
Fisher, P. A., 515
Fisher, S., 38, 424
Fiske, S. T., 8
Fite, P. J., 423
Fitness, J., 435
Fitzgerald, D.P., 406
Fitzgerald, J. M., 251–252
Fitzmaurice, G. M., 528
Fitzpatrick, L., 118
Fitzsimmons, C., 250, 254
Fivush, R., 244
Flaherty, J. H., 534
Flanagan, C., 321–322
Flanders, D., 146
Flannery, D., 223
Flavell, E. R., 217
Flavell, F. R., 217
Flavell, J. H., 200, 202–203, 217, 240–241, 400–402
Fleeson, W., 464
Fleming, J. S., 313
Fleming, L. E., 192
Fleming, S., 556
Fletcher, A. E., 189, 212
Fletcher, J. M., 318
Fletcher, K. L., 240, 518
Fletcher, P., 300
Flieller, A., 222
Flint, K. H., 149, 528
Flom, R., 371
Flook, L., 51, 487, 527
Floor, P., 302
Flores, E., 500
Florian, V., 549–550
Florsheim, P., 489
Flouri, E., 488
Flum, H., 347
Flynn, C., 509
Flynn, J. R., 264, 274, 277–278, 285
Flynn, M., 527
Flyvbjerg, B., 17–18
Foddy, M., 491
Foehr, U., 142
Fogassi, L., 299
Fogel, A., 51

Fogg, P., 23
Fok, A. K., 86
Foley, D., 155
Foley, E. P., 539
Foley, K., 562
Folke, S., 308
Fombonne, E., 512
Fonagy, P., 38, 447
Fong, G. T., 57, 392
Fong, L.S., 154
Fonseca, A. M., 359
Fontaine, N. M. G., 85, 421, 424
Fontana L., 161
Foorman, B. R., 317–318
Foos, P. W., 254
Foran, H. M., 497
Ford, E. S., 150
Ford, K. R., 346
Ford, T., 516, 522
Fordham, S., 321
Forestell, C. A., 174
Forgatch, M. S., 43, 495–496, 500
Forman, M. R., 144
Fornieles-Deu, A., 370
Forssell, S. L., 494
Förstl, H., 253, 256
Foss, J. W., 258
Foster, B., 557
Foster, G. D., 142
Foster, J. D., 23, 187
Foster, K., 172
Foster, S. N., 111
Fouquereau, E., 359
Fouts, H. N., 120
Fowler, J. W., 395. 428
Fowler, R. C., 207
Fowles, D. C., 419
Fox, H. C., 277, 280
Fox, M. K., 142
Fox, N. A., 337
Fox, S. E., 300
Fozard, J. L., 193
Fradley, E., 404
Fraga, M. F., 86
Fraley, R. C., 447, 449, 462–464, 559
Franchak, J. M., 168
Francis, D. J., 87, 318
Francis, E., 263
Francis, H. W., 175, 327
Francis, J., 93
Franck, K. L., 495
Frank, S. M., 195
Franke, B., 518
Franklin, C., 57
Franklin, N. T., 415
Franklin, S., 222
Franklin, Z., 169
Franko, D. L., 523
Franks, M. M., 491
Frans, E. M., 70
Franzetta, K., 387
Fraser, M. W., 125
Fraser, S. L., 105
Frateschi, L. J., 154
Fratiglioni, L., 531–533
Frattarelli, J. L., 113
Frattola, L., 194
Frawley, W., 205
Frayling, T., 159
Frederick, D. A., 156
Freedman, D. H., 44
Freedman, J., 300
Freedman, M., 312
Freedman-Doan, P., 323
Freeman, D., 419
Freeman, F. J., 350

Freeman, G. P., 349
Freeman, J. M., 140
Freeman, R., 290
Freeman, S. F. N., 290
Fremont, W. P., 32
Freud, S., 35–40
Freund, A. M., 349, 353, 356, 358, 360
Freund, L. S., 208
Frey, K. S., 340, 379
Freyd, J. J., 390
Frick, P. J., 421
Friedland, D. S., 357
Friedlmeier, W., 437
Friedman, H. S., 353
Friedman, J. M., 107
Friedman, L. J., 39–40
Friedman, M. S., 424, 459
Friedman, R. H., 357
Friedman, R. J., 423
Friedman, S. L., 448–449
Frier, B. M., 280
Fries, J. F., 158
Friesen, W. V., 438
Frieske, D., 257
Frieswijk, N., 349
Frigge, M. L., 70
Frijns, T., 459
Frith, U., 400
Fritz, A. S., 402
Froehlich, T. E., 517
Fromhoff, F. A., 244
Fromkin, J. B., 499
Fruyt, F. D., 357
Fry, C. L., 6
Fry, P. S., 360, 557
Fryar, C.D., 144
Fryer, R., 314–315
Fryer, S. L., 104
Fu, R., 341
Fu, X., 306
Fuerstenberg, E. A., 347
Fuglenes, D., 117
Fujimoto, K., 149
Fujimura, D., 173
Fujita, K., 191
Fukumoto, A., 415
Fulbright, R. K., 299, 317
Fuligni, A. J., 51, 151, 345, 424, 484 487
Fulker, D., 85, 423, 481
Fulkerson, J. A., 524
Fuller, S., 356
Fuller-Rowell, T., 561
Fulton, B. D., 519
Fulton, J. E., 149
Fung, H. H., 453
Funk, C. L., 82
Fuqua-Whitley, D. S., 521
Furberg, H., 523
Furman, E., 549
Furman, W., 441, 451, 456–457, 459, 482
Furrow, J. L., 428
Furstenberg, F. F., Jr., 6, 8, 389, 488

G
Gabbard, G. O., 35
Gable, L., 26
Gabrieli, J. D. E., 256, 438
Gadian, D. G., 235
Gage, F. H., 152
Gagliese, L., 545–546
Gagne, J. R., 80
Gagnon, H., 323–324
Gagnon, M. D., 489
Gaillard, M., 531
Gajdusek, D. C., 378
Galambos, N. L., 385

Gordon, A. R., 142
Gordon, B. N., 245, 384
Gordon, D. H., 220
Gordon, K. A., 175
Gordon, L. L., 244
Gordon, N. L., 488
Gordon-Salant, S., 193
Gordon-Salant, T., 193
Gori, M., 182
Gorman-Smith, D., 497
Gorrese, A., 460
Gosling, S. D., 5, 334
Goswami, U., 316
Gotlib, I. H., 5, 341, 415, 509, 515, 520
Gottesman, I. I., 70, 84–86, 89, 513
Gottfredson, L. S., 265, 279–280
Gottfried, A. E., 273, 286, 291, 313–314
Gottfried, A. W., 493
Gottlieb, G., 51, 68, 76, 86, 88, 120
Gottlob, L. R., 192
Gottman, J. M., 437, 485–486, 489
Goubet, N., 176, 238
Goudevenos, J. A., 150
Gould, D. C., 154–155
Gould, M. S., 528
Gourounti, K., 93
Gouttard, S., 512
Govarts, E., 110
Gover, G., 144
Gow, A. J., 78, 280
Gowen, L. K., 459
Goy, R. W., 376
Grabe, S., 156
Graber, J. A., 147–148
Grabill, C. M., 520
Gracia, E., 484
Grady, C. L., 255, 406
Grady, J. G., 252
Graf, D. L., 142
Graf, P., 234
Graham, A. M., 415
Graham, N., 531
Graham, S., 457
Graham-Bermann, S. A., 455
Gralinski, H., 339
Gralinski, J. H., 313
Granados, A., 380
Grand, A., 533
Grandison, K. J., 32
Grandjean, H., 533
Grandjean, P., 101, 109–110, 112–113
Granrud, C. E., 171
Grant, D., 117
Grant, K. E., 510
Grant, M. D., 154
Grant, T., 101
Graves, L., 142
Gray, A., 492
Gray, C., 286
Gray, G., 109
Gray, J. T., 244, 531
Gray, M. J., 546
Gray, N., 524
Gray, S. W., 275
Gray, W. M., 223
Gray-Little, B., 342, 346
Grayman-Simpson, N., 429
Graziano, P. A., 454
Grbich, C., 546
Gredebäck, G., 308
Green, C. E., 497
Green, C. R., 253
Green, M., 212, 551
Green, S. K., 460
Greenberg, J., 538
Greenberg, M. E., 324

Greenberg, M. T., 423
Greenberg, T., 528
Greenberger, E., 323–324, 493
Greendale, G. A., 193
Greene, J. D., 427
Greene, J. G., 154
Greene, J., 283
Greene, K., 223
Greene, S. M., 495
Greenfield, E. A., 429, 487
Greenfield, P. M., 300
Greenfield, R. A., 109
Greenhalgh, R., 120
Greenhill, L. L., 519
Greenhouse, S. W., 157
Greenough, W. T., 136, 157, 274
Greenson, J., 514
Greenway, R., 183
Greer, J. A., 559, 562
Gregory, A. M., 324, 424, 520
Greider, C., 160
Greisiger, R., 177
Grello, C. M., 387
Grenlich, F., 340
Gresham, F. M., 44
Greulich, F. K., 371, 373, 381
Greve, F., 277
Greve, W., 349
Greydanus, D. E., 525
Grieco, T. M., 175
Griffin, B., 357
Griffin, M. M., 291
Griffin, P., 562
Griffin, W. A., 495, 563
Griffin, Z. M., 325
Griffiths, D., 379
Griffiths, M. D., 187
Griggs, J., 488
Grigorenko, E. L., 273
Grigoryev, P., 435
Grilo, C. M., 82, 525
Grime, R. L., 426
Griskevicius, V., 146
Grizenko, N., 406
Groark, C. J., 448
Grodsky, A., 395
Grogan-Kaylor, A., 142
Groh, A. M., 447, 463
Grollman, E. A., 550
Grolnick, W. S., 436, 477
Gromoske, A. N., 43
Grontved, A. M., 194
Gropman, A. L., 71, 291
Grose-Fifer, J., 173–174
Grosjean, F., 312
Gros-Louis, J., 303
Gross, J. J., 243, 436, 438
Gross, M. S., 257
Grossberg, G. T., 533
Gross-Loh, C., 121
Grossman, A. W., 507, 510
Grossman, I., 406
Grossmann, K. E., 447, 463
Grotevant, H. D., 347, 447
Gruber, H., 242
Gruber-Baldini, A. L., 282
Grucza, R. A., 526
Gruen, R. S., 387
Grummer-Strawn, L. M., 121
Grunau, R. E., 488
Grunbaum, J. A., 150
Grundy, E., 490
Grunendahl, M., 530
Grusec, J. E., 418, 476
Grüters, A., 146
Grych, J. H., 496–497

Gu, H., 512
Gu, J., 158
Gu, Q., 144
Gu, W., 74
Guacci, N., 460
Guarnaccia, C. A., 562
Guarnaccia, P. J. J., 508
Guay, F., 340
Gudsnuk, K. M. A., 112
Guegan, J., 145
Gueldner, S. H., 281
Guerin, D. W., 273, 286, 336, 339
Guerra, N. G., 421, 423–425
Guerreiro, M., 253
Guerry, J. D., 455
Guilamo-Ramos, V., 392
Guimond, A. B., 346
Güler, O. E., 244
Gulko, J., 373
Gullberg, M., 299
Gullone, E., 437
Gundersen, C., 141
Gunn, J., 147
Gunnar, M. R., 447–448, 463, 515
Gunnarson, A. D., 177
Guo, G., 423
Gupta, A. K., 131
Gupta, M., 404
Gupta, S., 241
Guralnik, J. M., 155, 533
Gurba, E., 225
Gurland, B., 533
Gurung, R. A. R., 464
Gur-Yaish, N., 444
Guthrie, J., 154
Gutman, L. M., 318, 320–321
Gutmann, D., 392–393
Guttmacher Institute, 391
Guyenet, S., 149
Guyll, M., 527
Gweon, H., 403

H
Ha, J., 560
Haber, D., 355
Hack, M., 123
Hackett, G., 377
Haddow, J. E., 131
Hadwin, J. A., 38, 183
Haegerstrom-Portnoy, G., 190
Hafdahl, A. R., 342, 346
Hafetz, J., 369
Haffner, J., 337
Haffner, W. H. J., 109
Hagan, L. K., 379
Hagan, M. J., 563
Hagan, R., 374
Hagberg, B., 159
Hagberg, J. M., 156–157
Hagekull, B., 341
Hagemeister, A. K., 497
Hagen, E. W., 123
Hagerman, R. J., 71
Hagestad, G. O., 488
Haggart, N., 456, 459
Hagl, M., 562
Hahm, H. C., 389
Hahn, R. A., 521
Haidt, J., 427–428
Haight, B. K., 355
Haight, B. S., 355
Haight, W. L., 453
Haine, R. A., 560, 563
Hainline, L., 169–170, 182
Hains, S. M., 173

Hermans, H. J., 356
Hermelin, B., 267
Hermer, L., 172
Hernandez-Diaz, S., 101
Hernandez-Reif, M., 124
Heron, J., 113
Herrera, S., 497
Herrmann, E., 402, 412
Herrnstein, R. J., 285, 289
Hersen, M., 489
Hersh, R. E., 248
Hershberger, S. L., 53
Hertwig, R., 488
Hertzog, C., 12–13, 256–257, 283, 533
Heru, A. M., 521
Herzog, D. B., 254, 523
Hesketh, B., 357
Hess, P., 142
Hess, T. M., 406–407, 445–446
Hess, T., 255
Hesse, E., 445–446
Heston, L. L., 81
Hetherington, E. M., 85, 477, 494–496
Heutink, P., 518
Hewitt, B., 494
Hewitt, J. K., 81
Hewlett, B. S., 120–121
Heyman, R. E., 486, 497
Heymann, J., 493
Heymann, S. J., 7, 52, 493
Heyne, D. A., 32, 49
Hezlett, S. A., 279
Hibbert, J. R., 477
Hibbing, J. R., 82
Hickey, P. R., 72
Hickey, T., 358
Hicks, B. M., 369
Higgins, E. T., 311, 385
Higgins-D'Alessandro, A., 424
Higley, J. D., 87, 498
Hilden, K., 240
Hilgard, E. R., 245
Hill, A. J., 523
Hill, A. L., 291
Hill, A., 436
Hill, C., 291, 357
Hill, E. J., 493
Hill, J., 527
Hill, J. P., 385
Hill, N. E., 321–322
Hill, P. L., 352
Hill, R., 472
Hill, S. D., 336
Hill, S. E., 371
Hillier, T. A., 190
Hills, T., 303
Himes, J. H., 144
Himura, N., 423
Hindmarsh, P. C., 149, 379
Hinds, J. D., 560
Hinduja, S., 424
Hine, T., 8
Hines, D. A., 504
Hines, J. C., 254
Hines, P. M., 542
Hinshaw, S. P., 519
Hinson, J. T., 255
Hinton, J., 545
Hirschi, A., 346
Hirsh-Pasek, K., 304–305, 309, 453–454
Hitch, G. J., 234
Hjerling-Leffler, J., 274
Ho, A. Y., 457
Ho, R., 377
Hoare, C., 53
Hobbs, F. B., 157

Hochberg, M. C., 190
Hockley, C., 121
Hockly, C., 121
Hodapp, R. M., 290–291
Hodges, E. A., 255
Hodges, J., 448
Hodgkins, P., 518
Hodnett, E. D., 115, 118
Hoefnagels, C., 465
Hoegg, J., 186
Hoek, H. W., 522–523
Hoekstra, R. A., 513–514
Hof, P., 152–153
Hofer, C., 483
Hofer, J., 355
Hofer, S. M., 256
Hoff, E. V., 214, 304–308, 311
Hoffman, C., 360, 491
Hoffman, J. H., 389
Hoffman, K. L., 497
Hoffman, L. W., 493
Hoffman, M. L., 408, 414, 416–418
Hoffman, S. D., 391
Hoffman, S. I., 549
Hoffnung, M., 393
Hofman, A., 103, 109
Hofman, J. E., 457
Hofmann, S. G., 521
Hofmeyr, G. J., 115
Hofstra, M. B., 516
Hogan, M. J., 496
Hogg, K., 377
Hogström, L., 93
Hohm, E., 305
Hohm, F., 305
Holahan, C., 292
Holahan, J. M., 317
Holden, D. J., 240
Holden, G. W., 475–477, 480–482, 484, 493, 499, 501
Holen, A., 558
Holland, A. S., 449
Holland, J. L., 346
Holland, J. M., 561
Hollatz, A. L., 419
Hollenstein, T., 438
Hollich, G. J., 304–305
Hollins, M., 176
Hollon, S. D., 531
Hollowell, J. G., 131
Holm, K., 146
Holmbeck, G. N., 223, 482
Holmberg, J., 308
Holmes, A. E., 83, 146, 186
Holowka, S., 140
Holt, R. I., 131
Holzer, C. E., 530
Holzrichter, A. S., 301
Homeyer, L., 454
Homme, J. H., 524
Hommer D. W., 138
Honey, K. L., 119
Honeyman, M., 276
Hong, J. S., 424
Hongwanishkul, D., 406
Honk, J., 376
Honzik, M. P., 272
Hood, J. E., 390
Hood, J. F., 390
Hooker, K., 326
Hooper, C. J., 239, 248
Hooper, F. H., 226
Hooper, J. O., 226
Hooper, R., 447
Hooper, S. R., 71
Hoorens, S., 93
Hooven, C., 437

Hopfer, C. J., 81
Hopkins, B., 212
Hopkins, E. J., 453–454
Hopkins, M., 152
Hopkins, T. L., 369
Hopmeyer, A., 457
Hoppmann, C. A., 489
Horgan, R. P., 113
Horiuchi, S., 544
Horn, J. L., 265–266
Horn, K. H., 104
Horn, M. C., 530
Horn, S. P., 318
Hornberger, A. P., 357
Horne, R., 138
Horner, V., 44
Hornstra, G., 237
Horowitz, A., 190
Horowitz, L. M., 462
Horowitz, M. J., 558
Horswill, M. S., 191
Horwitz, S., 537
Hosman, C. M. H., 465
Houck, P. R., 519
Houdé, O., 204, 216
Hough-Eyamir, W. P., 300
House, J. D., 321
House, J. S., 357
House, R. A., 186
Houser, J. J., 457
Houshyar, S., 500
Houston, D. M., 303–304
Houts, R. M., 341, 451, 485
Houx, P. J., 256
Howe, D., 443
Howe, G. W., 357
Howe, M. L., 239–240, 244
Howe, N., 482
Howell, D. N., 106
Howell, K. K., 104
Howes, C., 374, 450
Howes, P., 447
Howieson, D. B., 532
Howlin, P., 514
Howson, C. P., 71
Hoyer, W. J., 254–256
Hoyme, H. E., 104
Hoza, B., 279, 519
Hrdy, S. B., 471
Hrebickova, M., 352
Hruda, L., 375
Hrychko, S., 406
Hsia, Y., 149
Hsieh, K., 489
Hsu, C. Y., 148, 323
Hsu, L. K. G., 523
Hsu, L. M., 350
Hu, V. W., 292, 511, 513–514
Huang, C-M., 152
Huang, F., 424
Huang, H., 173
Huang, M., 288
Hubbard, J. A., 17, 422
Hubel, D. H., 177
Hubert, H. B., 158
Huddleston, D. E., 13, 152
Hudson, B. O., 11
Hudson, J. A., 244–245
Hudson, L. M., 223
Hudziak, J. J., 423
Huesmann, L. R., 21, 420
Huff, S. M., 562
Hugh, M., 379
Hughes, D., 345–346
Hughes, E. K., 437
Hughes, F. M., 383

Hughes, J. P., 146
Huguley, S., 497
Huijbregts, S. C. J., 103
Huisman, M., 516
Huizink, A. C., 338
Hulme, C., 316
Hultman, C. M., 514
Hultsch, D. F., 256
Human Rights Watch, 493
Humen, E., 390
Hummert, M. L., 349
Hunkin, J. L., 160
Hünnerkopf, M., 241
Hunsberger, B., 410, 420, 426
Hunt, E., 324
Hunter, J. E., 279–280
Huntgeburth, U., 253, 256
Huntington, R., 524
Hurd, L. C., 156
Hurd, R. C., 560
Hure, A. J., 93
Hurst, A. J., 159
Hurst, K., 525
Hurst, S., 414
Hurt, E., 518
Huston, A. C., 7, 371
Huston, M., 494
Huston, T. L., 485
Hutchinson, I., 186
Hutter, I., 146
Huynh, V. W., 151
Hwang, I., 518
Hwang, P., 291
Hwang, S., 424
Hybels, C. F., 530
Hyde, J. S., 146–147, 156, 385, 368–369, 372, 387–388, 393–394, 486, 527
Hyde, K., 175
Hyde, M. J., 116
Hyson, M. C., 309

I

Iacoboni, M., 403
Iacono, W. G., 79, 341, 483
Ialongo, N. S., 275, 520
Iams, J., 107
Iarocci, G., 184
Iervolino, A. C., 376
Ikonomovic, M. D., 533
Imel, S., 326
Imperato-McGinley, J., 368, 378
Indian, R. W., 190
Ingersoll, B., 512
Ingoldsby, B. B., 485
Ingram, D. K., 161
Ingram, R. E., 509–510
Ingrassia, M., 450
Inhelder, B., 216–217, 219, 246, 224, 246
Inman, J. W., 143
Insurance Institute for Highway Safety, 191
International Human Genome Sequencing, 66
Inzlicht, M., 289
Ip, H. M., 121
Ippen, C. G., 551
Irons, G., 41
Irwin, J. D., 142
Isaacs, K. R., 157
Isabella, R. A., 446
Ishak, S., 181
Isingrini, M., 256
Islam, N., 18
Isles, A. R., 87
Ivanoff, J. G., 185
Ive, S., 523
Iverson, P., 173
Ivnik, R. J., 252–253

Izard, C. E., 434–435
Izquierdo, C., 7

J

Jaakkola, R., 549
Jaccard, J., 324, 392
Jack, F., 243–244
Jacklin, C. N., 369, 374
Jackson, C., 392
Jackson, J. S., 321, 430, 531
Jackson, K. L., 158
Jackson, P. W., 274
Jackson, V. A., 562
Jacobs, A., 375
Jacobs, H. S., 154
Jacobs, J. E., 224, 320, 342
Jacobs, M., 532
Jacobs, R. J., 395
Jacobs, S. C., 547
Jacobson, J. L., 105
Jacobson, K. C., 286
Jacobson, K., 192
Jacobson, S. W., 105
Jacobsson, L., 531
Jacobvitz, D., 498
Jaddoe, V. W., 103
Jaffa, T. ,525
Jaffe, J., 443
Jaffee, S. R., 425, 489
Jager, T., 439
Jagger, C., 367
Jaggli, N., 379
Jagnow, C. P., 174
Jain, E., 438
Jain, N. J., 107
Jakub, D. K., 557
Jakub, K. D., 557
Jambon, M., 417
James, J. B., 146, 335
James, S., 496
James, W., 168
Jamison, K. R., 554
Jampol, N. S., 416, 458
Jane Webb, S., 512
Janevic, M. R., 460
Jang, K. L., 333
Janicki-Deverts, D., 582
Jankowiak, W. R., 461
Jankowski, J., 272
Jannings, L. R., 241
Jansen, B. R. J., 243
Jansen, M. D., 492
Jansma, E. P. ,501
Janson, P. O., 93
Janus, C. L., 384
Janus, J. S., 384
Jaquish, G. A., 285
Järvelin, M. R., 105, 346
Jarvin, L., 268
Jarvis, P., 463
Jasinska, K., 312
Jasnow, M. D., 443
Jastrzembski, T. S., 251
Jaswal, R., 116
Jauregui, A., 185
Jayawardena, K. M., 497
Je, J. H., 159
Jean, R. T., 144
Jeavons, L., 275, 310
Jeffery, P. M., 118
Jeffery, R., 118
Jelenchick, L., 185
Jelicic, H., 425
Jelicic, M., 157
Jelliffe-Pawlowski, L. L., 109
Jemmott, J. B., 57, 392

Jemmott, L. S., 57, 392
Jenewein, J., 556
Jenkins, E., 291
Jenkins, F., 309, 322
Jenkins, J. J., 173
Jenkins, L., 326
Jenkins, S. R., 356–357
Jenkins, W. M., 318
Jennen-Steinmetz, C., 305
Jennings, K. D., 308–309
Jensen, A. R., 274–275, 279, 281, 285, 288–289
Jensen, P. S., 519
Jensen, T. K., 110
Jeong, H. S., 490
Jernigan, M., 26
Jessberger, S., 152
Jessell, T., 177
Jessor, R., 522
Jeste, D. V., 531
Jetha, M. K., 144
Jezzard, P., 301
Jimenez, D. E., 530
Jimenez, N. B., 419
Jina, E., 556
Jinks, A. L., 186
Jobes, D. A., 528
Jobin, J., 349
Jobse, J., 303
Jodoin-Krauzyk, J., 175
Joffe, K. M., 192
Joh, A. S., 181
Johansson, A., 308
Johansson, B., 281, 533
Johansson, M., 93
Johansson, S. E., 543
Johansson, T., 148
Johansson, U., 136
John, O. P. ,355, 487
Johnson, A. L. ,106
Johnson, C. A., 454, 485, 492, 499, 559
Johnson, D. J., 346
Johnson, D. R., 474, 492
Johnson, E., 161
Johnson, J. G., 312, 516, 559
Johnson, K., 541
Johnson, L. C., 121
Johnson, M. H., 96–97, 135, 169–171, 204, 512, 516
Johnson, M. J., 175
Johnson, M. K., 257, 356, 470
Johnson, R. L., 521
Johnson, S. C., 172
Johnson, S. M., 465
Johnson, S. P., 172
Johnson, T., 186
Johnson, V. E., 395–396
Johnson, W., 80, 280, 368
John-Steiner, V., 207
Johnston, K., 319
Johnston, L. D., 525–526
Johnston, P., 319
Joiner, R., 206
Joint Committee on Infant Hearing, 178
Jokela, M., 516
Joliot, M., 216
Jolles, J., 256
Jones, C., 352
Jones, E. J. H., 514
Jones, H. A., 519
Jones, J. R., 121
Jones, J., 525
Jones, K., 105
Jones, L., 117
Jones, P. W., 153
Jones, R., 518
Jones, S. S., 237

Jones, T., 433
Jones, W., 511
Jongsma, H. W., 237
Jonides, J., 341
Jönsson, F. U., 195
Joormann, J., 509, 515
Joosken, J., 303
Jordahl, T., 57
Jordan, A., 368
Joseph, S., 559–561
Jouriles, E. N., 497
Joy, M. E., 419
Joyce, A. S., 559
Joyce, J. J., 559
Joyner, K., 389, 459
Judd, T., 185
Judge, S., 448
Judge, T. A., 279–280, 356
Judy, B., 428
Juffer, F., 80, 448, 450, 465
Junaid, K. A., 141
Jungblut, P. R., 158
Jungeblut, A., 326
Juola, J. F., 192
Jurtz-Costes, B., 367
Jusczyk, P. W., 304
Jussim, L., 349
Justice, E. M., 241
Juul, A., 146, 110
Juvonen, J., 147–148

K

Kaakinen, M., 105, 346
Kabacoff, R. I., 489, 499
Kabeto, M. U., 490
Kabir, A. A., 117
Kabra, M., 131
Kaciroti, N., 145
Kadlec, K. M., 489
Kaffman, A. S., 87
Kagan, J., 336–337, 415, 444
Kahana, E., 428
Kahlenberg, S., 380
Kahn, R. L., 161, 253
Kahn, R. S., 517
Kahn, V., 336–337
Kail, R., 232, 248, 277
Kain, J., 319
Kainz, K., 310
Kajantie, E., 548
Kakuma, R., 534
Kalai, A., 521
Kalberg, W. O., 104
Kalil, A., 488
Kalinauskas, A., 406–407
Kalmijn, M., 489
Kalmuss, D., 486
Kalnok, M., 438
Kalra, G., 521
Kaltiala-Heino, R., 147
Kaltman, S., 554, 558
Kaltsas, G., 150
Kalverboer, A. F., 183
Kamakura, T., 340
Kamb, M., 108
Kaminester, D., 406
Kaminski, P. L., 554, 560
Kammeyer-Mueller, J. D., 356
Kamp Dush, C. M., 495
Kamphaus, R. W., 71, 288, 369
Kandel, E. R., 177
Kane, H. D., 265
Kane, J. B., 496
Kane, M. N., 395
Kanellopoulos, T. A., 103
Kann, L., 389

Kannass, K. N., 183
Kanner, L., 511
Kanwisher, N., 403
Kao, K., 105
Kaplan, D. S., 325
Kaplan, H. B., 325
Kaplan, J. S., 79
Kaplan, R. M., 543
Kappelman, M., 638
Kappes, M. E., 376
Kappes, M. H., 376
Kaprio, J., 140
Karakoc, E., 70, 514
Karantzas, G. C., 491
Karasik, L. B., 179, 181
Karbakhsh, M., 146
Karel, M. J., 531
Karg, K., 83
Karinen, P., 194
Karlawish, J., 27
Karmiloff-Smith, A., 204
Karney, B. R., 461
Karniol, R., 381
Karoly, L. A., 359
Karpov, Y. V., 203, 222
Karraker, A., 396
Karraker, K. H., 377
Kärtner, J., 337
Kasen, S., 516
Kashani, H. H., 146
Kashy, D. A., 524
Kaskie, B., 530
Kasl, S. V., 349, 547
Kasl-Godley, J., 533
Kaslow, N., 520
Kassi, E., 150
Kastenbaum, R. J., 538–539, 545, 548–550
Kastorini, C., 150
Kasworm, C. E., 258
Katagiri, K., 26
Katayama, T., 191
Katgert, T., 116
Kato, B. S., 160
Kato, S., 160
Katona, C., 531
Katsura, H., 351
Katusic, S. K., 517
Katz, L. F., 437
Katz, P. A., 383
Katzel, L. I., 155–156
Katzman, D. K., 523
Katzmarzyk, P. T., 149
Katz-Wise, S., 393, 486
Kaufman, A. S., 268, 281, 288
Kaufman, A. V., 491
Kaufman, J. C., 270, 276
Kaufman, J., 498
Kaufman, N. L., 268, 281, 288
Kaufman, S. B., 368
Kautiainen, H. J., 194
Kavanaugh, K., 483
Kavanaugh, R. D., 453
Kavosh, M. S., 146
Kaye, J. A., 532
Kaye, R. A., 395
Kaye, W., 524
Kayed, N. S., 171
Kazdin, A. E., 520–521
Kazemnejad, A., 153
Kazmi, H., 300
Kazura, K. L., 455
Keane, S. P., 454
Kearney, A. J., 44
Kearney, C. A., 32, 38, 46, 53
Keasey, C. B., 410
Keatinge, C., 526–528, 530

Keefer, C. H., 121
Keel, P. K., 522–524
Keen, R., 181
Keenan, K., 369, 423
Keesee, N. J., 556
Kehoe, C., 437, 464
Keightley, M. L., 406
Keijsers, L., 459
Keith, J., 6
Keizer, R., 492
Kelemen, W. L., 248
Kelishadi, R., 146
Kellam, S. G., 275, 520
Keller, B. B., 481
Keller, H., 294, 337
Keller, K. L., 141
Keller, M. B., 521
Keller, M. C., 507
Kelley, E., 514
Kelley, K. E., 101
Kelley-Buchanan, C., 106
Kellman, P. J., 166, 170
Kellogg, N. D., 384
Kelly, D. J., 168–171, 345
Kelly, J., 487, 495
Kelly, Y., 121
Kelsall, D. C., 194
Kelsey, S. F., 154
Kember, D., 327
Kemp, S., 251
Kempe, C. H., 498
Kempe, R. S., 498
Kempen, G. I. J. M., 157
Kemper, S., 157, 325
Kempermann, G., 152
Kemtes, K. A., 325
Kendall-Tackett, K. A., 390
Kendeou, P., 316
Kendler, K. S., 76, 386, 508
Kendrick, C., 481
Kenis, G., 533
Keniston, J. A., 6
Kennedy, C., 563
Kennedy, Q., 439
Kennedy, S., 472
Kennell, J., 118
Kenny, M. E., 456
Kenny, S. L., 203–204
Kensinger, E. A., 139
Kenward, B., 308
Kenyon, B. L., 549–550
Kenyon, D. B., 425
Keough, J., 288
Keppler, A., 447
Keren, M., 515
Kerka, S., 326
Kermoian, R., 172
Kern, M. L., 353
Kerns, K. A., 449, 451
Kerr, D. C. R., 416
Kerr, M., 458, 481
Keshteli, A. H., 146
Kessels, R. P. C., 256
Kessler, R. C., 386, 516, 518, 520, 530–531
Kestenbaum, R., 447
Kett, J. F., 8
Kettlewell, H. B. D., 63
Khaleque, A., 477
Khan, M. M., 190
Khazan, I., 471
Khodal, S., 146
Khoo, S. T., 563
Khoshnevisan, A., 176
Khoury, J. C., 107
Kiang, L., 346
Kiecolt, K. J., 497

Kurjak, A., 98
Kurkup, G., 369
Kurowski, C. O., 436
Kwak, J., 539
Kwak, K., 435
Kwan, L., 324
Kwan, V. S. Y., 352
Kwok, O., 424, 563
Kwong, M. J., 498

L
Labarthe, D. R., 149
Labinowicz, E., 220
Labonté, B., 87, 498
LaBounty, J., 410
Lacey, C., 156
Lachance, J. A., 368
Lachman, M. E., 21–23, 495
Ladd, G. W., 424, 455
Laderman, M., 530
Laflamme, D., 275
LaFranchi, S. H., 131
Lagercrantz, H., 173, 304
Lahiri, D. K., 533
Laible, D. J., 415
Laing, D. G., 186
Laird, R. D., 478
Lakatta, E. G., 156
Lalande, K. L., 558–559
Lamaze, F., 111
Lamb, C., 435
Lamb, M. E., 245, 474–475, 495
Lamberg, K., 512
Lambert, S. R., 177
Lamborn, S. D., 477, 484, 459
Lamere, T. G., 459
Lammlein, S. E., 358
LaMontagne, L. L., 559
Lampert, C., 524
Lampinen, P., 158
Lampl, M., 136
Lampman-Petraitis, C., 438
Lamy, D., 345
Lamy, P. P., 345
The Lancet, 512
Landau, S., 203
Landen, J., 149
Landers, K., 379
Landreth, G., 454
Landrigan, P. J., 110
Landry, S. H., 124–125, 286
Lane, J. D., 416
Lane, M. A., 161
Lang, F. R., 349, 358, 439, 460
Lang, S., 447
Langa, K. M., 253, 490
Lange, G., 242, 495
Langer, A., 172
Langer, E. J., 255, 350
Langevin, J. P., 406
Langfahl, E. S., 460
Langley, K., 113
Langley, L. K., 192
Langley-Evans, A. J., 113
Langley-Evans, S. C., 113
Långström, N., 70
Lannon, R., 306
Lanoë, C., 204, 216
Lanouette, N., 531
Lanphear, B. P., 517
Lanpher, B., 291
Lansford, J. E., 57, 422–423, 460, 473, 477, 495–496, 499, 501, 525–526
Lantos, J., 26
Lanza, S., 342
Lanzenberger, R., 187

LaPierre, L., 541
Laplante, D., 112
Lappin, S., 300
Lapsley, D. K., 223, 416
Larkina, M., 236
Larose, S., 456
LaRossa, R., 486
Larsen, J. T., 436
Larson, E. B., 115, 533
Larson, R. P., 251
Larson, R. W., 482
Larson, R., 323, 438
Larsson, H., 85
Larsson, I., 384
Larsson, M., 195
Larus, D. M., 243
Laska, M. N., 149
Lathi, R. B., 93
Lau, E. C., 74
Lauber, E. J., 185
Laucht, M., 305, 518
Laumann, E. O., 154
Laumann-Billings, L., 501
Laureys, S., 540
Laursen, B., 345–346, 459, 483–484
Lautenschlager, G., 254
Lautenschlager, N. T., 500
Lauterbach, M. D., 369
Lavner, J. A., 485
LaVoie, J. C., 344
Law, K. L., 103
Law, R. W., 495
Lawford, H., 456, 459
Lawlor, D. A., 280
Lawn, J. E., 108
Lawrence, C., 523
Lawson, K. R., 183
Lawton, M. P., 360
Laybutt, R., 87, 113
Lazarus, R. S., 436, 438
Le Blanc, M., 351
Le Goff, J., 345
Leaf, P. J., 530
Leaper, C., 374, 379
Lears, M., 382
Lebowitz, B. D., 530–531
Leckman, J. F., 441
Leclerc, C. M., 406
LeCompte, D. C., 256
Lecouteur, A., 513
Leddon, E., 306
Lederberg, A. R., 301
Lederman, S. A., 109
Lee, C., 175, 492
Lee, D. J., 192
Lee, E., 542
Lee, G. R., 492
Lee, J. M., 141, 145
Lee, J., 26, 389
Lee, K. E., 189
Lee, K. H., 123
Lee, K. S., 102
Lee, K., 168–170,173, 241, 245, 345, 404
Lee, M. R., 525
Lee, M., 525
Lee, N. R., 421
Lee, N. Y. L., 427
Lee, P. A., 144
Lee, R., 309
Lee, S. J., 43
Lee, S. W., 152
Lee, S. Y., 323
Lee, W. W., 351
Lee, Y., 311, 313
Leeb, R., 371
Leeder, E. J., 470

Leenarts, L. E. W., 501
Leeper, J. D., 491
Leerkes, E. M., 339, 441
Lee-Shin, Y., 453
Lefkowitz, E. S., 389, 489
Legare, C. H., 552
Leggett, E. L., 312–313
leGrange, D., 525
Lehman, D. R., 555, 560
Lehman, H. C., 284
Lehn, H., 518
Lehoux, P. M., 482
Leichtman, M. D., 244
Leikin, M., 311
Leinbach, M. D., 371, 374, 377, 379
Leirer, V., 250, 254
Leis, J. A., 6
Lejarraga, H., 136
Lekes, N., 323–324
LeMare, L. J., 406
Lemerise, F. A., 426
Lemery-Chalfant, K., 322
Lemire, R. J., 105, 107
Lemke, L., 267
Lenderts, S. E., 521
L'Engle, K. L., 392
Lengua, L. J., 495
Lenroot, R. K., 84, 421
Lenze, S., 521
Leo, A. J., 172
Leo, I., 170
Leon, D. A., 280
Leon, G. R., 522
Leonard, K. E., 106
Leondari, A., 550
Leong, D. J., 207–208
Lepore, J., 11
LePore, P. C., 323
Leritz, L. E., 278
Lerner, A. S., 453–454
Lerner, J. V., 425, 493
Lerner, M. D., 453–454
Lerner, M. J., 489
Lerner, R. M., 13, 51, 226, 425
Leroux, G., 204, 216
Leshikar, E. D., 152
Leskin, G. A., 448
Leslie, A. M., 400
Lester, D., 528
Lester, P., 448
Lettre, G., 130
Leung, A. K. C., 372
Leutwyler, B., 248
LeVay, S., 287
Leve, L. D., 379
Leveille, S., 155
Levenkron, S., 523
Levenson, R. W., 438, 489
Leventhal, B., 424
Lever, J., 156
Levett, K. M., 117
Levey, A. I., 144
Levin, A. V., 177
Levin, J. R., 248
Levine, A., 441
Levine, C., 347
Levine, P., 519
Levine, S. Z., 514
Levinson, D. J., 356, 499
Levinson, M. H., 356
Levinson, S., 41
Levitas, J., 436
Levit-Dori, T., 222
Levitt, M. J. ,460, 464
Levitt, P., 300
Levkoff, S., 359

Macartney, S., 7
Maccoby, E. E., 369–370, 373–374, 470, 476–477, 480
MacDonald, K., 471, 507
MacDonald, S., 53, 244
MacDorman, M. F., 112, 114, 117, 119, 138
MacGregor, G. A., 141
Machado, A., 50, 203
Maciejewski, P. K., 547, 556
Macintyre, S., 280
MacKenzie, G., 427
Mackey, R. A., 487
MacKinlay, R. J., 241
Mackler, J. S., 436
MacLean, K., 447–448
MacLeod, D., 318
MacLeod, J., 310
MacLeod, M. S., 254
MacMillan, D., 117
Macmillan, M., 38
Macomber, J., 172
MacPherson, S. E., 407
MacSweeney, M., 301
MacTurk, R. H., 309
MacWhinney, B., 312
Madden, D. J., 192, 254–255
Madden, P. A. F., 509, 527
Madden, V., 553
Maddocks, I., 546
Maddox, G. L., 157
Maddux, J. E., 308
Madsen, S. D., 456–457, 459
Maehr, M., 298
Maercker, A., 284
Maestripieri, D., 87, 498
Magai, C., 438, 463
Magliano, D. J., 150
Magnusson, D., 355
Magnusson, G., 70
Magori-Cohen, R., 138
Maguire-Jack, K., 43
Mahaffy, K. A., 347
Mahapatra, M., 426
Mahdavi, J., 424
Mahmut, M., 179
Maholmes, V., 448
Maiden, R. J., 353
Maier, E. H., 495
Maier, M. A., 313
Maier-Bruckner, W., 243
Maillet, M., 173
Main, K. M., 110
Main, M., 445–446, 449–450
Main, S. R., 319
Maire-Leblond, C., 238
Maisonet, M., 146
Maker, E., 538
Makin, J. W., 176
Makoroff, K., 499
Malaspina, D., 113
Malatesta, C. Z., 435–436, 438
Malcuit, G., 371, 475
Malec, J. F., 252
Maliken, A. C., 437
Malina, R. M., 144
Malinosky-Rummell, R., 499
Malley-Morrison, K., 501
Mallya, G., 142
Malmstrom, M., 543
Malone, P. S., 423, 477, 525–526
Malouf, M. A., 376
Manchester, J., 358
Mancini, A. D., 486, 555, 562
Mandalà, M., 175
Mandara, J., 346, 477–478
Mandeli, J., 395

Mandler, G., 234
Manganello, J. A., 43
Mangelsdorf, S. C., 436, 444, 447, 474
Manke, B., 477, 482
Manlove, J., 387, 390
Manly, J., 532
Manning, K., 253
Manning, W. D., 484
Mansi, G., 103
Mansoor, E., 106
Mäntylä, T., 241
Marceau, J. R., 174
Marceau, K., 147
March, J. S., 508, 531
Marchand, H., 225–226
Marchione, K. E., 317
Marcia, J. E., 344, 355
Marciano, D. L., 380
Marcoen, A., 340
Marcoulides, G. A., 313–314
Marcovitch, S., 212
Marcus, S., 525
Mare, R. D., 323
Marentette, P. F., 301
Mareschal, D., 204
Margand, N. A., 474, 476
Margolin, G., 422, 498–500
Margrett, J. A., 258
Marian, V., 312
Maring, B. L., 214
Marini, Z., 239
Markham, J. A., 274
Markides, K. S., 490
Markiewicz, D., 340, 456, 459
Markison, S., 194
Markman, A. B., 215
Markman, E. M., 305
Markman, H. J., 447, 485, 492
Markon, K. E., 84
Markowitz, J. C., 531
Markowitz, L. E., 391
Marks, N. E., 429
Marks, N. F., 487
Markstrom-Adams, C., 345–346
Markus, H. R., 9, 350–351
Marlier, L., 176
Marlowe, J., 425
Marois, R., 185
Marottoli, R. A., 191
Marrero, N. M., 141
Marrington, S. A., 191
Marschark, M., 175
Marsee, M. A., 421
Marsh, H. W., 340–341, 343
Marshal, M. P., 424, 459
Marshall, P. J., 313, 337
Marshall, W. A., 144
Marsiglio, W., 495
Marsiske, M., 12, 255, 258, 283
Marston, M., 109
Marti, C. N., 523, 525
Martin, A., 157
Martin, C. L., 371, 373–375, 380–382, 435, 452
Martin, G. B., 414
Martin, J. A., 107, 117, 476–480
Martin, J. M., 103, 342
Martin, J., 103, 252, 423, 481
Martin, M. J., 479–480
Martin, M., 281, 479–480, 530
Martin, N. G., 76, 292, 527
Martin, N. W., 292
Martin, N., 423, 523
Martin, P. D., 309
Martin, P., 159, 530
Martin, R. P., 319

Martin, S. E., 435
Martinengo, G., 493
Martinez, A., 423
Martinez, C. D., 446
Martinez, C. N., 380
Martinez, G. M., 56, 492
Martinez, G., 485
Martinez-Frias, M. L., 101
Martire, L. M., 359, 490–491
Martlew, M., 178
Martorano, S. C., 220
Martorell, G. A., 499
Martus, P., 146
Martz, J., 522
Maruff, P., 186
Maruna, S., 355
Marvin, R. S., 448, 482
Marwit, S. J., 350, 559
Marzolf, D., 436
Masaki, K., 155
Masataka, N., 301
Mascher, J., 26
Masciadrelli, B. P., 475
Mashek, D. J., 408
Mashoodh, R., 68, 86–87, 106
Masi, C. M., 464
Masiello, M., 424
Masliah, E., 152
Mason, B., 380
Mason, U., 172
Massey, S. G., 387, 459
Masson, G., 70
Masson, J. M., 70
Masten, A. S., 308, 517, 526, 553
Masters, W. H., 157, 395
Mastora, A., 550
Mastrogiannis, D. S., 107
Masur, E. F., 303
Masyn, K. E., 423
Matas, L., 444
Matchar, E., 23
Mather, M., 439
Matheson, C. C., 450, 453
Mathews, J., 323
Mathews, T. J., 103, 114, 119, 138
Matsuba, M. K., 428
Matthews, K. A., 138, 141, 154., 553
Mattis, J. S., 429
Mattock, K., 173
Matusov, E., 208
Maughan, B., 318, 420, 423, 488, 509
Maurer, A., 548
Maurer, D., 171, 177, 179, 182, 548
Maurer, J., 359
Maurice-Tison, S., 149
Maxon, E., 483
Maxwell, S. E., 342
May, P. A., 104
Mayberry, R. I., 175, 300, 301
Mayer, A., 404
Mayer, B., 337
Mayer, C., 7
Mayes, R., 514
Mayeux, L., 421, 454, 457
Mayhew, E. M. Y., 244–245
Maynard, R. A., 391
Mayo Clinic, 131, 253
Mayr, U., 439
Mayseless, O., 456
Mazursky, H., 486
Mazzocco, M. M., 368
Mbilinyi, L. F., 497
McAdams, D. P., 332, 334, 345, 355–356, 361
McAdams, P. P., 326
McAdoo, H. P., 286

McAlister, A. L., 404, 411
McArdle, J. J., 489
McAuley, E., 256
McCabe, E. R. B., 66, 86, 146
McCabe, L. L., 66, 86, 146
McCabe, M. P., 340, 523
McCadney, A., 520
McCall, R. B., 11, 19, 272, 448
McCance, D. R., 107
McCarthy, J. R., 552
McCarthy, M. E., 309
McCarthy, M. M., 300
McCartney, K., 79, 84, 146, 449
McCarton, C. M., 124, 274
McCarty, C. A., 508, 524
McCarty, F., 392
McCaul, E. J., 324
McClay, J., 423, 481
McClearn, G. E., 75, 78, 81–82, 155
McClintock, M. K., 132
McClintock, M., 384
McCloskey, L. A., 498
McClowry, S. G., 336, 339
McConkie-Rosell, A., 71
McConnell, M., 471
McCormick, M. C., 124
McCormick, W. C., 512, 533
McCowan, L., 113
McCoy, S., 193
McCoy, T. A., 141–142
McCoyd, J. L. M., 548–549, 553
McCrae, R. R., 285, 333, 341, 351–353, 361
McCrory, E. J. P., 421
Mccullough, A., 117
McCullough, B. M., 23
McCullough, C. M., 23
McCune, L., 304
McDermott, B., 525
McDonald, A., 96–97, 109
McDonald, J. A., 122
McDonald, K. L., 452, 455–456
McDonald, P. R., 171
McDonald, R., 497
McDonald, S., 356
McDonough, C., 306
McDowell, E. E., 539
McDowell, M. A., 146
McElhaney, K. B., 455, 478, 484
McFall, R. M., 11
McGaw, B., 21
McGee, C. L., 104
McGinley, J., 415
McGinley, M., 368
McGoldrick, M., 471–472, 496, 542
McGowan, P. O., 87, 498
McGrath, C., 316
McGrath, E. P., 314
McGrath, J. J., 70
McGrory, C., 231
McGue, M., 76, 79–80, 82, 341, 483, 524, 527
McGuffin, P., 71,75, 78–79, 81–83, 423, 527
McGuire, S., 482
McHale, J. L., 474
McHale, J. P., 471
McHale, S. J., 320, 322
McHale, S. M., 52, 379, 482–483, 485, 487
McInnes, L., 281
McIntosh, D. N., 404, 513
McIntosh, G. C., 113
McIntyre, H. D., 107
McIsaac, C., 459
McKenzie, S. O., 148
McKinney, P. M., 142
McKitrick, L. A., 258
McKnew, D. H., Jr., 520
McLanahan, S. S., 7, 476, 530

McLean, K. C., 345
McLoyd, V. C., 478
McMahon, S. D., 423
McManus, B., 387
McMenamy, J. M., 436
McNeill, D., 302
McNerney, E. K., 514
McQuillan, G., 391
McRae, K., 438
McShane, K., 414
Meade, C. S., 389
Meadows, L. A., 520
Meadows, S., 203
Meadows-Orlans, K. P., 190
Mealey, L., 507
Meaney, M. J., 68, 83, 86–87
Medin, D. L., 250, 426
Medina, J. J., 161
Medina, R. A., 258
Meeks, S., 530
Meeks, T. W., 531
Meeus, W. H. J., 345, 483
Meeuwsen, I. B. A. E., 155
Meheula, L., 13
Mehler, J., 299, 304
Meier, R. P., 301
Meijer, J., 206
Meilahn, E. N., 154
Meilman, P. W., 345
Meins, E., 404
Meir, E. I., 347
Melchior, J., 226
Melhem, N. M., 553
Mellinger, J. C., 326
Mellon, M. K., 175
Meltzer, H., 516, 522
Meltzer-Brody, S., 119
Meltzoff, A. N., 213, 237–238, 309, 403
Melz, H., 485
Melzer, D., 159
Melzi, G., 311
Memon, A., 245
Menacker, F., 117
Menaghan, E. G., 496
Mencl, E., 317
Mendle, J., 147, 459
Mendola, P., 145
Mendonca Lima, C. A., 531
Mendoza, B. L., 557
Mennella, J. A., 174, 176
Mensa, F. K., 147
Ment, L. R., 124
Mercer, J., 451
Meredith, P., 486
Merikangas, K. R., 520, 522
Merkle, K., 514
Merrick, E., 104
Merrick, J., 104
Merriwether, A. M., 387, 459
Mertesacker, B., 436
Merzenich, M. M., 318
Meschke, L. L., 388
Mesman, J., 516
Messer, D. J., 309
Messina, A., 424
Messinger, D., 513
Messinger-Rapport, B. J., 191
Mestas, M., 321
Metcalf, P., 542
Metcalfe, J., 248
Metzger, B. E., 107
Metzger, P. A., 546
Meulenbroek, O., 256
Meunier, J., 186
Meydani, M., 161
Meyer, F., 103, 455

Meyer, H., 298
Meyer, S., 415, 435
Meyer-Bahlburg, H. F., 376, 387
Meyerhoefer, C., 155
Meyer-Schiffer, P., 98
Mezulis, A. H., 527
Michel, M. K., 436
Mick, E., 518
Mickelson, K., 349
Middleton F., 518
Midgley, C., 321–322
Midlarsky, E., 428
Mielke, M., 283
Miell, D., 206
Mikulincer, M., 462–463, 559
Milburn, N., 463
Milgram, J. I., 489
Milionis, H. J., 150
Milki, A. A., 93
Milkie, M. A., 475, 486–487
Miller, A., 154, 311
Miller, G. E., 86, 455
Miller, H., 377
Miller, J. A., 73
Miller, J. G., 426
Miller, J. W., 499
Miller, J., 497
Miller, K. F., 246
Miller, M., 378
Miller, N. A., 74
Miller, P. H., 32, 54, 56, 167, 185, 199, 201, 203,
   240, 426, 477
Miller, R. A., 160
Miller, S. A., 14–15, 203, 286, 402, 404, 455, 477
Miller, S. C., 154
Miller, S., 525
Miller, T. R., 528
Miller-Johnson, S., 275, 310, 422, 454
Millheiser, L. S., 93
Mills, C. J., 313
Mills-Koonce, W. R., 446
Milofsky, E., 355
Milos, G., 522
Minear, S., 121
Mineka, S., 47
Mingroni, M. A., 277
Miniño, A. M., 542–543
Minnes, S., 106
Miralt, G., 552
Misa, T. J., 369
Mischel, W., 333, 341, 415
Mishori, R., 175
Mishra, G. D., 154
Misri, S., 488
Mitchell, A. A., 101
Mitchell, B. A., 487
Mitchell, J. E., 524–525
Mitchell, P., 335
Mitchell, S. L., 539
Mitnick, D. M., 486
Mitzner, T. L., 325
Miyake, K., 447, 484
Miyamoto, R. T., 175
Miyamura, T., 176
Miyawaki, K., 173
Mize, J., 454
Mizuta, I., 423
Mobbs, C., 152–153
Mock, S. E., 386
Modell, B., 71
Modi, A. C., 150
Modi, N., 116
Moehler, E., 337
Moen, P., 357
Moffitt, T. E., 80, 83, 85, 341, 343, 415, 420–421,
   423, 489, 499–500, 509, 520

Mohammad, K., 146
Mohammed, A. H., 274
Mohapatra, S., 98
Moilanen, I., 105, 346
Mokdad, A. H., 150
Molfese, V. J., 274, 286
Molina, B. S. G., 147, 519
Molina, G. B., 57
Moll, H., 414
Mollborn, S., 7
Molteni, R., 149
Monahan, K. C., 420, 458
Mondloch, C. J., 177, 182
Moneta, G., 482
Monette, J., 534
Money, J., 375–378, 387
Monk, C. E., 173–174
Monroe, S. M., 510
Monshouwer, H. J., 421
Monsour, A., 342
Montaze, M., 146
Montazeri, A., 153
Monteilh, C., 146
Montemayor, R., 342–343
Montero, P., 154
Montgomery, A., 154
Montgomery, M. J., 355
Monti, M. M., 540
Montie, J., 275
Moon, C., 173, 304
Moon, S. M., 292
Mooney-Somers, J., 494
Moore, A. A., 193
Moore, A. B., 427
Moore, A. T., 190
Moore, E. G. J., 288–289
Moore, G., 446
Moore, K. L., 102
Moore, M. K., 182, 213, 237
Moore, S. R., 459
Moorehouse, M. J., 493
Moors, A. C., 388
Mor, V., 562
Moraga, A. V., 534
Morales, J., 312
Moran, T. P., 311, 313
Morell, C. H., 193
Morelli, G. A., 451
Morelli, S. A., 427
Morello, C., 550
Morelock, M. J., 292
Moreno, F., 357
Moreno, M. A., 185
Morey, C. C., 357
Morgan, D. L., 464
Morgan, E. M., 386
Morgan, G. A., 444
Morgan, L. K., 174
Morgan, M., 119
Morgeli, H., 556
Mori, C. A., 67
Moriarty, D. G., 196
Moride, Y., 534
Morin, R., 26
Morina, N., 559
Morizot, J., 351
Morley, J. E., 534
Morrell, R. W., 257
Morris, J. T., 380
Morris, M. J., 87, 113
Morris, P. A., 51–53., 471
Morris, P., 8
Morris, R. G., 406–407
Morrongiello, B. A., 377
Morrow, B., 122
Morrow, C. E., 106

Morrow, D. G., 256, 283, 325
Morrow, D., 250, 256, 283, 325
Morrow, J. D., 160
Morse, C. A., 154, 463, 491
Morse, J. Q., 463, 491
Morsella, E., 38
Mortimer, J. T., 324., 356
Morton, B. G., 527
Morton, J., 171
Mory, M. S., 457
Moser, J. S., 311, 313
Moser, K., 357
Moses, L. J., 404
Moskey, E. G., 387–388
Moskovic, D. J., 153
Moss, M. S., 557
Moss, P., 514
Moss, S. Z., 557
Motzoi, C., 442, 455
Moulton, L. H., 109
Moum, T., 556
Mount, R. J., 175
Mounts, N. S., 459, 477, 484
Mouton, C. P., 554
Moye, J., 551
Mroczek, D. K., 352, 438
Mueller, E., 450
Muennig, P., 192
Muhamedrahimov, R. J., 448
Muir, D. W., 176
Mulatu, M. S., 357
Mullally, P. R., 350–351
Muller, M. T., 541
Müller, V., 247, 438
Mulsant, B. H., 531, 534
Mulvey, K. L., 416
Mumford, M. D., 278
Mundy, L., 414
Mundy, P. C., 335, 401
Munir, K., 512
Munro, E. R., 448
Munroe, R. L., 451
Munson, J., 514
Murayama, K., 315
Murdoch, A., 315
Muris, P., 337
Murnen, S. K., 380, 523
Murphy, B. A., 559
Murphy, B. P., 177
Murphy, C., 194–195, 337
Murphy, D. R., 193, 256, 553
Murphy, E. M., 497
Murphy, G., 291
Murphy, L. M., 458–459
Murphy, M. L. M., 455
Murphy, P. K., 5
Murphy, S. A., 556–557,
    559, 562
Murphy, S. L., 542–543
Murray, A. D., 287
Murray, C. I., 551
Murray, C., 285, 289
Murray, H., 174
Murray, I., 118
Murray, L., 119, 435, 447
Murray, M., 129
Murray-Close, D., 369
Murrin, C., 101
Musil, C. M., 488
Muster, A. J., 158
Mutran, E. J., 488
Muzikansky, A., 562
Mwamwenda, B. A., 222
Mwamwenda, T. S., 222
Myers, J. K., 530
Mylod, D. E., 486

N

Na, J., 406
Nachmani, J., 141
Nagamatsu, L. S., 153
Nagarajan, S. S., 317–318
Nagel, S. K., 493
Nagell, K., 305
Naglieri, J. A., 143
Nagy, G., 353
Naigles, L. G., 306
Naigles, L. R., 305
Naigles, L., 514
Nair, R. L., 479
Najman, J. M., 557
Nakamura, J., 284
Nanan, R. K., 174
Nanayakkara, A. R., 313
Nanez, J. E., 171
Nanney, M. S., 142
Narayan, M., 253
Nardi, A. H., 256
Nargeot, M. C. G., 531
Narvaez, D., 426, 428
Nash, A., 450
Näsi, T., 140
Nass, C., 13
National Center for Education Statistics,
    322, 324, 326
National Center for Health Statistics, 8, 103,
    528, 543
The National Child Development Study, 516
National Institute on Aging, 153, 532–533
National Osteoporosis Foundation, 158
National Reading Panel, 317
National Sleep Foundation, 150–151
Natsuaki, M. N., 527
Neal, A. R., 401
Neale, B. M., 518
Neale, M. C., 386
Nebes, R. D., 251, 531, 534
Neblett, E. W., Jr., 346
Nederend, S., 385
Neece, W. M., 358–359
Needham, A., 181
Needle, E., 324
Neiderhiser, J. M., 85, 147, 357, 480
Neighbors, H. W., 531
Neijstrom, E., 253
Neil, A., 113
Neimark, E. D., 224
Neimeyer, R. A., 556, 559, 561–562
Neisser, U., 243, 278, 280, 288–289
Nellett, G., 350
Nelson, C. A., 133, 136, 235, 300
Nelson, E. S., 428
Nelson, G., 310
Nelson, J. M., 428–429
Nelson, K. E., 316
Nelson, K., 244–245, 306–307, 404
Nelson, R. J., 153
Nelson, S. A., 416
Nelson, S. K., 486
Nemeroff, C. B., 521
Nemeroff, R., 428
Nemeth, R., 381
Neppl, T., 423
Neppl, T. K., 498
Nerenberg, L., 497
Nes, S. L., 206
Nesse, R., 531
Nesse, R. M., 555
Nesselroade, J. R., 155, 438–439
Nestle, M., 149
Nettelbeck, T., 268
Netzley, S. B., 380
Neubert, A. C., 149

Neufield, S. J., 435
Neugarten, B. L., 7, 10, 360
Neuhaus, R., 556
Neumann, D., 368
Neumark-Sztainer, D., 150, 342
Neville, B., 475
Neville, H. J., 301
Nevitt, M. C., 190
Nevitt, M., 158
New, M. I., 376
Newall, N. E., 313
Newby, P.K., 141
Newcomb, R., 390, 423
Newcombe, N. S., 244
Newcombe, R., 423
Newcorn, J. H., 519
Newell, A., 232
Newell, L., 171
Newell, W., 455
Newman, A. J., 301
Newman, J. L., 385
Newman, R., 306
Newman, T. N., 533
Newport, E. L., 312
Newsom, J. T., 464
Newsome, M., 304
Newsorn, M., 304
Neyer, F. J., 460
Nezlek, J. B., 460
Ng, E. L., 245
Ng, E. S., 189
Ng, K., 447
Ng, S. F., 87, 113
Ng, T. W. H., 357–358
Nguyen, H. T., 530
Nguyen, H. X., 346
Nguyen, S., 148
NICHD Early Child Care Research Network, 449
Nicholas, C., 119
Nicholls, D. E., 524
Nicholls, E. F., 86
Nichols, C., 558
Nichols, K. E., 418
Nichols, T. R., 147
Nicholson, T., 157
Nicolich, L. M., 452
Niebler, G., 518
Niegel, K., 119
Nielsen, M., 44–45
Nielson, N. L., 359
Nieuwenhuijsen, M., 110
Nigg, J. T., 524
Nijhuis, J. G., 237
Nikiforova, N. V., 448
Nikolic, J., 223
Nillson, L.-G., 254, 256
Nilsson, L., 256
Nilsson, M., 136
Niparko, J. K., 175
Nisbett, R. E., 264, 274, 285, 406
Nishimura, M., 177
Nishishiba, M., 464
Nishitani, S., 176
Nissen, C., 233
Nissilä, I., 140
Nissim, R., 545–546
Niv, S., 423
Nix, R. L., 316
Noble, K. D., 292
Noeker, M., 131
Noh, E. R., 493
Noh, S., 486
Noirhomme, Q., 540
Nolen-Hoeksema, S., 527–528, 530, 559
Noll, A., 74
Noll, J. G., 558

Noll, J., 265–266
Noll, R. B., 131
Noller, P., 486
Nomaguchi, K. M., 486
Nondahl, D. M., 192
Noone, J. H., 359
Noponen, T., 140
Noppe, I. C., 552
Noppe, L. D., 552
Norberg, K. E., 526
Norbury, C. F., 509, 512
Nordin, S., 194–195
Nores, M., 275
Norenzayan, A., 9
Norman, A., 244
Normandeau, J., 173
Norquist, G. S., 521
Norris, D. R., 487
Norris, J. E., 426
Norris, L., 256
Norris, S. P., 316
North, M. S., 8
Northstone, K., 141
Norton, T. R., 490–491
Notarius, C. I., 486
Nourhashemi, F., 533
Nouri, K., 146
Novak, D. C., 185
Nsamenang, A. B., 120
Nucci, L., 417, 424
Nugent, J. K., 121
Nulman, I., 104–105
Nurss, J. R., 280
Nusselder, W., 367
Nutt, R. L., 319
Nyberg, L., 254, 256
Nyborg, H., 279
Nye, C. D., 347
Nyqvist, K. H., 123
Nystrom, L. E., 427

O

O'Bleness, J. J., 415
O'Boyle, C., 377
O'Brien, B. A., 487
O'Brien, J., 101
O'Brien, L. T., 349
O'Brien, M., 339, 371, 375, 447, 486–487
O'Brien, P. M. S., 153
O'Connell, B., 302
O'Connell, P., 380
O'Connor, A.
O'Connor, B. P., 223, 464
O'Connor, G., 177
O'Connor, R. E., 316
O'Connor, T. G., 85, 423, 448, 481
O'Dempsey, T. J. D., 118
O'Donnell, W. T., 71
O'Donovan, M. C., 81
O'Halloran, C. M., 550
O'Hanlon, A. M., 380
O'Hara, N., 500
O'Hara, R. E., 57
O'Leary, C. M., 105
O'Loughlin, A., 531
O'Malley, P. M., 323, 525–526
O'Mara, A. J., 340
O'Mathúna, D. P., 131
O'Neil, A. K., 385
O'Neil, R., 493
O'Roak, B. J., 70, 514
O'Rourke, M., 545
O'Shaughnessy, E. S., 16
O'Shaughnessy, R., 524
Oakhill, J., 382

Oates, G., 357
Obel, C., 105, 346
Öberg-Blävarg, C., 195
Oberlander, S. E., 471
Oberlander, T. F., 488
Oberman, L. M., 403, 513
Obler, L. K., 325
Obradovic, J., 526
Oburu, P., 477
Ochs, E., 7, 303
Ochse, R., 276
Ochsner, K. N., 438
Oden, M. H., 292
Odendaal, H. J., 106
Odgers, C. L., 420, 425
Odouli, R., 107
Oehmke, J., 423
Oelkers-Ax, R., 337
Oepkes, D., 74
Ofstedal, M. B., 253
Ogbu, J. U., 26, 288, 321
Ogbuanu, I. U., 121
Ogden, C, L., 144
Ogletree, S. M., 380
Ogrodniczuk, J. S., 559
Ohman, A., 47
Øian, P., 117
Okagaki, L., 288
Oken, E., 136
Oldehinkel, A. J., 146–147
Olds, S. W., 121
Oles, P. K., 356
Olesen, S. C., 359
Olfson, M., 531
Oliver, B. R., 85
Oliver, P. H., 313–314
Oller, D. K., 178, 305
Olmstead, S. B., 387
Olowokure, B., 395
Olrick, J. T., 448
Olsen, J., 112, 428
Olsen-Cerny, C., 489
Olshan, A. F., 113
Olshansky, S. J., 160
Olson, B., 355
Olson, D. R., 216
Olson, J. M., 82
Olson, J., 303
Olson, S. L., 416
Oltjenbruns, K. A., 551
Olweus, D., 424
Omodei, D., 161
Onelov, E., 551
Ones, D. S., 279
Ong, A. D., 561
Onishi, K. H., 402
Ono, H., 492
Ono, Y., 333, 340
Ontai, L. L., 498
Onwuegbuzie, A. J., 287
Onwuteaka-Philipsen, B. D., 541
Oosterwegel, A., 340
Oppenheim, D., 416
Oppenheimer, J. D., 233
Oppenheimer, L., 340
Opwis, K., 242
Orlans, H., 194
Orloff, S. F., 562
Ormel, J., 146–147, 516
Ormrod, R. K., 390
Ornstein, P. A., 240, 245
Orobio de Castro, B., 421
Orpinas, P., 46
Orth, L. C., 319
Orth, U., 343, 348
Ortigo, K. M., 35

Sharpe, T. M., 524
Shaver, P. R., 462–463
Shaw, D., 316
Shaw, H., 524–525
Shaw, K., 520
Shay, J. W., 160
Shayer, M., 208
Shaywitz, B. A., 299, 317
Shaywitz, S. E., 317
Sheared, V., 326
Sheetz, M. J., 562
Sheffield, R. A., 421
Shekhar, S., 116
Shepard, B., 435–436
Shepard, R. J., 143
Shepard, R., 143
Shepard, T. H., 107
Sher, K. J., 6
Shera, D. M., 286
Sherer, S., 11
Sherman, A. M., 460
Sherman, S., 141
Sheu, C., 423
Shibley Hyde, J., 156
Shield, R., 562
Shiffrin, R. M., 232
Shigematsu, I., 109
Shih, M., 289
Shin, C., 527
Shin, L. M., 337
Shin, N., 346
Shiner, R. L., 336, 338, 341
Shiovitz-Ezra, S., 464
Ship, J. A., 194–195
Shirley, L., 275, 381
Shirtcliff, E. A., 515
Shisslak, C. M., 524
Shneider, A. E., 317
Shneidman, E. S., 545
Shneidman, L. A., 303
Shoda, Y., 333, 415
Shoham, V., 11
Shonk, S. M., 499
Shonkoff, J. P., 135
Shook, A., 312
Shore, C., 302
Shors, T. J., 153
Shreffler, K. M., 492
Shringarpure, R., 160
Shrout, P. E., 181
Shukla, D., 223
Shulman, S., 489
Shute, N., 521
Shweder, R. A., 351, 426
Siebold, C., 561
Siegal, M., 404, 417
Siegel, N. B., 390
Siegler, I. C., 360
Siegler, R. S., 245–246
Sigelman, C. K., 385
Sigman, M., 446, 511
Sigmundson, H. K., 378
Signorella, M. L., 382
Signorielli, N., 380
Silk, J. B., 302, 412, 414
Sill, M., 394–396
Silva, P. A., 489
Silventoinen, K., 145
Silver, R. C., 557
Silverman, A. B., 522
Silverman, I. W., 368, 408
Silverman, L. R., 457
Silverman, P. R., 552
Silverman, P. S., 560
Silverman, W. P., 291
Silverstein, M., 501

Sim, L. A., 534
Simcock, G., 238, 244
Simion, F., 171
Simmons, R. G., 148, 321, 342
Simon, H. A., 232, 270
Simon, L. S., 279
Simon, L. W., 279
Simonds, J., 338
Simonoff, E., 513
Simons, R. F., 422
Simons, R. L., 479, 481, 527
Simons-Morton, B. G., 527
Simonton, D. K., 284–285
Simpson, J. A., 146, 449
Simpson, J. L., 74
Simpson, L., 123
Simpson, R., 514
Sims, L., 323
Singer, B., 5
Singer, D. G., 453
Singer, L. T., 106
Singer, T., 254, 281
Singh, D., 187
Singh, P., 424
Sinigaglia, C., 403
Sinnott, J. D., 225
Sipe, T. A., 521
Sisk, C. L., 148, 524
Skinner, B. F., 252
Skinner, E. A., 551
Skinner, M. A., 489
Skotko, B. G., 74
Skow, C., 520
Skowronek, M. H., 518
Slaby, R. G., 421
Slade, L., 212
Slade, M. D., 349
Slaten, E., 489–490
Slater, A., 169–171
Slater, C. L., 355
Slater, R., 176
Slattery, M., 517
Slaughter, V., 404, 549–550
Slavick, J. T., 390
Slavkin, M., 394
Slep, A. M., 486, 497
Sliwinski, M., 281
Slobin, D. I., 307
Sloboda, Z., 527
Slora, E. J., 145
Slotkin, T. A., 103
Slusarcick, A. L., 324
Smagorinsky, P., 206
Smailes, E., 516
Small, B. J., 256
Small, M., 120
Small, S. G., 317
Smallish, L., 518
Smart, D., 480
Smart, J. L., 140
Smeeth, L., 189
Smetana, J. G., 417
Smiley, S. S., 247
Smit, F., 355
Smith Slep, A. M., 486, 497
Smith, A. D., 255
Smith, A. K., 518
Smith, C. H., 390
Smith, D. M., 490
Smith, E. P., 346
Smith, G. D., 101
Smith, G. E., 252
Smith, G. J. W., 452–454
Smith, K. E., 124
Smith, L. B., 180
Smith, L. G., 273

Smith, L., 187, 273
Smith, M. D., 482
Smith, P. K., 270, 424, 452
Smith, P., 278
Smith, S., 485
Smith, T., 489, 514
Smith, W., 190
Smithmyer, C. M., 422
Smitsman, A. W., 179
Smolak, L., 523
Smolkowski, K., 522
Smyer, M. A., 531
Smyke, A. T., 448
Snarey, J. R., 424, 426
Sneed, J. R., 354
Sneed, L., 123
Snidman, N., 336
Snow, C. E., 303, 307
Snow, D., 305
Snowdon, D., 161
Snowling, M. J., 316
So, K., 138
Sobolewski, J. M., 495–496
Sodian, B., 220, 241
Soederberg, L. M., 253, 325
Sogn, J., 93
Sohn, W., 141
Sokol, W. B., 416
Sokoloff, L., 157
Sokolovsky, J., 159, 161
Soler, M. J., 193
Solomon, F., 551
Solomon, J., 445
Solomon, S., 538
Soltys, F. G., 355
Somers, D. G., 489
Son, L. K., 248
Song, H., 152, 306
Song, J. W., 528–529
Song, J., 358
Song, L., 306
Sönksen, P. H., 131
Sonnega, J., 555
Sonntag, W. E., 161
Sonuga-Barke, E., 183, 448
Sorell, G. T., 460
Sorensen, A. B., 7
Sorensen, S., 490
Soriano, F. I., 423
Soriano-Mas, C., 133
Sorkhabi, N., 477
Sorri, M., 194
Soska, K. C., 168
Sostek, A. M., 26
Sosunov, A. A., 13, 152
Sotomayor, S., 331–332
Sotomi, O., 177
Sotoudeh, A., 146
Soussignan, R., 176
Span, P., 487
Spaniol, J., 254
Spar, D., 357
Sparks, A., 509, 512
Sparks, R. L., 315
Sparling, J. J., 310
Sparrow, R., 175
Sparrow, S. S., 268
Spear, L. P., 144, 522
Spearman, C., 265
Spector, F., 177
Speece, D. L., 316
Speece, M. W., 550
Spelke, E. S., 170, 172
Spence, I., 368
Spence, J. T., 325, 393
Spence, M. J., 173

Spencer, J. P., 441
Spencer, M. B., 345
Spencer, P. E., 301
Spencer, S., 288
Spera, C., 337
Sperling, M. B., 469
Sperry, S., 535
Spiby, H., 113, 122
Spicer, P., 361
Spiegel, C., 306
Spiegelman, D., 514
Spieler, D. H., 325
Spilich, G. J., 250
Spinath, B., 313
Spinath, F. M., 313
Spindler, A., 522
Spinrad, T. L., 336, 414, 419
Spiro, A., 135
Spitz, M. R., 144
Spitz, R. A., 515
Spitze, G., 487, 489
Spitznagel, E., 520
Spokane, A. R., 347
Spoth, R., 527
Spratling, M. W., 204
Sprecher, S., 461
Springen, K., 450
Springer, S., 140
Spruijt-Metz, D., 149
Spruyt, K., 138
Squire, L. R., 234
Sroufe, L. A., 444, 449, 498, 507
St. Clair, D., 113
St. George, D., 473, 497
St. Hilaire, A., 81
St. Jacques, P. L., 251
St. Petersburg–USA Orphanage Research Team, 448
Stacey, J., 475
Staff, J., 323, 356
Stager, C. L., 182
Stalets, M., 520
Stambrook, M., 550
Standing, T., 488
Stanfors, M., 486
Stanger, C., 336
Stanhope, N., 248
Stanley, S. M., 485, 492
Stanley-Hagen, M., 496
Stanovich, K. E., 222, 315
Stapp, J., 393
Starr, J. M., 280
Starr, R. H., 471
Statham, D. J., 527
Stattin, H., 458, 481
Staudinger, U. M., 12, 24, 254, 282–284, 358
Staudt, J., 224
Steele, C. M., 288
Steele, R., 556, 562
Steenbergen-Hu, S., 292
Steenland, K., 280
Stefano, J. L., 123
Steffen, L. M., 149
Steffens, D. C., 533
Stein, C. H., 490
Stein, D. J., 147
Stein, J. H., 147
Stein, R., 540
Steinberg, L., 144, 147, 321, 340, 459, 476, 477, 481, 484, 510, 522
Steinbrenner, G. M., 155–156
Steineck, G., 551
Steiner, J. E., 174
Stellern, S. A., 415
Stemler, S. E., 268
Stemp, P. S., 486
Stepanian, M. T., 406

Stephens, C., 359
Stephens, M. A. P., 490
Stephenson, H., 521
Stepp, L. S., 550
Stern, D., 442
Stern, M., 377
Stern, Y., 312
Sternberg, L., 264
Sternberg, M., 391
Sternberg, R. J., 461
Sternglanz, S. H., 383
Stettler, N. M., 437
Steurer, M. A., 98
Stevens, A. B., 258
Stevens, D. P., 326
Stevens, E., 173
Stevens, G., 312
Stevens, J. C., 253
Stevens, J. J., 318
Stevens, M. M., 551, 553
Stevens, M., 494
Stevens, W. D., 255
Stevenson, H. C., 346
Stevenson, H. W., 323
Stevenson, J., 183
Stevenson, R. J., 179
Steverink, N., 349
Stewart, A. J., 344, 355
Stewart, R. B., 482
Stewart, S., 141
Stice, E., 523–525
Stifter, C., 446
Stigler, J. W., 323
Stillion, J. M., 539
Stine, E. A. L., 325
Stine-Morrow, E. A. L., 253, 256, 283
Stipek, D. J., 275, 309, 313, 320
Stirling, S., 189
Stith, S. M., 498
Stobel-Richter, Y., 357
Stockman, M., 421
Stoddart, T., 385
Stolberg, U., 444
Stone, M. R., 458
Stone, R., 517
Stone, S., 519
Stone, W.L., 513
Stoner, G., 518
Stones, M. J., 157
St-Onge, M. P., 141
Stoolmiller, M., 76
Story, M., 142, 150
Stoyak, S., 553
Strait, L. B., 425
Strand, S., 265
Strange, W., 173
Straus, M. A., 497
Strauss, A. L., 545
Strauss, J., 549
Strayer, J., 355
Streissguth, A. P., 105–106
Streri, A., 182
Striano, T., 335
Stright, A. D., 394
Strigini, P., 113
Stringer, J. S., 109
Strober, M., 524
Stroebe, M., 547, 557–558
Stroebe, R., 556
Stroebe, W., 557
Strøm, I. F., 424
Strong, B., 461
Studenski, S. A., 156
Stuebing, K. K., 317
Stuewig, J., 424
Stump, J., 531

Stupnisky, R. H., 313
Sturla, E., 378
Stutz, H., 499
Styner, M., 512
Su, R., 347, 356
Sucato, G. S., 424, 459
Suchindran, C., 388
Suchowersky, O., 73
Sudhalter, V., 311
Sue, S., 507, 531
Sugden, K., 83, 85
Suh, C. S., 146
Suisman, J. L., 523–524
Suitor, J. J., 487, 489
Sulem, P., 70
Sulkava, R., 194
Sullivan, H. S., 441, 466
Sullivan, J., 520
Sullivan, M. W., 336
Sullivan, P. F., 523
Sullivan, S., 406
Sulloway, F. J., 299
Sumi, M., 185
Sumida, E., 499
Sun, F., 504
Sun, S. S., 146
Sun, Y., 468
Sunderland, T., 530
Sundet, J. M., 108
Sundquist, J., 543
Sundqvist, N., 179
Sung, S., 146
Super, C. M., 346
Super, D. E., 346
Surdulescu, G. L., 160
Susman, E. J., 147
Susser, E., 101, 113
Sussman, S., 458
Suter, J., 563
Sutherland, G. R., 70
Sutin, A. R., 353
Sutton, B. P., 256
Sutton-Brown, M., 73
Suwanlert, S., 508
Suzuki, A., 333
Suzuki, M., 159, 161
Svanborg, A., 395
Svartengren, M., 82, 252
Svedin, C., 384
Svetina, M., 217
Swain, J. E., 116
Swami, V., 462
Swamy, R., 98
Swan, D. C., 391
Swank, P. R., 124, 286
Swann, W. B., 334
Swanson, H. A., 191
Swanson, H. L., 255
Swanson, J. M., 101
Swanson, J., 322
Swanson, S. A., 522
Swarr, A. E., 147
Sweitzer, V. L., 412
Swendsen, J., 522
Swensen, L. D., 305
Swenson, L. P., 458
Swinson, T., 119
Switzer, F. S., 324
Sy, S. R., 323
Symons, D. K., 404
Szalacha, L., 357
Szatmari, P., 525
Szkrybalo, J., 371
Szoeke, C. E. I., 533
Szostak, J., 160
Szyf, M., 87

Tucker, K. L., 530
Tucker, P., 378
Tucker, R., 175
Tucker-Drob, E. M., 80
Tuckett, A., 327
Tuckey, M., 404
Tudor-Locke, C., 149
Tuer, M., 486
Tulandi, T., 93
Tullos, A., 215
Tuma, F. K., 521
Tun, P. A., 21–22, 193
Turan, B., 438–439
Turati, C., 171
Turchi, G., 117
Turecki, G., 87
Turiano, N., 352
Turiel, E., 385, 417
Turk-Charles, S., 360
Turkewitz, G., 173
Turkheimer, E., 80, 527
Turner, H. A., 390
Turner, J., 486
Turner, L. A., 248
Turner, P. J., 379
Turner, T. R., 380
Turnpenny, P. D., 66, 68, 70, 72, 74, 86
Tweed, R. G., 555
Tweed, T. S., 192
Twenge, J. M., 23, 367, 387
Twohey-Jacobs, J., 563
Tynelius, P., 82, 145
Tyre, P., 523
Tyson, D. F., 321–322
Tyson-Rawson, K. J., 553

U

U.S. Census Bureau, Population Division, 159
U.S. Department of Health and Human, 391
U.S. Department of Labor, 358, 366, 370
U.S.D.A. Factbook, 149
Ubel, P. A., 490
Uccelli, P., 306
Uchida, N., 191
Uchino, B. N., 464, 489
Uchronski, M., 367, 370
Udry, J. R., 459
Uematsu, S., 140
Ueno, K., 464
Uher, R., 516
Uhland, R. L., 326
Ulrich, B., 180
Umaña-Taylor, A. J., 345–346
Umberson, D., 489–490, 492, 557
Ungar, L., 427
Unger, E. R., 57, 391
Unger, J. B., 57
Ungvari, Z., 161
University of Copenhagen, 186
Uotinen, V., 359
Updegraff, K. A., 482
Updegraff, K., 379
Urbano, R. C., 178
Urbina, S., 268
Urdan, T., 321
Usher, J. A., 243
Usher-Seriki, K. K., 392

V

Vaca, V. L., 158
Vaccaro, B. G., 435
Vaden, N. A., 289
Vågerö, D., 357
Vaglio, S., 176
Vahia, I., 531
Vaillant, G. E., 355

Vaish, A., 412, 414
Valdes, A. M., 160
Valdez-Menchaca, M. C., 302
Valdimarsdottir, U., 551
Valente, T. W., 149
Valentino, K., 499
Valeri, S. M., 521
Valiente, C., 322, 483
Valkenberg, P. M., 13
Vallejo, A. N., 161
Vallin, J., 544
van Anders, S., 153
van Beijsterveldt, T. C. E. M., 513
van Berckelaer-Onnes, I. A., 511
Van Beurden, E., 141
van de Schoot, R., 345
Van den Berg, S. M., 107
Van den Bergh, B. R. H., 107
van den Boom, D. C., 339, 465
van den Bout, J., 557
van den Bree, M. B. M., 104, 112
van den Broek, P., 316
Van den Dries, L., 448
van den Hout, M., 563
van den Hove, D.,L.A., 533
van den Oever, J. M., 74
van der Ende, J., 516
van der Heide, A., 541
van der Heijden, P., 557, 559
van der Laan, P., 421
Van Der Lippe, T., 370
van der Loos, M., 78
van der Maas, H., 246
van der Maas, P. J., 541
van der Meer, A. L., 171
van der Vorst, H., 458
van der Wal, G., 107, 541
van der Wal, M. F., 107
van Doesum, K. T. M., 465
Van Ginneken, J. K., 146
van Goozen, S., 414
Van Hecke, A. V., 401
van Hees, Y., 112
van Hoeken, D., 523
van Hoof, A., 421
Van Horn, P., 551
Van Hulle, C., 414
van IJzendoorn, H. W., 455
van IJzendoorn, M. H., 21, 80, 445, 447–448, 463
van Kleeck, A., 316
Van Landeghem, P., 541
van Leeuwen, M., 285
Van Lieshout, C. F., 455
Van Oyen, H., 367
Van Paesschen, W., 235
Van Rossem, L., 121
Van Ryzin, M., 374
van Solinge, H., 359
Vance, J. C., 557
Vande Voort, J. L., 524
Vandell, D. L., 449–450
Vander Veur, S. S., 141–142
Vanderborght, M., 18
Vanderwerker, L. C., 556
VanDyke, R., 107
Vanhasselt, V. B., 489
Vanhaudenhuyse, A., 540
VanKim, N. A., 149
Vanneste, S., 256
Varea, C., 154
Vargas, L. A., 509
Vargas, M., 336
Vargha-Khadem, F., 140, 235, 300
Varley, J., 514
Varnum, M. E. W., 406
Vartanian, L. R., 223

Vartoukian, R., 245
Vaslamatzis, G., 93
Vasyukova, C., 251
Vaughan, R. C., 292
Vaughn, B. E., 455
Vazsonyi, A. T., 477
Vedantam, S., 521
Veenstra, R., 516
Veenstra-Vanderweele, J., 513
Veerman, J. W., 421
Velacott, C., 119
Velderman, M.K., 465
Vellas, B., 533
Vellutino, F. R., 317
Velting, D. M., 528
Vendlinski, M. K., 80
Venema, K., 514
Venkatraman, V., 152
Ventura, S. J., 56
Verbeek, P., 412
Verbrugge, R., 173
Verghese, J., 12
Verhaak, C. M., 93
Verhaar, H. J. J., 155
Verhaeghen, P., 5, 254–256
Verhey, F., 533
Verhulst, F. C., 146, 516
Verkade, R., 337
Verma, S., 323
Vermeulen, A., 154
Veroff, J., 325–326
Véronneau, M. H., 321
Veroude, K., 299
Verrillo, R. T., 195
Verrillo, V., 195
Verschueren, K., 340
Verweij, E. J., 74
Vesonder, G. T., 250
Veugelers, P. P., 103
Victor, A. M., 38
Victor, C. R., 554
Victor, J. D., 540
Vidal, F., 225
Videka-Sherman, L., 562
Viding, E., 85, 421
Viechtbauer, W., 352
Vietze, P. M., 309
Vihman, M. M., 304
Viljoen, K., 101
Villalobos, M., 417
Villalta, I., 525
Villatta, I. K., 525
Vinden, P. G., 404
Viner, R. M., 149, 524
Vining, E. P. G., 140
Vinokur, A. D., 357
Vishnevsky, T., 560
Visser, P. J., 533
Vita, A. J., 158
Vital-Durand, F., 170
Vitario, F., 455
Vitaro, F., 76–77
Vitiello, B., 519, 521
Vives, L., 70, 514
Vivian, D., 499
Voderholzer, U., 233
Vogel, S., 367, 537
Vogler, G. P., 80, 82
Vohr, B. R., 123, 175
Volkmar, F. R., 512–514
Volling, B. L., 482
von Eye, A., 425
von Gaudecker, H., 359
von Hofsten, C., 136, 180–182
von Oertzen, T., 247
Vondra, J., 498

Vondracek, F. W., 346, 356
Vonk, I. J. J., 521
Voorhees, C. C., 148
Vorster, J., 303
Voss, A., 254
Voss, H., 144
Voss, J. F., 250
Voss, K., 340
Voss, M. W., 153, 254, 256
Vouloumanos, A., 173
Voyer, D., 368
Vrangalova, Z., 386
Vreeling, F. W., 256
Vrsalovic, W. T., 336
Vuoksimaa, E., 140
Vuolo, M., 356
Vuorialho, A., 194
Vurpillot, E., 183–184
Vygotsky, L. S., 50, 200, 204, 206, 453

W

Wachlarowicz, M., 496
Wade, E., 528
Wadhwa, P. D., 101
Wadsworth, M. E., 551
Wadsworth, S. J., 292
Wadsworth, T., 394
Waechter, E. H., 551
Waffram, F., 112
Wagner, B., 563
Wagner, E., 414
Wagner, G. G., 438, 460
Wainryb, C., 416
Wainwright, R., 404
Waisbren, S. E., 73
Waite, L. J., 464, 489
Waiter, G. D., 403
Wake, M., 147
Wakefield, J. C., 556
Walden, B., 483
Waldenström, U., 118
Waldfogel, J., 309
Waldholz, M., 73
Waldman, I. D., 274, 423, 518
Waldman, I., 78, 81
Walk, R. D., 171
Walkenfeld, F. F., 404
Walker Payne, M., 553
Walker, C., 380
Walker, H., 86
Walker, L. J., 410, 426, 428
Walker, M., 553
Walker-Andrews, A. S., 182
Wall, S., 443
Wallace, C. S., 136, 274
Wallace, G. L., 512
Wallace, I. F., 272
Wallace, J. E., 357
Wallace, L. E., 479
Wallace, P. S., 181
Wallen, K., 392
Waller, E. M., 470–471
Wallis, C., 75
Wallman, L. M., 358–359
Walls, R. T., 346
Walrath, J., 123
Walsh, B. T., 525
Walsh, D., 531
Walsh, K. M., 159, 193
Walsh, P. V., 383
Walter, C. A., 545
Walters, L. H., 223
Walton, G., 288
Walton, K. E., 352
Wan, W., 146
Wancata, J., 531

Wandrei, M. L., 223
Wang, H. Y., 495
Wang, J. J., 190
Wang, J., 74
Wang, L., 341
Wang, M., 338
Wang, P. S., 531
Wang, Q., 484
Wang, S. H., 172
Wang, S. S., 160, 493
Wang, W., 475
Wang, X., 318
Wang, Z., 341
Ward, C. D., 173
Ward, D., 395
Ward, H., 448
Ward, R., 487
Ward, S. K., 347
Ware, J. H., 110
Warin, J., 381
Waring, S. C., 253
Warkentin, V., 336
Warneken, F., 414
Warner, C. B., 192, 488
Warren, J. R., 323
Warren, S. T., 71
Wartella, E. A., 18
Wartella, E., 309
Warwick, Z. S., 195
Washburn, J., 423
Wasik, B. H., 310
Wass, H., 557
Wasserman, A., 454
Wasserman, D., 530
Wasserman, M. S., 522
Wasserman, R. C., 145
Water, D., 301
Waterhouse, L., 110, 511–514
Waterman, A. S., 344, 347
Watermann, R., 321
Waters, C. S., 414
Waters, E., 444, 449
Watkins, E. R., 528
Watkins, K., 235, 300
Watkins, M. W., 273
Watson, J., 402
Watt, L. M., 355
Waxman, S. R., 217, 306
Way, N., 457
Wayne, A. J., 318
Weaver, J., 525
Weaver, S. R., 479
Webb, R. M., 292
Webb, S. J., 514
Weber, R. A., 460
Webster, J. D., 355
Webster, J., 119
Wechsler, D., 266
Wei, J. Y., 349
Weideman, R., 559
Weiffenbach, J. M., 194–195
Weihe, P., 109
Weihs, K., 357
Weinberg, R. A., 80, 274, 289
Weindruch, R., 161
Weiner, M. F., 533
Weinert, F. E., 220, 281–282
Weinfeld, M., 512
Weinfield, N. S., 450
Weingarten, G., 42
Weinraub, M., 443
Weinrott, M., 425
Weir, D. R., 253
Weisberg, D. S., 309
Weisberg, P., 46
Weisgram, E. S., 346

Weishampel, P., 106
Weisman, O., 138
Weisner, T. S., 482
Weiss, B., 508, 520
Weiss, D., 349, 353
Weiss, L. H., 477
Weiss, M., 185, 248, 336
Weiss, R. S., 546
Weiss, S. R., 157
Weiss, S., 356
Weissman, M. M., 530
Weisz, J. R., 508, 521
Weisz, J., 484
Weizman, A. O., 307
Welch, L. C., 562
Weller, A., 441
Wellman, H. M., 172, 402–403, 405
Wells, B. E., 387
Wells, K. B., 531
Wells, K. C., 423
Wells, K., 519
Welsh, D. P., 387
Welsh, J. A., 316
Welsh-Bohmer, K. A., 533
Wenner, J. A., 238
Wentzel, K. R., 455
Wentzel-Larsen, T., 424
Weon, B. M., 159
Werker, J. F., 173, 300
Werler, M. M., 101
Werner, E. A., 99
Werner, E. E., 125
Werner, H., 134
Werner, L. A., 173
Werth, J. L., 539, 541
West, G. L., 190
West, M. J., 303
West, R. F., 222
Westefeld, J. S., 520
Westen, D., 35
Westenberg, P. M., 49
Westerhof, G. J., 349
Westerlund, A., 171
Westermann, G., 204
Western, M., 494
Westhues, A., 310
Weston, D. R., 449
Westphal, L. M., 93
Wethington, E., 353
Wethington, H. R., 521
Wetle, T., 562
Wetzler, S. E., 251
Wewerka, S. S., 238
Weyandt, L. L., 517–518
Weyer, J. L., 563
Whalen, C. K., 369
Whalen, G., 103
Whalley, L. J., 277, 280
Wheeler, M. E., 369
Whiffen, V. E., 509
Whishaw, I. Q., 136, 181
Whitbeck, L. B., 357, 479
Whitbourne, S. B., 154–155, 158, 193
Whitbourne, S. K., 349, 354
White, C., 158
White, D. J., 395
White, D. L., 557
White, D., 395
White, J. B., 157
White, L. E., 255
White, L., 155
White, M. J., 316
White, R. L., 346
White, R. M. B., 479
Whitebread, D., 258
Whitehead, B. D., 486–487, 505

Subject Index

Antisocial behavior
coercive family environment theory, 422–423
combating, 424
emotions and, 421
prevention of, 424–425
social information processing model, 421–422
Anxiety, stranger, 443–444
Apgar test, 122–123
APOE4 gene, 78, 532
Arcuate fasciculus, 299
Artificial insemination, 93
ARTs. *See* Assisted reproductive technologies (ARTs)
Asperger syndrome, 511
Asphyxia, 116
Assimilation, 201
Assisted reproductive technologies (ARTs), 93
Associative play, 452
Attached infants
caregiver to infant, 442–443, 445–446
contextual issues, 447
day care and, 448–449
evolution and, 450
exploratory behavior and, 443
implications, 447–450
infant to caregiver, 443
later development and, 449–450
parenting styles and, 445–446
personality and, 446
relationship quality, 443–445
separations and, 448
social deprivation and, 447–448
types of, 442–445
Attachment
adolescent, 456
adult styles, 462–464
bereavement model, 546–548
contextual aspects, 447
dismissing style of, 462
disorganized-disoriented, 446
fears of, 443
later development and, 441
nature/nurture and, 440–441
oxytocin and, 441
parent–child, 451
parenting styles and, 445–446
quality of, 443–445
resistant, 443–444
secure, 443
theory, 440–441
therapies, 465
Attention
adult, 190
defined, 182
joint, 401
selective, 183
systematic, 183–184
Attention deficit hyperactivity disorder (ADHD), 71, 104
Attention span, 183–184
Authoritarian parents, 476–477
Authoritative parents, 477
Authority morality, 410, 420
Autism
Autism spectrum disorder (ASD), 511,
See autism.
brain functioning, 513
causes, 513–514
characteristics, 512
Down syndrome and, 400–401
DSM-5 criteria, 511
identification of, 511
outcomes, 514
prevalence of, 512
refrigerator moms, 513
theory of mind and, 400
treatment, 514

Autobiographical memory
adult, 251–252
beginning of, 243–245
Autonomy
adolescent achievement of, 484
development of, 40
shame and doubt *versus*, 354

B
Babbling, 304
Baby biographies, 11
Baby boom generation, 23
Bandura, Albert, theory of, 44–47
Bargaining, by dying, 545
Bayley Scales of Infant Development, 271–272
Behavior
antisocial, 420–425
exploratory, 443
gender role, 383
gender-typed, 374–375
inhibition, 336–337
neonate, 138
prosocial, 408, 413–414
school refusal, 40
sexual, 384, 388–392
Behavior rating scale, 271
Behavioral genetics studies.
See also Nature/nurture
breeding, 75
controversies, 86–88
intellectual ability findings, 79–80
molecular genetics and, 77–78
personality findings, 80–81
psychological disorder findings, 81
temperament findings, 80–81
twins and adoption, 76–77
Behaviorism, 41
Belief
desire and, 402
false, 402
Bereavement. *See also* Grief
attachment model of, 546–547
care during, 562–563
child, 551–552
defined, 546
dual-process model of, 547–548
family program, 563
posttraumatic growth, 560–561
Beta-amyloid, 531
Bias
IQ tests, 287–288
moral reasoning and, 425–428
Big Capitalize Five, 291
Bilingualism, 312
Binge–purge syndrome, 523
Bioecological model, 51–53
Biological aging, 5
Biological sex, 366
Birthing practices, 114–115
Blastocyst, 93
Blood sampling. *See* Maternal blood sampling
BMI. *See* Body mass index (BMI)
Bodily-kinesthetic intelligence, 267
Body mass index (BMI), 142
Bones
healthy, 158
infants, 135
Born to Learn, 310
Bottle feeding, 121
Bowlby, John. See also attachments
attachment theory, 440–441
attachment model of bereavement, 546–548
Brain
adolescent, 150
aging, 152–153

developmental stages, 95
drain, 150
early experience and, 177–178
fetal, 99
genetics and, 136
hippocampus, 235
language and, 299
lateralization of, 139–140
neural bases of memory, 234–235
neurogenesis of, 152–153
neurotransmitters in, 521
plasticity of, 136
thinking side, 139
Breast feeding, 121
Bronfenbrenner, Urie, theory of, 51–53
Bulimia nervosa, 523
Bullying, 424

C
Caloric restriction, 161
Camberwell Cohort, 291
Caregivers. *See* Parents
Carriers, 72
Cascade model of substance abuse, 526–527
Case studies
defined, 17
life-span development, 17
socialization, 418
Cataracts, 177
Catch-up growth, 130
Centenarians, 159
Centration, 215
Cephalocaudal principle, 134
Cesarean section, 116–117
Characteristic adaptations, 332
Chemical senses
adolescent, 186–188
aging and, 194–195
infants, 174, 176
Chemosensory irritation, 186
Child abuse
attention given to, 497
perpetuator profile, 497–498
victim profile, 499
Child effects model, 480–481
Childbirth
anoxia and, 116–117
changes in, 115–116
complications, 116–117
cultural factors, 118–119
father's experience, 120
hazards in, 116–117
medications, 117
mother's experience, 118–120
postponing, 473
stages of, 115
Child-directed speech, 303
Childhood
amnesia, 243
changing views of, 8–9
gene expression in, 87
growth during, 139
peers in, 441–442
psychological disorders in, 516
psychosexual development in, 36–38
psychosocial stages of, 39–40
sexuality, 383–384
Childhood gender nonconformity (CGN), 386
Children
academic achievement by, 311–313
attention development, 182–184
bereavement by, 551–552
classification problems, 217
conservation by, 214–216, 218
continuity of problems in, 516–517
creativity of, 274, 276

death concept of, 549–550
death of, 551, 556–557
depression in, 520–521
developing personality in, 341–342
discontinuity of problems in, 516–517
dynamic approach, 217
egocentrism of, 216
externalizing problems by, 516–517
friendships and, 455
gender differences in, 373–375
health of, 141–143
hearing-impaired, 175
inclusion problems, 217
intelligence of, 272–278
internalizing problems by, 516–517
logical thinking, 217–218
moral development, 416–419
overweight, 142–143
parental attachments, 451
peer networks, 451–452
physical behavior, 140–141
play by, 452–454
popularity of, 454–455
in poverty, 473
preschool, symbolic thinking, 214–218
psychological treatment for, 521
psychopathology in, 516–521
reading, learning to, 315–318
Santa Claus belief by, 215
self-esteem of, 340–341
sense of self, 339–340
seriation and, 218
sexual abuse of, 390
theory of mind and, 400–404
wellness of, 141–143
Chlamydia, 108
Chorion, 94
Chorionic villus sampling (CVS), 74
Chromosome abnormalities, 70–71
Chromosomes
characterization, 64–65
gender roles and, 375
Chronosystem, 52
Cigarette smoking. See Tobacco
Classical conditioning
defined, 41
principles of, 41
strengths of, 45–47
weaknesses of, 45–47
Class inclusion, 217
Classification problems, 217
Clinical method, 200
Cliques, 457
Cocaine, prenatal effects of, 106
Cochlear implants, 175
Codominance, 69
Coercive family environment theory, 422–423
Cognitive behavioral therapy, 520–521
Cognitive developmental theory. See also Social
    cognition development; Thought
adolescents and, 218–223
adults, 224–227
aging and, 226–227
childhood, 214–218
defined, 47
educational improvement from, 327
egocentrism, 216
gender differences, 380–381
identity formation and, 347–348
impairment, 253
infancy, 47
intelligence definition, 201–202
moral development, 408–410
origins of, 200
overlapping wave theory, 246
preschool children and, 217

sense of self and, 335–336
stages of, 48, 202, 211–213
strengths, 49–50
weaknesses, 49–50
Cognitive impairment. See Dementia
Cognitive reserve, 533
Cohort effects
circumvention of, 23–24
defined, 21
generational effects, 23
Collectivist cultures, 337, 341, 350–351, 447
Communality, 367
Comorbidity, 520
Companionate grandparents, 488
Compensation, memory and, 258
Complicated grief, 556
Computers
adolescents and the internet, 13
aging and, 21–22
computer-assisted instruction, 319
gender differences in, 369
internet addiction, 17
Conception, 64, 92–93
Concrete operations stage, 49
Conduct disorder, 420
Confidants, 464
Confidentiality, 27
Confluence approach, 271
Congenital malformations, 138
Conscience principles, 410
Conservation
forms of, 218
lack of, 214–217
transitivity and, 218
Conservation-of-liquid-quantity test, 215
Constructivism
defined, 47
intelligence and, 200–201
perception and, 166–167
Consummate love, 462
Contextual theories, 51
Continuing bonds, 558
Continuing education, 326–328
Continuity–discontinuity issue, 34
Contract, morality of, 410
Control of variables strategy (CVS), 222
Conventional morality, 409
Conventional reasoning, 421
Convergent thinking, 270
Cooing, 304
Cooperative play, 452
Coordination of secondary schemes, 213
Coparenting, 471
Corporal punishment.
    See Negative punishment
Corpus callosum, 139
Correlational method
culture and, 478
defined, 19
moral socialization and, 417–419
negative, 43–44
operant conditioning, 42–45
positive, 43–44
rival interpretations in, 20–21
Couvade, 120
Crawling, 179–180
Creative intelligence, 269
Creativity
childhood, 274–276
investment theory, 271
defined, 264, 270
divergent thinking in, 270–271
fostering, 278
IQ and, 274
older adults and, 284–285
Critical period, 101

Crossing over, 66
Cross-modal perception, 182
Cross-sectional designs, 21–22, 25
Crystallized intelligence, 265, 281
Culture. See also Subculture, sensitivity to
attachment and, 446
bioecological model and, 52
contextual aspects, 447
death and, 542
evolution of, 63–64
individualistic vs. collectivist, 337, 341,
    350–351, 447
labor experience and, 118
life expectancy and, 543–544
life span views, 5–6
math/science achievement and, 322–323
moral reasoning and, 425–426
parenting and, 478
perceptual preferences and, 178
self-conceptions and, 350–351
sensitivity to, 26
sexual maturation and, 144–146
thought and, 205
tools of, 50
Cumulative-deficit hypothesis, 274
Cystic fibrosis, 86
CVS. See Chorionic villus sampling (CVS)

D

Dai, 118
Darwin, Charles, 11–12
Data collection
defined, 15
methods, 16–17
Data, support from, 15
Dating, 459–460
Day care, 448–449
Deaf children
communication by, 404
language learning by, 300–301, 305
Deaf infants, 305
Defense mechanisms, 38
Death. See also Aging; Dying
adolescent, 141
adolescents' reaction to, 552–553
age-based causes, 543
attitudes toward, 541
bereavement and, 546–548
biological definitions of, 538–539
child, 551, 556–557
children's reaction to, 549–550
choices, 539–541
depression following, 555
experience of, 544–548
family context of, 554–557
grief work perspective, 557–559
infant, 548–549
LBW infants/babies, 123
parent, 557
partner/spouse, 554–556
social definition of, 541–542
Debriefing, 27
Decentration, 215
Decision/commitment, 461–462
Decontextualization, 222
Defense mechanisms, 38
Delay of gratification, 415
Delirium, 533
Demandingness–control parents, 476
Dementia. See also Alzheimer's disease (AD),
    Neurocognitive disorder
aging and, 531–534
causes of, 533–534
defined, 531
vascular, 534
Democratically accepted law, 410

unmarried couples, 491–492
violence in, 497–501
Family bereavement program, 563
Family life cycle
defined, 472
marital relationships in, 488–489
stages of, 472
Family stress model, 479
Family systems theory, 470
FAS. *See* Fetal alcohol syndrome (FAS)
Fast mapping, 306
Fathers
childbirth experience for, 120
infant relationship, 474–475
prenatal health and, 110–113
Fertilization process, 92
Fetal alcohol syndrome (FAS), 104–105
Fetal period
events of, 96–99
length of, 96
pattern differences, 99
Fetal programming, 100–101
Fine motor skills, 179
First words
errors in, 306
examples of, 306
meaningful, 305–307
prelude to, 304–305
vocabulary spurt and, 306
Fischer's dynamic skill framework, 209–210
Fluid intelligence, 265, 281
Flynn effect, 277–278
fMRI. *See* Functional magnetic resonance
imaging (fMRI)
Foreclosure status, 344
Formal operations stage, 48
Formal thought
adolescents, 222–223
adults, 222–223
Fragile X syndrome, 71
Fraternal twins, 67
Free radicals 160
Freud, Sigmund. *See also* Psychoanalytic theory
about, 35
theory of, 35–39
Friendships
adulthood, 464
childhood, 455
teen, 456–457
Functional grammar, 307
Functional magnetic resonance imaging
(fMRI), 16, 403
Fuzzy-trace theory, 244

G

Gain–stability-loss model, 5
Gays. *See* Homosexuals
Gender
behavior-associated, 374–375
defined, 366
importance of, 367
playmate selection and, 374
stereotypes, 372–374
Gender differences
aging parental caregivers, 491
autism, 513
body image, 146
changes in sexuality, 394–396
children, 372–384
depression, 530–531
early adult intimacy, 354–355
endocrine system, 131–132
identity formation, 344–345
infants, 370–372
meaningfulness of, 368–370
odor detection, 194

physical behavior, 140–141
retirement age, 359–360
sense of smell, 176
sexual maturation, 144–146
sexual morality, 388–389
substance abuse, 526
suicidality, 528
vocational development, 356
Gender identity, 371–374
Gender roles
adolescent, 385–392
attitudes, 393
biosocial theory of, 375–377
cognitive theories, 380–382
norms, 373–374
observational learning and, 379–380
sexuality, 394–396
social learning theory, 377–379
social roles and, 382–383
social labeling and, 377
stereotypes, 367–368
Gender segregation, 374
Gender typing, 372
Gene therapy, 86
Gene–environment. *See also* Nature/nurture
correlations, 84, 423
interactions, 83–84, 423
Gene expression, epigenetic effects on, 86
General event representations (GERs), 244
General similarities hypothesis, 368–370
Generations X and Y, 23
Generativity, 40
Genes
activity of, 86
APOE4, 532
defined, 9
disorders associated with, 72
dominant, 68–69
early experience and, 87
environmental influence, 68, 84–86
epigenetic effects on, 86
expression of, 68
influences of, 63, 67–68, 76–77
recessive, 68–69
sexual maturation and, 144
tongue-curl, 68
traits influence by, 68
Genetic abnormalities
screening for, 73–74
types of, 72–73
Genetic code
components of, 64–66
mapping of, 66
phenotype, 67–68
relatedness of, 66–67
sex determination and, 67
uniqueness of, 66–67
Genetics. *See also* Behavioral genetics studies; DNA
aging, 158–162
Alzheimer's disease, 532
anorexia, 523
autism, 514
brain development, 136–140
IQ scores and, 285–287, 289
molecular, 77–78
reproduction system and, 153
twin studies, 76
Genital herpes, 391
Genital warts, 391
Genotypes, 67
Germinal period, 93
GERs. *See* Scripts
Gibson, Eleanor
ecological theory of perception, 166–167
visual cliff, 171–172
grasping, 178

Giftedness, 291–292
Glaucoma, 189
Goal-corrected partnerships, 443
Gonorrhea, 391
Good boy, good girl morality, 409, 420
Goodness of fit, 338–339
Grammar
functional, 307
transformational, 308
universal, 299
Grandin, Temple, 401
Grandparents, 488
Grasping, 181
Grief. *See also* Bereavement
coping with, 559–560
death of child, 556–557
death of spouse, 554–556
succumbing to, 559–560
types, 557
Grief work perspective, 557–559
Gross motor skills, 179
Group-and-name trick, 242
Growth and development
adolescents, 143–151
building blocks of, 130–131
children, 139
endocrine system, 131–132
nervous system, 132–134
principles of, 134
Growth hormone, 131
Guided participation, 206

H

Habituation
infants, 168
memory and, 237–238
Harm, protection from, 27
Hayflick limit, 159
Head Start, 309
Health
adolescents, 148–151
children, 141–143
infant, 138–139
IQ and, 280
older adults, 157–158
Hearing
adolescents', 185–186
impairments, 175, 194
infants', 172–174
noise levels, 186
older adults, 192–193
Heavy metal exposure, 109–110
Hemophilia, 70, 72
Heredity. *See also* Genes
chromosome abnormalities in, 70–71
genetic code and, 64–67
genetic diagnosis/counseling, 72–75
inheritance and, 68–71
mutations and, 70
personality and, 352
Heritability
defined, 75
influences of, 80–81
traits, 81–82
Hippocampus, 235
Historical–cultural context, 13
HIV/AIDS, prenatal effects of,
108–109
Holland, John
person-environment fit theory of vocational
choice, 346
Holophrases, 305
Home Observation for Measurement
of the Environment (HOME),
286–287
Homogamy, 461

Homosexuality. *See also* sexual orientation.
  adolescent experimentation, 386–387
  dating, 459
  death and, 556
  defined, 386
  environmental factors, 386
  genes and, 76
Homosexuals
  death and, 556
  families, 493
  partnerships, 493, 556
Hormone replacement therapy (HRT), 154
Hormones. *See also specific hormone*
  female, 131–132
  gender roles and, 375–376
  male, 132
  sexual orientation and, 387
Hospice, 561
Hot flashes, 154
HRT. *See* Hormone replacement therapy (HRT)
Human Genome Project, 66
Humor, 222
Huntington's disease, 72–73
Hypotheses, 14
Hypothetical thinking, 219
Hypothetical–deductive reasoning, 220

I

Id, 36
Idea density, 162
Ideal self, 348–349
Identical twins, 66
Identification, 37
Identity
  concept of, 343
  crisis, 343
  defined, 332
  gender, 372–374
  role confusion *versus*, 40
  sense of, 343–348
Identity achievement status, 344
Identity formation
  developmental trends, 344–347
  ethnicity and, 345
  influences on, 347–348
Imaginary audience, 223
Imaginary companions, 214
Imitation, memory and, 236–237
Implantation process, 92
Implicit memory, 234
Incomplete dominance, 67
Indirect effects, 475
Individual principles of conscience, 410
Individual rights, 410
Individualistic cultures, 337, 341, 350–351 447
Induction, 417
Industry
  inferiority *versus*, 353
  sense of, 40
Infants. *See also* Attached infants; Neonates
  antisocial behavior, 414
  attachment fears of, 443
  audio capacities, 172–174
  autistic, 511–514
  behavioral inhibition, 336–337
  chemical senses, 174–176
  deaf, 305
  death of, 548–549
  depressed, 515
  depth perception, 171–172
  differential treatment of, 370–371
  early emotional development, 434–435
  early learning, effects of, 371
  effortful control in, 337
  empathy in, 413–414
  evoked potentials, 168
  exploratory instincts, 178

face recognition by, 172
feeding, 121
first words by, 305–307
gender differences in, 371
goodness of fit, 338–339
grasping by, 181
habituation, 168
health of, 138–139
hearing-impaired, 175
intelligence of, 271–272
intuitive theories, 172
language learning by, 308–309
locomotor development, 179, 181
memories, 236–238
moral development of, 413–416
motor skills, 180–182
negative alert in, 337–338
object organization by, 169–170
object permanence, 211–213
operant conditioning and, 168, 237–238
peer relations, 450
perception by, influences, 176–179
preferential looking by, 168
problem solving by, 238
prosocial behavior, 413–414
psychopathological disorders of, 510–515
reaching by, 181
rule distinguishing by, 417
sense of self, 335–336
sensorimotor stage, 211
sensory integration by, 182
sexuality of, 371–372
sleep-deprived, 138
speech perception, 173–174
states, 99
stranger anxiety in, 444
surgery in, 337–338
symbolic capacity and, 213
temperament, 336
theory of mind and, 400–401, 416
somaesthetic senses, 176
visual capacities, 168–172
wellness of, 138–139
Infertility
  defined, 93
  therapies, 93
Information-processing approach. *See also* Memory
    development
  adolescent, 247–248
  adult, 250–260
  children, 238–247
  defined, 232
  educational improvement from, 327
  infant, 236–238
  model of, 233
  principles of, 51
  problem solving, 236
  systems, 232–234
Informed consent, 27
In-group–out-group schema, 381
Inheritance
  breeding studies and, 75
  polygenic, 70
  sex-linked, 69–70
  single gene-pair, 68–69
Instincts, 36
Instrumental hedonism, 409, 420
Integration
  gender role theories, 382–383
  sensory, 182
Integrity, despair *versus*, 40, 355–356
Intellectual disability, 290–291
Intelligence. *See also* Cognitive developmental
    theory
  adolescent, 277
  adult, 279–280
  analytic, 268

behavioral genetics studies of, 79–80
bodily-kinesthetic, 267
children, 273–276
constructivism and, 200
creative, 268
crystallized, 265, 281
decline predictors, 281–282
defined, 264
development of, 201–202
early schooling and, 275
extremes of, 290–293
fluid, 265, 281
infant, 271–272
interpersonal, 267
intrapersonal, 267
linguistic, 267
logical–mathematical, 267
multiple theory of, 267
musical, 267
naturalist, 267
practical, 268
practical component, 268
psychometric approach, 265–267
research on, 327
spatial, 267
triarchic theory of, 268–270, 293
Intelligence quotient (IQ)
  age and, 280–281
  aging adults and, 283
  computation of, 266
  creativity and, 270, 275
  development of, 269
  emphasis of, 267
  environmental factors, 285–287, 289
  ethnicity and, 287–289
  factors influencing, 285–289
  Flynn effect, 277
  genetic factors, 285–287, 289
  giftedness and, 291
  group averages, 287
  health and, 280
  motivational differences, 288–289
  occupational success and, 279–280
  poverty and, 273–274
  race and, 287–288
  school achievement and, 278
  score stability, 273
  test bias, 287–288
Intergenerational transmission of parenting,
    498–499
Internal consistency, 15
Internal working models, 441, 463
Internet. See Computers.
Internet addiction, 17
Interpersonal intelligence, 267
Intimacy
  early, 354–355
  isolation *versus*, 40
  love and, 461–462
Intrapersonal intelligence, 267
Intuitive theories, 172
Invariant sequence, 48
In vitro fertilization, 93
Involved grandparents, 488
Isolation, intimacy *versus*, 40
IVF. *See* In vitro fertilization

J

Jaundice, 116
Joint attention
  characterization of, 335
  emergence of, 401
  language development and, 305
Junk DNA, 66
Juvenile delinquency
  aggression and, 423
  defined, 420

networks, 451–452
selection vs. socialization issue, 458, 527
Pendulum problem, 219–220
Perception
depth, 171–172
early influences, 176–179
factors influencing, 166–167
speech, 173–174
Perceptual salience, 214
Perinatal environment. *See also* Childbirth
cultural aspects, 114–115
cultural factors, 118–119
defined, 114
father's experience, 120
mother's experience, 118–120
resilience in, 125–126
risks, 125–126
Perinatologist, 115
Peripheral vision, 191
Permissive parents, 477
Permissiveness–restrictiveness parents, 476
Perseveration errors, 240
Persistent complex bereavement-related
disorder, 556
Personal distress, 506
Personal fable, 223
Personality. *See also* Temperament
adolescent, 342–348
adult, 348–360
aging and, 360
attachment style and, 447
basic concepts of, 332
Big Five, 333–334
changing, factors in, 352–353
children, 339–342
continuity in, 351–353
defined, 332
dimensions of, 351
discontinuity in, 351–353
dying and, 545
Erikson view, 353–356
mean changes, 352
ranking changes, 351–353
scale for, 334
theories of, 332–334
traits, 332
vocational development, 356–357
Personality development theory, 333–334
Perspective-taking skills, 405
Pesticide exposure, 110
Phallic stage, 36–38
Phenotypes, 67
Phenylketonuria (PKU), 72
Phonemes, 173
Phonics, 317
Phonological awareness, 316
Physical behavior, children, 140–141
Physiological measurements, 16–17
Piaget, Jean. *See also* Cognitive developmental
theory
challenges to, 203–205
contributions of, 202–203
moral development theory, 408–409
theory of, 47–49, 200
Vygotsky *versus*, 208
Pincer grasp, 181
Pitocin. *See* Oxytocin
PKU. *See* Phenylketonuria (PKU)
Placenta, 94
Placental barrier, 94
Plasticity
brain and, 136
defined, 12
Play
characterization, 452
frequency of, 452

imaginative, 452–453
importance of, 453–454
rule-governed, 453
social aspects of, 452
Playmate selection, 374
PMS. *See* Premenstrual syndrome (PMS)
Pollutants, prenatal effects of, 109–110
Polygenic inheritance, 70
Popularity, 454, 457
Positive effect, 439
Positive psychology, 561
Positive punishment, 43
Positive reinforcement, 42
Positive youth development, 425
Positron emission tomography (PET) scans, 235
Postconventional reasoning, 420
Posttraumatic growth, 560–561
Posttraumatic stress disorder, 390
Postformal thought, 225
Postpartum depression, 119
Poverty. *See* Socioeconomic status (SES)
Poverty of the stimulus (POTS), 300
Power assertion, 417
Practical component, 268
Practical intelligence, 268
Preconventional morality, 409, 421
Predicting moral action, 427–428
Preferential looking, 168
Pregnancy. *See also* Childbirth
age at, 110–112
emotional factors, 112
ethnic factors, 110–112
hormone, 132
miscarriage, 93
nutritional factors, 113
prenatal screenings, 73–75
racial factors, 110–112
teen, 56, 389–392
Preimplantation genetic diagnosis, 74
Premature infants, 123
Premenstrual dysphoric disorder (PDD), 153
Premenstrual syndrome (PMS), 153
Prenatal development
conception, 92–93
embryonic period, 94–96
fetal period, 96–99
germinal period, 93
screenings, 73–75
taste, 174–176
Prenatal environment
diseases and, 106–109
hearing in, 172–173
maternal factors, 110–113
overview of, 100
paternal factors, 113
pollutants and, 109–110
radiation and, 109
resilience in, 125–126
risks, 125–126
substance abuse and, 101–106
vulnerability of, 100
Preoccupied internal working model, 462
Preoperational stage, 48
Presbycusis, 193
Presbyopia, 189
Preschool, symbolic thinking, 48, 214
Pretend play, 401, 452
Primary circular reactions, 213
Primary emotions, 434
Primitive reflexes, 138
Private speech, 207
Proactive parenting strategies, 418
Problem solving
aging and, 257–258
children, 245–247
infant, 236

Procedural memory, 235
Production deficiency, 240
Progesterone, 132
Programmed theories, 158–160
Prosocial behavior, 408, 413–414
Prosody, 299
Proximodistal principle, 134, 179
Prozac, 521
Psychoanalytic theory
defense mechanisms, 38
instincts and, 35–36
learning theories *versus*, 44–45
moral development, 408
neo-Freudian, 39–41
personality, 332–333
perspective of, 54
psychic energy and, 36
psychosexual stages, 36–38
strengths of, 38
teen pregnancy and, 56
unconscious motives and, 36
weaknesses of, 38
Psychological development
adolescents, 146–147
adults, 156–157
defined, 5
Psychological disorders, 81
Psychometric approach, 265–267
Psychopathology. *See* Developmental
psychopathology
Psychosexual development
anal stage, 36–38
defined, 36
latency period, 38
oral stage, 36–37
phallic stage, 37–38
Psychosocial theory
early adult intimacy, 354–355
early conflicts, 354
midlife generativity, 355
old age integrity, 355
stages of, 37, 39–40, 353
Puberty
anorexia onset and, 523
defined, 143
physical signs of, 144–145
psychological aspects, 146–147
Punishment–and–obedience
orientation, 409
Pupil changes, 188–189

Q
Quantitative changes, 34
Quasi experiments, 19

R
Race. *See also* Ethnicity
academic achievement and, 321
death and, 542
depression and, 530–531
fetal health and, 110–112
IQ scores and, 287–289
religiousness and spirituality, 429–430
sexual maturation and, 144–145
suicide and, 528
Radiation, 109
Random assignment, 18–19
Random error theories of aging,
160–161
Raven Progressive Matrices Test, 265
Reaching, 181
Reactions
primary circular, 213
secondary circular, 213
tertiary circular, 213
Reactive attachment disorder, 448

Social cognition development
  adults, 406–407
  defined, 44
  perspective taking, 405–406
  principle of, 45–46
  self-description, 405–406
  theory of mind, 400–404
Social deprivation, 447–448
Social information processing
  model, 421–422
  skills, 421–422
Social interaction patterns, 460
Socialization
  case study, 418
  moral, 417–419
Social labeling, 377–378
Social learning theory
  gender roles, 377–381
  moral behavior, 410
  personality, 333
Social networks, 457–459
Social norms, 508–509
Social order–maintaining morality,
    410–420
Social perspective-taking skills, 405–406
Social play, 452
Social referencing, 435
Social responsiveness, 443
Social-role theory, 369–370
Sociocultural perspective
  culture, 205
  educational improvement from, 327
  origins of, 205
  principles of, 50
  social interaction, 206
  tool mediation, 206–209
  triarchic model and, 293
Socioeconomic status (SES)
  caregiving and, 473
  development and, 25–26
  IQ scores and, 287
  language learning and, 309
  parenting and, 478–479
Socioemotional selectivity theory,
    439, 460
Sociometric techniques, 454
Solitary play, 452
Somatic symptoms, 507
Sound production, 304
Spatial ability tasks, 369
Spatial intelligence, 267
Speech
  child-directed, 303
  perception, 173–174, 193–194
  private, 207
Spina bifida, 94
Spirituality
  age and, 429
  defined, 428
  morality and, 427–430
Spontaneous abortion, 93
Stage theories. See also Psychoanalytic theory;
    Psychosocial theory, Cognitive developmental
    theory
  cognitive developmental, 48
  developmental, 34–37
  dying, 544–546
  family life cycle, 472
  moral reasoning, 409–410
  perspective of, 54
  prenatal, 93–99
  psychosocial, 39–41, 353–354
Stagnation, generativity versus, 40
Standard deviation, 267
Stanford–Binet Intelligence Scale, 266, 268
Static thought, 216

Statistical deviance, 506
Stereotypes
  age-associated, 349–350
  gender roles, 367–368
  gender, acquiring, 372–373
  IQ scores and, 288–289
  rhythmic, 180
Sternberg, Robert
  investment model of creativity, 271
  successful intelligence, 270
  triarchic theory of intelligence, 268–270
  triarchic theory of love, 461–462
Stillbirths, 110
Stimulus, types of, 43
Storage, 233
Strange situation, 443, 445, 447–449, 456
Stranger anxiety, 444–445
Stress
  adolescents, 522
  diathesis and, 509–510
  maternal, 112
  menarche and, 146
  storm and, 12, 522
Striatum, 235
Storm and stress, 12, 522
Study skills, 242
Subculture, sensitivity to, 26
Substance use disorder
  adolescent, 525
  cascade model of, 526–527
  prenatal effects, 101–106
Suicidal behavior, 528–529
  warning signs, 529
Superego, 36
Surgency, 337
Survival reflexes, 136
Symbolic capacity, 213–214
Synapse, 133
Synchronized routines, 422–423
Syntactic bootstrapping, 305
Syntax, 298
Syphilis, 107–109, 391
Systems theories
  perspectives of, 54–55
  strengths of, 53
  teen pregnancy and, 57
  weaknesses of, 53

T
Talent, fostering, 278
Tanner scale, 144–145
Tasks
  explicit memory, 254
  familiar, 257–259
  theory of mind, 400–401
  timed, 252
  unfamiliar, 257–258
Taste
  acquired, 186
  adolescents and, 186
  foods, 195
  infants and, 173–174
  receptors, 187
Teens. See Adolescents
Telegraphic speech, 307–308
Telomeres, 160
Temperament. See also Personality
  behavioral genetics studies of, 80–81
  categories of, 339
  defined, 80
  infant, 336–339
  moral socialization and, 419
  types of, 336
Temperature
  infants and, 176
  older adults and, 196

Teratogens, 101
Termites, 292
Tertiary circular reactions, 213
Testosterone
  characterization, 95
  gender roles and, 377
Thalidomide, 101–102
Theories. See also specific theories
  function of, 32
  hypotheses versus, 14
  major perspectives, 32–34
Theory of mind
  belief–desire psychology, 402
  children and, 401
  desire psychology, 402
  infants, 416–417
  infants and, 401–402
  mirror neurons and, 403–404
  nature/nurture, 402–404
  primate studies, 402
  tasks, 400–401
Thinking side of brain, 139
Thought. See also Cognitive developmental
    theory
  abstract, 218–220
  convergent, 270
  culture and, 205
  dialectical, 225–226
  divergent, 270–271
  formal, 222–223
  hypothetical, 219
  identity formation and, 347–348
  postformal, 225
  relativistic, 225
  social interaction and, 206
  tools of, 206–207
Time-of-measurement effect, 23
Tinnitus, 185
Tobacco, 102–103
Tongue-curl gene, 68–69
Touch
  infants and, 176
  older adults and, 195
Traits
  defined, 332
  heritability of, 81
Transactional model, 481
Transformational grammar, 308
Transformational thought, 216
Transitivity, 218
Triangular theory of love, 461–462
Triarchic theory of intelligence, 268–270, 293
Trichomoniasis, 391
Trisomy 21. See Down syndrome
Trust versus mistrust stage, 353–354
Turner syndrome, 71, 130
Twin studies
  defined, 76
  estimating influences in, 76–77
  methods of, 76
  sexual orientation, 385–387

U
Ulnar grasp, 181
Unconscious motives, 35–36
Unexercised skills, 252
Underextension, 306
Understanding, emotional, 401
Undiscriminating social
    responsiveness, 443
Unemployment, 357
Unfamiliar tasks and, 257–258
Universal grammar, 299
Universality–context specificity, 34
Unoccupied play, 452
Unstimulating lifestyles, 282

Unwanted pregnancy among teens, 56
Utilization deficiency, 240

V
Varicocele, 93
Vascular dementia, 533
Vegetative states, 539
Verbal reports, 15
Vicarious reinforcement, 44
Violence. *See also* Domestic violence
    delinquency and, 423
    theories of, 421–423
Vision
    aging and, 188–192
    infants', 168–172
Vision problems
    disease, 190
    lens and, 189–190
    prevalence of, 188
    pupil and, 189–190
Visual accommodation, 169
Visual acuity, 168
Visual cliff, 171–172
Visual search skills, 192
Vocabulary
    size differences, 307
    spurt, 306

Vocations
    aging and, 358
    careers and, 356–357
    identity and, 345–348
    retirement and, 358–360
Vygotsky, Lev. *See also* Sociocultural
        perspective
    evaluation of, 207
    Piaget *versus*, 209
    theory of, 205–207

W
Walking, 180
Watson, John B., theory of, 41
Wechsler Adult Intelligence Scale
        (WAIS-IV) test, 266
Wechsler Intelligence Scale for Children
        (WISC-IV) test, 266
Wechsler Preschool and Primary Scale of
        Intelligence (WPPSI) test, 266
Wellness
    adolescents, 148–149
    children, 141–143
    infants, 138–139
    older adults, 157–158
Wernicke–Korsakoff's syndrome, 534
Widows/Widowers, 554–555

Wisdom
    age and, 283
    defined, 282
Words. *See also* First words
    basic order of, 300
    first words, 305–307
    segmentation of, 304
Working
    adolescents, 323–324
    mothers, 472–473
Working memory, 233

X
X chromosomes, 67, 69

Y
Y chromosome, 67, 95
Yearning, 547–548

Z
Zone of proximal development
    concept of, 210
    defined, 206
    language learning and, 302
Zygote
    defined, 64
    formation of, 64–65

SUMMARY OF PHYSICAL, COGNITIVE, PERSONAL, AND SOCIAL DEVELOPMENT ACROSS THE LIFE SPAN

Period	Physical Development	Cognitive Development
Infant (Birth to 2 years)	Brain rapidly grows and is pruned; physical growth is rapid. Reflexes are followed by more voluntary motor control; walking occurs at 1 year. Functioning senses are available at birth; there is an early ability to understand sensory information.	Sensorimotor period: Through senses and actions, infants acquire symbolic capacity and object-permanence concept. Cooing and babbling are followed by one-word and two-word sentences. Learning capacity and recognition memory are present from birth; recall improves with age.
Preschool child (2 to 5 years)	Rapid brain development continues. Coordination and fine motor skills improve. Perceptual abilities are good; attention span is short.	Preoperational stage: Thought is guided by perceptions rather than logic. Symbolic capacity (language acquisition and pretend play) blossoms. There are some limits in information-processing capacity, use of memory strategies, and reasoning.
School-age child (6 to 11 years)	Physical growth is slow; motor skills gradually improve. Children have increased ability to control attention and use the senses intelligently.	Concrete operations stage: Logical actions occur in the head; children master conservation. They also master fine points of language; memory strategies and problem solving with concrete objects improve. IQs begin to stabilize.
Adolescent (10 or 12 to 19 years)	Adolescents experience a brain spurt, a growth spurt, and attainment of sexual maturity. Physical functioning improves. Concern with body image is common.	Formal operations stage: Hypothetical and abstract thought emerge; scientific problem solving improves. Attention and information-processing skills continue to improve, linked to brain growth spurt.
Emerging adult and young adult (20 to 39 years)	This is the time of peak functioning, but a gradual decline in physical and perceptual capacities begins.	Intellectual functioning is mostly stable, and peak expertise and creative achievement often occur.
Middle-aged adult (40 to 64 years)	Physical declines become noticeable (e.g., some loss of endurance, need for reading glasses). Chronic illness increases. Menopause and male andropause occur.	Sophisticated cognitive skills develop, especially in areas of expertise. There is the possibility of growth beyond formal thought and gains in knowledge. Fluid intelligence may begin to decline, but crystallized knowledge is maintained well.
Older adult (65 years and older)	Physical declines continues; more chronic disease, disability, and sensory impairment are common; and reaction time slows. But there is also continued plasticity and reorganization of the brain in response to intellectual stimulation.	Declines in cognition are common but not inevitable. Slower learning, memory problems, declines in IQ and problem solving occur, especially if skills are rarely exercised, but crystallized intelligence holds up better than fluid.